July 11–15, 2015
Madrid, Spain

Association for Computing Machinery

Advancing Computing as a Science & Profession

GECCO'15

Proceedings of the 2015 Genetic and Evolutionary Computation Conference

Sponsored by:

ACM SIGEVO

Association for
Computing Machinery

Advancing Computing as a Science & Profession

The Association for Computing Machinery
2 Penn Plaza, Suite 701
New York, New York 10121-0701

ISBN: 978-1-4503-3472-3 (Digital)

ISBN: 978-1-4503-3882-0 (Print)

Additional copies may be ordered prepaid from:

ACM Order Department
PO Box 30777
New York, NY 10087-0777, USA

Phone: 1-800-342-6626 (USA and Canada)
+1-212-626-0500 (Global)
Fax: +1-212-944-1318
E-mail: acmhelp@acm.org
Hours of Operation: 8:30 am – 4:30 pm ET

Printed in the USA

Welcome from the General Chair

It is my pleasure to welcome you to Madrid for the 2015 Genetic and Evolutionary Computation Conference—GECCO 2015. This is a special year for several reasons. Firstly, sixteen years ago, in 1999, GECCO was born and held for the first time in Orlando, Florida, USA. So happy birthday sweet sixteen, GECCO! We are now in our teenage years, and still growing stronger. Second, thirty years ago the first ICGA, the International Conference on Genetic Algorithms, was held in 1985. Several people who attended that event are still with us today to bear witness to the strength of the (r)evolutionary ideas that were presented there. And last but not least, this year witnesses the highest ever proportion of women in the Organizing Committee, following the spirit of Women@GECCO.

This year's GECCO is comprised of 18 regular tracks, plus, for the second year, the Hot Off the Press (HOP) track, which offers authors of outstanding research recently published in journals and other conferences the opportunity to present their work to the GECCO community. Under the guidance of Editor-in-Chief Sara Silva, the Track Chairs and Program Committee have selected 182 out of the 505 submissions received in all tracks (excluding HOP) for oral presentation as full papers, resulting in an acceptance rate of 36%. Close to 100 short papers will be presented in the regular poster session. This year we also include an additional poster session, where late-breaking abstracts will be presented together with student papers.

A highlight of the conference is the keynote talks given by salient figures in the GECCO fields of interest. This year we wanted to enhance the experience by going back to our origins and have included a third talk from the Natural Sciences field. Our speakers and their subjects are

- Ricard Solé, "Re-designing nature with synthetic biology: from artificial ants and tissues to a new biosphere",
- Kate Smith-Miles, "Visualising the diversity of benchmark instances and generating new test instances to elicit insights into algorithm performance",
- Manuel Martín-Loeches, "Origins and evolution of human language: saltation or gradualism?".

Altogether 32 tutorials cover topics ranging from broad and introductory to specialized and at the frontier of current research. GECCO also hosts fifteen workshops, including several new ones as well as at least one that predates GECCO itself. Further high points include the 12th Annual "Humies" Awards for Human-Competitive Results, which are again generously supported by John Koza, and a record number of nine competitions, ranging from Art to Industry. Finally, Evolutionary Computation in Practice continues to be an important and integral part of GECCO, aiming at getting us in touch with the "real world".

All this would not have been possible without the hard work and dedication of the Organizing Committee over the past year. First of all a special mention is due to Sara Silva, who did a superb job of maintaining the high quality of the conference. Anabela Simões and Gisele Pappa ensured an interesting mixture of Tutorials and Workshops respectively, while Mike Preuss was in charge of finding challenging Competitions. Katia Rodríguez-Vázquez's efforts were devoted to that key component which ensures the conference's future development: the students. Şima Etaner Uyar and Pablo García-Sánchez made us reach the public via publicity and social media, and Juan Luis Jiménez-Laredo compiled all the useful information as Proceedings Chair. Thanks also go to the Track Chairs and the Program Committee for their careful reviewing of the large number of submissions received, and to the workshop chairs and tutorial presenters.

Good advice is worth more than gold and here my sincerest acknowledgement goes to the SIGEVO Business Committee, Pier Luca Lanzi and Jürgen Branke, to SIGEVO Officers Wolfgang Banzhaf, Una-May O'Reilly, Marc Schoenauer and Franz Rothlauf and to former GECCO chairs Dirk Arnold (2014) and Enrique Alba (2013). Thanks are also due to Roxane Rose and Cara Candler from ExecutivEvents, who have been in charge of logistical aspects and registration. Finally, a big hand to Iñaki Hidalgo and his team at the Universidad Complutense, who have ensured we all get the fullest Madrid experience.

Of course, all this effort would not make any sense without you, who are reading this right now, and all GECCO's attendees. So thanks to you too and I wish you all a productive and enjoyable conference!

Anna I Esparcia Alcázar
General Chair
Universitat Politècnica de València, Spain

A Word from the Chair of SIGEVO

Welcome to the Proceedings of GECCO 2015, the seventeenth GECCO, the "recombination" of the 24th International Conference on Genetic Algorithms (ICGA) and the 20th Genetic Programming Conference (GP). Our team this year are: Anna Esparcia-Alcazar serving as General Chair of GECCO 2015 and Sara Silva serving as Editor-in-Chief of the proceedings. Both have worked diligently since many months to prepare a high-quality event in Madrid and a lasting legacy in the form of these proceedings. The results of their and their team's effort can be seen in these pages.

We at SIGEVO are proud that GECCO is the *premiere* venue for presenting work in the area of Genetic and Evolutionary Computation world-wide. The quality of papers submitted to GECCO is very high, and GECCO has a rigorous paper selection process. Over the years we have steadily increased the selection pressure and improved the quality of selected papers. This means that only the best and most important work in Evolutionary Computation and related topics is presented at GECCO. Our conference is consistently ranked at the top of Evolutionary Computation conferences, exceeding in citation counts other venues and even well known journals.

If you were not able to attend GECCO 2015 in person, the Proceedings are in the ACM Digital Library; they are globally accessible and readily found, which benefits both readers and authors.

ACM SIGEVO

Members of ACM SIGEVO, the main sponsor of GECCO, continue to draw major benefits from joining ACM. First is a discount at SIGEVO sponsored conferences, at GECCO, for instance, as much as $100 per registrant. Members have, for a fee, access to the ACM Digital Library, a large and continuously growing resource for research in computing. Another key benefit is the outstanding newsletter SIGEVOlution produced by Pier Luca Lanzi and his excellent editorial board. If you want to access these proceedings and are not a member of SIGEVO, please consider joining (for the low price of $25/year for non-students, and $10/year for student members). This will help us a lot in promoting our community.

Involvement in ACM SIGEVO

SIGEVO became a Special Interest Group (SIG) of the ACM in 2005. ACM is the largest professional organization for Computer Science and considers its SIGs the lifeblood of its organization. We are governed by bylaws available on the SIGEVO web pages. There, you also find a list of members of the 18-member Executive Committee. I have served as chair of SIGEVO since 2011, together with a team of officers: Una-May O'Reilly (Vice-Chair), Marc Schoenauer (Secretary), and Franz Rothlauf (Treasurer). Our term ends this year and a new team (which might partially overlap with the current one) will be elected at our annual meeting in July. For me, however, it is time to say farewell as this will be the last GECCO as Chair. From the vintage point of 2015, I wish future GECCOs and ACM SIGEVO all the best.

Wolfgang Banzhaf
SIGEVO Chair
Department of Computer Science
Memorial University of Newfoundland

Table of Contents

TRACK: Artificial Immune Systems and Artificial Chemistries

TRACK: Artificial Life/Robotics/Evolvable Hardware

TRACK: Biological and Biomedical Applications

TRACK: Continuous Optimization

TRACK: Digital Entertainment Technologies and Arts

TRACK: Evolutionary Combinatorial Optimization and Metaheuristics

TRACK: Estimation of Distribution Algorithms

TRACK: Evolutionary Machine Learning

TRACK: Evolutionary Multiobjective Optimization

TRACK: Genetic Algorithms

TRACK: Generative and Developmental Systems

TRACK: Genetic Programming

TRACK: Integrative Genetic and Evolutionary Computation

TRACK: Parallel Evolutionary Systems

TRACK: Real World Applications

TRACK: Search-Based Software Engineering and Self-* Search

TRACK: Theory

GECCO'15 Organization

General Chair:	Anna I Esparcia-Alcázar *(Universitat Politècnica de València, Spain)*
Editor in Chief:	Sara Silva *(Universidade de Lisboa, Portugal)*
Proceedings Chair	Juan Luis Jiménez-Laredo *(Université du Havre, France)*
Local Chair	José Ignacio (Iñaki) Hidalgo *(Universidad Complutense de Madrid, Spain)*
Tutorials Chair:	Anabela Simões *(Instituto Politécnico de Coimbra, Portugal)*
Workshops Chair:	Gisele Pappa *(Universidade Federal de Minas Gerais, Brazil)*
Publicity Chair	A. Şima Etaner-Uyar *(Istanbul Technical University, Turkey)*
Competitions Chair:	Mike Preuss *(University of Münster, Germany)*
Students Chair:	Katya Rodríguez-Vázquez *(Universidad Nacional Autónoma de México)*
Social Media Chair	Pablo García-Sánchez *(Universidad de Granada, Spain)*
Late-breaking Abstracts Chair	Dirk Sudholt *(University of Sheffield, UK)*
Evolutionary Computation in Practice	Thomas Bartz-Beielstein *(FH Köln - Cologne University of Applied Sciences, Germany)* Jörn Mehnen *(University of Cranfield, UK)*
Local arrangements	Luis Hernández-Yáñez *(Universidad Complutense de Madrid, Spain)*
Business Committee	Jürgen Branke *(University of Warwick, UK)* Pier-Luca Lanzi *(Politecnico di Milano, Italy)*
SIGEVO Officers	Wolfgang Banzhaf, *Chair (Memorial University of Newfoundland, Canada)* Una-May O'Reilly, *Vice-chair (MIT, USA)* Marc Schoenauer, *Secretary (INRIA-Saclay, France)* Franz Rothlauf, *Treasurer (University of Mainz, Germany)*

GECCO 2015 Program Committee

Hussein Abbass *(UNSW@ADFA)*
Ashraf Abdelbar *(Brandon University)*
Ajith Abraham *(Machine Intelligence Research Labs)*
Giovanni Acampora *(Nottingham Trent University)*
Adnan Acan *(Eastern Mediterranean University)*
Andrew Adamatzky *(University of the West of England)*
Michael Affenzeller *(FH Hagenberg)*
Hernan Aguirre *(Shinshu University)*
Chang Wook Ahn *(Sungkyunkwan University)*
Barry Ahrens *(Nova Southeastern University)*
Enrique Alba *(University of Málaga)*
Kieran Alden *(University of York)*
Ricardo Aler *(Universidad Carlos III de Madrid)*
Eva Alfaro-Cid *(Instituto Tecnologico de Informatica)*
Shaukat Ali *(Simula Research Laboratory)*
Richard Allmendinger *(University College London)*
Nadia Alshahwan *(UCL)*
Sergio Jesus Alvarado Garcia *(CINVESTAV-IPN)*
Maria Joao Alves *(Faculty of Economics of University of Coimbra)*
Jhon Edgar Amaya *(UNET)*
Michele Amoretti *(University of Parma)*
Ng Amos *(University of Skövde)*
Sinha Ankur *(Aalto University School of Economics)*
Giuliano Antoniol *(Ecole Polytechnique de Montreal)*
Carlos Antunes *(DEEC-UC)*
Andrea Arcuri *(Simula Research Laboratory)*
Alfredo Arias Montaño *(IPN-ESIME)*
Takaya Arita *(Nagoya University)*
Ignacio Arnaldo *(MIT)*
Dirk V. Arnold *(Dalhousie University)*
Farshad Arvin *(University of Lincoln)*
Joshua E. Auerbach *(École Polytechnique Fédérale de Lausanne)*
Anne Auger *(INRIA)*
Mehmet Emin Aydin *(University of the West of England)*
Nizamettin Aydin *(Yildiz Technical University)*
Dogan Aydın *(Dumlupınar University)*
Raja Muhammad Atif Azad *(University of Limerick)*
Jaume Bacardit *(Newcastle University)*
Mohamed Bader-El-Den *(University of Essex)*
Golnaz Badkobeh *(University of Sheffield)*
Pedro J. Ballester *(Cancer Research Centre of Marseille)*
Wolfgang Banzhaf *(Memorial University of Newfoundland)*
Tiago Baptista *(CISUC, University of Coimbra)*
Helio J.C. Barbosa *(LNCC)*
Marcio Barros *(UNIRIO)*
Thomas Bartz-Beielstein *(Cologne University of Applied Sciences)*
Jeffrey K. Bassett *(Smithsonian Institute National Museum of Natural History)*
Matthieu Basseur *(Université d'Angers)*
Jacob Beal *(BBN Technologies)*
Slim Bechikh *(University of Michigan-Dearborn)*
Nacim Belkhir *(Thales Research&Technology)*
Peter J. Bentley *(University College London)*
James Bergstra *(University of Waterloo)*
Heder Bernardino *(DCC/UFJF)*
Matthias Bernt *(University Leipzig)*
Tom Bersano *(Google)*
Vincent Berthier *(Inria Tao)*
Eva Besada-Portas *(Universidad Compluntense de Madrid)*
Hans-Georg Beyer *(Vorarlberg University of Applied Sciences)*
Leonardo Bezerra *(IRIDIA, CoDE, ULB)*
Bir Bhanu *(University of California at Riverside, USA)*
Marco Biazzini *(INRIA - Bretagne Atlantique)*
Concha Bielza *(Technical University of Madrid)*
Benjamin Biesinger *(Vienna University of Technology)*
Mauro Birattari *(Université Libre de Bruxelles)*
Bernd Bischl *(TU Dortmund)*
Tim Blackwell *(Goldsmiths, University of London)*
Konstantinos Blekas *(University of Ioannina)*
Maria J. Blesa *(Universitat Politècnica de Catalunya - BarcelonaTech)*
Christian Blum *(University of the Basque Country)*
Josh Bongard *(University of Vermont)*
Mohammadreza Bonyadi *(The University of Adelaide)*
Lashon Booker *(The MITRE Corporation)*
Peter A.N. Bosman *(Centre for Mathematics and Computer Science)*
Alexandre Botazzo Delbem *(University of São Paulo)*

lydia boudjeloud *(LITA)*
Amine Boumaza *(Université de Lorraine / LORIA)*
Pascal Bouvry *(University of Luxembourg)*
Ollie Bown *(University of Sydney)*
Anthony Brabazon *(University College Dublin)*
Juergen Branke *(University of Warwick)*
Nicolas Bredeche *(ISIR, Université Pierre et Marie Curie)*
David E. Breen *(Drexel University)*
Karl Bringmann *(ETH Zurich)*
Dimo Brockhoff *(INRIA Lille - Nord Europe)*
Will Neil Browne *(Victoria University of Wellington)*
Alexander Brownlee *(University of Stirling)*
Lam Thu Bui *(Le Quy Don Technical University)*
Thang Bui *(Penn State Harrisburg, USA)*
Zdenek Buk *(Czech Technical University in Prague)*
Larry Bull *(University of the West of England)*
John A. Bullinaria *(University of Birmingham, UK)*
Paolo Burelli *(Aalborg University Copenhagen)*
Keki Mehernosh Burjorjee *(Brandeis University)*
Martin V. Butz *(University of Tübingen)*
Maxim Buzdalov *(ITMO University)*
Arina Buzdalova *(ITMO University)*
Aleksander Byrski *(AGH University of Science and Technology)*
Leticia Cagnina *(Universidad Nacional de San Luis)*
Xinye Cai *(Nanjing University of Aeronautics and Astronautics)*
David Cairns *(University of Stirling)*
Alexandre Campo *(Université Libre de Bruxelles)*
Angelo Cangelosi *(University of Plymouth)*
Nicola Capodieci *(University of Modena and Reggio Emilia)*
Bastos Filho Carmelo J A *(University of Pernambuco, Politechnic School of Pernambuco)*
Andre Carvalho *(USP)*
Mauro Castelli *(NOVA IMS, Universidade Nova de Lisboa)*
Alberto Castellini *(University of Verona, Italy)*
Pedro Castillo *(UGR)*
Nohe Ramon Cazarez-Castro *(Instituto Tecnologico de Tijuana)*
Sara Ceschia *(University of Udine)*
Uday Chakraborty *(University of Missouri)*
Pei-Chann Chang *(Yuan Ze University)*
Zeineb Chelly *(LARODEC, University of Tunis, Higher Institute of Management of Tunis)*
Tianshi Chen *(ICT, CAS)*
Ying-ping Chen *(National Chiao Tung University, TAIWAN)*
Yu-wang Chen *(Manchester Business School)*
Nick Cheney *(Cornell University)*
Marco Chiarandini *(University of Southern Denmark)*
Raymond Chiong *(The University of Newcastle)*
Siang Yew Chong *(University of Nottingham)*
Alexandre Adrien Chotard *(INRIA)*
Anders Christensen *(Instituto de Telecomunicações / ISCTE-IUL)*
Dominique Chu *(University of Kent, UK)*
Chung-Yao Chuang *(The Robotics Institute, Carnegie Mellon University)*
John Clark *(University of York)*
Maurice Clerc *(Independent Consultant)*
Jeff Clune *(University of Wyoming)*
Leandro Coelho *(Pontifical Catholic University of Parana)*
Carlos A. Coello Coello *(CINVESTAV-IPN)*
Mitch K. Colby *(Oregon State University)*
J. Manuel Colmenar *(Rey Juan Carlos University)*
Simon Colton *(Goldsmiths College)*
Brian Connelly *(University of Washington)*
Michael Cook *(Goldsmiths College, University of London)*
Oscar Cordon *(University of Granada)*
Ernesto Costa *(University of Coimbra)*
Lino António Costa *(University of Minho)*
M. Fernanda P. Costa *(University of Minho)*
Bart G.W. Craenen *(University of Edinburgh)*
Antoine CULLY *(ISIR)*
Ronan Cummins *(University of Cambridge)*
Sylvain Cussat-Blanc *(University of Toulouse)*
Steve Dahlskog *(Malmö University)*
Palle Dahlstedt *(University of Gothenburg / Chalmers University of Technology)*
David B. D'Ambrosio *(University of Central Florida)*
Duc-Cuong Dang *(University of Nottingham)*
Christian Darabos *(Dartmouth College)*
Angan Das *(Intel)*
Sanjoy Das *(Kansas State University)*
Dilip Datta *(Tezpur University)*
Rituparna Datta *(IIT Kanpur)*

Cornforth David *(UNSW@ADFA)*
Patrick De Causmaecker *(KU Leuven)*
Kenneth De Jong *(George Mason University)*
Luis Gerardo de la Fraga *(CINVESTAV)*
Luis de la Ossa *(Universidad de Castilla-La Mancha)*
Anthony Deakin *(University of Liverpool)*
Antonio Della Cioppa *(Natural Computation Lab - DIEM, University of Salerno)*
Aydin Demircioglu *(Ruhr-Universität Bochum)*
Bilel DERBEL *(INRIA USTL LIFL)*
Andre Deutz *(Leiden University)*
Clarisse Dhaenens *(LIFL / CNRS / INRIA)*
Gianni Di Caro *(IDSIA)*
Luca Di Gaspero *(University of Udine)*
Massimiliano Di Penta *(RCOST - University of Sannio)*
Victor Diaz Ramirez *(CITEDI-IPN)*
Yongsheng Ding *(Donghua University)*
Huy Dinh *(University of Tokyo)*
Michael J. Dinneen *(University of Auckland)*
Federico Divina *(Pablo de Olavide University)*
Benjamin Doerr *(Ecole Polytechnique)*
Christian Dominguez-Medina *(CIC-IPN)*
Stéphane Doncieux *(ISIR/UPMC)*
Alan Dorin *(Monash University)*
Bernabe Dorronsoro *(University of Cadiz)*
Rene Doursat *(Institut des Systemes Complexes, CNRS)*
León Dozal *(CICESE)*
Jan Drchal *(Department of Computer Science and Engineering, Faculty of Electrical Engineering, Czech Technical University)*
Martin Drozdik *(Shinshu University)*
Madalina Drugan *(AI-lab VUB)*
Jérémie Dubois-Lacoste *(IRIDIA, Université Libre de Bruxelles)*
Enrique Dunn *(University of North Carolina)*
Marc Ebner *(Ernst-Moritz-Universit\"at Greifswald, Germany)*
Aniko Ekart *(Aston University)*
Mohammed El-Abd *(American University of Kuwait)*
Emanuel Emil-Savan *(University of Manchester)*
Michael T. M. Emmerich *(LIACS)*
Andries P. Engelbrecht *(University of Pretoria)*
Anton V. Eremeev *(Omsk Branch of Sobolev Institute of Mathematics)*
Isabel Espirito Santo *(University of Minho)*
Fernando Esponda *(ITAM)*
Richard Everson *(University of Exeter)*
Muddassar Farooq *(Institute of Space Technology)*
Robert Feldt *(Dept of Computer Science and Engineering, Chalmers University of Technology)*
Serge Fenet *(Universite Lyon 1)*
Lavinia Ferariu *(Gheorghe Asachi Technical University of Iasi)*
Jose David Fernandez *(Université de Mons)*
Antonio J. Fernández Leiva *(University of Málaga)*
Juan Luis Fernandez Martinez *(Universidad de Oviedo)*
Paola Festa *(Universitá degli Studi di Napoli)*
Álvaro Fialho *(GE Global Research)*
Stefka Fidanova *(Institute of Information and Communication Technologies)*
Jonathan Edward Fieldsend *(University of Exeter)*
Grazziela Figueredo *(The University of Nottingham)*
Bogdan Filipic *(Jozef Stefan Institute)*
Steffen Finck *(Vorarlberg University of Applied Sciences)*
Andreas Fink *(Helmut-Schmidt-University)*
Asja Fischer *(Ruhr-University Bochum)*
Peter Fleming *(University of Sheffield)*
Gianluigi Folino *(ICAR-CNR)*
Carlos M. Fonseca *(University of Coimbra)*
James A. Foster *(University of Idaho)*
Alberto Franzin *(Université Libre de Bruxelles)*
Gordon Fraser *(University of Sheffield)*
Bernd Freisleben *(Universität Marburg)*
Alex A. Freitas *(University of Kent)*
Tobias Friedrich *(University of Jena)*
Charlie Frowd *(University of Winchester)*
Marcus R. Gallagher *(University of Queensland)*
Jose Enrique Gallardo *(Universidad de Málaga)*
Edgar Galvan *(Trinity College Dublin)*
Leo Galway *(University of Ulster)*
Luca Maria Gambardella *(IDSIA)*
Jose A. Gamez *(Universidad de Castilla-La Mancha)*
Xavier Gandibleux *(Université de Nantes)*
Pablo García Sánchez *(University of Granada)*
Carlos García-Martínez *(Univ. of Córdoba)*
Jose Garcia-Nieto *(University of Malaga)*
Alvaro Garcia-Piquer *(Institute of Space Sciences (IEEC-CSIC))*
Mario Garcia-Valdez *(Instituto Tecnologico de Tijuana)*
Simon Garnier *(New Jersey Institute of Technology)*

Deon Garrett *(Icelandic Institute for Intelligent Machines)*
Jason Gauci *(University of Central Florida)*
Shahin Gelareh *(University of Artois/ LGI2A)*
Arka Ghosh *(Indian Statistical Institute)*
Ioannis Giagkiozis *(The University of Sheffield)*
Raffaele Giancarlo *(University of Palermo)*
Jean-Louis Giavitto *(CNRS - IRCAM, UPMC, Inria)*
Christian Gießen *(DTU Compute, Technical University of Denmark)*
Rosalba Giugno *(University of Catania)*
Orazio Giustolisi *(Technical University of Bari)*
Adrien Goeffon *(LERIA, University of Angers)*
Chi-Keong Goh *(Rolls-Royce Singapore)*
Marco César Goldbarg *(Universidade Federal do Rio Grande do Norte)*
Brian W. Goldman *(Michigan State University)*
Juan A. Gomez-Pulido *(University of Extremadura)*
Ivo Gonçalves *(University of Coimbra)*
Wenyin Gong *(China University of Geosciences)*
Mario Graff *(Universidad Michoacana de San Nicolas de Hidalgo)*
Gary Greenfield *(University of Richmond)*
Julie Greensmith *(University of Nottingham)*
David Greiner *(Universidad de Las Palmas de Gran Canaria)*
Christian Grimme *(Münster University)*
Roderich Gross *(The University of Sheffield)*
Paul Grouchy *(University of Toronto Institute for Aerospace Studies)*
Feng Gu *(Kingston University, London)*
Andreia P. Guerreiro *(University of Coimbra)*
Frederic Guinand *(Université Le Havre)*
Walter J. Gutjahr *(University of Vienna)*
Evert Haasdijk *(VU University Amsterdam)*
Heiko Hamann *(University of Paderborn)*
Lutz Hamel *(University of Rhode Island)*
Ali Hamzeh *(Shiraz University)*
Said Hanafi *(university of Valenciennes)*
Hisashi Handa *(Kindai University)*
Jin-Kao Hao *(University of Angers - LERIA)*
Mark Harman *(UCL)*
Inman Harvey *(University of Sussex)*
Geir Hasle *(SINTEF)*
Erin Hastings *(University of Central Florida)*
Sabine Hauert *(MIT)*
Mark W. Hauschild *(University of Missouri-St. Louis)*
Shinpei Hayashi *(Tokyo Institute of Technology)*
Jun He *(University of Wales, Aberystwyth)*
Verena Heidrich-Meisner *(CAU Kiel)*
Tim Hendtlass *(Swinburne University of Technology)*
James Hereford *(Murray State University)*
Daniel Eduardo Hernandez *(CICESE)*
Carlos Hernández *(CINVESTAV-IPN)*
Arturo Hernández-Aguirre *(Centre for Research in Mathematics)*
Alfredo G. Hernández-Díaz *(Pablo de Olavide University)*
Malcolm Heywood *(Dalhousie University)*
Simon John Hickinbotham *(University of York, UK)*
Philip Hingston *(Edith Cowan University)*
Martin Holena *(Institute of Computer Science)*
John H. Holmes *(University of Pennsylvania)*
Gerard Howard *(CSIRO)*
Michael Hsiao *(Virginia Tech)*
Bin Hu *(Technische Universität Wien)*
Jianjun Hu *(University of South Carolina)*
Ting Hu *(Memorial University)*
Joost Huizinga *(University of Wyoming)*
Phil Husbands *(Sussex University)*
Frank Hutter *(UBC)*
David Andrei Iclănzan *(Sapientia Hungaryan University of Transylvania)*
Christian Igel *(Department of Computer Science, University of Copenhagen)*
Fumiya Iida *(ETH Zurich)*
Takashi Ikegami *(University of Tokyo)*
Manuel Iori *(University of Modena and Reggio Emilia)*
Hisao Ishibuchi *(Osaka Prefecture University)*
Juhos Istvan *(University of Szeged)*
David Jackson *(University of Liverpool)*
Cezary Z. Janikow *(UMSL)*
Thomas Jansen *(Aberystwyth University)*
Yue Jia *(UCL)*
Juan Luis Jimenez Laredo *(University of Le Havre)*
Yaochu Jin *(University of Surrey)*
Daniel Johannsen *(SAP Innovation Center)*
Ulf Johansson *(University of Borås)*
Colin Graeme Johnson *(University of Kent)*
Mark Johnston *(Victoria University of Wellington)*
Ayush Joshi *(University of Birmingham)*
Laetitia Jourdan *(INRIA Lille Nord Europe)*

Bryant Arthur Julstrom *(St. Cloud State University)*
Ata Kaban *(University of Birmingham)*
Michael Kampouridis *(University of Kent)*
Sindhya Karthik *(University of Jyväskylä)*
Ahmed Kattan *(UQU)*
Pascal Kerschke *(University of Münster)*
Gul Muhammad Khan *(NWFP University of Engineering and Technology)*
Vineet Khare *(Amazon Development Centre (India) Pvt ltd)*
Shuhei Kimura *(Tottori Universit)*
Timoleon Kipouros *(University of Cambridge)*
Michael Kirley *(University of Melbourne)*
Evan Kirshenbaum *(HP Labs)*
Joshua D. Knowles *(University of Manchester)*
Patrick Koch *(Cologne University of Applied Sciences, Institute of Computer Science)*
Mario Koeppen *(Kyushu Institute of Technology)*
Joanna Kolodziej *(Cracow University of Technology)*
Maciej Komosinski *(Poznan University of Technology, Institute of Computing Science)*
Wolfgang Konen *(Cologne University of Applied Sciences)*
Lysimachos Kontis *(University of Ioannina)*
Oliver Korb *(Cambridge Crystallographic Data Centre)*
Ilias Kotsireas *(WLU)*
Timo Kötzing *(MPI-INF)*
Miha Kovacic *(University Of Nova Gorica)*
Oliver Kramer *(University of Oldenburg)*
Jozef Kratica *(Mathematical Institute, Serbian Academy of Sciences and Arts)*
Oswin Krause *(University of Copenhagen)*
Gabriel Kronberger *(Unversity of Applied Sciences Upper Austria)*
Jiri Kubalik *(CTU Prague)*
Marvin Künnemann *(Max-Planck-Institut für Informatik)*
Gary Byron Lamont *(AF Institute of Technology)*
Jouni Lampinen *(University of Vaasa)*
Ricardo Landa *(Cinvestav Tamaulipas)*
Dario Landa-Silva *(University of Nottingham)*
William B. Langdon *(University College London)*
Pier Luca Lanzi *(Politecnico di Milano)*
Adriana Lara *(CINVESTAV-IPN)*
Raul Lara-Cabrera *(University of Malaga)*
Antonio LaTorre *(Universidad Politécnica de Madrid)*
Henry Lau *(The University of Hong Kong)*
Hoong-Chuin Lau *(Singapore Management University)*
Claire Le Goues *(Carnegie Mellon University)*
Pierrick Legrand *(Université de Bordeaux)*
Guillermo Leguizamon *(Universidad Nacional de San Luis)*
Joel Lehman *(The University of Texas at Austin)*
Per Kristian Lehre *(University of Nottingham)*
Kenji Leibnitz *(National Institute of Information and Communications Technology)*
Johannes Lengler *(ETH Zurich)*
Cazenille Leo *(Université Paris 7 Diderot - LIED Team)*
Coromoto Leon *(Universidad de La Laguna)*
Dan Lessin *(The University of Texas at Austin)*
Kwong Sak Leung *(The Chinese University of Hong Kong)*
Matthew Lewis *(The Ohio State University)*
Peter R. Lewis *(Aston University)*
Juan Carlos Leyva López *(Universidad de Occidente)*
Ke Li *(Michigan State University)*
Xianneng Li *(Waseda University, Japan)*
Xiaoou Li *(CINVESTAV-IPN)*
Feng Liang *(Nanyang Technological University)*
Yiwen Liang *(Wuhan University)*
Tianjun Liao *(IRIDIA)*
Antonios Liapis *(Center for Computer Games Research, IT University of Copenhagen)*
Peter Lichodzijewski *(Dalhousie University)*
Arnaud Liefooghe *(Université Lille 1)*
Steffen Limmer *(University Erlangen)*
Ping Ling *(Jiangsu Normal University)*
Piotr Lipinski *(Institute of Computer Science, University of Wroclaw, Poland)*
Andrei Lissovoi *(Technical University of Denmark)*
Bo Liu *(Academy of Mathematics and Systems Science, Chinese Academy of Sciences)*
Jialin Liu *(TAO, INRIA)*
Daniel Lobo *(Tufts University)*
Fernando G. Lobo *(University of Algarve)*
Daniele Loiacono *(Politecnico di Milano)*
Michael Lones *(Heriot-Watt University)*
Rui Lopes *(University of Coimbra)*
Antonio López-Jaimes *(Centro de Investigación y de Estudios Avanzados (CINVESTAV))*
Ilya Loshchilov *(INRIA, University Paris-Sud)*

Sushil Louis *(UNR)*
Nuno Lourenço *(Universidade de Coimbra)*
Jose A. Lozano *(University of the Basque Country)*
Manuel Lozano *(University of Granada (SPAIN))*
Emiao Lu *(Manchester Business School)*
Simon Lucas *(University of Essex)*
Simone A. Ludwig *(North Dakota State University)*
Francisco Luna *(University of Extremadura)*
J. M. Luna *(University of Cordoba, Spain)*
Wenjian Luo *(University of Science and Technology of China)*
Thibaut Lust *(UPMC)*
Robert J. Lygoe *(Ford Motor Co Ltd)*
Robert Lyon *(University of Manchester)*
Shingo Mabu *(Yamaguchi University)*
Penousal Machado *(University of Coimbra)*
Ana Maria Madureira *(Institute of Engineering - Polytechnic Institute of Porto)*
Domenico Maisto *(Institute for High Performance Computing and Networking, National Research Council of Italy (ICAR–CNR))*
Stephen Majercik *(Bowdoin College)*
Luigi Malago *(Shinshu University)*
Yazmin Maldonado *(Instituto Tecnologico de Tijuana)*
Pekka Malo *(Aalto University School of Business)*
Andrea Mambrini *(University of Birmingham)*
Bernard Manderick *(VUB)*
Jacek Mandziuk *(Faculty of Mathematics and Information Science, Warsaw University of Technology)*
Maszatul M. Mansor *(University of Sheffield)*
Luca Manzoni *(Università degli Studi di Milano-Bicocca)*
Elena Marchiori *(Radboud University)*
Ana Maria, Rocha *(University of Minho)*
Yannis Marinakis *(Technical University of Crete)*
Dietmar Maringer *(University of Basel)*
Luis Martí *(Pontifícia Universidade Católica do Rio de Janeiro)*
Andrew Martin *(Dept Biochem & Mol Biol, UCL)*
Simon Martin *(University of Stirling)*
Hector P. Martinez *(IT-Universitetet i København)*
Ivette C. Martinez *(Universidad Simon Bolivar)*
Franco Mascia *(Université Libre de Bruxelles)*
Antonio D. Masegosa *(University of Deusto)*
Igor V. Maslov *(EvoCo Inc)*
Shouichi Matsui *(SERL, CRIEPI)*
Giancarlo Mauri *(University Milano-Bicocca)*
Michalis Mavrovouniotis *(De Montfort University)*
Helmut A. Mayer *(University of Salzburg)*
James McDermott *(University College Dublin)*
Phil McMinn *(University of Sheffield)*
Nicholas Freitag McPhee *(University of Minnesota, Morris)*
Jorn Mehnen *(Cranfield University)*
David Meignan *(University of Osnabrück)*
Stephan Meisel *(Münster University)*
Nouredine Melab *(Université Lille 1)*
Alexander Melkozerov *(Tomsk State University of Control Systems and Radioelectronics)*
Rui Mendes *(CCTC/UM)*
Alexander Mendiburu *(University of the Basque Country UPV/EHU)*
Stefan Menzel *(Honda Research Institute Europe)*
Tim Menzies *(ComSci / NcState University)*
Jose M. Merigo Lindahl *(University of Barcelona)*
Olaf Mersmann *(TU Dortmund)*
Pablo Mesejo Santiago *(INRIA)*
Bernd, Meyer, *(Monash University)*
Silja Meyer-Nieberg *(Universitaet der Bundeswehr Muenchen)*
Efren Mezura-Montes *(University of Veracruz)*
Thomas Miconi *(The Neurosciences Institute)*
Martin Middendorf *(University of Leipzig)*
Risto Miikkulainen *(The University of Texas at Austin)*
Damjan Miklic *(University of Zagreb)*
Rob Mills *(University of Lisbon)*
Leandro Minku *(The Centre of Excellence for Research in Computational Intelligence and Applications, School of Computer Science, The University of Birmingham)*
Luis Miramontes Hercog *(Self-Organizing Solutions)*
Eduardo Reck Miranda *(University of Plymouth)*
Mustafa MISIR *(University of Freiburg)*
George Mitchell *(CCKF Ltd)*
Hans Jonas Fossum Moen *(Norwegian Defence Research Estblishment)*
Chilukuri K. mohan *(Syracuse University)*
Julian Molina *(University of Malaga)*
Jean-Marc Montanier *(BSC)*
Roberto Montemanni *(Dalle Molle Institute for Artificial Intelligence)*
Marco A. Montes de Oca *(University of Delaware)*

Antonio Mora *(Dpto. Arquitectura y Tecnología de Computadores)*
Melanie Moses *(University of New Mexico)*
Alison Motsinger *(North Carolina State University)*
Santiago Muelas *(DATSI - Facultad de Informática - Universidad Politécnica de Madrid)*
Nysret Musliu *(Vienna University of Technology)*
Amir Nakib *(Laboratoire LISSI)*
Kaname Narukawa *(Honda Research Institute Europe GmbH)*
Boris Naujoks *(Cologne University of Applied Sciences)*
Antonio Nebro *(University of Málaga)*
Roman Neruda *(Institute of Computer Science of ASCR)*
Frank Neumann *(The University of Adelaide)*
Hoai Nguyen Xuan *(Hanoi University, Vietnam)*
Miguel Nicolau *(University College Dublin)*
Julio Cesar Nievola *(PUCPR)*
Geoff Nitschke *(University of Cape Town)*
Marco Nobile *(Università degli Studi di Milano-Bicocca, Dipartimento di Informatica, Sistemistica e Comunicazione)*
Yusuke Nojima *(Osaka Prefecture University)*
Nasimul Noman *(University of Newcastle)*
Mel Ó Cinnéide *(National University of Ireland, Dublin)*
Charles Ofria *(Michigan State University)*
Choong Kun Oh *(U.S. Naval Research Laboratory)*
Tatsuya Okabe *(Honda Research Institute Japan)*
Markus Olhofer *(Honda Research Institute Europe GmbH)*
Pedro Oliveira *(University of Porto)*
Pietro S. Oliveto *(The University of Sheffield)*
Tomasz Oliwa *(The University of Georgia)*
Juan Luis Olmo *(University of Cordoba)*
Mohammed Omran *(Gulf University for Science & Technology)*
Michael O'Neill *(University College Dublin)*
Isao Ono *(Tokyo Institute of Technology)*
Colm O'Riordan *(NUI, Galway)*
Carlotta Orsenigo *(Politecnico di Milano)*
Julio Ortega *(Universidad de Granada)*
Eneko Osaba *(Deusto University)*
Fernando Otero *(University of Kent)*
Ali Ouni *(University of Montreal)*
Ben Paechter *(Edinburgh Napier University)*
Federico Pagnozzi *(Université Libre de Bruxelles)*
Leon Palafox *(The University of Arizona)*
Michael E. Palmer *(Stanford University)*
Wei Pang *(University of Aberdeen)*
Luis Paquete *(University of Coimbra)*
Victor Parque *(Toyota Technological Institute)*
Konstantinos Parsopoulos *(University of Ioannina)*
Philippe Pasquier *(SIAT - Simon Fraser University)*
Castillo Pedro *(UGR)*
Paola Pellegrini *(IRIDIA-CoDE ULB)*
Jose-Maria Peña *(Universidad Politécnica de Madrid)*
Kalin Penev *(Southampton Solent University)*
Leslie Perez Caceres *(Iridia - ULB)*
Steve Phelps *(University of Essex)*
Andrew Philippides *(University of Sussex)*
Martin Pilát *(Faculty of Mathematics And Physics, Charles University in Prague)*
Nelishia Pillay *(University of KwaZulu-Natal)*
Clara Pizzuti *(Institute for High Performance Computing and Networking - ICAR National Research Council of Italy - CNR)*
Daniel Polani *(University of Hertfordshire)*
Silvia Poles *(EnginSoft)*
Petrica Pop *(North University of Baia Mare, Romania)*
Elena Popovici *(Icosystem Corp)*
Daniel Porumbel *(CEDRIC, CNAM (Conservatoire National des Arts et Métiers))*
Petr Pošík *(Czech Technical University in Prague)*
Walter Potter *(University of Georgia)*
Simon Poulding *(Blekinge Institute of Technology)*
Matthias Prandtstetter *(AIT Austrian Institute of Technology GmbH)*
Steve Prestwich *(University College Cork)*
Jakob Puchinger *(AIT - Austrian Institute of Technology)*
Cesar Puente *(Universidad Autónoma de San Luis Potosi)*
Jose Miguel Puerta *(UCLM)*
William F. Punch *(Michigan State University)*
Robin Purshouse *(University of Sheffield)*
Jianlong Qi *(Ancestry.com)*
A. K. Qin *(RMIT University)*
Günther R. Raidl *(Vienna University of Technology)*
Marcus Christian Randall *(School of Information Technology, Bond University)*
Ranji S. Ranjithan *(North Carolina State Univ)*

Khaled Rasheed *(University of Georgia)*
Tapabrata Ray *(School of Aerospace, Civil and Mechanical Engineering)*
Tom Ray *(University of Oklahoma)*
Michael Raymer *(Wright State University)*
Mark Read *(University of Sydney)*
Patrick M. Reed *(Cornell University)*
Lewis Rhyd *(Cardiff University)*
Hendrik Richter *(HTWK Leipzig University of Applied Sciences)*
John Rieffel *(Union College)*
Maria Cristina Riff *(UTFSM)*
Wille Robert *(University of Bremen)*
Denis Robilliard *(LISIC, ULCO, Univ Lille-Nord de France)*
Peter Rockett *(Dept of Electronic & Electrical Engineering)*
Eduardo Rodriguez-Tello *(CINVESTAV,Tamaulipas)*
Philipp Rohlfshagen *(Schneider-Electric)*
Andrea Roli *(Alma Mater Studiorum Universita' di Bologna)*
Simona E. Rombo *(Dep. of Mathematics and Computer Science, University of Palermo)*
Carlos Romero *(Technical University of Madrid)*
Marc Roper *(University of Strathclyde)*
Brian J. Ross *(Brock University)*
Peter Ross *(Napier University)*
Franz Rothlauf *(University of Mainz)*
Jonathan Rowe *(University of Birmingham)*
Guenter Rudolph *(TU Dortmund University)*
Guenther Ruhe *(University of Calgary)*
Ruben Ruiz *(Polytechnic University of Valencia)*
Thomas Runkler *(Siemens AG)*
Conor Ryan *(University of Limerick)*
Ramon Sagarna *(University of the Basque Country)*
Erol Sahin *(Middle East Technical University)*
Houari Sahraoui *(DIRO, Univ. de Montreal)*
Jun Sakuma *(University of Tsukuba)*
Ziad Salem *(Graz University)*
Luciano Sanchez *(Universidad de Oviedo)*
Roberto Santana *(University of the Basque Country (UPV/EHU))*
Iván Santibáñez Koref *(Technical Univ. Berlin)*
Federica Sarro *(University College London)*
Hiroyuki Sato *(The University of Electro-Communications)*
Yuji Sato *(Hosei University)*
Fredéric Saubion *(University of Angers, France)*
Hideyuki Sawada *(Kagawa University, Japan)*
Robert Schaefer *(AGH University of Science and Technology)*
Massimiliano Schillaci *(STMicroelectronics)*
Manuel Schmitt *(University of Erlangen-Nuremberg)*
Marc Schoenauer *(INRIA)*
Peter Scully *(Aberystwyth University)*
Michele Sebag *(Université Paris-Sud)*
Carlos Segura *(Universidad de La Laguna)*
Lukas Sekanina *(Brno University of Technology, Czech Republic)*
Yann Semet *(Thales)*
Sandip Sen *(University of Tulsa)*
Kevin Seppi *(Brigham Young University)*
Martin Serpell *(University of the West of England)*
Marc Sevaux *(Université de Bretagne-Sud - Lab-STICC)*
Ugur Sezerman *(Sabancı University)*
Fatima Shaheen *(Loughborough University)*
Noor Shaker *(IT University of Copenhagen)*
Siddhartha Shakya *(Business Modelling & Operational Transformation Practice, BT)*
Jonathan Lee Shapiro *(University of Manchester)*
Yang Shengxiang *(De Montfort Unviersity)*
Pradyumn Kumar Shukla *(KIT)*
Patrick Siarry *(University of Paris-Est Créteil)*
Arlindo Silva *(Polytechnic Institute of Castelo Branco)*
Fernando Silva *(Instituto de Telecomunicações; BioISI, University of Lisbon)*
Kevin Sim *(Edinburgh Napier University)*
Moshe Sipper *(Ben-Gurion University)*
Alexei N. Skurikhin *(Los Alamos National Laboratory)*
Alice Smith *(Auburn University)*
Jim Smith *(University of the West of England)*
Tamara Smyth *(University of Califronia San Diego)*
Christine Solnon *(LIRIS, INSA de Lyon)*
Eduardo J. Solteiro Pires *(UTAD University)*
Andrea Soltoggio *(Loughborough University)*
Andy Song *(RMIT University)*
Victor Adrian Sosa Hernandez *(CINVESTAV-IPN)*
Humberto Sossa *(Instituto Politécnico Nacional)*
Jerffeson Souza *(State University of Ceara)*
Lee Spector *(Hampshire College)*
Giovanni Squillero *(Politecnico di Torino)*

Russell Standish *(High Performance Coders)*
Susan Stepney *(University of York)*
Sebastian Stich *(Université catholique de Louvain)*
Forrest Stonedahl *(Northwestern University)*
Umberto Straccia *(ISTI-CNR, Italy)*
Giovanni Stracquadanio *(University of Oxford)*
Thomas Stützle *(Université Libre de Bruxelles)*
Dirk Sudholt *(University of Sheffield)*
Ponnuthurai Suganthan *(NTU)*
Chaoli Sun *(Taiyuan University of Science and Technology)*
Yi Sun *(Google Inc)*
Andrew Michael Sutton *(Friedrich-Schiller-Universität Jena)*
Reiji Suzuki *(Nagoya University)*
Keiki Takadama *(UEC)*
Ricardo Takahashi *(Universidade Federal de Minas Gerais)*
El-Ghazali Talbi *(INRIA)*
Ying Tan *(Peking University)*
Kiyoshi Tanaka *(Shinshu University)*
Ivan Tanev *(Faculty of Engineering, Doshisha University)*
Ernesto Tarantino *(ICAR - CNR)*
Daniel R. Tauritz *(Missouri University of Science and Technology)*
Jorge Tavares *(Microsoft)*
Roberto Tavares *(UFSCAR)*
Tim Taylor *(University of London International Academy)*
Jürgen Teich *(University of Erlangen-Nuremberg)*
Hugo Terashima Marín *(ITESM - CSI)*
Andrea G. B. Tettamanzi *(Université de Nice Sophia Antipolis)*
Christof Teuscher *(Portland State University)*
Johannes Textor *(University of Utrecht)*
Fabien Teytaud *(University of Lille Nord de France)*
Ruck Thawonmas *(Ritsumeikan University)*
Lothar Thiele *(ETH Zurich)*
Dirk Thierens *(Utrecht University)*
Tommy Thompson *(University of Derby)*
Chuan-Kang Ting *(Department of Computer Science and Information Engineering, National Chung Cheng University)*
Peter Tino *(University of Birmingham)*
Renato Tinos *(University of São Paulo)*
Ashutosh Tiwari *(Cranfield University)*
Santosh Tiwari *(General Motors Company)*
Julian Togelius *(IT University of Copenhagen)*
Marco Tomassini *(University of Lausanne)*
Alberto Paolo Tonda *(INRA)*
Martin Trefzer *(University of York)*
Vito Trianni *(ISTC-CNR)*
Krzysztof Trojanowski *(Institute of Computer Science, Polish Academy of Sciences)*
Giuseppe A. Trunfio *(University of Sassari)*
Alexis Tsoukias *(Université Paris Dauphine)*
Elio Tuci *(Aberystwyth University)*
Matthias Tuma *(Ruhr-Universität Bochum)*
Tea Tusar *(Jozef Stefan Institute)*
Cem Celal Tutum *(Michigan State University)*
Jamie Twycross *(University of Nottingham)*
Man Chon U *(Las Vegas Sands Corporate)*
Roberto Ugolotti *(University of Parma)*
Paulo Urbano *(University of Lisbon)*
Neil Urquhart *(Edinburgh Napier University)*
Guillermo Valencia-Palomo *(Instituto Tecnologico de Hermosillo)*
H. Jaap Van den Herik *(Tilburg University)*
Leonardo Vanneschi *(NOVA IMS, Universidade Nova de Lisboa)*
Zdeněk Vašíček *(Brno University Of Technology)*
Igor Vatolkin *(TU Dortmund)*
Nadarajen Veerapen *(University of Stirling)*
Nubia Velasco *(Universidad de los Andes)*
Sebastian Ventura *(Universidad de Cordoba)*
Phillip Verbancsics *(Space and Naval Warfare Systems Center - Pacific)*
Sebastien Verel *(Université du Littoral Côte d'Opale)*
Silvia Vergilio *(Federal University of Paraná)*
Ana Viana *(INESC TEC, Polytechnic of Porto)*
Petra Vidnerova *(Institute of Computer Science of ASCR)*
Fernando J. Von Zuben *(Unicamp)*
Michael N. Vrahatis *(University of Patras)*
Tobias Wagner *(Institute of Machining Technology, TU Dortmund University)*
Rolf Wanka *(University of Erlangen-Nuremberg)*
Westley Weimer *(University of Virginia)*
Simon Wessing *(Technische Universität Dortmund)*
Peter Alexander Whigham *(University of Otago)*
David White *(University of Glasgow)*
Bartosz Wieloch *(Poznan University of Technology)*

Josh Wilkerson *(NAVAIR)*
Garnett Wilson *(Afinin Labs Inc)*
Stewart W. Wilson *(Prediction Dynamics)*
Manuel Wimmer *(Vienna University of Technology)*
Mark Wineberg *(University of Guelph)*
Stephan Winkler *(University Of Applied Sciences Upper Austria)*
Carsten Witt *(Technical University Of Denmark)*
M. L. Dennis Wong *(Swinburne University of Technology)*
John R. Woodward *(S T I R L I N G U N I)*
Alden H. Wright *(University of Montana)*
Borys Wrobel *(Adam Mickiewicz University)*
Annie S. Wu *(University of Central Florida)*
Huayang Xie *(Oracle New Zealand)*
Takeshi Yamada *(NTT Communication Science Labs)*
Lidia Yamamoto *(University of Strasbourg)*
Georgios Yannakakis *(IT University of Copenhagen)*
Wei-Chang Yeh *(National Tsing Hua University)*
Gary G. Yen *(Oklahoma State University)*
Shin Yoo *(University College London)*
Jason Yosinski *(Cornell University)*
Tian-Li Yu *(Taiwan Evolutionary Intelligence Lab)*
Tina Yu *(Memorial University)*
Yang Yu *(Nanjing University)*
Martin Zaefferer *(Cologne University of Applied Sciences)*
Amelia Zafra *(University of Cordoba)*
Payam Zahadat *(Artificial Life Lab, University of Graz)*
Daniela Zaharie *(West University of Timisoara)*
Fabio Zambetta *(RMIT University)*
Saúl Zapotecas Martínez *(CINVESTAV-IPN)*
Andreas Zell *(University of Tübingen)*
Zhu Zexuan *(Shenzhen University)*
Fu Zhang *(Mathworks)*
Mengjie Zhang *(Victoria University of Wellington)*
Yuanyuan Zhang *(University College London)*
Yanfei Zhong *(Wuhan university)*
Aimin Zhou *(Department of Computer Science, East China Normal University)*
Jayadeva *(Indian Institute of Technology, Delhi)*

GECCO 2015 Track Chairs

Track	Chairs
Ant Colony Optimization and Swarm Intelligence (ACO-SI):	Manuel López-Ibáñez *(Université Libre de Bruxelles)* Sanaz Mostaghim *(Otto von Guericke University of Magdeburg)*
Artificial Immune Systems and Artificial Chemistries (AIS-AChem):	Jon Timmis *(University of York)* Christine Zarges *(University of Birmingham)*
Artificial Life / Robotics / Evolvable Hardware (ALIFE):	Luis Correia *(University of Lisbon)* Terrence Soule *(University of Idaho)*
Biological & Biomedical Applications (BIO):	Mario Giacobini *(University of Torino)* Ryan Urbanowicz *(Dartmouth College)*
Continuous Optimization - Evolution Strategies & Evolutionary Programming (CO):	Youhei Akimoto *(Shinshu University)* Tobias Glasmachers *(Ruhr-University Bochum)*
Digital Entertainment Technologies & Arts (DETA):	Francisco Fernandez de Vega *(University of Extremadura)* Amy Hoover *(University of Malta)*
Estimation of Distribution Algorithms (EDA):	Pedro Larrañaga *(Technical University of Madrid)* Marta Soto *(Institute of Cybernetics, Mathematics & Physics)*
Evolutionary Combinatorial Optimization & Metaheuristics (ECOM):	Carlos Cotta *(University of Málaga)* Francisco B. Pereira *(Polytechnic Institute of Coimbra)*
Evolutionary Machine Learning (EML):	Julia Handl *(University of Manchester)* Jan Koutnik *(IDSIA)*
Evolutionary Multiobjective Optimization (EMO):	Antonio Gaspar-Cunha *(University of Minho)* Heike Trautmann *(University of Münster)*
Generative and Developmental Systems (GDS):	Jean-Baptiste Mouret *(University Pierre and Marie Curie)* Sebastian Risi *(IT University of Copenhagen)*
Genetic Algorithms (GA):	Ernesto Costa *(University of Coimbra)* Oliver Schuetze *(Cinvestav-IPN)*
Genetic Programming (GP):	Krzysztof Krawiec *(Poznan University of Technology)* Alberto Moraglio *(University of Exeter)*
Integrative Genetic & Evolutionary Computation (IGEC):	Julian F. Miller *(University of York)* Pawel Widera *(Newcastle University)*
Parallel Evolutionary Systems (PES):	Stefano Cagnoni *(University of Parma)* JJ Merelo *(University of Granada)*
Real World Applications (RWA):	Emma Hart *(Edinburgh Napier University)* Leonardo Trujillo *(Edinburgh Napier University)*
Search-Based Software Engineering & Self-* Search (SBSE-SS):	Marouane Keswsentini *(University of Michigan)* Gabriela Ochoa *(University of Stirling)*
Theory (THEORY):	Francisco Chicano *(University of Málaga)* Carola Doerr *(University Pierre and Marie Curie)*

An Improved Collaborative Filtering Recommendation Algorithm Based on Community Detection in Social Networks

Cen Cao
School of Computer Science and Engineering
Southeast University
Nanjing, China, 211189

Qingjian Ni *
School of Computer Science and Engineering
Southeast University
Nanjing, China, 211189
nqj@seu.edu.cn

Yuqing Zhai
School of Computer Science and Engineering
Southeast University
Nanjing, China, 211189

ABSTRACT

Recommendation algorithms in social networks have attracted much attention in recent years. Collaborative filtering recommendation algorithm is one of the most commonly used recommendation algorithms. Traditional user-based collaborative filtering recommendation algorithm recommends based on the user-item rating matrix, but the large amounts of data may cause low efficiency. In this paper, we propose an improved collaborative filtering recommendation algorithm based on community detection. Firstly, the user-item rating matrix is mapped into the user similarity network. Furthermore, a novel discrete particle swarm optimization algorithm is applied to find communities in the user similarity network, and finally Top-N items are recommend to the recommended user according to the communities. The experiments on a real dataset validate the effectiveness of the proposed algorithm for improving the precision, coverage and efficiency of recommendation.

Categories and Subject Descriptors

I.2.8 [**Artificial Intelligence**]: Problem Solving, Control Methods, and Search

Keywords

Collaborative filtering; community detection; user similarity network; discrete particle swarm optimization

1. INTRODUCTION

With the rapid growth of information on the internet, . To solve the problem of information overload, the researches on how do the users in the internet share their views on items, services and other users have received extensive attention. It is very difficult for people to find interested information, and recommendation systems appear to solve this problem [1]. Recommendation algorithms can effectively recommend the required information to users. Currently, recommendation algorithms have been widely used in Amazon, eBay, Facebook, etc.

Recommendation algorithms fall into two categories: collaborative filtering (CF) methods and content-based methods [2, 7]. And user-based collaborative filtering and item-based collaborative filtering are two typical collaborative filtering algorithms, and in this paper we choose user-based CF to recommend. User-based CF is oriented to users, and has a more emphasis on the social attributes of users [18]. Furthermore, User-based CF can be well applied in social networks. However, traditional user-based CF is based on the entire user-item network which involves large amounts of data. This leads to the problem of scalability, low recommendation efficiency and low recommendation quality. While collaborative filtering recommendation based on community detection can efficiently ease the problem of scalability and improve recommendation performance, and previous researches have shown promising results [9, 15, 17].

Although the issues of recommendation based on community detection have been discussed in many papers, existing methods are mostly used in unweighted networks, and can only detect two communities or a specified number of communities at a time. In most cases, these methods are suitable to small-scale networks, but can not be applied to social networks with large numbers of nodes. PSO algorithm has been widely applied in community detection problem [3, 16, 5]. Detecting community structures in complex networks with PSO algorithm does not need prior knowledge about the size of communities and the number of communities. Accordingly, we choose PSO algorithm to detect community structure in this paper. In this paper, we propose a novel community detection method based on discrete particle swarm optimization algorithms. In the discrete particle swarm optimization algorithm, an individual's position is closely connected with the network structure. The proposed algorithm redefines the update formulas of velocity and position according to the unique discrete representation of community detecting problem in the framework of basic PSO algorithm, and it can obtain the results without prior knowledge of the size of communities and the number of communities.

The rest of this paper is organized as follows: we provide our improved collaborative filtering recommendation algorithm based on community detection (CFCD-PSO) in

GECCO '15, July 11 - 16, 2015, Madrid, Spain
© 2015 ACM. ISBN 978-1-4503-3472-3/15/07...$15.00
DOI: http://dx.doi.org/10.1145/2739480.2754670

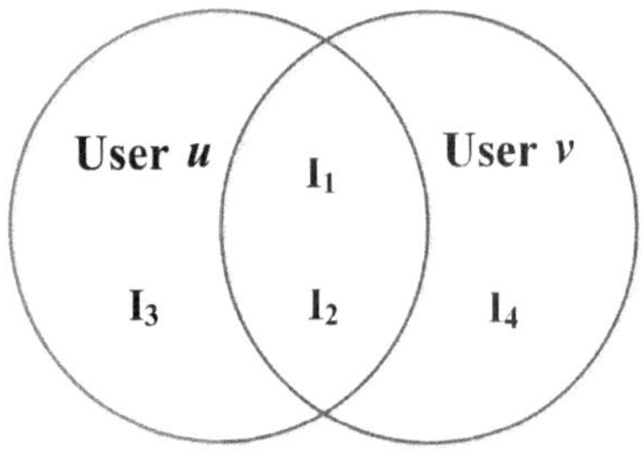

Figure 1: Schematic diagram of collaborative filtering algorithm.

Section 2. In Section 3 we address a novel discrete particle swarm optimization (NPSO) algorithm for community detection. Finally, we show the experiment results in Section 4 and present our conclusions and future work in Section 5.

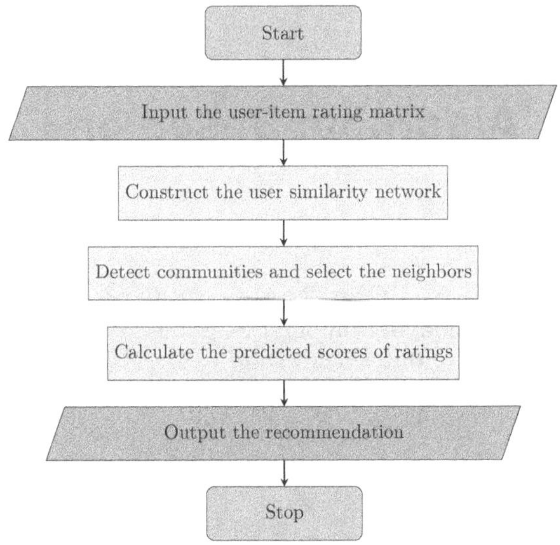

Figure 2: Framework of CFCD-PSO algorithm.

2. IMPROVED COLLABORATIVE FILTERING RECOMMENDATION ALGORITHM BASED ON COMMUNITY DETECTION

In this section, basic ideas of user-based collaborative filtering is first given to help understanding the motives of this work. The processes of the improved collaborative filtering recommendation algorithm based on community detection are then proposed.

2.1 Basic Ideas of User-based Collaborative Filtering

User-based CF algorithm was proposed by Goldberg *et al.* in 1992 [4]. The basic idea is that there are similarities between users, and if users have similar ratings on some items, then their ratings on other items are also similar. In [12], Donovan pointed out the similarity assumption is the basis of recommendation. Take Figure 1 as an example, user u and v both prefer item I_1 and I_2, then user u can recommend item I_3 to v and user v can recommend I_4 to u. User-based CF algorithm calculates the similarities between users based on the user-item rating matrix, finds the recommended user's neighbors, and predicts scores of recommended user's ratings on the items according to the neighbors' ratings. Finally, Top-N items which have not been rated by the recommended user and have the maximum predicted ratings will be recommended.

According to the basic ideas of user-based CF algorithm, this paper proposes an improved collaborative filtering recommendation algorithm based on community detection. The framework of CFCD-PSO algorithm is shown in Figure 2.

2.2 Construction of User Similarity Network

The user-item network in recommendation algorithms consists of user, item and rating information. As is shown in Figure 2.2, the upper network is the item network, representing the information of items. The underlying network is the user network, representing the information of users. Between the two networks is the user-item network, and the weights of the connections are the scores of ratings. The scores are integers in the range of $[1, 5]$, and 1 is the lowest, 5 is the highest.

The relationship between users, items and ratings in the user-item network can be expressed by a matrix. Assuming there are m users and n items in the user-item network, then the user-item rating matrix is as equation (1):

$$R = \begin{bmatrix} r_{11} & r_{12} & \dots & r_{1n} \\ r_{21} & r_{22} & \dots & r_{2n} \\ \dots & \dots & \dots & \dots \\ r_{m1} & r_{m2} & \dots & r_{mn} \end{bmatrix} \tag{1}$$

Where $r_{ij}(1 \leq i \leq m, 1 \leq j \leq n)$ is the rating from user i on item j.

Traditional user-based CF algorithm recommends items to users based on the user-item network, which has been discussed in Section 2.1. However, CFCD-PSO algorithm recommends based on communities, and a community is a social unit consisting of people with certain common interests. Therefore, CFCD-PSO algorithm should firstly maps the user-item network into the user similarity network. The user similarity network reflects the similarities between users, which are calculated by the user-item rating matrix. Many experiments have shown that Pearson correlation coefficient can present the similarities better [8]. The Pearson similarity between user u and v is calculated by equation (2).

$$sim(u, v) = \frac{\sum_{t \in I_{uv}} (r_{ut} - \overline{r_u})(r_{vt} - \overline{r_v})}{\sqrt{\sum_{t \in I_{uv}} (r_{ut} - \overline{r_u})^2 \sum_{t \in I_{uv}} (r_{vt} - \overline{r_v})^2}} \tag{2}$$

where I_{uv} is the collection of common items rated by user u and v, r_{ut} is the score rated by user u on item t, and $\overline{r_u}$ is the average score rated by user u. The user-user relation matrix can be derived from the similarities between users:

$$s_U = \begin{bmatrix} s_{11} & s_{12} & \dots & s_{1n} \\ s_{21} & s_{22} & \dots & s_{2n} \\ \dots & \dots & \dots & \dots \\ s_{n1} & s_{n2} & \dots & s_{nn} \end{bmatrix} \tag{3}$$

where $s_{ij}(1 \leq i, j \leq n)$ is the similarity between user i and user j. The user similarity network is shown in Figure 2.2.

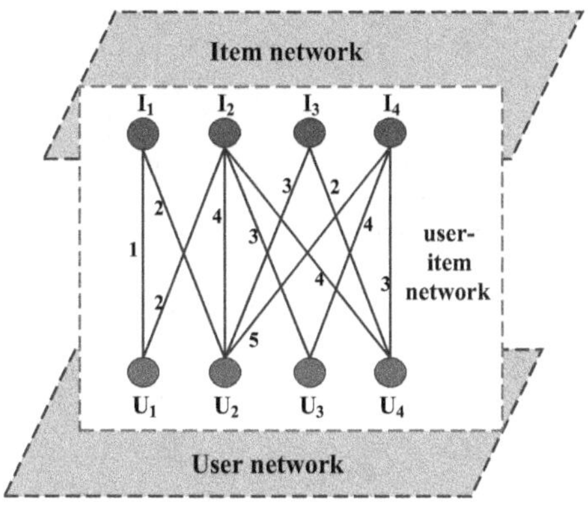

Figure 3: A schematic representation of user-item network.

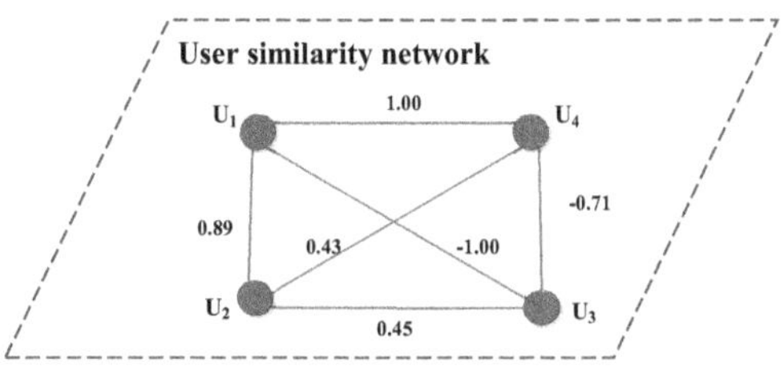

Figure 4: A schematic representation of user similarity network.

The nodes in the user similarity network represent the users, and the weights on the connections are similarities.

2.3 Selection of the Neighbors

After construction of user similarity network, a novel discrete particle swarm optimization algorithm is used to detect communities in the user similarity network, which will be discussed in Section 3. All the users will be detected into different communities, and users in the same community have a high similarity. Then in the neighbors search process, CFCD-PSO algorithm does not need to select from all the users but select from the users within the same community of the recommended user. Since the recommended user may belong to multiple communities, the neighbors should be merged if the recommended user appear in many communities simultaneously. This algorithm can narrow the search scope, reduce the computational time and improve the recommendation performance.

2.4 Calculation of the Predicted Scores of Ratings

Recommendation algorithms make recommendations based on the predicted ratings from the recommended user on the unrated items, and N items with the highest predicted score will be recommended. The predicted score of a rating from the recommended user u on item i is calculated by equation (4):

$$r_u(i) = \overline{r_u} + \frac{\sum_{u' \in U} sim(u,u')(r_{u't} - \overline{r_{u'}})}{\sum_{u' \in U} sim(u,u')} \quad (4)$$

where U is the collection of neighbors which are within the same community of the recommended user, and $sim(u,u')$ is the similarity between user u and u'.

In traditional user-based CF algorithm, calculating similarities between users and finding neighbors of the recommended user are carried out on the entire user-item network. While in CFCD-PSO algorithm, the above steps only perform in the communities. Since the number of neighbors reduces, the amount of computation has significantly reduced. In addition to improving the efficiency of recommendation, CFCD-PSO algorithm can also improve the precision and coverage of recommendation.

3. A NOVEL DISCRETE PARTICLE SWARM OPTIMIZATION ALGORITHM FOR COMMUNITY DETECTION

3.1 Encoding of Individuals in NDPSO Algorithm

Particle swarm optimization (PSO) algorithm were essentially inspired by a model of social interactions between independent birds seeking for food [6]. In PSO, a number of individuals fly in the search space with a velocity. Each individual's position is treated as a D-dimensional vector, such as $X_i = (x_{i1}, x_{i2}, \cdots, x_{iD})$. The best previous position of the ith individual is $P_i = (p_{i1}, p_{i2}, \cdots, p_{iD})$, and the best position found by the population is $P_g = (p_{g1}, p_{g2}, \cdots, p_{gD})$. Each individual evaluates the fitness function at its current position, and determines its movement by combining some aspect of its current position, its best previous position and the population's best position.

The encoding of the individual's each dimension represents the id of a node. If the value of the ith dimension is j, then node i and node j are in the same community. When initializing the population, each node finds its neighbors in the network according to the connections. The position of individual's i^{th} dimension is the id of a node randomly selected from the ith node's neighbors. Figure 5 shows an individual's encoding in NDPSO algorithm. An example of the user similarity network and the community detection results are shown in Figure 6.

3.2 Updating Methods of NDPSO Algorithm

The position of an individual is a community detection scheme consisting of all the nodes and their neighbors. All the schemes constitute a search space of the problem. The representation of an individual's velocity and position discussed in section 3.1 is a key problem in NDPSO algorithm. Another key problem is redefining the updating formulas of velocity and position according to the unique discrete representation of community detection problem in the framework of basic PSO algorithm. Shi and Eberhart introduced inertia weight ω into basic PSO algorithm [13]. The updating formulas of velocity and position are shown in equation (5) and (6):

$$v_{id} = \omega \otimes v_{id} \oplus c_1 \otimes (p_{id} \ominus x_{id}) \oplus c_2 \otimes (p_g \ominus x_{id}) \quad (5)$$

$$x_{id} = x_{id} \oplus v_{id} \quad (6)$$

The proposed NDPSO algorithm redefines the operation rules in the above updating formulas. The operation rules of velocity (V) and position (X) update formulas are defined as

Dimension	1	2	3	4	5	6	7	8	9	10	11	12	13	14
Position	2	3	2	3	6	7	8	5	6	7	13	11	12	12

Figure 5: An individual's encoding in NDPSO algorithm.

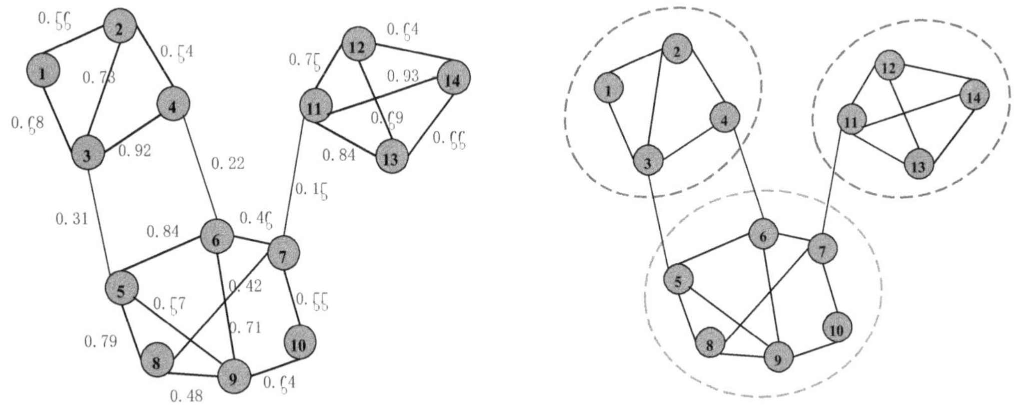

(a) User similarity network.

(b) Communities.

Figure 6: An example of the user similarity network and the community detection results.

follows:

Definition 1. (Operator ⊗). When velocity V is multiplied by a constant c, it will generate a random number within the range of $[0, 1]$. If the random number is less than c, then the result is V, otherwise the result is 0.

$$c \otimes V = \begin{cases} V, & rand(0,1) < c \\ 0, & others \end{cases} \tag{7}$$

Definition 2. (Operator ⊕). This operator can be applied in adding velocity and velocity or adding position and velocity. The result of adding V_1 and V_2 is either V_1 or V_2:

$$V_1 \oplus V_2 = \begin{cases} V_1, (V_1 \neq 0 \& V_2 = 0)\ or (V_1, V_2 \neq 0 \& rand(0,1) < 0.5) \\ V_2, others \end{cases} \tag{8}$$

When updating the individual's position, the current position is obtained by adding previous position and current velocity. If current velocity is 0, then the position stays unchanged. If current velocity does not equal to 0, then swap the position and velocity of the individual to update the position.

$$X_1 \oplus V_1 = \begin{cases} X_1, & V_2 = 0 \\ X_1 \leftrightarrow V_1, & V_1 \neq 0 \end{cases} \tag{9}$$

Definition 3. (Operator ⊖). This is the inverse operation of *Operator* ⊕, and it is suitable for the subtraction of two positions. When position X_1 is not equal to X_2, the result is X_1, otherwise the result is 0.

$$X_1 \ominus X_2 = \begin{cases} X_1, & X_1 \neq X_2 \\ 0, & X_1 = X_2 \end{cases} \tag{10}$$

where $rand(0, 1)$ is a random number within $(0, 1)$, ω and c are constants.

3.3 Fitness Function of NDPSO Algorithm

Newman proposed modularity to measure the quality of community structure in 2006 [11]. The value of modularity is in the range of [0,1], and large modularity represents obvious community structure. Since the user similarity network is a weighted network, we use the modularity in [10] as the fitness function:

$$Q = \frac{1}{2m} \sum_{ij} (A_{ij} - \frac{k_i k_j}{2m}) \delta(c_i, c_j) \tag{11}$$

where A_{ij} is edge weight between node i and j, $k_i = \sum_j A_{ij}$ is the sum of edge weights of node i, c_i is the community id of node i. When node i and j are in the same community, $\delta(c_i, c_j) = 1$, otherwise $\delta(c_i, c_j) = 0$.

3.4 CFCD-PSO Algorithm with NDPSO for Community Detection

After some iterations in NDPSO algorithm, the global best individual is obtained. Assuming the global best individual's position is P_g, if the value of P_{gi} is j, then merge node i and node j in the user similarity network. Furthermore, if the value of P_{gj} is k, then node i, j and k are in the same community. NDPSO algorithm will search from the first dimension to the last dimension of the global best individual's position, and the results of community detection are gotten after a certain number of searches (θ). When θ is small, the communities detected are fragmented, and there is a larger number of communities. On the contrary, there are much nodes in each community when θ is large. Hence, too large or too small value of θ can not achieve good results in community detection, and we should choose an appropriate value of θ. The steps of CFCD-PSO algorithm is shown in Algorithm 1.

Algorithm 1: CFCD-PSO algorithm.

Initialize the user-item matrix with information of users, items and ratings;
Calculate the similarities between users, and construct user similarity network;
Initialize a population of m individuals with random velocities and positions;
Set the iteration number *CurCount* to 1;
while *The termination condition is not satisfied* ($CurCount \neq TotalCount$) **do**
    Calculate each individual's fitness value;
    Update the best fitness and best position of the individual;
    Update the best fitness and best position of the population;
    Update the velocity and position of each individual;
    Iteration number (*CurCount*) increases 1;
Get the communities with defined number of searches (θ);
For each user, calculate the predicting score of items based on the user's neighbors within the same community;
Recommend items to users.

4. EXPERIMENT RESULTS AND ANALYSIS

4.1 Dataset and Evaluation Metrics

Movielens dataset is often used to verify the recommendation results. This dataset consists of 100,000 ratings from 943 users on 1682 movies, and the scores of ratings range from 1 to 5. Each user in this dataset has rated at least 20 movies. We split 80% and 20% of the data into training and testing data randomly. Five training sets and five testing sets will be generated. We repeat the experiments with each training and testing set and average the results.

In order to verify the performance of the proposed recommendation algorithm, we compare it with user-based CF algorithm in terms of precision, coverage and efficiency. Precision is to measure the accuracy of the predicted scores of ratings. Mean absolute error (MAE) is the most commonly used precision evaluation [14], which is defined in equation (12):

$$MAE = \frac{\sum_{i=1}^{N} |resultRate_i - testRate_i|}{N} \qquad (12)$$

where $resultRate_i$ is the predicted score of rating, $testRate_i$ is the score of rating in testing set, and N is the total number of ratings. Besides of precision, another evaluation metrics is coverage. In this paper, coverage of prediction is considered as the proportion of the number of ratings which can be predicted by the recommendation algorithm to the total number of ratings.

$$Coverage = \frac{N - failN}{failN} \times 100\% \qquad (13)$$

where $failN$ is the number of failure ratings and N is the number of total ratings. We also use the average runtime of predicting a rating to present the efficiency of the recommendation algorithm.

4.2 Results of Community Detection based on NDPSO Algorithm

In the experiments, population size is 20, total iteration number is 200, c_1 and c_2 are 0.7, and ω is 0.5. The results of community detection using NDPSO algorithm in different value of θ are shown in Table 1. When $\theta = 3, 4$, the 12 communities and 4 communities detected by NDPSO algorithm are shown in Figure 7 & 8. When $\theta = 5$, community 1 in the detection result is the same as community 1 in Figure 8, and community 2 is the merging result of community 2,3,4 in Figure 8.

4.3 Comparisons of User-based CF and CFCD-PSO Algorithm

We compare user-based CF and CFCD-PSO algorithms in the experiments. The number of common ratings (n) between the recommended user and the neighbors, the number of neighbors (K) in user-based CF, and the number of communities ($CNum$) in CFCD-PSO are the parameters in the comparison. The comparison results are shown in Table 2 and Figure 9 & 10 & 11.

As can be seen in Figure 9, the MAEs are in relation to the different number of common ratings, and our proposed algorithm performs better. Because of the high sparsity in user-item rating matrix, the number of co-rated users is very small. While larger number of common ratings can increase accuracy of similarity computation, and can get smaller MAE. In addition, Figure 10 illustrates the coverage of two algorithms. It can be seen that all the results of CFCD-PSO algorithm are higher than those of user-based CF algorithm. Furthermore, Figure 11 shows the average runtime to predict a rating. In the results, CFCD-PSO (CNum=2) has similar efficiency with user-based CF algorithm, and CFCD-PSO algorithm with 4 and 12 communities have the least runtime.

The comparisons show CFCD-PSO algorithm performs better than user-based CF algorithm. Because CFCD-PSO algorithm choose the neighbors within the same community, and the neighbors have very high similarity with the recommended user. Therefore CFCD-PSO algorithm can produce better predictions.

5. CONCLUSION AND FUTURE NETWORK

Recommendation algorithms aim to predict a user's interest on available products and services, which can deal with the problem of information overload. Collaborative filtering is the most commonly used recommendation technique and it mainly employs the user-item rating matrix.

In this paper, we proposed an improved collaborative filtering recommendation algorithm based on community detection which employs the user similarity network. This approach adopts a novel discrete particle swarm algorithm for community detection to reduce the amount of computation in neighbors selection, and then predicts scores of ratings based on communities. Through a series of experiments by Movielens dataset, we have shown our proposed algorithm has excellent performance in precision, coverage and efficiency of recommendation. In the future, we will validate that our proposed algorithm is an effective solution to scalability problem of recommendation.

Table 1: Results of community detection using NDPSO algorithm

θ	Number of communities	Number of users in each community
3	12	83, 57, 69, 143, 110, 278, 96, 31, 24, 29, 13, 20
4	4	136, 313, 69, 427
5	2	516, 427

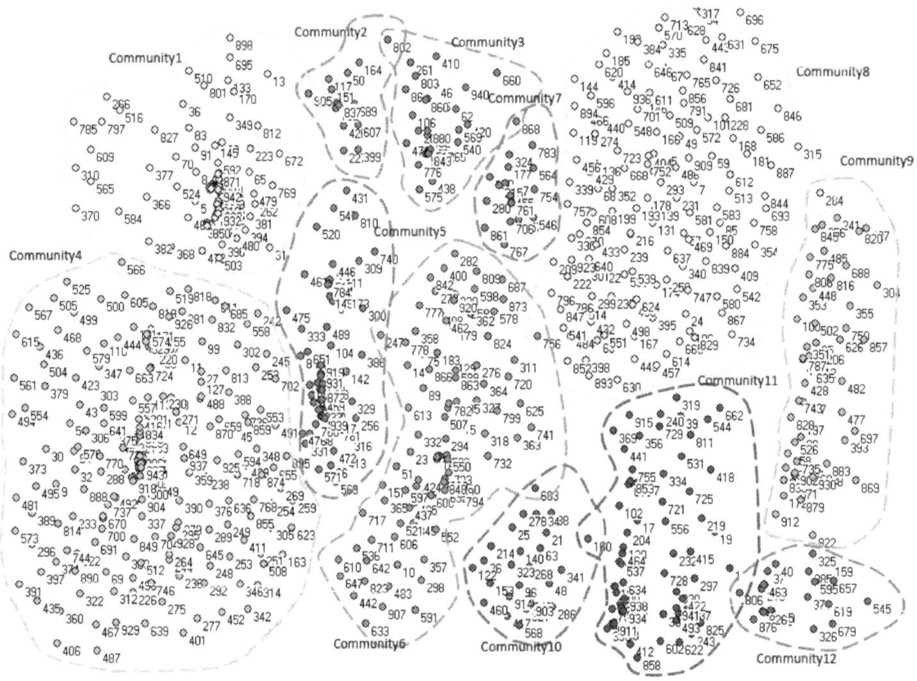

Figure 7: Results of community detection using NDPSO algorithm (12 communities)

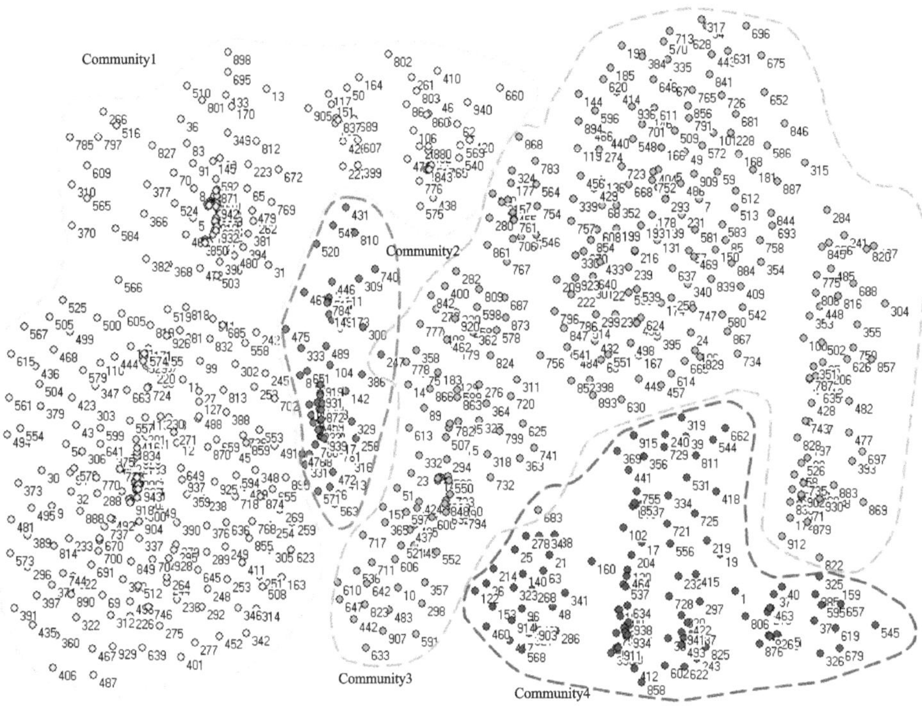

Figure 8: Results of community detection using NDPSO algorithm (4 communities)

Table 2: Comparisons of user-based CF and CFCD-PSO algorithms

Evaluations		User-based CF					CFCD-PSO		
		K=10	K=20	K=40	K=60	K=100	CNum=2	CNum=4	CNum=12
n>0	MAE	0.8596	0.8344	0.8069	0.7870	0.7502	0.7351	0.7462	0.7586
	Coverage(%)	17.14	26.50	43.35	58.10	71.17	88.40	95.05	96.33
	Runtime(s)	55.412	55.445	56.284	56.920	57.780	3.763	5.806	20.986
n>5	MAE	0.8256	0.7962	0.7798	0.7643	0.7375	0.7270	0.7380	0.7538
	Coverage(%)	30.73	45.67	62.04	85.57	93.49	93.51	98.86	99.55
	Runtime(s)	13.238	13.492	13.967	14.626	15.820	3.126	4.695	15.403
n>10	MAE	0.8170	0.7895	0.7684	0.7537	0.7360	0.7230	0.7331	0.7479
	Coverage(%)	39.96	54.68	71.07	89.98	93.67	94.39	98.85	99.60
	Runtime(s)	13.172	13.437	13.956	14.964	15.675	3.060	4.654	14.809
n>20	MAE	0.8095	0.7854	0.7618	0.7486	0.7407	0.7206	0.7299	0.7452
	Coverage(%)	51.61	66.35	79.43	86.56	88.26	94.82	98.68	99.60
	Runtime(s)	13.200	13.672	14.205	14.746	15.695	3.047	4.726	14.940

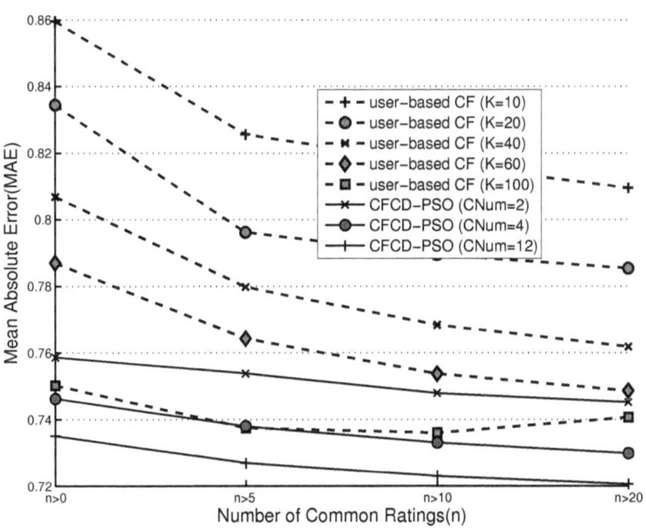

Figure 9: MAE of CFCD-PSO and user-based CF algorithms.

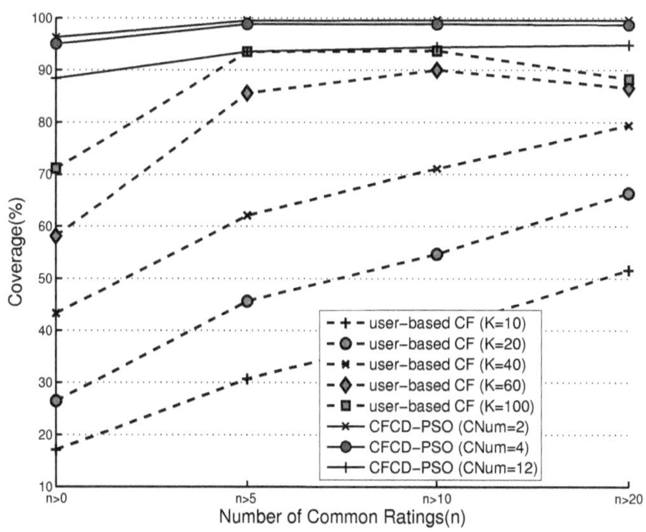

Figure 10: Coverage of CFCD-PSO and user-based CF algorithms.

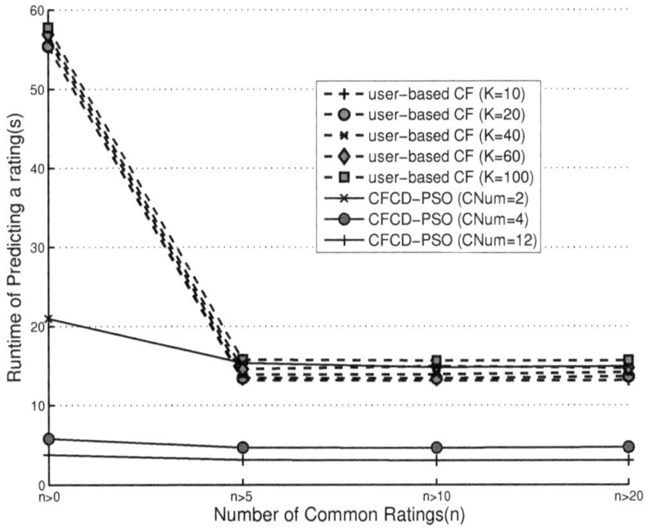

Figure 11: Efficiency of CFCD-PSO and user-based CF algorithms.

Acknowledgements

This paper is supported by National Natural Science Foundation of China (Grant No. 61170164).

6. REFERENCES

[1] G. Adomavicius and J. Zhang. Stability of recommendation algorithms. *ACM Transactions on Information Systems (TOIS)*, 30(4):23, 2012.

[2] X. Cai, M. Bain, A. Krzywicki, W. Wobcke, Y. S. Kim, P. Compton, and A. Mahidadia. Collaborative filtering for people to people recommendation in social networks. In *AI 2010: Advances in Artificial Intelligence*, pages 476–485. Springer, 2011.

[3] Y. Chen and X. Qiu. Detecting community structures in social networks with particle swarm optimization. In *Frontiers in Internet Technologies*, pages 266–275. Springer, 2013.

[4] D. Goldberg, D. Nichols, B. M. Oki, and D. Terry. Using collaborative filtering to weave an information tapestry. *Communications of the ACM*, 35(12):61–70, 1992.

[5] F. Huang and N. Xiao. Particle-swarm-optimization algorithm to discover network community. *Control Theory and Applications*, 28(9):1135–1140, 2011 (in Chinese).

[6] J. Kennedy. Particle swarm optimization. In *Encyclopedia of Machine Learning*, pages 760–766. Springer, 2010.

[7] P. Lops, M. De Gemmis, and G. Semeraro. Content-based recommender systems: State of the art and trends. In *Recommender systems handbook*, pages 73–105. Springer, 2011.

[8] L. Lü, M. Medo, C. H. Yeung, Y.-C. Zhang, Z.-K. Zhang, and T. Zhou. Recommender systems. *Physics Reports*, 519(1):1–49, 2012.

[9] P. A. Nandagawali and J. M. Patil. Community based recommendation system based on products. In *International Conference on Power, Automation and Communication (INPAC)*, pages 150–153. IEEE, 2014.

[10] M. Newman. Communities, modules and large-scale structure in networks. *Nature Physics*, 8(1):25–31, 2012.

[11] M. E. Newman. Modularity and community structure in networks. *Proceedings of the National Academy of Sciences*, 103(23):8577–8582, 2006.

[12] J. O'Donovan and B. Smyth. Trust in recommender systems. In *Proceedings of the 10th international conference on Intelligent user interfaces*, pages 167–174. ACM, 2005.

[13] R. Poli, J. Kennedy, and T. Blackwell. Particle swarm optimization. *Swarm intelligence*, 1(1):33–57, 2007.

[14] G. Shani and A. Gunawardana. Evaluating recommendation systems. In *Recommender systems handbook*, pages 257–297. Springer, 2011.

[15] C. Wongchokprasitti, P. Brusilovsky, and D. Parra-Santander. Conference navigator 2.0: community-based recommendation for academic conferences. 2010.

[16] D. Xiaodong, W. Cunrui, L. Xiangdong, and L. Yanping. Web community detection model using particle swarm optimization. In *Proceedings of the IEEE Congress on Evolutionary Computation (CEC)*, pages 1074–1079. IEEE, 2008.

[17] G. Zhao, M. L. Lee, W. Hsu, W. Chen, and H. Hu. Community-based user recommendation in uni-directional social networks. In *Proceedings of the 22nd ACM international conference on Conference on information and knowledge management*, pages 189–198. ACM, 2013.

[18] Z.-D. Zhao and M.-S. Shang. User-based collaborative-filtering recommendation algorithms on hadoop. In *Third International Conference on Knowledge Discovery and Data Mining*, pages 478–481. IEEE, 2010.

Parameter Estimation in Bayesian Networks Using Overlapping Swarm Intelligence

Nathan Fortier, John Sheppard, and Shane Strasser
Montana State University
Bozeman MT, 59717-3880
nathan.fortier@msu.montana.edu, john.sheppard@cs.montana.edu,
shane.strasser@cs.montana.edu

ABSTRACT

Bayesian networks are probabilistic graphical models that have proven to be able to handle uncertainty in many real-world applications. One key issue in learning Bayesian networks is parameter estimation, i.e., learning the local conditional distributions of each variable in the model. While parameter estimation can be performed efficiently when complete training data is available (i.e., when all variables have been observed), learning the local distributions becomes difficult when latent (hidden) variables are introduced. While Expectation Maximization (EM) is commonly used to perform parameter estimation in the context of latent variables, EM is a local optimization method that often converges to sub-optimal estimates. Although several authors have improved upon traditional EM, few have applied population based search techniques to parameter estimation, and most existing population-based approaches fail to exploit the conditional independence properties of the networks. We introduce two new methods for parameter estimation in Bayesian networks based on particle swarm optimization (PSO). The first is a single swarm PSO, while the second is a multi-swarm PSO algorithm. In the multi-swarm version, a swarm is assigned to the Markov blanket of each variable to be estimated, and competition is held between overlapping swarms. Results of comparing these new methods to several existing approaches indicate that the multi-swarm algorithm outperforms the competing approaches when compared using data generated from a variety of Bayesian networks.

Categories and Subject Descriptors

Swarm Intelligence [**Probabilistic Graphical Models**]: Bayesian Networks

1. INTRODUCTION

Bayesian networks are widely used models for reasoning under uncertainty that provide a compact representation of high-dimensional joint probability distributions. There are two categories of learning related to Bayesian networks, the first involves learning the structure of the network, while the second involves learning the parameters that define the local probability distributions of the network. In the case of complete data, parameter estimation is not difficult, but in practice training data is often incomplete and some hidden variables never have data.

GECCO '15, July 11 - 15, 2015, Madrid, Spain

DOI: http://dx.doi.org/10.1145/2739480.2754793

It is common for latent or hidden variables to be incorporated into Bayesian network models. Latent variables allow the network to encode unobserved effects and can drastically reduce the number of parameters used to specify the model. However, when latent variables are introduced to a Bayesian network, marginal probabilities can no longer be computed efficiently [14]. Also, since the likelihood of the parameters is no longer decomposable, conditional dependencies exist between the optimal parameters for the network's variables.

While several algorithms have been proposed for parameter estimation, these algorithms have a tendency to gravitate towards sub-optimal solutions, resulting in poor generalization for unseen test data, especially when estimating parameters for joint distributions with many conditional dependencies. Also, despite their effectiveness on complex search problems, few authors have applied population based search methods to the problem of parameter estimation.

We propose a new algorithm for latent variable parameter estimation in Bayesian networks based on particle swarm optimization (PSO). Our algorithm assigns a single swarm to each latent variable and its children. Each swarm learns the unknown parameters for the corresponding node's Markov blanket. Swarms with overlapping Markov blankets compete for inclusion in a global parameter set.

We hypothesize that, by assigning a swarm to the Markov blanket of a node, we can exploit conditional independence properties of the network to achieve better performance than single population search methods. To evaluate this hypothesis, we give a traditional single-swarm approach to parameter estimation and compare our multi-swarm approach to single-swarm PSO and several other existing approaches to parameter estimation. We also hypothesize that both of our PSO-based methods will yield results competitive with traditional and state-of-the-art methods based on methods that extend the Expectation-Maximization (EM) algorithm.

2. BACKGROUND

2.1 Bayesian Networks

A Bayesian network is a directed acyclic graph that represents a joint distribution over a set of variables [14]. In a

Bayesian network, each random variable is represented by a node, and edges between nodes represent conditional dependence relationships between the variables. Each root node encodes a prior probability distribution, while each non-root node encodes a probability distribution conditioned on the node's parents. In discrete Bayesian networks, these distributions are represented as conditional probability tables (CPT). For the variables in the network, the probability of any entry in the joint distribution can be computed using the chain rule:

$$P(X_1, ..., X_n) = \prod_{i=1}^{n} P(X_i | X_{i+1}, ..., X_n)$$

Using the local distributions specified by the network, which exploit conditional independence properties of the variables, the joint distribution can be represented equivalently as

$$P(X_1, \ldots, X_n) = \prod_{i=1}^{n} P(X_i | \text{Pa}(X_i)).$$

where $\text{Pa}(X_i)$ denotes the parents of X_i.

In a Bayesian network, the Markov blanket of a node consists of the node's parents, children, and children's parents. A variable X_i is conditionally independent of all other variables in the network given its Markov blanket.

$$\{X_i \perp (\mathbf{X} \backslash (\{X_i\} \cup MB(X_i))) \,|MB(X_i)\}$$

An example illustrating the concept of a Markov blanket is shown in Figure 1. Figure 1(a) shows the Markov blanket of d_3, Figure 1(b) shows the Markov blanket of d_5, and Figure 1(c) shows the Markov blankets of both d_3 and d_5. In the example, nodes in the Markov blanket of d_3 and nodes in the Markov blanket d_5 are shown with a dashed rectangle. In Figure 1(c) nodes that are in the Markov blankets of both d_3 and d_5 (namely c and d_4) are shown to be inside both dashed rectangles, thus indicating an overlap. We will exploit these overlaps later.

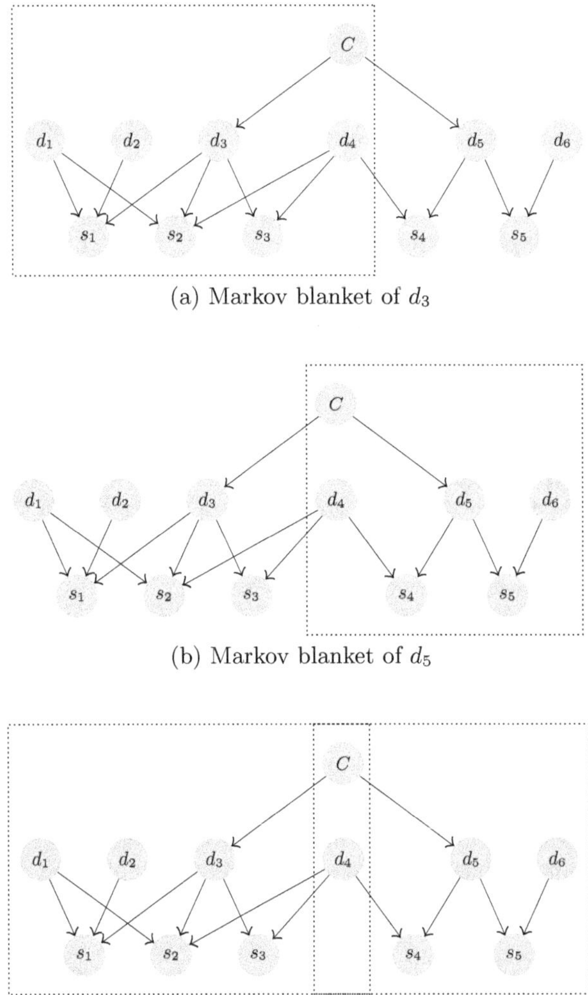

(a) Markov blanket of d_3

(b) Markov blanket of d_5

(c) Overlap of Markov blankets for d_3 and d_5

Figure 1: Markov blanket example

2.2 Particle Swarm Optimization

Particle Swarm Optimization is a population based search technique proposed by Kennedy and Eberhart [4] in 1995, which is inspired by the behavior of bird flocks and fish schools. The pseudocode for PSO is presented in Algorithm 1. In PSO, the population is initialized with a number of random solutions called particles. Each particle contains a position vector that encodes a potential solution in the search space and a velocity vector that defines how the particles will move through the search space. Each particle tracks the coordinates in the search space associated with the best solution it has found so far. These coordinates are called the personal best position of the particle and denoted p_i for the ith particle. The algorithm also keeps track of the overall best solution found so far by any particle in the swarm. This is called the global best position and is denoted p_g.

Typically, both position and velocity are defined as vectors of real numbers. The search process updates the position vector of each particle based on that particle's corresponding velocity vector. These velocity vectors are updated at each iteration based on the fitness of the states visited by the particles. Eventually all particles should move closer to a local optimum in the search space.

3. RELATED WORK

There have been prior methods applying swarm and evolutionary based methods to Bayesian networks. These methods include work like learning Bayesian network structures using Ant Colony Optimization [17] and abductive inference using PSO [8]. However, to our knowledge, no work has been published using PSO or multi-population methods for parameter estimation. In this next section, we discuss work related to parameter estimation and multi-population optimization algorithms

3.1 Parameter Estimation

A number of algorithms have been developed for parameter estimation. The most common algorithm for parameter estimation is Expectation Maximization (EM) [14]. The algorithm begins with an initially random parameter assignment and repeatedly executes the expectation and maximization steps. During the expectation step, the algorithm fills in the missing values using the current parameter estimates of the model. This way, a set of data can be generated with values corresponding, not only to the observable vari-

Algorithm 1 Particle Swarm Optimization

```
repeat
  for each particle position x_i ∈ P do
    Evaluate position fitness f(x_i)
    if f(x_i) > f(p_i) then
      p_i = x_i
    end if
    if f(x_i) > f(p_g) then
      p_g = x_i
    end if
    v_i = ωv_i + U(0, φ_1) ⊗ (p_i − x_i) + U(0, φ_2) ⊗ (p_g − x_i)
    x_i = x_i + v_i
  end for
until termination criterion is met
```

ables but to the hidden variables as well. The maximization step uses the resulting completed data set to find a new maximum likelihood estimate of the probability estimates for those hidden variables. Unfortunately, since the EM algorithm is a local search method, this process often converges to sub-optimal parameters and even small changes to the initial parameters can change the local optima found by the algorithm significantly. Also, the expectation step can often be computationally expensive since it must estimate the joint distribution for each data point.

Several authors have developed enhanced versions of EM in terms of both computational complexity and quality of learned parameters. In 1990 Wei and Tanner proposed a randomized EM algorithm in which the expectation step is approximated using Monte Carlo sampling [21]. In this approach, the data is completed by sampling from the conditional distribution of the missing data for each data point. The expectation is then approximated as the Monte Carlo average. The performance of Monte Carlo EM (MCEM) is often comparable to that of traditional EM and the algorithm has been shown to perform well even when a single sample is drawn for each data-point[2].

In 2002, Elidan *et al.* used data perturbation to improve upon the quality of the local maxima reached by EM [7]. Their algorithm allows EM to escape local maxima by perturbing the training data, thereby forcing the algorithm to explore new ascent directions. This work evaluates the effectiveness of both random data perturbation and adversarial data perturbation, in which the data is modified to directly challenge the current parameter estimates.

In 2005, Elidan and Friedman proposed the information bottleneck EM algorithm for learning both the parameters and the structure of Bayesian networks in the presence of incomplete data [6]. This approach is based on the information bottleneck framework and involves grouping observed variables by mutual information and then creating a hidden variable for each group.

More recently, EM has been combined with population based approaches to improve the quality of learned parameters. In 2006, Jank proposed a genetic algorithm version of EM (GAEM) based on MCEM. In this algorithm, each individual in the population encodes a set of parameter estimates. The fitness of an individual is the approximate probability of the data given the parameters as computed by a single iteration of MCEM[13].

Another variant of EM based on evolutionary computation was proposed by Mengshoel *et al.* in 2012 [15]. This algorithm is described as an age-layered EM (ALEM) approach that discards low likelihood runs before convergence. This algorithm maintains a population of individuals that represent EM runs. The population is then divided into a set of layers, each with a user-defined age limit. Once the number of iterations for an individual EM run exceeds this limit, the individual is removed from the layer and, if the likelihood of the data given the parameters is high enough, the individual is moved to the next layer.

3.2 Multi-population Algorithms

Several authors have proposed multi-population genetic algorithms (GA) [1, 19, 22, 23]. These include island models, in which several subpopulations are maintained by the genetic algorithm, and members of the populations are exchanged through a process called migration. These methods have been shown to obtain better quality solutions than traditional GAs [23] when applied to the problems of neural network parameter learning, the traveling salesman problem, and several deceptive problems proposed by Goldberg *et al.* [11]. Because the sub-populations maintain some independence, each island can explore a different region of the search space while sharing information with other islands through migration. This improves genetic diversity and solution quality [22].

Van den Bergh and Engelbrecht developed several multi-population PSO methods for training multi-layer feed-forward neural networks [20]. These methods include NSPLIT in which there is a single particle swarm for each neuron in the network, and LSPLIT in which there is a swarm assigned to each layer of the network. The authors claim that splitting the swarms in this way results in a finer-grained credit assignment, reducing the possibility of neglecting a potentially good solution for a specific component of the solution vector. The results obtained by Van den Bergh and Engelbrecht indicate that these algorithms outperform traditional PSO methods specifically on neural network training problems.

Recently a new distributed approach to improve the performance of the PSO algorithm has been explored where multiple swarms are assigned to overlapping subproblems. This approach is called Overlapping Swarm Intelligence (OSI) [10, 12, 16]. In OSI each swarm searches for a partial solution to the problem, and solutions found by the different swarms are combined to form a complete solution once convergence has been reached. Where overlap occurs, communication and competition take place to determine the combined solution to the full problem.

Haberman and Sheppard first proposed OSI as a method to develop an energy-efficient routing protocol for sensor networks that ensures reliable path selection while minimizing the energy consumption during message transmission [12]. In this approach a swarm is associated with each node in the sensor network, and each swarm consists of a particle for its corresponding node and the particles for all of the node's immediate neighbors. The particles encode the cost estimate of sending a messing along one of the outgoing edges of the node. Using this method, the swarm for a given node overlaps with its neighboring swarms. This algorithm was shown to be able to extend the life of the sensor networks and to perform significantly better than current energy-aware routing protocols.

Ganesan Pillai and Sheppard extended the OSI method to learn the weights of deep artificial neural networks [16].

This algorithm separates the structure of the network into paths where each path begins at an input node and ends at an output node. Each of these paths is associated with a swarm that learns the weights for that path of the network. A common vector of weights is maintained across all swarms to describe a global view of the network. This vector is created by combining the weights of the best particles in each of the swarms. This method was shown to outperform the backpropagation algorithm, a traditional single-swarm PSO algorithm, and both NSPLIT and LSPLIT on deep networks. A distributed version of this approach was developed subsequently by [10].

Following the success of OSI on training deep neural networks, Fortier *et al.* adapted the OSI to yield a method for both partial and full abductive inference in Bayesian Networks [8]. In this approach, multiple swarms are used to find the most probable state assignments for a Bayesian network given the evidence. Each node in the network is associated with a swarm that learns the state assignments for its Markov blanket. Swarms periodically communicate and compete for inclusion in the final set of most probable state assignments.

In 2014, a method for learning the structure of Bayesian classifiers was proposed by Fortier *et al.* [9]. In this work, a swarm is assigned to each node in the network, and the swarm learns the parent and child edges for that node. Swarms then compete for inclusion in a global network structure.

4. APPROACH

We describe two algorithms for parameter estimation in Bayesian networks using PSO. The first uses a traditional single swarm approach to solve the problem, while the second uses a multi-population variant of PSO based on OSI.

4.1 Traditional Particle Swarm Optimization

Since PSO has not been applied to parameter estimation in Bayesian networks, we have developed both a single swarm and and OSI-based approach to the problem, thus allows us to compare these two methods in terms of the quality of learned parameters. For the single swarm approach, each particle's position vector x_i is a d-dimensional vector of real numbers where $x_i \in [0,1]^d$, d is the number of unknown parameters in the network, and initially each component of x_i is drawn from a uniform probability distribution $U(0,1)$. Each value corresponds to a parameter in the conditional distribution of a missing variable or the child of a missing variable and the size if this vector is equal to the number of parameters to be estimated.

For some variable A in the network, let $x_{a|\text{Pa}(A)}$ be the value in a particle's position vector that encodes the likelihood of $A = a$ given some state assignment to the parents of A, $\text{Pa}(A)$. During fitness evaluation, $x_{a|\text{Pa}(A)}$ is normalized to compute the particle's estimate of the probability $P(a|\text{Pa}(A))$ as follows:

$$P(a|\text{Pa}(A)) = \frac{x_{a|\text{Pa}(A)}}{\sum_{a' \in A} x_{a'|\text{Pa}(A)}}$$

The parameters for each variable being learned can be computed from the particle's position in this way.

If a variable is present in the data and none of its parents are latent variables, we estimate its parameters directly based on frequency. Given some data-set D we can estimate any joint probability over the observed variables as

$$P(x_1, x_2, ..., x_n) = \frac{\sum_{d \in D} \mathbf{1}_d(x_1, x_2, ..., x_n) + \alpha}{|D| + \alpha z}$$

where

$$z = \prod_i^n |Val(X_i)|$$

In the above equations, $\mathbf{1}_d$ is an indicator function for a data point d, $Val(X)$ is the set of possible values for variable X, and $\alpha > 0$ is a smoothing parameter. Using the above joint probability estimate we can compute any conditional probability over a subset of the observed variables as follows:

$$P(x|\text{Pa}(x)) = \frac{P(x, \text{Pa}(x))}{P(\text{Pa}(x))}$$

Because these probabilities can be computed directly, PSO will not optimize the parameters for observed variables with no latent parents.

Once the parameters have been computed, each particle's fitness is evaluated. To compute the fitness of a set of parameters we use variable elimination to calculate the log likelihood of the data D given the parameters Θ.

$$L(D|\Theta) = \log P(D|\Theta). \tag{1}$$

Since performing variable elimination can be computationally expensive, it may be necessary to sample from the training data to obtain a smaller dataset S. The log likelihood of this reduced data set can then be used as the fitness function. Alternatively, an approximate inference method such as importance sampling can also be used. After computing the fitness for a particle, its position and velocity are updated as shown in Algorithm 1.

4.2 Overlapping Swarm Intelligence

We also developed a multi-swarm approach to parameter estimation based on OSI. In this approach, a swarm is assigned to each latent variable, and each child of a latent variable. Each variable's corresponding swarm learns the parameters associated with that variable's Markov blanket using PSO. This representation is advantageous since every node in the network is conditionally independent of all other nodes when conditioned on its Markov blanket.

Figure 2 shows an example network with a single hidden variable L where the nodes whose parameters are learned by a particular swarm are indicated by a dashed rectangle. For this network, the algorithm maintains three swarms: one for the hidden variable L, and one for each of its children, C and D. Figure 2(a) shows that parameters will be learned by swarm S_C, which covers nodes L and C; 2(b) shows that parameters will be learned by swarm S_D, which covers nodes L and D; and Figure 2(c) shows that parameters will be learned by swarm S_L, which in this case covers the nodes in $S_C \cup S_D$. If C and D had children, then S_C and S_D would have included those children while S_L would not. Note that the parameters associated with nodes A and B are not learned by any of the swarms, as these parameters can be estimated directly using the frequency based approach described in the previous section.

The pseudocode for our approach is shown in Algorithm 2. The algorithm is split into two main loops that are executed repeatedly until some termination criterion is met.

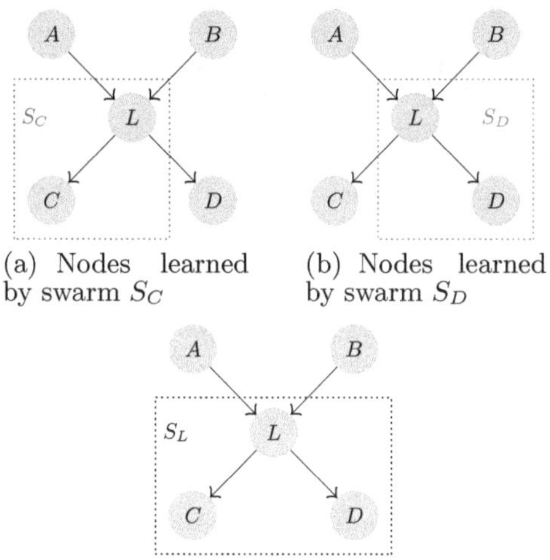

(a) Nodes learned by swarm S_C

(b) Nodes learned by swarm S_D

(c) Nodes learned by swarm S_L

Figure 2: Swarm assignment example

The first iterates over each of the swarms, evaluating the fitness of the corresponding particles, while the second holds a competition between the best particles in the swarms to update a global set of network parameters. This set of initially random global parameters is used for inter-swarm communication.

Each particle's position x_i is defined by a d-dimensional vector of continuous values where $x_i \in [0,1]^d$, where d is the number of parameters to be learned by the particle's swarm. Each position value encodes a likelihood value for the probability distribution of a node in the swarm's Markov blanket, thus each particle encodes the parameter estimates for part of the network. As in the traditional PSO algorithm, the log-likelihood of the data given the parameters is used to evaluate the fitness of each particle.

For some swarm s, let $M(s)$ be the set of variables in the Markov blanket associated with s. Let $\Theta_g = \{\theta_{g,v_1}, \ldots, \theta_{g,v_n}\}$ be the set of CPTs for all variables $v_1, \ldots, v_n$ in the network. Let $\Theta_p = \{\theta_{p,v} | v \in M(s)\}$ be the set of CPTs encoded by the position vector of particle p in swarm s. A new full parameter set $\Theta_{g,p}$ can be constructed by inserting Θ_p into Θ_g as follows:

$$\Theta_{g,p} = \Theta_p \cup \Theta_g \backslash \{\theta_{g,v} | v \in M(s)\}$$

We use the log likelihood of the data given the parameters $\Theta_{g,p}$ as the fitness for the particle p.

$$f(p) = L(D|\Theta_{g,p})$$

This function defines the fitness of particle p as the log likelihoods of the data given the global parameters Θ_g, when the parameter estimates encoded in p are substituted into Θ_g.

When multiple swarms learn the parameters for a given node, (such as c and d_4 in Figure 1) these swarms are said to overlap. After each iteration of the algorithm, overlapping swarms compete to determine which parameter estimates to include for each entry in the CPTs. This competition is held between the parameter estimates encoded in the personal best particles of each swarm. The parameters resulting in the highest log-likelihood are selected for inclusion in the global parameter set. Thus in the example presented in Figure 1, the swarms associated with d_3 and d_5 would compete to determine which parameter values are assigned to the nodes c and d_4.

Algorithm 2 Overlapping Swarm Intelligence

Randomly initialize Θ_g
Initialize particles in each swarm

repeat
  for each swarm s **do**
    for each particle, $p \in s$ **do**
      Construct $\Theta_{g,p}$
      Calculate particle fitness $f(p)$
      if $f(p) >$ p's personal best fitness **then**
        Update p's personal best position and fitness
      end if
      if $f(p) >$ the global best fitness **then**
        Update global best position and fitness for s
      end if
      Update p's velocity and position
    end for
  end for

  for each incomplete variable v in the network **do**
    Let the set of swarms $S = \{s | v \in MB(s)\}$
    for each parameter $z \in \theta_{g,x}$ **do**
      $z \leftarrow Compete(S, z)$
    end for
  end for
until termination criterion is met

return Θ_g

Algorithm 3 $Compete(S, z)$

$L_{best} \leftarrow -\infty$
for each swarm $s \in S$ **do**
  Let p_g be the most fit particle in s
  Let w_z be the parameter estimate for z within p_g
  Insert w_z into Θ_g
  if $L(D|\Theta_g) > L_{best}$ **then**
    $L_{best} \leftarrow L(D|\Theta_g)$
    $w_{best} \leftarrow w_z$
  end if
end for
return w_{best}

5. EXPERIMENTS

To test the performance of our algorithms, several experiments were performed using data generated from networks in the Bayesian Network Repository [18]. We compared our algorithms to four competing approaches to parameter estimation: EM, Monte-Carlo EM (MCEM), Genetic Algorithm EM (GAEM), and Age-Layered EM (ALEM) [13, 14, 15, 21].

5.1 Methodology

For these experiments, we chose networks with gradually increasing numbers of parameters to evaluate the effect of network complexity on performance, in terms of log likelihood. For each network, we used forward sampling to generate 2000 data points and then removed the data for some of the nodes, thereby simulating the presence of latent variables.

To evaluate the effect of latent variable structure on performance, we repeated the above sampling procedure for each network using two latent variable sets. The first set of data was generated using a latent variable architecture with a number overlapping Markov blankets, while the second was generated using latent variables with fewer overlapping Markov blankets. A cross-reference to the network information and latent variable configurations for the datasets is shown in Table 1. Datasets annotated with "O" were generated from networks with a greater number of overlapping latent variable structures, when compared to the datasets annotated with "I". We estimate the amount of overlap as the average number of nodes learned by each swarm:

$$\text{Overlap} = \frac{\sum_{s \in S} N(s)}{|S|}$$

where $N(s)$ is the number of nodes learned by swarm s. Note that since we are calculating Overlap based only on the swarms, this measure will differ on the same network depending on which variables are identified as being latent. We found that all of the networks with a greater number of overlapping latent variable structures had Overlap ≥ 3.

For our algorithm, six particles were assigned to each subswarm. For the other population based approaches, the total number of individuals was six times the number of incomplete nodes, to ensure that all population based algorithms had the same total number of individuals. For both swarm-based algorithms ϕ_1 and ϕ_2 were set to 1.49618, while ω was set to 0.7298. Eberhart and Shi empirically determined that these are good parameter choices for ω, ϕ_1, and ϕ_2 [5]. For MCEM, 400 samples were used during the expectation step.

To evaluate the effect of sampling from the dataset during fitness evaluation, we compared two versions of OSI. In the first, the entire training set was used during fitness evaluation, while the second version of OSI evaluated the parameters using a subset of the training data, containing $\frac{1}{3}$ of the original data points that were sampled at random during each fitness calculation. We denote the sampling based OSI algorithm as OSI-S.

To evaluate the performance of these algorithms, each data set was divided into training and testing data using a 5×2 cross-validation procedure, as recommended by Dietterich [3]. The log likelihoods for the best parameters found in each run were averaged over the runs for each algorithm. We compared the average log likelihoods of the algorithms using a paired t-test with a confidence interval of 95% to evaluate statistical significance.

5.2 Results

Table 2 shows the average log likelihoods for each algorithm and network configuration. Bold values indicate that the corresponding algorithm's performance is statistically significantly better than the competing algorithms. If two algorithms tied on the significance testing, both values are bolded.

On the networks with greater overlap, both OSI algorithms were statistically significantly better than all the other algorithms. OSI performed the best on Child-O, Alarm-O, Win95-O, and Hepar2-O networks while OSI-S did better on the Sachs-S and Insurance-O networks. MCEM was the worst performing algorithm on the Sachs-O and Hepar2-O networks. On the Child-O, Alarm-O, and Insurance-O, PSO was the worst performing algorithm while GAEM was the worst on the Win95-O network. Neither MCEM or GAEM outperform traditional EM on any of these networks.

On the networks with less overlap, OSI outperformed all other algorithms. However, while OSI and OSI-S were statistically significantly better than all the other algorithms on all networks, on the Alarm-I network, OSI was also statistically significantly than OSI-S. Additionally, OSI was only outperformed by OSI-S on the Insurance-I network. MCEM was the worst performing algorithm on the Sachs-I network while PSO performed the worst on the Child-I, Alarm-I, and Insurance-I network. For the Win95-I and Hepar-I networks, GAEM was the worst performing algorithm. EM was only outperformed by MCEM on the Hepar2-I network. On all other networks, EM outperformed MCEM and GAEM.

Finally, we observed that for three of the six networks, the gap between EM and OSI is much larger when the Markov blankets of the latent variables have greater overlap. Additionally, the performance of the OSI algorithms is worse when there was less overlap over the Markov blankets.

5.3 Discussion

The paired t-tests on the log likelihoods indicate that OSI performs better than the competing methods for all generated datasets. While PSO has consistently worse log likelihood than EM, OSI outperforms both EM and PSO on all datasets. Although ALEM managed to outperform traditional EM for most of the data-sets, the improvement was small compared that of OSI. Neither MCEM or GAEM outperform traditional EM, this is likely a result of the error introduced by the approximate Monte-Carlo based expectation step. The results also show that using a randomly sampled subset of the training data for fitness evaluation does not have a significant impact on the performance of OSI in terms of log likelihood for most datasets.

Although OSI outperforms EM and ALEM even when there is little overlap between the Markov blankets of latent variables, for half of the networks, the gap between the log likelihoods of OSI and EM were even larger when the latent variables had greater overlap between their Markov blankets. This is evidence that the improved performance obtained by OSI is due to the representation of each swarm being based on the Markov blankets and the corresponding competition that occurs between overlapping swarms. Recall that each variable is conditionally independent of all other variables in the network given its Markov blanket. By defining each variable's swarm to cover its Markov blanket, we ensure that the swarm learns the corresponding parameters for all variables upon which that variable may depend.

The difference in log-likelihood when overlap is varied is particularly large for the Sachs and Hepar2 networks. This may be because of the large difference in the overlap metric between the two configurations of the networks. However, we do not see similar results for the Win95 network, which has the most extreme difference in overlap between the two configurations. It appears that the effect of overlap on the performance of OSI could vary between networks, but further experiments must be performed to verify this claim and determine the effect of overlap on OSI's performance.

There are several additional advantages provided by our multi-swarm approach that may explain why our method outperforms competing approaches, even when there is little

Table 1: Network Statistics

Network	Params	Nodes	Label	Latent Variables	Overlap
Sachs	178	11	O	PKA, Raf, Erk	3.57
			I	PIP3, Raf, Erk	2.33
Child	230	20	O	LungParench, HypDistrib, HypoxiaInO2, ChestXray	3.00
			I	LVH, HypDistrib, Sick, CO2	2.11
Alarm	509	37	O	VENTLUNG, INTUBATION, SAO2, CATECHOL	3.20
			I	CO, VENTALV, LVEDVOLUME, VENTTUBE	2.64
Win95	574	76	O	NtGrbld, LclGrbld, DSLCLOK, AppData, DSNTOK	3.89
			I	TTOK, PSGRAPHIC, CmpltPgPrntd, AppDtGnTm, DSLCLOK	2.33
Insurance	984	27	O	CarValue, ThisCarCost, OtherCarCost, VehicleYear	3.67
			I	ThisCarCost, SeniorTrain, DrivQuality, Cushioning	2.75
Hepar2	1453	70	O	Obesity, Steatosis, RHepatitis, Hepatomegaly	3.89
			I	Obesity, Joints, Encephalopathy, Injections	2.40

Table 2: Comparison against other approaches

Network	EM	MCEM	GAEM	ALEM	PSO	OSI	OSI-S
Sachs-O	-5700.67	-7049.28	-6664.70	-5602.99	-6804.89	**-854.82**	**-834.18**
Child-O	-10598.31	-11706.62	-11477.23	-10519.32	-11751.61	**-3534.98**	**-3574.44**
Alarm-O	-11053.01	-13172.76	-13043.30	-10572.05	-13365.95	**-4797.21**	**-4811.59**
Win95-O	-8951.64	-9387.82	-9505.28	-8786.31	-5542.32	**-5194.31**	**-5814.35**
Insurance-O	-12316.01	-13774.30	-14577.78	-12209.57	-15622.23	**-7575.05**	**-7555.93**
Hepar2-O	-33329.08	-34504.95	-33970.11	-32704.60	-34105.81	**-19213.89**	**-19337.85**
Network	**EM**	**MCEM**	**GAEM**	**ALEM**	**PSO**	**OSI**	**OSI-S**
Sachs-I	-5168.45	−6515.06	-5946.70	-5173.73	-5979.34	**-3110.52**	**-3545.88**
Child-I	-10966.85	-11263.68	-11250.29	-10715.44	-11342.20	**-5118.27**	**-5499.05**
Alarm-I	-11037.85	-13585.07	-13541.31	-10749.36	-13995.45	**-4396.54**	-4761.65
Win95-I	-9294.90	-9792.64	-9861.66	-9081.66	-8630.77	**-5357.83**	**-5490.31**
Insurance-I	-12554.39	-14234.46	-14014.89	-12375.49	−15504.62	**-8942.22**	**-8855.79**
Hepar2-I	-31249.45	-31214.12	-31261.57	-31195.40	-31006.87	**-26198.50**	**-26719.78**

overlap between the Markov blankets of latent nodes. First, since the sub-swarms maintain independence, each swarm can explore a different region of the search space. Second, by splitting the swarms over the nodes of the network, we reduce the possibility of neglecting a potentially good parameter for a specific component of the global network's complete parameter set.

Also, since several swarms learn the parameters for a single variable, OSI allows for greater exploration of the search space and the competition between swarms ensures that the best parameter estimates found by the swarms are used in the global network. It is likely that this increased exploration contributes to the improved performance of OSI when compared to the EM algorithm, which is known to converge to local optima.

While these results are encouraging, more work must be done to empirically verify the effect of conditional dependencies on the optimal overlap structure. One area of improvement is the sampling procedure. It is possible that our the sampling procedure could result in some data points existing in both the training and testing data, thus introducing a bias into our results, but the number of times this occurred was small. In addition, since our goal is to parameterize the distribution with latent variables, one could argue that removing these data points would also bias the results negatively due to under-sampling. In addition, we are currently researching the effect of applying the OSI framework to other stochastic search techniques such as genetic algorithms, differential evolution, and simulated annealing to determine if the benefit of overlap is algorithm specific.

6. CONCLUSIONS

We have presented a swarm-based method for parameter estimation in Bayesian networks. In our approach, a swarm is associated with each hidden/latent variable in the network, and that swarm learns the parameters for its corresponding node. We compared our algorithm to several other approaches to parameter estimation, including a traditional single-swarm PSO. Our results indicate that OSI significantly outperforms the competing approaches on all of the datasets studied in terms of the log likelihood of the data given the parameters. Additionally, we found that, by sampling from the training data during fitness evaluation, we can reduce the computational burden of the algorithm without impacting the quality of learned parameters.

For future work, we will investigate the affect OSI parameters, such as the number particles per sub-swarm and how often competition is performed, have on OSI's performance. Additionally, the traditional OSI algorithm uses a sharing step in which the global solution is used to seed values in other sub-swarms. In this work, the sharing step was left out because it was found to dramatically decrease OSI's performance. More work is needed to investigate why OSI's performance decreased when OSI performed sharing.

Other areas of future work include investigating the existence of optimal swarm overlap structures. In the work presented here, we used the Markov blanket to derive OSI's sub-swarm architecture. We conjecture that, for many optimization problems, optimal OSI sub-swarm architectures exist related to the conditional dependence/epistatic properties of the underlying fitness landscape. We are exploring theoretical avenues to support this claim and are developing procedures to derive the swarm architectures based on a transformed representation of the optimization problem whereby we can determine each variable's Markov blanket. This would then allow us to know how to apply OSI to a large spectrum of optimization problems.

Finally, we are exploring how to use OSI to learn the structure of Bayesian networks. In all of the work presented in this paper, we assumed that the structure of the network was given; however, in many scenarios, the structure of the Bayesian network is unknown and must be learned from data. We plan to adapt OSI to the Bayesian structure learning problem, after which we can then use the work presented here as a way to learn the parameters for that structure. This will give us a OSI algorithm to learn a Bayesian network given only the data.

7. REFERENCES

[1] T. Belding. The distributed genetic algorithm revisited. In *Proceedings of the International Conference on Genetic Algorithms*, pages 114–121, 1995.

[2] G. Celeux and J. Diebolt. A stochastic approximation type EM algorithm for the mixture problem. *Stochastics: An International Journal of Probability and Stochastic Processes*, 41(1-2):119–134, 1992.

[3] T. G. Dietterich. Approximate statistical tests for comparing supervised classification learning algorithms. *Neural computation*, 10(7):1895–1923, 1998.

[4] R. Eberhart and J. Kennedy. A new optimizer using particle swarm theory. In *Proceedings of the Sixth International Symposium on Micro Machine and Human Science*, pages 39–43, 1995.

[5] R. C. Eberhart and Y. Shi. Comparing inertia weights and constriction factors in particle swarm optimization. In *Proceedings of IEEE Congress on Evolutionary Computation*, volume 1, pages 84–88, 2000.

[6] G. Elidan and N. Friedman. Learning hidden variable networks: The information bottleneck approach. In *Journal of Machine Learning Research*, pages 81–127, 2005.

[7] G. Elidan, M. Ninio, N. Friedman, and D. Shuurmans. Data perturbation for escaping local maxima in learning. In *Proceedings of the National Conference on Artificial Intelligence*, pages 132–139, 2002.

[8] N. Fortier, J. Sheppard, and S. Strasser. Abductive inference in bayesian networks using distributed overlapping swarm intelligence. *Soft Computing*, pages 1–21, 2014.

[9] N. Fortier, J. Sheppard, and S. Strasser. Learning bayesian classifiers using overlapping swarm intelligence. In *Proceedings of the IEEE Swarm Intelligence Symposium*, pages 1–8, 2014.

[10] N. Fortier, J. W. Sheppard, and K. G. Pillai. DOSI: Training artificial neural networks using overlapping swarm intelligence with local credit assignment. In *Proceedings of the Joint 6th International Conference on Soft Computing and Intelligent Systems (SCIS) and 13th International Symposium on Advanced Intelligent Systems (ISIS)*, pages 1420–1425, 2012.

[11] D. E. Goldberg and J. H. Holland. Genetic algorithms and machine learning. *Machine learning*, 3(2):95–99, 1988.

[12] B. K. Haberman and J. W. Sheppard. Overlapping particle swarms for energy-efficient routing in sensor networks. *Wireless Networks*, 18(4):351–363, 2012.

[13] W. Jank. The EM algorithm, its randomized implementation and global optimization: Some challenges and opportunities for operations research. In *Perspectives in operations research*, pages 367–392. Springer, 2006.

[14] D. Koller and N. Friedman. *Probabilistic graphical models: principles and techniques.* MIT press, 2009.

[15] O. J. Mengshoel, A. Saluja, and P. Sundararajan. Age-layered expectation maximization for parameter learning in bayesian networks. In *Proceedings of the Fifteenth International Conference on Artificial Intelligence and Statistics*, pages 984–992, 2012.

[16] K. G. Pillai and J. W. Sheppard. Overlapping swarm intelligence for training artificial neural networks. In *Proceedings of the IEEE Swarm Intelligence Symposium*, pages 1–8, April 2011.

[17] K. M. Salama and A. A. Freitas. Learning bayesian network classifiers using ant colony optimization. *Swarm Intelligence*, 7(2-3):229–254, 2013.

[18] M. Scutari. Bayesian network repository. http://www.bnlearn.com/bnrepository/, 2012.

[19] R. Tanese, J. Co-Chairman-Holland, and Q. Co-Chairman-Stout. Distributed genetic algorithms for function optimization. In *Proceedings of the International Conference on Genetic Algorithms*, pages 434–439. University of Michigan, 1989.

[20] F. van den Bergh and A. Engelbrecht. Cooperative learning in neural networks using particle swarm optimizers. *South African Computer Journal*, 26:94–90, 2000.

[21] G. C. Wei and M. A. Tanner. A monte carlo implementation of the EM algorithm and the poor man's data augmentation algorithms. *Journal of the American Statistical Association*, 85(411):699–704, 1990.

[22] D. Whitley, S. Rana, and R. Heckendorn. The island model genetic algorithm: On separability, population size and convergence. *Journal of Computing and Information Technology*, 7:33–48, 1999.

[23] D. Whitley and T. Starkweather. Genitor ii: A distributed genetic algorithm. *Journal of Experimental & Theoretical Artificial Intelligence*, 2(3):189–214, 1990.

Robustness of Ant Colony Optimization to Noise

Tobias Friedrich　Timo Kötzing　Martin S. Krejca　Andrew M. Sutton

Hasso Plattner Institute
University of Potsdam
Potsdam, Germany

ABSTRACT

Recently Ant Colony Optimization (ACO) algorithms have been proven to be efficient in uncertain environments, such as noisy or dynamically changing fitness functions. Most of these analyses focus on combinatorial problems, such as path finding.

We analyze an ACO algorithm in a setting where we try to optimize the simple OneMax test function, but with additive posterior noise sampled from a Gaussian distribution. Without noise the classical $(\mu + 1)$-EA outperforms any ACO algorithm, with smaller μ being better; however, with large noise, the $(\mu + 1)$-EA fails, even for high values of μ (which are known to help against small noise). In this paper we show that ACO is able to deal with *arbitrarily large* noise in a graceful manner, that is, as long as the evaporation factor ρ is small enough dependent on the parameter σ^2 of the noise and the dimension n of the search space ($\rho = o(1/(n(n+\sigma \log n)^2 \log n))$), optimization will be successful.

Categories and Subject Descriptors

F.2 [**Theory of Computation**]: Analysis of Algorithms and Problem Complexity

Keywords

Ant colony optimization; noisy fitness; theory; run time analysis

1. INTRODUCTION

Ant colony optimization (ACO) is a class of randomized general-purpose optimization algorithms inspired by the foraging behavior of ant colonies. ACO has been successfully applied as a heuristic technique for solving combinatorial optimization problems.

In real-world optimization problems, there is sometimes a large degree of uncertainty present due to the complexity of candidate solution generation, noisy measurement processes, and rapidly changing problem environments. Empirically, ACO seems particularly well-suited to uncertain problems due to its dynamic and distributed nature, and in some cases it can outperform classical state-of-the-art approaches on dynamic network routing problems [3]. We will focus on a version of the *Max-Min Ant System* (MMAS, [15]) applied to pseudo-Boolean optimization (i.e. optimization where solutions are coded as bit strings).

Jin and Branke [10] survey a number of sources of uncertainty that randomized search heuristics must often deal with in practice, (1) noisy objective functions, (2) dynamically changing problems, (3) approximation errors in the objective function, and (4) a requirement that an optimal solution must be robust to changes in design variables and environmental parameters that occur after optimization is complete. Arguably, the two most important sources of uncertainty are (1) and (2), namely, *stochastic* problems and *dynamic* problems (see also [1] for a recent survey). In stochastic problems, the objective function value of a search point follows a random distribution, and that distribution does not change over time. In dynamic problems, the evaluation of the fitness is deterministic but changes over time.

In order to address these practical issues, the theoretical analyses of randomized search heuristics under uncertainty has recently gained momentum. For example, a number of recent papers rigorously analyzed the performance of evolutionary algorithms in stochastic environments [2, 9]. For ant colony optimization, a series of papers considered the performance of ACO on single destination shortest paths (SDSP) problems with stochastic weights. This work was initiated by Sudholt and Thyssen [16] and later followed up by Doerr, Hota, and Kötzing [4], who showed that by augmenting the ant system with a re-evaluation strategy on the best-so-far solution, many of the difficulties with noise discovered in [16] could be overcome. Feldmann and Kötzing [7] recently showed that an ant system that uses a fitness-proportional update rule (called MMAS-fp) can efficiently optimize SDSP on graphs with stochastic weights. MMAS-fp is closer to systems that are used by practitioners [15] and is the ant system variant that we analyze in the current paper.

For the optimization of functions over bit strings, analyses of ACO suggest that it often performs worse than evolutionary algorithms and simple hill-climbers in a noise-free setting [13]. On the other hand, ACO can outperform evolutionary algorithms on dynamic problems [12, 14]. So far,

GECCO '15 July 11 - 16, 2015, Madrid, Spain

ISBN 978-1-4503-3472-3/15/07...$15.00

DOI: http://dx.doi.org/10.1145/2739480.2754723

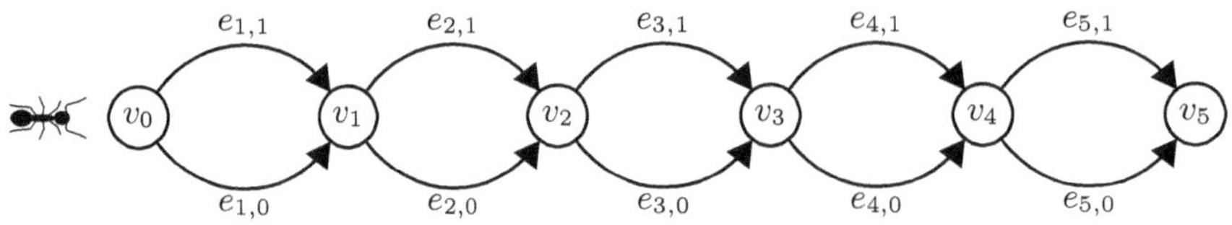

Figure 1: Construction graph for pseudo-Boolean optimization with $n = 5$ bits.

the question of how robust ACO is to noisy evaluation on pseudo-Boolean optimization remains unanswered.

The goal of this paper is to observe the robustness of ACO to noise on a simple objective function. In particular, we are interested in the *scalability* of the run time of the algorithm as a function of noise intensity (measured by variance). We study the algorithm on the well-known OneMax function, the most common starting point for rigorous analyses of randomized search heuristics. In Section 3 we show that robustness can be achieved for additive posterior noise from a Gaussian distribution: for all variances σ^2, there is a parameter setting such that MMAS-fp on OneMax $+\mathcal{N}(0, \sigma^2)$ is successful in time $\sigma^2 \cdot \text{poly}(n)$; thus, we say that MMAS-fp handles Gaussian noise *gracefully*. Such a graceful scaling cannot be achieved by the $(\mu + 1)$ EA, as shown in [8].

A similar statement holds for an ACO algorithm which does not impose nontrivial Max-Min bounds on the pheromone values. This is achieved by not relying on the standard technique of *pheromone freezing* employed by many early works on the mathematical analysis of ACO algorithms, but instead we show that all pheromones *drift* in the right direction (in particular, they will never be close to any pheromone bound on the wrong side of the spectrum); see Corollary 6.

In Section 4 we extend our findings to other noise models and show that we achieve the same robustness also in the presence of other additive noise distributions (which fulfill a certain restriction) as well as for the model of prior noise from [6]. We discuss our findings and conclude the paper in Section 5.

2. PRELIMINARIES

We consider optimizing pseudo-Boolean functions, i.e., functions of type $f\colon \{0,1\}^n \to \mathbb{R}$. In the following, n always denotes the dimension of the solution space $\{0,1\}^n$. For any bit string $x \in \{0,1\}^n$, $f(x)$ is called the *fitness of* x, and we are interested in finding a solution x^* such that $f(x^*)$ is maximal. The fitness function we are going to investigate is OneMax. This function simply returns the amount of ones in a bit string, i.e., $\text{OneMax}(x) = \|x\|_1$. So the unique optimum is the all ones string.

We consider, however, a noisy version of OneMax. The noise perturbing the actual function value will be a Gaussian distributed random variable D with mean 0 and variance σ^2 that is added to the OneMax value. More formally, $\text{OM}_{\sigma^2}(x) := \text{OneMax}(x) + D$ with $D \sim \mathcal{N}(0, \sigma^2)$.

2.1 Algorithms

Our main algorithm of interest is MMAS-fp *(Min-Max Ant System)*, an ACO algorithm with a so-called *fitness-proportional* update rule.

To find an optimal solution, MMAS-fp keeps a vector $\tau \in [\ell, u]^n$, the components of which are called *pheromones*, whereas $0 \leq \ell < 1/2$ and $1 \geq u > 1/2$ are the lower and upper bound for each pheromone, respectively. $\tau^{(t)}$ with $t \in \mathbb{N}$ denotes the pheromone vector in the t-th iteration of the algorithm.

MMAS-fp starts off with every pheromone $\tau_i^{(0)} = 1/2$ and iteratively generates solutions $x^{(t)} \in \{0,1\}^n$ until $x^{(t)}$ is optimal. These solutions $x^{(t)}$ are sampled accordingly to $\tau^{(t)}$ in the manner $\forall i\colon \Pr(x_i^{(t)} = 0) = \tau_i^{(t)} \wedge \Pr(x_i^{(t)} = 1) = 1 - \tau_i^{(t)}$. This is equivalent to a definition of using a simulated ant walk on the construction graph as shown in Figure 1. Afterward, the pheromone vector for the next iteration is updated accordingly to the fitness of the sampled solution, i.e.,

$$\tau_i^{(t+1)} := \begin{cases} \min\left\{\tau_i^{(t)}\left(1 - \rho\frac{f(x^{(t)})}{n}\right) + \rho\frac{f(x^{(t)})}{n}, u\right\} & : x_i^{(t)} = 0, \\ \max\left\{\tau_i^{(t)}\left(1 - \rho\frac{f(x^{(t)})}{n}\right), \ell\right\} & : x_i^{(t)} = 1, \end{cases}$$

for all $i \in \{1, \ldots, n\}$.

The parameter $\rho \in [0, 1]$ is the so-called *evaporation factor* and a parameter of the algorithm. Intuitively, it regulates the impact of the fitness of a sampled solution on the corresponding pheromone update.

Note that MMAS-fp does not keep a best-so-far solution but, instead, always updates its pheromone vector regardless of the quality of the solution sampled. The update is proportional to the fitness of each sampled solution, hence the suffix *fp*. If an updated pheromone is not capped due to the pheromone bounds, we speak of a *normal* update.

In the following, we will denote a pheromone vector $\tau^{(t)}$ simply as τ if we are not interested in t. Likewise, x denotes the solution sampled by τ, and τ' denotes the pheromone vector after the update according to x.

The other algorithm we consider is ACO-fp. It is a special case of MMAS-fp where $\ell = 0$ and $u = 1$, i.e., only trivial pheromone bounds are enforced.

2.2 Tools Used

The proofs in this paper rely heavily on *drift theory*, a tool that allows to give upper and lower bounds on the hitting times of randomly moving processes if there is a bias in the process's motion, the so-called *drift*.

We state two drift theorems that we are going to use in our proofs.

Theorem 1 (Multiplicative Drift [5]). *Let $(X_t)_{t\in\mathbb{N}}$ be non-negative random variables over $\mathbb{R}$, each with finite expectation, and let $T = \min\{t \mid X_t < 1\}$.*

Suppose there exists an $\varepsilon > 0$ such that, for all t,

$$\text{E}(X_t - X_{t+1} \mid X_t, t < T) \geq \varepsilon X_t \,.$$

Then

$$\text{E}(T \mid X_0) \leq \frac{1 + \ln X_0}{\varepsilon} \,.$$

Algorithm 1: MMAS-fp with $\rho \in (0,1]$, for optimizing $f\colon \{0,1\}^n \to \mathbb{R}$

for $i \in \{1,\ldots,n\}$ **do**
  $\tau_i \leftarrow \frac{1}{2}$;
while optimum not found **do**
  for $i \in \{1,\ldots,n\}$ **do**
    $x_i \leftarrow 0$ with probability τ_i, $x_i \leftarrow 1$ with probability $1-\tau_i$;
  for $i \in \{1,\ldots,n\}$ **do**
    if $x_i = 0$ **then**
      $\tau_i \leftarrow \min\left\{\tau_i\left(1-\rho\frac{f(x)}{n}\right)+\rho\frac{f(x)}{n}, u\right\}$;
    else
      $\tau_i \leftarrow \max\left\{\tau_i\left(1-\rho\frac{f(x)}{n}\right), \ell\right\}$;

Theorem 2 (Negative Drift [11]). *Let $(X_t)_{t\in\mathbb{N}}$ be random variables over $\mathbb{R}$, each with finite expectation, let $d > 0$, and let $T = \min\{t\colon X_t \geq d \mid X_0 \leq 0\}$. Suppose there are $s, 0 < s < d$ and $\varepsilon < 0$ such that, for all t,*

1. $\mathrm{E}(X_{t+1} - X_t \mid X_t, t < T) \leq \varepsilon$, *and*

2. $|X_t - X_{t+1}| < s$.

Then, for all $t \in \mathbb{N}$,

$$\Pr(T \leq t) \leq t \exp\left(-\frac{d|\varepsilon|}{16s^2}\right) .$$

The following proposition gives tail bounds for our noise $D \sim \mathcal{N}(0,\sigma^2)$ by using standard estimates of the complementary error function [17].

Proposition 3. *Let D be a zero-mean Gaussian random variable with variance σ^2. For all $t > 0$, we have*

$$\Pr(D < -t) = \frac{1}{2}\operatorname{erfc}\left(\frac{t}{\sigma\sqrt{2}}\right) \leq \frac{1}{2}\exp\left(\frac{-t^2}{2\sigma^2}\right) .$$

3. GAUSSIAN NOISE

In this section we are going to bound the run time of MMAS-fp for optimizing OM_{σ^2}, which will be denoted as f in the proofs.

First off, we bound the noise and thus the difference of two consecutive pheromones with high probability.

Lemma 4. *Consider MMAS-fp optimizing OM_{σ^2}. Then we can bound $|\tau_i - \tau_i'|$ for any pheromone τ_i with high probability as follows:*

$$|\tau_i - \tau_i'| \leq \frac{\rho}{n}(n + \mathcal{O}(\sigma \log n)) .$$

Proof. We make a case distinction for τ_i' and assume $\ell = 0$ and $u = 1$ since capping a pheromone would only make the difference smaller. Because of that, it does not even matter if a pheromone would exceed the bounds $[0,1]$.

1. $\tau_i' = \tau_i\left(1-\rho\frac{f(x)}{n}\right)$:

$$|\tau_i - \tau_i'| = \left|\tau_i - \tau_i\left(1-\rho\frac{f(x)}{n}\right)\right| = \frac{\rho}{n}|\overbrace{\tau_i}^{\leq 1} f(x)| \leq \frac{\rho}{n}|f(x)| .$$

2. $\tau_i' = \tau_i\left(1-\rho\frac{f(x)}{n}\right)+\rho\frac{f(x)}{n}$:

$$|\tau_i - \tau_i'| = \left|\tau_i - \left(\tau_i\left(1-\rho\frac{f(x)}{n}\right)+\rho\frac{f(x)}{n}\right)\right| = \frac{\rho}{n}|\overbrace{(\tau_i - 1)}^{\geq -1} f(x)| \leq \frac{\rho}{n}|f(x)| .$$

We bound $|f(x)| = \big|\|x\|_1 + D\big|$. By Proposition 3 we get:

$$\Pr(D > t) = \Pr(D < -t) \leq \frac{1}{2}\exp\left(-\frac{t^2}{2\sigma^2}\right) .$$

For $t = \omega(\sigma \log n)$ this probability is superpolynomially small. So we can bound $|f(x)| \leq n + \mathcal{O}(\sigma\log n)$ and get

$$|\tau_i - \tau_i'| \leq \frac{\rho}{n}(n + \mathcal{O}(\sigma \log n)) . \qquad \square$$

In the following, let $s = \rho(n + \mathcal{O}(\sigma \log n))/n$, i.e., the greatest difference between two consecutive pheromones, as stated by Lemma 4. We further assume the restrictions $\ell + s < 1/2 < u - s$ for the pheromone bounds.

Also, we always condition on the event that the noise does not exceed the bounds mentioned in the proof of Lemma 4, which holds with high probability in any polynomial number of steps of MMAS-fp. Other runs are discarded as fails.

Lemma 5. *Consider MMAS-fp optimizing OM_{σ^2}. Then, for all pheromone vectors, the drift of each pheromone $\tau_i = b \in [\ell + s, u - s]$ toward 1 is $-b(1-b)\rho/n$.*

Proof. We condition on an arbitrary pheromone vector τ where $\tau_i = b \in [\ell + s, u - s]$, thus, the pheromone is updated normally.

Let A denote the event that x_i was sampled as 1, and consider the expected value of τ_i'. Regardless of A, τ_i decreases. Only in the case of $\overline{A}$ it is additionally increased.

$$\begin{aligned}\mathrm{E}(\tau_i') &= \mathrm{E}\left(\tau_i\left(1-\rho\frac{f(x)}{n}\right)\right) + \mathrm{E}\left(\rho\frac{f(x)}{n} \,\middle|\, \overline{A}\right)\overbrace{\Pr(\overline{A})}^{=\tau_i} \\ &= b + b\frac{\rho}{n}\Big(\mathrm{E}(f(x) \mid \overline{A}) - \mathrm{E}(f(x))\Big) .\end{aligned}$$

We get the negative drift:

$$\begin{aligned}\mathrm{E}(\tau_i' - \tau_i) &= b + b\frac{\rho}{n}\Big(\mathrm{E}(f(x) \mid \overline{A}) - \mathrm{E}(f(x))\Big) - b \\ &= b\frac{\rho}{n}\Big(\mathrm{E}(n - \|x\|_0 + D \mid \overline{A}) - \mathrm{E}(n - \|x\|_0 + D)\Big) \\ &= b\frac{\rho}{n}\Bigg(n - \Big(1 + \sum_{\substack{j\\ j\neq i}} \tau_j\Big) - \Big(n - \big(b + \sum_{\substack{j\\ j\neq i}} \tau_j\big)\Big)\Bigg) \\ &= b(b-1)\frac{\rho}{n} \\ &= -b(1-b)\frac{\rho}{n} .\end{aligned}$$

$\square$

Corollary 6. *Consider MMAS-fp optimizing* OM_{σ^2}*, and let* $b \in [\ell, u]$*, with* $u \geq d$ *and* $d > 1/2 + s$ *being a constant. If* $\rho = o\big(nb(1-b)/\big((n+\sigma\log n)^2\log n\big)\big)$*, then each pheromone reaches values of at least* d *in polynomial time with only superpolynomially low probability.*

Proof. First, note that the drift of Lemma 5 is an upper bound on the drift for pheromones in $(u-s, u]$, in which case the additive term turns out to be smaller than it is in a normal update case.

We can therefore apply Theorem 2 by using the bound given in Lemma 4 and the negative drift of Lemma 5.

$$\begin{aligned}\Pr(T \leq t) &\leq t\exp\left(-\frac{\overbrace{\left(d-\frac{1}{2}\right)}^{>0}b(1-b)\frac{\rho}{n}}{16\frac{\rho^2}{n^2}(n+\mathcal{O}(\sigma\log n))^2}\right)\\ &= t\exp\left(-\frac{(d-\frac{1}{2})nb(1-b)}{16\rho(n+\mathcal{O}(\sigma\log n))^2}\right).\end{aligned}$$

This means that the probability for a single pheromone starting from $1/2$ to reach d in any polynomial amount of steps is superpolynomially small for $\rho = o\big(nb(1-b)/((n+\sigma\log n)^2\log n)\big)$, as given, if that pheromone is in $[\ell+s, u]$.

Now consider a pheromone to be in $[\ell, \ell+s)$. Even the best update could not get that pheromone above $1/2$ because $s = \rho(n+\mathcal{O}(\sigma\log n))/n = o(1)$ with ρ as given. So we can apply the above argumentation.

Note that $s = o(1) < d - 1/2$, as this is what we need to apply Theorem 2. □

Using a union bound argument, we can now say that none of the polynomially many pheromones reaches d as in Corollary 6 in polynomially many steps with high probability.

Lemma 7. *Consider MMAS-fp optimizing* OM_{σ^2} *with* $\rho = o\big(nb(1-b)/\big((n+\sigma\log n)^2\log n\big)\big)$*,* $\ell = o(1/n^2)$*, and* $u > 1/2 + s$*. Consider further that* $k \in [0,n] \cap \mathbb{N}$ *pheromones dropped below* $1/n$ *(*$\geq \ell + s$*). If at least one pheromone is at least* $1/n$*, then the drift of the sum of all pheromones* τ_{total} *is* $\Omega(\tau_{\text{total}}\rho/n^2)$*.*

Proof. In this proof we pessimistically assume pheromones below $1/n$ driftwise (and only driftwise!) as having reached ℓ. Note that, thus, there cannot be any positive drift if $k = n$ since none of the pheromones could drop any lower.

We split up the overall drift of the sum of all pheromones into the (positive) drift (toward 0) of the $n-k$ pheromones that are at least $1/n$ and into the (negative) drift of the k pheromones that are below $1/n$.

Let Y denote the index set of those former $n-k$ pheromones, Z the index set of the latter k, and let K be the event that exactly k pheromones are below $1/n$. The string x^y denotes the bit string consisting only of those elements of x whose index is in Y, and x^z is defined analogously with respect to Z. The sum of pheromones with index in Y is denoted by τ^y_{tot} and the sum of those with index in Z by τ^z_{tot}.

First, we have a look at the $n-k$ pheromones. Each of these pheromones drops and all of them which got a zero sampled for their respective bit position get at most a normal update (in the case of capped pheromones the drift would be even greater).

$$\begin{aligned}&\mathrm{E}(\tau^y_{\text{tot}} - \tau^{y\,\prime}_{\text{tot}} \mid \overbrace{K, \tau^y_{\text{tot}} = b}^{:=B})\\ &\geq \mathrm{E}\left(\tau^y_{\text{tot}} - \left(\tau^y_{\text{tot}}\left(1-\rho\frac{f(x)}{n}\right) + \|x^y\|_0\rho\frac{f(x)}{n}\right)\,\middle|\, B\right)\\ &= \frac{\rho}{n}\mathrm{E}\left(\tau^y_{\text{tot}}f(x) - \|x^y\|_0 f(x) \mid B\right)\\ &= \frac{\rho}{n}\Big(b\mathrm{E}(f(x) \mid B) - \mathrm{E}\left(\|x^y\|_0 f(x) \mid B\right)\Big).\end{aligned}$$

We give bounds for the expected values needed.

$$\mathrm{E}(f(x) \mid B) = \mathrm{E}(n - \|x\|_0 + D \mid B) = n - (b + k\ell),$$

and

$$\begin{aligned}\mathrm{E}(\|x^y\|_0 f(x) \mid B) &= \mathrm{E}(\|x^y\|_0(n - \|x\|_0 + D) \mid B)\\ &= n\mathrm{E}(\|x^y\|_0 \mid B) - \mathrm{E}(\|x^y\|_0\|x\|_0 \mid B)\\ &= nb - \mathrm{E}(\|x^y\|_0\|x\|_0 \mid B).\end{aligned}$$

Let a be a variable ranging over Y; j ranges over all pheromone indices. Let $[\cdot]$ denote the Iverson bracket (indicator function). We make use of Corollary 6.

$$\begin{aligned}&\mathrm{E}(\|x^y\|_0\|x\|_0 \mid B) = \mathrm{E}\left(\sum_a\sum_j [x_a = 0][x_j = 0]\,\middle|\, B\right)\\ &= \sum_a\sum_j \mathrm{E}\left([x_a = 0][x_j = 0] \mid B\right)\\ &= \sum_a\sum_{\substack{j\\ j\neq a}} \mathrm{E}\left([x_a = 0] \mid B\right)\mathrm{E}\left([x_j = 0] \mid B\right) +\\ &\quad\sum_a \mathrm{E}\left([x_a = 0][x_a = 0] \mid B\right)\\ &= \sum_a\sum_{\substack{j\\ j\neq a}} \tau_a\tau_j + \sum_a \tau_a\\ &= \sum_a \tau_a\sum_j \tau_j - \sum_a \tau_a^2 + \sum_a \tau_a\\ &= \sum_a \tau_a\sum_j \tau_j + \sum_a \tau_a(1 - \overbrace{\tau_a}^{\leq d})\\ &\geq b(b + k\ell) + (1-d)b.\end{aligned}$$

Now we can calculate the desired drift.

$$\begin{aligned}&\mathrm{E}(\tau^y_{\text{tot}} - \tau^{y\,\prime}_{\text{tot}} \mid B)\\ &\geq \frac{\rho}{n}\Big(b\left(n - (b + k\ell)\right) - \left(nb - b(b + k\ell) - (1-d)b\right)\Big)\\ &= \frac{\rho}{n}(1-d)b.\end{aligned}$$

For the negative drift, we have to look at τ^z_{tot} and $\tau^{z\,\prime}_{\text{tot}}$. All of the k pheromones where the corresponding bit position was sampled as 1 cannot drop any lower due to our assumption. The remaining of the k pheromones get a normal update in the best case:

$$\tau_{\text{tot}}^{z}{}' \le \|x^z\|_1\ell + \|x^z\|_0\left(\ell\left(1-\rho\frac{f(x)}{n}\right)+\rho\frac{f(x)}{n}\right)$$

$$= \overbrace{\|x^z\|_1\ell + \|x^z\|_0\ell}^{=k\ell} - \|x^z\|_0\ell\rho\frac{f(x)}{n} + \|x^z\|_0\rho\frac{f(x)}{n}$$

$$= k\ell + \frac{\rho}{n}(1-\ell)\|x^z\|_0 f(x)\ .$$

Thus we get:

$$\mathrm{E}(\tau_{\text{tot}}^{z} - \tau_{\text{tot}}^{z}{}' \mid B) \ge \mathrm{E}\left(k\ell - k\ell - \frac{\rho}{n}(1-\ell)\|x^z\|_0 f(x) \,\middle|\, B\right)$$

$$= -\frac{\rho}{n}(1-\ell)\mathrm{E}\left(\|x^z\|_0 f(x) \mid B\right)\ .$$

The remaining estimations follow analogously to the ones beforehand:

$$\begin{aligned}\mathrm{E}(\|x^z\|_0 f(x) \mid B) &= \mathrm{E}\left(\|x^z\|_0(n - \|x\|_0 + D) \mid B\right)\\ &= n\mathrm{E}(\|x^z\|_0 \mid B) - \mathrm{E}(\|x^z\|_0\|x\|_0 \mid B)\\ &= nk\ell - \mathrm{E}(\|x^z\|_0\|x\|_0 \mid B)\ .\end{aligned}$$

Note that a now refers to indices in Z.

$$\begin{aligned}\mathrm{E}(\|x^z\|_0\|x\|_0 \mid B) &= \sum_a \tau_a \sum_j \tau_j + \sum_a \tau_a(1-\tau_a)\\ &\ge k\ell(b + k\ell) + k\ell\,(1-d)\\ &= k\ell\,(b + k\ell + (1-d))\ .\end{aligned}$$

So we get the negative drift:

$$\mathrm{E}(\tau_{\text{tot}}^{z} - \tau_{\text{tot}}^{z}{}' \mid B) \ge -\frac{\rho}{n}(1-\ell)k\ell\,(n - b - k\ell - (1-d))\ .$$

Now we can look at the general drift:

$$\begin{aligned}&\mathrm{E}(\tau_{\text{total}} - \tau_{\text{total}}' \mid B)\\ &\ge \frac{\rho}{n}(1-d)b - \frac{\rho}{n}(1-\ell)k\ell\,(n - b - k\ell - (1-d))\\ &= \frac{\rho}{n}\left((1-d)b - (1-\ell)\left(nk\ell - bk\ell - k^2\ell^2 - (1-d)k\ell\right)\right)\ ,\end{aligned}$$

which we want to be positive.

Recall that we only consider $k \in [0, n-1] \cap \mathbb{N}$. We bound b by $(n-k)/n$ since all these pheromones are at least $1/n$.

Thus, we end up having:

$$(1-d)(n-k)/n - (1-\ell)\Big(nk\ell - (n-k)k\ell/n - k^2\ell^2 - (1-d)k\ell\Big)\ .$$

On inspection one sees that the highest order terms in the minuend are $n/n = 1$ and $-k/n$. Since we want to have a positive drift, $1 > k/n$ must hold. Because we are interested in $k \in [0, n-1] \cap \mathbb{N}$, this does hold.

The highest order term in the subtrahend is $-nk\ell$. It is absolutely largest for $k \in \Theta(n)$, i.e, $n^2\ell$. To avoid any conflict with 1, we need $1 \in \omega(n^2\ell)$, i.e.,

$$\lim_{n\to\infty} \frac{1}{n^2\ell} = \infty\ ,$$

which holds for $\ell = \mathrm{o}(1/n^2)$, as given. This results in the drift being in $\Omega(b\rho/n)$.

Since we want the drift to be expressed in terms of τ_{total}, we need $b\rho/n \ge \varepsilon\tau_{\text{total}}$ to hold for an $\varepsilon > 0$.

We can bound $\tau_{\text{total}} < b + k/n$ by pessimistically assuming all k pheromones below $1/n$ as being $1/n$. So we want $b\rho/n \ge \varepsilon(b + k/n)$ to hold for all valid values of b. This is equivalent to $1/\varepsilon \ge (n + k/b)/\rho$. To make k/b as large as possible we bound $b \le (n-k)/n$, and we get $1/\varepsilon \ge (n + nk/(n-k))/\rho$, where $k/(n-k)$ is maximal for $k = n-1$ (we do not consider $k = n$). This results in $\varepsilon = \mathcal{O}(\rho/n^2)$.

Overall, we finally get a drift of $\Omega(\tau_{\text{total}}\rho/n^2)$. □

Theorem 8. *Consider MMAS-fp optimizing* OM_{σ^2} *with* $\rho = \mathrm{o}(1/(n(n+\sigma\log n)^2\log n))$, $\ell = \mathrm{o}(1/n^2)$, *and* $u > 1/2 + s$. *The algorithm then finds the optimum after* $\mathcal{O}(n^2\log(n)/\rho)$ *steps with high probability.*

Proof. Let T denote the run time of the algorithm when the drift is positive, i.e., $T = \min\{t \in \mathbb{N} \mid \forall i\colon \tau_i^{(t)} < 1/n\}$.

According to Lemma 7, there is a positive drift of the pheromone sum toward 0 of at least $\tau_{\text{total}}\rho/n^2$.

With this multiplicative drift we get an upper bound on the expectation of T using Theorem 1:

$$\mathrm{E}\left(T \,\middle|\, \forall i\colon \tau_i^{(0)} = \frac{1}{2}\right) = \mathcal{O}\left(\frac{1+\log\frac{n}{2}}{\frac{\rho}{n^2}}\right) = \mathcal{O}\left(\frac{n^2\log n}{\rho}\right)\ .$$

Now assume that all pheromones dropped below $1/n$. The probability to sample the optimum now is $(1-1/n)^n \ge (1-1/n)/e$. Thus, the optimum will be sampled in expectation in $en/(n-1) = \mathcal{O}(1)$ many tries.

The overall expected run time is bounded above by the following worst case scenario: the algorithm needs $\mathcal{O}(n^2\log(n)/\rho)$ steps until all pheromones drop below $1/n$. Then the algorithm does not sample the optimum and all pheromones are set back to $1/2$ (that does not actually happen but we are looking at a worst case). As mentioned before, in this scenario, the algorithm would need $\mathcal{O}(1)$ tries to sample the optimum, once the pheromones are low enough. Hence, the algorithm hast to be restarted $\mathcal{O}(1)$ times.

Overall, this results in an expected run time in $\mathcal{O}(n^2\log(n)/\rho)$ with high probability due to us conditioning on the noise being bounded, as stated in Lemma 4. □

Corollary 9. *Consider ACO-fp optimizing* OM_{σ^2}. *If* $\rho = \mathrm{o}(1/(n(n+\sigma\log n)^2\log n))$, *the algorithm finds the optimum after* $\mathcal{O}(n^2\log(n)/\rho)$ *steps with high probability.*

Proof. Recall that the proof Lemma 4 is actually a proof for ACO-fp as well. We can thus argue analogously as in the proof of Theorem 8. The upper bound d is at most 1 because $d \le u \le 1$. The lower bound of $\ell = 0$ for ACO-fp satisfies $\ell = \mathrm{o}(1/n^2)$ as well. □

4. OTHER NOISE MODELS

In this section we consider the optimization of OneMax perturbed by other noise than additive posterior Gaussian noise.

4.1 Posterior Noise

We start with a generalization of Corollary 9 by taking non-Gaussian noise into account, i.e., we optimize OM_D with $\mathrm{OM}_D(x) := \|x\|_1 + D$ and D being a random variable (possibly not Gaussian).

Corollary 10. *Consider MMAS-fp optimizing* OM_D *with* $\ell = \mathrm{o}(1/n^2)$ *and* $u > 1/2 + s$*, where D is a random variable such that, for some* $t^* > 0$ *and all polynomials p, the following holds:*

$$\Pr(|D| > t^*) \leq 1 - \mathrm{o}\left(\frac{1}{p(n)}\right) . \tag{1}$$

If $\rho = \mathrm{o}(1/(n(n+t^*)^2 \log n))$*, then the algorithm finds the optimum after* $\mathcal{O}(n^2 \log(n)/\rho)$ *steps with high probability.*

Proof. The drifts of Lemmas 5 and 7 hold here as well since the noise is additive and posterior and, thus, it cancels out in expectation.

To be able to use Corollary 6, we need to bound $|f(x)|$ with high probability. Because of Equation (1) we can do so, and it follows that any pheromone τ_i reaches values of at least a constant $d > 1/2 + s$ with superpolynomially low probability for $\rho = \mathrm{o}(1/(n(n+t^*)^2 \log n))$.

We can now use an analogous argumentation as in Theorem 8, proving the proposition. □

Corollary 11. *Consider ACO-fp optimizing* OM_D*, where D is a random variable such that, for some* $t^* > 0$ *and all polynomials p, the following holds:*

$$\Pr(|D| > t^*) \leq 1 - \mathrm{o}\left(\frac{1}{p(n)}\right) .$$

If $\rho = \mathrm{o}(1/(n(n+t^*)^2 \log n))$*, then the algorithm finds the optimum after* $\mathcal{O}(n^2 \log(n)/\rho)$ *steps with high probability.*

Proof. We can use the same same proof as for Corollary 10 and argue as in the proof of Corollary 9 that we do not need the special pheromone bounds. □

4.2 Prior Noise

In this section we have a look at the noise model from [6], where $\mathrm{OM}_p(x) := \mathrm{OneMax}(\widetilde{x})$, whereas $\widetilde{x} = x$ with probability $(1-p)$, and $\widetilde{x} = x'$ with $d_{\mathrm{H}}(x, x') = 1$ for each such x' with probability p/n. That means that with probability p a single bit in x gets flipped uniformly at random.

Note that we can bound $|\tau_i - \tau_i'| \leq \rho$ in the same way as we did in the proof of Lemma 4 since $|f(x)| \leq n$. We again assume that $\ell + \rho < 1/2 < u - \rho$.

Lemma 12. *Consider MMAS-fp optimizing* OM_p*. Then, for all pheromone vectors, the drift of each pheromone* $\tau_i = b \in [\ell + \rho, u - \rho]$ *toward 1 is* $-b(1-b)(1-2p/n)\rho/n$*.*

Proof. As the noise does not have any influence on the update of the pheromones and we have a normal update, we get the same basic equation for the desired drift as in Lemma 5. Let A denote the event that x_i was sampled as 1, and condition on any pheromone vector τ where $\tau_i = b \in [\ell + \rho, u - \rho]$.

$$\mathrm{E}(\tau_i' - \tau_i) = b\frac{\rho}{n}\left(\mathrm{E}\left(f(x) \mid \overline{A}\right) - \mathrm{E}(f(x))\right) .$$

Let P denote the event that $\widetilde{x} = x'$ during the evaluation of f, i.e., a bit flipped, and let j and k range from 1 to n.

For $\mathrm{E}\left(f(x) \mid \overline{A}\right)$ we have

$$\begin{aligned}
&\mathrm{E}\left(f(x) \mid \overline{A}\right) \\
&= \mathrm{E}\left(f(x) \mid \overline{A}, \overline{P}\right)(1-p) + \mathrm{E}\left(f(x) \mid \overline{A}, P\right) p \\
&= \left(n - \left(1 + \sum_{\substack{j \\ j \neq i}}\right)\right)(1-p) + \\
&\quad \left(n - \sum_{\substack{k \\ k \neq i}} \frac{1}{n}\left(1 + (1-\tau_k) + \sum_{\substack{j \\ j \neq k \\ j \neq i}} \tau_j\right) - \frac{1}{n}\sum_{\substack{j \\ j \neq i}} \tau_j\right) p .
\end{aligned}$$

And for $\mathrm{E}(f(x) \mid \tau_i = b)$ we get

$$\begin{aligned}
&\mathrm{E}(f(x)) = \mathrm{E}\left(f(x) \mid \overline{P}\right)(1-p) + \mathrm{E}\left(f(x) \mid P\right) p \\
&= \left(n - \left(b + \sum_{\substack{j \\ j \neq i}} \tau_j\right)\right)(1-p) + \\
&\quad \left(n - \sum_{\substack{k \\ k \neq i}} \frac{1}{n}\left(b + (1-\tau_k) + \sum_{\substack{j \\ j \neq k \\ j \neq i}} \tau_j\right) - \right. \\
&\quad \left. \frac{1}{n}\left((1-b) + \sum_{\substack{j \\ j \neq i}} \tau_j\right)\right) p .
\end{aligned}$$

Thus we get

$$\begin{aligned}
&\mathrm{E}\left(f(x) \mid \overline{A}\right) - \mathrm{E}(f(x)) \\
&= -(1-b)(1-p) + \left(\frac{n-1}{n}(b-1) - \frac{1}{n}(b-1)\right) p \\
&= -(1-b)(1-p) - (1-b)\frac{n-2}{n} p \\
&= -(1-b)\left(1 - \frac{2}{n} p\right) .
\end{aligned}$$

Finally, we have a negative drift as desired:

$$\mathrm{E}(\tau_i' - \tau_i) = -b(1-b)\left(1 - \frac{2}{n} p\right)\frac{\rho}{n} .$$

□

Corollary 13. *Consider MMAS-fp optimizing* OM_p*, and let* $b \in [\ell, u]$*, with* $u \geq d$ *and* $d > 1/2 + \rho$ *being a constant. If* $\rho = \mathrm{o}\left(b(1-b)\left(1 - \frac{2}{n}p\right)/(n \log n)\right)$*, then each pheromone reaches values of at least d in polynomial time with only superpolynomially low probability.*

Proof. The proof is basically the same as the one of Corollary 6. Using again Theorem 2, for all $t \geq 0$, the following proposition holds for T as the hitting time of one pheromone reaching a value of at least d:

$$\begin{aligned}
\Pr(T \leq t) &\leq t \exp\left(-\frac{\left(d - \frac{1}{2}\right) b(1-b)\left(1 - \frac{2}{n}p\right)\frac{\rho}{n}}{16\rho^2}\right) \\
&= t \exp\left(-\frac{\left(d - \frac{1}{2}\right) b(1-b)\left(1 - \frac{2}{n}p\right)}{16\rho n}\right) .
\end{aligned}$$

The probability for a single pheromone starting from 1/2 to reach d in any polynomial amount of steps is superpolynomially small for $\rho = \mathrm{o}\left(b(1-b)\left(1 - \frac{2}{n}p\right)/(n \log n)\right)$. □

Again, a union bound argument gives us the guarantees of Corollary 13 for all pheromones.

Lemma 14. *Consider MMAS-fp optimizing* OM_p *with* $\rho = o\left(b(1-b)\left(1-\frac{2}{n}p\right)/(n\log n)\right)$, $\ell = o(1/n^2)$, *and* $u > 1/2 + \rho$. *Consider further that* $k \in [0,n] \cap \mathbb{N}$ *pheromones dropped below* $1/n$ $(\geq l+\rho)$. *If at least one pheromone is at least* $1/n$, *then the drift of the sum of all pheromones* τ_{total} *is* $\Omega(\tau_{\text{total}}\rho/n^2)$.

Proof. We are going to use the same notation as in the proof of Lemma 7. P shall, again, denote the event that the bit flip occurred.

As mentioned before, the kind of noise has no impact on the general form of the drifts. So for the $n-k$ pheromones we have

$$\mathrm{E}(\tau^y_{\text{tot}} - {\tau^y_{\text{tot}}}' \mid B) \geq \frac{\rho}{n}\Big(b\mathrm{E}(f(x) \mid B) - \mathrm{E}\left(\|x^y\|_0 f(x) \mid B\right)\Big).$$

The required expected values can now be calculated:

$$\begin{aligned}\mathrm{E}(f(x) \mid B) &= \mathrm{E}(f(x) \mid B, \overline{P})(1-p) + \mathrm{E}(f(x) \mid B, P)p \\ &= (n-(b+k\ell))(1-p) + (n - \mathrm{E}(\|x\|_0 \mid B, P))\,p\,.\end{aligned}$$

Furthermore, we get

$$\begin{aligned}\mathrm{E}(\|x\|_0 \mid B, P) &= \sum_i \frac{1}{n}\Big((1-\tau_i) + \sum_{\substack{j\\ j\neq i}} \tau_j\Big) \\ &= \frac{1}{n}\sum_i (1-\tau_i + b + k\ell - \tau_i) \\ &= \frac{1}{n}\sum_i (b+k\ell+1) - \frac{2}{n}\sum_i \tau_i \\ &= b + k\ell + 1 - \frac{2}{n}(b+k\ell)\,.\end{aligned}$$

This results in

$$\begin{aligned}\mathrm{E}(f(x) \mid B) &= (n-b-k\ell) + \\ &\qquad p\left(-n+b+k\ell+n-b-k\ell-1+\frac{2}{n}(b+k\ell)\right) \\ &= n-b-k\ell+p\left(\frac{2}{n}(b+k\ell)-1\right)\,.\end{aligned}$$

Now we get for $\mathrm{E}(\|x^y\|_0 f(x) \mid B)$

$$\mathrm{E}(\|x^y\|_0 f(x) \mid B) = nb - \mathrm{E}(\|x^y\|_0 \|\widetilde{x}\|_0 \mid B)\,,$$

and by using Corollary 13

$$\begin{aligned}&\mathrm{E}(\|x^y\|_0 \|\widetilde{x}\|_0 \mid B) \\ &= \sum_a \sum_{\substack{j\\ j\neq a}} \mathrm{E}\left([x_a = 0] \mid B\right)\mathrm{E}\left([\widetilde{x}_j = 0] \mid B\right) + \\ &\qquad \sum_a \mathrm{E}\left([x_a = 0] \mid B\right) \\ &= \sum_a \sum_{\substack{j\\ j\neq a}} \tau_a\left(\tau_j(1-p) + \tau_j p\frac{n-1}{n} + (1-\tau_j)\frac{p}{n}\right) + \sum_a \tau_a \\ &= \sum_a \sum_{\substack{j\\ j\neq a}} \tau_a\left(\tau_j\frac{n-2p}{n} + \frac{p}{n}\right) + \sum_a \tau_a \\ &= \frac{n-2p}{n}\sum_a \sum_{\substack{j\\ j\neq a}} \tau_a\tau_j + \frac{p}{n}\sum_a \sum_{\substack{j\\ j\neq a}} \tau_a + \sum_a \tau_a \\ &= \frac{n-2p}{n}\sum_a \sum_j \tau_a\tau_j - \frac{n-2p}{n}\sum_a \tau_a^2 + \\ &\qquad \sum_a \tau_a + \frac{p}{n}\sum_a \sum_{\substack{j\\ j\neq a}} \tau_a \\ &\overset{b\leq d}{\geq} \frac{n-2p}{n}b(b+k\ell) + \sum_a \tau_a\left(1-\frac{n-2p}{n}d\right) + b\frac{n-1}{n}p \\ &= \frac{n-2p}{n}b(b+k\ell) + b\left(1-\frac{n-2p}{n}d\right) + b\frac{n-1}{n}p\,.\end{aligned}$$

Thus we get

$$\begin{aligned}&\mathrm{E}(\|x^y\|_0 f(x) \mid B) \\ &\leq nb - \frac{n-2p}{n}b(b+k\ell) - b\left(1-\frac{n-2p}{n}d\right) - b\frac{n-1}{n}p\,.\end{aligned}$$

Now we can calculate the desired drift as follows.

$$\begin{aligned}&\mathrm{E}(\tau^y_{\text{tot}} - {\tau^y_{\text{tot}}}' \mid B) \\ &\geq \frac{\rho}{n}\left(b\left(n-b-k\ell+p\left(\frac{2}{n}(b+k\ell)-1\right)\right) - nb + \right. \\ &\qquad \left.\frac{n-2p}{n}b(b+k\ell) + b\left(1-\frac{n-2p}{n}d\right) + b\frac{n-1}{n}p\right) \\ &= \frac{\rho}{n}\left(nb - b(b+k\ell) - nb + b(b+k\ell) + b - \right. \\ &\qquad \left. b\frac{dn-2dp+p}{n}\right) \\ &\geq \frac{\rho}{n}b\,(1-d)\,.\end{aligned}$$

Regarding the negative drift we have

$$\mathrm{E}(\tau^z_{\text{tot}} - {\tau^z_{\text{tot}}}' \mid B) = -\frac{\rho}{n}(1-\ell)\mathrm{E}\left(\|x^z\|_0 f(x) \mid B\right)\,.$$

We also get

$$\begin{aligned}&\mathrm{E}(\|x^z\|_0 f(x) \mid B) = nk\ell - \mathrm{E}(\|x^z\|_0\|\widetilde{x}\|_0 \mid B) \\ &\leq nk\ell - \frac{n-2p}{n}k\ell(b+k\ell) + k\ell\left(1-\frac{n-2p}{n}d\right) + \\ &\qquad k\ell\frac{n-1}{n}p \\ &= k\ell\left(n - \frac{n-2p}{n}(b+k\ell+d) + 1 + \frac{n-1}{n}p\right)\,.\end{aligned}$$

Now we have the negative drift as follows

$$\begin{aligned}&\mathrm{E}(\tau^z_{\text{tot}} - {\tau^z_{\text{tot}}}' \mid B) \\ &\geq -\frac{\rho}{n}(1-\ell)k\ell\left(n - \frac{n-2p}{n}(b+k\ell+d) + 1 + \frac{n-1}{n}p\right).\end{aligned}$$

Taking all the parts together, we get the total drift

$$\begin{aligned}&\mathrm{E}(\tau_{\text{total}} - \tau'_{\text{total}} \mid B) \\ &\geq \frac{\rho}{n}b(1-d) - \frac{\rho}{n}(1-\ell)k\ell\Big(n - \frac{n-2p}{n}(b+k\ell+d) + \\ &\qquad 1 + \frac{n-1}{n}p\Big) \\ &= \frac{\rho}{n}\left(b(1-d) - (1-\ell)k\ell\Big(n - \frac{n-2p}{n}(b+k\ell+d) + \right. \\ &\qquad \left. 1 + \frac{n-1}{n}p\Big)\right)\,,\end{aligned}$$

which we want to be positive.

Again, we only consider $k \in [0, n-1] \cap \mathbb{N}$, and we use $b \geq (n-k)/n$. We thus end up having

$$(n-k)(1-d)/n - (1-\ell)k\ell\Big(n - \frac{n-2p}{n}(b + k\ell + d) + 1 + \frac{n-1}{n}p\Big).$$

The highest order terms are the same as in the proof of Lemma 7, and the drift is again $\Omega(b\rho/n)$. So we can conclude analogously. □

Theorem 15. *Consider MMAS-fp with $\rho = o(1/(n^3 \log n))$, $\ell = o(1/n^2)$, and $u > 1/2 + \rho$ or ACO-fp optimizing OM_p. Both algorithms then find the optimum after $\mathcal{O}(n^2 \log(n)/\rho)$ steps with high probability.*

Proof. The argumentation is exactly as in the proof of Theorem 8 or Corollary 9, respectively, but now we use Lemmas 12, 14, and Corollary 13. The value of ρ has to be changed accordingly using Corollary 13. □

5. DISCUSSION AND SUMMARY

In this work we saw that two simple ACO algorithms on OneMax scale gracefully with noise for Gaussian distributions, i.e., the run time depends only linearly on the variance of the noise. We get similar results for many other noise models and for different ACO algorithms, suggesting that ACO algorithms are generally good for dealing with noise (at least in settings where the underlying fitness function is simple enough, as in the case of OneMax). Many of these settings are not solvable by simple hill climbers [6].

The analysis of meta-heuristics such as ACO on noisy fitness functions is of particular interest because this is one particular area where very few tailored approaches exist for designing efficient algorithms.

One drawback of the ACO algorithms analyzed in this paper is that the variance of the noise must be known in order to correctly set the evaporation factor ρ. This problem can be bypassed as follows: guess a variance of 1 and run the algorithm until it has a constant success probability if the guess was correct. If the optimum was not found so far, double the guess and repeat. This standard doubling scheme leads to a *noise-oblivious* ACO algorithm with an expected run time of at most a constant factor away from the ACO which knows the noise in advance.

Acknowledgements

The research leading to these results has received funding from the European Union Seventh Framework Programme (FP7/2007-2013) under grant agreement no. 618091 (SAGE). We would like to thank the anonymous reviewers for their helpful comments.

6. REFERENCES

[1] L. Bianchi, M. Dorigo, L. Gambardella, and W. Gutjahr. A survey on metaheuristics for stochastic combinatorial optimization. *Natural Computing*, 8:239–287, 2009.

[2] D.-C. Dang and P. K. Lehre. Evolution under partial information. In *Proc. of GECCO'14*, pages 1359–1366, 2014.

[3] G. A. Di Caro, F. Ducatelle, and L. M. Gambardella. Theory and practice of Ant Colony Optimization for routing in dynamic telecommunications networks. In N. Sala and F. Orsucci, editors, *Reflecting interfaces: the complex coevolution of information technology ecosystems*, pages 185–216. Idea Group, 2008.

[4] B. Doerr, A. Hota, and T. Kötzing. Ants easily solve stochastic shortest path problems. In *Proc. of GECCO'12*, pages 17–24, 2012.

[5] B. Doerr, D. Johannsen, and C. Winzen. Multiplicative drift analysis. *Algorithmica*, 64(4):673–697, 2012.

[6] S. Droste. Analysis of the (1+1) EA for a Noisy OneMax. In *Proc. of GECCO'04*, pages 1088–1099, 2004.

[7] M. Feldmann and T. Kötzing. Optimizing expected path lengths with ant colony optimization using fitness proportional update. In *Proc. of FOGA'13*, pages 65–74, 2013.

[8] T. Friedrich, T. Kötzing, M. S. Krejca, and A. M. Sutton. The benefit of sex in noisy evolutionary search. `arXiv:1502.02793 [cs.NE]`, 2015.

[9] C. Gießen and T. Kötzing. Robustness of populations in stochastic environments. In *Proc. of GECCO'14*, pages 1383–1390, 2014.

[10] Y. Jin and J. Branke. Evolutionary optimization in uncertain environments—a survey. *IEEE Trans. on Evol. Comp.*, 9:303–317, 2005.

[11] T. Kötzing. Concentration of first hitting times under additive drift. In *Proc. of GECCO'14*, pages 1391–1397, 2014.

[12] T. Kötzing and H. Molter. ACO beats EA on a dynamic pseudo-boolean function. In *Proc. of PPSN'12*, pages 113–122, 2012.

[13] T. Kötzing, F. Neumann, D. Sudholt, and M. Wagner. Simple max-min ant systems and the optimization of linear pseudo-boolean functions. In *Proc. of FOGA'11*, pages 209–218. ACM, 2011.

[14] A. Lissovoi and C. Witt. MMAS versus population-based EA on a family of dynamic fitness functions. *Algorithmica*, 2015. (To appear).

[15] T. Stützle and H. H. Hoos. MAX-MIN Ant System. *Future Generation Computer Systems*, 16:889–914, 2000.

[16] D. Sudholt and C. Thyssen. A simple ant colony optimizer for stochastic shortest path problems. *Algorithmica*, 64:643–672, 2012.

[17] E. W. Weisstein. Erfc, 2015. From MathWorld–A Wolfram Web Resource. http://mathworld.wolfram.com/Erfc.html.

The Effect of Quantum and Charged Particles on the Performance of the Dynamic Vector-evaluated Particle Swarm Optimisation Algorithm

Mardé Helbig
University of Pretoria
Department of Computer Science
Hatfield, Pretoria, South Africa
mhelbig@cs.up.ac.za

Andries P. Engelbrecht
University of Pretoria
Department of Computer Science
Hatfield, Pretoria, South Africa
engel@cs.up.ac.za

ABSTRACT

Many problems in the real-world have more than one objective, with at least two objectives in conflict with one another. In addition, at least one objective changes over time. These kinds of problems are called dynamic multi-objective optimisation problems (DMOOPs). Studies have shown that both the quantum particle swarm optimisation (QPSO) and charged particle swarm optimisation (CPSO) algorithms perform well in dynamic environments, since they maintain swarm diversity. Therefore, this paper investigates the effect of using either QPSOs or CPSOs in the sub-swarms of the dynamic vector-evaluated particle swarm optimisation (DVEPSO) algorithm. These DVEPSO variations are then compared against the default DVEPSO algorithm that uses gbest PSOs and DVEPSO using heterogeneous PSOs that contain both charged and quantum particles. Furthermore, all of the aforementioned DVEPSO configurations are compared against the dynamic multi-objective optimisation (DMOPSO) algorithm that was the winning algorithm of a comprehensive comparative study of dynamic multi-objective optimisation algorithms. The results indicate that charged and quantum particles improve the performance of DVEPSO, especially for DMOOPs with a deceptive POF and DMOOPs with a non-linear POS.

Keywords

charged PSO; quantum PSO; heterogeneous PSO; dynamic vecor-evaluated PSO; dynamic multi-objective optimisation

1. INTRODUCTION

Optimisation problems with least two objectives, of which at least two are in conflict with one another and at least one objective changes over time, are called dynamic multi-objective optimisation problems (DMOOPs). An improvement in one objective leads to a worse value of the other objective. Therefore, these kinds of problems to do not have a single solution, but a set of optimal trade-off solutions. The goal of an algorithm trying to solve DMOOPs are to track the changing optimal trade-off solutions over time and to maintain a diverse set of optimal trade-off solutions.

The major issues particle swarm optimisation (PSO) algorithms have to face when dealing with dynamic problems, is an outdated memory and diversity loss [2]. Even though information obtained by the entities of the algorithm (for example a particle's best solution found so far or the swarm's best solution found so far for a PSO) were important information for a specific environment, once the environment changes this information may become invalid and misguide the search. In these cases the gathered information has become outdated. Re-evaluating the entities once a change has occurred in the environment addresses outdated memory. If the entities of the algorithm were converging on an optimal solution, the other entities will be attracted to the optimal solution. If the environment changes, the entities have already converged on the previous optimum and have lost their diversity. Therefore, their exploration ability will be limited. One way to address the loss of diversity is to re-initialise a percentage of the population. However, this will lead to information loss.

Research has shown that two variations of PSO work well when solving dynamic single-objective optimisation problem (DSOOP), since they maintain diversity. These two variations of PSO are the charged PSO (CPSO) and the quantum PSO (QPSO) [1, 2]. Greeff and Engelbrecht [9] introduced a co-operative PSO-based algorithm to solve DMOOPs, i.e. the dynamic vector evaluated particle swarm optimisation (DVEPSO) algorithm. DVEPSO introduces diversity after a change in the environment by re-initialising a percentage of the swarm. The goal of this paper is to investigate the performance of DVEPSO using:

- either the CPSO or QPSO as the sub-swarms, and
- heterogeneous PSO sub-swarms that contain both charged and quantum particles.

The rest of the paper is outlined as follows: Section 2 introduces background information that is required for the rest of the paper. Section 3 discusses the experimental setup and statistical analysis that was performed on the obtained data. The results are discussed in Section 4. Finally, conclusions are drawn in Section 5.

GECCO'15, July 11 - 15,2015, Madrid, Spain

DOI: http://dx.doi.org/10.1145/2739480.2754810

2. BACKGROUND

This section discusses dynamic multi-objective optimisation (DMOO), CPSO, QPSO and DVEPSO.

2.1 Dynamic Multi-objective Optimisation

A DMOOP does not have a single solution and it does have conflicting objectives (refer to Section 1). Therefore, an approach is required to compare the quality of two solutions with more than one dimension in the objective space, namely vector domination. A decision vector dominates another decision vector if and only if both solutions are at least equal in quality with regards to all objectives and the dominating decision vector is better than the other vector for at least one of the objectives. The term Pareto-optimal refers to the non-dominated decision vectors. The set of all Pareto-optimal decision vectors is referred to as the Pareto-optimal set (POS) and the set of corresponding objective vectors is called the Pareto-optimal front (POF).

The goals of an algorithm solving a multi-objective optimisation problem (MOOP) are to find a diverse set of solutions, and to find solutions as close as possible to the true POF. However, when solving a DMOOP, in addition to the two aforementioned goals, a dynamic multi-objective optimisation algorithm (DMOA) also has to track the POF over time.

2.2 Charged Particle Swarm Optimisation

Blackwell and Bentley [1] proposed the CPSO algorithm. CPSO is based on electrostatic laws and contains both neutral and charged particles. Each particle is assigned a charge value, with neutral particles obtaining a charge of zero and charged particles a charge greater than zero. Charged particles are repulsed from each other if they are within a specified distance from one another. Neutral particles behave in the same manner as particles of the standard PSO. However, charged particles' velocity include an additional accelleration term that incorporates the repulsion from other charged particles. Therefore, the neutral particles will move towards the best position of the entire swarm (gbest), while the charged particles will continue to explore the search space. The combination of both neutral and charged particles ensures that there is no diversity loss, even if a change in the environment occurs.

2.3 Quantum Particle Swarm Optimisation

The QPSO algorithm was proposed by Blackwell and Branke [2]. QPSO is based on a model of an atom and uses a quantum analogy for the dynamics of the charged particles. In QPSO, the orbiting electrons of an atom is replaced by a quantum cloud. The quantum cloud is a probability distribution that determines the position of the particle. Therefore, a percentage of the swarm is treated as a quantum cloud, that is randomised at each iteration in a spherical area with a specified radius, centered around the particle with the best position in the entire swarm (gbest). The particles that are not part of the quantum cloud, are neutral particles, and follow the standard PSO velocity and position updates. Furthermore, in contrast to the CPSO, the quantum particles (in the quantum cloud) do not repel from each other. QPSO maintains its diversity through the randomisation of the quantum cloud. The quantum particles explore the search space and the neutral particles refine the current solution (exploitation).

2.4 Dynamic Vector-evaluated Particle Swarm Optimisation

Parsopoulos *et al.* [21] introduced a co-operative PSO-based algorithm called vector evaluated particle swarm optimisation (VEPSO). In VEPSO the number of sub-swarms is equal to the number of objectives of the optimisation problem and each swarm optimises only one objective function. Knowledge is shared between the swarms, and this shared knowledge is then used to update the velocity of the particles.

VEPSO was extended for DMOO by Greeff and Engelbrecht [9], referred to as DVEPSO. Harrison and Engelbrecht [11] investigated the effect of using CPSO as sub-swarms in DVEPSO for DMOO. However, DVEPSO in that study did not use Pareto-dominance for the gbest update. Furthermore, the study was limited to DMOOPs, with the exception of dMOP3 [8] (refer to Section 3.2), that the default DVEPSO configuration used in this study has successfully solved [12]. For this study, the following default configuration of DVEPSO is used:

- A particle's new position is selected as the particle's new personal best position (pbest) if a particle's new position leads to a better objective function value than its current pbest. Only the objective function being optimised by the sub-swarm is taken into consideration for the pbest update, i.e. Pareto-dominance is not used.
- If a particle's new position dominates the current global best (gbest) position of the whole sub-swarm, the particle's position is selected as the new gbest. However, if a particle's new position is non-dominant with regards to the sub-swarm's current gbest, one of these two positions is randomly selected as the sub-swarm's new gbest.
- Each sub-swarm is a gbest PSO where the neighbourhood of the particle is defined as the whole sub-swarm.
- A specified number of particles, called sentry particles [5], are randomly selected and re-evaluated after the algorithm performed the specific iteration, but before the next iteration starts. If the sentry particle's fitness value differs after re-evaluation with more than a specificed value, the sub-swarm is notified that a change in the environment has occurred.
- If a change in the environment has occurred, 30% of the particles of the sub-swarm whose objective function has changed is randomly re-initialised. The particles of the sub-swarm(s) whose objective function did not change are not re-initialised. Furthermore, after a change in the environment has occurred, the archive is re-evaluated, i.e. non-dominated solutions in the archive that have become dominated are removed from the archive.
- A random knowledge sharing topology [10] is used to share knowledge between the sub-swarms. With a random topology, the selected sub-swarm can be another sub-swarm or the sub-swarm itself. The gbest of the selected sub-swarm that contains the shared knowledge is chosen using tournament selection.
- If the archive is full, a solution is removed from a crowded region in the archive.

2.5 Dynamic Multi-objective Particle Swarm Optimisation

Coello Coello and Salazar Lechuga [3] proposed multi-objective particle swarm optimisation (MOPSO) as one of the first PSO algorithms extended for multi-objective optimisation (MOO). MOPSO uses an archive to preserve elitism and selects the global guide from the archive. MOPSO was adapted for DMOO by Lechuga [19]. The source code of MOPSO was obtained from the authors of [19], adapted for DMOO according to [19] and extended using sentry particles to detect a change in the environment. This adapted version of MOPSO is referred to as dynamic MOPSO (DMOPSO) for the rest of the paper.

3. EXPERIMENTAL SETUP

This section discusses the experimental setup for the purposes of this paper. Section 3.1 discusses the algorithms that were used for this study. The benchmark functions and performance measures are discussed in Sections 3.2 and 3.3 respectively. The statistical tests that were performed on the obtained data are discussed in Section 3.4.

3.1 Algorithms

The following algorithm configurations were used for this study:

- The default DVEPSO configuration as discussed in Section 2.4. A study where DVEPSO was optimised for these benchmark functions [12] was used to select the default DVEPSO parameter values. Swarm sizes of 20 particles were used, the inertia weight was set to 0.72 and the accelleration coefficients (c_1 and c_2) were set to 1.49 [22].
- DVEPSO using CPSOs (refer to Section 2.2) as the sub-swarms. The parameters for QPSO were selected based on empirical studies in [1]. All charged particles had a charge magnitute of 16 and 50% of the swarm was charged particles and the other 50% neutral particles. The radii of repulsion were set to 1.0 and 30 respectively. The standard PSO parameters had the same values as the default DVEPSO, since these values lead to convergence[22].
- DVEPSO using QPSOs (refer to Section 2.3) as the sub-swarms. The parameters for QPSO were based on empirical studies [2]: the quantum cloud was set to 2 and 50% of the swarm were assigned to the quantum cloud. The standard PSO parameters had the same values as the default DVEPSO, since these values lead to convergence[22].
- DVEPSO using heterogeneous PSOs as the sub-swarms. The particles of the heterogeneous PSOs are randomly assigned a behaviour for their velocity and position updates, i.e. a behaviour is being either a particle of a CPSO or a particle of a QPSO. Therefore, the swarm has both charged and quantum particles. However, each of these particles can be neutral (refer to Sections 2.2 and 2.3). If a change in the environment occurs, each particle is then randomly assigned a new behaviour. The motivation for using a heterogeneous approach is to combined the benefits of both CPSO and QPSO into one swarm. Studies on using heterogeneous DVEPSO [18] indicated that this approach does improve the performance of DVEPSO. However, in previous studies the behaviour pool for position and velocity behaviours were much larger, incorporating various position and velocity update approaches. The focus of this study is however on only charged and quantum behaviours in the behaviour pool.
- DMOPSO as discussed in Section 2.5.

Each algorithm configuration was executed on each benchmark function for each environment for 30 independent runs of 1000 iterations each. The source code of DVEPSO, QPSO and CPSO is available in the opensource library CIlib (version 1.0) [20].

3.2 Benchmark Functions

Based on the analysis of DMOOPs in [17], four benchmark functions were selected of various DMOOP types [6] to compare the performance of DVEPSO configurations and DMOPSO. These functions include dMOP2$_{dec}$ [15], dMOP3 [8], HE2 [13], and HE7 [12, 17]. For each benchmark function the following severity of change (n_t) and frequency of change (τ_t) combinations were used: $n_t = 10$ and $\tau_t = 25$, $n_t = 10$ and $\tau_t = 50$, $n_t = 1$ and $\tau_t = 10$, and $n_t = 20$ and $\tau_t = 10$. Therefore, the algorithms were evaluated on 16 benchmark functions.

dMOP2$_{dec}$'s POF changes from convex to concave and vice versa over time. Furthermore, it has a deceptive POF, i.e. there is at least one local POF and the search space favours the local POF and not the global POF. dMOP3 has a convex POF and the variable that changes the spread of solutions changes over time. HE2 has a discontinuous POF, i.e. the POF consists of disconnected continuous pieces. HE7 has a POF that changes from convex to concave and vice versa over time, a non-linear POS, and each decision variable has a different POS.

These functions were selected since previous studies [12, 14] indicated that DVEPSO struggles with these specific benchmark functions.

3.3 Performance Measures

Based on an analysis of performance measures in [16], two performance measures were selected for this study, namely the alternative accuracy measure (acc_{alt}) [4], referred to in this article as *acc* (a low *acc* value indicates good performance). *acc* is measured as the absolute difference between the hypervolume (HV) of the true POF and the hypervolume of the approximated (found) POF at a specific time t. Stability (*stab*) [4] quantifies the effect of changes in the environment on *acc* of the DMOA (a low *stab* value indicates good performance).

The hypervolume value required for these two measures was calculated using the source code of Fonseca *et al* [7]. The reference vector used for the hypervolume calculations was calculated for each benchmark function and consisted of the worst objective function value for each dimension.

3.4 Statistical Analysis

For each DMOOP, for each environment, and for each performance measure wins and losses were calculated as proposed in [14].

For each time step just before a change in the environment occurred, the average performance measure value over 30 runs was calculated. A Kruskal-Wallis test was performed on these values obtained by the DVEPSO configurations and DMOPSO.

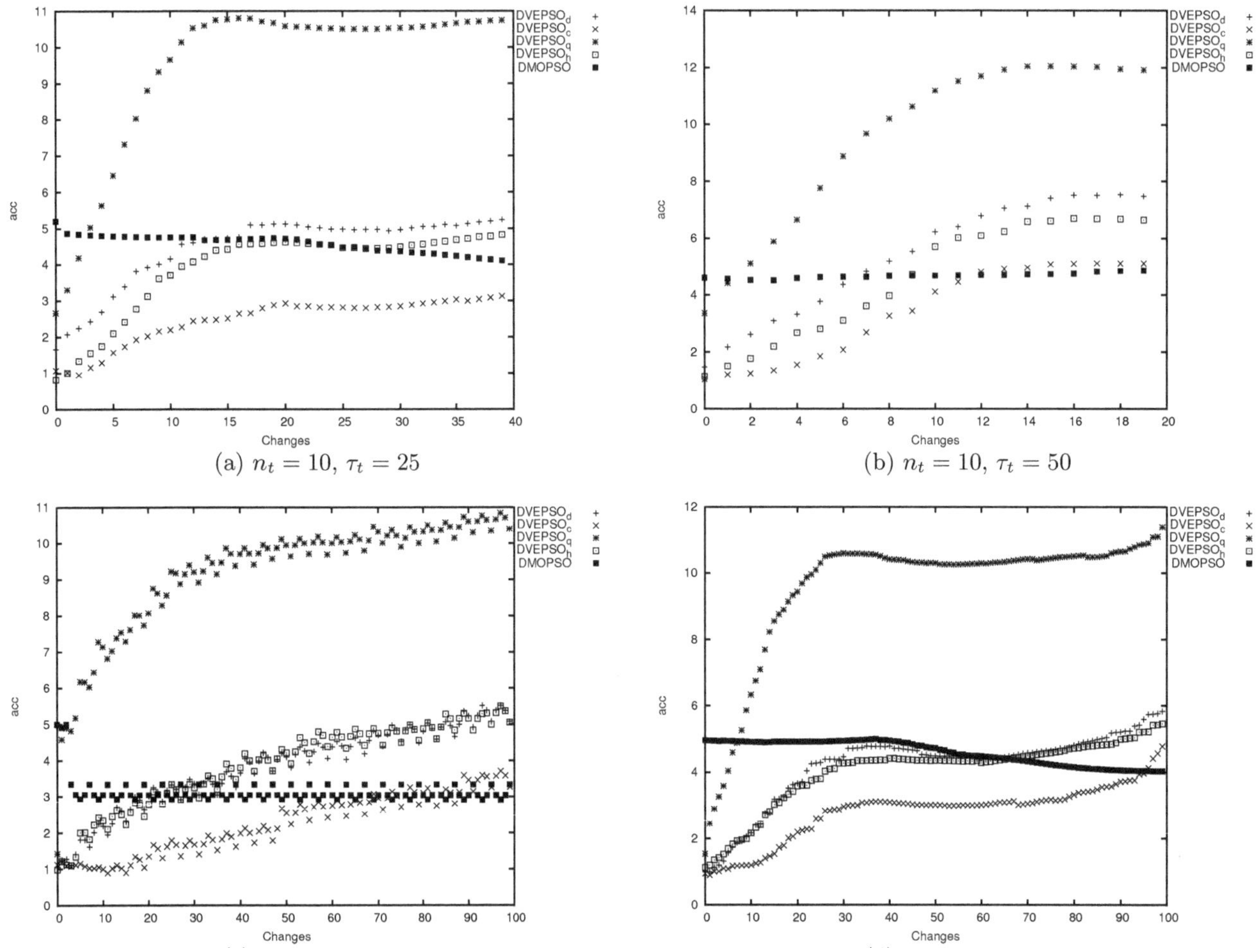

(a) $n_t = 10$, $\tau_t = 25$ (b) $n_t = 10$, $\tau_t = 50$

(c) $n_t = 1$, $\tau_t = 10$ (d) $n_t = 20$, $\tau_t = 10$

Figure 1: *acc* for the various environments obtained by DMOAs for HE7 for various n_t-τ_t combinations

If the Kruskal-Wallis test indicated a statistical significant difference between these performance measure values, a pair-wise Mann-Whitney U test was performed for each pair of DVEPSO configurations.

If a significant difference was indicated by the Mann-Whitney U test, wins and losses were awarded as follows: at each time step just before a change in the environment occurred, the average performance measure values of the two DMOAs were compared. The DMOA with the best performance measure value was awarded a win and the other DMOA was awarded a loss.

In order to ensure that a DMOA's performance on a specific DMOOP did not lead to skewed results, the number of wins and losses were normalised for each DMOOP. For all statistical tests a confidence level of 95% was used.

4. RESULTS

This section discusses the results obtained by the various DMOAs. The performance measure values are discussed in Section 4.1 and the statistical analysis of the results is discussed in Section 4.2. DVEPSO$_d$, DVEPSO$_c$, DVEPSO$_q$, DVEPSO$_h$ and DMOPSO refer to the default DVEPSO, charged DVEPSO, quantum DVEPSO, heterogeneous DVEPSO and dynamic MOPSO respectively.

4.1 Performance Measures

This section discusses the performance measure values obtained by the DMOAs. The average *acc* and *stab* values obtained for the various environments for HE7 are illustrated in Figures 1 and 2. Figures 1 and 2 show that the *acc* values and *stab* values obtained by DMOPSO do not vary much over time, remaining reasonably stable with a slight decrease for slowly changing environments ($n_t = 10$, $\tau_t = 25$) and environments that do not change severely ($n_t = 20$, $\tau_t = 10$). The *acc* and *stab* values of DVEPSO$_q$ increases over time, indicating that the performance of DVEPSO$_q$ deteriorates over time. In addition, DVEPSO$_q$ performs poorly on HE7, with high *acc* and *stab* values. Note that all other DVEPSO configurations experiences an increase in *acc* over time, but still performs well. Furthermore, DVEPSO$_c$ performed the best for HE7.

Figure 3 illustrates the average *acc* values obtained by the DMOAs for dMOP3. DMOPSO performed the best for *acc*, obtaining much better *acc* values than the other DMOAs for all environments. Furthermore, DMOPSO's *acc* values remained consistently low for all environments. For slowly changing environments ($\tau_t = 25$ and $\tau_t = 50$) DVEPSO$_q$ performed the worst. Furthermore, the *acc* values obtained by the DVEPSO configurations increases and decreases over

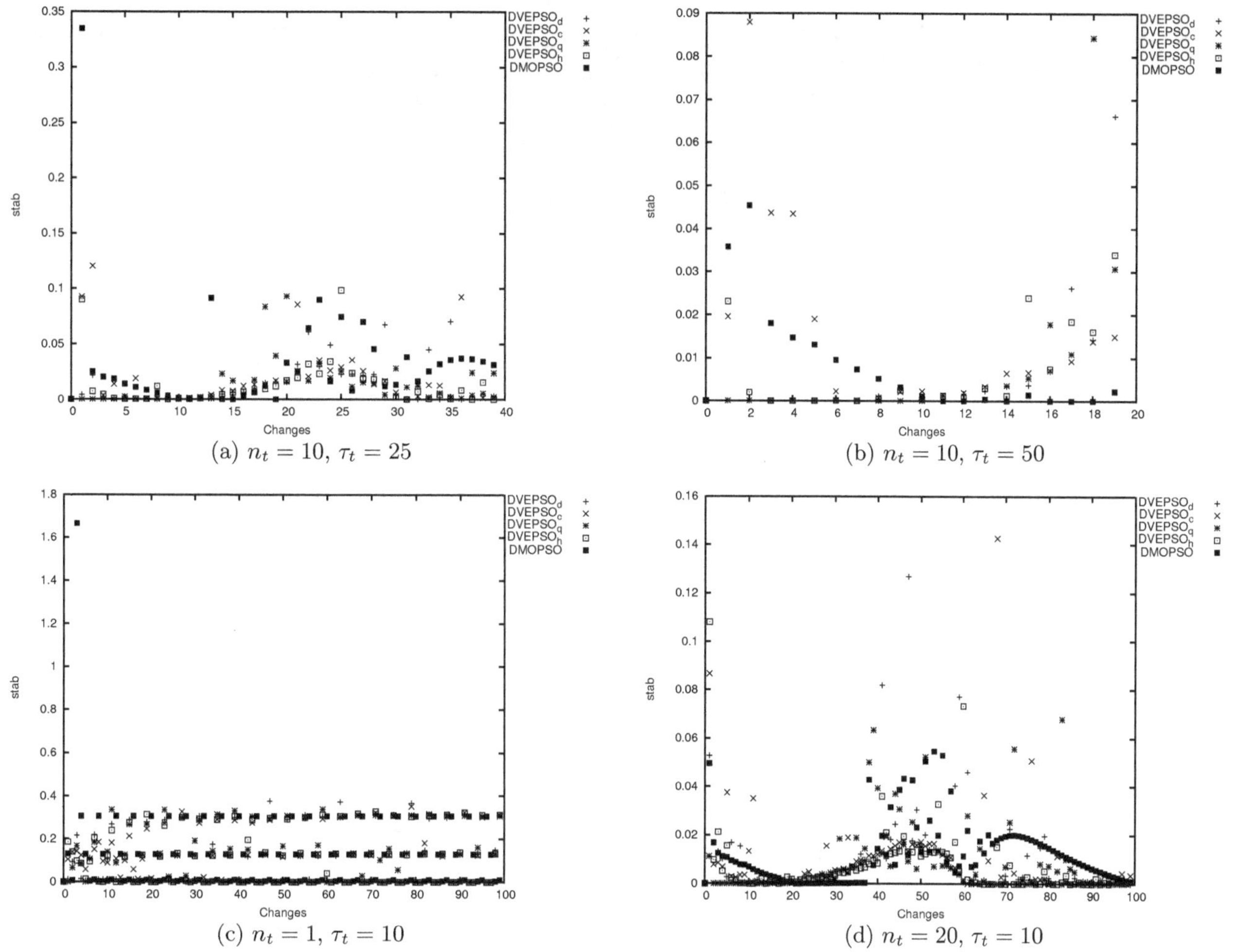

Figure 2: *stab* for the various environments obtained by DMOAs for HE7 for various n_t-τ_t combinations

time in faster changing environments ($\tau_t = 10$). The approximated POFs of the DMOAs for dMOP3 with $n_t = 10$, $\tau_t = 25$ (slowly changing environment) obtained over 30 runs are illustrated in Figure 4. Figure 4 shows that DMOPSO converged to the true POF, but DVEPSO$_h$ struggled to find solutions. The other DVEPSO configurations struggled to converge to the true POF, but did manage to obtain an approximated POF with a similar shape than the true POF.

4.2 Statistical Analysis

This section discusses the statistical analysis (refer to Section 3.4) that was performed on the obtained data. Tables 1 and 2 presents the wins and losses for each of the benchmark functions. In both tables, DV and DM refers to DVEPSO and DMOPSO respectively.

For dMOP3, DMOPSO performed the best, with regards to both *acc* and *stab* and performed the best in all environments. DVEPSO$_h$ was the second best performing algorithm in all environments, except slowly changing environments ($\tau_t = 50$) where it performed the worst. Measuring the performance of the algorithms over all environments, *DMOPSO* performed the best for both *acc* and *stab*. DVEPSO$_q$ performed the second best and DVEPSO$_c$ performed the worst. For *stab*, DVEPSO$_h$ was the best performing DVEPSO configuration, and DVEPSO$_q$ performed the worst.

For dMOP2$_{dec}$, DMOPSO performed the worst for all environments, and for both *acc* and *stab*. DVEPSO$_c$ performed the best for *acc*, and all DVEPSO configurations obtained more wins than losses for *acc*. For *stab* there is not much difference in the number of wins or losses assigned to the various algorithms. DVEPSO$_h$ performed the best for *stab*, and DMOPSO performed the worst.

For HE1, DMOPSO performed the best for *acc*, with DVEPSO$_h$ performing the worst. For *stab*, both DVEPSO$_d$ and DVEPSO$_h$ performed the best, and DMOPSO the worst. DMOPSO performed the best in all environments, while DVEPSO$_h$ obtained either the worst or second worst rank for all environments.

In contrast to HE1, when solving HE7, DVEPSO$_c$ performed the best for *acc* and DVEPSO$_q$ performed the best for *stab*.

Furthermore, DVEPSO$_c$ performed the best for all environments. However, DVEPSO$_q$ performed the worst in all environments.

Table 1: Overall wins and losses for dMOP3 and dMOP2$_{dec}$ obtained by the various DMOO algorithms

n_t-τ_t	Measure	Results	dMOP3 DMOO Algorithm					dMOP2$_{dec}$ DMOO Algorithm				
			DV$_d$	DV$_c$	DV$_q$	DV$_h$	DM	DV$_d$	DV$_c$	DV$_q$	DV$_h$	DM
all	*acc*	Wins	5.81	2.425	8.98	2.785	16.0	3.95	4.67	4.23	3.95	0.2
all	*acc*	Losses	8.19	11.575	5.02	11.215	0.0	0.05	0.33	0.77	0.05	15.8
all	*acc*	Diff	-2.38	-9.15	3.96	-8.43	16.0	3.9	4.34	3.46	3.9	-15.6
all	*acc*	Rank	3.0	5.0	2.0	4.0	**1.0**	2.0	**1.0**	4.0	2.0	5.0
all	*stab*	Wins	1.4	3.315	0.925	11.37	12.765	0.0	0.0	0.0	0.55	0.42
all	*stab*	Losses	9.3	8.355	9.855	1.83	0.435	0.0	0.0	0.0	0.42	0.55
all	*stab*	Diff	-7.9	-5.04	-8.93	9.54	12.33	0.0	0.0	0.0	0.13	-0.13
all	*stab*	Rank	4.0	3.0	5.0	2.0	**1.0**	2.0	2.0	2.0	**1.0**	5.0
10-25	all	Wins	1.85	0.1	2.825	3.275	7.425	1.0	1.0	1.0	1.0	0.0
10-25	all	Losses	4.1	4.85	3.125	3.275	0.125	0.0	0.0	0.0	0.0	4.0
10-25	all	Diff	-2.25	-4.75	-0.3	0.0	7.3	1.0	1.0	1.0	1.0	-4.0
10-25	all	Rank	4.0	5.0	3.0	2.0	**1.0**	**1.0**	**1.0**	**1.0**	**1.0**	5.0
10-50	all	Wins	2.0	1.0	3.0	0.0	4.0	0.95	0.95	0.95	0.95	0.2
10-50	all	Losses	2.0	3.0	1.0	4.0	0.0	0.05	0.05	0.05	0.05	3.8
10-50	all	Diff	0.0	-2.0	2.0	-4.0	4.0	0.9	0.9	0.9	0.9	-3.6
10-50	all	Rank	3.0	4.0	2.0	5.0	**1.0**	**1.0**	**1.0**	**1.0**	**1.0**	5.0
1-10	all	Wins	0.45	2.0	1.79	4.71	6.95	1.0	1.72	1.28	1.0	0.0
1-10	all	Losses	5.52	4.94	4.18	1.25	0.01	0.0	0.28	0.72	0.0	4.0
1-10	all	Diff	-5.07	-2.94	-2.39	3.46	6.94	1.0	1.44	0.56	1.0	-4.0
1-10	all	Rank	5.0	4.0	3.0	2.0	**1.0**	2.0	**1.0**	4.0	2.0	5.0
20-10	all	Wins	2.81	2.54	2.14	3.42	6.84	1.0	1.0	1.0	1.55	0.42
20-10	all	Losses	4.07	5.34	4.82	3.47	0.05	0.0	0.0	0.0	0.42	4.55
20-10	all	Diff	-1.26	-2.8	-2.68	-0.05	6.79	1.0	1.0	1.0	1.13	-4.13
20-10	all	Rank	3.0	5.0	4.0	2.0	**1.0**	2.0	2.0	2.0	**1.0**	5.0
all	all	Wins	7.21	5.74	9.905	14.155	28.765	3.95	4.67	4.23	4.5	0.62
all	all	Losses	17.49	19.93	14.875	13.045	0.435	0.05	0.33	0.77	0.47	16.35
all	all	Diff	-10.28	-14.19	-4.97	1.11	28.33	3.9	4.34	3.46	4.03	-15.73
all	all	Rank	4.0	5.0	3.0	2.0	**1.0**	3.0	**1.0**	4.0	2.0	5.0

Table 2: Overall wins and losses for HE1 and HE7 obtained by the various DMOO algorithms

n_t-τ_t	Measure	Results	HE1 DMOO Algorithm					HE7 DMOO Algorithm				
			DV$_d$	DV$_c$	DV$_q$	DV$_h$	DM	DV$_d$	DV$_c$	DV$_q$	DV$_h$	DM
all	*acc*	Wins	7.92	2.12	11.94	1.02	16.0	4.685	13.69	0.285	7.545	6.795
all	*acc*	Losses	8.08	12.88	4.06	13.98	0.0	7.315	0.31	15.715	4.455	5.205
all	*acc*	Diff	-0.16	-10.76	7.88	-12.96	16.0	-2.63	13.38	-15.43	3.09	1.59
all	*acc*	Rank	3.0	4.0	2.0	5.0	**1.0**	4.0	**1.0**	5.0	2.0	3.0
all	*stab*	Wins	2.375	2.365	1.945	2.375	0.57	2.465	1.61	2.115	1.86	3.705
all	*stab*	Losses	0.835	0.845	2.945	0.835	4.17	1.44	2.27	0.8	1.095	6.15
all	*stab*	Diff	1.54	1.52	-1.0	1.54	-3.6	1.025	-0.66	1.315	0.765	-2.445
all	*stab*	Rank	**1.0**	3.0	4.0	**1.0**	5.0	2.0	4.0	**1.0**	3.0	5.0
10-25	all	Wins	2.475	0.725	3.975	1.375	4.0	1.95	3.95	0.75	3.425	2.85
10-25	all	Losses	2.375	4.125	2.575	3.475	0.0	3.025	0.05	4.225	1.55	4.075
10-25	all	Diff	0.1	-3.4	1.4	-2.1	4.0	-1.075	3.9	-3.475	1.875	-1.225
10-25	all	Rank	3.0	5.0	2.0	4.0	**1.0**	3.0	**1.0**	5.0	2.0	4.0
10-50	all	Wins	1.95	0.9	3.0	0.15	4.0	1.0	2.0	0.1	1.0	0.9
10-50	all	Losses	2.05	3.1	1.0	3.85	0.0	1.0	0.0	3.9	0.0	0.1
10-50	all	Diff	-0.1	-2.2	2.0	-3.7	4.0	0.0	2.0	-3.8	1.0	0.8
10-50	all	Rank	3.0	4.0	2.0	5.0	**1.0**	4.0	**1.0**	5.0	2.0	3.0
1-10	all	Wins	3.21	1.18	3.94	1.2	4.0	1.76	4.28	0.03	1.75	4.15
1-10	all	Losses	2.3	3.33	2.4	3.31	2.19	2.23	0.71	3.97	2.24	2.82
1-10	all	Diff	0.91	-2.15	1.54	-2.11	1.81	-0.47	3.57	-3.94	-0.49	1.33
1-10	all	Rank	3.0	5.0	2.0	4.0	**1.0**	3.0	**1.0**	5.0	4.0	2.0
20-10	all	Wins	2.66	1.68	2.97	0.67	4.57	1.74	4.62	0.77	3.23	2.6
20-10	all	Losses	2.19	3.17	1.03	4.18	1.98	2.25	0.37	4.22	1.76	4.36
20-10	all	Diff	0.47	-1.49	1.94	-3.51	2.59	-0.51	4.25	-3.45	1.47	-1.76
20-10	all	Rank	3.0	4.0	2.0	5.0	**1.0**	3.0	**1.0**	5.0	2.0	4.0
all	all	Wins	10.295	4.485	13.885	3.395	16.57	7.15	15.3	2.4	9.405	10.5
all	all	Losses	8.915	13.725	7.005	14.815	4.17	8.755	2.58	16.515	5.55	11.355
all	all	Diff	1.38	-9.24	6.88	-11.42	12.4	-1.605	12.72	-14.115	3.855	-0.855
all	all	Rank	3.0	4.0	2.0	5.0	**1.0**	4.0	**1.0**	5.0	2.0	3.0

5. CONCLUSIONS

Both the charged particle swarm optimisation (PSO) and quantum PSO have performed well on dynamic optimisation problems, since they maintain diversity. Therefore, this paper investigated the effect of charged and quantum particles on the dynamic vector-evaluated PSO (DVEPSO). Various DVEPSO configurations and the dynamic multi-objective PSO (DMOPSO) algorithm were evaluated on benchmark functions with various characteristics.

The results show that the heterogeneous DVEPSO performed well for all functions, except HE1. For HE1, the quantum DVEPSO performed well. Furthermore, DMOPSO outperformed the DVEPSO configurations on dMOP3, where the variable that controls the spread of solutions changes

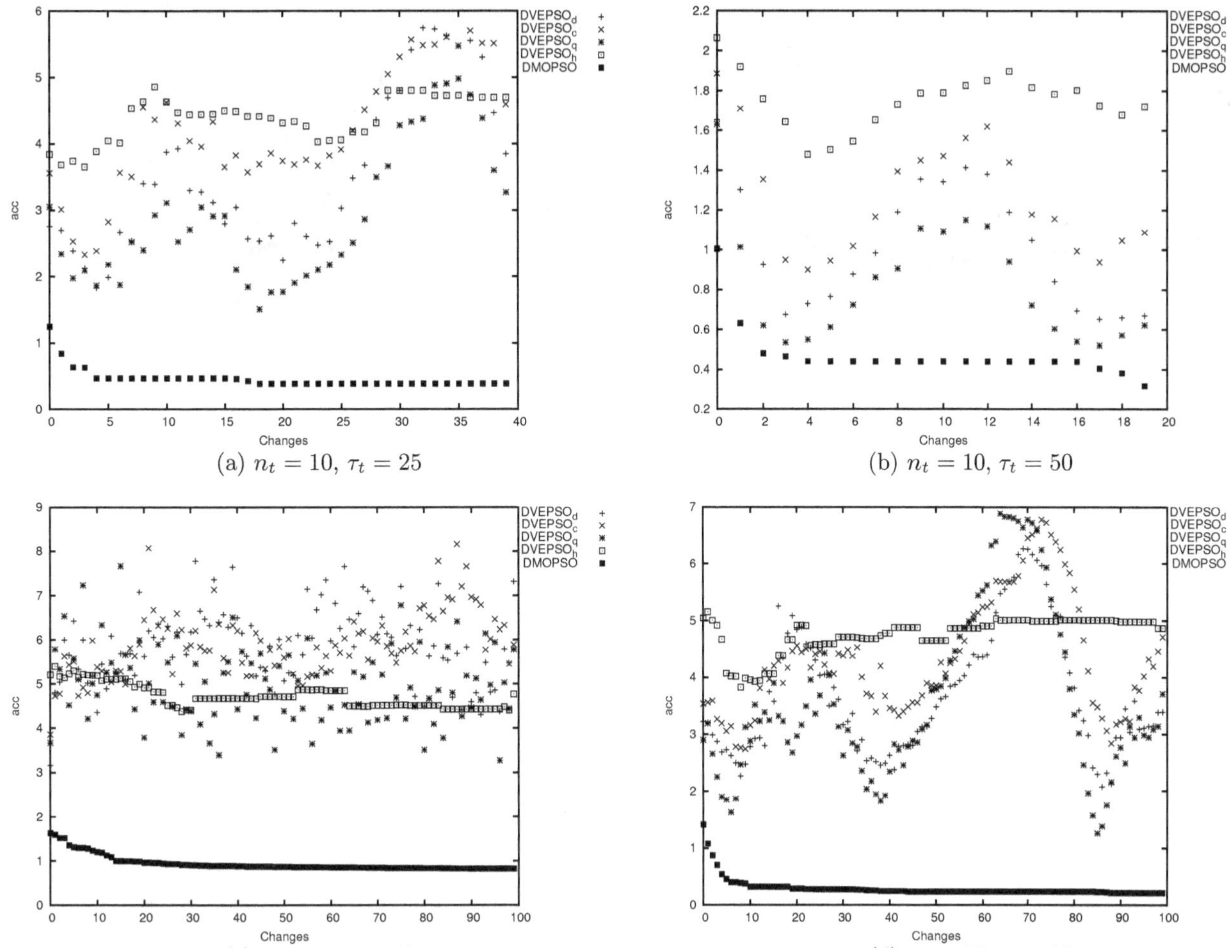

(a) $n_t = 10$, $\tau_t = 25$ (b) $n_t = 10$, $\tau_t = 50$

(c) $n_t = 1$, $\tau_t = 10$ (d) $n_t = 20$, $\tau_t = 10$

Figure 3: *acc* for the various environments obtained by DMOAs for dMOP3 for various n_t, τ_t combinations

over time. For dMOP2$_{dec}$ with a deceptive POF that changes from convex to concave and vice versa, the DVEPSO configurations outperformed DMOPSO for both *acc* and *stab*. For HE1, DMOPSO performed the best for *acc*, and the DVEPSO configurations outperformed DMOPSO on *stab*. For HE7, with a non-linear POS and where each decision variable has a different POS, the DVEPSO configurations outperformed DMOPSO on both *acc* and *stab*.

Therefore, more research is required to investigate the usage of heterogeneous PSOs (containing charged and quantum particles) as sub-swarms of DVEPSO to determine whether it will improve DVEPSO's robustness when solving dynamic multi-objective optimisation problems of various types in a wide range of environment types.

6. REFERENCES

[1] T. Blackwell and P. Bentley. Dynamic search with charged swarms. In *Proceedings of the Genetic and Evolutionary Computation Conference*, pages 19–26, New York, U.S.A., 9-13 July 2002.

[2] T. Blackwell and J. Branke. Multiswarms, exclusion, and anti-convergence in dynamic environments. *IEEE Transactions on Evolutionary Computation*, 10(4):459–472, August 2006.

[3] C.A. Coello Coello and M. Lechuga. MOPSO: a proposal for multiple objective particle swarm optimization. In *Proceedings of Congress on Evolutionary Computation*, volume 2, pages 1051–1056, 2002.

[4] M. Cámara, J. Ortega, and F. de Toro. A single front genetic algorithm for parallel multi-objective optimization in dynamic environments. *Neurocomputing*, 72(16–18):3570–3579, 2007.

[5] A. Carlisle and G. Dozier. Tracking changing extrema with adaptive particle swarm optimizer. In *Proceedings of World Automation Congress*, volume 13, pages 265–270, Orlando, Florida, U.S.A., June 2002.

[6] M. Farina, K. Deb, and P. Amato. Dynamic multiobjective optimization problems: test cases, approximations, and applications. *IEEE Transactions on Evolutionary Computation*, 8(5):425–442, October 2004.

[7] C. Fonseca, L. Paquete, and M. Lopez-Ibanez. An improved dimension-sweep algorithm for the hypervolume indicator. In *Proceedings of Congress on Evolutionary Computation*, pages 1157–1163, New York, U.S.A., July 2006. Source code available online

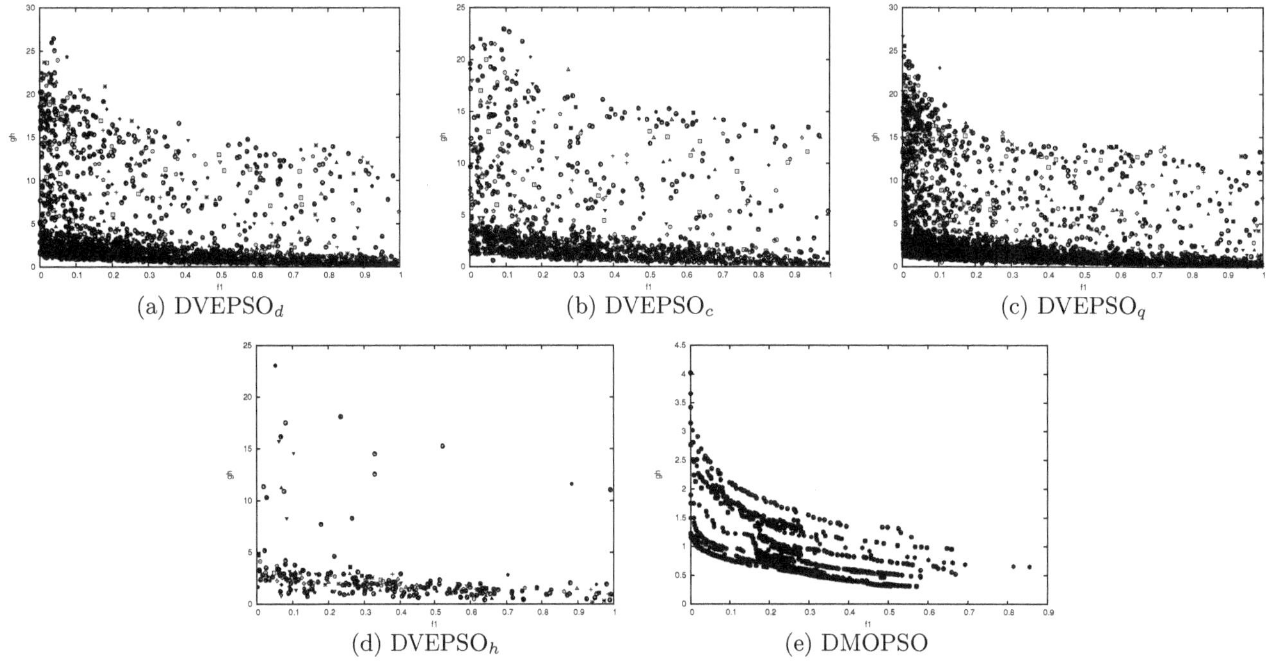

(a) DVEPSO_d (b) DVEPSO_c (c) DVEPSO_q

(d) DVEPSO_h (e) DMOPSO

Figure 4: Approximated POFs found by the DMOAs for dMOP3 with $n_t = 10$, $\tau_t = 25$

at: http://iridia.ulb.ac.be/~manuel/hypervolume. Last accessed on: 10 December 2013.

[8] C.-K. Goh and K. Tan. A competitive-cooperative coevolutionary paradigm for dynamic multiobjective optimization. *IEEE Transactions on Evolutionary Computation*, 13(1):103–127, February 2009.

[9] M. Greeff and A. Engelbrecht. Solving dynamic multi-objective problems with vector evaluated particle swarm optimisation. In *Proceedings of World Congress on Computational Intelligence (WCCI): Congress on Evoluationary Computation*, pages 2917–2924, Hong Kong, June 2008.

[10] M. Greeff and A. Engelbrecht. Dynamic multi-objective optimisation using PSO. In N. Nedjah, L. dos Santos Coelho, and L. de Macedo Mourelle, editors, *Multi-Objective Swarm Intelligent Systems*, volume 261 of *Studies in Computational Intelligence*, pages 105–123. Springer Berlin/Heidelberg, 2010.

[11] K. Harrison, B. Ombuki-Berman, and A. Engelbrecht. Dynamic multi-objective optimization using sharged vector evaluated particle swarm optimization. In *Proceedings of IEEE Congress on Evolutionary Computation*, pages 1929–1936, July 2014.

[12] M. Helbig. *Solving dynamic multi-objective optimisation problems using vector evaluated particle swarm optimisation.* PhD thesis, University of Pretoria, 2012.

[13] M. Helbig and A. Engelbrecht. Archive management for dynamic multi-objective optimisation problems using vector evaluated particle swarm optimisation. In *Proceedings of Congress on Evolutionary Computation*, pages 2047–2054, New Orleans, U.S.A., June 2011.

[14] M. Helbig and A. Engelbrecht. Analysing the performance of dynamic multi-objective optimisation algorithms. In *Proceedings of the IEEE Congress on Evolutionary Computation*, pages 1531–1539, Cancún, Mexico, June 2013.

[15] M. Helbig and A. Engelbrecht. Benchmarks for dynamic multi-objective optimisation. In *Proc. of IEEE Symposium Series on Computational Intelligence*, pages 84–91, Singapore, April 2013.

[16] M. Helbig and A. Engelbrecht. Performance measures for dynamic multi-objective optimisation algorithms. *Information Sciences*, 250:61–81, November 2013.

[17] M. Helbig and A. Engelbrecht. Benchmarks for dynamic multi-objective optimisation algorithms. *ACM Computing Surveys*, 46(3):37:1–37:39, 2014.

[18] M. Helbig and A. Engelbrecht. Heterogeneous dynamic vector evaluated particle swarm optimisation for dynamic multi-objective optimisation. In *IEEE Congress on Evoluationary Computation*, pages 3151–3159, July 2014.

[19] M. Lechuga. *Multi-objective optimisation using sharing in swarm optimisation algorithms.* PhD thesis, University of Birmingham, July 2009.

[20] G. Pamparà, A. Engelbrecht, and T. Cloete. CIlib: A collaborative framework for computational intelligence algorithms - Part I. In *Proceedings of World Congress on Computational Intelligence*, pages 1750–1757, Hong Kong, 1-8 June 2008. Source code available at: http://www.cilib.net. Last accessed on: 10 December 2013.

[21] K. Parsopoulos and M. Vrahatis. Recent approaches to global optimization problems through particle swarm optimization. *Natural Computing*, 1(2-3):235–306, 2002.

[22] F. v.d.Bergh and A. Engelbrecht. A study of particle swarm optimization particle trajectories. *Information Sciences*, 176(8):937–971, 2006.

Enhancing IACO$_{\mathbb{R}}$ Local Search by Mtsls1-BFGS for Continuous Global Optimization

Udit Kumar, Jayadeva, Sumit Soman *
Department of Electrical Engineering
Indian Institute of Technology
Delhi, India
jayadeva@ee.iitd.ac.in

ABSTRACT

A widely known approach for continuous global optimization has been the Incremental Ant Colony Framework ($IACO_{\mathbb{R}}$). In this paper, we propose a strategy to introduce hybridization within the exploitation phase of the $IACO_{\mathbb{R}}$ framework by using the Multi-Trajectory Local Search (Mtsls1) algorithm and Broyden-Fletcher-Goldfarb-Shanno (BFGS) algorithms. Our approach entails making a probabilistic choice between these algorithms. In case of stagnation, we switch the algorithm being used based on the last iteration. We evaluate our approach on the Soft Computing (SOCO) benchmark functions and present results by computing the mean and median errors on the global optima achieved, as well as the iterations required. We compare our approach with competing methods on a number of benchmark functions, and show that the proposed approach achieves improved results. In particular, we obtain the global optima in terms of average value for **14** out of **19** benchmark functions, and in terms of the median value for all SOCO benchmarks. At the same time, the proposed approach uses fewer function evaluations on several benchmarks when compared with competing methods, which have been found to use **54%** more function evaluations.

Categories and Subject Descriptors

G.1.6 [**Numerical Analysis**]: Optimization—*Unconstrained Optimization, Global Optimization, Gradient Methods*

Keywords

Incremental Ant Colony Optimization; Continuous Global Optimization; Local Search; Multi-trajectory local search; BFGS; Gradient Based Methods.

*Udit Kumar, Jayadeva, Sumit Soman are with the Department of Electrical Engineering, IIT Delhi. E-mail: udit.vlsi@gmail.com, jayadeva@ee.iitd.ac.in, sumit.soman@gmail.com, Web: http://jayadeva.net

GECCO '15, July 11 - 15, 2015, Madrid, Spain

 ISBN 978-1-4503-3472-3/15/07... $15.00
DOI: http://dx.doi.org/10.1145/2739480.2754689

1. INTRODUCTION

Ant Colony Optimization (ACO) has found applications in continuous global optimization [17,21]. The unified ACO approach by Liao et al. [14] and a novel pheromone update rule by Seçkiner et al. [19] have been prominent works in this direction. Work has also been done using the Bee Colony Optimization approach, notably by Liao et al. [12], Aydın et al. [2], Kıran et al. [9], Karaboga et al. [8] among others. Though many approaches towards continuous global optimization have been proposed, the search for an efficient algorithm, in terms of accuracy and speed, continues to be an area of active research.

The work presented in this paper is based upon the Incremental ACO ($IACO_{\mathbb{R}}$) framework, proposed by Liao et al. [13] and the Multi-Trajectory Local Search (Mtsls1) by Tseng et al. [24]. Conventional optimization algorithms have two phases of operation, exploration and exploitation. The exploration phase searches a larger space to find an optimal solution, which is further refined in the exploitation phase by searching a limited region. We have used $IACO_{\mathbb{R}}$ as exploration engine and offer a choice between using Mtsls1 and BFGS as the exploitation engine. A Probability Density Function (PDF) is used to generate new solutions; if the new solutions are found to be better than current best, then they replace the current best solution. Further, bound constraints [13] are handled by adaptive methods, which make decisions based on the current count of function evaluations. The key contribution of our work is that we propose a hybrid local search approach with the usage of Mtsls1 and BFGS. Also, the choice between using Mtsls1 and BFGS is based on information from the previous iteration in case there is stagnation due to a random choice of selection of either of the approaches. Hence, this hybrid local search enhances algorithm performance, by using a combination of approaches, as well as by avoiding stagnation in locally exploiting the search space.

We have used the SOCO benchmarks [6,23] for evaluating the performance of our approach. Specifically, our hybrid approach is able to find the global optima in terms of average value for **14** benchmark functions, and in terms of the median value **for all 19** SOCO benchmark functions.

The rest of the paper is organized as follows. Section 2 presents the discussion of the Mtsls1 approach, which is followed by a description of the BFGS approach in Section 3. Based on these, we present our hybrid approach incorporating Mtsls1 and BFGS in Section 4. The results and discussion on benchmark functions are presented in Section 5, followed by the conclusions in Section 6.

2. IACO$_{\mathbb{R}}$ AND MTSLS1

The original $ACO_{\mathbb{R}}$ approach for continuous optimization is a fixed-size solution archive technique which aims at iteratively improving the solution set. At each iteration, the algorithm constructs new solutions along each dimension of the function. This is done by estimating the multimodal PDF using weighted Gaussians. At the end of every iteration, the solutions are sorted in order of quality and the algorithm terminates when the global optima is found, or when specified termination criteria are satisfied.

An enhancement to the $ACO_{\mathbb{R}}$ algorithm is the $IACO_{\mathbb{R}}$, which uses a solution archive that increases in size over time. The initial archive is chosen to be relatively smaller in size, and an algorithm parameter (γ) is used to control the growth of the solution archive. Initially, new solutions are generated at random, and are then moved towards the best solution in the archive based on a weighted factor of the difference between the new and present best solution. Another interesting aspect of this algorithm is the manner in which solutions are chosen subsequently for generation of new solutions. This is done using a probability parameter $p \in [0, 1]$, which can be set to ensure that the only the best solutions at present can be used to generate new solutions.

The next stage of improvement comes from the incorporation of a local search procedure in the $IACO_{\mathbb{R}}$ algorithm, which is known as the $IACO_{\mathbb{R}} - LS$ [13]. The previous algorithms focused on the exploration phase to generate viable solutions. The next logical step was to perform exploitation, which would ensure faster convergence to better solutions. This led to the use of local search procedures, which started at the best solution determined by the exploration-intensive algorithms. Termination conditions for the local search included reaching a maximum number of iterations $Iter_{max}$, or when relative change between solutions found during subsequent iterations was lower than a specified tolerance τ. A parameter to prevent stagnation ($Siter_{max}$) at the local search level was also introduced. The details of implementation of $IACO_{\mathbb{R}} - LS$ can be found in [13].

The multi-trajectory local search, or Mtsls1 algorithm [24] exploits the search space across multiple paths. The approach has evolved to many variants, notable among which are the self-adaptive evolution by Zhao et al. [30], multi-objective optimization [25] and dynamic search trajectories by Snyman et al. [20].

The Mtsls1 algorithm searches from one dimension to another. The algorithm starts from an initial point and moves by a step size s along one dimension. This is illustrated in Figure 1 as movement from point a to b. Here, x_k represents the kth dimension of a point $x \in \mathbb{R}^n$, while f_n^x represents the value of the function f evaluated at a point x during the current dimension of local search. An update along a dimension is denoted as $\hat{x}$.

As a consequence of movement by s along a dimension, the change in the function value is evaluated, and if the function value is reduced, then the point obtained is used for optimization in next dimension. If the function value increases, then the algorithm goes back to the starting point and moves by $0.5 * s$ towards the negative direction (This is illustrated in Figure 1 as movement from point b to c). The function is then evaluated at the new point, and if the function value is less at c than point a, then point c is used as starting point in next dimension.

Though this algorithm performs well on many benchmark functions, there are enhancements possible in terms of the local-search technique used. We propose an approach where we offer a choice at the local-search level between the Mtsls1 and BFGS techniques. A primer to the BFGS approach is presented in the following section, followed by the motivation for our approach.

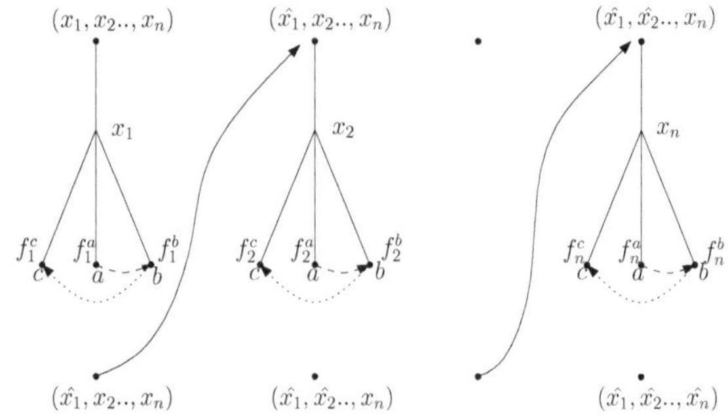

Figure 1: Mtsls1 search along one dimension from the first dimension to the last dimension

3. BFGS APPROACH

The Broyden-Fletcher-Goldfarb-Shanno (BFGS) [29] algorithm has been a classical optimization algorithm belonging to the class of approximate Newton methods. Along with several variants [10, 15, 26, 27], BFGS has been widely used in the domain of unconstrained optimization.

The basic sequence of steps followed in implementing the BFGS algorithm are as follows. It begins with an initial guess x_0 and an approximate Hessian B_0 for a function $f(x)$, and iterates until the point x_k converges. At each iteration, a direction p_k is chosen by solving $B_k p_k = -\nabla f(x_k)$, and line-search is performed to find a step-size α_k. The point is updated using $x_{k+1} = x_k + \alpha_k p_k$. The Hessian is updated as given by Equations (1)-(3).

$$s_k = \alpha_k p_k \tag{1}$$

$$y_k = \nabla f(x_{k+1}) - \nabla f(x_k) \tag{2}$$

$$B_{k+1} = B_k + \frac{y_k y_k^T}{y_k^T s_k} - \frac{B_k s_k s_k^T B_k}{s_k^T B_k s_k} \tag{3}$$

One of the concerns expressed in literature regarding the use of gradient-based methods for optimization is with regard to the technique used to compute the derivative. Salomon [18] opines that approximating the gradient is directly linked to the algorithm's ability to escape local minima. In case of evolutionary algorithms, there is a difference due to the techniques used for selecting population for the next generation. He states that *"If, however, the gradient is estimated by independent trials with a distance along each axis, the difference between both classes of algorithms almost vanishes."* We indicate here that our computations of gradient are based on approximating the derivative using central differences. We use the BFGS implementation available in the NLOPT library [7].

4. HYBRID LOCAL SEARCH USING MTSLS1 AND BFGS

As stated previously, our approach aims to combine the Mtsls1 approach and the BFGS method for local search.

This section begins with the motivation behind using the gradient and non-gradient based methods for continuous optimization problems, in the specific context of local-search, and proceeds to present the case which justifies the use of a hybrid variant of these approaches that would result in enhancements in reaching the optimal solutions.

We first consider the case of gradient-based algorithms such as the BFGS. The advantage obtained by using the BFGS algorithm is that it ensures quadratic convergence and also uses information from the previous iterations at every successive iteration. Recent works have been directed towards exploration of hybrid BFGS approaches. For instance, Li et al. [11] propose an approach combining BFGS with Particle Swarm Optimization (PSO) and illustrate promising results on benchmark datasets. Kafaki et al. [3] propose hybridization of Hestenes-Stiefel and Dai-Yuan approaches for unconstrained optimization problems. These works direct our motivation to develop a hybrid approach involving BFGS.

Further, it has been shown that gradient-based methods tend to perform better in several cases. This can be observed particularly in cases of convex and unimodal functions, where gradient based methods tend to quickly converge to the optimal values, and hence are suited to such kind of problems. On the other hand, non-gradient based methods may not be suitable in such situations or say may require large number of function evaluation. To give an example, on the SOCO benchmark function $F1$, which is a 50-dimensional function, BFGS requires only **620** iterations to converge to the optimal solution whereas Mtsls1 would take around 24070 iterations, this is shown in Figure 3.

Concretely, non-gradient based methods such as Mtsls1 are inherently designed to pursue multiple trajectories, and hence may not quickly reach the optimal value. Even though the speed of convergence may be compensated by use of these methods, it is advantageous to use them for multimodal functions, as they reach multiple optimal solutions within defined variable spaces. The trade-off in using such an approach exclusively is the increased number of function evaluations and also slower convergence rates towards the later iterations.

Based on these observations, we propose an hybrid local-search approach which incorporates both the gradient-based BFGS and non-gradient based Mtsls1 as part of the $IACO_{\mathbb{R}}-LS$ technique. Our approach offers a choice between selecting either of the two approaches, based on a probabilistically determined choice. In case this probabilistic choice fails to provide any improvement after a specific number of iterations, we switch the algorithm being used based on the algorithm used in the previous iteration. This ensures that our local-search approach does not stagnate, and also gives our approach an "adaptive" flavor.

The hybrid local search algorithm is shown in Figure 2. Here, we define a parameter $P(bfgs)$ which determines the probability of selecting the $BFGS$ algorithm for local search. There is a counter $ctr_{localsearch}$ which tracks the improvement in local search. If there is no improvement the counter is incremented by one. The hybrid local-search algorithm also uses a parameter $thresh_{localsearch}$, which helps in selecting a different local search algorithm when $ctr_{localsearch}$ crosses $thresh_{localsearch}$. The algorithm starts by checking the probability $P(bfgs)$; if this value is between zero and one, then we check whether the local search counter has not crossed the local search threshold $thresh_{localsearch}$, and then the BFGS algorithm is selected with probability $P(bfgs)$. If $P(bfgs)$ is zero, Mtsls1 is always selected in the local search, and if $P(bfgs)$ is one, then BFGS is always selected. In case of stagnation, where $ctr_{localsearch}$ exceeds the local search threshold counter, we switch the algorithm based on the algorithm used in the previous iteration. If BFGS was used, we choose Mtsls1, and vice-versa. When there is improvement, $ctr_{localsearch}$ is reset.

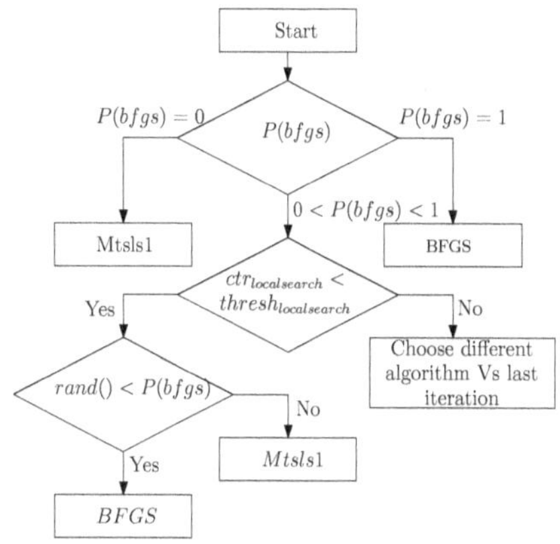

Figure 2: Hybrid algorithm approach

The consolidated algorithm for our approach is shown in Algorithm 1. Note here that our hybrid local-search approach, which was shown in Figure 2, is incorporated at Step 10 in the algorithm.

Algorithm 1 Hybrid $IACO_{\mathbb{R}}$ Algorithm

```
1: procedure HYBRID IACO_R(Probability (p), constant
   parameter (ζ), initial archive size (α), growth (γ), max-
   imum archive size (α_max), function tolerance (τ), maxi-
   mum iterations (Iter_max), maximum failure (Fail_max),
   maximum stagnation iterations (Siter_max), dimensions
   (N), termination criteria (Tc))        ▷ Algorithm parameters
2:     Initialize α solutions
3:     Evaluate initial solutions
4:     while (Tc not satisfied) do
5:         if (Fail_(i,best) < Fail_max) then
6:             Local search from Sol_best
7:         else if (Fail_(i,random) < Fail_max) then
8:             Local search from Sol_random
9:         end if
10:        if P(bfgs) == 0 then                ▷ Local Search
11:            Use Mtsls1
12:        else if P(bfgs) == 1 then
13:            Use BFGS                         ▷ Continued...
```

```
            else
                if ctr_localsearch < thresh_localsearch then
                    if rand() < P(bfgs) then
                        Use BFGS
                    else
                        Use Mtsls1
                    end if
                else
                    if Last iteration used Mtsls1 then
                        Use BFGS
                    else
                        Use Mtsls1
                    end if
                end if
            end if
            if No improvement in solution then
                Increment Fail_i
                Update ctr_localsearch
            end if
            if rand() < p then          ▷ Generate new solution
                Sample best Gaussian for each dimension
                if New soln is better then      ▷ Exploitation
                    Substitute new solution for Sol_best
                end if
            else
                for all j ∈ [1 : α] do          ▷ Exploration
                    Sample Gaussian along each dimension j
                    if new solution is better then
                        Substitute new solution for Sol_j
                    end if
                end for
            end if
            if Iter_curr is a multiple of γ and α < α_max then
        ▷ Archive Growth
                Initialize new solutions using S_new = S_new +
        rand() · (S_best − S_new)
                Add new solution to archive
                Increment α
            end if
            if ctr_globalsearch==Siter_max then        ▷ Restart
                Re-initialize solution set without S_best
            end if
        end while
    end procedure
```

5. STUDY AND DISCUSSION

We evaluate the performance of our approach by comparing its performance with the algorithms featured in SOCO benchmarks. For this purpose, we use the same 19 benchmark functions suite, shown in Table 1.

A brief description of the benchmark functions is in order. We used the 50 dimensional versions of the 19 SOCO functions. Functions $F1 - F6$ were originally proposed for the special session on large scale global optimization organized for the IEEE 2008 Congress on Evolutionary Computation (CEC 2008) [23], Functions $F7 - F11$ were proposed at the ISDA 2009 Conference. Functions $F12 - F19$ are hybrid functions that combine two functions belonging to $F1 - F11$. Some properties of the benchmark functions are listed in Table 1. The detailed description of these functions is available in [6, 16].

We applied the termination conditions used for SOCO, that is, the maximum number of function evaluations was $5000N$, where N is the number of dimensions in which the function is considered. All the investigated algorithms were run 25 times on each function. We report error values defined as $f(x) - f(x^*)$, where x is a candidate solution and x^* is the optimal solution. Error values lower than 10^{-14} (this value is referred to as 0-threshold) are approximated to 0. Our analysis is based on either the whole solution quality distribution, or on the median and average errors. For the evaluation of our $IACO_{\mathbb{R}}$-Hybrid approach, we use the algorithm parameters as indicated in Table 2 of [13]. Further, we use $P(bfgs)$ as 0.6 (determined using trial-and-error), and parameters for BFGS $x_{tol_{rel}} = x_{tol_{abs}} = 1e-7$, $f_{tol_{rel}} = f_{tol_{abs}} = 1e-15$ (for description of these parameters, the reader may refer to [7]). The value of $thresh_{localsearch}$ parameter is set to 2.

Table 1: Benchmark functions and their description. The last three columns indicate the modality, separability and rotation attributes of the respective functions.

ID	Name/Description	Uni/Multi	Sep.	***Rotated***
$F1$	Shift Sphere	U	Y	N
$F2$	Shifted Schwefel 2.21	U	N	N
$F3$	Shifted Rosenbrock	M	N	N
$F4$	Shifted Rastrigin	M	Y	N
$F5$	Shifted Griewank	M	N	N
$F6$	Shifted Ackley	M	Y	N
$F7$	Shifted Schwefel 2.22	U	Y	N
$F8$	Shifted Schefel 1.2	U	N	N
$F9$	Shifted Extended $F10$	U	N	N
$F10$	Shifted Bohachevsky	U	N	N
$F11$	Shifted Schafler	U	N	N
$F12$	$F9 + 0.25\ F1$	M	N	N
$F13$	$F9 + 0.25\ F3$	M	N	N
$F14$	$F9 + 0.25\ F4$	M	N	N
$F15$	$F10 + 0.25\ F7$	M	N	N
$F16$	$F9 + 0.5\ F1$	M	N	N
$F17$	$F9 + 0.75\ F3$	M	N	N
$F18$	$F9 + 0.75\ F4$	M	N	N
$F19$	$F10 + 0.75\ F7$	M	N	N

We compare our approach against reference algorithms used on the SOCO benchmark functions [13]. These include the differential evolution algorithm (DE) [22], the covariance matrix adaptation evolution strategy with increasing population size (G-CMA-ES) [1], the real-coded CHC algorithm (CHC) [4] and $IACO_{\mathbb{R}}$.

Table 2 shows the average error obtained using our approach (indicated in the column $IACO_{\mathbb{R}}$-Hybrid) on each of the 19 benchmark functions, and how it compares with other algorithms. We note that the new approach is able to achieve global optima for **14** benchmark function in terms of average solution and global optima on the SOCO benchmark functions.

Further, in terms of median error, our approach provides zero median error for **all** benchmark functions. This indicates that the hybrid approach gives good results on all functions, except for minor errors which may be attributed to the cases where the approach stagnates at local minima.

To estimate the overall difference in performance with other algorithms across the SOCO benchmark functions, we applied a Wilcoxon signed-ranks test [28]. The two-sided p-values of Wilcoxon matched-pairs signed-ranks test using $IACO_{\mathbb{R}}$ with BFGS and Mtsls1, along with other algorithms across 19 functions are presented in Table 4. The columns $(W+)$ and $(W-)$ denote the sum of signed ranks. The col-

Table 2: $IACO_{\mathbb{R}}$-Hybrid Average error on SOCO benchmark function (50D)

Function	DE	CHC	G-CMA	$IACO_{\mathbb{R}}$-Mtsls1	$IACO_{\mathbb{R}}$-BFGS	$IACO_{\mathbb{R}}$-Hybrid
F1	0.00E+00	1.67E-11	0.00E+00	0.00E+00	0.00E+00	**0.00E+00**
F2	3.60E-01	6.19E+01	2.75E-11	5.50E-13	0.00E+00	**0.00E+00**
F3	2.89E+01	1.25E+06	7.97E-01	8.17E+01	0.00E+00	**0.00E+00**
F4	3.98E-02	7.43E+01	1.05E+02	0.00E+00	4.08E+02	**0.00E+00**
F5	0.00E+00	1.67E-03	2.96E-04	0.00E+00	0.00E+00	**0.00E+00**
F6	1.43E-13	6.15E-07	2.09E+01	0.00E+00	1.91E+01	**0.00E+00**
F7	0.00E+00	2.66E-09	1.01E-10	0.00E+00	4.93E+03	**0.00E+00**
F8	3.44E+00	2.24E+02	0.00E+00	2.94E-05	0.00E+00	**0.00E+00**
F9	2.73E+02	3.10E+02	1.66E+01	0.00E+00	3.57E+02	**0.00E+00**
F10	0.00E+00	7.30E+00	6.81E+00	0.00E+00	1.51E+01	**0.00E+00**
F11	6.23E-05	2.16E+00	3.01E+01	0.00E+00	3.60E+02	**0.00E+00**
F12	5.35E-13	9.57E-01	1.88E+02	0.00E+00	6.08E+01	**0.00E+00**
F13	2.45E+01	2.08E+06	1.97E+02	3.03E+00	8.64E+01	8.77E-01
F14	4.16E-08	6.17E+01	1.09E+02	3.04E-01	3.49E+02	2.90E-02
F15	0.00E+00	3.98E-01	9.79E-04	0.00E+00	5.32E+02	**0.00E+00**
F16	1.56E-09	2.95E-09	4.27E+02	0.00E+00	1.48E+02	1.12E-03
F17	7.98E-01	2.26E+04	6.89E+02	6.19E+01	2.77E+02	1.84E-06
F18	1.22E-04	1.58E+01	1.31E+02	0.00E+00	1.42E+02	9.20E-01
F19	0.00E+00	3.59E+02	4.76E+00	0.00E+00	3.54E+01	**0.00E+00**

Table 3: $IACO_{\mathbb{R}}$-Hybrid Median error on SOCO benchmark function (50D)

Function	DE	CHC	G-CMA-ES	$IACO_{\mathbb{R}}$-Mtsls1	$IACO_{\mathbb{R}}$-BFGS	$IACO_{\mathbb{R}}$-Hybrid
F1	0.00E+00	1.63E-11	0.00E+00	0.00E+00	0.00E+00	**0.00E+00**
F2	3.29E-01	5.89E+01	2.64E-11	4.41E-13	0.00E+00	**0.00E+00**
F3	2.90E+01	1.33E+02	0.00E+00	4.83E+01	0.00E+00	**0.00E+00**
F4	1.51E-13	7.36E+01	1.08E+02	0.00E+00	4.09E+02	**0.00E+00**
F5	0.00E+00	1.32E-11	0.00E+00	0.00E+00	0.00E+00	**0.00E+00**
F6	1.42E-13	6.27E-07	2.11E+01	0.00E+00	1.91E+01	**0.00E+00**
F7	0.00E+00	1.40E-09	7.67E-11	0.00E+00	0.00E+00	**0.00E+00**
F8	3.54E+00	1.75E+02	0.00E+00	2.66E-05	0.00E+00	**0.00E+00**
F9	2.73E+02	3.08E+02	1.61E+01	0.00E+00	3.57E+02	**0.00E+00**
F10	0.00E+00	7.03E+00	6.71E+00	0.00E+00	1.53E+01	**0.00E+00**
F11	5.60E-05	1.12E-02	2.83E+01	0.00E+00	3.57E+02	**0.00E+00**
F12	5.27E-13	8.30E-11	1.87E+02	0.00E+00	5.95E+01	**0.00E+00**
F13	2.44E+01	6.90E+01	1.97E+02	6.79E-01	8.59E+01	**0.00E+00**
F14	2.58E-08	5.58E+01	1.05E+02	0.00E+00	3.55E+02	**0.00E+00**
F15	0.00E+00	6.05E-05	8.12E-04	0.00E+00	6.30E+00	**0.00E+00**
F16	1.51E-09	2.37E-09	4.22E+02	0.00E+00	1.48E+02	**0.00E+00**
F17	6.83E-01	7.89E+01	6.71E+02	6.50E+00	2.87E+02	**0.00E+00**
F18	1.20E-04	1.39E+01	1.27E+02	0.00E+00	1.40E+02	**0.00E+00**
F19	0.00E+00	4.20E+00	4.03E+00	0.00E+00	1.94E+01	**0.00E+00**

Table 4: Wilcoxon Signed-Ranks Tests with respect to IACO$_{\mathbb{R}}$-Hybrid approach

Algorithm	*Average Error*				*Median Error*			
	W+	W-	N	p-value	W+	W-	N	p-value
DE	73	18	13	0.0574	91	0	13	**0.0002**
CHC	186	4	19	**0.0003**	190	0	19	**0.0001**
G-CMA-ES	153	0	17	**0.0003**	120	0	15	**0.0001**
SOUPDE	81	24	14	0.0785	55	0	10	**0.002**
DE-D40+Mm	87	18	14	**0.0295**	36	0	8	**0.0078**
GODE	68	23	13	0.1272	78	0	12	**0.0005**
GaDE	39	16	10	0.2754	45	0	9	**0.0039**
jDElscop	31	14	9	0.3594	28	0	7	**0.0156**
MOS-DE	18	18	8	1.0000	15	0	5	0.0625
MA-SSW-Chains	147	24	18	**0.0074**	105	0	14	**0.0001**
RPSO-vm	119	17	16	**0.0084**	105	0	14	**0.0001**
Tuned IPSOLS	94	11	14	**0.0067**	55	0	10	**0.002**
EvoPROpt	190	0	19	**0.0001**	120	0	15	**0.0001**
EM323	78	27	14	0.1189	105	0	14	**0.0001**
VXQR1	86	5	13	**0.0024**	91	0	13	**0.0002**
IACOR-Mtsls1	28	8	8	0.1953	15	0	5	0.0625

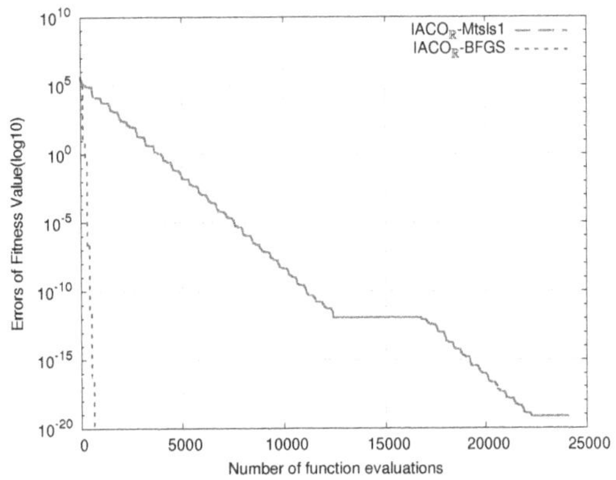

Figure 3: Function $F1$: Comparison of error of fitness value in Mtsls1 and BFGS. This is the case where both algorithm find global optimum.

umn (N) indicates represent number of instances for which there is a difference in the result between two algorithms.

A p-value greater than 0.05 indicates non-significant statistical difference [5]. In terms of average error, the performance of our approach is comparable to $IACO_{\mathbb{R}}$-Mtsls1 as the p-value is **0.1953** (> 0.05) and outperforms CHC, G-CMA-ES, DE-D40+Mmm, MA-SSW-Chains, RPSO-vm, Tuned IPSOLS, EvoPROpt and VXQR1 algorithms. In terms of median error, our approach performs better than all approaches considered, except MOS-DE and $IACO_{\mathbb{R}}$-Mtsls1 to which it is comparable.

We now provide specific examples from the SOCO benchmark functions in order to illustrate the performance of our approach. In Figure 3, it is seen that for the 50-dimensional function $F1$, both algorithms (Mtsls1 and BFGS) are able to independently find the global minima. However, the speed of BFGS leads to faster convergence, the reason for which can be attributed to that fact that the function is a spherical unimodal function. Hence it is easier for gradient-based algorithms to find the global minima on such functions.

In Figure 4, we show that for the function $F3$, Mtsls1 approach fails in finding the global minima, whereas the use of BFGS as well as our hybrid approach, are able to achieve optimal results.

One may opine that the reason for faster convergence is

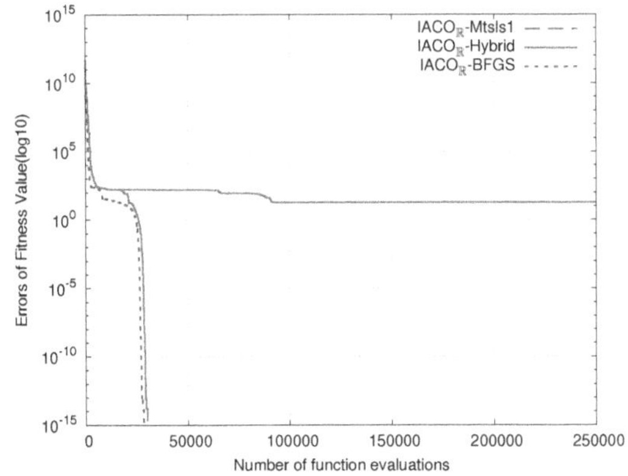

Figure 4: Function $F3$: Comparison of error of fitness value using all three approaches. In this case, BFGS algorithm finds the global optimum whereas the Mtsls1 algorithm fails.

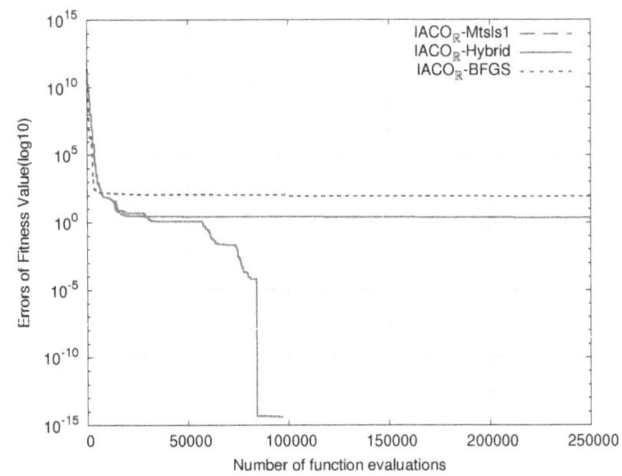

Figure 5: Function $F13$: Comparison of error of fitness value on all three approaches, indicating that the standalone use of the BFGS or Mtsls1 algorithm fails to find the global optimum, but our hybrid algorithm is able to attain the optimal solution.

the usage of BFGS algorithm, but we demonstrate that it may not always be true. In the case of benchmark functions $F13$ and $F17$, we find that both algorithms individually are not able to achieve global optima, whereas hybrid approach is successful. This is shown in Figures 5 and 6.

In Figure 7, we compare all the three approaches in terms of average number of function evaluations on the SOCO benchmark functions. We find that our hybrid approach takes less number of function evaluations on an average. It takes lower number of function evaluations than $IACO_{\mathbb{R}} - Mtsls1$ for **14** out of 19 functions and **16** out of 19 functions for $IACO_{\mathbb{R}} - BFGS$. Our hybrid approach outperforms both the approaches for 11 out of 19 functions, namely $F2, F4, F6, F7, F8, F10, F13, F14, F15, F17$ and $F19$. On an average (across benchmark functions), the reference approaches take 54% more function evaluations ($IACO_{\mathbb{R}}$-Mtsls1: 134464.7, $IACO_{\mathbb{R}}$-Hybrid: **87043.97**) than our approach.

We also show the box plots for the average and median error for using our approach against the other approaches in Figures 8 and 9. The vertical axis represents the error (average or median) on the 19 benchmark functions. In

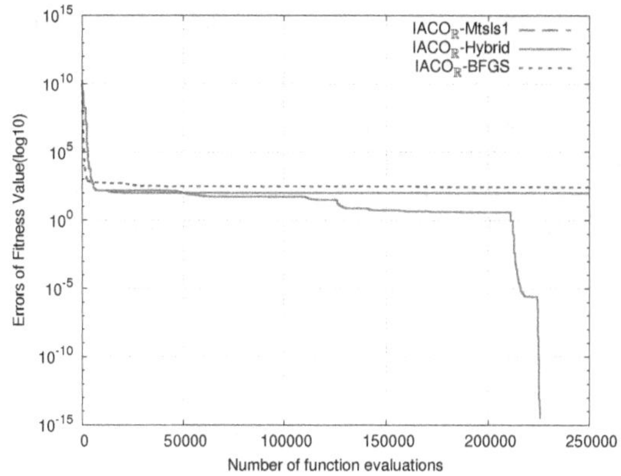

Figure 6: Function $F17$: Comparison of error of fitness values on all three approaches, , indicating that the standalone use of the BFGS or Mtsls1 algorithm fails to find the global optimum, but our hybrid algorithm is able to attain the optimal solution.

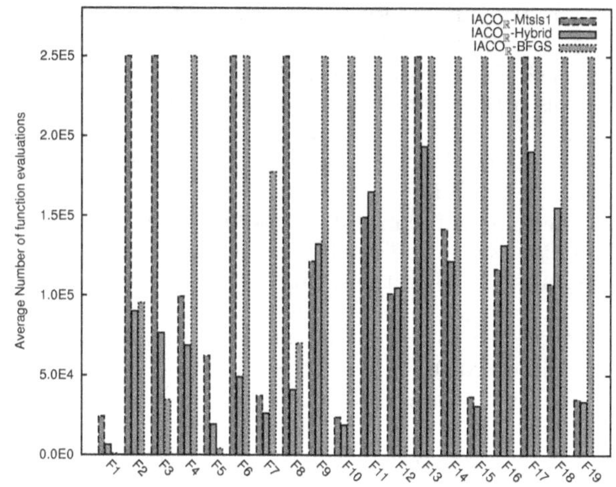

Figure 7: Comparison of average number of function evaluations used in all three approaches. Our hybrid approach uses fewer number of iterations, as can be seen from the bars in the plot.

case of average error shown in Figure 8, we observe that the performance of our hybrid approach is comparable to other approaches, whereas in case of median error, our approach outperforms the others, as shown in Figure 9.

6. CONCLUSION

This paper presented a hybrid approach using $IACO_\mathbb{R}$ for exploration and a choice between Mtsls1 and BFGS for exploitation (local-search). We presented the results of using this approach on functions from the SOCO benchmarks. Our hybrid approach is able to find the global optima in terms of average value for **14** benchmark functions, and in terms of the median value for **all** SOCO benchmark functions. The approach also gives improved results in terms of number of iterations on these benchmarks (the reference approaches use upto 54% more function evaluations on an average). We conclude that this approach is feasible for being used in applications involving continuous optimization. Future work in this direction would involve developing adaptive strategies by introducing parameters to make informed choices between the gradient and non-gradient based methods presented here, rather than simply making a probabilistic choice. This would enable to make improved and adaptive local decisions, which can provide better results when incorporated with the overall optimization algorithm.

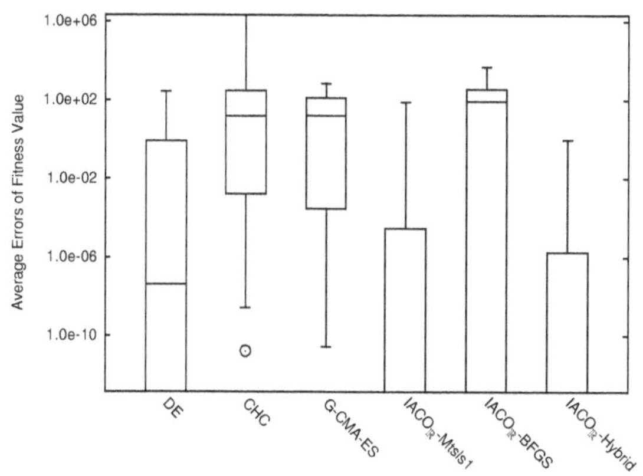

Figure 8: Box plot for average errors

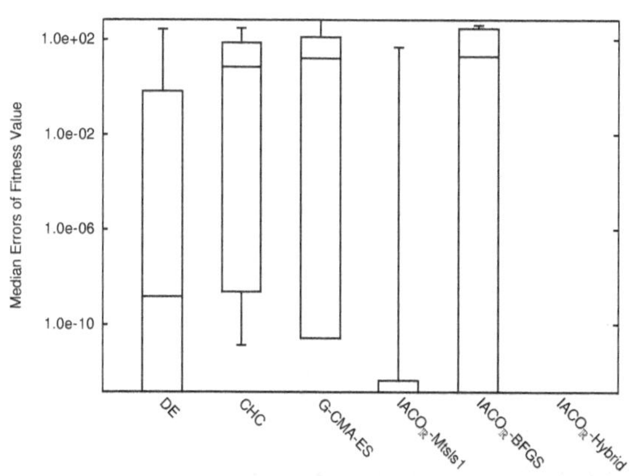

Figure 9: Box plot for median Errors

7. REFERENCES

[1] Anne Auger and Nikolaus Hansen. A restart CMA evolution strategy with increasing population size. In *Evolutionary Computation, 2005. The 2005 IEEE Congress on*, volume 2, pages 1769–1776. IEEE, 2005.

[2] Doğan Aydın, Tianjun Liao, Marco A Montes de Oca, and Thomas Stützle. Improving performance via population growth and local search: the case of the artificial bee colony algorithm. In *Artificial Evolution*, pages 85–96. Springer, 2012.

[3] Saman Babaie-Kafaki, Masoud Fatemi, and Nezam Mahdavi-Amiri. Two effective hybrid conjugate gradient algorithms based on modified BFGS updates. *Numerical Algorithms*, 58(3):315–331, 2011.

[4] Larry J Eshelman. chapter real-coded genetic

algorithms and interval-schemata. *Foundations of genetic algorithms*, 2:187–202, 1993.

[5] Ahmed Ezzat, Ashraf M Abdelbar, and Donald C Wunsch II. A bare-bones ant colony optimization algorithm that performs competitively on the sequential ordering problem. *Memetic Computing*, 6(1):19–29, 2014.

[6] F Herrera, M Lozano, and D Molina. Test suite for the special issue of soft computing on scalability of evolutionary algorithms and other metaheuristics for large scale continuous optimization problems. *URL: http://sci2s.ugr.es/eamhco/updated-functions1-19.pdf*, published 2010.

[7] Steven G Johnson. The NLopt nonlinear-optimization package, 2010.

[8] Dervis Karaboga, Beyza Gorkemli, Celal Ozturk, and Nurhan Karaboga. A comprehensive survey: artificial bee colony (ABC) algorithm and applications. *Artificial Intelligence Review*, 42(1):21–57, 2014.

[9] Mustafa Servet Kıran and Mesut Gündüz. A recombination-based hybridization of particle swarm optimization and artificial bee colony algorithm for continuous optimization problems. *Applied Soft Computing*, 13(4):2188–2203, 2013.

[10] Dong-Hui Li and Masao Fukushima. A modified BFGS method and its global convergence in nonconvex minimization. *Journal of Computational and Applied Mathematics*, 129(1):15–35, 2001.

[11] Shutao Li, Mingkui Tan, Ivor W Tsang, and JT-Y Kwok. A hybrid PSO-BFGS strategy for global optimization of multimodal functions. *Systems, Man, and Cybernetics, Part B: Cybernetics, IEEE Transactions on*, 41(4):1003–1014, 2011.

[12] Tianjun Liao, Doğan Aydın, and Thomas Stützle. Artificial bee colonies for continuous optimization: Experimental analysis and improvements. *Swarm Intelligence*, 7(4):327–356, 2013.

[13] Tianjun Liao, Marco A Montes de Oca, Dogan Aydin, Thomas Stützle, and Marco Dorigo. An incremental ant colony algorithm with local search for continuous optimization. In *Proceedings of the 13th annual conference on Genetic and evolutionary computation*, pages 125–132. ACM, 2011.

[14] Tianjun Liao, Thomas Stützle, Marco A Montes de Oca, and Marco Dorigo. A unified ant colony optimization algorithm for continuous optimization. *European Journal of Operational Research*, 234(3):597–609, 2014.

[15] Dong C Liu and Jorge Nocedal. On the limited memory BFGS method for large scale optimization. *Mathematical programming*, 45(1-3):503–528, 1989.

[16] Manuel Lozano, Daniel Molina, and Francisco Herrera. Editorial scalability of evolutionary algorithms and other metaheuristics for large-scale continuous optimization problems. *Soft Computing*, 15(11):2085–2087, 2011.

[17] Mohit Mathur, Sachin B Karale, Sidhartha Priye, VK Jayaraman, and BD Kulkarni. Ant colony approach to continuous function optimization. *Industrial & Engineering Chemistry Research*, 39(10):3814–3822, 2000.

[18] Ralf Salomon. Evolutionary algorithms and gradient search: similarities and differences. *Evolutionary Computation, IEEE Transactions on*, 2(2):45–55, 1998.

[19] Serap Ulusam Seçkiner, Yunus Eroğlu, Merve Emrullah, and Türkay Dereli. Ant colony optimization for continuous functions by using novel pheromone updating. *Applied Mathematics and Computation*, 219(9):4163–4175, 2013.

[20] JA Snyman and LP Fatti. A multi-start global minimization algorithm with dynamic search trajectories. *Journal of Optimization Theory and Applications*, 54(1):121–141, 1987.

[21] Krzysztof Socha and Marco Dorigo. Ant colony optimization for continuous domains. *European journal of operational research*, 185(3):1155–1173, 2008.

[22] Rainer Storn and Kenneth Price. Differential evolution–a simple and efficient heuristic for global optimization over continuous spaces. *Journal of global optimization*, 11(4):341–359, 1997.

[23] Ke Tang, Xın Yáo, Ponnuthurai Nagaratnam Suganthan, Cara MacNish, Ying-Ping Chen, Chih-Ming Chen, and Zhenyu Yang. Benchmark functions for the CEC 2008 special session and competition on large scale global optimization. *Nature Inspired Computation and Applications Laboratory, USTC, China*, 2007.

[24] Lin-Yu Tseng and Chun Chen. Multiple trajectory search for large scale global optimization. In *Evolutionary Computation, 2008. CEC 2008.(IEEE World Congress on Computational Intelligence). IEEE Congress on*, pages 3052–3059. IEEE, 2008.

[25] Lin-Yu Tseng and Chun Chen. Multiple trajectory search for unconstrained/constrained multi-objective optimization. In *Evolutionary Computation, 2009. CEC'09. IEEE Congress on*, pages 1951–1958. IEEE, 2009.

[26] Zhong Wan, Kok Lay Teo, XianLong Shen, and ChaoMing Hu. New BFGS method for unconstrained optimization problem based on modified armijo line search. *Optimization*, 63(2):285–304, 2014.

[27] Zengxin Wei, Gaohang Yu, Gonglin Yuan, and Zhigang Lian. The superlinear convergence of a modified BFGS-type method for unconstrained optimization. *Computational optimization and applications*, 29(3):315–332, 2004.

[28] Frank Wilcoxon. Individual comparisons by ranking methods. *Biometrics bulletin*, pages 80–83, 1945.

[29] SJ Wright and J Nocedal. *Numerical optimization*, volume 2. Springer New York, 1999.

[30] Shi-Zheng Zhao, Ponnuthurai Nagaratnam Suganthan, and Swagatam Das. Self-adaptive differential evolution with multi-trajectory search for large-scale optimization. *Soft Computing*, 15(11):2175–2185, 2011.

An Ant Colony Optimization Algorithm based on Scheduling Preference for Maximizing Working Time of Wireless Sensor Networks

Yu Liu[124], Wei-Neng Chen[1234], Xiao-Min Hu[245*], Jun Zhang[1234]
[1]School of Advanced Computing, Sun Yat-sen University, Guangzhou, China
[2]Key Lab. Machine Intelligence and Advanced Computing, Ministry of Education, China
[3]Collaborative Innovation Center of High Performance Computing, China
[4]Engineering Research Center of Supercomputing Engineering Software, Ministry of Education, China
[5]School of Public Health, Sun Yat-sen University, Guangzhou, China
* Corresponding Author, Email: huxiaom6@mail.sysu.edu.cn

ABSTRACT

Abstract—With the proliferation of wireless sensor networks (WSN), the issues about how to schedule all the sensors in order to maximize the system's working time have been in the spotlight. Inspired by the promising performance of ant colony optimization (ACO) in solving combinational optimization problem, we attempt to apply it in prolonging the life time of WSN. In this paper, we propose an improved version of ACO algorithm to get solutions about selecting exact sensors to accomplish the covering task in a reasonable way to preserve more energy to maintain longer active time. The methodology is based on maximizing the disjoint subsets of sensors, in other words, in every time interval, choosing which sensor to sustain active state must be rational in certain extent. With the aid of pheromone and heuristic information, a better solution can be constructed in which pheromone denotes the previous scheduling experience, while heuristic information reflects the desirable device assignment. Orderly sensor selection is designed to construct an advisable subset for coverage task. The proposed method has been successfully applied in solving limited energy assignment problem no matter in homogenous or heterogeneous WSNs. Simulation experiments have shown it has a good performance in addressing relevant issues.

Categories and Subject Descriptors

• **Mathematics of computing~Evolutionary algorithms** • *Hard ware~Sensor applications and deployments*

General Terms

Algorithms, Performance, Design, Experimentation

GECCO '15, July 11–15, 2015, Madrid, Spain
© 2015 ACM. ISBN 978-1-4503-3472-3/15/07...$15.00
DOI: http://dx.doi.org/10.1145/2739480.2754671

Keywords

Ant colony optimization algorithm; Wireless Sensors Network (WSN); maximize working time; schedule.

1. INTRODUCTION

With the rapid development and a wide range of application of embedding chips, Wireless Sensors Network has been applied in some aspects in technological and daily life. Sensors are tiny embedding devices which are commonly comprised of sensing component, signal transformer, transmitter and sources of energy supplying. These tiny embedding devices can detect surrounding environment, and gather quantified state changes of monitored objects, then transform changes to electrical signals and provide a corresponding output, transmit it to the control center (decision-making center) [17]. Owing to its practical properties, WSN has been widely applied in real-time monitoring field [1], [3], [8]-[9], [22]-[23],[25]-[26], [28] , such as smart home management [3], [26], natural disease prevention and control [28], environmental security tracking [4], [5], and some other domains [8],[25]. For instance, in security field, based on data gathered from sensors, we can judge whether there are some dangerous things will happen [9].

Since the main energy source of sensors is non-replaceable battery, in the same environment, the quality of performance of WSN mainly depends on the working time of systems. With this momentum, studies about how to use the fixed energy and prolong the working time of the whole system have been one of the most significant cases which scientists are committing them to studying. Recent days, some novel approaches have been brought up [2], [5], [7], [10]-[14], [16], [20]-[21], [27], [29], [32]-[33]. Among them, scheduling devices efficiently, choosing a minimal subset of sensors to achieve the coverage mission while the rest of sensors turn to sleep state to save energy, has shown a satisfying performance [10]-[12], [34]. Finally, in order to achieve longer working time, we need a function-well method to schedule active sensors, and to make the disjoint subsets of sensors which can accomplish covering job at its own as much as possible. With available usage counts of sensors changing, schedule scheme will updated simultaneously. It is a headache problem because sensors scheduling in the previous time interval may lay influence on choice making in the latter time interval. Therefore, how to maximize disjoint minimal subsets of sensors in the whole proceeding flow has been prone to a non-deterministic polynomial (NP) complete problem and exhaustive search is impossible.

Furthermore, depending on the types of sensors and different coverage scopes of devices, WSN can be categorized as homogeneous and heterogeneous wireless sensors network. In application reality, due to the complexity of the task, multiple sensors (e.g., chemical, pressure, humidity, thermal and fluid velocity sensor) are generally required to cooperate to achieve tasks. Diversity of sensors makes the solving of such issues become thornier. It is indispensable that taking different coverage radii of different sensors into consideration while scheduling sensors. Existing work on WSN typically assumes all sensors in system are identical, and uses Boolean Detect Model to express the relationship between the sensor and the target point [34]. Therefore some methods exist to progress the problem in homogeneous wireless sensor networks, researches on heterogeneous wireless sensor network have progressed at a slow pace. In this paper, equal attentions will be attached on these two kinds of networks. In the meantime, another model, Probability Detect Model is considered [6] which recently have been used by many papers [10], [13]. In the new model, a target point being covered by a sensor is measured with probability which do comply more with the application reality and turn the topologies between sensors and target points into mathematically formal representation.

However, how to schedule sensors efficiently is still a thorny problem. Recent studies have shown that the inherent characteristic of stochastic algorithms makes it essential in solving such problems in terms of influences of experimental results imposed by scheduling sequence. Particle swarm optimization (PSO) [13], genetic algorithm (GA) [34] and ant colony optimization (ACO) algorithms [10]-[11], [32]-[33], etc., have been applied in handling such a headache challenge. Among them, ACO has shown to be promising. Although existing work on this has progressed a lot, there still are some issues to be solved, e.g., basically, which factors put constraints on system working time, whether some favorable scheduling preference are waiting to be discovered, and how to construct a optimal solution though applying the ACO algorithm.

Ant colony algorithm was developed by Marco Dorigo [18]-[20], inspired by foraging behaviors of ants. Based on heuristic information and pheromone, an approximately optimal solution of the problem can be constructed. ACO algorithm has inherent advantages in terms of combinational optimization problem and variable-length coding. In order to solve different practical problems and reflect characteristics of specific issues, the key is how to choose heuristic information, initialize and update pheromone, and then optimize the conventional algorithm for the better performance. The existing methods for utilizing ACO algorithm to solve the Efficient Energy Coverage problem of WSNs focus on the issues of constructing heuristic information, pheromone and evaluation criterion [10], [11]. Nevertheless, scheduling order has been omitted, which is indispensable in scheduling cases. Therefore, this paper comprehensively analyzes how to improve performance of conventional ACO algorithm by introducing a novel scheduling sequence and changing the solution constructing space of an ant. As the well-known Cannikin Law say, how much of a bucket filled with water, does not depend on the highest piece of wood on the sides of casks, but rather depends on the shortest piece on the sides of casks. Hence, more attention should be put on the shortest piece of wood in the scheduling algorithm. In this paper, we try to find the key factors that are constraints for working time of the whole system. It is quite clear that the target points which are covered by few sensors become the shortest piece of wood. Therefore, all targets points will be sorted according to coverage ratio. The lower coverage ratio a target point have, the higher its priority level of scheduling preference is which the sensor node is selected to meet its coverage need.

In order to schedule sensors in a more reasonable and efficient way, system working time are divided into several minor time intervals. In the existing methods on how to construct an optimal schedule [10], [11], ACO algorithm is applied in constructing an optimal schedule scheme in the current time interval until no subset of sensors which could accomplish sensing task can be found, and then the past time intervals are the total working time of the whole system. In fact, there are defects in the above approach. It is well known that sensors scheduling in the previous time interval will affect schedule in the latter time interval. A least reasonable schedule in the previous time interval will shorten the total working time of the system. Therefore, we change solution constructing space of an ant. An ant constructs an integrated schedule about the whole working flow, though stigmergy between ants, some better solution for the whole schedule can be constructed.

The rest of this paper is organized as follows. Part Two explains some precondition definitions, for instance, problem definition, explanations about Probability Detect Model and priority level of scheduling preference. Part Three displays the details about the approach proposed in this paper. Simulation results are presented in Part Four to evaluate the effectiveness of the proposed approach. Part Five concludes the whole paper.

2. PRELIMINARY

In this section, we will have a deep introduction about some definitions about problem properties and computational formula in the proposed algorithm. Then we'll have a brief introduction about ant colony optimization.

2.1 Problem definition

In a common wireless sensor network, these are some target points in the monitored area. Some sensors are deployed to detect the changing states of the target points. On the ground of the places of sensors, WSN could be divided into unstructured WSN and structured one. In the structured WSN, all places of sensors are designed based on the places of target points in advance according to a particular topological algorithm. However, attempts to find a suitable placement are time-consuming and headache issues. At the same time, there are still some places where are full with dangerous or harmful objects out of reach. As a consequence, in this paper, assumed that wireless sensors network is unstructured, sensors are densely placed in the monitored area. It means the positions of sensors are random and there is no need to take complicated topological structure into consideration that is still unsolved. Apparently, unstructured WSN makes the formation for solution to the problem in a more clear way.

In the unstructured WSN, sensors are always redundant for all target points. In order to achieve the monitoring task, there is no need to activate all sensors. Choose a minimal and optimal subset of sensors which can accomplish the coverage task to be scheduled to be working state until some of them are energy drained or a better combination occurs while the remained sensor nodes turn to be sleeping mode. In the existing methods [30], the scheduled subset of sensors tends to continue working until some of them are energy drained that the subset of sensors can't achieve the coverage task. In a certain extent, there is much irrationality in the above approaches. With the decay of available usage counts of sensors, the previous scheduled subset may become little reasonable for the current time interval. Therefore, a new model is adopted by recent researches in which system time is divided into several minor time intervals, then according to a scheduling algorithm an optimal subset of sensors is scheduled for the current time interval and energy distribution of sensors. There are several assumption in the proposed algorithm, e.g. Sensors have fixed usage counts; active sensors consume once from available usage counts in a time interval. In every time interval, energy distribution of sensors is different, then an optimal of sensors scheduling for the current time interval are changing. When a new time interval starts, sensors should be scheduled again. As a prerequisite, the working subset of sensors must fulfill the coverage task. All things we need to do are maximizing the number of subsets of sensors to prolong working time of the whole system.

In the general case, considerating the working time of wireless sensors network, there are two issues need to be focused on. One is the sensing coverage issue and other is network connectivity. With the development of electronic technology, these above issues can be performed by sensors simultaneously. Coverage means active sensors can detect changes of states about all target points. The sensing coverage issue can be measured by the sensing radius of sensors and the distance between the sensor node and the target point. While the connectivity among devices demands all sensors form a well-communicating network and sensors can transmit information gathered to the control center. If the communication range r_c of devices is more twice than the sensing coverage radius r_s, it has been well proven that full coverage in target area infers well-connected communication between devices [4]. In this paper, this restriction is assumed to be satisfied on the ground that it is has become a technological requirement with progress in sensor technology.

In the problem scenario, formally, there are some target points $p_i(i=1,2,3\cdots N_p$, N_p is the number of target points) to be monitored the occurrence of events in the target area A. Some sensors s_j ($j=1,2,3\cdots N_s$, N_s is the number of sensors) are deployed to monitor the changes of states about target points.

2.2 Probability detect model

In Boolean Detect Model, sensor nodes are deemed to have a coverage radius; when Euclidean distance between the sensor node and the target point is more-or-equal than the covering radius of sensor, sensor can't detect anything about the target point, while the distance is less than the coverage radius, the sensor node can detect changes about the objective node. When dealing with heterogeneous sensors which different types of sensor nodes may occur, Boolean Detect Model are appeared with some defects and become unsuitable to handle cases about different coverage radii. In this paper, Probability Detect Model is considered [6] which recently have been adopted by many papers [13]. Probability Detect Model measures coverage problem with probability, every kind of sensors has two types of coverage radii, r_s and r_u, when Euclidean distance between the sensor node and the target point is less than r_s, the probability of the target point be detected is almost equal to 1, while distance is more than r_u, the probability is almost 0, when distance is within the range between r_s and r_u, the probability increases exponentially along with distance decreasing.

Mathematically, the probability that a sensor j detect the target point i can be written as follows:

$$p_{ij} = \begin{cases} 0, & if\ d_{ij} > r_u \\ e^{-a(d_{ij}-r_u)^m}, & if\ r_s < d_{ij} \le r_u \\ 1, & if\ d_{ij} \le r_s \end{cases} \qquad (1)$$

Where d_{ij} is symbolized the Euclidean distance between the senor j and the target point i.

A target point can be detected by many sensors with probability being more than zero. Nevertheless, being covered means the probability by which the target point is detected is more than a fixed parameter ε which is user-specified. Mathematically, the definition can be formalized as follows:

$$p_i = 1 - \prod_{s_t \subseteq s}(1 - p_{ij}) \ge \varepsilon \qquad (2)$$

Where S is the set of all sensors, $s_t \subseteq s$ is the set of sensors that is scheduled in the current time interval. In every time interval, this condition as above must be met by every target point.

Therefore, in every time interval, sensors are either active states or dormant states. The problem we are aimed to handle is turned to a binary-code programming, that is, for a specific sensor, whether to choose it to achieve the coverage task.

On the ground that every target point must meet the above demand about coverage quantified with probability, target points which are covered by few sensors will be constraints to the working time of systems. Once sensors are energy drained, they will have no available usage counts to be active then become unavailable for scheduling. Unreasonable scheduling sequence may make these sensors become too fewer sensors to cover it to meet the demand about coverage. Therefore, we define the coverage priority level of scheduling preference for every target point according to the Cannikin Law. Defining the coverage priority level on the ground of a numeric variable computed as follows:

$$x_i = \sum_{j=1}^{N_s} e_j p_{ij} \qquad (3)$$

Where e_j is the remained usage counts of sensor j can continue working, p_{ij} is the probability that sensor j detect the target point i and N_s is the number of all sensors. Therefore, x_i is a value which can reflect the being coverage ratio of the target point i. The smaller the value of x_i is, the higher the priority level of scheduling preference is which a sensor is selected to cover it.

2.3 The conventional ACO algorithm

In this subsection, we will have a brief introduction about ant colony optimization algorithm. ACO is a member of swarm intelligence algorithms, and is a kind of stochastic algorithms.

Inspired by the foraging behavior of ants, the ACO algorithm was initially proposed by Marco Dorigo [18]-[20]. An ant seeks to a path between its colony and the source of food. When the ant constructs a complete path, it deposits pheromone in the past edges. The next ant can construct better solution depend on pheromone on the paths and some random factors. After many ants completing the construction of paths, a shortest path between the source of food and the ant colony can be found through stigmergy between ants. Pheromones represent empirical experiences from those past individuals, while heuristic information that are random factors in the algorithm represent the desirability of exploring more possible paths and reflects the stoaschtic characteristics simultaneously. ACO first applied in solving the traveling salesman problem (TSP) [18]. A salesman wanders in a map with many cities to construct a shortest circuit which pasts all cities only once. Though the proceeding procedure of solving the TSP problem, we can have a clear understanding about ACO algorithm.

```
Algorithm 1: ACO algorithm for Traveling Salesman Problem

Input: information about cities
Output: the shortest circuit between cities

Let t=0
Set parameters: Nk, Nc, ρ
Initialize(dij , Pij)
While t< Nc do
// a new colony starts selection
    for each ant k=1,···,nk
    //a new solution for ant k starts
      do
        Add link(i, j) to path xk(t) based on equation (4)
      until a circuit between all cities accomplish
    if fk(t)<fbest fk(t)->fbest xk(t)->xbest
   update τij using equation (5)
t=t+1
Return the path xbest with the length fbest as the solution
```

Figure 1. Pseudocode flow of solving TSP with conventional ACO algorithm

Where N_c denotes the number of the colonies and N_k is the number of ants in each colony. $f^k(t)$ is the length and $x^k(t)$ is the path of the circuit constructed by the ant k in the colony t. x_{best} is the integrated path and f_{best} is the length of the shortest circuit.

When an ant chooses which edge to be joined into the path, selection is based on the heuristic information and the pheromone. Roulette Wheel Selection is usually applied in selection process. The probability of the ant on the city i choosing the city j to be the next city to reach is computed as follow:

$$p_{ij}^k(t) = \begin{cases} \dfrac{\tau_{ij}^\alpha(t)\eta_{ij}^\beta(t)}{\sum_{u \in \mathrm{N}_i^k(t)} \tau_{iu}^\alpha(t)\eta_{iu}^\beta(t)} & if\ j \in \mathrm{N}_i^k(t) \\ 0 & if\ j \notin \mathrm{N}_i^k(t) \end{cases} \quad (4)$$

Where $\tau_{ij}(t)$ is the pheromone and $\eta_{ij}(t)$ is the heuristic information on the link between i and j. α and β are parameters specified for the problem to balance the weight of pheromone and heuristic information, $\mathrm{N}_i^k(t)$ is the collection of the remained cities which have a link with city i but haven't been visited for the ant k in the colony t. When all ants in a colony have accomplished the construction of paths, pheromone will be updated, updating formula like this:

$$\tau_{ij}(t+1) = (1-\rho)\tau_{ij}(t) + \Delta\tau_{ij} \quad (5)$$

$$\Delta\tau_{ij} = \sum_{k=1}^{\mathrm{N}_k} \frac{1}{f^k(t)} \quad (6)$$

Where $f^k(t)$ is the distance of circuit constructed by ant k, and ρ is the decay ratio of pheromone. At the beginning of the algorithm, pheromone in each edge usually is initialized with an identical little random number or in some other ways.

In this scenario, heuristic information is set to the reciprocal of the distance of path constructed by the ant which is due to that a short path is expected to be found.

For a specified practical problem, It's critical that how to construct the pheromone and heuristic information.

3. MODEL DESCRIPTION

As introduced in the Part One, these are some factors to be constraints to working time of the whole system. For target points which are covered by few sensors, undoubtedly, they become the shortest pieces among influences for working time of the network. Therefore, more attentions must be put on those target points to avoid unreasonable schedule makes them couldn't be covered by enough sensors in the early time to shorten working time of the whole network.

To achieve a rational schedule and a maximal working time, according to the Cannikin Law theory, at the beginning of scheduling, coverage ratios of all target points will be computed and sorted in ascending order to find the shortest board. Sensors should be scheduled firstly to meet the coverage demand of target points which have a small coverage ratio computed as the formula (3). For every target point, a set of candidate sensors will be maintained, and a sensor will be selected from the candidate set to meet coverage task of the target point. Selection is made on the basis of probability which is computed as follows:

$$p_{ij}^s(t) = \begin{cases} \dfrac{\tau_{ij}(t)\eta_{ij}(t)}{\sum_{u \in \mathrm{N}_i^s(t)} \tau_{iu}(t)\eta_{iu}(t)} & if\ j \in \mathrm{N}_i^s(t) \\ 0 & if\ j \notin \mathrm{N}_i^s(t) \end{cases} \quad (7)$$

Where $\tau_{ij}(t)$ denotes the pheromone and $\eta_{ij}(t)$ denotes the heuristic information for sensor j is chose to cover the target point i. $\mathrm{N}_i^s(t)$ is the candidate set of sensors that remains several available usage times and can cover the target point i in the time interval t for the solution constructed by the ant s.

In this paper, pheromone τ_{ij} is set to the tendency that the target point i is mainly covered by the sensor j. We firstly initialize all pheromone with an identical value. After a colony of ants completing the construction of solutions, values of pheromone will be updated. The updating formula could be formalized like follows:

$$\tau_{ij}(t+1) = (1-\rho)\tau_{ij}(t) + \Delta\tau_{ij} \quad (8)$$

Pheromone evaporates with time elapsing and ρ is the decay ratio of pheromone.

$$\Delta\tau_{ij} = \sum_{s=1}^{n_k} \frac{n_{ij}}{n_s} \quad (9)$$

Where n_s is the total working time of the schedule constructed by the ant s, and η_{ij} is the number of times for sensor j is selected to meet the coverage task of target point i in all time intervals of the current solution constructed by the ant s. n_k is the number of ants in the current colony.

For a reason that a sensor which has more residual times for using and could cover more target points is preferable to be selected, the heuristic information for sensor j to cover the target point i is computed like this:

$$\eta_{ij}(t) = e_j(t) \cdot c_j \quad (10)$$

Where $e_j(t)$ is the residual times for using in the current time interval t and c_j is the number of target points that sensor j can cover. In different time interval, the usage counts for sensor j are changing all the time. Thus, when a new time interval starts, the value of $\eta_{ij}(t)$ need be updated.

After computing the choosing probability for all sensors, a 0.9-roulette wheel selection strategy is adopted to select a sensor from the candidate set of sensors. The 0.9-roulette wheel selection is an improved version from roulette wheel selection strategy. A random number p between 0 and 1 is produced, if p is less than 0.9, the sensor in candidate set which has the biggest choosing probability will be chose directly. If p is more or equal than 0.9, roulette wheel selection strategy will be applied to select a sensor from the candidate set. Obviously, the improved version speeds the running of the algorithm and reserves the stochastic characteristics.

The selected sensor doesn't only cover the current target point, but also cover other target points under coverage. Along with the sorted sequence of target points, sensors will be selected until all target points have reached the demand about coverage, otherwise, the above procedures will be repeated, then a sub-schedule for the current time interval completes. Available usage counts of sensors in the current sub-schedule will decrease, then the rank of all target points will updated. The above things are done over and over again until there isn't a set of sensors can accomplish the coverage task for all target points. The past working time intervals are the active time for the whole system in the solution constructed by the ant. Figure 2 has shown this process. Then, construction of solution by the current ant ends, and the next ant starts constructing new solution.

With multiple updating of pheromone, under the guide with richer experiences, a better scheduling scheme can be found.

In this paper, the selecting rule of conventional ACO is still observed. When wandering in the solution graph, choosing a direction to construct the solution simultaneously.

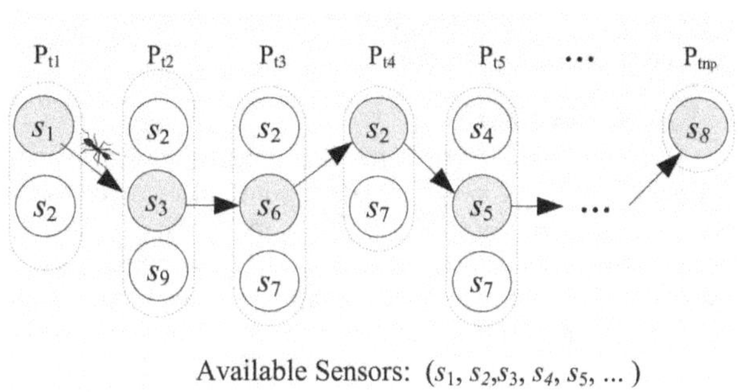

Fig 2. A simplified process of solution construction

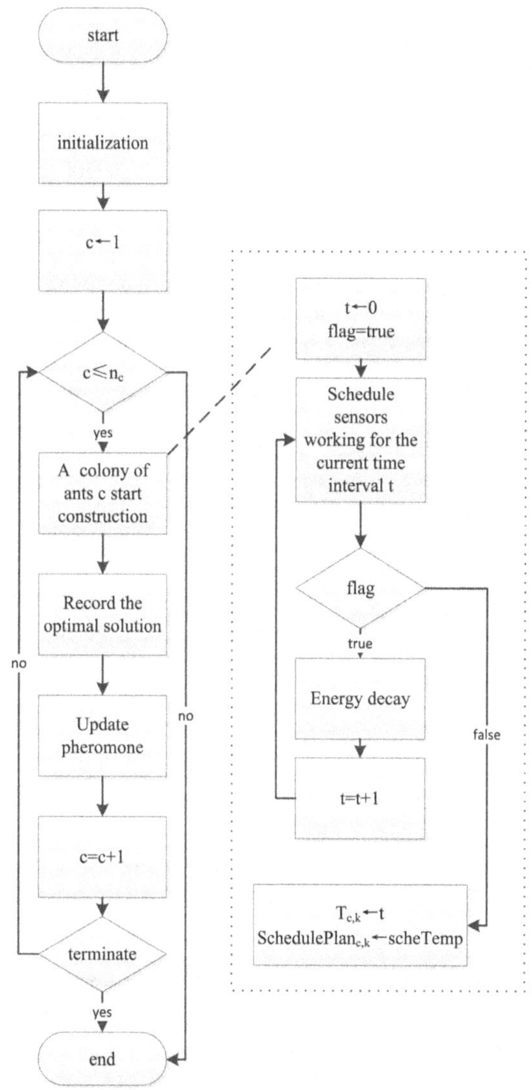

Fig. 3 The flow chart of the new proposed method

Every ant in the colony constructs an integrated solution independently. In other words, the constructing space for solutions by an ant is an integrated scheduling scheme for the whole network. Therefore, it is more possible to construct a better solution for the whole scheduling than an ant just constructs a partial solution.

In the Figure 3, an integrated proceeding flow for the new proposed approach will be shown.

4. SIMULATION

In this section, we present some experimental results to verify performance of the proposed approach. Since many methods have been proposed for maximizing the working time of wireless sensors network, a comparison between the new approach and the approach in [10] will be shown. Both of them apply the ACO to search a function-well scheduling scheme to prolong working time of WSN. For the new proposed approach, two improved aspects have been introduced, then, efficiency in application reality is verified in the homogeneous and heterogeneous WSN. The key point of comparison lies not only in the performance but the computational complexity.

4.1 Experimental conditions

We carried out two simulations to verify the performance of the proposed approach. In the first simulation, we compare working time of the network with the algorithm proposed in [10] applied in the homogeneous network. There are six different scenarios in first simulation, all scenarios are set in a background which sensors and target points are deposed at random in a 10m*10m square area. Table 1 shows the number of sensors and target points in different scenarios. There is only one type of sensors that we set parameters as follows: r_s=1.5m, r_u=6m, a=0.5 and m=0.5. All sensors have an initial using time of 10, if a sensor always keeps working state, it can sustain working ten time intervals. In all scenarios, we set identically for the number of ants, the number of colonies and the parameter ε and ρ as follows: NA=50, NC=200, ε=0.97, ρ=0.5. In every scenario, the algorithm runs thirty times for the same map. The settings about parameters are same as in previous ACB-SA algorithm in [10].

In the second simulation, experiments are conducted in heterogeneous WSNs. All sensors are belonged to different categories and have different coverage radii. In experiments, coverage radii are randomly generated. r_s ranges between 1m and 3m, and r_u ranges between 4m and 6m. This simulation was conducted in an extreme condition that sensors are densely deployed in the target area. The number of sensors and target points are set to 100 and 50. All other parameters are identical as above. Particularly, possibility of a sensor being chosen is computed as formula (7). The parameter α and β in conventional ACO are set to be equal to 1.

All experiments are carried out on the PC with Intel(R) Core(TM) i3-4150 CPU at 3.50GHz and RAM of 8 GB.

Table 1.The number setting in every scenario

scenario	Number of sensors	Number of target points
S1	100	10
S2	150	10
S3	200	10
S4	100	30
S5	150	30
S6	200	30

4.2 Performance comparison

Conducted the two simulations, a comparison about the average working time will show as follows as Table.2.

Table 2.experimental results

Homogenous case			
	New method	ACB-SA	t-test
S1	71.8	68.1	18.13591
S2	126.7	124.5	8.02814
S3	126.2	123.1	13.99126
S4	64.1	61.0	11.49643
S5	79.6	72.7	24.22337
S6	145.2	139.7	14.74179
Heterogeneous case			
Ss1	66.3	64.8	5.56976

The first and second column of numbers is the average working time of the two algorithms. From the Table 2, significant differences can be shown, compared with the approach in [10], in every scenario, the average working time achieved by the new approach is significantly longer than that achieved by the ACB-SA. Hence, the new proposed approach has a promising performance in scheduling the sensors to achieve longer working time. The efficiency not only works well in the homogeneous WSNs, but also in the heterogeneous WSNs.

4.3 Computational complexity analysis

A promising algorithm has many requirements from kinds of aspects. Other than achieving good performance, in reality, fewer time and space consume are needed to be take into consideration. In this part, we focus on the comparation of computational complexity between approach in [10] and the new proposed approach to illustrate the promising performance of the new proposed approach in a further aspect.

In the ACB-AS, a round of ACO algorithm is aimed to select an optimal schedule in a time interval. Therefore, its computational complexity can be measured as (*# of colonies*) ·(*# of ants*) · (*# of target points*). In the new proposed approach, an ant finish an integrated schedule scheme includes schedule in every time interval. Similarly, its computational complexity can be calculated as (*# of colonies*)· (*# of ants*) · (*# of target points*). Apparently, these two algorithms has same order of magnitude in the case of computational complexity. However, the new proposed algorithm has a more promising performance than the existing approaches.

5. CONCLUSION

In this paper, we propose a novel approach to solve the Efficient Energy Coverage problem by applying an improved ACO. Proved by several experiments, the approach has a better performance than the existing one in [10]. Applied two improvements in two aspects, working time of WSNs have been extended in a relatively large extent. First of all, difference between target points has been taken into consideration. Target points which restrict the whole lifecycle have been taken as a priority of scheduling preference.

Then, a round of ACO algorithm is applied in constructing an optimal solution not only for a time interval, but a whole solution for the network. Introduced by this strategy, it is more possible to construct an optimal solution for the whole scheduling.

The construction of pheromone and heuristic information are also adjusted to make them more instructional for constructing solutions.

6. ACKNOWLEDGEMENT

This work was supported in part by the National Science Foundation of China (NSFC) Projects No.61379061, No.61332002, No.61202130, in part by Natural Science Foundation of Guangdong No. S2013040014949, and in part by Specialized Research Fund for the Doctoral Programs No. 20120171120027, No. 20130171120016.

7. REFERENCES

[1] A. R. Al-Ali, I. Zualkernan, F. Aloul. 2010. "A mobile GPRS-sensors array for air pollution monitoring," *IEEE Sensors J.*, 10, 10, 1666-1671.

[2] C. Zhang, Y. Zhang, Y. Fang. 2010. "A coverage inference protocol for wireless sensor networks," *IEEE Trans. Mobile Comput.* 9, 6, 850-864.

[3] D. M. Han, J. H. Lim. 2010. "Design and implementation of smart home energy management systems based on zigbee," *IEEE Trans. Consumer Electronics*, 56, 3, 1417 – 1425.

[4] D. Tian, N.D. Georganas. 2004. Connectivity maintenance and coverage preservation in wireless sensor networks. In *2004. Canadian Conference on Electrical and Computer Engineering*. May 2004. IEEE. 1097 – 1100.

[5] F. Ren, J. Zhang, T. He, et al. 2011. "EBRP: Energy-Balanced Routing Protocol for Data Gathering in Wireless Sensor Networks", *IEEE Trans. Parall. Distrib. Systems*. 22, 12, 2108 – 2125.

[6] H. da S Araújo, R. Holanda Filho. 2010. "WSN Routing: An Geocast Approach for Reducing Consumption Energy," In *2010 IEEE Wireless Communications and Networking Conference (WCNC)*. April 2010. IEEE. 1 – 8.

[7] H. Guo, K. S. Low, H. A. Nguyen. 2011. "Optimizing the Localization of a Wireless Sensor Network in Real Time Based on a Low-Cost Microcontroller," *IEEE Trans. Industrial Electronics*. 58, 3, 741 – 749.

[8] J. P. Carmo, P. M. Mendes, C. Couto, et al. 2010. "A 2.4-GHz CMOS Short-Range Wireless-Sensor-Network Interface for Automotive Applications," *IEEE Trans. Industrial Electronic*. 57, 5, 1764 – 1771.

[9] J. Yick, B. Mukherjee, D. Ghosal. 2005. "Analysis of a prediction-based mobility adaptive tracking algorithm," In *Broadband Networks, 2005. BroadNets 2005. 2nd International Conference on,* October 2005, IEEE, 753-760.

[10] J. W. Lee, J. J. Lee. 2012. "Ant-Colony-Based Scheduling Algorithm for Energy-Efficient Coverage of WSN," *IEEE Sensors Journal*. 12, 10, 3036 – 3046.

[11] J.W. Lee, B.S. Choi, J. J. Lee. 2011. "Energy-Efficient Coverage of Wireless Sensor Networks Using Ant Colony Optimization with Three Types of Pheromones," *IEEE Trans. Industrial Informatics*. 7, 3, 419 – 427.

[12] J. Zhang, H. S. H. Chung, A. W. L. Lo, et al. 2009. "Extended Ant Colony Optimization Algorithm for Power Electronic Circuit Design," *IEEE Trans. Power Electronics*. 24, 1, 147 – 162.

[13] J. Chen, J. Li, S. He, et al.. 2010. "Energy-efficient coverage based on probabilistic sensing model in wireless sensor networks," *IEEE Communications Letters*, 14, 9, 833 – 835.

[14] J. V. V. Sobral, R. A. L. Rabelo, H. S. Araujo, et al.. 2013. "Automated design of fuzzy rule base using ant colony optimization for improving the performance in Wireless Sensor Networks," *In 2013 IEEE International Conference on Fuzzy Systems (FUZZ)*. July 2013. IEEE. 1 – 8.

[15] J. Chen, J. Li, L.H. Lai. 2013. "Energy-Efficient Intrusion Detection with a Barrier of Probabilistic Sensors: Global and Local," *IEEE Trans. Wireless Communications*. 12, 9, 4742 – 4755.

[16] K. K. Rachuri, C. Siva Ram Murthy. 2009. "Energy Efficient and Scalable Search in Dense Wireless Sensor Networks," *IEEE Trans. Computers*. 58, 6, 812 – 826.

[17] L.M. Borges, F. J. Velez, A.S Lebres. 2014. "Survey on the Characterization and Classification of Wireless Sensor Network Applications," *IEEE Communications Surveys & Tutorials*. 16, 4, 1860 – 1890.

[18] M. Dorigo, L. M. Gambardella. 1997. "Ant colony system: a cooperative learning approach to the traveling salesman problem," *IEEE Trans. Evolutionary Computation*. 1, 1, 53 – 66.

[19] M. Dorigo, V. Maniezzo, A. Colorni. 1996. "Ant system: optimization by a colony of cooperating agents." *IEEE Trans. Systems, Man, and Cybernetics, Part B: Cybernetics*. 26, 1, 29 – 41.

[20] M. Dorigo, M. Birattari, T. Stutzle. 2004. "Ant Colony Optimization for NP-Hard Problems." In *Ant Colony Optimization*. MIT Press. 153 – 222.

[21] M. C. Rodriguez-Sanchez, S. Borromeo, J. A. Hernández-Tamames. 2011. "Wireless Sensor Networks for Conservation and Monitoring Cultural Assets." *IEEE Sensors Journal*. 11, 6, 1382 – 1389.

[22] M. S. Pan, L. W. Yeh, Y. A.Chen, et al. 2008. "A WSN-Based Intelligent Light Control System Considering User Activities and Profiles." *IEEE Sensors Journal*. 8, 10, 1710 – 1721.

[23] N. P. Preve, E. N. Protonotarios. 2011. "An Integrated Sensor Web Grid Cyberimplementation for Environmental Protection." *IEEE Sensors Journal*. 11, 9, 1787 – 1794.

[24] N. Chen, W. N. Chen, Y. J. Gong, et al., "An Evolutionary Algorithm with Double-Level Archives for Multi-Objective Optimization," *IEEE Trans. Cybernetics*, in press.

[25] O. Mirabella, M. Brischetto. 2011. "A Hybrid Wired/Wireless Networking Infrastructure for Greenhouse Management." *IEEE Tran. Instrumentation & Measurement*. 60, 2, 398 – 407.

[26] P. Turaga, Y. A. Ivanov. 2011. "Diamond Sentry: Integrating Sensors and Cameras for Real-Time Monitoring of Indoor Spaces." *IEEE Sensors Journal*. 11, 3, 593 – 602.

[27] Q. Wang, K. Xu, G. Takahara, et al. 2007. "Transactions Papers - Device Placement for Heterogeneous Wireless Sensor Networks: Minimum Cost with Lifetime Constraints." *IEEE Trans. Wireless Communications*. 6, 7, 2444 – 2453.

[28] T. W. Davis, X. Liang, C. M. Kuo, et al. 2012. "Analysis of Power Characteristics for Sap Flow, Soil Moisture, and Soil Water Potential Sensors in Wireless Sensor Networking Systems." *IEEE Sensors Journal*. 12, 6, 1933 – 1945.

[29] W. N. Chen, J. Zhang, H. S. H. Chung, et al. 2010. "Optimizing Discounted Cash Flows in Project Scheduling—An Ant Colony Optimization Approach." *IEEE Trans. Systems,*

Man, and Cybernetics, Part C: Applications and Reviews. 40, 1, 64 – 77.

[30] W. N. Chen, J. Zhang, Y. Lin, et al. "Particle Swarm Optimization with an Aging Leader and Challengers", *IEEE Trans. Evolutionary Computation*, vol. 17, no. 2, pp. 241-258, 2013.

[31] W. N. Chen, J. Zhang, H. S. H. Chung, et al "A novel set-based particle swarm optimization method for discrete optimization problem," *IEEE Trans. Evolutionary Computation*, vol. 14, no. 2, pp. 278-300, 2010.

[32] X. M. Hu, J. Zhang, H. S. H. Chung, et al. 2009. "An Intelligent Testing System Embedded With an Ant-Colony-Optimization-Based Test Composition Method," *IEEE Trans. Systems, Man, and Cybernetics, Part C: Applications and Reviews*. 39, 6, 659 – 669.

[33] Y. Lin, J. Zhang, H. S. H. Chung, et al. 2012. "An Ant Colony Optimization Approach for Maximizing the Lifetime of Heterogeneous Wireless Sensor Networks," *IEEE Trans. Systems, Man, and Cybernetics, Part C: Applications and Reviews*. 42, 3, 408 – 420.

[34] Y. Li, X. Hu, J. Zhang. 2009. "A new genetic algorithm for the SET k-cover problem in wireless sensor networks," In *IEEE International Conference on Systems, Man and Cybernetics, 2009. SMC 2009.* San Antonio, TX, October 2009, IEEE, 1405 – 1410.

An Ant Colony Optimization Based Memetic Algorithm for the Dynamic Travelling Salesman Problem

Michalis Mavrovouniotis
Centre for Computational Intelligence (CCI)
School of Computer Science and Informatics
De Montfort University
Leicester LE1 9BH, UK
mmavrovouniotis@dmu.ac.uk

Felipe Martins Müller*
Technological Center
Department of Applied Computing
Federal University of Santa Maria
97105–900, Santa Maria, Brazil
felipe@inf.ufsm.br

Shengxiang Yang
Centre for Computational Intelligence (CCI)
School of Computer Science and Informatics
De Montfort University
Leicester LE1 9BH, UK
syang@dmu.ac.uk

ABSTRACT

Ant colony optimization (ACO) algorithms have proved to be able to adapt for solving dynamic optimization problems (DOPs). The integration of local search algorithms has also proved to significantly improve the output of ACO algorithms. However, almost all previous works consider stationary environments. In this paper, the $\mathcal{MAX}$-$\mathcal{MIN}$ Ant System, one of the best ACO variations, is integrated with the unstringing and stringing (US) local search operator for the dynamic travelling salesman problem (DTSP). The best solution constructed by ACO is passed to the US operator for local search improvements. The proposed memetic algorithm aims to combine the adaptation capabilities of ACO for DOPs and the superior performance of the US operator on the static travelling salesman problem in order to tackle the DTSP. The experiments show that the $\mathcal{MAX}$-$\mathcal{MIN}$ Ant System is able to provide good initial solutions to US and the proposed algorithm outperforms other peer ACO-based memetic algorithms on different DTSPs.

Categories and Subject Descriptors

G.2.1 [**Combinatorics**]: Combinatorial algorithms

Keywords

Ant colony optimization, Memetic computing, Local search, Dynamic Travelling salesman problem

1. INTRODUCTION

Ant colony optimization (ACO) algorithms have proved that they are powerful tools to provide near-optimal solutions for solving different combinatorial optimization problems, e.g., the travelling salesman problem (TSP) [6]. Traditionally, researchers have drawn their attention on stationary optimization problems, where the environment remains fixed during the execution of an algorithm. However, many real-world applications are subject to dynamic environments. Dynamic optimization problems (DOPs) are challenging since the aim of an algorithm is not only to find the optimum of the problem quickly, but to efficiently track the moving optimum when changes occur [16]. A change in a DOP may involve factors like the objective function, input variables, problem instance, constraints, and so on.

ACO algorithms have been originally designed for stationary optimization problems [5], e.g., to converge fast into an optimum or near-optimum solution, and may face a serious challenge to tackle DOPs. This is because, after a change, the pheromone trails of the previous environment may bias the population to search into an old optimum, making it difficult to track the moving optimum. As a result, ACO will not adapt well to dyanmic changes once the population converges into an optimum. Considering that DOPs can be taken as a series of stationary problem instances, a simple way to tackle them is to reinitialize the pheromone trails and consider every dynamic change as the arrival of a new problem instance which needs to be solved from scratch d_{ij} is the distance [13, 18]. However, this restart strategy is generally not efficient.

In contrast, once enhanced properly, ACO algorithms are able to adapt to dynamic changes since they are inspired from nature, which is a continuously changing process [1, 16]. Several strategies have been proposed and integrated with ACO to shorten the re-optimization time and maintain a high quality of the output efficiently, simultaneously. These strategies can be categorized as: increasing diversity after a change [13, 18]; maintaining diversity during the execution [7, 19]; and memory-based schemes [14, 15].

The integration of local search operations with ACO or other metaheuristics, which leads to the so-called memetic algorithms, has proved that the performance of these algorithms can be further improved regarding the solution quality [17, 22, 24]. This is because local search algorithms can better explore locally a neighbourhood in the search space than ACO. However, local search algorithms generate strong exploitation at the global level since they are optimizing to-

*Visiting professor at the Centre for Computational Intelligence (CCI), De Montfort University, Leicester, UK

GECCO '15, July 11 - 16, 2015, Madrid, Spain

DOI: http://dx.doi.org/10.1145/2739480.2754651

wards the optimum. Therefore, the use of ACO provides the exploration and the knowledge transfer needed to adapt to DOPs, whereas a local search algorithm improves the output. In this paper, we integrate an advanced local search operator, called unstringing and stringing (US) [12], which was proposed for the TSP, within ACO to address dynamic TSPs (DTSPs). The dynamic benchmark generator for permutation problems (DBGP) [20] is used to generate DTSPs in order to systematically analyze the investigated algorithms.

The rest of the paper is organized as follows. Section 2 describes the TSP and the construction of DTSP using the DBGP. Section 3 describes one of the best variations of ACO used for the experiments. Section 4 describes the proposed memetic framework for ACO algorithms. Section 5 gives the experimental results, including the statistical tests, and analysis. Finally, Section 6 concludes this paper with discussions on relevant future work.

2. TRAVELLING SALESMAN PROBLEMS

2.1 Problem Description

The TSP can be described as follows: given a collection of cities, the objective is to find the Hamiltonian cycle that starts from one city and visits each of the other cities once before returning to the starting city. Typically, the problem is modelled by a fully connected weighted graph $G = (N, A)$, where $N = \{v_0, \ldots, v_n\}$ is a set of nodes and $A = \{(v_i, v_j) \in N : i \neq j\}$ is a set of arcs. Each arc (v_i, v_j) is associated with a non-negative value d_{ij} which represents the distance between cities v_i and v_j.

Formally, the TSP is defined as follows. Let ψ_{ij} denote the binary decision variables defined as follows:

$$\psi_{ij} = \begin{cases} 1, & \text{if } (v_i, v_j) \text{ is covered in the tour,} \\ 0, & \text{otherwise,} \end{cases} \tag{1}$$

where $\psi_{ij} \in \{0, 1\}$. Then, the objective of the TSP is defined as follows:

$$f(x) = min \sum_{i=0}^{n} \sum_{j=0}^{n} d_{ij}\psi_{ij}, \tag{2}$$

where n is the number of cities and d_{ij} is the distance between cities v_i and v_j.

2.2 Dynamic Benchmark Generators

Over the years, several dynamic benchmark generators have been proposed for the DTSP that tend to model real-world scenarios, such as the DTSP with traffic factors [7, 19] and the DTSP with exchangeable cities [13, 14, 17]. These benchmark generators modify the fitness landscape, whenever a dynamic change occurs, and cause the optimum value to change.

In this paper, the recently proposed dynamic benchmark generator for permutation-encoded problems (DBGP)[1] is used [20], which can convert any stationary permutation-encoded benchmark problem instance to a DOP. The fitness landscape is not changed with DBGP, and thus, the optimum value (if known) remains the same. This is because DBGP shifts the population of the algorithm to search to a new location in the fitness landscape rather than modifying the fitness landscape as other benchmark generators do.

[1]Available from: http://www.tech.dmu.ac.uk/~syang/Codes/DBGP.zip

The main advantage of using the DBGP over other generators is that one can observe how close to the optimum an algorithm can perform when a dynamic change occurs. One can argue that since a DOP can be considered as a series of static problem instances, a direct way is to solve each problem instance to optimality, which may be non-trivial due to the $\mathcal{NP}$-hardness of most combinatorial optimization problems, especially for large-size problem instances [11]. It may be possible for small-size problem instances, but then the usefulness of benchmarking will be reduced.

The drawback of DBGP is that it sacrifices the realistic modelling of application problems for the sake of benchmarking. However, when comparing algorithms on the DTSP with traffic factors, the optimum value is unknown. Although such DOPs satisfy the modelling of a real-world scenario, using them leads to other problems. For example, one can see that one algorithm performs better than the others, but it may be the case that all algorithms converge far away from the actual optimum. Hence, with DBGP, apart from the comparison benefits described previously, it is also possible to assess the difficulty of a DOP. Particularly, in case all the algorithms perform far away from the optimum on a specific DOP, and closer to the optimum on another DOP, it gives an indication that the former DOP is more difficult to solve than the latter one.

2.3 Dynamic Test Environments

Considering the TSP description above, each city $i \in N$ has a location defined by (x, y) and each arc $(v_i, v_j) \in A$ is associated with a non-negative distance d_{ij}. Usually, the distance matrix of a problem instance is defined as $\mathbf{D} = (d_{ij})_{n \times n}$. DBGP generates the dynamic case as follows.

Every f iterations a random vector $\vec{V}(T)$ is generated that contains exactly $m \times n$ cities where $T = \lceil t/f \rceil$ is the index of the period of change, t is the iteration count of the algorithm, f determines the frequency of change, n is the size of the problem instance, and $m \in [0.0, 1.0]$ determines the magnitude of change. Then, a randomly re-ordered vector $\vec{U}(T)$ is generated that contains only the cities of $\vec{V}(T)$. In this way, exactly $m \times n$ pairwise swaps are performed in $\mathbf{D}$ using the two random vectors $(\vec{V}(T) \otimes \vec{U}(T))$, where "$\otimes$" denotes the swap operator.

3. ANT COLONY OPTIMIZATION

3.1 $\mathcal{MAX}$-$\mathcal{MIN}$ Ant System

The ACO metaheuristic consists of a population of μ ants that construct solutions and share their information among each other via their pheromone trails. The first ACO algorithm, i.e., the Ant System (AS) [3], was developed for solving the TSP. Many variations of the AS have been applied to address difficult optimization problems [6].

One of the best performing AS variations is the $\mathcal{MAX}$-$\mathcal{MIN}$ AS ($\mathcal{MM}$AS) [21]. Ants read pheromones in order to construct their solutions and write pheromones to store their solutions. Each ant k uses a probabilistic rule to choose the next city to visit. The decision rule of the kth ant to move from city v_i to city v_j is defined as follows:

$$p_{ij}^k = \frac{[\tau_{ij}]^\alpha [\eta_{ij}]^\beta}{\sum_{l \in \mathcal{N}_i^k} [\tau_{il}]^\alpha [\eta_{il}]^\beta}, \text{if } j \in \mathcal{N}_i^k, \tag{3}$$

where τ_{ij} and η_{ij} are the existing pheromone trail and the heuristic information available a priori between cities v_i and v_j, respectively. The heuristic information is defined as $\eta_{ij} = 1/d_{ij}$ where d_{ij} is defined as in Eq. (2). $\mathcal{N}_i^k$ is the neighbourhood of unvisited cities for ant k adjacent to city v_i. α and β are the two parameters which determine the relative influence of τ_{ij} and η_{ij}, respectively.

The pheromone trails in $\mathcal{MM}$AS are updated by applying evaporation as follows:

$$\tau_{ij} \leftarrow (1-\rho)\,\tau_{ij}, \forall (v_i, v_j), \tag{4}$$

where ρ is the evaporation rate which satisfies $0 < \rho \leq 1$, and τ_{ij} is the existing pheromone value. After evaporation, the best ant deposits pheromone as follows:

$$\tau_{ij} \leftarrow \tau_{ij} + \Delta\tau_{ij}^{best}, \forall (v_i, v_j) \in T^{best}, \tag{5}$$

where $\Delta\tau_{ij}^{best} = 1/C^{best}$ is the amount of pheromone that the best ant deposits and C^{best} defines the solution quality of tour T^{best}. The best ant that is allowed to deposit pheromone may be either the best-so-far, in which case $C^{best} = C^{bs}$, or the iteration-best, in which case $C^{best} = C^{ib}$, where C^{bs} and C^{ib} are the solution quality of the best-so-far ant[2] and the iteration best ant, respectively. Both update rules are used in an alternate way in the implementation [22].

The lower and upper limits τ_{min} and τ_{max} of the pheromone trail values are imposed. The τ_{max} value is bounded by $1/(\rho C^{bs})$, where C^{bs} is initially the solution quality of an estimated optimal tour and later on is updated whenever a new best-so-far ant solution quality is found. The τ_{min} value is set to $\tau_{min} = \tau_{max}/a$, where a is a constant parameter.

Since only the best ant is allowed to deposit pheromone, the population may quickly converge towards the best solution found in the first iteration. Therefore, the pheromone trails are occasionally reinitialized to the τ_{max} value to increase exploration. For example, whenever the stagnation behaviour[3] occurs or when no improved solution is found for a given number of iterations, the pheromone trails are reinitialized.

3.2 Response to Dynamic Changes

ACO algorithms are able to use knowledge from previous environments via their pheromone trails and can be applied directly to DOPs without any modifications [1, 18]. For example, when the changing environments are similar, the pheromone trails of the previous environment may provide knowledge to speed up the optimization process to the new environment. However, the algorithm needs to be flexible enough to accept the knowledge transferred from the pheromone trails, or eliminate the pheromone trails, in order to adapt well to the new environment. In particular, pheromone evaporation enables the algorithm to forget bad decisions made in previous iterations. When a dynamic change occurs, evaporation eliminates the pheromone trails of the previous environment from areas that are generated on the old optimum and helps ants to explore for the new optimum.

[2]The best-so-far ant is a special ant that may not necessarily belong to the current population of ants.

[3]Detected using λ-branching [10] that calculates the statistics regarding the distribution of the current pheromone trails.

Algorithm 1 ACO-based Memetic Framework

```
InitializePheromoneTrails
while (termination condition not satisfied) do
    ConstructSolutions
    UpdateBestAnts
    if (newBestAntFound is true) then
        ApplyLocalSearch
    end if
    UpdatePheromone
end while
```

In case the changing environments are different, then pheromone reinitialization may be a better choice rather than transferring the knowledge from previous pheromone trails [1, 13, 14, 18]. A detection mechanism is required to reinitialize the pheromone trails whenever a dynamic change occurs. The detection mechanism for the DTSPs generated by DBGP is straightforward. A single solution is required to be stored and re-evaluated every iteration. If there is a change to the tour cost, it indicates that a dynamic change has occurred [18].

4. ACO-BASED MEMETIC ALGORITHM

4.1 Memetic Framework

Generally, in ACO based memetic algorithms, when all ants construct solutions, the best-so-far ant after a dynamic change is selected to undergo local search improvements in dynamic environments. For example, in the memetic-ACO (M-ACO) proposed in [17], an adaptive version of the inver-over operator [23] is applied to the best ant for a predefined number of steps. The resulting ant replaces the selected best ant whenever the solution is improved.

The inver-over operator used in M-ACO does not consider any heuristic information as other operators (e.g., 2-opt or 3-opt [4]), hence it is not used for comparison in the experiments. Usually, heuristic based local search operators are applied to solutions until no further improvement is available. Therefore, there is no need to apply such operators to the best-so-far ant after a dynamic change in every iteration. Since local search operators are computational expensive, especially when the problem size is large, the computation time can be reduced when they are applied only when a new best-so-far ant is found (e.g., when the best ant of the current iteration is better than the best ant found from all previous iterations since the last dynamic change). The overall framework of proposed ACO-based memetic algorithms is given in Algorithm 1.

4.2 Local Search Operator

In this paper, we consider a more advanced local search operator previously proposed for the TSP, i.e., US [12]. This specific operator has been originally used for the stationary TSP with promising results when compared with other local search algorithms. In order to take advantage of the adaptation capabilities of ACO, the US operator considers the best solution constructed by ACO.

The US operator basically removes (unstringing) and inserts (stringing) cities from a tour into such position that improves the overall tour cost. It can work equally well to symmetric and asymmetric problems [8, 9]. In this paper, we consider only symmetric TSPs. Hence, to simplify the

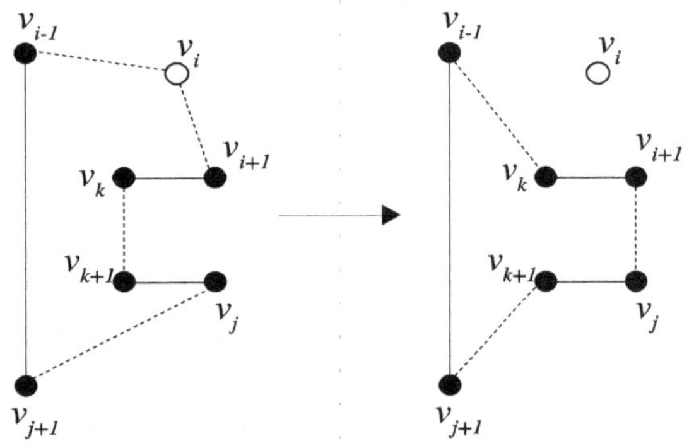

Figure 1: Illustration of Type I removal of v_i.

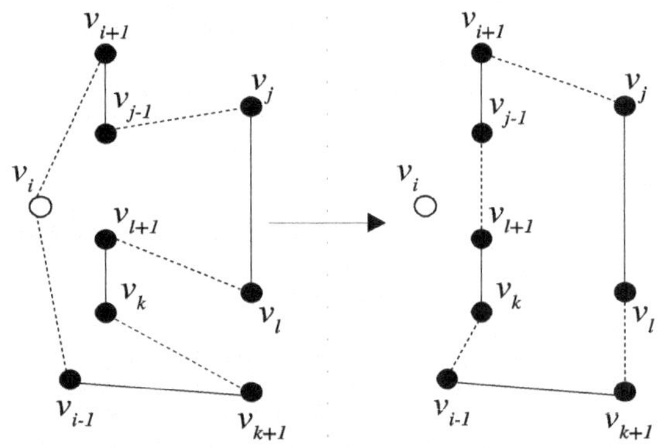

Figure 2: Illustration of Type II removal of v_i.

description of the US operator, we assume only this case, i.e., symmetric TSPs.

Suppose that we wish to insert v_x between any two vertices v_i and v_j. The main feature of the insertion procedure is that when a city v_x is inserted, it is not necessarily placed between two consecutive cities. However, after the insertion, these cities become adjacent to v_x. For a given orientation of a tour, consider v_k a city in the subtour from v_j to v_i and v_l a city in the subtour from v_i to v_j. We also consider for any vertex v_h on the tour, v_{h+1} its successor and v_{h-1} its predecessor. Since the potential number of choices for v_i, v_j and v_x could be large, we limit the search within a neighbourhood of a given size q (the suggested value is $q = 4$) as in most local search operators. Basically, the neighbours of a city v_j are the closest (e.g., the least distance) q successors and predecessors among all cities already included in the tour. The selection of the best place to insert a city in the tour is now constrained to the neighbourhood of each city involved in the alternative under consideration as well as the alternatives tested to the removal procedures.

More precisely, the unstringing procedure suggests two possible types of removals of v_i from the tour as shown in Figures 1 and 2, respectively.

- Type I Removal: Assume that v_j belongs to the neighbourhood of v_{i+1} and v_k belongs to the neighbourhood of v_{i-1}, with v_k being part of the subtour $(v_{i+1}, \ldots, v_{j-1})$. The removal of city v_i results in the deletion of arcs (v_{i-1}, v_i), (v_i, v_{i+1}), (v_k, v_{k+1}) and (v_j, v_{j+1}); and the insertion of arcs (v_{i-1}, v_k), (v_{i+1}, v_j) and (v_{k+1}, v_{j+1}). Also, the subtours $(v_{i+1}, \ldots, v_k)$ and $(v_{k+1}, \ldots, v_j)$ are reversed.

- Type II Removal: Assume that v_j belongs to the neighbourhood of v_{i+1}, v_k belongs to the neighbourhood of v_{i-1}, with v_k being part of the subtour $(v_{j+1}, \ldots, v_{i-2})$ and v_l belongs to the neighbourhood of v_{k+1}, with v_l being part of the subtour $(v_j, \ldots, v_{k-1})$. The removal of city v_i results in the deletion of arcs (v_{i-1}, v_i), (v_i, v_{i+1}), (v_{j-1}, v_j), (v_k, v_{k+1}) and (v_l, v_{l+1}); and the insertion of arcs (v_{i-1}, v_k), (v_{l+1}, v_{j-1}), (v_{i+1}, v_j) and (v_l, v_{k+1}). As above, the subtours $(v_{i+1}, \ldots, v_{j-1})$ and $(v_{l+1}, \ldots, v_k)$ are reversed.

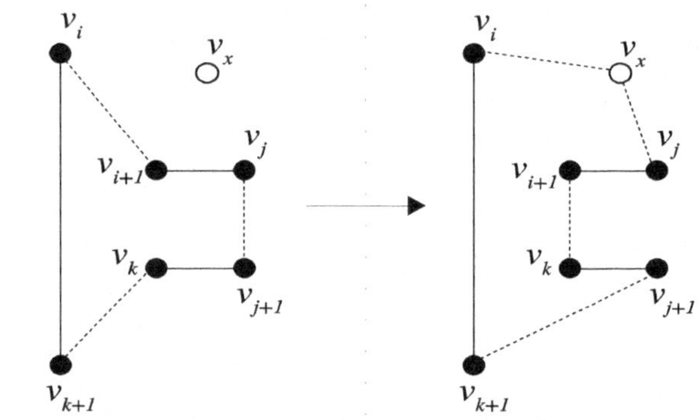

Figure 3: Illustration of Type I insertion of v_x between v_i and v_j.

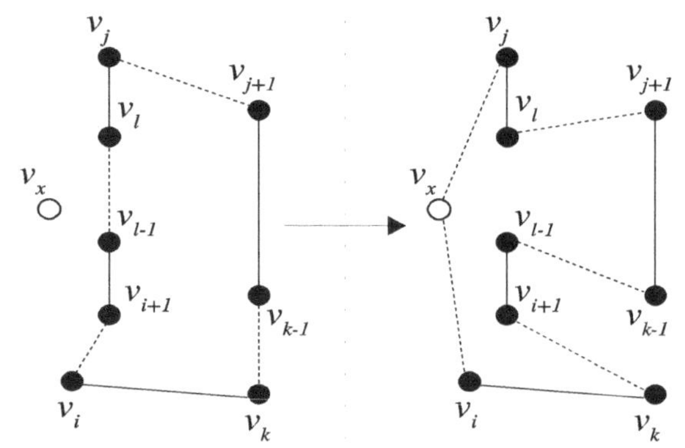

Figure 4: Illustration of Type II insertion of v_x between v_i and v_j.

The stringing procedure is basically the reverse of the unstringing procedure. Since there are two types of removals there are two corresponding types of insertions, as shown in Figures 3 and 4, respectively.

- Type I Insertion: Assume that $v_k \neq v_i$ and $v_k \neq v_j$. The insertion of v_x results in the deletion of arcs (v_i, v_{i+1}), (v_j, v_{j+1}) and (v_k, v_{k+1}); and the insertion of arcs (v_i, v_x), (v_x, v_j), (v_{i+1}, v_k) and (v_{j+1}, v_{k+1}). Also, the subtours $(v_{i+1}, \ldots, v_j)$ and $(v_{j+1}, \ldots, v_k)$ are reversed.

- Type II Insertion: Assume that $v_k \neq v_j$, $v_k \neq v_{j+1}$, $v_l \neq v_i$, and $v_l \neq v_{i+1}$. The insertion of v_x results in the deletion of arcs (v_i, v_{i+1}), (v_{l-1}, v_l), (v_j, v_{j+1}) and (v_{k-1}, v_k); and the insertion of arcs (v_i, v_x), (v_x, v_j), (v_l, v_{j+1}), (v_{k-1}, v_{l-1}) and (v_{i+1}, v_k). As above, the subtours $(v_{i+1}, \ldots, v_{l-1})$ and $(v_l, \ldots, v_j)$ are reversed.

In summary, the unstringing and stringing procedures described above are applied to the tour provided by ACO (i.e., the best-so-far ant) for local search improvements. The resulting solution is then used to deposit pheromone trails using Eq. (5). Note that the same pheromone update policy with $\mathcal{MM}$AS is used.

5. EXPERIMENTAL STUDY

5.1 Experimental Setup

In the experiments, we investigate the effects of having ACO providing its solutions rather than using randomly generated solutions for local search improvements, and compare the proposed ACO with the US operator over the existing integrations of ACO with the 2-opt and 3-opt operators. In particular, the performance of the following algorithms is investigated:

- $\mathcal{MM}$AS: no local search improvement is applied [21].
- $\mathcal{MM}$AS+2opt: the 2-opt operator is applied whenever a new best-so-far ant is found until there is no further improvement [22].
- $\mathcal{MM}$AS+3opt: the 3-opt operator is applied as in the $\mathcal{MM}$AS+2opt [22].
- $\mathcal{MM}$AS+US: the US operator is applied as in $\mathcal{MM}$AS+2opt and $\mathcal{MM}$AS+3opt for a fair comparison.
- $\mathcal{MM}$AS$_R$+US: the same algorithm as $\mathcal{MM}$AS+US but whenever an environmental change is detected the pheromone trails are reinitialized.
- Random+US: the US operator applied on random solutions rather than solutions generated by the ants.

All algorithmic parameters were set to commonly used values: $\alpha = 1$, $\beta = 5$, $\rho = 0.2$ and the number of ants was set to $\mu = 50$, except in $\mathcal{MM}$AS$_R$+US where $\mu = 49$ since one solution was used as a detector to detect dynamic changes.

DTSPs are generated from three stationary benchmark instances obtained from TSPLIB[4] using the DBGP generator described in Section 2. The frequency of change f was set to change every 10 and 100 algorithmic iterations indicating quickly and slowly changing environments, respectively, and the magnitude of change m was set to 0.1, 0.25, 0.5 and 0.75, indicating slightly, to medium, to severely changing environments, respectively. Totally, a series of 8 DTSPs were constructed from each stationary instance. For each ACO algorithm on a DTSP, 30 independent runs were executed on the same set of random seed numbers. For each run, 1000 iterations were allowed and an observation (i.e., the value of the best-so-far ant after a dynamic change) was recorded every iteration.

[4]Available from http://comopt.ifi.uni-heidelberg.de/software/TSPLIB95/

The modified *offline error* [2] was used to evaluate the overall performance of ACO algorithms, which is defined as:

$$\bar{E}_{offline} = \frac{1}{E}\sum_{i=1}^{E}\left(\frac{1}{R}\sum_{j=1}^{R} Err_{ij}\right), \tag{6}$$

where R is the number of runs, E is the number of iterations, and Err_{ij} is the best-so-far error value (i.e., the difference between the tour cost of the best-so-far ant and the optimum value for the fitness landscape) after a change in observation i of run j. Note that this measurement is compatible with DBGP because the optimal value (shown in Table 1) of each benchmark instance is known and remains the same during the environmental changes.

Moreover, the population diversity [19] was recorded as:

$$\bar{T}_{DIV} = \frac{1}{E}\sum_{i=1}^{E}\left(\frac{1}{R}\sum_{j=1}^{R} DIV_{ij}\right), \tag{7}$$

where R and E are defined in Eq. (6) and DIV_{ij} defines the diversity of the population in observation i of run j. For the DTSP, DIV_{ij} can be calculated as follows:

$$DIV_{ij} = \frac{1}{\mu(\mu-1)}\sum_{p=1}^{\mu}\sum_{q\neq p}^{\mu}\left(1 - \frac{c_{E_{pq}}}{n}\right), \tag{8}$$

where μ is the size of population, $c_{E_{pq}}$ is defined as the number of common edges between the solutions of ants p and q, and n is the number of cities.

5.2 Experimental Results and Analysis

The experimental results regarding the offline error of investigated algorithms for all DTSPs are presented in Table 1. The corresponding statistical results are presented in Table 2, where Kruskal–Wallis tests were applied, followed by posthoc paired comparisons using Mann–Whitney tests with the Bonferroni correction. In Table 2, the results are shown as "+", "−" and "∼" when the first algorithm is significantly better than the second one, when the second algorithm is significantly better than the first one, and when the two algorithms are not significantly different, respectively. In Figure 5, the dynamic offline error for slowly changing environments against the algorithmic iterations of $\mathcal{MM}$AS+2opt, $\mathcal{MM}$AS+3opt, $\mathcal{MM}$AS+US and $\mathcal{MM}$AS$_R$+US are plotted to better understand the behaviour of the ACO-based memetic algorithms. Figure 6 presents the population diversity of ACO algorithms for all DTSPs. From the experimental results, several observations can be drawn.

First, it can be observed that the performance of $\mathcal{MM}$AS is improved dramatically when integrated with local search algorithms for all DTSPs; see Table 1. This is natural because $\mathcal{MM}$AS performs global optimization and cannot be accurate to the output provided, whereas 2-opt, 3-opt and US perform local optimization and can locate the optimum in a given neighbourhood. $\mathcal{MM}$AS provides a good initial solution for local search algorithms since it may locate the neighbourhood that contains the global optimum or a near-optimum solution. This can be supported by the fact that $\mathcal{MM}$AS+US significantly outperforms Random+US in most DTSPs; see the comparisons of $\mathcal{MM}$AS+US ⇔ Random+US in Table 2. Basically, Random+US is a simple restart strategy whereas $\mathcal{MM}$AS+US is a guided restart strategy, respectively, of the US local search procedure that restarts the US operator for several times (iterations). Their

Table 1: **Offline error of ACO algorithms for different DTSPs where bold values indicate best results**

Algorithms & DTSPs	kroA100(Optimum=21282)				kroA150(Optimum=26524)				kroA200(Optimum=29368)			
$f = 10$, $m \Rightarrow$	0.1	0.25	0.5	0.75	0.1	0.25	0.5	0.75	0.1	0.25	0.5	0.75
$\mathcal{MM}$AS	1183	3107	3915	4123	2737	4846	5804	6003	3689	6196	7135	7393
$\mathcal{MM}$AS+2opt	341	1084	1253	1307	1122	1732	1891	1927	1400	2038	2205	2251
$\mathcal{MM}$AS+3opt	135	374	444	443	525	722	755	770	611	861	911	927
$\mathcal{MM}$AS+US	**100**	227	247	236	**524**	593	602	586	**586**	729	748	756
$\mathcal{MM}$AS$_R$+US	220	**225**	**223**	**229**	597	**591**	**583**	**582**	728	**727**	**728**	**723**
Random+US	272	286	302	286	621	622	616	605	832	821	839	836
$f = 100$, $m \Rightarrow$	0.1	0.25	0.5	0.75	0.1	0.25	0.5	0.75	0.1	0.25	0.5	0.75
$\mathcal{MM}$AS	419	844	1176	1329	1049	1810	2261	2353	1108	2052	2847	2939
$\mathcal{MM}$AS+2opt	190	408	662	692	716	1154	1344	1384	695	1237	1608	1641
$\mathcal{MM}$AS+3opt	100	201	334	366	446	627	708	730	450	705	838	885
$\mathcal{MM}$AS+US	**65**	**145**	189	213	**434**	**550**	558	555	**455**	**655**	725	752
$\mathcal{MM}$AS$_R$+US	164	146	**168**	**169**	573	574	lso **548**	**554**	688	666	**714**	**672**
Random+US	290	294	297	261	618	612	629	604	810	854	808	831

Table 2: **Statistical comparisons of ACO algorithms for different DTSPs.**

Algorithms & DTSPs	kroA100				kroA150				kroA200			
$f = 10$, $m \Rightarrow$	0.1	0.25	0.5	0.75	0.1	0.25	0.5	0.75	0.1	0.25	0.5	0.75
$\mathcal{MM}$AS+US $\Leftrightarrow$ $\mathcal{MM}$AS	+	+	+	+	+	+	+	+	+	+	+	+
$\mathcal{MM}$AS+US $\Leftrightarrow$ $\mathcal{MM}$AS+2opt	+	+	+	+	+	+	+	+	+	+	+	+
$\mathcal{MM}$AS+US $\Leftrightarrow$ $\mathcal{MM}$AS+3opt	+	+	+	+	~	+	+	+	~	+	+	+
$\mathcal{MM}$AS+US $\Leftrightarrow$ $\mathcal{MM}$AS$_R$+US	+	~	−	~	+	~	~	~	+	~	−	−
$\mathcal{MM}$AS+US $\Leftrightarrow$ Random+US	+	+	+	+	+	+	~	~	+	+	+	+
$f = 100$, $m \Rightarrow$	0.1	0.25	0.5	0.75	0.1	0.25	0.5	0.75	0.1	0.25	0.5	0.75
$\mathcal{MM}$AS+US $\Leftrightarrow$ $\mathcal{MM}$AS	+	+	+	+	+	+	+	+	+	+	+	+
$\mathcal{MM}$AS+US $\Leftrightarrow$ $\mathcal{MM}$AS+2opt	+	+	+	+	+	+	+	+	+	+	+	+
$\mathcal{MM}$AS+US $\Leftrightarrow$ $\mathcal{MM}$AS+3opt	+	+	+	+	~	+	+	+	~	~	+	+
$\mathcal{MM}$AS+US $\Leftrightarrow$ $\mathcal{MM}$AS$_R$+US	+	~	~	−	+	~	~	~	+	~	~	−
$\mathcal{MM}$AS+US $\Leftrightarrow$ Random+US	+	+	+	~	+	+	+	~	+	+	+	~

difference lies in that the pheromone trails in $\mathcal{MM}$AS+US provide a communication mechanism between the several restart points. Therefore, the search process is guided towards the promising areas of the search space.

Second, $\mathcal{MM}$AS+US performs better than $\mathcal{MM}$AS$_R$+US on DTSPs with $m = 0.1$ and $m = 0.25$; and they are comparable on DTSPs with $m = 0.5$ and $m = 0.75$. This is because when the changing environments are not similar $\mathcal{MM}$AS cannot adapt well as expected. The pheromone trails of the previous environment may not fit for the new environment hence the solution constructed by $\mathcal{MM}$AS and passed to US may lead the search process to a poor local optimum. This can be supported by the superior performance of $\mathcal{MM}$AS$_R$+US against $\mathcal{MM}$AS+US on DTSPs with $m = 0.75$; see the comparisons of $\mathcal{MM}$AS+US $\Leftrightarrow$ $\mathcal{MM}$AS$_R$+US in Table 2. In contrast, $\mathcal{MM}$AS+US significantly outperforms $\mathcal{MM}$AS$_R$+US in slightly changing environments, e.g., $m = 0.1$, where the adaptation via pheromone trails works as expected. $\mathcal{MM}$AS$_R$+US inherits the communication mechanism of $\mathcal{MM}$AS+US between the restart points as described above, but it is destroyed whenever a dynamic change occurs.

Third, $\mathcal{MM}$AS$_R$+US performs significantly better than $\mathcal{MM}$AS$_R$+2opt and $\mathcal{MM}$AS$_R$+3opt in all DTSPs. The strength of US procedure relies on the fact that it was designed to preserve or reverse subtours. Since ACO tends to find promising subtours (e.g., from the areas with high intensity of pheromone trails); when the US operator is applied to these solutions the promising subtours tend to be preserved whereas the remaining subtours are reversed. If we observe the US operator closely; taking the right choice for the cities and neighbourhood, we can see that it embodies 2-opt and 3-opt moves, but it outperforms both of them. In fact, US was also found to perform better than the Lin-Kernighan algorithm [12], which is one of the best performing algorithm for the TSP.

Fourth, the diversity is lower when local search operators are used (except on $\mathcal{MM}$AS$_R$+US where pheromone trails are reinitialized). This can be observed from Figure 6, where $\mathcal{MM}$AS maintains slightly higher diversity than $\mathcal{MM}$AS+2opt, $\mathcal{MM}$AS+3opt and $\mathcal{MM}$AS+US in almost all DTSPs. In contrast, Random+US always maintains higher diversity since random solutions are generated for the US operator. This shows that higher diversity may sometimes help in DTSPs with severely changing environments but may sometimes disturb the optimization in DTSPs with slightly changing environments.

6. CONCLUSIONS AND FUTURE WORK

In this paper, we integrate an advanced local search operator (i.e., US) with the $\mathcal{MM}$AS for dynamic environments. The aim of the integration is to take the advantage of the adaptation capabilities of $\mathcal{MM}$AS and the solution improvement of the US operator. The performance of this specific memetic algorithm is investigated on different DTSPs gen-

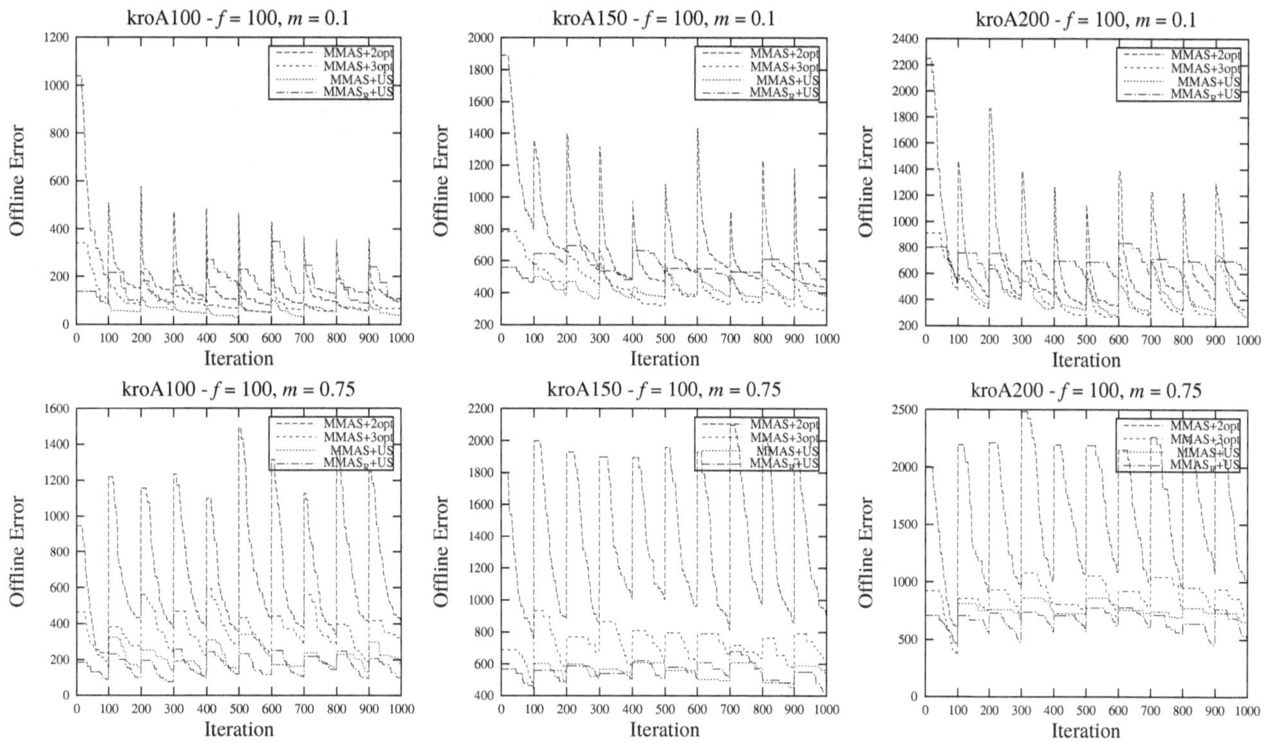

Figure 5: Dynamic offline error of ACO-based MAs in slowly changing DTSPs with $m = 0.1$ (top) and $m = 0.75$ (bottom).

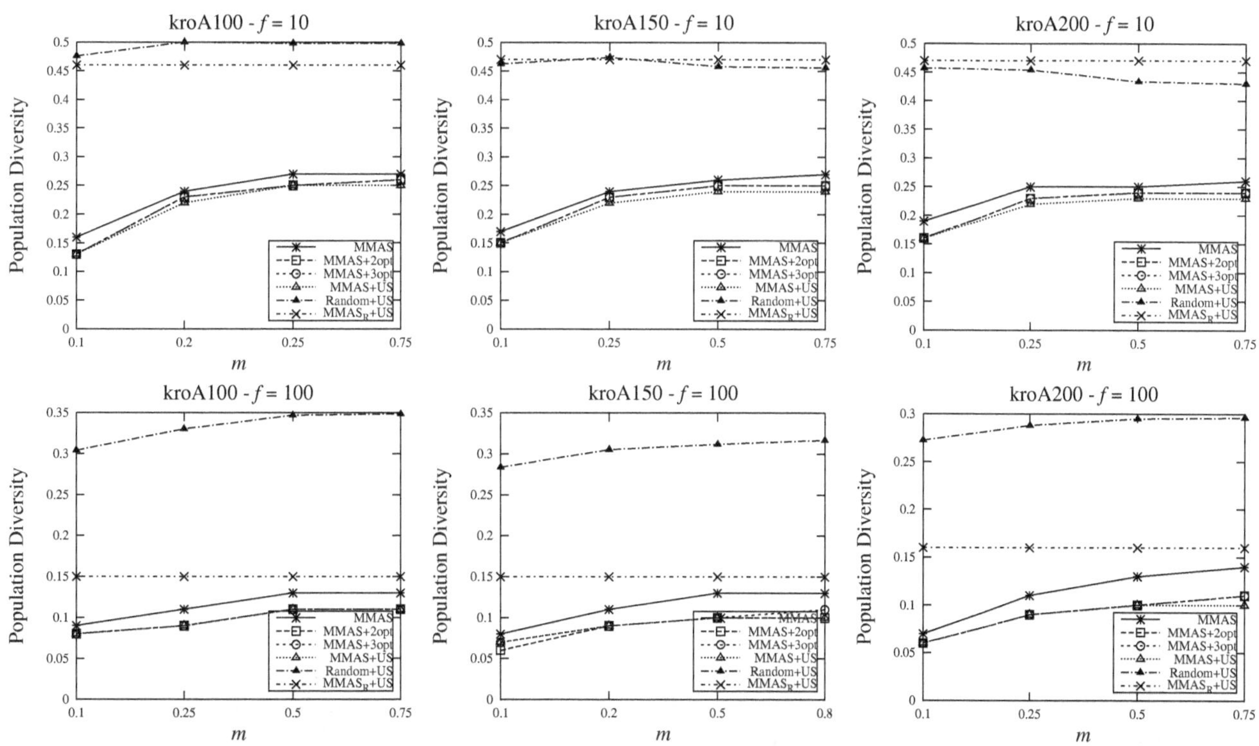

Figure 6: Population diversity of ACO algorithms for DTSPs with $f = 10$ (top) and $f = 100$ (bottom).

erated by the DBGP generator against other ACO-based memetic algorithms.

From the experimental results, the following conclusions can be drawn. First, local search operators improve significantly the performance of $\mathcal{MM}$AS in DTSPs. Second, the integration of $\mathcal{MM}$AS with US outperforms other memetic algorithms in all DTSP cases. Third, $\mathcal{MM}$AS provides good initial solutions to US in cases where adaptation is convenient (e.g., slightly changing environments); otherwise, a restart of $\mathcal{MM}$AS provides better initial solutions (e.g., severely changing environments).

A straightforward future work is to investigate the performance of $\mathcal{MM}$AS+US in asymmetric DTSPs since it is claimed that it performs equally well for stationary symmetric and asymmetric TSPs [8, 9]. Another future work is to apply the algorithm into more challenging DOPs that model real-world scenarios (e.g., DTSPs with traffic factors).

7. ACKNOWLEDGMENTS

This work was supported by the Engineering and Physical Sciences Research Council (EPSRC) of U.K. under Grant EP/K001310/1. Felipe M. Müller was partially supported by Coordenação de Aperfeiçoamento de Pessoal de Nivel Superior (CAPES), Brazil under grant BEX 2380/14-5.

8. REFERENCES

[1] D. Angus and T. Hendtlass. Ant colony optimisation applied to a dynamically changing problem. In T. Hendtlass and M. Ali, editors, *Developments in Applied Artificial Intelligence*, volume 2358 of *LNCS*, pages 618–627. Springer Berlin Heidelberg, 2002.

[2] J. Branke and H. Schmeck. Designing evolutionary algorithms for dynamic optimization problems. In A. Ghosh and S. Tsutsui, editors, *Advances in Evolutionary Computing*, Natural Computing Series, pages 239–262. Springer Berlin Heidelberg, 2003.

[3] A. Colorni, M. Dorigo, and V. Maniezzo. Distributed optimization by ant colonies. In F. Vaerla and P. Bourgine, editors, *Proceedings of the European Conference on Artificial Life*, pages 134–142. Elsevier Publishing, 1991.

[4] G. A. Croes. A method for solving traveling-salesman problems. *Operations Research*, 6(6):791–812, 1958.

[5] M. Dorigo, V. Maniezzo, and A. Colorni. Ant system: optimization by a colony of cooperating agents. *IEEE Transactions on Systems, Man, and Cybernetics, Part B: Cybernetics*, 26(1):29–41, 1996.

[6] M. Dorigo and T. Stützle. *Ant colony optimization.* MIT Press, London, England, 2004.

[7] C. Eyckelhof and M. Snoek. Ant systems for a dynamic TSP. In M. Dorigo, G. Di Caro, and M. Sampels, editors, *Ant Algorithms*, volume 2463 of *LNCS*, pages 88–99. Springer Berlin Heidelberg, 2002.

[8] P. M. França, M. Gendreau, G. Laporte, and F. M. Müller. The m-traveling salesman problem with minmax objective. *Transportation Science*, 29(3):267–275, 1995.

[9] P. M. França, M. Gendreau, G. Laporte, and F. M. Müller. A tabu search heuristic for the multiprocessor scheduling problem with sequence dependent setup times. *International Journal of Production Economics*, 43(2-3):79–89, 1996.

[10] L. M. Gambardella and M. Dorigo. Ant-Q: A reinforcement learning approach to the traveling salesman problem. In *International Conference on Machine Learning*, pages 252–260, 1995.

[11] M. Garey and D. Johnson. *Computer and intractability: A guide to the theory of NP–completeness.* Freeman, San Francisco, 1979.

[12] M. Gendreau, A. Hertz, and G. Laporte. New insertion and postoptimization procedures for the traveling salesman problem. *Operations Research*, 40(6):1086–1094, 1992.

[13] M. Guntsch and M. Middendorf. Pheromone modification strategies for ant algorithms applied to dynamic TSP. In E. Boers, editor, *Applications of Evolutionary Computing*, volume 2037 of *LNCS*, pages 213–222. Springer Berlin Heidelberg, 2001.

[14] M. Guntsch and M. Middendorf. Applying population based ACO to dynamic optimization problems. In M. Dorigo, G. Di Caro, and M. Sampels, editors, *Ant Algorithms*, volume 2463 of *LNCS*, pages 111–122. Springer Berlin Heidelberg, 2002.

[15] M. Guntsch, M. Middendorf, and H. Schmeck. An ant colony optimization approach to dynamic TSP. In *Proceedings of the 2001 Genetic and Evolutionary Computation Conference*, pages 860–867, 2001.

[16] Y. Jin and J. Branke. Evolutionary optimization in uncertain environments–a survey. *IEEE Transactions on Evolutionary Computation*, 9(3):303–317, 2005.

[17] M. Mavrovouniotis and S. Yang. A memetic ant colony optimization algorithm for the dynamic travelling salesman problem. *Soft Computing*, 15(7):1405–1425, 2011.

[18] M. Mavrovouniotis and S. Yang. Adapting the pheromone evaporation rate in dynamic routing problems. In A. Esparcia-Alcázar, editor, *Applications of Evolutionary Computation*, volume 7835 of *LNCS*, pages 606–615. Springer Berlin Heidelberg, 2013.

[19] M. Mavrovouniotis and S. Yang. Ant colony optimization with immigrants schemes for the dynamic travelling salesman problem with traffic factors. *Applied Soft Computing*, 13(10):4023–4037, 2013.

[20] M. Mavrovouniotis, S. Yang, and X. Yao. A benchmark generator for dynamic permutation-encoded problems. In C. Coello, V. Cutello, K. Deb, S. Forrest, G. Nicosia, and M. Pavone, editors, *Parallel Problem Solving from Nature - PPSN XII*, volume 7492 of *LNCS*, pages 508–517. Springer Berlin Heidelberg, 2012.

[21] T. Stützle and H. Hoos. MAX–MIN ant system and local search for the traveling salesman problem. In *Proceedings of 1997 IEEE International Conference on Evolutionary Computation*, pages 309–314, 1997.

[22] T. Stützle and H. H. Hoos. MAX–MIN ant system. *Future Generation Computer Systems*, 16(8):889–914, 2000.

[23] G. Tao and Z. Michalewicz. Inver-over operator for the TSP. In A. Eiben, T. Bäck, M. Schoenauer, and H.-P. Schwefel, editors, *Parallel Problem Solving from Nature - PPSN V*, volume 1498 of *LNCS*, pages 803–812. Springer Berlin Heidelberg, 1998.

[24] N. Ulder, E. Aarts, H.-J. Bandelt, P. van Laarhoven, and E. Pesch. Genetic local search algorithms for the traveling salesman problem. In H.-P. Schwefel and R. Männer, editors, *Parallel Problem Solving from Nature*, volume 496 of *LNCS*, pages 109–116. Springer Berlin Heidelberg, 1991.

Particle Swarm Optimization Based on Linear Assignment Problem Transformations

Luis Miguel Antonio
CINVESTAV-IPN,
Departamento de Computación
Av. IPN 2508. San Pedro Zacatenco
México D.F. 07300, MÉXICO
lmiguel@computacion.cs.cinvestav.mx

Carlos A. Coello Coello
CINVESTAV-IPN,
Departamento de Computación
Av. IPN 2508. San Pedro Zacatenco
México D.F. 07300, MÉXICO
ccoello@cs.cinvestav.mx

ABSTRACT

Particle swarm optimization (PSO) algorithms have been widely used to solve a variety of optimization problems. Their success has motivated researchers to extend the use of these techniques to the multi-objective optimization field. However, most of these extensions have been used to solve multi-objective optimization problems (MOPs) with no more than three objective functions. Here, we propose a novel multi-objective PSO (MOPSO) algorithm characterized by the use of a recent approach that transforms a MOP into a linear assignment problem (LAP), with the aim of being able to solve many-objective optimization problems. Our proposed approach, called LAP based PSO (LAPSO), adopts the Munkres assignment algorithm to solve the generated LAPs and has no need of an external archive. LAPSO is compared with respect to three MOPSOs which are representative of the state-of-the-art in the area: the Optimized Multi-Objective Particle Swarm Optimizer (OMOPSO) the Speed-constrained Multiobjective Particle Swarm Optimizer (SMPSO) and a variant of the latter that uses the hypervolume indicator for its leader selection scheme (SMPSOhv). Our results indicate that LAPSO is able to outperform the MOPSOs with respect to which it was compared in most of the test problems adopted, specially when solving instances with more than three objectives.

1. INTRODUCTION

Particle swarm optimization (PSO) is a metaheuristic inspired on the social behavior of birds within a flock [14]. Due to its simplicity and good performance, PSO has become a very popular approach to solve optimization problems and many different extentions to Multi-Objective Optimization have been reported in the specialized literature [28]. Most Multi-Objective Particle Swarm Optimizers (MOPSOs) adopt a selection process of the local and global best solutions based on Pareto dominance and the use of a crowding factor. However, it is now well-known that Pareto-based multi-objective evolutionary algorithms (MOEAs) do not perform properly when dealing with problems having more than three objectives (the so-called *many-objective optimization* problems) [11]. In such problems, the number of nondominated solutions significantly increases, making it difficult to generate new particles that dominate the previous ones, giving rise to the so-called *dominance resistance* [15, 26]. In this paper, we propose a novel MOPSO designed to solve many-objective optimization problems. We adopt an approach that transforms the original MOP into a linear assignment problem (LAP), recently presented in [19], in order to avoid the scalability problems of Pareto-based approaches. Our preliminary results indicate that our proposed approach is a very good alternative for solving many-objective optimization problems.

The remainder of this paper is organized as follows. Section 2 states the problem of our interest. The previous related work is discussed in Section 3. Section 4 describes our proposed approach and the experiments carried out to validate it. Finally, our conclusions and some possible paths for future work are drawn in Section 5.

GECCO'15, July 11-15, 2015, Madrid, Spain.

DOI: http://dx.doi.org/10.1145/2739480.2754789

2. THE MULTI-OBJECTIVE OPTIMIZATION PROBLEM

Formally, a multi-objective optimization problem (MOP) is defined as follows:

$$\text{minimize}\vec{f}(\vec{x}) = [f_1(\vec{x}), f_2(\vec{x}), \dots, f_k(\vec{x})]^T \quad (1)$$

subject to:

$$g_i(\vec{x}) \leq 0 \qquad i = 1, 2, \dots, m \quad (2)$$

$$h_i(\vec{x}) = 0 \qquad i = 1, 2, \dots, p \quad (3)$$

where k is the number of objective functions $f_i : \mathbb{R}^n \to \mathbb{R}$, $g_i, h_j : \mathbb{R}^n \to \mathbb{R}, i = 1, ..., m, j = 1, ..., p$ are the constraint functions of the problem and $\vec{x} = [x_1, x_2, \dots, x_n]^T$ the vector of decision variables. We thus wish to determine from the set Ω (where Ω is the feasible region) of all the vectors that satisfy (2) and (3) to the vector $\vec{x}^* = [x_1^*, x_2^*, \dots, x_n^*]^T$ of solutions that are *Pareto optimal* (those solutions in which one objective cannot be improved without worsening another).

3. PARTICLE SWARM OPTIMIZATION

In PSO, a group of candidate solutions is represented as a set of *particles* in a *swarm* [32]. Each particle has to adjust its flight trajectory into the search space according to a certain direction and keeping a certain *velocity*, given by its own previous flight experience and those of their neighboring particles in the swarm. PSO starts with a random initialization of each particle's position and velocity (particle's displacement) in decision variable space. Then, the velocity v and the position x of the each particle are updated at each step t according to the following equations:

$$\vec{v}_i(t) = w\vec{v}_i(t-1) + C_1 r_1(\vec{x}_{p_i} - \vec{x}_i) + C_2 r_2(\vec{x}_{g_i} - \vec{x}_i) \quad (4)$$

$$\vec{x}_i(t) = \vec{x}_i(t-1) + \vec{v}_i(t) \quad (5)$$

where x_{p_i} is the best solution that x_i has viewed so far, x_{g_i} is the best particle (also known as the leader) that the entire swarm or a certain pre-defined neighborhood has experienced, W is the inertia weight of the particle, which controls the impact of the previous velocity $v_i(t-1)$ on the movement of the particle, aimed to prevent swarm explosion (i.e., an uncontrolled increase of a particle's velocity), r_1 and r_2 are two uniformly distributed random numbers in the range $[0, 1]$ and C_1 and C_2 are the learning factors which control the effect of the personal and social influence. Particles in the swarm interact by defining a common set of links, which controls the exchange of information between particles, and is known as *swarm topology*. The set of particles informing the ith particle is defined as the particle's neighborhood, which in most cases includes the particle itself as a member. Traditional topologies for PSO include the gbest (star), lbest (circle), and von Neumann [13] topologies. Also, an adaptive random topology has been proposed. Here, each particle randomly informs K neighbors and itself (the same particle may be chosen several times), with K usually set to 3. In this topology, the connections between particles randomly change when the social optimum shows no improvement [3].

3.1 Multi-objective PSO algorithms

The successful application of PSO in a wide variety of single-objective optimization problems has made it very popular in recent years. However, in order to handle multiple objectives, PSO must be obviously modified. In most Multiple-Objective Particle Swarm Optimizers (MOPSOs), the major modifications to the basic PSO algorithm are the selection process of *pbest* and *gbest*. Among them, the differences lie on the number of selected global leaders and in the way in which they are selected [5]. Most of these approaches share the use of an external archive where the nondominated solutions found during the search are stored [27, 23, 28, 22]. The most commonly employed strategy is to use only one global leader randomly selected from the archive. Other works consider the use of a density estimator for selecting leaders from the archive, aiming to favor the spread of the computed approximation to the Pareto front. Next, we briefly describe some MOPSOs representative of the state-of-the-art in the area.

The first implementation of a MOPSO was proposed by Moore et al. [20]. Here, they used Pareto dominance for leader and personal best selection. Reddy et al. [12] proposed a MOPSO where the leader was randomly selected from an external archive where the best solutions found during the process were stored. The main target of this work was the use on an elitist-mutation-mechanism in combination with PSO. In [29] Santana et al. proposed a MOPSO which incorporates a *turbulence* (mutation) operator in addition to the crowding distance mechanism and a roulette wheel to select the social leader and to prevent an excessive number of nondominated solutions in the external archive. Another approach is the Optimized Multi-Objective Particle Swarm Optimizer (OMOPSO) [27]. This MOPSO selects a leader by means of a binary tournament based on the crowding value of the leaders. The maximum size of the set of leaders is fixed equal to the size of the swarm. After each generation, the set of leaders is updated, and so are the corresponding crowding values. If the size of the set of leaders is greater than the maximum allowable size, only the best leaders are retained based on their crowding value. The rest of the leaders are eliminated. OMOPSO adopts two mutation operators: uniform mutation and non-uniform mutation. The swarm is subdivided in three parts (of equal size). Each sub-part of the swarm adopts a different mutation scheme: the first sub-part uses no mutation at all, the second sub-part uses uniform mutation and the third sub-part adopts non-uniform mutation. With the use of these different operators, OMOPSO has the ability to explore and exploit the search space. It also adopts the concept of ϵ-dominance in order to fix the size of the external archive that contains the (nondominated) solutions that will be reported by the algorithm, so the size of the final external archive depends on the ϵ-value, which needs to be obtained from a pre-sampling process.

In [23] the Speed-constrained Multi-objective PSO (SMPSO) is presented. The authors of this approach adopt a control mechanism for particle's velocity that, instead of using upper and lower parameter values to limit the step size of the velocity, adopts a constriction coefficient obtained from a constriction factor χ, originally developed by Clerc and Kennedy in [4]. The following equations are adopted for this sake:

$$\chi = \frac{2}{2 - \varphi - \sqrt{\varphi^2 - 4\varphi}} \quad (6)$$

where

$$\varphi = \begin{cases} C_1 + C_2 & \text{if} \quad C_1 + C_2 > 4 \\ 0 & \text{if} \quad C_1 + C_2 \leq 4 \end{cases} \quad (7)$$

SMPSO also introduces a mechanism where the accumulated velocity of each variable (in each particle) is further bounded by means of the following velocity constriction equation:

$$v_i(t) = \begin{cases} \delta_i & \text{if} \quad v_i(t) > \delta_i \\ -\delta_i & \text{if} \quad v_i(t) \leq -\delta_i \\ v_i(t) & \text{otherwise} \end{cases} \quad (8)$$

where

$$\delta_i = \frac{upper\_limit_i - lower\_limit_i}{2} \quad (9)$$

So, the velocity of the particles is calculated according to eq. (4). The resulting velocity is then multiplied by the constriction factor and the resulting value is constrained using eq. (8). SMPSO uses a limited size external archive to store the non-dominated solutions found during the search. When the archive becomes full, the solutions with the smallest crowding distance are discarded. It also uses a turbulence operator by means of polynomial mutation, but it applies it to only 15% of the whole swarm. Later, a variant of SMPSO that uses the hypervolume indicator [36] to guide leader selection was presented in [22]. In this variant, called SMPSOhv, when the velocity of a particle has to be updated, two solutions are randomly selected from the archive, and the one contributing the most to the archive's hypervolume is selected as the leader. To apply this scheme, the external archive of non-dominated solutions is changed for an archive managed by the contribution of each solution to the value of this indicator.

There are some MOPSOs that consider the use of more than one particle from the archive as global leaders at the same time. An example is the approach described in [18], called Multi Leaders Multi Objective Optimization algorithm, which is an initial implementation of multiple leaders in guiding the particles' flight to search for optimum solutions. The multiple leaders' method is implemented by summing up all the distances between a particle and all of its leaders during the velocity update. Many other MOPSOs exist [24], but most of them are Pareto-based approaches and solve MOPs with no more than 3 objectives. Here, we propose a novel MOPSO which adopts the transformation of a MOP into a linear assignment problem (LAP), with the specific aim of solving many-objective optimization problems.

4. OUR PROPOSED APPROACH

As mentioned before, studies have shown that Pareto-based multi-objective evolutionary algorithms (MOEAs) do not perform properly when dealing with problems having more than three objectives (the so-called *many-objective optimization* problems) [11] and most MOPSOs' leader selection strategies are based on this same idea. Here, we propose to use an alternative selection mechanism which is not based on Pareto dominance or on any performance indicator. The algorithm presented here transforms the selection process into a linear assignment problem (LAP), which is solved using the *Munkres assignment algorithm* [17]. As evidenced in [19], the solution of this LAP allows convergence towards the true Pareto front and, at the same time, a good distribution of solutions along the Pareto front.

4.1 Linear assignment problem transformation

The matching or assignment problem is a fundamental class of combinatorial optimization problems [9, 21]. In its most general form, an assignment problem is the problem of choosing an optimal assignment of n to m of tasks, assuming that numerical ratings are incurred for each agent performing each task [17]. An optimal assigment is one which makes the sum of the agents' ratings for their tasks a maximum or minimum, according to the context of the problem. The Linear Assignment Problem (LAP) is the simplest of the assignment problems. In the canonical LAP, there are as many agents as tasks, and any agent can be assigned to perform any task. Formally, the LAP can be formulated as follows:

Let $A = \{a_1, ..., a_n\}$ and $T = \{t_1, ..., t_n\}$ be a set of agents and tasks with the same cardinality, given a cost function $C : A \times T \rightarrow \mathbb{R}$ and having $\Phi : A \rightarrow T$ as the set of all possible bijections between A and T, then a LAP can be expressed as follows :

$$\underset{\phi\in\Phi}{\text{minimize}} \sum_{a\in A} C(a, \phi(a)) \tag{10}$$

Usually, the cost function is also viewed as a squared real-valued matrix C with elements $C_{ij} = C(a_i, t_j)$, and the set Φ of all possible bijections between A and T as a set of assignment matrices $\mathcal{X}$. So, the LAP can be expressed as an integer linear program as follows:

$$\begin{aligned} \underset{x\in\mathcal{X}}{\text{minimize}} \quad & \sum_{i,j=1}^{n} C_{ij}x_{ij} \\ \text{subject to:} \quad & \sum_{i=1}^{n} x_{ij} = 1,\ \forall j \in \{1, .., n\}, \\ & \sum_{j=1}^{n} x_{ij} \leq 1,\ \forall i \in \{1, ..., n\}, \\ & x_{ij} \in \{0, 1\},\ \forall i, j \in \{1, ..., n\} \end{aligned} \tag{11}$$

In 1955, Harold W. Kuhn [17] proposed an algorithm for constructing a maximum weight perfect matching in a bipartite graph. This combinatorial optimization algorithm solves the assignment problem in polynomial time. Later on, James Munkres [21] reviewed Kuhn's work and made several important contributions to the theoretical aspects of the algorithm. He showed that Kuhn's algorithm is (strongly) polynomial and proposed an improved version of $O(n^3)$. The contribution of Munkres to the development of the Hungarian algorithm has led to the algorithm which is referred to as the Kuhn-Munkres or Munkres assignment algorithm. In [2], Bourgeois and Lassalle developed an extension for rectangular matrices which allows the algorithm to operate in assignment problems where the numbers of agents and tasks are unequal. Such extension can be formulated as follows: Given a $n \times m$ matrix (c_{ij}) of real numbers, find a set of k independent elements $[k = min(n, m)]$ so that the sum of these elements is minimum.

A linear assignment problem can be created from a MOP using the k-dimensional objective vectors from the individuals (solutions) in a MOEA. Since uniformly spread weight vectors in objective function space can be created, one can reformulate the MOP as follows: having n individuals and m vectors well-distributed in a $(k-1)$-dimensional unit simplex of the objective space, a cost can be incurred for each individual representing some vector in the Pareto Front approximation. So, the goal is to describe all regions covered by the n vectors using only m individuals in such a way that the total cost of the assignment is minimized. A cost matrix is then created such that it minimizes the total cost involved in retaining the solutions which are a good approximation of the Pareto Front. This procedure is described next.

First, the n vectors of objective values are normalized to reduce the current objective space to a unit hypercube. This is done in order to deal with non-commensurable objective functions. The maximum $\vec{z}^{max}$ and minimal $\vec{z}^{min}$ vectors are calculated for this purpose.

$$\begin{aligned} \vec{z}^{max} &= [z_1^{max}, ..., z_k^{max}]^T,\ z_i^{max} = \max_{j=1,...,2n} f_i(\vec{x}_j), i = 1, ..., k, \\ \vec{z}^{min} &= [z_1^{min}, ..., z_k^{min}]^T,\ z_i^{min} = \min_{j=1,...,2n} f_i(\vec{x}_j), i = 1, ..., k, \end{aligned} \tag{12}$$

where $f_i(\vec{x}_j)$ is the ith objective value of the jth solution in Q_g, and its normalized value $\tilde{f}_i(\vec{x}_j)$ is calculated as:

$$\tilde{f}_i(\vec{x}_j) = \frac{f_i(\vec{x}_j) - z_i^{min}}{z_i^{max} - z_i^{min}}, \quad j = 1, ..., n, \ i = 1, ..., k. \quad (13)$$

Let W be a set of m weight vectors uniformly scattered in objective space.

$$W \subset \mathbb{W} = \{\vec{w} \mid \vec{w} \in [0,1]^k, \sum_{i=1}^{k} w_i = 1\}, \ |W| = m, \quad (14)$$

The cost C_{rj} of assigning the individual $\vec{x}_j$ to the weight vector $\vec{w}_r$ is given by:

$$C_{rj} = \max_{i=1,\ldots,k} w_{ri} \times \tilde{f}_i(\vec{x}_j), \ r = 1, ..., n, \ j = 1, ..., n. \quad (15)$$

The matrix C indicates how each solution is suitable to represent each region of the Pareto Front approximation. The solution to our assignment problem is found by identifying the combination of values in C resulting in the smallest sum, subject to the following conditions:

- Exactly one value must be chosen in each row; this ensures that only one solution is assigned to each position on the Pareto Front.
- At most one value can be selected in each column; this ensures that no solution is assigned to more than one position.

The matrix C and the above conditions are formally represented by (11) as a linear programming problem. The solution to this problem is then obtained by the aforementioned Kuhn-Munkres algorithm for rectangular matrices [2]. The matrix that solves (11) represents the solutions assigned to each weight vector such that it minimizes the total cost of the assignment, allowing to retain the best solutions to approximate the Pareto Front.

4.2 Generation of weight vectors by Uniform Design

There exist several MOEAs [35, 25] that require the computation of a set of weight vectors uniformly scattered on a $(k-1)$-unit simplex to obtain solutions along the entire Pareto Front in a k-objective optimization problem. A variety of methods to obtain an evenly distributed subset of weights in a simplex are available in the specialized literature [8]. The simplex-lattice design method [30] is the approach that has been the most commonly adopted in MOEAs. However, at least three problems can be identified in this method [8]. First, the weight vectors are not uniformly distributed. Also, there are too many vectors at the boundary of the domain. Finally, the number of vectors generated increases nonlinearly with the number of objectives. Thus, if H divisions are considered along each objective, the total number of weight vectors (hence the population size) in a k-objective problem is given by: $\binom{H+k-1}{k-1}$. Some MOEAs have resorted to other methods to generate an arbitrary number of scattered weight vectors. In [25] a hypervolume-based weight vector generation is proposed. This method produces well-distributed vectors maximizing the hypervolume covered by them in objective space. Another approach was presented in [31], where the uniform design (UD) [8] and good lattice point (*glp*) [16] methods were combined to set the weight vectors. However, both the hypervolume and the *glp* method have a high computational cost when the number of objectives grows, which prevents their use in problems with many objectives.

Uniform design is a space filling design method that seeks experimental points to be uniformly scattered in the domain [8]. In uniform design, a set of points is considered uniformly spread throughout the entire domain if it has a small *discrepancy*, where discrepancy is a numerical measure of scattering. Fang and Wang [8] presented different methods for generating points that can be applied to the generation of a set of space-filling design points. Among them, the good lattice point (*glp*) method and Hammersley's method [10] excel. In [19] the authors propose to generate weight vectors using uniform design combined with Hammersley's method because this algorithm allows a more uniform distribution of the weight vectors over the space than the simplex-lattice method, and the population size of the MOEAs neither increases nonlinearly with the number of objectives nor considers a formulaic setting. Additionally, Hammersley's method provides a set of design points with low discrepancy similar to the *glp* method, but at a much lower computational cost [8].

Algorithm 1: Generation of weight vectors

```
Input  : number of objectives (k), number of weights (n)
Output: Set of weight vectors W
p ← array with the first k − 2 prime numbers;
U ← ∅;
for i = 1 to n do
    u_i1 ← (2i − 1)/2n;
    for j = 2 to k − 1 do
        u_ij ← 0;
        f ← 1/p_{j−1};
        d ← i;
        while d > 0 do
            u_ij ← u_ij + f × (d mod p_{j−1});
            d ← ⌊d/p_{j−1}⌋;
            f ← f/p_{j−1};
        end
    end
    U ← U ∪ {u};
end
W ← Apply transformation (19) to U;
```

Hammersley's method is based on the p-adic representation of natural numbers: Any positive integer m can be uniquely expressed using a prime base $p \geq 2$ as

$$m = \sum_{i=0}^{r} b_i \times p^i, \quad 0 \leq b_i \leq p-1, \quad i = 0, \ldots, r, \quad (16)$$

where $p^r \leq m < p^{r+1}$. Then, for any integer $m \geq 1$ with representation (16), let

$$y_p(m) = \sum_{i=0}^{r} b_i \times p^{-(i+1)}, \quad (17)$$

where $y_p(m) \in (0,1)$ and is known as the radical inverse of m base p. Let $k \geq 2$ and $p_1, \ldots, p_{k-1}$ be $k-1$ distinct prime numbers; then, the Hammersley set consisting of n points uniformly scattered on $[0,1]^k$ is given by

$$\vec{x}_i = \left[\frac{2i-1}{2n}, y_{p_1}(i), \ldots, y_{p_{k-1}}(i)\right]^T, \ i = 1, \ldots, n. \quad (18)$$

In [33], it was proposed the use of uniform design for experiments with mixture (UDEM). This method seeks points to be uniformly scattered in the domain $\mathbb{W}$ defined by (14). The authors employed the transformation method for the construction of such uniform design. This method requires a set of vectors $U = \{\vec{u}_i = [u_{i1}, ..., u_{i(k-1)}]^T, i = 1, ..., n\} \subset [0,1]^{k-1}$ with small discrepancy. In our proposal, Hammersley's method is used to obtain U and then to apply the next transformation:

$$
\begin{aligned}
w_{ti} &= (1 - u_{ti}^{\frac{1}{k-i}}) \prod_{j=1}^{i-1} u_{tj}^{\frac{1}{k-j}}, \quad i = 1, ..., k-1, \\
w_{tk} &= \prod_{j=1}^{k-1} u_{tj}^{\frac{1}{k-j}}, \quad t = 1, ..., n.
\end{aligned}
\tag{19}
$$

Then $\{\vec{w}_t = [w_{ti}, ..., w_{tk}]^T, t = 1, ..., n\}$ is a uniform design on $\mathbb{W}$. The pseudocode of the algorithm used to generate weight vectors is presented in Algorithm 1.

4.3 Description of the proposed approach

Making use of the LAP transformation, we propose a MOPSO that adopts an evolutionary model to select solutions based on the LAP transformation as described next. LAPSO starts with an initial swarm $S(0)$ of n particles and performs a random initialization of each particle's position and velocity (particle displacement) within decision variables space. The velocity v of each particle is updated at each step t according to eq. (4), where x_{p_i} is the best solution that x_i has viewed so far (in terms of the LAP transformation already described), and xg_i is the best particle within a defined neighborhood in terms of Pareto dominance. For this purpose, we adopted an adaptive random topology originally proposed in [3], which has been found to produce good results in the area of global optimization [34, 1]. Here, each particle randomly informs K neighbors and itself (the same particle may be chosen several times). In this topology, the connections among particles randomly change when the social optimum shows no improvement (we set $K = 3$). As there is evidence of the problems that an uncontrolled increase of velocity may cause [7], we adopt the velocity constriction mechanism of SMPSO described in Section 3.1. So, the inertia weight W, the two uniformly distributed random numbers r_1 and r_2 and the learning factors C_1 and C_2 (for the personal and social influence) were adopted, same as in SMPSO [23]. After the initialization, at each step t, we create a new swarm $S_2(t)$ of n particles from the actual swarm $S(t)$. Each particle will be created by means of eq. (5), where $v_i(t)$ is the velocity, computed as we just described. After that, a turbulence operation (mutation) will be applied to this new swarm and then each particle is evaluated according to the given MOP. Having both swarms, we form a set $CS_t = S(t) \cup S_2(t)$ of $2n$ posible solutions to the MOP. Then, a linear assignment problem is created using the k-dimensional objective vectors from CS_t (as explained in Section 4.1) and n weight vectors uniformly spread in objective function space are created as described in Algorithm 1. Then, a selection procedure based on the LAP transformation will be performed in order to select n particles from $CS(t)$ which are closer to the weight vectors and to solve the created LAP. These particles will form the next swarm $S(t+1)$. With this, there is no need of an external archive since the actual swarm always keeps the best solutions to the LAP and the members of the neighborhood for each particle are also in the swarm. This process is repeated until a stopping criterion is fulfilled. The whole procedure is summarized in Algorithm 2.

Algorithm 2: Linear assignment problem based PSO (LAPSO)

Input : MOP, swarm size n, maximum number of iterations t_{max}
Output: Solution set S

Generate initial swarm population $S(0)$ and their velocity values randomly;
Assign $k = 3$ neighbors to each particle in S;
Evaluate each particle in S;
$W \leftarrow$ Generate n weight vectors using Algorithm 1;
for $t = 1$ **to** t_{max} **do**
    $S_2(t) \leftarrow$ Generate new particles from S_t using (5) ;
    Apply turbulence operator to each individual in $S_2(t)$;
    Evaluate each individual from $S_2(t)$;
    if *social optimum shows no improvement* **then**
        recompute neighbors;
    end
    $CS_t \leftarrow S(t) \cup S_2(g)$;
    Compute $\vec{z}^{max}$ and $\vec{z}^{min}$ by (12) Normalize objectives of each solution in CS_t by (13);
    Generate the cost matrix C by (15) using CS_t and W;
    $\mathcal{I} \leftarrow$ Obtain the best assignment in C using the Hungarian Method;
    $S(t+1) \leftarrow \{\vec{x}_i \mid i \in \mathcal{I}, \vec{x}_i \in CS_t\}$;
    update velocity values using (4);
end

4.4 Experimental Results

We validated LAPSO comparing its performance with respect to the three aforementioned MOPSOs representative of the state-of-the-art in the area: OMOPSO [27], SMPSO [23] and SMPSOhv [22]. For the purposes of this study, we adopted the Deb-Thiele-Laumanns-Zitzler (DTLZ) test suite [6] with instances from three to ten objectives. In order to assess the performance of each MOPSO, we selected the hypervolume indicator [36], since this measure can differentiate between degrees of complete outperformance of two sets. The hypervolume is defined as the n-dimensional space that is contained by an n-dimensional set of points. When applied to multi-objective optimization, the n-dimensional objective values for solutions are treated as points for the computation of such space. That is, the hypervolume is obtained by computing the volume (in objective function space) of the nondominated set of solutions Q that minimize a MOP. For every solution $i \in Q$, a hypercube v_i is generated with a reference point W and the solution i as its diagonal corner of the hypercube:

$$
\mathcal{S} = Vol\left(\bigcup_{i=1}^{|Q|} v_i\right) \tag{20}
$$

The aim of this study is to identify which of the MOPSOs being compared is able to get closer to the true Pareto front using the same number of objective function evaluations and how they behave as the dimensionality of the MOP increases.

4.5 Parameterization

The parameters of each MOPSO used in our study were chosen in such a way that we could do a fair comparison. Thus, the same number of iterations and swarm size were adopted. For all MOPSOs, the mutation probability was set to $p_m = 1/l$, where l is the number of decision variables;

the distribution indexes for the polynomial mutation used by SMPSO, SMPSOhv and LAPSO were set as: $\eta_c = 20$ and $\eta_m = 20$. Different population sizes for each problem instance were used. For problems with 3 and 4 objectives the population size was set to 100. For problems having 5 objectives, the population size was set to 120. For problems with 6, 7, 8 and 9 objectives, a swarm size of 200 was used. Finally, for problems with 10 objectives, the swarm size was set to 220. The maximum number of iterations adopted for problems with 3 objectives was 100. In all other problems we used 300 iterations, regardless of their dimensionality. All other parameters, such as the learning factors and inertia weight, were set as the authors suggest for their respective approaches. The reference points $\vec{y}_{ref} = [y_1, \cdots, y_m]$ were $y_i = 1.5$ for DTLZ1to DTLZ6 and $y_i = 6.5$ for DTLZ7.

4.6 Discussion of Results

In our experiments, we obtained the hypervolume value over the 30 independents runs performed. Table 1 shows the average hypervolume of each of the MOPSOs being compared for each test problem adopted, as well as the results of the statistical analysis that we made to validate our experiments, for which we used Wilcoxon's rank sum. OMOPSO presented a poor performance in all problem instances having more than three objectives, since it couldn't produce solutions which dominate the reference points for the hypervolume computation used in our experimentes. It was only able to scale in DTLZ4 with at most five objetives and we can reject the null hypothesis (medians are equal) in all the cases. SMPSO produced competitive results for DTLZ4, DTLZ5 and DTLZ6, although it could not outperform LAPSO except for one case (DTLZ5 with 3 objectives), in which SMPSO presented a marginal improvement with respect to LAPSO, we cannot reject the null hypothesis in only two cases, DTLZ5 with 4 objectives and DTLZ7 with 3, which means that in these cases both algorithms have a similar behavior. Due to its high computational cost, a time limit of 12 hours for SMPSOhv's runs was used. As a result, SMPSOhv was no able to produce results for more than four objetives. In the comparisons using problems with three and four objectives, LAPSO was able to outperform SMPSOhv in DTLZ1, DTLZ3 and DTLZ7. Regarding the other test problems, LAPSO was able to produce very competitive results but at a significantly lower computational cost and has similar behavior, which means the null hypothesis cannot be rejected, in only three cases (DTLZ1, DTLZ3 and DTLZ7 with dimensions of 3, 4 and 3 respectively).

5. CONCLUSIONS AND FUTURE WORK

Here, we developed a novel MOPSO called LAPSO, which adopts a recent selection scheme originally proposed for MOEAs. LAPSO uses a selection based on the transformation of a MOP into an assignment problem. The implicit elitism associated with this scheme makes unnecessary the use of an external archive. Using a set of well-distributed points on a unit simplex, the obtained assignment problem is solved with the Munkres assignment algorithm. Our experimental results indicate that LAPSO outperforms OMOPSO and SMPSO in MOPs having from four up to ten objective functions and showed very competitive results with respect to SMPSOhv but at a significantly lower computational cost. In our future work, we intend to study other algorithms for solving the LAP and the use of other topologies for LAPSO.

6. ACKNOWLEDGMENTS

The first author acknowledges support from CONACyT and CINVESTAV-IPN to pursue graduate studies in Computer Science and would like to thank the ACM for the SIGEVO GECCO 2015 student travel grant. The second author gratefully acknowledges support from CONACyT project no. 221551.

7. REFERENCES

[1] M. R. Bonyadi and Z. Michalewicz. Spso 2011: Analysis of stability; local convergence; and rotation sensitivity. In *Proceedings of the 2014 Conference on Genetic and Evolutionary Computation*, GECCO '14, pages 9–16, New York, NY, USA, 2014. ACM.

[2] F. Bourgeois and J.-C. Lassalle. An Extension of the Munkres Algorithm for the Assignment Problem to Rectangular Matrices. *Commun. ACM*, 14(12):802–804, December 1971.

[3] M. Clerc. *Particle Swarm Optimization.* ISTE (International Scientific and Technical Encyclopedia), USA, 2006.

[4] M. Clerc and J. Kennedy. The particle swarm - explosion, stability, and convergence in a multidimensional complex space. *IEEE Transactions on Evolutionary Computation*, 6(1):58–73, Feb 2002.

[5] C. A. Coello Coello, D. A. Van Veldhuizen, and G. B. Lamont. *Evolutionary Algorithms for Solving Multi-Objective Problems.* Kluwer Academic Publishers, New York, May 2002. ISBN 0-3064-6762-3.

[6] K. Deb, L. Thiele, M. Laumanns, and E. Zitzler. Scalable Test Problems for Evolutionary Multiobjective Optimization. In A. Abraham, L. Jain, and R. Goldberg, editors, *Evolutionary Multiobjective Optimization. Theoretical Advances and Applications*, pages 105–145. Springer Berlin Heidelberg, USA, 2005.

[7] J. Durillo, A. Nebro, C. Coello Coello, J. Garcia-Nieto, F. Luna, and E. Alba. A Study of Multiobjective Metaheuristics When Solving Parameter Scalable Problems. *IEEE Transactions on Evolutionary Computation*, 14(4):618–635, August 2010.

[8] K. T. Fang and Y. Wang. *Number-Theoretic Methods in Statistics.* Chapman & Hall/CRC Monographs on Statistics & Applied Probability. Taylor & Francis, 1994.

[9] D. Gale and L. S. Shapley. College Admissions and the Stability of Marriage. *The American Mathematical Monthly*, 69(1):9–15, 1962.

[10] J. M. Hammersley. Monte-Carlo methods for solving multivariable problems. *Annals of the New York Academy of Sciences*, 86(3):844–874, 1960.

[11] H. Ishibuchi, N. Tsukamoto, and Y. Nojima. Evolutionary many-objective optimization: A short review. In *2008 Congress on Evolutionary Computation (CEC'2008)*, pages 2424–2431, Hong Kong, June 2008. IEEE Service Center.

[12] M. Janga Reddy and D. Nagesh Kumar. An efficient multi-objective optimization algorithm based on swarm intelligence for engineering design. *Engineering Optimization*, 39(1):49–68, 2007.

[13] J. Kennedy. Small worlds and mega-minds: effects of neighborhood topology on particle swarm performance. In *Proceedings of the 1999 IEEE*

Function	No. Obj	LAPSO HV	OMOPSO HV	LAPSO-OMOPSO P(H)	SMPSO HV	LAPSO-SMPSO P(H)	SMPSOhv HV	LAPSO-SMPSOhv P(H)
DTLZ1	3	3.347	0.000	0.000000 (1)	3.339	0.000000 (1)	3.335	0.386525 (0)
	4	5.053	0.000	0.000000 (1)	5.028	0.002348 (1)	5.037	0.000067 (1)
	5	7.540	0.000	0.000000 (1)	5.563	0.000000 (1)	–	–
	6	11.357	0.000	0.000000 (1)	7.625	0.000000 (1)	–	–
	7	17.054	0.000	0.000000 (1)	7.392	0.000000 (1)	–	–
	8	25.548	0.000	0.000000 (1)	11.892	0.000000 (1)	–	–
	9	38.429	0.000	0.000000 (1)	25.100	0.000000 (1)	–	–
	10	57.652	0.000	0.000000 (1)	48.215	0.000000 (1)	–	–
DTLZ2	3	2.750	1.684	0.000000 (1)	2.697	0.000000 (1)	2.791	0.000000 (1)
	4	4.559	0.000	0.000000 (1)	4.058	0.000000 (1)	4.631	0.000000 (1)
	5	7.127	0.000	0.000000 (1)	5.251	0.000000 (1)	–	–
	6	11.025	0.000	0.000000 (1)	7.925	0.000000 (1)	–	–
	7	16.721	0.000	0.000000 (1)	11.383	0.000000 (1)	–	–
	8	25.056	0.000	0.000000 (1)	16.646	0.000000 (1)	–	–
	9	37.704	0.000	0.000000 (1)	26.432	0.000000 (1)	–	–
	10	57.070	0.000	0.000000 (1)	19.386	0.000000 (1)	–	–
DTLZ3	3	2.768	0.000	0.000000 (1)	1.061	0.000000 (1)	2.740	0.000171 (1)
	4	4.266	0.000	0.000000 (1)	3.761	0.000000 (1)	4.067	0.579073 (0)
	5	5.928	0.000	0.000000 (1)	1.111	0.000000 (1)	–	–
	6	9.175	0.000	0.000000 (1)	0.606	0.000000 (1)	–	–
	7	11.201	0.000	0.000000 (1)	0.099	0.000000 (1)	–	–
	8	18.886	0.000	0.000000 (1)	0.124	0.000000 (1)	–	–
	9	30.319	0.000	0.000000 (1)	0.000	0.000000 (1)	–	–
	10	51.368	0.000	0.000000 (1)	1.333	0.000000 (1)	–	–
DTLZ4	3	2.715	2.570	0.000000 (1)	2.694	0.013268 (1)	2.733	0.010280 (1)
	4	4.540	4.435	0.000000 (1)	4.441	0.000000 (1)	4.577	0.000000 (1)
	5	7.135	5.861	0.000000 (1)	6.815	0.000000 (1)	–	–
	6	11.062	0.000	0.000000 (1)	10.626	0.000000 (1)	–	–
	7	16.755	0.000	0.000000 (1)	15.995	0.000000 (1)	–	–
	8	25.211	0.000	0.000000 (1)	23.776	0.000000 (1)	–	–
	9	37.860	0.000	0.000000 (1)	36.303	0.000000 (1)	–	–
	10	57.114	0.000	0.000000 (1)	55.753	0.000000 (1)	–	–
DTLZ5	3	2.027	2.012	0.000000 (1)	2.034	0.000000 (1)	2.036	0.000000 (1)
	4	2.837	0.000	0.000000 (1)	2.824	0.077272 (0)	2.833	0.000000 (1)
	5	4.146	0.000	0.000000 (1)	3.973	0.000000 (1)	–	–
	6	6.131	0.000	0.000000 (1)	5.862	0.000000 (1)	–	–
	7	9.118	0.000	0.000000 (1)	8.565	0.000000 (1)	–	–
	8	13.496	0.000	0.000000 (1)	12.718	0.000000 (1)	–	–
	9	20.033	0.000	0.000000 (1)	19.089	0.000000 (1)	–	–
	10	30.307	0.000	0.000000 (1)	29.167	0.000000 (1)	–	–
DTLZ6	3	2.019	0.893	0.000000 (1)	1.490	0.007810 (1)	1.898	0.000060 (1)
	4	2.855	0.000	0.000000 (1)	2.835	0.000000 (1)	2.889	0.000076 (1)
	5	4.154	0.000	0.000000 (1)	3.811	0.000000 (1)	–	–
	6	6.214	0.000	0.000000 (1)	5.631	0.000000 (1)	–	–
	7	9.175	0.000	0.000000 (1)	8.210	0.000000 (1)	–	–
	8	13.677	0.000	0.000000 (1)	12.258	0.000000 (1)	–	–
	9	20.187	0.000	0.000000 (1)	18.553	0.000000 (1)	–	–
	10	30.286	0.000	0.000000 (1)	27.517	0.000000 (1)	–	–
DTLZ7	3	148.430	66.120	0.000000 (1)	148.217	0.050009 (0)	148.257	0.128758 (0)
	4	789.868	0.000	0.000000 (1)	765.637	0.000003 (1)	788.868	0.000000 (1)
	5	4014.694	0.000	0.000000 (1)	3686.969	0.000000 (1)	–	–
	6	95892.612	0.000	0.000000 (1)	68725.215	0.000000 (1)	–	–
	7	96965.307	0.000	0.000000 (1)	65720.831	0.000000 (1)	–	–
	8	404852.438	0.000	0.000000 (1)	259361.361	0.000000 (1)	–	–
	9	1207098.816	0.000	0.000000 (1)	728523.513	0.026075 (1)	–	–
	10	6956918.762	0.000	0.000000 (1)	1203500.273	0.000000 (1)	–	–

Table 1: Average of the hypervolume indicator values of the results obtained for the DTLZ test problems. We show average values over 30 independent runs. The cells containing the best hypervolume value for each problem have a grey colored background. The P(H) columns show the results of the statistical analysis applied to our experiments using Wilcoxon's rank sum. P is the probability of observing the given result (the null hypothesis is true). Small values of P cast doubt on the validity of the null hypothesis. $H = 0$ indicates that the null hypothesis ("medians are equal") cannot be rejected at the 5% level. $H = 1$ indicates that the null hypothesis can be rejected at the 5% level.

Congress on Evolutionary Computation, volume 3, 1999.

[14] J. Kennedy and R. Eberhart. Particle swarm optimization. In *IEEE International Conference on Neural Networks*, volume 4, pages 1942–1948, Nov 1995.

[15] I. Kokolo, K. Hajime, and K. Shigenobu. Failure of Pareto-based MOEAs: Does Non-dominated Really Mean Near to Optimal? In *Proceedings of the Congress on Evolutionary Computation 2001 (CEC'2001)*, volume 2, pages 957–962, Piscataway, New Jersey, May 2001. IEEE Service Center.

[16] N. Korobov. The approximate computation of multiple integrals. *Doklady Akademii Nauk SSSR*, 124:1207–1210, 1959.

[17] H. W. Kuhn. The Hungarian Method for the Assignment Problem. *Naval Research Logistics Quarterly*, 2(1–2):83–97, Mar. 1955.

[18] K. S. Lim, S. Buyamin, A. Ahmad, and Z. Ibrahim. An improved leader guidance in multi objective particle swarm optimization. In *Modelling Symposium (AMS), 2012 Sixth Asia*, pages 34–39, May 2012.

[19] J. A. Molinet Berenguer and Carlos A. Coello Coello. Evolutionary Many-Objective Optimization Based on Kuhn-Munkres' Algorithm. In A. Gaspar-Cunha, C. H. Antunes, and C. Coello Coello, editors, *Evolutionary Multi-Criterion Optimization, 8th International Conference, EMO 2015*, pages 3–17. Springer. Lecture Notes in Computer Science Vol. 9019, Guimarães, Portugal, March 29 - April 1 2015.

[20] J. Moore, R. Chapman, and G. Dozier. Multiobjective particle swarm optimization. In *Proceedings of the 38th Annual on Southeast Regional Conference*, ACM-SE 38, pages 56–57, New York, NY, USA, 2000. ACM.

[21] J. Munkres. Algorithms for the Assignment and Transportation Problems. *Journal of the Society for Industrial and Applied Mathematics*, 5(1):32–38, Mar. 1957.

[22] A. J. Nebro, J. J. Durillo, and C. A. Coello Coello. Analysis of Leader Selection Strategies in a Multi-Objective Particle Swarm Optimizer. In *2013 IEEE Congress on Evolutionary Computation (CEC'2013)*, pages 3153–3160, Cancún, México, 20-23 June 2013. IEEE Press. ISBN 978-1-4799-0454-9.

[23] A. J. Nebro, J. J. Durillo, J. Garcia-Nieto, C. A. Coello Coello, F. Luna, and E. Alba. SMPSO: A New PSO-based Metaheuristic for Multi-objective Optimization. In *2009 IEEE Symposium on Computational Intelligence in Multi-Criteria Decision-Making (MCDM'2009)*, pages 66–73, Nashville, TN, USA, March 30 - April 2 2009. IEEE Press. ISBN 978-1-4244-2764-2.

[24] N. Padhye, J. Branke, and S. Mostaghim. Empirical Comparison of MOPSO Methods - Guide Selection and Diversity Preservation -. In *2009 IEEE Congress on Evolutionary Computation (CEC'2009)*, pages 2516–2523, Trondheim, Norway, May 2009. IEEE Press.

[25] D. H. Phan and J. Suzuki. R2-IBEA: R2 Indicator Based Evolutionary Algorithm for Multiobjective Optimization. In *IEEE Congress on Evolutionary Computation (CEC'2013)*, pages 1836–1845, 2013.

[26] R. C. Purshouse and P. J. Fleming. On the Evolutionary Optimization of Many Conflicting Objectives. *IEEE Transactions on Evolutionary Algorithms*, 11(6):770–784, December 2007.

[27] M. Reyes Sierra and C. A. Coello Coello. Improving PSO-Based Multi-objective Optimization Using Crowding, Mutation and ϵ-Dominance. In C. A. Coello Coello, A. Hernández Aguirre, and E. Zitzler, editors, *Evolutionary Multi-Criterion Optimization. Third International Conference, EMO 2005*, pages 505–519, Guanajuato, México, March 2005. Springer. Lecture Notes in Computer Science Vol. 3410.

[28] M. Reyes-Sierra and C. A. Coello Coello. Multi-Objective Particle Swarm Optimizers: A Survey of the State-of-the-Art. *International Journal of Computational Intelligence Research*, 2(3):287–308, 2006.

[29] R. Santana, M. Pontes, and C. Bastos-Filho. A multiple objective particle swarm optimization approach using crowding distance and roulette wheel. In *Intelligent Systems Design and Applications, 2009. ISDA '09. Ninth International Conference on*, pages 237–242, Nov 2009.

[30] H. Scheffé. Experiments with mixtures. *Journal of the Royal Statistical Society. Series B (Methodological)*, 20(2):344–360, 1958.

[31] Y.-Y. Tan, Y.-C. Jiao, H. Li, and X.-K. Wang. MOEA/D + uniform design: A new version of MOEA/D for optimization problems with many objectives. *Computers & Operations Research*, 40(6):1648–1660, June 2013.

[32] P. K. Tripathi, S. Bandyopadhyay, and S. K. Pal. An Adaptive Multi-Objective Particle Swarm Optimization algorithm with Constraint Handling. In B. K. Panigrahi, Y. Shi, and M.-H. Lim, editors, *Handbook of Swarm Intelligence. Concepts, Principles and Applications*, pages 221–239. Springer-Verlag, Berlin, Germany, 2011.

[33] Y. Wang and K. T. Fang. Number-Theoretic Method in Applied statistics (II). *Chinese Annals of Mathematics. Serie B*, 11:859–914, 1990.

[34] M. Zambrano-Bigiarini, M. Clerc, and R. Rojas. Standard particle swarm optimisation 2011 at cec-2013: A baseline for future pso improvements. In *Evolutionary Computation (CEC), 2013 IEEE Congress on*, pages 2337–2344, June 2013.

[35] Q. Zhang and H. Li. MOEA/D: A Multiobjective Evolutionary Algorithm Based on Decomposition. *IEEE Transactions on Evolutionary Computation*, 11(6):712–731, December 2007.

[36] E. Zitzler, D. Brockhoff, and L. Thiele. The Hypervolume Indicator Revisited: On the Design of Pareto-compliant Indicator Via Weighted Integration. In S. Obayashi, K. Deb, C. Poloni, T. Hiroyasu, and T. Murata, editors, *Evolutionary Multi-Criterion Optimization, 4th International Conference, EMO 2007*, pages 862–876, Matshushima, Japan, March 2007. Springer. Lecture Notes in Computer Science Vol. 4403.

Evolutionary Inheritance Mechanisms for Multi-criteria Decision Making in Multi-agent Systems

Ruby L. V. Moritz
Complex Systems and Parallel Computing Group
University of Leipzig
Germany
ruby.moritz@informatik.uni-leipzig.de

Martin Middendorf
Complex Systems and Parallel Computing Group
University of Leipzig
Germany
middendorf@informatik.uni-leipzig.de

ABSTRACT

In this paper we study the use of different evolutionary inheritance mechanisms for the adaptation of parameters in a multi-agent system where the agents have to solve tasks that are distributed within a dynamic environment. In the studied system the agents have to form teams to execute the tasks. Deciding which task to execute next is a multi-criteria decision problem for which the agents use different ranking schemes. Agents that have successfully executed several tasks can reproduce and pass the type of ranking scheme they have used and some corresponding parameter values to their successors. Three types of evolutionary mechanisms are compared: haploid, diploid, and haplo-diploid. The latter one is new for multi-agent systems. The focus of our simulation experiments is to study the influence of the different evolutionary mechanisms on the diversity of the agents and on the resulting efficiency of the multi-agent system for different dynamic environments.

Categories and Subject Descriptors

Computing methodologies [**Artificial intelligence**]: Distributed artificial intelligence—*Multi-agent systems*; Theory of computation [**Theory and algorithms for application domains**]: Machine learning theory—*Multi-agent learning*

Keywords

Multi-agent systems; Evolution strategies; Adaptation/self-adaptation; Swarm intelligence; Multi-criteria decision making

1. INTRODUCTION

In self-organized multi-agent systems the agents have to decide by themselves which task to execute next. This is difficult when the information that an agent has about the state of the system is limited. Then, the agent might use different criteria for its decision, and therefore is confronted with a multi-criterion decision making problem. A possible strategy is to use a ranking scheme for the different criteria. Which ranking scheme leads to a better success might depend on environmental factors. In dynamic systems the environmental factors can change over time. This can have an influence on the relative priority of the criteria. Therefore, it can be a challenge for the agents to find a good ranking scheme. Thus, it might be beneficial for the system when the decisions are based on different ranking schemes instead of a single one and when the system reacts to changes of the environment. One possible approach is that each agent uses its own individual ranking scheme.

In this paper we study the use of evolutionary inheritance mechanisms for the adaptation of ranking schemes and of the corresponding parameter values. Successful agents can reproduce and pass the respective values they applied to their successors. How this is done is defined by an evolutionary inheritance mechanism. The introduced inheritance mechanisms are inspired by evolutionary processes in nature that lead to an adaptivity of species. Three types of inheritance mechanisms are compared in this paper: haploid, diploid, and haplo-diploid. A haplo-diploid inheritance mechanism has, to the best of our knowledge, never been used for multi-agent systems.

In the multi-agent system that is used as a test system the agents have to solve multi-agent tasks that are distributed within a dynamic environment. The agents have to form teams to execute the multi-agent tasks. The focus of our simulation experiments is to study the influence of the different evolutionary mechanisms on the diversity of the agents and on the resulting efficiency of the multi-agent system with different dynamic environments.

A short introduction to inheritance mechanisms and their use in computer science is given in the next Section 2. The multi-agent system and the used inheritance mechanisms are described in Section 3. Experimental result are presented in Section 4 and conclusions are given in Section 5.

2. INHERITANCE MECHANISMS

Evolutionary principles like recombination, crossover, and mutation are used in computer science for a long time. Evolutionary algorithms are a prominent example. In evolutionary robotics the shape, movement, or interaction between robots has been designed by using evolutionary principles (for a recent review see [1]). Also as part of multi-agent systems such evolutionary principles have been used, e.g. in [11, 12, 14, 15]. However, most of the studies either focus on homogeneous swarms or on systems where each agent or robot evolves by itself, e.g. by using a neural network or a

GECCO '15, July 11 - 15, 2015, Madrid, Spain
© 2015 ACM. ISBN 978-1-4503-3472-3/15/07... $15.00
DOI: http://dx.doi.org/10.1145/2739480.2754773

genetic algorithm. Here, we are interested in a system inheritance, i.e. with a transfer of genetic material between the agents such that one agent can learn from other agents.

Inheritance in nature is often based on haploid mechanisms where each individual contains only a single copy of its genetic material. Haploidy is very efficient in the elimination of lethal genes, as they are immediately removed from the population by the death of the individual.

In contrast, diploid individuals carry two different copies of the genetic material. In case of a dominance-recessive relation between two copies of a gene (alleles) the dominant allele defines the phenotype of the individual while the recessive allele remains dormant. Thus, the individuals fitness is determined by the dominant alleles. When an individual reproduces, the recessive alleles are also multiplied. Hence, even 'bad' genetic material might remain in the population. The corresponding genetic diversity can lead to a higher adaptability which can be advantageous in dynamic systems. The concept of diploidy has already been used in genetic algorithms [4, 16]. It was shown that the higher diversity in the population can avoid premature convergence [7, 13, 5, 6]. A study of diploidy in neural networks showed that diploids had lower average fitness but a higher peak fitness in fixed environments. They were able to keep a genetic 'memory' that they could fall back on in changing environments with repetitive conditions [3]. The benefit of diploidy in dynamic multi-agent system has been studied in [2].

A third inheritance mechanism that occurs in nature is haplo-diploidy. In haplo-diploid species (e.g. bees, ants, or wasps) the males that hatch from unfertilized eggs are haploid while the females that origin from fertilized eggs are diploid. While the diploid females ensure a high diversity, the haploid males eliminate lethal alleles from the population – by dying. To the best of our knowledge, the concept of haplo-diploidy has not been used for evolutionary algorithms and evolutionary multi-agent systems.

3. MODEL

The designed multi-agent model is minimalistic with a small number of variable parameters in order to keep a general scenario that does not depend on assumptions from specific applications. A slightly similar multi-agent model where the agent have to solve a resource collection task has been studied in [8, 9]. However, different from this study, the agents in [8, 9] have no multi-criteria decision problem, there exists no inheritance mechanisms, and the agents have different capabilities. The focus of these papers was to study different strategies for the agents to form teams in a static [8] dynamic [9] environment and limited energy conditions.

The model consists of a 2-dimensional arena for a swarm of moving agents that are tasked with the collection of distributed resources. The collection of the resources on a location requires a specific number of agents and a specific amount of time. Each agent has only very limited information about the environment. However, an agent can asses information about its current location and has the ability to memorize information about a limited number of other locations which it has visited before. An agent can communicate with other agents in its vicinity and can build a team with them to cooperatively collect resources. The agents try to collect as many resources as possible. For this, a decentralized strategy is needed due to the limited capabilities of the agents.

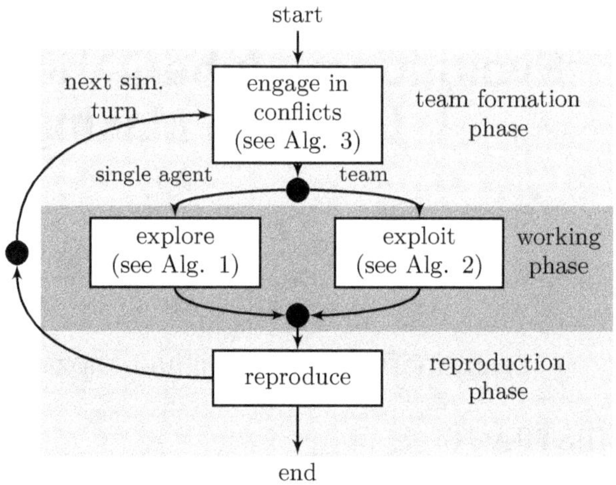

Figure 1: Flow diagram of the three phases making up a simulation turn. Black dots are points of synchronization.

Each agent is in one of two possible behavioral states: the *single agent state* (also called *exploration state*) and the *team state* (also called *exploitation state*). An agent in exploration state walks randomly around in order to find locations with good properties concerning the collection of resources. It will memorize the best locations it has found. In the exploitation phase a team of agents targets the best locations its members have memorized during their respective former exploration phase. Once a team has collected all resources at a location that was found by some member of the team, that team member leaves the team, erases its memory, and returns into the exploration state.

We investigate decentralized strategy that enable the agents to gather information about the environment and subsequently to use this information for collecting resources within teams. Obviously, this raises a couple of questions concerning the design of the agents behavior, most intriguingly:

1. Which locations should an agent memorize during the exploration phase?
2. How long should an agent explore?
3. Gathering more agents can be essential for the success of a team. When two teams meet and they both require more agents, which team is able to take agents from the other team?
4. Each team has several potential target locations: the locations memorized by its members. Which strategy should they use to choose the next target?

Since we investigate dynamic scenarios where there might not be one best strategy the system should adapt or evolve the strategies that the agents use. The details of the agent model are introduced in the following.

3.1 Environment

The agents are located in an environment that consists of a 2-dimensional torus F with $d \times d$ fields. Thus, the last field in every row and column is adjacent to the first field in its row respectively column. $A = \{a_1, \ldots, a_n\}$ is the set of agents. The size of a field equals the sensory range of an agent with respect to the resources. Hence, an agent on a field $f \in F$ can sense the amount of resources on f only. To collect resources a team of at least two or more agents has to be formed, i.e. a single agent cannot collect resources. All agents of a team are located on the same field. On each field at most one team of agents can collect resources at a time. Each team of agents can communicate only with a team or an agent that is located on the same field or one of the eight adjacent fields (Moore neighborhood). Hence, the communication range includes only the current field and its adjacent fields. Each agent has an orientation which points to one of the eight fields that are adjacent to its current field.

Each simulation is a sequence of simulation turns. During each simulation turn an agent or a team can move from its current field to an adjacent field. Besides its coordinates $(x(f), y(f))$, each field $f \in F$ has the following attributes

1. $r(f)$ denotes the amount of resources on f,
2. $a(f)$ is the required minimum size of a team to collect the resources on f,
3. $t(f)$ is the number of simulation turns that a team has to remain on f in order to collect the resources on f.

The attribute values of each field are chosen randomly and change each time their resources have been collected. Each simulation turn consists of three phases that are described in the next subsections: the team formation phase, the working phase, and the reproduction phase (see Figure 1).

3.2 Working Phase

During the working phase the single agents move around to explore their environment in search for good fields. Each team moves either towards its target field or, if it has already arrived there, collects resources.

Exploration State.

A single agent in the exploration state stores the following information on the best fields it has visited in its *field memory*: the location and attribute values of a field, and the time of visit. Whenever an agent moves onto a field f it can add information about f to its memory. However, due to the limited capacity of the memory the agent might need to discard information about another field. Each agent is confronted with a multi-criterion decision problem and has to consider the following four criteria (quality measures):

1. the amount of resources $r(f)$,
2. the number of required agents $a(f)$,
3. the resource collection time $t(f)$, and
4. the age of the gathered information.

Criterion 1 is to be maximized whereas the other criteria are to be minimized. The agents can use different ranking methods (as described in Section 3.5) to decide which of the fields they have visited to remember. Algorithm 1 shows the working phase of an agent that is in the exploration state.

When an agent has entered the exploration state it moves around to find good fields and to collect information about them. Therefore, it will refuse to become member of a team for *exploration time* many simulation turns. Afterwards, the agent tries to become member of a team to put the collected information to use. Before the end of its exploration time an agent is called *blocked agent*. Otherwise it is called a *free agent*, because it is free to join a team.

Exploitation State.

All members of a team share the same location and move together. Each team decides on a target field and moves towards it along a shortest path. Once a team arrived at its target field it tries to engage in the resource collection. It will fail if either the team is too small or another team is already working on the field. If a team can work on its field f, it remains there for $t(f)$ simulation turns to collect the available resources and then leaves f. Otherwise, the team leaves the field immediately. Either way i. the agent that provided the information on f leaves the team, ii. the team decides on a new target field f', and iii. moves to a neighbored field towards f' (see Algorithm 2).

Algorithm 1: Working phase: exploration state

```
choose random number ρ ∈ [0, 1]
if ρ < rotation probability then
    change orientation by 45°
move forward in the current orientation onto the
  adjacent field f'
if field memory M is full then
    rank all fields from M ∪ {f'}
    discard the field with lowest rank and place others
      in M
else
    add f' to M
```

Algorithm 2: Working phase: exploitation state

```
if team T is located on its target field f_T then
    if no other team works on f_T and |T| ≥ a(f_T)
      and counter < t(f_T) then
        work on target
        counter := counter + 1
        if counter = t(f_T) then
            increase personal and global collected
              resources by r(f_T)
            counter := 0
    else
        owner of f_T in T leaves the team
        choose next target field
        counter := 0
else
    move toward target field
```

3.3 Team Formation Phase

Whenever two teams (or free agents) are in each others sensing range, i.e. on adjacent fields or the same field, they can engage in a team formation event. A team that is too small to process its target field successfully, tries to get agents from the other team. Neither team wants to give away any of its agents and their field information. If both teams have enough agents they avoid a conflict, but in any other case they engage in a competition over their member agents (see Algorithm 3).

Of the many possible strategies to decide this conflict the agents apply a very archaic approach. Each agent a has a power *power*(a) that adds to the power *power*(T) of its team T , i.e., $power(T) = \sum_{a \in T} power(a)$. In a conflict between two teams T and T' team T wins iff

$$\rho \leq \frac{power(T)}{power(T) + power(T')}$$

Algorithm 3: Team formation during conflicts

if *T's exploration time has ended* **and** $|T| < a(f_T)$ **and** *T has not been part of a conflict in this simulation turn* **then**
  choose a team or agent T' randomly from all those teams and agents with the following properties:
    1. T' is in the Moore-neighborhood of T
    2. T' is not working on a field
    3. T' 's exploration time has ended
    4. T' was in no conflict during the current simulation turn
  choose a random number $\rho \in [0, 1]$
  if $\rho \leq power(T)/(power(T) + power(T'))$ **then**
    T takes $\min(|T'|, a(f_T) - |T|)$ agents from T'
  else
    T' takes $\min(|T|, a(f_{T'}) - |T'|)$ agents from T

where $\rho \in [0, 1]$ is a uniform random number. The additive power favors large teams over small teams. This way, fields that require many agents are also processed.

Let $x = \min(a(f_T) - |T|, |T'|)$, where f_T is the target field of T. Then x randomly chosen agents from T' are transferred to T if T wins. If $a(f_T) - |T| \leq |T'|$, T' is completely absorbed by T. A worst case scenario for T' is the loss of the agent that provided T' with the information about $f_{T'}$. Then T' is forced to choose another target field after it already invested time to move towards $f_{T'}$.

3.4 Choosing a Target Field

A team chooses a target field in the following situations:

(A) Agent a just finished its exploration phase and is in a conflict with team T. If a wins it gets agents from T and builds its own team. In this case a chooses one of the fields that it has memorized. The agent ignores the information of the newly acquired agents, as any other team would when it got new agents after a victory. Note that a leaves the team after the resources from its proposed field are collected, thus, returning into the exploration phase as soon as possible.

(B) Team T reached its target field. Independently of T's success in collecting resources on that field, it evicts the agent that provided the information and has to choose a new target field.

(C) Team T lost a conflict and lost the agent providing the information on the previous target field to the winner team.

In the latter two cases, team T choses its new target field among all fields memorized by all member agents. There are four objectives to consider in this decision.

1. The amount of resources $r(f)$ on the field f.
2. The likelihood $P(|T| \geq a(f_T))$ to have the required team size by the time the field is reached. This value is predicted by estimating the expected change of team size per simulation turn P_{growth}. In each simulation turn P_{growth} is computed anew with the following simple learning rule

$$P_{growth} = (1 - \alpha)P_{growth} + \alpha\Delta$$

where Δ is the change of team size during the last simulation turn and $0 < \alpha \leq 1$ is the growth learning rate. The required time of travel can be inferred from the minimum Euclidean distance $\Delta(f_c, f_T)$ between the current field f_c and the target field f_T

$$\Delta(f_c, f_T) = \left\| \begin{pmatrix} \frac{d}{2} - \left||x(f_c) - x(f_T)| - \frac{d}{2}\right| \\ \frac{d}{2} - \left||y(f_c) - y(f_T)| - \frac{d}{2}\right| \end{pmatrix} \right\|$$

where $\|x\|$ is the Euclidean norm of x. The agents derive an approximated probability for team T to have at least size $a(f_T)$ with

$$P(|T| \geq a(f_T)) = \max(0, \min(1, \psi(T, f_c)))$$
$$\psi(T, f_c) = 1 - \frac{a(f_T) - P_{growth}\Delta(f_c, f_T)}{2|T|}$$

Note, $|T| + P_{growth}\Delta(f_c, f_T)$ is the expected size of T after reaching f_T. If the expected team size equals the number of required agents $a(f)$, then $P(|T| \geq a(f_T)) = 0.5$.

3. The required time for a target field f_T is $\Delta(f_c, f_T) + t(f_T)$, i.e., the time to reach it and to collect the resources.
4. Once the resources of a field have been collected it regenerates. However, agents are not informed whether any of their memorized fields have regenerated since the time of visit. Thus, the more time has passed since an agent memorized the information the higher is the possibility that the information is deprecated.

All four criteria should be considered by the team when it chooses a new target field. Each agent ranks all fields in the field memory of all member agents with its personal ranking strategy. These ranks are averaged over all team members to infer the highest ranking field and set it as target field.

3.5 Ranking Methods

Each agent applies exactly one of the following four ranking methods at a time. Note, that these ranking methods have been used in [10] for different multi-objective optimization algorithms to select good solutions.

Dominance Depth Ranking.

The dominance depth ranking is based on the Pareto dominance relation. A field f is Pareto dominant over another field f' if f is not worse than f' in any criterion and is in at least one criterion better than f'. A dominance depth ranking sorts the set of fields by iteratively removing the set of non-dominated solutions from the whole set of solutions such that no field is dominated by any field of lower rank where all ranks are minimized. In case of incomparability the order is set randomly.

Weighted Ranking.

The weighted ranking uses a weight vector $w \in [0, 1]^k$, with $\sum_{i \in \{1,\dots,k\}} w_i = 1$, to compute a weighted sum over all criteria. It is individual for each agent. Let $f^{(j)}$ be the value of criterion $j \in \{1, \dots, k\}$ of field f. Note, that the negative value of the first criterion is used for $f^{(1)}$, as it needs to be maximized. A set of fields M is ranked with

$$s(f) = \sum_{j=1}^{k} \frac{w_i \left(f^{(j)} - \min_{f' \in M} f'^{(j)}\right)}{\max_{f' \in M} f'^{(j)} - \min_{f' \in M} f'^{(j)}}, \quad f \in M$$

such that the lower $s(f)$ is the higher is the rank of f.

WL Ranking.

This ranking method conducts pairwise comparisons of all fields in the set. A comparison can either have a winner and a loser, or is a tie. The field that has better values in more criteria than its competitor wins the comparison. If the number of criteria in which they are better is equal to the number of criteria in which they are worse, both fields are in a tie. A field is prioritized before another field if it either wins in more comparisons or, in case of equal number of won comparisons, loses less comparisons.

Points Ranking.

Similar to the WL ranking, all fields are compared to each other. The Points ranking gives a field two points for a victory and one point for a tie. The total number of points is used to rank the fields. If two or more fields have an equal number of points, their relative order is set randomly.

3.6 Evolutionary Processes

Instead of tuning the critical parameters in an exhaustive analysis and to avoid over fitting in dynamic environments, some of the critical parameters are learned in the multi-agent system by evolutionary mechanisms. Each agent has at least one set of chromosomes that contains the agents behavioral properties: *exploration time*, *power*, the applied ranking scheme, and weights for the weighted ranking scheme. An agent reproduces when it has collected a certain amount (defined by the *reproduction threshold*) of resources. To keep the number of agents constant each reproduction goes along with the death of a randomly chosen other agent. We consider three different inheritance mechanisms.

Haploid Inheritance.

A haploid agent a has one chromosome set. If a reaches the reproduction threshold it randomly choses an agent a' and overwrites the chromosome set of a'. During the copy process the chromosome set can mutate, such that a''s chromosome set is not identical to that of a. The chromosome set of a does not mutate. It is possible that a and a' are the same agent.

Diploid Inheritance.

Diploid agents have two chromosome sets but apply only one them. An agent a that reaches the reproduction threshold randomly chooses two other agents a' and a''. The four chromosome sets of a and a' replace those of a' and a'', such that a' and a'' have one chromosome set of a and a', respectively. The new chromosome sets of a' and a'' are shuffled, i.e. the genes are reallocated to the chromosome sets at random to simulate recombination. Afterwards the chromosome sets mutate and both a' and a''. Without loss of generality due to the recombination process, the first chromosome set is set as active chromosome set. The genotype of a remains unchanged throughout the whole procedure.

Haplo-Diploid Inheritance.

Haplo-diploid agents have two chromosome set, representing diploid females. If an agent a reaches the reproduction threshold it randomly choses two agents a' and a''. Both of these agents randomly replace one of their chromosome sets with one of the chromosome sets of a and then shuffle the genes between their chromosome sets, and mutate them.

In all three variants death is a random event. Instead of eliminating the weakest member of the swarm, a random agent is chosen. However, the best agents collect more resources and reproduce more frequently. This is similar to natural selection where fitter individuals reproduce more often but death typically strikes at random.

Table 1: Fixed parameters of all experiments.

Parameter	Definition	Values
	number of performed runs	50
d	arena size	50×50
	number of simulation turns	50 000
k	objectives	4
n	agents	100
	rotation probability	0.25
α	growth learning rate	0.2
	reproduction threshold	1
	memory size	5
	initial exploration time	10 sim. turns
$power$	initial power	10
w	random initial weights	$[0, 500]$
σ	mutation strength	1

Table 2: Different applied scenarios with the distributions that are used to set the field values and the regeneration rate (reg. rate).

	$r(f)$	$a(f)$	$t(f)$	reg. rate
1	exponential	even	even	0
2	even	exponential	even	0
3	even	even	exponential	0
4	even	even	even	100

Mutation.

The values for the traits *power*, *exploration time*, and the weights for the weighted ranking scheme mutate from one generation to the next. Mutation is achieved by choosing a random number ρ from a normal (Gaussian) distribution $N(0, \sigma)$, where 0 is the mean value and σ the variance. The current value of the trait is then in-/decreased by $\rho \in N(0, \sigma)$ such that $x' = \max(0, x + \rho)$ where x is the old value of a parameter and x' the new value. Note, that by varying σ the strength of the mutations is set and that values cannot decrease below zero.

4. EXPERIMENTAL RESULTS

Multiple scenarios are tested to analyze the agents behavior and the evolutionary processes under different environmental conditions.

4.1 Experimental Setting

The initial values for field properties $r(f)$, $a(f)$, and $t(f)$ are set randomly. The respective random values are taken either from an exponential distribution with $\lambda = 1$ or from an even distribution (details see Table 2). The values are chosen such that $r(f) \in [0, 1]$, $a(f) \in \{2, \ldots, 10\}$, $t(f) \in \{1, \ldots, 10\}$. When a field is regenerated its values are not reset with new random values but swapped with the values of another field. This procedure maintains the respective distributions of the parameters in the environment. This would not be the case when the parameters are simply initialized with new random values, because the teams prefer

Table 3: Correlations between objectives in different scenarios; (1) required time, (2) available resources, (3) required agents, (4) age of information as measured in the haploid system; values are presented only when statistically significant (Pearson correlation, p-values < 0.01).

	Scen. 1			Scen. 2			Scen. 3			Scen. 4		
	2	3	4	2	3	4	2	3	4	2	3	4
1	–	-0.15	0.37	0.09	-0.11	0.35	0.13	0.01	0.38	0.02	-0.07	0.30
2		0.11	0.17		0.09	0.18		0.10	0.20		0.02	-0.01
3			0.12			0.12			0.13			0.12

to collect resources of fields with good values. Parameter *regeneration rate* gives the number of fields that are picked at random in each simulation turn to be regenerated. Thus, the agents are confronted with a constantly changing environment and deprecating information.

At first we analyze four scenarios in Section 4.2 and then inspect the adaptability of the swarm in dynamic environments in Section 4.3. All results are based on measurements performed every 100 simulation turns. Table 1 gives an overview of the fixed parameter values applied in all experiments. Note, that the weights for the objectives are in $[0, 500]$ instead of $[0, 1]$. The weights are normalized for the ranking process but otherwise have these rather large values for their mutation process. Initially, the weights have a very large variance and and provide a very diverse starting point. The initial power and exploration time, though prone to the same mutation strength, have much smaller initial values. All agents start with the same initial power and exploration time in each experiment.

In the second type of experiments we analyze dynamic environments. A dynamic environment is defined by a periodic rotation between Scenarios 1 to 4. Three strengths of dynamics are considered depending on the time period between changes of scenarios (100, 1000, or 10 000 simulation turns).

4.2 Analysis of the Scenarios

Criteria Correlations.

In the four scenarios the distributions of the values for the parameters $r(f)$, $t(f)$, and $a(f)$ induce different strengths in the criteria correlations (see Table 3). While the correlation between the required time and the available resources is low or not significant, there are stronger correlations between the required time and the age of information. This phenomenon can be explained by the fact that new information is derived from fields that were recently visited by members of the team and that are still in close proximity. The older the information is, the larger can be the distance between the team and the respective field.

In most scenarios the correlation between the required time and the probability to have a sufficient team size is negative. This is due to the fact that a longer distance to the target field gives a team more possibilities to recruit more agents on their way there. This negative correlation subsides if the actual processing time $t(f)$ of a field has a larger impact on the required time than the distance the team has to travel because the values of $t(f)$ are exponentially distributed (Scenario 3).

The higher regeneration rate in Scenario 4 turns the otherwise positive correlation between required time and required agents into a slightly negative correlation. In Scenarios 1 to 3 the active choosing process of the agents inflicts a positive correlation – they prefer fields where both values are good over those where only one value is good. In Scenario 4, however, the agents have different priorities.

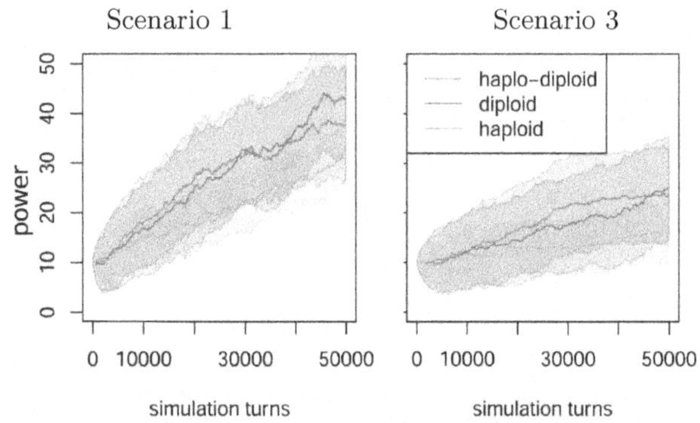

Figure 2: Power in different scenarios with average values and standard deviations.

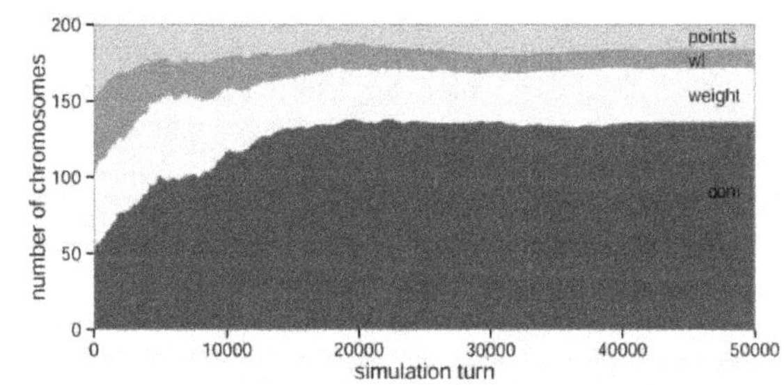

Figure 3: Distribution of the different ranking schemes in the haplo-diploid system for Scenario 2; Dominance Depth is abbreviated by 'dom'.

Power.

This parameter changes over time and is used to decide which team wins in case of a conflict and can assimilate agents of the other team into itself. Figure 2 shows how the average values of the power parameter develop in the different scenarios with the three inheritance mechanisms.

Initially, all agents have a power of ten. During the simulation run the power increases, as could be expected since more powerful agents can force other agents to join their team. This higher chance of having a sufficiently sized team when they reach their target field is obviously beneficial.

For the diploid and haplo-diploid inheritance mechanisms the standard deviation is higher as well as the speed of increasing the values than in the haploid inheritance mechanism. Scenario 1 appears to give a higher selective pressure on the power, that rises to average values of up to 40, whereas the values grow slower in the other scenarios (from 20 to 30) as represented by Scenario 3 in Figure 2.

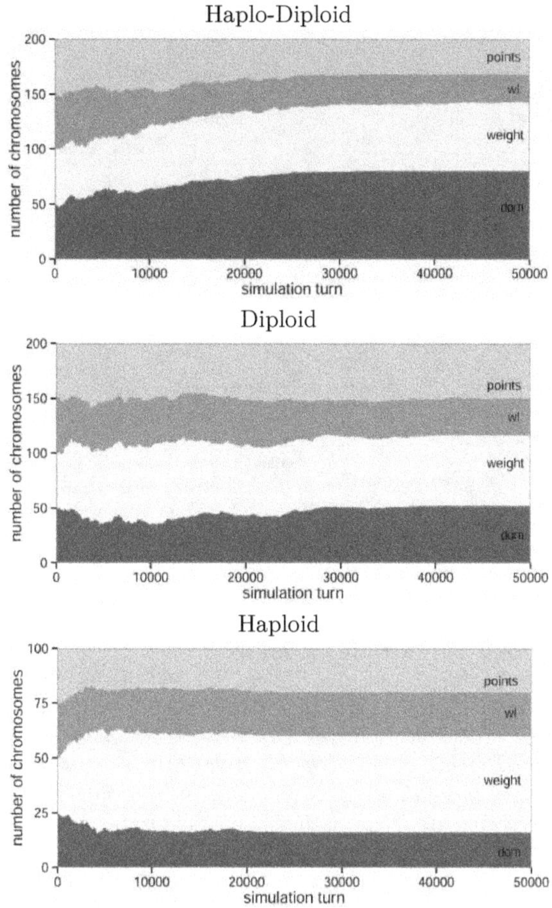

Figure 4: Distribution of the different ranking schemes in the different systems for Scenario 4; Dominance Depth is abbreviated by 'dom'.

Ranking schemes.

In Scenarios 1 - 3 the Dominance Depth ranking scheme dominates all systems regardless of their inheritance mechanisms by making up more than half of all ranking scheme chromosomes. The Weighted ranking is often second followed by the WL ranking scheme. The Points ranking scheme goes always extinct in systems with haplo-diploid and haploid inheritance in the first three scenarios. In diploid inheritance systems they have a marginally higher survival rate but are, on average over all runs, never more frequent then the Dominance Depth or Weighted ranking scheme. After 25 000 simulation turns the frequencies of the ranking schemes fluctuate only very little. Due to limited space we can only show an exemplary time series in Figure 3 which shows the abundances of the four different ranking schemes during the simulations with diploid inheritance in Scenario 2.

Scenario 4 induces a very different development (see Figure 4). None of the ranking schemes goes always extinct and no ranking scheme is on average clearly the most dominant in this scenario. However, in the following analysis it is shown that these systems are rarely mixed but typically dominated by one of the ranking schemes in each single simulation run.

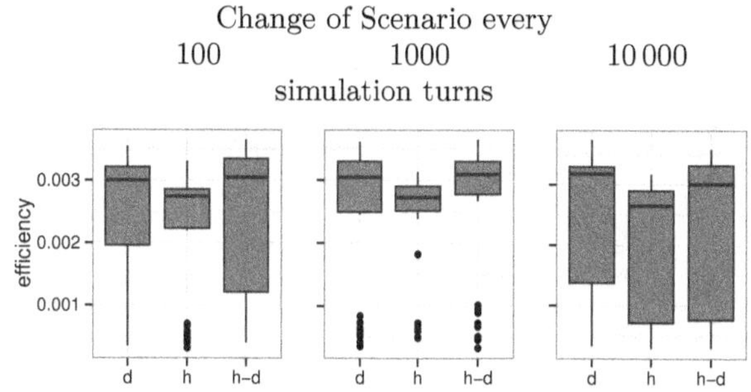

Figure 5: Efficiency (average collected resources per agent per simulation turn) in different dynamic systems with average values and standard deviations.

4.3 Diversity and Adaptability Analysis

A special focus in this analysis lies on the diversity and efficiency of the different inheritance mechanisms. To measure the diversity we applied the Shannon-Weaver index $H' = -\sum_{i=1}^{R} p_i \ln p_i$ where p_i is the proportional abundance of class $i \in \{1, \ldots, R\}$ with a total of R classes, defined by the ranking schemes of all chromosome sets in the system.

Figure 6 shows the development of the diversity in the dynamic settings. A change of scenario every 1000 or 10 000 simulation turns results in a decrease of diversity and promotes systems based on only one ranking scheme. With more frequent changes of scenarios the process of complete loss of diversity is faster. However, none of the different inheritance mechanism maintains more than one ranking scheme in the system until the end of the simulation. The haploid system is the fastest to converge and settle on a single ranking scheme, while the diploid and haplo-diploid system are slower.

Figure 5 shows the efficiency of the different inheritance mechanisms in the different dynamic systems. A Friedman-Nemenyi post-hoc analysis labels the difference in efficiency between the haplo-diploid and haploid system with scenario changes every 1000 simulation turns significant (p-value $<$ 0.01) as well as the differences between the diploid and haploid system with scenario changes every 10 000 simulation turns. A comparison of the efficiencies of the systems in the different scenarios shows that in Scenario 1 the diploid system has a significantly higher efficiency than the haploid system. In Scenario 3 both the diploid and haplo-diploid system are significantly better than the haploid system.

5. CONCLUSION

The use of evolutionary inheritance mechanisms for the adaptation of parameters in a multi-agent system has been studied. In the studied system the tasks are distributed within the environment and the agents have to form teams to execute the tasks. It is a multi-criterion decision problem for the agents to decide which task to execute next. For this they use different ranking schemes. Agents that have successfully executed several tasks can reproduce and pass the type of ranking scheme they have used and some corresponding parameter values to their successors. Three types of evolutionary inheritance mechanisms are compared: haploid, diploid, and haplo-diploid. The influence of different inheritance mechanisms on the efficiency of the multi-agent

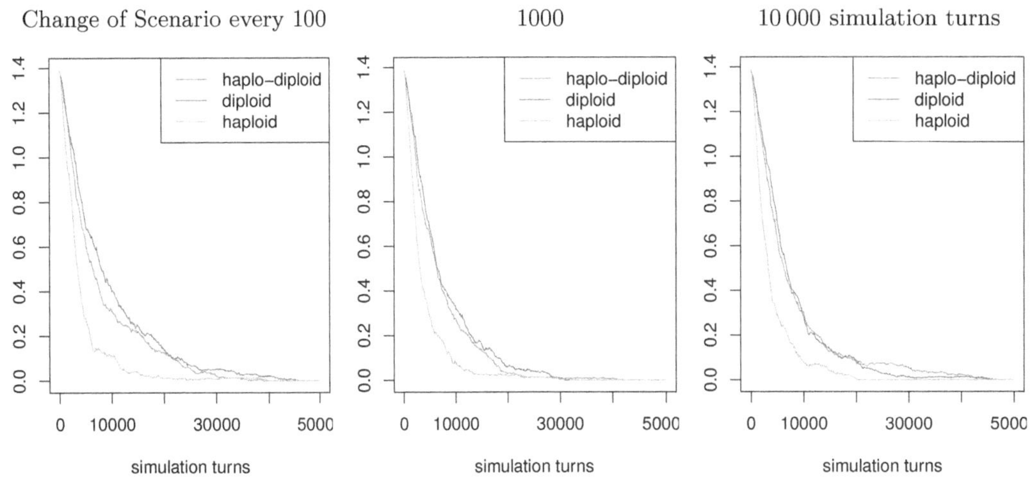

Figure 6: Diversity in different dynamic systems with average values and standard deviations.

system was inferred by simulation experiments for different dynamic environments. The results show that the diploid and haplo-diploid inheritance mechanisms could maintain a higher genetic diversity and thus a higher diversity of the ranking schemes that occur in the system. They also show tendencies to perform better than the haploid system. However, in the final state of the systems in nearly all experimental runs only one ranking scheme 'survived'. The fact that these final dominant ranking schemes are incoherently different ones in the different simulation runs indicates that a mixed system might be more beneficial, nevertheless.

6. ACKNOWLEDGMENTS

This work has been supported by the European Social Fund (ESF) and the Free State of Saxony within the junior research group „Schwarm-inspirierte Verfahren zur Optimierung, Selbstorganisation und Ressourceneffizienz".

7. REFERENCES

[1] J. C. Bongard. Evolutionary robotics. *Communications of the ACM*, 56(8):74–83, 2013.

[2] R. I. Bowers and E. Sevinç. Preserving variability in sexual multi-agent systems with diploidy and dominance. In *Engineering Societies in the Agents World VI*, pages 184–202. Springer, 2006.

[3] R. Calabretta, R. Galbiati, S. Nolfi, and D. Parisi. Two is better than one: a diploid genotype for neural networks. *Neural Processing Letters*, 4(3):149–155, 1996.

[4] D. E. Goldberg and R. E. Smith. Nonstationary function optimization using genetic algorithms with dominance and diploidy. In *ICGA*, pages 59–68, 1987.

[5] F. Herrera and M. Lozano. Adaptation of genetic algorithm parameters based on fuzzy logic controllers. *Genetic Algorithms and Soft Computing*, 8:95–125, 1996.

[6] K.-S. Leung, Q.-H. Duan, Z.-B. Xu, and C. Wong. A new model of simulated evolutionary computation-convergence analysis and specifications. *Evolutionary Computation, IEEE Transactions on*, 5(1):3–16, 2001.

[7] M. L. Mauldin. Maintaining diversity in genetic search. In *AAAI*, pages 247–250, 1984.

[8] R. L. Moritz and M. Middendorf. Self-organized cooperation between agents that have to solve resource collection tasks. In *Proc. IEEE Swarm Intelligence Symposium*, page 12, 2013.

[9] R. L. Moritz and M. Middendorf. Decentralized and dynamic group formation of reconfigurable agents. *Memetic Computing*, pages 1–15, to appear.

[10] R. L. Moritz, E. Reich, M. Schwarz, M. Bernt, and M. Middendorf. Refined ranking relations for selection of solutions in multi objective metaheuristics. *European Journal of Operational Research*, to appear.

[11] L. Panait and S. Luke. Cooperative multi-agent learning: The state of the art. *Autonomous Agents and Multi-Agent Systems*, 11(3):387–434, 2005.

[12] J. Pieter and E. D. de Jong. Evolutionary multi-agent systems. In *Parallel Problem Solving from Nature-PPSN VIII*, pages 872–881. Springer, 2004.

[13] J. C. Potts, T. D. Giddens, and S. B. Yadav. The development and evaluation of an improved genetic algorithm based on migration and artificial selection. *Systems, Man and Cybernetics, IEEE Transactions on*, 24(1):73–86, 1994.

[14] T. Shibata and T. Fukuda. Coordinative behavior by genetic algorithm and fuzzy in evolutionary multi-agent system. In *Robotics and Automation, 1993. Proceedings., 1993 IEEE International Conference on*, pages 760–765. IEEE, 1993.

[15] J. M. Whitacre, P. Rohlfshagen, A. Bender, and X. Yao. The role of degenerate robustness in the evolvability of multi-agent systems in dynamic environments. In *Parallel Problem Solving from Nature, PPSN XI*, pages 284–293. Springer, 2010.

[16] Y. Yukiko and A. Nobue. A diploid genetic algorithm for preserving population diversity – Pseudo-Meiosis GA. In *Parallel Problem Solving from Nature–PPSN III*, pages 36–45. Springer, 1994.

The Impact of Centrality on Individual and Collective Performance in Social Problem-Solving Systems

Diego Noble
Institute of Informatics
UFRGS
dvnoble@inf.ufrgs.br

Felipe Grando
Institute of Informatics
UFRGS
felipe.grando@inf.ufrgs.br

Ricardo M. Araújo
Centro de Desenvolvimento
Tecnológico UFPel
ricardo@inf.ufpel.edu.br

Luis C. Lamb
Institute of Informatics
UFRGS
luislamb@acm.org

ABSTRACT

In this paper, we analyze the dependency between centrality and individual performance in socially-inspired problem-solving systems. By means of extensive numerical simulations, we investigate how individual performance in four different models correlate with four different classical centrality measures. Our main result shows that there is a high linear correlation between centrality and individual performance when individuals systematically exploit central positions. In this case, central individuals tend to deviate from the expected majority contribution behavior. Although there is ample evidence about the relevance of centrality in social problem-solving, our work contributes to understand that some measures correlate better with individual performance than others due to individual traits, a position that is gaining strength in recent studies.

CCS Concepts

•Computing methodologies → *Network science;* Multi-agent systems; **•Human-centered computing** → **Social networks;**

Keywords

Social Problem-Solving; Network Organization; Centrality in Social Systems

1. INTRODUCTION

Agent-based social systems have long served as tools of research in social sciences. They hold a potential to improve our understanding of social institutions and organizations by offering a natural environment to study connectionist phenomena of social systems [1, 11, 14].

A fundamental endeavour in the investigation of social problem-solving systems is to understand the interplay between the social structure and system's performance [15, 22]. Among structural properties, *centrality* is one that has long been regarded as fundamental in a diverse set of social systems [4, 5, 7, 8, 13]. In the context of social problem-solving, recent evidence with human subjects suggests that centrality is positively correlated with individual's performance [19]. However, one may ask whether socially-inspired computational models of problem-solving corroborate this result.

This work's main objective is to investigate the role of centrality in social problem-solving systems. Using extensive numerical simulation, we compare how individual performance is related to four classical structural measures of centrality (degree, betweenness, closeness and eigenvector).

We employed four agent-based socially-inspired models of problem-solvers in order to have a diverse set of models. They are: the Particle Swarm Optimization model (PSO) [16, 23], the Memetic Network model [2], the Dynamic Search Range model (DSR) [21] and the Fully Informed Particle Swarm model (FIPS) [20]. All of these models have one common property which is the structured communication network. This network defines who should communication to whom, that is, who is connected to whom. Communication in these models plays a key role, for it allows agents to solve the problem collaboratively.

Our results show that central individuals usually get an advantage, but we show too, cases where exactly the opposite happens. All centralities agreed more or less about the relevance of position within the network to predict individual's contribution. Additionally, we exposed the influence of other important factors affecting individual's contribution, such as, individual's problem-solving traits (strategies) and problem's peculiarities. These results corroborate to recent evidence about individual's behavioral traits that are relevant to social problem-solving systems [15, 19, 22].

Next, we present essential information about related works, proceeded by the explanation of the experimental methodology and by the experimental results with associated discussion. We conclude addressing implications and limitations of this work's results and future directions.

GECCO '15, July 11–15, 2015, Madrid, Spain

DOI: http://dx.doi.org/10.1145/2739480.2754679

2. RELATED WORK

Centrality is an ambiguous concept in network studies. A central node in a network could be either a node with many connections or a well-connected node. Historically, several measures were developed in order to formalize this concept [5, 8, 13].

Freeman's original measures were based on three concepts: communication activity (degree, i.e. the number of connections), potential for control of communication (betweenness, i.e. the number of shortest paths between each pair of nodes that passes by the node being measured), and independence or efficiency (closeness, i.e. Inverse length of shortest path to all other nodes.).

Bonacich [5] proposes the eigenvector centrality[1] which captures the idea that a node connected to influential (powerful) nodes is also an influential node. The eigenvector centrality is similar to the degree centrality, but it reflects how much a node can communicate indirectly with other nodes in the network [6].

Since we are concerned with the relationship between centrality and individual performance, we proceed to present definitions of the measures of centrality that we shall use in our experiments.

Degree Centrality

The degree centrality of a node is simply defined as its number of connections. It reflects how much a node can communicate directly with other nodes, i.e. how much it is active in communication [13]. It has an absolute version (Equation (1), below) and a relative one (Equation (2), below), the former is a simple counting while the latter is the proportion of edges a node has compared to the maximum possible degree in the network. $a(p_i, pk)$ is 1 if there is an edge between nodes i and k and 0 otherwise.

$$C_D(p_k) = \sum_i^n a(p_i, p_k) \quad (1)$$

$$C_D^{'}(p_k) = \frac{C_D(p_k)}{n-1} \quad (2)$$

Betweenness Centrality

The betweenness centrality of a node p_k is the number of geodesic paths (shortest paths) between any two nodes p_i and p_j that passes by a node k, divided by the total number of shortest paths between i and j (Equation 3). A node with high betweenness centrality occupies a position where a high fraction of the network traffic passes by and, thus, has a high potential to control this flow. The relative form (Equation 4) divides the result by the maximum betweenness a node can have. Below, $g(p_i, p_j)$ is the number of shortest paths between nodes p_i and p_j while $g(p_i, p_j)(pk)$ is the number of shortest paths between nodes p_i and p_j that pass through node p_k.

$$C_B(p_k) = \sum_{i \neq k \neq j} \frac{g(p_i, p_j)(pk)}{g(p_i, p_j)} \quad (3)$$

$$C_B^{'}(p_k) = \frac{2C_B(p_k)}{n^2 - 3n + 2} \quad (4)$$

Closeness Centrality

The closeness centrality of a node is the inverse of the sum of the links in the shortest paths to all other nodes. Nodes with high closeness have low average distances to all other others. A close node may receive information in less time (assuming that the network flow uses shortest paths) than farther nodes. Its absolute form (5) and its relative form (6) are given below. Below, $dg(p_i, p_j)$ counts the number of links in the geodesic between nodes p_i and p_j.

$$C_C(p_k) = \sum_i^n dg(p_i, p_k) \quad (5)$$

$$C_C^{'}(p_k) = \frac{n-1}{C_C(p_k)} \quad (6)$$

Eigenvector Centrality

The eigenvector centrality is defined by the connections summed to all others nodes, weighted by their centralities [5]. The idea behind the eigenvector centrality is that a node that is connected to an influential node is also an influential node. The eigenvector centrality is similar to the degree centrality, but it reflects how much a node can communicate indirectly with other nodes in the network [6]. Equation 7 depicts the eigenvector centrality, where R is the adjacency matrix, λ is the eigenvalue, and e is the eigenvector.

$$C_E(pk) = \lambda e_{pk} = \sum_j^n R_{kj} e_{pj} \quad (7)$$

Betweenness and closeness centralities, considering network flow[2], are adequate only if the flow happens through shortest paths. This assumption implies that any flow has a source along with a destination and it fits perfectly some non-social scenarios such as package delivery. Degree and eigenvector centralities do not make use of shortest paths, but rather assume that flows are random walks [6].

Social systems are too heterogeneous to allow any general assumption about their flow. For example, gossip flow inside an organization may happen from one person to another (serial flow) and it may suffer slight changes as it flows through the network. Different behaviors, on other hand, may spread from one person to many others at he same time (parallel flow) as it is when a person yawns in front of an audience, transmitting that will to the others [6].

Social problem-solving happens when individuals seek to collaboratively solve a problem. Specifically, such collaborative endeavor is justified when there is evidence that communication among individuals improves collective performance despite each individual being capable of solving the problem alone.

Communication among individuals is of paramount relevance therefore. It must obey rules that are fundamentally different from rules used in e.g. evolutionary system. In social problem-solving systems, agents communicate directly when they have a social link, while in evolutionary systems, communication is usually performed indirectly by a stochastic breeding mechanism (as in genetic algorithms). The structure that emerges from such rules is known as the *social network* of the system and provides a natural structure where information is to flow.

[1]Defined by the connections summed to all others nodes, weighted by their degree centralities.

[2]Network flow in this context must be understood in broad sense of how things or information flow within a network and not in the sense of the graph-theoretical model used in the problem of maximum flow.

Investigations framing social systems as social problem-solving systems are abound. One of the earliest is the work of Bavelas and Barrett [4]. Bavelas and his group performed a series of social problem-solving experiments using small groups of people, concluding that network centrality was indeed linked to group performance. As investigations matured, often with contradictory results, Burgess [7] advised that results with social problem-solving at the time were not consistent nor cumulative.

In a more recent investigation, [15] investigated how humans solved collectively two constraint satisfaction problems: graph coloring and consensus. Their results gave evidence that long-distance connectivity, a structural network property, elicits opposing phenomena in the problems, making consensus easier and coloring harder. The authors observed that the position of an individual alone may not account for its influence on neighbors and that individual traits may play a more important role than previously thought. The authors suggest some benefits of broadening the research on social systems to include individual aspects instead of focusing solely on network structure.

The relation between individual's traits and centrality has not been well investigated yet. Our main objective is to analyze this interplay and determine how the most common centrality measures correlate with individual and collective outcomes. We proceed to explain the methodology employed.

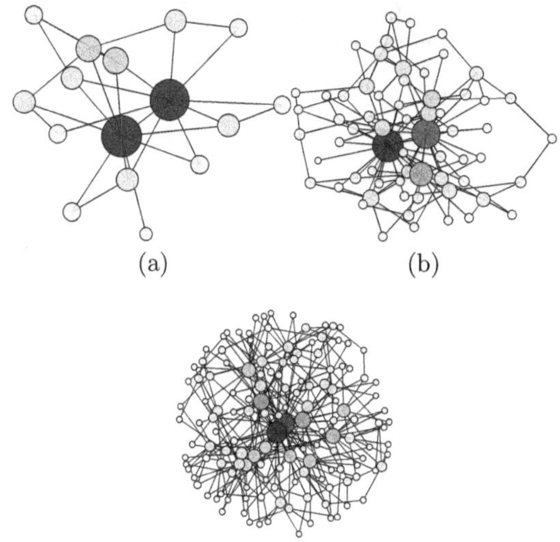

(a) (b)

(c)

Figure 1: Networks generated by the Barabási-Albert model where new nodes connect to $m = 2$ following a preferential attachment mechanism of connection. The network sizes were 16 (a), 64 (b), and 144 (c). The node size in these pictures is directly proportional to its degree.

3. METHODOLOGY

An agent-based social system can be seen as a group of interdependent, yet autonomous, agents who follow simple rules [14, 18]. Compared to humans, experiments with artificial agents have the advantage of being more easily controlled. This section exposes the design decisions we have taken to instantiate agent-based models used in this work.

The first decision pertains to the choice of an adequate network topology. While regular or random networks are often used in sociological studies, we need more realistic topologies where centrality is better distributed[3], so that one can observe central (few) and peripheral nodes (most). To generate such networks, we employed the generative network process developed by Barabási and Albert [3]. The process starts by adding one new node at each iteration and connecting this node to m other nodes.

The choice of the m nodes depends on their respective degree, the higher the degree, the higher the probability of being chosen. This way, the network grows through a mechanism of preferential attachment. The resulting centrality distribution resembles a power-law distribution, with few well-connected nodes (hubs) and the remaining nodes occupying intermediate and peripheral positions.

The population sizes used in experiments were of 16, 64 and 144 individuals (nodes). These values represent a small, an intermediate, and a big population size when one considers previous experimental works.

The next decision was to select the problem to be solved. We decided to frame problem-solving as a minimization problem of real-valued functions. We have chosen five functions, the Ackley function (here referenced as F1), the Griewank function (F2), the Rastrigin function (F3), the Rosenbrock function (F4) and the Sphere function (F5). By using a diversity of functions with different properties, regarding modality and separability, we hope to capture features of distinct real-world problems. Interested readers can refer to [17] for more detailed information about these functions. All functions were set to have 30 dimensions - i.e. 30 real-valued independent variables.

Later, we elaborate our measure of individual's performance (success of the agent). We consider two kinds of individual performance, one global and the other local. Global performance of a node is defined by the number of times it has found a solution which was better than the previous best solution held by the whole system (i.e. all nodes) — we call this the *individual global contribution*. The local performance is defined as the number of times that a node held a solution which was better than those held by any of its neighbors — we call this the *individual local contribution*.

Four agent-based models were used in the experiments: Particle Swarm Algorithm (PSO), the Fully Informed Particle Swarm (FIPS), an instance of Memetic Networks (MN) model, and the Dynamic Search Range (DSR). All models share a similar structure as depicted in Algorithm 1.

All these models satisfy the social problem-solving property we highlighted earlier: agents work better when they collaborate, despite being capable of solving the problem by themselves. They start initializing the population with random solutions, yielding a uniform distribution of solutions within the search space. After initializing the individuals' solutions, we connect them according to the Barabási-Albert model, using different random seeds for each independent trial. We also used a bi-dimensional periodic grid as control network – i.e. all agents have the same degree and have the same average distance from all nodes. Both network topologies were static.

[3]By a better distribution we mean a distribution where one can observe a rich spectra of nodes regarding their centralities.

Algorithm 1 Algorithm structure used by all models.

```
Input  : Population_size, stop_condition, Problem_size,
         m
Output: Solution_best

//Initialize the population with random solutions.
Population ←InitializePopulation
(Population_size,Problem_size)
//Establish social ties among individuals.
BarabasiAlbert (Population,m)
repeat
    foreach node ∈ Population do
        UpdateState (node,Problem_size)
        EvaluateState (node)
until stop_condition
Solution_best←RetrieveBestSolution (Population)
return Solution_best
```

Algorithm 2 UpdateState procedure of a particle. Operations $\{+, \times, -\}$are in the matrix notation.

```
Input : node,Problem_size
//UPDATE PARTICLE'S VELOCITY.
neighbor ← FINDBESTNEIGHBOR(node_neighbors)

V1 ← RANDOMVECTOR(min = 0.0, max = 2.05, size =
Problem_size)
V2 ← RANDOMVECTOR(min = 0.0, max = 2.05, size =
Problem_size)

Cognitive ←
node_best_previous_position − node_current_position
Social ←
neighbor_best_previous_position − node_current_position

node_velocity ← 0.7298 *
(node_velocity + (Cognitive × V1) + (Social × V2))
CHECKVELOCITYLIMITS(node_velocity)

//UPDATE PARTICLE'S POSITION.
node_solution ← node_solution + node_velocity
CHECKSOLUTIONLIMITS(node_solution)
```

With the individuals in place and the network ties formed, the models start their iterative stage, where each agent evaluates and updates its current solution according to its own search operations. After all individuals have updated and evaluated their state, the algorithm proceeds to the next round until the stop condition is found. We used 5000 rounds as the stop criterion and four decimal digits of precision.

In the PSO model, particles hold a velocity vector which they update at each iteration. This vector is used to update the particle's current position. It is calculated by summing over two components: the cognitive component, which points to the own particle's best previous position; and the social component, which points to the particle's best ranked neighbour's previous solution. After adding some perturbation to these components, the particle sums its velocity vector to its current solution. If this new solution is better evaluated than the previous best solution (used by the cognitive component), the particle updates its previous best solution.

Our PSO implementation follows Clerc and Kennedy's work (2002). This implementation is considered the canonical form of the PSO model [23]. Velocities are limited to the maximum absolute range of each variable in each dimension [10]. Any particle's solution component that leaves the boundary of the problem's space is set to the maximum valid value and its respective velocity component is reflected back by multiplying it by -1.0. The Algorithm 2 depicts the PSO algorithm we used. Note that most operations in pseudo-code are in the matrix notation to simplify understanding.

The first step is to find the particle's best ranked neighbour. The second is to generate two random vectors that will be multiplied by the cognitive and the social components. The cognitive component is given by the difference between the particle's previous best position visited and its current position, whereas, the social component is calculated from the difference from the position of the best ranked neighbour and the particle's current position. Both components are multiplied by the random vectors and summed. The resulting value is summed with the previous particle velocity, then it is multiplied by a constant $c = 0.7298$[4]. Afterwards, the model performs a double boundary check during each iteration: one on the velocity and other on the position. Finally, particles update their current solution with the new one and, if it is the case, update their best previous solution.

Among the PSO extensions, there is the Fully-Informed Particle Swarm (FIPS) by Mendes et al. (2004). The main difference is that FIPS's particles use the information from all of its neighbour particles to update their position, averaging over all possibilities instead of relying only on the best ranked neighbour as the canonical PSO. We can say that a FIPS particle receives more influence from its neighborhood than the other models.

The MN is a class of socially-inspired problem-solving models. It was developed to test the impact of social network topology on a system's performance [2]. The Memetic Networks are not exactly a model, but rather a meta-model with guidelines for the design of an agent-based problem-solving system. This model resembles the PSO model in the sense that both models make use of the social network concept to structure communication, but the exchange of information is made more explicit in MNs.

A MN makes use of the concept of memes, which are the cultural analogues of genes [9], to represent the basic units of information. Its dynamics arise from three simple rules: connection, aggregation and appropriation. The Memetic Networks (MN) model used here follows Noble et al. version [21] which in turn is inspired by Araújo and Lamb's version [2]. The Algorithm 3 depicts how a memetic node updates its current state. Note that the appropriation rule does not depend on any exogenous information and that the better ranked set of nodes include the node itself.

Each node in a memenet performs aggregation by condensing a pool of better ranked nodes. With this pool filled, the memetic node composes its solution by retrieving randomly memes from it, one at a time, and conserving their

[4]This constant is originally part of the model

Algorithm 3 UpdateState procedure of memetic node. Note that the appropriation rule is purely endogenous and the better ranked set of nodes include the node itself.

```
Input : node, Problem_size, Upper_limit, Lower_limit

//Aggregation rule.
Better_Neighbors ← RetrieveBetter(node_Neighbors) ∪ node
for i ← 1 to Problem_size do
    Chosen_Neighbor ← RandomChoose(Better_Neighbors)
    node_Solution[i] ← Chosen_Neighbor_Solution[i]

//Appropriation rule.
for i ← 1 to Problem_size do
    With 1/Problem_size probability
        node_Solution[i] ← Random(min = Lower_limit, max = Upper_limit)
```

Algorithm 4 UpdateState procedure of memetic node employing a R* appropriation (DSR). SRP stands for Social Relative Performance.

```
Input : node, Problem_size, Upper_limit, Lower_limit

//Aggregation rule.
Better_Neighbors ← RetrieveBetter(node_Neighbors)
for i ← 1 to Problem_size do
    Chosen_Neighbor ← RandomChoose(Better_Neighbors)
    node_Solution[i] ← Chosen_Neighbor_Solution[i]

//R* Appropriation rule.
SRP ← Count(Better_Neighbors)/Count(node_Neighbors)
Δ ← (|Upper_limit| + |Lower_limit|)/ 2 × (SRP) + α
for i ← 1 to Problem_size do
    With 1/Problem_size probability
        node_Solution[i] ← Random(min =
        node_Solution[i] − Δ, max = node_Solution[i] + Δ)
```

respective positions. The node's own solution is added to the pool to guarantee that its solution is not lost. The appropriation rule applies a small perturbation in order to introduce novel memes. As memes flow through a social network, they are likely to change their original form and the appropriation step incorporates such behavior, similarly to a mutation operator in Genetic Algorithms. A system where individuals only aggregate information would converge to a combination of the initial memes.

The Dynamic Search Range (DSR) model is an extension of the original Memetic Networks model that includes a fundamental human trait: the individual ability to adapt to the social context. The authors suggest the idea that individuals could be modeled as self-adaptive regarding their social problem-solving strategies [21]. The original idea stems from prior works that relate humans to motivated tacticians [12, 24]. In the context of social problem-solving, it represents an individual mechanism that balances exploration and exploitation during the search process.

To perform this balance, the individual relies on network's feedback information. If a majority of its neighbors hold better solutions, then this focal node expands its search range during the appropriation step. Hence, it can explore more of the search space in hope of increasing the likelihood of finding a better solution than the status quo. Otherwise, the node may gain little from intensifying the search around its relatively poor solution. The DSR model basically allows nodes to count how many neighbors are better than themselves and, with this information, adjust their search range during the appropriation step. Thus, the appropriation rule is not purely endogenous and is called R* appropriation [21]. The aggregation rule used here is the same used in the canonical MN.

The R* appropriation embodies the idea of social adaptation through a mechanism that controls the search range of the individual. This mechanism receives as input a ratio called Social Relative Performance (SRP) before performing any operation on the memes. The SRP is the ratio between the number of better ranked neighbors and the total number of neighbors. An SRP of 1.0 means that all neighbors of the node possess better solutions while a SRP of 0.0 means that no neighbor has a better solution. This value is multiplied by half the maximum interval for each meme. The resulting value is the search range for the node, being this interval centralized at the current meme so that the new solution is within this range. The α constant represents the minimum interval that a node with SRP of 0.0 is to search and for our experiments we used α as 0.0001 for all problems.

The more neighbours a node have, the more information it has to adjust its search range. That is because the SRP can assume a larger set of values. This observation has some parallel with real social systems in the sense that well connected nodes can make more informed decisions if they pay attention to how their peers are faring.

Our experiments were composed by 1000 independent trials for each configuration (model, problem, population size, network topology), calculating individuals' contributions - (global and local) and centrality values (degree, betweenness, closeness, eigenvector), normalized to the range [0, 1] as proposed by Freeman (1979) to allow comparison of different networks sizes.

Pearson's correlation was used to measure the degree of linear dependency between each contribution (global and local) and each centrality measure (degree, eigenvector, betweenness and closeness).

A correlation close to one indicates a strong relation between the individual centrality and its contribution to their peers or to the whole system. On the other hand, a correlation value close to minus one shows a strong inverse correlation (the higher is the contribution the more peripheral is the position of the individual in the network). Values near zero for correlation denote a nonexistent or weak correlation between the metrics.

4. RESULTS AND DISCUSSION

Experiments results are condensed in Table 1 and Table 2. The former regards global contribution, and the latter, local contribution. They show the averaged correlation grouped by the model and then by the problem, for each centrality measure. Each cell condenses three thousand experiment trials, being a thousand for each size of population.

Each pair composed by a model and a problem presented very distinct results. Nevertheless, we observed high positive correlations between local contribution and every centrality measure in the MN data. In this case, closeness was slightly better to estimate local contribution.

The DSR model showed high positive correlation between global contribution and every centrality measure, being the degree centrality slightly higher than the others. The PSO

Table 1: Pearson's Correlation Between Individual Global Contribution and Centrality.

Model	F	Betweeness	Closeness	Degree	Eigenvector
		Centrality			
MN	F1	0.38	0.40	0.40	0.40
	F2	0.37	0.39	0.39	0.39
	F3	0.45	0.47	0.48	0.48
	F4	0.33	0.35	0.35	0.36
	F5	0.38	0.39	0.40	0.40
Mean		0.38	0.40	0.40	0.41
Std.Dev.		0.0398	0.0392	0.0417	0.0391
DSR	F1	0.74	0.71	0.78	0.73
	F2	0.75	0.72	0.78	0.74
	F3	0.69	0.67	0.73	0.68
	F4	0.76	0.73	0.80	0.75
	F5	0.75	0.72	0.78	0.74
Mean		0.74	0.71	0.78	0.73
Std. Dev.		0.0240	0.0201	0.0219	0.0243
PSO	F1	0.45	0.47	0.48	0.48
	F2	0.44	0.46	0.47	0.47
	F3	0.38	0.39	0.40	0.40
	F4	0.62	0.65	0.66	0.67
	F5	0.73	0.77	0.78	0.78
Mean		0.52	0.55	0.56	0.56
Std. Dev.		0.1324	0.1404	0.1414	0.1431
FIPS	F1	0.43	0.22	0.36	0.33
	F2	0.25	0.03	0.17	0.15
	F3	-0.29	-0.46	-0.34	-0.39
	F4	-0.20	-0.46	-0.29	-0.33
	F5	-0.44	-0.72	-0.54	-0.58
Mean		-0.05	-0.28	-0.13	-0.16
Std. Dev.		0.3304	0.3459	0.3369	0.3457

Table 2: Pearson's Correlation Between Individual Local Contribution and Centrality.

Model	F	Betweeness	Closeness	Degree	Eigenvector
		Centrality			
MN	F1	0.72	0.82	0.79	0.81
	F2	0.72	0.82	0.79	0.81
	F3	0.76	0.85	0.83	0.83
	F4	0.68	0.79	0.75	0.77
	F5	0.72	0.83	0.79	0.81
Mean		0.72	0.82	0.79	0.80
Std. Dev.		0.0239	0.0194	0.0240	0.0203
DSR	F1	0.12	0.14	0.14	0.13
	F2	0.09	0.11	0.10	0.10
	F3	0.06	0.09	0.08	0.08
	F4	0.10	0.13	0.12	0.12
	F5	0.12	0.14	0.14	0.13
Mean		0.10	0.12	0.12	0.11
Std. Dev.		0.0230	0.0193	0.0223	0.0208
PSO	F1	0.23	0.23	0.24	0.23
	F2	0.22	0.22	0.23	0.23
	F3	0.24	0.27	0.25	0.27
	F4	0.62	0.65	0.66	0.67
	F5	0.74	0.78	0.80	0.80
Mean		0.41	0.43	0.43	0.44
Std. Dev.		0.2257	0.2367	0.2436	0.2428
FIPS	F1	0.02	-0.14	0.01	-0.09
	F2	-0.03	-0.19	-0.04	-0.13
	F3	-0.15	-0.32	-0.17	-0.25
	F4	-0.20	-0.36	-0.22	-0.31
	F5	-0.41	-0.70	-0.51	-0.57
Mean		-0.15	-0.34	-0.19	-0.27
Std. Dev.		0.1511	0.1971	0.1824	0.1675

model presented a moderate positive correlation between both kinds of contribution and all measures. The FIPS model had a weak negative correlation with all the measures, meaning that a central node is likely to contribute less than a peripheral node.

In addition, while DSR and MN did not present big differences in correlation values between different problems, a central position seems more strongly correlated in FIPS and PSO in the Sphere (F5) and the Rosenbrock (F4) problems. Moreover, standard deviations for FIPS correlation values are very high (close to 0.3 on most cases) while all other models are relatively low (close to 0.1), showing a strong noise and randomness inherent to FIPS model regarding individual's network position.

Another factor that can be highlighted is that local and global contribution, as we defined, resulted in diverse correlation values with the centrality measures, especially for MN and DSR models, indicating that it plays an important role on the analysis.

The strong negative correlations shown by FIPS model (especially with F5 problem, in both contributions measures) was an unexpected result. We hypothesize this happens because central FIPS particles receive high amounts of influence, impairing any possible convergence behavior. More importantly, it points that there is a strong dependence between the problems and how each individual solves it. Such strong dependence calls attention to hasty associations of centrality with individual success.

The results also call attention to the fact that very similar models, the MN and the DSR, presented distinct correlations for different kinds of contribution: centrality (all measures) is useful to predict the MN individual ratio of local contribution while in DSR it is useful to predict individual likelihood of global contribution. Central DSR nodes have more sources of information to balance their own exploration/exploitation rate, i.e. their problem-solving behavior, thus they had an advantage when in central positions. MN nodes being unable to change their exploration/exploitation balance, fared better locally only. It may be the case that when in central positions, thus in a high information flow position[5], a solver must be flexible to adapt its behavior and careful to select what information must be useful to achieve high global contribution rates. However, further investigation is required to confirm this hypothesis.

[5]Here information is meant in the broad sense, it can regarded as pieces of solution themselves as well as information about how neighbors solvers are faring.

We also tested whether centrality really accounted for differences in contribution rates. To do so, we measured the standard deviations of contributions of a control topology (Grid) and compared to the centralized networks generated using the Barabasi-Albert model (NBA). Table 3 shows the comparison. A small standard deviation means that contribution is uniformly distributed across the population at the end of the solving process.

Each cell of Table 3 presents an average over three thousand trials (a thousand for each size of population), except the third and sixth valued columns, which represent how much (percentage) is the NBA's standard deviation value higher than that of the Grid.

Table 3: Averaged Standard Deviation of Individuals' Contributions.

		Global Contribution			Local Contribution		
Model	F	Grid	NBA	%	Grid	NBA	%
MN	F1	1.10	1.26	14.25	13.62	33.32	144.68
	F2	1.09	1.25	14.66	13.69	33.35	143.55
	F3	1.21	1.45	19.34	13.16	37.24	182.90
	F4	1.10	1.21	10.67	14.06	29.61	110.66
	F5	1.08	1.25	15.26	13.69	33.31	143.37
DSR	F1	2.20	3.99	81.82	23.05	25.24	9.50
	F2	2.23	4.07	82.51	24.89	26.84	7.84
	F3	2.12	3.49	64.55	21.04	24.08	14.45
	F4	2.42	4.52	86.43	26.61	28.25	6.16
	F5	2.25	4.11	82.54	23.62	25.85	9.46
PSO	F1	3.62	3.84	6.08	45.58	40.08	-12.05
	F2	3.90	4.15	6.54	40.54	36.29	-10.49
	F3	7.23	6.79	-5.98	82.10	58.55	-28.68
	F4	16.75	21.77	29.97	43.81	54.97	25.47
	F5	9.60	16.28	69.51	25.87	42.87	65.70
FIPS	F1	2.45	3.91	59.61	64.00	137.69	115.13
	F2	3.61	5.79	60.68	71.74	129.81	80.96
	F3	3.98	7.48	87.91	127.48	185.36	45.40
	F4	6.02	16.37	171.91	53.31	114.53	114.84
	F5	10.79	50.28	365.80	11.46	56.98	397.15

The Grid presented lower standard deviation than the NBA topology whenever there was a high discrepancy between central nodes contribution and peripheral ones, and also, the correlation values between centrality measures and the individuals' contribution are more extreme (closer to -1.0 or 1.0).

The opposite is also true, when the disparity amid the networks standard deviation is low, correlation values between centrality measures and individuals' contribution are closer to zero — especially when NBA network standard deviation values are not more than 50% of the ones shown by the Grid network. It also shows that whenever there is a different behavior (being it an advantage or disadvantage) caused by individuals' positions, centrality measures are good to predict which individuals will contribute more.

Figure 2 depicts three trials samples taken from our experiments of different correlation values. The figure reinforces that centrality can be negatively correlated, weakly correlated and also positively correlated with individual contribution. These trials were picked to show extreme results and the variations found in our experimental data regarding centrality prediciton of success in social problem-solving.

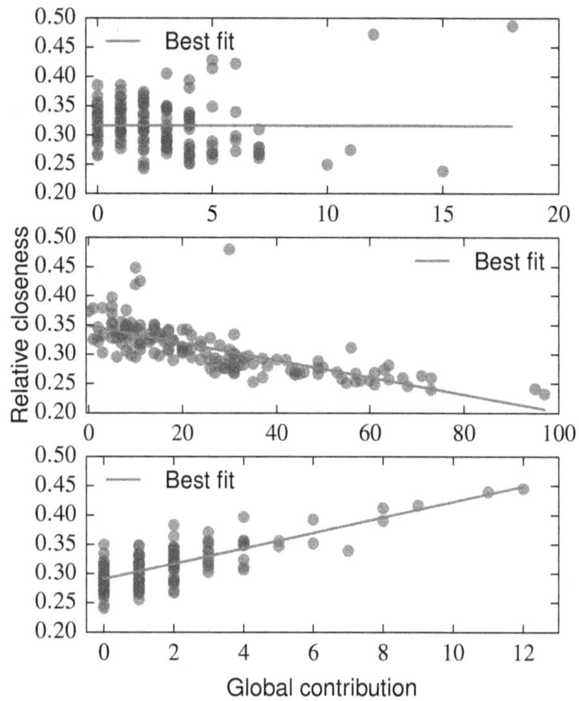

Figure 2: Sample trials depicting a close to zero correlation (FIPS, F4, population size 144), a negative correlation (-0.72, FIPS, F1, population size 144) and a positive correlation (0.79, DSR, F5, population size 144) respectively top-down.

In summary, specific cases demonstrate the disparity among different models and tell us that individual's traits and problem's features are more relevant than the network flow itself. Furthermore, this is a first step to identify how and when centrality is relevant and can be successful applied in social problem-solving context.

5. CONCLUSIONS

This main objective of this work was to investigate how centrality correlates with individual performance in social problem-solving systems. In order to do so we performed a series of experiments with agent-based models. These experiments sought to compare these models and understand the relationship between different centrality measures and individual performance.

The overall results present some of the difficulties in generalizing a centrality measure for very distinct problems and models, reinforcing that each kind of individual behavior and problem being solved are important factors to determine which individual will take more advantage from its position in the network. Sometimes central individuals get a substantial advantage over the others, but that cannot be assumed true for all the cases (we show one case where peripheral positions are advantageous).

In addition, we have shown that there is not a big difference between distinct centrality measures, probably because larger variations caused by the models and problems to overcome the measures variations and/or the power law network generation method excludes topologies of networks that will present larger divergence among centrality measures.

When nodes are able to systematically exploit their network positions, we observed that there is a higher correlation between centrality and individual's contribution. In this case, we observed that some measures have significantly better correlations than others. This suggests that one should not rely on only one centrality measure when investigating individual's performance in social problem-solving systems. We also provided evidence that central nodes tend to "collaborate" more with their neighbors, but that did not necessarily translated into higher global contribution (with the exception of the DSR model).

At the same time that socially-inspired models can help us determine the impact that network properties have at both the individual and the collective level, most previous research has focused on their application as optimizers. This contrasts with our investigation, which used them as research tools to investigate the complex phenomena of social systems. As recent experiments with humans suggest [15, 19, 22], we currently lack sophisticated and heterogeneous models which better correspond to real life scenarios. We believe that the results reported in this paper have contributed towards the development of more realistic models and research tools, as well as to show that some factors other than centrality are also relevant when dealing with social problem-solving.

Acknowledgements

This work is partly supported by the Brazilian Research Council CNPq and the CAPES Foundation.

6. REFERENCES

[1] R. M. Araújo and L. C. Lamb. Towards understanding the role of learning models in the dynamics of the minority game. In *16th IEEE International Conference on Tools with Artificial Intelligence (ICTAI 2004)*, pages 727–731. IEEE Computer Society, 2004.

[2] R. M. Araújo and L. C. Lamb. Memetic networks: analyzing the effects of network properties in multi-agent performance. In *AAAI Conference on Artificial Intelligence*, volume 1, pages 3–8. AAAI Press, 2008.

[3] A. Barabási and R. Albert. Emergence of Scaling in Random Networks. *Science*, 286(5439):509–512, Oct. 1999.

[4] A. Bavelas and D. Barrett. An Experimental Approach to Organisational Communication. *Personnel*, pages 366–371, Mar. 1951.

[5] P. Bonacich. Power and Centrality: A Family of Measures. *American Journal of Sociology*, 92(5):1170–1182, 1987.

[6] S. P. Borgatti. Centrality and network flow. *Social Networks*, 27(1):55–71, Jan. 2005.

[7] R. L. Burgess. Communication networks and behavioral consequences! *Human Relations*, 22(2):137–159, 1969.

[8] R. Burt. *Structural Holes: The Social Structure of Competition.* Harvard University Press, 1995.

[9] R. Dawkins. *The Selfish Gene.* Oxford University Press, 2006.

[10] R. Eberhart and Y. Shi. Comparing inertia weights and constriction factors in particle swarm optimization. In *IEEE Congress on Evolutionary Computation*, volume 1, pages 84–88, 2000.

[11] J. Epstein. *Generative Social Science: Studies in Agent-Based Computational Modeling.* Princeton Studies in Complexity. Princeton University Press, 2006.

[12] S. T. Fiske and S. E. Taylor. *Social Cognition.* McGraw-Hill, second edition, 1991.

[13] L. C. Freeman. A set of measures of centrality based on betweenness. *Sociometry*, 40(1):35–41, Mar. 1979.

[14] N. R. Jennings, K. P. Sycara, and M. Wooldridge. A roadmap of agent research and development. *Autonomous Agents and Multi-Agent Systems*, 1(1):7–38, 1998.

[15] S. Judd, M. Kearns, and Y. Vorobeychik. Behavioral dynamics and influence in networked coloring and consensus. *Proceedings of the National Academy of Sciences of the United States of America*, 2010.

[16] J. Kennedy and R. Eberhart. Particle swarm optimization. In *International Conference on Neural Networks*, volume 4, pages 1942–1948, 1995.

[17] J. J. Liang, A. K. Qin, P. Suganthan, and S. Baskar. Comprehensive learning particle swarm optimizer for global optimization of multimodal functions. *IEEE Transactions on Evolutionary Computation*, 10(3):281–295, 2006.

[18] M. W. Macy and R. Willer. From factors to actors: Computational sociology and agent-based modeling. *Annual Review of Sociology*, 28:143–166, 2002.

[19] W. Mason and D. J. Watts. Collaborative learning in networks. *Proceedings of the National Academy of Sciences of the United States of America*, 109(3):764–7699, Jan. 2012.

[20] R. Mendes, J. Kennedy, and J. Neves. The Fully Informed Particle Swarm: Simpler, Maybe Better. *IEEE Transactions on Evolutionary Computation*, 8(3):204–210, June 2004.

[21] D. Noble, L. Lamb, and R. Araújo. Modeling Adaptative Social Behavior in Collective Problem Solving Algorithms. In *IEEE International Conference on Self-Adaptive and Self-Organizing Systems*, pages 205–210, Sept. 2012.

[22] D. Noble, M. O. Prates, D. Bossle, and L. C. Lamb. Collaboration in social problem-solving: When diversity trumps network efficiency. In *AAAI Conference on Artificial Intelligence (AAAI-15)*, pages 1277–1283. AAAI Press, 2015.

[23] R. Poli, J. Kennedy, and T. Blackwell. Particle swarm optimization. *Swarm Intelligence*, 1(1):33–57, Aug. 2007.

[24] N. Schwarz. Warmer and more social: Recent developments in cognitive social psychology. *Annual Review of Sociology*, 24:239–264, 1998.

Input-to-State Stability Analysis on Particle Swarm Optimization

Daqing Yi
daqing.yi@byu.edu
Computer Science Dept.
Brigham Young University
Provo, UT, USA

Kevin D. Seppi
kseppi@cs.byu.edu
Computer Science Dept.
Brigham Young University
Provo, UT, USA

Michael A. Goodrich
mike@cs.byu.edu
Computer Science Dept.
Brigham Young University
Provo, UT, USA

ABSTRACT

This paper examines the dynamics of particle swarm optimization (PSO) by modeling PSO as a feedback cascade system and then applying input-to-state stability analysis. Using a feedback cascade system model we can include the effects of the global-best and personal-best values more directly in the model of the dynamics. Thus in contrast to previous study of PSO dynamics, the input-to-state stability property used here allows for the analysis of PSO both before and at stagnation. In addition, the use of input-to-state stability allows this analysis to preserve random terms which were heretofore simplified to constants. This analysis is important because it can inform the setting of PSO parameters and better characterize the nature of PSO as a dynamic system. This work also illuminates the way in which the personal-best and the global-best updates influence the bound on the particle's position and hence, how the algorithm exploits and explores the fitness landscape as a function of the personal best and global best.

Categories and Subject Descriptors

I.2.8 [**Artificial Intelligence**]: Problem Solving, Control Methods, and Search—*Heuristic methods*

Keywords

Particle Swarm Optimization; Input-to-State Stability

1. INTRODUCTION

Particle Swarm Optimization (PSO) is a popular and well-studied algorithm that was originally motivated by the flocking behaviors of birds and insects. Soon after its first publication it was discovered that the structure of the PSO algorithm is amenable to formal analysis using dynamical systems theory (sometimes referred to as dynamic systems) [5]. The use of this theory has informed the setting of parameters [16, 8], led to the proposal of new variants of the algorithm [5], and allowed for the analysis of the behavior of the algorithm [15], especially the behavior at stagnation, that is, when the algorithm fails to find better solutions [5].

While the study of the algorithm at stagnation is important and a significant first step, it only answers questions about the behavior at the point that PSO has degenerated into random search. At that point the algorithm can be mimicked by simply sampling from the appropriate distribution [12]. In this paper we extend the limited work that has been done to understand the behavior *before* stagnation, that is, when the unique mechanisms of PSO are directing the behavior of the algorithm.

By using a *feedback cascade model* we are able to include both what we refer to as the *position update* which comes from the PSO equations, but also the *input update*, that is, the effect of the personal and global best. This paper does so in contrast to prior work which focuses on the position update. A cascade model also allows us to make fewer assumptions in mapping from PSO to a dynamical system model. Using this model we are able to derive the conditions under which the process is input-to-state stable [9], prove bounds on both the particle motion and the mean of particle motion. The input-to-state stable conditions and the bounds can inform parameter adjustments and other properties that can, in turn, control the extent to which the algorithm explores or exploits the fitness landscape. This is especially valuable in the context of the design of future PSO variants.

The body of this paper is organized as described here. In section 3, we model the PSO dynamics as a feedback cascade system, which enables the input-to-state stability analysis. The definition of input-to-state stability (ISS) and its meaning in the context of PSO are also given. Section 4 shows that for particular parameter values, the position-update component of a particle is input-to-state stable. Using the ISS property we then give the bound on particle motion. We also use the ISS property in the context of the analysis of the moments (the mean and higher moments) of particle motion. In section 5, we use the ISS property to help analyze the dynamics of the particle. Using the ISS property of the input-update component, we can analyze the dynamics of the particle before and at stagnation.

GECCO '15, July 11–15, 2015, Madrid, Spain

 ISBN 978-1-4503-3472-3/15/07...$15.00

DOI: http://dx.doi.org/10.1145/2739480.2754782

2. RELATED WORK

Although the input-to-state stable analysis given in this paper can be applied to many versions of PSO, for this work we use the formulas from Kennedy's most recent definition of PSO[2] for the constricted position-update rule. The constricted position-update rule is

$$v_{ij}(k+1) = \chi[v_{ij}(k) + \phi^P u^P_{ij}(k)(x^P_{ij}(k) - x_{ij}(k)) + \phi^G u^G_{ij}(k)(x^G_{ij}(k) - x_{ij}(k))], \tag{1a}$$

$$x_{ij}(k+1) = x_{ij}(k) + v_{ij}(k+1). \tag{1b}$$

$x_{ij}(k)$ represents the position of particle i in dimension j at time k. Similarly, $v_{ij}(k)$ represents the velocity of particle i in dimension j also at time k. $x^G_{ij}(k)$ and $x^P_{ij}(k)$ are global best (actually the topology best or local best) and personal best positions observed by the swarm and the particle respectively. $u^G_{ij}(k)$ and $u^P_{ij}(k)$ are independent random values drawn from $[0,1]$. $\chi \in (0,1)$, ϕ^P and ϕ^G are algorithm parameters.

Due to the stochastic nature of the particle's path and the social interaction represented by the topology, the dynamics of the algorithm is hard to evaluate in general. Understanding how the particles move guides how to improve the algorithm design [1], particularly the stochastic factors in the velocity update of Equation (1a). However once a particle is no longer able to find improvements in x^G and x^P, it exhibits the *stagnation phenomenon* [6]. In this state the analysis is easier since there is no effect from the topology.

Previous work that assumes stagnation can be categorized into two groups each based on how the analysis treats the stochastic factors. The first approach is to ignore the stochastic factors. Using this simplification, the convergence of a particle at stagnation can be analyzed [5, 3]. The convergence trajectories can be estimated [17] and the conclusions are compared with empirical results [4]. By building a linear system model [14], the PSO algorithm can be viewed as a closed loop system and the convergence can be analyzed. Based on such a convergence analysis, parameters can be set for best effect [16].

The second approach for handling the stochastic factors is based on stochastic analysis. By taking the mean of the stochastic variables, the stochastic terms can be converted into constant terms. A convergence analysis of the mean and variance of a particle at stagnation can also be obtained by using the characteristic equation in a discrete-time model [8]. In a similar way, other moments can be computed [12, 13, 11]. Using the discrete-time system model of different moments, the equilibrium can be found. The stability requirements can be obtained from the norm by setting the root values of the characteristic equation to all be less than 1.

There is also some work that addresses the dynamics when a particle is not in the stagnation phase. The discrete-time dynamics of PSO, that is, the dynamics of particle trajectory, can be approximated using a continuous-time model [7]. Furthermore, the probability of convergence in time can be analyzed by viewing the update process as a random search process [18]. The process of particles reaching a local optimum has also been analyzed [15].

3. INPUT-TO-STATE STABILITY OF PSO

Input-to-state stability analysis consists of two parts:

- the decomposition of the PSO algorithm into components, and
- the input-to-state stability of each component.

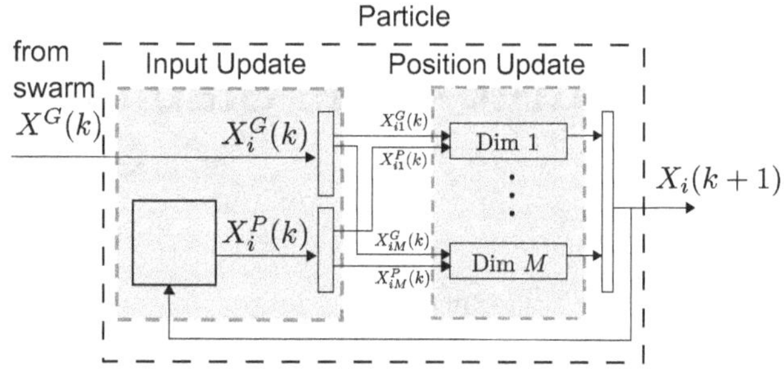

Figure 1: System structure of PSO

In this section, we model particle motion using a feedback cascade model. Then we review the definition of the input-to-state stability (ISS). We also explain why ISS should be applied to PSO.

3.1 Feedback Cascade Model

For the purpose of input-to-state stability analysis we decompose the PSO algorithm into components as shown in Figure 1. This decomposition is comprised of cascaded components (the input update, followed by the position update) and the feedback of the historical state. These two components are the *input-update component* for the global best ($x^G_i(k)$) and the personal best ($x^P_i(k)$), and the *position-update component* for particle position ($x_i(k+1)$), which depends on the inputs $x^G_i(k)$ and $x^P_i(k)$ as well as the previous position $x_i(k)$.

The properties of this system can be analyzed using the input-to-state stability of the position-update component and the input-update component. Given an input-to-state stable position-update component, we will see that the convergence of $x_i(k)$ depends on bounds on $x^G_i(k)$ and $x^P_i(k)$.

3.2 Input-to-state stability

Before reviewing the definition of input-to-state stability, we first introduce several types of functions [9].

- K-function $\mathbb{K}$: a function $\alpha : [0,a) \to [0,\infty)$ is continuous, strictly increasing and $\alpha(0) = 0$.
- K_∞-function $\mathbb{K}_\infty$: a function $\alpha : [0,a) \to [0,\infty)$ is a K-function and $\alpha(s) \to \infty$ as $s \to \infty$.
- KL-function $\mathbb{KL}$: a function $\beta : [0,a) \times [0,\infty) \to [0,\infty)$ satisfies:
    1. $\forall t \geq 0$, $\beta(\cdot, t)$ is a K-function;
    2. $\forall s \geq 0$, $\beta(s, \cdot)$ is decreasing and $\beta(s,t) \to 0$ as $t \to \infty$.

These functions are used to define input-to-state stability in Definition 1.

DEFINITION 1 (INPUT-TO-STATE STABLE [9]). *For x, a discrete-time system defined as follows:*

$$x(k+1) = f(x(k), u(k)), \tag{2}$$

with $f(0,0) = 0$ [1], *the system is* (globally) input-to-state stable *if there exist a KL-function β and a K-function γ*

[1]This means that $x = 0$ is an equilibrium of the 0-input system.

such that, for each input $u \in l_\infty^m$ and each $\xi \in \mathbb{R}^n$, it holds that $\forall k \in \mathbb{Z}^+$,

$$|x(k,\xi,u)| \leq \beta(|\xi|,k) + \gamma(\|u\|). \quad (3)$$

The $\beta()$ term in Equation (3) defines an initial bound with a decaying property. The $\gamma()$ term in Equation (3) defines a bound determined by the input. This means that the $\beta()$ term gradually decreases to zero and the position is bounded by a range determined by the bound on the input.

3.3 Importance of input-to-state stability

Under certain conditions the dynamics of complex systems can be understood by first decomposing the system into a set of individual input-to-state stable components. We will take this approach with PSO. Parallel combination of input-to-state stable components yields a combined structure that is also input-to-state stable [10]. In the case of PSO and as shown in Figure 1, if each component (representing a single dimension) is input-to-state stable, the position-update component which combines all the dimensions is also input-to-state stable. Thus we have Property 1.

PROPERTY 1. *The position-update component is input-to-state stable if the position update in each dimension is input-to-state stable.*

This simplifies the analysis of the system since it allows us to consider each dimension separately. The serial connection and the feedback connection also lead to some interesting property from input-to-state stability, which will be discussed in Section 5.

The input-to-state stability analysis also provides the tool for the analysis of the convergence of PSO and the analysis of bounds on particle motion. PSO is designed to strike an effective balance between *exploring* and *exploiting* a fitness landscape. A bound on a particle's state is an indicator of the nature of that balance. When this bound is large the particle is exploring. However, as a particle finishes exploring and reach stagnation, a particle's position should converge.

Input-to-state stability implies that the state of the system is bounded in a range determined by the bounds on the input. Before stagnation, when the personal best and global best values have not converged, we can expect only a loose bound on the particle state. These looser bounds reflect both what is know about the update process itself and what is know about the inputs to the update process, that is, the personal best and the global best.

We call the bounds on the global best and personal best the "exploit radius" and the bounds on the particle's position a "explore radius". The ratio of the explore radius to the exploit radius is determined by the parameters of the position-update component. However, if the personal best and global best converge to an estimated optimal position, the exploit radius falls to zero and the explore radius converges to a bound.

4. ANALYSIS OF INPUT-TO-STATE STABILITY IN PSO

We then show PSO satisfies the definition of input-to-state stability when the parameters of PSO are set in a requisite range. We also derive the bounds implied by the ISS property and use the ISS property in Section 5 to find bounds

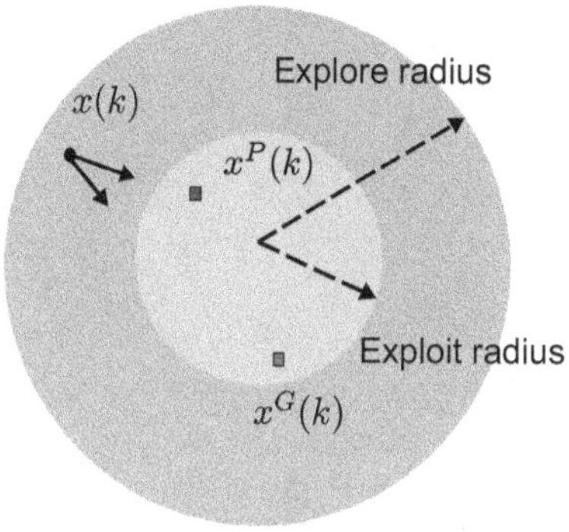

Figure 2: Exploration and exploitation.

on particle motion. Last, we will use ISS to analyze the moments (the mean and higher moments) of particle motion.

In our analysis of the PSO algorithm, we seek to understand how the particles converge to some position x^*, which is intended (not guaranteed) by the algorithm to be the global minimum position of the objective function.

For this analysis we use a one-dimension particle and extract the linear form of the position-update component. As noted above, the one dimensional case can be extended to many dimensions.

We begin our analysis of PSO input to state stability by rewriting the PSO equations in (1) in the following way:

$$X(k+1) = A(k)X(k) + B(k)U(k) \quad (4)$$

with

$$A(k) = \begin{bmatrix} \chi & -\chi\phi^G u^G(k) - \chi\phi^P u^P(k) \\ \chi & 1 - \chi\phi^G u^G(k) - \chi\phi^P u^P(k) \end{bmatrix}$$

and

$$B(k) = \begin{bmatrix} \chi\phi^G u^G(k) & \chi\phi^P u^P(k) \\ \chi\phi^G u^G(k) & \chi\phi^P u^P(k) \end{bmatrix}.$$

The system state is $X(k) = [v(k),\ x(k) - x^*]^T$, and the system input is $U(k) = [x^G(k) - x^*,\ x^P(k) - x^*]^T$ [2]. The convergence of this model means that $v(k) \to 0$ and $x(k) \to x^*$.

4.1 Conditions for input-to-state stability for position update in PSO

Using the definition of the PSO position update as given in Equation (4), PSO can be shown to be input-to-state stable as defined in definition 1.

THEOREM 1. *When $|\lambda_{\max}(A(k))| < 1$, the position-update component of PSO (4) is input-to-state stable.*

The proof follows the ISS-Lyapunov-function approach. The ISS-Lyapunov function, defined in Appendix 6.1, can be used to prove the input-to-state stability of a system and analyze the state bound[9]. The details of the proof are given in Appendix 6.2.

Note that in Equation (4), $[v(k),\ x(k) - x^*]^T = [0,\ 0]^T$ is an equilibrium position when the input $[x^G(k) - x^*,\ x^P(k) -$

[2]We use x^* to represent an equilibrium point to the system. In PSO, it can be a local optimum, a global optimum, or an estimated optimum. We use it as a reference point to check the bounds.

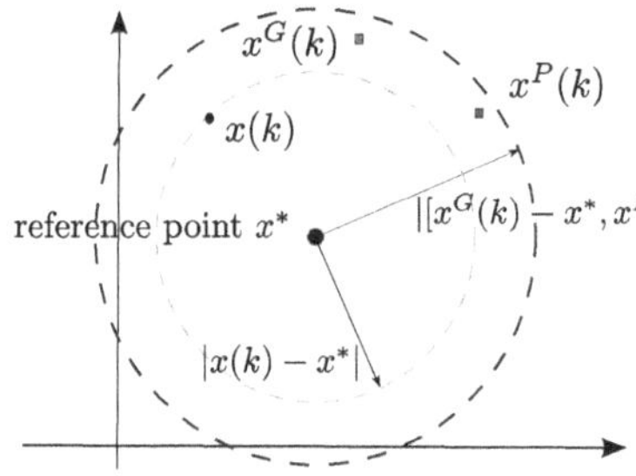

Figure 3: A bound on a particle's position by a reference point x^* from Equation (6). The ratio of two radii indicates γ.

$x^*]^T = [0,\ 0]^T$. Without loss of generality, for an arbitrary optimization problem x^* would typically not be at the origin. In such a problem, input-to-state stability means that the boundaries of $|v(k)|$ and $|x(k) - x^*|$ would be transformed and thus determined by $|x^G(k) - x^*|$ and $|x^P(k) - x^*|$, but the properties of ISS apply independent of where the function is centered.

Having shown that PSO is input-to-state stable we can now state a bound on particle position.

COROLLARY 1. *Given a bound on the input $||u||$ in the position-update component, we have the bound on the particle position from Equation* (4).

$$\forall k, |x(k) - x^*| \leq \max\left(|x(0) - x^*|, \gamma(|\left[x^G(k) - x^*,\ x^P(k) - x^*\right]^T|)\right), \tag{5}$$

in which $\gamma = \alpha_3^{-1} \circ \sigma$. ($\alpha_3$ and σ are defined in Appendix 6.2.)

PROOF. *This is obtained from Remark 3.7 in [9] and by choosing P be a symmetric identity matrix. Furthermore we drop the velocity part because $|x(k) - x^*| \leq |[v(k),\ x(k) - x^*]^T|$.* □

The max part is needed to account for the effect of the starting point, represented by the first parameter. Eventually the effect of the starting point no longer affects the system, formally:

$$\exists T, \forall k \geq T, |x(k) - x^*| \leq \gamma(|[x^G(k) - x^*,\ x^P(k) - x^*]^T|). \tag{6}$$

Figure 3 gives an example on how a particle's boundary is determined by the personal best and global best.

COROLLARY 2. *Let* $A(k) = \begin{bmatrix} \chi & -\chi\phi \\ \chi & 1 - \chi\phi \end{bmatrix}$, *in which* $\phi \in [0, \phi^{sup}]$, $\phi^{sup} = \phi^P + \phi^G$ *and* $\chi \in (0, 1)$. *When* $\phi^{sup} \in \left(0, \frac{2(1+\chi)}{\chi}\right)$, *the system* (4) *is input-to-state stable.*

The proof is given in Appendix 6.3.

Figure 4 shows the parameter space. The x-axis is $\phi^{sup} = \phi^P + \phi^G$ and the y-axis is χ. The stable region in dark blue is obtained from eigenvalue test on Theorem 1. The red boundary is obtained from Corollary 2. It indicates the equivalence of the results from Theorem 1 and Corollary 2.

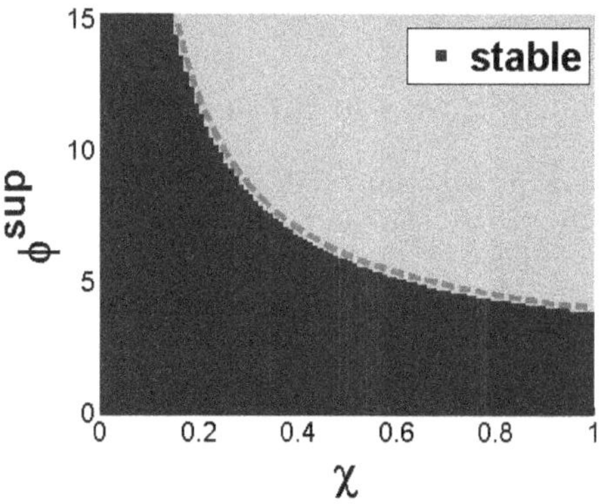

Figure 4: Parameter space

4.2 Moment Analysis

Using the same perspective of the feedback cascade system, the input-to-stable stability analysis can also be applied to moment analysis. Like the others [8, 11], we derive models for the statistical features (moments) of the particle's position at stagnation. In contrast to this prior work, input-to-state stability analysis can also provide bounds before a particle reaches stagnation.

We adopt the approach of Jiang, Luo & Yang [8] to construct an ISS model for the mean. Using that model $E(x(k))$ converges to

$$\hat{x} = \frac{\phi^P x^P + \phi^G x^G}{\phi^P + \phi^G}$$

in stagnation. If we treat $\hat{x}$ as a swarm average estimation on the optimum, we are interested in how $E(x(k))$ deviates from $\hat{x}$.

$$\begin{aligned}\begin{bmatrix} E(x(k+1)) - \hat{x} \\ E(x(k)) - \hat{x} \end{bmatrix} &= A_m \begin{bmatrix} E(x(k)) - \hat{x} \\ E(x(k-1)) - \hat{x} \end{bmatrix} \\ &+ B_m \begin{bmatrix} E(x^P(k)) - \hat{x} \\ E(x^G(k)) - \hat{x} \end{bmatrix},\end{aligned} \tag{7}$$

with

$$A_m = \begin{bmatrix} 1 + \chi - \frac{\chi\phi^P}{2} - \frac{\chi\phi^G}{2} & -\chi \\ 1 & 0 \end{bmatrix}$$

and

$$B_m = \begin{bmatrix} \frac{\chi\phi^P}{2} & \frac{\chi\phi^G}{2} \\ 0 & 0 \end{bmatrix}.$$

The convergence of $E(x(k))$ in stagnation is given in [8, 11]. Even without the stagnation assumption, the input-to-state stable analysis on Equation (7) indicates how $E(x(k))$ will deviate from $\hat{x}$ anytime we know how $E(x^G(k))$ and $E(x^P(k))$ deviate from $\hat{x}$. Stagnation is a simple case of knowing how $E(x^G(k))$ and $E(x^P(k))$ deviate from $\hat{x}$. This special case is discussed more later in this paper.

We now proceed to show the conditions that must hold for the mean model to be input-to-state stable.

THEOREM 2. *The system* (7) *is input-to-state stable, if* $|\lambda_{\max}(A_m)| < 1$.

PROOF. *The proof process is similar with Theorem 1, but we can get a constant symmetric positive definite Q_m from $A_m^T P A_m - P = -Q_m$.* □

Similar to Corollary 2, we have Corollary 3 for parameter selection on mean convergence. Note that when the condition in Corollary 2 is satisfied, the condition in Corollary 3 is also guaranteed. This means that when the system (4) is input-to-state stable, the mean dynamics (7) is also input-to-state stable.

COROLLARY 3. *Let* $A_m = \begin{bmatrix} 1+\chi-\frac{\chi\phi^P}{2}-\frac{\chi\phi^G}{2} & -\chi \\ 1 & 0 \end{bmatrix}$, *in which* $\phi \in [0, \phi^{sup}]$ *and* $\phi^{sup} = \phi^P + \phi^G$ *and* $\chi \in (0,1)$. *When* $\phi^{sup} \in \left(0, \frac{4(1+\chi)}{\chi}\right)$, *the system (7) is input-to-state stable.*

The proof is given in Appendix 6.4.

Similar to Corollary 1, we can use the Q_m to determine the state bound.

COROLLARY 4. *If the system (7) is input-to-state stable, we have a bound*

$\exists T, \forall k > T,$

$$|E(x(k)) - \hat{x}| \le \gamma_m \left| \left[E(x^P(k)) - \hat{x},\ E(x^G(k)) - \hat{x} \right]^T \right|, \tag{8}$$

with

$$\gamma_m = \frac{2\|A_m\|^2\|B_m\|^2 + \lambda_{min}(Q_m)^2\|B_m\|^2}{2(\lambda_{min}(Q_m))^3}. \tag{9}$$

In a similar way, we can apply the input-to-state stability analysis to the variance model [8] and higher order moment models [13].

5. IMPLICATIONS OF PARTICLE ISS

In this section, we add the input-update component that was first shown in Figure 1 and then analyze the convergence of particle position.

Since by Theorem 1 PSO is input-to-state stable, and therefore by Corollary 1 the stability of the cascade system depends on the output of the input-update component. We can say:

1. If the input-update component generates converging personal best and global best, the bound of the particle position will converge;
2. If the personal best and global best vary within a bound, the particle will converge within a bound;
3. If the personal best and global best become constant, the particle will converge within a bound.
4. If the personal best and global best are constant and the same, the particle will converge toward the global best.

By Theorem 2 and 4, we can make similar statements about the particle mean. As well, this boundary analysis could be applied to higher moments.

Furthermore, by Equation (5), we know that the convergence of a particle's position $x(k)$ to x^* depends on how $x^P(k)$ and $x^G(k)$ converge to x^* when the position-update component is input-to-state stable. In particular, the bound on the distance between a particle's position and x^* is determined by the initial distance $x(0) - x^*$, $x^P(k) - x^*$ and $x^G(k) - x^*$.

5.1 Stagnation

Since stagnation is defined as a state where a particle fails to find better positions, in stagnation $x^P(k)$ and $x^G(k)$ are constant in k, and can thus be represented as x^P and x^G respectively. If we assume that $u^P(k)$ and $u^G(k)$ are equivalent and constant, it can be stated that

$$\hat{x} = \frac{\phi^P x^P + \phi^G x^G}{\phi^P + \phi^G} \tag{10}$$

is an equilibrium point for stagnation as noted in previous work [5].

By Theorem 2, in stagnation the mean of the position will converge. Corollary 1 describes a bound on position as a function of the PSO parameters. Similarly, assuming that parameters are chosen that will also lead to the convergence of higher moments similar to previous work [8, 13], the pattern of particle movement at stagnation could be simulated by a distribution constructed to be consistent with PSO moment information[13].

By letting $x^* = \hat{x}$ be the reference point, and by Corollary 1, we can go beyond prior work and can identify a bound on PSO behavior at stagnation:

$$\exists T, \forall k > T, |x(k) - \hat{x}| \le \gamma_d |[x^P - \hat{x},\ x^G - \hat{x}]^T|, \tag{11}$$

with

$$\gamma_d = \frac{2\|A'\|^2\|B'\|^2 + \lambda_{min}(Q'))^2\|B'\|^2}{2(\lambda_{min}(Q'))^3}. \tag{12}$$

Particularly, when $x^P = x^G$, we have $\hat{x} = x^G = x^P$. By Equation (11) we know that $\exists T, x(T) = x^G$, which means $x(k) \to x^G$. Thus we have shown the convergence of PSO in stagnation without treating the random terms as constants required by the work described in Section 2.

5.2 Before stagnation

Input-to-state stable analysis also supports understanding the cases before stagnation. When the $x^P(k)$ and $x^G(k)$ are not constant, the system state depends on the property of the input-update component. The personal-best update is

$$x_i^P(k) = \arg \max_{x \in \{x_i(k), x_i^P(k-1)\}} f(x). \tag{13}$$

The global-best update is

$$x_i^G(k) = \arg \max_{x \in \{x_i(k), x_i^G(k-1)\}} f(x). \tag{14}$$

As in Figure 1, there exists a feedback cascade system structure for a particle. If we assume that there is another model for swarm information sharing, which implements the $x^G(k)$ update. Then in the particle, the $x^G(k)$ can be viewed as an input that is independent with the current particle state. The feedback loop uses the current state to update the $x^P(k)$. As in Equation (13) and (14), the input-to-state stability of the input-update component depends on $f(x)$, which indicates that the input-to-state stability relies on the shape of the fitness distribution. Assuming that the PSO parameters are set such that the position-update component is input-to-state stable, there are three cases in analyzing the dynamics of a particle.

- *When only the $x^G(k)$ is constant*
  This happens usually when a "good" global best is found. Thus the swarm stops finding better global

bests. The input from the swarm can be modeled as a constant factor of the system. However, the particle still finds new personal best positions and updates the personal best. The system dynamics of the particle is determined by the feedback state, which updates the personal best. In this process, $f(x^P) < f(x^G)$, otherwise, x^G will be updated. In this case, the two components form a feedback loop structure. The small gain theorem [9] can be used. If the multiplication of the gain factors of two components is less than 1, the system will still converge.

- *When only the $x^P(k)$ is constant*
This usually means that this particle is "stuck" in exploring a local region but some other particles are continuously finding new better position. Thus the global best is being updated. In this case, the feedback of the system does not impact the input-update component and thus nor does it impact the position-update component. In this case the system model can be simplified by ignoring the feedback. As a result, the system falls into only a serial cascade system because there is no feedback for this particle. If the input-update component is input-to-state stable, the serial connection of two input-to-state stable component is still input-to-state stable (it can be shown that a serial cascade of ISS components is also input-to-state stable [10]). Since this serial cascade system is input-to-state stable, the new position will be bounded somewhere around $x^G(k)$. This implies that the particle will converge toward the $x^G(k)$. If we have $f(x^G) > f(x^P)$, in the assumption of the continuity in the fitness space, when the particle gets closer to the global best, there exits some region that $f(x) > f(x^P)$. The x^P will start to change.

- *When both the $x^G(k)$ and $x^P(k)$ are not constant*
This usually means that both the particle and the swarm it belongs to keep on finding better positions. Thus both the particle updates the personal best and the swarm updates the global best. In this case, the input-to-state stability of the input-update component is harder to guarantee. However, if the change of $x^G(k)$ and $x^P(k)$ is bounded, the movement of the particle is still bounded by Corollary 1.

Generally, in the PSO, the dynamics of a particle switches in between these cases before eventually reaching the stagnation. Understanding the dynamics of the particles before stagnation supports the exploration and exploitation capability of particles in optimal search.

6. CONCLUSION

In this paper, we have decomposed the particle in the PSO algorithm into a feedback cascade model, which consists of input-update and position-update components. We introduce the input-to-state stability analysis to the position-update component. For an input-to-state stable position-update component, if the input to this component is bounded, the state is bounded; also if the input to the component converges, the state converges. The convergence of a particle in PSO is determined by the output of the input-update component, which are the personal best and global best. If they are in stagnation, the particle converges.

The analysis of a cascade structure used here can be applied to a wide range of PSO variants. In the cases that the same position-update component but different input-update components are used, the convergence and the boundary of the particles are determined by whether the input-update component generates converging or bounded personal best and global best. For variants that use a different position-update component, the ISS properties would need to be verified.

The ISS property of the input-update component depends on the fitness distribution. We provide several scenarios for the dynamics of the particle. We show that the optimal search process switches among these scenarios and how the input-to-state stability analysis should be applied into different scenarios.

Appendix

6.1 ISS-Lyapunov function

Using the definitions of a K-function and a KL-function in Section 3 we can define an ISS-Lyapunov function as follows, an ISS-Lyapunov function $V : \mathbb{R}^n \to \mathbb{R}_{\geq 0}$ satisfies:

1. $\exists \alpha_1, \alpha_2 \in \mathbb{K}$ such that $\forall \xi \in \mathbb{R}^n$, $\alpha_1(|\xi|) \leq V(\xi) \leq \alpha_2(|\xi|)$.
2. $\exists \alpha_3 \in \mathbb{K}_\infty, \sigma \in \mathbb{K}$ such that $\forall \xi \in \mathbb{R}^n, \forall \mu \in \mathbb{R}^m, V(f(\xi,\mu)) - V(\xi) \leq -\alpha_3(|\xi|) + \sigma(|\mu|)$.

6.2 Proof of Theorem 1

PROOF. Let P be an identity matrix. As $|\lambda_{\max}(A(k))| < 1$, we have $\|A^T(k)PA(k)\| \leq \|P\|\|A(k)\|^2 \leq \|P\||\lambda_{\max}(A(k))|^2 < \|P\|$. Because P is an identity matrix it is positive definite, and thus $A^T(k)PA(k)$ is positive definite or positive semi-definite by definition. So by positive definite ordering we have $A^T(k)PA(k) < P$.

Let $-Q(k) = A^T(k)PA(k) - P$. Since $A^T(k)PA(k) < P$ then $-Q(k) < 0$ furthermore $\exists Q' \forall k, Q(k) > Q' > 0$.

By the Lemma 3.5 in [9], if we can show that a proposed positive definite Lyapunov function is an ISS-Lyapunov function, the system is input-to-state stable.

Define a Lyapunov function

$$V(X(k)) = X^T(k)PX(k). \tag{15}$$

We can have $\lambda_{min}(P)|X(k)|^2 \leq V(X(k)) \leq \lambda_{max}(P)|X(k)|^2$ and $\lambda_{min}(P) = \lambda_{max}(P)$.

Let $\alpha_1(\xi) = \lambda_{min}\xi^2$ and $\alpha_2(\xi) = \lambda_{max}\xi^2$, we have $V(x)$ satisfying condition 1 of the ISS-Lyapunov function definition.

By applying Equation (4) to $V(X(k+1)) - V(X(k))$, we have

$$\begin{aligned}
&V(X(k+1)) - V(X(k)) \\
=&[X^T(k)A^T(k) + U^T(k)B^T(k)]P[A(k)X(k) + B(k)U(k)] \\
&- X^T(k)PX(k) \\
=&X^T(k)A^T(k)PA(k)X(k) + X^T(k)A^T(k)PB(k)U(k) \\
&+ U^T(k)B^T(k)PA(k)X(k) + U^T(k)B^T(k)PB(k)U(k) \\
&- X^T(k)PX(k)
\end{aligned} \tag{16}$$

As P is identity matrix, it is symmetric, thus

$$[X^T(k)A^T(k)PB(k)U(k)]^T = U^T(k)B^T(k)PA(k)X(k). \tag{17}$$

$V(X(k{+}1)), V(X(k)) \in \mathbb{R}$, we have $X^T(k)A^T(k)PB(k)U(k)$ and $U^T(k)B^T(k)PA(k)X(k)$ are both real value (like 1×1 matrix). Thus,

$$X^T(k)A^T(k)PB(k)U(k) = U^T(k)B^T(k)PA(k)X(k). \quad (18)$$

We then have

$$\begin{aligned} & V(X(k+1)) - V(X(k)) \\ =& - X^T(k)[A^T(k)PA(k) - P]X(k) \\ & + U^T(k)B^T(k)PB(k)U(k) \\ & + 2X^T(k)A^T(k)PB(k)U(k) \\ \leq & - X^T(k)Q'X(k) + U^T(k)B^T(k)PB(k)U(k) \\ & + 2X^T(k)A^T(k)PB(k)U(k) \end{aligned} \quad (19)$$

By applying matrix norm, we have

$$\begin{aligned} & V(X(k+1)) - V(X(k)) \\ \leq & - \lambda_{min}(Q')|X(k)|^2 + |B^T(k)PB(k)||U(k)|^2 \\ & + 2|A^T(k)PB(k)||U(k)||X(k)| \\ =& - \frac{1}{2}\lambda_{min}(Q')|X(k)|^2 + |B^T(k)PB(k)||U(k)|^2 \\ & - \frac{1}{2}\lambda_{min}(Q')|X(k)|^2 + 2|A^T(k)PB(k)||U(k)||X(k)| \\ =& - \frac{1}{2}\lambda_{min}(Q')|X(k)|^2 \\ & + \left(\frac{2|A^T(k)PB(k)|^2}{(\lambda_{min}(Q'))^2} + |B^T(k)PB(k)|\right)|U(k)|^2 \\ & - \frac{1}{2}\lambda_{min}(Q')[|X(k)|^2 - \frac{4|A^T(k)PB(k)|}{\lambda_{min}(Q')}|X(k)||U(k)| \\ & + \frac{4|A^T(k)PB(k)|^2}{(\lambda_{min}(Q'))^2}|U(k)|^2] \end{aligned} \quad (20)$$

By completing the square, we have

$$\begin{aligned} & V(X(k+1)) - V(X(k)) \\ \leq & - \frac{1}{2}\lambda_{min}(Q')|X(k)|^2 \\ & + \left(\frac{2|A^T(k)PB(k)|^2}{(\lambda_{min}(Q'))^2} + |B^T(k)PB(k)|\right)|U(k)|^2 \\ & - \frac{1}{2}\lambda_{min}(Q')\left(|X(k)| - \frac{2|A^T(k)PB(k)|}{\lambda_{min}(Q')}|U(k)|\right)^2 \\ \leq & - \frac{1}{2}\lambda_{min}(Q')|X(k)|^2 \\ & + \left(\frac{2\|A^T(k)PB(k)\|^2}{(\lambda_{min}(Q'))^2} + \|B^T(k)PB(k)\|\right)|U(k)|^2. \end{aligned} \quad (21)$$

Because $u^P(k) \in [0, 1]$, there exist an A' and B' such that $\|A(k)\| \leq \|A'\|$ and $\|B(k)\| \leq \|B'\|$. We have $\|A^T(k)PB(k)\| \leq \|A'\|\|P\|\|B'\|$ and $\|B^T(k)PB(k)\| \leq \|P\|\|B'\|^2$. Since the identity matrix P has $||P|| = 1$:

$$\begin{aligned} & V(X(k+1)) - V(X(k)) \\ \leq & - \frac{1}{2}\lambda_{min}(Q')|X(k)|^2 + \left(\frac{2\|A'\|^2\|B'\|^2}{(\lambda_{min}(Q'))^2} + \|B'\|^2\right)|U(k)|^2. \end{aligned} \quad (22)$$

Let

$$\alpha_3(\xi) = \frac{1}{2}\lambda_{min}(Q')\xi^2,$$

and

$$\sigma(\xi) = \left(\frac{2\|A'\|^2\|B'\|^2}{(\lambda_{min}(Q'))^2} + \|B'\|^2\right)\xi^2.$$

Thus we have $V(X(k+1)) - V(X(k))$ satisfying condition 2 of the ISS-Lyapunov function definition and so (15) is an ISS-Lyapunov function. Using Jiang's Lemma 3.5[9], the position-update component of PSO (Equation (4)) is input-to-state stable. □

6.3 Proof of Corollary 2

PROOF. Let $a = (1 + \chi) - \chi\phi$. The eigenvalues of $A(k)$ are

$$\lambda = \frac{a \pm \sqrt{a^2 - 4\chi}}{2}.$$

There can be two cases.

1. If $a^2 \geq 4\chi$, the eigenvalues are real number. We have $a \geq 2\sqrt{\chi}$ or $a \leq -2\sqrt{\chi}$.
   If $a \geq 2\sqrt{\chi}$, then $|\lambda_{\max}| < 1$ derives
   $$0 < \frac{a - \sqrt{a^2 - 4\chi}}{2} \leq \frac{a + \sqrt{a^2 - 4\chi}}{2} < 1.$$
   It means that $2\sqrt{\chi} \leq a < 1 + \chi$.
   If $a \leq 2\sqrt{\chi}$, then $|\lambda_{\max}| < 1$ derives
   $$-1 < \frac{a - \sqrt{a^2 - 4\chi}}{2} \leq \frac{a + \sqrt{a^2 - 4\chi}}{2} < 0.$$
   It means that $-(\chi + 1) < a \leq -2\sqrt{\chi}$.
2. If $a^2 < 4\chi$, the eigenvalues are complex number. We have $-2\sqrt{\chi} < a < 2\sqrt{\chi}$.
   $|\lambda_{\max}| < 1$ derives
   $$\frac{a^2}{4} + \frac{a^2 - 4\chi}{4} < 1.$$
   It means that $-2\sqrt{2(1 + \chi)} < a < 2\sqrt{2(1 + \chi)}$. Because $\sqrt{2(1 + \chi)} > 2\sqrt{\chi}$, we have $-2\sqrt{\chi} < a < 2\sqrt{\chi}$.

Combining these two cases, we have $-(1 + \chi) < a < 1 + \chi$. It equals to $\phi \in \left(0, \frac{2(1+\chi)}{\chi}\right)$. □

6.4 Proof of Corollary 3

PROOF. The proof is similar with that in Subsection 6.3. In this case, $a = (1 + \chi) - \frac{\phi}{2}\chi$. Similarly, we can have two cases and derive $-(1 + \chi) < a < 1 + \chi$. It equals to $\phi \in \left(0, \frac{4(1+\chi)}{\chi}\right)$. □

7. REFERENCES

[1] M. Bonyadi, Z. Michalewicz, and X. Li. An analysis of the velocity updating rule of the particle swarm optimization algorithm. *Journal of Heuristics*, 20(4):417–452, 2014.

[2] D. Bratton and J. Kennedy. Defining a standard for particle swarm optimization. In *Swarm Intelligence Symposium, 2007. SIS 2007. IEEE*, pages 120–127, April 2007.

[3] C. Cleghorn and A. Engelbrecht. A generalized theoretical deterministic particle swarm model. *Swarm Intelligence*, 8(1):35–59, 2014.

[4] C. Cleghorn and A. Engelbrecht. Particle swarm convergence: An empirical investigation. In *Evolutionary Computation (CEC), 2014 IEEE Congress on*, pages 2524–2530, July 2014.

[5] M. Clerc and J. Kennedy. The particle swarm - explosion, stability, and convergence in a multidimensional complex space. *Evolutionary Computation, IEEE Transactions on*, 6(1):58–73, Feb 2002.

[6] M. Clerc and E. R. Poli. Stagnation analysis in particle swarm optimisation or what happens when nothing happens. Technical report, 2006.

[7] J. Fernandez-Martinez and E. Garcia-Gonzalo. Stochastic stability analysis of the linear continuous and discrete pso models. *Evolutionary Computation, IEEE Transactions on*, 15(3):405–423, June 2011.

[8] M. Jiang, Y. Luo, and S. Yang. Stochastic convergence analysis and parameter selection of the standard particle swarm optimization algorithm. *Information Processing Letters*, 102(1):8 – 16, 2007.

[9] Z.-P. Jiang and Y. Wang. Input-to-state stability for discrete-time nonlinear systems. *Automatica*, 37(6):857 – 869, 2001.

[10] H. K. Khalil and J. Grizzle. *Nonlinear systems*, volume 3. Prentice hall New Jersey, 1996.

[11] R. Poli. Dynamics and stability of the sampling distribution of particle swarm optimisers via moment analysis. *J. Artif. Evol. App.*, 2008:15:1–15:10, Jan. 2008.

[12] R. Poli. Mean and variance of the sampling distribution of particle swarm optimizers during stagnation. *Evolutionary Computation, IEEE Transactions on*, 13(4):712–721, Aug 2009.

[13] R. Poli and D. Broomhead. Exact analysis of the sampling distribution for the canonical particle swarm optimiser and its convergence during stagnation. In *Proceedings of the 9th Annual Conference on Genetic and Evolutionary Computation*, GECCO '07, pages 134–141, New York, NY, USA, 2007. ACM.

[14] N. Samal, A. Konar, S. Das, and A. Abraham. A closed loop stability analysis and parameter selection of the particle swarm optimization dynamics for faster convergence. In *Evolutionary Computation, 2007. CEC 2007. IEEE Congress on*, pages 1769–1776, Sept 2007.

[15] M. Schmitt and R. Wanka. Particle swarm optimization almost surely finds local optima. In *Proceeding of the Fifteenth Annual Conference on Genetic and Evolutionary Computation Conference*, GECCO '13, pages 1629–1636, New York, NY, USA, 2013. ACM.

[16] I. C. Trelea. The particle swarm optimization algorithm: convergence analysis and parameter selection. *Information Processing Letters*, 85(6):317 – 325, 2003.

[17] F. van den Bergh and A. Engelbrecht. A study of particle swarm optimization particle trajectories. *Information Sciences*, 176(8):937 – 971, 2006.

[18] F. van den Bergh and A. P. Engelbrecht. A convergence proof for the particle swarm optimiser. *Fundam. Inf.*, 105(4):341–374, Dec. 2010.

A Set-based Comprehensive Learning Particle Swarm Optimization with Decomposition for Multiobjective Traveling Salesman Problem

Xue Yu[124], Wei-Neng Chen[1234*], Xiao-Min Hu[245], Jun Zhang[1234]

[1]School of Advanced Computing, Sun Yat-sen University, Guangzhou, China

[2]Key Lab. Machine Intelligence and Advanced Computing, Ministry of Education, China

[3]Collaborative Innovation Center of High Performance Computing, China

[4]Engineering Research Center of Supercomputing Engineering Software, Ministry of Education, China

[5]School of Public Health, Sun Yat-sen University, Guangzhou, China

* Corresponding Author, Email: chenwn3@mail.sysu.edu.cn

ABSTRACT

This paper takes the multiobjective traveling salesman problem (MOTSP) as the representative for multiobjective combinatorial problems and develop a set-based comprehensive learning particle swarm optimization (S-CLPSO) with decomposition for solving MOTSP. The main idea is to take advantages of both the multiobjective evolutionary algorithm based on decomposition (MOEA/D) framework and our previously proposed S-CLPSO method for discrete optimization. Consistent to MOEA/D, a multiobjective problem is decomposed into a set of subproblems, each of which is represented as a weight vector and solved by a particle. Thus the objective vector of a solution or the cost vector between two cities will be transformed into real fitness to be used in S-CLPSO for the exemplar construction, the heuristic information generation and the update of *pBest*. To validate the proposed method, experiments based on TSPLIB benchmark are conducted and the results indicate that the proposed algorithm can improve the solution quality to some degree.

Categories and Subject Descriptors

I.2.8 [**Artificial Intelligence**]: Problem Solving, Control Methods, and Search – *Heuristic methods.*

General Terms

Algorithms, Design, Experimentation.

Keywords

multiobjective traveling salesman problem (MOTSP); multiobjective evolutionary algorithm based on decomposition (MOEA/D); set-based particle swarm optimization (S-PSO).

GECCO '15, July 11 - 15, 2015, Madrid, Spain

 ISBN 978-1-4503-3472-3/15/07…$15.00

DOI: http://dx.doi.org/10.1145/2739480.2754672

1. INTRODUCTION

As one of the most famous combination optimization problems [1], the traveling salesman problem (TSP) is to find a Hamiltonian circuit with minimum length in a number of cities, that is, a salesman would like start from a home city to visit other cities once and only once and come back to his home city finally. The TSP has been proved as NP-hard [2]. Because of the simplicity to describe and hardness to solve, TSPs are commonly used as benchmarks to assess the performance of heuristics [3] and have been well research in many fields [4]-[7]. However, in reality some other kinds of cost except for distance have to be considered when dealing with a TSP, such as risk and time, thus the TSP becomes an MOTSP with more than one objectives to optimize. A MOTSP can be formulated as follows

$$\begin{aligned} &\min F(x) = (f_1(x), ..., f_m(x)) \\ &f_i(x) = \sum_{j=1}^{n-1} c^i_{x_j, x_{j+1}} + c^i_{x_1, x_n}, i = 1, ..., m \end{aligned} \quad (1)$$

where m is the number of objectives, n is the number of cities, $x = (x_1, ..., x_n)$ is a permutation of city indices, $C(i) = (c^i_{j,k})_{n\times n}$ is the ith cost matrix, $f_i(x)$ is the ith objective. It is worth noting that the objectives in (1) often conflict with each other, thus a single solution with every objective optimized is impossible to find. Like other multiobjective optimization problems (MOPs), a set of tradeoff solutions is usually found when developing an MOEA for dealing with an MOTSP. A prevailing way to make tradeoff in MOPs is based on Pareto dominance theory, where a *Pareto front* (*PF*) is found in the objective space (*Pareto set* (*PS*) in the decision space) [8].

Much effort has been devoted to solving MOTSPs and there are two approaches regularly adopted: 1) based on local search on multiobjective framework; 2) based on EAs and multiobjective framework. In the former case, the hybridization of decomposition and local search is developed in [9], where the Pareto local search is extended to solve MOTSPs. For the latter case, more applications can be found. For instances, the estimation of distribution algorithm (EDA) [10] is integrated into the decomposition framework to solve the multiobjective multiple traveling salesman problem in [11]; L. J. Ke etc. [12] proposed a multiobjective EA, namely MOEA/D-ACO, combining ant colony optimization (ACO) [13] and the multiobjective evolutionary algorithm based on decomposition (MOEA/D) [14];

[15] developed a multiobjective hybrid genetic algorithm (MO-HGA) for TFT-LCD module assembly scheduling that hybridizes with the variable neighborhood descent (VND) algorithm as a local search and TOPSIS evaluation technique to derive the best compromised solution.

Among all the popular EAs, the particle swarm optimization (PSO) is easy to implement as well as obtain pretty solutions when applied to optimize many problems. However, the conventional PSO was originally designed for solving continuous problems [16] and some strategies have been proposed to develop discrete PSO when using it to solve discrete problems [17]-[20]. Among those discrete strategies, the set-based particle swarm optimization (S-PSO) method proposed in [20] is effective and its validity for solving combinatorial optimization problems (COPs) have been proved on TSP and 0/1 knapsack problem benchmarks. Based on the S-PSO method, the representation scheme is carefully designed and the position and velocity of a particle are represented as a crisp set and a set with possibilities respectively. Then according to the update formulae of a variant PSO with extra mathematical operations defined for crisp sets and sets with possibilities, the discrete PSO evolves to solve some certain COPs. Like other heuristics for solving COPs, the local heuristic information is also important to the efficiency of S-PSO and should be carefully designed based on the characteristics of the COP to be solved.

To make S-PSO available for solving MOTSPs, a prevailing multiobjective framework based on decomposition, i.e. MOEA/D, is adopted in this paper to extend S-PSO to its multiobjective version. More specifically, we obtain the discrete comprehensive learning PSO (CLPSO) [21] based on S-PSO method, namely S-CLPSO and then extend S-CLPSO to its multiobjective version using the MOEA/D, donated as MOEA/D-S-CLPSO. In MOEA/D-S-CLPSO, an MOTSP is decomposed into several single-objective TSPs represented by different weight vectors, and each subproblem is optimized by a particle in S-CLPSO method using information from its neighboring particles. The neighboring particles of a particle are determined according to the distance between weight vectors of subproblems. Actually, the weight vector of a particle is also used in exemplar construction, local heuristic information generation and update of best-so-far solutions in S-CLPSO: 1) when constructing an exemplar for a particle, its weight vector is used to converted the objective vectors of two randomly-selected particles into two real values and the better one can be selected out by comparing the two real values during tournament selection. 2) The heuristic information will help to make decision when there are two cities can be taken as next node. However, there will be a cost vector instead of a single cost value between two cities. Through the product of a cost vector and the particle's weight vector, the cost vector is transformed into a single cost value and the comparison can be made easily on it. 3) In MOEA/D-S-CLPSO, the objective vectors of a particle's all neighboring particles are compared to update the particle's *pBest*, where the objective vector is transformed into a real value. To validate the proposed method, experiments based on TSPLIB benchmark are conducted and the results indicate that the proposed algorithm can improve the solution quality to some degree.

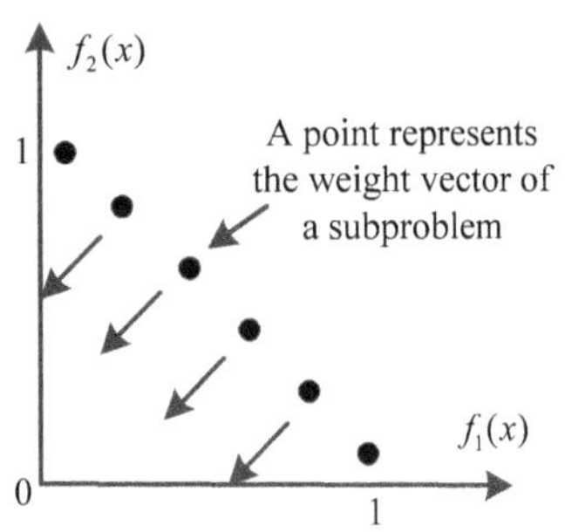

Figure 1. Example of a set of evenly distributed subproblem weight vectors

The rest of this paper is organized as follows. Section 2 reviews the MOEA/D framework. Section 3 introduces S-PSO method. In Section 4, the proposed MOEAD-S-CLPSO for solving MOTSP is presented. Experiments and comparison studies are shown in Section 5, and the conclusions are drawn in Section 6.

2. MOEA/D FREAMWORK

MOEA/D is a prevalent EA framework based on decomposition to solve MOPs. It decomposes an MOP into a number of scalar optimization subproblems and optimizes them simultaneously. Each subproblem is represented by a weight vector and optimized by combining the information from its several neighboring subproblems.

2.1 Decomposition Approaches

Several approaches are available to convert an MOP into a number of scalar optimization problems. The following two approaches are introduced in [8]:

1) *Weighted Sum Approach*

Considering a minimal MOP with m objectives, let $\lambda = (\lambda_1,...,\lambda_m)^T$ be a weight vector. Then the scalar optimization problem is defined as follows:

$$\text{minimize } g^{ws}(x \mid \lambda) = \textstyle\sum_{i=1}^{m} \lambda_i f_i(x), x \in \Omega \qquad (2)$$

2) *Chebyshev Approach*

In this approach, the scalar optimization problem is defined as follows:

$$\text{minimize } g^{te}(x \mid \lambda, z^*) = \max_{1 \le i \le m} \{\lambda_i \mid f_i(x) - z_i^* \mid\}, x \in \Omega \qquad (3)$$

where z^* is the reference point, i.e., $z_i^* = \min\{f_i(x) \mid x \in \Omega\}$.

2.2 Basic Ideas of MOEA/D

Actually, the following two main points in MOEA/D make it efficient as well as simple.

1) *Subproblem*: Each subproblem *i* is assigned with a specific weight vector λ_i, thus it's responsible for optimizing that direction of the MOP. Therefore, a set of well-distributed subproblem weight vectors will guarantee a good approximation of the *PF*. Usually, a set of evenly distributed subproblem weight vectors is used, that is, shown in Fig. 1., where $\lambda_i^j \ge 0$ for all $j = 1,...,m$ and $\sum_{j=1}^{m} \lambda_i^j = 1$.

2) *Neighborhood*: Each subproblem is optimized by only using its neighboring subproblems' information, which results in a lower computational complexity. In MOEA/D, the neighborhood *B*(*i*) of subproblem *i* with the weight vector λ_i is defined as a set of its

several closest weight vectors in all the subproblem weight vectors, i.e., $\{\lambda_1,...,\lambda_N\}$.

3. SET-BASED PSO

3.1 Continuous PSO

In the original PSO **Error! Reference source not found.**, the ith particle in the swarm maintains a velocity vector v_i and a position vector x_i , where $v_i, x_i \in R^n$ if the swarm is to search the global optimum in the n-dimensional space. In each iteration, the velocity and position of particle i are updated as follows:

$$v_i^j = wv_i^j + c_1 r_1^j (pBest_i^j - x_i^j) + c_2 r_2^j (\text{g}Best^j - x_i^j) \quad (4)$$

$$x_i^j = x_i^j + v_i^j \quad (5)$$

where $pBest_i$ is the best-so-far solution yielded by particle i, $gBest$ is the best-so-far solution obtained by the whole swarm, w, c_1, c_2 are parameters with great importance on the algorithm efficiency.

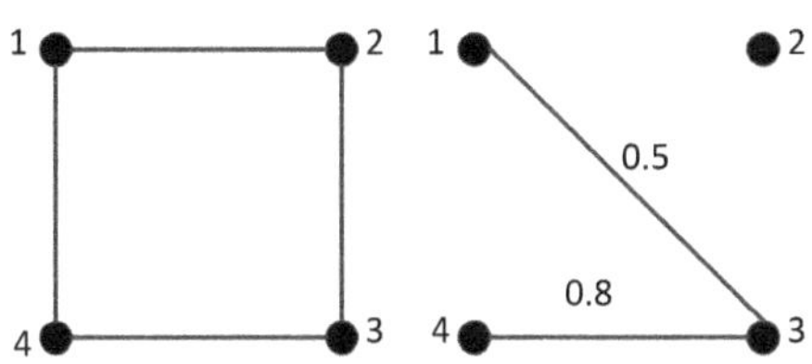

$X = \{(1,2),(2,3),(3,4),(1,4)\}$

$X^1 = \{(1,2),(1,4)\}, X^2 = \{(1,2),(2,3)\}$

$X^3 = \{(2,3),(3,4)\}, X^4 = \{(3,4),(1,4)\}$

$V = \{(1,3)/0.5,(3,4)/0.8\}$

$V^1 = \{(1,3)/0.5\}, V^2 = \{\}, V^4 = \{(3,4)/0.8\}$

$V^3 = \{(1,3)/0.5,(3,4)/0.8\}$

(a)

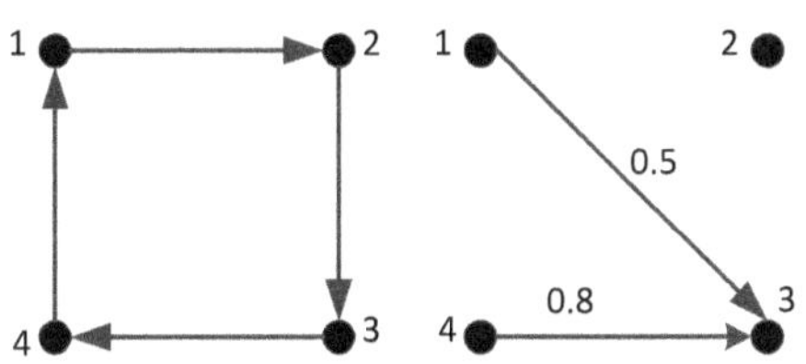

$X = \{(1,2),(2,3),(3,4),(4,1)\}$

$X^1 = \{(1,2)\}, X^2 = \{(2,3)\}$

$X^3 = \{(3,4)\}, X^4 = \{(4,1)\}$

$V = \{(1,3)/0.5,(4,3)/0.8\}$

$V^1 = \{(1,3)/0.5\}, V^2 = \{\}$

$V^3 = \{\}, V^4 = \{(4,3)/0.8\}$

(b)

Figure 2. Examples of the representation scheme for the TSP. (a) Scheme for the symmetric TSP. (b) Scheme for the asymmetric TSP.

Many variants of PSO have been proposed by researchers, and CLPSO is a representative one among them. In CLPSO, a novel learning strategy is used and the velocity of particle i is updated as follows:

$$v_i^j = wv_i^j + cr^j (pBest_{f_i(j)}^j - x_i^j) \quad (6)$$

where $f_i(j)$ is set as i or the better one of two randomly selected particles in a particularly probabilistic way. In other words, all particles' historical best information is used to update a particle's velocity [21].

3.2 S-PSO

To extend continuous PSOs to their discrete versions, the set-based PSO method is presented in [20]. Since a set-based representation scheme is applied in S-PSO, a particle's position X is redefined as a crisp set corresponding to a feasible solution to the problem and its velocity V is redefined as a set with possibilities, also, the updating operators of position and velocity are changed respectively.

To address the key concepts in S-SPO, a TSP instance with four nodes, indexed as 1,…,4, is taken as an example in the following.

1) *Representation scheme of X and V*: Usually, the set-based representation scheme of a particle's position and velocity for a discrete problem is intuitive to build up, whose design depends on the characteristics of a specific problem. To describe it figuratively, representations of X and V for the TSP is given in Figure 2.

2) *The velocity updating rules*: The concepts of a set with possibilities, the multiplication operator between a coefficient and a set with possibilities, the multiplication operator between a coefficient and a crisp set and the plus operator between two sets with possibilities are carefully defined in [20]. Based on those definitions, examples of all the arithmetic operators when updating particle i's for a symmetric TSP are given in Figure 3.

3) *Position updating*: After updating the velocity, particle i uses the new velocity V_i , its own position X_i to build a new position $NEWX_i$. Unlike the continuous cases, the positions in the discrete space must satisfy some constraints, for example, a feasible solution in TSP must be a permutation of all the city nodes. To ensure the feasibility of the new position, a constructive is used in S-PSO with extra constraint-checking mechanism or solution-repair mechanism. When constructing the jth dimension of $NEWX_i$, denoted as $NEWX_i^j$, particle i first learns from elements in $cut_\alpha(V_i^j)$, which is a set consists of all elements in V_i^j whose possibility is larger than a given threshold $\alpha \in [0,1]$. If there is no available element in $cut_\alpha(V_i^j)$, particle i reuses the elements in the previous X_i^j . If there is still no available element in X_i^j , it uses the other available elements to complete $NEWX_i^j$.

4. MOEA/D-S-CLPSO FOR MTSP

Consistent with the MOEA/D framework, MOEA/D-S-CLPSO decomposes a multiobjective optimization problem into a number of single-objective subproblems. Each particle with a certain representative weight vector is responsible for solving one subproblem, and it belongs to a neighborhood. Checking all the newly constructed solutions in the neighborhood, a particle updates its best-so-far $pBest$ if a better one is found in terms of its

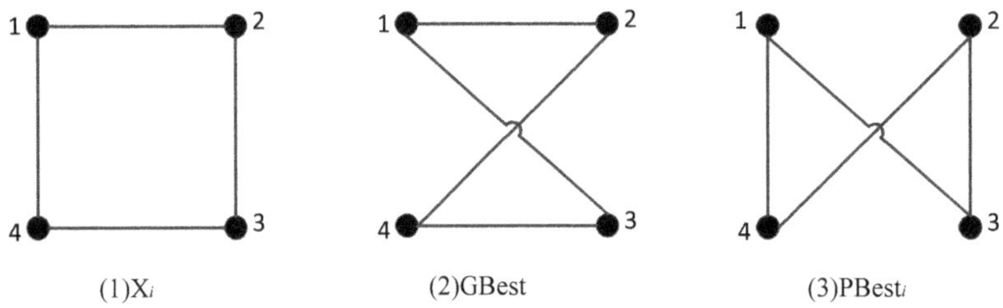

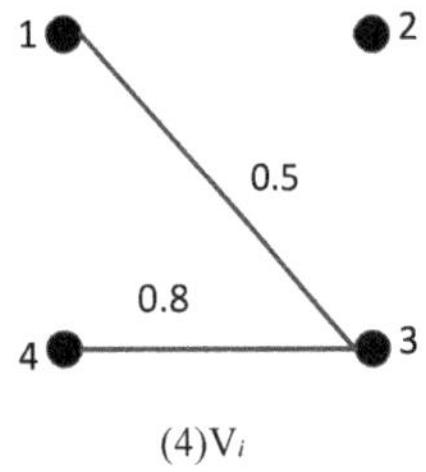

$(a) X_i = \{(1,2),(2,3),(3,4),(1,4)\}$
$(b) V_i = \{(1,3)/0.5,(3,4)/0.8\}$
$(c) GBest = \{(1,2),(1,3),(2,4),(3,4)\}$
$(d) PBest_i = \{(1,3),(1,4),(2,3),(2,4)\}$
$(e) \omega V_i^1 = \{(1,3)/0.35\}(\omega = 0.7)$
$(f) GBest^1 - X_i^1 = \{(1,3)\}$
$(g) PBest_i^1 - X_i^1 = \{(1,3),(1,4)\}$
$(h) c_1 r_1^1 (PBest_i^1 - X_i^1) = \{(1,3)/0.5,(1,4)/0.5\}(c_1 r_1^1 = 0.5)$
$(i) c_2 r_2^1 (GBest^1 - X_i^1) = \{(1,3)/0.7\}(c_2 r_2^1 = 0.7)$
$(j) V_i^1 = \{(1,3)/0.7,(1,4)/0.5\}$

Figure 3. Examples of all the arithmetic operators when updating particle i's for a symmetric TSP.

own objective. Meanwhile, exemplars for guiding each particle's evolution are constructed in CLPSO way, i.e., each dimension of a particle learns from itself or the better one from two particles randomly selected in the neighborhood according to the specific objective. A particle updates its velocity and position in the similar way in S-PSO except that the local heuristic information is closely related to the corresponding subproblem.

4.1 Initialization

Since the proposed MOEA/D-S-CLPSO consists of MOEA/D framework and S-CLPSO algorithm, the initialization preparations should be conducted from that two perspectives. For MOEA/D, the way of decomposing an MTSP into several subproblems (single-objective TSPs) and determining the neighboring subproblems of each subproblem should be defined, that is, the setting of weight vectors λs and the partition of neighborhoods according to λs. For S-CLPSO, the initialization of velocities and positions is important since the representation scheme of S-PSO changes along with the specific discrete problem.

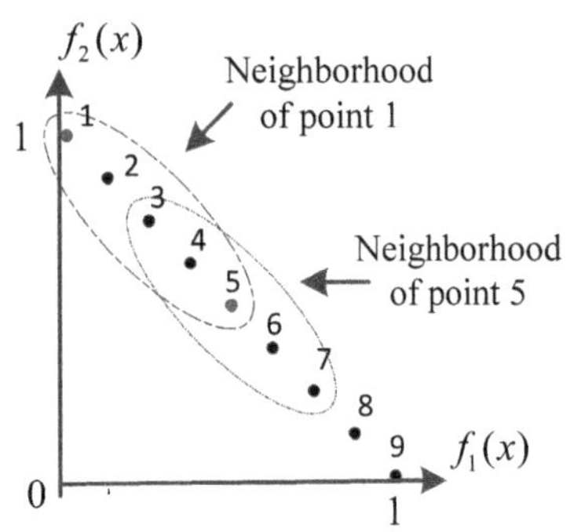

Figure 4. The neighborhoods of different points in if evenly-distributed

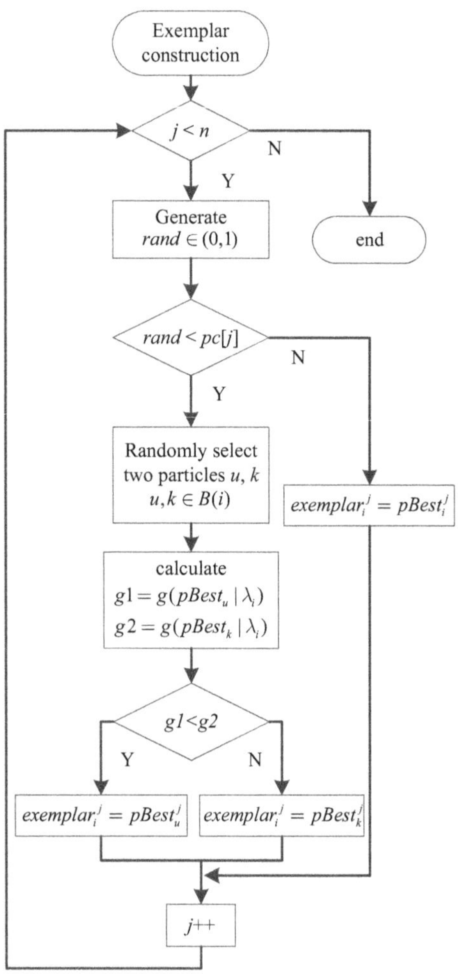

Figure 5. The algorithm of exemplar construction

1) *λs and neighborhoods*: In this paper, the evenly-distributed-like weight vectors are adopted and the neighborhoods are determined based the distances among weight vectors, that is, the neighborhood $B(i)$ of subproblem i with the weight vector λ_i is defined as a set of its several closest weight vectors in all the subproblem weight vectors, i.e., $\{\lambda_1,...,\lambda_N\}$. As for the setting of evenly-distributed-like weight vectors, more weight vectors are placed in the fringe compared with evenly-distributed weight vectors. In mathematics, take bi-objective weight vectors for example, there are F weight vectors in the form of $[1,0]^T$ and F weight vectors in the form of $[0,1]^T$ and the other (ps-2*F) weight vectors are evenly distributed in the way shown in Figure 1.

Why not just evenly-distributed weight vectors: As shown in Figure 4, assume the size of neighborhood is 5 and the number of weight vectors is 9, the neighboring points of point 1 all lay on its right except itself and the point 5 is its farthest neighbor, however, the neighboring points of point 5 lay on its left and right and the point 3 is one of its farthest neighbors. Then it is obvious that the distance between point 1 and point 5 is two times the distance between point 5 and point 3. If the distance between two weight vectors is too long, the subproblems represented by that two weight vectors will differ significantly and they should not learn from each other. Therefore, by placing more points in the fringe, the above problem can be overcome to some degree.

2) *Initialization of position and velocity*: For a TSP with n cities, each position of particle i is initialized as a permutation of n cities, i.e. a permutation of 1,...,n, since the position of a particle must be a candidate solution for that TSP. Then a position {(1,3),(3,2),(2,4),(1,4)} with n = 4 will represents a path that one starts from city 1, then go to city 3, then city 2, then city 4, then returns to the city 1. As for the velocity for particle i, we choose n edges from the complete topology of n cities and randomly generate a real value in [0,1] for each edge since the velocity in S-PSO is a set with possibilities. For example, a velocity can be {(1,2)/0.4, (1,3)/0.5, (2,4)/0.4, (2,3)/0.1}.

4.2 Exemplars construction in CLPSO way

As pointed out above, the dimension j of exemplar for particle i can be determined by k-tournament selection (k=2 in this paper). However, when dealing with multiobjective TSPs, the selection operator should be carefully designed due to the lack of single fitness value. Two obvious approaches can be used to select the better one: 1) based on dominance; 2) based on aggregation of multiobjective values. In the dominance-based way, it is common to find that the two randomly chosen particles not dominated by each other. Thus in this paper, the second approach has been adopted and the algorithm of exemplar construction for particle i is given in Figure 5.

4.3 Update operators

1) *Update of velocity*: The dimension j of particle i is updated in formula (7). Just as the example in the section VI. A, the $V_i^1=\{(1,2)/0.4,(1,3)/0.5\}$ and $X_i^1=\{(1,3),(1,4)\}$, assume that w=0.7, $cr^1=0.7$ an $exemplar_i=\{(1,4),(4,3),(3,2),(1,2)\}$, i.e., $exemplar_i^1=\{(1,4),(1,2)\}$, then according to the mathematical operations on crisp set and set of possibilities, the dimension j of new velocity is that $V_i^1=\{(1,2)/0.7,(1,3)/0.35\}$.

$$v_i^j = wv_i^j + cr^j(exemplar_i^j - x_i^j) \tag{7}$$

2) *Heuristic information and update of position*: When solving discrete combinatorial problems, the heuristic information is important and the bad use of heuristic information will result in terrible algorithm efficiency. For particle i, if the current node is city k and there are two cities u, l can be chosen as next node, then the better one should be selected out based on the heuristic information. In this paper, the multiple costs between two cities are aggregated into a real value (heuristic fitness) by the weight vector of particle i, i.e., the heuristic fitness from city k to city u is calculated as $HF_{k,u}=g(C_{k,u}\mid\lambda_i)$ where $C_{k,u}$ is costs vector from k to u, then the heuristic fitness is used as heuristic information the one with less heuristic fitness is better. The update of X is just in the S-PSO way, that is, when constructing the jth dimension of $NEWX_i$, denoted as $NEWX_i^j$, particle i first learns from elements in $cut_\alpha(V_i^j)$ firstly, then the elements in the previous X_i^j, then the other available elements. Whenever there are more than one elements available, the best one will be chosen according to their heuristic fitness values.

3) *Update of pBest*: According to the MOEA/D framework, the best-so-far solution of a particle should be updated by combining the information of its neighborhood. In MOEA/D-S-CLPSO, to update particle i's *pBest*, the best one of all new solutions generated by i's neighbors (including i itself). Still, the aggregation method is used for selection operator, that is, the one with minimal g value is selected where the g value is calculated based on the decomposition approach adopted in MOEA/D, i.e., $g(X_k)=g(X_k\mid\lambda_i), k\in B(i)$.

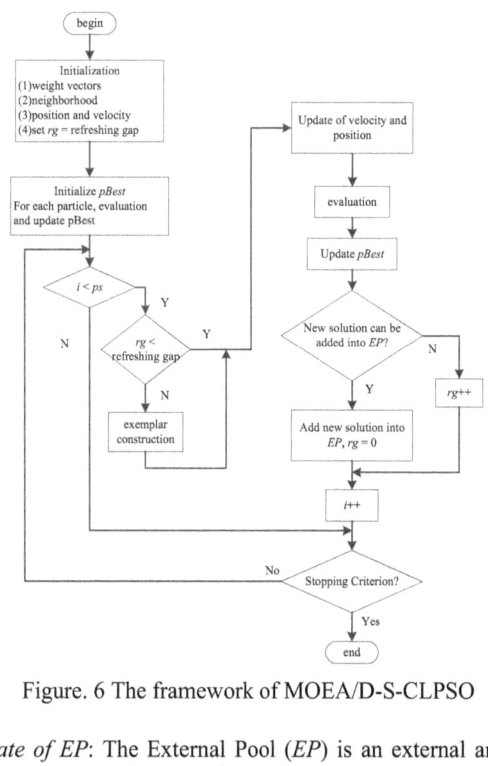

Figure. 6 The framework of MOEA/D-S-CLPSO

4) *Update of EP*: The External Pool (*EP*) is an external archive for saving all non-dominated solutions during the evolution. Whenever a new solution is generated by a particle, we check the dominance relationship between that solution and all the solutions in *EP*. If the new solution is not dominated by any solution in *EP*, then it is added into EP and all the solutions in *EP* dominated by

it will be deleted. Meanwhile, in the proposed MOEA/D-S-CLPSO, the refreshing value *rg* (used in CLPSO) of each particle will be updated according to the update of *EP*, that is, if the new solution generated by particle *i* is added into *EP* successfully then particle *i*'s refreshing value will be set to zero, otherwise, the value plus one. If the value is greater than or equals the refreshing gap, a new exemplar will be constructed for particle *i*.

4.4 Algorithm Framework

The main framework of MOEA/D-S-CLPSO is given in Figure 6, firstly we initialize weight vectors, neighborhoods, position and velocity for each particle and set *rg* value for refreshing gap for each particle, and then we evaluate each particle and initialize its *pBest*. After initialization, an iteration begins, that is, for each particle: construct exemplar if needed, then update velocity and position, evaluation, update *pBest* and *EP*. At the end of an iteration, the stopping criterion is checked, if stopping criterion is satisfied then the algorithm ends, otherwise a new iteration is started.

5. COMPARISON WITH MOEA/D-ACO

BicriterionAnt [22] is one of the best existing multiobjective ACOs on bi-objective TSP [23] [24], and MOEA/D-ACO has been proved to outperform BicriterionAnt significantly in [12]. Therefore, to assess the performance proposed in this paper, only comparison with MOEAD-ACO is made here.

5.1 Performance Metric

The inverted generational distance (IGD) is used to assess the performance of the algorithm proposed in this paper.

Let *P* be the *PF* approximated by an MOEA and *P** be a set of uniformly distributed points along the real *PF* of an MTSP, the IGD from *P** to *P* is defined as

$$IGD(P^*,P)=\frac{\sum_{\upsilon\in P^*}d(\upsilon,P)}{|P^*|} \tag{8}$$

where $d(\upsilon,P)$ is the minimum Euclidean distance between υ and the points in *P*. If *P** is large enough to approximate the real *PF*, the IGD value can measure the distance from *P* to the real *PF* to some degree. To have a low IGD value, points in *P* must be close to the real *PF* and well distributed in objective space without missing any part of the whole *PF*.

5.2 Experimental Setup

The 12 instances with corresponding *P**s from [25] are used in the experiments. The two algorithms are implemented in C++ and executed in the same environment (the source code of MOEA/D-ACO for TSP is provided by its authors and available in [26]).

The parameters of MOEA/D-ACO are set according to **Error! Reference source not found.**. Since MOEA/D-ACO with Chebyshev decomposition strategy performs better that with Weighted Sum strategy, only Chebyshev strategy for MOEA/D-ACO is included in experiments. In contrast, the Weighted Sum strategy is used for MOEA/D-S-CLPSO and the parameter settings of MOEA/D-ACO are as follows.

- Number of particles *ps* = 72
- Neighborhood size *T* = 12
- Max generations *maxgen* = 1000

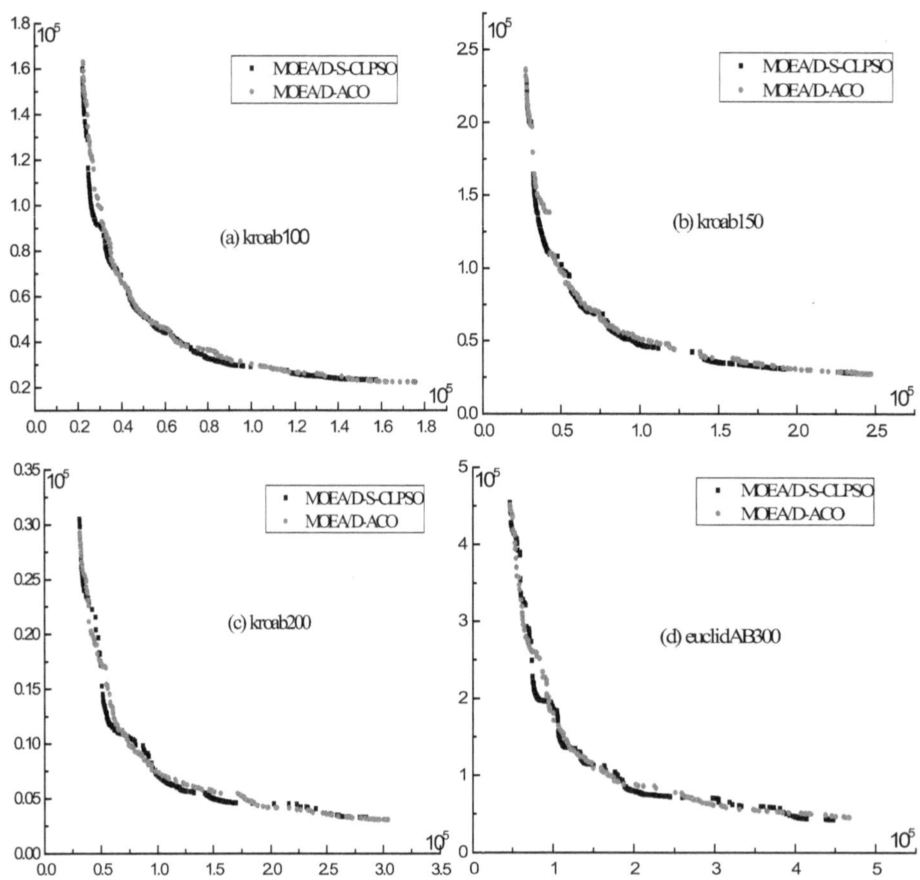

Figure 7. The best approximations with smallest IGD among 30 runs obtained by MOEA-S-CLPSO and MOEA/D-ACO on four TSP instances

Table 1. The IGD statistics obtained by two algorithms over 30 independent runs

Instances		MOEA/D-S-CLPSO			MOEA/D-ACO	
name	n	mean	std	W-test	mean	std
kroab100	100	2061.57	325.011	+	2332.04	189.226
kroac100	100	2216.75	270.048	+	2839.58	231.312
kroad100	100	1866.03	269.045	+	2419.98	162.166
kroae100	100	2030.45	301.114	+	2644.03	183.91
krobc100	100	1847.77	216.977	+	2853.49	256.169
krobd100	100	2041.95	293.867	+	2742.4	204.823
krobe100	100	2150.96	214.202	+	3016.27	236.163
kroab150	150	4382.99	658.298	—	4307.53	269.1
kroab200	200	6899.61	613.307	+	7266.96	309.189
euclidAB100	100	2106.46	268.593	+	3203.1	240.606
euclidAB300	300	13374.8	604.431	+	13789.6	432.348

W-test (Wilcoxon sighed-rand test) is made at the 5% significance level to compare the IGD values of MOEA/D-S-CLPSO and MOEA/D-ACO. "+" and "—" denote that the mean IGD value of the corresponding algorithm is significantly smaller (better) or larger (worse) than that of MOEA/D-ACO.

- F value for evenly-distributed-like weight vectors, $F = 5$
- Refreshing gap $ref\_g = 7$
- $pc[]$, $pc[i] = 0.1$ for each particle i
- $c = 2.0$, w linearly decrease within [0.4, 0.9]
- $\alpha = 0.001$ for obtaining α -cut of a set

All statistics are based on 30 independent runs. MOEA/D-ACO stops after 3000 generations with 24 ants and MOEA/D-S-CLPSO stops after 1000 generations with 72 particles, thus the same number of candidate solutions for each MOTSP instance are generated in each run.

5.3 Experimental results

The mean and standard deviation of IGDs obtained by MOEA/D-ACO and MOEA/D-S-CLPSO are summarized in Table 1. As shown in Table 1, mean IGD value obtained by MOEA/D-S-CLPSO is significantly smaller than that obtained by MOEA/D-ACO for almost all instances except for kroab150ab, i.e., MOEA/D-SCLPSO can approximates the *PF* better for those MOTSP instances.

However, it can't be ignored that the standard deviation values of MOEA/D-S-CLPSO are larger than MOEA/D-ACO's on all instances apart from krobc100 and krobe100, especially for kroab150, kroab200 and euclidAB300. Combining the results or IGDs' mean and standard deviation, we find that compared with MOEA/D-ACO, MOEA/D-S-CLPSO can achieve better approximations to *PF* for almost all instances but with poorer stability, it can't guarantee its solution quality in an arbitrary run.

For further discussion, the final approximations with smallest IGDs for four MOTSP instances, i.e., kroab100, kroab150, kroab200 and euclidAB300, over 30 runs are given in Figure 7. Although the quality differences between the two algorithms are hard to detect visually, it can be found that the solutions generated by MOEA/D-S-CLPSO are commonly denser in comparison with MOEAD-ACO. Meanwhile, it is clear that nearly all the approximations of two algorithms miss some parts of the real *PF*, which is not desired and hoped to be avoided in further study.

6. CONCLUSION

In this paper, a hybrid algorithm namely MOEA/D-S-CLPSO is proposed to solve multiobjective traveling salesman problems by aggregating the set-based CLPSO into the MOEA/D framework. In the hybrid algorithm, an MOTSP is decomposed into a set of single-objective subproblems and each particle is responsible for solving a specific subproblem in S-CLPSO way. Experiments in comparison with MOEA/D-ACO are designed to prove the validity of MOEA/D-S-CLPSO. The statistical results show that a better solution quality can be achieved by MOEA/D-S-CLPSO at most time but the quality can't be guaranteed due to poor stability. Also, the deficiency shared by the two algorithms is addressed in this paper.

7. ACKNOWLEDGEMENT

This work was supported in part by the National Science Foundation of China (NSFC) Projects No.61379061, No.61332002, No.61202130, in part by Natural Science Foundation of Guangdong No. S2013040014949, in part by Specialized Research Fund for the Doctoral Programs No. 20120171120027, No. 20130171120016, and in part by the Guangzhou Pearl River New Star of Science and Technology No. 151700098.

8. REFERENCES

[1] A. Schrijver, *Combinatorial Optimization: Polyhedra and Efficiency*. Berlin: Springer, 2003.

[2] R. Baraglia, J. Hidalgo, and R. Perego, "A hybrid heuristic for the traveling salesman problem," *IEEE Transactions on Evolutionary Computation*, vol. 5, no. 6, pp. 613 -622, 2001.

[3] F. Gao, A.-M. Zhou, and G.-X. Zhang, "An estimation of distribution algorithm based on decomposition for the multiobjective TSP," in *Inter. Conf. on Natural Comp. (ICNC 2012)*, May 2012, pp. 817-821.

[4] K. C. Tan, H. J. Tang, and S. S. Ge, "On parameter settings of Hopfield networks applied to traveling salesman

problems," *IEEE Trans. on Circuit and Systems I: Regular Papers*, vol. 52, no. 5, pp. 994-1002, 2005.

[5] J. W. Pepper, B. L. Golden, and E. A. Wasil, "Solving the traveling salesman problem with annealing-based heuristics: a computational study," *IEEE Trans on System, Man and Cybernetic*, vol. 32, no. 1, pp. 72-77, 2002.

[6] T. Weise, R. Chiong, J. Lassig, and K. Tang et al., "Benchmarking optimization algorithms: An open source framework for the traveling salesman problem," *IEEE Trans. on Comput. Intelli. Mag.*, vol. 9, no. 3, pp. 40-52, 2014.

[7] H. D. Nguyen, I. Yoshihara, K. Yamamori, and M. Yasunaga, "Implementation of an effective hybrid GA for large-scale traveling salesman problems", *IEEE Trans. Sys., Man, and Cyber.*, vol. 37, no. 1, pp. 92-99, 2007.

[8] K. Miettinen, *Nonlinear Multiobjective Optimization.* Boston, MAA: Kluwer, 1999.

[9] L. J. Ke, Q. F. Zhang, and R. Battiti, "Hybridization of Decomposition and Local Search for Multiobjective Optimization," IEEE Trans. On Cyber., vol. 44, no. 10, pp. 1808-1820, 2014.

[10] P. Larrañaga, and J. A. Lozano, *Estimation of Distribution Algorithms: A New Tool for Evolutionary Computation.* Norwell: Kluwer, 2001.

[11] V. A. Shim, K. C. Tan, and C. Y. Cheong, "A hybrid estimation of distribution algorithm with decomposition for solving the multiobjective multiple traveling salesman problem", *IEEE Trans. Sys., Man, and Cyber.*, vol. 42, no. 5, pp. 682-691.

[12] L. J. Ke, Q. F. Zhang, and R. Battiti, "MOEA/D-ACO: A multiobjective evolutionary algorithm using decomposition and AntColony," *IEEE Trans. on Cybernetics*, vol. 43, no. 6, pp. 1845-1859, 2013.

[13] M. Dorigo, V. Maniezzo, and A. Colorni, "Ant System: Optimization by a colony of cooperating agents," *IEEE Transactions on Systems, Man, and Cybernetics*, vol. 26, no. 1, pp. 29-41, 1996.

[14] Q. Zhang and H. Li, "MOEA/D: A multiobjective evolutionary algorithm based on decomposition," *IEEE Trans. Evol. Comp.*, vol. 11, no. 6, pp. 712-731, 2007.

[15] C. W. Chou, C. F. Chien, and M. Gen, "A Multiobjective Hybrid Genetic Algorithm for TFT-LCD Module Assembly Scheduling," *IEEE Trans. Auto. Sci. and Engineering*, vol. 11, no. 3, pp. 692-705, 2014.

[16] J. Kennedy and R. Eberhart, "Particle swarm optimization," in *Proc. IEEE. Conf. Neur. Net.*, Nov. 1995, pp. 1942-1948.

[17] Y. del Valle, G. Venayagamoorthy, S. Mohagheghi, J.-C. Hernandez, and R. Harley, "Particle swarm optimization: Basic concepts, variants and applications in power systems," *IEEE Transactions on Evolutionary Computation*, vol. 12, no. 2, pp. 171–195, 2008.

[18] M. Clerc, *Discrete Particle Swarm Optimization*, ser. New Optimization Techniques in Engineering. New York: Springer-Verlag, 2004.

[19] W. Pang, K.-P. Wang, C.-G. Zhou, L.-J. Dong, M. Liu, H.-Y. Zhang, and J.-Y. Wang, "Modified particle swarm optimization based on space transformation for solving traveling salesman problem," in *Proceedings of the International Conference on Machine Learning and Cybernetics*, vol. 4, 2004, pp. 2342–2346.

[20] W. N. Chen, J. Zhang, H. S. H. Chung, W. L. Zhong, W. G. Wu, and Y. H. Shi, "A novel set-based particle swarm optimization method for discrete optimization problems," *IEEE Trans. Evol. Comp.*, vol. 14, no. 2, pp. 278-300, 2010.

[21] J. J. Liang, A. K. Qin, P. N. Suganthan, and S. Bashar, "Comprehensive learning particle swarm optimizer for global optimization of multimodal functions," *IEEE Trans. Evol. Comp.*, vol. 10, no. 3, pp. 281-295, 2006.

[22] S. Iredi, D. Merkle, and M. Middendorf, "Bi-criterion optimization with multi colony ant algorithm," in *Proc. 1st Int. Conf. EMO*, 2001, pp. 359-372.

[23] C. Garcia-Martinez, O. Cordon, and F. Herrera, "A taxonomy and an empirical analysis of multiple objective ant colony optimization algorithms for the bi-criteria TSP," *Eur. J. Oper. Res.*, vol. 180, no. 1, pp. 116–148, Jul. 2007.

[24] I. Alaya, C. Solnon, and K. Ghedira, "Ant colony optimization for multiobjective optimization problems," in *Proc. 19th IEEE Int. Conf. Tools Artif. Intell.*, 2007.

[25] [Online]. Available: http://eden.dei.uc.pt/~paquete/tsp/

[26] [Online]. Available: http://dces.essex.ac.uk/staff/qzhang/

An Immuno-inspired Approach Towards Sentence Generation

Samir Kr Borgohain
Department of Computer Science &Engineering
National Institute of Technology,
Silchar (India)
+9134842242025
samirborg@gmail.com

Shivashankar B. Nair
Department of Computer Science &Engineering
Indian Institute of Technology Guwahati,
Guwahati (India)
+913612582356
sbnair@iitg.ernet.in

ABSTRACT
Though human beings comprehend, imbibe and subsequently generate syntactically and semantically correct languages, the manner in which they do so has hardly been understood or unearthed. Most of the current work to achieve the same is heavily dependent on statistical and probabilistic data retrieved from a large corpus coupled with a formal grammar catering to the concerned natural language. This paper attempts to portray a technique based on an analogy described by Jerne on how his theory of the Idiotypic Network could possibly explain the human language generation capability. Starting with a repertoire of unigrams (antibodies) weaned from a corpus available *a priori*, we show how these can be sequenced to generate higher order *n-grams* that depict full or portions of correct sentences in that language. These sentences or their correct portions form a network similar to the Idiotypic Network that in turn aid in the generation of sentences or portions thereof which are new to the corpus signifying the learning of new and correct sequences. The network is built based on a modified version of the dynamics suggested by Farmer et. al. The paper describes the related dynamics of the network along with the results obtained from a corpus.

Categories and Subject Descriptors
I. 2.7 [**Natural Language Processing**]: Language generation and Language models.

General Terms
Algorithms, Experimentation, Languages

Keywords
Sentence generation; Idiotypic network; Immune; Language processing

1. INTRODUCTION
The problem of processing natural language has been attacked from several frontiers. The earlier techniques used aformal grammar [1, 2, 3, 4] to start with and analysed whether the incoming sentences conformed to the rules of the grammar embedded *a priori*. A Context Free Grammar for instance, is defined by a vocabulary containing a set of non-terminals and a set of productions or transition rules. First an initial non-terminal is considered and is replaced by a set of productions. The productions are applied repeatedly until a terminal sequence of words is generated.

However, natural language with its rich set of virtually countless grammar rules cannot be accommodated by such methods. This forced researchers to try out corpus based statistical methods [2]. Statistical information derived from a large corpus of the language was used to find measures based on probability of the next word in a sequence. Most of these techniques use the term *n-grams* [1,2] where *n* is a non-zero positive integer and the *gram* represents a token or a word in the corpus. The *n-gram* model concentrates on local dependencies and also encodes linguistic information [1] like syntax, semantics, etc.The *n-gram* model is locally dependent because it takes the window size of *n* and predicts only by taking the context of *(n-1)* words. Further the model is trained using a corpus and because a corpus is always finite, some acceptable *n-grams* are bound to be omitted. Addition of smoothing techniques [5] to add non-zero probabilities to zero probability bigrams eases the issue to some extent.Although the empirical based language models [6] are capable of generating sentences, the complexity of a natural language makes it infeasible to generate all the rules within.

In this paper, we propose an immuno-inspired language processing model, a paradigm shift from the conventional techniques of language processing that, when given a set of correct sentences generates a network which in turn can emit new and correct ones. This technique does not suffer from data sparseness and there is no requirement of a grammar base or a large annotated or tagged corpus. The model opens up the possibility of understanding the working of the biological generative grammar [7].

2. LANGUAGE GENERATION IN HUMAN BEINGS
The manner of the origin and evolution of language and how human beings have over several thousands of years seamlessly conveyed their thought processes through language still remains unraveled. The works carried out by Knight, Studdert-Kennedy and Hurford [8], Hurford, Studdert-Kennedy and Knight [9], Harnard andSteklis[10] are notable. According to them, language has evolved in human beings due to their genetic traits. Two distinct schools of thought – one biological and the other based on cultural evolution – exist, which seek the answer to the origin of a language. The first school of thought proposes that human language originated due to biological evolution. Numerous experiments have been carried out by researchers on apes and

GECCO '15, July 11–15, 2015, Madrid, Spain
© 2015 ACM. ISBN 978-1-4503-3472-3/15/07...$15.00
DOI: http://dx.doi.org/10.1145/2739480.2754805

monkeys to make them learn a language but with hardly any success. On the contrary a human child of around five years of age or even less is capable of acquiring a language from its environment [11] with great ease. This observation led Chomsky [12] to argue that human beings are possibly innately equipped with a set of language rules that aid in the production of sentences.He defines a Universal grammar (UG) which is a formal system within the being and is capable of aligning words (or morphemes) into a pattern which could be grammatically correct or at least acceptable. According to Chomsky these grammatical rules are sort of hard-wired in the human brain. This theory of the existence of a UG is widely accepted by the research community [13,14]. Bickerton [15] describes of the possible existence of a *protolanguage* that exhibits a limited grammar without many of the features of modern day human languages. According to him, the emergence of a fully developed language is due to a sudden and discontinuous 'macro-mutation' of this *protolanguage*. Pinker and Bloom [16] reason that language evolution was a gradual process which possibly took a longperiod of time. Elman [17] questions the innateness of language and concludes that although language is innate the grammar is not encoded in the genomes but has resulted due to many interactions between the genes. Kirby [18] argues that cultural processes may have played a more significant role in the evolution of languages than as the result of evolution due to genes. According to him, languages are passed from one generation to the next resulting in the development of innately possible grammars. Cavalli-Sforza and Feldman [19] have also attempted to develop a general theory for the same, based on cultural evolution.

N. Jerne [7] advocated Chomsky's innateness of generative grammar and drew parallels between language and immunology. Jerne's theory states that the immune system is governed by a set of grammatical rules that allow the formation of new sentences (or antibodies). These antibodies form an interconnected lattice-work. Based on such a network, Jerne draws an analogy with Chomsky's theory of generative grammar that is innate and equally capable of generating new sentences that are recognized by a native speaker. Chomsky's generative grammar results in an "*open-ended*" number of sentences which Jerne correlates to the "*completeness*" of the antibody repertoire. Chomsky and Jerne, both believed [7, 12] that grammatical rules of a human language are carried forward by genomes from one generation to the next.

It is well known that a person fluent in a certain language can wax eloquently in that language. This proficiency makes it extremely difficult for the person to generate ill-formed sentences in the same language, spontaneously. One may thus infer that the person possibly generates a language-based Idiotypic network that impedes the generation of any incorrect language pathogens. With prolonged exposure to a language, a person seems to prototype an in-built immune network capable of distinguishing well-formed sentences and preventing or suppressing the generation of ill-formed ones. It is also interesting to note that grammar by itself is never taught in the initial phases of language learning by a human being. In many a case a person may speak a language fluently without having an iota of knowledge about its grammar. A child, for instance picks up a language very well, oblivious of the associated grammar. It is thus obvious that a collection of sentences, that constitute a corpus, is formed initially within the child. Subsequent sentence generation largely depends on the combinations of the words within this corpus and the inherent grammatical structures contained therein.

3. IMMUNO-INSPIRED LANGUAGE PROCESSING

The existing language models are based on the framework of linguistic rules and statistical methods. While the former rule-based language processing [21] relies heavily on grammatical rules the latter suffers from data sparseness [20]. A sizeable corpus is always necessary while applying the above two techniques of language processing.The immune inspired algorithms have found their use in diverse areas, a few of the notable areas being intrusion detection, pattern recognition and optimization [22]. Immune algorithms have been rarely used in language processing. Kumar and Nair [23] have used the negative selection algorithm [24] to check grammatical errors in English sentences. They treat grammatical errors as pathogens and try to build antibodies that can detect such errors. One of the drawbacks in this approach is the requirement of a large *annotated* corpus. Others have skirted this area by formulating spam filters by combining language with immune algorithm based classifiers [25].

This paper proposes a paradigm shift in the manner of language processing by working out an *Idiotypic Language Network*that, when provided with *n-grams* can eventually emit new and correct sentences.

4. OVERVIEW OF IDIOTYPIC NETWORK

In an immune system the primary role of antibodies is to eliminate the antigens, which constitute foreign substances like the virus, bacteria, etc., from the body. An antibody contains a *paratope* which allows itself to attach onto the *epitope* of an antigen.

According to the *Idiotypic network theory* postulated by Jerne [7], antibodies communicate with different antibodies to form a large scale network even in the absence of antigens [26]. An antibody has its specific antigenic determinant called an *idiotope* through which it binds to the *paratope* of another antibody.The schematic diagram representing Jerne's idiotypic network [7] is shown below as Figure 1.

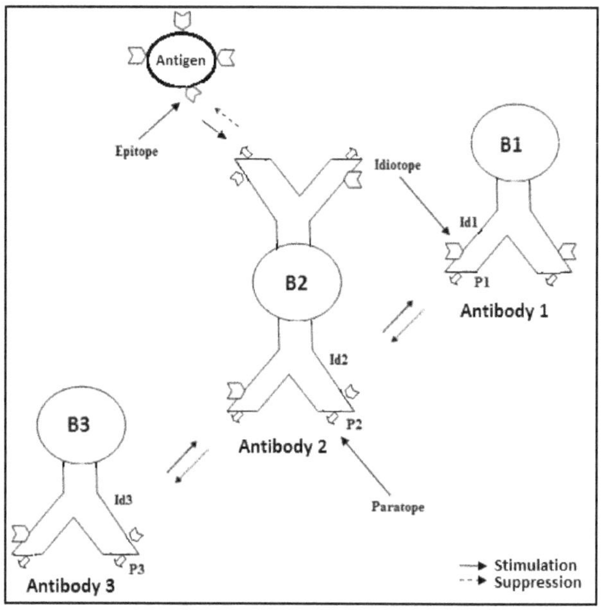

Figure 1. Jerne's Idiotypic Network [7]

The *idiotopeId1* of antibody *B1* binds to the *paratopeP2* of antibody *B2* and stimulates the latter. On the other hand, antibody *B2* recognizes *Id1* of antibody *B1* as an antigen and therefore suppresses antibody *B1*. Stimulations and suppressions between the antibodies, constitute the formation of an *idiotypic* network even in the absence of an antigen.

4.1 Modeling the idiotypic network

Farmer et. al[27] provide a mathematical model for the Idiotypic network which closely approximates its biological counterpart. The dynamics of the model consists of a set of differential equations that changes the concentration of the antibodies w.r.t stimulations and suppressions. The natural death of antibodies is also taken into account. The mathematical equation to calculate the concentration of ith antibody is given by

$$\frac{dx_i}{dt} = \sum_{j=1}^{N} M_{ji}x_j - \alpha_1 \sum_{j=1}^{N} M_{ij}x_j + \sum_{j=1}^{n} M_i y_j - \alpha_2 .x_i \quad (1)$$

where N is the number of antibodies and x_i(or x_j) is the concentration of antibody i(or j). The affinity between antibody j and antibody i is denoted by M_{ji} and the affinity between antibody i and the detected antigen is represented by M_i. The first and second terms on the R.H.S of the equation (1) denote the stimulations and suppressions from other antibodies while the third term represents the stimulation from the antigen. The fourth specifies the natural death of the antibody.

Jos'e Pacheco et. al [28] have proposed an Abstract Immune Systemalgorithm inspired by the Jerne's idiotypic network model and clonal selection wherein he ignores the antigens which results in a modified version of Farmer's equation given below –

$$\frac{dx_i}{dt} = \sum_{j=1}^{N} M_{ji}x_j - \alpha_1 \sum_{j=1}^{N} M_{ij}x_j - \alpha_2 .x_i \quad (2)$$

Researchers have employed various techniques to calculate the affinity values M_{ji} and M_i, depending on the problem at hand and the representation of entities viz. antibodies and antigens in immune algorithms. They have represented entities within, using binary strings, strings over finite set of alphabet (other than binary), real-valued vectors and even hybrid representations which contain continuous and categorical data [29].The concentrations of antibodies have been calculated using a non-linear differential equation [30]. Affinity which is the distance between two antibodies has been calculated using different algorithms such as Weighted kappa [31] and Kendall's Tau [32, 33]. Ishiguro et al. [34] have proposed a decentralized consensus-making system using Farmer's equation to calculate the concentration of affinities. The affinity values or degree of disallowance are calculated by using the following two equations.

$$M_{ji} = \frac{S_p^{Abj} + S_r^{Abi}}{S_{Abi}^{Abj}} \quad (3)$$

$$M_{ij} = \frac{S_p^{Abi} + S_r^{Abj}}{S_{Abi}^{Abj}} \quad (4)$$

where S_p^{Abj} and S_r^{Abj} denote the number of times penalty and reward signals were received when antibody Ab_j was selected. The denominator denotes the number of times when both Ab_j and Ab_i react with their specific antigens.

5. IDIOTYPIC LANGUAGE NETWORK (ILN)

5.1 A Typical ILN

In order to make the explanation simpler and lucid, we illustrate an ILN using an example. To start with, assume that a small child has heard and gathered a lexicon containing the following words as shown in Table 1. Using these words as a base, the child generates combinations that are subsequently uttered during a phase termed the training phase. The different combinations of words generated from these words could be looked upon as candidate antibodies (from the immunological perspective) and have been depicted in Figure 2.

Table 1. A small lexicon of words generated by the child

Sl. No.	Words learnt by the child
1	*went*
2	*I*
3	*home*
4	*all*
5	*alone*

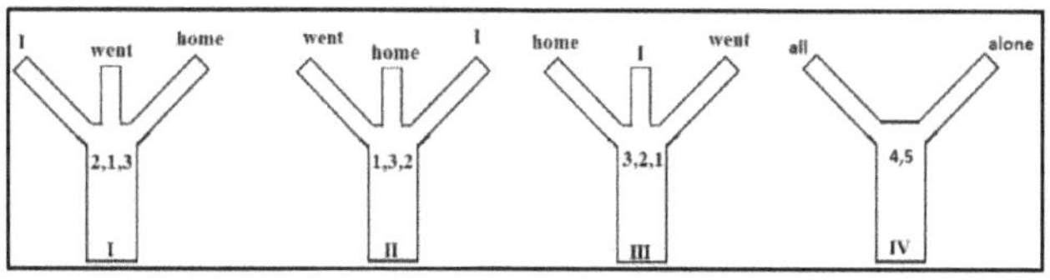

Figure 2. Randomly generated antibodies

During the training phase, the child picks antibodies randomly and utters them in some sequence. A human listener, assumed to be the tutor, verifies it and provides a reward or a penalty based on whether the sequence is correct or incorrect.

Let us now consider that the child uttered the following sequence of antibodies in the order - antibody#II followed by antibody# IV. The sequence that is generated is –

"went home Iall alone".

The tutor in turn informs that antibody#II is incorrect but antibody#IV is correct. The peers of antibody#II are I and III since they all contain the same words but in different orders. Since antibody#II is incorrect, it will be suppressed by I and III. This will ensure that amongst antibodies I, II and III, antibody#II will be selected more infrequently in subsequent times. Figure 3 represents the stimulations and suppressions that occur between the set of antibodies.

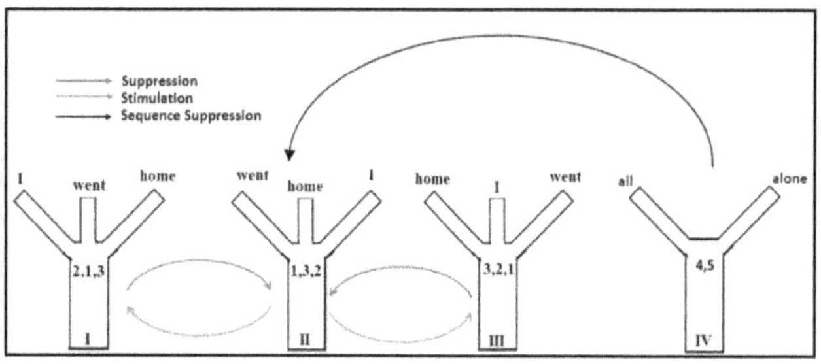

Figure 3. The stimulations and suppressions of antibodies

In Figure 3, the green coloured arrows represent the stimulations while the red ones indicate suppressions. The antibody#II is suppressed by both its peer antibodies numbered I and III as antibody#IIwas found to be incorrect. On the other hand, antibody#II stimulates both the antibodies numbered I and III. As a result, antibody#II will not be selected in the subsequent iteration as it is being suppressed and thus has effectively a lower concentration. The thick black arrow between antibody#IV and antibody#II with the arrow pointing to the latter indicates the suppression of the sequence viz. –<"*went home I*"> followed by <"*all alone*">.

Since a part of the sentence is wrong, the child once again attempts to correct the incorrect portion. If it chooses antibody# I to generate the following sequence: The sequence would then be expressed as -

I, IV →<u>*I went homeall alone*</u>

The tutor verifies and rewards the correct antibodies. This new information causes a change in the above network (Figure 3) of antibodies which is reflected in Figure 4. Here a new set of stimulations and suppressions are generated between antibodies I and III. Also since antibodies I and IV are correct, they stimulate one another which are shown by bidirectional arrows. This however means that "*I went home all alone*" and "*allalone I went home*" are correct at the moment. However, the latter will be rejected due to suppressions that will appear at a later stage when this incorrect sentence is generated.

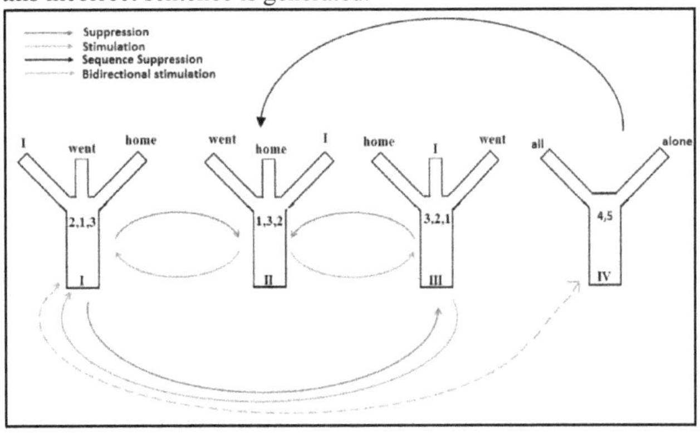

Figure 4.Addition of more stimulation and suppression links between the antibodies

At the end of the training phase, we find that an antibody network is established as a result of interactions between the antibodies. With the arrival of new antibodies which are randomly selected and created from the given lexicon, more such suppressions and stimulations will appear. It may be noted that over a period of time antibodies II, III and V will disappear since they will either be suppressed greatly (reduced concentration) or possibly because they will never be used (activated). Thus only antibodies I and IV will survive to generate two sentences viz. in the present stage of learning:

I went home.

I went home all alone.

This has been illustrated graphically in Figure 5 as an *idiotope-paratope* linkage between two antibodies.

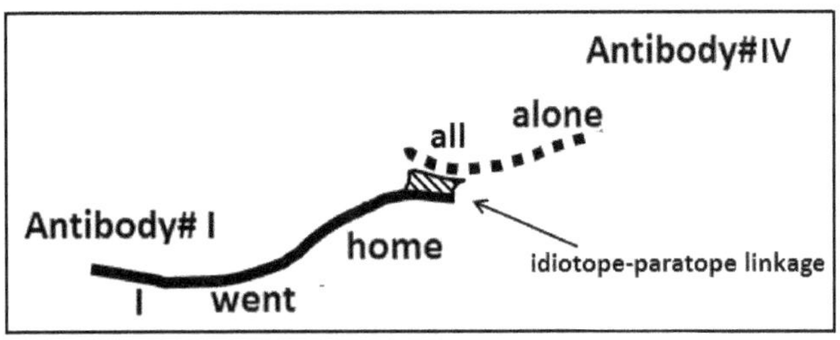

Figure 5. Two segments (antibodies)forming an *idiotope-paratope* linkage

With more words in the lexicon, the network would cater to the generation of more combinations and eventually retain only the correct ones. If we imagine the network in this manner where an antibody forms part of a sentence (a correct sequence of words) then antibodies could concatenate or adhere to parts of another antibody (*idiotope-paratope* like linkage) to make a complete and correct sentence. Thus a more complex set of sentences could be viewed as shown in Figure 6.

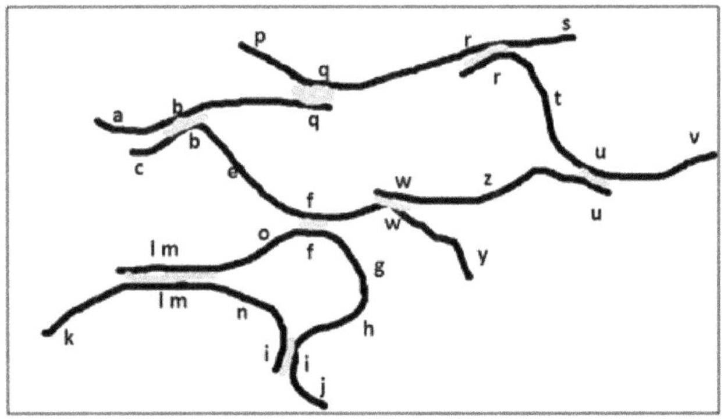

Figure 6. A complex ILN (Each alphabet designates a unique antibody viz. a word or a sequence of words)

In this figure, the green portions act as *joiners*or *bonds* or *idiotope-paratopelinkages*that fuse together two or more antibodies. Assuming the lowercase alphabet are actually valid words in the lexicon (or a sequence of words or n-grams), there could be many valid sentences that could now be generated from such a network; for e.g. *abq, abefghij, klmnij, klmofghij*and so on. The subsequent section deals with the dynamics that drive the formation and evolution of the ILN.

5.2 ILN Generation and Dynamics

The basic flow in the generation of an ILN is shown in Figure 7. Each of the components within has been described separately inthe following sections.

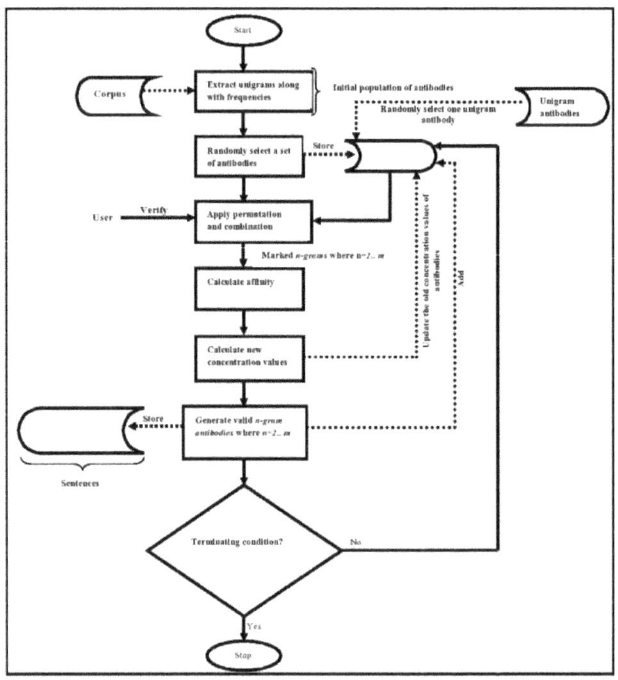

Figure 7. Architecture of the sentence generation model

a) Pre-processing: From a given corpus, unigrams are initially extracted along with their frequencies. The collection of all unigrams along with their frequencies forms the initial population of candidate antibodies and their respective concentrations.

b) Random selection of unigram antibodies: A set of random unigram antibodies are selected from the initial population. This random selection was done only to ensure that the processing time is not too high. It may be noted however that the entire population could be taken in. We thus start off by building a small ILN with this initial sub-population and eventually add more candidate antibodies to scale the derived ILN.

c) Permutation and Combination: The candidate antibodies stored in the selected population are permuted and combined in all possible ways to generate all probable *n-gram* antibodies where $n>1$. Some of the probable *n-gram* antibodies may not be correct. The user verifies the same and is appropriately marked at this stage of processing. The marked *n-gram* antibodies (both correct as well as incorrect ones) are preserved. The incorrect ones are preserved along with the correct ones because the correct *n-grams* fetch rewards whereas incorrect *n-grams* fetch penalties which are required for calculating the affinity values.

d) Affinity: The binding of an antibody to an antigen (or antibody) is known as affinity. The mutual affinity values of every marked bigram antibody with another in the same set are found. As a candidate bigram antibody is composed of two individual units i.e. unigram antibodies, each of the unigram antibodies are either rewarded or penalizedbased on their correctness. By using the reward and penalty parameters, the affinity between the antibodies is calculated. For our convenience, we have assumed that reward and penalty parameters will be represented using positive numerical values. Initially, both the reward and penalty parameters are initialized to 0. If an antibody receives a reward, the reward parameter is set to 2 otherwise the penalty parameter is set to 1. The same method is applied to calculate the affinity values for higher-order *n-gram* antibodies in the subsequent steps of the iteration. The equations (3) and (4) mentioned in sub-section 4.1 were tailored to calculate the mutual affinity values. The denominators in R.H.S. of the equations (3) and (4) term in the present context denote the degree of the strength of juxtaposition. If either antibody Ab_ifollowed by antibody Ab_jor antibody Ab_jfollowed by antibody Ab_iyield a correct bigram antibody, then theS_{Abi}^{Abj} =1. If these pairs of antibodies (Ab_i,Ab_j)followed by (Ab_j, Ab_i)generates a correct tetragram then the value of the denominator is taken to be less than unity in order to increase their mutual stimulations between the antibodies. Let us consider two randomly selected candidateantibodies viz. Ab_1=*a:12* and Ab_2=*lion:7* where Ab_1 and Ab_2 are the symbolic representations of the antibodies. The R.H.S terms are the actual unigram values along with their respective frequencies (concentrations). After permutation and combination, we get four bigram pairs namely (Ab_1, Ab_1), (Ab_1, Ab_2), (Ab_2, Ab_1) and (Ab_2, Ab_2). The pair (Ab_1, Ab_2) i.e. *a lion* is the only pair that is correct while the remaining three pairs are incorrect. Thus, for the pair (Ab_1, Ab_2), we have S_p^{Ab1}=0, S_r^{Ab1}=1, S_p^{Ab2}=0 and S_p^{Ab2}=1.By substituting the values in equations(3) and (4), we get the following affinity values M_{21} =1 and M_{12} =1. Also, we have M_{11} =1 and M_{22} =1.

e) Concentration: The affinity values are substituted in Farmer's equation to calculate the new concentration values of antibodies. The old concentration values of the antibodies are regularly updated with new ones. To make things clear, we take the same example as mentioned in sub-section 5.2 (d).By using Farmer's equation (1), the concentration values of antibodies Ab_1 and Ab_2 respectively can now be calculated. We have Ab_1 = 12, Ab_2=7, M_{12}=1, M_{21}=1, M_i=0 and y_i=0 (due to absence of antigen), $\alpha_1 = \alpha_2$ =0.1, N=2, n=0. If an antibody does not interact with any of the antibodies for a longer period of time, then its concentration value is decreased by using the death rate factor i.e. α_2. Otherwise, α_2 is ignored during the initial stages of calculation of concentrations.By replacing the values in the above equation (1), we have

$$\frac{dAb_1}{dt} = 151.2 \text{ and } \frac{dAb_2}{dt} = 152.4.$$

f) Generation of valid *n-gram* antibodies: A valid *n-gram* antibody is generated only when the probable bigram or higher-order *n-gram* antibodies are marked as correct and the individual units of the *n-gram* have concentration values higher than the pre-specified threshold. In sub-section 5.2 (e), we have seen that the new concentration values of Ab_1 and Ab_2 is 151.2 and 152.4 respectively. As the bigram pair (Ab_1, Ab_2) is correct and the concentration values of both the antibodies have increased, a new *n-gram* (bigram) antibody is generated viz. Ab_3= "*a lion*". The initial concentration value of the newly generated antibody *Ab3* is set to 1. It is likely that when Ab_3 interacts with other antibodies in future, its concentration value will increase. A copy of the newly generated *n-gram* antibody is added to the selected population of candidate antibodies. As a result the number of antibodies in the selected population increases. It now contains a mixture of unigrams and *n-gram* antibodies where $n>1$. After the completion of each iteration, again a single random antibody is selected from the initial population of the candidate antibodies and inducted into the selected population of mixed candidate antibodies. This is to introduce diversity in the selected population of candidate antibodies. Prior to induction of a new antibody, the older version of selected population of candidate antibodies has already participated in the training and has formed an ILN. The iteration continues until all the candidate antibodies in the initial population are exhausted or when the user terminates further generation.

g) Generation of New Sentences: In sub-section 5.2 (f),we have shown the process of generating new *n-gram* antibodies. An *n-gram* antibody is said to be valid if it is a syntactically and grammatically acceptable sentence or part thereof. This feature of finding valid *n-grams* is left to the user who verifies it manually. Only the grammatically *n-gram* antibodies where $n>2$ are stored separately and the collection of these *n-grams* forms the set of partial or complete sentences. The first and second term of Farmer's equation (1) represent the stimulations and suppressions from other antibodies. In section 5.2 (e), we have used Farmer's equation first to calculate the stimulation and suppression values between the antibodies and finally found the new concentration values of the antibodies. An ILN is thus formed due to the stimulations and suppressions. The ILN becomes a part of a larger network when more number ofantibodiesare introducedinto the system. Due to this reason the antibody population grows rapidly. To control the growth of the antibody population, measures are initiated to eliminate specific antibodies depending on a pre-specified threshold concentration value τ. The choice of value for τ plays a significant role. If τ is low, the rate of elimination of some candidate antibodies decreasesresulting in an increase inantibody population. A higher value ofτ increases the rate of elimination of antibodies resultingin the loss ofsome candidate antibodies that could have contributed to the construction of higher order *n-gram* antibodies. The choice of τ should be done judiciously and may requireseveral trials.The antibodies with concentration values greater than τ survive and become part of ILN.The ones having concentration values less than τ die and are thus flushed out from the network. In each of the iterations, we keep introducing a fresh supply of antibodies to the system. The existing antibodies that are part of the ILN, interact (based on the stimulations and suppressions) with these incoming antibodies. The incoming antibodies get stimulated and suppressed from other antibodies and as a result the existing ILN gets modified over the iterations.

6. RESULTS AND DISCUSSIONS

We have portrayed herein the results of the experiments based on an initial population of 80 unigram antibodies extracted from a small untagged corpus whose contents are shown in Table 2. The initial values of the parameters α_1 andα_2 wereset to 0.1.Since an antigen is absent in this case the value of $y_i$was set to 0.

Table 2. The contents of the corpus

Once upon a time there lived a lion in a forest. One day after a heavy meal, it was sleeping under a tree. After a while, there came a mouse and it started to play on the lion. Suddenly the lion got up with anger and looked for those who disturbed its nice sleep. Then it saw a small mouse standing trembling with fear. The lion jumped on it and started to kill it. The mouse requested the lion to forgive it. The lion felt pity and left it. The mouse ran away. On another day, the lion was caught in a net by a hunter. The mouse came there and cut the net. Thus it escaped. Thereafter, the mouse and the lion became friends. They lived happily in the forest afterwards. Moral: A friend in need is a friend indeed.

The list of nine randomly selected unigram antibodies along with their initial and new concentration values after six iterations of the training, are listed in Table 3. These nine antibodies comprise the selected population of candidate antibodies.

Table 3. The unigram antibodies and concentrations

Unigram antibodies	Initial concentrations (frequencies)	New concentrations calculated using equation 1
a	12	7948.674
lion	7	146117.08125
in	4	129472.252
there	4	60.8
lived	2	39.5
time	1	22.85
forest	1	22.85
upon	1	14.75
once	1	20839.359

The statistics of the number of valid *n-grams* generated at the end of the trainingare shown in Table 4. It is to be noted that these valid *n-grams* are added to the initially selected population of candidate antibodies. Thus, the updated selected population of candidate antibodies now contains a diverse population of antibodies (different types of *n-grams*).

Table 4. Statistics of *n-gram*antibodies generated after six iterations

Valid *n-gram* antibodies generated	Count
bigram antibodies	33
trigram antibodies	30
quadrigram antibodies	11
pentagram antibodies	9
hexagram antibodies	5
heptagram antibodies	3
octagram antibodies	2
n-gram (where N=9) antibodies	0
n-gram (where N=10) antibodies	1
n-gram (where N=11) antibodies	11

The partial listof correct and incorrect sentences that are generated after the training is shown in Table 5 and Table 6 respectively.

Table 5. Partial list of correct sentences generated after the training

Sl. No	Partial list of generated sentences which were correct
1	once upon a time there lived a lion in a forest
2	once in a forest there lived a lion
3	there lived a lion in a forest
4	there lived a lion
5	a lion lived in a forest
6	in a forest there lived a lion

Table 6. Partial list of incorrect sentences that are generated after the training

Sl. No	Partial list of generated sentences or portions thereof which were incorrect
1	a forest lived a lion
2	lion lived once in forest
3	there lived a forest
4	once in time a lion
5	once there forest lived a lion

When six numbersof sentences were generated from the updated selected population of candidate antibodies, a new unigram antibody was randomly selected from the initial population of candidate antibodies and added to the selected population of candidate antibodies. Table 7 and Table 8 show the list of correct and incorrect sentences generated after the addition of new unigram antibodies viz. "*was*"and "*sleeping*"with initial concentration values (frequencies) of 2 and 1 respectively.

Table 7. Partial list of correct sentences generated with the inclusion of new unigram antibodies "*was*" and "*sleeping*"

Sl. No	New unigram antibody with its initial concentration	Partial list of generated sentences which are correct
1		there was a lion
2		there was a forest
3	was:2	there was a lion in a forest
4		in a forest there was a lion
5		once upon a time there was a forest
6	sleeping:1	a lion was sleeping

Table 8. Partial list of incorrect sentences generated with the inclusion of new unigram antibodies "*was*" and "*sleeping*"

Sl. No	New unigram antibody with its initial concentration	Partial list of generated sentences which are incorrect
1	was:2	there lived a lion was in a forest
2		forest was a lion
3		once upon a time was a lion
4		once upon a time was a forest
5	sleeping:1	there lived a lion was sleeping in a forest
6		forest was sleeping
		lion in a forest was sleeping

Figure 8 shows a portion of the ILN when the whole of the corpus presented in Table 2 was used. The green bonds facilitate a change or jumping of tracks along the black lines while reading out the sentences contained in the network. The ILN is obviously yet to saturate since it carries a few incorrect sentences. By tracing out the paths of the ILN in Figure 8, we are able to generate the following sentences which are listed separately in Table 9.

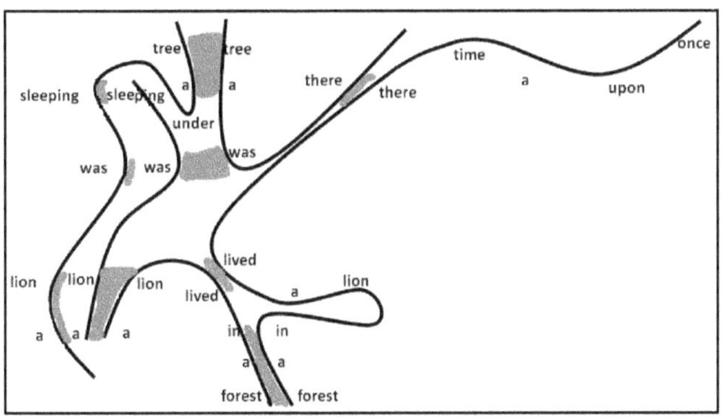

Figure 8. A portion of the ILN formed from the corpus in Table 2

Table 9. Partial list of generated sentences which were correct obtained from the ILN of Figure 8.

Sl. No	Partial list of generated sentences which were correct obtained from the ILN of Figure 8
1	once upon a time there lived a lion in a forest
2	a lion lived in a forest
3	a lion was sleeping
4	a lion was sleeping under a tree
5	once upon a time there was a tree

7. CONCLUSIONS

Using an existing corpus of words,wc have been able to generate anIdiotypicLanguage network (ILN) from initially disconnected *n-grams* that form metaphors for the antibodies.With this network, new correct sentences or parts thereof were generated. With more interaction or effective addition of new *uni-* or *n-grams* the network strengthens itself and generates newer sentences. The generation of the ILN throws light on the possible mechanism of the biologicalequivalent of the generative grammar. The verification process is currently being done by the human user who in turn delivers the reward and penalty. To make the system autonomously generate the ILN, a larger and correct corpus could be used for such verification. The generated sentences or parts thereof could be verified for their correctness if they exist within this larger corpus. This would be analogous to how a child who continuously reads several books (the larger and correct corpus) gains in his/her sentence generation capability.In future, we intend to emulate and use this immuno-inspired approach in a distributed manner as described in [35] to enable the system to learn and converge faster.

8. REFERENCES

[1] Rosenfeld, R. 2000. Two decades of statistical language modeling: where do we go from here?, Proceedings of the IEEE, 88(8), 1270-1288.

[2] Jurafsky, D. and Martin, J. H. 2009. Speech and Language Processing: An Introduction to Natural Language Processing, Speech Recognition, and Computational Linguistics, 2nd edition, Prentice-Hall.

[3] Sleator, D and Temperley, D. 1991. Parsing English with a link grammar. Technical Report CMU-CS-91-196, Computer Science Department, Carnegie Mellon University, Pittsburgh,PA.

[4] Lafferty, J. D, Sleator, D. and Temperley, D. 1992. Grammatical trigrams: a probabilistic model of link grammar. In Proceedings of the AAAI Fall Symposium on Probabilistic Approaches to Natural language, Cambridge, MA.

[5] Chen, S. F. and Goodman, J. T. 1999.An empirical study of smoothing techniques for language modeling. Computer, Speech and Language.

[6] Waterfall, H.R., Sandbank, B., Luca Onnis, L. and Edelman, S. 2010. An empirical generative framework for computational modeling of language acquisition. Journal of Child Language, 37, 671-703.

[7] Jerne, N. K. 1974. Towards a network theory of the immune system. Ann. Immunol. Paris, 125C, 373.

[8] Knight, Chris, Kennedy, M. S. and Hurford, J. 2000. Editors. The evolutionary emergence of language: Social function and the origins of linguistic form, Cambridge: Cambridge University Press.

[9] Hurford, James, Kennedy, M. S. and Knight, C. 1998 Editors. Approaches to the evolution of language, Cambridge: Cambridge University Press.

[10] Steklis, H. and Harnad, S. 1976. From hand to mouth: Some critical stages in the evolution of language Editors. Origins and Evolution of Language and Speech. Annals of the New York Academy of Sciences, Volume 280, pages 445—455.

[11] Cangelosi A. andParisi D. 2002. Computer simulation: A new scientific approach to the study of language evolution. In: Cangelosi A, Parisi D, editors. Simulating the evolution of language. Springer; London, pp. 3–28.

[12] Chomsky, N. 1972. Language and Mind. San Diego, Harcourt Brace Jovanovich.

[13] Slobin, D. I. 1979. Psycholinguistics. Gelnview, Illinois, Scott, Foresman and Company.

[14] Pinker, S. 1994. The Language Instinct, Penguin.

[15] Bickerton, D. 1990. Species and Language. Chicago, Chicago University Press.

[16] Pinker, S. and Bloom, P. 1992. Natural Language and Natural Selection. In The Adapted Mind. J. H. Barkow, L. Cosmides and J. Tooby (Eds.), Oxford University Press.

[17] Elman, J. L. 1999. The Emergence of Language: A Conspiracy Theory. In The Emergence of Language. B. MacWhinney (Ed.). Mahwah, New Jersey, Lawrence Erlbaum Associates: 1-28.

[18] Kirby, S. 1998. Fitness and the Selective Adaptation of Language. In Approaches to the Evolution of Language. J. R. Hurford, M. Studdert-Kennedy and C. Knight (Eds.), Cambridge University Press: 359-383.

[19] Cavalli-Sforza, L. L. and Feldman, M. W. 1978. Towards a Theory of Cultural Evolution. Interdisciplinary Review 3: 99-107.

[20] Peng, F. 2001. The sparse data problem in statistical language modeling and unsupervised word segmentation. PhD proposal, http://citeseer.ist.psu.edu/489036.html.

[21] Nadkarni, P.M, Ohno-Machado, L. and Chapman, W.W. 2011. Natural language processing: an introduction. J Am Med Inform Assoc. 18(5):544–51,DOI=http://10.1136/amiajnl-2011-000464.

[22] Zheng J, Chen Y. and Zhang W. 2010. A survey of artificial immune applications, Artificial Intelligence Review, Springer, Volume 34, Issue 1, pp 19-34.

[23] Kumar, A. and Nair, S. B. 2007. Artificial Immune Systems, 6th International Conference, ICARIS 2007, Santos, Brazil, Proceedings. Lecture Notes in Computer Science 4628, Springer, ISBN 978-3-540-73921-0 pp. 348 – 357.

[24] Forrest, S., Perelson, A., Allen, L. andCherukuri, R. 1994. Selfnonself discrimination in a computer. Proceedings of the IEEE Symposium on Security and Privacy, IEEE Computer Society Press, Los Alamitos.

[25] Yue, X., Abraham, A., Chi, Z-X., Hao, Y. Y. and Mo, H. 2007. Artificial immune system inspired behavior-based anti-spam filter, Soft Computing, 11, pp. 729-740.

[26] de Castro and L.N., Timmis, J. 1992. Artificial immune systems: A new computational intelligence approach, Springer, London.

[27] Farmer, J.D, Packard, N.H. and Perelson, A.S. 1986. The immune system, adaptation, and machine learning,Physica, vol. 22, pp. 187-204.

[28] Pacheco, J and Costa, J.F. 2007. The abstract immune system algorithm, 6th International Conference on Unconventional Computation, Kingston, Canada.

[29] Hart, E and Ross, P. 2005. The impact of the shape of antibody recognition regions on the emergence of idiotypic networks, International JournalofUnconventional Computing, 1 (3), pp. 281–313.

[30] Dipankar, D. and Fernando, N. 2008. Immunological Computation: Theory and Applications, Auerbach Publications.

[31] Harmer, P. G, Williams, P. D., Gnush and Lamont, G. 2002. An artificial immune system architecture for computer security applications. IEEE Transaction on Evolutionary Computation, 6(3), 252–280.

[32] Percus, J. K., Percus, O. E. and Perelson, A. S. 1993. Predicting the size of the T-cell receptor and antibody combining region from consideration of efficient self-nonself discrimination. Proceedings of National Academy of Sciences USA 90, Las Vegas, pp. 1691–1695.

[33] Balthrop, J. F., Esponda, Forrest S. and Glickman, M. 2002. Coverage and generalization in an artificial immune system. Proceedings of the Genetic and Evolutionary Computation Conference (GECCO 2002), pp. 3–10, Morgan Kaufmann Publishers, New York.

[34] Ishiguro, A., Shirai, Y., Kondo, T. and Uchikawa, Y. 1996. Immunoid: An architecture for behavior arbitration based on the immune networks, Proc. Int. Conf. Intelligent Robotics and Systems, pp.1730 -1738.

[35] Jha, S.S., Shrivastava, K. and Nair, S.B. 2013. On Emulating Real-world Distributed Intelligence using Mobile Agent based Localized Idiotypic Networks, The First International Conference on Mining Intelligence and Knowledge Exploration (MIKE 2013), Virudhunagar, India, Springer International Publishing, LNAI, Vol. 8284, pp. 487-498.

Distinguishing Adaptive Search From Random Search in Robots and T cells

G. Matthew Fricke
Computer Science Dept.
The University of New Mexico
Albuquerque, NM USA
mfricke@cs.unm.edu

Sarah R. Black
Dept. of Mathematics
The University of New Mexico
Albuquerque, NM USA
sarblack92@gmail.com

Joshua P. Hecker
Computer Science Dept.
The University of New Mexico
Albuquerque, NM USA
jhecker@cs.unm.edu

Judy L. Cannon
Dept. of Molecular Genetics and Microbiology
and Dept. of Pathology
The University of New Mexico
Albuquerque, NM USA
jucannon@salud.unm.edu

Melanie E. Moses
Depts. of Computer Science and of Biology
The University of New Mexico
Albuquerque, NM USA
Santa Fe Institute
melaniem@cs.unm.edu

ABSTRACT

In order to trigger an adaptive immune response, T cells move through lymph nodes (LNs) searching for dendritic cells (DCs) that carry antigens indicative of infection. We hypothesize that T cells adapt to cues in the LN environment to increase search efficiency. We test this hypothesis by identifying locations that are visited by T cells more frequently than a random model of search would suggest. We then test whether T cells that visit such locations have different movement patterns than other T cells. Our analysis suggests that T cells do adapt their movement in response to cues that may indicate the locations of DC targets. We test the ability of our method to identify frequently visited sites in T cells and in a swarm of simulated iAnt robots evolved to search using a suite of biologically-inspired behaviours. We compare the movement of T cells and robots that repeatedly sample the same locations in space with the movement of agents that do not resample space in order to understand whether repeated sampling alters movement. Our analysis suggests that specific environmental cues can be inferred from the movement of T cells. While the precise identity of these cues remains unknown, comparing adaptive search strategies of robots to the movement patterns of T cells lends insights into search efficiency in both systems.

Categories and Subject Descriptors

I.2.9 [**Artificial Intelligence**]: Robots—*Autonomous vehicles*; F.2.2 [**Theory of Computation**]: Nonnumerical Algorithms and Problems—*Sorting and searching*

GECCO '15, July 11 - 15, 2015, Madrid, Spain

DOI: http://dx.doi.org/10.1145/2739480.2754794

Keywords

swarm robotics; robot search; immunological search; evolutionary computation

1. INTRODUCTION

Identifying algorithms and behaviours for effective distributed search without centralized coordination is a challenging computational problem, particularly important for distributed systems such as wireless sensor networks and swarm robotics. Complex biological systems have evolved spectacularly successful decentralized collective search, exemplified by ant colonies and immune systems. Ant colonies with millions of individuals collectively forage in dynamic landscapes without hierarchy or centralized control; their decentralized foraging strategies have dominated resource consumption in challenging and dynamic environments across the globe for over 100 million years [22]. Immune systems comprised of trillions of cells differentiated into dozens of cell types are forced by an evolutionary arms race to rapidly find and eradicate previously unseen pathogens, with each cell acting independently of any centralized controller.

A goal of artificial immune systems is to emulate biological strategies in computational systems; however, the mechanisms that generate adaptive biological search are not always well understood. In this paper we use computational tools to infer whether certain cells of the immune system search randomly or whether they adapt to their search environment to search more efficiently. We then compare movement patterns during search in the immune system to decentralized search in robotic swarms whose behaviour was inspired by foraging ants. Our robots adapt to sensed features of their environment to improve search efficiency. Here we ask whether T cells similarly adapt to features of their environment during search. By studying both systems in the same framework, we gain insights into distributed search in both immunology and swarm robotics. Additionally, we improve our understanding of the movement patterns of searching T cells, thereby identifying potential mechanisms for distributed search in robotics.

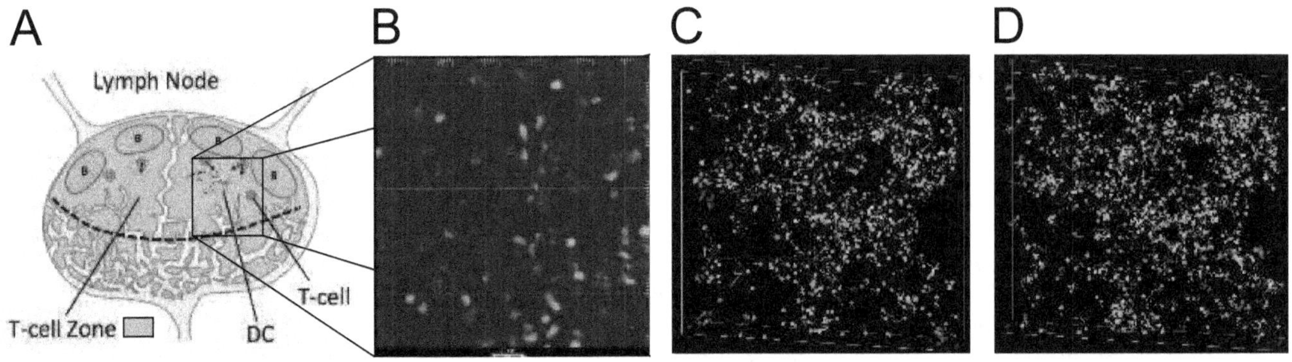

Figure 1: A) Diagram of a LN with T cell zone shown in blue. B) Observation field. 350 × 350 × 70μm 2PM image of a region in the T cell zone with T cells tagged with red and green dyes. C) Observed T cell tracks; simulated DCs are in cyan (discovered) and magenta (undiscovered), all other colours are T cell tracks. D) The model generated set of tracks; starting positions are the same as the observed T cells.

1.1 T cell Search for DCs in LNs

In this paper, we focus on a search process which is crucial for the initiation of an adaptive immune response: the search for antigen-bearing dendritic cells (DCs) by T cells in LNs. In order to mount an effective immune response, T cells must be activated in LNs (Fig.1A). Antigens are markers that identify particular pathogens, and each T cell matches a particular set of antigens. A DC presenting an antigen indicates that the corresponding pathogen has been encountered in the organism's tissues. T cell interactions with DCs displaying cognate antigen are necessary to trigger an adaptive immune response [15].

To facilitate T cell activation, T cells and DCs interact within the T cell zone of LNs. The T cell zone is on the order of 1 mm^3 in the inguinal mouse LNs we analyse. T cells and DCs are on the order of 10 μm in diameter, so each T cell must search a space 1 million times its own volume in each lymph node. In secondary lymphoid organs, DCs usually comprise between 1% and 5% of the T cell zone's total cell population. Each T cell interacts with as many DCs as possible in order to maximize the probability of detecting a matching antigen [17]. This imposes the need for efficient random search to mount an effective immune response.

Early response to infection depends on the rate at which DCs are encountered by T cells in the lymph node. The adaptive immune system is in an evolutionary arms race against an exponentially-growing pathogen population. That evolutionary pressure selects for efficient detection of, and response to, infection [11]. Therefore we hypothesise that evolutionary pressure has produced an efficient mechanism for bringing T cells and DCs together, providing a model that can be used for random robotic search and in which we can explore the efficiency of the observed T cell search.

Two-photon microscopy (2PM) has allowed a revolution in the observation and tracking of cell movement in intact tissues. We use 2PM to study T cell movement in a LN that has been excised from a mouse. In this ex vivo experiment, T cells remain alive and motile and their movement is visualized with 2PM. Laser light scanning through the ex vivo LN cause molecules bound to T cells to fluoresce at a particular wavelength. These fluorescence signals are are localized in 3-dimensions producing a position in space and time for individual T cells. Knowing the positions of T cells and the frame rate of image capture, we can also calculate T cell speeds and step lengths.

1.2 Adaptive and Stochastic Search Strategies

While 2PM provides abundant T cell movement data, it can be difficult to determine whether cells are responding to local information or are employing a purely stochastic search strategy. We describe a method of analysing search patterns in T cells that allows us to distinguish adaptive search from purely stochastic search.

Stochastic spatial search is a task common to biological and engineered agents. In environments where target distributions are unknown or change over time randomized search strategies are more effective than deterministic strategies [1, 19]. Here we identify two kinds of non-deterministic search strategies: adaptive strategies that change in response to features of their environment and purely stochastic strategies that do not. Searchers employing an adaptive strategy sample the distribution of targets as they are encountered and use the information gained to create an informed search strategy. For example *Escherichia coli* couple their flagella motility and sensors through an integrative feedback loop in their signal transduction network. This causes *E. coli* to either *tumble* or *run* in space depending on whether they are moving up or down a chemoattractant gradient. As a result *E. coli* tend to move to, and remain in, the most resource rich parts of their environment [3].

Searchers using purely stochastic strategies form a pattern of movement by sampling from probability density functions (PDFs) that govern turning angles and step lengths. For example, *Paenibacillus dendritiformis* posess internal clocks that allow changes in direction independent of environmental cues [4]. Viswanathan et al. characterized the movement of *Diomedea exulans* [21], and Humphries et al. described *Thalassarche melanophrys* [13] searching for pelagic prey as statistically driven, where the pattern of motion is fractal, that is the distribution of step lengths is similar at all scales, defined as a Lévy flight. Such search patterns are provably optimal when targets are rare and are not permanently depleted when discovered.

Motion in general can be described as a sequence of positions over time. We define *step length* to be the shortest distance between positions after merging all positions where the angle turned since the last position is less than 15°.

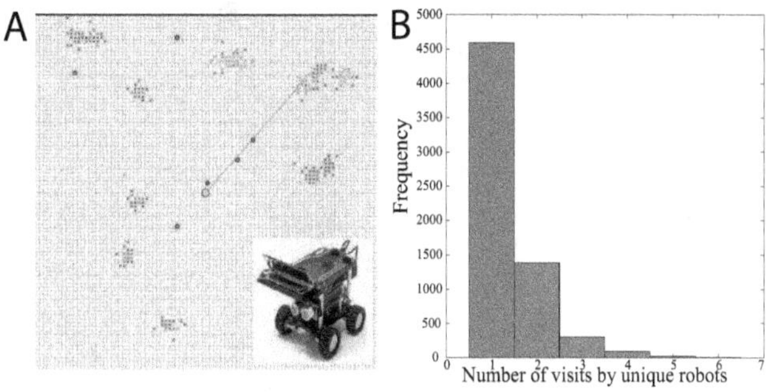

Figure 2: A) An image of an iAnt robot (inset) and a simulation of 6 iAnts foraging for clustered targets. B) Distribution of the number of different iAnt robots that visit each 8 cm^2 grid cell during the search phase of simulated foraging.

The mean squared displacement of a simple random walk (Brownian motion) grows as the square root of time and on 2-dimensional surfaces Brownian motion is space filling [20]. The result is a pattern of motion that is very *thorough* in that it visits all nearby locations eventually, but expands the search area (*extent*) relatively slowly. In contrast Lévy walks are less thorough but they are superdiffusive with displacement exceeding that of Brownian motion until the limit of ballistic (straight line) motion is reached. Brownian motion is therefore more efficient at finding local, densely packed targets. Lévy walks tend to be more efficient when targets are sparsely distributed in space [21]. The optimal tradeoff between thoroughness and extent depends, in part, on the distribution of targets.

Harris et al. [9] describe the movement patterns of T cells searching for *Toxoplasma gondii* and find that they are consistent with a Lévy flight. Our prior analysis of T cell movement in the LN also suggested a Lévy pattern of search, however more detailed analysis of additional data suggests the pattern of motion of T cells searching for DCs is a combination of a correlated random walk (CRW), and steps drawn from a lognormal PDF.

1.3 iAnt Robot Swarms

iAnt robots swarms provide a platform for experiments in biological search in an embodied robotic system [14]. iAnts are built from commodity parts including an ultrasonic rangefinder, a compass, and 2 cameras. An Arduino Uno microcontroller and iPod touch provide for onboard computation and sensor integration. (Fig. 2A, inset).

The robots implement an ant-inspired central place foraging algorithm (CPFA) that mimic colonies of seed-harvester ants using a combination of individual memory and pheromone trails to efficiently collect clustered resources and carry them to a central nest. The iAnt CPFA is based in field observations of seed harvester ants [5]. iAnt behaviour has several phases, including, and of primary significance to this work, adaptive and uninformed statistical random search phases. An agent-based simulation replicates the movement and sensing capabilities of these robots. A genetic algorithm (GA) evolves parameters that control the sensitivity threshold for triggering behaviours, the likelihood of transitioning from one behaviour to another, and the length of time each behaviour should last. In this work we analyse data from a simulation, which is carefully parametrised to reflect the behaviour, sensing, and navigation error of physical iAnt robots [10].

2. METHODS

2.1 T cell Observations

Lymph nodes (LNs) were prepared according to the protocol described previously by Matheu, Parker and Cahalan [16]. T cells were purified by nylon wool according to Allenspach et al. [2] and labelled with fluorescent dyes, and then between 5 and 10 million labelled T cells were injected intravenously into recipient mice. Fifteen to 18 hours later, after T cells migrated into LNs, the inguinal LNs were removed and recorded using two-photon microscopy (2PM). Imaging experiments were performed using the methods described in Fricke at al. [6]. This observation (Fig. 1B) provides the data needed to develop a statistical model of T cell search, informed the simulations of T cells search (Fig. 1D), and allow us to detect deviations between observation and simulation. We detail the analysis of the movement of 438 T cell tracks, consisting of 11,951 positions, in one experimental observation of a LN. We also provide summary statistics that characterize T cell movement in an additional 40 experimental LN observations.

2.2 T cell Model

In other work we built a simulation in which T cells move stochastically and match the statistical properties of observed T cell motion. Simulated T cells moved using a purely stochastic search derived from fitting probability density functions (PDFs) to the the observed T cell tracks using maximum likelihood estimation (MLE). Here the simulation serves as the null model (H_0) in which T cells do not adapt to their environment. The simulation is implemented as a continuous (floating-point) 3D model written in C++. Our observations have an average volume of 6.3×10^6 µm^3. T cell tracks were observed and recorded as 3D coordinate sequences within a bounding box defined by the visible section of the ex vivo lymph node. Simulations of the observed field were repeated 10 times. Searchers in the idealized model start at the same initial positions as the observed T cells, and exist in a volume equal to the observed field volume (Fig. 1). Each T cell track in a simulated field corresponded to a T cell track in the observed field. T cells in the simulated field were constrained to move a total distance equal to the distance covered by the observed T cells. A T cell was considered to have encountered a DC if the distance between a T cell and a DC was less than 10 µm. T cells and DCs were modelled as spheres with diameter 10 µm.

2.3 Identifying Hot Spots

The field was discretised into 8000 µm^3 voxels (the length of a voxel is 20 µm, approximately twice the diameter of a T cell). For each voxel in the field, we count how many times that location was visited by distinct T cell tracks. We defined *hot spots* as locations that are visited by more T cell tracks than would be predicted by the null model (H_0).

Hot spots were determined by the following method. We calculated the number of unique track visits to each location in each simulation, repeating the simulation of the observed LN 10 times. We then took the average of the maximum number of unique track visits to locations over the simulations. This is the H_0 prediction for the maximum number of visits to any location using a purely stochastic search. Let x be the maximum number of visits predicted by H_0. The locations in the observed LN were filtered so that only locations visited more than x times were identified as hot spots. Fig. 3A shows the distribution of the number of unique T cells that step into each voxel for the 10 simulations of one LN and the empirical observation from that same LN. In the LN shown in Fig. 3, any location visited 8 times or more was identified as a hot spot.

T cell tracks that visit any hot spot at any time during the observation were identified as hot tracks. We call all other tracks cold tracks.

2.4 Search in Robot Swarms

In this paper we analyse data from simulated iAnts, focusing on one aspect of adaptive iAnt foraging behaviour: robot movement during the search phase of foraging. iAnts have 2 search modalities: informed and uninformed correlated random walks (CRWs).

Search using an *uninformed walk*: the robot has no information about the location of targets. In this case it searches using a correlated random walk with fixed step size and direction θ_t at time t, defined by Equation 1:

$$\theta_t = \mathcal{N}(\theta_{t-1}, \sigma) \quad (1)$$

Where $\mathcal{N}(\mu, \sigma)$ is a Gaussian PDF with mean, μ, and standard deviation, σ. The standard deviation, σ, determines how correlated the direction of the next step is with the direction of the previous step. Robots initially search for resources using an uninformed correlated random walk, where σ is assigned a fixed value in Equation 2:

$$\sigma \leftarrow \omega \quad (2)$$

where the value of ω is evolved to maximize foraging efficiency by a genetic algorithm (GA).

Search using an *informed walk*: If the robot is informed about the location of resources (because of its own memory of previously discovered targets or because of pheromone communication from another robot), it searches using an informed CRW, where the standard deviation σ is defined by Equation 3:

$$\sigma = \omega + (4\pi - \omega)e^{-\lambda_{id} t} \quad (3)$$

The standard deviation of the successive turning angles of the informed random walk decays as a function of time t, producing an initially undirected and localized search that becomes more correlated over time. This time decay allows the robot to search thoroughly where it expects to find targets, but also to straighten its path, increase displacement, and so search more broadly if a target is not found. If the robot discovers a target, it transitions to sensing the local target density. The higher the local density of targets the higher the probability that the iAnt transitions to using an informed rather than an uninformed CRW.

2.5 iAnt GA and Experimental Design

We evolved a population of 100 simulated robot swarms for 100 generations, though convergence consistently occurred in fewer generations. Fitness was defined as the number of targets detected by the robot swarm in one hour of simulated time. We used the recombination and mutation described in our previous work [14]. Parameters were randomly initialized using independent samples for each swarm. Robots within a swarm used identical parameters throughout the hour-long simulation. During each generation of the GA, all 100 swarms underwent 8 fitness evaluations, each with different random placements of 256 targets into 4 clusters. A new random placement of targets was performed for each fitness evaluation.

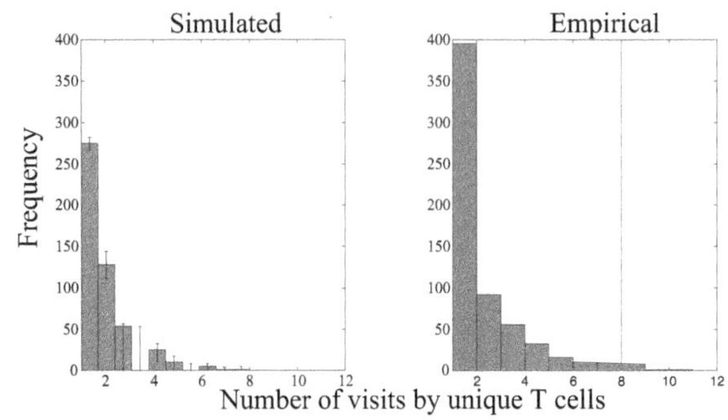

Figure 3: Distribution of the number of unique T cells that visit each of 800 voxels in space A) averaged over 10 simulations (standard deviations shown as error bars) and B) empirically in 1 observation window of a LN. Sites visited 10 or more times (indicated by the red line) are considered frequently visited hot spots.

At the end of each generation, the fitness of each swarm was the sum total of targets collected in the 8 runs of a generation. Deterministic tournament selection with replacement (tournament size = 2) was used to select 99 candidate swarm pairs. Each pair was recombined using uniform crossover and 10% Gaussian mutation with fixed standard deviation (0.05) to produce a new swarm population. We used elitism to copy the swarm with the highest fitness, unaltered, to the new population – the resulting 100 swarms made up the next generation.

We used the highest fitness parameter set from 10 runs of the GA to determine parameters in Equations 1, 2 and 3. We then ran experiments in simulation to generate iAnt movement data which we analysed and compared to T cell movement. All experiments were simulations of 6 iAnt robots searching for 256 targets arranged into 4 clusters. Physical iAnts have an $8\,\text{cm}^2$ detection area and explored a $100\,\text{m}^2$ area for 1 h. The simulated arena reproduces these dimensions.

3. RESULTS

3.1 Analysis of T cell Hot Spots

Our goal is to identify whether T cells modify their movement in response to local features of the lymph node (LN) environment, and if so, if those modifications appear to be adapted to increase search efficiency. First we identify hot spots that are visited by T cells more frequently than is expected by our null model. This expectation is produced by 10 repeated simulations that contain no adaptive movement (Fig. 3). We then characterize the movement of the T cell tracks that visit those hot spots to determine if T cells visiting hot spots move differently than T cells that do not visit hot spots.

The counts of unique T cells visiting each voxel are shown in Fig. 3. The hot spots of one LN along with the T cells that visited those hot spots are visualized in Fig. 4.

We calculated the step length distribution of the T cells

Table 1: **Comparison of the distribution of step lengths of hot T cell tracks (those that visit hot spots) and cold tracks (those that do not visit hot spots).** In order to compare the 514 hot tracks to the 4,998 cold tracks we randomly select five sets of 514 uniformly chosen tracks and show the 95% confidence interval (CI) for each cold track statistic. Bold table columns indicate hot track statistics (the median, variance, skew and kurtosis) that are outside of the 95% CI of cold tracks. While the mean step length for hot tracks does not fall out of the cold track 95% CI, the significantly smaller variance, skew and kurtosis of hot tracks reinforce that hot tracks are less heavy tailed than cold tracks and therefore exhibit a more Brownian pattern of motion.

	Mean	Median	Variance	Skew	Kurtosis
Hot Tracks	2.84 μm	**2.12 μm**	**8.71 μm²**	**5.37**	**54.8**
Cold Tracks	3.01±0.67 μm	1.71±0.0979 μm	182±129 μm²	17.2 ± 6.3	332 ± 221

Table 2: **Comparison of the distribution of step lengths of informed iAnts (those revisiting known resource locations) and uninformed iAnts (those searching without knowledge of resource locations).** The informed tracks have mean and median step lengths that are shorter than the 95% CI of uninformed tracks, while the variance, skew and kurtosis of hot tracks are within the 95% CI of uninformed tracks.

	Mean	Median	Variance	Skew	Kurtosis
Informed Tracks	**1.95 m**	**1.7 m**	2.6 m²	1.29	5.03
Uninformed Tracks	2.84±0.16 m	2.83±0.133 m	2.45±1.2 m²	1.08 ± 0.617	5.42 ± 1.18

that visit hot spots (shown in color in Fig. 4) and those that do not visit any hot spots (in gray).

T cell steps lengths are constructed by converting a sequence of positions in a T cell track into a sequence of vectors. For a particular track the angle between all consecutive vectors is calculated. Points at the intersection of vectors with angles of less than 15° are removed. The euclidean distance between remaining points is calculated to yield step lengths. Thus a step length is defined as persistent motion without deviation of more than 15°.

Longer step lengths indicate tracks that move in a persistent direction, while short step lengths indicate frequent turns (greater than 15 degrees). Tracks with a more symmetrical, closer to Gaussian, distribution of step lengths indicate Brownian motion which achieves a more thorough search of a local area, while a more skewed step length distribution is indicative of a Lévy walk which searches more broadly.

While Fig. 3 and Fig. 4 show data from only one LN, we increase our statistical power by repeating our hot spot analysis independently for each of 41 experimental observations of LN. The threshold for hot spots is specific to each observation because it depends on the number and initial location of T cells in each LN. We find that 14 of those 41 observations contain hot spots. We analyse the movement of the 514 hot T cell tracks, with 15,717 positions, in all 14 of those observations and 4,998 cold cell tracks, consisting of 157,193 positions, in Fig. 5.

Fig. 5 shows the distribution of step sizes for hot and cold T cell tracks. While the mean step length is similar for both classes of T cells, there is more skew in the cold tracks, suggesting more Lévy-like movement in cold tracks and more thorough Brownian search in hot tracks. The statistical differences between hot and cold T cell tracks are summarized in Table 1: the variance, skew and kurtosis of hot track step lengths are significantly smaller than the 95% confidence interval of cold track step lengths, indicating more Brownian motion in hot tracks.

Brownian motion around the hot spots is also suggested visually in Fig. 4. However not all T cells that visit hot spots have searched thoroughly. Instead, several relative straight paths are visible through the hot spots. Some of those cells travel straight into the hot spots and then search more thoroughly, and others appear to pass through the hot spots without stopping. Additionally, there are other locations not near identified hot spots where cells move in more Brownian motion. Thus, while there appears to be a trend toward more Brownian motion near hot spots, T cell tracks move in various ways, both near hot spots and away from hot spots.

3.2 Analysis of iAnt Robot Movement

While our analysis suggests more Brownian motion of T cells visiting hot spots, some cells in Fig. 4 wander across the hot spot with more persistent directional motion. To calibrate our hot spot detection approach, and to better understand how well differences in movement can be resolved, we conduct similar analysis of simulated iAnt robot data in which we can identify locations with search targets, and we can identify different behavioral states that govern movement.

Fig. 2B shows the distribution of the number of iAnt visits to each location in space: most cells are visited by only 1 iAnt, but a very small number of cells are visited by 5 or 6 iAnts. The distribution is highly skewed, similar to the distribution of T cell visits in Fig. 3B. The distribution of simulated non-adaptive T cells in Fig. 3A is also skewed, but less so.

Figures 6 and 7 show analysis of iAnt robot movement as they search for resources in their environment. In Fig. 6, we show locations visited by iAnts, in this case using a heatmap with red and yellow sites visited by the most iAnts, and blue and green sites visited by fewer iAnts. Superimposed on top of these hot spots are the clusters of tags for which the iAnts were searching.

Fig. 7 shows the step length distribution of iAnts as they search for targets using two different correlated random walk (CRW). Fig. 7 panel A shows iAnts searching in locations known to have resources (informed iAnts using Eqn. 3) while

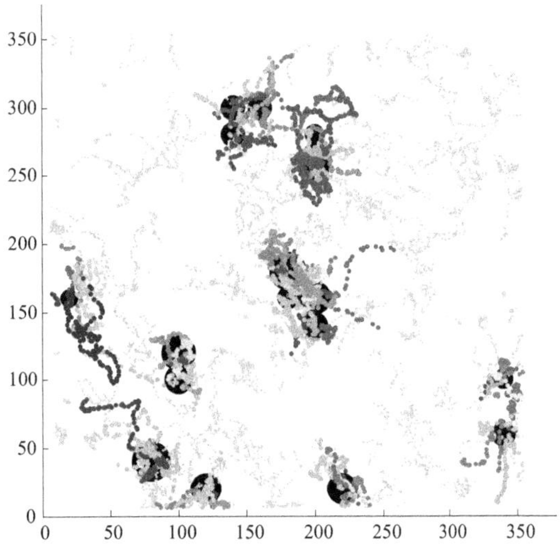

Figure 4: T cell tracks and hot spots from one observed LN. Black circles show hot spots, with circle size indicating the number of unique T cell tracks that visit that location. 124 T cells that visit hot spots are shown in colours (each track a different color) and 313 T cells that do not visit hot spots are shown in gray.

panel B shows iAnts searching at random without any information about resource locations (uninformed iAnts moving according to Eqn. 2).

For iAnts the difference in movement patterns between informed and uninformed search is evident in the statistically lower mean and median of the step length distribution (summarized in Table 2.) While informed iAnts take smaller steps, unlike T cells, the shape of the distribution is not different – the variance, skew and kurtosis of the step lengths of informed iAnts are within the 95% CI of uninformed iAnts.

Thus, iAnts that visit hot spots and T cells that revisit resource locations have different movement than iAnts and T cells that don't visit hot spots or known resource locations. However iAnts and T cells both differ in the distribibution of steps. In T cells this is reflected int the more Gaussian distribution of steps with a higher mean step length which in iAnts the step lengths become shorter.

4. CONCLUSIONS

We have identified hot spots as locations in the lymph node (LN) that are visited by T cells more often than would be expected by chance. T cells that visit those hot spots move differently: the distribution of step lengths is more normally distributed, indicative of more Brownian motion, while distribution of step lengths for other T cells is more skewed (potentially indicative of a Lévy walk) so that there is a greater chance of T cells taking a long step in a persistent direction. The more Brownian motion of T cells that visit hot spots may indicate more thorough local search, while the heavier-tailed distributions of T cells that do not visit hot spots suggests that those T cells move more broadly, perhaps searching for dispersed targets. These results demonstrate that T cells react to their environment in non-random ways, and more specifically, they suggest that T cells that visit hot spots search more thoroughly.

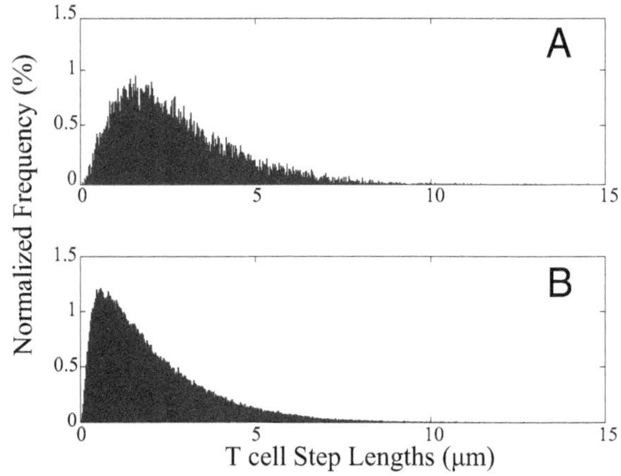

Figure 5: A) Step length distribution for T cell hot tracks and B) cold tracks.

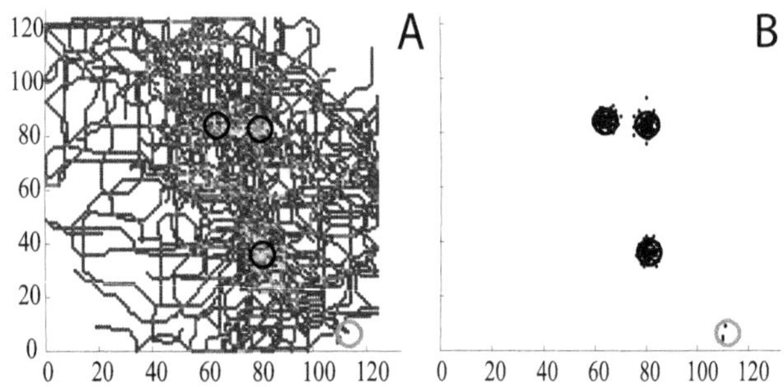

Figure 6: iAnt Search Pattern. A) iAnt tracks of six robots searching for tags. Blue spots were visited by 1 robot, red spots by 6 robots. B) The location of target clusters. Black circles indicate exploited targets. The grey circle correponds to a target cluster that was encountered but not exploited. Grid units are 8 cm.

The differences in the statistical properties of steps produced by T cells visiting hot spots and those that do not, suggest that T cells may adapt to an external cue in the environment to modify their search pattern. It is possible that T cells search more thoroughly when coming into direct contact with a dendritic cell (DC) or an high endothelial venule (HEV) (around which DCs tend to be clustered [8]), or they may respond to a chemical signal or chemokine released by DCs, HEVs or some other feature of the LN.

Given that T cells are selected to repeatedly contact DCs, and that DCs are often clustered in space (likely near the HEVs through which T cells enter the LN [8]), T cells that search areas with DCs more thoroughly may have more repeated contacts as well as contacts with more DCs.

An alternative explanation for hot spots could be that T cells are tracking fibroblastic reticular cells (FRCs), however, the more Brownian search around these points suggests that the tracks are searching thoroughly, not travelling along structures in the LN.

Our hypotheses about T cells are supported by our analysis of the movement of iAnt robots. iAnt movement is

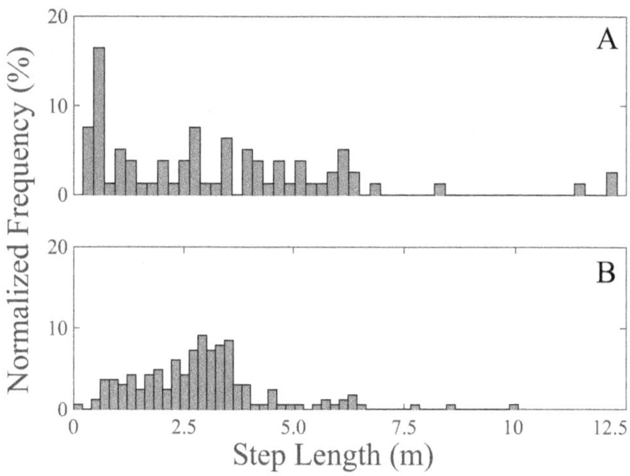

Figure 7: A) iAnts that are re-visiting previously identified tag locations. B) Step length distribution for iAnts that are searching randomly without information about previously identified tag locations. Each histogram divides the region between the minimum and maximum values into 50 equally spaced bins. The bar heights correspond to observed frequency normalized so that the sum over bars equals 100%.
.

governed by a set of ant-inspired search behaviours, with parameters tuned by a genetic algorithm (GA) to maximize the collection of resources [14]. In the experiments we analyse here, resources are clustered (in Fig. 6, in 4 large clusters) to mimic the clustered DCs targets of T cells. We validate the method of inferring target locations by correctly inferring the locations of iAnt robots using methods similar to those we use to infer T cell hot spots (Fig. 4). In addition to knowing a priori the location of target locations, we also know more about how iAnt movement behaviours adapt to their environment. iAnts are programmed to use an informed correlated random walk (CRW) with lower correlation among successive step directions when the iAnt is returning to a known target cluster location. This results in a different mean and median step length for informed vs uninformed iAnts (Fig. 7).

The nature of the adaptive movement in iAnts (lower mean and median step lengths for informed iAnts) is different than the hypothesized adaptation in hot T cell tracks (less skew in the distribution of step lengths indicating more Brownian search). However, in both cases, the informed iAnts and the hot T cell tracks appear to search more thoroughly then their uninformed counterparts.

This similarity in search behaviour between iAnts and T cells is noteworthy. iAnts were designed to mimic biological behaviours of foraging ants. Moses and Banerjee have suggested similarities in how ants and T cells search [18]. Despite differences in the search environments and the sensing abilities of the search agents, both T cells and iAnts change their movement in response to features of their environment. T cells (evolved by natural selection to find antigen-bearing DCs) and iAnts (evolved by GAs to collect targets) change their movement patterns to search more thoroughly when targets are nearby.

We identified hot spots in only 34% of our experiments, and in those experiments approximately 25% of T cells visited those locations. These are likely underestimates for two reasons. First, our test identifying hot spots is conservative–only those locations that were visited more frequently than by chance were identified as hot spots, but some locations with fewer visits could be clusters of DCs that happened not to be visited by many T cell tracks. Additionally, only a small number of T cells could be visualized during the experiments. Therefore there may be many more T cells overlapping in space than the ones we have identified. Not visualizing a hot spot may simply be a byproduct of the low density of T cells. In future experimental work we will identify DCs and T cells in the same lymph node to test our ability to identify hot spots.

Another limitation of our computational approach is that it may be difficult to clearly distinguish movement behaviours of T cells visiting hot spots, simply because many T cells move in variable ways–sometimes taking long persistent directional steps and sometimes searching thoroughly. Even for iAnts, which are specifically programmed to search more thoroughly where hot spots are identified, the difference in step distribution is difficult to detect statistically. While there is a clear shift in the average step length of informed iAnts, there is a broad range of steps lengths (up to 12 m) in informed and uninformed iAnts. Our prior experiments [6] show that an adaptive walk with small changes in turning angles (and therefore small changes in the step length distribution) can make a large difference (42.9%) in search efficiency. This suggests that subtle differences in T cell movement might generate important differences in how rapidly T cells encounter DCs.

Our T cell experiments also suggest new strategies for iAnt robots. It is possible that different T cells have different movement patterns, not necessarily because of reactions to the environment. Our iAnts are all programmed identically, and vary in response to information about the environment. The variability in T cell behaviour suggests that it is worth testing variation in search strategies among iAnts. Additionally, some have proposed that T cells move using a Lévy walk [9]. Prior analysis suggests that T cell movement is heavy-tailed (if not strictly Lévy) [6]. A heavy-tailed step distribution vs more Brownian motion (Fig. 5) provides an alternative model for thorough vs extensive search. One advantage of this approach over the current iAnt model described by Hecker at al. [10] (which increases turning angles of successive steps to achieve more thorough search) is that a Lévy-like walk might be tuned with fewer parameters. Additionally, there is substantial mathematical analysis of Lévy walk efficiency that may allow iAnts to tune their search based on analytical predictions of the most efficient walk for a given environment, without needing to evolve. Thus T cells may provide a simpler model of movement that may be more analytically tractable than the current iAnt central place foraging algorithm (CPFA).

Here we have identified similarities and differences in search behaviours of iAnts and T cells. Our analysis provides a computational hypothesis: that hot spots are locations of DC clusters or signaling molecules and that T cells adapt movement in response to sensing those environmental cues. Our future work will test this hypothesis experimentally by simultaneously visualizing fluorescent DCs and T cells in the same ex vivo LN. As we learn more about how T cells move and adapt as they search the LN environment, we can generate new iAnt search strategies to mimic these T cell search strategies. This will continue the cycle of computational analysis informing experimental design, and experimental observation informing our understanding of T cell search processes. As we improve our understanding of how T cells search, we identify additional mechanisms that computational approaches can emulate.

References

[1] E. U. Acar, H. Choset, Y. Zhang, and M. Schervish. Path planning for robotic demining: Robust sensor-based coverage of unstructured environments and probabilistic methods. *The International Journal of Robotics Research*, 22(7-8):441–466, 2003.

[2] E. J. Allenspach, P. Cullinan, J. Tong, Q. Tang, A. G. Tesciuba, J. L. Cannon, S. M. Takahashi, R. Morgan, J. K. Burkhardt, and A. I. Sperling. Erm-dependent movement of cd43 defines a novel protein complex distal to the immunological synapse. *Immunity*, 15(5):739–750, 2001.

[3] U. Alon, M. G. Surette, N. Barkai, and S. Leibler. Robustness in bacterial chemotaxis. *Nature*, 397(6715):168–171, 1999.

[4] A. Be'er, S. K. Strain, R. A. Hernández, E. Ben-Jacob, and E.-L. Florin. Periodic reversals in paenibacillus dendritiformis swarming. *Journal of bacteriology*, 195(12):2709–2717, 2013.

[5] T. Flanagan, K. Letendre, W. Burnside, G. Fricke, and M. Moses. Quantifying the effect of colony size and food distribution on harvester ant foraging. *PloS one*, 7(7):e39427, 2012.

[6] G. M. Fricke, F. Asperti-Boursin, J. Hecker, J. Cannon, and M. Moses. From microbiology to microcontrollers: Robot search patterns inspired by T cell movement. In *Advances in Artificial Life, ECAL*, volume 12, pages 1009–1016, 2013.

[7] G. M. Fricke, F. Asperti-Boursin, J. Hecker, J. Cannon, and M. Moses. Beyond lévy: Efficiency of t cell search in lymph nodes. (In review)

[8] M. Y. Gerner, P. Torabi-Parizi, and R. N. Germain. Strategically localized dendritic cells promote rapid t cell responses to lymph-borne particulate antigens. *Immunity*, 42(1):172–185, 2015.

[9] T. H. Harris, E. J. Banigan, D. A. Christian, C. Konradt, E. D. T. Wojno, K. Norose, E. H. Wilson, B. John, W. Weninger, A. D. Luster, et al. Generalized lévy walks and the role of chemokines in migration of effector cd8+ t cells. *Nature*, 486(7404):545–548, 2012.

[10] J. P. Hecker, K. Stolleis, B. Swenson, K. Letendre, and M. E. Moses. Evolving Error Tolerance in Biologically-Inspired iAnt Robots. In *ECAL 2013*, 2013.

[11] S. M. Hedrick. The acquired immune system-a vantage from beneath. *Immunity*, 21(5):607–616, 2004.

[12] J. H. Huang, L. I. Cárdenas-Navia, C. C. Caldwell, T. J. Plumb, C. G. Radu, P. N. Rocha, T. Wilder, J. S. Bromberg, B. N. Cronstein, M. Sitkovsky, et al. Requirements for t lymphocyte migration in explanted lymph nodes. *The Journal of Immunology*, 178(12):7747–7755, 2007.

[13] N. Humphries, H. Weimerskirch, N. Queiroz, E. Southall, and D. Sims. Foraging success of biological lévy flights recorded in situ. *Proceedings of the National Academy of Sciences*, 109(19):7169–7174, 2012.

[14] J. P. Hecker and M. E. Moses Beyond pheromones: Evolving error-tolerant, flexible, and scalable ant-inspired robot swarms. *Swarm Intelligence*, 9(1), 43–70, 2015.

[15] I. R. Mackay, F. S. Rosen, U. H. von Andrian, and C. R. Mackay. T-cell function and migration - two sides of the same coin. *New England Journal of Medicine*, 343(14):1020–1034, 2000.

[16] M. P. Matheu, I. Parker, and M. D. Cahalan. Dissection and 2-photon imaging of peripheral lymph nodes in mice. *Journal of Visualized Experiments: JoVE*, (7), 2007.

[17] H. P. Mirsky, M. J. Miller, J. J. Linderman, and D. E. Kirschner. Systems biology approaches for understanding cellular mechanisms of immunity in lymph nodes during infection. *Journal of theoretical biology*, 287:160–170, 2011.

[18] M. Moses and S. Banerjee. Biologically inspired design principles for scalable, robust, adaptive, decentralized search and automated response (radar). In *Artificial Life (ALIFE), 2011 IEEE Symposium on*, pages 30–37. IEEE, 2011.

[19] D. W. Stephens and J. R. Krebs. *Foraging theory.* Princeton University Press, 1986.

[20] S. J. Taylor. The hausdorff α-dimensional measure of brownian paths in n-space. In *Mathematical Proceedings of the Cambridge Philosophical Society*, volume 49, pages 31–39. Cambridge Univ Press, 1953.

[21] G. Viswanathan, F. Bartumeus, S. V Buldyrev, J. Catalan, U. Fulco, S. Havlin, M. Da Luz, M. Lyra, E. Raposo, and H. Eugene Stanley. Levy flight random searches in biological phenomena. *Physica A: Statistical Mechanics and Its Applications*, 314(1):208–213, 2002.

[22] E. O. Wilson and B. Hölldobler. The rise of the ants: a phylogenetic and ecological explanation. *Proceedings of the National Academy of Sciences of the United States of America*, 102(21):7411–7414, 2005.

5. ACKNOWLEDGEMENTS

The authors gratefully acknowledge financial support from NSF EF 1038682, DARPA P-1070-113237, NIH 1R01AI097202-01, the Spatiotemporal Modeling Center 1 P50 GM085273, and a James S. McDonnell Foundation grant for the study of Complex Systems. Thanks to the reviewers for many helpful suggestions.

Securing the Internet of Things with Responsive Artificial Immune Systems

Julie Greensmith
School of Computer Science
University of Nottingham
Wollaton Road
Nottingham, UK
NG8 1BB
julie.greensmith@nottingham.ac.uk

ABSTRACT

The Internet of Things is a network of 'smart' objects, transforming everyday objects into entities which can measure, sense and understand their environment. The devices are uniquely identifiable, rely on near field connectivity, often in embedded devices. The Internet of Things is designed to be deployed without human intervention or interaction. One application is the 'smart house', with components including household appliances, networked with the user able to control devices remotely. However, the security inherent in these systems is added as somewhat of an afterthought. One hypothetical scenario is where a malicious party could exploit this technology with potentially disastrous consequences, turning on a cooker remotely leading to digital arson. Reliance on standard methods is insufficient to provide the user with adequate levels of security, an area where AIS may be extremely useful. There are currently limitations with AIS applied in security, focussing on detection without providing automatic responses. This problem provides an opportunity to advance AIS in providing both an ideal scenario for testing their real-world application and to develop novel responsive AIS. A responsive version of the deterministic Dendritic Cell Algorithm will be proposed to demonstrate how responsive AIS will need to be developed to meet these future challenges through proposing the incorporation of a model of T-cell responses.

Keywords

Artificial Immune Systems; Internet of Things; Automated Responses; Security; Dendritic Cell Algorithm.

1. INTRODUCTION

The Internet of Things (IoT) is a network of smart objects, which will allow us to transform a multitude of everyday objects into entities which can measure, sense and understand their environment [15]. This differs from conventional computer networks as the devices are uniquely identifiable, rely on near field connectivity and RFID connections, and are frequently embedded devices. Most importantly, the IoT is also designed to be deployed without human intervention or human computer interaction. One such application of the IoT is the concept of the smart house, with components such as conventional household appliances becoming networked[23]. Refrigerators, cookers, washing machines, entertainment centres, and central heating systems will be able to communicate within a household network, opening up new networked functionality for these objects. The advantage to the user is to be able to control such devices remotely, such as turning on the cooker while on the way home from work, or communicating with their refrigerator to find out if it contains fresh milk. Energy usage within a house can be optimised, logging when users enter and leave a property, and indeed commercial products exist to make the deployment of the IoT a reality[14].

However, as with so many previous innovations in technology, the security inherent in novel systems is added as somewhat of an afterthought. It is not a great leap from a computer security perspective to hypothesise the situation where a malicious party could exploit this technology with potentially disastrous consequences. Obviously, in a conventional oven, a person needs physical access to the asset in order to control the machine. In a networked oven which can be controlled via the internet, it is possible to imagine the scenario where an unauthorised user could gain access remotely to the device, turning the empty cooker on to a high temperature at will. Overheating of the device leads to a fire risk, giving rise to a new threat, a form of digital arson. While this scenario may seem somewhat hypothetical, the vulnerability is tangible and is a feasible style of attack to perform, as the same access control methods for conventional networks are being integrated into the smart objects. Additionally, within the domestic setting, the responsibility of securing the network of smart objects will fall on the shoulders of the householder, who may not have sufficient security expertise to preserve the confidentiality, integrity and availability of this new style of network. Reliance on virtual private networks, high standards of access controls and encryption will be insufficient to provide the user with adequate standards of security for protecting our primary

GECCO '15, July 11–15, 2015, Madrid, Spain
© 2015 ACM. ISBN 978-1-4503-3472-3/15/07...$15.00
DOI: http://dx.doi.org/10.1145/2739480.2754816

assets, namely our homes [2]. What is required is novel security systems which can protect the IoT through automatically detecting and responding to malicious behaviour and intruders.

The potential role which Artificial Immune Systems (AIS) can play in providing protection for the IoT will be discussed in this positional paper. AIS have a long history of success within the computer security domain, including Negative Selection and the Dendritic Cell Algorithm [3], yet the so-called 'killer application' of AIS has so far remained elusive. The IoT is a potential fertile area in which to develop novel AIS due to the characteristics of these networks: having a composition of a large number heterogeneous embedded devices; the requirement to detect a multitude of different types of attack; the need for the detection to operate in a distributed environment; to be able to produce a range of different and reliable responses to the detection of malicious use. These characteristics synergise with the ideal properties of AIS of being distributed, adaptive, robust and error tolerant. Securing the IoT may have the potential to provide the ideal application area for AIS.

However, there is a significant limitation with current AIS in that the immune-inspired algorithms applied historically to computer security applications have focussed primarily on the detection of intruders, but have not been equipped with automated responses to the detection of a threat. In order to protect the IoT, it is imperative that the developed 'responsive' AIS is able to respond in addition to performing detection. This problem provides an opportunity to advance AIS on two fronts, in providing an ideal scenario for testing the real-world application of immune-inspired algorithms and the potential to develop novel responsive AIS. This is imperative for the protection of the IoT as the central concept is that the network runs and is self administrated without human intervention. In this paper a proof of concept style case study will be presented based on the 'smart house' scenario. Modifications are proposed to the danger-based deterministic Dendritic Cell Algorithm, used to demonstrate how a responsive AIS can be applied to protect this style of system. A discussion will be presented as to how future responsive AIS will need to be developed in order to meet the challenges presented by the need to secure the IoT. This includes how models of diversity in T-cell responses can be incorporated into immune-inspired security systems to make future AIS fit for this purpose.

The main contribution of this paper is to provide a case for support as to why IoT security is a suitable problem to be solved by AIS. In doing so we discuss the current issues inherent in security the Internet of Things in Section 2. A review of the use of AIS in security is provided in Section 4 where we examine how current immune inspired algorithms could be used in order to provide security for the IoT, and present how current AIS would need to be modified in order to become fit for this purpose. The Dendritic Cell Algorithm (DCA) is presented as an example, showing how a responsive component could be added and postulate how this novel AIS can be applied to IoT security.

2. THE INTERNET OF INSECURE THINGS

The IoT is an incredibly fast moving and technologically driven field. Like many previous innovations, the push towards fast deployment of the technology is outstripping the development of security measures for this new technology. Within the next decade both personal and business usage of the IoT will become unavoidable. It has been described as the extention of the Internet into the physical domain. This is achieved by adding the capability of sensing and remote communication to physically embedded devices. These networks contain large numbers of nodes, processing high volumes of data, communicating with centralised hubs which are used to extract knowledge from this data. The underlying concept of the IoT is to have a heterogeneous network of devices, which are small (or lightweight), rely on communicating through near field technology or RFID. Networks with these characteristics are not particulaly novel. Sensor networks, for example, can be deployed to have similar characteristics, and RFID technology is now extremely mature. The main difference is that devices enabled with this new technology will transform everyday objects into smart objects, equipped with sensing and processing abilities, and communication and control without the need for explicit human intervention.

What makes the IoT particularly interesting, especially from a security perspective, is that the networking capability is being incorporated into devices which were never previously envisioned to be part of a computer network. Computer hardware and software vendors are particularly aware of the security compromises and malware which exist and have evolved over time in computer security. As a result, security countermeasures like secure development processes, encryption, firewalls and anti-virus techniques are applied in order to mitigate against commonly found malware and to preserve the confidentiality of data and the privacy of users. Household appliance vendors see the IoT as a great opportunity to revolutionise the way in which we use their devices. However, such vendors do not have a history of appreciating the potential security risks associated with adding these novel features to appliances. Maintaining the security of a domestic IoT is also a challenge as the responsibility is placed on the home owner to manage and ensure the security of the IoT in this setting[17].

The incorporation of Internet technologies into the physical domain has implications for how we perceive and manage domestic access control. We currently rely on physical forms of access control and authentication to decide who has access to our homes and by extension who has access to the assets and artefacts contained within. For example, access to the temperature control on a household thermostat is controlled by physical means. We lock our doors and windows securing houses physically in order to prevent modification of any of the settings on the thermostat - if a person is physically not inside the property, they cannot modify the device. Transforming the thermostat into a networked object means that we now have a different paradigm of access control to manage for these previously non-networked devices. An extra layer of security must be added and managed effectively in order to prevent unauthorised or even malicious tampering with such devices.

Why would one tamper with the settings on a thermostat of a house? The consequence of turning the device down is not particularly dire, one's house would become cold, not necessarily a particular problem, but indeed would be an annoyance. However, the concept is that the transformation of the thermostat to become a smart object is not simply to provide remote control operations, but also stores data regarding user energy consumption, logging increases and decreases in thermostat activity[6]. In addition some systems like the Hive home heating controller interface [14] with the occupants smartphones, turning heating systems on and off depending on the users proximity to the home. Unauthorised access to this data, indicating if a property is vacant, opens up the risk of physical intrusion of property. Accidental misconfiguration by the system administrator, in this case the homeowner who is non-specialist in security, could lead to a compromise of the property.

A darker scenario is the networking to a domestic IoT of cooking devices including conventional ovens (either gas or electric) and microwave ovens. The advantage of adding this capability to these devices is that one is able to remotely turn them on and off and to a desired heat settings and cycles. It is a desirable thought for dinner to be cooked upon ones return home. As with the thermostat scenario, we currently protect access to the controls of these devices through physical means: it would require the physical penetration of a home in order to tamper with such devices. However, a networked cooker, should the access control be compromised a malicious party could turn on the device at will causing a serious fire hazard. This could pose a significant threat not only to the property itself and assets within but also to the occupants of the property.

Another case study of the abuse of a household device is a recent compromise of an internet baby monitor system. This system consists of a web-cam, microphone and speaker system, which is placed in sight of an infant for remote monitoring by the parent via a smartphone app[13]. The attacker was able to gain access through discovering that the root administration password for these devices was simply 'admin', and the IP and MAC address combination gave the device a discoverable signature. As a result the intruder was able to send an audio stream to the device, and was caught shouting obscenities to wake the sleeping infants. The hardware vendor stated that as the product was simply a web cam that security was not of paramount importance, demonstrating the prioritisation by vendors of features over security. While this attack was not life-threatning, the invasion of privacy for those involved was significant and disturbing.

Classical security techniques rely on encryption to preserve the confidentiality and integrity of computer systems and assets. Encryption relies on verified standards (such as SHA-2) being applied correctly in order to preserve the integrity of data. Computer networks, even in a domestic setting, rely on anti-virus software to detect spyware, botnets and keyloggers, and home users are now used to installing and maintaining this type of security measure. Business users and medium to large scale network administrators frequently rely on the application of signature-based intrusion detection systems[19] in order to detect unauthorised intruders within a network. Anomaly-based network intrusion detection systems depend on matching profiles of normal behaviour in comparison with current behaviour. Like signature-based systems, log files of alerts are generated and are subject to further analysis to determine the presence of an attacker and the effects that the intrusion has on the monitored system.

In the context of the domestic IoT, there are issues in applying these classical security paradigms. Modern encryption techniques would be needed for the smart objects to pass messages. The current proposed architectures often contain a centralised data analysis unit, and encryption would be required to pass and to verify the identity of the devices passing messages between each other and the centralised unit. The authentication of provably secure digital certificates between lightweight devices can be computationally expensive. Having a centralised unit for data analysis would also make an ideal point of attack to extrapolate knowledge of the status of the house. The centralised unit would need protection mechanisms akin to firewalls, anti-virus and intrusion detection technology. Yet, the administration of these techniques would pose a challenge for even the most techologically compentent home users. If classical intrusion paradigms like signature-based intrusion detection is used, analysis of the output of the system is complex and is not automatic. This would require significant eduction of the home user to be able to manage this problem. This also contravenes the central idea of the IoT which is to have minimal user involvement or human computer interaction.

3. AIS IN IOT: RELATED WORK

The relevance of AIS to IOT researchers has not gone unnoticed, and indeed we are starting to see a number of references stating as to how immune inspired components can be used in this type of network. In this section a short review of relevant recent work related to applying concepts in AIS to the IOT is given.

Chen *et al.* [2] propose what they describe as a 'security situation' for the IOT and have identified a role for AIS in their work. They propose the use of an AIS to survey and assess the levels of threats and their detection within the IOT. This is proposed as a modified version of clonal selection algorithms [5] adapted for this purpose. This variant of clonal selection consists of a detector pool which matches detectors - as antibodies, and threats - as antigen. This approach is combined with a set of memory detectors which are tuned to remember past threats. The system is designed to be deployed at the protocol, or datagram, layer of the IOT to analyse the network packets sent between devices. While this paper proposes a quite specific matching technique, it is unclear as to exactly what data could be used and how this could be tranformed for use within the IOT. We infer that they mean to perform detection attributes taken from the network datagrams which can be then mapped to antibody-antigen feature space. In contrast to what is proposed in this paper, the detection system is passive and does not produce a specific system-changing response. However a detection component may prove useful in the detection stage, as an assessment of threat severity, not just a binary judgement may be a useful asset to an IOT protection system.

Another proposition is provided by Ning and Liu [18] shows AIS components integrated with a multi-layer protection system, which also encompasses societal and human aspects to IOT security. In this paper, the authors motivate the need for a more sophisticated security mechanism for the IOT, due to the complexity of the problem, its distributed nature and the severe resource constraints on many 'smart object' devices. The authors highlight a particular IOT framework which they are interested in protecting produced in their previous research termed U2IOT, which aims to combine a cognitive, intelligent approach with a social component. In this propositional paper they subdivide the different security aspects into layers: information layer, a physical layer; and a management of security layer. Each layer allows for combining security between the components within the physical layer, covering the authentication and maintaining the integrity of the digital data within. Of particular interest is their proposal to use a multi-component immune based system at the heart of the physical layer security. It is envisioned that the immune based component will monitor and maintain the homeostasis of the system. They propose that an innate component could provide what they term 'basic barriers', including authentication mechanisms. Suspicious behaviour at the innate layer is flagged up and inspected more deeply by an adaptive layer, via the novel use of communication through artificial 'co-stimulation signals'. Details of implementation including what might trigger the costimulation signals are not given in this early stage of research, but it is interesting to see research combining immune algorithms within the IOT sphere.

More concrete research has been performed by Ding *et al.* [7] who give insight a to how self organisation can be used to monitor and maintain the IOT. This is based on an idea of hormone generation and diffusion throughout devices on the network. It is of interest because they produce an actual implementation of their system and show directly how a homeostatic monitoring system is useful in the management of nodes in such networks. While this is not directly related to the security properties of the IOT, it shows that a layer of automation and control is possible with the constrained resources of the devices, and that such a system is beneficial for the IOT.

4. APPLYING CURRENT AIS TO THE IOT

4.1 Desirable properties

It is a very *natural* idea to develop an Artificial Immune System (AIS) to protect and detect intruders in a computational system. Irun Cohen [3] described this scenario as the 'literal AIS', one where the artificial system attempts to solve a similar problem to the natural system. These are the immune inspired techniques which form the focus of this paper.

From an abstract perspective, the most sought after properties of an AIS [22] and of their corresponding application are as follows:

Robust: to be able to classify under imprecise and uncertain data conditions

Lightweight: to be able to process with low computational complexity

Error tolerant: to be able to function given error in input, giving rise to robustness

Adaptive: to be able to evolve and learn over the lifetime of the system, producing adaptive behaviours

Distributed: to process in a distributed manner, free from centralised control

Also in the abstract, these properties are desirable in constructing an AIS to protect devices on the IoT. The robustness would allow for nodes to pass incomplete and noisy data to the AIS for processing, yet good quality classification of the behaviour of devices could be performed. Due to the embedded nature of smart objects, with low processing power, and AIS would be useful if it had the desirable lightweight processing properties and did not consume large amounts of processing power to perform its operations. In a heterogeneous network like that proposed in the IoT where devices may be prone to sensor malfunction or incomplete data transmissions, a protection system needs to function despite the generation of errors by smart devices. Adaptivity in protecting the IoT is of high importance. As with any security application, it is an 'arms race' against so called zero-day attacks and the protection system needs to adapt to new and emerging threats. It also needs to be able to adapt to the conditions of a dynamically configurable network, with devices frequently added and disconnected. Finally the IoT is an inherently distributed system, with processing performed in a number of different locations, including on the smart objects themselves and in centralised analytic devices in addition to routers. Therefore, a distributed protection system would also be ideal to monitor such networks from multiple vantage points, without providing a single point of failure for an attacker wishing to compromise the integrity of the protection system. In summary, the perfect AIS is potentially suitable solution to a number of challenges pertaining to securing the IoT.

There are four main types of AIS categorised below:

- Negative Selection: a supervised learning classification algorithm, based on the thymic selection process of T-cell development to generate central tolerance, commonly applied to anomaly detection.
- Clonal Selection: a supervised data mining technique, based on the hypermutation properties of B-cells, commonly applied to optimization problems.
- Immune Networks: an unsupervised learning algorithm, based on a theoretical model in immunology involving the interaction between B-cell derived antibodies, used for both clustering and dynamic classification.
- Dendritic Cell Algorithm (DCA) : a semi-supervised classification algorithm, based on the signal processing and correlation properties of natural dendritic cells, applied to two-class classification in security applications.

Many current AIS contain one or more of the above properties, but AIS containing all of the above properties are rare. Such systems have been attempted, such as Fanelli's NETTriad[8]. These systems are difficult to reimplement, formally verify and the parameter space for their operation is difficult to tune. Each of the four main types of AIS capitalise on different combinations of the ideal properties. For example clonal selection algorithms[5] are adaptive through their hypermutation operators and affinity maturation properties, but are not particularly lightweight and can be computationally expensive. Negative selection [12] is also adaptive and contains a distributed population of artificial detectors, but is not particularly robust due to its one-shot learning system. It is also not particularly lightweight as theoretical results have shown [20]. Immune network approaches [4] capitalise on the distributed and adaptive properties and are perhaps the most suitable type of AIS to be applied directly to this problem, as they generally rely on producing robust and adaptive behaviours. Again, they can be computationally expensive. Finally, the Dendritic Cell Algorithm[10] has been shown to be lightweight in terms of computational complexity, has been applied previously to embedded devices. It is also shown to be robust and error tolerant, but it is not adaptive. Once the inputs have been categorised for the signal processing component, they do not adapt and as a result false negative classifications can arise.

4.2 Addendum: Responses

The desirable properties of an AIS were derived based on examining and abstracting the properties of the human immune system. One desirable property which is perhaps missing from this list is the human immune system's ability to generate appropriate responses to a given threat. The human immune system is highly sophisticated, containing many layers (physical, innate and adaptive). The two immune-inspired algorithms which have focussed on security application are Negative Selection and the Dendritic Cell Algorithm. Both of these types of AIS are primarily used to perform the detection of intruders in a computer network. Negative selection achieves this by producing a set of alerts to a system user, where the number of alerts generated must pass a set threshold in order to classify a network connection as anomalous. There is no automated response to disconnect the connection, throttle the packet rate or to delay the connection. In the Dendritic Cell Algorithm, the classical application is the classification of anomalous processes on a host machine. Anomaly scores are generated for running processes, to give the system administrator information to kill or to halt the processes.

This differs from the human immune system where the 'immunological synapse' exists between the adaptive and innate immune systems, with the specific function of controlling and generating appropriate effector responses. Large numbers of different type of T-lymphocyte have been characterised, each producing responses to detected pathogens in subtly different ways. T-cells also have responses which influence the behaviour of other T-cells, further fine tuning the human immune systems responses to detected threats. The most obvious mechansim of this differentiated response is in the production of T-helper Type 1 and Type 2 cells. The detection of different pathogens leads to different proportions of proliferations of these two types of cell. Type 1 cells increase in numbers upon the detection of bacterial pathogens, activating B-cells and the compliment system to produce specific types of antibody which bind to the pathogent to assist in elimiation of the bacteria. Type 2 cells are primarily involved in allergic responses, the detection of a totally different foreign body.

This model is a simplified example used to illustrate that the immune system produces different types of T-cell depending on the detected threat and is a gross oversimplification of the actual underlying immunology. Advances in immunology have shown that T-cell differentiation is a highly plastic process, with T-cells changing their effector function dynamically in response to a multitude of input signals. As the immunological evidence amasses however, it is now becoming feasible to construct a computational model of T-cell responses. If it is possible to produce abstract computation from this model, then it is also possible to abstract algorithmic properties.

The ideal situation would be to combine a model of immune responses with existing immune-inspired algorithms which explicity model the detection process. A powerful AIS can be conceived which not only detects a threat, but it is also able to dynamically produce and adapt appropriate responses. The field of AIS also contains a sub-field of computational modelling, which is now becoming mature using a variety of simulation techniques including Agent Based Modelling. The combination of having the immunological grounding for understanding immune responses combined with advances in computational immunology means that it may be, at least in principle, to captialise on the immune system's ability to generate responses and to conceptualise how this could be incorporated algorithmically. By doing this, it would be possible to create an AIS which is suitable for monitoring, managing and protecting machine-to-machine networks like the IoT, with numerous security related applications. It is worth considering that for future AIS frameworks, the ability to automatically and appropriately respond to a threat should become of equal consideration to the properties of adaptation and decenralisation.

In the next two sections, two aspects of AIS are considered with respect to their application to the security of the IoT: firstly the application of the Danger Theory to detecting malicious behaviour and the construction of responsive AIS in order to correct and mitigate the detected problems.

5. DETECTING DANGER IN THE IOT

5.1 The Danger Theory

The Danger Theory was proposed by Polly Matzinger in 1994 [16]. She stated that the immune system is controlled by the detection of damage to the body via the release of danger signals, not the detection of antigen structures or bacterial products. The danger theory also proposes that the cells of the innate immune system can actively suppress an immune response in the absence of danger in the tissue. This is mediated through the recognition of 'tissue context', derived from the balance between two types of cell death: necrosis and apoptosis.

Apoptosis or 'planned cell death' regulates growth and development. During apoptosis the cell's internal contents are gracefully degraded digesting the cell from the inside out. Dendritic Cells are sensitive to an increase in the signals of apoptosis and are attracted to the dying cell. Eventually the cell is found by a DC and ingested. If the cell is ingested by a DC, the proteins contained within the cell (termed self-antigen) are presented to the immune system in a 'safe' context, as the cell died as part of a normal process. The immune system is then tolerised to self-antigens with the same structure.

Not all cells die in this clean and controlled manner but through cell stress which can occur through irradiation, shock, lack of oxygen or pathogenic infection, leading to the death of the cell via necrosis. In necrosis the internal cell contents degrade chaotically and the cell membrane loses its integrity. Irregular fragments of DNA are produced and oxidised to become uric acid crystals, with heat shock proteins and other hydrophobic compounds released from the cell. Dendritic cells are sensitive to changes in concentration of the molecules released as a result of necrosis. Upon the detection of danger, the DC migrates from the tissue and presents any collected debris as antigen to T-cells, causing immune responses.

5.2 Uses in the IoT

The use of the Danger Theory in AIS was first proposed by Cayzer and Aickelin in 2002[1], where they suggested computer security applications for the theory. Danger signals could be generated as a result of unusual behaviour, having an algorithm which can detect *concentrations* of danger signal. A behaviour based approach could be beneficial for securing the IoT. In this scenario, smart objects could emit small datagrams or packets as used in the signalling networks in Ding *et al.*[7]. Instead of reflecting hormone concentrations, the network could transmit similar packets containing danger signals if their operational behaviour deviated from a defined normal, with an intelligent processing algorithm mapping the network behaviour to the signal concentration. To make the metaphor more powerful, a monitoring system could be implemented to analyse the origin and severity of the behaviour deviation.The monitoring system could then allocate more resources to investigating and responding to the behaviour deemed dangerous. This monitoring system would form the overall immune system protecting the network.

Just as in the human immune system, the emission of a single danger signal would be insufficient to generate an appropriate response, therefore the danger monitoring system would need to perform correlation across nodes in order to detect a potential threat. The deterministic DCA[11] is one candidate algorithm which could be used to provide the monitoring system, as it is designed to process a mapping of danger signals and is shown to have correlation properties. It is also lightweight and has been applied in embedded computing scenarios.

In the case of the domestic IoT, smart objects operating outside of normal parameters could release danger signals, to be detected by the monitoring AIS. In the case of a cooker, this is a literal danger signal, as if the oven is too hot, this could lead to a fire risk. The use of danger within computer security has historically been limited by difficulty in mapping what is *dangerous*, and so the use of an evolutionary method to train the system may be beneficial. The signals could be correlated with other behavioural attributes, such as if the occupants of the property are in residence or if the property is vacant. In the IoT, where the internet meets the physical world, this analogy is much stronger. In order to show the efficacy of this idea, a testbed network of the devices and a monitoring system would need to be created. Additionally, a set of attacks would also need to be generated in order to validate the approach. Unlike in network security, where attacks are *in the wild*, there is no library of IoT security attacks, and it would be extremely useful to generate such scenarios.

In applying the deterministic DCA, it would be challenging to find the correct mappings for signals (and the corresponding identifying antigen), as an additional learning component would have to be added in order to remove the 'semi' supervised component from this algorithm in order to make it fit for purpose. Adaptive analysis of protocol behaviour would need to be implemented to overcome this, and the challenge would be to achieve this in a suitably lightweigh manner. This would be complicated by the lack of standards developed for devices connected via the IoT, which would have practical implications for producing a system to protect the IoT enabled home. There would also be the additional complication of protecting the AIS itself from external attack, postulations of which are beyond the scope of this paper, but is an important concern nontheless. While it would be possible to apply the DCA for the detection of misbehaviour, again it underestimates the problem of constructing effective and reliable responses to the detected threats.

6. CONSTRUCTING RESPONSIVE AIS IN IOT SECURITY

The security of the IoT could be a potentially interesting and useful application of an immune-inspired monitoring system. However, this would require a rethink of how we derive, construct and apply AIS. AIS have thus far concentrated purely on small models of specific functions of specific cell types, for example the affinity maturation properties of clonal selection, or the danger signal processing mechanisms of the DCA. Single mechanisms are abstracted to solve single problems. However, the problem of security in the IoT has multiple problems which need to be adressed within the same monitoring system. This is the problem of both detecting malicious use and generating appropriate responses to recover and repair the system in response. A more integrated approach, combining multiple immune mechansims may be required in order to produce a successful application. This would allow for the AIS practitioner to capitalise on the diversity of problem solving mechanisms inherent in the human immune system. This could potentially lead to the development of much more powerful AIS. Multiple cell types are used to orchestrate specialised responses to specific threats in the human immune system. Therefore, AIS which combine multiple mechanisms will need to be developed to meet these challenges.

Multiple AIS could be combined using ideas from ensemble methods, bootstrapping different existing AIS together, as suggested by Chen *et al.* [2]. This would achieve AIS containing multiple cell types, but it may not solve the problem of producing both suitable and timely responses. This is because current AIS frequently focus on detection and do not provide the facility for automated responses as highlighted in previous sections. Indeed, in Forrest *et al.* [9], responses are produced alongside alerts based on activation thresholds, but the response was limited to 'drop packet' in practice. The heterogenous and complex nature of the IOT will call for a more sophisticated response mechanism, if it is required to eliminate the human in-the-loop.

Creating responsive AIS will not be a trivial process as to do so may involve increasing our understanding of the mechanisms in the human immune system, or combining elements of reinforcement learning. The immune mechanisms which may provide some answers are complex and therefore may require higher processing requirements when turned into algorithmic form. As previously stated, the ideal AIS to apply to this scenario must also be lightweight, and this must be a strong consideration when developing novel responsive AIS.

The methodology for achieving this must build on current innovations in AIS, including the recent advances in computational immunology including making use of simulation and also mathematical modelling. The proposed method for achieving immune responses would be the deep interdisciplinary study of the nature of T-cell effector responses. The role of a subtype of T-cell, the Th-17 cell may be pivotal, as this has the ability to prevent the immune system from producing a natural form of false positive. The plasticity of the T-cell response generated through its interaction with a DC[21], driven by the DCs response to danger signals. Models of DC and T-cell interaction could be constructed to provide the algorithmic basis for a responsive AIS, though further characterisation of this interaction is needed before a computationally feasible algorithm could be constructed.

One major consideration in developing a responsive AIS would be the protection of the system against denial of service attacks. If the system responds innappropriately, this could lead to the network becoming disabled. For example, this would be problematic if the IoT also encompasses a home security system. The potential exists for the responses themselves to be subverted and turned into an attack against the system. This is a problem that must be taken into consideration when developing such systems.

7. CONCLUSIONS

The development of AIS to be fit for purpose in protecting and maintaining the security of the IOT is an interesting challenge on two fronts. Firstly, the characteristics of the security issues lends itself to be an ideal problem space for AIS. This is because there is a strong mapping between the desirable properties of AIS, and the properties required to craft a suitable security system for the IoT in terms of robustness, decentralisation, error-tolerance, adaption and the need for lightweight embedded computation. As the amount of networked devices and the prevalence of the IoT increases, the need for such a security system will become paramount. It is also a domain in which classical security mechanisms will be challenging to manage, presenting an opportunity for more complex solutions such as AIS. Secondly it presents an interesting challenge in how we develop novel AIS in future, while having a defined scenario in which to test the novel AIS. The incorporation of responses into AIS, especially those involved in security, has the potential to provide a means of generating more powerful, more applicable algorithms with a defined niche.

There are a number of significant challenges to overcome in order to attack this problem from both an algorithmic and application perspective. The methodology used in order to attack this problem will be cruicial to its sucess, depending on input from a variety of disciplines including immunology, computational modelling, algorithm design, network security and smart object vendors. Coordination of interdisciplinary teams to perform the proposed research will also be a challenge, and a development framework would need to be put in place in order for this to be sucessful. Modelling frameworks must be employed and as a community, AIS may need to rethink how and what we define as an AIS. We also need to foster stronger links between the subfield of computational immunology and novel immune-inspired systems development, to make best use of the generated models. A strong theory component ensuring algorithmic rigour must also be used if the security community is to accept responsive AIS as a serious contender technqiue for protecting the IoT. Modification of existing AIS algorithms to include responses is the starting point, while research into the underlying immunology of effector responses and the development of the IoT continues. Past research in AIS has shown that algorithms like the DCA were developed with a target application in mind, which assisted in the development and testing of the novel algorithm, and a similar process could be beneficial in combining responsive AIS and the security of the IoT.

8. REFERENCES

[1] U. Aickelin and S. Cayzer. The danger theory and its application to artificial immune systems. In *Proceedings of the 1st International Conference on ARtificial Immune Systems (ICARIS 2002), Canterbury, UK*, pages 141–148, 2002.

[2] R. Chen, C. Liu, and L. Xiao. A security situation sense model based on artificial immune system in the internet of things. *Advanced Materials Research*, 403-408:2457–2460, 2012.

[3] I. R. Cohen. Real and artificial immune systems: computing the state of the body. *Nat Rev Immunol*, 07(07):569–574, 07 2007.

[4] L. N. de Castro and F. J. Von Zuben. Immune and neural network models: theoretical and empirical comparisons. *International Journal of Computational Intelligence and Applications*, 1(3):239–257, 2001.

[5] L. N. De Castro and F. J. Von Zuben. Learning and optimization using the clonal selection principle. *Evolutionary Computation, IEEE Transactions on*, 6(3):239–251, 2002.

[6] I. Dent, T. Craig, U. Aickelin, and T. Rodden. Variability of behaviour in electricity load profile clustering; who does things at the same time each day? In P. Perner, editor, *Advances in Data Mining*,

volume 8557 of *Lecture Notes in Computer Science*, pages 70–84, Heidelberg, 2014. Springer.

[7] Y. Ding, Y. Jin, L. Ren, and K. Hao. An intelligent self-organisation scheme for the internet of things. *IEEE Computational Intelligence Magazine*, pages 41–53, 2013.

[8] R. L. Fanelli. A hybrid model for immune inspired network intrusion detection. In *Artificial Immune Systems*, pages 107–118. Springer, 2008.

[9] S. Forrest, S. A. Hofmeyr, and A. Somayaji. Computer immunology. *Commun. ACM*, 40(10):88–96, Oct. 1997.

[10] J. Greensmith. *The Dendritic Cell Algorithm*. PhD thesis, University of Nottingham, 2007.

[11] F. Gu, J. Greensmith, and U. Aickelin. Theoretical formulation and analysis of the deterministic dendritic cell algorithm. *Biosystems*, 111 (2):127–135, 2013.

[12] S. A. Hofmeyr and S. Forrest. Architecture for an artificial immune system. *Evolutionary computation*, 8(4):443–473, 2000.

[13] http://www.economist.com/news/special-report/21606420-perils-connected-devices-home-hacked home.

[14] http://www.hivehome.com.

[15] G. Kortuem, F. Kawsar, D. Fitton, and V. Sundramoorthy. Smart objects as building blocks for the internet of things,. *IEEE Internet Computing*, 14(1):44–51, 2009.

[16] P. Matzinger. Tolerance, danger, and the extended family. *Annual review of immunology*, 12(1):991–1045, 1994.

[17] C. M. Medaglia and A. Serbanati. An overview of privacy and security issues in the internet of things. *The Internet of Things*, pages pp 389–395, 2010.

[18] H. Ning and H. Liu. Cyber-physical-social based security architecture for future internet of things. *Advances in Internet of Things*, 2:1–7, 2012.

[19] M. Roesch. Snort: Lightweight intrusion detection for networks. In *LISA*, volume 99, pages 229–238, 1999.

[20] T. Stibor, J. Timmis, and C. Eckert. A comparative study of real-valued negative selection to statistical anomaly detection techniques. In *Artificial Immune Systems*, pages 262–275. Springer, 2005.

[21] R. V. Sutavani, R. G. Bradley, J. M. Ramage, A. M. Jackson, L. G. Durrant, and I. Spendlove. Cd55 costimulation induces differentiation of a discrete t regulatory type 1 cell population with a stable phenotype. *The Journal of Immunology*, 191(12):5895–5903, 2013.

[22] J. Timmis. Artificial immune systems—today and tomorrow. *Natural Computing*, 6(1):1–18, 2007.

[23] R. Weber. Internet of things – new security and privacy challenges. *Computer Law and Security Review*, 26(1):23–30, 2010.

RAIS$_{\mathrm{TTP}}$ Revisited to Solve Relaxed Travel Tournament Problem

Elizabeth Montero*
Elizabeth.Montero@inf.utfsm.cl

María-Cristina Riff†
Maria-Cristina.Riff@inf.utfsm.cl

Universidad Técnica Federico Santa María
Avenida España 1680
Valparaíso, Chile

ABSTRACT

We are interested in methods and strategies that allow us to simplify the code of bio-inspired algorithms without altering their performance. In this paper, we study an artificial immune algorithm specially designed to solve Relaxed Traveling Tournament Problems which has been able to obtain new bounds for some instances of this problem. We use the EvoCa tuner to analyze the components of the algorithm in order to discard some parts of the code. The results show that the filtered algorithm is able to solve the instances as well as does the original algorithm, and with this code we have obtained new bounds for some instances of the problem.

Categories and Subject Descriptors

I.2.8 [**Problem Solving, Control Methods, and Search**]: Heuristic methods

Keywords

Tuning; Immune Algorithms; Code Refining

1. INTRODUCTION

In order to obtain a metaheuristic with good performance, we have to make several design decisions. The design process is usually iterative, and at each step, the involved components must be evaluated. On the other hand, the final code of the metaheuristic can be extremely complex. Thus, analyzing and understanding its results becomes difficult, and this is often a very time consuming task. Unexperienced designers usually tend to include more and more components during the iterative design process of a metaheuristic, without evaluating the usefulness of previously incorporated ones. Some previus work has been proposed in this area [13] motivating the importance of a proper definition of the metaheuristic design problem. As in [13] we propose to have a refining step, in order to help the designer to obtain a simpler design with similar performance. The motivation of this work is to analyze in-depth $RAIS_{TTP}$ (Artificial Immune System for the Relaxed Traveling Tournament Problem) which is an immune algorithm that has many components and which has been able to obtain new bounds for the relaxed traveling tournament problem[15]. Our goal is to refine $RAIS_{TTP}$ without loss performance (e.g. in terms of the solutions quality). It is important to remark that our goal is not to find the best solution to the relaxed traveling tournament problem, but to focus on the way to distinguish the components that are strictly required from the ones that are unnecessary in $RAIS_{TTP}$. We briefly revise published works related to this subject in section 2. In section 3 we formally define the Refining Metaheuristic Design (RMD) problem as configuration problem. After a brief description of the Relaxed Traveling Tournament Problem in section 4, we present the principal components of the immune algorithm $RAIS_{TTP}$ and we show how we use the Evolutionary Calibrator (EvoCa) [17] tuner that can work with categorical and numerical parameters in this RMD in section 6. We present the results of a set of experiments in section 7, as well as a statistical comparison between the results obtained using different versions of $RAIS_{TTP}$. Finally, we present the conclusions and future work in section 8. The contributions of this paper are: an in-depth analysis of the data generated by EvoCa to make better decisions to accomplish the refining design problem, a new version of the immune algorithm that solves RTTP and new bounds for the RTTP.

*Supported by Postdoctoral Fondecyt Project no. 3130754
†Supported by Fondecyt Project no. 1151456

GECCO '15, July 11 - 15, 2015, Madrid, Spain

DOI: http://dx.doi.org/10.1145/2739480.2754753

2. RELATED WORK

Most of the motivation of this work arises from literature on automated parameter tuning and algorithm configuration [9]. In automated algorithm configuration, the design space is defined by an algorithm scheme that contains a number of instantiable components, along with a discrete set of concrete choices for each of these. Some ideas have been proposed to use tuning methods for supporting metaheuristic design processes [13, 2]. We can also relate these approaches to hyper-heuristic methods [3], whose goal is to find a good design with sufficient quality.

On the other hand artificial immune algorithms have been widely applied to optimization problems the last two decades. Those applications include numerical optimization [19], constrained optimization problems [6], constraint satisfaction problems [18], combinatorial optimization problems: like traveling salesman [7] and job-shop scheduling [5]; multi-objective optimization [23] and dynamic optimization problems [22].

The traveling tournament problem is a real challenge to both complete and incomplete combinatorial optimization techniques. Best complete techniques are able to find the optimum for small instances of up to 10 teams [20]. Finding the optimum requires a long execution time. For bigger instances the most successful methods are those based on metaheuristics. A simulated annealing for TTP is proposed in [1] where reheats and a strategic oscillation strategy are used to vary the constraint weight parameter during the search. This method was very successful for solving TTP obtaining several of the best solutions so far. Tabu search [10], Ant colony optimization [21], immune algorithms [14] and hybrid methods [11] have also been proposed. In the field of hyper-heuristics, an ant based hyper-heuristic is introduced in [4] and a learning hyper-heuristic is given in [12]. Both obtaining good results. Best known optima for the Relaxed Traveling tournament are published on the Michael Trick website[1].

3. THE REFINING METAHEURISTIC DESIGN PROBLEM

We can identify two problems when designing metaheuristics: The on-the-fly metaheuristic design problem (OMD) and the post-design problem or refining metaheuristic design problem (RMD). The first one occurs during the design process and is about the decisions to make when building efficient metaheuristics. In this paper we are interested in the refining problem. The Refining Metaheuristic Design Problem (RMD) occurs during post-design of the metaheuristic when we are interested in simplifying its code without performance loss. RMD can be stated as follows: given M, a target algorithm or metaheuristic, a set of parameters for the algorithm and a set of input data. The RMD consists in finding a reduced code for the metaheuristic which gives, at least, the same performance with the same input data than M. Figure 1 illustrates both problems. For the OMD problem, when we are building `My Code` we evaluate the inclusion of new components to improve its performance. After this evaluation a current code `Ccode` is obtained, which can follow a new procedure of inclusion of new components. For the RMD problem when the code is finished, it follows an evaluation step in order to identify, when this is possible, an alternative code which uses a reduced number of its components but has at least the same performance. In this work we map RMD to a configuration problem, where new parameters are introduced to the algorithm in order to identify alternative designs for M. More formally,

DEFINITION 3.1. *Given a metaheuristic code M, an instance of the problem consists in a 6-tuple*

$$P = (M, S, \Theta, \Pi, \kappa_{max}, M'),$$

where S is the set of new binary parameters introduced in M that allows to either turn on or off some components. M' is the modified version of M that includes S. Θ is the configurations space for M'. Π is the set of input problem instances, $g(\theta, \Pi)$ is a function that computes the expected gain (e.g., the quality of the solutions) of running M' using instance $\pi \in \Pi$ when using configuration θ. κ_{max} is a time out after which all instances of M' will be terminated if they are still running.

Any configuration $\theta \in \Theta$ is a candidate configuration of P. The gain of a candidate configuration θ is given by:

$$G_P(\theta) = mean_{\pi \in \Pi}(g(\theta, \pi))$$

[1]http://mat.gsia.cmu.edu/TOURN/relaxed/

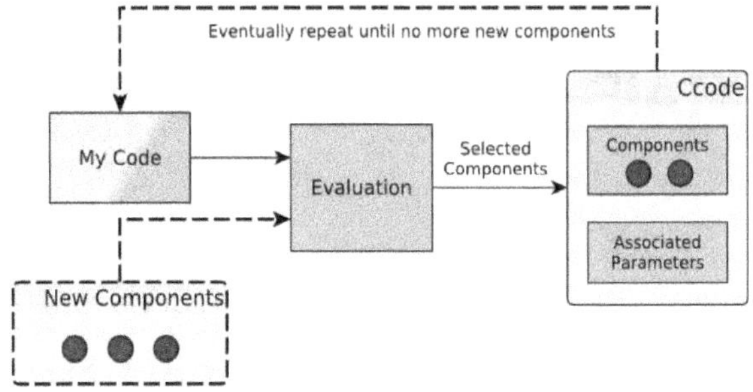

Figure 1: Illustration of the designing problems

This definition considers the mean of gain induced by $g(\theta, \pi)$, but any other statistic could be used instead (e.g. median, variance). Given G^M, the gain of metaheuristic M using its best parameter configuration, an alternative code defined by the configuration θ^* has a value $G_P(\theta)$ such that:

$$G_P(\theta^*) \geq G^M$$

We formally define an alternative design of the final metaheuristic code M as:

DEFINITION 3.2. *Given M a metaheuristic with a performance G^M and $M_1, \ldots, M_l$ alternative algorithms with performances $G_{M_1}(\theta_1), \ldots, G_{M_l}(\theta_l)$ for a maximization problem. M_i belongs to the* **set of alternative designs** *S_d, if and only if, $G_{M_i}(\theta_i) \geq G^M$. We define M_i as the* **best alternative design** *such that*

$$G_{M_i}(\theta_i) \geq G_{M_j}(\theta_j), \forall M_i, M_j \in S_d, i \neq j$$

During the post-design we are looking for a possible alternative code that allows the metaheuristic M' to solve the problems as M does with at least the same performance, but using a reduced number of its initial components. Given its stochastic nature, it is noteworthy to mention that the refined algorithm could show better performance than the initial one. Definitions are also applicable to minimization problems.

4. RELAXED TRAVELING TOURNAMENT

The Traveling Tournament Problem [8] (TTP) is a timetabling problem which involves two issues: the assignment feasibility (tournament structure) and optimization (reducing distance traveled by all teams). The objective is, given a number of teams N and a distance matrix $D_{i,j}$, to find a double round robin tournament which minimizes the distance traveled. The *trip length* constraint establishes the minimum and the maximum number of consecutive home/away matches allowed during the tournament. Usually, the lower and upper boundaries are one and three respectively.

A solution must also satisfy the following constraints:

- Constraint 1 [No repeaters]: Matches that involve the same pair of teams (i, j) must not take place in consecutive rounds.

- Constraint 2 [Mirrored]: The first half of the tournament should be a single round robin tournament, the second is obtained by mirroring the first one.

The double round robin structure requires $2(N-1)$ rounds, $N/2$ matches must take place every round, each pair of teams must play twice during the tournament exchanging homes, and all teams must play only one match every round.

The goal in the TTP is to find a compact schedule: the number of time slots is equal to the number of games each team plays. This forces every team to play in every time slot. In the Relaxed Traveling Tournament problem, the schedule is not required to be compact and teams are allowed to have a fixed number K of byes, hence RTTP schedule length is $2(N-1)+K$. Byes are ignored in determining the length of a home stand or road trip, and in determining whether a repeater has occurred. The higher the value of K the more flexibility to find solutions with lower distance traveled.

5. $RAIS_{TTP}$ ALGORITHM

In this section we introduce $RAIS_{TTP}$ artificial immune algorithm to solve the Relaxed TTP. For more details refer to [15] were $RAIS_{TTP}$ was introduced.

5.1 Representation

Considering a set of teams $S_T = \{T_1, \ldots, T_N\}$ of N teams, and a set of rounds $S_R = \{R_1, \ldots, R_M\}$ of M rounds, solutions are represented using a matrix TM_{NXM}, where the absolute value of each element $|tm_{ij}|$ indicates the opponent of team T_i in the round R_j. More precisely,

- $|tm_{ij}| \in \{1, \ldots, N\}$, with $|tm_{ij}| \neq i$

- $tm_{ij} > 0$ when the match is at home

- $tm_{ij} < 0$ when the match is away.

$RAIS_{TTP}$ approach considers constraints related to the double round robin stucture as hard constraints, and the moves take their satisfaction into account. The non structural constraints of *No repeaters* and *trip length* are managed by a penalization on the fitness function.

5.2 Fitness Function

In order to guide the algorithm to find good quality solutions which also satisfy the constraints, the algorithm uses equation 1 which computes the penalty function W_c for the constraint c. In this equation $\bar{d}$ is the average distance among teams and δ_c is the penalty factor associated to the dissatisfaction of the constraint c.

$$W_c = \bar{d} * (N-1) * \delta_c, \forall c = 1, 2. \quad (1)$$

Finally, equation 2 defines the fitness function F_{ttp}, considering all rounds, ϕ_i is the total traveled distance of team i and v_c is the number of violated non-structural constraints in a scheduling candidate.

$$F_{ttp} = \sum_{i=1}^{N} \phi_i + \sum_{c=1}^{2} v_c * W_c \quad (2)$$

5.3 $RAIS_{TTP}$ structure

$RAIS_{TTP}$ structure is shown in algorithm 1. Initial solutions are obtained using *"polygon method"* [16] to create single round robin structures (graph 1-factorization), that are mirrored and randomly assigned homes to complete the double round robin tournaments. Solutions are evaluated and cloned. cl_{rate} is the clonation rate which represents the percentage of the repertoire to be selected. Then, a set of clones is generated using the affinity proportional equation

$$C = \sum_{l=1}^{n} round\left(\frac{cl_{factor} * n}{l}\right),$$

where cl_{factor} is the clonal factor, n the repertoire size and l the antibody ranking. A hypermutation procedure is then performed. Hypermutation process is described in detail in section 5.5. Then, a new repertoire is created of the union between *Cells* and the hypermutated population P_c. The selection of cells does not only consider their fitness but it also considers their diversity. Diversity of each solution in P_c is measured by the average of the hamming distance between its home/away pattern and the home/away pattern of the solutions already members of the selected cells set. $r_{rate} * n$ new solutions are included each iteration.

Algorithm 1: $RAIS_{TTP}$

$Cells \leftarrow$ `InitializePopulation`(n) ;
$i \leftarrow 1$;
repeat
  `CalculateFitness` $(Cells)$;
  /*Select best $cl_{rate} * n$ antibodies from $Cells$*/
  $B_a \leftarrow$ `SelectBestAntibodies`$(cl_{rate} * n, Cells)$;
  /*Generate C clones of each antibody in B_a */
  $P_c \leftarrow$ `GenerateClones`(C, B_a) ;
  $P_c \leftarrow$ `Hypermutation`(P_c);
  $P_c \leftarrow P_c \cup Cells$;
  $Cells \leftarrow$ `DiversitySelection`(P_c, n);
  $Cells \leftarrow Cells+$ `GenerateNew`$(r_{rate} * n)$;
until *termination_condition*;
return;

5.4 Moves

The algorithm uses seven moves. *Swap Homes*, *Swap Rounds*, *Swap Teams*, *Partial Swap Rounds* and *Partial Swap Teams* have been proposed for a Simulated Annealing algorithm in [1]. *SwapByesMatches* and *GroupingAwayByes* were introduced in [14]. *GroupingAwayByes* is oriented to the reduction of traveling costs. As the cost of a team schedule corresponds to the cost of its away matches (trips), the idea is to try to group its trips to reduce the traveling costs.

- `SwapTeams`(T_i, T_j): Exchanges teams T_i and T_j matches, except for the ones which involve themselves.

- `SwapHomes`(T_i, T_j): Exchanges teams T_i and T_j matches home (matrix elements sign).

- `SwapRounds`(R_i, R_j): Exchanges rounds R_i and R_j schedules.

- `PartialSwapTeams`(T_i, R_j, R_k): Exchanges teams T_i and T_j matches for a round R_k.

- `PartialSwapRounds`(T_i,R_j,R_k): Exchanges round R_j match for R_k round match for a team T_i, .
- `SwapByesMatches`(T_i,T_j): Exchanges teams T_i and T_j from their current round to a new one were thay have a day off.
- `GroupingAwayByes` (T_i): Tries to group the trips of the team T_i using the byes in order to reduce the traveling costs.

5.5 Hypermutation procedure

In $RAIS_{TTP}$, the antibody ranking is used as a hypermutation level indicator. It determines the number of moves to apply to each clone. Algorithm 2 shows the procedure. It uses an exhaustive selection process from the solutions obtained by applying each of the six moves to the same candidate solution. The selected solution follows the `GroupingAwayByes` in order to try to improve it.

Algorithm 2: `Hypermutation`(P_c)

```
forall the s ∈ P_c do
    /*Ranking to determine hypermutation level */
    for x ← 1 to ranking do
        for y ← 1 to 6 do
            s*_y ← op_y(s);
        end
        sol ← Best(s*_1, ..., s*_6);
        s*_7 ←GroupingAwayByes(sol);
        if Better(s*_7, sol) then
            sol ← s*_7;
        end
    end
    s ← sol;
end
return;
```

6. REFINING $RAIS_{TTP}$

The goal of our experiments is to analyze which components of the hypermutation process are required. Thus, we evaluate the seven moves used by the $RAIS_{TTP}$ hypermutation procedure.

6.1 Refining strategy

In order to apply a tuner to this evaluation process we added seven parameters to $RAIS_{TTP}$. We have associated one binary parameter to each move. Algorithm 3 shows the pseudocode of our refining on hypermutation process.

In our approach the value of parameter $UseST$ indicates either to use or not use `SwapTeams`. The same is interpreted for parameters $UseSH$, $UseSR$, $UsePST$ $UsePSR$ $UseSBM$ and $UseGAB$ related to the remaining moves analyzed. For all these parameters a value 0 means that the associated move can be deleted from the code without loss performance.

From algorithm 3, the use of each move requires the evaluation of a new solution, hence, the more moves the $RAIS_{TTP}$ uses, the more computational effort is required for each iteration. In our approach we use EvoCa tuner in order to determine simpler codes than $RAIS_{TTP}$ requiring the same computational effort but having similar performance.

Algorithm 3: `Refining Hypermutation`(P_c)

```
forall the s ∈ P_c do
    /*Ranking to determine hypermutation level */
    for x ← 1 to ranking do
        for y ← 1 to 6 do
            /*Value of each binary parameter
              determines the use of related move */
            if UseOp_y then
                s*_y ← op_y(s);
            end
        end
        sol ← Best(s*_1, ..., s*_6);
        /*Value of parameter UseGAB determines
          the use of GroupingAwayByes             */
        if UseGAB then
            s*_7 ←GroupingAwayByes(sol);
        end
        if Better(s*_7, sol) then
            sol ← s*_7;
        end
    end
    s ← sol;
end
return;
```

6.2 Evolutionary Calibrator

EvoCa is an evolutionary algorithm that works with a population of parameter calibrations. It uses a wheel-crossover that constructs one child calibration from the whole population. The child replaces the worst calibration in the current population. It also uses a hill climbing procedure for mutation. The child generated by mutation replaces the second worst calibration in the current population, when a better parameter calibration is found. For a detailed description of EvoCa refer to [17].

7. EXPERIMENTS

In our experiments we use $RAIS_{TTP}$'s authors implementation. For these experiments we have considered the set of *National League* (NL) traveling tournament problem instances: $NL4$ to $NL16$ ranging from 4 to 16 teams. Moreover, we have considered experiments with $K = 1$, $K = 2$ and $K = 3$. We used EvoCa's authors implementation with a population of 10. Sources for our experiments are available in our website[2].

7.1 Tuning process

The tuning process considered a total of 10 parameter values to tune. Here, we tune 3 original $RAIS_{TTP}$ parameters defined by its authors: cl_{rate} represents the percentage of solutions to be selected for clonation, cl_{factor} is the clonal factor related to the amount of clones that will be generated from each solution and r_{rate} represents the percentage of new solutions included each iteration. The seven binary parameters previously defined were also tuned in this process. 20 independent tuning processes were executed in order to deal with stochastic nature of tuning method. Each tuning process considered the entire NL set of instances. A maximum budget of $10K$ $RAIS_{TTP}$ executions was fixed for each

[2]comet.informaticae.org

tuning process. Each $RAIS_{TTP}$ considered a termination criterion of $7K$ evaluations.

7.2 Results

Table 1 shows the results obtained in 20 different tuning processes. In each tuning process 10 parameter values were tuned. Seven of these parameter values can be considered design decisions and the remaining three are numerical parameter of $RAIS_{TTP}$. Hence, each tuning process can be seen as a competition between different design options (each one using proper $RAIS_{TTP}$ parameter values) and its output represents the best design decision with the best parameter values. It is important to point out that design decisions and tuning of $RAIS_{TTP}$ parameters can not be made independently because the determination of the final performance of $RAIS_{TTP}$ depends on the way they interact.

To calculate the gain $G_P(\theta)$ of these algorithms they were executed 100 times in each instance. For these experiments, the number of evaluations was fixed to $7K$ for $NL4$ and $NL6$, $210K$ for $NL8$, $NL10$, $NL12$ and $NL14$; and $1400K$ for $NL16$. Relative distance to best performance was calculated for each instance. Column $G_P(\theta)$ in table 1 shows the average of relative distance to best performance considering the entire set of instances. For a minimization problem the algorithm with lower gain value shows the best performance.

From table 1 we can observe that in 25% of cases the best design is not use `SwapRounds` and `SwapByesMatches` operators. The diversity of the results in the performance for this design is due to the stochastic nature of Evoca, because in different runs it identifies different parameter's values. However, each run uses different seeds and it follows an internal competition process among the set of the alternative designs. Thus, the selected design is the best option after the complete evaluation process of each run. We can also observe that the original design has been selected as the best of the run only once ($E1$). From these results we identify the design selected more times and from those designs $E12$ has the best parameter's values.

In order to obtain the best performance for the selected design a complete new tuning process could be done to obtain the three best numerical parameter values of the new design of $RAIS_{TTP}$. The tuning method used by the authors of $RAIS_{TTP}$ was an exhaustive one, where all possible values have been tested.

Table 3 compares the performance of algorithm $RAIS_{TTP}$ ($E12$) with the original $RAIS_{TTP}$ for each instance studied. For these experiments we executed $RAIS_{TTP}$ using values tuned by authors in [15] and shown in table 2. Table 3 shows the average and best performance of 100 independent executions of the original $RAIS_{TTP}$ versus $RAIS_{TTP}$ ($E12$). Last column shows the p-value of Wilcoxon signed rank test comparing the performance of both algorithms for each instance. Considering a confidence level of 95% statistically different performance is presented in bold face.

Table 2: Parameter values used in [15]

Instance	cl_{rate}	cl_{factor}	r_{rate}
All	1.0	1.0	0.3

From these results we can conclude that design $E12$ allows to simplify $RAIS_{TTP}$ algorithm finding no statistically significant difference in 12 cases and a statistical better performance in 9 cases.

Graphs in figures 2-7 show box-plots comparing the results of $RAIS_{TTP}$ and $RAIS_{TTP}(E12)$ considering $K=1$, $K=2$ and $K=3$ for each instance. We did not include a graph for $NL4$ because both $RAIS_{TTP}$ versions found always the same performance in this instance.

Here we can observe that for instances $NL6$-$NL10$ the performance of both versions of $RAIS_{TTP}$ are very similar, but in larger instances, $RAIS_{TTP}$ ($E12$) clearly outperforms the original design considering all values of K.

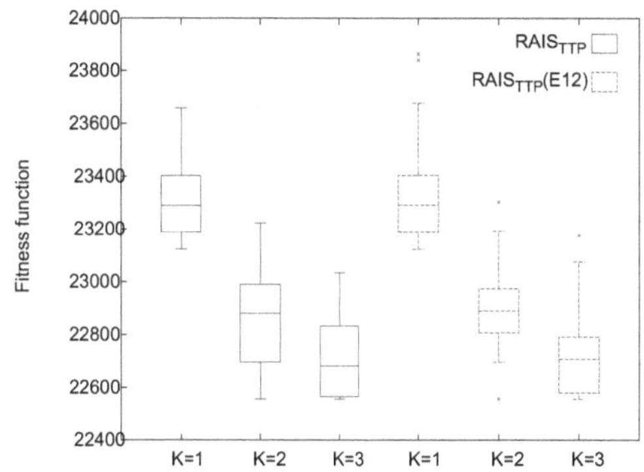

Figure 2: $RAIS_{TTP}$ versus $RAIS_{TTP}(E12)$ for $NL6$

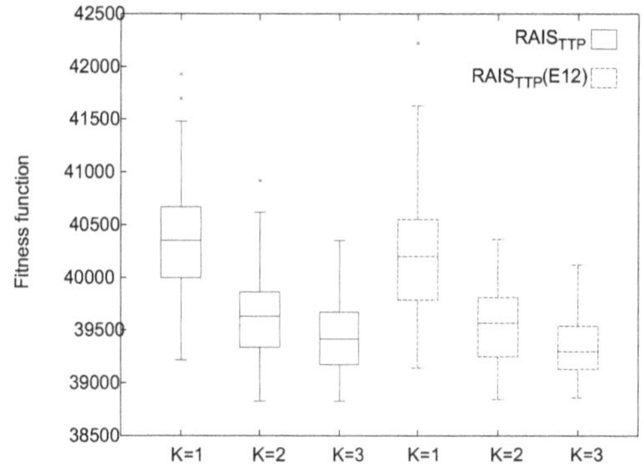

Figure 3: $RAIS_{TTP}$ versus $RAIS_{TTP}(E12)$ for $NL8$

Table 4 compares the performance of $RAIS_{TTP}$ ($E12$) with the best bounds published. Here, we can observe that the new design for $RAIS_{TTP}$ was able to find new bounds for $NL10$ with $K=1$ and $K=3$.

Graphs in figures 8 and 9 show convergence of $RAIS_{TTP}$ and $RAIS_{TTP}(E12)$ when they were able to find their best solutions in table 3. Logarithmic scale was used for x axis in order to improve the reading.

Figure 8 shows the best behaviour of each algorithm to solve $NL10$ with $K=1$. Because of each algorithm has shown its best behaviour using different seeds, the initial populations are different. We observe that $RAIS_TTP(E12)$ despite starting with poorer population is able to converge to a better solution than $RAIS_TTP(E12)$. $RAIS_TTP(E12)$ can perform a higher number of evaluations given its simplicity compared to the original algorithm.

Table 1: **Algorithms and their performances**

Id.	cl_rate	cl_factor	r_{rate}	$useST$	$useSH$	$useSR$	$usePST$	$usePSR$	$useSBM$	$useGAB$	$G_P(\theta)$
E0	0.90	0.80	0.32	1	0	0	1	1	0	1	1.96
E1	0.82	0.30	0.00	1	1	1	1	1	1	1	2.09
E2	1.00	0.20	0.30	1	1	1	1	1	0	1	2.19
E3	0.89	0.18	0.53	1	1	0	1	1	0	1	2.49
E4	0.60	1.00	0.40	1	1	0	1	1	1	1	1.09
E5	0.80	1.00	0.28	1	1	0	1	1	1	0	2.13
E6	1.00	1.00	0.20	1	1	0	0	1	0	1	1.19
E7	0.50	0.90	0.60	1	1	0	1	1	0	1	1.80
E8	0.40	0.90	0.05	1	1	0	1	1	0	1	0.85
E9	0.50	1.00	0.20	1	0	0	1	1	1	1	1.83
E10	0.84	0.90	0.50	1	1	1	1	1	0	0	2.37
E11	0.51	0.97	0.00	1	1	0	0	1	0	1	1.01
E12	**0.78**	**1.00**	**0.20**	**1**	**1**	**0**	**1**	**1**	**0**	**1**	**0.62**
E13	0.80	0.50	0.00	0	1	0	1	1	1	0	5.34
E14	0.84	0.65	0.56	1	1	0	1	1	0	1	1.77
E15	0.91	0.19	0.20	1	0	1	1	1	1	1	2.97
E16	0.80	0.40	0.50	1	1	0	1	1	1	0	3.52
E17	0.40	0.85	0.00	1	0	1	0	1	1	1	2.96
E18	1.00	0.90	0.00	1	1	1	1	1	0	1	0.87
E19	0.70	0.30	0.60	0	1	1	1	1	0	0	5.60
% usage				90	80	35	85	100	40	75	

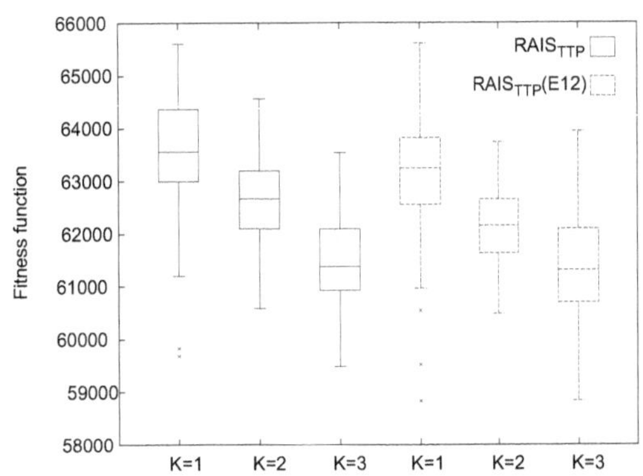

Figure 4: $RAIS_{TTP}$ **versus** $RAIS_{TTP}(E12)$ **for** $NL10$

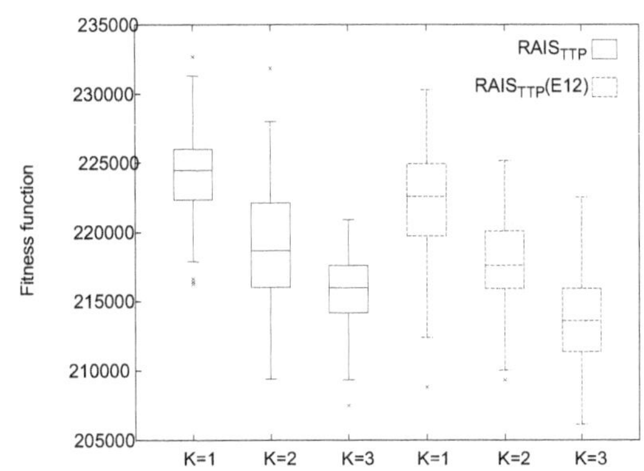

Figure 6: $RAIS_{TTP}$ **versus** $RAIS_{TTP}(E12)$ **for** $NL14$

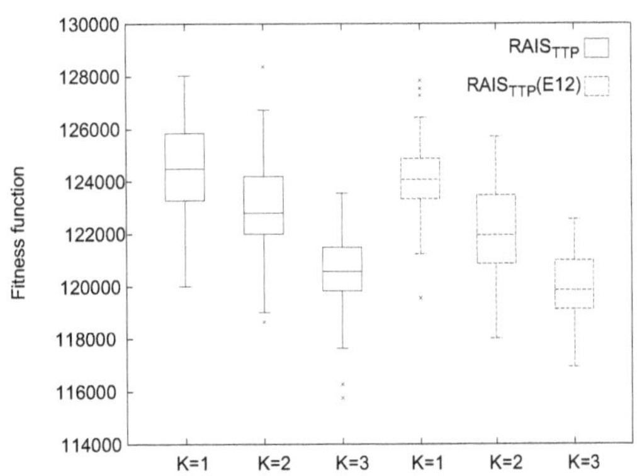

Figure 5: $RAIS_{TTP}$ **versus** $RAIS_{TTP}(E12)$ **for** $NL12$

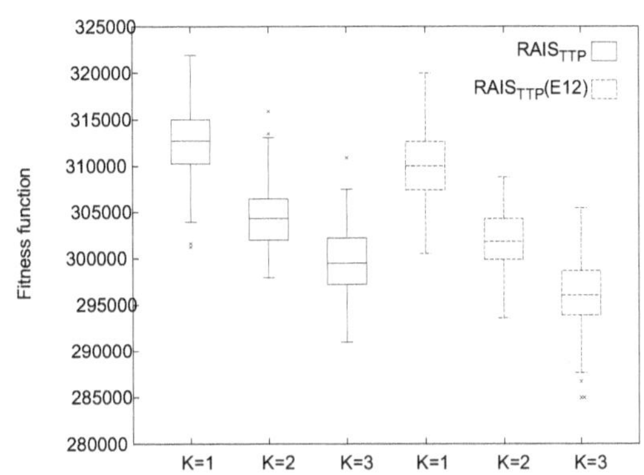

Figure 7: $RAIS_{TTP}$ **versus** $RAIS_{TTP}(E12)$ **for** $NL16$

Table 3: Performance comparison: $RAIS_{TTP}$ versus $RAIS_{TTP}(E12)$

Instance		$RAIS_{TTP}$ Average	$RAIS_{TTP}$ Best	$RAIS_{TTP}(E12)$ Average	$RAIS_{TTP}(E12)$ Best	p-value
NL4	K=1	8160.0	8160	8160.0	8160	-
	K=2	8160.0	8160	8160.0	8160	-
	K=3	8044.0	8044	8044.0	8044	-
NL6	K=1	23308.7	23124	23322.9	23124	0.75
	K=2	22861.9	22557	22895.9	22557	0.08
	K=3	22700.5	22557	22705.7	22557	0.89
NL8	K=1	40343.7	39218	40213.9	39142	0.09
	K=2	39625.1	38831	39569.9	38845	0.29
	K=3	39432.0	38831	39355.7	38859	0.08
NL10	K=1	63542.8	59686	**63160.8**	58825	**0.01**
	K=2	62653.7	60584	**62095.6**	60477	**0.00**
	K=3	61526.9	59486	61407.5	58834	0.48
NL12	K=1	124457.4	120016	124107.1	119570	0.08
	K=2	123027.6	118674	**122089.0**	118037	**0.00**
	K=3	120564.7	115755	**119955.7**	116942	**0.00**
NL14	K=1	224272.7	216236	**222197.0**	208823	**0.00**
	K=2	219010.7	209402	218020.0	209331	0.09
	K=3	215872.1	207495	**213782.1**	206134	**0.00**
NL16	K=1	312448.2	301232	**309895.2**	300531	**0.00**
	K=2	304606.7	297936	**301840.7**	293575	**0.00**
	K=3	299642.1	290998	**296065.9**	284982	**0.00**

Table 4: Performance of calibration $E12$

Instance		Best known	E12 Average	E12 Best
NL4	K=1	8160	8160.0	8160
	K=2	8160	8160.0	8160
	K=3	8044	8044.0	8044
NL6	K=1	22642	23322.9	23124
	K=2	22557	22895.9	22557
	K=3	22557	22705.7	22557
NL8	K=1	39128	40213.9	39142
	K=2	38761	39569.9	38845
	K=3	38670	39355.7	38859
NL10	K=1	59425	63160.8	**58825**
	K=2	59373	62095.6	60477
	K=3	59436	61407.5	**58834**
NL12	K=1	108629	124107.1	119570
	K=2	108629	122089.0	118037
	K=3	108629	119955.7	116942
NL14	K=1	183354	222197.0	208823
	K=2	183354	218020.0	209331
	K=3	183354	213782.1	206134
NL16	K=1	249477	309895.2	300531
	K=2	249477	301840.7	293575
	K=3	249477	296065.9	284982

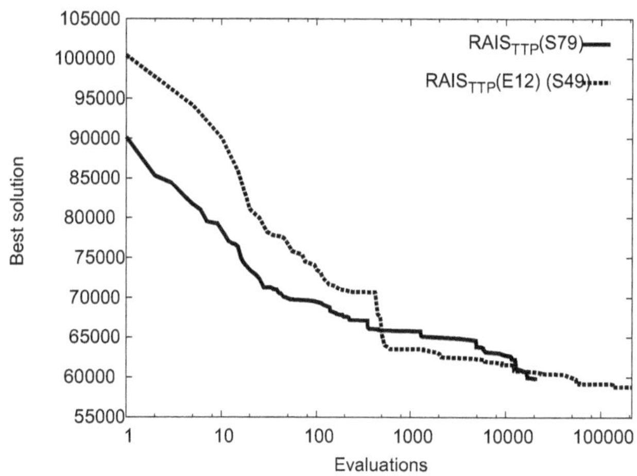

Figure 8: Convergence of $RAIS_{TTP}$ versus $RAIS_{TTP}(E12)$ for $NL10$ with $K = 1$

Figure 9 shows the convergence process for instance $NL10$ with $K = 3$. The same effect as in figure 8 can be noticed here. The use of moves `SwapRounds` and `SwapByesMatches` leads to a stagnation of the search , while $RAIS_{TTP}(E12)$ shows a similar behavior in first steps, but it is still able to obtain important improvements in the last steps of the search.

8. CONCLUSIONS AND FUTURE WORK

In this work we did an in-depth analysis of the immune algorithm $RAIS_{TTP}$, that was specially designed to solve instances of the relaxed travel tournament problem. We addressed the refining design problem, that is a post-design problem. We are interested in simplifying the $RAIS_{TTP}$ code without performance loss. From this study we have defined a simpler code ($RAIS_{TTP}$ ($E12$)) that shows no statistical significance difference in performance. Moreover, using this refined code we have obtained new bounds for the RTTP. The fact we have obtained a simpler algorithm does not mean that the original metaheuristic is not a good code. The classical incremental process of designing metaheuristics

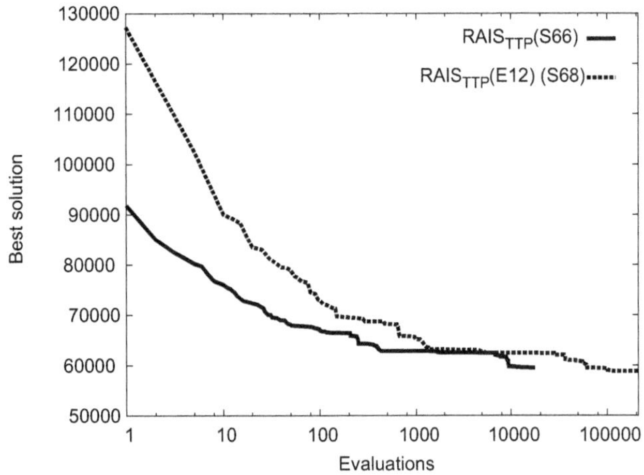

Figure 9: Convergence of $RAIS_{TTP}$ versus $RAIS_{TTP}(E12)$ for $NL10$ with $K = 3$

can produce a complex code, in which the interaction among many components is unknown. The key idea when searching for a refined code is to better understand the code behavior as well as the problem.

As future work we want to better analyze $RAIS_{TTP}$ using the refinement method to study new components in order to improve its performance in more complex instances.

Acknowledgment

We thank Mrs. Leslie Pérez-Cáceres for her support with $RAIS_{TTP}$ implementation.

9. REFERENCES

[1] A. Anagnostopoulos, L. Michel, P. V. Hentenryck, and Y. Vergados. A Simulated Annealing Approach to the Traveling Tournament Problem. *Journal of Scheduling*, 9(2):177–193, 2006.

[2] L. C. T. Bezerra, M. López-Ibáñez, and T. Stützle. Automatic design of evolutionary algorithms for multi-objective combinatorial optimization. In *PPSN*, volume 8672 of *LNCS*, pages 508–517. 2014.

[3] E. Burke, G. Kendall, J. Newall, E. Hart, P. Ross, and S. Schulenburg. Hyper-heuristics: An emerging direction in modern search technology. In *Handbook of Metaheuristics*, volume 57, pages 457–474. 2003.

[4] P.-C. Chen, G. Kendall, and G. Berghe. An ant based hyper-heuristic for the travelling tournament problem. In *IEEE Symposium on Computational Intelligence in Scheduling*, pages 19–26, 2007.

[5] C. A. Coello-Coello, D. Cortés-Rivera, and N. Cruz-Cortés. Use of an artificial immune system for job shop scheduling. In *Artificial Immune Systems*, volume 2787 of *LNCS*, pages 1–10. 2003.

[6] N. Cruz-Cortés, D. Trejo-Pérez, and C. A. Coello-Coello. Handling constraints in global optimization using an artificial immune system. In *Artificial Immune Systems*, volume 3627 of *LNCS*, pages 234–247. 2005.

[7] L. N. de Castro and F. J. V. Zuben. Learning and optimization using the clonal selection principle. *IEEE Transactions on Evolutionary Computation*, 6(3):239–251, 2002.

[8] K. Easton, G. Nemhauser, and M. Trick. The traveling tournament problem description and benchmarks. In *Principles and Practice of Constraint Programming*, volume 2239 of *LNCS*, pages 580–585, 2001.

[9] A. E. Eiben and S. K. Smit. Parameter Tuning for Configuring and Analyzing Evolutionary Algorithms. *Swarm and Evolutionary Computation*, 1(1):19–31, 2011.

[10] L. D. Gaspero and A. Schaerf. A composite-neighborhood tabu search approach to the traveling tournament problem. *Journal of Heuristics*, 13(2):189–207, 2007.

[11] A. Lim, B. Rodrigues, and X. Zhang. A simulated annealing and hill-climbing algorithm for the traveling tournament problem. *European Journal of Operational Research*, 174(3):1459–1478, 2006.

[12] K. V. M. Misir, T. Wauters and G. V. Berghe. A new learning hyper-heuristic for the traveling tournament problem. In *MIC 2009: The VIII Metaheuristics International Conference*, 2009.

[13] E. Montero and M.-C. Riff. Towards a method for automatic algorithm configuration: A design evaluation using tuners. In *PPSN*, volume 8672 of *LNCS*, pages 90–99. 2014.

[14] L. Pérez and M.-C. Riff. New bounds for the relaxed traveling tournament problems using an artificial immune algorithm. In *CEC*, pages 873–879, 2011.

[15] L. Pérez-Cáceres and M.-C. Riff. Solving scheduling tournament problems using a new version of clonalg. *Connection Science*, 27(1):5–21, 2015.

[16] C. C. Ribeiro and S. Urrutia. Heuristics for the mirrored traveling tournament problem. *European Journal of Operational Research*, 179(3):775–787, 2007.

[17] M.-C. Riff and E. Montero. A new algorithm for reducing metaheuristic design effort. In *CEC*, pages 3283–3290, Cancún, México, June 2013.

[18] M.-C. Riff, M. Zúñiga, and E. Montero. A graph-based immune-inspired constraint satisfaction search. *Neural Computing and Applications*, 19(8):1133–1142, 2010.

[19] J. Timmis, C. Edmonds, and J. Kelsey. Assessing the performance of two immune inspired algorithms and a hybrid genetic algorithm for function optimisation. In *CEC*, volume 1, pages 1044–1051, 2004.

[20] D. C. Uthus, P. J. Riddle, and H. Guesgen. Solving the traveling tournament problem with iterative-deepening a*. *Journal of Scheduling*, 15(5):601–614, 2012.

[21] D. C. Uthus, P. J. Riddle, and H. W. Guesgen. An ant colony optimization approach to the traveling tournament problem. In *GECCO*, pages 81–88. ACM, 2009.

[22] J. Walker and S. Garrett. Dynamic function optimisation: comparing the performance of clonalg and evolution strategies. In *Artificial Immune Systems*, volume 2787 of *LNCS*, pages 273–285, 2003.

[23] Z. Zhang. Immune optimization algorithm for constrained nonlinear multiobjective optimization problems. *Applied Soft Computing*, 7(3):840–857, 2007.

Evolving Robot Morphology Facilitates the Evolution of Neural Modularity and Evolvability

Josh C. Bongard
Dept. of Computer Science
University of Vermont
josh.bongard@uvm.edu

Anton Bernatskiy
Dept. of Computer Science
University of Vermont
anton.bernatskiy@uvm.edu

Ken Livingston
Dept. of Cognitive Science
Vassar College
livingst@vassar.edu

Nicholas Livingston
Robotics Laboratory
Vassar College
nilivingston@vassar.edu

John Long
Dept. of Biology
Vassar College
jolong@vassar.edu

Marc Smith
Dept. of Computer Science
Vassar College
mlsmith@vassar.edu

ABSTRACT

Although recent work has demonstrated that modularity can increase evolvability in non-embodied systems, it remains to be seen how the morphologies of embodied agents influences the ability of an evolutionary algorithm to find useful and modular controllers for them. We hypothesize that a modular control system may enable different parts of a robot's body to sense and react to stimuli independently, enabling it to correctly recognize a seemingly novel environment as, in fact, a composition of familiar percepts and thus respond appropriately without need of further evolution. Here we provide evidence that supports this hypothesis: We found that such robots can indeed be evolved if (1) the robot's morphology is evolved along with its controller, (2) the fitness function selects for the desired behavior and (3) also selects for conservative and robust behavior. In addition, we show that if constraints (1) and (3) are relaxed, or structural modularity is selected for directly, the robots have too little or too much modularity and lower evolvability. Thus, we demonstrate a previously unknown relationship between modularity and embodied cognition: evolving morphology and control such that robots exhibit conservative behavior indirectly selects for appropriate modularity and, thus, increased evolvability.

Categories and Subject Descriptors

I.2.9 [**Computing Methodologies**]: Artificial Intelligence-Robotics

Keywords

Artificial Intelligence, Robotics, Evolutionary Computation, Modularity, Evolvability, Embodied cognition, Artificial neural networks

GECCO '15, July 11–15, 2015, Madrid, Spain

DOI: http://dx.doi.org/10.1145/2739480.2754750

1. INTRODUCTION

In the field of evolutionary robotics [14, 10, 2], an evolutionary algorithm is typically employed to optimize the wiring diagram of the robot's neural controller and/or aspects of its morphology such that the robot exhibits some desired behavior. However, for complex robots with large numbers of artificial neurons, the number of possible connections between those neurons grows quadratically, requiring search over a very large space of candidate controllers. Another barrier to continued evolutionary improvement is that large, densely-connected neural controllers are notoriously difficult to evolve: any mutation to one part of the network tends to affect behavior at many other parts of the network.

Both of these reasons suggest that it would be desirable to evolve robots controlled by modular neural networks. However, it is unclear how to architect an evolutionary algorithm to evolve controllers with modularity suitable to the task the robot must perform.

Previous work has investigated evolving modular control if the task calls for it. In [13] however, the number and type of modules, as well as the connectivity pattern, were predetermined. Gruau [8] employed an indirect genotype to phenotype mapping that allowed for the construction of neural modules. However, this method requires an evolutionary operator for explicitly creating modules. In other work [3] an evolutionary operator could duplicate existing modules. The work presented here differs from all of these approaches in that it does not require such high-level operators: modules emerge (or dissipate) as local connectivity density gradually increases (or decreases) over evolutionary time.

The challenge of evolving modularity without pre-supposing the cognitive architecture of the controller, or explicitly having to formulate module-creating operators, is demonstrated in [4]. There, it was shown that HyperNEAT [17], a popular indirect encoding method, failed to evolve neural modularity on all but the simplest of problems.

Outside of evolutionary robotics, many recent projects have investigated the conditions under which structural modularity will evolve[1]. However, these approaches have investi-

[1]Structural modularity—in which dense connectivity exists within modules and few connections exist between modules—is distinguished from functionally modularity[20],

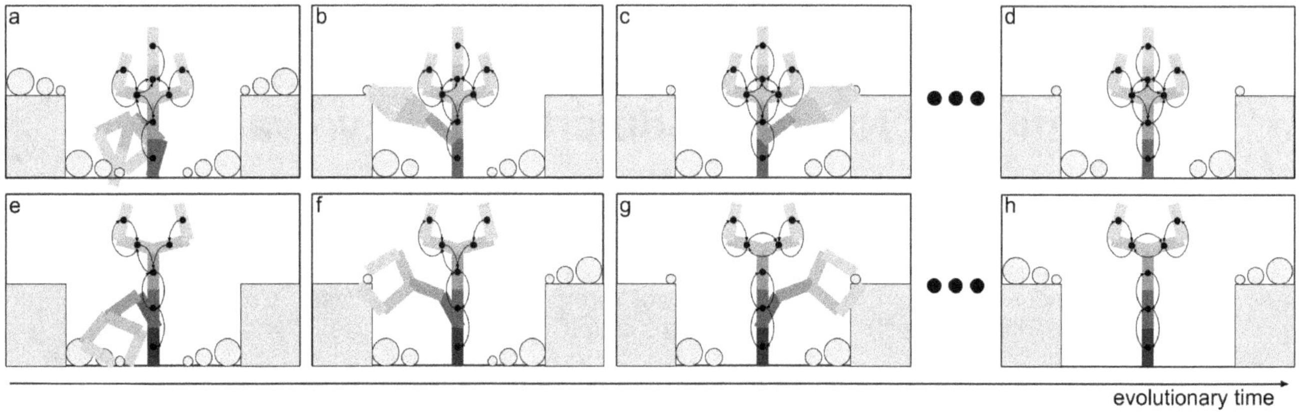

Figure 1: The hypothesized relationship between morphology, neural modularity, and evolvability. Two robot arms with different morphologies are evolved to move objects of different size onto two ledges: one arm supports a three-fingered gripper (a-d) while the other supports a two-fingered gripper (e-h). Both evolve the ability to grasp one object (a,e) and place it somewhere else (b,f). Later in evolutionary time, both evolve the ability to place two of the objects (c,g). During this second evolutionary phase, the second robot evolves a modular neural controller: synapses connect gripper motor neurons and other synapses connect the arm motor neurons, but there are no synapses connecting gripper and arm neurons (g). The first robot does not evolve neural modularity: its gripper and arm motor neurons do not become dissociated (c). This modularity renders the second arm more evolvable than the first such that it eventually evolves the ability to place all six objects (h).

gated modularity in a non-embodied context: in [9] and [5], a disembodied visual system must recognize combinations of familiar and unfamiliar patterns; in [6], gene regulatory networks were modeled without taking into account the effect that the cell's environment has on gene regulation.

In contrast, here we investigate the evolution of modular controllers in embodied agents and demonstrate a hitherto unknown relationship between modularity and adaptive behavior: evolving robot morphology along with control can lead to modular controllers which, in turn, increase the overall evolvability[2] of the population; however, if the robots' body plans are fixed, this evolvability cannot be achieved.

The robots evolve modular controllers because they experience a combination of directional selection and stabilizing selection. This combination of evolutionary pressures has been implicated as the driving force behind the evolution of modularity in biological organisms [19]. More recently, this theory was supported experimentally by observing the evolution of models of gene regulatory networks under these conditions [6].

In the same work [6], the link between modularity and evolvability was made clear: modular networks can rapidly produce novel combinations of previously- evolved gene activity patterns. Here, we demonstrate that robots with modular controllers are evolvable for similar reasons: such robots can recognize seemingly novel situations as novel combinations of familiar percepts. They are thus able to respond appropriately without having to evolve a novel response to this seeming novel situation.

in which a network exhibits several distinct functional pattens.

[2]Here we define the evolvability of a system as the average increase in fitness that can be achieved, given a fixed computational budget.

2. HYPOTHESIS

Our hypothesis is that robots with certain morphologies will experience directional selection acting on one part of their bodies and controllers, and stabilizing selection acting on another part of their bodies and controllers, as they evolve to perform some desired task. This combination of selection pressures will favor neural modularity that will in turn enable them to rapidly adapt when presented with novel combinations of familiar percepts: only slight evolutionary modification will be required in one or a few neural modules.

Fig. 1 provides a visual outline of the hypothesis we wish to test. Two robots with different morphologies evolve to perform an object pick-and-place task. The first robot's morphology does not experience the correct combination of selection pressures (Fig. 1a-b), does not evolve neural modularity (Fig. 1c), exhibits low evolvability, and fails to become increasingly adept at the task (Fig. 1d). The second robot happens to have the right morphology (Fig. 1e-f) that eventually leads to neural modularity (Fig. 1g) and increased evolvability (Fig. 1h).

Below, we demonstrate that this relationship between morphology, neural modularity and evolvability does indeed exist, at least for a simplified robot and task environment.

3. METHODS

This section outlines the robots, their task environments, their controllers, and the evolutionary algorithm we used to evolve them. All of the material for replicating the work described here is available at `http://git.io/vvH7r`.

3.1 The Robots

The robots used in this work are two dimensional, are composed of a three-segment arm (black lines in Fig. 2) and a hand composed of two, two-segment fingers (red and

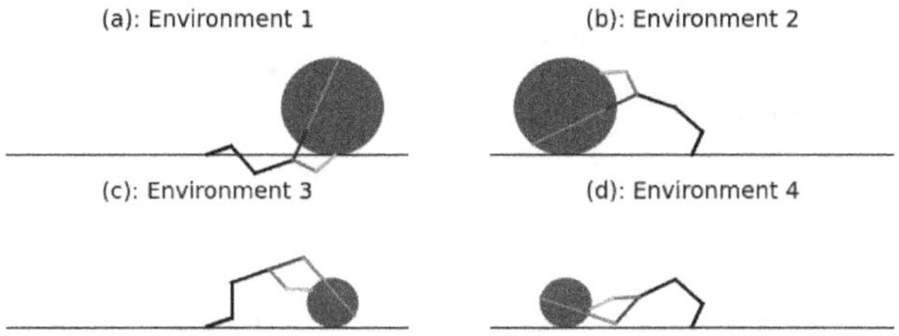

Figure 2: A typical evolved non-conservative pose. The robot's arm (black segments) and hand (red and green segments) reach a different pose in each environment.

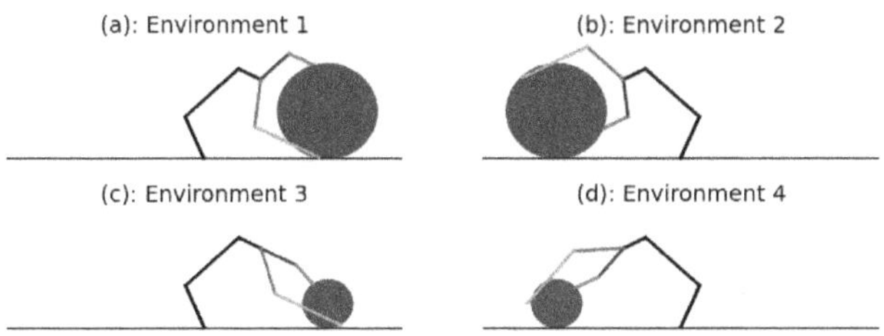

Figure 3: A typical evolved conservative pose. The hand reaches the same pose in environments 1 and 2, and environments 3 and 4. The arm reaches the same pose in environments 1 and 3, and environments 2 and 4.

green lines in Fig. 2), and are based on the robots investigated in [1]. Each of the seven segments can vary in length between $0.5u$ and $3.0u$[3]. Segments are attached by rotational hinge joints, each of which can take on one of four possible angles. The three arm joints can take any angle in $\{-70^o, -23.33^o, +23.33^o, +70^o\}$: negative and positive angles rotate the arm to the left and right, respectively. The left proximate phalange and right distal phalange can take any value in $\{-70^o, -46.67^o, -23.33^o, 0^o\}$; The right proximate phalange and left distal phalange can take any value in $\{0^o, 23.33^o, 46.67^o, 70^o\}$; These angle constraints for the hand ensure that it maintains claw-like poses and that the phalanges do not cross.

In the experiments in which the robot's morphology is evolved, a seven-element, floating-point valued vector $\mathbf{m}$ was evolved: element m_i in this vector encodes the length of the ith segment.

3.2 The Task Environments

The robots were evolved to grasp objects in four different environments. The first environment contained an object with radius $1u$ placed $2.5u$ to the right of the robot's base. The second environment contained an object with radius $1u$ placed $2.5u$ to the left of the robot's base. The third environment contained an object with radius $0.5u$ placed $2.5u$ to the right of the robot's base. The fourth environment contained an object with radius $0.5u$ placed $2.5u$ to the left of the robot's base. No collision detection and resolution was employed: the robot's segments could pass through the object. The robot and object were simulated in a kinematic simulation.

[3] u is a unitless measure of distance.

3.3 The Controllers

The robots were evolved with either a simple or random boolean network (RBN) controller.

Simple Control. The simple controller was encoded as a 4×7 matrix $\mathbf{C}$, in which the ith row encoded joint angles for the ith environment and the j column encoded angles for the jth joint. When the robot was 'controlled' by this simple controller, its joints were simply set to these angles and forward kinematics were used to compute the resulting pose of the robot. Fig. 2 displays a typical pose when the robot is evolved to grasp the four objects using this controller.

RBN Control. The RBN controller is composed of 14 binary neurons that can take on values in $\{-1, +1\}$. Each of the seven joints is assigned two of these neurons. The first six neurons are assigned to the three arm joints; the last eight neurons are assigned to the four hand joints. The four possible neuron value pairs $[-1, -1]$, $[-1, +1]$, $[+1, -1]$, and $[+1, +1]$ for each joint dictate which of its four possible angles it rotates to. Thus, each of the $2^{14} = 16,384$ possible states of the controller corresponds to a unique robot pose. Each controller is encoded as a 14×14 adjacency matrix $\mathbf{A}$. Elements in this matrix are trinary: $a_{ij} = +1$, $a_{ij} = -1$, and $a_{ij} = 0$ indicate that neuron i is connected to node j with an excitatory synapse, inhibitory synapse, or no synapse, respectively.

When a robot is placed into one of the four environments, the initial values of the neurons are set to indicate the size and position of the object in that environment. Thus, the robot can 'sense' its surroundings based on the neurons' initial values. Even-numbered neurons indicate object size: $n_0, n_2, \ldots, n_{12}$ are all set to $+1$ if the object is large and to -1 if the object is small. Odd-numbered neurons indicate object position: $n_1, n_3, \ldots, n_{13}$ are all set to $+1$ if the object is on the robot's right and to to -1 if the object is on the robot's left.

After setting the initial conditions, the RBN is updated three times using synchronous updating. The value of the ith neuron at time step t is set to

$$n_i^{(t)} = \sigma(\sum_{j=1}^{14} a_{ji} n_j^{(t-1)}) \quad (1)$$

where

$$\sigma(x) = \begin{cases} -1, & \text{if } x <= 0 \\ +1, & \text{otherwise} \end{cases} \quad (2)$$

The final values of the neurons are then used to set the robot's pose as described above. Fig. 3 displays a pose produced by an evolved RBN controller.

3.4 The Evolutionary Algorithm

We employed the Age-Fitness Pareto Optimization (AFPO) evolutionary algorithm [16] for all of the experiments reported here. AFPO is a multiobjective optimization method that periodically injects new genomes into the evolving population, and enables these younger genomes time to improve before being outcompeted in the population by older genomes with higher fitness. This enables older genomes trapped on local optima to periodically be displaced by younger genomes that, with time, evolve to higher fitness values. AFPO achieves this dynamic using the genome's age as one fitness objective.

Aside from age, genomes were also evolved to produce robots that could grasp objects, had modular controllers, and/or exhibited behavioral conservatism.

Grasping ability. Evolving robots could be exposed to one or more of the four environments shown in Fig. 2. In each environment, grasping ability was determined by how close the robot could get the tips of its fingers to the circumference of the object, and ensure that the fingertips touched on opposite sides of the objects.

In addition, the robot may have to exhibit grasping in the face of a perturbation: in some evaluations, after the initial values of the neurons have been set, one of the binary neuron values is flipped from +1 to −1 (or −1 to +1). The robot is expected to still exhibit successful grasping in the face of this perturbations.

A robot's grasping ability g was computed using

$$g = \sum_{r=0}^{14}\sum_{s=1}^{2}\sum_{p=1}^{2} g_{rsp}, \tag{3}$$

$$g_{rsp} = g_{rsp}^{(L)}\, g_{rsp}^{(R)}\, g_{rsp}^{(S)}, \tag{4}$$

$$g_{rsp}^{(L)} = \left(\frac{1}{1+d_{rsp}^{(L)}}\right), \tag{5}$$

$$g_{rsp}^{(R)} = \left(\frac{1}{1+d_{rsp}^{(R)}}\right), \tag{6}$$

$$g_{rsp}^{(S)} = \left(\frac{1}{1+d_{rsp}^{(S)}}\right), \tag{7}$$

$$d_{rsp}^{(S)} = |s_{rsp} - o_s|, \tag{8}$$

$$s_{rsp} = \sqrt{(x_{rsp}^{(L)} - x_{rsp}^{(R)})^2 + (y_{rsp}^{(L)} - y_{rsp}^{(R)})^2} \tag{9}$$

where

- $g = 0$ indicates that the robot failed completely in every environment, and $g = 15 \times 2 \times 2 = 60$ indicates that the robot grasped every object perfectly in every environment.
- g_{rsp} indicates the robot's ability to grasp during the rth perturbation, the sth object size, and the pth object position.
- For perturbation $r = 0$, no perturbation of the neurons' initial values in the robot's controller occurs. For $r = 1$ through $r = 14$, the initial value of the rth neuron is flipped.
- $s = 1$ indicates that the robot is in an environment in which the object is large; $s = 2$ indicates the object is small.
- $p = 1$ indicates that the robot is in an environment in which the object is on its right; $p = 2$ indicates the object is on its left.
- $g_{rsp} = 0$ indicates that the robot grasped the object in that environment poorly; $g_{rsp} = 1$ indicates it grasped it perfectly.
- $g_{rsp}^{(L)}$ (or $g_{rsp}^{(R)}$) indicate how close the robot's left fingertip (or right fingertip) got to the object's circumference, respectively.
- $d_{rsp}^{(L)}$ (or $d_{rsp}^{(R)}$) indicate the shortest distance between the robot's left fingertip (or right fingertip) and the object's circumference, respectively.
- $g_{rsp}^{(S)}$ denotes the spread of the robot's grasp: $g_{rsp}^{(S)} = 0$ indicates the robot's fingertips are touching the object's circumference at the same point (a poor grasp); $g_{rsp}^{(S)} = 1$ indicates the robot's fingertips are touching the object on opposite sides of its circumference (a good grasp).
- $d_{rsp}^{(S)}$ is the difference between the distance of the robot's fingertips—their spread (s_{rsp})—and the circumference of the sth object (o_s).
- Finally, $x_{rsp}^{(L)}$ and $y_{rsp}^{(L)}$ (and $x_{rsp}^{(R)}$ and $y_{rsp}^{(R)}$) denote the horizontal and vertical position of the robot's left (and right) fingertips.

During evolution, each robot was only exposed to the next environment if it achieved sufficiently good grasping in the current environment. The robot was allowed to behave in the next environment—and, thus, obtain higher fitness—if $g_{rsp} > 0.9$ and the robot's controller had settled into a fixed-point attractor. This latter stipulation ensures that the robot has not simply managed to bring its fingertips near the object during the third and final update of its controller but may move away from the object on subsequent updates.

Thus, more fit robots had to exhibit competency in a growing number of environments. Furthermore, as shown by the summation sequence in Eqn. (3), robots experienced changes in their environment in a particular order: they experienced a novel object position in environment 2 (Fig. 2b) and a novel object size in environment 3 (Fig. 2c).

Once a robot evolves to succeed in all four environments, it is evaluated again in the first environment, but now suffers a perturbation: the initial value of its first neuron is flipped. If successful there, the robot is evaluated a sixth time in environment 2 with a flipped first neuron value, and so on. Robots can thus be exposed up to a maximum of $15 \times 2 \times 2 = 60$ environments.

Controller modularity. The modularity of an evolved robot's controller was computed using

$$m = \frac{1 + d_{aa} + d_{hh}}{1 + d_{ah} + d_{ha}}, \tag{10}$$

$$d_{aa} = \frac{\sum_{a1=1}^{3}\sum_{a2=1}^{3} |a_{a1a2}|}{9}, \tag{11}$$

$$d_{hh} = \frac{\sum_{h1=4}^{7}\sum_{h2=4}^{7} |a_{h1h2}|}{16}, \tag{12}$$

$$d_{ah} = \frac{\sum_{a1=1}^{3}\sum_{h1=4}^{7} |a_{a1h1}|}{12}, \tag{13}$$

$$d_{ha} = \frac{\sum_{h1=4}^{7}\sum_{a1=1}^{3} |a_{h1a1}|}{12} \tag{14}$$

where d_{aa}, d_{hh}, d_{ah}, and d_{ha} denote the density of connectivity between the arm neurons, between the hand neurons, between the arm and hand neurons, and between the hand and arm neurons, respectively.

Thus m, like the more general modularity metric Q [12], measures the ratio of connection density within candidate modules, compared to connection density across modules[4].

[4]The Q modularity score was not employed here because of its computational overhead.

In this work we seek to measure specific modularity in the robot's controller: evolutionary dissociation between the arm neurons and the hand neurons.

Behavioral conservatism. It has been hypothesized [19] and shown experimentally in non-embodied systems [6] that structural modularity evolves when a system experiences stabilizing selection on one part of its phenotype and directional selection on another part. Here, we wished to select for robots that experience this kind of evolutionary pressure. We did so by formulating a measure c that gauges the amount of conservatism in a robot's evolved behavior:

$$c = \frac{c_a + c_h + c_r}{3}, \tag{15}$$

$$c_a = \left(\sum_{r=0}^{14} \sum_{s=1}^{2} \sum_{p_1=1}^{2} \sum_{p_2=1}^{2} \sum_{a=1}^{6} e_{rsp_1p_2} \left(n_a^{(rsp_1)} = n_a^{(rsp_2)} \right) \right) / e_p, \tag{16}$$

$$e_p = \sum_{r=0}^{14} \sum_{s=1}^{2} \sum_{p_1=1}^{2} \sum_{p_2=1}^{2} \sum_{a=1}^{6} e_{rsp_1p_2}, \tag{17}$$

$$c_h = \sum_{r=0}^{14} \sum_{s_1=1}^{2} \sum_{s_2=1}^{2} \sum_{p=1}^{2} \sum_{a=7}^{14} e_{rs_1s_2p} \left(n_h^{(rs_1p)} = n_h^{(rs_2p)} \right) / e_s, \tag{18}$$

$$e_s = \sum_{r=0}^{14} \sum_{s_1=1}^{2} \sum_{s_2=1}^{2} \sum_{p=1}^{2} \sum_{a=7}^{14} e_{rs_1s_2p}, \tag{19}$$

$$c_r = \sum_{r=1}^{14} \sum_{s=1}^{2} \sum_{p=1}^{2} \sum_{i=1}^{14} e_{rsp} \left(n_i^{(0sp)} = n_i^{(rsp)} \right) / e_r, \tag{20}$$

$$e_r = \sum_{r=1}^{14} \sum_{s=1}^{2} \sum_{p=1}^{2} \sum_{i=1}^{14} e_{rsp} \tag{21}$$

where

- $c = 0$ when the robot exhibits a different pose in every environment and under every perturbation. (Fig 2 shows a robot with this minimal conservatism.)
- $c = 1$ when the arm does the same thing in all environments in which the object is at the same position, the hand always does the same thing in all environments in which the object is the same size, and the overall robot does the same thing in the same environment, regardless of whether its initial state was perturbed or not. (Fig. 3 shows an evolved robot that achieves this: the hand reaches the same pose in environments 1 and 2 and environments 3 and 4, and the arm reaches the same pose in environments 1 and 3 and environments 2 and 4.)
- c_a measures the amount of similarity across arm poses for environments in which the object is on the same side,
- c_h measures the amount of similarity across hand poses for environments in which the object is the same size, and
- c_r measures the robot's robustness: how similar is the robot's overall pose when it experiences a perturbation compared to the same environment in which it does not experience a perturbation.
- $e_{rsp_1p_2}$ is equal to 1 if the robot was evaluated in the two environments rsp_1 and rsp_2, and the object had the same position in those environments ($p_1 = p_2$), and is equal to zero otherwise.
- $n_a^{(rsp_1)} = n_a^{(rsp_2)}$ is equal to 1 if arm neuron n_a holds the same value in a pair of environments with equal object positions, and zero otherwise.
- e_p denotes the number of environments with equally-positioned objects that the robot was evaluated in.
- $e_{rs_1s_2p}$ is equal to 1 if the robot was evaluated in the two environments rs_1p and rs_2p, and the object had the same size in those environments ($s_1 = s_2$), and is equal to zero otherwise.
- $n_h^{(rs_1p)} = n_h^{(rs_2p)}$ is equal to 1 if hand neuron n_h holds the same value in a pair of environments with equal object sizes, and zero otherwise. Finally,
- e_s denotes the number of environments with equally-sized objects that the robot was evaluated in.
- e_{rsp} is equal to 1 if the robot was evaluated in environment rsp and is equal to zero otherwise.
- e_r denotes the number of environments the robot was evaluated in.
- Finally, $n_i^{(0sp)} = n_i^{(rsp)}$ is equal to 1 if the ith neuron obtains the same final value in an environment in which the initial value of neuron r experienced no perturbation, and the same environment in which the initial value of neuron r was flipped, and zero otherwise.

Population initialization. Each population was seeded with 100 randomly-generated genomes. For robots evolved with simple controllers (experiment set 1 in Table 1), each genome was made up of one set of morphological parameters $\mathbf{m}$ and control parameters $\mathbf{C}$. For robots with fixed morphologies and RBN controllers (experiment sets 2, 4, and 6 in Table 1), each genome was comprised of an RBN adjacency matrix $\mathbf{A}$. For robots with evolved morphologies and evolved RBN controllers (experiment sets 3, 5, and 7 in Table 1), each genome comprised a set of morphological parameters $\mathbf{m}$ and an RBN adjacency matrix $\mathbf{A}$.

Randomly-generated $\mathbf{m}$ vectors were filled with random values drawn from $(0.5, 3.0)$ with a uniform distribution. Randomly-generated $\mathbf{C}$ matrices were filled with random angles drawn from the four possible angles for each joint. Randomly-generated $\mathbf{A}$ matrices were filled with $(2 \times 14 = 28)$ positive or negative edges, following the convention established in [6].

Selection. In each generation, each new genome was evaluated on the robot in as many environments as it was able to succeed in. Then, the Pareto front was calculated using the genome's age, grasping ability, controller modularity and/or behavioral conservatism, as shown in Table 1. All dominated genomes were then discarded. The population was refilled by selecting a non-dominated genome at random, copying it, mutating it, and placing it in an empty slot until the population size reached 99. The final empty slot was filled with a new randomly-generated genome with an age of zero.

Mutation. When $\mathbf{m}$ was mutated, zero (0.33 probability), one (0.33 probability) or two (0.34 probability) segment

Table 1: **Summary of experimental settings.**

Experiment set	Controller type	Morphology evolved?	Popn. size	Num of generations	Num of replicates	First objective	Second objective	Third objective	Environ-ments
1	Simple	yes	100	100,000	100	age	grasping		4
2	RBN	no	100	1,000,000	100	age	grasping		60
3	RBN	yes	100	1,000,000	100	age	grasping		60
4	RBN	no	100	1,000,000	100	age	grasping	modularity	60
5	RBN	yes	100	1,000,000	100	age	grasping	modularity	60
6	RBN	no	100	1,000,000	100	age	grasping	conservatism	60
7	RBN	yes	100	1,000,000	100	age	grasping	conservatism	60

lengths in $\mathbf{m}$ were mutated. The current value was replaced with a new random value drawn from $(0.5, 3.0)$ with a uniform probability.

When $\mathbf{C}$ was mutated, zero (0.33 probability), one (0.33 probability) or two (0.34 probability) angles in $\mathbf{C}$ were mutated. The current value was replaced with a new angle drawn from the four possible angles for that joint.

$\mathbf{A}$ was mutated with a bias toward two or three incoming edges, following [6]. Each neuron in a newly-copied controller was targetted for mutation with probability 0.05. If selected for mutation, the probability that an incoming synapse to n would be deleted is defined as

$$p(n) = \frac{4r_n}{4r_n + (14 - r_n)} \tag{22}$$

and the probability that a randomly-selected incoming edge will be added to n is defined as $q(n) = 1 - p(n)$. Here r_n denotes the in-degree of neuron n.

4. RESULTS

The settings for all of the experiments described in this section are summarized in Table 1.

In the first experiment, 100 trials were conducted in which the morphologies of robots were evolved along with their simple controllers. These robots were evolved only to grasp, did not experience perturbations, and each robot was exposed to all four environments. One hundred robots were collected by extracting the best robot from each trial. The resulting behavior for one of these robots is shown in Fig. 2. All 100 of these robots succeeded in all four environments: each achieved $g > 0.96$ (data not shown).

In the 100 trials comprising the second experiment, each trial was seeded with one of the 100 robots from the previous experiment. Then, RBN controllers were evolved in each trial to enable the fixed-morphology robot assigned to that trial to succeed at grasping in (up to) the 60 possible environments. The third experiment was conducted in the same manner, except that the trials began with randomly-generated morphologies, and those morphologies then evolved along with the controllers. The 100 best robots were collected from the second experiment and the third experiment; differences between their mean grasping ability (Fig. 4a), controller modularity (Fig. 4b), behavioral conservatism (Fig. 4c) and pose differences (Fig. 4d) are reported. (Pose difference is defined as the converse of behavioral conservatism: how different was the robot's arm pose in environments with objects in the same place; how different was the robot's hand pose in environments with objects of the same size; and how different was the robot's overall pose with or without initial perturbation.)

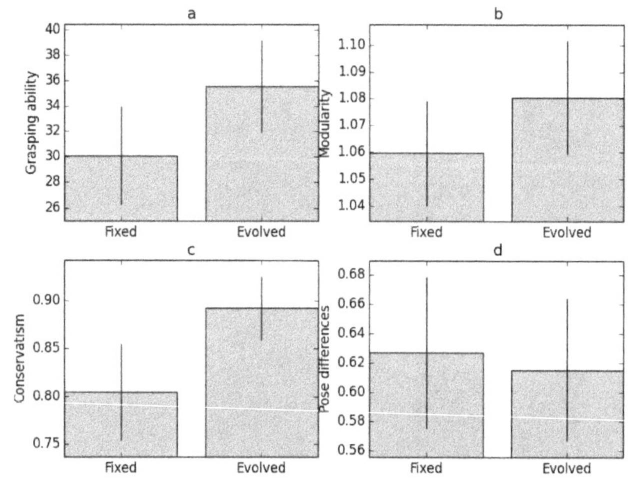

Figure 4: Relative performance of robots with fixed and evolved morphologies, when evolved to grasp the objects. Robots with evolved morphology exhibited (a) significantly better grasping ability (Mann-Whitney U-test, $p < 0.001$), (b) no significant difference in modularity, (c) significantly more behavioral conservatism (Mann-Whitney U-test, $p < 0.001$), and (d) no significant difference in the amount of pose differences. Error bars denote the 95% confidence intervals.

Two more experiments were conducted in which the robot's morphology was fixed or was allowed to evolve (experiment sets 4 and 5 in Table 1). In the 100 treatments involving a fixed-morphology robot (experiment set 4), the 100 morphologies evolved in experiment 1 were re-used. In these two experiments, the robots were evolved against the additional objective of controller modularity, in addition to grasping ability and genome age. The differences in mean grasping ability, controller modularity, behavioral conservatism and pose differences for the 100 best robots from each experiment are reported in Fig. 5.

A final pair of experiments were conducted (experiment sets 6 and 7 in Table 1) where, again, the robots' morphologies were held constant in the first set of 100 trials, and were allowed to evolve in the second set of 100 trials. The

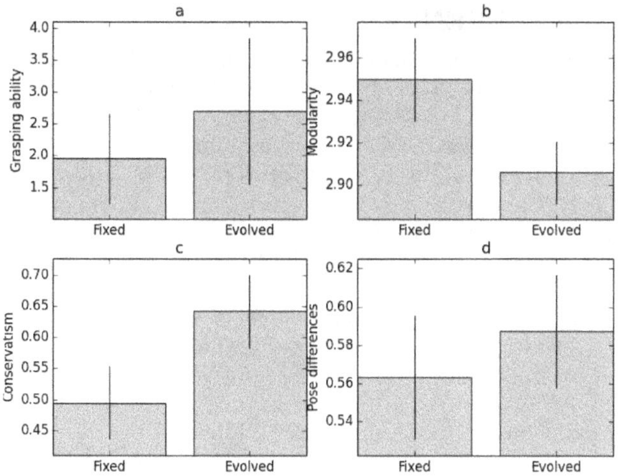

Figure 5: Relative performance of robots with fixed and evolved morphologies, when evolved to grasp the objects with highly modular controllers. Robots with evolved morphology exhibited (a) significantly better grasping ability (Mann-Whitney U-test, $p < 0.001$), (b) significantly lower modularity (Mann-Whitney U-test, $p < 0.001$), (c) significantly more behavioral conservatism (Mann-Whitney U-test, $p < 0.001$), and (d) no significant difference in the amount of pose differences.

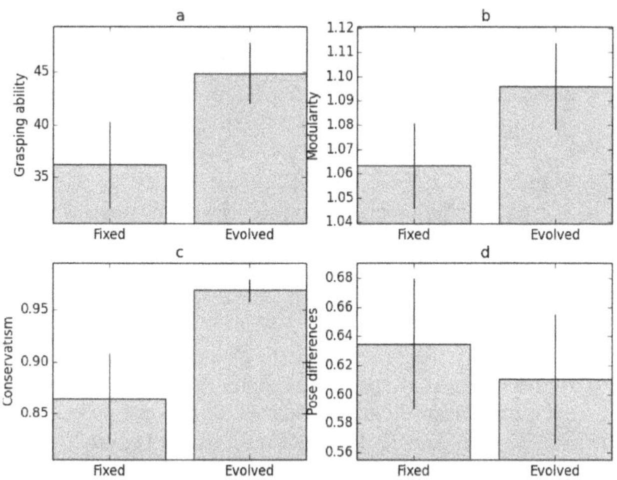

Figure 6: Relative performance of robots with fixed and evolved morphologies, when evolved to grasp the objects in a conservative manner. Robots with evolved morphology exhibited (a) significantly better grasping ability (Mann-Whitney U-test, $p < 0.001$), (b) significantly higher modularity (Mann-Whitney U-test, $p < 0.001$), (c) significantly more behavioral conservatism (Mann-Whitney U-test, $p < 0.001$), but (d) no significant difference in the amount of pose differences.

mean grasping ability, controller modularity, behavioral conservatism and pose differences for the 100 best robots from these two experiments are reported in Fig. 6.

5. DISCUSSION AND CONCLUSIONS

Fig. 4a indicates that evolving robot morphologies along with RBN controllers produces robots significantly more capable of grasping than robots with fixed morphologies, even though these latter robots are known to be capable of solving the task. Fig. 4b suggests why: evolution is able to find robot morphologies capable of grasping with more modular controllers than the controllers found for the fixed-morphology robots. However, the difference in neural modularity between the fixed- and evolved-morphology robots is not statistically significant.

This suggests that directly selecting for modular controllers may increase the evolvability of the evolving robots, enabling them to react appropriately to new environments which are novel combinations of familiar percepts. However, when both grasping and neural modularity are selected for performance decreased: exceedingly modular controllers are discovered (Fig. 5b) but at the expense of grasping ability: regardless of whether robots have fixed or evolved morphologies, few reach even the third or fourth environment (Fig. 5a).

We hypothesize that this is because evolution tends to maximize the interconnectivity among the hand neurons, and among the arm neurons. Such dense connectivity within neural modules likely makes the addition of new attractors corresponding to new useful hand (or arm) poses difficult. Indeed, the inability of dense networks to add attractors while preserving existing ones has been reported in [18]. An alternative explanation is that the multiobjective method employed here may have impaired this set of runs. In future work we will compare these results against those produced by a single-objective optimization method in which graping ability and neural modularity are multiplied together.

Returning to robots evolved only to grasp, there is another feature of the successful robots that was signficantly higher among the evolved-morphology robots than among those with fixed modularity, even though it was not selected for: the conservatism of their behavior (Fig. 4c). When conservatism is directly selected for along with grasping (Fig. 6), significantly better grasping is achieved (Fig. 6c), even though, due to the additional fitness objective of conservatism, selection pressure acting directly on grasping is weaker. Indeed, robots with evolved morphologies and controllers that were selected for grasping and conservatism yielded significantly better grasping that the robots produced by experiment sets two through six (Fig. 7).

The robots produced by selecting for grasping and conservatism also achieved significantly higher neural modularity (Fig. 6b), even though this trait was not directly selected for. These results, taken together, support the hypothesis outlined above: Under these particular pressures, and given the ability to mould the body of robots, evolution seems better able to find morphology and controller pairs that enable successful grasping such that the arm only attends to changes in object position and the hand only attends to changes in object size. Evolution accomplishes this by increasing neural modularity in such a way that arm and hand motor neurons become more independent (Fig. 6b).

This modularity then presumably enables robots to rapidly evolve in new environments, because the evolving arm modules and hand modules both react appropriately to a familiar object position and object size, respectively, even if those percepts appear in a novel combination. This can be seen

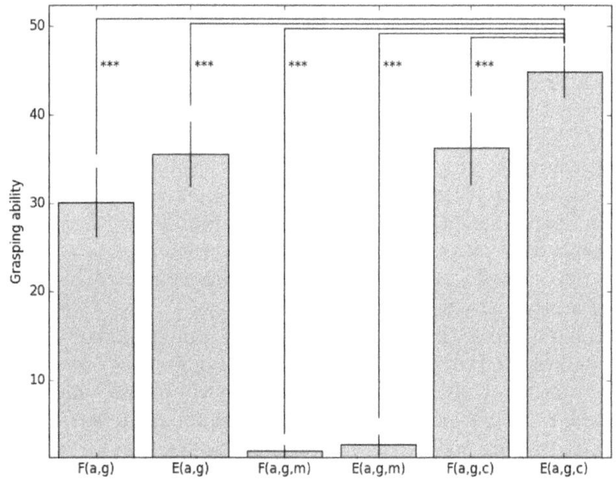

Figure 7: Comparative grasping abilities of evolved robots. $F(x)$ and $E(x)$ denote robots with fixed and evolved morphologies, respectively. (a, g) denote genomes evolved for age and grasping ability; (a, g, m) denote genomes evolved for age, grasping ability and neural modularity; (a, g, c) denote genomes evolved for age, grasping ability and behavioral conservatism.

in the evolved robot shown in Fig. 3: this robot employs the same hand pose in environment 4 as the one it evolved to succeed in environment 3, and it also employs the same arm pose in environment 4 as the one it evolved to succeed in environment 2.

This work thus suggests a new reason for why roboticists should pay careful attention to the design of a robot's mechanical structure. Even if a robot is designed in such a way that it is known to be capable of solving specific instances of a task, it may not be evolvable: poor design choices may inadvertently require additional learning or the evolution of new behaviors when presented with any new instance of the task. This work may also have implications for neuroscience. There is evidence that distinct regions of the brain come to reflect discrete structure out in the world [15]. However, brains also strike a balance between localized and distributed representations [11], which we also see in the modular but not extremely modular nature of our robot's evolved controllers. Finally, the demonstrated ability of the robots here to recognize novel combinations of familiar percepts could pave the way to robots capable of more flexible cognition through the establishment of compositional symbol grounding from motor patterns [7].

In future work we plan to scale up the complexity and physical realism of the robot and its task environment. Specifically, we wish to investigate whether in more challenging domains behavioral conservatism will be of increasingly utility such that it does not have to be directly selected for. Also, we plan to study robots which must act on their environment to draw out the invariant features that modules should evolve to deal with independently.

6. ACKNOWLEDGEMENTS

We thank Jodi Schwarz for many thoughtful discussions that contributed to the fruition of this project. This work was supported by NSF Awards PECASE-0953837 and INSPIRE-1344227 and DARPA award MSEE-FA8650-11-1-7155.

7. REFERENCES

[1] J. C. Bongard. Spontaneous evolution of structural modularity in robot neural network controllers. In *Procs of GECCO*, pages 251–258. ACM, 2011.

[2] J. C. Bongard. Evolutionary robotics. *Communications of the ACM*, 56(8):74–83, 2013.

[3] R. Calabretta, S. Nolfi, D. Parisi, and G. P. Wagner. Duplication of modules facilitates the evolution of functional specialization. *Artificial Life*, 6(1):69–84, 2000.

[4] J. Clune, B. Beckmann, P. McKinley, and C. Ofria. Investigating whether HyperNEAT produces modular neural networks. In *Procs of GECCO*, pages 635–642. ACM, 2010.

[5] J. Clune, J.-B. Mouret, and H. Lipson. The evolutionary origins of modularity. *Procs of the Royal Society B: Biological sciences*, 280(1755):20122863, 2013.

[6] C. Espinosa-Soto and A. Wagner. Specialization can drive the evolution of modularity. *PLoS Comp Biol*, 6(3):e1000719, 2010.

[7] A. Greco and C. Caneva. Compositional symbol grounding for motor patterns. *Frontiers in Neurorobotics*, 4, 2010.

[8] F. Gruau. Automatic definition of modular neural networks. *Adaptive Behaviour*, 3:151–183, 1994.

[9] N. Kashtan and U. Alon. Spontaneous evolution of modularity and network motifs. *PNAS*, 102(39):13773, 2005.

[10] J. Long. *Darwin's Devices*. Basic Books, 2012.

[11] B. Z. Mahon and A. Caramazza. What drives the organization of object knowledge in the brain? *Trends in Cognitive Sciences*, 15(3):97–103, 2011.

[12] M. E. Newman. Modularity and community structure in networks. *PNAS*, 103(23):8577–8582, 2006.

[13] S. Nolfi. Using emergent modularity to develop control systems for mobile robots. *Adaptive Behavior*, 3–4:343–364, 1997.

[14] S. Nolfi and D. Floreano. *Evolutionary Robotics*. MIT Press, Boston, MA, 2000.

[15] T. Orlov, T. R. Makin, and E. Zohary. Topographic representation of the human body in the occipitotemporal cortex. *Neuron*, 68(3):586–600, 2010.

[16] M. Schmidt and H. Lipson. Age-Fitness Pareto Optimization. *Genetic Programming Theory and Practice VIII*, pages 129–146, 2011.

[17] K. Stanley, D. D'Ambrosio, and J. Gauci. A hypercube-based encoding for evolving large-scale neural networks. *Artificial Life*, 15(2):185–212, 2009.

[18] C. Torres-Sosa, S. Huang, and M. Aldana. Criticality is an emergent property of genetic networks that exhibit evolvability. *PLoS Comp Bio*, 8(9):e1002669, 2012.

[19] G. Wagner, M. Pavlicev, and J. Cheverud. The road to modularity. *Nature Reviews Genetics*, 8(12):921–931, 2007.

[20] Y. Yamashita and J. Tani. Emergence of functional hierarchy in a multiple timescale neural network model: a humanoid robot experiment. *PLoS Comp Bio*, 4(11):e1000220, 2008.

Enhancing a Model-Free Adaptive Controller through Evolutionary Computation

Anthony J. Clark
Computer Science and Engineering
Michigan State University
East Lansing, MI, USA
ajc@msu.edu

Philip K. McKinley
Computer Science and Engineering
Michigan State University
East Lansing, MI, USA
mckinle3@msu.edu

Xiaobo Tan
Electrical and Computer Engineering
Michigan State University
East Lansing, MI, USA
xbtan@egr.msu.edu

ABSTRACT

Many robotic systems experience fluctuating dynamics during their lifetime. Variations can be attributed in part to material degradation and decay of mechanical hardware. One approach to mitigating these problems is to utilize an adaptive controller. For example, in model-free adaptive control (MFAC) a controller learns how to drive a system by continually updating link weights of an artificial neural network (ANN). However, determining the optimal control parameters for MFAC, including the structure of the underlying ANN, is a challenging process. In this paper we investigate how to enhance the online adaptability of MFAC-based systems through computational evolution. We apply the proposed methods to a simulated robotic fish propelled by a flexible caudal fin. Results demonstrate that the robot is able to effectively respond to changing fin characteristics and varying control signals when using an evolved MFAC controller. Notably, the system is able to adapt to characteristics not encountered during evolution. The proposed technique is general and can be applied to improve the adaptability of other cyber-physical systems.

Categories and Subject Descriptors

I.2.8 [**Artificial Intelligence**]: Problem Solving, Control Methods, and Search—*Control theory*

Keywords

adaptive control; model-free control; robotic fish; flexible materials; differential evolution

1. INTRODUCTION

Increasingly, robots are being deployed in complex and uncertain environments, where reaction and physical agility are essential to the completion of tasks. The adaptability and robustness exhibited by natural organisms has led to many *bio-inspired* approaches to robot design. For example, integration of soft and/or flexible materials into the morphology of a robot can partially compensate for actuation capabilities that are primitive relative to those of biological organisms [10]. Examples include the "whipping" action of a flexible fin on a robotic fish [3], shock absorption by flexible joints on a legged robot [19], and thrust generation by flexible wings on a robotic flying insect [23]. However, integrating flexible materials into a robot poses numerous challenges to controlling the system, since the flexibility of a structure affects the resulting forces and torques experienced during interactions with the environment [8]. Moreover, the properties of such components are likely to change over time due to degradation of materials and changing environmental conditions such as temperature. To produce effective locomotion, on-board controllers must account for these uncertainties.

One promising approach is *model-free* adaptive control (MFAC) [2, 20], intended for "gray box" situations where only partial, and possibly inaccurate, information is known. Like traditional adaptive control [6], this method attempts to minimize the error between desired and actual outcomes. However, instead of requiring a precise model of the system, an MFAC controller *learns* how to control a device by continually updating the link weights of an artificial neural network (ANN). Moreover, by saving recent error signals and using them as additional inputs to the ANN, MFAC controllers take advantage of state information, or so-called neural network memory. Although this is a general purpose control paradigm, the values of several parameters, as well as the structure of the ANN, need to be specified *a priori*, potentially limiting adaptability of the system. This raises the following questions. Is it possible to optimize an MFAC controller in order to enhance adaptability after deployment? And how can this be done such that the controller can account for changes in the robot morphology?

In this study we investigate the coupling of evolutionary computation with model-free adaptive control. Specifically, the differential evolution (DE) algorithm [14] is used to find *good* MFAC controller parameters that enable a robot to adapt during its lifetime to changes such as mechanical wear and material degradation. We apply this method to a simulated robotic fish that swims by means of a flexible caudal fin; an example of a target robot is shown in Figure 1. Equipping a robotic fish with a flexible caudal fin has been shown to improve efficiency with respect to thrust and power [3, 12]. However, the increase in performance introduces difficulty in controlling the system, particularly in a complex and highly nonlinear aquatic environment. Here, the ob-

GECCO '15, July 11 - 15, 2015, Madrid, Spain

ISBN 978-1-4503-3472-3/15/07...$15.00
DOI: http://dx.doi.org/10.1145/2739480.2754762

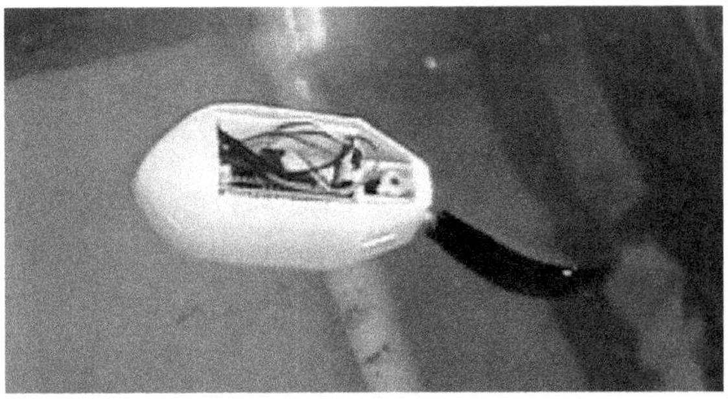

Figure 1: A prototype 3D-printed robotic fish with a flexible caudal fin.

jective for DE is to find MFAC parameters that enable the system to closely follow a desired reference signal (e.g., a desired swimming speed) while adapting to physical changes to the robotic fish caudal fin (e.g., changing fin flexibility).

The results of this initial study are promising. Compared to an MFAC controller with *typical* parameters, evolved solutions are better able to match desired reference speeds while also adapting to changes in fin characteristics. In addition, we view the pairing of adaptive control with evolutionary computation (EC) as mutually beneficial. First, EC techniques aid in finding effective control parameters, and second, the use of on-board adaptive control will help to address the reality gap [7]. Specifically, an adaptive controller should allow a robotic system to better handle disparities between simulation and reality, namely, unmodeled or poorly modeled dynamics. In this work, evolutionary optimization takes place in simulation during development in order to enhance the adaptability of the system after deployment. Our ongoing work applies this method to physical robots.

2. BACKGROUND AND RELATED WORK

Robotic Fish.

As an emerging class of embedded computing systems, robotic fish are anticipated to play an important role in environmental monitoring [15], inspection of underwater structures [5], and tracking of hazardous wastes and oil spills [22]. Similar to live fish, robotic fish accomplish swimming by deforming their bodies or fin-like appendages. This form of locomotion offers certain key advantages relative to traditional propeller-driven underwater vehicles. First, robotic fish are potentially more maneuverable, which is critical when operating in cluttered underwater environments [15]. Second, since robotic fish produce very little noise and exhibit wake signatures similar to live fish, they are less intrusive to aquatic ecosystems and offer stealth in security-related applications. Finally, with fin/body motions operating at relatively low frequencies (typically a few Hz), these systems are less likely to harm aquatic animals or become jammed with foreign objects.

Autonomy and adaptation are particularly important in aquatic environments, where human oversight is often limited, if not impossible. However, while studies of robotic fish have produced many advances over the past two decades [18, 1, 9, 15], robotic fish still do not approach their biological counterparts in terms of agility or robustness. Integrating flexible materials as fins, or as entire bodies, is one approach to improving the performance of robotic fish [16, 8]. For example, Clark et al. [3] demonstrated how a genetic algorithm can be utilized to optimize both morphological characteristics and control patterns. However, an equally important issue is how the system can adapt to changes that occur *after* deployment.

Adaptive Control.

Adaptive control is a well-established field of study for dealing with uncertainty in cyber-physical systems [6]. For example, in model reference adaptive control (MRAC), a reference model defines the desired response of the system and control laws are designed such that the controlled system is forced to behave as this reference model. However, reliance on a model of the target system makes it difficult to accommodate unexpected conditions for which the underlying reference model does not apply. In addition, the complexity associated with many physical systems, such as robots with flexible components, often renders the design of a model-based controller intractable or inconvenient.

Hou and Huang [4] first proposed the idea of *model-free* adaptive control (MFAC), based on the concept of a pseudo-partial-derivative and reliance on only system inputs and outputs. The MFAC approach we use in this study, proposed by Cheng [2], combines a traditional proportional controller with an adaptive ANN, as shown in Figure 2. As an input, the ANN receives a continuous error signal e, calculated as the difference between a desired reference input and the actual state of the robot (see Figure 3). The error signal is discretized at a sampling rate T_s, and then normalized between -1 and 1 using an error bound e_b. This normalized, discretized error signal, denoted E, is passed to the first input neuron, I_1, and then propagated to each subsequent input neuron at successive discrete sampling times. This process is repeated such that the N input neurons store the N most recent error signals E. By storing these values and using them as inputs to the ANN, MFAC controllers take advantage of state information. Additionally, at each sampling time, the input neuron values $(E_1..E_N)$ are fed forward to the ANN hidden neurons $(H_1..H_N)$ which in turn feed their values to the output neuron (V). The final output of the controller, u, is the sum of the value from a single output neuron and the current error signal, amplified by the controller gain K_c. Adding the current error signal to the network output improves the responsiveness of the controller. Specifically, any change in error will results in an immediate change in the controller's output. Hidden and output neurons are activated with a sigmoidal activation function.

The weights of links connecting the input layer to the hidden layer (w_{ij}) and from the hidden layer to the output neuron (h_j) are updated at each sample time. Learning rules were derived by minimizing the error signal [2]; specifically, the partial derivative of an objective function, based on the error signal, is taken with respect to the link weights. Formally, these rules are described by Equations 1 and 2:

$$\Delta w_{ij}(n) = \eta K_c e(n) q_j(n)(1 - q_j(n)) E_i(n) \sum_{k=1}^{N} h_k(n), \quad (1)$$

$$\Delta h_j(n) = \eta K_c e(n) q_j(n), \quad (2)$$

where (n) denotes the sample time and q_j refers the output of the jth hidden neuron. The number of recent error signals, N, as well as the rate at which link weights are updated (called the adaptive learning rate, η), are configurable.

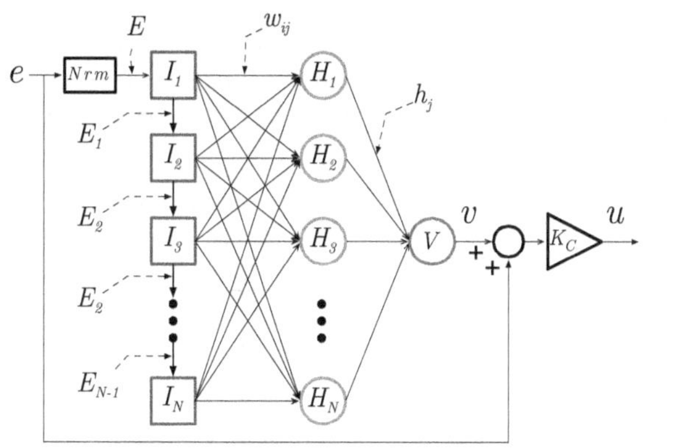

Figure 2: A graphical representation of the MFAC ANN. A continuous time error signal e is first normalized (Nrm block) and then propagated through the input neurons I_i. The ANN is then activated as a feed-forward network to produce an output v. The final controller output u is an amplified summation of v and e.

The magnitude of an MFAC controller output is adjustable through the controller gain value K_c.

Determining the optimal values of the MFAC parameters is challenging and depends on the application domain. In this study, we address this challenge with evolutionary computation. Specifically, we use the differential evolution (DE) algorithm [14] to optimize MFAC parameters (T_s, e_b, N, K_c, and η); the MFAC controllers govern a (simulated) robotic fish, which can have varying fin characteristics (i.e., fin length and fin flexibility). It is the job of an MFAC controller to adapt to these variations, which are meant to mimic changes in the caudal fin material that occur after deployment, in order to realize effective locomotion.

Before continuing, it is perhaps useful to distinguish the adaptive control process discussed in this paper from other forms of adaptive control. Specifically, a well-known method for realizing adaptability in autonomous robots is to introduce synaptic plasticity in ANNs. So-called *plastic* ANNs are able to strengthen or weaken their synapses by following a set of learning rules [17]. However, the objective for plastic ANNs is fundamentally different from that of the adaptive controllers employed in this paper. Specifically, plastic ANNs are meant to learn a new *behavior*, whereas the adaptive controller is regulating a desired control signal. For example, a plastic ANN may be used to dynamically change a swimming gait while an MFAC controller would be used to *maintain* a specific swimming speed.

3. METHODOLOGY

MFAC for Robotic Fish.

Figure 3 shows a block diagram of the MFAC controller with the robotic fish. The input to the entire system is a reference signal r, which can be any physical signal relating to the robotic fish. For this study, r refers to a *desired* speed, and the output of the robotic fish y is the *actual* (measured) speed. For physical experiments, speed can be measured by filtering and integrating accelerometer data. Generally, reference signals are generated by a higher-level module.

The controller's objective is to produce a control signal u such that y closely tracks r. That is, an effective controller

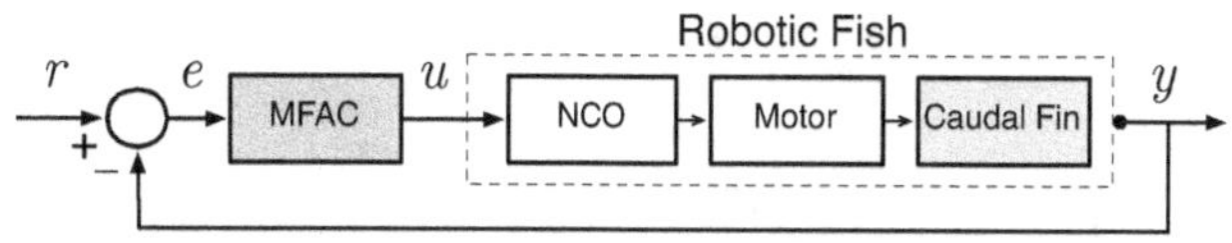

Figure 3: A block diagram of the MFAC controller and the robotic fish. Signals r and y denote the reference and measured speeds, respectively, e is the difference between reference and measured speeds, and u is the controller output.

will force the robotic fish to closely match the desired speed, and have little error e between y and r. For the robotic fish, u is a frequency of oscillation for the caudal fin motor, and a numerically controlled oscillator (NCO) generates a sinusoidal pattern at the given frequency. For this study, we have fixed the sinusoid's amplitude to 20°.

The motivating problem for this study is how to specify the MFAC parameters in such a way that they allow the controller to adapt to variations in caudal fin behavior. As a robotic fish's caudal fin undergoes regular wear and degradation it will begin to respond differently to motor commands, particularly if the fin is fabricated from flexible materials. Consequently, a static, non-adaptive feedback controller will begin to *detune*, leading to deteriorated performance. Additionally, an MFAC controller should be better able to handle noisy accelerometer data, although we do not consider noisy measurements in our simulations.

MFAC parameters are typically set based on expert knowledge. For example, the robotic fish that this study is based on has a maximum tail frequency of roughly 3.5 Hz. Cheng et al. [2] recommend for the sampling rate to be less than one-third of the period of the controlled system, or roughly 0.1 seconds for the robotic fish. The error bound used for normalization e_b can be set to near the maximum speed at which the robotic fish is expected to travel (i.e., 15 cm/s for the modeled robotic fish). A good starting point for the number of input and hidden neurons N is 3, as the ANN can interpret inputs as the current error and its first and second derivatives. This setup would roughly correspond to a PID algorithm, a widely used general-purpose feedback controller. Typical initial values for the gain K_c and the learning rate η are 1.0 and 0.8, respectively. In Section 4, we compare the performance of an MFAC controller implemented with these values to that of one with evolved values.

Simulation dynamics.

Simulation of the robotic fish is conducted in Simulink [13], enabling a straightforward translation of dynamic equations (described below) into simulation. A critical aspect of the simulation is modeling of the flexible caudal fin dynamics. The model used in this study, developed by Wang et al. [21], has proven to be both accurate and computationally efficient. Figure 4 depicts the modeled hydrodynamics. Wang's model assumes that all motions are constrained to a two-dimensional plane. Flexibility in the caudal fin is modeled as multiple rigid segments connected by springs and dampers. The spring constant between two consecutive segments determines how stiff or flexible the caudal fin behaves. The force acting on each fin segment f_i can be calculated independently, and the resulting thrust force F_T is simply a summation of all segment forces, including an additional force that acts at the tip of the final segment f_L.

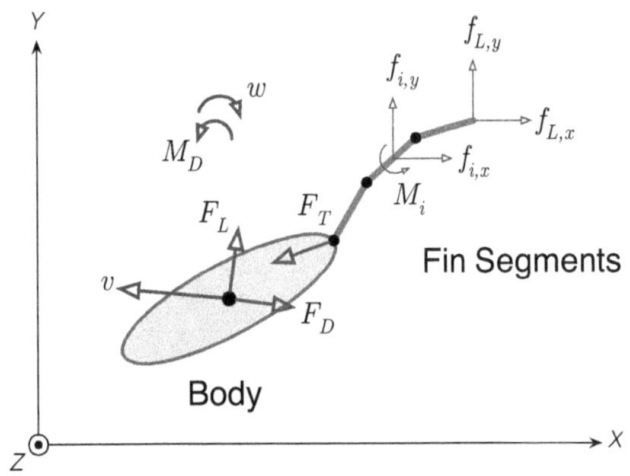

Figure 4: Graphical representation of the simulated hydrodynamics. Linear velocity v and angular velocity w are the result of thrust force F_T, drag force F_D, lift force F_L, and drag moment M_D. F_T is calculated as the sum of all forces acting on the fin segments.

The robotic fish prototype upon which this simulation is based (similar to that in Figure 1) is approximately 20 cm in length, including a 7.6 cm long tail fin of moderate flexibility made from a 3D-printed ABS plastic.

Differential evolution.

To enhance the adaptability of MFAC controllers we apply differential evolution (DE), a global optimization algorithm developed by Storn et al. [14]. DE was chosen because studies have shown that it will converge faster than real-valued genetic algorithms for problems similar to ours [11].

DE progresses in a fashion similar to other evolutionary algorithms. First, a population is randomly initialized. For this study, the population size is set to 50, which is the recommended value for a DE experiment with 5 evolving parameters (T_s, e_b, N, K_c, and η). Next, each individual is evaluated with a problem-specific fitness function. In this study, we employ two different fitness schemes. In the first, individuals are simulated for only one set of conditions, and fitness is assigned as the mean absolute error (MAE) (i.e., the average error between r and y). In the second, each individual is simulated under a variety of different conditions (varying caudal fin characteristics). Fitness is then assigned as the sum of the MAE for each set of conditions. Once each individual has been assigned fitness, the DE algorithm produces a new generation of individuals.

Mutation and crossover operators are where DE differs from conventional real-valued genetic algorithms. DE focuses on creating new individuals near the best member of the parent population. Each child is initialized as a linear combination of the best and at least two other randomly selected parents. During this recombination, the relative weight of the *best* parent to the random parents is referred to as the mutation factor and is configurable (0.8 in this study). The child is then crossed with the *base* parent (each parent is taken as the base in turn) using a configurable crossover rate (0.7 in this study). DE algorithm specifics, as well as a comparison with other evolutionary optimization algorithms, can be found in [11]. Using Storn's DE notation, the algorithm utilized for this study is denoted as DE/best/2/bin, where best signifies that all children are created around the previous generations best individual, 2 denotes that mutation is based on two individuals, and bin refers to a binary crossover operation.

MFAC parameters are allowed to evolve only within a certain range. The range for each parameter is listed in Table 1. These ranges are based on the typical MFAC parameters discussed earlier.

Parameter	Minimum	Maximum	Typical
T_s (s)	0.0	0.17	0.1
e_b (cm/s)	5.0	50.0	15.0
N	1	8	3
K_c	0.1	4.0	1.0
η	0.1	4.0	0.8

Table 1: Evolutionary range of MFAC parameters, as well as the typical values.

4. SINGLE-EVALUATION RESULTS

In this set of evolutionary experiments we evolve MFAC parameters under a single set of conditions. However, we first conduct a simulation of the robotic fish incorporating typical MFAC parameters (as listed in Table 1). Figure 5 shows results from this simulation. The task for the MFAC controller is to track a reference speed r (the orange, dashed line in Figure 5), which varies over time according to a predefined pattern. This reference speed, utilized during evolution and most test cases, is designed to contain periods requiring acceleration, deceleration, and sustaining a constant speed. Despite choosing parameters based on expert knowledge, the controller struggles to track (i.e., closely match) the reference speed. Ideally, in Figure 5 (and all similar figures) the solid blue line (y) would match the dashed orange line (r), and the error line (e) would remain at zero.

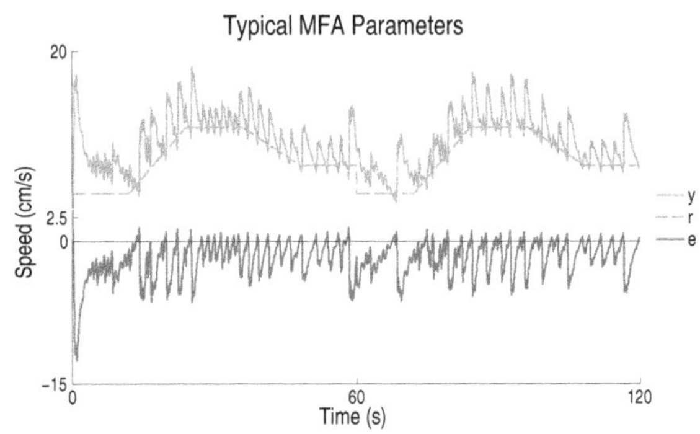

Figure 5: Results for an MFAC controller with typical parameters controlling a robotic fish. The dashed orange line denotes the reference speed r, the actual speed y of the robotic fish is the blue line, and the error e between these signals is red.

After the initial simulation using typical parameters, we conducted 20 replicate differential evolution (DE) experiments. Replicates are seeded with a unique number, and DE algorithm parameters are configured as described in Section 3. Each set of MFAC parameters (i.e., individual solutions) is evaluated under identical circumstances: it is simulated for 60 seconds with the same reference speed signal, and fitness is measured as the mean absolute error (MAE). All replicate experiments converge to similar fitness values within 150 generations.

As shown in Figure 6, solutions from the single-evaluation experiments perform the evolutionary task well (i.e., tracking the reference speed encountered during evolution for 60 seconds). However, even a slight change to this task, such as doubling the simulation to 120 seconds, causes a large change in performance. This behavior can be seen during the final 60 seconds of Figure 6, where simply repeating the reference signal results in poorer tracking and increased error. This experiment demonstrates that evolved solutions are incapable of adapting to new conditions while maintaining the same level of performance. More specifically, the evolved parameters appear to be *overfit*. The best solutions only work for the conditions encountered during evolution.

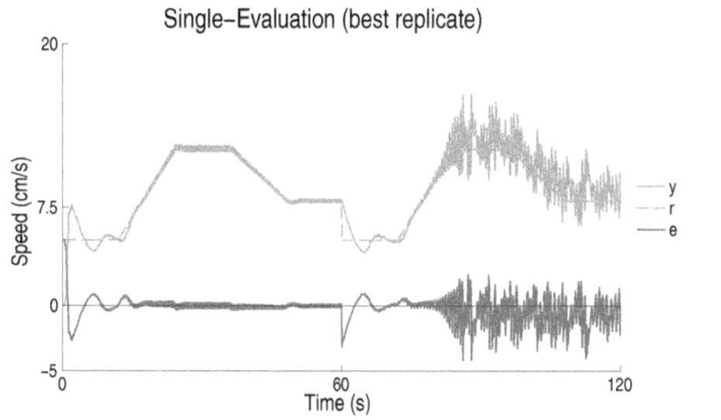

Figure 6: Results for the overall best (across all replicate experiments) single-evaluation solution simulated with default fin characteristics and the same reference signal utilized during evolution. The controller shows poor performance starting at the 80 second mark, and similar results were found in all replicate experiments.

5. MULTI-EVALUATION RESULTS

Given the results from Section 4, we conducted a second set of experiments in which fitness of each individual is based on its performance under *multiple* different conditions. The settings for these simulations, referred to as the 9-evaluation experiments, are listed in Table 2. In the table, *sim1* corresponds to the conditions used in the previous experiments. For each simulation, fin flexibility is set to: 100%, increased to 200%, or decreased to 50% of the default value. Likewise, the caudal fin length is set to: 100%, lengthened to 110%, or contracted to 90% of the default value.

Name	Flexibility	Length
sim1	100%	100%
sim2	200%	100%
sim3	50%	100%
sim4	100%	110%
sim5	200%	110%
sim6	50%	110%
sim7	100%	90%
sim8	200%	90%
sim9	50%	90%

Table 2: Fin characteristics for the 9-evaluations experiment.

Evaluating individuals under a variety of conditions is intended to eliminate the tendency of evolving overfit solutions. Experiencing multiple conditions also simulates how fins may change once deployed. For example, fin dynamics can change if the fin is damaged (e.g., cut) or encumbered by environmental entities (e.g., seaweed). Fitness is calculated as the summation of the MAE from each of the 9 60-second simulations. Evolving with this fitness function is meant to add an implicit objective to the fitness function: better solutions must be more adaptable.

Figure 7 shows the best solution from 20 replicates of the 9-evaluation experiments. Here, the controller continues to closely track the reference for 120 seconds, even though evolutionary evaluations are only 60 seconds in length. Figure 8 shows that tracking is accomplished by adjusting the fin's oscillating frequency in a pattern roughly matching that of the reference signal. Although this test indicates improvement over the single-evaluation experiment, it does not address the issue of adapting to different conditions.

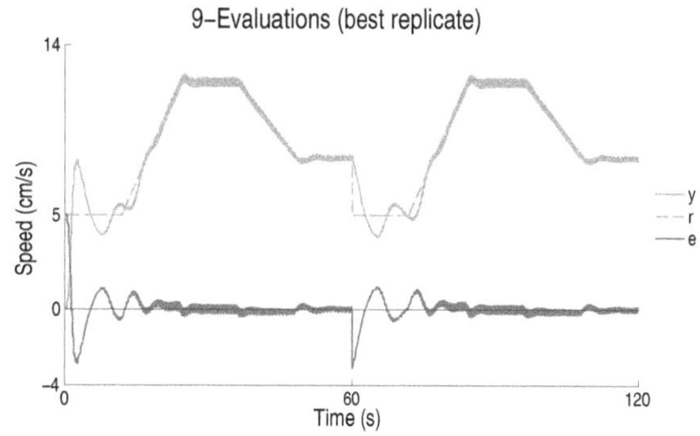

Figure 7: The overall best 9-evaluation solution evaluated on *sim1*. The MFAC controller is able to drive the robotic fish at the desired reference speed (r).

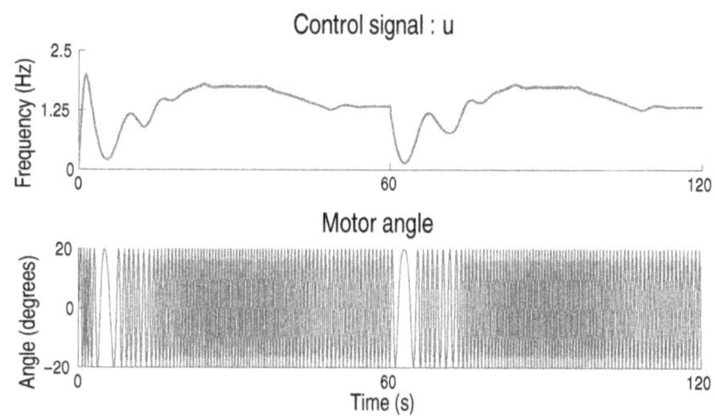

Figure 8: Control signal u and the resulting motor angle for the overall best 9-evaluation solution evaluated on *sim1*. The control signal trajectory roughly follows the reference signal.

Figure 9 depicts performance of the same solution when confronted with conditions that were *not* encountered during evolution. As shown, the controller is able to adapt to the novel fin lengths. This evolved MFAC controller should allow a robotic fish to maintain a certain level of performance even if the fin length changes during operation.

The fin can, however, reach lengths that cause the controller to lose its tracking ability. While fixing fin flexibility and the reference signal, we performed a sweep over a wide range of different fin lengths and found that the controller can maintain performance while caudal fin length is within a range of 60% to 137% of the default value. Effectively the caudal fin can be cut from 7.6 to 4.5 cm (or lengthened to

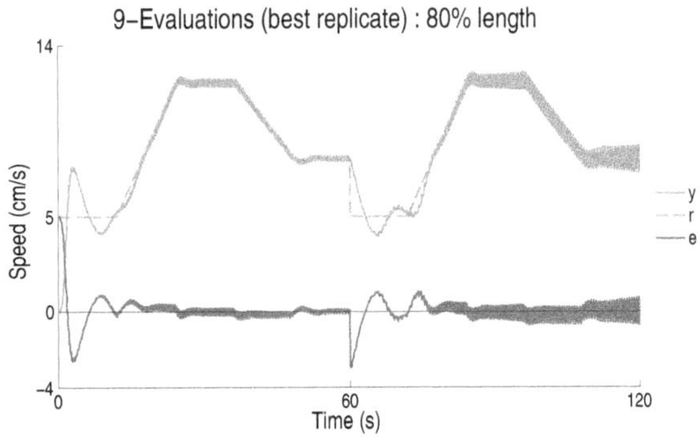

(a)

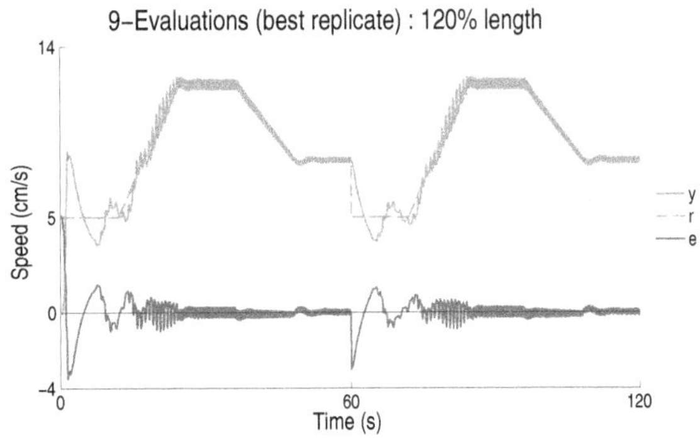

(b)

Figure 9: The overall best 9-evaluation solution tested against fin lengths that were not encountered during any of the evolutionary simulations. In (a) fin length is shortened to 80% of the default length, and in (b) fin length is lengthened to 120% of the default length. In both cases, the evolved controller is able to adapt to a novel fin length.

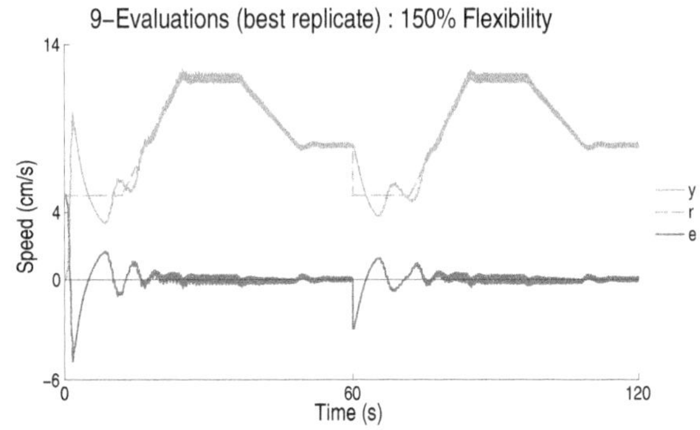

Figure 10: The overall best 9-evaluation solution evaluated with a fin that is 150% of the default fin flexibility. Evolved controllers were able to adapt to this novel value for flexibility.

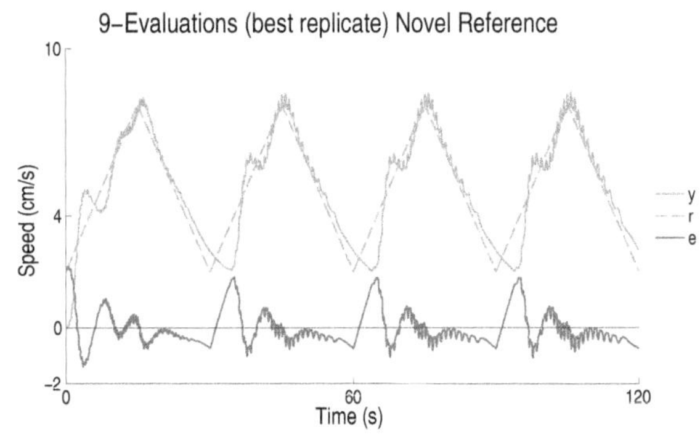

Figure 11: The overall best 9-evaluation solution simulated with default fin characteristics and a reference signal not encountered during evolution.

10.4 cm) without the controller losing its ability to drive the robotic fish at a desired speed. Values outside of this range cause a noticeable increase in the error signal.

Figure 10 shows that evolved controllers are also able to adapt to changes in fin flexibility. Similar to the fin length parameter sweep, we found upper and lower limits for fin flexibility changes. While keeping all other factors constant, the evolved MFAC controllers can maintain performance as long as flexibility remains within a range from 90% to 160% of the default value.

In addition to changes in fin characteristics, evolved controllers have the ability to adapt to different reference signals. Figure 11 demonstrates that an evolved controller is capable of tracking a novel pattern for the reference speed, in this case alternating periods of fast acceleration and deceleration. Additional test results (not shown) demonstrate that limits on the reference signal depend only on the limits of the robotic fish. Specifically, the adaptive controller will remain effective as long as the reference signal does not require speeds, accelerations, or decelerations that are impossible for the robotic fish. For example, if the reference signal changes too quickly, the robotic fish may not be physically capable of accelerating fast enough.

Figure 12 shows how the evolved controller handles simultaneous changes to both fin length and fin flexibility. For this test, fin length is set to values outside of the range encountered during all evolutionary simulations. For the test in 12(b), increasing the fin's length actually allows the evolved controller to adapt to a flexibility (80%) that would otherwise cause performance degradation. Specifically, a flexibility of 80% (of the default value) is beyond the lower limit found when flexibility was altered in isolation (i.e., the range of 90% to 160% mentioned previously). This is indicative of the complex interactions among material properties (e.g., flexibility and dimensions). Such interactions cause difficulties when designing a simple feedback controller, such as a PID controller, or a model-based controller that must account for all of the necessary dynamics. An evolved adaptive controller can automatically handle these complex interactions.

To further increase adaptability of an evolved MFAC controller (i.e., increase the range of fin characteristic variation while maintaining the same performance levels), the 9-evaluations experiments were repeated with larger variations from the default values. For instance, in *sim5* (refer to Table 2) the flexibility is set to 1000% of the default value, and length is increased to 200% of the default value. Likewise, in *sim9* flexibility is set to 10% of the default value, while length is decreased to 67% of the default value.

Although the evolved controller is generally still able to track r, the best solutions from all replicates performed worse, on all test cases, than previous solutions. Figure 13 shows an individual from the altered experiments.

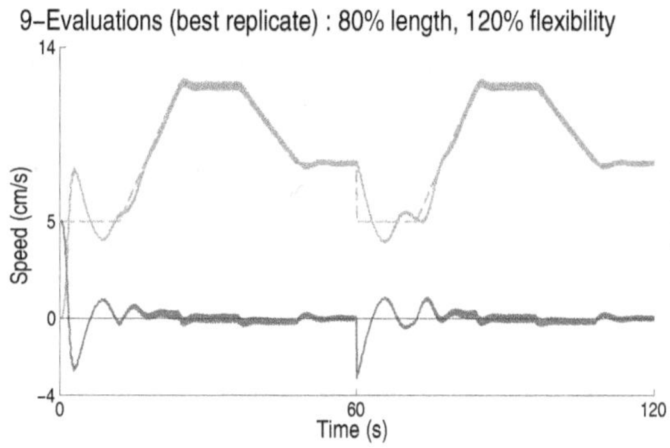

(a)

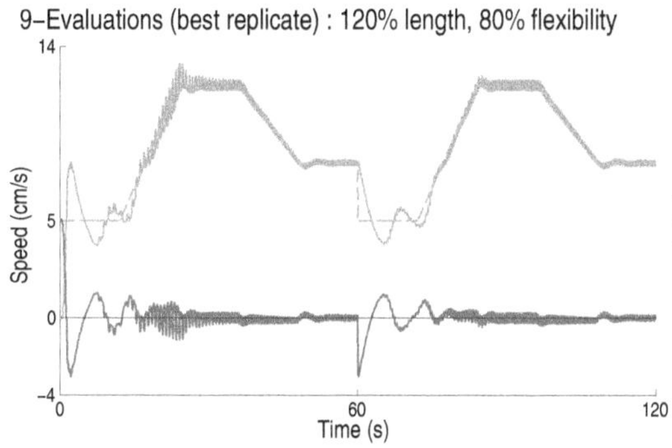

(b)

Figure 12: The overall best 9-evaluation solution tested against fin lengths and fin flexibilities that were not encountered during evolutionary simulations. In (a) fin length is shortened to 80% of the default length and the flexibility is increased to 120% of the default, and in (b) fin length is lengthened to 120% of the default length and fin flexibility is reduced to 80% of the default value.

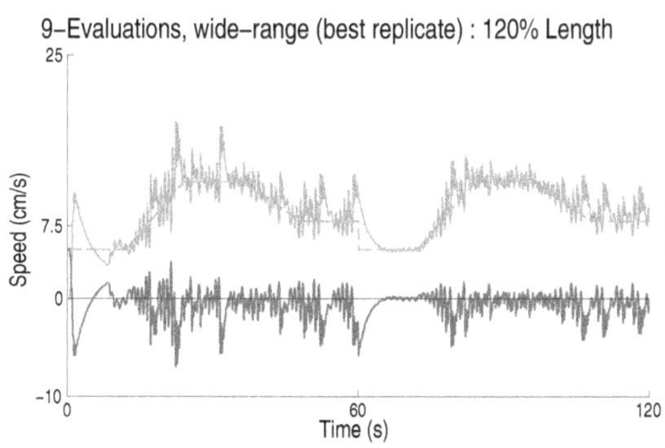

Figure 13: Performance of the best evolved solution from the altered 9-evaluations experiments tested with a fin length 120% of the default.

The primary reason for the MFAC's inability to adapt to large variations lies in how the dynamics change. Certain fin characteristics or combinations of characteristics cause the physical system to behave fundamentally differently. The basic MFAC presented in this study relies on the robotic system to be *direct-acting*. That is, as the MFAC controller output increases, the output from the controlled device must monotonically increase. Figure 14 depicts how changes to fin characteristics can alter the robotic fish's response to commands from the controller. Essentially, if fin characteristics vary beyond a certain threshold, the robotic fish may no longer behave as a direct-acting robotic system. This issue is most clearly demonstrated by the green, dotted curve (200%), which changes from direct to reverse-acting near 1.5 Hz, and then back to direct-acting near 3.5 Hz. A similar effect can be seen, to a lesser extent, for each of the curves. Even an optimized MFAC controller will be unable to cope with these highly varied dynamics.

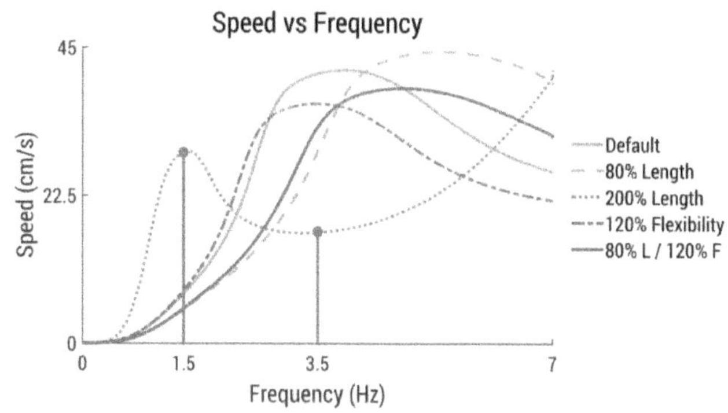

Figure 14: Speed vs. oscillating frequency for several different fin characteristics. For certain conditions increasing the frequency results in slower speeds.

6. CONCLUSION

In this study, we explored the integration of evolutionary computation and adaptive control. Specifically, we applied differential evolution to optimize the parameters of a model-free adaptive controller. The goal of evolution is to find a set of parameters that enable an MFAC controller to adapt to changes in fin characteristics (i.e., length and flexibility) and changes to the reference signal (e.g., faster/slower accelerations). Additionally, evolved MFAC controllers should be able to handle changes to the reference signal (i.e., different desired reference speeds).

Results show that evolving MFAC parameters against a single set of fin characteristics can produce a controller capable of achieving *good* fitness (i.e., specifically, low mean absolute error). However, these solutions do not produce a controller capable of adapting to changing fin characteristics. Next, the fitness function was modified to include a variety of different fin characteristics. The newly evolved controllers were tested under several different conditions, including scenarios in which the fin characteristics were outside the range experienced during evolution. This method succeeded in generating more adaptable controllers. Specifically, the best MFAC controllers were able to maintain close tracking as long as fin length remained within 60% to 137% of the default and fin flexibility remained within 90% to 160% of the default.

To explore the limits of this approach, the fitness function was again modified to include a larger variety of different characteristics. However, these experiments resulted in poorer performing controllers. Drastically varying the fin characteristics essentially creates a fundamentally different set of governing dynamics. Evolved controllers require the system to be either direct- or reverse-acting, which is not always the case when, for example, the fin is made to be too flexible; in such cases, increasing the control frequency results in slower speeds rather than faster. Even the most fit individuals were incapable of successful adaptation when subjected to such conditions.

We note that the MFAC controllers presented in this study are designed to handle a single-input, single-output (SISO) system. However, more complex MFAC controllers have been designed to accommodate multiple inputs and multiple outputs. In the future, we plan to extend the approach presented in this study to include tracking a desired reference heading while simultaneously tracking a reference speed. Doing so will produce controllers capable of more complex behaviors that incorporate both turning and forward locomotion. Adaptive techniques may also improve an evolved solution's ability to cross the reality gap, as all unmodeled and poorly modeled dynamics will be treated as variations and accounted for during adaptation. Although this study demonstrates adaptation in the aquatic domain, the proposed technique can be applied to similarly control the speeds of terrestrial robots, and more broadly to other cyber-phsyical system.

7. ACKNOWLEDGMENTS

The authors gratefully acknowledge the contributions and feedback on the work provided by Jared Moore, Jianxun Wang, and the BEACON Center at Michigan State University. This work was supported in part by National Science Foundation grants IIS-1319602, CCF-1331852, CNS-1059373, CNS-0915855, and DBI-0939454, and by Michigan State University.

8. REFERENCES

[1] J. M. Anderson and N. K. Chhabra. Maneuvering and stability performance of a robotic tuna. *Integr. Comp. Biol.*, 42:118–126, 2002.

[2] G. S. Cheng. Model-free adaptive (MFA) control. *Computing and Control Engineering*, 15(3):28–33, 2004.

[3] A. J. Clark, J. M. Moore, J. Wang, X. Tan, and P. K. McKinley. Evolutionary design and experimental validation of a flexible caudal fin for robotic fish. In *Proceedings of the Thirteenth International Conference on the Synthesis and Simulation of Living Systems*, pages 325–332, East Lansing, Michigan, USA, July 2012.

[4] Z. Hou and W. Huang. The model-free learning adaptive control of a class of SISO nonlinear systems. In *Proceedings of the 1997 American Control Conference*, volume 1, pages 343–344, 1997.

[5] F. S. Hover, R. M. Eustice, A. Kim, B. Englot, H. Johannsson, M. Kaess, and J. J. Leonard. Advanced perception, navigation and planning for autonomous in-water ship hull inspection. *International Journal of Robotics Research*, 31(12):1445–1464, 2012.

[6] P. Ioannou and J. Sun. *Robust Adaptive Control.* Dover Books on Electrical Engineering. Dover Publications, 2012.

[7] N. Jakobi, P. Husbands, and I. Harvey. Noise and the reality gap: The use of simulation in evolutionary robotics. In *Advances in Artificial Life, Lecture Notes in Computer Science*, volume 929, pages 704–720. Springer, 1995.

[8] E. Kanso and P. K. Newton. Passive locomotion via normal-mode coupling in a submerged spring-mass system. *Journal of Fluid Mechanics*, 641:205–215, 2009.

[9] K. H. Low and C. W. Chong. Parametric study of the swimming performance of a fish robot propelled by a flexible caudal fin. *Bioinspiration and Biomimetics*, 5(4):046002, 2010.

[10] C. Majidi. Soft robotics: A perspective – current trends and prospects for the future. *Soft Robotics*, 1:5–11, July 2013.

[11] N. Padhye, P. Bhardawaj, and K. Deb. Improving differential evolution through a unified approach. *Journal of Global Optimization*, pages 1–29, 2013.

[12] Y.-J. Park, U. Jeong, J. Lee, S.-R. Kwon, H.-Y. Kim, and K.-J. Cho. Kinematic condition for maximizing the thrust of a robotic fish using a compliant caudal fin. *IEEE Transactions on Robotics*, 28:1216–1227, 2012.

[13] Simulink: Dynamic system simulation for MATLAB, User's Guide. The MathWorks Inc., Natick, Massachusetts, USA, 1990-2013.

[14] R. Storn and K. Price. Differential evolution–a simple and efficient heuristic for global optimization over continuous spaces. *Journal of Global Optimization*, 11(4):341–359, 1997.

[15] X. Tan. Autonomous robotic fish as mobile sensor platforms: Challenges and potential solutions. *Marine Technology Society Journal*, 45(4):31–40, 2011.

[16] J. L. Tangorra, G. V. Lauder, I. W. Hunter, R. Mittal, P. G. A. Madden, and M. Bozkurttas. The effect of fin ray flexural rigidity on the propulsive forces generated by a biorobotic fish pectoral fin. *Journal of Experimental Biology*, 213:4043–4054, 2010.

[17] P. Tonelli and J.-B. Mouret. On the relationships between generative encodings, regularity, and learning abilities when evolving plastic artificial neural networks. *PloS ONE*, 8(11):e79138, 2013.

[18] M. S. Triantafyllou and G. S. Triantafyllou. An efficient swimming machine. *Scientific American*, 272:64, 1995.

[19] R. Van Ham, T. G. Sugar, B. Vanderborght, K. W. Hollander, and D. Lefeber. Compliant actuator designs. *IEEE Robotics & Automation Magazine*, pages 81–94, September 2009.

[20] V. VanDoren. *Techniques for adaptive control.* Butterworth-Heinemann, 2002.

[21] J. Wang, P. K. McKinley, and X. Tan. Dynamic modeling of robotic fish with a base-actuated flexible tail. *Journal of Dynamic Systems, Measurement and Control*, 137(1), August 2014.

[22] Y. Wang, R. Tan, G. Xing, J. Wang, and X. Tan. Accuracy-aware aquatic diffusion process profiling using robotic sensor networks. In *Proceedings of the 11th ACM/IEEE Conference on Information Processing in Sensor Networks*, pages 281–292, Beijing, China, 2012.

[23] R. J. Wood. The first takeoff of a biologically inspired at-scale robotic insect. *IEEE Transactions on Robotics*, 24(2):341–347, 2008.

Novelty-Based Evolutionary Design of Morphing Underwater Robots

Francesco Corucci
The BioRobotics Institute
Scuola Superiore Sant'Anna
Pisa, Italy
f.corucci@sssup.it

Marcello Calisti
The BioRobotics Institute
Scuola Superiore Sant'Anna
Pisa, Italy
m.calisti@sssup.it

Helmut Hauser
Department of Engineering Mathematics
University of Bristol
United Kingdom
helmut.hauser@bristol.ac.uk

Cecilia Laschi
The BioRobotics Institute
Scuola Superiore Sant'Anna
Pisa, Italy
c.laschi@sssup.it

ABSTRACT

Recent developments in robotics demonstrated that bioinspiration and embodiement are powerful tools to achieve robust behavior in presence of little control. In this context morphological design is usually performed by humans, following a set of heuristic principles: in general this can be limiting, both from an engineering and an artificial life perspectives. In this work we thus suggest a different approach, leveraging evolutionary techniques. The case study is the one of improving the locomotion capabilities of an existing bioinspired robot. First, we explore the behavior space of the robot to discover a number of qualitatively different morphology-enabled behaviors, from whose analysis design indications are gained. The suitability of novelty search – a recent open-ended evolutionary algorithm – for this intended purpose is demonstrated. Second, we show how it is possible to condense such behaviors into a reconfigurable robot capable of online morphological adaptation (morphosis, morphing). Examples of successful morphing are demonstrated, in which changing just one morphological parameter entails a dramatic change in the behavior: this is promising for a future robot design. The approach here adopted represents a novel computed-aided, bioinspired, design paradigm, merging human and artificial creativity. This may result in interesting implications also for artificial life, having the potential to contribute in exploring underwater locomotion "as-it-could-be".

CCS Concepts

•**Computing methodologies → Evolutionary robotics;** *Artificial life; Genetic algorithms;*

GECCO '15, July 11 - 15, 2015, Madrid, Spain

DOI: http://dx.doi.org/10.1145/2739480.2754686

Keywords

Computer aided/automated design; morphogenesis; artificial life; evolutionary robotics; genetic algorithms

1. INTRODUCTION

Legged robotics is notoriously a challenging field. As in other sub-fields of robotics, the bio-inspired approach turns out to be a very effective paradigm [13]. Working at different levels of abstraction and biomimetism, researchers produced a number of remarkably simple designs for legged robots, that are at the same time efficient and effective [8, 14, 7, 1].

Most of these robots (inspired by or contributing to the field of embodied intelligence [20]) draw from nature in order to facilitate the control: the idea is that, with a proper morphological design, the body can take over (at least partially) the role of the controller. Biological and bio-mechanical studies indeed demonstrated that the robust locomotion of most animals is, to a large extent, the result of self-stabilizing properties of their mechanical structure, see e.g. [9, 12]. As a consequence, most of the aforementioned robots feature a simple, periodic, open-loop control.

Having such a simple control, the morphological design becomes crucial to achieve an effective behavior leveraging the interaction with the environment. Nonetheless this design stage in robotics is usually performed by human experts, that carefully engineer such robots to achieve meaningful behaviors. This entails to take difficult decisions, selecting a single configuration over a whole range of possible solutions, in a design space whose dimension easily explodes also for the simplest robots. Often the path towards the final design is guided by a set of heuristic principles [19], and when experimental tests are performed to "optimize" the design for a given ecological niche, only a small portion of the design space can be explored due to practical limitations. In addition, when highly dynamic behaviors are targeted, the complex intertwining of physics phenomena ensure that the result of such a procedure will be, almost certainly, suboptimal.

In general this human intervention can limit the possible outcomes of a bioinspired design process. This appears to be true both from an engineering perspective (i.e. in building the best robot for a given environment or application) and from an artificial life perspective, e.g. in exploring "life-as-it-could-be" [15], producing real robots with surprising lifelike behaviors that deviate from those of biological creatures. Methods from evolutionary robotics [4] can come into play, as they demonstrated an enormous potential to produce complex, functional, lifelike morphologies in simulation (from the seminal work of Karl Sims [24] to more recent, exciting, demonstrations [6, 11, 2, 22]).

In this work our goal is not to evolve from scratch a completely new robot morphology, but rather to improve an existing one [1] by redesigning it, capitalizing elements of bioinspiration that resulted to be effective, but leveraging evolutionary algorithms to explore alternative solutions in a large design space. The emphasis is on morphology evolution in presence of a simple periodic open loop control. We aim at discovering a number of novel, self-stabilized, morphology-enabled, legged gaits with respect to the ones currently exhibited by the robot. Doing so, design indications can be gained by analyzing the evolved morphologies. The focus is thus different with respect to related works [28, 27, 3], in which the goal was mainly to evolve the control for a *fixed*, kinematically complex, robot morphology.

In order to further develop the potential use of morphology to achieve diverse behaviors in presence of a very simple control, we resort to another bioinspired concept: the one of *morphosis* or *morphing*, i.e. the possibility to control morphological adaptation online (a concept that is related to the broader one of morphological computation [10]). This behavior has been observed in biology [26] and preliminary work in this direction has also been done in robotics, mainly for the design of mechanical solutions enabling it [21, 16].

Our methodology attempts to automatically discover candidate morphologies to perform and exploit morphological adaptation online, in order to switch among diverse behaviors. Particularly, we are interested in investigating whether it is possible to trigger a macroscopic change in the behavior by modifying few (ideally one) morphological parameters. Successful examples of this kind of morphing will be presented, and the possibility to build a reconfigurable robot exploiting morphosis to switch among different behaviors is envisioned (e.g. switching from running to swimming to overcome an obstacle). Also, with respect to previous works following similar approaches [25] (focusing on the evolution of quasi-static gaits for terrestrial robots), the setting presented in this paper differs for several reasons. First, robots will evolve in water environment, in which, with respect to the terrestrial one, the importance of morphology is further stressed. As it will be shown, a slight morphological change has the potential to entail dramatic change in the resulting behavior. Second, the reference robot has the potential to perform dynamic multi-modal locomotion (e.g. crawling, running, hopping, swimming), an uncommon feature in legged robotic platforms. Third, we differ in the adopted methodology.

We propose the adoption of genetic algorithms (GA) in combination with a recently introduced evolutionary algorithm called *novelty search* [18] as a suitable tool to explore the behavior space of a robot. Its ability to produce a large and diverse set of solutions is highly desirable here, as it can potentially mitigate the transfer problem (offering more chances of success) when trying to translate some of the insights gained in this work in a future robotic prototype. To the best of our knowledge, this is the first time novelty search is applied for such a purpose. A method to analyze the results of the evolutionary run is also proposed, that allows the human designer to find candidate morphologies for morphing that are close in morphology space but far apart in behavior space. Eventually this procedure will allow us to design systematically robots that are geared for morphosis, exploiting embodiement to switch among different behaviors, thus being more adaptive and robust.

We propose this design flow as a general approach to mix bioinspired embodied robot design and evolutionary computation, i.e. human and machine skills and creativity. This methodology could potentially bring contributions to the more general field of artificial life, evolving novel artificial life forms that exploit some elements of bioinspiration (provided by humans) and suggesting more that are produced by the evolutionary process, possibly deviating from the starting biological model. As for bioinspired robot design, an advantage of this approach lies in the fact that the system can be improved by the evolutionary process while being exposed (in simulation) to the actual task and environment. This can potentially bring into the final design elements that were overlooked in the bioinspiration process or that (although not present in the reference biological model) could entail benefits in terms of performance or efficiency.

2. METHODS AND MATERIALS

2.1 Reference robot

Our case study will be the PoseiDRONE robot [1] (Fig. 1a), a multi-purpose, soft, underwater robot inspired by the octopus. The robot, composed for most part of soft materials, is made of three main units: a central body (meant for jet-propelled swimming, not relevant to this study), a legged module and a floating module. The legged module comprises four soft silicone limbs, each of which is attached to the rigid part of the robot via a thin, centrally embedded, flexible beam of steel. Each leg is actuated in feed-forward by a rotational motor via a three-bars mechanism, functionally inspired by the push-pull locomotion strategy of the octopus [7]. The mechanism translates a circular rotation of a crank into a pseudo-elliptical loop in the distal part of the leg (Fig. 1b), suitable for locomotion. The floating module can be inflated and deflated to change the robot density and to shift its center of buoyancy. This aspect is peculiar as it can be exploited to change the stance of the robot (e.g. to lift a pair of legs to achieve bipedal locomotion [5]) or to initiate dynamic phenomena (arising from the momentum between buoyancy acting on the center of buoyancy – CoB, and gravity acting at the center of mass – CoM) that can be exploited for locomotion. The robot demonstrates an effective, self-stabilized locomotion in water tank experiments, exhibiting two kinds of legged gaits, i.e. crawling and bipedal walking [1, 5] as configurations were varied. Particularly, mainly for practical reasons, only two morphological parameters were varied during experiments performed with the prototype, i.e. the inclination of the floating module with respect to the central body of the robot, and its inflation state, affecting the resulting robot density. By varying just these two parameters some qualitatively different behaviors were observed: however, by exploring the full morphological space, our work demonstrates that this robot could indeed exhibit

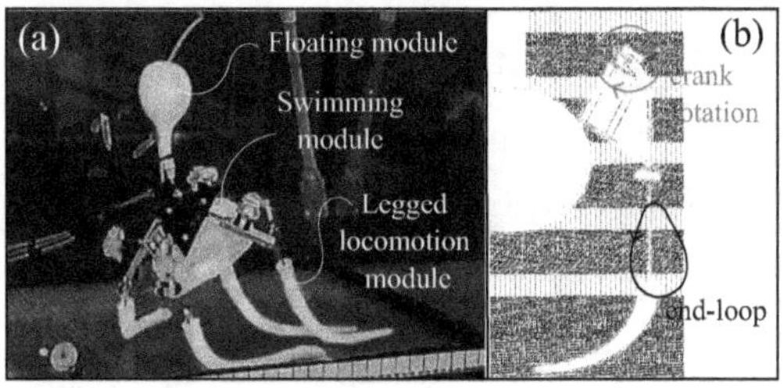

Figure 1: (a) The PoseiDRONE robot in a water tank, (b) detail of the leg mechanism.

a much wider range of morphology-enabled, multi-modal, dynamic behaviors.

2.2 Simulated model

Starting from the robot described in Sect. 2.1 a general model (Fig. 2) was developed and exploited to simulate alternative designs. An exhaustive description of the model is out of the scope of this paper (the interested reader can refer to [5]): in what follows only the most salient features will be reported. Given that the locomotion of the robot is mainly planar, the mathematical model describing its dynamics is planar too, thus featuring three degrees of freedom: the position of the CoM (x and y coordinates) and the pitch angle ϑ. Each leg is actuated by imposing a rotation of the corresponding crank around the center of rotation (CoR), at a given, constant, angular speed $\dot{\vartheta}_r$. The corresponding frequency is thus $f = \dot{\vartheta}_r/2\pi$, and it can be different for front and hind legs (f_{front}, f_{rear}). Moreover, an inter-leg phase shift $\phi_{interleg}$ can exist between the two legs of each pair (front and hind pairs), as well as a front to rear phase shift $\phi_{frontRear}$. From a dynamic point of view the soft legs are described as mass-less spring-damper systems. Each leg exerts to the ground elastic and damping forces proportional to the stiffness k and damping coefficient dr. In addition to gravity, the model describes specific dynamics of the underwater setting, such as buoyancy forces, fluid drag, and fluid dynamics effect induced by sculling movements of the legs [23]. The central body is approximated with a sphere of radius R: this simplifies the computation of relevant quantities such as the isotropic drag, body inertia and added mass. Finally, a second order foot slipping model is also present. The model embeds a considerable number of parameters (geometric, dynamic, related to materials, etc.) affecting the resulting behavior of the robot, whose complex interrelation is not easy to foresee. The ones that have been varied to explore the behavior space of the robot are listed in Tab. 1. The model was implemented and numerically solved in MATLAB®.

2.3 Optimization setup

The model described in Sect. 2.2 is used to explore the behavior space of the robot in simulation, by adopting genetic algorithms (GAs). To conduct such an exploration *novelty search* is suggested and adopted, operating on top of a standard genetic algorithm. To demonstrate the advantages of this approach for the present study, a conventional objective-based GA is first used to achieve a comparison baseline. In the next sections we will describe the two optimization approaches in more detail.

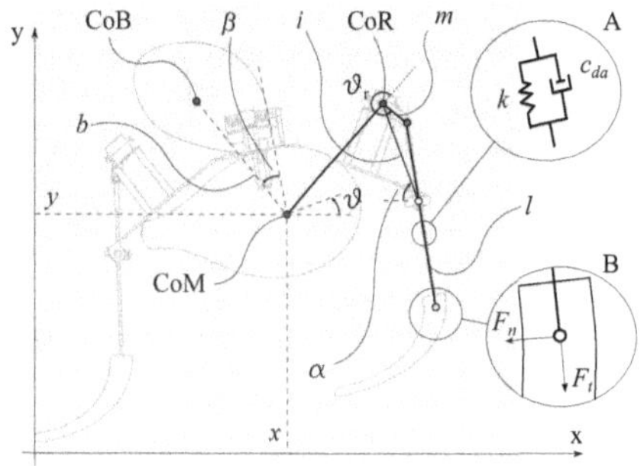

Figure 2: Schematic view of the robot showing the kinematic structure of the leg mechanism as well as some of the geometric and dynamic parameters. Legs are depicted in phase for simplicity. Detail A highlights parameters governing contact forces, while detail B highlights sculling forces that can be exploited for swimming.

2.3.1 Encoding

The structure of the artificial genome is the same for both settings (objective-based and novelty-based), embedding the geometric, actuation and materials parameters described in Tab. 1. Direct encoding is adopted, the resulting genome length being 24. Some parameters are expressed as multipliers of other quantities in such a way to embed necessary constraints into the encoding and impose only boundary constraints.

2.3.2 Experimental details

The model was allowed to run for $t_e = 25s$ for each genome. All the robots are dropped from a constant distance to the floor. If a robot falls (i.e. touches the ground with parts of the body other than feet) the event is detected and the simulation stops. Both the objective-based and the novelty-based settings rely on a standard GA implementation from MATLAB's Global Optimization Toolbox (real-coded linear constrained solver with bound constraints). Relevant GA parameters are listed in Tab. 2. All the processing was performed in MATLAB 2013b®. Each execution of the GA ran in parallel over 12 cores of a Workstation (Intel Xeon 3.07 GHz, 48GB RAM), for a total execution time of $\sim$ 48 h.

2.3.3 Objective-based GA

The objective-based setting serves as a baseline to highlight the benefits of novelty search in exploring the behavior space of a robot. The adopted fitness is based on the space traveled by each robot, normalized by a characteristic body length (BL). The problem was formulated as a minimum, and the fitness was thus defined as: $fitness = -|s_x/BL|$, where s_x is the abscissa of the CoM at the end of the simulation, and $BL = l_{front} + l_{rear}$. Falling robots receive a fixed positive penalty of 100, plus an additional penalty (the longer the time a robot managed to keep the balance, the lower the additional penalty): $P_{fall} = \lceil 100 + 5 \cdot (t_e - t_{fall}) \rceil$, where t_e is the total execution time and t_{fall} is the falling time.

2.3.4 Novelty-based GA

Novelty search [18] is a recently introduced open-ended approach to evolutionary computation. Instead of maximiz-

Table 1: Model parameters composing the genome and corresponding bounds. The indication "x2" means that two parameters of the described type are present, one for hind legs, one for front legs.

Parameter	Description	Bounds
	Geometry	
R	Radius of the central spherical body	$[0.05, 0.30]\ m$
β	Inclination of the CoB with respect to the medial plane	$[-90, +90]^\circ$
bR_{mul}	Multiplier determining the distance b between CoB and CoM ($b = bR_{mul} \cdot R$)	$[0, 3]$
$lMul$	x2 - Multiplier determining the length of the legs l $l = lMul \cdot (m + i)$	$[1, 2]$
$mMulI$	x2 - Multiplier determining the length of the cranks $m = min(mMulI \cdot i, mMulR \cdot R)$	$[0.01, 0.95]$
$mMulR$	x2 - Multiplier determining the length of the cranks (see above row)	$[0.01, 0.95]$
i	x2 - Distance of crank's CoR from the spherical joint	$[0.01, 0.40]\ m$
α	x2 - Inclination of leg's mechanisms	$[0, 120]^\circ$
	Actuation	
f	x2 - Rotation frequency of the cranks (the sign encodes the direction)	$[-3, 3]\ Hz$
$\phi_{interleg}$	Phase shift between legs of the same pair	$[0, 360]^\circ$
$\phi_{frontRear}$	Phase shift between frontal and rear legs	$[0, 360]^\circ$
	Materials	
λ_t	Tangential drag coefficient of the legs	$[0, 0.04]\ kg/m$
λ_n	Normal drag coefficient of the legs	$[0, 0.15]\ kg/m$
k	Stiffness of the legs	$[50, 400]\ N/m$
dr	Damping reduction factor $c_{da} = dr \cdot 2\sqrt{k\ M}$	$[0.1, 1.5]$
c_{sf}	Static friction coefficient	$[0.1, 1]$
c_{dfmul}	Dynamic friction coefficient multiplier ($c_{df} = c_{dfmul} \cdot c_{sf}$)	$[0.1, 0.9]$
ρ_r	Robot density	$[1010, 1400]\ \frac{kg}{m^3}$

Table 2: MATLAB GA settings.

Option	Value
$GenomeSize$	24
$PopulationSize$	800
$CrossoverFraction$	0.7
$EliteCount$	4
$TimeLimit$	Inf
$Generations$	70
$CreationOperator$	$gacreationuniform$
$SelectionOperator$	$gaselectionstochunif$
$CrossoverOperator$	$crossoverscattered$
$MutationOperator$	$mutationgaussian$

ing an explicit, task-based objective, it maximizes a novelty metric, that quantifies how novel an individual is with respect to others that have been previously observed. Instead of rewarding individuals performing *well*, the algorithm rewards individuals performing *differently*. Even in problems in which a clear objective can be defined, novelty search completely ignores the objective. Nevertheless, it was shown that this strategy is effective in several scenarios, and it is indeed capable of producing far better solutions with respect to settings in which the objective is explicitly defined. Proposers of this algorithm suggest [18] that this could be due to the fact that novelty search is most likely to reward counter-intuitive intermediate solutions that are not appealing for an objective-based algorithm, but that can, eventually, lead to a far better final solution.

Here we adopt novelty search to explore the space of morphology enabled behaviors of a robot. This idea is appealing for a number of reasons. First, it has the potential to encourage the production of diverse locomotion strategies with respect to the ones already implemented in the reference robotic prototype and, possibly, also with respect to the ones observed in nature. Second, it is capable of producing *several* alternative designs: this is highly attractive with respect to the possibility to cross the reality-gap. Having a number of various designs to test into the real world, potentially exploiting very different locomotion strategies, the chances to achieve a successful transfer from simulation to reality increase significantly. Third, it produces a potentially large set of alternative solutions in a single run, and without the need to specify each time hand-crafted fitness functions.

In order to apply novelty search to a problem, a *novelty score* must be defined for each individual, being the scalar quantity actually optimized by the algorithm. A possible procedure to compute such a score is to first map each individual into a features space, and then apply a novelty metric acting on such a space to quantify how novel an individual is with respect to previously observed ones. As for the novelty metric (essentially a sparseness metric), the average Euclidean distance to the k nearest neighbors is adopted as in related works [18]. It has to be noted that, for each individual, the k nearest neighbors are searched in a set that contains all the current population plus the so called *novelty archive* (a repository that keeps track of the most novel individuals discovered during evolution).

Features are domain-specific, and should be defined in such a way that by exploring novelty in the features space interesting behaviors can be instantiated. In our setting the behavior of each robot design is thus characterized by a vector $\boldsymbol{x}$ of locomotion-related behavioral features defined as $\boldsymbol{x} = (\overline{s_x}, \overline{s_y}, \overline{\delta_{front}}, \overline{\delta_{rear}}) \in \Re^4$, where $\overline{s_x}$ and $\overline{s_y}$ are, respectively, the normalized space traveled in the x and y directions, and $\overline{\delta_{front}}$ and $\overline{\delta_{rear}}$ are the mean duty factors of front and rear legs (i.e. the percentage of time legs stay in contact with the ground).

Resorting to the Euclidean distance, novelty search may be biased towards exploring features with a bigger magnitude, while overlooking those with a smaller one. In general this is not desirable, as the algorithm may completely ignore some of the features, ending up exploring just a portion of the behavior space. Therefore, before computing the novelty score (at the end of each epoch), the following normalization is applied to the behavior space: $\overline{x} = (x - x_{min})/(x_{max} - x_{min})$, where $\overline{x}$ is the normalized behavior vector, x_{min}, x_{max} are vectors containing, respectively, the minimum and maximum values for each feature, and the division is intended as an element-wise vector operation. Novelty search was implemented on top of MATLAB's GAs following the C++ reference implementation by Joel Lehman [17], the only difference being that in our setting the N_{add} most novel individuals of each generation are added to the novelty archive ($N_{add} = 0.025 \cdot PopulationSize$).

2.4 Morphing

2.4.1 Morphing among close morphologies

The output of the evolutionary run is expected to be a large set of different designs exhibiting diverse locomotion strategies, that we would like to embed into a reconfigurable morphing robot. The more morphological parameters must be changed to entail a relevant behavior switch, the more complex must be the robot to allow such a complete reconfiguration (e.g. in terms of additional actuators). It is thus important to understand whether it is possible to achieve a macroscopic variation in the behavior by changing the minimum number of parameters (ideally just one). In what follows, we propose a search procedure to identify robot designs that are close in the morphology space, but far apart in behavior space.

2.4.2 Searching for candidate morphologies

The output of novelty search comprised the final population and the novelty archive, the size of such a set being, in our experiments, of 2200 individuals. The question arises of how could we search for candidate morphologies to attempt morphing in such a big set. Here we propose the following procedure:

1. Normalize the genomes space (comprising the last population and the novelty archive) as explained in Sect. 2.3.4;
2. Perform a clustering procedure in morphology space (Sect. 2.4.3);
3. Select a number of promising clusters to analyze (e.g. in which the maximum speed is above a certain threshold);
4. Inside each of the promising clusters, rank individuals for their speed, and select one candidate for morphing;
5. For each of the selected candidates search, within the same cluster, for individuals that although being close in morphology space (e.g. differing in just one parameter) maximally differ in their behavior, i.e. are far apart in behavior space. Euclidean distance is employed to estimate proximity in such spaces. Among them, select the candidate(s) for morphing;
6. Start simulating one of the selected morphologies and trigger morphing at some point of the execution (multiple times, if multiple candidates were selected).

In this procedure the human designer actively re-enters into the design process, evaluating which behaviors are more interesting, either for morphing, or because they embed promising design configurations that are most likely to be transferable to the real world at a later stage.

2.4.3 Details on the clustering procedure

For the experiments reported in this paper, *agglomerative hierarchical clustering* was applied. This approach groups data at different scales, creating a cluster tree (also called *dendrogram*, Fig. 5). The procedure does not produce a single set of clusters, but instead a multi-level hierarchy that the designer can "cut" to achieve clustering at different scales. Standardized Euclidean distance was used to compute similarity, while agglomeration is based on unweighted average distance. Clustering functions from MATLAB® Statistics Toolbox were adopted.

2.5 Human-machine collaborative design

In the proposed methodology the human designer works together with the evolutionary algorithm and the other computational tools during the design process, in a sort of collaborative design process. The goal is to preserve the best from both worlds. The human designer first performs the conceptual work needed to apply bioinspiration in a proper manner. Clever bioinspired solutions devised by human designers in previous work (such as the leg mechanism and the presence of soft limbs) are not overlooked, but instead used to constrain the search space and simplify the job of the evolutionary algorithm in finding simple, functional, and effective robots. Also, constraining the algorithm to adopt technical solutions that have been already implemented in several prototypes ensures that evolved morphologies can be actually built. The novelty-based evolutionary algorithm then leverage these building blocks to explore different solutions in a "creative" way. It can play with the basic morphology of the robot in any conceivable way, possibly deviating (as we will show in Sect. 3) from the original biological model. In this sense this methodology can provide hints for alternative solutions with respect to the one observed in biology. The human designer then reenters the design process with the important task of searching for interesting solutions within the results of the evolutionary run.

3. RESULTS

3.1 Novelty-based vs. objective based GA

An extensive comparison between the objective-based and the novelty-based settings is beyond the scope of this work. Here we report some experimental results to support the idea that novelty search is suitable for the intended study, comparing typical runs performed with the two approaches.

First, our experiments confirm previous observations [18] suggesting that novelty search is indeed capable of outperforming objective-based algorithms even though it completely ignores the objective. Fig. 3 shows the best horizontal speed achieved at each generation by the two algorithms. Although for novelty search this quantity is only one of the four explored features (the others being vertical speed and mean duty factors of front and hind legs) and there is no pressure applied toward discovering faster robots, the algorithm outperforms the objective-based GA.

More relevant for our intended study is the comparison reported in Fig. 4, in which the four features are plotted for individuals produced by the two evolutionary runs. The objective-based GA produces individuals that are concentrated in a narrow region of the behavior space. It can be observed how the objective-based GA converges toward a bipedal robot running backward (duty factors of front legs

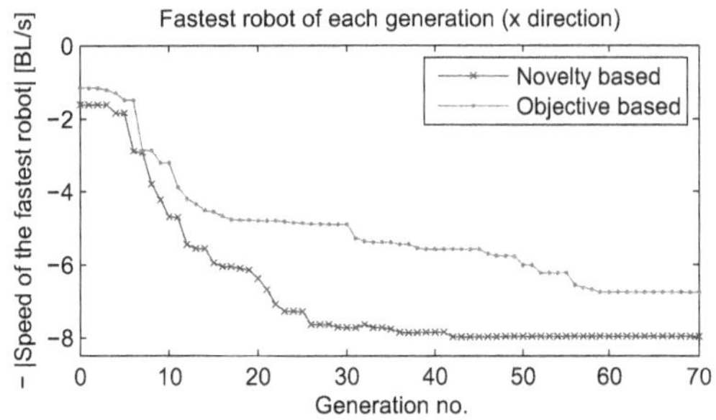

Figure 3: Speed of the fastest individual of each generation: comparison of the objective-based and novelty-based genetic algorithm. Novelty search finds faster individuals (compare absolute values).

are null for almost all individuals). Basically the algorithm returns *one* design, and individuals in the last run are mostly slight variations of the same design, exploiting the same locomotion principle. In contrast, novelty search seems to explore the four dimensional behavior space as intended, producing a heterogeneous population. Qualitatively different solutions can be observed. From the plot of space traveled, it can be observed how novelty search produces robots that travel not only forward and backward in the x direction, but also swim in all possible directions (in contrast with the objective-based setting, in which the space traveled in y never exceeds $1BL$). The production of qualitatively different solutions is confirmed by the plot of duty factors, in which robots can be observed that exhibit a wide range of behaviors (bipedal – on both pairs of legs, quadrupedal, etc.).

Results thus suggest that novelty search can be effective in exploring the behavior space of a robot and, as a consequence, its morphology space (given the marginal role of the control in our setting). The final population contains a rich repertoire of possible designs to search in. Hereafter the focus will thus be on analyzing results of the novelty-based evolutionary run.

3.2 Evolved morphologies and morphing experiments

We now analyze some of the designs extracted from the final population that, in addition to exhibiting interesting locomotion strategies, provided examples of successful morphing. Those designs are the result of the search procedure described in Sect. 2.4.2. Fig. 5 shows a typical dendrogram, resulting from clustering in morphology space. The cophenetic correlation coefficient – an index that measures how faithfully the clustering preserves the structure in the data – is 0.9043 (the closer to 1 the better). Fig. 6 details some of the most interesting designs. Configurations discovered by novelty search suggest different, multi-modal, locomotion strategies, each embedding possible design choices. For example, many designs suggest that, although being originally designed for walking and running, the leg mechanism is indeed particularly effective to achieve swimming by sculling. By keeping $m \approx i$ (as a reminder, m is the length of the crank, i is the distance between the crank's CoR and the spherical joint), the distal parts of the legs reach high speeds, thus generating high swimming forces. According to experimental data this appears as a particularly effective strategy, confirmed by the fact that the fastest

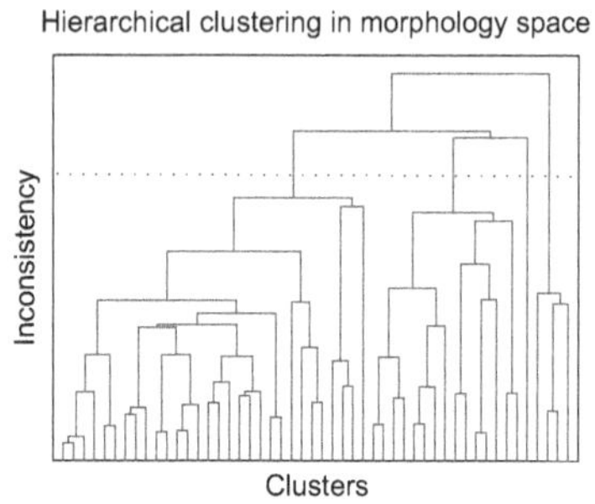

Figure 5: The dendrogram resulting from the clustering in morphology space, and a possible cut.

robot is indeed a swimming one. As for morphing, the diverse final population offers multiple alternatives to perform it, switching among qualitatively different behaviors. Examples of successful morphing are reported in Fig. 6. Note that in those examples varying just one parameter resulted to be enough to entail a macroscopic variation in the behavior (e.g. switching from running to swimming). Although here omitted for space constrains, an in-deep analysis of evolved behaviors reveals very elaborated solutions, regularities, and embodiement properties (e.g. effective locomotion leveraging passive dynamics). Finally, although evolved behaviors appear natural and life-like in many cases, lot of the evolved designs deviate from any conceivable biological model, therefore suggesting novel ways to locomote underwater.

4. CONCLUSIONS

Results confirm our hypothesis that novelty search is indeed a suitable tool to explore the behavior and morphology space of a robot. Also, the proposed methodology for human-machine collaborative design proved to be effective in order to design self-stabilized legged robots, mixing the strengths of both worlds. The human designer enters into the design process when conceptual work is needed to apply bioinspiration in a proper manner, as well as when results of an evolutionary process must be analyzed. On the other hand, the evolutionary algorithm is able to explore a huge behavior space, producing a wide range of effective alternative solutions. Morphing was also demonstrated, encouraging to build a reconfigurable robot exploiting self-stabilization to switch among different behaviors. In this regard it was also demonstrated that in water environment a single parameter is enough to determine macroscopic variations in the resulting behavior. From a design perspective, some of the most interesting parameters to exploit for morphing have been identified. Design indications were gained (as for example the suitability of the three-bar leg mechanism for performing sculling-based swimming) and more can still be gained by further analyzing evolved designs. From an artificial life perspective novel underwater "creatures" have been produced in simulation that exhibit surprising behaviors, in some cases resembling biological creatures, in some other completely deviating from biological examples.

Acknowledgments

This work is partly supported by RoboSoft - A Coordination Action for Soft Robotics (FP7-ICT-2013-C # 619319)

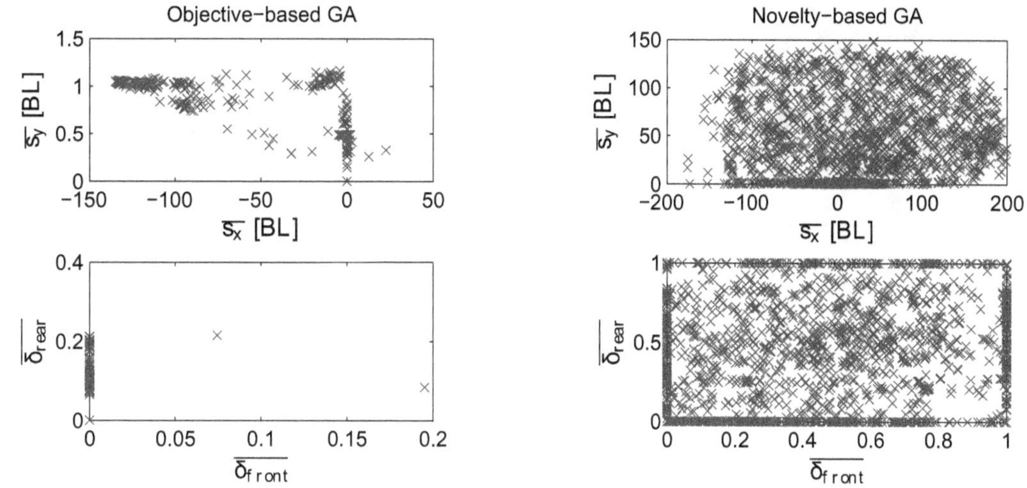

Figure 4: Behavioral space exploration: objective-based GA vs. novelty-based GA.

and by the Fondazione Livorno within the framework of the PoseiDRONE project Grant.

5. REFERENCES

[1] A. Arienti, M. Calisti, F. G. Serchi, and C. Laschi. Poseidrone: design of a soft-bodied ROV with crawling, swimming and manipulation ability. In *Proceedings of the MTS/IEEE OCEANS*. MTS/IEEE, 2013.

[2] J. E. Auerbach and J. C. Bongard. On the relationship between environmental and morphological complexity in evolved robots. In *Proceedings of the Fourteenth International Conference on Genetic and Evolutionary Computation*, pages 521–528. ACM, 2012.

[3] J. Bongard, V. Zykov, and H. Lipson. Resilient machines through continuous self-modeling. *Science*, 314(5802):1118–1121, 2006.

[4] J. C. Bongard. Evolutionary robotics. *Commun. ACM*, 56(8):74–83, Aug. 2013.

[5] M. Calisti, F. Corucci, A. Arienti, and C. Laschi. Bipedal walking of an octopus-inspired robot. In *Biomimetic and Biohybrid Systems*, pages 35–46. Springer, 2014.

[6] N. Cheney, R. MacCurdy, J. Clune, and H. Lipson. Unshackling evolution: evolving soft robots with multiple materials and a powerful generative encoding. In *Proceeding of the Fifteenth Annual Conference on Genetic and Evolutionary Computation*, pages 167–174. ACM, 2013.

[7] M. Cianchetti, M. Calisti, L. Margheri, M. Kuba, and C. Laschi. Bioinspired locomotion and grasping in water: the soft eight-arm octopus robot. *Bioinsp. Biomim.*, to appear, 2014.

[8] K. C. Galloway, G. C. Haynes, B. D. Ilhan, A. M. Johnson, R. Knopf, G. A. Lynch, B. N. Plotnick, M. White, and D. E. Koditschek. X-RHex: A highly mobile hexapedal robot for sensorimotor tasks. 2010.

[9] S. Grimmer, M. Ernst, M. Günther, and R. Blickhan. Running on uneven ground: leg adjustment to vertical steps and self-stability. *Journal of Experimental Biology*, 211(18):2989–3000, 2008.

[10] H. Hauser, R. M. Füchslin, and R. Pfeifer. *Opinions and Outlooks on Morphological Computation.* Zürich, 2014 - ISBN 978-3-033-04515-6.

[11] J. D. Hiller and H. Lipson. Evolving amorphous robots. In *ALIFE*, pages 717–724, 2010.

[12] F. Iida, J. Rummel, and A. Seyfarth. Bipedal walking and running with spring-like biarticular muscles. *Journal of Biomechanics*, 41(3):656–667, 2008.

[13] A. J. Ijspeert. Biorobotics: Using robots to emulate and investigate agile locomotion. *Science*, 346(6206):196–203, 2014.

[14] S. Kim, J. E. Clark, and M. R. Cutkosky. iSprawl: Design and tuning for high-speed autonomous open-loop running. *The International Journal of Robotics Research*, 25(9):903–912, 2006.

[15] C. Langton. *Artificial Life: An Overview.* A Bradford book. BRADFORD BOOK, 1997.

[16] J. C. Larsen, D. Brandt, and K. Stoy. Locokit: A robot construction kit for studying and developing functional morphologies. In *From Animals to Animats 12*, pages 12–22. Springer, 2012.

[17] J. Lehman. Novelty search C++ 1.0 - http://eplex.cs.ucf.edu/uncategorised/software, 2008.

[18] J. Lehman and K. O. Stanley. Abandoning objectives: Evolution through the search for novelty alone. *Evolutionary Computation*, 19(2):189–223, 2011.

[19] R. Pfeifer, F. Iida, and J. Bongard. New robotics: Design principles for intelligent systems. *Artificial Life*, 11(1-2):99–120, 2005.

[20] R. Pfeifer, M. Lungarella, and F. Iida. Self-organization, embodiment, and biologically inspired robotics. *Science*, 318(5853):1088–1093, 2007.

[21] H. V. Quy, G. Ramstein, F. Casanova, L. Aryananda, M. Hoffmann, F. I. Sheikh, and H. Hauser. Gait versatility through morphological changes in a new quadruped robot. In *5th International Symposium on Adaptive Motion of Animals and Machines*, 2011.

[22] J. Rieffel and S. Smith. A face-encoding grammar for the generation of tetrahedral-mesh soft bodies. In *ALIFE*, pages 414–420, 2010.

[23] M. Sfakiotakis, A. Kazakidi, N. Pateromichelakis, J. A. Ekaterinaris, and D. P. Tsakiris. Robotic underwater propulsion inspired by the octopus multi-arm swimming. In *Robotics and Automation (ICRA), 2012 IEEE International Conference on*, pages 3833–3839. IEEE, 2012.

[24] K. Sims. Evolving virtual creatures. In *Proceedings of the 21st annual conference on Computer Graphics and Interactive Techniques*, pages 15–22. ACM, 1994.

[25] B. G. Smith, C. M. Saaj, and E. Allouis. Evolving legged robots using biologically inspired optimization strategies. In *Robotics and Biomimetics (ROBIO), 2010 IEEE International Conference on*, pages 1335–1340. IEEE, 2010.

[26] J. T. Watson, R. E. Ritzmann, and A. J. Pollack. Control of climbing behavior in the cockroach, blaberus discoidalis. ii. motor activities associated with joint movement. *Journal of Comparative Physiology A*, 188(1):55–69, 2002.

[27] J. Yosinski, J. Clune, D. Hidalgo, S. Nguyen, J. Zagal, and H. Lipson. Evolving robot gaits in hardware: the hyperneat generative encoding vs. parameter optimization. In *Proceedings of the 20th European Conference on Artificial Life*, pages 890–897, 2011.

[28] V. Zykov, J. Bongard, and H. Lipson. Evolving dynamic gaits on a physical robot. In *Proceedings of Genetic and Evolutionary Computation Conference, Late Breaking Paper, GECCO*, volume 4, 2004.

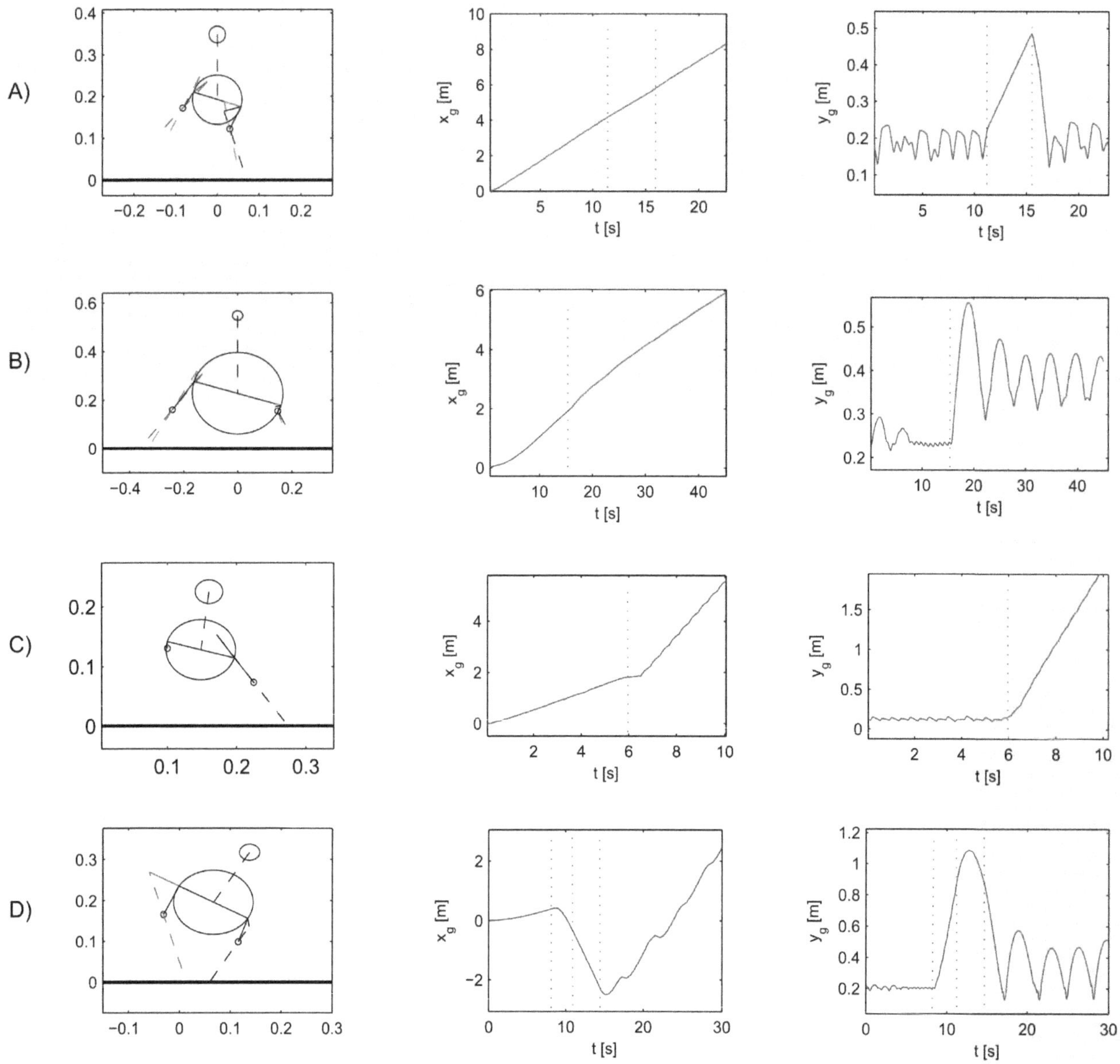

Figure 6: ***Simulation results: some of the evolved morphologies and examples of successful morphing.*** **Morphing from one morphology m_1 to another morphology m_2 is implemented as a gradual linear transformation in morphology space, occurring in a predefined time ($morphingTime$) A) A quadruped design resembling some kind of fast terrestrial quadruped (e.g. antelopes). The robot shows functional differentiation of front and hind legs. Hind legs provide powerful swimming strokes during the flight phase, modifying the ballistic trajectory of the robot and accelerating its descent towards the ground. Frontal legs absorb the subsequent impact, then releasing energy and making the robot bounce. Around $t = 11s$ the β parameter (Tab. 1) is decreased, with the effect of tilting the robot backward: the robot starts swimming. Shortly after $t = 15s$, β is brought back to the original value: the robot absorbs the impact with the ground and converges again toward a terrestrial gait. B) A bipedal robot that uses hind legs to push himself forward (front legs disappeared during evolution). Fluid resistance helps the robot to balance. At $t = 15s$ the length of the rear cranks is increased, entailing a change in the trajectory of rear feet. As a consequence the gait changes considerably. C) Another bipedal design, this time exploiting front legs to run (hind legs disappeared during evolution). Around $t = 6s$ the β parameter is decreased (similarly to A), tilting the robot backward: the robot starts to swim. D) This robot is tilted toward its front side, and exploits frontal legs to run. However, it has a functional pair of hind legs that, although being deactivated, appear to be optimized for swimming ($m \approx i$). Around $t = 8s$ rear legs are activated with a forward rotation: the robot inverts its motion and starts swimming backward. Around $t = 11s$ the β parameter is brought close to zero: this redirects the swimming propulsive action of rear legs, bringing the robot closer to ground. Around $t = 14.57s$ the rotation applied to hind legs is inverted: when the robot touches the ground, it converges to a hopping terrestrial gait. Other configurations are here omitted for space constraints.**

The Effect of Fitness Function Design on Performance in Evolutionary Robotics: The Influence of a Priori Knowledge

Mohammad Divband Soorati
Department of Computer Science,
University of Paderborn,
Zukunftsmeile 1, 33102 Paderborn, Germany
divband@mail.upb.de

Heiko Hamann
Department of Computer Science,
University of Paderborn,
Zukunftsmeile 1, 33102 Paderborn, Germany
heiko.hamann@uni-paderborn.de

ABSTRACT

Fitness function design is known to be a critical feature of the evolutionary-robotics approach. Potentially, the complexity of evolving a successful controller for a given task can be reduced by integrating a priori knowledge into the fitness function which complicates the comparability of studies in evolutionary robotics. Still, there are only few publications that study the actual effects of different fitness functions on the robot's performance. In this paper, we follow the fitness function classification of Nelson et al. (2009) and investigate a selection of four classes of fitness functions that require different degrees of a priori knowledge. The robot controllers are evolved in simulation using NEAT and we investigate different tasks including obstacle avoidance and (periodic) goal homing. The best evolved controllers were then post-evaluated by examining their potential for adaptation, determining their convergence rates, and using cross-comparisons based on the different fitness function classes. The results confirm that the integration of more a priori knowledge can simplify a task and show that more attention should be paid to fitness function classes when comparing different studies.

Categories and Subject Descriptors

I.2.2 [**Artificial Intelligence**]: Automatic Programming—*Program synthesis*

Keywords

evolutionary robotics; fitness function design

1. INTRODUCTION

Evolutionary robotics [16, 1] emerged with great early success and is meanwhile struggling to scale to more complex tasks. Recent reports on new methods such as novelty search [9, 10] and multi-objective evolution combined with methods generating behavioral diversity [12, 13, 3] seem to have high potential. Also the new emerging field of embodied online onboard evolution [5, 21, 8], that focuses on implementing evolutionary robotics as an embodied distributed system directly operating on a group of robots, is encouraging. Still, in all of these approaches the overall challenge of maximizing task complexity while minimizing necessary a priori knowledge persists. The idea of using little a priori knowledge in the design of either a behavioral distance measure or of a fitness function is motivated by a key advantage of evolutionary computation—it is a black-box optimizer [4]. As such, evolutionary computation is particularly suited for problems that are not well understood. The problem of defining a robot controller that generates a desired, reliable, and adaptive behavior is of that kind. However, in research of evolutionary robotics it seems to be tempting to put an effort in fitness function design. In preliminary experiments the researcher learns about specific features of the considered task, that is gaining a priori knowledge, and might consciously or unconsciously incorporate that knowledge into the fitness function. However, in an application of evolutionary robotics we would like to minimize the need for doing preliminary experiments and having to interpret them.

Nelson et al. [14] focus on that problem. They define the quality of an evolutionary-robotics approach as twofold: "the success of research is measured in the difficulty of tasks investigated, and the amount of a priori information needed to generate successful evolution of controllers capable of performing those tasks." While there is definitely a competition for more complex tasks in the community, the latter criterion of minimizing a priori knowledge seems neglected sometimes. In particular, a competition of minimizing a priori knowledge for similar tasks seems to be absent in evolutionary robotics literature except for a few directly related publications [17, 15] and a few other works that study fitness function design with strong focus on special domains [7, 6, 11]. It is also suggested by Nelson et al. [14]: "one particular ER effort might be considered an improvement over an earlier work if the later work required the use of much less a priori knowledge on the part of the researchers to evolve controllers for a similar task." In this paper, we report early results to fill this gap. An obvious challenge in this endeavor is to measure a priori knowledge. We follow the classification of fitness functions of Nelson et al. [14] to solve that issue. They define seven fitness function classes that are sorted according to the incorporated a priori knowledge.

GECCO '15, July 11 - 16, 2015, Madrid, Spain

ISBN 978-1-4503-3472-3/15/07...$15.00

DOI: http://dx.doi.org/10.1145/2739480.2754676

Here we focus on four of them: behavioral fitness functions (a priori knowledge incorporated: high), functional incremental fitness functions (moderately high), tailored fitness functions (moderate), and aggregate fitness functions (low). Unfortunately, classifying fitness functions according to this scheme is fuzzy and to some extent subjective. Hence, the challenge remains to define an objective measure of a priori knowledge, which is not solved within this work. However, the following study still allows for a structured approach. In alternative to the fitness function classification of Nelson et al. [14], there is also the classification of Nolfi and Floreano [16]. They define a 3-dimensional space along three axes: functional-behavioral, explicit-implicit, and external-internal. Relevant here is mostly the functional-behavioral aspect that classifies whether the fitness function defines detailed features (functional) or whether the fitness function defines abstract features (behavioral). Also the dimension explicit-implicit is of interest as it classifies basically the complexity of the fitness function (e.g., number of components). We prefer to use the approach of Nelson et al. [14] because it allows for a more detailed classification.

In this paper, we investigate a selection tasks and fitness functions. Over a month of computational time for the simulated evolutionary runs was invested. The results indicate a clear trend across the four investigated fitness function classes. Nonetheless, our findings are not easily generalized to all possible scenario of evolutionary robotics which cannot be achieved by giving a finite number of examples. However, a reliable mathematical formalism, which would allow to prove the generality of any result in evolutionary robotics, is also out of reach. Hence, our objective is not to naively generalize from our results. Instead we want to point to the significance of a priori knowledge and we want to show that more research has to be done to fill the benchmarking gap in the literature on this issue.

This paper is structured as follows. First, the fitness function classes are introduced in Sec. 2. Then, for each experimental task these fitness function classes are instantiated and explained (Sec. 3). After designing the experiments and simulation, in Sec. 4 the performance of the robot is investigated based on post-evaluation metrics, and the final ranking of the fitness functions is presented. We conclude with a short discussion and options for future work.

2. FITNESS FUNCTION CLASSES FOLLOWING NELSON ET AL.

Our study is based on the fitness function classes as defined by Nelson et al. [14]. The idea of this classification is to sort fitness functions according to the a priori knowledge that is involved in their design. As mentioned above, an objective measure of a priori knowledge is missing which complicates the classification of particular fitness functions. Still, it seems a viable approach based on the best methods that have been published so far. The classes in increasing order of required a priori knowledge are: aggregate, competitive and co-competitive, environmental incremental, tailored, functional incremental, behavioral, and training data fitness functions. In the following, we focus on the four classes only: aggregate fitness functions, behavioral fitness functions, tailored fitness functions, and functional incremental fitness functions.

Aggregate fitness functions (AFF) have the lowest degree of a priori knowledge and evaluate only *what* is achieved, that is, the completion of the task as the metric to select the best robots. The procedure of how the robot accomplishes a task is irrelevant. For example, the locomotion task of a bipedal robot can be described by an AFF that relies on traveled distance only. Such fitness functions are easy to design because they require little a priori knowledge and they are of low complexity. The drawback is obviously that there may be bootstrapping problems and there is no guidance for evolution through intermediate solutions.

Behavioral fitness functions (BFF) measure *how* the task is solved. Designing BFF hence requires a priori knowledge about options how the task can be solved. This way BFF also predetermine potential solutions and possibly exclude counterintuitive options. The design process for this type of fitness functions is relatively complex because it either requires good knowledge about effective solutions to the task or preliminary experiments that help to determine potential solutions.

Tailored fitness functions (TFF) combine elements of behavioral and aggregate fitness functions, that is, they combine BFF and AFF. Tailored fitness functions have a higher degree of complexity than AFF and BFF as they have several components that are typically multiplied or summed.

Functional incremental fitness functions (FIFF) are sets of fitness functions that are applied separately and gradually. The functions are applied in a series of distinct stages. The whole evolutionary process is divided into multiple intervals of generations in which only one fitness function holds. Therefore the number of fitness functions determines the number of such stages as well.

For the following experiments we need to define a particular fitness function for each task and class. All results are hence task-dependent and depending on the particular, chosen fitness function. We are interested in general conclusions, of course, and try to maximize the potential for generalizability by investigating three different tasks. Still, one could argue that our selections of fitness functions are beneficial for a certain fitness function class in individual cases and, hence, introduce a bias. To maximize the comparability of our examples, we define a structured and elaborated design strategy. First, the BFF are designed, second, the AFF. Then combinations of AFF and BFF define by design pattern the TFF. TFF combine AFF and BFF by multiplication. We make individual design decisions only for FIFF, whether the first stage starts with AFF followed by a phase with BFF or vice versa. Hence, the results within each task are easily comparable because they rely on the same fitness function components.

Besides the degree of a priori knowledge, the fitness functions can also be ordered according to their complexity. We do that in a simplistic approach. AFF have the simplest design process by considering task completion only. In contrast, BFF are complex to design. The remaining two classes are even more complex because they contain AFF and BFF as components (assuming an application scenario where we would need to define TFF and FIFF from scratch without using predefined AFF and BFF). FIFF requires the decision about the sequence of the components in addition to the component selection. Hence, it is considered as the most complex fitness function here. The order of complexity, starting with the lowest, is: AFF, BFF, TFF, and FIFF.

3. IMPLEMENTATION AND TASK-SPECIFIC FITNESS FUNCTIONS

We use the open-source simulator *Player/Stage*[1] to simulate a robot with differential drive that has 8 proximity sensors (6 to the front and 2 to the back) and 2 ambient light sensors (one at the front and one at the back). Our implementation is based on MultiNEAT [2] which is a portable software library implementing NEAT, a popular approach to optimize and complixify artificial neural networks [19, 20]. Using NEAT we start with simple network topologies that are then complexified during the evolutionary run. This process of complexification simplifies the approach to evolve controllers for tasks of different complexity. We evolve neural networks with 8 input neurons for the first task (obstacle avoidance) and 10 inputs for the two other tasks: 8 inputs s_i representing the input from the proximity sensors and two inputs (I_f and I_b) from the light sensors. There is a variable number of neurons on the hidden layer based on NEAT and two output neurons (speed of left and right wheel).

The total computation time was more than 112 days (30 generations × population of 30 × 3 evaluations with different initial positions × 3 repetitions each × 3 tasks × 4 fitness functions × 10 evolutionary runs × about 10 seconds for each evaluation) on evolving the best controllers even with a small number of generations. Therefore, we could run the experiments for 30 generations with a population size of 30, see Table 1 for all NEAT parameters. The controllers are evaluated for three different initial positions with different rotations. The simulation is non-deterministic due to variant time intervals between sensor readings in Player/Stage. Thus, the robot controller is simulated three times for each of these initial positions, totaling in nine evaluations. The assigned fitness is the average of these nine evaluations. All tasks use the same simulated rectangular arena of dimensions $2m \times 2m$, see Fig. 1a. The three initial positions are depicted with blue circles.

The tasks can be classified into three categories: movement (e.g., locomotion with obstacle avoidance), homing (e.g., goal homing), and object manipulation (e.g., object pushing) [18]. In the following experiments we focus on two of these categories (i.e., movement and homing) and instantiate three simple tasks: obstacle avoidance from movement category, goal homing, and periodic goal homing from the homing category. Our selection was motivated by requiring a coherent order of complexity among the tasks. This is guaranteed because the tasks of higher complexity contain the tasks of lower complexity as subtasks. Collision avoidance is part of the two other tasks. In the case of periodic goal homing, the robot needs to avoid the obstacles to reach a certain goal, hence, containing both other tasks. Next, we define the fitness function for each class and task based on the above mentioned design strategy.

3.1 Obstacle avoidance (OA)

One of the simplest tasks in evolutionary robotics is to evolve a collision avoidance behavior [16]. Avoiding collisions is of particular relevance in embodied evolution [22]. The idea is that the robot covers as much distance as possible (otherwise staying stopped is an optimal collision avoidance behavior) while minimizing collisions with walls and objects.

[1]http://playerstage.sourceforge.net

Parameter	Value
PopulationSize	30
CrossoverRate	0.75
DynamicCompatibility	True
MutateWeightsProb	0.9
CompatTreshold	2.0
WeightMutationMaxPower	5.0
YoungAgeTreshold	15
YoungAgeFitnessBoost	1.1
OverallMutationRate	0.33
WeightReplacementMaxPower	5.0
OldAgeTreshold	31
MutateWeightsSevereProb	0.5
MinSpecies	5
WeightMutationRate	0.75
MaxSpecies	25
MaxWeight	20
SurvivalRate	0.25
MutateAddNeuronProb	0.05
RouletteWheelSelection	True
MutateAddLinkProb	0.05
RecurrentProb	0.1
MutateRemoveLinkProb	0.05

Table 1: Used NEAT parameters.

For this task, BFF is based on the speed of both wheels and the inputs from the proximity sensors. This type of fitness function rewards behavioral features, that is, how the task is solved. First, the faster the robot moves the better it accomplishes the task. The first component is the average of the two wheel speeds averaged over time: $\bar{v}_l = \frac{1}{T}\sum_t v_l(t)$ and similarly for $\bar{v}_r$. Furthermore, maximal distance is covered by moving straight, that is, by avoiding rotations. The difference between the two speeds is minimized by defining $(1 - \sqrt{|\bar{v}_l - \bar{v}_r|})$ (square root gave best results in preliminary tests). The last component is $\frac{1}{\theta}\min_t(\min_i(s_i(t)))$ and rewards to stay far from obstacles. If any sensor detects an obstacle to be closer than an allowed distance, that is interpreted as a collision which needs to be penalized heavily. The threshold θ returns an extreme penalty of $\theta = 10^3$ if at least one collision occurred during the evaluation. Otherwise, we have $\theta = 1$. The behavioral fitness function for collision avoidance is defined by

$$F_{\text{bff}}^{\text{collAv}} = \left(\frac{\bar{v}_l + \bar{v}_r}{2}\right)(1-\sqrt{|\bar{v}_l - \bar{v}_r|})\frac{1}{\theta}\min_t(\min_i(s_i(t))). \quad (1)$$

For AFF, the focus is on task completion. Here we simply define the aggregate fitness function by the distance δ that the robot traveled during evaluation,

$$F_{\text{aff}}^{\text{collAv}} = \delta. \quad (2)$$

In the case of FIFF, a set of fitness functions is required. Following our design strategy we reuse the behavioral and aggregate fitness functions (eqs. 1 and 2), divide the evolution into two phases, and define the functional incremental fitness functions as a 2-tuple by

$$F_{\text{fiff}}^{\text{collAv}} = \{F_{\text{bff}}^{\text{collAv}}, F_{\text{aff}}^{\text{collAv}}\}. \quad (3)$$

We define TFF by the product of the behavioral and aggregate fitness function

$$F_{\text{fiff}}^{\text{collAv}} = F_{\text{bff}}^{\text{collAv}} F_{\text{aff}}^{\text{collAv}}. \quad (4)$$

3.2 Goal Homing (GH)

Goal homing is also a frequently investigated task in evolutionary robotics [14]. While in the collision avoidance task the robot's direction is not specified, the robot is now required to move as close as possible to a light source that is located in the middle of the arena. Finding the best path to the highest light intensity is the goal in this task. In simulation the light intensity is proportional to the inverse of the squared distance d between the robot's position and the arena center

$$I \propto \frac{1}{d^2}. \tag{5}$$

For all the following fitness functions, collisions are penalized by introducing a discount to the accumulated light intensity reward. For the time steps after the collision the light intensity is rewarded only by one half of the intensity.

In this task, the robot should approach the light quickly and then stay close to the light source. Hence, the robot should move fast, when it is far from the light, and it should stop moving, when it is close to the light. Hence, we reward the accumulated difference between intensity and traveled distance over all simulation steps. Based on empirical experience we add a weight $c = 5$ to increase the impact of light intensity relative to traveled distance. The behavioral fitness function is defined by

$$F_{\text{bff}}^{\text{gh}} = \sum_t \left| cI(t) - \Delta d(t) \right|, \tag{6}$$

whereas $I(t) = \frac{1}{2}(I_f + I_b)$ is the average of the detected light intensity in simulation step t and $\Delta d(t)$ is the robot's current speed. For the case of AFF, a simple function based on accumulated light intensity is defined by

$$F_{\text{aff}}^{\text{gh}} = \sum_t I(t). \tag{7}$$

For FIFF, we define two objectives: first approach the light and second avoid collisions. We reuse function $F_{\text{aff}}^{\text{collAv}} = \delta$ from eq. 2 (δ is traveled distance).

$$F_{\text{fiff}}^{\text{gh},1} = \sum_t I(t), \tag{8a}$$

$$F_{\text{fiff}}^{\text{gh},2} = F_{\text{aff}}^{\text{collAv}} = \delta \tag{8b}$$

The tailored fitness function is the product of behavioral and aggregate fitness function, defined by

$$F_{\text{tff}}^{\text{gh}} = \left(\sum_t I(t) \right) \left(\sum_t \left| cI(t) - \Delta d(t) \right| \right). \tag{9}$$

3.3 Periodic Goal Homing (PGH)

In periodic goal homing, the robot not only has to approach the light, but has to maximize the distance to the light again once it has been reached, and has to repeat that periodically. The robot should increase and then decrease the light intensity as much as possible. We divide the arena into two areas. A ring-shaped area A_1 (see Fig. 1c), containing all positions with intensities of $0.3 < I(t) < 0.7$ and an area A_2 that contains the remaining parts of the arena ($I(t) > 0.7$, $I(t) < 0.3$). The robot should traverse area A_1 as fast as possible. In addition, obstacle avoidance is imposed because the evaluation is stopped whenever the robot hits an obstacle. We define the behavioral fitness function

$$F_{\text{bff}}^{\text{pgh}} = \sum_t \varphi(t) \Delta d(t), \tag{10}$$

with $\varphi(t) = -1$ for $0.3 < I(t) < 0.7$ and $\varphi(t) = +1$ otherwise. φ penalizes spending time on A_1 and $\Delta d(t)$ is the robot's speed at time t, hence rewards moving fast on A_2.

For the case of AFF, we need a global feature that allows to determine whether the robot accomplishes its task well. From a number of options ranging from frequency analysis to measuring wavelengths, we pick the easily implemented option of the standard deviation σ that is directly calculated from the data acquired during the evaluation. Here, σ is a statistical function that gets the set of all light intensities $I = \{I(t) | \text{for all time steps } t\}$ as input and returns the standard deviation. A big standard deviation indicates a good periodic goal homing behavior. We define the aggregate fitness function

$$F_{\text{aff}}^{\text{pgh}} = \sigma(I). \tag{11}$$

We select two fitness functions to define the FIFF. Following our design strategy we would use the BFF and AFF but experiments showed that for this task that approach is ineffective (data not shown). Instead, we choose two AFFs of previous tasks (goal homing and collision avoidance), one rewards maximizing light intensity the other rewards movement.

$$F_{\text{fiff}}^{\text{pgh},1} = F_{\text{aff}}^{\text{gh},1} = \sum_t I(t), \tag{12a}$$

$$F_{\text{fiff}}^{\text{pgh},2} = F_{\text{aff}}^{\text{collAv}} = \delta. \tag{12b}$$

This way, the robot is assumed to move toward the light, but should keep moving. This is a rather rough way of defining the task but we follow our design strategy of reusing fitness functions for FIFF and not defining new components.

The tailored fitness function is the product of the behavioral and aggregate fitness functions, defined by

$$F_{\text{tff}}^{\text{pgh}} = F_{\text{bff}}^{\text{pgh}} F_{\text{aff}}^{\text{pgh}}. \tag{13}$$

These twelve fitness functions were used to evolve robot controllers for these three tasks. Our observations of the robots' behaviors indicate that the obtained best controllers were able to achieve a periodic behavior.

4. POST-EVALUATION AND READAPTATION TESTS

In the evolutionary runs with the above described twelve fitness functions we obtain a best controller from each evolutionary run. The evolutionary algorithm is effective and hence they are best relative to their fitness function for which they have been evolved. However, the question that we have to answer is how well they perform according to an objective performance measure because we want to know the best fitness function for each task. This is in itself a difficult problem, in fact, a self-referential problem because this objective performance measure is itself, of course, a fitness function. Therefore, we do a cross-comparison of each controller with each of the three fitness functions and for each task. Our aim is to come up with a conclusion about the effectiveness of our different fitness functions and in the end of the different fitness function classes. Three types of post-evaluations and adaptation tests were done. First, the best controllers were post-evaluated 30 times with each of the fitness functions (Sec. 4.1). Second, for the last populations the evolution was resumed with each of the fitness functions for a few generations to test for evolutionary adaption (Sec. 4.2). Third, for the last populations the evolution was resumed for each of the fitness functions in a new environment to test re-adaptation (walls added, Sec. 4.3).

4.1 Post-evaluations in cross-comparison

We have three tasks and four classes of fitness functions that help in evolving best controllers that accomplish each of these tasks. For each task, the best controllers are post-evaluated with the same environment again, but this time we evaluate them with all fitness functions. The idea is to do a full cross-comparison and to find the most effective fitness function class. FIFF cannot be investigated here because that would require to resume the evolution of populations to allow for a useful comparison, which is left for Sec. 4.2 and Sec. 4.3.

The results of our cross-comparisons between all tasks are shown in Fig. 1 (rows 2, 3, and 4). For each task (rows) we take the best controllers evolved using AFF (1st column), BFF (2nd column), and TFF (3rd column) and post-evaluate them against AFF (1st boxplot in each diagram), BFF (2nd boxplot), and TFF (3rd boxplot). For example, Fig. 1d shows the results for the best controllers evolved with AFF which are post-evaluated against AFF, BFF, and TFF. We compare the three fitness function classes based on their rank in each test. In order to rank the results, that were achieved by the different fitness functions, we applied significance tests based on the Wilcoxon rank sum test. Significantly different results ($p < 0.05$) receive different ranks while insignificant results receive the same rank. In the same example (Fig. 1d), lines with asterisks denote the significances in the data. All pairs of fitness functions are significantly different in this case. AFF is ranked the highest followed by TFF, while BFF is ranked the lowest. The first column in Tab. 2 represents the ranking in Fig. 1d. The second and third columns belong to the comparisons in Fig. 1e and Fig. 1f, respectively. After summing the ranks, the forth column denotes the overall ranking of the three fitness functions for obstacle avoidance. Tab. 3 shows the overall ranks for all of the tasks. By summing the ranks we see that TFF in total is ranked best. AFF and BFF compete basically on the same level but with a slight advantage for BFF (rank sum better by one).

4.2 Resuming evolution in the same environment

Next, we test how the populations, that were evolved with different fitness functions, adapt to new fitness functions when we resume evolution. We take the last population from each evolutionary run and resume evolution for 10 generations. This also allows to include the FIFF using both functions for 5 generations each.

For each fitness function we have a population of the last generation for each evolutionary run. We take these populations and continue to evolve them. For example, we take a population evolved with AFF and continue to evolve it for 10 generations with AFF. However, we also take a population evolved with AFF and resume evolution for 10 generations with BFF and similarly for all other cases of the cross-comparison. From each of the final populations after 10 generations we take the best controller for the following analysis.

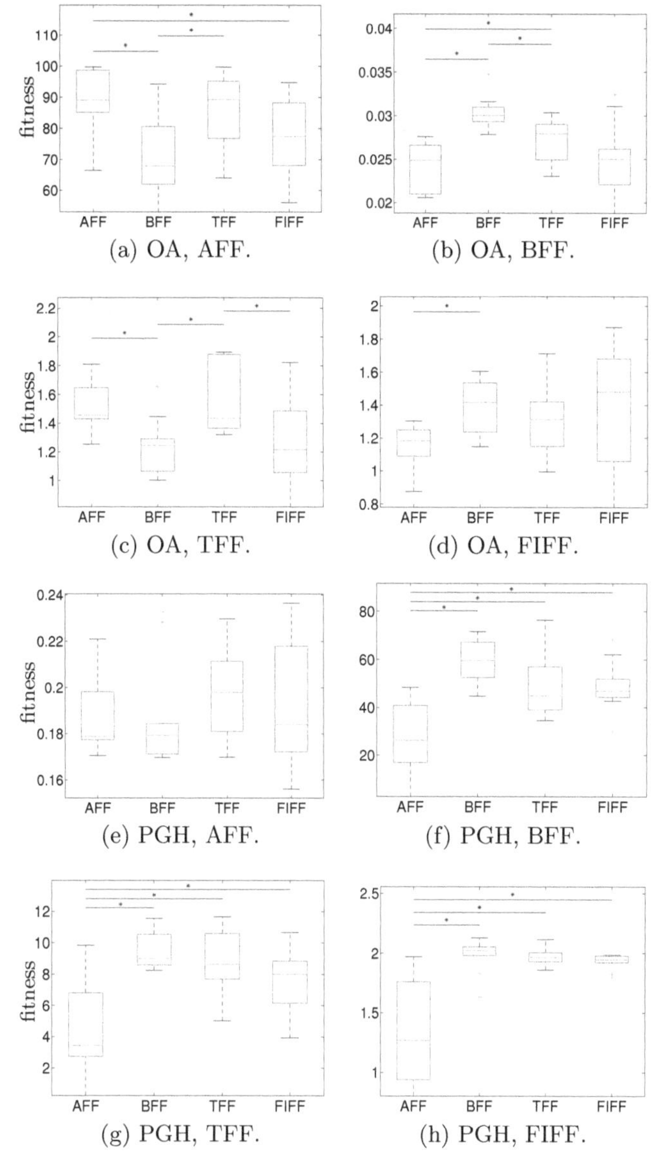

Figure 2: Best controllers for Obstacle Avoidance (OA, a-d) and Periodic Goal Homing (PGH, e-h) obtained by evolving with Aggregate Fitness Function (AFF), Behavioral Fitness Function (BFF), and Tailored Fitness Function (TFF) but then resume evolution with AFF, BFF, and TFF.

Fig. 2 gives the results for tasks OA and PGH only. Taking into account also the results for GH (not shown), Tab. 5 is computed for all tasks and fitness functions. As shown in the overall column of this table, TFF is best followed by BFF, AFF, and FIFF.

4.3 Re-adaptation, convergence rate, and full comparison

In the last part of this study, we test the potential for re-adaptation in the evolved populations. We evolve the population of controllers for 30 generations and then resume the

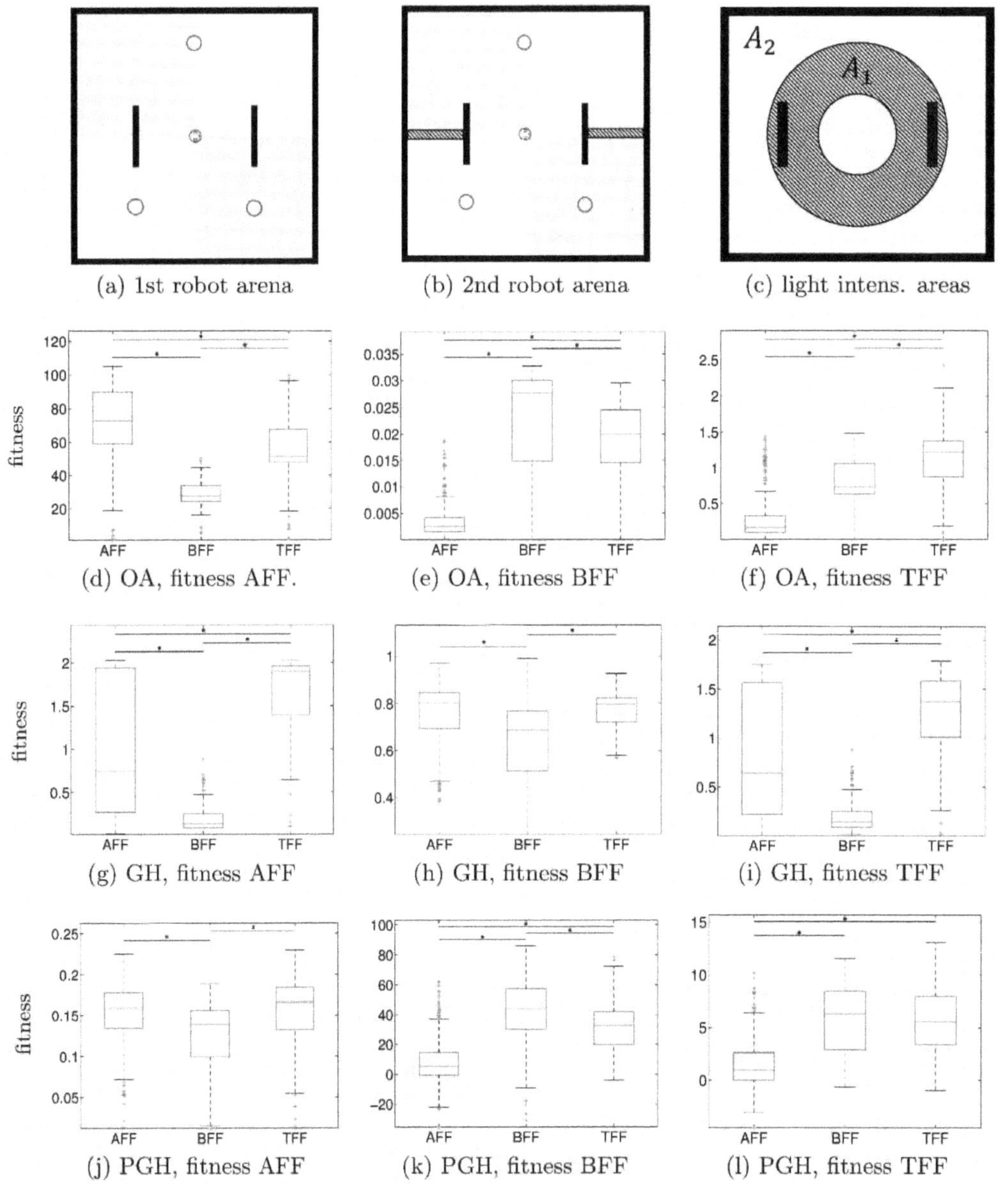

(a) 1st robot arena (b) 2nd robot arena (c) light intens. areas

(d) OA, fitness AFF. (e) OA, fitness BFF (f) OA, fitness TFF

(g) GH, fitness AFF (h) GH, fitness BFF (i) GH, fitness TFF

(j) PGH, fitness AFF (k) PGH, fitness BFF (l) PGH, fitness TFF

Figure 1: Simulated robot arenas, logically defined light intensity areas for Periodic Goal Homing (PGH), fitness of best controllers for Obstacle Avoidance (OA, 2nd row), Goal Homing (GH, 3rd row), and PGH (4th row) obtained by evolving with Aggregate Fitness Function (AFF, 1st boxplot in each figure), Behavioral Fitness Function (BFF, 2nd boxplot), and Tailored Fitness Function (TFF, 3rd boxplot) but post-evaluated with AFF (1st column), BFF (2nd column), and TFF (3rd column).

FF	AFF	BFF	TFF	Overall
AFF	1	3	3	3
BFF	3	1	2	2
TFF	2	2	1	1

Table 2: Detailed ranking of post-evaluation shown in Fig. 1d, e, and f only for obstacle avoidance.

FF	OA	GH	PGH	overall
AFF	3	2	2	3
BFF	2	3	1	2
TFF	1	1	1	1

Table 3: Overall ranking of post-evaluation.

evolution of the populations for another 10 generations in a changed environment (two walls added, shown in dashed pattern, Fig. 1b). The evolution is resumed with the same fitness function that was used for evolution before (no cross-comparison). The robot controllers have to re-adapt to accomplish their tasks. To check the ratio of re-adaptation after the change in the environment, we consider the median of the best fitness for each generation. b_g is the median of the best controllers' fitness from 10 evolutionary runs for generation g. To compare the maximum median values over generations before ($g \leq 30$) and after the change ($g > 30$), we define the ratio

$$R_r = \max_{30<g\leq 40}(b_g)\left(\max_{0\leq g\leq 30}(b_g)\right)^{-1}. \quad (14)$$

We are interested in finding fitness functions that score high on R and hence evolved adaptive controllers. For this test we give no boxplots but only the ranks, see Tab. 6. The overall ranks show that TFF is best in adapting to the new environment followed by BFF, AFF, and FIFF.

Finally, in a fourth test we investigate the rate of convergence because we are interested in the dependence of the optimization process speed on the fitness function classes. We define a visual evaluation of graphs to assign a value to the quality of convergence rate. For the measured functions $F_{\text{best}}(g)$ of best fitness over generations g, we measure the area below the curve and relate it to the overall area of the rectangle defined by $(0,0)$ and $(g_{\max}, F_{\text{best}}^{\max})$, which gives $g_{\max} \times F_{\text{best}}^{\max}$. Therefore, the convergence rate is defined as

$$R_c = \frac{1}{g_{\max} \times F_{\text{best}}^{\max}} \sum_{g=1}^{g_{\max}} F_{\text{best}}(g). \quad (15)$$

The investigation of all evolutionary runs gives the information in Tab. 4 that shows AFF as the best, followed by BFF, and TFF (FIFF not considered here). A summary of all results based on ranks from all of the tests is shown in Tab. 7. What we refer to as 'simplicity' in Tab. 7 is the inverse of complexity as defined in Sec. 2. We find that fitness

FF	OA	GH	PGH	overall
AFF	2	1	1	1
BFF	1	2	2	2
TFF	3	3	3	3

Table 4: Overall ranking of convergence rate.

FF	OA	GH	PGH	overall
AFF	2	2	4	3
BFF	2	4	1	2
TFF	1	1	2	1
FIFF	3	3	3	4

Table 5: Overall ranking of re-evolution.

FF	OA	GH	PGH	overall
TFF	1	1	3	1
BFF	3	2	2	2
AFF	4	3	1	3
FIFF	2	4	4	4

Table 6: Overall ranking of re-adaptation.

function classes that incorporate a lot of a priori knowledge, such as TFF and BFF, achieve higher performance across different tasks and across several performance features (post-evaluation, adaptation). The convergence rate of AFF is good but only because they achieve lower maximal values than BFF and TFF.

#	post-eval.	resumed evolution	re-adapted	conv. rate	simplicity
1	TFF	TFF	TFF	AFF	AFF
2	BFF	BFF	BFF	BFF	BFF
3	AFF	AFF	AFF	TFF	TFF
4	-	FIFF	FIFF	-	FIFF

Table 7: Final ranking of the fitness functions.

5. CONCLUSION

We have presented a study on how a priori knowledge in the design of the fitness function influences the performance of the evolutionary algorithm in evolutionary robotics. Although we face the problem of fuzzy and subjective definitions of a priori knowledge and fitness function classifications [14], we still get a clear result for the proposed examples. Fitness functions that include a high degree of a priori knowledge (here TFF and BFF) influence the performance positively. They help to simplify the evolution of a successful controller and hence simplify the chosen task. However, we also know that incorporating a high degree of a priori knowledge foils the dominant idea of evolutionary computation as a black-box optimizer. Therefore, there is a problem of comparability in evolutionary robotics. While there is a competition for more and more complex tasks in the community, more attention could possibly be paid to the amount of a priori knowledge included in the design of fitness functions. More studies on the same task with an effort on minimizing a priori knowledge could possibly be done to have a competition for minimal a priori knowledge, too. Furthermore, we require a more precise and objective measure of a priori knowledge.

Our study focuses on the standard approach of evolutionary robotics that requires the definition of a fitness function. There are also recent alternative approaches, such as novelty search [10] and multi-objective behavioral diversity [12, 13], that either substitute the fitness function with a measure for behavioral diversity or add behavioral diversity as an additional objective. Also called 'task-agnostic' approaches as discussed in [4]. However, the design of the behavioral distance measure might require an effort similar to the standard fitness function design challenge. For example, Mouret and Doncieux [13] discuss this analogy between fitness function design and the design of a measure for behavioral diversity: "More importantly, novelty search critically depends on a good behavior characterization to create a gradient. Researchers in ER used to craft fitness function to create a perfect fitness gradient; novelty search users have to craft the behavior distance to create a similar gradient. This last option may be easier for some problems but eventually some distances will be hard to define."

In future work we plan to do a similar study also for measures of behavioral diversity. In addition, we plan to extend the fitness function classification approach of Nelson et al. [14] to allow for a better motivation of chosen fitness functions. Furthermore a collection of results for a diverse set of fitness functions and measures of behavioral diversity for selected tasks, also including negative results, could prove to be helpful for the field.

Acknowledgment

Supported by EU-H2020 project 'florarobotica', no. 640959.

6. REFERENCES

[1] J. C. Bongard. Evolutionary robotics. *Communications of the ACM*, 56(8):74–83, 2013.

[2] P. Chervenski and S. Ryan. MultiNEAT, project website;. http://www.multineat.com/.

[3] S. Doncieux and J.-B. Mouret. Dynamic behavioral diversity. In *Proceedings of the 14th Annual Conference on Genetic and Evolutionary Computation (GECCO'12)*, pages 1453–1454. ACM, 2012.

[4] S. Doncieux and J.-B. Mouret. Beyond black-box optimization: a review of selective pressures for evolutionary robotics. *Evolutionary Intelligence*, 7(2):71–93, 2014.

[5] Á. E. Eiben, E. Haasdijk, and N. Bredeche. Embodied, on-line, on-board evolution for autonomous robotics. In P. Levi and S. Kernbach, editors, *Symbiotic Multi-Robot Organisms: Reliability, Adaptability, Evolution*, volume 7 of *Cognitive Systems Monographs*, pages 362–384. Springer, 2010.

[6] W. Fan, E. A. Fox, P. Pathak, and H. Wu. The effects of fitness functions on genetic programming-based ranking discovery for web search. *Journal of the American Society for Information Science and Technology*, 55(7):628–636, 2004.

[7] E. Fast, C. Le Goues, S. Forrest, and W. Weimer. Designing better fitness functions for automated program repair. In *Proceedings of the 12th Annual Conference on Genetic and Evolutionary Computation (GECCO'10)*, pages 965–972. ACM, 2010.

[8] E. Haasdijk and N. Bredeche. Controlling task distribution in MONEE. In *Advances In Artificial Life (ECAL'13)*, pages 671–678, 2013.

[9] J. Lehman and K. O. Stanley. Exploiting open-endedness to solve problems through the search for novelty. In S. Bullock, J. Noble, R. Watson, and M. A. Bedau, editors, *Artificial Life XI: Proceedings of the 11th International Conference on the Simulation and Synthesis of Living Systems*, pages 329–336. MIT Press, 2008.

[10] J. Lehman and K. O. Stanley. Improving evolvability through novelty search and self-adaptation. In *Proceedings of the 2011 IEEE Congress on Evolutionary Computation (CEC'11)*, pages 2693–2700. IEEE, 2011.

[11] C. López-Pujalte, V. P. Guerrero-Bote, and F. de Moya-Anegón. Order-based fitness functions for genetic algorithms applied to relevance feedback. *Journal of the American Society for Information Science and Technology*, 54(2):152–160, 2003.

[12] J.-B. Mouret and S. Doncieux. Using behavioral exploration objectives to solve deceptive problems in neuro-evolution. In *Proceedings of the 11th Annual Conference on Genetic and Evolutionary Computation (GECCO'09)*, pages 627–634. ACM, 2009.

[13] J.-B. Mouret and S. Doncieux. Encouraging behavioral diversity in evolutionary robotics: an empirical study. *Evolutionary Computation*, 20(1):91–133, 2012.

[14] A. L. Nelson, G. J. Barlow, and L. Doitsidis. Fitness functions in evolutionary robotics: A survey and analysis. *Robotics and Autonomous Systems*, 57:345–370, 2009.

[15] A. L. Nelson and E. Grant. Using direct competition to select for competent controllers in evolutionary robotics. *Robotics and Autonomous Systems*, 54(10):840–857, 2006.

[16] S. Nolfi and D. Floreano. *Evolutionary Robotics: The Biology, Intelligence, and Technology of Self-Organizing Machines*. MIT Press, 2000.

[17] I. G. Sprinkhuizen-Kuyper, R. Kortmann, and E. O. Postma. Fitness functions for evolving box-pushing behaviour. In A. van den Bosch and H. Weigand, editors, *Proceedings of the 12th Belgium–Netherlands Artificial Intelligence Conference (BNAIC'00)*, pages 275–282, 2000.

[18] C. Sprong. Common tasks in evolutionary robotics, an overview. Technical report, Faculty of Sciences, University of Amsterdam, Netherlands, 2011.

[19] K. Stanley and R. Miikkulainen. Evolving neural networks through augmenting topologies. *Evolutionary Computation*, 10(2):99–127, 2002.

[20] K. O. Stanley and R. Miikkulainen. Competitive coevolution through evolutionary complexification. *Journal of Artificial Intelligence Research*, 21(1):63–100, Jan. 2004.

[21] J. Stradner, H. Hamann, P. Zahadat, T. Schmickl, and K. Crailsheim. On-line, on-board evolution of reaction-diffusion control for self-adaptation. In C. Adami, D. M. Bryson, C. Ofria, and R. T. Pennock, editors, *Alife XIII*, pages 597–598. MIT Press, 2012.

[22] M. Wahby and H. Hamann. On the tradeoff between hardware protection and optimization success: A case study in onboard evolutionary robotics for autonomous parallel parking. In *Applications of Evolutionary Computation (EvoApplications 2015)*, volume 9028 of *Lecture Notes in Computer Science*, pages 759–770. Springer, 2015.

Decentralized Innovation Marking for Neural Controllers in Embodied Evolution

Iñaki Fernández Pérez
inaki.fernandez@loria.fr

Amine Boumaza
amine.boumaza@loria.fr

François Charpillet
francois.charpillet@inria.fr

Université de Lorraine, Loria UMR n° 7503, Vandœuvre-lès-Nancy, F-54500, France
CNRS, Loria UMR n° 7503, Vandœuvre-lès-Nancy, F-54500, France
Inria, Villers-lès-Nancy, F-54600, France

ABSTRACT

We propose a novel innovation marking method for Neuro-Evolution of Augmenting Topologies in Embodied Evolutionary Robotics. This method does not rely on a centralized clock, which makes it well suited for the decentralized nature of EE where no central evolutionary process governs the adaptation of a team of robots exchanging messages locally.

This method is inspired from event dating algorithms, based on logical clocks, that are used in distributed systems, where clock synchronization is not possible. We compare our method to odNEAT, an algorithm in which agents use local time clocks as innovation numbers, on two multi-robot learning tasks: navigation and item collection. Our experiments showed that the proposed method performs as well as odNEAT, with the added benefit that it does not rely on synchronization of clocks and is not affected by time drifts.

Categories and Subject Descriptors

I.2.6 [**Computing Methodologies**]: Artificial Intelligence—*Learning*

Keywords

Evolutionary robotics; Swarm robotics; Online algorithms; Artificial intelligence

1. INTRODUCTION

Evolutionary robotics (ER) deals with automatic robot behavior learning with techniques inspired from natural evolution [10]. Embodied ER [15] explores the idea of several agents simultaneously learning behaviors using evolutionary algorithms that the robots run onboard. It has been applied on different learning tasks, usually in the context of online multi-robot adaptation. Similarly to mainstream ER, agents' controllers are usually represented as neural networks (neuroevolution) that map sensor inputs to motor outputs, and the learning algorithm adapts the neural architecture and parameters such that the agents execute the correct behavior.

When evolving neural controllers, two different approaches are usually followed: on the one hand, adaptation can take place at the synaptic level, *i.e.* the evolutionary algorithm optimizes the weights of a fixed topology neural network. On the other hand, adaptation can also take place at the structural level of the controller, in which case the topology and the synaptic weights of the neural network are optimized simultaneously. Searching in this richer space of topologies and weight configurations allows for evolution of neural controllers with topologies adapted to the task and removes the need of hand-tuning the topology.

There exists a large body of work on the evolution of topology in neural networks [6, 14, 7]. However, many algorithms do not consider cross-over operators, since such operators, if not designed properly or if applied blindly, often tend to destruct functional building blocks. Among the algorithms that use cross-over, NEAT (NeuroEvolution of Augmenting Topologies) [14] introduced a simple gene marking scheme (called innovation numbers), where each element of the neural network (neurons and synapses) is uniquely identified and the chronological order of insertion of such elements is tracked, which allows to correctly recombine building blocks.

In our work, we are interested in Embodied Evolution (EE) to deal with a team of coexisting robots performing open-ended behavior learning, where robots are always adapting to the task at hand [2]. Each robot has an active genome that is locally broadcasted when robots cross each other, and an internal population, which corresponds to a local view of the population that is distributed across all robots. No robot has global knowledge of all genomes.

In the last years, several works have dealt with Embodied Evolution of neural robot controllers in general, usually limiting the evolution to the synaptic weights of fixed-topology neural networks. Recently, odNEAT (Online Distributed NEAT) [13] proposed a distributed version of NEAT in the context of Embodied Evolution. The algorithm uses high-resolution clocks at the robot level to mark structural innovations. However, such clocks may drift, thus requiring synchronization, especially if the robots are deployed for long periods of time, which is one of the objectives of EE. In a sense, this requirement is in contradiction with the distributed aspect of Embodied Evolution.

Our main motivation in the following work is to propose an algorithm to mark structural innovations that does not rely on a centralized clock or synchronizations. This algo-

GECCO '15, July 11 - 15, 2015, Madrid, Spain

DOI: http://dx.doi.org/10.1145/2739480.2754759

rithm that we name Gene Clocks (GC), is inspired from logical clock algorithms used in asynchronous distributed system models. By only using local exchanges and with a small computational and communication overhead, GC tracks the historical chronology of genes in the population. In this way the distributed nature of Embodied Evolution algorithms is preserved.

In the following sections, we will start by describing different algorithms that addressed neuroevolution of topologies in the embodied and distributed context and discuss the way innovations are marked. We will then detail our approach, and explain its links with asynchronous distributed system models and how innovation marking is performed in a distributed way. In section 4, we describe the experiments and discuss the results obtained. Finally, we present some open questions and research directions that could extend our work.

2. RELATED WORK

Several neuroevolution algorithms dealing with the evolution of neural topology along with the synaptic weights, have been proposed ([1], [6], [14]). Neural networks can be encoded as a set of neuron genes and connection genes. In this case, mutation operators usually add or remove neurons and connection genes with some probability, to introduce topological innovations in the neural networks. In this context, the goal of cross-over operators is to accurately combine the best functional characteristics, or building blocks, of two parent networks, to produce offspring that inherit these building blocks. This raises some problems (*e.g. Competing Conventions* problem [11]), because similar topologies can be represented with very different genetic encodings. Classical cross-over operators tend to be disruptive and break existing functional structures, thus hindering evolution. If cross-over is to be applied between two of such networks, their respective structural elements have to be matched and recombined correctly. This is the main reason why many topology-evolving neuroevolution algorithms do not use the cross-over operator [1].

NEAT [14] proposed an elegant solution to reduce the effect of the competing conventions problem and perform meaningful cross-over. The algorithm marks each new neuron or connection with an unique *innovation number*, which is a historical marker that identifies the new gene and keeps track of the chronology of its appearance in the evolutionary process. These innovation numbers are inherited by offspring networks. The purpose of innovation numbers is to detect the genes expressing the same neural elements between two genomes (genes having the same innovation number) without the need of matching the topology of the two networks. As such, the impact of the competing conventions problem is reduced, because genes having the same innovation number in two parent genomes are not repeated when applying cross-over. These historical markers are implemented in NEAT by keeping a global counter of innovations and sequentially assigning it to new genes in the genomes of the population. Furthermore, the algorithm uses a niching mechanism to divide the population in non-overlapping species, based on genotypic similarity. To promote topological diversity, NEAT uses intra-species fitness sharing, *i.e.* networks in the same niche share the same fitness. This results in the protection of new structures that could lead to fitter individuals but require time to optimize their parameters. The algorithm is a centralized offline EA with one global population initialized with minimal fully-connected perceptrons, and where all new genes can be tracked since all information is centralized.

When evolving both weight and topology in an EE context, the same problems raised in offline centralized setups (competing conventions, see above) occur. However, a global counter as in NEAT's innovation marking mechanism is not directly transferable to Embodied Evolution, because different robots cannot be simultaneously aware of each other's innovations. Two topology-evolving EE algorithms, and more specifically, two mechanisms to mark topological innovations in a distributed manner, have been proposed to date: odNEAT [13] and IM-(μ + 1) [12].

In IM-($\mu + 1$), each robot draws a random number (between 1 and 1000 in their experiments) to assign it as identifier of a new neuron gene added in any robot's genome. The authors state that, if the probability of drawing the same number, which is referred as an identifier collision, is sufficiently low, the system is overall not disturbed, and the impact of colliding innovation numbers is reduced by selection. Although this may be true in relatively short experiments with few robots, when dealing with long-term adaptation EE setups, this probability increases, and genealogy can not be tracked.

odNEAT (Online Distributed NeuroEvolution of Augmenting Topologies) translated NEAT characteristics to a distributed setup. Each local population is speciated based on a genotypic distance, and the genomes in a species share the fitness of the species, as in NEAT. Innovation markers are assigned using local, high-resolution timestamps. Robots mark new genes using their respective local clocks. Offspring are produced by selecting two parent genomes, recombining them as in NEAT, and mutating the result with some probability. Mutations either probabilistically add a new neuron, a connection or add a normal random variable to every weight in the network. The innovation numbers are used to sort the genes in a genome to facilitate the matching of common structures with another genome. As in NEAT, this alignment is used to distinguish between matching genes and non-matching genes in both genomes, either to compute a genotypic distance or to mate two parent genomes without repeating structures. According to the authors, the use of high-resolution timestamps practically guarantees identifier uniqueness and allows different robots to retain the chronology of the innovations across the distributed system.

Since odNEAT runs on all robots that are simultaneously evolving, their respective local clocks have a strong probability of drifting w.r.t. each other. This is specially true in open-ended long-term adaptation setups, where robots run for a long time and clock drifting may be considerably more important. In this case, innovation timestamps would not be coherent, and thus would not correctly keep track of the actual chronology of innovations. If odNEAT is to be run on physical robots, it would require a periodical clock synchronization between the robots, which may be impossible when robots are scattered.

3. ODNEAT WITH LOGICAL MARKERS

In our proposed innovation marking algorithm, we view an evolving set of robots in Embodied Evolution as a distributed computer system. In the asynchronous distributed system model [4], several interconnected processors communicate with each other and perform local computations in order to solve a common problem. Events in such systems consist of either local computations or message exchanges. In this work, we consider robots as processors, computational processes as the evolutionary process of each robot, events as topological innovations in the system and message exchange between processors as genome exchange between robots.

One of the fundamental problems in distributed systems is the dating and ordering of events. Since distributed processors do not have a common clock, ordering events w.r.t. each other requires a specific mechanism. Logical Clock algorithms (LC) [8] were proposed to identify and date events in the system in a decentralized way. In this mechanism, every processor has an unique identifier and a monotonically increasing local counter initialized to 0 to keep track of the events. When an internal event or a message exchange takes place, the event is marked with the current local counter and the counter is incremented by one. Whenever a processor receives a message, it updates its local counter with the maximum value between the received counter and its own. This way, events in the system can be ordered with respect to the moment they occurred. However, two events may have identical counters if they originated in two different processors and no communication took place between the two processors during the period in between events. These events are considered concurrent events. Whenever this case occurs, authors order the concurrent events by convention w.r.t. the processor identifier to define a total order between events in the system.

3.1 Decentralized Marking of Innovations

In our proposed method, each robot has a unique identifier, r, as well as a sequential *local innovation counter*, c_r, in the same manner as processors have identifiers and event counters in a distributed system. We consider innovation numbers as pairs $< r, c_r >$. Each robot increments its counter c_r by one each time a mutation adds a new gene, as processors do when they date events. When a robot broadcasts its active genome, all its topological innovations are marked with such innovation numbers.

Using these innovation numbers, genes in the genome can be ordered, based on their gene counters, since they keep a chronological sequence of the innovations on each individual robot. However, innovations originated in different robots can not be chronologically ordered since all robots maintain independent sequences of innovations. To palliate this issue, in addition to sending its active genome, a robot broadcasts its current c_r, and upon reception, robots update their respective c_r's with the maximum of the received value and their own, as it is done in LC. Concurrent innovations are still possible, *i.e.* two innovations with the same c_r, but originating in different robots that do not communicate in between. In this case, innovation numbers will be ordered by convention with respect to the robot's identifier so all robots sort genes in the exact same manner.

3.2 Evolutionary Algorithm

In our experiments, we use odNEAT as Embodied Evolution algorithm to evolve the topology and weights of neural networks. The main steps of the algorithm, that runs on every robot, are shown in Algorithm 1. At all times, each robot has an active genome that is initialized with a fully-connected single-layer perceptron. Robots locally broadcast their active genomes at every timestep, with a probability proportional to the fitness of the species of the genome (see below). Received genomes are stored in a limited-size local population, which also contains previous active genomes. When the population is full, the addition of a fit genome implies the removal of the worst genome in the population.

Each robot has an internal virtual energy level that is initialized to a default task-dependent value. This value represents the performance of the active controller in the task at hand, and it increases and decreases according to robot behavior. As such, the energy level measures how well a robot solves the given task. Every control cycle, a robot executes its active controller and updates its energy level according to its behavior. One of the inherent problems of EE is that evaluation is noisy, given that different controllers can be evaluated in very different conditions. For example, if a fit controller starts its evaluation surrounded by obstacles, its energy level will drop until it is able to escape the area. To alleviate this issue and record a more precise approximation of the actual performance, the robots periodically measure their respective energy levels at regular intervals. The energy measures are averaged to compute the controller's fitness $f_r(t)$ of robot r at instant t. Finally, whenever the energy level drops below a given threshold, a new offspring is produced and replaces the active genome, and the energy level is reset to its default initial value.

Algorithm 1: odNEAT algorithm run by every robot.

```
g_a ← random_genome()
//Add also to a new species
P ← {g_a}
e ← e_init
while True do
    if do_broadcast? then
        send(g_a, e, neighbors)
    forall the g ∈ received do
        if Tabu.approves(g) and P.accepts(g) then
            //Add also to corresponding species
            P ← P ⋃ {g}
            adjust_species_fitness()
    execute(g_a)
    e ← e + ΔE/Δt
    if e ≤ e_threshold and ¬ in_maturation_period then
        Tabu ← Tabu ⋃ {g_a}
        if random() < p_mate then
            p1, p2 ← select_parents(select_species())
            g_offsp ← mate(p1, p2)
        else
            g_offsp ← select_parent(select_species())
        if random() < p_mutate then
            g_offsp ← mutate(g_offsp)
        //Add also to corresponding species
        P ← P ⋃ {g_offsp}
        g_a ← g_offsp
        e ← e_init
```

To maintain diversity in local populations, genomes are divided into species based on a genotypic distance, *i.e.* the genomes in the population are grouped in non-overlapping species by genotypic similarity, and fitness sharing is applied in the same manner as in NEAT.

At each iteration, robots broadcast their active genome with a probability proportional to the fitness of the genome species. When a broadcast occurs, the robot's active genome, its current energy level, and c_r in the case of GC, are sent to all neighboring robots. If a given robot receives the same genome twice, the energy level is averaged with the previous value to provide a better estimator of the performance of the stored genome.

Whenever the energy level drops below the threshold, the active controller is replaced by a new genome generated as follows: First, a species is selected with a probability proportional to its average adjusted fitness. Then, with a probability p_{mate} two parents are selected within the chosen species and are recombined. Finally, the resulting offspring is mutated with a probability p_{mutate}. With a probability $(1-p_{mate})$, only one parent is selected from the species, and is mutated with probability p_{mutate}.

Mutation can be of 2 types, structural mutation and parameter mutation. Structural mutation includes adding a neuron with a probability p_{node} by splitting a random existing connection or adding a connection with probability p_{conn} between two random unconnected existing neurons. When adding a connection, there is a probability p_{recur} for this connection to be recurrent. On the other hand, concerning parameter mutation, there is a probability p_w of mutating all weights by adding a normal random variable with mean 0 and a standard deviation σ. Synaptic weights are maintained in $[-10, +10]$. The resulting offspring replaces the previous active genome, its energy level is reset to the default value, and the new genome starts being executed.

A new genome is given some time T_m to be executed and evaluated even if its energy level drops below the threshold level. This is known as maturation period [2], and it aims firstly at protecting potentially fit controllers that start their evaluation in difficult conditions, and secondly, at setting a lower bound to the time a given genome is evaluated to obtain a sufficiently accurate estimate of its performance.

Taking in account all the aforementioned variation probabilities, standard deviation of the weight mutation σ, the maturation time T_m, and the local population size, $|\mathbf{P}|$, we need to set values to 9 parameters. For that, we use a tuning procedure that is described in the next section.

odNEAT also maintains a tabu list to keep track of recent poor genomes, either genomes dropped because they depleted their energy, or the genomes that are not competitive enough and are dropped from the population because it was full. This is used to filter out received genomes that are similar to one or more individuals in the tabu list, before adding them to the local population, *i.e.* to avoid evaluating candidates similar to known poor solutions.

Both the tabu list filtering and the speciation mechanism rely on computing a genotypic distance, that is measured as follows:

$$d(g_1, g_2) = \frac{c_1 \cdot E}{N} + \frac{c_2 \cdot D}{N} + c_3 \cdot \overline{W} \qquad (1)$$

where $\overline{W}$ is the average of the weight difference between matching genes, *i.e.* genes corresponding to the same structural elements in g_1 and g_2. Non-matching genes are considered in two fashions, depending on the chronology of the compared genes: D is the number of *disjoint* genes, that is non-matching genes in the middle of the genome, and E is the number of *excess* genes, non-matching genes in the end of the largest genome. N is the number of genes of the largest of both genomes, and c_1, c_2, c_3 are coefficients weighting the relative importance of each of the three elements. The way to distinguish between matching, disjoint and excess genes consists in aligning two genomes using the innovation numbers presented above. Furthermore, the cross-over operator in odNEAT (as NEAT) also uses historical markers to distinguish between matching, disjoint and excess genes between two parent genomes (see [14] for details).

4. EXPERIMENTS

In our experiments, we compare the results of odNEAT using Gene Clocks and using timestamps as innovation numbers. Timestamps in a system where local clocks are synchronized allow for a perfect sorting of genes in a genome, provided that no drift occurs, whereas, in the case of concurrent innovations, GC sorts genes by convention. Our main hypothesis is that Gene Clocks approximate sufficiently the chronology of innovations to lead to performance levels similar to those obtained using timestamps while relying exclusively on local information and exchanges. Our experiments, presented below, corroborate this hypothesis, in terms of the quality of learned behaviors and in terms of the architecture of the evolved controllers.

4.1 Experimental Setup

We conducted our experiments on two well-studied tasks in ER [10], navigation with obstacle avoidance and item collection. In the navigation with obstacle avoidance task, robots must learn to move as fast and as straight as possible in a bounded environment, while avoiding both moving and static obstacles (other robots and walls). In the item collection task, food items are placed in the environment and robots must collect as many of them as possible.

We performed all our experiments in the RoboRobo simulator [3], which simulates a team of robots deployed in a bounded environment containing obstacles (black lines in Figure 1), as well as food items in the case of the item collection task (green circles). All robots have the same morphology, sensors and motors. 8 obstacle proximity sensors, that measure the distance to obstacles and other robots, are evenly distributed around the robot. An additional sensor measures the current energy level of the robot. In the case of the item collection task, robots perceive food using 8 additional food item sensors with the same range as the obstacle sensors. The robots move using two differential drive wheels. Being morphologically homogeneous, behavior difference between robots originates from having different controllers. A robot's neural controller is initialized with a bias neuron and as many inputs as there are sensors (9 in the case of navigation and 17 in the case of item collection). The two outputs of the neurocontroller correspond to the right and left wheel velocities.

An active genome's life cycle, or genome's evaluation, consists on executing it, updating the energy level and probabilistically broadcasting it to nearby robots, until its energy level is below a threshold. At this point, the genome is considered unfit to the task, and is replaced by a new one, generated as presented in Section 3.2. The energy level of the new genome is reset to the default value of 100 units, its maximal value being 200 units. A robot updates its energy level every control cycle as follows:

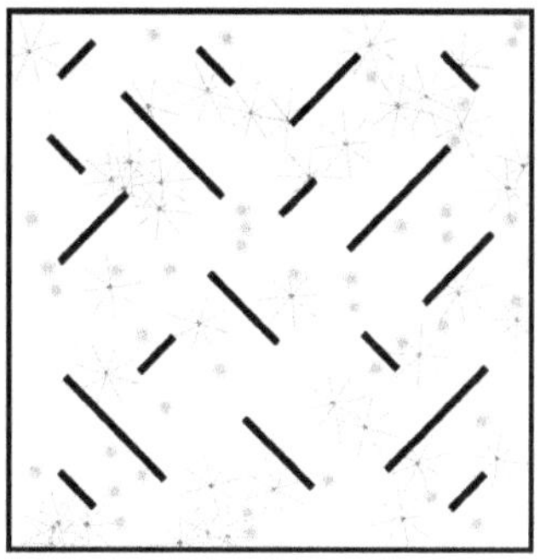

Figure 1: The simulation environment containing robots (red dots with thin hairlines representing sensors), obstacles (dark lines) and food items (green dots).

- **Navigation**:

$$\frac{\Delta E}{\Delta t} = f_n(|v_l + v_r| \cdot (1 - \sqrt{|v_l - v_r|}) \cdot (1 - d)) \quad (2)$$

  where v_l and v_r are the left and right wheel velocities and d is the distance to the closest obstacle. The f_n function is a linear mapping from the interval $[0, 1]$ to $[-1, 1]$. Thus, if a robot moves fast, straight and far from obstacles it will gain energy, and it will lose energy otherwise. This is the same energy update function in which odNEAT was studied [13], and it is inspired from [10].

- **Item collection**:

$$\frac{\Delta E}{\Delta t} = -0.1 + 10 \cdot c(t) \quad (3)$$

  where $c(t)$ is a boolean function indicating if an item was collected at t. At each time step, the robot loses 0.1 energy units, and when it picks up an item, it gains 10 units. In the experiments, 75 items are randomly placed in the environment. When a robot collects an item, it disappears, and a new one is randomly placed in the environment to keep the number of items constant.

In all experiments, 100 robots were deployed in the environment. Each robot runs Algorithm 1 for 40000 cycles in the navigation task and 60000 cycles in the collection task. We performed 64 independent runs for both innovation marking methods in both tasks. Every 100 cycles, we measure:

- The average fitness of all robots, or swarm fitness $F_s(t) = \frac{1}{|team|} \sum_{r \in team} f_r(t)$. It represents the overall performance of the evolving robots at instant t.

- The average number of species over the local populations of all robots. The number of species provides information on the overall topological diversity in the robots population.

- The average size of active controllers of all robots. In our work, we consider the number of connections and neurons as the size of a given neural controller. This gives an idea of the complexity of the evolved solutions.

In Embodied Evolution, the best fitness reached during evolution is not a reliable measure of the overall performance of the robots. Measures must emphasize the online nature of the algorithms, *i.e.* since robots adapt during the actual execution, an instantaneous measure would not be a reliable indicator of their performance. To consider this in the analysis of our experiments, we use the metrics of performance that were previously introduced in [5]. These metrics reflect information on the evolutionary process in general by integrating information spanning over time (see Figure 2).

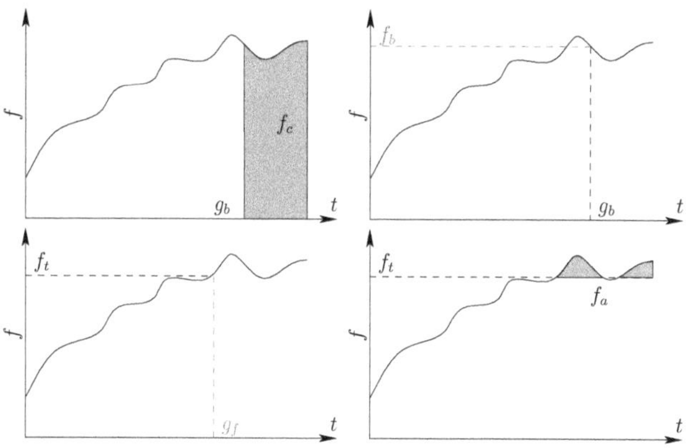

Figure 2: A pictorial description of the four comparison measures. From top to bottom and left to right: the average accumulated swarm fitness, f_c, the fixed budget swarm fitness, f_b, the time to reach target g_f, and the accumulated fitness above target, f_a.

In order to set the appropriate values for the 9 parameters of the algorithm (see 3.2), we performed a tuning procedure. For each task the parameters were independently tuned using Iterated Race for Automatic Algorithm Configuration (irace) [9], a parameter tuning algorithm that optimizes a given quality measure of complete runs of the evolutionary algorithm. The quality measure we used in irace is f_c, as presented above.

The tuning procedure was performed using timestamps as innovation numbers, and a total budget of 1200 runs was allotted to irace to find parameters maximizing f_c, for both tasks. At the end of these procedures, we obtain two sets of parameters, one for each task. All the experiments presented below used these sets of parameters, that are summarized in Table 1.

4.2 Results and analysis

In summary, we performed four experiments (two innovation marking mechanisms in two tasks), in order to test if our proposed method for innovation marking leads to similar results as the original timestamps-based mechanism of odNEAT. For each experiment, we performed 64 independent runs to provide statistically sound results. Figure 3 (resp. Figure 4) shows the swarm fitness F_s (the average fitness of the robots) during evolution, for both innovation marking algorithms in the navigation task (resp. the item collection task).

For the navigation task (Figure 3), both dating methods lead to the learning of proper behaviors, achieving around the end of the experiments values between 75% and 90% of the maximum level of swarm fitness (fixed in the exper-

Table 1: Summary of the tuned and fixed parameters of odNEAT in our experiments, as described in section 3.2.

	Tuned		Fixed	
	Navigation	Collection		
p_{mate}	0.842	0.212	c_1	0.5
p_{mutate}	0.154	0.244	c_2	1.5
p_w	0.575	0.559	c_3	0.4
p_{node}	0.057	0.422	$\#Robots$	100
p_{conn}	0.184	0.275	$\#Items$	75
p_{recur}	0.376	0.526		
σ	0.442	0.114		
T_m	19 cycles	27 cycles		
$\|\mathbf{P}\|$	5	7		

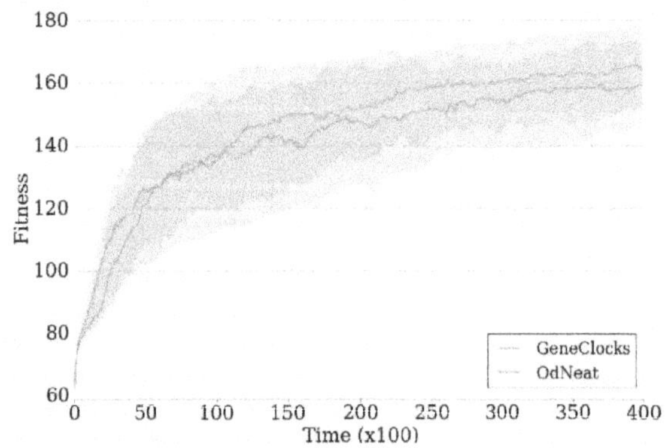

Figure 3: Swarm fitness, F_s, over time of the 64 runs for the navigation and obstacle avoidance task. The lines correspond to the median value between all runs, and the shaded areas show the interquartile range.

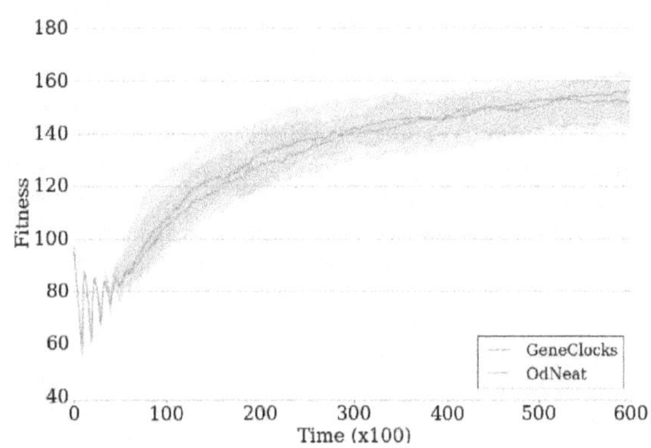

Figure 4: Same as Figure 3 for the item collection task.

iments at 200). Upon inspection of some of the evolved behaviors, we observed that, while having a limited range of perception, the robots are able to rapidly react to other incoming robots, avoid each other and keep moving straight and fast. As for the comparison between GC and the timestamp based dating method, the trend of F_s for both is roughly the same in median value and interquartile range.

Table 2: p-values of the Mann-Whitney two-sided tests between the four measures for Gene Clocks and timestamp-based dating mechanisms and both navigation and item collection tasks. The differences are not statistically significant for any comparison.

	f_c	f_b	t_f	f_a
Navigation	0.134	0.175	0.489	0.074
Collection	0.698	0.956	0.373	0.697

Similarly, in the item collection task (Figure 4) both experiments managed to evolve controllers that searched the environment and effectively collected items, with performances falling between 70% and 80% of the maximum value around the end of the experiments. When comparing GC to timestamps, we observe an even clearer overlap between the curves. The approximation of the global time with our decentralized method seems to have no impact with respect to the swarm fitness.

To further support this claim, we computed the four aforementioned measures on the 64 runs of each experiment. Box-and-whisker diagrams are presented in Figures 5 and 6 for each task. We performed two-sided Mann-Whitney tests comparing both dating mechanisms in both tasks, and over all four measures. The p-values of all tests are all over 0.05, *i.e.* there is no statistical difference between the dating methods with respect to any of the measures (see Table 2). This confirms our main hypothesis that Gene Clocks approximate a perfect innovation ordering sufficiently to have no impact on the reached fitness level.

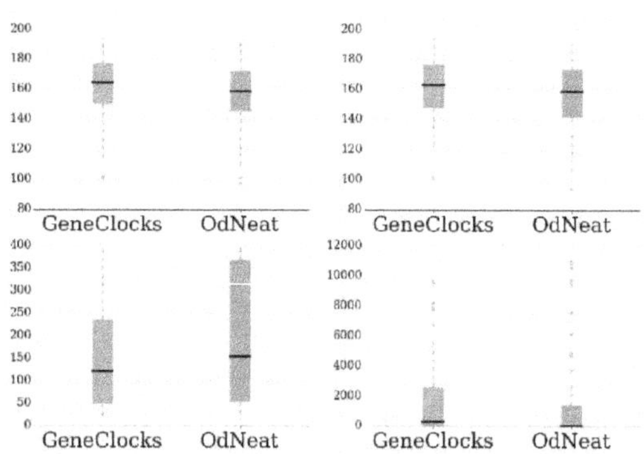

Figure 5: Performance measures of the 64 runs for the navigation task. From left to right and from top to bottom, f_c, f_b, t_f and f_a.

We also investigated the size of the architecture of evolved controllers and the size of the species in local populations to compare both methods in terms of the controllers they produce. The average number of species over time is presented in Figure 7 for the navigation task and in Figure 8 for the item collection task. The average size of the neural controller over time, measured as the sum of neurons and connections, is presented in Figures 9 (navigation) and 10 (item collection).

The average number of species per local population follows a similar trend over time in both methods, especially in the navigation task, in which they are almost undistinguishable.

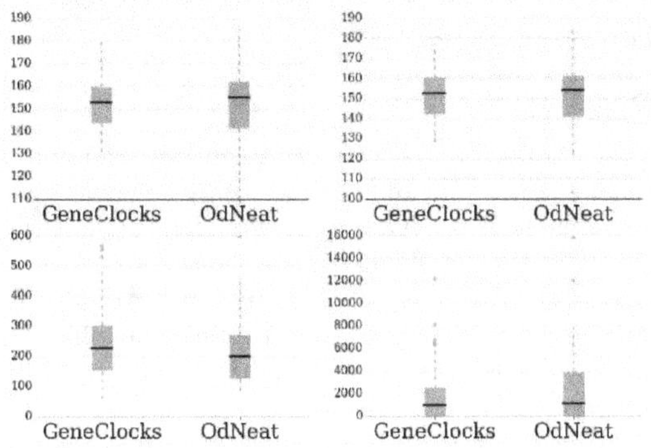

Figure 6: Same as Figure 5 for the collection task.

As for the item collection task, the median value (around 3.75 species per robot) is the same for both experiments, while the variance is slightly larger through evolution for the experiment with timestamps (interquartile range of around ± 0.40 species) than for GC (around ± 0.25 species). Although the difference is slim, the timestamps marking mechanism seems to induce slightly more variability w.r.t. the number of species. This suggests that the timestamps create more topological diversity in the local populations than our method that shows less variability. We believe that the cause for the disparity is related to innovations being sorted by convention during alignment in GC. In the experiments, the coefficients c_1 for excess genes, and c_2 for disjoint genes, used when computing genotypic distance, were set to 0.5 and 1.5 respectively, which means that excess genes have less impact on genome distance. Given that species are computed based on this value, one possible explanation for the lower dispersion of number of species with GC may be a bias towards alignments resulting in more genes at the end of the genome. Indeed, this requires further investigation regarding the effect that the coefficients have in the alignments resulting from the sorting using Gene Clocks.

With respect to size of the evolved controllers, the use of GC creates networks with around 3 ± 1.25 added connections or neurons in the navigation task, against around 2.25 ± 1 for the timestamp mechanism. In the item collection size, 3.75 ± 1 neural elements were added to controllers when using Gene Clocks, and 3 ± 0.8 in the case of the timestamps. GC learns controllers with approximately 0.75 more neural elements in both tasks. We computed the average accumulated size of the neural controllers during the last 10% of evolution (as for the swarm fitness above). The results in Figure 11 show that the difference between both dating methods is not statistically significant in both tasks (p-values > 0.9). This requires further investigation to ascertain if there is a bias induced by GC towards slightly larger networks compared to marking with a global clock shared by all robots.

We compared our proposed decentralized innovation marking method with the timestamps mechanism originally proposed for odNEAT in two multi-robot tasks, navigation with obstacle avoidance and item collection. The results comfort our motivation in proposing a completely decentralized innovation marking method that does not hinder the performance of the timestamp method, and that behaves in the same fashion. Furthermore, our method is completely decentralized, and only requires the addition of one integer to broadcasted genomes (the current robot's c_r), a considerably small communication overhead.

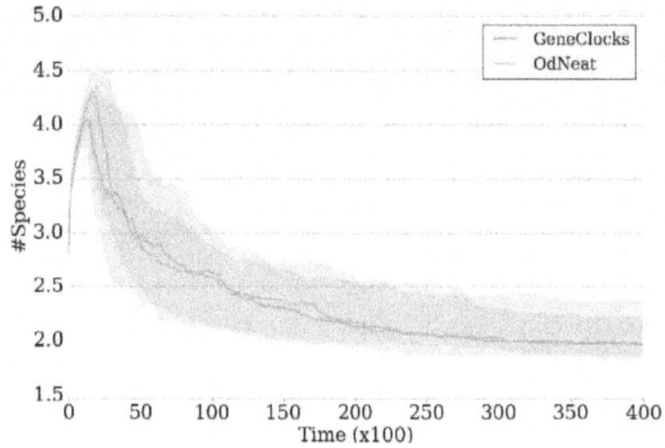

Figure 7: Mean number of species on all the robots, w.r.t. time, over the 64 runs for the navigation task.

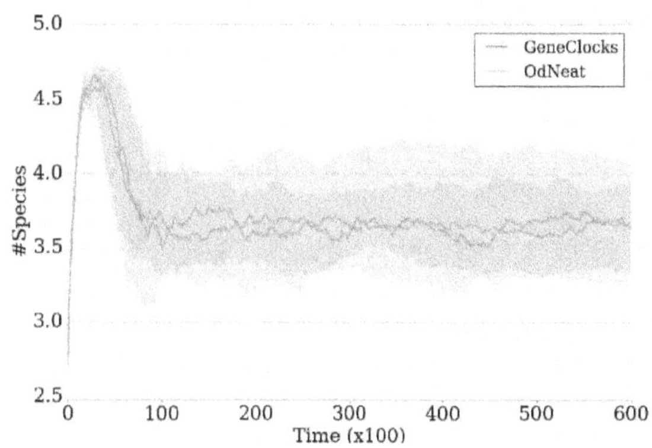

Figure 8: Same as Figure 7 for the collection task.

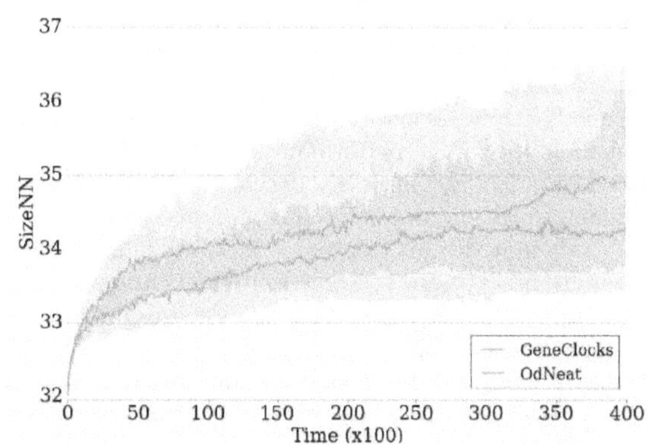

Figure 9: Mean size of the active neural controllers among the robots, measured as the sum of neurons and connections of active genomes, w.r.t. time, over the 64 runs for the navigation task.

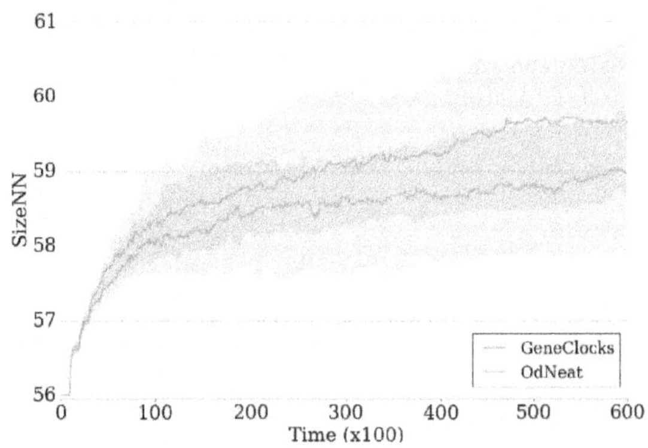

Figure 10: Same as Figure 9 for the collection task.

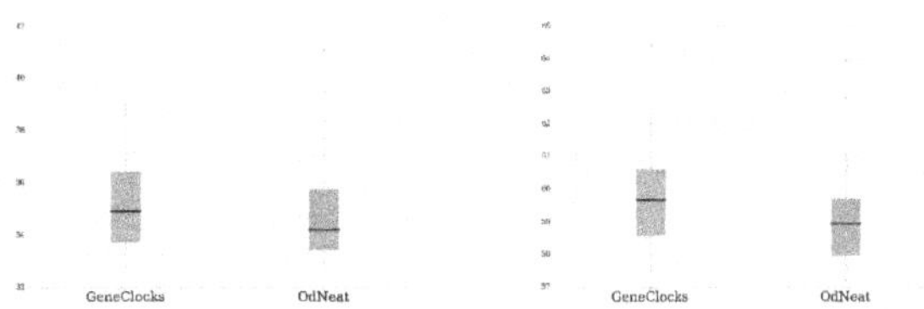

Figure 11: Controller size for the navigation task (left) and the item collection task (right).

5. CONCLUSION AND FUTURE WORK

In this article, we introduced Gene Clocks, a decentralized mechanism to mark genes with innovation numbers in embodied evolution of the topology and weights of neural controllers in a multi-robot distributed context. We have presented our experiments using odNEAT in two experiments involving 100 simulated robots: navigation with obstacle avoidance and item collection. We compared the performances obtained with GC to a method marking genes with local timestamps, which requires periodical synchronizations to be implemented on real robots. Both methods reach the same level of performances in the considered tasks, and the evolutionary dynamics are similar with respect to the number of species and the size of the controllers. In general terms, GC innovation numbers approximate the global time, leading to similar performances and dynamics, while being computed in a completely decentralized manner with a low communication and computational overhead.

One of our motivations to propose a decentralized mechanism to mark innovations in a distributed evolutionary robot system comes from the high cost, or even impossibility, of periodically synchronizing robots in such a framework. This is specially the case in large environments where robot encounters are rare, or more generally, in environments where the robot density is low. Future work aims at evaluating the scalability of the proposed method w.r.t. robot density to test if the innovation marking mechanism keeps functioning correctly when robot encounters are rare.

Innovation numbers contain information on the chronological relative age of genes in the genomes. We are interested in investigating if it is possible to further exploit this information to define more informed cross-over operators or genotypic distance measures.

6. REFERENCES

[1] Peter J Angeline, Gregory M Saunders, and Jordan B Pollack. An evolutionary algorithm that constructs recurrent neural networks. *Neural Networks, IEEE Transactions on*, 5(1):54–65, 1994.

[2] Nicolas Bredeche, Evert Haasdijk, and Agoston Eiben. On-line, on-board evolution of robot controllers. In *Artifical Evolution*, pages 110–121. Springer, 2010.

[3] Nicolas Bredeche, Jean-Marc Montanier, Berend Weel, and Evert Haasdijk. Roborobo! a fast robot simulator for swarm and collective robotics. *CoRR*, abs/1304.2888, 2013.

[4] George Coulouris, Jean Dollimore, Tim Kindberg, and Gordon Blair. *Distributed Systems: Concepts and Design*. Addison-Wesley, 5th edition, 2011.

[5] Iñaki Fernández Pérez, Amine Boumaza, and François Charpillet. Comparison of Selection Methods in On-line Distributed Evolutionary Robotics. In *ALIFE 14*, pages 282–289, New York, US, 2014.

[6] Frederic Gruau. Genetic synthesis of modular neural networks. In *GECCO'93*, pages 318–325. Morgan Kaufmann, 1993.

[7] Taras Kowaliw, Nicolas Bredeche, and Ren Doursat. *Growing Adaptive Machines: Combining Development and Learning in Artificial Neural Networks*. Springer Publishing Company, Incorporated, 2014.

[8] Leslie Lamport. Time, clocks, and the ordering of events in a distributed system. *Commun. ACM*, 21(7):558–565, July 1978.

[9] Manuel López-Ibáñez, Jérémie Dubois-Lacoste, Thomas Stützle, and Mauro Birattari. The irace package, iterated race for automatic algorithm configuration. Technical report, Université Libre de Bruxelles, Belgium, 2011.

[10] Stefano Nolfi and Dario Floreano. *Evolutionary Robotics*. MIT Press, 2000.

[11] J David Schaffer, Darrell Whitley, and Larry J Eshelman. Combinations of genetic algorithms and neural networks: A survey of the state of the art. In *COGANN-92*, pages 1–37. IEEE, 1992.

[12] Christopher Schwarzer, Florian Schlachter, and Nico K Michiels. Online evolution in dynamic environments using neural networks in autonomous robots. *International Journal On Advances in Intelligent Systems*, 4(3 and 4):288–298, 2012.

[13] Fernando Silva, Paulo Urbano, Luís Correia, and Anders Lyhne Christensen. odneat: An algorithm for decentralised online evolution of robotic controllers. *Evol. Comput.*, 2014. MIT Press. Available online.

[14] Kenneth O. Stanley and Risto Miikkulainen. Evolving neural networks through augmenting topologies. *Evol. Comput.*, 10(2):99–127, June 2002.

[15] Richard A. Watson, Sevan G. Ficici, and Jordan B. Pollack. Embodied evolution: Distributing an evolutionary algorithm in a population of robots. *Robotics and Autonomous Syst.*, 39:1–18, 2002. Elsevier.

Improving Survivability in Environment-driven Distributed Evolutionary Algorithms through Explicit Relative Fitness and Fitness Proportionate Communication

Emma Hart
School of Computing
Edinburgh Napier University
Edinburgh, Scotland, UK
e.hart@napier.ac.uk

Andreas Steyven
School of Computing
Edinburgh Napier University
Edinburgh, Scotland, UK
a.steyven@napier.ac.uk

Ben Paechter
School of Computing
Edinburgh Napier University
Edinburgh, Scotland, UK
b.paechter@napier.ac.uk

ABSTRACT

Ensuring the integrity of a robot swarm in terms of maintaining a stable population of functioning robots over long periods of time is a mandatory prerequisite for building more complex systems that achieve user-defined tasks. *mEDEA* is an environment-driven evolutionary algorithm that provides promising results using an implicit fitness function combined with a random genome selection operator. Motivated by the need to sustain a large population with sufficient spare energy to carry out user-defined tasks in the future, we develop an explicit fitness metric providing a measure of fitness that is relative to surrounding robots and examine two methods by which it can influence spread of genomes. Experimental results in simulation find that use of the fitness-function provides significant improvements over the original algorithm; in particular, a method that influences the frequency and range of broadcasting when combined with random selection has the potential to conserve energy whilst maintaining performance, a critical factor for physical robots.

Categories and Subject Descriptors

I.2.8 [**Artificial Intelligence**]: Problem Solving, Control Methods, and Search—*Heuristic methods*

Keywords

Evolutionary Robotics; Environment-driven; On-line Evolution

1. INTRODUCTION

Recent advances in technology both in hardware and software [8] have fuelled visions of swarms of robots being sent to remote or hazardous environments in which they will need to survive over long periods of time. Environments will be unknown and potentially dynamic, requiring autonomous adaptation by the swarm. This has led to a number of recent efforts to study evolution within a swarm as a mechanism for driving adaptation, as opposed to a mechanism for optimising an explicit fitness function, as is common in much work within evolutionary robotics. Montanier [12] notes that this step is in fact a pre-requisite to studying any kind of user-driven task behaviours within a robotic swarm in an open-environment, as the former cannot be achieved if the integrity of the swarm is compromised.

This type of evolution is often referred to as *environment-driven evolution* [2]. Typical approaches such as [14] remove the need for any central control, resulting in algorithms that perform distributed and online evolution. An additional feature of environment-driven algorithms is that no explicit fitness function is defined: instead, mate selection and reproduction depend on selection pressure provided only by the environment yet need to lead to stable populations. A recent example of this is the mEDEA algorithm (minimal Environment driven Distributed Evolutionary Adaptation) [3, 4, 5]. mEDEA relies on an implicit fitness function that results from two potentially conflicting motivations for a robot: an *extrinsic* motivation to cope with environmental constraints in order to maximise survival ability and an *internal* motivation to spread its genomes across the population in order to survive. A complex trade-off exists in which behaviours that maximise mating opportunities might negatively impact survival efficiency, e.g. failing to maintain stable energy levels; as a result, mEDEA (or an environment-driven EA) must find some equilibrium between the two states.

The original version of mEDEA exploited a simple strategy in which a robot continuously broadcast its genome — this can be received and stored by any robot currently within communication range. At the end of a generation, each robot makes a *random* selection from its set of stored genomes, applies a mutation operator, and then replaces its current genome, exactly as in a (1,1) Evolution Strategy [1]. Although there is no selection pressure on an individual basis, from a global perspective, the most widely spread genomes will be selected more often on average. While this achieved success in evolving stable populations in an open-ended environment, it is of interest to attempt to improve both the size of the swarms maintained and their net energy levels, in order that complex user-defined tasks can be added in future. It is reasonable to assume that spare energy, over and above that required to survive can be exploited to achieve complex tasks, whilst a large swarm offers more potential in terms of the tasks that might be accomplished.

Within mEDEA, the evolutionary mechanism differs from natural evolution that also drives adaptation in a number of

GECCO '15, July 11–15, 2015, Madrid, Spain

DOI: http://dx.doi.org/10.1145/2739480.2754688

respects. Firstly, there is no form or crossover — variation is provided only by a mutation operator — and hence the emphasis is on the spreading of *genomes* rather than *genes* as proposed by the Selfish Gene paradigm of Dawkins [7]. Secondly, as all robots broadcast their genome continuously and with fixed radius, each robot has an equal opportunity to pass on its genome, regardless of its quality. This latter point is clearly not true in many natural systems. In nature, an individual's chance of reproduction is related to its fitness relative to other individuals in its vicinity. Additionally, individuals mate selectively, choosing partners based on some estimation of their quality. Some species broadcast their quality through visual or behavioural displays: a peacock displays its tail feathers, a bird of paradise 'dances'. Fitter individuals can attract the attention of a greater number of potential mates.

Inspired by nature, we investigate the effect of introducing a relative fitness measure into mEDEA. A robot makes an estimate of its fitness to survive relative to those within its broadcast range, thereby maintaining the distributed nature of the algorithm. The value can be used in two ways:

- An individual robot can make an informed rather than random selection from the genomes it has received according to the relative fitness value
- The relative fitness value can be used to influence the broadcasting behaviour of a robot to provide a bias towards the spread of good genomes

The latter point changes the nature of the reproductive strategy used in mEDEA from a 'promiscuous' one in which there is indiscriminate broadcasting of a genome, to one in which the *spread* of a genome (and therefore the probability of it being collected) is dependent on its quality. Two novel methods for influencing broadcasting are introduced: the first causes the robot to adapt the probability with which it broadcasts based on its fitness. The second causes the robot to adapt the range over which it broadcasts its genome. As in the original version of mEDEA, robots still make a random selection from collected genomes; however, due to the biased broadcasting methods, on average good quality genomes are more likely to be collected than poorer ones.

Results for all approaches are compared to the original mEDEA algorithm. Experiments show that both methods perform equally well compared to the original algorithm. Note however that broadcasting in the physical world is an energy consuming operation; methods that reduce this energy in order to save battery by either reducing the range or frequency of broadcasting are likely to be of considerable benefit.

2. RELATED WORK

mEDEA was first proposed in [3]. The system was tested under two scenarios: the first evaluated mEDEA in an environment providing limited pressure in which energy is ignored and an agent survives as long as it collects at least one genome. In the second, environmental pressure is introduced by forcing robots to compete for limited resources in order to gain energy. The algorithm was demonstrated to be both efficient with regard to providing distributed evolutionary adaptation in unknown environments and robust to unpredicted changes in the environment. Furthermore, given its lightweight nature, it was predicted to be suitable for hardware and software setups that have limited computation.

Haasdijk *et al* [10] extended mEDEA so that in addition to surviving and operating reliably in an environment, a robot could also perform user-defined tasks. Survivor selection is driven by the environment, whereas parent selection is driven by task performance. Their new framework MONEE (Multi-Objective aNd open-Ended Evolution algorithm) showed that task-driven behaviour can be promoted without compromising environmental adaptation. Robots accumulate credit for accomplishing particular tasks — this credit value is transmitted along with a genome, and is utilised in a fitness function to select parents, replacing the random selection seen in mEDEA. The basic mEDEA setup is also altered by adding an 'egg' phase that occurs at periodic intervals: during this phase, the stationary robot collects genomes from passing robots — no genomes are collected whilst a robot is moving.

Perez *et al* [13] study the impact of adding explicit selection methods to the mEDEA algorithm in a task-driven scenario. They evaluate four selection methods that induce different intensities of selection pressure, using tasks that include obstacle avoidance and foraging, finding that higher selection pressure results in improved performances, especially in more challenging tasks.

Watson *et al.* [15] proposed an completely decentralised algorithm for embodied evolution (EE). In their Probabilistic Gene Transfer Algorithm (PGTA) robots exchange randomly selected genes through short range communication. The algorithm differs from other approaches in that is doesn't have a dedicated variation and replacement steps. Each robot holds a single genome of which only individual genes are replaced at runtime. Transmission frequency and gene acceptance are based on the explicit fitness value of the respective robot, which reflects its performance on a task.

Another strand of work of work worth mentioning is that of Stanley et al. [11] who introduced the notion of *Novelty Search* that promote the discovery of solutions that differ from the ones already evolved. Solutions are selected for novelty rather than objective fitness hence do not require an explicit fitness function; however, the algorithm requires global knowledge to calculate novelty hence cannot be used as described in a purely distributed evolutionary algorithm.

Our proposal provides a novel contribution to the line of work on mEDEA that started in [3] in adding an explicit fitness function that is defined in relation to survival ability rather than task performance, and using this to providing two methods of influencing the rate of spread of good genomes through the population. By providing a more robust mechanism for maintaining swarm integrity than previous work, we pave the way towards future work in which it is possible to add user-defined tasks to a swarm operating in an unknown environment, thereby increasing its utility.

3. ALGORITHM DESCRIPTION

mEDEA utilises an agent driven by a control architecture whose parameters are defined by the currently active genome. The genome defines the weights of an Elman recurrent neural network (RNN) consisting of 43 sensory inputs and 2 motor outputs (translational and rotational speeds). 8 ray-sensors are distributed around the robot's body. They detect the proximity to the nearest object, the presence of walls and other robots, whether it belongs to the same group and the relative orientation between the two robots. An energy level input feeds the current level into the network. A distance and angle sensor give the direction to the nearest energy token. The RNN has 1 hidden layer with 8 nodes, thus 434 weights are defined by the genome. This setup is adapted from [3]. The original mEDEA algorithm is defined in algorithm 1 — only the single step *broadcast()* is modified in this paper, therefore the reader is referred to [3] for a detailed description of the concepts that underpin its design and the specification of each of the other methods.

```
genome.randomInitialise();
while forever do
    if genome.isNotEmpty() then
        agent.load(genome);
    end
    for iteration = 0 to lifetime do
        if agent.isAlive() and genome.isNotEmpty()
        then
            agent.move();
            broadcast(genome);
        end
    end
    genome.empty();
    if genomeList.size() > 0 then
        genome =
        applyVariation(select_random(genomeList));
        if agent.isAlive() == false then
            agent.setAliveState(true);
        end
    end
    else
        agent.setAliveState(false);
    end
    genomeList.empty();
end
```

Algorithm 1: Pseudo code of the original mEDEA algorithm by Bredeche *et al.* [4]

In brief: for a fixed period, robots move according to their control algorithm, broadcasting their genome that is received and stored by any robot within range. At the end of this period, a robot selects a random genome from its list of collected genomes and applies a variation operator. This takes the form of a Gaussian random mutation operator, inspired from Evolution Strategies [1] which can be easily tuned through a σ parameter. Robots that have not collected any genomes become inactive, thus reducing the population size.

At the start of each generation, a robot is initialised with an energy E_0. Every time step, the energy value is decreased by one unit. Energy *tokens* are scattered in the environment. If a robot moves over a token, its energy is increased by an amount E_{token}. An robot with energy=0 remains stationary for the remainder of the generation.

The next section describes the proposed modifications to mEDEA algorithm that we dub $mEDEA_{rf}$ — mEDEA with relative fitness.

3.1 mEDEA$_{rf}$

A robot calculates an estimate of its own fitness to survive based on the balance between energy lost and energy gained, δ_E: this term is initialised to 0 at $t = 0$ and is decreased by 1 at each time-step, and increased by E_{token} if it crosses an energy token. Given δ_E, a robot calculates its fitness relative to the robots in a range r according to equation 1, where f_i' is the relative fitness of robot i at time t, $mean_{sub_i}$ is the mean δ_E of the robots within the subpopulation defined by all robots in range r of robot i, and sd_{sub_i} is the standard deviation of the δ_E of the subpopulation.

$$f_i'(t) = \frac{\delta_i(t) - mean_{sub_i}(t)}{sd_{sub_i}(t)} \tag{1}$$

Note that f_i' is defined in relation to the ability of the robot to *survive* in the environment; it records the net energy of a robot, accounting for energy expended and energy gained by locating tokens. It differs from the explicit task-driven fitness functions investigated by [13] that were concerned only with task-driven selection, i.e optimising performance on defined tasks; although one task investigated was a foraging task that involved collecting tokens in a similar manner to the one used here, the tokens did not influence robot survival in that they did not contribute to the energy of the robot and therefore its ability to stay alive.

The new explicit fitness function can be exploited in two ways: it can either be transmitted with a genome and used by an individual within a selection function or it can be used to influence the rate at which a genome is broadcast, thereby indirectly affecting its chances of being selected for reproduction. The two approaches are described below.

3.1.1 Explicit selection mechanisms

The $select_{random}(genomeList)$ method in mEDEA can easily be replaced with an informed selection method that uses the relative fitness measure to discriminate between genomes. We investigate three well-known selection strategies:
tournament-selection, roulette-wheel selection and an elitist select-best strategy.

3.1.2 Biasing broadcasting of genomes

Alternatively, the spread of genomes can be biased by adapting the *broadcast()* step in algorithm 1. In mEDEA, robots make a random selection from their list of collected genomes at the end of each generation. We propose two new methods, both of which bias the spread of genomes throughout the population in favour of higher quality ones based on a robot's estimation of its fitness f' relative to those in its immediate surroundings.

- *broadcast_radius()* adapts the range at which a robot broadcasts depending on f'
- *broadcast_probability()* broadcast at a fixed range r with the probability depending on f'

Given f_i', we define the probability of a robot broadcasting using equation 2 that simply describes a function that returns a probability 0 if f_i' is less than d_0, probability=1 if f_i' is greater than $d_{\max}$ standard deviations away from the mean, and linearly interpolated between 0 and 1 otherwise.

$$p_i(t) = \begin{cases} 0 & f_i'(t) <= d_0 \\ \frac{f_i'(t) - d_0}{d_{\max} - d_0} & d_0 \leq f_i'(t) < d_{\max} \\ 1 & f_i' \geq d_{\max} \end{cases} \tag{2}$$

For the *Broadcast_probability()* method, shown in *case*1 in algorithm 2, the probability $p_i(t)$ is used directly to determine whether a robot broadcasts. For *Broadcast_radius()*, the probability $p_i(t)$ is converted to a broadcasting range between 0 and a value $r_{\max}$ according to equation 3 — the higher the relative fitness, the greater the broadcast range.

Note that range increases with the square root of the probability in order to maintain a proportional increase in broadcast *area.*

$$r_i(t) = r_{\max} * \sqrt{p_i(t)} \tag{3}$$

Both methods result in robots that have higher relative fitness broadcasting their genome more than those with lower relative fitness, hence biasing the quality of genomes that a receiving robot collects. At the end of each generation, a random selection of genome is made from those collected as in mEDEA.

```
R ← all robots in simulation;
foreach robot i in R do
    N_i ← getRobotsWithinMaxRadius(R);
    if N_i > 0 then
        f'_i ← calculate fitness relative to N_i ;   // eq. 1
        p_i ← convert f'_i to probability;            // eq. 2
    else
        p_i = 0
    end
    switch exp do
        // vary probability
        case 1
            if p_i > rand() then
                broadcast(r_max, currentGenome, σ);
            end
        end
        // vary broadcast radius
        case 2
            r_i ← adjustRadius(p_i);                    // eq. 3
            foreach robot j in N_i do
                if distance(i,j) < r_i then
                    broadcast(r_i, currentGenome, σ);
                end
            end
        end
    endsw
end
```

Algorithm 2: Pseudo code of the algorithm that is executed at every discrete time step of the simulation.

4. EXPERIMENTS

Three sets of experiments were undertaken, exploring the effects of using the explicit selection mechanism, biasing spread of genomes through altering the broadcasting mechanism, and finally biasing spread *and* using explicit selection.

Explicit selection mechanisms.

The first set of experiments investigates the hypothesis that replacing the random selection method in mEDEA with a selection method that selects based on the relative fitness value will increase both the average δ_E of the population and number of robots alive N_{alive} at the end of the final generation when compared to the original mEDEA algorithm. Three selection methods are investigated: binary tournament, roulette-wheel and an elitist select-best. These experiments are labelled E1 (mEDEA), E1+t, E1+rw, E1+b to denote the different selection methods.

Biased broadcasting of genomes.

Experiments were designed to evaluate the following hypotheses:

1. Biasing the spread of genomes via adapting the *probability* that a robot broadcasts based on its relative fitness will improve the average δ_E of the population and N_{alive} compared to the original mEDEA algorithm.

2. Biasing the spread of genomes via adapting the *range* over which a robot broadcasts based on its relative fitness will improve the average δ_E of the population compared to the original mEDEA algorithm.

Note however that the new methods *broadcast_probability()* and *broadcast_range()* introduce *two* adaptations compared to the original algorithm: (1) the broadcast probability (and therefore range) is variable across the population and (2) the broadcast probability (and therefore range) is determined by *relative fitness.* Thus in order to show that any improvement in average δ_E can be attributed to the effect of introducing the *relative fitness* term rather than simply a random variation, we perform additional control experiments as follows:

Rather than calculating the relative fitness of a robot according to equation 1 using its own $\delta_i(t)$, we simply replace it with x_i — a random number drawn from a normal distribution with mean $\Delta(t)$ and $sd\Delta(t)$, where the Δ terms refer to the mean and standard deviation of the fitness of the *global* population (the global fitness is used simply to ensure that the random value is drawn from an appropriate range). New methods *broadcast_randomProbability()* and *broadcast_randomRange()* then use equations 2 and 3 as previously described.These methods are introduced merely to perform rigorous control experiments: we do not suggest that this method would be used in practice as it requires the calculation of a global parameter, contrary to the distributed nature of the algorithm.

Five different experiments are performed, where E1-E3 are controls and E4 and E5 evaluate the new methods.

- E1 records the mean δ_E of the robot population and the number of active robots at the end of the final generation using only the original version of mEDEA

- E2 records the same metrics as above using *broadcast_randomProbability()*

- E3 records the same metrics as above using *broadcast_randomRange().*

- E4 records the same metrics as above using *broadcast_probability().*

- E5 records the same metrics as above using *broadcast_range().*

4.1 Methodology

All experiments use Roborobo! by Bredeche et al. from [6], as in the original simulations described with mEDEA. Roborobo! is a multi-platform, highly portable, robot simulator for large-scale collective robotics experiments. With respect to other robotic simulators, Roborobo! combines (pseudo-)realistic modelling with fast-paced simulation and thus falls somewhere in-between very realistic frameworks such as Player/Stage [9] that tend to be very slow and agent-based tool such as MASON that are extremely simplified with respect to the environment. It focuses solely on large-scale swarms of robots in a 2D environment and is based on a Khepera/ePuck model and has already been used in more than a dozen published research papers mainly concerned with evolutionary swarm robotics, including environment-driven self-adaptation and distributed evolutionary optimization, as well as online onboard embodied evolution and embodied morphogenesis.

All parameters used in the experiments are given in table 1. Simulation parameters are based on the original papers. Experimental parameters were chosen following limited empirical tuning. The maximum broadcasting range requires sensible selection and should be chosen proportional to the arena size.

Simulation parameters	
Arena size	1024 pixel by 1024 pixel
Number of robots	100
Robot lifetime	1500 iterations
Food regrow time	500 iterations
Sensor range	32 pixel
Chromosome length	434
Experimental parameters	
Number of runs	30
Maximum generations	500
Number of energy tokens	800
Energy value of token	100
Start energy	1200
Maximum range $r_{\max}$	64
d_0	0
$d_{\max}$	2

Table 1: Simulation and Experimental Parameters for all experiments

5. RESULTS AND ANALYSIS

Explicit selection by individuals.

Results from the experiments E1, E1+t, E1+rw, E1+b in which the $select_{random}(genome\_list)$ method in algorithm 1 is replaced with a selection method are shown in figure 1, which compares the median[1] energy and agents alive over 30 repeated runs for each of the four experiments listed. Adding an explicit selection method based on a relative fitness value relating to the ability of another robot to survive over the generation has significant effect in the case of *roulette wheel* and *best* selection when compared to mEDEA. Both of these methods exert high selection pressure. In contrast, the low-pressure *tournament* selection method shows little difference to the random selection method of mEDEA. Wilcoxon rank-sum tests confirm that the roulette-wheel and best methods provide significantly different results for both energy and N_{alive}, while no significant difference is observed with the tournament selection method for either metric. The highest pressure selection method *best'* outperforms *roulette-wheel* with statistically significant results at the 0.05 significance level.

Biasing genome spread.

The next set of experiments examines the results of using the two new broadcasting methods, comparing results to the original mEDEA algorithm. Figure 3 clearly shows that experiments E4 and E5 that introduce the new broadcasting methods outperform both the original mEDEA algorithm and the two control experiments. A Wilcoxon rank-sum test with significance level $\alpha = 0.05$ showed that the difference

[1]as a Shapiro-Wilk test showed that the results were not normally distributed

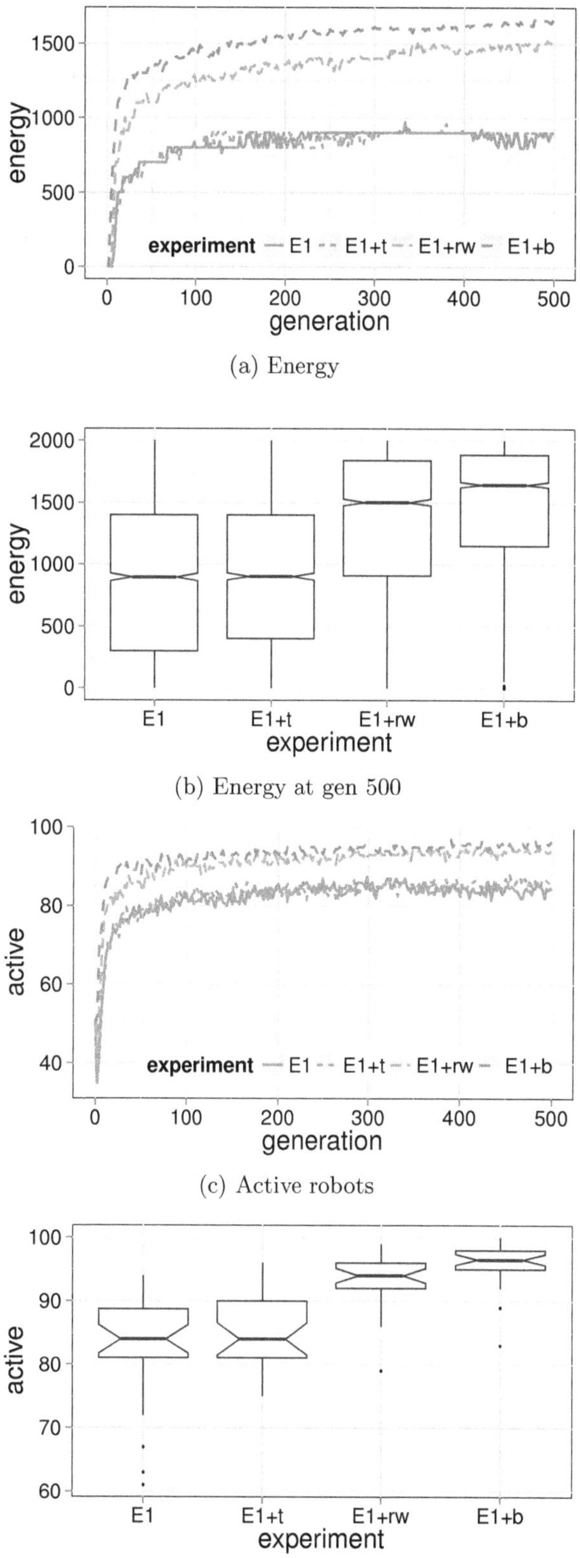

(a) Energy

(b) Energy at gen 500

(c) Active robots

(d) Active robots at gen 500

Figure 1: Explicit selection added to the mEDEA algorithm

in final energy at generation 500 for both E4 and E5 was statistically different to E1, E2 and E3, but that there is no statistical difference between E4 and E5. The fact that E4 and E5 differ significantly from controls E2 and E3 show that the differences in performance are not simply attributable to varying the broadcast rate or range, but must be related to the fact that the broadcast rate and range are adjusted according to the estimate of fitness f' calculated by each robot. A corresponding pattern is observed when examining the number of active robots. Plots (e) and (f) within figure 3 clearly show that the number of genomes broadcast significantly decreases with respect to the original methods, but that is compensated for using the higher environmental pressure achieved by adapting what is broadcast based on the quality estimate f'.

In the original mEDEA, as all robots broadcast indiscriminately at the same fixed range, a very weak selection pressure is created that results in genomes that have spread more widely having more chance of being selected if we consider the population as a whole. Behaviours that lead to a robot coming in contact with more robots will result more spreading of genomes and thus on average, a higher probability of generating future offspring. In contrast, the more discriminate methods of broadcasting proposed in this paper create higher selection-pressure: genomes that have higher relative fitness have more chance of being received by other robots than lower fitness ones and thus are more likely to be randomly selected.

Combining explicit selection with biased broadcasting.

Finally, we investigate the effect of combining explicit selection within an individual with biased broadcasting, testing each of the three selection methods in combination with E4 and E5. Figure 2 shows boxplots of the results obtained from using the two $mEDEA_{rf}$ variants and mEDEA. Each of the $mEDEA_{rf}$ variants is significantly better in terms of energy level and active robots compared to standard mEDEA using an explicit selection method, confirmed using a Wilcoxon Rank-Sum test with a significance level $\alpha = 0.05$.

In order to easily contrast the new methods to the original algorithm, figure 4 compares mEDEA, mEDEA+rw, and the two new broadcasting methods combined with roulette wheel selection and in table 2 we use the Wilcoxon test to compare pairs of experiments with and without explicit selection (indicated by $Ei + s$ Ei respectively). Statistically significant results are shown in bold.

The following comments can be made that summarise all experiments. Where claims are made, they are evidenced by data that is statistically significant as show in the table.

- Coupling the standard mEDEA algorithm with a high-pressure explicit selection method results in a more robust and sustainable population (higher energy and more alive robots) than the standard mEDEA. However, using a low-pressure explicit selection method does not result in any statistical difference.

- The new methods of biasing the spread of genomes based on relative fitness combined with a random selection method by individiual robts (E4, E5) result in a more robust and sustainable population than mEDEA (higher energy and more alive robots). However there are no discernible differences between the two new methods.

- Coupling the methods for biasing spread of genomes (E4, E5) with an explicit selection method by individuals robots improves on the standard mEDEA but in most cases does not provide any significant advantage over biasing the spread and using random selection,

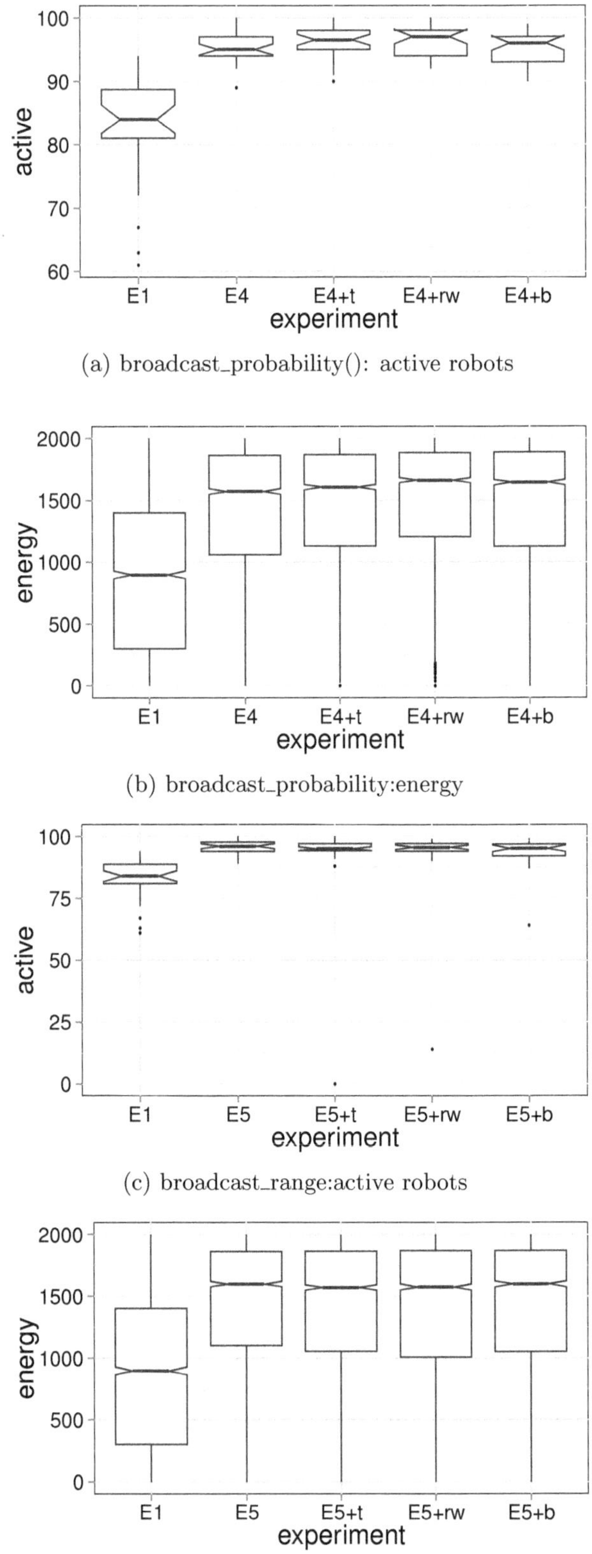

(a) broadcast_probability(): active robots

(b) broadcast_probability:energy

(c) broadcast_range:active robots

(d) broadcast_range():energy

Figure 2: Combining the biased broadcasting of genomes with explicit selection by individuals.

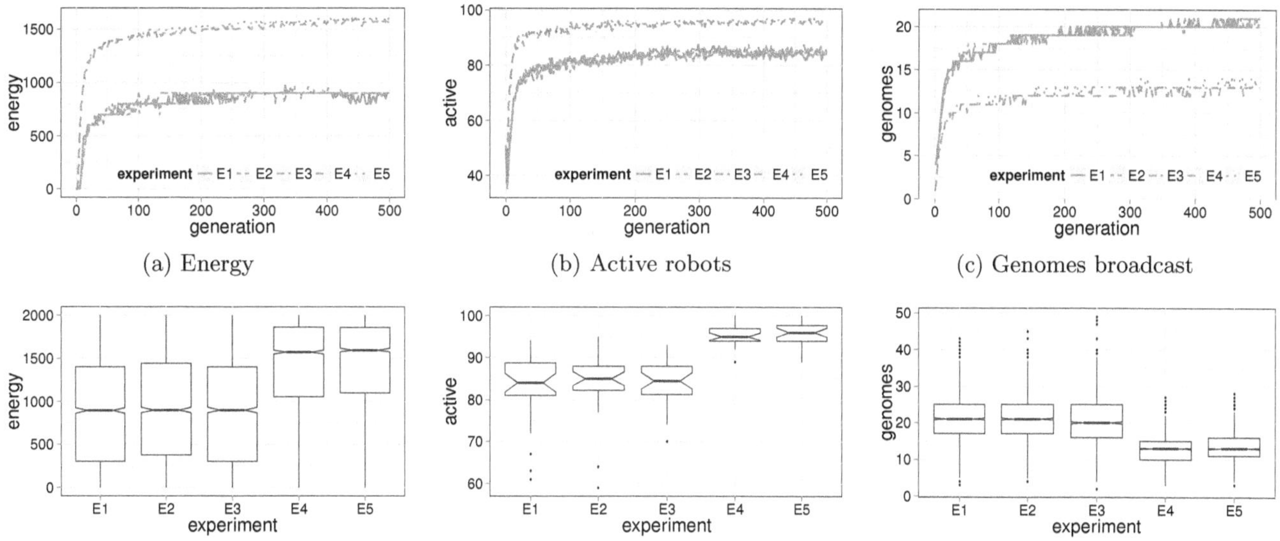

(a) Energy (b) Active robots (c) Genomes broadcast

(d) Energy at gen 500 (e) Active robots at gen 500 (f) Genomes broadcast at gen 500

Figure 3: mEDEA, control experiments and biased broadcasting: figures show the energy, number of active robots and genomes received for each of the experiments E1-E5

with the exception of improving energy levels in the case of $E4 + s$ when compared to E4 alone.

- Using roulette-wheel selection combined with standard mEDEA outperforms the two experiments in which the spread of genomes is biased but individuals apply random selection in terms of sustaining higher levels of energy within the population, but has no significant effect on the size of the sustained population. However, note that using the explicit selection method comes at a potentially high cost in terms of the number and range of broadcasts required to implement this when compared to the biased-broadcasting methods.

In summary, the results show that using mEDEA with a relative fitness function that either promotes spread of good genomes (via biasing what is transmitted) or promotes selection of genomes with high energy values (explicit selection) result in swarms that sustain high energy levels and high percentages of active robots when compared to the original version.

However, when considering real, physical robots, it should be clear that broadcasting comes with an overhead in terms of the energy required to communicate. Two factors influence the cost of broadcasting in energy terms — the number of broadcasts made and the broadcast range. For the explicit selection and *broadcast_range()* methods, the same number of broadcasts are made — however *broadcast_range()* results in a range of broadcast distances $\leq r_{\max}$, whereas the explicit selection method combined with mEDEA always broadcasts at $r_{\max}$, thus utilising greater energy. The *broadcast_probability()* method directly reduces the number of broadcasts made with respect to mEDEA as weaker robots broadcast less on average, thus saving energy. Hence, although both methods of influencing genome choice can provide similar results, the methods that modulate the broadcasting behaviours are preferable in reducing communication overhead. When considering real-robots this factor can have a significant impact on survival ability — in many real-life scenarios, the ability to prolong battery life by reducing energy usage might well be critical.

		E1	E4	E5
E4	Energy	**< 2.2e-16**		
	Alive	**3.079e-10**		
E5	Energy	**< 2.2e-16**	0.3521	
	Alive	**4.112e-10**	0.4885	
E1+s	Energy	**< 2.2e-16**	**2.13e-05**	**1.963e-07**
	Alive	**6.207e-08**	0.0684	0.1994
E4+s	Energy	**< 2.2e-16**	**1.227e-07**	**1.007e-05**
	Alive	**1.222e-10**	0.1076	0.2793
E5+s	Energy	**< 2.2e-16**	0.5267	0.1288
	Alive	**3.287e-09**	0.7715	0.7658

Table 2: p-values obtained from applying Wilcoxon's Rank Sum Test across pairs of experiments, including biased-broadcast only and biased broadcasting coupled with an explicit selection method

6. CONCLUSION AND FUTURE WORK

The paper has provided a number of extensions to an existing Environment Driven Evolutionary Adaptation algorithm — mEDEA. The goal of the work is to show that the integrity of the swarm can be maintained in a more robust manner than in the original work, while still retaining the original distributed and online flavour of the algorithm by using a fitness function that indicated fitness to survive. Having introduced the new fitness function, two new methods were described that adapted either the broadcast range or the probability of broadcasting of a robot, based on its estimate of its relative fitness.

This biases the spread of genomes through the population, with robots that are relatively fitter than their neighbours able to spread their genomes more effectively: individual robots perform a random selection from their store of (now biased) genomes. A thorough analysis of the experimental results shows that a considerable gain in performance is achieved, both in the number of active robots at the end of a fixed period of evaluation, and in the energy levels sustained by those robots.

The new fitness function was also evaluated within an explicit selection method. Experiments showed that this

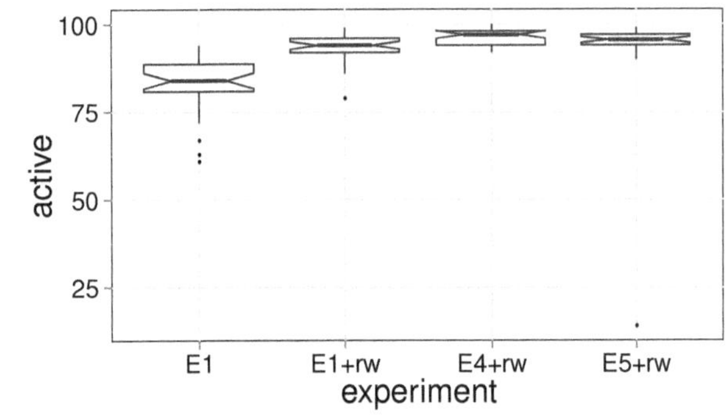

(a) Active robots at gen 500

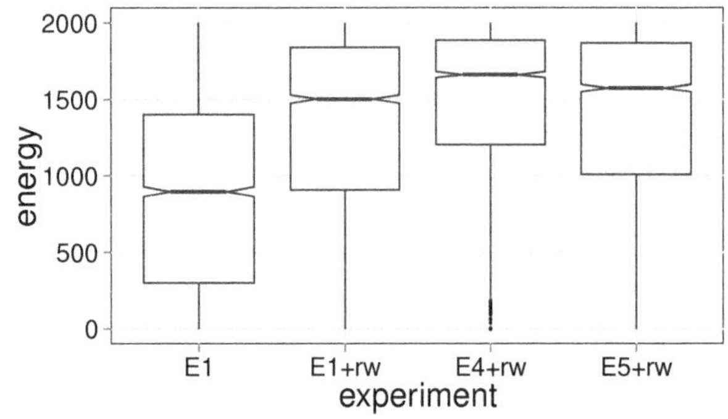

(b) Energy at gen 500

Figure 4: Comparison between vanilla mEDEA, mEDEA with explicit selection by individuals and $mEDEA_{rf}$ + explicit selection by individuals

also provided significant improvements over mEDEA, and slightly outperformed the biased broadcast methods in terms of energy sustained. However, as we described above, this comes with a higher cost than either of the biased broadcast methods in terms of the energy used in transmitting. This might be detrimental in a number of real-world scenarios and hence the lower energy-cost methods are preferred.

An obvious extension to this work will include accounting for the cost of broadcasting when calculating the net energy of a robot that is used by the fitness function, to test whether this will differentiate results from the two sets of experiments desribed in this paper. The results provide a robust platform for future experimentation in which user-defined tasks can be added to examine the effects of mixing environment and task driven evolution with a more robust swarm. Given the lightweight nature of the algorithm, an obvious way forward would also include testing on a real hardware platform in the near future.

Acknowledgements

The authors would like to thank Nicolas Bredeche for providing the improved version of Roborobo!, the base of the mEDEA algorithm implementation on which the experiments are based on and the inspirational discussions at the FOCAS summer school 2014.

7. REFERENCES

[1] H.-G. Beyer and H.-P. Schwefel. Evolution strategies – a comprehensive introduction. *Natural Computing*, 1:3–52, 2001.

[2] R. Bianco and S. Nolfi. Toward open-ended evolutionary robotics: evolving elementary robotic units able to self-assemble and self-reproduce. *Connection Science*, 16(4):227–248, 2004.

[3] N. Bredeche and J.-M. Montanier. Environment-driven embodied evolution in a population of autonomous agents. In R. Schaefer, C. Cotta, J. Kołodziej, and G. Rudolph, editors, *Parallel Problem Solving from Nature, PPSN XI*, volume 6239, pages 290–299, Krakov, Poland, 2010. Springer Berlin Heidelberg.

[4] N. Bredeche and J.-M. Montanier. Environment-driven Open-ended Evolution with a Population of Autonomous Robots. In *Evolving Physical Systems Workshop*, East Lansing, United States, 2012.

[5] N. Bredeche, J.-M. Montanier, W. Liu, and A. F. T. Winfield. Environment-driven distributed evolutionary adaptation in a population of autonomous robotic agents. *Mathematical and Computer Modelling of Dynamical Systems*, 18(1):101–129, Feb. 2012.

[6] N. Bredeche, J.-M. Montanier, B. Weel, and E. Haasdijk. Roborobo! a Fast Robot Simulator for Swarm and Collective Robotics, *CoRR*, abs/1304.2, Apr. 2013.

[7] R. Dawkins. *The Selfish Gene.* 1976.

[8] A. E. Eiben. Grand Challenges for Evolutionary Robotics. *Frontiers in Robotics and AI*, 1(4):74, June 2014.

[9] B. Gerkey, R. T. Vaughan, and A. Howard. The player/stage project: Tools for multi-robot and distributed sensor systems. In *Proceedings of the 11th International Conference on Advanced Robotics (ICAR 2003)*, number Icar 2003, pages 317–323, Coimbra, Portugal, 2003.

[10] E. Haasdijk, B. Weel, and A. E. Eiben. Right on the MONEE. In C. Blum, editor, *GECCO2015*, pages 207–214, Amsterdam, The Netherlands, 2013. ACM New York, NY, USA.

[11] J. Lehman and K. O. Stanley. Exploiting Open-Endedness to Solve Problems Through the Search for Novelty. In *Artificial Life XI*, pages 329–336. MIT Press, 2008.

[12] J.-M. Montanier. *Environment-driven Distributed Evolutionary Adaptation for Collective Robotic Systems.* PhD thesis, Université Paris Sud - Paris XI, Mar. 2013.

[13] I. n. F. Pérez, A. Boumaza, and F. Charpillet. Comparison of Selection Methods in On-line Distributed Evolutionary Robotics. In *ALife2014*, 2014.

[14] F. Silva, P. Urbano, S. Oliveira, and A. L. Christensen. odNEAT: An Algorithm for Distributed Online, Onboard Evolution of Robot Behaviours. In C. Adami, D. M. Bryson, C. Ofria, and R. T. Pennock, editors, *Artificial Life 13*, pages 251–258. MIT Press, July 2012.

[15] R. A. Watson, S. G. Ficici, and J. B. Pollack. Embodied Evolution: Distributing an evolutionary algorithm in a population of robots. *Robotics and Autonomous Systems*, 39(1):1–18, Apr. 2002.

Three-fold Adaptivity in Groups of Robots: The Effect of Social Learning

Jacqueline Heinerman
VU University Amsterdam
Amsterdam, The Netherlands
j.v.heinerman@vu.nl

Dexter Drupsteen
University of Amsterdam
Amsterdam, The Netherlands
dexter.drupsteen@gmail.com

A.E. Eiben
VU University Amsterdam
Amsterdam, The Netherlands
a.e.eiben@vu.nl

ABSTRACT

Adapting the control systems of robots on the fly is important in robotic systems of the future. In this paper we present and investigate a three-fold adaptive system based on evolution, individual and social learning in a group of robots and report on a proof-of-concept study based on e-pucks. We distinguish inheritable and learnable components in the robots' makeup, specify and implement operators for evolution, learning and social learning, and test the system in an arena where the task is to learn to avoid obstacles. In particular, we make the sensory layout evolvable, the locomotion control system learnable and investigate the effects of including social learning in the 'adaptation engine'. Our simulation experiments demonstrate that the full mix of three adaptive mechanisms is practicable and that adding social learning leads to better controllers faster.

Keywords

Evolutionary robotics; on-line evolution; individual learning; social learning; obstacle avoidance; neural networks

1. INTRODUCTION

The importance of adapting the control systems of robots on the fly in robotic systems of the future has been emphasised in for example [16] and [20]. Robots with adaptive controllers are able to adjust to circumstances not (fully) known in advance during their design time and/or when the circumstances, e.g. the environment or user preferences, change.

In this paper we adopt the conceptual framework presented in [13], distinguishing three types of adaption within population-based adaptive systems in general: evolution, lifetime learning and social learning. The differences between these mechanisms are based on distinguishing inheritable and learnable features of the individuals and postulating that inheritable properties do not change during an individuals lifetime, while learnable properties do. Consequently, we distinguish evolutionary operators that act on inheritable features and learning operators adjusting the learnable properties. Furthermore, we distinguish individual learning that can be done by a single individual alone and social learning that requires the exchange of knowledge between more individuals.

Obviously, the difference between inheritable and learnable properties depends on the application and the feasibility of implementing reproduction. This latter one is non-trivial when using real robots as the technology for truly embodied evolution is just emerging [8, 9, 22]. The motivation behind this paper is grounded in real robotics, envisioning robot populations that can adapt by all three mechanisms mentioned above. Therefore, we chose to base our experiments on real robots (e-puck), where we designate the sensory apparatus as inheritable/evolvable. This is technically feasible, because all robots actually do have all sensors, but depending on their 'genome' they may use only some of them. This makes the hardware makeup flexible enough for experimentation. In the meanwhile, this is also a sound design, where the minds of the robots (learnable controllers) must match their bodies (the evolvable sensory layout).

Given such a population of e-pucks we investigate the feasibility of integrating evolution, individual learning, and social learning in a global 'adaptation engine' and look more closely into social learning. In particular, we include a social learning mechanism that allows robots to share their individually learned controllers and test whether social learning works if the hardware of the robots (here: sensory layout) is different. In robot populations with homogeneous hardware we expect that sharing individually learned knowledge will improve adaptation. However, in populations with heterogeneous hardware this is not so obvious, because the learned controllers are, in principle, hardware specific. Thus, our experiments will seek answers to the following three questions:

1. What is the effect of social learning on the quality and speed of learning in a robot population with homogeneous sensory layout (no evolution)?
2. What is the effect of social learning on the quality and speed of learning in a robot population with heterogeneous sensory layout (no evolution)?
3. What is the effect of social learning on the quality and speed of learning in a robot population with evolving sensory layout?

GECCO '15, July 11–15, 2015, Madrid, Spain

DOI: http://dx.doi.org/10.1145/2739480.2754743

2. RELATED WORK

Evolutionary Robotics (ER) is a successful field with a history of a decade and a half [3, 12, 17, 7, 19]. The majority of work in ER employs a rather conventional evolutionary algorithm to evolve controllers, morphologies, or both for robots in some environment(s) in an off-line fashion. That is to say, the design time and the operational time of the robots are separated and evolution only takes place in the design stage. After deployment the robots are not evolving anymore.

In this paper we follow an alternative approach, that of on-line adaption as we will have evolution, individual learning, and social learning all take place during the operational period of the robots. On-line evolution in a population of robots has been first demonstrated in [21]. In this paper physical robots broadcast parameter values from the robot's control specification at a rate proportional to their fitness. Since then, multiple distributed setups have been proposed with and without the use of an explicit fitness function, see for example [5], [10], [15], and adding maturation time [24].

The main difference between existing work and the current paper is the use of a three-fold adaptation mechanism. Technically this means a separation between inheritable and learnable features and the corresponding evolutionary and learning operators, as explained in the Introduction. This distinction is not new per se, a distinction between genes and memes and genotypes and memotypes has been made earlier, for instance, in [14], [11], and [23]. It is interesting to note that social learning can be perceived as a Darwinian process in the memotype space with selection (of memes to send/receive) and recombination (of memes of the sender and the recipient). Individual learning can then be considered the informed mutation operator that changes the memotype of one individual.

Another cluster of related works concerns the evolvability of sensory layout, typically related to finding the best sensory layout to increase autonomy, adaptivity and a better understanding of how sensors evolve in nature [6]. Restricting the sensory layout to only the important sensors, results in a smaller search space and thus a faster learning process [1]. To our best knowledge, investigating the effect of social learning in this setup has not been done.

3. SYSTEM DESCRIPTION

We use e-puck robots as shown in Figure 1 in an arena with the task being obstacle avoidance. The performance of a robot measured over an evaluation time T is defined after [4] as follows:

$$f = \sum_{t=0}^{T} s_{trans} \times (1 - s_{rot}) \times (1 - v_{sens}),$$

where s_{trans} is the translational speed (not normalised) and s_{rot} the rotational speed (between 0 and 1). v_{sens} is the minimal distance to the nearest obstacle (between 0 and 1). In other words, the fitness is maximized when there is a straight movement and minimal sensory input.

3.1 Inheritable and learnable features

The e-puck is a small (7 cm) differential wheeled mobile robot that is equipped with 8 Infra-Red (IR) proximity sensors to be able to detect obstacles. We designate the sensory apparatus as inheritable/evolvable. Therefore, the *genotype* is an array with length 8 where g_i is 0 when sensor i is disabled and 1 if it is used. By definition, a genotype does not change during lifetime. Therefore, a genome can be seen as the ID of an individual and we consider the same e-puck with another genome another individual from the perspective of evolution. This implies that the lifetime of an individual is the period of having the same genome, i.e., the same sensory layout. Imposing another layout on a given e-puck will make it another individual for the evolutionary process.

Figure 1: The e-puck robot developed at the *École Polytechnique Fédérale de Lausanne* (EPFL).

The learnable controller of the robots, the *memotype* is a neural network (NN) with a variable number of input nodes depending on the genome, no hidden nodes, and two output nodes (motor speed values). This results in a maximum neural network size of 18 weights (including the bias node). The motors are activated based on a hyperbolic tangent activation function. A meme consists of information about the neural network structure and corresponding weights. Again by definition, learnable features can change during the lifetime of a given individual, but they are re-initialized if the genotype changes (assuming non-Lamarckian evolution).

3.2 Adaptive mechanisms

The general idea behind the integrated adaptation mechanism is as follows. Each individual –that is, a robot with a particular sensory layout as specified by its genotype– has a maximum lifetime, allocated at birth. This maximum lifetime can vary between the robots. This results in overlapping generations where the young robots can learn from the more experienced ones through the social learning mechanism. Time for learning and evolution is measured by the number of controller evaluations; the age of a robot is increased by one after every evaluation until the maximum lifetime is reached. Then a new genotype –hence, a new robot individual with a new sensory layout– is created. During a robots life several controllers are created and evaluated by the learning mechanisms.

The whole mechanism is outlined in Algorithm 1, the three adaptive mechanisms that form the components of the system are described in the subsequent subsections.

Algorithm 1 Pseudocode of the 3-fold adaptation method

```
while current evaluation < max. no. of evaluations
  for every generation
    set maximum lifetime of individual randomly
    if first generation or no genotypes collected
      initialize genotype randomly
    else
      select a mate from collected genotypes
      create child from mate and current genotype
    end if
    initialize memotype randomly
    while individual age < maximum lifetime
      choose action: individual learning /
      social learning / reevaluate champion
      broadcast genotype and fitness
      broadcast memotype if exceeding threshold
      receive genotypes and memotypes
    end while
  end for
end while
```

3.2.1 Evolution.

Genotypes are broadcasted to all other robots after every controller evaluation together with the fitness value. Robots are collecting these genotypes in their *genotype storage*. Only unique genes are stored here together with the corresponding fitness value. When the genome is already in storage, the fitness value will be replaced by the last obtained fitness value. When a robot's lifetime expires it picks a new genome through tournament selection from the genotype storage. Uniform crossover and mutation are performed on the genome of the tournament winner and the current genome of the robot. When a new genome is established, the genotype storage is cleaned an a new memotype is created where the weights of the neural network are uniform random initialized.

3.2.2 Individual Learning.

The method for individual learning can be any algorithm that can optimize neural networks efficiently. In our system it is a (1+1) Evolutionary Strategy based on [4]. The fitness function for this ES is the f defined in the beginning of this section. The algorithm works on the weights of the neural network that are mutated with a Gaussian noise $N(0, \sigma)$ whose σ value is doubled when the mutated controller (the so-called challenger) is not better than the current controller (the so-called champion). Before a controller is evaluated a recovery period is introduced. During this period, the robot can move, but the fitness is not being measured, so that the robot is able to recover from a difficult starting position. When a challenger has a higher fitness than the champion, the weights of the neural network are replaced resulting in a new controller.

3.2.3 Social Learning.

Memotypes are broadcasted to all other robots after every controller evaluation, provided that a minimum fitness threshold is exceeded. We have implemented a *low*, a *medium* and a *high* value for this, in particular, 10%, 20% or 30% of the theoretical maximum of the fitness function.[1] The place where memotypes from other robots are collected is called the *memotype storage*. A memotype is taken from the memotype storage in a *Last In First Out (LIFO)* order and combined with the current robots controller to create a challenger. To perform recombination the weights of the current controller are copied into the challenger. After that the challenger weights, now equal to the champion weights, are overridden by those of the collected meme if these weights are applicable to the current genome (i.e. the corresponding sensory layout). The resulting meme is thus a crossover between the champion and the challenger. After evaluation of the challenger, the challenger meme is either discarded, when the fitness is lower than the current champion, or promoted to the current champion.

During an evaluation, one of three possible actions are performed. The robot performs individual learning, social learning or reevaluates its current controller. The fitness value obtained by reevaluation is used to create a new fitness value for the current controller in combination with the old fitness value with an 20-80 weight distribution (where 80% is from the old fitness value). Reevaluation of a champion is necessary because of the noisy fitness function [2]. The proportion of number of executions between the three mentioned actions, individual learning, social learning and reevaluation, is a system parameter and thus can be tuned.

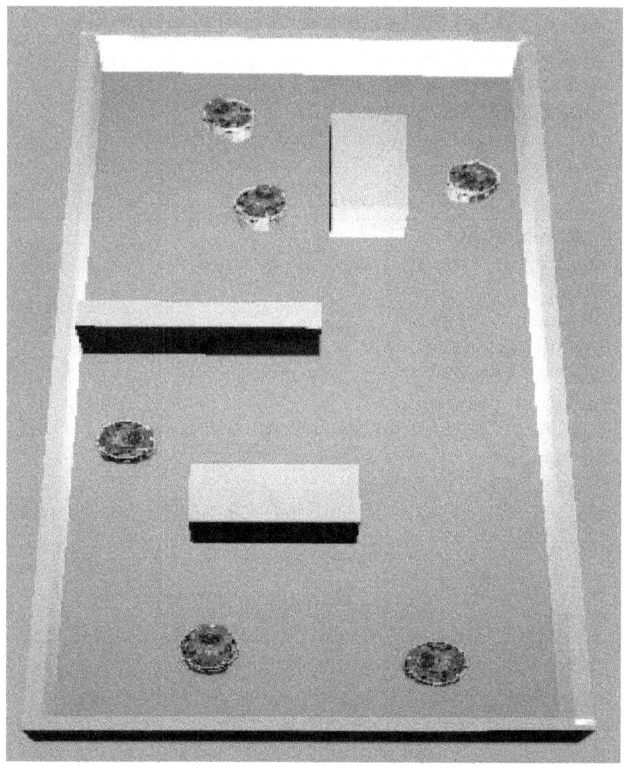

Figure 2: The Webots (version 7.4.2) environment where the group of six e-puck are simulated

[1] The maximum is calculated by assuming a robot moving in a perfectly straight line with no obstacles in sight for the full evaluation period. Let us note that the practically obtainable fitness values are around 40% of this maximum.

4. EXPERIMENTAL SETUP

We conduct our experiments [2] in a high quality simulator, Webots version 7.4.2. We limit the duration of simulations to 3 hours, because the batteries of the e-pucks do not last longer. The simulation environment is exhibited in Figure 2 showing 6 e-pucks. This is the amount of real e-pucks we have, such that we can validate the results in hardware.

The list of all relevant system parameters and the values used in the experiments is given below. When multiple parameter values are used for the experiments, the range is given.

System parameters

Parameter	Value
`Max. evaluations` Maximum number of evaluations in a run.	200 - 800
`Max. robot lifetime` Maximum lifetime of a robot initialized at birth.	100 - 200
`Evaluation duration` The duration of one evaluation measured in seconds. (Recovery time is 1.5 sec and actual evaluation is 8.75 sec).	10.25 sec
`Reevaluation rate` Chance that the champion is reevaluated.	0.2
`Challenger rate` Chance that a challenger is evaluated trough either social learning or individual learning.	0.8
`Social learning rate` Chance that a challenger is created by social learning.	0.3
`Individual learning rate` Chance that a challenger is created by individual learning.	0.7

Evolution

Parameter	Value
`Disable chance` Chance for each sensor to be disabled at birth.	0.3
`Tournament size` Size of tournament that is held among the collected genomes.	2
`Mutation chance` Change to enable/disable sensor after recombination.	0.05
`Maximum genotype memory` Maximum number of unique collected genomes.	5

Learning

Parameter	Value
`Weight range` Value of NN weights are between [-Weight range, Weight range].	4
`Sigma initial` Initial sigma value for mutating weights.	1
`Sigma maximum` Maximum sigma value.	4
`Sigma minimum` Mimimal sigma value.	0.01
`Maximum memotype memory` Maximal size of meme storage.	20

[2]The code for implementation is available on https://github.com/jvheinerman/three_fold_adaptivity_algorithm.

Fitness

Parameter	Value
`Reevaluation weight` Weight of champion fitness in reevaluation.	0.8
`Maximum fitness` Theoretical maximum fitness value.	22400
`Threshold` Percentage of maximum fitness to exceed before sending meme.	0-30%

5. EXPERIMENTAL RESULTS

We have arranged our experiments according to the main research questions listed in the Introduction. Thus, we conducted three series of runs under different conditions regarding the sensory layout of the robots. In each case, we compared the setup with individual learning only and that of individual and social learning together. Furthermore, we varied the threshold value that regulates the quality pressure in the social learning mechanism, cf. Section 3.2.3. This resulted in four social learning variants: no threshold at all, low, medium or high threshold. For every threshold value and the test without social learning 50 repetitions were executed with different random seeds.

In the first experiment all robots have the same layout: all eight proximity sensors are activated and there is no evolution in the genotype space. The duration of the run is 200 controller evaluations. The outcomes are displayed in Figure 3. The graph shows the average fitness (over the 50 repetitions) of the population. The plots clearly show the impact of social learning: it improves the speed of learning as well as the quality of the learned controllers. For every threshold value the average fitness increases with at least 30% (and up to 60%). It is interesting to note that social learning has a positive effect even if there is no threshold for broadcasting memotypes after every evaluation. This is good news, indicating that the method works even in cases where there is not enough information about optimal fitness values to establish a reasonable threshold. To validate this effect we re-plot the experimental results with the 95% confidence intervals for individual learning alone and social learning without threshold in Figure 4. We can see that the confidence intervals do not overlap, meaning a significant difference with the P value much less than 0.05 [18].

In the second experiment the robots have a different layout: each e-puck has different sensors that are activated. These layouts are randomly generated in the beginning of each experiment. The results are shown in Figure 5. In this case, social learning does not result in a much higher quality (average fitness increase is up to 30%), but it does make the learning process faster, reaching the same fitness levels in fewer evaluations then individual learning only. It is interesting to compare the setup with no threshold and with the high threshold. This shows that having no threshold causes a faster increase of the fitness function, while a high threshold results in higher fitness at the end of the 200 evaluations. This indicates that the threshold value can be used to calibrate the system according to user preferences: speed or quality.

In the third experiment the robots have an evolvable layout initialized randomly. To better investigate the effect of social learning we decided to use non overlapping genera-

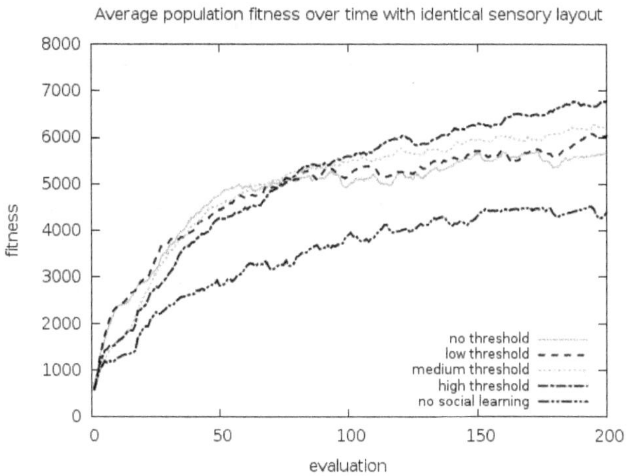

Figure 3: Average population fitness when the sensory layouts of the robots are identical. Time is measured by the number of evaluations (x-axis), fitness by the formula in Section 3 (y-axis). Averages are taken over 50 repetitions.

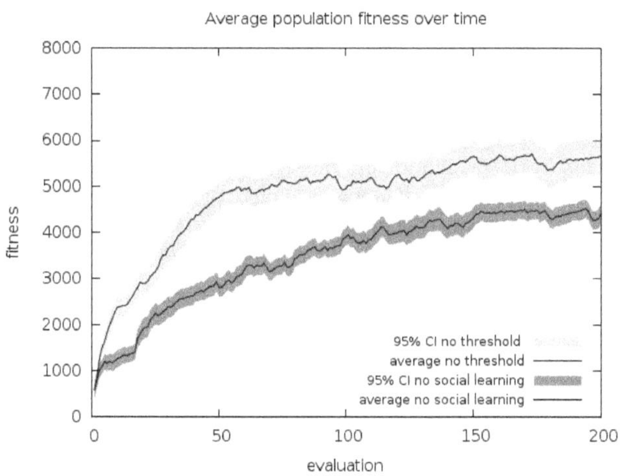

Figure 4: Average population fitness when the sensory layouts of the robots are identical including 95% confidence intervals.

tions, where every robot has the same age. The maximum lifetime is set at 100, i.e., every generation lasts for 100 evaluations, and we have 8 generations all together. Figure 6 displays the results. The first generation shows similar results to Figure 5. Again, we can clearly see a positive effect of social learning. The changes from generation to generation are subtle, but over the whole run we can see a trend: learning within a generation becomes faster.

To inspect the effect of evolution on the genotypes, that is, the sensory layout of the robots., we collected statistics about the status of the sensors that (on or off). The data shows that the number of sensors used decreases over time. The decrease is about 10 to 20 percent, compared to the number of active sensors in the beginning (which varies, depending on the random initialization). Evolution seems to

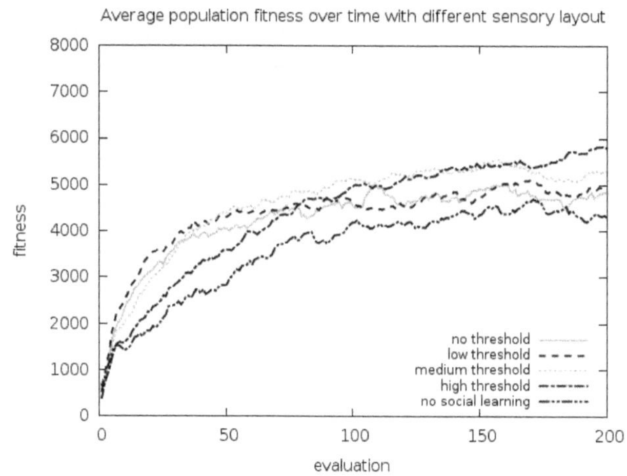

Figure 5: Average population fitness when the sensory layouts of the robots are different. Time is measured by the number of evaluations (x-axis), fitness by the formula in Section 3 (y-axis). Averages are taken over 50 repetitions.

discover that using fewer sensors is advantageous, because it makes the learning task easier. Furthermore, we could observe a difference between the usage of the front and the rear sensors. Intuitively, one would expect that rear sensors become obsolete because they are not necessary for detecting obstacles during forward locomotion. The data provides some confirmation for this, showing that the decrease in the usage of front sensors is lower (around 10%) than the drop for the rear sensors (around 15%). Figure 7 provides an illustration of these effects for two setups, the one with social learning and a low threshold and the one with social learning and a medium threshold.

6. CONCLUSIONS AND FURTHER WORK

In this paper we presented and investigated a three-fold adaptive mechanism based on evolution, individual and social learning to implement on the fly adaptation in a group of robots. The conceptual framework underlying this system is generic, based on distinguishing inheritable and learnable components in the robots makeup and specifying adequate evolutionary and learning operators. Such a system provides a new opportunity to investigate the mutual effects of all these adaptive mechanisms together – an option that existing systems do not offer.

We have implemented this three-fold system in a population of e-puck robots for investigating the effects of social learning. To this end, we designated the sensory apparatus as inheritable/evolvable and the NN-based controllers as learnable. The experiments clearly indicated the benefits of social learning: it makes the population learn faster and the quality of learned controllers higher. This effect is demonstrated under three different setups: for robots with identical sensory layout, for robots with different sensory layout and for robots with evolving sensory layout. We have also found that the social learning mechanism can be tuned for speed or controller quality by a simple parameter, the quality threshold maintained for sending around a robot's controller to others.

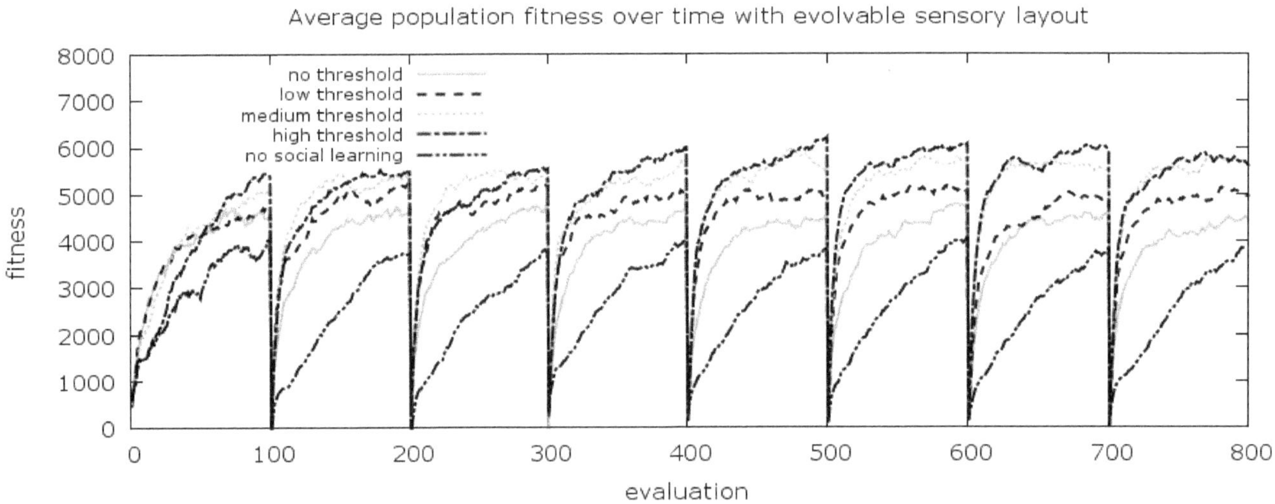

Figure 6: Average population fitness when the sensory layouts of the robots are evolving. Time is measured by the number of evaluations (x-axis), fitness by the formula in Section 3 (y-axis). Averages are taken over 50 repetitions. After 100 evaluations an evolutionary step takes place resulting in a new genotype (sensory layout) for the e-pucks and the controllers are re-initialized.

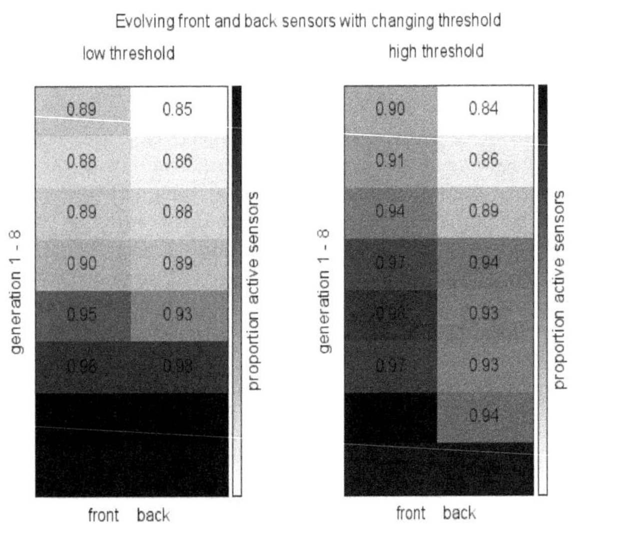

Figure 7: Evolution of the usage of front and rear sensors. The grayscale indicates the portion of active sensors w.r.t. the initial setting over time (black = 100%), the numbers show the exact figures.

Limited by the battery life of the real e-pucks we could only accommodate eight generations in the experiments with evolving sensory layouts. In general, this is not much on an evolutionary timescale, but we could observe a trend of a decreasing number of active sensors over generations.

All in all, our experiments represent a proof of concept, in the meanwhile they provide answers to the specific research questions within our implementation. Ongoing work concerns validation of these results in hardware, facing several challenges. Direct communication between e-pucks is not reliable enough for continuous and frequent broadcasting of memotypes. Extending the hardware with a Linux extension board will hopefully solve this problem. Further research will address tuning of the parameters, using multiple tasks and the use of different hardware, for example Thymio II robots.

7. ACKNOWLEDGMENTS

This work was made possible by the European Union FET Proactive Initiative: Knowing, Doing, Being: Cognition Beyond Problem Solving funding the Deferred Restructuring of Experience in Autonomous Machines (DREAM) project under grant agreement 640891.

8. REFERENCES

[1] K. Balakrishnan and V. Honavar. On sensor evolution in robotics. In *Proceedings of the 1st annual conference on genetic programming*, pages 455–460. MIT Press, 1996.

[2] H.-G. Beyer. Evolutionary algorithms in noisy environments: theoretical issues and guidelines for practice. *Computer Methods in Applied Mechanics and Engineering*, 186(2-4):239 – 267, 2000.

[3] J. Bongard. Evolutionary robotics. *Communications of the ACM*, 56(8):74–85, 2013.

[4] N. Bredeche, E. Haasdijk, and A. E. Eiben. On-line, on-board evolution of robot controllers. In P. Collet, N. Monmarché, P. Legrand, M. Schoenauer, and E. Lutton, editors, *Proceedings of the 9th international conference on Artificial evolution*, pages 110–121, Berlin, 2009. Springer.

[5] N. Bredeche, J.-M. Montanier, W. Liu, and A. F. Winfield. Environment-driven distributed evolutionary adaptation in a population of autonomous robotic agents. *Mathematical and Computer Modelling of Dynamical Systems*, 18(1):101–129, 2012.

[6] K. Dautenhahn, D. Polani, and T. Uthmann. Guest editors' introduction: Special issue on sensor evolution. *Artificial Life*, 7(2):95–97, 2001.

[7] S. Doncieux, N. Bredeche, and J.-B. Mouret, editors. *New Horizons in Evolutionary Robotics*, volume 341 of *Studies in Computational Intelligence*. Springer, 2011.

[8] A. E. Eiben. Grand challenges for evolutionary robotics. *Frontiers in Robotics and AI*, 1(4), 2014.

[9] A. E. Eiben. In Vivo Veritas: towards the Evolution of Things. In T. Bartz-Beielstein, J. Branke, B. Filipič, and J. Smith, editors, *Parallel Problem Solving from Nature – PPSN XIII*, volume 8672 of *LNCS*, pages 24–39. Springer, 2014.

[10] S. Elfwing, E. Uchibe, K. Doya, and H. Christensen. Biologically inspired embodied evolution of survival. In *2005 Congress on Evolutionary Computation (CEC'2005)*, volume 3, pages 2210–2216, Edinburgh, UK, 2005. IEEE Press, Piscataway, NJ.

[11] D. Federici. Combining genes and memes to speed up evolution. In *2003 Congress on Evolutionary Computation (CEC'2003)*, volume 2, pages 747–754, Edinburgh, UK, 2003. IEEE Press, Piscataway, NJ.

[12] D. Floreano, P. Husbands, and S. Nolfi. Evolutionary robotics. In B. Siciliano and O. Khatib, editors, *Springer Handbook of Robotics*, volume Part G.61, pages 1423–1451. Springer, 2008.

[13] E. Haasdijk, A. E. Eiben, and A. F. Winfield. *Individual, Social and Evolutionary Adaptation in Collective Systems*, chapter 12, pages 413–471. Pan Stanford, Singapore, 2013.

[14] F. Heylighen and K. Chielens. Cultural evolution and memetics. *Encyclopedia of complexity and System Science*, pages 1–27, 2008.

[15] R.-J. Huijsman, E. Haasdijk, and A. E. Eiben. An on-line on-board distributed algorithm for evolutionary robotics. In J.-K. Hao, P. Legrand, P. Collet, N. Monmarché, E. Lutton, and M. Schoenauer, editors, *Artificial Evolution, 10th International Conference Evolution Artificielle*, number 7401 in LNCS, pages 73–84. Springer, 2011.

[16] A. L. Nelson, G. J. Barlow, and L. Doitsidis. Fitness functions in evolutionary robotics: A survey and analysis. *Robotics and Autonomous Systems*, 57(4):345 – 370, 2009.

[17] S. Nolfi and D. Floreano. *Evolutionary Robotics: The Biology, Intelligence, and Technology of Self-Organizing Machines*. MIT Press, Cambridge, MA, 2000.

[18] M. E. Payton, M. H. Greenstone, and N. Schenker. Overlapping confidence intervals or standard error intervals: what do they mean in terms of statistical significance? *Journal of Insect Science*, 3(1):34, 2003.

[19] P. Vargas, E. D. Paolo, I. Harvey, and P. Husbands, editors. *The Horizons of Evolutionary Robotics*. MIT Press, 2014.

[20] J. H. Walker, S. M. Garrett, and M. S. Wilson. The balance between initial training and lifelong adaptation in evolving robot controllers. *IEEE Trans. Syst., Man, Cybern. B*, 36(2):423–432, 2006.

[21] R. A. Watson, S. G. Ficici, and J. B. Pollack. Embodied evolution: Distributing an evolutionary algorithm in a population of robots. *Robotics and Autonomous Systems*, 39(1):1–18, Apr. 2002.

[22] A. Winfield and J. Timmis. Evolvable robot hardware. In M. Trefzer and A. Tyrrell, editors, *Evolvable Hardware*, Natural Computing Series, pages 331–348. Springer, 2015.

[23] A. F. T. Winfield and M. D. Erbas. On embodied memetic evolution and the emergence of behavioural traditions in robots. *Memetic Computing*, 3(4):261–270, July 2011.

[24] S. Wischmann, K. Stamm, and F. Wörgötter. Embodied evolution and learning: The neglected timing of maturation. In F. Almeida e Costa, editor, *Advances in Artificial Life: 9th European Conference on Artificial Life*, volume 4648 of *Lecture Notes in Artificial Intelligence*, pages 284–293. Springer-Verlag, Lisbon, Portugal, September 10–14 2007.

Finding a Mate With No Social Skills

Chris Marriott
University of Washington
1900 Commerce Street
Tacoma, Washington
dr.chris.marriott@gmail.com

Jobran Chebib
University of Zürich
190 Winterthurerstrasse 8057
Zürich, Switzerland
jobran.chebib@ieu.uzh.ch

ABSTRACT

Sexual reproductive behavior has a necessary social coordination component as willing and capable partners must both be in the right place at the right time. While there are many known social behavioral adaptations to support solutions to this problem, we explore the possibility and likelihood of solutions that rely only on non-social mechanisms. We find three kinds of social organization that help solve this social coordination problem (herding, assortative mating, and natal philopatry) emerge in populations of simulated agents with no social mechanisms available to support these organizations. We conclude that the non-social origins of these social organizations around sexual reproduction may provide the environment for the development of social solutions to the same and different problems.

Categories and Subject Descriptors

I.2.11 [**Artificial Intelligence**]: Distributed Artificial Intelligence—*Multiagent systems*; I.6.6 [**Simulation and Modelling**]: Simulation Output Analysis

Keywords

evolution, sexual reproduction, social learning, herding, assortative mating, philopatry

1. INTRODUCTION

Finding a mate means coordinating the location in time and space of two willing participants. This social coordination problem (called the *encounter problem* by Gimelfarb [9]) can be solved by social species like humans through social behaviors like negotiation. There are many social behaviors that might support solutions to the encounter problem in humans and other species including herding [3, 11, 21, 23], philopatry [5, 10, 22], pair bonding [4], and assortative mating [2, 7, 9, 12, 13, 16, 25]. However, sexual reproduction is a ubiquitous phenomena and a compelling hypothesis is that not all sexually reproductive life are capable of coordinative social behaviors. We present evidence that social coordination can emerge around sexual reproduction in populations of agents with no social behaviors.

GECCO '15, July 11 - 15, 2015, Madrid, Spain

ISBN 978-1-4503-3472-3/15/07...$15.00

DOI: http://dx.doi.org/10.1145/2739480.2754804

For the purposes of our discussion we draw distinctions between social and non-social problems and social and non-social solutions to problems. We call a problem *social* if it involves the coordination of behavior of more than one individual. Sexual reproduction is a clear social problem since agents must coordinate their behavior in some way. This is in contrast to non-social problems that might be solved by a solitary agent without the coordination with others. Foraging for food is an example of a non-social problem.

A solution to a problem is *social* if the mechanisms that lead to the solution involve interaction between the individuals. Specifically, the focus is on the mechanisms used in the solution to the problem and whether those mechanisms involve interaction (exchange of information) between agents. A problem may be non-social but still have social solutions. Foraging can be solved by a solitary agent yet in many species social solutions are observed (e.g. eusocial insects or pack hunting animals).

Coordinated behavior between agents can arise due to the social forces of social influence or social learning [26, 27, 28]. However, it is well known that coordinated behavior can arise from non-social mechanisms as well [27]. This means that non-social solutions might be found for social coordination problems. In other words the social coordination problem of sexual reproduction can potentially be solved in non-social species by non-social mechanisms. We employed computer simulation to explore the nature of these non-social solutions following the hypothesis that sexual reproduction might serve as an evolutionary catalyst for the emergence of social behaviors in populations.

Our simulation involves agents that have no means of social interaction of any kind except sexual reproduction. To be clear, this means that agents cannot sense the presence or actions of other agents other than when seeking a mate. When seeking a mate they are aware only of the presence or lack of another willing mate. Thus the agents are not capable of social interaction ruling out social solutions to the coordination problem.

Even with these limitations we show that the agents solve the social problem of sexual reproduction through social organization like herding, natal philopatry, and assortative mating. This social coordination emerges due to the constraints that the coordination problem places on the behavior of sexual agents.

We conclude with a discussion of the role sexual reproduction plays in the emergence of social behaviors. We propose a common pathway in which sexual agents could become socially aware. The sexual coordination problem leads first to non-social solutions that have as their consequence social structure in the population. This social structure can serve as the environment in which social behaviors may emerge and potentially shift the non-social solution to a social solution by relying on social signals. We argue that the first steps down this pathway can occur if two conditions exist. First, breeding pair selection must be influenced by the spatial distribution of individuals in the population. Second, the spatial distribution of individuals in the population must be at least indirectly influenced by the genotype of the individuals.

2. MIMETIC PROCESSES

Following Whiten and Ham [27] we use the term *mimetic process* to mean "...[any process] whereby some aspect of the behavior of one animal, B, comes to be like that of another, A". There are many known mimetic processes classified by Whiten and Ham in three broad categories. The mimetic processes can be *non-social* in origin, arise from *social influence*, or arise from *social learning*.

Since we have limited the channels of social communication between the agents we are most interested in the non-social mimetic processes. Whiten and Ham identify four possible types of non-social mimetic processes: *convergence*, *common descent*, *mimicry*, and *individual learning*.

Convergence is an evolutionary mechanism by which individuals in similar evolutionary niches face similar selective pressures and thus may be selected to have convergent behavior profiles. In contrast, *common descent* is when the individuals have a shared ancestry and have inherited similar behavior profiles from that ancestry. *Mimicry* is another evolutionary mechanism that selects for behaviors that are similar to another group in order to blend into that group either for protection (i.e. camouflage, defensive mimicry) or to attract prey or mates. While this last mechanism implies an indirect "copying" behavior this is distinguished from social mechanisms in that mimicry is an evolutionary mechanism, not a mechanism of individual or social adaptation.

The last non-social mimetic process is not an evolutionary process. It is an *individual learning* process. This mimetic process occurs when two learning individuals are exposed to the same or similar learning environments and thus learn similar behaviors. This is another type of convergent process. Like evolutionary convergence above this mechanism operates on the fact that there are convergent solutions that will be found by the adaptive process independent of interaction between individuals. Learning convergence will play a minor role in the agents which are not capable of any significant ontogenetic development.

2.1 Herding

We use the term *herding* broadly to mean the tendency for individuals to group together in *herds* [3], *schools* [11], *flocks* [21], *swarms* [23], or the like. Herding behavior can be seen as a similar behavioral phenotype among the individuals of the herd. As a result herding behavior can be explained as occurring as a product of some mimetic process. Herding behavior can also be seen as a mechanism underlying mimetic processes. A herd will likely all eat, sleep, mate and migrate together and so they will be exposed to similar evolutionary and learning niches. Herding behavior can thus act as a mechanism underlying mimetic processes of evolutionary convergence and/or individual learning convergences for behaviors like foraging, nesting, and mating.

Further many of the social mimetic processes may also be supported by a herding behavior. Spending time with others is the precondition of social influence and social learning and thus herding behavior ensures this precondition is met. The social mechanisms that could be supported by a herd include behavioral contagion, exposure, stimulus enhancement, imitation, over-imitation, and emulation (see [27, 28] for more details on these social mechanisms).

Herding behavior is well known to be supported by a set of very few social rules ([3, 11, 21, 23] all use simple social rules to explain herding behavior). This simple and elegant solution has often served as an explanation of the wide variety of herding behaviors seen in nature and has become useful in analysis of this behavior. We wish to challenge an unspoken understanding that this elegant social solution is the only explanation of this organization. We show that herds can also form in non-social groups due to other forces.

2.2 Philopatry

Philopatry is the tendency for an individual to remain or return to common locations during its lifetime. *Territorial philopatry* (also called *territorial fidelity*) is the tendency to claim a territory or reuse specific navigation paths for travel. *Breeding site fidelity* is when individuals repeatedly breed at the same location. *Natal philopatry* is a particular type of breeding fidelity when an individual returns to the place of its birth for breeding [5, 10, 22].

As we might expect philopatry will commonly co-occur in populations that also display a degree of herding. It is hard to extract a causal relationship between this observance as we could in theory explain herding with reference to philopatric behaviors or vice versa. This again exposes that these behaviors are both the product of mimetic processes and can serve as supporting mechanisms of other mimetic processes.

Instead of discussing causation, we focus on whether non-social or social mimetic processes are at work when considering the philopatry observed. Some instances of philopatry may arise due to a social behavior, whereas others may be supported by non-social processes.

2.3 Assortative Mating

Assortative mating, commonly also known as *homogamy*, refers to non-random mating patterns. A random mating pattern asserts that all mating pairs are equally likely in a population. In many cases mate selection tends to result in a sorting of mates for similarity (and occasionally dissimilarity) along a number of phenotypic or genotypic dimensions. For instance assortative mating along size [2], age [8], appearance [13], or perceived fitness [13, 16] in general are all phenotypic assortments observed in nature. Genotypic assortment occurs when those that reproduce are closely related genetically and can often be a byproduct of phenotypic assortment. Genotypic assortment is also commonly cited as a cause of sympatric speciation [24].

Assortative mating is a shared behavior pattern among individuals and thus can be explained as a product of a mimetic process. Standard explanations of assortment in nature fall into both the social and non-social categories.

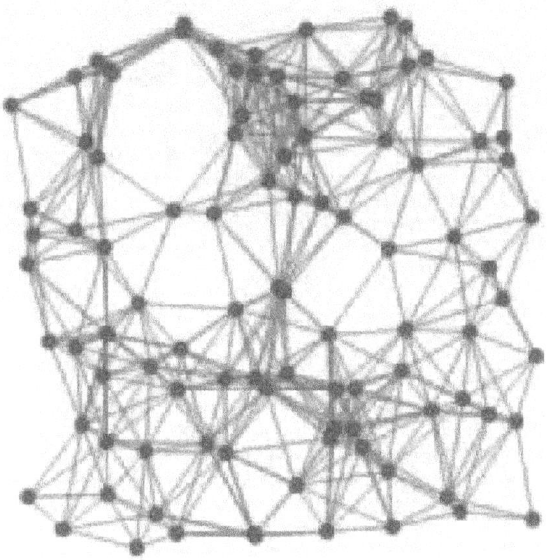

Figure 1: A typical random geometric network.

While it is commonly admitted that assortment may occur due to non-social processes [8, 12], biological studies have uncovered several social mechanisms of mate preference that can lead to assortment (see [12] for a survey of these cases). Nonetheless, Gimelfarb [9] shows that even when these mechanisms are in play it may still be the case that non-social forces explain the assortment.

Again, we can look for links between assortative mating and herding and philopatry. We find co-occurrence of these behaviors in nature and simulation. Common explanations of why species engage in dispersal of members is to avoid inbreeding that comes with philopatry [5, 10].

As in herding and philopatry, we can see that assortative mating may support mimetic processes like the non-social evolutionary processes of convergence and common descent. In individuals capable of social influence or social learning, assortative mating might lead to an assortative social learning structure as well [16].

3. MODEL

Our simulation consists of agents in a random geometric network [20] of resource sites. We select random geometric networks because they are representative of real space and are useful for understanding social networks [1]. See Figure 1 for an example environment. Each day the agents expend energy to move from site to site, forage for resources [19], and engage in mating. Energy in the simulation corresponds to the time an agent can spend doing activities. The resources gathered determines the energy the agent has for activities in the next day. The net daily energy gain or loss determines whether the agent lives or dies (if the energy is depleted) and whether the agent is capable of reproduction (if stored energy exceeds a threshold).

The possible behaviors of the agents are encoded in their genomes as a path of resource sites in the network (our model extends the model from [17] and a more detailed description of the simulation is available in [18]). Each day the agents select a sub-path of their genome that corresponds to a path of sites that can be visited with the energy they have available for that day and that maximizes their expected resource gain. This is carried out by locating all sites in the genome that correspond to the agent's current site and then tracing out sub-paths from the genome leading from those sites with total energy cost less than or equal to the agent's current energy. Finally, the path that appears to maximize the resource gain for the agent is selected. This selection depends on the current site of the agent so the behavior of the agent is determined by the coupling of its genotype with the environment. For the purposes of our analysis this daily selected path is the relevant phenotype of each agent.

Resource gathering at each site is determined by a learning task [17, 18]. Each gene in the genome of an agent corresponds to how a task is performed at a specific gathering site. Different alleles at each gene, corresponding to different ways a task is performed, determine how much energy must be used to gather resources at that site. Each site rewards a fixed constant number of resources on each attempt (unless depleted).

The agents can engage in sexual reproduction when they have an energy total above a reproduction threshold and can find another willing and able participant at the same site. Whether the agent will seek a mate at a site or not is also encoded at each gene in the genome. If an agent is seeking a mate at a site it will remain at the site for an extended period after gathering resources. If two agents are seeking mates at the same site at the same time and they are both above a sexual reproduction threshold then they will engage in sexual reproduction. If no mate is found then agents will wait until the next opportunity to mate or eventually engage in asexual reproduction.

In this experiment both the genotype and the phenotype can be expressed as a path in the network. We use the Levenshtein edit distance [14] to measure the distance between two paths in the graph. This gives us a means of measuring the genotypic and phenotypic difference between agents allowing us to track mating trends and behavioral similarity.

The genotypic and phenotypic difference between mates is measured to determine the degree of assortment in the population along these dimensions. The phenotypic difference between any two agents represents whether they visited different locations during the day. Two agents with identical behavioral phenotypes will visit all the same sites in the same order implying a herd like structure. We track pairwise phenotypic differences in the population and use this to track herding in the simulation.

We measure which sites are used by an agent for breeding and use this data to measure breeding site fidelity and natal philopatry. We measure the levels of breeding site reuse for agents and for sites over the duration of the simulation. We also classify breeders as philopatric if they have bred at the site of their birth (at least once). If it has only bred at sites other than its birth site then it is non-philopatric.

4. OBSERVATIONS

We run the simulations under experimental and control conditions. The experimental simulation consists of a population of agents all descended from a single agent. This facilitates a close observation of the emergence of sexual

Figure 2: Each large dark square along the diagonal represents a cluster of agents with the same daily activity, that is, a herd. This data shows 390 agents in a population after 10000 days of simulation.

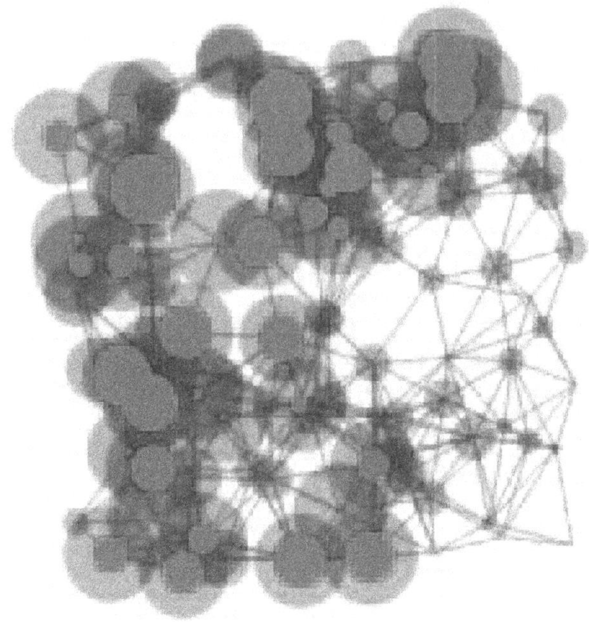

Figure 3: An example network of sites indicating the number of visits (blue) and occurrences of sexual reproduction (red) per site. The radius of the circle indicates the frequency on a logarithmic scale.

reproduction in the initially small asexual population. In contrast we compare this to control runs seeded with one hundred genetically random agents. The initial population of control runs are related only by chance and not by descent. This allows us to observe random mating patterns.

4.1 Experimental Runs

We seed the experimental runs with a single agent created by randomly generating a genome (we generate the path by simulating a random walk on the network [15]). This random agent is deposited in the environment and will not always be viable. The random agent will follow the random walk encoded in its genome until it finds a local optimum that maximizes resource gain. Assuming it can find an optimum that results in positive resource gain the agent will eventually asexually create offspring.

With high likelihood the agent and its offspring will select the same path from their similar genomes and thus will travel together. If along this shared path the agents spend time looking for a mate there is again a high chance of these periods overlapping leading to sexual reproduction. If these likely events do not occur due to a disruptive mutation, then there is often another chance for this lucky event to occur soon after with the same two agents, or with future asexual offspring. As a result the first sexual reproduction occurs soon after the first asexual offspring are born.

The first sexual reproduction event is usually between genotypically and phenotypically similar (if not identical) agents. As a result most of the agents created in the early stages have a high genetic similarity (depending on random mutations). Since they also all tend to be born in the same part of the environment they also tend to select the same or similar paths from their genome to express. Thus, the pair of identical movers quickly becomes a herd. Growth of the herd is usually exponential until the resource limits are reached and it cannot be sustained without mutation leading to emigration (see below).

Figure 2 shows the herd structure in one simulation as a heat map of phenotypic differences. Each row (and column) represents an agent. Each intersection in the heat map represents the difference between the daily activities of the two agents. The axes have been ordered the same way so the diagonal shows comparisons between an agent and itself. The ordering of agents has been selected by performing single link hierarchical clustering on the matrix of differences. Such a clustering groups similar agents together. In the heat map, black represents identical daily activities of the two agents and white expresses the maximum difference between two agents in the population. Shades of red show differences in between these extremes. Since similar agents are grouped together each large dark square around the diagonal represents a group of agents with the same or similar daily activities. These groups are interpreted as herds.

These herds are also observed to be philopatric from a number of different perspectives. It is common for agents to focus on one area of their genome over their life often repeating the same locally optimal path forwards and backwards. This can be seen as a strong territorial fidelity but is also an artifact of the simulation design. Since agents in the same herd will all repeat the same path this can also be seen as the territory of the herd or sub-population. This territorial social coordination is carried over in the herd from one generation to the next.

Breeding site fidelity within agents and within territorial herds is observed. Which sites are used by the herd emerge as social contingencies, but after being established become

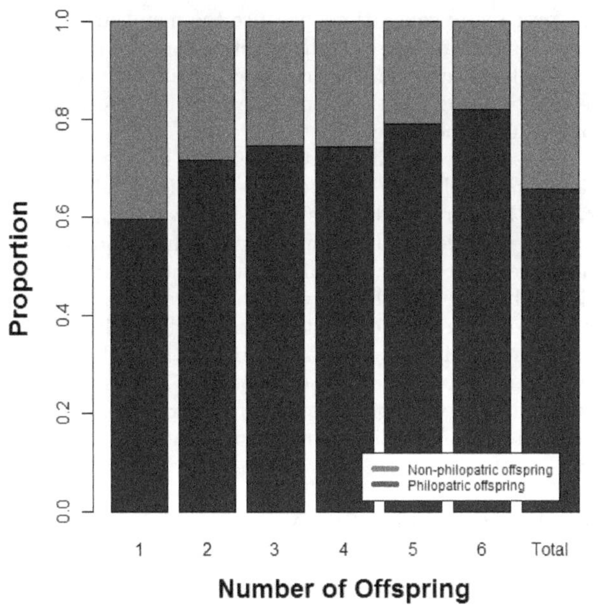

Figure 4: Percentages of philopatry among breeders in the population by number of children.

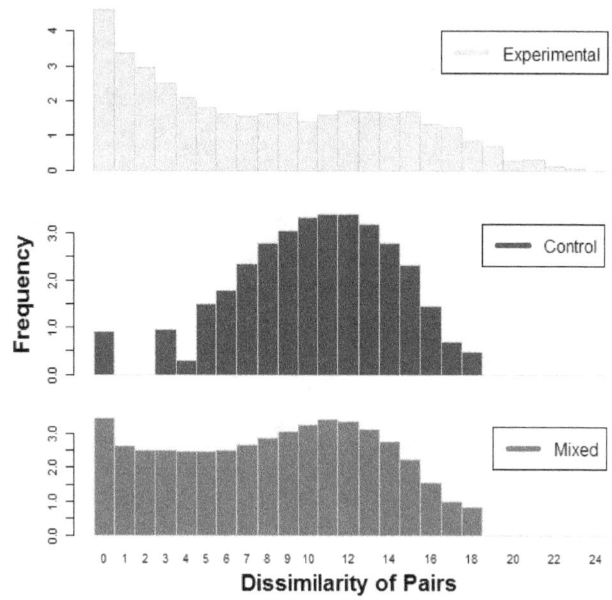

Figure 5: Histogram of parents by difference of daily activities. Top: All parents in runs of length 10000 days. Middle: Control agents breeding with each other. Bottom: Control agents breeding with their offspring.

characteristics of the herd's social structure. Figure 3 shows the example network from Figure 1 displaying the breeding sites used in a 10000 day run on that network. A dozen sites have been used as the primary breeding sites with other sites being used less frequently and many sites not being used for breeding at all. The frequency is on a logarithmic scale.

Among the common breeding sites are the birth sites of many of the herd members. An idealized herd might have a single breeding site at which all members of the herd were born. This herd would display a pure form of natal philopatry. Although an idealized herd is not observed there is evidence of natal philopatry in many agents. Figure 4 shows that 66% of parents engage in natal philopatry for some of their breeding events. Natal philopatry is also more common in agents that have more children.

Herding and philopatry are supported by a high degree of phenotypic and often genotypic similarity between agents in the same herd or using the same breeding site [18]. This leads to a tendency for agents within herds to breed with other agents from the same herd. This implies a large amount of phenotypic similarity should be expected between parents.

Levenshtein edit distance was used to measure the similarity between two paths in the network (representing the daily activities of the agents). Agents that have the same daily activities will have a measurement of zero (most similar). Each addition, deletion, or substitution of a site will increase the measurement of distance. Parents must have met sometime during the day to breed. Thus all parents must have at least some degree of phenotypic similarity.

Figure 5 is a histogram of the similarities of daily activities between parents. The top histogram shows the parents from over 100 runs of length 10000 on a logarithmic scale. The left most rank indicates parents with no difference between their daily activities. It can seen that the number of parents with no difference between them is orders of magnitude larger than even those with a single site difference in their daily activities. This frequency continues to decline as difference increases. The frequency levels out before dropping off completely near the maximal difference. Parents with large differences between them likely represent members of different herds that meet by chance and this data indicates that these meetings still occur with some regularity.

The shape of this distribution contrasts with a control group (see below) where the network is seeded with 100 random agents. Like the seed agents described above, their genomes (and thus daily activities) are generated by a random walker. This represents a case where agents have no genetic or phenotypic similarity to rely on to find mates. The middle histogram of Figure 5 shows the difference between parents that were lucky enough to find one another in this control group. The control agents when breeding with one another display a near normal distribution around the mean difference in the population.

After these control agents found one another they created offspring that were more genetically similar to their parents. The initial control agents would frequently breed with these offspring (ostensibly taking advantage of the genetic similarities). The bottom histogram of Figure 5 shows the differences among parents that had one initial control agent and a second agent that was a descendant of the initial control agents. Note that the shape of this histogram appears to be a hybrid of the shapes of the other two classes.

The above analysis is repeated for genetic difference between parents. In simulation genomes are typically much longer than daily activities. A typical seed agent has a genome that is four times longer than a typical phenotype and after evolution population genomes usually range from

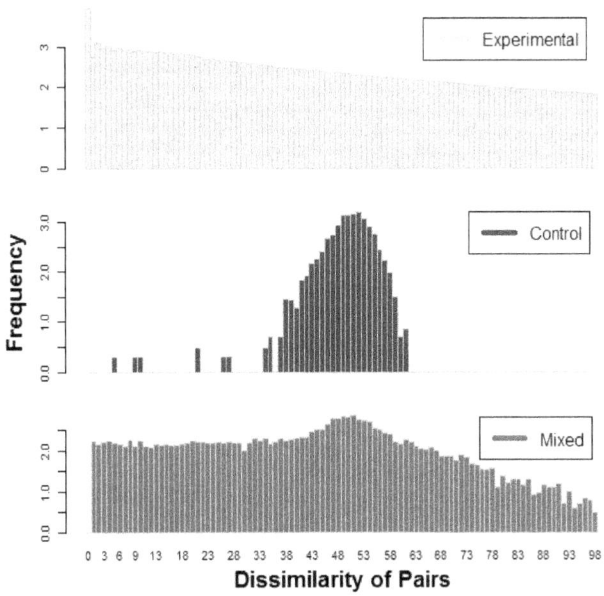

Figure 6: Histogram of parents by genetic difference. Top: All parents in runs of length 10000 days. Middle: Control agents breeding with each other. Bottom: Control agents breeding with their offspring.

the length of a typical phenotype to one thousand times the length of a typical phenotype in extreme cases. As a result we were curious if genetic assortment was also occurring due to the phenotypic assortment.

Figure 6 shows that there is a genetic assortment among the agents as well. The top histogram represents the genetic similarity between parents in 10000 day runs. This histogram shows a clear exponential decay in parent frequency as genetic difference increases (recall these plots are on a logarithmic scale). There is a gentler decay than when comparing phenotypes, but there is no leveling off. Part of this is due to genetic drift observed in the herds as time goes on [18].

As with the phenotypes, the contrast to the control population of random agents (middle histogram in Figure 6) shows a near normal distribution of parents around the mean of genetic difference among the random control population. Also similar to the phenotypic analysis, when the control population breeds with their descendants they begin a trend of assortment that is similar to the population of non-random agents (bottom histogram in Figure 6).

We propose that the primary mimetic process at work in these observations is common descent. Initially, the agents are all genetically similar because they are all copies of the first agent except for a few possible mutations. The coordination of behavior of the first few agents is ensured by their similar genetic heritage and that they occupy the same environment. As the simulation progresses and variation increases in the population common descent still plays a major role in coordinating the behavior of herd members.

Philopatry is also largely maintained through common descent. Breeding and birth sites are maintained in populations over many generations because the members that use those sites have maintained the genetic similarity that led to that site being used in the first place. Maintenance of this site as a breeding location is much easier than evolving as a group to use a new site.

The assortative mating patterns emerge for the same reasons. Initially all herd members are genetically alike so assortment is guaranteed. This is upset as variation is introduced by mutation and recombination. When a novel population emerges it either has migrated to a new spatial region or it has become out of sync with the breeding strategies of the old herd. In both cases it is more likely for herd members to breed with members of their own herd than others just because of proximity. The phenotypic assortment is assured and the genotypic assortment either exists naturally or is created after multiple generations of phenotypic assortment.

4.2 Control Population

The typical run in the simulation begins with a single seed agent that is randomly generated. In contrast to these runs, a control population is run with one hundred initial random agents. Each agent in this control population is randomly generated and thus all similarity is due to random chance. No agents in this initial population share common descent. It is presumed that all mating that occurs between these agents occurs due to a convergence of their breeding behaviors. Since these agents have not evolved, their common behaviors are due to a random convergence.

In the experimental runs described above the first sexual reproductive events come about through common descent. In control runs common descent can play no role. Instead of two agents traveling together, agents have chosen similar breeding sites (and times) coincidentally. A large number of agents in the control population have no offspring at all because they could not find partners.

The control population has the potential to breed either among itself or, like in the experimental runs, they can breed with their offspring. Offspring will regularly be more phenotypically similar to their parents than others from the initial population due to common descent (as above). Comparing the mating behavior of the initial population with other members of the initial population provides a distribution around the mean difference between agents in that population. This is the standard hypothesis of a random mating strategy. This strategy is quickly erased with their offspring in favor of an assortative strategy even among members of the initially random population.

After many agents in the control population have died out, it appears very similar to what is seen in the single agent seed runs (though usually at later stages). The sites where the coincidental meetings occur become likely locations for future breeding because of common descent. After the seed population is gone, all that can be seen are herds forming around the locations of the coincidental meetings. While initially varied, the members of the herds grow genetically more similar over generations due to assortment, which leads to a very similar dynamic as observed in experimental runs.

4.3 Mutation and Emigration

Another main difference between the experimental and control runs is the role that mutation plays in migration. Initializing the simulation with multiple agents will ensure that these agents cover more resource sites than a single agent. This gives more chances for success and so the population that emerges from the control population also tends to cover more resource sites. Note not all sites are guaranteed to be used as coincidental meetings dictate which and how many sites are eventually used by the herds.

In an experimental run, agents migrate to a different set of sites through mutation. For this to happen two conditions must be met. First, there must exist a sub-path of an agent's genome that maximizes resource gain better than the one currently used by the agent. Second, there must be a means for the agent to exploit this better region by moving through the environment to the new sites.

The first condition is commonly satisfied. A mutation in an unused portion of the genome could optimize that region increasing its resource gain. A mutation could occur in the used portion of the genome causing it to decrease its resource gain. The portion of the genome that is used by the agent is only guaranteed to be locally optimal and there is no reason to assume it is globally optimal.

The second condition is more challenging to achieve and we consider two cases. The easier case is when the new region of the genome and the old region of the genome share some overlapping sites. These sites can then serve as a way for the agent to move in its genome without having to move in the environment. When this type of adaptation occurs the new behavior will commonly still overlap with the old behavior and so members of the new herd and the old herd may interbreed. The more difficult case is when the new region of the genome and the old region of the genome do not share any overlapping sites. In this case there must also exist a region of the genome that can serve to bridge the two regions. We know this region exists because the genome is a single path, but in many cases the bridge may be smaller than the actual genetic path that links the two regions (because of overlapping sites as above). However, for the bridge to be used it must also be a region that is of greater resource gain to encourage the agent to leave its local optimum. This will often require a large number of fortuitous mutations and is not often observed in the simulations. However, due to the large number of agents found over the course of the simulation, populations do migrate in this fashion.

Migration of agents that results in successful populations often depends on the topology of the underlying random geometric network of sites. If two areas are separated by too few paths a genome may never evolve to cross into the isolated area. This is because mutation of the path in the network is modeled as a random walker on the network and random walkers will tend to accumulate in areas of higher edge density [15].

5. DISCUSSION

We attribute the successful sexual reproduction in the agents to non-social mimetic processes of convergence and common descent. Specifically common descent seems to be a strong force in the simulation ensuring the fidelity of behavior within breeding populations. Convergence seems to be a force that leads to the meeting and genetic exchange between populations that is important in maintaining genetic variation.

We believe that these non-social evolutionary forces will lead to similar mating dynamics whenever two conditions are satisfied. First, the occurrence of mating between members of a population depends on the spatial arrangement of members of the population. This is the social coordination problem (called the encounter problem by Gimelfarb [9]). This requirement seems very ubiquitous in the natural world, but is often omitted in simulation. Second, the genotype must influence the spatial arrangement of members of the population. If it does not, then agents are merely random walkers and this random behavior cannot be selected for or against. This influence can be direct or indirect requiring environmental interaction.

In the agents, the genome has a strong influence on the spatial distribution as it encodes paths in space directly. We expect that other types of genomes may also lead to these social organizations. In particular, we have considered another type of agent that encodes transition probabilities to move to a new site based on its current site. We would expect that these agents might evolve to display herding, philopatry, and assortative mating and we plan to test this important hypothesis in the future as we also encourage others to test this hypothesis.

Finding evidence that supports this hypothesis would help to explain the ubiquity of sexual reproduction in the natural world even in the absence of social mechanisms of coordination of individuals. All members of sexual species (animal or non-animal) must coordinate their sexual reproduction in real space. So we must assume that our first condition holds for these species. It is reasonable to assume that the genomes of many forms of life are attuned to certain environments. Even if the population in question is not capable of locomotion the survival rates of individuals exposed to different environments could lead to differential distributions of individuals by their genotypes and their phenotypes. We suggest that this is enough to support the types of organization seen in our agents. However, we also believe that these behaviors exist on a spectrum and that populations that have less genetic influence on spatial distribution will likely display these behaviors also to a lesser degree. All that is necessary for a population to survive is that these behaviors are strong enough to support continued reproduction.

We also believe that non-social mimetic processes can lead to social mimetic processes because our simulation shows that social organization can emerge from non-social processes in sexually reproductive populations. In particular, the organizational abilities of herding, philopatry, and assortative mating all ensure that a certain social structure emerges in the population. This social structure can then serve as the environment in which social interaction can evolve. This might mean that the non-social mimetic processes that lead to social organization may be replaced by social mimetic processes that support that same or similar organization.

For instance, a herd that has emerged due to non-social mimetic processes provides the environment in which agents are regularly exposed to other members of the herd. We have seen that mutation may take an agent away from the herd in these cases. While this may lead to successful emigration, it often leads to death. Agents that become socially inclined to stay near the herd would be insulated from the negative effects of these mutations and might not be selected against in some environments. As a result the herd can move from being non-socially organized to being socially organized (likely shifting the dynamics of the population).

This is one possible case of what we call a scaffolding of social behaviors around sexual reproduction (Dennett[6] calls this phenomena ratcheting). The scaffolding process would provide a common pathway for populations to evolve social behaviors from non-social ones due to the constraints of sexual reproduction. If such a scaffolding effect is possible we would expect it to be present in a wide range of sexual organisms. It may be the process that has led to the many examples of social processes in nature including human beings. As future work we intend to expand the simulation discussed to test this hypothesis by exploring conditions under which a scaffolding of social behaviors around sexual reproduction can be encouraged or discouraged.

6. CONCLUSION

We have argued that under two conditions a non-social evolving population has the means to organize itself for the purposes of solving the social coordination problem of sexual reproduction. Given that sexual reproduction in a population is constrained by the spatial distribution of individuals, and as long there is a genetic influence on the spatial distribution of individuals, we suggest social coordination will emerge around sexual reproduction.

This social organization's only purpose may be to support sexual reproduction and may remain non-social in origin in many populations. However, we suggest that in some populations this social organization can serve as scaffolding of social behaviors by providing the social environment for these behaviors.

7. REFERENCES

[1] A. Antonioni, S. Bullock, and M. Tomassini. Reds: an energy-constrained spatial social network model. In *The Fourteenth Conference on the Synthesis and Simulation of Living Systems*. MIT Press, 2014.

[2] G. Arnqvist, L. Rowe, J. Krupa, and A. Sih. Assortative mating by size: patterns in water striders a meta-analysis of mating. *Evolutionary Ecology*, 10:265–284, 1996.

[3] A. V. Banerjee. A simple model of herd behavior. *The Quarterly Journal of Economics*, pages 797–817, 1992.

[4] C. Carter and E. Keverne. The neurobiology of social affiliation and pair bonding. *Hormones, Brain and Behavior, Five-Volume Set*, 2002.

[5] T. Clutton-Brock and D. Lukas. The evolution of social philopatry and dispersal in female mammals. *Molecular Ecology*, 21(3):472–492, 2012.

[6] D. Daniel. *Darwin's dangerous idea.* New York: Simon and Schuster, 1995.

[7] S. De, S. K. Pal, and A. Ghosh. Genotypic and phenotypic assortative mating in genetic algorithm. *Information Sciences*, 105(1):209–226, 1998.

[8] M. Ferrer and V. Penteriani. A process of pair formation leading to assortative mating: passive age-assortative mating by habitat heterogeneity. *Animal Behaviour*, 66(1):137–143, 2003.

[9] A. Gimelfarb. Processes of pair formation leading to assortative mating in biological populations: dynamic interaction model. *Theoretical population biology*, 34(1):1–23, 1988.

[10] P. J. Greenwood. Mating systems, philopatry and dispersal in birds and mammals. *Animal behaviour*, 28(4):1140–1162, 1980.

[11] Y. Inada. Steering mechanism of fish schools. *Complexity international*, 8:1–9, 2001.

[12] Y. Jiang, D. I. Bolnick, and M. Kirkpatrick. Assortative mating in animals. *The American Naturalist*, 181(6):E125–E138, 2013.

[13] M. Kirkpatrick. Sexual selection by female choice in polygynous animals. *Annual Review of Ecology and Systematics*, pages 43–70, 1987.

[14] V. I. Levenshtein. Binary codes capable of correcting deletions, insertions, and reversals. In *Soviet physics doklady*, volume 10, pages 707–710, 1966.

[15] L. Lovász. Random walks on graphs: A survey. *Combinatorics, Paul erdos is eighty*, 2(1):1–46, 1993.

[16] R. D. Mare. Five decades of educational assortative mating. *American sociological review*, pages 15–32, 1991.

[17] C. Marriott and J. Chebib. The effect of social learning on individual learning and evolution. In *The Fourteenth Conference on the Synthesis and Simulation of Living Systems*, pages 736–743. MIT Press, 2014.

[18] C. Marriott and J. Chebib. Emergence-focused design in complex system simulation. In *European Conference on Artificial Life*, 2015.

[19] G. Mobus. Foraging search: Prototypical intelligence. In *Proceedings of the Conference of the American Institute of Physics*, pages 592–605. Institute of Physics Publishing, 2000.

[20] M. Penrose. *Random geometric graphs*, volume 5. Oxford University Press Oxford, 2003.

[21] C. W. Reynolds. Flocks, herds and schools: A distributed behavioral model. *ACM Siggraph Computer Graphics*, 21(4):25–34, 1987.

[22] J. A. Sedgwick and T. Grubb Jr. Site fidelity, territory fidelity, and natal philopatry in willow flycatchers (empidonax traillii). *The Auk*, 121(4):1103–1121, 2004.

[23] D. Sumpter and D. Broomhead. Shape and dynamics of thermoregulating honey bee clusters. *Journal of theoretical Biology*, 204(1):1–14, 2000.

[24] S. Via. Sympatric speciation in animals: the ugly duckling grows up. *Trends in Ecology & Evolution*, 16(7):381–390, 2001.

[25] A. Weis, J. Winterer, C. Vacher, T. Kossler, C. Young, and G. LeBuhn. Phenological assortative mating in flowering plants: the nature and consequences of its frequency dependence. *Evolutionary Ecology Research*, 7(2):161–181, 2005.

[26] A. Whiten. Primate culture and social learning. *Cognitive Science*, 24:477–508, 2000.

[27] A. Whiten and R. Ham. On the nature and evolution of imitation in the animal kingdom: reappraisal of a century of research. *Advances in the Study of Behavior*, 21:239–283, 1992.

[28] A. Whiten, N. McGuigan, S. Marshall-Pescini, and L. M. Hopper. Emulation, imitation, over-imitation and the scope of culture for child and chimpanzee. *Philosophical Transactions of the Royal Society of London: Biological Sciences*, 364:2417–2428, 2008.

Novelty Search for Soft Robotic Space Exploration

Georgios Methenitis[*]
Centrum Wiskunde & Informatica (CWI)
Amsterdam, The Netherlands
Georgios.Methenitis@cwi.nl

Daniel Hennes
Advanced Concepts Team
European Space Agency (ESTEC)
Noordwijk, The Netherlands
Daniel.Hennes@esa.int

Dario Izzo
Advanced Concepts Team
European Space Agency (ESTEC)
Noordwijk, The Netherlands
Dario.Izzo@esa.int

Arnoud Visser
University of Amsterdam
Amsterdam, The Netherlands
A.Visser@uva.nl

ABSTRACT

The use of soft robots in future space exploration is still a far-fetched idea, but an attractive one. Soft robots are inherently compliant mechanisms that are well suited for locomotion on rough terrain as often faced in extra-planetary environments. Depending on the particular application and requirements, the best shape (or body morphology) and locomotion strategy for such robots will vary substantially. Recent developments in soft robotics and evolutionary optimization showed the possibility to simultaneously evolve the morphology and locomotion strategy in simulated trials. The use of techniques such as generative encoding and neural evolution were key to these findings. In this paper, we improve further on this methodology by introducing the use of a novelty measure during the evolution process. We compare fitness search and novelty search in different gravity levels and we consistently find novelty–based search to perform as good as or better than a fitness–based search, while also delivering a greater variety of designs. We propose a combination of the two techniques using fitness–elitism in novelty search to obtain a further improvement. We then use our methodology to evolve the gait and morphology of soft robots at different gravity levels, finding a taxonomy of possible locomotion strategies that are analyzed in the context of space-exploration.

CCS Concepts

•Computing methodologies → Artificial intelligence; Evolutionary robotics; Search methodologies; Control methods;

[*]Based on the master's thesis [1], work conducted under the supervision of both the University of Amsterdam and the Advanced Concepts Team (ESTEC).

GECCO '15, July 11 - 15, 2015, Madrid, Spain

DOI: http://dx.doi.org/10.1145/2739480.2754731

Keywords

Soft Robotics; Locomotion; Novelty Search; CPPN; CPPN-NEAT; VoxCAD; Space Exploration

1. INTRODUCTION

Robotic exploration of extraterrestrial bodies is a challenging endeavour that requires the deployment of advanced technological solutions. The Huygens descent on Titan, the landing of Philae on the comet 67P/Churyumov-Gerasimenko or the daily accounts of the three martian rovers Spirit, Opportunity and Curiosity are incredible achievements that were made possible by our ever increasing technological capabilities. One challenge, in all of these missions, is that of mobility. Advanced mobility solutions for exoplanetary rovers are the subject of active research. It is not uncommon in this research field to find ideas drawing inspiration from biology. For example, this was the case for the Mars tumbleweed exploration concept [2, 3], the lunar ALI exploration concept [4], or the many legged robots, inspired by insect locomotion, that are being studied in the context of exoplanetary exploration. The locomotion strategy and the body morphology of these robots, though closely related, were not co-designed and were treated as rather uncoupled entities. In this work, we are interested in investigating the possibility to simultaneously design the morphology and the gait of robots as to adapt their locomotion to different extraterrestrial environments defined by different terrain types and gravity strengths. The effects of gravity, slopes, and stiffness on the gaits evolved by a quadruped robot in dynamic walking and running was researched in [5, 6]. Hildebrand gait diagrams [7] were employed to analyze gaits and prove their stability under varying planetary conditions. The robot morphology, though, was kept fixed and only the leg lengths and the controller were subject to optimization. The simultaneous optimization of gaits and morphology, using evolutionary techniques is, though, possible. In the work of Sims [8] a generative (or indirect) encoding was used to enable the evolution of virtual creatures adapted for jumping, walking or swimming. The idea has been a source of inspiration for a large number of later works and recently, the practical possibility to evolve soft material robots [9] able to produce locomotion has been proved. The evolution of soft structures in a virtual environment was later also studied

Figure 1: Soft robots can be actuated through air pressure tubes (top-left), pressure variations (top-right), or internal explosions (bottom-left). Autonomously actuated soft robot [20], it is able to withstand extreme temperatures and variant terrain types (bottom-right).

in [10] where a powerful generative encoding, CPPNs [11], was used to generate soft voxel-formed three dimensional structures, coupled with the use of NEAT algorithm which ensures the increasing complexity of the networks produced. The interest of soft robotics [12, 13] for space exploration has been recently well defined by Lin, Leisk and Trimmer [14] and summarized in three points: a) intrinsically safe (rather than "control safe") b) morph-able (size-changing and versatile) and c) gravity independent (able to move in any orientation). Having no rigid parts in their design (See Fig. 1), the degrees of freedom of a soft robot are infinite and the possible ways of motion can become extremely rich and hard to control. In this paper we build upon previous work [10] first improving significantly the methodology by considering the evolutionary process as driven by novelty [15, 16, 17, 18] rather than by fitness. A similar idea was investigated in [19] in the context of rigid robots and proved to result in a far more exploratory algorithm in the space of morphologies. We then obtain a further performance boost combining novelty search with fitness–elitism and we use the resulting algorithm to evolve a number of robots and locomotion patterns adapted to different planetary conditions. Given the extreme complexity of the task and the early research stages of the tools used, we are not as much interested in the practical use of the designs evolved as in their use to inspire future advanced robotic exploration missions.

2. BACKGROUND

We start by introducing VoxCad, the open source simulator used throughout this study to analyze soft robot morphologies and locomotion strategies. Shape and structure of the studied robots are expressed using a generative encoding technique and evolved using a neuro-evolutionary algorithm called CPPN-NEAT. In particular, we follow the approach detailed in previous work [10] and briefly summarize the key aspects of the resulting setup here.

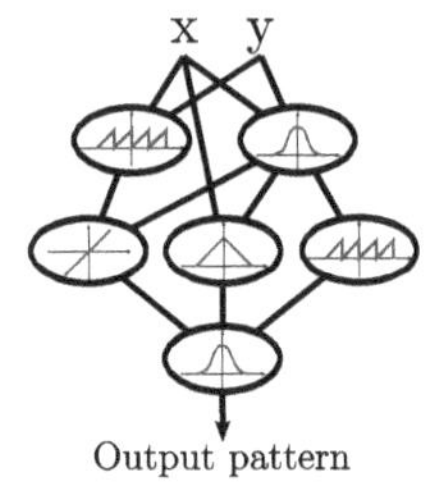

Figure 2: Compositional pattern-producing networks have identical network structure with artificial neural networks while they make use of a canonical set of activation functions.

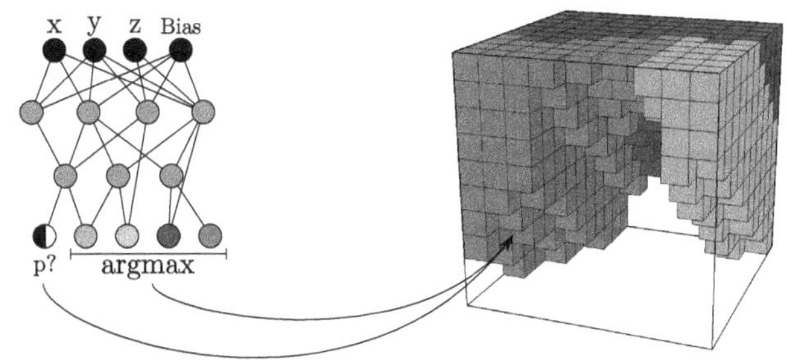

Figure 3: Each genotype (CPPN) is queried for every coordinate inside the lattice, its outputs determine the presence of a voxel and the type of its material.

2.1 VoxCad simulator

VoxCad [21] is a simulator targeted to mimic the physics of soft material, while accurately reflecting deformations and interactions. The workspace is represented as a 3D-lattice, where each voxel is of a certain material type. Materials can be actuated (i.e. expansion or contraction) by an external trigger. External actuation is achieved by varying the temperature of the environment and thus exploiting the various material properties. Modifying the material properties results in soft or hard material that either does (active) or does not react (passive) to temperature variations.

2.2 Generative encoding

We use the technique of Compositional Pattern-Producing Networks (CPPNs) [11] as a generative encoding to produce morphologies (i.e. shape and structure) of simulated soft robots. CPPNs are artificial neural networks with an extended set of activation functions. The set of activation functions can include repetitive, symmetrical, and linear functions; an example is depicted in Figure 2. The CPPNs are queried for every coordinate of the lattice space to form a soft robot shape as well as to define the distribution of the materials. The input nodes (neurons) of the CPPN are assigned to normalized coordinates:[1] $x, y, z \in [-1, 1]$. The output of the network defines if the queried voxel is enabled and which material is used. The generative encoding of voxelyzed soft robots through CPPNs is shown in Figure 3.

[1]Therefore, the morphology can be sampled at different lattice resolutions.

2.3 CPPN-NEAT

As CPPNs are artificial neural networks, yet with a richer set of activation function, we can deploy neuro-evolutionary algorithms to evolve these networks. Specifically, we use a technique called NeuroEvolution of Augmenting Topologies (NEAT) [22] with minor modifications in order to be applicable to CPPNs, the resulting algorithm is known as CPPN-NEAT [11]. During evolution, CPPN-NEAT modifies not only the weights, but also the structure of the network and the activation functions. As such, the number of hidden layers and neurons does not need to be fixed in advance.

3. METHODOLOGY

As outlined in the previous section, the use of soft robot simulator (VoxCad) and generative encoding in combination with neuro-evolution through CPPN-NEAT paves the way for successfully evolving complex morphologies for soft robots. However, in previous work [10], the diversity of evolved creatures was limited. Different locomotion profiles were predominantly the result of including secondary costs (e.g., cost for actuated voxels or voxel connections) in the fitness function. We now describe our approach based on *novelty search* that ensures intrinsic diversity without the need for a "hand-coded" objective that is subjective to the designers domain knowledge and may not generalize to exoplanetary environments with a variety of gravity levels. In addition, we describe how fitness–elitism can be incorporated in novelty search to combine the best of both worlds.

3.1 Novelty search

Unlike traditional fitness–based search, novelty search [15, 16, 17, 18] is an alternative way of optimization. Novelty search, evaluates new candidates with respect to their "novelty" when compared to all previously found solutions and not based on an objective function. The "novelty" measure is defined in the behavior space, which is a function of the phenotype. As an example, one can think of the behavior as the trajectory of a robot controlled by a neural network. A "novel" candidate will exhibit a trajectory that differs from all previously recorded trajectories (i.e. in the behavior space) and novelty is not determined by the difference in the weights of the neural network (i.e the genome search space).

For a behavior x, a novelty measure $f(x)$ determines how different the specific behavior is in respect to a set of other behaviors $\mathcal{S}$. We follow the definition in [15, 16], where the novelty measure is defined as *sparseness* measuring the average distance from the k–closest behaviors:

$$f(x) = \frac{1}{k}\sum_{i=1}^{k} dist(x, \mathcal{S}_i) \ , \qquad (1)$$

where S is a sorted set of the closest behaviors and $dist$ is a distance function between two behaviors.

In the context of soft robots, we define a behavior as the way the robot interacts with the environment during a VoxCad simulation run. Every aspect of the soft robot movement that can be observed, can also be used to describe the behavior. It is expected that behaviors that indirectly contain fitness–related information (i.e. displacement) will be more successful in terms of the original fitness function. Figure 4 presents all behaviors used for novelty computation during our study, in addition to behaviors that relate to displacement, e.g., trajectories and pace, we also include others that do not have this obvious relation, e.g., number of voxels touching the ground, kinetic energy, and pressure. For all recorded behavior metrics a constant sampling rate ensures that all signals have the same length. Furthermore, the discrete Fourier transformation of one dimensional signals was used to define other behavior types. The dominant frequencies of the pace, voxels touching the ground, pressure, and kinetic energy are expected to be descriptive of the locomotion strategies the evolved soft robots exhibit.

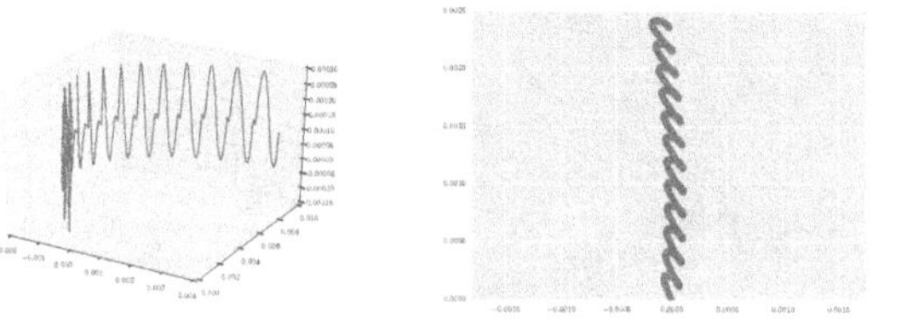

(a) Three and two dimensional trajectories of the soft robots.

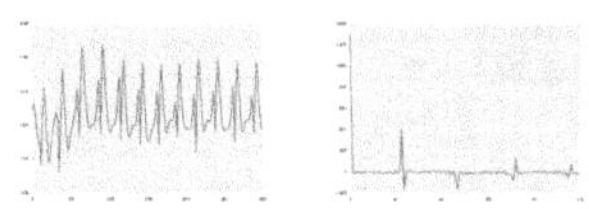

(b) Pace and discrete Fourier transformation of the same signal.

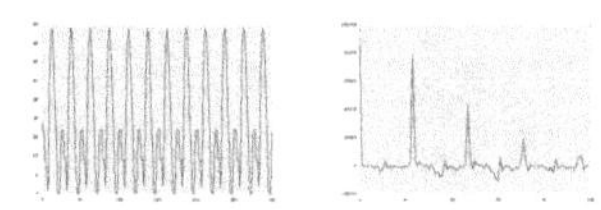

(c) Voxels touching the ground and discrete Fourier transformation of the same signal.

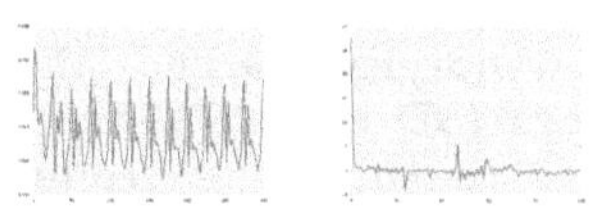

(d) Maximum pressure and discrete Fourier transformation of the same signal.

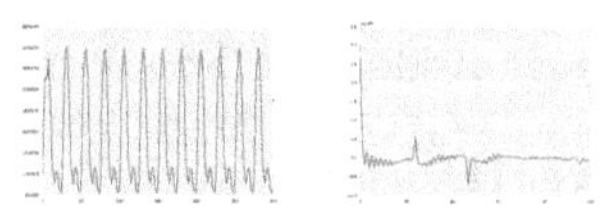

(e) Kinetic energy and discrete Fourier transformation of the same signal.

Figure 4: Observed behaviors of the soft robots used for the sparsity computation in novelty search.

In order to compute the novelty measure (see Equation (1)) for a trajectory behavior, we need to define the distance function $dist$. By definition, all trajectories start at the origin and trajectory points are sampled at the same constant rate. Trajectories are rotated so that the average over all trajectory points falls on the x–axis, thus resulting in a rotation–invariant measure. Hence, the difference in two behaviors $\mathcal{S}_i$ and $\mathcal{S}_j$ can be computed as the sum over the point absolute differences between the corresponding trajectories $\boldsymbol{t}_i$ and $\boldsymbol{t}_j$:

$$\mathcal{S}_i = \boldsymbol{t}_i = t_{i,1}, t_{i,2}, \ldots, t_{i,N} \qquad (2)$$

$$\mathcal{S}_j = \boldsymbol{t}_j = t_{j,1}, t_{j,2}, \ldots, t_{j,N} \qquad (3)$$

$$dist(\mathcal{S}_i, \mathcal{S}_j) = \boldsymbol{t}_i - \boldsymbol{t}_j = \sum_{k=1}^{N} \|t_{i,k} - t_{j,k}\| \qquad (4)$$

where N is the number of sampled coordinate points. In the same way we can define the distance between other types of behaviors and subsequently compute the sparseness (see Equation (1)) a.k.a the novelty measure. For the discrete Fourier transformation of the one dimensional signals only the absolute difference in the first twenty coefficients is measured.

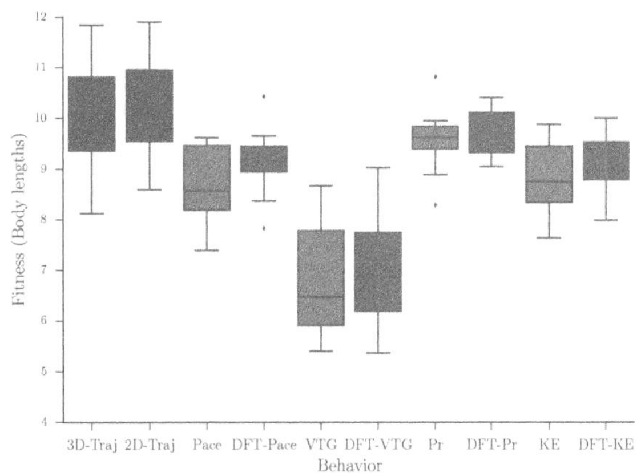

Figure 5: Boxplots of the champion fitness under 10 variant defined behaviors for novelty search. Blue are trajectory type behaviors (3D and 2D), green are 1D signals (pace, voxels touching the ground (VTG), pressure (Pr), and kinetic energy (KE)). Red is the discrete Fourier transformation (DFT-<type>) of the 1D signals.

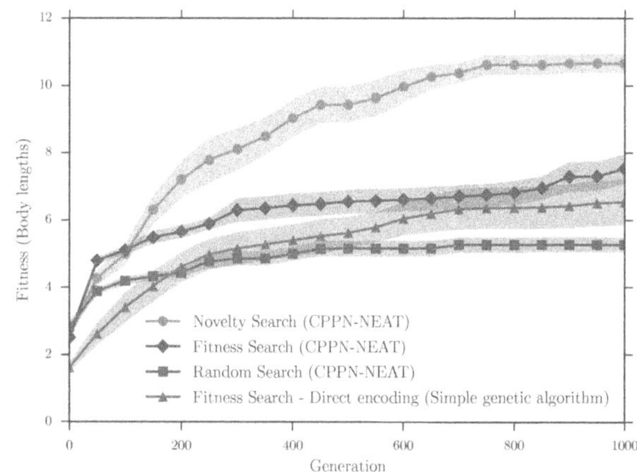

Figure 6: Comparison of simple genetic algorithm (direct encoding) against novelty-fitness-random search with generative encoding. Best fitness so far averaged over 10 runs, deviation error is shown by the shaded part.

3.2 Fitness–elitism in novelty search

While novelty search promotes diversity by rewarding novel individuals, elitism ensures that the best genetic material is passed on from generation to generation. In particular, we introduce elitism in CPPN-NEAT by carrying–over the best individual of each species so that they can contribute with their beneficial genes later in the evolutionary process. We distinguish between fitness–elitism, where the "best" individuals are selected based on the fitness function and novelty–elitism, where the individuals with the highest sparseness are protected from modification. When combining fitness–elitism with novelty search, the fittest individual is carried over to the next generation and serves in the gene pool to possibly spawn novel yet fit individuals thus combining the best of both worlds, process similar to novelty–based multiobjectivization [23]. Going forward, we deploy novelty search with and without fitness–elitism to study the effectiveness of this approach.

3.3 Experimental setup

Each experiment consists of 10 runs with the following fixed settings. The population size is set to 30 individuals and the maximum number of generations per run is set to 1000. Due to the extremely computationally demanding simulations, not all experiments could be carried out using a VoxCad lattice of $10 \times 10 \times 10$, where applicable deviating dimensions are indicated. We use two externally activated materials with non-zero and opposite thermal expansion coefficients, colored Red and Green. The two additional materials represent non-actuated tissue, representing soft tissue (Cyan voxels) with a five times smaller elastic modulus of their material than hard tissue (Blue voxels). For neuroevolution we use the HyperNEAT[2] package; all parameter settings of CPPN-NEAT are the same as detailed in [10].

[2]HyperNEAT `v4.0 C++` by J. Gauci code (url: https://github.com/MisterTea/HyperNEAT)

Details about the experimental setup, source code, and a wiki page on how to reproduce experiments can be found in the project's repository[3].

4. RESULTS

Pure novelty search is compared with respect to the fitness measure (displacement of soft robots in body-lengths) to fitness–based search. Different behavior types are used to investigate the effects on performance of novelty search. In addition we explore the effect of fitness–elitism when combined with novelty search. Lastly, the performance of both methods, novelty and fitness–based search, are investigated for several levels of gravity. Evolved candidate solutions show how environmental conditions can have significant effect on the morphologies and the locomotion strategies of soft robots.

4.1 Behavior selection

Figure 5 illustrates the performance achieved by novelty search for the 10 behavior types. In particular, what is shown is the fitness in body-lengths of the champion of the whole evolution for 10 independent runs for a lattice size 7^3. Both trajectory–type behaviors achieve the best performance with regards to the fitness measure, with a small difference in favor of 2D over 3D trajectories. The rest of the behavior metrics apart from VTG and DFT-VTG are close as far as the final performance of the evolution is concerned. One reason they fail to meet the trajectories' performance is the fact that although they keep track of cues that can describe the performance of the robot (e.g., displacement and speed), they cannot encode the direction of motion. Soft robots that have a circular trajectory can exhibit fast locomotion, in this case though, the measured displacement from their initial position remains low. Counting the number of voxels of a soft robot that touched the ground at every sampling step of the simulation does not hold any information as to how fast the robot is moving. A fast moving robot that

[3]http://tinyurl.com/Soft-Robots-Novelty-Search

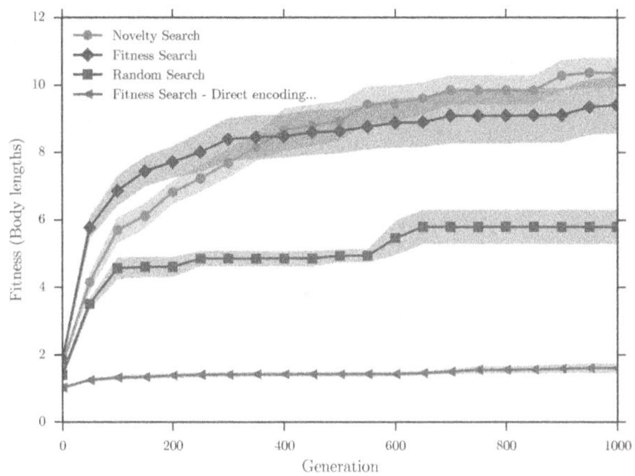

Figure 7: Simple genetic algorithm against novelty-fitness-random search with generative encoding. Best fitness so far averaged over 10 runs.

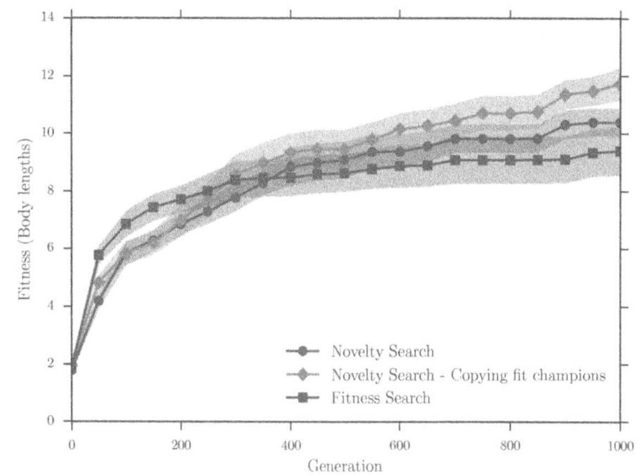

Figure 8: Best fitness so far, novelty search with and without copying *fit* champions (fitness–elitism), and fitness search, averaged over 10 runs.

is hopping can have a similar behavior to a hopping robot that stays in the same position. In contrast, the trajectory behavior of these robots would show a large difference.

4.2 Performance comparison

To compare the performance achieved by novelty search, its performance is set side by side with fitness–based search (normalized body-length displacement of the soft robot's center of mass from its initial position), random search, and finally a simple genetic algorithm[4] with direct encoded genomes. The same experiment held under two different simulation settings (i.e. for lattice size 5^3 and 10^3). Note, that the first three methods are referring to a generative encoding evolved by CPPN-NEAT and using selection with respect to novelty, fitness, and random selection. The last method uses a direct encoded genome driven by fitness within a simple genetic algorithm. Two dimensional trajectories are used by novelty search in order to describe the novelty in the behavior space through the sparseness measure.

Figure 6 presents the results for the small lattice (i.e. 5^3). The average best displacement so far is presented alongside the deviation error. Note, the difference between novelty search and the other methods. Using the two dimensional trajectories of the soft robots, novelty search visits optimal solutions that none other method reaches. Local optima can prevent fitness–based search to achieve the performance of novelty search. Encoding limitations in direct encoding cannot lead to optimal solutions for this settings. In the case of random search, having neither the information about their fitness, nor the driving force of novelty search that seeks for novel behaviors, it fails to evolve any successful locomotion strategy. The only reason random search in CPPN-NEAT achieves a displacement of ~ 5 body-lengths, is the powerful generative encoding. The simple genetic algorithm approach performs better than using random selection with an indirect encoding. Structural regularity and symmetry does not show all of its advantages in this small lattice setting.

For larger lattices, it is expected that generative encoding will prove its merits over the direct encoding scheme [10, 11]. More complicated morphologies can be produced (morphology space for 10^3 lattice resolution: 9.3×10^{698}). Furthermore, the space of behaviors, for instance two dimensional trajectories, becomes larger since more complex soft robots can achieve higher displacement and more advanced strategies for locomotion. These higher resolution morphologies can achieve life–like locomotion. Figure 7 illustrates the performance (i.e. best displacement so far) of the four different methods in these higher resolution settings. Results reassure that novelty search achieves higher fitness (> 1 body-length) on average against fitness–based search. Nevertheless, the effect is not as strong as in the previous experiment. Both methods succeed to evolve the soft robot structure with the highest fitness found in all experiments (~ 14 body-lengths). Novelty search behaves more constant in evolving individuals with high fitness in all runs, on the other hand most of individual runs of fitness–based search are being trapped in low fitness local optima, trying to optimize specific individuals without trying to explore deeply the fitness landscape like novelty search successfully does. The high difference between random evolution and novelty search proves that seeking novel behaviors in novelty search cannot be considered as a random search. The superiority of generative encoding (i.e. CPPN) over direct encoding can be clearly observed. Regularity in shape morphologies provides advantages that result in more efficient motion.

4.3 Fitness–elitism in novelty search

The reason that novelty search is considered such a revolutionary search method is because it finds solutions for deceptive problems, where the fitness landscape is not a straightforward function. At each generation of novelty search, novel behaviors that are also fit with regards to the objective of the problem are discovered. Mutations of these solutions will yield in behaving similarly to their ancestors, resulting in similar behaviors. Thus, the novelty value of these individuals will be declined as similar behaviors will contribute in a denser area in the behavior space. Eventually, these solutions will stop being selected, and evolution will not have the chance of carrying their genes along. Mutations and other genetic operations can optimize these fit individuals

[4]The GAlib C++ library [24] used for the implementation of this method. Source code used from [10].

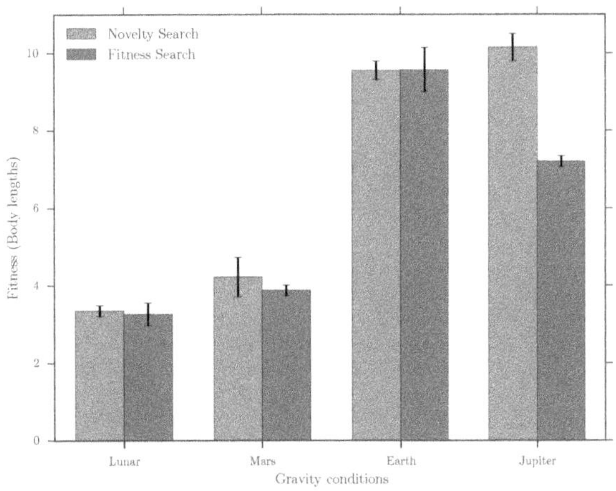

Figure 9: Novelty search performs better or equally good than fitness–based search in all gravity conditions tested.

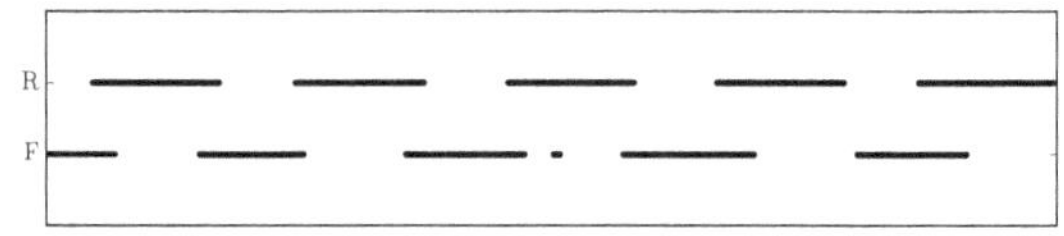

(a) Two-legged soft robot.

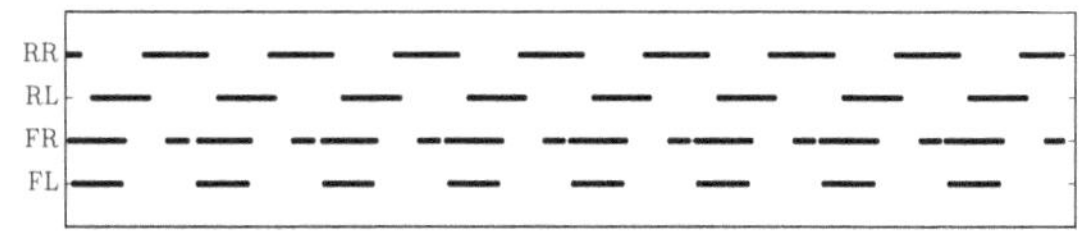

(b) Four-legged soft robot.

Figure 10: Hildebrand diagrams of two evolved soft robots for Earth's gravity acceleration. Timing of impacts between legs and the ground.

more. These individuals (with high fitness values) can be seen as *stepping stones* [16] towards more optimized versions of themselves. Being blind to the objective function, novelty search will eventually stop producing new individuals out of them, which will lead to promising individuals being unable to survive through the evolution process. Figure 8 illustrates the gain in performance when fitness–elitism is used in novelty search method compared with the pure novelty and fitness–based search methods.

5. EVOLVING SOFT ROBOTS FOR SPACE EXPLORATION

Gravity conditions heavily affect the evolution of soft robots in our set-up. The interaction between the robot body and the environment biases the selection towards chromosomes that are able to produce robot bodies that efficiently interact with the terrain at the considered gravity strength. We experiment with both methods discussed, novelty and fitness–based search, presenting some interesting resulted body morphologies and locomotion strategies evolved for specific gravity accelerations using a large lattice size (10^3). For the novelty search method we select the two dimensional trajectories of the soft bodies as the behavior metric defining the novelty of each individual. Due to the computational time demand of the simulations especially in lower gravity accelerations (longer simulation trials are needed to observe the locomotion strategy of hopping soft robots), a lower lattice size is used to approximate the performance of both methods under different gravity strengths. Figure 9 presents the performance of novelty and fitness–based search for four different gravity levels using a lattice size 7^3.

Soft robots on Lunar's gravity

Locomotion strategies evolved under Lunar gravity showed that only hopping gaits can produce effective locomotion. Low gravity makes it challenging for the soft body structures to grip on the ground surface and evolve different strategies than hopping. The morphology of each hopper differs. A C-shaped hopper soft robot (see Fig. 11a) evolved in these settings. Additional experiments showed that lower actuation frequencies for the soft materials contribute in the evolution of stable locomotion strategies, while higher frequencies cannot produce decent motion for the soft bodies.

Soft robots on Mars' gravity

The locomotion effectiveness on Mars is higher when compared to Lunar, the higher gravity acceleration makes it possible for the virtual soft robots to evolve other kind of gaits using legged bodies (see Fig. 11b). Note that the C-shaped hopper soft robot mostly uses passive materials apart from its upper body where all the active material are located. Its upper part alone generates enough motion to hop efficiently. What is observed in the morphologies evolved at lower gravity levels is that the use of a lower number of active voxels can still produce decent locomotion. Apart from hopping strategies, other motion behaviors were observed including legged soft robots.

Soft robots on Earth's gravity

On higher gravity levels familiar locomotion strategies emerge. In Figure 10 we show the Hildebrand diagram for two of the creatures evolved under Earth gravity, where we note characteristics remarkably similar to biped and quadruped locomotion used by animals on Earth. Interesting animal-like gaits are visualized in Fig. 11c. These results suggest an encouraging connection between our set-up and the locomotion strategies of living organisms evolved on Earth for thousands of years. Tumbleweed-like locomotion (see Fig. 11d) has also emerged at this gravity level under novelty search, producing rolling soft robots that can locomote efficiently. Tumbleweed is also a concept of low-cost exploration that has inspired robot designers for Mars' missions in the past [2] and has been already deployed in Antarctica for testing purposes by NASA.

Soft robots on Jupiter's gravity

Moving on to higher gravity levels, i.e. on Jupiter (assuming a stable surface), heavier structures can use galloping as a strategy for their locomotion. Galloping is again consid-

(a) Lunar's gravity: C-shaped hopper (novelty search)

(b) Mars' gravity: 2-legged C-shaped hopper (novelty search)

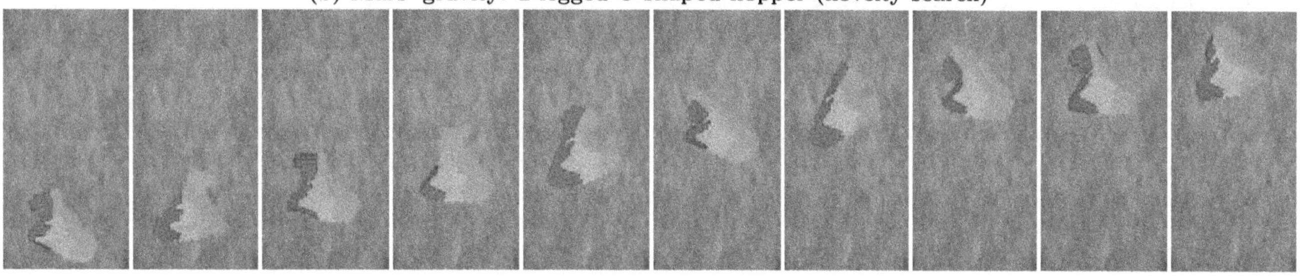

(c) Earth's gravity: *Top view*, 4-legged animal like locomotion (fitness search)

(d) Earth's gravity: Tumbleweed-like locomotion (novelty search)

(e) Jupiter's gravity (Assuming a stable surface): C-shaped hopper (novelty search)

Figure 11: Locomotion strategies evolved in variant gravity conditions.

ered to be an effective way of moving in such a high gravity, whereas thicker legs are evolved to withstand the high gravitational force. Push-pull worm-like locomotion can also produce decent velocities for soft robots. Finally, hoppers have also evolved in this setting (performing short hops), while using more actuated materials (see Fig. 11e) than the hopping soft robots presented earlier for lower gravity accelerations.

6. DISCUSSION AND OUTLOOK

In all our experiments, both novelty search and fitness search evolved soft bodies able to efficiently move in the considered environment. However, the performance with regard to the fitness defined (i.e. displacement of the body in body-lengths) was equal or higher for novelty search in all experiments. One would expect novelty to deliver more diversity, at the cost of a lower fitness function; novelty does not know about fitness and a method well targeted to improve fitness is likely to deliver better results. This was not the case and we found that the creatures evolved with novelty are also able to move faster than the ones that were evolved to move fast. Previous work [19] in a try to evolve walking three dimensional virtual creatures used the evolved morphology of the creatures to describe their behavior. Although, comparing the morphology of the evolved soft robots is similar to comparing the chromosome (CPPN) of each individual. Behaviors that describe the morphology of the evolved robots have failed [19], since search is then forcing new types of morphologies without caring about the actual target of the evolution, which was the efficient locomotion. Therefore, only the comparison of the observed behavior in the phenotype level can lead the evolution towards more complex behaviors.

Some interesting general observations can be made. To start with, low gravity levels seem not to allow for a great variety of gaits. Hopping seems to be the predominant strategy followed by most evolved creatures. Higher gravity levels, instead, allow for more complicated behaviors to emerge and legged locomotion starts to became favorable. At Earth gravity levels, gaits remarkably similar to animal-like motion appear, increasing our confidence in the simulation set-up. Second, the greater variety of creatures evolved using novelty search, allow for rolling tumbleweed-like [2] robots, quadruped and biped robots, hoppers as well as odd creatures to emerge.

Beyond its purely inspirational value, we believe that this methodology, if improved and refined, can be of direct use for the design of soft robotic rovers. Extreme temperature fluctuations, for example on asteroids or comets, could trigger passive actuated materials to perform a designed movement. Although the VoxCad simulator could not be used to simulate the extreme environment of asteroids or comets, it is an interesting idea for further research. The rotation of the celestial body (e.g., with a period as short as a few hours) would then create a cyclic temperature profile having an extreme excursion and thus actuating the soft robot locomotion. This would result, if the soft robot was evolved in such an extreme environment, into a slow crawl of the robot leading to an extremely useful exploratory behavior that could deliver incredible scientific data.

7. CONCLUSIONS

We introduced the use of a diversity seeking method, novelty search, in evolutionary soft robotics. We found that well defined behavior metrics can lead novelty search to outperform traditional fitness–based search. Novelty search not only improved the performance and the diversity in the fitness space, but also contributed to a larger variety of morphologies. Finally, both techniques were used to evolve soft robots in four different gravity levels, showing interesting results and the possibility of influencing future robotic designs for planetary exploration.

8. REFERENCES

[1] Georgios Methenitis. Evolution of Soft Robots by Novelty Search. Master's thesis, University of Amsterdam, The Netherlands, 2014.

[2] Jeffrey Antol, Philip Calhoun, John Flick, Gregory Hajos, Richard Kolacinski, David Minton, Rachel Owens, and Jennifer Parker. Low cost mars surface exploration: the mars tumbleweed. Technical report, 2003.

[3] Tomi Ylikorpi, Aarne Halme, Peter Jakubik, Jussi Suomela, and Mika Vainio. Biologically inspired solutions for robotic surface mobility. In *Proceedings of 8th ESA Workshop on Advanced Space Technologies for Robotics and Automation*, pages 2–4, 2004.

[4] PE Clark, SA Curtis, ML Rilee, and SR Floyd. Ali (autonomous lunar investigator): Revolutionary approach to exploring the moon with addressable reconfigurable technology. In *36th Annual Lunar and Planetary Science Conference*, volume 36, page 1217, 2005.

[5] Evangelos G Papadopoulos, Ioannis Kontolatis, Iosif S Paraskevas, and Leopold Summerer. Ariadna study: Space gaits. Technical report, 2013.

[6] Ioannis Kontolatis, Dimitrios Myrisiotis, Iosif Paraskevas, Evangelos Papadopoulos, Guido de Croon, and Dario Izzo. Quadruped optimum gaits analysis for planetary exploration. In *12th Symposium on Advanced Space Technologies in Robotics and Automation.*

[7] M. Hildebrand. Vertebrate locomotion: An introduction: How does an animal's body move itself along? *BioScience*, 39(11):764–765, 1989.

[8] Karl Sims. Evolving virtual creatures. In *Proceedings of the 21st annual conference on Computer graphics and interactive techniques*, pages 15–22. ACM, 1994.

[9] Jonathan Hiller and Hod Lipson. Automatic design and manufacture of soft robots. *Robotics, IEEE Transactions on*, 28(2):457–466, 2012.

[10] Nick Cheney, Robert MacCurdy, Jeff Clune, and Hod Lipson. Unshackling evolution: evolving soft robots with multiple materials and a powerful generative encoding. In *Proceeding of the fifteenth annual conference on Genetic and evolutionary computation conference*, pages 167–174. ACM, 2013.

[11] Kenneth O Stanley. Compositional pattern producing networks: A novel abstraction of development. *Genetic programming and evolvable machines*, 8(2):131–162, 2007.

[12] Deepak Trivedi, Christopher D Rahn, William M Kier, and Ian D Walker. Soft robotics: Biological inspiration, state of the art, and future research. *Applied Bionics and Biomechanics*, 5(3):99–117, 2008.

[13] Rolf Pfeifer, Max Lungarella, and Fumiya Iida. The challenges ahead for bio-inspired'soft'robotics. *Communications of the ACM*, 55(11):76–87, 2012.

[14] H. Lin, G.G. Leisk, and B.A. Trimmer. Soft robots in space: A perspective for soft robotics. *Acta Futura*, 6:69–79, 2013.

[15] Joel Lehman and Kenneth O Stanley. Exploiting open-endedness to solve problems through the search for novelty. In *ALIFE*, pages 329–336, 2008.

[16] Joel Lehman and Kenneth O Stanley. Abandoning objectives: Evolution through the search for novelty alone. *Evolutionary computation*, 19(2):189–223, 2011.

[17] Joel Lehman and Kenneth O Stanley. Revising the evolutionary computation abstraction: minimal criteria novelty search. In *Proceedings of the 12th annual conference on Genetic and evolutionary computation*, pages 103–110. ACM, 2010.

[18] Sebastian Risi, Sandy D Vanderbleek, Charles E Hughes, and Kenneth O Stanley. How novelty search escapes the deceptive trap of learning to learn. In *Proceedings of the 11th Annual conference on Genetic and evolutionary computation*, pages 153–160. ACM, 2009.

[19] Joel Lehman and Kenneth O Stanley. Evolving a diversity of virtual creatures through novelty search and local competition. In *Proceedings of the 13th annual conference on Genetic and evolutionary computation*, pages 211–218. ACM, 2011.

[20] Michael T Tolley, Robert F Shepherd, Bobak Mosadegh, Kevin C Galloway, Michael Wehner, Michael Karpelson, Robert J Wood, and George M Whitesides. A resilient, untethered soft robot. *Soft Robotics*, 1(3):213–223, 2014.

[21] Jonathan Hiller and Hod Lipson. Dynamic simulation of soft heterogeneous objects. *arXiv preprint arXiv:1212.2845*, 2012.

[22] Kenneth Stanley and Risto Miikkulainen. Evolving neural networks through augmenting topologies. *Evolutionary computation*, 10(2):99–127, 2002.

[23] Jean-Baptiste Mouret. Novelty-based multiobjectivization. In *New Horizons in Evolutionary Robotics*, pages 139–154. Springer, 2011.

[24] Matthew Wall. Galib: A c++ library of genetic algorithm components. *Mechanical Engineering Department, Massachusetts Institute of Technology*, 87:54, 1996.

An Embodied Approach for Evolving Robust Visual Classifiers

Karol Zieba
University of Vermont
Department of Computer Science
Burlington, Vermont 05401
kzieba@uvm.edu

Josh Bongard
University of Vermont
Department of Computer Science
Burlington, Vermont 05401
jbongard@uvm.edu

ABSTRACT

Despite recent demonstrations that deep learning methods can successfully recognize and categorize objects using high dimensional visual input, other recent work has shown that these methods can fail when presented with novel input. However, a robot that is free to interact with objects should be able to reduce spurious differences between objects belonging to the same class through motion and thus reduce the likelihood of overfitting. Here we demonstrate a robot that achieves more robust categorization when it evolves to use proprioceptive sensors and is then trained to rely increasingly on vision, compared to a similar robot that is trained to categorize only with visual sensors. This work thus suggests that embodied methods may help scaffold the eventual achievement of robust visual classification.

Categories and Subject Descriptors

I.2.m.c [**Artificial Intelligence**]: Evolutionary computing and genetic algorithms; I.2.9 [**Computing Methodologies**]: Artificial Intelligence - Robotics

Keywords

Evolutionary Computation; fitness; deception; scaffolding

1. INTRODUCTION

Categorization is an important aspect of intelligence [12], but fundamental disagreement exists as to how an artificial agent should do so, and how biological organisms acquire this ability.

One can partition categorization strategies into non-embodied and embodied approaches. In the non-embodied approach, an agent is presented with some stimuli and must signal which category the perceived object belongs to. In the embodied approach, the robot or organism must interact with its environment to generate useful percepts for categorization [1, 3, 22].

GECCO '15, July 11–15, 2015, Madrid, Spain
© 2015 ACM. ISBN 978-1-4503-3472-3/15/07 ... $15.00
DOI: http://dx.doi.org/10.1145/2739480.2754788

The disagreement about which of these two approaches to categorization is superior stems from the fact that humans are equally adept at both: one can nearly instantaneously visually recognize a friend at a distance or rapidly pick out a desired key from one's pocket just by handling a set of them.

Deep learning methods have recently demonstrated an excellent ability to recognize objects belonging to familiar categories using the non-embodied approach [2, 13]. These methods are able to handle input images with very high dimensionality because they are provided with millions of training images. However, despite these successes, recent work [21, 16] has demonstrated that these methods can fail on images that, from a human observer's perspective, clearly do not contain the object claimed to exist in the image.

Embodied approaches to categorization offer an advantage over non-embodied approaches in that the learner may choose how to manipulate objects such that spurious differences between objects in the same class, including orientation and position, are reduced. In addition, the learner may act to increase the differences between objects belonging to different classes: if edged objects are to be distinguished from round objects, the learner may alter her grasp of an object to confirm the existence (or absence) of an edge. It has even been shown that, given an appropriate morphology, a robot may reduce intra-category differences and increase inter-category differences as a side effect of actions that are not directed towards explicit object manipulation [20].

Evolutionary algorithms have been employed previously to enable a robot to perform this active categorical perception (ACP). Beer [1] reported an agent that achieves ACP simply by moving relative to objects in its environment without touching them, while Tuci [22] and Bongard [3] reported robots that achieved ACP by physically manipulating objects. Furthermore, Bongard [3] demonstrated that evolving robot morphology along with control facilitated the evolution of ACP, presumably because evolution could more readily discover grasping strategies that reduced intra-category differences and exaggerated inter-category differences. However, to date, no evolutionary approaches have show that tactile experiences predispose certain strategies to be robust in novel situations.

Outside of evolutionary robotics, Fitzpatrick *et al.* [10] presented work in which robots learn to visually classify objects based on their physical interactions with them. However, the robots were pre-programmed to explicitly detect correlations between proprioceptive and visual features. Here we describe a similar approach, but do not require that the robot detect similarities between different sensor modalities. Instead, we employ scaffolding to gradually wean a robot off sensors that require physical contact and onto visual sensors that do not.

Scaffolding, a concept brought to robotics from developmental psychology [18], facilitates learning by initially exposing the learner to simpler tasks, and only exposing her to more challenging versions of the tasks gradually. Our use of scaffolding to swap one sensor modality in for another differs from most usages of scaffolding in robotics, in which the robot is exposed to increasingly more challenging task environments [8, 17, 19], or in which the robot's morphology itself scaffolds the acquisition of adaptive behavior [5, 4].

Here, we demonstrate a robot evolved to achieve active categorical perception using action and proprioception, which successfully reduces spurious intra-category differences. During subsequent evolution, these robots are challenged to rely increasingly on vision and allowed to rely less on proprioception, which gradually transitions the robot from ACP to visual classification. We demonstrate that the resulting robots retain the action that reduced intra-category differences and thus exhibit robust visual classification when exposed to novel visual scenes.

The next section describes this method in more detail. Sect. 3 reports our results, and the final section provides some discussion and concluding remarks.

2. METHODS

We first describe the task for our robot. We proceed to describe the robot's body and controller architecture. We then describe the robot's sensor modalities. This is followed by a description of how scaffolding is employed to wean categorizing robots off proprioception and force them to rely increasingly on vision alone. We also elaborate on the various environments the robots were trained in. We conclude this section by describing how we measured the robustness of the evolved robots when forced to categorize in previously unseen environments. All material for replicating the work described here is available at http://git.io/vfYYP

2.1 Task

The robot we are evaluating is tasked with classifying the size of a cylinder within its grasp. Two cylinder sizes are presented to each robot. These cylinders vary in their radius: the larger one's radius is 50% larger than the smaller one. The larger cylinder's radius was 30% of each of the robot's arm segments in length.

2.2 Robot Morphology

The robot's morphology (Figure 1) is planar and is comprised of five body segments connected together with four, one degree-of-freedom hinge joints. The bulk of the robot is comprised of its chassis, which is locked in place for the present study. The two arms are each connected to the chassis at slightly different heights to allow them to slide past each other if their grip flexes sufficiently far inward. Each arm is composed of an upper and lower segment. These segments are attached with a hinge joint that rotates the two arm segments through the horizontal plane, with a range of motion constrained to $[-90^o, +90^o]$. The upper segment is attached to the chassis with a second hinge joint that rotates the entire arm relative to the chassis through the range $[-90^o, +90^o]$. The initial pose of the robot, as shown at the

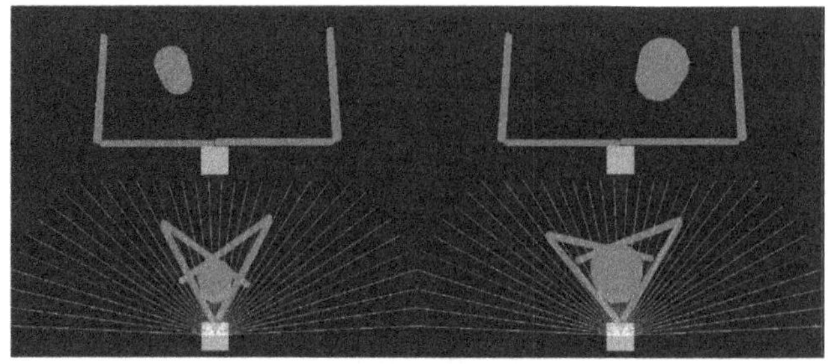

Figure 1: Each of the four frames show the robot under different environments. The top frames depict the start of simulations with a small object and a large object respectively. The bottom frames exhibit the rays the robot uses to see objects after the robot has gripped the objects during its simulation, with the slightly darker ray depicting the center of each eye.

top of Figure 1, is considered to set the four joint angles to default values of $0\,^\circ$.

Each of the four joints are equipped with a motor that applies a torque to the joint proportional to the difference between the joint's current angle and the desired angle output by the robot's controller. The robot is equipped with four proprioceptive sensors, which report the current angle of each joint.

Vision is, in the most fundamental sense, an instantaneous perception of remote objects. For this experiment we chose not to simulate vision, but rather to simulate a simpler set of distance sensors. Distance sensors operate much like visual ones, but instead of detecting variations in colors they detect variations in distance. Furthermore, like vision, distal sensors can be high resolution. Vision here is thus approximated using four sets of 'eyes', which point at -67.5^o, -22.5^o, $+22.5^o$, and $+67.5^o$ relative to the forward facing direction, arbitrarily considered to be 0°.

Each eye is composed of a fan of nine rays equally spaced ($5\,^\circ$) apart. At each time step a cast ray returns a value linearly proportional to the distance between the source of the ray and the first point of collision. A maximum value is returned if the ray is unobstructed. The rays' values are then averaged and normalized to provide four visual inputs to the controller. A visual input value of -1 indicates a large object right in front of the sensor while $+1$ indicates there is no object within range of that eye. A higher resolution of rays was not used due to the linearly increasing computational cost of casting rays.

The following equation shows the setup of each of they vision sensors. The term N is the number of rays. The term R is the length of each of the rays. The subscript o refers to the origin of the ray and the subscript c refers to the point of first collision.

$$\begin{aligned} d_r &= \sqrt{(x_{r,o} - x_{r,c})^2 + (y_{r,o} - y_{r,c})^2 + (z_{r,o} - z_{r,c})^2} \\ v &= \frac{1}{N} \sum_{r=1}^{N} \begin{cases} 2\frac{d_r}{R} - 1 & \text{if ray } r \text{ collides} \\ 1 & \text{otherwise} \end{cases} \end{aligned} \quad (1)$$

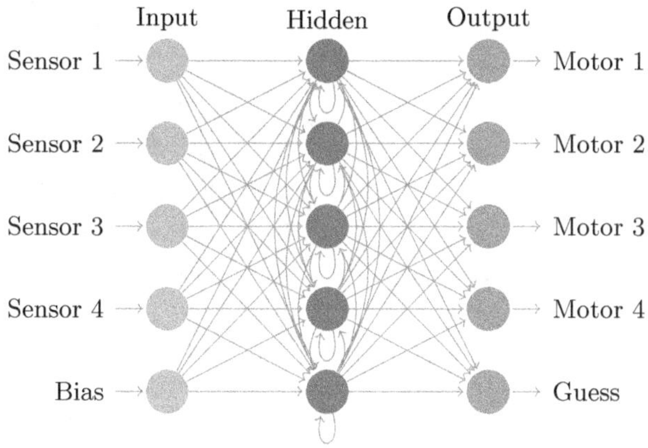

Figure 2: Neural Network of Controller

2.3 Controller

The robot's controller is a synchronous, deterministic, and real-valued neural network. Figure 2 reports its architecture, where each layer is fully connected to the succeeding layer. The middle (hidden) layer is also fully recurrent, obtaining inputs from all five input and five hidden neurons. The output layer's five neurons feed directly from the hidden layer. Four of the five input neurons were designated as sensor inputs. The fifth input neuron was a bias neuron permanently set to the maximum neuron value of one. Four of the five output neurons were used to control the joint motors. The final output neuron is the guess neuron, which was used for object categorization but did not influence the motion of the robot. At each time step the input neurons were encoded with the current sensor values. Each hidden neuron was then updated using:

$$h_i^{(t+1)} = \text{erf}\left(\sum_{j=1}^{5} n_j^{(t+1)} w_{j,i} + \sum_{j=1}^{5} h_j^{(t)} w_{j,i}\right) \quad (2)$$

where n_j and h_j are the jth input and hidden neurons, respectively, $w_{j,i}$ is the synaptic weight connecting neuron j to neuron i, and this weighted sum is normalized to a value in $[-1, +1]$ using the Gauss error function. Synaptic weights were restricted to the range $[-1, +1]$.

The output neurons were updated using:

$$o_i^{(t+1)} = \text{erf}\left(\sum_{j=1}^{5} h_j^{(t+1)} w_{j,i}\right) \quad (3)$$

After the network was updated, the values of the four motor neurons were scaled to values in $[-90^o, +90^o]$ and then translated into torques by the motors, proportional to how far the current angle was from the desired angle.

During the evolutionary runs in which the robot is weaned off proprioception and on to vision, some mixture of proprioception and vision is supplied to the sensor neurons, rather than feeding increasingly less proprioception to four sensor neurons and increasingly more vision to an additional four sensor neurons. In this way evolution does not need to learn to ignore or value sets of weights over the evolutionary run.

2.4 Evolutionary Algorithm

The Covariance Matrix Adaptation Evolution Strategy [11] (CMA-ES) was chosen as the real-valued optimization method. In all evolutionary trials, only the synaptic weights in the robot's controller were evolved. All aspects of the robot's cognitive architecture and morphology remained fixed. CMA-ES evolved 75 synaptic weights, each constrained to $[-1, 1]$. The initial synapses vector was initialized with uniformly random weights in the bounded range. CMA-ES specific parameters included initializing each run with a σ of 0.25 and a default of 16 fitness evaluations per generation. Each evaluation was composed of multiple simulations in which the robot was confronted with different objects placed at different positions. All other unmentioned parameters were kept at the default settings. Since we utilized CMA-ES as a function minimizer, our experiment attempted to minimize the error of the robot's guess as to which class the object currently in front of it belonged to. We shall use the term evolutionary run to refer to the process of evolving (training) our controllers for a given set of environments and sensor modality.

2.5 Environments

The environment of the robots differ primarily through the position and size of the cylinder presented in each simulation. Each robot's controller for a given sensor modality was simulated a specific number of times, which we define as an evaluation. During training the objects were placed as described below and shown in Figure 3 for each 6-simulation evaluation. The horizontal and vertical environments were chosen because they constrained the training data to one dimension. The alternating environment was chosen because it did not place both a large and a small cylinder at the same positions. Additionally, we also investigated how controllers evolved when exposed to fewer (4) and more (8) simulations. The evaluation types include:

Horizontal (H4, H6, H8) The objects were placed across the X axis such that both sizes were tried at each unique position.

Vertical (V4, V6, V8) The objects were placed across the Z axis such that both sizes were tried at each unique position.

Alternating (A4, A6, A8) The objects were placed in a two-object deep rectangle, alternating large and small objects, each object with their own unique position.

Testing The objects were placed on a Cartesian plane over 78 positions for a total of 156 simulations.

2.6 Sensor Modalities and Scaffolding

2.6.1 *Proprioception (P)*

Robots evaluated under this sensor modality only utilized their proprioceptive sensors (joint angles) as inputs to their controller for the entirety of training and testing.

2.6.2 *Vision (V)*

Robots evaluated under this sensor modality only utilized their vision sensors (four eyes composed of distal rays) as inputs to their controller for the entirety of training and testing.

2.6.3 *Scaffolding*

Although scaffolding is a common method employed in robotics [8, 17, 19, 5, 4], we employed it here in a novel way.

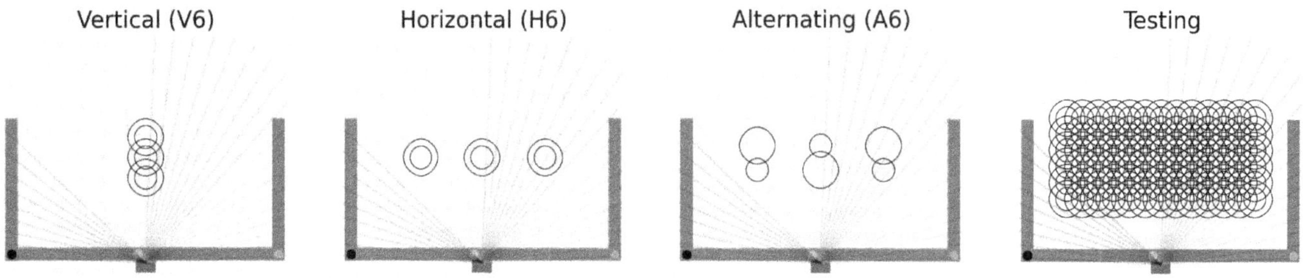

Figure 3: This figure depicts the initial positions for the cylinders under various environments. Additionally, the thick red lines indicate the initial position of the robot's limbs. The filled circles represent the locations of the joints. The circle and ray colors correspond to the ordered pairs of sensors combined during the ontological scaffolding: the teal outer joint on the right arm corresponds to the rightmost eye's rays.

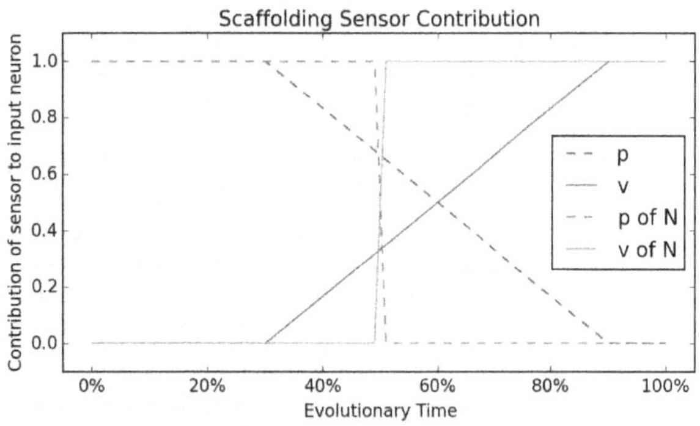

Figure 4: The relative contribution of proprioception (P) and vision (V) to a robot's input over the course of an evolutionary run that is scaffolded. This parameter is then used in each simulation as seen in Figure 5.

During the evolutionary process, the robot is forced to rely progressively less on proprioception and progressively more on vision to perform categorization. Three different types of scaffolds were attempted and reported here. For each scaffolding type, a single parameter linearly descends from one to zero over the course of an evolutionary run and dictates how much proprioceptive input the robot has access to (blue line in Figure 4). A second parameter climbs from zero to one over the course of an evolutionary run and dictates how much visual input the robot has access to (green line in Figure 4). During testing, the controllers evolved using scaffolding were tested identically to the controllers evolved using the Vision (V) sensor modality.

During scaffolded evolutionary runs the robot could rely only on proprioception during the initial 30% of training. The next 60% of training time caused a constant linear decrease in the scaffold. During the final 10% of training, the robot could only rely on vision. Each robot evaluation was provided with a fraction that was zero during the first 10% of training, some value in [0, 1] during the next 60% of training, and one for the last 10% of training. This value was used to tune the three scaffolding schedules described next.

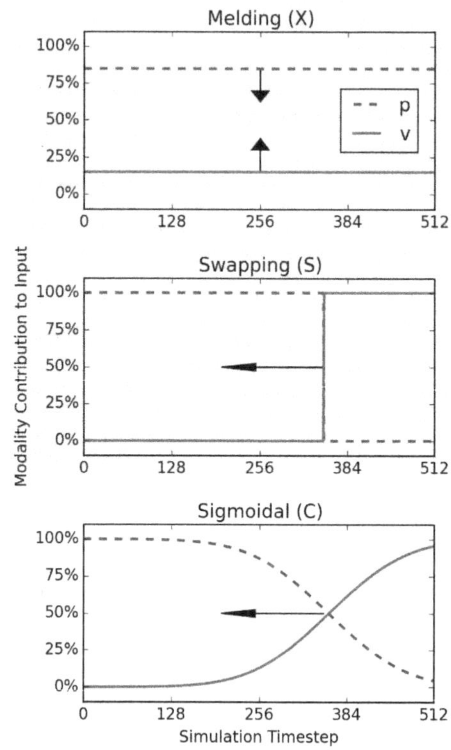

Figure 5: Changes in contribution of proprioception (P) and vision (V) during the evaluation of a single controller. The lines represent ontological scaffolding, or the scaffolding that occurs over one simulation of the robot. The arrows represent how the relative contribution of proprioception and vision change as the evolutionary run proceeds. The movement in the direction of the arrows, as described in Figure 4, represents evolutionary scaffolding.

Melding (X) During the evaluation of an individual robot, the values arriving at the sensor neurons were an admixture of the four proprioceptive and the four visual sensors (Fig. 5a). The proportions of both sensor modalities gradually changed over evolutionary time: robots in the first generation obtained 100% proprioceptive input and 0% visual input, robots halfway through an evolutionary run received roughly 50% proprioceptive input and 50% visual input, and robots in the final generation received 100% visual input.

Swapping (S) Partway through the evaluation of a single robot, its input would switch from proprioception to vision (Fig. 5b). The point at which this swap would occur changed over evolutionary time: robots in the first generation received only proprioceptive input, robots halfway through an evolutionary run received proprioceptive input for the first 256 time steps and visual input for the last 256 time steps, and robots in the last generation received only visual input.

Sigmoidal (C) A sigmoidal smoothing function was used to determine the amount of contribution of vision and proprioception to the input layer during any single time step of the evaluation (Fig. 5c). The shape of this sigmoid was altered over the course of an evolutionary run such that the contribution of proprioception dropped more precipitously—and the amount of visual input increased more precipitously—later during the evolutionary run. Essentially, this scaffold is a combination of the other two scaffolds.

None (N) For the first half of evolutionary time the robot's controller solely received input from its proprioceptive sensors. For the second half of evolutionary time the robot's controller solely received input from its vision sensors.

In the case of the sigmoidal smoothing function the contribution of vision to the value of the input neurons is shown in equation 4. The term g represents the current generation in the evolutionary run out of G generations. The term t represents the time step in the simulation out of T time steps.

$$c_v = \frac{\text{erf}\left[4\left(\frac{g}{G}+2\frac{t}{T}-1\right)-2\right]+1}{2} \tag{4}$$

2.7 Fitness

Each simulation lasted 512 time steps in the Bullet Physics Engine[7]. The final 10% of values of the controller's guess neuron were recorded and used to compute the controller's fitness. The guess neuron's values were compared against the cylinder's class label (-0.5 for small and 0.5 for large) to obtain a difference. This difference is averaged over the time steps to become our error:

$$e = \frac{1}{C}\sum_{c=1}^{C}\frac{1}{T}\sum_{t=0.9T}^{T}|g_{c,t}-r_c| \tag{5}$$

where C represents the number of cylinders placed and T represents the total number of time steps for an evaluation. $g_{c,t}$ denotes the value of the guess neuron when the robot is simulated under environment c and r_c denotes the relative radius of the object in environment c. ($r = -0.5$ for the small object and $r = 0.5$ for the large objects.) In this way an error of zero indicates perfect and stable categorization over the last 5% of the robot's evaluation period. Importantly, the category values were not set to the extrema of the neuron's output range (-1 and +1) because this made the robot's task too easy: instead, it had to hold each guess neuron steady at the correct value for a protracted period of time.

The robot morphology and task were formulated such that there were at least four types of movement that could be used to manipulate objects. The robot could choose to not move objects by extending its joints outward. The robot could open one of its arms while closing the other to slide objects which come into contact with the closing arm away from it. The robot could close its inner joints while keeping its outer joints relatively open, leading to the object becoming trapped in a diamond-like arm pattern. Finally, the robot could fully close both arms, leading to the object becoming trapped in a triangle formed by the arms. (Figure 1) We found that the controller rarely changed its motion strategy partway through a simulation.

2.8 Tests

After evolution, we assessed how robustly a robot could categorize when simulated in novel environments. To do so, we extracted the controller with the lowest training error obtained during the final 10% of the generations from each evolutionary run. This robot was denoted as that run's representative. The representative controllers were then presented with the Testing environment as shown in Fig. 3. In these test evaluations the robots were only allowed to use the visual sensors for categorization. The only exception were those runs in which only proprioception was allowed during training; these robots were allowed to use only proprioception during testing. As during training, testing error was calculated using Equation (5), but averaged over 156 simulations instead of four, six, or eight simulations.

In the next section we investigate the intra- and inter-category distances between objects caused by the robot's movement. The following equations describe these values. In each case I and J represent the number of large and small objects, respectively.

$$D_{\text{intra}} = \frac{2\sum_{i=1}^{I}\sum_{j=i+1}^{I}\sqrt{(x_i-x_j)^2+(z_i-z_j)^2}}{I(I-1)} + \frac{2\sum_{i=1}^{J}\sum_{j=i+1}^{J}\sqrt{(x_i-x_j)^2+(z_i-z_j)^2}}{J(J-1)} \tag{6}$$

$$D_{\text{inter}} = \frac{1}{IJ}\sum_{i=1}^{I}\sum_{j=1}^{J}\sqrt{(x_i-x_j)^2+(z_i-z_j)^2} \tag{7}$$

3. RESULTS

In this section we report on a total of $3 \times 3 \times 6 \times 50 = 2250$ evolutionary runs. We evolved the robot's controllers against every environment: the combination of object position (horizontal, vertical, and alternating) and simulation count (4, 6, 8). Robots had six modalities: just proprioceptive input (P), just visual input (V), or evolved against one of the four scaffolding strategies (N, S, X, C). For each of the 54 combinations of object positioning, simulation count, and scaffolding strategy, we performed 50 evolutionary runs. For robots trained against four, six, and eight objects, they were evolved for 40,000, 60,000, and 80,000 robot simulations, respectively. This provided every evolutionary run with the same number of evaluations.

The average testing errors for the representative controllers is reported in Table 1. A robot whose strategy would be to randomly guess the size of its cylinders would have a test error of 0.5. When we refer to robots as memorizing we mean that their test error is high; these robots have overfitted the training examples and therefore cannot perform well on the generalized test set.

In most cases, the robots trained with vision (column 'V' in Table 1) memorized more than robots trained using one of the scaffolds (columns 'N' through 'C' in Table 1). How-

	P	V	N	X	S	C
A8	0.16**	0.24	0.23	0.21	0.22	0.19*
H8	0.14***	0.23	0.21	0.21	0.24	0.21
V8	0.16***	0.27	0.25	0.25	0.32	0.27
A6	0.21***	0.31	0.27	0.22***	0.27	0.25**
H6	0.20	0.22	0.25	0.22	0.26*	0.21
V6	0.23***	0.41	0.35**	0.30***	0.34***	0.35***
A4	0.36	0.35	0.34	0.37	0.36	0.39
H4	0.20***	0.36	0.26***	0.26***	0.28***	0.24***
V4	0.20***	0.41	0.34*	0.35*	0.34**	0.36*

Table 1: Test errors for 50 runs over the different object counts. positions, and sensor modalities. The asterisks designate p values below 0.05, 0.01, and 0.001 for one through three asterisks respectively. p values were calculated by applying a t-test to the average test errors of vision when compared to other those of the other sensor modalities for each of the environments.

ever, robots trained with proprioception and then tested using proprioception also memorized on occasion: these robots obtained similarly high testing error as the robots trained and tested with vision in environments H6 and A4. This result implies that although the task may seem sufficiently simple that categorization using proprioception always results in robust categorization in unseen environments, there are movement strategies that evolve for which this is not the case. In this case, the P solutions evolved behaviors that would swing the arms asymmetrically, utilizing feedback from the objects' positions to complete the task of deciding their size.

4. DISCUSSION

It was found that many scaffolded robots evolved to rely on proprioception early during an evolutionary run. These ACP-evolved behaviors contributed to contributed to the evolution of subsequent controllers that exhibited robust visual categorization in novel environments. This is indicated by the significantly lower testing error obtained by many of the scaffolding schedules (X, S, and C) compared to the runs in which only vision was available (V). The behavior exhibited by one of these robustly-categorizing robots is illustrated in Figure 1. As can be seen, this robot's evolved behavior of closing its arms together has the effect of moving objects at different positions to the same position directly in front of the robot. This has the result of reducing differences in irrelevant properties of the object; here, such an irrelevant difference is the different positions of the objects.

In contrast, a robot that does not move will generate no difference in sensor signatures during different object placements if it relies on proprioception for categorization, and very different sensor signatures if it relies on vision. Neither bode well for robust categorization in unseen environments. In the former case, the robot will not be able to successfully categorize even under training environments. In the latter case, there is a danger that the robot will memorize the training environments and fail to generalize to any unseen environments. This highlights the importance of motion for active categorical perception and that proprioception is more likely to lead to active behaviors: a blind robot must move and contact objects in order to categorize them.

4.1 Scaffolding success through motion

For the experiment set involving vertical arrangement of six object positions (V6), we obtained some of our most successful results. Since the training set consisted of closely positioned objects, vision-evolved controllers had a natural tendency to memorize with little movement. As shown in Figure 6 both the proprioception and all of the scaffolded runs resulted in significantly more motion during testing. This indicates that when vision favors passive behaviors that do not involve object manipulation, then scaffolding can be a good way to bias search toward movement-based categorization. This movement-bias is retained while the robot transitions to vision, and results in increased robustness of the eventual visual classifier.

One of the primary indicators for whether a controller would generalize was the extent to which it manipulated the object. As shown in Figure 6, the motion induced by the vision-based controllers is significantly lower than any observed in the scaffolded runs. Memorization combined with the lack of motion is the reason that the visual classifier was only able to successfully categorize objects inside the range of its training positions.

The scaffolding process can therefore lead to robust visual classifiers. The efficacy of scaffolding indeed increased as the training set grew increasingly sparse (eight objects are reduced to six and then four in Table 1) and accordingly the amount of computational effort available was increasingly restricted (from 80,000 robot simulations to 60,000 to 40,000).

4.2 Scaffolding success in other cases

We also investigated the effect of scaffolding when the visual classifier's motion was not significantly different from robots that relied on proprioception. This was the case for the A8 training regimen, as shown in Figure 7. However, even in this case, the C scaffolding schedule achieved significantly lower test error than pure vision.

The reason for this is that motion is not a meaningful metric in and of itself. A robot may evolve to move its arms a great deal and push the objects away from it in ways that exaggerate the irrelevant feature of object position.

To distinguish between helpful and unhelpful motion, we can look at intra-category and inter-category distances. Intra-category distance, the average distance between the final position of an object and every other object in its category, would be low for the behavior shown in Figure 1 as the objects would be pulled to about the same location. Since objects are getting pulled close regardless of size, we would expect to see inter-category distance, the average distance between an object and every other object not in its category, to also decrease a similar amount.

Because the radii of the objects are different, we do not expect inter-category distances to be lower than intra-category distances as the centers of the two object sizes would be in marginally different places (25% of the small object's radius) when the objects are flush against the robot's chassis. For unhelpful movement, objects may be pushed away from a swinging arm or not moved at all: both intra-category and inter-category distances should thus remain high. The results in Figure 7 show that the scaffolds that were most successful have intra-category and inter-category differences that are low, like those for proprioception. The unsuccessful scaffold (S) characteristically evolved higher intra-category

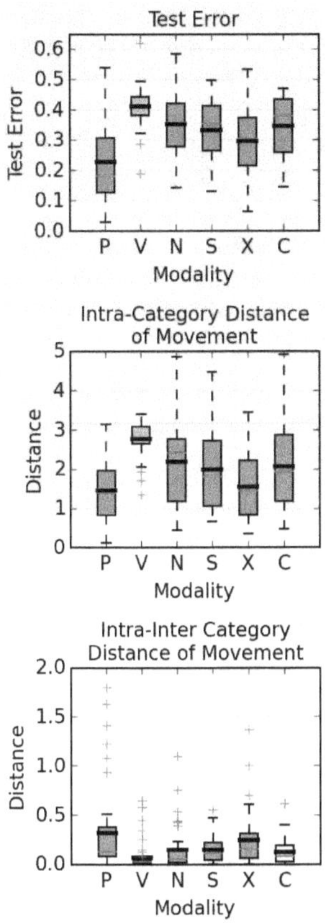

Figure 6: Statistics of V6-trained controllers over 60,000 simulations per run. We define motion as the average euclidean distance between the beginning and ending positions of the objects during testing simulations. The light blue boxplot represents vision. Green boxplots for each subplot are significantly different than vision at a p level of 0.05. The horizontal red lines designate medians and the thick horizontal black lines designate the mean. In the intra and inter-category graphs the horizontal yellow lines designate what the distances would be if the test objects were not perturbed. The boxplot's whiskers represent the 25th and 75th percentiles.

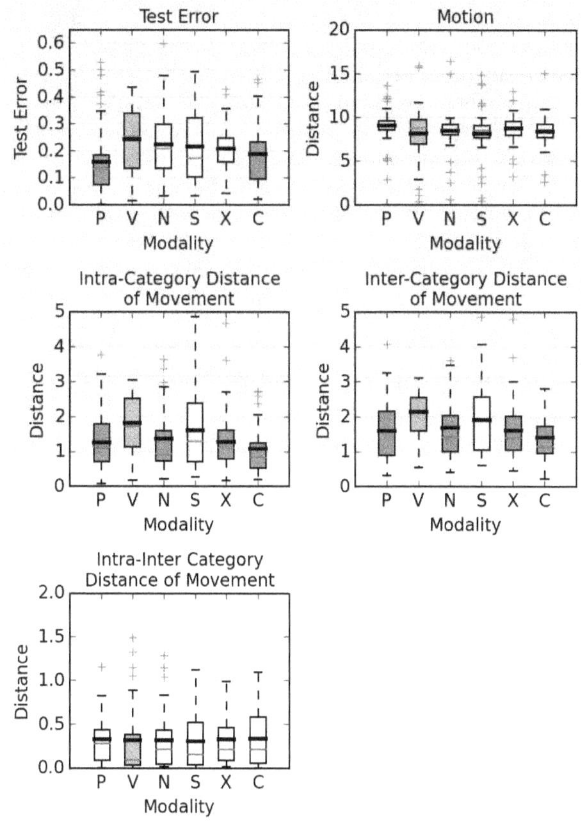

Figure 7: Statistics of A8-trained controllers over 80,000 simulations per run.

and inter-category behavior, which were more in line with the same metrics for the pure vision runs (V).

From this, it seems likely that the best predictor of whether a particular run will produce robust visual classifiers is whether the difference between intra-category and inter-category distances is magnified by motion induced by the robot's limbs. Indeed this is what is observed in the results from the V6 training regimen (Figure 6).

The types of movements that the scaffolds can help instigate is therefore also an important component of whether they lead to robust visual categorization, and the signature of whether motion is helpful is if it reduces the separation between intra-category and inter-category differences.

4.3 Scaffolding Issues

As shown in Table 1, both the vertical and horizontal environments' scaffolds lead to relatively better generalizers as we provide fewer training positions, and therefore less computational power. This highlights vision's inclination towards memorization. In the case of the alternating object positions, a different pattern emerges. In the case of A4, neither proprioception nor any of the scaffolds have significantly different means; proprioception becomes just as much a memorizer as vision. This explains the lack of success of the scaffolds; they do not have a robust categorization strategy from which to begin weaning the robot off proprioception. However, as we add computational power and complexity through A6 and A8, proprioception-based robots memorize less. Even as the environments exhibit greater variation and vision-based controllers memorize, proprioception based controllers resist memorization and are thus still able to be scaffolded. This indicates that even when problems are not constrained to a single dimension of position, there may be success through sensor scaffolding. The underlying pattern for success is whether proprioception can evolve and then pass these successful grasping behaviors to vision. The grasping behaviors that work are the ones that collapse the state space by reducing intra-category and inter-category distances.

When comparing our four scaffolds, none of the scaffolds had a clear and universal advantage over any other. The positive aspect of this is that scaffolding strategies are a manual process that the experiment designer must consider. On the other hand, we still have little insight into the underlying intricacies of applying different scheduling scaffolds.

5. CONCLUSIONS AND FUTURE WORK

Here we have demonstrated how, through action, a robot may be gradually transitioned from active categorical perception to visual classification.

Direct successors to this research revolve around improving the efficacy of scaffolding. We believe that the current method presented in this paper can potentially benefit from further optimizations. These potential investigations include spending more time evolving proprioceptive behaviors and limiting evolution's ability to move away from ACP-evolved grasping behaviors. Another angle of approach would be provide each evolutionary run with a randomized set of initial positions to evolve with. Other future work might include evolving classifiers that utilize both touch and vision concurrently, or a system that learns to map sensors to neural inputs concurrently with the scaling of its neural weights.

The results presented here and previously in [3], when taken together, suggest a pathway for uniting the two sister disciplines of evolutionary robotics and developmental robotics. Work in evolutionary robotics tends to focus on how control and morphology can be gradually shaped by evolutionary pressures to enable successful achievement of a task [6]. In developmental robotics, the focus is often on how an individual robot gradually acquires greater behavioral competency as its sensory and motor systems complexify or become less constrained [15].

If these two approaches were combined in future work, evolution may explore different kinds of developmental transitions from embodied to non-embodied categorization, beyond the four manually-devised transitions we studied here. Evolved transitions that enable a more efficient transition from proprioception to vision during the robot's lifetime would confer an evolutionary advantage on it, thus leading to the evolution of increasingly efficient transitions. This better reflects biological evolution, which evolves developmental trajectories from infant to adult forms, rather than fixed traits. Such a combined evolutionary and developmental approach may discover evolved transitions that are more efficient and effective than the manually-devised developmental transition studied here.

Furthermore, in previous work [3] it was shown that evolving morphology can facilitate the acquisition of active categorical perception in robots. Thus, evolving morphology may further empower evolution to discover useful control, morphology and action combinations that lead to efficient transitions from embodied to non-embodied categorization.

It may also be applicable to other aspects of cognition. For example, it may be possible to automatically evolve embodied language understanding [9] or embodied symbol manipulation [14], and then automatically and gradually transition these competencies to abstract reasoning about language or symbols.

6. REFERENCES

[1] R. D. Beer. The dynamics of active categorical perception in an evolved model agent. *Adaptive Behavior*, 11(4):209–243, 2003.

[2] Y. Bengio. Learning deep architectures for AI. *Foundations and Trends® in Machine Learning*, 2(1):1–127, 2009.

[3] J. Bongard. The utility of evolving simulated robot morphology increases with task complexity for object manipulation. *Artificial Life*, 16(3):201–223, 2010.

[4] J. Bongard. Morphological and environmental scaffolding synergize when evolving robot controllers: artificial life/robotics/evolvable hardware. In *Proceedings of the 13th annual conference on Genetic and Evolutionary Computation*, pages 179–186. ACM, 2011.

[5] J. Bongard. Morphological change in machines accelerates the evolution of robust behavior. *Proceedings of the National Academy of Sciences*, 108(4):1234–1239, 2011.

[6] J. C. Bongard. Evolutionary robotics. *Communications of the ACM*, 56(8):74–83, 2013.

[7] E. Coumans et al. Bullet Physics Library, version 2.82. http://bulletphysics.org, 2014.

[8] M. Dorigo and M. Colombetti. Robot Shaping: Developing Autonomous Agents Through Learning. *Artificial Intelligence*, 71(2):321–370, 1994.

[9] M. H. Fischer and R. A. Zwaan. Embodied language: A review of the role of the motor system in language comprehension. *The Quarterly Journal of Experimental Psychology*, 61(6):825–850, 2008.

[10] P. Fitzpatrick, G. Metta, L. Natale, S. Rao, and G. Sandini. Learning about objects through action: initial steps towards artificial cognition. In *IEEE Intl Conf on Robotics and Automation*, volume 3, pages 3140–3145. IEEE, 2003.

[11] N. Hansen. Cma evolution strategy, 1.1.05. https://www.lri.fr/ hansen/cmaes_inmatlab.html, 2014.

[12] S. Harnad. To cognize is to categorize: Cognition is Categorization. *Handbook of Categorization in Cognitive Science*, pages 20–45, 2005.

[13] G. E. Hinton. Learning multiple layers of representation. *Trends in Cognitive Sciences*, 11(10):428–434, 2007.

[14] G. Lakoff and R. E. Núñez. *Where mathematics comes from: How the embodied mind brings mathematics into being*. Basic Books, 2000.

[15] M. Lungarella, G. Metta, R. Pfeifer, and G. Sandini. Developmental robotics: a survey. *Connection Science*, 15(4):151–190, 2003.

[16] A. Nguyen, J. Yosinski, and J. Clune. Deep neural networks are easily fooled: High confidence predictions for unrecognizable images. *IEEE CVPR*, 2015.

[17] S. Perkins and G. Hayes. *Robot shaping: Principles, methods and architectures*. 1996.

[18] J. Plumert and P. Nichols-Whitehead. Parental scaffolding of young children. *Developmental Psychology*, 32(3):523–32, 1996.

[19] L. M. Saksida, S. M. Raymond, and D. S. Touretzky. Shaping robot behavior using principles from instrumental conditioning. *Robotics and Autonomous Systems*, 22(3):231–249, 1997.

[20] C. Scheier and R. Pfeifer. Classification as sensory-motor coordination. In *Advances in Artificial Life*, pages 657–667. Springer, 1995.

[21] C. Szegedy, W. Zaremba, I. Sutskever, J. Bruna, D. Erhan, I. Goodfellow, and R. Fergus. Intriguing properties of neural networks. *International Conference on Learning Representations*, 2014.

[22] E. Tuci, G. Massera, and S. Nolfi. Active categorical perception of object shapes in a simulated anthropomorphic robotic arm. *IEEE Transactions on Evolutionary Computation*, 14(6):885–899, 2010.

An Analysis of Integration of Hill Climbing in Crossover and Mutation operation for EEG Signal Classification

Arpit Bhardwaj
Indian Institute of Technology Indore
Indore, India
phd12110102@iiti.ac.in

Aruna Tiwari
Indian Institute of Technology Indore
Indore, India
artiwari@iiti.ac.in

M.Vishaal Varma
Indian Institute of Technology Indore
Indore, India
cs1100121@iiti.ac.in

M.Ramesh Krishna
Indian Institute of Technology Indore
Indore, India
ee1100220@iiti.ac.in

ABSTRACT

A common problem in the diagnosis of epilepsy is the volatile and unpredictable nature of the epileptic seizures. Hence, it is essential to develop Automatic seizure detection methods. Genetic programming (GP) has a potential for accurately predicting a seizure in an EEG signal. However, the destructive nature of crossover operator in GP decreases the accuracy of predicting the onset of a seizure. Designing constructive crossover and mutation operators (CCM) and integrating local hill climbing search technique with the GP have been put forward as solutions. In this paper, we proposed a hybrid crossover and mutation operator, which uses both the standard GP and CCM-GP, to choose high performing individuals in the least possible time. To demonstrate our approach, we tested it on a benchmark EEG signal dataset. We also compared and analyzed the proposed hybrid crossover and mutation operation with the other state of art GP methods in terms of accuracy and training time. Our method has shown remarkable classification results. These results affirm the potential use of our method for accurately predicting epileptic seizures in an EEG signal and hint on the possibility of building a real time automatic seizure detection system.

CCS Concepts

•Computing methodologies → Genetic programming; *Continuous space search;*

Keywords

Genetic Programming; Epilepsy; Crossover; Mutation; Fitness Function; Hill Climbing Search

GECCO '15, July 11 - 15, 2015, Madrid, Spain

DOI: http://dx.doi.org/10.1145/2739480.2754710

1. INTRODUCTION

One of the most studied problem in machine learning is the Multi class classification [1]. It involves predicting the value of a categorical attribute based on the values of other attributes. Evolutionary algorithms (EA) are a class of computational techniques inspired by the Darwin's theory of natural evolution to solve the real life complex problems [2,3]. Genetic Programming (GP) [4] is an evolutionary learning methodology that offers a great potential for classification. GP is essentially considered to be a variant of genetic algorithms (GA) [4] that uses a complex representation language to codify individuals. GP is a very flexible heuristic technique that makes it very convenient to represent complex patterns in the form of trees and graphs, therefore working with various operations and functions become easier. Since GP is a search and optimization algorithm, it can be easily employed as a search algorithm for generating a classifier. The goal of GP is the evolution of computer programs [5]. A population of computer programs, which are feasible solutions to a given optimization problem are evolved by means of Darwinian principle of survival of fittest. A set of biologically inspired operations such as reproduction, crossover and mutation are used in evolving these computer programs. Reproduction [4], which replicates the principle of natural selection, selects and copies the best individuals to the next generation. In mutation, a node or a subtree of a chosen individual is supplanted by a randomly generated node or a subtree. Mutation is helpful in bringing diversity among individuals. Crossover combines two individuals to produce a new individual (offspring). The idea behind crossover is that the newly generated offspring might be better than both of the parents if it acquires required characteristics from each of the parent individuals. These operations are undergone in evolution by a user-defined probability for each operations.

The Crossover and Mutation operations could be sometimes devastating in nature [6], as the totally arbitrary choice in crossover and mutation couldn't guarantee the best choice, which ultimately results in decrease in classification accuracy. These operations are responsible for destroying good subprograms in evolved programs during the later stage of evolution. So, there is a need to find a better way to perform crossover and mutation operations in GP. Including

Hill Climbing search [7], a simple heuristic search method, with crossover and mutation operation could produce better individuals and improves classification accuracy. In Hill Climbing, a random solution is generated, and this process is iterated until a better solution is found. In this paper, we focus on integrating the Hill Climbing technique in crossover and mutation operator to the EEG signal classification, by proposing a novel Hybrid crossover and mutation operator, and analyze its improvements in terms of classification accuracy and computational time.

The most important application of EEG signal classification is the detection of Epileptic seizures in human brain [8]. The Human brain is the most complex and magnificent organ in the human body, and as a matter of fact, it is so complicated that it remains an exhilarating frontier. In short, the brain serves as the seat of human consciousness and dictates the behaviors that enables us to survive [9]. Electroencephalography [10] is the measurement of the continuous brain-wave patterns, or electrical activity of the brain and the chronicler of disorders of the nervous system. An EEG [11] is a recording of electrical signals from the brain with the placement of small metal discs called electrodes positioned on the human scalp. The changes and voltages in these electric signals are measured in terms of voltage fluctuations of brain. In recent years, EEG techniques are growing popular among researchers for the investigation of epileptic seizures in particular. These techniques may prove as quintessential tools when used in conjunction with more prevalent neuropsycological tests.

Epilepsy [12] is a critical neurological brain disorder originating from temporary abnormal discharges of the brain electrical activity, leading to uncontrollable movements and tremblings. It is a neurological condition in which an individual experiences prolonged abnormal bursts of electrical discharges in the brain and is characterized by unexpected recurrent seizures. A detailed analysis of the EEG records could provide a valuable insight in predicting seizures. Until now, the exact cause of epilepsy in individuals is unknown and the mechanisms that involved behind the seizures are little understood. Thus, efforts towards its diagnosis and treatment are of significant importance. Developing automatic seizure detection methods [13] is of great significance and can serve as first-rate clinical tools for the scrutiny of EEG data in a more unprejudiced and computationally coherent manner, since visual inspection for discriminating EEG signals is time consuming, imprecise and high costly, especially in the case of long-term recordings.

The classification of EEG signals into seizure and non-seizure using Genetic Programming is prominent in developing real time seizure detection systems, as we can attain high classification accuracies using GP. Integration of Hill Climbing in the crossover and mutation operation makes it feasible to achieve such high classification accuracies. In the previous paper [14], we proposed Constructive Crossover and Mutation Operator for Genetic Programming, which integrates the hill climbing with crossover and mutation operation. In this paper we propose a new Hybrid Crossover and Mutation operation and compare with the existing methods of GP in classifying the EEG signals.

The remainder of this paper is organized as follows: Section 2 overviews the essential background of the approach. It describes about the Empirical Mode Decomposition, Life Cycle of GP and Related work. Section 3 describes the proposed work, section 5 presents and analyses the experimental results and finally Section 6 draws conclusion and future work directions.

2. BACKGROUND

This section describes the essential background for this approach, which includes the Empirical Decomposition for Feature extraction, life cycle of Genetic Programming, the standard crossover and Mutation operation, the constructive crossover and mutation operation and also details the related work.

An epileptic seizure can be fore casted by classifying the incoming EEG signal into seizure and non-seizure. The below mentioned is the chronological approximation of the ongoing implementation done for building a real time Epileptic Seizures detection system.

- Extraction of Brain signal Input.
- Pre-Processing the extracted EEG signals using Empirical Mode Decomposition.
- Classification of EEG signals using Genetic Programming.
- Build a Real Time Epileptic Seizure Detection System.

2.1 Empirical Mode decomposition

The feature extraction process is carried out using Empirical Mode Decomposition. The method Empirical Mode Decomposition (EMD) was initially proposed by Huang et al [15] which instructs to decompose a non linearly stationary signal into a superposition of natural modes, each of which could be easily analyzed for their instantaneous frequencies and bandwidths. Bajaj et al [16] proposed the use of Empirical mode decomposition to extract the features to classify the EEG signal.

EMD is a method of breaking down a signal without leaving the time domain introduced for analysis of nonlinear and non- stationary signals. EMD decomposes any given data into intrinsic mode functions (IMF) [15] that are not set analytically and are rather determined by an analyzed sequence alone, each successive IMF contains lower frequency oscillations than the preceding one. On completion of this process, it would generate a set of bandwidth parameters which are attributed as features for the Genetic Programming (GP) classifier. A typical implementation of EMD for decomposition of an EEG signal involves the following steps:

- Calculation of IMF for each iteration using EMD on EEG signals.
- Apply Hilbert transform on the calculated IMF's during each iteration.
- Generation of a Bandwidth parameters viz. Frequency parameter and the Amplitude parameter as the features for the classifier from the Hilbert Transform.

These Bandwidth parameters constitute the input parameters for the Genetic Programming classifier. During the feature extraction, we select five IMF's from each EEG signal and remove the residue. In sum, a total of 10 features from each EEG signal (two from each IMF's) are extracted and chosen as input to the GP classifier.

2.2 Life Cycle of Genetic Programming

GP evolves a population of computer programs, which are feasible solutions to a given optimization problem, using the Darwinian principle of survival of the fittest. It works on a principle, for instance, if there exists several entities in a nature, the fitter entities survive and evolve at a higher rate; less fitter individuals survive, if at all at a lower rate. It is an extension of the Genetic Algorithms and was substantiated, endorsed and developed into a practical tool by John Koza [4] amongst a whole range of possible evolutionary algorithms. GP is a very flexible heuristic technique that makes it very convenient to represent complex patterns in the form of trees and graphs, therefore working with various operations and functions becomes easier. Each individual in the population is represented as a tree with functions and terminals pertinent to a given problem. The evolutionary GP life cycle is detailed as follows:

1. Generate the initial random population.
2. Evaluate the fitness measure of each individuals using training data.
3. Evolve the individuals to get a new generation using reproduction, crossover and mutation.
4. Terminate the GP process on finding a best individual, or else go to step 2 and repeat the process

2.3 Crossover and Mutation Operation

2.3.1 *Standard Crossover*

In standard crossover operation [17], two parent individuals are selected from the population for the crossover operation. A crossover point is then randomly selected in each of the two parents, then the subtrees below the crossover points are exchanged and two new child individuals are spawned. The two new generated children are then transferred to the next generation.

2.3.2 *Standard Mutation*

In standard Mutation, an individual is selected from the population and a node or subtree is randomly chosen and replaced with a randomly generated node or subtree.

2.3.3 *Constructive Crossover*

In constructive crossover [14], a local hill climbing is integrated with the crossover operation. Here individuals are split into N_r and N_c for reproduction and crossover respectively. Initially, the N_r individuals undergo reproduction. After the reproduction, the remaining N_c individuals undergo constructive crossover, where individuals are made into pairs and are subjected to perform the crossover operation. The generated offspring from selected couples are compared with the parents in terms of fitness. While comparing, if it is known that the offspring are better than their parents in terms of fitness, they are accepted. Otherwise they are rejected and the process is repeated till we get two individuals better than parent. In this manner, the local hill climbing method is integrated with the crossover operation and is repeated for all N_c individuals and generated offspring are placed in Crossover Offspring Table (COT). A COT is a table in which we store the offspring generated from the crossover operations in such a way that the offspring having the highest fitness remain in the first row, the second highest fitness offspring in second row and so on. The top $N_c r$ offspring in terms of fitness, the globally prime offspring, are present on the top $N_c r$ positions in the Crossover Offspring Table (COT) and the remaining lower level offspring in COT are deleted. The remaining N_m individuals are selected for mutation operation.

2.3.4 *Constructive Mutation*

In the constructive mutation [14], the individuals, left after reproduction and crossover operations are chosen to generate better offspring while compared to their parents by applying hill climbing search. We randomly choose a subtree in a parent and replace it with a newly generated subtree and repeat this process till we get better offspring than parent.The benefit of employing this constructive mutation technique is that the destructive nature of mutation operation is reduced by transferring the better individuals than parents to next generation and also the constructive mutation provide a wider exploration of the search space, help in not sticking in local optima. The individuals, who are not good at producing better offspring than parents during crossover are altered in this constructive subtree mutation operation.

The aim of the constructive crossover and mutation operation is to find children with better fitness and improve the classification accuracy.

2.4 Related Work

Till now, a numerous methods have been proposed to classify an EEG signal into seizure and non-seizures in order to prognosticate epileptic seizures. Panda et al [18] produced different features, such as energy, entropy and standard deviation from wavelet transformation to classify epileptic EEG signals using support vector machine (SVM). Liang et al [19] used combination of complexity analysis and spectrum analysis and entropy features. Ocak [20] proposed fourth-level wavelet packet decomposition for several frequency bands to differentiate normal and epileptic EEG signals. A wide range of feature extraction methods are proposed which are used in conjunction with a very renowned classification technique Artificial neural network (ANN), to detect the epileptic seizures [21–25]. More recently, a new technique for classification was proposed which used Empirical Mode Decomposition and LS-SVM to differentiate between seizure and non-seizure EEG signals [16]. Here, the features are extracted by decomposing the EEG signal into a set of IMF's and then are fed into LS-SVM classifier. However, Recently, evolutionary algorithms have been emerged as a promising technique for classification of medical data [26]. Genetic Programming, developed by John Koza [4] could be used for the EEG signal classification. Castelli et al. [27] introduced a new GP system that uses the concept of semantics to improve search effectiveness. Arpit et al. [14] presented the concept of Constructive Crossover and Mutation, where a local hill climbing search was integrated with the crossover and mutation operation to improve classification accuracy. However, this method does not guarantee the best solution.

The goal of this paper is to propose a hybrid crossover and mutation operator, which finds the best children generated from the parent and reduce the computational time to reach the desired accuracy. In this paper, we compare and analyze the proposed hybrid crossover and mutation operation, which uses both standard crossover and local hill climbing crossover operation.

3. PROPOSED WORK

Here, we propose to investigate the variations in the standard GP process and Constructive Crossover and Mutation GP [14] process and its applications in the epileptic seizure detection. In the proposed Hybrid Crossover and Mutatation Genetic Programming (HCM-GP) method, we eliminate the randomness of crossover operation and reduce the computational time by introducing a novel hybrid crossover operator. We bring in diversity among individuals by introducing hybrid mutation operator. The flow chart of the proposed HCM-GP method is shown in the Fig 1

3.1 Hybrid Crossover Operation

The proposed Hybrid Crossover could be regarded as the blend of standard crossover and the constructive crossover operation. In the constructive crossover, a local hill climbing technique is integrated with the crossover to improve the classifier. But introduction of constructive crossover leads to decrease in the computational speed, as a great deal of time is spent in selection of better offspring. In order to significantly reduce the computational time, we introduced the hybrid crossover operation.

In our proposed method, we select the best fitness N_r individuals from the total population for *reproduction*, the next N_c individuals for the crossover and the remaining N_m individuals for the mutation. Among the N_c individuals for the crossover, individuals are randomly chosen between standard crossover and local hill climbing crossover. The split up of individuals into 50-50 between hill climbing and standard crossover has shown promising results while experimenting the proposed crossover operation. Individuals selected for the local hill climbing crossover are made into pairs and are subjected to perform the crossover operation to generate offspring. Here, the generated offspring is calculated for its fitness measure and is compared with its parents. If the parents have higher fitness value than the offspring, crossover is again repeated on the offspring. Else the offspring are transfered to the next generation. Here, we limit the number of crossover iterations to 20 [28] in order to avoid infinite loops, particularly when we are unable to generate a better offspring. The local hill climbing crossover is similar to the constructive crossover. The remaining individuals perform the standard crossover operation and generate their offspring to maintain the diversity. Hence, we ensure that the classifiers with higher fitness are transferred to the next generation, while maintaining the diversity among the population. The proposed hybrid crossover, which is categorized as a blend of hill climbing and standard crossover is better than the standard crossover, because it applies global elitism to some extent, by selecting the best individuals from a set of combinations, while simultaneously bringing the diversity among those individuals. The hybrid crossover is better than the constructive crossover because it does not take large amounts of computational time unlike constructive crossover.

3.2 Hybrid Mutation Operation

In the proposed hybrid mutation operator, we apply a hill climbing search on the N_m individuals, left after reproduction and crossover operations to generate better offspring while compared to their parents. In the constructive mutation operation, the low performing individuals in the crossover are brought to the mutation, where as in the hybrid mutation, we assign a fixed number of N_m individuals to the mutation operation after the fitness evaluation ie., prior to the crossover operation. Here, a random subtree was replaced with a newly generated random subtree. This process is repeated till we reach an individual with better fitness value. The benefit of employing this hybrid mutation technique is that the destructive nature of mutation operation is eliminated by transferring the better individuals to next generation. Moreover, This hybrid mutation technique doesn't make the searching of the solution to stuck in local optima. And the other advantage is about the selection, where the parents of mutation are chosen subsequent to the crossover and reproduction operation, as a result providing a scope for the low fitness offspring to survive in the evolutionary world.

Algorithm 1 Algorithm for Hybrid Crossover

Begin
Generate initial classifier population (k).
Randomly select fixed percentages of the initial population for crossover crossover (P_c), mutation (P_m) and reproduction (P_r).
Select N_c individuals, based on fitness measure, after the reproduction.
Split the N_c individuals into two groups randomly.
On one half, apply Hill Climbing
for all Selected half of the Individuals **do**
    Take the parent pair and generate two better offspring from them by applying hill climbing search.
    Place the top offspring (includes the parents if they have a superior fitness after 20 attempts).
end for
On the other half, apply Standard crossover
for all Selected half of the Individuals for standard crossover **do**
    Take the parent pair and generate offspring from using standard crossover.
end for
The resulting N_c offspring will advance to the next generation.

Algorithm 2 Algorithm for Hybrid Mutation

Generate initial classifier population (k).
Take the individual (N_m) which are left after reproduction and crossover operations.
for all mutation individual (N_m) **do**
    Apply Hill Climbing method, that is take the parent and generate child from them till we get better child than parent by replacing a subtree with a newly generated subtree.
end for
Transfer the individuals to the next generation.

All in all, the introduction of these variations in the GP life cycle is essential for the EEG signal classification, as it greatly reduces the computational time. Hence, the proposed hybrid crossover and mutation can be employed as an auxiliary tool for the neurologists to determine onsets

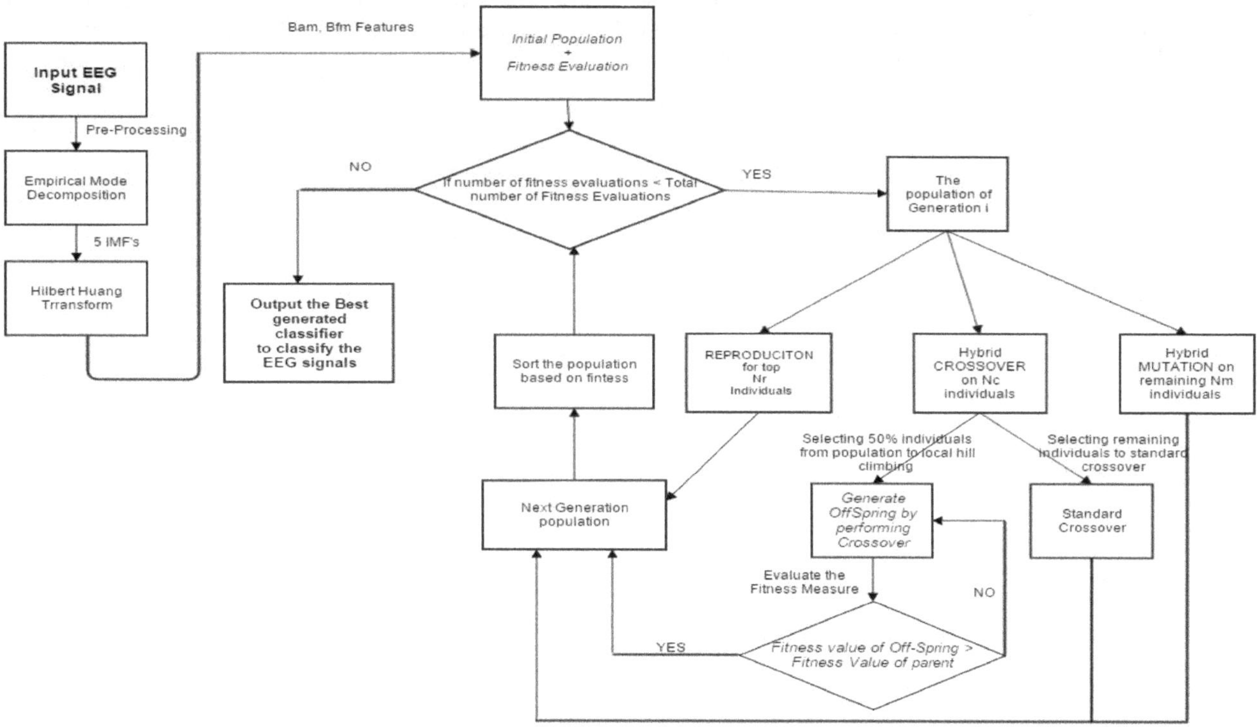

Figure 1: Flow Chart of the proposed Hybrid Crossover and Mutation GP

of seizures in analyzing 24 hr EEG recordings. In the next section, we demonstrate the results of the hybrid crossover and mutation operation and analyze the integration of hill climbing in the existing and proposed methods.

4. RESULTS AND DISCUSSIONS

This section presents the experimental results of the proposed Hybrid Crossover and Mutation. We analyze the effect of integration of local hill climbing in crossover and mutation by comparing the HCM-GP method with the existing ST-GP and CCM-GP methods.

4.1 Dataset Description

An EEG dataset, which is available on-line [29] was used for training, testing and evaluation of our method. In this dataset, the signals were recorded with a *128-channel* amplifier system as an average common reference. The analog data were digitized at 173.61 samples per second by a 12 bit A/D resolution with band-pass filter settings of 0.53-40 Hz (12 dB/oct). The dataset comprises of five different sets (denoted Z, O,N, F and S), each containing 100 signal channel EEG segments of 23.6 sec. duration. These signals were carefully chosen and cut out from continuous multi-channel EEG recordings after removing artifacts caused due to eye and muscle moments and power line interference. EEG signals in sets O and Z have been recorded from healthy volunteers through external surface electrodes using the standardized 10-20 electrode placement scheme. The volunteers were relaxed in an awake state with eyes open (set Z) and closed (set O). Sets F and N are obtained in seizure free intervals. Set F acquired from epileptogenic zone of the brain shows focal interictal activity; set N extracted from hippocampal formation of the opposite hemisphere of the brain hints the non-focal interictal activity, and set S were obtained from within the epileptic zone of a seizure activity. On an overall, Sets N, F and S originated from an EEG register of presurgical diagnosis. Sets Z and O are portrayed as Normal, sets N and F as interictal and Set S corresponds to an ictal State (Seizure). Here, The sets Z, O, N and F are combined and called as **Non-Seizure**, while the set S as **Seizure**. The goal of this experiment is to classify between seizure and non-seizure.

4.2 Performance Measures

The existing and proposed methods are evaluated by computing statistical parameters sensitivity, specificity and accuracy. Moreover, we also used Confusion matrix and ROC Curve for comparing the methods.The definitions of these performance measures are as follows:

1. **Accuracy:** Accuracy is the measure of the ability of the classifier to accurately classify the patterns.

$$Accuracy = \frac{TP + TN}{TP + TN + FP + FN} \times 100 \quad (1)$$

2. **Sensitivity:** Sensitivity is the fraction of correctly detected positive patterns to the total number of actual positive patterns.

Table 1: Confusion matrix

	Predicted Positive	Predicted Negative
Actual Positive	True Positive (TP)	False Negative (FN)
Actual Negative	False Positive (FP)	True Negative (TN)

$$Sensitivity = \frac{TP}{TP + FN} \times 100 \quad (2)$$

3. **Specificity:** Specificity is the fraction of correctly detected negative patterns to the total number of actual negative patterns.

$$Specificity = \frac{TN}{TN + FP} \times 100 \quad (3)$$

4. **Time required**: It is the time required to find the best individual.

5. **Confusion matrix**: Confusion matrix consists of information about actual and predicted classifications performed by a classifier. A confusion matrix used for our classifier, generally for two class problems is shown in Table 1.

6. **ROC curve** [30] is a fundamental diagnostic test evaluation and an excellent way to compare the performance of diagnostic tests. It is a two dimensional measure for the performance of classification and gives a complete sensitivity/specificity report. It also play an important role in comparing our test to the perfect test. ROC curve is plotted with *1-specificity* on the x-axis to *Sensitivity* on the y-axis.

4.3 Experimental Results

An important aspect underlying the HCM-GP method is that, it could be successfully modified to automatically detect highly suspicious seizure activities in brain through real time detection. In order to evaluate the performance of the methods, the dataset was divided into training and testing in several combinations namely 50-50, 60-40, 70-30 and 10-fold cross validation. Table 2 shows the partition into training and testing dataset for the classification into non-seizure and seizure (ZONF-S).

Table 2: Training and Testing dataset for the classification of EEG signals into Seizure and Non Seizure (ZONF-S)

Training-Testing Partition (%)	No. of samples in the set: Training Samples	ZONF	S	Testing Samples	ZONF	S
50-50	250	200	50	250	200	50
60-40	300	240	60	200	160	40
70-30	350	280	70	150	120	30
10-fold Cross Validation	450	360	90	50	40	10

Since, we are interested in investigating the integration of local hill climbing in GP life cycle, we analyzed the HCM-GP with Standard GP [4] and CCM-GP method [14], in terms of statistical parameters. The confusion matrix for the methods using various training-testing partitions are given in table 3.

Table 3: Confusion matrices for classifiers used for classification of EEG signals into Seizure and Non Seizure for different training-testing data

Classifier		50-50 ZONF	50-50 S	60-40 ZONF	60-40 S	70-30 ZONF	70-30 S	10 fold cross validation ZONF	10 fold cross validation S
ST-GP	ZONF	188	12	148	12	114	6	38	2
	S	8	32	3	37	3	27	2	8
CCM-GP	ZONF	196	4	156	4	118	2	39	1
	S	4	46	3	37	3	27	1	9
HCM-GP	ZONF	198	2	158	2	119	1	39	1
	S	1	49	1	39	1	29	0	10

(Column groups: Validation Techniques (Testing data).)

Table 4: Comparison of HGP method with ST-GP and CCM-GP in terms of Performance measures

Method	Validation Technique	Sensitivity Min	Sensitivity Max	Specificity Min	Specificity Max	Accuracy Min	Accuracy Max	Time Required Min	Time Required Max
ST-GP	50-50	93.5	94.5	83.45	84.45	91.5	93	7.6	8.21
	60-40	92	94.5	92	94	92	94.5	8.09	9.10
	70-30	93.65	95.85	81	83	91.5	94.5	8.56	9.95
	10 fold cross validation	94	95.5	80	82	92	94.5	9.42	10.45
CCM-GP	50-50	95.5	98.65	90	93	95.5	97.5	5.50	6.26
	60-40	97	98.4	91.6	93.5	96	97.5	6.1	6.45
	70-30	97.85	99.5	89.5	92	96.65	97.75	6.95	7.45
	10 fold cross validation	97	98.5	90.5	92.5	96	97.5	7.65	8.13
HCM-GP	50-50	98.5	99.5	98.6	99.35	98.85	99.5	2.35	2.59
	60-40	98.875	99.45	98.5	98.85	98.75	99.65	3.12	3.48
	70-30	99.10	99.75	98.24	99.05	98.65	99.68	3.30	3.59
	10 fold cross validation	98.85	99.25	99.5	100	99.5	100	4.10	5.10

(Column groups: Performance Measures.)

The sensitivity, specificity and accuracy and training time of the methods are quantified, noted and are shown in Table 4.

We also plotted the ROC curve using the above results. Fig 2 shows the ROC curve and area under the ROC curve for 50-50 training-testing data.

The above results demonstrate that our proposed method has achieved better classification accuracy than the other methods. It is also clear from the result, that our method requires lesser amount of time to reach the desired accuracy.

The high classification accuracy of our HCM-GP method compared to the other GP methods and consequentially we can affirm that this outweighs the standard GP and CCM-GP methods and we suggest that it can be used as a diagnostic decision support mechanism in the treatment of epilepsy patients. In our method, We integrated the local hill climbing in our crossover and mutation operation, which removed the randomness of the crossover operation and also guarantees a better solution, because it choses a better offspring than the parents, which inevitably increases the classification accuracy.

It is found that our method outperforms the Standard GP and CCM-GP methods. Our method improves the overall accuracy and speed by a fair amount. The standard GP can be destructive in nature. In standard crossover and mutation, rather than generating a offspring with better fitness, it could produce offspring with lesser fitness and transfer them to next generation. The CCM-GP acheived better accuracy than the Standard GP, its performance is low while com-

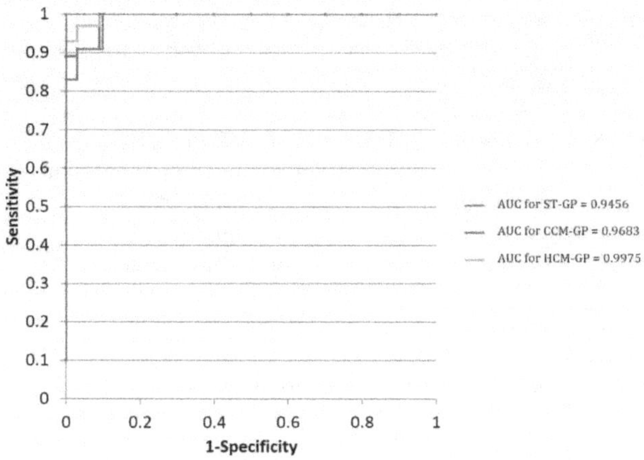

Figure 2: ROC Curve for 50-50 training-testing data

pared to HCM-GP. In CCM-GP, as all the individuals left after the reproduction undergo local hill climbing during the crossover, it takes a great deal of time to reach the desired accuracy. As, a result the CCM-GP method is time consuming, which is not ideal for real time detection of seizure. The proposed Hybrid Crossover searches for the best solution, in least possible time by merging both the standard crossover and constructive crossover. The Hybrid Mutation is responsible for improving the low performing individuals by bringing diversity among them.

Hence we can conclude that, though the integration of local hill climbing provides better solution, it is often time consuming, which is a major drawback for the CCM-GP method. Hence, we should be wise while integrating the hill climbing technique with the crossover and mutation. The proposed HCM-GP method, which uses local hill climbing on half of the individuals, still consumes a bit longer time than the Standard GP. But this is small price to pay, if it can significantly improve the classification performance. This makes the proposed HCM-GP framework a suitable tool to assist the experts by facilitating analysis of a patient's information and decreasing the time and effort required to accurately diagnose their patients.

5. CONCLUSION

An effectual real time detection of epileptic seizures is of paramount importance in clinical diagnosis of epilepsy. Genetic Programing has a huge potential in classifying the EEG signals to detect these epileptic seizures. Integration of local hill climbing technique with the crossover and mutation operations removes the destructive nature of crossover operation and improves the GP life cycle. However, we have to overcome a few limitations of the hill climbing search in order to build an effectual real time seizure detection system. The goal of this paper was to analyze the integration of local hill climbing method with crossover and mutation and to help overcome its limitations. The goal was successfully achieved by proposing hybrid Crossover and Mutation (HCM) operation. The purpose of the hybrid crossover and mutation is to attain the desired accuracy in least possible time. This approach uses the both Standard GP and CCM-GP. In the Hybrid Crossover, the first half of the individuals undergo conventional crossover operation, while the other half of the individuals undergo constructive crossover operation, where individuals which are only better than their parents are transfered to the next generation. The individuals which are left after the hybrid crossover and reproduction undergo hybrid mutation operation, where again a local hill climbing search is integrated with the mutation.

This approach was examined and compared with Standard GP and CCM-GP on a benchmark EEG signal dataset. The results suggest that the new approach outperformed the standard GP, while spending a bit longer time that the Standard GP. The new proposed operator achieves better classification accuracy in lesser time while compared to the CCM-GP. We can infer that the proposed HCM-GP method is considered as an efficient way to classify EEG signals and an inspiration for further developments in this area.

5.1 Future Work

Although this method improves the crossover and mutation operation and subsequently the GP life cycle, but still it does not provide a feasible solution.

The goal of this paper is to demonstrate the proposed HCM-GP and to analyze the integration of hill climbing with crossover and mutation with respect to EEG signal classification.So, the proposed method was only examined on EEG signal dataset and was not examined on other wider application tasks. We will further investigate this new classification approach on more general and wider range of pattern recognition problems such as Alzheimer's and Parkinson's diseases, breast cancer and diabetes detection and diagnosis in the future.

6. REFERENCES

[1] G. Tsoumakas and I. Katakis, "Multi-label classification: An overview," *Dept. of Informatics, Aristotle University of Thessaloniki, Greece*, 2006.

[2] Z. Michalewicz, *Genetic algorithms+ data structures= evolution programs*. Springer Science & Business Media, 1996.

[3] K. C. Tan, T. H. Lee, and E. F. Khor, "Evolutionary algorithms for multi-objective optimization: performance assessments and comparisons," *Artificial intelligence review*, vol. 17, no. 4, pp. 251–290, 2002.

[4] J. R. Koza, *Genetic Programming: vol. 1, On the programming of computers by means of natural selection*. MIT press, 1992, vol. 1.

[5] ——, "Genetic evolution and co-evolution of computer programs," *Artificial life II*, vol. 10, pp. 603–629, 1991.

[6] K. Yong11, "Improving crossover and mutation for adaptive genetic algorithm," *Computer Engineering and Applications*, vol. 12, p. 027, 2006.

[7] U.-M. O'Reilly and F. Oppacher, "Program search with a hierarchical variable length representation: Genetic programming, simulated annealing and hill climbing," in *Parallel Problem Solving from NatureâĂŤPPSN III*. Springer, 1994, pp. 397–406.

[8] M. During and D. Spencer, "Extracellular hippocampal glutamate and spontaneous seizure in the conscious human brain," *The lancet*, vol. 341, no. 8861, pp. 1607–1610, 1993.

[9] M. D. Bownds and D. Bownas, *The biology of mind: Origins and structures of mind, brain, and consciousness.* Fitzgerald Science Press Bethesda, MD, 1999.

[10] S. Sanei and J. A. Chambers, *EEG signal processing.* John Wiley & Sons, 2008.

[11] M. Teplan, "Fundamentals of eeg measurement," *Measurement science review*, vol. 2, no. 2, pp. 1–11, 2002.

[12] P. Gómez-Gil, E. Juárez-Guerra, V. Alarcón-Aquino, M. Ramírez-Cortés, and J. Rangel-Magdaleno, "Identification of epilepsy seizures using multi-resolution analysis and artificial neural networks," in *Recent Advances on Hybrid Approaches for Designing Intelligent Systems.* Springer, 2014, pp. 337–351.

[13] A. Subasi, "Eeg signal classification using wavelet feature extraction and a mixture of expert model," *Expert Systems with Applications*, vol. 32, no. 4, pp. 1084–1093, 2007.

[14] A. Bhardwaj, A. Tiwari, M. V. Varma, and M. R. Krishna, "Classification of eeg signals using a novel genetic programming approach," in *Proceedings of the 2014 conference companion on Genetic and evolutionary computation companion.* ACM, 2014, pp. 1297–1304.

[15] N. E. Huang, Z. Shen, S. R. Long, M. C. Wu, H. H. Shih, Q. Zheng, N.-C. Yen, C. C. Tung, and H. H. Liu, "The empirical mode decomposition and the hilbert spectrum for nonlinear and non-stationary time series analysis," *Proceedings of the Royal Society of London. Series A: Mathematical, Physical and Engineering Sciences*, vol. 454, no. 1971, pp. 903–995, 1998.

[16] V. Bajaj and R. B. Pachori, "Classification of seizure and nonseizure eeg signals using empirical mode decomposition," *Information Technology in Biomedicine, IEEE Transactions on*, vol. 16, no. 6, pp. 1135–1142, 2012.

[17] R. Poli and W. B. Langdon, "On the search properties of different crossover operators in genetic programming," *Genetic Programming*, pp. 293–301, 1998.

[18] R. Panda, P. Khobragade, P. Jambhule, S. Jengthe, P. Pal, and T. Gandhi, "Classification of eeg signal using wavelet transform and support vector machine for epileptic seizure diction," in *Systems in Medicine and Biology (ICSMB), 2010 International Conference on.* IEEE, 2010, pp. 405–408.

[19] S.-F. Liang, H.-C. Wang, and W.-L. Chang, "Combination of eeg complexity and spectral analysis for epilepsy diagnosis and seizure detection," *EURASIP Journal on Advances in Signal Processing*, vol. 2010, p. 62, 2010.

[20] H. Ocak, "Optimal classification of epileptic seizures in eeg using wavelet analysis and genetic algorithm," *Signal processing*, vol. 88, no. 7, pp. 1858–1867, 2008.

[21] I. Güler and E. D. Übeyli, "Adaptive neuro-fuzzy inference system for classification of eeg signals using wavelet coefficients," *Journal of neuroscience methods*, vol. 148, no. 2, pp. 113–121, 2005.

[22] N. F. Güler, E. D. Übeyli, and İ. Güler, "Recurrent neural networks employing lyapunov exponents for eeg signals classification," *Expert Systems with Applications*, vol. 29, no. 3, pp. 506–514, 2005.

[23] K. Aslan, H. Bozdemir, C. Şahin, S. N. Oğulata, and R. Erol, "A radial basis function neural network model for classification of epilepsy using eeg signals," *Journal of medical systems*, vol. 32, no. 5, pp. 403–408, 2008.

[24] L. Guo, D. Rivero, J. Dorado, J. R. Rabunal, and A. Pazos, "Automatic epileptic seizure detection in eegs based on line length feature and artificial neural networks," *Journal of neuroscience methods*, vol. 191, no. 1, pp. 101–109, 2010.

[25] L. Guo, D. Rivero, and A. Pazos, "Epileptic seizure detection using multiwavelet transform based approximate entropy and artificial neural networks," *Journal of neuroscience methods*, vol. 193, no. 1, pp. 156–163, 2010.

[26] K. C. Tan, Q. Yu, C. Heng, and T. H. Lee, "Evolutionary computing for knowledge discovery in medical diagnosis," *Artificial Intelligence in Medicine*, vol. 27, no. 2, pp. 129–154, 2003.

[27] M. Castelli, L. Vanneschi, and S. Silva, "Semantic search-based genetic programming and the effect of intron deletion," *Cybernetics, IEEE Transactions on*, vol. 44, no. 1, pp. 103–113, 2014.

[28] M. Zhang, X. Gao, and W. Lou, "A new crossover operator in genetic programming for object classification," *Systems, Man, and Cybernetics, Part B: Cybernetics, IEEE Transactions on*, vol. 37, no. 5, pp. 1332–1343, 2007.

[29] R. G. Andrzejak, K. Lehnertz, F. Mormann, C. Rieke, P. David, and C. E. Elger, "Indications of nonlinear deterministic and finite-dimensional structures in time series of brain electrical activity: Dependence on recording region and brain state," *Physical Review E*, vol. 64, no. 6, p. 061907, 2001.

[30] A. P. Bradley, "The use of the area under the roc curve in the evaluation of machine learning algorithms," *Pattern recognition*, vol. 30, no. 7, pp. 1145–1159, 1997.

Evolution Strategies for Exploring Protein Energy Landscapes

Rudy Clausen
Dept of Computer Science
George Mason University
Fairfax, VA 22030
rclausen@gmu.edu

Emmanuel Sapin
Dept of Computer Science
George Mason University
Fairfax, VA 22030
esapin@gmu.edu

Kenneth De Jong
Dept of Computer Science
George Mason University
Fairfax, VA 22030
kdejong@gmu.edu

Amarda Shehu*
Dept of Computer Science
George Mason University
Fairfax, VA 22030
amarda@gmu.edu

ABSTRACT

The focus on important diseases of our time has prompted many experimental labs to resolve and deposit functional structures of disease-causing or disease-participating proteins. At this point, many functional structures of wildtype and disease-involved variants of a protein exist in structural databases. The objective for computational approaches is to employ such information to discover features of the underlying energy landscape on which functional structures reside. Important questions about which subset of structures are most thermodynamically-stable remain unanswered. The challenge is how to transform an essentially discrete problem into one where continuous optimization is suitable and effective. In this paper, we present such a transformation, which allows adapting and applying evolution strategies to explore an underlying continuous variable space and locate the global optimum of a multimodal fitness landscape. The paper presents results on wildtype and mutant sequences of proteins implicated in human disorders, such as cancer and Amyotrophic lateral sclerosis. More generally, the paper offers a methodology for transforming a discrete problem into a continuous optimization one as a way to possibly address outstanding discrete problems in the evolutionary computation community.

Categories and Subject Descriptors

J.3 [**Computer Applications**]: Life and Medical Sciences; I.6.3 [**Computing Methodologies**]: Simulation and Modeling—*Applications*

*Corresponding Author

GECCO '15, July 11 - 15, 2015, Madrid, Spain

 ISBN 978-1-4503-3472-3/15/07...$15.00
DOI: http://dx.doi.org/10.1145/2739480.2754692

Keywords

evolution strategies; protein modeling; energy landscape.

1. INTRODUCTION

The focus on important diseases of our time has prompted many experimental labs to resolve and deposit functional structures of disease-involved proteins in structural databases such as the Protein Data Bank (PDB) [4]. Research in the wet laboratory has shown that proteins involved in some of the most complex human diseases, such as cancer, assume different functional structures and shift between them to modulate their biological function [11]. In disease, changes have occurred to the underlying chemical composition of a protein; namely, particular amino acids in the protein's amino-acid sequence have mutated from the healthy or wildtype (WT) version into a variant version. Variations in sequence have been related with human oncogenicity in proteins such as H-Ras and occurrence of familial Amyotrophic lateral sclerosis (ALS) in proteins such as SOD1.

The availability of structure data on disease-involved proteins opens up an interesting direction for experimentally-assisted or guided protein modeling research. Important questions remain unanswered that protein modeling can address. While wet-laboratory investigations can catch healthy and diseased-versions of a protein in different stable structures under physiological conditions, such investigations cannot provide information on the underlying energy landscape of the protein under investigation. While structures stable enough to be caught in the wet laboratory are associated with minima in the energy landscape, the location of such minima is unknown. In particular, the location of the global optimum is not known, as experimental techniques are more limited than computation in their ability to probe the structure space. Extracting information on the energy landscape and the location of the global optimum is important for two reasons. First, such information can help understand which of the experimentally-determined functional structures reside at the global optimum and are thus most stable. Second, the discovery of the global optimum can point to functional regions of the energy landscape that have yet to be probed in the wet laboratory. In both cases, precious insight is obtained into the biological function of disease-involved proteins.

There is a growing body of protein modeling research in the evolutionary computation (EC) community. The main focus of evolutionary algorithms (EAs) has been on the *de novo* structure prediction problem (PSP), where no information is assumed to be available on the functional structure(s) of a given protein amino-acid sequence. These algorithms are limited to small proteins ($\leq$ 70 amino acids long) in their applicability [7, 20, 8, 13, 32, 6, 3, 14, 10] and are increasingly shown to be outperformed by domain-specific algorithms originating in the computational biology community with respect to their ability to discover functional structures [5, 31, 16, 34, 30, 23].

While progress has been made recently [24, 25, 26], EAs for PSP are limited in their utility for protein modeling research. Their assumption that only sequence information and no structural information is available on a protein is invalidated on proteins that play a central role in human diseases. Such proteins are also typically longer than the cases that EAs for PSP can currently handle. While current EAs can typically handle short protein chains $\leq$ 70 amino acids long, many interesting proteins have lengths of at least 100 amino acids. The variable space of these proteins is too high-dimensional for exploration. Exploiting any available information on where the relevant regions of this space are is beneficial, but the current challenge is how to do so. Thus, the challenge for EAs in this new subdomain in protein modeling research is how to make use of the functional structures found for a protein in its healthy and diseased forms in the wet laboratory.

The subfield of algorithms originating in the computational biology community for guided exploration of a protein's fitness landscape is also sparse. Some local search algorithms that are initiated from a given structure and explore the space in the vicinity of the initial structure exist [9, 33, 29]. Running times of these algorithms vary from a few hours to a few days on one CPU. In principle, these algorithms can be run in a restart mode, initiated from different structures, to explore the fitness landscape. However, their computational demands would also increase in this new setting, and their ability to populate regions of the space with no experimentally-available structures is questionable, given that they fundamentally control computational cost by limiting their exploration in a neighborhood around the initial structure.

For these reasons, in this paper we focus on how to make structure-guided exploration for protein modeling amenable to evolution strategies. In essence, one is provided with a discrete setting, where domain experts (wet-laboratory investigators) have revealed a set of fit individuals. One direction of research can elect to focus on the design of an effective representation and effective reproductive operators over the individuals.

In this paper, we propose a novel direction. We provide a transformation of the discrete setting into a continuous optimization one. In essence, the collection of experimentally-available functional structures for healthy and diseased versions of a protein are subjected to a dimensionality reduction technique. The technique reveals the underlying variable space, its axes, number of dimensions, shape of the space, and bounds. Once a continuous variable space is defined, evolution strategies for continuous stochastic optimization can then be readily employed. In particular, here we showcase the ability to apply the Covariance Matrix Adaptation Evolution Strategy (CMA-ES). Several adaptations have to be introduced to properly initialize the algorithm and accurately compute fitness. The reason we choose CMA-ES here is that CMA-ES has been shown effective for difficult non-linear non-convex black-box optimization problems in continuous domains with anywhere from 3 to 100 variables. CMA-ES has yielded competitive results for local and global optimization [18, 17, 2] and is now a well-established method with many different application domains [12, 27, 19].

The analysis in this paper focuses on understanding the performance of CMA-ES on this new problem. The analysis shows that CMA-ES is capable of rapidly exploring the structure space and converging to the global optimum on different test cases. In some test cases, the algorithm is able to reveal which functional structures caught in the wet-laboratory reside in the global optimum of the fitness landscape and are thus thermodynamically more stable. In others, the algorithm reveals new information on the location of the global optimum, thus suggesting further experimentation in the wet-laboratory to probe unknown functional regions of the structure space.

The contributions of this paper go beyond the specific application domain on structure-guided exploration for protein modeling research. More generally, what this paper introduces is a methodology for transforming a discrete problem into a continuous one. While here we show a proof-of-concept on a needed subfield in protein modeling research, the applicability of this methodology extends to to other problems in protein modeling, such as protein-ligand and protein-protein binding and modeling of protein dynamics in folding and more. Even more generally, ideas introduced here may allow making progress in addressing challenging discrete optimization problems regarding evolution of finite state machines, neural networks, and more. What would be typically thought of as discrete problems can in principle be converted to continuous optimization problems. An approach that captures the underlying structure of the variable space, which we realize here through a statistical analysis of examples provided from domain experts, may allow re-introducing powerful evolution strategies capable of handling challenging continuous optimization problems.

2. METHODS

We first describe the transformation from a discrete problem into a continuous optimization one in detail. Next we describe our adaptation of CMA-ES to make use of the proposed transformation.

2.1 Tranformation from a Discrete to Continuous Setting

The transformation from a discrete to a continuous setting makes use of a linear dimensionality reduction technique to expose the underlying variable space. In this particular application setting, we are provided with experimentally-available functional structures of a protein. These are extracted from the PDB in the form of PDB entries, and each PDB entry lists the x, y, z coordinates of all atoms that constitute the amino acids of a protein. Figure 1(a) draws the structure of a short protein chain of 21 amino acids to illustrate the atom composition of a protein. A protein consists of backbone or skeleton comprised of N, CA, C, and O atoms. Each amino acid shares these atoms, and they repeat in a serial fashion. A bond connects the N of one amino acid to the O of the other amino acid, thus providing the amino-acid chain. The CA atom is the central carbon atom in each amino acid that connects to the side-chain group of atoms that are found in each amino acid. Effectively, side chains dangle off the backbone like beads in a necklace. Different structures can exist for the same protein chain, as the backbone is highly deformable. Some functional structures of two proteins that are used as test cases in this paper are shown in Figure 1. Only the backbone chain is shown in each of these functional structures, in blue, for ease of visibility.

The transformation we employ here extracts only the CA atoms of each structure obtained for a protein from the PDB. So, the x, y, z coordinates of the CA atoms of each of n functional structures collected for a protein from the PDB are deposited into a data matrix of n columns and $3m$ rows, where m is the number of CA atoms in the protein. The first column, corresponding arbitrarily to the first structure, is used as reference. All other columns are modified through a technique known as optimal fit [22] to remove differences due to rigid-body transformations. The resulting data matrix is then centered, removing the average x, y, and z coordinate of each CA atom from each entry, and then multiplied by $\frac{1}{\sqrt{n-1}}$. The matrix is then subjected to the lapack [1] *dgesvd* procedure, which provides a singular value decomposition of the matrix as a product $U \cdot \Sigma \cdot V^T$ (also known as a Principal Component Analysis – PCA [21]).

The columns of the U matrix, known as the principal components (PCs), are the new orthogonal axes over which the data has been projected. These axes are vectors of $3m$ entries, with entries $3 \cdot i$, $3 \cdot i + 1$, and $3 \cdot i + 2$ providing the x, y, z displacements for the CA of the ith amino acid in the protein. The diagonal of the Σ matrix contains the singular values, which are the square roots of the eigenvalues corresponding to each of the PCs. The *dgesvd* routine provides the PCs in the order of largest to smallest singular value. Analysis of the corresponding eigenvalues, as described in section 3, allows selecting a subset of PCs to consider as variables to represent an individual.

2.2 Adaptation of CMA-ES

CMA-ES follows an iterative process, where individuals in a generation are sampled from a multivariate normal distribution in R^n and then fit individuals are selected to update the multivariate normal distribution and covariance matrix. Details on CMA-ES are available in [17].

We introduce two adaptations to CMA-ES. The first adaptation concerns the initialization of the multivariate normal distribution. Since the data matrix to which PCA is applied is centered, the distributions of projections of the experimentally-available structures onto the PCs have a mean of 0. Standard deviations for each of the normal distributions along each of the PCs/variables are set at twice the standard deviations of the projections of experimentally-available structures; the resulting distributions have been confirmed to cover all experimentally-available structures are covered.

The second adaptation concerns evaluating sampled individuals. The individuals in a CMA-ES generation are not actual protein structures. They are points in a multi-dimensional PC-space. However, we want to associate with each of them a fitness that is measured through a sophis-

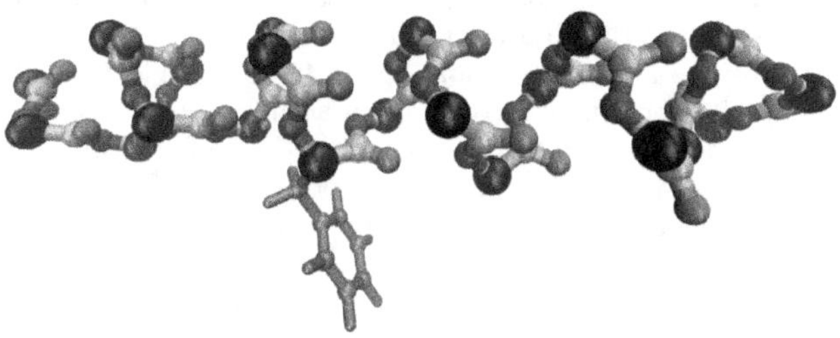

(a)

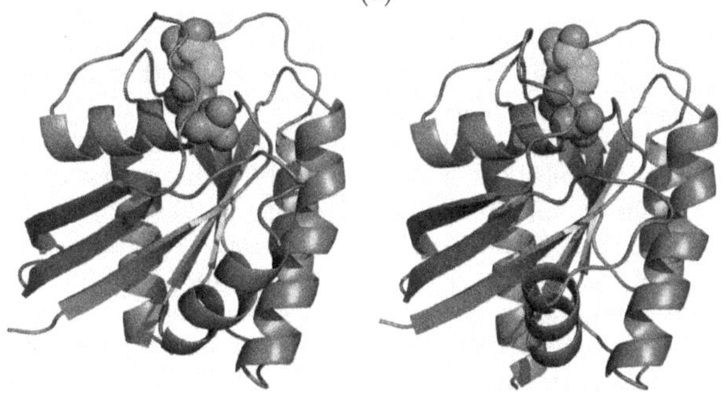

(b1) (b2)

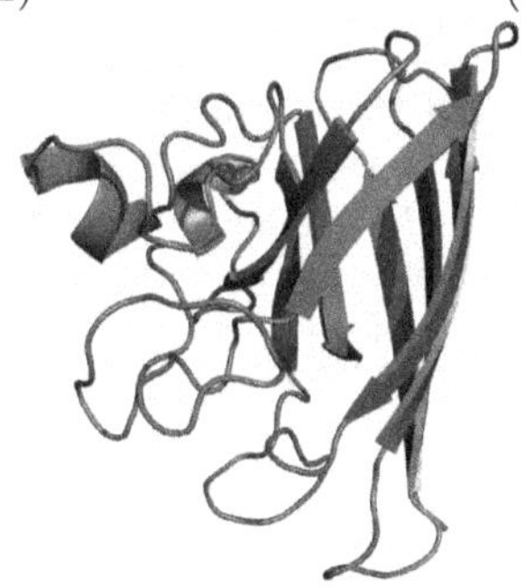

(c)

Figure 1: (a) illustrates a short protein chain of 21 amino acids. The main atoms, N, CA, C, and O, are shown for each amino acid. These atoms constitute the backbone chain of a protein and effectively provide the skeleton of a protein structure. Side-chain atoms for each amino acid dangle off the CA atom. The CA atom, which is the central atom in each amino acid, is drawn larger and in black. Side chain atoms are shown for only one amino acid here, drawn thinner and in gray, to illustrate their connetivity to the CA atom of an amino acid. (b)-(c) show two fit individuals (functional structures) for the healthy version of the H-Ras protein, corresponding to PDB entries (b1) 1qra and (b2) 4q21. Repectively, these represent the On (ligand-binding) and Off (non ligand-binding) states of H-Ras. (c) shows a fit individual for the healthy version of the SOD1 protein corresponding to PDB entry 1hl4. Structures are drawn in blue with Pymol [28]. For H-Ras, the ligand with which the protein interacts is drawn, as well, with ligand amino acids drawn as red and yellow spheres.

ticated all-atom energy function such as Rosetta *score12* (available in the open-source Rosetta structure prediction package [5]). The goal is to have the fitness landscape to correspond to the all-atom protein energy landscape, so that conclusions and observations made have biological significance. This requires recovering an actual protein structure with all-atom detail from an individual. The following technique is used. First, the x, y, z coordinates of all m CA atoms for an individual are recovered from an individual I represented through less than $3m$ variables through the operation $I \cdot U^T + A$, where the A vector contains the average x, y, z coordinates for each CA atom (this average vector was used to center the data matrix for PCA, as described above). Once the coordinates of CA atoms are recovered for an individual, a detailed all-atom structure can be then be computed. First, coordinates of the all backbone atoms can be filled in with statistics-based algorithms such as BBQ [15], which is one of the top backbone reconstruction protocols in protein modeling. Then, side-chain packing algorithms can be used to obtain optimal configurations of side-chain atoms of each amino acid given the backbone coordinates of the amino acids The *relax* protocol in the open-source Rosetta structure prediction package is used for this purpose. This protocol is easily integrated into CMA-ES, as it is open source.

2.3 Implementation Details

CMA-ES is run for 100 generations, and population size is set at 500. This takes $47-55$ hours on a CPU for CMA-ES. CMA-ES implemented in C/C++ and run on a 16 core red hat linux box with 3.2GhZ HT Xeon CPU and 8GB RAM. Analysis that looks into robustness of the algorithm uses 5 independent runs.

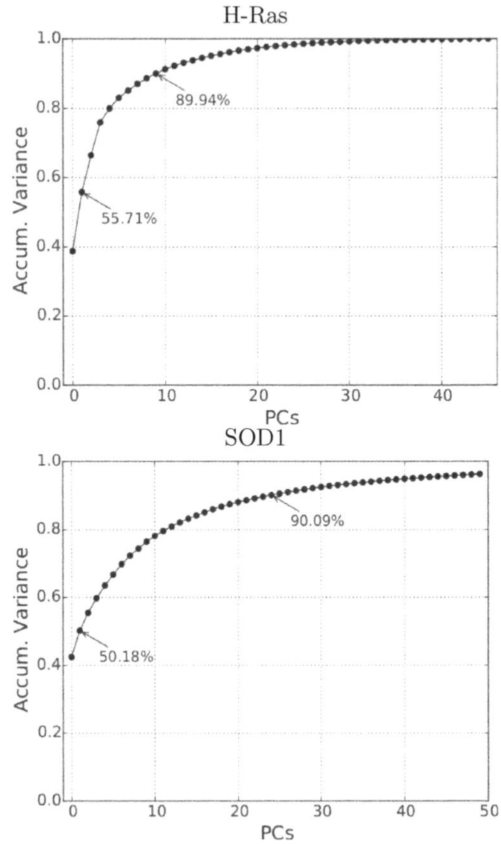

Figure 2: The accumulation of variance over the PCs is shown for H-Ras and SOD1. The accumulated variance at 2 PCs and 10 PCs is annotated.

3. RESULTS

Test Cases: Performance is evaluated on 6 test cases. These include the WT and 3 variants of the H-Ras protein and the WT and one variant of the SOD1 protein. The variants of H-Ras are G12V, G12D, and Q61L; in G12V, for instance, the glycine amino acid at position 12 has been replaced with a valine amino acid in the variant. The variant considered for SOD1 is A4V, where the alanine amino acid at position 4 in the sequence has been replaced with a valine amino acid. These variants are linked to human diseases. In particular, the H-Ras variants are known to be oncogenic, whereas the SOD1 A4V variant is found in familial ALS.

Data Preparation: Experimentally-available structures of WT and variants of H-Ras and SOD1 are collected from the PDB. Variants with more than 3 amino-acid changes are discarded. PDB entries with missing internal amino acids are discarded, as well. This leaves 86 structures, each 166 amino acids long, for H-Ras and 186 structures, each 150 amino acids long, for SOD1. PCA is applied to each dataset, as described in section 2, to obtain the underlying variables for the WT and variants of H-Ras and SOD1.

Experimental Setup: The analysis focuses on the convergence of CMA-ES, as well as understanding where and how CMA-ES converges on the fitness landscape. The latter information is compared with the location of experimentally-available functional structures on the landscape. The performance of CMA-ES in terms of convergence

3.1 PCA is Effective to Elucidate Underlying Variables

Figure 2 demonstrates that PCA is an effective dimensionality reduction tool for exposing the underlying variables for protein systems studied here. Figure 2 draws the accumulation of variance over the PCs as sorted by largest to smallest corresponding eigenvalue. Note that the eigenvalue obtained for a PC measures the variance of data projected on that PC. By sorting PCs from largest to smallest eigenvalue, one can estimate through $\frac{\sum_{i=1,\ldots,i=j} e_i}{\sum_{i=1,\ldots,N} e_i}$ the data variance that can be preserved if data are represented as j-dimensional vectors of entries that are projections over PC_1, ..., PC_j. In particular, Figure 2 shows that over 50% of the variance is preserved when employing only 2 PCs. In order to determine an optimal number of PCs that can be used as variables in the new PC-based representation, a variance threshold of 90% is used. This is reached at 10 PCs for H-Ras and 25 PCs for SOD1. That is, the number of variables in the representation used by the algorithms here is 10 for H-Ras WT and its variants and 25 for SOD1 WT and its variant.

3.2 CMA-ES Convergence

Two measurements are tracked across each of the 100 generations. The first concerns fitness improvement, measured as the difference in best fitness from generation i to generation $i+1$ (we note that low *score12* values are considered high fitness). Figure 3 shows this analysis on two selected test cases, H-Ras WT and SOD1 WT.

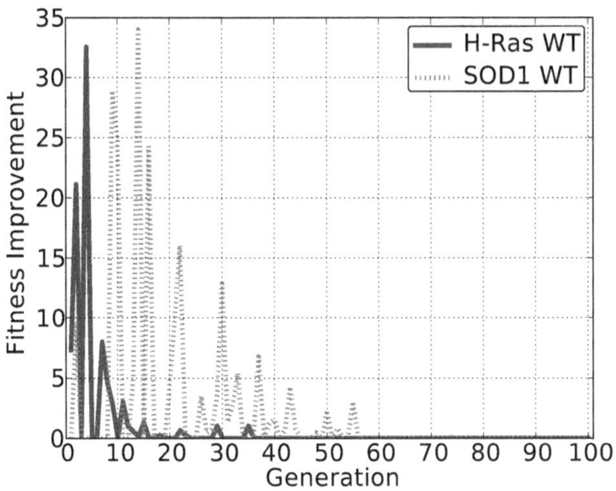

Figure 3: The fitness improvement from generation i to generation $i+1$ are tracked across the 100 generations.

The second measurement tracked across 100 generations concerns diversity, which is measured as the average Euclidean distance over all pairs of individuals in a population is tracked and plotted in Figure 4(a)-(b) for each of the 6 test cases. This analysis shows that CMA-ES converges quickly, within generation 20 in all H-Ras WT and variant test cases. For SOD1, where the variable space has twice the number of dimensions of that of H-Ras, convergence is reached at generation 40. These results are supported by the analysis on fitness improvement.

3.3 Detailed Analysis of CMA-ES

The convergence of CMA-ES is studied in greater detail. For two selected test cases, H-Ras WT and SOD1 WT, the two-dimensional gaussians over PC1 and PC2 are tracked over a few of the generations, starting with the initial generation and ending with the generation where CMA-ES is considered to have converged. Figure 5(a)-(b) draws these gaussians and individuals that constitute 2/3 of the population for each of the selected generations. The results show, as expected, narrowing of the distributions and movements of the means towards particular regions in the variable space.

To better illustrate where in the space CMA-ES converges, Figure 6(a)-(b) color-codes the gaussians by the average fitness of the corresponding population and draws only the locations of the experimentally-available structures in the PC1-PC2 projection of the variable space. These results show that the average fitness improves, as expected, and the generation where CMA-ES converges exposes which structures found in the wet laboratory constitute the global optimum of the fitness landscape. This discovery is important, as it reveals important information about landscape. In particular, for H-Ras WT, the experimentally-available structures, whose positions align well with the gaussian of the generation where CMA-ES converges, are considered to be the functional On state of H-Ras. In other words, CMA-ES has discovered that the On state of H-Ras WT is at the global optimum in the fitness landscape and is thus

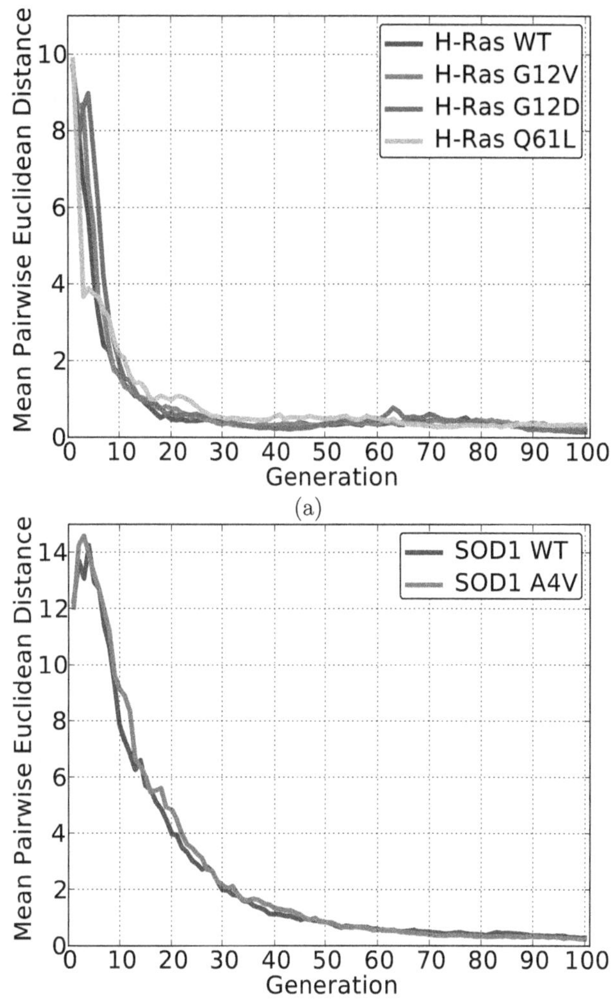

Figure 4: The average pairwise Euclidean distance is tracked across the 100 generations for H-Ras WT and its variants in (a) and SOD1 WT and its variant in (b).

more thermodynamically stable than other experimentally-determined structural states of H-Ras. On SOD1, the additional rendering of projections of the crystal structures shows that CMA-ES has converged to a distribution comprised of two distinct clusters of conformations. These largely cover the crystal structures known for SOD1 and further illustrates the ability of CMA-ES to capture these favorable regions of the SOD1 conformational space upon convergence even when initiated from a wide gaussian. In particular, the results for SOD1 illustrate that there are two equally energetically-favorable regions of the conformational space, pointing to two possibly equally stable structural states for the SOD1 WT.

While not shown here, CMA-ES run on H-Ras variants converges to the same location as for the WT. This indicates that on both healthy and diseased versions of the H-Ras protein the global optimum is the same and contains the On state probed in the wet laboratory. This finding provides insight into what may be the reason for misfunction in the H-Ras variants. It is not that the variants lose

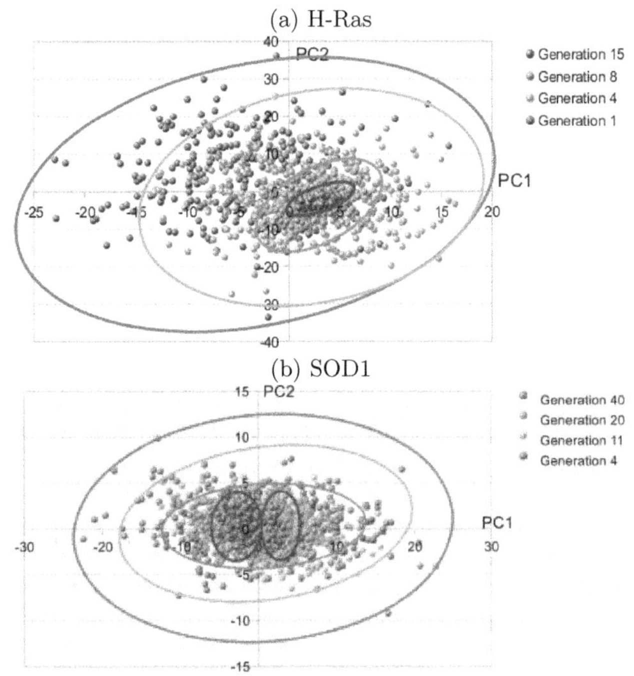

Figure 5: (a)-(b) illustrate the gaussians over PC1 and PC2 for H-Ras WT in (a) and SOD1 WT in (b) for 4 selected generations. The selected generations include the first and the one where CMA-ES is considered to have converged. Drawn points are 2/3 of the population in each selected generation.

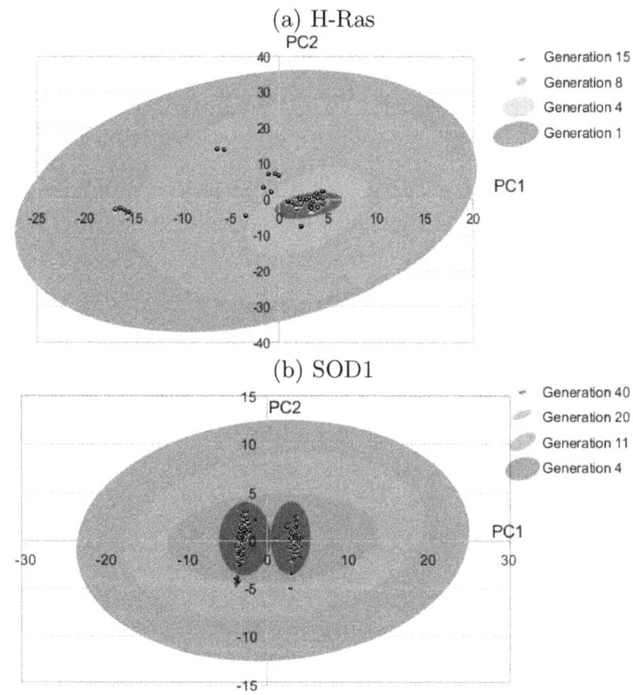

Figure 6: (a)-(b) Gaussians are now color-coded by the average fitness of corresponding population. A red-to-blue color scheme is used to indicate low-to-high fitness. The points drawn are projections of the X-ray structures on PC1 and PC2.

the ability to access the On state. Instead, possible barriers in the landscape may prevent them from switching from the Off to the On state at the same rate as the WT. This finding provides guidance for what further studies can investigate. On the other test cases, SOD1 WT and variant, CMA-ES reveals a global optimum that is different from the location of experimentally-available structures. This finding suggests CMA-ES proposes the existence of novel functional structures not yet captured in the wet laboratory.

In summary, this detailed analysis reveals that CMA-ES is effective and is able both to reproduce current knowledge, as in the case of H-Ras, and generate novel insight, as in the case of SOD1.

3.3.1 Restart Analysis of CMA-ES

Here the variability in when and where CMA-ES converges is studied in greater detail. In particular, two test cases are selected, H-Ras WT and SOD1 WT, and on each case CMA-ES is run 5 times. It is important to note that while the definition of the initial gaussian that initializes CMA-ES is the same on each independent run, the actual individuals sampled may be different, and thus the other gaussians of following populations can vary. Table 1 reports the mean and standard deviation of the mean of the gaussians over PC1 and PC2 in the generation where CMA-ES converges. The results in Table 1 demonstrate that CMA-ES is robust, as the standard deviations of the two tracked quantities are small.

4. CONCLUSION

This work has introduced a novel direction of research on evolution strategies for exploring protein energy landscapes. In particular, the exploitation of experimental data is proposed to guide EAs for protein modeling research. An interesting setup is proposed in this paper, where a discrete problem is transformed into a continuous optimization one. In particular, rather than pursue research on reproductive operators for three-dimensional protein structures, this work has instead focused on extracting information from a collection of experimentally-available structures on the underlying variables of the space, as well as the value ranges for these variables. Dimensionality reduction is used to extract such variables, which allows framing the problem as a continuous optimization one and employing both standard and novel evolutionary strategies for exploration.

One of the main observations in this paper is that this interesting exploitation of experimentally-available data allows the application and adaptation of powerful EAs such as CMA-ES. The results presented in this paper show that CMA-ES is effective, converges fast, and is able to reveal interesting information regarding the energy or fitness landscape of a protein under study. While the algorithm is essentially seeded only with information on what the initial shape and bounds of the variable space are, it manages to quickly find the global optimum of the landscape. Comparing the location of the optimum with the locations of the experimentally-available structures allows revealing which structures reside on the global optimum and which ones do not. In particular, for one of the proteins studied here, CMA-ES reveals that structures captured when the protein is in its On state are indeed of better fitness than other ones. This insight allows understanding that the On

Table 1: CMA-ES is run 5 times on two selected test cases, Ras WT and SOD1 WT. Where CMA-ES has reached convergence in terms of the means μ_{PC1} and μ_{PC2} of the normal distributions on PC1 and PC2 are tracked. Means and standard deviations of these two quantities over the 5 separate runs are reported here.

Test case	$\mu_{\mu_{PC1}}$ ($\sigma_{\mu_{PC1}}$)	$\mu_{\mu_{PC2}}$ ($\sigma_{\mu_{PC2}}$
H-Ras WT	3.32 (0.11)	-2.96 (0.14)
SOD1 WT	-2.45 (0.17)	6.39 (0.07)

state has higher thermodynamic stability than other structural states of H-Ras, thus revealing precious information on the function of H-Ras. For another test case, the algorithm reveals a global optimum that is further from the location of experimentally-available structures. This finding suggests further experimentation is needed in the wet laboratory to probe unknown functional regions of the structure space.

The work presented in this paper opens the way for several directions of further research. First, the interesting transformation here from a discrete problem into a continuous one may prompt more EC researchers to pursue novel evolution strategies for exploration and mapping of protein fitness landscapes. Other approaches beyond linear dimensionality reduction may be pursued.

The work presented here falls in the category of non black-box optimization algorithms that exploit existing knowledge about a problem. The exploitation of already-available information, as in the form of experimentally-available structures here, is an important direction to ground and guide optimization algorithms in a possibly very high-dimensional space. In particular, the combination of experiment and computation is an important direction that is bound to reveal more accurate biological insight onto the energy landscapes and thus function of protein molecules.

While this paper has focused on a protein modeling application, the setup introduced here to convert a discrete problem into a continuous optimization one may inspire progress in addressing challenging discrete optimization problems concerning evolution of finite state machines, neural networks, and more.

5. ACKNOWLEDGMENTS

This work is supported in part by NSF CCF No. 1421001, NSF IIS CAREER Award No. 1144106, and the Thomas F. and Kate Miller Jeffress Memorial Trust Award.

6. REFERENCES

[1] E. Anderson, Z. Bai, J. Dongarra, A. Greenbaum, A. McKenney, J. Du Croz, S. Hammerling, J. Demmel, C. Bischof, and D. Sorensen. Lapack: A portable linear algebra library for high-performance computers. In *Proceedings of the 1990 ACM/IEEE Conference on Supercomputing*, Supercomputing '90, pages 2–11, Los Alamitos, CA, USA, 1990. IEEE Computer Society Press.

[2] A. Auger and N. Hansen. A restart cma evolution strategy with increasing population size. In *IEEE Congress on Evolutionary Computation (CEC)*, pages 1769–1776. IEEE, 2005.

[3] D. Becerra, A. Sandoval, D. Restrepo-Montoya, and L. Nino. A parallel multi-objective ab initio approach for protein structure prediction. In *IEEE Intl Conf Bioinf and Biomed (BIBM)*, pages 137–141. IEEE, 2010.

[4] H. M. Berman, K. Henrick, and H. Nakamura. Announcing the worldwide Protein Data Bank. *Nat Struct Biol*, 10(12):980–980, 2003.

[5] P. Bradley, K. M. Misura, and D. Baker. Toward high-resolution de novo structure prediction for small proteins. *Science*, 309(5742):1868–1871, Sep 2005.

[6] J. Calvo, J. Ortega, and M. Anguita. Comparison of parallel multi-objective approaches to protein structure prediction. In *J Supercomputing*, pages 253–260. CITIC UGR Univ Granada, Dept Comp Architecture & Comp Technol, Granada, Spain, 2011.

[7] C. Chira, D. Horvath, and D. Dumitrescu. An Evolutionary Model Based on Hill-Climbing Search Operators for Protein Structure Prediction. *Evolutionary Computation, Machine Learning and Data Mining in Bioinformatics*, pages 38–49, 2010.

[8] Cutello, V, G. Morelli, G. Nicosia, M. Pavone, and G. Scollo. On discrete models and immunological algorithms for protein structure prediction. *Natural Computing*, 10(1):91–102, 2011.

[9] B. L. de Groot, D. M. van Aalten, R. M. Scheek, A. Amadei, G. Vriend, and H. J. Berendsen. Prediction of protein conformational freedom from distance constraints. *Proteins: Struct Funct Genet*, 29(2):240–251, 1997.

[10] R. Faccioli, I. N. da Silva, L. O. Bortot, and A. Delbem. A mono-objective evolutionary algorithm for Protein Structure Prediction in structural and energetic contexts. In *IEEE Congress on Evolutionary Computation (CEC)*, pages 1–7. IEEE, 2012.

[11] A. Fernández-Medarde and E. Santos. Ras in cancer and developmental diseases. *Genes Cancer*, 2(3):344–358, 2011.

[12] C. Gagné, M. Beaulieu, J. NAND Parizeau, and S. Thibault. Human-competitive lens system design with evolution strategies. *Applied Soft Computing*, 8(4):1439–1452, 2008.

[13] M. Garza-Fabre, G. Toscano-Pulido, and E. Rodriguez-Tello. Locality-based multiobjectivization for the HP model of protein structure prediction. In *Intl Conf on Genet and Evol Comput (GECCO)*. 2012. ACM.

[14] M. M. Goldstein, E. E. Fredj, and R. B. R. Gerber. A new hybrid algorithm for finding the lowest minima of potential surfaces: approach and application to peptides. *J Comput Chem*, 32(9):1785–1800, July 2011.

[15] D. Gront, S. Kmiecik, and A. Kolinski. Backbone building from quadrilaterals: a fast and accurate algorithm for protein backbone reconstruction from

alpha carbon coordinates. *J Comput Chem*, 28(29):1593–1597, 2007.

[16] J. Handl, J. Knowles, R. Vernon, D. Baker, and S. C. Lovell. The dual role of fragments in fragment-assembly methods for de novo protein structure prediction. *Proteins: Struct Funct Bioinf*, 80(2):490–504, 2012.

[17] N. Hansen and S. Kern. Evaluating the cma evolution strategy on multimodal test functions. In *Intl Conf on Parallel Problem Solving from Nature (PPSN)*, pages 282–291, 2004.

[18] N. Hansen and A. Ostermeier. Completely derandomized self-adaptation in evolution strategies. *Evolutionary Computation*, 9(2):159–195, 2001.

[19] O. Ibañez, L. Ballerini, O. Cordón, S. Damas, and J. Santamaria. An experimental study on the applicability of evolutionary algorithms to craniofacial superimposition in forensic identification. *Information Sciences*, 179(3):3998–4028, 2009.

[20] M. K. Islam, M. Chetty, and M. Murshed. Novel Local Improvement Techniques in Clustered Memetic Algorithm for Protein Structure Prediction. In *IEEE Congress on Evolutionary Computation (CEC)*, pages 1003–1011. IEEE, Apr. 2011.

[21] D. G. Luenberger. *Introduction to Linear and Nonlinear Programming*. Addison-Wesley, 1973.

[22] A. D. McLachlan. A mathematical procedure for superimposing atomic coordinates of proteins. *Acta Crystallogr A*, 26(6):656–657, 1972.

[23] K. Molloy, S. Saleh, and A. Shehu. Probabilistic search and energy guidance for biased decoy sampling in ab-initio protein structure prediction. *IEEE/ACM Trans Bioinf and Comp Biol*, 10(5):1162–1175, 2013.

[24] B. Olson, K. A. D. Jong, and A. Shehu. Off-lattice protein structure prediction with homologous crossover. In *Intl Conf on Genet and Evol Comput (GECCO)*, pages 287–294, New York, NY, 2013. ACM.

[25] B. Olson and A. Shehu. Multi-objective stochastic search for sampling local minima in the protein energy surface. In *ACM Conf on Bioinf and Comput Biol (BCB)*, pages 430–439, Washington, D. C., September 2013. ACM.

[26] J. Santos, P. Villot, and M. Dieguez. Emergent protein folding modeled with evolved neural cellular automata using the 3d hp model. *J of Comp Biol*, 21(11):823–845, 2014.

[27] J. Schaub, K. Mauch, and M. Reuss. Metabolic flux analysis in escherichia coli by integrating isotopic dynamic and isotopic stationary 13c labeling data. *Biotechnol Bioeng*, 99(5):1170–1185, 2008.

[28] L. Schrödinger. The PyMOL molecular graphics system, version 1.3r1, August 2010.

[29] A. Shehu, C. Clementi, and L. E. Kavraki. Modeling protein conformational ensembles: From missing loops to equilibrium fluctuations. *Proteins: Struct Funct Bioinf*, 65(1):164–179, 2006.

[30] A. Shehu and B. Olson. Guiding the search for native-like protein conformations with an ab-initio tree-based exploration. *Intl J Robot Res*, 29(8):1106–1127, 2010.

[31] A. Shmygelska and M. Levitt. Generalized ensemble methods for de novo structure prediction. *Proc Natl Acad Sci USA*, 106(5):94305–95126, 2009.

[32] A.-A. Tantar, N. Melab, and E.-G. Talbi. A grid-based genetic algorithm combined with an adaptive simulated annealing for protein structure prediction. *Soft Computing*, 12(12):1185–1198, 2008.

[33] S. A. Wells. Geometric simulation of flexible motion in proteins. *Methods Mol Biol*, 1084:173–192, 2014.

[34] D. Xu and Y. Zhang. Ab initio protein structure assembly using continuous structure fragments and optimized knowledge-based force field. *Proteins: Struct Funct Bioinf*, 80(7):1715–1735, 2012.

Metabolic Design And Engineering Through Ant Colony Optimization

Stephen Lincoln
Department of Chemical and Biomolecular Engineering, University of Connecticut, Storrs, CT, USA
191 Auditorium Road
Storrs, CT 06226 USA
stephen.lincoln@uconn.edu

Ian Rogers
Department of Chemical and Biomolecular Engineering, University of Connecticut, Storrs, CT, USA
191 Auditorium Road
Storrs, CT 06226 USA
ian.rogers@uconn.edu

Ranjan Srivastava
Department of Chemical and Biomolecular Engineering, University of Connecticut, Storrs, CT, USA
191 Auditorium Road
Storrs, CT 06226 USA
srivasta@engr.uconn.edu

ABSTRACT

Due to the vast search space of all possible combinations of reaction knockouts in *Escherichia coli*, determining the best combination of knockouts for over-production of a metabolite of interest is a computationally expensive task. Ant colony optimization (ACO) applied to genome-scale metabolic models via flux balance analysis (FBA) provides a means by which such a solution space may feasibly be explored. In previous work, the Minimization of Metabolic Adjustment (MoMA) objective function for FBA was used in conjunction with ACO to identify the best gene knockouts for succinic acid production. In this work, algorithmic and biological constraints are introduced to further reduce the solution space. We introduce Stochastic Exploration Edge Reduction Ant Colony Optimization, or STEER-ACO. Algorithmically, ACO is modified to refine its search space over time allowing for greater initial coverage of the solution space while ultimately honing on a high quality solution. Biologically, a heuristic is introduced allowing the maximum number of knockouts to be no greater than five. Beyond this number, cellular viability becomes suspect. Results using this approach versus previous methods are reported.

Categories and Subject Descriptors
J.3 [**Life and Medical Science**]: Biology and genetics

General Terms: Algorithms.

GECCO '15, July 11 - 15, 2015, Madrid, Spain

ACM 978-1-4503-3472-3/15/07...$15.00
DOI: http://dx.doi.org/10.1145/2739480.2754817

Keywords: Metabolic modeling, computational biology, metabolic engineering, ant colony optimization, genome-scale, flux balance analysis, systems biology

1. INTRODUCTION

The production of molecules and biomaterials from microorganisms is a well-established practice in industrial settings, as well as bench scale experiments. For example, active pharmaceutical ingredients (APIs) that are too complex or too costly to be produced via classic organic chemistry reactions can be synthesized via metabolically engineered microorganisms due to the high value of the API of interest and low cost and low quantity of reactants needed by the engineered microorganism [10]. Another example is the production of hydrogen with *Escherichia coli.* Recent studies have been conducted for utilizing the cheap and abundant substrate glycerol to produce biofuel, or hydrogen gas. The production of H_2 via *E. coli* is of growing interest because H_2 can be used directly as a reactant in fuel cells and does not contribute to greenhouse gas emissions. H_2 also reduces the need for fossil fuel sources and can be created by *E. coli* via waste generated from agriculture and industry. However, gene insertions and deletions must be made into the wild-type *E. coli* in order to maximize the production of H_2 to feasible levels [24].

Determining the best gene knockouts and insertions to produce a molecule or biomaterial of interest in *E. coli* is a computationally and theoretically difficult task. Genome-scale metabolic models have become a powerful computational tool for simulating an organism's metabolism under a given set of genetic and environmental constraints. The term "genome-scale" simply refers to how the metabolic network is constructed. The genome annotation of an organism is used to identify genes that catalyze metabolic reactions. If such a gene is present, the metabolic reaction it catalyzes is inferred to be present. In this way, it is possible to create a genome-scale metabolic model [4; 9; 14; 15].

Attempts have been made to predict and analyze gene and reaction knockouts in metabolic networks using genome-scale metabolic modeling [16]. As an example, the genome-scale metabolic model of *E. coli, iJR904*, has 1075 reactions, 761 metabolites, and 904 genes, and models are constantly being updated as new genes, kinetic information, and thermodynamic information is discovered [17; 18]. If the number of reactions knocked out is limited to three in *iJR904*, there are on the order of 10^9 different combinations of reactions to knock out. Increasing the maximum number of knockouts to five increases the number of possible combination to 10^{15}, and six to the order of 10^{18}. It is apparent that computational time and power become a concern as the number of knockouts is increased.

There are a number of *in silico* simulation programs to identify the best knockouts. For example, OptKnock [5] has been used to identify triplets of knockouts for overproduction of 1-butanol, 1-propanol, and 1,3-propanediol in *E. coli* in previous work [12]. However, this method is computationally expensive. For more five or more knockouts at a time, computations may take several hours to days on standard computing hardware.

Most approaches to modeling metabolism at the genome-scale use flux balance analysis (FBA) to analyze resulting fluxes based on the knockouts [3; 11; 13; 19]. The term "fluxes" refers to the throughput or "flux" of a metabolite through a given reaction pathway. Due to the number of equations and variables in an FBA model, the system is underdetermined. To calculate flux values, optimization theory is used where an objective function regarding how the cell will grow is postulated. The most commonly used objective function is maximization of growth rate. The premise for this objective function is that the cells that grow the fastest would be the most competitive. Thus those cells would be selected by evolution to be the dominant strain. However, when carrying out genetic engineering, the network that nature evolved is disrupted, casting doubt on the use of such an objective for genetically engineered organisms. To overcome this issue, another objective function has been proposed which states that the genetically engineered cell will attempt to distribute its metabolic resources in a manner similar to the wild type because that is how it evolved. This idea is referred to as "minimization of metabolic adjustment" or MoMA [20]. The MoMA concept may be formulated as a quadratic programming problem, which then may be solved to return reasonable flux distributions and identify more realistic best knockout sets. However, while MoMA can predict how metabolic resources will be distributed in genetically engineered organisms, it does not predict what genes should be knocked out to optimize production of a metabolite.

In this work, we propose a new method to identify the best sets of gene knockouts for metabolite production. Specifically we combine MoMA with ant colony optimization (ACO). We refer to this method as Stochastic Exploration Edge Reduction Ant Colony Optimization (STEER-ACO). A similar ACO/MoMA approach has recently been attempted [6]. However, the STEER-ACO algorithm improves on the previous work in several ways. The newly developed algorithm refines the search space over time to converge better solutions, as well as avoiding large reductions in the growth rate of *E. coli* by using the growth rate as a heuristic factor. It avoids a pre-processing step reduced the metabolic network that was used in the older algorithm, which had the potential to generate false positives and false negative knockouts. In addition, we have ported MoMA to Python and implemented our algorithm in Python while utilizing a Redis database system setting the stage for parallelization of the algorithm in the future. It is anticipated that this will further reduce the computational time required.

To evaluate the STEER-ACO algorithm, succinic acid production from genetically engineered *E. coli* was used as a case study. Succinic acid was chosen for two primary reasons. First, succinic acid is an important compound in industrial processes, ranging from food and pharmaceutical products, surfactants and detergents, green solvents and biodegradable plastics, and ingredients to stimulate animal and plant growth [25]. In addition, numerous studies on maximization of succinic acid production in *E. coli* have been performed, providing a large body of experimental data to compare with.

2. METHODS

2.1 Minimization of Metabolic Adjustment (MoMA)

MoMA is a constraint based programming method FBA which was first introduced by Daniel Segre, Dennis Vitkup, and George M. Church in 2002 [20]. One of the core principles of FBA is that the metabolic network of an organism of interest, such as *E. coli,* is assumed to be at steady state, which is strictly true for cells growing in chemostats and approximately true for cells growing in exponential phase [14; 23]. Under such conditions, the mass balance for each metabolite in the metabolic network of reactions must be zero. This can be denoted by the equation

$$\boldsymbol{S} \cdot \boldsymbol{v} = \boldsymbol{0} \qquad (1)$$

Where **S** is the stoichiometric coefficient matrix of size *m x n* where *m* is the number of metabolites, and *n* is the number of reactions in the network. ***v*** is the vector of fluxes in the network. The system is also bound to a set of constraints for the amount of nutrients available to the system, as well as the theoretical minimum and maximum fluxes supported by the system, such that

$$\boldsymbol{a_i} \leq \boldsymbol{v_i} \leq \boldsymbol{b_i} \qquad (2)$$

Linear programming (LP) is used to determine each flux for the wild-type microorganism using the system described above. After the system is solved with the objective of maximizing biomass growth, MoMA is used in order to determine the new fluxes in the system once a reaction, or set of reactions is knocked out. This is simulated in MoMA by setting the lower and upper bounds for the knocked out flux to zero. MoMA then uses quadratic programming (QP) to determine the network's new fluxes, under the assumption that the mutant flux distribution will be as close to the wild-type's flux distribution as possible. In other words, the goal is to determine a flux vector, ***x*** in which the Euclidian distance is as close as possible to the wild-type flux vector ***w***:

$$\boldsymbol{D} = \sqrt{\sum_{i=1}^{N} (\boldsymbol{w_i} - \boldsymbol{x_i})^2} \qquad (3)$$

D is the distance between the wild-type flux ***(w)*** and mutant flux ***x*** and **N** is the number of optimal points.

Since MoMA uses QP in order to solve the system, the goal is to minimize the standard QP problem

$$f(x) = L \cdot x + \frac{1}{2}x^T Qx \qquad (4)$$

Such that the vector L is of length **N** and the matrix Q is of size NxN. Q is used to define the linear and quadratic objective function, and x^T represents the transpose of x. Since minimizing D in Equation (3) is the same as minimizing its square and constants can be omitted from the objective function, **Q** can be set to an $N \times N$ unit matrix and L can be set to $-w$, where $w = v^{wt}$.

2.2 Ant Colony Optimization (ACO)

Ant Colony Optimization is a subset of swarm intelligence that is based on the behavior of ant colonies foraging for food. Ants communicate indirectly by depositing pheromone trails that decay over time in their environment while foraging. Although ants randomly choose a path to take, there is a greater probability to take a path that contains a large amount of pheromones. This allows ants to converge towards the shortest path to food in an autocatalytic reinforcement process [22]. The metaheuristic that governs ACO is as follows:

Set parameters, initialize pheromone trails
While termination condition not met **do**
  Construct solutions
  Apply local search (optional)
  Update Pheromones
End

The choice of solutions is guided stochastically with bias from the pheromone trails. The optional local search is performed to improve upon known solutions by locally searching the solution space, and is usually included in most ACO algorithms in order to improve upon known good solutions [7].

2.3 Stochastic Exploration Edge Reduction Ant Colony Optimization (STEER-ACO)

Although previous work has applied ACO/MoMA hybrid techniques [6] to determining the best sets of reaction knock outs in *E. coli* for succinic acid production, the approach used a completely stochastic search for knockout combinations based off of known viable reaction knock out candidates. In addition, the growth rate of mutant *E. coli* was not taken into account as a factor in engineering the final organism. The STEER-ACO algorithm is proposed as improvement to the previous approach based on both algorithmic and biological strategies. STEER-ACO consists of three stages

1. Initialization
    a. Bias generation
2. Solution Generation/Deletion
    a. Determine solution/path
    b. Update pheromone trails
    c. Forget bad solutions
3. Solution Examination

2.3.1 Initialization

During the initialization phase, the growth rate and flux of interest is determined and returned using LP FBA. Then each reaction is knocked out one at a time and the growth rate and flux of interest is determined using MoMA. If the growth rate is 0, the knockout is deemed lethal and removed from the selection of reactions that may be knocked out during solution generation. Otherwise, the value of the flux of interest is stored for that particular knockout in order to calculate the bias term that allows the algorithm to converge onto a better solution over time. Each viable knockout is stored as a key in a Redis database with the values of the current pheromone trail value, flux of interest from MoMA, growth rate returned from MoMA, and probability associated with choosing the solution. The value returned from MoMA is stored so that if an ant picks a known solution, MoMA would not have to be run again simply to return the QP value; it could just be grabbed from the database to speed up the algorithm. Besides being open source and easy to use, Redis was chosen for solution storage for two primary reasons:

1. Storing solutions with Redis is fast due to its in-memory storage
2. Redis allows for easy parallelization of STEER-ACO

The pheromone trail value is generated using the equation

$$\textit{Pheromone amount} = \tau^{\alpha}\eta^{\beta} \qquad (5)$$

Where τ represents the flux of interest value such that

$$\tau_i = \begin{cases} \frac{v_{mut}}{v_{wt}} \; if \; v_{wt} \neq 0 \\ v_{mut} \; otherwise \end{cases} \qquad (6)$$

which is done to normalize the value returned from MoMA. The value for η was the growth rate for the knockout, and α and β are constants to influence the strength of each term. The growth rate was used for η to allow a higher probability of choosing solutions that have both a good growth rate and good flux of interest, which is one of the ways STEER-ACO integrates the algorithm and biological knowledge. It is also one of the ways in which STEER-ACO differs from previous work. In addition, by defining η this way, it also allows for STEER-ACO to score a solution with very high flux of interest value with a subpar growth rate as a good solution, as long as the growth rate is not too poor.

2.3.2 Bias Generation

Each viable single reaction knockout has its flux of interest value stored into an array. At the end of initialization, the array is divided by its sum in order to determine probabilities associated with selecting a particular gene to knock out during solution generation. In other words, each viable flux has a probability of being selected if an ant chooses to find a new solution; the higher the value from Equation (7) below, the higher the probability it has of being chosen.

2.3.3 Solution Generation

At the beginning of each epoch of solution generation, all of the current keys, or solutions, present in the Redis database are returned with their pheromone value. The probability of choosing a particular known solution, denoted p_i, is calculated for each solution:

$$p_i = \frac{\tau_i^\alpha \eta_i^\beta}{\sum_{i=1}^{K} \tau_i^\alpha \eta_i^\beta} \quad (7)$$

where **K** is the total number of known solutions

2.3.4 Determine solutions/paths

For each ant in the system, there exists a probability denoted as ω to choose a new path based on the list of known solutions. This value is set high initially and decreases as the number of epochs increases. The purpose of this gradual decrease of ω is to encourage ants to explore new solutions initially, then converge on to known good solutions as time goes on. If an ant chooses a new solution, a knockout is chosen from the list of viable knockouts generated during initialization. This knockout is determined using a uniform random distribution initially in order to exhaust the search space. However, after the ants have gone through half of the allowed epochs, the knockout is chosen based on the bias determined during initialization. In other words, knockout candidates that return both a good flux value of interest and growth rate have a higher chance of being selected as time goes on.

Once a new knockout is selected, a random key is returned from the Redis database and the knockout is added to it to form a new solution. If the key already has the maximum amount of knockouts allowed, a knockout is removed based on the bias term calculated initially. Therefore, knockouts that generate a lower flux value of interest and growth rate compared to other knockouts in the solution have a higher probability to be removed and replaced. Finally, if the ant does not choose a new solution with a probability of **1- ω**, a known solution is selected from the Redis database by the probability described in Equation (7).

2.3.5 Update Pheromone Trails and Solution Deletion

After all the ants have chosen a path, the pheromone trails are updated

$$\tau_i \leftarrow (1-\rho)\tau_i + \sum_k \tau_i^k = (1-\rho)\tau_i + n\tau_i \quad (8)$$

Where **ρ** is the pheromone evaporation coefficient, and τ_i^k is the amount of pheromone deposited on solution ***i*** by the ***k***^***th*** ant, which simply reduces to $n\tau_i$ where ***n*** is the amount of ants that selected the solution. After all the pheromone trails have been updated, the solutions in the database are iterated through, and old solutions are deleted. A solution is forgotten and deleted if the **τ** of the solution is less than τ_{min}. A maximum tau is also set. See **Figure 1** for the algorithm flowchart.

Table 1. Parameters used for each trial of STEER-ACO

Parameter	Value
α	1
β	1.5
ρ	0.65
ω	0.7
Max Epochs	100
Num. Ants	200
Max Knockouts	5
τ_{min}	0.01
τ_{max}	100

2.3.5 Solution Examination

At the end of the maximum epochs allowed, the solutions in the database are sorted according to the amount of pheromone deposited at each solution. The top five results are returned according to the amount of pheromone deposited. The top five most common knockouts are also put into a separate knockout set and run through MoMA. Results that are deemed best return the largest succinic acid production, while sub-optimal results are defined as any combination of knockouts that produce a moderate amount of succinic acid with a high growth rate close to the wild-type growth rate.

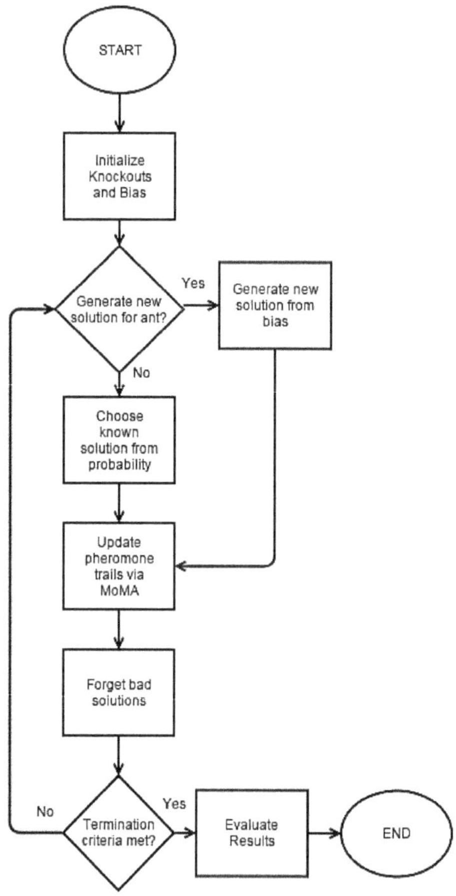

Figure 1. Flowchart for STEER-ACO algorithm

3. SIMULATIONS

The latest edition of dataset *iJR904* for *E. coli* was used [18], which contains 1075 reactions, 761 metabolites, and 904 genes, as well as gene to protein to reaction (GPR) information. For each calculation of the wild-type fluxes as well as MoMA simulations, the glucose uptake rate was set to 10 mmol $gDW^{-1}hr^{-1}$. The wild-type growth rate for the model was found to be 0.9219 h^{-1}. The objective was kept at maximizing biomass growth, while the τ value returned from MoMA was set to succinic acid production. Unlike previous work, there was no preprocessing done on the dataset in order to retain the complete model. Although this will increase the computational time, the average time required to achieve the algorithms best solution is 8.4 minutes under current settings shown in **Table 1** for five knockouts. More importantly, the potential for false positive and false negatives is reduced by leveraging the use of the entire metabolic network rather than an abridged, albeit more tractable, version. Additionally, plans to parallelize STEER-ACO and utilize PyCUDA GPU programming will significantly decrease the computational time, so preprocessing to remove reactions and metabolites was deemed unnecessary.

The number of maximum epochs was set to 100 in order to allow enough iterations to exhaust the search space, but still converge on a good solution. The number of ants was set to 200, or about 0.2 of the total number of reactions. Simulations using more ants took more computation time and did not return a better solution. In order to take advantage of parallelization and GPU programming in future work, MoMA was ported to Python v2.7.9 utilizing CPLEX v12.6 with Python bindings for LP and QP calculations. The STEER-ACO algorithm was written in Python 2.7.9 utilizing Numpy v1.9.0. All solutions were stored in a Redis database utilizing Python bindings (v2.9.1). The model from the database was parsed into CPLEX [1] using COBRA v0.2.1 [8]. All simulations were performed on Ubuntu 12.04.5 LTS with an Intel Core 2 Duo 2.0 GHz processor and 4 GB of DDR2 RAM.

4. RESULTS

Previous approaches used an older model of *iJR904*, and the model was preprocessed. Thus those results are not directly comparable to the results presented here. To compare results generated by STEER-ACO with previous studies, the top three triplet knockouts generated by those older studies were input into MoMA using the updated, unprocessed *iJR904* model, with the results shown in **Table 2.** STEER-ACO was run 20 times, with the top five results returned for each trial shown in **Table 3**.

Table 2. Top three triplet knockouts returned from previous studies using updated & unprocessed model *iJR904*

Reactions Knocked Out	Succinic Acid Production (mmol gDW^{-1} h^{-1})	Growth Rate (h^{-1})
G6PDH2r PDH SUCD1i	2.8542	0.1139
FUM G6PDH2r PDH	2.6463	0.1162
FUM G6PDH2r PYK	2.2042	0.1244

The top five results of all the trials are listed in **Table 4.** The top ten most common knockouts for the top five sets over 20 trials were found as seen in **Figure 2.**

STEER-ACO not only performed better in terms of succinic acid production, but growth rate as well. The best solution returned from STEER-ACO had a succinic acid production and growth rate of 3.5815 mmol $gDW^{-1}h^{-1}$ and 0.1270 h^{-1} respectively. In comparison, the best result from the older algorithm had a succinic acid production rate of 2.8542 mmol $gDW^{-1}h^{-1}$ and growth rate of 0.1139 h^{-1} based on the knockouts they predicted. This is a 25.5% increase in succinic acid production, and 11.5% increase in growth rate. Even the fifth best solution returned from STEER-MOMA had an 11.5% increase in growth rate while producing approximately the same amount of succinic acid as compared to the best solution returned using the approach described in the previous studies.

Table 3. Top five sets of three knockouts returned from STEER-ACO from unprocessed model *iJR904*

Reactions Knocked Out	Succinic Acid Production (mmol gDW^{-1} h^{-1})	Growth Rate (h^{-1})
ACt2r GLCDe SUCD4	3.5815	0.1270
ACt2r SUCD4 XYLt2	3.5466	0.1273
ACNML EX_ac_(e) SUCD4	3.5466	0.1287
EX_ac_(e) Kt2r SUCD4	3.5285	0.1287
DBTSr SUCD1i PTAr	2.8288	0.1363

Given the speed at which the STEER-ACO ran, it was feasible to explore a larger knockout space. Based on our experimental experience, the viability of *E. coli* generally degraded significantly once more than five knockouts were made. A five knockout limit was thus decided upon. When comparing the predictions of STEER-ACO for five knockouts to previous work that had only three knockouts, STEER-ACO predicted genetic modifications that yielded higher levels of succinic acid. This result is unsurprising given that five knockouts provide substantially more flexibility relative to three knockouts if one is able to effectively take advantage of it. What is surprising, however, is that even with five knockouts, STEER-ACO predicts growth rates higher than previous studies did with three knockouts. The best solution returned from SEARCH-ACO had a succinic acid production and growth rate of 5.1206 mmol $gDW^{-1}h^{-1}$ and 0.1393 h^{-1} respectively, shown in **Table 4**. This is a 79.4% increase in succinic acid production and a 22.3% increase in growth rate.

The fifth best solution returned from STEER-MOMA had a 51.8% increase in succinic acid production rate and 22.5% increase in growth rate as compared to the best solution obtained using the previous study's results. This result is surprising because it would be expected that as more succinic acid is produced, few metabolic resources would be available to for cellular growth. However, it appears that by incorporating the growth rate into the value of **η**, it was possible to identify high succinic acid production rates while maintaining relatively high growth rates. Maintaining high growth rates in cell culture is important in the biotech industry for a variety of reasons [21]. Such a result indicates the potential usefulness and value of the STEER-ACO algorithm.

Table 4. Top five sets of five knockouts returned from STEER-ACO from unprocessed model *iJR904*

Reactions Knocked Out	Succinic Acid Production (mmol $gDW^{-1} h^{-1}$)	Growth Rate (h^{-1})
ACt2r EX_leu_L_(e) NMNAT SUCD1i TALA	5.1206	0.1393
EX_ac_(e) FUM G6PDH2r SUCD4 TMPKr	4.5951	0.1253
EX_ac_(e) FUM G6PDH2r GUAPRT SUCD4	4.5889	0.1256
EX_ac_(e) EX_no2_(e) G6PDH2r PYRt2r SUCD4	4.5779	0.1277
EX_ac_(e) MTHFC RNDR3 SUCD1i SUCD4	4.3329	0.1224

The remainder of the analysis focuses on data collected from the simulations and optimization using the five knockout systems. In an attempt to create better set of knockouts, the top five most common knockouts are put into a separate set and run through MoMA, which returned a growth rate of 0.8450 h^{-1} and succinic acid production rate of 0.9317 mmol $gDW^{-1}h^{-1}$, which falls under a sub-optimal knockout set due to the moderate succinic acid production and high growth rate.

An acetic acid transport export reaction was found to be present in all of the top five knockouts combinations. In terms of the TCA cycle, this theoretically allows more acetic acid to be fed into the TCA cycle via acetyl-CoA. In addition, fumarase and succinate dehydrogenase are the most frequently knocked out reactions and appear in all of the top five knockouts. As seen in **Figure 3**, this disallows key reactions that consume succinic acid in the TCA cycle.

Table 5. Genes associated with each set of top five reactions. Note that all reactions starting with "EX" refer to transport reactions or "exchange/export fluxes" were resources are taken up by the cell or secreted from the cell.

Reactions Knocked Out	Gene Name
ACt2r	-
EX_leu_L_(e)	-
NMNAT	nadD
SUCD1i	sdh
TALA	talA or talB
EX_ac_(e)	-
FUM	fum
G6PDH2r	zwf
SUCD4	sdh
TMPKr	thiL
EX_ac_(e)	-
FUM	fumA or fumC or fumB
G6PDH2r	zwf
GUAPRT	gpt or hpt
SUCD4	sdhD, sdhC, sdhA, sdhB
EX_ac_(e)	-
EX_no2_(e)	-
G6PDH2r	zwf
PYRt2r	-
SUCD4	sdh
EX_ac_(e)	-
MTHFC	folD
RNDR3	nrd
SUCD1i	sdh
SUCD4	sdh

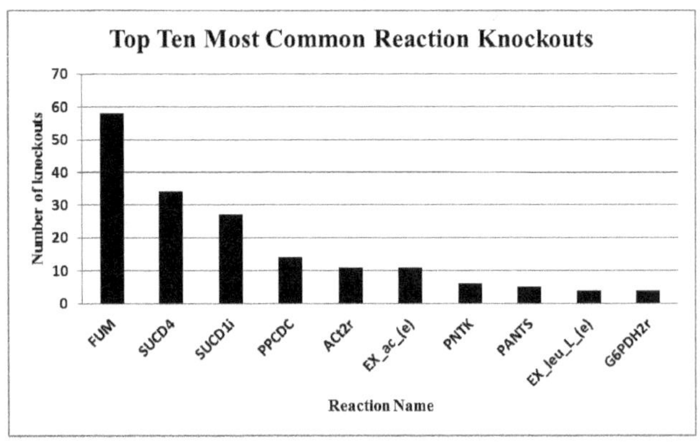

Figure 2. Top ten most common knockouts for overproduction of succinic acid in *E. coli iJR904* found in the top five results for 100 trials.

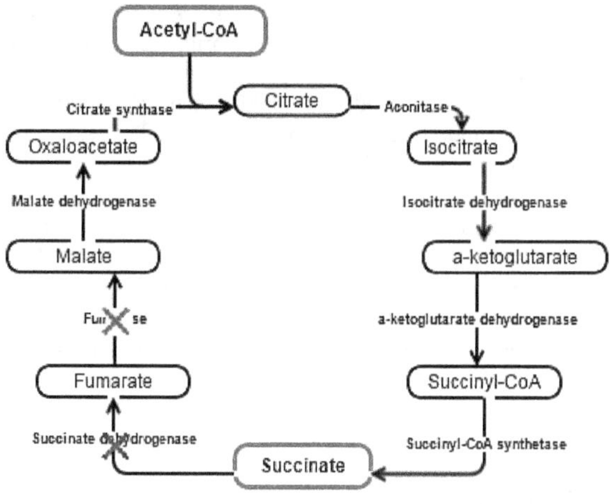

Figure 3. Basic TCA cycle diagram. Knocking out acetate exporters, succinate dehydrogenase, and fumarase allows for overproduction of succinic acid

Although fumarase was present in only two of the five top results, it is present in nearly every sub-optimal knockout set. In the sub-optimal sets, the growth rate is closer to the wild-type growth rate of 0.9219 h^{-1} but the succinic acid production is lower than in the best sets presented in **Table 3**. In the case of fumarase, it was present in 58 of the 100 top knockout sets, which includes the best and sub-optimal sets. The average succinic acid production and growth rate for the sets that contained fumarase were 1.6777 mmol $gDW^{-1}h^{-1}$ and 0.5731 h^{-1} respectively. This is further demonstrated for each of the top ten reaction knockouts in **Table 5.** In general, if a reaction knockout has a higher average succinic acid production rate, it has a lower growth rate due to the majority of the carbon available to the *E. coli* being shunted towards the succinic acid synthesis rather than production of biomass. The genes catalyzing the reactions that were recommended to be knocked out are shown in **Table 4**.

Table 5. The average succinic acid production rate and growth rate for all knockout sets containing each reaction

Reaction Name	Average Succinic Acid Production (mmol $gDW^{-1}h^{-1}$)	Average Growth Rate (h^{-1})
FUM	1.6777	0.5731
SUCD4	2.6715	0.2210
SUCD1i	2.7725	0.2096
PPCDC	0.8838	0.8434
ACt2r	6.1650	0.3074
EX_ac_(e)	3.6132	0.1908
PNTK	0.8857	0.8452
PANTS	0.8863	0.8453
EX_leu_L_(e)	2.6929	0.3202
G6PDH2r	4.3057	0.1324

5. CONCLUSION

This work focused on implementation of STEER-ACO in order to determine the best reaction knockouts to be performed for overproduction of succinic acid in *E. coli* model *iJR904*. This algorithm differs from the previous ACO/MoMA hybrid methods developed by *Chong et. al.* in that while the solution space is searched in a completely stochastic manner in the first iterations of the algorithm, it refines the search space over time towards favorable solutions or edges. This is performed with a bias towards favorable single reaction knockouts determined in the initialization phase of the algorithm, as well as a probability of local search that decays over time. The top five predicted best knockouts in five sets of twenty runs not only had a higher succinic acid production rate, but a higher growth rate as well when compared to reaction knockouts reported from *Chong et. al.*. This is due in part by using the growth rate as a heuristic factor in determining the amount of pheromone to be deposited on a solution, as well as the bias towards favorable knockouts as time goes on. This allows for solutions that return a high succinic acid production rate and a reasonable growth rate. It also allows for identification of sub-optimal solutions that return a moderate succinic acid production rate and growth rate close to the wild type, which is important if growth rate is an important factor.

In addition, good solutions can be converged upon in just over eight minutes for up to a maximum of five reaction knockouts. The methods described in this work can be applied to any flux of interest, such as H_2 production for biofuel or API's for pharmaceutical use. Furthermore, predictions made by STEER-ACO may be used as a guideline for wet laboratory experiments to guide overproduction of a molecule or biomaterial of interest, especially because custom reaction and constraints easily be inserted into the *in silico* model and replicated *in vitro*.

This algorithm is still in its early stages of development. In the future, the algorithm will be further optimized for speed and performance. This will be accomplished by parallelization across multiple CPU's, as well as utilizing PyCUDA for GPU programming, which can achieve 20x-2000x performance increase [2]. This will eliminate the need for any preprocessing of the model to cut down computation time, and allow for more ants and iterations for exhaustion of the search space and convergence on best solutions.

6. ACKNOWLEDGMENTS

This material is based upon work supported by the National Science Foundation under Grant No. 1137249.

7. REFERENCE

[1] CPLEX Optimizer. In *CPLEX Optimization Studio* IBM.

[2] 2015. GPU Accelerated Computing with Python. In *CUDA ZONE* NVIDIA.

[3] Bautista, E.J., Zinski, J., Szczepanek, S.M., Johnson, E.L., Tulman, E.R., Ching, W.M., Geary, S.J., and Srivastava, R., 2013. Semi-automated Curation of Metabolic Models via Flux Balance Analysis: A Case Study with Mycoplasma gallisepticum. *PLoS Comput Biol 9*, 9 (Sep), e1003208. DOI= http://dx.doi.org/10.1371/journal.pcbi.1003208.

[4] Becker, S.A., Feist, A.M., Mo, M.L., Hannum, G., Palsson, B.O., and Herrgard, M.J., 2007. Quantitative prediction of cellular metabolism with constraint-based

models: the COBRA Toolbox. *Nat Protoc 2*, 3, 727-738. DOI= http://dx.doi.org/10.1038/nprot.2007.99.

[5] Burgard, A.P., Pharkya, P., and Maranas, C.D., 2003. Optknock: a bilevel programming framework for identifying gene knockout strategies for microbial strain optimization. *Biotechnol Bioeng 84*, 6 (Dec 20), 647-657.

[6] Chong, S.K., Mohamad, M.S., Mohamed Salleh, A.H., Choon, Y.W., Chong, C.K., and Deris, S., 2014. A hybrid of ant colony optimization and minimization of metabolic adjustment to improve the production of succinic acid in Escherichia coli. *Comput Biol Med 49*(Jun), 74-82. DOI= http://dx.doi.org/10.1016/j.compbiomed.2014.03.011.

[7] Dorigo, M., Birattari, M., and Stutzle, T., 2006. Ant colony optimization. *Computational Intelligence Magazine, IEEE 1*, 4, 28-39.

[8] Ebrahim, A., Lerman, J.A., Palsson, B.O., and Hyduke, D.R., 2013. COBRApy: COnstraints-Based Reconstruction and Analysis for Python. *BMC Syst Biol 7*, 74. DOI= http://dx.doi.org/10.1186/1752-0509-7-74.

[9] Feist, A.M. and Palsson, B.O., 2008. The growing scope of applications of genome-scale metabolic reconstructions using Escherichia coli. *Nat Biotechnol 26*, 6 (Jun), 659-667. DOI= http://dx.doi.org/10.1038/nbt1401.

[10] Keasling, J.D., 2010. Manufacturing molecules through metabolic engineering. *Science 330*, 6009 (Dec 3), 1355-1358. DOI= http://dx.doi.org/10.1126/science.1193990.

[11] Latendresse, M., Krummenacker, M., Trupp, M., and Karp, P.D., 2012. Construction and completion of flux balance models from pathway databases. *Bioinformatics 28*, 3 (Feb 1), 388-396. DOI= http://dx.doi.org/10.1093/bioinformatics/btr681.

[12] Ohno, S., Furusawa, C., and Shimizu, H., 2013. In silico screening of triple reaction knockout Escherichia coli strains for overproduction of useful metabolites. *J Biosci Bioeng 115*, 2 (Feb), 221-228. DOI= http://dx.doi.org/10.1016/j.jbiosc.2012.09.004.

[13] Orth, J.D., Thiele, I., and Palsson, B.O., 2010. What is flux balance analysis? *Nat Biotechnol 28*, 3 (Mar), 245-248. DOI= http://dx.doi.org/10.1038/nbt.1614.

[14] Palsson, B.O., 2006. *Systems Biology: Properties of Reconstructed Networks*. Cambridge University Press, New York.

[15] Price, N.D., Reed, J.L., and Palsson, B.O., 2004. Genome-scale models of microbial cells: evaluating the consequences of constraints. *Nat Rev Microbiol 2*, 11 (Nov), 886-897.

[16] Reed, J.L. and Palsson, B.O., 2003. Thirteen years of building constraint-based in silico models of Escherichia coli. *J Bacteriol 185*, 9 (May), 2692-2699.

[17] Reed, J.L., Vo, T.D., Schilling, C.H., and Palsson, B.O., 2003. An expanded genome-scale model of Escherichia coli K-12 (iJR904 GSM/GPR). *Genome Biol 4*, 9, R54.

[18] Schellenberger, J., Park, J.O., Conrad, T.M., and Palsson, B.O., 2010. BiGG: a Biochemical Genetic and Genomic knowledgebase of large scale metabolic reconstructions. *BMC Bioinformatics 11*, 213. DOI= http://dx.doi.org/10.1186/1471-2105-11-213.

[19] Schilling, C.H., Edwards, J.S., Letscher, D., and Palsson, B.O., 2000. Combining pathway analysis with flux balance analysis for the comprehensive study of metabolic systems. *Biotechnol Bioeng 71*, 4, 286-306.

[20] Segre, D., Vitkup, D., and Church, G.M., 2002. Analysis of optimality in natural and perturbed metabolic networks. *Proc Natl Acad Sci U S A 99*, 23 (Nov 12), 15112-15117. DOI= http://dx.doi.org/10.1073/pnas.232349399.

[21] Shuler, M.L. and Kargi, F., 2001. *Bioprocess Engineering: Basic Concepts*. P T R Prentice Hall, Englewood Cliffs.

[22] Solnon, C., 2010. *Ant colony optimization and constraint programming*. Wiley Online Library.

[23] Stephanopoulos, G.N., Aristidou, A.A., and Nielsen, J., 1998. *Metabolic Engineering: Principles and Methodologies*. Academic Press, San Diego.

[24] Tran, K.T., Maeda, T., Sanchez-Torres, V., and Wood, T.K., 2015. Beneficial knockouts in Escherichia coli for producing hydrogen from glycerol. *Appl Microbiol Biotechnol*(Jan 8). DOI= http://dx.doi.org/10.1007/s00253-014-6338-7.

[25] Zeikus, J., Jain, M., and Elankovan, P., 1999. Biotechnology of succinic acid production and markets for derived industrial products. *Appl Microbiol Biotechnol 51*, 5, 545-552.

Evolutionary Optimization of Cancer Treatments in a Cancer Stem Cell Context

Ángel Monteagudo
Department of Computer Science
University of A Coruña
Campus de Elviña s/n, 15071 A Coruña (Spain)
angel.minsua@udc.es

José Santos
Department of Computer Science
University of A Coruña
Campus de Elviña s/n, 15071 A Coruña (Spain)
santos@udc.es

ABSTRACT

We used evolutionary computing for optimizing cancer treatments taking into account the presence and effects of cancer stem cells. We used a cellular automaton to model tumor growth at cellular level, based on the presence of the main cancer hallmarks in the cells. The cellular automaton allows the study of the emergent behavior of the multicellular system evolution in different scenarios defined by the predominance of the different hallmarks. When cancer stem cells (CSCs) are modeled, the multicellular system evolution is additionally dependent on the CSC tumor regrowth capability because their differentiation to non-stem cancer cells. When a standard treatment is applied against non-stem (differentiated) cancer cells, different effects are present depending on the strategy used to eliminate these non-stem cancer cells. We used Differential Evolution to optimize the treatment application strategy in terms of intensity, duration and periodicity to minimize the final outcome of tumor growth and regrowth.

Categories and Subject Descriptors

F.1 [**Theory of Computation**]: Computation by abstract machines—*Unbounded-action devices*

Keywords

Cellular automata, Cellular behavior, Cancer growth modeling, Cancer hallmarks, Cancer stem cells, Cancer treatment, Differential evolution

1. INTRODUCTION

Cancer is a complex collection of distinct genetic diseases united by different hallmarks (traits that govern the transformation of normal cells to malignant cells). Hanahan and Weinberg described these hallmarks in their 2000 article [14] and its update in 2011 [15]. In these articles the authors described six essential alterations: self-sufficiency in growth signals, insensitivity to growth-inhibitory (antigrowth) signals, evasion of programmed cell death (apoptosis), limitless replicative potential, sustained angiogenesis, and tissue invasion. In the update [15] the authors included two more hallmarks: reprogramming of energy metabolism and evasion of immune destruction, that emerged as critical capabilities of cancer cells. Moreover, the authors described two enabling characteristics or properties of neoplastic cells that facilitate acquisition of hallmark capabilities: genome instability and tumor-promoting inflammation (mediated by immune system cells recruited to the tumor site).

The interaction among cells generates an emergent behavior, that is, a behavior present in systems whose elements interact locally, providing a global behavior which is not possible to explain from the behavior of a single element, but rather from the interactions of the group [2]. Cellular Automata (CA) were the most used tool in Artificial Life to study and characterize the emergent behavior [16][18]. A cellular automaton is defined by a set of rules that establishes the next state of each of the sites of a grid environment given the previous state of this site and the states of its defined neighborhood, where the states can be associated with the cell states in the intended simulations of tumor growth.

Thus, with respect to the classical models based on the use of differential equations [21], the approaches relying on cellular automata models make easy the modeling at cellular level, where the state of each cell is described by its local environment. Previous works have used the CA capabilities for different purposes in tumor growth modeling [10][11][23][24], including some previous works which have used CA models based on the presence of hallmarks [1][3][30]. For example, Abbott et al. [1] and Spencer et al. [30] were interested in what sequences of mutations are most likely to produce a tumor behavior. Basanta et al. [3] used a CA model based on the Hanahan and Weinberg hallmarks, focusing their work on analyzing the effect of different environmental conditions on the sequence of acquisition of phenotypic traits. In previous works we also used CA to model the behavior of cells when the hallmarks are present and in the avascular phase, with a different aim to those previous works, since they focused on the study of the multicellular system dynamics in terms of emergent behaviors that can be obtained, analyzing the relative importance of different hallmarks [26][27] and the capability of Cancer Stem Cells (CSCs) and hallmarks to generate tumor growth and regrowth in different conditions [19][20].

The cancer stem cell theory states that a small fraction of cancer cells is responsible for tumor growth and relapse [12].

GECCO '15, July 11–15, 2015, Madrid, Spain
 ISBN 978-1-4503-3472-3/15/07...$15.00
DOI: http://dx.doi.org/10.1145/2739480.2754640

These CSCs have been shown to have various characteristics in common with stem cells, like the capacity to divide indefinitely [33]. The importance of the presence of these cells is because, if current treatments of cancer do not properly destroy enough CSCs, the tumor will probably reappear [7]. In fact, CSCs are relatively resistant to standard cytotoxic and irradiation therapies since, for example, cytotoxic therapies affect rapidly proliferating cells, whereas evidence suggests that only a small fraction of CSCs actively proliferate.

Since CSCs have an important contribution in possible regrowth behavior of a tumor, we can analyze the effects of different cancer treatment strategies taking into account CSC presence. Since the best possible treatment implies the optimal determination of different parameters like intensity and its period of application, we used an evolutionary optimization by means of Differential Evolution to determine the best strategy for the application of a treatment. For this objective, first, in Section 2 we summarize the main aspects of the tumor growth model used and based on the presence of the hallmarks, together with a basic explanation of the well-known method of Differential Evolution used for the optimization. In Section 3 we detail the results of the optimizations for the treatment strategies, focusing the analyses on the reasons of the resulting optimal strategies with respect to future tumor relapses. Finally, in Section 4 we briefly discuss the results of the methodology and experiments.

2. METHODS

2.1 Event model for tumor growth simulation

We followed the event model used by Abbott et al. [1] in their study of the likely sequences of precancerous mutations that end in cancer, to simulate the behavior of cells when different hallmarks are acquired, as previously exposed in more detail in our previous works [20][27].

In the simulation each cell resides in a site in a 3D lattice and has an artificial "genome" that indicates if any of five different hallmarks are activated as consequence of mutations. The mutations occur when a cell divides: a hallmark is acquired with a hallmark mutation rate ($1/m$) defined by the parameter m (default value $m = 100000$ as in [1][3][30]). We have considered five hallmarks: *Self-Growth (SG)*, *Ignore Growth Inhibit (IGI)*, *Evasion of Apoptosis (EA)*, *Effective Immortality (EI)* and *Genetic Instability (GI)*.

Although Abbott et al. [1] considered the hallmark angiogenesis (ability to stimulate blood vessel construction), in our work metastasis (cancer cells invade other tissues and spread to other organs) and angiogenesis are not considered, as we are interested in the first avascular phases of tumorigenesis. Thus, every cell has its genome which consists of five binary hallmarks (SG, IGI, EA, EI and GI) plus two parameters particular to each cell: Parameters *telomere length* (tl) and *hallmark mutation rate* ($1/m$) can change their values in a particular cell over time. The cell's genome is inherited by the daughter cells when a mitotic division occurs.

In the modeling mitoses are scheduled between 5 and 10 time iterations in the future for simulating the variable duration of the cell life cycle (between 15 and 24 hours), as indicated in Figure 1. Taking into account these time intervals, each iteration represents an average time of 2.6 hours, so, for example, every 1000 iterations in the simulation imply an average time of 15.5 weeks.

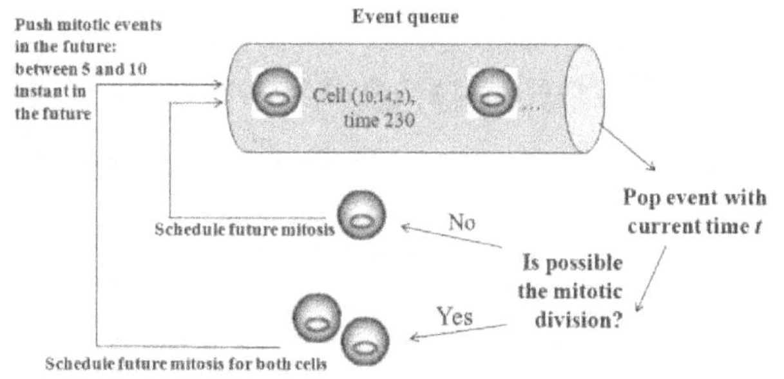

Figure 1: Scheme of the event model used in the simulation.

The main aspects of the model can be summarized in the following steps, that additionally define the implications of the acquisition of the different hallmarks:

Start: The simulation can begin with only one healthy cell at the center of the grid, as in most previous works [1][3][7][23] or with the grid full of healthy cells. Mitoses are scheduled for the initial cells (push a mitotic event in an event queue between 5 and 10 time iterations in the future).

After the new daughter cells are created, mitosis is scheduled for each of them, and so on. Each mitotic division is carried out by copying the genetic information (the hallmark status and associated parameters) of the cell to an unoccupied adjacent space in the grid. Random errors occur in this copying process, so some hallmarks can be activated, taking into account that once a hallmark is activated in a cell, it will be never repaired by another mutation [1].

In terms of complex systems, the emergent growth behaviors are independent of the initial condition regarding the initial number of healthy cells, with the only difference of the required iterations to obtain a stable behavior [26][27].

Pop event: The events are ordered on event time. Pop event from the event queue with the highest priority (the nearest in time).

Random cell death test: Cells undergo random cell death with low probability ($1/a$ chance of death, default value $a = 1000$) because of several causes.

Genetic damage test: The larger the number of hallmark mutations, the greater the probability of cell death (n/e, being n the number of hallmarks acquired and e a parameter with default value 10). If "Evade apoptosis" (EA) is ON, death as consequence of the genetic damage is not applied.

Mitosis tests:

1. **Replicative potential checking**: If the telomere length (tl) is 0, the cell dies, unless the hallmark "Effective immortality" (Limitless replicative potential, EI) is mutated (ON). The initial default telomere length is 50 which is decreased with every cell division.

2. **Growth factor checking**: As in [1][3][30], cells can perform divisions only if they are within a predefined spatial boundary, which represents a threshold in the concentration of growth factor; beyond this area (95% of the inner space in each dimension in our simulations, which represents 85.7% of the 3D grid inner space) growth signals are too faint to prompt mitosis (unless hallmark SG is ON).
3. **Ignore growth inhibit checking**: If there are not empty cells in the neighborhood, the cell cannot perform a mitotic division. Following the simulation used in [1][30], if the hallmark "Ignore growth inhibit" (IGI) is ON, then the cell competes for survival with a neighbor cell and with a likelihood of success ($1/g$, default value $g = 30$).

If the three tests indicate possibility of mitosis:

- Increase the hallmark mutation rate ($1/m$) if genetic instability (GI) is ON, by a factor i (default value $i = 100$ as in [1][3]).
- Add mutations to the new cells according to hallmark mutation rate ($1/m$).
- Decrease (one unit) telomere length in both cells.
- Push events. Schedule mitotic events (push in event queue) for both cells: Mother and daughter, with the random times in the future.

If mitosis cannot be applied:

- Schedule a mitotic event (in queue) for mother cell.

2.2 Cancer Stem Cell modeling

CSCs have been shown to have various characteristics in common with stem cells, like the capacity to divide indefinitely [33]. Additionally, these CSCs present resistance to apoptosis and they present heterogeneity, i.e. potential for multidirectional differentiation [12]. CSC theory states that the small fraction of these cells is responsible for tumor growth and relapse. We followed the CSC simulation used by Enderling and Hahnfeldt [7] regarding their differentiation. Thus, CSCs will divide symmetrically, with a low probability ($p_s = 0.01$ in [7]) or asymmetrically (with probability $1 - p_s$) to produce a CSC and a non-stem cancer cell (Differentiated Cancer Cell - DCC). In addition, CSCs have the hallmarks *effective immortality* (EI) and *evade apoptosis* (EA) given their defining properties.

Moreover, in our simulation, in the asymmetric division, the differentiated non-stem cancer cell acquires (randomly) one of the hallmarks considered in our modeling as well as the initial telomere length which defines its finite replicative potential. In the simulations, beginning with the grid full of healthy cells, we will introduce a low number of CSCs in the inner area with growth factor to check their effect on the behavior of the multicellular system evolution. In several cancer types, such proportion of identified CSCs varies, being, for example, about 2.5% in colon cancer population [25] and 1-5% of primary tumors in human mammary carcinomas [17].

Algorithm 2.1: DIFFERENTIAL EVOLUTION(*Population*)

```
for each Individual ∈ Population
  do {Individual ← INITIALIZERANDOMPOSITIONS()
repeat
 for each Individual x ∈ Population
   do { x1, x2, x3 ← GETRANDOMINDIVIDUAL(Population)
        // must be distinct from each other and x
        R ← GETRANDOM(1, n) // the highest possible
        // value n is the dimensionality of the problem to be
        // optimized
        for each i ∈ 1 : n
        // Compute individual's potentially new position
        // y = [y1, ..., yn]
          do { ri ← GETRANDOM(0, 1)// uniformly in
               // open range (0,1)
               if ((i = R) || (ri < CR))
                  yi = x1i + F(x2i − x3i)
               else yi = xi
        if (f(y) ≤ f(x))  x = y
        // replace x with y in Population
until TERMINATIONCRITERION()
return (GETLOWESTFITNESS(Population))
// return candidate solution
```

2.3 Differential Evolution

Differential Evolution (DE) [22] is a population-based search method. DE creates new candidate solutions by combining existing ones according to a simple formula of vector crossover and mutation, and then keeping whichever candidate solution has the best score or fitness on the optimization problem at hand. The central idea of the algorithm is the use of difference vectors for generating perturbations in a population of vectors. This algorithm is specially suited for optimization problems where possible solutions are defined by a real-valued vector. The basic DE algorithm is summarized in the pseudo-code of Algorithm 2.1.

Differential Evolution needs a reduced number of parameters to define its implementation. The parameters are F or differential weight and CR or crossover probability. The weight factor F (usually in $[0, 2]$) is applied over the vector resulting from the difference between pairs of vectors (x_2 and x_3). CR is the probability of crossing over a given vector of the population (target vector x) and a "donor" vector created from the weighted difference of two vectors ($x_1 + F(x_2 - x_3)$) [6]. We used the "binomial" crossover (specified in the pseudo-code of Algorithm 2.1), for defining the value of the "trial" vector (y) in each vector component or position i [6]. Finally, the index R guarantees that at least one of the parameters (genes) will be changed in such generation of the trial solution.

Finally, the selection operator maintains constant the population size. The fitness of the trial vector ($f(y)$) and the target vector ($f(x)$) are compared to determine which one survives for the next generation: If the new trial vector yields an equal or lower (better) value of the objective function, it replaces the corresponding target vector in the next generation; otherwise the target vector is retained [6]. Thus, the fitness of the best solution of the population is improved or remains the same through generations.

By combining different mutation and crossover operators various schemes have been designed. The usual variants or schemes of DE choose the base vector x_1 randomly (variant $DE/rand/1/bin$, where 1 denotes the number of differences involved in the construction of the mutant or donor vector and bin denotes the crossover type) or as the individual with the best fitness found up to the moment (x_{best}) (variant $DE/best/1/bin$). To avoid the high selective pressure of the latter, we used a tournament to pick the vector x_1, which also allows us to easily establish the selective pressure by means of the tournament size.

As Feoktistov [8] indicates, the fundamental idea of the algorithm is to adapt the step length ($F(x_2 - x_3)$) intrinsically along the evolutionary process. At the beginning of generations the step length is large, because individuals are far away from each other. As the evolution goes on, the population converges and the step length becomes smaller and smaller, providing this way an automatic balance in the search.

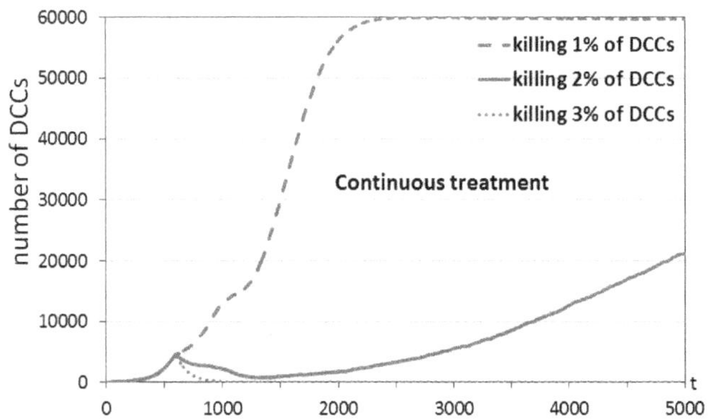

Figure 2: Evolution of the number of DCCs through time iterations when continuous treatments that kill 1%, 2% and 3% of the DCCs are applied in every time iteration.

3. RESULTS

3.1 Examples of treatment strategies

We selected different scenarios to show the implications of different treatment strategies when CSCs are present. We considered ideal treatments in the sense that these only kill cancer cells, although this does not change the reasoning and conclusions drawn from the experiments. The grid size was 64000 (40 sites in each dimension), the simulations begin with the grid full of healthy cells except the incorporated CSCs, from the beginning, in the inner area with growth factor. These CSCs correspond to a 5% of the grid size. We also selected a representative example in which differentiated tumor cells (DCCs) have a high invasion potential in the surrounding tissue, as we used $g = 5$. This means that cells that acquire the hallmark *ignore growth inhibit* (IGI) have a high probability ($1/g$) to escape the contact inhibition mechanism. Cervical cancer is an example [14]. Moreover, since the parameter m determines the probability of acquisition of hallmarks and consequently the onset of a tumor behavior, we used $m = 1000$ to obtain tumor development behaviors without using a large number of iterations. Nevertheless, the conclusions and CSC implications commented here are independent of the particular scenario considered regarding the relevance of the hallmarks.

Figure 2 shows an example where continuous treatments are applied in every iteration. The treatments are applied from iteration 600, in order to give DCCs the opportunity to growth in number. When a treatment that kills 1% or 2% of the DCCs is applied in every time iteration, the number of DCCs is not controlled enough, ending with an increase of DCCs that will cover the full grid. On the contrary, when a treatment that kills 3% of the DCCs is applied in every time iteration, the number of DCCs is controlled to a minimum through time.

As an opposite strategy, Figure 3 shows a run where a discontinuous and periodic treatment is applied. The treatment kills the 100% of the DCCs every 600 iterations. The problem with this strategy is that the regrowth of DCCs is faster with respect to a situation without treatment application, such as the initial increase of DCCs. The 2D snapshots shown at the bottom of Figure 3 explain the reason. These snapshots correspond to a central plane that crosses the grid, which provide more information than the 3D representation as these show the internal distribution of the cells. For example, at $t = 3000$, all DCCs are eliminated, so there are empty sites that are filled in few iterations with mostly healthy cells. Nevertheless, because of these empty sites, the few CSCs (shown with enlarged size) had more opportunities to proliferate and differentiate, generating a few DCCs (see snapshots at $t = 3020$ and $t = 3025$) that can produce a fast increase of a tumor bulk. In a normal situation, given the few possibilities for CSCs to proliferate (the grid is almost full), the increase of DCCs is slower. This fast increase is well documented in many cancer treatment applications [29][32]. So, this effect must be taken into account in treatment applications, trying to difficult CSC proliferation and differentiation.

Figure 4 now shows an "average" strategy between these two extreme cases. The treatment is applied periodically, again every 600 time iterations, but killing only 5% of DCCs in each time iteration. Moreover, the treatment is maintained during 150 time iterations. Figure 4 shows that now, when the treatment stops after such 150 iterations, the increase of the regrowth is slower with respect to the previous case. The reason can be guessed looking at the snapshots at the bottom of Figure 4. For example, the snapshot at $t = 3020$ shows that the CSCs are immediately surrounded by healthy cells, given the very few free sites produced as consequence of the low-intensity treatment, so the CSCs had no so many opportunities to proliferate and differentiate as in the previous case. So, this seems a good strategy, trying to difficult CSC proliferation through low-intensity treatments.

Figure 5 illustrates the intensity used during each treatment application, measured as the percentage of DCCs killed in each iteration. This Figure shows the accumulative treatment intensity as consequence of the application of previous treatment strategies, that is, the summation of the intensity of the treatment during the intervals of its application. In Figure 5 we considered the intensities as probabilities of killing a DCC, so these are in the interval [0,1] in each iteration.

In the cases corresponding to the periodic treatments previously considered, logically the accumulative intensity follows a linear progression. With the discontinuous treatments, the accumulative intensity is increased in the par-

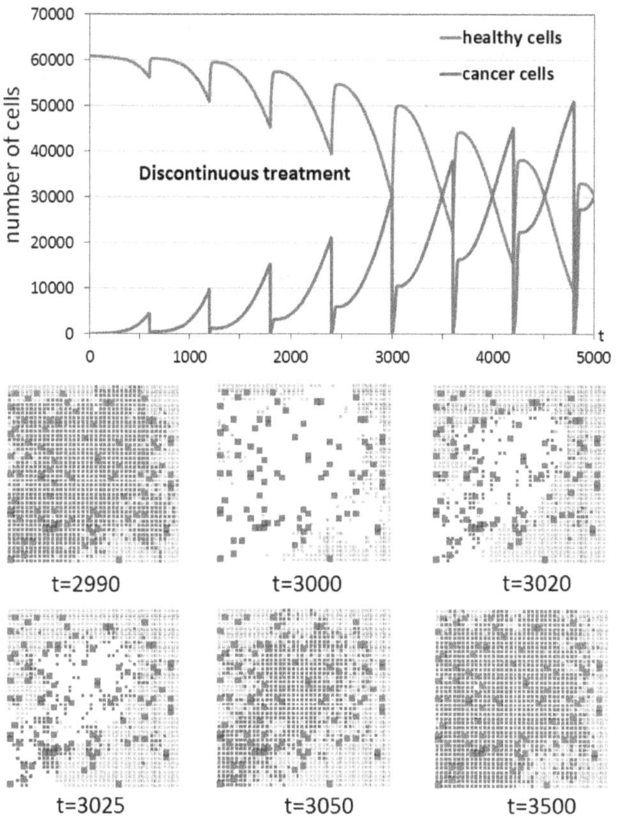

Figure 3: Evolution of the number of DCCs through time iterations when a periodic discontinuous treatment is applied (Every 600 time iterations killing the 100% of the DCCs in such iterations). The bottom part shows 2D snapshots of the central part of the grid at given time iterations (Colors: Gray - healthy cells, Blue - DCCs, Red-enlarged size - CSCs).

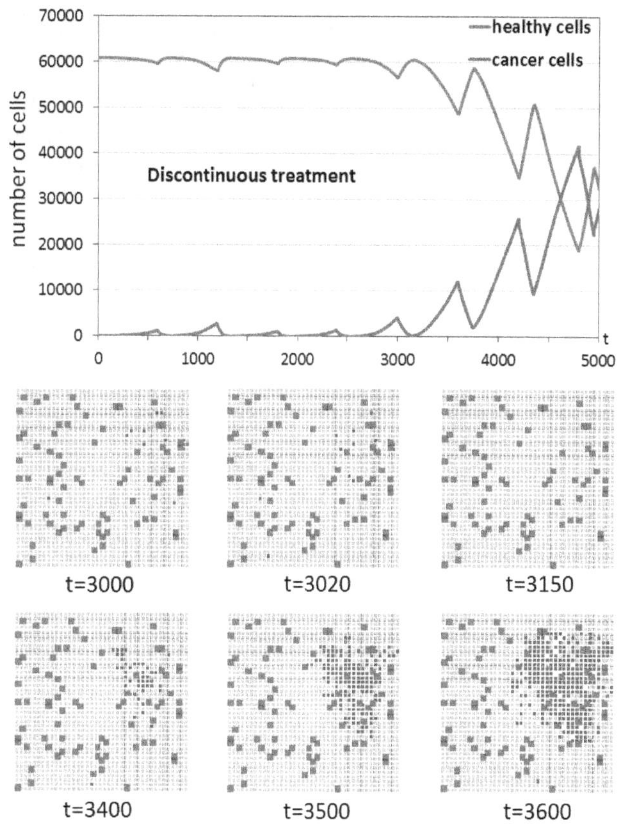

Figure 4: Evolution of the number of DCCs through time iterations when a periodic discontinuous treatment is applied (Every 600 time iterations killing the 5% of the DCCs during the next 150 iterations). The bottom part shows 2D snapshots of the central part of the grid at given time iterations.

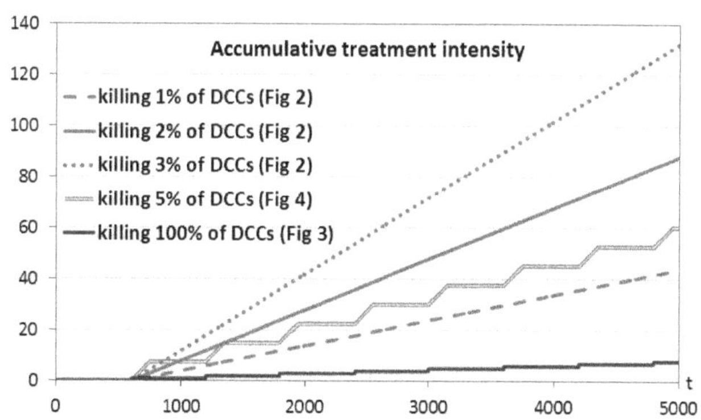

Figure 5: Accumulative treatment intensity across iterations with different treatment strategies of previous Figures.

ticular iterations the treatments are applied. Figure 5 and previous Figures (Figs. 2-4) show the different behaviors in both features (number of final DCCs and accumulative treatment intensity): The continuous treatment that kills 3% of DCCs in each iteration has the number of DCCs controlled at the cost of high treatment intensity. The discontinuous periodic treatment with high intensity (Figure 3) has a lower value in the accumulative treatment intensity but has a poorer control of the final number of DCCs (as consequence of the fast regrowth of DCCs). Finally, the periodic treatment that kills 5% of DCCs in each iteration, maintained during 150 time iterations (Figure 4) has a better control over the final DCCs (with respect to the previous case, Fig. 3) but a higher accumulative intensity. In order to find out what strategy would be the best regarding these objectives, we applied the evolutionary methodology to optimize the treatment taking into account such objectives or measures.

3.2 Treatment strategy optimizations

We can first begin with the use of the evolutionary algorithm to try to optimize a single treatment application. The first test implies the optimization regarding the intensity of application of a conventional treatment (chemotherapy or radiotherapy) that kills DCCs as well as its duration. We used the previous scenario with high invasion potential of cells with the hallmark IGI acquired, with a 5% of incorporated CSCs. The genotypes include the encoding of both parameters (intensity and duration) in the interval [-1,1], while the encoded values are decoded in the interval [0%,100%] for the intensity of the treatment, meaning that a number of DCCs corresponding to such percentage are killed in each iteration. The DCCs subject to be killed are randomly selected. For the duration of the treatment we used an ample range [0,600] (which corresponds to an interval [0,65 days]), meaning that the treatment with the encoded intensity of the first parameter is maintained such number of iterations.

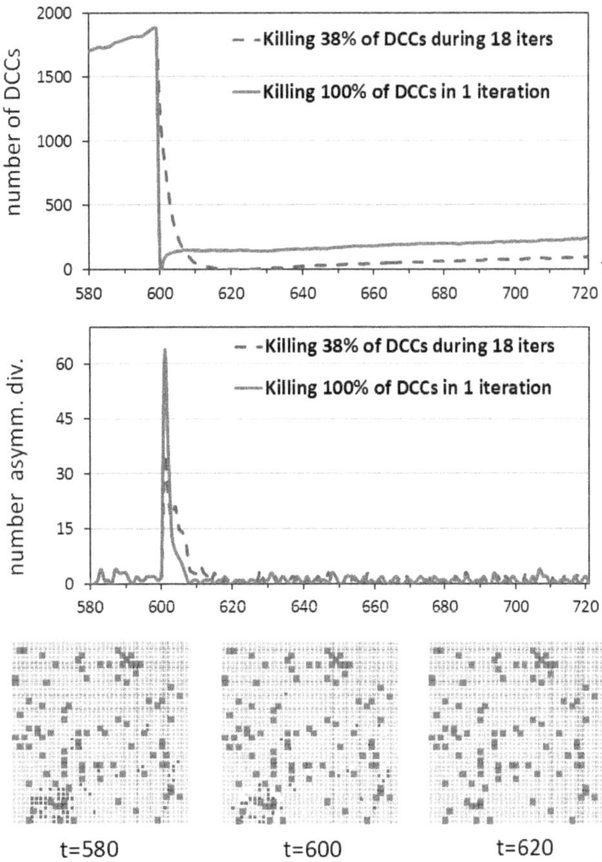

Figure 6: Multicellular system evolution when a best evolved treatment is applied, with its intensity and duration optimized. Treatments begin in time iteration $t = 600$. In the example, the best evolved treatment kills 38% of DCCs in the next 18 time iterations. A high-intensity treatment that kills the 100% of DCCs only at $t = 600$ is included for comparison. Upper part: Evolution of DCCs through time iterations. Middle part: Evolution of the number of CSC asymmetric divisions. Bottom Part: 2D snapshots of the central part of the grid corresponding to the multicellular system evolution at particular time iterations when the best evolved treatment is applied.

For the fitness function we used a simple formula, which takes into account two terms: First, the final number of DCCs after a given number of iterations (100) once the treatment is stopped. Second, the intensity used during the treatment application. This second aspect is not easy to measure, but we can assume it is related to the summation of the percentage of DCCs killed in each iteration (as illustrated in previous examples and Figure 5). Treatments always begin at time iteration $t = 600$. This means, for example, that a high-intensity treatment which kills 100% of DCCs in one iteration is equivalent to a treatment that kills 1% of DCCs during 100 iterations. The fitness is a weighted summation of both terms (0.01·final number of DCCs + treatment intensity, with the weights tuned so that both terms have close values in best individuals). Finally, the fitness of each encoded parameter set is averaged with 5 independent runs of the multicellular system.

We used DE with a population of 50 individuals, with standard values for the other parameters in DE: $CR = 0.9$ and $F = 0.9$ [31], whereas the size of the tournament to choose the base vector was 8% of the population, which implies a low selective pressure when selecting such vector to disturb (Section 2.3). The evolutions were run for 50 generations using again a grid size of 64000 sites. For this test we used the parameters previously commented ($g = 5$ and $m = 1000$ while the rest of hallmark parameters were set to their standard values) and, as indicated, the encoded treatments begin at time iteration $t = 600$. Because of the different duration of the encoded treatments, the simulation time of each treatment is variable. Given the high requirements in processing time for the simulation of the multicellular system, using an Intel Core i3 processor at 3.33 GHz and 4 Gytes of main memory, the average computing time for each DE generation was 36 minutes.

Figure 6 shows the behavior with one of the best strategies found by the evolutionary algorithm, with an intensity of 38% and duration of 18 iterations (1.95 days). The upper part corresponds to the evolution of the number of DCCs. We included a high-intensity treatment for comparison, which kills the 100% of DCCs only at time iteration $t = 600$. The middle graph illustrates the number of CSC asymmetric divisions in both cases, which is incremented when CSCs have more opportunities to proliferate during the treatment administration. Finally, the bottom subfigures show again 2D snapshots of central sections of the grid at three time iterations when the best evolved treatment was applied. The snapshots show that, even with this treatment intensity that generates a few empty sites (see snapshot at $t = 600$) so the surrounding CSCs can take advantage for their proliferation and differentiation, the maintained treatment eliminates those DCCs in the next few iterations. All the best evolved treatments follow this pattern avoiding high intensities: the average intensity of the best evolved treatments was 32.3% (standard deviation 5.1) in 10 independent DE runs, while the average duration was 26.4 iterations (standard deviation 9.3).

In a second test we used DE for the optimization of three parameters of a treatment: the previous two (intensity and duration), together with the period of application of the treatment. As in the previous case, the treatment intensity, once decoded, can vary in the interval [0%,100%]. Now, the period of application can vary in the interval [0,600], meaning that the treatment is periodically repeated with the period indicated with such value. The other parameter, the duration of the treatment in each application, is dependent on the period of application. This parameter is encoded again in the interval [-1,1], but decoded taking into account the encoded value of the period of application. For example, if the encoded value for the period represents 500 time iterations and the encoded value for the duration is 0 (middle value in the interval [-1,1]), then the duration is 250 time iterations in each application. The other DE parameters are the same as in the previous test. We used simulations of the multicellular system with a minimum of 3000 time iterations, so every encoded treatment strategy is applied several times to determine the fitness. Given the higher number of time iterations in the evaluation of each encoded solution, the average computing time per generation is now 237 minutes, using the same population size (50) and computing platform as in the previous test.

As in the previous case, the fitness is defined as the same weighted sum of the intensity of the treatment and the final number of DCCs after 100 time iterations of its cessation. The first term is measured again as the intensity used across the whole period since the beginning of the treatment application, taking into account that all treatments are applied after time iteration $t = 600$ in order to have an initial and significant increase of DCCs.

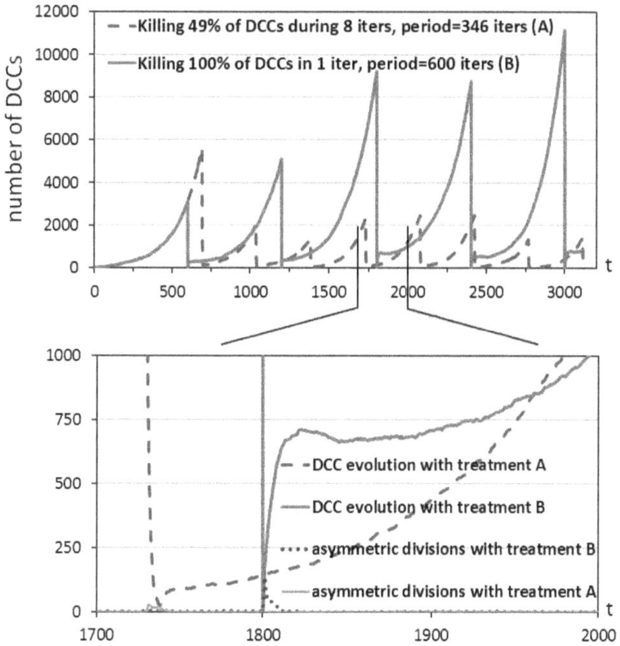

Figure 7: Multicellular system evolution when a best evolved treatment is applied, with its period, intensity and duration optimized. Treatments do not begin before time iteration $t = 600$. In the example, the best evolved treatment kills 49% of DCCs during 8 time iterations and a period of 346 iterations (treatment A). A high-intensity treatment that kills the 100% of DCCs every 600 iterations is included for comparison (treatment B). Upper part: Evolution of DCCs through time iterations. Bottom Part: Interval of time iterations enlarged for a more detailed view of the effect of the treatment strategies on next DCC progression. This bottom Figure also includes the number of CSC asymmetric divisions with the two treatments.

Figure 7 now shows the behavior with one of the best evolved strategies, with an intensity of 49%, a period of application of 346 (37.5 days) and a duration of 8 iterations (21 hours). Again, the graph includes, for comparison, a high-intensity treatment that kills the 100% of DCCs in only one iteration, being periodically applied with a period of 600 time iterations. Figure 7 includes an enlarged view of a particular interval of the multicellular system evolution, between time iterations 1700 and 2000, which denotes the same effect previously explained: A high-intensity treatment promotes CSC proliferation and differentiation (as shown with the higher number of CSC asymmetric divisions in the bottom part of Figure 7), so there is a posterior high increase of DCCs. Note that this enlarged view shows that, after the fast increase of DCCs, their progression is more stable in next iterations. This is because in the CSC asymmetric divisions the new DCCs acquire randomly one of the five hallmarks and only the hallmark IGI provides an immediate advantage for fast proliferation. Thus, more time iterations are necessary so that a sufficient number of DCCs acquire such hallmark to begin again an increase in their number. On the contrary, the evolved periodic and discontinuous treatment makes more difficult CSC differentiation, so the future regrowth of DCCs is slower and consequently it is easier to control DCC increase.

4. DISCUSSION AND CONCLUSIONS

We used a cellular automaton to model tumor growth at cellular level, based on the presence of the main cancer hallmarks in the cells. The abstract model of cancer hallmarks allows an analysis of the multicellular system in terms of emergent behaviors. Without the need to deepen in the gene level (oncogenes or suppressor genes that can activate a hallmark), the abstract model of hallmarks permits a systemic view of the emergent tumor growth behavior, in line with Savage's comment: "the recent focus on genetics and pathways in individual cells has caused many researchers to neglect the systemic view" [28].

In the present work we used the model to analyze the implications of treatment strategies taking into account the presence of CSCs, using evolutionary computing to establish the best strategies of treatment applications considering the regrowth capacity of such CSCs. We emphasize the difference of our work and aim with respect to standard treatment strategies. For example, an usual treatment like FOLFOX4 protocol [9] was demonstrated effectiveness against regrowth in phase II of colon cancer [5]. This is a chemotherapy treatment in which drugs are used to kill the cancer cells. Mostly two or more drugs are used in combination which proves to be more effective. In FOLFOX chemotherapy, drugs used are Fluorouracil 5FU, Folinic acid (Leucovorin) and Oxaliplatin. Typically the treatment is composed of 12 phases or cycles, each one 14 days length. These types of protocols were experimentally tested and tuned to shrink the tumor bulk. Nevertheless, no treatment analyses took into account, with an exhaustive study, the effect of possible future relapses (regrowths). So, computational experiments, even with the simplifications performed, can go a step ahead with respect to in vitro and in vivo analyses, and additionally allow explaining the reasons of the resultant behaviors.

Since we considered different terms in the fitness, it is obvious that we could use a multi-objective approach for searching the Pareto Set of non-dominated individuals regarding, for example, the treatments that minimize the total intensity applied and the treatments that minimize the final number of DCCs (with obvious optimal strategies). Nevertheless, we first tackled the problem with the mono-objective approach to analyze the implications of the presence of CSCs and the main aspects that can define a treatment strategy.

It is also obvious that other treatment strategies can be considered, such as applications with increasing or decreasing intensities through time. Although we used a particular scenario of relevance of hallmarks, and consequently the treatment parameters are optimized for that scenario, the implications of CSC presence are general: In contrast with the main current attempts to CSC control focused on alternatives for CSC elimination and induction of CSC differentiation [4][13], our analyses show that treatments should be maintained during very few days, avoiding high intensities and, consequently, with longer periods than the ones used in standard treatments. This is always with the aim to make more difficult CSC proliferation and consequently their differentiation in order to minimize their future effect on a possible tumor regrowth.

5. ACKNOWLEDGMENTS

This work was funded by the Ministry of Economy and Competitiveness of Spain (project TIN2013-40981-R).

6. REFERENCES

[1] R. Abbott, S. Forrest, and K. Pienta. Simulating the hallmarks of cancer. *Artificial Life*, 12:617–634, 2006.

[2] C. Adami. *Introduction to artificial life.* Telos-Springer Verlag, 1998.

[3] D. Basanta, B. Ribba, E. Watkin, B. You, and A. Deutsch. Computational analysis of the influence of the microenvironment on carcinogenesis. *Mathematical Biosciences*, 229:22–20, 2011.

[4] K. Chen, Y.-H. Huang, and J.-L. Chen. Understanding and targeting cancer stem cells: therapeutic implications and challenges. *Acta Pharmacologica Sinica*, 34:732–740, 2013.

[5] Colon Cancer Stages, http://www.cancer.gov/cancertopics/pdq/treatment/colon/HealthProfessional/page3.

[6] S. Das and P. Suganthan. Differential evolution: A survey of the state-of-the-art. *IEEE Transactions on Evolutionary Computation*, 15(1):4–31, 2011.

[7] H. Enderling and P. Hahnfeldt. Cancer stem cells in solid tumors: Is 'evading apoptosis' a hallmark of cancer? *Prog. Biophys. Mol. Bio.*, 106:391–399, 2011.

[8] V. Feoktistov. *Differential Evolution: In Search of Solutions.* Springer, New York, USA, 2006.

[9] FOLFOX4:http://www2.mdanderson.org/depts/oncolog/articles/10/10-oct/10-10-compass.html.

[10] P. Gerlee and A. Anderson. An evolutionary hybrid cellular automaton model of solid tumour growth. *Journal of Theoretical Biology*, 246(4):583–603, 2007.

[11] J. Gevertz, G. Gillies, and S. Torquato. Simulating tumor growth in confined heterogeneous environments. *Phys. Biol.*, 5(3):1–10, 2008.

[12] J. Gil, A. Stembalska, K. Pesz, and M. Sasiadek. Cancer stem cells: the theory and perspectives in cancer therapy. *J App Genet*, 49(2):193–199, 2008.

[13] L. Han, S. Shi, T. Gong, Z. Zhang, and X. Sun. Cancer stem cells: therapeutic implications and perspectives in cancer therapy. *Acta Pharmacol. Sin.*, 3(2):65–75, 2013.

[14] D. Hanahan and R. Weinberg. The hallmarks of cancer. *Cell*, 100:57–70, 2000.

[15] D. Hanahan and R. Weinberg. Hallmarks of cancer: The next generation. *Cell*, 144(5):646–674, 2011.

[16] A. Ilachinski. *Cellular automata. A discrete universe.* World Scientific, 2001.

[17] H. Korkaya, A. Paulson, F. Iovino, and M. Wicha. HER2 regulates the mammary stem/progenitor cell population driving tumorigenesis and invasion. *Oncogene*, 27(47):6120–6130, 2008.

[18] C. Langton. Life at the edge of chaos. In *Artificial Life II, Addison-Wesley*, pages 41–49, 1992.

[19] A. Monteagudo and J. Santos. Cancer stem cell modeling using a cellular automaton. *Lecture Notes in Computer Science*, 7931:21–31, 2013.

[20] A. Monteagudo and J. Santos. Studying the capability of different cancer hallmarks to initiate tumor growth using a cellular automaton simulation. Application in a cancer stem cell context. *BioSystems*, 1:46–58, 2014.

[21] M. Patel and S. Nagl. *The role of model integration in complex systems. An example from cancer biology.* Springer-Verlag, 2010.

[22] K. Price, R. Storn, and J. Lampinen. *Differential Evolution. A Practical Approach to Global Optimization.* Springer - Natural Comp. Series, 2005.

[23] K. Rejniak and A. Anderson. Hybrid models of tumor growth. *WIREs Syst Biol Med*, 3:115–125, 2010.

[24] B. Ribba, T. Alarcon, K. Marron, P. Maini, and Z. Agur. The use of hybrid cellular automaton models for improving cancer therapy. *Proc. ACRI 2004, LNCS*, 3305:444–453, 2004.

[25] L. Ricci-Vitiani, D. Lombardi, E. Pilozzi, M. Biffoni, M. Todaro, C. Peschle, and R. De Maria. Identification and expansion of human colon-cancer-initiating cells. *Nature*, 445(7123):111–115, 2007.

[26] J. Santos and A. Monteagudo. Study of cancer hallmarks relevance using a cellular automaton tumor growth model. *Proceedings PPSN 2012 - Parallel Problem Solving from Nature - Lecture Notes in Computer Science*, 7491:489–499, 2012.

[27] J. Santos and A. Monteagudo. Analysis of behaviour transitions in tumour growth using a cellular automaton simulation. *IET Systems Biology doi: 10.1049/iet-syb.2014.0015*, pages 1–13, 2014.

[28] N. Savage. Modelling: Computing cancer. *Nature*, 491:S62–S63, 2012.

[29] A. Sottoriva, J. Verhoeff, T. Borovski, S. McWeeney, L. Naumov, J. Medema, P. Sloot, and L. Vermeulen. Cancer stem cell tumor model reveals invasive morphology and increased phenotypical heterogeneity. *Cancer Research*, 70(1):46–56, 2010.

[30] S. Spencer, R. Gerety, K. Pienta, and S. Forrest. Modeling somatic evolution in tumorigenesis. *PLoS Computational Biology*, 2(8):939–947, 2006.

[31] R. Storn and K. Price. Differential evolution - a simple and efficient heuristic for global optimization over continuous spaces. *Journal of Global Optimization*, 11(4):341–359, 1997.

[32] V. Vainstein, O. Kirnasovsky, Y. Kogan, and Z. Agur. Strategies for cancer stem cell elimination: Insights from mathematical modeling. *Journal of Theoretical Biology*, 298:32–41, 2012.

[33] D. Wodarz and N. Komarova. Can loss of apoptosis protect against cancer? *Trends in Genetics*, 23(5):32–41, 2012.

A Repair Method for Differential Evolution with Combined Variants to Solve Dynamic Constrained Optimization Problems

María-Yaneli Ameca-Alducin, Efrén Mezura-Montes and Nicandro Cruz-Ramírez
Artificial Intelligence Research Center, University of Veracruz
Xalapa, Veracruz, México
yaneliameca@gmail.com, {emezura,ncruz}@uv.mx

ABSTRACT

Repair methods, which usually require feasible solutions as reference, have been employed by Evolutionary Algorithms to solve constrained optimization problems. In this work, a novel repair method, which does not require feasible solutions as reference and inspired by the differential mutation, is added to an algorithm which uses two variants of differential evolution to solve dynamic constrained optimization problems. The proposed repair method replaces a local search operator with the aim to improve the overall performance of the algorithm in different frequencies of change in the constrained space. The proposed approach is compared against other recently proposed algorithms in an also recently proposed benchmark. The results show that the proposed improved algorithm outperforms its original version and provides a very competitive overall performance with different change frequencies.

CCS Concepts

•**Computing methodologies** → **Genetic algorithms;**
•**Mathematics of computing** → *Continuous functions;*

Keywords

Differential Evolution; Constraint-handling; Dynamic optimization

1. INTRODUCTION

Constrained optimization problems have been successfully solved by Evolutionary Algorithms (EAs) [6, 12, 16]. Nevertheless, among the current trends which have attracted the interest of researchers and practitioners is the presence of dynamism in the fitness function and/or the constraints of the optimization problem [13, 18]. This type of problems is known as the Dynamic Constrained Optimization Problem (DCOP) [17, 18, 20, 22]. A DCOP can be seen as a search problem where its fitness landscape and feasible region change through time. In their original versions, EAs were not designed to deal with dynamic search spaces because they lacked mechanisms to detect search space changes [18, 17]. Without loss of generality, a DCOP can be defined as to:

Find $\vec{x}$, at each time t, which:

$$\min_{\vec{x}\in F_t\subseteq[L,U]} f(\vec{x},t)$$

where $t \in N^+$ is the current time,

$$[L,U] = \{\vec{x} = (x_1, x_2, ..., x_D)|L_i \leq x_i \leq U_i, i = 1 \ldots D\}$$

is the search space,
subject to:

$$F_t = \{\vec{x}|\vec{x} \in [L,U], g_i(\vec{x},t) \leq 0, i = 1 \ldots m,$$
$$h_j(\vec{x},t) = 0, j = 1 \ldots p\}$$

is called the feasible region at time t.

$\forall\vec{x} \in F_t$ if there exists a solution $\vec{x}^* \in F_t$ such that $f(\vec{x}^*,t) \leq f(\vec{x},t)$, then $\vec{x}^*$ is called a feasible optimal solution and $f(\vec{x}^*,t)$ is called the feasible optima value at time t.

Four types of DCOPs are defined: i) a static objective function and static constraints (i.e. a static constrained optimization problem), ii) a dynamic objective function and static constraints, iii) a static objective function and dynamic constraints, and iv) a dynamic objective function and dynamic constraints.

In the specialized literature on DCOPs, the Genetic Algorithm (GA) is the most popular EA, where different mechanisms to deal with fitness landscape and feasible region changes have been considered, such as diversity maintenance [4, 5, 17] and solution repair [18, 20, 22]. On the other hand, recent meta-heuristic approaches like the Dynamic Constrained T-Cell (DCTC), which is inspired by the T-Cell model of the immune system[2], has been used to tackle DCOPs. Another bio-inspired algorithm recently adapted to solve DCOPs is the Gravitational Search Algorithm (GSA), where a repair mechanism [22, 24] was also considered. Furthermore, in [21], an algorithm that combined Differential Evolution (DE) and a repair method was proposed in order to produce better results. In another DE-based algorithm, the combination of two DE variants, called Dynamic Differential Evolution with Combined Variants (DDECV), was proposed to solve DCOPs [1]. Among its added mechanisms there was a local search operator to promote convergence to

GECCO '15, July 11 - 15, 2015, Madrid, Spain
© 2015 ACM. ISBN 978-1-4503-3472-3/15/07...$15.00
DOI: http://dx.doi.org/10.1145/2739480.2754786

the dynamic feasible region of the also dynamic search space. However, such operator showed some limitations to generate feasible solutions after a change [1]. On the other hand, the above mentioned repair methods require feasible solutions as reference to convert infeasible solutions into feasible ones. This is the main motivation of this paper, where a novel repair method, which does not require feasible solutions to operate, and inspired by the differential mutation operator, is proposed to promote a better overall performance of the approach. A set of experiments focused on the frequency of the change in the search space are carried out, because the repair method has an important role for the algorithm to recover after a change. The results obtained are compared against several state-of-the-art approches to solve DCOPs.

The rest of the paper is divided as follows: Section 2 details DDECV, while Section 3 introduces the proposed repair method. Section 4 presents the experiments and results obtained by the algorithm in a benchmark recently proposed [18]. Finally, Section 5 includes the conclusions and directions regarding future research.

2. DDECV ALGORITHM

DDECV is based on the combination of two well-known DE variants, DE/rand/1/bin (base variant) and DE/best/-1/bin (alternative variant) [1]. DE is a stochastic search algorithm based on a set of solutions called vectors [23]. Such set is called population and each one of its vectors can be represented as: $\vec{x}_{i,G}$, $i = 1, \ldots, NP$, where $\vec{x}_{i,G}$ is vector i at generation G, and NP represents the population size. For both variants, each target vector $\vec{x}_{i,G}$ generates one trial vector $\vec{u}_{i,G}$ by using a mutant vector $\vec{v}_{i,G}$. For DE/rand/1/bin, the mutant vector is computed as in Equation 1, where $\vec{x}_{r0,G}$, $\vec{x}_{r1,G}$, and $\vec{x}_{r2,G}$ are vectors chosen at random from the current population ($r0 \neq r1 \neq r2 \neq i$. $\vec{x}_{r0,G}$ is known as the base vector and $\vec{x}_{r1,G}$, and $\vec{x}_{r2,G}$ are the difference vectors. $F > 0$ is a scale factor defined by the user. For DE/best/1/bin the mutant vector is generated as in Equation 2, where the only difference is the fact that the base vector is the best solution in the current population (represented as $\vec{x}_{best,G}$).

$$\vec{v}_{i,G} = \vec{x}_{r0,G} + F(\vec{x}_{r1,G} - \vec{x}_{r2,G}) \tag{1}$$

$$\vec{v}_{i,G} = \vec{x}_{best,G} + F(\vec{x}_{r1,G} - \vec{x}_{r2,G}) \tag{2}$$

After the mutant vector $\vec{v}_{i,G}$ is generated, for the two DE variants discussed in this paper, it is combined with the target vector $\vec{x}_{i,G}$ by applying a crossover operator as shown in Equation 3.

$$u_{i,j,G} = \begin{cases} v_{i,j,G} & \text{if}(rand_j \leq CR) \text{ or } (j = J_{rand}) \\ x_{i,j,G} & \text{otherwise} \end{cases} \tag{3}$$

where $CR \in [0, 1]$ defines the similarity between the trial vector and the mutant vector, $rand_j$ generates a random number between 0 and 1, and $j \in \{1, \ldots, D\}$ is the j-th variable of the D- dimensional vector. $J_{rand} \in [1, D]$ is an integer random number which ensures that at least one element of the mutant vector is copied to the trial vector so as to prevent copies of the target vector.

To end the process, the best vector, based on fitness, between the target and trial vector is chosen for the next generation as follows:

$$\vec{x}_{i,G+1} = \begin{cases} \vec{u}_{i,G} & \text{if}(f(\vec{u}_{i,G}) \leq f(\vec{x}_{i,G})), \\ \vec{x}_{i,G} & \text{otherwise} \end{cases} \tag{4}$$

DDECV, wich will be explained in detail so as to get a self-contained paper, has three main elements: (1) change detection, (2) exploration promotion, and (3) convergence promotion. The last is the source of motivation of this research and will be detailed later. Firstly, the change detection and the exploration promotion mechanisms are described below.

The change detection mechanism consists of solution reevaluation [25, 9]. At each generation, the first trial vector and the trial vector at the middle of the current population are evaluated and their objective function values and constraints values are compared against their previous values. If any value is different, an indicator is activated. Lastly, the best vector in the current population is stored in a memory file, called the memory population. This memory keeps promising solutions that can be used after a change. The goal of using the first vector and the one located at the middle of the population is to decrease the chances of missing a change during a given generation. The pseudocode of the change detection mechanism is detailed in Algorithm 1.

Algorithm 1 Change_detection_mechanism

Require: $\vec{x}_{i,t-1}$
Evaluate $\vec{x}_{i,t}$ at time t
if any value is not the same as those of its previous evaluation **then**
  Copy the best vector in the population $\vec{x}_{best,t}$ to the memory population
  Reevaluate all vectors in the current population and also in the memory population
  $eval = eval + current\_population\_size + memory\_population\_size$
end if

The exploration promotion mechanism is activated after a successful change detection (see Algorithm 1), and here is where the two DE variants are switched because DDECV starts by using DE/rand/1/bin. However, after the change detection, DE/best/1/bin is used instead for a number of generations defined by the user (Gen_{best}) and the F value is increased (expanded F) during the same period of time so as to promote exploration [14]. Furthermore, considering that DE/best/1/bin is used, the best vector (which will be the base vector for the differential mutation) can be chosen from either the current population or the memory population. The exploration promotion mechanism is outlined in Algorithm 2.

To add more diversity to the population, a number of IB randomly generated solutions, called immigrants [26], are added to the population at the end of each generation. However, the number of immigrants is increased (IA) during the DE/best/1/bin operation so as to increase the diversiy after a change. The worst individuals are replaced by the immigrants to keep the population size fixed.

The set of three feasibility rules proposed by Deb [7] are used in DDECV as selection criteria in Equation 4 and also

Algorithm 2 Exploration_promotion_mechanism

if counter for using DE/best/1/bin < Gen_{best} **then**
  Generate $\vec{u}_{i,t}$ with Equation 2 with expanded F value and Equation 3
else
  Generate $\vec{u}_{i,t}$ with Equations 1 and 3
end if
return $\vec{u}_{i,t}$

every time the best vector is selected. The rules are the following:

1. Between two feasible vectors, the one with the best objective function value is selected.
2. If one vector is feasible and the other one is infeasible, the feasible vector is selected.
3. If both vectors are infeasible, the one with the lowest sum of constraint violation is selected.

Finally, the convergence promotion is carried out by a local search operator [10], which is applied to a randomly chosen vector $\vec{x}_{rand,t}$ from the current population. A randomly chosen variable from $\vec{x}_{rand,t} = (x_{rand,1,t}, \ldots, x_{rand,D,t})$ is added with a random value $\delta \in [0, 1]$. Such value is also substracted to the variable, then two neighbors are generated. The interval $[0, 1]$ is suitable for the benchmark used in this work, but it can be changed for other problems. The best vector, based on the three feasibility criteria above mentioned, among the original vector and the two neighbors is chosen as the new starting point. The process is repeated ILS (Iterations for Local Search) times, (user-defined parameter). The vector obtained by this mechanism replaces the worst vector in the current population (see Algorithm 3).

Algorithm 3 Convergence_promotion_mechanism

Require: $\vec{x}_{rand,t}$
for $c \leftarrow 1$ to ILS **do**
  $\delta = random(0, 1)$
  $\vec{x}_{N_i+,t} = \vec{x}_{rand,t}$
  $\vec{x}_{N_i-,t} = \vec{x}_{rand,t}$
  Select randomly one variable $x_{rand,j,t}$ of $\vec{x}_{rand,t}$
  $x_{N_i+,j,t} += \delta$
  $x_{N_i-,j,t} -= \delta$
  $\vec{x}_{rand,t}$=best($\vec{x}_{rand,t}$, $\vec{x}_{N_i+,t}$, $\vec{x}_{N_i-,t}$)
end for
Replace the worst vector in the population with $\vec{x}_{rand,t}$

The pseudocode of the complete DDECV for solving DCOPs [1] is detailed in Algorithm 4.

Algorithm 4 DDECV algorithm

G=0
Create a randomly-generated initial population $\vec{x}_{i,G}\, \forall i, i = 1, \ldots, NP$
Evaluate each $\vec{x}_{i,G}\, \forall i, i = 1, \ldots, NP$
$eval = eval + NP$
while $eval \leq Max\_eval$ **do**
  for $i \leftarrow 1$ to NP **do**
    if $i = 1$ or $i = NP/2$ **then**
      Change_detection_Mechanism ($\vec{x}_{i,G}$) {Algorithm 1}
      $eval = eval + 1$
    end if
    $\vec{u}_{i,G}$ = Exploration_promotion_mechanism {Algorithm 2}
    $eval = eval + 1$
    if $f(\vec{u}_{i,G})$ is better than $f(\vec{x}_{i,G})$ based on the feasibility rules **then**
      $\vec{x}_{i,G+1} = \vec{u}_{i,G}$
    else
      $\vec{x}_{i,G+1} = \vec{x}_{i,G}$
    end if
  end for
  Add IA or IB immigrants to the current population and evaluate them
  $eval = eval + IA(or + IB)$
  Convergence_promotion_mechanism {Algorithm 3}
  $eval = eval + 2 * ILS$
  $G = G + 1$
end while

3. DDECV+ REPAIR

Recalling from Section 1, the usage of repair methods has been reported as constraint-handlers for DCOPs. The main idea of a repair method is the use of a set with only feasible solutions to serve as reference for infeasible solutions of the current population and help them to become feasible [15, 18, 20, 21, 22].

In this work a novel but simple repair method is proposed and added to DDECV (DDECV + Repair). The main difference with respect to other repair methods lies in the fact that DDECV + Repair does not use feasible vectors as reference, it is just based on the differential mutation operator. For each infeasible vector, three new and temporal vectors are generated at random with the only aim to apply the differential mutation operator (see Equation 1) as if a mutant vector is created in DE. At each generation, before the application of the selection operator based on the feasibility rules (see Equation 4) between the target and trial vectors, if the trial vector is infeasible, the repair method is applied until it is repaired or Repair_Limit attempts are computed. This can be seen in Algorithm 5. Considering the fact that only the constraints are evaluated to check the feasibility of a vector, the evaluations computed by the repair method are not considered in the total evaluations made by the proposed algorithm.

DDECV + Repair does not consider the convergence promotion of its former version and the repair method is used instead. The details of DDECV + Repair are shown in Algorithm 6, where the repair method is remarked in boldface.

Algorithm 5 Repair_Method

Require: $\vec{u}_{i,G}$ {trial vector}
$counter = 0$
while $\vec{u}_{i,G}$ is infeasible and $counter \leq$ Repair_Limit **do**
  Generate three random vectors ($\vec{u}_{r0,G}$, $\vec{u}_{r1,G}$ and $\vec{u}_{r2,G}$)
  $\vec{u}_{i,G} = \vec{u}_{r0,G} + F(\vec{u}_{r1,G} - \vec{u}_{r2,G})$
  $counter = counter + 1$
end while
Return $\vec{u}_{i,G}$

Table 1: Main features of the test problems [18].

Problem	Obj. Function	Constraints	DFR	SwO	bNAO	OICB	OISB	Path
g24_u	Dynamic	No Constraints	1	No	No	No	Yes	N/A
g24_1	Dynamic	Static	2	Yes	No	Yes	No	N/A
g24_f	Static	Static	2	No	No	Yes	No	N/A
g24_uf	Static	No Constraints	1	No	No	No	Yes	N/A
g24_2*	Dynamic	Static	2	Yes	No	Yes and No	Yes and No	N/A
g24_2u	Dynamic	No Constraints	1	No	No	No	Yes	N/A
g24_3	Static	Dynamic	2-3	No	Yes	Yes	No	N/A
g24_3b	Dynamic	Dynamic	2-3	Yes	No	Yes	No	N/A
g24_3f	Static	Static	1	No	No	Yes	No	N/A
g24_4	Dynamic	Dynamic	2-3	Yes	No	Yes	No	N/A
g24_5*	Dynamic	Dynamic	2-3	Yes	No	Yes and No	Yes and No	N/A
g24_6a	Dynamic	Static	2	Yes	No	No	Yes	Hard
g24_6b	Dynamic	Static	1	No	No	No	Yes	N/A
g24_6c	Dynamic	Static	2	Yes	No	No	Yes	Easy
g24_6d	Dynamic	Static	2	Yes	No	No	Yes	Hard
g24_7	Static	Dynamic	2	No	No	Yes	No	N/A
g24_8a	Dynamic	No Constraints	1	No	No	No	No	N/A
g24_8b	Dynamic	Static	2	Yes	No	Yes	No	N/A

DFR	Number of disconnected feasible regions
SwO	Switched global optimum between disconnected regions
bNAO	Better newly appear optimum without changing existing ones
OICB	Global optimum is in the constraint boundary
OISB	Global optimum is in the search boundary
Path	Indicate if it is easy or difficult to use mutation to travel between feasible regions
Dynamic	The function is dynamic
Static	There is no change
*	In some change periods, the landscape either is a plateau or contains infinite number of optima and all optima (including the existing optimum) lie in a line parallel to one of the axes

Algorithm 6 DDECV+Repair algorithm

G=0
Create a randomly-generated initial population $\vec{x}_{i,G}\ \forall i, i = 1, \ldots, NP$
Evaluate each $\vec{x}_{i,G}\ \forall i, i = 1, \ldots, NP$
$eval = eval + NP$
while $eval \leq Max\_eval$ **do**
  for $i \leftarrow 1$ to NP **do**
    if $i = 1$ or $i = NP/2$ **then**
      Change_detection_Mechanism ($\vec{x}_{i,G}$) {Algorithm 1}
      $eval = eval + 1$
    end if
    $\vec{u}_{i,G}$ = Exploration_promotion_mechanism {Algorithm 2}
    if $\vec{u}_{i,G}$ is infeasible **then**
      Repair_Method($\vec{u}_{i,G}$) {Algorithm 5}
    end if
    $eval = eval + 1$
    if $f(\vec{u}_{i,G})$ is better than $f(\vec{x}_{i,G})$ based on the feasibility rules **then**
      $\vec{x}_{i,G+1} = \vec{u}_{i,G}$
    else
      $\vec{x}_{i,G+1} = \vec{x}_{i,G}$
    end if
  end for
  Add IA or IB immigrants to the current population and evaluate them
  $eval = eval + IA(or + IB)$
  $G = G + 1$
end while

4. EXPERIMENTS AND RESULTS

4.1 Experimental setup

DDECV + Repair was tested on eighteen benchmark problems. The main features of those problems are summarized in Table 1 and the details can be found in [18, 19]. The results obtained by DDECV + Repair were compared with those from state-of-the-art EAs in dynamic constrained optimization: (1) a GA with elitism, nonlinear ranking parent selection, arithmetic crossover and uniform mutation (GAElit) [18], (2) a GA similar to GAElit but with random immigrants (RIGAElit) [18], (3) another version of GAElit but with hypermutation (HyperMElit) [18], (4) a GA with a traditional repair mechanism (GA + Repair) [18], (5) a traditional differential evolution with an also traditional repair mechanism (DE + Repair)[21], (6) the gravitational search algorithm with a traditional repair mechanism (GSA + Repair) [22], and (7) the original DDECV [1] to analyze the particular effect of the proposed repair method in this algorithm.

Table 2 shows the settings for the benchmark problems. Different change frequencies were tested (500, 1000 and 2000 evaluations), with a medium objective and constraint function change severity as suggested in [18]. DE + Repair and GSA + Repair were compared with 1000 evaluations as change frequency because no results were found for the remaining frequencies. The parameter values used by DDECV and DDECV + Repair are listed in Table 3 and were taken from [1] (with the exception of Repair_Limit).

The offline error [3] was employed to measure the performance of DDECV + Repair. The offline error is defined as the average of the sum of errors in each cycle divided by the sum of the number of cycles. The offline error is always greater than or equal to zero. This latter value indicates a perfect performance [17]. This measure is defined as:

Table 2: Parameter values for the test problems taken from [18]

Number of runs	50
Number of changes	12
Frequency change	500, 1000, 2000 Evals.
Obj. function severity k	0.5
Constraint severity S	20

Table 3: DDECV and DDECV + Repair parameter values taken from [1]

Pop size	25
Crossover	CR = 0.8399
F before change	F = 0.9644
F after change	FA = 1.0820
Immigrants before change	IB = 5
Immigrates after change	IA = 3
Gen_{best}	16
Iterations for local search	ILS = 8 (only DDECV)
Repair_Limit	100 (only DDECV + Repair)

$$offline\_error = \frac{1}{n}\sum_{j=1}^{n} e(j)$$

where n is the number of cycles so far and $e(j)$ denotes the best error since the last change gained by the algorithm at cycle j (see the next Equation).

$$e(j) = |f(\vec{x}^*, t) - f(\vec{x}, t)|$$

where $f(\vec{x}^*, t)$ denotes the feasible global optima at time t and $f(\vec{x}, t)$ is the best solution found at generation G.

4.2 Results

The average and standard deviation values of the offline error obtained per each compared algorithm in the set of eighteen test problems are presented in Tables 4, 5, and 6 for change frequencies of 500, 1000 and 2000 evaluations, respectively.

The statistical validation for all test functions was computed with the non-parametric 95%-confidence Friedman test and a post-hoc test (Bergmann-Hommels) [8]. Non-parametric tests were adopted because the samples of runs did not fit to a Gaussian distribution based on the Kolmogorov-Smirnov test.

It was observed from the results in Table 4 (500 evaluations for a change), and from the Friedman and Bergmann - Hommels tests, that DDECV + Repair outperformed all the compared algorithms but DDECV (i.e. no significant differences in the complete set of test problems were observed). Because of this, the 95%-confidence Wilcoxon test was used to determine statistical differences per each test problem between DDECV + Repair and DDECV. Based on such results, DDECV + Repair outperformed DDECV in fourteen test problems (g24_f, g24_2, g24_3, g24_3b, g24_3f, g24_4, g24_5, g24_6a, g24_6b, g24_6c, g24_6d, g24_7, g24_8a, g24_8b), while the original DDECV outperformed DDECV + Repair in four test problems (g24_u, g24_uf, g24_2u and g24_1). The main feature of the first three test problems

Table 4: Average and standard deviation offline error values obtained by DDECV + Repair and the compared algorithms with a change frequency of 500 evaluations. Significant best results, based on the 95%-confidence Wilcoxon test between DDECV and DDECV+Repair are remarked in boldface.

Algorithms	Functions		
	G24_u	G24_1	G24_f
GAElit	0.184(±0.035)	0.641(±0.057)	0.175(±0.083)
RIGAElit	0.235(±0.025)	0.496(±0.046)	0.266(±0.051)
HyperMElit	0.163(±0.026)	0.52(±0.065)	0.209(±0.053)
GA+Repair	0.500(±0.059)	0.264(±0.024)	0.077(±0.011)
DDECV	**0.082(±0.011)**	**0.109(±0.067)**	0.075(±0.019)
DDECV+Repair	0.086(±0.009)	0.117(±0.015)	**0.048(±0.009)**
	G24_uf	G24_2	G24_2u
GAElit	0.091(±0.022)	0.372(±0.05)	0.132(±0.017)
RIGAElit	0.125(±0.02)	0.325(±0.037)	0.146(±0.024)
HyperMElit	0.091(±0.012)	0.364(±0.043)	0.115(±0.016)
GA+Repair	0.358(±0.018)	0.298(±0.036)	0.354(±0.029)
DDECV	**0.010(±0.005)**	0.162(±0.032)	**0.065(±0.005)**
DDECV+Repair	0.016(±0.005)	**0.137(±0.008)**	0.088(±0.008)
	G24_3	G24_3b	G24_3f
GAElit	0.375(±0.049)	0.631(±0.084)	0.252(±0.058)
RIGAElit	0.436(±0.048)	0.545(±0.051)	0.264(±0.048)
HyperMElit	0.404(±0.05)	0.557(±0.088)	0.244(±0.051)
GA+Repair	0.063(±0.008)	0.184(±0.019)	0.035(±0.008)
DDECV	0.087(±0.024)	0.225(±0.07)	0.071(±0.025)
DDECV+Repair	**0.062(±0.008)**	**0.147(±0.012)**	**0.028(±0.007)**
	G24_4	G24_5	G24_6a
GAElit	0.646(±0.075)	0.367(±0.029)	1.038(±0.157)
RIGAElit	0.542(±0.047)	0.287(±0.035)	0.534(±0.05)
HyperMElit	0.573(±0.075)	0.324(±0.039)	0.694(±0.071)
GA+Repair	0.143(±0.015)	0.196(±0.024)	0.616(±0.074)
DDECV	0.233(±0.081)	0.195(±0.033)	0.267(±0.114)
DDECV+Repair	**0.143(±0.012)**	**0.140(±0.014)**	**0.083(±0.016)**
	G24_6b	G24_6c	G24_6d
GAElit	0.631(±0.057)	0.666(±0.052)	0.664(±0.075)
RIGAElit	0.436(±0.039)	0.443(±0.029)	0.512(±0.057)
HyperMElit	0.535(±0.039)	0.543(±0.051)	0.584(±0.041)
GA+Repair	0.567(±0.048)	0.518(±0.038)	0.475(±0.038)
DDECV	0.145(±0.029)	0.173(±0.048)	0.414(±0.083)
DDECV+Repair	**0.098(±0.01)**	**0.090(±0.011)**	**0.196(±0.015)**
	G24_7	G24_8a	G24_8b
GAElit	0.441(±0.053)	0.356(±0.028)	0.807(±0.056)
RIGAElit	0.565(±0.068)	0.405(±0.028)	0.758(±0.064)
HyperMElit	0.430(±0.062)	0.355(±0.028)	0.710(±0.071)
GA+Repair	0.134(±0.017)	0.341(±0.032)	0.380(±0.068)
DDECV	0.156(±0.038)	0.292(±0.035)	0.332(±0.108)
DDECV+Repair	**0.134(±0.023)**	**0.257(±0.031)**	**0.189(±0.033)**

(g24_u, g24_uf, g24_2u) is that they are unconstrained, and the fourth one (g24_1) has a disconnected feasible region. The better performance of the original DDECV in the first three test problems can be understood due to the fact that the local search used as convergence promotion (see Algorithm 3) is precisely designed to improve good solutions faster and the whole search space is feasible on those problems. However, in presence of constraints, DDECV + Repair clearly performed better (except in test problem g24_1).

Table 5: Average and standard deviation offline error values obtained by DDECV + Repair and the compared algorithms with a change frequency of 1000 evaluations. Significant best results, based on the 95%-confidence Wilcoxon test between DDECV and DDECV+Repair are remarked in boldface.

Algorithms	Functions		
	G24_u	**G24_1**	**G24_f**
GAElit	0.106(±0.035)	0.459(±0.057)	0.154(±0.083)
RIGAElit	0.149(±0.025)	0.346(±0.046)	0.178(±0.051)
HyperMElit	0.111(±0.026)	0.384(±0.065)	0.149(±0.053)
GA+Repair	0.468(±0.059)	0.226(±0.024)	0.041(±0.011)
DE+Repair	0.099(±0.01)	0.151(±0.024)	0.039(±0.022)
GSA+Repair	0.049(±0.004)	0.132(±0.015)	0.029(±0.012)
DDECV	0.050(±0.006)	0.109(±0.033)	0.029(±0.010)
DDECV+Repair	**0.039(±0.007)**	**0.061(±0.01)**	**0.021(±0.006)**
	G24_uf	**G24_2**	**G24_2u**
GAElit	0.063(±0.022)	0.288(±0.050)	0.073(±0.017)
RIGAElit	0.069(±0.02)	0.246(±0.037)	0.091(±0.024)
HyperMElit	0.053(±0.012)	0.253(±0.043)	0.068(±0.016)
GA+Repair	0.218(±0.018)	0.281(±0.036)	0.294(±0.029)
DE+Repair	0.057(±0.019)	0.191(±0.014)	0.141(±0.012)
GSA+Repair	0.047(±0.009)	0.182(±0.019)	0.196(±0.012)
DDECV	**0.004(±0.002)**	0.126(±0.030)	0.054(±0.004)
DDECV+Repair	0.009(±0.002)	**0.062(±0.006)**	**0.036(±0.001)**
	G24_3	**G24_3b**	**G24_3f**
GAElit	0.289(±0.049)	0.457(±0.084)	0.158(±0.058)
RIGAElit	0.308(±0.048)	0.386(±0.051)	0.167(±0.048)
HyperMElit	0.243(±0.05)	0.394(±0.088)	0.128(±0.051)
GA+Repair	0.156(±0.008)	0.171(±0.019)	0.025(±0.008)
DE+Repair	0.091(±0.012)	0.121(±0.019)	0.013(±0.009)
GSA+Repair	0.028(±0.004)	0.076(±0.009)	0.009(±0.007)
DDECV	0.057(±0.018)	0.134(±0.033)	0.032(±0.011)
DDECV+Repair	**0.046(±0.006)**	**0.084(±0.006)**	**0.010(±0.002)**
	G24_4	**G24_5**	**G24_6a**
GAElit	0.453(±0.075)	0.266(±0.029)	0.674(±0.157)
RIGAElit	0.421(±0.047)	0.240(±0.035)	0.333(±0.050)
HyperMElit	0.426(±0.075)	0.248(±0.039)	0.491(±0.071)
GA+Repair	0.211(±0.015)	0.236(±0.024)	0.431(±0.074)
DE+Repair	0.121(±0.021)	0.121(±0.011)	0.047(±0.009)
GSA+Repair	0.073(±0.012)	0.153(±0.013)	0.033(±0.003)
DDECV	0.131(±0.032)	0.126(±0.019)	0.215(±0.067)
DDECV+Repair	**0.088(±0.011)**	**0.078(±0.008)**	**0.036(±0.005)**
	G24_6b	**G24_6c**	**G24_6d**
GAElit	0.408(±0.057)	0.441(±0.052)	0.510(±0.075)
RIGAElit	0.309(±0.039)	0.325(±0.029)	0.342(±0.057)
HyperMElit	0.390(±0.039)	0.394(±0.051)	0.456(±0.041)
GA+Repair	0.427(±0.048)	0.390(±0.038)	0.354(±0.038)
DE+Repair	0.101(±0.012)	0.790(±0.010)	0.910(±0.011)
GSA+Repair	0.047(±0.003)	0.045(±0.004)	0.037(±0.007)
DDECV	0.108(±0.016)	0.128(±0.025)	0.288(±0.055)
DDECV+Repair	**0.041(±0.010)**	**0.041(±0.01)**	**0.079(±0.006)**
	G24_7	**G24_8a**	**G24_8b**
GAElit	0.316(±0.053)	0.266(±0.028)	0.662(±0.056)
RIGAElit	0.416(±0.068)	0.304(±0.028)	0.598(±0.064)
HyperMElit	0.315(±0.062)	0.279(±0.028)	0.608(±0.071)
GA+Repair	0.181(±0.017)	0.496(±0.032)	0.391(±0.068)
DE+Repair	0.033(±0.009)	0.217(±0.033)	0.227(±0.039)
GSA+Repair	0.018(±0.002)	0.202(±0.041)	0.192(±0.034)
DDECV	**0.106(±0.022)**	0.141(±0.025)	0.151(±0.058)
DDECV+Repair	0.107(±0.011)	0.138(±0.015)	**0.074(±0.025)**

The results in Table 5 (1000 evaluations for a change) show that DDECV + Repair outperformed most of the compared algorithms with the exception of DDECV and GSA + Repair based on the Friedman and Bergmann - Hommels tests. Due to this, the 95%-confidence Wilcoxon test was used again to validate statistical differences per each test problem between DDECV + Repair and DDECV (the same comparison was not made against GSA + Repair because the results per each independent run were not available). According to those results, DDECV + Repair provided better results in fifteen test problems (g24_u, g24_1, g24_f, g24_2, g24_2u, g24_3, g24_3b, g24_3f, g24_4, g24_5, g24_6a, g24_6b, g24_6c, g24_6d, g24_8b) and the original DDECV was better in two test problems (g24_uf, g24_7). The first problem (g24_uf) is unconstrained, and the second one (g24_7) has a disconnected feasible region. In test problem g24_8a no significant differences were observed.

Table 6: Average and standard deviation offline error values obtained by DDECV + Repair and the compared algorithms with a change frequency of 2000 evaluations. Significant best results, based on the 95%-confidence Wilcoxon test between DDECV and DDECV+Repair are remarked in boldface.

Algorithms	Functions		
	G24-u	**G24-1**	**G24-f**
GAElit	0.065(±0.011)	0.332(±0.074)	0.092(±0.052)
RIGAElit	0.110(±0.014)	0.235(±0.038)	0.106(±0.037)
HyperMElit	0.072(±0.015)	0.289(±0.053)	0.084(±0.042)
GA+Repair	0.262(±0.04)	0.055(±0.012)	0.023(±0.006)
DDECV	0.030(±0.008)	0.066(±0.018)	0.016(±0.016)
DDECV+Repair	**0.023(±0.003)**	**0.036(±0.010)**	**0.011(±0.004)**
	G24-uf	**G24-2**	**G24-2u**
GAElit	0.032(±0.010)	0.183(±0.024)	0.049(±0.008)
RIGAElit	0.047(±0.015)	0.168(±0.023)	0.057(±0.011)
HyperMElit	0.028(±0.008)	0.172(±0.037)	0.044(±0.012)
GA+Repair	0.164(±0.054)	0.147(±0.022)	0.171(±0.040)
DDECV	**0.002(±0.001)**	0.071(±0.016)	0.031(±0.002)
DDECV+Repair	0.005(±0.001)	**0.035(±0.007)**	**0.018(±0.001)**
	G24-3	**G24-3b**	**G24-3f**
GAElit	0.164(±0.033)	0.320(±0.058)	0.072(±0.032)
RIGAElit	0.208(±0.026)	0.262(±0.024)	0.100(±0.026)
HyperMElit	0.168(±0.029)	0.288(±0.048)	0.082(±0.036)
GA+Repair	0.019(±0.004)	0.044(±0.009)	0.010(±0.003)
DDECV	0.032(±0.008)	0.078(±0.015)	0.017(±0.006)
DDECV+Repair	0.036(±0.002)	**0.063(±0.009)**	**0.006(±0.001)**
	G24-4	**G24-5**	**G24-6a**
GAElit	0.333(±0.074)	0.196(±0.026)	0.408(±0.050)
RIGAElit	0.309(±0.037)	0.174(±0.022)	0.236(±0.026)
HyperMElit	0.287(±0.067)	0.182(±0.019)	0.287(±0.036)
GA+Repair	0.044(±0.009)	0.111(±0.023)	0.300(±0.054)
DDECV	0.073(±0.014)	0.081(±0.011)	0.103(±0.032)
DDECV+Repair	**0.057(±0.005)**	**0.041(±0.004)**	**0.020(±0.004)**
	G24-6b	**G24-6c**	**G24-6d**
GAElit	0.274(±0.028)	0.282(±0.033)	0.318(±0.059)
RIGAElit	0.210(±0.025)	0.213(±0.027)	0.242(±0.027)
HyperMElit	0.234(±0.019)	0.249(±0.034)	0.281(±0.030)
GA+Repair	0.306(±0.030)	0.287(±0.042)	0.263(±0.024)
DDECV	0.053(±0.008)	0.063(±0.013)	0.139(±0.027)
DDECV+Repair	**0.026(±0.005)**	**0.022(±0.004)**	**0.044(±0.003)**
	G24-7	**G24-8a**	**G24-8b**
GAElit	0.217(±0.047)	0.232(±0.023)	0.499(±0.048)
RIGAElit	0.303(±0.043)	0.269(±0.017)	0.496(±0.042)
HyperMElit	0.253(±0.036)	0.237(±0.013)	0.463(±0.052)
GA+Repair	0.050(±0.015)	0.247(±0.020)	0.136(±0.035)
DDECV	0.062(±0.014)	0.072(±0.032)	0.078(±0.032)
DDECV+Repair	**0.057(±0.005)**	0.075(±0.015)	**0.041(±0.012)**

As it can be seen in Table 6 (2000 evaluations for a change) and based on the Friedman and Bergmann - Hommels tests, DDECV + Repair outperformed all the compared algorithms, except DDECV. As in the previous two cases, the 95%-confidence Wilcoxon test was used to determine statistical differences per each test problem between DDECV + Repair and DDECV. It was observed in the results that DDECV + Repair outperformed DDECV in fifteen test problems (g24_u, g24_1, g24_f, g24_2, g24_2u, g24_3b, g24_3f, g24_4, g24_5, g24_6a, g24_6b, g24_6c, g24_6d, g24_7, g24_8b) and the original DDECV was better in just one test problem (g24_uf). The main feature of this problem is that it is unconstrained. In test problems g24_3 and g24_8a no significant differences were observed.

Finally, to get insights of the effectiveness of the repair method, the averages of successful applications, where a successful application means that a feasible solution was obtained from an infeasible one, for each test problem, and for each frequency, are reported in Table 7. In all the constrained problems the simple repair method based on the differential mutation, and with no help of feasible solutions, was very successful, even in those problems where the offline error was not as good as expected (i.e. test problems with a disjoint feasible region). Such good performance may be due to the fact that the feasible region of the original static test problem (g24) [11], which is the base of all the benchmark, covers about 79% of the whole search space.

Table 7: Average successful application of the proposed repair method with change frequency of 500, 1000 and 2000 evaluations. Only constrained problems are included.

Functions	Frequencies		
	500 Evals	1000 Evals	2000 Evals
g24_1	1.0	1.0	1.0
g24_f	1.0	1.0	1.0
g24_2	1.0	1.0	1.0
g24_3	0.99	0.99	0.99
g24_3b	0.99	0.99	0.99
g24_3f	0.99	0.99	0.99
g24_4	0.99	0.99	0.99
g24_5	0.99	0.99	0.99
g24_6a	1.0	1.0	1.0
g24_6b	1.0	1.0	1.0
g24_6c	1.0	1.0	1.0
g24_6d	1.0	1.0	1.0
g24_7	0.99	0.99	0.99
g24_8b	1.0	1.0	1.0

5. CONCLUSIONS

A simple repair method based on the differential mutation operator was proposed and added to the DDECV algorithm to solve dynamic constrained optimization problems. The main difference of the repair method is that it does not require feasible solutions to operate. Instead, random solutions are generated to apply the differential mutation operator a number of attempts defined by the user. Such repair method replaced the convergence promotion mechanisms in the original DDECV. DDECV + Repair was tested in a recently proposed benchmark with eighteen test problems at different change frequency values (500, 1000 and 2000 evaluations). The offline error was the value adopted to measure the performance of the proposed improved algorithm. Six algorithms (including GAs, DE, GSA, some of them with traditional repair methods), besides the original DDECV version, were used for comparison purposes.

The overall results showed that DDECV + Repair improved the results of its previous version and also outperformed most of the compared al gorithms, regardless of the change frequency. The exception was with a frequency of 1000 evaluations, where DDECV + Repair was as good as GSA + Repair. However, GSA + Repair uses a traditional repair method which requires feasible solutions, while the proposed algorithm only uses the differential mutation with random solutions for the same purpose. Finally, some difficulties to get good offline error values were found in test problems with a disjoint feasible region.

For future work, the repair method will be re-visited so as to (1) analyze the negative effect of a disjoint feasible region, and (2) add it some knowledge to improve its performance. Finally, other test problems with smaller feasible regions will be sought so as to test the repair method in those situations.

6. ACKNOWLEDGMENTS

The authors acknowledge the valuable help and comments provided by Prof. Swagatam Das. The first author acknowledges support from the Mexican Council for Science and Technology (CONACyT) to pursue graduate studies at the University of Veracruz. The second author acknowledges support from CONACyT through project No. 220522.

7. REFERENCES

[1] M.-Y. Ameca-Alducin, E. Mezura-Montes, and N. Cruz-Ramirez. Differential evolution with combined variants for dynamic constrained optimization. In *Evolutionary Computation (CEC), 2014 IEEE Congress on*, pages 975–982, July 2014.

[2] V. Aragón, S. Esquivel, and C. Coello. Artificial immune system for solving dynamic constrained optimization problems. In E. Alba, A. Nakib, and P. Siarry, editors, *Metaheuristics for Dynamic Optimization*, volume 433 of *Studies in Computational Intelligence*, pages 225–263. Springer Berlin Heidelberg, 2013.

[3] J. Branke and H. Schmeck. Designing evolutionary algorithms for dynamic optimization problems. In A. Ghosh and S. Tsutsui, editors, *Advances in Evolutionary Computing*, Natural Computing Series, pages 239–262. Springer Berlin Heidelberg, 2003.

[4] H. Cobb. An investigation into the use of hypermutation as an adaptive operator in genetic algorithms having continuous, time-dependent nonstationary environments. Technical report, Naval Research Lab Washington DC, 1990.

[5] H. Cobb and J. Grefenstette. Genetic algorithms for tracking changing environments. In S. Forrest, editor, *ICGA*, pages 523–530. Morgan Kaufmann, 1993.

[6] C. A. Coello Coello. Theoretical and Numerical Constraint Handling Techniques used with Evolutionary Algorithms: A Survey of the State of the Art. *Computer Methods in Applied Mechanics and Engineering*, 191(11-12):1245–1287, January 2002.

[7] K. Deb. An efficient constraint handling method for genetic algorithms. *Computer Methods in Applied Mechanics and Engineering*, 186(24):311–338, 2000.

[8] J. Derrac, S. García, D. Molina, and F. Herrera. A practical tutorial on the use of nonparametric statistical tests as a methodology for comparing evolutionary and swarm intelligence algorithms. *Swarm and Evolutionary Computation*, 1(1):3–18, 2011.

[9] M. du Plessis. *Adaptive Multi-Population Differential Evolution for Dynamic Environments*. PhD thesis, Faculty of Engineering, Built Environment and Information Technology, University of Pretoria, April 2012.

[10] S. Hernandez, G. Leguizamon, and E. Mezura-Montes. A hybrid version of differential evolution with two

differential mutation operators applied by stages. In *Evolutionary Computation (CEC), 2013 IEEE Congress on*, pages 2895–2901, 2013.

[11] J. J. Liang, T. Runarsson, E. Mezura-Montes, M. Clerc, P. Suganthan, C. A. Coello Coello, and K. Deb. Problem definitions and evaluation criteria for the CEC 2006 special session on constrained real-parameter optimization. Technical report, Nanyang Technological University, Singapore, December, 2005.

[12] E. Mezura-Montes, editor. *Constraint-Handling in Evolutionary Optimization*, volume 198 of *Studies in Computational Intelligence*. Springer-Verlag, 2009.

[13] E. Mezura-Montes and C. A. C. Coello. Constraint-handling in nature-inspired numerical optimization: Past, present and future. *Swarm and Evolutionary Computation*, 1(4):173–194, 2011.

[14] E. Mezura-Montes, M. E. Miranda-Varela, and R. del Carmen Gómez-Ramón. Differential evolution in constrained numerical optimization. an empirical study. *Information Sciences*, 180(22):4223–4262, 2010.

[15] Z. Michalewicz and G. Nazhiyath. Genocop iii: a co-evolutionary algorithm for numerical optimization problems with nonlinear constraints. In *Evolutionary Computation, 1995., IEEE International Conference on*, volume 2, pages 647–651 vol.2, Nov 1995.

[16] Z. Michalewicz and M. Schoenauer. Evolutionary Algorithms for Constrained Parameter Optimization Problems. *Evolutionary Computation*, 4(1):1–32, 1996.

[17] T. Nguyen, S. Yang, and J. Branke. Evolutionary dynamic optimization: A survey of the state of the art. *Swarm and Evolutionary Computation*, 6(0):1 – 24, 2012.

[18] T. Nguyen and X. Yao. Continuous dynamic constrained optimization: The challenges. *IEEE Transactions on Evolutionary Computation*, 16(6):769–786, 2012.

[19] T. Nguyen and X. Yao. Evolutionary optimization on continuous dynamic constrained problems - an analysis. In S. Yang and X. Yao, editors, *Evolutionary Computation for Dynamic Optimization Problems*, volume 490 of *Studies in Computational Intelligence*, pages 193–217. Springer Berlin Heidelberg, 2013.

[20] T. T. Nguyen and X. Yao. Benchmarking and solving dynamic constrained problems. In *Evolutionary Computation, 2009. CEC '09. IEEE Congress on*, pages 690–697, 2009.

[21] K. Pal, C. Saha, and S. Das. Differential evolution and offspring repair method based dynamic constrained optimization. In B. Panigrahi, P. Suganthan, S. Das, and S. Dash, editors, *Swarm, Evolutionary, and Memetic Computing*, volume 8297 of *Lecture Notes in Computer Science*, pages 298–309. Springer International Publishing, 2013.

[22] K. Pal, C. Saha, S. Das, and C. Coello-Coello. Dynamic constrained optimization with offspring repair based gravitational search algorithm. In *Evolutionary Computation (CEC), 2013 IEEE Congress on*, pages 2414–2421, 2013.

[23] K. Price, R. Storn, and J. Lampinen. *Differential Evolution A Practical Approach to Global Optimization*. Natural Computing Series. Springer-Verlag, 2005.

[24] E. Rashedi, H. Nezamabadi, and S. Saryazdi. Gsa: A gravitational search algorithm. *Information Sciences*, 179(13):2232 – 2248, 2009.

[25] H. Richter. Detecting change in dynamic fitness landscapes. In *Evolutionary Computation, 2009. CEC '09. IEEE Congress on*, pages 1613–1620, 2009.

[26] Y. Shengxiang. Memory-based immigrants for genetic algorithms in dynamic environments. In *Proceedings of the 2005 conference on Genetic and evolutionary computation*, GECCO '05, pages 1115–1122, New York, NY, USA, 2005. ACM.

Towards an Augmented Lagrangian Constraint Handling Approach for the (1+1)-ES

Dirk V. Arnold
Faculty of Computer Science
Dalhousie University
Halifax, Nova Scotia
Canada B3H 4R2
dirk@cs.dal.ca

Jeremy Porter
Faculty of Computer Science
Dalhousie University
Halifax, Nova Scotia
Canada B3H 4R2
jporter@cs.dal.ca

ABSTRACT

We consider the problem of devising an approach for handling inequality constraints in evolution strategies that allows converging linearly to optimal solutions on sphere functions with a single linear constraint. An analysis of the single-step behaviour of the $(1+1)$-ES shows that the task of balancing improvements in the objective with those in the constraint function is quite delicate, and that adaptive approaches need to be carefully designed in order to avoid failure. Based on the understanding gained, we propose a simple augmented Lagrangian approach and experimentally demonstrate good performance on a broad range of sphere functions as well as on moderately ill-conditioned ellipsoids with a single linear constraint.

Categories and Subject Descriptors

I.2.8 [**Problem Solving, Control Methods, and Search**]; G.1.6 [**Optimization**]: Constrained Optimization

Keywords

Stochastic black-box optimization; constraint handling; penalty method; augmented Lagrangian; evolution strategy

1. INTRODUCTION

Evolutionary algorithms (EAs) are often devised with unconstrained optimization problems in mind. When facing constrained problems, mechanisms that govern the behaviour of the algorithms when infeasible candidate solutions are generated need to be incorporated. The primary challenge when developing constraint handling techniques is to design them in such a way that the ability of the algorithm to successfully adapt its internal parameters is not impaired. Mezura-Montes and Coello Coello [15] present a survey of constraint handling techniques proposed for use in EAs.

Most often, when new constraint handling techniques for EAs are introduced, they are evaluated by applying them to sets of test functions designed to pose difficulties reflective of a wide range of problems that the algorithms may encounter. Nonlinear and multimodal objective functions, nonlinear constraint functions, very small feasible regions, and varying numbers of constraints active at the location of the optimal solution are all typically included. Examples of test sets include that by Michalewicz and Schoenauer [16] as well as the set used in a benchmarking competition held at the 2006 *IEEE Congress on Evolutionary Computation* [12]. While yielding valuable information regarding the relative capabilities of different algorithms, the numerical results obtained are not usually useful for analyzing reasons for failure of an algorithm to attain an optimal solution, or, if an optimal solution is found, determining whether it was located efficiently.

Work with the goal of developing an understanding of the impact of constraint handling on the adaptation behaviour of EAs includes that of Schwefel [19] as well as of Arnold et al. [4, 1, 2, 3] and Hellwig and Arnold [8]. They consider the adaptation of the step size of basic evolution strategies applied to linear problems with a single linear constraint as well as a linear problem with a conically shaped feasible region where the optimal solution lies at the apex of the cone. The work shows that convergence to nonstationary points may occur due to the premature reduction of the step size as a result of constraint handling, irrespective of whether a success probability based technique, mutative self-adaptation, or cumulative step size adaptation are employed. The impact of the constraint handling technique is qualitative in that for the simple problems considered, premature convergence can under some conditions be avoided.

As an optimal solution does not exist, linear problems with a single linear constraint cannot serve as global models of practical optimization problems. The simplest nonlinear problems are quadratic ones with a positive definite Hessian matrix. Kramer and Schwefel [11] employ a sphere function with a single linear constraint for evaluating the performance of several constraint handling techniques for evolution strategies. Even though the search space is only two-dimensional, very large numbers of function evaluations are required to arrive at solutions of the desired accuracy.

We argue that an effective constraint handling approach for EAs must result in linear convergence on quadratic minimization problems with positive definite Hessian matrix and a single linear constraint. Moreover, the rate of convergence should be inversely proportional to the dimension of the problem and not too far below that achieved on the

GECCO '15, July 11 - 15, 2015, Madrid, Spain
© 2015 ACM. ISBN 978-1-4503-3472-3/15/07...$15.00
DOI: http://dx.doi.org/10.1145/2739480.2754813

corresponding unconstrained problem. Perhaps surprisingly, commonly used EAs for constrained optimization often fail to meet those requirements. An approach that in experiments does appear to result in linear convergence on convex quadratic objective functions with a single linear constraint is a variant of the $(1+1)$-CMA-ES [9] for constrained optimization proposed by Arnold and Hansen [5]. The algorithm adapts the covariance matrix governing the distribution of offspring candidate solutions in such a way that variances in directions where infeasible candidate solutions are encountered are reduced. As a consequence of the resulting transformation of the search space, premature convergence due to low success probabilities associated with small constraint angles can be avoided. However, the computational cost of adapting the full covariance matrix may be prohibitive if the dimension of the problem is large.

In this paper, we consider the problem of developing a variant of the $(1+1)$-ES that achieves linear convergence on convex quadratic optimization problems with a single linear constraint *without* the need to adapt the covariance matrix of the mutation distribution. For reasons outlined in Section 2 we employ an augmented Lagrangian approach to convert the constrained problem into a sequence of unconstrained ones. Related work in evolutionary computation is also reviewed. By analyzing the single-step behaviour of the $(1+1)$-ES with added Lagrangian and penalty terms on constrained sphere functions in Section 3, we derive requirements that a successful strategy for adapting the penalty parameter and Lagrange factor must fulfill. We then propose an adaptation strategy and in Section 4 experimentally test the resulting algorithm on constrained sphere functions as well as on moderately ill-conditioned ellipsoidal functions with a single linear constraint. Section 5 concludes with a brief discussion of the expected challenges encountered when attempting to make the algorithm suitable for optimization in the presence of more than a single constraint and proposed future work.

2. BACKGROUND AND RELATED WORK

Constraint handling techniques for EAs provide ways of weighting the degree to which constraints are either satisfied or violated against the objective function value of a candidate solution for the purpose of selection. Mezura-Montes and Coello Coello [15] divide constraint handling techniques into several classes, including feasibility rules, penalty based techniques, and those that use ideas from multiobjective optimization. Penalty based techniques are among the oldest and replace the problem of optimizing an objective function subject to one or more constraints with the unconstrained problem of optimizing a sequence of objectives that incorporate the original objective as well as penalties for violating constraints. Most often, the modified objective is the sum of the original one and as many penalty terms as there are constraints, each weighted with its own penalty parameter. Barbosa et al. [6] provide a recent review of adaptive penalty techniques (i.e., of penalty techniques that adapt their penalty parameters in response to the candidate solutions generated during the search).

Adaptive penalty techniques (as well as other constraint handling techniques for EAs) are almost always based on heuristics, with little or no analysis of their behaviour. Nocedal and Wright [17] provide a discussion of penalty techniques in the context of numerical optimization, and they provide conditions under which convergence to optimal solutions can be guaranteed. Quadratic penalty techniques generally suffer from ill-conditioning as penalty parameters need to tend to infinity. This form of ill-conditioning can be avoided by using penalty terms based on the ℓ^1-norm rather than quadratic ones, but at the cost of introducing sharp ridges in the modified objective function. While EAs do not require smoothness of the objective, the difficulty of successfully adapting step sizes in the presence of sharp ridges is well known [14].

Another commonly used approach for solving constrained optimization problems is based on the Karush-Kuhn-Tucker conditions. Assuming that the objective function $f : \mathbb{R}^n \to \mathbb{R}$ as well as the constraint functions $g_i : \mathbb{R}^n \to \mathbb{R}$, $i = 1, \dots, m$, are continuously differentiable at the location of the optimum and that certain regularity conditions are satisfied, the problem of minimizing $f(\mathbf{x})$ subject to the constraints $g_i(\mathbf{x}) \leq 0$ for $i = 1, \dots, m$ can be solved by introducing Lagrange function $h : \mathbb{R}^{n+m} \to \mathbb{R}$ with

$$h(\mathbf{x}, \boldsymbol{\lambda}) = f(\mathbf{x}) + \sum_{i=1}^{m} \lambda_i g_i(\mathbf{x}) \ , \tag{1}$$

where $\boldsymbol{\lambda} = (\lambda_1, \dots, \lambda_m)^{\mathrm{T}}$ is the vector of nonnegative Lagrange factors. The ith term in the summation has the effect of adding a penalty for solutions that violate the ith constraint, but also to add a "reward" for those solutions that satisfy it. Locally optimal points of the constrained optimization problem are stationary points of the Lagrange function. Lagrangian relaxation techniques iterate the process of optimizing the Lagrange function with respect to $\mathbf{x}$ while adapting the Lagrange multipliers $\boldsymbol{\lambda}$ between iterations.

Augmented Lagrangian approaches combine the objective from Eq. (1) with additional quadratic penalty terms, resulting in objective

$$h(\mathbf{x}, \boldsymbol{\lambda}, \mu) = f(\mathbf{x}) + \sum_{i=1}^{m} \psi\left(g_i(\mathbf{x}), \lambda_i, \mu\right) \ , \tag{2}$$

where

$$\psi(g, \lambda, \mu) = \begin{cases} \lambda g + \dfrac{\mu g^2}{2} & \text{if } \lambda + \mu g \geq 0 \\ -\dfrac{\lambda^2}{2\mu} & \text{otherwise} \end{cases}$$

and the penalty parameter μ as well as the Lagrange factors are nonnegative. That objective is optimized with respect to $\mathbf{x}$ in each iteration. The penalty parameter increases between iterations (though not necessarily to infinity as in the absence of the Lagrangian terms, thus avoiding the ill-conditioning). Also between iterations, the Lagrange factors are updated according to

$$\lambda_i \leftarrow \max(0, \lambda_i + \mu g_i(\mathbf{x})) \tag{3}$$

(i.e., Lagrange factors increase if the corresponding constraints are violated and they decrease otherwise). Nocedal and Wright [17] provide a derivation and deeper discussion.

In a number of instances, Lagrangian relaxation and augmented Lagrangian approaches have been used in the context of EAs. Tahk and Sun [21] devise a coevolutionary approach based on an augmented Lagrangian formulation and evaluate the performance of their algorithm on four nonlinear, constrained test problems. Their approach employs an evolution strategy with mutative self adaptation, but requires an external schedule for lower-bounding the step size of the algorithm in order to be able to avoid premature stagnation.

Chrzanowska-Jeske et al. [7] use a Lagrangian relaxation based approach for constructing nonslicing VLSI floor plans with soft modules. The algorithm does not address the problem of adapting the step size used for the updates of the Lagrange factors and is not evaluated on test functions other than the VLSI layout problem.

Yoon et al. [22] use an evolution strategy to evolve Lagrange factors in a Lagrangian relaxation based approach for the 0/1 multiple knapsack problem. They do not evaluate their approach on optimization problems other than the combinatorial one.

Srivastava and Deb [20] present a genetic algorithm based augmented Lagrangian method for constrained optimization. Their algorithm relies on large populations and an effective local search procedure. It has not been evaluated for whether the Lagrange factors and penalty parameter converge to optimal values.

Long et al. [13] employ an augmented Lagrangian approach in the context of differential evolution. In an outer loop, the Lagrange factors and penalty parameters are updated. In an inner loop, the resulting unconstrained optimization problem is addressed using differential evolution. The update of the penalty parameters (and thus the step size for the update of the Lagrange factors) follows a fixed geometric schedule.

The analysis in the following section shows that an adaptive update of the penalty parameter μ, which controls the step size used in the update of the Lagrange factors in the augmented Lagrangian approach, is required to achieve good performance across functions with different scales.

3. ANALYSIS AND ALGORITHM

Throughout this section we consider the problem of minimizing the sphere function

$$f(\mathbf{x}) = a\mathbf{x}^{\mathrm{T}}\mathbf{x}$$

subject to constraint

$$g(\mathbf{x}) = c + \mathbf{b}^{\mathrm{T}}\mathbf{x} \leq 0\ ,$$

where $f, g : \mathbb{R}^n \to \mathbb{R}$ and $a > 0$. Due to the rotational symmetry of the problem and the invariance to coordinate rotations of the algorithm to be considered, we can without loss of generality assume that $\mathbf{b} = (b, 0, \ldots, 0)^{\mathrm{T}}$, i.e., that the constraint normal coincides with the x_1 axis or its negative.

Using quadratic completion, the augmented Lagrange function from Eq. (2) can for the problem at hand be written as

$$h(\mathbf{x}, \lambda, \mu) = \begin{cases} (\mathbf{x} - \mathbf{x}^*)^{\mathrm{T}} \mathbf{A} (\mathbf{x} - \mathbf{x}^*) + d & \text{if } \lambda + \mu g(\mathbf{x}) \geq 0 \\ a\mathbf{x}^{\mathrm{T}}\mathbf{x} - \dfrac{\lambda^2}{2\mu} & \text{otherwise,} \end{cases} \tag{4}$$

where matrix

$$\mathbf{A} = a\mathbf{I}_{n\times n} + \frac{\mu}{2}\mathbf{b}\mathbf{b}^{\mathrm{T}}$$

is symmetric and positive definite, $\mathbf{I}_{n\times n}$ is the $n \times n$ identity matrix,

$$\mathbf{x}^* = -\frac{\lambda + \mu c}{2a + \mu b^2}\mathbf{b}\ , \tag{5}$$

and

$$d = \frac{(2\lambda + \mu c)ac - \lambda^2 b^2/2}{2a + \mu b^2}\ .$$

In the case that $\lambda + \mu g(\mathbf{x}) \geq 0$, for given μ and λ the augmented Lagrange function is thus a convex quadratic function in $\mathbf{x}$ with condition number $1 + \mu b^2/(2a)$ of its Hessian matrix and with its centre at $\mathbf{x} = \mathbf{x}^*$. In the case that $\lambda + \mu g(\mathbf{x}) < 0$, it is convex quadratic in $\mathbf{x}$ with condition number 1 and its centre at $\mathbf{0}$. For given μ, the Karush-Kuhn-Tucker conditions are satisfied for Lagrange factor

$$\lambda_{\mathrm{opt}} = \begin{cases} \dfrac{2ac}{b^2} & \text{if } c \geq 0 \\ 0 & \text{otherwise} \end{cases} \tag{6}$$

and

$$\mathbf{x}_{\mathrm{opt}} = \begin{cases} -\dfrac{c\mathbf{b}}{b^2} & \text{if } c \geq 0 \\ \mathbf{0} & \text{otherwise,} \end{cases} \tag{7}$$

which is the location of the optimal solution of the constrained optimization problem.

3.1 Analysis

Consider the case that $c \geq 0$ (i.e., that the constraint is active at the optimal solution). We strive to derive necessary criteria that a (1 + 1)-ES with an augmented Lagrangian constraint handling approach much satisfy in order to achieve linear convergence to the solution described by Eqs. (6) and (7) at a rate similar to that attained on the unconstrained sphere.

The update rule for λ in Eq. (3) stipulates that whenever the second case in Eq. (4) is encountered, the Lagrange factor will be set to zero in the following iteration. Linear convergence of λ to $\lambda_{\mathrm{opt}} > 0$ thus implies that after a sufficiently large number of iterations, the objective function "seen" by the strategy will be that from the first case in Eq. (4).

For given parental candidate solution $\mathbf{x} \in \mathbb{R}^n$ and step size $\sigma > 0$, an offspring candidate solution $\mathbf{y}$ is generated by sampling a multivariate normal distribution with mean $\mathbf{x}$ and covariance matrix $\sigma^2\mathbf{I}_{n\times n}$. Due to the spherical symmetry in dimensions $2 \ldots, n$ we can assume without loss of generality that the parental candidate solution is located such that $\mathbf{x} = (x_1, R, 0, \ldots, 0)^{\mathrm{T}}$, where R is the distance from the optimal solution in the space spanned by the x_2 through x_n axes. Omitting the explicit dependence of the Lagrange function on λ and μ and assuming that enough iterations have passed for $\lambda + \mu g(\mathbf{y}) \geq 0$ to hold, the objective function value at location $\mathbf{y}$ is thus

$$\begin{aligned} h(\mathbf{y}) &= h(\mathbf{x} + \sigma\mathbf{z}) \\ &= a\sum_{i=1}^{n}(x_i + \sigma z_i)^2 + \lambda\left[\sum_{i=1}^{n} b_i(x_i + \sigma z_i) + c\right] \\ &\quad + \frac{\mu}{2}\left[\sum_{i=1}^{n} b_i(x_i + \sigma z_i) + c\right]^2, \end{aligned}$$

where mutation vector $\mathbf{z} = (z_1, \ldots, z_n)^{\mathrm{T}}$ is drawn from a multivariate normal distribution with mean zero and unit covariance matrix. Taking into account the location of the parental candidate solution and assuming that $\lambda + \mu g(\mathbf{x}) \geq 0$

it follows that

$$h(\mathbf{y}) = h(\mathbf{x}) + 2\sigma a x_1 z_1 + 2R\sigma a z_2 + \sigma^2 a \sum_{i=1}^{n} z_i^2 + \lambda\sigma b z_1 + \mu\sigma b(c + b x_1) z_1 + \mu\sigma^2 b^2 z_1^2/2 \ .$$

Introducing normalized step size $\sigma^* = \sigma n/R$, omitting terms that decrease faster than linearly with n, and letting

$$\Xi = x_1 + \frac{b}{2a}\left(\lambda + \mu g(\mathbf{x})\right) \quad (8)$$

yields

$$h(\mathbf{y}) \approx h(\mathbf{x}) + \frac{2R^2 a}{n}\left[\sigma^* \frac{\Xi}{R} z_1 + \sigma^* z_2 + \frac{\sigma^{*2}}{2}\right] \quad (9)$$

for the value of the augmented Lagrangian function at the location of the offspring candidate solution.

The $(1+1)$-ES replaces the parental candidate solution with the offspring if and only if the term in square brackets in Eq. (9) is nonpositive. The signs of the first and second of the three terms in the square brackets, which depend linearly on the normalized step size, depend on the realizations of z_1 and z_2. The sign of the third term, which depends quadratically on the normalized step size, is always nonnegative.

In order to be able to achieve stochastic linear convergence of the $(1+1)$-ES, the step size σ and the Lagrange factor λ and penalty parameter μ must be controlled such that:

1. The normalized step size follows a stationary distribution and falls in the evolution window [18].
2. Ξ/R follows a stationary distribution and has values of unit order of magnitude.

The first requirement ensures that for a not insignificant number of offspring the sum of the first two terms in the square brackets in Eq. (9) is negative and outweighs the third, and that the resulting steps that are made are of a not insignificant length. The second requirement ensures that progress made in the direction of the constraint normal is in lockstep with progress in the remaining $n-1$ dimensions, and that the algorithm does not converge to the optimum in the latter space while stagnating in the former.

Equations (8) and (9) highlight the main difficulty in designing an algorithm for updating the Lagrange factor and penalty parameter. While R tends to zero as the optimal solution is approached, for $c > 0$ neither of the two terms in Eq. (8) does. To achieve values of Ξ/R that avoid premature convergence in either the one- or the $(n-1)$-dimensional subspaces of the search space, λ and μ must be adapted such that the two terms comprising Ξ increasingly cancel each other out. Only if the contributions from the objective, Lagrangian, and penalty terms in Eq. (4) are weighted such that the combination of their gradients has similar magnitude in both subspaces can the $(1+1)$-ES succeed.

According to Eq. (8), changes to $\lambda + \mu g(\mathbf{x})$ must differ in magnitude from changes to x_1 by a factor of approximately $2a/b$. As neither a nor b are available to the algorithm and both can assume arbitrary values, any non-adaptive setting for the magnitude of changes to μ and λ that is appropriate for some problem will fail for another one that differs from the former only by a multiplicative factor in either the objective or the constraint functions.

3.2 Algorithm

Based on the insights gained, we now propose an augmented Lagrangian approach for solving optimization problems with a single inequality constraint using the $(1+1)$-ES. The state of the algorithm is determined by parental candidate solution $\mathbf{x} \in \mathbb{R}^n$, step size $\sigma > 0$, Lagrange factor $\lambda \geq 0$, and penalty parameter $\mu > 0$. Each iteration of the algorithm consists of the steps summarized in Fig. 1 and discussed in what follows.

In each iteration, the algorithm computes a single offspring candidate solution $\mathbf{y} \in \mathbb{R}^n$ by generating standard normally distributed vector $\mathbf{z} \in \mathbb{R}^n$ and adding $\sigma\mathbf{z}$ to the parental candidate solution $\mathbf{x}$. The offspring candidate solution replaces the parent if and only if it is non-inferior in terms of the augmented Lagrangian function from Eq. (4).

The step size of the algorithm is under control of the 1/5th rule [18] as implemented by Kern et al. [10]. That is, we multiply the step size σ by $2^{1/n}$ each time an offspring is accepted, and we multiply it by $2^{-1/(4n)}$ otherwise. As a result, the step size is unchanged in the mean if one out of every five offspring candidate solutions is successful.

In contrast to typical augmented Lagrangian approaches that increase the penalty parameter μ and adapt the Lagrange factor λ only after an accurate solution for the current values of those parameters has been found, we choose to adapt both parameters after every successful step. As in Eq. (3), the Lagrange factor is updated according to

$$\lambda \leftarrow \max(0, \lambda + \mu g(\mathbf{y})) \ . \quad (10)$$

As a result, it is increased (and thus infeasible candidate solutions penalized more) upon accepting an infeasible candidate solution; it is decreased (unless it is zero already) whenever an offspring replaces the parent.

It remains to develop an update rule for the penalty parameter μ. That update is critical for the success of the algorithm as according to Eq. (10), μ controls the rate at which the Lagrange factor λ is adapted. Jointly, μ and λ determine the location $\mathbf{x}^*$ of the optimal solution to the augmented Lagrangian according to Eq. (5). Too large a value of μ results in large changes of the objective seen by the $(1+1)$-ES between iterations and in an unnecessarily ill-conditioned problem. Too small a value of μ results in small changes of $\mathbf{x}^*$ between iterations and the danger of premature stagnation of the strategy. In order for the algorithm to converge linearly at a rate close to that attainable on unconstrained sphere functions, the penalty parameter μ must take on values of order of magnitude $2a/b^2$. It follows from the discussion below that this choice of μ is necessary for the second term in Eq. (8) to be able to converge to a value that cancels out the first.

Neither a nor b are available to the algorithm, making it impossible to simply set μ to a value in the vicinity of $2a/b^2$. Instead, we propose an update mechanism based on the (observable) changes in the values of the augmented Lagrangian and constraint functions. As the range of potentially optimal values for the penalty parameter is very large, we will develop an update rule that multiplies the current value of μ with constants either greater or less than 1, depending on whether it is to be increased or decreased. As a result, exponential growth and decay of the penalty parameter can be achieved.

Linear convergence at a rate close to that attainable in the unconstrained case requires values of σ^* of unit order

1. Generate offspring candidate solution

$$\mathbf{y} = \mathbf{x} + \sigma\mathbf{z}$$

where $\mathbf{z} \in \mathbb{R}^n$ is standard normally distributed.

2. Compute

$$\Delta g = g(\mathbf{y}) - g(\mathbf{x})$$

and

$$\Delta h_{\mathbf{x}} = h(\mathbf{y}, \lambda, \mu) - h(\mathbf{x}, \lambda, \mu)$$

where h is the augmented Lagrangian from Eq. (4).

3. If $\Delta h_{\mathbf{x}} \leq 0$ then update the state variables as follows:

$$\lambda \leftarrow \max(0, \lambda + \mu g(\mathbf{y}))$$

$$\mu \leftarrow \begin{cases} \mu\chi^{1/4} & \text{if } \mu g^2(\mathbf{y}) < k_1|\Delta h_{\mathbf{x}}|/n \text{ or } k_2|\Delta g| < |g(\mathbf{x})| \\ \mu\chi^{-1} & \text{otherwise} \end{cases}$$

$$\mathbf{x} \leftarrow \mathbf{y}$$

$$\sigma \leftarrow \sigma 2^{1/n} .$$

Otherwise, update the step size according to

$$\sigma \leftarrow \sigma 2^{-1/(4n)} .$$

Figure 1: Single iteration of the $(1+1)$-ES with augmented Lagrangian constraint handling for a single inequality constraint.

of magnitude. Much smaller values would result in slow progress, larger ones in divergence of the strategy. As a result, it follows that $R \approx n\sigma$ and according to Eq. (9), changes in h due to changes in $\mathbf{x}$ are of order of magnitude

$$|\Delta h_{\mathbf{x}}| = |h(\mathbf{y}, \lambda, \mu) - h(\mathbf{x}, \lambda, \mu)| \propto n\sigma^2 a . \quad (11)$$

From Eq. (4), changes in h due to changes in λ and μ are

$$\begin{aligned} \Delta h_{\lambda,\mu} &= h(\mathbf{y}, \lambda + \Delta\lambda, \mu + \Delta\mu) - h(\mathbf{y}, \lambda, \mu) \\ &= g(\mathbf{y})\Delta\lambda + g^2(\mathbf{y})\Delta\mu/2 . \end{aligned}$$

According to Eq. (10), $\Delta\lambda = \mu g(\mathbf{y})$ after sufficiently many iterations. Due to the multiplicative update of μ, $\Delta\mu$ is proportional to μ. Thus, it follows that $|\Delta h_{\lambda,\mu}| \approx \mu g^2(\mathbf{y})$. Absolute values $|g(\mathbf{x})|$ of the constraint function must converge linearly to zero. As the change $\Delta g = g(\mathbf{y}) - g(\mathbf{x})$ in the value of the constraint function from one successful iteration of the algorithm to the next is of order of magnitude σb, this implies that

$$|\Delta h_{\lambda,\mu}| \approx \mu g^2(\mathbf{y}) \propto \mu\sigma^2 b^2 . \quad (12)$$

According to Eqs. (11) and (12), the desired term $2a/b^2$ is implicit in the ratio $|\Delta h_{\mathbf{x}}|/(n\mu g^2(\mathbf{y}))$. Small values of that ratio indicate that changes in the value of the augmented Lagrangian are primarily due to changes in λ and μ, and that μ should be decreased. Conversely, large values of the ratio indicate that changes in the value of the augmented Lagrangian are dominated by changes in the value of the objective, and that μ should be increased in order to avoid premature stagnation. A simple update rule for μ is thus to increase μ whenever $\mu g^2(\mathbf{y}) < k_1|\Delta h_{\mathbf{x}}|/n$ for some constant k_1, and to decrease it otherwise.

The simple update rule for μ thus derived can be observed to often work well; however, it is unstable and not sufficient to ensure linear convergence under all conditions tested. The rule breaks down and leads to premature stagnation when values of μ decrease too fast, in which case the second of the conditions identified in Section 3.1 is violated. Premature stagnation results in small changes to the value of the constraint function that rapidly decrease in magnitude. To avoid premature stagnation, we thus increase μ whenever $k_2|\Delta g| < |g(\mathbf{x})|$ for some constant k_2. In order to strike a balance between steps where changes to the value of the augmented Lagrangian function are dominated by changes to λ and μ and those where they are not, we update the penalty parameter according to

$$\mu \leftarrow \begin{cases} \mu\chi^{1/4} & \text{if } \mu g^2(\mathbf{y}) < k_1|\Delta h_{\mathbf{x}}|/n \text{ or } k_2|\Delta g| < |g(\mathbf{x})| \\ \mu\chi^{-1} & \text{otherwise} \end{cases} \quad (13)$$

where $\chi > 1$ is a constant. As a result, the distribution of μ will be stationary if on average, in four out of every five steps the condition for the first case in Eq. (13) is satisfied.

4. EVALUATION

In order to evaluate the augmented Lagrangian mechanism for the (1+1)-ES, we consider constrained sphere functions as well as moderately ill-conditioned ellipsoidal functions with a single linear constraint. In all of what follows, settings $k_1 = 3$, $k_2 = 5$, and $\chi = 2^{1/4}$ have been used. Larger values of χ would allow adapting μ faster, which is advantageous in situations where that parameter is initially set to a very poor value, but at the cost of a loss of stability and increased fluctuations in μ once near optimal values have been reached.

For each combination of parameter settings, we have conducted 99 runs using double-precision floating point numbers. We say that target accuracy has been reached when a candidate solution $\mathbf{x}$ with either $(f(\mathbf{x}) - f(\mathbf{x}_{\text{opt}}))/f(\mathbf{x}_{\text{opt}}) < 10^{-8}$ or with $\|\mathbf{x} - \mathbf{x}_{\text{opt}}\|/\|\mathbf{x}_{\text{opt}}\| < 10^{-4}$ has been attained. Sample runs shown below are those that required the median number of function evaluations to achieve target accuracy.

4.1 Constrained Sphere

Figure 2 shows sample runs of the $(1+1)$-ES with augmented Lagrangian constraint handling on sphere functions with a single linear constraint for dimension $n = 10$. Parameter a scaling the objective function as well as parameters b and c determining the location of the constraint plane as well as the magnitude of the gradient of the constraint function are as indicated. All runs have been initialized with $\mathbf{x} = (1, \ldots, 1)^{\mathrm{T}}$, $\sigma = \mu = 1$, and $\lambda = 0$. The figure shows the evolution of the distance $\|\mathbf{x} - \mathbf{x}_{\text{opt}}\|$ from the optimal solution given in Eq. (7), the distance $|\lambda - \lambda_{\text{opt}}|$ of the Lagrange factor from its optimal value given in Eq. (6), and the value of the penalty parameter μ. For comparison, the distance $\|\mathbf{x} - \mathbf{x}_{\text{opt}}\|$ from the optimal solution for corresponding runs on unconstrained sphere functions is included as well.

Values of μ are initially far too small in the second and far too large in the third case shown in Fig. 2. Nonetheless, it can be seen from the figure that in all cases considered, values of the penalty parameter converge to within about an order of magnitude of $2a/b^2$. The initial bump in μ values in the fourth case is a result of the initial candidate solution being deep within the infeasible region. Once values of μ in

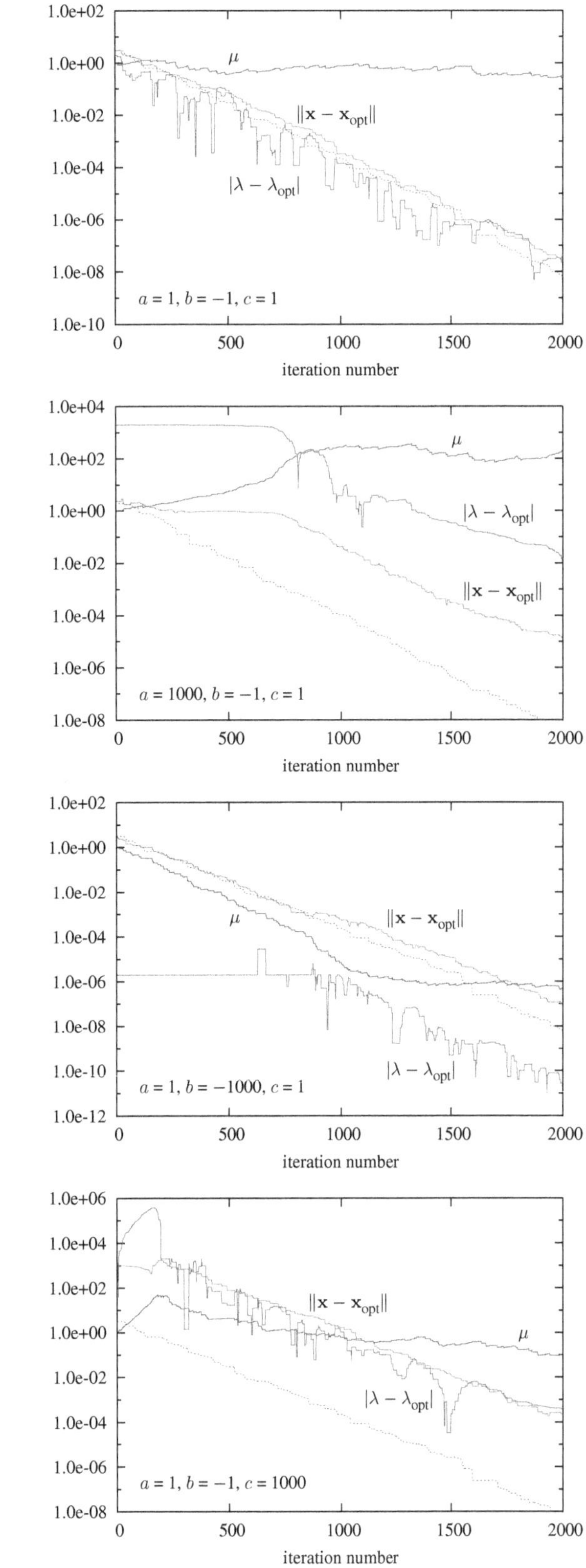

Figure 2: Sample runs of the $(1+1)$-ES with augmented Lagrangian constraint handling on linearly constrained sphere functions. The thin dotted line shows values of $\|\mathbf{x}-\mathbf{x}_{\mathbf{opt}}\|$ for the unconstrained case.

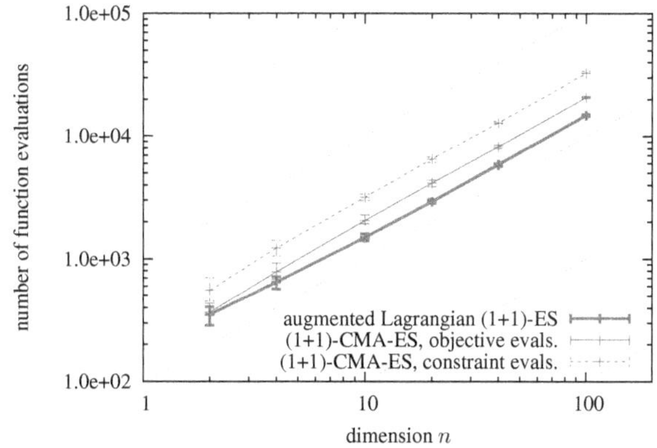

Figure 3: Number of function evaluations required to reach target accuracy on the linearly constrained sphere function with $a=-b=c=1$. Results shown are for the $(1+1)$-ES with augmented Lagrangian constraint handling (bold red line) and the $(1+1)$-CMA-ES, which handles constraints through active covariance matrix adaptation (thin green lines). The data points represent median values, and the error-bars the 10th and 90th percentiles from 99 independent runs. The thin dotted lines represent linear growth.

the vicinity of optimal ones have been attained, the strategy appears to converge linearly and at a rate not far below that achieved in the unconstrained case.

Figure 3 compares the performance of the $(1+1)$-ES with augmented Lagrangian constraint handling with that of the $(1+1)$-CMA-ES, which handles constraints through active covariance matrix adaptation [5]. The linearly constrained sphere function with $a=-b=c=1$ is considered. The values shown represent the median numbers of function evaluations, along with the 10th and 90th percentiles, required to achieve target accuracy plotted against the problem dimension n. Notice that while the $(1+1)$-ES with augmented Lagrangian constraint handling uses as many constraint function evaluations as it uses objective function evaluations, the $(1+1)$-CMA-ES computes objective function values only for feasible candidate solutions. All runs are initialized as described above, except that initial candidate solutions are drawn randomly from the feasible subregion of $[-100,100]^n$. The change has been made as the $(1+1)$-CMA-ES requires feasible initial candidate solutions. It can be seen that for both strategies, the numbers of function evaluations required to reach target accuracy appear to grow linearly with n. It can also be seen that for all but the smallest values of n, the $(1+1)$-CMA-ES requires about 40% more objective function evaluations and more than twice as many constraint function evaluations compared to the $(1+1)$-ES with augmented Lagrangian constraint handling.

4.2 Constrained Ellipsoid

We have also evaluated the performance of the $(1+1)$-ES with augmented Lagrangian constraint handling on moderately ill-conditioned ellipsoidal objective functions

$$f(\mathbf{x})=\sum_{i=1}^{n} a^{(i-1)/(n-1)} x_i^2$$

with a single linear constraint $c+\mathbf{b}^{\mathrm{T}}\mathbf{x} \leq 0$. Traces from sample runs in Fig. 4 are for $a = 10$, the cases that the normal vector $\mathbf{b}$ of the constraint plane coincides with the eigenvectors $\mathbf{v}_{\min}$ and $\mathbf{v}_{\max}$ that are associated with the smallest and largest eigenvalues of the Hessian of the objective, respectively, and values of c as indicated. As for the sphere function, it appears that linear convergence at a rate not far below that attained in the unconstrained case is achieved, and that after an initial adaptation period the distribution of μ values is stationary.

The numbers of objective and constraint function evaluations required to reach target accuracy plotted against the condition number a of the objective function's Hessian are shown in Fig. 5. Runs use constraints with $\mathbf{b}$ being a random unit vector and $c = 1$. Unsurprisingly, while the numbers of function evaluations required by the $(1+1)$-CMA-ES are relatively unaffected by the parameter a, ill-conditioning results in much larger numbers of function evaluations required by the $(1+1)$-ES with augmented Lagrangian constraint handling. It is interesting to note though that in those cases where a is not too large and n not too small, the $(1+1)$-ES with augmented Lagrangian constraint handling locates near optimal solutions faster than the $(1+1)$-CMA-ES, opening up the possibility that an augmented Lagrangian constraint handling approach in the $(1+1)$-CMA-ES may outperform the approach from [5].

5. DISCUSSION AND CONCLUSIONS

To conclude, we believe that linearly constrained quadratic problems should be among the first test cases for any constraint handling technique proposed for use in EAs. Failure to achieve linear convergence to the optimal solution in those relatively simple test cases does not bode well for the algorithms' ability to find optimal solutions to more difficult problems.

An analysis of the single-step behaviour of the $(1+1)$-ES on sphere functions with a single linear constraint has shown that the task of balancing progress in optimizing the objective function with that of minimizing constraint violations is nontrivial. When adapting Lagrange factors and penalties, the magnitude of the updates to the former must change in lockstep with the rate at which the strategy converges. Penalty parameters must be adapted carefully to achieve good performance. Employing an augmented Lagrangian approach in the $(1+1)$-ES, we have proposed a simple technique for adapting the Lagrange factor and penalty parameter for the case that only a single constraint is present. The approach has been seen to result in linear convergence on linearly constrained spherical as well as moderately ill-conditioned ellipsoidal functions.

In order to develop the proposed strategy into a useful algorithm for solving general constrained black-box optimization problems, it needs to be adapted to accommodate multiple constraints. However, generalizing the update rule for the penalty parameter in Eq. (13) to situations where a greater number of goals needs to be balanced is less than straightforward. Equation (8) turns into a combination of more than two terms with potentially widely varying coefficients, and it appears likely that some form of memory beyond that in the algorithm proposed here will be required. Further future work will explore the usefulness of the augmented Lagrangian approach in an evolution strategy performing covariance matrix adaptation.

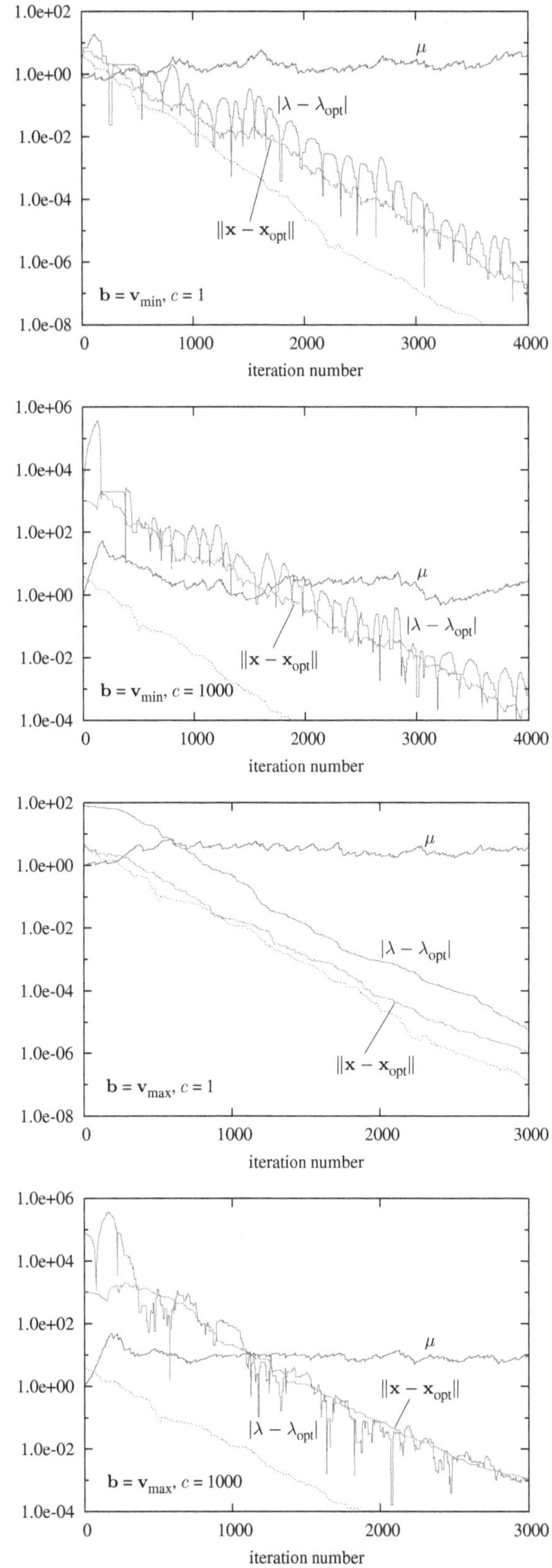

Figure 4: Sample runs of the $(1+1)$-ES with augmented Lagrangian constraint handling on linearly constrained ellipsoid functions. The thin dotted line shows values of $\|\mathbf{x}-\mathbf{x}_{\mathrm{opt}}\|$ for the unconstrained case.

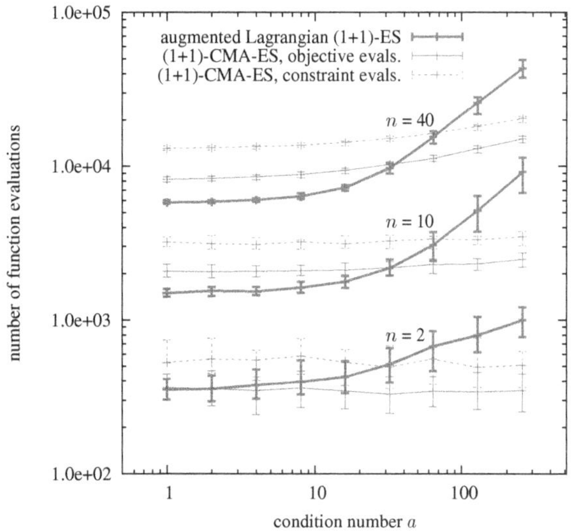

Figure 5: Number of function evaluations required to reach target accuracy on linearly constrained ellipsoidal functions with $c = 1$ and random b. Results shown are for the $(1+1)$-ES with augmented Lagrangian constraint handling (bold red lines) and the $(1+1)$-CMA-ES, which handles constraints through active covariance matrix adaptation (thin green lines). The data points represent median values, and the errorbars the 10th and 90th percentiles from 99 independent runs.

ACKNOWLEDGEMENTS

This research was supported by the Natural Sciences and Engineering Research Council of Canada (NSERC).

6. REFERENCES

[1] D. V. Arnold. On the behaviour of the $(1, \lambda)$-σSA-ES for a constrained linear problem. In C. A. Coello Coello et al., editors, *Parallel Problem Solving from Nature — PPSN XII*, pages 82–91. Springer, 2012.

[2] D. V. Arnold. Resampling versus repair in evolution strategies applied to a constrained linear problem. *Evolutionary Computation*, 22(3):389–411, 2013.

[3] D. V. Arnold. On the behaviour of the $(1, \lambda)$-ES for conically constrained linear problems. *Evolutionary Computation*, 22(3):503–523, 2014.

[4] D. V. Arnold and D. Brauer. On the behaviour of the $(1+1)$-ES for a simple constrained problem. In G. Rudolph et al., editors, *Parallel Problem Solving from Nature — PPSN X*, pages 1–10. Springer, 2008.

[5] D. V. Arnold and N. Hansen. A $(1+1)$-CMA-ES for constrained optimisation. In *Genetic and Evolutionary Computation Conference*, pages 297–304. ACM Press, 2012.

[6] H. J. C. Barbosa, A. C. C. Lemonge, and H. S. Bernadino. A critical review of adaptive penalty techniques in evolutionary computation. In R. Datta and K. Deb, editors, *Evolutionary Constrained Optimization*, pages 1–27. Springer, 2015.

[7] M. Chrzanowska-Jeske, G. Greenwood, and B. Wang. Combining evolution strategies with Lagrangian relaxation for constructing nonslicing VLSI floorplans with soft modules. In *IEEE Congress on Evolutionary Computation*, pages 1261–1266. IEEE Press, 2002.

[8] M. Hellwig and D. V. Arnold. Comparison of constraint handling mechanisms for the $(1, \lambda)$-ES on a simple constrained problem. *Evolutionary Computation*, 2015. to appear.

[9] C. Igel, T. Suttorp, and N. Hansen. A computational efficient covariance matrix update and a (1+1)-CMA for evolution strategies. In *Genetic and Evolutionary Computation Conference*, pages 453–460. ACM Press, 2006.

[10] S. Kern, S. D. Müller, N. Hansen, D. Büche, J. Ocenasek, and P. Koumoutsakos. Learning probability distributions in continuous evolutionary algorithms — A comparative review. *Natural Computing*, 3(1):77–112, 2004.

[11] O. Kramer and H.-P. Schwefel. On three new approaches to handle constraints within evolution strategies. *Natural Computing*, 5(4):363–385, 2006.

[12] J. J. Liang, T. P. Runarsson, E. Mezura-Montes, M. Clerc, P. N. Suganthan, C. A. Coello Coello, and K. Deb. Problem definitions and evaluation criteria for the CEC 2006 Special Session on Constrained Real-Parameter Optimization. Technical report, Nanyang Technological University, Singapore, 2006.

[13] W. Long, X. Liang, Y. Huang, and Y. Chen. A hybrid differential evolution augmented Lagrangian method for constrained numerical and engineering optimization. *Computer-Aided Design*, 45(12):1562–1574, 2013.

[14] S. Meyer-Nieberg and H.-G. Beyer. Why noise may be good: Additive noise on the sharp ridge. In *Genetic and Evolutionary Computation Conference*, pages 511–518. ACM Press, 2008.

[15] E. Mezura-Montes and C. A. Coello Coello. Constraint-handling in nature-inspired numerical optimization: Past, present, and future. *Swarm and Evolutionary Computation*, 1(4):173–194, 2011.

[16] Z. Michalewicz and M. Schoenauer. Evolutionary algorithms for constrained parameter optimization problems. *Evolutionary Computation*, 4(1):1–32, 1996.

[17] J. Nocedal and S. J. Wright. *Numerical Optimization*. Springer, 2nd edition, 2006.

[18] I. Rechenberg. *Evolutionsstrategie — Optimierung technischer Systeme nach Prinzipien der biologischen Evolution*. Friedrich Frommann Verlag, 1973.

[19] H.-P. Schwefel. *Numerical Optimization of Computer Models*. Wiley, 1981.

[20] S. Srivastava and K. Deb. A genetic algorithm based augmented Lagrangian method for computationally fast constrained optimization. In B. K. Panigrahi et al., editors, *Swarm, Evolutionary, and Memetic Computing*, pages 330–337. Springer, 2010.

[21] M.-J. Tahk and B.-C. Sun. Coevolutionary augmented Lagrangian methods for constrained optimization. *IEEE Transactions on Evolutionary Computation*, 4(2):114–124, 2000.

[22] Y. Yoon, Y.-H. Kim, and B.-R. Moon. An evolutionary Lagrangian method for the 0/1 multiple knapsack problem. In *Genetic and Evolutionary Computation Conference*, pages 629–635. ACM Press, 2005.

Global Line Search Algorithm Hybridized with Quadratic Interpolation and Its Extension to Separable Functions

Petr Baudiš
Czech Technical University in Prague
Fac. of Electrical Eng., Dept. of Cybernetics
Technická 2, 16627 Prague 6, Czech Republic
baudipet@fel.cvut.cz

Petr Pošík*
Czech Technical University in Prague
Fac. of Electrical Eng., Dept. of Cybernetics
Technická 2, 16627 Prague 6, Czech Republic
petr.posik@fel.cvut.cz

ABSTRACT

We propose a novel hybrid algorithm "Brent-STEP" for univariate global function minimization, based on the global line search method STEP and accelerated by Brent's method, a local optimizer that combines quadratic interpolation and golden section steps. We analyze the performance of the hybrid algorithm on various one-dimensional functions and experimentally demonstrate a significant improvement relative to its constituent algorithms in most cases. We then generalize the algorithm to multivariate functions, proposing a scheme to interleave evaluations across dimensions to achieve smoother and more efficient convergence. We experimentally demonstrate the highly competitive performance of the proposed multivariate algorithm on separable functions of the BBOB benchmark. The combination of good performance and smooth convergence on separable functions makes the algorithm an interesting candidate for inclusion in algorithmic portfolios or hybrid algorithms that aim to provide good performance on a wide range of problems.

CCS Concepts

•Mathematics of computing → Solvers; Nonconvex optimization; •Computing methodologies → Continuous space search;

Keywords

Black-box optimization, Line search, Separable functions, Hybrid algorithm

1. INTRODUCTION

Continuous black-box optimization concerns finding a minimum of a function with no accessible analytical form. One class of multivariate functions investigated regarding black-box optimization are *separable* functions — that is, functions that can be decomposed such that $f(\vec{x}) = \sum_i f_i(x_i)$.

*Contact author

GECCO '15, July 11 - 15, 2015, Madrid, Spain

ISBN 978-1-4503-3472-3/15/07...$15.00

DOI: http://dx.doi.org/10.1145/2739480.2754717

For some very hard separable functions, exploiting separability is the only way to quickly find the minimum.[1] A natural idea to optimize such functions is to use univariate optimization algorithms on individual dimensions. In [10], Brent's method (as implemented in MATLAB `fminbnd` function) and the STEP algorithm were used to separately optimize the function along each dimension. Brent's method was shown to be fast in case of unimodal functions, but due to its local nature it fails on multimodal functions. The global STEP method was able to solve both the uni- and multimodal functions, but needed much larger number of function evaluations. Moreover, their multidimensional variants were constructed inefficiently: the dimensions were optimized sequentially, one by one. As a result, the optimization process made hardly any significant progress until the algorithm started to optimize the last dimension. Another disadvantage of this solution is that the user must specify additional parameter, the budget for individual line searches.

Although these algorithms rely on the function separability and despite the above disadvantages, both of these methods proved to be useful in algorithmic portfolios [1] and hybrid algorithms [8] that strive to be successful on a broad range of functions, including the separable ones.

This paper builds on the above mentioned methods, and provides the following contributions:

1. We combine Brent's method and STEP into a single algorithm which converges faster than STEP (in many cases, it is almost as fast as Brent's method), while it preserves the global search ability of STEP (thus solving a larger proportion of functions than Brent's method, and often doing it faster).

2. We suggest a better way of making a multidimensional variant of this method. As opposed to solving the 1D problem in all dimensions sequentially, we propose to interleave the steps in individual dimensions, updating the full coordinates of sampled points based on results obtained in other dimensions so far.

The paper is organized as follows: In Sec. 2 we describe our hybrid univariate optimization algorithm and its multivariate extension. In Sec. 3 we outline our experimental setup for benchmarking both univariate and multivariate optimization performance, and in Sec. 4 we present and analyze the benchmark results. We conclude and outline future work in Sec. 5.

[1] A good example is the Skew Rastrigin-Bueche (f4) in the BBOB benchmark [3, 6].

2. ALGORITHM PRESENTATION

The algorithm proposed in this paper is a hybrid of two techniques: Brent's method and STEP. Algorithms based on these two methods belong to the best performing BBOB-2009 algorithms for the class of separable functions [5]. Let us first shortly review the two methods. We will then outline the approach to combine them and consequent required modifications to the individual methods. Finally, we will consider extending them from univariate to multivariate optimization without optimizing dimensions one by one.

2.1 Brent's Method

Brent's method [2] is a classic local line search method enriching a golden section search with quadratic interpolation (QI) to speed up its convergence on functions with continuous second derivative. Detailed description of this standard algorithm can be found in [12, Sec. 10.2]. Its implementation is also part of many scientific toolboxes (see e.g. function `fminbnd` in MATLAB or `minimize_scalar` in scipy.optimize).

In each iteration of the Brent's method, a parabola is interpolated through the three best-so-far sampled points. The point at the minimum of the parabola is considered for the next sample, provided that it passes a convergence criterion which (roughly speaking) ensures that the samples converge to a single point by the virtue of each sample being closer to the minimum best-so-far point than to the other two.[2] If the point is not accepted, a golden section step splits the interval between the best-so-far point and the domain bound which contained the proposed point.

2.2 STEP

STEP [7] is the acronym of "Select the Easiest Point". It is a global line search method which iteratively divides the initial domain into increasing number of intervals by evaluating a point in the middle of one of them. The interval to be split into halves is chosen on the basis of its *difficulty* which estimates how hard it will be to find an improvement by sampling from that particular interval.

To estimate the difficulty of (finding an improvement inside) an interval, a quadratic model is used. Assume that a particular interval is defined by 2 previously sampled and evaluated boundary points, (x_1, f_1) and (x_2, f_2). A parabola $y(x)$ is estimated such that it intersects both boundary points and improves the best solution so far (f_{BSF}), such that $y(x) = y_{\min} = f_{\text{BSF}} - \epsilon$ for some $x \in [x_1, x_2]$. The minimal curvature required for such a quadratic function is used as the *interval difficulty.*

2.3 Hybrid Brent-STEP Algorithm

The proposed hybrid combines Brent's and STEP methods in a *divide and conquer* manner. Both methods divide intervals into smaller parts. If possible, a step of local Brent's method is applied in a chosen search space part. If Brent's method does not seem to be profitable, a step of the global STEP method is applied.

In any time instant, the division of the search space into intervals is given by a sequence of points $(x_1, \ldots, x_N)$, $x_1 < x_2 < \ldots < x_N$. All these points are evaluated, their function values are $(f_1, \ldots, f_N), f_i = f(x_i)$. Each pair of successive x-values defines an interval, each triple of successive x-values defines a so-called *neighboring intervals pair* (NIP). There are thus $N - 1$ intervals, and $N - 2$ NIPs.

Our hybrid algorithm repeatedly inspects the available intervals bounded by points sampled so far, checks if Brent's iteration seems profitable (see below) in any NIP, and falls back to the STEP method to perform a global optimization step if that is not the case.

Brent's branch: Since each NIP is defined by 3 evaluated points, it is easy to check if these points bracket a minimum (that is, $f_i > f_{i+1} < f_{i+2}$). In that case it is possible to use quadratic interpolation to find an estimate of the minimum inside this NIP. Among all the NIPs which bracket a minimum, we choose the NIP with the best estimated minimum.[3] If the estimated minimum is nonnegligibly better than the best solution so far ($y_{\min} \le f_{\text{BSF}} - \epsilon$), we make an iteration of Brent's method. Whereas the original Brent's method used the three best-so-far points for QI, we use the three NIP boundary points instead as we can apply Brent's step in a different NIP in each iteration.[4]

STEP branch: If there is no NIP promising to improve the best solution, we perform an iteration of the STEP method — i.e. the interval with the lowest difficulty is selected and a point in the middle of the interval is sampled.

This process is repeated until a solution of sufficient quality is found, the function evaluation budget is exhausted, or until there is no interval sufficiently large to be halved. A high-level description of this process is presented as Alg. 1.

Let us reiterate that this algorithm uses two different quadratic models for two different purposes:

1. In Brent's method, to estimate the profitability of using a QI step inside a NIP, the quadratic model is fit to three points (interval boundaries). The estimated minimum value of the parabola is used to judge whether it will be profitable to sample in this NIP; if so, the coordinate of the minimum is used as the next sampling point.

2. In STEP, to estimate the suitability of an interval to be split, the difficulty of an interval is computed by fitting a parabola in such a way that it must pass through both points defining that interval, and its minimum must lie on the level $f_{\text{BSF}} - \epsilon$ somewhere in that interval. The coefficient of the quadratic term is then used as a measure of interval difficulty; the coordinate of the minimum is not used in any way.

In some cases (e.g. the f_{14} function shown below), Brent's method will zone in on the optimum, but eventually the expected improvement (as estimated by the quadratic interpolation) will become insufficient, and Brent's method is interrupted (although it would still be profitable to continue with the local search). The algorithm switches to STEP which will never sample the interval again (never triggering a possible Brent's method restart) because its difficulty

[2] In fact, there are more sample acceptance tests and the convergence criterion uses a heuristical time delay, but this is not relevant in our application.

[3] Unimodal functions will typically have only a single NIP bracketing a minimum.

[4] Considering the standard description of Brent's method, e.g. in [12], we use a modified variable assignment as follows: variables a and b are set to the boundary points of a NIP, x is set to the third point inside the NIP, w and v are set to the better and worse of a and b, respectively, u is set to x, and e is set to the size of the smaller interval in the pair.

Algorithm 1: Univariate Brent-STEP algorithm

Input: f – function to be optimized, $X = (x_i, f_i)_{i=1}^{3}$ – three evaluated points, such that x_1 and x_3 are lower and upper boundary, respectively, k – the period of unconditionally triggering Brent's iteration.

Output: $(x_{\text{BSF}}, f_{\text{BSF}})$ - estimate of the minimum.

begin
- $t \longleftarrow 0$
- $(x_{\text{BSF}}, f_{\text{BSF}}) \longleftarrow$ best of X.
- **while** *termination criteria are not met* **do**
  - $t \longleftarrow t + 1$
  - $B \longleftarrow$ choose the NIPs bracketing a minimum.
  - $i, y_{\min} \longleftarrow$ find the most promising NIP in B.
  - **if** $y_{\min} \leq f_{\text{BSF}} - \epsilon$ *or* $mod(t, k) = 0$ **then**
    - $x_s \longleftarrow$ sample from NIP i using Brent's iteration.
  - **else**
    - $i \longleftarrow$ find interval with lowest difficulty.
    - $x_s \longleftarrow$ sample the middle point of interval i.
  - $f_s \longleftarrow f(x_s)$
  - $(x_{\text{BSF}}, f_{\text{BSF}}) \longleftarrow$ update BSF using (x_s, f_s) if needed.
  - Incorporate (x_s, f_s) into X such that $x_1 < x_2 < \ldots < x_N$.

measure is too unfavorable. Therefore, as an important relaxation of the conditions above, every k iterations we allow an iteration of Brent's method even if it is not estimated as a sufficient improvement to f_{BSF}.

2.4 Multivariate Generalization

As we already mentioned, solving D-dimensional separable problem as D independent 1D problems is a plausible idea, but not very efficient. Rate of convergence and especially its steadiness would be much improved if the solvers in individual dimensions could cooperate. Steady convergence from the beginning is especially important for expensive optimization scenarios and in portfolios with online algorithm selection based on performance within the same run.

The sequential multivariate versions of Brent's method and STEP (in [10] denoted as LSfminbnd and LSstep, respectively) worked in the following way. A random point was first chosen in the search space; we call this point *a context* (and this is the only stochastic part of the algorithm). The fitness function was then optimized along the first axis taking all the other coordinate values from the context. After the optimization in the first dimension was finished, the first coordinate of the context was updated to the best solution found during the univariate search. The same process was then repeated for all the remaining dimensions.

We extend this approach by interleaving the individual univariate solvers. A single dimension is chosen in a round-robin fashion, and the algorithm associated with that dimension performs a single iteration. If an improvement Δf_{BSF} of the best-so-far solution is found, the context is updated and propagated to all the other univariate solvers immediately to update their states. Moreover, each other solver updates (by function separability) the function values of all the points sampled so far by Δf_{BSF}.

A related STEP "semi-interleaving" method was used in the HCMA algorithm [8], but the context was updated only after a complete pass through all dimensions, which allowed the hybrid algorithm to test the separability of the function.

It is worth noting that we extensively experimented with various dimension selection strategies [9] "smarter" than round-robin, especially based on the minimal interval difficulty, but the improvement compared to the round-robin strategy was insignificant.

3. EXPERIMENTAL PROCEDURE

To study the behavior of the Brent-STEP (B-S) algorithm in *univariate search* in contrast to its constituent methods[5] (Brent and STEP), we evaluated the BBOB benchmark functions with scalar arguments, even though they are typically used for multivariate benchmarking; most of them can be successfuly used this way. We do not consider functions 8, 9, 17, 18, 19, 20 and 24 since these cannot be evaluated with scalar argument or yield a constant function. We also do not detail results for 1D versions of functions 2, 3, 11, 12, and 13, which are very similar in shape and results to some of the other reference functions which are part of the comparison.

To test *multivariate performance*, we compared the proposed interleaved multivariate Brent-STEP method (NDsqistep) with

- the interleaved version of the STEP method (NDstep), which should reveal the benefit of hybridizing STEP with Brent's method,
- the non-interleaved versions of Brent (LSfminbnd) and STEP (LSstep) as submitted for BBOB-2009 [10], which shall reveal the benefit of interleaving the interations in individual dimensions, and
- HCMA [8] which is a competitive hybrid algorithm combining BFGS, STEP and a CMA-ES variant (and uses semi-interleaved STEP on separable functions until non-separability is detected).

These algorithms are compared on the whole testbed again.

We ran experiments according to [4] on the benchmark functions given in [3, 6]. We used the BBOB2015 set of instances for conducting benchmarks.

We follow the STEP algorithm settings as described in [10], in particular we set $\epsilon = 10^{-8}$. To facilitate continued Brent runs on functions with poor STEP convergence as described above, we unconditionally trigger the Brent's method every $k = 10$ iterations. The algorithms are wrapped in a multistart strategy that performs a random restart if the algorithm did not yield an improving result for 2000 iterations.

4. RESULTS AND DISCUSSION

First, we show results of the hybrid Brent-STEP algorithm on various univariate functions and analyze its performance relative to the constituent algorithms. Next, we turn to the multivariate case and compare the performance of Brent-STEP as we proposed it to other previously published algorithms focused on separable functions.

[5]We used our own Python STEP implementation for benchmarking STEP and the `bounded` scalar minimization method of SciPy 0.14.0 for benchmarking Brent's method.

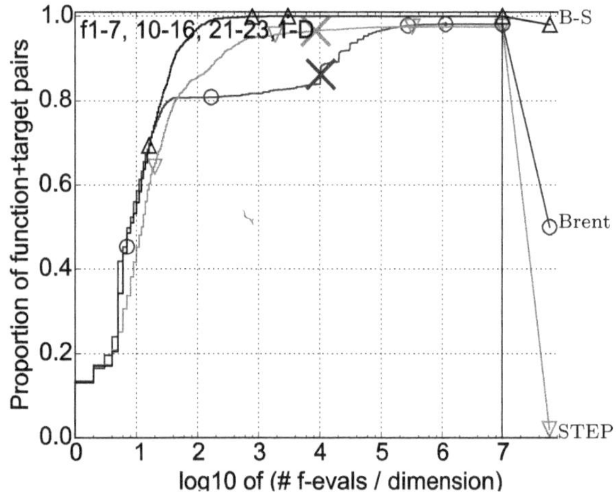

Figure 1: Bootstrapped empirical cumulative distribution of the number of objective function evaluations (FEvals) for 50 targets in $10^{[-8..2]}$ for all considered univariate functions.

The **expected running time (ERT)**, used in the figures and tables, depends on a given target function value, $f_t = f_{opt} + \Delta f$. It is computed over all relevant trials as the number of function evaluations executed during each trial while the best function value did not reach f_t, summed over all trials, and divided by the number of trials that actually reached f_t [4, 11]. **Statistical significance** is tested with the rank-sum test for a given target Δf_t using, for each trial, either the number of needed function evaluations to reach Δf_t (inverted and multiplied by -1), or, if the target was not reached, the best Δf-value achieved, measured only up to the smallest number of overall function evaluations for any unsuccessful trial under consideration.

4.1 Univariate Experiments

The empirical cumulative distribution function (ECDF) of ERT across all considered functions is shown in Fig. 1; the ECDF on individual functions is compared in Figure 2.

We can immediately observe that even though there are many functions for which either STEP or Brent exhibits some pathological behavior and has difficulty converging, the Brent-STEP algorithm converges on all of the considered functions, and moreover is always better than the worse of the constituent methods. The hybrid algorithm is therefore robust in this regard.

Looking at each of the detailed functions, we can notice three modes of behavior — either the hybrid algorithm closely matches the performance of the better of the methods (functions 1, 5, 7, 10, 14, 16, 21 and 22), it lags behind the better of the methods (only function 6), or the two methods cooperate in harmony on speeding up the search (highly multi-modal functions 4, 15, 23).

In case of function 6, we can observe that it is almost flat on one side of the optimum but very steep on the other side. Our modification of Brent does not perform well in this case since instead of the three best-so-far points, we fit the parabola through the three bracketing NIP boundary points. While the three best-so-far points would all lie on the flat side of the optimum, the rightmost NIP boundary

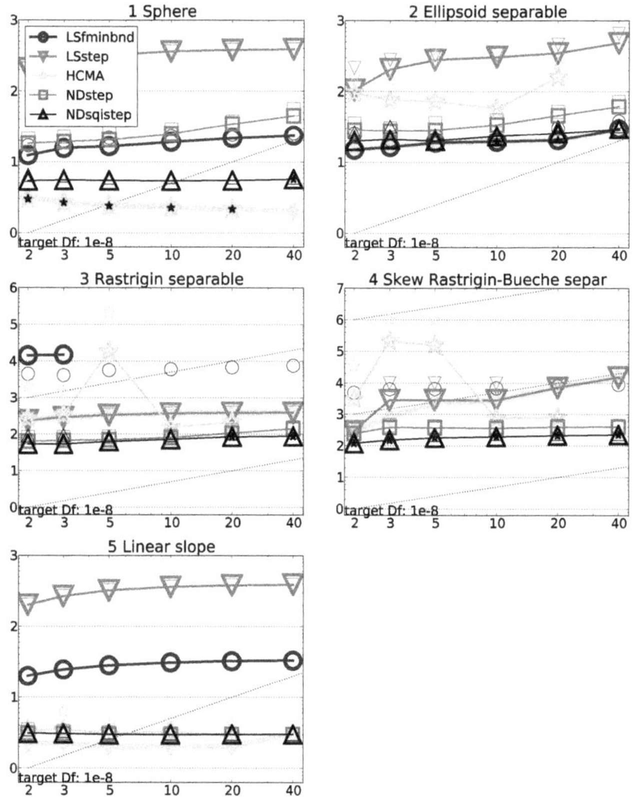

Figure 3: Expected running time (ERT in number of f-evaluations as $\log_{10}$ value), divided by dimension for target function value 10^{-8} versus dimension. Slanted grid lines indicate quadratic scaling with the dimension. Different symbols correspond to different algorithms given in the legend of f_1. Light symbols give the maximum number of function evaluations from the longest trial divided by dimension. Black stars indicate a statistically better result compared to all other algorithms with $p < 0.01$ and Bonferroni correction number of dimensions (six). Legend: ○:LSfminbnd, ▽:LSstep, :HCMA, □:NDstep, △:NDsqistep

remains at the steep side, causing repeated overshooting of the fitted parabola minimum to the flat side. Brent-STEP still converges and is faster than plain STEP, though.

The beneficial interplay of the two methods is most apparent on function 23, which has many local optima. The Brent algorithm, as a very local method, will always slide into the local optimum near the middle of the domain, while the STEP method will not explore the optima sufficiently. The combination of both methods enables simultaneous exploration of all local optima by Brent, with dynamic preference to spending evaluations on the most promising one.

4.2 Multivariate Experiments

The multivariate results are presented in Fig. 3 (expected running time — ERT scaling), Fig. 5 (convergence rate across many instances — ECDF) and in Tables 1 and 2. To highlight the effect of smooth convergence thanks to the interleaved dimension evaluation, we also show ERT scaling plotted for the "expensive" BBOB scenario in Figure 4, where

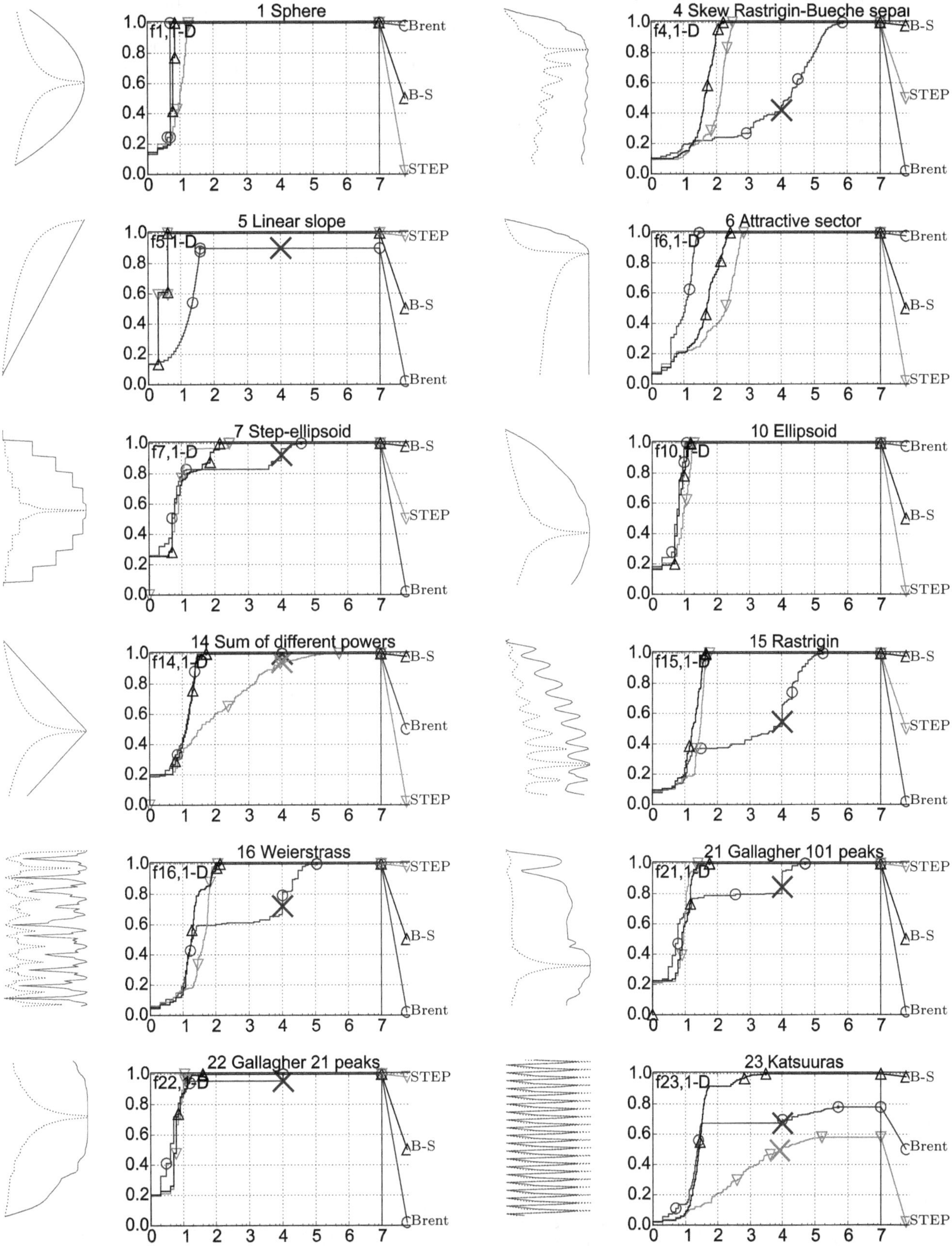

Figure 2: Bootstrapped empirical cumulative distribution (ECDF) of the number of objective function evaluations (FEvals) for 50 targets in $10^{[-8..2]}$ for each of the detailed univariate functions. The horizontal axis shows $\log_{10}$ number of FEvals required to reach the proportion of targets marked on the vertical axis. Near each ECDF graph is also shown a sketch (rotated sideways) of the corresponding univariate function in its whole domain; the dashed line shows the function log-scaled.

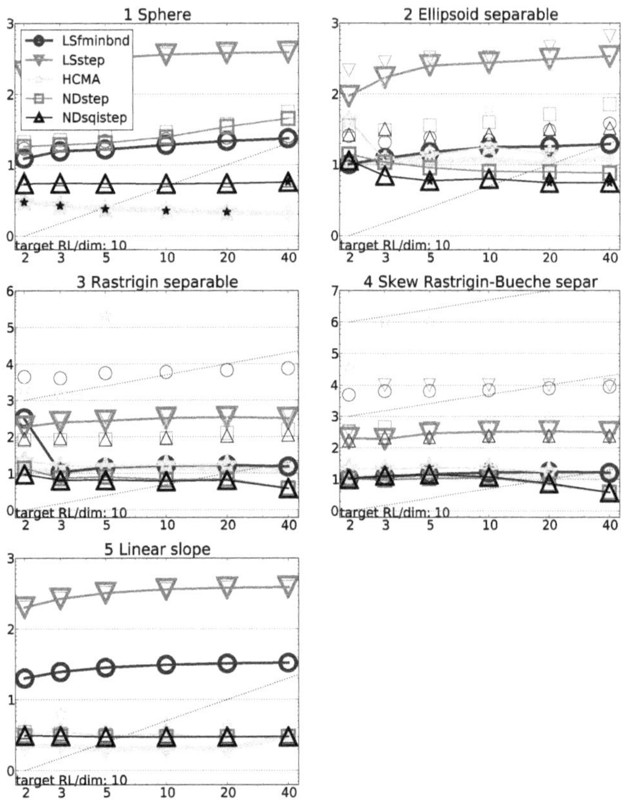

Figure 4: Expected running time (ERT in number of f-evaluations as $\log_{10}$ value) divided by dimension versus dimension. The target function value is chosen such that the bestGECCO2009 artificial algorithm just failed to achieve an ERT of $10 \times \mathrm{DIM}$. Different symbols correspond to different algorithms given in the legend of f_1. Light symbols give the maximum number of function evaluations from the longest trial divided by dimension. Black stars indicate a statistically better result compared to all other algorithms with $p < 0.01$ and Bonferroni correction number of dimensions (six). Legend: ○:LSfminbnd, ▽:LSstep, :HCMA, □:NDstep, △:NDsqistep

a substantial progress right from the beginning of the optimization is highly important.

Let us shortly discuss the results of HCMA. Figure 5 shows it has an advantage in the beginning of the search. The margin is caused by the use of BFGS method, which helps HCMA to optimize f1 very quickly (see Figs. 3 and 4). It also helps the method to quickly reach some less demanding targets on other functions. From this point of view, HCMA has a considerable advantage. On the other hand, being a general method aimed also at non-separable functions, HCMA must carefully decide whether it will use STEP or other constituent methods; this is not the case for the other methods with the assumption of independence hard-wired. From this point of view, HCMA has a significant disadvantage for comparison on separable functions.

The difference of NDstep (interleaved) to LSstep (non-interleaved) is predictable — NDstep converges comparably smoothly as apparent from the ECDF figure, and with lower ERT as there is no need to preemptively spend the whole alotted budget in each dimension.

Moving from STEP to Brent-STEP in multivariate case (the NDsqistep algorithm) has effects consistent with the univariate behavior — it always (except f5) improves the STEP variant, and on f2, where Brent's method dominated, it performs comparably.

Thanks to smooth convergence, the ERT for expensive scenario targets is also improved; on all non-trivial separable functions, the Brent-STEP algorithm improves the BBOB-2009 baseline.

5. CONCLUSION

We have reviewed two popular line search methods (Brent and STEP) that represent the BBOB-2009 baseline for performance on separable functions. We have introduced a new hybrid algorithm "Brent-STEP" combining these two methods non-trivially and demonstrated that on univariate and separable functions the hybrid algorithm in general outperforms both of them, in the univariate case often by a wide margin, and that it is behaving robustly even when one of the constituent methods is failing to converge.

Separable functions are not a very common class in practice, but we envision inclusion of the proposed algorithm in other hybrid methods (akin to HCMA introduced above) and in algorithm portfolios to efficiently handle the case of separable or near-separable functions. Even on non-separable functions, a short run of Brent-STEP might for example serve to generate an initial population for a followup evolutionary (or other optimization) algorithm run. To facilitate this direction of research, we are making our implementation of the algorithm available as open source.[6]

We consider efficient usage of Brent-STEP in larger algorithm ensembles to be the main course of future work. Brent-STEP also exhibits suboptimal performance in case of some pathologically shaped functions (see f6 above), that could be improved by some heuristic tweaks.

Acknowledgement

This work was supported by the Grant Agency of the Czech Technical University in Prague, grant No. SGS14/194/OHK3 /3T/13.

6. REFERENCES

[1] B. Bischl, O. Mersmann, H. Trautmann, and M. Preuß. Algorithm selection based on exploratory landscape analysis and cost-sensitive learning. In *Proceedings of the 14th annual conference on Genetic and evolutionary computation*, pages 313–320. ACM, 2012.

[2] R. Brent. Algorithms for minimization without derivatives. *Prentice-Hall series in automatic computation*, 1973.

[3] S. Finck, N. Hansen, R. Ros, and A. Auger. Real-parameter black-box optimization benchmarking 2009: Presentation of the noiseless functions. Technical Report 2009/20, Research Center PPE, 2009. Updated February 2010.

[4] N. Hansen, A. Auger, S. Finck, and R. Ros. Real-parameter black-box optimization benchmarking

[6]https://github.com/pasky/step

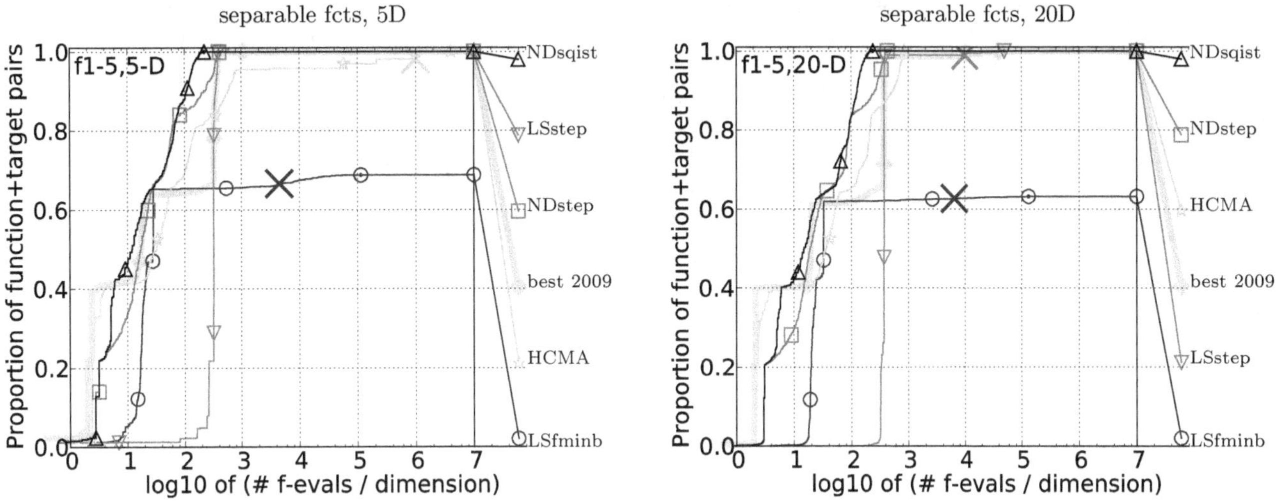

Figure 5: Bootstrapped empirical cumulative distribution of the number of objective function evaluations divided by dimension (FEvals/DIM) for 50 targets in $10^{[-8..2]}$ for all separable functions in 5-D and 20-D. The "best 2009" line corresponds to the best ERT observed during BBOB 2009 for each single target.

Δf_{opt}	1e1	1e0	1e-1	1e-2	1e-3	1e-5	1e-7	#succ
f1	11	12	12	12	12	12	12	15/15
LSfminb	6.0(2)	6.3(2)	6.7(3)	6.7(3)	6.8(2)	6.8(2)	6.8(2)	15/15
LSstep	92(46)	121(0.0)	129(17)	132(0.0)	132(0.1)	132(0.1)	132(0.1)	15/15
HCMA	**1.1**(0)$^{\star 2}$	**0.98**(0)$^{\star 4}$	**0.98**(0)$^{\star 4}$	**0.98**(0)$^{\star 4}$	**0.98**(0)$^{\star 4}$	**0.98**(0)$^{\star 4}$	**0.98**(0)$^{\star 4}$	15/15
NDstep	1.6(0.2)	2.1(0.1)	2.8(0.1)	3.5(0.1)	4.2(0.2)	5.6(0.1)	6.8(0.3)	15/15
NDsqist	1.6(0.1)	1.9(0.2)	2.1(0.3)	2.2(0.2)	2.2(0.1)	2.2(0.2)	2.2(0.2)	15/15
Δf_{opt}	1e1	1e0	1e-1	1e-2	1e-3	1e-5	1e-7	#succ
f2	83	87	88	89	90	92	94	15/15
LSfminb	1(0.2)	1(0.1)	1(0.1)	1(0.1)	1(0.1)	1(0.1)	**1**(0.2)	15/15
LSstep	16(3)	16(0.9)	16(2)	15(2)	15(2)	15(2)	15(0.1)	15/15
HCMA	1.5(0.1)	1.6(0.2)	1.8(0.2)	2.0(0.2)	2.2(0.3)	2.5(0.3)	2.8(0.2)	15/15
NDstep	0.72(0.1)$_{\downarrow 4}$	0.81(0.0)$_{\downarrow 3}$	0.88(0.1)	0.97(0.1)	1.1(0.1)	1.2(0.1)	1.4(0.1)	15/15
NDsqist	**0.56**(0.1)$^{\star}_{\downarrow 4}$	**0.59**(0.1)$^{\star 3}_{\downarrow 4}$	**0.63**(0.1)$^{\star 3}_{\downarrow 4}$	**0.72**(0.1)$^{\star 3}_{\downarrow 3}$	**0.79**(0.2)$^{\star 2}_{\downarrow 2}$	**0.90**(0.2)	1.0(0.2)	15/15
Δf_{opt}	1e1	1e0	1e-1	1e-2	1e-3	1e-5	1e-7	#succ
f3	716	1622	1637	1642	1646	1650	1654	15/15
LSfminb	1(1)	52(49)	∞	∞	∞	∞	∞ *2e4*	0/15
LSstep	2.2(3e-3)	1(8e-3)	1(0.0)	1(0.0)	1(9e-3)	1(0.0)	1(8e-3)	15/15
HCMA	0.29(0.2)	3.0(2)	55(44)	54(43)	55(0.1)	55(320)	55(86)	15/15
NDstep	0.12(0.0)	**0.12**(0.0)	**0.14**(0.0)	**0.15**(0.0)	**0.16**(0.0)	**0.17**(0.0)	0.20(0.0)	15/15
NDsqist	**0.09**(0.0)$_{\downarrow}$	0.13(0.0)	0.16(0.0)	0.17(0.0)	0.17(0.1)	0.18(0.0)	**0.18**(0.0)	15/15
Δf_{opt}	1e1	1e0	1e-1	1e-2	1e-3	1e-5	1e-7	#succ
f4	809	1633	1688	1758	1817	1886	1903	15/15
LSfminb	7.8(4)	∞	∞	∞	∞	∞	∞ *2e4*	0/15
LSstep	2.0(7e-3)	1(7e-3)	1(0.0)	1(0.0)	1(0.0)	1(0.1)	1(0.1)	15/15
HCMA	0.29(0.2)$_{\downarrow 3}$	74(263)	457(1482)	439(2134)	425(688)	410(663)	406(0.2)	13/15
NDstep	**0.14**(0.0)$_{\downarrow 4}$	0.24(0.1)$_{\downarrow 4}$	0.40(0.1)	0.53(0.1)	0.61(0.1)	0.88(0.1)	0.94(0.1)	15/15
NDsqist	0.15(0.1)$_{\downarrow 4}$	**0.21**(0.1)$_{\downarrow 4}$	**0.29**(0.1)*	**0.29**(0.1)$^{\star 3}$	**0.30**(0.1)$^{\star 4}$	**0.32**(0.1)$^{\star 4}$	**0.40**(0.1)$^{\star 4}$	15/15
Δf_{opt}	1e1	1e0	1e-1	1e-2	1e-3	1e-5	1e-7	#succ
f5	10	10	10	10	10	10	10	15/15
LSfminb	13(3)	14(0)	14(0)	14(0)	14(0)	14(0)	14(0)	15/15
LSstep	141(40)	160(0.1)	160(0.1)	160(0.1)	160(0.1)	160(0.1)	160(0.1)	15/15
HCMA	**1.3**(0.1)$^{\star 2}$	**1.4**(0.2)	1.5(0.3)	1.5(0.2)	1.5(0.3)	1.5(0.2)	1.5(0.2)	15/15
NDstep	1.5(0.1)	1.5(0.1)	**1.5**(0.1)	**1.5**(0.1)	**1.5**(0.1)	**1.5**(0.1)	**1.5**(0.1)	15/15
NDsqist	1.5(0.1)	1.5(0.1)	**1.5**(0.1)	**1.5**(0.1)	**1.5**(0.1)	**1.5**(0.1)	**1.5**(0.1)	15/15

Table 1: Expected running time (ERT in number of function evaluations) divided by the respective best ERT measured during BBOB-2009 in dimension 5. The ERT and in braces, as dispersion measure, the half difference between 90 and 10%-tile of bootstrapped run lengths appear for each algorithm and target, the corresponding best ERT in the first row. The different target Δf-values are shown in the top row. #succ is the number of trials that reached the (final) target $f_{\text{opt}} + 10^{-8}$. The median number of conducted function evaluations is additionally given in *italics*, if the target in the last column was never reached. Entries, succeeded by a star, are statistically significantly better (according to the rank-sum test) when compared to all other algorithms of the table, with $p = 0.05$ or $p = 10^{-k}$ when the number k following the star is larger than 1, with Bonferroni correction by the number of instances.

Δf_{opt}	1e1	1e0	1e-1	1e-2	1e-3	1e-5	1e-7	#succ
f1	43	43	43	43	43	43	43	15/15
LSfminb	9.3(2)	10(1)	10(1)	10(1.0)	10(1)	10(1.0)	10(1)	15/15
LSstep	164(14)	175(2)	176(2)	177(0.0)	177(0.0)	177(0.0)	177(0.0)	15/15
HCMA	**1.00**(0.0)^{*4}	**1.0**(0.0)^{*4}	**1.0**(0.0)^{*4}	**1.0**(0.0)^{*4}	**1.0**(0.0)^{*4}	**1.0**(6e-3)^{*4}	**1.0**(6e-3)^{*4}	15/15
NDstep	2.1(0.1)	2.8(0.1)	3.6(0.1)	4.4(0.1)	5.1(0.0)	6.7(0.1)	8.3(0.1)	15/15
NDsqist	1.9(0.1)	2.3(0.1)	2.5(0.3)	2.5(0.3)	2.5(0.2)	2.5(0.3)	2.5(0.3)	15/15
Δf_{opt}	1e1	1e0	1e-1	1e-2	1e-3	1e-5	1e-7	#succ
f2	385	386	387	388	390	391	393	15/15
LSfminb	1(0.1)	1(0.0)	1(0.1)	1(0.1)	1(0.1)	**1**(0.1)	**1**(0.0)	15/15
LSstep	17(0.7)	17(0.4)	17(0.4)	17(0.0)	17(0.2)	17(0.2)	17(0.2)	15/15
HCMA	1.3(0.0)	1.5(0.1)	1.7(0.1)	1.8(0.1)	2.1(0.2)	2.4(0.2)	2.8(0.3)	15/15
NDstep	0.69(0.0)$_{\downarrow4}$	0.78(0.0)$_{\downarrow4}$	0.88(0.2)	0.95(0.1)	1.1(0.1)	1.2(0.0)	1.4(0.1)	15/15
NDsqist	**0.59**(0.1)$^{\star2}_{\downarrow4}$	**0.65**(0.1)$^{\star3}_{\downarrow4}$	**0.69**(0.1)$^{\star3}_{\downarrow4}$	**0.79**(0.1)$^{\star2}_{\downarrow4}$	**0.87**(0.1)$^{\star3}_{\downarrow3}$	1.0(0.2)	1.1(0.1)	15/15
Δf_{opt}	1e1	1e0	1e-1	1e-2	1e-3	1e-5	1e-7	#succ
f3	5066	7626	7635	7637	7643	7646	7651	15/15
LSfminb	∞	∞	∞	∞	∞	∞	∞ *1e5*	0/15
LSstep	1.5(0.1)	1(1e-3)	1(2e-3)	1(2e-3)	1(2e-3)	1(1e-3)	1(2e-3)	15/15
HCMA	0.26(0.0)$_{\downarrow4}$	0.37(0.1)$_{\downarrow4}$	0.46(0.1)$_{\downarrow4}$	0.47(0.1)$_{\downarrow4}$	0.49(0.1)$_{\downarrow4}$	0.51(0.1)$_{\downarrow4}$	0.53(0.1)	15/15
NDstep	**0.12**(0.0)$_{\downarrow4}$	**0.15**(0.0)$_{\downarrow4}$	0.19(0.0)$_{\downarrow4}$	0.20(0.0)$_{\downarrow4}$	0.21(0.0)$_{\downarrow4}$	0.22(0.0)$_{\downarrow4}$	0.23(0.0)$_{\downarrow4}$	15/15
NDsqist	0.14(0.0)$_{\downarrow4}$	0.16(0.0)$_{\downarrow4}$	**0.19**(0.1)$_{\downarrow4}$	**0.19**(0.0)$_{\downarrow4}$	**0.20**(0.0)$_{\downarrow4}$	**0.20**(0.0)$_{\downarrow4}$	**0.21**(0.1)$_{\downarrow4}$	15/15
Δf_{opt}	1e1	1e0	1e-1	1e-2	1e-3	1e-5	1e-7	#succ
f4	4722	7628	7666	7686	7700	7758	1.4e5	9/15
LSfminb	∞	∞	∞	∞	∞	∞	∞ *1e5*	0/15
LSstep	1.6(8e-4)	1(4e-3)	1(5e-3)	1(7e-3)	1(9e-3)	1(0.0)	1(1)	9/15
HCMA	0.42(0.1)$_{\downarrow4}$	0.67(0.0)	0.90(0.1)	1.1(0.1)	1.5(0.1)	1.8(0.2)	0.11(0.0)	15/15
NDstep	0.19(0.0)$_{\downarrow4}$	0.30(0.1)$_{\downarrow4}$	0.46(0.1)$_{\downarrow4}$	0.60(0.1)	0.72(0.1)	0.86(0.1)	0.05(8e-3)	15/15
NDsqist	**0.18**(0.1)$_{\downarrow4}$	**0.29**(0.1)$_{\downarrow4}$	**0.31**(0.0)$^{\star3}_{\downarrow4}$	**0.32**(0.0)$^{\star4}_{\downarrow4}$	**0.33**(0.0)$^{\star4}_{\downarrow4}$	**0.36**(0.1)$^{\star4}_{\downarrow4}$	**0.02**(3e-3)$^{\star4}_{\downarrow4}$	15/15
Δf_{opt}	1e1	1e0	1e-1	1e-2	1e-3	1e-5	1e-7	#succ
f5	41	41	41	41	41	41	41	15/15
LSfminb	16(0.4)	16(6e-3)	16(0)	16(0)	16(0)	16(0)	16(0)	15/15
LSstep	185(5)	187(2)	187(0.0)	187(0.0)	187(0.0)	187(0.0)	187(0.0)	15/15
HCMA	**1.2**(0.1)^{*4}	**1.4**(0.4)	**1.4**(0.4)	**1.4**(0.3)	**1.4**(0.4)	**1.4**(0.4)	**1.4**(0.2)	15/15
NDstep	1.5(0.0)	1.5(0.0)	1.5(0.0)	1.5(0.0)	1.5(0.0)	1.5(0.0)	1.5(0.0)	15/15
NDsqist	1.5(0.0)	1.5(0.0)	1.5(0.0)	1.5(0.0)	1.5(0.0)	1.5(0.0)	1.5(0.0)	15/15

Table 2: Expected running time (ERT in number of function evaluations) divided by the respective best ERT measured during BBOB-2009 in dimension 20. The ERT and in braces, as dispersion measure, the half difference between 90 and 10%-tile of bootstrapped run lengths appear for each algorithm and target, the corresponding best ERT in the first row. The different target Δf-values are shown in the top row. #succ is the number of trials that reached the (final) target $f_{\text{opt}} + 10^{-8}$. The median number of conducted function evaluations is additionally given in *italics*, if the target in the last column was never reached. Entries, succeeded by a star, are statistically significantly better (according to the rank-sum test) when compared to all other algorithms of the table, with $p = 0.05$ or $p = 10^{-k}$ when the number k following the star is larger than 1, with Bonferroni correction by the number of instances.

2012: Experimental setup. Technical report, INRIA, 2012.

[5] N. Hansen, A. Auger, R. Ros, S. Finck, and P. Pošík. Comparing results of 31 algorithms from the black-box optimization benchmarking BBOB-2009. In *Workshop Proceedings of the Genetic and Evolutionary Computation Conference (GECCO 2010)*. ACM Press, 2010.

[6] N. Hansen, S. Finck, R. Ros, and A. Auger. Real-parameter black-box optimization benchmarking 2009: Noiseless functions definitions. Technical Report RR-6829, INRIA, 2009. Updated February 2010.

[7] S. Langerman, G. Seront, and H. Bersini. Step: The easiest way to optimize a function. In *Proceedings of the First IEEE Conference on Evolutionary Computation*, pages 519–524, 1994.

[8] I. Loshchilov, M. Schoenauer, and M. Sebag. Bi-population cma-es agorithms with surrogate models and line searches. In *Proceedings of the 15th annual conference companion on Genetic and evolutionary computation*, pages 1177–1184. ACM, 2013.

[9] P. Pošík and P. Baudiš. Dimension selection in axis-parallel Brent-STEP method for black-box optimization of separable continuous functions. In *Proceedings of the 2015 Conference on Genetic and Evolutionary Computation Companion*, New York, NY, USA, 2015. ACM. Accepted for publication.

[10] P. Pošík. BBOB-benchmarking two variants of the line-search algorithm. In *GECCO '09: Proceedings of the 11th annual conference companion on Genetic and evolutionary computation conference*, pages 2329–2336, New York, NY, USA, 2009. ACM.

[11] K. Price. Differential evolution vs. the functions of the second ICEO. In *Proceedings of the IEEE International Congress on Evolutionary Computation*, pages 153–157, 1997.

[12] W. T. Vetterling, S. A. Teukolsky, and W. H. Press. *Numerical recipes in C (2nd edition)*. Press Syndicate of the University of Cambridge, 1992.

Detecting Funnel Structures by Means of Exploratory Landscape Analysis

Pascal Kerschke
Information Systems and Statistics
University of Münster
kerschke@uni-muenster.de

Mike Preuss
Computational Intelligence Group
TU Dortmund
mike.preuss@tu-dortmund.de

Simon Wessing
Computational Intelligence Group
TU Dortmund
simon.wessing@tu-dortmund.de

Heike Trautmann
Information Systems and Statistics
University of Münster
trautmann@wi.uni-muenster.de

ABSTRACT

In single-objective optimization different optimization strategies exist depending on the structure and characteristics of the underlying problem. In particular, the presence of so-called funnels in multimodal problems offers the possibility of applying techniques exploiting the global structure of the function. The recently proposed Exploratory Landscape Analysis approach automatically identifies problem characteristics based on a moderately small initial sample of the objective function and proved to be effective for algorithm selection problems in continuous black-box optimization. In this paper, specific features for detecting funnel structures are introduced and combined with the existing ones in order to classify optimization problems regarding the funnel property. The effectiveness of the approach is shown by experiments on specifically generated test instances and validation experiments on standard benchmark problems.

CCS Concepts

•Mathematics of computing → Exploratory data analysis; *Continuous optimization;* **•Computing methodologies →** *Supervised learning by classification;*

Keywords

Fitness landscapes, Working principles of evolutionary computing, Machine learning, Exploratory Landscape Analysis, Funnel Structure, Optimization, Feature Selection

1. INTRODUCTION

Let us assume we need to find a very good solution for an unknown real-valued black-box optimization problem that is most likely multimodal. Then, we can imagine two extreme cases: a) all the peaks are well distributed over the search space so that knowing one of them does not at all help to find another one, or b) the peaks are partly superimposed and pile up to a huge mountain, with the global optimum to be found on top of it. Turning this problem upside down from a maximization to a minimization problem results in a so-called funnel, and we can presume that knowing some optima within a funnel *does* help to find even better ones because this resembles a *global structure* that can be exploited. The Rastrigin function is a well-known benchmark problem that possesses this property. Examples for the possible topologies are shown in Fig. 1.

In this work, we do not investigate how large the benefit of knowing the global structure of a problem actually is. This surely depends on many factors, and especially on the available optimization algorithms. However, when we have to select a suitable optimization algorithm, this knowledge will undoubtedly have an advantage. In order to obtain knowledge about the global structure of an unknown problem, we suggest to apply *Exploratory Landscape Analysis* (ELA).

The basic idea of ELA is to compute many simple, so-called low-level features based on a relatively small sample of evaluated search points, and then to use feature selection and classification methods in order to estimate the high-level properties of an optimization problem. The approach has been introduced in [20] and extended in [7], and it turned out that multimodality and global structure are among the most important high-level properties that help to differentiate between problem classes. A more detailed ELA description is following in §2.

In this work, we review the existing literature on optimization of funnel problems (§1.1), and define some new features that shall be suitable for funnel detection in §2. Employing also existing ELA features, we establish funnel classifiers on a set of generated problems in §3. The new classifiers are then tested on the BBOB problem suite and also on a set of disc packing problems in order to check if they are transferrable in §4. Given they still work, we have evidence that the classifiers can also be applied successfully to other related optimization problems.

To our knowledge, this is the first attempt that explicitly tries to classify an unknown problem from the continuous domain according to its global structure (funnel or not) by means of a limited sample of search points.

GECCO '15 July 11–15, 2015, Madrid, Spain

ISBN 978-1-4503-3472-3/15/07...$15.00

DOI: http://dx.doi.org/10.1145/2739480.2754642

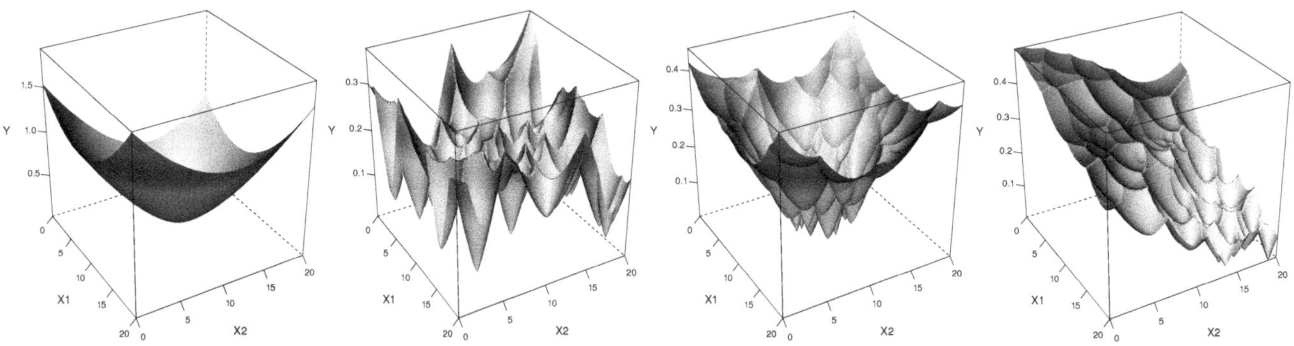

Figure 1: Generated test instances with different topologies. The first panel shows a unimodal problem. The other three have 40 local optima each. The second has a completely random structure. The third resembles a simple funnel, in which the best optima are clustered around the center of the search space. For the last one, there exists a linear trend from $(0,0)^T$ to $(20,20)^T$.

1.1 Funnel Structure Optimization

It is not exactly defined what constitutes a funnel structure. Lunacek and Whitley [19] survey several possible definitions, which basically all focus on two problem properties, namely the distribution of optima and the correlation of their objective values. The importance of the former aspect for problem difficulty was already recognized by Törn and Zilinskas [27, p. 11], although without using the term "funnel". Addis and Locatelli [3] develop a more detailed characterization of problem landscapes, by defining three levels of local optima, based on a graph structure. However, their theory is not applicable to real-world problems, because the necessary information is not available.

In combinatorial optimization, a common approach to solve funnel problems is iterated local search (ILS) [18]. ILS is a very simple concept, whose core idea is to restart local search from perturbations of previously found local optima. Examples for funnel problems in combinatorial optimization are the traveling salesperson problem, scheduling problems, or MAX-SAT [18].

Addis et al. [4] propose *monotonic basin hopping* (MBH) as optimization algorithm for real-valued funnel problems. MBH is a special case of the general basin hopping framework [28]. This algorithm is basically the real-valued equivalent to ILS. In [2], this approach is extended by embedding the MBH method into a random restart mechanism. As a local search component for their MBH, Addis et al. [4] favor sequential quadratic programming.

Also the CMA-ES is known to exhibit a good performance on funnel problems if the population size μ is chosen large enough [15, 19]. On problems without funnel structure, the large μ is not as helpful, instead a high number of random restarts is more important there. The "increasing population size" heuristic (IPOP) is an attempt to get rid of μ as an external parameter, by starting with a small μ and doubling it at every restart of CMA-ES [5]. Consequently, this approach is especially successful on funnel problems and does not harm too much on unimodal problems. Examples of problems in real-valued optimization, which supposedly are of the funnel type, are disc packing (DP, see §4.2), molecular conformation problems [28], or space trajectory planning [2].

2. ELA BASICS AND NEW FEATURES

Exploratory Landscape Analysis aims at characterizing the problem landscape and deriving rules for determining how problem properties influence algorithm performance. The final goal is an accurate prediction of the best suited algorithm for an arbitrary optimization problem based on the computed features. During the last years, important steps into this direction for single-objective optimization problems have been made. Experimental low-level features were introduced based on systematic sampling of the decision space in [20]. Six low-level feature classes were proposed (each containing several subfeatures), i.e. measures related to the distribution of the objective function values (y-Distribution), estimating meta-models such as linear or quadratic regression models on the sampled data (Meta-Model) and the level of convexity (Convexity). Furthermore, local searches are conducted starting at the initial design points (Local Search), the relative position of each objective value compared to the median of all values is investigated (Levelset), and numerical approximations of the gradient or the Hessian represent the class of curvature features (Curvature). It was shown in [20] that these features relate well to expert-defined high-level features such as the degree of multimodality, global structure, separability, variable scaling, search space homogeneity, basin-sizes, global to local contrast, and plateaus. Additional, conceptually similar features were introduced in [22, 1, 21]. In [7], a representative portfolio of four optimization algorithms was constructed from the complete list of BBOB 2009/2010 candidates. Based on the low-level features a sufficiently accurate prediction of the best suited algorithm within the portfolio for each function was achieved.

Recently, the feature set was extended based on the cell mapping concept in [17] by which a finite subdivision of the domain in terms of hypercubes is constructed. Function properties are then reflected by features comparing samples of different cells in order to assess local and global function characteristics. As these features can operate on the same initial design as the ELA features the cell mapping features come at no additional cost. It could be shown that the new properties especially improve the ELA feature set as in [20] in terms of an accurate mapping to a subset of the high-level features, i.e. the degree of multimodality and global structure. However, a meaningful application is so far limited to low-dimensional search spaces.

To detect if a problem exhibits a funnel structure, Lunacek and Whitley proposed to calculate a feature called "dispersion" [19]. As for all the features used in this paper, it is necessary to first draw a sample of the search space, for instance randomly uniform. The idea is to compare the sample's average pairwise distance with the same measure for a subset of the best solutions of this sample. The size of this subset may be determined by a parameter.

2.1 Features for Global Structure Recognition

Nearest-Better Clustering (NBC) is a recent heuristic for recognizing single peaks of a multimodal landscape. It is employed in its current form in [23] within the NEA2 algorithm, and we take over some of its general ideas in order to define features that should be helpful for recognizing funnel problems.

Using the same notation as in [24], we denote the distance to the nearest neighbor of a search point $\vec{x}$ from a population $\mathcal{P}$ with

$$d_{\text{nn}}(\vec{x}, \mathcal{P}) = \min(\{\text{dist}(\vec{x}, \vec{y}) \mid \vec{y} \in \mathcal{P} \setminus \{\vec{x}\}\}) \quad (1)$$

and the distance to the nearest better neighbor ($f(\vec{x})$ stands for the objective function value that corresponds to $\vec{x}$) as

$$d_{\text{nb}}(\vec{x}, \mathcal{P}) = \min(\{\text{dist}(\vec{x}, \vec{y}) \mid f(\vec{y}) < f(\vec{x}) \wedge \vec{y} \in \mathcal{P}\}). \quad (2)$$

We base our new features on the set of all nearest neighbor distances within the population

$$\mathcal{D}_{\text{nn}} = \{d_{\text{nn}}(\vec{x}, \mathcal{P}) \mid \vec{x} \in \mathcal{P}\} \quad (3)$$

and, accordingly, the set of all nearest-better distances

$$\mathcal{D}_{\text{nb}} = \{d_{\text{nb}}(\vec{x}, \mathcal{P}) \mid \vec{x} \in \mathcal{P}\} \quad (4)$$

with $d_{\text{nb}}(\vec{x}^*, \mathcal{P}) := d_{\text{nn}}(\vec{x}^*, \mathcal{P})$ for $\vec{x}^* = \arg\min(\{f(\vec{x}) \mid \vec{x} \in \mathcal{P}\})$, because for the best element in $\mathcal{P}$, no better neighbor exists.

Based on these two sets, we define five features. These are not made up arbitrarily; for each feature, we have an intuition of what it should measure, but at the same time we can assume that the formulation we choose is not unique. Features with approximately the same meaning can be constituted differently.

$$\text{nbf1} = \frac{\text{sd}(\mathcal{D}_{\text{nn}})}{\text{sd}(\mathcal{D}_{\text{nb}})} \quad (5)$$

divides the two standard deviations of the sets. In case the problem is very multimodal, $\mathcal{D}_{\text{nb}}$ should have a tendency to contain more extreme elements and $\text{sd}(\mathcal{D}_{\text{nb}})$ should be much larger than $\text{sd}(\mathcal{D}_{\text{nn}})$. On a unimodal problem or if a strong global structure exists, the nearest-better distances shall not be very different from the nearest-neighbor distances and the feature should be almost 1.

$$\text{nbf2} = \frac{\text{mean}(\mathcal{D}_{\text{nn}})}{\text{mean}(\mathcal{D}_{\text{nb}})} \quad (6)$$

inherits the overall idea of nbf1, but uses the mean values instead of the standard deviations.

$$\text{nbf3} = \text{cor}(\mathcal{D}_{\text{nn}}, \mathcal{D}_{\text{nb}}) \quad (7)$$

measures the Pearson correlation between the two sets. The expectation is that in a funnel setting, the correlation should be high, whereas in a random peaks setting, it should be much lower.

The fourth feature depends on the quotient of an individual's nearest-neighbor and nearest-better distances:

$$\mathcal{Q}_{\text{nn/nb}} = \left\{ \frac{d_{\text{nn}}(\vec{x}, \mathcal{P})}{d_{\text{nb}}(\vec{x}, \mathcal{P})} \,\middle|\, \vec{x} \in \mathcal{P} \right\}. \quad (8)$$

$$\text{nbf4} = \frac{\text{sd}(\mathcal{Q}_{\text{nn/nb}})}{\text{mean}(\mathcal{Q}_{\text{nn/nb}})} \quad (9)$$

thereby represents the coefficient of variation of the previously defined set $\mathcal{Q}_{\text{nn/nb}}$, which should be larger for random peak landscapes (because variation of the quotients should be higher).

$$\text{nbf5} = -\text{cor}(\{(\deg^-(\vec{x}), f(\vec{x})) \mid \vec{x} \in \mathcal{P}\}) \quad (10)$$

relates the indegree $\deg^-(\vec{x})$ of search points in the nearest-better graph (the number of search points for which a certain search point is the nearest better point) to their objective values. The reasoning behind is that in a funnel landscape, the best optima should have a large number of incoming connections whereas in a random peaks landscape, the better optima should have only few.

3. FEATURE SELECTION ON GENERATOR PROBLEMS

3.1 Problem Generator and Methodology

To train our classifier, we need some functions which are guaranteed to exhibit the mentioned structural features. Consequently, we are using a test problem generator to create the attributes artificially. This approach is recommended by Eiben and Jelasity [11]. Important aspects for us are the adjustability of the problem dimension, the number of optima, and of course the global topology. The employed generator combines unimodal functions to obtain a multimodal problem. The exact formulas are described in [29]. Similar approaches also appear in other problem generators [12]. The resulting surfaces are differentiable almost everywhere and the exact locations of the optima are known. Different landscapes can be produced by controlling the correlation between the depth of the unimodal functions and their position. Fig. 1 shows some results of this generator for $n = 2$ decision variables. Note that the generated instances look different every time, because the generating function is stochastic.

For our experiments, we used the generator to create a training data set, which contains instances of four values of $n \in \{2, 3, 5, 10\}$, ten different amounts of peaks (20, 40, ..., 200) and three versions of underlying topologies (*linear*, *funnel* and *random*). In addition, each of those instances was generated with five different starting seeds in order to respect the variability of the problem generator. In consideration of the stochasticity of some of the landscape features, we also replicated each instance ten times, resulting in a total of 6,000 instances. Such a duplication of instances is essential when dealing with stochastic features, as this allows for a comparison of the variability of a feature (and thereby reduces the effect of an outlier) on the very same problem instance.

On each of those instances, we computed a total of 29 features: 24 ELA features (12 Levelset, 9 Meta-Model, 3 y-Distribution, [20]), as well as our five NBC features (§2.1). All of those features are based on an initial design, consisting

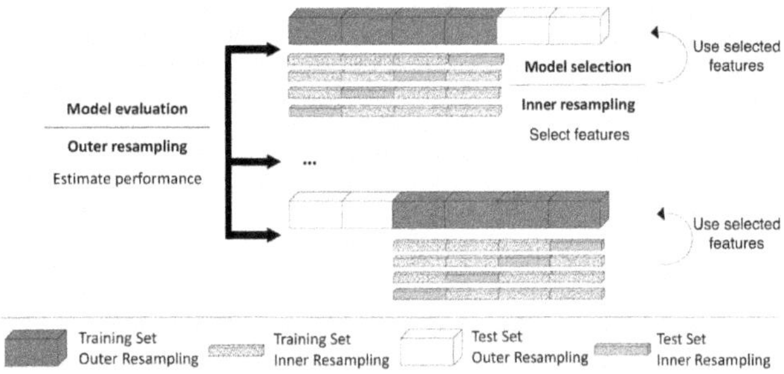

Figure 2: Feature selection based on nested resampling, cf. [17].

of $500 \times n$ observations, and therefore no additional function evaluations are required. In addition, a second feature set was generated, consisting of the 29 features above, supplemented by 16 dispersion features, whose idea is basically adapted from [19]. We therefore compared the arithmetic mean as well as the median of the pairwise distances of the entire data to the same measurement of the $\alpha\%$ best observations (w.r.t. the objective value), with $\alpha \in \{2, 5, 10, 25\}$. The comparison itself is employed by either using the quotient or the difference of the two measurements.

Based on the two previously introduced training data sets, we were able to train various models, using different classifiers, namely a classification tree (*rpart*, [9]), a random forest (*rf*, [8]), consisting of 500 classification trees, and kernel versions of k-nearest neighbors (*kknn*, [16]) and support vector machines (*ksvm*, [10]).

Although we first introduced the classes *random*, *linear* and *funnel*, we will actually make it a 2-class problem, because *linear* problems can be considered as a small subgroup of *funnel* problems. Therefore, we integrated the former one into the latter class, even though this leads to an uneven set of classes (67% *funnel* and 33% *random*).

In order to avoid overfitting to the data, we reduced the set of features per classifier, by conducting a forward-backward-feature selection, supported by a nested 10-fold cross-validation as shown in Fig. 2. For the outer cross-validation, we divided our data set into ten blocks of 600 observations each, where all ten replications that belong to the same instance were located within the same block. Then, nine of the ten blocks, i.e., 5,400 instances, were used to find the best subset of features over those instances. This is done by starting with an empty set of features and iteratively adding or removing a feature from that set until the performance of the model, which is trained on that set, does not improve. That performance itself is again evaluated with a 10-fold cross-validation – the so-called inner resampling. The feature set, which resulted in the best performance will then be trained on all 5,400 instances and evaluated on the remaining 600 instances. This approach is repeated ten times, so that the model performance was evaluated on each of the ten blocks exactly once. Using that approach, we receive ten different models – one per fold. However, as we are only interested in a single model, we use all 6,000 instances and all the features, which were selected within at least two of the ten folds, to train another model on the complete data. As we were using four different classifiers and two versions of initial feature sets, we received a total of eight models. The entire feature selection, modeling and performance evaluation was performed using the statistical software R [25] and the R-package mlr [6].

Problem		Settings		Classification method			
group	spec.	CV	disp.	rf	kknn	rpart	ksvm
model	funnel	yes	no	2.4%	5.9%	5.1%	3.0%
model	random	yes	no	16.4%	11.9%	20.9%	15.0%
model	total	yes	no	7.1%	7.9%	10.4%	7.0%
model	funnel	no	no	0.0%	0.0%	1.2%	1.4%
model	random	no	no	0.0%	0.0%	11.5%	10.9%
model	total	no	no	0.0%	0.0%	4.7%	4.5%
BBOB	funnel	no	no	5.2%	6.2%	2.1%	0.0%
BBOB	random	no	no	6.1%	68.3%	7.5%	86.5%
BBOB	total	no	no	5.4%	16.6%	3.0%	14.4%
DP	2–10	no	no	80/10	30/60	80/10	60/30
DP	11–30	no	no	200/0	0/200	0/200	0/200
model	funnel	yes	yes	3.2%	4.7%	5.1%	4.3%
model	random	yes	yes	15.0%	11.1%	17.5%	16.8%
model	total	yes	yes	7.1%	6.8%	9.2%	8.5%
model	funnel	no	yes	0.0%	0.0%	1.2%	1.0%
model	random	no	yes	0.0%	0.0%	12.5%	8.2%
model	total	no	yes	0.0%	0.0%	5.0%	3.4%
BBOB	funnel	no	yes	12.4%	6.3%	14.5%	0.0%
BBOB	random	no	yes	0.8%	67.9%	5.0%	99.6%
BBOB	total	no	yes	10.4%	16.6%	12.9%	16.6%
DP	2–7	no	yes	90/0	40/50	50/40	80/10
DP	8–30	no	yes	200/0	20/180	0/200	200/0

Table 1: Comparison of the misclassification rates and predictions (random / funnel) for the four classifiers, based on two different feature sets (with / without dispersion features) and evaluated on all three data sets. Our recommended model is highlighted in red.

3.2 Modelling Results

Tab. 1 summarizes the results of the four classifiers. At this stage, all entries but those related to validation experiments on the BBOB function set and disc packing instances (see §4) are relevant to assess model quality. The column *CV* indicates whether the misclassification errors based on 10-fold cross-validation or for a classifier trained on the whole problem set are reported. The latter functions as a prediction model for so far unknown function instances. The results are further distinguished regarding the integration of the dispersion features [19] into the candidate feature set. Total misclassification errors are supplemented by respective information for the two considered classes individually so that the balance between the prediction accuracies in both classes can be assessed.

The total misclassification rates for all entries are quite moderate, i.e. at most roughly 10 % which indicates that the considered features provide a suitable basis for the considered classification task. In general, the misclassification rates w.r.t. the *random* class exceed the respective ones for the *funnel* class by some orders of magnitude. Thus, the classifiers have a certain bias towards predicting a funnel structure.

We decided against the inclusion of the dispersion features though at first sight no substantial differences in the modeling results become obvious. However, those models perform worse on the validation sets in terms of balanced errors within the two classes and also w.r.t. total misclassification rates (§4). The final classifier recommendation marked in red, i.e. the decision tree *rpart*, as well results from such

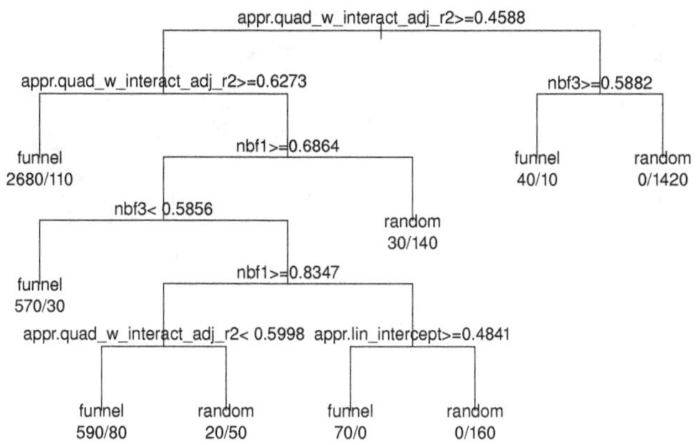

Figure 3: The final rpart-model, i.e. the tree which was built on all observations of the generator problems, but with a reduced feature set. The latter consists of the four features that were selected during the feature selection process, i.e., the features that are shown in the upper panel of Fig. 4.

considerations supplemented by the fact that model complexity and thus computation times are lowest compared to the other classifiers. Additionally, the decision tree can be nicely visualized as shown in Fig. 3. Here, the tree trained on the whole function set without cross-validation is provided as it serves as the final prediction model for the application to BBOB and disc packing later on. Crucial features are those provided by the Meta-Model ELA features (beginning with "appr" in the figures). Especially the one that fits a quadratic regression model with interactions intuitively has a strong relation to global structure. Two nearest-better features play an important role as well, i.e. nbf1 and nbf3. Interestingly, a very small and meaningful subset (four features) out of the whole feature set is sufficient to provide a highly accurate classification.

Fig. 4 visualizes feature importance for the cross-validated *rpart*. The red color reflects features which were used at least seven times in the final classification tree. The displayed feature set is restricted to features which were selected at least twice. Surprisingly, the problem dimensionality is very relevant in the CV-setting while it is not included in the final decision tree. Further analyses – in which the dimensionality was not considered as a possible feature – have shown that it can be replaced by other features characterizing the funnel structure of the problem's landscape.

For illustration purposes, the respective importance plot in case the feature set is supplemented by the dispersion features is given in the lower part of the figure. It can be seen that problem dimensionality clearly is the most important feature now, while the dispersion features are ranked next. Nearest-better features are partly selected within the CV iterations. Thus, it can be concluded that in case the dispersion features are neglected, the combination of meta-model features and nearest-better features completely capture the corresponding information and additionally also diminish the role of problem dimensionality.

4. VALIDATION AND APPLICATION

In order to assess the quality of our models, we evaluate their performances on two other well-known research

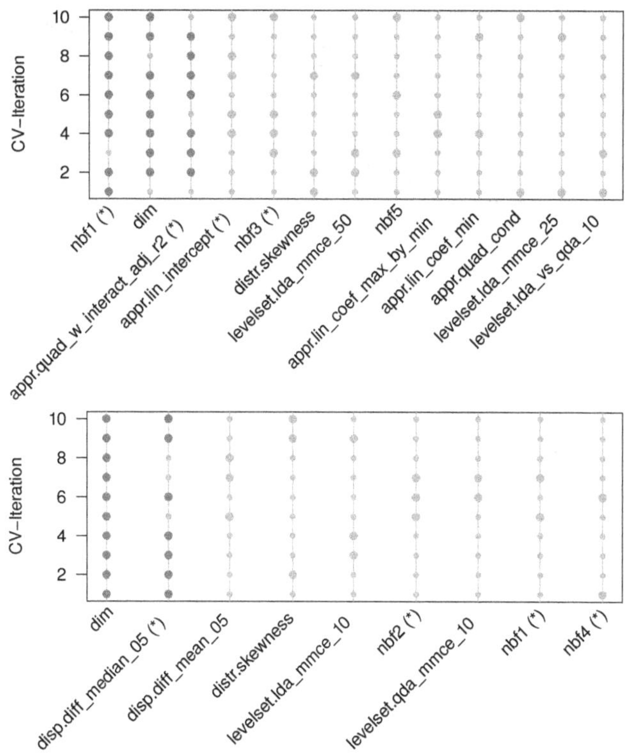

Figure 4: Feature importance plots for the 10-fold CV of the classification tree (top: without dispersion; bottom: with dispersion). Only features that were chosen at least twice are plotted. The ones selected at least seven times are shown in red, those of the final classification tree are marked with (*).

applications: the benchmark for continuous black-box optimization problems (BBOB [13, 14]) and disc packing problems [4].

4.1 Validation on BBOB Problems

The BBOB set consists of 24 continuous functions, which claim to cover a broad variety of function types. In previous works (e.g. [7]), the functions were examined w.r.t. various properties, such as the multimodality and global structure. We used that information to manually assign the topology of the BBOB functions, as shown in Tab. 2. Afterwards, we employed our classifiers to predict that topology. Therefore, a test set of the BBOB functions, consisting of all 24 functions and four dimensions $n \in \{2, 3, 5, 10\}$, was created. For each function, 15 instances were generated, which differ from each other due to rotation, scaling and shifts. Finally, all instances were replicated ten times in order to handle the stochasticity of some of the features. Then, the eight models were used to predict for each of those 14,400 instances, whether it is rather *random* or *funnel*.

The previously discussed Tab. 1 also presents the classification errors of our classifiers on the BBOB function set in relation to Tab. 2. Only four of the 24 functions shall be considered as of random topology, all others (including the many unimodal functions) possess one or several (functions 20 and 24) funnels. Given that we only apply classifiers that have been trained on a different set of test cases, the error rates are very good. We can observe two trends:

#	Function	multi-modality	global structure	funnel/ random
1	Sphere	none	strong	funnel
2	Ellipsoidal separable	none	strong	funnel
3	Rastrigin separable	high	strong	funnel
4	Bueche-Rastrigin	high	strong	funnel
5	Linear Slope	none	strong	funnel
6	Attractive Sector	none	strong	funnel
7	Step Ellipsoidal	none	strong	funnel
8	Rosenbrock	low	strong	funnel
9	Rosenbrock rotated	low	strong	funnel
10	Ellipsoidal high-cond.	none	strong	funnel
11	Discus	none	strong	funnel
12	Bent Cigar	none	strong	funnel
13	Sharp Ridge	none	strong	funnel
14	Different Powers	none	strong	funnel
15	Rastrigin multi-modal	high	strong	funnel
16	Weierstrass	high	med.	random
17	Schaffer F7	high	med.	funnel
18	Schaffer F7 ill-cond.	high	med.	funnel
19	Griewank-Rosenbrock	high	strong	funnel
20	Schwefel	med.	deceptive	funnel
21	Gallagher 101 Peaks	med.	none	random
22	Gallagher 21 Peaks	low	none	random
23	Katsuura	high	none	random
24	Lunacek bi-Rastrigin	high	weak	funnel

Table 2: Classification of the noiseless BBOB functions into the two high-level properties multimodality and global structure. In addition, each function was assigned the label funnel or random – based on expert knowledge.

- Except for the *kknn* method (where they are comparable), the results for the feature set without dispersion features are clearly better than for the one including those.
- For both feature sets, the *kknn* and *ksvm* based classifiers fail badly in recognizing random peak topologies.

This naturally narrows our choice down to *random forest* or *rpart* based classifiers on the set without dispersion features. The misclassification rates for both are similar with a slight advantage for the *rpart* based classifier. The advantage of the latter lies in the much faster computation and simpler structure. The choice made in §3.2 therefore also holds true for the BBOB problem classification task.

4.2 Application to Disc Packing

The general task of sphere packing problems is to arrange a given number of non-intersecting spheres with equal radius in a container so that the radius becomes maximal. A special case of this problem in $\mathbb{R}^2$ is to arrange discs in a square. If d is the number of discs, the dimensionality of the corresponding optimization problem is $n = 2d$. There is only one problem instance per dimension.

Globally optimal solutions for this problem, taken from [26], are shown in Fig. 5. These optima are not unique, as the arrangement of discs can be mirrored or rotated without changing the objective value. Additionally, discs which are not in contact with others or the boundary can also be moved without affecting the objective value. Addis et al. argue that disc packing problems possess a funnel structure, similar to the closely related molecular conformation problems [4, 28]. Apart from the symmetries, the funnel property probably stems from the fact that the optimal arrangements contain some regularity, causing locally optimal solutions to have a lot in common with the global ones. We therefore use these problems as an additional test case to apply our classifiers. However, it is known that the funnel property becomes more prevalent with increasing number of discs. Apart from the 2-disc case where the problem has only very few optima, a small number of discs does not result in a clear funnel structure. Therefore, as the turning point in the number of discs leading to a funnel structure is not exactly known, we do not report misclassification rates here but rather investigate the behaviour of the classifiers in order to support the general tendency described.

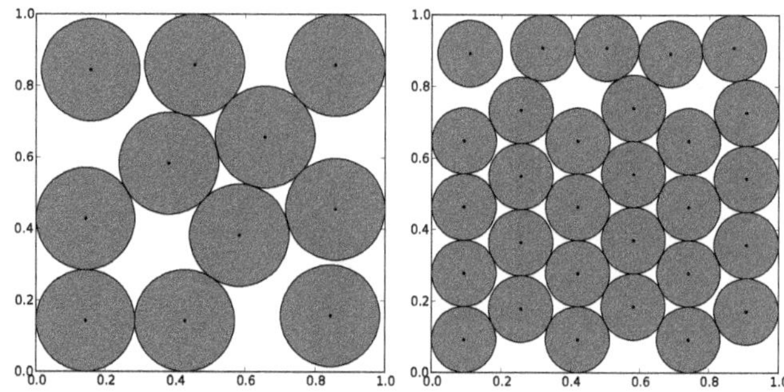

Figure 5: Optimal solutions for the disc packing problems with 11 and 29 discs. The coordinates of the disc centers determine the maximally possible radius.

For this test problem, we created 290 instances – ten replications for any number of discs between two and 30. Then we used all eight classifiers to predict the topology. Interestingly, all replications that belong to the same number of discs were predicted into the same category. The exact amount of predictions into *random* / *funnel* for each of the models is shown in Tab. 1.

As expected, the funnel topology only emerges in higher dimensions as shown in Tab. 3, which shows the predictions of the classifiers that do not use the dispersion features. The 2-disc problem was always classified as a *funnel* problem, whereas the next problems usually were classified as *random*. With the exception of the random forest, all higher-dimensional problems were predicted to be *funnel* problems. In general, the models based on dispersion features tend to have a strong bias regarding predicting random structures in this setting, especially the random forest and *ksvm*. These mixed results do not contradict the findings of Addis et al. [4], because they only regard problems with 50 discs or more.

5. CONCLUSIONS

As main result of this work we can state that we have established classifiers for experimentally detecting from a small sample, if an unknown black-box optimization problem has the funnel property, a previously unsolved problem. This resembles the first, necessary step for performing (optimization) algorithm selection as we assume that this information can be exploited to speed up the optimization (see the discussion in §1.1). The recommended classifier employs the *rpart* method, which results in a very simple tree with very few features (only four in our case). It is thus easy to interpret the model, and at the same time it provides us with highly accurate and well balanced predictions.

Discs	random forest	kknn	rpart	ksvm
2	funnel	funnel	funnel	funnel
3	random	random	random	random
4	random	random	random	random
5	random	random	random	random
6	random	funnel	random	random
7	random	funnel	random	random
8	random	funnel	random	random
9	random	funnel	random	funnel
10	random	funnel	random	funnel
11–30	random	funnel	funnel	funnel

Table 3: Class predictions of our classifiers on the disc packing problems (without dispersion features).

The newly introduced nearest-better features obviously capture important information concerning the problem type (*funnel* or *random*) and therefore seem to be at least as valuable as the dispersion features. All these results have been validated on two additional test sets (BBOB functions and disc packing problems) that have not been used during training. We thus have reason to assume that our classifiers can also be of use for other real-valued optimization problems.

However, the fact that the more sophisticated classifiers exhibit a worse performance than the simple ones is a hint that the training of the classifiers could be still improved. In the future, it probably would be advisable to extend the training set for the feature selection task, to rule out any overfitting. Ways to do this would be extending the test problem generator to model a broader class of functions or including other test problems from different sources.

Although the nearest-better features seemed superior so far, it may be also promising to investigate into further variants of the dispersion feature. Especially for measuring the diversity of the involved sets, several other options exist [24]. Additionally, it would of course be nice to further reduce the employed sample size for computing any features, which is currently $500n$. First experiments have indicated promising results as features, which were computed on smaller initial designs, led to comparable models. Consequently, we aim at further investigating this issue within future work.

Regarding the final goal of generating an algorithm selection model for unknown test problems, the funnel property could be included into the respective feature set. By this means, the modeling procedure becomes sequential in nature. At first our proposed model will be used to predict if a funnel structure is present for all candidate training instances. Afterwards, this feature can be integrated into the algorithm selection modeling phase (see e.g. [7]). Therefore, promising perspectives regarding the analysis of the influence on algorithm performance exist.

6. ACKNOWLEDGMENTS

Heike Trautmann and Pascal Kerschke acknowledge support by the European Center of Information Systems (ERCIS). In addition, this work was supported by the French national research agency (ANR) within the project "NumBBO - Analysis, Improvement and Evaluation of Numerical Blackbox Optimizer" (ANR-12-MONU-0009-03).

7. REFERENCES

[1] T. Abell, Y. Malitsky, and K. Tierney. Features for exploiting black-box optimization problem structure. In G. Nicosia and P. Pardalos, editors, *Learning and Intelligent Optimization*, Lecture Notes in Computer Science, pages 30–36. Springer, 2013.

[2] B. Addis, A. Cassioli, M. Locatelli, and F. Schoen. A global optimization method for the design of space trajectories. *Computational Optimization and Applications*, 48(3):635–652, 2011.

[3] B. Addis and M. Locatelli. A new class of test functions for global optimization. *Journal of Global Optimization*, 38(3):479–501, 2007.

[4] B. Addis, M. Locatelli, and F. Schoen. Disk packing in a square: A new global optimization approach. *INFORMS Journal on Computing*, 20(4):516–524, 2008.

[5] A. Auger and N. Hansen. A restart CMA evolution strategy with increasing population size. In *IEEE Congress on Evolutionary Computation (CEC)*, volume 2, pages 1769–1776, 2005.

[6] B. Bischl, M. Lang, J. Richter, J. Bossek, L. Judt, T. Kuehn, E. Studerus, and L. Kotthoff. *mlr: Machine Learning in R.* R package version 2.3.

[7] B. Bischl, O. Mersmann, H. Trautmann, and M. Preuss. Algorithm selection based on exploratory landscape analysis and cost-sensitive learning. In *Proceedings of the 14th Annual Conference on Genetic and Evolutionary Computation*, GECCO '12, pages 313–320. ACM, 2012.

[8] L. Breiman. Random forests. *Machine learning*, 45(1):5–32, 2001.

[9] L. Breiman, J. Friedman, C. J. Stone, and R. A. Olshen. *Classification and regression trees.* CRC press, 1984.

[10] C. Cortes and V. Vapnik. Support-vector networks. *Machine learning*, 20(3):273–297, 1995.

[11] A. E. Eiben and M. Jelasity. A critical note on experimental research methodology in EC. In *IEEE Congress on Evolutionary Computation (CEC)*, volume 1, pages 582–587, 2002.

[12] M. Gallagher and B. Yuan. A general-purpose tunable landscape generator. *IEEE Transactions on Evolutionary Computation*, 10(5):590–603, 2006.

[13] N. Hansen, A. Auger, S. Finck, and R. Ros. Real-parameter black-box optimization benchmarking 2009: Experimental setup. Technical Report RR-6828, INRIA, 2009.

[14] N. Hansen, A. Auger, S. Finck, and R. Ros. Real-parameter black-box optimization benchmarking 2010: Experimental setup. Technical Report RR-7215, INRIA, 2010.

[15] N. Hansen and S. Kern. Evaluating the CMA evolution strategy on multimodal test functions. In *Parallel Problem Solving from Nature - PPSN VIII*, volume 3242 of *Lecture Notes in Computer Science*, pages 282–291. Springer, 2004.

[16] K. Hechenbichler and K. Schliep. Weighted k-nearest-neighbor techniques and ordinal classification. 2004.

[17] P. Kerschke, M. Preuss, C. Hernández, O. Schütze, J. Sun, C. Grimme, G. Rudolph, B. Bischl, and H. Trautmann. Cell mapping techniques for

exploratory landscape analysis. In A. Tantar et al., editors, *EVOLVE — A Bridge between Probability, Set Oriented Numerics, and Evolutionary Computation V*, volume 288 of *Advances in Intelligent Systems and Computing*, pages 115–131. Springer, 2014.

[18] H. R. Lourenço, O. C. Martin, and T. Stützle. Iterated local search: Framework and applications. In M. Gendreau and J.-Y. Potvin, editors, *Handbook of Metaheuristics*, volume 146 of *International Series in Operations Research & Management Science*, pages 363–397. Springer, 2010.

[19] M. Lunacek and D. Whitley. The dispersion metric and the CMA evolution strategy. In *Proceedings of the 8th Annual Conference on Genetic and Evolutionary Computation*, GECCO '06, pages 477–484. ACM, 2006.

[20] O. Mersmann, B. Bischl, H. Trautmann, M. Preuss, C. Weihs, and G. Rudolph. Exploratory landscape analysis. In *Proceedings of the 13th annual conference on Genetic and evolutionary computation*, GECCO '11, pages 829–836. ACM, 2011.

[21] R. Morgan and M. Gallagher. Using landscape topology to compare continuous metaheuristics: A framework and case study on EDAs and ridge structure. *Evolutionary Computation*, 20(2):277–299, 2012.

[22] M. A. Muñoz, M. Kirley, and S. K. Halgamuge. A meta-learning prediction model of algorithm performance for continuous optimization problems. In C. A. C. Coello et al., editors, *Parallel Problem Solving from Nature - PPSN XII*, volume 7491 of *Lecture Notes in Computer Science*, pages 226–235. Springer, 2012.

[23] M. Preuss. Improved topological niching for real-valued global optimization. In *Applications of Evolutionary Computation*, volume 7248 of *Lecture Notes in Computer Science*, pages 386–395. Springer, 2012.

[24] M. Preuss and S. Wessing. Measuring multimodal optimization solution sets with a view to multiobjective techniques. In *EVOLVE - A Bridge between Probability, Set Oriented Numerics, and Evolutionary Computation IV*, volume 227 of *Advances in Intelligent Systems and Computing*, pages 123–137. Springer, 2013.

[25] R Core Team. *R: A Language and Environment for Statistical Computing.* R Foundation for Statistical Computing, Vienna, Austria, 2013.

[26] E. Specht. http://www.packomania.com, Retrieved: 2 Feb 2015.

[27] A. Törn and A. Zilinskas. *Global Optimization*, volume 350 of *Lecture Notes in Computer Science*. Springer, 1989.

[28] D. J. Wales and H. A. Scheraga. Global optimization of clusters, crystals, and biomolecules. *Science*, 285(5432):1368–1372, 1999.

[29] S. Wessing, M. Preuss, and G. Rudolph. Niching by multiobjectivization with neighbor information: Trade-offs and benefits. In *IEEE Congress on Evolutionary Computation (CEC)*, pages 103–110, 2013.

A New Repair Method For Constrained Optimization

Patrick Koch
Cologne University of Applied Sciences,
51643 Gummersbach, Germany
patrick.koch@fh-koeln.de

Samineh Bagheri
Cologne University of Applied Sciences,
51643 Gummersbach, Germany
samineh.bagheri@fh-koeln.de

Wolfgang Konen
Cologne University of Applied Sciences,
51643 Gummersbach, Germany
wolfgang.konen@fh-koeln.de

Christophe Foussette
divis intelligent solutions GmbH,
44277 Dortmund, Germany
foussette@divis-gmbh.de

Peter Krause
divis intelligent solutions GmbH,
44277 Dortmund, Germany
krause@divis-gmbh.de

Thomas Bäck
Leiden University, LIACS
2333 CA Leiden, The Netherlands
T.H.W.Baeck@liacs.leidenuniv.nl

ABSTRACT

Nowadays, constraints play an important role in industry, because most industrial optimization tasks underly several restrictions. Finding good solutions for a particular problem with respect to all constraint functions can be expensive, especially when the dimensionality of the search space is large and many constraint functions are involved. Unfortunately function evaluations in industrial optimization are heavily limited, because often expensive simulations must be conducted. For such high-dimensional optimization tasks, the constraint optimization algorithm COBRA was proposed, making use of surrogate modeling for both the objective and the constraint functions.

In this paper we present a new mechanism for COBRA to repair infill solutions with slightly violated constraints. The repair mechanism is based on gradient descent on surrogates of the constraint functions and aims at finding nearby feasible solutions. We test the repair mechanism on a real-world problem from the automotive industry and on other synthetic test cases. It is shown in this paper that with the integration of the repair method, the percentage of infeasible solutions is significantly reduced, leading to faster convergence and better final results.

Categories and Subject Descriptors

G.1.6 [**Optimization**]: Constrained optimization

Keywords

Optimization; Constrained optimization; Radial basis function; Infeasibility repair

GECCO '15, July 11 - 15, 2015, Madrid, Spain

© 2015 ACM. ISBN 978-1-4503-3472-3/15/07... $15.00

DOI: http://dx.doi.org/10.1145/2739480.2754658

1. INTRODUCTION

Real-world optimization problems are often subject to constraints, restricting the feasible region to a smaller subset of the search space. It is the goal of constraint optimizers to avoid infeasible solutions and to stay in the feasible region, in order to converge to the optimum. However, the search in constraint black-box optimization can be difficult, since knowledge about the size of the feasible region and the fitness landscape is usually unknown. This problem even turns out to be harder, when only a limited number of function evaluations is allowed for the search. However, in industry good solutions are requested in very restricted timeframes. An example is the well-known benchmark MOPTA 2008 [1].

In the past different strategies have been proposed to handle constraints. E. g., repair methods try to guide infeasible solutions into the feasible area. Penalty functions give a negative bias to the objective function value, when constraints are violated. Many constraint handling methods are available in the scientific literature, but often demand for a large number of function evaluations (e. g., results in [2, 3]). Up to now, only little work has been devoted to *efficient* constraint optimization (severely reduced number of function evaluations). A possible solution in that regard is to use *surrogate models* for the objective and constraint functions respectively. While the real function might be expensive to evaluate, evaluations on the surrogate functions are often much faster. As an example for this approach, the solver Constrained Optimization by Radial Basis Function Approximation (*COBRA*) was proposed by Regis [4] and outperforms many other algorithms on a large number of benchmark functions.

In this paper we analyze the COBRA algorithm and reveal its strengths and weaknesses. We extend the algorithm by a specific new repair method. Therefore we have defined the following research questions:

(H1) Can a repair mechanism for infeasible solutions help to achieve a faster convergence and smaller standard deviations as compared to the original COBRA algorithm proposed by Regis [4] without repair?

(H2) Does the proposed repair mechanism perform better

than other state-of-the-art repair mechanisms like the one proposed by Chootinan and Chen [5]?

(H3) How often is the repair successful?

1.1 Related work

Following the surveys about constraint handling given by Michalewicz and Schoenauer [6], Eiben and Smith [7], Coello Coello [8] and Kramer [9] several approaches are available to handle constraints:

i) unconstrained optimization with a penalty added to the fitness value for infeasible solutions

ii) repair algorithms to resolve constraint violations during the search

iii) multi-objective optimization, where the constraint functions are defined as additional objectives

iv) stochastic ranking, where solutions are lexically ranked according to their performance in constraint or fitness values in a comparison with other offspring in a certain number of sweeps.

A frequently used approach to handle constraints is to incorporate static or dynamic penalty terms in order to stay in the feasible region [8, 9, 10]. Penalty functions can be very helpful for solving constrained problems, but their main drawback is that they often require additional parameters for balancing the fitness and penalty terms. Repair algorithms have been mainly proposed in the context of combinatorial optimization problems (see e. g., Xiao et al. [11], Mühlenbein [12], Orvosh and Davis [13], Tate and Smith [14]), where special-purpose repair heuristics are designed anew for each problem. For continuous problems Chootinan and Chen [5] use numerically derived gradient information of the constraint evaluations for repairing infeasible solutions.

Other techniques handle constraints by optimizing constraint functions and objective function separately in a lexical order [15, 16]. Stochastic ranking [17] is another example of this approach. Also multi-objective optimization algorithms have been designed for constraint-based optimization, considering the constraint functions as additional objectives [17, 18]. Beyer and Finck [19] propose an extension of CMA-ES which allows to handle special types of constraints successfully.

In the field of model-assisted optimization algorithms for constrained problems, Support Vector Machines (SVMs) have been used by Poloczek and Kramer [20]. They make use of SVMs as a classifier for predicting the feasibility of solutions, but achieve only slight improvements. Powell [21] proposes COBYLA, a direct search method which models the objective and the constraints by linear functions. Recently, Regis [4] developed COBRA, an efficient solver that makes use of Radial Basis Function (RBF) interpolation, and outperforms most algorithms in terms of required function evaluations on a large number of benchmark functions.

In this paper we analyze a new implementation of COBRA in R [22], which allows easy adaptation of certain components of the algorithm. In Sec. 2 we present the problem and the algorithm in more detail. In Sec. 3 we perform a thorough experimental study on analytical test functions and on a real-world benchmark function MOPTA 2008 [1]. The results are discussed in Sec. 4 and we give conclusive remarks in Sec. 5.

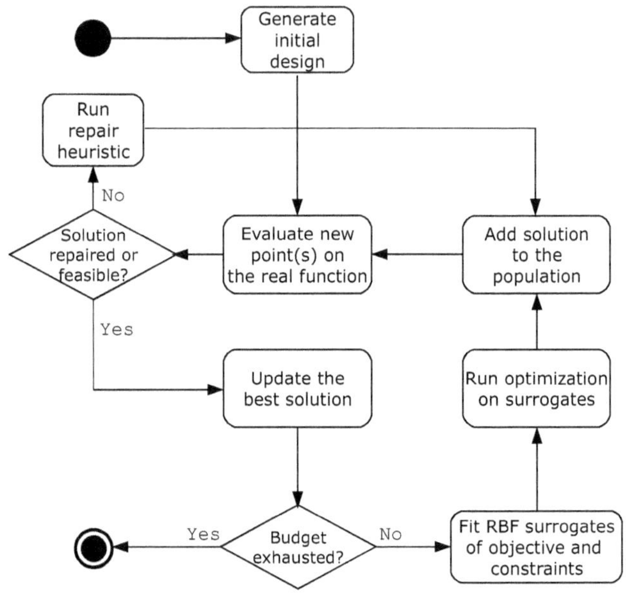

Figure 1: Flowchart of the COBRA algorithm.

2. METHODS

2.1 Constrained Optimization by Radial Basis Function Approximation

A constrained optimization problem can be defined by the minimization of a real-valued objective function f subject to constraint functions $s_1, \ldots, s_m$:

$$\begin{array}{lll} \text{Minimize} & f(\vec{x}), & \vec{x} \in \mathbb{R}^d \\ \text{subject to} & s_i(\vec{x}) \leq 0, & i = 1, 2, \ldots, m \end{array}$$

In this paper we always consider minimization problems. Maximization problems can be transformed to minimization problems without loss of generality.

Constrained Optimization by Radial Basis Function Approximation (COBRA) was proposed by Regis [4]. The main idea of this method is to use approximations of the objective function and the constraint functions for saving real function evaluations. This can be especially beneficial for industrial optimization problems where function evaluations are expensive. Internally, COBRA uses radial basis function interpolation for modeling the objective and constraints. In each iteration k the solution $\vec{x}^{(k)}$ to be evaluated on the real function f is the result of an optimization performed on the RBF surrogates consisting of surrogates of the objective and the constraint functions.

Fig. 1 presents a flowchart of the algorithm. In the beginning an initial population or design is generated for building the initial RBF models. The initial solutions can be selected, e. g., by classical design of experiments (DoE) [23]. Another option is to perform an initial local search with a limited number of function evaluations using an unconstrained optimizer (e. g., Hooke & Jeeves pattern search [24]). The sequence of points in this local search is then used as the initial design. During this local search, we penalize infeasible solutions with a simple penalty function.

The resulting RBF surrogates from the initial design are used to find the next iterate to be evaluated on the real function. Therefore, a sequential search is performed on the surrogate functions. The best point obtained from this search is referred to as *infill point* in the remainder of this paper. Note that only the infill points are evaluated on the real function. This makes the algorithm efficient in terms of saving real function evaluations. If the infill point is better than the current best solution, the best solution is replaced by the infill point. In any case the RBF models are updated using the new information. In the next round a new search on the updated surrogate functions is performed. These steps are repeated, until the the budget for the optimization exceeds a given limit.

Distance requirement cycle.
A distance requirement is integrated in COBRA which defines how closely a new infill solution may approach the previous ones. The idea is to avoid frequent updates in the direct neighbourhood of the best solution at present. The distance requirement can be passed by the user as external parameter. This parameter is a *vector* of distance requirements whose elements are cyclically reused. In each iteration COBRA checks as additional constraint the distance of the proposed infill solution to all previous infill points. If this constraint is not fulfilled, COBRA handles this as a normal constraint violation, e. g., the solution becomes infeasible. The distance requirement cycle is a clever idea, since the user can allow for switching between exploration and exploitation of the search space.

Uncertainty of constraint predictions.
COBRA aims at finding feasible solutions by extensive search on the surrogate functions. However, as the RBF models are probably not exact especially in the initial phase of the search, a regularization factor is added to the predicted constraint values. As a consequence, solutions evaluated on the RBF models are only feasible, if they are not too close to the constraint boundary. In other words, the regularization factor would correct small errors of too optimistic constraint models, and thereby forces the algorithm to more likely create feasible infill solutions.

2.2 Repairing infeasible solutions

In this paper we propose a new repair mechanism RI-2 for reducing the constraint violation of infill solutions obtained from the internal optimization algorithm. We compare the method with the algorithm of Chootinan and Chen [5].

2.2.1 RI-2

A repair mechanism for real-valued constraints can benefit from using gradient information of the constraint functions. If the gradient is not available analytically – as in the case of black-box constraints – it can be calculated numerically. This can be however too costly in the case of expensive black-box functions. Within the COBRA framework we take advantage of the surrogate functions and calculate the gradient *on the constraint surrogates* at no extra cost.

Before we describe our repair algorithm RI-2 in formal details, we have a look at two instructive examples:

A typical situation as it may arise with multiple constraints is shown in Figure 2. For simplicity we show only two violated constraints here, but the same idea applies for multiple violated constraints as well. The green and blue arrow show the negative gradient direction for the green and blue constraint, resp. The length of each arrow is q times larger than the estimated distance to the constraint boundary, where $q > 1$ is a parameter of the algorithm. Two or more such arrows form a parallelepiped. Our repair algorithm RI-2 draws m_{max} random points from this parallelepiped (red points) and tests whether they are feasible on the constraint surrogates. One of these surrogate-feasible points is selected (according to some quality measures detailed below) and returned.

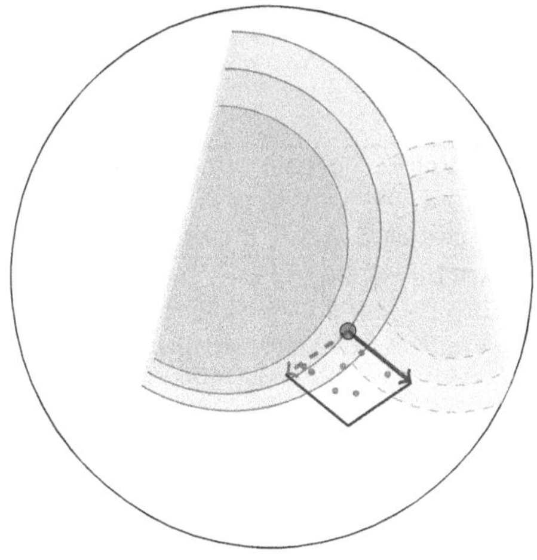

Figure 2: Repair strategy in the case of two constraints (blue-solid and green-dashed). The white area is the feasible region.

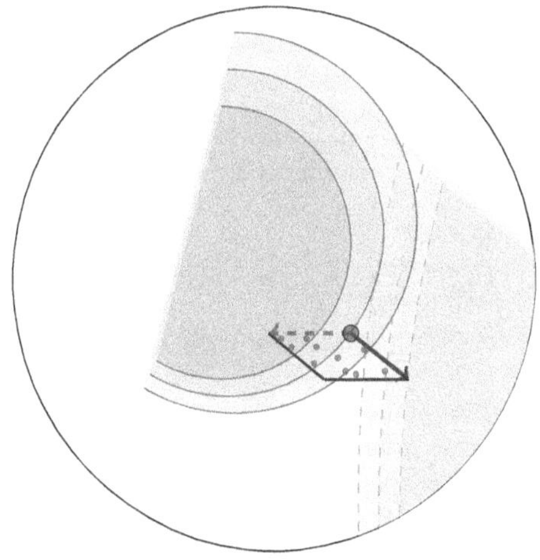

Figure 3: Repair strategy in the case of one violated constraint (blue-solid) and one constraint (green-dashed) being ϵ-infeasible.

A second typical situation is shown in Fig. 3: Here the current infill point violates only the blue constraint. But a correction along the direction of the blue arrow would make the new point infeasible in the second constraint (green). We define a point $\vec{x}$ to be **ϵ-feasible** in constraint s_i if

$$s_i(x) + \epsilon \leq 0.$$

Otherwise it is said to be **ϵ-infeasible**. As a solution to the problem in Fig. 3 we propose to treat all constraints which are ϵ-infeasible as violated constraints. Then we have again a blue and a green arrow forming a parallelepiped. Among the random realizations in this parallelepiped (red points) a feasible point can be found.

Algorithm 1 Repair algorithm RI-2. Input: an infeasible point $\vec{x} \in \mathbb{R}^d$ and its true constraint vector $\vec{s}(\vec{x}) \in \mathbb{R}^m$. Output: a suggestion $\vec{x} + \vec{\Delta}$ of a nearby feasible point.

1: **function** RI-2($\vec{x}, \vec{s}(\vec{x})$)
2: Set $\mathbf{E}$ to the $d \times d$ identity matrix
3: $\vec{g}^{(k)}$: gradient at $\vec{x}$ of the k'th surrogate
4: I: set of ϵ-infeasible constraints for $\vec{x}$.
5: Calculate for each constraint $k \in I$:

$$\vec{\Delta}^{(k)} = -\frac{s_k(\vec{x}) + \epsilon}{\|\mathbf{E}\vec{g}^{(k)}\|^2}\mathbf{E}\vec{g}^{(k)} \tag{1}$$

6: $\vec{\Delta} = \text{BestRandomRealization}(\vec{\Delta}^{(k)})$
7: Check if $\vec{x} + \vec{\Delta}$ is outside the search region in any dimension D. If so, then set the D'th diagonal element(s) of $\mathbf{E}$ to zero and repeat from Step 5.
8: **return** $(\vec{x} + \vec{\Delta})$
9: **end function**
10:
11: **function** BestRandomRealization($\vec{\Delta}^{(k)}$)
12: $R = \{\}$
13: **for** $m = 1, \ldots, m_{max}$ **do**
14: Draw $|I|$ random coefficients $\alpha_k \in [0, q]$
15: $R = R \cup \{\sum_{k \in I} \alpha_k \vec{\Delta}^{(k)}\}$
16: **end for**
17: $S = \{\vec{r} \in R \mid \vec{x} + \vec{r}$ is ϵ-feasible on *all* surrogates$\}$
18: **if** $S \neq \{\}$ **then**
19: $\vec{r}^{(bst)}$ = member of S with minimal length
20: **else**
21: n_v = minimum number of violated constraints
22: $T = \{\vec{r} \in R \mid \vec{x} + \vec{r}$ has n_v violated constraints$\}$
23: $\vec{r}^{(bst)}$ = member of T with lowest max(violation)
24: **end if**
25: **return** $\vec{r}^{(bst)}$
26: **end function**

The complete description of our repair algorithm RI-2 is given in Algorithm 1. The algorithm has three parameters ϵ, q and m_{max}. Note that all constraint calculations are done on the surrogate models, so no extra evaluations of the true constraint functions are needed inside RI-2.

The step $\vec{\Delta}^{(k)}$ in Eq. (1) is designed as follows: If s_k were the only violated constraint and if it were a linear function, then $\vec{\Delta}^{(k)}$ would bring us directly to the border of ϵ-feasibilty in s_k. If the nearest border point is outside the search region, then we move with the help of matrix $\mathbf{E}$ to another border point which is just inside the search region (Fig. 4).

Among the random realizations the best point is selected according to these rules: (a) If ϵ-feasible solutions exist, then select the one closest to $\vec{x}$. This should change the objective value as little as possible. (b) If not, select among the solutions with the mimumum number of violated constraints the one with lowest maximum violation.

2.2.2 *Chootinan Repair*

A repair method based on derivatives of the constraint functions has been also proposed by Chootinan and Chen [5]. They calculate the gradients of all violated constraints similar to RI-2 and put them into a matrix $\nabla_x V$. Then the

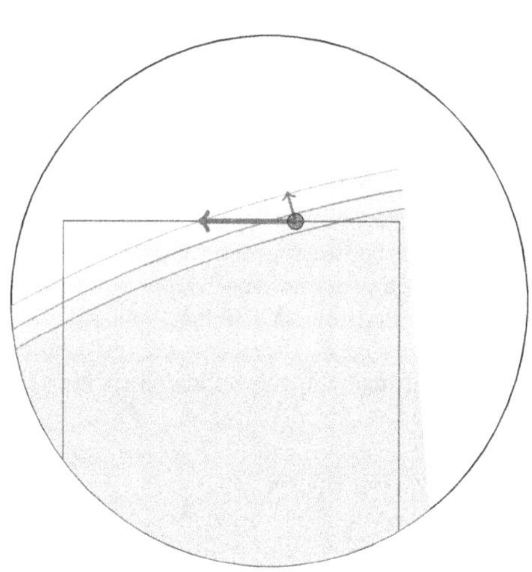

Figure 4: Strategy for staying in the search region: The current point (grey) is infeasible and on the boundary of the search space (black rectangle). Thus, a move in the negative gradient direction (thin arrow) is forbidden. The solution: project out the forbidden dimension(s) (matrix E) and make a larger move in the allowed direction (thick arrow).

Moore-Penrose inverse or pseudoinverse $(\nabla_x V)^+$ is taken. In each time step t the infeasible solution is updated by adding the pseudoinverse $(\nabla_x V)^+$ at infill point $\vec{x}^{(t)}$ times the constraint violations $\Delta\vec{V}$ at $\vec{x}^{(t)}$:

$$\vec{x}^{(t+1)} = \vec{x}^{(t)} + (\nabla_x V)^+ \cdot \Delta\vec{V} \tag{2}$$

This is iterated until $\vec{x}^{(t+1)}$ becomes feasible or until its change drops below a predefined threshold η.

The main difference between Chootinan and Chen's repair method and RI-2 is the different update of the search point. While RI-2 tries to explore new points in the feasible parallelepiped, Chootinan and Chen's update procedure can result in larger steps in the search space. Although this can lead to quick fixes of constraint violations, it can also induce possible new violations of constraint functions. In this paper we undertake a comparison between Chootinan and Chen's repair and RI-2.

3. EXPERIMENTAL ANALYSIS

3.1 Test functions

3.1.1 *MOPTA 2008*

The MOPTA 2008 benchmark (MOPTA08) by Jones [1] is a substitute for high-dimensional real-world problems encountered in the automotive industry: It is a problem with $d = 124$ dimensions and with 68 constraints. The problem should be solved within $1860 = 15 \cdot d$ function evaluations which in reality refers to one month of computation time on a high-performance computer.

3.1.2 *G-problem test suite*

For further evaluation we use popular benchmark functions, namely the G-problem test suite described in [6]. The underlying functions differ in dimension ($d = 2, \ldots, 20$), type of objective function (linear, quadratic, nonlinear) and number and type of constraints ($m = 1, \ldots, 9$). Since these functions are often used in the scientific literature for analyzing constrained-based solvers, they provide a good analytical testbed for our algorithms.

3.1.3 Experimental setup

Each experiment was repeated 10 times in the case of MOPTA08 and 30 times in the case of the G-problems, each time with a different random seed.

The initial design was either obtained from sampling LHS random points for the G-functions or from an initial optimization run using Hooke & Jeeves pattern search with additional penalty term for the MOPTA08 benchmark. The other parameters for COBRA (distance requirement cycle and others) were taken from the best setting COBRA-LOCAL in Regis' original work [4].

We compare three repair options: our algorithm RI-2, the method of Chootinan (CHO) [5] and no repair. The RI-2 algorithm was used with parameters $q = 3, \epsilon = 10^{-4}$ and $m_{max} = 1000$. The CHO algorithm was used with parameter $\eta = 10^{-5}$.

In our experiments we used the COBYLA [21] implementation from the *nloptr* R package version version 1.0.4. [1] With this implementation, some of our runs resulted in occasional "freezes" of the COBYLA-optimizer, making it necessary to implement a stopping mechanism in case of this undesirable behaviour. For statistical convenience we did not include these incomplete runs, but set up new runs until 10 or 30 runs for MOPTA08 or the G-problems, resp., were completed.

3.2 Results

3.2.1 MOPTA 2008

COBRA-R with the new initial design method (taking the iterates from local search with Hooke & Jeeves, cf. Sec. 2.1) shows in Fig. 5 a clear benefit for the first 500 iterations as compared to the initial design from Regis' COBRA (diamond symbols in Fig. 5, COBRA-LOCAL from [4]).

But after the initial design, our first solution (Fig. 5, red curve *COBRA-R w/o repair*) got stuck and only after 1500 iterations there was some progress to a mediocre mean objective function value 236. We noticed however that COBYLA was making steady progress on the objective function, but always with slightly infeasible solutions. This can be seen in Fig. 6 where we plot the best objective value when allowing each constraint to be violated up to 0.5%. Now the red curve comes much closer to the optimum.

This led us to the development of the repair algorithm RI-2. The repair algorithm improves the performance of COBRA-R a lot, as the curve *COBRA-R with repair [RI-2]* in Fig. 5 shows. This curve is remarkable for two reasons: (a) The best feasible solution improves dramatically fast in the first 1000 iterations, leading to objective value 226 at iteration 1000, significantly better than Regis' result. (b) The results are pretty stable with respect to random initial conditions of 10 runs: In Fig. 5 both the standard deviations and the spans between best and worst solution are much smaller than for the other COBRA-R curves.

We look now with more detail into the repair results: An inspection of the iterates shows that the repair algorithm

[1] http://cran.r-project.org/web/packages/nloptr/index.html

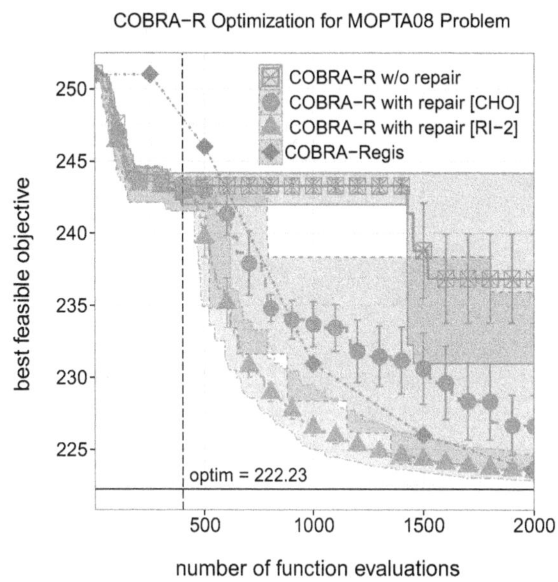

Figure 5: COBRA-R optimization performance for MOPTA08 problem. Every point represents the mean of ten independent runs. The ribbons around the curves indicate the best and the worst run. Error bars indicate standard deviations.

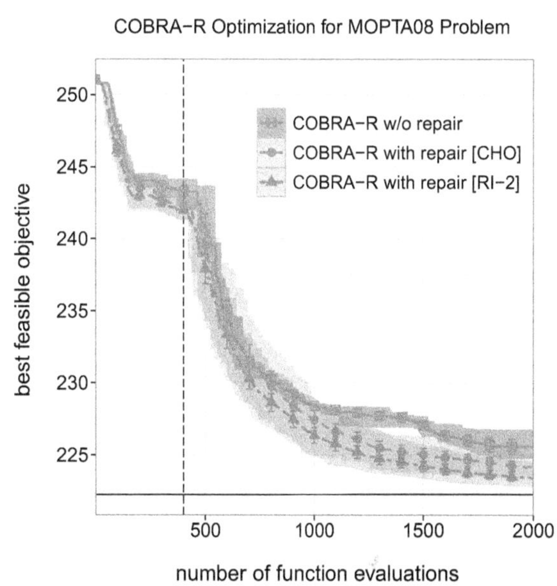

Figure 6: COBRA-R optimization performance if we allow an infeasibility tolerance of 0.5%.

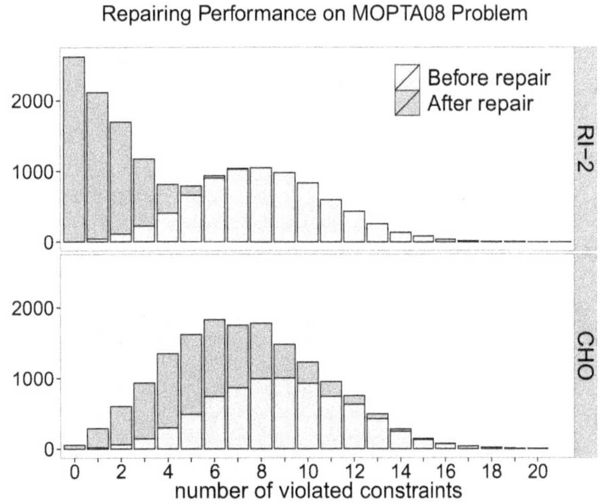

Figure 7: Number of violated constraints for MOPTA08 benchmark with 68 constraints. For each infill point entering and leaving the repair method we count its number of violated constraints. The bars are stacked.

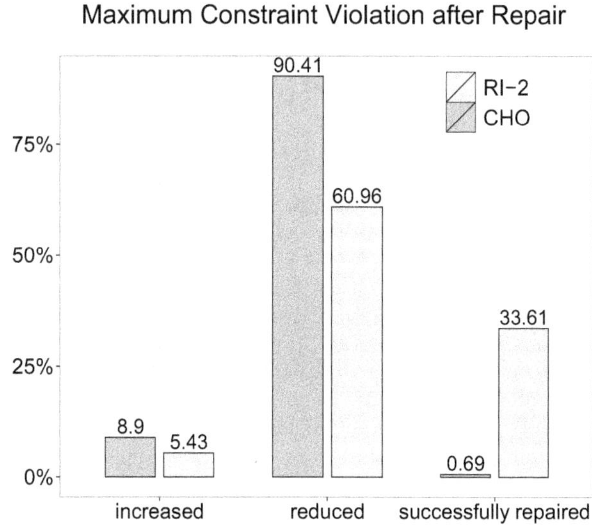

Figure 8: Comparing the performance of different repair methods on maximum violation for MOPTA08 problem. More than 30% of RI-2 repair calls contribute a fully feasible point. The success rate of CHO is less than 1%.

is called roughly every second iteration. This means that COBYLA produces mostly infeasible solutions.

How can these infeasible solutions be characterized? It is seen in Fig. 7 that the number of violated constraints is pretty large: 8-9 violated constraints on average and some extreme cases with up to 18 violated constraints. (The number of ϵ-infeasible constraints may be even higher.) This means that each repair algorithm faces a tough constraint satisfaction problem to be solved. Algorithm RI-2 very often reduces the number of violated constraints to zero or to a small number, while the method of Chootinan (CHO) only seldomly succeeds in doing this.

Figure 8 shows the success of repair on MOPTA08: While both methods, RI-2 and CHO, only rarely increase the maximum violation, RI-2 is much better in producing feasible solutions (successfully repaired > 30%) than CHO (< 1%).

3.2.2 G-problem test suite

In our previous work [25] we have studied the G-problem test suite in detail and compared COBRA-R on this test suite with other state-of-the-art constraint optimization algorithms [5],[17],[21]. The main result was that COBRA-R could achieve on all G-problems a performance similar to the other algorithms, but needed only a fraction of true function evaluations (fe) grace to the surrogate models: 50–360 fe for COBRA-R as compared to 6 000–350 000 fe for [5],[17]). The only exception was problem G02 where COBRA-R did not achieve good results, because the objective function in 20 dimensions has many local peaks and is not modelled well by the surrogate functions. We therefore exclude G02 from the following comparison.

Here we concentrate on the comparison of the different repair options on the G-problem test suite. Table 1 shows the results: Three problems are significantly better solved with repair, three are better solved without repair and three problems are indifferent. Among the two repair algorithms RI-2 is always equal or better than CHO.

The significance was tested with the Wilcoxon signed rank sum test (Table 2), which is a paired test on the 30 pairs with different seeds. In Table 3 we count the significant wins and losses and find slight advantages for RI-2 over *no repair* over Chootinan.

Table 1 shows in addition the repair success probability $p_{success}$, i. e. the probability that an infeasible solution becomes feasible on all true constraints after repair. On most G-problems the method RI-2 has a significantly larger $p_{success}$ than CHO (with the exception of problem G06).

4. DISCUSSION

4.1 Repairing infeasible solutions

4.1.1 MOPTA 2008

The results in Sec. 3.2.1 on MOPTA08 show that a repair mechanism is urgently needed in the case of COBRA-R with COBYLA as internal optimizer. The reason can be traced back to COBYLA (in combination with COBRA-surrogates): COBYLA produces mostly solutions which are very good in objective value, but slightly infeasible. It has to be noted that the Regis' original COBRA implementation [4] does not need a repair mechanism on the same benchmark because it uses another optimizer (MATLAB's `fmincon`, an interior point optimizer).

But the extra repair effort needed for COBYLA has a payoff: In conjunction with repair method RI-2 we see a faster convergence in Fig. 5, i. e. after 1000 true function evaluations RI-2 reaches a better feasible objective value than Regis' COBRA [4].

The repair method CHO fails on the MOPTA08 benchmark. Why is this the case? – A closer inspection of the results in Fig. 9 shows that CHO often reduces the maximum

Table 1: Comparison of different repair options (RI-2: our algorithm, CHO: Chootinan [5], none) on the G-problem test suite. median(dev): median of the deviation from the optimal objective value in 30 runs, $p_{success}$: probability that a repair attempt results in a feasible solution. Numbers in bold face: significantly better than other options in same row.

repair	RI-2	CHO	none	RI-2	CHO
	median(dev)			$p_{success}$	
G01	7.5E-05	7.5E-05	7.5E-05	**1.000**	0.000
G03	8.5E-02	6.8E-02	**4.1E-02**	**1.000**	0.483
G04	**2.3E-07**	1.4E-05	2.3E-06	**0.976**	0.281
G05	3.0E-04	2.9E-04	3.0E-04	**0.452**	0.296
G06	2.1E-03	2.7E-03	2.1E-03	0.006	**0.103**
G07	2.4E-06	2.4E-06	**5.4E-07**	**0.391**	0.195
G08	**7.1E-07**	1.3E-06	2.3E-06	**0.774**	0.418
G09	4.0E-05	2.1E-05	**6.8E-06**	**0.873**	0.395
G10	**8.7E-02**	**8.7E-02**	3.5E-01	0.196	0.172

Table 2: Wilcoxon rank sum test, paired, one sided, significance level 5%. Repair methods: RI-2, CHO: Chootinan [5], RN: *no repair*.

test	for problem
RI-2 significantly better than CHO	G04, G08
CHO significantly better than RI-2	G03, G09
RN significantly better than RI-2	G07, G09
RN significantly better than CHO	G04, G07, G09
RI-2 significantly better than RN	G04, G08, G10
CHO significantly better than RN	G08, G10

violation largely, but either it leaves a small reminiscent in some of the initially violated constraints or it repairs the violated constraints, but has in the end some other constraints violated which were feasible initially. It may be that method CHO would benefit from the concept of ϵ-feasibility as well, but we did not test this.

As a consequence of the lower probability of successful repair for method CHO, the span between best and worst solution is larger in this case than it is for method RI-2 (Fig. 5).

4.1.2 G-problem test suite

On most G-problems we get with repair method RI-2 a significantly higher success rate $p_{success}$ than with CHO (Table 1). But the overall effect of the repair is not that important for the final deviation from the optimum as in the MOPTA08 benchmark: We see cases where the final deviation is nearly the same in all three cases (e. g. G05, G06) and cases where we see higher deviation despite a higher success rate (G09). Sometimes the reason is that in contrast to MOPTA08 only few iterations of the G-problems require a repair. On the other hand, there are also cases where the repair gives a significant improvement (G04, G08, G10).

Table 3: Significant wins and losses on the 5%-level for the G-problem test suite.

method	significant wins	significant losses	delta
RI-2	5	4	1
none	5	5	0
CHO	4	5	-1

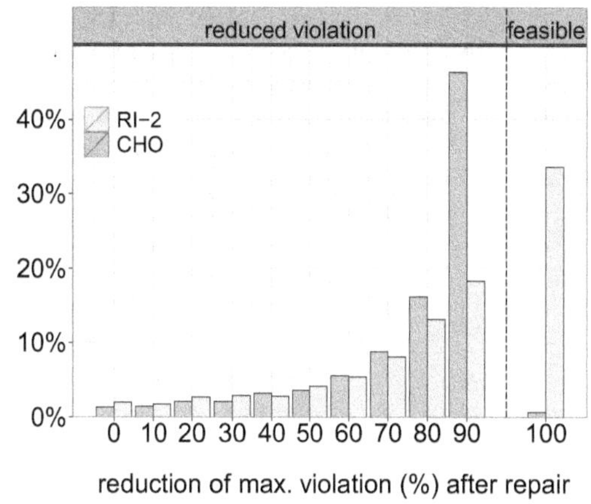

Figure 9: Reduction of maximum constraint violation

Why is it that in some cases the *no repair* method is better than RI-2 or CHO (G03, G07, G09)? – This result, surprising at first sight, is due to the fact that we allow only very few true function evaluations (50–360). If repair does not help to find better feasible objective values, then the fact that a considerable amount of function evaluations is devoted to repair can lead to a deterioration of the overall result. If we increase the number of function evaluations, the winning margin of *no repair* would decrease or even vanish.

A final note: The results on the G-problems with repair method CHO may differ from the results in Chootinan's original work [5]. This is because we use method CHO in the context of COBRA, while [5] has embedded it in a GA optimization scheme using more evaluations on the real function.

5. CONCLUSION

In this contribution we have studied various solvers for constrained optimization problems under severely limited budgets. Regis' COBRA method [4] based on surrogate models was re-implemented in R with a new internal optimizer COBYLA. We could confirm that COBRA leads to good results within few function evaluations on a variety of constrained optimization problems. In contrast to [4], we needed a repair method for infeasible solutions in the MOPTA08 benchmark. We proposed a new repair method (RI-2), which performed well on MOPTA08. It led in conjunction with COBYLA to the same asymptotic result as in [4], but with a faster rate of convergence. At the same time, RI-2 reduces the standard deviation as compared to the runs without repair. Thus we can give a positive answer to our research question (H1) on the MOPTA08 benchmark.

In a direct comparison of our new repair mechanism RI-2 with another gradient-based strategy CHO [5], we found both repair methods to perform similarly on the G-problem test-suite, where the number of constraints is relatively small. But on the MOPTA08 benchmark with its large number of constraints, the situation changes: RI-2 has a significantly higher success rate for solving constraint violations (Fig. 8), so that we can give a positive answer to research question (H2). It was shown that both repair operators RI-2 and CHO often decrease the intensity of constraint violations (Fig. 7 and 8). However, RI-2 is capable to transfer an infeasible solution into a feasible solution in more than 30% of the operator calls, whereas CHO has a very low success rate of less than 1% (cf. research question (H3)). Our discussion came to the conclusion that probably the notion of ϵ-feasibility is responsible for this beneficial effect. Since RI-2 performs all calculations on the surrogate models, it does not cost any extra function evaluations. The repair method RI-2 is not restricted to COBRA, it can be applied to any optimization algorithm with surrogate models.

6. REFERENCES

[1] D. Jones, "Large-scale multi-disciplinary mass optimization in the auto industry," in *Conference on Modeling And Optimization: Theory And Applications (MOPTA), Ontario, Canada*, 2008, pp. 1–58.

[2] T. Runarsson and X. Yao, "Stochastic ranking for constrained evolutionary optimization," *IEEE Transactions on Evolutionary Computation*, vol. 4, no. 3, pp. 284–294, 2000.

[3] O. Kramer and H.-P. Schwefel, "On three new approaches to handle constraints within evolution strategies," *Natural Computing*, vol. 5, no. 4, pp. 363–385, 2006.

[4] R. Regis, "Constrained optimization by radial basis function interpolation for high-dimensional expensive black-box problems with infeasible initial points," *Engineering Optimization*, vol. 46, no. 2, pp. 218–243, 2013.

[5] P. Chootinan and A. Chen, "Constraint handling in genetic algorithms using a gradient-based repair method," *Computers & Operations Research*, vol. 33, no. 8, pp. 2263–2281, 2006.

[6] Z. Michalewicz and M. Schoenauer, "Evolutionary algorithms for constrained parameter optimization problems," *Evolutionary Computation*, vol. 4, no. 1, pp. 1–32, 1996.

[7] A. Eiben and J. Smith, *Introduction to evolutionary computing*. Springer, 2003.

[8] C. Coello Coello, "Constraint-handling techniques used with evolutionary algorithms," in *Proc. 14th International Conference on Genetic and Evolutionary Computation Conference (GECCO)*. ACM, 2012, pp. 849–872.

[9] O. Kramer, "A review of constraint-handling techniques for evolution strategies," *Applied Computational Intelligence and Soft Computing*, vol. 2010, pp. 1–11, 2010.

[10] E. Mezura-Montes and C. Coello Coello, "Constraint-handling in nature-inspired numerical optimization: past, present and future," *Swarm and Evolutionary Computation*, vol. 1, no. 4, pp. 173–194, 2011.

[11] J. Xiao, Z. Michalewicz, L. Zhang, and K. Troja nowski, "Adaptive evolutionary planner/navigator for mobile robots," *IEEE Transactions on Evolutionary Computation*, vol. 1, no. 1, pp. 18–28, 1997.

[12] H. Mühlenbein, "Parallel genetic algorithms in combinatorial optimization," in *Computer Science and Operations Research*, O. Balci, R. Sharda, and S. Zenios, Eds. Pergamon, 1992, pp. 441–456.

[13] D. Orvosh and L. Davis, "Using a genetic algorithm to optimize problems with feasibility constraints," in *Proc. 1st IEEE Conference on Evolutionary Computation*. IEEE, 1994, pp. 548–553.

[14] D. Tate and A. Smith, "A genetic approach to the quadratic assignment problem," *Computers & Operations Research*, vol. 22, no. 1, pp. 73–83, 1995.

[15] T. Takahama and S. Sakai, "Constrained optimization by applying the alpha-constrained method to the nonlinear simplex method with mutations," *IEEE Trans. Evolutionary Computation*, vol. 9, no. 5, pp. 437–451, 2005.

[16] ——, "Learning fuzzy control rules by alpha-constrained simplex method," *Systems and Computers in Japan*, vol. 34, no. 6, pp. 80–90, 2003.

[17] T. Runarsson and X. Yao, "Search biases in constrained evolutionary optimization," *IEEE Transactions on Systems, Man, and Cybernetics, Part C: Applications and Reviews*, vol. 35, no. 2, pp. 233–243, 2005.

[18] A. H. Aguirre, S. B. Rionda, C. A. Coello Coello, G. L. Lizárraga, and E. M. Montes, "Handling constraints using multiobjective optimization concepts," *International Journal for Numerical Methods in Engineering*, vol. 59, no. 15, pp. 1989–2017, 2004.

[19] H.-G. Beyer and S. Finck, "On the design of constraint covariance matrix self-adaptation evolution strategies including a cardinality constraint," *IEEE Trans. Evolutionary Computation*, vol. 16, no. 4, pp. 578–596, 2012.

[20] J. Poloczek and O. Kramer, "Local SVM constraint surrogate models for self-adaptive evolution strategies," in *KI 2013: Advances in Artificial Intelligence*. Springer, 2013, pp. 164–175.

[21] M. Powell, "A direct search optimization method that models the objective and constraint functions by linear interpolation," in *Advances In Optimization And Numerical Analysis*. Springer, 1994, pp. 51–67.

[22] R Core Team, *R: A Language and Environment for Statistical Computing*, R Foundation for Statistical Computing, Vienna, Austria, 2013. [Online]. Available: http://www.R-project.org/

[23] R. Fisher, "Design of experiments," *British Medical Journal*, vol. 1, no. 3923, 1936.

[24] C. Kelley, *Iterative methods for optimization*. SIAM, 1999, vol. 18.

[25] P. Koch, S. Bagheri, W. Konen, C. Foussette, P. Krause, and T. Bäck, "Constrained optimization with a limited number of function evaluations," in *Proc. 24. Workshop Computational Intelligence*, F. Hoffmann and E. Hüllermeier, Eds. Universitätsverlag Karlsruhe, 2014, pp. 119–134.

A CMA-ES with Multiplicative Covariance Matrix Updates

Oswin Krause
Department of Computer Science
University of Copenhagen
Copenhagen, Denmark
oswin.krause@di.ku.dk

Tobias Glasmachers
Institut für Neuroinformatik
Ruhr-Universität Bochum
Bochum, Germany
tobias.glasmachers@ini.rub.de

ABSTRACT

Covariance matrix adaptation (CMA) mechanisms are core building blocks of modern evolution strategies. Despite sharing a common principle, the exact implementation of CMA varies considerably between different algorithms. In this paper, we investigate the benefits of an exponential parametrization of the covariance matrix in the CMA-ES. This technique was first proposed for the xNES algorithm. It results in a multiplicative update formula for the covariance matrix. We show that the exponential parameterization and the multiplicative update are compatible with all mechanisms of CMA-ES. The resulting algorithm, xCMA-ES, performs at least on par with plain CMA-ES. Its advantages show in particular with updates that actively decrease the sampling variance in specific directions, i.e., for active constraint handling.

Categories and Subject Descriptors

[**Continuous Optimization**]

Keywords

evolution strategies, covariance matrix adaptation, CMA-ES, multiplicative update, exponential coordinates

1. INTRODUCTION

Evolution Strategies (ES) are randomized direct search algorithms suitable for solving black box problems in the continuous domain, i.e., minimization problems $f : \mathbb{R}^d \to \mathbb{R}$ defined on a d-dimensional real vector space. Most of these algorithms generate a number of normally distributed offspring in each generation. The efficiency of this scheme, at least for unimodal problems, crucially depends on online adaptation of parameters of the Gaussian search distribution $\mathcal{N}(m, \sigma^2 C)$, namely the global step size σ and the covariance matrix C. Adaptation of the step size enables linear convergence on scale invariant functions [4], while covariance matrix adaptation (CMA) [10] renders the asymptotic convergence rate independent of the conditioning number of the Hessian in the optimum of a twice continuously differentiable function.

The most prominent algorithm implementing the above principles is CMA-ES [10, 8, 12]. Nowadays there exists a plethora of variants and extensions of the basic algorithm.

A generic principle for the online update of parameters (including the search distribution) is to maximize the expected progress. This goal can be approximated by adapting the search distribution so that the probability of the perturbations that generated successful offspring in the past are increased. This is likely to foster the generation of better points in the near future.[1]

The application of the above principle to CMA means to change the covariance matrix towards the maximum likelihood estimator of successful steps. To this end let $\mathcal{N}(m, C)$ denote the search distribution, and let $x_1, \dots, x_\mu$ denote successful offspring. The maximum likelihood estimator of the covariance matrix generating step $\delta_i = x_i - m$ is the rank-one matrix $\delta_i \delta_i^T$. All CMA updates of CMA-ES are of the generic form $C \leftarrow (1-c) \cdot C + c \cdot \delta\delta^T$, which is a realization of this technique keeping an exponentially fading record of previous successful steps δ. CMA-ES variants differ in which step vectors enter the covariance matrix update. Early variants were based on cumulation of directions in an evolution path vector p_c and a single rank-one update of C per generation [10]. Later versions added a rank-μ update based on immediate information from the current population [8].

A different perspective on CMA techniques is provided within the framework of information geometric optimization (IGO) [14], in particular by the natural evolution strategy (NES) approach [17, 16]. It turns out that the rank-μ update equation can be derived from stochastic natural gradient descent of a stochastically relaxed problem on the statistical manifold of search distributions. This more general perspective opens up new possibilities for CMA mechanisms, e.g., reparameterizing the covariance matrix in exponential form as done in the xNES algorithm [7]. This results in an update equation with the following properties: a) the update is *multiplicative*, in contrast to the standard additive update, b) it is possible to leave the variance in directions orthogonal to all observed steps unchanged, and c) even when performing "active" (negative) updates the covariance matrix is guaranteed to remain positive definite.

In this paper we incorporate the exponential parameteri-

[1]This statement holds only under (mild) assumptions on the regularity of the fitness landscape, which remain implicit, but may be violated, e.g., in the presence of constraints.

GECCO '15, July 11–15, 2015, Madrid, Spain

ISBN 978-1-4503-3472-3/15/07...$15.00

DOI: http://dx.doi.org/10.1145/2739480.2754781

zation of the covariance matrix into CMA-ES. We derive all mechanisms found in the standard CMA-ES algorithm in this framework, demonstrating the compatibility of cumulative step size adaptation and evolution paths (two features missing in xNES) with exponential coordinates. The new algorithm is called xCMA-ES. Its performance on standard (unimodal) benchmarks coincides with that of CMA-ES, however, in addition it benefits from neat properties of the exponential parameters, which show up prominently when performing active CMA updates with negative weights, e.g., for constraint handling.

In the next section we recap CMA-ES and xNES. Based thereon we present our new xCMA-ES algorithm. In section 3 its performance is evaluated empirically on standard benchmarks. We demonstrate the superiority for special tasks involving active CMA updates.

2. ALGORITHMS

In this section we provide the necessary background for our new algorithm before introducing the xCMA-ES. We will cover the well-known CMA-ES algorithm as well as xNES, both with a focus on the components required for our own contribution. In the following algorithms, a few implementation details are not shown, e.g., the eigen decomposition of C required for sampling as well as for the computation of the inverse matrix square root $C^{-1/2}$.

2.1 CMA-ES

The Covariance Matrix Adaptation Evolution Strategy (CMA-ES) [10, 12] is the most prominent evolution strategy in existence. It comes in many variants, e.g., with extensions for handling of fitness noise [9] and multi-modality [5]. Here we describe what can be considered a baseline version, featuring non-elitist (μ, λ) selection, cumulative step size control (CSA), and two different types of covariance matrix updates, namely a rank-1 update based on an evolution path, and the so-called rank-μ update based on the survivors of environmental truncation selection.

The state of CMA-ES is given by the parameters $m \in \mathbb{R}^d$, $\sigma > 0$, and $C \in \mathbb{R}^{d \times d}$ of its multi-variate normal search distribution $\mathcal{N}(m, \sigma^2 C)$, as well as by the two evolution paths $p_s, p_c \in \mathbb{R}^d$. Pseudo-code of a basic CMA-ES is provided in algorithm 1. The algorithm has a number of tuning constants, e.g., the sizes of parent and offspring population μ and λ, the various leaning rates, and the rank-based weights $w_1, \dots, w_\mu$. For robust default settings for the different parameters we refer to [12].

In each generation, CMA-ES executes the following steps:

1. Sample offspring $x_1, \dots, x_\lambda \sim \mathcal{N}(m, \sigma^2 C)$. This step is realized by sampling standard normally distributed vectors $z_1, \dots, z_\lambda \in \mathbb{R}^d$, which are then transformed via $x_i \leftarrow m + \sigma A z_i$, where A is a factor of the covariance matrix fulfilling $AA^T = C$. It can be computed via a Cholesky decomposition of C, however, the usual method is eigen decomposition since this operation is needed anyway later on.
2. Evaluate the offspring's fitness values $f(x_1), \dots, f(x_\lambda)$. This function call is often considered a black box, and it is assumed that its computational cost is substantial, usually exceeding the internal computational complexity of the algorithm.

Algorithm 1: CMA-ES

```
Input: m, σ
C ← I
while stopping condition not met do
    // sample and evaluate offspring
    for i ∈ {1, ..., λ} do
        x_i ← N(m, σ²C)
    end
    sort {x_i} with respect to f(x_i)
    // internal update (paths and parameters)
    m' ← Σ_{i=1}^{μ} w_i x_i
    p_s ← (1 − c_s) · p_s + sqrt(c_s(2 − c_s)μ_eff) · C^{−1/2}(m' − m)
    p_c ← (1 − c_c) · p_c + sqrt(c_c(2 − c_c)μ_eff) · (m' − m)/σ
    C ← (1 − c_1 − c_μ) · C + c_1 · p_c p_c^T
          + c_μ · Σ_{i=1}^{μ} w_i ((x_i − m)/σ) ((x_i − m)/σ)^T
    σ ← σ · exp( (c_s/D_σ) · ( ||p_s||/χ_d − 1 ) )
    m ← m'
end
```

3. Sort the offspring by fitness. Post-condition: $f(x_1) \leq f(x_2) \leq \cdots \leq f(x_\lambda)$.
4. Perform environmental selection: keep $\{x_1, \dots, x_\mu\}$, discard $\{x_{\mu+1}, \dots, x_\lambda\}$, usually the worse half.
5. Update the evolution path for cumulative step size adaptation: the path p_s is an exponentially fading record of steps of the mean vector, back-transformed by multiplication with the inverse matrix square root $C^{-1/2}$ into a coordinate system where the sampling distribution is a standard normal distribution. This path is supposed to follow a standard normal distribution.
6. Update the evolution path for covariance matrix adaptation: the path p_c is an exponentially fading record of steps of the mean vector divided (corrected) by the step size. This path models the movement direction of the distribution center over time.
7. Update the covariance matrix: a new matrix is obtained by additive blending of the old matrix with a rank-one matrix formed by the path p_c and a rank-μ matrix formed by successful steps of the current population.
8. Update the step size: the step size is changed if the norm of p_s indicates a systematic deviation from the standard normal distribution. Note (for later reference) that this update has a multiplicative form, involving the exponential function.
9. Update the mean: discard the old mean and center the distribution on a weighted mean of the new parent population.

2.2 xNES

The exponential natural evolution strategy (xNES) algorithm [7] is a prominent member of the family of natural evolution strategies (NES) [17, 16]. While exhibiting all properties of an evolution strategy, it is derived as a stochastic natural gradient descent method on the statistical manifold of search distributions, an approach that is best understood as an instance of information geometric optimization [14]. NES was found to have close relations to CMA-ES [1, 7].

The NES family of algorithms is derived as follow. Let $\{P_\theta \,|\, \theta \in \Theta\}$ denote a family of search distributions with

Algorithm 2: xNES

```
Input: m, σ
B ← I
while stopping condition not met do
    // sample and evaluate individuals
    for i ∈ {1,...,λ} do
        z_i ← N(0, I)
        x_i ← m + σ · B z_i
    end
    sort {(z_i, x_i)} with respect to f(x_i)
    // internal update (SNGD step)
    G_δ ← Σ_{i=1}^{λ} u_i · z_i
    G_M ← Σ_{i=1}^{λ} u_i · (z_i z_i^T − I)
    G_σ ← tr(G_M)/d
    G_B ← G_M − G_σ · I
    m ← m + η_m · σB · G_δ
    σ ← σ · exp(η_σ/2 · G_σ)
    B ← B · exp(η_B/2 · G_B)
end
```

parameters θ, where Θ is a differentiable manifold. The most prominent example are multivariate Gaussian distributions $P_\theta = \mathcal{N}(m, C)$ with parameters $\theta = (m, C)$ and density $p_\theta(x)$. The algorithm aims to solve the optimization problem

$$\min_\theta F(\theta) = \mathbb{E}_{x \sim P_\theta}\left[f(x)\right]$$

which is lifted from points x to distributions P_θ. The gradient of $\nabla_\theta F(\theta)$ is $\int f(x) \nabla \log(p_\theta(x)) \mathrm{d}x$ (given that the integral converges in an open set around θ). It is intractable in the black box model, however, it can be approximated by the Monte Carlo estimator

$$G(\theta) = \frac{1}{\lambda} \sum_{i=1}^{\lambda} f(x_i) \nabla \log(p_\theta(x_i))$$

with samples $x_i \sim P_\theta$. These samples correspond to the offspring population of an ES. The update $\theta \leftarrow \theta - \gamma \cdot G(\theta)$ (with learning rate $\gamma > 0$) amounts to minimization of F with stochastic gradient descent (SGD).

This update is unsatisfactory in the context of NES since it depends on the chosen parameterization $\theta \mapsto P_\theta$ (see [14], and refer to [16, 6] for further shortcomings). In the case of optimizing P_θ, the question which direction to follow has a canonical answer. This is because $\{P_\theta \mid \theta \in \Theta\}$ is a statistical manifold (a manifold the points of which are distributions) with an intrinsic Riemannian information geometry induced by KL-divergence [17, 16, 14]. The gradient w.r.t. the intrinsic geometry, pulled back to the parameter space Θ, is known as the *natural gradient*, usually denoted by $\tilde{\nabla}_\theta F(\theta)$. It is obtained from the plain gradient as

$$\tilde{\nabla}_\theta F(\theta) = \mathcal{I}(\theta)^{-1} \cdot \nabla_\theta F(\theta) \enspace ,$$

since the Fisher information matrix $\mathcal{I}(\theta)$ is the metric tensor describing the intrinsic geometry. It is estimated in a straightforward manner by $\mathcal{I}(\theta)^{-1} G(\theta)$. The update

$$\theta \to \theta - \gamma \cdot \mathcal{I}(\theta)^{-1} G(\theta)$$

is known as stochastic natural gradient descent (SNGD).

Several different implementations of this general scheme have been developed with a focus on computational aspects [15]. It is common to replace "raw" fitness values $f(x_i)$ with rank-based utility values u_i that turn out to correspond exactly to the weights w_i of CMA-ES.

The xNES algorithm supersedes earlier developments with two novel approaches. The first of these is to perform the NES update in a *local* parameterisation $\theta \mapsto P_\theta$ for which the Fisher matrix is the identity matrix, which saves its computation or estimation and in particular its (numerical) inversion. The second technique is a parameterization of the positive definite covariance matrix involving the matrix exponential, which allows for an unconstrained representation of the covariance matrix.

Covariance matrices are symmetric and positive definite $d \times d$ matrices. Symmetric matrices form the $\frac{d(d+1)}{2}$ dimensional vector space $\mathcal{S}_d$. The requirement of positive definiteness adds a non-linear constraint. Let $\mathcal{P}_d$ denote the open sub-manifold of positive definite symmetric matrices. Then the parameter space takes the form $(m, C) = \theta \in \Theta = \mathbb{R}^d \times \mathcal{P}_d$.

Note that this space is not closed under subtraction, and also not under addition of terms from $\mathcal{S}_d$ (e.g., (natural) gradients). When performing an additive update of the covariance matrix of the form $C \leftarrow C - \gamma \cdot \Delta$, e.g., an SGD step, then a large enough step $\gamma \cdot \Delta$ can result in a violation of the positivity constraint.[2]

Possible workarounds are line search for a feasible step length or more elaborate constraint handling techniques. A conceptually easier and more elegant solution is to parameterize the manifold $\mathcal{P}_d$ with a vector space and perform SGD on this new parameter space. This is exactly the role of the matrix exponential $\exp : \mathcal{S}_d \to \mathcal{P}_d$, which is a diffeomorphism (a bijective, smooth mapping with smooth inverse).

The exponential map for matrices is in general defined in terms of the power series expansion $\exp(M) = \sum_{n=0}^{\infty} \frac{1}{n!} M^n$, mapping general $d \times d$ matrices to the general linear group of invertible $d \times d$ matrices. For symmetric matrices it can be understood in terms of a spectral transformation. Let $M = UDU^T$ with U orthogonal and D diagonal denote the eigen decomposition of M, then it is easy to see from the power series formula that it holds $\exp(M) = U \exp(D) U^T$. The exponential of a diagonal matrix is simply the diagonal matrix consisting of the scalar exponentials of the diagonal entries. Hence the matrix exponential corresponds to exponentiation of the eigen values, mapping general to positive eigen values and thus $\mathcal{S}_d$ to $\mathcal{P}_d$.

The xNES algorithm uses a special coordinate system for θ, centered into the current search distribution. Let (m, C) denote the parameters of the current search distribution, and let A denote a factor of the covariance matrix C, fulfilling $AA^T = C$. We introduce local coordinates $(\delta, M) = \theta \in \Theta = \mathbb{R}^d \times \mathcal{S}_d$ (hence now Θ forms a vector space, which is in particular closed under addition) so that $(\delta, M) = (0, 0)$ represents the current distribution, and new distribution parameters (m', A') are represented as

$$(\delta,\, M) \mapsto (m',\, A') = \left(m + A\delta,\, A \exp\left(\frac{1}{2} M\right)\right) \enspace .$$

The coordinates are chosen so that the Fisher matrix is the identity: $\mathcal{I}(0, 0) = \mathrm{I}$. Hence the coordinates are orthonormal

[2]This problem does not appear with standard CMA-ES updates where positive semi-definite matrices are added to a positive definite matrix, the result of which is always positive definite.

w.r.t. the intrinsic geometry. Plain and natural gradient coincide.

Despite the seemingly complicated derivation of xNES involving stochastic natural gradient on a statistical manifold and a non-linear coordinate system based on the matrix exponential, its update equations are surprisingly simple. The complete pseudo-code is given in algorithm 2.

In this implementation the covariance matrix factor A is represented as $A = \sigma B$, where the transformation matrix B fulfills $\det(B) = 1$. In the chosen exponential coordinates the determinant corresponds to the trace (see computation of G_σ and G_B in the algorithm). The parameters m, σ, and B can be updated with independent SNGD steps, potentially with different learning rates.

The parameters of the xNES algorithm are the sample (population) size λ, the learning rates η_m, η_σ, and η_B, as well as the rank-based weights $u_1, \dots, u_\lambda$. Population size and weights essentially follow the settings of CMA-ES, with the deviation to subtract the mean from the weights. This leads to the weights $u_i = w_i - 1/\lambda$, resulting in negative weights for individuals that simply don't enter the CMA-ES due to truncation selection. The mean learning rate has the canonical value $\eta_m = 1$, which results in the exact same mean update as in CMA-ES [1, 7], while the other learning rates were empirically tuned, see [7].

Note that due to the use of the matrix exponential in xNES the updates of σ and B have exactly the same form. In contrast to CMA-ES, the covariance matrix update of xNES is multiplicative in nature. We argue that conceptually this is a desirable property since σ (scale) and B (shape) both describe complementary properties of the covariance matrix $C = \sigma^2 BB^T$, and they enter the sampling process in a similar way, namely by left-multiplication with the standard normally distributed random vectors z_i. In fact, the exponential parameterization seems to be canonical since it allows for a clear separation of the scale component σ and the shape component B of the search distribution as *linear* sub-spaces of Θ, see also [7].

2.3 Efficient Multiplicative Update

While the multiplicative update rule of the xNES guarantees positive definiteness of the covariance matrix, the matrix exponential in itself is usually a computationally expensive operation. In the following we show that the update can be implemented efficiently with time complexity $\mathcal{O}(d^2\lambda)$, which coincides with the complexity of the additive update of the CMA-ES. Thus the computational difference between the updates is merely a constant.

LEMMA 1. *Consider a matrix $G = \sum_{i=1}^{\lambda} u_i(z_i z_i^T - \mathrm{I})$ built from $\lambda < d$ vectors $z_i \in \mathbb{R}^d$, weights $u_i \in \mathbb{R}$, and a positive definite symmetric matrix $C \in \mathbb{R}^{d\times d}$ for which a decomposition $C = AA^T$ is available. Then the term*

$$A \exp(G) A^T$$

can be computed with time complexity $\mathcal{O}(\lambda d^2 + \lambda^2 d + \lambda^3)$.

PROOF. The proof has two parts. In the case that $\sum_{i=1}^{\lambda} u_i = 0$, this reduces to $G = \sum_{i=1}^{\lambda} u_i z_i z_i^T$. We first take a look at the case that $\bar{u} = \sum_{i=1}^{\lambda} u_i \neq 0$. Then we have

$$\begin{aligned} \exp(G) &= \exp\left(-\bar{u}\mathrm{I} + \sum_{i=1}^{\lambda} u_i z_i z_i^T\right) \\ &= \exp(-\bar{u}\mathrm{I}) \exp\left(\sum_{i=1}^{\lambda} u_i z_i z_i^T\right) \\ &= \exp(-\bar{u}) \exp\left(\sum_{i=1}^{\lambda} u_i z_i z_i^T\right) \end{aligned}$$

The second step holds since $-\bar{u}\mathrm{I}$ commutes with $\sum_{i=1}^{\lambda} u_i z_i z_i^T$. We can thus assume w.l.o.g. that $G = \sum_{i=1}^{\lambda} u_i z_i z_i^T$, which includes the case $\bar{u} = 0$. Because of $\mathrm{rank}(G) \leq \lambda$ we can find an eigen decomposition of $G = QDQ^T$ with $Q \in \mathbb{R}^{d\times\lambda}$ and $D \in \mathbb{R}^{\lambda\times\lambda}$ in $\mathcal{O}(\lambda^2 d + \lambda^3)$ time[3]. With this decomposition the matrix exponential can be rewritten as

$$\begin{aligned} \exp(G) &= \left(\mathrm{I} - QQ^T\right) + Q\exp(D)Q^T \\ &= \mathrm{I} + Q\left(\exp(D) - \mathrm{I}\right)Q^T \ . \end{aligned}$$

The first equality holds because $\exp(G)$ maps all 0-eigenvalues of G to 1, which leads to the first term. Insertion of the result into the term of interest yields

$$\begin{aligned} A\exp(G)A^T &= A\left[\mathrm{I} + Q\left(\exp(D) - \mathrm{I}\right)Q^T\right]A^T \\ &= AA^T + AQ\left(\exp(D) - \mathrm{I}\right)(AQ)^T \\ &= C + AQ\left(\exp(D) - \mathrm{I}\right)(AQ)^T \end{aligned}$$

We can compute $K = AQ \in \mathbb{R}^{d\times\lambda}$ in $\mathcal{O}(\lambda d^2)$ and $C + K\left(\exp(D) - \mathrm{I}\right)K^T$ in $\mathcal{O}(\lambda d^2)$ time. □

The lemma implies that if a decomposition $C = AA^T$ is available then the update $C \leftarrow A\exp(G)A^T$, or $C \leftarrow C + K\left(\exp(D) - \mathrm{I}\right)K^T$ in the notation of the proof, can now be seen as a rank-λ update to C. It can be computed significantly faster than a full eigen decomposition of C. Typically, as $\lambda = \mathcal{O}(\log(d))$, the runtime costs are dominated by the $\mathcal{O}(\lambda d^2)$ operations of the matrix multiplications, which leads to the same runtime complexity as the additive matrix update. If A was a Cholesky-factor then it could be updated efficiently in $\mathcal{O}(d^2\lambda)$ operations as well, without requiring to store or compute C first [13]. If A has been computed through an eigenvalue decomposition then there is currently no fast algorithm known to perform the update of the eigenvalue decomposition, and recomputing it from C has time complexity $\Theta(d^3)$, dominating the overhead of the exponential update.

2.4 xCMA-ES

In this section we show that exponential coordinates for the covariance matrix are compatible with all mechanisms of CMA-ES. Consequently, we incorporate this technique into the CMA-ES algorithm, resulting in a new method called exponential CMA-ES, or *xCMA-ES* for short.

[3]This can be achieved by first applying a QR-decomposition on the matrix $Z = (z_1, \dots, z_\lambda)$ which yields a $\lambda \times d$-matrix B with $BB^T = I$ and $BGB^T = K \in \mathbb{R}^{\lambda\times\lambda}$ in $O(\lambda d^2)$. An eigenvalue decomposition of $K = VDV^T$ can then be performed in $O(\lambda^3)$ and $Q = B^T V$.

The xCMA-ES algorithm features all techniques found in CMA-ES, but in addition incorporates the multiplicative covariance matrix update of the xNES algorithm. This means that xCMA-ES is equipped with two evolution paths, one for cumulative step size control, and one for the rank-one covariance matrix update. Notably, xCMA-ES comes with explicit step size control, while in xNES the step size is updated with the same mechanism as the shape component of the covariance matrix, with the only difference that the learning rates can be decoupled. For xCMA-ES we follow the proceeding of CMA-ES and do not decouple these parameters explicitly (i.e., the scale of the covariance matrix is allowed to drift).

The beauty of this construction is that all mechanisms of standard CMA-ES are naturally compatible with the exponential parameterization of the covariance matrix. In particular, the updates of the evolution paths and the step size do not require any changes.

The stochastic natural gradient component $\sum_{i=1}^{\lambda} u_i \cdot (z_i z_i^T - \mathrm{I})$ of xNES deserves particular attention. This matrix is—up to scaling—the quantity entering the matrix exponential. It consists of a weighted sum of outer products of steps in the "natural" coordinate system of the standard normally distributed samples z_i minus their expected value, which (for standard normal samples) is the identity matrix. Note that due to $\sum_i u_i = 0$ the weighted identity matrices cancel each other out. Also note that in first order Taylor approximation around the origin the matrix exponential reduces to $\exp(M) \approx \mathrm{I} + M$, resulting in the exact rank-μ update of CMA-ES [1, 7, 14].

Hence it is natural to incorporate the rank-one update of CMA-ES into the multiplicative update by adding the term $c_1 \cdot (pp^T - \mathrm{I})$ to the term entering the matrix exponential, where $p = C^{-1/2} p_c$ is the evolution path transformed back to the coordinate system of standard normally distributed samples.

A disadvantage of the mean-free weights u_i in the xNES algorithm is that the computed steps G_δ are only mean-free with respect to the *estimated* mean $\hat{z} = \frac{1}{\lambda} \sum_{i=1}^{\lambda} z_i$ as

$$G_\delta = \sum_{i=1}^{\lambda} u_i \cdot z_i = \sum_{i=1}^{\lambda} \left(w_i - \frac{1}{\lambda} \right) \cdot z_i = \sum_{i=1}^{\lambda} w_i \cdot z_i - \hat{z} \ ,$$

thus adding additional noise to the update. By replacing $\hat{z}$ by the true (zero) mean, we achieve a better estimate—the original CMA-ES update[4].

These changes applied to CMA-ES define the basic xCMA-ES algorithm. Its pseudo-code is found in algorithm 3.

As noted above, when using identical weights and learning rates, in first order approximation the multiplicative update in xCMA-ES coincides with the additive update in standard CMA-ES. Both updates rely on a rank-$(\lambda+1)$ matrix[5] formed by the outer products of the sampling steps and the evolution path p_c. An interesting conceptual difference between additive and multiplicative update is that the additive update shrinks the variance in all directions orthogonal to the $\lambda + 1$ update vectors by a factor of $1 - c_1 - c_c$, while the multiplicative update leaves these variance components untouched. In our opinion the latter better reflects the fact that no information was observed about these directions. Also, by means of subtraction of the identity (the expected value) from the positive semi-definite weighted sum of outer products, it is natural for the multiplicative update to (multiplicatively) *grow or shrink* the variance in a specific direction. In contrast, the additive update can only (additively) *grow* the variance in a specific direction, while shrinking works only through global shrinking and subsequently growing all other directions, which can be slow.

Algorithm 3: xCMA-ES

Input: m, σ
$C \leftarrow \mathrm{I}$
while *stopping condition not met* **do**
  // sample and evaluate offspring
  for $i \in \{1, \dots, \lambda\}$ **do**
    $z_i \leftarrow \mathcal{N}(0, \mathrm{I})$
    $x_i \leftarrow m + \sigma \cdot \sqrt{C} z_i$
  end
  sort $\{(z_i, x_i)\}$ with respect to $f(x_i)$
  // internal update (paths and parameters)
  $m' \leftarrow \sum_{i=1}^{\lambda} (u_i + \frac{1}{\lambda}) x_i$
  $p_s \leftarrow (1 - c_s) \cdot p_s + \sqrt{c_s(2 - c_s)\mu_{\text{eff}}} \cdot C^{-1/2}(m' - m)$
  $p_c \leftarrow (1 - c_c) \cdot p_c + \sqrt{c_c(2 - c_c)\mu_{\text{eff}}} \cdot \frac{m' - m}{\sigma}$
  $Z \leftarrow c_1 \cdot \left[C^{-1/2} p_c p_c^T C^{-1/2} - \mathrm{I} \right] + c_\mu \cdot \sum_{i=1}^{\lambda} u_i z_i z_i^T$
  $C \leftarrow C^{1/2} \exp(Z) C^{1/2}$
  $\sigma \leftarrow \sigma \cdot \exp\left(\frac{c_s}{D_\sigma} \cdot \left(\frac{\|p_s\|}{\chi_d} - 1 \right) \right)$
  $m \leftarrow m'$
end

This problem was mitigated to some extent with so-called active covariance matrix updates [2, 11]. In an active update step the algorithm subtracts an outer product from the covariance matrix, an operation that must carefully ensure the positive definiteness of the result, e.g., by means of line search or finely tuned learning rates. In contrast, the multiplicative update operates on an unconstrained problem and hence can never result in an invalid configuration.

2.5 Constraint Handling

A powerful constraint handling mechanism for the $(1, \lambda)$-CMA-ES was introduces in [3]. In principle, the same mechanism can be applied to the non-elitist, population-based standard formulation of CMA-ES. The simple yet highly efficient approach amounts to performing active CMA updates for steps resulting in infeasible offspring, effectively reducing the variance in the direction of the constraint normal, while suspending step size adaptation.

The corresponding mechanism for xCMA-ES is essentially the same, namely to perform a standard update with negative weight, but of course without a need for constraining the step size. There is a subtle difference to the elitist setting considered in [3]: with non-elitist selection it is in principle possible for infeasible offspring to enter the new parent population, namely if more than $\lambda - \mu$ offspring happen to be infeasible—this can indeed be observed in experiments. Then the algorithm can get caught in a random walk through the infeasible region. To avoid this effect we propose to make the weights adaptive to the number of infeasible offspring as follows. We first compute the standard

[4]with both update choices, μ_{eff} is the same and computed from the w_i.

[5]In standard CMA-ES the rank is even reduced to $\mu + 1$ due to truncation selection effectively setting the weights of discarded offspring to zero.

weights w_i of CMA-ES. Infeasible offspring are treated as worst, generally obtaining low weights. For the active CMA update we subtract a constant from the weights of infeasible offspring, which is set to $\frac{0.4}{\lambda}\sum_i w_i$. Then we normalize the absolute values of the weights to one (by dividing all weights by $\sum_i |w_i|$), compute μ_{eff} based on these weights, and then make them mean free by subtracting $\frac{1}{\lambda}\sum_i w_i$. Finally, the parameters $c_s, d_\sigma, c_1, c_c, c_\mu$ are recomputed based on the new weights.

Finally, we ensure that the mean m stays in the feasible region by finding the minimum $k \in \mathbb{N}_0$ such that

$$m + \gamma^k(m' - m) , \qquad (1)$$

where we set $\gamma = 2/3$.

3. EXPERIMENTS

In this section we perform an empirical evaluation of xCMA-ES and compare it to CMA-ES. This comparison highlights the effect of the exponential covariance matrix parameters and the resulting multiplicative covariance matrix update. In particular, we aim to answer the following questions:

1. Does the exponential update impact black box performance?
2. How do active covariance updates perform in exponential form?

In order to answer the first question we perform experiments on the same standard benchmark sets as used for the xNES algorithm [7].

Due to lack of a fair baseline for comparison we cannot provide a good answer for the second question. However, we demonstrate that active updates work qualitatively as desired in a constraint optimization setting. As the CMA-ES is tuned on a large number of benchmark functions, ranking stability over speed, it is not hard to find parameters which beat it on a smaller set of functions. Thus tuning the parameters of the xCMA-ES on a small set of function would lead to an unfair benchmark. To avoid this situation we avoid tuning altogether and instead resort to the default parameters of CMA-ES which are given in table 1. This choice is justified by the similarity of the update rules, especially in the settings of small dimensionality with the conservative learning rates of CMA-ES.

constant	value
λ, μ	$4 + \lfloor 3\log(d) \rfloor$, $\lambda/2$
c_s	$\frac{\mu_{\text{eff}}+2}{d+\mu_{\text{eff}}+5}$
c_c	$\frac{4+\mu_{\text{eff}}/d}{d+4+2\mu_{\text{eff}}/d}$
c_1	$\frac{2}{(d+1.3)^2+\mu_{\text{eff}}}$
c_μ	$\min\left\{1 - c_1, 2\frac{\mu_{\text{eff}}-2+1/\mu_{\text{eff}}}{(d+2)^2+2\mu_{\text{eff}}/2}\right\}$
D_σ	$1 + c_s + 2\max\{0, \sqrt{\frac{\mu_{\text{eff}}-1}{d+1}} - 1\}$
w_i	$\frac{\max\{0,\log(\lambda/2-1)-\log(i-1)\}}{\sum_{j=1}^{\lambda}\max\{0,\log(\lambda/2-1)-\log(i-1)\}}$

Table 1: Constants used for the CMA-ES and xCMA-ES algorithms

3.1 Black Box Performance

To assess the black box performance of xCMA-ES, we compare it to CMA-ES on the set of benchmark functions used in [7]. We run both algorithms for 100 trials on each function for each dimensionality $d \in \{4, 8, 16, 32, 64\}$ until a target value f_{stop} is reached. We chose as initial step size for all functions $\sigma = \frac{1}{\sqrt{d}}$. We report the median of the required function evaluations over the successful trials for both algorithms. A trial is considered successful if the algorithm converges to the right optimum(which is only an issue on Rosenbrock). The function descriptions and the values of f_{stop} are given in table 2. The results of the experiments are given in Figure 1.

name	$f(x)$	f_{stop}
SharpRidge	$-x_1 + 100\sqrt{\sum_{i=2}^{d} x_i^2}$	-1000
ParabRidge	$-x_1 + 100\sum_{i=2}^{d} x_i^2$	-1000
Rosenbrock	$\sum_{i=1}^{d-1} 100(x_{i+1} - x_i^2)^2 + (1 - x_i)^2$	10^{-14}
Sphere	$\sum_{i=1}^{d} x_i^2$	10^{-14}
Cigar	$\alpha x_1^2 + \sum_{i=2}^{d} x_i^2$	10^{-14}
Discus	$x_1^2 + \alpha\sum_{i=2}^{d} x_i^2$	10^{-14}
Ellipsoid	$\sum_{i=1}^{d} \alpha^{\frac{i}{d-1}} x_i^2$	10^{-14}
Schwefel	$\sum_{i=1}^{d}\left(\sum_{j=1}^{i} x_i\right)^2$	10^{-14}
DiffPowers	$\sum_{i=1}^{d} \lvert x_i\rvert^{2+10\frac{i-1}{d}}$	10^{-14}

Table 2: The formulas for the benchmark functions. The default value $\alpha = 10^{-6}$ was used in all experiments.

The results show that both algorithms perform equally well on all functions, showing nearly no differences between the algorithms, with a minimal (maybe insignificant and surely irrelevant) edge for xCMA-ES.

3.2 Constraint Handling

Due to a lack of a non-elitist CMA-ES variant with a constraint handling mechanism based on (active) covariance matrix updates we can not provide a strong baseline algorithm for comparison with xCMA-ES. To obtain a reasonable baseline we constrain the mean of CMA-ES to never leave the feasible region with the same mechanism as proposed for xCMA-ES (see equation (1)). The standard selection operator is already capable of handling constraints to some extent when treating infeasible offspring as worse than feasible ones. The only differences between the baseline CMA-ES and xCMA-ES are the additive update vs. the multiplicative update with active constraint handling.

As a benchmark problem we use the constrained sphere function proposed in [3]:

$$\min_x \|x\|^2 - m \qquad \text{s.t } x_i \geq 1, i = 1, \ldots, m$$

The optimum x^* has components $x_i^* = 1$ for $i \leq m$ and $x_i^* = 0$ for $i > m$. The difficulty of this problem is twofold: In the vicinity of the optimum only a fraction of 2^{-m} of the space it feasible—hence the problem gets harder with growing number of constraints. At the same time, while approaching the optimum the gradient of the objective function in the unconstrained components towards zero vanishes. To counteract this trend the algorithm must reduce the variance of its sampling distribution in the subspace spanned by all constraint normals—a task for which active CMA updates are supposed to be helpful. We perform 100 runs of both algorithm in $d = 16$ and $d = 32$ dimensions with $m \in \{2, 4, \ldots, d/2\}$ constraints.

The results are given in figure 2. A plot of an example run with $d = 32$ and $m = 4$ is given in figure 3 showing the

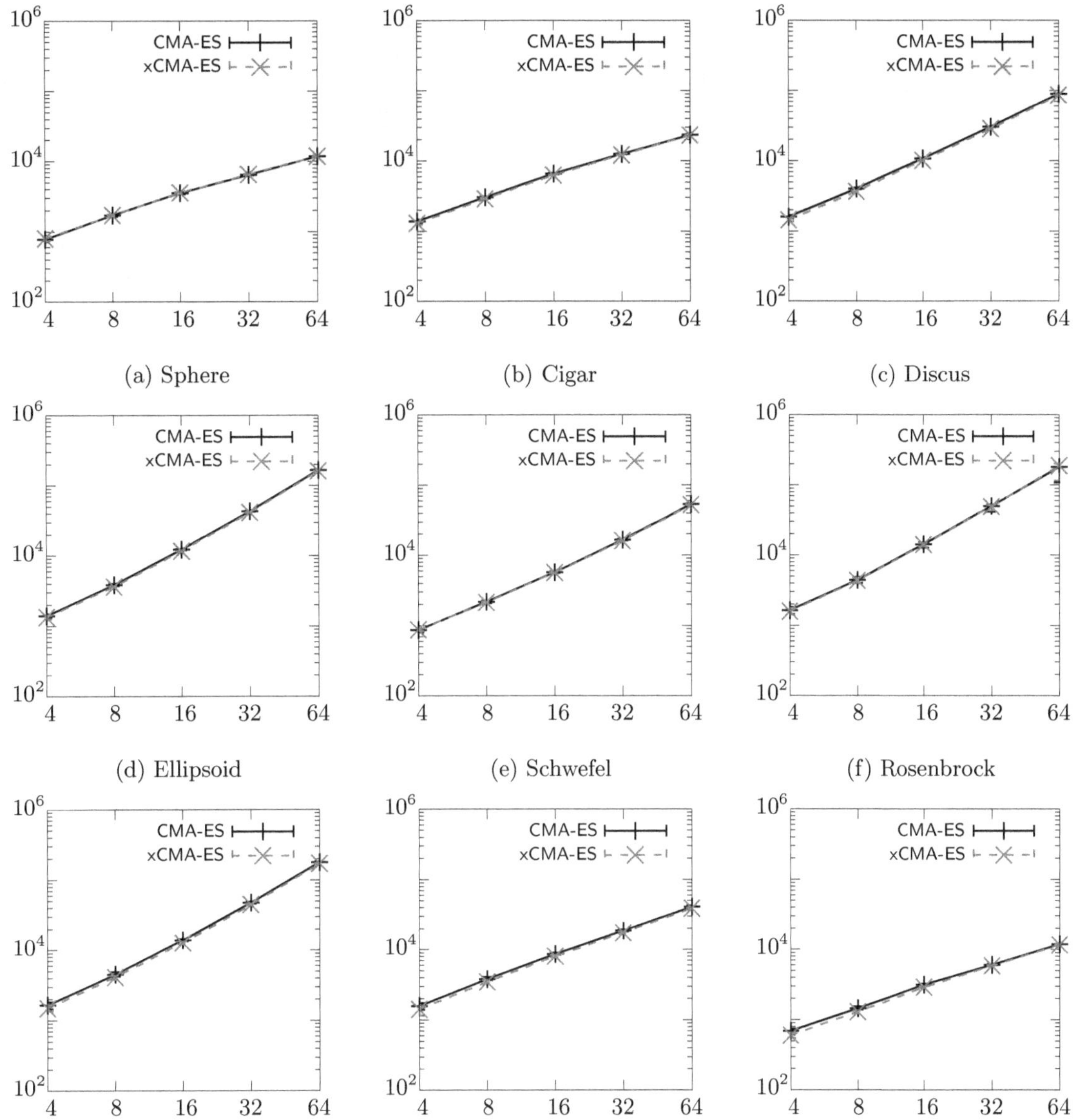

(a) Sphere (b) Cigar (c) Discus

(d) Ellipsoid (e) Schwefel (f) Rosenbrock

(g) DiffPowers (h) SharpRidge (i) ParabRidge

Figure 1: Median number of black box function evaluations over problem dimension of CMA-ES and xCMA-ES on nine standard benchmark problems. Due to low spread, the 25% and 75% quantile indicators are nearly invisible.

function values of the best point in the sampled population as well as the current step-size.

It turns out that xCMA-ES is always faster then the baseline CMA-ES. Moreover, CMA-ES became unstable with increasing m and in the case $d = 32$ and $m = 16$ fails to converge in all 100 runs. The plot in figure 3 shows this instability already for $m = 4$ constraints.

4. CONCLUSION

We have incorporated a new type of covariance matrix update into the CMA-ES algorithm. This multiplicative update stems from the xNES algorithm. It guarantees positive definiteness of the covariance matrix even with negative update weights. The resulting algorithm features all mechanisms of CMA-ES and is hence called xCMA-ES.

We showed that its performance on standard benchmarks is nearly indistinguishable from that of the CMA-ES. We demonstrated that, despite the application of the matrix exponential, it is possible to implement the multiplicative update with a time complexity of only $O(d^2\lambda)$.

We further investigated an extension of the algorithm for constrained optimization problems and showed that by a simple use of negative weights xCMA-ES outperforms the CMA-ES. This demonstrates the benefits of the multiplicative update.

Acknowledgements

Oswin Krause acknowledges support from the Danish National Advanced Technology Foundation through the project "Personalized breast cancer screening".

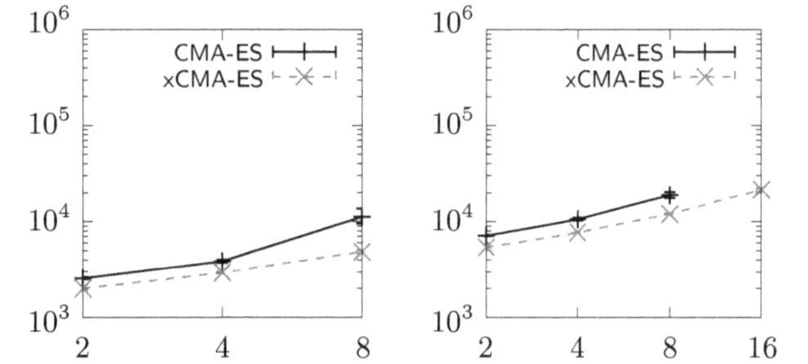

(a) $d = 16$ (b) $d = 32$

Figure 2: Number of iterations (generations) necessary to reach the target objective value of 10^{-12} over the number m of constraints for the constrained sphere problems in $d = 16$ and $d = 32$ dimensions. The value for CMA-ES at $d = 32$ and $m = 16$ is missing because the algorithm failed in all 100 runs.

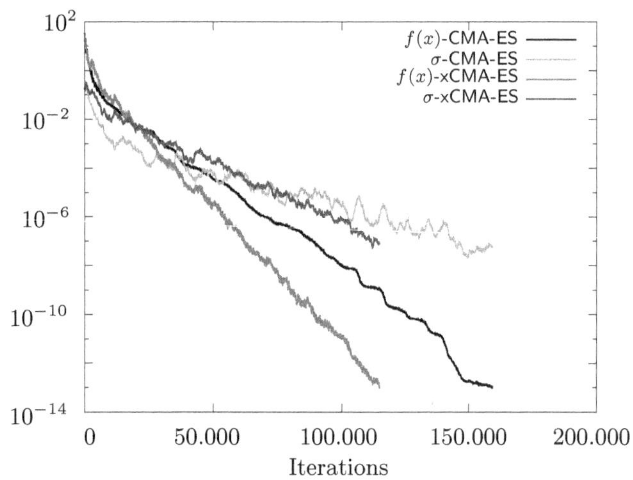

Figure 3: Plot of a single run of the CMA-ES and xCMA-ES algorithms on the constrained Sphere function with $d = 32$ and $m = 4$. Plotted are function value and step length over generations.

5. REFERENCES

[1] Y. Akimoto, Y. Nagata, I. Ono, and S. Kobayashi. Bidirectional Relation between CMA Evolution Strategies and Natural Evolution Strategies. In *Parallel Problem Solving from Nature (PPSN)*, 2010.

[2] D. V. Arnold and N. Hansen. Active covariance matrix adaptation for the (1+1)-CMA-ES. In *Proceedings of the 12th annual conference on Genetic and Evolutionary Computation (GECCO)*, pages 385–392. ACM, 2010.

[3] D. V. Arnold and N. Hansen. A (1+1)-CMA-ES for constrained optimisation. In *Proceedings of the Genetic and Evolutionary Computation Conference (GECCO 2012)*, pages 297–304. ACM, 2012.

[4] A. Auger. Convergence results for the $(1, \lambda)$-SA-ES using the theory of φ-irreducible Markov chains. *Theoretical Computer Science*, 334(1–3):35–69, 2005.

[5] A. Auger and N. Hansen. A restart CMA evolution strategy with increasing population size. In B. McKay et al., editors, *The 2005 IEEE International Congress on Evolutionary Computation (CEC'05)*, volume 2, pages 1769–1776, 2005.

[6] H.-G. Beyer. Convergence Analysis of Evolutionary Algorithms that are Based on the Paradigm of Information Geometry. *Evolutionary Computation*, 22(4):679–709, 2014.

[7] T. Glasmachers, T. Schaul, Y. Sun, D. Wierstra, and J. Schmidhuber. Exponential natural evolution strategies. In *Proceedings of the Genetic and Evolutionary Computation Conference (GECCO)*, 2010.

[8] N. Hansen, S. D. Müller, and P. Koumoutsakos. Reducing the time complexity of the derandomized evolution strategy with covariance matrix adaptation (CMA-ES). *Evolutionary Computation*, 11(1):1–18, 2003.

[9] N. Hansen, S. P. N. Niederberger, L. Guzzella, and P. Koumoutsakos. A Method for Handling Uncertainty in Evolutionary Optimization with an Application to Feedback Control of Combustion. *IEEE Transactions on Evolutionary Computation*, 13(1):180–197, 2009.

[10] N. Hansen and A. Ostermeier. Completely derandomized self-adaptation in evolution strategies. *Evolutionary Computation*, 9(2):159–195, 2001.

[11] G. A. Jastrebski and D. V. Arnold. Improving evolution strategies through active covariance matrix adaptation. In *Evolutionary Computation, 2006. CEC 2006. IEEE Congress on*, pages 2814–2821. IEEE, 2006.

[12] S. Kern, S. D. Müller, N. Hansen, D. Büche, J. Ocenasek, and P. Koumoutsakos. Learning probability distributions in continuous evolutionary algorithms–a comparative review. *Natural Computing*, 3(1):77–112, 2004.

[13] O. Krause and C. Igel. A More Efficient Rank-one Covariance Matrix Update for Evolution Strategies. In J. He, T. Jansen, G. Ochoa, and C. Zarges, editors, *Foundations of Genetic Algorithms (FOGA)*. ACM Press, 2015. accepted for publication.

[14] Y. Ollivier, L. Arnold, A. Auger, and N. Hansen. Information-geometric optimization algorithms: a unifying picture via invariance principles. *arXiv preprint arXiv:1106.3708v3*, 2014.

[15] Y. Sun, D. Wierstra, T. Schaul, and J. Schmidhuber. Stochastic Search using the Natural Gradient. In *International Conference on Machine Learning (ICML)*, 2009.

[16] D. Wierstra, T. Schaul, T. Glasmachers, Y. Sun, J. Peters, and J. Schmidhuber. Natural evolution strategies. *Journal of Machine Learning Research*, 15:949–980, 2014.

[17] D. Wierstra, T. Schaul, J. Peters, and J. Schmidhuber. Natural Evolution Strategies. In *Proceedings of the Congress on Evolutionary Computation (CEC)*. IEEE Press, 2008.

Dichotomy Guided Based Parameter Adaptation for Differential Evolution

Xiao-Fang Liu, Zhi-Hui Zhan* (Corresponding Author), Jun Zhang

Department of Computer Science, Sun Yat-sen University, Guangzhou, P. R. China, 510275

Key Laboratory of Machine Intelligence and Advanced Computing, Ministry of Education, P.R. China

Collaborative Innovation Center of High Performance Computing, National Univ. of Defense Tech., China

Engineering Research Center of Supercomputing Engineering Software, Ministry of Education, P.R. China

*zhanzhh@mail.sysu.edu.cn

ABSTRACT

Differential evolution (DE) is an efficient and powerful population-based stochastic evolutionary algorithm, which evolves according to the differential between individuals. The success of DE in obtaining the optima of a specific problem depends greatly on the choice of mutation strategies and control parameter values. *Good* parameters lead the individuals towards optima successfully. The increasing of the success rate (the ratio of entering the next generation successfully) of population can speed up the searching. Adaptive DE incorporates success-history or population-state based parameter adaptation. However, sometimes *poor* parameters may improve individual with small probability and are regarded as successful parameters. The *poor* parameters may mislead the parameter control. So, in this paper, we propose a novel approach to distinguish between *good* and *poor* parameters in successful parameters. In order to speed up the convergence of algorithm and find more "*good*" parameters, we propose a dichotomy adaptive DE (DADE), in which the successful parameters are divided into two parts and only the part with higher success rate is used for parameter adaptation control. Simulation results show that DADE is competitive to other classic or adaptive DE algorithms on a set of benchmark problem and IEEE CEC 2014 test suite.

Categories and Subject Descriptors

I.2.8 [**Artificial Intelligence**]: Problem Solving, Control Methods, and Search – *Heuristic methods.*

General Terms

Algorithms, Performance, Design, Experimentation

Keywords

Adaptive parameter control; dichotomy-guided; differential evolution; evolutionary optimization

GECCO '15, July 11 - 15, 2015, Madrid, Spain

© 2015 ACM. ISBN 978-1-4503-3472-3/15/07…$15.00

DOI: http://dx.doi.org/10.1145/2739480.2754646

1. INTRODUCTION

Differential evolution (DE) is a stochastic evolutionary algorithm, which is designed for real parameter optimization problems [1]. Optimization is a challenging area in mathematics. DE has been extensively studied and has been applied to lots of practical problems because of its relative simplicity and competitiveness [2][3]. However, the search performance of DE algorithms depends greatly on control parameter settings [4] such as population size *NP*, scaling factor *F*, and crossover rate *CR*. The optimal settings of these parameters are problem-dependent. A great amount of research work analyzes the effects of these parameters and proposes some suggestion of suitable parameters. The trial-and-error method for tuning the control parameters usually requires tedious optimization trials, so many adaptive or self-adaptive mechanisms have been proposed to update the control parameters during the evolutionary process [5][6][7][8][10][11], with adaptive selection of mutation strategies [9][12][13], and dynamic population size selection [14][15][16][17] to update the control parameters during the evolutionary process. The adaptive and self-adaptive mechanisms outperformed the classical DE algorithms in terms of the rate of convergence for many benchmark problems.

The mechanisms of adaptive parameter control can be categorized into three classes [18] as: deterministic parameter control in which parameters are changed based on deterministic rules such as the time-dependent change of the mutation rates proposed by Holland [19], adaptive parameter control based on learning from evolution process [9], and self-adaptive parameter control in which parameters are associated with individuals and undergo recombination. Adaptive parameter control mechanism updates the parameters according to the historic successful experience [10] or the current population state [20][21]. The successful parameters are believed to direct the individuals towards optima in the next generation. Some success history experience based adaptive parameter control strategies have been proposed.

JADE is a well-known effective DE algorithm which uses a novel mutation strategy called current-*p*best/1 and an external archive for storing the inferior solutions. Each individual has its own parameters *F* and *CR* which are generated by probability distribution of Cauchy and Gaussian based on μ_F and μ_{CR}, respectively. Therein, μ_F and μ_{CR} are updated generation by generation according to the historical accumulation and the *F* and *CR* values of the successful individuals in current generation. Since the excellent performance of JADE, some extension researches on JADE have been proposed. In order to improve the reliability of JADE, Peng et al. [22] modify the control parameter adaptation strategy of JADE by adding a weighting strategy and apply a "restart with knowledge transfer" strategy to guide the subsequent search. Yang et al. [23] applied JADE to optimize the weight vector in adaptive weighting process for large scale optimization problems. Gong et al. [24] proposed an approach combining strategy adaptation mechanism with JADE for numerical optimization. In order to improve the robustness of JADE, Tanabe et al. [25] proposed Success-History based Adaptive DE (SHADE), an improved version of JADE based on a historical record of successful parameter settings. In each generation, SHADE selects μ_F and μ_{CR} from the memory of a diverse set of parameters randomly and updates the memory according to the successful parameters with a weighting strategy.

JADE updates the control parameters according to all the successful parameters in the last generation, which may include some *poor* parameters. That is, some parameters may be not good themselves, but the individual successes in improving the solution quality, mainly due to other factors rather than parameters. These *poor* parameters, however, may disturb the parameter adaptive control process. The weighting strategy at the ratio of improvement is one way to reduce the noise. Abandoning the *poor* and remaining the *good* is another way. In this paper, we proposed a different approach, Dichotomy-guided adaptive DE (DADE), which is a variant of JADE. DADE divides the successful F and CR into two parts according to the mean μ_F and μ_{CR} of last generation, respectively. Instead of based on all the successful F and CR like in JADE, the update of μ_F and μ_{CR} only related to the part with higher success rate. The population is divided into two parts according to the mean of F and CR, and the success rate is considered as the ratio of the number of individuals successfully entering the next generation to the number of individuals in this part.

The contributions of this work are:

1) Propose the idea of quality discrimination of successful parameters. The *good* parameters are distinguished from the *poor* parameters.
2) Propose a novel dichotomy-guided adaptive approach to select the *good* parameters from all the successful parameter for parameter adaptive process. The *poor* parameters are abandoned.

The rest of the paper is organized as follows. In Section 2, we review the base DE algorithm. Section 3 introduces some adaptive DE algorithms and JADE algorithm, which is the base of our algorithm. Section 4 develops DADE in detail. Experiments are carried out in Section 0 and test results are compared with other algorithms. Finally, conclusions are summarized in Section 6 and future work is highlighted.

2. DIFFERENTIAL EVOLUTION

As a branch of evolutionary algorithm, DE [1], first proposed by Storn and Price, is an effective and efficient global optimization algorithm. Just like genetic algorithm, DE performs mutation, crossover, and selection on population. The initial population $\{x_{i,0} = (x_{1i}, x_{2i}, \dots, x_{D,i}) | i = 1, 2, \dots, NP\}$ is randomly generated according to a uniform distribution on the search space as (1), where NP represents the size of population and D is the dimension of problem.

$$x_{j,i} = x_{j,\min} + \mathrm{rand}(0,1) \cdot (x_{j,\max} - x_{j,\min}) \quad (1.)$$

where $x_{j,\min}$ and $x_{j,\max}$ are the predefined lower and upper bounds of the jth dimension, rand(0,1) is a random number in range [0,1]. Then DE generates new population by mutation, crossover, and selection operations repeatedly until reaching the terminal condition. The operations are described below.

Mutation: At each generation g, a mutant vector $v_{i,g}$ is created by mutation operation for each individual $x_{i,g}$. The five frequently used mutation strategies are listed as follows:

DE/rand/1

$$v_{i,g} = x_{r1,g} + F \cdot (x_{r2,g} - x_{r3,g}) \quad (2.)$$

DE/rand/2

$$v_{i,g} = x_{r1,g} + F \cdot (x_{r2,g} - x_{r3,g}) + F \cdot (x_{r4,g} - x_{r5,g}) \quad (3.)$$

DE/best//1

$$v_{i,g} = x_{\mathrm{best},g} + F \cdot (x_{r1,g} - x_{r2,g}) \quad (4.)$$

DE/best/2

$$v_{i,g} = x_{\mathrm{best},g} + F \cdot (x_{r1,g} - x_{r2,g}) + F \cdot (x_{r3,g} - x_{r4,g}) \quad (5.)$$

DE/current-to-best/1

$$v_{i,g} = x_{i,g} + F \cdot (x_{\mathrm{best},g} - x_{i,g}) + F \cdot (x_{r1,g} - x_{r2,g}) \quad (6.)$$

where the indices $r1$, $r2$, $r3$, and $r4$ are distinct random integers selected from $[1, 2, \dots, NP]$. The factor F is a positive control parameter for scaling the difference vectors. The base vector $x_{\mathrm{best},g}$ is the individual with best fitness in generation g. The above mutation strategies can be generalized by DE/-/k scheme, where k is a positive integer representing the number of difference vectors. $v_{i,g}$ combines a base vector with k difference vectors multiplied by F.

Crossover: In order to enhance the diversity of the population, a binomial crossover operation forms a trial vector $u_{i,g} = (u_{1,i,g}, u_{2,i,g}, \dots, u_{D,i,g})$ as:

$$u_{j,i,g} = \begin{cases} v_{j,i,g}, & \text{if } \mathrm{rand}(0,1) \le CR \text{ or } j = j_{\mathrm{rand}} \\ x_{j,i,g}, & \text{otherwise} \end{cases} \quad (7.)$$

where rand(0,1) is a uniform random number on the interval [0,1], and j_{rand} is a uniform integer selected from $[1, 2, \dots, D]$, which is used to ensure that trial vector has at least one component different from $x_{i,g}$. The crossover probability $CR \in [0,1]$ is another control parameter corresponding to the average fraction of vector components inherited from trial vector.

Selection: To determine the new individual surviving in the next generation g+1, the trial vector $u_{i,g}$ is compared to the target vector $x_{i,g}$. The vector with better fitness enters the next generation. For example, for a minimization problem, the selected vector is given by:

$$x_{i,g+1} = \begin{cases} u_{i,g}, & \text{if } f(u_{i,g}) \le f(x_{i,g}) \\ x_{i,g}, & \text{otherwise} \end{cases} \quad (8.)$$

where $f(x)$ is the fitness evaluation function.

3. RELATED WORK

This section briefly reviews some adaptive DE algorithms that dynamically update control parameters as the evolutionary search proceeds.

3.1 SaDE

Qin et al. [9] proposed SaDE to simultaneously implement four mutation strategies "DE/rand/1/bin", "DE/rand-to-best/2/bin", "DE/rand/2/bin", and "DE/current-to-rand/1". The probability of applying four mutation strategies to generate trial vector is adapted based on their success rate in the past LP (a constant) generations. The more suitable mutation strategy for the problem under consideration contributes more at different learning stages. In addition, the scaling factors F are independently generated by normal distribution $N(0.5, 0.3)$ for different individuals in the current population at each generation. It shows that this scheme keeps both the local (with smaller F value) and global search (with larger F value) ability to generate potentially good mutation vectors throughout the evolution process. The crossover probabilities are randomly generated in range [0,1] according to normal distribution with mean CRm and standard deviation 0.1 for each 5 generations. The mean CRm of different strategies are calculated according to the successful CR which are used for the corresponding strategy. At each generation, the CR values associated with the trial vectors entering the next generation are recorded. After LP generations, CRm is recalculated according to the recorded CR values.

3.2 jDE

Brest et al. [8] proposed a new version of self-adaptive DE, jDE, which uses the classic DE/rand/1/bin strategy. The key idea is that the better values of control parameters lead to better individuals, which are more likely to survive and produce offspring, so that the *good F* and *CR* are propagated to the next generation. The population size is fixed but the control parameters F_i and CR_i of each individual are updated during the optimization. At the beginning, F_i of each individual is set as 0.5 and CR_i as 0.9. Instead of generating F_i and CR_i by normal distributions and updating CRm by recorded successful values in SaDE, jDE regenerated F_i and CR_i with probabilities τ_1 by uniform distributions on [0.1,0.9] and [0,1], respectively. The rules for self-adapting control parameters F and CR are quite simple. Experimental results suggest that jDE performs better than DE/rand/1/bin.

3.3 JADE

In this subsection, we describe JADE [10], which is the basis of our algorithm DADE. Its main features are a new mutation strategy current-to-*p*best/1, parameter adaptation, and adoption of external archive.

3.3.1 Currrent-to-pbest/1

Current-to-best/1 strategy uses a greedy mechanism, directing the trial vectors towards the best individual in the population. The greedy strategy leads to the quick convergence to local optimum. Current-to-best/1 strategy performs well on unimodal problems, but poorly on multimodal problems. In view of the fast convergence but less reliable performance of current-to-best strategy, Zhang et al. [10] proposed the current-to-*p*best strategy with p greediness as:

$$v_{i,g} = x_{i,g} + F_i \cdot (x_{pbest,g} - x_{i,g}) + F_i \cdot (x_{r1,g} - x_{r2,g}) \qquad (9.)$$

where $x_{pbest,g}$ is randomly selected from the top $NP \times p$ ($p \in [0,1]$) individuals in generation g, $r1$ and $r2$ are random integers in range of $[1, 2, \ldots, NP]$ different from i and $p$best. F_i is the F parameter of individual i. Current-to-best is the special case of (9) when p is $1/NP$. For each dimension j, if $v_{j,i,g}$ is outside the bounds of $[x_{j,\min}, x_{j,\max}]$, the component is set to be the middle of the violated bounds and the corresponding component of the target vector as:

$$\begin{aligned} v_{j,i,g} &= (x_{j,i,g} + x_{j,\min})/2, if\ v_{j,i,g} < x_{j,\min} \\ v_{j,i,g} &= (x_{j,i,g} + x_{j,\max})/2, if\ v_{j,i,g} > x_{j,\max} \end{aligned} \qquad (10.)$$

3.3.2 Parameter adaptation

Each individual has its own F_i and CR_i parameters, which are generated by probability distribution as:

$$CR_i = \text{randn}_i(\mu_{CR}, 0.1) \qquad (11.)$$

$$F_i = \text{randc}_i(\mu_F, 0.1) \qquad (12.)$$

where $\text{randn}_i(\mu_{CR}, 0.1)$, $\text{randc}_i(\mu_F, 0.1)$ are the random number generated according to normal distribution of $(\mu_{CR}, 0.1)$ and Cauchy distribution of $(\mu_F, 0.1)$. CR_i is truncated to [0, 1]. If $CR_i > 1$ or < 0, CR_i is set as 1 or 0. F_i is truncated to (0,1]. F_i is truncated as 1 when $F_i > 1$ and regenerated when $F_i \leq 0$. Both μ_{CR} and μ_F are initialized to 0.5 at the beginning, and updated at the end of each generation. The F_i and CR_i generated trial vectors entering the next generation successfully at the current generation are recorded in the set S_F and S_{CR} respectively. The uF and uCR are calculated according to the successful F and CR as:

$$\mu_{CR} = (1-c) \cdot \mu_{CR} + c \cdot \text{mean}_A(S_{CR}) \qquad (13.)$$

$$\mu_F = (1-c) \cdot \mu_F + c \cdot \text{mean}_L(S_F) \qquad (14.)$$

where c is a predefined constant between 0 and 1, $\text{mean}_A(S_{CR})$ is the arithmetic mean of CR in S_{CR}, and $\text{mean}_L(S_F)$ is the Lehmer mean as:

$$\text{mean}_L(S_F) = \frac{\sum_{F \in S_F} F^2}{\sum_{F \in S_F} F} \qquad (15.)$$

3.3.3 External Archive

In order to make use of the promising progress direction information, the inferior solutions $x_{i,g}$ which did not enter the next generation are recorded in an archive A. Define the current population as P. In the current-to-*p*best/1 with archive, $r2$ in Eq.(9) is randomly selected from the union, P ∪ A, of the population and archive. Archive is empty at the beginning, and then the inferior solutions are added into it for each generation. The maximal size of archive is set as NP. If the archive is full, the new member replaces the randomly selected member in archive.

4. DICHOTOMY-GUIDED ADAPTIVE DE

Good F and *CR* guide the individual towards the optimum. JADE updates μ_F and μ_{CR} according to the successful S_F and S_{CR} to move towards *good F* and *CR* values slowly. In order to speed up the parameter update process to get more *good F* and *CR*, we proposed a dichotomy-guided adaptive DE (DADE), a variant of JADE which uses a different parameter adaptation mechanism based on dichotomy-guided. In DADE, the F and CR in S_F and S_{CR} are divide into two parts. In contrast to JADE, which uses all the successful F and CR values to guide parameter adaptation, DADE picks a part of successful parameters with higher success rate to guide control parameter adaptation as search progresses. The individuals of the whole population are divided into two parts according to the mean of F and CR which are used to generate F and CR, the part with higher success rate is selected to update parameter. The success rate is defined as the ratio of the number of individuals successfully entering the next generation to the number of individuals in this part.

ALGORITHM I. PSEUDO CODE OF MEAN OF *F* AND *CR* UPDATE IN DADE

Algorithm 1: Update μ_F and μ_{CR} in DADE

```
c = MINC + (MAXC-MINC)*fes/FES
If S_CR≠∅ and S_F≠∅ then
  For i = 1 to | S_CR|
    If CR_i ≤ μ_CR then CR_i→L_SCR
    If CR_i ≥ μ_CR then CR_i→R_SCR
  For i = 1 to | S_F|
    If F_i ≤ μ_F then F_i→L_SF
    If F_i ≥ μ_F then F_i→R_SF
  If || L_SCR |/| L_PCR |-| R_SCR |/| R_PCR | |>C_CR then
    If | L_SCR |/| L_PCR | ≥ | R_SCR |/| R_PCR | then
      μ_CR =(1-c)·μ_CR +c·mean_A(L_SCR)
    Else
      μ_CR =(1-c)·μ_CR +c·mean_A(R_SCR)
  Else
      μ_CR =(1-c)·μ_CR +c·mean_A(S_CR)

  If || L_SF |/| L_PF |-| R_SF |/| R_PF ||>C_F then
    If | L_SF |/| L_PF | ≥ | R_SF |/| R_PF | then
      μ_F =(1-c)·μ_F +c·mean_L(L_SF)
    Else
      μ_F =(1-c)·μ_F +c·mean_L(R_SF)
  Else
    μ_F =(1-c)·μ_F +c·mean_L(S_F)
Else
μ_F and μ_CR remain unchanged
```

ALGORITHM II. PSEUDO CODE OF DADE ALGORITHM

Algorithm 2: DADE algorithm

```
// Initialization phase
  g=0; μ_F = 0.5; μ_CR = 0.5; A = ∅
  Initialize population P_0 = {x_1,0, x_2,0, …, x_NP,0} randomly;
// Main loop
  While the termination criteria are not met do
    S_CR=∅, S_F =∅ , L_PF=∅, R_PF=∅, L_PCR=∅, R_PCR=∅;
    For i = 1 to NP do
      F_i = randc_i(μ_F,0.1);
      CR_i = randn_i(μ_CR,0.1);
      If F_i ≤ μ_F then F_i→L_PF
      If F_i ≥ μ_F then F_i→R_PF
      If CR_i ≤ μ_CR then CR_i→L_PCR
      If CR_i ≥ μ_CR then CR_i→R_PCR
      Generate trial vector u_i,g by current-to-pbest/1/bin
      If f(x_i,g) ≤ f(u_i,g) then
        x_i,g+1 = x_i,g
      Else
        x_i,g+1 = u_i,g, x_i,g→A, CR_i→S_CR, F_i→S_F
      End if
    End for
    Randomly remove solutions from A so that |A|≤NP
    Update μ_F and μ_CR (Algorithm 1);
    g ++;
  End
```

4.1 Dichotomy-Guided Parameter Adaption

The key idea of dichotomy guided parameter adaption is to move the mean μ_F and μ_{CR} for F and CR towards the part with higher success rate. In each generation, the control parameters CR_i and F_i used by each individual are generated by Eqs.(10) and (11) according to the procedure described above for JADE in Section 3. As with JADE, S_F and S_{CR} record the successful F and CR in the current generation. All F and CR of the entire population are recorded in P_F and P_{CR}. At the end of each generation, S_F and S_{CR} are divided into two parts by μ_F and μ_{CR}. If F is smaller than μ_F, F is inserted into the L_{SF}. If F is larger than μ_F, F is inserted into R_{SF}. If F is equal to μ_F, F is inserted into both L_{SF} and R_{SF}. Similar to S_F, the S_{CR} are also divided into two parts L_{SCR} and R_{SCR} which record the small and large CR respectively. The same dichotomy is applied on the P_F and P_{CR} of the population, which produces L_{PF} and R_{PF}, L_{PCR} and R_{PCR}, respectively. The update of μ_{CR} and μ_F is as:

$$\mu_{CR}=\begin{cases}(1-c)\cdot\mu_{CR}+c\cdot\text{mean}_A(L_{SCR}),\text{ if }|L_{SCR}|/|L_{PCR}|\ge|R_{SCR}|/|R_{PCR}|\\(1-c)\cdot\mu_{CR}+c\cdot\text{mean}_A(R_{SCR}),\text{otherwise}\end{cases}\quad(16.)$$

$$\mu_{F}=\begin{cases}(1-c)\cdot\mu_{F}+c\cdot\text{mean}_L(L_{SF}),\text{ if }|L_{SF}|/|L_{PF}|\ge|R_{SF}|/|R_{PF}|\\(1-c)\cdot\mu_{F}+c\cdot\text{mean}_L(R_{SF}),\text{otherwise}\end{cases}\quad(17.)$$

$$c=\text{MINC}+(\text{MAXC}-\text{MINC})*fes/\text{FES}\quad(18.)$$

where MINC and MAXC are constant, which are set as 0.01 and 0.1 in this paper. FES is the max function evaluation number throughout the searching process, and *fes* is the current function evaluation times used at the current time. c is a parameter in [0.01,0.1], increases linearly with increasing of function evaluation number. $|L_{SCR}|$ is the number of elements in L_{SCR}, $\text{mean}_A(L_{SCR})$ is the usual arithmetic mean, mean_L is the Lehmer mean as Eq.(14). Both μ_F and μ_{CR} are initialized to 0.5 at the beginning. The pseudo code of update process is described in Algorithm I. If the success rate of two part of L_{SF} and R_{SF} is near, the selection of anyone part may cause the misleading of F and CR. So in order to lessen the risk of misleading, we add a threshold C_F and C_{CR} to control the selection. Only when the difference of success rate between left and right is larger than the threshold, Eqs.(16) and (17) are carried out to calculate μ_F and μ_{CR}. Otherwise, all the F and CR in S_F and S_{CR} are used to calculate μ_F and μ_{CR} as Eqs.(13) and (14).

4.2 Overall Algorithm

The overall DADE algorithm is shown in Algorithm II. The procedure of DADE is the same as JADE except for the adaptation of parameters. DADE adopts the current-to-*p*best/1 strategy. The individuals of the population are generated randomly in the searching space. After the initialization, in each generation, F_i of individual i is generated by Cauchy distribution of mean μ_F and CR_i is generated by normal distribution of mean μ_{CR}. Both μ_F and μ_{CR} are initialized to 0.5 at the beginning. For each individual, trial vector is generated by crossover and mutation operations. Then the vector with better fitness value between trial and target vectors is selected and enters the next generation. At the end of each generation, the μ_F and μ_{CR} are updated according to the dichotomy approach described in Algorithm I. The parameters are divided into two parts and the part with higher success rate is selected to calculate μ_F and μ_{CR}. DADE regenerates new population repeatedly until reaching the terminal conditions. The population size is fixed throughout the evolutionary process.

5. EXPERIMENTS AND COMPARISIONS

5.1 Experimental Settings

In this section, DADE is applied to minimize a set of 42 scalable benchmark functions of dimensions D = 30 chosen from [26][27][28] and [29], as shown in Table I. The benchmark functions of f_1-f_{12} have an optimal value f^*=0, which have different characteristics. f_1-f_4 are continuous unimodal functions. f_5 is the Rosenbrock function which is unimodal functions for 2 dimension but multimodal for high dimension. f_6 is a discontinuous step function, and f_7 is a noisy quartic function. f_8 is separable multimodal functions. f_9-f_{12} are nonseparable multimodal functions. The last 30 functions are taken from the CEC 2014 competition [29]. F_1-F_3 are rotated unimodal function, F_4-F_{16} are simple multimodal functions, F_{17}-F_{22} are

TABLE I. TEST FUNCTIONS OF DIMENSION D

Name	Test functions	Initial range
Sphere	$f_1(x)=\sum_{i=1}^{D} x_i^2$	$[-100,100]^D$
Schewefel 2.22	$f_2(x)=\sum_{i=1}^{D}\lvert x_i\rvert+\prod_{i=1}^{D}\lvert x_i\rvert$	$[-10,10]^D$
Schewefel 1.2	$f_3(x)=\sum_{i=1}^{D}\left(\sum_{j=1}^{i} x_j\right)^2$	$[-100,100]^D$
Schewefel 2.21	$f_4=\max_i\{\lvert x_i\rvert\}$	$[-100,100]^D$
Rosenbrock	$f_5(x)=\sum_{i=1}^{D-1}\left[100\left(x_{i+1}-x_i^2\right)^2+\left(x_i-1\right)^2\right]$	$[-30,30]^D$
Step	$f_6(x)=\sum_{i=1}^{D}\lfloor x_i+0.5\rfloor^2$	$[-100,100]^D$
Noisy Quaric	$f_7(x)=\sum_{i=1}^{D} i x_i^4+rand[0,1)$	$[-1.28,1.28]^D$
Rastrigin	$f_8(x)=\sum_{i=1}^{D}\left[x_i^2-10\cos(2\pi x_i)+10\right]$	$[-5.12,5.12]^D$
Ackley	$f_9=-20\exp(-0.2\sqrt{\frac{1}{D}\sum_{i=1}^{D}x_i^2})-\exp(\frac{1}{D}\sum_{i=1}^{D}\cos(2\pi x_i))+20+e$	$[-32,32]^D$
Griewank	$f_{10}(x)=\frac{1}{4000}\sum_{i=1}^{D}x_i^2-\prod_{i=1}^{D}\cos(\frac{x_i}{\sqrt{i}})+1$	$[-600,600]^D$
Penalized	$f_{11}(x)=\frac{\pi}{D}\{10\sin^2(\pi y_1)+\sum_{i=1}^{D-1}(y_i-1)^2[1+10\sin^2(\pi y_{i+1})]+(y_D-1)^2\}+\sum_{i=1}^{D}u(x_i,10,100,4)$ where $y_i=1+\frac{1}{4}(x_i+1)$ and $u(x_i,a,k,m)=\begin{cases}k(x_i-a)^m & x_i>a\\ 0 & -a\le x_i\le a\\ k(-x_i-a)^m & x_i<-a\end{cases}$	$[-50,50]^D$
	$f_{12}=0.1\{\sin^2(3\pi x_1)+\sum_{i=1}^{D-1}(x_i-1)^2[1+\sin^2(3\pi x_{i+1})]$ $+(x_D-1)^2[1+\sin^2(2\pi x_D)]\}+\sum_{i=1}^{D}u(x_{i,}5,100,4)$	$[-50,50]^D$
Shifted and Rotated, hybrid , composition functions	F_1-F_{30}: The 30 functions from the IEEE CEC 2014 special session and competition [29]	$[-100,100]^D$

hybrid functions, and F_{23}-F_{30} are composition functions. Obviously, the last 30 functions are much more complex.
DADE is compared with two other adaptive DE algorithms SaDE and jDE, the classic DE/rand/1/bin. For fair comparison, we set the parameters of DADE to be fixed, p = 0.05 and MINC=0.01, MAXC=0.1, C_F=0.3 and C_{CR}=0.15 in all simulation. We follow the parameter settings in the original paper of JADE [10], SaDE [9], jDE [8]. The parameters of DE/rand/1/bin are set to $F = 0.5$ and $CR = 0.9$.

In all simulations, we set the population size NP to be 100 for 30D problems. All algorithms runs in 50 times for each function. The results reported are the mean of 50 runs. For clarity, the results of the best and second best algorithms are marked in **boldface** and *italic*, respectively. In addition, we use Wilcoxon's rank sum test at $\alpha = 0.05$ to evaluate the statistical significance of the results. The ≈,+, - indicate whether a given algorithm performed significantly not different (≈), better(+) or worse(-) compared to DADE according the Wilcoxon rank-sum test.

5.2 Experimental Results

5.2.1 *Classic Functions: f_1-f_{12}*

The mean and standard deviation of the results obtained by each algorithm for f_1-f_{12} are summarized in Table II. These statistics are calculated at the end of the optimization. As shown in Table II, DADE performs the best or the second best in all functions. For f_1 and f_2, DADE performs best compared with JADE, jDE, SaDE, and DE. Compare with jDE, DADE performs better on 10 functions except for f_6 and f_9. DADE obtains better results on 7 functions than SaDE, while the results of the other functions are not significantly different. For DE, DADE performs better on 9 functions except for 3 functions which are not significantly different. So, we can conclude that DADE performs better than jDE, SaDE, and DE. Compared with JADE, DADE performs better on functions f_1 and f_2 but worse on 3 functions f_3, f_4, and f_7. DADE takes only part of the successful F and CR values to update the mean μ_F and μ_{CR} while JADE use all successful F and CR. DADE performs better than JADE on f_1 and f_2, which

TABLE II. EXPERIMENTAL RESULTS OF 30-DIMENSIONAL PROBLEMS F_1-F_{12}, AVERAGED OVER 50 INDEPENDENT RUNS

≈,+, - indicates whether a given algorithm performed significantly not different, better or worse compared to DADE according the Wilcoxon rank-sum test

fun	Gen	DADE		JADE		jDE		SaDE		DE/rand/1/bin	
		Mean	Std	Mean	Std	Mean	Std	Mean	Std	Mean	Std
f1	1500	**1.81E-77**	4.34E-77	*2.58E-59(-)*	1.15E-58	1.26E-28(-)	1.25E-28	5.93E-38(-)	1.13E-37	7.85E-14(-)	9.31E-14
f2	2000	**4.49E-50**	1.18E-49	2.46E-20(-)	1.68E-19	9.02E-24(-)	6.60E-24	5.50E-25(-)	1.23E-24	1.16E-09(-)	7.86E-10
f3	5000	*6.02E-72*	1.29E-71	**2.73E-86(+)**	1.15E-85	8.31E-14(-)	1.35E-13	1.49E-44(-)	1.05E-43	5.54E-11(-)	8.40E-11
f4	5000	*7.73E-56*	3.72E-55	**2.05E-65(+)**	5.16E-65	7.99E-01(-)	9.55E-01	2.44E-19(-)	5.30E-19	5.28E-01(-)	9.63E-01
f5	20000	*1.60E-30*	5.12E-30	7.97E-02(≈)	5.64E-01	1.59E-01(-)	7.89E-01	3.99E-01(-)	1.21E+00	**3.47E-31(≈)**	2.45E-30
f6	1500	**0.00E+00**	0.00E+00	**0.00E+00(≈)**	0.00E+00	**0.00E+00(≈)**	0.00E+00	**0.00E+00(≈)**	0.00E+00	**0.00E+00(≈)**	0.00E+00
f7	3000	*7.56E-04*	2.64E-04	**6.97E-04(+)**	3.68E-04	3.41E-03(-)	8.16E-04	1.88E-03(-)	6.92E-04	4.60E-03(-)	1.23E-03
f8	5000	**0.00E+00**	0.00E+00	**0.00E+00(≈)**	0.00E+00	**0.00E+00(≈)**	0.00E+00	**0.00E+00(≈)**	0.00E+00	6.75E+01(-)	3.22E+01
f9	2000	**3.41E-15**	0.00E+00	**3.41E-15(≈)**	0.00E+00	*7.89E-15(-)*	1.73E-15	**3.41E-15(≈)**	0.00E+00	9.26E-08(-)	3.92E-08
f10	3000	*7.23E-21*	1.87E-20	1.48E-04(≈)	0.00E+00	**1.08E-21(-)**	7.67E-21	2.96E-04(-)	1.46E-03	1.97E-04(≈)	1.39E-03
f11	1500	**1.57E-32**	2.78E-48	**1.57E-32(≈)**	1.66E-47	8.77E-30(-)	1.20E-29	**1.57E-32(≈)**	1.66E-47	7.17E-15(-)	5.56E-15
f12	1500	**1.35E-32**	5.57E-48	**1.35E-32(≈)**	8.29E-48	8.47E-29(-)	1.07E-28	**1.35E-32(≈)**	8.29E-48	4.38E-14(-)	3.46E-14
+(better than DADE)				2		0		0		0	
-(worse than DADE)				3		10		7		9	
≈(no sig.)				7		2		5		3	

TABLE III. SUCCESS RATE AND SEARCH SPEED COMPARISONS ON 30-DIMENSIONAL PROBLEMS $f1$-$f12$

fun	Acceptable accuracy		DADE	JADE	jDE	SaDE
f1	1E-6	SR	**100**	**100**	**100**	**100**
		FEs	**22503**	25580	49996	33106
		Rank	1	2	4	3
f2	1E-6	SR	**100**	**100**	**100**	**100**
		FEs	**35266**	44078	65232	52438
		Rank	1	2	4	3
f3	1E-6	SR	**100**	**100**	**100**	**100**
		FEs	100036	**62324**	289720	111152
		Rank	2	**1**	4	3
f4	1E-6	SR	**100**	**100**	0	**100**
		FEs	73893	**61670**	N/A	172498
		Rank	2	**1**	4	3
f5	1E-6	SR	**100**	98	96	90
		FEs	143366	**104438**	536256	199920
		Rank	**1**	2	3	4
f6	0	SR	**100**	**100**	**100**	**100**
		FEs	**10733**	11588	21942	14722
		Rank	**1**	2	4	3
f7	1E-2	SR	**100**	**100**	**100**	**100**
		FEs	29733	**28744**	103474	53178
		Rank	2	**1**	4	3
f8	1E-6	SR	**100**	**100**	**100**	**100**
		FEs	147996	116920	**102216**	132116
		Rank	4	2	**1**	3
f9	1E-6	SR	**100**	**100**	**100**	**100**
		FEs	**32693**	37716	73174	48982
		Rank	**1**	2	4	3
f10	1E-6	SR	**100**	96	**100**	96
		FEs	**24596**	29172	53458	36431
		Rank	**1**	3	2	4
f11	1E-6	SR	**100**	**100**	**100**	**100**
		FEs	**20543**	24012	44762	29700
		Rank	**1**	2	4	3
f12	1E-6	SR	**100**	**100**	**100**	**100**
		FEs	**22520**	25964	48746	31876
		Rank	**1**	2	4	3
Avg_Rank			**1.38**	1.69	3.23	2.92

shows that some *F* and *CR* disturb the parameter adaptive control.

In Table III, we summarize the success rate (SR) of each algorithm and the average number of function evaluations over successful runs (FEs). An experiment is considered as successful if the best solution is found with acceptable accuracy. FEs and SR are useful to compare the convergence rate (in successful runs) and reliability of different algorithms. The ranks in the table are evaluated based on the descending order of the success rates and the ascending order of FEs. From Table III, we find that all the algorithm perform high success rate on most functions. In particular, DADE 100% successfully finds the acceptable solutions on all functions. Only DADE can find achieve the near-global optimum for f_5, while JADE, jDE, and SaDE sometimes fails to obtain the optimum. From the aspect of search speed, DADE and JADE uses a smaller FEs to reach the acceptable solution than jDE and SaDE. DADE ranks the first and is the fastest in most of the functions. For all the multimodal nonseprable functions f_5 and f_9-f_{12}, DADE ranks the first and performs the best. Overall, DADE performs the best on most functions in f_1-f_{12}. The results show that the dichotomy guided parameter adaptive approach speeds up the search process, and move to *good* *F* and *CR* quickly.

5.2.2 IEEE CEC 2014 Competition: F_1-F_{30}

Table IV compares on the five algorithms on IEEE CEC 2014 competition function set. All the functions are shifted, rotated, hybrid, or composition functions. These functions are difficult for most of the optimization algorithms. It can be seen that no algorithm is able to obtain a near-global optimum on all functions. DADE obtains better results on more functions. DADE performs better than JADE, jDE, SaDE, and DE on 10, 20, 20, and 20 functions, respectively. Conversely, JADE, jDE, SaDE, and DE perform better than DADE on 5, 4, 7, and 8 functions, respectively. Overall, DADE performs the best. For simple functions F_1-F_{16}, DADE performs better on 6 but worse than JADE on 3 functions. And DADE performs better than JADE on hybrid functions F_{17}-F_{22} especially for F_{18}, F_{20}, and F_{21}. For compose functions, DADE performs worse than JADE on F_{28} and F_{29} but better on F_{26} and an equivalent effect on other functions. DADE outperforms JADE on simple and hybrid functions, but not on composition functions on more occasions.

6. CONCLUSION

This paper proposed DADE, a dichotomy-guided based adaptive DE which extends JADE. DADE takes only higher success rate part of the successful *F* and *CR* to update the mean μ_F and μ_{CR} to get more *good* parameters. DADE was shown to outperform JADE, jDE, SaDE, and DE/rand/1/bin on most cases

TABLE IV. EXPERIMENTAL RESULTS OF 30-DIMENSIONAL PROBLEMS F_1-F_{30}, AVERAGED OVER 50 INDEPENDENT RUNS

fun	DADE		JADE		jDE		SaDE		DE/rand/1/bin	
	Mean	Std	Mean	Std	Mean	Std	Mean	Std	Mean	Std
F1	**2197.59**	2373.15	*2334.58(-)*	1417.61	83957.9(-)	86118.3	87778.9(-)	64379.6	82601.1(-)	92570
F2	1.23E-14	1.43E-14	1.95E-14(≈)	1.33E-14	3.41E-15(+)	9.33E-15	**0(+)**	0	*3.41E-15(+)*	9.33E-15
F3	6.63E-14	2.15E-14	0.000369(-)	0.001803	1.82E-14(+)	2.68E-14	**0(+)**	0	*7.96E-15(+)*	1.99E-14
F4	*2.01E-13*	4.55E-13	**7.47E-14(+)**	2.90E-14	11.8499(-)	23.221	0.945987(-)	5.20477	1.54154(-)	8.92808
F5	*20.309*	0.0448103	**20.2896(+)**	0.030424	20.3635(-)	0.0347005	20.8342(-)	0.0584629	20.913(-)	0.0492376
F6	**0.520859**	1.25853	9.51302(-)	2.11086	8.97849(-)	5.17562	*4.61054(-)*	7.50528	4.78853(-)	2.42099
F7	4.17E-14	5.57E-14	*2.01E-14(≈)*	4.38E-14	9.09E-14(-)	4.59E-14	**0(+)**	0	0.00014 (≈)	0.00104596
F8	**0**	0	**0(≈)**	0	0.0198992(≈)	0.140708	1.08613(-)	1.78133	127.885(-)	23.7552
F9	**18.9327**	3.13409	26.9342(-)	4.59556	44.032(-)	6.77148	120.631(-)	8.98442	178.66(-)	11.0678
F10	**0.00902167**	0.011832	0.009797(≈)	0.012034	3.60701(-)	3.54782	395.372(-)	78.1793	3949.23(-)	718.258
F11	**1571.45**	235.326	1656.61(≈)	209.396	2809.69(-)	301.751	5864.01(-)	331.763	6790.67(-)	295.158
F12	*0.29049*	0.0438903	**0.258242(+)**	0.04569	0.497145(-)	0.0705661	1.7974(-)	0.232437	2.3848(-)	0.248515
F13	**0.168534**	0.0232873	*0.21185(-)*	0.03296	0.288649(-)	0.0386808	0.293576(-)	0.0368541	0.36334(-)	0.0380017
F14	**0.226569**	0.034456	*0.236031(≈)*	0.032342	0.305864(-)	0.0385814	0.269278(-)	0.0296651	0.267298(-)	0.0295258
F15	*3.1928*	0.442603	**3.06125(≈)**	0.415325	5.79822(-)	0.564672	11.6375(-)	0.969501	15.5367(-)	1.0396
F16	**9.16391**	0.384313	*9.33009(-)*	0.432232	10.3873(-)	0.345541	12.3589(-)	0.200787	12.6395(-)	0.261038
F17	1240.11	362.124	*1196.01(≈)*	331.88	1530.1(≈)	981.534	**1043.72(+)**	314.034	1474(-)	168.889
F18	80.8564	30.2393	147.674(-)	453.766	**18.4001(+)**	9.85452	90.5753(-)	25.3154	*53.0875(+)*	7.21286
F19	**4.54948**	0.975606	*4.62783(≈)*	0.788838	5.4887(-)	0.715036	5.75106(-)	0.509561	5.03464(-)	0.6568
F20	*22.9696*	77.2491	2793.38(-)	2444.79	**12.3273(-)**	3.56416	37.1735(-)	7.75455	32.9986(-)	7.49414
F21	**294.969**	133.987	15951.5(-)	59467.3	*303.584(≈)*	198.642	786.735(-)	200.888	683.399(-)	150.878
F22	144.494	56.3702	143.033(≈)	61.9006	142.043(≈)	58.9894	*122.325(+)*	45.0506	**75.1894(+)**	68.9857
F23	**315.244**	5.78E-14	**315.244**(≈)	4.02E-13	**315.244**(≈)	4.16E-13	**315.244**(≈)	3.60E-13	**315.244**(≈)	4.02E-13
F24	224.703	2.35238	224.913(≈)	2.15984	225.343(-)	1.85919	*223.865(≈)*	0.902074	**216.895(+)**	10.3466
F25	204.257	1.12724	203.823(≈)	1.10005	203.369(+)	0.646241	*203.275(+)*	1.13723	**202.634(+)**	0.119261
F26	**100.168**	0.027169	102.171(-)	13.9746	100.29(-)	0.0461031	100.294(-)	0.0372848	100.342(-)	0.041282
F27	*327.274*	45.8999	336.618(≈)	46.5475	391.229(-)	24.2412	**321.56(+)**	37.4329	351.65(-)	56.7135
F28	*817.208*	49.724	**786.422(+)**	42.283	825.959(≈)	19.222	835.533(-)	32.5592	823.013(-)	25.3954
F29	**733.661**	16.7342	175687(+)	1.25E+06	830.088(-)	78.4253	760.115(-)	38.1916	699189(+)	2.39E+06
F30	*1663.12*	619.812	1682.65(≈)	699.958	2528.91(-)	921.983	1774.41(≈)	921.505	**1408.09(+)**	751.981
	+(better than DADE)		5		4		7		8	
	-(worse than DADE)		10		20		20		20	
	≈		15		6		3		2	

≈,+, - indicates whether a given algorithm performed significantly not different (≈), better(+) or worse(-) compared to DADE according the Wilcoxon rank-sum test.

of 12 benchmark functions and 30 complex functions of CEC 2014 competition. Although DADE may find the near solution as JADE, DADE uses a smaller function evaluation times than JADE. DADE runs faster on most functions. The dichotomy guided approach moves the parameter towards the part with higher success rate, and speeds up the searching process. The experiment results show that the idea of taking part of successful F and CR for parameter control is reasonable. Only taking the *good* parameters for the parameter update process, the algorithm speeds up. There are some *poor* F and CR of successful individual which may disturb parameter control.

Further research work includes 1) analyzing the parameter control process further; 2) finding other methods to pick the *good* F and CR for parameter adaptive control.

7. ACKNOWLEDGMENTS

This work was supported in part by the National Natural Science Foundations of China (NSFC) with No. 61402545, the Natural Science Foundations of Guangdong Province for Distinguished Young Scholars with No. 2014A030306038, the Project for Pearl River New Star in Science and Technology, Guangzhou, China, the Fundamental Research Funds for the Central Universities, the NSFC Key Program with No. 61332002, the NSFC for Distinguished Young Scholars with No. 61125205, and the National High-Technology Research and Development Program (863 Program) of China No.2013AA01A212.

8. REFERENCES

[1] R. Storn and K. Price, "Differential Evolution – A Simple and Efficient Heuristic for global Optimization over Continuous Spaces," *J. Glob. Optim.*, vol. 11, no. 4, pp. 341–359, Dec. 1997.

[2] Y. L. Li, Z. H. Zhan, Y. J. Gong, W. N. Chen, J. Zhang, and Y. Li, "Differential evolution with an evolution path: A DEEP evolutionary algorithm," *IEEE Trans. on Cybernetics*, DOI:10.1109/TCYB.2014.2360752, 2014.

[3] Z. H. Zhan and J. Zhang, "Enhance differential evolution with random walk," in *Proc. Genetic Evol. Comput. Conf.*, Philadelphia, America, Jul. 2012, pp. 1513-1514.

[4] S. Das and P. N. Suganthan, "Differential Evolution: A Survey of the State-of-the-Art," *IEEE Tran. Evol. Comput.*, vol. 15, no. 1, pp. 4–31, 2011.

[5] M. M. Ali and A. Törn, "Population set based global optimization algorithms: Some modifications and numerical studies," *Comput. Oper. Res.*, vol. 31, no. 10, pp. 1703–1725, 2004.

[6] M. G. H. Omran, A. Salman, and A. P. Engelbrecht, "Self-adaptive differential evolution," *in Proc. Comput. Intell. Security*, Lecture Notes in Artificial Intelligence 3801. 2005, pp. 192–199

[7] Z. H. Zhan and J. Zhang, "Self-adaptive differential evolution based on PSO learning strategy," in *Proc. Genetic Evol. Comput. Conf.*,Portland, America, Jul., 2010, pp. 39-46..

[8] J. Brest, S. Greiner, B. Boskovic, M. Mernik, and V. Zumer, "Self-Adapting Control Parameters in Differential Evolution: A Comparative Study on Numerical Benchmark Problems," *IEEE Tran. Evol. Comput.*, vol. 10, no. 6, pp. 646–657, 2006.

[9] A. K. Qin, V. L. Huang, and P. N. Suganthan, "Differential Evolution Algorithm with Strategy Adaptation for Global Numerical Optimization," *IEEE Tran. Evol. Comput.*, vol. 13, no. 2, pp. 398–417, 2009.

[10] J. Zhang and A. C. Sanderson, "JADE: Adaptive differential evolution with optional external archive," *IEEE Tran. Evol. Comput.*, vol. 13, no. 5, pp. 945–958, 2009.

[11] S. M. Islam, S. Das, S. Ghosh, S. Roy, P. N. Suganthan, "An Adaptive Differential Evolution Algorithm With Novel Mutation and Crossover Strategies for Global Numerical Optimization" *IEEE Trans. Syst., Man, Cybern. B, Cybern.*, vol. 42, no. 2, pp. 482-500, Apr. 2012.

[12] R. Mallipeddi, P. N. Suganthan, Q. K. Pan, M. F. Tasgetiren, "Differential evolution algorithm with ensemble of parameters and mutation strategies" *Applied Soft Computing*, vol. 11, no. 2, pp. 1679-1696, Mar. 2011.

[13] Y. Wang, Z. X. Cai, Q. F. Zhang, "Differential evolution with composite trial vector generation strategies and control parameters" *IEEE Tran. Evol. Comput.*, vol. 15, no. 1, pp. 55-66, Feb. 2011.

[14] J. Teo, "Exploring dynamic self-adaptive populations in differential evolution," *Soft Comput. A Fusion Found. Methodol. Applicat.*, vol. 10, no. 8, pp. 673–686, 2006.

[15] J. Brest and M. S. Mauèec, "Population size reduction for the differential evolution algorithm," *Appl. Intell.*, vol. 29, no. 3, pp. 228–247, Dec. 2008.

[16] Z. H. Zhan and J. Zhang, "Co-evolutionary differential evolution with dynamic population size and adaptive migration strategy," in *Proc. Genetic Evol. Comput. Conf.*.,Dublin, Ireland, Jul., 2011, pp. 211-212.9.

[17] R. A. Sarker, S. M. Elsayed, T. Ray, "Differential evolution with dynamic parameters selection for optimization problems" *IEEE Tran. Evol. Comput.*, vol. 18, no. 5, pp. 689-707, Oct. 2014.

[18] A. E. Eiben and J. E. Smith, Introduction to Evolutionary Computing. Berlin, Germany: Springer, 2003.

[19] J. H. Holland, *Adaptation in Natural and Artificial Systems*. Ann Arbor, MI: The University of Michigan Press, 1975.

[20] Z. H. Zhan, J. Zhang, Y. Li, and H. Chung, "Adaptive particle swarm optimization," *IEEE Transactions on Systems, Man, and Cybernetics--Part B*, vol. 39, no. 6, pp. 1362-1381, Dec. 2009.

[21] W. J. Yu, M. Shen, W. N. Chen, Z. H. Zhan, Y. J. Gong, Y. Lin, O. Liu, J. Zhang, "Differential Evolution With Two-Level Parameter Adaptation", *IEEE Trans. Cybern.*, vol. 44, no. 7, pp. 1080-1099, Jul. 2014.

[22] F. Peng, K. Tang, G. Chen, and X. Yao, "Multi-start JADE with knowledge transfer for numerical optimization," in *IEEE CEC*, 2009, pp. 1889–1895.

[23] Z. Yang, J. Zhang, K. Tang, X. Yao, and A. C. Sanderson, "An adaptive coevolutionary differential evolution algorithm for large-scale optimization," in *Proc. IEEE CEC*, 2009, pp. 102–109.

[24] W. Gong, Z. Cai, C. X. Ling, and H. Li, "Enhanced differential evolution with adaptive strategies for numerical optimization," *IEEE Trans. On Systems, Man, and Cybernetics, Part B*, vol. 41, no. 2, pp. 397–413, 2011.

[25] R. Tanabe and A. Fukunaga, "Success-History Based Parameter Adaptation for Differential Evolution," in *IEEE CEC*, 2013, pp. 71–78.

[26] X. Yao, Y. Liu, and G. Lin, "Evolutionary programming made faster," *IEEE Trans. on Evol. Comput.*, vol. 3, no. 2, pp. 82–102, Jul. 1999.

[27] Z. H. Zhan, J. Zhang, Y. Li, and Y. H. Shi, "Orthogonal learning particle swarm optimization," *IEEE Transactions on Evolutionary Computation*, vol. 15, no. 6, pp. 832-847, Dec. 2011.

[28] Y. H. Li, Z. H. Zhan, S. J. Lin, J. Zhang, and X. N. Luo, "Competitive and cooperative particle swarm optimization with information sharing mechanism for global optimization problems," *Information Sciences*, vol. 293, no. 1, pp. 370-382, 2015.

[29] J. J. Liang, B. Y. Qu, P. N. Suganthan, "Problem Definitions and Evaluation Criteria for the CEC 2014 Special Session and Competition on Single Objective Real-Parameter Numerical Optimization," in *Proc. IEEE Congr. Evol. Comput.*, 2014.

Towards an Analysis of Self-Adaptive Evolution Strategies on the Noisy Ellipsoid Model: Progress Rate and Self-Adaptation Response

Alexander Melkozerov
Department of Television and Control
Tomsk State University
of Control Systems
and Radioelectronics
Lenin ave. 40, 634050 Tomsk, Russia
ame@tu.tusur.ru

Hans-Georg Beyer
Research Center Process and Product
Engineering
Department of Computer Science
Vorarlberg University of Applied Sciences
Hochschulstr. 1, A-6850 Dornbirn, Austria
hans-georg.beyer@fhv.at

ABSTRACT

This paper analyzes the multi-recombinant self-adaptive evolution strategy (ES), denoted as $(\mu/\mu_I, \lambda)$-σSA-ES on the convex-quadratic function class under the influence of noise, which is referred to as noisy ellipsoid model. Asymptotically exact progress rate and self-adaptation response measures are derived (i.e., for $N \to \infty$, N – search space dimensionality) for the considered objective function model and verified using experimental ES runs.

Categories and Subject Descriptors

I.2.6 [**Artificial Intelligence**]: Learning—*parameter learning*; G.1.6 [**Numerical Analysis**]: Optimization

Keywords

Evolution strategy, ellipsoid model, noise, self-adaptation, progress rate, mutation strength

1. INTRODUCTION

Theoretical analysis of evolutions strategies (ES) is an area of active research, where much of the recent effort has been devoted to the extension of the range of the test functions analyzed, including particular cases of the positive definite quadratic forms (PDQFs) [4]. The general case of the PDQF, referred to as general ellipsoid model, has been treated in [7, 5], where asymptotically exact quadratic progress rate and self-adaptation rate formulae have been obtained for the self-adaptation evolutionary strategy with intermediate recombination (the $(\mu/\mu_I, \lambda)$-σSA-ES). Based on these results, the expected value dynamics of the ES have been derived and in turn the optimal learning parameter, which provides for the highest possible convergence rate, has been calculated analytically.

Still, the aforementioned analysis has been done for the noise-free ellipsoid model which does not allow to account for noisy distortions of the objective function values often arising in practical optimization tasks. The aim of this paper is to extend the analysis of the $(\mu/\mu_I, \lambda)$-σSA-ES to the case of the noisy ellipsoid model and derive the corresponding local progress measures.

The paper is organized as follows. First, the noisy ellipsoid model to be analyzed is presented followed by the description of the the $(\mu/\mu_I, \lambda)$-σSA-ES algorithm. The noisy progress measures are introduced in Section 2, where their outcome is also compared with results of one-generation experiments. Section 3 is devoted to the self-adaptation response function, which is derived for the noisy ellipsoid model and tested for validity by comparison with the $(\mu/\mu_I, \lambda)$-σSA-ES experimental runs. Finally, the obtained results are discussed in the conclusion.

1.1 Noisy Ellipsoid Model

The consideration of noisy fitness environments is of particular importance because noise often arises in practical optimization tasks. For example, the objective function may depend on noisy physical measurements or computer simulations with simplified models. In both cases, the ES observes a noise-disturbed $F_{\text{noisy}}(\mathbf{y})$ value. The *perceived* fitness [3] $F_{\text{noisy}}(\mathbf{y})$ consists of an *ideal* noise-free fitness influenced by the noise term. Therefore, the noisy ellipsoid model is defined as

$$F_{\text{noisy}}(\mathbf{y}) = \sum_{i=1}^{N} a_i y_i^2 + \sigma_\epsilon(\mathbf{y}) Z, \quad \mathbf{y} \in \mathbb{R}^N, \quad a_i > 0, \qquad (1)$$

where $\sigma_\epsilon(\mathbf{y})$ is the *noise strength*, or standard deviation of the noise term, and Z is a random variate. Eq. (1) is a noise-disturbed model where the noise term represents random influence of such factors as measurement errors, approximations, or calculations with limited accuracy.

From a number of noise models considered for the ES analysis [1], it is assumed in this work that the distribution of Z is Gaussian, i.e., $Z \sim \mathcal{N}(0,1)$ and $\mathcal{N}(0,1)$ is a standard normally distributed random variate.

GECCO'15 July 11–15, 2015, Madrid, Spain

DOI: http://dx.doi.org/10.1145/2739480.2754800

1.2 ES Algorithm

The $(\mu/\mu_I, \lambda)$-σSA-ES algorithm is presented in Alg. 1. Note that a symbol with superscript (g) is used to refer to a value in a given generation g, $g = 0, 1, \ldots, g_{max}$. The subscript l after a symbol refers to a value associated with the lth offspring, $l = 1, 2, \ldots, \lambda$.

Algorithm 1 The algorithm of the $(\mu/\mu_I, \lambda)$-σSA-ES

1 $\sigma^{(0)} \leftarrow \sigma_{init}$, $\mathbf{y}^{(0)} \leftarrow \mathbf{y}_{init}$, $g \leftarrow 0$
2 **do**
3   **for** $l = 1, \ldots, \lambda$ **begin**
4     $\tilde{\sigma}_l \leftarrow \sigma^{(g)} e^{\tau \mathcal{N}_l(0,1)}$
5     $\tilde{\mathbf{z}}_l \leftarrow \mathcal{N}_l(\mathbf{0}, \mathbf{I})$
6     $\tilde{\mathbf{y}}_l \leftarrow \mathbf{y}^{(g)} + \tilde{\sigma}_l \tilde{\mathbf{z}}_l$
7     $\tilde{F}_l \leftarrow F(\tilde{\mathbf{y}}_l)$
8   **end**
9   $\tilde{\mathbf{F}}_{sort} \leftarrow \text{sort}\left(\tilde{F}_{1\ldots\lambda}\right)$
10   $\sigma^{(g+1)} \leftarrow \frac{1}{\mu}\sum_{m=1}^{\mu} \tilde{\sigma}_{m;\lambda}$
11   $\mathbf{y}^{(g+1)} \leftarrow \frac{1}{\mu}\sum_{m=1}^{\mu} \tilde{\mathbf{y}}_{m;\lambda}$
12   $g \leftarrow g + 1$
13 **until** termination criterion fulfilled

The parental mutation strength $\sigma^{(0)}$ and the parental parameter vector, or *parental centroid* $\mathbf{y}^{(0)}$ are initialized in line 1. λ offspring are generated from line 3 to line 8 in the following way. For each offspring, the mutation of $\sigma^{(g)}$ is performed in line 4 using the log-normal operator $e^{\tau \mathcal{N}_l(0,1)}$, where $\mathcal{N}_l(0, 1)$ is a $(0, 1)$ normally distributed random scalar. The learning parameter τ in the log-normal operator controls the self-adaptation rate. In line 5, direction of the mutation vector $\tilde{\sigma}_l \tilde{\mathbf{z}}_l$ is determined by means of a $(0, 1)$ normally distributed random vector $\mathcal{N}_l(\mathbf{0}, \mathbf{I})$. The offspring parameter vector $\tilde{\mathbf{y}}_l$ is generated in line 6 and used in the calculation of the objective function value $\tilde{\mathrm{F}}_l$ in line 7.

After creation, λ offspring are ranked according to their $\tilde{F}_l$ values in line 9. The recombination of offspring mutation strengths and parameter vectors is performed in lines 10–11 in order to obtain a new parental mutation strength $\sigma^{(g+1)}$ and a new parental parameter vector $\mathbf{y}^{(g+1)}$. The subscript $m; \lambda$ refers to the mth-best of λ offspring (the mth-smallest for minimization).

In line 13, the termination criterion is checked. If it is fulfilled, the current parental parameter vector is considered an approximation of the optimizer of the objective function $F(\mathbf{y})$. Otherwise, the algorithm returns to line 2.

2. NOISY PROGRESS RATE

First, a noisy version of the $(\mu/\mu_I, \lambda)$-σSA-ES progress rate, defined as

$$\varphi_i = \mathrm{E}\left[y_i^{(g)} - y_i^{(g+1)} | \mathbf{y}^{(g)}\right], \tag{2}$$

is derived which is used in the noisy quadratic progress rate formula obtained next.

Noise-disturbed objective function evaluations influence the $(\mu/\mu_I, \lambda)$-σSA-ES selection process because the offspring ranking depends on the perceived fitness $F_{\text{noisy}}(\mathbf{y})$. The influence of the noise on the selection is modeled by the noisy local quality change introduced in the following definition. Note that the noise-free local quality change definition

$$Q_{\mathbf{y}}(\mathbf{x}) := F(\mathbf{y} + \mathbf{x}) - F(\mathbf{y}) \tag{3}$$

can not be adapted to the noisy case by substitution of $F(\mathbf{y})$ with $F_{\text{noisy}}(\mathbf{y})$ because it leads to an incorrect formula with the noise term included twice. The $(\mu/\mu_I, \lambda)$-σSA-ES evaluates the objective function of each individual only once (as it uses the "comma"-selection which discards individuals from the previous generation), therefore, $Q_{\text{noisy}}(\mathbf{x})$ must contain one noise term.

Let $\mathbf{y}$ be the ES parental parameter vector and $\mathbf{x}$ be a mutation vector applied to it (cf. line 6 in Alg. 1). Then the noisy local quality change is defined as [6]

$$Q_{\text{noisy}}(\mathbf{x}, \mathbf{y}) := Q_{\mathbf{y}}(\mathbf{x}) + \sigma_\epsilon(\mathbf{y} + \mathbf{x})\mathcal{N}(0, 1), \tag{4}$$

where $Q_{\mathbf{y}}(\mathbf{x})$ is the noise-free local quality change given by Eq. (3) and $\sigma_\epsilon(\mathbf{y} + \mathbf{x})$ is the noise strength.

The noise strength $\sigma_\epsilon(\mathbf{y})$ in (4) may represent different noise models including the constant non-normalized noise model as well as the constant normalized noise model. However, for the latter it will be assumed that $\sigma_\epsilon(\mathbf{y}^{(g)}) \simeq \sigma_\epsilon(\tilde{\mathbf{y}}_l)$, which states that the noise strength values of the parental individual and offspring are sufficiently close to each other (this holds exactly for $N \to \infty$ or sufficiently small mutation steps). Using Eq. (4), the progress rate formula for the $(\mu/\mu_I, \lambda)$-σSA-ES on the noisy ellipsoid model is obtained in the next section.

2.1 Progress Rate φ

The derivation steps for the noisy progress rate formula are analogous to the noise-free case presented in [7] taking into account that $Q_{\text{noisy}}(\mathbf{x}, \mathbf{y})$ is used in place of $Q_{\mathbf{y}}(\mathbf{x})$. The resulting formula for the progress rate of the $(\mu/\mu_I, \lambda)$-ES along the ith axis of the noisy ellipsoid model (1) without dominating[1] coefficients a_i is

$$\varphi_i(\sigma) \simeq \frac{2\sigma c_{\mu/\mu,\lambda} y_i a_i}{\sqrt{\sigma_\epsilon^2/\sigma^2 + \sum_{j=1}^{N} 2a_j^2\left(2y_j^2 + \sigma^2\right)}}, \tag{5}$$

where the progress coefficient $c_{\mu/\mu,\lambda} := e_{\mu,\lambda}^{1,0}$ is a special case of generalized progress coefficients

$$e_{\mu,\lambda}^{a,b} = \frac{\lambda - \mu}{\sqrt{2\pi}^{a+1}}\binom{\lambda}{\mu}\int_{-\infty}^{+\infty}(-t)^b e^{-\frac{a+1}{2}t^2} \times (1 - \Phi(t))^{\lambda-\mu-1}\Phi(t)^{\mu-a}\mathrm{d}t, \tag{6}$$

The derivation of Eq. (5) is sketched in Appendix A.

Since the noise strength $\sigma_\epsilon(\mathbf{y})$ in general case depends on the parameter vector $\mathbf{y}$ of an individual, it is normalized in order to obtain formula invariant to the position in the search space. Departing from the normalization used for the sphere model [6] $\sigma_\epsilon^* = \sigma_\epsilon N/\left(2(R^{(g)})^2\right)$ (where $R^{(g)}$ is the distance to the optimizer at generation g), the following generalization is used for the noise strength normalization on the ellipsoid model

$$\sigma_\epsilon^* = \sigma_\epsilon \sum_{i=1}^{N} a_i \Big/ \left(2\sum_{j=1}^{N} a_j^2 y_j^2\right). \tag{7}$$

[1]This assumption guarantees that the Lindeberg condition is fulfilled and the central limit theorem can be used in the limit $N \to \infty$.

Applying it together with the mutation strength normalization

$$\sigma^{*(g)} = \sigma^{(g)} \sum_{i=1}^{N} a_i / \sqrt{\sum_{i=1}^{N} a_i^2 y_i^{(g)2}} \tag{8}$$

to the noisy progress rate (5) yields

$$\varphi_i(\sigma^*) \simeq \sigma^* c_{\mu/\mu,\lambda} a_i y_i / \left(\sqrt{1 + (\sigma_\epsilon^*/\sigma^*)^2} \sum_{j=1}^{N} a_j \right), \tag{9}$$

where the assumption

$$\frac{(\sigma^*)^2}{2} \cdot \frac{\sum_{j=1}^{N} a_j^2}{\left(\sum_{j=1}^{N} a_j\right)^2} \ll 1 \tag{10}$$

has been used. The assumption (10) is valid for sufficiently small σ^* values. For the cases $a_i = i, i^2$, it is fulfilled if $(\sigma^*)^2/N \ll 1$. The term $\sigma_\epsilon^*/\sigma^*$ in Eq. (9) is referred to as *noise-to-signal ratio*

$$\vartheta = \sigma_\epsilon^*/\sigma^*. \tag{11}$$

After the progress rate normalization

$$\varphi_i^* := \varphi_i \sum_{j=1}^{N} a_j \tag{12}$$

and substitution of ϑ, the normalized progress rate of the $(\mu/\mu_I, \lambda)$-ES on the noisy ellipsoid model reads

$$\varphi_i^*(\sigma^*) \simeq \sigma^* c_{\mu/\mu,\lambda} a_i y_i \frac{1}{\sqrt{1+\vartheta^2}}. \tag{13}$$

Eq. (13) shows that the noisy objective function evaluations negatively influence the $(\mu/\mu_I, \lambda)$-ES progress rate: The larger is the noise-to-signal ratio ϑ, the smaller is the progress rate. Note that Eq. (13) has the same deficiencies as its noise-free counterpart [7] $\varphi_i^*(\sigma^*) = \sigma^* c_{\mu/\mu,\lambda} a_i y_i$, in that it does not measure the approach toward the optimizer. To this end, the second-order y_i^2 term must be taken into account. Due to these reasons, Eq. (13) is used exclusively as a part of the noisy quadratic progress rate formula obtained in the next section.

2.2 Quadratic Progress Rate φ^{II}

The quadratic progress rate φ_i^{II} is defined as

$$\varphi_i^{II} = \mathrm{E}\left[\left(y_i^{(g)}\right)^2 - \left(y_i^{(g+1)}\right)^2 | \mathbf{y}^{(g)} \right]. \tag{14}$$

The expression for φ_i^{II} on the noisy ellipsoid model (1) is derived by considering expectations of the respective product moments. Using the derivation steps for the noise-free quadratic progress rate from [5], one obtains for the noisy case the same equation

$$\varphi_i^{II} = 2 y_i \varphi_i - \frac{2}{\mu^2} E_1 - \frac{1}{\mu^2} E_2, \tag{15}$$

which includes the noisy progress rate φ_i given by Eq. (5) and the product moments E_1 and E_2. The sums of product moments E_1 and E_2 for the noisy case are provided in Appendix B. Inserting Eq. (49) and (50) into (15) yields the quadratic progress rate formula

$$\varphi_i^{II}(\sigma) \simeq 2 y_i \varphi_i(\sigma) - \frac{\sigma^2}{\mu} \left[1 + \left((\mu-1) e_{\mu,\lambda}^{2,0} + e_{\mu,\lambda}^{1,1} \right) \frac{a_i^2 y_i^2}{\frac{\sigma_\epsilon^2}{4\sigma^2} + \sum_{j=1}^{N} a_j^2 \left(y_j^2 + \frac{\sigma^2}{2} \right)} \right], \tag{16}$$

where the progress rate $\varphi_i(\sigma)$ is given by (5) and the progress coefficients $e_{\mu,\lambda}^{2,0}$ and $e_{\mu,\lambda}^{1,1}$ are calculated using (6).

Applying to Eq. (16) the mutation strength normalization (8), taking into account the assumption (10) and the progress rate normalization (12) leads to

$$\varphi_i^{II*}(\sigma^*) \simeq 2 y_i \varphi_i^*(\sigma^*) - \frac{(\sigma^*)^2}{\mu \sum_{j=1}^{N} a_j} \left[\sum_{j=1}^{N} a_j^2 y_j^2 + \left((\mu-1) e_{\mu,\lambda}^{2,0} + e_{\mu,\lambda}^{1,1} \right) \frac{a_i^2 y_i^2}{1+\vartheta^2} \right], \tag{17}$$

where $\varphi_i^*(\sigma^*)$ is given by (13).

As expected, the noisy quadratic progress rate formula (17) yields for $\vartheta = 0$ the corresponding noise-free equation obtained in [5]. For $\vartheta > 0$, the gain term $2 y_i \varphi_i^*(\sigma^*)$ is decreased by a factor of $1/\sqrt{1+\vartheta^2}$ (cf. Eq. (13)). Interestingly, the second part in the loss term in Eq. (17), i.e., the last factor in the second line of (17) also gets smaller with increasing ϑ.

A simplified φ_i^{II*} formula can be obtained from Eq. (17) by discarding the expression $\left((\mu-1) e_{\mu,\lambda}^{2,0} + e_{\mu,\lambda}^{1,1} \right) a_i^2 y_i^2$ in the loss term

$$\varphi_i^{II*}(\sigma^*) \simeq 2\sigma^* c_{\mu/\mu,\lambda} a_i y_i^2 \frac{1}{\sqrt{1+\vartheta^2}} - \frac{(\sigma^*)^2}{\mu \sum_{j=1}^{N} a_j} \sum_{j=1}^{N} a_j^2 y_j^2. \tag{18}$$

Denormalization of Eq. (18) yields

$$\varphi_i^{II}(\sigma) \simeq \frac{2\sigma c_{\mu/\mu,\lambda} a_i y_i^2}{\sqrt{(1+\vartheta^2) \sum_{i=1}^{N} a_i^2 y_i^2}} - \frac{\sigma^2}{\mu}, \tag{19}$$

where $\vartheta^2 = \sigma_\epsilon^2 / \left(4\sigma^2 \sum_{i=1}^{N} a_i^2 y_i^2 \right)$. Eq. (19) is a rough approximation of Eq. (17), and its validity is checked in the next section by means of one-generation experiments.

2.3 One-Generation Experiments

In this section, the procedure for one-generation experiments is employed to compare the theoretical predictions of Eqs. (13), (17) and (18) with experimental results. In the experimental code, an important implementation detail is the noise strength denormalization: Due to the assumption $\sigma_\epsilon(\mathbf{y}^{(g)}) \approx \sigma_\epsilon(\tilde{\mathbf{y}}_l)$, the parental parameter vector $\mathbf{y}^{(g)}$ is used to denormalize σ_ϵ^* and the resulting single σ_ϵ participates in the $\tilde{F}_l$ calculation for all offspring.

First, the progress rate φ_i formulae (13) and (5) are checked in Fig. 1 using the $(3/3_I, 10)$-ES one-generation experiments for $a_i = 1$ and $a_i = i$. The experimental settings are $\sigma_\epsilon^* = 10$, $G = 10^6$ and $\mathbf{y}^{(0)} = \mathbf{1}$. Each point in Fig. 1 represents the mean of 100 one-generation experiments, while bars depict their standard deviations. φ_1^*/a_1 points for $N = 400$, $a_i = i$ are not shown due to large deviations.

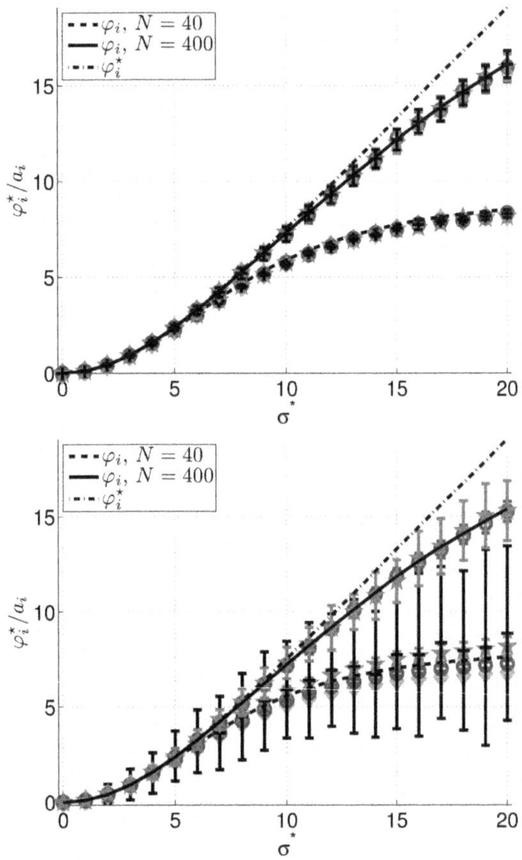

Figure 1: One-generation experiments for the $(3/3_I, 10)$-ES for $a_i = 1$ (upper figure) and $a_i = i$ (lower figure), $\sigma_\epsilon^* = 10$. Curves depict theoretical predictions of Eq. (13) (dash-dot lines) and (5) (dashed curves for $N = 40$ and solid curves for $N = 400$, $y_i = 1$), while points represent experimental results: $+$ φ_1^*/a_1, $\star$ $\varphi_{N/4}^*/a_{N/4}$, $\circ$ $\varphi_{N/2}^*/a_{N/2}$ and $\diamond$ φ_N^*/a_N.

In Fig. 1, the first-order φ_i^* results (dash-dot lines) obtained using Eq. (13) are depicted. Note that φ_i^* lines for $N = 40$ and $N = 400$ coincide due to the φ_i^*/a_i normalization. In comparison to the noise-free case, φ_i^* values are smaller since noisy objective function evaluations reduce the progress rate of the $(\mu/\mu_I, 10)$-ES. For small σ^*, the reduction is particularly large because the ES generates new offspring which lie close to the parental individuals and the difference between the ideal fitness values is dominated by the noise term (cf. Eq. (1)). Experimental φ_i^* mean values match theoretical curves for the same ranges of σ^* values as in the noise-free case. That is, errors due to assumptions used in the derivation of φ_i^* formulae do not increase for the noisy ellipsoid model and both Eqs. (13) and (5) remain asymptotically exact.

In Fig. 2, the quadratic progress rate φ_i^{II*} formula (17) and its approximation (18) are compared with the results of one-generation experiments. The experimental settings $G = 10^6$ and $\mathbf{y}^{(0)} = \mathbf{1}$ are the same as in the φ_i experiments. The results of the $(3/3_I, 10)$-ES one-generation experiments for $a_i = 1$ and $a_i = i$ are shown in Fig. 2.

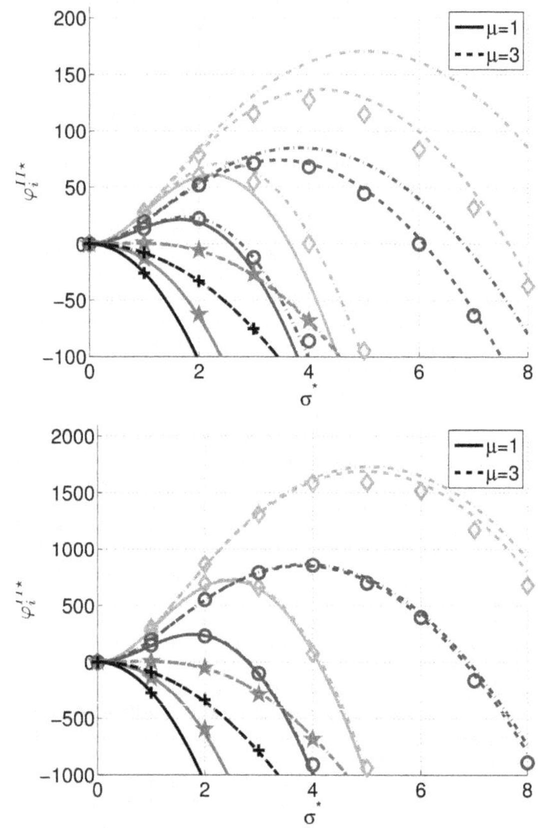

Figure 2: One-generation experiments for the $(3/3_I, 10)$-ES for $N = 40$ (upper figure) and $N = 400$ (lower figure), $\sigma_\epsilon^* = 2$. The solid curves and dashed curves depict theoretical predictions of Eq. (17) for $\mu = 1$ and $\mu = 3$, respectively, while points represent experimental results for $N = 40$ and $N = 400$ ($y_i = 1$): $+$ φ_1^{II*}/a_1, $\star$ $\varphi_{N/4}^{II*}/a_{N/4}$, $\circ$ $\varphi_{N/2}^{II*}/a_{N/2}$ and $\diamond$ φ_N^{II*}/a_N. Dot-dash curves show the results of the simplified formula (18).

According to the results depicted in Fig. 2, the quadratic progress rate approximation using Eq. (17) improves for $N = 400$ (lower figure) in comparison with $N = 40$ (upper figure) as solid and dashed curves corresponding to Eq. (17) are situated closer to the experimental points in the former case. This observation is in accordance to the fact that simplifications based on the assumption $N \to \infty$ have been made during the derivation of Eq. (17). Still, the experimental behavior is correctly reproduced in the $N = 40$ case as well: the $\varphi_i^{II*}(\sigma^*)$ dependency has the characteristic form with a maximum, after which the negative loss terms in φ_i^{II*} prevail over the positive gain term. The results of the simplified Eq. (18) (dot-dash curves) approach the curves corresponding to Eq. (17) for sufficiently small σ^* and replicate the functional dependency of Eq. (17) for larger σ^* values. Thus, Eq. (18) can be regarded as an upper bound estimate of the quadratic progress rate of the $(\mu/\mu_I, \lambda)$-ES on the noisy ellipsoid model.

3. THE SELF-ADAPTATION RESPONSE

The self-adaptation response (SAR) function is defined as the expected relative mutation strength change from the generation g to $(g+1)$

$$\psi = \mathrm{E}\left[\left(\sigma^{(g+1)} - \sigma^{(g)}\right)/\sigma^{(g)} \mid \mathbf{y}^{(g)}, \sigma^{(g)}\right]. \quad (20)$$

The derivation steps for the SAR formula are similar to the noise-free case presented in [7]. One obtains for the $(\mu/\mu_I, \lambda)$-σSA-ES on the noisy ellipsoid model (1)

$$\psi(\sigma) \simeq \tau^2 \left(\frac{1}{2} + e^{1,1}_{\mu,\lambda} \frac{\sum_{i=1}^{N} 2a_i^2\left(2y_i^2 + \sigma^2\right)}{\frac{\sigma_\epsilon^2}{\sigma^2} + \sum_{i=1}^{N} 2a_i^2\left(2y_i^2+\sigma^2\right)} - c_{\mu/\mu,\lambda}\sigma \frac{2\sum_{i=1}^{N} a_i}{\sqrt{\sigma_\epsilon^2/\sigma^2 + \sum_{i=1}^{N} 2a_i^2(2y_i^2+\sigma^2)}} \right), \quad (21)$$

where the progress coefficients $c_{\mu/\mu,\lambda} = e^{1,0}_{\mu,\lambda}$ and $e^{1,1}_{\mu,\lambda}$ are special cases of generalized progress coefficients (6) and τ is the learning parameter (cf. line 4 in Alg. 1). A very short sketch of the derivation of Eq. (21) is presented in App. C.

Applying to Eq. (21) the normalization (8) and taking into account the assumption (10) yields

$$\psi(\sigma^*) \simeq \tau^2 \left(\frac{1}{2} + e^{1,1}_{\mu,\lambda} \frac{1}{1+\vartheta^2} - c_{\mu/\mu,\lambda}\sigma^* \frac{1}{\sqrt{1+\vartheta^2}} \right). \quad (22)$$

Similar to the case of the noise-free SAR function [7], the normalized noisy SAR formula (22) has the same form as the normalized SAR function obtained in [9] for the $(\mu/\mu_I, \lambda)$-σSA-ES on the noisy sphere model. That is, Eq. (22) generalizes the previously published result to the class of noisy ellipsoid models (1) by introducing an appropriate mutation strength normalization.

3.1 One-Generation Experiments

In Fig. 3, the results of one-generation experiments are shown for the $(3/3_I, 10)$-σSA-ES with initial parameter vector $\mathbf{y}^{(0)} = \mathbf{1}$, learning parameter $\tau = 1/\sqrt{N}$ on the sphere model $a_i = 1$ and ellipsoid model with coefficients $a_i = i$ and $a_i = i^2$. Each point represents the mean of 10 one-generation experiments, while the corresponding standard deviations are smaller than the size of the data points and not shown. Note that the ψ values on the vertical axis are multiplied by N. Due to the mutation strength normalization (8), experimental points for $a_i = 1$, $a_i = i$ and $a_i = i^2$ coincide for the $N = 400$ case.

The experimental results in Fig. 3 are presented for 4 noise strength values (from the bottom group of curves to the top: solid curves for $\sigma^*_\epsilon = 1$, curves with longer dashes for $\sigma^*_\epsilon = 5$, solid curves for $\sigma^*_\epsilon = 10$, and curves with shorter dashes for $\sigma^*_\epsilon = 20$, respectively). The experimental points in Fig. 3 match the theoretical curves based on Eqs. (22) (single black curves) and (21) (groups of 3 curves with different colors) for sufficiently small σ^* values. These borderline σ^* values increase for larger N (cf. the upper figure for $N = 40$ and the lower figure for $N = 400$) due to the assumption $N \to \infty$ used in the analysis. As expected, the curves corresponding to Eq. (21) lie closer to the experimental points than the curves depicting the simplified Eq. (22) with the difference more pronounced for the smaller $N = 40$. The approximation quality appears to improve with increasing noise (compare, for example, the lower curves for $\sigma^*_\epsilon = 1$ with the upper curves for $\sigma^*_\epsilon = 20$). This issue does not stem from the better approximation for the larger noise strength, but is due to smaller SAR values for higher noise strengths and can be resolved with appropriate normalization.

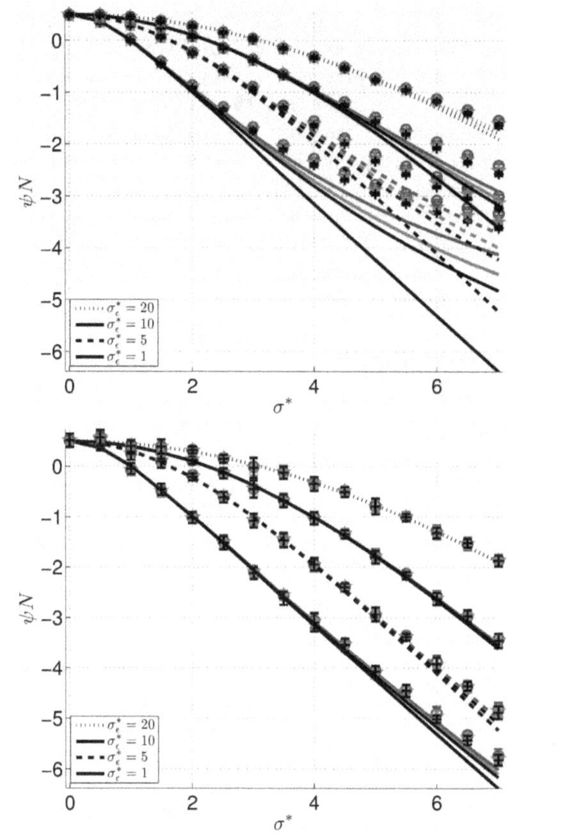

Figure 3: One-generation experiments for the $(3/3_I, 10)$-σSA-ES for $N = 40$ (upper figure) and $N = 400$ (lower figure), $y_i = 1$, $\tau = 1/\sqrt{N}$, $\sigma^*_\epsilon = 1, 5, 10, 20$ from the bottom group of curves to the top. Curves depict theoretical predictions of Eqs. (22) and (21), respectively, multiplied by N, while points represent experimental results for $N = 40$ and $N = 400$: $+$ $a_i = 1$, $\star$ $a_i = i$, $\circ$ $a_i = i^2$.

4. SUMMARY AND CONCLUSIONS

The analysis of the $(\mu/\mu_I, \lambda)$-σSA-ES on the noisy ellipsoid model (1) between two consecutive generations has been performed. To this end, an asymptotically exact noisy progress rate (9) and noisy quadratic progress rate (17) have been derived along with corresponding simplified formulae (13) and (18), respectively. Comparison with experiments showed that the obtained formula predicts the noisy progress rate of the $(\mu/\mu_I, \lambda)$-ES satisfactorily even for the $N = 40$ case despite of the $N \to \infty$ assumption used in the derivations.

As one can conclude from the experimental results, the SAR function is satisfactorily approximated by Eq. (22) for small mutation strength values. Since the $(\mu/\mu_I, \lambda)$-σSA-

ES in the steady state usually yields $\sigma^*_{\text{st}} = 0, \ldots, 2.5$, this behavior should not pose a problem even for $N = 40$. For smaller N, a more precise Eq. (21) can be used, although one should keep in mind that the assumption $N \to \infty$ has been used in the derivation of the SAR function.

Following the steps of the noise-free analysis further, the continuation of the work will be the formulation of a time discrete system describing the evolutionary dynamics of the $(\mu/\mu_I, \lambda)$-σSA-ES. Solutions of this system will lead to an analytical formula for the optimal learning parameter of the self-adaptive ES on the noisy ellipsoid model.

Acknowledgments

This work was supported by the Austrian Science Fund FWF under grants P19069-N18 and P22649-N23. The work of A. Melkozerov was supported by the state contract 8.1802. 2014/K of the Russian Ministry of Education and Science (software development), the RFBR grant 14-29-0925 (analytic derivations), and the RSF grant 14-19-01232 (numerical experiments) in the TUSUR University.

5. REFERENCES

[1] Arnold, D.V. and Beyer, H.-G. A general noise model and its effects on evolution strategy performance. *IEEE Trans. Evol. Comp.*, 10(4) (2006), 380–391.

[2] Arnold, D.V. *Noisy Optimization with Evolution Strategies.* Kluwer, Dordrecht, 2002.

[3] Arnold, D.V. and Beyer, H.-G. Performance analysis of evolution strategies with multi-recombination in high-dimensional search spaces disturbed by noise. *Theoretical Computer Science*, 289 (1) (2002), 629–647.

[4] Beyer, H.-G. and Finck, S. Performance of the $(\mu/\mu_I, \lambda)$-σSA-ES on a class of PDQFs. *IEEE Trans. Evol. Comp.*, 14 (3) (2010), 400–418.

[5] Beyer, H.-G. and Melkozerov, A. The dynamics of self-adaptive multi-recombinant evolution strategies on the general ellipsoid model. *IEEE Trans. Evol. Comp.*, 18(5) (2014), 764–778.

[6] Beyer, H.-G. *The Theory of Evolution Strategies.* Natural Computing Series. Springer, Heidelberg, 2001.

[7] Melkozerov, A. and Beyer, H.-G. On the analysis of self-adaptive evolution strategies on elliptic model: first results. In *GECCO'10*, pp. 369–376, ACM, 2010.

[8] Melkozerov, A. and Beyer, H.-G. *On the Derivation of the Progress Rate and Self-Adaptation Response for the $(\mu/\mu_I, \lambda)$-σSA-ES on the Noisy Ellipsoid Model* (Technical Report TR 2015/01). Vorarlberg University of Applied Sciences, PPE, Dornbirn, Austria, 2015.

[9] Meyer-Nieberg, S. *Self-Adaptation in Evolution Strategies.* PhD thesis, University of Dortmund, CS Department, Dortmund, Germany, 2007.

APPENDIX

A brief outline of steps necessary to obtain the progress rate and the SAR formulae is presented in the following. For a detailed treatment it is referred to [8].

A. NOISY PROGRESS RATE

The goal of this section is to determine the $(\mu/\mu_I, \lambda)$-ES progress rate along the ith axis of the noisy ellipsoid model. Following the approach introduced in [7], the ES progress along each axis is considered separately. That is, the noisy progress rate along the ith axis of the ellipsoid model (1) is defined as (2) leading to

$$\varphi_i = \frac{1}{\mu}\sum_{m=1}^{\mu} \mathrm{E}\left[y_i^{(g)} - \left(\tilde{y}_i^{(g)}\right)_{m;\lambda} |\mathbf{y}^{(g)}\right], \tag{23}$$

where the subscript $m;\lambda$ refers to the mth-best of the λ offspring. To simplify notation, indices (g) are omitted in the following derivations. Introducing the mutation vector $\mathbf{x}_l = \tilde{\sigma}_l \tilde{\mathbf{z}}_l$ (note that σ is fixed and $\mathbf{x}_l = \sigma\tilde{\mathbf{z}}_l$ in the progress rate analysis due to the assumption $\tau \overset{N\to\infty}{\to} 0$) yields [7]

$$\varphi_i = -\frac{1}{\mu}\sum_{m=1}^{\mu}\int_{-\infty}^{\infty} x p_{m;\lambda}(x|\mathbf{y})\,\mathrm{d}x. \tag{24}$$

The density of induced order statistics $p_{m;\lambda}(x|\mathbf{y})$ in (24) has been obtained in [7] for $N \to \infty$ and reads

$$p_{m;\lambda}(x|\mathbf{y}) = \frac{\lambda!}{(m-1)!(\lambda-m)!} p_x(x) \int_{-\infty}^{+\infty} p_Q(q|x,\mathbf{y}) \times P_Q(q|\mathbf{y})^{m-1}\left[1 - P_Q(q|\mathbf{y})\right]^{\lambda-m} \mathrm{d}q, \tag{25}$$

where $p_Q(q|x,\mathbf{y})$ is the conditional density and $P_Q(q|\mathbf{y})$ is the cumulative distribution function to be determined below. Plugging (25) into (24), changing the order of integration and denoting the inner integral by

$$I_i(q|\mathbf{y}) := \int_{-\infty}^{+\infty} x p_x(x) p_Q(q|x,\mathbf{y})\,\mathrm{d}x, \tag{26}$$

the progress rate formula (24) reads

$$\varphi_i = -\frac{1}{\mu}\sum_{m=1}^{\mu}\frac{\lambda!}{(m-1)!(\lambda-m)!}\int_{-\infty}^{+\infty} I_i(q|\mathbf{y}) \times P_Q(q|\mathbf{y})^{m-1}\left[1-P_Q(q|\mathbf{y})\right]^{\lambda-m}\mathrm{d}q. \tag{27}$$

To determine $P_Q(q|\mathbf{y})$, the normal approximation is used

$$P_Q(q|\mathbf{y}) \simeq \Phi\left(\frac{q - \mathrm{E}\left[Q_{\text{noisy}}(\mathbf{x},\mathbf{y})\right]}{\mathrm{D}\left[Q_{\text{noisy}}(\mathbf{x},\mathbf{y})\right]}\right), \tag{28}$$

where $\mathrm{E}\left[Q_{\text{noisy}}(\mathbf{x},\mathbf{y})\right]$ is the expectation and $\mathrm{D}\left[Q_{\text{noisy}}(\mathbf{x},\mathbf{y})\right]$ is the standard deviation of the noisy local quality change (4). Inserting the expansion of $Q_{\mathbf{y}}(\mathbf{x})$ into Eq. (4) yields

$$Q_{\text{noisy}}(\mathbf{x},\mathbf{y}) = \sum_{j=1}^{N} a_j\left(2y_jx_j + x_j^2\right) + \sigma_\epsilon \mathcal{N}(0,1), \tag{29}$$

where x_j are the components of the mutation vector $\mathbf{x}$. The expectation of $Q_{\text{noisy}}(\mathbf{x},\mathbf{y})$ is equal to the expectation of the noise free $Q_{\mathbf{y}}(\mathbf{x})$

$$\mathrm{E}\left[Q_{\text{noisy}}(\mathbf{x},\mathbf{y})\right] = \sigma^2 A_0,\ A_n := \sum_{j\neq n}^{N} a_j. \tag{30}$$

To determine $\mathrm{D}\left[Q_{\text{noisy}}(\mathbf{x},\mathbf{y})\right]$, $Q_{\text{noisy}}(\mathbf{x},\mathbf{y})$ is written down as a sum of noise-free components and the noisy term $Q_{\text{noisy}} = \sum_{j=1}^{N}\left(Q_{\mathbf{y}}\right)_j + \sigma_\epsilon\mathcal{N}(0,1)$, where each component $\left(Q_{\mathbf{y}}\right)_j$ is defined as $\left(Q_{\mathbf{y}}\right)_j := a_j\left(2y_jx_j + x_j^2\right)$. $\mathrm{D}\left[Q_{\text{noisy}}(\mathbf{x},\mathbf{y})\right]$ is calculated then by means of the variances

$$\mathrm{D}^2\left[Q_{\text{noisy}}(\mathbf{x},\mathbf{y})\right]=\sum_{j=1}^{N}\mathrm{D}^2\left[(Q_{\mathbf{y}})_j\right]+\sigma_\epsilon^2, \quad (31)$$

where $\mathrm{D}^2\left[(Q_{\mathbf{y}})_j\right]$ has been obtained in [7] $\mathrm{D}^2\left[(Q_{\mathbf{y}})_j\right] = 2a_j^2\sigma^2\left(2y_j^2+\sigma^2\right)$. The standard deviation of Q_{noisy} is

$$\mathrm{D}\left[Q_{\text{noisy}}(\mathbf{x},\mathbf{y})\right]=\sigma\sqrt{B_0+\sigma_\epsilon^2/\sigma^2},\ B_n:=\sum_{j\neq n}^{N}2a_j^2\left(2y_j^2+\sigma^2\right). \quad (32)$$

After inserting (30) and (32) into (28) the conditional probability distribution reads

$$P_Q(q|\mathbf{y})\simeq\Phi\left(\left(q-\sigma^2A_0\right)/\left(\sigma\sqrt{B_0+\sigma_\epsilon^2/\sigma^2}\right)\right). \quad (33)$$

The conditional density in Eq. (25) is calculated analogously to the noise free case [7]

$$p_Q(q|x,\mathbf{y})\simeq\frac{1}{\sqrt{2\pi}\mathrm{D}\left[Q_{\text{noisy}}\right]}\exp\left[-\frac{1}{2}\left(\frac{q-\mathrm{E}\left[Q_{\text{noisy}}\right]}{\mathrm{D}\left[Q_{\text{noisy}}\right]}\right)^2\right], \quad (34)$$

except that the noisy local quality change Q_{noisy} is used. First, the ith summand of (29) is taken out and the substitution $x_i=\sigma z_i$ is used. Next, under the assumption that $|\sigma z_i|\ll|2y_i|$ for $\sigma\to0$, a rough $Q_{\text{noisy}}(\mathbf{x},\mathbf{y})$ approximation is introduced

$$Q_{\text{noisy}}(\mathbf{x},\mathbf{y})\approx2a_iy_ix_i+\sum_{j\neq i}^{N}a_j\left(2y_jx_j+x_j^2\right)+\sigma_\epsilon\mathcal{N}(0,1). \quad (35)$$

The validity of (35) is verified experimentally. Keeping $x_i = x$ fixed (since this is the condition, $\mathrm{D}^2[x]=0$) yields

$$\mathrm{E}\left[Q_{\text{noisy}}(\mathbf{x},\mathbf{y})\,|x\right]=2a_iy_ix+\sigma^2A_i. \quad (36)$$

and

$$\mathrm{D}^2\left[Q_{\text{noisy}}(\mathbf{x},\mathbf{y})\,|x\right]=\sigma^2\sum_{j\neq i}^{N}2a_j^2\left(2y_j^2+\sigma^2\right)+\sigma_\epsilon^2, \quad (37)$$

which leads to $\mathrm{D}\left[Q_{\text{noisy}}(\mathbf{x},\mathbf{y})\,|x\right]=\sigma\sqrt{B_i+\sigma_\epsilon^2/\sigma^2}$. Inserting (36) and $\mathrm{D}\left[Q_{\text{noisy}}(\mathbf{x},\mathbf{y})\,|x\right]$ into (34) results in

$$p_Q(q|x,\mathbf{y})\simeq\frac{1}{\sqrt{2\pi}\sigma\sqrt{B_i+\sigma_\epsilon^2/\sigma^2}}\times\exp\left[-\frac{1}{2}\left(\frac{q-2a_iy_ix-\sigma^2A_i}{\sigma\sqrt{B_i+\sigma_\epsilon^2/\sigma^2}}\right)^2\right]. \quad (38)$$

Inserting (33) and (38) into (26) and substituting $t=x/\sigma$ yields

$$I_i(q|\mathbf{y})\simeq\frac{1}{2\pi\sqrt{B_i+\sigma_\epsilon^2/\sigma^2}}\int_{-\infty}^{\infty}t\mathrm{e}^{-\frac{1}{2}t^2}\times\exp\left[-\frac{1}{2}\left(\frac{q-2y_ia_i\sigma t-\sigma^2A_i}{\sigma\sqrt{B_i+\sigma_\epsilon^2/\sigma^2}}\right)^2\right]\mathrm{d}t. \quad (39)$$

Further an integral formula from [6] is applied to (39) and the result is simplified by neglecting σ^2a_i and σ^2 terms under assumption that the resulting error is negligible for $N\to\infty$. Inserting the result and (33) into Eq. (27), setting $s=\frac{q-\sigma^2A_0}{\sigma\sqrt{B_0+\sigma_\epsilon^2/\sigma^2}}$ and rearranging the resulting equation leads to an equation, where the sum is substituted by an integral [6]. Using the substitution $v=1-\Phi(t)$ and exchanging the order of integration leads to

$$\varphi_i\simeq\frac{2\sigma y_ia_i}{\sqrt{B_0+\sigma_\epsilon^2/\sigma^2}}\frac{\lambda-\mu}{2\pi}\binom{\lambda}{\mu}\int_{t=-\infty}^{t=\infty}\mathrm{e}^{-t^2}\times\left(1-\Phi(t)\right)^{\lambda-\mu-1}\left(\Phi(t)\right)^{\mu-1}\mathrm{d}t. \quad (40)$$

Comparing the resulting integral with (6), the coefficient $c_{\mu/\mu,\lambda}=e_{\mu,\lambda}^{1,0}$ is recognized leading to the final formula (5).

B. NOISY QUADRATIC PROGRESS RATE

The product moments E_1 and E_2 in the noisy quadratic progress (15) are given by [5]

$$E_1=\sigma^2\mathrm{E}\left[\sum_{l=2}^{\mu}\sum_{k=1}^{l-1}z_{k;\lambda}z_{l;\lambda}|\mathbf{y}\right],\ E_2=\sigma^2\mathrm{E}\left[\sum_{m=1}^{\mu}z_{m;\lambda}^2|\mathbf{y}\right], \quad (41)$$

where the $z_{k;\lambda}$ noisy order statistics correspond to the j-components of the mutation vector $\mathbf{x}_{k;\lambda}$ producing the kth best offspring $\tilde{\mathbf{y}}_{k;\lambda}=\mathbf{y}+\mathbf{x}_{k;\lambda}=\mathbf{y}+\tilde{\sigma}_{k;\lambda}\mathbf{z}_{k;\lambda}$. The kth best offspring is ranked according to its objective function value $\tilde{F}(\tilde{\mathbf{y}}_{k;\lambda})$ which depends on the random vector $\mathbf{z}_{k;\lambda}=\mathcal{N}(\mathbf{0},\mathbf{I})$. Since the progress rate analysis is performed for small τ ($\tau\to\infty$), it follows that $\tilde{\mathbf{y}}_{k;\lambda}=\mathbf{y}+\sigma\mathbf{z}_{k;\lambda}$.

To compute E_1 and E_2, the local quality change is considered first. Its expansion leads to

$$Q_{\text{noisy}}(\mathbf{x},\mathbf{y})=2\sigma a_jy_j\left(z_j\right)_{k;\lambda}+2\sigma\sum_{i\neq j}^{N}a_iy_i\left(z_i\right)_{k;\lambda}+\sigma^2\sum_{i=1}^{N}a_i\left(z_i\right)_{k;\lambda}^2+\sigma_\epsilon\mathcal{N}(0,1). \quad (42)$$

Dividing both sides by $2\sigma a_jy_j$ and introducing the quotient $Q_{\text{noisy}}(\mathbf{x},\mathbf{y})/2\sigma a_jy_j=:v_{k;\lambda}$ yields

$$v_{k;\lambda}=\left(z_j\right)_{k;\lambda}+\sum_{i\neq j}^{N}\frac{a_iy_i}{a_jy_j}\left(z_i\right)_{k;\lambda}+\frac{\sigma}{2}\sum_{i=1}^{N}\frac{a_i}{a_jy_j}\left(z_i\right)_{k;\lambda}^2+\frac{\sigma_\epsilon}{2\sigma a_jy_j}\mathcal{N}(0,1). \quad (43)$$

Equation (43) is a sum of the random variate $\left(z_j\right)_{k;\lambda}$, two sum expressions and a noise term. For $N\to\infty$, the central limit theorem can be applied to the second and third term in (43) yielding an approximate normal distribution

$$v_{k;\lambda}=\left(z_j\right)_{k;\lambda}+\mathcal{N}\left(\frac{\sigma\sum_{i=1}^{N}a_i}{2a_jy_j},\frac{1}{a_j^2y_j^2}\left(\sum_{i\neq j}^{N}a_i^2y_i^2+\frac{\sigma^2}{2}\sum_{i=1}^{N}a_i^2+\frac{\sigma_\epsilon^2}{4\sigma^2}\right)\right). \quad (44)$$

The kth random variate $\left(z_j\right)_{k;\lambda}$ in Eq. (44) corresponds to the kth best $Q_{\text{noisy}}(\mathbf{x},\mathbf{y})$ value which is proportional to $v_{k;\lambda}$. Considering the second term in Eq. (44) as a noise term, the variates $\left(z_j\right)_{k;\lambda}$ can be identified as noisy order statistics or concomitants of $v_{k;\lambda}$.

The sums of product moments of $(z_j)_{k;\lambda}$ have been calculated in [5]

$$E_1 = \mu(\mu-1)\frac{\sigma^2}{2}\rho^2 e^{2,0}_{\mu,\lambda},\ E_2 = \mu\sigma^2\left(1+\rho^2 e^{1,1}_{\mu,\lambda}\right), \tag{45}$$

where ρ is the correlation coefficient [2]

$$\rho = 1/\sqrt{1+\beta^2}. \tag{46}$$

As follows from Eq. (44), the variance β^2 in (46) is expressed as

$$\beta^2 = \frac{1}{a_j^2 y_j^2}\left(\sum_{i\neq j}^{N} a_i^2 y_i^2 + \frac{\sigma^2}{2}\sum_{i=1}^{N} a_i^2 + \frac{\sigma_\epsilon^2}{4\sigma^2}\right). \tag{47}$$

Thus the correlation coefficient ρ for the noisy case reads

$$\rho = |a_j y_j| / \sqrt{\frac{\sigma_\epsilon^2}{4\sigma^2} + \sum_{i=1}^{N} a_i^2\left(y_i^2 + \frac{\sigma^2}{2}\right)}. \tag{48}$$

Inserting Eq. (48) into Eqs. (45), the final formulae for the expectations of product moments are obtained

$$E_1 \simeq \mu(\mu-1)\frac{\sigma^2}{2}\frac{a_j^2 y_j^2 e^{2,0}_{\mu,\lambda}}{\frac{\sigma_\epsilon^2}{4\sigma^2} + \sum\limits_{i=1}^{N} a_i^2\left(y_i^2 + \frac{\sigma^2}{2}\right)}, \tag{49}$$

$$E_2 \simeq \mu\sigma^2\left(1 + \frac{a_j^2 y_j^2 e^{1,1}_{\mu,\lambda}}{\frac{\sigma_\epsilon^2}{4\sigma^2} + \sum\limits_{i=1}^{N} a_i^2\left(y_i^2 + \frac{\sigma^2}{2}\right)}\right). \tag{50}$$

C. THE NOISY SAR FUNCTION

The derivation of the SAR formula for the $(\mu/\mu_I,\lambda)$-σSA-ES on the noisy ellipsoid model follows the analysis steps for its noise-free counterpart described in [7]. The starting point is the integral representation of the SAR function [7]

$$\psi(\sigma) = \frac{1}{\mu}\sum_{m=1}^{\mu}\int_0^{\infty}\left(\frac{\tilde{\sigma}-\sigma}{\sigma}\right) p_{m;\lambda}(\tilde{\sigma}|\sigma)\,\mathrm{d}\tilde{\sigma}, \tag{51}$$

where $p_{m;\lambda}(\tilde{\sigma}|\sigma)$ is the density of induced order statistics. The $p_{m;\lambda}(\tilde{\sigma}|\sigma)$ formula reads [7]

$$p_{m;\lambda}(\tilde{\sigma}|\sigma) = \frac{\lambda!}{(m-1)!(\lambda-m)!} p_\sigma(\tilde{\sigma}|\sigma)\int_{-\infty}^{\infty} p_Q(q|\tilde{\sigma}) \times P_Q(q|\sigma)^{m-1}\left(1-P_Q(q|\sigma)\right)^{\lambda-m}\mathrm{d}q, \tag{52}$$

where $p_\sigma(\tilde{\sigma}|\sigma)$ is the distribution density [6]

$$p_\sigma(\tilde{\sigma}|\sigma) = \frac{1}{\sqrt{2\pi}\tau\tilde{\sigma}}\exp\left[-\frac{1}{2}\left(\frac{\ln(\tilde{\sigma}/\sigma)}{\tau}\right)^2\right]. \tag{53}$$

The conditional probability distribution $P_Q(q|\sigma)$ is calculated using the formula

$$P_Q(q|\sigma) \simeq \int_0^{\infty}\Phi\left(\frac{q-\tilde{\sigma}^2 A_0}{\tilde{\sigma}\sqrt{\tilde{B}_0 + \sigma_\epsilon^2/\tilde{\sigma}^2}}\right)p_\sigma(\tilde{\sigma}|\sigma)\mathrm{d}\tilde{\sigma}, \tag{54}$$

where $\tilde{B}_0 = \sum\limits_{j=0}^{N} 2a_j^2\left(2y_j^2+\tilde{\sigma}^2\right)$. For sufficiently small τ, the integral in (54) can be approximated by [6] $P_Q(q|\sigma) \simeq \Phi\left(\frac{q-\mathrm{E}[\sigma]}{\mathrm{D}[\sigma]}\right)$, where the expectation $\mathrm{E}[\sigma] = \sigma^2 A_0$ and the standard deviation $\mathrm{D}[\sigma] = \sigma\sqrt{B_0+\sigma_\epsilon^2/\sigma^2}$ have been calculated in Section A. Inserting these results yields

$$P_Q(q|\sigma) \simeq \Phi\left(\frac{q-\sigma^2 A_0}{\sigma\sqrt{B_0+\sigma_\epsilon^2/\sigma^2}}\right) \tag{55}$$

Approximating $p_Q(q|\tilde{\sigma})$ as normal distribution yields

$$p_Q(q|\tilde{\sigma}) \simeq \frac{1}{\sqrt{2\pi}\mathrm{D}[Q_{\text{noisy}}|\tilde{\sigma}]}\exp\left[-\frac{1}{2}\left(\frac{q-\mathrm{E}[Q_{\text{noisy}}|\tilde{\sigma}]}{\mathrm{D}[Q_{\text{noisy}}|\tilde{\sigma}]}\right)^2\right]. \tag{56}$$

The expectation $\mathrm{E}[Q_{\text{noisy}}(\mathbf{x},\mathbf{y})|\tilde{\sigma}]$ and standard deviation $\mathrm{D}[Q_{\text{noisy}}(\mathbf{x},\mathbf{y})|\tilde{\sigma}]$ can be obtained similarly to results in Section A. Taking into account these results, one obtains

$$p_Q(q|\tilde{\sigma}) \simeq \frac{1}{\sqrt{2\pi}\tilde{\sigma}\sqrt{\tilde{B}_0+\sigma_\epsilon^2/\tilde{\sigma}^2}}\exp\left[-\frac{1}{2}\left(\frac{q-\tilde{\sigma}^2 A_0}{\tilde{\sigma}\sqrt{\tilde{B}_0+\sigma_\epsilon^2/\tilde{\sigma}^2}}\right)^2\right]. \tag{57}$$

Inserting Eqs. (57) and (55) into (52) and Eq. (52) into (51) yields

$$\psi \simeq \frac{1}{\mu}\sum_{m=1}^{\mu}\int_0^{\infty}\left(\frac{\tilde{\sigma}-\sigma}{\sigma}\right)\frac{\lambda!}{(m-1)!(\lambda-m)!}p_\sigma(\tilde{\sigma}|\sigma) \times \frac{\sigma}{\tilde{\sigma}}\sqrt{\frac{B_0+\sigma_\epsilon^2/\sigma^2}{\tilde{B}_0+\sigma_\epsilon^2/\tilde{\sigma}^2}}\int_{-\infty}^{\infty}\frac{1}{\sqrt{2\pi}}\mathrm{e}^{-\frac{1}{2}\left(\frac{\sigma\sqrt{B_0+\sigma_\epsilon^2/\sigma^2}s - A_0\left(\tilde{\sigma}^2-\sigma^2\right)}{\tilde{\sigma}\sqrt{\tilde{B}_0+\sigma_\epsilon^2/\tilde{\sigma}^2}}\right)^2} \times \Phi(s)^{m-1}\left(1-\Phi(s)\right)^{\lambda-m}\mathrm{d}s\mathrm{d}\tilde{\sigma}, \tag{58}$$

where the substitution $s = \left(q-\sigma^2 A_0\right)/\left(\sigma\sqrt{B_0+\sigma_\epsilon^2/\sigma^2}\right)$ has been employed.

The sum in (58) can be expressed by an integral representation of the incomplete regularized beta function. After a further transformation and an exchange of the integration order one ends up with a triple integral

$$\psi \simeq \frac{\lambda-\mu}{\sqrt{2\pi}}\binom{\lambda}{\mu}\int_0^{\infty}\left(\frac{\tilde{\sigma}-\sigma}{\sigma}\right)p_\sigma(\tilde{\sigma}|\sigma) \times \frac{1}{\sqrt{2\pi}}\int_{p=-\infty}^{p=+\infty}\mathrm{e}^{-\frac{1}{2}p^2}\left(1-\Phi(p)\right)^{\lambda-\mu-1}\Phi(p)^{\mu-1} \times \frac{\sigma\sqrt{B_0+\sigma_\epsilon^2/\sigma^2}}{\tilde{\sigma}\sqrt{\tilde{B}_0+\sigma_\epsilon^2/\tilde{\sigma}^2}}\int_{s=-\infty}^{s=p}\mathrm{e}^{-\frac{1}{2}\left(\frac{\sigma\sqrt{B_0+\sigma_\epsilon^2/\sigma^2}s-A_0\left(\tilde{\sigma}^2-\sigma^2\right)}{\tilde{\sigma}\sqrt{\tilde{B}_0+\sigma_\epsilon^2/\tilde{\sigma}^2}}\right)^2}\mathrm{d}s\mathrm{d}p\mathrm{d}\tilde{\sigma}, \tag{59}$$

where the innermost integral can be expressed by the CDF of the normal distribution. This CDF is expanded into a Taylor series about σ including the linear term. After that step, the remaining integral can be determined using formulae obtained in [9]. Thus, one finally obtains the SAR function (21)

$$\psi(\sigma) \simeq \frac{\tau^2}{2} + e^{1,1}_{\mu,\lambda}\frac{B_0}{B_0+\sigma_\epsilon^2/\sigma^2}\tau^2 - c_{\mu/\mu,\lambda}\frac{2A_0\sigma}{\sqrt{B_0+\sigma_\epsilon^2/\sigma^2}}\tau^2 + \mathcal{O}\left(\tau^4\right). \tag{60}$$

Sample Reuse in the Covariance Matrix Adaptation Evolution Strategy Based on Importance Sampling

Shinichi Shirakawa
University of Tsukuba
1-1-1 Tennodai, Tsukuba, Ibaraki, Japan
shirakawa@iit.tsukuba.ac.jp

Youhei Akimoto
Shinshu University
4-17-1 Wakasato, Nagano City, Nagano, Japan
y_akimoto@shinshu-u.ac.jp

Kazuki Ouchi
Aoyama Gakuin University
5-10-1 Fuchinobe, Chuo-ku, Sagamihara-shi, Kanagawa, Japan
kzk0520.cb@gmail.com

Kouzou Ohara
Aoyama Gakuin University
5-10-1 Fuchinobe, Chuo-ku, Sagamihara-shi, Kanagawa, Japan
ohara@it.aoyama.ac.jp

ABSTRACT

Recent studies reveal that the covariance matrix adaptation evolution strategy (CMA-ES) updates the parameters based on the natural gradient. The rank-based weight is considered the result of the quantile-based transformation of the objective value and the parameters are adjusted in the direction of the natural gradient estimated by Monte-Carlo with the samples drawn from the current distribution. In this paper, we propose a sample reuse mechanism for the CMA-ES. On the basis of the importance sampling, the past samples are reused to reduce the estimation variance of the quantile and the natural gradient. We derive the formula for the rank-μ update of the covariance matrix and the mean vector update using the past samples, then incorporate it into the CMA-ES without the step-size adaptation. From the numerical experiments, we observe that the proposed approach helps to reduce the number of function evaluations on many benchmark functions, especially when the number of samples at each iteration is relatively small.

Categories and Subject Descriptors

G.1.6 [**Numerical Analysis**]: Optimization—*Global optimization*

Keywords

Importance Sampling; Natural Gradient; Covariance Matrix Adaptation Evolution Strategy; Information Geometric Optimization

1. INTRODUCTION

The covariance matrix adaptation evolution strategy (CMA-ES) [6, 7] is a comparison-based stochastic search algorithm for continuous optimization. The CMA-ES controls the mean vector and the covariance matrix of the multivariate normal distribution, from which candidate solutions are sampled. At each iteration it samples candidate solutions, then they are evaluated on the problem and their ranking is computed. The parameter of the distribution $\mathcal{N}(m, \sigma^2 C)$ are updated by using the candidate solutions and their ranking, so that the candidate solutions tend to converge towards the optimum of the problem at a geometric rate. Since it does not explicitly use the objective value, the CMA-ES is invariant to the order-preserving transformation of the objective function, $f \mapsto g \circ f$, where $f : \mathbb{R}^d \to \mathbb{R}$ is an objective function and $g : \mathbb{R} \to \mathbb{R}$ is any increasing function. Invariances to the order-preserving transformation of the objective function and to the linear transformation of the search space enable the CMA-ES to efficiently solve non-convex, non-separable and ill-conditioned problems [8].

Recent studies [2,5,10] reveal that some components of the CMA-ES, namely m-update and the rank-μ C-update, are regarded as the stochastic natural gradient ascent [4]. Ollivier et al. [10] have proposed a generalized framework of the stochastic search method for black-box optimization problems on an arbitrary search space, called information geometric optimization (IGO). The IGO framework includes not only the rank-μ update CMA-ES but also a binary optimization algorithm called population-based incremental learning (PBIL) as instantiations with different probability models. The IGO framework provides a mathematical interpretation of the weighted recombination, based on which we develop a novel technique in this paper.

In the IGO framework, the objective function (to be minimized, w.l.o.g.) is transformed into the utility function on the basis of the quantile of the objective value under the sampling distribution. The objective of the parameter update is considered to maximize the expected utility function over the sampling distribution, and the parameters are updated in its steepest ascent direction. With respect to the KL-divergence, the steepest ascent direction is known to be given by the so-called natural gradient [4], which is computed by the product of the inverse Fisher information matrix and the gradient. The natural gradient is estimated by Monte-Carlo using the candidate solutions sampled from the current distribution. Larger sample size typically results in higher accuracy (lower variance) of the natural gradient estimate, requires less iterations, but it costs more function evaluations.

GECCO '15, July 11 - 15, 2015, Madrid, Spain

DOI: http://dx.doi.org/10.1145/2739480.2754704

To accurate the natural gradient estimate without any additional function evaluations and accelerate the search, we consider *reusing* the candidate solutions of past iterations. In the CMA-ES and the IGO setting, the samples drawn at past iterations are discarded. If we just reuse the samples from past iterations without the modification of the update, it will introduce a bias to the Monte-Carlo estimate of the natural gradient since the past distributions are different from the current distribution. However, if the past distributions are close to the current distribution, the past samples can be useful to estimate the natural gradient. Reusing the past samples is natural and widely used in the evolutionary computation, for instance, the $(\mu + \lambda)$-ES, though their purpose differs from ours.

In this paper, we propose a sample reuse mechanism for the CMA-ES based on the importance sampling. We derive the formula to estimate the utility values (recombination weights) and the natural gradient by using the samples from the mixture of the current and past distributions. Theoretically it does not introduce any bias in the estimation and is expected to reduce the estimation variance. We derive the formula of the rank-μ update of the covariance matrix and the mean vector update with the sample reuse, then incorporate rank-one update into this mechanism.

The rest of the paper is organized as follows. In Section 2 we overview the CMA-ES, the IGO, and an existing sample reuse mechanism called importance mixing [13, 14]. In Section 3, we introduce the importance sampling in the IGO framework and derive the update formula for the rank-μ update CMA-ES. In Section 4, we evaluate the performance of the CMA-ES with and without the proposed sample reuse mechanism. We also compare the proposed strategies with the importance mixing. In Section 5, we summarize the contribution and discuss the future work.

2. RELATED ALGORITHMS

2.1 The CMA-ES without CSA

The covariance matrix adaptation evolution strategy (CMA-ES) [6, 7] maintains the Gaussian distribution $\mathcal{N}(m, \sigma^2 C)$, from which the candidate solutions are sampled. It repeats sampling, evaluation and update of the parameters of the distribution. At each iteration the CMA-ES generates the λ candidate solutions x_i for $i = 1, \cdots, \lambda$. Their objective values are evaluated and the ranking of each solution is computed. The parameters of the Gaussian distribution is updated by using the current candidate solutions and their ranking. The Gaussian distribution in the CMA-ES is parameterized with a mean vector $m \in \mathbb{R}^d$ and a covariance matrix $\sigma^2 C$, where $\sigma \in \mathbb{R}_>$ is called global step-size and $C \in \mathbb{R}^{d \times d}$ is a positive-definite symmetric matrix. These parameters are updated by the different update rules, the weighted recombination for m, the rank-μ and rank-one update for C, and the cumulative step-size adaptation (CSA) for σ. Here, we only explain the update rules of m and C since we consider the CMA-ES without CSA to investigate the basic effect of the proposed approach in this paper. Therefore, w.l.o.g., we assume $\sigma = 1$.

Let $\mathrm{rk}(x_i^t)$ be the ranking of x_i^t among the λ candidate solutions with respect to f. The weight is assigned to each solution according to its ranking. Each weight defined in [7] is

$$w_i = \frac{\max(0, \ln(\frac{\lambda+1}{2}) - \ln(i))}{\sum_{j=1}^{\lambda} \max(0, \ln(\frac{\lambda+1}{2}) - \ln(j))} \tag{1}$$

and the weight $w_{\mathrm{rk}(x_i^t)}$ is assigned to each solution x_i^t.

The mean vector m is updated by

$$m^{t+1} = m^t + c_m \sum_{i=1}^{\lambda} w_{\mathrm{rk}(x_i^t)} (x_i^t - m^t), \tag{2}$$

where c_m is the learning rate for m and usually $c_m = 1$. The update rule of the covariance matrix C consists of two components: rank-one update and rank-μ update. The rank-one update accelerates the update of the covariance matrix using the evolution path which is the cumulation of the consecutive steps. The evolution path for the rank-one update, p_c, is updated with the following formula

$$p_c^{t+1} = (1 - c_c) p_c^t + \sqrt{c_c (2 - c_c) \mu_{\mathrm{eff}}} \sum_{i=1}^{\lambda} w_{\mathrm{rk}(x_i^t)} (x_i^t - m^t), \tag{3}$$

where c_c is the cumulation parameter for the evolution path and $\mu_{\mathrm{eff}} = (\sum_{i=1}^{\lambda} w_i^2)^{-1}$. Then, the update rule of the covariance matrix C with the rank-one and rank-μ update is

$$C^{t+1} = C^t + \underbrace{c_1 (p_c^{t+1} (p_c^{t+1})^{\mathrm{T}} - C^t)}_{\text{rank-one update}} + \underbrace{c_\mu \sum_{i=1}^{\lambda} w_{\mathrm{rk}(x_i)} \left((x_i^t - m^t)(x_i^t - m^t)^{\mathrm{T}} - C^t \right)}_{\text{rank-}\mu\text{ update}}, \tag{4}$$

where c_1 and c_μ are the learning rates of the rank-one and rank-μ updates for C, respectively. The rank-one update enlarges the eigenvalue of C corresponding to the direction of the evolution path, and the rank-μ update is considered the natural gradient ascent of the expectation of the transformed objective function as described in Section 2.2. The CMA-ES described above with $c_1 = 0$ is called the pure rank-μ update CMA-ES.

2.2 Information Geometric Optimization

Given a probability model $p_\theta(x)$ on $\mathbb{X}$ with the parameter $\theta \in \Theta$, the IGO [10] transforms the original minimization problem of $f : \mathbb{X} \to \mathbb{R}$ to the maximization of $J_{\theta^t} : \Theta \to \mathbb{R}$ at each iteration and performs the so-called natural gradient ascent. The function J_{θ^t} depends on the parameter θ^t at each iteration. It is the expected value of the utility $W_{\theta^t}^f(x)$ that is a nonlinear and non-increasing transformation of the objective function f.

The utility function[1], $W_\theta^f(x)$, is defined by using the quantile of $f(x)$ under $x \sim p_\theta$. Let $w : [0, 1] \to \mathbb{R}$ be a non-increasing function, $q_\theta^{\leqslant}(x) = P_\theta[y : f(y) \leqslant f(x)]$ represent the probability of sampling a better point than x from p_θ, and $W_\theta^f(x) = w(q_\theta^{\leqslant}(x))$. Then, $J_{\theta^t}(\theta)$ is defined as the expectation of the utility over the distribution p_θ, namely,

$$J_{\theta^t}(\theta) = \int W_{\theta^t}^f(x) p_\theta(x) \mathrm{d}x.$$

The natural gradient, $\tilde{\nabla} J_{\theta^t}(\theta)$, is given by the product of the inverse of the Fisher information matrix $F(\theta)$ and the vanilla gradient $\nabla J_{\theta^t}(\theta)$, i.e., the vector of the partial derivative w.r.t. each parameter, which can be written as

$$\tilde{\nabla} J_{\theta^t}(\theta) = \int W_{\theta^t}^f(x) \tilde{\nabla} l(\theta; x) p_\theta(x) \mathrm{d}x. \tag{5}$$

[1]This definition assumes the probability of getting the same objective value among different samples is 0. This assumption holds only if the Lebesgue measure of the level set of the objective function is 0, and it is no problem in most practical cases. The rigorous formulation that allows the same objective value is explained in [10].

Here, $\tilde{\nabla} l(\theta; x) = F^{-1}(\theta)\nabla l(\theta; x)$ is the natural gradient of the log-likelihood $l(\theta; x) = \ln p_\theta(x)$.

In practice, the integral in (5) cannot be computed analytically since the objective function is black-box, and have to be estimated by Monte-Carlo using the samples drawn from $p_{\theta^t}(x)$. Replacing the expectation in (5) with the arithmetic average over the samples $x_i \sim p_{\theta^t}$, we have

$$\tilde{\nabla} J_{\theta^t}(\theta^t) \approx \frac{1}{\lambda}\sum_{i=1}^{\lambda} W^f_{\theta^t}(x_i)\tilde{\nabla} l(\theta^t; x_i) \ .$$

We also need to estimate the utility $W^f_{\theta^t}(x_i) = w(q^{\leqslant}_{\theta^t}(x_i))$ for each x_i. Since $q^{\leqslant}_{\theta^t}(x_i)$ is the probability of sampling a better point than x_i from p_{θ^t}, it can be approximated by using the number of better point than x_i among the λ samples drawn from p_{θ^t}, namely $(\mathrm{rk}(x_i) - 1/2)/\lambda$. Then, the utility $W^f_{\theta^t}(x_i)$ is approximated by $\hat{w}(x_i) = w((\mathrm{rk}(x_i) - 1/2)/\lambda)$. With this approximation, we have an estimate of (5) at θ^t as $\tilde{\nabla} J_{\theta^t}(\theta^t) \approx \lambda^{-1}\sum_{i=1}^{\lambda} \hat{w}_i \tilde{\nabla} l(\theta^t; x_i)$. Then, we obtain the parameter update

$$\theta^{t+1} = \theta^t + \eta \sum_{i=1}^{\lambda} \frac{\hat{w}_i}{\lambda}\tilde{\nabla} l(\theta^t; x_i) \ , \tag{6}$$

where η denotes the learning rate and $\hat{w}_i = \hat{w}(x_i)$ for simplicity.

The pure rank-μ update CMA-ES ($c_1 = 0$ in (4)) is considered an instantiation of the IGO algorithm. Given the multivariate Gaussian distribution $\mathcal{N}(m, C)$ parameterized by $\theta = (m, C)$, the parameter update (6) in the IGO algorithm is equivalent to (2) and (4) if $c_m = c_\mu, c_1 = 0$, and any function w such that $w((i-1/2)/\lambda) = \lambda w_i$ for w_i defined in (1).

2.3 Importance Mixing

An idea of reusing previously generated solutions has been introduced in [13, 14], called importance mixing. It creates the set of points that can be considered as taken from the current distribution p_{θ^t}. Provided a population of λ points drawn from $p_{\theta^{t-1}}$, it accepts each point x in the population with probability $\min\{1, (1-\alpha)p_{\theta^t}(x)/p_{\theta^{t-1}}(x)\}$ into new population. Let $\lambda' \leqslant \lambda$ be the number of accepted points. Then, sample a point x from p_{θ^t} and accept it with probability $\max\{\alpha, 1 - p_{\theta^{t-1}}(x)/p_{\theta^t}(x)\}$ into the new population and repeat this procedure until $\lambda - \lambda'$ points are accepted. Then, the new population is considered as being distributed as p_{θ^t}. Since this idea is introduced to reduce the number of points for which the function value is evaluated at each iteration, the estimation variance of the natural gradient does not necessarily lessen. In Section 4, we compare the proposed strategies with the importance mixing. The parameter α called the minimal refresh rate is set to $\alpha = 0$ to reduce the function evaluations as much as possible in the experiments.

3. SAMPLE REUSE IN THE CMA-ES

In this section, we propose a sample reuse mechanism for the CMA-ES based on the importance sampling that is a technique to estimate the expectation over a probability distribution by using samples drawn from a different probability distribution. We mix the current and past samples as drawn from the mixture of the current and past distributions, and estimate the natural gradient by Monte-Carlo with the samples from the mixture.

3.1 Importance Sampling

Suppose that we have $K + 1$ probability distributions p^k ($k = 0, 1, \dots, K$) and λ independent samples x^k_i ($i = 1, \dots, \lambda$) from each probability distribution p^k. Our objective here is to estimate the expectation $\int g(x)p^0(x)\mathrm{d}x$ by using $\lambda(K+1)$ samples x^k_i. In the CMA-ES, p^0 and p^k corresponds to the current distribution and the distribution of previous kth iteration. The simplest way is to apply the Monte-Carlo estimate by using only the samples x^0_i from p^0,

$$\frac{1}{\lambda}\sum_{i=1}^{\lambda} g(x^0_i) \tag{7}$$

implying that we discard all the other samples x^k_i ($k \geqslant 1$) despite that they may help to estimate the quantity more accurately. To utilize all the possible samples, we employ the idea of importance sampling.

Let $\bar{p}$ be the mixture $\bar{p}(x) = (K+1)^{-1}\sum_{k=0}^{K} p^k(x)$. One can rewrite the expectation as

$$\int g(x)p^0(x)\mathrm{d}x = \int g(x)\frac{p^0(x)}{\bar{p}(x)}\bar{p}(x)\mathrm{d}x \tag{8}$$

Considering the set of points x^k_i to be sampled from $\bar{p}$, we can approximate the RHS of the above equality by the average

$$\frac{1}{\lambda(K+1)}\sum_{k=0}^{K}\sum_{i=1}^{\lambda} g(x^k_i)\frac{p^0(x^k_i)}{\bar{p}(x^k_i)} \ . \tag{9}$$

It is an unbiased estimator of (8) shown in [11,15], i.e., the expected value of (9) equals to (8). In this way, we can utilize all the possible samples without introducing any bias and expect that this leads to more accurate estimation than the simple Monte-Carlo using only x^0_i. This is the key idea of our work. Note that the case $K = 0$ recovers (7).[2]

3.2 Sample Reuse in the IGO

We introduce (9) in the IGO framework to estimate the natural gradient $\tilde{\nabla} J_{\theta^t}(\theta^t)$ using the samples x^{t-k}_i ($i = 1, \dots, \lambda$) from the current and past K distributions, p^{t-k} ($k = 0, 1, \dots, K$). Let $\bar{p}(x) = (K+1)^{-1}\sum_{k=0}^{K} p^{t-k}(x)$.

First, we need to estimate $W^f_{\theta^t}(x^{t-k}_i) = w(q^{\leqslant}_{\theta^t}(x^{t-k}_i))$. By definition, we can write $q^{\leqslant}_{\theta^t}(x^{t-k}_i)$ in the form of (8) with $g(x) = \mathbb{I}\{f(x) \leqslant f(x^{t-k}_i)\}$, where $\mathbb{I}\{\cdot\}$ indicates the indicator function. Then, we can apply the formula (9) to estimate $q^{\leqslant}_{\theta^t}(x^{t-k}_i)$ and we obtain

$$\sum_{l=0}^{K}\sum_{j=1}^{\lambda}\frac{\mathbb{I}\{f(x^{t-l}_j) \leqslant f(x^{t-k}_i)\}}{\lambda(K+1)}\frac{p^t(x^{t-l}_j)}{\bar{p}(x^{t-l}_j)} =: \bar{q}(x^{t-k}_i) \ . \tag{10}$$

Given w, the estimate $\hat{w}^{t-k}_i$ of the weight value $W^f_{\theta^t}(x^{t-k}_i)$ for each x^{t-k}_i is computed as

$$\hat{w}^{t-k}_i = w\left(\bar{q}(x^{t-k}_i)\right) \ . \tag{11}$$

Next we estimate the natural gradient (5) using (11). The natural gradient (5) at θ^t is of the form (8) with $g(x) = W^f_{\theta^t}(x)\tilde{\nabla} l(\theta^t; x)$.

[2] One can create a different unbiased estimator that uses all the possible samples. Instead of considering the mixture $\bar{p}$, one computes $K+1$ unbiased estimator $\lambda^{-1}\sum_{i=1}^{\lambda} g(x^k_i)p^0(x^k_i)/p^k(x^k_i)$ and averages them, resulting in

$$\lambda^{-1}(K+1)^{-1}\sum_{k=0}^{K}\sum_{i=1}^{\lambda} g(x^k_i)p_0(x^k_i)/p_k(x^k_i).$$

This is also an unbiased estimator of (8). We can prove that (9) has a smaller estimation variance than this estimator, which is also claimed by [11, 12]. Therefore, we employ (9).

With an approximation of $W^f_{\theta^t}(x_i^{t-k})$ for each i and k defined in (11), we can apply the formula (9) and obtain the estimate of $\tilde{\nabla} J_{\theta^t}(\theta^t)$ as

$$\frac{1}{\lambda(K+1)} \sum_{k=0}^{K} \sum_{i=1}^{\lambda} \hat{r}(x_i^{t-k}) \tilde{\nabla} l(\theta^t; x_i^{t-k}) \ , \qquad (12)$$

where $\hat{r}(x_i^k) = \hat{w}_i^k p_{\theta^t}(x_i^k)/\bar{p}(x_i^k)$. We remark that the proposed estimator (12) as well as the original estimator (the second term on the RHS of (6)) is biased; its expectation differs from (5) since the same samples are used to estimate $W^f_{\theta^t}$ and $\tilde{\nabla} J_{\theta^t}$, but they are consistent; the bias vanishes and both estimates converge to (5) w.p.1 as $\lambda \to \infty$. See Remark 2 of [1] for the impact of the bias.

3.3 Sample Reuse in the CMA-ES

We introduce the importance sampling to the CMA-ES described in Section 2.1. More precisely, we replace the mean vector update (2) and the rank-μ update of the covariance matrix in (4) with novel ones using the samples from the current and past K iteration.

As discussed in Section 2.2, the pure rank-μ update CMA-ES is considered as an instantiation of the IGO algorithm with the multivariate Gaussian distribution. Therefore, we can simply replace the second term on the RHS of (2) and the rank-μ update of the covariance matrix in (4) with the novel natural gradient estimate (12). All we need is to choose the function w. We choose $w(s) = -2\ln(2s)\mathbb{I}\{s \leqslant 1/2\}$, since w_i defined in (1) is considered as an approximation of $w((i-1/2)/\lambda)$ for large λ. The weight value $\hat{w}_i^{t-k}$ in (12) is given by (11) with this w. Then, we obtain the update rules for the mean vector and the covariance matrix as

$$m^{t+1} = m^t + c_m \sum_{k=0}^{K} \sum_{i=1}^{\lambda} \frac{\hat{r}(x_i^{t-k})}{\lambda(K+1)} (x_i^{t-k} - m^t), \qquad (13)$$

$$C^{t+1} = C^t + c_\mu \sum_{k=0}^{K} \sum_{i=1}^{\lambda} \frac{\hat{r}(x_i^{t-k})}{\lambda(K+1)} \cdot ((x_i^{t-k} - m^t)(x_i^{t-k} - m^t)^{\mathrm{T}} - C^t). \qquad (14)$$

Note that if $K = 0$, (13) and (14) is equivalent to (2) and (4) with $c_1 = 0$, except that $\hat{w}_i^t/\lambda$ is different from w_i defined in (1). In the preliminarily experiments we have observed that the sum of $\hat{w}_i^t/\lambda$ tends to be smaller than one when $K = 0$, whereas the sum of w_i is always one. Its impact is observed in the next section.

We combine the rank-one update to (14). We simply add the second term on the RHS of (4) to (14). To update the evolution path, we solely uses the current samples and use $w_{\mathrm{rk}(x_i^t)}$ as the weight for each x_i^t rather than $\hat{w}_i^t$. It means, the evolution path is updated as it is done in (3). Since the evolution path itself accumulates the past information, the rank-one update is considered utilizing the past samples. Therefore, the proposed algorithm exploits the past information in different ways to update the covariance matrix, and we expect the synergy.

To implement the proposed method, one needs to keep the mean vectors and the covariance matrices of the past K distributions to compute the likelihood ratio $p_{\theta^t}(x_i^{t-k})/\bar{p}(x_i^{t-k})$, which requires $O(Kd^2)$ additional memory space. For efficient and numerically stable computation, we keep the log-likelihood of each point, $l_i^{k,l} = \ln p_{\theta^{t-k}}(x_i^{t-l})$, for each $i = 1, \dots, \lambda$ and $k, l = 0, \dots, K$, which requires $O(\lambda K^2)$ additional space. The likelihood ratio is then computed as $p_{\theta^t}(x_i^{t-k})/\bar{p}(x_i^{t-k}) = (K+1)(\sum_{l=0}^{K} \exp(l_i^{l,k} - l_i^{0,k}))^{-1}$. Then the computational complexity at each iteration is $O(\lambda K d^2)$.

4. EXPERIMENTS AND RESULTS

In this section, we evaluate the proposed approach on a standard benchmark functions. We consider the following four variants of the CMA-ES using the past solutions:

(A) Reuse-*m*, *C* The parameters are updated using (13) and (14).

(B) Reuse-*C* The covariance matrix is updated using (14), while the mean vector is updated by (2), only current samples are used and the rankings are computed among the current samples as in the standard CMA-ES.

(C) Reuse-*m*, *C* + rank-one The rank-one update is incorporated into Algorithm (A), as is described in Section 3.3.

(D) Reuse-*C* + rank-one The rank-one update is incorporated into Algorithm (B).

For these four variants, we observe the effect of K and the population size λ. Moreover, we compare them with the pure rank-μ update CMA-ES with and without importance mixing and the hybrid of the rank-one and rank-μ update.

4.1 Experimental Procedure

Our benchmark set consists of Sphere, Rosenbrock, Ellipsoid, Cigar, Ackley, Bohachevsky, Schaffer, and Rastrigin functions[3]. The global optimum is located at $[1, \cdots, 1]^{\mathrm{T}}$ for Rosenbrock function and $[0, \cdots, 0]^{\mathrm{T}}$ for the other functions, where the optimal value is 0. The problem dimension d of each benchmark function is set to 20 and 40.

The initial mean vector m^0 of the Gaussian distribution is drawn uniform randomly from $[a, b]^d$ for each run, and the covariance matrix is initialized by $C^0 = \sigma^2 I$, where $\sigma = (b-a)/2$. The range is set to $[1, 5]^d$ for Sphere, Ellipsoid, Cigar, and Rastrigin functions, $[-2, 2]^d$ for Rosenbrock function, $[1, 30]^d$ for Ackley function, $[1, 15]^d$ for Bohachevsky function, and $[10, 100]^d$ for Schaffer functions, according to [3]. The evolution path p_c is initialized to the zero vector.

Each run is terminated and regarded as success when the best objective value reaches smaller than 10^{-10}. On the other hand, the run is terminated and regarded as failure after $d \times 10^6$ function evaluations, or when the minimal eigenvalue of the covariance matrix reaches 10^{-30}, except for Schaffer function, where the minimal eigenvalue is set to 10^{-60}. For each setting we conduct 50 independent runs.

Different population sizes (sample size) λ and K are tested. For Sphere, Rosenbrock, Ellipsoid, and Cigar functions, $\lambda \in \{4 + \lfloor 3\ln d \rfloor, 0.2d, 0.4d, 0.8d, d, 2d, 4d, 8d, 16d\}$. For the other multimodal functions, $\lambda = 2\lfloor 2^{i/2-1}\lambda_{\mathrm{base}} \rfloor$ for $i = 0, 1, \cdots, 7$ with $\lambda_{\mathrm{base}} = 2\ln d, d, 2d, 10d$ for Ackley, Bohachevsky, Schaffer, and Rastrigin functions, respectively. In preliminary experiments we have observed the failure with high probability when $\lambda \leqslant \lambda_{\mathrm{base}}$. The number of iterations for sample reuse is $K = 0, 1, 3, 5, 7, 9$. As is mentioned in Section 3.3, $K = 0$ leads to parameter updates slightly different from the standard mean vector update and the rank-μ update.

Following [7], we set the learning rates as follows:

$$c_m = 1, \quad c_c = \frac{4 + \mu_{\mathrm{eff}}/d}{\lambda + 4 + 2\mu_{\mathrm{eff}}/\lambda}, \quad c_1 = \frac{2}{(d+1.3)^2 + \mu_{\mathrm{eff}}}, \qquad (15)$$
$$c_\mu = \min\left(1.0 - c_1, \frac{2(\mu_{\mathrm{eff}} - 2 + 1/\mu_{\mathrm{eff}})}{(d+2)^2 + 2\mu_{\mathrm{eff}}/2}\right).$$

[3]The definition of each benchmark function can be found in [3, 9].

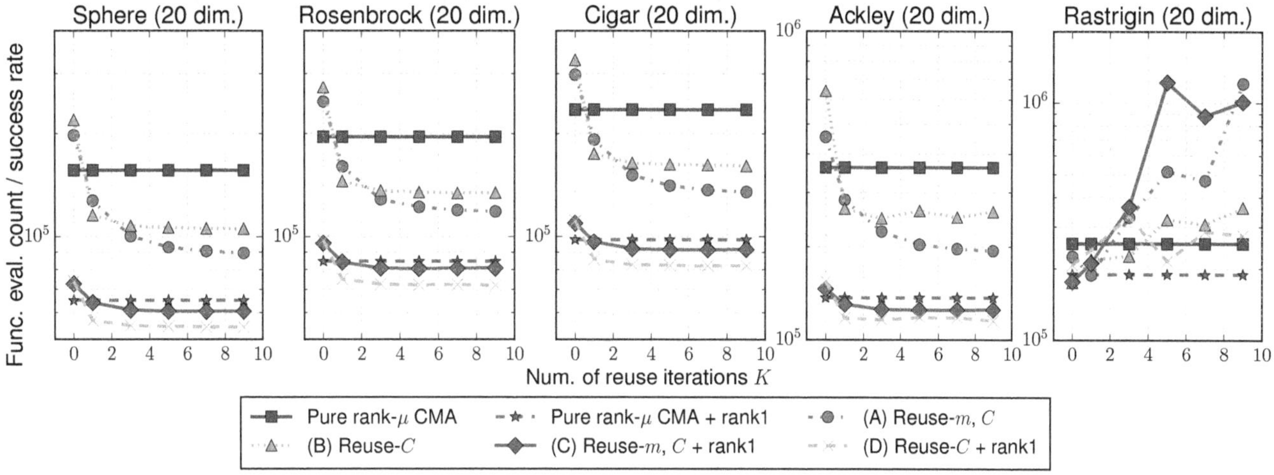

Figure 1: Average number of function evaluations divided by the success probability are shown on 20 dimensional problems. The default population size is used for Sphere, Rosenbrock, and Cigar functions and $\lambda = 2\lfloor 2\lambda_{\text{base}} \rfloor$ for Ackley and Rastrigin functions.

Note that for Algorithms (A) and (B), the learning rate for the rank-one update, c_1, is set to 0 and we do not update the evolution path.

4.2 Results and Discussion

Figure 1 shows the average number of function evaluations over the successful runs divided by the success probability on 20 dimensional functions for six algorithms: the pure rank-μ update CMA-ES ($c_1 = 0$ in Section 2.1), the hybrid update CMA-ES (described in Section 2.1), and Algorithms (A)–(D). The default population size $\lambda = 4 + \lfloor 3 \ln d \rfloor$ is used for Sphere, Rosenbrock, and Cigar functions and $\lambda = 2\lfloor 2\lambda_{\text{base}} \rfloor$ for Ackley and Rastrigin functions. The result on Ellipsoid function is very similar to that on Cigar function, and the results on Bohachevsky and Schaffer functions are similar to that on Ackley function. Moreover, we have observed a similar trends on K on the 40 dimensional functions. E.g., with the default population size, the pure rank-μ update CMA-ES and Algorithm (A) with $K = 5$ spend 7.5×10^5 and 3.8×10^5 function evaluations to solve 40 dimensional Sphere function, respectively. Their results are omitted due to the space limitation.

Figures 2 and 3 show the average number of function evaluations over the successful runs divided by the success probability on 20 dimensional problems. The performance of the pure rank-μ update CMA-ES, the pure rank-μ update CMA-ES with importance mixing, and the pure rank-μ update CMA-ES with sample reuse (Algorithm (A): Reuse-m, C with $K = 0, 1, 3, 5$) for different population sizes are shown in Figure 2. The results of the hybrid update CMA-ES, and the CMA-ES with sample reuse (Algorithm (D): Reuse-C with rank-one with $K = 0, 1, 3, 5$) for different population sizes are shown in Figure 3.

Figure 4 illustrates the transition of the sum of the products of the weight and the likelihood ratio $s_t^k = (1/\lambda)\sum_i \hat{r}(x_i^k)$ for the current ($k = t$) and past samples ($k = t-1, \ldots, t-3$) in a typical run. The results of Algorithm (A) and (B) with $K = 3$ and the default population size on 20 dimensional Sphere function are shown. Smaller values for $t - k$ iteration indicate either that the samples from $t - k$ iteration are away from the current distribution and the likelihood ratios are small, or that the samples from $t - k$ iteration are low in the ranking and small or zero weight values are assigned to them. Remark also that the sum of the coefficients does not amount to 1, as we have mentioned in Section 3.3.

Figure 5 displays the typical behaviors of Algorithm (A) with the default population size on 20 dimensional Sphere, Rosenbrock, and Ellipsoid functions and Algorithm (D) with $\lambda = 160$ on 20 dimensional Rosenbrock function. The results of both $K = 0$ and $K = 5$ are monitored.

4.2.1 *Impact of K*

We observe from Figure 1 that the performances of Algorithms (A)–(D) improve more or less monotonically as K increases for all but Rastrigin function. The algorithms with sample reuse (A and B or C and D) outperform the one without sample reuse (the pure rank-μ update CMA-ES or the hybrid update CMA-ES, respectively) already with $K = 1$, where the current and previous populations are used. We see the improvement over K up to 7 in Algorithm (A), whereas the improvement is observed for K up to 3 in Algorithms (B)–(D). The reason that the performance is saturated for large K is because the likelihood ratios for old samples tend to be small since past distributions are away from the current distribution and newer samples tend to have better function values, resulting that very small weights are assigned to very old samples. On Rastrigin function, a large K value tends to lead to low success rate. This defect is less visible when λ becomes larger as it is seen in Figures 2 and 3.

From Figure 5, the speedup by the sample reuse ($K = 5$ over $K = 0$) is seen not only at the convergence stage but also at the adaptation stage.

4.2.2 *Impact of λ*

When the population size is relatively large, we observe from Figures 2 and 3 that the sample reuse is not helpful very much to reduce the number of function evaluations. For large λ, we expect that the natural gradient estimate in (2) and (4) is relatively accurate and the effect of the sample reuse is less emphasized. Moreover, since the learning rate c_μ defined in (15) becomes larger as λ increases, leading to a big change of the probability distribution, the likelihood ratios for the past samples will be small. Therefore, the sample reuse does not help when λ is relatively large. We can observe the same effect of large λ for Algorithms (B) and (C) as well.

On Rosenbrock function, the sample reuse turns out to lead to failure in the case of $\lambda > 10^2$. As we see in Figure 5, the mean vector needs to move from the origin towards the global optimum.

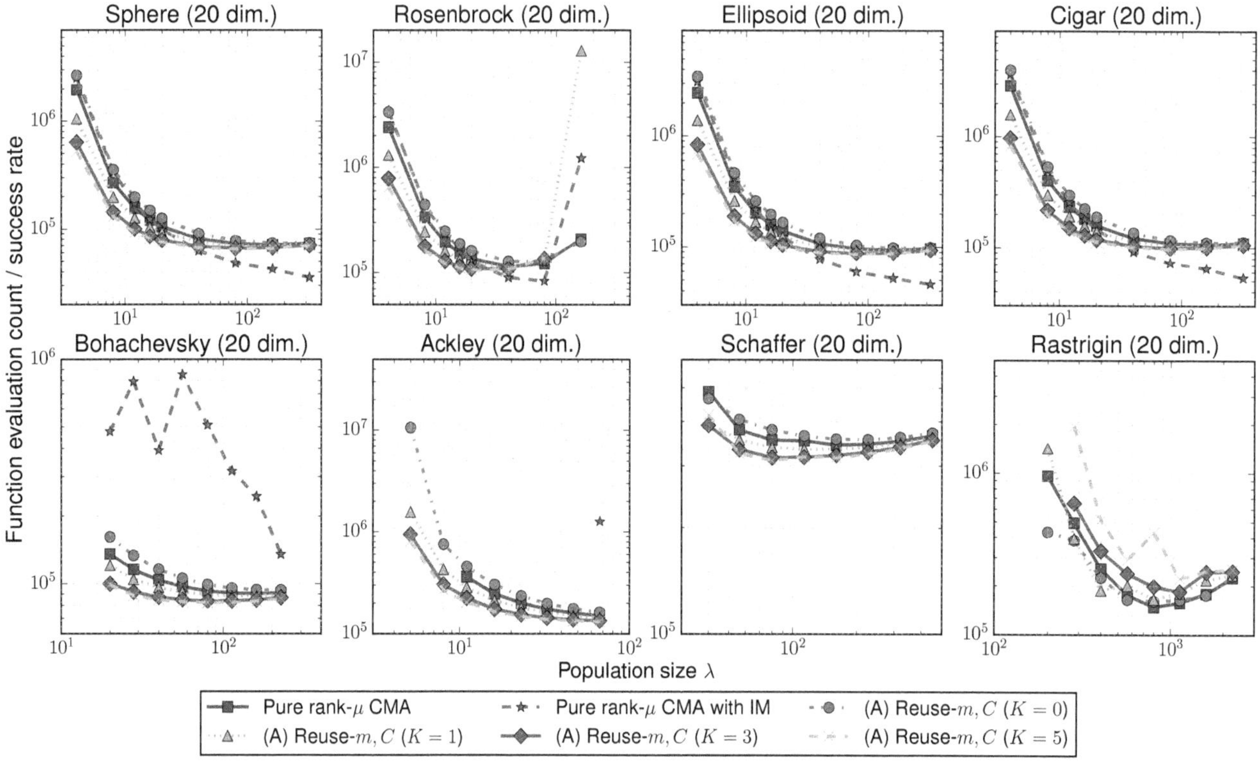

Figure 2: Average number of function evaluations divided by the success probability versus population size λ of the pure rank-μ update CMA-ES without and with importance mixing (IM), and the rank-μ update CMA-ES with sample reuse (Algorithm (A) for $K = 0, 1, 3, 5$) on 20 dimensional problems. Missing data implies the failure.

In the case of $\lambda = 160$ and $K = 5$, we observe that the eigenvalues of the covariance matrix tends to be smaller compared to the case of $K = 0$ during the movement of the mean vectors. Smaller eigenvalues of the covariance matrix leads to producing shorter steps, $x - m$, resulting in slow movement of the mean vectors.[4]

4.2.3 Sample reuse in the pure rank-μ update

Comparing Algorithms (A) and (B) in Figure 1, we find that Algorithm (B) is better for $K = 1$ but Algorithm (A) reaches better performance for larger K. The reason is observed in Figure 4, where the sums of the coefficients, $\hat{r}(x_i^k)$, which appears in (13) and (14), are more or less equal for $k = t, \dots, t-3$ in Algorithm (A), whereas the sums for $k = t$ and $t - 1$ amount to higher values than the ones for $k = t-2$ and $t-3$ in Algorithm (B). This indicates that the past samples are used to estimate the natural gradient in Algorithm (A) as well as the current samples, whereas mostly the current and previous samples are used and the older samples has less impact in Algorithm (B). In Algorithm (A), the mean vector is updated by using the proposed update (13), where the natural gradient is estimated with smaller variance than the one estimated in the original update (2). Then, the mean vector less fluctuates and the likelihood ratios are likely to be relatively large for the past samples.

[4]Empirically, we observe that a larger population size itself leads to smaller eigenvalues. Since more samples are used in the case of $K = 5$, compared to the case of $K = 0$, the reason of adapting a smaller covariance matrix may be the same reason.

4.2.4 Sample reuse in the hybrid update

Each variant of the algorithms is improved by introducing the rank-one update as seen in Figure 1. While the sample reuse for m update results in better performance when the covariance matrix is solely updated by the rank-μ update, the standard m update leads to faster convergence when the rank-one update is incorporated. As discussed in Section 4.2.3, the proposed m update (13) tends to have less fluctuation in a subspace that are less sensitive in function value such as the first axis for Cigar function. Then the evolution path will not be long in this subspace, while it should be in the example of Cigar function so that the covariance matrix learns the principle axis. The standard m update does not disturb the rank-one update and the speedup is achieved by the sample reuse in the rank-μ update.

Comparing the performance on Rastrigin function shown in Figures 2 and 3, we notice that Algorithm (D) is less suffered from a large value of K than Algorithm (A). This may be because the past samples have less effect in Algorithm (D) for the reason partially observed in Figure 4.

Figure 3 shows that smallest λ leads to the least performance difference between different K values in Algorithm (D) for the unimodal functions, while the difference between different K values becomes pronounced for smaller λ in Algorithm (A), shown in Figure 2. The learning rate c_1 for the rank-one update has a relatively large value for a small population size compared with the learning rate c_μ for the rank-μ update, then the impact of the rank-one update is dominative.

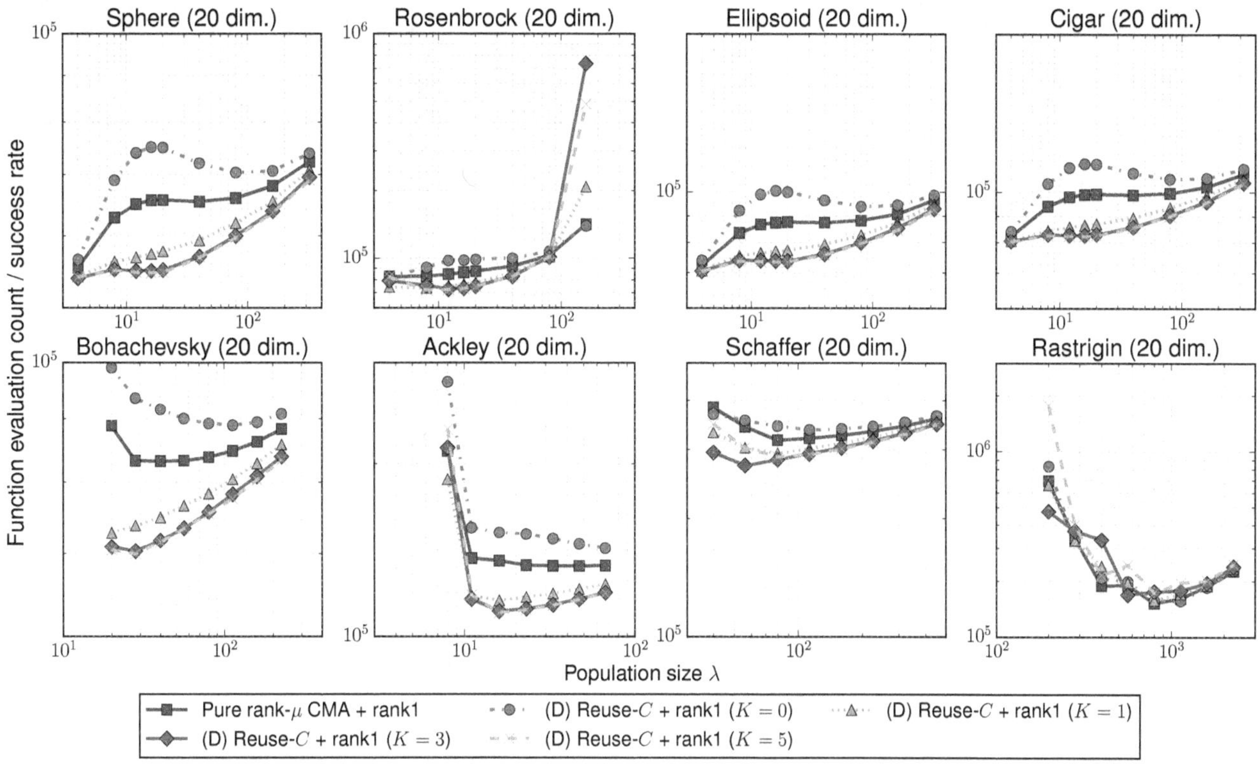

Figure 3: Average number of function evaluations divided by the success probability versus population size λ of the pure rank-μ update CMA-ES with rank-one update, and the CMA-ES with sample reuse (Algorithm (D) for $K = 0, 1, 3, 5$) on 20 dimensional problems.

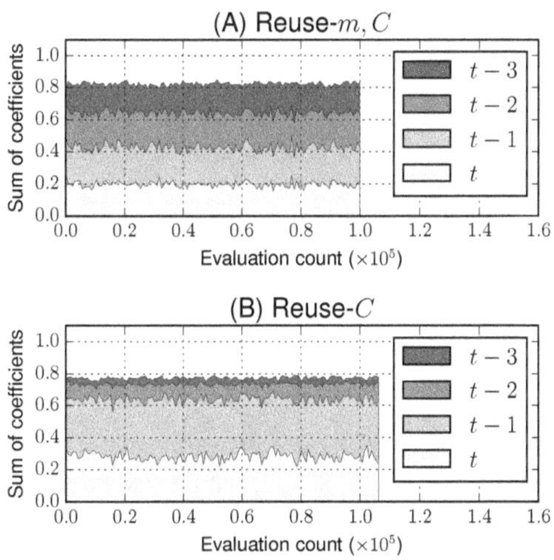

Figure 4: Transition of the sum of the coefficients (the products of the weight and the likelihood ratio) for the current and past samples, $s_t^k = 1/\lambda \sum_i \hat{r}(x_i^k), k = t, \ldots, t-3$, on 20 dimensional Sphere function for Algorithm (A) and (B) with $K = 3$ and the default population size. The moving average with window size 11 is computed for smoothing.

4.2.5 *Comparison with importance mixing*

When introducing the importance mixing in the pure rank-μ update CMA-ES, the performance on the unimodal functions are improved. The improvement is emphasized when λ is relatively large as is seen in Figure 2. The performance is better than Algorithm (A) for $\lambda \geqslant 320$. On the other hand, it is likely to be trapped by local minima on the multimodal functions. The motivation of the importance mixing is to reduce the number of function evaluations by reusing the sample and not to estimate the natural gradient more precisely. In fact, the estimate of the natural gradient will be less accurate since the number of samples drawn from the current distribution is less than λ.

Combining the rank-one update and the importance mixing, it ceases working properly when the refresh rate $\alpha = 0$. By tuning α, the unimodal functions can be solved. However, the α needs to be tuned dependently of λ. Moreover, it does not work well on the multimodal functions.

5. CONCLUSION

We have proposed the sample reuse technique based on the importance sampling to improve the accuracy of the estimate of the natural gradient in the CMA-ES. The quantile based utility function and then the natural gradient are estimated using the mixture of the current and last K populations. This has been realized thanks to the mathematical formulation of the rank-based selection proposed in the IGO framework. From the experiments, we have found that the sample reuse is effective both for the mean vector and the covariance matrix update in the pure rank-μ update CMA-ES. On the other hands, when the rank-one update is employed with rank-μ update (i.e., hybrid update), the sample reuse for the mean vector update disturbs the evolution path. The best performance is achieved by the variant that updates the mean vector without the sample reuse and combines the rank-one update and the rank-μ update using the sample reuse, where the reasonable choice for K seems to be $K \leqslant 3$.

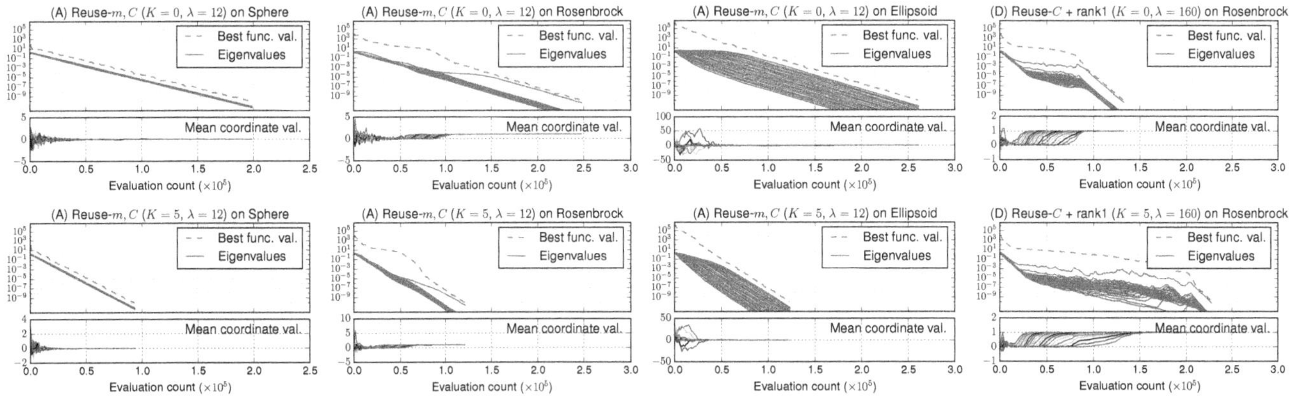

Figure 5: The best objective function value, eigenvalues of C, and each coordinate of m with $K = 0$ (top) and $K = 5$ (bottom) are shown for Algorithm (A) with the default population size on 20 dimensional Sphere (1st column), Rosenbrock (2nd column), and Ellipsoid (3rd column) functions and Algorithm (D) with $\lambda = 160$ on 20 dimensional Rosenbrock (4th column) function.

Larger K values tend to lead to failure on Rastrigin function. We have investigated the effect of K on 20 and 40 dimensional problems and observed a similar trend. More study on the effect of K should be done on higher dimensional problems.

The step-size adaptation is not introduced in the paper. In the CMA-ES, the step-size adaptation improves the efficiency and the robustness of the algorithm drastically. For instance, it can solve 20 dimensional Ellipsoid function within 2×10^4 function evaluations with the default population size, whereas the proposed algorithm needs at least 7×10^4 function evaluations. However, since this leads to a fast change of the distribution, the likelihood ratio for the past populations will be very small and the past population cannot contribute the natural gradient estimate. Therefore, we expect that the proposed sample reuse mechanism, as it is, is not effective when the step-size adaptation is employed. We may need a modification to effectively reuse the past samples.

6. REFERENCES

[1] Y. Akimoto, A. Auger, and N. Hansen. Convergence of the Continuous Time Trajectories of Isotropic Evolution Strategies on Monotonic C^2-composite Functions. In *Problem Solving from Nature-PPSN XII*, pages 42–51, 2012.

[2] Y. Akimoto, Y. Nagata, I. Ono, and S. Kobayashi. Bidirectional Relation between CMA Evolution Strategies and Natural Evolution Strategies. In *Parallel Problem Solving from Nature –PPSN XI*, volume 6238 of *LNCS*, pages 154–163. Springer, 2010.

[3] Y. Akimoto, J. Sakuma, I. Ono, and S. Kobayashi. Functionally Specialized CMA-ES : A Modification of CMA-ES Based on the Specialization of the Functions of Covariance Matrix Adaptation and Step Size Adaptation. In *Proceedings of the Genetic and Evolutionary Computation Conference (GECCO '08)*, pages 479–486, 2008.

[4] S. Amari. Natural Gradient Works Efficiently in Learning. *Neural Computation*, 10(2):251–276, 1998.

[5] T. Glasmachers, T. Schaul, Y. Sun, D. Wierstra, and J. Schmidhuber. Exponential Natural Evolution Strategies. In *Proceedings of the Genetic and Evolutionary Computation Conference (GECCO '10)*, pages 393–400, 2010.

[6] N. Hansen. The CMA Evolution Strategy: A Comparing Review. In J. A. Lozano, P. Larrañaga, I. n. Inza, and E. Bengoetxea, editors, *Towards a New Evolutionary Computation*, volume 192 of *Studies in Fuzziness and Soft Computing*, pages 75–102. Springer, 2006.

[7] N. Hansen and A. Auger. Principled Design of Continuous Stochastic Search: From Theory to Practice. In Y. Borenstein and A. Moraglio, editors, *Theory and Principled Methods for Designing Metaheustics*, Natural Computing Series, pages 145–180. Springer, 2014.

[8] N. Hansen, A. Auger, R. Ros, S. Finck, and P. Pošík. Comparing Results of 31 Algorithms from the Black-Box Optimization Benchmarking BBOB-2009. In *Proceedings of the Genetic and Evolutionary Computation Conference (GECCO '10) Companion*, pages 1689–1696, 2010.

[9] N. Hansen and A. Ostermeier. Completely Derandomized Self-Adaptation in Evolution Strategies. *Evolutionary Computation*, 9(2):159–195, 2001.

[10] Y. Ollivier, L. Arnold, A. Auger, and N. Hansen. Information-Geometric Optimization Algorithms: A Unifying Picture via Invariance Principles. *eprint arXiv:1106.3708v2*, 2011.

[11] C. R. Shelton. Policy Improvement for POMDPs Using Normalized Importance Sampling. Technical Report AI Momo 2001-002, MIT AI Lab., 2001.

[12] C. R. Shelton. Policy Improvement for POMDPs Using Normalized Importance Sampling. In *Proceedings of the Seventeenth Conference on Uncertainty in Artificial Intelligence (UAI '01)*, pages 496–503, 2001.

[13] Y. Sun, D. Wierstra, T. Schaul, and J. Schmidhuber. Efficient Natural Evolution Strategies. In *Proceedings of the Genetic and Evolutionary Computation Conference (GECCO '09)*, pages 539–546, 2009.

[14] Y. Sun, D. Wierstra, T. Schaul, and J. Schmidhuber. Stochastic Search Using the Natural Gradient. In *Proceedings of the 26th International Conference on Machine Learning (ICML '09)*, pages 1161–1168, 2009.

[15] E. Veach and L. J. Guibas. Optimally Combining Sampling Techniques for Monte Carlo Rendering. In *Proceedings of the 22nd Annual Conference on Computer Graphics and Interactive Techniques (SIGGRAPH '95)*, pages 419–428, 1995.

Extended Differential Grouping for Large Scale Global Optimization with Direct and Indirect Variable Interactions

Yuan Sun
Department of Mechnical Engineering
The University of Melbourne
Parkville, Australia
yuans2@student.unimelb.edu.au

Michael Kirley
Department of Computing and Information Systems
The University of Melbourne
Parkville, Australia
mkirley@unimelb.edu.au

Saman K. Halgamuge
Department of Mechnical Engineering
The University of Melbourne
Parkville, Australia
saman@unimelb.edu.au

ABSTRACT

Cooperative co-evolution is a framework that can be used to effectively solve large scale optimization problems. This approach employs a divide and conquer strategy, which decomposes the problem into sub-components that are optimized separately. However, solution quality relies heavily on the decomposition method used. Ideally, the interacting decision variables should be assigned to the same sub-component and the interdependency between sub-components should be kept to a minimum. Differential grouping, a recently proposed method, has high decomposition accuracy across a suite of benchmark functions. However, we show that differential grouping can only identify decision variables that interact directly. Subsequently, we propose an extension of differential grouping that is able to correctly identify decision variables that also interact indirectly. Empirical studies show that our extended differential grouping method achieves perfect decomposition on all of the benchmark functions investigated. Significantly, when our decomposition method is embedded in the cooperative co-evolution framework, it achieves comparable or better solution quality than the differential grouping method.

Categories and Subject Descriptors

G.1.6 [**Numerical Analysis**]: Optimization

Keywords

Variable interaction, problem decomposition, cooperative co-evolution, large scale global optimization

1. INTRODUCTION

Evolutionary algorithms (EAs) are meta-heuristics that can be used to solve a wide range of optimization problems. However, when the problem has a large number of decision variables – *large scale global optimization* – it becomes difficult for an EA to find the optimal solution [8, 22].

GECCO '15, July 11 - 15, 2015, Madrid, Spain
© 2015 ACM. ISBN 978-1-4503-3472-3/15/07…$15.00
DOI: http://dx.doi.org/10.1145/2739480.2754666

Cooperative co-evolution (CC) [16] has been used with some successes when tackling large scale global optimization (eg. [12]). In CC, the optimization problem is divided into sub-components that are evolved independently. The final solution is a concatenation of representatives from each of the sub-components. In the original paper by Potter et al. [16], it was shown that the CC genetic algorithm was able to solve separable optimization problems, however it was ineffective on non-separable problems. These results may in part be attributed to the fact that the CC approach did not take variable interactions into consideration when allocating decision variables to sub-components.

When using a CC framework, it has been shown that the overall performance is correlated with the decomposition method used [1, 12]. Ideally, the interacting decision variables should be assigned to the same sub-component and the interdependence between sub-components should be kept to a minimum. Unfortunately, identifying the interacting variables in many optimization problems is non-trivial.

Recently, Omidvar et al. [12] proposed a decomposition method – *differential grouping* (DG) – that can be used when allocating decision variables to sub-components when using the CC framework. Results from detailed numerical simulation experiments indicate that the DG method had high decomposition accuracy on most of the benchmark functions investigated [20]. However, on some benchmark functions, such as the Rosenbrock functions, the decomposition accuracy was very low. This suggests that the decomposition method described did not cover all forms of decision variable interactions.

In this paper, we investigate the effects of interactions between decision variables and decomposition methods within the CC framework. We start by considering the form of decision variable interaction in optimization problems such as the Rosenbrock functions. We suggest that there are two distinct types of variable interactions as shown in Figure 1. In Type I interactions, the variables interact directly eg. x_1 and x_2 (or x_2 and x_3) interact directly. In Type II interactions, the variables have a form of indirect interaction eg. x_1 and x_3 are linked by x_2. The formal definition of these two types of variable interactions will be given in Section 3. We show that DG can only capture Type I interactions and fails to capture Type II interactions between decision

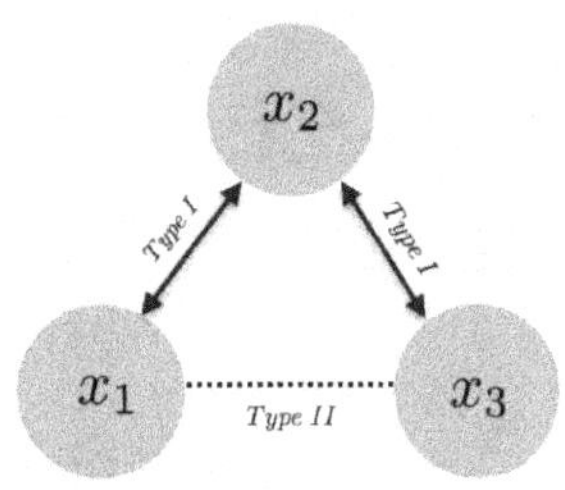

Figure 1: Two types of decision variable interaction. Type I: two variables interact directly with each other. Type II: two variables interact indirectly, that is they are linked via a third variable.

variables. We hypothesize that this is the reason why DG performs poorly on the Rosenbrock functions.

We propose an eXtended Differential Grouping (XDG) method to cater for the different forms of variable interactions. In XDG, after allocating decision variables that interact directly to nominated sub-components, "overlaps" between sub-components are identified. That is, when an overlap is observed, the sub-components that contain the same decision variables are merged. This searching–merging technique is employed to capture Type II interaction between decision variables. The efficacy of the XDG is evaluated using the benchmark functions from the CEC'2010 special session on large scale global optimization [20]. The experimental results show that XDG achieves perfect decomposition on all of the benchmark functions. We then embed XDG into the CC framework to solve large scale optimization problems. Empirical studies show that on the benchmark functions with Type II interactions, the proposed approach achieves significantly better results than the CC with standard DG. On the benchmark functions without Type II interactions, the proposed approach achieves comparable results with the CC with standard DG.

The remainder of this paper is organized as follows. Section 2 discusses the related work. Section 3 shows the limitation of DG and proposes an extension to address this limitation. Section 4 sets up the experiments and analyses the experimental results. Section 5 concludes the paper.

2. RELATED WORK

In this section, we briefly describe studies related to variable interaction within an evolutionary computation context. We also summarize well-known decomposition methods used within the CC framework, before describing the DG method in detail.

Investigating the effects of interactions between "bits" or decision variables – epistasis or linkage – in genetic algorithm research has a long history (see [4]). The original motivation behind much of this work, was to improve the design and effectiveness of the genetic operators. For example, specific crossover operators allow a set of interacting binary variables to be inherited together in the evolutionary process, such as the model used in the messy GA [3], fast messy GA [5], gene expression messy GA [7]. Significantly, there is work describing the level of epistasis and problem difficulty. For example, papers describing epistasis variance [2], epistasis correlation [17] and entropic epistasis [18] have been used to quantify the variable interactions and problem difficulty.

In the continuous optimization domain, many studies have examined the effects of variable interactions and used this to guide the evolution trajectory. For example, estimation of distribution algorithms [9] build a probabilistic model based on the promising candidate solutions and updates the model during each generation. The population for the next generation is sampled from the probabilistic model. In the covariance matrix adaptation - evolutionary strategy [6], the population evolves with the mean and covariance matrix of the promising candidate solutions. In each generation, the mean and covariance matrix are calculated from the promising candidate solutions. The population for the next generation is sampled from the mean and covariance matrix.

In the CC framework, the decomposition methods that are typically used are based on some measures of decision variable interaction. Perhaps the simplest decomposition method is random grouping [23]. In the random grouping decomposition method, decision variable allocations are exchanged (or modified) a few times to increase the probability of assigning interacting decision variables into the same sub-component. However, it has been shown that when the number of interacting variables is greater than two, it is unlikely to put all of them into the same sub-component [13].

Perturbation methods, which include LINC-R [10], LIMD [11], CCVIL [1], differential grouping [12], and delta grouping [14] can also be used when allocating decision variables to sub-components. Perturbation methods identify interaction between two decision variables by adding a small perturbation to the decision variables and detecting the changes in the fitness values. However, these methods are sensitive to the computational errors in the system.

In the DG method introduced by Omidvar et al. [12], interactions between decision variables are identified according to the following rule: if

$$\Delta_{x_i} f(\vec{X})|_{x_i=a,x_j=b_1} \neq \Delta_{x_i} f(\vec{X})|_{x_i=a,x_j=b_2}, \tag{1}$$

then x_i and x_j are interacting decision variables, where

$$\Delta_{x_i} f(\vec{X}) = f(\ldots, x_i + \delta, \ldots) - f(\ldots, x_i, \ldots). \tag{2}$$

In DG, when changes in f caused by adding a perturbation to x_i varies for different values of x_j, then x_i and x_j are interacting decision variables.

3. EXTENDED DIFFERENTIAL GROUPING

In this section, we define two types of interactions between decision variables and show that the DG method can only identify one type of interaction. An extension of DG, which we refer to as XDG, is proposed to address this limitation.

In Figure 1, we illustrate two alternative forms of variable interactions between decision variables. In Type I, two variables interact directly with each other. In Type II, two variables are linked via a third decision variable. We call the former *direct interaction* and the latter *indirect interaction*. The formal definition of interacting types is listed below:

DEFINITION 1. *In an objective function $f(\vec{X})$, decision variables x_i and x_j interact directly with each other if $\exists$ a candidate solution $\vec{x}_*$, s.t.*

$$\left.\frac{\partial f}{\partial x_i \partial x_j}\right|_{\vec{x}_*} \neq 0, \tag{3}$$

denoted by $x_i \nleftrightarrow x_j$. Decision variables x_i and x_j interact indirectly with each other if for all candidate solutions,

$$\frac{\partial f}{\partial x_i \partial x_j} = 0, \tag{4}$$

and $\exists$ a set of decision variables $\{x_{k1}, \ldots, x_{kt}\} \subset \vec{X}$, s.t. $x_i \leftrightarrow x_{k1} \leftrightarrow \ldots \leftrightarrow x_{kt} \leftrightarrow x_j$. Decision variables x_i and x_j are independent with each other if for all candidate solutions, (4) holds and $\nexists$ a set of decision variables $\{x_{k1}, \ldots, x_{kt}\} \subset \vec{X}$, s.t. $x_i \leftrightarrow x_{k1} \leftrightarrow \ldots \leftrightarrow x_{kt} \leftrightarrow x_j$.

Consider the following example to further explain this definition:

EXAMPLE 1. *In the objective function: $f(\vec{X}) = (x_1 - x_2)^2 + (x_2 - x_3)^2 + x_4^2$, $\vec{X} \in [-1, 1]^4$, x_1 and x_2 interact directly with each other (Type I), x_1 and x_3 interact indirectly with each other (Type II), x_1 and x_4 are independent.*

THEOREM 1. *In an objective function $f(\vec{X})$, if (4) holds, then*

$$\Delta_{x_i} f(\vec{X})|_{x_i=a, x_j=b_1} = \Delta_{x_i} f(\vec{X})|_{x_i=a, x_j=b_2}, \tag{5}$$

where $\Delta_{x_i} f(\vec{X})$ is defined in (2).

PROOF. If (4) holds, integrating (4) with respect to x_j, we can obtain:

$$\frac{\partial f}{\partial x_i} = \int 0 \mathrm{d}x_j = g(\vec{X_k}), \tag{6}$$

where $\vec{X_k} \subset \vec{X}$, $x_j \notin \vec{X_k}$, $g(\vec{X_k})$ is a function of $\vec{X_k}$. That states $\partial f / \partial x_i$ is not a function of x_j. Therefore $\forall\ x_i$,

$$\left.\frac{\partial f}{\partial x_i}\right|_{x_j=b_1} = \left.\frac{\partial f}{\partial x_i}\right|_{x_j=b_2}. \tag{7}$$

That is

$$\left.\frac{\Delta_{x_i} f(\vec{X})}{\delta}\right|_{x_j=b_1} = \left.\frac{\Delta_{x_i} f(\vec{X})}{\delta}\right|_{x_j=b_2}. \tag{8}$$

Thus,

$$\Delta_{x_i} f(\vec{X})|_{x_j=b_1} = \Delta_{x_i} f(\vec{X})|_{x_j=b_2} \tag{9}$$

is true for all x_i. Thus, (5) is obtained. □

In an objective function, if x_i and x_j interact indirectly with each other, then (4) holds. According to Theorem 1, (5) holds. DG will classify x_i and x_j as independent. Therefore, DG can not capture indirect interaction (Type II) between decision variables. This is the main limitation of DG.

Now consider a second example:

EXAMPLE 2. *In the objective function: $f(\vec{X}) = (x_1 - x_2)^2 + (x_2 - x_3)^2$, $\vec{X} \in [-1, 1]^3$, x_1 and x_3 interact indirectly with each other (Type II). However, DG classifies x_1 and x_3 as independent.*

PROOF. On the one hand,

$$\begin{aligned}\Delta_{x_1} f(\vec{X})|_{x_1=a, x_3=b_1} &= (a+\delta-x_2)^2 + (x_2-b_1)^2 \\ &-(a-x_2)^2 - (x_2-b_1)^2 = (a+\delta-x_2)^2 - (a-x_2)^2.\end{aligned} \tag{10}$$

On the other hand,

$$\begin{aligned}\Delta_{x_1} f(\vec{X})|_{x_1=a, x_3=b_2} &= (a+\delta-x_2)^2 + (x_2-b_2)^2 \\ &-(a-x_2)^2 - (x_2-b_2)^2 = (a+\delta-x_2)^2 - (a-x_2)^2.\end{aligned} \tag{11}$$

Algorithm 1 XDG

```
Require: f, d, ub⃗, lb⃗, ϵ
1: IM ← zeros(d − 1, d) // IM: Interaction Matrix
2: sep_var ← [] //sep_var: separable variables
3: for i = 1 to d do
4:   groups(i) = {i}
5:   X⃗1 ← lb⃗
6:   X⃗2 ← X⃗1
7:   X⃗2(i) ← ub⃗(i)
8:   Δ1 ← f(X⃗1) − f(X⃗2)
9:   for j = i + 1 to d do
10:    if IM(i, j) = 0 then
11:      X⃗1(j) ← (ub⃗(j) + lb⃗(j))/2
12:      X⃗2(j) ← (ub⃗(j) + lb⃗(j))/2
13:      Δ2 ← f(X⃗1) − f(X⃗2)
14:      if |Δ1 − Δ2| > ϵ then
15:        IM(i, j) ← 1
16:        groups(i) ← groups(i) ∪ {j}
17:      end if
18:    else
19:      groups(i) ← groups(i) ∪ {j}
20:    end if
21:  end for
22:  for p, q ∈ groups(i) & p < q do
23:    IM(p, q) ← 1
24:  end for
25: end for
26: while the number of variables in groups is not d do
27:   for p, q ∈ {1 : num(groups)} & p < q do
28:     if groups(p) ∩ groups(q) ≠ ∅ then
29:       groups(p) ← groups(p) ∪ groups(q)
30:       delete groups(q)
31:     end if
32:   end for
33: end while
34: for i = 1 to num(groups) do
35:   if length(groups(i)) = 1 then
36:     sep_var ← sep_var ∪ group(i)
37:     delete groups(i)
38:   end if
39: end for
40: groups ← groups ∪ {sep_var}
41: return groups
```

Therefore,

$$\Delta_{x_1} f(\vec{X})|_{x_1=a, x_3=b_1} = \Delta_{x_1} f(\vec{X})|_{x_1=a, x_3=b_2}. \tag{12}$$

DG classifies x_1 and x_3 as independent. □

Can this limitation be addressed? Definition 1 states that under the condition (4), if a set of decision variables can be found to link x_i and x_j together, x_i and x_j interact indirectly with each other. Inspired by this, we propose the XDG method (see in Algorithm 1) to address this limitation.

In Algorithm 1, the inputs are: f is the objective function; d is the dimensionality; $\vec{ub}$ and $\vec{lb}$ are the upper bounds and lower bounds of decision variables; ϵ is the threshold to identify direct interaction between decision variables.

There are three main stages in the XDG method. The first stage is to identify direct interaction between decision variables (line 3 to line 25). The second stage is to identify

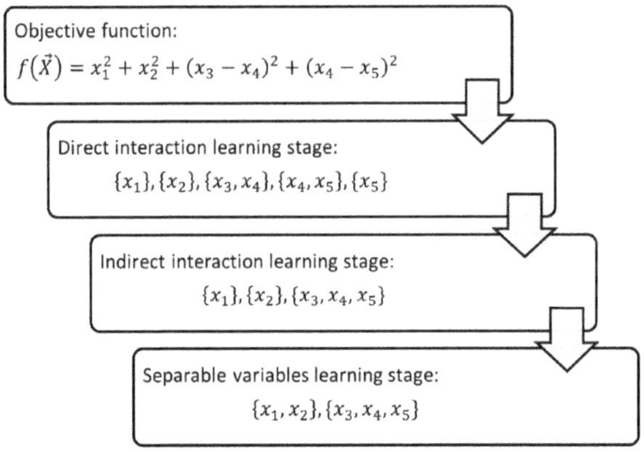

Figure 2: The decomposition processes used in XDG for a sample objective function. In the direct interaction learning stage there are 5 sub-components. In the indirect interaction learning stage the number of sub-components is reduced to 3. The separable variable learning stage results in 2 sub-components.

indirect interaction between decision variables (line 26 to line 33). The third stage is to group all of separable decision variables into the same sub-component (line 34 to line 40).

The first stage begins with the algorithm identifying all of the decision variables that interact directly with x_1, and placing them in the first sub-component with x_1. Note that the pairwise decision variables in the same sub-component are not needed to be examined again in the following procedure (line 22 to line 24). For example, if x_1 directly interacts with x_3 and x_4, we already know x_3 interacts with x_4, therefore, they do not need to be examined again in the following procedures. Secondly, the algorithm examines the direct interaction between x_2 and all of the other decision variables except x_1, for x_1 and x_2 have been examined in the previous procedure. This process is conducted for all decision variables and d sub-components are formed.

The technique used to identify direct interaction is the same as in the original DG method (line 5 to line 8, line 11 to line 17). To examine direct interaction between x_i and x_j, all decision variables are initialized to the lower bound of the search space in the vector of $\vec{X}_1$ (line 5). $\vec{X}_2$ is the same with $\vec{X}_1$ except for the i_{th} value, which is set to the upper bound of the search space (line 6 and line 7). The algorithm calculates the difference between the fitness values at $\vec{X}_1$ and $\vec{X}_2$, denoted by Δ_1 (line 8). Then the j_{th} value of $\vec{X}_1$ and $\vec{X}_2$ are set to the center of the search space. And the algorithm calculates the difference between the fitness values at $\vec{X}_1$ and $\vec{X}_2$ again, denoted by Δ_2 (line 11 to line 13). If the difference between Δ_1 and Δ_2 is greater than the threshold ϵ, x_i and x_j are classified as direct interaction.

In the second stage, the algorithm searches for overlaps between the d sub-components formed in the first stage. If the same decision variable appears in two sub-components, the algorithm merges the two sub-components (line 28 to line 31). This process is repeated until all sub-components are disjoint. Note that when all sub-components are disjoint, the total number of variables in all sub-components is equal to d. This is employed as the stopping criterion of the second stage (line 26).

In the third stage, the algorithm counts the number of decision variables in each sub-component. If it is equal to 1, the algorithm places the decision variable into the separable variable sub-component. Note that placing all separable variables into the same sub-component is arbitrary, which may not be the best decomposition method. However, we follow the approach used in DG to group separable variables in this way. The algorithm returns all of the sub-components as the output.

To further expand on the processing stages, consider Example 3 and Figure 2.

EXAMPLE 3. *Take the objective function:* $f(\vec{X}) = x_1^2 + x_2^2 + (x_3 - x_4)^2 + (x_4 - x_5)^2$, $\vec{X} \in [-1, 1]^5$ *as an example. The three stages of XDG on the objective function is illustrated in Figure 2.*

4. EXPERIMENTS

In this section, detailed numerical experiments are conducted to investigate the efficacy of XDG. Two research questions guide the experimental design:

Q1. Can the proposed XDG method address the limitation of the DG method identified in Section 3?

Q2. Can the proposed XDG method outperform the DG method when it is embedded in a CC framework for large scale optimization problems?

4.1 Methodology

To answer the two research questions, benchmark functions from the CEC'2010 special session on large scale global optimization [20] are used. This benchmark suite was also used to evaluate the DG method in [12]. The suite consists of 20 benchmark functions with 5 categories:

1. fully separable functions (f_1 to f_3);
2. partially separable functions with 1 non-separable sub-component (f_4 to f_8);
3. partially separable functions with 10 non-separable sub-components (f_9 to f_{13});
4. partially separable functions with 20 non-separable sub-components (f_{14} to f_{18});
5. fully non-separable functions (f_{19} to f_{20}).

The dimensionality of the 20 benchmark functions is $d = 1000$, and the number of decision variables in each sub-component is 50.

To investigate Q1, our XDG method is tested on the 20 benchmark functions. The threshold ϵ was set to 10^{-1}. (If not specified $\epsilon = 10^{-1}$ in the rest of the paper). Other values of ϵ (10^{-3} and 1) were used to test the sensitivity of XDG. Two metrics were employed to evaluate the performance of XDG: one is the number of function evaluations used to decompose the problem; the other is the accuracy of grouping of the interacting variables into the same sub-component. The performance of XDG is compared with the performance of DG. The value 10^{-3} is selected as the threshold ϵ for DG, as suggested in [12]. If not specified, all the parameter selections are consistent with the original paper. Note that the parameter settings for XDG and DG are different. For DG, $\epsilon = 10^{-3}$ performs better than $\epsilon = 10^{-1}$, as

Table 1: Decomposition results of XDG and DG on the 20 large scale benchmark functions. XDG and DG values are separated by "/".

Function	Sep Vars	Non-sep Vars	Non-Sep Groups	Extended Differential Grouping ($\epsilon = 10^{-1}$) / Differential Grouping ($\epsilon = 10^{-3}$)					
				Captured Sep Vars	Captured Non-sep Vars	Formed Non-sep Groups	Misplaced Vars	Function Evaluations	Grouping Accuracy
f_1	1000	0	0	1000/1000	0/0	0/0	0/0	1001000/1001000	100%/100%
f_2	1000	0	0	1000/1000	0/0	0/0	0/0	1001000/1001000	100%/100%
f_3	1000	0	0	1000/1000	0/0	0/0	0/0	1001000/1001000	100%/100%
f_4	950	50	1	0/33	50/50	1/10	0/0	80526/14554	100%/100%
f_5	950	50	1	950/950	50/50	1/1	0/0	998648/905450	100%/100%
f_6	950	50	1	950/950	50/50	1/1	0/0	998648/906332	100%/100%
f_7	950	50	1	950/248	50/34	1/4	0/16	998648/67742	100%/68%
f_8	950	50	1	0/134	50/45	2/5	0/5	121658/23286	100%/90%
f_9	500	500	10	500/500	500/500	10/10	0/0	977480/270802	100%/100%
f_{10}	500	500	10	500/500	500/500	10/10	0/0	977480/272958	100%/100%
f_{11}	500	500	10	500/501	500/499	10/10	0/1	978528/270640	100%/99.8%
f_{12}	500	500	10	500/500	500/500	10/10	0/0	977480/271390	100%/100%
f_{13}	500	500	10	500/131	500/159	10/34	0/341	1000154/50328	100%/31.8%
f_{14}	0	1000	20	0/0	1000/1000	20/20	0/0	953960/21000	100%/100%
f_{15}	0	1000	20	0/0	1000/1000	20/20	0/0	953962/21000	100%/100%
f_{16}	0	1000	20	0/4	1000/996	20/20	0/4	956286/21128	100%/99.6%
f_{17}	0	1000	20	0/0	1000/1000	20/20	0/0	953960/21000	100%/100%
f_{18}	0	1000	20	0/78	1000/230	20/50	0/770	999340/39624	100%/23%
f_{19}	0	1000	1	0/0	1000/1000	1/1	0/0	3998/2000	100%/100%
f_{20}	0	1000	1	0/33	1000/287	1/241	0/713	1001000/155430	100%/28.7%

shown in [12]. This is the reason why we select 10^{-3} instead of 10^{-1} as the ϵ value for DG.

To investigate Q2, we use the DECC cooperative coevolution algorithm/framework used by Omidvar et al. [12]. DECC uses SaNSDE [24] to optimize each sub-component. The population size was set to 50. The maximal number of function evaluations is set to 3×10^6, divided between the decomposition phase and the evolutionary optimization phase. The performance of XDG was compared with DG and delta grouping [14], where each decomposition method was incorporated into the DECC. These three algorithms are denoted by DECC-XDG (DECC with XDG), DECC-DG (DECC with DG) and DECC-D (DECC with delta grouping). For each algorithm, 25 independent runs are conducted for each benchmark function. The mean and standard deviation of the best solutions found in the fixed number of function evaluations are recorded to evaluate the performance of the algorithms. The two-sided Wilcoxon test with the confidence interval of 95% is used to determine the best performance from the 3 algorithms in a pairwise fashion.

4.2 Performance of XDG

In this section, we analyse the decomposition results of XDG on 20 benchmark functions. We compare the results from XDG with the decomposition results of DG. We also analyse the sensitivity of XDG to the parameter ϵ.

The decomposition results of XDG and DG on the 20 benchmark functions are presented in Table 1, which are separated by "/". The different categories of benchmark functions are separated by the double lines. The first 4 columns are the details for each benchmark function, and the last 6 columns are the results of the decomposition methods on each benchmark function. Specifically, the ninth column records the number of function evaluations used by XDG/DG to decompose each benchmark function. The last column records the accuracy of XDG/DG when grouping interacting variables into the same sub-component on each benchmark function.

Table 1 shows that XDG outperforms DG. In terms of grouping accuracy, XDG achieves 100% accuracy on all of the 20 benchmark functions. DG achieves 100% accuracy only on 13 benchmark functions. On functions f_{18} and f_{20}, the grouping accuracy of DG is very low (less than 30%). Note that the number of function evaluations used by XDG is equal or larger than the number used by DG. The extra function evaluations are used to identify indirect interaction between decision variables.

The first category of the 20 benchmark functions (See Section 4.1) contains three fully separable functions (f_1 to f_3). Both XDG and DG successfully identify all of the 1000 decision variables as separable. Note that the function evaluations used by XDG/DG on the three separable functions are the same, which is 1001000/1001000.

Category 2 consists of 5 partially separable functions (f_4 to f_8). Each function contains one non-separable group with 50 decision variables. On function f_5 f_6 and f_7, XDG successfully identifies all of the 50 interacting variables and 950 separable variables. On function f_4, XDG identifies all of the 1000 decision variables as interacting variables. It may seem odd that we still report the grouping accuracy as 100%. The reason is that XDG (or DG) only focuses on grouping interacting variables. As long as all of the interacting variables are grouped into the same sub-component, the grouping accuracy is 100%. This criterion is suggested in [12]. On function f_8, XDG forms two non-separable groups, one with 50 interacting variables and one with 950 separable variables. Note that XDG (or DG) automatically places all of the separable variables into the same sub-component. Therefore, the unexpected grouping of 950 separable variables will not affect the final decomposition result on f_8. DG also achieves perfect decomposition on f_5 and f_6. On f_7, the number of interacting variables identified by DG is 34 out of 50. Therefore the grouping accuracy of DG on f_7 is 68%. On f_8, the grouping accuracy of DG is 90%, with 45 out of 50 interacting variables successfully identified.

Category 3 functions (f_9 to f_{13}) contain 10 non-separable sub-components, each with 50 interacting decision variables. The number of separable and non-separable decision variables are both 500 in each function. On all of the 5 functions, XDG successfully identifies the 500 separable decision vari-

Table 2: Decomposition results of XDG with different values of threshold ϵ on 20 benchmark functions. The results of $\epsilon = 1$ and the results of $\epsilon = 10^{-3}$ are separated by "/".

Function	Sep Vars	Non-sep Vars	Non-Sep Groups	Extended Differential Grouping ($\epsilon = 1$)/ Extended Differential Grouping ($\epsilon = 10^{-3}$)					
				Captured Sep Vars	Captured Non-sep Vars	Formed Non-sep Groups	Misplaced Vars	Function Evaluation	Grouping Accuracy
f_1	1000	0	0	1000/1000	0/0	0/0	0/0	1001000/1001000	100%/100%
f_2	1000	0	0	1000/1000	0/0	0/0	0/0	1001000/1001000	100%/100%
f_3	1000	0	0	1000/1000	0/0	0/0	0/0	1001000/1001000	100%/100%
f_4	950	50	1	0/0	50/50	1/1	0/0	80526/80526	100%/100%
f_5	950	50	1	950/950	50/50	1/1	0/0	998648/998648	100%/100%
f_6	950	50	1	950/950	50/50	1/1	0/0	998648/998648	100%/100%
f_7	950	50	1	950/0	50/50	1/1	0/0	998648/45290	100%/100%
f_8	950	50	1	0/0	50/50	2/2	0/0	121658/1216586	100%/100%
f_9	500	500	10	500/500	500/500	10/10	0/0	977480/977480	100%/100%
f_{10}	500	500	10	500/500	500/500	10/10	0/0	977486/ 977480	100%/100%
f_{11}	500	500	10	1000/500	0/500	0/10	500/0	1001000/977482	0%/100%
f_{12}	500	500	10	500/500	500/500	10/10	0/0	977480/977480	100%/100%
f_{13}	500	500	10	500/4	500/50	10/2	0/450	1000154/ 573776	100%/10%
f_{14}	0	1000	20	0/0	1000/1000	20/20	0/0	953960/953960	100%/100%
f_{15}	0	1000	20	0/0	1000/1000	20/20	0/0	953978/ 953960	100%/100%
f_{16}	0	1000	20	1000/0	0/1000	0/20	1000/0	1001000/953968	0%/100%
f_{17}	0	1000	20	0/0	1000/1000	20/20	0/0	953960/ 953960	100%/100%
f_{18}	0	1000	20	0/0	1000/50	20/1	0/950	999340/ 171370	100%/5%
f_{19}	0	1000	1	0/0	1000/1000	1/1	0/0	3996/3996	100%/100%
f_{20}	0	1000	1	0/0	1000/1000	1/1	0/0	1001000/ 705698	100%/100%

ables and 10 non-separable groups, each with 50 interacting variables. DG also achieves perfect decomposition on f_9, f_{10} and f_{12}. On f_{11}, DG only misplaces 1 non-separable decision variable. On f_{13}, DG forms 34 non-separable groups. The number of interacting decision variables correctly identified is 159. Note that f_{13} is a Rosenbrock function, which contains examples of indirect interaction (Type II). It also shows that DG can not capture indirect interaction between decision variables. For this reason, DG may break one non-separable group into several groups. For example, in the function: $f(\vec{X}) = (x_1 - x_2)^2 + (x_2 - x_3)^2 + (x_3 - x_4)^2$, there is only one non-separable group: $\{x_1, x_2, x_3, x_4\}$. However DG will form two non-separable groups: $\{x_1, x_2\}$ and $\{x_3, x_4\}$. This is why DG forms 34 non-separable groups on f_{13}.

Category 4 functions (f_{14} to f_{18}) contain 20 non-separable groups, each with 50 interacting decision variables. XDG achieves perfect decomposition on all of the 5 functions. DG achieves 100% grouping accuracy on f_{14} f_{15} and f_{17}. On f_{16}, DG unexpectedly classifies 4 interacting variables as separable. Function f_{18} is another function with indirect interaction. DG forms 50 non-separable groups. The number of interacting decision variables correctly identified is 230. Therefore, the grouping accuracy of DG on f_{18} is 23%, which is very low. Note that the function evaluations used by XDG on all of the 5 functions are around one million, which is much greater than the function evaluations used by DG (around twenty thousand).

Category 5 consists of two fully non-separable functions with 1000 interacting decision variables (f_{19} and f_{20}). XDG successfully assigns all of the 1000 interacting variables into the same sub-component. DG also achieves 100% grouping accuracy on f_{19}. However on f_{20}, DG only correctly identifies 287 interacting decision variables. Note that f_{20} is also a Rosenbrock function. The number of function evaluations used by XDG and DG on f_{19} are both small. However on f_{20}, the number of function evaluations used by XDG is about 6 times greater than that used by DG.

In sum, DG achieves high grouping accuracy on most of the benchmark functions. However, it performs poorly on functions with indirect interaction, such as f_7 f_{13} f_{18} and f_{20}. XDG achieves 100% grouping accuracy on all of the 20 benchmark functions. It can successfully identify both direct interaction and indirect interaction. Therefore, the extension in XDG can address the limitation of the standard DG. However, XDG is more computational expensive than DG as it requires computational resources to identify indirect interaction between decision variables. This represents a classic trade-off between accuracy and efficiency.

The parameter ϵ is the threshold to classify pairwise decision variables as direct interaction or independent. The larger the ϵ is, the more likely the interacting decision variables are classified as independent. However, if the ϵ is too small, the independent decision variables may be classified as interacting due to the computational errors in the system. Table 2 presents the grouping results of XDG with $\epsilon = 1$ and $\epsilon = 10^{-3}$, which are separated by "/".

According to Table 1 and Table 2, the grouping results of XDG with $\epsilon = 1$ are the same with $\epsilon = 10^{-1}$ on the 20 benchmark functions except f_{11} and f_{16}. On f_{11} and f_{16}, XDG identifies all of the decision variables as separable variables. The reason may be that f_{11} and f_{16} are very smooth functions. The fitness difference between two candidate solutions in the search space is less than 1. Therefore, $\epsilon = 1$ is too large to identify interacting variables.

When $\epsilon = 10^{-3}$, the grouping accuracy of XDG on 18 out of 20 benchmark functions is 100%. On function f_{13}, two non-separable groups are formed with only 50 interacting decision variables correctly identified. The reason for this may be that the computational errors in the system is large compared with the value of ϵ: 10^{-3}. XDG unexpectedly assigns some separable decision variables into the non-separable group. Besides, the 10 groups of non-separable decision variables are assigned to the same group. Note that the second stage of XDG is to learn indirect interaction. An unexpected grouping of interacting decision variables in the first stage may result in two non-separable groups merged as one. It will cause a rapid deterioration of the grouping accuracy. Similar results can be found with f_{18}, where XDG places all of the 20 groups of interacting decision variables into the same group. Therefore, the grouping accuracy of XDG on f_{18} is 5%.

In sum, the selection of ϵ should not be too large or too small. A large value of ϵ will fail to identify some of the interacting decision variables. A small value of ϵ will result in fault grouping of interacting decision variables. The value 10^{-1} is used for XDG in the rest of the paper.

4.3 DECC Comparison

This section analyses the experimental results of the DECC algorithm with our proposed extended differential grouping method, DECC-XDG, on the 20 benchmark functions. The performance of DECC-XDG is compared with DECC-DG and DECC-D.

On fully separable functions, DECC-D outperforms DECC-DG and DECC-XDG significantly. The reason may be that DG and XDG put all of the separable decision variables into the same sub-component. When the number of separable variables is large (hundreds and thousands), it may not be a good choice to place all of the separable variables into the same sub-component [21, 19]. An alternative decomposition approach could be to treat each separable variable as one sub-component, however, such an approach is not ideal. The intermediate decomposition between these two extreme cases has been shown to be more efficient [15]. Another reason may be that the number of function evaluations used by DECC-XDG or DECC-DG in the decomposition phase is too large, resulting in few function evaluations left for the evolutionary optimization phase. According to Table 1, the number of function evaluations used by DECC-XDG/DG in the decomposition phase is 1001000, which is approximately equal to 1/3 of the maximal number of function evaluations (3×10^6). Note that the performances of DECC-XDG and DECC-DG on the 3 separable functions are almost the same.

On f_8, f_{13}, f_{18} and f_{20}, DECC-XDG outperforms DECC-DG significantly. Note that all the of four functions have indirect interaction between decision variables. XDG achieves perfect decomposition on the four benchmark functions, while the decomposition accuracy of DG is low according to Table 1. Although the number of function evaluations used by DECC-XDG in the decomposition phase is greater than that of DECC-DG (See Table 1), DECC-XDG still significantly outperforms DECC-DG on the four benchmark functions. For f_{18}, DECC-XDG used 25 times the number of function evaluations used by DECC-DG in the decomposition phase. However, the mean of the best solutions found by DECC-XDG is 2.60e+03, while the mean of the best solutions found by DECC-DG is 1.44e+10. The former is much better than the latter, which demonstrates the effectiveness of the extension in XDG. It also shows that an ideal decomposition can significantly improve the performance of a CC algorithm.

On functions without indirect interactions such as f_{15}, f_{16}, f_{17}, DECC-XDG achieves the same or slightly worse results than DECC-DG. Note that the decomposition accuracy achieved by DECC-XDG and DECC-DG are both the same on these functions. However the number of function evaluations used by DECC-XDG in the decomposition phase is much greater than that of DECC-DG. Therefore, the number of function evaluations left for DECC-XDG to optimize each sub-component is much less than that of DECC-DG.

On function f_{20}, DECC-XDG successfully places all of the 1000 interacting decision variables into the same sub-component. However, the quality of the best solution found by DECC-XDG is worse than that of DECC-D. It may be an indication that assigning all of the interacting decision variables into the same sub-component may not be a good decomposition method when the number of interacting variables is large.

Table 3: The comparison between the performances of DECC-XDG, DECC-DG and DECC-D on the 20 benchmark functions. The significant better performances are highlighted in bold (Wilcoxon test with $\alpha = 0.05$)

Func	Num	DECC-XDG	DECC-DG	DECC-D
f_1	Mean	2.23e+04	1.12e+04	**4.07e-24**
	Std	8.01e+04	3.37e+04	1.75e-23
f_2	Mean	4.44e+03	4.42e+03	**2.82e+02**
	Std	1.64e+02	1.59e+02	2.40e+01
f_3	Mean	1.66e+01	1.67e+01	**1.52e-13**
	Std	4.12e-01	3.05e-01	8.48e-15
f_4	Mean	**7.84e+11**	4.63e+12	4.12e+12
	Std	1.67e+11	1.35e+12	1.46e+12
f_5	Mean	**1.68e+08**	1.98e+08	2.48e+08
	Std	1.74e+07	4.58e+07	4.79e+07
f_6	Mean	**1.63e+01**	**1.62e+01**	5.34e+07
	Std	3.28e-01	2.82e-01	8.79e+07
f_7	Mean	**1.39e+03**	1.63e+04	6.89e+07
	Std	2.61e+03	8.93e+03	4.96e+07
f_8	Mean	**4.78e+05**	2.51e+07	1.09e+08
	Std	1.32e+06	2.54e+07	4.87e+07
f_9	Mean	1.12e+08	**5.60e+07**	6.13e+07
	Std	1.13e+07	6.59e+06	6.28e+06
f_{10}	Mean	**5.31e+03**	**5.22e+03**	1.29e+04
	Std	1.55e+02	1.28e+02	2.27e+02
f_{11}	Mean	1.04e+01	9.94e+00	**1.55e-13**
	Std	1.15e+00	9.57e-01	8.19e-15
f_{12}	Mean	1.24e+04	**2.83e+03**	4.30e+06
	Std	2.32e+03	9.92e+02	1.79e+05
f_{13}	Mean	**1.21e+03**	5.35e+06	**1.19e+03**
	Std	2.25e+02	4.89e+06	5.02e+02
f_{14}	Mean	5.83e+08	3.43e+08	**1.93e+08**
	Std	4.11e+07	2.23e+07	1.06e+07
f_{15}	Mean	**5.91e+03**	**5.84e+03**	1.60e+04
	Std	7.56e+01	8.93e+01	4.24e+02
f_{16}	Mean	1.81e-08	**7.32e-13**	1.70e+01
	Std	1.57e-09	4.62e-14	8.48e+01
f_{17}	Mean	1.26e+05	**3.99e+04**	7.48e+06
	Std	7.47e+03	1.80e+03	4.03e+05
f_{18}	Mean	**1.41e+03**	1.44e+10	3.32e+03
	Std	1.88e+02	2.50e+09	7.09e+02
f_{19}	Mean	**1.59e+06**	1.72e+06	2.32e+07
	Std	4.96e+04	6.83e+06	5.56e+06
f_{20}	Mean	5.55e+05	6.69e+10	**1.18e+03**
	Std	1.75e+06	9.24e+09	8.25e+01

5. CONCLUSION

In this paper, we have investigated the effects of decision variable interaction and decomposition methods within the cooperative co-evolution framework. We have described two alternative types of variable interactions – direct interaction and indirect interaction – that may appear in the decision variable space of large scale optimization problems. Importantly, we have shown that the state-of-art decomposition method DG can not capture indirect interaction, and this in turn can be used to explain relatively poor performance on some of the benchmark functions. As a result, we have introduced an extended differential grouping method, XDG, to address this limitation. Results from comprehensive numerical simulation experiments clearly illustrated that XDG can achieve perfect decomposition on all of the benchmark functions investigated. When XDG was embedded within a cooperative co-evolutionary framework, it achieves significantly better performance than DECC-DG and DECC-D on the benchmark functions with indirect interaction. It also achieves comparable performance with DECC-DG on the benchmark functions without indirect interaction.

6. ACKNOWLEDGMENT

The authors would like to thank Xiaodong Li for providing the source code of the differential grouping method and the DECC algorithm on the website.

7. REFERENCES

[1] W. Chen, T. Weise, Z. Yang, and K. Tang. Large-scale global optimization using cooperative coevolution with variable interaction learning. In *Lecture Notes in Computer Science*, pages 300–309, 2010.

[2] Y. Davidor. Epistasis variance: Suitability of a representation to genetic algorithms. *Complex Systems*, 4:369–383, 1990.

[3] D. Goldberg, B. Korb, and K. Deb. Messy genetic algorithms: Motivation, analysis, and first results. *Complex systems*, 3:493–530, 1989.

[4] D. E. Goldberg. *Genetic Algorithms in Search, Optimization, and Machine Learning*, volume Addison-We. 1989.

[5] D. E. Goldberg, K. Deb, H. Kargupta, and G. Harik. Rapid Accurate Optimization of Difficult Problems Using Fast Messy Genetic Algorithms. *Proceedings of the Fifth International Conference on Genetic Algorithms,(Urbana, USA)*, pages 56–64, 1993.

[6] N. Hansen. Reducing the time complexity of the derandomized evolution strategy with covariance matrix adaptation (CMA-ES). *Evolutionary computation*, 11(1):1–18, 2003.

[7] H. Kargupta. The performance of the gene expression messy genetic algorithm on real test functions. *Proceedings of IEEE International Conference on Evolutionary Computation*, 1996.

[8] Y. Liu, X. Yao, Q. Zhao, and T. Higuchi. Scaling up fast evolutionary programming with cooperative coevolution. *Proceedings of the 2001 Congress on Evolutionary Computation*, 2, 2001.

[9] H. Mühlenbein, J. Bendisch, and H. M. Voigt. From recombination of genes to the estimation of distributions II. Continuous parameters. *Parallel Problem Solving from Nature - PPSN IV. Springer Berlin Heidelberg*, pages 188–197, 1996.

[10] M. Munetomo and D. Goldberg. A genetic algorithm using linkage identification by nonlinearity check. *IEEE SMC'99 Conference Proceedings. 1999 IEEE International Conference on Systems, Man, and Cybernetics*, 1, 1999.

[11] M. Munetomo and D. E. Goldberg. Linkage identification by non-monotonicity detection for overlapping functions. *Evolutionary computation*, 7:377–398, 1999.

[12] M. Omidvar, X. Li, Y. Mei, and X. Yao. Cooperative co-evolution with differential grouping for large scale optimization. *IEEE Transcations on Evolutionary Computation*, 18(3):378–393, 2014.

[13] M. N. Omidvar, X. Li, Z. Yang, and X. Yao. Cooperative co-evolution for large scale optimization through more frequent random grouping. In *IEEE Congress on Evolutionary Computation*, 2010.

[14] M. N. Omidvar, X. Li, and X. Yao. Cooperative co-evolution with delta grouping for large scale non-separable function optimization. In *IEEE Congress on Evolutionary Computation*, 2010.

[15] M. N. Omidvar, Y. Mei, and X. Li. Optimal Decomposition of Large-Scale Separable Continuous Functions for Cooperative Co-evolutionary Algorithms. *IEEE Congress on Evolutionary Computation*, 2014.

[16] M. Potter and K. D. Jong. A cooperative coevolutionary approach to function optimization. *Parallel Problem Solving from Nature - PPSN III*, pages 249 – 257, 1994.

[17] S. Rochet, G. Venturini, M. Slimane, and E. E. Kharoubi. A critical and empirical study of epistasis measures for predicting GA performances: a summary. *Artificial evolution*, 1998.

[18] D.-I. Seo and B.-R. Moon. An information-theoretic analysis on the interactions of variables in combinatorial optimization problems. *Evolutionary computation*, 15:169–198, 2007.

[19] Y.-j. Shi, H.-f. Teng, and Z.-q. Li. Cooperative Co-evolutionary Differential Evolution for Function Optimization. In *Advances in Natural Computation*, pages 1080–1088. 2005.

[20] K. Tang, X. Yáo, and P. Suganthan. Benchmark functions for the CEC'2010 special session and competition on large scale global optimization. *Rapport technique, USTC, Nature Inspired Computation and Applications Laboratory*, (1):1–23, 2010.

[21] F. VandenBergh and A. Engelbrecht. A Cooperative Approach to Particle Swarm Optimization. *Evolutionary Computation, IEEE Transactions on*, 8:225–239, 2004.

[22] T. Weise, R. Chiong, and K. Tang. Evolutionary Optimization: Pitfalls and Booby Traps. *Journal of Computer Science and Technology*, 27(5):907–936, Nov. 2012.

[23] Z. Yang, K. Tang, and X. Yao. Large scale evolutionary optimization using cooperative coevolution. *Information Sciences*, 178(15):2985–2999, Aug. 2008.

[24] Z. Yang, K. Tang, and X. Yao. Self-adaptive differential evolution with neighborhood search. In *2008 IEEE Congress on Evolutionary Computation, CEC 2008*, pages 1110–1116, 2008.

Interactively Evolving Compositional Sound Synthesis Networks

Björn Jónsson
IT University of Copenhagen
Copenhagen, Denmark
bangsi@bthj.is

Amy K. Hoover
University of Malta
Msida, Malta MSD 2080
amy.hoover@gmail.com

Sebastian Risi
IT University of Copenhagen
Copenhagen, Denmark
sebr@itu.dk

ABSTRACT

While the success of electronic music often relies on the uniqueness and quality of selected timbres, many musicians struggle with complicated and expensive equipment and techniques to create their desired sounds. Instead, this paper presents a technique for producing novel timbres that are evolved by the musician through interactive evolutionary computation. Each timbre is produced by an *oscillator*, which is represented by a special type of artificial neural network (ANN) called a *compositional pattern producing network* (CPPN). While traditional ANNs compute only sigmoid functions at their hidden nodes, CPPNs can theoretically compute *any* function and can build on those present in traditional synthesizers (e.g. square, sawtooth, triangle, and sine waves functions) to produce completely novel timbres. Evolved with NeuroEvolution of Augmenting Topologies (NEAT), the aim of this paper is to explore the space of potential sounds that can be generated through such *compositional sound synthesis networks* (CSSNs). To study the effect of evolution on subjective appreciation, participants in a listener study ranked evolved timbres by personal preference, resulting in preferences skewed toward the first and last generations. In the long run, the CSSN's ability to generate a variety of different and rich timbre opens up the intriguing possibility of evolving a complete CSSN-encoded synthesizer.

1. INTRODUCTION

While many electronic musicians strive to produce novel timbres for their pieces [9, 18], traditional sound synthesis requires extensive expertise [4]. Inspired by analog oscillators, most digital synthesizers produce periodic combinations of sine, sawtooth, square, and triangle waves [14] that are controlled and manipulated by the user. Because setting synthesizer parameters is complicated, amateur musicians typically default to expert-determined settings to find compelling sounds, thereby limiting the possible novelty of discovered timbres.

GECCO '15, July 11 - 15, 2015, Madrid, Spain

DOI: http://dx.doi.org/10.1145/2739480.2754796

To alleviate expertise required by the user and also permit discovery of novel sounds, the approach in this paper is helps users evolve the waveforms through interactive evolutionary computation (IEC) [30]. Each timbre is represented by a special type of artificial neural network called a *compositional pattern producing network* (CPPN; 28), which unlike traditional artificial neural networks can compute any function at its hidden nodes. CPPNs can not only compute the standard sine, sawtooth, square, and triangle waves present in analog synthesizers, but can also add new functions to theoretically produce novel timbres. The sound producing CPPNs introduced in this paper, called *compositional sound synthesis networks* (CSSNs) are then evolved through NeuroEvolution of Augmenting Topologies (NEAT). Each CSSN can complexify over generations (i.e. add and mutate existing functions and weights), which can result in a more personalized CSSN space. By evolving CSSN topologies, users can find and explore a rich space of potential sounds.

Experiments in this paper are designed to explore the perceived quality of evolved timbres produced by CSSNs. In a listener study participants are asked to rank five related timbres from different generations in the same evolutionary run. Results indicate that preference is dependent on the particular user, but that first and later generations are preferred. Section 2 describes previous approaches to sound synthesis with evolutionary computation while section 3 discuss generating timbres with CSSNs. Sections 4 describe the experiment and listener study. Results are presented in 5 and discussed in sections 6 and 7.

2. BACKGROUND

This section introduces previous approaches in evolving sounds and provides background on CPPNs, NEAT, and wavetable oscillators, the foundations of CSSNs.

2.1 Evolutionary Computation and Sound Generation

Timbre choice often influences musical mood and a listener's perception of quality, and is therefore an important consideration for composers and electronic music producers. While most digital audio workstations provide sound banks from which composers can choose, enhancing these sounds is is often left to the user. Because producing desirable sounds is a complex process requiring the optimization of potentially hundreds of parameters [3], several approaches reproduce existing sounds electronically by evolving and optimizing these parameters. For instance, with a given synthesizer, parameters can be evolved to transform a synthesized waveform into target waveforms [12, 20, 16]. Similarly, other methods evolve these waveforms directly [17, 19, 1, 7]. While these approaches can potentially help musicians to create synthesized sounds for music production, they rely on matching existing sounds rather than exploring the space of entirely new sounds.

Interactive evolutionary computation (IEC) is a popular method for evolving art and music [5, 30]. Instead of relying on fitness functions designed by developers, users make their own aesthetic decisions by rating candidate individuals. With IEC users can evolve music and sounds [11, 3, 15], images [26], and visuals for video games [24, 8, 10, 23]. For example in MutaSynth [3], timbres are encoded as arrays of floats where each gene represents a synthesizer parameter. Users interactively evolve these sounds by both listening to the generated sound and inspecting a visual representation. Parameters are similarly evolved for the CSound synthesis engine in Johnson [15].

In most approaches, users can explore a sound space that is produced by an external synthesizer whose parameters are interactively evolved. Instead, the approach in this paper allows users to interactively evolve wave forms that are themselves generated by a composition of functions rather than strings of parameter settings.

2.2 CPPNs and NEAT

Because timbres are in essence patterns generated from a composition of different functions, in this paper they are represented by compositional pattern producing networks (CPPNs; 28), which are a special type of artificial neural network (ANN) that can compute any activation function at its hidden nodes. In addition to the sigmoid activation functions present in traditional ANNs, CPPNs (shown in Figure 1a) also incorporate sine, linear, and Gaussian activation functions that can bias toward certain types of regularities (e.g. repetition, repetition with variation, bilateral symmetry, etc.). Additionally, CPPNs are typically applied across a broader range of possible inputs like coordinates of a two-dimensional space, therefore allowing them to produce e.g. two-dimensional images (Figure 1b).

In this paper, CPPNs are evolved with *NeuroEvolution of Augmenting Topologies* (NEAT; 27), which was originally designed to solve complex control and decision tasks. NEAT begins evolution with a minimal network topology and complexifies through evolution by adding and mutating connections and nodes to the evolving network. CPPNs evolved in this way have generated picture patterns in Picbreeder [26], musical voices in MaestroGenesis [11], flowers in Petalz [24, 23], and weapon visuals in the video game Galactic Arms Race [8]. Inspired by the quality of results from these approaches, this paper explores the space of one-dimensional sound waves created by CPPNs and searched with NEAT. By representing timbres through hidden node activation functions inherited from analog sound synthesis, CPPNs can in principle reproduce and elaborate on traditional waveforms to produce novel timbres.

2.3 Constructing Wavetables

The patterns produced by CPPNs are the basis to create playable wavetable oscillators in this paper. Wavetables are popular in digital sound synthesis and are in essence an array of N values, where each value represents the oscillator's amplitude at a particular point in the cycle (Figure 2).

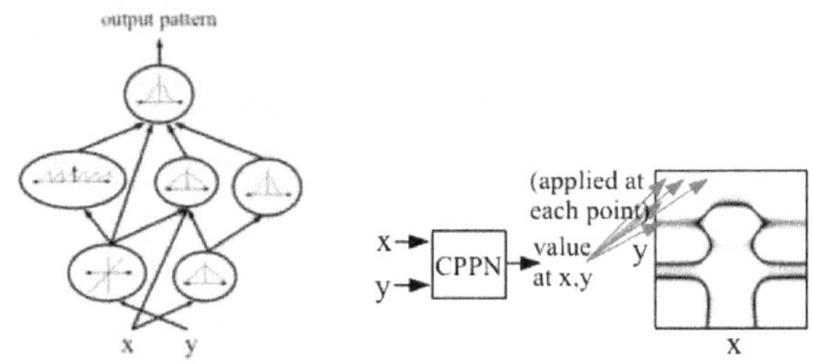

(a) CPPN (b) CPPN to Image

Figure 1: Compositional Pattern Producing Networks. (a) CPPNs can use a variety of different functions like sigmoids, Gaussian, sine and many others in contrast to more traditional ANNs with sigmoid activation functions (b) The CPPN example in this figure inputs two arguments x and y that are interpreted as coordinates in two-dimensional space. Applying the CPPN to all the coordinates and drawing them with an ink intensity determined by its output results in a two-dimensional image.

While wavetables are sometimes described as "the sequence of numbers that represent a single cycle of a regular, periodic waveform" [22] others describe it as a technique for stepping through a series of periodic waveforms (in a table) for the duration of each note played [13]. Like analog oscillators, this paper represents wavetables as a single, arbitrary waveform that are playable in a periodic fashion.

The waveforms for building wavetable oscillators can come from a variety of sources. For instance, some are pre-processed and pre-recorded. A recent, notable example of a such a synthesizer is *Animoog*, whose "diverse library of timbres is derived from analog waveforms captured from classic Moog oscillators, both vintage and modern, and run through ...high-end outboard and analog signal processors" [21], thus delivering some of the desired qualities of analog hardware synthesizers to the more affordable digital domain.

Some audio synthesis applications help users create wavetable oscillators by allowing users to draw arbitrary waveforms freely by hand. Others employ techniques from vector graphics to shape the periodic waveforms, such as BÃl'zier curves such as the *DIN Is Noise* synthesizer [25]. These methods challenge the ability to apply visual imagination to the process of shaping interesting timbres. Instead of designing waveforms directly, the new approach presented in this paper lets the user interactively evolve such waveforms, which are encoded by CPPNs. These waveforms are then automatically converted into playable wavetable oscillators.

While there appear to be no previous applications of CPPN-NEAT to create wavetable oscillators (CSSNs), a previous approach evolves soundtrack patterns with CPPN-NEAT [31] and guitar effect pedals [6].

3. APPROACH

The approach presented here focuses on the CSSN representation for sound synthesis and provides an initial investigation into the space of timbres evolved through NEAT. To facilitate the exploration of the space of CSSN timbres, populations of waveforms are presented to the user and evolved through IEC.

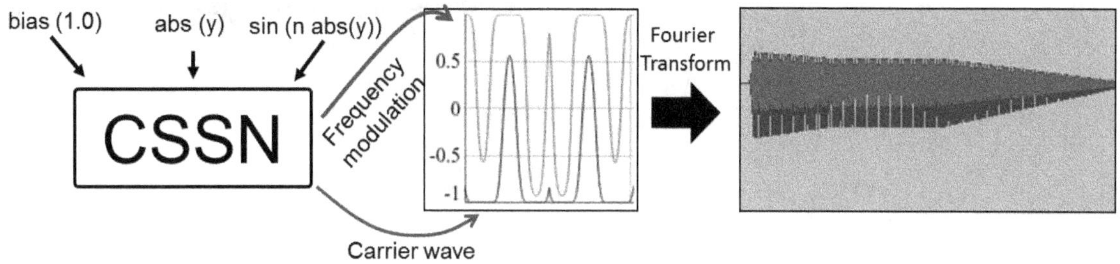

Figure 3: Compositional Sound Synthesis Network. The CSSN has three inputs and two outputs. It receives the absolute values of numbers in a sequence that represents a single cycle of a waveform, and periodic inputs as sine waves produced from multiples of the numbers in that same sequence. The two CSSN outputs allow the assembly of a simple *frequency modulation* synthesizer, in which the modulator output can affect the oscillation frequency of the carrier oscillator output.

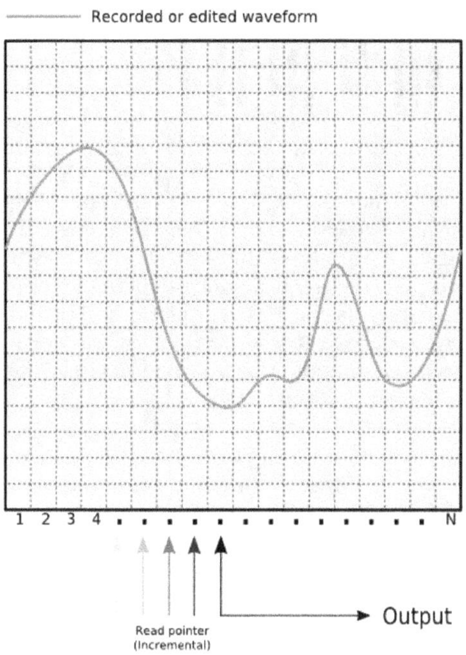

Figure 2: Wavetable Oscillator. This figure shows the basic structure of a wavetable oscilator. Retrieved from http://upload.wikimedia.org/wikibooks/en/4/4b/SSWavetable.png.

The hope of this novel approach is that the generated waveforms reveal interesting timbres that can be serve as unique building blocks for the assembly of novel synthesizers while potentially offering a viable alternative to previous wavetable construction approaches. Additionally, IEC approaches have the unique potential to provide continual improvement in the perceived quality of additional musical voices [11].

The next sections explain the underlying CPPN-based representation in more detail, followed by a description of the interactive framework called *Breedesizer*.

3.1 CPPN Waveform Synthesis

A crucial aspect of generating timbres in this paper is the representation, which is based on CPPNs. CPPNs are particularly suited to produce structured waveforms because of their ability to generate patterns with important regularities such as symmetry and repetition [28, 26]. A fundamental difference between the timbre-encoding CPPNs in this paper and the CPPNs employed in Picbreeder (Figure 1) is that they work with one-dimensional instead of two-dimensional inputs to the networks.

The novel approach presented here is called a *compositional sound synthesis network* (CSSN), an extension of CPPNs to generate playable wavetable oscillators. The current CSSN implements sine, cosine, and inverse tangent activation functions, but further exploration will likely benefit from including a wider variety of functions in the set, such as those representing the classic analog waveforms (e.g. Sawtooth, Square and Triangle).

An overview of the approach is shown in Figure 3. The CSSN is queried with one-dimensional input y that represent each sample of the waveform to be generated. The numbers are in a sequence that represents a single cycle of a periodic waveform between -1 and 1. To ensure continuity between the ends of the waveforms, the absolute value of y is provided as input instead of y directly. To produce repetition in CSSN outputs, $sin(n \times abs(y))$ is fed into an additional input node, with an adjustable integer value n to allow different frequencies of repetition. Removing the application of the absolute value function on the y values passed to the sine wave calculation can result in discontinuous waveforms that may produce unpleasant or interesting timbres.

Each CSSN has two outputs to allow for the assembly of a simple *frequency modulation* (FM) [2] synthesizer; one output modulates the oscillation frequency of the carrier oscillator produced by the second output. The modulated FM synthesis produces a richer timbre than the unmodulated carrier oscillator. Figure 4 shows example waveforms created by different CSSNs with and without symmetry enabled. The underlying encoding is able to elaborate on the repeating sine input, the most fundamental building block of sounds in this paper, and produce personalized oscillators.

To create playable wavetable oscillators from the arbitrary waveforms produced by the CSSN, their signal data is decomposed to its constituent frequencies by a Fourier transform. The results of this process is a table of coefficients in a Fourier series, which represent the partials of a periodic waveform. The FM synthesizer are constructed in con-

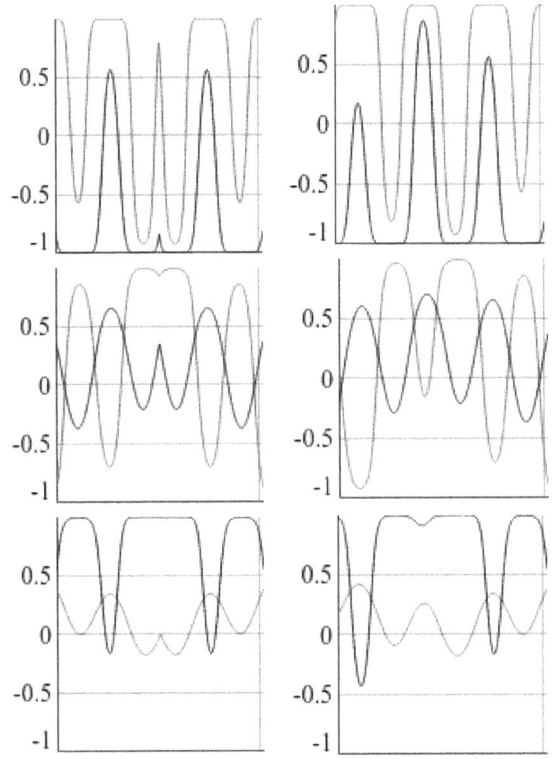

(a) Symmetric (b) Non-symmetric

Figure 4: Example Timbres Produced by Compositional Sound Synthesis Networks (CSSNs). This figure shows two waveforms produced by the same CSSN, either with inputs restricted to absolute values (a), or with those restrictions lifted from the periodic input node (b). The green curves represent the carrier wave and the blue curves represent the frequency modulation wave.

nection with each wavetable oscillator under consideration. This is accomplished by forming two periodic waveforms as outputs from the evolved CPPN, where each is used to construct its own wavetable oscillator; one is acting as a modulator of the timbre produced by the other carrier output.

Using the Web Audio API[1], those Fourier coefficients are transformed into a periodic wave, or a wavetable, which can have arbitrary harmonic content. The bigger the table (or sample size), the closer the approximation by the Fourier transform, and the size is adjustable in the user interface with a default of 1024.

More waveforms could easily be added as additional outputs to the CSSN and be used as building blocks of other audio synthesis techniques. The simple FM synthesis approach described here provides a glimpse into the possibilities of using this technique to arrange more complex synthesizers.

3.2 The IEC Application: Breedesizer

Breedesizer is written in HTML and JavaScript and is readily accessible in common web browsers without additional setup overheads of traditional software plug-ins. The program is publicly available at http://bthj.is/breedesizer.

[1]http://webaudioapi.com/

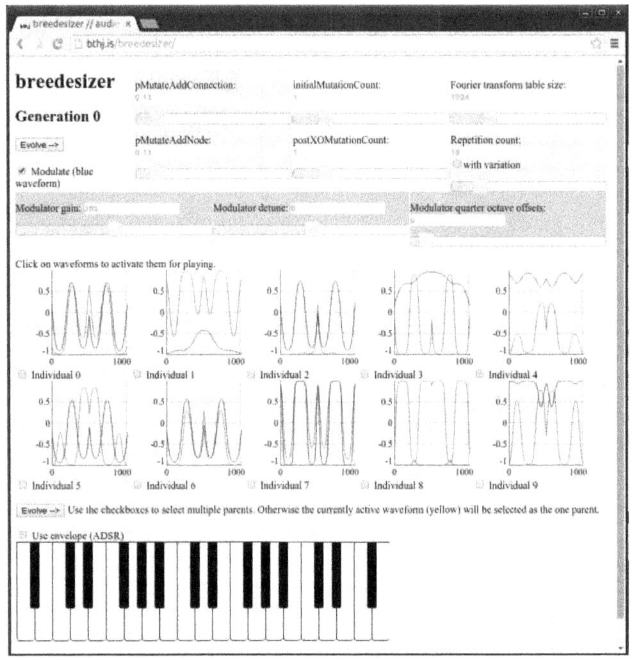

Figure 5: Breedesizer User Interface. Breedesizer allows the user to evolve CSSN-encoded musical timbres through IEC. A variety of different sliders can adjust mutation rates and the frequency of the periodic input to the CSSN or enable/disable FM modulation. Ten individuals are displayed at once to the user. Each waveform can be listened to by clicking on it or playing the virtual keyboard.

Breedesizer is built on the CPPN-NEAT implementation of the Worldwide Infrastructure for Neuroevolution (WIN)[2] solution, which allows them to run in a web browser.

A screenshot of the Breedesizer user interface is shown in Figure 5. The interface presents one population of ten waveforms at a time, which are produced by the CSSN-encoding described in Section 3.1. The ten waveforms at the beginning of each IEC session are created randomly. Future generations are based on mating parents selected from the current population and mutating their offspring. Mutations in the CSSNs modify the connections weights or add nodes and new connections with a low probability.

Each waveform presented can be enabled for playback by clicking on it. An on-screen musical keyboard can be clicked with a pointing device to play different notes with the selected oscillator. The keys of a desktop computer's QWERTY keyboard can also be clicked to play different notes.

In lessen user fatigue, each waveform instantly plays one short note when clicked (C3 at 130.813 Hz), for the duration of one quarter note at 120 BPM, 500 ms. The continuous playing of a selected MIDI song while auditioning the timbres of the different oscillators is still under development.

Mutation probabilities are adjustable in the user interface with two sliders, one for the probability of adding a connection and another for adding a node. A slider is also present for adjusting how many times to mutate each individual.

[2]http://winark.org/, a proposed framework for turning any evolutionary domain into an online interactive platform [29]. The modules are compiled with the Component[3]

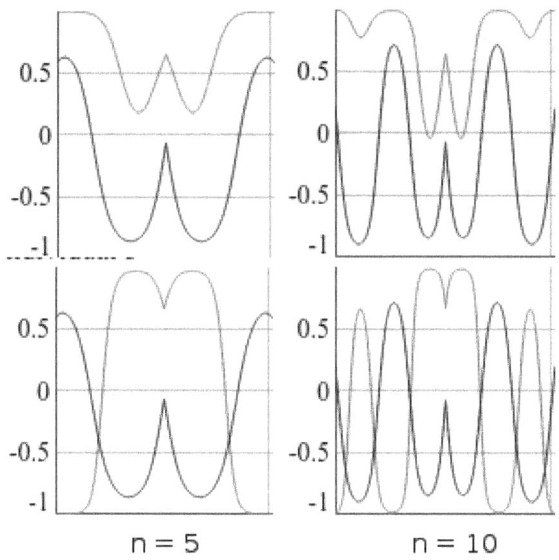

Figure 6: Varying the Periodic CSSN Input. By varying the periodic frequency input into the CSSN different but functionally related waveforms can be created.

Initially, this value is set to five to produce a large variety of different timbres for the first generation, and then reduced to a value of one.

The frequency of the periodic wave input is adjustable with a slider in the user interface, updating the waveform drawings in real time as the slider values are changed. This option allows the user to hear different timbre textures from each CSSN. An example of two waveform variations produced by the same CSSN with different periodic input frequencies is shown in Figure 6.

Three additional sliders are present in the user interface, for adjusting parameters to the FM synthesis configuration. The first sliders change the amplitude of the modulator, controlling its effect on the carrier wave. The second slider enables the detuning of the modulator wave, which is per default set to the same frequency as the carrier. Slightly detuning the modulator frequency produces an audible and often interesting phase change between the oscillators, with a loop between an in-phase and out-of-phase state. The third slider changes the modulator frequencies by multiples of the carrier frequency, where each slider step corresponds to $\frac{carrier\_frequency}{4}$.

The presence of those sliders can be considered as contrary to the primary aim of the presented IEC environment, which is to enable non-experts to discover interesting synthesized sounds; the adjustments of the optional parameters does benefit from familiarity with the fundamentals of frequency modulation synthesis. However, those knowledge-demanding sliders are present in the user interface nonetheless, as the optional addition of FM synthesis (via a checkbox) from the output of each CSSN, is considered an important example of the possible uses for CPPN-NEAT beyond the mere formation of waveforms to base wavetable oscillators on. Additionally, the adjustment of those parameters is important for the appreciation of the expressive power that FM synthesis has to offer.

To provide a familiar synthesizer characteristic and allowing played notes to start and stop less abruptly, an ADSR envelope (Attack-Decay-Sustain-Release) can optionally be enabled while playing the musical keyboard.

4. EXPERIMENT

The main focus of this paper is to explore whether IEC allows an effective exploration of the search space induced by CSSN-encoded timbres. Additionally, the hope is that the quality of timbres should increase as evolution progresses. This section describes the IEC experiment in which the authors evolved timbres interactively and the listener study designed to elucidate its results.

4.1 Experimental Parameters

The CSSN probability of adding a new connection or a new node is set to 0.13 and the probability of changing a weight is 0.7. These parameters were found through prior experimentation. Population size is 10 per generation. The activation functions for each hidden neuron in the CSSNs are chosen from the canonical set of Gaussian, Bipolar sigmoid, sine and linear, each with a 0.25 probability of being added. The ADSR envelope is enabled for the study presented here, resulting in timbres that start and end smoothly by ramping up the volume at the beginning and then bringing it down at the end of the waveform.

4.2 Interactively Evolving Timbres

To study whether the CSSN can create a variety of novel timbres through IEC the authors evolved waveforms for 45 generations through the interface described in Section 3.1. The experiment is designed to provide insight into what type of sounds the CSSN can generate and what are the challenges faced when evolving timbres in this way.

While the particular run of interactive evolution reported in this paper is anecdotal, the hope is that it can nevertheless provide deeper insights into the particular interactions between IEC and CSSN-generated timbres. Most runs exhibited similar dynamics and features in the evolved sounds.

4.3 Listener Study

To explore whether timbres can increase in perceived quality over time, 26 users ranked five clips of Beethoven's "FÃijr Elise" played by related timbres from different generations in the same evolutionary lineage. The survey was administration through SurveyMonkey (www.surveymonkey.com) and advertised through the ISMIR mailing list and colleagues of the authors. The survey reads:

> Below are five clips of Beethoven's FÃijr Elise. Each one is played by a different instrument or timbre. Each clip differs only in the instrument being heard. Please rank your preferences from Most Favorite to Least Favorite.

5. RESULTS

This section presents the results of interactively evolving timbres by the authors and the insights from the listener study. The CSSN-generated sounds, which also serve as the basis for the listener study, are available through the survey on SurveyMonkey: https://www.surveymonkey.com/s/TZX6DJ6. The corresponding generations for the wavefiles in the survey are C=0, B=3, E=20, A=36, and D=45.

Generation	Mean	Std. Dev
0	3.15	1.08
3	2.34	1.26
20	2.07	1.19
36	3.38	1.16
45	3.92	1.09

Table 1: Average Scoring of Survey Participants.

5.1 Evolving Timbres

The initial population of waveforms, presented in the Breedesizer interface, already provides an interesting variety of timbres. The miscellaneity of waveforms initially presented can be attributed to the high number of mutations performed on the individuals created from the population seeds, but the interestingness of the timbres can be attributed to the representational properties of CPPNs.

Figure 7 shows a lineage of timbre evolution of generations 0, 3, 20, 36, and 45. Evolution through the first generations commonly produces more variety of timbres with a similar perceived quality. Individuals that emerge around and after generation four can produce less pleasing sounds than their predecessors and continued evolution can show little or no improvement for the immediately following generations. It may seem like the initial production of variety has stopped, as monotonic timbres of inferior quality are produced over several successive generations.

This period of apparent deterioration, or stagnation at best, gives the user performing the IEC little incentive to continue the evolution, but if he or she perseveres, interesting individuals can emerge again after generation 20. The increase in variety and perceived quality is commonly maintained beyond that point and the timbres can be perceived as fuller, with lesser resemblance of a tin can sound. This increase in richness of the produced sounds can be attributed to subtle nuances that begin to appear in the waveforms, as especially apparent in the blue waveform of Figure 7d.

The pattern of perceived timbre quality during the IEC process is reflected in the user study, discussed next.

5.2 Listener Study Results

The results from the 26-person listener study are shown in Figure 8 and summarized in Table 1. Participants commonly preferred the sounds from the first generation to those from the immediately following generations. However, starting from generation 20 the sounds consistently increase in perceived listener appreciation. Importantly, generation 45 is judged significantly higher than generations 0 to 20 ($p < 0.05$; Student's t-test). Thus the participants felt some overall progression from the initial generation to the last, even though the timbres first decreased in perceived quality.

Interestingly, while similar experiments in evolving musical accompaniments through IEC showed a consistent increase in perceived listener appreciation [11], results from the timbre evolution and listener study are less clear. For instance, first generations in timbre evolution show little or no improvement and the sounds can sometimes first deteriorate in perceived quality before they improve.

The main result is that the CSSN can eventually generate rich and full timbres through IEC that are appreciated by the survey participants. Future work will facilitate and accelerate this process.

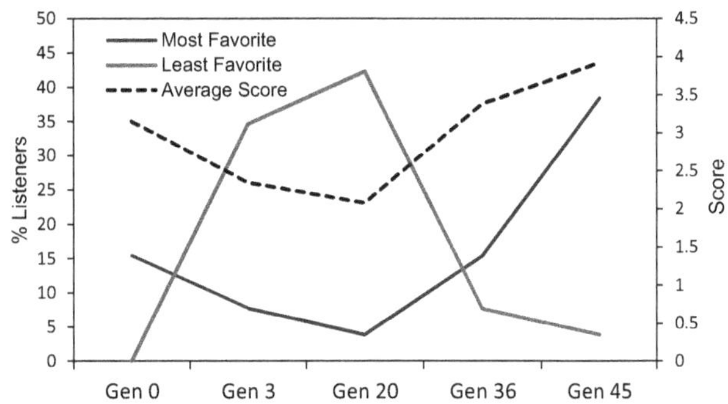

Figure 8: Perceived Quality by Survey Participants. This figure shows the average rating and the percentage of listeners rating the song either as their most or least favorite. The main result is that the participants commonly preferred the sounds from the first generation to those from the immediately following generations, and sounds produced beyond generation 20 are favored still more.

6. DISCUSSION AND FUTURE WORK

The representational properties of CPPNs to form periodic waves enables the presented CSSN approach to produce a variety of timbres. In this way, CSSNs offer a viable alternative to more traditional wavetable construction methods such as free-form drawing or shaping BÃĽzier curves by hand. Future work aims to compare the spaces of timbres that can be produced with these approaches to further explore the structure of the presented search space.

Furthermore, collaborative effort in the evolutionary process, in which users can branch off each others work in a fashion similar to that offered by Picbreeder [26], could help overcome the lack of incentive given by the initial periods of evolutionary stagnating. Fatigue sets soon in, especially when dealing with sound, and a user with âĂIJfresh earsâĂİ could be more likely to have the extra patience needed to steer the evolution in an interesting direction.

Future work will also focus on leveraging the CSSN's ability to create a wider variety of different sounds. Exploration in the space of single waveforms output from each CSSN can be of limited interest, while using multi-waveforms to construct more complex synthesis configurations may prove to be more interesting and fruitful.The CSSN approach can easily be extended to output more waveforms, which would be different but still functionally related. The additional FM synthesis output in this paper showed how such an addition can make the produced timbres more interesting. Other audio synthesis techniques are based on the combination of many periodic waveforms, both for timbre and control, and they could provide interesting search spaces for exploration. Additionally, CSSNs could output waveforms for each entry in a wavetable, and one additional waveform to define a curve guiding the sweeps through the series of periodic waveforms in this table, similar to wavetable synthesis.

Eventually, whole synthesizer configurations (i.e. where oscillator outputs flow through filters and are affected by control signals) could be evolved. Instead of specifying activation functions, each network node would designate one component of the synthesizer while the weights on connections between nodes would define the strength of interaction between the components.

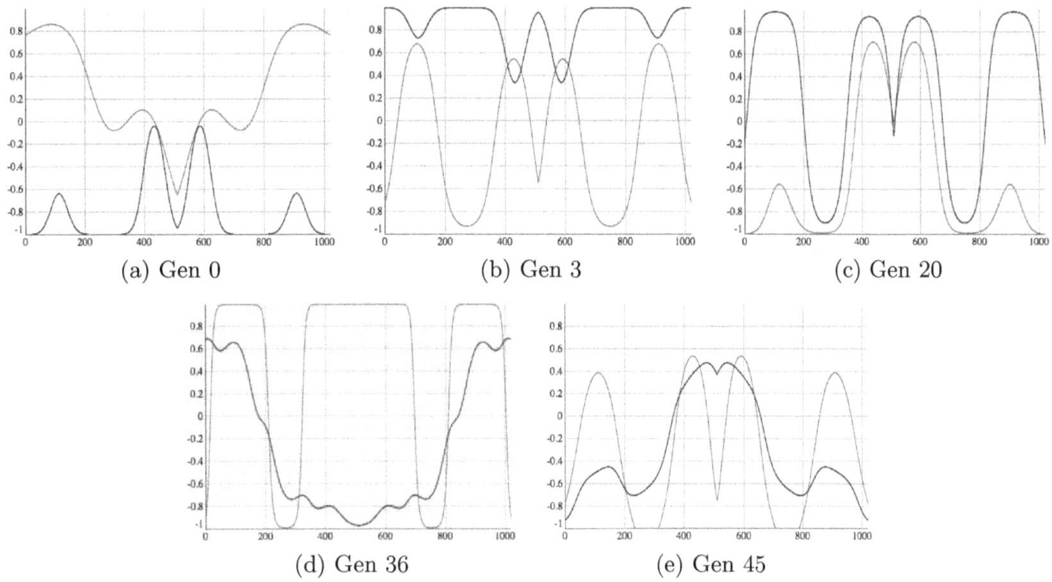

(a) Gen 0 (b) Gen 3 (c) Gen 20

(d) Gen 36 (e) Gen 45

Figure 7: Evolutionary Timbre Sequence. One lineage of timbre waveforms evolved through successive generations. The blue curves represent the carrier wave, or timbre as it would be heard without FM synthesis, and the green curves represent the frequency modulation wave, which is in effect when FM synthesis is enabled. Only one parent is selected for each generation in this evolution example.

The CSSN presented in this paper enables a variety of different applications, thus opening up a new research direction in sound synthesis.

7. CONCLUSION

This paper presented a novel method for sound synthesis, called compositional sound synthesis networks (CSSNs). The CSSN representation is explored with a new application called Breedesizer that allows users to interactively evolve CSSN-encoded sounds. The benefit of the CSSN representation is that it enables the generation of arbitrary waveforms, thereby offering a viable alternative to traditional methods of sound synthesis. Users can elaborate on CSSN-generated timbres through Breedesizer, allowing an amateur composer to generate novel and rich sounds. Future work will focus on extending the approach presented in this paper to evolve CSSNs that output a multitude of different waveforms and eventually complete synthesizers.

8. ACKNOWLEDGMENTS

The research is supported in part by the FP7 ICT project C2Learn (project no: 318480). Special thanks to Paul A. Szerlip who assisted with the CPPN-NEAT implementation of the Worldwide Infrastructure for Neuroevolution (WIN).

References

[1] Caetano, M. F., Manzolli, J., and Zuben, F. J. V. Interactive control of evolution applied to sound synthesis. In *FLAIRS Conference* (2005), 51–56.

[2] Chowning, J. M. The synthesis of complex audio spectra by means of frequency modulation. *Computer Music Journal* (1977), 46–54.

[3] Dahlstedt, P. Creating and Exploring Huge Parameter Spaces: Interactive Evolution as a Tool for Sound Generation. In *Proceedings of the 2001 International Computer Music Conference* (2001), 235–242.

[4] Dahlstedt, P. Evolution in creative sound design. In *Evolutionary Computer Music*. Springer, 2007, 79–99.

[5] Dawkins, R. *The Blind Watchmaker.* Longman, Essex, U.K., 1986.

[6] DeBoer, S. M., and Stanley, K. O. Systems and methods for inducing effects in a signal, Dec. 3 2013. US Patent 8,600,068.

[7] Garcia, R. A. Growing sound synthesizers using evolutionary methods. In *Proceedings ALMMA 2001: Artificial Life Models for Musical Applications Workshop,(ECAL 2001)* (2001).

[8] Hastings, E. J., Guha, R. K., and Stanley, K. O. Evolving Content in the Galactic Arms Race Video Game. In *Proceedings of the IEEE Symposium on Computational Intelligence and Games (CIG 2009)*, IEEE (2009), 241–248.

[9] Hill, B. Breaking down the breakdown: The use of timbres in contemporary dance music sub-genres. In *Proceedings of the Australasian Computer Music Conference (ACMC 2005)* (2005).

[10] Hoover, A. K., Cachia, W., Liapis, A., and Yannakakis, G. N. Audioinspace: Exploring the creative fusion of generative audio, visuals and gameplay. In *Evolutionary and Biologically Inspired Music, Sound, Art and Design* (2015), 101–112.

[11] Hoover, A. K., Szerlip, P. A., and Stanley, K. O. Functional scaffolding for composing additional musical voices. *Computer Music Journal 38*, 4 (2014), 80–99.

[12] Horner, A., Beauchamp, J., and Haken, L. Machine tongues xvi: Genetic algorithms and their application to fm matching synthesis. *Computer Music Journal* (1993), 17–29.

[13] Howell, S. Origins of wavetable, s&s and vector synthesis. http://www.soundonsound.com/sos/feb06/articles/qa0206_1.htm. Accessed: January 21 2015.

[14] Jenkins, M. *Analog Synthesizers : Understanding, Performing, Buying–From the Legacy of Moog to Software Synthesis*. Taylor and Francis, 2009.

[15] Johnson, C. G. Exploring sound-space with interactive genetic algorithms. *Leonardo 36*, 1 (2003), 51–54.

[16] Lai, Y., Jeng, S.-K., Liu, D.-T., and Liu, Y.-C. Automated optimization of parameters for fm sound synthesis with genetic algorithms. In *International Workshop on Computer Music and Audio Technology* (2006).

[17] Macret, M., and Pasquier, P. Automatic design of sound synthesizers as pure data patches using coevolutionary mixed- typed cartesian genetic programming. In *Proceedings of the Genetic and Evolutionary Computation Conference (GECCO 2014)* (2014).

[18] Manning, P. *Electronic and Computer Music*. Oxford University Press, 2004.

[19] Manzolli, J., Jr., A. M., Fornari, J., and Damiani, F. The evolutionary sound synthesis method. In *Proceedings of the Ninth ACM International Conference on Multimedia*, ACM (2001), 585–587.

[20] McDermott, J., Griffith, N. J. L., and O'Neill, M. Evolutionary computation applied to the control of sound synthesis. In *Applications of Evolutionary Computing*, vol. 4974 of *Lecture Notes in Computer Science* (2008).

[21] Moog Music Inc. Animoog (product page). http://www.moogmusic.com/products/apps/animoog-0. Accessed: January 22 2015.

[22] Reid, G. Thor demystified 11: The wavetable oscillator part 1. https://www.propellerheads.se/blog/tutorials/thor-demystified-11-the-wavetable-oscillator-part-1/. Accessed: January 21 2015.

[23] Risi, S., Lehman, J., D'Ambrosio, D., Hall, R., and Stanley, K. Petalz: Search-based procedural content generation for the casual gamer. *Computational Intelligence and AI in Games, IEEE Transactions on PP*, 99 (2015), 1–1.

[24] Risi, S., Lehman, J., D'Ambrosio, D. B., Hall, R., and Stanley, K. O. Combining search-based procedural content generation and social gaming in the petalz video game. In *Proceedings of the Artificial Intelligence and Interactive Digital Entertainment Conference (AIIDE 2012)*, AAAI Press (Menlo Park, CA, 2012).

[25] Sampath, J. DIN Is Noise synthesizer. http://dinisnoise.org/. Accessed: January 21 2015.

[26] Secretan, J., Beato, N., D'Ambrosio, D. B., Campbell, A. R. A., Folsom-Kovarik, J. T., and Stanley, K. O. Picbreeder: A case study in collaborative evolutionary exploration of design space. *Evolutionary Computation 19*, 3 (2011), 373–403.

[27] Stanley, K., and Miikkulainen, R. Evolving neural networks through augmenting topologies. *Evolutionary computation 10*, 2 (2002), 99–127.

[28] Stanley, K. O. Compositional pattern producing networks: A novel abstraction of development. *Genetic Programming and Evolvable Machines 8*, 2 (2007), 131–162.

[29] Szerlip, P., and Stanley, K. O. Steps toward a modular library for turning any evolutionary domain into an online interactive platform. In *ALIFE 14: The Fourteenth Conference on the Synthesis and Simulation of Living Systems*, vol. 14 (2014), 726–733.

[30] Takagi, H. Interactive evolutionary computation: fusion of the capabilities of ec optimization and human evaluation. *Proceedings of the IEEE 89*, 9 (Sep 2001), 1275–1296.

[31] Ye, J., and Chen, S. SoundBreeder with MultiNEAT. http://web.cs.swarthmore.edu/~meeden/cs81/s14/papers/AndyLucas.pdf. Accessed: January 19 2015.

Darwin's Avatars: a Novel Combination of Gameplay and Procedural Content Generation

Dan Lessin
ITU Copenhagen
Copenhagen, Denmark
dles@itu.dk

Sebastian Risi
ITU Copenhagen
Copenhagen, Denmark
sebr@itu.dk

ABSTRACT

The co-evolution of morphology and control for virtual creatures enables the creation of a novel form of gameplay and procedural content generation. Starting with a creature evolved to perform a simple task such as locomotion and removing its brain, the remaining body can be employed in a compelling interactive control problem. Just as we enjoy the challenge and reward of mastering helicopter flight or learning to play a musical instrument, learning to control such a creature through manual activation of its actuators presents an engaging and rewarding puzzle. Importantly, the novelty of this challenge is inexhaustible, since the evolution of virtual creatures provides a way to procedurally generate content for such a game. An endless series of creatures can be evolved for a task, then have their brains removed to become the game's next human-control challenge. To demonstrate this new form of gameplay and content generation, a proof-of-concept game—tentatively titled *Darwin's Avatars*—was implemented using evolved creature content, and user tested. This implementation also provided a unique opportunity to compare human and evolved control of evolved virtual creatures, both qualitatively and quantitatively, with interesting implications for improvements and future work.

Categories and Subject Descriptors

I.2.6 [**Artificial Intelligence**]: Learning—*connectionism and neural nets*; I.6.8 [**Simulation and Modeling**]: Types of Simulation—*animation*; I.2.1 [**Artificial Intelligence**]: Applications and Expert Systems—*games*; I.3.7 [**Computer Graphics**]: Three-Dimensional Graphics and Realism—*animation*

Keywords

evolved virtual creatures; artificial life; muscle drives; physics-based character animation; procedural content generation

GECCO '15, July 11–15, 2015, Madrid, Spain
© 2015 ACM. ISBN 978-1-4503-3472-3/15/07...$15.00
DOI: http://dx.doi.org/10.1145/2739480.2754749

(a) User view of the game.

(b) Volunteers playtesting the human vs. human version of the game.

Figure 1: Proof-of-concept game implementation. See video at http://youtu.be/p42wPQ3FYLU .

1. INTRODUCTION

This paper describes a new form of gameplay and a corresponding method of procedural content generation [17, 19, 5] which are made possible by evolutionary computation. The fundamental gameplay mechanism is a complex non-intuitive problem: How to control a physically simulated three-dimensional creature by manually activating its muscles.

The core content of the game—the creature to be controlled—is generated procedurally using a muscle-driven evolved virtual creature (EVC) system like the one described in Lessin et al. [6]. Due to this close coupling between the core gameplay mechanics (learning to control an unfamiliar creature) and the associated method for procedural content generation (evolving virtual creatures), the game's entertainment value is inherently vibrant, novel, and open ended. The implementation, mechanics, and procedural generation of content for the game—referred to here as *Darwin's Avatars*—are described in Section 3.

An additional benefit of this game system is that it permits the co-evolved controllers for these creature bodies to be compared to human control techniques. By seeing the ways in which human and evolved controllers differ (both in strategy and ability), we may be able to produce better evolved controllers. In Section 5, the results of such a comparison (both quantitative and qualitative) are presented, using data collected across multiple trials, users, and creatures. Useful implications of these comparisons are discussed in Section 6.

2. BACKGROUND

Before the presentation of the new system, relevant related work–both in terms of implementation and gameplay–will be described in this section.

2.1 EVC System

The EVC method at the heart of this new system of gameplay and content generation is an adaptation of Sims' original work [16], with a few small changes as well as some novel features. That method is described next.

Evolutionary Algorithm

A conventional evolutionary algorithm is used, with elitism, fitness-proportionate selection, and rank selection [8]. In addition, the most challenging tasks employ shaping [20, 3]. Fitness is evaluated in a physically simulated virtual environment implemented with NVIDIA PhysX [10].

Morphology

As in Sims' original work, creature morphology is described by a graph-based genotype, with graph nodes representing body segments, and graph edges representing joints between segments (Figure 2). By starting at the root and traversing the graph's edges, the phenotype is expressed. Reflexive edges as well as multiple edges between the same node pair are allowed, making it possible to define recursive and repeated body substructures easily. In addition, as in Sims' work, body symmetry is made readily available to evolution, with only a single mutation required to produce it. In this implementation, all PhysX primitives are available for use as body segments: boxes, spheres, and capsules. Joints between segments may be of most of the types offered by PhysX, specifically: fixed, revolute, spherical, prismatic, and cylindrical. In contrast to the typical technique of separately evolving explicit joint limits, most limitations on joint movement are provided implicitly by creature structure through natural collisions between adjacent segments.

In addition to the typical segments and joints, the implementation of the underlying EVC system also evolves muscle drives, described next.

Muscles

In a break with traditional evolved virtual creature systems, which typically use forces exerted directly at joints, the underlying EVC system of this paper uses simulated muscles as actuators [7]. Muscles are rendered as lines (as seen in Figures 4-6), with color from white to red indicating the degree

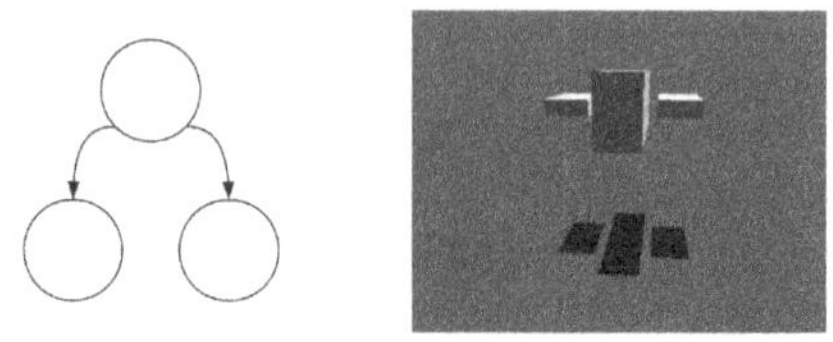

(a) Simple topology.

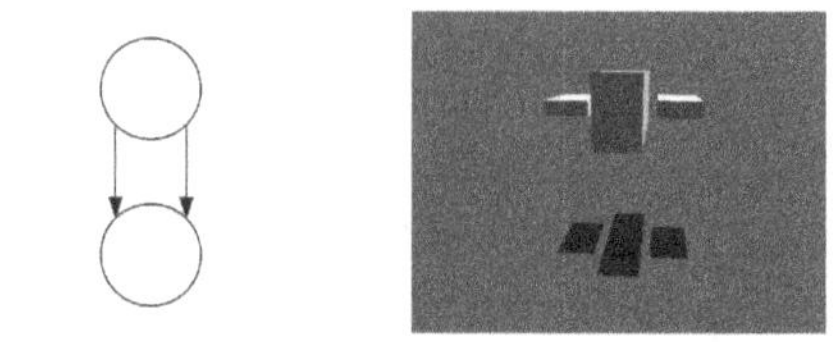

(b) Multiple edges for repeated substructures.

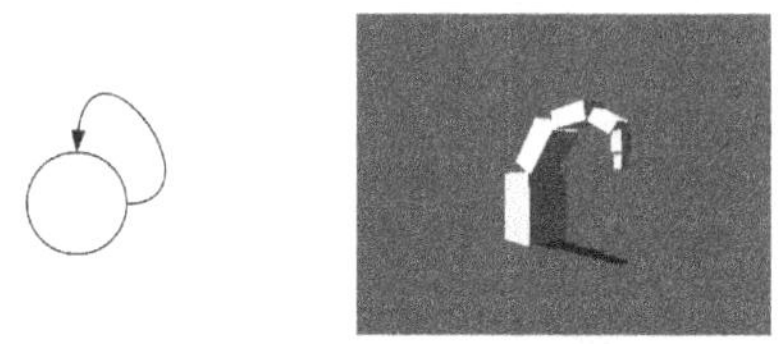

(c) Reflexive edge for recursive structure.

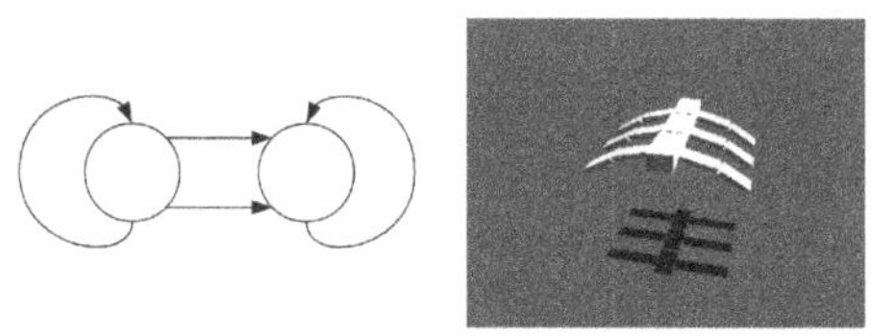

(d) Multiple and reflexive edges together.

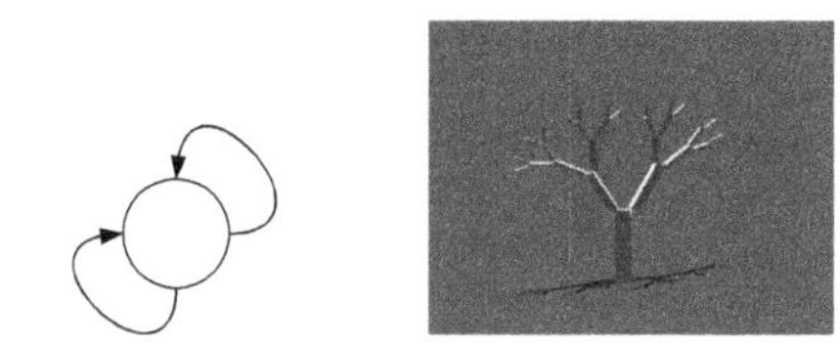

(e) Multiple reflexive edges.

Figure 2: Hand-designed genotype/phenotype pairs (after those of Sims [16]) demonstrate the encoding power of EVC systems like the one employed in this paper.

of activation, from zero to full, respectively. Each muscle is defined by two attachment points on adjacent segments, along with a maximum strength value. In simulation, the muscle is implemented as a spring, with muscle activation modifying the spring constant. In addition to acting as an effector, each muscle also produces a proprioceptive feedback signal based on its current length. For each muscle, two nodes are added to the brain: one that accepts an input to set the muscle's activation, and another that makes the muscle's proprioceptive output signal available to the rest of the brain.

Control

In a manner which is again very similar to that of Sims, creature control is provided by a brain composed of a set of nodes connected by wires (as in Figure 3). Nodes receive varying numbers of input wires, and use their inputs to compute an output value (always in the range [0,1]) which may be sent to other wires. Signals originate from sensors in the body as well as certain types of internal brain nodes, travel through the network of internal nodes and wires, and ultimately control the operation of actuators (muscles) in the physically simulated body. For each step of physical simulation, control signals move one step through the brain.

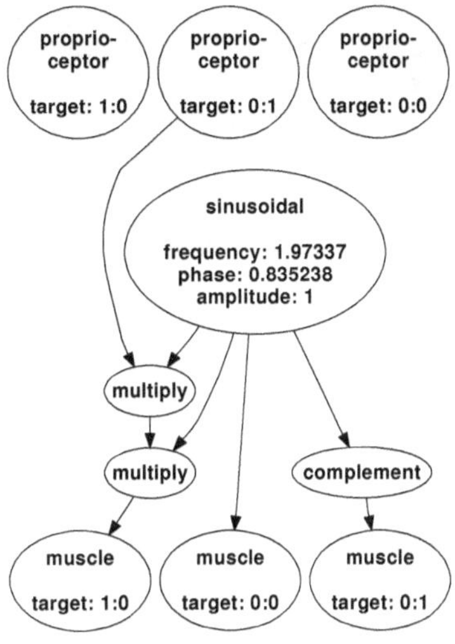

Figure 3: An EVC control network, co-evolved with a body for locomotion.

In addition to the special node types for muscles and their associated proprioceptors (described above), the following node types are allowed: sinusoidal, complement, constant, scale, multiply, divide, sum, difference, derivative, threshold, switch, delay, and absolute difference.

2.2 Related Work

The gameplay presented here, while novel, is not without precedent. The most obvious and closely related example is Bennett Foddy's online game *QWOP*[1] [2]. In QWOP, the user is presented with a two-dimensional physically simulated human runner whose muscles are controlled by pressing Q, W, O, and P on the keyboard. This work is useful in that it demonstrates the viability of gameplay which uses manual keyboard control of physically simulated muscles. The primary difference between the new system and QWOP is that this new control challenge is deeper and open ended, since it takes place in an unlimited supply of novel creatures produced through evolution. In addition, this evolutionary process provides viable automatic control systems for the creatures, making them available as competitors or teaching models.

Also of note, *Incredipede*[2] demonstrates the rewarding gameplay challenge of non-intuitive creature control (again in 2-D), although in this case, morphology can vary. This variability of body and control are at the heart of that game's entertainment value, serving to demonstrate the worth of the same gameplay challenge in the new system presented here. In Incredipede, however, morphological novelty is added by the player through a manual creature construction process, in contrast to the automated mechanism of procedural content generation described in this paper.

[1]http://www.foddy.net/Athletics.html
[2]http://www.incredipede.com

With respect to human vs. evolved control of physically simulated creatures, QWOP was recently the subject of such a comparison [12]. While not yet able to compete with human QWOP champions [11], their system is described by the authors as the first autonomous evolution of successful QWOP gaits.

When applied to games, procedural content generation (PCG) allows game elements (e.g. maps, textures, items, quests, etc.) to be generated algorithmically rather than through direct human design [19, 5]. This approach can reduce design costs and can also benefit players by providing them unique experiences every time they play. In particular, evolutionary computation and other search-based approaches [19] can enable the design of new content outside the scope of a fixed space of rules.

An example of PCG applied to video games is Galactic Arms Race (GAR [4]), in which weapons are evolved automatically based on user behavior. Further examples include Avery et al. [1], who evolved several aspects of a tower defense game, Shaker et al. [15] who evolved levels for the platform game Super Mario Bros., Risi et al. [13], whose game *Petalz* allows players to breed an unlimited variety of virtual flowers, and Togelius et al. [18], who experimented with evolving the rules of the game itself.

While the potential of PCG in competitive gaming is now well established [4, 9, 14], this paper presents the first example of PCG-generated EVCs for game content. The promise of this new approach is that it could supply a novel and unlimited stream of interesting creatures for the player to master.

3. THE GAME: DARWIN'S AVATARS

This paper's primary contribution is a new and powerful combination of gameplay and content generation. The fundamental challenge of the game is to manually control the muscles of a novel creature to achieve a certain task. In this proof-of-concept implementation, the challenge is a race, either against another human user, or against an evolved controller.

In this section, this system is presented in detail. First, the game's method of procedural content generation is described. Second, the mechanics of the game implementation are presented. Finally, the results of a human vs. human playtesting trial of the game are given.

3.1 Procedural Generation of Game Content

The game described above derives its entertainment value from the user's mastery of an unfamiliar control problem. In other games (e.g., QWOP and Incredipede) this challenging unfamiliarity is either fixed or the result of a user-controlled construction process. In contrast, this new game's corresponding procedural content generation is both open-ended and automatic, providing the user with an essentially inexhaustible source for the challenge at the heart of its gameplay.

To produce novel creatures for the user to control, an EVC system (Section 2.1) is run, with fitness corresponding to what will be the user's goal during gameplay. In the game described in this paper, for example, the creatures are the result of evolution for a locomotion task. Typically, ten runs might be started in parallel (with different random seeds), each with population size 100. These might evolve for 500 generations, with the winner from each run examined for both fitness success and aesthetic suitability. Approximately half of these runs might be expected to yield useful results.

Because the body is co-evolved with a successful control mechanism, two important aims are achieved: First, it is demonstrated that useful control of the evolved body is possible. If the body were merely evolved on its own, creatures might result which had no possibility of successful control. Second, the existence of an evolved control system for each creature makes a non-player character available, enabling a single user to compete against—or learn by example from—the evolved brain.

3.2 Game Mechanics

Drawing upon the bodies evolved as described in Section 3.1, users are presented with three creatures, each with a different body plan, muscle structure, and likely locomotion style. The first creature (Figure 4) has three muscles, and typically moves by raising and lowering its heavy front limb to generate a fast jumping gait. The second creature (Figure 5) has four muscles controlling sphere limbs in a body which is symmetrical from front to back. This creature is more challenging to control, as its body makes it as easy to move backward as it is to move forward. It is also possible to tip over with this creature's morphology, although recovery seems always to be possible. The third creature (Figure 6) has the most complex body, with seven segments and six muscles, which are typically used in a familiar (and slower-paced) quadrupedal gait.

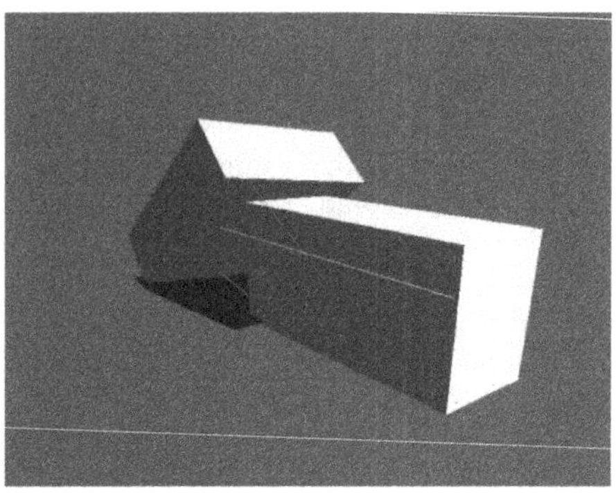

Figure 4: Creature type A: two segments, three muscles.

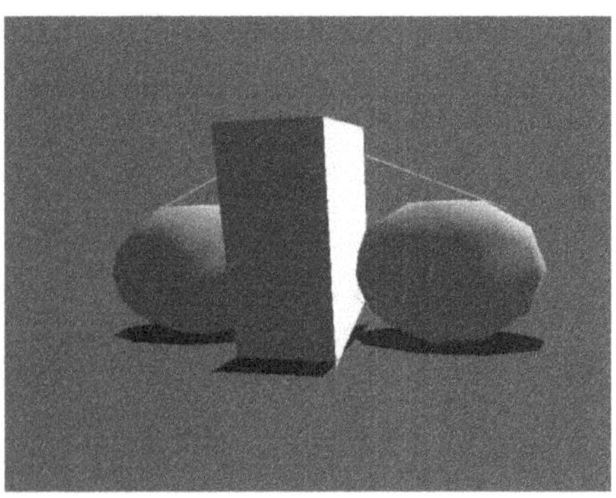

Figure 5: Creature type B: three segments, four muscles.

Once the creature is selected, the user is presented with the set of keys which will control their character. These keys are selected in a fixed yet essentially arbitrary order, with multiple players having a matching pattern of keys in the right and left halves of the keyboard. This non-intentional ordering of muscles and keys is appropriate to the fundamental gameplay challenge of learning a non-intuitive interface to creature control, and it may also be required if the game is to take advantage of the open-ended generation of content provided by the EVC system. Keys control muscle activation directly, with a key being up or down at any point in time corresponding to zero or full activation of a muscle, respectively. Keys controlling muscles function independently, allowing them to be activated in arbitrary overlapping patterns.

Figure 6: Creature type C: seven segments, six muscles.

Two copies of the chosen creature are presented in a side-by-side pair of tracks (Figure 1a), with one creature controlled by player 1, and the other controlled by either player 2 or the creature's original evolved brain, as selected by the user. In this implementation, the tracks were straight, and creatures were prevented from leaving them by invisible physically simulated walls.

At a key press, the start timer counts down to zero, and the race begins. Time and distance are tracked for each creature, until both creatures have reached the end of the tracks or the time limit is reached. The time limits (10, 15, and 20 seconds for creatures A, B, and C, respectively) are based on the evolved controller's known speed for the current creature, with approximately double that time used as a limit in this implementation. When the race ends, each player's speed is presented. Speed is computed as positive or negative distance covered from the start point, divided by time to reach the end of the track (or the limit time, if the end of the track was not reached).

4. HUMAN VS. HUMAN USER EXPERIENCE

In preliminary human-vs.-human playtesting (four users, five matches with each of the three creatures, in the order A, B, C), the value of the proposed gameplay mechanics appear to have been validated. While some users may find direct competition against an evolved brain discouraging due to the mismatch in speed (see Section 5.2), most appear to enjoy the human-versus-human version of the game. As would be expected, such a one-on-one competition tends to reduce frustration, providing real hope for success as long as both players are at a similar level. For example, in the sequence of contests shown in Figure 7, the players are close enough in skill that user 012, while worse on average, is still within reach of user 011's speed, even surpassing it in the fourth run. During testing, many players displayed great curiosity about their scores and relative rankings, suggesting an interest in performance, accomplishment, and competition that bodes well for a motivated and rewarding gameplay experience.

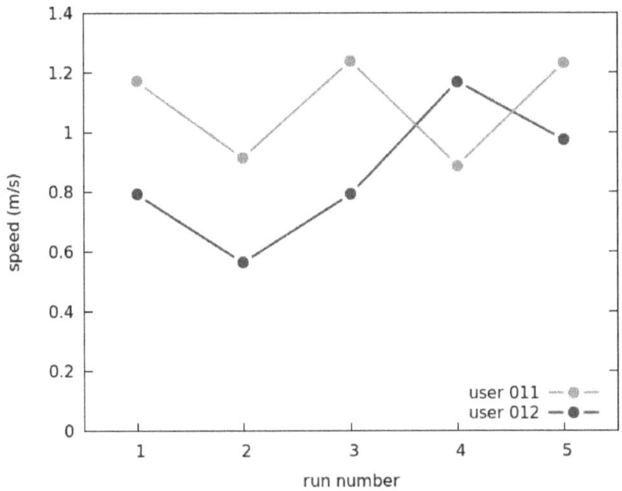

Figure 7: A competitive sequence of five runs of human vs. human competition using the A-type creature.

Also of note, there is evidence for an increase in skill with practice, even over as little as the five runs allowed for each creature type during playtesting. Table 1 illustrates the change in mean speed between the first and fifth run for each creature, using data collected as described in Section 5. While only creature type C's increase is statistically significant ($p < 0.01$, using two-tailed, paired t-test), all three types show an increase in the mean that is at least suggestive.

Creature Type	Run 1 Mean	Run 1 SD	Run 5 Mean	Run 5 SD	p
A	0.4121	0.1651	0.6023	0.2986	0.1591
B	0.1988	0.1293	0.2424	0.0711	0.3930
C	0.1818	0.0543	0.3049	0.1265	0.0088

Table 1: Change in mean speed for each creature type between first and last run of playtesting, along with standard deviations and p (computed using a two-tailed, paired t-test).

This type of learning and accomplishment provides the player with satisfaction, increasing the player's enjoyment and the game's viability. And note that this core aspect of the game's entertainment value—the challenge and satisfaction of improving at a novel control task—is exactly what is extended by the game's corresponding procedural content generation solution.

5. HUMAN VS. EVOLVED-CONTROL RESULTS

In addition to producing the coupled game mechanics and content generation described above, the manual control of muscles in evolved virtual creatures provides a new way to compare human and evolved control of EVCs. In this section, both qualitative differences in control strategy and quantitative differences in resulting speed are presented.

These results are derived from single-player user tests by seven volunteers. In each user test, five runs were performed for each of the three creature types (first A, then B, then C), with both final speed and muscle-activation patterns recorded for each run.

5.1 Qualitative Comparison

For qualitative comparison of human and evolved controllers, patterns of recorded muscle activation are compared. A useful way to present such patterns is as a variation on a spectrogram, with each row corresponding to a single muscle's activation over time. In Figures 8-10, a spectrogram for the final user run of each creature type is presented (in green), along with a spectrogram from that creature's evolved controller (in red).

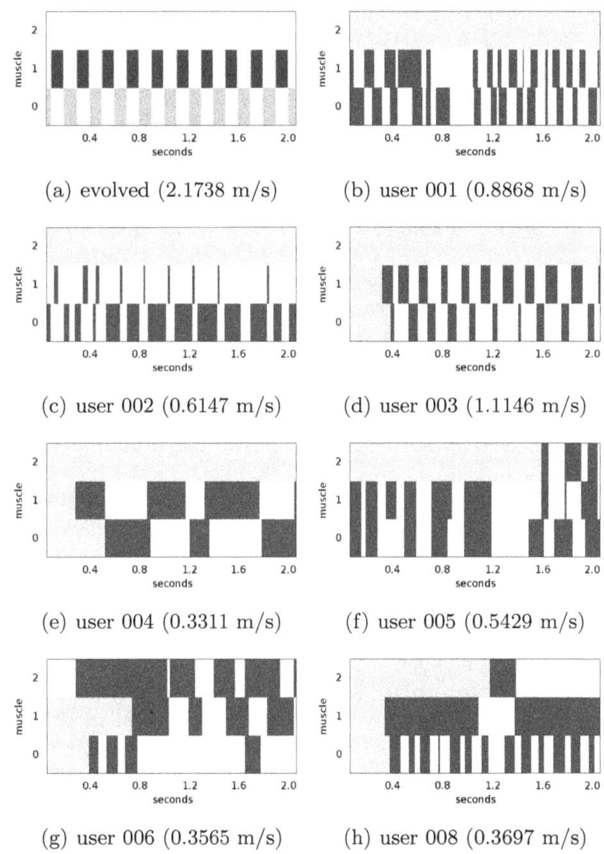

(a) evolved (2.1738 m/s) (b) user 001 (0.8868 m/s)

(c) user 002 (0.6147 m/s) (d) user 003 (1.1146 m/s)

(e) user 004 (0.3311 m/s) (f) user 005 (0.5429 m/s)

(g) user 006 (0.3565 m/s) (h) user 008 (0.3697 m/s)

Figure 8: Creature type A: muscle-activation spectrograms, with corresponding speeds.

For the A-type creature (Figure 8), human control strategies are similar to that of the evolved controller. Users tend to employ the same two muscles as the evolved controller, and many also replicate its simple alternating pattern, as well. The user pattern most similar to the evolved solution (Figure 8d) was also the fastest human example for that run (1.1146 m/s), although still far from the evolved controller's mean for that creature (2.3281 m/s). Beyond differences in control technique, another reason for lower human scores which is indicated in these spectrograms is that many users do not begin activating muscles until a fraction of a second after the run begins, while the evolved controllers start without any delay.

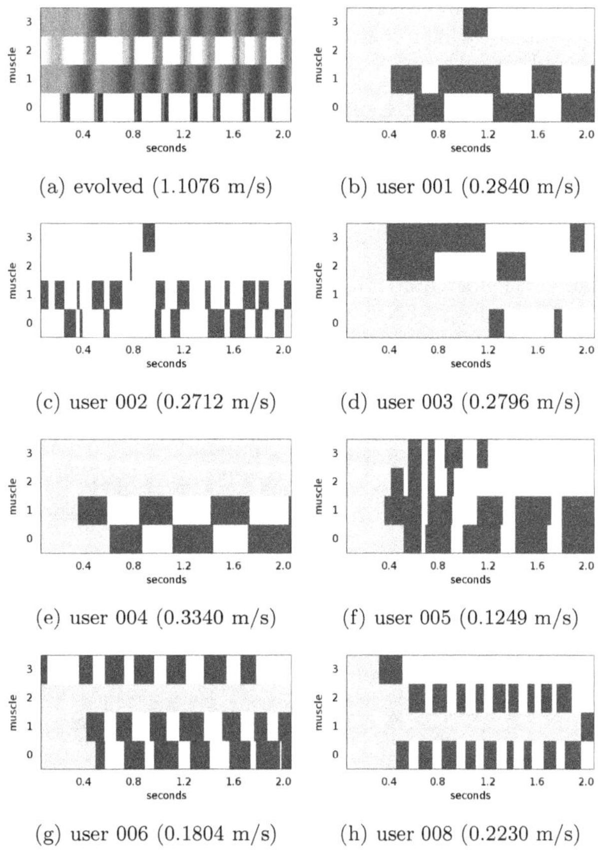

(a) evolved (1.1076 m/s) (b) user 001 (0.2840 m/s)

(c) user 002 (0.2712 m/s) (d) user 003 (0.2796 m/s)

(e) user 004 (0.3340 m/s) (f) user 005 (0.1249 m/s)

(g) user 006 (0.1804 m/s) (h) user 008 (0.2230 m/s)

Figure 9: Creature type B: muscle-activation spectrograms, with corresponding speeds.

For the B-type creature (Figure 9), most human activation patterns differ significantly, both from each other and from the evolved controller, and none are particularly successful compared to the evolved solution. Although its importance is not proven, this evolved controller makes the most obvious use of continuous activation values—something not available to a human user through the keyboard interface (as discussed in Section 6). This may be one reason why human users find this creature particularly challenging. Another difficult aspect of controlling this creature originates in its morphology: Because its body is symmetrical from front to back, it just as easy for it to move backwards as forwards, with some users even achieving a negative speed during evaluation runs.

For the C-type creature (Figure 10), there is again great variety in timing and muscles used, both among human and evolved results. In this creature, however, human control has finally begun to compete with evolved control. Interestingly for this creature, the human control pattern most visually similar to the evolved one (Figure 10b, 0.2983 m/s) is not nearly the fastest. Instead, it is the pattern of Figure 10c, using very different muscles and timing from the evolved

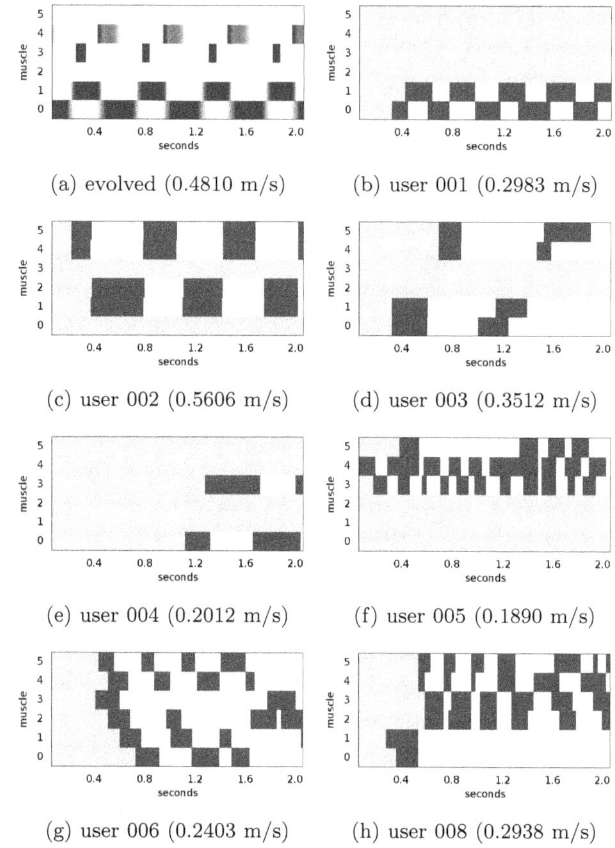

(a) evolved (0.4810 m/s) (b) user 001 (0.2983 m/s)

(c) user 002 (0.5606 m/s) (d) user 003 (0.3512 m/s)

(e) user 004 (0.2012 m/s) (f) user 005 (0.1890 m/s)

(g) user 006 (0.2403 m/s) (h) user 008 (0.2938 m/s)

Figure 10: Creature type C: muscle-activation spectrograms, with corresponding speeds.

solution, which scores best, reaching 0.5606 m/s, beating the evolved controller's mean of 0.5515 m/s.

5.2 Quantitative Comparison

For quantitative comparison of human and evolved control of EVCs, the same human test data is examined with respect to locomotive speed. Figures 11-13 illustrate human-controlled speed vs. evolved-controller speed for each of the three creature types. For each creature, data for seven test subjects over five runs are plotted, with mean, standard deviation, and best result indicated for each run. For comparison, seven runs of the evolved creature are similarly recorded and graphed. For each of the three creature types, evolved controllers score better in mean and best result during every run, but there are some important differences worth noting.

For creature types A and B, humans were not competitive with the evolved solution throughout the recorded trials. The best human score remained well below the evolved-controller mean for all such runs. Given the limited number of runs, however, and real-world examples of human control-task learning (consider learning to play the piano, or compete in Olympic gymnastics), it is not unreasonable to think that a human player might be competitive with an evolved controller, if given enough time to practice.

With creature type C, however, human performance was much closer to evolved performance throughout, with the best human controller once approaching the evolved-controller

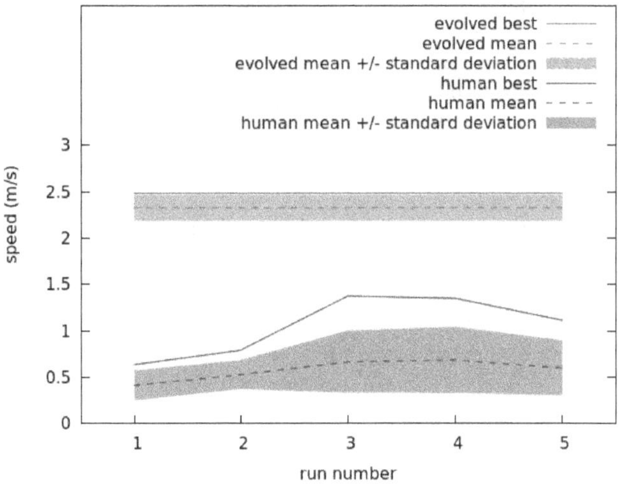

Figure 11: Comparison of evolved and human controller speeds for creature type A.

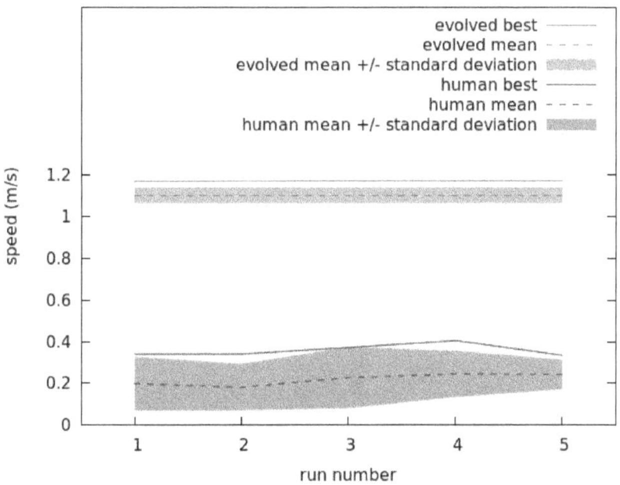

Figure 12: Comparison of evolved and human controller speeds for creature type B.

mean, and once even exceeding it. In fact, the last run for this type showed both the highest mean and highest best score for human controllers, with a statistically-significant indication of increasing score between the first and last runs for this creature (as described in Section 4 and Table 1). With human results approaching evolved results and shown to be still increasing, C-type creature results seem to offer humanity's best hope for matching or surpassing evolved controllers for the virtual creatures examined here.

6. DISCUSSION AND FUTURE WORK

The results of Section 5's comparison between human and evolved controllers have some interesting implications, and suggest potentially valuable future work. One important observation is that humans may be able to produce usable (although likely slower) control strategies in a significantly shorter wall-clock time than evolution—on the order of minutes for humans versus hours or more for evolution. Another

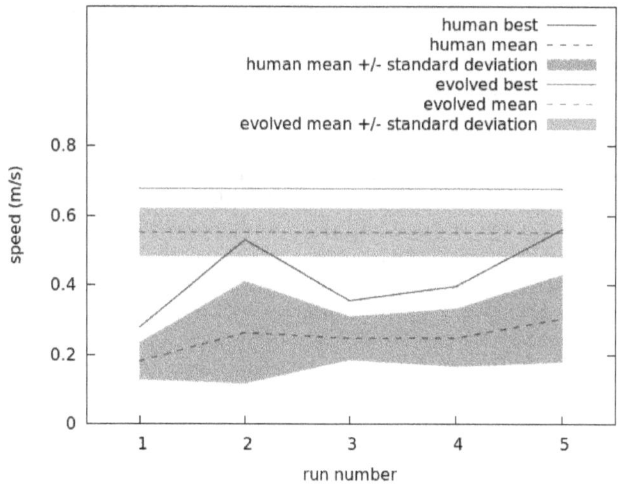

Figure 13: Comparison of evolved and human controller speeds for creature type C.

important observation is that human and evolved controllers often use very different techniques, with even the most competitive human controller differing greatly in strategy from the evolved controller for the same creature. This suggests the potential for a productive transfer of knowledge from human user to evolution. For example, evolved solutions could be rewarded for their similarity to successful human play traces, just as a teacher might instruct a student on technique when learning a physical skill. The proper combination of human and evolved skill could potentially lead to better solutions than either might have achieved alone, and seems worthy of future study.

Another important topic worthy of discussion is the difference in possible activation patterns between human and evolved controllers in the system this paper describes. As in typical EVC systems, the evolved controllers studied here generate continuous activation signals, while human users are limited to a binary signal for each muscle, owing to the keyboard interface. For human-vs.-human competition, this limitation may be acceptable, since useful control was shown to be possible with such discrete input, and because both players have this constraint in common. For human-vs.-evolved competitions or comparisons, however, it is unknown if this limitation contributed to the observed difference in achievement between the two types of control. To resolve this issue, future evolved controllers could be forced to produce binary muscle activation signals by applying a threshold filter to their outputs. Then, identical human and evolved activation patterns would be possible, placing human and machine on equal footing in both gameplay and research comparisons.

Another interesting difference between human and evolved controllers is the input that each receives. Although not all EVCs in this implementation use it, they have the potential to employ proprioceptive signals based on the current length of their muscles. This information is not directly available to the human user. Similarly, human users have access to a visual representation of the creature in simulation, providing them with information not available to the evolved controller (e.g.: the orientation, position, and velocity of many body segments; or which parts of the creature are in contact with the ground). While it is not clear which of these might confer a larger advantage, or whether the differences are significant at all, it is at least worth noting the difference.

On the topic of future work, one important step would be more deeply exploring the potential for evolution of new creatures and online interaction. In a full version of the game, great value might be added by allowing users to evolve their own creatures, trade them with each other, and compete against each other online.

Another potentially valuable extension to this initial experiment would be the addition of different tasks. Any action that EVCs can be evolved to perform (jumping, climbing, swimming, fighting, etc.) might serve as a rewarding new control challenge for the game.

7. CONCLUSION

This paper has presented *Darwin's Avatars*—a novel combination of gameplay and procedural content generation made possible by evolutionary computation. Although similar physical control challenges have already proven successful in previous games, this new game adds the novel elements of three-dimensional creatures and creatures which are unfamiliar without being constructed by the user. Preliminary playtesting showed that these gameplay mechanics have the potential to be entertaining and challenging, offering users the opportunity for learning and close competition. And importantly, this system's inherent ability to generate the core ingredient of its gameplay—novel control challenges, in its unlimited supply of newly evolved creatures—makes for a unique and compelling new combination. In addition, the game's core mechanic of human control of muscles in EVCs made it possible to compare human and evolved controllers, providing some initial insight into how these two types of controller compare numerically, how they may differ in terms of technique, and potential improvements and future work implied by these differences.

8. REFERENCES

[1] P. Avery, J. Togelius, E. Alistar, and R. van Leeuwen. Computational intelligence and tower defence games. In *Evolutionary Computation (CEC), 2011 IEEE Congress on*, pages 1084–1091. IEEE, 2011.

[2] B. Foddy. Qwop [flash game](2008). Technical report, Retrieved 11-6-13 from http://www. foddy. net/Athletics. html, 2013.

[3] F. Gomez and R. Miikkulainen. Incremental evolution of complex general behavior. *Adaptive Behavior*, 5:317–342, 1997.

[4] E. J. Hastings, R. K. Guha, and K. O. Stanley. Automatic content generation in the galactic arms race video game. *IEEE Transactions on Computational Intelligence and AI in Games*, 1(4):245–263, 2010.

[5] M. Hendrikx, S. Meijer, J. Van Der Velden, and A. Iosup. Procedural content generation for games: A survey. *ACM Transactions on Multimedia Computing, Communications, and Applications (TOMCCAP)*, 9(1):1, 2013.

[6] D. Lessin, D. Fussell, and R. Miikkulainen. Open-ended behavioral complexity for evolved virtual creatures. In *Proceeding of the Fifteenth Annual Conference on Genetic and Evolutionary Computation Conference*, GECCO '13, pages 335–342, New York, NY, USA, 2013. ACM.

[7] D. Lessin, D. Fussell, and R. Miikkulainen. Trading control intelligence for physical intelligence: Muscle drives in evolved virtual creatures. In *Proceedings of the Genetic and Evolutionary Computation Conference (GECCO) 2014*, 2014.

[8] M. Mitchell. *An Introduction to Genetic Algorithms.* MIT Press, Cambridge, MA, USA, 1998.

[9] C. Pedersen, J. Togelius, and G. N. Yannakakis. Modeling player experience for content creation. *IEEE Transactions on Computational Intelligence and AI in Games*, 2(1):54–67, 2010.

[10] A. PhysX. Ageia, 82 pioneer way, suite 118, mountain view, ca 94041, 2008.

[11] R. Ramachandra. Fastest 100m run, qwop (flash game). *Guinnes World Records*, 2013.

[12] S. Ray, V. S. Gordon, and L. Vaucher. Evolving qwop gaits. In *Proceedings of the 2014 conference on Genetic and evolutionary computation*, pages 823–830. ACM, 2014.

[13] S. Risi, J. Lehman, D. D'Ambrosio, R. Hall, and K. Stanley. Petalz: Search-based procedural content generation for the casual gamer. *Computational Intelligence and AI in Games, IEEE Transactions on*, PP(99):1–1, 2015.

[14] N. Shaker, G. N. Yannakakis, and J. Togelius. Towards automatic personalized content generation for platform games. In *Proceedings of Artificial Intelligence and Interactive Digital Entertainment (AIIDE-10)*. AAAI Press, 2010.

[15] N. Shaker, G. N. Yannakakis, J. Togelius, M. Nicolau, and M. O'Neill. Evolving personalized content for Super Mario Bros using grammatical evolution. In *Proceedings of the Artificial Intelligence and Interactive Digital Entertainment Conference (AIIDE 2012)*, Menlo Park, CA, 2012. AAAI Press.

[16] K. Sims. Evolving virtual creatures. In *Proceedings of the 21st annual conference on Computer graphics and interactive techniques*, SIGGRAPH '94, pages 15–22, New York, NY, USA, 1994. ACM.

[17] J. Togelius, A. J. Champandard, P. L. Lanzi, M. Mateas, A. Paiva, M. Preuss, and K. O. Stanley. Procedural Content Generation: Goals, Challenges and Actionable Steps. In S. M. Lucas, M. Mateas, M. Preuss, P. Spronck, and J. Togelius, editors, *Artificial and Computational Intelligence in Games*, volume 6 of *Dagstuhl Follow-Ups*, pages 61–75. Schloss Dagstuhl–Leibniz-Zentrum fuer Informatik, Dagstuhl, Germany, 2013.

[18] J. Togelius and J. Schmidhuber. An experiment in automatic game design. In *Computational Intelligence and Games, 2008. CIG'08. IEEE Symposium On*, pages 111–118. IEEE, 2008.

[19] J. Togelius, G. N. Yannakakis, K. O. Stanley, and C. Browne. Search-based procedural content generation: A taxonomy and survey. *IEEE Transactions on Computational Intelligence and AI in Games*, 3(3):172–186, 2011.

[20] J. Urzelai, D. Floreano, M. Dorigo, and M. Colombetti. Incremental robot shaping. *Connection Science*, 10:341–360, 1998.

Open Loop Search for General Video Game Playing

Diego Perez[*]
diego.perez@ovgu.de

Jens Dieskau
jens.dieskau@st.ovgu.de

Martin Hünermund
martin.huenermund@gmail.com

Sanaz Mostaghim
sanaz.mostaghim@ovgu.de

Simon M. Lucas
sml@essex.ac.uk

ABSTRACT

General Video Game Playing is a sub-field of Game Artificial Intelligence, where the goal is to find algorithms capable of playing many different real-time games, some of them unknown a priori. In this scenario, the presence of domain knowledge must be severely limited, or the algorithm will overfit to the training games and perform poorly on the unknown games of the test set. Research in this area has been of special interest in the last years, with emerging contests like the General Video Game AI (GVG-AI) Competition. This paper introduces three different open loop techniques for dealing with this problem. First, a simple directed depth first search algorithm is employed as a baseline. Then, a tree search algorithm with a multi-armed bandit based tree policy is presented, followed by a Rolling Horizon Evolutionary Algorithm (RHEA) approach. In order to test these techniques, the games from the GVG-AI Competition framework are used as a benchmark, evaluation on a training set of 29 games, and submitting to the 10 unknown games at the competition website. Results show how the general game-independent heuristic proposed works well across all algorithms and games, and how the RHEA becomes the best evolutionary technique in the rankings of the test set.

Categories and Subject Descriptors

I.2 [**Computing Methodologies**]: Artificial Intelligence, Learning

Keywords

Games; Decision Making; Genetic Algorithms

1. INTRODUCTION

Research in Game AI traditionally presents algorithms that play a particular game, counting on heuristics tailored to them. These heuristics are usually designed manually by some expert in these specific games, and are used to guide the search to states with high chances of victory.

General Game Playing (GGP) and General Video Game Playing (GVGP), on the other hand, drive research to algorithms that play a set of significantly different games, even some of them unknown a priori. Therefore, the presence of specific domain knowledge is limited or almost non-existent. The main challenge of GGP and GVGP is that the agent needs to be general enough to learn the structure of any game, guide the search to relevant states of the search space, and be able to adapt to a wide variety of situations in the absence of game-dependent heuristics. The idea of having general agents that are able to deal with a large variety of situations is one of the most important goals of AI [19].

One of the first attempts to develop and establish a GGP framework was carried out by the Stanford Logic Group of Stanford University, when they organized the first Association for the Advancement of Artificial Intelligence (AAAI) GGP competition in 2005 [6]. GGP focuses mainly on 2-player board games, where each player must provide an action after 1s of "thinking time". In contrast, GVGP proposes playing real-time single-player games, where the time budget for a move is measured in milliseconds. Recently, a GVGP framework and competition has been carried out by Perez et al. [17]. Interestingly, both GGP and GVGP competitions have shown the proficiency of Monte Carlo Tree Search (MCTS) methods, the winner of several editions of these contests. For instance, CADIA-Player (by Hilmar Finnsson [5]), was the first MCTS based approach to be declared winner of the 2007 AAAI GGP competition, followed by Ary, another MCTS approach developed by J. Méhat and T. Cazenave [12] that won the 2009 and 2010 editions. In the case of GVG-AI, the winner of the only edition of the competition (2014) was Adrien Couëtoux with an Open Loop MCTS approach (OLETS) [17].

However, to the knowledge of the authors of this paper, no research has been done on Rolling Horizon Evolutionary Algorithms (RHEA) for GVGP. This paper addresses this, proposing a combination of an evolutionary algorithm with a game tree search, and compares it with other tree search methods. Additionally, this paper proposes a game-independent GVGP heuristic that focuses on maximizing the exploration of the level played by the agent. Last but not least, this paper analyzes the hazards posed by stochastic real-time games to action-decision making, and the advantages of using an open loop approach to deal with these. Most of the agents submitted to the GVG-AI Competition were based on closed loop techniques [17].

This paper is structured as follows. Section 2 presents the benchmark used for this research. Then, Section 3 explains the concepts behind the agents proposed in this paper, such as game tree search, open loop and RHEA. Section 4 describes the algorithms used for

[*]The first four authors are with the Faculty of Computer Science at the Otto von Guericke University, Magdeburg, Germany. Simon M. Lucas is with the Computer Science and Electronic Engineering School at the University of Essex, Colchester, UK.

GECCO '15, July 11–15, 2015, Madrid, Spain
© 2015 ACM. ISBN 978-1-4503-3472-3/15/07...$15.00
DOI: http://dx.doi.org/10.1145/2739480.2754811

the experimental study, detailed in Section 5. Finally, Section 6 draws some final conclusions and lines for future work.

2. THE GVG-AI FRAMEWORK

The General Video Game Playing competition and framework (GVG-AI) is inspired by the Video Game Description Language (VGDL), a framework designed by Ebner et al. [4] and developed by Tom Schaul [22] for GVGP in Python (*py-vgdl*). In VGDL, *objects* interact in a two-dimensional rectangular space, with associated coordinates, and have the ability to interact (collide) with each other. VGDL defines an ontology that allows the generation of real-time games and levels with simple text files.

The GVG-AI framework is a Java port of py-vgdl, re-engineered for the GVG-AI Competition by Perez et al. [17], which exposes an interface that allows the implementation of controllers that must determine the actions of the player (also referred to as the *avatar*). The framework provides a *forward model* and information regarding the state of the game to the controllers. The VGDL definition of the game is, however, not provided, so it is the responsibility of the agent to determine the nature of the game and the actions needed to achieve victory.

A controller in the GVG-AI framework can spend 1s of initialization time before a game starts, and 40ms for each game step, where a move to execute in the game must be returned. During each one of these calls, the agent receives information about the current state of the game, such as the current time step, game score, current victory condition (game *won*, *lost* or *ongoing*) and the list of available actions in the game (variable from game to game, these can be moving *left*, *right*, *up* or *down*, and a generic *use* action). Information about the observations in the level (other sprites in the game) and history of avatar events (collisions between the avatar and other sprites) is also provided. The GVG-AI framework includes several sample controllers. The most relevant to our research are *SampleGA* (a simple RHEA), and *SampleMCTS* and *SampleOLMCTS* (closed and open loop MCTS approaches, respectively).

The GVG-AI framework featured in the first edition of the GVG-AI Competition in 2014, held in the IEEE Computational Intelligence in Games Conference in Dortmund (Germany), and the second edition will be held in the Genetic and Evolutionary Computation Conference (GECCO) 2015 in Madrid (Spain). At the time of the writing of this paper, 29 games of the framework have been made public (20 used in the competition, plus 9 created after the contest), which form the training game set used for the experiments described in this paper. 10 more games, unknown to all participants, are held in the server. Contestants can submit their controllers to this server in order to play these secret games. This set of 10 games is used as a test set for this research. All games vary in many different aspects, such as winning conditions, number and types of non-player characters, scoring mechanics and even in the available actions for the agent. Examples of known games are *Sokoban*, *BoulderDash*, *Zelda*, *Frogger*, *Digdug* and *Pacman*. The full list of games, sample controllers, results and rules of the competition can be found on the website[1] and in [17].

The results of the 2014 GVG-AI Competition show that this problem is far from trivial. The winner of the contest achieves a rate of victories, in the test set, of 51.2%, and only 2 more entries were able to obtain a rate higher than 30%. The way that entries are ranked, however, is not by the percentage of victories across this set of 10 games. Instead, controllers are sorted (for each game) by the highest number of games won, the highest total sum of game scores (as a tie-breaker), and finally the minimum time spent in total (as a second tie-breaker). Points are then awarded to them according to this order, following a Formula-1 score system (25, 18, 15, 12, 10, 8, 6, 4, 2 and 1 points; entries beyond the 10th position obtain 0 points). The winner is determined by the sum of points across all games, using the number of first, second, etc. positions to break possible ties.

[1] http://www.gvgai.net

3. BACKGROUND

This section introduces the main techniques behind the algorithms presented in this paper, such as game tree search, open loop approaches and RHEA.

3.1 Game Tree Search

Tree Search (TS) is one of the most employed types of techniques for action-decision making in games. Tree search techniques are iterative approaches originally employed for 2-player board games such as Chess, Checkers or Go. Research in this type of algorithms has advanced the state of the art from initial approaches such as Minimax or $\alpha - \beta$ search [20] to Monte Carlo Tree Search (MCTS) [3, 2]. This and other tree search algorithms are currently applied to a wide range of games, including games of uncertain information, general game playing, single-player games and real-time games.

A tree search algorithm builds a *game tree* with game states as nodes and actions as edges, with the current game state as the root of the tree. One of the most important components needed by a tree search algorithm is a *generative* or *forward model*, in order to be able to simulate actions before making a final decision about the move to make. In particular, a forward model is able to produce a state s' from a state s when an action a is taken ($a \in A(s)$ is one of the possible actions from the state s).

When the tree reaches a terminal state (where the game is over), it is possible to determine if the game was won or lost. However, in some cases, terminal states are so far ahead in the future that they are not reachable by simulations (this happens, for instance, in real-time games, a subject of study in this paper). In this situation, the algorithm defines a Simulation Depth D, that limits the number of moves that are performed from the current state, and a *heuristic* function, which evaluates a non-terminal state.

In either case, the evaluation of a game state allows statistics to be stored in the nodes of the tree regarding how good or bad certain actions are, and therefore bias the action selection process and tree growth towards the most promising parts of the search space. Examples of statistics that are usually stored are: how often each move is played from a given state ($N(s, a)$), how many times any move is played from there ($N(s)$) and the empirical average of the rewards obtained when choosing action a at state s ($Q(s, a)$).

This information allows the agent to make decisions at two levels. First, for each iteration of the algorithm, decisions must be made while navigating the tree (a procedure known as *Tree Policy*, that determines actions to take from a given state). Difference policies are used in the literature, such as ϵ-greedy (with $1 - \epsilon$ probability, the best action from a state is chosen; otherwise, another action is picked uniformly at random) or Upper Confidence Bound 1 (UCB1) , introduced by Kocsis [9] and shown in Equation 1:

$$a^* = \underset{a \in A(s)}{\arg\max} \left\{ Q(s, a) + C \sqrt{\frac{\ln N(s)}{N(s, a)}} \right\} \quad (1)$$

This equation finds an action a that maximizes the UCB1 equation, designed to provide a balance between exploration of the different actions available, and exploitation of the most promising action found so far. $Q(s, a)$ is the exploitation term, while the second term (weighted by a constant C) is the exploration term. If the rewards $Q(s, a)$ are normalized in the range $[0, 1]$, a commonly used value for C in single-player games is $\sqrt{2}$. The value of C is application dependant, and it may vary from game to game. Additionally, when $N(s, a) = 0$ for any of the possible actions from s, the action a must be chosen before UCB1 can be applied. This tree selection policy has become very popular because of the success of MCTS, concretely in the Upper Confidence Bounds for Trees version of the algorithm (UCT, [9]).

Secondly, a decision has to be made about the action to take when the iterations have finished (a limit imposed, for instance, by a time budget in real-time games). This policy, known as *Recommendation Policy*, can be implemented in different ways, such as selecting the action that leads to the highest reward found, the one with the highest average reward, the one with the maximum number of visits, or simply applying the UCB1 Equation 1.

3.2 Open versus Closed Loop Tree Search

In deterministic scenarios, a game tree can contain future states in its nodes that mimic perfectly the states that will be found when performing an action or sequence of actions (*Closed Loop* tree search). Additionally, once a new node is added to the tree, there is no need to generate such state again, and the algorithm can traverse the tree during the tree policy phase without spending time in using the forward model again from the previous pair (s, a).

However, this aspect changes when considering stochastic scenarios, as this poses the problem of not knowing how believable the states reached after a simulated move are. In the general case, given a state s and a set of actions $A(s)$, if the action $a \in A(s)$ is selected, one may assume that the state s' obtained using the forward model is drawn from an unknown probability distribution. Consequently, storing a state in a node could be detrimental: the state generated when the node was added to the tree might not be representative of the most probable s' found after applying a from s. Furthermore, even if it were, the search performed from that node in the tree would be biased by one instance of all possible states s'.

Ideally, in order to deal with this scenario, the algorithm should sample each one of the available actions a *sufficient* number of times, and create as many children as future states found. In practice, however, the combination of nodes that the tree would contain by applying this procedure grows exponentially. Additionally, the limited time budget available in real time games draws this solution infeasible.

An approximate solution to this problem is to use an *Open Loop* approach. The idea is that the nodes do not store the states, but only the statistics. Obviously, this forces the use of the forward model every time the algorithm chooses an action during the tree policy. However, now the statistics gathered are representative of the set of states found after applying an action a from s. In other words, the tree stores statistics derived from executing a sequence of actions from a given state (open loop case), and not from a sequence of pairs (s, a) (closed loop). More information about open versus closed loop control can be found in [23].

Another important detail about tree search is the way the information is kept. Typically, an algorithm runs during the allowed time budget and, at the end, selects an action to apply in the real game guided by the recommendation policy. This process is repeated during several game steps until the game ends. All controllers employed in this research keep this information from one game cycle to the next, as the data from the node that follows the chosen action can be reused. This node becomes the new root, and its siblings are discarded, as they can no longer be reached. Figure 1 shows an explanatory diagram of this procedure.

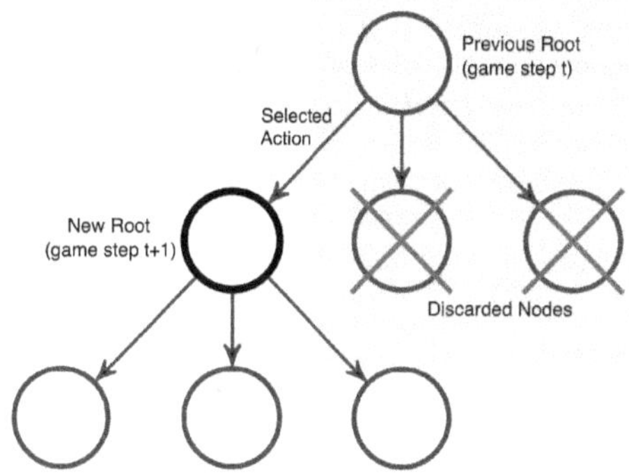

Figure 1: Changing the root node from a previous game step.

3.3 Rolling Horizon Evolutionary Algorithms

Rolling Horizon Evolutionary Algorithms (RHEA) are a suitable alternative to Tree Search for action-decision making in real-time games. Traditionally, Evolutionary Algorithms (EA) are used in conjunction with a simulator to train a controller offline, and then use the already evolved controller to play the game. This is a technique not only used in games [11], but also in other problems [8] or in the domain of Artificial Life [1].

RHEA approaches, however, employ evolution in a similar way to how it is done in tree search, using a forward model to evaluate a sequence of actions. The agent evolves a plan (a sequence of actions) during some predefined time budget, and then selects the first action of the best individual as the move to play in the real game. This type of approach is called "Rolling Horizon", as planning is performed at every time step, up to a determined point in the future, as far as the length of the individual (or plan).

It is worthwhile mentioning that this approach, by definition, is an open loop approach, as the states found during the search are not stored or reused in any way. The evaluation of each individual consists of applying the sequence of actions, and assigning as fitness the value given by the evaluation of the state reached at the end. It is possible to find usages of RHEA in the literature in deterministic games, as in S. Samothrakis and S. Lucas [21] in the Mountain Car problem, or Perez et al. [16] in the Physical Travelling Salesman Problem.

A possible usage of RHEA in stochastic scenarios could be to evaluate each individual several times, and assign as fitness the average of these evaluations. However, the same problem seen in tree search affects RHEA in real-time games: the limited time budget does not permit running too many evaluations. This paper proposes the combination of RHEA and Tree Search, while keeping the benefits of open loop search, in one of the algorithms presented (see Section 4.4).

4. CONTROLLERS

This section explains the different controllers used for the experiments described later in Section 5. All these algorithms build a game tree without storing the states in the nodes (i.e., they implement open loop search, as explained in Section 3.2) and reusing the subtree in the next step. Additionally, all algorithms use the same heuristic to evaluate states (see Section 4.1) and the same recommendation policy (described in Section 4.2).

Algorithm 1 Pseudocode of the heuristic

```
1:  procedure HEURISTIC(state, avatar, pheromones)
2:      p ← avatar.position
3:      reward ← 0
4:      if HasPlayerWon(state) then
5:          reward ← HIGH_VALUE
6:      if HasPlayerLost(state) then
7:          reward ← −HIGH_VALUE
8:      reward ← reward+ GetGameScore(state)
9:      if OppositeActions(avatar) then
10:         reward ← reward − PEN_OA
11:     if BlockedMovement(avatar) then
12:         reward ← reward − PEN_BM
13:     reward ← reward − pheromones[p.x][p.y]
14:     return reward
```

4.1 Heuristic

All controllers presented in this study follow the same heuristic, whose objective is to guide the search and evaluate states found during the simulations. Note that this a domain independent heuristic, as it has been designed without any domain knowledge from specific games. Algorithm 1 shows how the different components of the heuristic are combined together.

The heuristic is a combination of several factors. First of all, the end condition of the game is checked (lines 4 to 7). When a game ends, the player may have won or lost the game. If any of these two scenarios is met, a very high or low reward is assigned to the score respectively.

Then, the reward is modified by adding the current score of the game (line 8) and subtracting two penalties (lines 9 to 12):

- *Opposite Actions:* None of the algorithms tested impose any restriction about the movements available, other than the actions allowed by each game on each state. In some cases, it is possible to perform two consecutive contrary movements, such as moving *Right* after *Left* or vice-versa. With the exception of some rare cases where this is a good thing to do, this redundancy is unnecessary. Thus, a penalty PEN_{OA} is subtracted from the reward when this happens. The value of PEN_{OA} is set to 0.1, determined after a trial and error process.

- *Blocked Movement:* It is possible that one of the available movement actions in a state does not change the avatar's position in a determined situation (i.e. moving against a static wall). When this happens in the state reached, the reward receives a penalty PEN_{BM} set to -100, a value determined by trial and error.

Another possibility to these penalties would have been to deny some actions from being chosen, similar to pruning branches in tree search. However, penalties permit to achieve a similar effect with a lower computational cost, which is a valuable resource in real-time games. Additionally, this sort of *soft pruning* does not completely avoid an action from being selected, allowing some exploration through that node anyway. Also, there are some minor cases where taking these actions may be beneficial, such as dodging an bullet or not moving at all.

The last component of the heuristic is a nature-inspired technique based on *pheromone* trails, that works as a *potential field* [24] for the avatar. In the implementation presented in this paper, the avatar secretes repelling pheromones. These pheromones spread into the neighbouring area, defined as the grid cells above, below, on the right and on the left of a given position. The amount of pheromone contained in a given cell is a value between 0 and 1, and it decays with time. Figure 2 shows an example of a pheromone diffusion in one game step, where the avatar is located at the center.

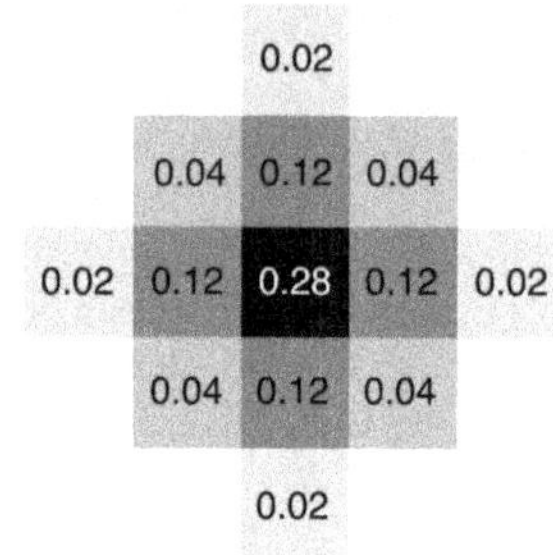

Figure 2: Pheromone diffusion.

The amount of pheromone on each cell is updated at every state as shown in Equation 2:

$$\begin{aligned} pheromones_{i,j} &= \rho_{df} \times \rho_{\phi} + \\ &= (1 - \rho_{df}) \times \rho_{dc} \times pheromones_{i,j} \end{aligned} \quad (2)$$

where i and j are coordinates in the level board, and ρ_{ϕ} is the ratio of pheromone trail in the neighbouring cells divided by the number of neighbouring cells (note that the edges of the level might limit the amount of neighbours). $\rho_{df} \in (0,1)$ defines the value of diffusion of the pheromone in the current game step, and $\rho_{dc} \in (0,1)$ indicates the decay of the value at each game step. After some experimental testing, these values have been set to $\rho_{df} = 0.4$ and $\rho_{dc} = 0.99$, providing a balance between global and local exploration (higher and lower values, respectively).

The pheromone diffusion algorithm creates a high concentration of pheromones in the close proximity of the current and recent positions of the avatar. As defined in the heuristic (see line 13), the value of the pheromone is subtracted from the reward. Hence, the heuristic will give less value to those states with positions where the avatar is, or has been in recent time steps, aiming to increase the exploration of the level. Interestingly, this exploration technique is similar to the one developed independently (and almost simultaneously) by Nielsen et al. [13].

Summarizing, the heuristic employed to evaluate states rewards high game score or victory, plus favouring those actions that allow a larger exploration of the level the avatar is playing.

4.2 Recommendation Policy

The recommendation policy of the algorithms described in this paper selects the action a, so it maximizes the value $R(s,a)$ calculated for each one of the children of the current state s. Equation 3 shows how the value $R(s,a)$ is obtained[2]:

$$R(s,a) = w_r \times R_{max}(s,a) + (1 - w_r) \times Q(s,a) \quad (3)$$

$R(s,a)$ is a weighted sum between $R_{max}(s,a)$ and the average of rewards obtained from state s after applying a (this is, $Q(s,a)$). $R_{max}(s,a)$ is described in Equation 4 as the maximum value of $R(s',a')$, where s' is the state reached from s after applying a, and a' is each one of the actions available from s'.

[2]In order to adhere to the nomenclature used in the literature, we will keep using s when referring to states, even when the statistics are held in the nodes that (in open loop) do not store the state s.

$$R_{max}(s,a) = max_{a' \in A(s')} R(s',a') \quad (4)$$

The weight w_r has been set to 0.5 by trial and error. This policy gives more weight to those states nearer in the future, and it is inspired by the One-pass Exponential Weighted Average [10].

4.3 Tree Search Approaches

Two different tree search approaches have been used in the experimental study:

- **DBS:** A Directed Breadth First Search (DBS) algorithm has been implemented as our first tree search approach. The objective of this simple algorithm is to serve as a baseline controller for comparison with the other two. Starting from the current state, a child node is created for each one of the available actions. The tree is then traversed depth level after depth level until a terminal game state is reached, or the time budget runs out. The tree search is *directed* because it evaluates the children in order, according to the highest average reward $Q(s, a)$. When this process finishes, the action to take in the game is selected by the recommendation policy described in Section 4.2.
- **UCB1-TS:** The second tree search approach proposed in this paper uses the UCB1 Equation 1 as tree policy, instead of following the child with the highest average reward. The algorithm grows the game tree iteratively up to a determined simulation depth D, adding a new node to the tree at each iteration. All states found during the navigation of the tree are evaluated with the heuristic described in section 4.1. When the time budget is exhausted, the move to make is chosen by the recommendation policy from Section 4.2.

4.4 RHEA

As with the tree search algorithms, it is important that the RHEA is implemented in an *anytime* fashion (i.e. that it can be stopped at any time, yielding a valid solution). In order to avoid having long evaluation times, where a whole population is evaluated at once, the algorithm proposed here evaluates one new individual per generation. If this new individual is found better than the worse one of the population, the latter is replaced by the former. This assures that the best individuals are always kept in the population.

The population has a size T, and its individuals are encoded as strings of actions with a determined length L, which establishes how far into the future the plan is performed. Generation of new individuals is performed in two different ways: by the recombination of two different individuals from the population, or by the mutation of one of them. Recombination of two individuals is performed by applying uniform crossover. Mutation replaces one gene of the individual, chosen uniformly at random, with a new value, also determined randomly. A parameter α defines the probability of choosing one of the two breeding methods at each generation.

In both cases, the selection of individuals is performed by an approach similar to non-linear ranking [18], but using a Gaussian function instead of a Polynomial one. All individuals of the population are ranked according to their fitness value, and selected for reproduction by using Gauss Selection [7]. Two different selection mechanisms were tried in a pre-experimental process:

- Normal Gauss Selection: A random value is drawn from a Gauss distribution and mapped to the ranked population.
- P-Gauss Selection: With probability $P = 0.5$, the best individual of the population is selected. Otherwise, a normal Gauss Selection is employed.

After some initial testing, P-Gauss Selection proved to provide better solutions, and therefore it was chosen for the experiments detailed in Section 5.

Fitness values are calculated by executing the sequence of actions of the individual using the forward model, until all actions are executed or a final game state is reached. While evaluating an individual, a tree is generated with the actions performed. When a new sequence of actions is executed from the current state (i.e. from the root of the tree), new nodes will be added to the tree accordingly. When some of these sequences are repeated in different individuals, the tree nodes will be reused to gather the stored statistics. Therefore, the evaluation of the individuals of the population is used to generate a game tree, similar to the ones employed by the tree search approaches. This provides the algorithms with a way of calculating statistics about the actions taken, as well as reusing information from one game step to the next by keeping the game tree, as described before in Figure 1.

The fitness function proposed in this paper maximizes the average of the $Q(s, a)$ values of all nodes visited during the evaluation of the individual. This allows not only the state of the game reached after the sequence of actions has been executed to be taken into account, but also valuing intermediate states. Alternative options, such as using only the reward of the state reached at the end of the evaluation, would not take advantage of the statistics stored in the game tree: note that the last state is only visited more than once if two or more individuals with exactly the same sequence of actions are evaluated.

5. EXPERIMENTAL STUDY

5.1 Experimental Setup

A thorough experimental study has been performed to analyze the quality of the algorithms presented in this paper. For the RHEA approach, the parameters tested are the breeding parameter ($\alpha = \{0.00, 0.25, 0.50, 0.75, 1.00\}$), the individual length (L = 2 to 7) and the population size ($T = \{5, 20, 100\}$).

For the UCB1-TS, the parameters tested are the simulation depth (D = 1 to 7) and the value of the constant C for UCB1 (see Equation 1; $C = \{0.00, 0.33, 0.67, 1.00, 1.33, 1.67, 2.00\}$).

All configurations have been tested 10 times on each one of the 5 levels of the 29 games from the training set of the GVG-AI framework (Intel Xeon CPU E3-1245, 3.40GHz and 32GB of memory). Therefore, each algorithm has played 1450 games, with the exception of DBS, which has played each level 100 times (thus playing a total of 14500 games), and has no parameters to tune.

Finally, the DBS controller and the best configurations found for RHEA and UCB1-TS, have been submitted to the GVG-AI competition website for its evaluation in the test set (that contains 10 unknown games) in order to compare these approaches with other entries from the contest. According to the rules of the competition, the server executes each controller 10 times on each one of the 5 levels of the 10 games from this set.

5.2 Results on the Training Set

Table 1 shows the average (with standard error of the averages) of the percentage of games won by UCB1-TS, for the configurations tested for this algorithm. As can be seen, higher values of the UCB1 constant C seem to provide a higher rate of victories. The right-most column shows an increment of this measure as C approaches to 2.00. This implies that a higher exploration in the search space tends to provide better results. Actually, the worst average of results is obtained with C = 0.00, which effectively

UCB1 Constant C	Simulation Depth D							
	1	2	3	4	5	6	7	Avg.
0.00	36.23 (0.54)	38.62 (0.38)	38.97 (0.19)	38.62 (0.53)	38.90 (0.48)	38.90 (0.28)	39.03 (0.33)	38.47 (0.17)
0.33	37.32 (0.1)	40.75 (0.48)	44.93 (0.38)	44.58 (0.3)	44.24 (0.34)	44.86 (0.26)	44.10 (0.32)	42.97 (0.14)
0.67	35.68 (0.49)	39.86 (0.27)	44.72 (0.34)	44.72 (0.44)	43.63 (0.33)	44.10 (0.39)	43.49 (0.12)	42.31 (0.17)
1.00	36.57 (0.31)	40.20 (0.3)	45.48 (0.4)	44.31 (0.31)	42.87 (0.37)	43.76 (0.47)	44.31 (0.44)	42.50 (0.15)
1.33	36.78 (0.37)	40.68 (0.27)	44.79 (0.14)	44.79 (0.27)	44.17 (0.44)	43.42 (0.34)	43.69 (0.29)	42.62 (0.12)
1.67	35.68 (0.52)	40.61 (0.33)	44.79 (0.16)	44.86 (0.36)	43.08 (0.45)	43.76 (0.38)	44.04 (0.41)	42.40 (0.15)
2.00	35.81 (0.48)	40.27 (0.3)	**46.16 (0.35)**	45.54 (0.28)	43.49 (0.36)	44.04 (0.26)	43.69 (0.26)	42.71 (0.13)
Avg.	36.30 (0.54)	40.14 (0.38)	44.26 (0.32)	43.92 (0.43)	42.91 (0.46)	43.26 (0.42)	43.19 (0.44)	42.00 (0.35)

Table 1: Average (Standard Error) of the percent of games won by UCB1-TS. Best result in bold font.

Individual length L	Breeding parameter α					
	0.00	0.25	0.50	0.75	1.00	Avg.
2	24.65 (0.32)	41.36 (0.71)	40.13 (0.49)	38.97 (0.36)	40.20 (0.15)	37.06 (0.25)
3	26.78 (0.45)	42.39 (0.54)	43.35 (0.76)	42.73 (0.59)	**44.59 (0.47)**	39.97 (0.35)
4	29.38 (0.36)	43.35 (0.33)	44.10 (0.32)	44.24 (0.19)	44.04 (0.39)	41.02 (0.2)
5	30.27 (0.48)	42.05 (0.51)	42.53 (0.34)	42.60 (0.65)	42.39 (0.58)	39.97 (0.32)
6	28.15 (0.36)	42.94 (0.37)	43.15 (0.53)	43.90 (0.45)	43.42 (0.37)	40.31 (0.26)
7	29.31 (0.68)	41.50 (0.65)	42.60 (0.57)	43.08 (0.41)	42.60 (0.56)	39.82 (0.36)
Avg.	28.09 (0.57)	42.27 (0.67)	42.64 (0.65)	42.59 (0.57)	42.87 (0.54)	39.69 (0.26)

Table 2: Average (Standard Error) of the percent of games won by RHEA ($T = 5$). Best result in bold font.

Individual length L	Breeding parameter α					
	0.00	0.25	0.50	0.75	1.00	Avg.
2	35.34 (0.41)	41.37 (0.29)	39.79 (0.43)	39.86 (0.56)	39.52 (0.43)	39.17 (0.26)
3	39.31 (0.57)	44.93 (0.45)	44.99 (0.55)	44.86 (0.43)	44.04 (0.35)	43.63 (0.39)
4	38.21 (0.25)	44.10 (0.55)	45.27 (0.53)	45.41 (0.26)	46.36 (0.34)	43.87 (0.24)
5	38.49 (0.41)	**47.26 (0.45)**	46.37 (0.16)	45.68 (0.59)	47.05 (0.3)	44.97 (0.24)
6	36.50 (0.49)	44.93 (0.58)	45.41 (0.39)	45.96 (0.46)	46.98 (0.44)	43.95 (0.29)
7	36.30 (0.61)	46.23 (0.21)	44.31 (0.4)	44.59 (0.34)	45.27 (0.38)	43.34 (0.24)
Avg.	37.36 (0.59)	44.80 (0.54)	44.36 (0.53)	44.39 (0.57)	44.87 (0.48)	43.16 (0.24)

Table 3: Average (Standard Error) of the percent of games won by RHEA ($T = 20$). Best result in bold font.

means that the tree policy follows greedily the best child of a node at each movement within the tree.

Regarding the simulation depth (D), there seems to be an optimal spot (among the values tested for D) at $D = 3$, with a slightly worse rate of victories when this value is increased, and definitely worse results when D is set to 1 or 2. This result suggests that an intermediate number of steps from the current state (not too short, not too long) produces higher rates of victories in the 29 games tested. Note that the longer the simulation depth, the smaller the amount of iterations that can be performed by UCB1-TS in the available time budget. Therefore, an intermediate value of D conveys a good equilibrium between how long the algorithm simulates into future states and the number of iterations, which give a higher confidence in the statistics stored in the nodes of the tree.

The best average of victories obtained by UCB1-TS corresponds to the best values of these two parameters, providing a rate of 46.16% of victories, with a standard error of 0.35. For a comparison with the other algorithms, the percentage of games won by UCB1-TS considering all configurations tested is 42.00% with a standard error of 0.35.

Tables 2, 3 and 4 show the averages (with standard errors) of each configuration tested for the RHEA approach, employing population sizes of 5, 20 and 100, respectively. There are some general conclusions that can be drawn by analyzing the results obtained by this algorithm.

The first aspect worth noticing is that a small population produces lower victory rates, with averages when $T = 5$ around 3 or 4 points lower than population sizes of 20 and 100. The results between $T = 20$ and $T = 100$ are similar, with a slightly higher

Individual length L	Breeding parameter α: 0.00	0.25	0.50	0.75	1.00	Avg.
2	41.43 (0.33)	40.95 (0.39)	40.00 (0.36)	40.55 (0.60)	39.79 (0.25)	40.54 (0.24)
3	44.99 (0.49)	44.79 (0.45)	45.34 (0.31)	45.82 (0.27)	46.09 (0.33)	45.41 (0.23)
4	43.22 (0.32)	45.13 (0.08)	46.91 (0.51)	46.78 (0.35)	**47.39 (0.3)**	45.89 (0.19)
5	40.68 (0.55	44.38 (0.37)	46.64 (0.38)	46.36 (0.37)	46.44 (0.41)	44.90 (0.26)
6	39.52 (0.35)	44.11 (0.51)	45.48 (0.52)	45.41 (0.44)	45.54 (0.43)	44.01 (0.28)
7	38.76 (0.34)	43.90 (0.51)	43.15 (0.23)	42.94 (0.33)	43.56 (0.34)	42.46 (0.22)
Avg.	41.43 (0.51)	43.88 (0.49)	44.56 (0.50)	44.64 (0.51)	44.80 (0.44)	43.87 (0.21)

Table 4: Average (Standard Error) of the percent of games won by RHEA ($T = 100$). Best result in bold font.

victory rate for $T = 100$. This again suggests that a higher exploration of the search space is better for the controller.

Limiting ourselves to analyzing the results obtained for $T = 20$ and 100, it can be observed that a good individual length is again (as it happened with UCB1-TS) a good compromise between how far a sequence of actions simulates into the future and the amount of evaluations that can be performed during a game cycle (longer sequences imply that fewer individuals can be evaluated in the time budget). In this case, intermediate values of L such as 5 (for $T =$ 20) and 4 (for $T = 100$) seem to perform best.

Regarding the breeding parameter, the differences on performance are small when $\alpha > 0.00$. A priori, it seemed obvious that a value of $\alpha = 0.00$ would not achieve very good results, as the only way of creating new individuals does not generate any new genetic material by mutation. However, it is still interesting to analyze the results obtained. For $T = 100$, the results are around 10 points better when $\alpha = 0.00$ in $T = 5$, and close to 4 points higher than in the $T = 20$ case. This is of course due to a higher variety of individuals in a population with a larger size.

Nevertheless, it is clear that setting α to 0.00 is not an optimal strategy, because the best results are found when $\alpha = 0.25$ and $L = 5$ for $T = 20$ (47.26 with a standard error of 0.45), and $\alpha = 1.00$ and $L = 4$ for $T = 100$ (47.39 with a standard error of 0.3). The average of victories in all experiments run with the RHEA approach is 42.2 (0.42).

The experiments performed with DBS provide an average of 39.0 (0.38) of games won, significantly lower than the other two approaches. Table 5 compares the results of all algorithms tested in this study, showing the average (with standard error), minimum and maximum rates of victories of all runs of each approach. Both UCB1-TS and RHEA are clearly better than DBS, with the evolutionary approach slightly ahead of the best tree search technique in terms of average of victories.

Finally, in a game per game basis, the results suggest that the games where the proposed techniques fail more often are those where the rewards are delayed far in the future.

5.3 Results on the Test Set

The top configurations of each controller have been submitted for testing to the GVG-AI competition's website server (Intel Core i5, 2.90GHz, and 4GB of memory), so they can be ranked according to the contest rules as described at the end of Section 2. This ranking awards those controllers that play better across the set of 10 unknown games of the competition. The controllers submitted are DBS (its *username* in the server - and in Figure 3 - is *TeamTopbug_HR*), UCB1-TS (*TeamTopbug_RL*) with $D = 3$ and $C = 2.00$, and RHEA with $T = 100$, $L = 4$ and $\alpha = 1.00$ (*TeamTopbug_NI*).

	Min	Average (Std. Err)	Max
DBS	36.3	39.0 (0.38)	41.1
UCB1-TS	35.7	42.0 (0.35)	46.2
RHEA	24.7	42.2 (0.42)	47.4

Table 5: Percent of games won by DBS, UCB1-TS and RHEA.

Figure 3 shows the three algorithms in the rankings with the first entries submitted to the competition (for the sake of space, the bottom 15 entries are not included in this figure). As can be seen, the RHEA (*TeamTopbug_NI*) approach obtains more points than the UCB1-TS algorithm, getting a better result in 9 of the 10 games of the set. The evolutionary approach obtains 44.8% of victories in this game, while the two tree approaches get around 41.0%. The winner of the 2014 competition, still the first entry at the time of writing of this paper, achieves a rate of victories of 51.2%.

Compared to the other entries of the competition, our evolutionary approach ranks 4th, obtaining the best overall result in two games of the set. It is worthwhile highlighting that our RHEA controller is the best evolutionary approach found in the rankings; the other entries in Figure 3 are variants of MCTS, the second best EA controller is ranked 14th, and the sample Genetic Algorithm (GA) controller supplied with the framework is in 18th position.

6. CONCLUSIONS AND FUTURE WORK

This paper presents several approaches for general video game playing in real-time games. Concretely, it proposes two tree search algorithms and a RHEA combined with the generation of a game tree search. All these approaches are open loop planning algorithms, as they do not rely on specific states found by the forward model, but on the statistics gathered after executing sequences of actions. This paper also proposes a general purpose heuristic, with no game-dependent knowledge, employed to play up to 39 different real-time games.

The results obtained in this paper allow several conclusions to be drawn about the algorithms tested. First, regarding the tree search techniques, the experimental study shows the advantage of using a tree policy that finds a balance between exploration of the search space and exploitation of the best action found so far, tested across a large set of games. The proposed RHEA algorithm obtains very good results in the set of unknown 10 games of the GVG-AI competition, becoming the highest ranked evolutionary approach. All algorithms tested rank in the top third of the rankings, which suggests that the common heuristic employed (that maximizes level exploration) works well across algorithms and games.

Potential future work of this research may include exploration of other values for the parameters tested. For instance, initial tests show that larger values of simulation depth ($\sim$ 20) behave extremely well in some of the games tested, although more thorough experimental work is needed to analyze this.

Additionally, other techniques found in the literature may help to further improve the results obtained in this research, such as the

Rank	Username	# Wins	G-1	G-2	G-3	G-4	G-5	G-6	G-7	G-8	G-9	G-10	Total
1	adrienctx	256/500	**25**	0	**25**	0	12	4	15	10	**25**	1	**117**
2	emergence	189/500	12	**25**	6	0	15	0	12	0	8	**25**	**103**
3	JinJerry	216/500	15	1	18	**25**	2	0	18	8	10	4	**101**
4	TeamTopbug_NI	224/500	4	1	12	4	**25**	10	10	**25**	2	6	**99**
5	psuko	208/500	18	8	15	15	4	2	1	12	15	0	**90**
6	TeamTopbug_RL	204/500	2	1	0	2	18	1	6	18	0	12	**60**
7	sampleOLMCTS Sample	160/500	10	15	0	0	8	18	0	6	0	0	**57**
8	TeamTopbug_HR	202/500	1	1	0	0	10	6	8	15	0	10	**51**
9	sampleMCTS Sample	158/500	0	12	1	0	6	**25**	0	2	0	0	**46**

Figure 3: Results of the three algorithms in the test set of the GVG-AI 2014 Competition.

use of macro-actions [15] to reduce the search space and effectively enjoy a longer time budget for action decision. Another possibility is to address the problem with Multi-Objective Optimization techniques (both evolutionary and tree-search based) [14]. An approach that takes the victory condition, the maximization of the game score and the exploration of the level as separate but complimentary objectives, seems to be a viable alternative.

7. REFERENCES

[1] R. Beer and J. Gallagher. Evolving Dynamical Neural Networks for Adaptive Behavior. *Adaptive behavior*, 1(1):91–122, 1992.

[2] C. Browne, E. J. Powley, D. Whitehouse, S. Lucas, P. I. Cowling, P. Rohlfshagen, S. Tavener, D. Perez, S. Samothrakis, and S. Colton. A Survey of Monte Carlo Tree Search Methods. *IEEE Transactions on Computational Intelligence and AI in Games*, 4:1:1–43, 2012.

[3] G. M. J.-B. Chaslot, S. Bakkes, I. Szita, and P. Spronck. Monte-Carlo Tree Search: A New Framework for Game AI. In *Proceedings of the Artificial Intelligence for Interactive Digital Entertainment Conference*, pages 216–217, 2006.

[4] M. Ebner, J. Levine, S. Lucas, T. Schaul, T. Thompson, and J. Togelius. Towards a Video Game Description Language. *Dagstuhl Follow-up*, 6:85–100, 2013.

[5] H. Finnsson and Y. Björnsson. CADIA-Player: A Simulation Based General Game Player. *IEEE Transactions on Computational Intelligence and AI in Games*, 1:1–12, 2009.

[6] M. Genesereth, N. Love, and B. Pell. General Game Playing: Overview of the AAAI Competition. *AI Magazine*, 26:62–72, 2005.

[7] D. E. Goldberg and K. Deb. A comparative analysis of selection schemes used in genetic algorithms. In *Foundations of Genetic Algorithms*, pages 69–93. M. Kaufmann, 1991.

[8] F. Gomez and R. Miikkulainen. Solving Non-Markovian Control Tasks with Neuroevolution. In *International Joint Conference on Artificial Intelligence*, volume 16, pages 1356–1361. Lawrence Erlbaum Associates LTD, 1999.

[9] L. Kocsis and C. Szepesvári. Bandit Based Monte-Carlo Planning. *Machine Learning: ECML*, 4212:282–293, 2006.

[10] J. Loveless, S. Stoikov, and R. Waeber. Online Algorithms in High-Frequency Trading. *Comm. ACM*, 56(10):50–56, 2013.

[11] S. Lucas and G. Kendall. Evolutionary Computation and Games (Invited Review). *IEEE Computational Intelligence Magazine*, 1(1):10–18, February 2006.

[12] J. Méhat and T. Cazenave. A Parallel General Game Player. *KI - Künstliche Intelligenz*, 25:43–47, 2011.

[13] T. Nielsen, G. Barros, J. Togelius, and M. Nelson. General Video Game Evaluation using Relative Algorithm Performance Profiles. In *EvoApplications*, 2015.

[14] D. Perez, S. Mostaghim, S. Samothrakis, and S. Lucas. Multi-Objective Monte Carlo Tree Search for Real-Time Games. *IEEE Transactions on Computational Intelligence and AI in Games*, pp:1–13, DOI: 10.1109/TCIAIG.2014.2345842, 2014.

[15] D. Perez, E. J. Powley, D. Whitehouse, P. Rohlfshagen, S. Samothrakis, P. I. Cowling, and S. Lucas. Solving the Physical Travelling Salesman Problem: Tree Search and Macro-Actions. *IEEE Transactions on Computational Intelligence and AI in Games*, 6:1:31–45, 2013.

[16] D. Perez, S. Samothrakis, S. Lucas, and P. Rohlfshagen. Rolling Horizon Evolution versus Tree Search for Navigation in Single-Player Real-Time Games. In *Proceedings of the Conference on Genetic and Evolutionary Computation (GECCO)*, pages 351–358, 2013.

[17] D. Perez, S. Samothrakis, J. Togelius, T. Schaul, S. Lucas, A. Couëtoux, J. Lee, C.-U. Lim, and T. Thompson. The 2014 General Video Game Playing Competition. *IEEE Transactions on Computational Intelligence and AI in Games*, page (to appear) DOI: 10.1109/TCIAIG.2015.2402393, 2015.

[18] H. Pohlheim. Ein genetischer Algorithmus mit Mehrfachpopulationen zur numerischen Optimierung. *at-Automatisierungstechnik*, 43(3):127–135, 1995.

[19] S. J. Russell. Rationality and Intelligence. *Artificial Intelligence*, 1:57–77, 1997.

[20] S. J. Russell and P. Norvig. *Artificial Intelligence: A Modern Approach*. Pearson Education, 2003.

[21] S. Samothrakis and S. Lucas. Planning Using Online Evolutionary Overfitting. In *UK Workshop on Computational Intelligence*, pages 1–6. IEEE, 2010.

[22] T. Schaul. A Video Game Description Language for Model-based or Interactive Learning. In *Proceedings of the IEEE Conference on Computational Intelligence in Games*, pages 193–200, Niagara Falls, 2013. IEEE Press.

[23] R. Weber. *Optimization and Control*. University of Cambridge, 2010.

[24] W. Zhe, K. Q. Nguyen, R. Thawonmas, and F. Rinaldo. Adopting Scouting and Heuristics to Improve the AI Performance in Starcraft. *Proceedings of the Innovations in Information and Communication Science and Technology IICST 2013*, pages 155–164, Sept. 2013.

Solving Interleaved and Blended Sequential Decision-Making Problems through Modular Neuroevolution

Jacob Schrum
Dept. of Mathematics and Computer Science
Southwestern University
Georgetown, TX 78626 USA
schrum2@southwestern.edu

Risto Miikkulainen
Department of Computer Science
The University of Texas at Austin
Austin, TX 78712 USA
risto@cs.utexas.edu

ABSTRACT

Many challenging sequential decision-making problems require agents to master multiple tasks, such as defense and offense in many games. Learning algorithms thus benefit from having separate policies for these tasks, and from knowing when each one is appropriate. How well the methods work depends on the nature of the tasks: Interleaved tasks are disjoint and have different semantics, whereas blended tasks have regions where semantics from different tasks overlap. While many methods work well in interleaved tasks, blended tasks are difficult for methods with strict, human-specified task divisions, such as Multitask Learning. In such problems, task divisions should be discovered automatically. To demonstrate the power of this approach, the MM-NEAT neuroevolution framework is applied in this paper to two variants of the challenging video game of Ms. Pac-Man. In the simplified interleaved version of the game, the results demonstrate when and why such machine-discovered task divisions are useful. In the standard blended version of the game, a surprising, highly effective machine-discovered task division surpasses human-specified divisions, achieving the best scores to date in this game. Modular neuroevolution is thus a promising technique for discovering multimodal behavior for challenging real-world tasks.

Categories and Subject Descriptors

I.2.1 [**Artificial Intelligence**]: Applications and Expert Systems—*Games*; I.2.6 [**Artificial Intelligence**]: Learning—*Connectionism and neural nets*

Keywords

Games, Neural networks, Multi-objective optimization

GECCO '15, July 11 - 16, 2015, Madrid, Spain

DOI: http://dx.doi.org/10.1145/2739480.2754744

1. INTRODUCTION

Discovering intelligent agent behavior automatically for complex environments is an important goal for Artificial Intelligence. Such behavior is needed in both real-world robots and virtual environments. However, most interesting domains consist of multiple tasks, each requiring different behavior. Such behavior is multimodal, because distinct behavior is required in each task. Learning such behavior is difficult, and even harder when individual tasks overlap.

This paper presents a new way of identifying tasks for complex domains, and applies several methods of constructing modular policies for such domains using evolved neural networks (i.e. neuroevolution). Tasks are defined by partitioning the state space such that the frequency of transitions between tasks is low. This approach is then complimented by using domain semantics to define predicates (based on high-level domain features) that identify each task.

When distinctions between tasks are clear, the tasks are interleaved. A learning agent can then split up a domain by dedicating separate policies to each task. When distinctions are not clear, the tasks are blended. In such domains, it is sensible to identify the prominent tasks, and treat the domain as a blend of these representative tasks. However, to succeed in such domains, agents need the freedom to discover their own task divisions.

This paper builds on recent research in Ms. Pac-Man using evolved neural networks [24]. To support multiple tasks, networks have separate output modules to represent different behaviors. Previous research required evolution to discover how to use these modules, but this paper also allows a human designer to specify how modules are used in each task, in a style similar to Multitask Learning [7]. This extension makes it possible to identify the costs and benefits of discovering task divisions automatically. Another new contribution is that these methods are compared not only in the original Ms. Pac-Man, where the tasks are blended, but also in an interleaved version of the game. This extension makes it possible to determine where each approach is most effective.

The conclusion is that while a variety of approaches work well in the interleaved version, agents in the original blended version need the freedom to discover their own task division in order to succeed. When given such freedom, the most effective task divisions discovered are sometimes surprising: A luring strategy is learned, which uses one module to gather all ghosts close together, so that another module can quickly escape to a power pill, allowing the first module to easily capture the ghosts. Such a task division is not obvious to a human designer a priori, demonstrating the power of the modular neuroevolution approach.

2. RELATED WORK

Domains requiring multimodal behavior are common in both robotics and simulated environments, and various approaches have been implemented to deal with such domains.

For complex tasks, it is common to combine controllers into a hierarchy. Such hierarchies can be hand-designed [5] or learned. For example, Togelius's [31] evolved subsumption architecture was used in EvoTanks [30] and Unreal Tournament [32], and Stone's [27] Layered Learning was applied to RoboCup Soccer. Recently, Lessin et al. [18] used a human-designed hierarchical syllabus to evolve complex behavior for virtual creatures. Though effective, these approaches require a programmer to divide the domain into constituent tasks and develop effective training scenarios for each.

Hierarchical Reinforcement Learning (HRL) also produces hierarchical controllers consisting of multiple sub-controllers. Early HRL research required the hierarchy to be human-specified [10], but methods now exist for learning it as well [11]. Most HRL techniques are based on the formalism of Semi-Markov Decision Processes (SMDPs), which was first used to develop partial control policies called options [29]. Similar techniques, e.g. skills [16] and activities [3], also fit this formalism. The methods in this paper can also be cast in the SMDP formalism, but they do not depend on it. Therefore, a simpler formalization is presented in the next section.

Several evolutionary approaches to learning multimodal behavior simply focus on discovering modular policies. One approach is to associate components of the architecture automatically with specific functionality. For instance, Calabretta et al. [6] evolved neural networks to control robots using a duplication operator, which copies one output neuron with all of its connections and weights. The network then has two outputs for the same actuator, and needs to arbitrate between them. Such arbitration is performed by selector units: For each actuator, the output neuron with the highest corresponding selector unit activation controls the actuator for that time step.

A similar approach is Module Mutation [23, 24], which introduces groups of neurons rather than individual neurons. A single Module Mutation adds enough output neurons to define a new policy, plus an additional neuron to arbitrate between modules. The behavior-defining neurons are called policy neurons, and the one arbitration neuron per module is called a preference neuron. Preference neurons are similar to the selector units of Calabretta et al. [6]. Since Module Mutation is used in this paper, it is discussed further in Section 4.3 on learning methods.

Other researchers have developed modular networks with a more general concept of a module [8, 13], i.e. a cluster of interconnected neurons with few connections to neurons in other clusters. Such modular networks can also be created using generative and developmental methods [19, 33, 12]. These methods evolve modular neural networks assuming that having different modules handle different parts of the task makes optimization easier. Compared to these approaches, the modular networks of this paper create clear task divisions in which it is always known which module is responsible for an agent's actions.

Modular policies have also been explored in Genetic Programming (GP). An early example is Koza's Automatically Defined Functions [17], which encapsulate portions of a program tree that can potentially be reused. A similar GP technique is Adaptive Representation through Learning [22], which culls modules from program trees based on differential parent/child fitness.

All of these techniques face the same challenge of having to break a domain into separate tasks. The next section presents a new way of identifying tasks within a domain.

3. TASK DIVISIONS

This section first describes the Markov Decision Process (MDP) formalism that is the basis of Reinforcement Learning (RL) problems [28]. This formalism is then used to specify a way of identifying individual tasks. The nature of the task division is used to distinguish between domains where tasks are interleaved vs. blended.

3.1 Markov Decision Process

An MDP is a formal description of a domain in terms of the results of taking certain actions in certain states. Specifically, an MDP is a tuple $(\mathcal{S}, \mathcal{A}, \mathcal{P}, \mathcal{R})$, where $\mathcal{S}$ is the state space, $\mathcal{A}$ is the set of actions, $\mathcal{P}$ is the transition function, and $\mathcal{R}$ is the reward function. The transition function is defined as $\mathcal{P} : (\mathcal{S} \times \mathcal{A} \times \mathcal{S}) \rightarrow [0, 1]$ where $\mathcal{P}(s, a, s')$ returns the probability of reaching state s' immediately after performing action a in state s. The reward function provides the agent with feedback on how well it is performing. Typical RL formulations use scalar rewards, but $\mathcal{R}$ can be extended to multiple objectives: $\mathcal{R} : (\mathcal{S} \times \mathcal{A}) \rightarrow \mathbb{R}^N$ is defined such that $\mathcal{R}(s, a)$ returns a tuple of the expected immediate rewards in each objective for performing action a in state s. This tuple has length N, the number of objectives.

The commonly used discount factor γ is excluded from this definition because only episodic domains are considered in this paper. As a result, the goal of an agent is to maximize the sum of rewards in each objective throughout the course of an episode. An episode is an evaluation period with definite start and end points, which allows rewards to be safely weighted equally without emphasizing early rewards in favor of later rewards [28]. For use in an evolutionary algorithm, the sum of rewards in each objective is treated as a different fitness function subject to multiobjective optimization.

The next sections use this definition of MDPs to explain the concepts of interleaved and blended tasks.

3.2 Interleaved Tasks

A collection of T interleaved tasks for an MDP is defined as a partition of its state space $\{\mathcal{S}_1, \ldots, \mathcal{S}_T\}$. By the definition of a partition, $\mathcal{S}$ is the union of these sets, which are pairwise disjoint:

$$\mathcal{S} = \bigcup_{i=1}^{T} \mathcal{S}_i \text{ and} \tag{1}$$

$$\forall i, j \in \{1, \ldots, T\}(\mathcal{S}_i = \mathcal{S}_j \vee \mathcal{S}_i \cap \mathcal{S}_j = \varnothing). \tag{2}$$

Importantly, each state is in exactly one task because all tasks cover $\mathcal{S}$, but are disjoint from each other. However, not all partitions are meaningful. For the concept of interleaved tasks to be useful, an agent should mostly remain in each task for an extended period before switching to another, so that its actions can have a useful impact in each task. In other words, the proportion of task switches to total time spent in the domain should be small. A low rate of thrashing back and forth between tasks indicates that a domain consists of a few important tasks that partition the state space. Of course, frequency of task switches also depends on a policy $\pi : \mathcal{S} \rightarrow \mathcal{A}$ (assuming the policy is deterministic), but because state transitions are stochastic, even the policy does not completely dictate which states are visited. The sequence of states visited within an episode determines the number of task transitions it contains. Therefore, an episode e consisting of m states can be defined as the sequence of visited states $s_1, s_2, \ldots, s_m$. Given this definition of an episode, the thrashing rate τ_e of episode e is defined as

$$\tau_e = x_e / m, \tag{3}$$

where x_e is the number of task transitions in e. The number of task transitions can be formally defined as the cardinality, or size, of the set of states in the episode where the next state is in a different task:

$$x_e = |\{s_i | s_i \in \mathcal{S}_j \wedge s_{i+1} \in \mathcal{S}_k \wedge j \neq k\}|, \quad (4)$$

where $i \in \{1, \ldots, m-1\}$, and therefore refers to any state before the last state, and $j, k \in \{1, \ldots, T\}$, so that each refers to one of the T tasks in the MDP. In other words, each time adjacent states of the episode are in different tasks, one task transition is tallied. From τ_e, the *domain's* thrashing rate $\bar{\tau}$ is defined as the average τ_e across all possible e. For a domain to have distinct interleaved tasks, $\bar{\tau}$ must be low.

Calculating $\bar{\tau}$ may not be possible, but a rough estimate is enough to determine whether a partition of the state space creates interleaved tasks. The lower $\bar{\tau}$ is, the more likely a domain can be usefully labelled as having interleaved tasks. The interleaved domain used in this paper has a thrashing rate less than 0.01, as will be explained in Section 5.1.

Although the thrashing rate provides a way of identifying the states in each task, the intuitive notion of a task is that each one has some distinct semantic properties that are clear to someone who understands the domain. In a domain with interleaved tasks, some obvious set of semantic properties should correspond to the structurally defined tasks that result in a low $\bar{\tau}$. Each task should have a predicate that is true for all states in that task, and false for all other states. Formally, $\psi_1, \ldots, \psi_T : \mathcal{S} \to \{\top, \bot\}$ are semantic predicates for the T tasks in the MDP for which each state satisfies one and only one semantic predicate:

$$\forall i \in \{1, \ldots, T\} \forall s \in \mathcal{S}_i(\psi_i(s) = \top) \text{ and} \quad (5)$$

$$\forall i, j \in \{1, \ldots, T\} \forall s \in \mathcal{S}_i(i \neq j \to \psi_j(s) = \bot). \quad (6)$$

These predicates allow any task i to be defined as the subset of $\mathcal{S}$ that satisfies ψ_i: For any predicate on states $\psi : \mathcal{S} \to \{\top, \bot\}$, define that predicate's task as the set of states that satisfy it:

$$\Phi(\psi) = \{s \in \mathcal{S} | \psi(s) = \top\}. \quad (7)$$

For the set of predicates above that satisfy properties 5 and 6, $\Phi(\psi_i) = \mathcal{S}_i$ for all $i \in \{1, \ldots, T\}$. Generally, an initial guess at suitable predicates should lead to the desired low thrashing rate.

However, predicates with properties 5 and 6 are not easy to define in domains with blended tasks, described next.

3.3 Blended Tasks

Interleaved tasks are defined in terms of the structure of the state space, which in turn depends on the transition function. However, it is also desirable for states in the same task to share high-level properties linked to semantic predicates. Unfortunately, it is sometimes hard to partition the state space of a domain with respect to such properties. In fact, sets of states in which different semantic properties hold may not be disjoint. The region where such properties overlap blends the properties of different tasks.

Assume that m distinct semantic predicates $\psi_1, \ldots, \psi_m$ are identified in some domain, but that

$$\exists i, j \in \{1, \ldots, m\}(i \neq j \wedge \Phi(\psi_i) \cap \Phi(\psi_j) \neq \varnothing). \quad (8)$$

That is, the set of m predicates does not satisfy properties 5 and 6 because the resulting tasks are not disjoint. It is possible to choose new predicates specifically designed to address the overlap, by replacing every two predicates ψ_x, ψ_y whose tasks overlap with three new predicates $\phi_x, \phi_y, \phi_{xy}$:

$$\phi_x(s) = \psi_x(s) \wedge \neg\psi_y(s), \quad (9)$$

$$\phi_y(s) = \psi_y(s) \wedge \neg\psi_x(s), \quad (10)$$

$$\phi_{xy}(s) = \psi_x(s) \wedge \psi_y(s). \quad (11)$$

These new predicates split up states into those that only satisfy ψ_x, those that only satisfy ψ_y, and those that satisfy both.

If every state satisfies at least one of the initial m predicates, iterating this process creates a set of predicates that generate disjoint tasks. If the thrashing rate between the resulting tasks is sufficiently low, then they are interleaved.

However, such a proliferation of predicates ignores the fact that some states have properties from multiple tasks. An alternative is to treat regions of intersection as blended regions between tasks. This view allows a learning agent to focus on major distinctions between tasks rather than micromanage different behaviors for many small but similar tasks. At least two semantic predicates ψ_p, ψ_q that satisfy the following properties are required:

$$\exists s \in \mathcal{S}(\psi_p(s) \wedge \neg\psi_q(s)), \quad (12)$$

$$\exists s \in \mathcal{S}(\psi_q(s) \wedge \neg\psi_p(s)), \quad (13)$$

$$\exists s \in \mathcal{S}(\psi_q(s) \wedge \psi_p(s)). \quad (14)$$

In other words, the tasks defined by ψ_p and ψ_q are not disjoint, but neither is a subset of the other. As a result, the states not in the intersection correspond to specific tasks, and the states in the intersection are in the blended region between those two tasks.

In domains with blended tasks, it becomes important for an agent to decide what role to take on at any given time. There may be clear goals in regions of a specific task, but in the blended region there are often multiple competing goals. If an agent can discover its own task division, it can more easily learn which goals to pursue in such regions. However, learning methods that easily allow for different modes of behavior in different tasks are needed in both blended and interleaved domains. Such methods are described next.

4. LEARNING METHODS

Evolutionary multiobjective optimization is used to evolve controllers for MDPs with multiple tasks. The evolved individuals are neural networks, and modular architectures are used to encourage multimodal behavior.

4.1 Evolutionary Multiobjective Optimization

Because different tasks can have different goals, domains requiring multimodal behavior may have multiple objectives. Therefore, a principled way of dealing with multiple objectives is needed. Such a framework is provided by the concepts of Pareto dominance and optimality:

Pareto Dominance: Vector $\vec{v} = (v_1, \ldots, v_N)$ dominates $\vec{u} = (u_1, \ldots, u_N)$ iff

$$\forall i \in \{1, \ldots, N\}(v_i \geq u_i) \text{ and} \quad (15)$$

$$\exists i \in \{1, \ldots, N\}(v_i > u_i). \quad (16)$$

Pareto Optimality: A set of points $\mathcal{A} \subseteq \mathcal{F}$ is Pareto optimal iff it contains all points such that $\forall \vec{x} \in \mathcal{A} \neg\exists \vec{y} \in \mathcal{F}$ such that $\vec{y}$ dominates $\vec{x}$. The points in $\mathcal{A}$ are non-dominated, and make up the non-dominated Pareto front of $\mathcal{F}$.

These definitions indicate that one solution dominates another if it is strictly better in at least one objective and no worse in the others. The best solutions are not dominated by any other solutions, and make up the Pareto front of the search space. The next best individuals are those that would be in a recalculated Pareto front if the actual Pareto front were removed first. Layers of Pareto fronts can be defined by successively removing the front and recalculating it for the remaining individuals. Solving a multiobjective optimization problem involves approximating the first Pareto front as best as possible. This paper accomplishes this goal using Non-dominated Sorting Genetic Algorithm II (NSGA-II [9]).

NSGA-II uses ($\mu + \lambda$) elitist selection favoring individuals in higher Pareto fronts of the current population over those in lower fronts. Within a given front, individuals that are more distant from others in objective space are favored by selection so that the algorithm explores diverse trade-offs.

Applying NSGA-II to a problem produces a population containing an approximation to the Pareto front. This approximation set potentially contains multiple solutions. Usually, this set must be analyzed to determine which solutions fulfill the needs of the user, but for the domains in this paper (whose objectives are described in Section 5.2), a specific objective weighting (based on Ms. Pac-Man game score) is available which reduces two objectives to a single score. Evolution on this single objective could also be used, but optimizing with multiple objectives instead of one is appealing because it can improve search by helping avoid local optima [14].

NSGA-II is indifferent as to how solutions are represented. This paper uses NSGA-II to evolve artificial neural networks.

4.2 Neuroevolution

Neuroevolution is the simulated evolution of artificial neural networks. All behavior in this paper is learned via a version of NEAT (Neuro-Evolution of Augmenting Topologies [26]), a constructive neuroevolution method that has been successful in many RL domains [15, 25].

NEAT networks start with no hidden neurons, and are modified by three mutation operators during evolution. Weight mutation perturbs the weights of existing network connections, link mutation adds new connections between existing nodes, and node mutation splices new nodes along existing connections. NEAT also features an efficient method of topological crossover between networks.

The variant of NEAT used in this paper is Modular Multiobjective NEAT[1] (MM-NEAT [24]), which distinguishes itself from NEAT by incorporating NSGA-II, and providing several methods for creating networks with multiple output modules, described next.

4.3 Modular Networks

MM-NEAT networks allow for multiple output modules. Each such module defines a different control policy. A new feature of MM-NEAT in this paper is the ability to arbitrate between modules based on a human-specified division, i.e. via Multitask networks. As in previous research, arbitration can also be based on preference neurons. In preference neuron networks, evolution must discover how to use the modules. Using Module Mutation, evolution must also settle on an appropriate number of modules. Each of these approaches is evaluated in this paper.

Multitask networks were first proposed by Caruana [7] for supervised learning using neural networks and backpropagation. One network has multiple modules, and each module corresponds to a different task (Fig. 1b). Each module is trained on data for its corresponding task, but because hidden-layer neurons are shared by all outputs, knowledge common to all tasks can be stored in the hidden layer. This approach speeds up supervised learning of multiple tasks because knowledge shared across tasks is only learned once, rather than learned independently multiple times.

Multitask Learning is a powerful technique, but the individual tasks need to be identified a priori (the specific divisions used in Ms. Pac-Man are discussed in Section 5.2). Appropriate task divisions are not always obvious, and obvious divisions may actually hurt learning. Therefore, Multitask Learning will only be useful if its task division is appropriate. When tasks are blended, it is hard to provide an appropriate division. To discover better task divisions, a means of learning how to arbitrate between tasks is needed.

Preference neurons make module arbitration without a human-specified task division possible. Each module has policy neurons for defining behavior and a preference neuron that outputs the network's preference for using that module's policy neurons (Fig. 1c). Whenever inputs are presented to the network, the module whose preference neuron output is highest specifies the network's output.

Preference neurons partition the state space into one set per output module, though there is no requirement that these sets are interleaved tasks in terms of the thrashing rate $\bar{\tau}$ between them. However, preference neuron networks have the capacity to evolve such a task division if it is useful.

This architecture assumes that a designer specifies the number of modules. However, evolution can also discover how many modules are needed by adding modules gradually, using Module Mutation.

Module Mutation is any structural mutation operator that adds a new output module to a neural network. An indefinite number of modules may be added in this way. Such networks depend on preference neurons for module arbitration. New populations start with a single module and a preference neuron that only becomes relevant after more modules are added (Fig. 1d). Each Module Mutation adds a new set of policy neurons and a new preference neuron.

Different versions of Module Mutation exist [23, 24]. This paper uses MM(D), for *duplicate*, because each new module duplicates the behavior of an existing module. For every link into a policy neuron in the original module, a duplicate link into the corresponding policy neuron of the new module is created, and it has the same source neuron and link weight as the link being copied (Fig. 1e). After MM(D), a network will behave the same as before, but evolution can then modify the new structure, so that module behavior diverges. However, links to the new module's preference neuron are not copied from the parent module. Rather, the new preference neuron has a single link with a random source and weight, to encourage the module to be used in different circumstances.

MM(D) and the other modular approaches described so far are evaluated in domains with interleaved tasks and blended tasks, as described next.

5. EXPERIMENTS

The domains used for evaluation are two variants of the classic video game Ms. Pac-Man. This game requires multimodal behavior because enemy agents are sometimes threats, and sometimes sources of points. Most of the modular architectures described above were applied to the original, blended version of Ms. Pac-Man [24], in which a mixture of edible and threat ghosts can be present at the same time. However, the interleaved version of the domain, in which such mixtures never occur, is new, and seeing these results side-by-side gives new insight into when and why certain types of modular networks are successful. This section describes both blended and interleaved variants of Ms. Pac-Man, then describes experiments in both domains.

5.1 Ms. Pac-Man

Ms. Pac-Man (1981) is among the most popular video games of all time. Its gameplay is simple, yet requires complex strategies for success. A popular platform for Ms. Pac-Man research is the simulator for the Ms. Pac-Man vs. Ghosts competitions[2] [21],

[1]Download at http://nn.cs.utexas.edu/?mm-neat. Download includes source code for all experiments presented in this paper.

[2]http://www.pacman-vs-ghosts.net/

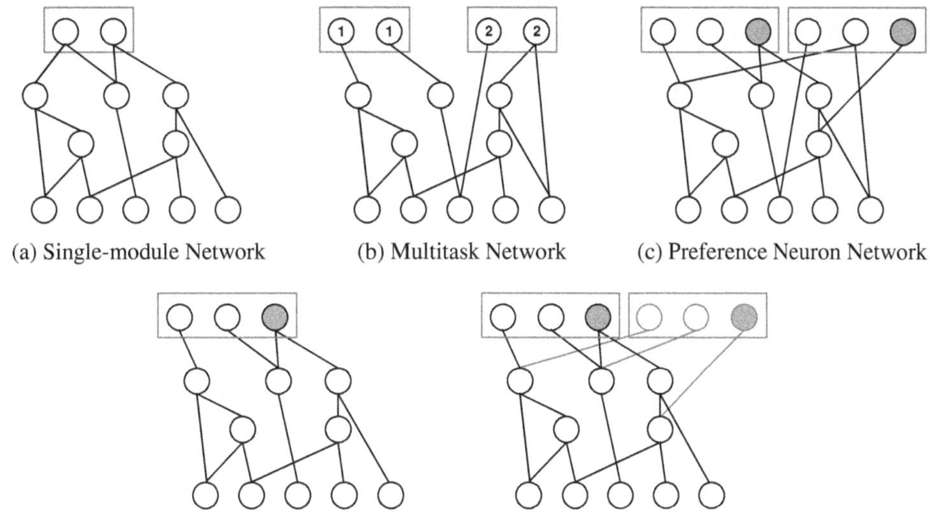

(a) Single-module Network (b) Multitask Network (c) Preference Neuron Network

(d) Before Module Mutation (e) Module Mutation Duplicate

Figure 1: Modular Networks: These example networks are designed for a domain where two policy neurons define the behavior of an agent. Inputs are at the bottom, and each output module is contained in its own red box. (a) Standard neural network with just one module. (b) Multitask network with two modules, each consisting of two policy neurons. A human-specified task division indicates when to use Policy 1 vs. Policy 2. (c) A fixed network with two modules that uses preference neurons (colored gray) to determine which module to use. (d) A starting network in a population where Module Mutation is enabled. It has one module, and an irrelevant preference neuron. (e) After MM(D), the network gains a new module with policy neurons linked to the same neuron sources with the same link weights as policy neurons in the module that was duplicated. However, the new preference neuron is linked to a random source with a random weight so that the new module is used in different situations. After MM(D), both the pre-existing and newly added preference neurons become relevant. Extra modules allow these networks to learn multimodal behavior more easily by associating a different module with each behavioral mode.

which includes a standard `Legacy` ghost team that approximates the original ghosts.

In Ms. Pac-Man, each of four mazes contains several pills and four power pills. Ms. Pac-Man moves around, eating pills she comes in contact with, all of which must be eaten to clear a level. Each pill earns 10 points, and each power pill 50 points.

Each maze starts with four hostile ghosts in a lair near the center of the maze. They come out one by one and pursue Ms. Pac-Man according to different algorithms. If a ghost touches Ms. Pac-Man, she dies and the episode ends. However, if Ms. Pac-Man eats a power pill, then for a limited time she can eat the ghosts. The 1st, 2nd, 3rd, and 4th ghosts eaten in sequence are worth 200, 400, 800, and 1600 points, respectively. The maximum score is achieved by eating all four ghosts after each power pill. This goal becomes more challenging in each subsequent level, because edible time decreases as the level increases, but it is still achievable because edible ghosts move at half speed.

If ghosts were always all edible or all threatening, this domain would provide a clear example of interleaved tasks: one task predicate satisfied when any ghost was edible, and the other when any ghost was a threat. An upper bound on $\bar{\tau}$ for this interleaved domain can be calculated by realizing that each power pill can cause two task transitions: ghosts become edible, then go back to being threats. Some amount of time has to pass before Ms. Pac-Man can reach a power pill, and once she eats one she is guaranteed to survive for the entire edible time, which is 200 in the first maze. Therefore, for every two task transitions, over 200 time steps must pass. Thus, an upper bound for the thrashing rate is $2/200 = 0.01$. This bound will hold despite the fact that the edible time decreases to 145 by the fourth level. It takes over 1,000 time steps simply to eat all pills in one of the mazes, and dodging ghosts causes further delays. Therefore, the extra time steps required to beat preceding levels more than cancels out the decrease in edible time.

However, sometimes ghosts of both types are in the maze at the same time. After a ghost is eaten it returns to the lair for a short time before reemerging as a threat, which can happen before the edible time has expired for the other ghosts. Therefore, there are situations with both threat and edible ghosts, each at different positions relative to Ms. Pac-Man, which put the competing goals of survival and ghost eating at odds with each other. This set of states represents the blended region between the threat and edible tasks. Thus, Ms. Pac-Man is a game with blended tasks.

However, the game can be modified to have strictly interleaved tasks by confining eaten ghosts to the lair until either all ghosts have been eaten, or the edible time has expired. This change creates a new domain that shows the relative benefits of different types of modular policies in domains with interleaved vs. blended tasks. Although the two domains are slightly different, each requires multimodal behavior to succeed. The next section explains how experiments in these domains are conducted.

5.2 Experimental Setup

Neural networks are evolved in the manner described by Schrum and Miikkulainen [24], details of which are provided below. Networks are evaluated with sensor information corresponding to each available movement direction on each time step in order to produce a single output value for each direction. Ms. Pac-Man moves in the direction with the highest network output.

There are both direction-oriented sensors and sensors that are not direction-oriented, i.e. ones providing the same reading for each direction. Direction-oriented distances measure the shortest path to objects of interest starting in a particular direction and continuing without reversing. Distances have a maximum of 200, and all sensors are scaled to $[0, 1]$.

The direction-oriented sensors are: distances to the nearest pill, power pill, and junction, the maximum numbers of pills and junctions within 30 steps, distances to the 1st, 2nd, 3rd, and 4th closest ghosts, whether each ghost is approaching, whether a directional path to each ghost contains junctions, and the Options From Next Junction (OFNJ). OFNJ looks at the next junction in a given direction, and counts the number of subsequent junctions that can be safely reached from the first junction without reversing. The safety of a route can be determined by taking all agent distances into account and conservatively assuming ghosts will follow the shortest path to the target junction. Additionally, the blended game has a sensor for whether each ghost is edible, which is not needed in the interleaved version because a single sensor provides this information about all ghosts.

The remaining sensors are not direction-oriented: a constant bias, the proportions of remaining pills, power pills, edible ghosts, and edible time, and Boolean sensors indicating whether any ghost is edible, whether there are four threats outside the lair, and whether Ms. Pac-Man is within 10 steps of a power pill.

These sensors are used to evolve Ms. Pac-Man controllers with separate pill and ghost objectives. The pill score is the number of pills eaten, including power pills. The ghost score gives points proportional to the score that would be received for each ghost eaten: the 1st, 2nd, 3rd, and 4th ghosts are worth 1, 2, 4, and 8 points, respectively. Evaluation in Ms. Pac-Man is noisy because the ghost movement is non-deterministic, so each neural network is evaluated 10 times; fitness scores are the average scores across evaluations. Although these objectives are used during evolution, the final results are evaluated in terms of game score.

Because 10 episodes per network are costly, an episode will end after the fourth maze is cleared, and an 8,000 time step per level limit is imposed, after which point Ms. Pac-Man dies.

In both the interleaved and blended versions of the game, populations of networks with one module (`1M`), two modules (`2M`), and three modules (`3M`) are evolved. Modular networks use preference neurons to decide which module to use on each time step. Populations that start with one module, but can add more via `MM(D)`, are also evaluated. These approaches were previously evaluated in the blended Ms. Pac-Man game, but not in the interleaved version.

Multitask networks require human-specified task divisions. In the interleaved game, the Multitask (`MT`) approach has one module each for the edible and threat tasks. In the blended game, two Multitask approaches are used. The two module (`MT2`) approach uses one module when any ghost is edible, and another module otherwise, and the three module (`MT3`) approach uses separate modules when all ghosts are either threats or edible, and the third module when there is a mix of both types. `MT3` treats the blended region between tasks as its own task.

Populations of each type are evolved 30 times for 200 generations each, with a population size of 100. The mutation rates are: 5% chance of weight perturbation per link, 40% chance of a new link, and 20% chance of a new node. In MM(D) runs, Module Mutation is applied to 10% of offspring. The crossover rate is 50%. These settings lead to the results described in the next section.

5.3 Results

In general, modular networks perform well in both the interleaved and blended domains, while `1M` performs the worst. Multitask approaches handle interleaved tasks well, but perform poorly when tasks are blended.

Figure 2a shows how in the interleaved domain, `2M`, `3M`, `MM(D)` and `MT` all quickly achieve higher scores than `1M`. In the final generation, each of these modular approaches has much higher scores than `1M`. Figure 2b shows how in the blended domain, methods using preference neurons (`MM(D)`, `3M` and especially `2M`) reach scores much higher than those achieved by the Multitask methods (`MT2` and `MT3`) and `1M`. The modular approaches that use preference neurons are all better than `1M` and the Multitask approaches. The high performance of preference neuron approaches is consistent with previous work, but the poor performance of Multitask networks is an interesting new result.

These results indicate that while human-specified and machine-learned task divisions can both handle interleaved tasks well, human-specified task divisions have difficulty with blended tasks. This result holds when the blended region is treated as its own task, as with `MT3`.

These results are statistically verified by post-learning evaluations of the champions from each run. Each was evaluated 1,000 times in the game, and the resulting average scores were compared. In each domain, Kruskal-Wallis tests verify that the learning algorithms perform differently, and pairwise Mann-Whitney U post tests with Bonferroni error correction identify significant differences between specific pairs. Specifically, there are differences between methods in the interleaved domain ($H = 37.02, df = 4, N = 30, p \approx 1.8 \times 10^{-7}$), and post tests reveal that all modular approaches are significantly better than `1M` ($p < 0.05$), but not different from each other. There were also significant differences between methods in the blended domain ($H = 49.69, df = 5, N = 30, p \approx 1.6 \times 10^{-9}$), but these post tests indicate that while `2M`, `3M`, and `MM(D)` are significantly better than `1M` and `MT2`, only `2M` and `3M` are significantly better than `MT3` ($p < 0.05$).

These post-learning evaluations also reveal the types of task divisions learned by each champion. Average scores are plotted against the usage of the most used module in Figures 2c and 2d. Color-coded movies[3] of the module usage are observed to determine the role of each module. Similar divisions emerge in both versions of the game. However, certain divisions do not work as well in blended tasks as they do in interleaved tasks.

A common strategy in both domains is to dedicate one module to dealing with edible ghosts (roughly 20% of the time) and another to threat ghosts (roughly 80%). This strategy is mandated by `MT` in the interleaved domain, and approximated in different ways by `MT2` and `MT3` in the blended domain (the 20% that `MT3` dedicates to edible ghosts is split across two modules). The `2M`, `3M`, and `MM(D)` networks also learn a pure threat/edible strategy in the interleaved domain, and an approximation of it in the blended domain. In particular, preference neurons in the blended domain do not switch modules as soon as ghost states change, but switch modules strategically based on the number and proximity of ghosts of different types. Sometimes, these networks will even thrash back and forth between modules as they dodge threat ghosts until they find an opening to chase an edible ghost. Despite the thrashing, these strategies are still a form of threat/edible strategy.

However, threat/edible strategies earn higher scores in the interleaved domain than in the blended domain. More importantly, their scores are noticeably higher than most `1M` scores in the interleaved domain, whereas threat/edible and `1M` scores mostly overlap in the blended domain.

There is another, surprising strategy that emerges in both domains. Only networks using preference neurons can develop it, because it involves a task division that is not obvious: Networks use one module about 95% of the time to deal with threat and edible ghosts, but the remaining 5% dictates what Ms. Pac-Man does when surrounded by threat ghosts. Specifically, the most-used module eats pills while threat ghosts chase her, but sometimes the ghosts surround Ms. Pac-Man. At this point, the least-used module

[3]Available at http://nn.cs.utexas.edu/?interleaved-pm and http://nn.cs.utexas.edu/?blended-pm

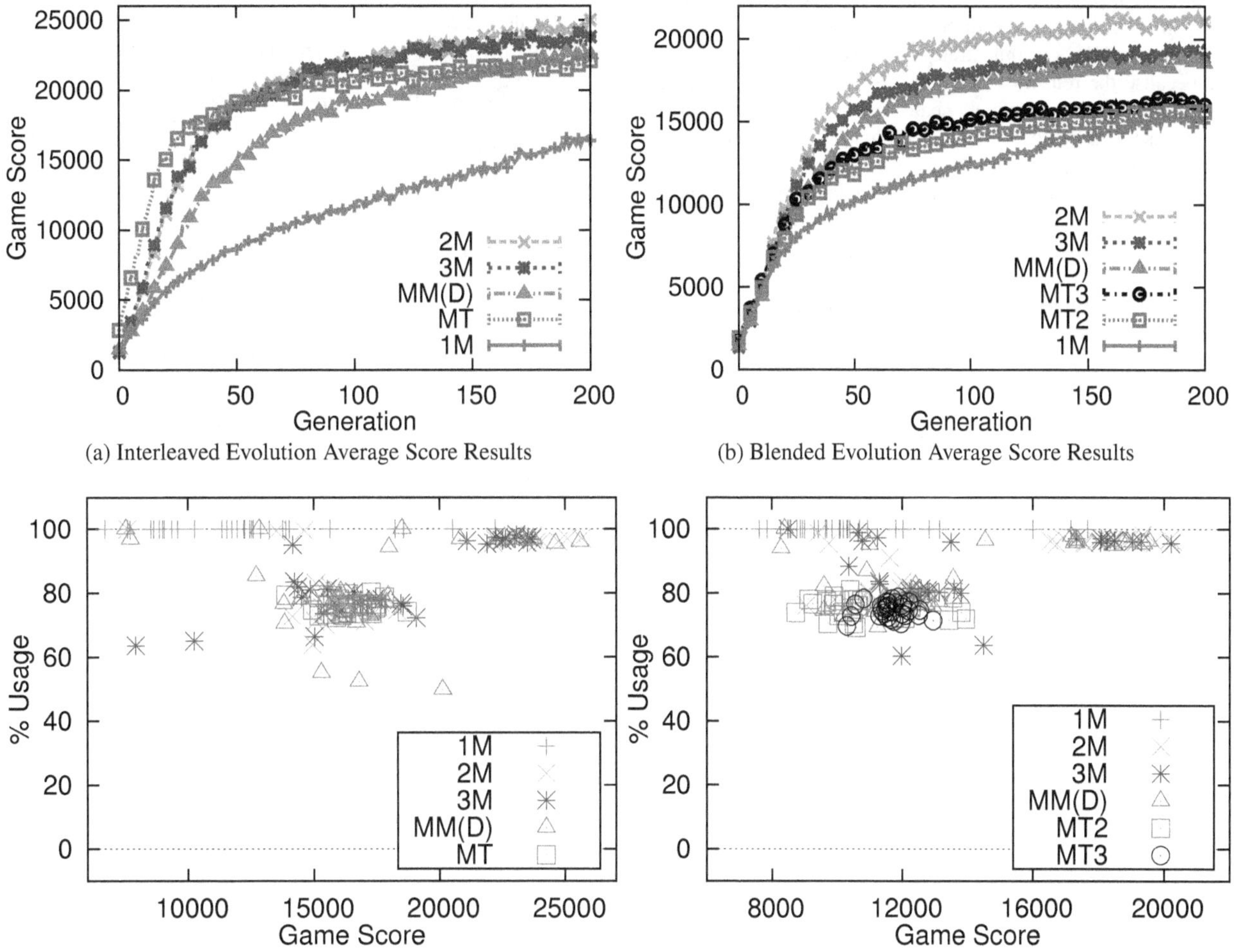

(a) Interleaved Evolution Average Score Results

(b) Blended Evolution Average Score Results

(c) Interleaved Primary Module Usage Post Results

(d) Blended Primary Module Usage Post Results

Figure 2: Results During Evolution and Post-Learning Evaluations For Both Interleaved and Blended Domains. Average champion scores across 30 runs of evolution are shown for (a) interleaved and (b) blended domains. Interleaved scores are generally higher because this version of the game is easier. Most modular approaches perform well in both domains, but Multitask networks only perform well in the interleaved domain. Multitask performance in the blended domain is close to that of `1M`, which performs poorly in both domains. Post-learning evaluations in both the (c) interleaved and (d) blended domains clarify the difference. Average scores of each champion across 1,000 evaluations are plotted on the x-axis, and the percentage of time steps that each champion used its most-used module across all evaluations is plotted on the y-axis. The middle cluster in each figure corresponds to champions using a threat/edible task division, while the cluster in the top-right of each figure corresponds to a luring strategy. The gap between threat/edible and luring scores in the blended domain is larger than the corresponding gap in the interleaved domain, thus highlighting the importance of being able to discover custom task divisions in a domain with blended tasks. Videos of each evolved behavior are available in the interleaved (http://nn.cs.utexas.edu/?interleaved-pm) and blended (http://nn.cs.utexas.edu/?blended-pm) domains.

kicks in to help Ms. Pac-Man escape. Often this behavior happens near a power pill, which then makes it easy for Ms. Pac-Man to first eat the power pill, and then all ghosts. The overall behavior learned is thus a *luring* behavior, and it greatly increases the ghost score. Although champions in both domains evolve luring behavior, it is more vital in the domain with blended tasks, where the score gap between luring behavior and threat/edible behavior is larger.

A final curious result is that preference neuron networks rarely make use of three or more modules. In particular, it is not clear why `3M` or `MM(D)` networks do not develop a luring strategy with the most-used module split up into one module for edible ghosts and one for threat ghosts. The `3M` networks evolve to ignore one module, and `MM(D)` networks either stop adding modules beyond the second, or mostly ignore their few additional modules. Of course, even though a three-module division seems to make sense from a human perspective, the successful two-module luring networks show that it is not necessary. The luring networks with just two modules are apparently easier for evolution to discover than networks that behave similarly, but have more modules, possibly because of the extra coordination effort required.

6. DISCUSSION

Similar behaviors were developed in the interleaved and blended domains, but the resulting scores are different. A threat/edible division makes sense in the interleaved domain, because the two tasks are sharply divided. Luring behavior earns higher scores in this domain, but the difference is small because a simple threat/edible division already makes it easy to eat a lot of ghosts. Because all ghosts are edible at the same time, advanced planning is not needed to assure that ghosts are eaten before threats return, which would disrupt the simple strategy of pursuing the edible ghosts wherever they are.

In contrast, luring behavior is strongly needed in the blended domain. In this domain, the threat/edible split is better than using a single module, but this strategy will often fail to eat many ghosts because the return of threat ghosts disrupts it. Luring behavior allows ghosts to be quickly eaten once they become edible, which means that a mix of threat and edible ghosts are encountered less often; luring agents spend less time in the blended region between tasks. In other words, evolution discovered a task division that makes the blended domain behave more like an interleaved domain, which makes Ms. Pac-Man more successful.

In the blended domain—the standard Ms. Pac-Man—the scores achieved by the luring strategy are better than those achieved by other techniques, such as Genetic Programming [1, 4], Monte-Carlo Tree Search [2], and Ant Colony Optimization [20]; see Schrum and Miikkulainen [24] for a detailed comparison.

The results in this paper show how the choice of a learning technique should fit the type of task division. Human-specified task divisions, such as those employed by Multitask networks, work fine in an interleaved domain, but poorly in one with blended tasks. If Multitask networks were explicitly programmed to dedicate a module to luring, then they could perhaps achieve similar success. Note, however, that this task division was not obvious a priori, nor is it clear how to implement it a posteriori.

Though preference neuron networks automatically evolve good task divisions, it could be useful in future work to incorporate the formalism from Section 3 into MM-NEAT to discover appropriate task divisions more quickly and/or reliably.

Regardless, this paper not only reaffirms that letting evolution discover its own task divisions is a promising technique for domains with multiple tasks, but also identifies properties of domains that make different modular architectures more likely to succeed.

7. CONCLUSION

This paper demonstrates how behavior can be divided effectively into separate tasks in sequential decision-making problems. Two kinds of domains were identified—interleaved and blended—and modular neuroevolution techniques were used to solve them. The results in two variants of Ms. Pac-Man showed that while human-specified task divisions work well in interleaved domains, they are difficult to properly specify for blended domains. Machine discovery of multimodal behavior is therefore a promising approach to challenging sequential decision-making problems.

8. ACKNOWLEDGMENTS

This research was supported in part by NSF grants DBI-0939454, IIS-0915038, and SBE-0914796, and by NIH grant R01-GM105042.

9. REFERENCES

[1] A. M. Alhejali and S. M. Lucas. Evolving Diverse Ms. Pac-Man Playing Agents Using Genetic Programming. In *UKCI*, 2010.

[2] A. M. Alhejali and S. M. Lucas. Using Genetic Programming to Evolve Heuristics for a Monte Carlo Tree Search Ms Pac-Man Agent. In *CIG*, pages 65–72. IEEE, 2013.

[3] A. G. Barto and S. Mahadevan. Recent Advances in Hierarchical Reinforcement Learning. *Discrete Event Dynamic Systems*, pages 41–77, 2003.

[4] M. F. Brandstetter and S. Ahmadi. Reactive Control of Ms. Pac Man Using Information Retrieval Based on Genetic Programming. In *CIG*, pages 250–256. IEEE, 2012.

[5] R. A. Brooks. A Robust Layered Control System for a Mobile Robot. *Robotics and Automation*, 2(10), 1986.

[6] R. Calabretta, S. Nolfi, D. Parisi, and G. Wagner. Duplication of Modules Facilitates the Evolution of Functional Specialization. *ALife*, 6(1):69–84, 2000.

[7] R. A. Caruana. Multitask Learning: A Knowledge-based Source of Inductive Bias. In *ICML*, pages 41–48, 1993.

[8] J. Clune, J.-B. Mouret, and H. Lipson. The Evolutionary Origins of Modularity. *Royal Society B*, pages 20122863–20122863, 2013.

[9] K. Deb, A. Pratap, S. Agarwal, and T. Meyarivan. A Fast and Elitist Multiobjective Genetic Algorithm: NSGA-II. *Evolutionary Computation*, 6:182–197, 2002.

[10] T. G. Dietterich. The MAXQ Method for Hierarchical Reinforcement Learning. In *ICML*, 1998.

[11] B. Hengst. Discovering Hierarchy in Reinforcement Learning with HEXQ. In *ICML*, pages 243–250, 2002.

[12] J. Huizinga, J.-B. Mouret, and J. Clune. Evolving Neural Networks That Are Both Modular and Regular: HyperNeat Plus the Connection Cost Technique. In *GECCO*, pages 697–704. ACM, 2014.

[13] N. Kashtan and U. Alon. Spontaneous Evolution of Modularity and Network Motifs. *National Academy of Sciences*, 102(39):13773–13778, 2005.

[14] J. D. Knowles, R. A. Watson, and D. Corne. Reducing Local Optima in Single-Objective Problems by Multi-objectivization. In *EMO*, pages 269–283. Springer, 2001.

[15] N. Kohl and R. Miikkulainen. Evolving Neural Networks for Strategic Decision-Making Problems. *Neural Networks, Special issue on Goal-Directed Neural Systems*, 2009.

[16] G. Konidaris and A. Barto. Skill Discovery in Continuous Reinforcement Learning Domains using Skill Chaining. In *NIPS*, pages 1015–1023, 2009.

[17] J. R. Koza. *Genetic Programming II: Automatic Discovery of Reusable Programs*. MIT Press, 1994.

[18] D. Lessin, D. Fussell, and R. Miikkulainen. Open-Ended Behavioral Complexity for Evolved Virtual Creatures. In *GECCO*, pages 335–342. ACM, 2013.

[19] J.-B. Mouret and S. Doncieux. MENNAG: A Modular, Regular and Hierarchical Encoding for Neural-networks Based on Attribute Grammars. *Evolutionary Intelligence*, 2008.

[20] G. Recio, E. Martín, C. Estébanez, and Y. Sáez. AntBot: Ant Colonies for Video Games. *TCIAIG*, 4(4):295–308, 2012.

[21] P. Rohlfshagen and S. M. Lucas. Ms Pac-Man versus Ghost Team CEC 2011 Competition. In *CEC*, pages 70–77. IEEE, 2011.

[22] J. P. Rosca. Generality Versus Size in Genetic Programming. In *GP*, pages 381–387. MIT Press, 1996.

[23] J. Schrum and R. Miikkulainen. Evolving Multimodal Networks for Multitask Games. *TCIAIG*, 4(2):94–111, 2012.

[24] J. Schrum and R. Miikkulainen. Evolving Multimodal Behavior With Modular Neural Networks in Ms. Pac-Man. In *GECCO*, pages 325–332. ACM, 2014.

[25] K. O. Stanley, B. D. Bryant, I. Karpov, and R. Miikkulainen. Real-Time Evolution of Neural Networks in the NERO Video Game. In *National Conference on Artificial Intelligence*, 2006.

[26] K. O. Stanley and R. Miikkulainen. Evolving Neural Networks Through Augmenting Topologies. *Evolutionary Computation*, pages 99–127, 2002.

[27] P. Stone and M. Veloso. Layered Learning. In *ECML*, pages 369–381. Springer Verlag, 2000.

[28] R. S. Sutton and A. G. Barto. *Reinforcement Learning: An Introduction*. MIT Press, Cambridge, MA, 1998.

[29] R. S. Sutton, D. Precup, and S. P. Singh. Between MDPs and Semi-MDPs: A Framework for Temporal Abstraction in Reinforcement Learning. *Artificial Intelligence*, 112(1-2):181–211, 1999.

[30] T. Thompson, F. Milne, A. Andrew, and J. Levine. Improving Control Through Subsumption in the EvoTanks Domain. In *CIG*, pages 363–370. IEEE, 2009.

[31] J. Togelius. Evolution of a Subsumption Architecture Neurocontroller. *Intelligent and Fuzzy Systems*, pages 15–20, 2004.

[32] N. van Hoorn, J. Togelius, and J. Schmidhuber. Hierarchical Controller Learning in a First-Person Shooter. In *CIG*, pages 294–301. IEEE, 2009.

[33] P. Verbancsics and K. O. Stanley. Constraining Connectivity to Encourage Modularity in HyperNEAT. In *GECCO*, pages 1483–1490. ACM, 2011.

Controlling Crowd Simulations using Neuro-Evolution

Sunrise Wang
sunrisewng@gmail.com

James E. Gain
jgain@cs.uct.ac.za

Geoff S. Nitschke
gnitschke@cs.uct.ac.za

Department of Computer Science
University of Cape Town
Cape Town, South Africa

ABSTRACT

Crowd simulations have become increasingly popular in films over the last decade, appearing in large crowd shots of many big name block-buster films. An important requirement for crowd simulations in films is that they should be directable both at a high and low level. As agent-based techniques allow for low-level directability and more believable crowds, they are typically used in this field. However, due to the bottom-up nature of these techniques, to achieve high level directability, agent-level parameters must be adjusted until the desired crowd behavior emerges.

As manually adjusting parameters is a time consuming and tedious process, this paper investigates a method for automating this, using Neuro-Evolution. To this end, the Conventional Neuro-Evolution (CNE), Covariance Matrix Adaptation Evolutionary Strategy (CMA-ES), Neuro-Evolution of Augmenting Topologies (NEAT), and Enforced Sub Populations (ESP) algorithms are compared across a variety of representative crowd simulation scenarios. Overall, it was found that CMA-ES generally performs the best across the selected simulations.

Categories and Subject Descriptors

I.2.11 [**Artificial Intelligence**]: Multiagent systems

Keywords

Entertainment and media; Simulation optimization; Genetic algorithms; Multi-agent systems; Neural networks

1. INTRODUCTION

The short film *Stanley and Stella in: Breaking the Ice*, shown at the Electronic Theater at SIGGRAPH '87, showcased the revolutionary idea that complex group behavior can be achieved by providing simple local rules to the agents within the group, as opposed to using some set of enforced global rules. Accompanying this short film was a technical paper detailing the technique used to simulate the flocking behavior [21].

Much work has since been done on Crowd Simulations. These can be roughly divided into two groups. *Agent-based* [29, 19] techniques aim to simulate behavior at an agent level, with the aggregate crowd behavior being emergent. *Group-based* [20, 24] techniques aim to simulate behavior at a group level, with the individual agent behaviors being chosen so as to adhere to the rules of the group.

Agent-based techniques have the benefit that the agent behaviors are much more heterogeneous, leading to more believable scenes. Additionally, the behaviors of individual agents within the crowd can be directed. Group-based techniques, on the other hand, have the advantage of being less computationally costly to simulate, allowing for both larger crowds and interactive simulation speeds. The aggregate behavior of crowds can also be directed much more easily than with agent-based methods, which require the adjustment of agent-level parameters in order to obtain the desired emergent group behavior [25].

Crowd simulations have become increasingly popular in films in the last decade, appearing in a plethora of movies such as *The Lord of the Rings Trilogy*, *World War Z*, *Ratatouille*, and *Inception*. Directors need these crowd simulations to be both controllable and believable [25]. Group-based techniques are not a viable choice as they often have overly homogeneous behaviors, which leads to less believability, and lack low-level directability since the simulation occurs at a group level. Thus, agent-based simulations are used. However, this requires artists to perform the time consuming and tedious work of adjusting agent parameters until the desired crowd behavior emerges.

In order to alleviate this burden, it is possible to automate the adjustment of these parameters. This can be achieved with various machine learning algorithms. We investigate one such technique in this context, namely *Neuro-Evolution* (NE), which uses *Evolutionary Algorithms* (EAs) to train *Artificial Neural Networks* (ANNs). We apply NE in order to derive crowd behaviors that accomplish given tasks. That is, agent controllers are ANNs adapted with EAs such that crowd behavior conforming to user specifications is evolved. NE has the advantage that it does not require a specific rule-set for agent behaviors, allowing for an easier authoring process.

Due to the variety of NE methods, and to the dearth of work that applies NE to achieve user specified goals in the context of crowd simulations designed for film [27], it is unknown which algorithm yields the best results.

GECCO '15, July 11 - 15, 2015, Madrid, Spain

DOI: http://dx.doi.org/10.1145/2739480.2754715

The contribution of this paper is to present a preliminary comparative study for various NE methods applied to representative crowd simulation tasks. The objective is to ascertain if there is a single NE method that is appropriate for automating crowd behavior design. Given the diversity of tasks tested, NE method efficacy is measured as the best achieved fitness after a set number of fitness evaluations. The NE methods investigated are Conventional Neuro-Evolution (CNE) [28], Covariance Matrix Adaptation Evolutionary Strategy (CMA-ES) [11], Enforced Sub-populations (ESP) [10], and Neuro-Evolution of Augmenting Topologies (NEAT) [22]. These methods were chosen in order to cover a range of different types of algorithms. Our results show CMA-ES to be the best performing algorithm across our simulation scenarios.

2. BACKGROUND AND RELATED WORK

2.1 Controlling Crowd Simulations

Methods for controlling crowd simulations can be separated into two categories, high-level and low-level control [25]. Low-level control deals with directing individual agents within the scene. This is typically achieved by either modifying the variables associated with task or motor outputs [4], or by building up a state tree for an agent, and then traversing it to find the desired final state of the agent [9].

High-level control involves controlling the aggregate behavior of the crowd. Various group-based techniques have been successfully applied for such high-level control. For example, flow or potential fields can be used to steer agents towards desirable areas, whilst steering them away from undesirable areas [26, 6], whereas crowd configurations can be controlled through the traversal of motion graphs that depict group, instead of agent configurations [15]. Additionally, while not considered full crowd simulation systems, corridor-based path planning algorithms [13, 3] also represent a group-based approach to controlling group motion.

Agent-based techniques are also capable of providing high-level crowd control, typically by using an additional phase to learn the best parameters for achieving the desired behaviors. As an example, Anderson et al. [2] applied high-level control to bird-flock movement. This was achieved by performing a forward simulation of the flock, as well as a series of backward simulations that precisely satisfy the user provided constraints. The backward simulation most similar to the forward simulation was then chosen as the final output. In another method [12], the agent controllers are represented using fuzzy controllers, with the membership functions of these controllers being adjusted using Particle Swarm Optimization [14] in order to satisfy a fitness function representing the desired final crowd behavior.

Despite its success, the method of Anderson et al. [2] suffers from only being able to control the movement of crowds. Additionally, it only works with bird flocks as it uses a bird-flock specific *wander* element to measure the similarities between simulations. Jacka's method [12], whilst being much more general, is reliant on the artist constructing a well designed fuzzy controller structure in order for the training to be successful. NE is a promising alternative to these techniques as it is general, but also does not require the complex authoring process of fuzzy controllers, as users are merely required to specify the ANN structure, and the desired crowd behaviors.

2.2 Crowd Simulations in Neuro-Evolution

Crowd simulations fall into the large field of Multi-Agent Systems (MASs) [23], which have to take into account factors such as cooperation or competition between the agents, agent communication, and role specialization. These factors can be divided along two axes, namely *communicative versus non-communicative* and *homogeneous versus heterogeneous* [23].

There have been several studies of MASs in NE, such as Bryant and Miikkulainen's [5] work on role specialization of agents using homogeneous teams, which found that agents can learn to have adaptive role specialization dependent on their local context, and Yong and Miikkulainen's [30] work where ANN controllers learn to communicate via stigmergy, the act of implicitly communicating through perceived changes in the environment.

These works show that it is possible to use both homogeneous teams and stigmergy when dealing with communication and team composition in the design of our simulations. Both are desired as they allow for significant reductions in the problem dimensionality.

2.3 Neuro-Evolution Algorithms

NE methods can be divided up into three categories: single population fixed topology; cooperative co-evolution; and topology and weight evolving ANNs (TWEANNs) [7, 22, 18]. In order to test the viability of using NE to control crowd simulations, we select and compare a well-established algorithm from each category, in addition to *Conventional Neuro-Evolution* (CNE) [28], which is used as a benchmark to determine if the performance of more complex algorithms is significantly better.

CNE [28] is the simplest of the NE methods used, where a single population of fixed topology ANNs is evolved. These ANNs are represented as vectors of real numbers, with each real number corresponding to a weight within the ANN.

A different single population fixed topology approach is the Covariance Matrix Adaptation Evolutionary Strategy (CMA-ES) [11]. Much like CNE, CMA-ES also represents the ANNs as real valued vectors, however, it differs in the generation of offspring. Offspring are produced in CMA-ES through sampling a multi-variate distribution, with the covariance matrix, step size, and mean being iteratively updated so that the distribution covers high fitness areas of the search space.

The cooperative co-evolution algorithm selected is Enforced Sub-populations (ESP) [10]. In ESP, multiple sub-populations of real valued vectors representing neurons are evolved, as opposed to a single population of ANNs. In order to evaluate the fitness of these neurons, a neuron is selected from each sub-population to form an ANN, which can then get evaluated. The fitness obtained by this ANN is then shared across all participating neurons. Additionally, each neuron is evaluated multiple times in order to remove noise.

Neuro-Evolution of Augmenting Topologies (NEAT) [22] is the selected TWEANN. In NEAT, both the structures and the weights of a single population of ANNs are evolved. The evolution of the ANN structures is achieved by mutation operators that add connections or nodes, and the evolution of the weights which is achieved by mutating connection weights, and by reproduction, where the weight of the better performing parent is chosen. NEAT also makes use of complexification, which initializes the ANNs to their simplest

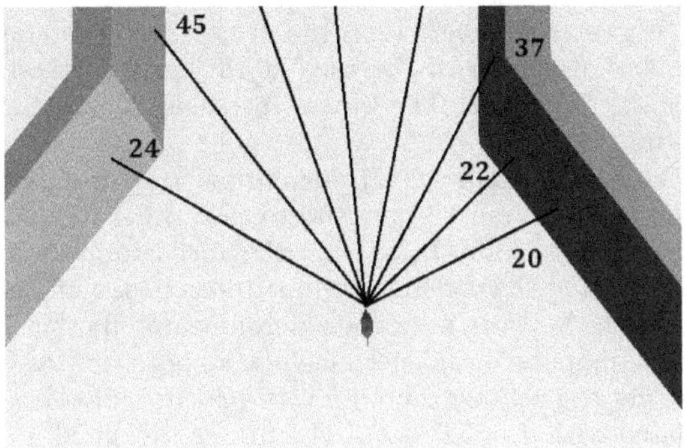

Figure 1: An agent's vision is simulated by casting rays, and returning the distance to the closest intersected object for each ray.

structure at the start of training, and speciation, which separates sufficiently different ANNs into different species, in order to protect structural innovations and minimize structure size.

All of the algorithms selected for comparisons are direct encoding methods [8], where the genotype has a direct mapping to the ANNs. A different approach would be to use generative encodings [8], where genotypes are interpreted using some set of rules in order to obtain the ANNs. Although comparing generative encodings lies outside the scope of this paper, it remains a promising direction for future investigation.

3. METHOD

Our system is divided up into three sub-systems: Neuro-Evolution, Simulation, and Rendering. The NE sub-system is responsible for loading the initial ANN structure and for running the NE methods, the simulation sub-system evaluates the fitnesses of candidate solutions sent from the NE sub-system within a given simulation scenario, and the rendering sub-system is responsible for visualizing a given simulation with a candidate solution and for loading 3D models.

Full results and source code used for this paper can be found in our online repository[1]. Additionally, videos of the various simulation scenarios can be found on our YouTube channel[2].

3.1 Controlling Agents

Each agent performs four steps every simulation cycle in order to update its behavior. It first *perceives* its local environment, using aspects such as vision (figure 1), agent velocity, and agent goals. The agent's ANN controller is then *evaluated* using its perception as input values. We use Fully connected Feed-Forward ANNs as our chosen ANN type as we found that they performed sufficiently, thus eliminating the need for using more complex ANN types. The output values of the ANN are then passed back to the agent, which then *interprets* them to determine what actions should be performed. Finally, the agent *acts* according to these instructions.

[1]https://bitbucket.org/igorawratu/ne-algorithm-comparison-paper

[2]https://www.youtube.com/channel/UCInMj1UK-1XXEo-RLidNrtw

3.2 Team composition

We use a homogeneous per species approach when assigning ANN controllers to agents, where all agents within a species use the same ANN controller. These species are used to represent different agent types, such as mice and robots, or different desired roles, such as defenders and attackers. The homogeneous teams approach is beneficial to crowd simulations as it allows for better search space scalability, as simulations can consist of tens to hundreds of thousands of agents. Species allow for simulations to have different agent types with differing inputs and outputs, and to have the same types of agents adopt different roles.

3.3 Fitness Evaluation

The fitness function of a given simulation is represented as a set of objectives, encoding the desired behaviors for the crowd. Examples of these objectives are reaching a physical goal location, or having a specific amount of agents alive at the end of a battle.

In order to evaluate a candidate solution, a simulation is run for a specified amount of time with the given solution, with the crowd's behavior being evaluated against the given objectives. After the simulation has completed, these objectives are then combined as a weighted sum in order to obtain the final fitness value. Fitness function weightings were obtained through exploratory experiments.

4. EXPERIMENT

Our crowd simulation testbed consists of eight different scenarios: Car Bridge Crossing; Car Race; Car Crash; War Robot Battle; Mouse Escape; Space-Ship Turnback; Space-Ship Obstacle; and Space-Ship Obstacle Field. Four different agent types were used in these scenarios, namely: Car, War-Robot, Mouse, and Space-Ship. This section elaborates on these scenarios and agents, as well as the parameters and experimental setup for our tests.

4.1 Agents

There are four different agent types used in our simulations. The **Car** agent is an agent that moves in a two-dimensional plane, with the ANN controller determining both its linear and angular acceleration. In order to simulate this agent's vision, eight rays are cast uniformly around the Car, thus simulating aspects such as rear and side-view mirrors.

Much like the Car agent, the **Mouse** agent's movement is also two-dimensional, with the ANN determining both its linear and angular acceleration. The Mouse agent also has the additional behavior that it can sense if there is an obstacle in front of it, and if so, it will come to a halt. The vision of this agent is simulated by casting eight rays in a cone in front of the Mouse.

The **War Robot** agent is another agent whose movement is on a two-dimensional plane, with the ANN controlling the linear and angular accelerations of the agent. The war-robot is also capable of sensing if there is an enemy in front of it, and if there is, it will fire and destroy it. The vision of this agent is similar to the Car agent, where rays are cast uniformly around the agent. However, it differs in that in addition to distance, the type of obstacle is also returned, with possible types being friendly, neutral, and enemy.

The **Space Ship** agent moves in three-dimensional space, with the ANN controller determining its x and y angular acceleration (allowing it to rotate around both x and y axis), and its linear acceleration. Although it is typical for these types of agents to also rotate around the z axis, we eliminated this as we found that the agents evolved a visually unpleasant behavior, where they achieved the desired objectives very inefficiently by spiraling towards the goals. The vision of this agent is simulated by casting rays in a forward facing 5x5 grid.

In addition to vision, the agents are also provided with a variety of other inputs. However, as these inputs are simulation specific, they will be discussed in section 4.2. Additionally, all ANN controllers have six hidden nodes, which was found to work consistently well (we experimented with ANNs with 0 to 10 nodes). However, no hidden nodes were used for the initial ANN structure when using NEAT, to allow complexification.

4.2 Simulations

There are a total of eight different simulations used in our tests. While these simulations are not representative of all possible crowd simulation use cases in films, they do provide a reasonably diverse set with which to evaluate NE.

A set of common objectives were used across all of our simulations:

- D - The sum of the distances of all the agents to their final goal at the end of a simulation;
- A - Accumulated angular velocities of all agents throughout the simulation, used to eliminate oscillating agent movement;
- C - Total number of collisions occurring throughout the simulation;
- P - Difference between desired and actual population size of a crowd.

In addition to these, there are a couple of specific objectives, which are further explained within their respective simulation sections.

We also define a fitness threshold for each simulation. This threshold represents what a candidate solution's fitness should achieve in order to display acceptable behavior in the given simulation. These thresholds were obtained by viewing the simulations at various fitnesses, and then selecting a value close to an acceptable simulation's achieved fitness.

In the **Car Bridge Crossing (CBC)** simulation, ten Car agents starting in a wide area are tasked to cross a narrow bridge area within 10 seconds whilst avoiding collisions with both the environment and other agents. The Car agents, in addition to vision, also provide the ANN with their current position, the finish line that they must cross, current linear velocity, and current angular velocity. The fitness of a genotype is calculated using $f = 2D + 2C + A$. The acceptable fitness threshold of this simulation is 100.

In the **Car Race (CR)** simulation, ten Car agents are tasked to complete a race course within 13 seconds while avoiding collisions, where the agent at the back must comeback and win the race. The Car agents are provided with additional inputs in the form of position, the points defining the finishing line, velocity, the desired winner's position, and a flag specifying whether or not they are the desired winner. The fitness for this simulation is calculated using $f = C + D + 20W$ where W is the distance of the underdog to the actual winner of the race at the time the first Car crosses the finish line. The fitness threshold defined for this simulation is 250.

In the **Car Crash (CC)** simulation, two groups of 10 Cars each are initialized opposite to each other in a narrow corridor, with the aim being that they need to move to the opposite end of the corridor within 10 seconds, while avoiding collisions between both the environment and other Cars. Additional inputs for an agent include its position, the finish line for its respective group, and its velocity. The fitness is calculated with $f = 5D + C$. The fitness threshold for this simulation is 250.

In the **War Robot Battle (WRB)** scenario, two groups of 40 War Robot agents are tasked to battle each other for 10 seconds. One group is initialized behind various buildings, whereas the other is initialized in an open field. The aim of this simulation is to have between nine and 11 agents left on each side at the end of the simulation. The additional inputs for the War Robot agents are position and velocity. The fitness for this simulation is calculated using $f = C + 20P$. The fitness threshold defined for this simulation is 150.

In the **Mouse Escape (ME)** simulation, thirty-five Mouse agents are tasked to escape from five robot agents, with the aim of there being between 11 and 13 Mouse agents escaping by the end of a 15 second simulation, with the rest of the mice having been killed by the robots. The Mouse agents are initialized on one side of the environment, behind various buildings which act as cover, and have to cross a finish line situated at the opposite end of the environment in order to count as having escaped. The Mouse agents have additional inputs of position, linear velocity, and the finishing line. The War Robot agents have additional inputs of position and velocity. The fitness of the simulation is calculated by using $f = 4D + 25P + C$. Fitnesses under 100 are regarded as acceptable for this simulation.

In the **Space Ship Turn back (SSTB)** simulation, 40 Space Ship agents are tasked to move towards a goal sphere, which is initialized behind their starting position, within 10 seconds. In order to enforce cohesion amongst the crowd, an extra goal sphere with a significantly larger radius is used. Although it is also possible to instead use the sum of the distances to the crowd centroid as an objective, we found using the extra goal spheres to be a much simpler method. The Space Ship agents are provided the additional inputs in the form of current agent position, position of the goal spheres, current linear velocity, and the magnitude of their angular velocity. The fitness for this simulation is calculated using $f = 10C + 2G_1 + 2G_2 + 0.2A$ where G_1 is the goal sphere and G_2 is the extra goal sphere used to enforce cohesion. The fitness threshold for this simulation is 750.

The **Space Ship Obstacle (SSO)** simulation is identical to the Space Ship turn back simulation, with the exception of the goal spheres and the environment. The goal spheres are placed in front of the agent, with a large obstacle in between the goal point and the agent starting positions. Additionally, the fitness threshold of this simulation is higher than that of the turnback simulation due to the presence of the extra obstacle, leading it to be defined at 1000.

Table 1: Mean fitness after 20,000 fitness evaluations achieved by the NE methods across the various simulations. Bolded fitness values achieved better values than the fitness threshold. Acceptable thresholds for each simulation can be found in section 4.2.

Simulation	NEAT	CMA-ES	CNE	ESP
CBC	**7.87**	**60.14**	**3.35**	**43.14**
CC	946.78	389.03	752.48	935.16
CR	401.85	**147.59**	**171.34**	265.68
ME	**17.82**	**5.64**	**1.70**	**7.75**
WRB	**72.09**	**74.39**	**90.2**	**108.72**
SSTB	**428.63**	**47.8**	**203.21**	**101.93**
SSO	1262.45	**773.99**	1273.87	2190.49
SSOF	**891.21**	**675.13**	**847.42**	1031.02

Table 2: Mann-Whitney U test p-values of the various algorithms when compared to the algorithm that achieved the lowest mean after 20,000 fitness evaluations in each simulation scenario. N/A is used to signify the algorithm with the lowest mean.

Simulation	NEAT	CMA-ES	CNE	ESP
CBC	9.5e-4	0.21	N-A	2.2e-3
CC	1.1e-10	N-A	3.8e-9	1.6e-11
CR	1.1e-10	N-A	0.47	6.6e-5
ME	2.4e-7	3.1e-6	N-A	4e-5
WRB	N-A	0.39	1.6e-4	7.7e-10
SSTB	6e-11	N-A	1.8e-8	2.5e-8
SSO	3.7e-10	N-A	6.2e-5	5.4e-10
SSOF	4.5e-8	N-A	2.8e-4	4.1e-7

Table 3: Mean execution times of the NE algorithms across the various simulation scenarios when evolved for 20,000 fitness evaluations.

Simulation	NEAT	CMA-ES	CNE	ESP
CBC	280.1s	305.3s	231.3s	241.4s
CC	514.1s	602.5s	538.9s	531.1s
CR	385.8s	1402.1s	372.2s	356.4s
ME	1356.6s	2590.8s	955.6s	961.4s
WRB	2671.1s	5671.2s	2612.1s	2659.7s
SSTB	1086.4s	2201.4s	1013.4s	1017.7s
SSO	1062.5s	2185.8s	1021.3s	1000.1s
SSOF	1261.9s	2383.5s	1256.2s	1170.1s

The **Space Ship Obstacle Field (SSOF)** simulation is identical to the Space Ship obstacle simulation, with the exception of there being a field of small obstacles instead of one large one. The fitness threshold of this simulation is defined at 1000.

4.3 Parameters and Operators

The operators used for our experiments are: Linear Rank-Based Selection for CNE, NEAT, and ESP; Blend crossover for CNE and ESP with $\alpha = 0.5$ and a crossover probability of 0.8; and Gaussian weight mutation for CNE, NEAT, and ESP, with a mutation probability of 0.2, and a mutation probability of 0.02 for CNE and ESP, and 0.8 for NEAT. Additionally, the add node and add connection mutation probabilities for NEAT were 0.03 and 0.05 respectively, and the compatibility threshold was set at 0.5. We used populations of 100 for CNE and NEAT, and sub-populations of 50 with each neuron being evaluated 5 times for ESP, with 5% elitism for CNE, ESP, and NEAT. We used an initial step size of 0.2 for CMA-ES. We run burst mutation on an ESP sub-population after it has stagnated, which we detect by seeing if it has not improved after 20 generations. These operators were determined through preliminary experiments.

4.4 Experimental Setup

Each of the four NE methods were run for 20,000 fitness evaluations 30 times each on every simulation, with the best fitness obtained by each algorithm being sampled every 10 fitness evaluations. We then plot the averages of the fitness values obtained, using the one-tailed Mann Whitney U test [16] to test if the distributions are significantly different using a confidence interval of 95% and a significance threshold of p=0.05.

5. RESULTS AND DISCUSSION

As shown in tables 1 and 2, CMA-ES was found to either perform the best, or perform comparably to the best algorithm. The one exception is the Mouse Escape simulation. However, this simulation proved very easy for all algorithms to learn, with the differences in mean fitness being negligible. One problem that we found with CMA-ES is that its computational cost far exceeds the other three algorithms on problems with higher dimensions, with thethe mean time taken to execute CMA-ES being between 2-4 times that of the other three[3] (table 3) on some of the simulations. This increased computational cost is mainly due to the Eigen-decomposition step of the algorithm, which is $O(n^3)$. In order to verify this we used CMA-ES in a simulation where 4 agents were tasked to complete a race track within a given time limit, with the team setups being heterogeneous, 1 ANN for every 2 agents, and homogeneous. The execution times found for these team compositions were 3689.02s, 1398.85s, and 283.86s respectively.

CNE performed above expectations and achieved the best mean fitness for two out of eight of the simulations. It was also one the second best performing algorithm for four out of eight of the simulations. This high performance was mainly unexpected due to its simplicity, and to it achieving poorer results than the other algorithms in previous works [22, 10]. In addition to the algorithm's high task performance, it is also the least computationally intensive, leading to it being an attractive option for evolving ANN controllers to control crowd behaviors. One issue with CNE is that its task performance deteriorated on higher dimensional problems. This may lead to it performing poorly in more heterogeneous team setups, however, further investigation is required.

NEAT's task performance was average compared to the other algorithms, often being either the second or third best performer. One unique benefit to NEAT, however, is that it is not necessary to predetermine an effective ANN structure, as both structure and weights are evolved.

ESP was shown to be the worst performing algorithm in our simulations. On the other hand, as shown in figure 2, ESP is often still improving at the end of our preset 20,000 fitness evaluation limit. Thus it may be possible that it will perform significantly better given longer evolution run times. This is most likely due to our use of sub-population

[3]Processor: i5-3570 @ 3.4GHz

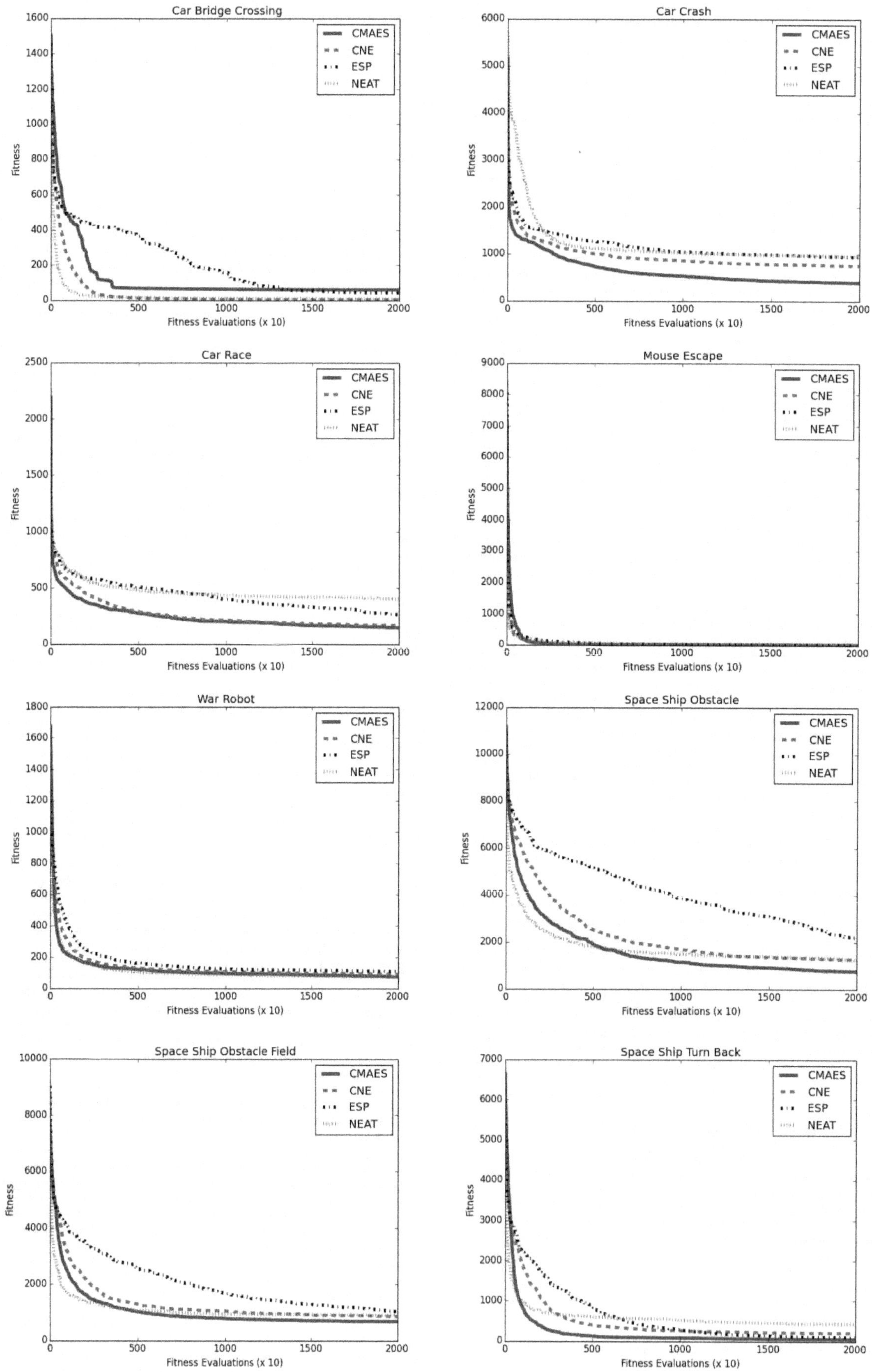

Figure 2: Mean fitness values of the NE methods across the various simulation scenarios using a population of 30 samples throughout 20,000 fitness evaluations for each simulation

sizes of 50 with five fitness evaluations per neuron, causing ESP to run for less than half the number of generations of NEAT and CNE, and less than 10 times the amount of generations of CMA-ES for the same number of fitness evaluations. Additionally, ESP's performance increased relative to the other algorithms on higher dimensional problems, such as the space-ship turn back scenario, possibly due to its cooperative nature. This increased performance makes ESP a worthwhile avenue of investigation when researching more heterogeneous controller setups.

Of the eight test simulations, we found that the Car Bridge Crossing, Mouse Escape, Space-Ship Turn Back, and War Robot Battle scenarios to be the easiest to evolve effective controllers for, with all the algorithms ultimately achieving acceptable final crowd behaviors. Scenarios of moderate difficulty were the Space-Ship Obstacle, Space-Ship Obstacle Field, and the Car Race simulation as only 1-3 algorithms (depending on the actual simulation) were able to achieve the target fitness thresholds for those scenarios.

The one simulation that all algorithms struggled with is the Car Crash scenario, with none of the algorithms able to achieve a mean fitness below the threshold. The difficulty of learning this simulation is due to the close proximity of the agents, as well as the extremely narrow corridor, resulting in the agents having to evolve near perfect movement in order to avoid collisions. One way to deal with this is to have an ANN controller for each group as opposed to a single ANN controller for both groups, which would allow each group of agents to adopt different avoidance strategies.

In addition to dealing with the Car Crash scenario, investigating more heterogeneous controller setups is also desirable for generating more diverse behaviors amongst agents, as we found that in certain simulations with sparse environments, such as the War Robot Battle, agents tend to adopt very homogeneous behaviors. This is undesirable for films as it leads to the crowds being less believable. This issue can be attributed to many of the ANN inputs being the same, resulting in identical outputs for multiple agents. We hypothesize that using more heterogeneous controller setups may result in more heterogeneous behaviors, leading to more believable scenes. Additionally, this would also allow for the use of pareto-based multi-objective optimization to evolve differing but optimal agents [1]. This is achieved by selecting sufficiently different candidate solutions on the pareto-front as agent controllers for the simulation.

A different approach to achieve more heterogeneous behavior is to instead employ a hierarchical model [20, 17], where an agent's high level goals and cognition are separated from their low level motor functionalities. The ANN would then control the cognitive-level functions of the agents, as opposed to the direct motor behaviors as in our current simulations. This approach may allow for more complex agent behaviors, whilst keeping the problem dimensionality low. However, the additional behavioral layers could result in the crowds being more difficult to control.

6. CONCLUSIONS AND FUTURE WORK

This paper evaluated the task performance of Conventional Neuro-Evolution (CNE), Covariance Matrix Adaptation Evolutionary Strategy (CMA-ES), Neuro-Evolution of Augmenting Topologies (NEAT), and Enforced Sub-populations (ESP) in the domain of controlling emergent crowd behaviors for film across eight different simulation scenarios. Overall, we found that CMA-ES achieves the best task performance. However, it comes at the cost of computational complexity, as it performs significantly slower than the other three algorithms on higher-dimensional scenarios. For this reason, it may be desirable to instead use CNE, which combines good task performance and cheap computation cost. Nonetheless, we found that CNE's mean fitness is poorer in our higher dimensional scenarios relative to lower-dimensional ones. Thus, further investigation is required in order to determine how well it performs on higher dimensionality problems.

Future directions of research include investigating more heterogeneous controller setups, exploring various generative encoding NE methods, performing user evaluations on the believability of the generated crowds, using pareto-based multi-objective optimization in order to generate more heterogeneous behaviors, and investigating the use of NE with more hierarchical agent behavior models.

7. ACKNOWLEDGMENTS

This research was funded by the National Research Foundation, the Centre for High Performance Computing and Triggerfish Animation Studios under THRIP Grant TP2011071600004.

8. REFERENCES

[1] A. Agapitos, J. Togelius, S. M. Lucas, J. Schmidhuber, and A. Konstantinidis. Generating diverse opponents with multiobjective evolution. In *Proceedings of the IEEE Symposium on Computational Intelligence and Games, 2008. CIG'08.*, pages 135–142. IEEE, 2008.

[2] M. Anderson, E. McDaniel, and S. Chenney. Constrained animation of flocks. In *Proceedings of the 2003 ACM SIGGRAPH/Eurographics symposium on Computer animation*, pages 286–297. Eurographics Association, 2003.

[3] O. B. Bayazit, J.-M. Lien, and N. M. Amato. Roadmap-based flocking for complex environments. In *Proceedings of the 10th Pacific Conference on Computer Graphics and Applications*, pages 104–113. IEEE, 2002.

[4] B. M. Blumberg and T. A. Galyean. Multi-level direction of autonomous creatures for real-time virtual environments. In *Proceedings of the 22nd annual conference on Computer graphics and interactive techniques*, pages 47–54. ACM, 1995.

[5] B. D. Bryant and R. Miikkulainen. Neuroevolution for adaptive teams. In *Proceedings of the 2003 congress on evolutionary computation*, volume 3, pages 2194–2201, 2003.

[6] S. Chenney. Flow tiles. In *Proceedings of the 2004 ACM SIGGRAPH/Eurographics symposium on Computer animation*, pages 233–242. Eurographics Association, 2004.

[7] D. Dasgupta and D. R. McGregor. Designing application-specific neural networks using the structured genetic algorithm. In *International Workshop on Combinations of Genetic Algorithms and Neural Networks, 1992., COGANN-92.*, pages 87–96. IEEE, 1992.

[8] D. Floreano, P. Dürr, and C. Mattiussi. Neuroevolution: from architectures to learning. *Evolutionary Intelligence*, 1(1):47–62, 2008.

[9] J. Funge, X. Tu, and D. Terzopoulos. Cognitive modeling: knowledge, reasoning and planning for intelligent characters. In *Proceedings of the 26th annual conference on Computer graphics and interactive techniques*, pages 29–38. ACM Press/Addison-Wesley Publishing Co., 1999.

[10] F. J. Gomez and R. Miikkulainen. Solving non-markovian control tasks with neuroevolution. In *Proceedings of the International Joint Conferences on Artificial Intelligence*, volume 99, pages 1356–1361, 1999.

[11] N. Hansen and S. Kern. Evaluating the cma evolution strategy on multimodal test functions. In *Parallel Problem Solving from Nature-PPSN VIII*, pages 282–291. Springer, 2004.

[12] D. Jacka. *High-Level Control of Agent-based Crowds by means of General Constraints.* PhD thesis, University of Cape Town, 2009.

[13] A. Kamphuis and M. H. Overmars. Finding paths for coherent groups using clearance. In *Proceedings of the 2004 ACM SIGGRAPH/Eurographics symposium on Computer animation*, pages 19–28. Eurographics Association, 2004.

[14] J. Kennedy. Particle swarm optimization. In *Encyclopedia of Machine Learning*, pages 760–766. Springer, 2010.

[15] Y.-C. Lai, S. Chenney, and S. Fan. Group motion graphs. In *Proceedings of the 2005 ACM SIGGRAPH/Eurographics symposium on Computer animation*, pages 281–290. ACM, 2005.

[16] H. B. Mann, D. R. Whitney, et al. On a test of whether one of two random variables is stochastically larger than the other. *The annals of mathematical statistics*, 18(1):50–60, 1947.

[17] N. Pelechano, J. M. Allbeck, and N. I. Badler. Controlling individual agents in high-density crowd simulation. In *Proceedings of the 2007 ACM SIGGRAPH/Eurographics symposium on Computer animation*, pages 99–108. Eurographics Association, 2007.

[18] J. C. F. Pujol and R. Poli. Evolving the topology and the weights of neural networks using a dual representation. *Applied Intelligence*, 8(1):73–84, 1998.

[19] F. Qiu and X. Hu. Modeling group structures in pedestrian crowd simulation. *Simulation Modelling Practice and Theory*, 18(2):190–205, 2010.

[20] S. Raupp Musse and D. Thalmann. Hierarchical model for real time simulation of virtual human crowds. *IEEE Transactions on Visualization and Computer Graphics*, 7(2):152–164, 2001.

[21] C. W. Reynolds. Flocks, herds and schools: A distributed behavioral model. In *Proceedings of the 14th Annual Conference on Computer Graphics and Interactive Techniques*, pages 25–34, New York, NY, USA, 1987. ACM.

[22] K. Stanley and R. Miikkulainen. Evolving neural networks through augmenting topologies. *Evolutionary computation*, 10(2):99–127, 2002.

[23] P. Stone and M. Veloso. Multiagent systems: A survey from a machine learning perspective. *Autonomous Robots*, 8(3):345–383, 2000.

[24] D. Thalmann, H. Grillon, J. Maim, and B. Yersin. Challenges in crowd simulation. In *2009 International Conference On Cyberworlds*, number EPFL-CONF-159013, pages 1–12, 2009.

[25] D. Thalmann, C. Hery, S. Lippman, H. Ono, S. Regelous, and D. Sutton. Crowd and group animation. In *ACM SIGGRAPH 2004 course notes*, page 34. ACM, 2004.

[26] A. Treuille, S. Cooper, and Z. Popović. Continuum crowds. In *ACM Transactions on Graphics (TOG)*, volume 25, pages 1160–1168. ACM, 2006.

[27] S. Wang, J. Gain, and G. Nitschke. Comparing crossover operators in neuro-evolution with crowd simulations. In *Proceedings of the IEEE Congress on Evolutionary Computation (CEC)*, pages 2298–2305. IEEE, 2014.

[28] A. P. Wieland. Evolving neural network controllers for unstable systems. In *Proceedings of the International Joint Conference on Neural Networks.*, volume 2, pages 667–673. IEEE, 1991.

[29] H. Yeh, S. Curtis, S. Patil, J. van den Berg, D. Manocha, and M. Lin. Composite agents. In *Proceedings of the 2008 ACM SIGGRAPH/Eurographics Symposium on Computer Animation*, pages 39–47. Eurographics Association, 2008.

[30] C. H. Yong and R. Miikkulainen. Coevolution of role-based cooperation in multiagent systems. *IEEE Transactions on Autonomous Mental Development*, 1(3):170–186, 2009.

Hyperheuristics Based on Parametrized Metaheuristic Schemes

José-Matías Cutillas-Lozano
Departamento de Informática y Sistemas
Universidad de Murcia, Spain
josematias.cutillas@um.es

Domingo Giménez
Departamento de Informática y Sistemas
Universidad de Murcia, Spain
domingo@um.es

Francisco Almeida
ETS Ingeniería Informática
Universidad de La Laguna
Tenerife, Spain
falmeida@ull.es

ABSTRACT

The use of a unified parametrized scheme for metaheuristics facilitates the development of metaheuristics and their application. The unified scheme can also be used to implement hyperheuristics on top of parametrized metaheuristics, selecting appropriate values for the metaheuristic parameters, and consequently the metaheuristic itself. The applicability of hyperheuristics to efficiently solve computational search problems is tested with the application of local and global search methods (GRASP, Tabu Search, Genetic algorithms and Scatter Search) and their combinations to three problems: a problem of optimization of power consumption in operation of wells, the determination of the kinetic constants of a chemical reaction and the maximum diversity problem. The hyperheuristic approach provides satisfactory values for the metaheuristic parameters and consequently satisfactory metaheuristics.

Categories and Subject Descriptors

I.2.8 [**Artificial Intelligence**]: Problem Solving, Control Methods, and Search—*Heuristic methods*

Keywords

Hyperheuristics, Parametrized metaheuristics, Electricity consumption, Kinetic constants determination, Maximum Diversity Problem

1. INTRODUCTION

The basic idea of a hyperheuristic is to build new algorithms for problem solving by combining known (meta)heuristics in ways that allow each to compensate, to some extent, for the weaknesses of others [2, 3, 13]. They are methods that work with a search space of heuristics. Different (meta)heuristics or (meta)heuristics components can be selected, generated or combined to solve a given optimization problem in different ways [6]. Usually, there is a clear separation between the high-level hyperheuristic and the set of low level (meta)heuristics or components of these. The work of the high-level strategy is to guide the search intelligently and adapt according to the success or failure of the low-level (meta)heuristics or combinations of (meta)heuristics during the search process.

The ideas of (meta)heuristic optimization often appear in the literature as methods for automatic algorithm configuration with different approaches: methods to set the values of algorithm parameters; instantiation of possible algorithms by repeated application of the rules defined by a grammar [12]; and strategies describing the process of instantiating grammars in terms of parameters [7, 11]. Some of these strategies are model-guided and can explore the solution space efficiently by discarding the least promising elements from a statistical point of view [8]. Algorithm parameters can be numerical or categorical; in the latter case allowing the combination of different heuristic components to form a specific algorithm for a particular problem. Heuristics can be fine-tuned later with other numeric-type parameters, so creating flexible and highly configurable algorithmic frameworks.

Our approach provides an algorithmic configuration using numeric-type parameters which are called from a set of basic functions within a common framework of metaheuristics. It differs from other approaches based on genetic programming guided by grammars, where algorithmic code is modified (optimized) or parts of it (functions) are instantiated by categorical parameters. In a previous work [1], the use of a parametrized scheme of metaheuristics allowed us to choose easily between different types of metaheuristics or combinations of metaheuristics simply by selecting satisfactory values for the parameters in the scheme. The main contribution of this work is to facilitate the implementation of hyperheuristics by using a unified parametrized scheme. A criterion based on the fitness is used to automatically select good metaheuristics from certain training instances.

Three problems are used as test cases: a problem of electricity consumption in exploitation of wells (PECEW), a problem of determination of the kinetic constants of a chemical reaction (PKICO) and the maximum diversity problem (MDP). The first and second problems were optimized by applying the metaheuristic scheme [4, 5], so the results with the application of the hyperheuristic approach introduced here can be compared with earlier results in which the metaheuristics are tuned with the parametrized scheme. Furthermore, MDP is a widely studied problem, and the applica-

GECCO '15, July 11 - 16, 2015, Madrid, Spain

DOI: http://dx.doi.org/10.1145/2739480.2754641

tion of our hyperheuristic approach to this problem allows us to compare the results with those of well established metaheuristics.

The rest of the paper is organized as follows. Section 2 summarizes the ideas of the common parametrized scheme for metaheuristics on top of which the development of hyperheuristics is studied. In section 3, the ideas of hyperheuristics based on metaheuristic schemes are presented. Section 4 summarizes the optimization problems used as test case. Section 5 shows the experimental results. Section 6 concludes the paper and offers some future research lines.

2. A PARAMETRIZED SCHEME FOR METAHEURISTICS

The use of a unified parametrized scheme for metaheuristics facilitates the development of metaheuristics and their application. The scheme (Algorithm 1) considers a set of basic functions whose instantiation determines the particular metaheuristic that is being implemented. The same implementations of the basic functions can be used in different methods, and different metaheuristics can be instantiated with the same pattern. The scheme is also valid as a generic mechanism for hybridization. However, selecting the appropriate values of the *Metaheuristic parameters* ($ParamX$ in the algorithm) to apply a satisfactory metaheuristic to a particular problem can be difficult and is computationally demanding. The selection of these values can be made through a hyperheuristic method, which could in turn be developed with the same parametrized metaheuristic scheme.

Algorithm 1 parametrized metaheuristic scheme

```
Initialize(S,ParamIni)
while ( not EndCondition(S,ParamEnd)) do
  SS=Select(S,ParamSel)
  SS1=Combine(SS,ParamCom)
  SS2=Improve(SS1,ParamImp)
  S=Include(SS2,ParamInc)
end while
```

We summarize particuar implementations of the functions of the parametrized scheme and present the common parameters for the basic metaheuristics considered: Greedy Randomized Adaptive Search Procedure (GRASP), Scatter Search (SS), Tabu Search (TS) and Genetic algorithms (GA). We also consider the possibility of reusing basic functions:

- `Initialize`: $INEIni$ elements are generated, and a subset with $FNEIni$ elements is selected for the iterations. Some initial elements are improved. A parameter $PEIIni$ indicates the percentage of elements to be improved, and the intensity of the improvement is represented by $IIEIni$. $STMIni$ is used for the extension of Tabu short-term memory in the initialization improvement.
- `EndCondition`: The end condition is common to the different metaheuristics. It consists of a maximum number of iterations ($MNIEnd$) or a maximum number of iterations without improving the best solution ($NIREnd$).
- `Select`: The elements are grouped into two sets, the best and worst according to the objective function. The number of best elements is $NBESel$ and that of worst elements $NWESel$.
- `Combine`: The total number of elements to obtain by combination is $2{\cdot}(NBBCom + NBWCom + NWWCom)$, where the parameters represent the number of combinations of the best with the best elements, the number of the best with the worst and the number of the worst with the worst.
- `Improve`: As in the improvement in the initialization, $PEIImp$, $IIEImp$ and $SMIImp$ represent the percentage of elements to be improved, the intensification of the improvement and the short-term memory in the improvement of the elements generated in the combination; and $PEDImp$, $IDEImp$ and $SMDImp$ represent the corresponding values in a diversification.
- `Include`: The $NBEInc$ best elements are maintained in the reference set, and the others are selected from the remaining elements. $LTMInc$ is a Tabu parameter (long-term memory) that allows the tracking of individuals most frequently explored.

The set of metaheuristic parameters is the union of the six sets of parameters of the basic functions. Thus, we have a set of 20 parameters with which it is possible to experiment to hybridize, mix and adapt the metaheuristics to the target problem.

3. HYPERHEURISTICS BASED ON PARAMETERIZED METAHEURISTIC SCHEMES

The parametrized scheme of metaheuristics is used for the implementation of hyperheuristics, which work by searching the metaheuristic space determined by the values of the metaheuristic parameters, and which can in turn use the same metaheuristic scheme for hyperheuristics development. In the hyperheuristic an individual or element is represented by an integer vector $MetaheurParam$ that encodes the set of parameters that characterizes a metaheuristic. The number and meaning of the parameters is determined by the basic metaheuristics integrated in the scheme, the implementation of the basic functions and the parameters that can be varied in the functions. With those considered in the previous section, an element in the hyperheuristic has 20 components, with values in ranges which depend on the possible values of the parameter and also on some restrictions imposed on the hyperheuristic to reduce the search space. The set of individuals constitutes the reference set, which means a set of metaheuristics, with each metaheuristic being the combination/hybridation of basic metaheuristics. The fitness value in the hyperheuristic for an element $MetaheurParam$ is based on that obtained when the metaheuristic with the parameters in $MetaheurParam$ is applied to the problem for which the metaheuristic is been obtained. The objective is to minimize (or maximize) the fitness function and so obtain the combination of the metaheuristic parameters which gives the best fitness function for different instances of the problem. There are different possibilities for the fitness function computation, depending on whether it is applied to a single instance or to several instances, and whether a single execution or more are considered. We decided to calculate the fitness with several problem inputs in one execution (FitSP1E), which allows us to reduce the dependence on the input and the increase in the execution time, by applying the metaheuristics to only one input, and changing the input during the hyperheuristic application. The same problem is used in each iteration, but the problem to which the metaheuristics are applied changes for different iterations or groups of iterations. The main problem is that the relative classification of the metaheuristics would depend on the input to which each is applied, and a re-application of some of the metaheuristics may be necessary to obtain a new classification.

The characteristics of the basic functions of the algorithm for hyperheuristics are commented on:

- `Initialize`: Due to the high computational cost of hyperheuristics, the number of elements in the initial set and in the reference set is normally smaller than for metaheuristics. So, the application of local search methods or methods with small populations are preferable. Valid random elements are generated, with different ranges for the different parameters, and with shorter ranges than for metaheuristics.
- `EndCondition`: The end condition may be common to that of metaheuristics, but the limits on the numbers of iterations will be lower.
- `Select`: The selection of elements is made as for metaheuristics. The only difference is the fitness function used to classify the elements.
- `Combine`: As with metaheuristics, pairs of best, worst and best-worst elements can be combined, but the combination is normally problem-dependent, so satisfactory combinations for the metaheuristic selection problem should be obtained. There are various possibilities, but only the combination by groups of parameters was considered. For example, $GroupIni = \{INEIni, FNEIni, STMIni\}$, $GroupImpIni = \{PEIIni, IIEIni\}$, etc, and groups of parameters were selected from the ascendants to generate the descendants.
- `Improve`: This works in the same way as for metaheuristics, but with lower values of the parameters.
- `Include`: The only differences with metaheuristics are the fitness function for selection of the best elements, and a lower value of the parameter for the Tabu long-term memory.

As in the case of metaheuristics, the set of hyperheuristic parameters is the union of the six sets of parameters of the basic functions in the scheme. Thus, we have a set of 20 parameters with which we can experiment and apply the hyperheuristics to select good metaheuristics.

4. TEST CASE PROBLEMS USED IN THE EXPERIMENTS

We summarize here the optimization problems that have been used as test cases to show the usefulness of the hyperheuristic based on the parametrized metaheuristic scheme. Readers interested in a deeper knowledge of the problems and of metaheuristics applied to them should consult the references indicated below. The first and second problems were chosen because we had experience and some technical knowledge and experimental data of them, and the third was chosen with the aim of applying our methodology to a widely known problem with which we could compare the results obtained.

4.1 A problem of electricity consumption in exploitation of wells (PECEW)

The cost-minimization problem [5] used as a test case is briefly explained. We consider a water system consisting of a series of pumps (B) of known power, located in wells, that draw water flow along a daily time range R. The total flow is the sum of the flows contributed by each well. The pumps may be running or idle at a given time. The pumps operate electrically and the electricity has a daily cost which should be minimal:

$$C_e = \sum_{i=1}^{R} \sum_{j=1}^{B} T_i P_j N_i X_{ij} \tag{1}$$

where T_i is the cost of the electricity in the range i; P_j is the electric power consumed by the pump j; N_i is the number of hours of pump operation in the time slot i; and X_{ij} represents a binary element of a matrix with values 1 or 0 for pump on or off. Five constraints related to the technical development of the operations of pumping and water transmission have been taken into account. These restrictions are: demand satisfaction, minimum flow maintenance, compliance with maximum exploitation volumes for each well, maintaining the average conductivity below the limit and compliance with maximum depths of dynamic levels. An element is represented by the binary matrix, X, of size $B \cdot R$, which encodes the set of pumps distributed in different time slots.

4.2 Determination of the kinetic constants of a chemical reaction (PKICO)

The kinetic of dissolution of calcium carbonate is a function of the concentration of the various carbonate species in the solution and, therefore, a function of the partial pressure of carbon dioxide and pH. A model for the dissolution of calcium carbonate was developed in [14]. Depending on the value of the pH, there are four different ways in which the dissolution of calcium carbonate occurs: by reaction with acetic acid, by reaction with carbonic acid, and by the hydrolysis reaction (the fourth path may be neglected in the pH range considered). Therefore the variation of moles of calcium over time is:

$$\begin{aligned} \frac{1}{V}\frac{dN_{Ca^{2+}}}{dt} &= -k_1 a^{n_1}\left[H_3O^+\right]^{n_2} \\ &\quad -k_2 a^{n_3}\left[H_2CO_3\right]^{n_4} - k_3 \end{aligned} \tag{2}$$

where k_1, k_2 and k_3 are the combined reaction rate constants, n_1, n_2, n_3 and n_4 are the reaction orders, and a is the area of the tablet, which is known. The integration of the equation for a certain value of time, t_j, gives the increase of calcium in the solution as a function of the concentrations of protons and carbonic acid.

The values of the parameters can be approached with metaheuristics. An individual is represented by a real vector of size seven. The ranges of values for the constants are set following empirical criteria. Every time we have to evaluate the fitness of an individual, we must solve the whole chemical system. The calculation of the fitness function is presented in algorithm 2, where we have a loop of N time intervals that calculates the value of each variable of the chemical problem for next time instant $i+1$ depending on the value of the variable in the previous instant i.

Algorithm 2 Calculation of the fitness function for an individual

```
Calculate Fitness(k1, k2, k3, n1, n2, n3, n4):
for i = 0 -> N do
  Calculate at instant i:
  [Ca^{2+}], a, [H3O^+], [HCO^-], [H2CO3],
  pH_cal, Δ[Ca^{2+}], [CH3COOH], [CH3COO^-]
  Fitness = Fitness + (pH_exp,i - pH_cal,i)^2
end for
```

When performing the simulations, there are two constraints that should be met by both the kinetic constants and the problem variables: the main reaction path should be respected in each pH range, and all the concentrations of chemical species must be positive in each experimental point.

4.3 Maximum Diversity Problem (MDP)

The maximum diversity problem (MDP) consists of selecting a subset of m elements from a set of n elements so that the sum of the distances between the chosen elements is maximized. The definition of distance between elements depends on the specific applications [10]. In most applications, it is assumed that each element can be represented by a set of attributes. Considering s_{ik} as the state or value of the k-th attribute of element i, where $k = 1, ..., K$. Then the distance between elements i and j could be defined as:

$$d_{ij} = \sqrt{\sum_{k=1}^{K} (s_{ik} - s_{jk})^2} \quad (3)$$

In this case, d_{ij} is simply the Euclidean distance between i and j. The distance values are then used to formulate the MDP as a quadratic binary problem [9], where variable x_i takes the value 1 if element i is selected and 0 otherwise, $i = 1, ..., n$:

$$\textbf{Maximize} \quad \sum_{i=1}^{n-1} \sum_{j=i+1}^{n} d_{ij} x_i x_j \quad (4)$$

subject to

$$\sum_{i=1}^{n} x_i = m,$$

$$x_i = \{0, 1\}, \qquad 1 \le i \le n \quad (5)$$

5. EXPERIMENTAL RESULTS

The validity of the methodology is analyzed by applying it to the optimization problems. This work focuses on analyzing the applicability of hyperheuristics and their suitability as a general optimization tool, independent of the input, in terms of fitness for several test inputs.

Since the hyperheuristics are developed using the parametrized scheme of metaheuristics, it suffices to fix the metaheuristic parameters of the hyperheuristic (we call them hyperheuristic parameters) to specific values. In table 1 we can see the three types of hyperheuristics that will serve us as a reference for selecting good metaheuristics:

Table 1: Values of the hyperheuristic parameters used for the selection of metaheuristics. Hybrid Hyperheuristic (Hhy), Reduced Hybrid Hyperheuristic (Hre) and Genetic Algorithm based Hyperheuristic (Hge).

	INEIni	FNEIni	PEIIni	IIEIni	STMIni	NBESel
Hhy	20	20	50	5	5	10
Hre	5	5	50	3	2	3
Hge	20	20	0	0	0	20

	NWESel	NBBCom	NBWCom	NWWCom	PEIImp	IIEImp
Hhy	10	15	20	15	50	5
Hre	2	2	3	2	50	3
Hge	0	10	0	0	0	0

	SMIImp	PEDImp	IDEImp	SMDImp	NBEInc	LTMInc
Hhy	5	10	5	5	10	5
Hre	2	10	5	2	3	5
Hge	0	10	5	0	20	0

- We have chosen a mid-size hybrid hyperheuristic (Hhy), with some decisions taken to reduce the execution time: small populations, intensification at each point where they are in the metaheuristic scheme but with improvement of approximately half of the elements and a not very intensified improvement.
- The hyperheuristic with a genetic algorithm approach (Hge) also works with a small population and improvement is made only in the diversification, which means the elements obtained with mutations are improved to reduce the possibility of their rapid death. The values of the Tabu parameters are set to zero.
- Because the execution time of the genetic approach is much lower than that with the hybrid approach, a reduced hybrid hyperheuristic (Hre) is also considered. It has the same parameters as the previous hybrid hyperheuristic but with lower values for many of them in order to reduce the execution time.

To verify the effectiveness of the hyperheuristics, it seems reasonable to compare the fitness obtained with the metaheuristic selected by the hyperheuristics with those obtained with some pure metaheuristics applied directly to the optimization problem. Instances of the parameters corresponding to the four basic metaheuristics considered have been chosen. In previous works [4, 5] we have experimented in depth with hybrid metaheuristics to obtain the most efficient one for the problems PECEW and PKICO. Therefore, it also seems appropriate to compare the best results obtained with the best hybrid metaheuristic for those problems with those obtained with the hyperheuristic, which is applied here for the first time to MDP, for which the results with the hyperheuristic are compared with those of basic metaheuristics.

Table 2 shows the values selected for the parameters for the four basic metaheuristics and the best hybrid metaheuristics (combinations of the four pure metaheuristics) obtained for PECEW in [5] (Mhy1) and for PKICO in [4]

(Mhy2). The best hybrid metaheuristic for MDP (Mhy3) has also been considered. For this problem no short-term memory was selected for Tabu because the implementation of the improvement function does not require it to work efficiently, and only the long-term memory parameter was considered for Tabu. The values of the metaheuristic parameters are in general higher than the corresponding values for the hyperheuristics, because the application of a metaheuristic requires much lower execution time than that of a hyperheuristic.

Table 2: Values of the parameters for the four pure metaheuristics and the hybrid metaheuristics (Mhy1, Mhy2 and Mhy3).

	INEIni	FNEIni	PEIIni	IIEIni	STMIni	NBESel
GR	200	1	100	50	0	0
GA	100	100	0	0	0	100
SS	100	20	100	50	0	10
TS	200	1	100	10	5	1
Mhy1	200	50	100	50	10	25
Mhy2	50	15	100	15	2	8
Mhy3	50	15	100	15	0	8

	NWESel	NBBCom	NBWCom	NWWCom	PEIImp	IIEImp
GR	0	0	0	0	0	0
GA	0	50	0	0	0	0
SS	10	90	100	90	100	5
TS	0	0	0	0	100	5
Mhy1	25	90	100	90	100	5
Mhy2	7	15	20	15	100	5
Mhy3	7	15	20	15	100	5

	SMIImp	PEDImp	IDEImp	SMDImp	NBEInc	LTMInc
GR	0	0	0	0	0	0
GA	0	10	5	0	100	0
SS	0	0	0	0	10	0
TS	5	0	0	0	1	20
Mhy1	10	10	5	10	25	30
Mhy2	2	20	5	2	8	3
Mhy3	0	20	5	0	8	0

In principle, any values of the parameters can determine a metaheuristic, but it is preferable to establish ranges that allow us to compare the results obtained with the application of the hyperheuristic with those obtained with pure metaheuristics. Therefore, the hyperheuristic will select metaheuristic parameters for each function of the scheme in the ranges of values presented in table 3 for PECEW and PKICO, where we consider that the lower values greater or equal to zero are preferable for some parameters in most cases. For MDP, lower values for the ranges were fixed in order to reduce the execution time. The EndCondition parameters were fixed to 1000 and 10 for PECEW, and a limit of ten iterations was fixed for the other problems.

To study the application of hyperheuristics to the problems considered, the following instances were used: for PECEW ($B-R$), 10-3, 10-6, 20-3, 20-6, 40-3 and 40-6; for PKICO, S1 to S6; and for MDP, n25_m7, n15_m12, n30_m12, n50_m5, n50_m15, n100_m40, n200_m60 and n300_m60.

Several possibilities for the fitness function were discussed. The basic idea is to apply the hyperheuristic to a number of instances of the problem and verify that the metaheuristics obtained give good results when applied to other instances of the problem. Only the fitness calculated with FitSP1E

Table 3: Lower and upper limits of the metaheuristic parameters for the selection of individuals by the hyperheuristics.

	INEIni	FNEIni	PEIIni	IIEIni	STMIni	NBESel
Lower	5	5	0	1	0	2
Upper	200	100	100	20	15	100

	NWESel	NBBCom	NBWCom	NWWCom	PEIImp	IIEImp
Lower	2	5	5	5	0	1
Upper	100	100	100	100	100	20

	SMIImp	PEDImp	IDEImp	SMDImp	NBEInc	LTMInc
Lower	0	0	1	0	2	0
Upper	15	100	10	15	100	15

was considered: only one execution is carried out, and the instance or problem size is varied in each iteration. This provides a large reduction in the execution time and reduces problem dependence.

Figure 1 shows the results of the application of metaheuristics automatically selected from hyperheuristics (using FitSP1E) to the three sizes of PECEW, PKICO and MDP used for the tests. Fitness of the first and second problems is minimized and that of the third is maximized. The quotients of the fitness of each metaheuristic with respect to the best for each problem size are shown. The quotient was chosen because it allows better visualization of the results. The best fitness is usually obtained by directly applying to each problem size some of the three hyperheuristic configurations in table 1. The fitnesses are also compared with those with the application of the metaheuristics with the parameters in table 2. The last entries in the figure represent the mean of the fitness quotient with respect to the best fitness for each problem size.

On average, for problems PECEW and PKICO, metaheuristics obtained appreciably improve the results achieved by applying the pure metaheuristics, and they provide fitness values that are close to the best obtained when applying the hyperheuristic to the validation problems directly. For MDP the differences are not so large, possibly because the metaheuristics are already highly optimized and the hyperheuristic has less effect on improving fitness. Significantly, the metaheuristic obtained by the genetic hyperheuristic returns very good fitness and reduced execution times for the three problems.

Another way to verify the need for a hyperheuristic is to compare it with previous results and see if it improves what was obtained in terms of fitness. In the last column of table 4 we present the results obtained by applying the best (hybrid) metaheuristic (Mhy1, Mhy2 and Mhy3 in table 2) that we obtained in previous studies to three different problem sizes of PECEW, PKICO and MDP. We can see that in all cases the three hyperheuristic configurations improve these results.

Finally, in figure 2, a statistical summary of the means obtained by applying different metaheuristic algorithms to two sizes of the problems is presented. The results are grouped into sets with a variable number of points in each set (between six and twelve). The sets are obtained by the direct application of the three hyperheuristic configurations (H),

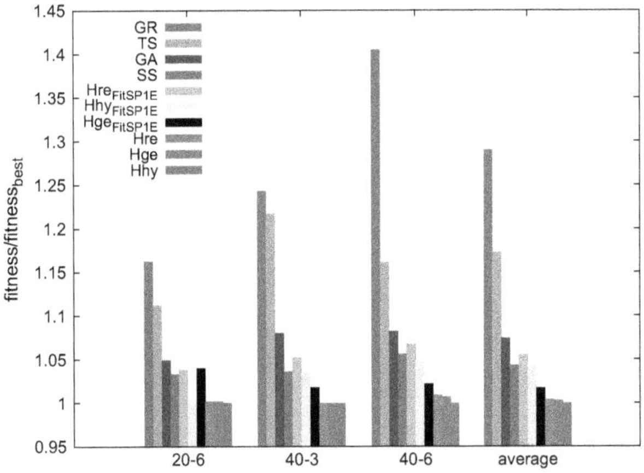

(a) PECEW

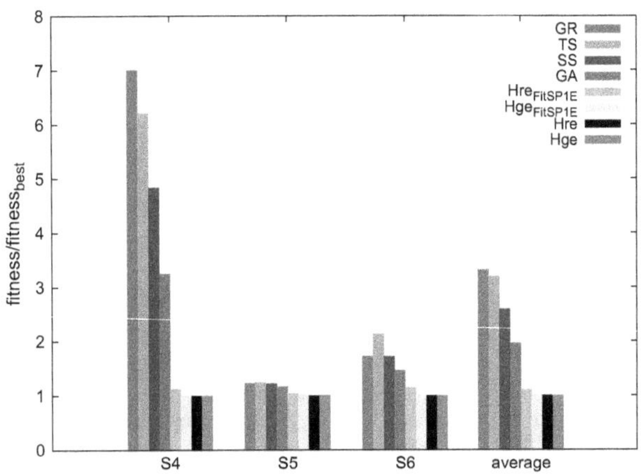

(b) PKICO

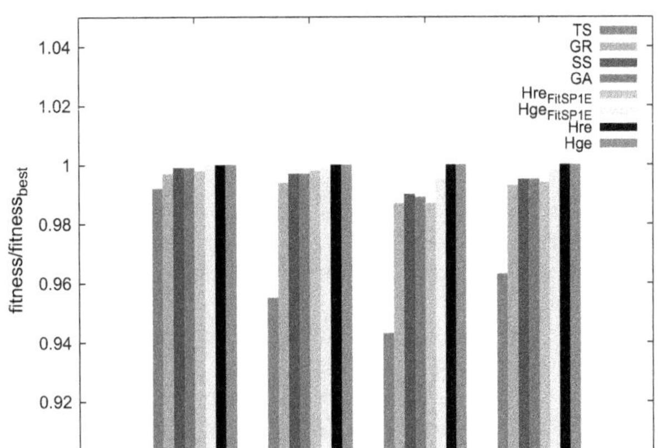

(c) MDP

Figure 1: Quotient of fitness with respect to the best fitness, for various sizes of (a) PECEW, (b) PKICO and (c) MDP, for the four pure metaheuristics, with the optimum hybrid metaheuristics selected by the hyperheuristics for variable problems in one execution (FitSP1E), and with the direct application of the hyperheuristics to each problem. Fitness of first and second problems is minimized and the third is maximized.

Table 4: Comparison of the fitness obtanined when executing the hyperheuristic configurations directly to three test instances of PECEW (a), PKICO (b) and MDP (c) with those obtained when applying the best hybrid metaheuristic (Mhy). Fitness of first and second problems is minimized and the third is maximized.

	Hhy	Hge	Hre	Mhy1
20-6	2421.89	2426.37	2426.37	2515.22
40-3	4685.18	4685.18	4685.18	4760.00
40-6	4598.05	4629.18	4638.37	4786.65
Average	3901.71	3913.58	3916.64	4020.62

(a) PECEW

	Hre	Hge	Mhy2
S4	0.8937	0.8931	1.7600
S5	3.8209	3.8311	4.0178
S6	1.3023	1.3022	1.7953
Average	2.0055	2.0088	2.5243

(b) PKICO

	Hre	Hge	Mhy3
n100m40	4142	4142	4140
n200m60	9437	9437	9419
n300m60	9689	9689	9634
Average	7756	7756	7731

(c) MDP

that of metaheuristics obtained from hyperheuristics (M-H), the application of instances of the best metaheuristic (B-M) not automatically selected (combinations Mhy in table 2), and that of the four pure metaheuristics (P-M). A relatively small number of points was considered in some cases because of the high execution time in some algorithms with very small variances. For PECEW, the problem sizes are grouped into categories by number of pumps, so, for example, PECEW_20 includes instances of size 20-3 and 20-6. The Kruskal-Wallis test revealed statistical differences in the means for all the groups of problems considered.

A deeper analysis between the groups within each set of problem sizes was made. The Wilcoxon rank sum test with continuity correction was applied at a significance level $\alpha = 0.05$. The algorithm performing best for a particular data set is indicated by a symbol $+$. Algorithms against which it is statistically superior are indicated by a $-$, and $\sim$ represents that there was no difference in the means. Table 5 shows that the best algorithm in all cases was the hyperheuristic (H) applied directly to each instance, except B-M and M-H applied to instances PECEW_20, and B-M applied to instances MDP_n100m40.

As our interest is to test the applicability of metaheuristics obtained automatically from hyperheuristics (M-H) against metaheuristics not automatically obtained (B-M and P-M), we applied the Wilcoxon test, taking M-H as control group. Table 6 shows that for PKICO, the M-H group is significantly better than the others; for PECEW, M-H is better than P-M and equal to B-M; and for MDP, M-H is equal to the others for the two sizes studied.

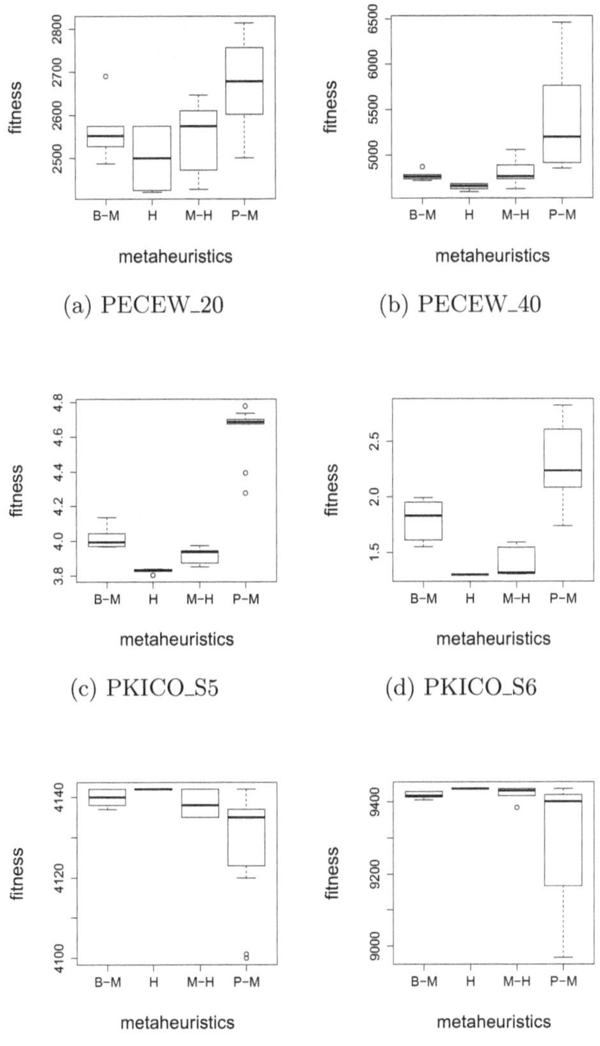

(a) PECEW_20 (b) PECEW_40

(c) PKICO_S5 (d) PKICO_S6

(e) MDP_n100m40 (f) MDP_n200m60

Figure 2: Statistical summary of the fitness means obtained by applying different metaheuristic algorithms to two sizes of the problem PECEW (a and b), PKICO (c and d) and MDP (e and f). Fitness of first and second problems is minimized and the third is maximized. Four sets of algorithms were considered: the direct application of the three hyperheuristic configurations (H), the set of metaheuristics obtained from hyperheuristics (M-H), the application of the best metaheuristics not automatically selected (B-M), and the set of the four pure metaheuristics (P-M).

Table 5: Results of the Wilcoxon rank sum test at a significance level $\alpha = 0.05$ for two groups of test instances of PECEW (a), PKICO (b) and MDP (c). The means of each set are given. Fitness of first and second problems is minimized and the third is maximized.

instance	B-M	H	M-H	P-M
20	2564.06∼	2499.54+	2545.20∼	2673.44−
40	4773.33−	4653.52+	4808.26−	5382.86−

(a) PECEW

instance	B-M	H	M-H	P-M
S5	4.0178−	3.8291+	3.9206−	4.6414−
S6	1.7953−	1.3023+	1.3997−	2.2873−

(b) PKICO

instance	B-M	H	M-H	P-M
n100m40	4140∼	4142+	4138−	4129−
n200m60	9419−	9437+	9423−	9304−

(c) MDP

Table 6: Results of the Wilcoxon rank sum pairwise test at a significance level $\alpha = 0.05$, to compare the B-M and P-M sets with the reference set M-H, for the groups of instances specified in table 5.

instance	B-M	P-M
20	∼	−
40	∼	−

(a) PECEW

instance	B-M	P-M
S5	−	−
S6	−	−

(b) PKICO

instance	B-M	P-M
n100m40	∼	∼
n200m60	∼	∼

(c) MDP

6. CONCLUSIONS AND FUTURE WORK

Hyperheuristics have been developed satisfactorily using a unified parametrized scheme for metaheuristics that facilitates their development and their application by reusing the basic functions. The implementation of these functions are basically the same as with the metaheuristics.

The applicability of the parametrized metaheuristic scheme for hyperheuristics development has been tested with the application of local and global search methods (GRASP, Tabu Search, Genetic algorithms and Scatter Search) and their combinations to three problems: a problem of optimization of power consumption in operation of wells, the determination of the kinetic constants of a chemical reaction and the maximum diversity problem. The results allow us to verify that our hyperheuristic is a good automatic optimization tool, which makes it easy to obtain satisfactory values for the metaheuristic parameters and, consequently, satisfactory metaheuristics.

On average, the best results for the three problems studied in terms of fitness when applying metaheuristics selected from hyperheuristics are obtained from the genetic hyperheuristic with the methodology of several problem inputs in one execution. In general, hyperheuristics significantly improve the results of applying pure metaheuristics and also improve the fitness resulting from the application of the best known hybrid metaheuristic in many cases.

Future research could apply the hyperheuristic methodology to other optimization problems, even very widely studied ones, to compare our approach with other hyperheuristic implementations. The inclusion of parallelism in the hyperheuristic could also be interesting to reduce execution times as far as possible.

7. ACKNOWLEDGMENTS

Partially supported by the Spanish Ministry of Education and Science, TIN2012-38341-C04-03, and the Spanish High-Performance Computing Network on Parallel Heterogeneus Architectures (CAPAP-H). The authors gratefully acknowledge the computer resources and assistance provided by the Barcelona Supercomputing Center.

8. REFERENCES

[1] F. Almeida, D. Giménez, J.-J. López-Espín, and M. Pérez-Pérez. Parameterised schemes of metaheuristics: basic ideas and applications with Genetic algorithms, Scatter Search and GRASP. *IEEE Trnsactions on Systems, Man and Cybernetics, Part A: Systems and Humans*, 43(3):570–586, 2013.

[2] E. K. Burke, M. Hyde, G. Kendall, G. Ochoa, E. Ozcan, and J. R. Woodward. *A Classification of Hyper-heuristic Approaches*, volume 146, pages 449–468. Springer, 2010. In Michel Gendreau, Jean-Yves Potvin, editors, Handbook of Meta-heuristics.

[3] E. K. Burke, M. Gendreau, M. R. Hyde, G. Kendall, G. Ochoa, E. Özcan and R. Qu. *Hyper-heuristics: a survey of the state of the art*, volume 64(12), pages 1695–1724. 2013. In Journal of the Operational Research Society.

[4] J.-M. Cutillas-Lozano and D. Giménez. Determination of the kinetic constants of a chemical reaction in heterogeneous phase using parametrized metaheuristics. In *ICCS*, pages 787–796, 2013.

[5] L.-G. Cutillas-Lozano, J.-M. Cutillas-Lozano, and D. Giménez. Modeling shared-memory metaheuristic schemes for electricity consumption. In *DCAI*, pages 33–40, 2012.

[6] F. Glover and G. A. Kochenberger. *Handbook of Metaheuristics*. Kluwer, 2003.

[7] F. Hutter, H. H. Hoos, K. Leyton-Brown, and T. Stützle. ParamILS: An Automatic Algorithm Configuration Framework. *J. Artif. Intell. Res. (JAIR)*, 58:267-306, 2009.

[8] F. Hutter, H. H. Hoos, and K. Leyton-Brown. Sequential Model-Based Optimization for General Algorithm Configuration. In *LION*, pages 507–523, 2011.

[9] C. C. Kuo, F. Glover, and K. S. Dhir. Analyzing and modeling the maximum diversity problem by zero-one programming. *Decision Sciences*, 24(6):1171–1185, 1993.

[10] R. Martí, M. Gallego, A. Duarte, and E. G. Pardo. Heuristics and metaheuristics for the maximum diversity problem. *J. Heuristics*, 19(4):591–615, 2013.

[11] F. Mascia, M. López-Ibáñez, J. Dubois-Lacoste, and T. Stützle. From Grammars to Parameters: Automatic Iterated Greedy Design for the Permutation Flow-Shop Problem with Weighted Tardiness. In *LION*, pages 321–334, 2013.

[12] F. Mascia, M. López-Ibáñez, J. Dubois-Lacoste, and T. Stützle. Grammar-based Generation of Stochastic Local Search Heuristics Through Automatic Algorithm Configuration Tools. *IRIDIA, Université Libre de Bruxelles*, number 2013-015, December 2013.

[13] E. Ozcan, B. Bilgin, and E. Korkmaz. A comprehensive analysis of hyper-heuristics. *Intelligent Data Analysis*, 12(1):3–23, 2008.

[14] L. N. Plummer, T. M. L. Wigley, and D. L. Parkhurst. The kinetics of calcite dissolution in CO_2–water systems at 5 to 60 $^\circ C$ and 0.0 to 1.0 atm CO_2, American Journal of Science 278, 1978, pp. 179–216.

Global vs Local Search on Multi-objective NK-Landscapes: Contrasting the Impact of Problem Features

Fabio Daolio
Shinshu University
fdaolio@shinshu-u.ac.jp

Arnaud Liefooghe
Univ. Lille, CRIStAL, Inria
arnaud.liefooghe@inria.fr

Sébastien Verel
Univ. du Littoral Côte d'Opale
verel@lisic.univ-littoral.fr

Hernán Aguirre
Shinshu University
ahernan@shinshu-u.ac.jp

Kiyoshi Tanaka
Shinshu University
ktanaka@shinshu-u.ac.jp

ABSTRACT

Computationally hard multi-objective combinatorial optimization problems are common in practice, and numerous evolutionary multi-objective optimization (EMO) algorithms have been proposed to tackle them. Our aim is to understand which (and how) problem features impact the search performance of such approaches. In this paper, we consider two prototypical dominance-based algorithms: a global EMO strategy using an ergodic variation operator (GSEMO) and a neighborhood-based local search heuristic (PLS). Their respective runtime is estimated on a benchmark of combinatorial problems with tunable ruggedness, objective space dimension, and objective correlation (ρMNK-landscapes). In other words, benchmark parameters define classes of instances with increasing empirical problem hardness; we enumerate and characterize the search space of small instances. Our study departs from simple performance comparison to systematically analyze the correlations between runtime and problem features, contrasting their association with search performance within and across instance classes, for both chosen algorithms. A mixed-model approach then allows us to further generalize from the experimental design, supporting a sound assessment of the joint impact of instance features on EMO search performance.

1. MOTIVATIONS

Despite the increasing number of available heuristics for evolutionary multi-objective optimization, the understanding of their search dynamics is comparatively less advanced than in the single-objective case. This knowledge is all the more valuable in a black-box scenario, where such approaches are mostly adopted. Finding what makes a problem hard, which features have an influence on algorithm performance, and how that changes across different algorithm and problem classes, are relevant and still open challenges in multi-objective optimization.

Following [17], we precisely investigate the impact of instance features on search performance. We decline this research question in three complementary sub-questions: (i) how strongly are features associated to performance? (ii) what performance change is to be expected when varying each feature? (iii) what is the relative importance of features in explaining the performance variance? We consider a global and a local EMO heuristics and try to highlight the differences and similarities in the behavior of both algorithm classes, with respect to a set of relevant problem features. As such, the emphasis is more on making inferences, e.g. [8], rather than making predictions, e.g. [11]. Hence, this work attempts to provide both insightful understandings and methodological suggestions.

We introduce the experimental setup of our analysis in Section 2, in particular the considered problems, ρMNK-landscapes [24], and the search algorithms, namely the global simple EMO optimizer (GSEMO) [14] and the Pareto local search (PLS) [21], of which we measure the estimated runtime to find a $(1+\varepsilon)-$approximation of the Pareto set. In Section 3, we examine the performance of GSEMO and PLS depending on the ruggedness, the objective space dimension, and the objective correlation of ρMNK-landscapes. In Section 4, we provide an overview of the features that characterize the hardness of problem instances, relating to the difficulties randomized search heuristics might have to face. Via a correlation and regression analysis, we are able to point out how such features influence the performance of global and local search algorithms like GSEMO and PLS. The last section concludes the paper.

2. INGREDIENTS

2.1 Multi-objective Optimization

We are interested in maximizing a black-box objective function vector $f : X \rightarrow Z$, that maps any solution from the solution space $x \in X$ to a vector in the objective space $z \in Z$, with $Z \subseteq \mathbb{R}^M$, such that $z = f(x)$. We assume that the solution space is a discrete set $X = \{0,1\}^N$, where N is the problem size, i.e. the number of binary (zero-one) variables. An objective vector $z \in Z$ is dominated by an objective vector $z' \in Z$, denoted by $z \prec z'$, iff for all $i \in \{1,\ldots,M\}$ $z_i \leqslant z'_i$, and there is a $j \in \{1,\ldots,M\}$ such that $z_j < z'_j$. Similarly, a solution $x \in X$ is dominated by a solution $x' \in X$ iff $f(x) \prec f(x')$. An objective vector $z^\star \in Z$ is non-dominated if there does not exist any objective vector $z \in Z$ such that $z^\star \prec z$. A solution $x^\star \in X$ is non-dominated, or Pareto-optimal, if $f(x)$ is non-dominated. The set of Pareto-optimal solutions is the Pareto set (PS) ; its mapping in the objective space is the Pareto front (PF). One of the main challenges in multi-objective optimization is to identify the Pareto set/front, or a good approximation of it, for large-size and difficult problems.

2.2 ρMNK-Landscapes

The family of ρMNK-landscapes constitutes a problem-independent model used for constructing multi-objective multimodal land-

GECCO '15, July 11 - 15, 2015, Madrid, Spain

DOI: http://dx.doi.org/10.1145/2739480.2754745

scapes with objective correlation [24]. They extend single-objective NK-landscapes [12] and multi-objective NK-landscapes with independent objective functions [1]. Candidate solutions are binary strings of size N, i.e. the solution space is $X = \{0,1\}^N$. The objective function vector $f = (f_1, \ldots, f_i, \ldots, f_M)$ is defined as $f : \{0,1\}^N \to [0,1]^M$ such that each objective function f_i is to be maximized. As in the single-objective case, each separate objective function value $f_i(x)$ of a solution $x = (x_1, \ldots, x_j, \ldots, x_N)$ is an average value of the individual contributions associated with each variable x_j. Indeed, for each objective f_i, $i \in \{1, \ldots, M\}$, and each variable x_j, $j \in \{1, \ldots, N\}$, a component function $f_{ij} : \{0,1\}^{K+1} \to [0,1]$ assigns a real-valued contribution for every combination of x_j and its K *epistatic interactions* $\{x_{j_1}, \ldots, x_{j_K}\}$. These f_{ij}-values are uniformly distributed in the range $[0,1]$. Thus, the individual contribution of a variable x_j depends on its value and on the values of $K < N$ other variables $\{x_{j_1}, \ldots, x_{j_K}\}$. The problem can be formalized as follows.

$$\begin{aligned} \max \quad & f_i(x) = \frac{1}{N} \sum_{j=1}^{N} f_{ij}(x_j, x_{j_1}, \ldots, x_{j_K}) && i \in \{1, \ldots, M\} \\ \text{s.t.} \quad & x_j \in \{0,1\} && j \in \{1, \ldots, N\} \end{aligned}$$

In this work, the epistatic interactions, i.e. the K variables that influence the contribution of x_j, are set uniformly at random among the $(N-1)$ variables other than x_j, following the random neighborhood model from [12]. By increasing the number of epistatic interactions K from 0 to $(N-1)$, problem instances can be gradually tuned from smooth to rugged. In ρMNK-landscapes, f_{ij}-values additionally follow a multivariate uniform distribution of dimension M, defined by an $M \times M$ positive-definite symmetric covariance matrix (c_{pq}) such that $c_{pp} = 1$ and $c_{pq} = \rho$ for all $p, q \in \{1, \ldots, M\}$ with $p \neq q$, were $\rho > \frac{-1}{M-1}$ defines the objective correlation degree; see [24] for details. The positive (respectively negative) data correlation ρ decreases (respectively increases) the degree of conflict between the objective function values. The same correlation coefficient ρ is then defined between all pairs of objectives, and the same epistatic degree K and epistatic interactions are set for all the objectives.

2.3 Multi-objective Search Heuristics

In this paper, we consider two randomized search heuristics for ρMNK-landscapes: (i) global SEMO (GSEMO) [14], a simple elitist steady-state *global* EMO algorithm (see Algorithm 1); and (ii) Pareto local search (PLS) [21], a population-based multi-objective *local* search (Algorithm 2). Both algorithms maintain an *unbounded* archive A of mutually non-dominated solutions. This archive is initialized with one random solution from the solution space. Then, at each iteration, one solution is selected at random from the archive $x \in A$. In GSEMO, each binary variable from x is independently flipped with rate $\frac{1}{N}$ in order to produce an offspring solution x'. The archive is then updated by keeping the non-dominated solutions from $A \cup \{x'\}$. In PLS, the solutions located in the neighborhood of x are evaluated. Let $\mathtt{N}(x)$ denote the set of solutions located at a Hamming distance 1. The non-dominated solutions from $A \cup \mathtt{N}(x)$ are stored in the archive, and the current solution x is then tagged as *visited* in order to avoid a useless revaluation of its neighborhood. This process is iterated until a stopping condition is satisfied. While for GSEMO there does not exists any explicit stopping rule [14], PLS has a natural stopping condition which is satisfied when all solutions from the archive are tagged as *visited*.

In other words, while PLS is based on the exploration of the whole 1-bit-flip neighborhood from x, GSEMO rather uses an ergodic operator, i.e. an independent bit-flip mutation. This means

Algorithm 1: GSEMO

Choose an initial solution x_0 uniformly from X;
$A \leftarrow \{x_0\}$;
repeat
  Select an element x out of A uniformly;
  Create x' by flipping each bit of x with a rate $1/N$;
  $A \leftarrow$ non-dominated solutions from $A \cup \{x'\}$;
until *success* $\vee$ *maxeval*;

Algorithm 2: PLS

Choose an initial solution x_0 uniformly from X;
$A \leftarrow \{x_0\}$;
repeat
  Select a non-visited element x out of A uniformly;
  Create $\mathtt{N}(x)$ by flipping each bit of x in turns;
  Flag x as visited;
  $A \leftarrow$ non-dominated solutions from $A \cup \mathtt{N}(x)$;
until *all-visited* $\vee$ *success* $\vee$ *maxeval*;

that there is a non-zero probability of reaching any solution from the solution space at every GSEMO iteration. This makes GSEMO a *global* optimizer rather than a *local* optimizer as PLS. In this paper, we are interested in the running time, in terms of a number of function evaluations, until an $(1+\varepsilon)-$approximation of the Pareto set is identified and is contained in the internal memory A of the algorithm, subject to a maximum budget of function evaluations.

2.4 Estimated Expected Running Time (`ert`)

Let ε be a constant value such that $\varepsilon \geqslant 0$. The (multiplicative) ε-dominance relation ($\preceq_\varepsilon$) can be defined as follows. For $x, x' \in X$, x is ε-dominated by x' ($x \preceq_\varepsilon x'$) iff $f_i(x) \leqslant (1+\varepsilon) \cdot f_i(x')$, $\forall i \in \{1, \ldots, m\}$. A set $X^\varepsilon \subseteq X$ is an $(1+\varepsilon)-$approximation of the Pareto set if for any solution $x \in X$, there is one solution $x' \in X^\varepsilon$ such that $x \preceq_\varepsilon x'$. This is equivalent to finding an approximation set whose multiplicative epsilon quality indicator value with respect to the (exact) Pareto set is lower than $(1+\varepsilon)$, see e.g. [25]. Interestingly, under some general assumptions, there always exists an $(1+\varepsilon)$-approximation, for any given $\varepsilon \geqslant 0$, whose cardinality is both polynomial in the problem size and in $\frac{1}{\varepsilon}$ [20].

Following a conventional methodology from single-objective continuous black-box optimization [3], we measure algorithm performance in the expected number of function evaluations to identify an $(1+\varepsilon)-$approximation. However, as any heuristic, GSEMO or PLS can either succeed or fail to reach an accuracy of ε in a single run. In case of success, we record the number of function evaluations until an $(1+\varepsilon)-$approximation was found. In case of failure, we simply *restart* the algorithm at random. Thus we obtain a "*simulated running time*" [3] from a set of independent trials on each instance. Such performance measure allows us to take into account both the success rate $p_s \in (0,1]$ and the convergence speed of the algorithm with restarts. Precisely, after $(t-1)$ failures, each one requiring T_f evaluations, and the final successful run of T_s evaluations, the total runtime is $T = \sum_{i=1}^{t-1} T_f + T_s$. By taking the expectation and by considering independent trials as a Bernoulli process stopping at the first success, we have:

$$\mathbb{E}[T] = \left(\frac{1-p_s}{p_s}\right) \mathbb{E}[T_f] + \mathbb{E}[T_s]$$

In our case, the success rate p_s is estimated with the ratio of suc-

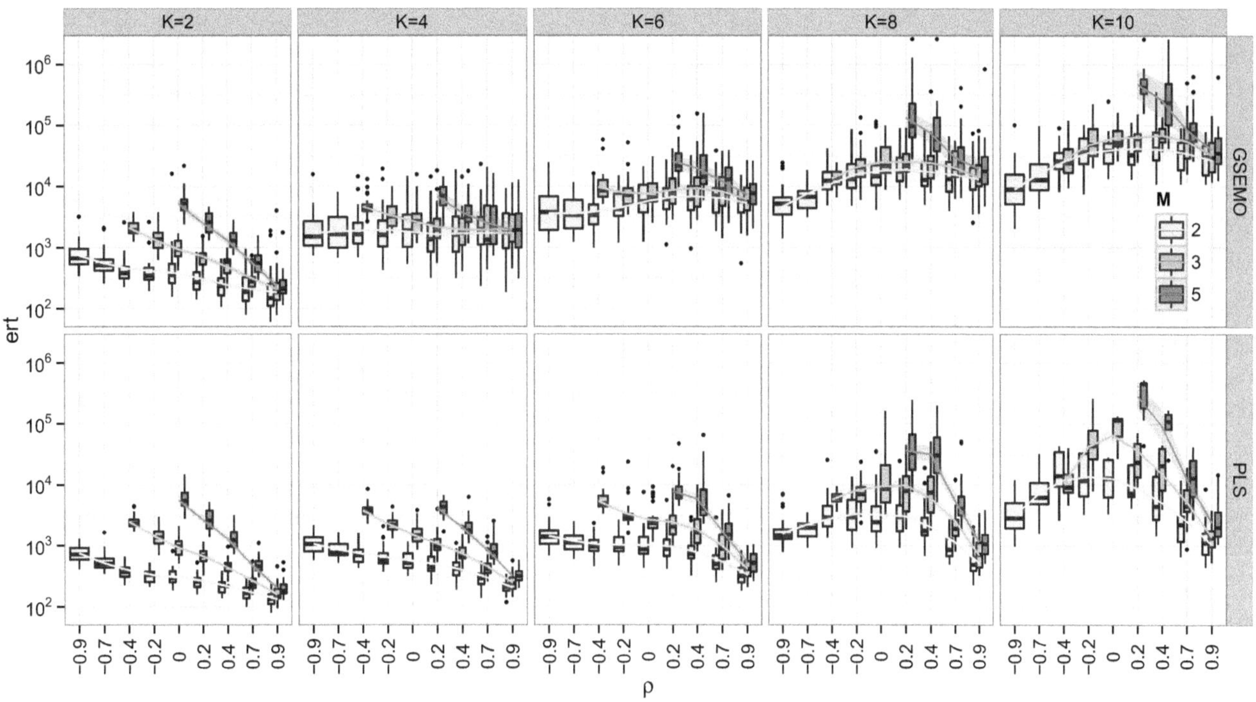

Figure 1: distribution of estimated runtime *ert* (y-axis, fixed log-scale) w.r.t. to objectives correlation ρ (x-axis) for both algorithms (see facets right labels). Results are grouped by problem non-linearity K (see facets top labels) and by number of objectives M (see legend). Box-and-whisker plots give median and inter-quantile range; LOESS smooth curves show trends.

cessful runs over the total number of executions ($\hat{p}_s$), the expected running time for unsuccessful runs $\mathbb{E}[T_f]$ is set as a constant limit on the number of function evaluation calls T_{max}, and the expected running time for successful runs $\mathbb{E}[T_s]$ is estimated with the average number of function evaluations performed by successful runs:

$$\texttt{ert} = \left(\frac{1-\hat{p}_s}{\hat{p}_s}\right) T_{max} + \frac{1}{t_s}\sum_{i=1}^{t_s} T_i$$

where t_s is the number of successful runs, and T_i is the number of evaluations for successful run i. For more details, we refer to [3].

3. EXPERIMENTAL ANALYSIS

3.1 Experimental Setup

We consider ρMNK-landscapes with an epistatic degree $K \in \{2, 4, 6, 8, 10\}$, an objective space dimension $M \in \{2, 3, 5\}$, and $\rho \in \{-0.9, -0.7, -0.4, -0.2, 0.0, 0.2, 0.4, 0.7, 0.9\}$, such that $\rho > \frac{-1}{M-1}$, as objective correlation. The problem size is set to $N = 18$ in order to enumerate the solution space exhaustively. A set of 30 different landscapes are independently generated at random for each parameter combination ρ, M, and K. They are made available at the following URL: http://mocobench.sf.net.

The target is set at $\varepsilon = 0.1$. The time limit is set to $T_{max} = 2^N \cdot 10^{-1} < 26\,215$ function evaluations without identifying an $(1+\varepsilon)-$approximation. Each algorithm is executed 100 times *per* instance. From these 100 repetitions, the success rate and the expected number of evaluations for successful runs, hence the expected runtime on the given instance, are estimated. For the comparative analysis, we only consider pairwise-complete cases, i.e. instances that have been solved by both algorithms. This brings the total number of available observations to 2 874 *per* algorithm.

3.2 Exploratory Analysis

The expected runtime (`ert`) distribution across the experimental blocks that are defined by each combination of benchmark parameters is presented in Figure 1. For both algorithms, the `ert` clearly increases with the ruggedness (K) and the number of objectives (M), whereas the trend w.r.t. the objective correlation (ρ) is a bit more complex. Indeed, for a small K and a large M, the `ert` decreases when ρ increases. On the contrary, for large K, problem instances seem to get harder when the objectives are independent ($\rho \approx 0$) rather than anti-correlated ($\rho < 0$), despite the fact that the cardinality of the Pareto set (PS) gets higher in such cases [24]. This gives rise to the inverted u-shape observed on the right side of the figure, which is particularly pronounced for PLS. Actually, we observed that the ε-value of random approximation sets follows a similar u-shaped trend w.r.t. objective correlation. Also, this ε-value tends to increase with K. This holds for approximation sets containing a constant number of randomly generated solutions. Moreover, we know from [24] that the number of Pareto local optimal solutions increases with K and decreases with ρ. This could explain the relative advantage of PLS on problem instances with positively correlated objectives. Notice also that the opposite is true for the connectedness of the PS: the smaller K, the larger ρ, the more clustered are Pareto optimal solutions in the solution space.

Figure 2 displays the runtime aggregated over all the instance parameters (ρ, M, K) but one. We clearly see that PLS is significantly outperforming GSEMO overall, and in particular for positively correlated objectives. In fact, the runtime of PLS is shorter than that of GSEMO for 88% of the instances; compared to PLS, on average GSEMO requires more than 17 000 additional function evaluations to identify a 1.1−approximation of the PS. The performance dif-

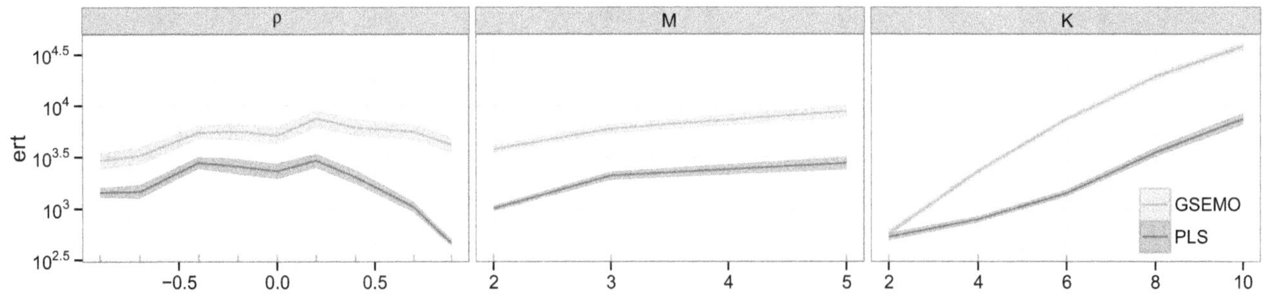

Figure 2: interaction plots between the average estimated runtime ert (y-axis, log-scale) and the benchmark parameters: objective correlation ρ (left), the number of objectives M (center), and the problem non-linearity K (right, see titles). Results are grouped by algorithm (see legend). The average (lines) and is 0.95 confidence interval (shaded areas) are evaluated through bootstrapping.

ference between the two algorithms seems to be constant, except for large ρ and w.r.t. K. Notably, the ruggedness of the underlying single-objective objective functions appears to have the highest impact on the search performance. In particular, the ruggedness seems to have more impact on the performance of GSEMO than PLS. In general, finding an $(1+\varepsilon)-$approximation becomes harder as the number of objectives grows and much harder for highly-rugged instances, whereas the trend w.r.t. objective correlation is less clear, more algorithm-dependent.

In the next section, we list the problem features that are *intuitively* impacting the performance of dominance-based search heuristics for the class of ρMNK-landscapes, and we *explicitly* assess their separate and joint effect on the runtime of PLS and GSEMO.

4. FEATURE-BASED ANALYSIS

4.1 Characterizing Problem Difficulty

Besides the benchmark parameters defining ρMNK-landscapes, a total of twelve general-purpose problem features are summarized in Table 1; they can be classified into the following three groups:

(i) Features related to the Pareto set (PS) includes the number of non-dominated solutions, the number of supported solutions [9], and the hypervolume of the Pareto front, setting the reference point to the origin.

(ii) Features related to the distance and the connectedness of Pareto optimal solutions includes the average and the maximum distance between any pair of solutions from the PS, the number of clusters relative to the PS size, the proportional size of the largest cluster, and the minimum distance to consider such that all solutions belong to the same cluster. The distance measure is here taken as the Hamming distance between binary strings, which is directly related to the *bit-flip* neighborhood operator.

(iii) Features related to multimodality or ruggedness of the landscape includes the number of Pareto local optimal (PLO) solutions, the length of a single-solution Pareto hill-climbing that iteratively accepts a dominating neighbor until a PLO is found, as well as the autocorrelation of hypervolume of single solutions or of their neighborhood sets (local hypervolume), along a random walk. The random walk length is set to $\ell = 10^4$, and the neighborhood is the *1-bit-flip*.

Obviously, since some of those features require the solution space to be enumerated exhaustively, they are not practical for a performance prediction purpose. However, we decided to include them

Table 1: Summary of ρMNK-landscape benchmark parameters and problem instance features investigated in the paper.

	Benchmark parameters (3)
K	Number of variable (epistatic) interactions
M	Number of objective functions
ρ	Correlation between the objective values
	Problem instance features (12)
`npo`	Number of solutions from the PS [1, 13]
`supp`	Proportion of supported solutions in the PS [13]
`hv`	Hypervolume [25] of the PS [1]
`avgd`	Avg. dist. between solutions from the PS [16]
`maxd`	Max. dist. between solutions from the PS [13]
`ncomp`	Relative number of clusters in the PS [23]
`lcomp`	Proportional size of the PS largest cluster [15]
`dconn`	Minimal distance to connect the PS [23]
`nplo`	Number of Pareto local optima [22]
`ladapt`	Length of adaptive walk [24]
`corhv`	Autocorrelation of solution hypervolume [16]
`corlhv`	Autocorrelation of local hypervolume [16]

in order to examine their impact on the algorithm performance. For a more comprehensive explanation of those features and their intercorrelation, we refer to [16]. In the next section, we relate the value of those features for enumerable ρMNK-landscapes to the performance of both GSEMO and PLS.

4.2 Correlation Analysis

A first assessment of the dependency of the search performance on instance features can be done through visual inspection of scatter plots, supported by a correlation analysis. Naturally, *correlation* does not imply *causation*, and we do not draw any *direct* link between each considered feature and the algorithm runtime, even if in our case the eventual link could only go in one direction. Instead, we restrict ourself to measure the association of each feature to the performance metric (`ert`). We quantify this dependency strength via the Kendall's τ statistic [18]. This rank-based nonlinear correlation measure is based on the ordering of all possible pairs, and its value is proportional to the difference between the number of concordant and discordant pairs among all possible pairwise comparisons. As such, when the null hypothesis of mutual independence ($H_0 : \tau = 0$) is rejected, τ can be directly interpreted as the prob-

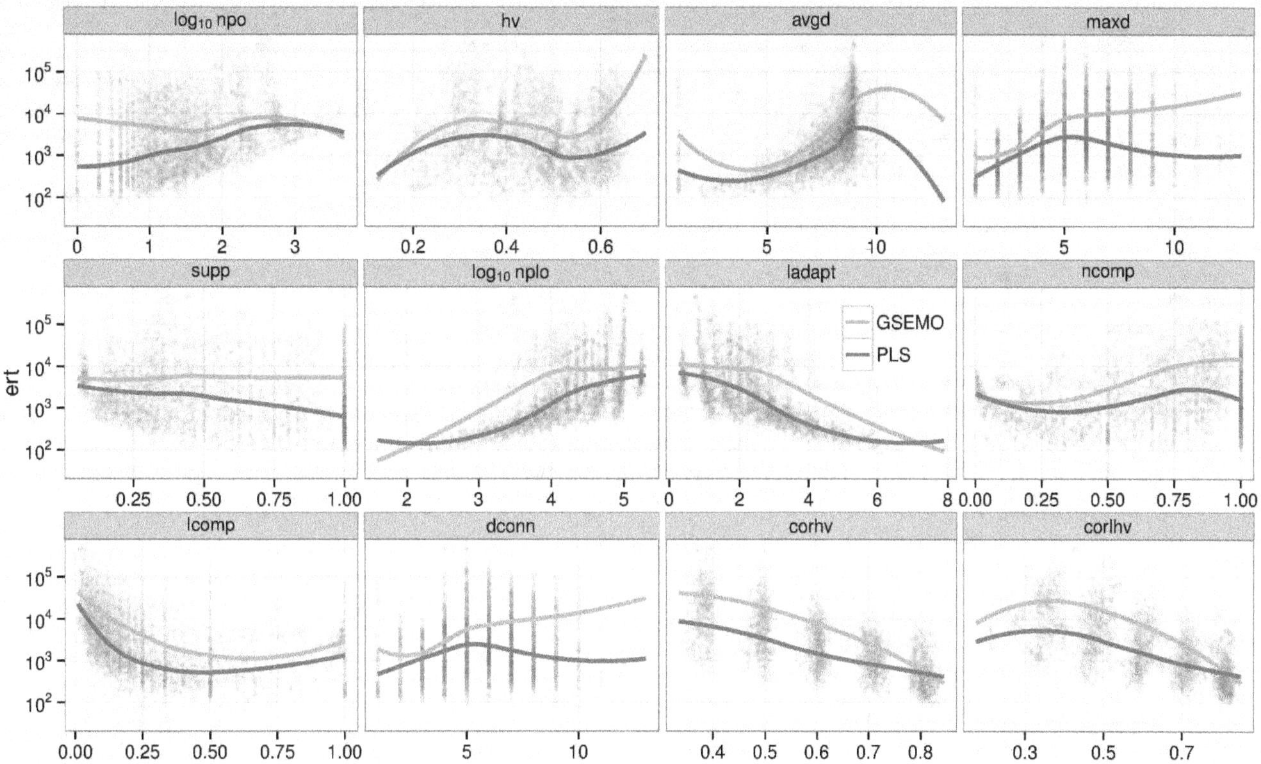

Figure 3: interaction plots between the average estimated runtime ert (y-axis, fixed logscale) and the instance features (x-axis, see facets titles). Results are grouped by algorithm (see legend). Lines represent a locally-fitted polynomial function (LOESS).

ability of observing agreement ($\tau > 0$) or disagreement ($\tau < 0$) between the ranks of paired values.

The scatter plots and the regressions (with local polynomial fitting) of the average running time of both algorithms as a function of the instance features are provided in Figure 3. In addition, Kendall's τ coefficients are given by the red points in Figure 4. For both algorithms, the average distance between Pareto optimal solution (`avgd`) is highly positively correlated with `ert`: the larger this distance, the longer the running time. On the contrary, both ruggedness-related features based on measures of hypervolume autocorrelation (`corhv`, `corlhv`), and one feature related to the connectedness, i.e. the size of the largest cluster in the PS (`lcomp`), are highly negatively correlated. As expected, ruggedness and connectedness play a major role for both algorithms: the runtime decreases with `corhv` and `corlhv`, and when a large number of Pareto optimal solutions are clustered in the solution space.

Some features have a different impact on the two algorithms, possibly highlighting their respective strengths and weaknesses. In particular, the runtime of PLS increases with the number of Pareto optimal solutions and with the number of PLO solutions. Contrastingly, the scatter plots show that having a high number of PLO has less impact on GSEMO than PLS. Moreover, the runtime of GSEMO is correlated with three others features related to the connectedness of the PS (`maxd`, `ncomp`, `dconn`). Indeed, the relations between Pareto optimal solutions have a large effect on the runtime of GSEMO, especially when the distance between those solutions is large. Surprisingly, the runtime of PLS does not increase when non-dominated solutions are disconnected.

However, we have to be careful when drawing conclusions by aggregating data from different areas of the instance parameters space, since feature values and their range depend, in turn, on the levels of ρ, M, and K. This can be visually appreciated in Figure 3: the autocorrelation measures `corhv` and `corlhv`, for example, are clearly clustered around five levels that actually correspond to the different K-values. Similarly, we are able to distinguish three clusters in the hypervolume metric `hv`, which actually follow the objective space dimension M.

Therefore, we deepen the analysis by evaluating the correlation *within* the instance groups defined by each possible combination of the $\langle\rho, M, K\rangle$-values under study. Black points and lines in Figure 4 display the average τ-value within groups, together with the confidence interval associated to the mean. By comparing them with red points, we can clearly notice how data aggregation slightly enhances the correlation statistic in the `corhv` and `corlhv` case, leading to the same inference nonetheless. On the contrary, although hypervolume is very weakly associated with runtime overall, and that its impact is contradictory between GSEMO and PLS, group results are more consistent, showing a strong positive association between `ert` and `hv` for both algorithms. Unfortunately, as for features related to the connectedness of the PS, our confidence on the average correlation within groups is too low to make further comments, mainly due to the fact that, in many cases, we could not reject the null hypothesis of mutual independency at the group level. Nevertheless, the previous observations on data blocks and their possible effect motivate the remainder of our analysis.

4.3 Regression Analysis

In this section we aim to quantify the impact of instance features, and possibly disentangle their individual contribution to the performance variance, by taking into account the dependency among

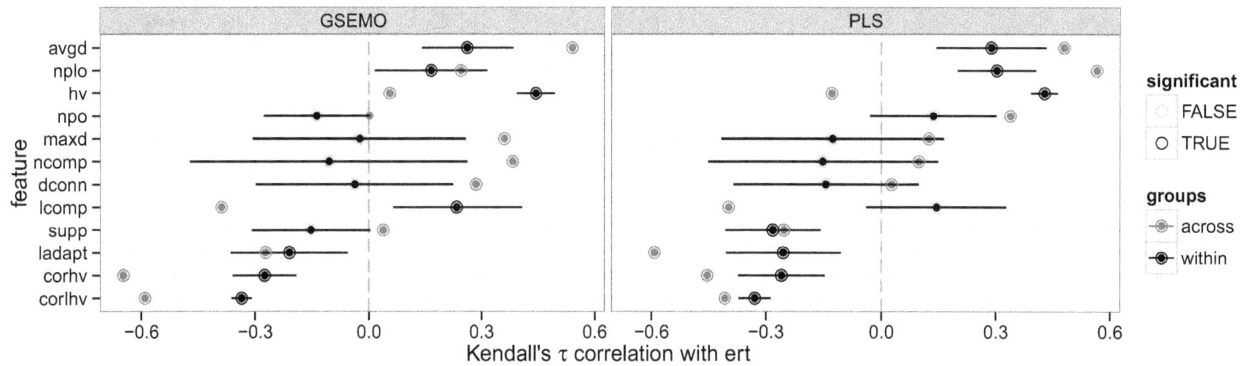

Figure 4: performance-feature association. Points give Kendall's τ statistic for the correlation between runtime and instance feature, evaluated on the whole set of instances (red) or within instance groups (black, see left legend). Group averages, 0.95 confidence intervals, and significance, are estimated with a t-test considering only statistics that were already significant at the group level. Group and overall significance are based on Kendall's test $p-$value at the 0.05 level ($H_0 : \tau_i = 0$) [18].

measurements that is induced by the experimental plan. Our goal is precisely to generalize from it as much as possible, in order to make inferences about the effect and relative importance of features.

4.3.1 Linear Mixed-Model

Let y_i be the log-transformed expected runtime (`ert`) on the i-th problem instance. We treat y_i as an observation from a random variable Y with expectation $\mathbb{E}(Y) = \mu$, i.e. $y_i = \mu + \varepsilon_i$ where ε_i are taken to be independent, identically distributed, and zero-mean.

In a classical multilinear regression, we would model μ as a linear combination of p predictors, notably (a subset of) the p problem instance features that we can measure. Thus, the performance observation on instance i can be written as:

$$y_i = \beta_0 + \sum_{k=1}^{p} \beta_k x_{ki} + \varepsilon_i \qquad \varepsilon_i \sim \mathcal{N}(0, \sigma^2)$$

where ε_i is the usual random term, i.e. the regression residual. In this model, performance observations are supposed to be i.i.d. from a normal distribution $y_i \sim \mathcal{N}(\mu, \sigma^2)$. However, as discussed in the previous sections, our observations are mostly clustered around the different combinations of benchmark parameters; see Figure 1. In fact, a simple linear regression on a dummy categorical predictor having a different level for each combination of ρ, M, and K, would explain 84.51% and 86.85% of the `ert` variance of GSEMO and PLS, respectively.

Since we rather want to investigate the impact of instance features, we need to decompose that global performance variance into what is due to the grouping of benchmark parameters, from which we would like to generalize, and what is due to the randomness involved in the instance generation process; namely for ρMNK-landscapes, the epistatic interaction links and their contributions to the objective values. That conveys the feature variance within the blocks of our experimental design. To this end, instead of fitting an independent regression model for each instance group, we build a linear mixed-model with random effects for experimental blocks. In such framework, the performance on instance i from group j can then be modelled as:

$$y_{ij} = \beta_0 + \sum_{k=1}^{p} \beta_k x_{kij} + \alpha_j + \varepsilon_{ij} \qquad \varepsilon_{ij} \sim \mathcal{N}(0, \sigma^2)$$

where α_j are i.i.d random variables, with $\alpha_j \sim \mathcal{N}(0, \sigma_\alpha^2)$ denoting the group effect. By doing so, we suppose that features have the same impact across groups; in linear terms, constant (*fixed*) slopes and *random* intercepts. Notice that estimates $\hat{\beta}$ and residuals ε will likely not be the same as in the previous model. Notice also that performance observations are now i.i.d. *conditionally* on the grouping factor $y_{ij}|\alpha_j \sim \mathcal{N}(\mu+\alpha_j, \sigma^2)$, whereas the unconditional model $y_{ij} \sim \mathcal{N}(\mu, \sigma^2 + \sigma_\alpha^2)$ carries a dependency between measurements on the same group and yields the aforementioned variance decomposition [8].

The usual approach to estimate the parameters of the unconditional model is the restricted maximum likelihood method; see [5, 10] for theoretical and implementation details. In the following, we present the results of such estimation on the full model comprising all instance features and for both algorithms. In particular, each estimated β_i is tested against the null hypothesis $H_0 : \beta_i = 0$, whereas as for the group effect we only need to check $H_0 : \sigma_\alpha^2 = 0$. In the multilinear framework, the regression coefficients that are statistically significant allow us to assess the runtime effect of each feature conditionally on all the others and, given the random effect formulation, across experimental blocks.

Finally, in order to assess the accuracy of a regression model, the conventional R^2 (ratio of variance explained by the regression) can be extended by taking into account the variance decomposition that is specific to mixed-models [19]. We obtain a *marginal* R^2 yielding the proportion of variance explained by instance features, and a *conditional* R^2 which, despite its name, gives the proportion of variance explained by the entire model, i.e. including the random effect of benchmark parameter combinations. Marginal and conditional R^2 are respectively 0.617 and 0.919 for the regression modelling GSEMO's `ert`, respectively 0.482 and 0.911 for PLS.

4.3.2 Predictors Effect Size

We report in Figure 5 the values of the regression coefficients estimated from the mixed-model. In a multilinear regression, each coefficient β_i predicts the change in the conditional mean of the response variable after a unitary change of the corresponding covariate x_i. As such, higher values correspond, visually, to steeper slopes of the partial regression lines where the given predictor is the only covariate and all other predictors remain constant. This simple interpretation motivates the choice of a multilinear model.

For both algorithms, the features having the highest individual impact on the runtime are the hypervolume (`hv`) and its autocorrelation measures (`corhv` and `corlhv`, in order of importance).

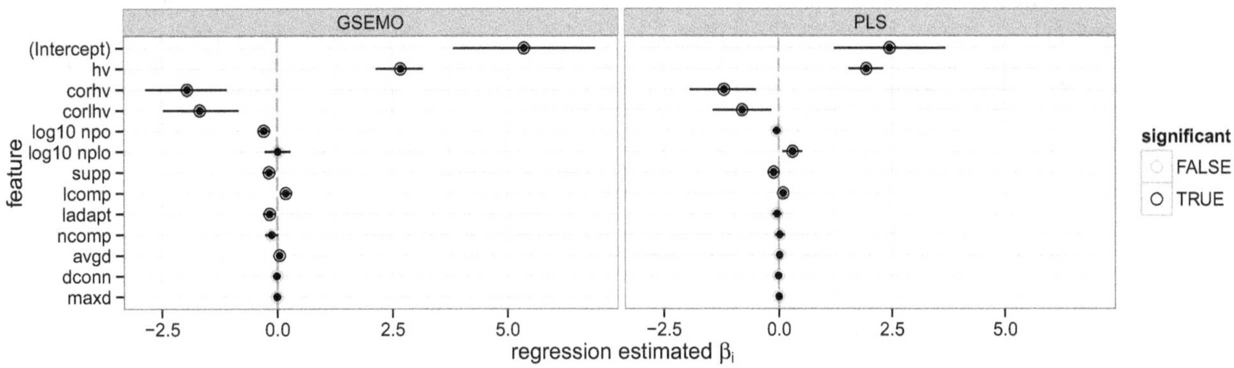

Figure 5: conditional impact of instance features on $\log_{10}$ expected runtime in a linear mixed-model. Points and bars give, respectively, the estimates and 0.95 confidence intervals of model parameters for intercept and fixed effects β_i ($H_0 : \beta_i = 0$) [5].

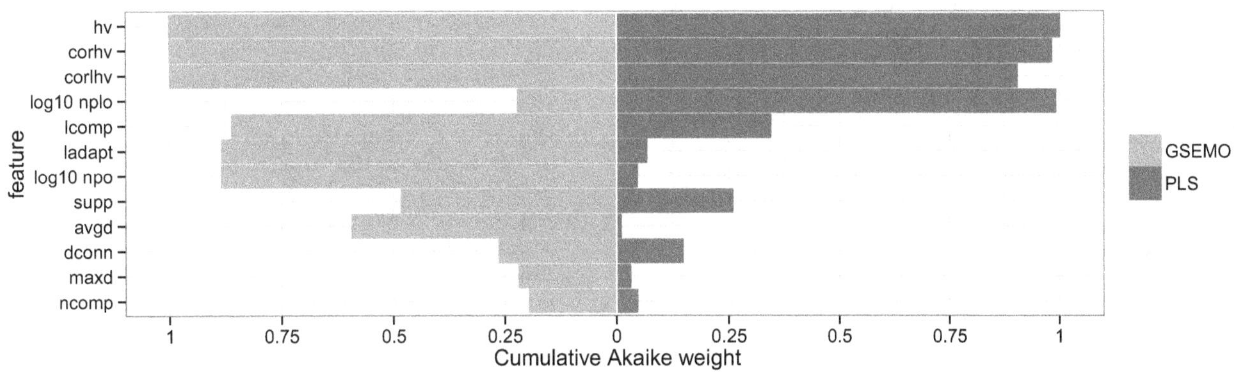

Figure 6: relative importance of instance features as performance predictors in a linear mixed-model. Each bar displays, among all 2^p possible models, the sum of the Akaike's weights of the $2^{(p-1)}$ models including the given feature [4].

For GSEMO, the number of Pareto optimal solutions has a significant effect on estimated runtime, the larger `npo` the shorter `ert`, whereas we cannot reject the hypothesis that the number of PLO solutions has no effect on GSEMO's `ert`. Still, the effect size of the length of an adaptive walk (`ladapt`), which is a good estimator of `nplo` [24], is significant for GSEMO. Conversely, the opposite is true for PLS. Once again, the relative size of the largest connected component of the PS (`lcomp`) impacts the performance of both algorithm. However, when controlling for all other features (i.e. conditionally on all other predictors), we find that an increase in the PS connectedness yields an increase in the expected runtime. Surprisingly also, the number of supported solutions (`supp`) is a significant predictor for both algorithms, even if none of them explicitly exploits this feature during the search process. Finally, despite being one of the features with the highest correlation to `ert`, the average distance between non-dominated solutions (`avgd`) has little impact on GSEMO and no significant impact on PLS.

4.3.3 *Relative Importance of Predictors*

Variable importance is commonly assessed via feature selection. However, stepwise selection can be misleading: intercorrelated predictors have a confounding effect on each other, but what the multilinear regression tries to measure is precisely the effect of one variable *controlling* for the others (i.e. fixing all the others), which leads to a poor estimation in the presence of collinearity. In an information theoretical framework, the Akaike Information Criterion (AIC) [2] measures the relative quality of a model on a given dataset, not in terms of accuracy, but in terms of likelihood, i.e. the relative distance to the unknown true mechanism generating the observed data. The difference in AIC-values between two models can then be used to estimate the strength of evidence for one model against the other. On a set of alternate models, AIC differences can be transformed into so-called Akaike weights, which can be directly interpreted as the probability for each model to be the "best" one, conditionally on the considered set of models [6]. In this context, instead of performing feature selection, variable importance can be better assessed by making inference from all candidate models [7]. We perform an exhaustive search in the space of all 2^p models we can build with our p predictors. The sum of Akaike weights for the $2^{(p-1)}$ models that contain a given predictor, can give us an estimation of the relative importance of that particular variable.

Results are reported in Figure 6: `hv`, `corhv`, and `corlhv` are strong explanatory features for both models, albeit in different order of relative importance. For GSEMO, `npo`, `ladapt`, and `lcomp` can also be considered as important features, whereas `nplo` is the second most-important predictor of PLS runtime.

5. CONCLUSIONS

In this paper we investigated the impact of problem characteristics on the performance of two simple dominance-based multiobjective search heuristics. More particularly, we analyzed the expected runtime of GSEMO and PLS to identify a $(1+\varepsilon)$−approximation of the Pareto set for enumerable ρMNK-landscapes. Beyond a more conventional performance assessment of competing algorithms, we studied the correlations between algorithm performance and a set of relevant problem features. We contrasted their association with algorithm runtime, within and across instance classes. By building a mixed-model regression taking into account the experimental design, we were able to make more general inferences about the impact of problem features, their relative importance, as well as similarities and differences between both algorithms in this respect. Notably, the global hypervolume indicator value and its local autocorrelation measures, which are related to the ruggedness of the fitness landscape, have the strongest impact for both algorithms. In addition, as expected, our analysis reveals that the runtime of PLS appears to be largely affected by the landscape multimodality, here defined as the number of Pareto local optimal solutions. Moreover, the Pareto set cardinality plays a more important role for GSEMO than for PLS. At last, the features reflecting the connectedness of the Pareto set are important predictors for the runtime of GSEMO, which navigates the search space with an ergodic variation operator. On the contrary, the same features have a non-significant effect on the performance of PLS, which is constrained by the exploration of a finite neighborhood.

A similar analysis on other problem classes and large-size instances, with computationally affordable features, would allow us to further understand and gain more knowledge about the main difficulties that EMO algorithms have to face, and eventually to predict their expected performance.

Acknowledgments

This work was partially supported by the Japanese-French JSPS project "Global Research on the Framework of Evolutionary Solution Search to Accelerate Innovation" (2013-2016), and by the Japanese-French JSPS-Inria project "Threefold Scalability in Any-objective Black-Box Optimization" (2015-2017).

6. REFERENCES

[1] H. E. Aguirre and K. Tanaka. Working principles, behavior, and performance of MOEAs on MNK-landscapes. *Eur J Oper Res*, 181(3):1670–1690, 2007.

[2] H. Akaike. Information theory as an extension of the maximum likelihood principle. In *Second International Symposium on Information Theory*, pages 267–281. Akademinai Kiado, 1973.

[3] A. Auger and N. Hansen. Performance evaluation of an advanced local search evolutionary algorithm. In *Evolutionary Computation, 2005. The 2005 IEEE Congress on*, volume 2, pages 1777–1784. IEEE, 2005.

[4] K. Bartoń. *MuMIn: Multi-Model Inference*, 2014. R package version 1.12.1.

[5] D. Bates, M. Mächler, B. Bolker, and S. Walker. Fitting linear mixed-effects models using lme4. *arXiv preprint arXiv:1406.5823*, 2014.

[6] K. P. Burnham and D. R. Anderson. *Model selection and multimodel inference: a practical information-theoretic approach*. Springer Science & Business Media, 2002.

[7] K. P. Burnham and D. R. Anderson. Multimodel inference understanding aic and bic in model selection. *Sociological methods & research*, 33(2):261–304, 2004.

[8] M. Chiarandini and Y. Goegebeur. Mixed models for the analysis of optimization algorithms. In *Experimental Methods for the Analysis of Optimization Algorithms*, volume 1, page 225. Springer, 2010.

[9] M. Ehrgott. *Multicriteria optimization*. Springer, 2005.

[10] J. J. Faraway. *Extending the linear model with R: generalized linear, mixed effects and nonparametric regression models*. Texts in Statistical Science. Chapman & Hall/CRC, 2005.

[11] F. Hutter, L. Xu, H. H. Hoos, and K. Leyton-Brown. Algorithm runtime prediction: Methods & evaluation. *Artificial Intelligence*, 206:79–111, 2014.

[12] S. A. Kauffman. *The Origins of Order*. Oxford University Press, 1993.

[13] J. Knowles and D. Corne. Instance generators and test suites for the multiobjective quadratic assignment problem. In *Evolutionary Multi-Criterion Optimization (EMO 2003)*, volume 2632 of *LNCS*, pages 295–310. Springer, 2003.

[14] M. Laumanns, L. Thiele, and E. Zitzler. Running time analysis of evolutionary algorithms on a simplified multiobjective knapsack problem. *Nat Comput*, 3(1):37–51, 2004.

[15] A. Liefooghe, L. Paquete, and J. R. Figueira. On local search for bi-objective knapsack problems. *Evol Comput*, 21(1):179–196, 2013.

[16] A. Liefooghe, S. Verel, H. Aguirre, and K. Tanaka. What makes an instance difficult for black-box 0–1 evolutionary multiobjective optimizers? In *International Conference on Artificial Evolution (EA 2013)*, volume 8752 of *LNCS*, pages 3–15, 2013.

[17] A. Liefooghe, S. Verel, F. Daolio, H. Aguirre, and K. Tanaka. A feature-based performance analysis in evolutionary multiobjective optimization. In *Evolutionary Multi-Criterion Optimization*, volume 9019 of *LNCS*, pages 95–109. Springer, 2015.

[18] A. McLeod. *Kendall: Kendall rank correlation and Mann-Kendall trend test*, 2011. R package version 2.2.

[19] S. Nakagawa and H. Schielzeth. A general and simple method for obtaining r2 from generalized linear mixed-effects models. *Methods in Ecology and Evolution*, 4(2):133–142, 2013.

[20] C. H. Papadimitriou and M. Yannakakis. On the approximability of trade-offs and optimal access of web sources. In *Symposium on Foundations of Computer Science (FOCS 2000)*, pages 86–92, 2000.

[21] L. Paquete, M. Chiarandini, and T. Stützle. Pareto local optimum sets in the biobjective traveling salesman problem: An experimental study. In *Metaheuristics for Multiobjective Optimisation*, volume 535 of *Lecture Notes in Economics and Mathematical Systems*, chapter 7, pages 177–199. Springer, 2004.

[22] L. Paquete, T. Schiavinotto, and T. Stützle. On local optima in multiobjective combinatorial optimization problems. *Ann Oper Res*, 156(1):83–97, 2007.

[23] L. Paquete and T. Stützle. Clusters of non-dominated solutions in multiobjective combinatorial optimization: An experimental analysis. In *Multiobjective Programming and Goal Programming*, volume 618 of *LNMES*, pages 69–77. Springer, 2009.

[24] S. Verel, A. Liefooghe, L. Jourdan, and C. Dhaenens. On the structure of multiobjective combinatorial search space: MNK-landscapes with correlated objectives. *Eur J Oper Res*, 227(2):331–342, 2013.

[25] E. Zitzler, L. Thiele, M. Laumanns, C. M. Foneseca, and V. Grunert da Fonseca. Performance assessment of multiobjective optimizers: An analysis and review. *IEEE Trans. Evol. Comput.*, 7(2):117–132, 2003.

On the Empirical Scaling Behaviour of State-of-the-art Local Search Algorithms for the Euclidean TSP

Jérémie Dubois-Lacoste
Université libre de Bruxelles
(ULB), IRIDIA
jduboisl@ulb.ac.be

Holger H. Hoos
University of British Columbia
(UBC)
hoos@cs.ubc.ca

Thomas Stützle
Université libre de Bruxelles
(ULB), IRIDIA
stuetzle@ulb.ac.be

ABSTRACT

We present a thorough empirical investigation of the scaling behaviour of state-of-the-art local search algorithms for the TSP; in particular, we study the scaling of running time required for finding optimal solutions to Euclidean TSP instances. We use a recently introduced bootstrapping approach to assess the statistical significance of the scaling models thus obtained and contrast these models with those recently reported for the Concorde algorithm. In particular, we answer the question whether the scaling behaviour of state-of-the-art local search algorithms for the TSP differs by more than a constant from that required by Concorde to find the first optimal solution to a given TSP instance.

1. INTRODUCTION

The TSP is one of the best-known combinatorial optimisation problems, and its pivotal role in the development and assessement of new algorithmic ideas could hardly be overestimated. Until recently, the state of the art in exact and inexact TSP solving has been defined by two long-standing incumbents: Concorde [2] and the Lin-Kernighan heuristic (LKH) [4, 5]. In 2013, Nagata and Kobayashi introduced EAX [13] – a new evolutionary algorithm for the TSP that makes use of an improved version of the edge assembly crossover operator [12] to achieve an effective recombination of sub-tours. Their empirical results suggest that EAX tends to perform better than the latest version of LKH and hence represents an improvement in the state of the art in inexact TSP solving. A recent study by Kotthoff *et al.* confirmed that, on aggregate, EAX performs better than LKH across a broad range of Euclidean TSP instances, but that EAX does not dominate LKH, in that there is a substantial number of instances on which LKH reaches tour qualities known to be optimal (from previous runs of Concorde) substantially faster [10].

In what follows, we study the empirical performance of EAX and LKH in more detail. In particular, we investigate the scaling of the median running time required by these state-of-the-art inexact TSP solvers for finding solutions to 2-dimensional Euclidean TSP instances that are known to be optimal (from previous, typically much longer runs of Concorde). We focus on 2D Euclidean TSP instances, since they constitute arguably the most widely studied special case of the general TSP, and because 2D instances occur in many practical applications [1, 3]. Our study is inspired by recent results we obtained on the empirical scaling of Concorde's running time on Euclidean TSP instances with instance size (number of cities), n, according to which median running time closely follows a function of the form $a \cdot b^{\sqrt{n}}$ [8]. Furthermore, in this previous study, we reported log-normal distributions of running time over sets of instances and showed that Concorde's performance on structured 2D Euclidean TSP instances generally agrees well with the scaling model derived from random uniform Euclidean (RUE) instances.

Specifically, in this work, we are interested in answering the following questions:

1. How does the performance of state-of-the-art inexact TSP solvers scale with instance size?
2. How does the performance scaling of these solvers compare to that of the state-of-the-art exact TSP solver, Concorde?
3. Are there qualitative differences between the performance scaling of EAX and LKH?
4. How does the variation of performance across sets of TSP instances of the same size compare between EAX, LKH and Concorde?

Regarding Questions 1 and 2, as we will show, there are interesting qualitative differences between the scaling behaviour of Concorde and that of EAX and LKH. In particular, while the scaling of running time for EAX and LKH is consistent with the same two-parameter root-exponential model, $a \cdot b^{\sqrt{n}}$, previously established for Concorde, there is clear evidence that the scaling parameter b is significantly lower for EAX and LKH (when an appropriate restarting mechanism is used). Furthermore, regarding Question 3, there is weak evidence that the performance of EAX might scale better with instance size than that of the latest version of LKH. Finally, regarding Question 4, unlike in the case of Concorde, the running times of EAX and LKH are not log-normally distributed for fixed instance size, and the distributions for EAX are distinctly multi-modal. Still, we found no evidence for substantially different scaling between the median and higher quantiles of these distributions.

GECCO '15, July 11–15, 2015, Madrid, Spain
© 2015 ACM. ISBN 978-1-4503-3472-3/15/07...$15.00
DOI: http://dx.doi.org/10.1145/2739480.2754747

The remainder of this article is structured as follows. In Section 2, we introduce the instance sets, the algorithms and the analysis methods we used. We present our experimental results in Section 3. Finally, in Section 4, we discuss our results and their implications before closing with a brief outlook on future work.

2. INSTANCES, ALGORITHMS, METHODS

2.1 Benchmark instances

We performed experiments on Euclidean TSP instances stemming from two primary sources: RUE instances of various sizes and real-world instances from TSPLIB and from http://www.math.uwaterloo.ca/tsp/data/.

The RUE instances were generated by placing uniformly at random n points in a $100\,000 \times 100\,000$ square and computing the Euclidean distances between the points, using the `portgen` generator from the 8th DIMACS implementation challenge on the TSP. We produced 1000 instances for each instance size $n \in \{500, 600, .., 2000\}$ and 100 instances for each $n \in \{2500, 3000, 4000, 4500\}$. In previous studies, we have determined optimal solutions for most of these instances, using Concorde [2], the best performing exact algorithm for the TSP [8]; since these computations are very expensive, we used the same instances and optimal solutions.

2.2 Helsgaun's Lin-Kernighan heuristic

Helsgaun's variant of the Lin-Kernighan heuristic (LKH) represents a major advance in inexact TSP solving, and for many years, it was the uncontested state-of-the-art method for finding high-quality solutions to a large variety of TSP instances [4, 5]. The Lin-Kernighan (LK) heuristic is a variable-depth search method that generates complex local search moves by heuristically constructing a sequence of edge exchanges. Helsgaun's variant of LK is based on exchange sequences using five [4] or more edge exchanges [5]. The iterated version of the LKH algorithm restarts the local search process from new solutions that are obtained by solution perturbations, which are performed using either a random k-exchange move or a special walk strategy. Furthermore, an approximation of the Held-Karp lower bound is used to obtain small candidate sets for the local search steps.

For our experiments, we used the most recent version 2.0.7 of LKH, as well as the earlier version 1.3. After observing stagnation behaviour in LKH 1.3 and LKH 2.0.7 (which, from here on, we refer to as LKH 2), we enhanced both versions with a restart mechanism (for details see Section 2.4). Apart from the additional restart mechanism, LKH 1.3 was run with its default parameter setting. LKH version 2 comes with example parameter files for tackling TSPLIB instance `pr2392`, where the default parameter settings are modified to include patching of cycles during the search for improving moves (setting `PATCHING_A = 2` and `PATCHING_C = 3`). We compared these recommended settings to the default parameter settings for LKH 2, which would switch this patching of cycles off. As the default settings resulted in worse performance in solving `pr2392`, we used the modified parameters for all further experiments with LKH 2.

2.3 GA with edge assembly crossover

In recent years, several high-performing evolutionary algorithms for the TSP have been proposed [11]. The most successful lines of research mainly dealt with the integration of high-performance local search algorithms into so-called memetic algorithms and the development of specialized recombination operators. The most successful outcome of this work are the evolutionary algorithms integrating variants of edge assembly cross-over – a recombination operator that combines the edges of two parent solutions trying to add only few, short edges not found in any of the two parents [12].

The first such algorithm known to have reached the performance of LKH, and hence state-of-the-art performance, in finding very high quality solutions to a broad range of Euclidean TSP instances (as considered in our work) is EAX, the genetic algorithm by Nagata & Kobayashi [13]. In a nutshell, EAX exploits improved local and global variants of the edge assembly cross-over operator, specific diversity preservation techniques that uses edge entropy measures in the population replacement scheme, and initialization of the population by local optimization. (For a detailed description of the algorithm and the operators, we refer the reader to the original publication by Nagata & Kobayashi [13].)

Computational results by Nagata & Kobayashi indicate that on many large Euclidean TSP instances, EAX performs better than LKH 2; specifically, they reported that on 50 out of 57 TSPLIB, VLSI and National instances of sizes between 4 461 and 60 000 cities, EAX produced statistically significantly better solutions than LKH in shorter computation times [13]. (Our experiments comparing EAX to LKH 2 shed further light on their relative performance.)

In what follows, we used EAX with its default parameter settings, as specified in the publically available code, using a population size of 100 (which appeared to be sufficient for the instance sizes we tackled) and 30 offspring generated for each attempt of recombining two parent tours (applying the EAX recombination operator repeatedly to two given parent solutions allows to generate several different offspring). The original version of EAX does not support termination upon reaching a given solution quality and used a complex termination criterion to end runs. We modified this version to terminate upon reaching a target solution quality (in our experiments always set to the known optima for the given instances) and to restart whenever the original termination criterion is met, as discussed in more detail in the following.

2.4 Restarts

In this work, we examine the scaling behavior of LKH and EAX for reaching optimal solutions on RUE instances. Ideally, as a pre-requisite, we should ensure that LKH and EAX find an optimal solution in each run. Unfortunately, it is known that even high-performing local search algorithms can be prone to stagnation behaviour [14, 7]. As it happens, this holds for the two high-performance TSP algorithms we consider here. It is clearly seen from the run-time distributions shown in Figure 1 for EAX (all running times were measured on the reference machines specified in Section 2.5).

In fact, especially EAX exhibits a very particular run-time behaviour: It typically requires a relatively high initialisation time until the search process starts producing very high-quality solutions, but once it does, even better solutions are frequently found quite rapidly. However, some runs of EAX are terminated prematurely, based on a built-in, complex criterion. Clearly, the behaviour of EAX can be improved by restarting the search rather than terminating it. Similarly,

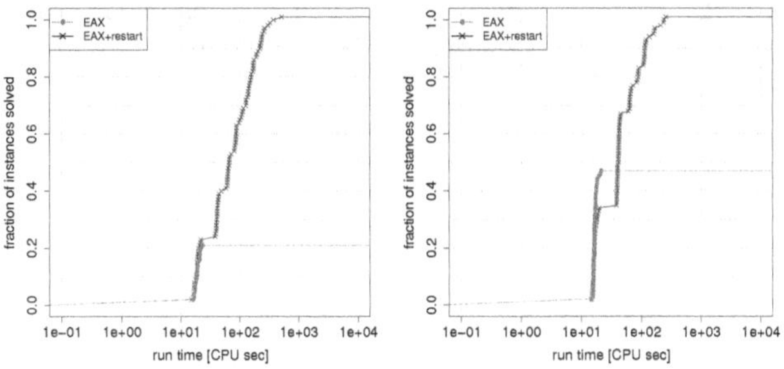

Figure 1: Distributions of running times over multiple independent runs of EAX with and without restart on two RUE instances of size 1500.

we observed stagnation behaviour that could be remedied using a restart mechanism for both versions of LKH.

Based on these observations, we modified the original EAX to perform restarts whenever its original termination criterion is met, and to terminate only when a given target solution quality or CPU time cutoff is reached. In the following, we simply refer to this variant as EAX. Furthermore, we augmented LKH 1.3 and LKH 2 with a mechanism that would trigger a restart when during n iterations, where n is the size of the TSP instance to be solved, no improved solution has been found. From here on, whenever we refer to LKH 1.3 and LKH 2, we mean their versions with restarts.

2.5 Computing environment and experimental setup

We performed all algorithm runs used in our experiments on a cluster of computing nodes equipped with a 2.0 GHz eight-core AMD 6128 processor and 2×12MB L2/L3 cache as well as 16GB RAM each, running Cluster Rocks Linux 6.0/CentOS 6.3. The programmes were compiled with gcc 4.4.6 (using optimization flag `-O3` and run on a single CPU core, as the implementations are all fully sequential. We ran Concorde on those same machines, to ensure comparability of results. We further note that the machines are similar to those used in our previous analysis of the scaling of Concorde's running time [8].

For each of the instances that were solved to optimality by Concorde[1] we performed 10 independent runs of each of LKH 1.3, LKH 2.0.7 and EAX. We chose cutoff times that ensured that all runs of these algorithms were always successful in producing an optimal solution. From those sets of 10 runs per instance and algorithm, we computed median CPU times for each algorithm and instance. All further analysis were performed based on those performance measurements.

2.6 Scaling analysis

To study the scaling of EAX and LKH with instance size n, we considered quantiles (particularly, the median) of the distributions of running times obtained for sets of RUE instances with various fixed values of n. Following [8], we considered the following three 2-parameter scaling models:

- exponential: $Exp[a,b](n) = a \cdot b^n$
- polynomial: $Poly[a,b](n) = a \cdot n^b$
- square-root exponential: $SRExp[a,b](n) = a \cdot b^{\sqrt{n}}$

Our scaling analysis was performed using performance data for EAX, LKH 2 and LKH 1.3 on instance sizes $n = 500, 600, \ldots, 1500$ (the so-called support for our models); specifically, we fitted each scaling model on 11 data points, one for each instance size. The fitting was performed using the nonlinear least-squares Marquardt-Levenberg algorithm implemented by the 'fit' command of the *gnuplot* software.

To asses the degree to which the predictions made by our scaling models are affected by the precise sets of instances in our support, we employed the bootstrapping procedure introduced by Hoos [6] and that we used in our previous study of Concorde [8]: we generated $m = 1000$ samples of algorithm performance data for each instance size in the support (using uniform random sampling with replacement), and for each of these bootstrap samples, we fitted our scaling model to obtain m sets of performance predictions for the large challenge instance sizes. From these sets of predictions, we generated bootstrap confidence intervals for confidence level $\alpha = 0.95$, resulting in an interval $CI = [Q(0.5 - \alpha/2), Q(0.5 + \alpha/2]$, where $Q(x)$ denotes the x-quantile of the distribution of the predicted performance values.

3. EXPERIMENTAL RESULTS

3.1 Performance correlation

As a first step in our analysis, we examined the correlation of the median running times among our three inexact solvers and between these and Concorde. Figure 2 shows scatter plots between running times for pairs of solvers for $n = 1500$; results for other n look quite similar and are summarised by the correlation coefficients shown in Table 1. We note that the correlation of the running times of Concorde and the inexact solvers is very low, as can be seen from the scatter plots for Concorde *vs* EAX (top plot) and LKH 2 (second from top), as well as from the low correlation coefficients of 0.0925 and 0.1716, respectively (*cf.* Table 1). More surprisingly, the performance correlation between EAX and LKH 2 (but also LKH 1.3, not shown here) is also very low, as seen from the third scatter plot in Figure 2 (the corresponding correlation coefficient is 0.0611). Only for the two versions of LKH, performance correlation is somewhat higher (bottom-most plot, correlation coefficient 0.512), but still surprisingly low, considering the overall conceptual similarity between LKH 2 and LKH 1.3.

These results suggest that we have no reason to expect the performance of these TSP algorithms to show the same scaling behaviour (in contrast to a hypothetical situation where performance correlations at different instance sizes had been very tight). Consistent with recent work by Kotthoff *et al.* [10], our results also clearly demonstrate the potential for achieving performance gains using portfolio techniques, such as algorithm selection. On the instance sizes we considered, as well as on structured instances (see Section 4), we found no evidence that the performance of any of our three inexact solvers would be dominated by any of the others, even as n is growing. However, we did see some evidence suggesting that, in terms of simply finding high-quality solutions to Eu-

[1]For instance sizes up to $n = 3000$, all instances were solved to optimality; for larger instance sizes, we mention the details where relevant.

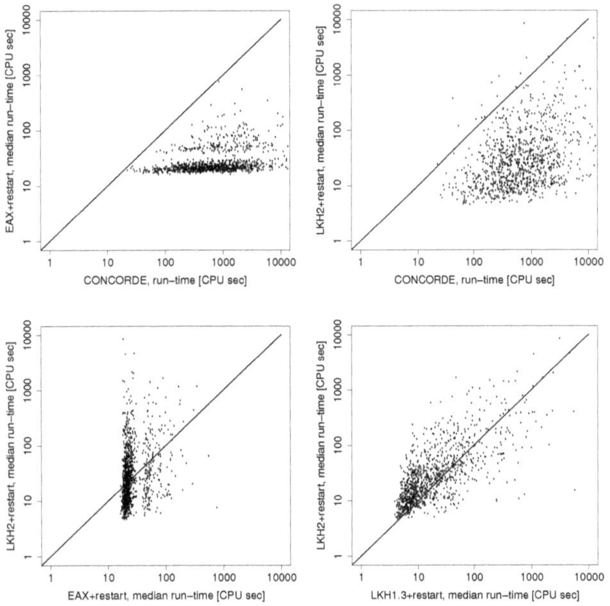

Figure 2: Median running time of Concorde *vs* EAX (top left), Concorde *vs* LKH 2 (top right), EAX *vs* LKH 2 (bottom left) and LKH 1.3 vs LKH 2 (bottom right) on RUE instances, $n = 1500$.

clidean TSP instances, for large n, Concorde performs worse than the inexact solvers (data not shown).

3.2 Empirical scaling on small instances

As a first step of our the scaling analysis, we visually examined the scaling of the median and the 0.1 and 0.9 quantiles, $Q(0.1)$ and $Q(0.9)$, of the distributions of (median) running times over RUE instance sets for $n \in \{500, \ldots 1500\}$, which are the same instances used in a previous analysis (support data) [8]. As can be seen in Figure 3, all three solvers show roughly linear median scaling curves in a log-log plot, indicating close to polynomial scaling. For both versions of LKH, the scaling curves for $Q(0.9)$ are roughly parallel to that for the median, which indicates a constant factor between the corresponding running times, and hence suggests that scaling on the hardest instances is not worse than observed for the median. For EAX, on the other hand, there is a strong increase in $Q(0.9)$ between $n = 900$ and $n = 1100$, after which the scaling curves seem to become parallel again. The main reason for this is that for increasing n, EAX requires restarts on an increasing fraction of the instances to solve them to optimality, while small instances are often solved without restarting the search process. The high initialization time incurred by EAX, thus, causes multiple modes to appear in its running time distributions, which in turn induces the observed scaling of $Q(0.9)$ (and other high quantiles). Further insights into this behavior are given in Section 3.5. The 0.1 quantile for EAX is very close to the median, as a large fraction of the instances (especially for small n) are solved without restarting. For LKH 2 and LKH 1.3, $Q(0.1)$ is significantly lower than the median, but seems to be scaling similarly.

Next, we fitted our three two-parameter scaling models to the median running times from this support data. Table 3 shows the root mean square error (RMSE) for each of the models we fitted. In all cases, the exponential models give the worst fit, that is, they have the highest RMSE values. For both variants of LKH, the best fit is obtained from the root-exponential model, while for EAX, the polynomial model has the lowest RMSE. Table 2 shows the best-fit models obtained for each algorithm. The base b of the root-exponential model of LKH 2 is smaller ($b = 1.18264$) than in the case of LKH 1.3 ($b = 1.19592$), indicating better scaling behaviour of LKH 2. The exponent of the polynomial model for EAX is $b = 1.95417$, indicating slightly less than quadratic scaling of median running time with instance size.

Table 2: Best-fit scaling models (*i.e.*, those with minimal RMSE), as specified in Section 2.6.

Algorithm	Best-fit model	a	b
EAX	Poly	1.38225e-05	1.95417
LKH 2	SRexp	0.03481	1.18264
LKH 1.3	SRexp	0.01362	1.19592

Table 3: RMSE of scaling models on support data.

Model	RMSE		
	EAX	LKH 2	LKH 1.3
Poly	0.10306	0.54834	0.37975
Exp	0.78518	0.58083	0.29718
SRexp	0.43369	0.44632	0.27701

3.3 Performance scaling on larger instances

Next, we assessed the predictive power of our models by comparing predicted and observed performance on larger instances sizes (challenge data), with $n \in \{2500, \ldots 4500\}$. In this context, we encountered a difficulty, in that for $n > 3000$, we do not have optimal tour lengths for all TSP instances, since Concorde (even with the 7 CPU day running time cutoff that was used in [8]) was unable to solve some instances. Considering the lack of tight performance correlation between Concorde and the solvers considered here (see Section 3.1), some of those instances might be easy for EAX or LKH. Therefore, there is uncertainty about the precise location of the medians of the running time distributions at each such n, and we can only provide bounds on those medians instead. These bounds are based on the best and worst case scenarios, in which all instances unsolved by Concorde are easiest or hardest, respectively, for the algorithm in question. We note that these are not confidence intervals, since we can guarantee the actual median running times to lie within them. (As we will discuss further in Section 4, there may be ways to tighten or collapse those bounds, but they would come at considerable computational cost.)

From the resulting intervals for observed medians, we derived lower and upper bounds on the RMSEs for all models, which are given in Table 4. From these bounds, we observed that, for all three solvers, the exponential scaling model agrees least with the observed performance values, as in all cases it has by far highest RMSE intervals. For EAX and LKH 1.3, the root-exponential scaling model agrees best with observed performance, while for LKH 2, the polynomial model shows the smallest bounds on RMSE. We note how these results differ from the conclusions drawn based

Table 1: Pearson correlation coefficient between running times of EAX, LKH 2, LKH 1.3 and Concorde (Crd) on sets of RUE instances of size n.

n	500	600	700	800	900	1000	1100	1200	1300	1400	1500	2000	2500	3000	3500	4000	4500
EAX, LKH 1.3	0.0943	-0.001	0.0805	0.0476	-0.001	0.0766	0.0269	0.0205	0.0716	0.0343	0.0454	0.0646	0.0951	0.1771	0.1724	-0.0226	0.0457
EAX, LKH 2	0.2191	0.0052	0.0788	0.092	0.0022	0.0337	0.0492	0.066	0.0903	0.0258	0.0611	0.0834	0.4793	0.2714	0.1609	0.2761	0.1277
EAX, Crd	0.2038	0.2153	0.2688	0.076	0.0861	0.1364	0.1426	0.1556	0.1687	0.0798	0.0925	0.1582	0.4825	0.1343	0.1545	0.1407	0.0522
LKH 1.3, LKH 2	0.4518	0.6032	0.382	0.1564	0.3777	0.145	0.7311	0.273	0.5551	0.5083	0.512	0.3855	0.405	0.3824	0.6478	0.5681	0.4582
LKH 1.3, Crd	0.1667	0.087	0.1722	0.0464	0.0532	0.0308	0.1097	0.0961	0.0405	0.1821	0.163	0.11	0.2101	0.0349	0.3144	0.0489	-0.0278
LKH 2, Crd	0.4608	0.0577	0.1251	0.0726	-0.0044	0.0235	0.0921	0.2034	0.1135	0.0748	0.1716	0.0934	0.6921	0.2203	0.0569	0.2693	-0.0299

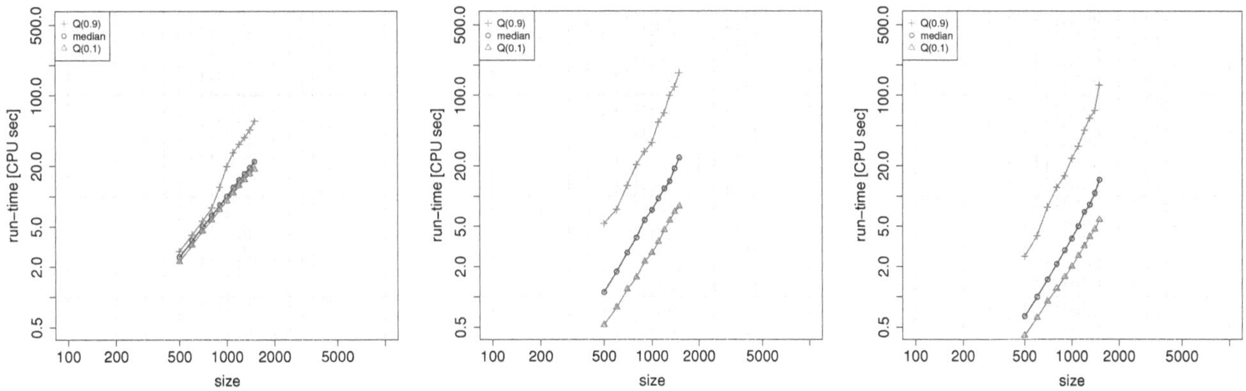

Figure 3: Empirical scaling of median, $Q(0.1)$ and $Q(0.9)$ running time of EAX (left), LKH 2 (middle) and LKH 1.3 (right) on RUE instance sets.

Table 4: RMSE for scaling models from Section 3.2 on challenge data.

Model	RMSE
	EAX
Poly	[103.6738, 328.7718]
Exp	[1738.077, 1979.996]
SRexp	[8.760844, 158.3214]
	LKH 2
Poly	[114.694, 488.5378]
Exp	[13944.76, 14365.05]
SRexp	[516.7933, 930.916]
	LKH 1.3
Poly	[642.3105, 1613.221
Exp	[12046.95, 13052.59]
SRexp	[101.087, 778.7793]

on performance observed on support data only; the reason for this lies likely in somewhat different scaling of algorithm performance for small n.

3.4 Statistical assessment of scaling models

As first observed by Hoos [6], model fits can substantially depend on the samples of instances for each n used as support data. Therefore, we statistically assess model predictions using the bootstrap method outlined in Section 2.6. Because of the uncertainty in our observed median running times discussed earlier, this assessment is slightly more involved. In the following, we say that a scaling model is *inconsistent* with observed data of the interval formed by the bounds on the observed medians described in Section 3.3 if it is disjoint from the bootstrap confidence interval for predicted running times; we say that a scaling model is *consistent* with observed data, if the interval for observed medians overlaps with, but is not fully contained within the bootstrap confidence interval for predicted running times; we say that a scaling model is *strongly consistent* with observed data, if the interval for observed medians is fully contained within the bootstrap confidence interval for predicted running times.

As can be seen in Table 5, for EAX and both versions of LKH, the exponential models are almost all inconsistent with our observations (with the only exception being LKH 2 for $n = 2000$) and should therefore be dismissed. For EAX, the polynomial model is also inconsistent with our observations, while the root-exponential model is consistent for $n \geq 3500$. For LKH 2, the root-exponential model is strongly consistent with the observed performance for $n = 2000$ but inconsistent for larger n, while the polynomial model is inconsistent up to $n = 4000$ and consistent for $n = 4500$, but with relatively small overlap between the intervals. For LKH 1.3, the root-exponential model is consistent with our observations, and even strongly consistent for n up to 4000; the polynomial model, on the other hand, is inconsistent for all n.

In summary, among the models considered here, the root-exponential model best explains scaling behaviour observed for EAX and LKH 1.3, while the scaling for LKH 2 seems to lie somewhere between the polynomial and the root-exponential model. Specifically, LKH 1.3 most likely shows root-exponential scaling of median running time with instance size n, while LKH 2 seems to perform slightly better than suggested by the root-exponential model with some possibility of polynomial scaling for sufficiently large n; EAX likely

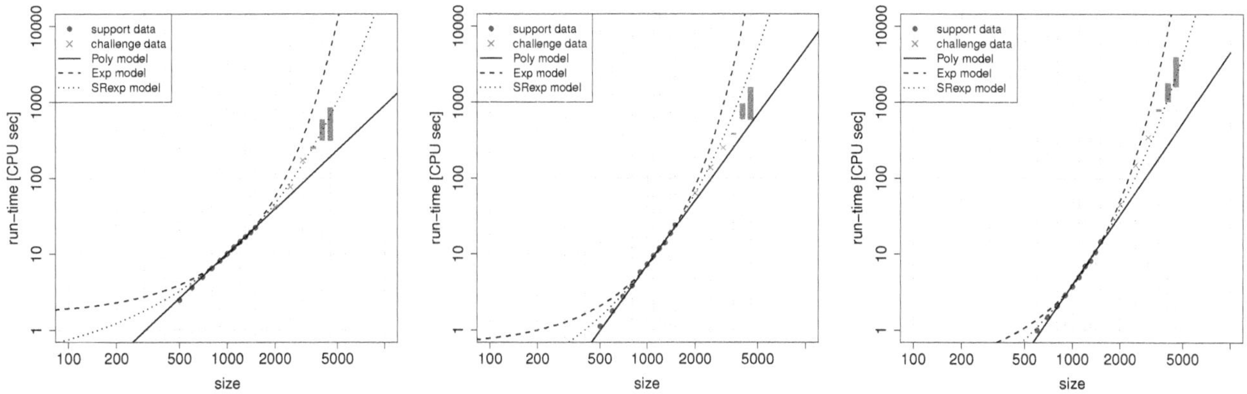

Figure 4: Scaling models of median running time (fitted on support data) and observed data for sets of larger challenge instance for EAX (left), LKH 2 (middle) and LKH 1.3 (right).

Table 6: Confidence intervals for parameter values for scaling models fitted on bootstrapped support data.

Best-fit model	a	b
	EAX	
Poly	[1.27095e-05, 1.60351e-05]	[1.93245, 1.96595]
Exp	[1.58004, 1.62804]	[1.00176, 1.00180]
SRexp	[0.22357, 0.23809]	[1.12461, 1.12681]
	LKH 2	
Poly	[1.10147e-08, 9.25764e-09]	[2.74510, 3.09874]
Exp	[0.47657, 1.00000]	[1.00206, 1.00265]
SRexp	[0.02201, 0.04205]	[1.17617, 1.19873]
	LKH 1.3	
Poly	[1.07808e-09, 9.25297e-10]	[3.01844, 3.54762]
Exp	[0.18548, 0.29762]	[1.00255, 1.00296]
SRexp	[0.00560, 0.01455]	[1.19302, 1.22686]
	Concorde	
Poly	[8.69e-11, 8.44e-9]	[3.46, 4.11]
Exp	[6.71, 11.21]	[1.00292, 1.00334]
SRexp	[0.115, 0.373]	[1.2212, 1.2630]

scales root-exponentially for sufficiently large n, with a small possibility of polynomial scaling.

Our bootstrap scaling analysis also produces confidence intervals for the model parameters. As seen in Table 6, EAX scales substantially better than LKH 2, which, in turn, scales somewhat better than LKH 1.3 (as one would expect). Compared to the confidence intervals for the parameters of the root-exponential scaling model for Concorde reported in [8] and also shown in the table, EAX and LKH 2 show significantly better scaling than Concorde, and LKH 1.3 seems to scale slightly better (although the respective confidence intervals for the scaling parameter b overlap minimally).

3.5 Performance variation for fixed instance size

In Figure 5, we show distributions of median running time per instance over sets of RUE instances of a fixed size. We clearly observe that distributions for EAX are multi-modal. Closer examination revealed that this is a consequence of the fact that the complex restart mechanism fails to com-

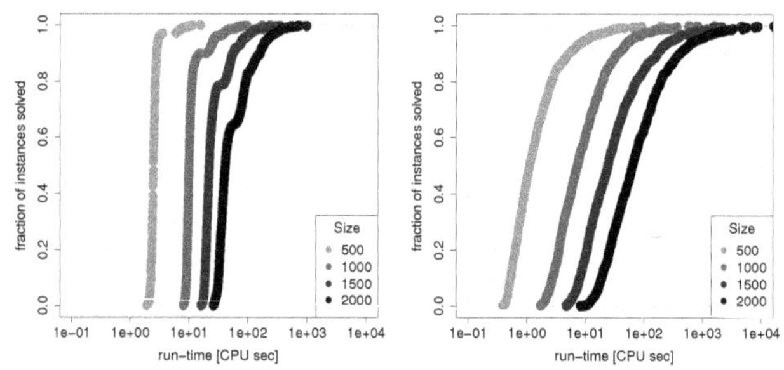

Figure 5: Cumulative distribution functions of running time for EAX (left) and LKH 2 (right) over sets of RUE instances. The plot for LKH 1.3 (not shown here) looks qualitatively similar to that for LKH 2.

pletely avoid stagnation behaviour. As n grows, the fraction of instances that can be solved without restart drops, while the fraction of instances that do require restarts increases. Each mode (visible as a 'hump' in the empirical CDF) corresponds to a set of instances for which a specific number of restarts has been performed. Still, from examining the right tails of the CFDs, there is no clear evidence that the running time for the most difficult instances increases faster than observed at median difficulty, once restarts are required. This is consistent with what we observed earlier, in Section 3.2.

The situation for LKH is qualitatively different: Here, the distributions of median running time across instances for fixed n show no sign of multi-modality, indicating that the restart mechanism we added to the original implementations of LKH 1.3 and LKH 2 does not suffer from the type of stagnation found in EAX. Again, there is no evidence that the higher quantiles of these distributions scale worse than the median. However, different from the situation from Concorde, where the distributions were characterised as log-normal [8], here, we find distributions that deviate from log-normality, as clearly evident from the fact that the CDFs, shown in the semi-log plot, are not point-symmetrical (as all log-normal distributions would be).

Table 5: Bootstrap confidence intervals for predicted median running times, obtained from scaling models fitted on bootstrapped support data.

size	Poly model	Exp model	Root-exp model	observed (corrected) median
		EAX		
2000	[38.36, 39.26]	[55.28, 56.87]	[45.46, 46.62]	41.45
2500	[59.05, 60.87]	[133.48, 139.32]	[84.51, 87.57]	76.34
3000	[84.01, 87.12]	[322.12, 341.19]	[148.03, 154.79]	170.79
3500	[113.18, 117.97]	[777.61, 835.37]	[247.87, 261.36]	[243.59, 260.79]
4000	[146.48, 153.38]	[1877.36, 2045.64]	[400.44, 425.62]	[313.49, 589.76]
4500	[183.92, 193.35]	[4532.43, 5009.62]	[628.24, 672.96]	[311.17, 844.59]
		LKH 2		
2000	[48.75, 58.89]	[62.43, 93.83]	[59.59, 72.93]	62.64
2500	[90.08, 117.75]	[175.50, 351.54]	[140.75, 189.98]	137.02
3000	[148.70, 207.19]	[493.34, 1312.54]	[305.19, 451.79]	249.37
3500	[226.89, 334.09]	[1386.78, 4914.56]	[621.91, 1001.17]	[379.97, 382.77]
4000	[327.52, 505.51]	[3898.22, 18466.95]	[1208.54, 2098.30]	[594.94, 951.26]
4500	[451.91, 728.46]	[10957.83, 69105.15]	[2255.56, 4205.25]	[581.69, 1553.86]
		LKH 1.3		
2000	[31.40, 41.92]	[49.05, 68.61]	[38.70, 52.34]	45.1002
2500	[61.70, 92.38]	[175.60, 299.54]	[98.44, 153.35]	142.2693
3000	[106.99, 175.92]	[629.27, 1315.31]	[229.61, 405.85]	328.0472
3500	[170.76, 302.96]	[2255.04, 5777.80]	[497.01, 996.14]	[768.9041, 814.4542]
4000	[256.17, 486.24]	[8081.02, 25262.33]	[1019.59, 2296.28]	[1023.6704, 1822.6779]
4500	[366.26, 738.27]	[28958.66, 110454.73]	[2003.86, 5031.37]	[1630.5511, 3970.6894]

4. DISCUSSION

The results from our scaling analysis clearly rule out pure exponential scaling of the median running time required by any of the three high-performance state-of-the-art TSP solvers we studied, EAX, LKH 2 and LKH 1.3 (all equipped with restart mechanisms) to find optimal solutions of RUE instances. This is not surprising, since Concorde, which also proves optimality when run to completion, has also been shown to have more benign scaling behaviour than a simple exponential function on this widely studied type of TSP instances [8]. In fact, Concorde's median scaling of running time with instance size appears to closely follow $a \cdot b^{\sqrt{n}}$ with $a \in [0.115, 0.373]$ and $b \in [1.2212, 1.2630]$. Therefore, one would expect the scaling behaviour of high-performance inexact TSP solvers to be no worse.

In fact, our study provided evidence consistent with the hypothesis that EAX and LKH 1.3 show scaling of the same fundamental type as Concorde, albeit with smaller constants b. Our analysis is complicated by the fact that for $n > 3000$, provably optimal solutions to some RUE instances could not be obtained. This limitation also applies to an earlier study [8], but has less impact there, where the missing data points do not affect the medians used in the scaling analysis. Because the algorithms we studied here are inexact, and their performance does not correlate tightly with Concorde, we can merely bound the median running times for any set that contains instances unsolved by Concorde. As a result, even though the bootstrap confidence intervals obtained for the predictions made using our three families of models do not overlap for the most part, our observations are not entirely inconsistent with the hypothesis of polynomial scaling of the LKH 2 variant. However, considering the relatively small overlap of the interval between our bounds for the median running times on our challenge data and the respective bootstrap confidence intervals, we believe that polynomial scaling may not be very likely.

Assuming root-exponential scaling for all three inexact solvers (note that for LKH 2 the root-exponential scaling seems to overestimate actual media run-times), it becomes interesting to compare the parameters of the respective scaling models, and in particular, the parameter b, which mostly determines the scaling behaviour. We say that an algorithm A scales better than an algorithm B if, and only if, we have reason to believe that the b value of the scaling model for A is lower than that for B. Our analysis clearly suggests that, in this sense, EAX scales better than LKH 2 ($b \in [1.1246, 1.1268]$ *vs* $b \in [1.1762, 1.1987]$), which in turn scales likely better than LKH 1.3 ($b \in [1.1930, 1.2268]$). As one would expect, EAX and the current version of LKH scale better than Concorde ($b \in [1.2212, 1.2630]$), and the same is likely the case for LKH 1.3. This provides solid evidence in support of common experience suggesting that when tackling very large TSP instances, inexact algorithms are the only feasible means to obtain optimal or near-optimal solutions.

Our readers may object that comparing the scaling of an exact solver with that of an inexact solver is misleading, since after all, the exact solver will find optimal solutions possibly long before being able to complete a proof of optimality; however, recent empirical results suggest that, at least for Concorde on Euclidean TSP instances like the ones studied here, this tends to not be the case, as the fraction of Concorde's overall running time spent before an optimal solution is first encountered approaches 1 as n increases [9]. This implies that the median running time required by Concorde for first finding an optimal solution (without completing a proof of optimality) scales somewhat *worse* than its overall running time (although asymptotically, the scaling would become indistinguishable).

Naturally, we were interested to see whether the predictions obtained from the scaling models for RUE instances were consistent with the running times observed by the inexact solvers we considered on structured TSP instances, such as the ones in TSPLIB or the VLSI and National sets from http://www.math.uwaterloo.ca/tsp/data/. We found that LKH 2 and EAX found optimal solutions for most of these instances in the size range we considered for RUE within running times quite consistent with our predictions. However, in a few cases, both solvers had substantial difficulties in finding the optimal solutions. This concerns in particular the TSPLIB instances `fl3795`, `u2319` and, to a lesser extent, `fl1577`. For these instances, either optimal solutions could not be found at all (notably, for `fl3795`), or solving times where orders of magnitude larger as would be expected from the confidence intervals obtained from our root-exponential models. One reason for these discrepancies lies in the fact that the structure of those instances is markedly different from those found in RUE and many other types of 2D Euclidean TSP instances, in that they contain a small number of well-separated, large clusters of cities or cities that are arranged in a grid pattern. We note that, although these instances are difficult for EAX or LKH, they are not necessarily hard to solve for other TSP solvers based on stochastic local search [14].

Our analysis could be extended in three directions. Firstly, it would be nice to reduce the uncertainty in analysis arising from the instances for which optimal solutions are not known. This could be done by attempting even longer runs for Concorde, although, considering the cutoff of 7 CPU days used to determine the optimal solutions used here, it is unclear how effective this would be. Another possibility would be to perform multiple long runs of Concorde on these instances using different pseudo-random number seeds, since it is known that running times can vary significantly with seeds. Yet another option would be run extensive experiments with cutting-edge inexact solvers to create pseudo-optimal solutions, and to then use these as a basis for scaling analysis. Although this may introduce errors, as these solution may in fact not be optimal, the very high performance of EAX and LKH 2 with restarts we observed when solving large RUE instances suggests that the incidence of such errors should be very small.

Secondly, we may build scaling models from support sets consisting of larger instances sizes, to reduce the possible impact of changes in the scaling behaviour as the instances become reasonably challenging. To asses the extent to which such impact may have coloured our findings, we have repeated our scaling analysis using the instance sets for $n = \{1000, 1100, 1200, 1400, 1500, 2000\}$ as the support data for fitting scaling models and found that the qualitative results remain similar, although the confidence intervals for model predictions and model parameters tend to be smaller.

Finally, we note that the inexact solvers we studied all have parameters that impact their performance and may affect scaling behaviour. To investigate to which extent optimising these parameters (or the heuristic mechanisms they control) may not only improve performance, but also the scaling of performance with instance size, is an interesting direction for future work.

Acknowledgments. This research and its results have been made possible through funding from the COMEX project (P7/36) within the Interuniversity Attraction Poles Programme of the Belgian Science Policy Office. HH acknowledges funding through an NSERC Discovery Grant. TS acknowledges support from the Belgian F.R.S.-FNRS, of which he is a Senior Research Associate.

5. REFERENCES

[1] D. Applegate, R. E. Bixby, V. Chvátal, and W. J. Cook. *The Traveling Salesman Problem: A Computational Study.* Princeton University Press, Princeton, NJ, 2006.

[2] D. Applegate, R. E. Bixby, V. Chvátal, and W. J. Cook. Concorde TSP solver. http://www.math.uwaterloo.ca/tsp/concorde.html, 2014. Version visited last on 15 April 2014.

[3] W. J. Cook. *In Pursuit of the Traveling Salesman.* Princeton University Press, Princeton, NJ, 2012.

[4] K. Helsgaun. An effective implementation of the Lin-Kernighan traveling salesman heuristic. *European Journal of Operational Research*, 126:106–130, 2000.

[5] K. Helsgaun. General k-opt submoves for the Lin-Kernighan TSP heuristic. *Mathematical Programming Computation*, 1(2–3):119–163, 2009.

[6] H. H. Hoos. A bootstrap approach to analysing the scaling of empirical run-time data with problem size. Technical Report TR-2009-16, University of British Columbia, June 2009. Available on-line at http://www.cs.ubc.ca/ hoos/Publ/Hoos09.pdf.

[7] H. H. Hoos and T. Stützle. *Stochastic Local Search—Foundations and Applications.* Morgan Kaufmann Publishers, San Francisco, CA, 2005.

[8] H. H. Hoos and T. Stützle. On the empirical scaling of run-time for finding optimal solutions to the traveling salesman problem. *European Journal of Operational Research*, 238(1):87–94, 2014.

[9] H. H. Hoos and T. Stützle. On the empirical time complexity of finding optimal solutions *vs* proving optimality for Euclidean TSP instances. *Optimization Letters*, 2015, DOI: 0.1007/s11590-014-0828-5.

[10] L. Kotthoff, P. Kerschke, H. H. Hoos, and H. Trautmann. Improving the state of the art in inexact TSP solving using per-instance algorithm selection. In C. Dhaenens, L. Jourdan, and M.-E. Marmion, editors, *Proceedings of Learning and Intelligent OptimizatioN Conference, LION 9, Lille, France*, January 2015.

[11] P. Merz and B. Freisleben. Memetic algorithms for the traveling salesman problem. *Complex Systems*, 13(4):297–345, 2001.

[12] Y. Nagata and S. Kobayashi. Edge assembly crossover: A high-power genetic algorithm for the traveling salesman problem. In T. Bäck, editor, *ICGA*, pages 450–457. Morgan Kaufmann Publishers, San Francisco, CA, 1997.

[13] Y. Nagata and S. Kobayashi. A powerful genetic algorithm using edge assembly crossover for the traveling salesman problem. *INFORMS Journal on Computing*, 25(2):346–363, 2013.

[14] T. Stützle and H. H. Hoos. Analysing the run-time behaviour of iterated local search for the travelling salesman problem. In P. Hansen and C. Ribeiro, editors, *Essays and Surveys on Metaheuristics*, Operations Research/Computer Science Interfaces Series, pages 589–611. Kluwer Academic Publishers, Boston, MA, 2001.

Approximate Approaches to the Traveling Thief Problem

Hayden Faulkner, Sergey Polyakovskiy, Tom Schultz, Markus Wagner
Optimisation and Logistics
School of Computer Science
University of Adelaide, Australia

ABSTRACT

This study addresses the recently introduced Traveling Thief Problem (TTP) which combines the classical Traveling Salesman Problem (TSP) with the 0-1 Knapsack Problem (KP). The problem consists of a set of cities, each containing a set of available items with weights and profits. It involves searching for a permutation of the cities to visit and a decision on items to pick. A selected item contributes its profit to the overall profit at the price of higher transportation cost incurred by its weight. The objective is to maximize the resulting profit.

We propose a number of problem-specific packing strategies run on top of TSP solutions derived by the Chained Lin-Kernighan heuristic. The investigations provided on the set of benchmark instances prove their rapidity and efficiency when compared with an approximate mixed integer programming based approach and state-of-the-art heuristic solutions from the literature.

Categories and Subject Descriptors

G.1.6 [**Optimization**]: Miscellaneous; I.2.8 [**Problem Solving, Control Methods, and Search**]: Scheduling

Keywords

Traveling thief problem; local search; multi-component problems

1. INTRODUCTION

Recently, a new benchmark problem called the Traveling Thief Problem (TTP)has been introduced [3] in an attempt to provide an abstraction of problems with multiple interdependent components. The underlying idea of TTP is to combine the Traveling Salesman Problem (TSP) and the Knapsack Problem (KP). They both have been intensively studied for many years and are the core problems in the field of optimization. The TTP comprises a thief stealing items with weights and profits from a number of cities. The thief uses a knapsack of limited capacity and pays rent for it depending on the overall travel duration. To make the two components interdependent, the speed of the thief is made dependent (non-linearly) on the weight of the items picked so far. The thief has to visit all cities once and collect items so that the overall profit is maximized. While it is possible to generate solutions for the TTP by combining solutions for the individual components, such approaches do not necessarily result in near-optimal solutions: (1) each solution for the TSP hinders the best quality that can be achieved in the KP component because of the impact on the profit that is a function of travel time, and vice versa (2) each solution for the KP component influences the tour time for TSP as different items impact the speed of travel differently due to the variability of the weights of items.

A range of different approaches to the problem have been developed recently. For example, Mei et al. [6] focus on large TTP instances with relatively simple approaches. They analyze the computational complexity of different algorithms and suggest asymptotic speed-ups. The resulting algorithm significantly outperforms the three iterative and constructive algorithms originally presented in [10]. Bonyadi et al. [4] are the first to attempt to solve both components of the TTP in parallel, instead of sequentially. The authors design a co-evolutionary approach called CoSolver in which modules responsible for either the TSP part or the KP part communicate with each other. The proposed CoSolver outperforms a heuristic similar to the constructive heuristic SH from [10]. Mei et al. [7] also investigate a co-evolutionary approach and compare it to a memetic algorithm, with the result of the memetic algorithm outperforming the co-evolutionary one.

Recently, Polyakovskiy et al. [11] investigated a non-linear knapsack problem that occurs when packing items along a fixed route and taking into account travel time. They address the complexity of the problem and show that even the capacity unconstrained version is $\mathcal{NP}$-hard. Subsequently, they propose exact and approximate mixed integer programming (MIP) solutions that are able to produce (near-) optimal results for instances of a moderate size.

Despite the state-of-the-art techniques there remains potential for TTP-specific algorithms based on different paradigms. In this article, we provide a set of structurally diverse algorithms to effectively solve the entire range of existing TTP instances.

This article is set out as follows. In Section 2 we outline the important features of the Traveling Thief Problem. In Section 3 we describe our three local search routines, based on which we construct heuristic searches in Section 4. Sec-

GECCO '15, July 11 - 15, 2015, Madrid, Spain
© 2015 ACM. ISBN 978-1-4503-3472-3/15/07...$15.00
DOI: http://dx.doi.org/10.1145/2739480.2754716

tion 5 adopts the MIP based approximate approach of [11] and yields another high-quality technique. In Section 6, we present and compare their results with the state-of-the-art solutions. We finish with some concluding remarks.

2. TRAVELING THIEF PROBLEM

In the following, we first describe the TTP as defined in [10]. Given is a set of cities $N = \{1, \ldots, n\}$ and a set of items $M = \{1, \ldots, m\}$ distributed among the cities. The distance d_{ij} between any pair of cities $i, j \in N$ is known. Every city i, except the first one, contains a set of items $M_i = \{1, \ldots, m_i\}$, $M = \bigcup_{i \in N} M_i$. Each item k positioned in the city i is characterized by its profit p_{ik} and weight w_{ik}, thus the item $I_{ik} \sim (p_{ik}, w_{ik})$. The thief must visit each of the cities exactly once starting from the first city and returning back to it in the end. Any item may be selected in any city as long as the total weight of collected items does not exceed the capacity W. A renting rate R is to be paid per each time unit taken to complete the tour. Respectively, υ_{max} and υ_{min} denote the maximal and minimum speeds that the thief can move. The goal is to find a tour, along with a packing plan, that results in the maximal profit.

To set up the objective function precisely, let $y_{ik} \in \{0, 1\}$ be a binary variable equal to one when the item k is selected in the city i. In addition, let W_i denote the total weight of collected items when the thief leaves the city i. Therefore, the objective function for a tour $\Pi = (x_1, \ldots, x_n)$, $x_i \in N$ and a packing plan $P = (y_{21}, \ldots, y_{nm_i})$ has the following form:

$$Z(\Pi, P) = \sum_{i=1}^{n} \sum_{k=1}^{m_i} p_{ik} y_{ik} - R \left(\frac{d_{x_n x_1}}{\upsilon_{max} - \nu W_{x_n}} + \sum_{i=1}^{n-1} \frac{d_{x_i x_{i+1}}}{\upsilon_{max} - \nu W_{x_i}} \right) \quad (1)$$

where $\nu = \frac{\upsilon_{max} - \upsilon_{min}}{W}$ is a constant value defined by input parameters. The minuend is the sum of all packed items' profits and the subtrahend is the amount that the thief pays for the knapsack's rent equal to the total traveling time along Π multiplied by R.

A brief numeric example of the TTP problem is provided in Figure 1 [10]. Each node but the first has an assigned set of items. Let us assume that the maximum weight $W = 3$, the renting rate $R = 1$ and υ_{max} and υ_{min} are set as 1 and 0.1, respectively. Then the optimum objective value $Z(\Pi, P) = 50$ for $\Pi = (1, 2, 4, 3)$ and $P = (0, 0, 0, 1, 1, 0)$. Specifically, the thief collects no items traveling from city 1 to city 3 via cities 2 and 4. Therefore, this part of the tour has a cost of 15. In the city 3 only items I_{32} and I_{33} are picked up, resulting in a total profit of 80. However, on the way from city 3 back to city 1 the thief's knapsack has a weight of 2. This reduces the speed and results in an increased cost of 15. Consequently, the final objective value is $Z(\Pi, P) = 80 - 15 - 15 = 50$.

3. LOCAL SEARCH ROUTINES

In this section, we discuss a number of routines used to elaborate a packing plan for a given permutation of the cities Π. We assume that a TSP tour Π is the outcome of the call of the Chained Lin-Kernighan heuristic [2][1]. A packing routine is applied to construct an initial packing which is further enhanced by a set of local search procedures.

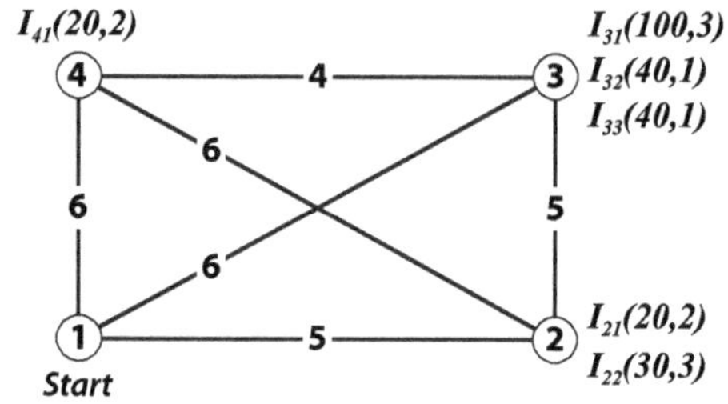

Figure 1: Illustrative Example [10]

3.1 Packing Routine

For greedy heuristics, it is common to utilize a goodness measure of the elements of a problem to make a decision. Here, we provide our packing heuristic algorithm with a scoring function which generates a score s_{ik} for item k placed in city i as:

$$s_{ik} = \frac{p_{ik}}{w_{ik} \times d_i},$$

where d_i is the distance from city i to the end of a given tour Π. The function incorporates a trade-off between a distance that item I_{ik} is to be carried over, its weight and its profit. Depending on a particular instance, it might be beneficial to strengthen the influence of one or more variables of the function. In this scope, we introduce exponents applied to the weight and the profit of an item to manage their impact. Thus, the function takes the following form:

$$s_{ik} = \frac{p_{ik}^{\alpha}}{w_{ik}^{\alpha} \times d_i}.$$

Our preliminary study shows that keeping the exponent of a distance low relative to the exponents of other two variables results in the best objective values. Therefore, we omit using an exponent for the distance variable. Moreover, using the same value for the exponents of the profit and weight variables often achieves the higher objective values when compared to varying exponents between the variables.

Algorithm 1 depicts our knapsack packing routine. The constructing process starts by giving a score to each item, and then subsequently sorting the entire set M of the items in non-decreasing order based on their scores. Then, the algorithm instantiates the control parameters. Since evaluating the objective function (1) is time-consuming, especially when complicated by the size of an instance, we introduce a parameter μ controlling the frequency of the objective value recomputation. Thus, the objective value is only evaluated each time μ items have been included for a possible packing. The value of μ is initialized in relation to the number of items m as $\mu = \lfloor m/\tau \rfloor$, where τ is a given integer constant. In addition, the current and the best packing plans P and P^* respectively, are initialized as empty sets. Finally, the best objective value found so far is set to $-\infty$.

Having been initialized, the algorithm starts the iterative solution construction process by considering the first item $I_1 \in M$ with the largest score. At each iteration k, item k is added to P if there remains enough free space in the knapsack. Every time μ items have been considered, the routine computes the objective value Z. When Z is improved, μ remains the same and the best objective value Z^* is updated

[1]As available at http://www.tsp.gatech.edu/concorde/downloads/downloads.htm

Algorithm 1
Packing Routine PACK (Π,α)

```
compute score for each of the items I_m ∈ M
sort the items of M in non-decreasing order of their scores
set the frequency μ = ⌊m/τ⌋
set the current packing plan P = ∅ and W' = 0
set the best packing plan P* = ∅
set best objective value Z* = −∞
set the counter k = 1 and set k* = 1
while (W' < W) and (μ > 1) do
    if (W' + w_k ≤ W) then
        add item I_k ∈ M to the packing plan P = P∪{I_k}
        set W' = W' + w_k
        if (k mod μ = 0) then
            compute the objective value Z = Z(Π, P)
            if (Z < Z*) then
                restore the packing plan P = P*
                set k = k* and update W'
                set μ = ⌊μ/2⌋
            else
                update the best packing plan with P* = P
                set k* = k and Z* = Z
    set k = k + 1
return P
```

Algorithm 2
Iterative Packing Routine PACKITERATIVE (Π,c,δ,q)

```
obtain P_l by PACK (Π,c − δ) and compute Z_l = Z(Π, P_l)
obtain P_m by PACK (Π,c) and compute Z_m = Z(Π, P_m)
obtain P_r by PACK (Π,c + δ) and compute Z_r = Z(Π, P_r)
set the best packing plan P* = ∅
set the counter i = 1
while i ≤ q do
    if (Z_l > Z_m) and (Z_r > Z_m) then
        if (Z_l > Z_r) then
            set Z_m = Z_l, c = c − δ and P* = P_l
        else
            set Z_m = Z_r, c = c + δ and P* = P_r
    else if (Z_l > Z_m) then
        set Z_m = Z_l, c = c − δ and P* = P_l
    else if (Z_r > Z_m) then
        set Z_m = Z_r, c = c + δ and P* = P_r
    δ = δ/2;
    obtain P_l by PACK (Π,c−δ) and compute Z_l=Z(Π,P_l)
    obtain P_r by PACK (Π,c+δ) and compute Z_r=Z(Π,P_r)
    set i = i + 1
    if (Z_l − Z_m < ε) and (Z_r − Z_m < ε) then break
return P*
```

Algorithm 3
BITFLIP (Π,P)

```
set Z* = Z(Π, P)
set P* = P
for each item I_m ∈ M do
    if I_m ∉ P* then
        add item I_m, P = P* ∪ {I_m}
    else
        remove item I_m, P = P* \ {I_m}
    compute the objective value Z(Π, P)
    if Z > Z* then
        set Z* = Z
        set P* = P
return P*
```

accordingly. However, as soon as the packing plan P yields $Z < Z^*$, the previous packing plan P^* is restored and the algorithm returns back to consider the items again starting with item $I_k \in M$. In addition, the frequency μ is halved. This strategy helps to identify the moment when no further solution improvement is possible while keeping the algorithm computationally fast. The heuristic terminates either when no further improvement is possible or the limit value of 1 is reached for μ.

To reach a better packing performance, we run the packing routine routine PACK (Π,α) iteratively for different values of the exponent α. Algorithm 2 explains the structure of the solution process. The algorithm PACKITERATIVE (Π,c,δ,q) is fed by the starting exponent value $c \in \mathbb{R}_+$, and a deviation value $\delta \in \mathbb{R}_+$ which defines the current studying interval for potential exponent values as $(c-\delta, c+\delta)$. In addition, an integer q is given as a limit on the number of iterations. The algorithm starts with evaluating objective values obtained by PACK (Π,α) in case of $\alpha = c$ and in cases of two terminal values $\alpha = c - \delta$ and $\alpha = c + \delta$. At each iteration, the algorithm compares the corresponding objective values Z_l, Z_m and Z_r, and selects the further interval for investigation. Specifically, it switches its attention to smaller values if $(Z_l > Z_m) \wedge (Z_l > Z_r)$ or to larger values if $(Z_r > Z_m) \wedge (Z_r > Z_l)$. Subsequently, the routine updates the best packing plan P^* found so far. In addition, it narrows the potential interval for a search setting $\delta = \delta/2$ and changes the current exponent value c to $c - \delta$ or $c + \delta$, depending on which produces the largest objective value. The searching process continues until the number of iterations performed reaches its limit or improvement in the objective value is less than ϵ, where ϵ is a small threshold constant.

3.2 Bitflip

The previously presented packing approach is not guaranteed to find a globally optimal TTP solution as (1) it does not modify the tours, and (2) the packing plan it finds may not necessarily be optimal for a given tour. Therefore, we present two local search operators to complement the packing plan generation from Section 3.1.

The BitFlip operator is a simple greedy hillclimber with a low runtime. Its pseudocode is shown in Algorithm 3. The operator iteratively evaluates the outcome of flipping each bit position corresponding to item $I_m \in M$ in the packing plan P. If flipping a bit improves the objective value ($Z > Z^*$), the change is kept, otherwise P remains unchanged. A single iteration of the operator ends when all bit flips have been attempted once. Multiple passes can result in further improvement of the objective value.

3.3 Insertion

The insertion operator takes advantage of the situation where a valuable item at a particular city is picked up early and it is worth trying to delay the item pickup by modifying the tour Π. Figure 2 shows an example where city x_2 is inserted later in the tour, after city x_7. In this case the result is a slightly longer tour, however the items at x_2 are now later in the tour and hence contribute a lower carrying cost.

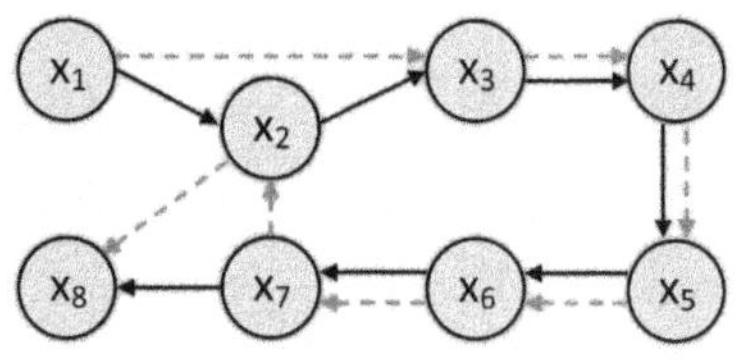

Figure 2: A graphical example of insertion: The solid black line represents the initial tour option, while the red dashed line represents a modified tour where city x_2 has been inserted after city x_7. The red tour can have a higher objective score due to a valuable (but heavy) picked item at city x_2.

Algorithm 4
INSERTION (Π,P)

```
for a = n → 1 do
    compute Z = Z(Π, P)
    for b = a − 1 → 1 do
        set Π* = Π
        insert city x_a between x_b and x_{b−1} in tour Π*
        compute Z* = Z(Π*, P)
        if Z* > Z then
            set Z = Z*
            set Π** = Π*
        if b = 1 then
            set Π = Π**
return Π
```

There is a tradeoff between increasing the tour length and hence travel time and carrying cost for all items before the insertion point, and decreasing the carrying cost of the items of the inserted city. The insertion pseudocode is shown in Algorithm 4. The operator searches over all cities in reverse tour order ($x_n \rightarrow x_1$), evaluating the effect of inserting each city at all positions before its own position in the tour Π^*. If an insertion for a city x_a is found that produces a greater objective value than (1) the current tour Π and (2) all other insertions for Π^*_a, then the tour is stored as Π^{**}. Once the tour has been completely checked for better positions for x_a then Π^{**} becomes the new tour Π and the process begins with the next city x_{a-1}. Again, multiple passes can result in further improvement of the objective value.

Note that in typical good solutions to the TTP many items are picked up towards the end of the tour. The intuition is that it is not too harmful to the overall objective value if items are picked up late, since the speed of the thief is typically low at that point in time. We begin our insertions at the end of the tour since this is a time consuming search operation for very large instances.

4. LOCAL SEARCH ALGORITHMS

In order to isolate the effects of the different search routines, we first define a set of straight-forward local search algorithms. All algorithms use the Chained Lin-Kernighan heuristic (CLK) to generate an initial TSP tour:

- Heuristic S1: run CLK, then PACKITERATIVE;
- Heuristic S2: run CLK, then PACKITERATIVE, then repeat BITFLIP until converged;
- Heuristic S3: run CLK, then PACKITERATIVE, then (1+1)-EA;
- Heuristic S4: run CLK, then PACKITERATIVE, then repeat INSERTION until converged;
- Heuristic S5: repeat S1 until time is up.

Because BITFLIP and INSERTION are deterministic, we can stop the heuristics S2 and S4 once the objective value does not change.

(1+1)-EA is a simple alternative to the greedy BITFLIP, which was previously used in [10]: given a packing plan, we flip each item with probability $1/m$. If the TTP solution with the new packing plan has a higher objective value, we use it as the next starting point. We terminate it once the CPU time is used up.

Since we expect the different routines to be able to escape each others local optima, we also define the following slightly more complex heuristics:

- Heuristic C1: run CLK, then PACKITERATIVE, then repeat "one BITFLIP pass, one INSERTION pass" until converged;
- Heuristic C2: run CLK, then PACKITERATIVE, then repeat "one BITFLIP pass, one (1+1)-EA pass, one INSERTION pass";
- Heuristic C3: run CLK until 10% of the time is used, then apply PACKITERATIVE, select the best of those, then "one BITFLIP pass, one INSERTION pass";
- Heuristic C4: run CLK until 10% of the time is used, then apply PACKITERATIVE, select the best of those, then "one BITFLIP pass, one (1+1)-EA pass, one INSERTION pass";
- Heuristic C5: repeat C1 until time is up;
- Heuristic C6: repeat C2 until time is up.

The heuristics C1 and C2 are straight-forward extensions of S2 and S4, with the hope that the two routines complement each other. Heuristics C3 and C4 use 10% of their CPU time to sample better starting points. This allows us to investigate the benefits of a better starting point over performing more iterations of the routines. Lastly, C5 and C6 are the restart variants of C1 and C2, with which we can observe the advantage of restarts to make the best use of the available computation time.

Note that we limit (1+1)-EA to 10,000 iterations in these complex heuristics, whereas it is unlimited in the simple ones. In addition, note that we decided to execute only single passes of BITFLIP and INSERTION per iteration due to their computational complexity. With this interleaving of the two routines, none of them will use a disproportionate amount of time. This is important particularly for the instances in which there are a large number of cities and items.

5. PACKING ITEMS WITH A MIP BASED APPROACH

When a tour is given, the two MIP based approaches of Polyakovskiy and Neumann [11] are able to solve the residuary knapsack packing part either exactly or approximately. Obtaining the optimal solution is costly in regard to running time as it requires the use of a linearization technique to handle the non-linear terms in the objective function. As an alternative, the piecewise linear approximation technique can be used. In this case, each of the non-linear terms is represented by the function $t(v) = 1/v$ which is subsequently approximated by a set of straight line segments. The computational experiments presented in [11] show that the approximate approach yields a tight approximation within only 1% of the optimal packing plan.

For our MIP-based approach, we adopt the approximative technique and run it on top of the Chained Lin-Kernighan heuristic [2] as a tour generator. The final solution for a particular instance results from the following iterative process. Each iteration starts with computing a distinct tour Π as a result of the TSP heuristic. Then, we run the approximative solver for the KP component. Firstly, the primal order $\Pi = (x_1, x_2, \ldots, x_n)$ is considered. Specifically, the set of items M is refined to exclude any existing unprofitable and compulsory items according to the pre-processing scheme as prescribed in [11]. Then the resulting non-linear knapsack problem on the reduced set of items is solved as the linear mixed 0-1 program named NKP^a_τ, where τ is the number of equal-sized line segments and is used to manage the precision of the approximation. Secondly, the reversed order $\overline{\Pi} = (x_1, x_n, \ldots, x_2)$ is investigated for which the pre-processing scheme and NKP^a_τ are performed again. Thus, we obtain through each iteration two feasible solutions based on either Π or $\overline{\Pi}$. Afterwards, we start the next iteration with a new tour. We consider the best solution found by this iterative process within a given time limit to be the output of this approach.

6. EXPERIMENTAL INVESTIGATIONS

In this section, we investigate the effects of the different local search routines and compare our approaches with existing ones.

6.1 Experimental Setup

As mentioned above, we use the comprehensive set of TTP instances from Polyakovskiy et al. [1, 10] for our investigations. The two components of the problem are balanced in such a way that the near-optimal solution of one sub-problem does not dominate over the optimal solution of another sub-problem.

The characteristics of the 9,720 instances vary widely, and we outline the most important ones in the following:[2]

- The instances have 51 to 85,900 cities, based on instances from the TSPlib by Reinelt [12];
- For each TSP instance, there are three different types of knapsack problems: *uncorrelated*, *uncorrelated with similar weights* and *bounded strongly correlated* types, where the latter has been shown to be difficult for different types of knapsack solvers in [5, 10];
- For each TSP and KP combination, the number of items per city (referred to as an *item factor*) is $F \in \{1, 3, 5, 10\}$. Note that all cities of a single TTP instance have the same number of items, except for the first city (which is also the last city), where no items are available;
- For each instance, the renting rate R that links both subproblems is chosen in such a way that at least one TTP solution with zero negative objective value exists;
- Lastly, for each TTP configuration 10 different instances exist where the knapsack capacity is varied.

[2]For a more detailed description, we refer the interested reader to [1, 10].

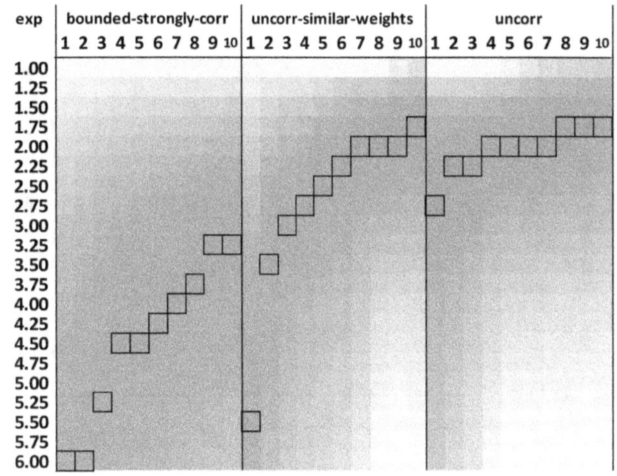

Figure 3: Heat-map of objective values for different values of α, averaged over the same 50 tours for each of the thirty instances of pcb3038_n9111. Greener (darker) squares indicate higher objective values and boxes represent the best.

From the set of 9,720 TTP instances, we select 72 as a representative subset to cover small, medium, and large size instances with different characteristics:

- six different numbers of cities (spread out roughly logarithmically): 195, 783, 3038, 11849, 33810, 85900;
- two different numbers of items per city: 3, 10;
- all three different types of knapsacks;
- two different sizes of knapsacks (capacities): 3 and 7 times the size of the smallest knapsack.

We run all algorithms for a maximum of 10 minutes per instance, except for the MIP-based approach which we run for 8 hours on the instances with $n \in \{33810, 85900\}$ cities. Due to their randomized nature, we perform 30 independent repetitions of the algorithms on each instance. All computations of heuristics S1–S5 and C1–C6 are performed on machines with Intel Xeon E5430 CPUs (2.66GHz), on Debian Linux 4.7.2, with Java SE RE 1.7.0. All computations of our MIP-based appproach were performed on machines with AMD Opteron 6348 CPUs (2.8GHz) on Red Hat Linux 4.4.7, with IBM ILOG CPLEX 12.6.

We assess the quality of the algorithms using the following approach. For each instance, we consider the best solution found to be a lower bound on the achievable objective value. Then, we take the average of the 30 results produced by an algorithm and then compute the ratio between that average and the best objective value found, which gives us the approximation ratio. This ratio allows us to compare the performances across the chosen set of instances, since the objective values vary across several orders of magnitude.

6.2 Impact of the Exponent in the Packing Routine

In the following, we investigate the performance of the packing approaches from Section 3.1. First, in an attempt to uncover the best performing values for α for varying instances, we carry out an experimental study with objective values being calculated and averaged over 100 unique tours using values $e \in [1, 6]$ at 0.25 intervals.

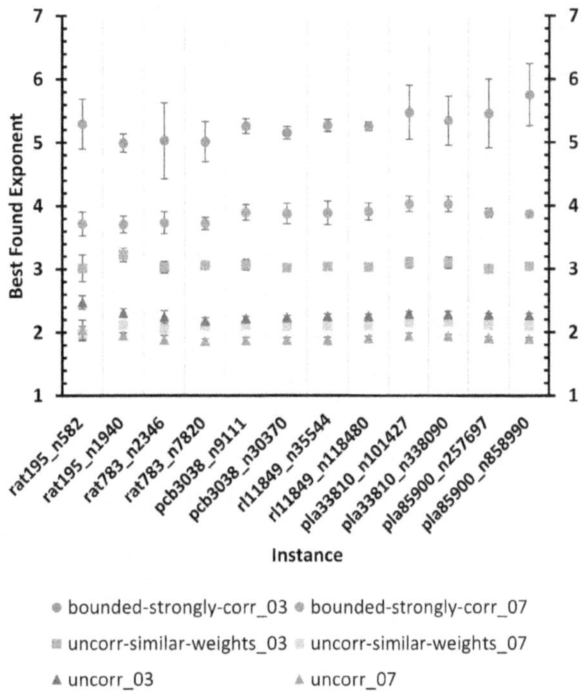

Figure 4: The best performing exponent values averaged over 50 tours for varying instances and instance types.

Figure 3 is a heat-map from the study for the pcb3038_n9111 instances.[3] It is easy to see that (1) there appears to be a single best performing exponent for each instance, and (2) there is also an optimal trend-line curve for instances of the same type that stars at high exponents for small knapsacks and ends at smaller exponents for larger knapsacks. This heat-map is representative of heat-maps for other instances. Across all instances, the trend-lines are dependent on the knapsack types (bounded-strongly, uncorr-similar, uncorr).

In order to quickly determine well performing exponents, we use PACKITERATIVE. Based on previous experiments, we use the starting exponent $c = 5$ and the sampling spread $\delta = 2.5$. To limit the runtime of Algorithm 2, we limit the number of iterations $q = 20$ and use $\epsilon = 0.1$. We show the best performing exponents in Figure 4. What we can observe in Figure 3 is now visible across all 72 instances: the best performing exponents for the uncorrelated ones are significantly smaller than those for the instances with bounded and strongly correlated items.

Interestingly, the best performing exponents for certain classes of TTP instances are in very narrow ranges, e.g. for all instances with uncorrelated weights. For the instances with bounded and strongly correlated items, however, the best performing exponents vary significantly.

Further investigation into these trends is necessary to fully understand why they exist and what particularities of an instance affect the value of the optimal exponent.

6.3 Results and Discussion

In the following, we will show and analyse the performance of the different heuristics on the 72 instances. We compare

[3]Only here we consider the wider range of knapsack sizes 1–10 to better show the trends.

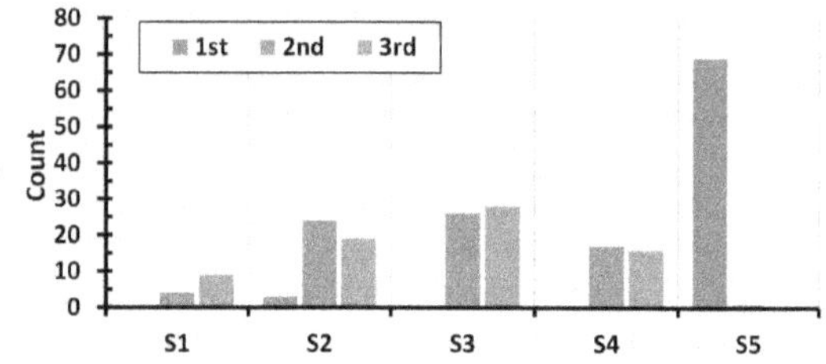

Figure 6: Results of S1–S5: ranking across the 72 instances.

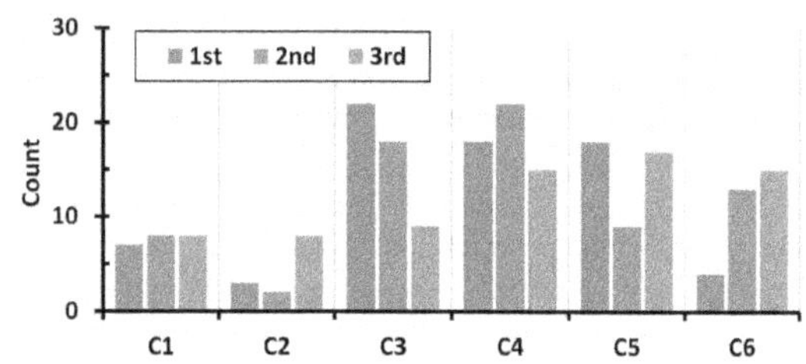

Figure 7: Results of C1–C6: ranking across the 72 instances.

our heuristics S1–S5, C1–C6, and MIP based heuristic with the heuristic MATLS [6] and with the three heuristics presented in [10]. Note that the study in [6] already shows that MATLS outperforms these three on large instances.

In Table 1 we list all achieved average ratios. Due to space constraints, we only show in this table the results of algorithms with an average approximation ratio $\geq 96\%$. Thus, the three approaches from [10] are missing in the table, as are S2–S4. S1 remains as an important baseline for our analyses. In addition, we show in Figure 5 for all 16 approaches the number of times that a heuristic achieved the best, second best, and third best average ratio.

A closer look into the results yields surprising insights. First, let us look into our group of simple heuristics S1–S5. In Figure 6 we show the number of times that a particular approach performed on average either best or second best in this group. We can see that S5 clearly outperforms our other simple heuristics when it comes to the number of times that its average is the highest. The runner-ups are S2–S4, which shows that all three routines BITFLIP, (1+1)-EA and INSERTION perform well on instances for which the others do not. In particular the performance of S4 shows that modifications of the tours need to be considered in addition to modifications of the packing plans. Note that the dominating performance of S5 is a first indicator of the importance of the initial TSP tour for the final objective value.

Next, for the analysis of the complex heuristics, let us recall that C3 and C4 sample several starting points in comparison to C1 and C2, and that C5 and C6 are the restart variants of C1 and C2. In Figure 7 we show again the number of times that an approach achieved either the best, second best, or third best average objective value in this group. We can see that C3 and C4 perform best, which we attribute to the fact that both select the best from several TTP solution candidates for the subsequent hill-climbing. The restarting algorithms C5 and C6 perform better than the single-iteration ones, however, they do not perform as well as algorithms C3 and C4 that can explore more TSP tours. Again, the performance of the algorithms that sample more tours indicates that the TSP tours are of high importance.

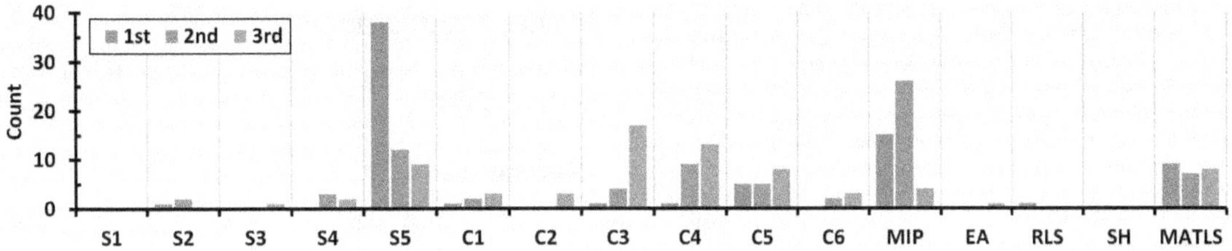

Figure 5: Results for all approaches: ranking across the 72 instances. Shown are the number of times an algorithm's approximation ratio is best, second best, or third best on an instance.

Interestingly, it is possible to directly compare the effects of resampling tours and of hill-climbing based on a good initial solution: C3/C4 contain S5, even though it is limited to just 10% of the overall computation time. A look into Table 1 reveals that the resampling strategy is the more successful one, since S5 achieves an average approximation ratio of 98.2%, whereas C3 and C4 achieve only about 97%.

Since PACKITERATIVE requires only a small number of evaluations, it is very quick compared to the traditional iterative TTP approaches that are allowed to use up to 10 minutes. For example, the runtimes of PACKITERATIVE ranges from 15-60 milliseconds for the instances with 195 cities and 1.2-13 seconds for instances with 11,849 cities, to 18-110 seconds for the instances with 85,900 cities. Since S1 performs only a single iteration of PACKITERATIVE, we can compare the performance of this basic step with the other approaches in Table 1.

As we can observe in the approximation ratios of S1 and S5, the impact of initial tours on the final solution quality can be significant. On many instances, the restart approach of S5 outperforms any other complex approach. This strongly indicates that, even though the local search routines are problem-specific, their effect is limited. Given our short computation time budget, even the iterative MIP approach achieves just comparable performance.

The results also show that the routines BITFLIP and INSERTION can help to improve the solutions, in particular when we compare the ratios of the complex algorithms C1–C6 with that of S1. The drawback of these routines, however, is their computational complexity. To increase their effectiveness, fast and particular heuristics are necessary to prevent the exhaustive search that both routines currently perform.

Additional noteworthy observations include, amongst others:

- The mixed-integer approach performs second best on average, if we do not consider the instances with n =85,900 cities.
- MATLS cleary outperforms our approaches on a few instances. On average, however, it is not amongst the best-performing algorithms.

Since generating tours can be very time consuming for very large problem instances, it would be an obvious improvement to pre-compute many TSP tours and to randomly pick from these. In practice, the decision to pre-compute can be reasonable, in cases where the locations of delivery or pick-up spots rarely change. In fact, a large number of slightly different tours can be achieved by running CLK multiple times. To investigate this further, we repeatedly run CLK: if the number of cities n <1,000 then we run it 10,000 times, if $1{,}000 \leq n < 10{,}000$ we run it 1,000 times, and if $n \geq 10{,}000$ we run the heuristic 100 times (see Figure 8). In particular for TSP instances that are based on electronic circuits, which exhibit regular grid like arrangements, often the final tours are identical with the exception of a few nodes that then belong to earlier or later parts of the tour.

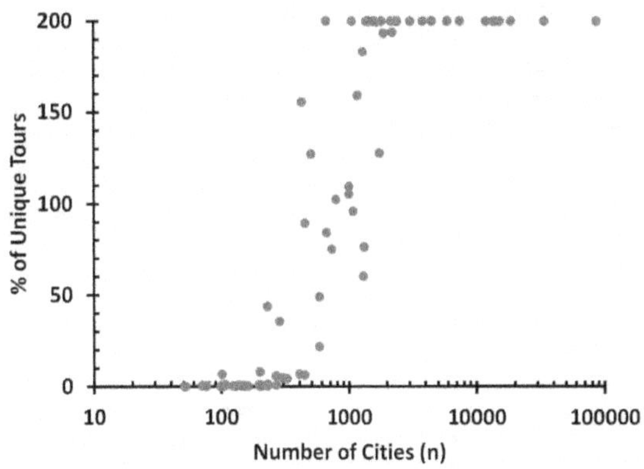

Figure 8: Percentage of unique tours found in repeated Lin-Kernighan runs. Percentages >100 are possible as a single TSP tour can be used in two different directions for TTP purposes.

Summarizing the results the following conclusion can be made: while problem understanding can help, it is surprising how well a greedy approach with low computational complexity performs compared to more complex ones.

7. CONCLUDING REMARKS

As discovered from the literature and as observed in our experiments, there does not yet seem to be a single best algorithm paradigm for the TTP. So far, constructive heuristics, simple and complex hill-climbers, and also more sophisticated co-evolutionary approaches have been applied to the TTP. With each study, more successful approaches are identified however further investigation is needed to enable understanding to solve the TTP. The interdependence of the TTP is rarely considered, and minimally problem-specific local searches that alternate between solving the TSP and KP components perform best.

It appears that the near future in TTP research will mostly be driven by experiments. Maybe research similar to that in [8, 9, 13], where the difficulty of TSP instances is systematically analyzed, will contribute to the theoretical understanding of the TTP. Computational complexity analyses of simple approaches on simple instances may also provide insights.

n	m	t	F	S1	S5	C3	C4	C5	C6	MIP	MATLS
195	582	bsc	3	88.1	99.6	99.4	99.4	99.6	99.5	100	96.3
			7	88.0	99.2	99.2	99.2	99.2	99.2	99.2	95.6
		unc	3	98.2	99.2	99.3	99.3	99.3	99.3	99.3	99.5
			7	99.2	99.9	100	100	100	100	100	99.8
		usw	3	96.1	98.6	99.0	98.9	99.3	99.0	99.5	98.5
			7	98.2	99.1	99.2	99.2	99.3	99.2	99.3	99.2
	1940	bsc	3	89.6	99.9	99.9	99.9	99.9	99.9	100	98.3
			7	89.2	97.7	97.1	97.5	97.7	97.6	98.1	97.0
		unc	3	96.0	99.1	98.7	98.7	99.3	99.1	99.1	99.0
			7	96.3	98.6	97.7	97.7	98.7	98.5	98.8	99.2
		usw	3	88.4	91.3	91.3	91.6	91.5	91.7	91.4	97.0
			7	92.6	96.3	95.6	95.6	96.4	96.0	96.9	99.4
783	2346	bsc	3	97.8	99.7	99.4	99.4	99.6	99.4	99.7	96.6
			7	95.5	99.3	98.7	98.6	99.1	98.8	99.0	96.6
		unc	3	95.9	98.9	98.5	98.5	98.8	98.5	98.7	98.8
			7	96.3	97.9	97.6	97.7	97.9	97.7	97.8	98.6
		usw	3	95.3	99.1	99.2	99.2	99.5	99.3	99.5	98.7
			7	96.0	99.7	99.6	99.5	99.8	99.5	99.7	98.7
	7820	bsc	3	98.0	99.7	99.6	99.7	99.4	99.5	99.8	94.8
			7	97.0	99.5	99.4	99.4	99.3	99.1	99.5	94.5
		unc	3	96.8	99.3	99.2	99.1	99.2	98.7	99.3	98.5
			7	97.9	99.5	99.4	99.3	99.3	99.1	99.4	99.0
		usw	3	96.0	99.3	99.6	99.6	99.4	99.0	99.6	97.7
			7	95.9	99.3	99.2	99.2	99.2	98.4	99.4	98.1
3038	9111	bsc	3	97.9	99.5	99.1	99.1	98.1	98.0	99.1	93.9
			7	97.6	99.4	99.0	99.0	97.7	97.4	98.8	94.4
		unc	3	98.0	99.7	99.4	99.4	98.5	98.0	99.5	99.0
			7	98.3	99.7	99.5	99.4	98.9	98.5	99.6	99.4
		usw	3	97.0	99.1	99.2	99.1	97.2	97.2	99.2	98.2
			7	97.6	99.6	99.3	99.2	98.4	97.7	99.3	99.0
	30370	bsc	3	98.1	99.6	99.3	99.3	99.0	99.0	99.3	96.7
			7	97.0	99.2	98.7	98.8	98.6	98.2	98.9	95.8
		unc	3	97.1	99.6	99.2	99.1	98.9	98.8	99.3	99.0
			7	97.8	99.5	99.3	99.3	99.2	98.9	99.3	99.2
		usw	3	94.8	98.9	98.2	98.3	97.6	97.6	98.6	98.3
			7	96.2	99.1	98.6	98.4	98.5	97.9	98.6	98.6
11849	35544	bsc	3	97.1	99.2	98.4	98.6	97.3	97.4	97.5	93.5
			7	96.7	98.9	97.9	98.1	96.6	96.7	96.7	93.9
		unc	3	97.4	99.0	98.4	98.5	97.6	97.8	98.0	98.4
			7	97.9	99.5	98.9	99.0	98.0	98.3	98.4	99.3
		usw	3	96.3	98.6	97.8	98.0	96.2	96.5	97.2	97.6
			7	97.1	99.0	98.5	98.5	97.0	97.3	97.3	98.7
	35544	bsc	3	96.7	99.0	98.4	98.3	96.9	97.0	97.9	93.6
			7	96.2	99.2	98.1	98.3	96.2	96.4	97.4	94.0
		unc	3	97.2	99.2	98.6	98.7	97.4	97.6	98.3	98.4
			7	97.4	99.2	98.6	98.4	97.9	97.8	98.5	98.8
		usw	3	95.3	98.3	97.8	97.8	95.6	95.9	97.1	97.6
			7	96.2	98.9	98.1	98.0	96.7	96.7	97.9	98.5
33810	101427	bsc	3	91.3	97.9	95.5	94.0	93.9	92.0	98.3	94.4
			7	91.0	97.9	94.2	95.3	93.8	91.7	96.5	94.1
		unc	3	70.6	73.5	71.4	71.5	71.2	70.9	73.3	75.8
			7	95.1	98.2	96.4	96.0	95.3	95.5	99.9	98.4
		usw	3	90.4	97.5	93.7	93.3	92.5	91.8	96.2	95.9
			7	92.2	98.0	94.7	93.9	93.9	93.5	98.1	97.4
	338090	bsc	3	92.2	97.3	93.8	93.3	92.5	92.4	99.1	93.9
			7	92.6	97.1	94.9	94.3	92.6	93.3	96.9	94.6
		unc	3	94.7	98.3	95.3	95.5	95.8	95.0	97.8	98.0
			7	95.0	98.4	96.0	96.1	96.2	95.7	98.5	98.7
		usw	3	91.3	97.7	93.5	92.8	92.1	92.3	98.3	96.4
			7	93.9	98.3	94.4	95.1	94.1	94.6	99.5	98.3
85900	338090	bsc	3	95.8	98.3	96.3	95.8	95.9	96.4	97.6	-
			7	96.1	97.8	96.8	95.9	96.3	97.1	98.4	-
		unc	3	97.4	98.9	94.2	94.1	97.8	97.7	-	-
			7	97.6	98.6	95.6	95.4	98.0	98.2	98.1	-
		usw	3	95.1	97.6	92.6	92.3	96.1	95.2	-	-
			7	95.8	97.4	93.4	93.3	96.4	96.0	97.9	-
	858990	bsc	3	95.9	96.8	96.2	97.1	95.6	96.3	-	-
			7	96.6	97.2	97.0	97.6	96.6	96.3	-	94.1
		unc	3	97.6	97.5	92.1	92.0	97.6	97.3	-	-
			7	97.9	97.9	94.6	94.5	97.8	97.7	-	98.5
		usw	3	95.7	97.5	91.8	92.7	96.3	95.3	-	-
			7	96.6	96.9	93.2	93.2	96.5	96.3	-	97.9
avg				95.2	98.2	97.0	96.9	96.9	96.8	87.2	84.9
avg^{-85900}				95.0	98.3	97.5	97.4	97.0	96.8	98.1	97.0

Table 1: Approximation ratios achieved. n is the number of cities, m the number of items, t stands for the three KP types, and F stands for the KP size. **avg** is the average ratio achieved across all 72 instances, **avg**$^{-85900}$ across the top 60 instances.

Acknowledgements

This work has been supported by the ARC Discovery Project DP130104395.

References

[1] TTP Test Data. See http://cs.adelaide.edu.au/~optlog/research/ttp.php.

[2] D. Applegate, W. J. Cook, and A. Rohe. Chained Lin-Kernighan for large traveling salesman problems. *INFORMS Journal on Computing*, 15(1):82–92, 2003.

[3] M. R. Bonyadi, Z. Michalewicz, and L. Barone. The travelling thief problem: The first step in the transition from theoretical problems to realistic problems. In *IEEE Congress on Evolutionary Computation (CEC)*, pages 1037–1044. IEEE, 2013.

[4] M. R. Bonyadi, Z. Michalewicz, M. R. Przybylek, and A. Wierzbicki. Socially inspired algorithms for the travelling thief problem. In *Genetic and Evolutionary Computation Conference (GECCO)*, pages 421–428, New York, NY, USA, 2014. ACM.

[5] S. Martello, D. Pisinger, and P. Toth. Dynamic programming and strong bounds for the 0-1 knapsack problem. *Management Science*, 45(3):414–424, Mar. 1999.

[6] Y. Mei, X. Li, and X. Yao. Improving efficiency of heuristics for the large scale traveling thief problem. In *Simulated Evolution and Learning (SEAL)*, volume 8886 of *LNCS*, pages 631–643. Springer, 2014.

[7] Y. Mei, X. Li, and X. Yao. On investigation of interdependence between sub-problems of the travelling thief problem. *Soft Computing*, pages 1–16, 2014.

[8] O. Mersmann, B. Bischl, H. Trautmann, M. Wagner, J. Bossek, and F. Neumann. A novel feature-based approach to characterize algorithm performance for the traveling salesperson problem. *Annals of Mathematics and Artificial Intelligence*, 69(2):151–182, 2013.

[9] S. Nallaperuma, M. Wagner, and F. Neumann. Parameter prediction based on features of evolved instances for ant colony optimization and the traveling salesperson problem. In *Parallel Problem Solving from Nature PPSN XIII*, volume 8672 of *LNCS*, pages 100–109. Springer, 2014.

[10] S. Polyakovskiy, M. R. Bonyadi, M. Wagner, Z. Michalewicz, and F. Neumann. A comprehensive benchmark set and heuristics for the traveling thief problem. In *Genetic and Evolutionary Computation Conference (GECCO)*, pages 477–484. ACM, 2014.

[11] S. Polyakovskiy and F. Neumann. Packing while traveling: Mixed integer programming for a class of nonlinear knapsack problems. In *Integration of AI and OR Techniques in Constraint Programming*, volume 9075 of *LNCS*, pages 330–344. Springer, 2015.

[12] G. Reinelt. TSPLIB - A Traveling Salesman Problem Library. *ORSA Journal on Computing*, 3(4):376–384, 1991.

[13] K. Smith-Miles, J. van Hemert, and X. Y. Lim. Understanding TSP difficulty by learning from evolved instances. In *Learning and Intelligent Optimization (LION)*, pages 266–280. Springer, 2010.

A Genetic Algorithm for Scheduling Electric Vehicle Charging

Jorge García-Álvarez
Dept. of Computer Science
University of Oviedo
Gijón, Spain
jgarcia-alvarez@outlook.com

Miguel A. González
Dept. of Computer Science
University of Oviedo
Gijón, Spain
mig@uniovi.es

Camino R. Vela
Dept. of Computer Science
University of Oviedo
Gijón, Spain
crvela@uniovi.es

ABSTRACT

This paper addresses a problem motivated by a real life environment, in which we have to schedule the charge of electric vehicles in a parking, subject to a set of constraints, with the objective of minimizing the total tardiness. We consider both the static version of the problem, where we know in advance the arrival time, charging time and due date of every vehicle, and also the dynamic version of it. We design a genetic algorithm with some components specifically tailored to deal with the problem. In the experimental study we evaluate the proposed algorithm in a benchmark set taken from the literature, and we also compare it against the state-of-the-art showing that our proposal is significantly better.

Categories and Subject Descriptors

I.2.8 [**Artificial Intelligence**]: Problem Solving, Control Methods, and Search—*Heuristic methods, Scheduling*

Keywords

Time-tabling and scheduling; Genetic algorithms; Heuristics; Combinatorial optimization; Dynamical optimization

1. INTRODUCTION

The number of electric vehicles (EVs) has increased in last years. They could have a very positive impact on the economies of the countries and also in the environment, reducing the dependence on oil. In addition, the energy stored in electric vehicles can be used as an auxiliary source of electrical energy storage [8] to regulate voltage profiles and power of the network, and compensate for fluctuations in renewable energy generation [1]. In this way, EVs can contribute to the efficient use of energy. However, the use of large fleets of EVs may overload the grid due to the high charging time batteries. As it is noted in the report of the European Distribution System Operators for Smart Grids [2], one of the challenges in electric vehicle technology is the development of intelligent control systems for charging that avoid peak demand. The charging of vehicles can be scheduled to take place at times of low consumption and thus balance the electrical needs when vehicles are parked for long periods of time. In fact, a number of charging control systems have already been proposed [3] [10] that, in some cases, try to fill the overnight valley in order to reduce daily cycling and operational cost.

In this paper we face the problem presented and defined in [6], which consists in scheduling the charging of a large number of electric vehicles so that the user demands are met. Calculating a schedule that maximizes user satisfaction can be a very difficult problem to solve due to the physical constraints of charging stations and the existence of contracts with electrical companies that provide a limited amount of energy. The origin of this problem is inspired by a real project in which users require the charge of their electric vehicles while they are parked in their private parking spaces. Each parking space has a single connection to a three-phase line that has certain restrictions. Not all EVs can be charged simultaneously because the power supply is limited and must be balanced between the three lines, thus a suitable control policy is needed to define the intervals for charging vehicles during the time they are stationed [11]. In [6] the authors define this problem and propose an algorithm for solving its dynamic version. Their Problem Decomposition (PD) approach is based on decomposing the problem in three instances of the one machine sequencing problem with variable capacity, and these instances are solved with a method based on a dispatching rule.

However, the problem has a great complexity, and even if heuristic schedulers are able to obtain reasonable solutions, metaheuristics are better suited for obtaining good results. In fact, a number of metaheuristic approaches can be found in the literature to solve similar problems, as for example particle swarm optimization [12]. In [4] we can find a review of different strategies, algorithms and methods to implement smart charging control systems.

In particular, genetic algorithms (GAs) have the ability to work with huge search spaces and allow to exploit any kind of heuristic knowledge from the problem domain, and by doing so, they are actually competitive with the most efficient methods in scheduling. In this paper we present a GA with operators designed specifically for this problem. We propose an scheduler algorithm which incorporates a procedure to fix some inefficient charging time assignments that may appear due to the constraint of maximum imbalance

GECCO '15, July 11–15, 2015, Madrid, Spain

DOI: http://dx.doi.org/10.1145/2739480.2754695

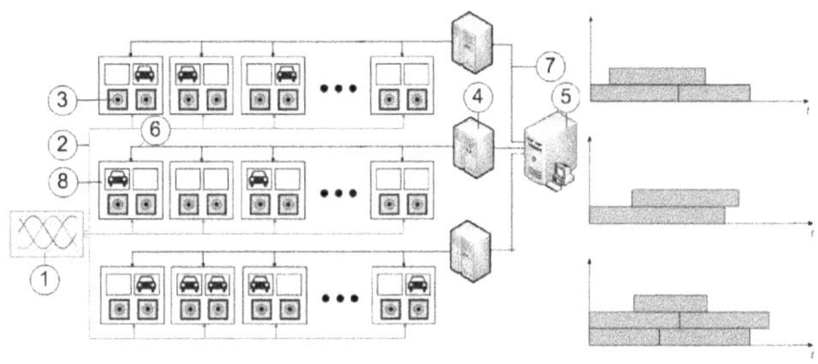

Figure 1: General structure of the distribution net of the charging station. (1) power source, (2) three-phase electric power, (3) charging points, (4) masters, (5) server with database, (6) communication RS 485, (7) communication TCP/IP, (8) slaves. The Gantt Chart in the right side shows the charging schedule of the vehicles in each line.

between any two lines. We also propose some crossover operators tailored for this problem and we prove that one of them obtains significantly better results than standard operators. Additionally, we define a mutation operator for this problem and a way of generating a diverse initial population.

We are considering two versions of the problem: the static version in which we know in advance the arrival times, charging times and due dates of all the vehicles, and the dynamic version in which we do not have that information. We will see that both versions of the problem are relevant. We conducted an experimental study to analyze our proposal and to compare it against the state-of-the-art, and also to discuss the difference in solving the static and dynamic problems.

The remainder of the paper is organized as follows. In the next section we summarize the aspects of the charging station. Then, we describe the problem and the algorithm to solve it. Finally, we report the results of the experimental study and give conclusions and ideas for future research.

2. THE CHARGING STATION

In this section we summarize the main features of the electrical structure and the operation mode of the charging station. These elements are detailed in [11]. Figure 1 shows a schema of the distribution net of the charging station. We have to remark that we had no choice over its design, which was motivated by simplicity and economic reasons. The net is feeded by a three-phase source of electric power. In the model considered here, each line feeds a number of charging points. The station has 180 spaces (60 in each line), each one having a charging point which may be in two states: active or inactive. When it is active it is connected to the net and transfers energy at a constant rate (2.3 Kw).

The operation of the station is controlled by a distributed system comprising one master in each line and a number of slaves. Each user has one space assigned. It is important to remark that the user has to be the owner or renter of its stall and he cannot use the space of another user. This restriction makes the scheduling problem harder to solve as each stall is connected to one of the three lines of the three phase feeder and so keeping the balance constraints may not be easy. When entering the station, the user connects his vehicle to the charging point and provides the charging time, as well as an expected time, or due date, for taking the vehicle away. These values are used by the control system to schedule the vehicle, i.e., to establish a starting time.

There are some constraints that must be satisfied for the station to work properly. For example, although there are 180 spaces available, not all the charging points in these spaces can be activated at the same time. In practice there is a maximum number of vehicles N, which depends on the contracted power, that can be charging (active) at the same time in a given line. Also, due to electro-technical and economical reasons, the power consumption in the three lines must be balanced. This condition is considered as a maximum imbalance between any two lines.

In this paper we consider a simplified model of the charging station that makes the following assumptions: the user never takes the vehicle away before the declared due date and the battery does not get completely charged before the charging time indicated by the user. Even though they are unrealistic assumptions, the model could be easily adapted to deal with these situations.

In principle, each time a new vehicle enters the facility and requires charging, the current schedule may get unfeasible and so a new schedule should be built. However, in order to avoid the system to collapse if many of such events are produced in a very short period of time, new schedules are computed at most at time intervals of length ΔT. To this end, every ΔT time units a supervisor program, running on the server, checks for the events produced in the last interval. If at least one event was produced, then the scheduler is launched to obtain a new feasible schedule which is applied from this time on. In the real environment, ΔT is set at two minutes.

3. PROBLEM FORMULATION

The problem defined in [6] may naturally be considered as a dynamic problem due to the fact that in a real scenario, the arrival of the vehicles is not known in advance. However, in this paper we will consider both static and dynamic versions as it is interesting to compare the difficulty of solving each version. Moreover, the study of the static version of the problem can give some insights about how to solve the dynamic version more efficiently and also gives information about how much the solution to the dynamic problem can still be improved. We borrow the problem formulation from [6], which is detailed in the following subsections.

3.1 The static problem

Considering that we know in advance the arrival times of the vehicles, their charging times and due dates, we can formalize the static version of the problem.

In an instance of the static version of the problem, there are three lines $L_i, 1 \leq i \leq 3$, each one with n_i charging points. $N > 0$ is the maximum number of charging points that can be active at the same time in each line. The line L_i receives a number of M_i vehicles $v_{i1}, \ldots, v_{iM_i}$ from a time 0 up to a planning horizon. Each vehicle v_{ij} is characterized by an arrival time $t_{ij} \geq 0$, a charging time $p_{ij} > 0$ and a time at which the user is expected to take the vehicle away, or due date, $d_{ij} \geq t_{ij} + p_{ij}$ by which the battery of the vehicle should be completely charged.

The goal is to obtain a feasible schedule, i.e. to assign starting times to the decision variables st_{ij} for each v_{ij}, $1 \leq i \leq 3$, $1 \leq j \leq M_i$, so that the following constraints are satisfied and the evaluation function is minimized:

1. All vehicles must start charging after the arrival time.

$$\forall v_{ij}, \quad st_{ij} \geq t_{ij} \tag{1}$$

2. No preemption is allowed, so a vehicle v_{ij} can not be disconnected before its charging time C_{ij} is reached.

$$C_{ij} = st_{ij} + p_{ij} \tag{2}$$

3. The number of active charging points in a line at a given time can not exceed N.

$$\max N_i(t) \leq N, \quad t \geq 0; 1 \leq i \leq 3 \tag{3}$$

where $N_i(t)$ denotes the number of charging points of line L_i which are active at a time t.

4. The maximum imbalance between any two lines L_i and L_j is controlled by the parameter Δ.

$$\max \left(\frac{|N_i(t) - N_j(t)|}{N} \right) \leq \Delta, \quad t \geq 0; 1 \leq i, j \leq 3 \tag{4}$$

The objective function that should be minimized is the total tardiness, defined as

$$\sum_{i=1}^{3} \sum_{j=1}^{M_i} \max(0, C_{ij} - d_{ij}) \tag{5}$$

3.2 The dynamic problem

An instance of the dynamic problem can be given as a sequence of instances $P_1, P_2, \ldots, P_n$. Each P_k is defined by a set of vehicles that demand charging at a given time, but have not yet started to charge, along with some vehicles that may have already started to charge but are still charging.

In a more formal definition, we can consider that a set of vehicles $\{v_{i1}, \ldots, v_{ia_i}, \ldots, v_{im_i}\}$ are given in an instance P_k at a time T_k in each line L_i, $1 \leq i \leq 3$. Each vehicle v_{ij} has a charging time p_{ij} and has a due date d_{ij}. The vehicles $v_{i1}, \ldots, v_{ia_i}$ are already active, as they started to charge at a time $st_{ij} < T_k$, $1 \leq j \leq a_i$ and have not yet finished, i.e., $C_{ij} = st_{ij} + p_{ij} > T_k$. While the vehicles $v_{ia_i+1}, \ldots, v_{im_i}$ have not yet started to charge. So, in the iteration k, the capacity of the line L_i to charge new vehicles, denoted $M_i^k(t)$ is given by

$$M_i^k(t) = N - \sum_{j=1}^{a_i} X_{ij}(t), \quad t \geq T_k \tag{6}$$

where

$$X_{ij}(t) = \begin{cases} 1, & \text{if } t < C_{ij} \\ 0, & \text{if } t \geq C_{ij} \end{cases} \tag{7}$$

The goal of an instance P_k is to obtain a feasible schedule such that all vehicles can be charged, even if no new vehicles arrive after T_k. This requires assigning starting times st^*_{ij} to all vehicles unscheduled at time T_k so that all constraints naturally derived from the static problem are satisfied. Notice that a given vehicle may get different values for st^*_{ij} in subsequent iterations while it does not start charging. However, once it starts, it can not longer be rescheduled. The evaluation function to minimize is again the total tardiness.

4. SOLVING THE DYNAMIC PROBLEM

Algorithm 1 follows the approach presented in [6] and shows the procedure to solve the dynamic version of the problem, where ΔT represents the length of the time interval at which a new event may be expected (two minutes in the real setting). The algorithm iterates every ΔT, so in each T_k, a new instance P_k is created if any vehicle has arrived since T_{k-1}. This instance is solved by the genetic algorithm and the new solution S' replaces the current one from T_k on. If no vehicle has arrived between T_{k-1} and T_k then the current solution remains valid until the next iteration. This means that the vehicles start charging at the times st^*_{ij} given in the current solution S', and therefore $st_{ij} = st^*_{ij}$ and $C_{ij} = st_{ij} + p_{ij}$ in the final solution S.

Algorithm 1 Solving the dynamic version of the problem

Require: A problem instance P and the time interval ΔT
  $S \leftarrow \varnothing$; $S' \leftarrow \varnothing$; $k = 1$; $T_{k-1} = 0$; $T_k = T_{k-1} + \Delta T$;
  while Not all vehicles have been scheduled **do**
    if A new vehicle v_{ij} has arrived at a time $t = t_{ij} \in [T_{k-1}, T_k)$ **then**
      Generate a new instance P_k with all vehicles v_{ij} such that $t_{ij} < T_k$ and that have not yet started charging along with all vehicles still charging at time T_k;
      Calculate a solution S' for instance P_k; {i.e. define starting times $st^*_{ij} \geq T_k$ for the vehicles of P_k that are not yet charging}
    end if
    Establish S' as the solution for the time interval $[T_k, T_{k+1})$; i.e., for each $st^*_{ij} \in S'$ such that $T_k \leq st^*_{ij} < T_{k+1}$, set $st_{ij} = st^*_{ij}$ in the final schedule S;
    $k = k + 1$; $T_k = T_{k-1} + \Delta T$;
  end while
  return The schedule S;

5. GENETIC ALGORITHM

Algorithm 2 describes the GA proposed in this paper. The initial population is generated by a combination of random and heuristic chromosomes. Then, the algorithm iterates over a number of generations until the stopping criterion is satisfied. In each iteration, a new generation is built from the previous one by applying selection, crossover, mutation and replacement operators. The termination criterion is satisfied when the best chromosome of the population is not improved during a consecutive number of generations, or also if we find a solution with zero tardiness. In the following subsections we detail the different components of the GA.

5.1 Chromosome representation and evaluation

To codify chromosomes we have decided to use a permutation of the vehicles. We have also considered a matrix representation, but the experimental results were worse.

To create a schedule S from a permutation V, the idea is to sequentially schedule all vehicles of V, choosing for each vehicle the earliest starting time such that all constraints are met with respect to the previously scheduled vehicles. However, the constraint of maximum imbalance between any two lines may lead to some undesirable assignments of charging times. This is clarified with the following example.

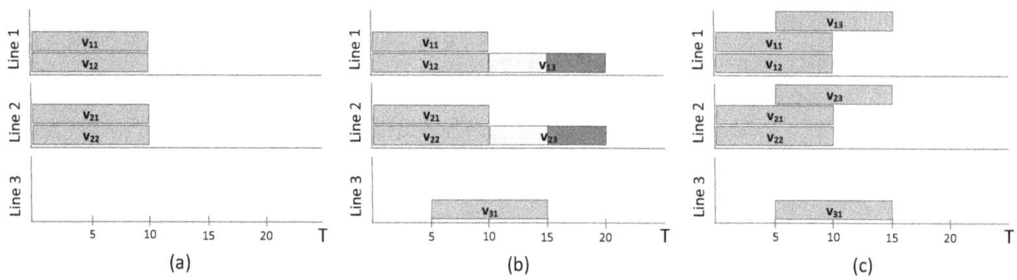

Figure 2: Example to illustrate the scheduler algorithm

Algorithm 2 The genetic algorithm

Require: A problem instance P
  Generate the initial population;
  while Not termination criterion is satisfied **do**
    Group all chromosomes randomly in pairs;
    Apply the crossover operator to each pair with probability *cr_prob*;
    Apply the mutation operator to each line of every offspring with probability *mut_prob*;
    Evaluate all new chromosomes;
    Choose chromosomes for the next generation with the replacement strategy;
  end while
  return The schedule S from the best chromosome;

Consider a problem with three vehicles (v_{11}, v_{12}, v_{13}) in L_1, three vehicles (v_{21}, v_{22}, v_{23}) in L_2 and one vehicle (v_{31}) in L_3. Arrival time is 0 for all vehicles except for v_{31}, being $t_{31} = 5$. Charging time is 10 for all vehicles. Due date is 10 for vehicles v_{11}, v_{12}, v_{21}, v_{22}, and 15 for vehicles v_{13}, v_{23}, v_{31}. The maximum number N of active charging points in any line is 3 and the maximum imbalance parameter Δ is 2/3 (therefore, at any given time point there should be at most a difference of two vehicles between any two lines).

Consider the permutation $(v_{11}, v_{12}, v_{21}, v_{22}, v_{13}, v_{23}, v_{31})$ and the partial schedule where the first four vehicles have already been scheduled (see Figure 2(a)). In this situation, when vehicles v_{13} and v_{23} are to be scheduled, both need to be scheduled at time 10 because if they are scheduled at time 5 then the maximum imbalance constraint with respect to line 3 is violated. Afterwards, v_{31} can be scheduled at time 5 and the result is the schedule of Figure 2(b) with tardiness 10 (we mark in red the portion of the charging time that surpasses the due date). However, notice that the scheduling of v_{31} breaks the previous "imbalance lock" in lines 1 and 2, and now both v_{13} and v_{23} could be reassigned to start charging at time 5, as indicated in Figure 2(c), to obtain a solution with no tardiness.

This example motivates us to design our scheduler algorithm so that vehicles can be reassigned in the following way. When we schedule the charging of a vehicle v' in line L' with charging time p' we choose the minimum starting time t' that fulfills all constraints. Then, we check if this new assignment breaks a previous imbalance lock, i.e. before the assignment of v' no vehicle could be scheduled in some other line because of the maximum imbalance with respect to line L', but after the assignment of v' it is possible to do it.

Algorithm 3 Scheduler algorithm

Require: A permutation of vehicles V
  $S \leftarrow \varnothing$;
  while S contains less vehicles than V **do**
    Let v' be the leftmost vehicle in V such that $v' \notin S$;
    Let t' be the minimum starting time for v' that fulfills all constraints, L' its line and p' its charging time;
    if the assignment of v' in the interval [t', t'+p'] breaks a previous imbalance lock **then**
      Unschedule (i.e. remove from S) all vehicles of lines different from L' such that its starting time is $\geq t'$;
    end if
    Schedule v' (i.e. append v' at the end of S) with starting time t';
  end while
  return The schedule S;

Formally, we can define that an assignment of a feasible starting time t' to a vehicle v' breaks a previous imbalance lock if and only if before the assignment it holds that $\exists t \in [t', t' + p')$ and $\exists i \in \{1, 2, 3\}, i \neq L'$ such that $\frac{N_i(t)+1-N_{L'}(t)}{N} > \Delta$, and after the assignment, with $N_{L'}$ updated in $[t', t' + p')$, it holds that $\frac{N_i(t)+1-N_{L'}(t)}{N} \leq \Delta$.

If this occurs, we propose to unschedule all vehicles of lines different from line L' such that its charging time starts at a time $\geq t'$, so that they may be rescheduled again with an earlier starting time. Therefore, as now the vehicles may be unscheduled, instead of sequentially scheduling all vehicles in V, we opted to schedule the leftmost vehicle from V such that its not yet scheduled (or has been unscheduled). Algorithm 3 shows the details of the procedure. Notice that the resulting schedule is always feasible.

Figure 3 shows a graphical representation of a schedule for an instance with 180 vehicles. We show the charging intervals for all vehicles assigned to each line, while in the bottom of the figure we report the maximum imbalance level among the lines. Cars that finished charging before their due date are colored in green, while cars that finished after their due date are colored in yellow and red (in red the portion after the due date, i.e. the tardiness of the vehicle).

5.2 Initial population

To create a diverse initial population we propose to use a combination of two dispatching rules together with some random chromosomes. One third of the population is created with each technique.

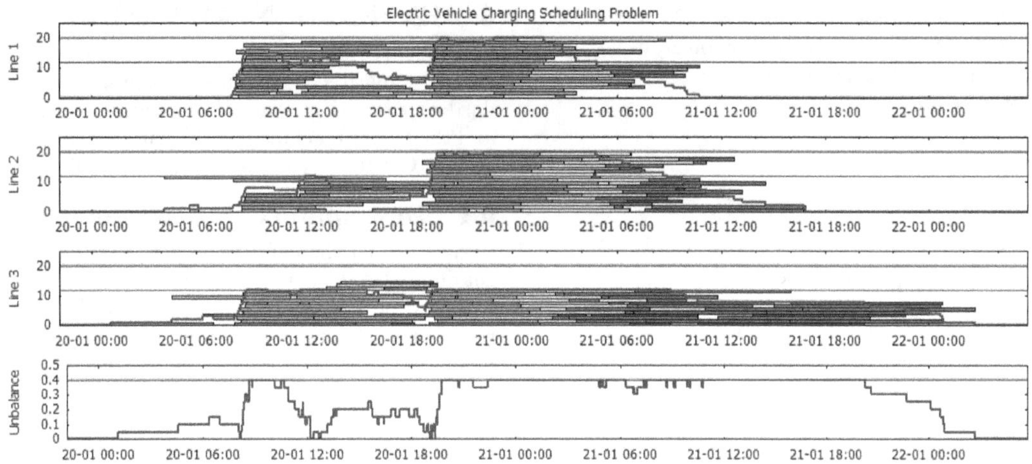

Figure 3: Example of a problem schedule. Green intervals represent charging times of vehicles that finish before their due date. Yellow and red intervals represent charging times of vehicles that finish after their due date (in yellow the portion before the due date and in red the portion after the due date, i.e. the tardiness of the vehicle).

The first dispatching rule is the Due Date rule, which sorts the vehicles in increasing order of its due date d_{ij}.

The second is the Apparently Tardiness rule, which is an adaptation of the rule used in [6]. This rule was used in many papers (see for example [9]) and is well-known for its effectiveness when minimizing tardiness. We propose to adapt this rule as follows: let $\Gamma(\alpha)$ be the earliest starting time for an unscheduled vehicle in the partial schedule α built so far. Then for all unscheduled vehicles that can start at $\Gamma(\alpha)$ a selection probability is calculated as

$$\Pi_j = \frac{1}{p_j} \exp\left[\frac{-\max(0, d_j - \Gamma(\alpha) - p_j)}{g\overline{p}}\right] \tag{8}$$

where $\overline{p}$ is the average charging time of vehicles and g is a look-ahead parameter to be fixed empirically, which is set here to 0.25 based on the experiments performed in [6]. The rule sorts all the vehicles in ascendent order of Π_j.

These two rules are deterministic but we need to create diverse chromosomes. Therefore, to select the next vehicle to be appended to the chromosome, firstly we sort the vehicles with the corresponding dispatching rule and then we perform a tournament selection. To this end, we randomly select a number $tSize$ of vehicles and we add to the chromosome the best of the chosen vehicles according to the ordering given by the dispatching rule. The tournament size $tSize$ is a relevant parameter, as if it is too large very similar chromosomes will be produced, whereas too small tournament sizes may result in almost random chromosomes.

5.3 Selection and replacement strategies

In the selection phase all chromosomes are grouped into pairs, and then the crossover operator is applied to each pair to produce two offspring solutions, which can then be modified by the mutation operator. Then, the replacement strategy is used to choose the chromosomes that will advance to the next generation. For each pair of parents and its two offspring, we choose the best two chromosomes such that they have a different tardiness. In this way we preserve the diversity avoiding to choose two identical chromosomes. Also notice that the best solution of a generation is always equal or better than the best solution of the previous generation. In case that the two parents and their two offspring have all the same tardiness, we choose two of them randomly.

5.4 Crossover operator

The crossover operator should generate chromosomes that inherit good characteristics of their parents and hopefully improve the value of the fitness function. In this paper we define three different crossover operators that combine two parents (P_1 and P_2) to produce two offspring (O_1 and O_2).

The first one is denoted *LEX* (Line Exchange Crossover), and it starts randomly selecting one line L_i. Then, it assigns to the offspring O_1 all vehicles of L_i in the same order as they appear in P_2, and the vehicles of the remaining two lines in the same order as in P_1. To create O_2 the vehicles of L_i are taken from P_1 and the remaining vehicles from P_2.

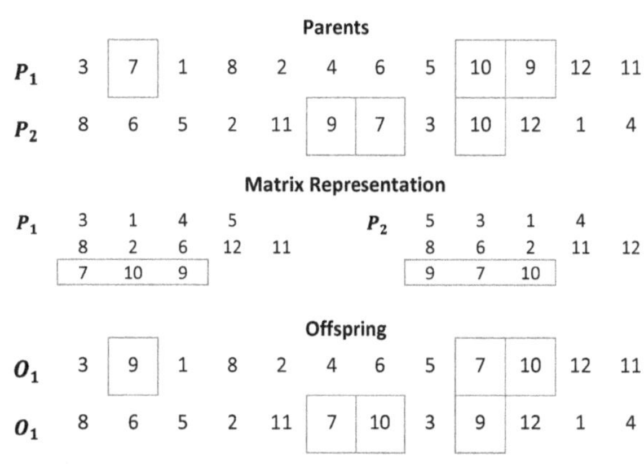

Figure 4: Example of *LEX*. Line 3 is randomly selected and its vehicles are exchanged in the offspring.

The second operator, denoted *SBX* (Starting-time Based Crossover) randomly selects a time t_0. Then, O_1 is created with all vehicles of P_1 such that they start charging before t_0. The chromosome is completed with the remaining vehicles in the same order as they appear in P_2. O_2 is created similarly.

Figures 4 and 5 show examples of operators LEX and SBX respectively. In these examples, the conversion from vector to matrix is performed with illustrative purposes only, as in practice it is not necessary.

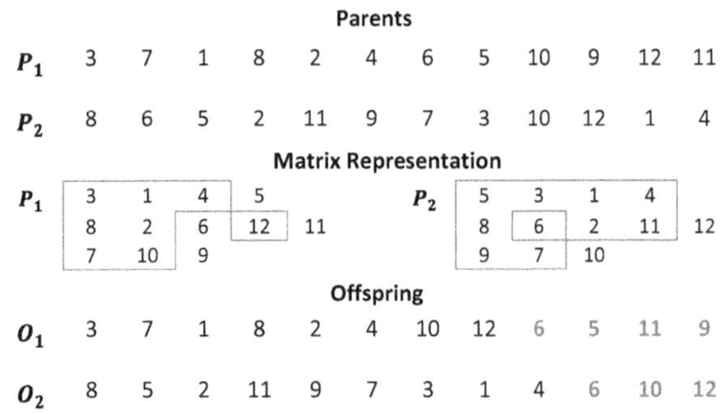

Figure 5: Example of SBX. Starting times of vehicles in P_1 are $\{0,0,0,0,0,7,10,10,0,10,7,11\}$ and in P_2 are $\{0,10,0,0,7,0,0,5,9,12,0,7\}$. Time $t_0 = 9$ is randomly selected, and then all vehicles that start charging before t_0 are taken from one parent and the remaining vehicles are taken from the other parent.

We also consider the standard one-point crossover operator (denoted $1PX$), which randomly chooses a position in the chromosome, and creates O_1 by choosing all vehicles of P_1 before that position, and completes O_1 by adding the remaining vehicles in the same relative order as in P_2. For creating O_2 the parents reverse their roles.

LEX and SBX are specifically designed to solve our particular problem and hence we expect that they are more efficient than the standard one-point crossover operator $1PX$.

Notice that no repairing mechanisms for infeasible solutions are needed, as the resulting chromosomes are evaluated (after the mutation step) by the scheduler algorithm detailed in Section 5.1, which always produces feasible schedules.

5.5 Mutation operator

The mutation operator should improve the diversity of the population and introduce new schemata into the chromosomes. We propose an operator that given a schedule, each line is mutated with some probability. If some line L_i is mutated, the operator selects a random subset of consecutive vehicles of that line, and randomly shuffles the order of these vehicles. Figure 6 shows an example of this operator in which one of the lines of the schedule is mutated.

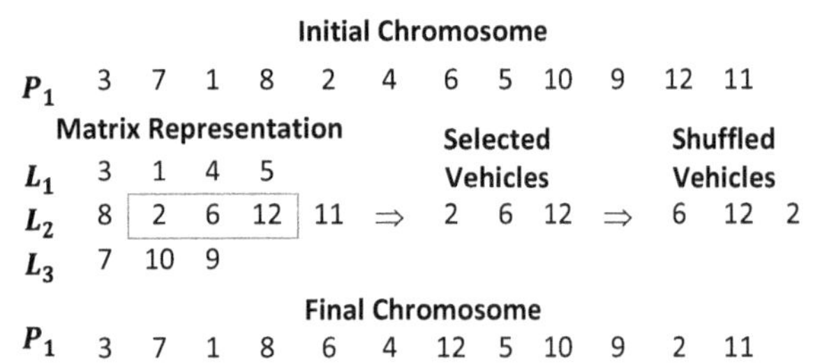

Figure 6: Example of the mutation operator. Each line is mutated with some probability (only L_2 in this example). A random subset of consecutive vehicles of the line is shuffled.

6. EXPERIMENTAL RESULTS

We have conducted an experimental study to evaluate our proposal and to compare it with the state-of-the-art in standard benchmarks. The GA has been implemented in C++ and the target machine is a PC with a Xeon E5520 processor and 24 GB RAM running Linux (SL 6.0).

6.1 Description of the benchmark set

We consider the benchmark set proposed in [6], where the charging station is installed in a car park with 180 spaces, with a time horizon of one day and different profiles of arrival times, demands and due dates based on the expected behavior of the users in some weekdays.

Two types of instances are defined. In type 1 instances 60 vehicles arrive at each line L_i along the day and demand charging, while in type 2 instances 108 vehicles arrive in L_1, 54 in L_2 and 18 in L_3, i.e., 60%, 30% and 10% respectively. So, in the later case we may expect that the scheduling algorithm has to control many situations of imbalance among the lines in order to build a feasible schedule. We also consider different values for the imbalance parameter Δ (0.2, 0.4, 0.6 and 0.8) and for the maximum number of vehicles that can be charging at the same time in a line N (20, 30 and 40). 30 instances were generated for each combination of type, Δ and N, so we have a total of 720 instances.

6.2 GA parameter settings

Firstly we have conducted a preliminary study to set some of the parameters of the GA. We have considered a set of 24 instances, in particular the first one of each combination of parameters. We have set the population size at 200 chromosomes and the stopping condition at 25 generations without improving the best solution found so far, or also if we find a solution with zero tardiness. These values are reasonable and by using them the computational time is adequate. Then, we tested different values for the remaining GA parameters, i.e. crossover probability, mutation probability for each line of the schedule, and tournament size for the dispatching rules used to create the initial population. Table 1 shows a summary of the tested values, indicating in bold the configuration that achieved the best average results.

Table 1: Values tested in the parameter tuning. Bold values indicate the best configuration found.

Parameter	Values tested
cr_prob	0.6, **0.8**, 1
mut_prob	0, **0.1**, 0.3
tSize	4, **8**, 12, 16

This configuration results in reasonable convergence patterns, as shown in Figure 7, which details the evolution of the best and average tardiness of the population for one run on an instance of *Type* 1, $N = 20$ and $\Delta = 0.2$.

6.3 Comparison of the crossover operators

In this section we compare the crossover operators LEX, SBX and $1PX$ described in Section 5.4. Again, experiments were made in 24 instances: the first instance of each combination of parameters. GA is executed 30 times for each instance to obtain statistically significant results. Table 2 shows the results, in particular the average tardiness values grouped by instance type in both the static and dynamic

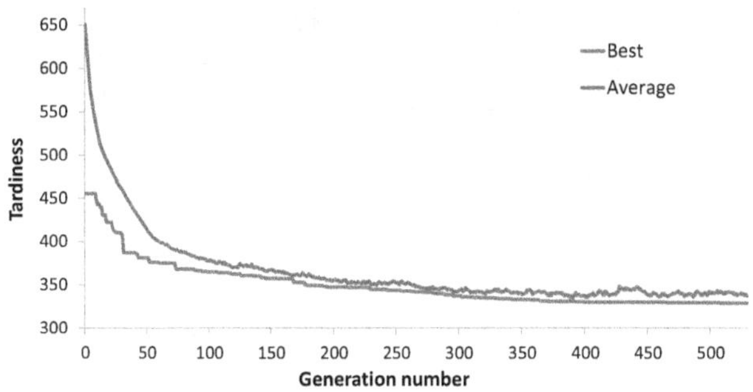

Figure 7: Evolution of the best and average tardiness of the population depending on the generation number, for one run on an instance of *Type* 1, $N = 20$ and $\Delta = 0.2$.

problems. We notice that *SBX* operator always obtains the best results, while *LEX* operator seems the worst option.

To further compare the quality of the proposed crossover operators, we have done some statistical tests to analyze differences between them. Following [5], since we have multiple-problem analysis, we have used non-parametric statistical tests. First, we have run a Shapiro-Wilk test to confirm the non-normality of the data. Then we have used paired Wilcoxon signed rank tests to compare the average values in all the 48 instances considered (24 for the static problem and 24 for the dynamic one). In all these tests, the level of confidence used was 95% and the alternative hypothesis was "the difference between the errors of operator *SBX* and the other operator is smaller than 0". The *p*-values obtained with these tests (*LEX*: 1.061e-08, *1PX*: 0.0001584) show that there exist statistically significant differences between *SBX* and the other proposed operators in these instances.

We believe that *SBX* obtains better results than *1PX* because it is based on the phenotype instead of the genotype, and therefore it captures better the particular issues of our problem. On the other hand, *LEX* obtains worse results probably because the created offspring is too similar to their parents and hence the diversity of the population is lower.

6.4 Comparison with the state-of-the-art

In this section we compare the GA (using *SBX* operator) with the state-of-the-art method in this problem, which is the Problem Decomposition approach (*PD*) proposed in [6]. In this case we consider the full benchmark, i.e. the 720 instances in both the static and dynamic versions of the problem. Again, our GA is run 30 times for each instance and the best and average tardiness (in hours) are registered.

Table 3 shows the results of these experiments. We report, for each group of 30 instances, the sum of the tardiness of all 30 instances. It is remarkable that our GA obtains better average tardiness values than *PD* in all groups of instances in both the static and dynamic versions of the problem.

To further compare GA and *PD*, as similarly done in Section 6.3, we have run a Shapiro-Wilk test to confirm the non-normality of the data and then a paired Wilcoxon signed rank test to compare the average tardiness values obtained by GA and *PD* results in the 720 considered instances in the dynamic problem (which is arguably the most fair comparison). The *p*-value obtained from these tests (lower than 2.2e-16) show that there exist statistically significant differ-

Table 2: Comparison between the proposed crossover operators in a set of 24 instances. We report the average tardiness in hours of 30 runs, grouped by instance type.

Ins.	Static			Dynamic		
	LEX	*SBX*	*1PX*	*LEX*	*SBX*	*1PX*
Type1	56.34	55.27	55.67	73.24	71.79	72.11
Type2	1157	1113	1118	1129	1119	1121

ences between GA and *PD*, and then we can conclude that GA is significantly better than the state-of-the-art.

It is also essential to discuss computational times, as the algorithm is intended to be run in a real scenario. In the static problem the average time is 93 seconds per run, although the time varies depending on the instance parameters. In fact, instances with $\Delta = 0.2$ generally take more time because the imbalance constraints are much more restrictive and the problem is more difficult to solve. In the dynamic problem the average time is 325 seconds. However, this number accounts for the total running time along the 24-hour period. As the algorithm is run every two minutes, it is run 720 times in a 24-hour period, and therefore the average running time is only 0.45 seconds. Again, this number depends on the instance parameters, but in the worst case the average time is 2.75 seconds and so we can conclude that the algorithm is appropriate in a real-world setting.

In Table 3 we can also observe that the genetic algorithm reaches much better tardiness values for the static version than for the dynamic one. Although in absolute terms the reduction is similar in type 1 and type 2 instances, the improvements are specially remarkable in type 1 instances, as in relative terms the average reduction is nearly of 50%. We think that type 2 instances offer less room for improvement, as the difference of vehicle arrivals in each line (60% in L_1, 30% in L_2 and 10% in L_3) makes much more difficult to improve the schedule because of the imbalance constraints. Anyway, we can conclude that GA is able to exploit all the extra information about arrival times, charging times and due dates to reach better solutions.

7. CONCLUSIONS

In this work we addressed the problem of scheduling the charging of electric vehicles and we developed a genetic algorithm that obtains competitive results. The problem is defined in [6] and it is motivated by a real environment in which a number of vehicles may require charge from an electric system installed in a garage. The environment has a number of constraints, as a maximum number of vehicles that can be charged simultaneously and also imbalance constraints among the three lines of the three-phase electric feeder. We have considered two versions of the problem: the static version and the dynamic one. In the static version we know in advance the arrival time, charging time and due date of every vehicle, whereas in the dynamic version we do not have these data.

We have proposed a genetic algorithm with some operators specifically designed to efficiently deal with our problem. We have analyzed our proposal and compared it with the state-of-the-art algorithm for this problem, which is the Problem Decomposition approach proposed in [6], obtaining significantly better results. The scheduler algorithm, the crossover and mutation operators and the way of gen-

Table 3: Comparison of our GA with the state-of-the-art algorithm PD. Each value corresponds to the sum of the tardiness (in hours) of the 30 instances of each group.

Instance N	Δ	PD	GA (Static) Best	GA (Static) Avg.	GA (Dynamic) Best	GA (Dynamic) Avg.
Type 1						
20	0.2	7720	5250	5442	6744	7142
	0.4	4240	2616	2680	3844	3977
	0.6	3849	2260	2300	3494	3569
	0.8	3807	2204	2239	3435	3502
30	0.2	1782	931	997	1262	1412
	0.4	490	80	92	343	375
	0.6	458	37	50	302	319
	0.8	458	35	49	300	317
40	0.2	646	337	364	464	511
	0.4	28	0	0	4	6
	0.6	9	0	0	3	3
	0.8	9	0	0	3	3
Avg.		1958	1146	1184	1683	1761
Type 2						
20	0.2	127614	123167	124380	123746	124599
	0.4	46254	44675	45263	45049	45461
	0.6	23008	20957	21206	21771	22075
	0.8	14808	12888	13031	14107	14337
30	0.2	72460	70304	71129	70825	71462
	0.4	21427	20378	20630	21043	21321
	0.6	8079	7093	7188	7837	8007
	0.8	4501	3551	3607	4325	4408
40	0.2	46096	44618	45216	45031	45455
	0.4	10932	9883	10011	10593	10799
	0.6	3520	2870	2917	3432	3518
	0.8	1659	888	923	1524	1569
Avg.		31696	30106	30458	30773	31084

erating a diverse initial population are contributions of this work, and we think that the good performance of the overall algorithm is due to them.

We have seen that the tardiness obtained while solving the static version of the problem is much lower than that of the dynamic version. This leads us to think that there may be better ways of dealing with the dynamic problem. Maybe if we could anticipate some car arrivals (for example having a probability distribution of the arrival of cars depending on the time of the day), then we may avoid some bottlenecks and hence schedule the cars in a more effective way. This may be the subject of further research.

We also plan to compare our results with those reported in [7]. Additionally, it would be interesting to design new and improved crossover operators for this problem, as well as compare them with other well-known operators from the literature, as for example PMX (Partially Matched Crossover) or CX (Cycle Crossover). Another research line could be designing local search methods to combine with the GA in order to improve its results.

Finally, we plan to consider additional characteristics of the real problem. For example, the users may pick up the vehicle before the declared due date, or the battery may get fully charged before the expected charging time p_{ij}. It would also be interesting to consider that the contracted power changes over time or that the vehicles can be charged at non constant rate.

8. ACKNOWLEDGMENTS

This research has been supported by the Spanish Government under research project TIN2013-46511-C2-2-P.

9. REFERENCES

[1] D. Dallinger. *Plug-in Electric Vehicles Integrating Fluctuating Renewable Electricity*. Kassel University Press, 2013.

[2] EDSO. Position paper on electric vehicles charging infrastructure. Technical report, European Distribution system Operators for Smart Grids (EDSO), 10 April 2012.

[3] L. Gan, U. Topcu, and S. Low. Optimal decentralized protocol for electric vehicle charging. *IEEE Transaction on Power Systems*, 28(2):940–951, 2013.

[4] J. García-Villalobos, I. Zamora, J. San Martín, F. Asensio, and V. Aperribay. Plug-in electric vehicles in electric distribution networks: A review of smart charging approaches. *Renewable and Sustainable Energy Reviews*, 38:717–731, 2014.

[5] S. García, A. Fernández, J. Luengo, and F. Herrera. Advanced nonparametric tests for multiple comparisons in the design of experiments in computational intelligence and data mining: Experimental analysis of power. *Information Sciences*, 180:2044–2064, 2010.

[6] A. Hernandez-Arauzo, J. Puente, M. A. Gonzalez, R. Varela, and J. Sedano. Dynamic scheduling of electric vehicle charging under limited power and phase balance constraints. In *Proceedings of the 7th Scheduling and Planning Applications Workshop (SPARK 2013)*, pages 1–8, 2013.

[7] A. Hernandez-Arauzo, J. Puente, R. Varela, and J. Sedano. Electric vehicle charging under power and balance constraints as dynamic scheduling. *Computers & Industrial Engineering*, Accepted Manuscript (unedited version) available online: 13-APR-2015. DOI: 10.1016/j.cie.2015.04.002, 2015.

[8] J. Kang, S. J. Duncan, and D. N. Mavris. Real-time scheduling techniques for electric vehicle charging in support of frequency regulation. *Procedia Computer Science*, 16:767–775, 2013.

[9] S. Kaplan and G. Rabadi. Exact and heuristic algorithms for the aerial refueling parallel machine scheduling problem with due date-to-deadline window and ready times. *Computers & Industrial Engineering*, 62(1):276–285, 2012.

[10] Z. Ma, D. Callaway, and I. Hiskens. Decentralized charging control of large populations of plug-in electric vehicles. *IEEE Transactions on Control Systems Technology*, 21(1):67–78, 2013.

[11] J. Sedano, M. Portal, A. Hernandez Arauzo, J. Villar, J. Puente, and R. Varela. Sistema de control autónomo para distribución de energía en una estación de carga de vehículos eléctricos: diseño y operación. Technical report, Instituto Tecnológico de Castilla y León ITCL, 2012.

[12] J. Yang, L. He, and S. Fu. An improved pso-based charging strategy of electric vehicles in electrical distribution grid. *Applied Energy*, 128:82–92, 2014.

Predicting Heuristic Search Performance with PageRank Centrality in Local Optima Networks

Sebastian Herrmann
Department of Information Systems and Business Administration
University of Mainz, Germany
s.herrmann@uni-mainz.de

Franz Rothlauf
Department of Information Systems and Business Administration
University of Mainz, Germany
rothlauf@uni-mainz.de

ABSTRACT

Previous studies have used statistical analysis of fitness landscapes such as ruggedness and deceptiveness in order to predict the expected quality of heuristic search methods. Novel approaches for predicting the performance of heuristic search are based on the analysis of local optima networks (LONs). A LON is a compressed stochastic model of a fitness landscape's basin transitions. Recent literature has suggested using various LON network measurements as predictors for local search performance.

In this study, we suggest PageRank centrality as a new measure for predicting the performance of heuristic search methods using local search. PageRank centrality is a variant of Eigenvector centrality and reflects the probability that a node in a network is visited by a random walk. Since the centrality of high-quality solutions in LONs determines the search difficulty of the underlying fitness landscape and since the big valley property suggests that local optima are not randomly distributed in the search space but rather clustered and close to one another, PageRank centrality can serve as a good predictor for local search performance. In our experiments for NK-models and the traveling salesman problem, we found that the PageRank centrality is a very good predictor for the performance of first-improvement local search as well as simulated annealing, since it explains more than 90% of the variance of search performance. Furthermore, we found that PageRank centrality is a better predictor of search performance than traditional approaches such as ruggedness, deceptiveness, and the length of the shortest path to the optimum.

Categories and Subject Descriptors

F.2.m [**Analysis of Algorithms and Problem Complexity**]: Miscellaneous; G.2.2 [**Discrete Mathematics**]: Graph Theory—*Network Problems*; I.2.8 [**Artificial Intelligence**]: Problem Solving, Control Methods, and Search—*Heuristic methods*

GECCO '15, July 11 - 15, 2015, Madrid, Spain

ISBN 978-1-4503-3472-3/15/07...$15.00

DOI: http://dx.doi.org/10.1145/2739480.2754691

Keywords

Fitness landscape analysis, search difficulty, pagerank centrality, local optima networks, NK-landscapes, traveling salesman problem.

1. INTRODUCTION

Most evolutionary search concepts use intensification during search. A common concept for intensification is to apply some kind of local search that applies incremental changes to a solution candidate and prefers solutions with a higher solution quality. Standard examples in evolutionary search that rely on local search are hill climbing, simulated annealing [14], and genetic algorithms, in particular evolutionary strategies or evolutionary programming. A downside of local search is its tendency to get stuck in local optima [9]. Thus, using only local search alone usually does not guarantee finding the global optimum. As local search is a core of many heuristic optimization approaches, predicting the performance of local search [10] is relevant for the process of selecting an appropriate algorithm for a given problem and also for the design of search techniques [18, 24].

Most approaches for predicting the performance of local search use the concept of fitness landscapes [28]. The fitness landscape of a problem instance is defined by the solution candidates, their neighborhood structure (defined by the used search operator), and the fitness of the solution candidates. In general, two solutions are adjacent if they can be transformed into each other by an incremental change, that is, a single local search step. Often, structural properties of the resulting landscape are used for predicting algorithm performance. For instance, the more rugged a fitness landscape is, the higher the probability that an algorithm gets stuck in a local optimum [25].

Local Optima Networks (LONs) can be used for the statistical network analysis of fitness landscapes [19]. In general, a LON is a stochastic and compressed representation of a fitness landscape, where the vertex set (nodes) of the LON represents the landscape's local optima. In a LON, there is a directed edge between two nodes A and B if a local search step directly transforms one solution in node A's basin of attraction into another solution that lies in node B's basin of attraction. The basin of attraction of a local optimum is the set of solution candidates from which the focal local optimum can be reached using a number of local search steps (no diversification steps are allowed). Each edge of a LON is weighted by the number of possible transitions between the two basins of attraction.

LONs have already been used successfully to predict the

performance of heuristic optimization methods using local search. For example, [5] predicted the run-time performance of iterated local search in Kauffman's NK landscapes [13]. The authors proposed four different network metrics as predictors, of which the average length of the shortest paths to the optimum had the highest accuracy for predicting performance ($R^2 \approx 0.5$). These results are promising and inspired us to conduct further research on predicting search performance by network analysis of LONs.

In network analysis, the concept of centrality describes how important or influential a node is—depending on the network's linkage structure and the focal node's location [7]. The Eigenvector centrality is a measurement of the centrality of a node in a network. It is based on random walks on the network graph, where nodes and edges can be revisited multiple times [2]. A prominent implementation of the Eigenvector centrality is Google's PageRank algorithm [3]. The PageRank value of a node (originally defined for a network of web pages) corresponds to the probability that a random surfer would visit this node/web page [6].

Thus, in this paper, we study whether the PageRank centrality of the global optimum in the LON is a valuable predictor of performance for local-search based metaheuristics. As a performance measure, we use the probability of finding the global optimum (success rate) and the average number of function evaluations (run-time). We performed a series of experiments on scalable test problems (Kauffman's NK landscapes) and a representative of a combinatorial optimization problem (symmetric traveling salesman problem). We found that the PageRank centrality of an instance's global optimum is a good predictor of the probability that the global optimum can be located by (i) stochastic hill climbing and (ii) simulated annealing.

The high accuracy of PageRank centrality at predicting the performance of local search can be explained by the structure of the LON that models the problem's fitness landscape. The weighted edges in a LON describe possible transition paths of local search. Along the edges, local search can switch between two basins of attraction. Thus, the performance of a local search process highly depends on whether the path between the local optima in a LON leads to the global optimum. If many paths lead to the global optimum, the performance of the local search is high; if there are only a few paths, local search can hardly make its way to the global optimum, leading to low performance. For instance, if the number of edges (transition probabilities) are equal between all local basins of attraction, there is no inherent trajectory in such a landscape that leads local search towards the optimum and we expect a low probability of finding the global optimum. In contrast, the probability to find the global optimum is high if the LON's linkage structure supports the convergence into the optimum's basin. This explanation is in line with the findings for many combinatorial optimization problems, where a "big valley structure" [1] can be observed. In many of such problems, local optima are not randomly distributed in the search space; rather they are clustered. Thus, most local optima are close to each other and the global optima is usually not isolated in the search space; rather it is surrounded by all the local optima. Big valley properties have been observed for the TSP [1] and other problem types.

Our paper is structured as follows: In section 2, we describe the local-search mechanism used for our experiments (hill climbing and simulated annealing). In section 3, we introduce a formal definition of a fitness landscape, the neighborhood structure, basins of attraction and some commonly used landscape features. In section 4, we give a formal definition of the concept of Local Optima Networks. Section 5 deals with the calculation of PageRank Centrality and its application in LONs. In section 6, we describe our experiment setup and the problem types used (NK-model, TSP). We present our results in section 7 and draw our conclusions in section 8.

2. LOCAL SEARCH ALGORITHMS

This section briefly reviews the two variants of heuristic optimization methods used as representatives for local search-based methods: hill climbing and simulated annealing.

2.1 Hill Climbing

Hill climbing is a straightforward and rather simple application of local search. Let S be the solution space, i.e. the set of all valid problem solutions. The function $f : S \rightarrow \mathbb{R}_{\geq 0}$ assigns a fitness value to each $s \in S$. Hill climbing starts with a randomly selected solution $s_0 \in S$. Then, in iterative steps, the algorithm selects a random solution s_{i+1} from the neighborhood of s_i. The neighborhood $N(s)$ is the set of solutions that can be reached by performing an incremental change to s. In first-improvement hill climbing (fi-hc), a random solution is selected from the neighborhood; if it is better than the existing solution, it replaces the existing solution (algorithm 1). Hill Climbing performs incremental changes until no further improvement can be achieved or a fixed limit of iterations has been reached.

Algorithm 1 First-Improvement Hill Climbing

Require: Solution space S, Fitness function $f(S)$, Neighborhood function $N(S)$
Choose initial random solution $s_0 \in S$
i ← 0
repeat
  choose random $s_{i+1} \in N(s_i)$
  if $f(s_i) < f(s_{i+1})$ **then**
    $s_i \leftarrow s_{i+1}$
  end if
  $i \leftarrow i + 1$
until s_{i+1} is local optimum
return s_{i+1}

We use first-improvement hill climbing as a representative of a basic local search method since it is well-understood and often used.

2.2 Simulated Annealing

The major drawback of hill climbing is that it can get stuck in a local optimum [9]. Simulated annealing (SA) [14] is a method inspired by statistical mechanics that has the ability to overcome local optima. It is based on an analogy with cooling down a liquid to a solid substance. Algorithm 2 gives the basic principle of SA using a fixed cooling schedule for a maximization problem.

SA always accepts better solutions; solutions with a lower fitness are accepted with probability $\frac{e^{-|f(s_i)-f(s_{i+1})|}}{T_i}$. Thus, the probability of accepting worse solutions decreases with

Algorithm 2 Simulated Annealing

Require: Solution space S, Fitness $f(S)$, Neighborhood $N(S)$, Initial Temperature T_0, Cooling Rate α

Choose random initial solution $s_0 \in S$
$i \leftarrow 0$
repeat
  choose random $s_{i+1} \in N(s_i)$
  if $(f(s_i) < f(s_{i+1}))$ **then**
    $s_i \leftarrow s_{i+1}$
  else if $\frac{e^{-|f(s_i)-f(s_{i+1})|}}{T_i} \geq rand(0,1)$ **then**
    $s_i \leftarrow s_{i+1}$
  end if
  $T_{i+1} \leftarrow \alpha \times T_i$
  $i \leftarrow i+1$
until s_{i+1} is global optimum or i > iteration limit
return s_{i+1}

a higher fitness difference $|f(s_i) - f(s_{i+1})|$ and a lower temperature T_i. For the temperature $T \rightarrow 0$, SA becomes first-improvement hill climbing.

The parameters initial temperature T_0 and cooling rate α must be set problem-specific. A rule of thumb for a proper starting temperature is to randomly select a number of solutions and to set $T_0 \approx \sigma(f(s))...2\sigma(f(s))$ (where σ is the standard deviation). A proper setting for the cooling is $\alpha \in (0.9, 0.999)$ [15]. For our experiments, we randomly sampled 1000 solutions s_i before each SA run and set the initial temperature to $T_0 = 1.5 \times \sigma(f(s_i))$. For all runs, we set $\alpha = 0.97$.

3. FITNESS LANDSCAPE ANALYSIS

3.1 Neighborhood Structure

A fitness landscape [28] is a triplet of a search space S, fitness function f, and neighborhood structure $N(S)$. There is a set of valid solution candidates $s \in S$. The evaluation function $f : S \rightarrow \mathbb{R}_{\geq 0}$ assigns a fitness value to each $s \in S$. The neighborhood function $N : S \rightarrow \mathcal{P}(S)$ assigns a set of neighbors $N(s)$ (which is a subset of S) to every $s \in S$. The neighborhood determines the position of each s in the landscape [23]. Furthermore, we define a distance function between two solutions s_0 and s_1 as

$$d : (s_0, s_1) \rightarrow \mathbb{N}_0, s_0 \wedge s_1 \in S. \quad (1)$$

The distance function depends on the search operator used. Usually, the application of a local search operator creates a new solution s_1 with distance $d_{s_0,s_1} = 1$ to the original solution s_0. Using distances, we can define the neighborhood function as

$$N : s_0 \rightarrow \{s_1 \in S \mid s_1 \neq s_0 \wedge 0 < d(s_0, s_1) \leq d_{\max}\}. \quad (2)$$

Most local search uses a low constant value for $d_{\max}$ (like $d_{\max} = 1$). Other heuristic methods (like variable neighborhood search) vary $d_{\max}$ during run-time to obtain higher diversification and to escape from a local optimum by using perturbation steps. This results in changes in the landscape during the run of the algorithm, and makes static analyses more difficult. Since most operators of local-search based techniques are based on simple metrics—e.g. Hamming distance—it is generally accepted to study a landscape defined by a fitness function and one or several induced distances [22].

3.2 Definition of Local Optima

A fitness landscape can have one or more local optima. A local optimum is a solution that has no superior neighbors ("top of the hill"). For a maximization problem, we define a function

$$N_{\text{sup}}(s) = \{n \in S \mid n \in N(s) \wedge f(n) > (f(s)\} \quad (3)$$

which returns the neighbors of a solution $s \in S$ that have a superior fitness. Thus, the set

$$LO = \{lo \in S \mid N_{\text{sup}}(lo) = \{\}\}. \quad (4)$$

contains all solutions that have no neighbors with superior fitness, which is equivalent to the set of local optima. LO also contains the global optimum.

3.3 Landscape Features

Many concepts that can be used for the prediction of performance focus on the structural properties of fitness landscapes. Kallel [12] provides a well-elaborated collection of such features. In the literature, two of the frequently used concepts to help predict performance are ruggedness [27] and deceptiveness [11]. The idea of ruggedness is that the smoother the landscape is, the more easily heuristic search methods can find the global optimum. Ruggedness is usually measured as the correlation of fitness values between neighboring solutions (nearest-neighbor-correlation).

A landscape is deceptive if the structure of the search space leads local search approaches away from the global optimum. A measurement for deceptiveness is the correlation between the fitness of the solutions and their distance to the global optimum [11]. For the calculation of fitness-distance correlation, the global optimum must be known in advance.

3.4 Basins of Attraction

Basins of attraction are an important concept for the analysis of fitness landscapes. Each local (and global) optimum has a basin of attraction, which is defined as the set of solution candidates from which local search can converge to the local optimum ("way-points that lead to the top of the hill"). Identifying the basins is a prerequisite for the calculation of LONs. They depend on the selection-rule of the hill-climbing algorithm [20].

The function

$$B : lo \rightarrow \mathcal{P}(S \backslash LO) \quad (5)$$

assigns a set of solutions P (which represent the basin) to each local optimum $lo \in LO$. First-improvement hill climbing uses a stochastic selection rule and accepts all better neighboring solutions. Hence a solution can belong to more than one basin. The attractor function $Attr : s \rightarrow s < LO$ returns the set of local optima for each solution candidate. A local optimum is solely attracted by itself, s.t. $|Attr(lo)| = 1 \ \ \forall \ lo \in LO$. To determine the probability that a solution s belongs to the basin of the local optimum lo, we assume that all optima are equally strong attractors. The probability then depends on the number of attractors:

$$p_{\text{bas}}(s, lo) = \begin{cases} \frac{1}{|Attr(s)|} & \text{if } s \in B(lo) \wedge lo \in LO \\ 0 & \text{else.} \end{cases} \quad (6)$$

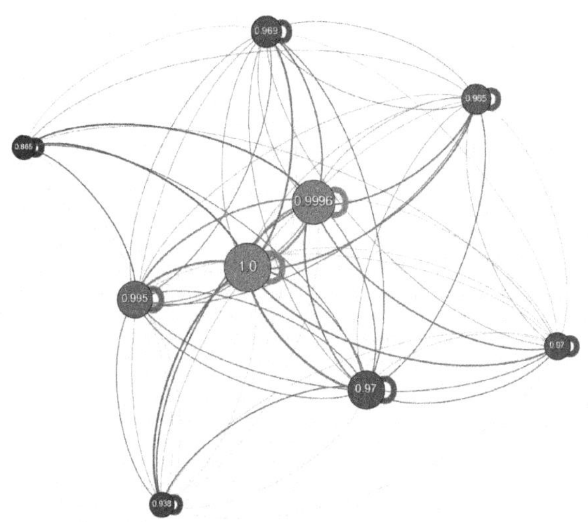

Figure 1: LON of a TSP instance. Node label and color indicate the fitness value. Node thickness and arrangement (the higher the PageRank, the more central the node position) represent PageRank centrality. Thickness of arcs indicates their weight, i.e., the transition probability between the local optima's basins of attraction.

4. LOCAL OPTIMA NETWORKS

The concept of Local Optima Networks (LONs) has been introduced for the purpose of conducting a statistical network analysis on fitness landscapes [19]. LONs have been inspired by the study of energy landscapes in chemical physics [26]. The basic idea is to construct a network in which a landscape's local optima represent the nodes in the network graph. Let our graph representation be $G = (V, A)$. The vertex set $V = LO$ contains all local optima (including the global optima) of the fitness landscape.

A is the set of arcs. There is a weighted arc from a local optimum lo_0 to a local optimum lo_1 if local search can pass from the basin of attraction $B(lo_0)$ to the basin $B(lo_1)$. For such a transition, both basins must be connected s.t. a solution in $B(lo_1)$ with a high fitness is a neighbor to a solution in $B(lo_0)$ with a lower fitness. The more such connections between two basins exist, the higher the transition probability between their corresponding local optima is, and the higher the arc weight is.

We use the following rule-set for the calculation of arcs: the probability to perform a move from any solution s_0 to another solution s_1 depends on the number of superior neighbors of s_0. First-improvement hill climbing (fi-hc) selects a random neighbor with superior fitness. Thus the probability to move from s_0 to s_1 can be calculated as

$$p(s_0, s_1) = \frac{1}{|N_{\text{sup}}(s_0)|}. \tag{7}$$

The probability to move from any solution s_0 to the basin of attraction of any local optimum $lo_1 \in LO$ depends on (i) the probability to move from s_0 to a new solution in $B(lo_1)$ and (ii) the probability that the new solution belongs to $B(lo_1)$. Thus, the conditional probability to select any superior neighbor s_1 that belongs to a different basin $B(lo_1)$ can be calculated as

$$p(s_0, s_1 | s_1 \in B(lo_1)) = \frac{1}{|N_{\text{sup}}(s_0)|} \times p_{bas}(s_1, lo_1), \tag{8}$$

To determine the probability that the algorithm moves from s_0 to any solution in the basin of lo_1, we iterate over all superior neighbors of s_0 that can be members of $B(lo_1)$ and sum up the conditional probabilities that the algorithm moves from s_0 to one of these solutions:

$$p(s_0, B(lo_1)) = \sum_{s_i:\{s | s \in N_{\text{sup}}(s_0) \wedge s \in B(lo_1)\}} [p(s_0, s_1 | s_1 \in B(lo_1))]. \tag{9}$$

To calculate the arc weights of the LON, which is the overall probability to move from one basin $B(lo_0)$ to another basin $B(lo_1)$, we sum up the probabilities of all $s_i \in B(lo_0)$ to move from s_i to $B(lo_1)$. Each probability is weighted by the probability that s_i belongs to $B(lo_0)$. The total probability is given by the ratio between that sum and the sum of probabilities of all solutions that belong to basin $B(lo_0)$:

$$p(B(lo_0), B(lo_1)) = \frac{\sum_{s_i \in B(lo_0)} [p_{\text{bas}}(s_i, lo_0) \times p(s_i, lo_1)]}{\sum_{s_i \in B(lo_0)} [p_{\text{bas}}(s_i, lo_0)]}. \tag{10}$$

Using this function, we can calculate the transition probabilities between all basins, and thus the weights of arcs between all local optima in the LON:

$$A_{i,j} = p(B(i), B(j)) \quad \forall\, i, j \in LO. \tag{11}$$

A is a stochastic matrix. The total probability of the outgoing links, i.e., the sum of the arc weights is

$$\sum_{i:LO} A_{i,j} = 1 \quad \forall\, j \in LO. \tag{12}$$

Local Optima are self-connected by the probability that the search algorithm remains in the current basin. Figure 4 shows an example of a LON for a TSP instance with eight cities.

5. PAGERANK CENTRALITY

The centrality of nodes is a meaningful concept in graph theory and network analysis. With the help of centrality, we can identify important or influential nodes in a network [2]. Modeling the *world wide web* as a network, where web pages are nodes and links to other web pages are (directed) edges, Google was the first search engine that used the centrality of nodes for assessing the relevance and importance of web sites.

To calculate a website's centrality, Google have been using the concept of PageRank [3], which is a variant of the Eigenvector centrality. The PageRank is based on the model of a surfer who is randomly visiting WWW pages. The surfer starts at a random page and then follows one of its links to another page and so forth. After following a number of links, the surfer randomly selects a new page (e.g., by typing the address into the browser's address field). Based on the model of the random surfer, the PageRank value of a website indicates the probability that a page is visited by the surfer. Incoming links from other websites increase the centrality of a page. However, PageRank also takes into account the importance of the linking sources. An incoming link from an important page can increase the relevance of a website more than numerous links coming from rather unimportant sites. Moreover, a website with many outgoing links contributes less to the importance of a linked page than a website with fewer outgoing links (given that both linking pages are equally important). Thus, three factors determine the PageRank of a web page: the number of links a page receives, the number of outgoing links of the linking pages and the PageRank of the linking pages. For detailed information on the calculation of the PageRank, we refer to [6].

To calculate the PageRank of websites, it is first necessary to represent the linkage structure as an adjacency matrix A that models the existence of links between two nodes. Then, A is normalized into a transition matrix Π that contains the probabilities of moving from one node (page) to another. Π is a stochastic matrix, since all rows and columns sum up to 1. To calculate the PageRank of the nodes of a LON, we use the transition matrix A as defined in (11). Since A is already a normalized, stochastic matrix, we set $\pi = A$.

A problem of the PageRank model is that a random surfer could get trapped in a node that has no outgoing links. The solution to this problem is that a surfer—having stayed on a page for some time—loses interest and types in a random address in the browser field. The transition matrix for this behavior is the teleportation matrix E that contains identical rows of uniform probability vectors. The convex combination of Π and E results in the transition matrix (also called *Google Matrix*)

$$G = \alpha \times \Pi + (1 - \alpha) \times E. \tag{13}$$

α is a damping factor, where $1 - \alpha$ is the probability that a random surfer stops following links and visits a random page instead. A typical value is $\alpha = 0.85$, which says that a surfer chooses a random page after about five link clicks. Since local search uses no perturbation operators (e.g., by randomly selecting a new solution from a wider neighborhood), we ignore this behavior and set $\alpha = 1$.

Then, the PageRank centrality of all nodes (local optima) is given by the vector P, such that

$$P = G \times P. \tag{14}$$

P is the Eigenvector of Π, and there is a unique solution for P if the real square matrix Π has positive components and is irreducible, i.e., it is a strongly connected graph [8, 21]. The transition matrix of a LON has positive transition probabilities and the nodes are—by our empirical observation—strongly connected for instances of the NK-model and the TSP.

P contains the PageRank centralities of local optima in the graph. Consequently, we define P_{opt} as the PageRank value of the global optimum s_{opt}.

6. EXPERIMENTAL SETTING

For our study, we assessed the correlation between the performance of local search methods (first-improvement hill climbing (fi-hc) and simulated annealing (SA)) and the PageRank centrality of the global optimum for the NK-model and the Traveling Salesman Problem (TSP).

6.1 NK-Model

The NK-model [13] is a combinatorial optimization problem that is frequently used in organizational theory, complex systems and evolutionary computation. Each instance of the model can be generated by the two parameters N and K. Each solution $s \in S$ consists of N binary decision variables, forming a search space of $|S| = 2^N$ possible states. Every combination of bits is a valid solution and has an assigned score. Each problem instance has one unique global optimum.

Instances of the NK-model are tunably difficult as there are adjustable interdependencies between the decision variables: for a given solution, each decision variable contributes to the overall score. The level of contribution depends on the variable's own state and on the state of some other preselected variables. These co-variables are randomly assigned in the process of generating a problem instance. The parameter K determines the number of co-variables per decision variable and thus the complexity of an instance. A value of $K = 0$ results in a problem solvable in linear time. $K = N - 1$ leads to a maximally difficult problem, where each decision variable can only be set to the optimal value if all other $N - 1$ co-variables are considered. In general, problem difficulty increases with higher values of K.

The distance between two binary solutions $x, y \in S$ is calculated as the Hamming-distance $d(x, y) = \sum_{i=0}^{n} |x_i - y_i|$, i.e., the number of bits that are set to different values when comparing two solutions. For both search algorithms (fi-hc as well as SA), we assumed that two solutions x, y are neighbors if their Hamming distance equals one ($d_{\max} = 1$). Then, a local search step flips exactly one bit of the current solution.

6.2 Traveling Salesman Problem (TSP)

The TSP is a well-studied and well-understood $\mathcal{NP}$-hard combinatorial optimization problem [17]. Given a set of n cities C and a pairwise symmetric distance matrix D_{ij}, the objective of the symmetric TSP is to find the Hamiltonian tour with minimum length. The Hamiltonian tour visits each city exactly once.

We studied instances of a symmetric TSP with Euclidean distances and used an order-based representation for the solutions. This encoding assigns to each city an index from the set $C = \{0, 1, .., n-1\}$ and each tour is a permutation of the indices. For a tour of n cities, there are $(n-1)!$ different permutations. This encoding is redundant since each solution tour is represented by $2N$ genotypes (N rotations and two directions) [4]. We reduced the size of the search space by a factor N by removing all rotated solutions. Since we did not remove the symmetric solutions, each instance contains two global optima. We normalized and transformed all instances to a maximization problem such that $f(s_{\text{opt}}) = 1.0$ and $f(s_{\min}) = 0.0$.

To be able to represent an instance of the TSP as a fitness landscape, we had to assign a unique integer number to each solution in the search space. In order to number the permutations, we used a scheme introduced by Lehmer [16]. We used standard 2-opt moves as the local search operator. Thus, a single move "deletes two nonadjacent edges of the current tour and then reconnects the two resulting paths into a new tour" [1]. The distance between two solutions x and y is the minimum number of 2-opt moves necessary to transform x into y.

6.3 Experiments

For each problem (NK-model and TSP), we generated 500 problem instances. For the NK-model, we used $N = 12$ decision variables. The parameter K was randomly chosen with $K \in (2, ...10)$. The considered TSP instances was of size $n = 8$. The size of our problem instances was relatively low, since the computational effort for the experiments grows factorially by the problem size n.

To be able to measure the PageRank centrality of the global optimum in the LON, we extracted the fitness landscape and the LON for each problem instance. Overall, we calculated the following measures:

1. ρ_{nn}: the ruggedness of the fitness landscape measured by the Pearson correlation between the fitness of nearest neighbors [27],
2. ρ_{fd}: the deceptiveness of the landscape measured by the Pearson correlation between fitness and distance to the global optimum [11],
3. P_{opt}: the PageRank of the global optimum in the LON.

ρ_{nn} and ρ_{fd} were determined by a random sample of 1,000 solutions per problem instance. The PageRank centrality of the peak P_{opt} was calculated using the NetworkX Library[1]. Since we assumed no perturbation, we set the damping factor to $\alpha = 1$.

For each problem instance, we performed 1,000 independent runs of first-improvement hill-climbing and simulated annealing (both with random initial solutions). For each instance, we measured search performance by

1. the success rate (p_s), which is defined as the percentage of runs that find the global optimum, and
2. the average number of fitness evaluations T_s necessary to find the global optimum. For the calculation of $avg(T_s)$, we considered only the runs that found the global optimum.

We assessed the quality of the different predictor metrics by the determination coefficient (R^2) of a linear regression model between predictor metric and empirical performance over all problem instances.

7. RESULTS

7.1 Performance of Local Search Methods

In a first step, we studied the performance of the two local search heuristics, first-improvement hill-climbing (fi-hc) and simulated annealing (SA). We measured their performance using success rate p_s and average running time $avg(T_s)$. For the NK-model, the average success rate was $p_s = 0.099$ for fi-hc and $p_s = 0.187$ for SA, resp. For the TSP, $p_s = 0.154$ for fi-hc and $p_s = 0.442$ for SA. Figure 2 compares the performance of fi-hc and SA. In this figure, we show the average performance (p_s and $avg(T_s)$) of SA over the average performance of fi-hc for the NK-model (top) and TSP (bottom). Each data point represents the performance of both algorithms for a single problem instance. In general, SA shows a better performance than fi-hc. This is expected, since SA can escape from a local optimum. Along with a higher p_s, SA needs more fitness evaluations than fi-hc.

7.2 Evaluation of Predictive Quality

We studied the quality of our metrics to predict the performance of the two search algorithms in both problem types.

[1] http://networkx.github.io/

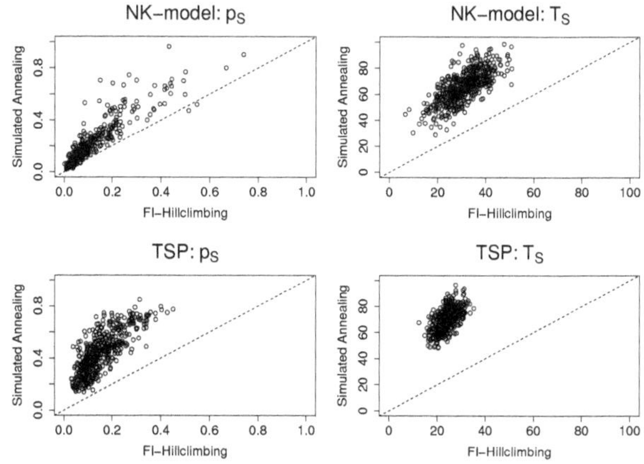

Figure 2: The performance of First-Improvement Hill Climbing over the performance of Simulated Annealing for 500 instances of the NK-model (top) and TSP (bottom). In this figure, we show the success rate (left) and the running time (right).

Table 1 gives an overview of the results of our experiments. We determined the coefficient of determination (R^2) for each combination of predictor metric, performance metric, search method and problem type. For instances of the NK-model, the PageRank P_{opt} of the global optimum explains more than 90% of the variance of the success rates of both fi-hc and SA. The correlation between running time and P_{opt} is much lower since only about 30%-50% of the variance is explained. The benchmark predictors nearest-neighbor correlation ρ_{nn} and fitness-distance correlation ρ_{fd} have a much lower predictive power since the $R^2 \approx [0.4, 0.6]$ for success rate and $R^2 \approx [0.1, 0.3]$ for running time.

For TSP, we observe similar numbers: the explanatory power of the standard metrics ρ_{nn} and ρ_{fd} ranges from 0% to 20%. In contrast, the PageRank explains around 65%-75% of the variance of p_s and between 35%-60% of $avg(T_s)$. In summary, the PageRank is a good predictor for the expected success probability of local search approaches like fi-hc and SA.

	FI Hill Cimbing		**SA**	
Performance	p_s	$avg(T_s)$	p_s	$avg(T_s)$
NK-model				
ρ_{nn}	0.475	0.139	0.587	0.374
ρ_{fd}	0.37	0.101	0.541	0.306
P_{opt}	0.906	0.307	0.916	0.537
TSP				
ρ_{nn}	0.006	0.003	0.001	0.001
ρ_{fd}	0.11	0.043	0.273	0.001
P_{opt}	0.757	0.605	0.646	0.338

Table 1: R^2 for NK-model and TSP

We will now take a closer look at the predictive quality of PageRank for the different search methods and problem types. Figure 3 plots p_s (left) and $avg(T_s)$ (right) over the PageRank of the global optimum for fi-hc (top) and SA (bottom). All results are for the NK-model. Each dot represents the average performance of the particular search method in a single problem instance over the PageRank centrality of the global optimum in the corresponding LON. The plots reveal a high correlation between PageRank and success rate. For running time (right), the correlation is lower. Figure 4 plots the same numbers for the TSP instances. We observed the following characteristics of the results:

1. For both the NK-model and TSP, the PageRank explains almost the total variance of success rate. This also holds for different values of K in the NK-model. This result is due to the fact that the transition matrix in the LON is a stochastic approximation of the moves of local search algorithms in the fitness landscape. The LON graph induces a finite-state Markov Chain, and the PageRank vector corresponds to the chain's stationary distribution [6]. Since the success rate is the probability of finding the global optimum, the scalar value of the global optimum in the PageRank Vector of the LON approximates the success rate.
2. The PageRank explains more variance of success rate in the NK-model than in the TSP. We explain this by the implementation of our TSP-model: due to the nature of the symmetric TSP, there are two local optima, reducing the significance of prediction.
3. The prediction of success rate is similar for fi-hc and SA in the NK-model. For the TSP, the correlation between PageRank and success rate of fi-hc is slightly higher than for SA. An explanation for this effect could be that the success rate and its variance are in general higher for SA than for fi-hc, leading to a loss of predictive power.
4. In the NK-model, the PageRank explains less of the variance of the running time of fi-hc than of SA. We explain this by the higher success rate of SA. Since only successful runs were considered in the run-time evaluation, the sample size of SA is higher than that of fi-hc. Furthermore, the plots indicate that the relationship between PageRank and $avg(T_s)$ is non-linear. In such a case, our linear regression model has only limited significance.
5. In the TSP, the PageRank explains more of the variance of the running time of fi-hc than SA. This could be due to the stochastic nature of SA, which accepts fitness deterioration with a decreasing probability. This behavior is not modeled in the transition probabilities of LONs.

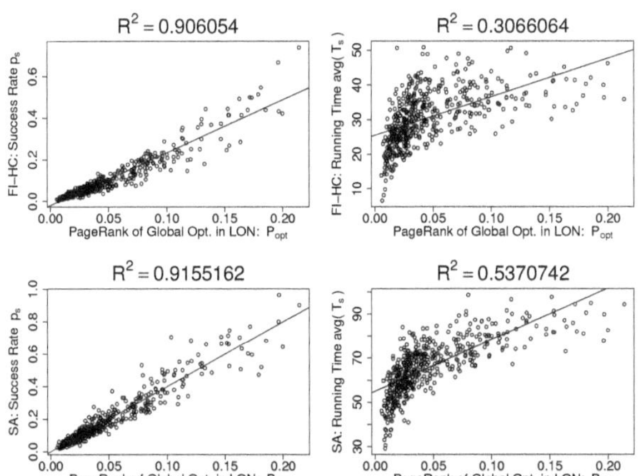

Figure 3: PageRank over performance of FI-Hill Climbing (top) and SA (bottom) for the NK-model. We plot success rate (left) and running time (right).

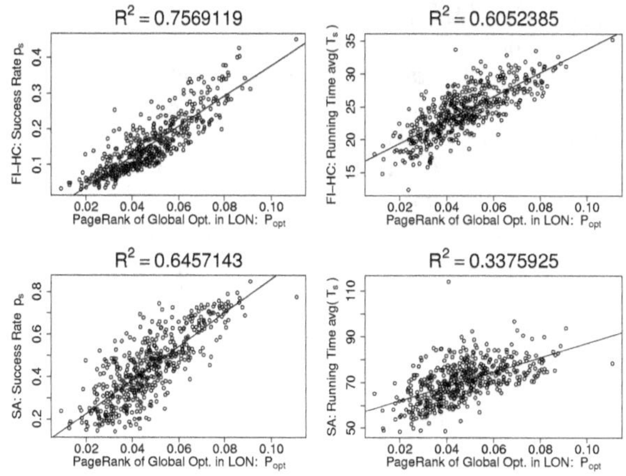

Figure 4: PageRank over performance of FI-Hill Climbing (top) and SA (bottom) for TSP. We plot success rate (left) and running time (right).

8. CONCLUSIONS

We suggest that the PageRank of the global optimum in a Local Optima Network is a predictor of the expected performance of local search heuristics like first improvement local search and simulated annealing. A comparison of PageRank with standard predictors like ruggedness and deceptiveness shows a much higher predictive power. For the NK-model and TSP, the PageRank explains around 90% of the variance of performance. The explanatory power of the PageRank is also higher than the average length of the shortest paths to the optimum, which has been suggested by [5] and explains around 50% of the variance.

The PageRank centrality is a good predictor of local search performance since LONs are a good approximation for the computationally expensive extraction of Markov Chain models from fitness landscapes. The PageRank vector provides the stationary distribution of all local optima and, thus, can be used as a proper predictor for finding the high-quality solutions. Furthermore, many combinatorial optimization problems have a "big valley structure" [1], where local optima are not randomly distributed in the search space, but rather, are clustered. Thus, most local optima are close to each other and the global optimum is usually not isolated in the search space; rather, it is surrounded by all the local optima. Thus, the PageRank of the global optimum in a LON is a good proxy of performance for many simple search methods based on local search.

A limitation of the PageRank is that it works well if local search is the main search operator; however, with an increasing amount of diversification, its predictive power becomes lower since it does not take into account non-intensifying search steps. Another limitation is the computational effort for the extraction of basins. Even though we used only small problem instances for our experiments, we hope that our findings can be extrapolated onto larger problems. In addition, we suggest that future research should focus on studying other metrics which can serve as approximations for PageRank Centrality. Finally, we suggest as future work to test our results with the alternative model of LONs with escape edges.

9. REFERENCES

[1] K. D. Boese, A. B. Kahng, and S. Muddu. A new adaptive multi-start technique for combinatorial global optimizations. *Operations Research Letters*, 16(2):101–113, 1994.

[2] S. P. Borgatti. Centrality and network flow. *Social Networks*, 27(1):55–71, Jan. 2005.

[3] S. Brin and L. Page. The anatomy of a large-scale hypertextual Web search engine. *Computer Networks and ISDN Systems*, 30(1-7):107–117, Apr. 1998.

[4] S. Choi and B. Moon. Normalization for Genetic Algorithms With Nonsynonymously Redundant Encodings. *IEEE Transactions on Evolutionary Computation*, 12(5):604–616, 2008.

[5] F. Daolio, S. Verel, G. Ochoa, and M. Tomassini. Local optima networks and the performance of iterated local search. *Proceedings of the fourteenth international conference on Genetic and evolutionary computation conference - GECCO '12*, page 369, Oct. 2012.

[6] M. Franceschet. PageRank: standing on the shoulders of giants. *Communications of the ACM*, 54(6):92, June 2011.

[7] L. C. Freeman. *The Development of Social Network Analysis.* Createspace, 2004.

[8] G. Frobenius. Über Matrizen aus nicht negativen Elementen. *Sitzungsberichte Preussische Akademie der Wissenschaft, Berlin*, pages 456–477, 1912.

[9] F. Glover. Future paths for integer programming and links to artificial intelligence. *Computers & Operations Research*, 13(5):533–549, Jan. 1986.

[10] J. He, C. Reeves, C. Witt, and X. Yao. A note on problem difficulty measures in black-box optimization: classification, realizations and predictability. *IEEE Transactions on Evolutionary Computation*, 15(4):435–43, Jan. 2007.

[11] T. Jones and S. Forrest. Fitness Distance Correlation as a Measure of Problem Difficulty for Genetic Algorithms. *Proceedings of the Sixth International Conference on Genetic Algorithms*, 1995.

[12] L. Kallel, B. Naudts, and C. R. Reeves. Properties of Fitness Functions and Search Landscapes. In L. Kallel, B. Naudts, and A. Rogers, editors, *Theoretical Aspects of Evolutionary Computing*, Natural Computing Series, pages 175–206. Springer Berlin Heidelberg, 2001.

[13] S. Kauffman and S. Levin. Towards a General Theory of Adaptive Walks on Rugged Landscapes. *Journal of theoretical Biology*, pages 11–45, 1987.

[14] S. Kirkpatrick, C. D. Gelatt, and M. P. Vecchi. Optimization by simulated annealing. *Science (N.Y.)*, 220(4598):671–80, May 1983.

[15] P. J. M. Laarhoven and E. H. L. Aarts. *Simulated Annealing: Theory and Applications.* Kluwer Academic Publishers, Norwell, MA, USA, 1988.

[16] D. H. Lehmer. Teaching combinatorial tricks to a computer. In *Proceedings of the Symposium on Applied Mathematics and Combinatorial Analysis.*, 1960.

[17] J. K. Lenstra and a.H. Rinnooy Kan. Complexity of Vehicle Routing and Scheduling Problems. *Networks*, 11:221–227, 1981.

[18] K. M. Malan and A. P. Engelbrecht. Fitness Landscape Analysis for Metaheuristic Performance Prediction. In H. Richter and A. Engelbrecht, editors, *Recent Advances in the Theory and Application of Fitness Landscapes*, pages 103–129. Springer, 2014.

[19] G. Ochoa, M. Tomassini, S. Vérel, and C. Darabos. A study of NK landscapes' basins and local optima networks. In *Proceedings of the 10th annual conference on Genetic and evolutionary computation - GECCO '08*, page 555, New York, 2008. ACM Press.

[20] G. Ochoa, S. Verel, and M. Tomassini. First-improvement vs. best-improvement local optima networks of nk landscapes. *PPSN'10 Proceedings of the 11th international conference on Parallel problem solving from nature*, I:104–113, 2010.

[21] O. Perron. Zur Theorie der Matrices. *Mathematische Annalen1*, 64(1):248–263, 1907.

[22] E. Pitzer and M. Affenzeller. A Comprehensive Survey on Fitness Landscape Analysis. In J. Fodor, R. Klempous, and C. P. Suárez Araujo, editors, *Recent Advances in Intelligent Engineering Systems*, volume 378 of *Studies in Computational Intelligence*, pages 161–191. Springer, Berlin and Heidelberg, 2012.

[23] C. M. Reidys and P. F. Stadler. Combinatorial Landscapes. *SIAM Review*, 44(1):3–54, Jan. 2002.

[24] F. Rothlauf. *Design of modern heuristics: Principles and application.* Springer, Berlin and Heidelberg, 2011.

[25] P. F. Stadler. Landscapes and their correlation functions. *Journal of Mathematical Chemistry*, 20(1):1–45, 1996.

[26] F. H. Stillinger. A topographic view of supercooled liquids and glass formation. *Science (N.Y.)*, 267(5206):1935–9, Mar. 1995.

[27] E. Weinberger. Correlated and Uncorrelated Fitness Landscapes and How to Tell the Difference. *Biological cybernetics*, 336:325–336, 1990.

[28] S. Wright. The roles of mutation, inbreeding, crossbreeding, and selection in evolution. In *Proceedings of the 6th International Congress of Genetics*, pages 356–366, 1932.

Generator Start-up Sequences Optimization for Network Restoration Using Genetic Algorithm and Simulated Annealing

Paul Kaufmann
Department of CS
University of Paderborn, Germany
paul.kaufmann@gmail.com

Cong Shen
Department of EE and CS
University of Kassel, Germany
cong.shen82@yahoo.de

ABSTRACT

In the domain of power grid systems, scheduling tasks are widespread. Typically, linear programming (LP) techniques are used to solve these tasks. For cases with high complexity, linear system modeling is often cumbersome. There, other modeling approaches allow for a more compact representation being typically also more accurate as non-linear dependencies can be captured natively.

In this work, we focus on the optimization of a power plant start-up sequence, which is part of the network restoration process of a power system after a blackout. Most large power plants cannot start on their own without cranking energy from the outside grid. These are the non-black start (NBS) units. As after a blackout we assume all power plants being shut down, self-contained power plants (black start (BS) units), such as the hydroelectric power plants, start first and boot the NBS units one after each other. Once a NBS unit is restored, it supports the restoration process and because an average NBS unit is much larger than a BS unit, NBS unit's impact on the restoration process is typically dominant. The overall restoration process can take, depending on the size of the blackout region and the damaged components, some hours to weeks. And as the blackout time corresponds directly to economic and life losses, its reduction, even by some minutes, is worthwhile.

In this work we compare two popular metaheuristics, the genetic (GA) and simulated annealing (SA) algorithms on start-up sequence optimization and conclude that an efficient restoration plan can be evolved reliably and, depending on the implementation, in a very short period of time allowing for an integration into a real-time transmission system operation tool.

1. INTRODUCTION

With better and cheaper communication and monitoring capabilities the modern electric power systems became more and more flexible and robust. However, the risk of a total power system blackout is still present and with the increasing share of renewable energy sources even on the rise. A power system blackout can cause dramatic consequences. Recent power system blackouts (for instance, the Northeast America blackout in 2003 [6], the Japan power system collapse caused by an earthquake in 2011 [1] and the Northern, Eastern and Northeast India power system blackout in July 2012 [8]) have demonstrated that an efficient power system restoration plan is of utmost importance.

For an optimized generator start-up sequence, multiple approaches have been investigated. In [11], the generator start-up sequence is formalized as a mixed integer linear programming problem. However, while optimizing the start-up sequence the paper considers only the temporal constraints. Important performance indexes such as the power increasing rate, capacity, reliability and node importance degree of an NBS power plant are neglected. As performance indexes are often rated differently regarding their relevances by human experts, using them as a part of the goal function requires harmonization. This can be done by the the analytic hierarchy process and vague sets, as presented in [12] or by the fuzzy Choquet integral operator and group decision making, as done in [5] and [4].

A very similar problem to the generator start-up sequence optimization is the optimization of restoration paths, where a rebooted power plant starts powering up neighboring loads. This is the subsequent step after restoring power plants and has been investigated in [2] by reformalizing the process as an combinatorial problem and making it input to a quantum-inspired evolutionary algorithm. In [9] the restoration path selection has been solved by using a multi-objective evolutionary algorithm giving the system operator different solutions that are maximizing the load shedding and minimizing the switching operations. The similarity of restoration path and generator start-up sequence optimization comes not only from the fact that the two tasks are closely interleaved during the restoration process. Their encodings and the algorithmic approaches for solving them are very similar. Combining generator start-up sequence and restoration path optimization into a single task would allow for better solutions. However, the search space grows exponentially. To achieve appropriate computing times decomposition of the algorithmic components can be required.

The entire restoration process is dynamic, composing of many subproblems and is inherently multi-objective. Its formalization as a single and monolithic optimization task would allow for high-quality solutions but would also be very

GECCO '15, July 11 - 16, 2015, Madrid, Spain
© 2015 ACM. ISBN 978-1-4503-3472-3/15/07...$15.00
DOI: http://dx.doi.org/10.1145/2739480.2754647

likely not fast enough for making decisions within minutes. Decomposing the restoration process into tasks handled by metaheuristics allows for computing potential decisions immediately, continuously improving their quality. New status information can easily make its way into the running optimization process as well as help avoiding a full optimization restart, which can be necessary when using linear programming techniques. The contribution of this paper is therefore a study of a metaheuristic-friendly encoding for capturing the generator start-up sequence, analysis of appropriate operators such as perturbation/mutation and recombination, first work towards efficient multi-objective evolutionary optimization of generator start-up sequences, and the comparison of two popular methods for combinatorial challenges, the Simulated Annealing and Genetic Algorithm.

The paper is organized as follows: Section 2 describes the generator start-up sequence formulation with its constraints and the objective function. Section 3 sketches the employed optimization algorithms, their parameters and operators. Section 4 presents the methodological approach of the work, shows the data set and the performance metrics, investigates the inner mechanisms of the proposed operators and finally compares Simulated Annealing and the Genetic Algorithms on generator startup sequence optimization. Finally, Section 5 concludes the analysis, summarizing the restrictions and outlining current and future efforts.

2. FORMULATION OF GENERATOR START-UP PROCEDURE

In this section, we introduce a simplified boot sequence model of a power plant and present constraints as well as objective functions for the overall optimization problem.

2.1 Temporal BS Unit Boot Sequence Model

A generator start-up sequence begins with booting all NB units. NB units can boot independently. As soon as there is energy in the grid, the first NBS unit starts booting which draws energy from the grid for some time. When there is enough free energy available again, the next NBS unit is started, and so on. Fig. 1 illustrates an example for a booting procedure for a grid with one BS and one NBS unit. Fig. 1 (a) shows the output power of a BS unit during the restoration process. Starting at $t^{\mathrm{BS}}_{\mathrm{start}}$, denoted as t_0 in the total available grid power diagram in Fig. 1 (c), the BS unit initiates its internal components for $t^{\mathrm{BS}}_{\mathrm{prep}}$ units of time. Then, at the time point $t_1 = t^{\mathrm{BS}}_{\mathrm{start}} + t^{\mathrm{BS}}_{\mathrm{prep}}$, the BS unit starts injecting energy into the grid and increases its output power linearly for $t^{\mathrm{BS}}_{\mathrm{inc}}$ time units until reaching 90% of the maximal output power $P^{\mathrm{BS}}_{\mathrm{max}}$ at $t_7 = t^{\mathrm{BS}}_{\mathrm{start}} + t^{\mathrm{BS}}_{\mathrm{prep}} + t^{\mathrm{BS}}_{\mathrm{inc}}$. As a general rule, the maximal output of BS and NBS units is assumed to be 90% of their rated power due to reserve power for frequency and voltage control. The capacity of a unit is defined as the sum of the rated and cranking powers. The cranking power of a BS unit is set to be zero. A closed form of a BS unit output function during restoration is:

$$P^{\mathrm{BS}}_{\mathrm{out}}(t) = \begin{cases} 0 & \text{if } t < t^{\mathrm{BS}}_{\mathrm{start}} + t^{\mathrm{BS}}_{\mathrm{prep}} =: t_1 \\ \frac{0.9 \cdot P^{\mathrm{BS}}_{\mathrm{max}}}{t^{\mathrm{BS}}_{\mathrm{inc}}}(t - t_1) & \text{if } t_1 \leq t < t_1 + t^{\mathrm{BS}}_{\mathrm{inc}} =: t_7 \\ 0.9 \cdot P^{\mathrm{BS}}_{\mathrm{max}} & \text{else.} \end{cases} \quad (1)$$

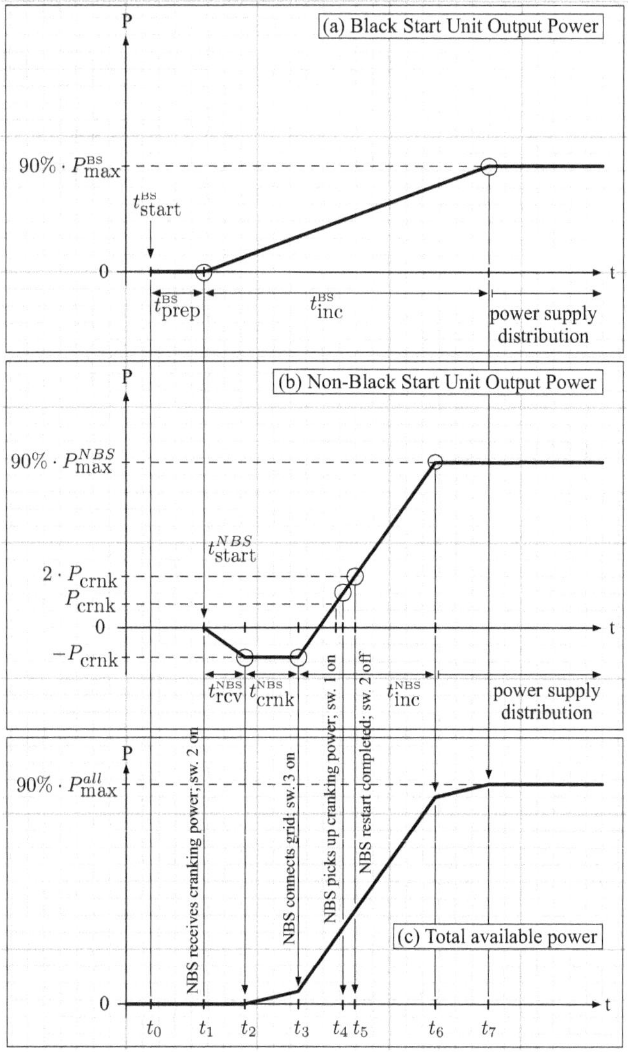

Figure 1: Temporal model of the boot process of a grid with one BS and one NBS unit.

2.2 Temporal NBS Unit Boot Sequence Model

Fig. 2 illustrates the simplified interconnect between a generator of an NBS unit and the outer grid. Three power flows can be identified in this figure. In the regular operation mode the energy produced by the generator, presented by a circle with a sine wave inside, is flowing through a transformer, presented by three overlapping circles, and a closed switch no. 3 to the outside grid. Additionally, part of the produced energy flows through the same transformer and the closed switch no. 1 to NBS unit's own ancillary devices. Switch no. 2 is open. This way, the NBS unit can produce and consume it's own cranking power, which is the regular case in normal operation conditions.

In case an NBS unit is currently booting and producing not enough power to supply its ancillary devices, it needs support form the grid. This can be realized by enabling a third power flow from the grid over the second transformer, presented by two overlapping circles, and the closed switch no. 2. The correct switching sequence during a start up is presented at the bottom of Fig. 2 and will be explained

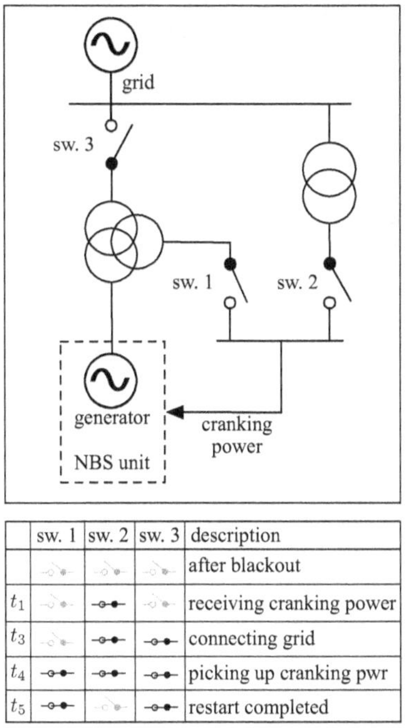

Figure 2: Temporal model of the boot process of a NBS unit.

later on in this section. Last thing to mention is that any switch operation can cause electrical fluctuations. Therefore, switch operations need a synchronization phase and some time period after the switching point to ensure that frequency and voltage fluctuations are coming back to normal values. This, and other electrical properties such as over-voltage problems caused by self-excitation and energizing unload transmission lines, frequency control during the load restoration, and cold load pick up inrush have to be either validated before starting or checked during the optimization procedure. In our previous work we have already presented handling these requirements in an optimization algorithm [10, 9]. Therefore, we will skip this, as the focus of the current work is to find good performing encodings, operators and optimization algorithms for generator start-up sequence optimization. In our future work, we will incorporate electric checks into the optimization challenge.

The boot procedure of the NBS unit is shown in Fig. 1 (b) and is modeled as follows:

1. After a blackout, we assume all NBS units being disconnected from the grid. All three switches of an NBS unit are open in Fig. 2. If some NBS unit is selected for restoration, it closes first switch no. 2 and starts consuming cranking energy from the grid. In Fig. 1 this happens at $t_1 = t^{\mathrm{NBS}}_{\mathrm{start}} = t^{\mathrm{BS}}_{\mathrm{start}} + t^{\mathrm{BS}}_{\mathrm{prep}}$. For simplicity, we assume that the NBS unit consumes the entire free energy of the grid but at most P_{crnk}.

2. As the BS unit increases its output power linearly from 0, its output reaches P_{crnk} after $t^{\mathrm{NBS}}_{\mathrm{rcv}}$ time units at $t_2 = t^{\mathrm{NBS}}_{\mathrm{start}} + t^{\mathrm{NBS}}_{\mathrm{rcv}}$. From now on, the NBS units consumes P_{crnk} for $t^{\mathrm{NBS}}_{\mathrm{crnk}}$ time units until $t_3 = t^{\mathrm{NBS}}_{\mathrm{start}} + t^{\mathrm{NBS}}_{\mathrm{rcv}} + t^{\mathrm{NBS}}_{\mathrm{crnk}}$. In our optimization set up we assume that consuming cranking power will not be interrupted. In a more realistic model this event should also be considered adding some penalty time to $t^{\mathrm{NBS}}_{\mathrm{crnk}}$.

3. After consuming cranking power for $t^{\mathrm{NBS}}_{\mathrm{crnk}}$ time units and energizing its ancillary devices, the NBS unit synchronizes to the grid, closes the switch no. 3 and starts producing it's own power as well as injecting it into the grid. Switch no. 2 stays closed until the NBS unit produces enough energy to power its own ancillary devices. For the same reason switch no. 1 stays open.

4. After the NBS unit is able to produce more energy than its own ancillary devices consume, it closes the switch no. 1 at t_4 preparing to power its ancillary devices by itself.

5. If the output power of the NBS unit reaches some security margin, in our case we set this to twice the amount of the cranking power, the NBS unit opens the switch no. 2. From this moment on, the NBS unit produces all the energy it requires to operate by itself and does not rely anymore on the energy from the outside grid. In Fig. 1 (b) this happens at t_5. The switch positions reach also their regular configuration.

6. Finally, after injecting energy for $t^{\mathrm{NBS}}_{\mathrm{inc}}$ time units the NBS unit reaches at $t_6 = t_3 + t^{\mathrm{NBS}}_{\mathrm{inc}}$ 90% of it's rated power and enters the normal operation conditions. The power produced by the NBS unit is available as cranking power to other NBS units.

A closed form formulation of the output power function $P^{\mathrm{NBS}}_{\mathrm{out}}$ of a NBS unit is presented in the equation below. In contrast to $P^{\mathrm{BS}}_{\mathrm{out}}$, which depends only on the input parameter time, $P^{\mathrm{NBS}}_{\mathrm{out}}$ depends also on the available power of the system, which in our case is $P^{\mathrm{BS}}_{\mathrm{out}}$, and the time point where this system power gets available: $t^{\mathrm{NBS}}_{\mathrm{start}} = t^{\mathrm{BS}}_{\mathrm{start}} + t^{\mathrm{BS}}_{\mathrm{prep}} = t_1$. With this, $P^{\mathrm{NBS}}_{\mathrm{out}}(t, P_{\mathrm{in}}, t^{\mathrm{NBS}}_{\mathrm{start}})$ amounts to

$$P^{\mathrm{NBS}}_{\mathrm{out}} = \begin{cases} 0 & \text{if } t < t^{\mathrm{NBS}}_{\mathrm{start}} =: t_1 \\ -P_{\mathrm{in}} & \text{if } t_1 \leq t < t_1 + t^{\mathrm{NBS}}_{\mathrm{rcv}} =: t_2 \\ -P_{\mathrm{crnk}} & \text{if } t_2 \leq t < t_2 + t^{\mathrm{NBS}}_{\mathrm{crnk}} =: t_3 \\ \frac{0.9(P^{\mathrm{NBS}}_{\mathrm{max}} + P_{\mathrm{crnk}})(t - t_3)}{t^{\mathrm{NBS}}_{\mathrm{inc}}} - P_{\mathrm{crnk}} & \text{if } t_3 \leq t < t_3 + t^{\mathrm{NBS}}_{\mathrm{inc}} =: t_6 \\ 0.9 \cdot P^{\mathrm{NBS}}_{\mathrm{max}} & \text{else.} \end{cases} \quad (2)$$

2.3 Combined Start-up Model

The total power in the system during the booting process is a sum of $P^{\mathrm{BS}}_{\mathrm{out}}$ and $P^{\mathrm{NBS}}_{\mathrm{out}}$ and is illustrated in Fig. 1 (c). Since after t_3 the NBS unit can send its power to the network, the ramp rate between t_3 and t_6 equals the sum of the output powers of the BS and NBS units. The NBS unit reaches 90% of the nominal output at t_6 and the ramp rate reduces to the output power increasing rate of the BS unit. After t_7, the BS unit also reaches 90% of its nominal value completing the booting process of this example.

In a larger network model with several BS and NBS units, the NBS unit start sequence determines the temporal booting procedures of the power plants. We have developed a corresponding simulator that takes as input a given power network with generators and their characteristics as well as an NBS start-up sequence and computes the development of the overall power and the overall restoration time of the power grid. The operation time of switches and switch insulators is neglected as this time is short compared to the total restoration time.

2.4 Constraints

Following constraints have to be respected during the restoration process:

1. Each NBS unit should be able to start. This criteria is relaxed in this work to: All BS units have to have enough accumulated power P^B to restart any of the NBS units with the cranking power of P_{crnk}: $P^B \geq P_{\text{crnk}}$.
2. An NBS unit should receive its cranking power $P_{\text{crnk},i}$ uninterrupted for at least T_i^{min} time to be able to start. We assume this constraint to be valid in the simulation. For real situations one has to check, whether there is always enough cranking power in the grid between t_2 and t_3, adding otherwise penalty time of m hours to the restoration process of an NBS unit.
3. Since cranking power is consumed mainly by induction motors, it is important to ensure that node voltages and the network frequency lie in acceptable ranges when BS units send cranking power to NBS units.

The benchmarks used in this work are constructed such that the constraints hold. However, we have implemented and used run-time constraint checks detecting invalid solutions and rendering their fitness insufficient in our previous work [9, 10].

2.5 Objective Function

The two most important goals of the restoration process are to maximize the reliability of the generator start-up sequence, which essentially means minimizing the possibility that the power system collapses again during the boot process, and to minimize the booting time for the generator start-up sequence.

Given N as the number of NBS units, a generator start-up sequence is defined as $s = (s_1, s_2, \ldots, s_N), 1 \leq s_i \leq N, s_i \neq s_j$ if $i \neq j$, where the indices s_i refer to individual NBS units. Based on the reliability index $r[s_i]$ of a single generator, we can express the reliability $R(s)$ of a generator start-up sequence s as:

$$R(s) = \left[\sum_{i=1}^{N}\left[1-(i-1)\frac{1}{N}\right]\right]^{-1}\left[\sum_{i=1}^{N}\left[r[s_i]\left(1-(i-1)\frac{1}{N}\right)\right]\right]$$
$$= \frac{2}{N+1}\sum_{i=1}^{N}\left[r[s_i]\left(1-\frac{i-1}{N}\right)\right]. \tag{3}$$

The first part of Eqn. 3 is for normalization and the second presents the non-normalized reliability.

Consider as an example a grid with $N = 4$ NBS units with reliability indices of $r[\text{NBS}_1] = 0.9$, $r[\text{NBS}_2] = 0.95$, $r[\text{NBS}_3] = 0.8$ and $r[\text{NBS}_4] = 0.7$. For the starting sequence $s = (\text{NBS}_1, \text{NBS}_2, \text{NBS}_3, \text{NBS}_4)$ the non-normalized reliability amounts to $0.9 \cdot 1 + 0.95 \cdot (1 - 0.25) + 0.8 \cdot (1 - 2 \cdot 0.25) + 0.7 \cdot (1 - 3 \cdot 0.25) = 2.1875$ and the normalized reliability $R(s)$ is given by $\frac{2.1875}{2.5} = 0.875$. The generator start up sequence $s' = (\text{NBS}_2, \text{NBS}_1, \text{NBS}_3, \text{NBS}_4)$ results in an overall reliability of $R(s') = \frac{2.2}{2.5} = 0.88$. Thus, the second sequence should be preferred over the first as the chance for a brake-down during the booting process is lower.

Along with the reliability, the booting time for a generator start-up sequence is the second criteria. The optimization goal is to arrange the generator start-up sequences such that the reliability R is maximized and the restoration time T is minimized. We define a single-objective goal function by linearly weighting and aggregating the reliability $R(s)$ and the restoration time $T(s)$ as:

$$F_{R,T}(s) = \frac{1}{2}\left(R(s) + \left(1 - \frac{T(s)}{T_{\max}}\right)\right), \tag{4}$$

where $T_{\max}$ is set slightly larger than the worst case time effort for all power plants.

The selection of an aggregated and not a Pareto-based fitness function has the following reasons: For a fair comparison we would like to employ the same goal function definition for all candidate optimization algorithms. A linear combination of the objective functions is the easiest way to achieve this and is used in this work. A common Pareto-based goal function is ongoing work.

Table 1: Temperature control strategies. T_0, T_N, and t are the start, terminal, and current temperatures. N is the number of SA iterations.

$T_t^{(1)}$	$\leftarrow T_0 - \frac{T_0 - T_N}{N}$
$T_t^{(2)}$	$\leftarrow T_0 \left(\frac{T_n}{T_0}\right)^{\frac{t}{N}}$
A B $T_t^{(3)}$	$\leftarrow \frac{(T_{\text{start}} - T_{\text{end}})(N+1)}{N}$ $\leftarrow T_{\text{start}} - A$ $\leftarrow \frac{A}{t+1} + B$
$T_t^{(4)}$	$\leftarrow 0.5(T_0 - T_N)(1 + \cos(\frac{\pi t}{N})) + T_N$
$T_t^{(5)}$	$\leftarrow 0.5(T_0 - T_N)(1 - \tanh(\frac{10t}{N} - 5)) + T_N$
$T_t^{(6)}$	$\leftarrow \frac{T_0 - T_N}{\cosh(\frac{10t}{N})} + T_N$
$T_t^{(7)}$	$\leftarrow T_0 \exp(-\frac{1}{N} \ln(\frac{T_0}{T_N}) t)$
$T_t^{(8)}$	$\leftarrow T_0 \exp(-\frac{1}{N^2} \ln(\frac{T_0}{T_N}) t^2)$

3. ALGORITHMS, ENCODINGS AND OPERATORS

3.1 Simulated Annealing (SA)

Simulated Annealing (SA) is a trace-based algorithm iterating from one solution to the other by means of a perturbation operator. Unlike Hill Climbing (HC), SA may also accept worse solutions at a rate, reciprocal to the functional qualities of the current and the derived solutions. Also unlike the Metropolis Algorithms, this rate reduces over time letting the SA account for the state of the optimization run. The rational behind this is that at the beginning SA globally searches for regions with a good potential for local and global optima while towards the end the perturbation horizon is tightened for locally exploiting a region in a HC manner. The implementation of a contracting neighborhood definition is realized by a temperature parameter T_t, which is reduced during an SA run gradually. There are, however applications benefitting from episodic "reheating" of T, such as floorplanning in chip design. In our experiments we have exhaustively evaluated eight temperature control strategies. They are presented in Tab. 1.

In our implementation we have realized the regular SA

algorithm. The only variations are that the size of a temperature level, the period between updating T_t is set to one and the rejection factor, which is the number of iterations without a change of the current solution, to ∞. These parameters have had marignal impact during our experiments.

3.2 Generator Start-up Encoding

The encoding of a power plant boot sequence is done as a string of unique numbers. The numbers are identifying the power plants. The order of numbers in the string indicates, which power plant to boot first, second, and so on. With this encoding, SA's perturbation and GA's mutation operators can be implemented canonically by swapping two numbers in the sequence, as presented in Fig. 3. The encoding remains correct after such a modification.

While this kind of encoding allows for a simple implementation of SA and EA operators, it has also the drawback of a potentially high epistasis. (High) Epistasis denotes an effect where changing some bits in the encoding of a solution (dramatically) impacts on the way some other bits in the encoding are evaluated by the goal function. A high epistatic encoding shows often no regularities, letting the perturbation/mutation and recombination operators having almost random impact on the goal function. Unfortunately, many combinatorial optimization problems have high-epistatic encodings. Despite the potential for high epistasis, Sec. 4 shows that the presented perturbation/mutation and the uniform order-based recombination work well with this encoding.

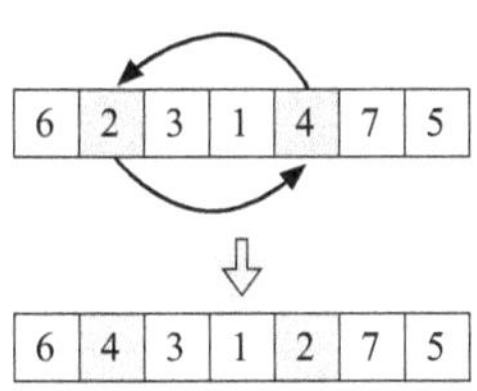

Figure 3: Perturbation / Mutation operator and power plant boot sequence definition.

3.3 Genetic Algorithm (GA)

In this work we use the standard Genetic Algorithm scheme where new population of individuals are derived from the old population in a loop where each time two parent individuals are selected by a 2-tournament selection, recombined and the off-spring individuals mutated. The recombination and mutation probabilities define, how frequently the individuals are modified instead of just cloning them. For instance, a mutation probability of 0.5 let the mutation operator return the original solution in 50% of the cases, returning a mutated individual otherwise. The recombination and mutation rates, on the opposite, specify the percentage of the gene material that is going to be modified. Before starting the GA loop, best 5% but at least one individual is copied to the new population.

3.4 The Recombination Operator

SA and GA share the same problem encoding and the perturbation/mutation operator. To realize global search behavior, GA uses additionally a recombination operator. Because ordered sequences are a widely used encoding model for many real world applications including the traveling sales-

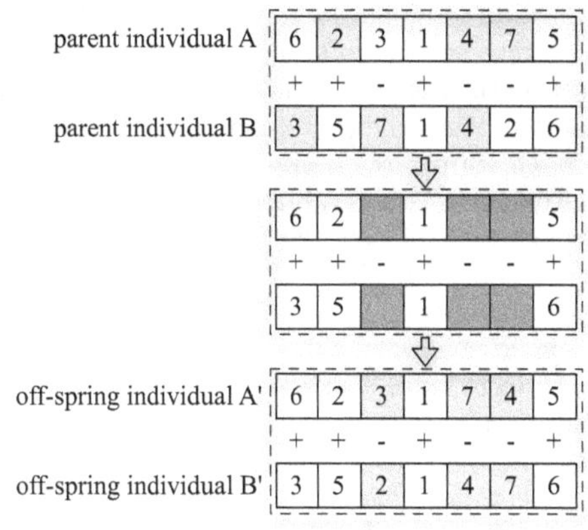

Figure 4: Uniform Order-Based Crossover: transplanting ordered subsets. A "-" denotes a gene selected for recombination. A set of genes selected for recombination in chromosome A: "3", "4", and "7" are reshuffled according to the order of these genes in chromosome B: "3", "7", and "4".

man problem, some previous work has been done on meaningful recombination operators for this kind of representations. We have selected the uniform order-based crossover, which decides according to a uniform probability distribution for each gene (power plant number), whether to recombine or not. Then, these genes are not transferred to a second chromosome (start-up sequence encoding) but reordered in the original chromosome according to the sorting of these genes in the second chromosome. This way, ordered structures are transferred between chromosomes without producing incorrect encodings. An example is shown in Fig. 4. Recombined genes are marked by a "-", other genes by a "+". Genes selected for recombination in chromosome A are 3, 4, and 7. Their sequence in chromosome B is 3, 7, and 4. Thus, these three genes are reordered in chromosome A to 3, 7, 4. The chromosome A' shows the resulting solution. The same procedure is applied also to chromosome B. There, 7, 4, and 2 have to be reshuffled according to their order in chromosome A: 2, 4, and 7. The resulting chromosome B' is shown at the bottom of Fig. 4.

4. ANALYZING GENERATOR START-UP OPTIMIZATION

This section presents the evaluation methodology and metrics, analyzes good operator configurations, investigates optimization algorithm parameterizations, and finally compares Simulated Annealing and Genetic Algorithms on the task of generator start-up sequence optimization.

4.1 Evaluation Methodology and Metrics

GA and SA are randomized algorithms. Therefore, for each algorithm parameterization GA and SA have been executed 30 times with varying random seeds. The algorithm runs have been terminated after 100000 fitness evaluations and evaluated regarding the mean, standard deviation, first, second (median), and third quartiles as well as peak values. To compute these numbers, the best functional quality from each of the 30 runs has been extracted. In case of SA, the best solution is stored in a separate variable and printed out on exit. Elitism-based GA, on contrary, never forgets the best solution and propagates it into the final population, where it also gets printed out.

Once best performing SA and GA configurations have been found, the best functional qualities of the 30 runs for each of the algorithms are checked for statistical similarities using the two-tailed Mann-Whitney (MW) U and the two-tailed Kolmogorov-Smirnov (KS) tests at the significance level of $\alpha = 0.05$. The MW U test checks the hypothesis whether two independent samples come from distributions with equal medians. The KS test distinguishes between H0="Two independent sequences A and B follow the same distribution" and HA="Two independent sequences A and B follow different distributions."

Finally, we compare SA and GA regarding their computation times. For this task, the Computational Effort (CE) metric is a popular approach computing a bound on fitness evaluations to reach some optimization goal f_g at a specific probability z [3]. CE also computes the number of fitness evaluations after which an optimization run has to be restarted, avoiding stuck in local optima. In our investigation, we set z to 99% and f_g to 0.67. f_g is selected such that most of SA and GA configurations reach this functional quality, allowing for an precise comparison using the CE metric.

4.2 Data Test Case Setup

For first investigations we have used the New England 39 test case network defined in [7]. It is a greatly simplified model of a real network case consisting of 39 busses with 10 synchronous generators. We have extended this benchmark by additional 47 generators, which are parameterized similar to the 10 original generators. This network sizes are not uncommon to transmission and medium voltage distribution grids. However, much larger networks are also relevant and susceptible to a total blackout.

All restoration parameters of the test benchmark are presented in Tab. 2. The table columns show the power plant index, its type, the power increasing rate, the cranking power, the restart time, the rated power, and reliability. The cranking power is set uniformly to 20% of the rated power. Older power plants may need more and modern power plants less cranking power. The restart time denotes the preparation time (t^{BS}_{prep}) for black and cranking power receiving time (t^{NBS}_{crnk}) for non black start units.

4.3 Evaluating Operators

In first experiments we would like to get the intuition on how successful the perturbation/mutation and recombination operators are throughout the optimization process and how many genetic material the operators are modifying. We have configured a GA scheme setting the perturbation/mutation and recombination probabilities to 1.0 and the perturbation/mutation and recombination rates to randomly values between 0.0 and 1.0 sampled anew each time an operator is executed. Population sizes have been set to 4, 8, 16, 32, 64, and 128. The results are presented in Fig. 5 an Fig. 6 and are common to all GA parameterizations. Fig. 5 (a) presents the success rates and the amount of modified genetic material for the mutation operator. As expected, mutating even large amount of genes in the initial search phase often improves the functional quality. The distribution of modified genetic material, which corresponds to the perturbation/mutation rate, follows roughly $\exp(-x)$.

Table 2: Column 1: generator index, 2: generator type (1=BS, 2=NBS), 3: power increasing rate [MW/min], 4: cranking power (P_{crnk}) [MW], 5: restart time (BS: t_{prep}, NBS: t_{crnk}) [min], 6 - rated power (P_{max}) [MW] (NBS: 5 · cranking power), 7 - reliability.

1	2	3	4	5	6	7
1	1	6.4	NA	10	90	0.89
2	2	6.4	70	10	70/0.2	0.93
3	2	5.6	110	12	110/0.2	0.73
4	2	6.8	90	20	90/0.2	0.94
5	2	5.8	70	20	70/0.2	0.96
6	2	6.2	70	25	70/0.2	0.78
7	2	4.9	120	20	120/0.2	0.76
8	2	4.2	50	15	50/0.2	0.69
9	2	6.6	95	10	95/0.2	0.76
10	2	4.6	89	25	89/0.2	0.86
11	2	5.8	95	18	95/0.2	0.83
12	2	3.2	50	40	40/0.2	0.89
13	2	5.6	60	50	50/0.2	0.98
14	2	4.2	40	46	40/0.2	0.93
15	2	2.2	30	30	30/0.2	0.92
16	2	6.1	60	50	60/0.2	0.83
17	2	5.2	60	40	60/0.2	0.78
18	2	3.4	40	40	40/0.2	0.96
19	2	1.6	18	20	18/0.2	0.73
20	2	6.2	60	50	60/0.2	0.91
21	2	3.3	40	40	40/0.2	0.92
22	2	3.1	35	36	35/0.2	0.86
23	2	2.3	25	28	25/0.2	0.84
24	2	3.2	50	40	50/0.2	0.88
25	2	6.8	66	57	66/0.2	0.98
26	2	6.2	60	50	60/0.2	0.94
27	2	6.3	66	57	66/0.2	0.98
28	2	2.8	36	38	36/0.2	0.95
29	2	5.8	70	48	70/0.2	0.85
30	2	4.6	18	65	18/0.2	0.78
31	2	7.2	60	67	60/0.2	0.77
32	2	2.3	40	89	40/0.2	0.87
33	2	5.1	35	87	35/0.2	0.68
34	2	9.3	25	43	25/0.2	0.78
35	2	3.2	50	34	50/0.2	0.92
36	2	5.8	66	56	56/0.2	0.97
37	2	7.2	60	23	60/0.2	0.63
38	2	2.3	66	45	66/0.2	0.87
39	2	5.8	36	56	36/0.2	0.86
40	2	7.8	70	23	70/0.2	0.83
41	2	5.3	66	56	66/0.2	0.97
42	2	7.8	36	67	36/0.2	0.87
43	2	6.8	70	67	70/0.2	0.92
44	2	3.6	18	56	18/0.2	0.95
45	2	4.2	60	53	60/0.2	0.98
46	2	5.3	40	67	40/0.2	0.91
47	2	6.1	35	36	35/0.2	0.93
48	2	2.3	25	45	25/0.2	0.97
49	2	8.2	50	46	50/0.2	0.87
50	2	3.8	66	89	66/0.2	0.86
51	2	5.2	60	56	60/0.2	0.83
52	2	6.3	66	56	66/0.2	0.87
53	2	7.8	36	89	36/0.2	0.92
54	2	5.8	70	56	70/0.2	0.91
55	2	4.3	66	45	66/0.2	0.73
56	2	3.8	36	76	36/0.2	0.86
57	2	6.8	70	56	70/0.2	0.88

Table 3: Perturbation / Mutation mechanism: The number of perturbed / mutated gene pairs is uniformly sampled from the presented table. These gene pairs are selected randomly and the genes are swapped.

1	1	1	1	1	1	1	2	2	2	3	5

After about 20000 fitness evaluations the distribution of successfully modified gene material stabilizes, allowing us to define the perturbation/recombination operator that samples its perturbation/mutation rate uniformly from the table presented in Tab. 3.

When analyzing the success behavior of the recombination operator, apart from the expected gradual reduction of the success probability over the time, no obvious behavior in the amount of the modified genes can be observed in Fig. 5 (b). However, when looking more precisely at the distribution of the recombined genes, as presented in Fig. 6 for the GA experiment with 16 individuals in a population and for the optimization interval between 10000 to 20000 fitness evaluations, the distribution becomes clear. The recombination operator is more successful when configured to recombine small and large amount of genes. The effect of the recombination operator is not symmetric. While recombining a small amount of genes, the effect of the recombination operator is very similar to the mutation operator. But recombining a lot of genes copies large and consolidated parts of a chromosome to the offspring individual at a slightly different position. This behavior comes close to shifting large parts of a chromosome around. Later experiments show that the recombination operator helps GA to excel when configured at the recombination rate of around 90%.

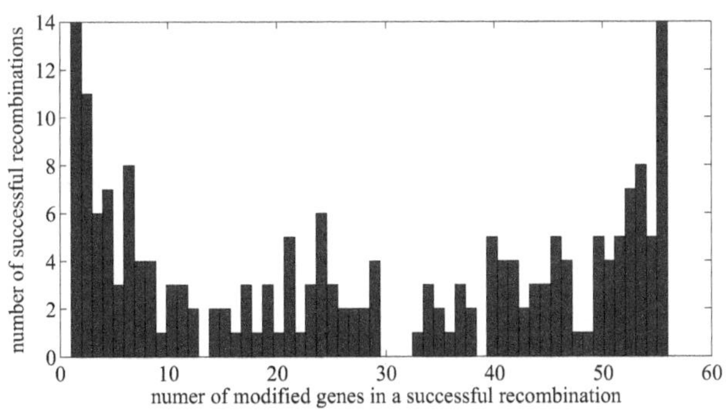

Figure 6: Distribution of modified genetic material for successful recombination operations between fitness evaluations 10000 and 20000.

4.4 Parametrizing GA and SA

After have identified good perturbation/mutation and recombination parameters, we have exhaustively tested SA and GA. SA was evaluated for all possible temperature range combinations between $T_{\text{start}} = 1000, 100, 10, 1, 0.1, 0.01, 0.001$ and $T_{\text{stop}} = 10, 1, 0.1, 0.001, 0.0001$ with $T_{\text{start}} > T_{\text{stop}}$ and regarding all eight cooling schemes. In total, 176 SA experiments with 30 SA runs each have been executed. GA have been first executed for all mutation and recombination probability combinations between 0.01, 0.1, 0.2, 0.3, 0.4, 0.5, 0.6, 0.7, 0.8, 0.9, and 0.99 and population sizes of 4, 10, 20, 50, and 100. Higher mutation and recombination rates in combination with 20 individuals in a population showed best performances. Therefore, GA parameterization were refined in final experiments to all mutation and recombination probability combinations between 0.90, 0.92, 0.93, 0.94, 0.95, 0.96, 0.97, 0.98, 0.99 and 0.999 and a population size of 20. In total, 705 GA experiments with 30 GA runs each have been executed.

Table 4: Results

	SA	GA
Peak value	0.68342	0.68311
Mean±SD	$0.68199{\pm}1.2e^{-3}$	$0.67841{\pm}1.5e^{-3}$
1st Quartile	0.68139	0.67762
Median	0.68234	0.67835
3rd Quartile	0.68300	0.67963
MW U test, p-value	$1.6947e^{-09}$	
KS test, p-value	$1.1088e^{-08}$	
CE at $f_g = 0.67$	14501	6237
CE restart after	14501	6237

4.5 Comparing GA and SA

Tab. 4 presents the evaluation of best SA and GA configurations. SA achieves the best peak performance of 0.683423 when started at $T_{\text{start}} = 10.0$, $T_{\text{stop}} = 0.0001$ and the cooling scheme 3. GA achieves a peak performance of 0.683112 with the recombination probability/rate of 0.9 and the mutation probability of 0.9. While SA is slightly ahead of GA, similar peak values indicate that the exhaustive parameter tuning was able explored the most promising GA and SA parameter combinations.

The second group of lines in Tab. 4 summarizes the figures for the SA and GA configurations with best average finesses. For this, SA has to be configured with $T_{\text{start}} = 0.001$, $T_{\text{stop}} = 0.0001$ and the cooling scheme 6 and GA with the recombination probability/rate of 0.9 and the mutation probability of 0.999. The table figures show that while the standard deviations for both algorithms are compact and similar, the distance between the means amounts for 0.004. The distances for the medians and the quartiles are differing also for 0.003 to 0.004, underlying the disparity of performances. While the differences seem to be marginal, the MW U and the KS tests reject the h_0 hypothesis with very low p-values. Interestingly, the CE for SA is more than twice as large as for GA. This could indicate that SA is able to steadily improve the best solution even in the final search phase while the GA is fast in the beginning. In our Matlab implementation a regular Intel i7 notebook processor requires a second to compute 500 fitness values. To evolve solution with a functional quality of 0.67 and above with a probability of 99%, on average 12 seconds are therefore needed. However, implementing the optimization algorithms using C or C++ and parallelizing the GA can reduce the computation time significantly.

The best CE value achieved by SA amounts for 6201 fitness evaluations at $T_{\text{start}} = 1.0$, $T_{\text{stop}} = 0.0001$ and the cooling scheme 3. This is similar to the best GA figures

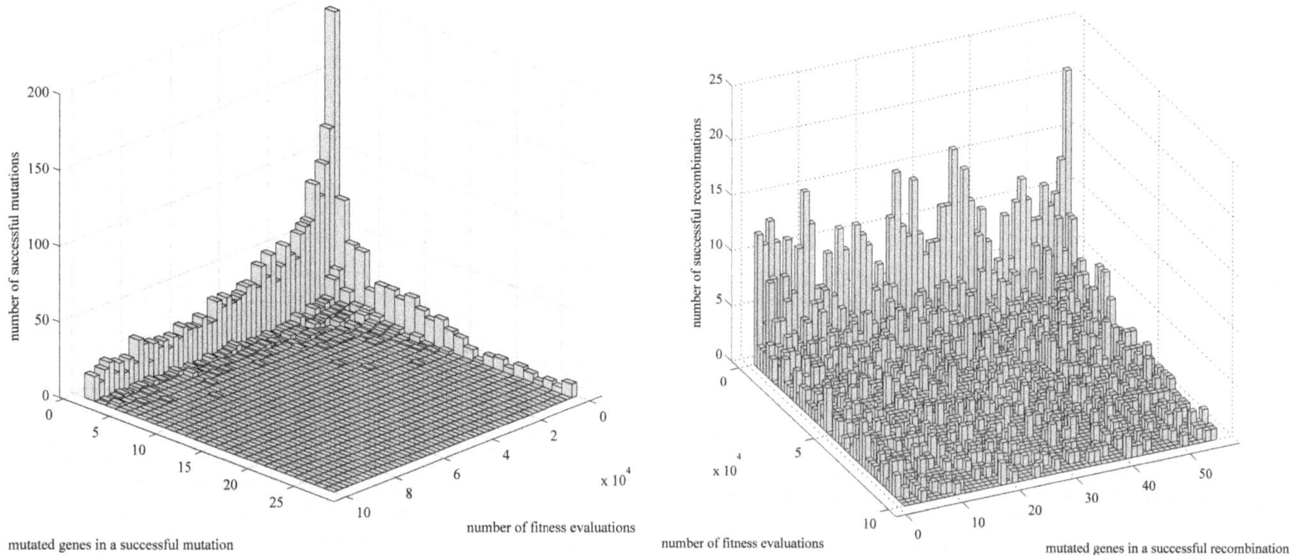

(a) Mutation operator (b) Recombination operator

Figure 5: Number of successful executions of the perturbation/mutation and recombination operators and the distribution of the genetic material modified during this executions.

indicating again, that given similar or identical operators and problem encodings, the exhaustive parameter tuning was able to find for each of the optimization algorithms a parameterization allowing to reach similar peak values.

5. CONCLUSION

This paper investigates on the task of power plant boot scheduling, encoding models, operators and nature-inspired metaheuristics. The insights we have gained in our work are that SA and GA are highly effective for generator start-up sequence optimization with suitable computation times for real-time control systems for network restoration. Additionally, while epistasis is very likely a problem of the presented encoding, the uniform order-based crossover seems to work very well.

In ongoing and future work, we will implement a Pareto-based MOEA using the operators presented in this paper, try to mathematically formalize the restoration procedure more precisely, improve the execute time, and compare the algorithms to linear programming approaches.

6. REFERENCES

[1] M. Bruch, V. Münch, M. Aichinger, M. Kuhn, M. Weymann, and G. Schmid. Power Blackout Risks. *Allianz*, 2011.

[2] J. Hou, Z. Xu, Z. Y. Dong, and K. P. Wong. Permutation-based Power System Restoration in Smart Grid Considering Load Prioritization. *Electric Power Components and Systems*, 42(3-4):361–371, 2014.

[3] J. Koza. *Genetic Programming: On the Programming of Computers by Means of Natural Selection.* MIT Press, 1992.

[4] W. Liu and Z. Lin. Analysis and Optimization of the Preferences of Decision-Makers in Black-Start Group Decision-Making. *IET Generation, Transmission & Distribution*, 7:pp.14–23, 2012.

[5] W. Liu, Z. Lin, and F. Wen. Intuitionistic Fuzzy Choquet Integral Operator-based Approach for Black-start Decision-making. *IET Generation, Transmission & Distribution*, 6:378–386, 2012.

[6] New York Independent System Operator. Interim Report on the August 14, 2003 Blackout. *Harvard Kennedy School*, 2004.

[7] North American Rockwell Corporation and Edison Electric Institute. *On-line Stability Analysis Study: RP90-1.* North American Rockwell Information Systems Company, October 12, 1970.

[8] Power Systems Engineering Research Center. Selected Information About The July 31 Blackout in India Affecting the Northern and Eastern Regions. *Arizona State University*, 2012.

[9] C. Shen, P. Kaufmann, and M. Braun. A New Distribution Network Reconfiguration and Restoration Path Selection Algorithm. In *Power Systems Computation Conference (PSCC)*. IEEE, 2014.

[10] C. Shen, P. Kaufmann, and M. Braun. Optimizing the Generator Start-up Sequence After a Power System Blackout. In *IEEE Power and Energy Society General Meeting (IEEE GM)*, 2014.

[11] S. Wei and L. Chen-Ching. Optimal Generator Start-Up Strategy for Bulk Power System Restoration. *IEEE Transactions on Power Systems*, 26(3):1357–1366, 2011.

[12] S. Zeng, Z. Lin, and F. Wen. A New Approach for Power System Black-Start Decision-Making With Vague Set Theory. *International Journal of Electrical Power & Energy Systems*, 34:114–120, 2012.

A Sequence-based Selection Hyper-heuristic Utilising a Hidden Markov Model

Ahmed Kheiri
University of Exeter
College of Engineering, Mathematics and Physical Sciences
Streatham Campus, Harrison Building
Exeter EX4 4QF, UK
a.kheiri@exeter.ac.uk

Ed Keedwell
University of Exeter
College of Engineering, Mathematics and Physical Sciences
Streatham Campus, Harrison Building
Exeter EX4 4QF, UK
e.c.keedwell@exeter.ac.uk

ABSTRACT

Selection hyper-heuristics are optimisation methods that operate at the level above traditional (meta-)heuristics. Their task is to evaluate low level heuristics and determine which of these to apply at a given point in the optimisation process. Traditionally this has been accomplished through the evaluation of individual or paired heuristics. In this work, we propose a hidden Markov model based method to analyse the performance of, and construct, longer sequences of low level heuristics to solve difficult problems. The proposed method is tested on the well known hyper-heuristic benchmark problems within the CHeSC 2011 competition and compared with a large number of algorithms in this domain. The empirical results show that the proposed hyper-heuristic is able to outperform the current best-in-class hyper-heuristic on these problems with minimal parameter tuning and so points the way to a new field of sequence-based selection hyper-heuristics.

Categories and Subject Descriptors

I.2.8 [**Artificial Intelligence**]: Problem Solving, Control Methods, and Search—*Heuristic methods*

Keywords

Hyper-heuristic, Cross-domain, Computational Design

1. INTRODUCTION

A *hyper-heuristic* performs a search over the space of heuristics which operate directly on the space of solutions, for solving computationally hard problems [4]. It conducts exploration of the search space of heuristics complying with the limitations exposed by the *domain barrier*, which does not allow any problem dependent information to pass through to the high-level where the hyper-heuristic components reside. This feature enables the reuse of their components and themselves on other problem domains without any change. Even though the term hyper-heuristic was coined in the early 21st century [7], the idea of combining the different existing heuristics to exploit their strengths dates back to 1960s [8, 12]. Two categories of hyper-heuristics can be defined, namely, *selection* hyper-heuristics and *generation* hyper-heuristics. Selection hyper-heuristics function by selecting and applying a heuristic from a set of low level heuristics followed by a move acceptance criterion to decide whether to accept or reject the new solution (Figure 1), while generation hyper-heuristics aim to generate new heuristics by understanding the characteristics of the input heuristics. Hyper-heuristics can be further distinguished by their feedback mechanisms and they can incorporate online learning, offline learning or no learning at all. The online learning hyper-heuristic learns from feedback during the search process, whereas the offline learning hyper-heuristic learns before the actual search starts [4]. This work focuses on the development of a novel online learning selection hyper-heuristic utilising a hidden Markov model to analyse sequences of heuristics. The performance of the hyper-heuristic is assessed through HyFlex [19], a software tool for facilitating the testing of hyper-heuristics. HyFlex provides implementations of six problem domains each with its own problem instances and relevant problem-specific information such as low level heuristics, providing scientists with a means to benchmark their algorithms and therefore solely focus on the hyper-heuristic development. The cross domain heuristic search over the six HyFlex problem domains was the CHeSC competition in 2011[1].

Traditional selection hyper-heuristics consider single heuristics (e.g. simple random and random permutation hyper-heuristics [7]) or heuristic pair performance (e.g. choice function hyper-heuristic [7]) when determining the heuristic to select (and execute) next. Several previously proposed hyper-heuristics have attempted to produce sequences of heuristics. The sequences of heuristics in these studies are usually predetermined in an offline manner such as in iterated local search [15] which applies a sequence of mutational heuristics (diversification) followed by hill climbers (intensification). Before CHeSC 2011 started, it is reported in [3] that the best performing hyper-heuristic on HyFlex was an approach based on an iterated local search which applies a set of low level heuristics in a predefined sequence. The current state-of-the-art hyper-heuristic and the winner

GECCO '15, July 11–15, 2015, Madrid, Spain
© 2015 ACM. ISBN 978-1-4503-3472-3/15/07...$15.00
DOI: http://dx.doi.org/10.1145/2739480.2754766

[1]http://www.asap.cs.nott.ac.uk/chesc2011/

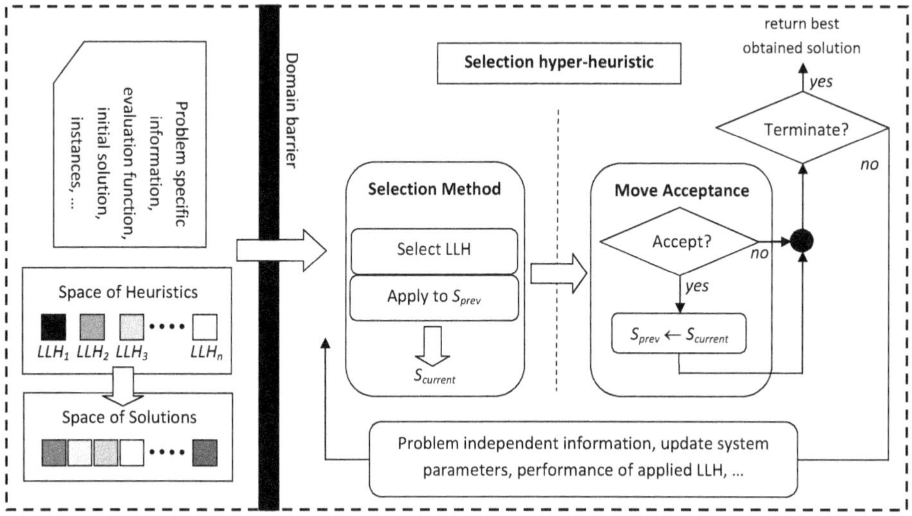

Figure 1: Selection hyper-heuristic framework

of CHeSC 2011, known as AdapHH [17], uses a technique to discover relay hybridised heuristics during part of the search process. The number of combined heuristics is fixed and maintained in a first-in-first-out manner. Other top performing approaches in CHeSC 2011 include the rank 2 algorithm VNS-TW [13], which is based on variable neighbourhood search and applies a predefined sequence of shaking heuristics then hill-climber heuristics; rank 3 was ML [14] which is based on a self-adaptive meta-heuristic using multiple cooperating agents to determine adequate sequences of local search heuristics; rank 4 was PHUNTER [6] which attempts to balance the *diversification* and *intensification* sequence of heuristics; and rank 5 was EPH [16] which evolves population of prefixed sequence of heuristics by employing *diversification* and *intensification* scheme. Soon after the competition, CHeSC 2011 became a benchmark for evaluating the performance and generality level of a selection hyper-heuristic for subsequent algorithms. These include [11], where an improved choice function hyper-heuristic is proposed, which uses heuristic pair performance. The results revealed the success of the approach when compared to the traditional choice function [7]; and [5, 1], where a set of successful iterated local search algorithms for cross-domain search are proposed.

In contrast to the above approaches, this work introduces a new method known as sequence-based selection hyper-heuristic (SSHH), inspired by the hidden Markov model (HMM) [2], at which each low level heuristic, analogous to a state in the HMM, has a transition probability matrix to move to another state and emission probability matrices to determine the parameters for each low level heuristic and the acceptance strategy. The HMM approach is able to both analyse the sequence of heuristics and generate sequences of any size for use in optimisation. The automatic generation of probability matrices linking low level heuristics, acceptance strategy and heuristic parameters ensures that many fewer parameters have to be set to operate the technique. The analysis of higher order (e.g. greater than 2) heuristic sequences in this way using a hidden Markov model is also unprecedented in the literature. Although a very recent technique using an HMM exists [21], it represents solutions as states rather than low level heuristics as proposed here. The proposed approach records the search process as a sequence of pairs of heuristic application in an online fashion, and processes this information to inform the selection of the next heuristic to apply in the optimisation. It does not explicitly enforce the *diversification* and *intensification* phases, but rather discovers and learns these sequences automatically. The HyFlex framework is used to evaluate this new hyper-heuristic and to compare with many of the state-of-the-art approaches shown above. In later experimentation we show the HMM-sequence based technique improves upon all the entries to this contest, demonstrating that it can improve on the state-of-the-art in this field, with many fewer parameters to optimise than competing techniques.

The paper is structured as follows. Section 2 provides briefly the background of HyFlex and CHeSC 2011. Section 3 describes the novelty and all algorithmic components of the proposed hyper-heuristic. Section 4 presents the results of the proposed method on HyFlex problems and discusses the generality of the approach. Section 5 provides the conclusions of the study.

2. HYFLEX

HyFlex (**Hy**per-heuristics **Flex**ible framework) [19] is an object oriented software framework written in Java providing an implementation of six problem domains and encapsulating the problem specific information such as solution representations, solution constructions, low level heuristics and evaluation functions. HyFlex currently provides an implementation of boolean satisfiability (SAT), 1D bin packing (BP), personnel scheduling (PS), permutation flowshop (PFS), travelling salesman problem (TSP), and vehicle routing problem (VRP). In each HyFlex problem, four types of perturbative low level heuristics are defined: (i) *mutational* which perturbs a solution randomly, (ii) *ruin and re-create* which destroys a given solution partially and then rebuilds the deleted parts, (iii) *hill climbing* that incorporates an iterative improvement process and returns a non-worsening solution, and (iv) *crossover* which creates a new solution by exchanging and recombining parts from two solutions. Each low level heuristic is associated with a problem and heuristic dependent parameter, controlled by the user and taking a value in the range [0,1]. HyFlex was used in the Cross-domain Heuristic Search Challenge (CHeSC) in 2011, to determine the hyper-heuristic that works well across the different HyFlex problem domains. Competitors are invited to submit their hyper-heuristics to the HyFlex framework for evaluation. The organisers conducted 31 runs for each competing algorithm for five selected instances from each problem domain. Each run is limited to 600 seconds based on the organisers' machines. The methodology followed to rank the algorithms was inspired by the Formula One system. In each instance, the median values of the 31 runs of each algorithm are calculated, and the top eight algorithms based on the median values take the score 10, 8, 6, 5, 4, 3, 2 and 1 points, respectively. These points are summed across the 30 instances for each algorithm. The approach that scores the maximum is deemed the winner. Table 1 summarises the total number of low level heuristics and the indexes of each low level heuristic for each heuristic category. Twenty competitors submitted their algorithms to CHeSC 2011. The description of the twenty competing algorithms and the results are provided in the CHeSC 2011 competition website.

Table 1: The total number of low level heuristics and the distribution of heuristic types

problem domains	SAT	BP	PS	PFS	TSP	VRP
no. of heuristics	11	8	12	15	13	10
mutational	0-5	0,3,5	11	0-4	0-4	0,1,7
ruin & re-create	6	1,2	5-7	5,6	5	2,3
hill climbing	7,8	4,6	0-4	7-10	6-8	4,8,9
crossover	9,10	7	8-10	11-14	9-12	5,6

3. METHODOLOGY

The traditional iterative selection hyper-heuristic passes a solution through a heuristic selection process to decide on a heuristic to apply from a fixed set of low level heuristics and then a move acceptance process to accept or reject the newly created solution at each step. The selection process has traditionally been accomplished through the evaluation of individual or paired heuristics. Empirical evidence [20] shows that the traditional selection hyper-heuristic framework may lead to the mutational heuristics being ignored. Hence, several hyper-heuristic frameworks have been proposed to combine a set of mutational and hill climber heuristics by invoking a mutational heuristic first followed by a hill climber [20]. These frameworks are explicitly encouraging a diversifying (exploring of the search space) phase followed by an intensifying (exploiting of the accumulated search experience) phase. Here we propose a sequence-based selection hyper-heuristic utilising a hidden Markov model which is relatively simple to implement and achieves robustness by automatically adjusting itself to the problem domain. The method is also able to use its probability matrices to adapt to changing search characteristics over time. For example, a problem might be best solved in the initial stages by a certain sequence of heuristics selected from the heuristics pool, but as the nature of the optimisation problem changes over time, the sequence will also need to change, necessitating the online approach. The developed method differs markedly from standard selection hyper-heuristic approaches in that it is able to *observe* recent sequences of operations and so is able to learn sequences of heuristics that generate good solutions. The algorithm 1 provides the pseudocode of the proposed hyper-heuristic.

In this method, the sequences of low level heuristics are generated and analysed using hidden Markov model (HMM) [2]. The hidden states of an HMM correspond to the low level heuristics. Initially, each low level heuristic (state) has an initial probability to be selected (Algorithm 1, Line 1). Each low level heuristic has three probability matrices associated with it: An acceptance strategy emission probability matrix to associate heuristics with acceptance strategy, a heuristic parameter emission probability matrix to determine the parameters for each low level heuristic and a transition probability matrix to determine the probability of moving from one heuristic to another during the optimisation (Algorithm 1, Lines 2-4). Initially, all probabilities are distributed equally (Algorithm 1, Line 8). At the first step, an initial low level heuristic will be selected (Algorithm 1, Line 12).

The next low level heuristic, acceptance strategy (AS) and heuristic parameter (p) are chosen based on probabilities provided in the matrices (Algorithm 1, Lines 15-17), using a roulette wheel selection strategy. They are added to a record for later processing (Algorithm 1, Line 18). Recall that each low level heuristic in HyFlex is associated with a problem and heuristic dependent parameter (denoted as p), controlled by the user and taking a value in the range [0,1]. We discretised the choices for the control parameters provided in HyFlex into 11 different parameters: {0.0, 0.1, 0.2, 0.3, 0.4, 0.5, 0.6, 0.7, 0.8, 0.9, 1.0}, whereas for the acceptance strategy there are only two options: {1, 2}. The selected heuristic with the selected parameter will be applied to the candidate solution to produce a new solution (Algorithm 1, Line 19). If the acceptance strategy is 1, then the move acceptance method will be invoked and the emission and transition probability matrices are updated (Algorithm 1, Lines 20-28). Otherwise, the move acceptance method will not be applied meaning that the next low level heuristic will be applied on the new solution regardless of the quality of the new solution. The latter strategy helps the search to discover new regions in the search space. The move acceptance method uses the previous solution before applying the recorded recent sequence of heuristics (i.e. the solution which was returned the last time the move acceptance method was called) and the current (candidate) solution and then returns one of these two solutions (Algorithm 1, Line 21). To maximise the likelihood of generating best solutions, emission and transition probability matrices are updated only if the candidate solution is better than the best recorded solution (Algorithm 1, Lines 23-26). To update the matrices (Algorithm 1, Line 25), the scores of the three matrices corresponding to the recorded previous and next heuristics, acceptance strategies and heuristic parameters are increased by 1. The probability of selection in any of the matrices is $score_p / \sum_{\forall k}(score_k)$. The above methods are iteratively applied until a set of termination criteria is satisfied (Algorithm 1, Line 29).

Figure 2 illustrates an example of how the developed method would work on 3 low level heuristics. For simplicity, we consider only three possible heuristic parameters: {0.0, 0.1,

Algorithm 1: Sequence-based Selection Hyper-heuristic

```
Let I: initial state distribution;
Let A: state transition probabilities;
Let B: acceptance strategy emission probabilities;
Let C: heuristic parameter emission probabilities;
Let S_prev: previous solution;
Let S_curr: current solution;
Let S_best: best obtained solution;
I, A, B, C ← Initialise();
S_prev ← S_initial;
S_curr ← S_prev;
S_best ← S_prev;
llh_curr ← Select(I);
repeat
    llh_prev ← llh_curr;
    llh_curr ← Select(A, llh_prev);
    AS ← Select(B, llh_curr);
    p ← Select(C, llh_curr);
    record.Add(llh_prev, llh_curr, AS, p);
    S_curr ← Apply(S_curr, llh_curr, p);
    if AS == 1 then
        S_prev ← MoveAcceptance(S_prev, S_curr);
        S_curr ← S_prev;
        if S_curr isBetterThan S_best then
            S_best ← S_curr;
            UpdateScores(A, B, C, record);
        end
        record.Clear();
    end
until TerminationCriteriaSatisfied();
```

0.2}. The initial matrices and the updated matrices after 5 iterations are shown in the figure. At the first iteration, LLH2 is selected with selection parameter $p = 0.2$ and acceptance strategy $AS = 1$ and applied on an initial solution ($S_{initial}$). The newly generated solution (S_1) is rejected by the move acceptance method and therefore the next low level heuristic will be applied on $S_{initial}$. The matrices are not updated because the best obtained solution has not been improved. LLH1 with $p = 0.1$ and $AS = 1$ are selected next and applied on $S_{initial}$. The new solution (S_2) is accepted by the move acceptance method and its quality is better than the best obtained solution, and therefore, the scores of moving from LLH2 to LLH1, the heuristic parameter $p = 0.1$ and the acceptance strategy $AS = 1$ of LLH1 are increased by 1. LLH3 with $p = 0.0$ and $AS = 2$ are selected next and applied on S_2 generating new solution S_3. Nothing is updated and the move acceptance method is not invoked because $AS = 2$. We move to the next iteration where LLH1 with $p = 0.1$ and $AS = 1$ are selected and applied on S_3 generating new solution S_4. The move acceptance method compares S_4 with S_2 to decide whether to accept or reject S_4. In this example, S_4 is accepted and because its quality is better than the best obtained solution (which was S_2) the scores of moving from LLH1 to LLH3, the heuristic parameter $p = 0.0$ and the acceptance strategy $AS = 2$ of LLH3 are increased by 1; and also the scores of moving from LLH3 to LLH1, the heuristic parameter $p = 0.1$ and the acceptance strategy $AS = 1$ of LLH1 are increased by 1. LLH1 with $p = 0.2$ and $AS = 1$ are selected next and applied on S_4. The new solution (S_5) is accepted by the move acceptance method, but its quality is not better than the best obtained solution, hence, the matrices are not updated.

When trained for a sufficient number of iterations on the problem, those sequences of operations that are more likely to produce the best solutions will automatically be learned. The two emissions and transition probability matrices create a model of the optimisation process conducted thus far and the likelihood for of the optimisation being in state (low level heuristic) i at time n given the recent application of heuristics, heuristic parameters and acceptance strategies can be calculated thus:

$$L(i, n) = L(i, n-1) \times a_{llh_{n-1}.llh_n} \times e^1(p) \times e^2(AS) \quad (1)$$

where $L(i, n-1)$ is the likelihood of the previous state (low level heuristic) in the automaton, a is the probability of transition from one low level heuristic to another, e^1 is the probability of the emission of heuristic parameter p for llh_n, and e^2 is the probability of the emission of acceptance strategy AS for llh_n. Given the example in Figure 2 and according to the roulette wheel selection strategy, one can say that LLH3 with $AS = 2$ and $p = 0.0$ has the greatest probability to be selected next, followed by LLH1 with $AS = 1$ and $p = 0.1$.

4. EMPIRICAL RESULTS

In this section, the results of the proposed sequence-based selection hyper-heuristic approach, denoted as SSHH, are presented. There is still a debate going on the usefulness of crossover in the evolutionary algorithm community [10, 18]. Considering that we have proposed a single point based search framework, crossover operators provided in HyFlex are ignored by our method during the experiments, since crossover requires two solutions as input. Investigating how to best utilise all low level heuristics, including crossover operators within sequence-based selection hyper-heuristic would be of interest as future work. The experiments are performed on an i7-4770K CPU at 3.50GHz with 16GB RAM. A benchmarking software tool developed by the organisers of CHeSC is used to report the time our machine should take which is equivalent to 600 seconds of the organisers' machine. This program reported that a single run of our machine should terminate after 346 seconds which was implemented as the convergence criterion. The move acceptance criterion (only called when $AS = 1$) employed in this work accepts all improving moves by default; non-improving moves are accepted if the objective value of the candidate solution is less than a threshold. The threshold equals the objective function value of the best recorded solution plus a value (T). The value of T is set to 30, and is decreased by 2 in case no improvements in the current best obtained solution are found for 15 consecutive seconds. Note that if the integer part of the objective value is already 0, then T is added to the decimal part. For example, if the objective value is 0.0325 and $T = 30$ then the threshold would be 0.0355. The parameter setting for T of 30 has been set after a small number of preliminary experiments.

To compare the performance of the SSHH against the CHeSC 2011 competitors, 31 trials across five CHeSC instances from boolean satisfiability (SAT), one dimensional bin packing (BP), personnel scheduling (PS), permutation flow shop (PFS), travelling salesman problem (TSP) and vehicle routing problem (VRP) problem domains are performed. Table 2 provides the scores of SSHH and CHeSC 2011 competing algorithms based on the Formula One scoring system with respect to the median values across all CHeSC 2011 instances. The proposed SSHH ranks top with

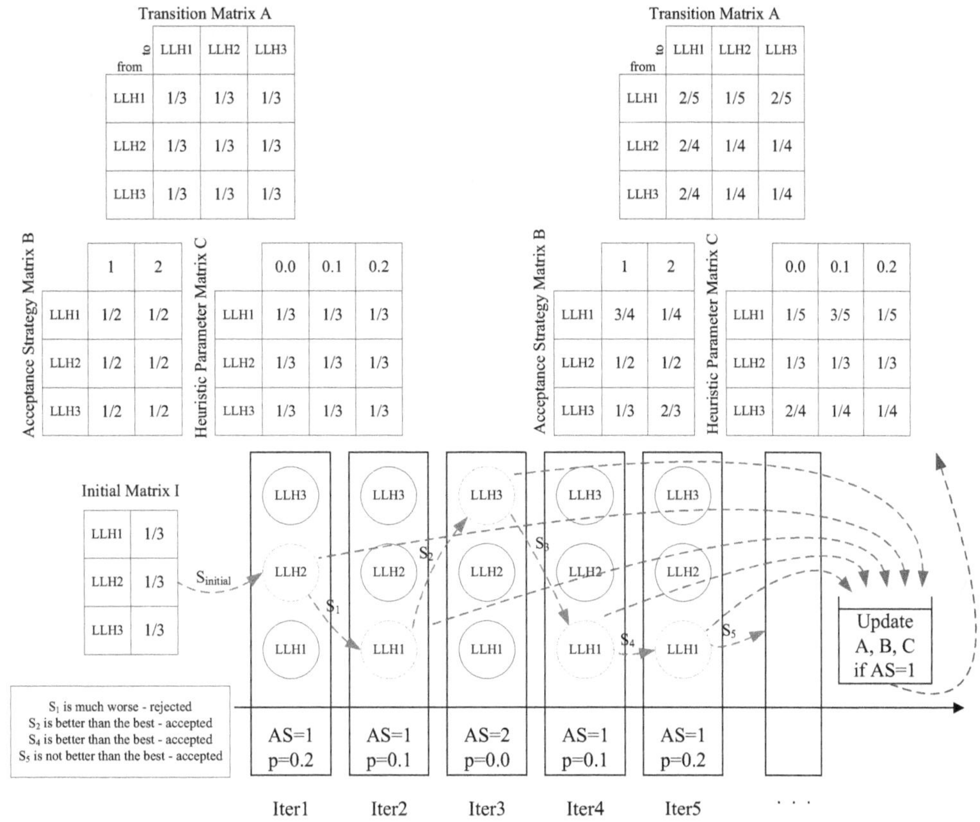

Figure 2: Sequence-based Selection Hyper-heuristic

a total score of 165.10, beating all other entries to the competition including the current best performer, AdapHH. SSHH is the best in SAT, BP and TSP problem domains. In the PS and VRP problem domains, it still performs well compared to the CHeSC approaches, but in the PFS problem domain, its performance is not as good as on the other problem domains. Interestingly, by examining the competing methods, the proposed SSHH performs better than the Markov chain hyper-heuristic (MCHH-S), that uses the Markov property, on all HyFlex problem domains. Further analysis of the behaviour of SSHH can be seen in Figure 4.

Figure 3 presents the boxplots of the normalised median objective function values of each competing method and SSHH for each instance for SAT, BP, PS, PFS, TSP and VRP problem domains. The median objective function values are normalised to a value in the range [0,1] as suggested in [9]. The normalisation is used to unify the scales of the objective function values. The following formula is employed for the normalisation:

$$n = \frac{m(i) - m_b(i)}{m_w(i) - m_b(i)} \tag{2}$$

where $m(i)$, for a given method, is the median objective function value of 31 runs on instance i, $m_b(i)$ is the best median objective function value of 31 runs obtained by any method on instance i, and $m_w(i)$ is similar but for the worst.

Due to space restrictions, we only provide analysis for three problem domains: BP, PS and TSP. Figure 4 provides the average utilisation rate of each heuristic considering only moves which improve on the best-of-run solution from 10 runs while solving an arbitrary instance from each problem domain. The figure also provides the probabilities of the emissions and transitions for each low level heuristic. Some of the low level heuristics do not seem to contribute to the best-of-run solutions. For example, LLH11 in PS does not contribute to the improvement of the best solutions. Fur-

Table 2: Scores of SSHH and CHeSC 2011 competing algorithms across six domains

Method	SAT	BP	PS	PFS	TSP	VRP	Overall
SSHH	39.10	45.00	22.50	3.50	41.00	14.00	165.10
AdapHH	30.43	38.00	8.00	37.00	34.75	14.00	162.18
VNS-TW	30.93	2.00	35.50	33.50	12.75	5.00	119.68
ML	10.00	8.00	29.50	39.00	10.00	21.00	117.50
PHUNTER	7.00	2.00	11.50	8.00	22.75	32.00	83.25
EPH	0.00	6.00	9.00	21.00	29.75	11.00	76.75
HAHA	26.43	0.00	23.00	3.50	0.00	13.00	65.93
NAHH	10.50	15.00	1.00	22.00	10.00	6.00	64.50
KSATS-HH	20.35	9.00	7.00	0.00	0.00	21.00	57.35
ISEA	3.50	23.00	14.50	3.50	7.00	3.00	54.50
HAEA	0.00	1.00	1.00	8.00	8.00	25.00	43.00
ACO-HH	0.00	16.00	0.00	9.00	7.00	1.00	33.00
GenHive	0.00	10.00	6.50	7.00	2.00	6.00	31.50
SA-ILS	0.25	0.00	16.00	0.00	0.00	4.00	20.25
XCJ	3.50	11.00	0.00	0.00	0.00	5.00	19.50
AVEG-Nep	9.50	0.00	0.00	0.00	0.00	8.00	17.50
DynILS	0.00	9.00	0.00	0.00	8.00	0.00	17.00
GISS	0.25	0.00	8.00	0.00	0.00	6.00	14.25
SelfSearch	0.00	0.00	2.00	0.00	2.00	0.00	4.00
MCHH-S	3.25	0.00	0.00	0.00	0.00	0.00	3.25
Ant-Q	0.00	0.00	0.00	0.00	0.00	0.00	0.00

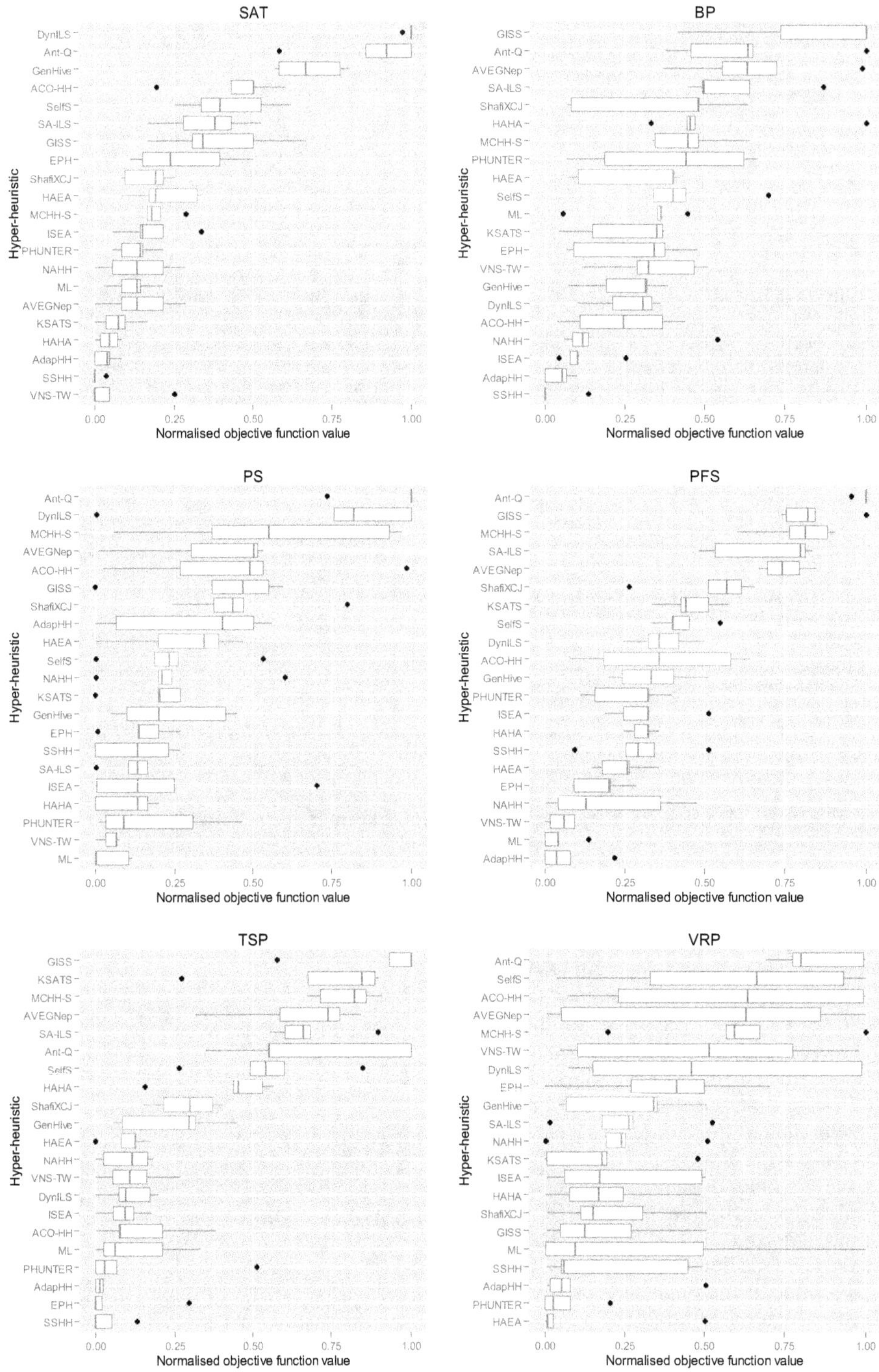

Figure 3: Boxplots of the normalised median objective function values of SSHH and CHeSC 2011 hyper-heuristics per each HyFlex problem domain over five CHeSC instances

thermore, a number of the low level heuristics are only useful when combined with other sequence of heuristics. For example, LLH0, LLH1 and LLH5 in TSP do not make improvement in their own, but the majority of the improvements in TSP are due to combining these heuristics (mutational and ruin & re-create heuristics) with LLH8 (hill climber). Interestingly, and by examining the transition matrix, LLH8 does not improve the best-of-run solutions unless combined with these heuristics. These types of sequences, which are automatically discovered by the proposed approach, have been previously suggested in the literature [15] by applying perturbation first (e.g. mutational heuristics) to explore the search space followed by the intensification phase (e.g. hill climbers) to exploit the accumulated search experience, but until now, this has been done manually. In BP, the sequence LLH4-LLH6-LLH2-LLH6 seems to generate most of the improvements, an interesting finding. However, in the case of the PS problem domain, such heuristic sequences were rarely identified. This is likely to be due to the fact that the low level heuristics (in particular the hill-climbers) associated with the PS problem domain are slow, and therefore there was not enough time to learn and detect the good sequences. In general, the probabilities of the heuristic parameters are distributed equally. However, in BP large values are slightly preferable. Most of the low level heuristics in BP use acceptance strategy 2 meaning that the search is largely exploratory for this problem. For the TSP problem domain, it is observed that the most successful low level heuristic in this problem (LLH8 - hill climber) favours the first acceptance strategy and acts as an intensification process, while the other heuristics (particularly LLH0, LLH1 and LLH5) prefer the second acceptance strategy for the purposes of diversification.

5. CONCLUSION

In this paper a new sequence-based selection hyper-heuristic inspired by a hidden Markov model has been proposed. The method has been shown to successfully optimise a number of combinatorial optimisation problems. The proposed approach is the best general purpose hyper-heuristic for heuristic search across a number of different HyFlex problem domains, achieving improved performance over established state-of-the-art hyper-heuristics such as AdapHH. A key further point is that the SSHH approach requires only one parameter (the threshold in the move acceptance method) to be set as opposed to AdapHH that has over 45 parameters[2]. The adaptive iteration limited list-based threshold move accepting method used in AdapHH allows diversification only if the intensification phase does not yield any improvements for a predefined number of iterations. Our method discovers and learns automatically when to move from intensification to diversification and vice versa. The additional power of this approach comes from the fact that it is capable of discovering sequences of heuristics and automatically identifying the relationship between the heuristic selected, its heuristic parameter and acceptance strategy in addition to its relationship with other low level heuristics on the problem. One further advantage of the method is that the probabilities learned by the model are easily accessible and can be analysed to determine what has been learned about the search space and relationships between low level heuristics, heuristic parameters and acceptance strategy. Our initial observations showed that the performance of selection hyper-heuristics may vary depending on the choice of the low level heuristics, and that not all the heuristics contribute to the improvement of a candidate solution during part of the search process unless they are applied in combination with sequences of heuristics. The proposed approach begins from a naïve state where the nature of the low level heuristics is not known, yet its adaptive characteristics lead automatically to the discovery of useful sequences of mutational heuristics followed by hill climbers. These findings are supported by results from other studies [15]. Further work on this analysis will investigate how these probabilities change over time and their interaction with known features in the problem landscape.

[2]http://code.google.com/p/generic-intelligent-hyper-heuristic/

6. ACKNOWLEDGMENTS

This work was supported by EPSRC grant EP/K000519/1.

7. REFERENCES

[1] S. Adriaensen, T. Brys, and A. Nowé. Fair-share ILS: a simple state-of-the-art iterated local search hyperheuristic. In D. V. Arnold, editor, *Proceedings of the 2014 Conference on Genetic and Evolutionary Computation (GECCO '14)*, pages 1303–1310, New York, NY, USA, 2014. ACM.

[2] L. E. Baum and T. Petrie. Statistical inference for probabilistic functions of finite state Markov chains. *The Annals of Mathematical Statistics*, 37(6):1554–1563, 12 1966.

[3] E. K. Burke, T. Curtois, M. R. Hyde, G. Kendall, G. Ochoa, S. Petrovic, J. A. V. Rodríguez, and M. Gendreau. Iterated local search vs. hyper-heuristics: towards general-purpose search algorithms. In *IEEE Congress on Evolutionary Computation (CEC '10)*, pages 1–8, 2010.

[4] E. K. Burke, M. Gendreau, M. Hyde, G. Kendall, G. Ochoa, E. Özcan, and R. Qu. Hyper-heuristics: a survey of the state of the art. *Journal of the Operational Research Society*, 64(12):1695–1724, 2013.

[5] E. K. Burke, M. Gendreau, G. Ochoa, and J. D. Walker. Adaptive iterated local search for cross-domain optimisation. In *Proceedings of the 13th Annual Conference on Genetic and Evolutionary Computation (GECCO '11)*, pages 1987–1994, New York, NY, USA, 2011. ACM.

[6] C. Y. Chan, F. Xue, W. H. Ip, and C. F. Cheung. A hyper-heuristic inspired by pearl hunting. In Y. Hamadi and M. Schoenauer, editors, *Learning and Intelligent Optimization*, Lecture Notes in Computer Science, pages 349–353. Springer Berlin Heidelberg, 2012.

[7] P. Cowling, G. Kendall, and E. Soubeiga. A hyperheuristic approach to scheduling a sales summit. In E. Burke and W. Erben, editors, *Practice and Theory of Automated Timetabling III*, volume 2079 of *Lecture Notes in Computer Science*, pages 176–190. Springer Berlin Heidelberg, 2001.

[8] W. B. Crowston, F. Glover, G. L. Thompson, and J. D. Trawick. *Probabilistic and parametric learning combinations of local job shop scheduling rules.* 117. Defense Technical Information Center, 1963.

[9] L. Di Gaspero and T. Urli. Evaluation of a family of reinforcement learning cross-domain optimization heuristics. In Y. Hamadi and M. Schoenauer, editors, *Learning and Intelligent Optimization*, Lecture Notes in Computer Science, pages 384–389. Springer Berlin Heidelberg, 2012.

[10] B. Doerr, E. Happ, and C. Klein. Crossover can provably be useful in evolutionary computation. In *Proceedings of the 10th Annual Conference on Genetic and Evolutionary Computation (GECCO '08)*, pages 539–546, New York, NY, USA, 2008. ACM.

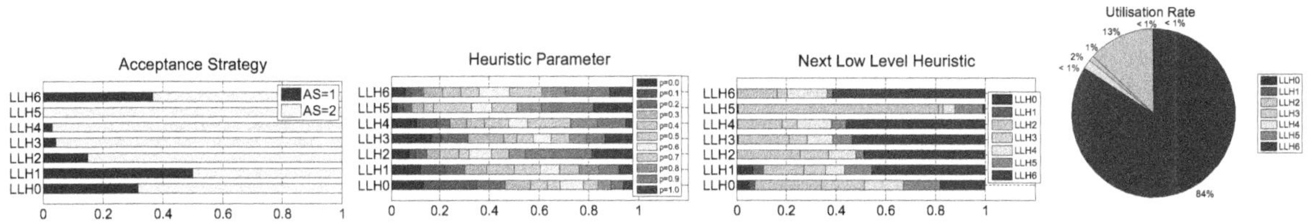

(a) BP

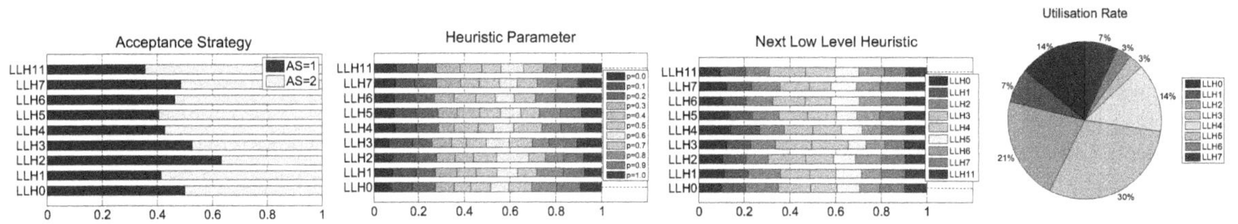

(b) PS

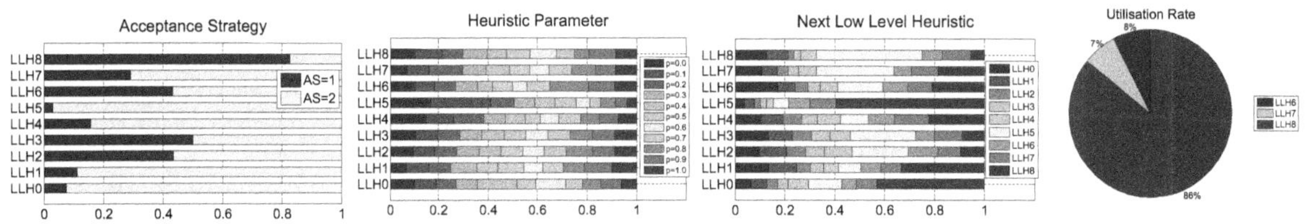

(c) TSP

Figure 4: Mean emission and transition probabilities and utilisation rate of each low level heuristic considering only moves which improve on the best-of-run solution from 10 runs while solving an arbitrary instance from each problem domain

[11] J. H. Drake, E. Özcan, and E. K. Burke. An improved choice function heuristic selection for cross domain heuristic search. In C. A. C. Coello, V. Cutello, K. Deb, S. Forrest, G. Nicosia, and M. Pavone, editors, *Parallel Problem Solving From Nature (PPSN XII)*, volume 7492 of *Lecture Notes in Computer Science*, pages 307–316. Springer Berlin Heidelberg, 2012.

[12] H. Fisher and G. L. Thompson. Probabilistic learning combinations of local job-shop scheduling rules. In J. F. Muth and G. L. Thompson, editors, *Industrial Scheduling*, pages 225–251, New Jersey, 1963. Prentice-Hall, Inc.

[13] P.-C. Hsiao, T.-C. Chiang, and L.-C. Fu. A VNS-based hyper-heuristic with adaptive computational budget of local search. In *IEEE Congress on Evolutionary Computation (CEC '12)*, pages 1–8, 2012.

[14] M. Larose. A hyper-heuristic for the CHeSC 2011. In *The 53rd Annual Conference of the UK Operational Research Society (OR53)*, 2011.

[15] H. R. Lourenço, O. C. Martin, and T. Stützle. Iterated local search: framework and applications. In M. Gendreau and J.-Y. Potvin, editors, *Handbook of Metaheuristics*, volume 146 of *International Series in Operations Research and Management Science*, pages 363–397. Springer US, 2010.

[16] D. Meignan. An evolutionary programming hyper-heuristic with co-evolution for CHeSC11. In *The 53rd Annual Conference of the UK Operational Research Society (OR53)*, 2011.

[17] M. Misir, K. Verbeeck, P. De Causmaecker, and G. Vanden Berghe. A new hyper-heuristic implementation in HyFlex: a study on generality. In J. Fowler, G. Kendall, and B. McCollum, editors, *Proceedings of the 5th Multidisciplinary International Scheduling Conference: Theory and Application (MISTA2011)*, pages 374–393, 2011.

[18] M. Mitchell, J. H. Holland, and S. Forrest. When will a genetic algorithm outperform hill climbing. In J. D. Cowan, G. Tesauro, and J. Alspector, editors, *Advances in Neural Information Processing Systems 6*, pages 51–58. Morgan Kaufmann, 1994.

[19] G. Ochoa, M. Hyde, T. Curtois, J. A. Vazquez-Rodriguez, J. Walker, M. Gendreau, G. Kendall, B. McCollum, A. J. Parkes, S. Petrovic, and E. K. Burke. HyFlex: a benchmark framework for cross-domain heuristic search. In J.-K. Hao and M. Middendorf, editors, *Evolutionary Computation in Combinatorial Optimization*, volume 7245 of *Lecture Notes in Computer Science*, pages 136–147. Springer Berlin Heidelberg, 2012.

[20] E. Özcan, B. Bilgin, and E. E. Korkmaz. A comprehensive analysis of hyper-heuristics. *Intelligent Data Analysis*, 12(1):3–23, 2008.

[21] W. Van Onsem, B. Demoen, and P. De Causmaecker. HHaaHMM: a hyper-heuristic as a hidden Markov model. http://www.hyflex.org/chesc2014/, 2014.

Evaluation of a Multi-Objective EA on Benchmark Instances for Dynamic Routing of a Vehicle

Stephan Meisel
Dept. of Information Systems
University of Münster, Germany
stephan.meisel@uni-muenster.de

Christian Grimme
Dept. of Information Systems
University of Münster, Germany
christian.grimme@uni-muenster.de

Jakob Bossek
Dept. of Information Systems
University of Münster, Germany
bossek@uni-muenster.de

Martin Wölck
Dept. of Information Systems
University of Münster, Germany
martin.woelck@uni-muenster.de

Günter Rudolph
Dept. of Computer Science
TU Dortmund Univ., Germany
guenter.rudolph@tu-dortmund.de

Heike Trautmann
Dept. of Information Systems
University of Münster, Germany
trautmann@uni-muenster.de

ABSTRACT

We evaluate the performance of a multi-objective evolutionary algorithm on a class of dynamic routing problems with a single vehicle. In particular we focus on relating algorithmic performance to the most prominent characteristics of problem instances. The routing problem considers two types of customers: mandatory customers must be visited whereas optional customers do not necessarily have to be visited. Moreover, mandatory customers are known prior to the start of the tour whereas optional customers request for service at later points in time with the vehicle already being on its way. The multi-objective optimization problem then results as maximizing the number of visited customers while simultaneously minimizing total travel time. As an a-posteriori evaluation tool, the evolutionary algorithm aims at approximating the related Pareto set for specifically designed benchmarking instances differing in terms of number of customers, geographical layout, fraction of mandatory customers, and request times of optional customers. Conceptional and experimental comparisons to online heuristic procedures are provided.

Categories and Subject Descriptors

I.2.8 [**Artificial Intelligence**]: Problem Solving, Control Methods, and Search—*Heuristic methods*; G.1.6 [**Numerical Analysis**]: Optimization

Keywords

Transportation; Metaheuristics; Online algorithms; Multi-objective optimization; Combinatorial optimization

GECCO '15, July 11 - 15, 2015, Madrid, Spain

ISBN 978-1-4503-3472-3/15/07...$15.00

DOI: http://dx.doi.org/10.1145/2739480.2754705

1. INTRODUCTION

Many real-world vehicle routing problems are of dynamic nature [20]. As one of the most prominent examples of dynamic routing of a vehicle, we consider the case where customer requests are not known in advance but are revealed in the course of time while the vehicle already is on its way. In practice both decisions about accepting dynamic customer requests for service and decisions about routing the vehicle are made in real-time. To this end decision makers typically rely on decision rules that they apply each time a new request occurs (see, e.g., [16]). However, real-time vehicle routing necessarily suffers from the fact that decisions are made without information about all customer requests being known. As a consequence, optimal decisions will rarely occur, and the problem of a-priori selection of the best decision rule is hard.

Yet one way of gradually gaining insights into the performance of decision rules consists of assessing applied rules in retrospect. In this paper we provide two fundamental means that enable such an assessment, provided that the decision maker pursues the two competing objectives of maximization of served requests and of minimization of travel distance.

On the one hand, we apply a multi-objective evolutionary algorithm for approximating the Pareto-front of a-posteriori solutions. The set of Pareto efficient a-posteriori solutions of a given problem instance may serve as a point of reference for solutions resulting from application of any real-time decision rule. On the other hand, we take into account the fact that algorithmic performance often strongly depends on the specific problem instance at hand. Therefore we carefully design and generate a set of benchmarking problem instances that systematically cover realizations of the most relevant problem characteristics.

The two main contributions of the present work are the new benchmarking instances that we propose as well as our analysis of the behavior of the evolutionary algorithm with respect to the different instances of the benchmarking set.

The following Section 2 provides a summary of related work, before Section 3 mathematically defines the class of routing problems we consider. Section 4 illustrates the approach we propose for generating a set of benchmarking instances of the class of routing problems. Section 5 introduces the multi-objective evolutionary algorithm. Finally, Section 6 provides computational results that illustrate the performance of the evolutionary algorithm with respect to the set of benchmarking instances. Section 7 concludes the paper.

2. RELATED WORK

Most of the existing works in the literature only consider the single objective of maximizing the number of customers visited within a given amount of time. The single vehicle problem with optional customers is frequently addressed as "orienteering problem" (e.g. [10]). A survey on different kinds of orienteering problems is provided in [21]. Although it has been recognized that orienteering problems should be formulated as bi-objective optimization problems [15], it can be concluded [7] that subsequent work (e.g. [5]) avoided dealing with true bi-objective formulations and aimed at minimization of the sum of total distance traveled and penalties for unvisited customers.

Publications that deal with a bi-objective formulation of the orienteering problem are rare. In [2] the ϵ-constraint approach is used to approximate the Pareto frontier by solving a series of single-objective problems where one of the two objectives is transformed into a constraint with varying bound ϵ. The solution of a series of single-objective problems is also necessary for the approximation schemes proposed in [8] which are proven to provide a Pareto-ϵ-approximation of the efficient set of solutions.

In contrast to the two preceding works the approach proposed in [13] explicitly solves the bi-objective formulation of the orienteering problem. Their method determines a high quality approximation of the efficient Pareto-frontier by two main steps. First an NSGA-II based multi-objective evolutionary algorithm is applied for generating a set of initial solutions. These solutions serve as starting points for an ejection chain process with two sets of neighborhood moves. A computational comparison with an iterated ϵ-constraint implementation of a state-of-the-art meta-heuristic for the single-objective orienteering problem shows that the method has advantages as the problem size increases.

To our knowledge, the approach of [13] so far is the only one that solves the bi-objective version of an orienteering problem without transformations to (a series of) single-criterion problems. Therefore it may be considered as most related to our approach, however time windows are not considered. Our problem scenario differs from traditional orienteering problems with time windows [14] as follows: the lower bound of a customer's time window does not represent the earliest point in time at which the vehicle may arrive at this customer's location; instead, the lower bound of a customer's time window represents the earliest point in time at which the vehicle may leave the preceding customer location. As a consequence, a comparison to previous work is hardly possible and new benchmark problems have to be developed. Thus, the few existing benchmark problems for orienteering problems with time windows [21] will not be included here as those would have to be adapted for our purposes and moreover lack a systematic generation procedure.

3. PROBLEM CLASS

Each problem instance of the benchmarking set proposed in the following Section 4 belongs to the class of vehicle routing problems defined in this section. An instance comprises one single vehicle and a set $C = \{1, 2, \ldots, N\}$ of locations, where location $i = 1$ is the start depot and location $i = N$ is the end depot of the vehicle. Travel distances d_{ij} between any pair (i, j) of locations are both known and deterministic, and one unit of travel distance corresponds to one unit of time. At time $t = 0$, the vehicle is located at $i = 1$ and at the end of the tour the vehicle must reach $i = N$.

The set $C\setminus\{1, N\}$ of customers consists of both the subset C^m of mandatory customers and the subset C^o of optional customers, where $C^m \cap C^o = \emptyset$. Mandatory customers request for service before time $t = 0$ and must necessarily be visited once by the vehicle. Each optional customer i issues one service request at a particular point in time $t_i > 0$ and must immediately be either accepted for service or rejected. Note that rejecting a customer typically saves travel time, and that in practice such a customer will become a mandatory customer of the following day.

Maximization of customer satisfaction clearly suggests accepting all optional customers. On the other hand, however, satisfying all requests typically implies high costs in terms of a long overall travel distance. In order to make an appropriate trade-off between maximization of customer satisfaction and minimization of travel costs both of these objectives are considered simultaneously.

The resulting bicriteria problem to be solved for determination of ideal a-posteriori solutions may be described by means of the following Equations 1a-1h:

$$\min\Big((|C| - \sum_{i\in C} x_i^c), (\sum_{(i,j)\in E} d_{ij}x_{ij}^r)\Big) \tag{1a}$$

$$s.t. \quad x_i^c = 1 \qquad \forall i \in C \setminus \{C^o\}, \tag{1b}$$

$$\sum_{(i,j)\in\phi^+(i)} x_{ij}^r = x_i^c \qquad \forall i \in C \setminus \{N\}, \tag{1c}$$

$$\sum_{(k,i)\in\phi^-(i)} x_{ki}^r = x_i^c \qquad \forall i \in C \setminus \{1\}, \tag{1d}$$

$$\sum_{(k,i)\in\phi^-(i)} (y_{ki} + d_{ki}x_{ki}^r) \le \sum_{(i,j)\in\phi^+(i)} y_{ij} \qquad \forall i \in C \setminus \{1\}, \tag{1e}$$

$$\sum_{(i,j)\in\phi^+(i)} (y_{ij} - t_i x_{ij}^r) \ge \sum_{(k,i)\in\phi^-(i)} d_{ki}x_{ki}^r \qquad \forall i \in C, \tag{1f}$$

$$y_{ij} \in \mathbb{N}_0 \qquad \forall (i,j) \in E, \tag{1g}$$

$$x_{ij}^r, x_i^c \in \{0,1\} \qquad \forall (i,j) \in E, \forall i \in C \tag{1h}$$

Three types of decisions are involved. For each location $i \in C$, decision x_i^c indicates whether or not the request of customer i has been accepted or not. Decisions x_{ij}^r determine whether or not the road link connecting locations i and j is part of the vehicles ideal route. Note that we assume that all locations of C are connected with each other, and that distances between any pair i, j of locations are symmetric. The set of all road links connecting any pair (i, j) is referred to as E. Set $\phi^+(i)$ (set $\phi^-(i)$) contains all road links that are going out of (or into) location i. Each of the variables y_{ij} equals zero if link (i, j) is not part of the solution, i.e., $y_{ij} = 0$ if $x_{ij}^r = 0$. In case of $x_{ij}^r = 1$, variable y_{ij} denotes the point in time at which the vehicle arrives at location i.

Our goal is minimization of both the number of unserved customers and the total distance traveled by the vehicle (Equation 1a). Equation 1b ensures that both depots as well as all mandatory customers $i \in C^m$ will be visited before returning to N. Equations 1c and 1d ensure that the vehicle leaves $i = 0$, reaches $i = N$ and visits each customer with an accepted request exactly once.

Equation 1e makes sure that the vehicle never arrives at location i before it's predecessor k (according to the route) has been visited and the distance d_{ki} has been traveled. As a consequence we have $y_{ki} \leq y_{ij}$ with j representing the successor of i. Additionally, Equation 1f ensures that the vehicle is never allowed to leave the preceding location k for moving on to i before i has actually issued a service request. Note that the claim of Equation 1f reflects the conditions present in a real-time setting.

Against the background of the vehicle routing literature, the proposed model represents a bicriteria orienteering problem. In the following Section we provide an approach to generating a set of benchmarking problem instances of the class of vehicle routing problems defined by Equations 1a-1h.

4. BENCHMARKING SET GENERATION

Our experimental study is based on a specifically designed set of 600 problem instances. The generated instances differ in the number of customers $n \in \{50, 100, 200, 400\}$ (including both start and end depot), the number of clusters $n_c \in \{1, 2, 3, 5, 10\}$ and the fraction of optional customers $f \in \{0.25, 0.5, 0.75\}$, representing a variety of typical scenarios for the VRP.

We started by generating a single geographical layout for each combination of the number of customers and the number of clusters. Single cluster instances consist of randomly placed customers in the euclidean plane, starting with a bounding box of $[0, 100]^2$ for $n = 50$ and doubling the bounding box sides on doubling the number of customers. The generation of instances with two or more clusters follows a more sophisticated procedure: 1) We generate a latin hypercube design (LHS) of size n_c in two dimensions to get reasonable cluster centers. The space-filling property of LHS designs ensures, that the cluster centers are highly distributed in the available space and avoids overlapping of clusters. 2) We then sample random points from a multivariate Gaussian distribution using the corresponding cluster center coordinates as the mean vector and the euclidean distance to the nearest cluster center as the variance.

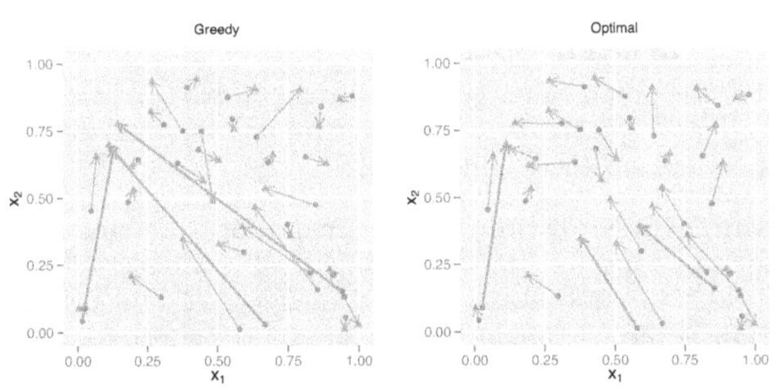

Figure 1: Greedy point matching (left) and optimal point matching (right). The three longest distances between assigned points are highlighted with bold arrows.

Moreover, we adopt the concept of *morphing* instances first introduced by [17] and later improved in [18], using a convex combination of point coordinates of two instances to generate instances in between the original ones [18]. However, we further improved the underlying point matching algorithm, which determines points of both instances, which should be combined. Recognizing that point matching on instances of the same size is equivalent to an assignment problem in bipartite graphs, we substituted the greedy approach used in [18] with a procedure, which makes use of a linear programming solver and finds the optimal point matching regarding to euclidean distance. The superiority of our point matching approach is depicted in Figure 1 by way of example.

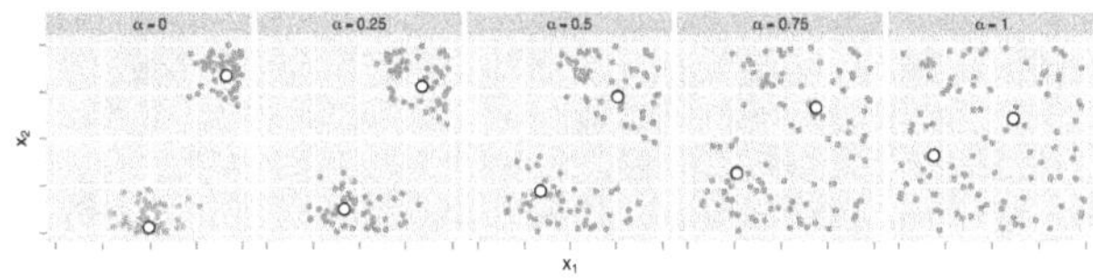

Figure 2: Example: Morphing of a clustered instance with two clusters and a random instance of equal size with two depots in each case for different morphing coefficients α.

An example of our morphing approach is visualized in Figure 2, morphing an instance with two clusters with a random instance. We observe a smooth and natural transition of one instance into another for increasing morphing coefficient α ($\alpha \in \{0, 0.25, 0.5, 0.75, 1\}$), with $\alpha = 0$ and $\alpha = 1$ representing the original instances.

We used the enhanced morphing algorithm – handling depots and customers separately – to generate instances in between the random instance and the instance with five clusters for each cluster size and corresponding instance size, resulting in 15 further geographical layouts. An overwiew of all generated geographies is given in Figure 3.

As a next step, we assigned request times to a fraction of f ($f \in \{0.25, 0.5, 0.75\}$) customers randomly for each of our 40 geographies (5 random plus 20 clustered plus 15 morphed), increasing the number of optional customers stepwise. The request times were sampled from an Exponential distribution with the rate parameter set accordingly. We started with a maximal arrival limit of 400 time units for instances with 50 customers and doubled the arrival limit for instances next in size each time. This process was repeated five times with different seeds for the random number generator to get different realizations of the underlying Poisson process.

We wrapped up the implementation of instance generation and enhanced morphing in the R package *netgen* [3].

5. MULTIOBJECTIVE APPROACH

In order to experimentally evaluate the considered routing problem instances regarding their complexity for multi-objective problem solving approaches as well as for evaluating the principal capabilities of multi-objective evolutionary algorithms to tackle this problem, we apply NSGA-II [4] as widely accepted algorithmic framework for our study. Starting with an initial population of size μ, the algorithm performs an evolutionary loop consisting of generating μ offspring solutions by variation, ranking the union set of parents and offspring regarding non-domination, and finally creating a new parental population by adding better ranked solutions until it contains μ or more individuals. If the new

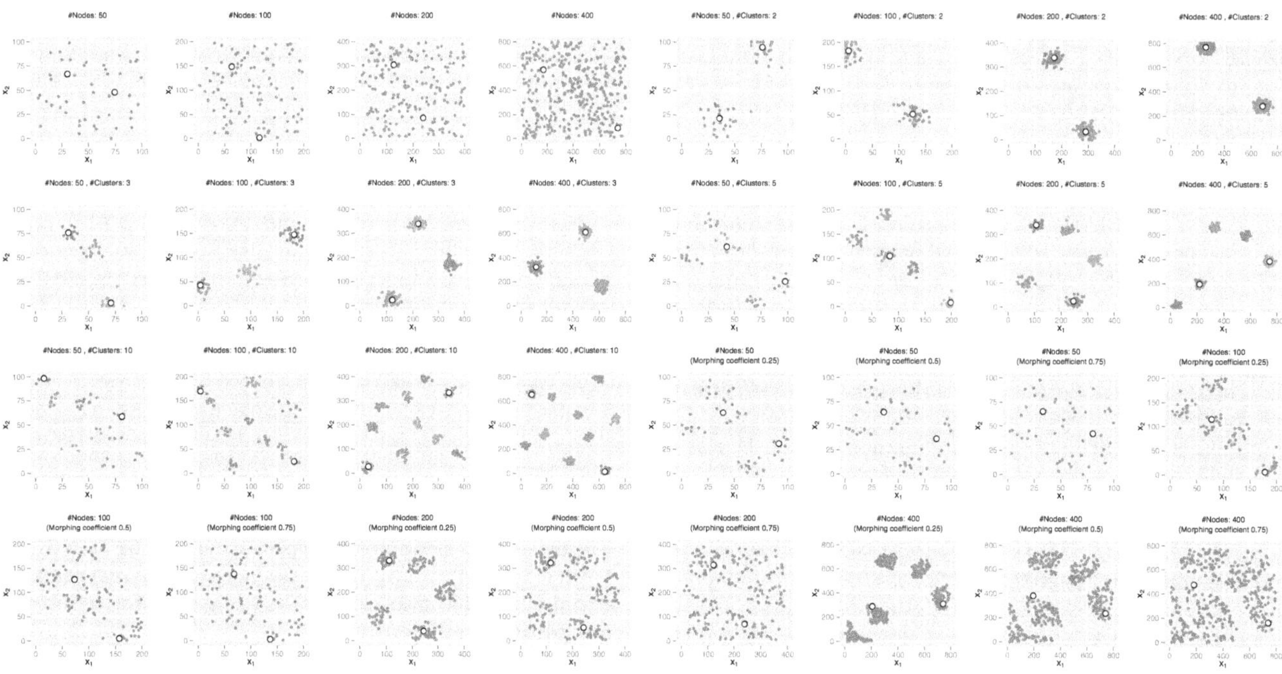

Figure 3: Overwiew of generated geographies.

population size is larger than μ, solutions with worst rank and smallest crowding distance [4] are removed. In the following we briefly explain the instantiation of the algorithmic framework in terms of solution encoding, variation operators, and integration of local search.

A solution to the vehicle routing problem as defined in Section 3 has several components: a subset of customers from C must be selected, while simultaneously an optimal tour for visiting those customers has to be determined. Thus, the encoding of a solution candidate consists of a permutation string and a binary string both of length $N-2$. The permutation string encodes the sequence of visits to all customers, while the binary string $B = (b_2, \ldots, b_{N-1}) \in \{0,1\}^{N-2}$ indicates for each customer $i \in C \setminus \{1, N\}$ whether it is visited ($b_i = 1$) or not ($b_i = 0$). This encoding disregards the start ($i = 1$) and end ($i = N$) depots, which are always part of the tour. We additionally introduce a probability encoding for each position in the binary string as strategy parameters to distinguish between the subsets C^m and C^o of C. Herein, we assign a flip probability $p_i \in [0,1]$ for each element in the binary string. If $p_i = 0$, the value of b_i never changes throughout the variation process. This way we denote customers from C^m as obligatory. A probability $0 < p_i \leq 1$ indicates a certain variability of value b_i, denoting dynamic customers from C^o.

With this encoding scheme a tour can be constructed from the permutation string by only considering the active customers. Fig. 4 shows two exemplary solutions for a problem with six customers (start and end depots are excluded from the encoding) and different activation states. In the left scenario only customers 3 and 4 are active resulting in a tour that only visits those customers. In the right scenario customers 3, 4, and 5 are active. The tours result from the permutations, with sequences $4 \rightarrow 3$ (left) and $5 \rightarrow 3 \rightarrow 4$ (right).

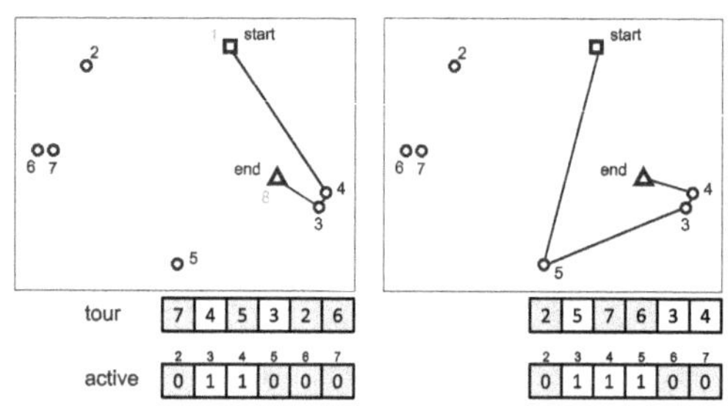

Figure 4: Exemplary encoding of two (Pareto-optimal) solutions for a routing problem instance with six customers, two of those active in the left and three active in the right case.

5.1 Variation operators

For the proposed encoding consisting of two chromosomes we combined common variation operators to specialized mutation and crossover building blocks.

Swap/Flip-Mutation: The permutation chromosome is varied by repeated pairwise swapping of randomly selected entries. This is controlled by parameter $\sigma_p \in \mathbb{N}$ which determines the maximum number of swaps performed. The actual number of swaps is drawn uniformly random from $\{0, \ldots, \sigma_p\} \subset \mathbb{N}$. Simultaneously, the binary string undergoes a flip mutation, where each position $b_i \in \{0,1\}$ in the string is flipped with probability $p_i \in [0,1]$ taken from the strategy parameters.

PMX/One-Point-Crossover: The crossover of two solutions is performed with Partially Mapped Crossover (PMX) for the permutation string and with One-Point-Crossover for the binary string. In PMX offspring is generated by interchanging a sub-sequence of the parental solutions and repairing violations to the permutation [19]. One-Point-Crossover recombines offspring by splitting up the binary string at a random position and alternately connecting the parts.

Note, during mutation no repair of infeasible solutions is needed. While swap mutation only changes the order of visits to customers, i.e. the tour, flip mutation influences tour length by activating and deactivating customers. During evaluation, if an active customer's order is not yet available due to a later request time, the vehicle remains waiting at the previous customer and the waiting time is added to tour length. Thus, inefficient tours containing long waiting times are punished during selection and removed on the long run.

5.2 Integration of Local Search

In addition to variation operators we integrate local search—especially for optimizing tour length—into NSGA-II. Instead of starting with a random initial solution set we applied 2-OPT local search to the initial population. Additionally, 2-OPT is repeatedly activated after variation. 2-OPT local search optimizes tour length by removing edge crossings from a tour. It is based on the insight, that in euclidean graphs planar tours are more cost-efficient than non-planar. In our implementation we apply the steepest descent variant of 2-OPT, which performs the most effective interchange of edges per step.

6. EXPERIMENTS

In this section we briefly describe the evaluation settings before showing and discussing experimental results.

6.1 Experimental Setup

We applied NSGA-II with the described variation operators and 2-OPT local search. However, the parameter settings for population size, variation operators, and number of function evaluations depends on the considered instance size (i.e. number of customers contained). As problem instance sizes systematically double (see Section 4), we applied the same approach to a basic set of good parameters.[1] In Table 1 we show generally formulated parameter settings and denote the instance sizes with $K = 0$ when comprising 50 customers up to $K = 3$ when comprising 400 customers. Experiments were repeated 10 times with independent random initialization. The chosen amount of basic function evaluations resembles approximately 120s running time of the algorithm implementation[2] on a Intel i7-3667U CPU machine at 2.5GHz with 8GB RAM. This makes the running time comparable with the maximum time allowed for the applied real-time decision rules executed in CPLEX.

Table 1: General algorithm parameters' scheme.

Parameter	Setting
Population size	$\mu = 100 \cdot 2^K$
Swap number	$\sigma_p = 2 \cdot 2^K$
Flip probability	$\frac{1}{N-2}$
Function evaluations	$\nu = 6,500,000 \cdot 2^K$
Initial local search	$0.1 \cdot \nu$
Internal local search	$0.01 \cdot \nu$, only 65 times per run

[1]This setting yielded best behavior for several considered test instances of comprising 50 customers.

[2]Implemented in the jMetal framework [6].

For comparison we consider two real-time decision rules, both of which are similar to rules that have been discussed in the literature (see, e.g., [16]). Each rule makes decisions about acceptance of new customer requests as well as about revision of the routing plan at each point in time a new customer request occurs. An acceptance decision is made by maximizing the number of newly accepted customers subject to a predefined overall time horizon. Decisions about plan revisions are then made by solving an open travelling salesman problem with all customers that have already been accepted but not visited yet. Note that this approach essentially pursues the single objective of maximizing the number of served customers at each point in time, with the second objective being represented in terms of a constraint that limits the total amount of travel time available.

The fact that the overall time horizon is predefined allows for the decision rules to strategically include waiting times into the route, where the idea is that allocating a certain amount of waiting time at specific customer locations will eventually reduce the overall distance travelled. Decisions about waiting time allocation are made if the vehicle has just arrived at a customer location, or if the vehicle currently waits and a new request appears. In particular, we consider the following two decision rules:

Distributed Waiting (DW): Waiting decisions are made such that the total amount of currently available waiting time is distributed equally among all customer locations of the current planned route. The amount of time to be spent at customer locations is recalculated as soon as a new customer request is accepted.

Drive First (DF): The vehicle only waits at its current customer location if both waiting time is available and the planned route only contains the end depot.

We apply each rule to each of the problem instances featuring either 50 or 100 locations. In order to approximate the set of Pareto efficient solutions with a given pair of instance and decision rule, we vary the predefined total amount of travel time and solve the instance several times. For each instance we start with a time horizon that merely allows for serving all customers C^m, i.e., that leads to rejection of all optional customers. We then increase the time horizon with a step size of ten time units until the time horizon is sufficiently long for also serving all customers C^o. Both the orienteering problem and the travelling salesman problem occuring at each decision time are solved optimally by a branch-and-cut procedure.

6.2 Indicators

For evaluation of experimental results we applied some standard as well as some specifically designed indicators, which are briefly described in the following paragraphs.

Hypervolume.

For determining the algorithms' performance on the evaluated instances, we applied the hypervolume indicator [22] which measures the normalized hypervolume enclosed by a non-dominated solution front and a given reference point. The reference point is determined as nadir point for each problem instance considering all NSGA-II and CPLEX results. Additionally, the utopia point is determined from the same set of solutions fronts. Both utopia and nadir points are used for normalizing the hypervolume.

Empirical Attainment Function.
The Empirical Attainment Function [9] allows the statistical interpretation of stochastic multi-objective algorithms by mapping the results of repeated algorithm runs to so called $k\%$-attainment surfaces. Each $k\%$-surface partitions the objective space in two areas: the area which is dominated by $k\%$ solution sets over all runs and the area, which is not dominated. Consequently, the best solutions obtained over all runs form the 0%-surface, while the worst solutions from all runs form the 100%-surface. In our evaluation we always also provide the 50%-surface as median.

Coverage.
For the defined vehicle routing problem the number of elements in the Pareto-front (PF) is determined by the number of optional customers: $|PF| = |C^o| + 1$. Given a non-dominated solution set $\mathcal{X}$ as result of applying algorithm A, this value can be used to define the coverage of the solution front as ratio

$$cov_A = \frac{|\mathcal{X}|}{|C^o| + 1}.$$

Obviously, this indicator does not provide information on the convergence behavior of algorithm A but indicates to what extent tour solutions for all (optional) customer configurations are found.

Determinism.
In order to make some statement on the algorithmic challenge posed by a problem instance topology, we define a measure which considers problem characteristics as well as solution quality: with T_A denoting the longest tour (travel time) in the non-dominated solution set after application of algorithm A,

$$Det_A = 1 - \frac{\max\{t_i \mid i \in C^o\}}{T_A}$$

is called the *determinism* of the instance under A. This measure relates the latest service request over all optional customers (instance property) to the longest tour in the non-dominated solution set. Clearly, the longest tour (largest travel time) will always exceed the latest service request. Thus determinism ranges in $0 < Det_A \leq 1$. In this range, determinism can be seen as a kind of approximation factor for the solution element with only mandatory customers. The lower Det_A is, the closer to the determined tour's end the last service request is dispatched.

A very specific variant of this indicator can be defined as purely instance related: instead of considering the longest tour of an algorithm solution set, we compute the optimal tour length T_{OPT} for all (mandatory and optional) customers in C without respecting service requests. We term this indicator

$$Det_{OPT} = 1 - \frac{\max\{t_i \mid i \in C^o\}}{T_{OPT}}.$$

This indicator specifically shows for $0 < Det_{OPT} \leq 1$ that the optimal travel time T_{OPT} exceeds the last service request. For $Det_{OPT} \leq 0$ the last service request appears after the lower bound for travel time.

In order to compute T_{OPT} as shortest paths from start to end depots, the Concorde solver [1] for the (symmetric) Travelling Salesperson Problem (STSP) was used. As mentioned, we assumed, that there are no dynamic requests and thus all the customers are mandatory. Since the problem of finding an optimal hamiltonian path differs slightly from the TSP, we applied two transformations to the distance matrix. First, we replaced the two depots with a dummy depot. The outgoing edges of this dummy node contain the distances of the start depot and the edge weights of the ingoing edges correspond to the edge weights of the end depot. However, the distance matrix is not symmetric anymore and hence the generated TSP problem is asymmetric (ATSP). Since Concorde is specially designed for the symmetric TSP we used a reformulation af the ATSP as a STSP by doubling the number of customers [12], i.e., adding another dummy customer for each customer. The resulting STSP was solved to optimality with Concorde. The tours for the ATSP were obtained by removing the dummy customers from the optimal STSP tour and and finally the optimal hamiltonian path was extracted by "cutting" the tour at the dummy depot [11]. Figure 5 shows some exemplary paths for some of our benchmark instances.

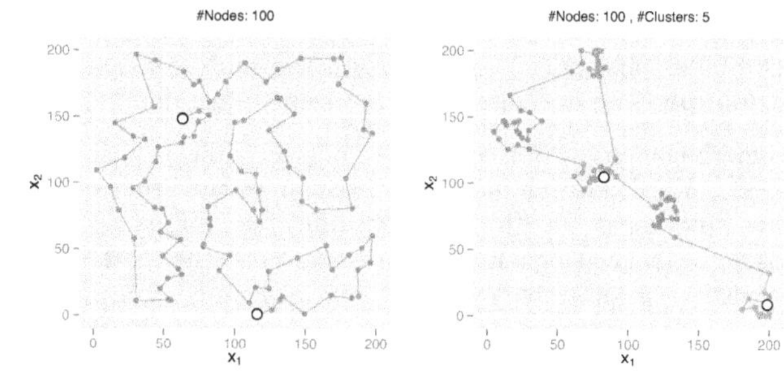

Figure 5: Examples for optimal hamiltonian pathes from start to end depot on different geographies of our benchmarking set.

6.3 Results

The indicators introduced in Section 6.2 are used to analyze problem characteristics in relation to EA behavior. Indicator values can be compared over all instances as they were designed in a normalized way such that the scaling is independent from the individual instance characteristics. At first, the relationship of both determinism indicators is investigated in Figure 6. A clear structure is visible when labeling the points regarding the underlying instance size. Of course the Det_{EA} indicator always exceeds Det_{OPT} as

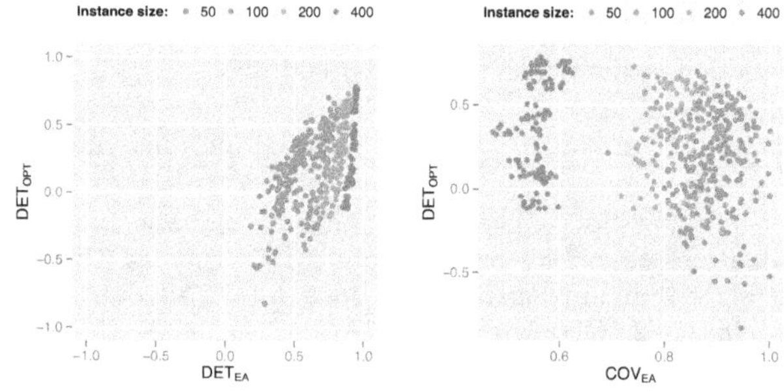

Figure 6: Det_{EA} (left) resp. cov_{EA}(right) vs. Det_{OPT} for all considered instances. Color labels indicate the instance size.

the maximum tour length of the evolutionary algorithm is always longer than the optimal solution for all nodes disregarding the request times. The extent of the difference increases with the instance size as larger problems are more difficult to solve for the EA. The same effect is visible in case Det_{OPT} is related to cov_{EA}(see right part of 6). Clearly, for higher instance sizes the fraction of approximated Pareto optimal solutions on the front decreases. Contrarily, Det_{OPT} is hardly influenced by the instance size which reflects that our request time settings were chosen in a reasonable way.

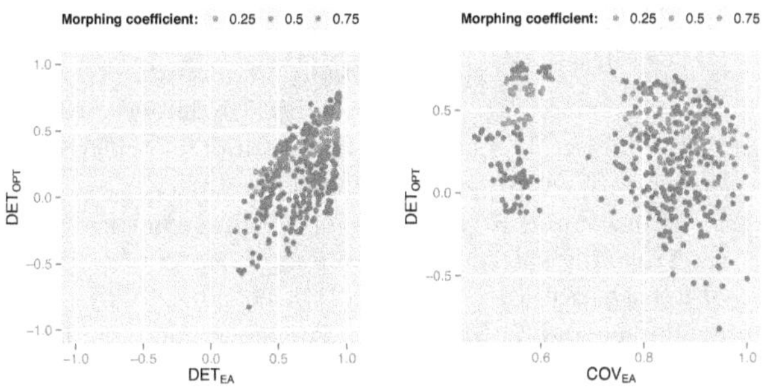

Figure 7: Det_{EA} (left) resp. cov_{EA}(right) vs. Det_{OPT} for all considered instances. Color labels indicate the morphing coefficient.

The topology of the instances influences the problem and EA characteristics. More specifically, Det_{OPT} simultaneously increases with the morphing coefficient (Figure 7, left). Thus, the optimal open TSP solution is higher for more randomly structured instances. The number of clusters has an impact on Det_{OPT} (Figure 8, left) such that random instances lead to higher open TSP solutions. Smallest respective values result from the smallest number of clusters which is intuitive as short paths are present within the clusters. In Figure 7, Det_{OPT} shows a smooth transition between clustered and random instances. Contrarily, cov_{EA} is not influenced by the morphing coefficient (Figure 7, right) while Det_{EA} has a slight tendency that the problem becomes less deterministic with decreasing morphing coefficient, i.e., for stronger clustered instances.

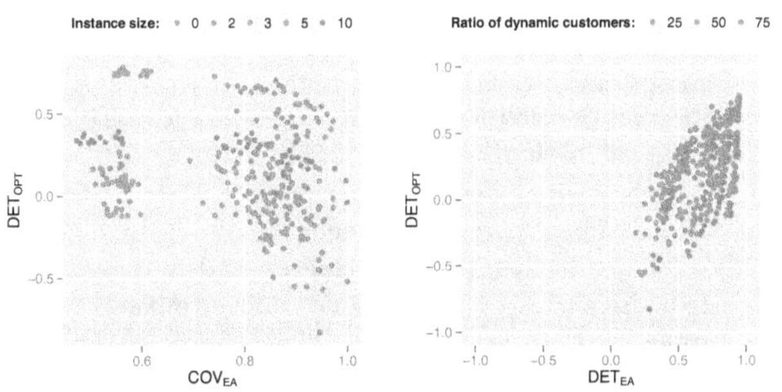

Figure 8: cov_{EA}(left) resp. Det_{EA} (right) vs. Det_{OPT}. Color labels indicate the number of clusters resp. the fraction of dynamic customers. In the left figure the morphed instances are neglected as the number of clusters is not assigned here.

Of course, the fraction of dynamic customers is only of interest for investigating the EA behaviour as the open TSP solution does not take into account the request times. From Figure 8 (right) we can conclude that within a specific instance size (see Fig. 6 for relating the labels) a higher fraction of dynamic customers increases the EA determinism. Due to the increasing tour uncertainty coming along with a higher fraction of dynamic customers, tour lengths tend to be higher than for a larger number of mandatory customers.

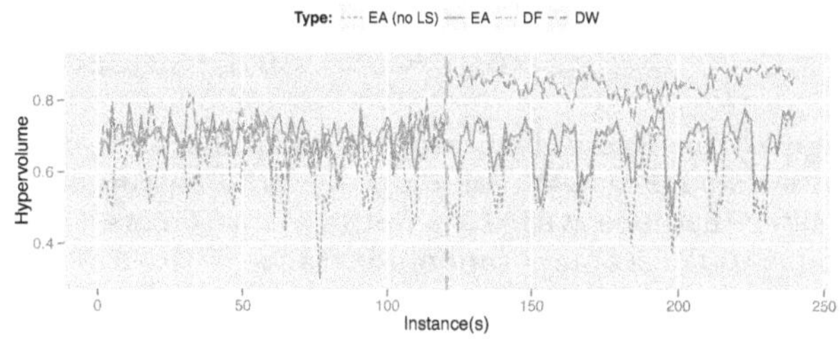

Figure 9: Dominated Hypervolume of the EA (with and w/o local search) and DF / DW solutions for instances of size 50 (left part) and 100 (right part). For the evolutionary algorithm, the average of all ten runs is shown.

In order to assess the EA performance on individual instances the Dominated Hypervolume indicator (HV) is used. Though the EA performance increases with higher HV values, the indicator level is only roughly comparable across instances due to the nature of the underlying normalization (see Section 6.2) but has to be evaluated in comparison to other approaches. Here, we relate it to the single-objective real-time (SORT) decision rules briefly discussed in Section 6.1. As the computational requirements of the latter approaches heavily increases with the instance size as well – due to a desired fine discretization of the Pareto front – with the number of optional customers, the former solutions are only available for instance sizes 50 and 100. Figure 9 shows the corresponding HV values. For the smallest instance size of 50, the EA and the SORT rules are comparable, while the EA often even provides better results than SORT. For the subsequent instance size of 100, the SORT solutions outperform the EA which gives the impression that performance difference increases with instance size. However, the SORT rules have to be conducted for each desired point on the Pareto front separately which eventually leads to enormous computation times and are thus not reasonably applicable for bigger instance sizes. Contrarily, the EA approximates the complete Pareto front in a single run and might perform better with higher budget of function evaluations and tuned parameter settings.

This potential can also be observed Figure 9 which shows the benefit of applying local search in the EA compared to applying a pure EA without local search mechanisms. Additionally, Figure 10 exemplarily shows the difference in approximation quality of EA and SORT solutions. In instances of size 50, SORT solutions range in the attainment area of the EA, while in 100 customer instances the optimization of (long) tours with many customers often causes the major difference in HV performance. Specifically designed and adjusted operators and superior local search mechanisms could help to overcome this issue. However, the focus is not on algorithm tuning at this stage but rather understanding EA behavior related to instance characteristics.

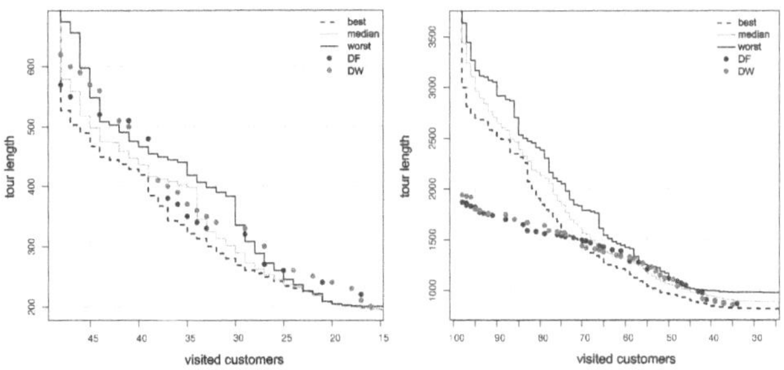

Figure 10: Exemplary attainment plots of EA results and DF / DW solutions for a 50 customers 2 cluster instance with 75% optional customers (left) and a 100 customers random instance with 75 % optional customers (right).

7. CONCLUSIONS

In this paper, we addressed a class of vehicle routing problems with two competing objectives. In order to establish the ground for following analysis, we carefully designed and created a set of benchmark instances for this problem class. Characteristics of these instances are experimentally investigated by applying a well-established multi-objective evolutionary approach. First results show different aspects of the benchmark problems' topologies like number of customers, dynamism, and number of clusters to be gradually influential onto algorithm performance. Furthermore, a closer look into the comparison of EA results and ILP-based methods highlights the potential of EAs to provide good solution sets in a single run for small problem instances. The comparison also reveals the need for application of alternative (evolutionary) multi-objective approaches and for integration of more sophisticated local search mechanisms. Thus, this paper may be considered as fundamental work proposing a valid set of benchmarking instances, and allowing for insights into algorithmic challenges posed by the considered problem class. Starting from this, more rigorous analysis of the benchmarking set as well as algorithm tuning and development are promising future directions of research.

8. REFERENCES

[1] D. Applegate, W. Cook, S. Dash, and A. Rohe. Solution of a min-max vehicle routing problem. *INFORMS J. on Computing*, 14(2):132–143, 2002.

[2] J.-F. Berube, M. Gendreau, and J.-Y. Potvin. An exact ε-constraint method for bi-objective combinatorial optimization problems: Application to the traveling salesman problem with profits. *Eur. J. Oper. Res.*, 194(1):39–50, 2009.

[3] J. Bossek. *netgen: Network Generator for Combinatorial Graph Problems*, 2015. R package v1.0.

[4] K. Deb, A. Pratap, S. Agarwal, and T. Meyarivan. A fast and elitist multiobjective genetic algorithm: NSGA–II. *IEEE Transactions on Evolutionary Computation*, 6(2):182–197, 2002.

[5] M. Dell'Amico, F. Maffioli, and P. Vaerbrand. On prize-collecting tours and the asymmetric travelling salesman problem. *International Transactions in Operational Research*, 2(3):297–308, 1995.

[6] J. Durillo and A. Nebro. jMetal: A Java framework for multi-objective optimization. *Advances in Engineering Software*, 42:760–771, 2011.

[7] D. Feillet, P. Dejax, and M. Gendreau. Traveling salesman problems with profits. *Transportation Science*, 39(2):188–205, 2005.

[8] C. Filippi and E. Stevanato. Approximation schemes for bi-objective combinatorial optimization and their application to the tsp with profits. *Computers & Operations Research*, 40(10):2418–2428, 2013.

[9] C. Fonseca and P. Fleming. On the performance assessment and comparison of stochastic multiobjective optimizers. In H.-M. Voigt et al., editors, *Parallel Problem Solving from Nature, PPSN IV*, pages 584–593. Springer Berlin Heidelberg, 1996.

[10] B. L. Golden, L. Levy, and R. Vohra. The orienteering problem. *Nav. Res. Log.*, 34(3):307–318, 1987.

[11] M. Hahsler and K. Hornik. Tsp – Infrastructure for the traveling salesperson problem. *Journal of Statistical Software*, 23(2):1–21, December 2007.

[12] R. Jonker and T. Volgenant. Transforming asymmetric into symmetric traveling salesman problems. *Oper. Res. Lett.*, 2(4):161–163, November 1983.

[13] N. Jozefowiez, F. Glover, and M. Laguna. Multi-objective meta-heuristics for the traveling salesman problem with profits. *Journal of Math. Modelling and Algorithms*, 7(2):177–195, 2008.

[14] M. G. Kantor and M. B. Rosenwein. The orienteering problem with time windows. *The Journal of the Operational Research Society*, 43(6):629–635, 1992.

[15] C. P. Keller and M. Goodchild. The multiobjective vending problem: A generalization of the traveling salesman problem. *Environ. Planning B: Planning Design*, 15(2):447–460, 1988.

[16] S. Meisel. *Anticipatory Optimization for Dynamic Decision Making*, Springer New York, 2011.

[17] O. Mersmann, B. Bischl, J. Bossek, H. Trautmann, M. Wagner, and F. Neumann. Local search and the traveling salesman problem: A feature-based characterization of problem hardness. In Y. Hamadi and M. Schoenauer, editors, *Proc. LION 6*, pages 115–129. Springer, 2012.

[18] O. Mersmann, B. Bischl, H. Trautmann, M. Wagner, and F. Neumann. A novel feature-based approach to characterize algorithm performance for the traveling salesman problem. *Annals of Mathematics and Artificial Intelligence*, 69:151–182, 2012.

[19] Z. Michalewicz. *Genetic Algorithms + Data Structures = Evolution Programs*. Springer, Berlin, 3rd ed., 1999.

[20] V. Pillac, M. Gendreau, C. Guéret, and A. L. Medaglia. A review of dynamic vehicle routing problems. *Eur. J. Oper. Res.*, 225(1):1–11, 2013.

[21] P. Vansteenwegen, W. Souffriau, and D. Van Oudheusden. The orienteering problem: A survey. *Eur. J. Oper. Res.*, 209(1):1–10, 2011.

[22] E. Zitzler, L. Thiele, M. Laumanns, C. M. Fonseca, and V. G. da Fonseca. Performance assessment of multiobjective optimizers: An analysis and review. *IEEE Transactions on Evolutionary Computation*, 7(2):117–132, 2003.

A Dispatching rule based Genetic Algorithm for Order Acceptance and Scheduling

Su Nguyen
Department of Industrial and Systems Engineering
International University, VNUHCM
Ho Chi Minh City, Vietnam
npbsu@hcmiu.edu.vn

Mengjie Zhang
Evolutionary Computation Research Group
Victoria University of Wellington
Wellington, New Zealand
mengjie.zhang@ecs.vuw.ac.nz

Kay Chen Tan
Department of Electrical and Computer Engineering
National University of Singapore, Singapore
eletankc@nus.edu.sg

ABSTRACT

Order acceptance and scheduling is an interesting and challenging scheduling problem in which two decisions need to be handled simultaneously. While the exact methods are not efficient and sometimes impractical, existing meta-heuristics proposed in the literature still have troubles dealing with large problem instances. In this paper, a dispatching rule based genetic algorithm is proposed to combine the advantages of existing dispatching rules/heuristics, genetic algorithm and local search. The results indicates that the proposed methods are effective and efficient when compared to a number of existing heuristics with a wide range of problem instances.

Categories and Subject Descriptors

I.2 [**Computing Methodologies**]: [Artificial Intelligence]

Keywords

genetic algorithm, scheduling, local search

1. INTRODUCTION

Order acceptance and scheduling (OAS) is an important task in make-to-order (MTO) production systems. In OAS, the goal is to determine whether to accept or reject orders from customers to optimise the use of the limited capacity of the shop based on process information and revenues of the orders. OAS is motivated by practical situations in MTO companies such as customised packing material producers [22] or logistic systems where order selection is important to effectively utilise the available capacity [5].

Simultaneously dealing with acceptance and scheduling decisions is necessary to have a proper assessment of the influences of orders on the production activities in the shop. OAS is more challenging than the traditional scheduling problems [1, 2, 3, 7, 16, 28, 38] since not only does the processing sequence of orders need to be determined, but also the combination of accepted orders must be decided. In this case, the quality of OAS solutions depends strongly on how well both acceptance and scheduling decisions are made since independently optimising each decision does not ensure to lead to optimal complete solutions. Because of its computational complexity, finding optimal solutions is challenging and sometimes impractical. Ghosh [10] proved that OAS is NP-hard and previous works have shown that exact methods can only find optimal solutions for small instances [30, 5]. Therefore, a number of studies have been conducted to develop meta-heuristics [26, 22, 5] to deal with this problem. These heuristics showed promising results and they are computationally less expensive than exact methods [30].

However, the large search space of OAS still makes the existing heuristics less efficient as the problem size (number of orders) increases. In order to handle this issue, we proposed a new dispatching rule based genetic algorithm (DRGA) for OAS. Different from previous meta-heuristics which represent OAS solution as an sequence of orders, the proposed method here represents the OAS solution as a sequence of dispatching rules to be applied during the scheduling construction process. By using this approach, we allow genetic algorithm to handle a much smaller search space (especially when the problem size is large). One drawback with this approach is that the new search space may not guarantee to contain the optimal solution. In order to handle this issue, we employ a local search heuristic to refine the solution obtained by DRGA.

Here are three research objectives of this paper:

- Develop a new dispatching rule based genetic algorithm for OAS,
- Integrate local search heuristics into the proposed DRGA,
- Compare the proposed approach with other meta-heuristics proposed in the literature.

The rest of the paper is organised as follows. The background for OAS problems and the literature related to methodologies to solve OAS problems are given in Section 2. The description of the proposed approach is shown in Section 3. The experimental results and analysis are provided in Section 4. Section 5 concludes the paper and discusses some directions for future studies.

GECCO '15, July 11 - 15, 2015, Madrid, Spain

© 2015 ACM. ISBN 978-1-4503-3472-3/15/07... $15.00

DOI: http://dx.doi.org/10.1145/2739480.2754821

2. BACKGROUND

This section first describes the OAS problem investigated in the paper. Then, we briefly review studies related to dispatching rule based meta-heuristics for scheduling problems.

2.1 OAS in the single machine environment

This study focuses on the OAS in the single machine shop with n customer orders. The goal of OAS is to determine which orders within the n orders are accepted (must be processed and delivered) and how the accepted orders are scheduled to optimise certain performance measures. Each order has a release time r_j, a processing time p_j, a due date d_j, a weight/penalty w_j, a maximum revenue e_j, and a deadline $\bar{d}_j$. A specific setup time s_{ij} for order j is incurred if order j is processed immediately after order i (s_{0j} is the setup time of order j in the case that order j is processed first). If the order is completed before the due date d_j, the revenue rev_j obtained from order j is the maximum revenue e_j. Otherwise, rev_j is the remaining revenue after deducting the penalty caused by the tardiness $T_j = \max(0, C_j - d_j)$ from e_j, where C_j is the completion time of order j. Generally, the revenue obtained by an order j can be calculated by $rev_j = e_j I_j - w_j T_j$ in which I_j is 1 if order j is accepted; and 0 otherwise. If orders are finished after their deadline $\bar{d}_j$, no revenue is gained. This problem is the same as those in [22] and [5]. This paper focuses on maximsing the total revenue $\text{TR} = \sum_{j \in \mathbb{A}} rev_j$ where $\mathbb{A}$ is the set of accepted orders.

Different methods have been proposed in the literature to deal with OAS. Slotnick and Morton [30] investigated OAS in a single machine environment without preemption and with the total revenue as the objective (which includes costs caused by order lateness). An exact branch and bound method and two heuristic procedures were proposed for this problem. The myopic heuristic was shown to be suitable for the problem in terms of effectiveness and efficiency as compared to the branch and bound method. Nguyen et al. [18] proposed another branch and bound algorithm for OAS with dependent setups [5], which showed to be much more efficient as compared to solving the MILP of OAS with CPLEX. However, the proposed methods can only found optimal solutions for OAS problems with the number of orders fewer than 25. Slotnick and Morton [31] further investigated the case where costs are caused by tardiness instead of lateness. Ghosh [10] showed that OAS is NP-hard and proposed two pseudo-polynomial time algorithms and approximate methods to deal with some special cases of this problem. Rom and Slotnick[26] proposed a hybrid genetic algorithm (GA) with local search heuristic to handle the same problem which showed promising results. In the proposed GA method, a solution is an array of real numbers (priorities) to determined the sequence in which orders are processed (orders that do not increase profit will be rejected).The OAS problem with setup costs as a major factor (due dates and penalty costs are ignored) was later considered by Huang et. al. [14]. In their study, they developed an algorithm for this problem by formulating it as resource-constrained profitable tour problem.

Oguz et al. [22] investigated OAS with sequence dependent setup times in printing operations for a customised packing material producer. They also developed a mixed integer linear programming (MILP) formulation for the problem. Since optimal solutions can only be obtained for a limited number of orders, Oguz et al. [22] proposed ISFAN, a heuristic based on simulated annealing to find near optimal solutions for the problem. Casaret et al. [5] proposed a tabu search (TS) method to handle the same problem and the experimental results showed that the proposed TS method outperformed ISFAN especially for instances with a large number of orders.

OAS in two-machine flowshop was investigated by Wang et al. [35, 36]. Mestry et al. [17] proposed a branch and price approach for order acceptance and capacity planning for MTO operations. OAS problems in the job shop environment have also been investigated by Wester et al. [37] and Roundy et al. [27]. Different from studies previously discussed, Wester et al. [37] performed a simulation to evaluate different order acceptance strategies when orders arrive according to some stochastic process over time. Roundy et al. [27] examined acceptance decisions when an order arrives to determine whether the production system has the capacity. A comprehensive review of OAS is provided by Slotnick [29].

2.2 Dispatching rule based meta-heuristics

Dispatching rules are a simple heuristic to generate solutions for scheduling problems. Normally, a dispatching rule use a priority function to prioritize jobs or orders that need to be processed. The job or order with the highest priority is selected to be processed next. Because of their simplicity and ease of implementation, dispatching rules have been used to handle many scheduling problems [24].

One key limitation of dispatching rules is that they only examine one particular solution and no improvement mechanism (as in meta-heuristics) is employed. Some efforts to combine both meta-heuristics and dispatching rules into the same framework have also been proposed in the literature. Storer et al. [32] proposed a hill climbing method to assign heuristics/dispatching rules into different scheduling windows. Even though it is promising, the method was still restricted to known dispatching rules and their linear combinations, which may flexible enough to solve hard JSS problems. Similarly, Dorndorf and Pesch [8] employed GA to determine the optimal applications of local decision rule sequences. Two GA methods are proposed in their paper. The first method search for the optimal sequence of dispatching rules to handle the conflicting operations in each decision moment of the Giffler and Thompson algorithm [11]. The second one was used to control the selection of nodes in the enumeration tree of the shifting bottleneck heuristic [24]. The experimental results suggested that the proposed methods can find better solutions compared to some existing heuristics such as the shifting bottleneck heuristic and simulated annealing. Hart and Ross [12] developed a hybrid GA method which is quite similar to the dispatching rules based GA proposed by Dorndorf and Pesch [8], except that the methods to calculate the set of conflicting operations are also encoded into the gene. This method was quite promising compared to other similar methods in the literature. However, the choice of suitable dispatching rules to deal with different objectives still requires a lot of preliminary works.

Zhou et al. [39] introduced a general method based on genetic algorithm and dispatching rules to solve a static JSS problems and showed that the proposed method was better than the pure genetic algorithm. Different from those proposed in [12] and [8], this method encoded the dispatching

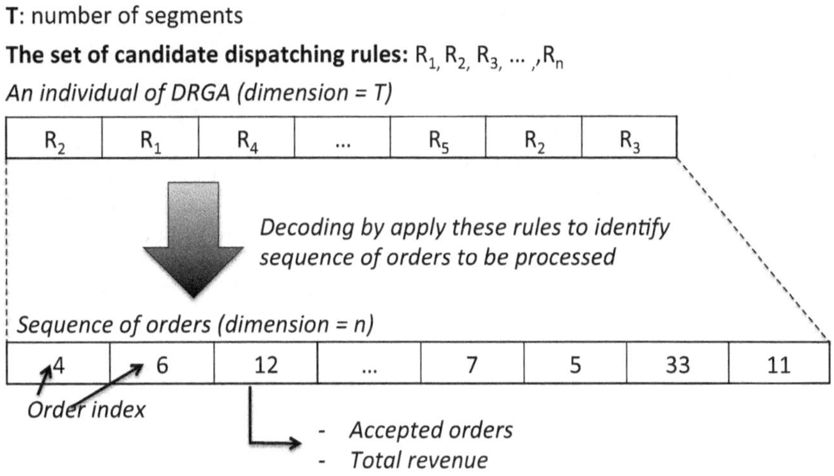

Figure 1: Decoding a DRGA individual.

rules for each machine in combination with the first job to be scheduled on that machine. This gives the proposed method more flexibility as compared to other similar methods. Even though the proposed hybrid GA provided solutions that are inferior to those obtained in [15], it was still very promising since it is capable of solving a variety of scheduling problems without major redesign. More recently, Vázquez-Rodríguez and Petrovic [34] introduced a new dispatching rule based GA for the multi-objective JSS problem. In their algorithm, they encoded both dispatching rules and the number of successive steps that these rules were applied. The proposed representation showed very good performance on a wide range of problem instances. For other similar methods, the reader is referred to [6], [23] and [25].

A number of dispatching rules have been applied to the OAS problems. Casaret et al. [5] examined a modified ATCS rule and two other rules based on the revenue-load ratio of orders. The experiments show that these dispatching rules perform poorly as compared to other meta-heuristics. Nguyen et al. [21, 18] applied genetic programming to automatically design new and effective dispatching rules OAS. The results suggested that the generated rules are quite competitive but there is still a gap in quality between dispatching rules and (effective) meta-heuristics. In this paper, we try to combine the advantages of dispatching rules and meta-heuristics to solve OAS.

3. DISPATCHING RULE BASED GENETIC ALGORITHM FOR OAS

The goal of this study is to develop a new DRGA for OAS. The overall algorithm of the proposed DRGA is shown in Figure 2. Similar to common GAs, our DRGA starts by initialising a population. In each generation, an individual p_i is applied to generate a solution for the OAS instance. The quality/fitness of p_i is the total revenue from the obtained solution. A local search heuristic is also applied to further enhance the quality of the obtained solution. After all individuals are evaluated, genetic operators are applied to generate new population.

```
Inputs: read the OAS instance

randomly initialise the population P ← {p_1, ..., p_N}
set p* ← null and fitness(p*) = −∞
generation ← 0
while generation ≤ maxGenerations do
    for all p_i ∈ P do
        fitness(p_i) ← generate OAS solution with p_i
        if fitness(p_i) > fitness(p*) then
            p* ← p_i
            fitness(p*) ← fitness(p_i)
        end if
        refine the solution obtained from p_i
    end for
    P ← apply genetic operators to P
    generation ← generation + 1
end while
```

Figure 2: DRGA for OAS.

3.1 Representation

The representation of DRGA is illustrated in Figure 1 and Figure 3. Instead of identifying the sequence of orders to be processed as used in previous studies, we divide the OAS solution into a number of segments. Orders processed in each segment will be determined by a particular dispatching rule instead of defining the sequence of orders explicitly. As shown in Figure 1, **T** segments are considered and **T** corresponding dispatching rules from a set of candidate rules that need to be determined. Therefore, the dimension of DRGA solutions is **T**. By applying rules in DRGA individual, we will generate a sequence of orders to be processed, which can be used to determined the set of accepted orders and their corresponding total obtained revenue. DRGA individuals are randomly initialised in the first generation by randomly selecting a rule for each segment.

Each rule in the DRGA will determine the sequence of n' orders. It is noted that $n = n' \times \mathbf{T}$. The sequence of orders in this all segments will be determined by using the algorithm in Figure 4. This algorithm aims to construct active schedules [11, 24] to avoid wasting the available capacity of the machine and reduce the search space of the optimising methods. Rejected orders in this construction procedure are the orders that are removed from Ω in line 8. In this algorithm, line 6 is the most important since it decides the processing sequence as well as the acceptance/rejection of orders. The rules in DRGA will be used to determine next processed orders j in line 6.

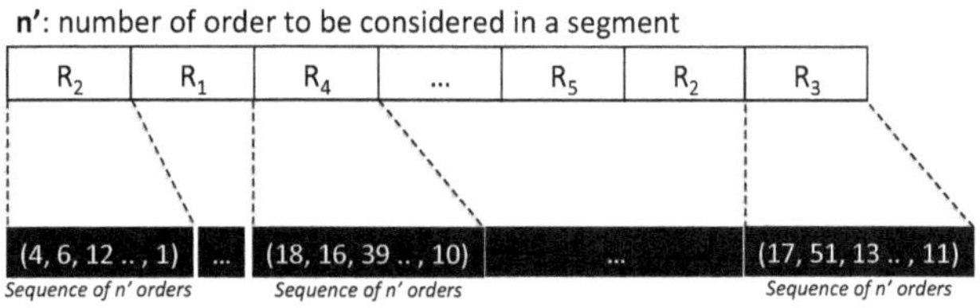

Figure 3: Representation of DRGA solutions.

3.2 Candidate dispatching rules

To use the representation proposed above, one important issue is to find a set of candidate dispatching rules. Here are five rules we will used in our algorithm:

1. Earliest due date (EDD) [24]: $priority = -d_j$
2. Slack (SL) [24]: $priority = t - d_j$, where t is the moment when a decision need to be made
3. Revenue-load ratio (RLR1) [5]: $e_j/(p_j + s_j^{avg})$, where s_j^{avg} is the average setup time of order j
4. Revenue-load ratio (RLR2) [5]: $e_j/(p_j + s^{prev,j})$ where $prev$ is the index of previous processed order
5. Composite slack/revenue [18]:
   $priority = \frac{e_j/\bar{d}_j}{h \times p_j - s_{prev,j} \min(t-d_j,0)}$

   The behaviour of this rule can be summarised as follows.

   - If two orders have equivalent values of slack ($t - d_j$) and processing/setup times, the order with a higher revenue and closer deadline will be processed first.
   - If two orders have similar revenue and deadline, setup time is ignored when they are late ($t > d_j$). If they are early, the one with the smaller setup time and slack will have higher priority.

   The coefficient h is used to control the importance of processing time as compared to setup times and slacks. From our experiments, $h = 7.5$ provides reasonable results across different OAS instances.

```
1: let Ω ← {1, 2, ..., n} is the set of candidate orders
2: current time t ← 0, and index of previous processed
   order i ← 0
3: while Ω is not empty do
4:     let earliest completion time t(Ω) ←
   min_{∀j∈Ω} { max{r_j, t} + s_ij + p_j }
5:     obtain Ω' ← {j ∈ Ω | r_j < t(Ω)}
6:     determine the next order j ∈ Ω' to be processed
7:     update t ← max{r_j, t} + s_ij + p_j and i = j
8:     remove orders that cannot finish before their
   deadlines d̄_j from Ω
9: end while
```

Figure 4: Generate active schedule.

3.3 Genetic operators

We will employ reproduction, crossover and mutation as genetic operators in our proposed algorithm. For reproduction, an individual is selected and copied directly to the next generation based on its fitness without any modification. For crossover, we using uniform crossover. It means that when two parents are selected for crossover, the children will be generated by randomly selecting the rule applied for each segment from either parent. We apply this crossover approach as it is simple to implement and it also ensures a good diversity for the population. As compared to the representation in previous studies, the proposed representation here helps simplify the crossover as the permutation of orders will not be violated. Similarly, the mutation can be simply performed by randomly changing the rule applied to a segment.

3.4 Local search heuristic

To enhance the quality of solutions found by DRGA, an iterated greedy heuristic is applied. From the obtained sequence of orders S (as shown in Figure 5), α orders will be randomly removed. Then each removed order will be reinserted (based on the order they are removed) into the partial solution S'. The insert position where S' has the highest total revenue will be used to update S'. The heuristic stops when the set of removed orders $\bar{S}$ is empty. It is easy to see that the complexity of this heuristic depends on the parameter α because it will determine the number of partial solutions we have to reevaluated. From the pilot experiments, we select $\alpha = 3$ as it gives us the most robust results.

3.5 Parameter settings

Table 1 shows the parameters used in our experiments. As the search space has been significantly reduced with the new representation, the population size is kept reasonably low to save more computational budgets for the local search heuristic. Selection in the DRGA algorithm is tournament selection with tournament size of 3. $Maxstep_I G_i nd$ is the number of times the iterated greedy search in Figure 5 is applied to the newly obtained solutions from DRGA. The best solution obtained in the generation is further refined with $Maxstep_I G_b est$ applications of the iterated greedy search.

4. RESULTS

The solutions obtained by DRGA is compared to those found by ISFAN [22], MILP, m-ATCS, and TS [5].

4.1 Datasets

To examine the effectiveness of the proposed DRGA and other methods, they are applied to solve the benchmark instances from Casaret et al. [5]. These instances are generated based on tardiness factor τ and due date range R. For

Table 1: Parameters of the proposed GP system

Parameter	Value
Population Size	20
Crossover rate	80%
Mutation rate	10%
Reproduction rate	10%
Tournament size	3
Generations	50
α	3
$MaxstepIGind$	20
$MaxstepIGbest$	200
$Numberofsegments$ **T**	10

```
1: let S ← {s_1, s_2, ..., s_n} is sequence in which orders will be processed
2: S' ← remove α orders from S; S̄ is the set of removed orders
3: while S̄ is not empty do
4:     select s_i in S̄ in the order it is removed in step 2
5:     insert s_i into S' at the position such as that S' provides the highest total revenue
6:     remove s_i from S̄
7: end while
8: return S'
```

Figure 5: Iterated Greedy Search.

an instance, processing times p_j and revenues e_j are randomly generated from the interval $[0, 20]$, and setup times are from $[1, 10]$. Release times r_j are randomly generated from $[0, \tau p_T]$, where p_T is the total processing time of all orders. Due dates are $d_j = r_j + \max_{i=0,1,\ldots,n}\{s_{ij}\} + \max\{slack, p_j\}$, where $slack$ is generated from $[p_T(1-\tau-R/2), p_T(1-\tau+R/2)]$. Deadlines are generated by $\bar{d}_j = d_j + Rp_j$ and weights are calculated as $w_j = e_j/(\bar{d}_j - d_j)$ to ensure that the revenue gained from an order becomes 0 at its deadline. The test bed contains different sets (each has 10 instances) generated from different combinations of τ and R and the number of orders n.

4.2 Comparison

For each dataset with a fixed number of orders n, each method is applied to 250 instances (classified into 25 subsets based on 5 different tardiness factors τ and due date ranges R [5]). Due to the space of this paper, we will not present all detailed results for each subset. As discussed previously, instances with the number of orders fewer than 25 can be solved optimally with branch and bound [21], we only consider instances with more than 25 orders here. The effectiveness of each method is measured by the absolute percentage error which is $100 \times (UB - TR)/UB$ where UB is the upper bound found by CPLEX [5, 22] and TR is the total revenue of the solution found by each method. It is noted that the method with lower average absolute percentage errors is better.

Tables 2–4 show the % deviation obtained by all methods. We only show the computational times of TS and DRGA as they are the much faster than other methods (except for mATCS which is a dispatching rule). From the results, it is very clear that TS and DRGA are much better than MILP, mATCS, and ISFAN. In many instances with low τ and R, the % deviations from TS and DRGA can be 2 to 5 times lower than those of ISFAN. For the dataset with $n = 25$, $\tau = 0.9$ and $R = 0.9$ which MILP (with CPLEX) can still handle reasonably well, DRGA can find the solutions that are very close to those of MILP (which are mostly optimal). This shows that DRGA is capable of finding very near optimal solutions for OAS.

The computational times of TS and DSRGA are negligible with n fewer than or equal to 25. TS is a slightly faster than DRGA with $n = 50$ but the difference is not very significant. As we solve the instances with $n = 100$, DRGA is more efficient than TS in most instances and it is also easy to see that the computational times of DRGA are very stable. The reason is that DRGA use the dispatching rules based representation where the search space did not change as the number of orders increases. Therefore, the parameters of DRGA are not necessarily changed as TS does [5] when n changes.

DRGA outperforms TS in most cases in terms of minimum, average, and maximum % deviations. For the instances with low τ, the gap between DRGA is not very clear because both DRGA and TS can find the near optimal solutions quite effectively. However, as we closely examine the searching process of DRGA, these solutions can be found in very early generations. It suggests that DRGA with the support of a good set of candidate dispatching rules can identify potential solutions very quickly. In the instances with $n = 100$, DRGA outperforms TS for most combinations of τ and R except for cases with $\tau = 0.5, 0.7$, where they performed similar.

In general, DRGA has successfully combined the advantages of existing dispatching rules and the local search heuristics to efficiently and effectively find near optimal solutions for OAS. Because of the balance in this combination, the computational times of DRGA are also stable. For $n = 50, 100$, we can see that DRGA tends to be slightly slower as τ increase. It is because the dispatching rules are not very effective in these cases (see [18] for more discussions) and the more efforts are needed from the local search heuristics to enhance the quality of the obtained solutions.

4.3 Further discussions

Dispatching rule based meta-heuristics is an simple and effective approach to utilising the advantages of existing heuristics and search techniques to solve scheduling problems. One important issue that has not been discussed in detail here is the choice of suitable set of dispatching rules as it decides that the search space that DRGA will explore. Although there are a number of dispatching rules proposed in the literature, their behaviours are still not fully investigated and their combinations have not been analysed carefully. Therefore, finding good combinations of dispatching rules is not easy. For new scheduling problems where existing dispatching rules or heuristics are limited, it will be even more tricky. Fortunately, in the last decades, hyper-heuristics [4, 9, 33, 13, 19, 20] have emerged as an power way for automated design of heuristics. Many effective and unknown dispatching rules have been discovered by the proposed hyper-heuristics. We believe that using hyper-heuristics to help designing a set of suitable dispatching rules will be an promising approach to enhancing the effectiveness of dispatching rule based meta-heuristics in the future. This is also an good

Table 2: % Deviations from upper bound of total revenue ($n = 25$)

τ	R	MILP			mATCS			ISFAN			TS				DRGA			
		min	avg	max	min	avg	max	min	avg	max	min	avg	max	Time (s)	min	avg	max	Time (s)
0.1	0.1	8	12	19	9	14	20	4	8	12	1	4	6	1	2	3	4	1
	0.3	6	13	23	6	16	32	3	7	11	2	3	6	1	1	2	6	1
	0.5	5	7	9	3	12	21	3	7	11	1	2	4	1	1	1	3	1
	0.7	1	5	11	5	13	23	2	5	9	0	1	4	1	0	1	3	1
	0.9	1	4	10	2	8	24	1	6	10	0	1	2	1	0	1	2	1
0.3	0.1	9	15	24	13	19	29	5	9	12	2	4	5	1	2	3	5	1
	0.3	7	11	20	7	18	24	7	10	12	3	5	7	1	2	3	5	1
	0.5	2	5	8	10	18	26	5	7	10	2	3	6	1	2	2	3	1
	0.7	1	5	9	8	17	32	6	11	24	1	2	6	1	1	2	5	1
	0.9	11	18	27	6	16	27	5	9	18	0	2	4	1	0	1	3	1
0.5	0.1	6	10	17	12	19	29	7	11	14	3	6	7	1	2	4	7	1
	0.3	4	9	13	11	21	29	6	11	17	3	5	9	1	2	5	8	1
	0.5	3	10	17	8	20	30	8	13	20	2	5	8	1	1	5	6	1
	0.7	2	8	13	17	26	38	7	13	17	2	6	11	1	2	4	7	1
	0.9	6	20	42	16	28	49	6	15	25	1	4	7	1	1	3	7	1
0.7	0.1	2	10	19	12	20	26	10	18	27	3	9	18	1	1	8	16	1
	0.3	8	12	17	18	26	33	9	17	23	7	10	14	1	5	9	13	1
	0.5	7	13	21	26	33	43	13	19	26	7	12	15	1	6	10	14	1
	0.7	2	9	15	15	29	40	9	15	21	2	8	14	1	2	7	12	1
	0.9	0	10	17	8	29	53	10	17	24	3	10	15	1	1	8	14	1
0.9	0.1	0	0	0	4	12	20	0	8	25	0	1	6	1	0	1	5	1
	0.3	0	0	0	10	17	22	1	5	8	0	1	1	1	0	1	1	1
	0.5	0	3	12	14	27	45	1	12	44	0	4	12	1	0	2	12	1
	0.7	0	7	22	17	29	45	0	13	31	1	8	25	1	1	7	21	1
	0.9	0	6	21	20	30	58	2	13	32	1	7	22	1	1	6	20	1

Table 3: % Deviations from upper bound of total revenue ($n = 50$)

τ	R	MILP			mATCS			ISFAN			TS				DRGA			
		min	avg	max	min	avg	max	min	avg	max	min	avg	max	Time (s)	min	avg	max	Time (s)
0.1	0.1	9	24	81	9	15	20	6	8	12	1	2	3	1	1	2	3	3
	0.3	7	16	22	9	15	18	7	9	12	1	2	4	1	1	2	3	3
	0.5	11	17	25	6	13	19	5	8	10	1	2	2	1	1	1	2	3
	0.7	9	13	18	7	14	24	4	9	22	0	2	16	1	0	2	16	3
	0.9	2	10	27	1	4	10	4	7	11	0	1	2	1	0	0	0	3
0.3	0.1	13	24	33	11	16	24	8	11	13	2	3	3	2	2	3	4	3
	0.3	18	28	48	11	20	30	9	12	15	3	4	5	1	2	3	4	3
	0.5	18	24	33	9	18	33	8	11	15	1	3	5	1	1	2	4	3
	0.7	13	20	26	5	14	24	7	11	18	0	1	3	1	0	1	2	3
	0.9	13	21	34	3	17	26	8	9	11	1	1	3	1	0	1	2	3
0.5	0.1	29	28	31	13	20	27	10	14	19	3	4	5	1	3	4	5	4
	0.3	25	42	86	18	25	30	11	16	20	3	6	8	1	3	5	7	4
	0.5	17	31	44	15	25	34	7	16	21	2	4	8	1	2	4	8	4
	0.7	10	21	38	12	24	31	9	15	18	2	3	5	1	1	3	6	4
	0.9	8	18	22	17	27	35	6	15	19	0	3	6	1	0	2	5	4
0.7	0.1	13	21	25	17	22	30	12	16	21	4	7	9	1	4	5	7	4
	0.3	11	18	23	16	24	33	11	16	20	4	7	11	2	4	7	10	4
	0.5	13	29	52	23	33	46	14	19	22	7	9	13	2	6	8	12	4
	0.7	9	21	28	24	31	35	12	19	29	2	9	18	1	3	8	15	4
	0.9	14	19	26	19	29	41	17	21	28	4	10	18	1	4	9	14	4
0.9	0.1	8	14	18	17	24	30	12	17	22	8	13	18	1	8	12	19	4
	0.3	11	16	22	21	32	42	18	23	28	12	16	21	1	9	14	18	4
	0.5	5	15	21	33	39	45	18	21	26	7	16	20	1	4	13	19	4
	0.7	9	17	25	26	37	46	17	27	72	8	14	21	1	7	13	18	4
	0.9	14	21	30	24	36	44	16	22	29	11	14	19	1	10	13	17	4

Table 4: % Deviations from upper bound of total revenue ($n = 100$)

τ	R	MILP			mATCS			ISFAN			TS				DRGA			
		min	avg	max	min	avg	max	min	avg	max	min	avg	max	Time (s)	min	avg	max	Time (s)
0.1	0.1	37	44	56	9	15	19	8	9	13	1	2	3	17	1	1	2	15
	0.3	42	51	88	11	17	20	7	9	10	2	2	3	17	1	1	2	15
	0.5	43	51	60	11	14	19	6	9	11	1	1	3	11	1	1	1	15
	0.7	46	54	60	5	11	16	6	9	12	0	1	1	6	0	1	1	15
	0.9	38	60	70	0	6	11	8	12	16	0	1	1	4	0	0	0	15
0.3	0.1	52	62	68	15	19	24	10	12	13	1	3	4	22	2	3	4	15
	0.3	52	64	75	15	18	23	11	13	17	2	3	5	20	1	3	4	15
	0.5	56	66	76	14	18	21	10	14	17	1	2	4	17	2	2	3	15
	0.7	63	73	84	15	20	32	12	14	15	1	2	3	9	1	1	1	15
	0.9	47	66	82	10	15	18	9	13	17	1	1	2	8	0	1	1	15
0.5	0.1	71	77	87	17	22	24	12	16	18	2	4	5	26	3	5	7	15
	0.3	47	61	86	17	23	28	12	15	18	3	4	6	29	4	4	6	15
	0.5	56	70	88	20	24	31	14	17	19	3	4	5	21	3	4	6	15
	0.7	55	71	92	10	23	34	13	17	21	2	3	4	16	1	3	4	15
	0.9	48	66	100	15	24	36	12	18	24	1	2	5	12	1	2	4	15
0.7	0.1	49	67	86	17	22	28	13	17	19	3	5	6	34	4	6	8	15
	0.3	45	57	66	18	24	34	13	17	21	4	7	11	27	4	6	9	15
	0.5	46	55	65	20	26	37	14	18	24	4	6	13	22	4	7	15	15
	0.7	42	60	76	22	31	38	16	19	23	3	7	13	26	5	8	12	16
	0.9	39	53	64	23	31	37	15	18	24	5	8	13	18	4	7	10	16
0.9	0.1	31	37	48	18	22	25	14	17	20	7	9	12	29	6	9	12	16
	0.3	28	40	50	25	31	36	16	20	26	7	14	17	26	8	12	16	16
	0.5	23	38	54	25	33	39	19	21	25	11	16	18	22	11	14	19	16
	0.7	27	38	48	26	36	40	15	21	24	11	15	20	23	10	14	16	16
	0.9	27	35	39	28	35	40	13	21	28	11	16	22	17	8	13	19	16

opportunity to unify offline methods (i.e, learning) and online methods (i.e., optimising) into a framework to handle hard computational problems.

5. CONCLUSIONS

This paper proposed a new dispatching rule based genetic algorithm for OAS. The proposed method focuses on combining the advantages of existing dispatching rules and the search mechanism of genetic algorithm and the local search heuristic. The search space from the proposed representation is much smaller than that from the existing metaheuristic especially when the problem size increases. The experimental results showed that the proposed method is effective and efficient as compared to other meta-heuristics in the literature.

The proposed method is very promising but there are still a number of issues that need to be investigated. As the success of this method relies on the choice of dispatching rules, the search mechanism of DRGA, and the applications of the local search heuristic, we need to understand thoroughly how they influence the overall performance. Future studies also need to look at the possibility to create the links between automated heuristics design and DRGA in order to design an effective method to deal with not only OAS but also other scheduling problems.

6. REFERENCES

[1] A. Allahverdi, J. N. Gupta, and T. Aldowaisan. A review of scheduling research involving setup considerations. *Omega*, 27(2):219–239, 1999.

[2] U. Bilge, M. Kurtulan, and F. Kirac. A tabu search algorithm for the single machine total weighted tardiness problem. *European Journal of Operational Research*, 176(3):1423–1435, 2007.

[3] W. Boejko, J. Grabowski, and M. Wodecki. Block approach-tabu search algorithm for single machine total weighted tardiness problem. *Computers & Industrial Engineering*, 50(1-2):1–14, 2006.

[4] E. Burke, M. Hyde, G. Kendall, G. Ochoa, E. Ozcan, and J. Woodward. Exploring hyper-heuristic methodologies with genetic programming. In C. Mumford and L. Jain, editors, *Computational Intelligence*, volume 1 of *Intelligent Systems Reference Library*, pages 177–201. Springer Berlin Heidelberg, 2009.

[5] B. Cesaret, C. Oguz, and F. S. Salman. A tabu search algorithm for order acceptance and scheduling. *Computers & Operations Research*, 39(6):1197–1205, 2012.

[6] T. C. Chiang, Y. S. Shen, and L. C. Fu. A new paradigm for rule-based scheduling in the wafer probe centre. *International Journal of Production Research*, 46(15):4111–4133, 2008.

[7] F. F. Choobineh, E. Mohebbi, and H. Khoo. A multi-objective tabu search for a single-machine scheduling problem with sequence-dependent setup times. *European Journal of Operational Research*, 175(1):318–337, 2006.

[8] U. Dorndorf and E. Pesch. Evolution based learning in a job shop scheduling environment. *Computers and Operations Research*, 22(1):25–40, 1995.

[9] C. D. Geiger, R. Uzsoy, and H. Aytug. Rapid modeling and discovery of priority dispatching rules: An autonomous learning approach. *Journal of Heuristics*, 9(1):7–34, 2006.

[10] J. B. Ghosh. Job selection in a heavily loaded shop. *Computers & Operations Research*, 24(2):141–145, 1997.

[11] B. Giffler and G. L. Thompson. Algorithms for solving production-scheduling problems. *Operations Research*, 8:487–503, 1960.

[12] E. Hart and P. Ross. A heuristic combination method for solving job-shop scheduling problems. In *Proceedings of the 5th International Conference on Parallel Problem Solving from Nature*, PPSN V, pages 845–854, 1998.

[13] T. Hildebrandt, J. Heger, and B. Scholz-Reiter. Towards improved dispatching rules for complex shop floor scenarios: a genetic programming approach. In *GECCO'10: Proceedings of the 12th Annual Conference on Genetic and Evolutionary Computation*, pages 257–264, 2010.

[14] S. Huang, M. Lu, and G. Wan. Integrated order selection and production scheduling under mto strategy. *International Journal of Production Research*, 49(13):4085–4101, 2011.

[15] S. Kreipl. A large step random walk for minimizing total weighted tardiness in a job shop. *Journal of Scheduling*, 3:125–138, 2000.

[16] Y. H. Lee, K. Bhaskaran, and M. Pinedo. A heuristic to minimize the total weighted tardiness with sequence-dependent setups. *IIE Transactions*, 29(1):45–52, 1997.

[17] S. Mestry, P. Damodaran, and C.-S. Chen. A branch and price solution approach for order acceptance and capacity planning in make-to-order operations. *European Journal of Operational Research*, 211(3):480–495, 2011.

[18] S. Nguyen, M. Zhang, and M. Johnston. A sequential genetic programming method to learn forward construction heuristics for order acceptance and scheduling. In D. Liu, A. Hussain, Z. Zeng, and N. Zhang, editors, *2014 IEEE Congress on Evolutionary Computation (CEC)*, pages 1824–1831. IEEE Press, Piscataway, NJ, 2014.

[19] S. Nguyen, M. Zhang, M. Johnston, and K. C. Tan. A coevolution genetic programming method to evolve scheduling policies for dynamic multi-objective job shop scheduling problems. *CEC'12: IEEE Congress on Evolutionary Computation*, pages 3332–3339, 2012.

[20] S. Nguyen, M. Zhang, M. Johnston, and K. C. Tan. A computational study of representations in genetic programming to evolve dispatching rules for the job shop scheduling problem. *IEEE Transactions on Evolutionary Computation*, 17(5):621–639, 2013.

[21] S. Nguyen, M. Zhang, M. Johnston, and K. C. Tan. Learning reusable initial solutions for multi-objective order acceptance and scheduling problems with genetic programming. In *EuroGP'13: Proceedings of the 16th European Conference on Genetic Programming*, pages 157–168, 2013.

[22] C. Oguz, F. Sibel Salman, and Z. Bilginturk Yalcin. Order acceptance and scheduling decisions in make-to-order systems. *International Journal of Production Economics*, 125(1):200–211, 2010.

[23] S. Petrovic, C. Fayad, D. Petrovic, E. Burke, and G. Kendall. Fuzzy job shop scheduling with lot-sizing. *Annals of Operations Research*, 159:275–292, 2008.

[24] M. L. Pinedo. *Scheduling: Theory, Algorithms, and Systems*. Springer, 3rd edition, 2008.

[25] S. G. Ponnambalam, V. Ramkumar, and N. Jawahar. A multiobjective genetic algorithm for job shop scheduling. *Production Planning and Control*, 12(8), 2001.

[26] W. O. Rom and S. A. Slotnick. Order acceptance using genetic algorithms. *Computers & Operations Research*, 36(6):1758–1767, 2009.

[27] R. Roundy, D. Chen, P. Chen, M. Cakanyildirim, M. B. Freimer, and V. Melkonian. Capacity-driven acceptance of customer orders for a multi-stage batch manufacturing system: models and algorithms. *IIE Transactions*, 37(12):1093–1105, 2005.

[28] M. Selim Akturk and D. Ozdemir. An exact approach to minimizing total weighted tardiness with release dates. *IIE Transactions*, 32(11):1091–1101, 2000.

[29] S. A. Slotnick. Order acceptance and scheduling: A taxonomy and review. *European Journal of Operational Research*, 212(1):1–11, 2011.

[30] S. A. Slotnick and T. E. Morton. Selecting jobs for a heavily loaded shop with lateness penalties. *Computers & Operations Research*, 23(2):131–140, 1996.

[31] S. A. Slotnick and T. E. Morton. Order acceptance with weighted tardiness. *Computers & Operations Research*, 34(10):3029–3042, 2007.

[32] R. H. Storer, S. D. Wu, and R. Vaccari. New search spaces for sequencing problems with application to job shop scheduling. *Management Science*, 38(10):1495–1509, 1992.

[33] J. C. Tay and N. B. Ho. Evolving dispatching rules using genetic programming for solving multi-objective flexible job-shop problems. *Computer & Industrial Engineering*, 54:453–473, 2008.

[34] J. A. Vázquez-Rodríguez and S. Petrovic. A new dispatching rule based genetic algorithm for the multi-objective job shop problem. *Journal of Heuristics*, 16(6):771–793, 2010.

[35] X. Wang, X. Xie, and T. Cheng. A modified artificial bee colony algorithm for order acceptance in two-machine flow shops. *International Journal of Production Economics*, 2012. DOI:10.1016/j.ijpe.2012.06.003.

[36] X. Wang, X. Xie, and T. Cheng. Order acceptance and scheduling in a two-machine flowshop. *International Journal of Production Economics*, 2012. DOI:10.1016/j.ijpe.2012.08.020.

[37] F. A. W. Wester, J. Wijngaard, and W. R. M. Zijm. Order acceptance strategies in a production-to-order environment with setup times and due-dates. *International Journal of Production Research*, 30(6):1313–1326, 1992.

[38] W. H. Yang. Survey of scheduling research involving setup times. *International Journal of Systems Science*, 30(2):143–155, 1999.

[39] H. Zhou, W. Cheung, and L. C. Leung. Minimizing weighted tardiness of job-shop scheduling using a hybrid genetic algorithm. *European Journal of Operational Research*, 194(3):637–649, 2009.

Minimizing Regular Objectives for Blocking Permutation Flow Shop Scheduling: Heuristic Approaches

Nouha Nouri
Ecole Supérieure des Sciences
Economiques et Commerciales de Tunis,
University of Tunis, Tunisia
nouri.nouha@yahoo.fr

Talel Ladhari
College of Business,
Umm Al-Qura University,
Umm Al-Qura, Saudi Arabia
talel_ladhari2004@yahoo.fr

ABSTRACT

The objective of this work is to present and evaluate meta-heuristics for the blocking permutation flow shop scheduling problem subject to regular objectives. The blocking problem is known to be NP-hard with more than two machines. We assess the difficulty level of this problem by developing two population-based meta-heuristics: Genetic Algorithm and Artificial Bee Colony algorithm. The final goal is to measure the performance of these proposed techniques and potentially contribute in possible improvements in the blocking benchmark instances. Furthermore, computational tests carried out on randomly generated test problems show that the approaches consistently yields good solutions in a moderate amount of time. Finally, an updated list of best-known solutions for the Taillard's and Ronconi and Henriques's benchmark is exposed: new best-known solutions for the blocking flow shop scheduling problem with makespan, total flow time, and total tardiness criteria are found.

Categories and Subject Descriptors

I.2.8 [**Computing Methodologies**]: Problem Solving, Control Methods, and Search - *heuristic methods, scheduling*

Keywords

Combinatorial optimization; GA; ABC; Empirical study

1. INTRODUCTION

Scheduling problems belong to the class of combinatorial optimization problems with the issue of finding a solution that optimizes some fixed criteria and satisfies all technological constraints. The most intensively studied scheduling problem is the permutation flow shop. It is one of the first machine scheduling models that has been explored since the publication of Johnson's paper for solving the two machine flow shop problem [18]. Its mainly goal is to specify the sequence of jobs for processing on a specific set of machines that minimizes some criterion. It is assumed that the sequence in which each machine processes all jobs is identical on all machines. The commonly used optimization measure is the makespan (C_{max}) which defines the time at which the last job in the sequence is completed and leaves the system. This problem with makespan criterion is denoted as $F|prmu|C_{max}$, using the $\alpha|\beta|\gamma$ notation of Graham et al. [14]. Various other scheduling features have been studied and analyzed in the literature: the total flow time, the maximum lateness, the maximum tardiness, the maximum earliness, and other similar criteria. All the above objective functions are so-called regular performance measures (measure that is always improved by reducing job completion time). Anyway, it is commonly assumed whatever the objective that buffer storage capacity between machines is limitless. Consequently, if we imagine no intermediate buffer exists between machines, then the problem becomes a blocking permutation flow shop (BFSP) [36]. Since there are no buffers in the shop, a job has to stay on a machine until its next machine is free. This classical blocking situation is called 'Release when Starting Blocking (RSb)'. One of the pioneering works on this problem is [30] who showed that the $F2|blocking|C_{max}$ problem may be reduced to a special case of the traveling salesman problem which may be resolved in polynomial time using the famous Gilmore and Gomory algorithm [11]. For $m > 2$ the problem is proved to be strongly NP-hard [15]. As well, the same problem with total flow time criteria and two machines is strongly NP-hard [33]. The two-machine flow shop tardiness case is also NP-hard [21].

Heuristic algorithms used in the literature may be broadly divided into constructive and improvement heuristics. Among the proposed constructive heuristics for the BFSP with makespan criterion, we may refer to the Profile Fitting (PF) [23]; the far-famed NEH (Nawaz-Enscore-Ham) [25] (made up of two phases: creation of the initial sequence of the jobs and the iterative insertion procedure); the minmax (MM), the combination of MM and NEH (MME), and the combination of PF and NEH (PFE) [34]. For the BFSP with total flow time criterion we refer to the modified NEH heuristic called NEH-WPT [39] where the superiority of NEH-WPT over NEH is proved. In [36], a constructive heuristic and a GRASP-based heuristic are settled for the BFSP with total tardiness criterion. Regarding the improvement heuristics, we may refer to the heuristic used to minimize the cycle time in a blocking flow shop [1] which can also be employed to the BFSP under makespan criterion. As well, the Genetic Algorithm (GA) proposed in [5] to solve large size flow

GECCO '15, July 11 - 16, 2015, Madrid, Spain
 ISBN 978-1-4503-3472-3/15/07...$15.00
DOI: http://dx.doi.org/10.1145/2739480.2754638

shop problems deals with the blocking problem as a special case. Subsequently, in [35] authors proposed (Ron) algorithm based on blocking-lower bound that out performs algorithms presented in their earlier studies. In [13], a fast Tabu search (TS) and an improved TS algorithms (TS+M) based on multi-moves technique are exposed. More recently, the reference [38] proposed a Hybrid Discrete Differential Evolution (HDDE) algorithm for the $Fm|blocking|C_{max}$. Computational results demonstrated that HDDE algorithm not only out performs TS and TS+M algorithms but also gets better results than the Hybrid Differential Evolution (HDE) algorithm [29]. We refer also to the reference [31] where an Iterated Greedy (IG) algorithm is proposed which makes use of the insertion method of the NEH heuristic.
Meanwhile, in [39] a hybrid modified global-best Harmony Search (hmgHS) algorithm is proposed for solving the blocking problem with the total flow time criterion. Similarly, in [40] the hmgHS algorithm is submitted under the same problem and was proven its superiority over the IG [31]. Later, a Discrete Artificial Bee Colony algorithm (DABC_D) is proposed [10] and compared with several other powerful algorithms, including DABC proposed in [37] (denoted by DABC_T), HDDE, and the IG algorithm.Three other effective hybrid DABC algorithms are proposed in [16]. As well, by combining the respective advantages of Artificial Immune Systems (AIS) and the annealing process of Simulated Annealing (SA), an effective Revised AIS (RAIS) algorithm is proposed minimizing the makespan [22]. The computational results showed that the heuristic provide better performances than the leading approaches for all problem sizes. In [26], a three-phase algorithm for the $Fm|blocking|C_{max}$ is presented: higher efficiencies of the algorithm over the IG algorithm. In [41] a Discrete Particle Swarm Optimization algorithm with self-adaptive diversity control is proposed to solve the same problem. After that, a high performing Memetic Algorithm (MA) for the blocking problem minimizing makespan is appeared [27], where a constructive heuristic is presented (combining PF and NEH) and a memetic algorithm is proposed based on path-relinking based crossover and a referenced local search. At last, in [8], a chaos-induced discrete self organizing migrating algorithm is applied to the blocking problem and tested on the Taillard problem sets. Unlikely, there is a great work dedicated to developing both exact and heuristic algorithms for both makespan and total flow time criteria, it seems that little work has dealt with the total tardiness criterion until recently. In particular, using the LBNEH method suggested in [2], Armentano and Ronconi [3] proposed a Tabu Search procedure to obtain an initial solution for their heuristic. In [36], a new NEH-based method called (FPDNEH) and a Greedy Randomized Adaptive Search Procedure(GRASP) were proposed. As well, in reference [32] an efficient Iterated Local Search algorithm (ILS) coupled with a Variable Neighborhood Search (VNS) is exposed to minimize the tardiness measure.
In this paper we propose a genetic algorithm (GA) and an Artificial Bee Colony Algorithm (ABC) to solve the BFSP under three regular objectives. Algorithms are hybridized with a local search technique to enhance the quality of the generated solutions. Computational experiments are done using two well known benchmark sets: Taillard, and Ronconi and Henriques. Accordingly, the rest of this paper is organized as follows: In Section 2 we briefly introduce the BFSP problem. We describe in Section 3 our blocking algorithms. The experiments results and the concluding remarks are reported in Section 4 and Section 5, respectively.

2. PROBLEM DESCRIPTION

We consider the blocking problem minimizing discretely the makespan, the total flow time, and the total tardiness criteria in the M-machine permutation flow shop environment. The problem can be defined as follows. At time 0, there are N independent jobs to be sequentially processed on M machines, having no intermediate buffers. All jobs follow the same route in the machines. Since there is no buffer between each successive pair of machines, intermediate queues of jobs waiting in the system for their next operation are not allowed. Therefore, a job cannot leave a machine until the next machine downstream is free. This blocking situation prevents processing of other jobs on the blocked machine. We call down the following assumptions to define the BFSP:

- There is precisely one task corresponding to the processing of job i ($i = 1, 2, ..., N$) on each machine j ($j = 1, 2, ..., M$) which requires a processing time p_{ij}, and may have a given due date D_i which is the time point at which the job should finish.
- Each job may be processed on only one machine at any time, and each machine can process only one job at a time.
- Jobs are ready for processing at the beginning and have no precedent constraints among them. Preemption is not allowed.

Considering the above-mentioned assumptions, the objectives is to find out a sequence for processing all jobs on all machines so as to singly minimize the maximum completion time, the total flow time, and the total tardiness.
According to the classifications mentioned in Graham et al. [14] , the blocking instances considered in this study are as follows: $Fm|block|C_{max}$, $Fm|block|\sum C_j$, and $Fm|block|\sum T_j$ representing respectively the BFSP with makespan, total completion time, and total tardiness criteria.
Let: $\Pi := (\pi_1, \pi_2, ..., \pi_N)$ be a solution for the problem, where π_i denotes the ith job in the considered sequence; $d_{\pi_i,j}$ ($i = 1, 2, ..., N; j = 0, 1, 2, ..., M$) represents the departure time of job π_i on machine j, where $d_{\pi_i,0}$ denotes the time job π_i starts its processing on the first machine. The corresponding values of makespan of Π may then be calculated in $O(nm)$ as $C_{max}(\Pi) = C_{\pi_N,M}(\Pi)$, where $C_{\pi_i,M} = d_{\pi_i,M}$ is the completion time of job π_i on machine M that can be calculated using the following expressions presented in [28]:

$$d_{\pi_1,0} = 0 \quad (1)$$

$$d_{\pi_1,j} = \sum\nolimits_{k=1}^{j} p_{\pi_{1,k}} \qquad j = 1, 2, ..., M-1 \quad (2)$$

$$d_{\pi_i,0} = d_{\pi_{i-1},1} \qquad i = 2, ..., N \quad (3)$$

$$\begin{aligned} d_{\pi_i,j} &= Max\{d_{\pi_i,j-1} + p_{\pi_i,j}, d_{\pi_{i-1},j+1}\} \\ & i = 2, ..., N; j = 1, 2, ..., M-1 \end{aligned} \quad (4)$$

$$d_{\pi_i,M} = d_{\pi_i,M-1} + p_{\pi_i,M} \qquad i = 1, 2, ..., N \quad (5)$$

Using again the above recursion, we may also calculate the total flow time (TFT) and the total tardiness (TT) as follows: $TFT(\Pi) = \sum_{i=1}^{n}(C_{\pi_i,M})$, and $TT(\Pi) = \sum_{i=1}^{n}(T_i)$

where $T_i = max\{0, (C_{\pi_i} - D_i\})$. We choose to calculate the due dates D_i following the Total Work Content (TWK) rule [4]: $D_i = \tau \times (\sum_{j=1}^{M}(p_{\pi_i,j}))$. τ is the due date tightness factor and $\sum_{j=1}^{M}(p_{\pi_i,j})$ is the total processing time of job π_i on all machines. τ is taken in the range [1-3] to make the job's due date loose, medium or tight randomly.

3. THE GENETIC ALGORITHM

Initially proposed by Holland [17], the GA is a randomized global search and an iterative method holding a population of PS solutions. Members of the population are entities (chromosomes) of specific length defining the quality of the solution. Variation into the population is introduced using operators as selection, mutation and crossover. The selection operator randomly picks some members from the population. The mutation operator avoid the loss of information by randomly inverting bits in the solutions, while the crossover generates new solutions by mating two or more selected parents to give descendants for the next generation. After producing new solutions, the fittest solutions survive and reach the next generation while the others are deleted. The population grows over generations until some stopping criterion is reached. In the following we describe all parameters and operators used in the proposed GA for the BFSP under some fixed criterion: the procedures involved at each step are explained.

3.1 Solution Representation and Population Initialization

A solution is encoded into a string of numbers consisting of a job-permutation list of N jobs. The job-permutation list indicate the order in which the jobs are processed in machines. Now, to guarantee an initial population with certain quality and diversity, the blocking GA (BGA) takes advantage of the NEH-WPT and NEH-MK heuristics with some minor modifications to produce two different solutions as two first members in the population ([39],[24]). The NEH-WPT heuristic is made up of two phases. In the constructive phase, a sequence is generated by sorting jobs in increasing order of their total processing times: we affect higher priorities for jobs with less total processing times. Next, the constructed solution is subjected to an iterative process for improving without any specified explicit tie-breaking criterion for when two-insertion positions give the same objective value. We have used the minimization of the total idle time of machines (TIT)[7]:

$$TIT = \sum_{j=1}^{M}(IT_j) \quad where \quad IT_j = d_{Nj} - d_{1,j-1} - \sum_{i=1}^{N} p_{ij} \quad (6)$$

So that, the sequence with the lowest idle time for the machines is selected (time associated with waiting). If there is still a tie, randomly select the best sequence. Moreover, an improved version of the insert-neighborhood based speed-up method developed in [38] is used to further reduce the computational time needed to find the better neighbors.

In parallel, the NEH-MK heuristic is performed to construct the next member in the population. The ordering sequence in stage 1 is the same as in NEH-WPT. In stage 2, once a job is placed in the best position in the partial sequence, all the others are mixed and reinserted once again. In the original forme of the NEH-MK, authors do not consider internal sequences that may have better quality, and retain only the final sequence. We choose to do so in our modified heuristic to better enhance solutions. So, when a partial solution is generated, we save it. Then we remix jobs: the obtained solution is compared to the saved one and we retain at the end the better one. Meanwhile, a pair wise-based local search is evolved to improve once more the final solution. We performed this method based again on the insert-neighborhood based speed-up method.

The remaining $(PS-2)$ members of the population are randomly and differently generated: If a solution is different from all the existing ones, Then keep it in the population; Else generate one other. Details on the Modified NEH-MK are depicted as following:

Heuristic Mod-NEH-MK

Stage 1: Arrange the jobs in increasing order of the sum of their processing times on all machines to obtain the first sequence $\Pi = (\pi_1, \pi_2, ..., \pi_N)$.

Stage 2: The first two jobs of Π are taken: two partial sequences are generated and evaluated. The best sequence is chosen and settled as the current partial sequence. Let $K = 3$.

Stage 3: Insert the job π_K in the best position of the current partial sequence based on the speed-up method, and consider the generated sequence as the current partial sequence.

Stage 4: Save a copy of the current partial sequence as a Π_{cop}.

Stage 5: Mix the jobs π_1 till π_{K-1}, and form the new sequence $\Pi' = (\pi'_1, \pi'_2, ..., \pi'_{K-1})$. Let $X = 1$.

Stage 6: Remove the job π'_X from the current partial sequence, and reinsert it in the best position based on the speed-up method. Consider this best partial sequence as the current partial sequence Π'_{cop}.

Stage 7: If $X = K - 1$, Then: compare Π_{cop} and Π'_{cop}, and save the best one, Then skip to ***Stage 8***. Else, increment X and skip to ***Stage 6***.

Stage 8: If $K = N$, Then skip to ***Stage 9***. Else, increment K and skip to ***Stage 3***.

Stage 9: Pick among the current partial sequence and all of its neighbors which are generated by a pair-wise exchange in this sequence the best and final solution.

After producing the initial population, the second step in the algorithm is to evaluate the fitness of each produced solution. Indeed, each solution has a specific fitness or an affinity function that comes from the objective value fixed for the BFSP. This function may be defined as $Fit_i = \frac{1}{O(\Pi)}$: the sequence with the largest function value has the best fitness (the minimum objective value). We use two ranking methods to pick out elite solutions which will be selected for either mutation or crossover. The first method is the roulette wheel selection: each solution is interpreted as a fragment of the wheel such that the size of this fragment is proportional to the fitness. The second procedure is the tournament selection where two solutions are selected randomly from the population, and the one with higher fitness is chosen as parent. These techniques are repeated as long as parents have to be selected. In this work, the probabilities of performing the roulette and tournament are fixed to 0.5 and 0.5 respectively.

3.2 Crossover operator and Mutation

After the selection, a crossover operator exchanges the information of the selected parents to generate promising children. We consider two versions of the operator for the BFSP,

namely the two-point and multi-parent crossover. The two-point operator is applied with a probability P_c to two distinct selected solutions. Two children are engendered. As a multi-parent crossover, we focus on diagonal based crossover [6]. It is a technique which divides the sequence into blocks by the number of parents, and then forms a new complete chromosome using the scanning order. During the search process and at each generation, if there is redundant solutions then the diagonal crossover is used to clean the population and replace these solutions by new individuals. The number of parents is set up as 3 in later experiments. More details on diagonal-based crossover can be found in [6].
Besides, each individual will be mutated to explore its neighboring solutions by using the shift mutation operator. In shift change, a job at a fixed position in the list is deleted and inserted at another position. These two positions are randomly selected. The probability of performing the shift mutation is P_m.

3.3 Final BGA algorithm

To summarize, the complete BGA algorithm for solving the exposed problem has the following scheme:

Algorithm BGA

Stage 1: Initialize the parameters: PS, P_c, P_m, and MCN

Stage 2: Generate the initial population: apply the modified NEH-WPT and the modified NEH-MK to produce the two first solutions, the rest are generated randomly and differently.

Stage 3: Test the population: calculate the objective function value $O(\Pi)$ for each solution (fitness), then store the best-solution.

Stage 4: Select parents based on the roulette wheel and the tournament selection techniques.

Stage 5: Apply the two-point crossover operator depending on the crossover rate P_c to generate new solutions.

Stage 6: Apply the mutation operator depending on the mutation rate P_m to enhance the quality of the new produced solutions.

Stage 7: Apply the multi-parent crossover based on the diagonal operator to generate once again new solutions. Store them in interne.

Stage 8: Search for redundant solutions, and replace them based on solutions of ***Stage 7***. Fulfill the population if needed based on the best-achieved so far solutions.

Stage 9: Update best-solution.

Stage 10: If the given termination criterion is satisfied, return the best-solution; Otherwise go back to ***Stage 4***.

In the coded versions, the algorithm is stopped when it reach the maximal cycle number of generation MCN.

4. THE ARTIFICIAL BEE COLONY ALGORITHM FOR THE BFSP

The ABC algorithm is a new swarm intelligence based approaches [19] originally designed for continuous function optimization. The artificial bees are sorted into three groups: employed, onlooker, and scout bees. The number of onlookers and employed bees corresponds to the number of food sources SN surrounding the hive. At the start, the algorithm generates randomly initial population of solutions, which are then randomly assigned to the employed bees and evaluated. Later, the population iterates the search processes of the employed, onlooker and scout bees. The employed or onlooker bee produces new solutions by modifying probabilistically their current solutions, and tests their fitness value. When all the employed bees end the search process, they share out information with the onlooker bees. The onlooker bee checks these information and picks a food source with a probability related to its nectar quantity. If a solution is not improved after a fixed number of $Limit$ trial, that solution is neglected by its employed bee. In the following we describe all parameters and operators used in the proposed ABC for the BFSP under some fixed criterion.

4.1 Population initialization

We initialize the population which consists a set of food sources. 'x' initial solutions are obtained using the PF-NEH(x) heuristic developed in [26]. So, while jobs are being arranged in an increasing order of the sum of their processing times at the first stage of the PF-NEH(x) algorithm, x solutions are produced iteratively where at each iteration of the algorithm the first ranked job is picked from the initial jobs ordering and then a finite solution is constructed based on both the PF method and the NEH's insertion-stage. Only the last λ jobs in the sequence produced by the PF method undergo the NEH's insertion-stage. The remaining $(SN-x)$ members of the colony are randomly generated.
Meanwhile, to improve the quality of the initial explored food sources, we perform the referenced local search technique as in [26]: it iteratively moves in the neighbor solutions until a local optimum is reached. A speed-up method is used to reduce the computational time needed for searching. The steps in the referenced local search are described in the following:

Procedure Referenced local search(Π, Π^{ref})

Stage 1: While (Π is improved)

For $i = 1$ ***To*** N ***Do***

- Let $\Pi' = \Pi$
- Find the job π_i^{ref} in Π', and remove it.
- Test π_i^{ref} in all the possible slots of Π'.
- Insert π_i^{ref} in the slot resulting the lowest objective value.
- If $O(\Pi') < O(\Pi)$ Then $\Pi = \Pi'$.

End For

Stage 2: Return the sequence Π

End Referenced local search

4.2 Employed bee phase

Now, having assigned randomly initial solutions to PS employed bees, candidate solutions are to be explored based on the path relinking approach [12]. In this paper, the path relinking starts from an incumbent solution to be enhanced and stops when there is no other possible movements to reach the target solution. A solution is initial if $\Phi \geq 0$, else it is a target. Besides, if no intermediate solutions exist then the current solution is kept and so not improved.
When a new solution is found for an employed bee, and its fitness value is better refined than that of the incumbent solution, then the employed bee memorizes the new position and reset its trial counter; else the parameter $trial_i$ of the incumbent solution is incremented by one.

4.3 Onlooker bee phase

To improve once more the quality of the colony, each onlooker bee selects a solution of an employed bee and tries to modify it. This selection is performed using the roulette wheel selection operator. Besides, the referenced local search based on the speed-up method is used again to explore neighboring solutions for each onlooker bee. The referenced sequence is randomly chosen. If the new explored solution is better, then the incumbent one is erased and the new explored solution by the local search technique becomes a new individual in the colony. Else, its trial is incremented.

4.4 Scout bee phase

The scout bee phase is evoked to replace if exists the discarded solution by the employed or onlooker bee during the last *Limit* number of trials, and generates new one by applying the insertion-based local search [10] to the best solution in the colony. This technique receives a permutation as input and then tries to explore all possible permutations those obtained by inserting jobs in different positions from their original places. There is exactly one scout bee who produces at most one solution at each iteration of the search process. After completing the three main phases of the ABC algorithm, the population is cleaned by identifying redundant solutions that will be replaced with randomly generated solutions.

4.5 Final BABC algorithm

As resumed in the following scheme, the complete Blocking ABC algorithm (BABC) runs in three basic steps: Initialization, position updating and termination.

Algorithm BABC

- ***Stage 1:*** Initialization:
  1. *Set* the parameters: SN, PS, $Limit$, and MCN.
  2. *Generate* the initial population: apply the PF-NEH(x) heuristic to produce 'x' initial solutions, the rest are generated randomly. *Set* $trial_i = 0, i : 1, 2, ..., SN$
  3. *Test* the population: calculate the objective function value $O(\Pi)$ for each solution (fitness), Then store the best-solution.
- ***Stage 2:*** Iterative process
  $cycle = 1$; ***Repeat***

  Employed Bees phase For $i = 1, 2, ..., PS$ Repeat
  1. *Produce* a new solution Π_i^* for the ith employed bee who is associated with the solution Π_i using the path relinking procedure;
  2. *Evaluate* the new solution Π_i^*: If Π_i^* is better than or equal to Π_i, Then *set* $\Pi_i = \Pi_i^*$;
  3. If Π_i has not been improved, Then *Increment* its trial by 1

  Onlooker Bees phase For $i = 1, 2, ..., PS$ Repeat
  1. *Select* a solution Π_i for the ith onlooker bee using the roulette wheel selection;
  2. *Generate* a new solution Π_i^* for the ith onlooker bee using the referenced local search;
  3. *Evaluate* the new solution Π_i^*: If Π_i^* is better than or equal to Π_i, Then *Set* $\Pi_i = \Pi_i^*$;
  4. If Π_i has not been improved, Then *Increment* its trial by 1

  Scout bee phase
  1. *Pick* the abandoned solution, if exists, during the last limit number of trails: *Define* i as the solution Π_i with the maximum trial;
  2. *Replace* Π_i based on the best solution on the population by applying the insertion-based local search, and *Set* its trial to 0;

  Overlapping solutions
  1. *Search* for redundant solutions, and replace them based on randomly generated one;
- **Memorize** the best solution achieved so far; $Cycle = Cycle + 1$; ***Until*** $cycle = MCN$
- **Return** the best solution found so far;

5. COMPUTATIONAL EXPERIMENTS

This section describes how we evaluate the performance of the proposed algorithms. Metaheuristics were coded in Visual C++ and run on an Intel Pentium IV 2.4 GHz PC with 512 MB of memory. A comprehensive experimental evaluations are presented based on the well-known flow shop benchmark set of Taillard. This benchmark set is composed of 12 subsets of given problems with the size ranging from 20 jobs and 5 machines to 500 jobs and 20 machines, and each subset consists of 10 instances. We treat them as the blocking flow shop problems with makespan and total flow time criterion. Each instance is independently executed ten replications, and in each replication the relative percentage deviation (RPD) is computed as follows:

$$RPD(A) = \frac{(Sol^A - Sol^{Min})}{Sol^{Min}} \times 100 \qquad (7)$$

where, Sol^A defines the value of the objective function reached by the algorithm A, $A \in \{BGA, BABC\}$; and Sol^{Min} defines the minimum objective value obtained among the two algorithms. We can see that the smaller the RPD is, the better result the algorithm produces. The average RPD (ARPD) over 10 replications for each problem size is also given as a statistic for the solution quality. To deal with the total tardiness criterion, we consider test problems generated by Ronconi and Henriques [36]. There are five groups of job sizes: 20, 50, 100, 200, and 500. In each job subset (20,50,100), they have 5, 10, and 20 machines to process the jobs, respectively. The job subset (200) has 10 and 20 machines, and the job subset (500) has only 20 machines to process the jobs. Ten different matrices of processing times were generated for each of the 12 sizes. Likewise, each algorithm is tested with a medium-sized set of 75 randomly generated instances.

This test set is produced following the procedure explained in Taillard where $N \in \{10, 20, 50, 70, 100\}$ and $M \in \{3, 5, 7\}$. For each of those matrices, four scenarios were built. The scenarios represent different configurations for the due dates [36]. The related processing times are given by a discrete uniform distribution as $p_{ij} \in U[1, 99]$ as usual in the scheduling literature. There is exactly five instances generated for each combination of N and M. The due dates are produced following the TWK rule as explained earlier where the due date tightness factor is taken in between [1,3].
On the basis of a set of preliminary experiments, best results were achieved using the specified parameter values for the BGA and BABC algorithms as in Table 1. It was noticed that when MCN, PS, SN or P_c is increased, better solutions may be generated at the expense of superior computational time.

Table 1: Parameter values used for the blocking algorithms after calibration

Parameter	MCN	PS	P_c	P_m	SN	$Limit$
Value	100	50	0.8	0.1	50	5

Table 2: Performance comparisons on randomly generated instances under makespan criterion (ARPD)

Inst	BGA	BABC
10×3	0,000%	0,000%
10×5	0,000%	0,000%
10×7	0,000%	0,000%
20×3	0,000%	0,000%
20×5	0,000%	0,000%
20×7	0,000%	0,000%
50×3	0,000%	0,037%
50×5	0,006%	0,033%
50×7	0,006%	0,058%
70×3	0,000%	0,103%
70×5	0,000%	0,154%
70×7	0,000%	0,189%
100×3	0,000%	0,123%
100×5	0,000%	0,238%
100×7	0,000%	0,344%
Average	0,001%	0,085%

5.1 Computational results for the randomly generated problem sets

Randomly generated instances were created to show the difference of the performances between the compared algorithms and judge their qualities. When tardiness criterion is considered, we choose to take τ in between the interval [1,3] such to make randomly the job due date loose, medium or tight respectively. So, the makespan, the total flow time, and the total tardiness values of the best-found solutions for these instances were recorded. The average RPD has been calculated for each set under a fixed criterion (Table 2, Table 3 and Table 4). We shall remarque that these tables reveal that under these instances the proposed algorithms behave in the same way under the three criteria. The BABC is outperformed by the BGA: whatever the objective the heuristics behave in similar way.

In the next subsection, the proposed algorithms are evaluated by comparing the results with some other effective metaheuristics presented in the literature for the blocking problem under the three cited measures including the GA, DPSO, IG, RAIS, ABC, and others.

5.2 Comparison with metaheuristics under makespan criterion

Table 5 summarizes the results of comparison of the algorithms under the makespan criterion. The effectiveness of the reported methods against the MA [27], DPSO [41], DABC [10], IG [31], HDDE [38], and the RAIS [22] was measured by listing the ARPDs values, where Sol^{Min} defines the best-known solution provided by [31]. The above table reveals that MA, DPSO, DABC, IG, HDDE, and RAIS are significantly outperformed by our algorithms for middle or large-scale instance sizes. For the small-scale instance sizes, the proposed algorithms obtain similar results with the compared ones. The total ARPD for all the 120 instances treating the BGA and the BABC are -0,678% and -0,654%, respectively. Whereas, for MA, DPSO, DABC, IG, HDDE, and RAIS the values are -0,559%, 1,321%, -0,240%, 0,000%, 0,882%, and -0,315%, respectively. DPSO is the worst algorithm with the largest overall RPD value. The negative average RPD values indicate an enhancement to the best-known solution reported in the literature: these improvements occur in all Taillard's instances from (50×5) to (500×20) test sets.

Table 3: Performance comparisons on randomly generated instances under total flow time criterion (ARPD)

Inst	BGA	BABC
10×3	0,000%	0,000%
10×5	0,000%	0,000%
10×7	0,000%	0,000%
20×3	0,000%	0,032%
20×5	0,000%	0,035%
20×7	0,000%	0,038%
50×3	0,000%	0,007%
50×5	0,000%	0,008%
50×7	0,000%	0,004%
70×3	0,000%	0,008%
70×5	0,000%	0,005%
70×7	0,000%	0,005%
100×3	0,000%	0,002%
100×5	0,000%	0,002%
100×7	0,000%	0,001%
Average	0,000%	0,010%

Table 4: Performance comparisons on randomly generated instances under total tardiness criterion (ARPD)

Inst	BGA	BABC
10×3	0,000%	0,000%
10×5	0,000%	0,000%
10×7	0,000%	0,000%
20×3	0,000%	0,010%
20×5	0,000%	0,057%
20×7	0,000%	0,089%
50×3	0,000%	0,007%
50×5	0,000%	0,007%
50×7	0,000%	0,014%
70×3	0,000%	0,005%
70×5	0,000%	0,004%
70×7	0,000%	0,008%
100×3	0,000%	0,002%
100×5	0,000%	0,002%
100×7	0,00%	0,004%
Average	0,000%	0,014%

5.3 Comparison with metaheuristics under total flow time criterion

Table 6 summarizes the results of the comparison of the algorithms under the total flow time criterion. The effectiveness of the reported methods against the hmghs [39], hDABC [16], and the IG [20] was measured by listing again the ARPDs values, where Sol^{Min} defines the best-known solution reported by [39]. As we can see, the above table reveals that hmgHS, hDABC, and IG are significantly outperformed by the proposed algorithms. The total ARPD for all the 120 instances concerning the BGA and BABC are -2,279% and -2,274%, respectively. Whereas, for hmgHS, hDABC, and IG the values are 0,000%, -0,389%, and -1,171%, respectively.

Table 5: ARPD on Taillard instances under makespan criterion

Inst	RAIS	MA	IG	DPSO	HDDE	DABC	BGA	BABC
20 × 5	0,000%	0,000%	0,000%	0,000%	0,000%	0,000%	0,000%	0,000%
20 × 10	0,000%	0,000%	0,000%	0,011%	0,000%	0,000%	0,000%	0,000%
20 × 20	0,000%	0,000%	0,000%	0,000%	0,000%	0,000%	0,000%	0,000%
50 × 5	-0,192%	-0,083%	0,000%	1,075%	0,779%	-0,202%	-0,288%	-0,226%
50 × 10	-0,197%	-0,202%	0,000%	1,255%	0,532%	-0,335%	-0,374%	-0,329%
50 × 20	-0,004%	-0,220%	0,000%	1,294%	0,351%	-0,278%	-0,236%	-0,211%
100 × 5	-0,818%	-0,360%	0,000%	1,348%	1,778%	-0,051%	-0,877%	-0,842%
100 × 10	-0,882%	-0,699%	0,000%	1,522%	1,013%	-0,877%	-0,964%	-0,930%
100 × 20	-0,712%	-0,709%	0,000%	1,843%	0,858%	-1,142%	-0,920%	-0,883%
200 × 10	-0,329%	-0,565%	0,000%	2,942%	2,494%	0,000%	-0,612%	-0,595%
200 × 20	-0,629%	-1,488%	0,000%	1,830%	1,240%	0,000%	-1,146%	-1,136%
500 × 20	-0,015%	-2,388%	0,000%	2,726%	1,538%	0,000%	-2,716%	-2,694%
Average	-0,315%	-0,559%	0,000%	1,321%	0,882%	-0,240%	-0,678%	-0,654%

Table 6: ARPD on Taillard instances under total flow time criterion

Inst	hmghs	IG	hDABC	BGA	BABC
20 × 5	0,000%	-0,001%	-0,001%	-0,001%	-0,001%
20 × 10	0,000%	0,000%	0,000%	0,000%	0,000%
20 × 20	0,000%	0,000%	0,005%	-0,133%	-0,133%
50 × 5	0,000%	-0,992%	-0,202%	-1,602%	-1,582%
50 × 10	0,000%	-0,585%	-0,255%	-1,209%	-1,190%
50 × 20	0,000%	-0,267%	-0,111%	-1,230%	-1,224%
100 × 5	0,000%	-2,966%	-0,690%	-4,251%	-4,262%
100 × 10	0,000%	-1,814%	-0,297%	-4,064%	-4,055%
100 × 20	0,000%	-1,464%	-0,437%	-3,539%	-3,538%
200 × 10	0,000%	-2,503%	-0,789%	-4,328%	-4,327%
200 × 20	0,000%	-1,479%	-0,624%	-4,129%	-4,129%
500 × 20	0,000%	-1,983%	-1,264%	-2,861%	-2,842%
Average	0,000%	-1,171%	-0,389%	-2,279%	-2,274%

The above observations attest that our blocking algorithms obtain better solutions than the leading algorithms since they improve the results for all instance.

5.4 Comparison with metaheuristics under total tardiness criterion

Table 7 summarizes the results of the comparison of the algorithms under the total tardiness criterion. The effectiveness of the reported methods against the GRASP metaheuristic [36] and the GA based on the path relinking technique GA_PR [9] was measured by listing again the ARPDs values, where Sol^{Min} defines the total tardiness value obtained by GRASP algorithm. Based on the above table, the BGA and BABC obtained the same results as the GRASP in 49 and 53 problems, respectively. These performances are much more better than those obtained by GA_PR (124 problems). We report the average of improvement percentage of each class with 10 problems. The BGA and BABC obtained the highest improvement for test instances with N*M = 200*10 (-16,336% and -22,833%) and N*M = 500*20 (-10,695% and -29,064%). The lowest values of improvement of the algorithms were for problems with N*M = 20*20 (-0,837% and -1,144%). An overall average improvement of -4,534% and -9,563% were achieved by BGA and BABC, respectively.

6. CONCLUSIONS

This paper proposes a GA and an ABC algorithms for dealing with the flow shop problem with blocking in order to minimize three fixed criteria. From all previously tests, it is concluded that the proposed algorithms are effective and efficient. Computational tests carried out on randomly generated test problems show that the approaches consistently yields good solutions with a bite advantage for the GA algorithm. These facts establish BGA and BABC as a new state-of-the-art heuristics for the BFSP: they obtained a lower average RPD values than the others did. So, an updated list of best-known solutions for the Taillard's and Ronconi and Henriques's benchmark is found.

7. REFERENCES

[1] I. Abadi, N. Hall, and C. Sriskandarajah. Minimizing cycle time in a blocking flowshop. *Operations Research*, 1:177–80, 2000.

[2] V. Armentano and D. Ronconi. Tabu search for total tardiness minimization in flowshop scheduling problems. *Computers and Operations Research 26*, 3:219–235, 1999.

[3] V. Armentano and D. Ronconi. Minimizaçâo do tempo total de atraso no problema de flowshop com buffer zero através de busca tabu. *Gestao and Produçao 7*, 3:352–363, 2000.

[4] K. Baker and J. Bertrand. An investigation of due date assignment rules with constrained tightness. *J. Oper. Manage*, 3:109–120, 1981.

[5] V. Caraffa, S. Ianes, T. Bagchi, and C. Sriskandarajah. Minimizing makespan in a flowshop using genetic algorithms. *International Journal of Production Economics*, 2:101–15, 2001.

[6] S. Chen, M. Chen, P. Chang, and V. Mani. Multiple parents crossover operators: A new approach removes the overlapping solutions for sequencing problems. *Applied mathematical modelling*, 37:2737–2746, 2013.

[7] R. Companys. Note on the blocking flow shop problem. *Working Paper, http://upcommons.upc.edu /e-prints/handle/2117/420*, pages 1–28, 2009.

[8] D. Davendra, M. Bialic-Davendra, R. Senkerik, and M. Pluhacek. Scheduling the flow shop with blocking problem with the chaos-induced discrete self organising migrating algorithm. *Proceedings 27th European Conference on Modelling and Simulation*, 2013.

[9] T. de O. Januario, J. E. C. Arroyo, and M. C. O. Moreira. *Nature Inspired Cooperative Strategies for Optimization (NICSO 2008)*. Springer Berlin Heidelberg, 2009.

[10] G. Deng, Z. XU, and X. Gu. A discrete artificial bee colony algorithm for minimizing the total flow time in the blocking flow shop scheduling. *Chinese Journal of Chemical Engineering*, 20:1067–1073, 2012.

[11] P. Gilmore and R. Gomory. Sequencing a one state variable machine: a solvable case of the traveling salesman problem. *Operations Research*, 5:655–79, 1964.

[12] F. Glover and M. Laguna. Tabu search. *Kluwer Academic Publishers, Boston*, 1997.

[13] J. Grabowski. and J. Pempera. The permutation flowshop problem with blocking. a tabu search approach. *Omega*, 3:302–11, 2007.

[14] R. Graham, E. Lawler, J. Lenstra, and K. Rinnooy. Optimization and approximation in deterministic

Table 7: ARPD on Ronconi and Henriques's instances under total tardiness criterion

Inst	Scenario 1			Scenario 2			Scenario 3			Scenario 4			All Scenario		
	GA_PR	BGA	BABC	GA_PR	BGA	BABC	GA_PR	BGA	BABC	GA_PR	BGA	BABC	GA_PR	BGA	BABC
20*5	-3,774%	-6,455%	-6,293%	-1,166%	-2,068%	-1,781%	-1,969%	-2,806%	-2,688%	-1,625%	-2,386%	-2,179%	-2,134%	-3,429%	-3,236%
20*10	-1,175%	-2,37%	-2,257%	-2,404%	-3,279%	-3,192%	-1,436%	-1,92%	-1,871%	-1,347%	-1,889%	-1,843%	-1,590%	-2,364%	-2,291%
20*20	-1,576%	-1,999%	-1,979%	-0,544%	-0,901%	-0,884%	-0,486%	-0,662%	-0,652%	-0,74%	-1,012%	-0,994%	-0,837%	-1,144%	-1,127%
50*5	-9,437%	-13,471%	-13,291%	0,000%	-2,051%	-2,09%	-4,014%	-5,078%	-5,045%	-3,138%	-4,014%	-3,962%	-4,147%	-6,154%	-6,097%
50*10	-8,372%	-13,257%	-13,133%	-10,517%	-17,166%	-16,966%	-3,169%	-4,538%	-4,507%	-1,701%	-4,274%	-4,194%	-5,940%	-9,809%	-9,700%
50*20	-2,958%	-7,065%	-7,003%	-2,347%	-5,025%	-4,992%	-2,128%	-3,162%	-3,151%	-1,531%	-2,416%	-2,414%	-2,241%	-4,417%	-4,390%
100*5	-11,033%	-15,226%	-15,113%	-4,449%	-4,776%	-4,776%	-0,573%	-2,108%	-2,075%	-0,628%	-4,421%	-4,409%	-4,171%	-6,633%	-6,593%
100*10	-6,606%	-10,455%	-10,407%	25,378%	6,803%	6,854%	-2,268%	-3,37%	-3,349%	-3,45%	-4,758%	-4,738%	3,263%	-2,945%	-2,910%
100*20	-4,477%	-11,651%	-11,632%	-11,545%	-25,327%	-25,299%	-1,444%	-3,145%	-3,135%	-0,727%	-2,583%	-2,572%	-4,548%	-10,676%	-10,660%
200*10	-5,616%	-15,283%	-15,284%	-57,059%	-58,364%	-58,357%	-1,154%	-7,769%	-7,768%	-1,516%	-9,914%	-9,914%	-16,336%	-22,833%	-22,831%
200*20	-4,964%	-15,922%	-15,918%	-10,747%	-29,637%	-29,556%	-2,383%	-8,291%	-8,29%	-2,034%	-7,309%	-7,308%	-5,032%	-15,290%	-15,268%
500*20	-6,255%	-20,19%	-20,189%	-30,471%	-54,021%	-54,02%	-2,46%	-16,133%	-16,132%	-3,594%	-25,911%	-25,91%	-10,695%	-29,064%	-29,063%
Average	-5,52%	-11,112%	-11,042%	-8,823%	-16,318%	-16,255%	-1,957%	-4,915%	-4,889%	-1,836%	-5,907%	-5,870%	-4,534%	-9,563%	-9,514%

sequencing and scheduling: a survey. *Annals of Discrete Mathematics*, 5:287–362, 1979.

[15] N. Hall and C. Sriskandarajah. A survey of machine scheduling problems with blocking and no-wait in process. *Operations Research*, 44:510–25, 1996.

[16] Y.-Y. Han, J. Liang, Q.-K. Pan, J.-Q. Li, H.-Y. Sang, and N. Cao. Effective hybrid discrete artificial bee colony algorithms for the total flowtime minimization in the blocking flowshop problem. *Int J Adv Manuf Technol*, 67:397–414, 2013.

[17] H. Holland. Adaptation in natural and artificial systems. *University of Michigan Press, Ann Arbor*, 1975.

[18] S. Johnson. Optimal two- and three-stage production schedules with setup time included. *Naval Research Logistics Quarterly*, 1:61–8, 1954.

[19] D. Karaboga. An idea based on honeybee swarm for numerical optimization. *Technical Report TR06, Erciyes University, Engineering Faculty, Computer Engineering Department*, 2005.

[20] D. Khorasanian and G. Moslehi. An iterated greedy algorithm for solving the blocking flow shop scheduling problem with total flow time criteria. *International Journal of Industrial Engineering and Production Research*, 23:301–308, 2012.

[21] C. Koulamas. The total tardiness problem: Review and extensions. *OR*, 42:1025–1041, 1994.

[22] S. Lin and K. Ying. Minimizing makespan in a blocking flowshop using a revised artificial immune system algorithm. *Omega*, 41:383–389, 2013.

[23] S. McCormick, M. Pinedo, S. Shenker, and B. Wolf. Sequencing in an assembly line with blocking to minimize cycle time. *OR*, 37:925–935, 1989.

[24] G. Moslehi and D. Khorasanian. Optimizing blocking flowshop scheduling problem with total completion time criterion. *Computers and Operations Research*, 40:1874–1883, 2013.

[25] M. Nawaz, J. Enscore, and I. Ham. A heuristic algorithm for the m-machine, n-job flow-shop sequencing problem. *Omega*, 11:91–95, 1983.

[26] Q. Pan and L. Wang. Effective heuristics for the blocking flowshop scheduling problem with makespan minimization. *Omega*, 2:218–29, 2012.

[27] Q. Pan, L. Wang, H. Sang, J. Li, and M. Liu. A high performing memetic algorithm for the flowshop scheduling problem with blocking. *IEEE Transactions on Automation Science and Engineering*, 10:741–756, 2013.

[28] M. Pinedo. Scheduling: theory, algorithms, and systems. *Pretice Hall. U.A.S*, 2008.

[29] B. Qian, L. Wang, D. Huang, W. Wang, and X. Wang. An effective hybrid de-based algorithm for multi-objective flowshop scheduling with limited buffers. *Computers and Operations Research*, 1:209–3, 2009.

[30] S. Reddi and C. Ramamoorthy. On the flow-shop sequencing problem with no wait in process. *Operational Research Quarterly*, 3:323–31, 1972.

[31] I. Ribas, R. Companys, and X. Tort-Martorell. An iterated greedy algorithm for the flowhsop scheduling problem with blocking. *Omega*, 3:293–301, 2011.

[32] I. Ribas, R. Companys, and X. Tort-Martorell. An efficient iterated local search algorithm for the total tardiness blocking flow shop problem. *International Journal of Production Research*, 51:5238–5252, 2013.

[33] H. Rock. Some new results in flow shop scheduling. *Zeitschrift fur Operations Research*, 28:1–16, 1984.

[34] D. Ronconi. A note on constructive heuristics for the flowshop problem with blocking. *International Journal of Production Economics*, 87:39–48, 2004.

[35] D. Ronconi. A branch-and-bound algorithm to minimize the makespan in a flowshop problem with blocking. *Annals of Operations Research*, 1:53–65, 2005.

[36] D. Ronconi and L. Henriques. Some heuristic algorithms for total tardiness minimization in a flowshop with blocking. *Omega*, 2:272–81, 2009.

[37] M. Tasgetiren, Q. Pan, P. Suganthan, and A. Chen. A discrete artificial bee colony algorithm for the total flow time minimization in permutation flow shops. *Inform. Sci.*, 16:3459–3475, 2011.

[38] L. Wang, Q. Pan, P. Suganthan, W. Wang, and Y. Wang. A novel hybrid discrete differential evolution algorithm for blocking flowshop scheduling problems. *Computers and OperationalResearch*, 3:509–20, 2010.

[39] L. Wang, Q. Pan, and M. Tasgetiren. Minimizing the total flow time in a flowshop with blocking by using hybrid harmony search algorithms. *Expert Syst. Appl*, 12:7929–7936, 2010.

[40] L. Wang., Q. Pan, and M. Tasgetiren. A hybrid harmony search algorithm for the blocking permutation flowshop scheduling problem. *Comput. Ind. Eng.*, 1:76–83, 2011.

[41] X. Wang and L. Tang. A discrete particle swarm optimization algorithm with self-adaptive diversity control for the permutation flowshop problem with blocking. *Applied Soft Computing*, 12:652–662, 2012.

Tunnelling Crossover Networks

Gabriela Ochoa
Department of Computing Science and Mathematics
University of Stirling
Stirling, FK9 4LA, Scotland
goc@cs.stir.ac.uk

Francisco Chicano
E.T.S. Ingeniería Informática
University of Málaga
Andalucía Tech, Spain
chicano@lcc.uma.es

Renato Tinós
Department of Computing and Mathematics
University of São Paulo
Ribeirão Preto, SP, Brazil
rtinos@ffclrp.usp.br

Darrell Whitley
Department of Computer Science
Colorado State University
Fort Collins, CO, USA
whitley@cs.colostate.edu

ABSTRACT

Local optima networks are a recent model of fitness landscapes. They compress the landscape by representing local optima as nodes, and search transitions among them as edges. Previous local optima networks considered transitions based on mutation; this study looks instead at transitions based on deterministic recombination. We define and analyse networks based on the recently proposed partition crossover for k-bounded pseudo-Boolean functions, using NKq landscapes as a case study. Partition crossover was initially proposed for the travelling salesman problem, where it was found to "tunnel" between local optima, i.e., jump from local optimum to local optimum. Our network analysis shows that this also happens for NK landscapes: local optima are densely connected via partition crossover. We found marked differences between the adjacent and random interaction NK models. Surprisingly, with the random model, instances have a lower number of local optima on average, but their networks are more sparse and decompose into several clusters. There is also large variability in the size and pattern of connectivity of instances coming from the same landscape parameter values. These network features offer new insight informing why some instances are harder to solve than others.

Categories and Subject Descriptors

I.2.8 [**Artificial Intelligence**]: Problem Solving, Control Methods, and Search

Keywords

Local Optima Network; Partition Crossover; Hill Climbing; Local Search; Fitness Landscapes; NK-landscapes

GECCO '15, July 11–15, 2015, Madrid, Spain

DOI: http://dx.doi.org/10.1145/2739480.2754657

1. INTRODUCTION

The number and distribution of local optima are fundamental features of fitness landscapes that can impact the performance of heuristic optimisation methods. In his seminal work [7], F. Glover states: "*Perhaps the most conspicuous limitation of a heuristic method for problems involving discrete alternatives is the ability to become trapped at a local optimum*".

Local Optima Networks (LONs) are a recent network-based model of combinatorial fitness landscapes capturing the structure and topology of local optima [12, 13, 16, 17]. They represent the local optima of the underlying optimisation problem as vertices; and as edges, possible transitions among them using a given search operator. Local optima networks were inspired by work in physics where *energy surfaces* are modelled as complex networks [6]. Modelling landscapes as networks introduces a new set of metrics to analyse computational search spaces and the possibility of visualising them [9, 10]. Previous work on local optima networks considered transitions among optima based on mutation operators; both binary and permutation spaces have been studied [5, 13]. The main contribution of this article is to instead consider transitions based on recombination.

Specifically, we consider the partition crossover recently proposed for k-bounded pseudo-Boolean functions (i.e., real-valued functions over binary strings where the interactions between variables is bounded by a constant k) [15]. NK landscapes, MAX-kSAT, and several graph optimisation problems, such as MAX-CUT, are examples of these functions. This class of functions is relevant to evolutionary computation, combinatorial optimisation, and machine learning.

Partition Crossover (PX) was first introduced for the travelling Salesman Problem (TSP) [19]. The operator exploits the fact that two "parent" solutions can be decomposed into a number of partial solutions or sub-tours (i.e., tours compressing a subset of the cities). Each partial solution is linearly independent from the other partial solutions, which means that each partial solution can be evaluated independently. For a specific pairing of parents, partial solutions are also modular so that one partial solution from one parent can replace a partial solution from another parent so as to always yield a feasible offspring.

Whitley et al. [19] have also shown that when partition crossover is used to recombine parent solutions that are local optima, the offspring are also local optima with a high probability (around 80% for TSP instances). There are two reasons for this. (i) PX generates offspring that are guaranteed to be "piecewise" locally optimal: no single partial solution that is inherited form a parent can be improved by local search, because every partial solution has already been optimized by local search, and each partial solution is inherited as a unit during recombination. Thus, the only way that local search can improve an offspring is by discovering an improving move that alters two or more partial solutions. This rarely happens, which may be explained by a more subtle secondary factor. (ii) PX is respectful and transmits edges from the parent solutions. *Transmission* means all of the edges in the offspring are inherited from the parents, while *respect* that all shared edges in the parents are also inherited by the offspring. In the TSP it is the *edges* that are inherited from the parents that impacts the evaluation of the offspring. Thus, if the parents are locally optimal and have a very good evaluation, the offspring will also likely have a very good evaluation, which increases the likelihood that the offspring will also be locally optimal. In a recent paper, Tinós, Whitley and Chicano [15] have shown that a similar decomposition exists for NK landscapes into partial solutions that are modular and which can be independently evaluated. They also demonstrated the effectiveness of PX, and again showed that when it is applied to parents that are locally optimal, the offspring are always locally optimal in a restricted hyperplane subspace, and are usually local optimal in the full search space as well.

This paper defines and analyses local optima networks where the transitions among optima are based on the application of PX over binary spaces such as NK landscapes, but the results may be extended to MAX-kSAT and other pseudo-Boolean problems. More specifically, the primary contributions of the paper are the following:

1. Definition of the mathematical object XLON (crossover local optima networks) with a case study considering PX.
2. Implementation of an effective algorithm for constructing the networks following recent developments which exploit the structure of k-bounded additive fitness functions, leading to fast deterministic hill-climbing [3].
3. Statistical analysis and visualisation of the extracted networks.
4. Empirical evidence indicating that the number of local optima is not necessarily a reliable indicator of search difficulty in combinatorial optimisation.

2. NK LANDSCAPES

Our study considers the NKq ('quantized' NK) family of landscapes [11], one of several models adding tunnable neutrality to the standard Kauffman's NK model [8].

NK landscapes are defined as a real stochastic function f on binary strings $x \in \mathbb{B}^N$, $f : \mathbb{B}^N \to \mathbb{R}$. The value of K determines how many other bits in the string interact with each bit x_i. These bit interactions can be expressed as sub-functions, f_i, where each sub-function takes $K+1$ bits as input. These K interacting bits can either be the nearest neighbours (adjacent model) or selected uniformly at random (random model). The fitness (evaluation) function is given by:

$$f(x) = \sum_{i=1}^{N} f_i(x|_{mask_i}), \tag{1}$$

where $mask_i$ selects the $k = K+1$ bits that will be accessed by sub-function f_i. In practice, the mask can be dropped in as much as it is inherent in the definition of sub-function f_i. In the standard model, the codomain values for each sub-function f_i are randomly generated real numbers from $[0,1]$. In NKq landscapes, the fitness contributions are instead integers drawn from the range $[0,q)$. This allows solutions with the same fitness (i.e., landscapes with neutrality). Our study considers a value of $q = 100$, which produces discrete landscapes with a very low degree of neutrality. Future work will study partition crossover local optima networks for neutral landscapes of the type that are common in MAX-kSAT problems.

It should also be noted that while NK landscapes are the focus of the current study, the methods used here and the partition crossover operator can be applied to all pseudo-Boolean functions with closed form evaluation functions. Just as every SAT problem can be expressed as a MAX-kSAT problem, every pseudo-Boolean function with an algebraic evaluation function can be expressed as a quadratic pseudo-Boolean function [1]. Thus, it should be noted that NK landscapes where $K = 1$ are also quadratic pseudo-Boolean functions (i.e., $k = 2$). Future work should explore what happens to the fitness landscape when NK landscapes with larger values of K are converted into quadratic pseudo-Boolean functions where $k = 2$ ($K = 1$).

3. PARTITION CROSSOVER (PX)

Under partition crossover, the evaluation of the offspring can be directly obtained from partial evaluations of components found in the parents. For NK landscapes, components are sets of differing bits in the parent solutions with interactions within the sets but no interactions among sets. If the differing bits found in the two parents can be partitioned into q components, partition crossover can be used to find the best of 2^q possible offspring. This is done at $O(N)$ cost per recombination. If the parents are locally optimal, any offspring must be locally optimal in a (more restricted) hyperplane subspace.

Given a subset of variables z of f, we would like to find a partition π of z such that f can be additively decomposed into $|\pi|$ sub-functions g_i for $i = 1$ to $|\pi|$, where each g_i depends on the variables in the subset π_i but does not depend on the variables in $z - \pi_i$.

We will use the *Variable Interaction Graph* (VIG) proposed by Chicano et. al. [3], where the vertices of the graph are the N variables, and two variables (vertices) are connected by an edge if they appear together in the same sub-function f_i. Note that we can potentially remove additional edges from the Variable Interaction Graph if the variable interactions do not result in a nonlinear interaction; this can be determined by taking the Walsh transforms of the sub-functions: if i and j appear together in any Walsh coefficient that is non-zero, edge $e(v_i, v_j)$ is added to the VIG, otherwise it can be removed. However, in most cases, variables that appear together in some sub-function also have a nonlinear interaction.

We are interested in how partition crossover can be used to partition the VIG.

PROPOSITION 1 ([15]). *For any pseudo-Boolean function with VIG G, V the set of variables of f and z a subset of V. The most fine grain partition π of z that additively decomposes f is given by:*

$$f(x) = c + \sum_{i=1}^{|\pi|} g_i(x|_{mask_i}), \qquad (2)$$

where $\pi_i \subseteq mask_i$, $(z - \pi_i) \cap mask_i = \emptyset$ and the constant c does not depend on any variable in z, is the partition induced by the connected components in the subgraph $G[z]$.

Proposition 1 defines the most fine grain way to additively decompose f when we are interested in separating the variables in a subset z. In partition crossover the set of variables z in which we are interested is the set of differing variables in the two parent solutions. Thus, instead of the VIG of the function f, it will be useful in the following to work with a reduced graph: the *recombination graph.* Prior to applying partition crossover it is necessary to construct the VIG, but the same VIG is common to all recombinations for the same objective function.

DEFINITION 1 (RECOMBINATION GRAPH [15]). *Let $f : \mathbb{B}^N \to \mathbb{R}$ be a pseudo-Boolean function with Variable Interaction Graph G and $x, y \in \mathbb{B}^N$ two solutions. We define the recombination graph of function f for solutions x and y as $G[x \oplus y]$ (where $\oplus$ denotes the exclusive OR bitwise operation), that is the subgraph of G composed of the variables in which x and y differ.*

The first step of the operator is to transfer all common bits to the offspring. Next, using the two parents x and y, determine the recombination graph and use Breadth First Search to find the connected components of the recombination graph. These connected components form a partition of the set of variables in $x \oplus y$ (the differing bits in the parent solutions).

Having determined the partition of variables in $x \oplus y$, test the two assignments from the two parents. Since this only includes non-shared assignments to variables, the solutions from the two parents will be complements. Proposition 1 ensures that we can write f as a linear sum of sub-functions g_i where each one depends on the variables in one component π_i and not the others. Select the assignment in each connected component that results in the best evaluation for the corresponding sub-function g_i.

THEOREM 1. **The Partition Crossover Theorem [15]:** *For any k-bounded pseudo-Boolean function f, if the recombination graph of f for solutions x and y contains q connected components, then partition crossover returns the best of 2^q solutions; including the parent solutions.*

We will use the following sub-functions to illustrate the VIG and the construction of a recombination graph. In this case, $N = 10$ and K=2 (k=3). The sub-functions are as follows:

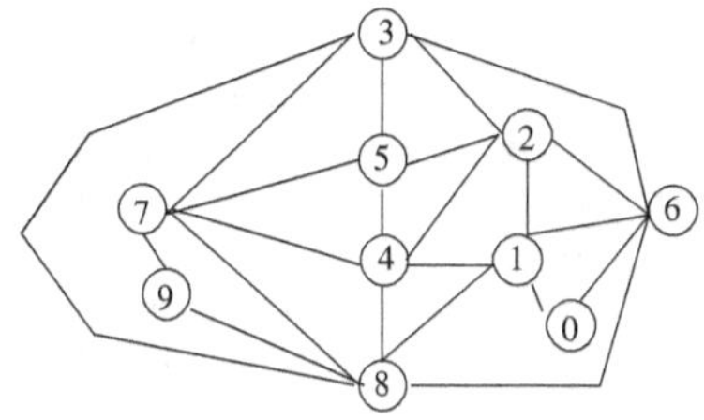

The Variable Interaction Graph

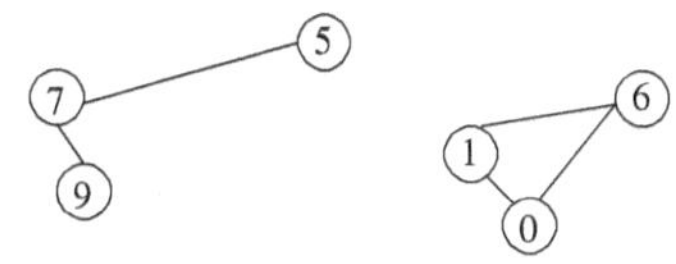

The decomposed Recombination Graph

Figure 1: The upper graph is the Variable Interaction Graph (VIG) of the sample function. When recombining the solutions 0000000000 and 1100011101, the vertices and edges associated with shared variables 2, 3, 4, 8 are deleted to yield the recombination graph which is shown below the VIG. If the recombination graph can be partitioned into q connected components, then recombination is guaranteed to return the best of 2^q possible offspring. In this example, there are only two components.

$f_0(x_0, x_1, x_6)$ $f_1(x_1, x_4, x_8)$ $f_2(x_2, x_3, x_5)$ $f_3(x_3, x_2, x_6)$
$f_4(x_4, x_2, x_1)$ $f_5(x_5, x_7, x_4)$ $f_6(x_6, x_8, x_1)$ $f_7(x_7, x_3, x_5)$
$f_8(x_8, x_7, x_3)$ $f_9(x_9, x_7, x_8)$

Each function yields a set of 4 nonlinear Walsh coefficients. Assume all of the Walsh coefficients are non-zero. This means that every pair of variables that appear together in some sub-function are connected by an edge in the VIG. This set of sub-functions results in the VIG shown in Figure 1.

Assume we wish to recombine two solutions 0000000000 and 1100011101; the variables are numbered from 0 to 9 from left to right. These two solutions reside in the hyperplane subspace **000***0* because these zero bits are shared in common by the parents. If the parents are locally optimal solutions, then any offspring are provably locally optimal in the reduced hyperplane subspace (but may or may not be locally optimal in the full search space).

From the VIG, we will generate the recombination graph by deleting the variables that share a common value assignment. The edges connected to the variables with common values are also deleted. We next ask if deleting these variables and edges "partitions" the recombination graph. In our example, the variables with shared values are 2, 3, 4 and 8. The variables that have different assignments are 0, 1, 5, 6, 7 and 9. The recombination graph is partitioned into two independent subgraphs, as illustrated in the lower graph in Figure 1. This means a new evaluation function can be constructed:

$$g(x) = c + g_1(x_5, x_7, x_9) + g_2(x_0, x_1, x_6)$$

For any string that resides in the subspace **000***0*, $f(x) = g(x)$, therefore $g(x)$ can be used to evaluate any offspring produced from the parent strings using partition crossover. Furthermore, in the example shown here, all offspring that are produced by partition crossover must also be locally optimal for the sub-functions g_1 and g_2.

In general, for every subgraph in the recombination graph, there will exist a sub-function g_i and every offspring generated by partition crossover will be locally optimal with respect to every sub-function g_i. In most cases, the offspring will also be locally optimal in the full search space. If the offspring is not a local optima in the full search space, the offspring can only be improved by first flipping one of the bits that was shared in common by the parents (meaning that one cannot flip any bit evaluated by a sub-functions g_i to obtain an improvement.)

4. CROSSOVER NETWORKS (XLON)

In order to produce the crossover networks, PX is applied to solutions that are locally optimal. To find a useful recombination graph, two parent solutions must share a significant number of bits in common. Random solutions tend to have fewer bits in common compared to parents that are local optima. Partition crossover is both deterministic and greedy. Given two parents, it deterministically generates the recombination graph, and then greedily returns the best possible partial solution for every sub-function g_i. In some cases, the best possible offspring is one of the parents.

In the XLON model, the nodes will be the set of all local optima in the landscape with respect to a given neighbourhood. As neighbourhoods, we will consider the Hamming distance 1 and 2 neighbourhoods (i.e., 1-flip and 2-flip). Directed edges will go from parents to their offspring using partition crossover. Formal definitions and the algorithmic procedure to construct the networks are detailed below.

4.1 Definitions

A fitness landscape [14] is a triplet $(S, \mathcal{N}, f)$ where S is a set of potential solutions i.e., a search space, $\mathcal{N} : S \longrightarrow 2^S$, a neighbourhood structure, is a function that assigns to every $s \in S$ a set of neighbours $\mathcal{N}(s)$, and $f : S \longrightarrow \mathbb{R}$ is a fitness function that can be pictured as the *height* of the corresponding solutions.

In our study, the search space is $\mathbb{B}^N$, i.e. the space of binary strings of length N, so its size is 2^N. As neighbourhoods, we consider the Hamming distance 1 and 2 neighbourhoods, that is, the set of all solutions at most Hamming distance 1 or 2, respectively from the current solution.

Vertices (V): Is the set of local optima in the search space. A local optimum, which is taken to be a maximum here, is a solution s' such that $\forall s \in \mathcal{N}$, $f(s) \leq f(s')$. Local optima are exhaustively obtained with Algorithm 1.

PX Edges (E_{PX}): Is the set of directed edges between parents and offspring after partition crossover. Specifically, there is an edge $e_{x,z}$ between local optima x and z in V if x is member of a crossover pair producing z. Either z is a local optimum directly after applying crossover, or it is the result of improving the offspring with a next improvement hill-climber. Multiple edges are possible between a pair of vertices (x, z) when z is produced by more than one crossover pair involving x. Partition crossover is not always possible, that is, for some pairs of local optima no new offspring is produced and the operator returns the best parent. This can happen for two reasons. (i) There is no partition of the VIG (Figure 1) for a pair of parents. (ii) Recombination is possible, but one of the two parents is better than any offspring. These unsuccessful pairings are not captured in the network-based model; there are no self-loops in the network.

Crossover Local Optima Network ($XLON$): Is the graph $XLON = G(V, E_{PX})$ where nodes are the local optima V, and edges E_{PX} link parents to offspring after partition crossover. The network is directed, without self-loops, and can have multiple edges.

4.2 Construction

The construction of the crossover networks proceeds in two steps: (i) all the vertices (i.e., the set V of local optima) are identified, (ii) all the pairs of local optima are recombined with partition crossover. That is, if $nv = |V|$ is the number of vertices, all the $nv \times (nv - 1)/2$ pairs are considered. If the resulting offspring after crossover is not one of the parents, then two directed edges are added to the network, both ending in the resulting local optimum and starting from each of the parents. Most successful crossover pairs produce local optima (between 70% and 90% in our study, as can be seen in rows named p_{px} in Table 2). To further increase the number of local optima an efficient deterministic next-ascent hill climber is started from the non-optima offspring.

4.2.1 Local optima identification

In order to efficiently identify all the local optima in the search space we use the concept of *Score* as defined in [3]. We will use $S_i(x)$ to denote the change in the objective function when we move from solution x to the one obtained from x by flipping the i-th bit. Formally:

$$S_i(x) = f(x \oplus 1_i) - f(x), \quad (3)$$

where $\oplus$ denotes the exclusive OR bitwise operation and 1_i denotes a binary string with 1 in the i-th bit and 0 in the other bits. A solution x will be a local optimum if there is no Score $S_i(x)$ greater than zero (we are maximising). Algorithm 1 describes this procedure.

Algorithm 1 Identification of local optima (V)

Output: V (set of local optima)
$V \leftarrow \emptyset$
for $x \in \mathbb{B}^n$ **do**
  if $S_i(x) \leq 0$ for all $1 \leq i \leq n$ **then**
    $V \leftarrow V \cup \{x\}$
  end if
end for

Two aspects of the implementation of Algorithm 1 make it very efficient. First, the Scores are computed from scratch only for the first solution, and thereafter, they are stored in a vector and updated incrementally. Second, solutions are explored following a Gray code order; the move from one solution to the next in the sequence flips only a single bit. Under this scenario, we can use the algorithms proposed by Chicano *et al.* [3], Whitley and Chen [18] or Chen *et al.* [2] to update the Score vector in constant time for pseudo-Boolean problems with bounded epistasis. Thus, the complexity of running Algorithm 1 in an NK landscape is $O(2^N)$, proportional to the size of the search space. It is worth mentioning that these speed ups allow the exhaustive exploration of larger landscapes than was possible before. Our study considers N values up to 30, while a maximum of $N = 18$ was considered in previous mutation based local optima network studies for NK landscapes [13, 17].

4.2.2 Network construction

Once all the local optima are identified, the edges are computed following Algorithm 2, which uses the partition crossover proposed by Tinós *et al.* [15], and the next improvement deterministic hill-climber proposed by Chicano *et al.* [3]. Two local optima x and z are connected by an edge $e_{x,z}$ if z can be obtained from x by applying partition crossover to x and another solution y and then running the hill-climber to reach z.

Algorithm 2 Network construction

```
Input: V
Output: XLON = G(V, E_PX)
for {x,y} ⊆ V do {All pairs of local optima}
    w ← PartitionCrossover(x,y)
    z ← HillClimber (w)
    if z ≠ x and z ≠ y then
        E_PX ← E_PX ∪ {(x,z),(y,z)}
    end if
end for
```

5. NETWORK ANALYSIS

Our study considers both random and adjacent NKq landscapes. Random NKq landscapes are NP-hard problems. However, the adjacent NK landscapes can be solved to optimality in polynomial time. In the adjacent NK landscapes, two adjacent sub-functions, f_i and f_{i+1} share $k - 1 = K$ variables.

NKq landscapes were generated for values of $q = 100$, $K \in \{2, 3\}$, and $N \in \{20, 25, 30\}$. In addition, Hamming distance neighbourhoods of size $r \in \{1, 2\}$ were considered. When $r = 1$ the neighbourhood is the standard bit flip neighbourhood. Up to two bits are flipped when $r = 2$, yielding the Hamming distance 2 neighbourhood. Since the local optima networks with $r = 2$ were small and very sparsely connected, most of the network analysis is done for $r = 1$. $N = 20$ still allows easy visual inspection, and 30 is (approximately) the maximum size for which the networks can be extracted in reasonable time. K values of 2 and 3 produced networks which are not too sparse and have a small number of connected components. Larger values of K produced sparsely connected networks, specially for the random model, which indicates that finding successful partition crossover pairs (i.e., pairs producing offspring different than their parents) is harder as K increases.

A first approach to analyse the structure of a network is often to visualise it. Software for analysing and visualising networks is currently available in various languages and environments. Here we use the R statistical language together with the igraph package [4]. Figure 2 illustrates two examples of local optima networks for the studied NKq landscapes with $r = 1$ and adjacent (left plot) and random interaction (right plot). Nodes are local optima, their area is proportional to fitness and the global optimum is highlighted in red (darker color). Edges link parents to offspring after partition crossover. Dark (black) edges indicate those cases where the result of crossover was not a local optimum and thus required improvement with hill-climbing. Notice that this only happens in few cases. Our statistical analysis revealed than 70% to 90% of the edges represent local optima obtained directly after partition crossover, with the percentage being higher for the adjacent model (rows named p_{px} in Table 2).

The networks in Figure 2 illustrate a marked difference we observed between the random and adjacent NK models. Networks for the adjacent model have on average a larger number of nodes under the Hamming distance 1 neighbourhood ($r = 1$), are densely connected and feature a single or a very small number of connected components. On the other hand, networks for the random model have on average fewer nodes, tend to be sparser, and decompose into several clusters.

Visualisation is only useful for small networks, we therefore turn to the statistical analysis of larger networks. Since the mid-1990s, there has been an explosion of interest in networks and network-based approaches to the modelling and analysis of complex systems. Among the many features and metrics that can be collected from complex networks [9], we selected only a few after some preliminary experiments, including those that better distinguish among the landscape classes, and intuitively may impact the dynamic of search (Table 1).

Table 1: Selected metrics.

nv	Number of vertices (local optima).
ne	Number of edges.
$\bar{f}$	Average fitness of local optima.
nc	Number of connected components (or clusters).
$\bar{\delta}$	Average in-degree (incoming edges).
p_{px}	Proportion of edges where the offspring was a local optimum immediately after PX.

For each landscape parameter set 30 instances were generated (with different random seeds) and their recombination local optima networks extracted following the procedure described in Section 4.2. Table 2 summarises the network metrics as mean and standard deviation values ($\bar{X}_\sigma$) on the select sets of landscape parameters (i.e., $N \in \{20, 25, 30\}$, $K \in \{2, 3\}$, and $q = 100$) and the two interaction models: adjacent and random. The first half of the table shows the landscapes for $K = 2$, while the bottom half those with $K = 3$. The top part of each half of Table 2 shows the metrics for a Hamming neighbourhood of radius $r = 1$, while the bottom part for $r = 2$. For $r = 2$ only the 3 most basic network metrics, namely number of nodes and edges (nv, ne) and the average fitness of local optima, are shown as these are small and sparse networks.

As expected, for a fixed K the number of local optima (nv) increases steadily with increasing N. Similarly, for a fixed N, the number of local optima increases rapidly with increasing K. What is surprising is that the number of local optima is consistently (i.e., for all landscape parameters) larger for the adjacent model as compared to the random model for a Hamming distance 1 neighbourhood. To the best of our knowledge this has not been reported before.

The box plots in Figure 3 show the distribution of the number of local optima across the 30 instances for a selected landscape class, namely $N = 20, K = 3$. Each plot reports the two models (adjacent and random). The top plot refers

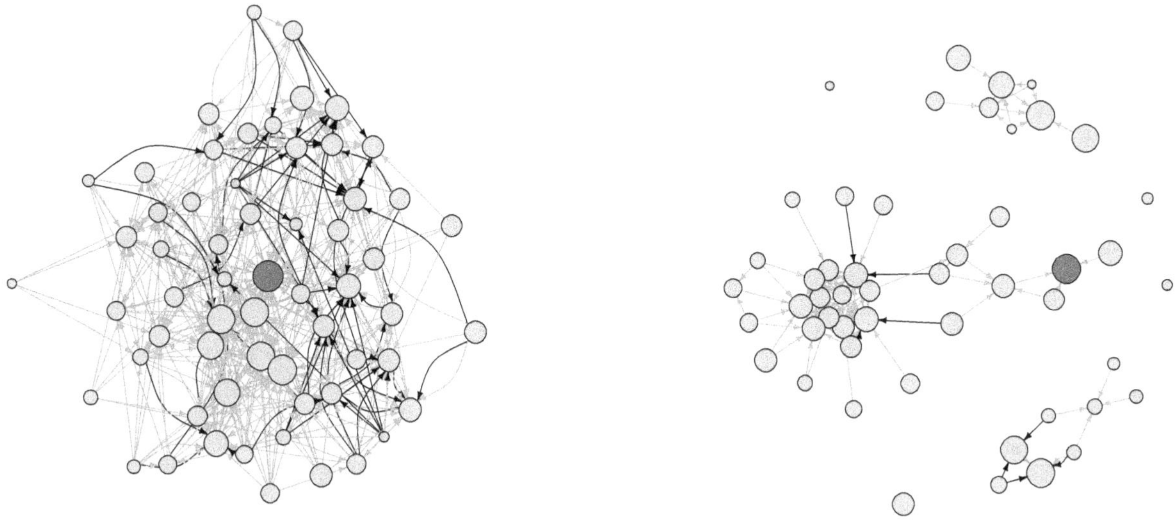

Figure 2: PX local optima networks for two selected instances with values $N = 20$, $K = 2$, $q = 100$. Nodes are local optima and edges connect parents to offspring after partition crossover (black edges indicate PX followed by hill-climbing). Vertex area is proportional to their fitness and the global optimum is highlighted in red (darker color). Left: Adjacent model, the network has 60 nodes and features a single connected component. Right: Random model, the network has 50 nodes (local optima) and features 7 connected components, 4 of which are isolated nodes.

to the Hamming distance 1 neighbourhoods ($r = 1$) and the bottom plot to distance 2 ($r = 2$). The number of local optima is substantially lower for $r = 2$, but their average fitness is higher as can be seen in Table 2 (rows $\bar{f}$ and $\bar{f}_{r=2}$).

The number of local optima is often considered to correlate with problem difficulty. However, this is not necessarily the case as our results indicate. The number of local optima is higher for the adjacent model and the distance 1 neighbourhood (Figure 3, top plot). But we know that: (i) the adjacent NK landscapes admit a polynomial time solution; (ii) empirical results indicate that a simple GA using partition crossover can easily find the global optimum for adjacent NK landscapes [15]. This is also confirmed by the experiments reported in section 6. Furthermore, when a Hamming distance 2 neighbourhood ($r = 2$) is used on exactly the same problems, there are more local optima for the random NK landscapes when $r = 2$ (Figure 3, bottom plot). Thus, while the adjacent NK landscapes yield more local optima for $r = 1$, most of these are "weak" local optima and disappear when $r = 2$.

The number of edges also clearly separates the adjacent from the random model. Networks are more densely connected for the adjacent model, which indicates a larger number of successful crossover pairs in this case. For $r = 2$, networks are sparsely connected (have a low number of edges), specially for the random model. The remaining 3 network features, number of components (nc), average in-degree ($\bar{\delta}$) and proportion of crossover pairs producing local optima (p_{px}), were only computed for $r = 1$. These metrics also clearly separate the two landscape models.

On one hand, the adjacent model shows an average number of components very close to one or even exactly one (i.e., a single connected component) for the larger networks ($N \in \{25, 30\}, K = 3$), and a noticeable higher average in-degree ($\bar{\delta}$), indicating that each node is produced by a larger number of crossover pairs. For both values of K the proportion of edges directly producing local optima after crossover (p_{px}) is higher. On the other hand, the random model reveals a much higher number of connected components, close to 100 on average for the landscapes with $K = 3$; and the in-degrees ($\bar{\delta}$) are around an order of magnitude lower as compared to those for the respective adjacent landscapes. For both values of K the proportion of edges directly producing local optima after crossover (p_{px}) is lower.

Our analysis suggests that the adjacent model is easier to solve by a PX-based GA as compared to the random model, despite the former producing a larger number of local optima on average. We hypothesise that search difficulty for a PX-based algorithm on the random model is related to the decomposition of the network into clusters and the low average in-degree.

6. ALGORITHM PERFORMANCE

An empirical study was conducted on the largest instances used in the network analysis, i.e., with $N = 30$, the two values of $K \in \{2, 3\}$ and the two landscape models. The hybrid genetic algorithm using partition crossover implemented in [15] was used. This implementation applies bit-flip local search with first improvement to random solutions in order to generate the initial population. Elitism is used to preserve

Table 2: Network metrics (as described in Table 1) for both random and adjacent NKq landscapes with $N \in \{20, 25, 30\}$ and $q = 100$. Top: $K = 2$. Bottom: $K = 3$. For each set of landscape parameters, results are mean and standard deviations ($\bar{X}_\sigma$) of 30 networks produced with different random seeds. Unless otherwise stated metrics refer to local optima networks with a Hamming distance neighbourhood $r = 1$.

	$N=20$		$N=25$		$N=30$	
	Adjacent	*Random*	*Adjacent*	*Random*	*Adjacent*	*Random*
$K=2$						
nv	$69.87_{32.61}$	$58.30_{27.30}$	$216.40_{120.86}$	$166.53_{98.53}$	$705.87_{545.48}$	$448.53_{254.65}$
ne	$688.83_{556.39}$	$179.73_{206.19}$	$6869.47_{7291.94}$	$1950.50_{2473.02}$	$80106.23_{139938.45}$	$12683.70_{13913.89}$
$\bar{f}$	$1363.88_{47.95}$	$1352.47_{46.60}$	$1701.84_{55.19}$	$1680.77_{72.68}$	$2045.08_{58.09}$	$2033.94_{82.76}$
nc	$1.47_{0.68}$	$8.40_{5.61}$	$1.60_{0.50}$	$4.90_{3.12}$	$1.43_{0.50}$	$2.57_{2.08}$
$\bar{\delta}$	$8.36_{3.54}$	$2.46_{1.73}$	$25.24_{12.30}$	$8.64_{6.26}$	$75.53_{51.18}$	$21.37_{13.80}$
p_{px}	$0.87_{0.08}$	$0.81_{0.13}$	$0.90_{0.07}$	$0.80_{0.11}$	$0.88_{0.08}$	$0.77_{0.08}$
$nv_{r=2}$	$6.20_{3.43}$	$6.97_{2.86}$	$10.57_{7.99}$	$13.60_{6.91}$	$14.70_{10.63}$	$23.57_{15.01}$
$ne_{r=2}$	$5.00_{6.90}$	$0.87_{2.40}$	$23.57_{43.88}$	$4.60_{7.39}$	$47.43_{63.44}$	$21.23_{34.04}$
$\bar{f}_{r=2}$	$1450.73_{68.80}$	$1419.58_{59.02}$	$1805.54_{69.20}$	$1764.67_{78.27}$	$2173.37_{62.41}$	$2129.01_{91.14}$
$K=3$						
nv	$265.20_{86.40}$	$171.53_{350.78}$	$1105.97_{505.38}$	$648.33_{172.17}$	$4386.40_{2274.61}$	$2452.20_{803.55}$
ne	$3730.63_{2088.81}$	$154.80_{146.32}$	$77707.70_{69844.47}$	$2176.80_{2519.51}$	$1321295.27_{1298347.89}$	$27912.10_{28985.72}$
$\bar{f}$	$1346.84_{36.88}$	$1341.50_{39.92}$	$1676.01_{43.18}$	$1670.23_{41.44}$	$2004.21_{44.46}$	$2002.88_{44.95}$
nc	$1.90_{0.10}$	$88.50_{24.95}$	$1.17_{0.38}$	$111.53_{55.92}$	$1.10_{0.31}$	$83.37_{58.24}$
$\bar{\delta}$	$12.96_{3.88}$	$0.80_{0.61}$	$60.13_{23.23}$	$3.10_{2.65}$	$245.87_{111.32}$	$10.42_{7.21}$
p_{px}	$0.81_{0.07}$	$0.74_{0.12}$	$0.80_{0.06}$	$0.69_{0.09}$	$0.79_{0.05}$	$0.68_{0.07}$
$nv_{r=2}$	$15.90_{5.78}$	$23.10_{7.05}$	$36.80_{15.74}$	$53.67_{13.49}$	$67.87_{39.60}$	$128.67_{46.54}$
$ne_{r=2}$	$11.83_{9.63}$	$0.30_{1.02}$	$120.20_{93.54}$	$8.80_{17.23}$	$514.33_{523.32}$	$57.07_{146.34}$
$\bar{f}_{r=2}$	$1450.55_{47.64}$	$1411.43_{46.77}$	$1795.34_{55.11}$	$1761.92_{42.94}$	$2154.87_{55.59}$	$2111.62_{52.77}$

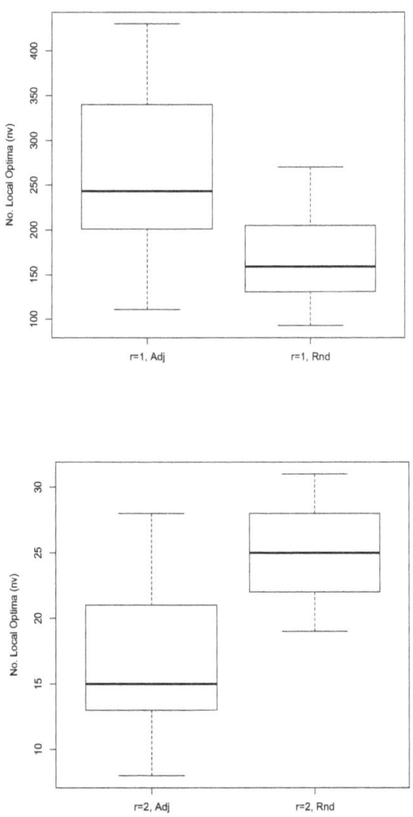

Figure 3: Distribution of the number of local optima for NKq landscapes with $N = 20, K = 3$, and Hamming distance neighborhoods $r \in \{1, 2\}$

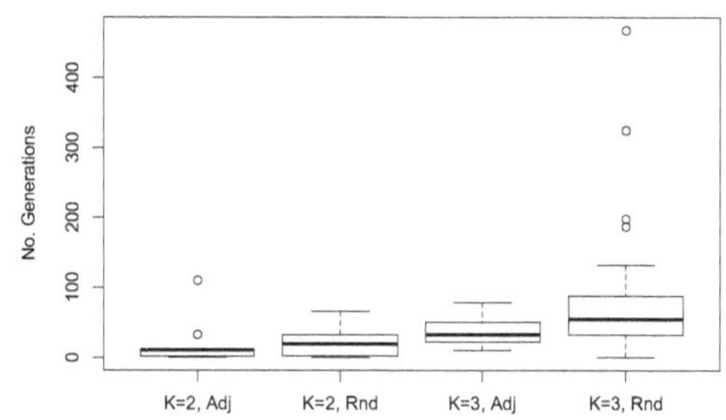

Figure 4: Distribution of the number of generations to find the global optima for a hybrid GA ruling on NKq landscapes with $N = 30$, $K \in \{2, 3\}$ and the two epistatic models.

the current best solution, while binary tournament selection is used to select parents for crossover and mutation. The population size was set to 10 individuals, given the small search spaces.

Instances are small and the global optimum was quickly found in all of them. Therefore, performance differences among landscape classes were not easy to assess. Figure 4 shows box-plots with the distribution of the number of generations before finding the global optimum when running the hybrid GA on the four landscape classes indicated. The values summarise the medians of 50 runs on each of the 30 instances for each landscape class. The number of generations to find the optimum is shorter for the adjacent model as compared to the random model (for both values of K), despite the former having a larger number of local optima.

7. CONCLUSIONS

We defined and analysed local optima networks with edges based on the recently proposed partition crossover for pseudo-Boolean optimisation, using the NKq landscape as a case study. Our network analysis revealed that for fixed N and K parameters and the 1-flip neighbourhood, the adjacent epistatic model produces much larger networks (i.e., with a larger number of local optima) as compared with the random model. It is well known that the adjacent model is easier to solve, which indicates that the number of local optima in a landscape is not necessarily a reliable indicator of difficulty. Our study of networks with Hamming distance 2 neighbourhood ($r = 2$) revealed that this reverses, i.e., the number of local optima for the random model is higher than for the adjacent model. Thus, while the adjacent NK landscapes yield more local optima for $r = 1$, most of these are "weak" local optima and disappear when $r = 2$.

The empirical results also show that the crossover networks for the random model are more sparsely connected than for the adjacent model. This means partition crossover does not as easily move between all local optima on random NK landscapes.

Future work will study crossover local optima networks for larger instances (by adequate sampling of the search space) and other combinatorial optimisation problems. The ultimate goal is to have a deeper understanding of the topological features of combinatorial search spaces over different search operators, which can help to predict performance and improve the design of heuristic search algorithms.

Acknowledgments

G. Ochoa acknowledges funding from the Engineering and Physical Sciences Research Council, UK (EPSRC) grant number EP/J017515. F. Chicano acknowledges funding from project number 8.06/5.47.4142 in collaboration with the VSB Technical University of Ostrava, UMA/FEDER FC14-TIC36, Universidad de Málaga, Campus de Excelencia Internacional Andalucía Tech and the Spanish Ministry of Education (grant CAS12/00274).

8. REFERENCES

[1] E. Boros and P. L. Hammer. Pseudo-boolean optimization. *Discrete Applied Mathematics*, 123(1-3):155 – 225, 2002.

[2] W. Chen, D. Whitley, D. Hains, and A. Howe. Second order partial derivatives for NK-landscapes. In *Genetic and Evolutionary Computation Conference (GECCO)*, pages 503–510, New York, NY, USA, 2013. ACM.

[3] F. Chicano, D. Whitley, and A. M. Sutton. Efficient identification of improving moves in a ball for pseudo-boolean problems. In *Genetic and Evolutionary Computation Conference (GECCO)*, pages 437–444. ACM, 2014.

[4] G. Csardi and T. Nepusz. The igraph software package for complex network research. *InterJournal*, Complex Systems:1695, 2006.

[5] F. Daolio, S. Verel, G. Ochoa, and M. Tomassini. Local optima networks of the quadratic assignment problem. In *Proceedings of the IEEE Congress on Evolutionary Computation, CEC 2010*, pages 1–8. IEEE Press, 2010.

[6] J. P. K. Doye. The network topology of a potential energy landscape: a static scale-free network. *Physical Review Letter*, 88:238701, 2002.

[7] F. Glover. Future paths for integer programming and links to artificial intelligence. *Computers and Operations Research*, 13(5):533 – 549, 1986.

[8] S. Kauffman and S. Levin. Towards a general theory of adaptive walks on rugged landscapes. *Journal of Theoretical Biology*, 128:11–45, 1987.

[9] M. E. J. Newman. The structure and function of complex networks. *SIAM Review*, 45:167–256, 2003.

[10] M. E. J. Newman. *Networks: An Introduction.* Oxford University Press, Oxford, UK, 2010.

[11] M. E. J. Newman and R. Engelhardt. Effect of neutral selection on the evolution of molecular species. *Proc. R. Soc. London B*, pages 1333–1338, 1998.

[12] G. Ochoa, M. Tomassini, S. Verel, and C. Darabos. A study of NK landscapes' basins and local optima networks. In *Proceedings of the Genetic and Evolutionary Computation Conference, GECCO 2008*, pages 555–562. ACM, 2008.

[13] G. Ochoa, S. Verel, F. Daolio, and M. Tomassini. Local optima networks: A new model of combinatorial fitness landscapes. In H. Richter and A. Engelbrecht, editors, *Recent Advances in the Theory and Application of Fitness Landscapes*, volume 6 of *Emergence, Complexity and Computation*, pages 233–262. Springer Berlin Heidelberg, 2014.

[14] P. Stadler. Fitness landscapes. *Biological evolution and statistical physics*, pages 183–204, 2002.

[15] R. Tinós, D. Whitley, and F. Chicano. Partition crossover for pseudo-boolean optimization. In *Proceedings of FOGA*, 2015. (to appear).

[16] M. Tomassini, S. Verel, and G. Ochoa. Complex-network analysis of combinatorial spaces: The NK landscape case. *Physical Revview E*, 78(6):066114, 2008.

[17] S. Verel, G. Ochoa, and M. Tomassini. Local optima networks of NK landscapes with neutrality. *IEEE Transactions on Evolutionary Computation*, 15(6):783–797, 2011.

[18] D. Whitley and W. Chen. Constant time steepest descent local search with lookahead for NK-landscapes and MAX-kSAT. In *Genetic and Evolutionary Computation Conference (GECCO)*, pages 1357–1364, 2012.

[19] D. Whitley and A. Hains, D.and Howe. Tunneling between optima: partition crossover for the TSP. In *Proc. of GECCO'09*, pages 915–922, 2009.

Fighting the Symmetries: The Structure of Cryptographic Boolean Function Spaces

Stjepan Picek
Faculty of Electrical Engineering and Computing
University of Zagreb, Croatia
stjepan@computer.org

R. I. (Bob) McKay
Comp. Sci. & Eng.
Seoul National University, Korea and Australian National University, Australia
rimsnucse@gmail.com

Roberto Santana
Comp. Sci. & Artif. Intell.
U. of the Basque Country
San Sebastian, Spain
roberto.santana@ehu.es

Tom D. Gedeon
Comp. Sci.
Australian National University
Canberra, Australia
tom@cs.anu.edu.au

ABSTRACT

We explore the problem space of maximum nonlinearity problems for balanced Boolean functions, examining the symmetry structure and fitness landscapes in the most common (bit string) representation. We present theoretical analyses of well understood aspects, together with detailed enumeration of the 4-bit problem, sampling of the 6-bit problem based on known optima, and sampling of the 8-bit problem based on its fittest known solutions.

We show that these problems have many more symmetries than is generally noted, with implications for crossover and for distributional methods. We explore the large-scale plateau structure of the problem, with similar implications for local search. We show that symmetries yield additional information that may yield more effective search methods.

Categories and Subject Descriptors

I.2.8 [**Computing Methodologies**]: Artificial Intelligence—*Problem Solving, Control Methods, and Search*

Keywords

Evolutionary Computation; Cryptographic Boolean Function; Fitness Landscape; Symmetry

1. INTRODUCTION

Boolean functions possessing good cryptographic properties are a key resource for information security – the difficulty is to find them. While finding a function that satisfies only a single property is not so difficult, finding a function that satisfies several properties can pose a challenging task requiring search. To date, the success of search methods in cryptography has been more limited than we might wish.

We consider the problem of maximizing nonlinearity of balanced Boolean functions (BN). It has known optimal solutions for 4- and 6-argument problems; the 8-argument problem has a proven upper bound for nonlinearity of 118 [2]. It is believed to be achievable, but the best found so far is 116 [13]. BN is among the simplest of the Boolean cryptographic problems, most others being refinements imposing further restrictions on the acceptable functions; thus, improved methods should extend to a wide range of problems.

We analyze two difficulties of the most common (bit string) representation. We present a fairly classical fitness landscape analysis, supplementing it with an analysis of the symmetries of the space, revealing additional structure and showing how it may be useful for search. Better understanding should lead either to better representations, or to better evolutionary operators within the bit string representation. We partially analyze the difficulties theoretically, and extend this by empirical analysis. The 4-argument problem is small enough to be exhaustively enumerated, but is very different from higher-order problems, yielding limited illumination (almost all functions are optimal, with very small regions of sub-optimal solutions, whereas by the time one comes to 8-argument functions optima are vanishingly rare). Thus we also stochastically sample regions of the 6-argument problem based on known optima, and sample regions of the 8-argument problem based on known high-fitness regions.

We emphasize that we are not studying the bit string representation as the "right" representation for search – our analysis shows that it has substantial problems for search. However it is the representation in which the problem is naturally defined – and is therefore simple to analyze. Any other representation should cover this space to guarantee that it does not exclude optima, so analyses in this representation can help to illuminate others as well. This deeper analysis will support a more structured search for better representations and operators that may allow us to extend to substantially larger functions. Many of the issues we identify here, especially of symmetries, are equally present in other representations – just more deeply hidden.

We next present background on the search problem, on

GECCO '15, July 11 - 15, 2015, Madrid, Spain
 ISBN 978-1-4503-3472-3/15/07...$15.00
DOI: http://dx.doi.org/10.1145/2739480.2754739

symmetry operators in Boolean function spaces, and on symmetries and fitness landscapes in evolutionary computation (Section 2). We then present a theoretical analysis of the problem (Section 3), emphasizing the symmetry structure, and extending with some basic observations on the fitness landscape. A brief description of a complete sampling of the 4-argument function space follows in Section 4, followed by a detailed comparison of random samples from the 6-argument space with "known-good" samples from shortest paths to known optima (Section 5). Section 6 repeats this analysis with 8-argument functions, but (since optima of this problem are currently not known) use examples of the next highest fitness level as surrogates. We sum up the knowledge gained from this research, and discuss how it may be applied, in Section 7.

2. BACKGROUND

2.1 Boolean Cryptographic Functions

We first introduce our notational conventions. The inner product of two vectors $\vec{x}$ and $\vec{y}$, denoted as $\vec{x} \cdot \vec{y}$, is defined as $\vec{x} \cdot \vec{y} = \oplus_{i=1}^{n} x_i y_i$. "$\oplus$" represents addition modulo 2 (logical XOR). The set of all n-tuples over the field $\mathbb{F}_2$ is denoted by $\mathbb{F}_2^n$, where $\mathbb{F}_2$ is the Galois field of two elements. A Boolean function of n arguments is any function $f : \mathbb{F}_2^n \rightarrow \mathbb{F}_2$. The Hamming weight (HW) of a vector $\vec{x} \in \mathbb{F}_2^n$, is the number of non-zero positions in the vector.

A Boolean function f on $\mathbb{F}_2^n$ can be uniquely represented by its truth table, a vector $(f(\vec{0}), ..., f(\vec{1}))$ containing the values of f, over its lexicographically ordered arguments [2].

The Walsh transform W_f is a Boolean analogue of the Fourier transform, and like it uniquely represents each function; its components measure the correlation between $f(\vec{x})$ and the linear functions $\vec{a} \cdot \vec{x}$ [2]. It can be written as

$$W_f(\vec{a}) = \sum_{\vec{x} \in \mathbb{F}_2^n} (-1)^{f(\vec{x}) \oplus \vec{a} \cdot \vec{x}}. \qquad (1)$$

A **balanced** Boolean function $bal(f)$ has Hamming weight 2^{n-1} [2]. The **nonlinearity** $nonlin(f)$ of a Boolean function f can be expressed in terms of the Walsh coefficients [2]:

$$nonlin(f) = 2^{n-1} - \frac{1}{2} max_{\vec{a} \in \mathbb{F}_2^n} |W_f(\vec{a})|. \qquad (2)$$

Sarkar and Maitra [19] derived a bound for nonlinearity of Boolean functions; for the special case of balanced functions with even number of inputs, it has the form

$$nonlin(f) \leq 2^{n-1} - 2^{\frac{n}{2}-1} - 2^{t+1}, \qquad (3)$$

for $n = 8$ and $t = 0$ this gives an upper bound of 118. Here, t represents the correlation immunity value [19].

For further details about Boolean functions and their cryptographic properties, we refer readers to [2].

2.2 Boolean Function Space Operators

In studying Boolean functions for circuit design, Slepian [21] introduced two operators (argument permutation and negation) which are symmetries on the space, relating them to Todd's earlier study [22] of the symmetry groups of regular polytopes. Golomb [5] extended them with a third symmetry (result complementation), and further studied the resulting symmetry group. Edwards [3] studied these operators in the context of hardware synthesis, extending them with a further two operators (argument XOR and result XOR), also both symmetries and thus of relevance to our work. All except result XOR preserve the properties defining the BN problem, and thus are symmetries, not merely of the space, but of the problem.

2.3 Symmetries in Stochastic Search

Symmetric fitness landscapes have long been seen as difficult for evolutionary algorithms (EAs), because of the confusion they induce. There are two main effects:

1. The assumption underlying crossover is that the regions between fit instances are more likely to contain fitter instances. Symmetries imply multiple regions of equivalent fitness, undermining this justification. For the vast number of symmetries in Boolean cryptographic function spaces, stochastic symmetry breaking is unlikely to ameliorate this.

2. Naudts, van HoyWeghen and colleagues have noted [14, 24] that for value symmetries, in specific types of problem spaces (decomposable over neighborhoods), different regions can converge to incompatible neighborhood optima, leading to deep local optima in the global fitness landscape.

More recently, Santana et al. [18] showed that suitably structured algorithms can take advantage of other kinds of symmetries (variable symmetries) to reduce problem difficulty. The five classes of symmetries mentioned earlier generate a huge number of symmetries in the balanced nonlinearity fitness landscape; since all but one generator are variable symmetries, so there is some hope for progress. Even the lone value symmetry may not pose as severe a problem as it does in Ising problems, because the fitness function for balanced nonlinearity is not obviously decomposable, so the symmetries may not generate deep local optima.

More generally, symmetry breaking has been studied in some detail in local search methods; Prestwich and Roli [17] presents a useful way into this literature.

2.4 Fitness Landscape Analysis

Fitness landscape analysis has been a useful tool to investigate different facets of problem difficulty for EAs. We use concepts from fitness landscape analysis to study the defining characteristics of fitness landscapes in the BN problem and the role of symmetries. We briefly review some relevant results.

For a given fitness function $f : E \rightarrow \mathcal{R}$, a landscape Λ for f can be defined [11] as a triple $\Lambda = (E, f, d)$ where $d : E \times E \rightarrow \mathcal{R} \cup \{\infty\}$ for which is required that: i) $d(\mathbf{s}, \mathbf{t}) \geq 0$, ii) $d(\mathbf{s}, \mathbf{t}) \Leftrightarrow \mathbf{s} = \mathbf{t}$, iii) $d(\mathbf{s}, \mathbf{u}) \leq d(\mathbf{s}, \mathbf{t}) + d(\mathbf{t}, \mathbf{u})$. A neighborhood relation in E can be defined in terms of the distance d, as $\mathbf{t} \in N(\mathbf{s}) \Leftrightarrow d(\mathbf{s}, \mathbf{t}) = 1$.

Issues addressed by fitness landscape analysis include:

- Identifying criteria describing the landscape complexity (e.g. isolation, multimodality, ruggedness) and measures to quantify search difficulty for EAs [7, 8, 9, 11].

- Parameterized fitness landscape models [1, 4, 6].

- Topological analysis of neighborhood connectivity of the landscape [15, 23, 26].

Several measures to quantify search difficulty have been proposed [7, 8, 10], aiming to predict the behavior of EAs. However, our survey of this area did not reveal any similar metrics for the amount of symmetry or its impact on search. In the absence of a deeper characterization, we use the total number of symmetries as a surrogate for the difficulty caused by symmetry. It reflects the symmetry breaking needed for crossover to work as a smooth operator rather than a macro-mutation, and the reduction in search space size to expect from "factoring out" symmetries.

Parameterized fitness landscape models have been extensively investigated in EAs [1, 6, 16, 25], the NK-landscape [12] having been used to study the behavior of many EAs. These studies have usually focused on the role of epistasis in the complexity of a fitness function. NK-landscapes are generated by random sampling of the parameters defining local functions, making the emergence of symmetric relationships between variables unlikely. We have found no reports of parameterized fitness landscape models designed to evaluate the effect of symmetry.

In network characterizations of combinatorial fitness landscapes [15, 23, 25], combinatorial landscapes are viewed as graphs, with each vertex denoting a solution and each edge the effect of an operator. Some properties of the landscape can be extracted from statistical analysis of these networks. A critical question in such analysis is the definition of the neighborhood. Although we do not explicitly conduct a network-based analysis of the Boolean function landscape, we use neighborhoods to analyze the distance between symmetric solutions and the distribution of feasible (balanced) solutions.

We have found few examples of works where the analysis of the fitness landscapes consider the impact and potential use of the symmetries in the problem. One such is [20], where the authors investigate fitness landscapes of dynamical systems aiming at the identification of variable symmetries that serve to propose variable aggregation methods for problem simplification. However, it seems of limited relevance here, as the BN problem is neither dynamic nor decomposable in anything like the required form.

3. THEORETICAL ANALYSIS

3.1 Problem Definition

The requirement is to search the space of balanced Boolean functions of N arguments (represented by the vector of output values ordered lexicographically over the inputs) for a function of maximum nonlinearity. The "balanced" part of the problem definition is a constraint that can be handled either as a sudden-death mechanism or a penalty function (in which case the imbalance is included as part of the fitness function). We formally define the penalty-function method; the mathematics of sudden-death is readily derivable from it. Using the standard notation for the Boolean space as $2 = \{0, 1\}$, the search space is thus the set 2^{2^N}. We analyze using the Manhattan distance δ over the space. We define:

$$\begin{aligned}
\textbf{nonlin}(f) &= \min_{\textbf{affine } f_1 \in 2^{2^N}} \delta(f, f_1) && (4)\\
\textbf{imbal}(f) &= \text{abs}(|x : f(x) = 1| - |x : f(x) = 0|) && (5)\\
&= \min_{\textbf{balanced } f_1 \in 2^{2^N}} 2 \times \delta(f, f_1)\\
\textbf{fit}(f) &= \max_{f \in 2^{2^N}} \{\textbf{nonlin}(f) - \textbf{imbal}(f)\} && (6)
\end{aligned}$$

Although the upper bound of nonlinearity for balanced Boolean functions in 8 variables from equation 3 is 118, the best known value as of January 2015 is 116 [13]. The final solution must satisfy the constraint $\textbf{imbal}(f) = 0$. The search space size for a penalty approach is 2^{2^N} (i.e. for $N = 4, 6, 8$ respectively $2^{16}, 2^{64}, 2^{256}$); for the sudden-death approach (i.e. balanced functions only) it is $C^{2^N}_{2^{N-1}}$ (i.e. approximately $2^{14}, 2^{61}, 2^{252}$, using the notation C^r_n for the binomial coefficient). In the next subsection, we study the numerous known symmetries on this space; among those we describe, there are respectively at least $(2^{14}, 2^{34}, 2^{63})$ and at most $(2^{19}, 2^{41}, 2^{72})$, expected to be nearer the upper end of the range for larger N.[1] There are sufficiently many to have a very substantial impact on the search space. Without careful study, the impact is likely to be negative: crossover may merely randomly jump between symmetry classes, and thus act effectively as a macromutation; with so many symmetry classes, stochastic symmetry breaking is not likely to be completed within reasonable computational time. But it may also be positive: from the perspective of two symmetric individuals in a search using mutation and crossover, the search space looks identical. Hence if we could find a way to search symmetry classes of functions rather than functions themselves, the search complexity may be very substantially reduced. By a symmetry class, we mean a partition of the function space under the equivalence relation induced by the symmetries.

3.2 Symmetries in the Problem Space

3.2.1 Definitions

We define the following second-order functions on the integer space 2^{2^N} (for any permutation $\pi : N \to N$, $f \in 2^{2^N}$, $i \in N$, and all $\vec{x} \in 2^N$):

$$\begin{aligned}
\sigma_\pi : 2^{2^N} \to 2^{2^N} &: & \sigma_\pi(f)(\vec{x}) &= f(\pi(\vec{x})) && (7)\\
\sigma_{\neg x_i} : 2^{2^N} \to 2^{2^N} &: & \sigma_{\neg x_i}(f)(\vec{x}) &= f(\vec{x}_{\neg i}) && (8)\\
\sigma_{\neg y} : 2^{2^N} \to 2^{2^N} &: & \sigma_{\neg y}(f)(\vec{x}) &= \neg f(\vec{x}) && (9)\\
\sigma_{x_i \oplus = x_j} : 2^{2^N} \to 2^{2^N} &: & \sigma_{x_i \oplus = x_j}(f)(\vec{x}) &= f(\vec{x}_{i \oplus = j}) && (10)\\
\sigma_{y \oplus = x_i} : 2^{2^N} \to 2^{2^N} &: & \sigma_{y \oplus = x_i}(f)(\vec{x}) &= f(\vec{x}) \oplus x_i && (11)
\end{aligned}$$

where $\vec{x}_{i \oplus = j}$ denotes $\vec{x}$ with x_i replaced by $x_i \oplus x_j$ and $\vec{x}_{\neg i}$ denotes $\vec{x}$ with x_i negated.

[1]The total number of symmetries on any set of size S is 2^S; we are restricting the symmetries by invariance requirements (balance, distance), reducing the total – but not necessarily to less than S. However, the maximum symmetry class size under the combination of all permitted symmetries is, of course, bounded above by S.

3.2.2 Symmetry Properties

PROPOSITION 3.1. *All σ_π, $\sigma_{\neg x_i}$, $\sigma_{\neg y}$, $\sigma_{x_i \oplus = x_j}$ and $\sigma_{y \oplus = x_i}$ are bijections.*

PROOF. *$\sigma_{\neg x_i}$, $\sigma_{\neg y}$, $\sigma_{x_i \oplus = x_j}$ and $\sigma_{y \oplus = x_i}$ are idempotent, while $\sigma_\pi^{-1}(f)(\vec{x}) = f(\pi^{-1}(\vec{x}))$.* □

They thus generate a subgroup of the full symmetry group $\mathfrak{S}_{2^{2^N}}$ on 2^{2^N} symbols. However, as we shall see later, $\sigma_{y \oplus = x_i}$ does not preserve balance, so we are most interested in the subgroup $\mathfrak{B}_N$ generated by σ_π, $\sigma_{\neg x_i}$, $\sigma_{\neg y}$ and $\sigma_{x_i \oplus = x_j}$. Elements in the subgroup generated by σ_π, $\sigma_{\neg x_i}$ and $\sigma_{\neg y}$ can be uniquely represented in the form $\sigma_\pi \circ \sigma_{\neg x_{i_1}} \circ \ldots \circ \circ \sigma_{\neg x_{i_1}} \circ \sigma_{\neg y}$, and hence $|\mathfrak{B}_N|$ is at least $2^{N+1} \times N!$. Strictly, the σ_π are superfluous among the generators, since they are generated by two-cycles $\sigma_{x_i \leftrightarrow x_j}$ and $\sigma_{x_i \leftrightarrow x_j} = \sigma_{x_i \oplus = x_j} \circ \sigma_{x_j \oplus = x_i} \circ \sigma_{x_i \oplus = x_j}$ because of idempotency of $\oplus$; we include them to clarify the relationship with earlier work.

PROPOSITION 3.2. *$F(N,N) \leq |\mathfrak{B}_N| \leq 2^{N+1} F(N,N)$, where $F(N,N)$ is the number of nonsingular square Boolean matrices of size $N \times N$.*

PROOF. *Since the $\sigma_{x_i \oplus = x_j}$ symmetries subsume the σ_π, we only need to consider three cases:*

1. *There are two $\sigma_{\neg y}$ symmetries*
2. *There are 2^N $\sigma_{\neg x_i}$ symmetries*
3. *Each $\sigma_{x_i \oplus = x_j}$ corresponds to a nonsingular $N \times N$ Boolean matrix. The number of square Boolean matrices of size N and rank k is normally denoted $F(N,k)$ (of course we are interested in $F(N,N)$).*

If the three groups of symmetries were completely orthogonal, the total number would be $2^{N+1} F(N,N)$. However, there is some overlap because of Boolean identities, specifically those of the form $\neg(x_1 \oplus \ldots \oplus x_m) = \neg(x_1) \oplus \ldots \oplus \neg(x_m)$. Since $\neg$ and $\oplus$ are both balanced operators, these are the only relevant identities; we need to factor these from the total, which we have not yet achieved. Nevertheless, there must be at least as many symmetries in total as there are $\sigma_{x_i \oplus = x_j}$ symmetries, and since the Boolean identities are relatively sparse, we expect the order of the total to be much closer to the upper bound than the lower. □

There is no known formula for $F(N,N)$, but directly computed values are available for $N \leq 8$ [28], and estimates based on stochastic sampling for $2^N \leq 2.5 \times 10^6$ [27].

PROPOSITION 3.3. *σ_π, $\sigma_{\neg x_i}$, $\sigma_{\neg y}$ and $\sigma_{x_i \oplus = x_j}$ preserve Manhattan distance, in the sense that*

$$\begin{aligned}
\delta(\sigma_\pi(f_1), \sigma_\pi(f_2)) &= \delta(f_1, f_2) \\
\delta(\sigma_{\neg x_i}(f_1), \sigma_{\neg x_i}(f_2)) &= \delta(f_1, f_2) \\
\delta(\sigma_{\neg y(f_1)}, \sigma_{\neg y(f_2)}) &= \delta(f_1, f_2) \\
\delta(\sigma_{x_i \oplus = x_j}(f_1), \sigma_{x_i \oplus = x_j}(f_2)) &= \delta(f_1, f_2) \\
\delta(\sigma_{y \oplus = x_i}(f_1), \sigma_{y \oplus = x_i}(f_2)) &= \delta(f_1, f_2) \qquad (12)
\end{aligned}$$

and hence so does every $\sigma \in \mathfrak{B}_N$

PROOF. *The three symmetries that affect only the function arguments (i.e. $\sigma_\pi, \sigma_{\neg x_i}, \sigma_{x_i \oplus = x_j}$) merely re-order the output vector; since they re-order f_1 and f_2 the same way, they do not change the Manhattan distance. $\sigma_{\neg y}$ negates the output vectors of both, again leaving the Manhattan distance unchanged. $\sigma_{y \oplus = x_i}$ preserves differences and equalities between output vector locations of f_1 and f_2 (i.e. it either changes both, or leaves both unchanged), again preserving Manhattan distance.* □

PROPOSITION 3.4. *σ_π, $\sigma_{\neg x_i}$, $\sigma_{\neg y}$, $\sigma_{x_i \oplus = x_j}$ and $\sigma_{y \oplus = x_i}$ (and hence all $\sigma \in \mathfrak{B}_N$) preserve linearity, in the sense that if $f \in 2^{2^N}$ is linear, then so is $\sigma(f)$.*

PROOF. *Trivial except for $\sigma_{\neg x_i}$ and $\sigma_{x_i \oplus = x_j}$; because we already have access to σ_π, we can assume wlog (by argument re-ordering) that we are applying $\sigma_{\neg x_1}$ to the function $a_0 \oplus (a_1 \wedge x_1) \oplus \ldots \oplus (a_N \wedge x_N)$. But*

$\sigma_{\neg x_1}(a_0 \oplus (a_1 \wedge x_1) \oplus \ldots \oplus (a_N \wedge x_N))$

$$\begin{aligned}
&= a_0 \oplus (a_1 \wedge \neg x_1) \oplus \ldots \oplus (a_N \wedge x_N) \\
&= a_0 \oplus (a_1 \wedge (1 \oplus x_1)) \oplus \ldots \oplus (a_N \wedge x_N) \\
&= a_0 \oplus ((a_1 \wedge 1) \oplus (a_1 \wedge x_1)) \oplus \ldots \oplus (a_N \wedge x_N) \\
&= (a_0 \oplus (a_1 \wedge 1)) \oplus (a_1 \wedge x_1)) \oplus \ldots \oplus (a_N \wedge x_N) \\
&= (a_0 \oplus (a_1 \wedge 1)) \oplus (a_1 \wedge x_1)) \oplus \ldots \oplus (a_N \wedge x_N)
\end{aligned}$$

which is of linear form. For $\sigma_{x_i \oplus = x_j}$, we can assume that we are applying $\sigma_{x_1 \oplus = x_2}$ to the function $a_0 \oplus (a_1 \wedge x_1) \oplus \ldots \oplus (a_N \wedge x_N)$. But

$\sigma_{x_1 \oplus = x_2}(a_0 \oplus (a_1 \wedge x_1) \oplus \ldots \oplus (a_N \wedge x_N))$

$$\begin{aligned}
&= a_0 \oplus (a_1 \wedge (x_1 \oplus x_2)) \oplus \ldots \oplus (a_N \wedge x_N) \\
&= a_0 \oplus ((a_1 \wedge x_1) \oplus (a_1 \wedge x_2)) \oplus (a_2 \wedge x_2) \oplus \ldots \\
&= a_0 \oplus (a_1 \wedge x_1) \oplus ((a_1 \wedge x_2) \oplus (a_2 \wedge x_2)) \oplus \ldots \\
&= (a_0 \oplus \neg a_1) \oplus (a_1 \wedge x_1) \oplus (0 \wedge x_2) \oplus \ldots \oplus (a_N \wedge x_N) \\
&\qquad \text{if } a_1 = a_2 \\
&= a_0 \oplus (a_1 \wedge x_1) \oplus (1 \wedge x_2) \oplus \ldots \oplus (a_N \wedge x_N) \\
&\qquad \text{if } a_1 \neq a_2
\end{aligned}$$

which in either case is of linear form. □

PROPOSITION 3.5. *σ_π, $\sigma_{\neg x_i}$, $\sigma_{\neg y}$ and $\sigma_{x_i \oplus = x_j}$ (and hence all $\sigma \in \mathfrak{B}_N$) preserve balance, in the sense that if $f \in 2^{2^N}$ is balanced, then so is $\sigma(f)$. However $\sigma_{y \oplus = x_i}$ does not (in general) preserve balance.*

PROOF. *All except $\sigma_{\neg y}$ and $\sigma_{y \oplus = x_i}$ simply permute the output vector, hence do not change balance. $\sigma_{\neg y}$ inverts the output vector, preserving balance. However $\sigma_{y \oplus = x_i}(f_i) = \vec{0}$; f_i is balanced, but $\vec{0}$ is not.* □

Thus $\sigma_{y \oplus = x_i}$ are of limited interest for problems requiring balanced functions, or in general for problems where balance is included in the fitness function. However, the $\sigma_{y \oplus = x_i}$ transformations may be important in analysis of problems not requiring balance.

COROLLARY 3.6. *All $\sigma \in \mathfrak{B}_N$ preserve the fitness function, in the sense that for $f \in 2^{2^N}$, $\mathbf{fit}(\sigma(f)) = \mathbf{fit}(f)$.*

Note that the symmetric regions are not, in general, disjoint. Specifically, the functions $\vec{0}$ and $\vec{1}$ are fixpoints for all the base symmetries except $\sigma_{\neg y}$ (which, of course, has no fixpoints since by definition it inverts every $f \in 2^{2^N}$). All the σ_π, $\sigma_{\neg x_i}$ and $\sigma_{x_i \oplus = x_j}$ have other fixpoints, but they differ for each symmetry.

3.2.3 Determining Symmetry

Golomb [5] provided a method to determine whether two Boolean functions were symmetric under his three symmetry classes ($\sigma_\pi, \sigma_{\neg x_i}, \sigma_{\neg y}$) by finding a canonical version of each (they are in the same symmetry classes only if they have the same canonical version). Its incremental process of determining the order of variables renders it reasonably efficient. It may be relatively straightforwardly extended to $\sigma_{x_i \oplus = x_j}$ symmetries, but unfortunately at the cost of efficiency: although it may be possible to find speedups, a direct implementation requires generating and testing all possible symmetric mappings, clearly at the limits of feasibility for 6-bit functions, and far beyond for 8-bit. Practically, we cannot fully test for symmetry in the absence of an algorithm breakthrough. But the isomorphism between neighborhoods gives a quite effective asymmetry test: since the neighborhoods of symmetric points are necessarily isomorphic, we can simply test the neighborhoods for isomorphism; any failure of isomorphism guarantees that the points are not symmetric.

3.3 The Fitness Landscape

3.3.1 Neighborhoods

The full 2^{2^N} search space and its balanced subspace have isotropic neighborhoods (that is, the search space looks the same everywhere, except for balance and distance to the linear functions). It is easiest to think about the neighborhood structure from a simple function – for example $f_{\frac{1}{2}}$, the function whose first half is all 1s, and second half all zeros. For the full search space, the number of functions at distance d is just $C_d^{2^N}$ (i.e. the number of ordered subsets of 2^N of size d); for the balanced subspace, the distance of a balanced function from $f_{\frac{1}{2}}$ is just twice the number of zeros in the first half. So of course, there are no balanced functions at any odd distance, and at any even $2d < N$, the number of balanced functions at that distance is $(C_d^{2^{N-1}})^2$ (considering the two halves of the function separately for counting).

3.3.2 Fitness and Distance

Theoretical analysis of the fitness landscape is difficult (which is why we concentrate on empirical analysis here). However, we can immediately conclude that one step of distance can change the balance and nonlinearity by at most one (hence the maximum gradient is at most 2). For the balanced search space, balance is fixed at zero, hence the minimum step (of length 2) can change the nonlinearity by at most 2, so that the maximum gradient is 1.

4. COMPLETE SAMPLING

Table 1: Symmetry Classes and Fitness Groups

Lexicographically Smallest Member	Class Size	Fitness	Group Size
0000000011111111	30	0	30
0000000101111111	1 800	2	1 920
0001011001101011	120	2	
0000001100111111	840	4	10 920
0000001101011111	7 360	4	
0000001101111101	1 942	4	
0000011101111001	602	4	
0001011001101110	176	4	

The 4-argument space is relatively small, so we can completely sample it. In Table 1, the vast majority of instances have maximum fitness; the only exceptions are linear functions and their nearest neighbors. This is so different from the situation with the functions of interest (8 or more arguments) that little useful can be inferred.

The symmetry classes are slightly more informative: they are very large (and for functions with more arguments will be even larger). To ignore the effects of these symmetries is to make the problem unnecessarily hard.

5. SAMPLING WITH KNOWN OPTIMA

Because we are able to reliably find optima for 6-argument functions, our analysis can be based on them. Table 2 shows the histogram of fitness. Although optimal fitness is attainable even with random search, the difference from the 4-argument case could not be more stark. The vast bulk of individuals have fitness between 18 and 22, and the fall-off in density from fitness 24 to fitness 26 is precipitous, so that there is an immense plateau effect.

Any reasonable algorithm readily attains a fitness of 22, so the major interest is how to move from fitness 22 to the much scarcer 26 fitness. We examined the neighborhood structure of two different classes of individuals. The first class consisted of 10^6 random individuals. The second class was formed by taking a number of known optima (of fitness 26), and then finding all linear functions at distance 26 from them. Any balanced path between such a linear function and the corresponding optimum forms a shortest path for search; we would like to know whether individuals on such "good" paths differ from random individuals. So we sampled all individuals along a random selection of such paths.[2] To reduce bias, we deleted all duplicates from the data set.

From the arguments in Section 3, the neighborhood structure is a key property. Each balanced individual has 1024 balanced neighbors, which we sampled, counting the number of neighbors of lower, equal or higher fitness (since the only possible fitness differences are $-2, 0, 2$, this completely characterizes the local neighborhood). We are mainly interested in the fit end of this spectrum, so we present the results only for fitnesses above 20, and only for structures with a sample proportion above 1%. Both samples considered the neighborhoods of 10^6 individuals.

The most obvious feature of Table 3 is the difference in neighborhood structures: shortest-path individuals have far more higher-fitness neighbors.[3] This seems likely to be helpful in search, breaking the vast monotonous landscape of fitness 20 and 22 individuals: the proportion of fitter neighbors (which can be estimated from small samples of neighbors) may be a better guide to search than fitness.

There are other interesting consequences. There are at least seven different symmetry classes of optima, and some of the optima are relatively well connected (as many as 44 neighboring optima). Random fitness 24 individuals rarely have neighboring optima, but those from shortest paths (which are guaranteed to have at least one optimal neighbor) often have substantially more. Overall, there is a wide plateau of fitness-24 individuals, highly connected to each other (but

[2]Note that these optima, resulting from a specific search algorithm, may not be a random selection of all optima.

[3]Around the 1% cutoff, the presence/absence of neighborhood structures in the table may reflect random fluctuations.

Table 2: Randomly Sampled Fitness counts and Proportions

Args	6		No. of Samples			3.7×10^6				
Fitness	0-8	10	12	14	16	18	20	22	24	26
Count	0	13	202	2 855	28 365	198 563	958 591	2 029 228	482 121	62
Ratio	0	<0.001	<0.001	0.001	0.008	0.054	0.259	0.548	0.130	<0.001
Args	8		No. of Samples			2.6×10^6				
Fitness	0-78	80	82	84	86	88	90	92	94	96
Count	0	2	14	31	109	428	1 568	5 093	15 200	42 312
Ratio	0	<0.001	<0.001	<0.001	<0.001	<0.001	<0.001	0.002	0.006	0.016
Fitness	98	100	102	104	106	108	110	112	114-118	
Count	112 889	262 058	523 355	777 046	656 813	194 808	8 266	8	0	
Ratio	0.043	0.101	0.201	0.299	0.253	0.075	0.003	<0.001	0	

even more highly connected to a larger plateau of fitness 22 individuals), with rare spikes up to fitness-26 optima. What is still not clear (and because of the very large neighborhood structure – close to a million for two steps – computationally almost impossible to test) is whether the fitness-24 individuals are fully connected to each other (or at least, whether every plateau is connected to an optimum), or whether there may be local optima.

6. SAMPLING IN HIGH FITNESS AREAS

Table 2 also shows the histogram of fitness of 8-argument functions. The trend for 6-argument functions is amplified. The vast bulk of individuals have fitness between 100 and 106, and again there is a precipitous fall-off in density from fitness 110 on, with random sampling virtually never attaining a fitness beyond 112.

We conducted a similar comparison between random and high-fitness-path individuals as for the 6-argument functions, again using a sample size of 10^6; the high-fitness-paths were generated from individuals of fitness 116. We cannot show tabular detail due to space restrictions, but there was an amplification of the phenomenon observed with 6-argument functions, that functions on a path to a high-fitness region have many more neighbors of higher fitness than random functions of the same fitness. Relative to the 6-argument case, there has been a very rapid increase in the number of different neighborhood structures (a proxy for number of symmetry classes). In our 6-argument samples, we saw a total of under 1 000 different neighborhoods. In the 8-argument samples, we saw over 47 000 in the random sample, and 13 600 in the path-based sample.

7. CONCLUSIONS

7.1 Summary

Landscape theory and the experimental results show that an important reason for difficulty in this problem is the immense size of the apparently featureless plateaus. Symmetry analysis reveals a second difficulty, that the immense number of symmetries render crossover merely a macromutation until the symmetries have been broken: if we rely on stochastic breaking, this will not happen quickly. There is little evidence of the more usual causes of evolutionary search difficulty. The very large neighborhoods make it computationally infeasible to confirm with certainty, but it appears that deception and local optima are not prominent features. The gradient, while weak, is smooth, with no abrupt changes in fitness. In short, were it not for the very large plateau size and the ineffectiveness of crossover, this would appear an easy problem.

7.2 Symmetries and their Implications for Search

From a fitness landscape perspective, there is little further to be done: the problem is simply one of scale. However our symmetry analysis may yield better approaches. We see at least five options:

1. The symmetry methods of [18] dramatically improved the search performance even for relatively low numbers of symmetries. However in the form used there, they required space proportional to the number of symmetries, so may be infeasible for this problem.

2. Knowing the symmetries, may help to design representations collapsing them. This ideal solution requires a flash of insight that has not yet arrived.

3. In principle, we could search the very much smaller (and less plateaued) space of canonical representatives of each symmetry class, but to be feasible this would require faster methods for finding the canonical representatives than we have at present.

4. While the plateaus are very large, they are not featureless. The proportion of improving neighbors can distinguish different classes, and shows strong indications as a useful feature for search. It is not difficult to envisage algorithms based on this, using sub-samples of the neighborhood to give a search direction even in regions of limited fitness change. It may even be better to move to neighbors with the same fitness but more neighbors of high fitness than to move directly to neighbors of higher fitness.

5. Knowing the symmetries can permit us to bias stochastic symmetry breaking to encourage it to happen faster. We could use a kind of anti-fitness-sharing (rewarding individuals for being more similar – but not too similar). In such an algorithm, we might also incorporate estimates of the number of improving neighbors as a component of the fitness function.

8. ACKNOWLEDGMENTS

This research was supported by the National Research Foundation of Korea Grant funded by the Korean Government (NRF-2012-013-NRF-2012S1A2A1A01031076). The ICT at Seoul National University provided research facilities for this study. R. Santana acknowledges support from the

Table 3: Random and Shortest Path Neighborhood Structures (6-Argument Functions), Sample Sizes 10^6

Random Sample						Sample from Shortest Path					
Fitness	Better	Worse	Equal	Count	Proportion	Fitness	Better	Worse	Equal	Count	Proportion
22	68	234	722	5 593	0.010	22	106	234	684	1 103	0.011
22	88	234	702	5 526	0.010	22	108	234	682	1 037	0.011
22	164	121	739	7 350	0.013	22	109	234	681	1 390	0.014
22	165	121	738	6 335	0.012	22	169	233	622	1 089	0.011
22	166	121	737	7 203	0.013	22	204	121	699	1 784	0.019
22	167	121	736	10 221	0.019	22	205	121	698	2 666	0.028
22	168	121	735	11 126	0.020	22	206	121	697	2 397	0.025
22	169	121	734	8 290	0.015	22	207	121	696	1 734	0.018
22	203	121	700	5 514	0.010	22	208	121	695	2 463	0.026
22	204	121	699	7 041	0.013	22	250	121	653	2 436	0.025
22	205	121	698	9 947	0.018	22	251	121	652	3 414	0.035
22	206	121	697	11 777	0.021	22	252	121	651	2 635	0.027
22	207	121	696	11 882	0.022	22	253	121	650	1 458	0.015
22	208	121	695	9 700	0.018	22	254	121	649	2 652	0.028
22	209	121	694	8 013	0.015	22	255	121	648	2 328	0.024
22	251	121	652	8 012	0.015	22	256	121	647	3 181	0.033
22	252	121	651	6 217	0.011	22	257	121	646	1 270	0.013
22	254	121	649	6 461	0.012	22	258	121	645	1 031	0.011
22	255	121	648	6 329	0.012	22	303	121	600	2 273	0.024
22	256	121	647	5 918	0.011	22	305	121	598	5 119	0.053
						22	306	121	597	3 308	0.034
						22	307	121	596	6 016	0.062
						22	308	121	595	1 688	0.018
						22	309	121	594	1 942	0.020
						22	311	121	592	1 288	0.013
						22	313	121	590	3 114	0.032
						22	314	121	589	1 246	0.013
						22	369	121	534	4 623	0.048
						22	371	121	532	2 400	0.025
						22	441	121	462	1 176	0.012
24	0	662	362	2 257	0.017	24	1	578	445	367	0.023
24	0	661	363	2 416	0.019	24	1	490	533	536	0.034
24	0	660	364	3 175	0.024	24	1	488	535	488	0.031
24	0	659	365	3 202	0.025	24	1	486	537	236	0.015
24	0	658	366	2 588	0.020	24	1	389	634	203	0.013
24	0	657	367	1 796	0.014	24	1	387	636	530	0.034
24	0	653	371	1 380	0.011	24	1	273	750	284	0.018
24	0	586	438	1 897	0.015	24	2	491	531	691	0.044
24	0	585	439	1 604	0.012	24	2	489	533	672	0.043
24	0	584	440	2 837	0.022	24	2	389	633	1 328	0.085
24	0	583	441	2 647	0.020	24	2	387	635	790	0.051
24	0	582	442	1 837	0.014	24	2	273	749	427	0.027
24	0	580	444	1 676	0.013	24	3	387	634	386	0.025
24	0	579	445	1 546	0.012	24	3	273	748	328	0.021
24	0	578	446	2 540	0.020	24	4	273	747	2 425	0.155
24	0	577	447	3 551	0.027	24	4	272	748	667	0.043
24	0	576	448	5 436	0.042	24	5	144	875	416	0.027
24	0	575	449	4 008	0.031	24	6	273	745	270	0.017
24	0	574	450	2 377	0.018	24	12	272	740	825	0.053
24	0	499	525	1 317	0.010	24	16	272	736	1 268	0.081
24	0	494	530	2 037	0.016						
24	0	490	534	1 663	0.013						
24	0	489	535	2 861	0.022						
24	0	488	536	4 503	0.035						
24	0	487	537	6 411	0.049						
24	0	486	538	4 396	0.034						
24	0	387	637	3 962	0.030						
24	0	386	638	1 354	0.010						
24	0	385	639	1 822	0.014						
24	1	387	636	1 688	0.013						
26	0	1 022	2	4	0.235	26	0	1 022	2	1	0.063
26	0	1 020	4	5	0.294	26	0	1 012	12	1	0.063
26	0	1 012	12	2	0.118	26	0	1 008	16	1	0.063
26	0	1 008	16	2	0.118	26	0	1 004	20	2	0.125
26	0	1 004	20	2	0.118	26	0	980	44	11	0.688
26	0	996	28	1	0.059						
26	0	980	44	1	0.059						

Saiotek and Research Groups 2013-2018 (IT-609-13) programs (Basque Government), and TIN2013-41272P (Ministry of Science and Technology of Spain). We thank Claude Carlet from the University of Paris 8 for his very thorough examination of our manuscript and invaluable feedback. We also thank Brian M. Scott for pointing out the relationship between the number of $\sigma_{x_i \oplus = x_j}$ symmetries and $F(N, N)$.

9. REFERENCES

[1] H. Aguirre and K. Tanaka. Genetic algorithms on NK-landscapes: Effects of selection, drift, mutation, and recombination. *Applications of Evolutionary Computing*, pages 131–142, 2003.

[2] C. Carlet. Boolean Functions for Cryptography and Error Correcting Codes. In Y. Crama and P. L. Hammer, editors, *Boolean Models and Methods in Mathematics, Computer Science, and Engineering*, pages 257–397. Cambridge University Press, New York, NY, USA, 1st edition, 2010.

[3] C. R. Edwards. The application of the Rademacher–Walsh transform to boolean function classification and threshold logic synthesis. *Computers, IEEE Transactions on*, 100(1):48–62, 1975.

[4] M. Gallagher and B. Yuan. A general-purpose tunable landscape generator. *Evolutionary Computation, IEEE Transactions on*, 10(5):590–603, 2006.

[5] S. Golomb. On the classification of boolean functions. *Circuit Theory, IRE Transactions on*, 6(5):176–186, 1959.

[6] M. W. Hauschild and M. Pelikan. Network crossover performance on NK landscapes and deceptive problems. In *Proceedings of the 12th annual conference on Genetic and evolutionary computation (GECCO-2010)*, pages 713–720. ACM, 2010.

[7] L. Hernando, A. Mendiburu, and J. A. Lozano. An evaluation of methods for estimating the number of local optima in combinatorial optimization problems. *Evolutionary computation*, 21(4):625–658, 2013.

[8] J. Horn. *Genetic Algorithms, Problem Difficulty, and the Modality of Fitness Landscapes.* PhD thesis, University of Illinois at Urbana-Champaign, Urbana, IL, July 1995.

[9] T. C. Jones. *Evolutionary Algorithms, Fitness Landscapes and Search.* PhD thesis, University of New Mexico, Alburquerque, 1995.

[10] T. C. Jones and S. Forrest. Fitness distance correlation as a measure of problem difficulty for genetic algorithms. In L.J.Eshelman, editor, *Proceedings of the Sixth International Conference on Genetic Algorithms*, pages 184–192, 1995.

[11] L. Kallel, B. Naudts, and R. Reeves. Properties of fitness functions and search landscapes. In L. Kallel, B. Naudts, and A. Rogers, editors, *Theoretical Aspects of Evolutionary Computing*, pages 177–208. Springer, 2000.

[12] S. A. Kauffman. *The origins of order: Self-organization and selection in evolution.* Oxford university press, 1993.

[13] S. Maitra and E. Pasalic. Further constructions of resilient boolean functions with very high nonlinearity. *Information Theory, IEEE Transactions on*, 48(7):1825–1834, Jul 2002.

[14] B. Naudts and J. Naudts. The effect of spin-flip symmetry on the performance of the simple GA. In *Parallel Problem Solving from Nature, PPSN V*, pages 67–76. Springer, 1998.

[15] G. Ochoa, M. Tomassini, S. Vérel, and C. Darabos. A study of NK landscapes' basins and local optima networks. In *Proceedings of the 10th annual conference on Genetic and evolutionary computation (GECCO-2008)*, pages 555–562. ACM, 2008.

[16] M. Pelikan, K. Martin, D. E. Goldberg, M. V. Butz, and M. Hauschild. Performance of evolutionary algorithms on NK landscapes with nearest neighbor interactions and tunable overlap. In *Proceedings of the Genetic and Evolutionary Computation Conference GECCO-2009*, pages 851–858, New York, NY, USA, 2009. ACM.

[17] S. Prestwich and A. Roli. Symmetry breaking and local search spaces. In *Integration of AI and OR Techniques in Constraint Programming for Combinatorial Optimization Problems*, volume 3524 of *Lecture Notes in Computer Science*, pages 273–287. Springer, 2005.

[18] R. Santana, R. I. McKay, and J. A. Lozano. Symmetry in evolutionary and estimation of distribution algorithms. In *Evolutionary Computation (CEC), 2013 IEEE Congress on*, pages 2053–2060. IEEE, 2013.

[19] P. Sarkar and S. Maitra. Nonlinearity bounds and constructions of resilient boolean functions. In M. Bellare, editor, *CRYPTO*, volume 1880 of *Lecture Notes in Computer Science*, pages 515–532. Springer, 2000.

[20] M. Shpak, P. Stadler, G. P. Wagner, and L. Altenberg. Simon-Ando decomposability and fitness landscapes. *Theory in Biosciences*, 123(2):139–180, 2004.

[21] D. Slepian. On the number of symmetry types of boolean functions of n variables. *Canad. J. Math*, 5(2):185–193, 1953.

[22] J. Todd. The groups of symmetries of the regular polytopes. *Mathematical Proceedings of the Cambridge Philosophical Society*, 27(02):212–231, 1931.

[23] M. Tomassini, S. Vérel, and G. Ochoa. Complex-network analysis of combinatorial spaces: The NK landscape case. *Physical Review E*, 78(6):066114, 2008.

[24] C. Van Hoyweghen, B. Naudts, and D. E. Goldberg. Spin-flip symmetry and synchronization. *Evolutionary Computation*, 10(4):317–344, 2002.

[25] S. Verel, P. Collard, and M. Clergue. Where are bottlenecks in NK fitness landscapes? In *Evolutionary Computation, 2003. CEC'03. The 2003 Congress on*, volume 1, pages 273–280. IEEE, 2003.

[26] S. Verel, G. Ochoa, and M. Tomassini. Local optima networks of NK landscapes with neutrality. *Evolutionary Computation, IEEE Transactions on*, 15(6):783–797, 2011.

[27] T. Voigt and G. M. Ziegler. Singular 0/1-matrices, and the hyperplanes spanned by random 0/1-vectors. *Combinatorics, Probability and Computing*, 15(03):463–471, 2006.

[28] M. Živković. Classification of small (0, 1) matrices. *Linear algebra and its applications*, 414(1):310–346, 2006.

On the Impact of Local Search Operators and Variable Neighbourhood Search for the Generalized Travelling Salesperson Problem

Mojgan Pourhassan
Optimisation and Logistics
School of Computer Science
The University of Adelaide
Adelaide, SA 5005, Australia
mojgan.pourhassan@adelaide.edu.au

Frank Neumann
Optimisation and Logistics
School of Computer Science
The University of Adelaide
Adelaide, SA 5005, Australia
frank.neumann@adelaide.edu.au

ABSTRACT

The generalized travelling salesperson problem is an important NP-hard combinatorial optimization problem where local search approaches have been very successful. We investigate the two hierarchical approaches of Hu and Raidl [9] for solving this problem from a theoretical perspective. We examine the complementary abilities of the two approaches caused by their neighbourhood structures and the advantage of combining them into variable neighbourhood search. We first point out complementary abilities of the two approaches by presenting instances where they mutually outperform each other. Afterwards, we introduce an instance which is hard for both approaches, but where a variable neighbourhood search combining them finds the optimal solution in polynomial time.

Categories and Subject Descriptors

F.2 [**Theory of Computation**]: Analysis of Algorithms and Problem Complexity

Keywords

Generalized Travelling Salesperson Problem; Local Search; Variable Neighbourhood Search; 2-OPT; Combinatorial Optimisation.

1. INTRODUCTION

Metaheuristics [6] such as local search, simulated annealing and various types of evolutionary algorithms have been successfully applied to a wide range of problems from combinatorial optimization. Despite their large practical success, it is very difficult to understand how and why they work on important classes of problems.

One of the best known local search approaches is the Lin-Kernighan heuristic for the well-known Travelling Salesperson problem (TSP). This heuristic is built on the classical 2-opt operator for the TSP. While extremely successful, it is still very hard to understand the success of these approaches from a theoretical perspective. Theoretical results on different types of metaheuristics for the TSP have been presented in [4, 12, 17] and the impact of different local search strategies and their combination with evolutionary algorithms on different types of problems have been analysed in [15, 16] by rigorous runtime analyses. The runtime analysis of metaheuristics has provided a lot of rigorous new insights into the working principles of these algorithms and we refer the reader to the three books [13, 1, 10] for comprehensive presentations. Despite this progress and the advancement of methods for analysing metaheuristics, understanding and analysing the run of even simple metaheuristics on classical problems such as run of local search on TSP remains challenging, and obtaining theoretical results that match practical experience is to a large extend an open problem.

With this paper, we contribute to the theoretical understanding of local search methods for the generalized travelling salesperson problem (GTSP). The problem is given by a set of cities with distances between them. Furthermore, the cities are divided into clusters and the goal is to find a tour of minimal cost that visits one city from each cluster exactly once. Different heuristic approaches for the GTSP have been presented in recent years [7, 14, 5, 9]. We investigate the two hierarchical approaches for solving the GTSP presented in [9]. Both approaches construct an overall solution based on an upper and lower level. The *Cluster-Based* approach uses a permutation on the clusters in the upper level and finds the best node selection based on that permutation on the lower layer. The *Node-Based* approach selects a spanning node for each cluster and then works on finding the best permutation of the chosen nodes. Hu and Raidl [9] have combined the two approaches into a variable neighbourhood search algorithm and shown that this leads to a high performing algorithm for the GTSP.

We investigate the two approaches from a theoretical perspective and point out complementary abilities. Our aim is to show situations where one of the approaches gets stuck in a local optimum and the other approach is able to perform well and achieves an optimal solution. This gives a deeper insight into the working principles of these two common approaches and highlights their complementary abilities. To gain these structural insights, our instances should be simple enough for theoretical treatment. As we are con-

GECCO '15, July 11 - 15, 2015, Madrid, Spain

 ISBN 978-1-4503-3472-3/15/07…$15.00
DOI: http://dx.doi.org/10.1145/2739480.2754656

sidering hierarchical approaches working with two solution layers, it is very difficult to argue in general about the run of metaheuristics on these problems. The only runtime analysis that we are aware of is the analysis of simple evolutionary algorithms in the context of bilevel optimization for the generalized minimum spanning tree problem [2] and the generalized travelling salesperson problem [3] in the context of parameterized complexity which shows that evolutionary algorithms using a cluster-based approach perform well for these problems if the number of clusters is small. We concentrate on instances with a small number of clusters to get further insights into hierarchical approaches for the GTSP. In particular, we present instances where the two approaches mutually outperform each other. Furthermore, we present an instance where both local search approaches are not able to achieve an optimal solution, but a combination of them into a variable-neighbourhood search reaches an optimal solution.

The outline of the paper is as follows. Section 2 introduces the problem and the algorithms that are subject to our investigations. In Section 3, we introduce a hard instance for the Cluster-Based approach which is easy to solve for Node-Based approach. Section 4 includes an instance easy for Cluster-Based approach and difficult for Node-Based approach and Section 5 introduces the third instance which is difficult for both of them but an algorithm that combines the two approaches can solve it easily. Finally, we finish with some concluding remarks in Section 6.

2. PROBLEM AND ALGORITHMS

We consider the generalized travelling salesperson problem (GTSP) which can be described as follows. The input is given by a (un)directed complete graph $G = (V, E, c)$ with $n = |V|$ nodes, a cost function $c\colon E \to \mathbb{R}^+$ on the edges, and a partitioning of V into m clusters $V_1, V_2, \ldots, V_m$. The goal is to find a cycle of minimum cost that visits exactly one node from each cluster.

A solution for this problem consists of two parts. A set of *spanning nodes* $P = \{p_1, p_2, \ldots, p_m\}$ where $p_i \in V_i$, and a Hamiltonian tour on the graph $G[P] = G(P, \{e \in E \mid e \subseteq P\})$ induced by P, i.e. the graph consisting of the spanning nodes and all edges between them. Following [9], we present a candidate solution as $S = (P, \pi)$ where $P = \{p_1, \ldots, p_m\}$ is the spanning node set and $\pi = (\pi_1, \ldots, \pi_m)$ is a permutation of the given clusters. Let p_{π_i} be the chosen node for cluster V_{π_i}, $1 \leq i \leq m$. Then the cost of a solution $S = (P, \pi)$ is given by

$$c(S) = c(p_{\pi_m}, p_{\pi_1}) + \sum_{i=1}^{m-1} c(p_{\pi_i}, p_{\pi_{i+1}}).$$

2.1 Cluster-Based Local Search

In the Cluster-Based approach, constructing the permutation of clusters constitutes the upper layer and the node selection is done in the lower layer.

Let $\pi = (\pi_1, \cdots, \pi_m)$ be a permutation of the m clusters. The 2-opt neighbourhood of π is given by

$$\begin{aligned} N(\pi) \;=\; & \{\pi' \mid 1 \leq i < j \leq m, \\ & \pi' = (\pi_1, \cdots, \pi_{i-1}, \pi_j, \pi_{j-1}, \cdots, \pi_i, \pi_{j+1}, \cdots, \pi_m)\} \end{aligned}$$

The cluster-based local search (CBLS) algorithm working with this neighbourhood structure is given in Algorithm 1.

Algorithm 1 Cluster Based Local Search (CBLS)

```
Choose a permutation π = (π_1, ..., π_m).
Find the optimal set of spanning nodes P with respect
    to π to obtain the solution S = (P, π).
for π' ∈ N(π) do
    Find an optimal set of nodes P' = {p'_1, ..., p'_m} with
    respect to π' to obtain the solution S' = (P', π').
    if c(S') < c(S) then
        S = S'
        GO TO 3
    end if
end for
```

Algorithm 2 Node Exchange Neighbourhood Local Search (NEN-LS)

```
Choose P = {p_1, p_2, ..., p_m},  p_i ∈ V_i.
Let π be the permutation of clusters obtained by per-
    forming a 2-opt local search on G[P] and S = (P, π) be
    the resulting solution.
for P' ∈ N'(P) do
    Let π' be the permutation of clusters obtained from
    π by performing a 2-opt local search on G[P'] and
    S' = (P', π') be the resulting solution.
    if c(S') < c(S) then
        S = S'
        GO TO 3
    end if
end for
```

CBLS starts with an initial permutation of clusters. At each step, a new permutation π' is selected from the 2-opt neighbourhood of π, where π is the current permutation of clusters. Then the lower layer uses the shortest path algorithm given in [11] to find the best spanning node set. The runtime of the algorithm to compute an optimal set of spanning nodes for a given permutation using this algorithm is $O(n^3)$.

The new solution $S' = (P', \pi')$ replaces the old one $S = (P, \pi)$ if it is of less cost and the algorithm terminates if no better permutation can be found in the 2-opt neighbourhood of the current solution π.

2.2 Node-Based Local Search

In the Node-Based approach, selection of the spanning nodes is done in the upper layer and the lower level consists of finding a shortest tour on the spanning nodes.

Given a spanning nodes set P, the node exchange neighbourhood $N'(P)$ is defined as

$$\begin{aligned} N'(P) \;=\; & \{P' \mid \; P' = \{p_1, \cdots, p_{i-1}, p'_i, p_{i+1}, \ldots, p_m\}, \\ & p'_i \in V_i \setminus \{p_i\}, 1 \leq i \leq m\} \end{aligned}$$

Note that the lower level involves solving the classical TSP; therefore, poses in general an NP-hard problem on its own. For our theoretical investigations, we consider two algorithms NEN-LS and NEN-LS*. NEN-LS computes a permutation on the lower level using 2-opt local search and is therefore not guaranteed to reach an optimal permutation π for a given spanning node set P. NEN-LS* uses an optimal solver to find an optimal permutation π for a given spanning node set P. Such a permutation can be obtained in time $O(m^2 2^m)$ using dynamic programming programming [8] and is practical if the number of clusters is small. We use NEN-

Algorithm 3 Node Exchange Neighbourhood Local Search* (NEN-LS*)

Choose $P = \{p_1, p_2, \cdots, p_m\}, \quad p_i \in V_i$.
Find a minimum-cost permutation π for $G[P]$ and let $S = (P, \pi)$ be the resulting solution.
for $P' \in N'(P)$ **do**
  Find a minimum-cost permutation π' for $G[P']$ and let $S' = (P', \pi')$ be the resulting solution.
  if $c(S') < c(S)$ **then**
    $S = S'$
    GO TO 3
  end if
end for

Algorithm 4 Variable Neighborhood Search (VNS)

Choose an initial solution $S = (P, \pi)$.
$l = 1$
while $l \leq 2$ **do**
  for $S' \in N_l(S)$ **do**
    if $c(S') < c(S)$ **then**
      $S = S'$
      GO TO 3
    end if
  end for
  $l = l + 1$
end while

LS* and show where it gets stuck in local optima even if the travelling salesperson problem on the lower level is solved to optimality.

NEN-LS and NEN-LS* (see Algorithms 2 and 3) start with a spanning node set P and search for a good or optimal permutation with respect to P. Then each solution $P' \in N'(P)$ together with its permutation π' is considered and $S' = (P', \pi')$ replaces the current solution $S = (P, \pi)$ if it is of smaller cost. Both algorithms terminate if there is no improvement possible in the neighbourhood $N'(P)$ of the current solution P.

2.3 Variable Neighbourhood Search

Now we describe the combination of two approaches into variable neighbourhood search. We use a general variable neighbourhood scheme which explores different neighbourhood structures. The algorithm uses the two neighbourhood structures of CBLS and NEN-LS.

Let $S = (P, \pi)$ be a solution to the GTSP. We define the two neighbourhoods N_1 and N_2 based on the 2-opt neighbourhood N and the node exchange neighbourhood N' as

- $N_1(S) = \{S' = (P', \pi') \mid \pi' \in N(\pi), P' =$ optimal set of nodes with respect to $\pi'\}$
- $N_2(S) = \{S' = (P', \pi') \mid P' \in N'(P), \pi' =$ order of clusters obtained by 2-opt from π on $G[P']\}$

Combining the two local searches of Cluster-Based approach and Node-Based approach is done by alternating between N_1 and N_2. N_1 is the first neighbourhood to be searched and N_2 is used when a local optimum has been found with respect to N_1. The resulting variable neighbourhood search (VNS) algorithm is given in Algorithm 4.

3. BENEFITS OF NEN-LS

In this section, we present an instance of the problem that can not be solved by CBLS. In contrast to this, NEN-LS finds an optimal solution in polynomial time.

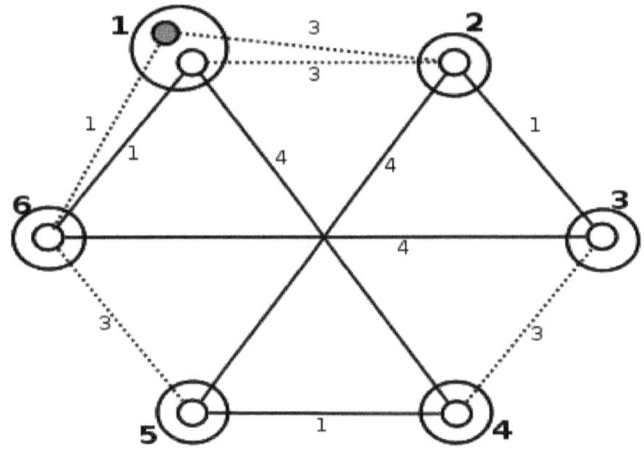

Figure 1: An instance of the problem, easy for Node-Based approach and hard for Cluster-Based approach

We consider the undirected graph, $G_1 = (V, E)$ which is illustrated in Figure 1. The graph has n nodes and 6 clusters V_i, $1 \leq i \leq 6$. Cluster V_1 contains $n/12$ white and $n/12$ grey nodes. We denote by V_{1W} the subset of white nodes and by V_{1G} the subset of grey nodes of cluster V_1. Each other cluster V_j, $2 \leq j \leq 6$, consists of $n/6$ white nodes. The node set $V = \cup_{i=1}^{6} V_i$ of G_1 is given by the nodes of the different clusters.

The edge set E consists of 4 types of edges which we define in the following.

- Type A: Edges of this kind have a cost of 1. All edges between clusters 2 and 3, and between clusters 4 and 5 and also between clusters 6 and 1, are of this kind.

$$A = \{\{v_i, v_j\} \mid (v_i \in V_{1W} \cup V_{1G} \wedge v_j \in V_6) \vee (v_i \in V_2 \wedge v_j \in V_3) \vee (v_i \in V_4 \wedge v_j \in V_5)\}$$

- Type B: Edges of this kind have a cost of 3. All edges connecting the nodes of cluster 1 to cluster 2 are of this type. So are the edges that connect nodes of cluster 3 to 4 and cluster 5 to 6.

$$B = \{\{v_i, v_j\} \mid (v_i \in V_{1W} \cup V_{1G} \wedge v_j \in V_2) \vee (v_i \in V_3 \wedge v_j \in V_4) \vee (v_i \in V_5 \wedge v_j \in V_6)\}$$

- Type C: Edges of this kind have a cost of 4. All edges between nodes of cluster 2 and 5 and also between clusters 3 and 6 are of this type. All edges that connect white nodes of the first cluster to nodes of the forth cluster are also of this type.

$$C = \{\{v_i, v_j\} \mid (v_i \in V_{1W} \wedge v_j \in V_4) \vee (v_i \in V_2 \wedge v_j \in V_5) \vee (v_i \in V_3 \wedge v_j \in V_6)\}$$

- Type D: Edges of this kind have a large cost of 100. All edges other than those of type A or B or C in this complete graph are of Type D. Note that the edges between grey nodes of the first cluster and the nodes of the forth cluster are also of this type.

$$D = \quad E \setminus \{A \cup B \cup C\}$$

Figure 1 shows the important connections of the nodes of this graph. For simplicity, we have drawn only one node for each group of similar nodes with similar edges in the picture.

We say that a permutation $\pi = (\pi(1), \dots, \pi(n))$ visits the cities in consecutive order iff $\pi(i+1) = (\pi(i) \mod n) + 1$, $1 \le i \le n$ and say that $\pi = (\pi(1), \dots, \pi(n))$ visits the cities in reverse-consecutive order iff $\pi(i) = (\pi(i+1) \mod n) + 1$, $1 \le i \le n$

PROPERTY 1. *For the instance G_1, each solution visiting the clusters in consecutive or reverse-consecutive order is optimal.*

PROOF. The graph consists of 6 clusters which implies that 6 edges are needed for a tour. The least costly edges are of type A, which are available only between 3 pairs of clusters. Therefore, the maximum number of edges of this type that can be used in a tour is 3. The second least costly type of edge is B with weights of 3. This implies that no tour can be shorter than $3 \cdot 1 + 3 \cdot 3 = 12$. Each solution with a permutation in consecutive or reverse-consecutive order uses exactly three edges of weight 1 and three edges of weight 3 which implies a cost of 12 and is therefore optimal. □

THEOREM 2. *Starting with the solution consisting of all the white nodes and the permutation $\pi = (1, 4, 5, 2, 3, 6)$, CBLS is not able to achieve any improvement.*

PROOF. Starting with all white nodes and a permutation $\pi = (1, 4, 5, 2, 3, 6)$, the solution contains three Type-A edges of cost 1 and three Type-C edges of cost 4. This implies a total cost of 15 which is not optimal. The edges belonging to this tour are marked solid in Figure 1. We claim that this solution is locally optimal, i.e. can not be improved by a 2-opt step.

When a 2-opt move is performed, depending on the different types of edges that are removed from the current tour, we show that the resulting tours have costs greater than 15.

Note, that all 3 edges of cost 1 are already used in the current permutation which implies no additional edge of cost 1 can be added. We inspect the different 2-opt steps with respect to the edges that are removed.

- If two edges of type A which have cost of 1 are removed, two other edges need to be added and the least costly edges that can be added have a weight of 3. This makes the total cost of the resulting solution to be at least $15 - 2 \cdot 1 + 2 \cdot 3 = 19$ which is greater than 15.
- If one edge of type A (weight 1) and one edge of type C (weight 4) are removed, again with the minimum two edges of cost 3 that are added, the total cost is at least $15 - 1 - 4 + 2 \cdot 3 = 16$ which is greater than 15.
- For removing two edges of Type C, there are three options:
  - Remove the edge between cluster 1 and cluster 4 and also the edge between cluster 2 and cluster 5. This 2-opt results in permutation $\pi' = (1, 5, 4, 2, 3, 6)$ which adds two edges of type D to the solution, making the total cost greater than 15.
  - Remove the edge between cluster 1 and cluster 4 and also the edge between cluster 3 and cluster 6. This 2-opt results in permutation $\pi' = (1, 3, 2, 5, 4, 6)$ which also adds two edges of type D to the solution, making the total cost greater than 15.
  - Remove the edge between cluster 2 and cluster 5 and also the edge between cluster 3 and cluster 6. This 2-opt results in permutation $\pi' = (1, 4, 5, 3, 2, 6)$ which also adds two edges of type D to the solution, making the total cost greater than 15.

We have shown that no 2-opt step is accepted which completes the proof. □

In contrast to the negative result for CBLS, we show that NEN-LS is able to reach an optimal solution when starting with the same solution.

THEOREM 3. *Starting with $\pi = (1, 4, 5, 2, 3, 6)$, NEN-LS finds an optimal solution for the instance G_1 in $O(nm^2)$ steps.*

PROOF. Starting with a solution with only white nodes and the permutation of $\pi = (1, 4, 5, 2, 3, 6)$, the lower level is already locally optimal using the arguments in the proof of Theorem 2. This implies that the solution does not change unless a grey note in cluster V_1 is selected.

Let $P = \{p_1, \cdots, p_6\}$ be the current set of spanning nodes. Selecting a grey node p_1' for cluster V_1 leads to the set of spanning nodes $P' = \{p_1', p_2, \cdots, p_6\}$. P' in combination with the the current permutation $\pi = (1, 4, 5, 2, 3, 6)$ has a total cost of 111 as there is one edge of type D with cost 100. We now show that starting from this solution and performing a 2-opt local search on the lower level results in an optimal solution.

In order to accept a new permutation on the lower level a solution of cost at most 111 has to be obtained. We do a case distinction according to the different types of edges that are removed in a 2-opt operation. If we only remove edges of type A and C, we reach a solution with total cost of greater than 111 using the arguments in the proof of Theorem 2. Hence, we only need to consider the case where at least one edge of type D is removed.

- There are two possibilities of removing one edge of type D and one of the edge of type C leading to the permutations $\pi' = (1, 5, 4, 2, 3, 6)$ and $\pi'' = (1, 3, 2, 5, 4, 6)$. Both have two edges of type D which implies a total cost of greater than 111 and are therefore rejected.
- Considering the case of removing the edge of type D and one of the edges of type A, the only applicable 2-opt move leading to a different permutation results in the permutation $\pi' = (1, 2, 5, 4, 3, 6)$. The resulting solution has cost 16 and is therefore accepted.

Considering $\pi' = (1, 2, 5, 4, 3, 6)$, the only acceptable 2-opt move leads to the global optimum $\pi_{opt} = (1, 2, 3, 4, 5, 6)$. The runtime is bounded by $O(nm^2)$ as it takes $O(n)$ time on the upper level to selected a grey node. Furthermore, each lower level optimization is bounded by $O(m^2)$ as either permutations are locally optimal with respect to the spanning nodes or there are at most two improvements of the permutation in the case that a grey node of cluster V_1 is selected. □

4. BENEFITS OF CBLS

We now consider a situation where NEN-LS* finds it hard to obtain an optimal solution and CBLS with the same starting solution obtains an optimum in polynomial time. The instance $G_2 = (V, E)$ is illustrated in Figure 2. There are m clusters where $m > 2$, and all the clusters contain only 2 nodes; one white and one black. We refer to the white and black nodes of cluster i, $1 \leq i \leq m$, by v_{iW} and v_{iB}, respectively. We call cluster V_1 the costly cluster as edges connecting this cluster are more costly than edges connecting the other clusters. The edge set E of G_2 is partitioned into 4 different types.

- Type A: Edges of this type have a weight of 1. All connections between white nodes of different clusters except cluster V_1 are of this type.

$$A = \quad \{\{v_{iW}, v_{jW}\} \mid 2 \leq i, j \leq m\}$$

- Type B: Edges of this type have a weight of 2. All connections between black nodes of different clusters are of this type.

$$B = \quad \{\{v_{iB}, v_{jB}\} \mid 1 \leq i, j \leq m\}$$

- Type C: Edges of this type have a weight of m. All edges between white node of the costly cluster and white nodes of other clusters are of this type.

$$C = \quad \{\{v_{1W}, v_{iW}\} \mid 2 \leq i \leq m\}$$

- Type D: Edges of this type have a weight of m^2. All other edges in this complete graph, which consist of all edges between a white and a black node, are of this type.

$$\begin{aligned} D = &\quad E \setminus \{A \cup B \cup C\} \\ = &\quad \{\{v_{iW}, v_{jB}\} \mid 1 \leq i, j \leq m\} \end{aligned}$$

We first claim that the optimal solution consists of only black nodes. Then we bring our main theorems on the runtime behaviour of solving this instance with the two mentioned approaches.

PROPERTY 4. *For the graph G_2 any solution containing all black nodes is optimal.*

PROOF. A solution that contains only black nodes has m edges of type B and therefore total cost of $2m$.

Choosing a combination of black and white nodes implies a connection of type D and therefore a solution of cost at least m^2. Choosing all white nodes implies 2 edges of cost m connected to cluster V_1 and $m-2$ edges of cost 1. Hence, the total cost of such a solution is $2m+(m-2)$ which implies that a solution selecting all black nodes is optimal. □

We now show that CBLS always finds an optimal solution due to selecting an optimal spanning nodes in time $O(n^3)$.

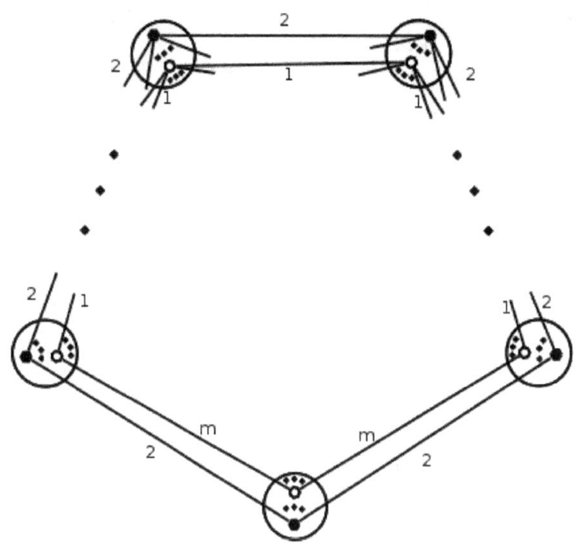

Figure 2: Graph G_2

THEOREM 5. *Starting with an arbitrary permutation π, CBLS finds an optimal solution for G_2 by choosing the optimal spanning node set P for π in time $O(n^3)$.*

PROOF. As mentioned in Property 4, visiting black nodes of the graph in any order is a globally optimal solution. For each permutation π the optimal set of nodes is given by all black nodes and found when constructing the first spanning node set. Such a set P is constructed in time $O(n^3)$ by the shortest path algorithm given in [11]. □

In contrast to the positive result for CBLS, NEN-LS* is extremely likely to get stuck in a local optimum if the initial spanning node set is chosen uniformly at random. Note, that NEN-LS* even uses an exact solver for the lower layer.

THEOREM 6. *Starting with a spanning node set P chosen uniformly at random, NEN-LS* gets stuck in a local optimum of G_2 with probability $1 - e^{-\Omega(n)}$.*

PROOF. Selecting $P = \{p_1, \cdots, p_m\}$ uniformly at random, the expected number of white nodes is $\frac{n}{2}$. Using Chernoff bounds, the number of white nodes is at least $n/4$ with probability $1 - e^{-\Omega(n)}$. The same applies to the number of black nodes.

Since connecting white nodes to black nodes is costly, the lower layer selects a permutation which forms a chain of white nodes and a chain of black nodes connected to form a cycle by only two edges of type D.

Let p_1 be the selected node of the costly cluster V_1. If p_1 is initially white, the lower layer places it at one border between the black chain and the white chain to avoid using one of edges of type C. This situation is illustrated in Figure 3. If p_1 is initially black, then the initial solution would look like Figure 4.

CLAIM 7. *Starting with a random initial solution, for all the clusters $V_i, 2 \leq i \leq m$; a change from black to white is improving while no change from white to black is improving.*

PROOF. As mentioned earlier, a random initial solution has a chain of black nodes and a chain of white nodes.

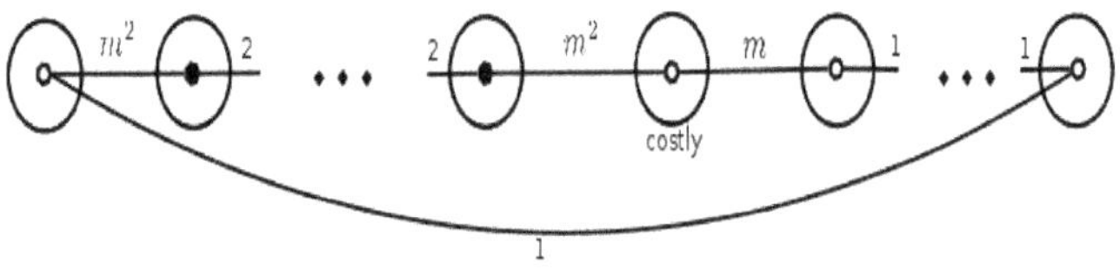

Figure 3: The initial solution for G_2 if a white node is selected for the costly cluster V_1

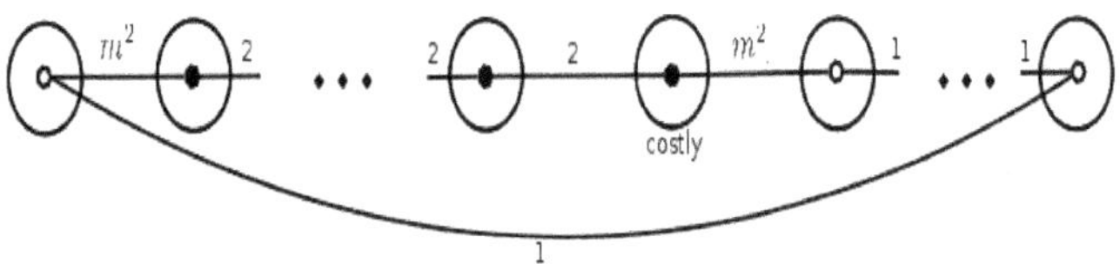

Figure 4: A possible solution for G_2 if a black node is selected for the costly cluster V_1

Changing a black node $p_i, i \neq c$ to white results in shortening the chain of black nodes by removing an edge of type B and cost 2, while the chain of white nodes gets longer by adding an edge of type A and cost 1. The new solution is hence improved in terms of fitness and accepted by the algorithm. On the other hand, the opposite move increases the cost of the solution; therefore in a cluster $V_i, i \neq c$ a change from white to black cannot happen.

The number of selected white nodes for clusters $V_i, i \neq 1$ never decreases; therefore, at all time during the run of the algorithm we have both chains of black nodes and white nodes, until all the black nodes change to white. □

CLAIM 8. *As long as there is at least one cluster V_i, $i \neq 1$ for which the black node is selected, a change from white to black is accepted for cluster V_1 and the opposite change is rejected.*

PROOF. Since there is at least one cluster $V_i, i \neq 1$, for which the black node is selected, we know that the current solution and the new solution both have a chain of black nodes and a chain of white nodes. If the white node of cluster V_1 is selected in the current solution, changing it to black shortens the chain of white nodes with removing the edge of type C while increases the number of black nodes by adding an edge of type B. This move is accepted because the new solution is improved in terms of cost. The result is illustrated in Figure 4. Using similar arguments, if the black node of cluster V_1 is selected in the current solution, changing it to white is rejected because it increases the cost. □

Using Claim 7 we can conclude that all nodes $p_i, i \neq 1$ gradually are changed to white in the local search that is performed in the NEN. For p_1:

- If p_1 is initially black, it remains black until all other p_is change to white. At this point p_1 is the only black node in the solution and is connected to two white nodes with edges of type D and cost m^2 as illustrated in Figure 5. If it changes to white, these two edges are removed and two edges of type C and cost m are added to the solution (Figure 6). This change is accepted because two edges of cost m are less costly than two edges of cost m^2.
- If p_1 is initially white,

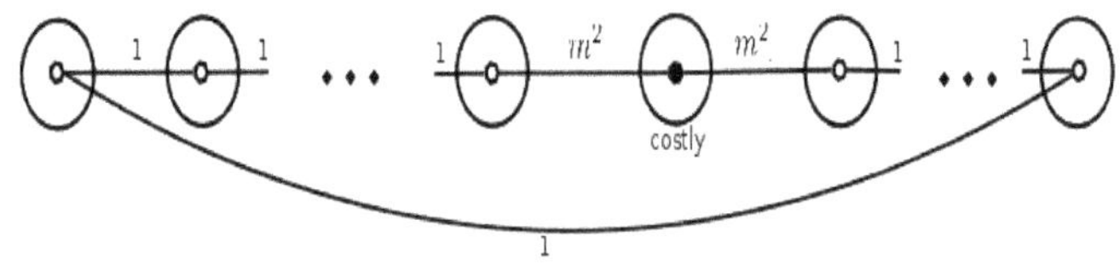

Figure 5: All other clusters change to white one by one

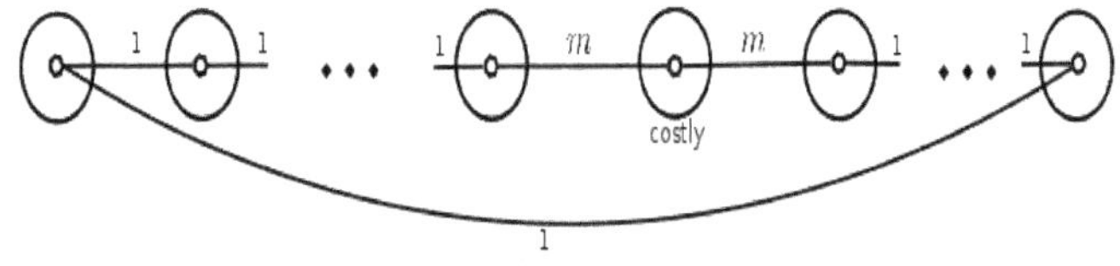

Figure 6: Local Optimum for G_2

  - If it happens to change to black, it remains black until all other p_is change to white, at which point p_1 also changes to white.
  - If all other p_is change to white before trying a black node for p_1, then it never changes to black.

This eventually results in a local optimum with all white nodes selected. The algorithm only needs to traverse the clusters on the upper layer only twice which gives $O(m)$ iterations on the upper layer for the algorithm to get stuck in a local optimum. In the first traverse, for all the clusters the white node will be selected except for the costly cluster V_1 for which the black node will be selected. In the second traverse, that only black node will also change to white. □

5. BENEFITS OF VNS

In this section we introduce an instance of the problem for which both of the mentioned neighbourhood search algorithms fail to find the optimal solution. Nevertheless, the combination of these approaches as described in Algorithm 4 results in finding the global optimum.

We consider the undirected graph G_3 shown in Figure 7 which has 6 clusters each containing $n/6$ nodes. There are three kinds of nodes in this graph: white, grey and black. The first cluster consists of $n/12$ black, $n/24$ white, and $n/24$ grey nodes. All other clusters contain $n/12$ white and $n/12$ black nodes. We refer to the set of white, black and grey nodes of cluster V_i by V_{iW}, V_{iB}, andV_{iG}, respectively.

There are 5 types of edges in this graph, 4 of which are quite similar to the 4 types of the instance in Section 3. The other type, named type D below, includes the edges between two consecutive black nodes with a cost of 1.5.

- Type A: Edges of this type have a cost of 1.

$$\begin{aligned} A = \{\{v_i, v_j\} \mid \quad & (v_i \in V_{1W} \cup V_{1G} \wedge v_j \in V_{6W}) \\ \vee \quad & (v_i \in V_{2W} \wedge v_j \in V_{3W}) \\ \vee \quad & (v_i \in V_{4W} \wedge v_j \in V_{5W})\} \end{aligned}$$

- Type B: Edges of this type have a cost of 3.

$$\begin{aligned} B = \{\{v_i, v_j\} \mid \quad & (v_i \in V_{1W} \cup V_{1G} \wedge v_j \in V_{2W}) \\ \vee \quad & (v_i \in V_{3W} \wedge v_j \in V_{4W}) \\ \vee \quad & (v_i \in V_{5W} \wedge v_j \in V_{6W})\} \end{aligned}$$

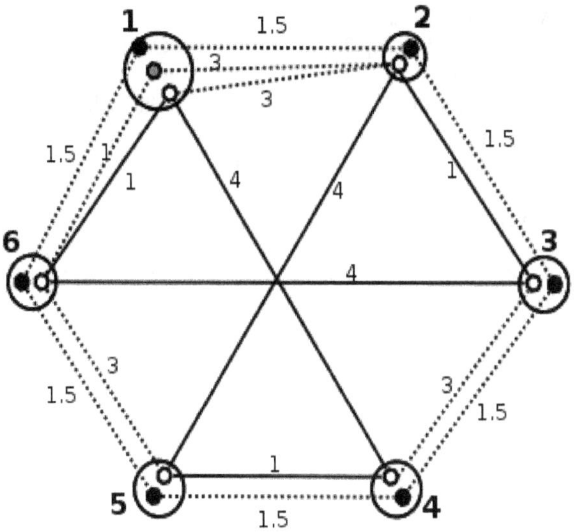

Figure 7: Graph G_3 showing one node of each type for each cluster and omitting edges of cost 100.

- Type C: Edges of this type have a cost of 4.

$$C = \{\{v_i, v_j\} \mid \quad (v_i \in V_{1W} \wedge v_j \in V_{4W}) \vee (v_i \in V_{2W} \wedge v_j \in V_{5W}) \vee (v_i \in V_{3W} \wedge v_j \in V_{6W})\}$$

- Type D: Edges of this type have a cost of 1.5.

$$D = \{\{v_i, v_j\} \mid \quad (v_i \in V_{kB} \wedge v_j \in V_{(k+1)B} \ , \ 1 \le k \le 5) \vee (v_i \in V_{6B} \wedge v_j \in V_{1B})\}$$

- Type F: Edges of this kind have a large cost of 100. All edges other than those of type A or B or C or D in this complete graph are of Type F. Note that the edges between grey nodes of the first cluster and the white nodes of the forth cluster are also of this type.

$$F = \quad E \setminus \{A \cup B \cup C \cup D\}$$

We now show that an optimal solution visits a black node from each cluster in consecutive or reverse-consecutive order.

PROPERTY 9. *The optimal solution for the graph G_3 is visiting all black nodes with the consecutive or reverse-consecutive order.*

PROOF. There are three kinds of nodes in this graph; white, grey and black. Any solution that contains black and one other kind of node has at least two edges of type F and weight 100 which makes the total cost of that solution more than 200. A solution that visits all black nodes in consecutive or reverse-consecutive order has 6 edges of type D and a total cost of 9. On the other hand, if we consider only white and grey nodes, our graph is the same as the instance of Section 3 with the optimal solution of cost 12. Therefore, visiting all black nodes with the cost of 9 is the optimal solution. □

We now show that the algorithms CBLS and NEN-LS may get stuck in a local optimum.

THEOREM 10. *Starting with a spanning node set P consisting of only white nodes and the permutation $\pi = (1, 4, 5, 2, 3, 6)$, CBLS and NEN-LS get stuck in a local optimum of G_3.*

PROOF. We first show that the mentioned initial solution is a local optimum for CBLS. The cost of this solution is 15 which is less than any of the edges between black nodes and white or grey nodes which are of type F. Therefore, any solution consisting of two kinds of nodes, black and another kind, cannot be accepted after this solution. Considering only white and grey nodes, the permutation $\pi' = (1, 2, 3, 4, 5, 6)$ is better than the current one, but as we saw in Theorem 2 of Section 3 this order can not be achieved with Algorithm 1. A solution consisting of all the black nodes is less costly only if they are visited in the optimal order of $\pi' = (1, 2, 3, 4, 5, 6)$ which is exactly the same permutation that is better for white nodes as well. As we discussed, this permutation is not achievable by searching the 2-opt neighbourhood of the current solution and the Cluster-Based approach can not find it.

Now we investigate the behaviour of NEN-LS which performs a local search based on the Node-Based approach for this instance. We show that this algorithm finds another locally optimal solution. Starting with the initial solution that is specified in the theorem, all black nodes can not be selected in one step and trying any one of the black nodes is rejected, because using two edges of type F are inevitable which makes the solution worse than the initial solution. The only spanning node set left in the NEN has the grey node of the first cluster. For this selection of nodes, the 2-opt TSP solver of the lower layer finds the optimal order of clusters similar to what we described in Theorem 3 of Section 3 which form a solution of cost 12. From this point any Node-Exchange-Neighbourhood search fails to find a better solution. □

Using the combination of the two hierarchical approaches by variable-neighbourhood search allows us to escape these local optima. As a result VNS obtains an optimal solution when starting with the same solution as investigated in Theorem 10.

THEOREM 11. *Starting with a spanning node set P consisting only of white nodes and the $\pi = (1, 4, 5, 2, 3, 6)$, VNS obtains an optimal solution in time $O(n^3)$.*

PROOF. This approach is supposed to start with Cluster-Based algorithm and alternate between the two algorithms whenever CBLS is stuck in a locally optimal solution. As we saw, from the initial solution, Algorithm 1 can not find any better solutions, because the initial solution is a local optimum for that algorithm. Finding this out requires searching all the 2-opt neighbourhood which can be done in constant time, because the number of clusters is fixed. Then NEN-LS manages to find another solution with the permutation of $\pi' = (1, 2, 3, 4, 5, 6)$. This can also be done in polynomial time as we described in Theorem 3 of Section 3. Then CBLS uses this as a starting solution. As $\pi' = (1, 2, 3, 4, 5, 6)$ is an optimal permutation the optimal set of nodes P consisting of all black nodes is found in time $O(n^3)$ on the lower layer. □

The investigations of this section have pointed out where a combination of the two hierarchical approaches into variable neighbourhood search gives a clear benefit to the optimization process as it is crucial for escaping local optima of the two single approaches.

6. CONCLUSION

Local search approaches have been shown to be very successful for solving the generalized travelling salesperson problem. We have investigated two common hierarchical representations together with local search neighbourhoods from a theoretical perspective. By presenting instances where they mutually outperform each other, we have gained new insights into the complimentary abilities of the two approaches. Furthermore, we have presented and analysed a class of instances where combining the two approaches into a variable-neighbourhood search helps to escape from local optima of the single approaches.

Acknowledgements

The research leading to these results has received funding from the Australian Research Council (ARC) under grant agreements DP130104395 and DP140103400.

7. REFERENCES

[1] A. Auger and B. Doerr. *Theory of Randomized Search Heuristics: Foundations and Recent Developments.* World Scientific Publishing Co., Inc., 2011.

[2] D. Corus, P. K. Lehre, and F. Neumann. The generalized minimum spanning tree problem: a parameterized complexity analysis of bi-level optimisation. In C. Blum and E. Alba, editors, *Genetic and Evolutionary Computation Conference, GECCO '13, Amsterdam, The Netherlands, July 6-10, 2013*, pages 519–526. ACM, 2013.

[3] D. Corus, P. K. Lehre, F. Neumann, and M. Pourhassan. A parameterized complexity analysis of bi-level optimisation with evolutionary algorithms. *CoRR*, abs/1401.1905, 2014.

[4] M. Englert, H. Röglin, and B. Vöcking. Worst case and probabilistic analysis of the 2-opt algorithm for the TSP. *Algorithmica*, 68(1):190–264, 2014.

[5] M. Fischetti, J. J. Salazar González, and P. Toth. A branch-and-cut algorithm for the symmetric generalized traveling salesman problem. *Operations Research*, 45(3):378–394, 1997.

[6] M. Gendreau and J.-Y. Potvin. *Handbook of Metaheuristics.* Springer Publishing Company, Incorporated, 2nd edition, 2010.

[7] G. Gutin and D. Karapetyan. A memetic algorithm for the generalized traveling salesman problem. *Natural Computing*, 9(1):47–60, 2010.

[8] M. Held and R. M. Karp. A dynamic programming approach to sequencing problems. In *Proceedings of the 1961 16th ACM National Meeting*, ACM '61, pages 71.201–71.204, New York, NY, USA, 1961. ACM.

[9] B. Hu and G. R. Raidl. Effective neighborhood structures for the generalized traveling salesman problem. In J. I. van Hemert and C. Cotta, editors, *EvoCOP*, volume 4972 of *Lecture Notes in Computer Science*, pages 36–47. Springer, 2008.

[10] T. Jansen. *Analyzing Evolutionary Algorithms - The Computer Science Perspective.* Natural Computing Series. Springer, 2013.

[11] D. Karapetyan and G. Gutin. Efficient local search algorithms for known and new neighborhoods for the generalized traveling salesman problem. *European Journal of Operational Research*, 219(2):234–251, 2012.

[12] T. Kötzing, F. Neumann, H. Röglin, and C. Witt. Theoretical analysis of two ACO approaches for the traveling salesman problem. *Swarm Intelligence*, 6(1):1–21, 2012.

[13] F. Neumann and C. Witt. *Bioinspired Computation in Combinatorial Optimization:Algorithms and Their Computational Complexity.* Springer-Verlag New York, Inc., New York, NY, USA, 1st edition, 2010.

[14] P. C. Pop and S. Iordache. A hybrid heuristic approach for solving the generalized traveling salesman problem. In N. Krasnogor and P. L. Lanzi, editors, *GECCO*, pages 481–488. ACM, 2011.

[15] D. Sudholt. Hybridizing evolutionary algorithms with variable-depth search to overcome local optima. *Algorithmica*, 59(3):343–368, 2011.

[16] D. Sudholt. Parametrization and balancing local and global search. In F. Neri, C. Cotta, and P. Moscato, editors, *Handbook of Memetic Algorithms*, volume 379 of *Studies in Computational Intelligence*, pages 55–72. Springer, 2012.

[17] A. M. Sutton, F. Neumann, and S. Nallaperuma. Parameterized runtime analyses of evolutionary algorithms for the planar Euclidean traveling salesperson problem. *Evolutionary Computation*, 22(4):595âĂŞ628, 2014.

Towards the User Equilibrium in Traffic Assignment Using GRASP with Path Relinking

Gabriel de O. Ramos
Instituto de Informática
Universidade Federal do Rio Grande do Sul
Porto Alegre, RS, Brazil
goramos@inf.ufrgs.br

Ana L. C. Bazzan
Instituto de Informática
Universidade Federal do Rio Grande do Sul
Porto Alegre, RS, Brazil
bazzan@inf.ufrgs.br

ABSTRACT

Solving the traffic assignment problem (TAP) is an important step towards an efficient usage of the traffic infrastructure. A fundamental assignment model is the so-called User Equilibrium (UE), which may turn into a complex optimisation problem. In this paper, we present the use of the GRASP metaheuristic to approximate the UE of the TAP. A path relinking mechanism is also employed to promote a higher coverage of the search space. Moreover, we propose a novel performance evaluation function, which measures the number of vehicles that have an incentive to deviate from the routes to which they were assigned. Through experiments, we show that our approach outperforms classical algorithms, providing solutions that are, on average, significantly closer to the UE. Furthermore, when compared to classical methods, the fairness achieved by our assignments is considerably better. These results indicate that our approach is efficient and robust, producing reasonably stable assignments.

CCS Concepts

•**Theory of computation** → **Optimization with randomized search heuristics;** *Exact and approximate computation of equilibria;* •**Computing methodologies** → *Artificial intelligence; Search methodologies; Modeling and simulation;*

Keywords

traffic assignment, user equilibrium, metaheuristics, GRASP

1. INTRODUCTION

Efficient urban mobility has shown to be a major challenge towards smart cities. Traditional approaches for dealing with arising traffic issues include increasing the physical capacity of existing traffic infrastructure. Such approaches, however, have proven unsustainable from many perspectives. Moreover, as stated by the Braess' paradox [4], expanding the infrastructure's capacity may lead to a deterioration in the traffic performance. Against this background, ways of making a more efficient use of the existing infrastructure have been increasingly studied. Among such ways, traffic assignment is a particularly relevant one.

Traffic assignment represents an important step towards modelling and simulating transportation systems. Specifically, the traffic assignment problem (TAP) addresses how to efficiently connect the physical infrastructure (supply) and the vehicles[1] that are going to use it. In other words, by solving the TAP one can promote a more efficient use of the currently available traffic infrastructure.

Solving the TAP, however, is not a trivial task. As a first attempt, one may consider assigning vehicles to their corresponding shortest routes. However, such an approach may lead to the concentration of vehicles in a small number of roads (a.k.a. links), which might incur in huge congestions. The problem is also unlikely to be overcome by simply creating alternative routes. Due to the limited availability of resources (links), different routes may share the same links. In other words, the problem is more related to how to efficiently *spread* the traffic than with the number of routes to be used itself. Precisely, solving the TAP means distributing the vehicles into the road network regarding their origins and destinations (a.k.a. OD pairs) in order to minimise some associated cost (e.g., travel time, money expenses, polluting emissions). Therefore, the TAP is essentially an optimization problem.

Two fundamental traffic assignment models have been developed to solve the TAP: system optimal (SO) and user equilibrium (UE). In an SO approach, one seeks to find an assignment that minimises the travel costs on a global level, i.e., it describes the system at its best operation. However, minimising the global cost may lead to increasing the cost of some users. Consequently, some users may have an incentive to deviate from the routes to which they were assigned. Hence, an SO solution may be infeasible in practice. The UE approach, on the other hand, describes solutions from the users' behaviour point of view. In essence, in a UE configuration, every user is assigned to one of the best available routes for its OD pair. Along these lines, the advantage of a UE solution (over an SO one) is that users have no incentive to deviate from the routes they were assigned to. Thus, the UE configuration is more likely to be pursued in practice by the drivers than an SO one.

Many methods have been proposed for solving the TAP using one or both models described before, each with its strengths and weaknesses. What must be clear, however,

[1]Henceforth, we use the terms vehicle and driver alternately.

GECCO '15, July 11 - 15, 2015, Madrid, Spain
© 2015 ACM. ISBN 978-1-4503-3472-3/15/07...$15.00
DOI: http://dx.doi.org/10.1145/2739480.2754755

is that in both approaches the search space can be huge and solving the problem optimally may be infeasible. To this respect, an alternative that has drawn attention is the development of methods capable of finding approximate solutions to the TAP. Specifically, the use of heuristics in the TAP has shown a promising direction.

In this paper, we approach the TAP in terms of UE with the GRASP+PR algorithm. GRASP+PR stands for the Greedy Randomised Adaptive Search Procedure algorithm embodied with the Path Relinking mechanism. GRASP is a heuristic search algorithm that greedily builds independent solutions and improve them with local search. The PR mechanism is used to increase the diversity of solutions. We propose a novel representation of solutions, which allows the modelling of TAP in terms of the UE. Through such a representation, GRASP+PR can be used to minimise the number of vehicles that are assigned to non-least cost routes, thus enhancing the assignments' fairness. To the best of our knowledge, this is the first approach to address the UE by minimising the amount of vehicles on non-least cost routes. Our proposal is empirically evaluated, and shown to provide solutions that are, on average, considerably fairer and closer to the UE than those from classical methods. Such results show that our approach is efficient, providing reasonably stable assignments.

The present work is organised as follows. Basic concepts are introduced in Section 2. A brief overview of related work and the GRASP+PR algorithm are presented in Sections 3 and 4, respectively. The problem modelling and the use of GRASP+PR in our approach are detailed in Section 5. The evaluation of our proposal is shown in Section 6. Concluding remarks and future directions are presented Section 7.

2. TRAFFIC ASSIGNMENT

In this section, the basic concepts surrounding traffic assignment are presented. For a more comprehensive overview the reader is referred to [16, chapter 10] or [3, chapter 4].

A road network can be represented as a directed graph $G = (N, L)$, where the set N of nodes represents the intersections, and the set L of directed links represents the roads between intersections. Each link $l_k \in L$ has an associated cost c_k, which is given as a function of some of its attributes, like length, speed limit, capacity, load/flow (of vehicles), etc. The cost of a link represents some sort of measure, like travel time, money expenses, polluting emissions, etc.

The flow of vehicles in a network (the demand) is based on the amount of trips made between different origins and destinations. Let T_{ij} be the demand for trips between origin i and destination j, i.e., the number of vehicles that need to reach j from i. The set of all such demands is represented by an origin-destination (OD) matrix $T = \{T_{ij} \mid \forall i, j \in N,\ i \neq j,\ T_{ij} \geq 0\}$. A trip is made by means of a route $R \subseteq L$, which is a sequence of links that connects an origin to a destination. The cost C_R of a given route R can be obtained by summing up the costs of the links that comprise it, as in Equation (1).

$$C_R = \sum_{l_k \in R} c_k \tag{1}$$

In order to compute the cost of the links, the concept of volume-delay functions (VDF) needs to be introduced. A VDF is a well-known abstraction used to express the delay (cost) of a link depending on the volume (flow) of vehicles on it. In other words, VDFs provide a means to study how the flow affects the cost on a link. Such a concept is important because the TAP is typically studied in a macroscopic level, i.e., the vehicles movement is considered in an abstract way. A VDF takes as input the flow of vehicles within a link and, based on the characteristics of such link (e.g., length, capacity, etc.), returns a cost on it. A simple VDF is presented in Equation (2), with t_k and f_k representing, respectively, the free flow travel time (minimum travel time when the link is not congested), and the number of vehicles on link $l_k \in L$. This particular VDF represents the travel time on link k, which is increased by 0.02 for each vehicle/hour of flow.

$$c_k(f_k) = t_k + 0.02 \times f_k \tag{2}$$

As previously stated, two fundamental models to solve the TAP are System Optimal (SO) and User Equilibrium (UE). Recall that an SO assignment describes the system as its best operation. On the other hand, UE stands for the traffic condition stated by the Wardrop's first principle: "under equilibrium conditions traffic arranges itself in congested networks such that all used routes between an OD pair have equal and minimum costs while all unused routes have greater or equal costs" [22]. We refer the reader to [11] for the mathematical formulation of these models. That said, although the SO model may seem the most efficient one, it has the disadvantage that some users may have no incentive to actually follow the routes to which they were assigned. In fact, some users would change their routes to those with minimum cost. Thus, the UE model has shown a more realistic way of assigning routes to vehicles.

The UE model can be analytically stated as an optimization problem. However, this model has the drawback of not being solvable algebraically, except for very simple scenarios. Hence, providing approximate solutions to the problem has shown a promising direction. Before advancing to this topic, some traditional methods need to be introduced.

In general, methods for the TAP involve two steps [16]: (i) using a set of rules to identify desirable routes (e.g., the fastest) in each OD pair (this is usually performed by shortest path algorithms), and (ii) assigning suitable portions of the OD trips to these routes so that a given objective is achieved. It should be noted, however, that the desirability of a given route may vary due to congestion effects. Specifically, desirable routes may become less attractive than others as the flow on their links increase. On this basis, the two steps above are generally performed iteratively, until a given (non-iterative) convergence criterion is achieved.

The simplest traffic assignment method is known as *all-or-nothing*, which perform the task without accounting for congestion effects. Specifically, the all-or-nothing method selects the shortest route for each OD pair, and then assigns the entire corresponding flow to that route. This approach, however, is quite naïve, since assigning all vehicles to the same routes (one per OD pair) can lead to congestions. Although this method is of low interest in practice, it has been used by more sophisticated methods. Furthermore, it may be useful as an upper bound.

More sophisticated methods for traffic assignment are iterative ones, which account for congestion. One of these methods is the so-called *incremental assignment*. The incremental assignment method iteratively loads proportional fractions p_n (with $\sum_n p_n = 1$) of the demand into the lowest cost routes (one for each OD pair). A new set of lowest cost

Algorithm 1: Pseudocode of MSA (adapted from [16])

1 select an initial set of current link costs (usually free-flow travel times); initialise the flow of every link k: $f_k = 0$; set $n = 0$;

2 create an auxiliary all-or-nothing assignment based on current link costs, obtaining a set of auxiliary flows F;

3 calculate the current flow of every link k as: $f_k^n = (1-\psi)f_k^{n-1} + \psi F_k$, with $\psi \in [0,1]$;

4 for every link k, update the cost c_k based on the flow f_k^n; if the predefined stop criterion was achieved, then stop; otherwise proceed to step 2;

routes is created (using the all-or-nothing assignment) on every iteration based on the costs resulting from the flows accumulated on previous iterations. A typical set of values for p_n is $\{0.4, 0.3, 0.2, 0.1\}$. This method, however, does not have convergence guarantees, because, once a flow is assigned, it cannot be changed from one iteration to another.

Another iterative method that accounts for congestion effects is the *method of successive averages* (MSA). MSA iteratively generates an all-or-nothing assignment, and changes a fraction ψ of the previous iteration's assignment according to the all-or-nothing one. This method is repeated until a given stop criterion is achieved. To be precise, the flow at the n-th iteration is a linear combination of the flow at the $(n-1)$-th iteration and an auxiliary flow resulting from an all-or-nothing assignment in the n-th iteration. The MSA can be formalised as in Algorithm 1. It has been shown [20] that MSA produces solutions convergent to the UE when $\psi = 1/n$ (with $n \to \infty$). However, this method may take many iterations, especially in more complex scenarios, thus being very inefficient.

3. RELATED WORK

Many approaches have been proposed to solve the TAP from many perspectives. Broadly speaking, we can classify these approaches into two fronts: global, when the assignment is performed by a central authority in charge of this process; and individual, when each vehicle is responsible for choosing its own route. In this section we present some relevant works on each of these fronts, starting with the former.

A genetic algorithm for the TAP is presented in [2] and [6], aiming at computing the SO. In these approaches, each vehicle has a corresponding position in the chromosome, and the value within this position corresponds to one among k predefined routes (regarding the vehicle's OD pair) to which the vehicle can be assigned. The main difference between these two approaches lies in the way the traffic is simulated: in [2] the simulation is macroscopic, whereas in [6] it is microscopic. As opposed to the macroscopic settings that we have seen so far, in a microscopic simulation the vehicles' movement is considered in detail (speed, gap between vehicles, etc.). Although microscopic simulation is more realistic, it is much more complex to handle. Despite of that difference, both approaches present good results regarding the purpose to which they were proposed. The UE, however, is not addressed by these approaches. Moreover, the size of the neighbourhood resulting from the proposed modelling is excessively large.

The TAP is approached from a game theoretic point of view in [1]. In this approach, the problem is modelled as a population game, where each population (i.e., vehicles from the same OD pair) has a probability vector (a.k.a. strategy) representing its possible routes. A genetic algorithm is used to evolve the strategy profiles, aiming at the UE. Results show that the UE may be achieved under certain mutation rates. However, this approach considers just three populations.

The TAP is indirectly addressed by means of the toll booth problem (TBP) in [5]. The TBP consists in selecting links to charge tolls so that drivers have a monetary incentive to spread over the network. In this sense, by putting tolls in some links, one can induce drivers to act on behalf of the social welfare, bridging the gap between the UE and SO. In this work, a biased random-key genetic algorithm is used to accomplish this task. However, this approach depends on a high number of tolls to achieve good results, what may be impractical to deploy. Moreover, charging tolls is not a popular alternative from the drivers' viewpoint.

In [21], a genetic algorithm is presented for optimising traffic signal settings. Basically, on each iteration of the algorithm, the evolved traffic signal settings are used as input for a modified version of MSA. The aim here is to jointly optimize the traffic signal settings and the TAP. This approach, however, is more focused on the former problem.

A fuzzy-based route choice model was proposed in [14] to tackle the uncertainties regarding the drivers' decision making. The basic idea is to maintain routes' cost predictions in a fuzzy set, thus representing knowledge imprecisions and traffic uncertainties. On the basis of such representation, the model allows the association of a degree of attractiveness with each route. This work, however, is more concerned with tackling the uncertainties of the process than with the assignment optimality.

In [18], a percentile-based route choice model is used to account for the travel time budgets of drivers. The employed model assumes that drivers make decisions with respect to the route travel time distributions collected from past experiences. In this approach, the focus is on identifying the amount of time that each vehicle must allocate to its trip in order to reach its destination on time. However, this approach does not compute the SO nor the UE.

Regarding the aforementioned second front, agent-based approaches have shown to be a natural way of modelling traffic problems. The work of [8] presents an Inverted Ant Colony Optimization (IACO) algorithm for minimising the SO in a decentralised, microscopic way. IACO is a variant of the ACO algorithm in which pheromone repels, instead of attracting, ants. To this respect, vehicles deposit pheromone into the roads they travel, and avoid travelling through congested ones. The objective is to keep routes as diverse as possible. However, the pheromone needs to be kept by a central authority, which is a quite strong requirement for such a distributed system. Moreover, this work does not provide any statement on the optimality of the solutions.

A game-theoretic approach is also used in [10], where an evolutionary version of the minority game is employed. In this work, each driver has a set of strategies used to predict the links occupancy based on historic data. Each driver scores its strategies based on occupancy and travel times previously experimented by themselves. However, this approach assumes that historic network information is available to all drivers. Furthermore, the approach was validated in a quite simple scenario.

A number of recent agent-based approaches make use of reinforcement learning algorithms to promote route choice in a distributed fashion. Some examples include: [19] using learning automata; and [13] using Q-learning and considering how a single agent impact the global performance. In these approaches, the drivers know their OD pairs but do not know their routes a priori. In this sense, intersections are decision points, where drivers can decide what link to take next. This kind of *en-route* decision allows the drivers to account for the variability in their travel times due to their peers' decisions. The objective here is to compute the SO. However, as previously discussed, the SO is not realistic when the behaviour of selfish drivers is being considered.

The impact of different levels of information in the route choice process has increasingly attracted attention. The idea here is to provide an understanding on how the demand reacts to traffic information. Some works that study the impact of traffic information in the drivers' route choice behaviour are: [7], in which neural networks were used to predict the compliance level of drivers who receive traffic suggestions; and [17], where a fuzzy-based system is used to predict the route behaviour of drivers who are provided with traffic information. However, the focus of these approaches is on the impact of the traffic information itself, and none of them is assessed in terms of UE or SO.

Therefore, as can be seen, many approaches discussed here do not fully address the UE. Moreover, most approaches presented here for the UE are suitable for small scenarios only. An exception is the work of [5], which on the other hand has a strong dependence on a high number of tools.

4. THE GRASP+PR ALGORITHM

4.1 Greedy Randomised Adaptive Search Procedure

GRASP is a multistart greedy metaheuristic introduced in [9]. Basically, GRASP works as follows: at each iteration a greedy randomised solution is built from scratch and a local search procedure is used to improve it. GRASP is multistart in a sense that iterations are independent among themselves, i.e., the knowledge acquired in previous iterations is not used in the subsequent ones. With regard to the final result, since the algorithm is multistart, the best solution found so far is stored and returned in the end of the execution. We now present some basic concepts, slightly adapted to the context of the current work.

The problem to be addressed by GRASP is defined by a ground set $E = \{e_1, \dots, e_{|E|}\}$, a set of feasible solutions $F \subseteq 2^E$, and an objective function $\phi : 2^E \to \mathbb{R}$. A solution $S \in F$ is typically represented by a vector over the ground set E. Considering a minimisation problem, the aim is to find an optimal solution $S^* \in F$ such that $\phi(S^*) \leq \phi(S), \forall S \in F$. The definitions of ground set, objective function, and feasible solutions are specific to each problem. In this regard, one possible representation of the TAP would be: E as the set of drivers, ϕ as the travel cost and F as all possible assignments.

In a greedy heuristic, solutions are built progressively: at each step, a single element of the ground set is selected and included in the solution under construction, until a feasible[2] solution is obtained. The selection process evaluates how much the inclusion of each element increases the solution cost. Based on such evaluation, a common selection strategy is the α-greedy, in which one selects among the α% best elements uniformly at random.

It must be remarked that the greedily generated solutions may not be optimal, thus a local search procedure is employed by GRASP to improve them. A local search works by successively applying small changes in a solution until a (local) optimum is reached. Each such change is called a *movement*, and each solution produced by a single movement is called a *neighbour*. The *neighbourhood* of a solution S is the set $N(S) \subseteq F$. A solution S is said to be a local optimum if $\phi(S) \leq \phi(S'), \forall S' \in N(S)$. Different strategies can be employed to guide the local search. A common strategy is known as *best improvement*, in which the search is restricted to the best neighbourhood $B(S) = \{S' \in N(S) \mid \phi(S') < \phi(S)\}$, and a best neighbour is selected uniformly at random.

4.2 Path Relinking

The path relinking (PR) mechanism was initially proposed in [12] within the context of tabu search. Broadly speaking, PR explores the trajectory between an initial and a target solution. The result of PR is the best solution found in the traversed trajectory.

Some definitions are necessary. Let S_s and S_t be the initial and target solutions. The distance $\Delta(S_s, S_t)$ between two given solutions measures how many movements are necessary to transform one into the other. The PR mechanism works by exploring a directed neighbourhood $D(S_s) = \{S' \in N(S_s) \mid \Delta(S', S_t) < \Delta(S_s, S_t)\}$. A common strategy here is also the best improvement. In this sense, the search is performed from S_s to S_t and takes at most $\Delta(S_s, S_t)$ iterations.

In the context of GRASP, the PR mechanism is applied at every iteration, after the local search procedure is applied to the incumbent solution S. A set P of reference solutions is maintained. This set can be seen as a kind of memory, and it is defined to store the best and more diverse solutions found so far. From this set, a solution S_t can be selected as target. A common selection strategy here is to select a solution S' from P with probability proportional to $\Delta(S, S')$. This strategy gives priority to farthest targets, thus promoting a higher coverage of the search space. GRASP+PR was introduced in [15].

5. TRAFFIC ASSIGNMENT WITH GRASP+PR

5.1 Modelling

5.1.1 Solution Encoding and Evaluation

A solution S for the TAP represents an assignment of vehicles into routes. Recall that the demand is represented by an OD matrix $T = \{T_{ij} \mid \forall i, j \in N, i \neq j, T_{ij} > 0\}$, where T_{ij} is the demand for trips between origin i and destination j. A trip is made through a route $R \subseteq L$. In this work, we limit the available routes for each OD pair to the k shortest ones, among which the demand must be partitioned. Let $R_{ij} = \{R_{ij}^1, \dots, R_{ij}^k\}$ be the set of k shortest routes between

[2]Infeasible solutions may also be produced. Our approach, however, prevent them to occur (as shown in Section 5). Thus, we omit such concept to simplify the notation.

origin i and destination j. These sets are computed considering free flow travel times, and this process can be performed by the KSP algorithm [23].

Given the above definitions, a natural approach is to represent the problem as a vector of integers (as in [2, 6]), where the value in the i-th position identifies the route to which the i-th vehicle was assigned. In such a representation, however, the size of a solution is equal to the total demand, which may be huge. On this regard, in this paper we employ a more compact solution representation, where vehicles are grouped by OD pair and route. Specifically, a solution S is a matrix of size $|T| \times k$, where rows represent OD pairs, and columns represent the available routes for these OD pairs. A value on position $S[ij][r]$ represents the amount of vehicles from T_{ij} assigned to route R_{ij}^r. Observe that the r-th route from two distinct OD pairs are obviously not the same. Based upon such representation, the size of a solution is $\Theta(|T| \times k)$, which is lower than of the representation in [2, 6].

The solution evaluation is defined in terms of the UE. Remark that, under UE, drivers are assigned to the least cost routes, thus having no incentive to deviate from such assignment. In this sense, we measure the performance of an assignment by counting how many vehicles were *not* assigned to their respective least cost routes, i.e., we measure those that would have an incentive to deviate from the assignment. The value of a solution S can be formalised by $\phi : S \to \mathbb{N}$ as in Equation (3), where $R_{ij}^* = \min_{R \in R_{ij}} C(R)$ represents any[3] least cost route of the OD pair ij under assignment S. In the function, the farther the solution is from the UE, the higher its value, and a value 0 means the UE itself. Thus, the objective here is to minimise ϕ. It is worth noting that minimising ϕ promotes fairer assignments, since fewer drivers are assigned to routes worse than those of their peers.

$$\phi(S) = \sum_{T_{ij} \in T} \sum_{R_{ij}^r \in R_{ij}} \begin{cases} S[ij][r] & \text{if } C(R_{ij}^r) > C(R_{ij}^*) \\ 0 & \text{otherwise} \end{cases} \quad (3)$$

5.1.2 Neighbourhood

We now define the neighbourhood of a given solution S. Recall that a neighbour is obtained by performing a single movement in the solution. A movement here is characterised by moving a single vehicle from any route $R_{ij}^r \in \{R_{ij}^r \in R_{ij} \mid C(R_{ij}^r) > C(R_{ij}^*)\}$ to R_{ij}^*. This means that at most $k-1$ movements can be done for each of the $|T|$ OD pairs. Thus, the number of neighbours is $O(|T| \times k)$ (we omit the proof due to the space limitation). Observe that, as the value of solutions approaches zero (the UE), the number of least cost routes increases, and, consequently, the number of neighbours decreases.

Two interesting properties of the present modelling must be highlighted. The first is that infeasible solutions are automatically avoided. An infeasible solution would have either a non-natural number (in any position) or a total demand different from that of the OD matrix. However, a movement consists in changing the route of a single vehicle, thus the demand does not change, and empty routes can only receive vehicles. The second property is that our neighbourhood definition avoids redundant neighbours. The definition would otherwise allow redundant neighbours if the movement of *each* vehicle from route R_{ij}^r to route R_{ij}^* were considered in particular. In this case, such neighbours would be redundant because, from the solution definition perspective, they would represent exactly the same solutions.

[3] As many routes may have the same cost, we refer to R_{ij}^* as any least cost route. Ties are broken at random.

Algorithm 2: Overview of implemented GRASP+PR

```
Input: MaxIterations        // number of iterations
       α                    // due to the α-greedy strategy
       β                    // size of the reference set
       γ                    // probability of uniform solutions
S ← initialise best solution so far;
P ← initialise with β uniform solutions;
for i ∈ {1, ..., MaxIterations} do
    S' ← { GreedySolution(α)   with prob. 1 − γ
         { UniformSolution()   otherwise          ;
    S' ← LocalSearch(S');
    S'' ←sample a solution from P;
    S' ← PathRelinking(S', S'');
    S' ← LocalSearch(S');
    if φ(S') < φ(S) then
        S ← S';
    end
    P ← update reference set with S';
end
return S;
```

5.2 Methods

A general overview of our GRASP+PR approach is presented in Algorithm 2.

5.2.1 Solution Generation

In GRASP, solutions are generated in a randomised greedy way. However, to prevent any bias in the generation procedure, we also allow solutions to be generated uniformly. These two procedures are used alternately, according to parameter γ: a solution is greedily generated with probability $(1-\gamma)$, or uniformly generated with probability γ. Both procedures are described next.

In the greedy procedure, the ground set E has one element for each OD pair and route (considering its k routes). Let $E_{ij}^r \in E$ be the element corresponding to route r of OD pair ij, and let its cost be the amount that $\phi(S)$ would increase if $S[ij][r]$ were incremented by 1. Given this, the process starts with an empty solution S. On each iteration of the procedure, the cost of every element in E is updated and the α-greedy strategy is used to select (uniformly at random) one among the α% best such elements. After the element of the ground set is selected, the corresponding position in the solution is incremented by 1. This process is repeated until all vehicles are assigned to a route, thus preventing the predefined demand from being exceeded.

The uniform generation procedure is much simpler. The process also starts with an empty solution S. Consider an OD pair ij, its demand T_{ij}, and the corresponding set of routes R_{ij}. Let $U_{ij} = \{0, u_2, \ldots, u_k, T_{ij}\}$ be a sorted set, where $u_2, \ldots, u_k$ correspond to $k-1$ natural numbers in the interval $[0, T_{ij})$, generated uniformly at random. The solution is defined as $S[ij][r] = U_{ij}[r+1] - U_{ij}[r]$ for every route r of OD pair ij. This process is performed for every OD pair. The result is a feasible assignment, with demands distributed uniformly at random among the available routes.

5.2.2 Local Search and Path Relinking

Once a solution is generated, a local search procedure is applied to reach its corresponding local optimum. Specifically, given a solution S, the procedure explores its best neighbourhood $B(S)$ using the best improvement strategy. The process is performed until the local optimum is reached.

The PR mechanism is performed at each iteration, after the local search procedure. As previously mentioned, PR explores the trajectory between two given solutions. In this sense, let S be the incumbent solution, $\Delta(S, S')$ the distance between two given solutions, and P be the set of reference solutions. A target solution S_t is selected from P with probability proportional to $\Delta(S, S_t)$, i.e., the greater the distance to the incumbent solution, the higher the probability of being selected. Once a solution is selected, PR employs a best improvement search strategy to traverse from S to S_t. The best solution found in such traverse is returned, and a local search is also applied on it.

Concerning the reference set, its size is limited to keep at most β solutions. In this sense, P is maintained as follows. Initially, P is populated with β uniformly generated solutions. Next, on each iteration of GRASP, an incumbent solution S can replace another in P if its cost is lower than the worst in P, i.e., if $\phi(S) < \max_{S' \in P} \phi(S')$. In this case, S replaces the solution $S' = \arg\min_{S' \in P} \Delta(S, S')$, i.e., the one which is closest to him. This update mechanism on the reference set is performed at the end of each iteration.

6. EMPIRICAL EVALUATION

6.1 Experiments

Our approach is evaluated in a non-trivial road network introduced in the exercise 10.1 of [16] (henceforth OW). The OW network is shown in Figure 1, where the numbers on links represent their free flow travel time (in minutes). This scenario has four OD pairs: AL, AM, BL, and BM, with a demand of 600, 400, 300, and 400 vehicles, respectively. The cost of the links is obtained by means of the simple VDF in Equation (2), though more sophisticated ones could be used as well.

The performance of solutions is measured by means of Equation (3), introduced in present work. An additional, classical, performance metric, namely that of Equation (4), is also employed here. This latter metric accounts for the relative cost of travel times of non-least cost routes (further details in [16]). Hereafter, we refer to equations (3) and (4) as ϕ and δ, respectively. Remark that both ϕ and δ measure how far a given solution is from the UE. Finally, the average travel time (*avg-tt* hereafter, measured in minutes) is employed as a third performance metric. For the three metrics, the lower the resulting value, the better.

$$\delta(S) = \frac{\sum_{T_{ij} \in T} \sum_{R_{ij}^r \in R_{ij}} S[ij][r] \times (C(R_{ij}^r) - C(R_{ij}^*))}{\sum_{T_{ij} \in T} T_{ij} \times C(R_{ij}^*)} \quad (4)$$

Experiments were set up as follows. The set of shortest routes is generated only once, using the KSP algorithm [23]. These sets of routes are presented in Table 1, for $k = 4$. Regarding the parameters configurations for GRASP+PR, different combinations of values for these were tested. For each such combination, 30 repetitions were performed, where a repetition corresponds to a single execution of the algorithm with 1000 iterations. This calibration process is presented in Appendix A and the best configuration found was $k = 4$, $\alpha = 0.2$, $\beta = 20$, and $\gamma = 0.5$. The results of such configuration were selected for further analysis in the next subsection.

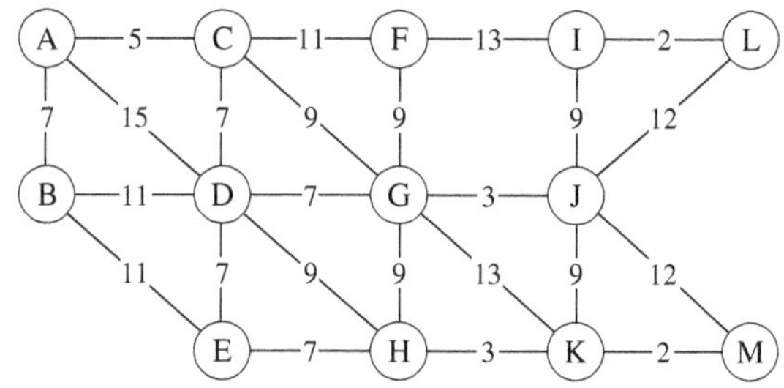

Figure 1: OW road network (adapted from [16]).

Table 1: Set of $k = 4$ shortest routes per OD pair

OD	Route 1	Route 2	Route 3	Route 4
AL	ACGJIL	ACGJL	ACFIL	ACDGJIL
AM	ACDHKM	ACGJKM	ACGHKM	ADHKM
BL	BDGJIL	BDGJL	BACGJIL	BACGJL
BM	BEHKM	BDHKM	BDEHKM	BEDHKM

Our approach is compared against the MSA, introduced in Section 2, with $\psi = 1/n$. In the case of MSA, no repetitions were needed since it is deterministic. We note that MSA has converged in around 450 iterations. Student's t-tests were applied to compare our approach against MSA. In this sense, henceforth, any claim that one approach is better than the other is supported by such tests at the 5% significance levels, except when otherwise stated. We omit the p-values due to the lack of space.

6.2 Results and Discussion

The performance of GRASP+PR along iterations is presented in Figure 2. In the plot, results represent the average and standard deviation over 30 repetitions. Recall that the incumbent solution is the one generated in the current iteration of the algorithm, whereas the best solution so far is the one that shall be returned at the end of the algorithm. As can be seen, the average value of incumbent solutions varies considerably. This happens because of the independent, randomised nature of the solutions generation process. On the other hand, it can also be seen that both the average value of incumbent solutions and the best so far decrease with time. This is due to the path relinking mechanism, which keeps

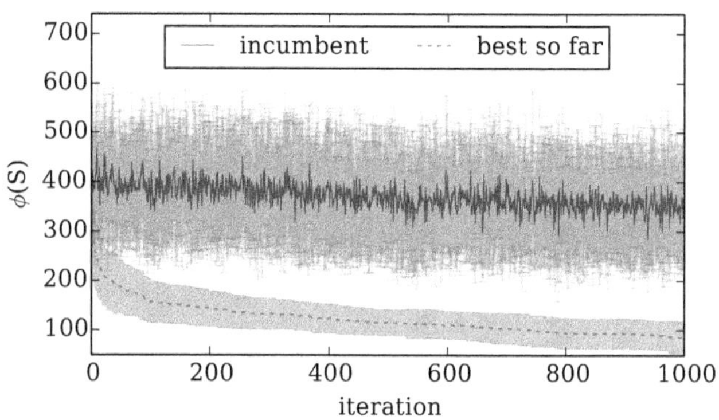

Figure 2: Average performance of GRASP+PR along iterations. Shaded lines represent the standard deviation.

Table 2: Performance comparison per OD pair and overall

	MSA			GRASP+PR		
OD	ϕ	δ	*avg-tt*	ϕ	δ	*avg-tt*
AL	215	**0.0001**	71.21	**23.37 (31.53)**	0.0011 (0.002)	**68.39 (0.52)**
AM	194	0.0032	**65.74**	**28.60 (30.71)**	**0.0007 (0.001)**	74.56 (0.56)
BL	62	0.0020	69.35	**13.87 (24.08)**	**0.0010 (0.002)**	**66.19 (0.64)**
BM	67	**0.0001**	**62.13**	**20.17 (16.42)**	0.0012 (0.001)	69.67 (0.53)
Overall	538	0.0053	**67.46**	**86.00 (32.56)**	**0.0039 (0.002)**	69.75 (0.20)

a kind of memory by means of the reference set. In this regard, the knowledge from previous iterations is exploited to improve the incumbent solutions.

The comparison of our approach against MSA is shown in Table 2, in terms of ϕ, δ, and *avg-tt* . Results are presented by OD pair as well as overall. In the case of GRASP, each result represents the average over 30 repetitions, thus standard deviations are also shown (in parenthesis). The best results for each combination of OD pair and metric are shown in bold.

Initially, consider the overall results. It can be observed that, on average, the solutions provided by GRASP+PR are considerably closer to the UE than those by MSA. In other words, our assignments are fairer than those of MSA. This is due to our problem formulation, which minimises the number of vehicles assigned to non-least cost routes. On the other hand, the solution yielded by MSA has a lower average travel time. However, the point here is that our approach is concerned with approximating the UE, not minimising the average travel costs. In fact, this latter is the focus of SO, not UE. The advantage of MSA in the *avg-tt* metric can be explained by its structure: it works by iteratively changing the route of a dwindling portion of the demand in order to narrow the gap among the vehicles' travel times. However, from the UE definition, minimising travel time per se is not the main objective.

Now, consider the results per OD pair. Considering the metric ϕ, GRASP+PR clearly outperforms MSA. The reason here is obvious: our approach was designed to minimise ϕ. In this same sense, it would be natural to expect MSA outperforming GRASP+PR in the *avg-tt* metric. However, it can be seen that each algorithm outperforms the other in half of the cases, and the same holds for the δ metric. For the *avg-tt* metric, one can see that our approach performed better in the pairs going to L, whereas MSA performed better in the pairs going to M. These differences are due to the structure of the approaches, and to the specific road network under consideration here. In the case of δ, however, it can be observed that our approach fared better in the OD pairs AM and BL. Assigning routes to these two OD pairs is more difficult since all of their routes overlap in at least one link. On the other hand, MSA presented better results for the OD pairs AL and BM, whose sets of available routes have no overlapping links between them. Thus, such results show that our approach provides fairer assignments, and, at least for the OW network, is more robust than MSA.

Regarding the *avg-tt* metric, some additional aspects (not shown here in their totality) can be analysed. The average difference between the best and worst routes of each OD pair is useful to measure the level of unfairness of an assignment. In our approach, this difference accounts for 4.38 (1.9) minutes, whereas in MSA it accounts for 7.39 minutes. When considering the best and worst routes over all OD pairs, in our approach this difference is of 12 (1.5) minutes, whilst in MSA it is of 22 minutes. As seen, the level of unfairness achieved by our approach is lower than of MSA. This means that, compared to MSA, the level of unfairness obtained by our approach has less impact on the vehicles. Furthermore, the number of vehicles that actually suffer from such unfairness is considerably lower in our assignments, as shown through the ϕ metric.

Summing up, the results achieved by our approach demonstrate its efficiency, fairness, and robustness to approximate the UE of the TAP. Despite the heuristic nature of our approach, it became evident that our solutions are much fairer and closer to the UE than those provided by the MSA. Indeed, the results obtained by our approach are, on average, 26% (δ metric) and 84% (ϕ metric) better than those of MSA. Furthermore, regarding the best solution found by our approach over all iterations, its values were only $\phi = 17$ and $\delta = 0.000916$. Naturally, the results presented here correspond to the OW network and may not hold for specific road networks. Such a fact, however, does not invalidate the generality of our results, since the OW network presents the same problems of other bigger road networks, such as congestions, routes overlapping, multiple OD pairs, etc.

7. CONCLUSIONS

Solving the traffic assignment problem (TAP) is an important step towards an efficient usage of the traffic infrastructure. In this paper, we presented the use of the GRASP+PR metaheuristic to approximate the user equilibrium (UE) of the TAP. A novel performance metric was introduced, which measures the amount of vehicles assigned to non-least cost routes. Through experiments, we show that our approach outperforms the well-known method of successive averages (MSA), providing solutions that are, on average, significantly closer to the UE. Furthermore, our approach has shown to provide assignments that are considerably fairer than those of MSA.

In spite of the satisfactory results achieved, there is still space for improvements. We have introduced a performance metric and showed that other metrics can also be employed. An interesting approach here would be to employ a multi-objective method in order to optimise several functions at the same time. Another interesting direction would be to model the UE in a disaggregate, agent-based nature. Such direction would lead to more realistic assignment methods from the drivers' point of view. Improving the process for generating the set of routes would also be useful. Some ideas in this direction include: allowing a variable number of routes per OD pair (or even per vehicle), and updating the set of routes periodically based on costs from previous iterations. Minor improvements include investigating other strategies for neighbourhood exploration, solutions construction, and path relinking.

8. ACKNOWLEDGMENTS

We thank the reviewers for their valuable comments. The authors are partially supported by CAPES and CNPq.

9. REFERENCES

[1] A. L. C. Bazzan. Co-evolution of the dynamics in population games: the case of traffic flow assignment. In *Proc. of the 14th An. Conf. on Genetic and Evol. Comp. (companion)*, pages 43–50, 2012. ACM.

[2] A. L. C. Bazzan, D. Cagara, and B. Scheuermann. An evolutionary approach to traffic assignment. In *2014 IEEE Symp. on Comp. Intel. in Vehicles and Transp. Systems (CIVTS)*, SSCI, pages 43–50, 2014.

[3] A. L. C. Bazzan and F. Klügl. *Introduction to Intelligent Systems in Traffic and Transportation.* Morgan and Claypool, 2013.

[4] D. Braess, A. Nagurney, and T. Wakolbinger. On a paradox of traffic planning. *Transportation Science*, 39(4):446–450, 2005.

[5] L. S. Buriol, M. J. Hirsh, P. M. Pardalos, T. Querido, M. G. Resende, and M. Ritt. A biased random-key genetic algorithm for road congestion minimization. *Optimization Letters*, 4:619–633, 2010.

[6] D. Cagara, A. L. C. Bazzan, and B. Scheuermann. Getting you faster to work: A genetic algorithm approach to the traffic assignment problem. In *Proc. of the 16th GECCO (comp.)*, pages 105–106, 2014. ACM.

[7] H. Dia and S. Panwai. Modelling drivers' compliance and route choice behaviour in response to travel information. *Journal of Nonlinear Dynamics*, 49(4):493–509, 2007.

[8] J. C. Dias, P. Machado, D. C. Silva, and P. H. Abreu. An inverted ant colony optimization approach to traffic. *Engineering Applications of Artificial Intelligence*, 36(0):122–133, 2014.

[9] T. A. Feo and M. G. Resende. A probabilistic heuristic for a computationally difficult set covering problem. *Operations Research Letters*, 8(2):67–71, 1989.

[10] S. M. Galib and I. Moser. Road traffic optimisation using an evolutionary game. In *Proc. of the 13th GECCO (companion)*, pages 519–526, 2011. ACM.

[11] C. Gawron. *Simulation-based traffic assignment.* PhD thesis, University of Cologne, Cologne, Germany, 1998.

[12] F. Glover. *Interfaces in Computer Science and Operations Research*, chap. Tabu Search and Adaptive Memory Programming – Advances, Applications and Challenges, pages 1–75. Springer, 1997.

[13] R. Grunitzki, G. de O. Ramos, and A. L. C. Bazzan. Individual versus difference rewards on reinforcement learning for route choice. In *2014 Brazilian Conf. on Intelligent Systems (BRACIS)*, pages 253–258, 2014.

[14] V. Henn. Fuzzy route choice model for traffic assignment. *Fuzzy Sets and Sys.*, 116(1):77–101, 2000.

[15] M. Laguna and R. Martí. Grasp and path relinking for 2-layer straight line crossing minimization. *INFORMS Journal on Computing*, 11(1):44–52, 1999.

[16] J. Ortúzar and L. G. Willumsen. *Modelling Transport.* John Wiley & Sons, 3rd edition, 2001.

[17] S. Peeta and J. Yu. A hybrid model for driver route choice incorporating en-route attributes and real-time information effects. *Net. and Sp. Econ.*, 5:21–40, 2005.

[18] A. J. Pel and A. J. Nicholson. Network effects of percentile-based route choice behaviour for stochastic travel times under exogenous capacity variations. In *Proc. of the 16th IEEE ITSC*, pages 1864–1869, 2013.

[19] G. de O. Ramos and R. Grunitzki. An improved learning automata approach for the route choice problem. In Koch, Meneguzzi, and Lakkaraju, eds., *Agent Technology for Intelligent Mobile Services and Smart Societies*, volume 498 of *CCIS*, pages 56–67. Springer, 2015.

[20] Y. Sheffi. *Urban Transportation Networks: Equilibrium Analysis With Mathematical Programming Methods.* Prentice-Hall, Englewood Cliffs, USA, 1984.

[21] H. Varia, P. Gundaliya, and S. Dhingra. Application of genetic algorithms for joint optimization of signal setting parameters and dynamic traffic assignment for the real network data. *Research in Transportation Economics*, 38(1):35–44, 2013.

[22] J. G. Wardrop. Some theoretical aspects of road traffic research. In *Proceedings of the Institute of Civil Engineers*, volume 2, pages 325–378, 1952.

[23] J. Y. Yen. Finding the k shortest loopless paths in a network. *Management Science*, 17(11):712–716, 1971.

APPENDIX

A. PARAMETERS TUNING

Here we present a brief analysis on the values defined for the parameters involved in our approach. The test scenario is the same as in Section 6, namely the OW network. Regarding the parameters, the following values were defined for each of them: $k = \{4, 10\}$, $\alpha = \{0.2, 0.5, 0.8\}$, $\beta = 20$, $\gamma = \{0.2, 0.5, 0.8\}$. The number of iterations per execution of the algorithm was set to 1000 in all cases. To improve the accuracy of results, each combination of parameters was repeated 30 times.

The present scenario characterises a factorial experiment, where factors are represented by the parameters, levels by the parameter's values, and the response variable corresponds to the value of solutions. In this sense, the factorial analysis of variation (ANOVA) test was employed to check for statistic equivalence of the parameters' values. In ANOVA, a null hypothesis is formulated for each factor, stating that its different levels produce the same mean response, i.e., all values of the given parameter produce the same results on average. The alternative hypothesis is that not all levels produce the same mean response. All tests here were applied at the 5% significance levels.

The resulting p-values for factors k, α, and γ, were 2×10^{-16}, 0.6323, and 4.6×10^{-16}, respectively. This means that no significant differences among the values of parameter α were detected. In this sense, we adopt $\alpha = 0.2$. On the other hand, the null hypothesis was rejected for parameters k and γ. We go forward on these factors, and apply a post-hoc test, namely the Student's t-test. Starting with parameter k, the null hypothesis is the same as before, but with the alternative hypothesis stating that $k = 4$ produces better solutions than $k = 10$. The p-value is 2.2×10^{-16}, meaning that $k = 4$ is better. Indeed, the average value of solutions when $k = 4$ is 93.90 ± 33.09, which is much lower than the 503.78 ± 59.76 of $k = 10$. Now, for parameter γ, we fix $\alpha = 0.2$ and $k = 4$. One test is then applied for each pair of values for γ. The resulting p-values 3.3×10^{-5}, 5×10^{-8}, and 0.1593, indicate that, respectively, $\gamma = 0.5$ is better than $\gamma = 0.2$, $\gamma = 0.8$ is better than $\gamma = 0.2$, and that $\gamma = 0.5$ and $\gamma = 0.8$ are equivalent. Thus, we adopt $\gamma = 0.5$ to provide a good balance between greedy and uniform solutions.

Guiding Evolutionary Search with Association Rules for Solving Weighted CSPs

Madalina Raschip
University of Neuchâtel,
Switzerland
madalina.raschip@unine.ch

Cornelius Croitoru
Alexandru Ioan Cuza
University of Iasi, Romania
croitoru@info.uaic.ro

Kilian Stoffel
University of Neuchâtel,
Switzerland
kilian.stoffel@unine.ch

ABSTRACT

Weighted constraint satisfaction problems are difficult optimization problems that could model applications from various domains. Evolutionary algorithms are not the first option for solving such type of problems. In this work, the evolutionary algorithm uses the information extracted from the previous best solutions to guide the search in the next iterations. After the archive of previous best solutions has been sufficiently (re)filled, a data mining module is called to find association rules between variables and values. The generated rules are used to improve further the search process. Different methods of applying the association rules are investigated. Computational experiments are done on academic and real-world problem instances. The obtained results validate the approach and show that it is competitive with existing approaches in literature.

Categories and Subject Descriptors

I.2.8 [**Artificial Intelligence**]: Problem Solving, Control Methods, and Search—*Heuristic methods*

Keywords

Weighted constraint satisfaction problems; Evolutionary computation; Association rules

1. INTRODUCTION

A large number of problems in artificial intelligence and in other domains can be formulated as constraint satisfaction problems (CSP) [6]. A CSP is defined by a set of variables, each associated with a domain of possible values, and a set of constraints imposed on them. The problem is to find an assignment of variables such that all constraints are satisfied, or to specify if such an assignment does not exist. Finding a solution to a constraint satisfaction problem is a NP-hard task. When real-world problems are translated into this framework, we have to deal with different types of knowledge like costs, preferences, uncertainties. In order to cope with over-constrained problems in which it is impossible to satisfy all the constraints simultaneously, the weighted constraint satisfaction problems (WCSP) framework [24] has been promoted. A WCSP is an extension of the classical CSP by allowing the constraints to be weighted, representing in this way the preferences among them. The problem is an optimization problem which asks to minimize the total cost of the weights. A wide range of applications from domains like resource allocation, combinatorial auctions, probabilistic reasoning are modeled under this framework.

Evolutionary computation methods [10], as general-purpose algorithms, were employed to solve problems from various domains, including constraint satisfaction problems [4] and data mining [7]. The performance of the evolutionary algorithms for constraint solving can be improved by combining them with other techniques [12], [8].

The fields of constraint programming and data mining interact [21]. Constraint programming techniques are used to specify desirable properties of the patterns or clusters to be identified in the data mining process. On the other hand, data mining techniques can be applied to automatically acquire new information from data and experiments. For example, the frequent patterns identified by data mining algorithms are exploited to reduce table constraints [9]. In the current paper the two fields are joined under the evolutionary computing framework.

There are numerous hybrid approaches in literature that use data mining techniques to improve the search [13]. Data mining could be used for example to evaluate or to initialize the solutions, to manage the population of individuals, to set up the parameters of a specific metaheuristic. Population-based incremental learning algorithm [2] is a metaheuristic that is based on the incorporation of data mining and which works with dynamic knowledge. The method uses a probability vector which characterizes high fitness solutions to build new solutions.

In this paper, the search experience, materialized in an archive of previous best individuals, guides the evolutionary algorithm. The proposed approach generates association rules from the archive of individuals to improve the quality of the next individuals. Two ways of taking benefit from the information stored by the association rules are verified: as a separate step, applying the rules on the whole population of individuals after the call of the genetic operators, or inside the genetic operators. A procedure of escaping from local optimum which uses the generated association rules was added to the approach.

GECCO '15, July 11 - 15, 2015, Madrid, Spain

ISBN 978-1-4503-3472-3/15/07...$15.00

DOI: http://dx.doi.org/10.1145/2739480.2754757

The paper is organized as follows. Section 2 presents the general aspects related to weighted constraint satisfaction problems and association rules mining. In Section 3 the hybrid evolutionary approach is described. The experimental results are given in Section 4. Section 5 concludes the paper and identifies possible future work.

2. TECHNICAL BACKGROUND

2.1 Weighted Constraint Satisfaction Problems

A constraint satisfaction problem (CSP) is a triple $(\mathcal{X}, \mathcal{D}, \mathcal{R})$ where $\mathcal{X} = (x_1, ..., x_n)$ is a set of variables, $\mathcal{D} = (D_1, ..., D_n)$ is a set of domains for variables, and $\mathcal{R}$ is a set of constraints between variables. The constraints define simultaneous assignments of variables to values. A solution of a CSP is a complete instantiation of variables with values from their domains such that all constraints are satisfied. The usual task in a CSP is to find a solution or to prove that there is no solution.

Denote by $x_i \leftarrow a$ the assignment of value a to variable x_i. A tuple is a set of assignments to variables $(x_{i_1} \leftarrow a_{i_1}, ..., x_{i_k} \leftarrow a_{i_k})$. The scope of a tuple t, noted $var(t)$, is the set of variables $(x_{i_1}, ..., x_{i_k})$ assigned by the tuple. A cost function f over $S \subseteq \mathcal{X}$ associates costs to tuples such that $var(t) = S$.

In a weighted constraint satisfaction problem (WCSP), the set of constraints is replaced by a set of cost functions to express preferences among tuples. A WCSP is a quadruple $\mathcal{P} = (\mathcal{X}, \mathcal{D}, \mathcal{F}, K)$ where $\mathcal{X}$ is the set of variables, $\mathcal{D}$ is the set of domains, $\mathcal{F}$ is the set of cost functions and K is the bound on the maximum acceptable cost of solutions. The set $\mathcal{F}$ defines the objective function,

$$F(X) = \sum_{f \in \mathcal{F}} f(X)$$

A solution is a complete assignment X such that $F(X) < K$. The task is to find a solution with minimum cost. The value K is used to tighten the solution, if a certain degree of quality is desired.

2.2 Approaches for solving WCSPs

Common approaches for solving WCSPs involve combinations of search and inference algorithms. Deterministic approaches are based on the Branch-and-Bound procedure which maintains different levels of consistency [5] or uses constraint processing to boost the search [15]. Real life scenarios require high quality solutions in a short amount of time. Approximation methods have the advantage of providing good solutions in a finite period of time. The drawback is that there is no guarantee of the optimality. Local search methods applied for solving constraint satisfaction are present in literature. Hill-climbing algorithms like Min-conflicts [18] and GSAT [14] achieve better results than systematic search on large instances. For the case of WCSPs, simple metaheuristics like tabu search [20] or hybrid metaheuristics were proposed. The method from [16] follows the Variable Neighborhood Decomposition Search scheme, where neighborhoods are obtained by unfixing a part of a solution. For searching a neighborhood, the approach makes a partial tree search combined with constraint propagation. The approaches from [12] and [8] are different hybrid methods that use the bucket elimination procedure to assign values to variables in the recombination operator.

2.3 Association rules mining

Let $\mathcal{I}$ be a set of literals, called itemsets, and $\mathcal{T}$ be a set of transactions. Each transaction T is a set of itemsets such that $T \subseteq \mathcal{I}$. The support of an itemset X, denoted by $supp(X)$, is the proportion of transactions in $\mathcal{T}$ that contain X. An association rule is an implication $X \Rightarrow Y$, where $X, Y \subset \mathcal{I}$, $X \cap Y = \emptyset$. X is the antecedent of Y and Y is the consequent of the rule.

The support of a rule $X \Rightarrow Y$ is the percentage of transactions that contain all items of X:

$$supp(X \Rightarrow Y) = supp(X)$$

The confidence of a rule $X \Rightarrow Y$ estimates the probability that a transaction which contains the itemset X, will also have the itemset Y:

$$conf(X \Rightarrow Y) = \frac{supp(X \cup Y)}{supp(X)}$$

The problem of mining association rules is to generate association rules between itemsets that have the confidence and support parameters greater than some specified values. The first step in solving this problem is to find the itemsets which satisfy the imposed limitations. The second step is to use the itemsets to generate association rules. One of the most known approach for solving the first step is the Apriori algorithm [1]. The way the Apriori algorithm works can be summarized in:

- find the items with support at least equal to the minimum support value
- the candidate generation phase: for each subsequent step $i \geq 2$, join itemsets with $i - 1$ items found in the previous step with individual itemsets
- the evaluation phase: keep the itemsets that have sufficient support; they will become the seed for the next step.

The process continues until no itemsets are found. The most expensive step is the candidate generation phase because it generates large numbers of subsets. Improvements over the Apriori algorithm were described in literature; for example, the FP-growth algorithm [11] which eliminates the candidate generation phase.

3. HYBRID EVOLUTIONARY APPROACH

This section describes the new hybrid approach that uses a data mining module to guide the search of the evolutionary algorithm. The approach follows the general scheme of a genetic algorithm. Besides the standard components of an evolutionary algorithm, the method stores an archive of best individuals found in the previous iterations. The archive contains the best chromosomes from each iteration since the last application of the mining algorithm. An individual is added to the archive if it is better than the worst individual from the archive.

The archive of individuals represents the database of transactions and each individual is an itemset to be used by the association rules mining algorithm. An individual is an assignment of variables. Therefore, an item is an assignment of a variable x_i with a value a, i.e. a pair (x_i, a). The archive is filled with individuals until a specified criterion is satisfied, for example after a sufficient number of replacements.

When this criterion is satisfied, a data mining step follows. A mining algorithm is applied on the archive to construct association rules in order to characterize the best individuals. In this way, the approach generates descriptions of the highest encountered peaks of the fitness landscape. The data mining algorithm will find association rules between variables and values. The algorithm used for mining association rules is the Apriori algorithm [1]. We have selected this algorithm because the archive of individuals is not large and because of its simplicity. The returned association rules are sorted first by confidence and then, eventually, by another, problem specific, criterion. Only a subset of the best rules is maintained. After the generation of the rules, the archive is emptied. The association rules are renewed once the established percentage of individual replacements is exceeded.

The association rules are used at each step of the algorithm, except for some evident cases. At the beginning of the algorithm, before the call of the data mining algorithm, there is no generated rule. Two methods of using the association rules are considered: in a "raw", unaltered way, and using the patterns generated by the rules. In the first case, the rules are applied on the population of individuals after the call of the genetic operators. In the second case, the rules are used inside the genetic operators to generate new individuals. By using this division, we can verify which learning method is better: the one that takes into account the context, or the one where the context does not matter. The description of the two cases is done in the next subsection.

3.1 The application of the association rules

3.1.1 Unaltered case

The main scheme of the genetic approach, following a generational model, for the first case, is given in Algorithm 1. Each iteration, a population of individuals is modified using the standard genetic operators. The association rules are applied to all individuals in the population, after the application of the operators. The idea of modifying the population of individuals according to the extracted rules is to improve the guidance of the search.

The application of an association rule to an individual include the following steps, described in Algorithm 2. The approach verifies which association rules can be applied and only the rules that can modify the individual are selected. From this set, the rule that satisfies a certain, problem specific, criterion is chosen next and applied. The application of a rule assume changing the values of the chromosome with the corresponding ones from the consequent part of the rule. Given a rule r, we denote by $LHS(r)$ and $RHS(r)$ the antecedent and respectively the consequent of the rule.

For the weighted constraint satisfaction problems the criterion can be the minimum number of constraint violations, for example. Another criterion could be the length of the rule. We denote by the length the number of pairs (x_i, a) found in the antecedent and the consequent of the rule. In our implementation we have used a combination of these two criteria. The same approach is used to sort the rules, after the call of the mining algorithm.

The application of the association rules performs exploitation of the search space as well as the selection operator,

```
Input: a WCSP (𝒳, 𝒟, ℱ, K)
k ← 0;
archive ← ∅;
generate initial population P(k);
evaluate individuals in P(k);
while stop criterion is not satisfied do
    k ← k + 1;
    selection of P(k) from P(k − 1) ;
    alter P(k) using crossover and mutation;
    apply association_rules on P(k);
    if updating association rules step then
        association_rules ← Apriori(archive);
        delete archive;
    if local optima then
        association_rules ← Apriori(archive);
        apply non-rules, constructed from
        association_rules, on P(k);
        delete archive;
    evaluate individuals in P(k);
    add best individuals to archive;
return best solution found;
```

Algorithm 1: The hybrid evolutionary algorithm (GAARs)

while the genetic operators maintain exploration. A good balance between exploration and exploitation must be achieved.

3.1.2 Mutation operator

Genetic algorithms work better if information from the problem to be solved is included in the algorithm. One possibility is through the genetic operators. For the WCSP, the classical mutation operator changes probabilistically the value of a variable with a random one from the domain. A method for the value selection, based on the best patterns previously found is described in the following. The goal is to choose the most promising value. The value is selected randomly, with a probability that depends on a learning factor and a heuristic factor. The first factor evaluates the learnt desirability of assigning the value evaluated from the generated association rules. The second factor evaluates the quality of the value.

Formally, the selection value procedure is given next. Let x_j be the variable to be assigned. The probability to select the value v for variable x_j is defined proportionally to the attraction capability of this value with respect to all candidate values $w \in D_j$:

$$p(x_j \leftarrow v) = \frac{[\tau(x_j \leftarrow v)]^\alpha [\eta(x_j \leftarrow v)]^\beta}{\sum_{w \in D_j} [\tau(x_j \leftarrow w)]^\alpha [\eta(x_j \leftarrow w)]^\beta}$$

where $\tau(x_j \leftarrow v)$ is the learning factor of the assignment $x_j \leftarrow v$, $\eta(x_j \leftarrow v)$ is the heuristic factor, and α and β are the parameters for their relative weights. The learning factor $\tau(x_j \leftarrow v)$ computes the number of appearances of the assignment $x_j \leftarrow v$ in the set of generated association rules. The heuristic factor $\eta(x_j \leftarrow v)$ is equal to the number of violated conflicts by the assignment $x_j \leftarrow v$. The procedure is inspired by ant colony optimization techniques [25]. The mutation operator applies the precedent procedure with a certain probability, otherwise the standard mutation is used.

```
Input: an individ assign, a set of rules rules
// 1.  select the rules that can be applied and
    can modify the individual
sr ← ∅;
foreach r ∈ rules do
    selected ← true;
    foreach (i, v) ∈ LHS(r) do
        if v ≠ assign[i] then selected ← false;
    if selected then
        foreach (i, v) ∈ RHS(r) do
            if v = assign[i] then selected ← false;
        if selected then add r to sr;

// 2.  select the rule which satisfies a
    (problem-specific) criterion
r ← selectRule(sr);
// 3.  apply the rule on individ
foreach (i, v) ∈ RHS(r) do
    assign[i] ← v
```

Algorithm 2: Application of an association rule

3.2 Local optimum

The evolutionary algorithm can be trapped in local optimum and then fails to explore new areas. For example, if the best solution does not change within a large number of iterations or the mining algorithm was not called for a large period of time. A specific technique for escaping from these optima, based on the generated association rules is proposed. This method tries to forget the rules previously learned, rules that are not able to produce further improvements. It is described in the following steps:

1. call the data mining algorithm to find the current association rules
2. apply *non-rules*: change the values of the variables that appear in the consequent part of the rule with randomly generated ones from the corresponding domains. This step requires first to check which rules can be applied.
3. make empty the archive of individuals.

The approach differs from a randomly restarting procedure. Only the learned patterns are changed.

3.3 Features of the hybrid approach applied to WCSPs

An individual is represented by an array of values, equal in dimension with N, the number of variables from the WCSP. The position i in the array correspond to the variable x_i. The values for each variable x_i are generated from the corresponding domain D_i. The fitness function is equal to the sum of the cost functions f and must be minimized. The crossover operator exchanges information between chromosomes. A standard operator, like the uniform crossover can be used. The mutation operator replaces the value of a variable x_i with a random value from the domain D_i.

The data mining algorithm finds associations and relationships between variables and their values. An example of an association rule r is the following:

$$r : \{(1,0),(3,1)\} \to (4,1)$$

where a binary-WCSP with N equal to 5 is considered. The rule specifies that if we have the following assignments $x_1 = 0$ and $x_3 = 1$ then it is likely to also have $x_4 = 1$.

3.4 Related work

Some similar approaches that use association rules within metaheuristics are present in literature. In [23] the oil collecting vehicle routing problem is solved with an evolutionary algorithm that includes a data mining module. The module discovers frequent contiguous sequences which guide the construction of individuals. In [3] a memetic algorithm that extracts an interval for the decision variables is described. The resulted information helps the mutation operator. In [17] an approach called *Learnable Evolution Model* is proposed. The evolutionary computation process does not assume the existence of the selection and genetic operators, instead it relies on machine learning techniques to evolve individuals. The method searches for rules that could explain the differences between the better and the worse individuals in the population. All these approaches are different from the proposed one. The rules are not used to construct individuals, like in [23]. The new approach verifies which association rules (and "non-rules") can be applied on an individual. Unlike [3], when the rules are used inside the mutation operator, a distribution of probability which takes into account the frequency of the values in the generated patterns is computed. In contrast with the new approach, the Learnable Evolution Model does not require the existence of the natural evolution mechanism.

4. EXPERIMENTAL RESULTS

4.1 Problem instances

The computational experiments were done on instances from academic and real world problems. Instances from the graph coloring, max-cut and radio link frequency assignment (RLFAP) problems were selected. All these problems can be represented as WCSPs. For example, the RLFAP consists in assigning frequencies, from limited spectral resources, to a set of radio links. The assignment must be done such that there is a minimum of interference between links. The assignments must satisfy some constraints, physical constraints or certain regulations. The problem can be modeled as a binary WCSP where each forbidden tuple has associated a penalty cost.

The problem instances were downloaded from the SoftCSP repository [1]. The optimal solutions were found with the open-source toulbar2 solver [2], the winner of Max-CSP 2008 competition [22]. Toulbar2 uses a Branch and Bound algorithm that maintains local consistency during the search. There was no time limit imposed on the solver to find the solutions.

4.2 Parameter settings

In order to validate the experimental results, we have compared the new approach with the standard genetic algorithm and with an evolutionary algorithm enhanced with the breakout mechanism [19]. The core idea of using the breakout mechanism is to reduce the probability of getting stuck in a local minimum. The algorithm uses the notion of

[1]http://carlit.toulouse.inra.fr/SoftCSP/Files/cflibtars
[2]http://mulcyber.toulouse.inra.fr/projects/toulbar2

nogoods, where a nogood tuple is a disallowed assignment. Initially, each nogood has associated a weight (in our case, the cost value). The sum of the weights of the matched nogoods are added to the evaluation function. When the evolutionary algorithm is trapped in a local minimum, the weights for the nogoods found in the current optimum are increased with their cost values. This process will cause the algorithm to find the variables that must change their values in order to reduce the cost. The same idea is implemented in the microgenetic iterative descend method, one of the best evolutionary approaches to solve constraint satisfaction problems [4]. An improved version of the breakout evolutionary algorithm which has a supplementary mechanism of forgetting some of the learned nogoods was considered here. For an old nogood the procedure decreases the weight.

All genetic algorithms have the following settings: the population size equal to 100 individuals, a tournament size of 2 for the tournament selection operator, the crossover probability of 0.8, and the mutation probability of $1/N$. The special mutation procedure is applied with a probability of 0.75 and α and β equal to 2, respectively 10. The evolutionary algorithm is trapped in a local minimum when the best solution does not change for the last 50 iterations and if the Apriori algorithm have not been called for the same, equal number of iterations (for the hybrid approach). The archive size is equal to 50 individuals and the mining algorithm is applied after the archive was replaced with new individuals for 6 times. The Apriori algorithm was called with a support value of 0.2 and a confidence of 0.8. From 100 rules extracted with the Apriori algorithm, 50 rules are preserved after sorting. The number of non-rules applied on each individual was of $0.2N$. The evolutionary algorithm is stopped when the number of iterations exceed 1000.

We have conducted the experiments on an Intel Core i5-3470S CPU, 2.90GHz x 4, with 8 GB under Linux.

4.3 Results

Table 1 reports the mean values and the standard deviation found by the genetic algorithms for the selected WCSP instances. The results of the evolutionary algorithms are the average values over 30 runs. The GAARs denotes the genetic algorithm where the association rules are applied on individuals, and GAARm stands for the genetic algorithm that uses the rules inside the mutation operator. The results for the genetic algorithm with the breakout scheme were included in the column GABR. The column opt reports the solution obtained by the WCSP solver. A statistical comparison using the non-parametric Wilcoxon signed rank test is made to compare the standard genetic algorithm and each of the hybrid approaches. A significance level of 0.05 was used.

The hybrid method obtains statistically better results than the simple genetic algorithm in the majority of cases for the selected instances. The highest improvements are obtained for the max-cut and the radio link frequency assignment problem instances. Three instances of the graph coloring problem are solved exactly. For this case, the standard genetic algorithm finds good solutions and there is less space for enhancements. The GAARm algorithm works better than the GAARs hybrid version for almost all of the graph coloring and RLFAP problem instances. For the max-cut problem the situation reversed. The hybrid versions are more robust than the standard genetic algorithm in general and they scale well with increasing dimension (see for example the max-cut distributions).

The breakout genetic algorithm has better results only for two instances of the graph coloring problem than the proposed approaches. The results of the hybrid methods in these cases are comparative with the results of the breakout genetic algorithm. For the majority of the RLFAP instances the breakout algorithm cannot improve over the standard genetic algorithm.

Figure 1 illustrates the evolution of the best cost during the run of the standard and hybrid algorithms for a problem instance from the max-cut and RLFAP distributions. Each plot is obtained as an average over 15 runs for each algorithm and it uses a logarithmic scale for the x-axis. The

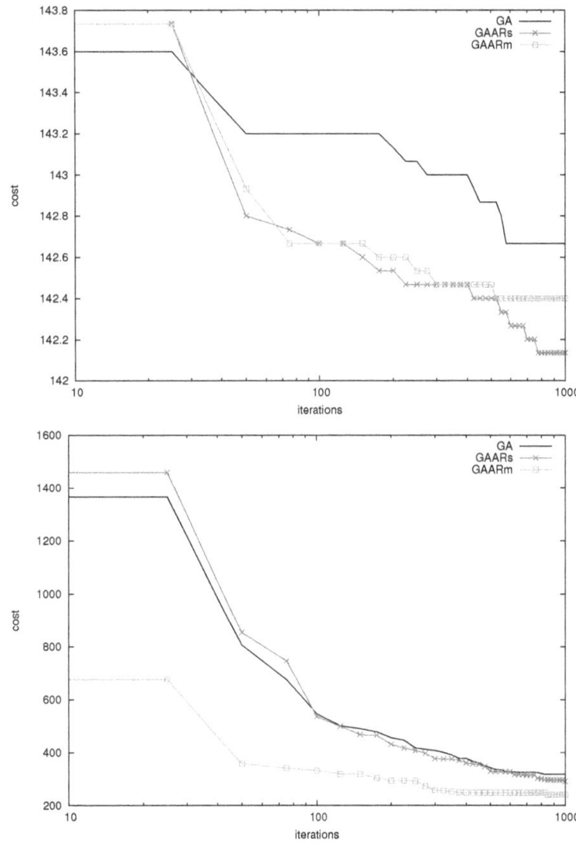

Figure 1: The evolution of the genetic algorithms for the maxcut30_340 and the sub0 problem instances

most improvements are produced in the first iterations for all algorithms. The hybrid approaches have a higher convergence rate than the standard genetic algorithm for the max-cut problem instance, while for the RLFAP instance only the GAARm has this property.

We measure next the average number of the constraint checks of the genetic algorithms. Figure 2 shows these values for the graph coloring and the radio link frequency assignment problem instances. The figure does not contain the values for the breakout algorithm because it is the same as for the standard genetic algorithm. The number of constraint checks of the hybrid GAARm version is higher compared with the other two approaches, the simple genetic algorithm and the

Table 1: The mean and the standard deviation of the algorithms for the WCSP instances. The column t shows the results of the statistical comparison between standard GA and the hybrid approaches, GAARs respectively GAARm. The sign + indicates a better performance for at least one of the hybrid methods.

Distribution	(N, D, R)	GA	GAARs	GAARm	t	GABR	opt
			Graph coloring				
geom30a_3	(30,3,81)	11.27 ± 0.44	11 ± 0	11 ± 0		11 ± 0	11
geom30a_4	(30,4,81)	4 ± 0	4 ± 0	4 ± 0		4 ± 0	4
geom40_2	(40,2,78)	22.5 ± 0.56	22.2 ± 0.4	22.23 ± 0.42	+	22.1 ± 0.3	22
geom40_3	(40,3,78)	7.3 ± 0.46	7.07 ± 0.25	7 ± 0		7 ± 0	7
myciel5g_3	(47,3,236)	19.26 ± 1.63	18.2 ± 1.4	17.93 ± 1.41	+	17.3 ± 0.97	16
myciel5g_4	(47,4,236)	4.9 ± 0.7	4.53 ± 0.56	4.23 ± 0.42	+	4.6 ± 0.61	4
			Max-CUT				
maxcut30_330	(30,2,660)	136.27 ± 1.18	135.3 ± 0.53	135.47 ± 0.56	+	135.33 ± 0.47	135
maxcut30_340	(30,2,680)	142.53 ± 0.88	142 ± 0	142.13 ± 0.43	+	142.13 ± 0.34	142
maxcut30_350	(30,2,700)	148.3 ± 0.7	148 ± 0	148.07 ± 0.36	+	148.1 ± 0.4	148
maxcut40_440	(40,2,880)	171.37 ± 2.41	170.5 ± 1.28	170.03 ± 1.14	+	170.37 ± 1.11	169
maxcut40_460	(40,2,920)	182.27 ± 2.16	180.9 ± 0.79	180.97 ± 0.87	+	181.3 ± 1.16	180
maxcut40_480	(40,2,960)	192.7 ± 2.1	191.6 ± 1.23	191.6 ± 1.17	+	191.73 ± 1.26	191
			RLFAP (celar6)				
sub0	(16,44,207)	332.93 ± 88.65	325.47 ± 110.99	210.93 ± 49.54	+	300.53 ± 89.27	159
sub1	(14,44,300)	3240.1 ± 183.63	3206.53 ± 239.6	2897.73 ± 154.35	+	3316.3 ± 239.34	2669
sub1-24	(14,24,300)	3036.46 ± 276.67	3026.37 ± 204.89	2811.33 ± 137.2	+	3023.3 ± 195.83	2656
sub2	(16,44,353)	3661.73 ± 305.16	3618.57 ± 396.76	3263.73 ± 255.13	+	3704 ± 319.26	2746
sub3	(18,44,421)	4101.13 ± 244.23	3963.43 ± 374.67	3603.83 ± 254.21	+	4153.8 ± 326.4	3079
sub4	(22,44,477)	4365.36 ± 366.31	4308.07 ± 350.16	3920.83 ± 221.74	+	4539.93 ± 4531.41	3230
sub4-20	(22,20,477)	3540.2 ± 479.5	3583.67 ± 388.74	3321.23 ± 352.29	+	3679.57 ± 335.32	2716

GAARs especially for the RLFAP instances. The reason is that the GAARm approach computes for each value to be used in the mutation operator the sum of new constraint violations. The results for the GAARs are almost similar with the standard GA, the small differences come from the fact that GAARs uses as a measure of rules efficiency the sum of cost functions of the partial assignment associated with the rule.

Table 2 shows, in average, the time spent by algorithms for finding the solutions (in seconds), for the max-cut and RLFAP problem instances. The table also includes the percent of time the hybrid methods spend for generating the association rules. The time comparison between the solver and the evolutionary approaches is not fair. The evolutionary algorithms are stopped after a number of iterations has been exceeded. They do not guaranty to find the optimum. The solver finds the optimal solutions, but in a large period of time in almost all cases. The time of the evolutionary algorithms does not exceed a few seconds. The time differences between the evolutionary approaches and the solver are more evident for the max-cut problem instances. The differences in time between the standard genetic algorithm and the GAARs algorithm are small for the RLFAP distributions. When compared with the GAARm, the differences are larger. With respect to the percent of time from the mining algorithm, the hybrid approaches spend more time with the Apriori algorithm for the max-cut problem instances. These distributions have a higher number of variables.

4.3.1 *Dependence on components*

To evaluate further the importance of the approaches components we have performed a comparison of the new methods with the following algorithms:

- the standard genetic algorithm which uses the association rules only for the generation of non-rules (the method is denoted further by GAnonr)
- the standard genetic algorithm which uses a random restarting technique for escaping from local minimum (GArr)
- the standard genetic algorithm with the mutation operator modified like this: assign the value from the domain that minimizes the sum of the cost functions of the unsatisfied constraints (GArw).

Figure 3 shows the confidence intervals of the mean for a graph coloring and a RLFAP problem instance. The GAnonr has a good performance, even better than GAARs for the graph coloring instance. The application of the rules at each step seems to be too rigid. The probabilistic greedy selection of the value from GArw is beneficial for one problem, while not for the other. A better strategy for escaping from local optima could bring improvements.

5. CONCLUSIONS AND FUTURE WORK

The paper verifies if by including information from previous iterations into the evolutionary search process, the performance of the evolutionary algorithm is boosted. New methods of using association rules mined from previous best solutions to improve the quality of the current individuals are described. In order to lead the search to promising areas, the population of chromosomes is changed by applying the generated rules either as a stand-alone module or inside the genetic operators. In the first case, for each individual the best rule according to the heuristic information criterion, the number of constraint violations, and the length is selected

Table 2: **The time used by the algorithms for solving the max-cut and the RLFAP WCSP instances**

Distribution	t(Toulbar2)	t(GA)	t(GAARs)	%time(Apriori)	t(GAARm)	%time(Apriori)
Max-CUT						
maxcut30_330	7.28	1.88	3.26	34.98	3.5	31.83
maxcut30_340	10.78	1.91	3.23	33.1	3.51	30.85
maxcut30_350	13.42	1.96	3.23	31.93	3.51	30.16
maxcut40_440	61.72	2.42	6.13	56.99	5.78	50.42
maxcut40_460	104.7	2.84	6.41	57.23	6.18	51.59
maxcut40_480	138.46	2.98	6.4	55.82	6.2	49.89
RLFAP						
sub0	0.06	0.63	0.88	8.99	4.76	2.14
sub1	3.96	0.99	1.06	4.35	7.03	1.57
sub1-24	1.28	0.85	1.04	3.66	3.97	1.36
sub2	4.14	1.07	1.23	5.71	7.74	1.47
sub3	11.3	1.37	1.49	6.29	8.23	2.18
sub4	15.8	1.45	1.96	14.5	9.13	4.62
sub4-20	0.56	1.41	1.95	16.59	5.18	8.9

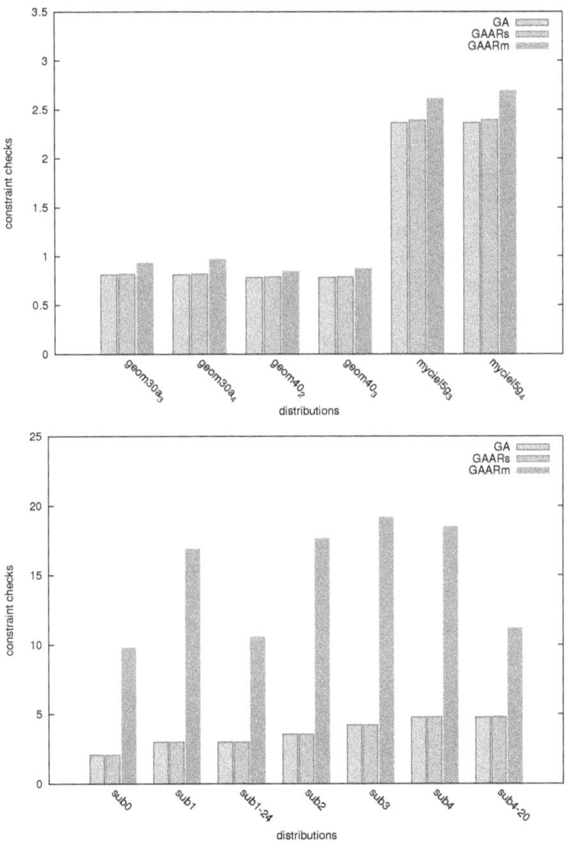

Figure 2: The average number of constraint checks (10^7 order) for a) the graph coloring and b) the RL-FAP problem instances

and then applied. In the second case, in the mutation operator, the patterns corresponding to the association rules help select values for variables. A new procedure of escaping from local optimum which uses the generated association rules is described. Computational results show improvements over the standard evolutionary algorithm. The new methods are competitive with existing approaches on academic and real-world problem instances.

In conclusion, the main contributions of the paper consist in the new way of using the association rules to guide the evolutionary search. Future work is needed to analyze the approach on other problem instances. When dealing with a higher number of variables, a different approach for finding association rules it might be necessary. It is desirable to modify "online" the rules, when the content of the archive is changed. Other improvements may relate to a different schema of using the association rules focused on the idea of learning from failures, or the implementation of a parallel version of the approach.

6. ACKNOWLEDGMENTS

This research is supported by the Sciex Fellowship no. 13.323.

7. REFERENCES

[1] R. Agrawal and S. Ramakrishnan. Fast algorithms for mining association rules. In *Proceedings of 20th International Conference of Very Large Data Bases (VLDB)*, volume 1215, pages 487–499, 1994.

[2] S. Baluja. Population-based incremental learning: A method for integrating genetic search based function optimization and competitive learning. Technical Report CMU-CS-94-163, Pittsburgh, PA, USA, 1994.

[3] J. Chia, C. Goh, K. Tan, and V. Shim. Memetic informed evolutionary optimization via data mining. *Memetic Computing*, 3(2):73–87, 2011.

[4] B. Craenen, A. Eiben, and J. van Hemert. Comparing evolutionary algorithms on binary constraint satisfaction problems. *IEEE Transactions on Evolutionary Computation*, 7(5):424–444, 2003.

[5] S. de Givry, M. Zytnicki, F. Heras, and J. Larrosa. Existential arc consistency: Getting closer to full arc consistency in weighted csps. In *Proceedings of the 19th International Joint Conference on Artificial Intelligence*, IJCAI'05, pages 84–89, 2005.

[6] R. Dechter. *Constraint processing.* Morgan Kaufmann, 2003.

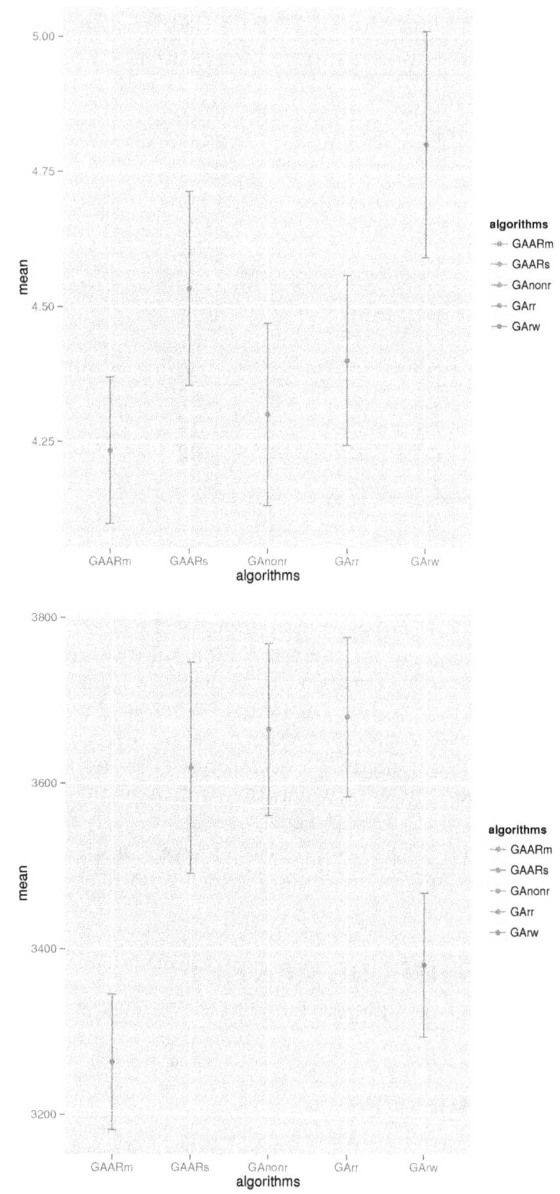

Figure 3: A comparison of different evolutionary approaches for myciel5g4 and sub2 problem instances

[7] A. A. Freitas. A survey of evolutionary algorithms for data mining and knowledge discovery. In *Advances in Evolutionary Computing*, pages 819–845. 2003.

[8] J. E. Gallardo, C. Cotta, and A. J. Fernández. Solving weighted constraint satisfaction problems with memetic/exact hybrid algorithms. *Journal of Artificial Intelligence Research*, 35(1):533–555, 2009.

[9] N. Gharbi, F. Hemery, C. Lecoutre, and O. Roussel. Sliced table constraints: Combining compression and tabular reduction. In *Integration of AI and OR Techniques in Constraint Programming*, pages 120–135. Springer, 2014.

[10] D. E. Goldberg. *The design of innovation: Lessons from and for competent genetic algorithms.* Kluwer Academic Publishers, Norwell, MA, USA, 2002.

[11] J. Han, J. Pei, and Y. Yin. Mining frequent patterns without candidate generation. In *Proceedings of ACM SIGMOD International Conference on Management of Data*, volume 29, pages 1–12, 2000.

[12] M. Ionita, C. Croitoru, and M. Breaban. Incorporating inference into evolutionary algorithms for max-csp. In *Hybrid Metaheuristics*, pages 139–149. Springer, 2006.

[13] L. Jourdan, C. Dhaenens, and E.-G. Talbi. Using datamining techniques to help metaheuristics: A short survey. In *Hybrid Metaheuristics*, pages 57–69. Springer, 2006.

[14] K. Kask and R. Dechter. Gsat and local consistency. In *Proceedings of the 14th International Joint Conference on Artificial Intelligence - Volume 1*, IJCAI'95, pages 616–622, 1995.

[15] J. Larrosa and R. Dechter. Boosting search with variable elimination in constraint optimization and constraint satisfaction problems. *Constraints*, 8(3):303–326, 2003.

[16] S. Loudni and P. Boizumault. Combining vns with constraint programming for solving anytime optimization problems. *European Journal of Operational Research*, 191(3):705 – 735, 2008.

[17] R. Michalski. Learnable evolution model: Evolutionary processes guided by machine learning. *Machine Learning*, 38(1-2):9–40, 2000.

[18] S. Minton, M. D. Johnston, A. B. Philips, and P. Laird. Minimizing conflicts: a heuristic repair method for constraint satisfaction and scheduling problems. *Artificial Intelligence*, 58(1-3):161 – 205, 1992.

[19] P. Morris. The breakout method for escaping local minima. In *Proceedings of the 11th National Conference on Artificial Intelligence*, pages 40–45, 1993.

[20] K. Nonobe and T. Ibaraki. An improved tabu search method for the weighted constraint satisfaction problem. *Infor-Information Systems and Operational Research*, 39(2):131–151, 2001.

[21] L. D. Raedt, S. Nijssen, B. O'Sullivan, and P. V. Hentenryck. Constraint programming meets machine learning and data mining. *Dagstuhl Reports*, 1(5):61–83, 2011.

[22] M. Sanchez et al. Max-csp competition 2008: toulbar2 solver description. *Proceedings of the 3rd International CSP Solver Competition*, pages 63–70, 2008.

[23] H. Santos, L. Ochi, E. Marinho, and L. Drummond. Combining an evolutionary algorithm with data mining to solve a single-vehicle routing problem. *Neurocomputing*, 70(1):70–77, 2006.

[24] T. Schiex, H. Fargier, and G. Verfaillie. Valued constraint satisfaction problems: Hard and easy problems. In *Proceedings of the 14th International Joint Conference on Artificial Intelligence - Volume 1*, IJCAI'95, pages 631–637, 1995.

[25] C. Solnon. Ants can solve constraint satisfaction problems. *IEEE Transactions on Evolutionary Computation*, 6(4):347–357, 2002.

A Novel Diversity-based Evolutionary Algorithm for the Traveling Salesman Problem

Carlos Segura
Center for Research in Mathematics A.C.
Guanajuato, Mexico
carlos.segura@cimat.mx

Salvador Botello Rionda
Center for Research in Mathematics A.C.
Guanajuato, Mexico
botello@cimat.mx

Arturo Hernández Aguirre
Center for Research in Mathematics A.C.
Guanajuato, Mexico
artha@cimat.mx

S. Ivvan Valdez Peña
Center for Research in Mathematics A.C.
Guanajuato, Mexico
ivvan@cimat.mx

ABSTRACT

The Traveling Salesman Problem (TSP) is one of the most well-known NP-hard combinatorial optimization problems. In order to deal with large TSP instances, several heuristics and metaheuristics have been devised. In this paper, a novel memetic scheme that incorporates a new diversity-based replacement strategy is proposed and applied to the largest instances of the TSPLIB benchmark. The novelty of our method is that it combines the idea of transforming a single-objective problem into a multi-objective one, by considering diversity as an explicit objective, with the idea of adapting the balance induced between exploration and exploitation to the various optimization stages. In addition, the intensification capabilities of the individual learning method incorporated in the memetic scheme are also adapted by taking into account the stopping criterion. Computational results show the clear superiority of our scheme when compared against state-of-the-art schemes. To our knowledge, our proposal is the first evolutionary scheme that readily solves an instance with more than 30,000 cities to optimality.

Categories and Subject Descriptors

I.2.8 [**Computing Methodologies**]: Artificial Intelligence—*Problem Solving, Control Methods and Search* Heuristic Methods

Keywords

Diversity Preservation; Traveling Salesman Problem; Evolutionary Algorithms; Memetic Algorithms

GECCO '15, July 11 - 15, 2015, Madrid, Spain

DOI: http://dx.doi.org/10.1145/2739480.2754802

1. INTRODUCTION

The Traveling Salesman Problem (TSP) is one of the most popular NP-hard combinatorial optimization problems [7]. Given a complete weighted graph, the goal in the TSP is to find a Hamiltonian cycle with the least weight, i.e. a cycle of minimum cost that visits every city. The TSP received its name from the field of logistics. Specifically, it refers to a situation where a traveling salesman must make a round of all the cities in a set and return to the initial position. However, the TSP is probably so popular because it does not only appear in logistics, but also in several different practical applications [7], such as in genome sequencing, chip design and telescope slewing.

Given the complexity and interest of the TSP, several different methods have been devised to deal with it [7]. Some exact approaches [2], such as those based on branch and cut, have been used to solve some large TSP instances. The concorde tool [3] is probably one of the most popular exact tools for the TSP. The largest non-trivial instance solved by concorde consists of 85,900 cities. However, this tool requires a huge amount of computational time and it has not been able to solve other smaller instances [3]. Thus, several approximation techniques have also been devised. These include various heuristics and metaheuristics [2]. In the 80s and 90s, a large number of constructive heuristics were defined [7]. In addition, several improvement heuristics have been devised [7]. In the 2-opt local search, neighbor solutions are created by eliminating two edges and reconnecting the two resulting paths in a different way. This can be generalized to k-opt moves, where k edges are interchanged. Finally, the Lin-Kernighan family of heuristics (LK) —which is the one incorporated into our proposal— is based on conducting a restricted search for larger values of k. These heuristics yield high-quality approximations for large instances in a relatively small amount of time. However, when tighter approximations are required, metaheuristics are used.

Practically every popular metaheuristic has been adopted to tackle the TSP. For instance, Iterated Local Search (ILS) [4], and Evolutionary Algorithms (EAs) [30] have been used. Trajectory-based metaheuristics attain high-quality solutions on reasonable timescales. However, when longer times are admissible, population-based metaheuristics are usually preferred. In fact, some of the best-known solutions for several instances of the TSP have been obtained with EAs [12]. Some of the first successful applications of EAs to the TSP were steady-state schemes that relied in the replace-worst (RW) strategy [27]. In these cases, diversity can be prematurely lost. This drawback can be avoided with the application of diversity-preservation schemes and larger instances can be considered [9, 23]. In fact, the LKH tool [11], which is one of the most efficient tools for dealing with large TSP instances, incorporates an EA that explicitly manages diversity. The LKH tool has reported the best-known solutions for several instances [1].

In recent years, several new methods for dealing with diversity have appeared [31], with those that take diversity into account as an alternative objective and use multi-objective schemes gaining considerable popularity [25]. In this paper, we propose an extension of these techniques and apply them to the TSP. Specifically, we propose a new replacement strategy that combines the idea of transforming a single-objective problem into a multi-objective one, by considering diversity as an explicit objective, with the idea of adapting the balance induced between exploration and exploitation to the various optimization stages. The aim of the paper is two-fold. First, to study the generality and suitability of this kind of diversity management scheme. Second, to improve on the best results reported by state-of-the-art EAs for the TSP. Our experimental validation with some of the largest instances of the TSPLIB benchmark [22] shows the clear benefits of the new model. In fact, to the best of our knowledge, this is the first EA that reports the optimal solution for *pla33810*, an instance that consists of 33,810 cities.

The rest of the paper is organized as follows. A discussion of some of the most important methods for maintaining proper diversity in EAs is given in Section 2. Section 3 offers a review of the literature on the application of EAs to the TSP. In Section 4 the new diversity-based replacement scheme, as well as the rest of the details of our memetic algorithm, are described. Section 5 is devoted to presenting our experimental validation. Some EAs not-based on diversity, as well as the EA of the LKH tool, are used to validate our scheme. Finally, our conclusions and some lines of future work are given in Section 6.

2. DIVERSITY PRESERVATION IN EVOLUTIONARY ALGORITHMS

Premature convergence is one of the most important drawbacks of many population-based metaheuristics [28]. Most of the techniques for dealing with premature convergence are based on directly or indirectly managing the diversity of the population [31]. These methodologies range from general techniques to ad-hoc heuristics. In this section, we briefly review some of the most popular general techniques, placing special emphasis on those techniques that, as our proposal, modify the replacement strategy.

During the 90s, considerable efforts were devoted to devising new parent selection schemes where the selection pressure might be controlled. However, some studies found that parent selectors were not able to maintain proper diversity *per se* [5] even if relatively large populations were used. The population model has also been studied with the aim of improving diversity preservation in EAs. In these schemes, some recombination restrictions are imposed by taking into account the positions of the individuals in the population. These modifications have important effects on diversity [1]. Other popular schemes [31] include those based on imposing mating restrictions and on adapting the variation stage. In the aforementioned schemes, diversity is controlled indirectly, thus complicating the task of adapting the schemes to the requirements of different problems and stopping criteria. In fact, such an indirect management approach is known to cause performance drawbacks in some cases [26].

Some techniques that rely on modifying the replacement phase have also been devised. The basic principle behind these schemes is that by diversifying the survivors, more exploration can be induced. The reason for this is two-fold. First, if the diversity of a given population is large, it means that several regions of the search space are maintained. Second, most crossovers tend to be explorative operators when distant individuals are involved. In our opinion, introducing the diversity preservation mechanism into the survivor selection stage is highly promising. We base this on the fact that while the variation and parent selection stages make decisions that affect the current generation — creation of the offspring —, the survivor selection mechanism makes decisions that might have a more drastic effect on the whole optimization process.

One of the first studies into this topic resulted in Cavicchio's *preselection scheme*, which was extended to create the *crowding* methods [31]. Several other replacement strategies that promote diversity have been proposed since then. One of the most popular is the *clearing* [21] strategy, which can be regarded as an extension of fitness sharing. Another state-of-the-art alternative is the method devised in [14] (CD/RW — Contribution to Diversity / Replace Worst), where a new individual enters the population by replacing another that is worse both in quality and diversity contribution. If such an individual is not found, a *replace-worst* strategy (RW) is applied, i.e., the worst individual in the population is deleted if it is worse than the newly generated individual.

Finally, another quite popular alternative is to explicitly consider diversity as an objective and apply a multi-objective optimization scheme [6]. In these methods, the auxiliary objective is a measure of the diversity introduced by each individual considered in the population. Several different ways of calculating the auxiliary objective have been proposed [25]. One of the most popular is probably the *distance to the closest neighbor* (DCN) metric [6]. In DCN, the auxiliary objective of a given individual is calculated as its distance to the closest member of the population. In addition, it was shown that a replacement phase where the DCN is calculated by taking into account only the members that have already been selected to survive is preferred [24]. In this paper, we propose a new replacement phase that is an extension of the method devised in [24].

3. EVOLUTIONARY ALGORITHMS FOR THE TSP

The application of EAs to the TSP has a long history [32]. In this section, we briefly review three of the areas that have seen the most intense research efforts: the development of

[1]http://www.akira.ruc.dk/~keld/research/LKH/

crossover schemes, the hybridization of improvement heuristics and metaheuristics, and diversity control.

The 80s and 90s saw the appearance of a large number of papers on recombination operators [27]. Among others, basic variants of the well-known maximal preservative crossover (MPX) [18], edge assembly crossover (EAX) [19] and edge recombination crossover (ERX) [32] were devised. While many other recombinations appeared, these three are some of the most widely used nowadays because they are adjacency-based crossovers, i.e., they emphasize preserving the edges of their parents, which has been shown to be a truly beneficial feature [30].

In the TSP, the crossover operators can be divided into two classes: those that use local problem-dependent information and those that do not. The former are greedy schemes that take into account the cost of the different edges to create better tours. The latter are simpler operators that, due to the absence of greedy operations, induce greater levels of diversity. Note that several extensions of the above operators have also been devised. For instance, a greedy variant of the ERX (Edge-T) was developed [29]. Edge-T not only includes a greedy strategy, but also encourages the alternation of parents in edge inheritance with the aim of increasing diversity. Nowadays, it is not clear whether using greedy or non-greedy strategies is preferred. In fact, both kinds of crossovers have attained the best-known solutions for different instances [20, 12]. In the case of greedy crossovers, hybridization is not usually required [12]. However, considering that some of the most powerful greedy variants [12] incorporate local searches to connect certain intermediate subtours, the conceptual difference between this scheme and hybrid methods is not so significant. Alternatively, when non-greedy crossovers are taken into account, hybrid methods are required to deal with large instances [20]. The LKH tool features the ERXT operator. This operator is a variant of the Edge-T that does not include the greedy operations.

A closely related approach to crossover is the *iterative partial transcription* (IPT) [17]. Similarly to crossover operators, IPT combines two tours with the aim of generating a new, shorter tour. Particularly, IPT identifies parts of the tours that can be exchanged without compromising the feasibility of the newly generated tour. The main drawback is that depending on the tours under consideration, no suitable parts might be identified. In these cases, no changes are made. As a result, IPT should not be used as a crossover. However, in some other cases, impressive improvements can be obtained. This is why in some EAs, as in the one incorporated in the LKH tool, in addition to a traditional crossover scheme, IPT is also incorporated. Specifically, new offspring created with the ERXT are then combined with all the members of the population using IPT. Since this method yields significant improvements, our scheme also incorporates it.

The study and implementation of hybrid schemes for the TSP is another very active area of research. Some of the first memetic algorithms incorporated simple improvement heuristics such as the 2-opt or 3-opt [16]. Subsequently, more complex schemes, especially those based on the LK heuristic, were adopted. Nowadays, the iterated LK (ILK) — which is a variant of ILS — has shown to be one of the best trajectory-based metaheuristics for the TSP. In several cases [20], ILK has been used as the individual-learning scheme in memetic algorithms. It is this scheme, specifically the variant incorporated in LKH, that we have adopted in our paper. Note that this variant is a special case of ILS. Usually, in ILS once a local optimum is found, a perturbation is done. However, in the LKH implementation, a new random tour is created. Then, the local search applied to this tour is biased by the best solution found in the current iteration of ILS. Specifically, k-opt moves in which the first edge to be broken belongs to the best solution found in the current iteration of ILS are not investigated. This attracts the solution towards the current zone being explored. In addition, the search restrictions produce a faster local search. Finally, note that since ILK incorporates mechanisms to create new edges, EAs without the presence of mutation can be used [30].

Some of the first successful EAs applied to the TSP were based on the GENITOR scheme [32], meaning that high levels of intensification were induced. However, some proposals where diversity was taken into account were also devised, showing the advantages of diversifying the search. The first methods applied were very basic. For instance, in ASPARAGOS [9] structured populations were used, while in [23] a method based on hashes to avoid clones was presented. In addition, some other classical diversity management strategies, such as fitness sharing, restarting, multi-chromosomal cramping, large populations and crowding, have been considered [23]. Note that some of these methods rely on functions capable of determining a real-valued measure of the distance between two given tours. Thus, several metrics to measure these distances have been devised [15]. These research efforts have revealed the benefits of taking diversity into account when designing EAs for the TSP. In fact, ASPARAGOS was the best evolutionary strategy for many years [16].

Most current EAs for the TSP include certain actions to control diversity [16, 11]. In fact, nowadays most of the general techniques devised for dealing with the balance between exploration and exploitation have been tested with the TSP. In addition, some techniques specifically designed for the TSP have also appeared. In several cases, structured populations are taken into account, though they are usually combined with other approaches. For instance, in [20] it is used with crowding, while in [13] diversity is taken into account when accepting immigrants. Mating restrictions are also quite popular. For instance, in [30], heterogeneous paring selections are promoted. Combining diversity and the length of the tour in the fitness function has also yielded quite promising results for large instances [12]. In these types of proposals, different entropy-based metrics have been used to measure the diversity. The LKH tool incorporates the CD/RW method and clone avoidance. In this case, the distance between two given individuals is calculated using the k-OPT metric [15]. In this metric, the number of different edges in both individuals is counted. Note that this operation can be completed in linear time with respect to the number of cities in the instance. Finally, we would like to note that while controlling diversity by considering it as an additional optimization objective has gained popularity in recent years [25], we are not aware of the application of this kind of method to the TSP.

4. OUR PROPOSAL

In our new proposal we incorporate a novel replacement strategy (Algorithm 1) in a memetic scheme (Algorithm 2) that applies readily available operators. This section describes both schemes.

Algorithm 1 MULTI_DYN survivor selection scheme

```
CurrentMembers = Population ∪ Offspring
Best = Individual with best f(x) in CurrentMembers
NewPop = { Best }
CurrentMembers = CurrentMembers - { Best }
while (|NewPop| < N) do
    Calculate DCN of CurrentMembers, considering as reference NewPop
    D = D_I - D_I * T_Elapsed / T_End
    Penalize(CurrentMembers, D)
    ND = Non-dominated individuals in CurrentMembers (without repetitions) according to the two defined objectives
    Selected = Randomly select an individual from ND
    NewPop = NewPop ∪ Selected
    CurrentMembers = CurrentMembers - {Selected}
end while
Population = NewPop
```

Algorithm 2 Pseudocode of the Memetic Scheme

```
Initialization: Generate an initial population with N individuals with the initialization incorporated in the LKH tool
Local Search: Apply ILS to every individual in the population
Survivor selection initialization: Initialize D_I
while (the stopping criterion is not fulfilled) do
    Mating selection: select 2 × N parents with binary tournaments
    Crossover: Apply the ERXT to generate N new individuals
    Local Search: Adapt the local-search strength and apply ILS to the offspring population
    Combination: Try to combine each new individual with every member of the current population using the IPT method
    Survivor selection: Apply the MULTI_DYN scheme to select N survivors
end while
```

4.1 Diversity-based Replacement Strategy

Our proposal builds on the multi-objective replacement strategy presented in [24] (MULTI) and modifies it with the aim of avoiding certain drawbacks. The MULTI strategy operates as follows. First, the population of the previous generation and the offspring are combined in a temporary set. Then, the best individual, i.e., the tour with the lowest length, is selected to form part of the new population. Then, until the new population is filled with N individuals, the following steps are executed. First, the distance to closest neighbor (DCN) objective is calculated. The k-OPT metric is used to calculate the distances in our case. The calculation considers the currently selected individuals as the reference, i.e., for each pending individual, the distance to the nearest individual previously selected is taken into account. Then, considering the individuals that have not been selected, the non-dominated front is calculated. The two objectives considered are the tour length and the DCN. The tour length should be minimized whereas the DCN should be maximized. This front is computed as a set with no repetitions. Finally, a non-dominated individual is randomly selected to survive. While survivor selections similar to this one have been successful in other cases [25], initial experimentation with long executions in the TSP revealed that this scheme is not appropriate. The reason is that it can accept very close tours even in the initial phases and tends to create clusters of distant tours that are maintained throughout the execution. Since the number of clusters maintained is neither large nor adaptive, schemes capable of inducing larger levels of diversity are required for long executions.

The main advantage of the newly devised replacement strategy (MULTI_DYN) is that the balance between exploration and exploitation is dynamically adjusted based on the given stopping criterion. Thus, the stopping criterion, as well as the elapsed time, are used as inputs to the replacement strategy. This way, for shorter stopping criteria, MULTI_DYN induces a faster reduction in diversity than for longer stopping criteria. One of the basic principles behind MULTI_DYN (Algorithm 1) is that individuals that contribute too little to diversity —the contribution is measured with the DCN value— should not survive regardless of their tour length. In our approach, individuals whose DCN value is lower than a value D are penalized by setting their tour length to a very low quality value. Specifically, we set it to the maximum value representable in a *long* data type. Then, individuals are ranked taking into account the modified values. While this approach is quite logical, one of the key choices is how to evaluate whether an individual contributes enough or not, i.e., how to set the value of D, which should depend on the optimization stage. Specifically, this value should be reduced as the stopping criterion is approached. In our scheme, the initial D_I value is set by calculating the maximum distance appearing between any two individuals of the initial population and dividing it by two. Note that in most instances, global and local optima share a large number of edges [16], which is why we decided to initialize D_I in this way. This induce a high but not exceedingly large exploration in the initial phases. In our initial experiments we also used some larger values related to the number of cities, though this resulted in higher levels of fruitless exploration. Subsequently, a linear reduction of D is done during the execution. The reduction is calculated in such a way that by the end of the execution, the resulting value is 0, meaning that in the final stages our proposal behaves as MULTI. In this paper, the stopping criterion is set based on time. Thus, if T_{End} is the number of seconds allocated to the run and $T_{Elapsed}$ is the elapsed time, D can be calculated as $D = D_I - D_I * \frac{T_{Elapsed}}{T_{End}}$.

4.2 Memetic Algorithm

The newly proposed EA (MULTI_DYN-MA - Algorithm 2) is quite similar to the one incorporated in the LKH tool. Initially, N individuals are generated. So as to start with solutions that are already fit, completely random solutions are not used. Instead, they are generated with the initialization procedure used in LKH [10] and the ILS variant of the LKH tool is applied to them. Note that the initialization scheme does not produce very high-quality solutions. However, since promising edges are selected, the time invested in the local search is reduced. Afterwards, the maximum distance between individuals is calculated with the aim of initializing the D_I value, as described above. Finally, a set of generations is evolved until the stopping criterion is fulfilled. In each generation the parents are selected through binary

Table 1: Results obtained by the different schemes in the long-term

	MULTI_DYN-MA		RW-MA		ELL_GEN-MA		LKH-MA	
	Mean	SR	Mean	SR	Mean	SR	Mean	SR
RL5915	**565530**	**100%**	565542.8	76.6%	565542.8	76.6%	**565530**	**100%**
RL5934	**556045**	**100%**	**556045**	**100%**	**556045**	**100%**	**556045**	**100%**
PLA7397	**23260728**	**100%**	**23260728**	**100%**	**23260728**	**100%**	**23260728**	**100%**
RL11849	**923288**	**100%**	**923288**	**100%**	**923288**	**100%**	**923288**	100%
USA13509	**19982859**	**100%**	19983011.2	60%	19983053.5	60%	**19982859**	**100%**
BRD14051	**469386.1**	**63.3%**	469391.9	10%	469389.2	10%	469388.3	23.3%
D15112	**1573084**	**100%**	1573120.4	6.6%	1573100.2	6.6%	1573084.2	96.6%
D18512	**645242.2**	0%	645248	3.3%	645242.6	3.3%	645243.4	**6.66%**
PLA33810	**66049417**	**76.6%**	66052783.2	10%	66050892.1	10%	66052732.5	0%
PLA85900	**142399695.8**	0%	142402714.9	0%	142400081.4	0%	142400364.8	0%

tournaments, the ERXT operator is applied to create N new individuals, and ILS is used to improve each generated individual. Since ILS already perturbs solutions, mutation is not used. Note that ILS accepts a parameter (*MoveType* in LKH) to define the strength of the local search. The default value of this parameter in the LKH tool is 5. In order to increase the number of generations evolved in our EA, we adapt this value. Specifically, in the first third of the execution it is set to 3; in the second third it is set to 4; and finally in the last third it is set to 5. In addition, the IPT scheme is used to combine each new individual with every member of the population. If a better tour is generated, this new tour replaces the offspring. Finally, the survivors are selected with the MULTI_DYN scheme.

5. EXPERIMENTAL EVALUATION

In this section, the experiments conducted with our new scheme (MULTI_DYN-MA) are described. The analyses were performed with the 10 largest instances of the TSPLIB benchmark [22]. Their sizes range from 5,915 to 85,900 cities. Tests were run in the cluster "El Insurgente" at CIMAT. In consists of bi-processor nodes with 32Gb RAM. Each processor is an Intel(R) Xeon(TM) CPU E5-2620 at 2.10GHz. Since stochastic algorithms were considered, each execution was repeated 30 times and comparisons were carried out by applying a set of statistical tests, following some of the recommendations given in [8]. Specifically, the following tests were applied, assuming a significance level of 5%. First, for each instance, a multiple-comparison among all methods was done with the Friedman's test. In the cases where the p-value was lower than the established significance level, the following pair-wise comparisons were carried out. First, a *Shapiro-Wilk test* was performed to check whether or not the values of the results followed a Gaussian distribution. If so, the *Levene test* was used to check the variances for homogeneity. If samples had equal variances, an ANOVA *test* was done; if not, a *Welch test* was performed. For non-Gaussian distributions, the *Kruskal-Wallis* test was used to test whether samples were drawn from the same distribution. In this work, the sentence "algorithm A is better than algorithm B" means that the differences between them are statistically significant, and that the mean and median obtained by A are lower than the mean and median achieved by B.

In order to show the benefits of the new model, three additional algorithms were executed. In two of them, the only difference with respect to MULTI_DYN-MA is the replacement strategy. In the RW-MA scheme, the RW strategy is used, while in the ELL_GEN-MA method a generational replacement with elitism is considered, i.e. in each generation $N-1$ new individuals are created. These new individuals and the best from the previous generation are then selected to survive. The aim of including these two schemes is to show the advantages of the MULTI_DYN replacement strategy. Finally, the state-of-the-art EA included in the LKH tool (LKH-MA) was also taken into account. The main difference with respect to MULTI_DYN-MA is the way in which diversity is managed in the replacement strategy. Note that LKH-MA applies the CD/RW strategy, which resorts to the use of the RW strategy in some cases. This means that in the long term, diversity can be greatly reduced. In addition, this scheme does not adapt the strength of the local search.

We divided our experiments into two sections. Given that maintaining higher levels of diversity is usually helpful, especially for long-term executions, in our first analyses we focus on the long long-term behavior of these algorithms. In any case, analyzing the convergence properties and the behavior in other phases is also helpful in providing a better insight into the behavior of the different schemes. Our second analyses are based on this principle.

5.1 Analysis of the long-term behavior

Our first experiments were focused on analyzing the long-term behavior of the various schemes. Specifically, in the 5 smallest instances, the stopping criterion was set to 4 days, while in the largest instances it was set to 10 days. While we do not report comparisons in base of the generations, it is interesting to remark that for the smallest instances more that 5,000 generations could be evolved, while in the largest ones about 300 were evolved. In the schemes considered in this paper, two parameters have to be set: the population size and the number of perturbations done in each iteration of the ILS. These were set experimentally to 50 and 25, respectively. Note that the behavior of the ILS in the LKH tool can be slightly modified with a large number of parameters. In our experiments we used the default values. Similarly, other ways of initializing D_I might be tested. We are aware that even better results might be obtained by properly tuning these parameters. However, given the computational cost associated with these tasks, such a study is beyond the scope of this paper.

Table 1 shows, for each scheme, the mean obtained for every TSP instance. Other important information, such as the median of the results, is not shown due to space limitations, but similar conclusions can be drawn for the median. Since the optimal tours of these instances are known, we also report the success rate (SR), i.e. the probability of

Table 2: **Statistical comparison of the different methods**

	MULTI-DYN MA		RW MA		ELL_GEN MA		LKH MA	
	↑	↓	↑	↓	↑	↓	↑	↓
RL5915	2	0	0	2	0	2	2	0
USA13509	2	0	0	2	0	2	2	0
BRD14051	3	0	0	3	1	2	2	1
D15112	2	0	0	3	1	2	2	0
D18512	1	0	0	3	1	0	1	0
PLA33810	3	0	0	2	2	1	0	2
PLA85900	1	0	0	2	1	0	0	0
Total	14	0	0	17	6	9	9	3

attaining the optimal solution. The clear superiority of the MULTI_DYN-MA is readily apparent. In fact, the mean success rate for MULTI_DYN-MA is 73.9%, which is larger than that attained by any other scheme. Specifically, LKH-MA, ELL_GEN-MA and RW-MA yielded means of 62.6%, 48.2% and 46.6% respectively. In addition, MULTI_DYN-MA attained the lowest mean in every instance. Notice that the largest differences arise in some of the largest instances, meaning that properly managing diversity is more helpful when dealing with large instances. Also worth noting is the fact that MULTI_DYN was able to achieve the optimal tour in the *pla33810* instance. To our knowledge, this is the first EA to achieve this accomplishment. Note that RW-MA and ELL_GEN-MA also obtained the optimal tours in some executions. However, they obtained lower success rates. Given that LKH-MA was not able to achieve the optimal solution, we hypothesized that adapting the local search strength might yield the most important improvements. As a result, we incorporated the adaptation strength into LKH-MA and executed the new scheme with the *pla33810* instance. While the results indeed improved in this case, the success rate only increased to 30%, meaning that, as expected, additional benefits come from the MULTI_DYN replacement strategy. In addition, it is important to note that in most cases MULTI_DYN-MA provides important benefits in terms of the mean achieved. However, when compared to ELL_GEN-MA in the *d18512* and *pla85900* instances, the differences diminish. In fact, in these two cases, the differences between MULTI_DYN-MA and ELL_GEN-MA are not statistically significant. The reasons have to do with the convergence properties in these problems and are analyzed in the next section.

Finally, the results were also subjected to statistical tests, as shown in Table 2. For each instance where the Friedman's test rejected the null hyphotesis, the column with the ↑ shows the number of cases where the method listed in the corresponding column is better than the other methods in the pairwise comparisons. Similarly, the column with the ↓ shows the number of cases where the model is worse. The only method that was not statistically inferior in any instance was the MULTI_DYN-MA, demonstrating once again its superiority. Due to space constraints, the p-values are not reported but they were quite low. For instance, in the case of the BRD14051, the maximum p-value obtained in the comparisons where MULTI_DYN-MA was taken into account was lower than 10^{-5}.

5.2 Analysis of the convergence properties

One of the advantages of explicitly controlling the diversity in EAs is that premature convergence might be avoided.

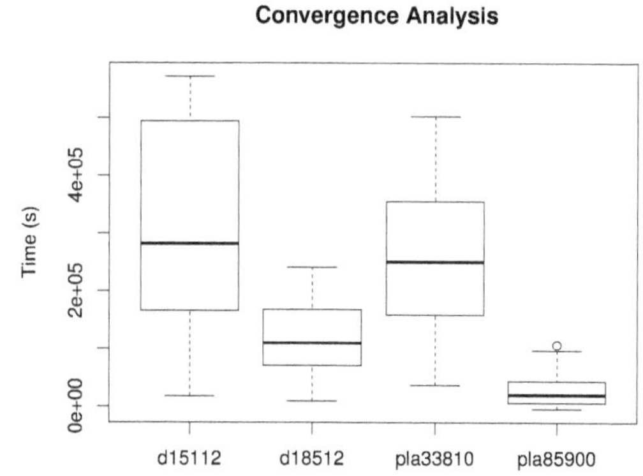

Figure 1: Box-plots of the time elapsed since the last improvement in ELL_GEN-MA

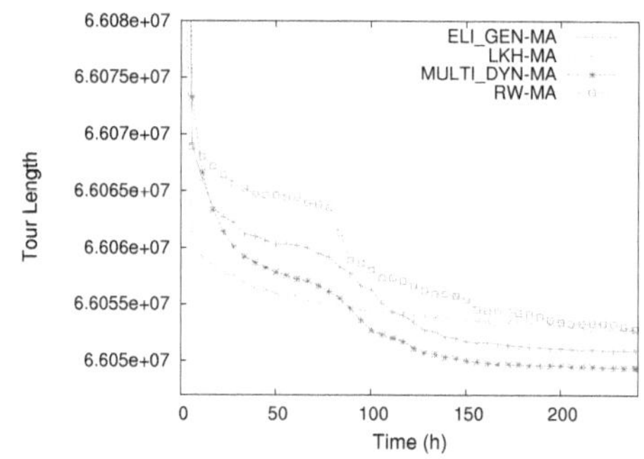

Figure 2: Evolution of tour length in the pla33810 instance

In the previous analyses, we saw how in two of the instances (D18512 and PLA85900) our new proposal did not provide significant benefits when compared to ELL_GEN-MA. In order to shed some light on the reasons behind this behavior, we re-executed ELL_GEN-MA with the four largest instances using the seeds that did not provide the optimal solution. In these executions, we stored the time elapsed between the last improvement made during the execution and the end of the execution. Figure 1 shows the box-plots of these times. We can clearly see that these times are short in D18512 and PLA85900, meaning that in these instances, premature convergence did not appear even after 10 days of execution. The reason is that the results were not very close to the optimal values, even after such a long execution time. Thus, in order to profit from explicitly controlling diversity, longer executions are needed. However, in the two other instances tested (D15112 and PLA33810), it is clear that premature convergence is appearing in ELL_GEN-MA. As a result, in these instances the advantages of using the MULTI_DYN-MA are more significant, both in terms of the success rate and of the mean values attained.

In addition, it is quite interesting to show the evolution of the best tour found for the different schemes. Figures 2 and 3 show how the tour length evolved for the schemes considered in the PLA33810 and PLA85900 instances, respectively. In the case of the PLA33810 intance, the MULTI_DYN-MA suffers from slow convergence in the first phases of the optimization, as expected. However, maintaining such a large diversity allows for better exploration of the different regions,

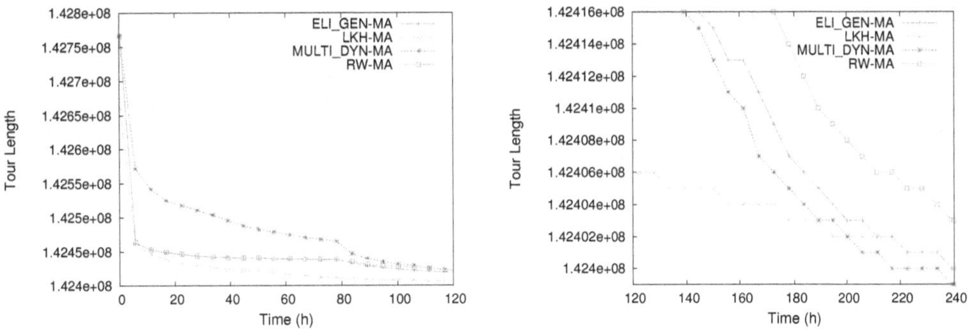

Figure 3: Evolution of tour length in the pla85900 instance

and in the long-term the benefits are clear. Also note that LKH-MA has the faster convergence. The reasons for this are two-fold. First, the strength of the local search is not adapted. Second, in large instances, LKH-MA relies too much on the RW strategy. As a result, it quickly loses diversity. In fact, in the two largest instances, differences between the results obtained by LKH-MA and RW-MA are not statistically significant. The PLA85900 instance exhibits similar effects, some of them more clearly. In the first phases, we see that the convergence in MULTI_DYN-MA is very slow. In fact, after 120 hours, MULTI_DYN-MA reports the worst tours. The time invested in the LK heuristics grows exponentially, meaning that in the longest instances much fewer generations are evolved. In addition, more promising zones can be detected because the search space is larger, meaning that much more time might be required to reach the optimal solution. In fact, in this case we can see that even after 240 hours, no scheme has converged. Also note that in spite of the initial slow convergence, MULTI_DYN-MA attains the lowest mean at the end of the executions. In any case, since the differences between the results of MULTI_DYN-MA and ELI_GEN-MA are not significant, it seems that longer executions are required in order to profit from the application of the MULTI_DYN-MA scheme. However, since these executions are already very long, parallelizing this EA seems quite promising. Finally, we would like to note that, to our knowledge, the mean achieved by MULTI_DYN-MA for the PLA85900 instance is the lowest value reported by an EA.

6. CONCLUSIONS

The TSP is one of the most challenging and studied combinatorial optimization problems. Several different schemes have been devised to address the TSP, including a large number of heuristics and metaheuristics. Among these methods, population-based schemes such as EAs have yielded quite promising results. Several studies have revealed that by properly managing the diversity induced by these methods, larger instances can be handled. In this paper, a new diversity-based memetic scheme for the TSP has been devised. The most important contribution is a novel replacement strategy that accepts the stopping criterion as a parameter, the goal being to properly alter the balance between exploration and exploitation. The realization of this idea is based on the application of certain principles that arise in the multi-objective field. This strategy has been integrated with state-of-the-art crossovers and local search operators. In addition, the strength of the local search is adapted. The new scheme has been compared against state-of-the-art EAs with the largest instances of the TSPLIB benchmark. The results show the clear superiority of our proposal. However, some instances were identified whose results were similar to those obtained by other schemes. The reason is that in these cases, convergence is not obtained even after a 10-day execution runtime. Even in these cases, however, by properly altering the balance between exploration and exploitation, the results reported by our proposal are not inferior. Thus, the newly devised scheme has yielded better or similar results than any other scheme in every instance tested. Two of the most important achievements of the new scheme are the following: the PLA33810 instance has been solved to optimality and, to our knowledge, the mean reported for the PLA85900 is lower than any mean reported by any other state-of-the-art EAs.

Since we have shown that for the largest instances, convergence is not obtained even after 10 days, one of the future lines of research is to develop a parallel scheme to handle even larger instances. We might first develop a straightforward master-slave scheme. Then, in order to be able to profit from a larger number of processors, we would like to parallelize it with an island-based approach. However, prior to implementing it, the implications that integrating structured populations into our proposals have on diversity should be studied. Finally, since there are several other crossovers and local search operators that have yielded high-quality solutions, new designs incorporating some of these schemes might be in order.

Acknowledgments

The first author acknowledges the financial support from CONCYTEG as part of the plan "Investigadores Jóvenes - DPP-2014" (project 14-IJ-DPP-Q182-11).

7. REFERENCES

[1] E. Alba. *Parallel Metaheuristics: A New Class of Algorithms*. Wiley series on parallel and distributed computing. Wiley-Interscience, 2005.

[2] S. Anbuudayasankar, K. Ganesh, and S. Mohapatra. Survey of methodologies for tsp and vrp. In *Models for Practical Routing Problems in Logistics*, pages 11–42. Springer International Publishing, 2014.

[3] D. Applegate, R. Bixby, V. Chvátal, and W. Cook. Available at www.tsp.gatech.edu.

[4] D. Applegate, W. Cook, and A. Rohe. Chained lin-kernighan for large traveling salesman problems. *INFORMS J. on Computing*, 15(1):82–92, Jan. 2003.

[5] T. Blickle and L. Thiele. A Comparison of Selection Schemes used in Evolutionary Algorithms. *Evolutionary Computation*, 4(4):361–394, 1996.

[6] L. T. Bui, H. A. Abbass, and J. Branke. Multiobjective optimization for dynamic environments. In *2005 IEEE Congress on Evolutionary Computation*, volume 3 of *CEC'05*, pages 2349 – 2356 Vol. 3, 2005.

[7] W. Cook. *In Pursuit of the Traveling Salesman: Mathematics at the Limits of Computation.* Princeton University Press. Princeton University Press, 2012.

[8] J. Derrac, S. García, D. Molina, and F. Herrera. A practical tutorial on the use of nonparametric statistical tests as a methodology for comparing evolutionary and swarm intelligence algorithms. *Swarm and Evolutionary Computation*, 1(1):3 – 18, 2011.

[9] M. Gorges-Schleuter. ASPARAGOS an Asynchronous Parallel Genetic Optimization Strategy. In *Proceedings of the Third International Conference on Genetic Algorithms*, pages 422–427, San Francisco, CA, USA, 1989. Morgan Kaufmann Publishers Inc.

[10] K. Helsgaun. An effective implementation of the lin-kernighan traveling salesman heuristic. *European Journal of Operational Research*, 126:106–130, 2000.

[11] K. Helsgaun. General k-opt submoves for the lin-kernighan tsp heuristic. *Mathematical Programming Computation*, 1(2-3):119–163, 2009.

[12] K. Honda, Y. Nagata, and I. Ono. A parallel genetic algorithm with edge assembly crossover for 100,000-city scale tsps. In *2013 IEEE Congress on Evolutionary Computation (CEC)*, pages 1278–1285, June 2013.

[13] C. Li, J. Wang, X. Yan, and G. Hu. Subpopulation diversity based accepting immigrant in distributed evolutionary algorithms. In *Parallel and Distributed Systems (ICPADS), 2013 International Conference on*, pages 422–423, Dec 2013.

[14] M. Lozano, F. Herrera, and J. R. Cano. Replacement strategies to preserve useful diversity in steady-state genetic algorithms. *Information Sciences*, 178(23):4421 – 4433, 2008. Including Special Section: Genetic and Evolutionary Computing.

[15] K.-T. Mak and A. J. Morton. Distances between traveling salesman tours. *Discrete Applied Mathematics*, 58(3):281 – 291, 1995.

[16] P. Merz and B. Freisleben. Memetic algorithms for the traveling salesman problem. *Complex Systems*, 13:297–345, 2001.

[17] A. Möbius, B. Freisleben, P. Merz, and M. Schreiber. Combinatorial optimization by iterative partial transcription. *Phys. Rev. E*, 59:4667–4674, Apr 1999.

[18] H. Mühlenbein. Evolution in Time and Space - The Parallel Genetic Algorithm. In *Foundations of Genetic Algorithms*, pages 316–337, San Francisco, CA, USA, 1991. Morgan Kaufmann.

[19] Y. Nagata and S. Kobayashi. Edge Assembly Crossover: A High-power Genetic Algorithm for the Travelling Salesman Problem. In T. Bäck, editor, *Proceedings of the Seventh International Conference on Genetic Algorithms (ICGA97)*, pages 450–457, San Francisco, CA, 1997. Morgan Kaufmann.

[20] H. D. Nguyen, I. Yoshihara, K. Yamamori, and M. Yasunaga. Implementation of an effective hybrid ga for large-scale traveling salesman problems. *IEEE Transactions on Systems, Man, and Cybernetics, Part B*, 37(1):92–99, 2007.

[21] A. Petrowski. A clearing procedure as a niching method for genetic algorithms. In *Proceedings of IEEE International Conference on Evolutionary Computation 1996 (CEC'96)*, pages 798–803, May 1996.

[22] G. Reinelt. TSPLIB - A Traveling Salesman Problem Library. *ORSA Journal on Computing*, 3(4):376–384, Nov. 1991.

[23] S. Ronald. Preventing Diversity Loss in a Routing Genetic Algorithm with Hash Tagging. *Complexity International*, 2, 1995.

[24] C. Segura, C. Coello, E. Segredo, G. Miranda, and C. León. Improving the diversity preservation of multi-objective approaches used for single-objective optimization. In *2013 IEEE Congress on Evolutionary Computation (CEC)*, pages 3198–3205, June 2013.

[25] C. Segura, C. A. Coello Coello, G. Miranda, and C. León. Using multi-objective evolutionary algorithms for single-objective optimization. *4OR*, 11(3):201–228, 2013.

[26] C. Segura, C. A. Coello Coello, E. Segredo, and C. León. An analysis of the automatic adaptation of the crossover rate in differential evolution. In *2014 IEEE Congress on Evolutionary Computation (CEC'14)*, pages 459–466, July 2014.

[27] T. Starkweather, S. McDaniel, K. Mathias, D. Whitley, and C. Whitley. A comparison of genetic sequencing operators. In R. Belew and L. Booker, editors, *Proceedings of the Fourth International Conference on Genetic Algorithms*, pages 69–76, San Mateo, CA, 1991. Morgan Kaufman.

[28] E.-G. Talbi. *Metaheuristics: From Design to Implementation.* Wiley Publishing, 2009.

[29] C.-K. Ting. Improving edge recombination through alternate inheritance and greedy manner. In J. Gottlieb and G. Raidl, editors, *Evolutionary Computation in Combinatorial Optimization*, volume 3004 of *Lecture Notes in Computer Science*, pages 210–219. Springer Berlin Heidelberg, 2004.

[30] H.-K. Tsai, J.-M. Yang, Y.-F. Tsai, and C.-Y. Kao. An evolutionary algorithm for large traveling salesman problems. *Trans. Sys. Man Cyber. Part B*, 34(4):1718–1729, Aug. 2004.

[31] M. Črepinšek, S.-H. Liu, and M. Mernik. Exploration and exploitation in evolutionary algorithms: A survey. *ACM Computing Surveys*, 45(3):35:1–35:33, July 2013.

[32] L. D. Whitley, T. Starkweather, and D. Fuquay. Scheduling problems and traveling salesmen: The genetic edge recombination operator. In *Proceedings of the 3rd International Conference on Genetic Algorithms*, pages 133–140, San Francisco, CA, USA, 1989. Morgan Kaufmann Publishers Inc.

A Visual Method for Analysis and Comparison of Search Landscapes

Sebastian Volke
Leipzig University
Institut für Informatik
PF 100920, D-04009 Leipzig
volke@informatik.uni-leipzig.de

Dirk Zeckzer
Leipzig University
Institut für Informatik
PF 100920, D-04009 Leipzig
zeckzer@informatik.uni-leipzig.de

Gerik Scheuermann
Leipzig University
Institut für Informatik
PF 100920, D-04009 Leipzig
scheuermann@informatik.uni-leipzig.de

Martin Middendorf
Leipzig University
Institut für Informatik
PF 100920, D-04009 Leipzig
middendorf@informatik.uni-leipzig.de

ABSTRACT

Combinatorial optimization problems and corresponding (meta-)heuristics have received much attention in the literature. Especially, the structural or topological analysis of search landscapes is important for evaluating the applicability and the performance of search operators for a given problem. However, this analysis is often tedious and usually the focus is on one specific problem and only a few operators. We present a visual analysis method that can be applied to a wide variety of problems and search operators. The method is based on steepest descent walks and shortest distances in the search landscape. The visualization shows the search landscape as seen by the search algorithm. It supports the topological analysis as well as the comparison of search landscapes. We showcase the method by applying it to two different search operators on the TSP, the QAP, and the SMTTP. Our results show how differences between search operators manifest in the search landscapes and how conclusions about the suitability of the search operator for different optimizations can be drawn.

CCS Concepts

•Mathematics of computing → Optimization with randomized search heuristics; •Human-centered computing → Information visualization;

Keywords

Combinatorial optimization, Local search, Fitness landscapes, Empirical study

GECCO '15, July 11–15, 2015, Madrid, Spain

DOI: http://dx.doi.org/10.1145/2739480.2754733

1. INTRODUCTION

A frequent class of optimization problems are *combinatorial* optimization problems, where an optimal solution has to be found from a finite set of solutions. Typically, the solution space grows exponentially in the problem size. Therefore, exhaustive search by complete enumeration is only possible for very small problem instances.

Local search algorithms [15] use search operators to construct a neighborhood among the solutions. They traverse the emerging search landscape in order to find locally optimal solutions. The topological complexity of the search landscape, e.g., indicated by the number of and the distance between local minima, the average length of search paths, or the probability of finding a good local minimum, depends on the interaction between the search operator and the optimization function. Optimization is much easier in search landscapes with simpler topology. Thus, an optimization problem can be solved by finding a search operator that induces a preferably simple search landscape.

The analysis of search landscapes is crucial in identifying well-performing search operators. In this paper, we present a method for analyzing search landscapes that is based on approximating the search landscape using random samples and steepest descent walks together with a visualization system that shows the topology of the solutions found by the sampling process. The method does not depend on a specific problem and thus is widely applicable. The visualization system fosters the interpretation of the analysis results. In particular, the visualization of the search landscape shows how the search algorithms perceives the optimization problem. We apply the method to instances of the TSP, the QAP, and the SMTTP and compare the performance of two different search operators on these problems.

2. SEARCH LANDSCAPES

2.1 Definition

Discrete combinatorial optimization addresses the selection of the best solution out of a finite *set of solutions* X of a problem instance. Usually, a *cost function* $f : X \rightarrow \mathrm{R}$

is used to model the quality of solutions: $x \in X$ is better than $y \in X$ if $f(x) < f(y)$. Solving the optimization problem is equivalent to finding the global minimum of f. Here, we are particularly interested in permutation problems, i.e., optimization problems where the set of solutions is a set of permutations of a given size, or a subset thereof. In the following, the length n of a permutation is referred to as the *problem size*. Many practically relevant permutation problems are NP-hard [9]. The relevant problems for this paper are discussed in Section 2.3.

Local search methods incrementally improve initial solutions until no further improvement can be achieved, i.e., until a local minimum is reached. Thereby, the *neighborhood* defines the search candidates for every solution. Formally, we define a neighborhood as a mapping $N : X \rightarrow 2^X$ that associates every solution with a set of neighbor solutions. In practice, the neighborhood is often implemented by use of a *search operator*. Following Schiavinotto et al. [24], we define a search operator Δ as a collection of operator functions $\delta : X \rightarrow X$ such that $y \in N(x) \iff \exists \delta \in \Delta$ with $\delta(x) = y$. The set of solutions together with the search operator form the *neighborhood graph* $G_{X,N} = (X, E_N)$. Thereby, the set of directed edges is defined as $E_N = \{(x,y)|x,y \in X \wedge y \in N(x)\} = \{(x,y)|x,y \in X \wedge \exists\delta \in \Delta : y = \delta(x)\}$. In particular, we consider search operators that give rise to connected and symmetric neighborhood graphs. Because the vertex set is the set of solutions, the cost function f can be considered a function on the vertex set of the neighborhood graph. Thus, the *search landscape* $S_{f,X,N} = (G_{X,N}, f)$ is formed.

The topological structure of the search landscape characterizes the difficulty of the search. Interesting properties are the number of local minima, the number of paths leading to these minima, or the lengths of these paths. The cost function f has an important influence on the complexity of the topology. Some problems give rise to much more complex search landscapes than others. However, also the search operator determines the topology, as it defines the connectivity within the landscape. Thus, complexity may also arise when the search operator does not fit the optimization problem well.

Depending of the size of the search operator—the operators defined in [24] have $|\Delta| \in O(n)$ or $|\Delta| \in O(n^2)$—the search landscape has $O(n!)$ nodes and $O(n^p n!)$ edges. This makes it impossible to search the complete graph except for very small n. Therefore, analysis approaches have been developed that use only parts of the landscape. One approach generates a representative sampling of the landscapes [17], i.e., it extracts a subset of solution with the same overall properties as the whole set of solutions. Other approaches consider search paths (steepest descent paths and descending random walks) and analyze their properties [8, 22, 26]. A *path* $\mathbf{p}$ *of length* l is a sequence of solutions $\mathbf{p} = [p_1 p_2 \dots p_l]$ with $p_{i+1} \in N(p_i)$ for all $1 \leq i < l$. A *descending path* is a path $\mathbf{p}$ with $f(p_{i+1}) < f(p_i)$. Naturally, descending paths can only be extended as long as a better neighbor exists. In particular, descending paths end in local minima. For *steepest descent paths* we require additionally that $p_{i+1} = \min_{f(p)}\{p \in N(p_i)\}$. Of special interest are shortest paths within the landscape, especially their length. We define the distance $d_\Delta(x,y)$ between $x, y \in X$ as the length of a shortest path between x and y, i.e., as the minimal number of applications of operator functions $\delta \in \Delta$ that are necessary to transform x into y. For many operators, there exist efficient algorithms to compute the distance between two solutions or at least a good approximation for this distance [24].

2.2 Proximate Optimality Principle

The *Proximate Optimality Principle* (POP) states, that "good solutions at one level are likely to be found 'close to' good solutions at an adjacent level" [7, 11]. In the case of local search algorithms, it can be translated as such: good local minima are likely to be found "close to" each other. Thereby, closeness or proximity can be expressed by means of the search operator distance.

This formulation of the POP does by no means hold for every search landscape. If it holds, the result will be one or several clear accumulations of local minima within a small part of the search landscape. If this is the case, like for the Traveling Salesman Problem [8, 26], it is very beneficial for the search process and can be exploited. Therefore, we are particularly interested in investigating whether the POP holds for a search operator on given problems.

2.3 Optimization Problems

In the following, we define the three NP-complete optimization problems that we consider in this paper. The *Symmetric Traveling Salesman Problem* (STSP) is to find for n given locations and distances $d_{ij} = d_{ji}$ between locations $1 \leq i,j \leq n$ the shortest round-trip that visits all locations. A round-trip can be considered as a permutation π where $\pi(i)$ is the location at position i of the round-trip. The length of the tour is $f_{TSP}(\pi) = \sum_{i=1}^{n-1} d_{\pi(i),\pi(i+1)} + d_{\pi(n),\pi(1)}$.

The *Quadratic Assignment Problem* (QAP) requires n facilities to be assigned to n locations. Given are distances $d_{ij} = d_{ji}$ between two locations $1 \leq i,j \leq n$ and the amount of exchange $e_{kl} = e_{lk}$ between two facilities $1 \leq k,l \leq n$. An assignment of facilities to locations is a permutation π, where facility k is assigned to location $\pi(k)$. Then a permutation is searched that minimizes $f_{QAP}(\pi) = \sum_{k=1}^{n}\sum_{l=1}^{n} e_{kl} \cdot d_{\pi(k),\pi(l)}$.

The *Single Machine Total Tardiness Problem* (SMTTP) is to find an optimal, sequential schedule of n jobs. Each job i has a processing time $p_i > 0$ and a due date $d_i > 0$. A schedule is a permutation π where job i is scheduled at position $\pi(i)$. Then, the completion time of job i is $C_i(\pi) = \sum_{\pi(j) \leq \pi(i)} p_j$. The tardiness of job i is $T_i(\pi) = \max\{0, C_i(\pi) - d_i\}$. A schedule π is searched that minimizes $f_{SMTTP}(\pi) = \sum_{i=1}^{n} T_i$.

2.4 Search Operators

The following two operators are of particular interest and will server as examples throughout the paper. The *2-opt operator* Δ_{2opt}, also known as 2-edge exchange operator, is a well established search operator for TSP ([5, 16]). Basically, it disentangles a route by eliminating edge crossings. Formally, the application of this operator corresponds to the reversal of a subsequence of a (circular) permutation. The corresponding distance between to permutations is called reversal distance. Unfortunately, the decision version of the problem to determine the reversal distance (or a corresponding shortest transformation between two solutions—also called the *sorting by reversal* problem) is NP-hard. However, the *bond distance* provides a good approximation for it: the number of edges is counted that are not in common between the two tours. This yields a maximal possible bond distance of n. The bond distance differs from the reversal distance at most by factor 2 as proven by Boese [2].

The *interchange operator* $\Delta_X = \{\delta_X^{ij} | 1 \leq i < j \leq n\}$ is the set of transpositions

$$\delta_X^{ij}(\pi) = (\pi_1 \dots \pi_{i-1} \pi_j \pi_{i+1} \dots \pi_{j-1} \pi_i \pi_{j+1} \dots \pi_n)$$

for a permutation $\pi = (\pi_1 \dots \pi_n)$. The distance between two permutations with respect to Δ_X can be determined by $d_{\Delta_X}(\pi, \pi') = n - c(\pi^{-1} \circ \pi')$ (see [24] for details). Thereby, $c(\pi)$ is the number of cycles of the permutation π, and π^{-1} is the inverse permutation, i.e., $\pi \circ \pi^{-1} = identity$. A permutation has at least one cycle, so that the maximal interchange distance is $n - 1$.

3. RELATED WORK

The analysis of search landscapes is an active area of research, e.g., [7, 8, 10, 15, 21, 22, 26]. Stadler and Schnabl [26] analyzed the auto-correlation function along random walks to gain insight into the shape of the landscape. Fonlupt et al. [8] also analyzed random walks as well as steepest descent walks, but mostly regarding their lengths. Primarily, they investigated the distribution of operator distances between local minima of the search landscape. Both of these papers focus on the TSP and also restrict their analysis to the 2opt operator. We consider our work a generalization of these approaches in that we extend their method and also expand the scope of the investigation to other optimization problems and other search operators. Additionally, we complement our method with a visualization that is tailored towards the analysis of the results.

There exist several sampling-based approaches for analyzing search landscapes since full enumeration is often infeasible because of the size of the landscape. Random sampling provides uninformed samples with unknown distribution within the landscape. Khor [17] presents a method based on Wang-Landau sampling that captures a representative subset of the search landscape. In particular, these subsets allow for reasoning about the distribution of cost values within the landscape. However, in this paper our main concern is the connectivity and relation among the local minima. We achieve this by considering a number of local search paths rather than unconnected solutions throughout the search landscape.

Flamm et al. [6] published an important work about the topological structure of landscapes and introduced the barrier tree. This work has been used in the analysis and visualization of combinatorial optimization [1, 14, 27, 28]. However, all of these methods require the set of all solutions below a certain cost threshold to be available. Therefore, they can only be applied to search landscapes of relatively small problems instances (see Section 2). Furthermore, no branch-and-bound techniques (as used by Hallam and Prügel-Bennett [14]) that would allow for efficient reduction of the search space are available for permutation problems in general. Our proposed approach does not result in a rigorous representation of the topology of the search landscape, but is applicable to problem instances that cannot be exhaustively searched. Instead of a tree representation of the search landscape, we derive visualizations that allow to draw conclusions about the shape of the search landscape from a small subset of it. A very similar approach has been presented by McCandlish [20] for the visualization of evolutionary landscapes. He uses an approximation of the number of evolutionary generations between individuals to obtain a transition or distance matrix. Afterward, he does an Eigendecomposition of this matrix to project the individuals into 2D space while preserving their evolutionary distance.

Halim et al. [13] propose a visualization system called "Viz" that facilitates the analysis of local search behavior. They create a search landscape representation by means of a 2D embedding of important landmarks from searches in the landscape, based on the Hamming distance function between the landmarks. Then, search runs are plotted as trajectories in this depiction. The focus of the system is the analysis of search algorithms, not on the search landscape itself. Furthermore, the fixed distance function introduces a gap between the perceived search space and the actual behavior of the search strategy. In contrast, we use distance functions that match the search operator in order to visualize the search landscape as seen by the search strategy.

4. ANALYSIS METHOD

The goal of our approach is to enable the topological analysis of search landscapes. The approach should be applicable to problem instances of arbitrary size. Further, it should not be specific to a certain problem type or search operator. Thus, the comparison of search landscapes of different problem instances, different search operators, and even different problems should be enabled. Thereby, the type of the problem should not need to be restricted. In particular, we do not rely on the existence of efficiently enumerable solution subsets or branch-and-bound techniques.

Our approach consists of two parts. In Section 4.1, the sampling of the search landscape providing representative data is described. The topological visualization (Section 4.2) uses this data enabling to address the goals and to perform the tasks in an effective and efficient manner.

4.1 Sampling of the Search Landscape

Analyzing the complete search landscape is infeasible for all but small problem instances (up to a problem size of about 15 for permutation problems). Instead, we analyze the properties of chosen solutions as well as of walks within the search landscape. Our analysis approach follows closely the approach of Fonlupt et al. [8, 22] and to some extend the one of Stadler and Schnabl [26].

We obtain a set of initial solutions, called *samples*, by generating random permutations using Knuth shuffles [18]. Then, we obtain a number of *search paths* by tracing each sample to a local minimum. Thereby, we use steepest descent paths that associate every solution with exactly one local minimum. The length of the search path provides information about the closeness of the minima to the samples.

We also obtain two additional sets of solutions from the search paths. First, we have the set of found *local minima*. Since multiple steepest descent paths may end at the same local minimum, the number of found local minima is equal to or less than the number of samples.

Second, we have the solutions on the search paths between the samples and the local minima. Since the lengths of search paths scale with the problem size [8], this can be a large amount of solutions. Adding all of them to the visualization would results in visual clutter. Therefore, we represent each path by its *median solution*.

We obtain information about the connectivity and the adjacency within the search landscape by computing the dis-

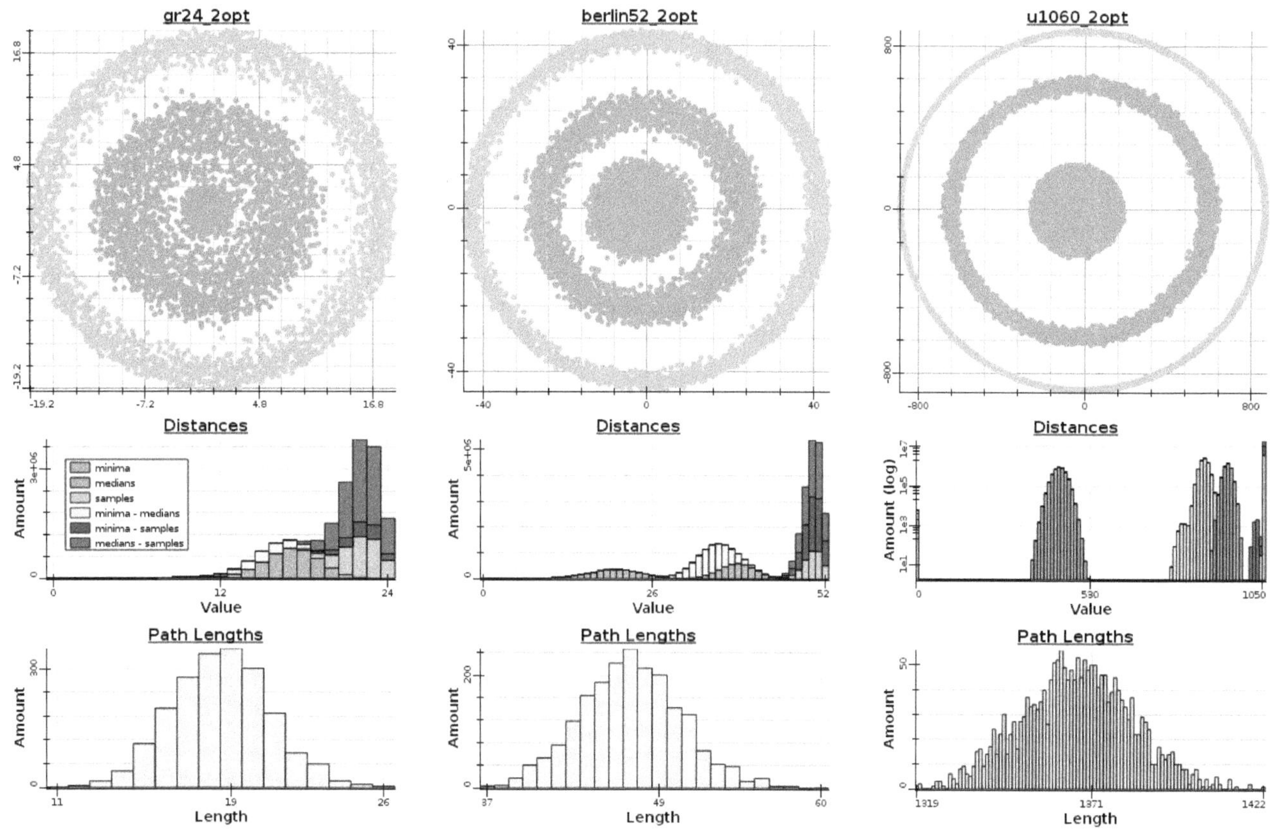

Figure 1: 2-opt search landscapes for three TSP instances from the TSPlib. The number in the problem names indicates the problem size. In the top row, the layout of the search landscapes is shown. Minima are shown in green, medians in light blue, and the samples (initial solutions) in orange. A clear, crater-like appearance can be seen. In the middle row, the distribution of the distances is shown. Colors correspond to the top row. The short distances between the local minima are clearly visible. In the bottom row, the distribution of the path lengths is plotted.

tance with respect to the search operator between any two solutions from all three sets (i.e., the samples, the corresponding local minima, and the corresponding median solutions). This results in six groups of distances. Based on knowledge about the search operator (e.g., the maximal distance or diameter of the search landscape, and the global distribution of distances), conclusions about the location and mutual proximity of local minima within the search landscape can be drawn [8]. Furthermore, the length of the search paths can be contrasted against the theoretical diameter of the search landscape.

Discussion.

Arguably, Knuth shuffles do not generate samples that represent the search landscape well in general [17]. During our experiments we found that only a small range of cost values is found by this sampling method and local minima or solutions near local minima are rarely encountered. However, random permutations are often used to initialize local search or simulated annealing methods. Therefore, our sampling method is in agreement with common optimization techniques. Because of that, we did not incorporate more elaborate sampling methods into our analysis.

Some analysis approaches (e.g., Stadler and Schnabl [26]) use random descending walks rather then steepest descent paths. These can be computed faster, because the neighborhood of each solution along the path does not need to be expanded completely. However, random walks typically can map each solution to several local minima. It is more straightforward to create a topological partition of the search landscape into basins around local minima using steepest descents [6] than using random descending walks [25]. There is also a close connection between steepest descent and the barrier tree [6]. Therefore, we preferred to use steepest descent in our method.

4.2 Visualization of the Search Landscape

In the following, we outline a visualization system that facilitates the understanding of the search landscape based on the extracted solutions (Section 4.1). For every solution we have a permutation and the associated cost value. Additionally, the distance between any two solutions is known. We propose using (stacked) bar charts of histograms [30] and scatterplots [12] for presenting the data. A detailed discussion of design alternatives and the design choices made are presented in a companion paper [29].

The distribution of the paths' length is shown using bar charts (e.g., bottom row of Figure 1). Histograms are very well suited for the analysis of single attributes.Thereby, the range of possible values is partitioned into equally-sized bins

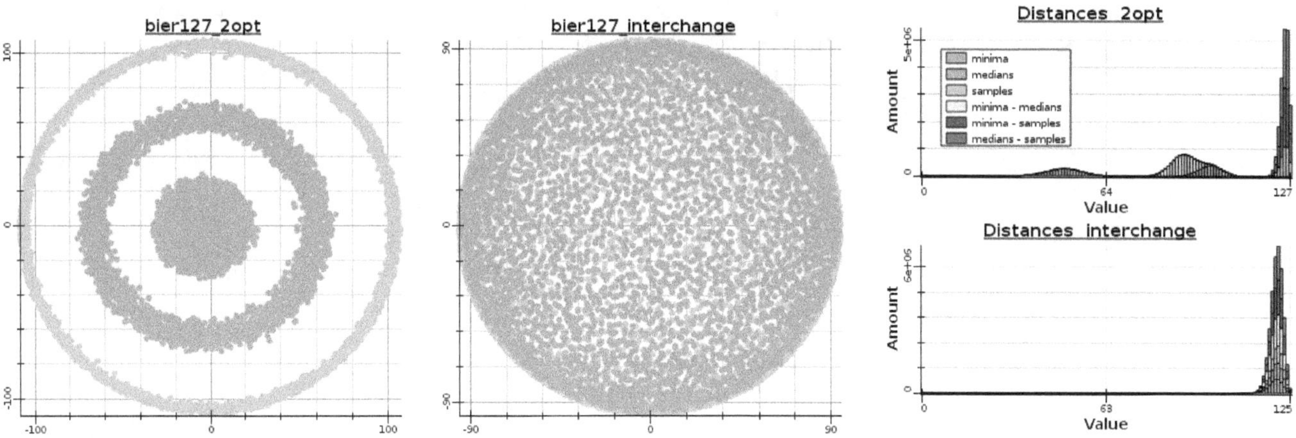

Figure 2: Juxtaposition of the layouts (left image and center image) and the distance distributions (right images) of the search landscape of the Bier127 problem for the 2-opt operator and the interchange operator. The search landscape from the interchange operator reveals much less structure, and the distances within all groups of solutions are almost maximal.

and the number of data values in every bin is counted. The bins are represented by bars in a two-dimensional plot. The position of the bar on the x-axis corresponds to the range of the bin, while the height of the bar (y-axis) corresponds to the number of elements in the bin. Altogether, this results in a so-called bar chart.

The distances between the solutions are represented using stacked bar charts and scatterplots. In the stacked bar chart (e.g., the middle row of Figure 1), six groups of distances are shown: distances within one class of solutions (3), and distances between two of these classes (3). For each group of distances, its histogram is computed. Stacking the histograms then yields the stacked bar chart. Thereby, each group of distances is assigned a particular color, e.g., green for the group of distances between minima, and yellow for the group of distances between minima and median solutions. The color assignment is shown in a legend.

For showing the distances, the stacked bar charts are complemented by a visual depiction of the search landscape (e.g., top row of Figure 1). Therefore, we exploit that the distances between the solutions carry topological information. The constructed visualization should preserve the distances and the topological properties as good as possible. Thereby, the topological proximity is approximated by the spatial proximity in the plot. To do so, the solutions are mapped onto the 2D plane such that the Euclidean distances between the points in the plane approximates the distances within the search landscape. This mapping is achieved using a metric Multidimensional Scaling technique [4], in particular, a variant of the Shepard-Kruskal algorithm that simulates a spring force model is applied. Initially, all solutions are placed at random positions in the 2D plane. Each solution exerts a force on every other solution according to the deviation of the Euclidean distance to the operator distance (for details see [29]). Then, all solutions are moved, so that the overall force is minimized. This is repeated until an equilibrium or a maximal number of iterations is reached. The resulting layout is shown in a 2D scatterplot. The same colors assigned to the solution classes for depicting the stacked bar charts are used for coloring the points in the scatterplot.

5. RESULTS

The search landscapes obtained by applying the 2opt and the interchange operator to TSP, QAP, and SMTTP were analyzed. The results of this analysis are presented next.

5.1 TSP

The TSP is a classical benchmark problem for which well-established results are available [8, 26]. Analyzing the search landscapes of the 2opt operator on all instances of the TSPlib [23] up to a problem size 1048 using our method confirmed these results. Figure 1 shows the result for three example problems of different sizes. Similar images have been obtained for all other test instances. The local minima (green) form a cluster in the center of the search landscape layout (Figure 1, top row). From the stacked bar charts, we can see, that the distances between the local minima are $\frac{1}{3}$ to $\frac{1}{2}$ of the problem size (Figure 1, middle row). Given the definition of the bond distance (cf. Section 2.4), this means that each two local minima have $\frac{1}{2}$ to $\frac{2}{3}$ inter-city connections in common. This conformance is unexpectedly high. Furthermore, we can see that the distances between the samples (orange) are almost maximal and that there is a large distance between the samples and the local minima (dark blue). The average path length is slightly smaller than the diameter of the search landscape. This indicates, that 2opt converges relatively straight to local minima.

Further, we compared the search landscapes of two different search operators (2opt and interchange operator). Figure 2 shows a juxtaposition of both search landscapes for instance Bier127 from the TSPlib, which is representative for the other instances from the TSPlib. When using the interchange operator, the search paths are longer on average and the found local minima (green) are not located close each other. Instead, there are almost maximal distances both between the samples (orange) as well as between the local minima (green). This results in a very different landscape layout that reveals little structure.

5.2 QAP

We applied our method to all instances of the QAPlib [3]. Results for two instances are shown in Figure 3 as an ex-

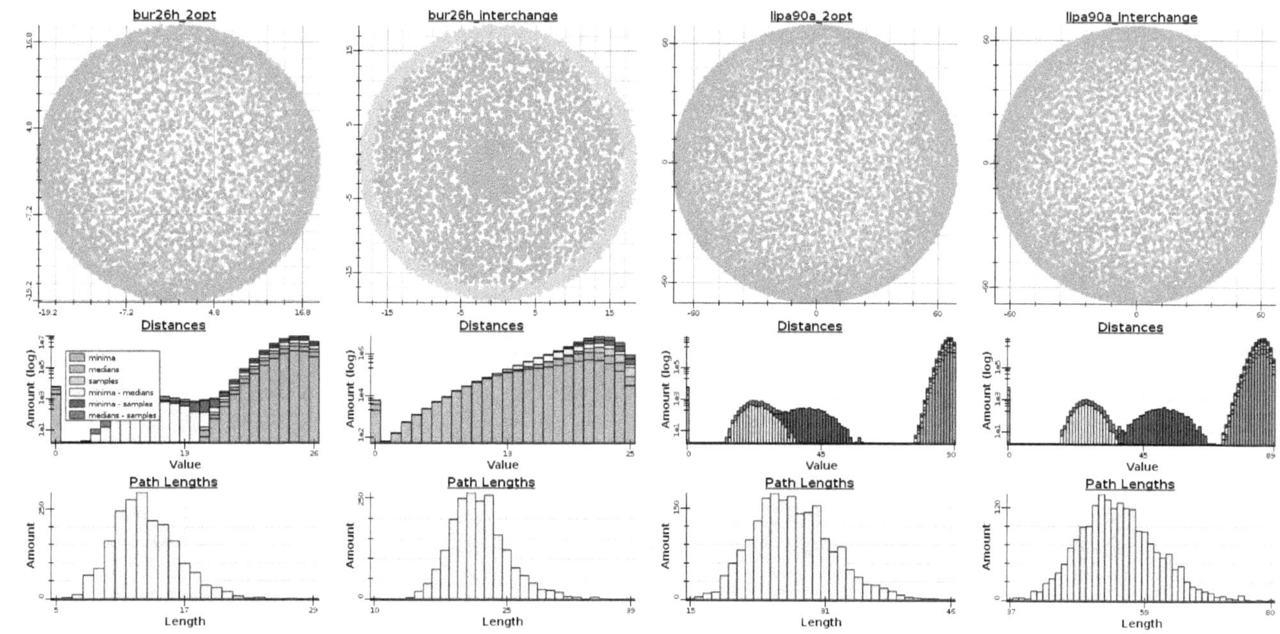

Figure 3: Search landscapes of two instances from the QAPlib for the 2opt operator and the interchange operator. The number in the problem names indicates the problem size. The search landscape layout is shown in the top row. Minima are shown in green, medians in light blue and the samples (initial solutions) in orange. In the middle row, the distribution of the distances is shown. Colors correspond to the top row. At the bottom, histograms of the search path length distributions are shown.

ample. Different from the TSP, we typically did not find the characteristic crater-like structure in the QAP. Usually, as can be seen in the search landscape layouts in Figure 3, top row, the local minima (green) are scattered throughout the landscape. Distances between solutions of the same group are nearly maximal almost without exception. In many problem instances, e.g., the lipa90a instance (see right images in Figure 3), there is no visual difference between the search landscapes of both operators. However, the interchange operator produces longer search paths (cf. path length histograms in the bottom row of Figure 3). The path length bar charts show that for some instances the local minima are close to the samples, less than half of the diameter of the search landscape (first, third, and fourth column of Figure 3). Interestingly, in some instances a subset of the found local minima (green) are grouped together when using the interchange operator (cf. the second column in Figure 3), whereas others remain scattered throughout the landscape. This can also be seen by the two peaks in the distribution of distances between local minima in the histogram. Such a grouping of local minima does not exist for the 2opt operator in any of the instances of the QAPlib.

5.3 SMTTP

For the analysis of the SMTTP, we generated various test instances of size 100. Both, the job lengths as well as the due dates were determined randomly. The processing times were chosen uniform randomly between 1 and 100. In the following, T denotes the sum of all processing times, i.e., the total processing time of the schedule. The due dates where generated according to two parameters r (range length) and $\widetilde{d}$ (mean due date). Thereby, the due dates were chosen uniformly from the interval $\left[T\cdot(\widetilde{d}-\frac{r}{2}), T\cdot(\widetilde{d}+\frac{r}{2})\right]\cap[0,T]$. The larger $\widetilde{d}$ is the earlier are the due dates, so that the total tardiness increases.

Figure 4 shows the search landscapes of the 2opt operator and the interchange operator for four selected instances. We found that the due date parameter $\widetilde{d}$ has a strong influence on the characteristics of the search landscape. If the mean due date is low, almost no structure is visible (top row). As can be seen in the bottom row of Figure 4, this changes when the mean due date increases. Then, a clear separation between local minima (green) and initial solutions (orange) can be seen, forming a crater-like structure similar as for the TSP with 2opt (cf. Figure 1). This structure is already visible in the search landscapes of the interchange operator at smaller due date values than in the landscapes of the 2opt operator. The range length appears to have an influence on the sharpness of the crater. Larger distances within the crater are possible when the range length is small.

6. DISCUSSION

We found the results of Fonlupt et al. [8] about 2opt on the TSP confirmed by our experiments. The "massif central" that is mentioned both by Fonlupt (and Stadler [26]) is clearly visible in the layout of the search landscapes. The distances of $n/3-n/2$ between the local minima (cf. Figure 1) are in accordance with Fonlupt's findings as are the average lengths of the steepest descent paths. All this indicates that the POP holds for the TSP with the 2opt operator.

When applying the interchange operator to the TSP, we obtain longer search paths and the search landscape layouts reveal almost no structure. This confirms intuitively that

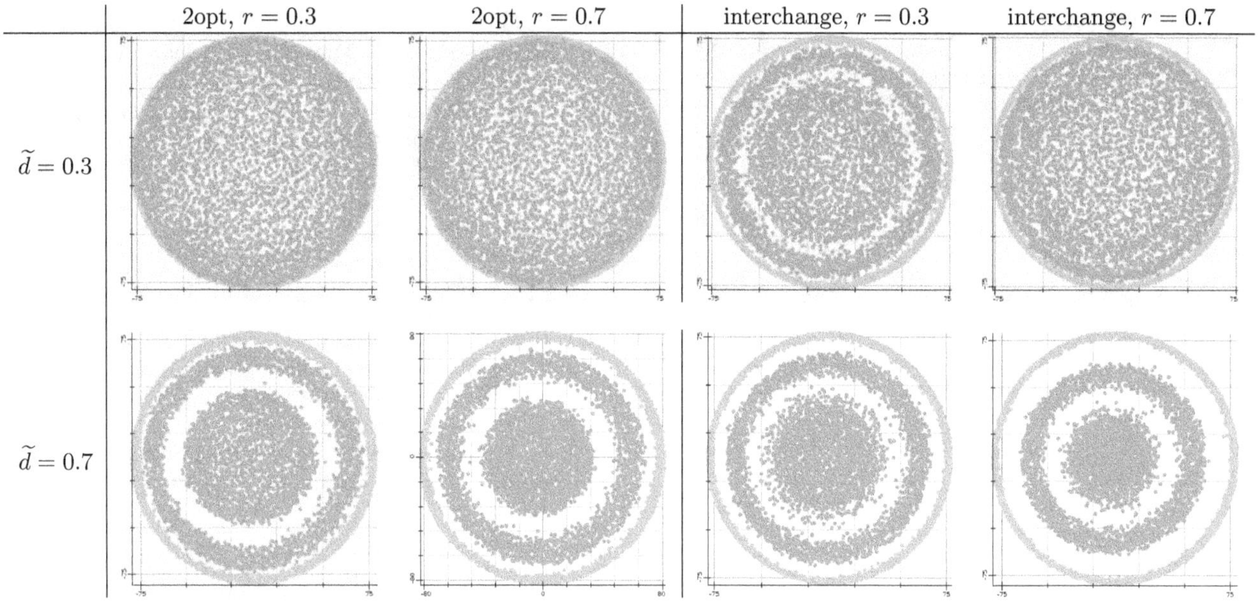

Figure 4: Randomly generated instances of the SMTTP with size 100. r is the relative length of the due dates interval and $\tilde{d}$ is the mean due date. The layouts of the search landscapes of the 2opt operator and the interchange operator are shown. Local minima are shown in green, medians in light blue and the samples (initial solutions) in orange.

steepest descent using the 2-opt operator is more efficient than using the interchange operator [19, 26]. Our interpretation is that the missing structure makes the TSP harder when using the interchange operator. In any case, the POP does not hold for the interchange operator on the TSP.

In contrast to the TSP, we did not find much structure in the landscapes of the QAP with our method. Moreover, algorithms are prone to get stuck in local minima that are close to the sample points, which can be induced from the short length of the search paths compared to the distances of the minima and the diameter of the search landscape. The interchange operator leads to longer search paths in comparison to the 2opt operator. Furthermore, in some instances, at least some structure among the local minima was present in the landscapes of the interchange operator. From that we conclude that the interchange operator seems to fit the QAP better than the 2opt operator. However, even for the interchange operator there is no clear clear indication that the POP holds. This indicates that the QAP is a harder problem than the TSP.

The results in the previous section show that the difficulty of the SMTTP clearly depends on the mean due date. The later the mean due date, the higher the tardiness and the more crater-like the landscape. This indicates that the POP holds and that the problem is potentially easier to solve. A reason for this may be the asymmetry in the cost function of the SMTTP, because of the cut-off of negative tardiness. The higher the overall tardiness is, the smaller is the overall cut-off. Thus, changes in the schedule are reflected to a greater extend by changes in the cost function. Also—in contrast to the TSP—the crater-like structure is more pronounced for the interchange operator compared to the 2opt operator, especially for small mean due dates $\tilde{d}$ and small ranges r. This indicates that for SMTTP, search algorithms based on the interchange operator might produce better results than those based on the 2opt operator.

7. CONCLUSIONS AND FUTURE WORK

We presented an analysis method for search landscapes that is applicable to permutation problems without restrictions, as well as to many different search operators. It uses steepest descent paths from random solutions within the search landscape to reveal topological properties of the landscape. The method is in accordance with and extends previous work on search landscapes [7, 8, 22, 26]. It includes a visualization system [29] based on visualization of statistical data as well as on a topological visualization of the search landscape. This supports the interpretation of the search landscape. We applied the method to instances of the TSP, the QAP, and the SMTTP. Our findings confirm previous work on the TSP and common assumptions about the relation between TSP, QAP, and SMTTP. Furthermore, we showed the influence of two due date parameters on the difficulty of the SMTTP and presented indications that the interchange operator is better suited for search algorithms for QAP and SMTTP than the 2opt operator.

Our findings suggest, that a more complete study that covers more search operators might reveal interesting insights into these well-known problems. In particular, a search operator that leads to crater-like structures in the QAP landscapes would be worth finding.

Sophisticated metaheuristics combine multiple search operators. Therefore, it is interesting future work to investigate how our approach can be extended to such cases.

8. ACKNOWLEDGMENTS

This work was partly supported by European Social Fund (ESF App.No.100098251).

9. REFERENCES

[1] S. Bin, S. Volke, G. Scheuermann, and M. Middendorf. Comparing the Optimization Behaviour of Heuristics with Topology Based Visualization. In A.-H. Dediu, M. Lozano, and C. Martín-Vide, editors, *Theory and Practice of Natural Computing*, volume 8890 of *Lecture Notes in Computer Science*, pages 47–58. Springer, 2014.

[2] K. D. Boese. *Models for Iterative Global Optimization.* PhD thesis, University of California at Los Angeles, CA, USA, 1996.

[3] R. Burkard, S. Karisch, and F. Rendl. QAPLIB – A Quadratic Assignment Problem Library. *Journal of Global Optimization*, 10(4):391–403, 1997.

[4] T. Cox and M. Cox. *Multidimensional Scaling.* CRC Press, 2010.

[5] G. A. Croes. A method for solving traveling salesman problems. *Operations Research*, 6:791–812, 1958.

[6] C. Flamm, I. L. Hofacker, P. F. Stadler, and M. T. Wolfinger. Barrier Trees of Degenerate Landscapes. *Z. Phys. Chem.*, 216:1–19, 2002.

[7] C. Fleurent and F. Glover. Improved Constructive Multistart Strategies for the Quadratic Assignment Problem Using Adaptive Memory. *INFORMS Journal on Computing*, 11(2):198–204, Feb. 1999.

[8] C. Fonlupt, D. Robilliard, P. Preux, and E.-G. Talbi. Fitness Landscapes and Performance of Meta-Heuristics. In *Meta-Heuristics: Advances and Trends in Local Search Paradigms for Optimization*, pages 257–268. Kluwer, 1999.

[9] M. R. Garey and D. S. Johnson. *Computers and Intractability: A Guide to the Theory of NP-Completeness.* W. H. Freeman, 1979.

[10] J. Garnier and L. Kallel. How to Detect All Maxima of a Function. In *Theoretical Aspects of Evolutionary Computing*, pages 343–370. Springer, 2001.

[11] F. Glover and M. Laguna. *Tabu Search.* Kluwer, 1997.

[12] G. Grinstein, M. Trutschl, and U. Cvek. High-Dimensional Visualizations. In *Proceedings of the VII Data Mining Conference KDD Workshop 2001*, pages 7–19. ACM Press, 2001.

[13] S. Halim, R. H. C. Yap, and H. C. Lau. Viz: A Visual Analysis Suite for Explaining Local Search Behavior. In *User Interface Software and Technology*, pages 57–66, 2006.

[14] J. Hallam and A. Prügel-Bennett. Large Barrier Trees for Studying Search. *IEEE Trans. Evolutionary Computation*, 9(4):385–397, 2005.

[15] H. H. Hoos and T. Stützle. *Stochastic local search: Foundations & applications.* Elsevier, 2004.

[16] D. S. Johnson. Local optimization and the Traveling Salesman Problem. In M. S. Paterson, editor, *Automata, Languages and Programming*, volume 443 of *Lecture Notes in Computer Science*, pages 446–461. Springer, 1990.

[17] S. Khor. Search space analysis with Wang-Landau sampling and slow adaptive walks. *CoRR*, abs/1112.5980, 2011.

[18] D. E. Knuth. *The Art of Computer Programming, Volume 2 (3rd Ed.): Seminumerical Algorithms.* Addison-Wesley, 1997.

[19] S. Lin and B. W. Kernighan. An Effective Heuristic Algorithm for the Travelling-Salesman Problem. *Operations Research*, 21:498–516, 1973.

[20] D. M. McCandlish. Visualizing fitness landscapes. *Evolution*, 65(6):1544–1558, 2011.

[21] E. Pitzer and M. Affenzeller. A Comprehensive Survey on Fitness Landscape Analysis. In J. Fodor, R. Klempous, and C. Suárez Araujo, editors, *Recent Advances in Intelligent Engineering Systems*, volume 378 of *Studies in Computational Intelligence*, pages 161–191. Springer, 2012.

[22] P. Preux, D. Robilliard, C. Fonlupt, R. M. Karp, and J. M. Steele. Fitness Landscapes of Combinatorial Problems and the Performance of Search Algorithms, 1997.

[23] G. Reinelt. TSPLIB—A Traveling Salesman Problem Library. *ORSA Journal on Computing*, 3(4):376–384, 1991.

[24] T. Schiavinotto and T. Stützle. A Review of Metrics on Permutations for Search Landscape Analysis. *Computer and Operations Research*, 34(10):3143–3153, October 2007.

[25] B. Stadler and P. Stadler. Combinatorial vector fields and the valley structure of fitness landscapes. *Journal of Mathematical Biology*, 61(6):877–898, 2010.

[26] P. F. Stadler and W. Schnabl. The landscape of the traveling salesman problem. *Physics Letters A*, 161(4):337 – 344, 1992.

[27] S. Volke, S. Bin, D. Zeckzer, M. Middendorf, and G. Scheuermann. Visual analysis of discrete particle swarm optimization using fitness landscapes. In H. Richter and A. Engelbrecht, editors, *Recent Advances in the Theory and Application of Fitness Landscapes*, volume 6 of *Emergence, Complexity and Computation*, pages 487–507. Springer, 2014.

[28] S. Volke, M. Middendorf, M. Hlawitschka, J. Kasten, D. Zeckzer, and G. Scheuermann. dPSO-Vis: Topology-based Visualization of Discrete Particle Swarm Optimization. *Computer Graphics Forum*, 32(3):351–360, 2013.

[29] S. Volke, D. Zeckzer, M. Middendorf, and G. Scheuermann. Visualizing topological properties of the search landscape of combinatorial optimization problems. Accepted for presentation at *Topology-Based Methods in Visualization 2015* (Annweiler, Germany, May 20. – 22., 2015). Final version for workshop proceedings currently under review.

[30] L. Wilkinson. *The Grammar of Graphics.* Springer, 1999.

Kernels of Mallows Models for Solving Permutation-based Problems

Josu Ceberio
Department of Computer Science and Artificial Intelligence, University of the Basque Country UPV/EHU
20018 Donostia, Spain
josu.ceberio@ehu.es

Alexander Mendiburu
Department of Computer Architecture and Technology, University of the Basque Country UPV/EHU
20018 Donostia, Spain
alexander.mendiburu@ehu.es

Jose A. Lozano
Department of Computer Science and Artificial Intelligence, University of the Basque Country UPV/EHU
20018 Donostia, Spain
ja.lozano@ehu.es

ABSTRACT

Recently, distance-based exponential probability models, such as Mallows and Generalized Mallows, have demonstrated their validity in the context of estimation of distribution algorithms (EDAs) for solving permutation problems. However, despite their successful performance, these models are unimodal, and therefore, they are not flexible enough to accurately model populations with solutions that are very sparse with regard to the distance metric considered under the model.

In this paper, we propose using kernels of Mallows models under the Kendall's-τ and Cayley distances within EDAs. In order to demonstrate the validity of this new algorithm, Mallows Kernel EDA, we compare its performance with the classical Mallows and Generalized Mallows EDAs, on a benchmark of 90 instances of two different types of permutation problems: the quadratic assignment problem and the permutation flowshop scheduling problem. Experimental results reveal that, in most cases, Mallows Kernel EDA outperforms the Mallows and Generalized Mallows EDAs under the same distance. Moreover, the new algorithm under the Cayley distance obtains the best results for the two problems in terms of average fitness and computational time.

Categories and Subject Descriptors

G.2 [**Discrete Mathematics**]: Combinatorics; I.2.8 [**Artificial Intelligence**]: Problem Solving, Control Methods, and Search—*Heuristic algorithms*; G.3. [**Probability and Statistics**]: Distribution functions

Keywords

Permutation problems; estimation of distribution algorithms; Mallows model; Kernels

1. INTRODUCTION

GECCO '15, July 11–15, 2015, Madrid, Spain

DOI: http://dx.doi.org/10.1145/2739480.2754741

Estimation of Distribution Algorithms (EDAs) [24, 27, 31, 33] constitute a powerful evolutionary algorithm for solving combinatorial optimisation problems. Based on machine learning techniques, at each generation, EDAs estimate a joint probability distribution associated with the set of most promising individuals, trying to explicitly express the interrelations between the different variables of the problem. Sampling the probabilistic model learnt in the previous generation, a new population of solutions is created. The algorithm stops iterating and returns the best solution found across the generations when a certain stopping criterion is met, such as a maximum number of generations, homogeneous population, or lack of improvement in the solutions. Based on this general framework, many works in the literature confirm the good performance of EDAs in the solution of artificial and real-world problems [4, 22, 29, 30, 39, 38]. In [36], MATEDA-2.0 was introduced, a matlab package for EDAs.

Despite their success in the last few decades, EDAs, up to recently, were not extensively developed for solving permutation based combinatorial optimisation problems [6]. In this sense, Ceberio et al. [10] published the first work that introduces in EDAs a probability model defined directly in the space of permutations. In that work, a *distance-based exponential probability model* called the Mallows model [13, 28] was studied to solve the permutation flowshop scheduling problem (PFSP) [18]. In [7], the authors introduced the Generalized Mallows model under the Kendall's-τ distance [14] in EDAs, which, combined with other optimisation strategies, outperformed the state-of-the-art algorithms for the PFSP. In the same research line, in [11], the Plackett-Luce model demonstrated remarkable performance when solving the linear ordering problem [12].

Despite their success, probability models, such as Mallows and Generalized Mallows, are unimodal models. As a consequence, they are able to provide accurate distributions when the solutions in the population have similar characteristics, i.e. they are close to each other with regard to the distance-metric considered under the model. However, these models are not flexible enough to accurately model populations of solutions that are very sparse.

As a result, a number of papers in the literature have proposed using mixtures of probability models since they allow to model a heterogeneous population by modelling it as a collection of sub-populations of solutions with similar characteristics. In this research line, Murphy et al. [32] extended the use of mixtures using distance-based models to deal with heterogeneous rank data, and Lee and Yu [26] proposed an extension of distance-based models using new weighted distance measures.

Similarly, in the field of EDAs, many works proposed to use mixtures of probability models: Peña et al. [34] presented mixture models based on Bayesian networks, Bosman and Thierens [3] proposed the algorithmic framework MIDEA for multi-objective optimisation using mixture distributions, Santana et al. [37] introduced mixtures of Kikuchi approximations, and recently, Gao [16] proposed mixtures of multivariate T-distributions and mutation-based multi-objective EDAs. Finally, with the aim of improving the performance of distance-based probability model EDAs, Santamaria et al. [35] introduced Mixtures of Generalized Mallows models in EDAs, which obtained good results when compared with the base line algorithm. However, the large computational cost and the numerical errors that may appear in the learning step of the model (related to the use of Expectation-Maximization and the small values dealt with), hinder the application of mixtures in large size instances.

In this paper, we take the idea of mixtures of distance-based probability models to the limit by calculating as many Mallows models as individuals in the selected population of solutions. This type of models, known as kernel models, permit to estimate a probability distribution on top of each solution. Particularly, we study kernels of Mallows models under the Kendall's-τ distance, introduced by Lebanon and Mao [25], and also introduce kernels of Mallows models under the Cayley distance. As a result, we present the Mallows Kernel EDA (MKEDA).

For the sake of providing an experimental framework to evaluate MKEDA, we generated an artificial benchmark of 90 large-size instances of the Quadratic Assignment Problem (QAP) [23] and the Permutation Flowshop Scheduling Problem (PFSP) [1, 2] (45 instances of each). In order to demonstrate the validity of MKEDA, we compare it with the baseline Mallows EDA (MEDA) and Generalized Mallows EDA (GMEDA) on both distances. Conducted experiments discover different behaviors with regard to the distance employed under the model. As regards Kendall's-τ, GMEDA still performs better than MKEDA. On the contrary, under the Cayley distance, MKEDA is systematically better than MEDA and GMEDA. Furthermore, this last new algorithm outperforms the rest of the algorithms considered in the experimental study in terms of average fitness and computational time for the QAP and PFSP.

The remainder of the paper is organised as follows: in the next section, permutation-based problems are introduced. Then, in Section 3, Mallows and kernels of Mallows models are introduced. Next, in Section 4, the Mallows Kernel EDA is presented. Afterwards, in Section 5, an experimental study of MEDA, GMEDA and MKEDA under the Kendall's-τ and Cayley distances is carried out. Finally, some conclusions and ideas for future work are presented in Section 6.

2. PERMUTATION-BASED PROBLEMS

Permutation-based problems are combinatorial optimisation problems whose solutions can be naturally represented as a *permutation*. A permutation is understood as a bijection σ of the set of natural numbers $\{1,\ldots,n\}$ onto the set $\{1,\ldots,n\}$. Usually, permutations are represented in the classic one-line notation, i.e., as an ordered list of the set $\{1,\ldots,n\}$. We say that item j is in position i when $\sigma(i)=j$. Alternatively, σ^{-1} denotes the inverse of the permutation σ, and $\sigma^{-1}(j)$ stands for the position of item j in σ. Note that by definition, for any permutation $\sigma \in \mathbb{S}_n$, $\sigma(i) \neq \sigma(j)$ for all $i \neq j$.

A permutation-based problem consists of finding the best solution for a *fitness function* f:

$$\begin{array}{rccc} f: & \mathbb{S}_n & \longrightarrow & \mathbb{R} \\ & \sigma & \longmapsto & f(\sigma) \end{array}$$

where $\mathbb{S}_n$ stands for the search space of solutions and is formed by $n!$ permutations of size n (*symmetric group*). In order to optimise f, one has to find a solution $\sigma^\star \in \mathbb{S}_n$ with minimum *fitness value* (in the case of a minimization problem), that is, $f(\sigma^\star) \leq f(\sigma)\ \ \forall \sigma \in \mathbb{S}_n$.

Obviously, behind the permutation nature of the solutions, each different problem has its particular challenges that need to be dealt with individually. Thus, it is dangerous to extrapolate the conclusions drawn from one problem to the whole class. In this sense, in this paper, we have chosen two problems that are known due to their hardness: the Quadratic Assignment Problem (QAP) [23] and the Permutation Flowshop Scheduling Problem (PFSP) [1, 2].

2.1 Quadratic Assignment Problem

The QAP [23] is the problem of allocating a set of facilities to a set of locations, with a cost function associated to the distance and flow between the facilities. The objective is to assign each facility to a location such that the total cost is minimized. Specifically, we are given two matrices with real values $\mathbf{D}=[d_{i,j}]_{n\times n}$ and $\mathbf{H}=[h_{k,l}]_{n\times n}$, where $d_{i,j}$ is the distance between location i and location j, and $h_{k,l}$ is the flow between facility k and facility l. Given n facilities, the solution of the QAP is codified as a permutation σ, where $\sigma(i)=j$ represents that the facility j is allocated in the i-th location. The fitness value of any solution σ is calculated by the following function:

$$f(\sigma)=\sum_{i=1}^{n}\sum_{j=1}^{n} d_{i,j}h_{\sigma(i),\sigma(j)}$$

2.2 Flowshop Scheduling Problem

In the PFSP [1, 2] n jobs ($i=1,\ldots,n$) have to be scheduled on m machines ($j=1,\ldots,m$) in such a way that a given criterion is minimized. A job consists of m operations and the j-th operation of each job must be processed on the j-th machine for a given specific processing time without interruption. The processing times are given by the matrix $\mathbf{P}=[p_{i,j}]_{n\times m}$ of non-negative numbers. Every job is available at time zero and, at a given time, a job can start on the j-th machine when its $(j-1)$-th operation has finished on machine $(j-1)$, and machine j is idle.

A solution for the PFSP is codified as a permutation σ of n jobs, where $\sigma(i)$ is the job scheduled in the i-th position. For instance, for $n=3$, the sequence $\sigma=231$ denotes that job 2 is scheduled in the first position, i.e. $\sigma(1)=2$, job 3 is scheduled second, and job 1 is scheduled third.

Inversely to the previous problems, different criteria have been proposed when optimising the PFSP. In this paper, we focus on the total flow time (TFT) which measures the sum of the times that each job remains in the flowshop. Given a permutation σ of jobs, the TFT is defined as

$$f(\sigma) = \sum_{i=1}^{n} c_{\sigma(i),m} \quad (1)$$

where $c_{\sigma(i),m}$ stands for the completion time of job $\sigma(i)$ at machine m. The completion time of job $\sigma(i)$ on machine j, $c_{\sigma(i),j}$, is recursively calculated as

$$c_{\sigma(i),j} = \begin{cases} p_{\sigma(i),j} & i = j = 1 \\ p_{\sigma(i),j} + c_{\sigma(i-1),j} & i > 1, j = 1 \\ p_{\sigma(i),j} + c_{\sigma(i),j-1} & i = 1, j > 1 \\ p_{\sigma(i),j} + \max\{c_{\sigma(i-1),j}, c_{\sigma(i),j-1}\} & i > 1, j > 1 \end{cases} \quad (2)$$

where $p_{\sigma(i),j}$ stands for the processing time required by job $\sigma(i)$ on machine j.

3. KERNELS OF MALLOWS MODELS

The Mallows model [28] is a distance-based exponential probability model over permutation spaces. Under this model, the probability value of every permutation $\sigma \in \mathbb{S}_n$ depends on two parameters: a spread parameter θ, and the distance to a central permutation σ_0, which is calculated by a distance-metric D on permutations. Formally, the Mallows model is defined as

$$P(\sigma) = \frac{e^{-\theta D(\sigma,\sigma_0)}}{\psi(\theta)} \quad (3)$$

where $\psi(\theta)$ denotes the normalisation constant. When $\theta > 0$, the central permutation σ_0 is the permutation with the highest probability value, and the probability of the other $n! - 1$ permutations exponentially decreases with the distance to σ_0 (and the spread parameter θ) (see Fig. 1). When $\theta = 0$, we obtain the uniform distribution.

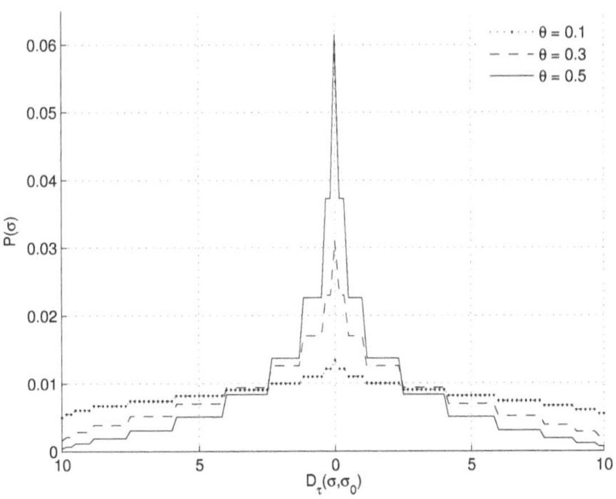

Figure 1: The Mallows model.

The distance metric the Mallows model is traditionally coupled with in the literature is the Kendall's-τ distance [14, 15]. Denoted as $D_\tau(\sigma, \pi)$, it counts the number of pairs of items for which σ and π have opposing ordering. An equivalent definition for Kendall's-τ is the minimum number of adjacent transpositions needed to bring σ^{-1} into π^{-1}:

$$D_\tau(\sigma, \pi) = |\{(i,j) : i < j, (\sigma(i) < \sigma(j) \wedge \pi(i) > \pi(j)) \\ \vee (\pi(i) < \pi(j) \wedge \sigma(i) > \sigma(j))\}|$$

Kendall's-τ has the *right invariant* property since $D_\tau(\sigma, \pi) = D_\tau(\sigma\gamma, \pi\gamma)$ for every permutation $\gamma \in \mathbb{S}_n$, where $\sigma\gamma$ stands for the composition of the permutations σ and γ, and is defined as $\sigma\gamma(i) = (\sigma \circ \gamma(i)) = \sigma(\gamma(i))$. Thus, by *right invariance*, when $\gamma = \pi^{-1}$, $D_\tau(\sigma, \pi)$ can be simplified as $D_\tau(\sigma\pi^{-1}, e)$ (also denoted as $D_\tau(\sigma\pi^{-1})$), where e stands for the identity permutation $e = 123\ldots n$.

In the particular case of Kendall's-τ, the distance is decomposed as

$$D_\tau(\pi) = \sum_{j=1}^{n-1} V_j(\pi),$$

such that $V_j(\pi) = \sum_{i=j+1}^{n} I[\pi(j) > \pi(i)]$, where $I[cond]$ equals 1 when the condition *cond* equals true, and 0 otherwise. Basically, $V_j(\pi)$ is the number of positions of the permutation on the right of j with values smaller than $\pi(j)$. It follows from the definition that $V_j(\pi)$ ranges from 0 to $n - j$ for $1 \leq j < n$.

As a result, the normalisation constant $\psi(\theta)$, which if calculated naively requires $n!$ sums, can be simplified as the product of $n - 1$ terms,

$$\psi(\theta) = \prod_{j=1}^{n-1} \psi_j(\theta) = \prod_{j=1}^{n-1} \frac{1 - \exp(-\theta(n-j+1))}{1 - \exp(-\theta)} \quad (4)$$

In addition to the Kendall's-τ distance, recently, another metric on permutations, the Cayley distance, has been introduced in this context [19]. The Cayley distance, $D_c(\sigma, \pi)$, counts the minimum number of swaps (not necessary adjacent) that have to be performed to transform σ into π. When the reference permutation is the identity, e, the number of swaps equals n minus the number of *cycles* of σ. A cycle is understood as a closed walk of elements in the permutation such that for every $1 \leq i, j \leq n$ for which $\sigma(i) = j$ is true, then i and j are in the same cycle. The Cayley distance $D_c(\sigma)$ is also decomposed as the sum of $n - 1$ terms

$$D_c(\sigma, \pi) = \sum_{j=1}^{n-1} X_j(\sigma\pi^{-1})$$

where $X_j(\sigma\pi^{-1})$ is binary and $X_j(\sigma\pi^{-1}) = 0$ if j is the largest item in its cycle in $\sigma\pi^{-1}$.

Under this distance, the normalization constant $\psi(\theta)$, is formalized as

$$\psi(\theta) = \prod_{j=1}^{n-1} \psi_j(\theta) = \prod_{j=1}^{n-1} (n-j)\exp(-\theta) + 1 \quad (5)$$

As stated in [25], the Mallows model, and in a lesser degree the Generalized Mallows model, suffer from several drawbacks. Their unimodal assumption is often too restrictive, which may lead the EDA to poor performances when the samples in the population have similar fitness but at the same time are far from each other for the metric considered under the model. However, it is precisely the unimodality and symmetry of the Mallows model make it a good choice to be used as a kernel [25].

In non-parametric statistics, and in kernel density estimation, a *kernel* is a non-negative function used to estimate the probability density function f of a sample with an unknown density function. Its general expression is:

$$\hat{f}(x) = \frac{1}{mh}\sum_{i=1}^{m} K\left(\frac{x-x_i}{h}\right) \quad (6)$$

where $h > 0$ is the smoothing parameter, x_i $(i = 1, \ldots, m)$ is the sample, and $K()$ stands for the kernel function which integrates to one in $(-\infty, \infty)$. In our case, we will use the Mallows model as the kernel function, and the θ parameter will be used to control the smoothness. So, the kernel distribution is

$$P(\sigma) = \frac{1}{m}\sum_{i=1}^{m} \frac{1}{\psi(\theta_i)} e^{-\theta_i D(\sigma,\sigma_i)} \quad (7)$$

where m is the number of kernels in the probability model, and σ_i and θ_i are, respectively, the central permutation and the spread parameter associated to the Mallows model of the i-th kernel.

4. MALLOWS KERNEL EDA

Based on the general framework defined for EDAs, Alg. 1 shows the pseudocode for the Mallows Kernel EDA. At each step of the algorithm, one kernel will be defined for each selected solution, using that solution as the central permutation of the model, together with the corresponding θ. Then, new solutions will be sampled from each kernel using the methods explained in [5, 7, 8] for the Mallows models under the Kendall's-τ and Cayley distances. Particularly, $(M-1)/N$ solutions are sampled from each kernel, when N corresponds to the number of kernels and M stands for the size of the population.

Regarding the spread parameters, in order to enhance the exploration/exploitation abilities of the model, we set an adaptive interval of values for the θ parameters as stated in [5]. The aim of this interval is to avoid extreme shapes of the model. When θ is close to 0, the Mallows model is close to the uniform distribution. Inversely, when θ is very high, the probability of the central permutation is close to 1. In both cases, the expected improvement of the EDAs by sampling models of these characteristics is very remote. Due to this, at the beginning of the process, the interval of θ values is set to $[\theta_{lower},\theta_{upper}]$. Then, at every iteration at which the best solution is not improved, the lower bound is increased by 0.1 to encourage exploitation. On the contrary, every time that a better solution is found, the lower bound is set to 0.01. The upper bound remains fixed throughout the optimization.

5. EXPERIMENTS

In order to conduct this experimentation, we designed an artificial benchmark of instances since the existing ones contain instances of irregular sizes and types. Particularly, we generated 45 QAP instances of sizes $\{100, 150, 200, 250, 300, 350, 400, 450, 500\}$ and 45 PFSP instances of sizes $\{50, 100, 200, 250, 300, 350, 400, 450, 500\}$[1].

[1]Both sets of instances, as well as the source codes, can be obtained from http://www.sc.ehu.es/ccwbayes/members/jceberio/home/publications.html

Algorithm 1 Pseudocode of Mallows Kernel EDA

1. $D_0 \leftarrow$ Generate M individuals at random.
2. t $\leftarrow$ 1.
3. Initialize $\theta_{\mathbf{lower}}$ and $\theta_{\mathbf{upper}}$.
4. **Do**
5. $D_{t-1} \leftarrow$ Evaluate individuals.
6. $D_{t-1}^{Se} \leftarrow$ Select $N \leq M$ individuals from D_{t-1}.
7. Build N kernels of Mallows models from D_{t-1}^{Se} and $\theta_{\mathbf{lower}}$.
8. Sample $(M-1)/N$ individuals from each kernel to create the new population.
9. Update $\theta_{\mathbf{lower}}$.
10. **Until** Stopping criterion is met

We compare six different EDAs: the Mallows and Generalized Mallows EDAs under the Kendall's-τ ($Mken$ and $GMken$) and Cayley ($Mcay$ and $GMcay$) distances (implemented following the indications in[5]), and Mallows Kernel EDAs also for both distances ($Kken$ and $Kcay$). We followed the parameter settings detailed in [5]:

- Population size: $10n$.
- Selected individuals: n.
- Selection type: truncation.
- Sampled individuals: $10n - 1$.
- All the kernels will use the same θ_{lower} and θ_{upper} values.
- Stopping criterion: a maximum number of $1000n^2$ evaluations.

Initially, θ is set to θ_{lower}. Different θ_{lower} and θ_{upper} values have been used for each problem size (n), looking for those values that assign probabilities of 0.5 and 0.9 to the central permutation. Tables 1 and 2 show the θ_{lower} and θ_{upper} values for each problem size n under the Kendall's-τ and Cayley distances.

Table 1: θ_{lower} and θ_{upper} values for the Kendall's-τ distance for the different problem sizes n.

n	θ_{lower}	θ_{upper}	n	θ_{lower}	θ_{upper}
50	4.3	6.1	300	6.2	8.0
100	5.0	6.7	350	6.3	8.1
150	5.4	7.2	400	6.4	8.2
200	5.6	7.5	450	6.5	8.3
250	5.8	7.7	500	6.6	8.4

All the algorithms have been implemented in the C++ programming language. The experimentation was conducted on a cluster of 20 nodes, each of them equipped with two Intel Xeon X5650 CPUs and 48GB of memory.

5.1 Results

Each *algorithm - instance* pair was run 10 times. The performance measure employed in our study is the average

Table 2: θ_{lower} and θ_{upper} values for the Cayley distance for the different problem sizes n.

n	θ_{lower}	θ_{upper}	n	θ_{lower}	θ_{upper}
50	7.6	9.4	300	11.1	13
100	8.8	10.8	350	11.3	13.3
150	9.5	11.6	400	11.5	13.6
200	10.2	12.2	450	11.9	13.8
250	10.6	12.6	500	12.1	14

relative percentage deviation (ARPD):

$$ARPD = \frac{\left(\frac{1}{10}\sum_{i=1}^{10} \text{Algorithm}_i\right)}{\text{Best}} - 1$$

where Algorithm_i denotes the solution found by the algorithm in the ith repetition, and Best stands for the best solution obtained throughout the whole experimental study by any of the EDAs[2]. The lower the ARPD value, the better the performance. Fig. 2 summarizes the ARPD results obtained throughout the experiments.

With regard to the Kendall's-τ distance, K_{ken} obtains better results than M_{ken} in most cases, but GM_{ken} outperforms both in all the instances. In the case of the Cayley distance, K_{cay} beats M_{cay} and GM_{cay} systematically, either on the QAP or PFSP.

5.2 Statistical test

In order to state whether there exist statistical differences among the algorithms on each problem, we applied the non-parametric Friedman's test to the ARPD results obtained by MEDA, GMEDA and MKEDA under the Kendall's-τ and Cayley distances separately on the QAP and PFSP. A level $\alpha = 0.05$ of significance was set. The statistical test pointed out that for both problems there exist significant differences (with a p-value below 0.001) between the six algorithms. Following the recommendation of Garcia et al. [17] for such cases, we applied the Shaffer's static procedure to carry out all the pairwise comparisons between the algorithms. Again, we fixed the significance level to $\alpha = 0.05$. Results are summarised in the critical difference diagrams in Figs. 3 and 4.

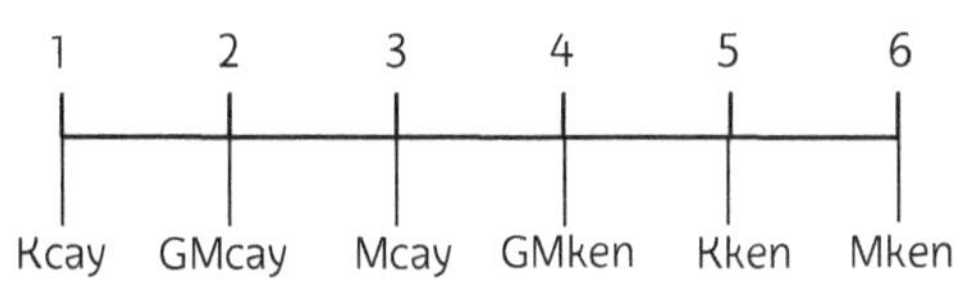

Figure 3: Critical difference diagram of the algorithms on the QAP.

The statistical test concludes that:

- in the case of the Cayley distance, K_{cay} is the preferred algorithm, followed by GM_{cay} and M_{cay},
- with regard to the Kendall's-τ distance, GMEDA obtains better results followed by K_{ken} and M_{ken}.

[2]Note that the instances optimised in this work have been generated for this experimental study, and, therefore, there are no best-known solutions with which to compare.

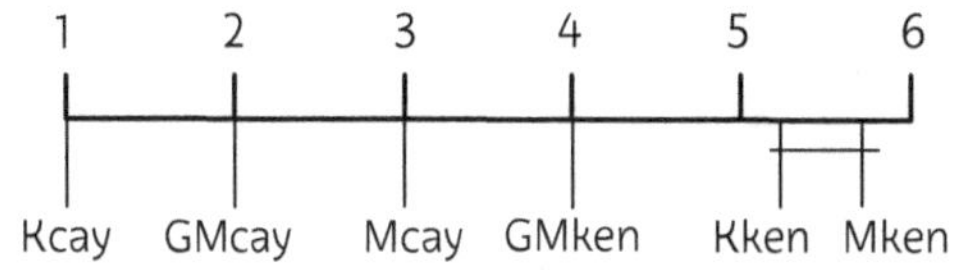

Figure 4: Critical difference diagram of the algorithms on the PFSP.

From a more general perspective, the MKEDA under the Cayley distance (K_{cay}) is the algorithm that performs the best for both problems. On the contrary, the MEDA under the Kendall's-τ (M_{ken}) is that which performs the worst.

Actually, results reveal that, for both problems, the Cayley distance is systematically preferred to the Kendall's-τ distance. In fact, in a recently published review of distances for the Mallows and Generalized Mallows EDAs [9], the authors argue that the Cayley distance induces *landscapes* that are smoother than those generated by the Kendall's-τ distance. As a result, the algorithm performs better. In this sense, it would be interesting to see in further studies whether such conclusions could be extended to the behaviour of MKEDAs.

5.3 Computational cost

In order to study the computational effort required by the compared algorithms to perform $1000n^2$ evaluations, in Fig. 5, we introduce the computational time (in seconds) consumed by the six EDAs.

On one hand, looking at the units in the y-axis, we appreciate that the EDAs under the Cayley distance are significantly faster than their counterparts under the Kendall's-τ distance. This is motivated principally by the time complexity associated to the sampling method of each of the distances, which is $O(n)$ for Cayley and $O(n^2)$ for Kendall's-τ.

On the other hand, we observe that the computation time of MEDA and GMEDA increases dramatically with n, whereas MKEDA discovers a more moderate tendency. Note that the learning step in MEDA and GMEDA implies calculating the central permutation and estimating the spread parameter(s), both processes being very time consuming. Inversely, in MKEDA, the parameters are set directly, and therefore the algorithm results much faster.

6. CONCLUSIONS AND FUTURE WORK

In previous works, distance-based probability models have demonstrated successful performances in the context of EDAs. However, these type of models are not flexible enough to accurately model populations of solutions that very sparse according to the distance metric employed under the model. With the aim of improving the performance of EDAs on permutation problems, in this paper we proposed Mallows Kernel EDA (MKEDA). This novel algorithm implements kernels of Mallows models within EDAs.

In order to demonstrate its validity, we run MKEDA under the Kendall's-τ and Cayley distances, and compared it with MEDA and GMEDA on a benchmark of 90 instances of the QAP and PFSP. Conducted experiments revealed that using kernel models, instead of the classical Mallows and Generalized Mallows models, better results can be obtained.

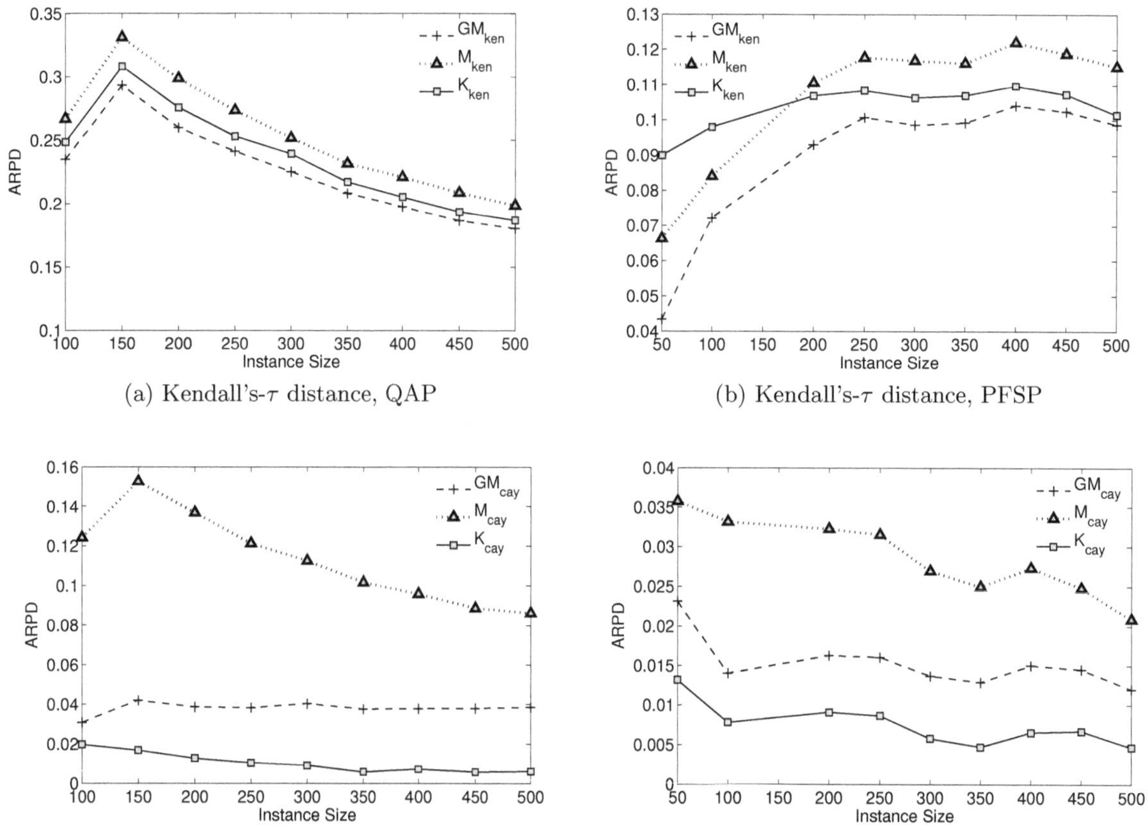

(a) Kendall's-τ distance, QAP

(b) Kendall's-τ distance, PFSP

(c) Cayley distance, QAP

(d) Cayley distance, PFSP

Figure 2: ARPD results of GMEDA, MEDA and Kernel EDA, under the Cayley and Kendall's-τ distances when solving the QAP and PFSP.

Moreover, the statistical test points out that MKEDA under the Cayley distance is the best performing algorithm (among those compared) for the QAP and PFSP. Furthermore, the analysis of the computational cost reveals that it is also the fastest algorithm.

Before bringing this paper to a close, there are some comments that are worth outlining for future research. On one hand, in the view of the outstanding performance of MKEDAs, especially under the Cayley distance, new state-of-the-art algorithms could be developed for the QAP and PFSP on the basis presented in this work. On the other hand, many parameters of MKEDA have been adjusted with out any previous experimentation. In this sense, performing a proper parameter tuning, and exploring new strategies to adjust the smoothing parameter θ, in a similar manner to the temperature parameter in simulated annealing, could provide further improvements. Finally, the work in this paper could be extended to other problems, such as the linear ordering problem [12], and also to other distances, such as Ulam [21] or Hamming [20].

7. ACKNOWLEDGMENTS

This work has been partially supported by the Saiotek and Research Groups 2013-2018 (IT-609-13) programs (Basque Government), TIN2013-41272P (Ministry of Science and Technology), COMBIOMED network in computational bio-medicine (Carlos III Health Institute), and by the NICaiA Project PIRSES-GA-2009-247619 (European Commission).

8. REFERENCES

[1] A. Allahverdi, C. Ng, T. Cheng, and M. Y. Kovalyov. A survey of scheduling problems with setup times or costs. *European Journal of Operational Research*, 187(3):985 – 1032, 2008.

[2] K. Baker. *Introduction to sequencing and scheduling*. Wiley, 1974.

[3] P. A. N. Bosman and D. Thierens. Mult-objective optimization with diversity preserving mixture-based iterated density estimation evolutionary algorithms. *Internation Journal of Approximate Reasoning*, 31(3):259–289, 2002.

[4] A. E. I. Brownlee, M. Pelikan, J. A. W. McCall, and A. Petrovski. An application of a multivariate estimation of distribution algorithm to cancer chemotherapy. In C. Ryan and M. Keijzer, editors, *Proceedings of the 10th Genetic and Evolutionary Computation Conference*, GECCO '08, pages 463–464, 2008.

[5] J. Ceberio. *Solving Permutation Problems with Estimation of Distribution Algorithms and Extensions Thereof*. PhD thesis, Faculty of Computer Science, University of the Basque Country, December 2014.

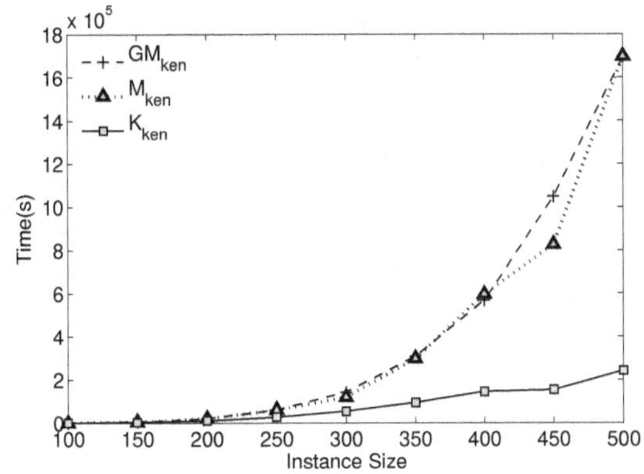

(a) Kendall's-τ distance, QAP

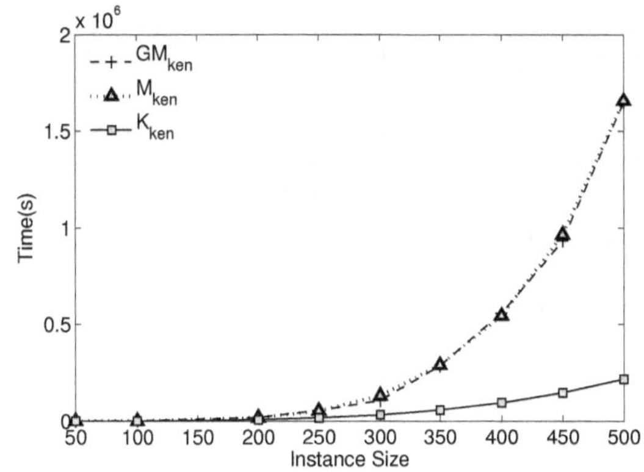

(b) Kendall's-τ distance, PFSP

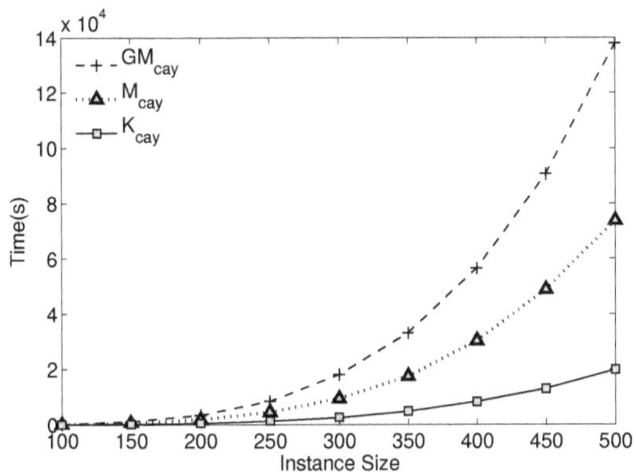

(c) Cayley distance, QAP

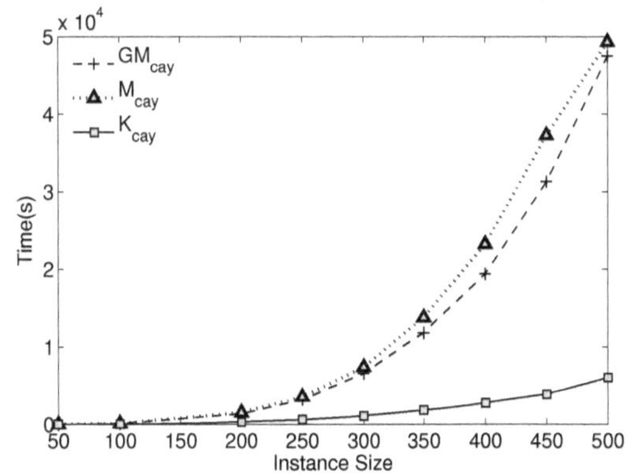

(d) Cayley distance, PFSP

Figure 5: Computational cost in seconds need to perform $1000n^2$ evaluations with MEDA, GMEDA and MKEDA, under the Kendall's-τ and Cayley distances when solving the QAP and PFSP.

[6] J. Ceberio, E. Irurozki, A. Mendiburu, and J. A. Lozano. A review on Estimation of Distribution Algorithms in Permutation-based Combinatorial Optimization Problems. *Progress in Artificial Intelligence*, 1(1):103–117, January 2012.

[7] J. Ceberio, E. Irurozki, A. Mendiburu, and J. A. Lozano. A Distance-based Ranking Model Estimation of Distribution Algorithm for the Flowshop Scheduling Problem. *IEEE Transactions on Evolutionary Computation*, 18(2):286 – 300, April 2014.

[8] J. Ceberio, E. Irurozki, A. Mendiburu, and J. A. Lozano. Extending distance-based ranking models in estimation of distribution algorithms. In *Proceedings of the 2014 IEEE Congress on Evolutionary Computation*. IEEE, July 2014.

[9] J. Ceberio, E. Irurozki, A. Mendiburu, and J. A. Lozano. A review of distances for the Mallows and Generalized Mallows estimation of distribution algorithms. *Computational Optimization and Applications*, March 2015.

[10] J. Ceberio, A. Mendiburu, and J. A. Lozano. Introducing the Mallows Model on Estimation of Distribution Algorithms. In B.-L. Lu, L. Zhang, and J. T. Kwok, editors, *Proceedings of International Conference on Neural Information Processing (ICONIP)*, Lecture Notes in Computer Science, pages 461–470. Springer, 2011.

[11] J. Ceberio, A. Mendiburu, and J. A. Lozano. The Plackett-Luce Ranking Model on Permutation-based Optimization Problems. In *Proceedings of the 2013 IEEE Congress on Evolutionary Computation*, pages 494 – 501, June 2013.

[12] J. Ceberio, A. Mendiburu, and J. A. Lozano. The Linear Ordering Problem Revisited. *European Journal of Operational Research*, 241(3):686–696, 2014.

[13] D. E. Critchlow, M. A. Fligner, and J. S. Verducci. Probability models on rankings. *Journal of Mathematical Psychology*, 35(3):294 – 318, 1991.

[14] M. Fligner and J. Verducci. Multistage ranking models. *Journal of the American Statistical Association*, 83(403):892–901, 1988.

[15] M. A. Fligner and J. S. Verducci. Distance based ranking Models. *Journal of the Royal Statistical Society*, 48(3):359–369, 1986.

[16] B. Gao. *Estimation of Distribution Algorithms for single- and multi-objective optimization*. PhD thesis, School of Mathematics and Physics, The University of Queensland, 2014.

[17] S. Garcia, D. Molina, M. Lozano, and F. Herrera. A study on the use of non-parametric tests for analyzing

the evolutionary algorithms' behaviour: a case study on the CEC'2005 Special Session on Real Parameter Optimization. *Journal of Heuristics*, 15(6):617–644, 2009.

[18] J. Gupta and J. E. Stafford. Flow shop scheduling research after five decades. *European Journal of Operational Research*, 169(3):699–711, 2006.

[19] E. Irurozki, B. Calvo, and J. A. Lozano. Sampling and learning Mallows and Generalized Mallows models under the Cayley distance. Technical report, University of the Basque Country UPV/EHU, 2014.

[20] E. Irurozki, B. Calvo, and J. A. Lozano. Sampling and learning the mallows and weighted mallows models under the Hamming distance. Technical report, University of the Basque Country UPV/EHU, 2014.

[21] E. Irurozki, J. Ceberio, B. Calvo, and J. A. Lozano. Mallows model under the ulam distance: a feasible combinatorial approach. In *Workshop Book 2014 NIPS Conference*, Montreal, Quebec, Canada, December 2014.

[22] S. Jiang, A. Ziver, J. Carter, C. Pain, A. Goddard, S. Franklin, and H. Phillips. Estimation of Distribution Algorithms for nuclear reactor fuel management optimisation. *Annals of Nuclear Energy*, 33(11-12):1039–1057, 2006.

[23] T. C. Koopmans and M. J. Beckmann. Assignment Problems and the Location of Economic Activities. Cowles Foundation Discussion Papers 4, Cowles Foundation for Research in Economics, Yale University, 1955.

[24] P. Larrañaga and J. A. Lozano. *Estimation of Distribution Algorithms: A New Tool for Evolutionary Computation*. Kluwer Academic Publishers, 2002.

[25] G. Lebanon and Y. Mao. Non-Parametric Modeling of Partially Ranked Data. *Journal of Machine Learning Research (JMLR)*, 9:2401–2429, 2008.

[26] P. H. Lee and P. L. H. Yu. Mixtures of weighted distance-based models for ranking data. In *IEEE Proceedings of COMPSTAT'2010*, pages 517–524, August 2010.

[27] J. A. Lozano, P. Larrañaga, I. Inza, and E. Bengoetxea. *Towards a New Evolutionary Computation: Advances on Estimation of Distribution Algorithms (Studies in Fuzziness and Soft Computing)*. Springer-Verlag New York, Inc., Secaucus, NJ, USA, 2006.

[28] C. L. Mallows. Non-null ranking models. *Biometrika*, 44(1-2):114–130, 1957.

[29] J. McCall, A. E. I. Brownlee, and S. Shakya. Applications of distribution estimation using markov network modelling (DEUM). In S. Shakya and R. Santana, editors, *Markov Networks in Evolutionary Computation*, pages 193–207. Springer, 2012.

[30] A. Mendiburu, J. Miguel-Alonso, J. A. Lozano, M. Ostra, and C. Ubide. Parallel EDAs to create multivariate calibration models for quantitative chemical applications. *Journal of Parallel and Distributed Computing*, 66(8):1002–1013, 2006.

[31] H. Mühlenbein and G. Paaß. From Recombination of Genes to the Estimation of Distributions I. Binary Parameters. In *Lecture Notes in Computer Science 1411: Parallel Problem Solving from Nature - PPSN IV*, pages 178–187, 1996.

[32] T. B. Murphy and D. Martin. Mixtures of distance-based models for ranking data. *Computational Statistics & Data Analysis*, 41(3-4):645–655, Jan. 2003.

[33] M. Pelikan, D. E. Goldberg, and F. G. Lobo. A survey of optimization by building and using probabilistic models. *Computational Optimization and Applications*, 21(1):5–20, 2002.

[34] J. M. Peña, J. A. Lozano, and P. Larrañaga. Globally multimodal problem optimization via an estimation of distribution algorithm based on unsupervised learning of Bayesian networks. *Evolutionary Computation*, pages 43–66, 2005.

[35] J. Santamaria, J. Ceberio, R. Santana, A. Mendiburu, and J. Lozano. Introducing mixtures of Generalized Mallows in estimation of distribution algorithms. In *X Congreso Español de Metaheuristicas, Algoritmos Evolutivos y Bioinspirados - MAEB 2015*, pages 19–25, Mérida-Almendralejo, Spain, February 2015.

[36] R. Santana, C. Bielza, P. Larranaga, J. A. Lozano, C. Echegoyen, A. Mendiburu, R. Armananzas, and S. Shakya. Mateda-2.0: Estimation of distribution algorithms in matlab. *Journal of Statistical Software*, 35(7):1–30, 2010.

[37] R. Santana, P. Larrañaga, and J. A. Lozano. Mixtures of Kikuchi approximations. In J. Fürnkranz, T. Scheffer, and M. Spiliopoulou, editors, *Machine Learning: ECML 2006*, volume 4212 of *Lecture Notes in Computer Science*, pages 365–376. Springer Berlin Heidelberg, 2006.

[38] R. Santana, P. Larrañaga, and J. A. Lozano. Protein folding in simplified models with Estimation of Distribution Algorithms. *IEEE Transactions On Evolutionary Computation*, 12(4):418–438, 2008.

[39] M. R. Soto, A. Ochoa, Y. González-Fernández, Y. Milanés, A. Álvarez, D. Carrera, and E. Moreno. Vine estimation of distribution algorithms with application to molecular docking. In S. Shakya and R. Santana, editors, *Markov Networks in Evolutionary Computation*, pages 175–190. Springer, 2012.

Simplified Runtime Analysis of Estimation of Distribution Algorithms

Duc-Cuong Dang
ASAP Research Group
School of Computer Science
University of Nottingham
duc-cuong.dang
@nottingham.ac.uk

Per Kristian Lehre
ASAP Research Group
School of Computer Science
University of Nottingham
perkristian.lehre
@nottingham.ac.uk

ABSTRACT

Estimation of distribution algorithms (EDA) are stochastic search methods that look for optimal solutions by learning and sampling from probabilistic models. Despite their popularity, there are only few rigorous theoretical analyses of their performance. Even for the simplest EDAs, such as the Univariate Marginal Distribution Algorithm (UMDA) which assumes independence between decision variables, there are only a handful of results about its runtime, and results for simple functions such as OneMax are still missing.

In this paper, we show that the recently developed *level-based theorem* for non-elitist populations is directly applicable to runtime analysis of EDAs. To demonstrate this approach, we derive easily upper bounds on the expected runtime of the UMDA.

Categories and Subject Descriptors

F.2 [**Theory of Computation**]: Analysis of Algorithms and Problem Complexity

Keywords

Runtime Analysis, Level-based Analysis, Estimation of Distribution Algorithm

1. INTRODUCTION

Estimation of Distribution Algorithm (EDA) [15] is a relatively new paradigm in Evolutionary Computation. Unlike traditional approaches of Evolutionary Algorithms (EAs) that work with explicit evolutionary/genetic operators such as mutation, recombination and selection, an EDA will attempt to build probabilistic models for solution sampling so that the probability of creating an optimal solution through the sampling is high. The algorithm often starts with a specific probabilistic model, which is gradually updated through selected solutions of intermediate samplings.

GECCO '15, July 11 - 15, 2015, Madrid, Spain

ISBN 978-1-4503-3472-3/15/07...$15.00

DOI: http://dx.doi.org/10.1145/2739480.2754814

Over the recent years, many variants of EDAs have been proposed, along with theoretical investigations on their convergence and scalability [11, 13, 18, 20, 21, 22, 23]. However, rigorous runtime analysis results for this particular class of algorithms on discrete domain are still sparse. The first analysis of this kind was conducted in [8] for the compact Genetic Algorithm (cGA) [12] on linear functions. cGA is one of the simplest EDAs which assume no dependence between decision variables. On bitstrings of length n, cGA uses a Poisson binomial distribution parametrised by a probability vector $(p_i)_{i\in[n]}$ as the probabilistic model. In each generation, the cGA generates two solutions and uses the best one to update the probability vector via a learning rate parameter $1/K$. Without any proper margin for each p_i, cGA can eventually end up with a distribution that can never generate an optimal solution, i. e., a premature convergence. Therefore, the runtimes for cGA on OneMax and BinVal functions which were reported in [8] are conditioned on the event that this does not occur. Very recently, the benefits of cGA in noisy environment were proven using runtime arguments in [10].

Another simple EDA is the Univariate Marginal Distribution Algorithm (UMDA) which was analysed in a series of papers [1, 2, 3, 4]. UMDA was proposed in [17], assuming as the cGA independence between decision variables. However, the UMDA samples a real population of solutions and uses the selected solutions to create a new vector $(p_i)_{i\in[n]}$ in each generation. The initial result of [2] was provided for LeadingOnes and a harder function known as TrapLeadingOnes under the so-called "no-random-error" assumption and with a sufficiently large population. The assumption was lifted due to the technique presented in [4]. Nevertheless, the analysis assumes an unrealistically large population size, leading in overall to a too high bound on the expected runtime. Note also that there are two versions of the algorithm based on whether or not margins are imposed to p_i, the difference between the two in terms on time complexity for various functions are discussed in [3]. More interestingly, [1] showed that UMDA without margins beats the (1 + 1) EA on a particular function called SubString. However, it is not recommended to use UMDA without margins in practice, as the algorithm can always end up with a premature convergence.

To summarise, there are very few rigorous runtime results for cGA and UMDA, the two simplest EDAs. The analytical techniques used in those analyses are often complex, e. g., relying on the machinery of Markov chain theory, and the results only hold under extra assumptions. Even more surprisingly, we could not find any results for UMDA on the OneMax function, a classic benchmark function used when initiating runtime analysis of new algorithms. This is very contrast to our current understanding of EAs, of which over the past decades [19], many rigorous runtime results have been shown for various settings, from the single-individual approach as the (1+1) EA or RLS to population-based ones like $(\mu+1)$ EA, or even Genetic Algorithms (GA) [5]. One contributing factor behind these advances for EAs may have been the development of appropriate analytical techniques such as *drift analysis* or *fitness-level* method (e.g., see [14] for an overview).

Motivated by the above facts, this paper derives the runtime of UMDA with margins and truncation selection on the two standard functions OneMax and LeadingOnes by a straightforward argument. We make no extra assumptions about the optimisation process. Our runtime results will be stated in terms of number of solution evaluations. This is made possible by the recently developed level-based method [5] which describes the search process at a high level of abstraction, akin to an estimation of distribution algorithm. The method is applicable to any search process which samples new solutions independently from a distribution that only depends on the current generation.

The remainder of the paper is organised as follows. In the next section, we give the formal description of the UMDA. Next, we describe the two methods, *level-based* analysis, and Feige's bound which are our main analytical tools. Then the results for LeadingOnes and OneMax are presented with straightforward proofs. Finally some conclusions are drawn.

2. ALGORITHM

We consider the optimisation of functions $f : \mathcal{X} \to \mathbb{R}$ over the Boolean hypercube $\mathcal{X} = \{0,1\}^n$. If $P \in \mathcal{X}^\lambda$ is a population of λ solutions, let $P(k,i)$ denote the value in the i-th bit position of the k-th solution in P. The Univariate Marginal Distribution Algorithm (UMDA) with (μ,λ)-truncation selection is defined in Algorithm 1. As a common practice in runtime analysis community, algorithms hereby are written without specifying the stopping condition. That is because we will mainly focus on computing the first point in time that an optimal solution is conceived.

Algorithm 1 UMDA

1: Initialise the vector $p_0 := (1/2,\dots,1/2)$.
2: **for** $t = 0,1,2,\dots$ **do**
3: **for** $k = 1$ to λ **do**
4: Sample the k-th individual $P_t(k,\cdot)$ according to

$$P_t(k,i) \sim \text{Bernoulli}(p_t(i)) \text{ for all } i \in [n].$$

5: **end for**
6: Sort the population P_t according to f.
7: Calculate a new vector p_{t+1} from P_t according to

$$p_{t+1}(i) := \begin{cases} \frac{m}{\mu} & \text{if } X_i < m \\ \frac{X_i}{\mu} & \text{if } m \le X_i \le \mu - m \\ 1 - \frac{m}{\mu} & \text{if } \mu - m < X_i, \end{cases}$$

for all $i \in [n]$, where $X_i := \sum_{k=1}^{\mu} P_t(k,i)$.
8: **end for**

The algorithm has three parameters, the parent population size μ, the offspring population size λ, and a parameter $m < \mu$ controlling the size of the margins. It is necessary to set $m > 0$ to prevent a premature convergence, e.g., without this margin a $p_t(i)$ can goes to a non-optimal fixation, this prevents further exploration and causes an infinite runtime. Based on insights about optimal mutation rates in the (1+1) EA, we will use the parameter setting $m = \mu/n$ in the rest of this paper.

3. TECHNIQUES

3.1 Level-based Analysis

The level-based theorem for analysis of population-based algorithms is a general tool that provides upper bounds on the expected runtime of a wide class of meta-heuristics applied to various optimisation scenarios. For example, it has been used to study genetic algorithms with crossover [5], and evolutionary algorithms subject to uncertain optimisation, such as noise or missing information [6, 7].

The theorem applies to any search process that can be represented in the algorithmic scheme shown in Algorithm 2. It is assumed that the algorithm at any time $t \ge 0$ has a population P_t of λ individuals in some search space $\mathcal{X}$. The algorithm generates the next population P_{t+1} by sampling independently λ times from a probability distribution $D(P_t)$ which is parameterised by the current population P_t. As such, the algorithmic scheme can be considered as a generic estimation of distribution algorithm (EDA) which evolves a sequence of probability distributions $(D_t)_{t\ge0}$ where $D_t = D(P_t)$. In particular, it is immediately clear that the UMDA in Algorithm 1 is a special case of this algorithmic scheme. The probability distribution $D(P_t)$ is computed in steps 6-7, and is defined for any search point $x \in \{0,1\}^n$ by

$$\Pr(Y = x) = \prod_{j=1}^{n} p_t(j)^{x_j} (1 - p_t(j))^{1-x_j}.$$

Note that in the compact genetic algorithm (cGA) and some other randomised search heuristics such as ant colony optimisation (ACO), the sampling distribution D_t does not only depend on the current population, but also on additional information, such as pheromone values. The level-based theorem does not apply to such algorithms.

Algorithm 2 Population Algorithm with Sampling

Require:
Finite state space $\mathcal{X}$,
Configurable probability distribution D over $\mathcal{X}$
$P_0 \sim \text{Unif}(\mathcal{X}^\lambda)$
for $t = 0,1,2,\dots$ **do**
for $k = 1$ to λ **do**
$P_{t+1}(k) \sim D(P_t)$.
end for
end for

The level-based theorem assumes that the search space has been partitioned into a sequence of levels $A_1,\dots,A_{m+1}$, such that the last level contains all the search points that are considered optimal solutions to the problem. If it can be shown that the distribution $D(P_t)$ is biased towards higher levels in a way that will be made precise below, the theorem provides upper bounds on the expected time to obtain solutions in the final level A_{m+1}. To simplify the writing, we use A_j^+ to denote all levels after A_j in the sequence, or $A_j^+ := \cup_{i=j+1}^{m+1} A_i$.

THEOREM 1. *Given a partition $(A_1, \ldots, A_{m+1})$ of $\mathcal{X}$, define $T := \min\{t\lambda \mid |P_t \cap A_{m+1}| > 0\}$ to be the first point in time that elements of A_{m+1} appear in P_t of Algorithm 2. If there exist parameters $z_1, \ldots, z_m, z_* \in (0,1]$, $\delta > 0$, a constant $\gamma_0 \in (0,1)$ and a function $z_0 : (0, \gamma_0) \to \mathbb{R}$ such that for all $j \in [m]$, $P \in \mathcal{X}^\lambda$, $y \sim D(P)$ and $\gamma \in (0, \gamma_0)$ we have*

(C1) $\Pr\left(y \in A_j^+ \mid |P \cap A_{j-1}^+| \geq \gamma_0 \lambda\right) \geq z_j \geq z_*$

(C2) $\Pr\left(y \in A_j^+ \mid |P \cap A_{j-1}^+| \geq \gamma_0 \lambda, |P \cap A_j^+| \geq \gamma\lambda\right) \geq z_0(\gamma) \geq (1+\delta)\gamma$

(C3) $\lambda \geq \frac{2}{a} \ln\left(\frac{16m}{ac\varepsilon z_*}\right)$ *with* $a = \frac{\delta^2 \gamma_0}{2(1+\delta)}$, $\varepsilon = \min\{\delta/2, 1/2\}$ *and* $c = \varepsilon^4/24$

then $\mathbf{E}[T] \leq \frac{2}{c\varepsilon}\left(m\lambda(1 + \ln(1 + c\lambda)) + \sum_{j=1}^{m} \frac{1}{z_j}\right)$

Informally, the two first conditions require a relationship between P and the distribution $D(P)$. In condition (C1), the theorem demands a certain probability z_j of creating an individual at level $j+1$ when some fixed portion γ_0 of the population is already at level j (or higher). Condition (C2) requires that in the fixed portion, the number of individuals at levels strictly higher than j (if those exist) tends to increase, e.g. by a multiplicative factor of $1+\delta$. The last condition (C3) requires a sufficiently large population size. When all the conditions are satisfied, an upper bound on the expected runtime (defined in terms of sampled/evaluated solutions) of the algorithm to reach A_{m+1} is guaranteed.

3.2 Feige's Inequality

To show that Condition (C1) and (C2) in the level-based theorem are satisfied, it will become necessary to compute lower bounds on the probability $\Pr(Y \geq j+1)$ where Y represents the level of an individual sampled from $D(P_t)$. It is often non-trivial to compute this probability directly, hence we resort to tail bounds that can be expressed in terms of the expectation of Y. While most tail inequalities provide upper bounds on $\Pr(Y \geq j+1)$, we will make use of a general result due to Feige to compute lower bounds [9]. The theorem is usually presented in the following form.

THEOREM 2. *Let $X_1, \ldots, X_n$ be non-negative, independent random variables with expectations $\mu_1, \ldots, \mu_n$ such that $\mu_i \leq 1$ for all i, define $X = \sum_{i=1}^n X_i$ and $\mu = \mathbf{E}[X]$. It holds for every $\delta > 0$ that*

$$\Pr(X < \mu + \delta) \geq \min\left\{\frac{1}{13}, \frac{\delta}{1+\delta}\right\}$$

For our purposes, it will be more convenient to use the following variant.

COROLLARY 3. *Let $Y_1, \ldots, Y_n$ be n independent random variables with support in $[0,1]$ and finite expectations, define $Y = \sum_{i=1}^n Y_i$ and $\mu = \mathbf{E}[Y]$. It holds for every $\delta > 0$ that*

$$\Pr(Y > \mu - \delta) \geq \min\left\{\frac{1}{13}, \frac{\delta}{1+\delta}\right\}$$

PROOF. For each i, define $x_i = 1 - Y_i$. It is clear that X_i also has support in $[0,1]$ and $\mathbf{E}[X_i] \leq 1$. Let $X = \sum_{i=1}^n X_i$, then $X = n - Y$ and $\mathbf{E}[X] = n - \mathbf{E}[Y] = n - \mu$. It follows from Theorem 2 that

$$\begin{aligned}\Pr(Y > \mu - \delta) &= \Pr(n - X > \mu - \delta) \\ &= \Pr(n - \mu + \delta > X) \\ &= \Pr(X < \mathbf{E}[X] + \delta) \\ &\geq \min\left\{\frac{1}{13}, \frac{\delta}{\delta+1}\right\}. \quad \square\end{aligned}$$

4. RUNTIME ANALYSIS ON LEADINGONES

As a warm-up example, and to illustrate the ease of use of our methods, we consider the standard benchmark function

$$\text{LEADINGONES}(x) = \sum_{i=1}^{n}\prod_{j=1}^{i} x_j,$$

where the objective is to maximise the number of leading one-bits in the bitstring. It is well-known that the expected optimisation time of the (1+1) EA on LEADINGONES is $\Theta(n^2)$, and that this is optimal for the class of unary unbiased black-box algorithms [16]. In this analysis, we do not require Feige's inequality.

THEOREM 4. *The Univariate Marginal Distribution Algorithm (UMDA) with offspring population size $\lambda \geq b\ln(n)$ for some constant $b > 0$, parent population size $\mu = \gamma_0\lambda$ for any constants $\gamma_0 \leq \frac{1}{(1+\delta)13e}$ and $\delta > 0$, and margin $m = \mu/n$ has expected optimisation time $\mathcal{O}(n\lambda\ln(\lambda) + n^2)$ on LEADINGONES.*

PROOF. We apply Theorem 1 with the parameter $\gamma_0 := \mu/\lambda$, and use the canonical level-partition given by

$$A_j := \{x \in \{0,1\}^n \mid \text{LEADINGONES}(x) = j\}.$$

In the following, we let Y denote the level of a sampled individual, or equivalently the number of leading one-bits in the solution. We first develop a generic bound on $\Pr(Y \geq j+1)$ which does not depend on γ. Then we use this bound to show that conditions (C1) and (C2) of Theorem 1 are satisfied.

For any population P_t, there exists an integer $j \geq 0$ and a real number $\gamma \in [0, \mu/\lambda)$ such that $|P_t \cap A_{j-1}^+| \geq \gamma_0\lambda = \mu$ and $|P_t \cap A_j^+| = \gamma\lambda < \mu$. In other words, among the μ best individuals in the current population, there are $\gamma\lambda$ individuals with a fitness at least $j+1$ and at least μ individuals with a fitness at least j. Hence

$$X_i = \mu \quad \text{and} \quad p_t(i) = 1 - 1/n \qquad \text{if } 1 \leq i \leq j.$$

Therefore,

$$\begin{aligned}\Pr(Y \geq j+1) &= \prod_{i=1}^{j+1} p_t(i) &(1)\\ &= \left(1 - \frac{1}{n}\right)^j p_t(j+1) &(2)\\ &\geq \frac{p_t(j+1)}{e}. &(3)\end{aligned}$$

If $\gamma = 0$, then none of the best μ individuals in the population has a one-bit in position $j+1$ and

$$X_{j+1} = 0 \quad \text{and} \quad p_t(j+1) = 1/n.$$

Condition (C1) can therefore be satisfied by choosing the same parameter $z_j = z_* = 1/(en)$ for all levels j.

If $\gamma > 0$, then among the best μ individuals in the population, there are $\gamma\lambda$ individuals with a one-bit in position $j+1$, and $\mu-\gamma\lambda$ individuals with a zero-bit in position $j+1$. Therefore,

$$X_{j+1} = \gamma\lambda \quad \text{and} \quad p_t(j+1) = \frac{\gamma\lambda}{\mu}.$$

It follows that

$$\Pr(Y \geq j+1) \geq \frac{p_t(j+1)}{e} = \frac{\gamma\lambda}{\mu e} \geq (1+\delta)\gamma$$

because the population size is $\lambda \geq (1+\delta)e\mu$. Condition (C2) is therefore satisfied.

Given that δ and γ are constants, the parameters a, ε and c are also constants. Furthermore, $1/z_* \in \text{poly}(n)$. Therefore, there must exist a constant b such that condition (C3) is satisfied whenever $\lambda \geq b\ln(n)$.

All three conditions are now satisfied, and the theorem implies that the UMDA has expected optimisation time

$$\mathcal{O}\left(n\lambda\ln(\lambda) + \sum_{j=1}^{n-1}\frac{1}{z_j}\right) = \mathcal{O}\left(n\lambda\ln(\lambda) + n^2\right). \quad \square$$

5. RUNTIME ANALYSIS ON ONEMAX

We now turn to another classical benchmark problem,

$$\text{ONEMAX}(x) = \sum_{i=1}^{n} x_i,$$

where the objective is to maximise the number of one-bits in the bitstring. It is well-known that the (1+1) EA solves this problem in expected time $\Theta(n\ln n)$, and this is optimal for the class of unary, unbiased black-box algorithms. While this problem may appear simpler than LEADINGONES, runtime analysis of UMDA on this problem is a much bigger challenge because the probability distribution induced by the UMDA follows a less clear trajectory than in the LEADINGONES problem. Surprisingly, no previous runtime analysis of UMDA seems available for ONEMAX. We demonstrate that the expected runtime can be obtained relatively easy with our methods. To obtain lower bounds on the tail of the level-distribution, we make use of the Feige inequality.

THEOREM 5. *The Univariate Marginal Distribution Algorithm (UMDA) with offspring population size $\lambda \geq b\ln(n)$ for some constant $b > 0$, parent population size $\mu = \gamma_0\lambda$ for any constants $\gamma_0 \leq \frac{1}{(1+\delta)13e}$ and $\delta \in (0,1)$, and margins $m = \mu/n$, has expected optimisation time $\mathcal{O}(n\lambda\ln\lambda)$ on ONEMAX.*

PROOF. We will use the canonical partition $(A_0, \ldots, A_n)$ given by

$$A_j := \{x \in \{0,1\}^n \mid \text{ONEMAX}(x) = j\}$$

Furthermore, we use the parameter $\gamma_0 := \mu/\lambda$, and let Y be the level of a sampled individual (or equivalently the number of one-bits in the sampled solution).

The probabilities (or components) of p_t can be categorised into three groups. Probabilities at the upper margin $1 - 1/n$, probabilities at the lower margin $1/n$, and intermediary probabilities in the closed interval $[1/\mu, 1-1/\mu]$. Due to linearity of the fitness function, the components of p_t can be rearranged without changing the distribution of Y. We can therefore assume w.l.o.g. the rearrangement so that there exists integers $k, \ell \geq 0$ satisfying

$$\begin{aligned}
1 \leq X_i < \mu \quad &\text{and} \quad p_t(i) = X_i/\mu && \text{if } 1 \leq i \leq k,\\
X_i = \mu \quad &\text{and} \quad p_t(i) = 1 - 1/n && \text{if } k < i \leq k+\ell, \text{and}\\
X_i = 0 \quad &\text{and} \quad p_t(i) = 1/n && \text{if } k+\ell < i.
\end{aligned}$$

By these assumptions, it follows that

$$\sum_{i=k+1}^{k+\ell} X_i = \mu\ell \quad \text{and} \quad \sum_{i=k+\ell+1}^{n} X_i = 0. \tag{4}$$

In the following, we define $Y_{i,k}$ to be the number of sampled one-bits due to the subset $(p_t(i), \ldots, p_t(k))$ of components. For any population P_t, there exists an integer $j \geq 0$ and a real number $\gamma \in [0, \mu/\lambda)$ such that $|P_t \cap A^+_{j-1}| \geq \gamma_0\lambda = \mu$ and $|P_t \cap A^+_j| = \gamma\lambda < \mu$. In other words, among the μ best individuals in the current population, there are $\gamma\lambda$ individuals with a fitness at least $j+1$ and at least μ individuals with a fitness at least j. Hence, the total number of one-bits among the fittest μ individuals must satisfy

$$\sum_{i=1}^{n} X_i \geq \gamma\lambda(j+1) + (\mu - \gamma\lambda)j = \gamma\lambda + \mu j. \tag{5}$$

Combining Eqs. (4) and (5) when $k \geq 1$ give

$$\mathbf{E}[Y_{1,k}] = \sum_{i=1}^{k} p_t(i) = \frac{1}{\mu}\sum_{i=1}^{k} X_i \geq \frac{\gamma\lambda}{\mu} + j - \ell. \tag{6}$$

We first consider the case when $\gamma > 0$. This condition implies that among the best μ individuals in the population, there exists both individuals with at least $j+1$ one-bits and individuals with exactly j one-bits. Hence, there must exist at least one index i such that the probability $p_t(i)$ is not at one of the margins. Therefore $k > 0$ which allows us to use Eq. (6). Together with Feige's inequality, we get

$$\begin{aligned}
\Pr(Y_{1,k} \geq j - \ell + 1) &= \Pr\left(Y_{1,k} > j - \ell + \frac{\gamma\lambda}{\mu} - \frac{\gamma\lambda}{12\mu}\right)\\
&\geq \Pr\left(Y_{1,k} > \mathbf{E}[Y_{1,k}] - \frac{\gamma\lambda}{12\mu}\right)\\
&\geq \min\left\{\frac{1}{13}, \frac{\frac{\gamma\lambda}{12\mu}}{\frac{\gamma\lambda}{12\mu} + 1}\right\}\\
&= \min\left\{\frac{1}{13}, \frac{\gamma\lambda}{\gamma\lambda + 12\mu}\right\}\\
&\geq \frac{\gamma\lambda}{13\mu}.
\end{aligned}$$

The probability of sampling an individual with at least $j+1$ one-bits in the next generation is therefore bounded from below by

$$\begin{aligned}\Pr(Y \geq j+1) &\geq \Pr(Y_{1,k} \geq j-\ell+1)\Pr(Y_{k+1,k+\ell}=\ell)\\ &\geq \frac{\gamma\lambda}{13\mu}\left(1-\frac{1}{n}\right)^{\ell}\\ &\geq \frac{\gamma\lambda}{13e\mu}\\ &\geq (1+\delta)\gamma.\end{aligned}$$

Consider now the case where $\gamma = 0$. We need to consider two sub-cases, either $k = 0$ or $k \geq 1$. If $k = 0$, then with our assumption, the j first probabilities are at the upper margin $1 - 1/n$, and the last $n - j$ probabilities are at the lower margin $1/n$. In order to obtain a search point with $j + 1$ one-bits, it is sufficient to sample exactly j one-bits in the first j positions and exactly one one-bit in the last $n - j$ positions. Hence, we have

$$\begin{aligned}\Pr(Y \geq j+1) &\geq \Pr(Y_{1,j}=j)\Pr(Y_{j+1,n}\geq 1)\\ &\geq \left(1-\frac{1}{n}\right)^{j}\left(\frac{n-j}{n}\right)\left(1-\frac{1}{n}\right)^{n-j-1}\\ &= \left(1-\frac{1}{n}\right)^{n-1}\left(\frac{n-j}{n}\right)\\ &\geq \left(\frac{n-j}{en}\right).\end{aligned}$$

In the sub-case where $k > 0$, we note from Eq. (6) that

$$\mathbf{E}[Y_{2,k}] = \mathbf{E}[Y_{1,k}] - p_t(1) \geq j - \ell - p_t(1)$$

Again, by Feige's inequality, we get

$$\begin{aligned}\Pr(Y_{2,k} \geq j-k) &= \Pr(Y_{2,k} > j-\ell-p_t(1)-(1-p_t(1)))\\ &\geq \Pr(Y_{2,k} > \mathbf{E}[Y_{2,k}]-(1-p_t(1)))\\ &\geq \min\left\{\frac{1}{13},\frac{1-p_t(1)}{2-p_t(1)}\right\}\\ &> \frac{1-p_t(1)}{13}.\end{aligned}$$

The probability of sampling an individual with at least $j + 1$ one-bits in this configuration can now be bounded from below as

$$\begin{aligned}&\Pr(Y \geq j+1)\\ &\quad > \Pr(Y_1=1)\Pr(Y_{2,k}\geq j-\ell)\Pr(Y_{k+1,k+\ell}=\ell)\\ &\quad\geq \left(\frac{p_t(1)(1-p_t(1))}{13}\right)\left(1-\frac{1}{n}\right)^{\ell}\\ &\quad\geq \left(\frac{(1/\mu)(1-1/\mu)}{13}\right)\left(1-\frac{1}{n}\right)^{\ell} \geq \frac{1}{14e\mu}.\end{aligned}$$

The last inequality holds for $\mu \geq 14$, which in turn only requires n to be larger than some constant. Hence, in the case when $\gamma = 0$, we get

$$\begin{aligned}\Pr(Y \geq j+1) &\geq \min\left\{\frac{1}{14e\mu},\frac{n-j}{en}\right\}\\ &\geq \frac{n-j}{14e\mu(n-j)+en} =: z_j.\end{aligned}$$

Clearly, there exists a z_* with $1/z_* \in \text{poly}(n)$ such that $\Pr(Y \geq j+1) \geq z_*$ for all $j \in [n-1]$. Condition (C2) is therefore satisfied.

Finally, we consider condition (C3) regarding the population size. The parameters δ and $\gamma_0 = \mu/\lambda$ are constants with respect to n, therefore the variables a, ε and c in condition (C3) are also constants, and $1/z_* \in \text{poly}(n)$. Hence, there must exist a constant $b > 0$ such that condition (C3) is satisfied when $\lambda \geq b\log(n)$.

To conclude, the expected optimisation time is

$$\begin{aligned}&\mathcal{O}\left(n\lambda\ln(\lambda)+\sum_{j=1}^{n-1}\frac{1}{z_j}\right)\\ &\qquad= \mathcal{O}\left(n\lambda\ln(\lambda)+14e\mu n+\sum_{j=0}^{n-1}\frac{en}{n-j}\right)\\ &\qquad= \mathcal{O}(n\lambda\ln\lambda). \quad \square\end{aligned}$$

6. CONCLUSION

Runtime analysis has become one of the standard approaches to theoretical analysis of evolutionary algorithms. Runtime results are available for a large number of algorithms and problems. Runtime analysis provides valuable insight into the behaviour of an algorithm, as it shows how the efficiency of the algorithm depends on its parameters and the characteristics of the fitness landscape.

However, with a few exceptions, runtime analyses have so far largely been unavailable for estimation of distribution algorithms (EDAs). An analysis has seemed elusive, even for apparently simple settings such as UMDA on ONEMAX. Many of the techniques that were developed to analyse evolutionary algorithms such as the (1+1) EA, do not transfer to the more complex EDAs. Mathematical simplifications that have been employed in theoretical studies of EDAs, such as infinite population size or time going to infinite, do not yield meaningful results in the context of runtime.

This paper shows that the *level-based technique* which was recently introduced to analyse population-based evolutionary algorithms is directly applicable to runtime analysis of estimation of distribution algorithms. In particular, the technique applies to any estimation of distribution algorithm where the sampling distribution can be computed from the current population. We demonstrate this new approach by analysing the expected runtime of the univariate marginal distribution algorithm (UMDA) on standard benchmark functions. In particular, for the LEADINGONES problem, we show a significantly improved upper bound on the runtime. Furthermore, we analyse the expected runtime on ONEMAX, a problem that has been remained open for a very long time.

The significance of this work lies in the relatively ease with which these results were obtained. Previous runtime analyses of EDAs have been highly involved, even in simple settings, preventing studies of more interesting scenarios. We believe that the new technique could make it possible to analyse the runtime of more complex EDAs and more challenging fitness landscapes.

Acknowledgements

The research leading to these results has received funding from the European Union Seventh Framework Programme (FP7/2007-2013) under grant agreement no 618091 (SAGE).

7. REFERENCES

[1] Tianshi Chen, Per Kristian Lehre, Ke Tang, and Xin Yao. When is an estimation of distribution algorithm better than an evolutionary algorithm? In *Proceedings of the IEEE Congress on Evolutionary Computation, CEC 2009*, pages 1470–1477, 2009.

[2] Tianshi Chen, Ke Tang, Guoliang Chen, and Xin Yao. On the analysis of average time complexity of estimation of distribution algorithms. In *Proceedings of the IEEE Congress on Evolutionary Computation, CEC 2007*, pages 453–460, 2007.

[3] Tianshi Chen, Ke Tang, Guoliang Chen, and Xin Yao. Rigorous time complexity analysis of univariate marginal distribution algorithm with margins. In *Proceedings of the IEEE Congress on Evolutionary Computation, CEC 2009*, pages 2157–2164, 2009.

[4] Tianshi Chen, Ke Tang, Guoliang Chen, and Xin Yao. Analysis of computational time of simple estimation of distribution algorithms. *IEEE Trans. Evolutionary Computation*, 14(1):1–22, 2010.

[5] Dogan Corus, Duc-Cuong Dang, Anton V. Eremeev, and Per Kristian Lehre. Level-based analysis of genetic algorithms and other search processes. In *Proceedings of Parallel Problem Solving from Nature - PPSN XIII*, pages 912–921, 2014.

[6] Duc-Cuong Dang and Per Kristian Lehre. Evolution under partial information. In *Genetic and Evolutionary Computation Conference, GECCO'14*, pages 1359–1366, 2014.

[7] Duc-Cuong Dang and Per Kristian Lehre. Efficient optimisation of noisy fitness functions with population-based evolutionary algorithms. In *(To appear) Foundations of Genetic Algorithms XIII, FOGA'15*, 2015.

[8] Stefan Droste. A rigorous analysis of the compact genetic algorithm for linear functions. *Natural Computing*, 5(3):257–283, 2006.

[9] Uriel Feige. On sums of independent random variables with unbounded variance, and estimating the average degree in a graph. In *Proc. of the 36th STOC*, pages 594–603, 2004.

[10] Tobias Friedrich, Timo Kötzing, Martin Krejca, and Andrew M. Sutton. The benefit of sex in noisy evolutionary search. *CoRR*, abs/1502.02793, 2015.

[11] Cristina González, Jose Antonio Lozano, and Pedro Larrañaga. Analyzing the PBIL algorithm by means of discrete dynamical systems. *Complex Systems*, 12:465–479, 2000.

[12] Georges R. Harik, Fernando G. Lobo, and David E. Goldberg. The compact genetic algorithm. *IEEE Trans. Evolutionary Computation*, 3(4):287–297, 1999.

[13] Markus Höhfeld and Günter Rudolph. Towards a theory of population-based incremental learning. In *Proceedings of the IEEE Congress on Evolutionary Computation, CEC 1997*, pages 1–5, 1997.

[14] Thomas Jansen. *Analyzing Evolutionary Algorithms - The Computer Science Perspective.* Natural Computing Series. Springer, 2013.

[15] Pedro Larrañaga and Jose A. Lozano, editors. *Estimation of Distribution Algorithms: A New Tool for Evolutionary Computation*, volume 2 of *Genetic Algorithms and Evolutionary Computation.* Springer, 2002.

[16] Per Kristian Lehre and Carsten Witt. Black-Box Search by Unbiased Variation. *Algorithmica*, 64(4):623–642, 2012.

[17] H. Mühlenbein and G. Paaß. From recombination of genes to the estimation of distributions i. binary parameters. In Hans-Michael Voigt, Werner Ebeling, Ingo Rechenberg, and Hans-Paul Schwefel, editors, *Parallel Problem Solving from Nature - PPSN IV*, volume 1141 of *Lecture Notes in Computer Science*, pages 178–187. Springer Berlin Heidelberg, 1996.

[18] Heinz Mühlenbein. The equation for response to selection and its use for prediction. *Evolutionary Computation*, 5(3):303–346, 1997.

[19] Pietro Simone Oliveto, Jun He, and Xin Yao. Time complexity of evolutionary algorithms for combinatorial optimization: A decade of results. *International Journal of Automation and Computing*, 4(3):281–293, 2007.

[20] Martin Pelikan, Kumara Sastry, and David E. Goldberg. Scalability of the bayesian optimization algorithm. *Int. J. Approx. Reasoning*, 31(3):221–258, 2002.

[21] Jonathan L. Shapiro. Drift and scaling in estimation of distribution algorithms. *Evolutionary Computation*, 13(1):99–123, 2005.

[22] Qingfu Zhang. On the convergence of a factorized distribution algorithm with truncation selection. *Complexity*, 9(4):17–23, 2004.

[23] Qingfu Zhang and Heinz Mühlenbein. On the convergence of a class of estimation of distribution algorithms. *IEEE Trans. Evolutionary Computation*, 8(2):127–136, 2004.

Optimization by Pairwise Linkage Detection, Incremental Linkage Set, and Restricted / Back Mixing: DSMGA-II

Shih-Huan Hsu
Taiwan Evolutionary Intelligence Laboratory
Department of Electrical Engineering
National Taiwan University
r02921076@ntu.edu.tw

Tian-Li Yu
Taiwan Evolutionary Intelligence Laboratory
Department of Electrical Engineering
National Taiwan University
tianliyu@ntu.edu.tw

ABSTRACT

This paper proposes a new evolutionary algorithm, called DSMGA-II, to efficiently solve optimization problems via exploiting problem substructures. The proposed algorithm adopts pairwise linkage detection and stores the information in the form of dependency structure matrix (DSM). A new linkage model, called the incremental linkage set, is then constructed by using the DSM. Inspired by the idea of optimal mixing, the restricted mixing and the back mixing are proposed. The former aims at efficient exploration under certain constrains. The latter aims at exploitation by refining the DSM so as to reduce unnecessary evaluations. Experimental results show that DSMGA-II outperforms LT-GOMEA and hBOA in terms of number of function evaluations on the concatenated/folded/cyclic trap problems, NK-landscape problems with various degrees of overlapping, 2D Ising spin-glass problems, and MAX-SAT. The investigation of performance comparison with P3 is also included.

Categories and Subject Descriptors

I.2 [**Artificial Intelligence**]: Problem Solving, Search.

Keywords

Genetic Algorithm; Estimation-of-Distribution Algorithm; Linkage Learning; Model Building.

1. INTRODUCTION

Since the importance of linkage and problem decomposition has been addressed in the field of evolutionary computation [12], many algorithms that adopt linkage learning have been developed. In 2003, Yu *et al.* [29] borrowed the concept of DSM from the organization theory and proposed DSMGA. One of its key mechanisms is pairwise linkage detection. The linkage information is then stored in a DSM and can be later used to construct different linkage models, such as the building-block (BB) graph [27,28]. In 2010, Thierens *et al.* proposed the optimal mixing operator (OM) and adopted it in the LT-GOMEA [3,22,23]. Unlike most traditional selection-crossover combination in GAs, the decision-making in OM is noise-free and hence results in a much smaller population-sizing requirement than most estimation-of-distribution algorithms. Combined with the linkage-tree model, the linkage tree genetic algorithm (LTGA) family has shown strong optimization ability on a wide range of problems [15,21,24]. However, LT may not be the most proper linkage model for problem decomposition—recent researches involves LT pruning [4,26] and more expressive linkage models such as LN [3]. In this paper, we propose a new evolutionary algorithm. The proposed algorithm adopts the pairwise linkage detection from DSMGA and uses it to construct a new linkage model called the incremental linkage set (ILS). Inspired by the idea of OM, we propose two recombination operators, the restricted and the back mixing. Combining the DSM linkage information, ILS, and the two new mixing operators, the proposed algorithm empirically demonstrates stronger optimization ability than the LT-GOMEA and few other algorithms on the concatenated trap, folded trap, cyclic trap with overlapping, the NK-landscape problems with various degrees of overlapping, Ising spin-glass problems, and MAX-SAT.

The remainder of this paper is organized into three main parts. The first part revisits researches that are directly related to this paper. The second part details DSMGA-II and its operators. The third part describes the experiments and demonstrates the results, and finally conclusion follows.

GECCO '15, July 11 - 15, 2015, Madrid, Spain
© 2015 ACM. ISBN 978-1-4503-3472-3/15/07...$15.00
DOI: http://dx.doi.org/10.1145/2739480.2754737

2. RELATED WORKS

In standard genetic algorithms, problems can be solved effectively and efficiently if solutions are mixed adequately. To match different kinds of problem structures, many techniques for building tunable models have been developed during the past decade. This section describes two important researches that we incorporated in our works.

2.1 Dependency Structure Matrix Genetic Algorithm (DSMGA)

Borrowed from the concept of organization theories, the dependency structure matrix genetic algorithm (DSMGA) utilizes DSM and clustering algorithms to detect interactions among variables. A DSM is essentially an adjacent matrix where each entry represents the pairwise information between two variables. The building-block information is then extracted by clustering the DSM. With the building-block information, DSMGA adopts building-block wise crossover instead of traditional gene-wise crossover. Such mechanisms have shown to be beneficial to the search efficiency due to fewer disruptions of subsolutions.

2.2 Optimal Mixing (OM)

OM was first proposed as the recombination operator of the recombinative/gene-pool optimal mixing evolutionary algorithm [23]. OM applies function evaluation during the recombination and take the change only if the fitness value improves. OM somewhat acts like building-block wise local search with interchangeable models. Models are usually described as the family of subsets (FOS) [23]. An FOS contains subsets of a certain set S. Each subset of FOS may appear more than once. The set S contains all problem variable indexes, *i.e.*, $\{1, 2, \ldots, \ell\}$. An FOS $\mathcal{F}$ can be written as an ordered set $\langle \boldsymbol{F}^1, \boldsymbol{F}^2, \ldots, \boldsymbol{F}^{|\mathcal{F}|} \rangle$ where $\boldsymbol{F}^i \subseteq S$, i $\in \{1, 2, \ldots, |\mathcal{F}|\}$. Moreover, every problem variable index is contained in at least one subset in $\mathcal{F}$ to ensure that every linkage is used in mixing operators. OMEAs are superior to most GAs in many aspects. One of the noticeable properties is that a much smaller population size is required for optimization because of the noise-free decision-making in terms of the population sizing [9]. Furthermore, OM operators are capable of dealing with problems with overlapping structures efficiently with certain FOS [3].

3. DSMGA-II

The following section gives details of the dependency structure matrix genetic algorithm II (DSMGA-II). Roughly speaking, DSMGA-II is the extension of DSMGA combined with the idea of OM and several new operators for improvement. We first introduce its framework. The concept of DSM construction and incremental linkage set are described then, and finally two mixing operators are shown — the restricted mixing and the back mixing. Note that all the algorithms in this paper are assumed to solve maximization problems for ease of expression.

3.1 Framework of DSMGA-II

The major components of DSMGA-II are linkage information retrieval via pairwise detection, expressive linkage model construction, and efficient mixing that balance between exploration and exploitation. The idea of pairwise linkage detection can be backtracked as early as LINC and LIMD [16], and is then adopted during model building in DSMGA. Original LTGA does not adopt pairwise linkage detection until a later work [18] which shows the pairwise approximation outperforms the original. Similar to DSMGA, DSMGA-II adopts pairwise detection due to its resistance of sampling noise. The algorithm first utilizes pairwise linkage detection and stores the information in DSM. After the building-block information is obtained, the mixing operators then proceed with incremental linkage set, which can be seen as a specific type of FOS. In addition, since local search has shown to be beneficial to EDAs [5], a bit-flipping local search operator is therefore performed right after the initialization of population to improve the quality of model building. The DSM is updated at the beginning of each generation with the after-selection population. The selection is tournament selection with the selection pressure 2 according to the suggested results in [31]. To prevent from overfitting due to frequent model building, the algorithm updates DSM once every $O(\ell)$ generations. Note that the population after-selection is only used for updating the DSM; the rest of algorithm proceeds with the original population.

Algorithm 1: DSMGA-II

```
P: population, ℓ: problem size D: DSM, L: incremental
linkage set, R: constant

randomly initialize population P
P ← RunLocalSearch(P)
while ¬ShouldTerminate do
    S ← TournamentSelection(P, s)
    D ← UpdateMatrix(S)
    for k = 1 to R do
        I ← random permutation from 1 to |P|
        for i = 1 to |P| do
            (P_{I_i}, L_s) ← RestrictedMixing(P_{I_i})
            P ← BackMixing(P_{I_i}, L_s)
return the best instance in P
```

The pseudo-code is given in Algorithm 1. Each operator is detailed in the following sections. The population is denoted by $\mathcal{P}$, with the chromosomes $P_1, \ldots, P_{|\mathcal{P}|}$, the problem size is ℓ, and the after-selection population is $\mathcal{S}$. R is a constant proportional to ℓ. The DSM is denoted by $\mathcal{D}$. $\mathcal{I} = \langle I_1, I_2, \ldots I_{|\mathcal{P}|} \rangle$ is a random permutation of $\{1, 2, \ldots |\mathcal{P}|\}$, and the incremental linkage set is denoted by $\mathcal{L}$, which is a set of masks and is elaborated in the following section. Each iteration of the "while" loop corresponds to a generation, and the algorithm terminates when the optimal solution appears.

3.2 Linkage Learning Model: ILS

DSM is a graph representation of the dependency between two variables, where each entry e_{ij} is the measure of dependency between nodes i and j. Entries can be real numbers or integers. The greater the e_{ij} is, the more significant measure between nodes i and j is. Once the matrix is constructed, the information can be interpreted as a graph, where vertices are the variables and edges are the measures of dependency.

Definition 1. (*Maximum-weight connected subgraph*, **MWCS**) *Given an undirected graph $G = (V, E)$ with edge weights $w : E \rightarrow \mathbb{R}$. MWCS is a complete subgraph $G' = (V', E')$ of G, (i.e., $V' \subseteq V$, $E' \subseteq E$, $\forall u, v \in V' \Rightarrow (u, v) \in E'$) such that $\sum_{e \in E'} w(e)$ is maximum.*

In this paper, pairwise dependency is measured by the mutual information [13], which can be calculated as follows:

$$I(X;Y) = \sum_{y \in Y} \sum_{x \in X} p(x, y) \log \frac{p(x, y)}{p(x)\, p(y)} , \quad (1)$$

where X and Y are two random variables, and x and y are outcomes of the random variables respectively. $p(x, y) = p(x)p(y)$ if X and Y are independent, and thus $I(X;Y)$ equals to 0.

Many clustering algorithms for DSM have been proposed. LTGA [22] applies a hierarchical clustering technique with normalized variation of information to build the linkage tree model of population. The clustering technique was further simplified by using pairwise linkage information with average linkage clustering to achieve efficient computation without apparent drawbacks [23].

We simply use mutual information as the dependency measure, which is the same as that of DSMGA. However, instead of clustering variables, we look for a specific subgraph called approximated maximum-weight connected subgraph (AMWCS) to construct the model. The concept of AMWCS is similar to MWCS [1, 14], but AMWCS is constructed by greedy approach. The algorithm initializes an AMWCS from a certain vertex and iteratively adds one vertex that is most related to the current AMWCS into AMWCS with average mutual information. The vertex for insertion in each iteration is chosen by the following equation:

$$j = \underset{j \in C'}{\text{argmax}} \frac{1}{|C|} \sum_{k \in C} I(j, k) , \quad (2)$$

where C is the set of vertices in the current AMWCS and C' is the set of all vertices but those in C.

Definition 2. (*Incremental linkage set*, **ILS**)
ILS is an FOS $\mathcal{F} = \langle \boldsymbol{F}^1, \boldsymbol{F}^2, \ldots, \boldsymbol{F}^{|\mathcal{F}|} \rangle$ *that satisfies* $\forall i, j \in \{1, 2, \ldots, |\mathcal{F}|\},\ i < j \Rightarrow \boldsymbol{F}^i \subset \boldsymbol{F}^j$.

The incremental linkage set is a specific type of FOS which consists of the AMWCSs after every iteration of insertion, thus the size of each element sequentially increases by 1 in this case. According to the results in [27], one of the keys to achieve efficient recombination on problems with overlapping structures is that every pair of building-blocks should have a substantially high enough probability to be mixed. Therefore, a vertex is first randomly chosen as the initial AMWCS. For instance, consider a problem with length 5, and the vertex 3 was randomly chosen from $\{1, 2, 3, 4, 5\}$ at first (Figure 1). After 4 iterations, the vertices were inserted into AMWCS in the order of 3–1–5–4–2, and the incremental linkage set $\mathcal{L} = \langle\{3\}, \{3, 1\}, \{3, 1, 5\}, \{3, 1, 5, 4\}, \{3, 1, 5, 4, 2\}\rangle$. Note that ILS is an ordered set.

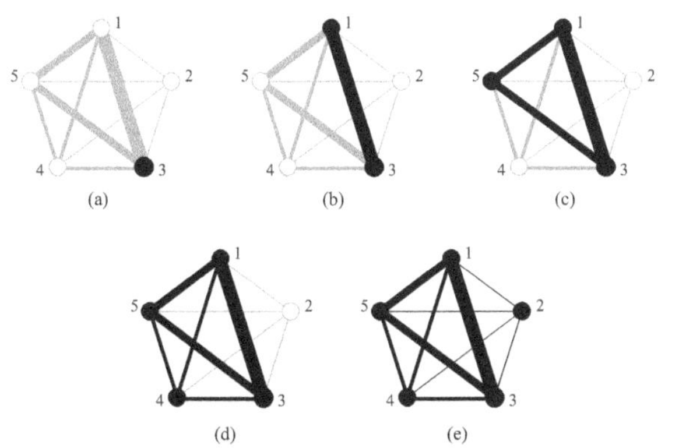

Figure 1: (a) to (e) shows the AMWCS in each iteration. The vertices represent variables and the gray edges represent the dependency measure between pairs. The larger the measure is, the wider the edge is. Black vertices and edges represent the determined AMWCS.

3.3 Restricted and Back Mixing

DSMGA-II adopts two mixing operators: the restricted mixing and the back mixing. Unlike canonical genetic algorithms (GAs), DSMGA-II does not actually generate offspring by recombination of parent solutions. Instead, it applies the restricted mixing to flips bits with the masks. Each mask is essentially a set of indexes that indicates which variables should be considered together during mixing operations. Relatively large mutual information implies that the corresponding bits are different from that of other solutions in current population. In other words, the bit will not be flipped if it converges to the same value. Also, when two solutions exchange subsolutions with certain mask, each allele may not actually vary because of the same subsolutions, especially for the population that is getting on for convergence. Although this drawback may not increase the number of function evaluations (NFE), it is still time-consuming. The flipping process however ensures that every trial is different. To sum up, the restricted mixing starts from choosing a receiver for the trial solution. Subsolutions in the trial solution are flipped with masks in ILS from small size to large size, and the change is preserved if the fitness does not decrease as well as the trial solution is unique in population. Once the solution improves, the restricted mixing terminates.

Moreover, in terms of building-block supply [9], we believe that proper subsolutions exist in current population. Accordingly, the restricted mixing also terminates when the complementary pattern of receiver does not exist in the current population. This can also be seen as a mixing between receiver and the chromosome which contains the complementary pattern of receiver, and this is the reason for calling this operation restricted mixing. The pseudo-code for the restricted mixing is given in Algorithm 2. The population is denoted by $\mathcal{P}$ with problem size ℓ. The incremental linkage set $\mathcal{L} = \langle L_1, L_2, \ldots, L_{|\mathcal{L}|}\rangle$. P_L is the pattern of chromosome P selected with mask L. P'_L is the complementary pattern of P_L. T is the trial solution, and the evaluation function is f. C is the set of vertices in AMWCS.

Algorithm 2: Restricted Mixing

```
𝒫: population, ℓ: problem size,
C: set of vertices in AMWCS
ℒ: incremental linkage set, f: evaluation function,
T: trial solution
Input: P : receiver
AMWCS ← random number from 1 to ℓ
while P'_C ∈ 𝒫 do
    ℒ ← ℒ ∪ C
    join the nearest vertex into AMWCS
for i = 1 to |ℒ| do
    T ← P
    T_{L_i} ← T'_{L_i}
    if f(T) ≥ f(P) and T ∉ 𝒫 then
        P ← T
        return (P, L_i)
```

Figure 2 is an example of the restricted mixing. Consider an ILS, a population $\mathcal{P} = \{P_1, P_2, \ldots, P_5\}$, and a receiver $P = P_4$.

After the restricted mixing finishes, the successfully flipped receiver during the restricted mixing becomes the donor

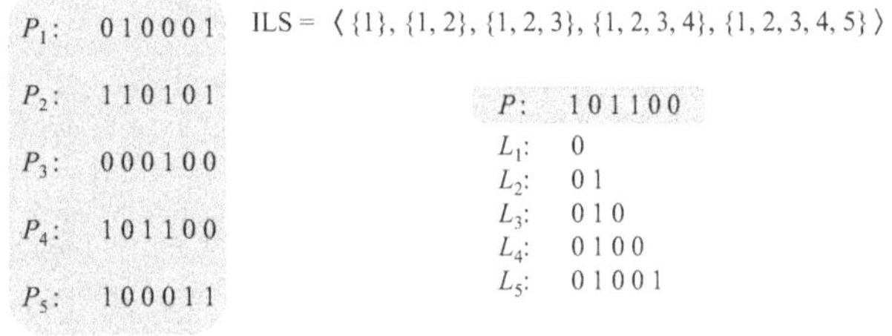

Figure 2: An example of the restricted mixing. Population $\mathcal{P}$ is on the left, and receiver $P = P_4$ is on the right. The complementary pattern with the first mask $\{1\}$ of receiver is 0, which exists in chromosome 1 and 3. With the second mask $\{1, 2\}$, the complementary pattern is 01, which exists in chromosome 1 only, and so on. However, the complementary pattern with the fifth mask $\{1, 2, 3, 4, 5\}$ is 01001, which does not exist in any chromosome of the population. Therefore, the last mask that should be utilized is the fourth one.

Algorithm 3: Back Mixing

$\mathcal{P}$: population, f: evaluation function, T: trial solution
E: set of candidate solutions
Input: D : donor, L: mask

```
improved ← false
for j = 1 to |P| do
    T ← P_j
    T_L ← D_L
    if f(T) > f(P_j) then
        P_j ← T
        improved ← true
    else
        if f(T) = f(P_j) then
            E ← E ∪ {T}
if ¬improved then
    accept all solutions in E
return P
```

---

of the back mixing. Every chromosome in the population is then mixed with the flipped pattern, and the change is adopted only if the fitness is improved. Note that the acceptance criterion is different from the restricted mixing. Real-world problems may contain various landscapes such as plateaus and basins, where solutions are of equal qualities and difficult to explore. Many operators have been developed to deal with such difficulties, such as the forced improvements (FI) [3]. However, diversity issue should be handled carefully. The back mixing tempts to substitute every solution with the same allele fragment, and it causes a strong drift effect if side walks (changes taken for equal fitness) are allowed. In contrast, if the acceptance criterion is set to strict fitness improvement, more evaluations are needed in order to jump out of the plateaus. Either case decreases the performance. Therefore, the acceptance criterion for the back mixing is set to strict fitness improvement as default, and side walks are allowed only if no solution is improved with the default setting during the back mixing. The pseudo-code for the back mixing is given in Algorithm 3.

Note that the implementation is slightly different from the above to alleviate the computational burden. In short, the idea behind this operator is graph refining to reduce unnecessary evaluations. The empirical results suggest that the back mixing is able to deal with both plateaus and diversity issues, which is detailed in Section 4.3.

4. TEST PROBLEMS AND EXPERIMENTS

This section first describes the benchmark problems used in this paper. The setup of the experiments is then given, and followed by experimental results and discussions.

4.1 Optimization Problems

In our research, six types of linkage benchmark problems are considered, including four classic linkage-underlying problems and two real-world problems. In the following context, the number of variables in the test function is referred to as the problem size, denoted by ℓ, and a chromosome is denoted as a vector $\mathbf{x} = (\mathbf{x}_1, \mathbf{x}_2, \ldots, \mathbf{x}_\ell)$.

Concatencted trap

The concatencted trap is composed of m additively separable trap functions, and each of which contains k variables [6]. The number of variables of the concatenated trap function is $m \cdot k$. It is well-known that the problem can only be efficiently solved when the underlying structure is detected and preserved while mixing [25]. Its fitness is as follows:

$$f_{m,k}^{trap}(\mathbf{x}) = \sum_{i=1}^{m} f_k^{trap}\left(\sum_{j=i\cdot k-k+1}^{i\cdot k} \mathbf{x}_j\right), \tag{3}$$

where

$$f_k^{trap}(u) = \begin{cases} 1 & \text{if } u = k, \\ \frac{k-1-u}{k} & \text{otherwise.} \end{cases} \tag{4}$$

Cyclic trap

The cyclic trap is composed of overlapping trap functions with wraparound [30]. The fitness function is given as follows:

$$f_{m,k}^{cyclic}(\mathbf{x}) = \sum_{i=1}^{m} f_k^{trap}\left(\sum_{j=i\cdot(k-1)-k+2}^{i\cdot(k-1)+1} \mathbf{x}_j\right), \tag{5}$$

where

$$f_k^{trap}(u) = \begin{cases} 1 & \text{if } u = k, \\ \frac{k-1-u}{k} & \text{otherwise.} \end{cases} \tag{6}$$

and

$$\mathbf{x}_j = \mathbf{x}_{j-\ell}, \text{ if } \ell < j \leq 2\ell. \tag{7}$$

In the cyclic trap, the linkage information needs to be carefully taken care of. Take a 12-bit cyclic trap with $k = 5$ as an example. Although the size of the subfunction is 5, the fitness of 111110000000 (one correct subsolution, $f = 2.2$) is lower than that of 000000000000 (all incorrect subsolutions, $f = 2.4$). One may of course increases the sizes of masks during recombination; however, the risk of doing so is the increase of the number of trials and hence NFE increases.

Folded trap

There are many variants of folded trap [10], and we use the bipolar deceptive function with $k = 6$ in our experiment.

The folded trap contains two global optima and many local optima. The key difficulty of this problem is that local optima reside on plateaus, and hence the exploration over plateaus needs to be performed. However, unnecessary exploration, such as from $11111*\ldots*$ to $00000*\ldots*$, increases NFE. Additionally, the folded trap is symmetric. Any preference toward 0s or 1s does not help find the global optimum. The fitness function with $k=6$ is described as follows:

$$f^{folded}_{m,k=6}(\mathbf{x}) = \sum_{i=1}^{m} f^{folded}_{k=6}\left(\sum_{j=i\cdot k-k+1}^{i\cdot k} \mathbf{x}_j\right), \quad (8)$$

where

$$f^{folded}_{k=6}(u) = \begin{cases} 1 & \text{if } |u-3| = 3, \\ 0.8 & \text{if } |u-3| = 0, \\ 0.4 & \text{if } |u-3| = 1, \\ 0 & \text{if } |u-3| = 2. \end{cases} \quad (9)$$

NK-landscape

The NK-landscape functions are composed of overlapped, randomly generated subfunctions [20]. There are three parameters of the function: ℓ, k, and s, where ℓ is the problem size, k is the number of neighbors of one gene, and s is the step size, the offset of two adjacent subfunctions. The function of the NK-landscape is given as follows:

$$f^{NK}_{\ell,k,s}(\mathbf{x}) = \sum_{i=0}^{(\ell-k-1)/s} f^{subNK}_{k,i}(\mathbf{x}_{i\cdot s+1}, \mathbf{x}_{i\cdot s+2}, \ldots \mathbf{x}_{i\cdot s+k+1}), \quad (10)$$

where $f^{subNK}_{k,i}$ are subfunctions subject to the constraint that $f^{subNK}_{k,i}(\mathbf{x}) \in [0,1]$ for any valid input $\mathbf{x}$. The NK-landscape functions are commonly considered as general cases of problems due to its random problem landscapes. One may change the degree of overlapping of NK-landscape by varying the step size s.

Ising spin-glass

The Ising spin-glass is a well known problem of statistical mechanics. Given a set of variables that represent spins, each one is in one of two states of $\{+1,-1\}$. For any two adjacent spins i and j, there is an coupling constant J_{ij}. The objective is to find a state of spins called *ground state* for given constants J_{ij} that minimizes the energy of system. The energy (fitness) function is given as follows:

$$f^{spin}_{n}(\mathbf{x}) = -\sum_{i,j=0}^{n} \mathbf{x}_i\mathbf{x}_j J_{ij}\ . \quad (11)$$

We consider a special case of spin-glass in our experiments: The spins are arranged on 2-D grid with each spin interacts with only four nearest neighbors on the grid, and the coupling constants contain only two values, $J_{ij} \in \{+1,-1\}$. Ising spin-glass systems are usually studied due to their particular properties, such as symmetry (*i.e.*, the fitness remains unchanged when swapping 0 and 1) and several plateaus.

MAX-SAT

The maximum satisfiability problem (MAX-SAT) was the first problem proven to be NP-complete. The problem consists of a series of *logical and* clauses, where each clause is a series of *logical or* variables. Each variable represents either a predicate or a negation of a predicate. The MAX-SAT problem can be described as following conjunctive normal form (CNF) formula:

$$F = \bigwedge_{i=1}^{m}\left(\bigvee_{j=1}^{k_i} l_{ij}\right), \quad (12)$$

where m is the number of clauses, k_i is the number of literals in the i-th clause, l_{ij} is the j-th literal in the i-th clause, which corresponds to a gene in the chromosome. The fitness of $\mathbf{x}$ is the number of clauses in F that are satisfied under the interpretation $\mathbf{x}$. For our experiments, we use the Uniform Random-3-SAT instances from SATLIB* with all satisfiable clauses.

4.2 Experiment Setup

Since DSMGA-II incorporates the concepts from DSMGA and OM, it is intuitive to compare DSMGA-II with them. However, original DSMGA [29] does not deal with problems with overlapping structures. Even combined with other techniques [27, 30], DSMGA still cannot rival DSMGA-II and hence is left out in this paper. Concerning GOMEAs, several different linkage models have been proposed [3, 4] since the original one, but the improvements are merely marginal, and LT-GOMEA is still considered as state-of-the-art.

Furthermore, we also compare DSMGA-II with the hierarchical Bayesian optimization algorithm (hBOA) [19] since it is a milestone and is often compared with in recent EDA researches. Finally, the parameter-less population pyramid (P3) [11] has shown outstanding performance and worths comparing with. However, P3 is extraordinary from the traditional EA framework, which makes designing a fair comparison virtually impossible. Hence we leave the comparison to the end of this section.

Traditionally, most researches utilize a bisection procedure [17] to find the minimum population size that is sufficiently large for a certain number of consecutive successful convergences; the required NFE at that population size is then used as the performance measure. However more than often, such minimum population sizing does not yield the minimum NFE as desired, and the differences vary for different algorithms.

For fair comparisons, we adopt an adaptive sweeping procedure to find the minimum NFE. The procedure starts by sweeping the population size through a reasonable range with a predefined step. The average NFE is then recorded over a certain number of consecutive successful hits. If the algorithm fails to converge to the global optimum with the population size, NFE is recorded as infinity. The sweeping range is then narrowed around the population size that yields the minimum NFE with a smaller step. The procedure iterates until the sweeping range becomes small enough. In this paper, the requirement is 10 consecutive successful hits, the initial population size is 10, the initial step size is 30 and then is divided by 2 for each iteration, and procedure terminates when the sweeping range is within 5% of the population size. For each problem, the results are averaged over 100 independent runs.

The experimental settings of algorithms are follows. The selection pressures of DSMGA-II, LT-GOMEA, and hBOA

*http://www.satlib.org/

are set to 2. In DSMGA-II, the model building is performed once every $\ell/50$ generations. In this paper, LT-GOMEA stands for the version with forced improvements [4], implemented by the inventors of GOMEA†. Also, LT-GOMEA is performed without local searcher, because its efficiency evidentially decreases by doing so [2].

For the NK-landscape problem, we choose NK-S1 (the highest degree of overlapping), S3 and S5 (non-overlapping) (*i.e.*, parameter s = 1, 3, 5) with 100 randomly generated instances each, and parameter n is set to 4. In this way, we can check how degrees of overlapping affect the performances of the algorithms. For the concatenated trap and the cyclic trap, the subfunction size k is set to 5, and the k of folded trap is set to 6.

4.3 Results and Discussions

On all problems that we considered, DSMGA-II requires the least NFE than that of others. In the following sections, the results of traditional EAs are detailed at first, and the comparison with P3 is then given.

As shown in Figure 3, the results indicate that the differences between DSMGA-II and others become larger as the degree of overlapping decreases. The back mixing spends a few function evaluations on refining the graph at first. As the linkage information becomes clearer, the correct subsolution stands out, and the back mixing makes it quickly dominate the population. This makes the algorithm more efficient. However, if the problem structures are severely overlapped, the graph refining process is prolonged and thus NFE increases.

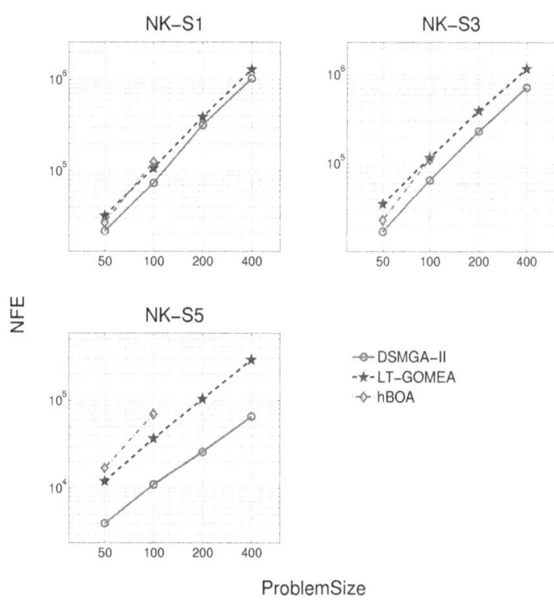

Figure 3: Scalability of DSMGA-II, LT-GOMEA and hBOA on NK-landscape problems with various degrees of overlapping.

The results also demonstrate that DSMGA-II is capable of handling problems with overlapping structures, even for the randomly generated problem landscapes. This is indicative that ILS model expresses overlapping relations well. A possible scenario of model building is shown in the Figure 4.

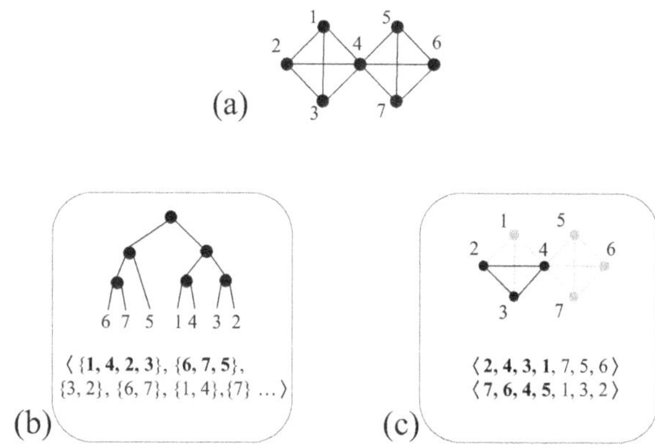

Figure 4: A snapshot of model building. (a) is the real structure of problem with vertex 4 overlapped. (b) is a LT model constructed from (a), and (c) is an ILS model with some possible AMWCS constructing sequences. Both LT and ILS model capture the problem structure. However, mask {4, 5, 6, 7} occurs in ILS within a single generation, while LT can only obtains this mask in later generations by rebuilding the model.

The results of various types of deceptive problems are shown in Figure 5. For the concatenated trap, the slope of DSMGA-II decreases as the problem gets larger.

For the cyclic trap, the scalability of all algorithms appears very similar, with DSMGA-II being lower by a constant factor. As mentioned in Section 4.1, the cyclic trap cannot be solved efficiently merely with the correct problem decomposition. The usage of linkage information is also the key. ILS automatically extends the mask for trials and stops on first successful recombination to avoid spending unnecessary function evaluations, while many other EAs utilize the linkage models determined by certain thresholds, which are sensitive to the parameter settings.

The folded trap contains a large number of local optima that reside on plateaus. Performing an efficient search without losing too much diversity is the key to conquer such difficulty. The back mixing leads to drift of subsolutions as necessary, and the restricted mixing checks if the trial solution is unique in population to keep diversity. DSMGA-II as a result shows the good ability on dealing with attractions without trading efficiency for diversity.

For Ising spin-glass problems, the slope of DSMGA-II decreases as the problem gets larger (Figure 6). This is probably because the problems contain a large number of plateaus, where the advantages of DSMGA-II hold. The overall time spent in fitness evaluations appears to grow polynomially as $O(n^3)$ for DSMGA-II, which is close to the best known results of problem-specific algorithm for Ising sping-glass [7,8]. For MAX-SAT problems, NFE of DSMGA-II still grows exponentially although it requires the fewest function evaluations.

As mentioned before, P3 differs from traditional EAs, and a fair comparison is difficult. P3 does not need a predetermined population size; instead, it increases the population one-by-one when needed until it hits the global optimum.

†http://homepages.cwi.nl/~bosman/source_code.php

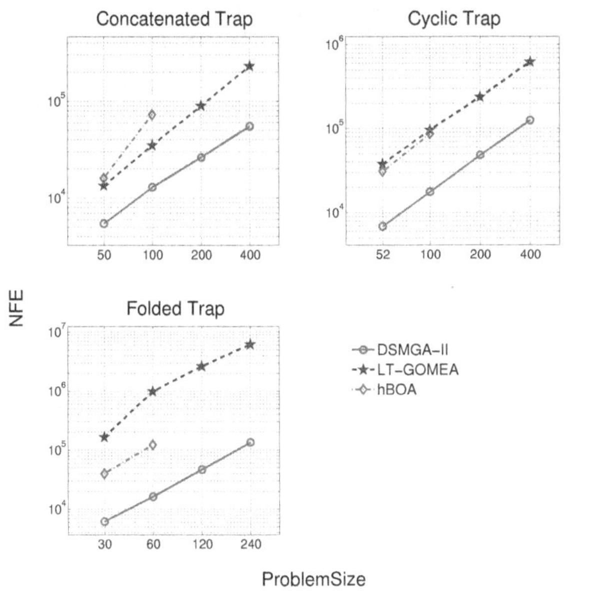

Figure 5: Scalability of DSMGA-II, LT-GOMEA and hBOA on the problems of deceptive variants.

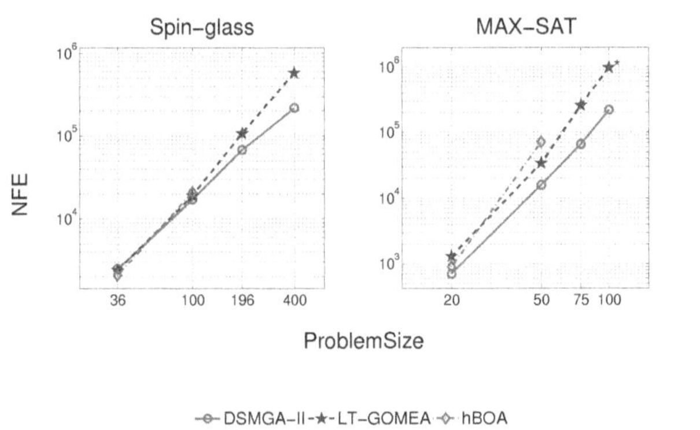

Figure 6: Scalability of DSMGA-II, LT-GOMEA and hBOA on Spin-glass and MAX-SAT (*LT-GOMEA fails to reach the global optima for two instances with $\ell = 100$ on MAX-SAT).

In traditional EA framework, the above situation is similar to a sweeping procedure with step size of 1, and the convergence requirement is merely 1 successful hit of the global optimum. However, this is still not a fair comparison by doing so, since P3 accumulates the NFE, while tradition EA framework does not when determining the population size. To sum up, the requirement of 10 consecutive successful hits favors P3, while merely 1 successful hit favors traditional EAs. Therefore, we cannot figure out a better way to compare DSMGA-II with P3 but listing results under both 10- and 1-hit requirements. Here we only show the results for the largest problems in Table 1.

5. CONCLUSION

This paper proposes a new evolutionary algorithm with linkage learning, called DSMGA-II. Similar to DSMGA, it adopts pairwise linkage detection and stores the information in a DSM. The linkage information is then used to construct a newly proposed linkage model, the incremental linkage set (ILS), which is expressive for problems with both overlapping and non-overlapping structures. Inspired by OM, the restricted mixing and the back mixing are designed to balance between exploration and exploitation. For each receiver, the restricted mixing chooses specific donors according to ILS constructed from the global information instead of random. The back mixing further refines the DSM using promising subsolutions and hence reduces unnecessary function evaluations. Empirical results shows that DSMGA-II outperforms many black-box optimization algorithms such as LT-GOMEA, hBOA and P3 in terms of the number of function evaluations without compromising the scalability on several benchmark problems, including concatenated trap, folded trap, cyclic trap with overlapping, the NK-landscape problems with various degrees of overlapping, Ising spin-glass and MAX-SAT.

As for future work, we would like to test DSMGA-II on problems with hierarchical structures. Also, one may think of several possible improvements, such as modifying the starting position of ILS or the receiver choosing in the back mixing, and we would like to investigate them. Finally, it is important to analyze DSMGA-II from the theoretical perspective to fully understand its strength and weakness.

Our C++ implementation for DSMGA-II is available at http://teilab.ee.ntu.edu.tw/resources/.

Problems	DSMGA-II		P3
	10-hit	1-hit	
Concatenated trap, $\ell = 400$	54	36	71
Cyclic trap, $\ell = 400$	125	66	143
Folded trap, $\ell = 240$	134	117	6831
NK-S1, $\ell = 400$	877	408	1900
NK-S3, $\ell = 400$	537	323	2103
NK-S5, $\ell = 400$	61	53	400
Ising spin-glass, $\ell = 400$	223	159	183
MAX-SAT, $\ell = 100$	208	68	151
			unit: k

Table 1: Required NFE for the largest test problems of DSMGA-II and P3.

6. ACKNOWLEDGMENT

The authors would like to thank the support by Ministry of Science and Technology in Taiwan under Grant No. MOST 103-2221-E-002-177-MY2-1.

7. REFERENCES

[1] E. Álvarez-Miranda, I. Ljubić, and P. Mutzel. *The maximum weight connected subgraph problem.* Springer, 2013.

[2] P. A. Bosman and D. Thierens. The roles of local search, model building and optimal mixing in evolutionary algorithms from a bbo perspective. *Proceedings of the Genetic and Evolutionary Computation Conference (GECCO 2011)*, pages 663–670, 2011.

[3] P. A. Bosman and D. Thierens. Linkage neighbors, optimal mixing and forced improvements in genetic algorithms. *Proceedings of the Genetic and Evolutionary Computation Conference (GECCO 2012)*, pages 585–592, 2012.

[4] P. A. Bosman and D. Thierens. More concise and robust linkage learning by filtering and combining linkage hierarchies. *Proceedings of the Genetic and Evolutionary Computation Conference (GECCO 2013)*, pages 359–366, 2013.

[5] W.-M. Chen, C.-Y. Hsu, T.-L. Yu, and W.-C. Chien. Effects of discrete hill climbing on model building forestimation of distribution algorithms. *Proceedings of the Genetic and Evolutionary Computation Conference (GECCO 2013)*, pages 367–374, 2013.

[6] K. Deb and D. Goldberg. Sufficient conditions for deceptive and easy binary functions. *Annals of Mathematics and Artificial Intelligence*, 10(4):385–408, 1994.

[7] A. Galluccio and M. Loebl. A Theory of Pfaffian Orientations I: Perfect Matchings and Permanents. *The Electronic Journal of Combinatorics*, 1997.

[8] A. Galluccio and M. Loebl. A theory of pfaffian orientations. ii. t-joins, k-cuts, and duality of enumeration. *Electronic Journal of Combinatorics*, 6(1):7, 1999.

[9] D. E. Goldberg, K. Deb, and J. H. Clark. Genetic algorithms, noise, and the sizing of populations. *Complex Systems*, 6:333–362, 1991.

[10] D. E. Goldberg, K. Deb, and J. Horn. Massive multimodality, deception, and genetic algorithms. *Urbana*, 51:61801, 1992.

[11] B. W. Goldman and W. F. Punch. Parameter-less population pyramid. *Proceedings of the Genetic and Evolutionary Computation Conference (GECCO 2014)*, pages 785–792, 2014.

[12] J. H. Holland. *Adaptation in Natural and Artificial Systems*. MIT Press, 1992.

[13] S. Kullback and R. A. Leibler. On information and sufficiency. *The Annals of Mathematical Statistics*, 22(1):79–86, 1951.

[14] H. F. Lee and D. R. Dooly. Decomposition algorithms for the maximum-weight connected graph problem. *Naval Research Logistics (NRL 1998)*, 45(8):817–837, 1998.

[15] N. H. Luong, H. La Poutré, and P. A. Bosman. Multi-objective gene-pool optimal mixing evolutionary algorithms. *Proceedings of the Genetic and Evolutionary Computation Conference (GECCO 2014)*, pages 357–364, 2014.

[16] M. Munetomo and D. E. Goldberg. Identifying linkage groups by nonlinearity/non-monotonicity detection. *Proceedings of the Genetic and Evolutionary Computation Conference (GECCO 1999)*, 1:433–440, 1999.

[17] M. Pelikan. *Hierarchical Bayesian optimization algorithm*. Springer Berlin Heidelberg, 2005.

[18] M. Pelikan, M. W. Hauschild, and D. Thierens. Pairwise and problem-specific distance metrics in the linkage tree genetic algorithm. *Proceedings of the Genetic and Evolutionary Computation Conference (GECCO 2011)*, pages 1005–1012, 2011.

[19] M. Pelikan, M. Pelikan, D. E. Goldberg, and D. E. Goldberg. Hierarchical boa solves ising spin glasses and maxsat. *Proceedings of the Genetic and Evolutionary Computation Conference (GECCO 2003)*, pages 1271–1282, 2003.

[20] M. Pelikan, K. Sastry, D. E. Goldberg, M. V. Butz, and M. Hauschild. Performance of evolutionary algorithms on nk landscapes with nearest neighbor interactions and tunable overlap. *Proceedings of the Genetic and Evolutionary Computation Conference (GECCO 2009)*, pages 851–858, 2009.

[21] K. L. Sadowski, P. A. Bosman, and D. Thierens. On the usefulness of linkage processing for solving max-sat. *Proceedings of the Genetic and Evolutionary Computation Conference (GECCO 2013)*, pages 853–860, 2013.

[22] D. Thierens. The linkage tree genetic algorithm. *Proceedings of Parallel Problem Solving from Nature: Part I (PPSN 2010)*, pages 264–273, 2010.

[23] D. Thierens and P. A. Bosman. Optimal mixing evolutionary algorithms. *Proceedings of the Genetic and Evolutionary Computation Conference (GECCO 2011)*, pages 617–624, 2011.

[24] D. Thierens and P. A. Bosman. Hierarchical problem solving with the linkage tree genetic algorithm. *Proceedings of the Genetic and Evolutionary Computation Conference (GECCO 2013)*, pages 877–884, 2013.

[25] D. Thierens and D. E. Goldberg. Mixing in genetic algorithms. *Urbana*, 51:61801, 1993.

[26] S.-M. Wang, Y.-F. Tung, and T.-L. Yu. Investigation on efficiency of optimal mixing on various linkage sets. *Evolutionary Computation (CEC 2014)*, pages 2475–2482, 2014.

[27] T. Yu, D. E. Goldberg, K. Sastry, C. F. Lima, and M. Pelikan. Dependency structure matrix, genetic algorithms, and effective recombination. *Evolutionary Computation*, 17(4):595–626, 2009.

[28] T.-L. Yu and D. E. Goldberg. Conquering hierarchical difficulty by explicit chunking: Substructural chromosome compression. *Proceedings of the Genetic and Evolutionary Computation Conference (GECCO 2006)*, pages 1385–1392, 2006.

[29] T.-L. Yu, D. E. Goldberg, A. Yassine, and Y.-p. Chen. A genetic algorithm design inspired by organizational theory: Pilot study of a dependency structure matrix driven genetic. *Proceedings of Artificial Neural Networks in Engineering (ANNIE 2003)*, pages 327–332, 2003.

[30] T.-L. Yu, K. Sastry, and D. E. Goldberg. Linkage learning, overlapping building blocks, and systematic strategy for scalable recombination. *Proceedings of the Genetic and Evolutionary Computation Conference (GECCO 2005)*, pages 1217–1224, 2005.

[31] T.-L. Yu, K. Sastry, D. E. Goldberg, and M. Pelikan. Population sizing for entropy-based model building in discrete estimation of distribution algorithms. *Proceedings of the Genetic and Evolutionary Computation Conference (GECCO 2007)*, pages 601–608, 2007.

An Estimation of Distribution Algorithm based on the Natural Gradient and the Boltzmann Distribution

Ignacio Segovia-Domínguez
Center for Research in Mathematics
Guanajuato, México
ijsegoviad@cimat.mx

Arturo Hernández-Aguirre
Center for Research in Mathematics
Guanajuato, México
artha@cimat.mx

ABSTRACT

This paper introduces an Estimation of Distribution Algorithm (EDA), in which the parameters of the search distribution are updated by the natural gradient technique. The parameter updating is guided via the Kullback-Leibler divergence between the multivariate Normal and the Boltzmann densities. This approach makes sense because it is well-known that the Boltzmann function yields a reliable model to simulate particles near to optimum locations.

Three main contributions are presented here in order to build an effective EDA. The first one is a natural gradient formula which allows for an update of the parameters of a density function. These equations are related to an exponential parametrization of the search distribution. The second contribution involves the approximation of the developed gradient formula and its connection to the importance sampling method. The third contribution is a parameter update rule which is designed to control the exploration and exploitation phases of the algorithm.

The proposed EDA is tested on a benchmark of 16 problems and compared versus the XNES and iAMaLGaM algorithms. The statistical results show that the performance of the proposed method is competitive and it is the winner in several problems.

Categories and Subject Descriptors

G.1.6 [**Optimization**]: Unconstrained optimization; G.1.2 [**Approximation**]: Special function approximations; G.3 [**Probability and statistics**]: Multivariate statistics

Keywords

Estimation of Distribution Algorithm, Boltzmann Distribution, Natural Gradient, Optimization

1. INTRODUCTION

A common approach of the Evolutionary Algorithm technique (EA) consists in taking simulations from a statistical function, which fits the optimum locations; e.g. EDAs, ES, IGO, et cetera. In order to improve the search process of the EAs based on statistical models, a large effort has been made to enhance the modelling of the search space [6] [11] [16]. The previous use can be tackled by adding new information into the parameter estimation of density functions. This paper introduces contributions in this trend by building a natural gradient based EDA and developing a Boltzmann based natural gradient.

The EDAs adapt the parameters of a search distribution in order to favour the most promising regions. Thus, the EDA focuses the probability mass around optimum locations. However, it is well-known that this approach presents several issues through the optimization process [11]. For instance, the spread of population is reduced too early and the typical parameter estimation assumes that the individuals have equal probability. Our proposal overcomes the previous issues by adapting the parameter estimation via the natural gradient approach.

The natural gradient approach has been successfully applied to Evolutionary Strategies (ES) and Information Geometric Optimization algorithms (IGO) [4] [6] [18]. These methods adapt the parameters of a search distribution via a vector calculated in the parameter space. This vector, so-called natural gradient, provides the steepest ascent direction of a parameter space with a certain underlying structure. So, the parameter updating ensures the simulation of new individuals in promising regions. A typical natural gradient is pointing to the direction of higher expected fitness. Here, we propose another approach based on the Boltzmann distribution of the fitness function.

This paper presents a new EDA capable of simulating individuals in promising regions. This proposal involves the prediction of the exploration and the exploitation phases; i.e. the enlargement or reduction of the spread of the search distribution according to the gathered information. It is controlled via the natural gradient proposed in this paper. Additionally, the way we adapt a natural gradient into the EDA approach might be transferable to other EAs.

The organization of the paper is as follows. Section 2 provides the basics of the natural gradient approach. Section 3 introduces a Boltzmann based natural gradient. Section 4 develops an estimator for the natural gradient proposed in the previous section. Section 5 presents an EDA based on the natural gradient and the Boltzmann distribution. Section 6 is dedicated to testing the proposed EDA against two algorithms from literature. Finally, Section 7 provides some concluding remarks.

GECCO '15, July 11 - 15, 2015, Madrid, Spain

DOI: http://dx.doi.org/10.1145/2739480.2754803

2. THE NATURAL GRADIENT APPROACH

Many stochastic optimisation methods tackle the black-box optimisation problems, $\mathcal{F}(\vec{x})$, by iteratively updating a density function $Q(\vec{x};\vec{\theta})$, so that any new sample has more chances to improve the fitness values of actual individuals. In this context, the natural gradient provides a straightforward way to adapt the parameters $\vec{\theta}$ of the search distribution $Q(\vec{x};\vec{\theta})$.

THEOREM 1. *The steepest ascent direction of a function $J(\vec{\theta})$ in a Riemannian space is given by*

$$\widetilde{\nabla J}(\vec{\theta}) = G^{-1}(\vec{\theta})\nabla J(\vec{\theta}) \quad (1)$$

where G^{-1} is the inverse of the Riemannian metric tensor G and $\nabla J(\vec{\theta})$ is the conventional gradient.

The direction $\widetilde{\nabla J}(\vec{\theta})$ stated in theorem 1 is usually named as the natural gradient of $J(\vec{\theta})$ in the Riemmanian space [5]. So, any vector calculated by (1) provides the steepest direction of a parameter space with a certain underlying structure. It suggests an iterative procedure to search the optimum on $J(\vec{\theta})$ by an ascent algorithm as follows

$$\vec{\theta}_{t+1} = \vec{\theta}_t + \eta\widetilde{\nabla J}(\vec{\theta}_t), \quad (2)$$

where the step size η might be allowed to change at every iteration [2].

Since the stochastic methods use samples from a density function to optimise the objective function $\mathcal{F}(\vec{x})$, the updating rule presented in Eq. (2) must be adapted accordingly. Firstly, it is known that the Riemmanian structure of the parameter space of a statistical model is defined by its Fisher information matrix $\mathbf{F}$ [3]; i.e. the Riemmanian structure G can be replaced by $\mathbf{F}$. Secondly, the function $J(\vec{\theta})$ to be optimized in the density parameter space must be determined. The Natural Evolution Strategie (NES) method applies a straightforward definition for $J(\vec{\theta})$ by

$$J_E(\vec{\theta}) = \mathbb{E}_Q[\mathcal{F}(\vec{x})] = \int \mathcal{F}(\vec{x})Q(\vec{x};\vec{\theta})\,d\vec{x}. \quad (3)$$

Thus, NES uses a natural gradient to update the parameters of the search distribution in the direction of higher expected fitness. Additionally the gradient of $J_E(\vec{\theta})$ can be written as

$$\nabla_{\vec{\theta}}J_E(\vec{\theta}) = \int \mathcal{F}(\vec{x})[\nabla_{\vec{\theta}}\log Q(\vec{x};\vec{\theta})]\,Q(\vec{x};\vec{\theta})\,d\vec{x} \quad (4)$$

and approximated as

$$\nabla_{\vec{\theta}}J_E(\vec{\theta}) \approx \frac{1}{N}\sum_{k=1}^{N}\mathcal{F}(\vec{x}_k)\nabla_{\vec{\theta}}\log Q(\vec{x}_k;\vec{\theta}) \quad (5)$$

because of the so-called log-likelihood trick and the Monte Carlo approximation [17]. It leads to formulate the natural gradient ascent method by

$$\vec{\theta}_{t+1} = \vec{\theta}_t + \eta\mathbf{F}^{-1}\nabla_{\vec{\theta}}J_E(\vec{\theta}), \quad (6)$$

where $\mathbf{F}$ represents the Fisher information matrix.

Because of Eq. (6) is a valid updating rule to any parametric distribution, it is looks tempting to utilize any available density from literature. But, many parametric distributions do not have a closed-form expression of the Fisher information matrix. On the other hand, even the typical multivariate Gaussian function presents an issue to update the covariance matrix via the natural gradient ascent method. However, a technique to avoid the computation of the Fisher matrix of the multivariate Gaussian distribution is emphasized below because our proposal takes advantage of this idea [9].

Let us assume $Q(\vec{x};\vec{\theta})$ is a multivariate normal density $\mathcal{N}(\vec{\mu},\mathbf{\Sigma})$ and $\mathbf{\Sigma} = \mathbf{C}\mathbf{C}^{\mathsf{T}}$. Also, suppose that $\vec{x}_k = \vec{\mu} + \mathbf{C}\vec{z}_k$ where $\vec{z}_k$ is an outcome of $\mathcal{N}(\mathbf{0},\mathbf{I})$. The idea consists in a suitable transformation of the global coordinate system to a local coordinate system. This change of coordinates causes the actual search distribution $\mathcal{N}(\vec{\mu},\mathbf{\Sigma})$ to match with a standard normal distribution $\mathcal{N}(\mathbf{0},\mathbf{I})$. As a consequence, the updating rule for the parameters is written as

$$(\vec{\delta},\mathbf{L}) \mapsto (\vec{\mu}_{new},\mathbf{C}_{new}) = (\vec{\mu} + \mathbf{C}\vec{\delta}, \mathbf{C}\exp(\mathbf{L}/2)) \quad (7)$$

where 'exp' represents an exponential map between matrices. Note that, if there is no update in the parameter of the density, i.e. $(\vec{\delta} = \mathbf{0}, \mathbf{L} = \mathbf{0})$, then the new parameters are the original ones. Also, the gradient $\nabla_{\vec{\theta}}J_E(\vec{\theta})$ and the natural gradient $\widetilde{\nabla J_E}(\vec{\theta})$ are equal when $\vec{\delta} = \mathbf{0}$ and $\mathbf{L} = \mathbf{0}$. As a consequence, this change of coordinates allows to compute the natural gradient without the calculus of the Fisher information matrix because

$$\nabla_{\vec{\delta}=\mathbf{0}}\log Q(\vec{x};\vec{\delta},\mathbf{L}=\mathbf{0}) = \vec{z} \quad (8)$$

and

$$\nabla_{\mathbf{L}=\mathbf{0}}\log Q(\vec{x};\vec{\delta}=\mathbf{0},\mathbf{L}) = \frac{1}{2}(\vec{z}\vec{z}^{\mathsf{T}} - \mathbf{I}). \quad (9)$$

So, the updating equation for each parameter can be written as follows

$$\vec{\mu}_{new} = \vec{\mu} + \frac{\eta}{N}\mathbf{C}\left(\sum_{k=1}^{N}\mathcal{F}(\vec{x}_k)\cdot\vec{z}\right) \quad (10)$$

$$\mathbf{C}_{new} = \mathbf{C}\exp\left(\frac{\eta}{4N}\sum_{k=1}^{N}\mathcal{F}(\vec{x}_k)\cdot(\vec{z}_k\vec{z}_k^{\mathsf{T}} - \mathbb{I})\right). \quad (11)$$

The previous proposal has been successfully used in evolutionary computation [1] [17] [18]. The next sections develop a new proposal for parameter updating of the Gaussian distribution based on the natural gradient approach and the Boltzmann density.

3. A NATURAL GRADIENT RELATED TO THE BOLTZMANN DENSITY

Equations (10) and (11) produce new parameters according to the direction of higher expected fitness. Additionally this proposal shows interesting characteristics and good performance [15]. However, criticism arises due to the fact that the function $J_E(\vec{\theta})$ can produce unstable estimates mainly because the expected value can be influenced by outliers [4] [6].

Following we propose a function $J(\vec{\theta})$ based on the divergence between the search distribution $Q(\vec{x};\vec{\theta})$ and the Boltzmann density

$$P(\vec{x};\beta) = \frac{\exp(\beta\mathcal{G}(\vec{x}))}{Z_P}. \quad (12)$$

The parameters of Eq. (12) must satisfy that $\beta \geq 0$ and $\mathcal{G}(\vec{x})) \geq 0$. Additionally the normalisation constant Z_P ensures that $P(\vec{x};\beta)$ is a density function.

The Boltzmann density allows for the simulation of samples near optimum locations. It is a very interesting characteristic, but it can not be explicitly used in black-box optimisation because the fitness formula is required in the energy function $\mathcal{G}(\vec{x})$ [11]. A way to overcome this issue consists in approximating the Boltzmann function via a measure between probability distributions. In this context, our proposal is stated in Eq. (13).

$$\begin{aligned} J_D(\vec{\theta}) &= -D_{KL}(Q(\vec{x};\vec{\theta})||P(\vec{x};\beta)) \\ &= -\int Q(\vec{x};\vec{\theta}) \log \frac{Q(\vec{x};\vec{\theta})}{P(\vec{x};\beta)}\, d\vec{x} \end{aligned} \tag{13}$$

The main difference with previous proposals is that another density function is considered. Note that the minus sign is added in order to ensure that $J_D(\vec{\theta})$ is a maximization problem. Although the Kullback-Leibler divergence is used to facilitate the calculus developed below, other measures between probability distributions might be utilized.

The gradient of $J_D(\vec{\theta})$ can be written as

$$\begin{aligned} \nabla_{\vec{\theta}} J_D(\vec{\theta}) &= -\int Q(\vec{x};\vec{\theta}) \nabla_{\vec{\theta}} \log Q(\vec{x};\vec{\theta})\, d\vec{x} \\ &\quad - \int \log Q(\vec{x};\vec{\theta}) \nabla_{\vec{\theta}} Q(\vec{x};\vec{\theta})\, d\vec{x} \\ &\quad + \int \log P(\vec{x};\beta) \nabla_{\vec{\theta}} Q(\vec{x};\vec{\theta})\, d\vec{x} \\ &= -\int [\nabla_{\vec{\theta}} \log Q(\vec{x};\vec{\theta})] Q(\vec{x};\vec{\theta})\, d\vec{x} \\ &\quad - \int \log Q(\vec{x};\vec{\theta}) [\nabla_{\vec{\theta}} \log Q(\vec{x};\vec{\theta})] Q(\vec{x};\vec{\theta})\, d\vec{x} \\ &\quad + \int \log P(\vec{x};\beta) [\nabla_{\vec{\theta}} \log Q(\vec{x};\vec{\theta})] Q(\vec{x};\vec{\theta})\, d\vec{x} \end{aligned} \tag{14}$$

when the so-called log-likelihood trick is used. A final reduction shows a few similarities with the gradient stated in Eq. (4), see Eq. (15).

$$\nabla_{\vec{\theta}} J_D(\vec{\theta}) = \int \log \left(\frac{P(\vec{x};\beta)}{\mathrm{e} \cdot Q(\vec{x};\vec{\theta})} \right) [\nabla_{\vec{\theta}} \log Q(\vec{x};\vec{\theta})] Q(\vec{x};\vec{\theta})\, d\vec{x} \tag{15}$$

The logarithmic function in Eq. (15) is applied on the ratio $P(\vec{x};\beta)/(\mathrm{e} \cdot Q(\vec{x};\vec{\theta}))$, where $\mathrm{e} = \exp(1)$. In fact, it shows a connection with importance sampling technique because the importance weight $P(\vec{x};\beta)/Q(\vec{x};\vec{\theta})$ is embedded in the gradient $\nabla_{\vec{\theta}} J_D(\vec{\theta})$. Also, the logarithmic function associates different weights to each simulation according to the probability of being sampled from the Boltzmann density; only importance weights above $1/\mathrm{e}$ have a positive value. These observations suggest that $\nabla_{\vec{\theta}} J_D(\vec{\theta})$ has a completely different performance in comparison with $\nabla_{\vec{\theta}} J_E(\vec{\theta})$.

Although $\nabla_{\vec{\theta}} J_D(\vec{\theta})$ is defined for any search distribution $Q(\vec{x};\vec{\theta})$, a few issues might arise when applying the provided formula. The next section presents an efficient way to estimate the natural gradient w.r.t $J_D(\vec{\theta})$ based on the importance sampling technique, the Monte Carlo method and an exponential parameterization.

4. THE NATURAL GRADIENT ESTIMATION

Despite the described $\nabla_{\vec{\theta}} J_E(\vec{\theta})$ and $\nabla_{\vec{\theta}} J_D(\vec{\theta})$ come from different sources, both gradients show strong similarities and straightforward connections. In fact, the only difference between these is the factor-term which multiplies $\nabla_{\vec{\theta}} \log Q(\vec{x};\vec{\theta}) \cdot Q(\vec{x};\vec{\theta})$. Following a natural gradient estimator is proposed, which takes advantage of these connections, and a graphical comparison is performed versus a typical approach.

Before providing an estimate for $\nabla_{\vec{\theta}} J_D(\vec{\theta})$ an issue must be tackled: the normalization constant Z_P of the Boltzmann density is unknown, mainly because the energy function $\mathcal{G}(\vec{x})$ depends on the unknown fitness function $\mathcal{F}(\vec{x})$. In this case, a trick based on importance sampling without normalisation can be used.

Let us write the involved density functions as $P(\vec{x};\beta) = \widetilde{P}(\vec{x};\beta)/Z_P$ and $Q(\vec{x};\vec{\theta}) = \widetilde{Q}(\vec{x};\vec{\theta})/Z_Q$, where $\widetilde{P}(\vec{x};\beta) = \exp(\beta\mathcal{G}(\vec{x}))$, $Q(\vec{x};\vec{\theta}) \propto \widetilde{Q}(\vec{x};\vec{\theta})$, $\int \widetilde{Q}(\vec{x};\vec{\theta})\, d\vec{x} = Z_Q > 0$ and $\int \widetilde{P}(\vec{x};\beta)\, d\vec{x} = Z_P > 0$. Here, the ratio $P(\vec{x};\beta)/Q(\vec{x};\vec{\theta})$ is expressed as

$$\begin{aligned} \frac{P(\vec{x};\beta)}{Q(\vec{x};\vec{\theta})} &= \left(\frac{Z_Q}{Z_P}\right) \widetilde{W}(\vec{x};\vec{\theta},\beta) \\ &= \left(\frac{1}{\int \widetilde{W}(\vec{x};\vec{\theta},\beta) Q(\vec{x};\vec{\theta})\, d\vec{x}} \right) \widetilde{W}(\vec{x};\vec{\theta},\beta) \end{aligned} \tag{16}$$

where $\widetilde{W}(\vec{x};\vec{\theta},\beta) = \widetilde{P}(\vec{x};\beta)/\widetilde{Q}(\vec{x};\vec{\theta})$ [12]. Since the samples $\vec{x}_1, ..., \vec{x}_k, ..., \vec{x}_N \sim Q(\vec{x};\vec{\theta})$ then the Monte Carlo method allows to approximate equation (16) as

$$\frac{P(\vec{x};\beta)}{Q(\vec{x};\vec{\theta})} \approx \frac{\widetilde{W}(\vec{x};\vec{\theta},\beta)}{\frac{1}{N}\sum_{k=1}^{N} \widetilde{W}(\vec{x}_k;\vec{\theta},\beta)}. \tag{17}$$

Eq. (17) provides a simple way to avoid the computation of the normalisation constant Z_P. In the same vein Eq. (15) can be approximated via the Monte Carlo technique because of the last term $Q(\vec{x};\vec{\theta})$ [14]. With this in mind, let us express the approximation for $\nabla J_D(\vec{\theta})$ as follows

$$\nabla_{\vec{\theta}} J_D(\vec{\theta}) \approx \frac{1}{N}\sum_{i=1}^{N} \log \left(\frac{N \cdot \widetilde{W}(\vec{x}_i;\vec{\theta},\beta)}{\mathrm{e} \cdot \sum_{k=1}^{N} \widetilde{W}(\vec{x}_k;\vec{\theta},\beta)} \right) \nabla_{\vec{\theta}} \log Q(\vec{x}_i;\vec{\theta}). \tag{18}$$

A first glance over the estimates in Equations (5) and (18) suggests a slight difference in computational complexity. Furthermore the estimate of $\nabla J_D(\vec{\theta})$ introduces an extra parameter β which plays an important role in stochastic optimisation. Below a further analysis is developed by choosing a multivariate normal density as the search distribution $Q(\vec{x};\vec{\theta})$.

4.1 The multivariate Normal distribution

Although the developed approximation for $\nabla J_D(\vec{\theta})$ works to any parametric search distribution, the special case with respect to a multivariate Gaussian function deserves extra attention.

Please assume that $Q(\vec{x};\vec{\theta}) = \mathcal{N}(\vec{x};\vec{\mu},\mathbf{\Sigma})$, then the function $\widetilde{W}(\vec{x};\vec{\mu},\mathbf{\Sigma},\beta)$ can be expressed as

$$\begin{aligned} \widetilde{W}_{\mathcal{N}}(\vec{x}) &= \widetilde{W}(\vec{x};\vec{\mu},\mathbf{\Sigma},\beta) \\ &= \exp\left(\beta\mathcal{G}(\vec{x}) + \frac{1}{2}(\vec{x}-\mu)^{\mathsf{T}}\mathbf{\Sigma}^{-1}(\vec{x}-\mu) \right). \end{aligned} \tag{19}$$

So, the logarithmic function in Eq. (18) is applied on exponential terms. Although it seems that the numerical limits could be exceeded when the exponential term is calculated, a further analysis shows stability computation up to dimension $d = 100$. Let us consider that the maximum exponent-value to avoid numerical issues is above 300, i.e. exp(300) still is a valid number to be computed, despite it depending on the machine-precision. Since the power in $\widetilde{W}_{\mathcal{N}}(\vec{x})$ consists of $\beta\mathcal{G}(\vec{x})$ and $\frac{1}{2}(\vec{x}-\mu)^{\mathsf{T}}\mathbf{\Sigma}^{-1}(\vec{x}-\mu)$, each term must be separately analysed. Notice that $(\vec{x}-\mu)^{\mathsf{T}}\mathbf{\Sigma}^{-1}(\vec{x}-\mu) \sim \chi^2_{(d)}$; thus if $d = 100$ it is very unlikely to get a value above 300. On the other hand, the energy function $\mathcal{G}(\vec{x})$ is intimately related to the fitness function $\mathcal{F}(\vec{x})$, which means that large values of the fitness function might produce large energy values. To avoid this issue the next energy function is proposed

$$\mathcal{G}(\vec{x}_k) = \frac{g(\vec{x}_k)}{\max(g(\vec{x}_1), ..., g(\vec{x}_N))} \quad \text{where } g(\vec{x}_k) = \mathcal{F}(\vec{x}_k) - \min(\mathcal{F}(\vec{x}_1), ..., \mathcal{F}(\vec{x}_N)). \tag{20}$$

Note that the maximum value for $\mathcal{G}(\vec{x}_k)$ according to Eq. (20) is 1. As a consequence, only the parameter β might produce a power above 300. Thus, we strongly recommend $\beta \leq 50$ in order to avoid numerical issues (anyway in practical applications this value for β is not an issue).

Another consequence of the similarities between the natural gradient discussed in Section 2 and our proposal, is that the latest can also avoid the computation of the Fisher information matrix. So, recalling the discussed change of coordinate system, then the term $\nabla_{\vec{\theta}} \log Q(\vec{x};\vec{\theta})$ in Eq. (18) is reduced as in Equations (8) and (9). It allows us to write the updating equations for each parameter as

$$\vec{\mu}_{new} = \vec{\mu} + \frac{\eta}{N}\mathbf{C}\left(\sum_{i=1}^{N} \log\left(\frac{N \cdot \widetilde{W}_{\mathcal{N}}(\vec{x}_i)}{\mathrm{e} \cdot \sum_{k=1}^{N} \widetilde{W}_{\mathcal{N}}(\vec{x}_k)}\right) \cdot \vec{z}_i\right) \tag{21}$$

and

$$\mathbf{C}_{new} = \mathbf{C}\exp\left(\frac{\eta}{4N}\sum_{i=1}^{N} \log\left(\frac{N \cdot \widetilde{W}_{\mathcal{N}}(\vec{x}_i)}{\mathrm{e} \cdot \sum_{k=1}^{N} \widetilde{W}_{\mathcal{N}}(\vec{x}_k)}\right)(\vec{z}_i\vec{z}_i^{\mathsf{T}} - \mathbf{I})\right) \tag{22}$$

where $\mathbf{\Sigma} = \mathbf{C}\mathbf{C}^{\mathsf{T}}$, $\vec{z}_i = \mathbf{C}^{-1}(\vec{x}_i - \vec{\mu})$, $\widetilde{W}_{\mathcal{N}}(\vec{x}_i)$ is defined in Eq. (19) and the step size should satisfy $\eta \geq 0$.

4.2 A graphical comparison

This section is dedicated to graphically analysing the behaviour of two natural gradients: 1) the developed by expected fitness, and 2) our proposal based on the divergence Kullback-Leibler between the Gaussian and the Boltzmann distributions.

Among the typical natural gradient approaches in literature, the exponential natural evolution strategy (XNES) is selected for a visual comparison [9]. This method computes the natural gradient via an exponential parameterization of the multivariate Gaussian distribution. Also, it utilises a rank-based utility function $\mathcal{U}(\vec{x})$ instead of the usual fitness function $\mathcal{F}(\vec{x})$; which is a notable difference versus our proposal.

The experiments are performed on the Sphere problem; notice that a change of sign must be applied in order to effectively use the Eq. (20). The simulation procedure randomly generates 300 particles, i.e. the sample size is $N = 300$.

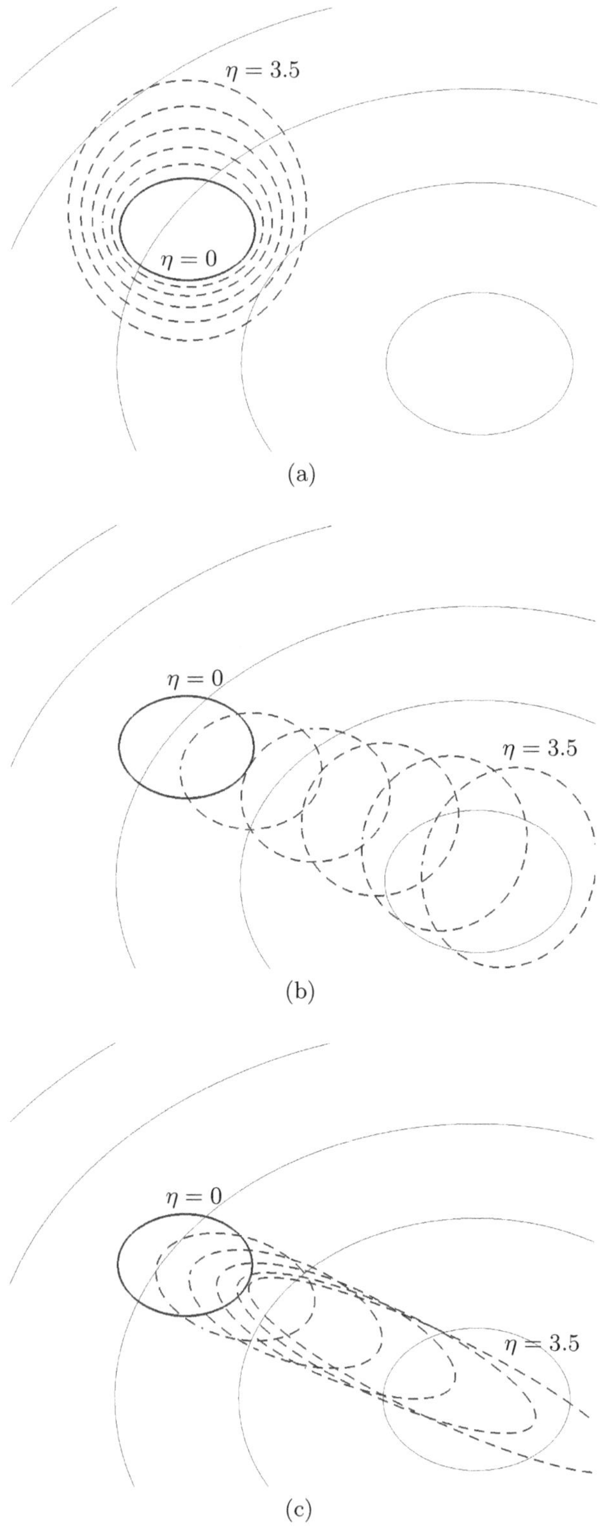

Figure 1: Examples of Gaussian Densities obtained by two different Natural Gradients. Top two Figures come from our approach. (a) $\widetilde{\nabla J}_D(\vec{\theta})$ with $\beta = 1/10$. (b) $\widetilde{\nabla J}_D(\vec{\theta})$ with $\beta = 10$. (c) $\widetilde{\nabla J}_E(\vec{\theta})$ from xNES.

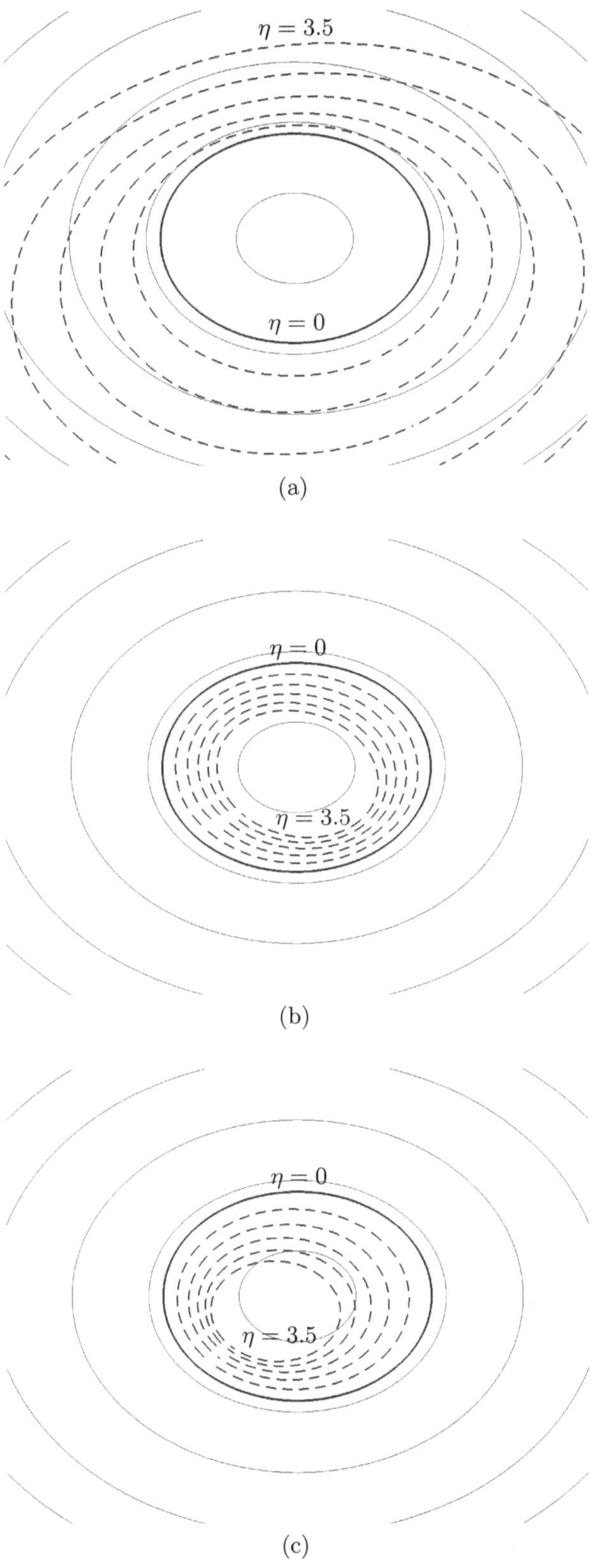

Figure 2: Examples of Gaussian Densities obtained by two different Natural Gradients. Top two Figures come from our approach. (a) $\widetilde{\nabla J}_D(\vec{\theta})$ with $\beta = 1/10$. (b) $\widetilde{\nabla J}_D(\vec{\theta})$ with $\beta = 10$. (c) $\widetilde{\nabla J}_E(\vec{\theta})$ from xNES.

Two different experiments were executed: 1) sampling at a medium distance from the global optimum, and 2) sampling around the global optimum. Figures 1 and 2 show the obtained parameters using different step sizes in the direction of the natural gradients. Following, the results of both experiments are commented on in detail.

Experiment 1
Initial parameters: $\vec{\mu} = [-5, 3]^\mathsf{T}$ and $\mathbf{\Sigma} = \mathbf{I}$.
Figure 1 shows the results of this experiment. Figures 1-(b) and 1-(c) look similar because the parameter $\beta = 10$ encourages the reduction of the spread of the Boltzmann density and tends to focus the probability mass around the best individuals. It is contrary to the observations in Figure 1-(a) where a larger step size enlarges the covariance matrix of the Gaussian distribution. Also, these observations are interesting because they mean that our proposal can modify the parameters in a similar way to the classic natural gradient of expected fitness.

Experiment 2
Initial parameters: $\vec{\mu} = [0, 0]^\mathsf{T}$ and $\mathbf{\Sigma} = \mathbf{I}$.
Figure 2 shows the results of this experiment. Once again Figures 2-(b) and 2-(c) show similar behaviour; both are focusing the Gaussian distribution on a smaller area around the global optimum. On the other hand, the parameter $\beta = 1/10$ encourages the increment of the spread of the Boltzmann density. As a consequence, in Figure 2-(a) the multivariate Gaussian distribution covers a bigger area according to the step size. This behaviour might be very useful to avoid being trapped in local optimum locations.

The previous experiments suggest that our proposal is capable of managing the exploration and exploitation phases. Note that, it is a desirable attribute to build effective evolutionary algorithms and maintain the diversity of the population [8] [16]. The next section is dedicated to building an Estimation of Distribution Algorithm (EDA) based on the natural gradient developed through the previous sections.

5. THE NATURAL GRADIENT BASED EDA

The Estimation of Distribution Algorithms (EDAs) fit a multivariate density function on regions near optimum locations; so that any new sample might be near the global optimum. However, it is well-known that the EDA approach might reduces the spread of population too early [13]. The EDA presented below deals with similar issues by effectively using the gathered information through the optimisation process. In addition, some of the ideas presented here can be applied in the general EDA context.

This section introduces our proposal named Natural Gradient based Estimation of Distribution Algorithm (NAGEDA), see Figure 3. The algorithm exploits the developed updating rules for the parameters $\vec{\mu}$ and $\mathbf{\Sigma} = \mathbf{C}\mathbf{C}^\mathsf{T}$. The central idea consists in the computation of a search distribution capable of predicting the location of optimum regions. Here, the Natural Gradient estimator developed in sections 3 and 4 plays an important role.

The NAGEDA starts with a random population, which is utilised to compute the fitness values $\mathcal{F}(\vec{x}_i)$ and the energy values $\mathcal{G}(\vec{x}_i)$. Note that Eq. (20) is a valid formula to find the maximum values of the fitness function $\mathcal{F}(\vec{x})$. But, the minimization problems should be attained via $\mathcal{F}(\vec{x}) =$

$-\mathcal{F}(\vec{x})$. Then, the whole set of individuals $\mathcal{P}^{(t)}$ is used to compute the maximum likelihood estimates $\vec{\mu}$ and $\mathbf{\Sigma}$. Additionally, a repair technique is applied to the estimate $\mathbf{\Sigma}$, line 7. This technique replaces the eigenvalues below 10^{-100} by setting the minimum value to 10^{-100}; as a consequence the matrix $\mathbf{\Sigma}$ is built again. Next, the initial matrix $\mathbf{C}$ is computed via a singular value decomposition of $\mathbf{\Sigma}$. It allows for the estimate of the vectors $\vec{z}_i$; note that $\vec{z} \sim \mathcal{N}(\mathbf{0}, \mathbf{I})$. Hence, the proposed natural gradient is computed to update the parameters $\vec{\mu}$ and $\mathbf{\Sigma}$, line 10. Next, new individuals are simulated from the updated multivariate Gaussian density. Since the set $\mathcal{P}_S^{(t)}$ could have better individuals than the actual population, the next population $\mathcal{P}^{(t+1)}$ is chosen by $\mathcal{P}^{(t)} \cup \mathcal{P}_S^{(t)}$. This step adds the necessary selective pressure to maintain the improvement of the population. This algorithm only needs to update the variables β and η, but an auto-adaptive rule is added for this purpose, lines 16-24.

```
1: Initialize t ← 0, N, S_s, β ← 10 and η ← 1/10
2: P^(t) ← U(Domain)                              ▷ First population
3: Evaluate F(x_i)
4: Compute G(x_i) by Eq. (20)
5: while (Stop condition is not reached) do
6:     Estimate μ and Σ via maximum likelihood
7:     Σ ← RepairMethod(Σ)
8:     Compute [U, S^2, U^T] = Σ and C = U(S^2)^(1/2)
9:     Compute z_i = C^(-1)(x_i − μ)
10:    Estimate μ_new and C_new by Eq. (21)-(22)
11:    P_S^(t) ← S_s individuals from Q(x; μ_new, C_new C_new^T)
12:    P_S^(t) ← Reinsertion(P_S^(t))
13:    Evaluate F(x_j) and G(x_j) of P_S^(t)
14:    P^(t+1) ← Best N individuals of P^(t) ∪ P_S^(t)
15:    M_s ← |P^(t+1) ∩ P_S^(t)|                  ▷ Number of survivors
16:    ε = | M_s/S_s − 0.5 |                      ▷ Absolute value-factor
17:    if 2M_s > S_s then                         ▷ Exploitation
18:        η = (1 + ε)η
19:        β = 10
20:    else                                       ▷ Exploration
21:        η = η/(1 + ε)
22:        β = 1/10
23:    end if
24:    if η ≤ 10^(-300) then η = 1 end if
25:    t ← t + 1
26: end while
27: Return the elite individual in P^(t)
```

Figure 3: Pseudocode of the proposed EDA: Natural Gradient based Estimation of Distribution Algorithm (NAGEDA).

The auto-adaptive rule for the variables β and η is based on the intersection between the sets $\mathcal{P}^{(t+1)}$ and $\mathcal{P}_S^{(t)}$. The number of survivors M_s is the number of new samples that are preserved from the current generation to the next one. This quantity allows for the control of the exploration and exploitation phases. If most of the new simulations are within the next population, the algorithm changes to the exploitation phase, contrary to an unsuccessful sampling. In addition, the step size of the natural gradient estimate is also adapted according to the number of survivor individuals. Here, the η value is increased in the exploitation phase, opposite to the exploration phase.

Since the simulation method might build samples outside the search domain, a re-insertion technique is added, line 12. Let $\gamma_k = l_k^{upper} - l_k^{lower}$ be the domain length in dimension k, where l_k^{upper} and l_k^{lower} are the upper bound and lower bound in dimension k. For each dimension, the new sample $\vec{y} = (y_1, \cdots, y_k, \cdots, y_d)$ is tested/replaced by

- if $y_k > l_k^{upper}$ then $a = (y_k - l_k^{upper})/\gamma_k$ and $y_k = l_k^{upper} - \gamma_k(a - \lfloor a \rfloor)$
- if $y_k < l_k^{lower}$ then $a = (l_k^{lower} - y_k)/\gamma_k$ and $y_k = l_k^{lower} + \gamma_k(a - \lfloor a \rfloor)$

which ensures any new individual is inside the domain.

An empirical study of NAGEDA suggests that its performance dependens on the population size N. We found an equation to increase N according to the dimension size d. Similar to well-known literature [7], a regression method is applied to obtain the equation $N = \exp(\lambda + 0.01 \cdot d) \cdot d$; where the best value for λ depends on the problem. Here we suggest $\lambda = 1.4$ for unimodal problems, $\lambda = 1.5$ for multimodal problems and $\lambda = 1.9$ for the Rosenbrock problem. Since the sample size is not as critical as the population size, the chosen sample size is $S_s = \lceil M_s/5 \rceil$.

6. EXPERIMENTS

This section is dedicated to testing our algorithm versus two state of the art methods: 1) the exponential Natural Evolution Strategy (xNES), and 2) the Incremental Adapted Maximum-Likelihood Gaussian Model Iterated Density Estimation Evolutionary Algorithm (iAMaLGaM) [9] [7]. The first algorithm applies the natural gradient approach in evolutionary strategies, while the second one is capable of adapting the multivariate Gaussian density in an efficient way to avoid premature convergence.

$\mathcal{F}$	NAME	U/M	$\mathcal{F}(\vec{x}^*)$	x_i^*	DOMAIN
$\mathcal{F}_1$	Sphere	U	0	0	$x_i \in [-600, 300]^d$
$\mathcal{F}_2$	Schwefel 1.2	U	0	0	$x_i \in [-20, 10]^d$
$\mathcal{F}_3$	Trid	U	Λ_f	Λ_x	$x_i \in [-d^2, d^2]^d$
$\mathcal{F}_4$	Zakharov	U	0	0	$x_i \in [-20, 10]^d$
$\mathcal{F}_5$	Ellipsoid	U	0	0	$x_i \in [-20, 10]^d$
$\mathcal{F}_6$	Cigar Tablet	U	0	0	$x_i \in [-20, 10]^d$
$\mathcal{F}_7$	Two Axes	U	0	0	$x_i \in [-20, 10]^d$
$\mathcal{F}_8$	Exponential	U	-1	0	$x_i \in [-1, 0.5]^d$
$\mathcal{F}_9$	Rosenbrock	M	0	1	$x_i \in [-20, 10]^d$
$\mathcal{F}_{10}$	Ackley	M	0	0	$x_i \in [-20, 10]^d$
$\mathcal{F}_{11}$	Griewangk	M	0	0	$x_i \in [-600, 300]^d$
$\mathcal{F}_{12}$	Cos. Mixture	M	$-0.1d$	0	$x_i \in [-1, 0.5]^d$
$\mathcal{F}_{13}$	Levy-Montalvo 1	M	0	-1	$x_i \in [-20, 10]^d$
$\mathcal{F}_{14}$	Levy-Montalvo 2	M	0	1	$x_i \in [-20, 10]^d$
$\mathcal{F}_{15}$	Levy 8	M	0	-1	$x_i \in [-20, 10]^d$
$\mathcal{F}_{16}$	Bohachevsky	M	0	0	$x_i \in [-20, 10]^d$

Table 1: Search domain, modality (U/M), global minimum and names of the test problems [10]. The expressions $\Lambda_f = -d(d+4)(d-1)/6$ and $\Lambda_x = i(d+1-i)$ are taken when $\mathcal{F}_3$ is in use.

A suitable set of problems is chosen in order to perform an adequate comparison, see Table 1. The source code is provided by the homepage of the authors. So, the parameters of each competitor-algorithm are the default ones. The experiments contrast the error $\mathcal{F} - \mathcal{F}^*$ reached for each method,

$\mathcal{F}$	NAGEDA	xNES	ρ
$\mathcal{F}_1$	**100.00**	**100.00**	
	9.05e-9±8.00e-10	8.81e-9±1.09e-9	1.95e-1
	3.62e+4±2.51e+2	5.98e+4±5.81e+2	**1.00e-4**
$\mathcal{F}_2$	**100.00**	**100.00**	
	8.95e-9±9.47e-10	8.97e-9±9.25e-10	8.96e-1
	2.94e+4±3.52e+2	5.60e+4±6.00e+2	**1.00e-4**
$\mathcal{F}_3$	**100.00**	**100.00**	
	8.87e-9±7.82e-10	9.03e-9±8.15e-10	3.14e-1
	3.73e+4±3.08e+2	6.19e+4±4.63e+2	**1.00e-4**
$\mathcal{F}_4$	**100.00**	**100.00**	
	8.76e-9±9.38e-10	9.07e-9±7.20e-10	6.80e-2
	2.98e+4±4.04e+2	6.80e+4±3.11e+3	**1.00e-4**
$\mathcal{F}_5$	**100.00**	94.00	
	8.72e-9±1.09e-9	1.58e-8±3.38e-8	1.22e-1
	3.84e+4±2.83e+2	1.31e+5±0.00e+0	**1.00e-4**
$\mathcal{F}_6$	**100.00**	0.00	
	9.02e-9±8.39e-10	2.61e+0±3.74e+0	**1.00e-4**
	3.99e+4±3.53e+2	3.00e+5±0.00e+0	**1.00e-4**
$\mathcal{F}_7$	**100.00**	0.00	
	8.84e-9±1.06e-9	1.05e+2±6.16e+1	**1.00e-4**
	3.97e+4±3.49e+2	3.00e+5±0.00e+0	**1.00e-4**
$\mathcal{F}_8$	**100.00**	74.00	
	8.90e-9±1.02e-9	1.58e-1±2.70e-1	**2.00e-4**
	2.13e+4±2.22e+2	1.40e+5±0.00e+0	**1.00e-4**
$\mathcal{F}_9$	**100.00**	**100.00**	
	8.75e-9±9.96e-10	9.13e-9±8.32e-10	**3.96e-2**
	1.18e+5±3.76e+3	**1.06e+5±5.37e+3**	**1.00e-4**
$\mathcal{F}_{10}$	**100.00**	**100.00**	
	9.26e-9±6.02e-10	9.50e-9±5.06e-10	**3.40e-2**
	5.49e+4±2.68e+2	9.13e+4±5.62e+2	**1.00e-4**
$\mathcal{F}_{11}$	**100.00**	**100.00**	
	8.52e-9±1.09e-9	9.11e-9±6.95e-10	**3.00e-3**
	3.67e+4±3.38e+2	5.39e+4±4.30e+2	**1.00e-4**
$\mathcal{F}_{12}$	**100.00**	28.00	
	8.91e-9±1.05e-9	1.70e+0±2.07e+0	**1.00e-4**
	2.89e+4±6.58e+2	2.38e+5±0.00e+0	**1.00e-4**
$\mathcal{F}_{13}$	**100.00**	**100.00**	
	8.76e-9±9.62e-10	9.09e-9±7.72e-10	6.61e-2
	2.65e+4±1.20e+3	4.39e+4±4.71e+2	**1.00e-4**
$\mathcal{F}_{14}$	**100.00**	**100.00**	
	8.99e-9±8.97e-10	8.89e-9±9.86e-10	5.71e-1
	2.92e+4±2.82e+2	4.93e+4±4.85e+2	**1.00e-4**
$\mathcal{F}_{15}$	**100.00**	**100.00**	
	9.12e-9±8.55e-10	8.91e-9±8.95e-10	2.28e-1
	2.91e+4±1.56e+3	4.81e+4±4.41e+2	**1.00e-4**
$\mathcal{F}_{16}$	**100.00**	82.00	
	8.94e-9±7.49e-10	1.52e-1±3.51e-1	**3.50e-3**
	3.64e+4±3.88e+2	1.06e+5±0.00e+0	**1.00e-4**

Table 2: Comparison between NAGEDA (our approach) and xNES methods in 30 dimensions. The winner is marked in boldface according to a non-parametric bootstrap test. Further details in section 6.

$\mathcal{F}$	NAGEDA	iAMaLGaM	ρ
$\mathcal{F}_1$	**100.00**	**100.00**	
	9.05e-9±8.00e-10	8.88e-9±8.03e-10	2.85e-1
	3.62e+4±2.51e+2	3.85e+4±5.11e+2	**1.00e-4**
$\mathcal{F}_2$	**100.00**	**100.00**	
	8.95e-9±9.47e-10	8.92e-9±1.00e-9	8.69e-1
	2.94e+4±3.52e+2	3.15e+4±4.52e+2	**1.00e-4**
$\mathcal{F}_3$	**100.00**	**100.00**	
	8.87e-9±7.82e-10	8.65e-9±1.18e-9	2.65e-1
	3.73e+4±3.08e+2	4.01e+4±6.22e+2	**1.00e-4**
$\mathcal{F}_4$	**100.00**	**100.00**	
	8.76e-9±9.38e-10	8.87e-9±8.47e-10	5.23e-1
	2.98e+4±4.04e+2	3.31e+4±4.61e+2	**1.00e-4**
$\mathcal{F}_5$	**100.00**	**100.00**	
	8.72e-9±1.09e-9	9.05e-9±7.94e-10	8.26e-2
	3.84e+4±2.83e+2	4.54e+4±1.94e+3	**1.00e-4**
$\mathcal{F}_6$	**100.00**	**100.00**	
	9.02e-9±8.39e-10	8.88e-9±8.19e-10	3.75e-1
	3.99e+4±3.53e+2	4.70e+4±2.00e+3	**1.00e-4**
$\mathcal{F}_7$	**100.00**	**100.00**	
	8.84e-9±1.06e-9	8.93e-9±9.44e-10	6.29e-1
	3.97e+4±3.49e+2	5.45e+4±2.13e+3	**1.00e-4**
$\mathcal{F}_8$	**100.00**	**100.00**	
	8.90e-9±1.02e-9	8.75e-9±8.18e-10	4.18e-1
	2.13e+4±2.22e+2	2.25e+4±4.12e+2	**1.00e-4**
$\mathcal{F}_9$	**100.00**	**100.00**	
	8.75e-9±9.96e-10	8.87e-9±9.31e-10	5.25e-1
	1.18e+5±3.76e+3	**1.07e+5±7.64e+3**	**1.00e-4**
$\mathcal{F}_{10}$	**100.00**	**100.00**	
	9.26e-9±6.02e-10	9.51e-9±3.73e-10	**1.44e-2**
	5.49e+4±2.68e+2	**5.19e+4±5.14e+2**	**1.00e-4**
$\mathcal{F}_{11}$	**100.00**	**100.00**	
	8.52e-9±1.09e-9	8.83e-9±8.75e-10	1.19e-1
	3.67e+4±3.38e+2	**3.51e+4±4.79e+2**	**1.00e-4**
$\mathcal{F}_{12}$	**100.00**	**100.00**	
	8.91e-9±1.05e-9	8.88e-9±9.15e-10	8.68e-1
	2.89e+4±6.58e+2	3.22e+4±1.42e+4	1.18e-1
$\mathcal{F}_{13}$	**100.00**	**100.00**	
	8.76e-9±9.62e-10	8.79e-9±1.06e-9	9.00e-1
	2.65e+4±1.20e+3	**2.56e+4±4.30e+2**	**1.00e-4**
$\mathcal{F}_{14}$	**100.00**	**100.00**	
	8.99e-9±8.97e-10	8.82e-9±1.00e-9	3.64e-1
	2.92e+4±2.82e+2	**2.86e+4±4.59e+2**	**1.00e-4**
$\mathcal{F}_{15}$	**100.00**	**100.00**	
	9.12e-9±8.55e-10	8.88e-9±8.47e-10	1.53e-1
	2.91e+4±1.56e+3	**2.80e+4±4.38e+2**	**1.00e-4**
$\mathcal{F}_{16}$	**100.00**	**100.00**	
	8.94e-9±7.49e-10	9.08e-9±7.07e-10	3.45e-1
	3.64e+4±3.88e+2	4.54e+4±2.10e+4	**3.90e-3**

Table 3: Comparison between NAGEDA (our approach) and iAMaLGaM methods in 30 dimensions. The winner is marked in boldface according to a non-parametric bootstrap test. Further details in section 6.

where $\mathcal{F}^*$ is the best fitness value found by an algorithm. The methods are executed 50 times for each test problem. Also, the algorithms are stopped when either: a maximum number of $10000 \cdot d$ evaluations or an error $\mathcal{F} - \mathcal{F}^* < 1 \times 10^{-8}$ is reached. Additionally the population size and sample size of the NAGEDA are modified by the equations provided in section 5.

Tables 2 and 3 summarize the comparison between our proposal and the competitors. These tables present the percentage of success rate, reached fitness values and needed number of evaluations, mean and standard deviation for each algorithm in 30 dimensions. The last column shows a nonparametric bootstrap test with precision $\alpha = 0.05$ by comparing the mean values. If ρ is boldface, there is statistical evidence of the difference between two algorithms. Furthermore, the winner is marked in boldface.

NAGEDA versus xNES

The results in Table 2 show that the NAGEDA has better performance than the xNES, even in the unimodal problems. Also, it is confirmed by a non-parametric bootstrap test on the number of function evaluations. A notable difference in the mean values can be confirmed by a visual comparison. This surprising result is mainly because the developed natural gradient is capable of adapting the parameters of the search distribution towards exploration and exploitation phases.

NAGEDA versus iAMaLGaM
Table 3 shows that both algorithms reached the precision requested for all test problems. However, there are significant differences in several problems. There is statistical evidence to confirm that the NAGEDA requires fewer number of function evaluations than iAMaLGaM to reach the desired precision in unimodal problems. On the other hand, in 6 out of 8 functions the iAMaLGaM shows better performance than the NAGEDA for the multimodal problems. Despite these facts being supported by the statistical testing, a visual comparison shows a slight difference between the mean values of the needed evaluations.

The comparisons discussed above show that the NAGEDA has better performance than the xNES in all the test functions. Despite the first one requiring a higher population size than the second algorithm, we can conclude that the NAGEDA uses the gathered information in an efficient way. On the other hand, NAGEDA and iAMaLGaM show a similar performance in most of the benchmark problems.

7. CONCLUSIONS

This paper proposes a natural gradient based on the Kullback-Leibler divergence between a search distribution and the Boltzmann distribution. An analysis of the developed formulae show a strong relationship between our proposal and a typical natural gradient based on the expected fitness. This fact allows us to reuse some ideas and methods from literature, mainly from the NES and the Monte Carlo approaches. Additionally the behaviour of our proposal can be explained via the importance sampling technique.

When the search distribution is set to the multivariate Gaussian distribution, the computational complexity of the natural gradient estimation is reduced. This is because it allows us to use an exponential parameterization for avoiding the computation of the Fisher information. Although the developed natural gradient estimate seems more complex than the typical one, a visual study exhibits that the first one has interesting properties related to the exploration and exploitation phases.

A natural gradient based EDA (NAGEDA) is introduced in order to apply the ideas presented in this paper. Also, a comparison is performed versus two successful algorithms: xNES and iAMaLGaM. Statistical results support that NAGEDA is competitive with state of the art algorithms, mainly because the proposed natural gradient allows for the control of the exploration and exploitation phases.

Future work will contemplate an auto-adaptive population size and additional enhancement techniques to reduce the number of function evaluations. Moreover, notice that the main contributions developed in this paper can be extended to other evolutionary algorithms.

8. REFERENCES

[1] Y. Akimoto, A. Auger, and N. Hansen. Comparison-Based Natural Gradient Optimization in High Dimension. In *Genetic and Evolutionary Computation Conference*, Vancouver, Canada, July 2014. ACM.

[2] S. Amari. Natural Gradient Works Efficiently in Learning. *Neural Computation*, 10(2):251–276, Feb. 1998.

[3] S. Amari and H. Nagaoka. *Methods of Information Geometry*, volume 191 of *Translations of Mathematical Monographs*. Oxford University Press, 2000.

[4] L. Arnold, A. Auger, N. Hansen, and Y. Ollivier. Information-Geometric Optimization Algorithms: A Unifying Picture via Invariance Principles. Technical report, Cornell University Library, 2011.

[5] K. Arwini and C. Dodson. *Information Geometry: Near Randomness and Near Independence*. Number 1953 in Lecture Notes in Mathematics. Springer, 2008.

[6] H. Beyer. Convergence Analysis of Evolutionary Algorithms that are based on the Paradigm of Information Geometry. *Evolutionary Computation*, 22(4):679–709, Dec. 2014.

[7] P. A. N. Bosman, J. Grahl, and D. Thierens. Benchmarking Parameter-free Amalgam on Functions with and Without Noise. *Evololutionary Computation*, 21(3):445–469, Sept. 2013.

[8] T. Friedrich, N. Hebbinghaus, and F. Neumann. Comparison of Simple Diversity Mechanisms on Plateau Functions. *Theoretical Computer Science*, 410(26):2455–2462, June 2009.

[9] T. Glasmachers, T. Schaul, Y. Sun, D. Wierstra, and J. Schmidhuber. Exponential Natural Evolution Strategies. In *Genetic and Evolutionary Computation Conference*, 2010.

[10] M. Jamil and X.-S. Yang. A Literature Survey of Benchmark Functions for Global Optimization Problems. *CoRR*, abs/1308.4008, 2013.

[11] P. Larrañaga and J. A. Lozano, editors. *Estimation of Distribution Algorithms: A New Tool for Evolutionary Computation*. Kluwer, Boston, MA, 2002.

[12] A. B. Owen. *Monte Carlo Theory, Methods and Examples*. In progress, available online, 2013.

[13] P. Pošík. Preventing Premature Convergence in a Simple EDA via Global Step Size Setting. In G. Rudolph, T. Jansen, N. Beume, S. Lucas, and C. Poloni, editors, *PPSN X*, volume 5199 of *Lecture Notes in Computer Science*, pages 549–558. Springer Berlin Heidelberg, 2008.

[14] C. Robert and G. Casella. *Monte Carlo Statistical Methods*. Springer-Verlag, Secaucus, NJ, USA, 2005.

[15] T. Schaul. Benchmarking Exponential Natural Evolution Strategies on the Noiseless and Noisy Black-box Optimization Testbeds. In *Workshop, Genetic and Evolutionary Computation Conference*, Philadelphia, PA, 2012.

[16] M. Črepinšek, S. Liu, and M. Mernik. Exploration and Exploitation in Evolutionary Algorithms: A Survey. *ACM Comput. Surv.*, 45(3):35:1–35:33, July 2013.

[17] D. Wierstra, T. Schaul, T. Glasmachers, Y. Sun, J. Peters, and J. Schmidhuber. Natural Evolution Strategies. *Journal of Machine Learning Research*, 15:949–980, 2014.

[18] S. Yi, D. Wierstra, T. Schaul, and J. Schmidhuber. Stochastic Search Using the Natural Gradient. In *Proceedings of the ICML*, pages 1161–1168, New York, NY, USA, 2009. ACM.

Theoretical Perspective of Convergence Complexity of Evolutionary Algorithms Adopting Optimal Mixing

Yu-Fan Tung
Taiwan Evolutionary Intelligence Laboratory
Department of Electrical Engineering
National Taiwan University
r02921044@ntu.edu.tw

Tian-Li Yu
Taiwan Evolutionary Intelligence Laboratory
Department of Electrical Engineering
National Taiwan University
tianliyu@ntu.edu.tw

ABSTRACT

The optimal mixing evolutionary algorithms (OMEAs) have recently drawn much attention for their robustness, small size of required population, and efficiency in terms of number of function evaluations (NFE). In this paper, the performances and behaviors of convergence in OMEAs are studied by investigating the mechanism of optimal mixing (OM), the variation operator in OMEAs, under two scenarios—one-layer and two-layer masks. For the case of one-layer masks, the required population size is derived from the viewpoint of initial supply, while the convergence time is derived by analyzing the progress of sub-solution growth. NFE is then asymptotically bounded with rational probability by estimating the probability of performing evaluations. For the case of two-layer masks, empirical results indicate that the required population size is proportional to both the degree of cross competition and the results from the one-layer-mask case. The derived models also indicate that population sizing is decided by initial supply when disjoint masks are adopted, that the high selection pressure imposed by OM makes the composition of sub-problems impact little on NFE, and that the population size requirement for two-layer masks increases with the reverse-growth probability.

Categories and Subject Descriptors

F.2.m [**Analysis of Algorithms and Problem Complexity**]: Miscellaneous; I.2.8 [**Artificial Intelligence**]: Problem Solving, Control Methods, and Search—*Heuristic methods*

Keywords

Optimal Mixing; Convergence Complexity; Population Sizing; Convergence Time; Number of Function Evaluations

1. INTRODUCTION

The importance of convergence analysis of evolutionary algorithms cannot be overemphasized. Without theoretical support, the empirical findings cannot be generalized, and the development of new mechanism lacks direction. However, due to the stochastic nature, the analyses of evolutionary algorithms (EAs) are difficult, and hence are either inaccurate and incomplete or come much later than the debut of the algorithm. For example, the concept of the simple GA was proposed around the late 1960s. Accurate facetwise models for the population sizing and the convergence time were not proposed until the late 1990s [4, 16, 10, 8, 6]. Similarly, the technique of model building in estimation of distribution algorithms (EDAs) has been developed since the late 1990s, and complexity analysis of model building, the kernel of EDA, appeared in the field about ten years later [11, 18].

Recently, the optimal mixing operator (OM), proposed by Thierens and Bosman, has drawn much attention for its robustness and performance [1, 15]. Utilizing the intermediate results during variation, mixing with OM is considered noise-free decision making, which greatly reduces the required population size and boosts the performance. The performance of OM significantly depends on the linkage sets [1, 7]. Recent researches involve using the CP index [17] and filtering/combining linkage hierarchies [2] to decide whether a given mask is promising during optimization. However, those techniques have been developed with little theoretic support.

The goal of this paper is to analyze the convergence complexity of EAs adopting OM, also called OMEAs, when various linkage models are adopted. In particular, we focus on deriving analytical models for the required population size, the convergence time, and the number of function evaluations (NFE). Among many OMEAs, the analyses in this paper suit best the scenario of GOMEA [14] since our study heavily uses probabilistic models.

For the rest of this paper, the background is first briefly introduced in Section 2. In the scenario of one-layer masks, complexity models are proposed in Section 3. The results are then extended to two-layer masks in Section 4, followed by conclusion.

GECCO '15, July 11 - 15, 2015, Madrid, Spain
© 2015 ACM. ISBN 978-1-4503-3472-3/15/07...$15.00
DOI: http://dx.doi.org/10.1145/2739480.2754685

2. BACKGROUND

In this section, background knowledge of this paper is provided. Since the behavior of OMEAs depends on the linkage sets, we first formally define the family of subsets and the associated notations. Using the notations, the test problems used in this paper are then described. We then give a brief introduction to GOMEA, which is the research scenario of this paper. Finally, since the concept of initial supply is highly related to our work, it is also addressed.

2.1 Family of Subsets

In OMEAs, variables are mixed according to linkage sets to ensure adequate mixing while preventing loss of promising partial solutions. The family of subsets [13], denoted by $\mathcal{F}$, is a general model of linkage sets. Before defining the FOS we introduce the necessary notations. We denote the length of chromosome by ℓ, and the population size by n. Variables in one chromosome, also called genes, can be expressed in a vector $\vec{x} = \langle x_1, \ldots, x_\ell \rangle$. The notation $|\vec{x}|$ denotes the number of elements in $\vec{x}$. The natural number set is denoted by $\mathbb{N}$. Using these notations the FOS is defined as follows.

DEFINITION 1. *For any integer $\ell \in \mathbb{N}$, S_ℓ is an* **index set** *which consists of all integers from 1 to ℓ. Subsets of S_ℓ are called* **masks**.

$$S_\ell = \{1, 2, \ldots, \ell\}.$$

DEFINITION 2. *For an index set S_ℓ, $\mathcal{F}$ is a* **family of subsets (FOS)** *with the following two properties.*

1. *$\mathcal{F}$ is an ordered set consisting of masks.*
$$\mathcal{F} = \langle \mathbf{F}^1, \mathbf{F}^2, \ldots, \mathbf{F}^{|\mathcal{F}|} \rangle,$$
$$\text{where } \mathbf{F}^i \subseteq S_\ell, 1 \leq i \leq |\mathcal{F}|.$$

2. *The union of all masks in $\mathcal{F}$ is the index set.*
$$\bigcup\nolimits_{\mathbf{F}^i \in \mathcal{F}} \mathbf{F}^i = S_\ell.$$

Take $\ell = 3$ as an example. The index set $S_3 = \{1, 2, 3\}$. Sets such as $\{1\}$, $\{2, 3\}$, and $\{1, 2, 3\}$ are all masks of S_3. $\langle \{1, 2\}, \{2, 3\} \rangle$, $\langle \{2, 3\}, \{1, 2\} \rangle$, and $\langle \{1, 2\}, \{2, 3\}, \{1, 2\} \rangle$ are three different FOSs of S_3. $\langle \{1, 2\}, \{2\} \rangle$ is not a valid FOS of S_3, since no mask contains 3. Note that the masks in FOS are in order, and there may be duplicated masks.

During OM, variables are mixed according to the elements in FOS. The operation can be viewed as a variable-wise mask operation, so elements in FOS are called masks. For a chromosome C, the variables selected according to a mask M are denoted by C_M.

Some special FOSs are further defined as follows.

DEFINITION 3. *For an index set S_ℓ and an integer k dividing ℓ, a* **homogeneous FOS** *$\mathcal{F}_k$ is defined as*

$$\mathcal{F}_k = \langle \mathbf{F}^1, \mathbf{F}^2, \ldots, \mathbf{F}^{\ell/k} \rangle,$$

$$\text{where } \mathbf{F}^i = \{\pi_j \,|\, (i-1) \cdot k < j \leq i \cdot k\}.$$

$\vec{\pi} = \langle \pi_1, \pi_2, \ldots, \pi_\ell \rangle$ can be any permutation of the index set S_ℓ. In other words, $\mathcal{F}_k$ is an FOS consisting of ℓ/k disjoint masks, and every mask contains k indexes. Since the locations of variables should not affect the behavior of optimization, we use the permutation notation to eliminate the dependency of variable locations.

DEFINITION 4. *The* **concatenated homogeneous FOS** *can be defined below.*

$$\mathcal{F}_{k_1, \ldots, k_a} = \mathcal{F}_{k_1} \parallel \mathcal{F}_{k_2} \parallel \cdots \parallel \mathcal{F}_{k_a},$$

where $\parallel$ is the concatenation operator, which concatenates the elements in the sets while preserving the order.

Take the case $\ell = 6$ as an example. $\langle \{1, 5\}, \{2, 4\}, \{3, 6\} \rangle$, $\langle \{2, 4, 5\}, \{1, 3, 6\} \rangle$, and $\langle \{1, 2, 3, 4, 5, 6\} \rangle$ are three valid homogeneous FOSs. They can be denoted by $\mathcal{F}_2$, $\mathcal{F}_3$, and $\mathcal{F}_6$ respectively. A valid concatenation of them is $\mathcal{F}_{3,6,2} = \langle \{2, 4, 5\}, \{1, 3, 6\}, \{1, 2, 3, 4, 5, 6\}, \{1, 5\}, \{2, 4\}, \{3, 6\} \rangle$.

2.2 Test Problems

The analyses and experiments are based on three maximization problems. By successful optimization we mean that the global optimum is found. The first problem is onemax:

$$f_{onemax}(\vec{x}) = u(\vec{x}),$$

where $u(\vec{x})$ is the number of 1s in $\vec{x}$. Onemax is trivial, but optimization performance on onemax indicates how well an algorithm deals with fully separable problems.

The second problem is one instance of the Royal Road functions [9], the structure of which can be characterized by an FOS $\mathcal{F}$:

$$f_{royal}(\vec{x}) = \sum_{\forall \mathbf{F}^i \in \mathcal{F}} R(\vec{x}_{\mathbf{F}^i}), \tag{1}$$

where

$$R(\vec{x}) = \begin{cases} 1 & \text{if } u(\vec{x}) = |\vec{x}|, \\ 0 & \text{otherwise.} \end{cases}$$

Note that $\vec{x}_{\mathbf{F}}$ is the part of $\vec{x}$ indicated by a mask $\mathbf{F}$, and $|\vec{x}|$ denotes the numbers of elements in $\vec{x}$. Motivation of using the Royal Road function is introduced in Section 3.3.

The third problem is the deceptive-trap problem [3], which can also be characterized by an FOS $\mathcal{F}$:

$$f_{trap}(\vec{x}) = \sum_{\forall \mathbf{F}^i \in \mathcal{F}} T(\vec{x}_{\mathbf{F}^i}),$$

where

$$T(\vec{x}) = \begin{cases} 1 & \text{if } u(\vec{x}) = |\vec{x}|, \\ 0.9 \cdot \frac{|\vec{x}| - 1 - u(\vec{x})}{|\vec{x}| - 1} & \text{otherwise.} \end{cases}$$

The deceptive-trap function is also commonly used for benchmark and is known for its deceptive nature. Local hill climbing does not lead to the global optimum when solving trap problems.

Note that although these problems are all binary-encoded, our results can be applied to χ-ary problems.

2.3 GOMEA

GOMEA [14] is one of the first proposed OMEAs and can be integrated with arbitrary FOS. In this paper, we focus on the variation operator of GOMEA, which is named gene-pool optimal mixing (GOM). The pseudocode of GOM can be expressed in Algorithm 1. Utilizing this operator, the pseudocode of GOMEA can be expressed in Algorithm 2. The population is denoted by $\mathcal{P} = \{P_1, \ldots, P_n\}$, and the offspring are denoted by $\{O_1, \ldots, O_n\}$. Optimization halts if the population converges to one instance. In this paper, all experiments are done with an implementation of GOMEA. For the experiments that need to determine the minimal required population size, a bisection procedure [12] is adopted.

In practice, linkage detection techniques are applied to generate FOS. In our scenario, this step is omitted. We manually determine the FOS before optimization to prevent unnecessary noise. We also disable the function of mutation in all of our experiments, which is the same as the scenario in the canonical GOMEA.

Algorithm 1: Genepool Optimal Mixing

```
Input  : f: fitness function, R: receiver,
         P: population, F: FOS
Output: O: offspring
O ← R //Copy to the offspring
B ← R //Copy to a buffer
for i = 1 to |F| do
    r ← random number from 1 to |P|
    D ← P_r //Select the donor
    B_{F^i} ← D_{F^i} //Get the fragment of the donor
    if f(B) ≥ f(O) then
        O_{F^i} ← B_{F^i} //Adopt the change if improved
    else
        B_{F^i} ← O_{F^i} //Reset the buffer if not improved
return O
```

Algorithm 2: GOMEA

```
Input  : f: fitness function, n: population size,
         F: FOS
Output: optimization solution
randomly generate n instances for P
while ¬ShouldTerminate(P) do
    for i = 1 to n do
        O_i ← GenepoolOptimalMixing(f, P_i, P, F)
    for i = 1 to n do
        P_i ← O_i
return the best instance in P
```

2.4 Population Sizing

For genetic algorithms (GAs), the supply model was proposed based on the concept of ensuring an adequate supply of partial solutions. GAs find the global optimum by mixing the segments of it, which must exist in the initial population. Consider a χ-ary problem which can be decomposed into m parts, and each of them contains k variables. Since GAs are stochastic processes, we can never guarantee the existence of all partial solutions. Instead, we consider a tolerable probability α of not having a partial solution in the initial population. By approximating α by $1/m$, the reciprocal of number of subproblems, Goldberg *et al.* derived a minimal required population size in this scenario [6]:

$$n = \chi^k \left(k \ln \chi + \ln m\right). \tag{2}$$

There are other population-sizing models for GAs. Goldberg *et al.* proposed one by considering that larger population leads to higher probability of making correct decisions [4]. Harik *et al.* proposed another model by making an analogy between selection in GAs and the gambler's ruin problem [8]. These models give different estimations of the required population size. In this paper, we find out that the supply model is a proper estimator for OMEAs.

3. ONE-LAYER MASKS

To begin our study, we first focus on the scenario so-called one-layer masks where FOS consists of disjoint masks. Three assumptions are made in this section. First, we only focus on problems which can be fully separated into subproblems. Second, we assume that the problem structures are perfectly identified before optimization. Discussion on not well-identified problems is in next section. Third, we assume the global optimum is unique in every problem. For problems with multiple global optimums, we expect smaller required population due to smaller need of initial supply.

3.1 Population Sizing

The required population size can be estimated from the viewpoint of initial supply. Consider a set containing k variables which are χ-ary, in correspondence to a mask with k indexes. We assume that the optimal state of the set is unique, which is part of the unique global optimum. A set is considered as correct if it is of optimal state, and is incorrect otherwise. The probability of the set being correct after uniformly random initialization is χ^{-k}. Since the variables are exchanged using the corresponding mask, they are always tied together during mixing. Therefore no new pattern is created after mixing.

Since the masks reflect the decomposed subproblems, correct sets are never replaced, and eventually dominate the population. Hence the population converges to the optimal state for the mask if and only if at least one correct set exists initially. For a mask of size k, the probability that at least one set of initial variables is correct among the population is

$$p_{correct} = 1 - \left(1 - \chi^{-k}\right)^n.$$

EA finds the global optimum if and only if every subproblem contains correct sets initially, the probability of which is

$$p_{success} = \prod_{\forall \mathbf{F}^i \in \mathcal{F}} \left(1 - \left(1 - \chi^{-|\mathbf{F}^i|}\right)^n\right). \tag{3}$$

If the tolerable failure rate of EA is α, solving $p_{success} = 1-\alpha$ yields the required population size n.

A special case of Equation 3 is that all masks are equal-sized, which means $|\mathbf{F}^i| = k$, $i = 1, 2, \ldots, m$. Therefore the equation can be rewritten as

$$1 - \alpha = p = \left(1 - \left(1 - \chi^{-k}\right)^n\right)^m. \tag{4}$$

This result is verified empirically in Figure 1. We can see that the experiment values are accurately estimated.

Equation 4 also leads to the required population size:

$$n = \frac{\ln\left(1 - (1-\alpha)^{\frac{1}{m}}\right)}{\ln\left(1 - \chi^{-k}\right)}. \tag{5}$$

Note that $0 < \frac{1}{m} \leq 1$ in Equation 5. To derive the complexity of n, we consider a convex function $f(x) = (1-\alpha)^x$, where $x \in (0, 1]$. Two inequalities can be derived:

$$(1-x) f(0) + x f(1) \geq f(x) \geq f(0) + x f'(0)$$

Let $x = \frac{1}{m}$ and take natural log, we have

$$\frac{\ln \frac{1}{1-\alpha}}{m} \leq 1 - (1-\alpha)^{\frac{1}{m}} \leq \frac{\alpha}{m},$$

$$\ln\left(c_1 \frac{1}{m}\right) \geq \ln\left(1 - (1-\alpha)^{\frac{1}{m}}\right) \geq \ln\left(c_2 \frac{1}{m}\right),$$

where c_1 and c_2 are some constants.

To compare the optimization cost of problems with different sizes, we assume that the problems have similar structures, which implies they are encoded in the same way (χ

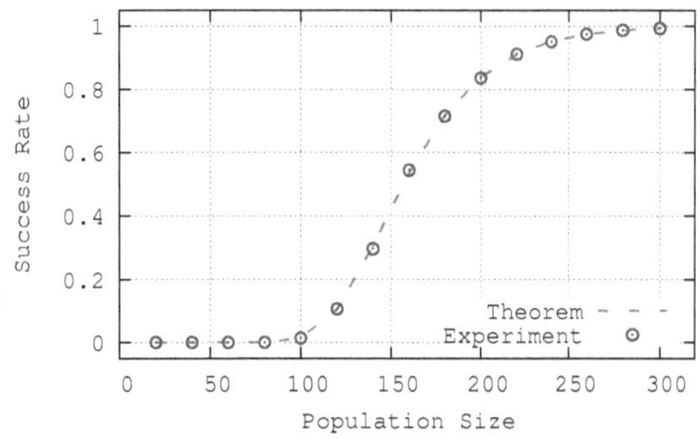

Figure 1: Success rate for various population sizes with $\ell = 500$ and $k = 5$. Experiments are repeated 10^4 times. The maximum absolute error is 1.03%.

is constant), and the adopted masks are similar (k is constant). The tolerable failure rate α should not vary with the problem size. By fixing α, χ, and k, asymptotically tight bound for Equation 5 with regarding to m can be derived:

$$\Theta(n) = \Theta\left(\ln\left(1-(1-\alpha)^{\frac{1}{m}}\right)\right) = \Theta(\ln m).$$

The complexity matches the supply model in Equation 2, which also leads to $n = \Theta(\ln m)$. In contrast, models concerning decision making suggest population sizing from $\Theta(\sqrt{m})$ to $\Theta(m)$ [4, 8]. By comparing the complexities, we verified that the concept of supply suits well for OMEAs, while others do not.

3.2 Convergence Time

The study of convergence time, the number of generations for OMEAs to converge, involves two parts. The case of a single mask is first studied, and the result of which is then extended to two-layer masks.

For the one-mask case, denote the mask size by k and the generation number by t, starting with $t = 0$. t increases 1 after each generation. Define p_t as the proportion of correct sets among all chromosomes. p_0 can be approximated by its expected value, χ^{-k}. We estimate the convergence time by modeling the growth of p_t.

In GOMEA, two candidates are selected as the donor and receiver, and the former tries to donate part of its bit pattern to the latter. The receiver takes the donation only if its fitness does not decrease, so a correct set never accepts an incorrect one. On the contrary, incorrect receiver becomes correct once the donor is correct. Since the expected number of incorrect chromosomes in generation t is $n(1-p_t)$, the expected gain in the number of correct sets after one generation is $n(1-p_t) \cdot Pr(\text{donor is correct}) = np_t(1-p_t)$. Note that changes are made on the offspring instead of receiver, so p_t remains constant until the end of the current generation. Thus we get the iterative equation:

$$np_{t+1} - np_t = n \cdot p_t \cdot (1-p_t). \quad (6)$$

For $t \in \mathbb{N}_0 = \mathbb{N} \cup \{0\}$, denote $1 - p_t$ by q_t, and we have

$$q_t - q_{t+1} = (1-q_t)\, q_t,$$

$$q_t^2 = q_{t+1}.$$

Along with $q_0 = 1 - p_0 = 1 - \chi^{-k}$, we get

$$p_t = 1 - q_t = 1 - \left(1-\chi^{-k}\right)^{2^t}, t \in \mathbb{N}_0. \quad (7)$$

Although the solution to Equation 6 is derived, no t satisfies $p_t = 1$, because we approximate p_t by its expected value. Since p_t represents the proportion of correct instances in the population with n candidates, the greatest value of p_t less than 1 is $1 - 1/n$. Since the expected time for p_t to reach $1 - 1/n$ is less than the convergence time, we derive a lower bound for the latter by solving $p_{t_{conv}} > 1 - 1/n$.

To estimate the lower bound t_L, we approximate p_t by a continuous function $p(t)$, which treats t as a real number. From Equation 7, we set

$$p(t) = 1 - q(t) = 1 - \left(1-\chi^{-k}\right)^{2^t}, t \geq 0. \quad (8)$$

Note that $p(t) = p_t$ for $t \in \mathbb{N}_0$. Solving $p(t_{conv}) > 1 - \frac{1}{n}$ yields

$$t_{conv} > t_L = \log_2\left(\frac{\ln\left(\frac{1}{n}\right)}{\ln\left(1-\chi^{-k}\right)}\right). \quad (9)$$

The result can be further extended to multiple disjoint masks. Since the problem is separable, convergence in one position does not interfere with that in another position. Convergence time is thus dominated by the variable set with the longest convergence time.

Assume that the chromosome consists of m sets of variables, convergence time of which are $t_{conv,1}, \ldots, t_{conv,m}$ respectively. We have $t_{conv} = \max_i(t_{conv,i})$. According to Equation 9, smaller initial proportion leads to longer convergence time. For the case that each set contains k variables, we can approximate the maximum of $t_{conv,i}$ by finding the convergence time of the set with least initial correct instances. Let $X_1, \ldots, X_m$ be m independent and identically distributed random variables following the binomial distribution $B\left(n, \chi^{-k}\right)$.* Denote the first order statistic by $X_{(1)} = \min_i(X_i)$. Let $E[X_{(1)}] = x_{(1)}$. Hence for multiple masks we have

$$t_{conv} > t_L = \log_2\left(\frac{\ln\left(\frac{1}{n}\right)}{\ln\left(1-\frac{x_{(1)}}{n}\right)}\right). \quad (10)$$

The lower bound we derived is verified with results on the onemax problem. Figure 2 shows the case of one mask, where the lower bound is from Equation 9. The case of multiple disjoint masks is shown in Figures 3 and 4, where the lower bound is from Equation 10.

The proposed lower bound strictly bounds the empirical results. For large n, $1 - 1/n$ approaches 1. Since the lower bound is derived by solving $p(t_L) = 1 - 1/n$, the lower bound should be close to the convergence time for large population. This can be verified in Figures 2 and 4. Since an almost converged population is likely to converge in one more generation, the lower bound is about one generation below experiment results.

In the case of multiple masks, we find out that the convergence time decreases while n increases when n is small. This

*$B(n,p)$ denotes the distribution with the pmf $Pr(x) = \begin{cases} \frac{n!}{(n-x)!x!}p^x(1-p)^{n-x} & x \in \{0,1,\ldots,n\}, \\ 0 & \text{otherwise.} \end{cases}$

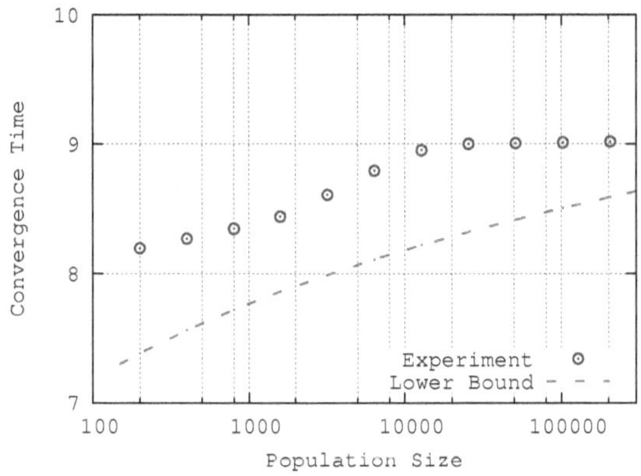

Figure 2: Convergence time with one mask of size 5. For population size ranging from 200 to 204800, the maximum difference between experiment values and the lower bound is 0.81 generations. The difference decreases for large population.

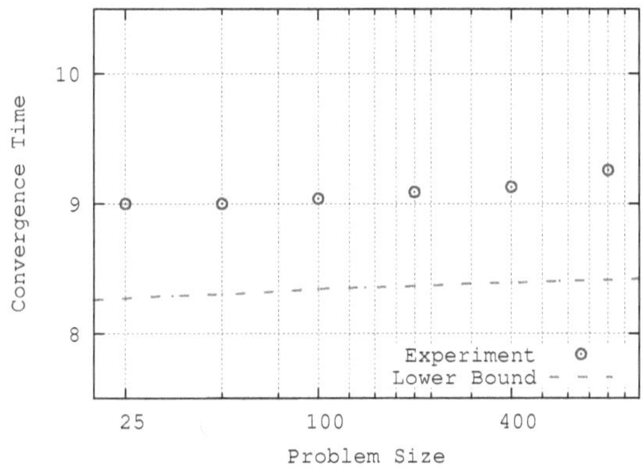

Figure 3: Convergence time for $n = 10000$. For problem size ranging from 25 to 800, the maximum difference is 0.85 generations.

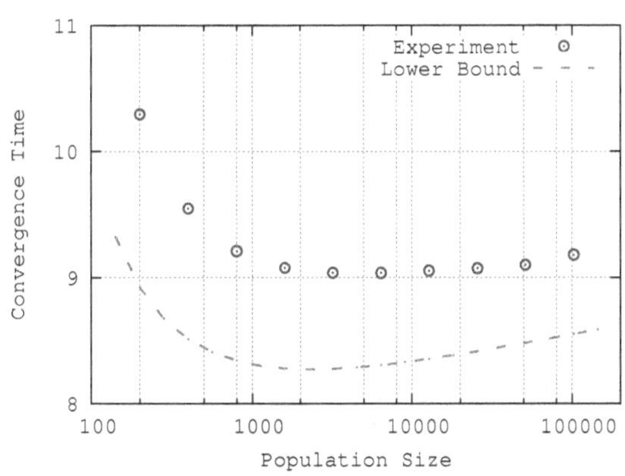

Figure 4: Convergence time for $\ell = 100$ with masks of size 5. For population size ranging from 200 to 102400, the maximum difference between experiment values and the lower bound is 1.37 generations. The difference decreases for large population.

is mainly because of the $\frac{x_{(1)}}{n}$ term in Equation 10. According to the central limit theorem, the first order statistics of the proportion of correct instances increases and approaches χ^{-k} when n grows. When n is large, the $\ln\left(\frac{1}{n}\right)$ term dominates the lower bound, making it increase when n grows. This phenomenon is verified in Figure 4.

3.3 Number of Function Evaluations

The function evaluations of OMEAs consist of two parts. The first is those during the initialization, and the second is those during OM. Therefore the total NFE is

$$n_{fe} = n + n_{fe,OM}. \tag{11}$$

We then model $n_{fe,OM}$ for the case of a single size-k mask.

As before, the proportion of correct subsolutions in the population at generation t is p_t. Under the assumption of unique global optimum, $\chi^k - 1$ subsolutions are not optimal. Denote each of their densities in the population by $q_t^{(1)}, \ldots, q_t^{(\chi^k-1)}$, respectively. In this generation, a receiver only needs to be evaluated when it differs from the donor. Therefore the probability that a receiver needs the evaluation is

$$e_t = 1 - p_t^2 - \left(q_t^{(1)}\right)^2 - \left(q_t^{(2)}\right)^2 - \cdots - \left(q_t^{(\chi^k-1)}\right)^2. \tag{12}$$

We already have the approximation of p_t in Equation 7. Since $q_t^{(1)}, \ldots, q_t^{(\chi^k-1)} \in [0,1]$, we have

$$\frac{\left(\sum_{i=1}^{\chi^k-1} q_t^{(i)}\right)^2}{\chi^k - 1} \leq \sum_{i=1}^{\chi^k-1} \left(q_t^{(i)}\right)^2 \leq \left(\sum_{i=1}^{\chi^k-1} q_t^{(i)}\right)^2.$$

With the condition that

$$\sum_{i=1}^{\chi^k-1} q_t^{(i)} = 1 - p_t,$$

Equation 12 leads to

$$1 - p_t^2 - \frac{(1-p_t)^2}{\chi^k - 1} \geq e_t \geq 1 - p_t^2 - (1-p_t)^2. \tag{13}$$

The required NFE can be approximated by

$$n_{fe,OM} = \sum_{t=0}^{\infty} n \cdot e_t = n \sum_{t=0}^{\infty} e_t.$$

By expanding the summation, we can derive the upper and lower bounds of n_{fe}. For the upper bound, there is no closed form. Since $\sum_{t=0}^{\infty}\left(1 - p_t^2 - \frac{(1-p_t)^2}{\chi^k-1}\right)$ is a function of k if p_t is approximated by Equation 7, we denote it by a function $U(k)$, where $U(k)$ is a function from $\mathbb{N}$ to $\mathbb{R}$. $\mathbb{N}$ is the natural number set, and $\mathbb{R}$ is the real number set. Here the variable χ is considered constant. So we have

$$n_{fe,OM} \leq n \cdot U(k).$$

There is a closed form of the lower bound:

$$\sum_{t=0}^{\infty}\left(1 - p_t^2 - (1-p_t)^2\right) = \sum_{t=0}^{\infty}\left(2q_t - 2q_t^2\right)$$

$$= \sum_{t=0}^{\infty}\left(2q_t - 2q_{t+1}\right) = 2q_0.$$

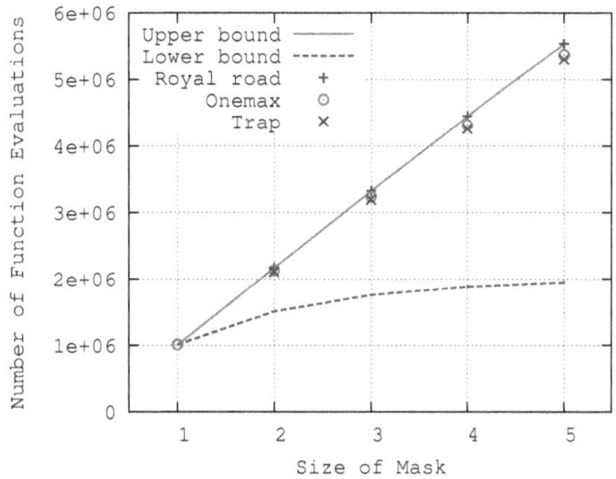

Figure 5: n_{fe} with different sizes of masks. Each FOS contains 100 masks, and the population size is fixed at 10^4. Note that the Royal Road, the onemax, and the trap function are identical for $k = 1$.

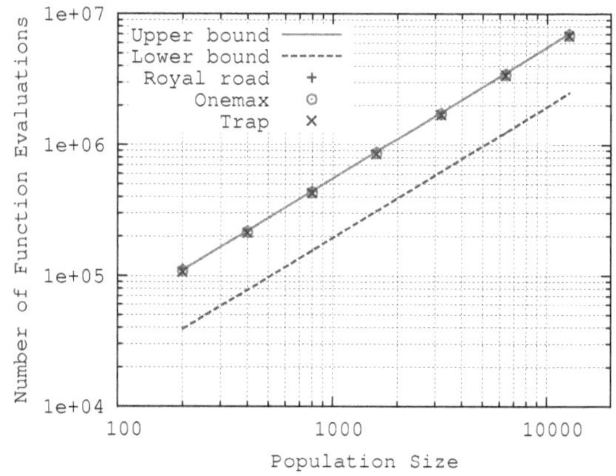

Figure 6: n_{fe} with different sizes of population. $m = 100$ and $k = 5$ for the test problems.

This yields

$$n_{fe,OM} \geq n \cdot 2q_0 = n \cdot 2\left(1 - \chi^{-k}\right) = n \cdot L(k),$$

where $L(k) = 2\left(1 - \chi^{-k}\right)$. Hence the NFE can be bounded by

$$n \cdot U(k) \geq n_{fe,OM} \geq n \cdot L(k).$$

The results can be extended to arbitrary number of masks, m. Since all of our masks are disjoint, evaluations of them are independent to each others. So the total NFE is the summation of all required NFEs for each mask. Therefore we get

$$n \cdot \sum_{\forall \mathbf{F}^i \in \mathcal{F}} U\left(\left|\mathbf{F}^i\right|\right) \geq n_{fe,OM} \geq n \cdot \sum_{\forall \mathbf{F}^i \in \mathcal{F}} L\left(\left|\mathbf{F}^i\right|\right),$$

or equivalently,

$$n + n \cdot \sum_{\forall \mathbf{F}^i \in \mathcal{F}} U\left(\left|\mathbf{F}^i\right|\right) \geq n_{fe} \geq n + n \cdot \sum_{\forall \mathbf{F}^i \in \mathcal{F}} L\left(\left|\mathbf{F}^i\right|\right). \quad (14)$$

For the special case that the sizes of all masks are equal, we have

$$n \cdot (1 + mU(k)) \geq n_{fe} \geq n \cdot (1 + mL(k)), \quad (15)$$

where k is the size of every mask, and m is the number of masks.

The problem nature affects the required number of evaluations. In Equation 15, the equality of upper bound holds when $q_t^{(1)} = q_t^{(2)} = \cdots = q_t^{(\chi^k - 1)}$. Consider one of our test problems, the Royal Road function. By definition, all suboptimals in one subproblem (the $R(\vec{x})$ in Equation 1) contribute equally to the fitness. Because all suboptimals are equally competitive during OM, proportions of all suboptimal instances are roughly equal. Since the equality of upper bound holds, this problem costs more function evaluations than others do.

The results are verified in the following experiments. Figure 5 shows NFE with masks of various sizes. Figure 6 shows the result with various population sizes. The theoretical values are from Equation 15.

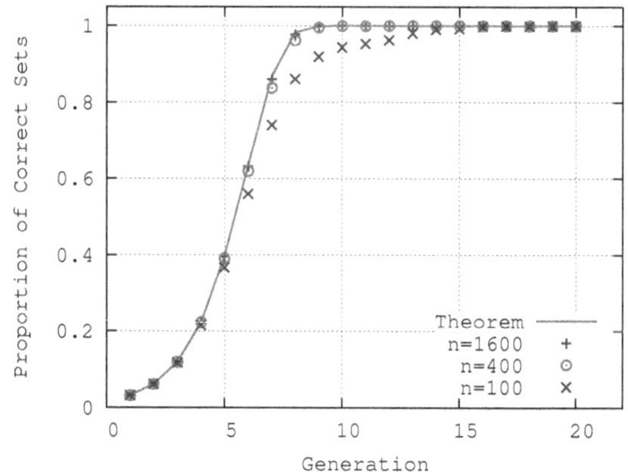

Figure 7: p_t for various population sizes. The problem is a 500-bit onemax problem, with masks of size 5. We can see smaller n leads to slower convergence.

In these two experiments, we have made some observations. First, the lower bound is generally far from experiment results when there are multiple suboptimals, since we derive the lower bound by ignoring the cost of comparison between suboptimals in Equation 13. Second, NFE of the Royal Road function exceeds the upper bound by 2.17% when $n = 200$ and by 0.02% when $n = 12800$ in Figure 6. We believe that the reason is as follows. The estimation of p_t deriving from the expected value while p_t is discrete is the reason. For small n, the approximation is inaccurate. This is verified in Figure 7, which indicates that smaller population leads to slower convergence, implying additional consumption in function evaluations. This explains why NFE is slightly underestimated, especially when n is small. Third, NFE of the Royal Road problem is always the greatest, and NFE of the trap problem is always the least. This verifies that the subproblem affects the NFE, yet the difference is subtle. Last, the upper bound seems a proper estimator for the NFE for all test problems, with relative error less than 5%. We infer that the high mask-wise selection pressure of OM quickly filters out the incorrect sets, and therefore the convergence behavior is not much affected from the subproblem structures.

k	$Pr(X_1 > X_0)$	$Pr(X_1 = X_0)$	$Pr(X_1 < X_0)$	p_{rg}
2	75%	25%	0%	25%
3	69%	25%	6%	31%
4	66%	23%	11%	34%
5	64%	22%	14%	36%

Table 1: Comparison of two random variables X_1 and X_0. Larger k yields larger p_{rg}, which is the probability that $X_1 \leq X_0$.

4. TWO-LAYER MASKS

In this section, we extend our study to two-layer masks as the first step to multi-layer masks. Multi-layer masks are usually adopted since in practice most problem structures are unknown and not fully separable. In this section, we focus on the onemax problem with FOS in the form $\mathcal{F}_{k,1}$ with $k > 1$. Note that the FOS is defined in Definition 4.

The population converges to the global optimum if and only if all the variables converge to 1s. For an index i, consider all the variables $\vec{x}_i$ in every chromosomes. There are n variables with this index. We use the notation p to denote the proportion of 1s in these n variables.

Since masks in a homogeneous FOS do not share common variables, exactly one mask in $\mathcal{F}_k$ and one mask in $\mathcal{F}_1$ contain i. When mixing with one-bit masks, 1s never change to 0s, but this is not the case of k-bit masks. Since the fitness is evaluated when all k variables are exchanged, the overall fitness never decreases, but some variables can be ruined. For example, the pattern `101` overwrites `010` when a 3-bit mask applies to them, since the fitness increases by 1. However, the second variable in `010`, which is one, is overwritten by a zero. For a certain index, if all n variables with the index in the population become 0s, the optimization fails.

This phenomenon can be further quantified from the viewpoint of probability. By the assumption of random initialization, $p = 2^{-1}$ in binary-coded problems. For a set of k variables covered by a k-bit mask, the number of 1s in the set can be expressed as a random variable. If the first variable is zero, the random variable X_0 follows the Binomial distribution $B(k-1, 2^{-1})$. Recall that k is an integer greater than one. If the first variable is one, the random variable is $X_1 = 1 + X_0$. Consider a variable $\vec{x}_i$ equals to 0 in the donor and equals to 1 in the receiver. $\vec{x}_i$ in the receiver becomes 0 with probability $Pr\,(X_1 \leq X_0)$, which we called the reverse-growth probability, p_{rg}. The probabilities are calculated using the Binomial distribution and shown in Table 1. We can see larger k leads to larger p_{rg}.

The required population size varies when adopting various FOSs. The concept of cross competition explains this phenomenon [5]. Cross competition is first introduced to derive an upper bound for the selection pressure in GA. To prevent cross-competitive failure, the selection pressure must satisfy

$$s < n\frac{\ln(1-p_0)}{\ln\alpha},$$

where s is the selection pressure, p_0 is the probability that a correct bit is preserved into the next generation, and α is a threshold, which means optimization is likely to fail when $\alpha\ell$ variables are incorrectly converged. After some modification, we obtain

$$n > \frac{s\cdot\ln\alpha}{\ln(1-p_0)}. \tag{16}$$

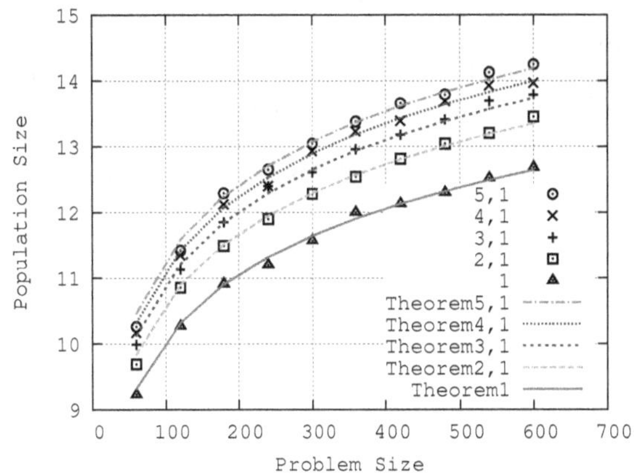

Figure 8: Required population size for various FOS. Theoretical values of $\mathcal{F}_{k,1}$ are estimated by curve fitting as multiple of that of $\mathcal{F}_1$. The maximum relative error among all estimations is 2.0%.

Although in the scenario of GOMEA, the situation is different, but the similar concept applies. Larger k leads to larger p_{rg}, which then leads to lower probability that a correct bit is preserved. In other words, larger k yields smaller p_0. By assuming that s and α do not vary much with k, the RHS of Equation 16 increases when k increases. This means that the lower bound of population size increases. In other words, the required population increases if k increases when adopting $\mathcal{F}_{k,1}$.

The following experiments are conducted to verify the above hypothesis. For various lengths of problems, different FOSs are adopted to solve the onemax problem. These FOSs are $\mathcal{F}_{5,1}$, $\mathcal{F}_{4,1}$, $\mathcal{F}_{3,1}$, $\mathcal{F}_{2,1}$, and $\mathcal{F}_1$. The result is shown in Figure 8, indicating that optimization using $\mathcal{F}_{k,1}$ with larger k requires larger population. Furthermore, a proportional relationship exists between the required population size for $\mathcal{F}_{k,1}$ and $\mathcal{F}_1$, while the latter can be approximated by Equation 5. From this observation, the theoretical values of required population for $\mathcal{F}_{k,1}$ are obtained by fitting the experiment values to a constant multiple of that of $\mathcal{F}_1$. According to the results, masks which cover multiple separable subproblems are not beneficial from the viewpoint of population size.

5. CONCLUSION

In this paper, we derived the convergence models of OMEAs for one-layer and two-layers masks. For problems with separable structures, behaviors of GOMEA with masks corresponding to the structures were analyzed. The required population size was accurately estimated from the viewpoint of initial supply. Analyzing the growth of sub-solution led to the convergence-time model. The NFE was then estimated. These three models were verified empirically, and the values of relative error among all experiments were less than 5%. For multi-layer disjoint masks, a special case with two-layer masks was studied. We found that the concept of cross competition explains the growth in the required population sizes.

As for future work, we would like to extend our results to multi-layer masks by quantifying the effect of cross competition and by investigating the growth of subsolutions iteratively. Hopefully, we would be able to analyze the behavior of OMEAs with full linkage tree, which is a special case of multi-layer FOS. Furthermore, since this paper is limited by the assumptions we made, we would like to study the case with weaker assumptions.

The major contributions of this paper reside in the derivations of the population-sizing, the convergence-time, and the NFE models for OMEAs with one-layer and two-layer masks. Our models are empirically verified and the relative errors of our estimators are small. In addition, our models lead to the following insightful findings. First, for the case of one-layer masks, the required population size is decided by initial supply rather than decision making. This explains why OMEAs generally require relatively small populations compared to EDAs. Second, NFE for the test problems is very close to the proposed upper bound, by which we infer that the mask-wise selection pressure of OM quickly filter out non-optimum subsolutions, making the subproblem composition insignificant. Third, for two-layer masks, the required population size is proportional to that of the one-layer masks, and the ratio is positively related to the reverse-growth probability.

6. ACKNOWLEDGMENTS

The authors would like to thank the support by Ministry of Science and Technology in Taiwan under Grant No. MOST 103-2221-E-002-177-MY2-1.

7. REFERENCES

[1] P. A. Bosman and D. Thierens. Linkage neighbors, optimal mixing and forced improvements in genetic algorithms. *Proceedings of the Genetic and Evolutionary Computation Conference (GECCO-2012)*, pages 585–592, 2012.

[2] P. A. Bosman and D. Thierens. More concise and robust linkage learning by filtering and combining linkage hierarchies. *Proceedings of the Genetic and Evolutionary Computation Conference (GECCO-2013)*, pages 359–366, 2013.

[3] K. Deb and D. E. Goldberg. Analyzing deception in trap functions. *Proceedings of the Second Workshop on Foundations of Genetic Algorithms (FOGA-1992)*, 2:98–108, 1992.

[4] D. E. Goldberg, K. Deb, and J. H. Clark. Genetic algorithms, noise, and the sizing of populations. *Complex Systems*, 6:333–362, 1991.

[5] D. E. Goldberg, K. Deb, and D. Thierens. Toward a better understanding of mixing in genetic algorithms. *Urbana*, 51:61801, 1992.

[6] D. E. Goldberg, K. Sastry, and T. Latoza. On the supply of building blocks. *Proceedings of the Genetic and Evolutionary Computation Conference (GECCO-2001)*, pages 336–342, 2001.

[7] B. W. Goldman and D. R. Tauritz. Linkage tree genetic algorithms: variants and analysis. *Proceedings of the Genetic and Evolutionary Computation Conference (GECCO-2012)*, pages 625–632, 2012.

[8] G. Harik, E. Cantú-Paz, D. E. Goldberg, and B. L. Miller. The gambler's ruin problem, genetic algorithms, and the sizing of populations. *Evolutionary Computation*, 7(3):231–253, 1999.

[9] M. Mitchell, S. Forrest, and J. H. Holland. The royal road for genetic algorithms: Fitness landscapes and GA performance. *Proceedings of the First European Conference on Artificial Life*, pages 245–254, 1992.

[10] H. Mühlenbein and D. Schlierkamp-Voosen. Predictive models for the breeder genetic algorithm: I. Continuous parameter optimization. *Evolutionary Computation*, 1(1):25–49, 1993.

[11] M. Pelikan, K. Sastry, and D. E. Goldberg. Scalability of the Bayesian optimization algorithm. *International Journal of Approximate Reasoning*, 31(3):221 – 258, 2002.

[12] K. Sastry. *Evaluation-relaxation schemes for genetic and evolutionary algorithms*. PhD thesis, University of Illinois at Urbana-Champaign, 2001.

[13] D. Thierens. Linkage tree genetic algorithm: First results. *Proceedings of the 12th Annual Conference Companion on Genetic and Evolutionary Computation*, pages 1953–1958, 2010.

[14] D. Thierens and P. A. Bosman. Optimal mixing evolutionary algorithms. *Proceedings of the Genetic and Evolutionary Computation Conference (GECCO-2011)*, pages 617–624, 2011.

[15] D. Thierens and P. A. Bosman. Hierarchical problem solving with the linkage tree genetic algorithm. *Proceedings of the Genetic and Evolutionary Computation Conference (GECCO-2013)*, pages 877–884, 2013.

[16] D. Thierens and D. E. Goldberg. Mixing in genetic algorithms. *Proceedings of the Fifth International Conference on Genetic Algorithms (ICGA-1993)*, pages 38–47, 1993.

[17] S.-M. Wang, Y.-F. Tung, and T.-L. Yu. Investigation on efficiency of optimal mixing on various linkage sets. *Proceedings of the 2014 IEEE International Conference on Evolutionary Computation*, pages 2475–2482, 2014.

[18] T.-L. Yu, K. Sastry, D. E. Goldberg, and M. Pelikan. Population sizing for entropy-based model building in discrete estimation of distribution algorithms. *Proceedings of the Genetic and Evolutionary Computation Conference (GECCO-2007)*, pages 601–608, 2007.

Ant Colony and Surrogate Tree-Structured Models for Orderings-Based Bayesian Network Learning

Juan I. Alonso-Barba
Computing Systems Dept.
UCLM
Albacete, Spain
juanignacio.alonso@uclm.es

Luis de la Ossa*
Computing Systems Dept.
UCLM
Albacete, Spain
luis.delaossa@uclm.es

Olivier Regnier-Coudert
IDEAS Research Institute
Robert Gordon University
Aberdeen, Scotland
o.regniercoudert@rgu.ac.uk

John McCall
IDEAS Research Institute
Robert Gordon University
Aberdeen, Scotland
j.mccall@rgu.ac.uk

José A. Gámez
Computing Systems Dept.
UCLM
Albacete, Spain
jose.gamez@uclm.es

José M. Puerta
Computing Systems Dept.
UCLM
Albacete, Spain
jose.puerta@uclm.es

ABSTRACT

Structural learning of Bayesian networks is a very expensive task even when sacrifying the optimality of the result. Because of that, there are some proposals aimed at obtaining relative-quality solutions in short times. One of them, namely Chain-ACO, searches an ordering among all variables with Ant Colony Optimization and a chain-structured surrogate model, and then uses this ordering to build a Bayesian network by means of the well-known K2 algorithm.

This work is based on Chain-ACO. We evaluate the impact of using a tree-structured surrogate model instead of a chain to evaluate orderings during the search. Moreover, we propose a variation of the way K2 builds the network, which consists of allowing some changes in the positions of the variables whenever they such changes not produce a cycle. This modification of the process may improve the score of the final network, without (almost) any additional cost.

Keywords

Bayesian Network Learning, Ant Colony Optimization, Surrogated Models

1. INTRODUCTION

Structural learning of Bayesian networks (BNs) from data is a complex task. Besides finding an optimal solution is an *NP-hard* problem, most algorithms require high execution times even for the search of approximate solutions. Because of that, and despite the existence of some optimal and suboptimal algorithms, the design of efficient methods is still an interesting topic [24], [1], [23].

*Corresponding author.

GECCO '15, July 11 - 15, 2015, Madrid, Spain

DOI: http://dx.doi.org/10.1145/2739480.2754806

Some of the proposals aimed at improving the efficiency of the learning process are based on the search of a topological ordering among variables, as it is possible to build a Bayesian network from an ordering in a relatively efficient way with the *K2* algorithm [8], or some of its modifications [1]. The advantages of this approach in relation with the direct search in the space of directed acyclic graphs are, mainly, a more efficient exploration of the search space, the avoidance of cycle detection, and the reduction in the number of local optima [23], [1].

As the search space of orderings is also exponential in the number of variables, it is common the use of different metaheuristics to find solutions also with this kind of representation [19], [1], [23], [12], [13], [5].

Even when algorithms use orderings and metaheuristics, they may require to build a network to evaluate each candidate solution (ordering).

In [26], the authors present an algorithm which use a surrogate model for evaluating the orderings during the search. This evaluation function returns the score of the *chain-like BN* compatible with the ordering, being this faster than building an unconstrained network. By means of *Ant Colony Optimization* (ACO) [6] and this evaluation scheme, the algorithm finds a reduced set of orderings that, afterwards, are used to build the final network with *K2*.

The idea underlying this algorithm is that a chain with high fitness contains "good" arcs -in terms of score- between pairs of variables, and these arcs will appear in the optimal network. This algorithm compares well with its counterpart, which uses *K2* to evaluate each ordering. However, the use of chains as surrogate models is very restrictive, and this fixed structure should not be the best to search for high quality orderings.

This article bases on the algorithm described above, and presents a variation, *Tree-ACO*, which uses the score of the best tree that can be built from an ordering as surrogate model. Although the tree structure is also bivariate, it considers more pairwise dependencies than the chain, whereas the complexity of its construction is almost the same.

Furthermore, it is possible to modify the way that *K2* (*K2M* in this work) builds the final network from the selected ordering. We propose and use a method which tries to optimize the process by carrying out some modifications in the ordering in such a way that, although the optimal set of parents of each node is calculated only once, the number of *candidate* parents is maximized. This way, the score of resulting network is always better (or equal in the worst case) than the score which would be obtained without any modification of the ordering. Nevertheless, the additional cost of this modification is almost nil.

As shown by the experimental results, the proposal based on using trees as surrogates improves the results obtained when using chains. Moreover, the way that the final network is built from the ordering found by the search algorithm produces a further improvement. Despite the fact that both improvements are significant, experiments show that the impact in the execution times are minimum.

The paper is divided into five sections besides this introduction. Section 2 describes the algorithm presented in [26], as well as the parameters and variations used in this study. Afterwards, Section 3 introduces the *Tree-ACO* algorithm, and Section 4 describes in detail the optimized method for the construction of the final network. The experimental study of the algorithms is carried out in Section 5 and, last, Section 6 presents the conclusions extracted from this work and possible lines of future work.

2. THE CHAIN-ACO ALGORITHM

There are several proposals of ACO algorithms for Bayesian network learning [11], [13], [21], [10], [22]. The use of this metaheuristic is due to the fact that it allows incorporating heuristic information, which is useful to guide the search.

In [26], the authors propose two ACO algorithms that search a topological ordering among variables. One of them, namely *K2ACO*, follows the approach of the algorithms presented in [13], i.e., each candidate ordering is evaluated by building the best compatible network with K2, and then getting the score of such network.

The other proposal presented in [26], namely *Chain-ACO*, follows a different approach, and aims at reducing the search and learning time. Instead of evaluating an ordering by means of building the compatible network, it builds the compatible *chain-like BN* and obtains its score.

The idea underlying this algorithm is that chains with high score will tend to contain links present in the optimal network. From the point of view of evolutionary computation, the chain is considered a *surrogate* model of the evaluation function [20].

The base of the algorithm used in [26] is the general purpose algorithm *Ant Colony System* described in [6]. The problem is represented by means of a fully connected graph, where each node i corresponds to a variable X_i, and each solution (ordering) corresponds with a path which traverses all nodes once.

Next, this section describes the generic parts of *Ant Colony System* and, afterwards, the *Chain-ACO* algorithm.

2.1 Ant Colony System

Ant colony system (ACS) [6] is one of the most basic ACO algorithms. In ACS, ants build paths according to a transition rule that, as in the rest of ACO algorithms, considers both the heuristic information and the amount of pheromone of each arc. It also uses a parameter, q_0, which determines when the election of a step is made in either a deterministic or a random way. These are the main components of the algorithm.

- The matrices $\tau(i,j)$ and $\eta(i,j)$.

They represent, respectively, the amount of pheromone (memoristic information) and the heuristic information associated to the arc $i \to j$.

- *Transition rule.*

If the ant is located in the node i (corresponding to variable X_i), the next node in the path, namely s, is chosen by means of:

$$s = \begin{cases} arg\ \underset{j \in J_k(i)}{max} \{\tau(i,j)\eta(i,j)^\beta\} & \text{if } q < q_0 \\ P_k(i) & \text{otherwise,} \end{cases}$$

in such a way that $\beta(>0)$ is a parameter which determines the relative importance of the pheromone, and q is a random number in $[0,1]$.

If $q < q_0$, then ant k chooses that node which maximizes $\tau(i,j)\eta(i,j)^\beta$ (combination of heuristic and pheromones), being $J_k(i)$ the set of nodes (variables) not visited by the ant yet.

If $q \geq q_0$, node s is obtained by sampling $P_k(i)$. According to this function, the probability of ant k moving from node i to node s is expressed as:

$$p_k(i,s) = \begin{cases} \frac{\tau(i,s)\eta(i,s)^\beta}{\sum_{j \in J_k(i)} \tau(i,j)\eta(i,j)^\beta} & \text{if } s \in J_k(i) \\ 0 & \text{otherwise.} \end{cases}$$

- *Pheromone update.*

Ant Colony System describes two rules for pheromone update.

The first of them is the *local update rule*, and implies that every time an ant moves from i to j, the pheromone level $\tau(i,j)$ moves towards its initial value, τ_0:

$$\tau(i,j) \leftarrow (1-\rho)\tau(i,j) + \rho \cdot \tau_0\,,\ (0 < \rho)$$

On the other hand, every time that the algorithm completes an iteration, all arcs in the best path, namely S^+, are updated. The amount of pheromone deposited on each arc is function of the fitness of the solution represented by the path, and is expressed as $\Delta(Ev(S^+))$.

This update rule, namely *global update rule*, is expressed as:

$$\tau(i,j) \leftarrow (1-\alpha)\tau(i,j) + \alpha \cdot \Delta(Ev(S^+))\,,\ (\alpha < 1).$$

2.2 Chain-ACO

2.2.1 The K2M Algorithm

In [1], the authors describe the algorithm *K2M*, which is a variation of the algorithm *K2* [8] for structural learning of Bayesian networks given a topological ordering.

K2M uses the *BDEu* [16] metric, which is decomposable and locally consistent [7]. The first property, decomposability, implies that the metric of the complete network is the result of adding the individual metric of each node. That is, let D be a data set, $\mathcal{G}$ a directed acyclic graph with n variables, and $Pa_{\mathcal{G}}(X_i)$ the set of parents of variable X_i in $\mathcal{G}$. The score (BDeu) of the network is obtained as:

$$f(\mathcal{G} : \mathcal{D}) = \sum_{i=1}^{n} f_D(X_i, Pa_{\mathcal{G}}(X_i)),$$

where $f_D(X_i, Pa_{\mathcal{G}}(X_i))$ is the individual score of the variable X_i given its parents in $\mathcal{G}$.

As *K2* does, *K2M* builds the network by determining, for each variable, the parent set which is compatible with the given ordering. In *K2*, this is done by *greedy* process which adds a candidate parent at each step. However, *K2M* allows the *arc delete* operation to this process, which then turns into a *local search*. Because of that, and due to the local consistency property as well, the resulting network is, asymptotically, a *minimal I-Map (minimal Independence Map)* of the original probability distribution, as it is demonstrated in [1].

2.2.2 The Chain-ACO Algorithm

Several components necessary for the complete definition of an ACO algorithm directly depend on the problem being solved. Concretely, the weight of the heuristic information, the initial amount of pheromone on each arc, and the rules for pheromone update (the global one in the case of *Ant Colony System*), are problem-dependent. Therefore, besides the way of evaluating each ordering, *Chain-ACO* must specify all these aspects. Next, all of them are detailed.

- *Heuristic information associated to each edge.*

Given two variables i and j, the original implementation of *Chain-ACO* establishes the weight of the heuristic component in the edge $i \rightarrow j$ from $\frac{1}{|f_D(X_j, \{X_i\})|}$.

This measure tend to give more heuristic weight to variables with greater individual score. Because of that, as it is done in [11] and [13], this scheme can be modified so that $\eta(i, j)$ is function of the increment of score induced by adding the arc $X_i \rightarrow X_j$ to the network. In the case of *Chain-ACO*, the improvement is measured in relation with the score of variable X_j without parents. This is:

$$\eta(i, j) = max\{f_D(X_j, \{X_i\}) - f_D(X_j, \emptyset), 0\}$$

The difference of scores relates the improvement with the heuristic weight directly. However, this improvement might even be negative. As this would cause a wrong behavior of the algorithm, we have fixed a minimum value $\eta(i, j) = 0$.

- *Initial amount of pheromones on each arc.*

There is a key factor when fixing the initial pheromone level: According to the transition rule of *ACS*, the probability of including $i \rightarrow j$ depends on the product $\tau(i, j)\rho(i, j)^{\beta}$. This implies that, given several alternatives (possible choices for j), the election depends on the relative level of pheromone among them, and not on their absolute values. Therefore, and regardless of the initial pheromone level, the influence of the pheromone in the exploration process is determined by means of the updating rules.

Because of that, and in order to gain more control over the rest of parameters (which is a *critical aspect of ACO*), we fixed $\tau_0 = 1$ for our implementation of *Chain-ACO*.

- *Global update.*

As mentioned above, the global pheromone update is a function of the best solution found on each iteration of the algorithm (S^+). In structural learning of Bayesian networks, the magnitude of this score, as well as the range of values that different solutions can take, is very variable. Thus, a difference δ between the scores of two networks could be insignificant when working over a particular dataset, and very high for another one.

In order to deal with this problem, the function regulating the update, Δ, considers the improvement obtained with S^+ in relation to the score of the network with no edges, $S^{\emptyset}$. Additional experiments, generating 50 random chains for each data set used in this work, and comparing their score with $S^{\emptyset}$, show values for $S^+/S^{\emptyset}$ between 0.96 and 1.2.

On the other hand, the amount of pheromone added must be proportional to the number arcs leaving the node, i.e., proportional to the number of variables.

According to both considerations, the function regulating the global update rule has been defined as:

$$\Delta(Ev(S^+)) = \left(\frac{S^{\emptyset}}{S^+} - 1\right) * n.$$

3. THE TREE-ACO ALGORITHM

The use of a bivariate model as surrogate in the context of Bayesian network learning is based on the fact that, in most cases, the parent which maximizes the (bivariate) score for a certain variable, is frequently included in the optimal parent set of such variable.

Chain-ACO is based on that idea. In order to evaluate an ordering during the search, it calculates the score of the compatible *chain-like Bayesian network*. However, this surrogate model loses a lot of information, as given a variable, its best parent could be any other preceding it, and not just the previous one. Because of that, it seems more reasonable that the individual score for each variable is obtained by *assigning as its only parent the best among all preceding variables*, i.e., using as surrogate model for the evaluation of an ordering the best compatible *tree-like Bayesian network*. This way, the evaluated arcs are more likely to appear in the network learnt from the ordering, and the score of the tree provides more information on the score of the network.

Table 1 shows the results of an experiment which confirms this hypothesis. For each one of the 7 databases used in this work (whose details are described in Section 5) we generated 500 random orderings. Then, for each ordering, we calculated the score of the chain compatible, the score of best tree, and their correlations with the score of the network obtained with *K2M*, which would correspond to the real evaluation.

As can be noticed, the correlation among the score of the best chain and the network obtained for a certain ordering is, generally, low. In some cases, even negative. This does not happen, however, with the correlation between the score of the best tree obtained from an ordering and the one from the compatible network. In such a case, all correlations are high, as even the lowest one, 0.55 is significant.

Table 1: Correlation between both surrogate models for ordering evaluation and the score of the network obtained with *K2M* (500 Random orderings for each database)

	Chain vs K2M	Tree vs K2M
Alarm	0.07	0.59
Barley	0.03	0.55
Child	0.13	0.88
Hailfinder	-0.11	0.90
Insurance	0.22	0.62
Mildew	-0.01	0.85
Munin	0.04	0.80

The algorithm *Tree-ACO* is similar to *Chain-ACO*, but uses a tree as surrogate model to evaluate orderings. The estimation of a tree does not require the calculation of any additional statistic, as all bivariate statistics are calculated and stored at the beginning.

3.1 Some comments on the heuristic function.

The heuristic information used by *Chain-ACO* to calculate the probability of transition from a node i to another j, $\eta(i, j)$, aims at including the best possible arc to the chain at each step. Thus, it considers $f_D(X_j, \{X_i\}) - f_D(X_j, \emptyset)$, i.e., the improvement induced by adding $X_i \rightarrow X_j$ in relation with the score of X_j without any parent.

However, when using a tree as surrogate model - and even considering the final network - this approach might not be the most suitable. Hence, once i is included in the ordering, any arc $X_i \rightarrow X_j$, such that X_j has not been visited yet, can be included in the final tree or network. Because of that, we can conclude that given two variables X_i and X_j, what is really important is their relative position in the ordering (and not their absolute positions).

On the other hand, and due to the properties of the metric:

$$f_D(X_j, \{X_i\}) - f_D(X_j, \emptyset) = f_D(X_i, \{X_j\}) - f_D(X_i, \emptyset)$$

that is, when no other arc exist, the improvement induced by $i \rightarrow j$ is the same as the improvement induced by $j \rightarrow i$. Therefore, the improvement induced by the relative position of two variables really depends on the rest of variables.

We tested several schemes for determining $\eta(i, j)$. As any variable preceding j in the ordering can be parent of j, we considered measures as the difference between the score obtained for X_j with its best parent in the ordering, and the score with its best parent among all variables; the improvement produced by using X_j as potential parent of the rest of variables; or combinations of both measures. *Surprisingly*, none of the tested heuristics improved the original proposal (the one used in *Chain-ACO*).

Because of that, we tested a simpler approach. By means of *K2M*, and without any ordering restriction, we obtained the optimal set of parents for each variable. Afterwards, we counted the number of times that each variable appears in the optimal set of parents of some other. The heuristic weight was obtained then as a function of this number. Therefore, the variables more *"valuable"* as parents will tend to appear before in the ordering. Concretely, if $countMP(X_j)$ is the number of times that X_j is included in the optimal set of parents of other variable:

$$\eta(i, j) = 1 + countMP(X_j) * n \quad \forall i.$$

4. OPTIMIZED K2M PROCEDURE

The algorithms presented before search for an ordering by ACS, and then use *K2M* to build the final network. This is done, as in *K2* by determining the optimal set of parents of each variable given the ordering.

During this process, the ordering is not modified. However, the results obtained by *K2M* can be improved by carrying out some small variations in the positions of the variables while building the network.

The procedure consists of searching the optimal set of parents for each variable sequentially, starting from the last one. Therefore, when processing the variable X_i, each variable appearing afterwards in the ordering must already have been processed. The set of parents of X_i is obtained then in four steps:

1. X_i is moved to the position previous to the first of its children in the ordering (all variables appearing after X_i have already been processed). That would not generate any cycle, but would allow all variables located between X_i and its first child to be parents of X_i. Figure 1 shows an example of this step.
2. The set of parents of X_i is obtained with *K2M*.
3. Once its parents have been obtained, X_i is moved just next to its last parent in the ordering. This would not create any cycle, and would allow X_i to be a part of the optimal set of parents of each variable located between its current and its original position. Figure 3 shows an example of this step.
4. Additionally, and as it is done in step 3, all children of X_i can be moved backwards in the ordering just next to their last parent.

The cost of this procedure is practically nil, as it only requires to check the tables storing parents and children of each node, and the set of parents for each variable is only calculated once. However, it may induce an improvement on the results, as *in the worst case* it would obtain the same network than *K2M*.

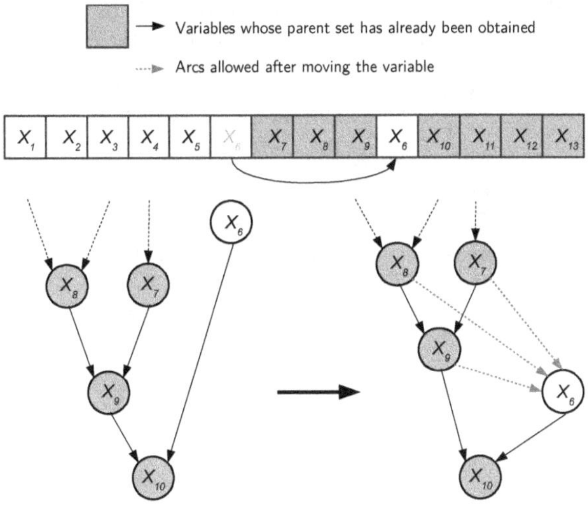

Figure 1: Step 1 of the optimized K2M. The first children of X_6 is X_{10}. X_6 can be moved forward, just before X_{10}, without creating any cycle. That would allow any of the variables X_7, X_8, or X_9 to be included in the set of parents of X_6.

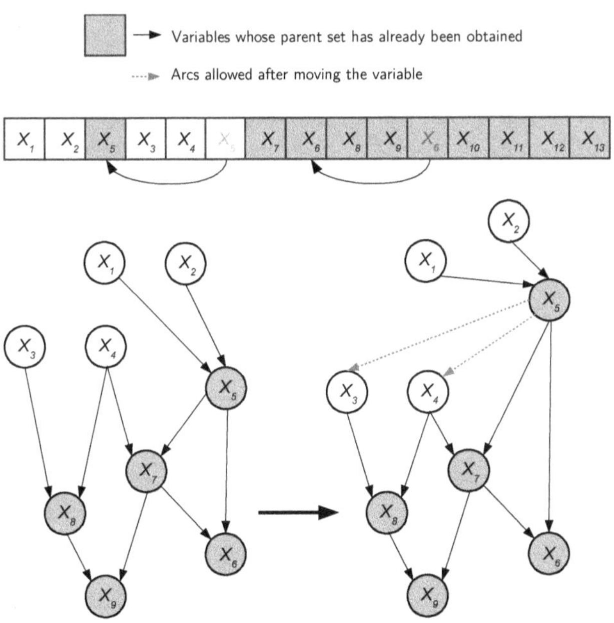

Figure 2: Step 3 of the optimized K2M. The last parent of X_5 is X_2. In the original ordering, X_5, can not be considered neither as parent of X_3 nor of X_4. However, moving X_5 just after X_2 does not create any cycle, and allows X_5 to be parent of both X_3 and X_4. In case of X_6, its movement just after X_7 does not create any cycle, but neither produces any improvement, as the parents of X_8 and X_9 have already been calculated.

5. EXPERIMENTAL EVALUATION

5.1 Datasets

In order to test and compare the different proposals described in this paper, we generated datasets from seven networks with different sizes and characteristics: *Alarm* [3], *Barley* [18], *Child* [9], *Hailfinder* [17], *Insurance* [4], *Mildew* [17] and Munin1 [2], all of them frequently used in related works.

Table 2 shows the information about these networks. As can be noticed, some of them represent domains defined with few variables, as *Alarm* and *Child*, whereas another, *Munin1*, models complex domains defined over hundreds of variables.

From each network, we obtained the corresponding data set by sampling 5000 instances.

Table 2: Bayesian networks used on the experimental evaluation. For each one of them we report: number of variables and arcs; average, minimum and maximum number of states for each variable; and maximum number of parents and children.

	Var.	Arc.	Mean St.	Min-Max St.	Max. Pa./ Ch.
Alarm	37	46	2.84	2-4	4/5
Barley	48	84	8.77	2-67	4/5
Child	20	25	3.00	2-6	2/7
Hailfinder	56	66	3.98	2-11	4/16
Insurance	27	52	3.30	2-5	3/7
Mildew	35	46	17.60	3-100	3/3
Munin 1	189	282	5.26	1-21	3/15

5.2 Evaluation of the algorithms

All algorithms have been tested with the same parameter configuration, which is detailed in Table 3. The parameter setting was done by preliminary experimentation over *Chain-ACO*, trying to get the best results for this algorithm.

Table 3: Parameters used in the different ACO algorithms.

Ants :	5
Iterations :	5000
q_0 :	0.5
β :	2
ρ :	0.1
α :	0.5
τ_0 :	1

All algorithms –*Chain-ACO*, *Tree-ACO* and the version which uses the optimized version of *K2M*, *Tree-ACO(Opt)*– have been run 30 times over each one of the datasets. Table 4 shows the average score (*BDEu*) for each case. The best result for each dataset has been marked in bold.

Table 4: Score (BDeu) obtained with the algorithms. Average for 30 runs.

Dataset	Chain-ACO	Tree-ACO	Tree-ACO(OPT)
Alarm	-50134.38	-49550.77	**-49463.31**
Barley	-300863.87	-296433.77	**-294377.59**
Child	-62536.78	-62459.62	**-62414.03**
Hailfinder	-255294.72	-254022.59	**-253869.18**
Insurance	-70276.05	-68932.23	**-68645.86**
Mildew	-263023.86	-259759.50	**-259750.99**
Munin1	-252662.83	-246180.59	**–242567.69**

The results in Table 4 are clear, as *Tree-ACO(OPT)* gets the best score for all problems, and *Tree-ACO* improves *Chain-ACO* for all problems too. Nevertheless, we performed a Friedmad test [15] with $\alpha = 0.05$, as suggested in [14]. The returned p-value, $9.1188e-04$, indicates statistical differences among the algorithms.

Table 5 shows the results for pairwise comparisons. We performed a Wilcoxon test [25], with $\alpha = 0.05$. As can be noticed, there are also statistical differences between all pairs of algorithms.

Table 5: Pairwise comparisons for score (BDeu)

		p-value	win	tie	loss
Tree-ACO(OPT)	Tree-ACO	2.3438e-02	7	0	0
Tree-ACO(OPT)	Chain-ACO	2.3438e-02	7	0	0
Tree-ACO	Chain-ACO	2.3438e-02	7	0	0

The first conclusion that can be drawn from the results is that *Tree-ACO* clearly outperforms *Chain-ACO*. Table 1 (Section 3) showed that the score of the tree obtained from an ordering is highly correlated with the score of the network learnt from the same ordering. However, besides using a tree as surrogate model, the proposed algorithm incorporated some changes in the way of incorporating the heuristic information. Some the improvement of *Tree-ACO* over *Chain-ACO* can also be due to the heuristic information. We have compared *Tree-ACO* with another version of the same algorithm which uses the same scheme for heuristic than *Chain-ACO*, namely *Tree-ACO(OldH)*. The results can be seen in Table 6. We carried out a Wilcoxon test with $\alpha = 0.05$ and it reported no statistical difference between both algorithms (p-value=$2.8906e-01$). Therefore, it seems that the way heuristic is incorporated is not a key issue for the algorithm (although it must be incorporated, according to some side experimentation).

In relation with the optimized *K2M* procedure, it is also clear that, as expected, the algorithm *Tree-ACO(OPT)* outperforms *Tree-ACO* (Table 5), as in the worst case the results must be the same.

As one of the main goals of this work was the design of efficient learning algorithms, we have also compared execution times. Table 7 shows the execution times (milliseconds - average over 30 runs) for each algorithm-dataset. Friedman test shows statistical differences between execution times in the algorithms (p-value = $3.8050e-03$).

Table 6: All results (BDeu) obtained for both versions of Tree-ACO. Average for 30 runs.

Dataset	Tree-ACO	Tree-ACO(OldH)
Alarm	**-49550.77**	-49951.59
Barley	**-296433.77**	-297195.74
Child	-62459.62	**-62294.38**
Hailfinder	-254022.59	**-253962.54**
Insurance	**-68932.23**	-69744.98
Mildew	-259759.5	**-259757.**0
Munin1	-246180.59	**-246158.88**

Table 7: Execution times(milliseconds) for all algorithms. Average for 30 runs.

Dataset	Chain-ACO	Tree-ACO	Tree-ACO(OPT)
Alarm	**931.50**	1253.10	1253.20
Barley	**1493.90**	2256.83	2242.30
Child	**289.30**	377.67	376.73
Hailfinder	**1922.47**	2643.33	2770.30
Insurance	**528.97**	671.90	698.93
Mildew	**856.83**	1139.47	1180.30
Munin1	**20750.60**	30140.10	33425.60

Again, we have carried out pairwise comparisons. The Wilcoxon test shows statistical differences between *Chain-ACO* and both *Tree-ACO* algorithms. However, there is no statistical difference in execution times between *Tree-ACO* and *Tree-ACO(OPT)*. This is an important result, as *Tree-ACO(OPT)* clearly improved *Tree-ACO* in terms of score.

Table 8: Pairwise comparison for execution times

		p-value	win	tie	loss
Tree-ACO	Tree-ACO(OPT)	**7.8125e-02**	5	0	2
Chain-ACO	Tree-ACO	2.3438e-02	7	0	0
Chain-ACO	Tree-ACO(OPT)	2.3438e-02	7	0	0

Lastly, Table 7 shows that differences between execution times of *Chain-ACO* and *Tree-ACO* are important for some problems. However, it is worth pointing out that the procedure used to calculate the heuristic information required to get the optimal parent set of each variable, prior to the execution of the ACO algorithm, is costly in terms of time, but some of the parent sets obtained can be re-used in the final network.

Moreover, as shown before, the scores obtained by *Tree-ACO* would not be statistically different if using other heuristic incorporation scheme, as in *Tree-ACO(OldH)*. In this case, the execution times are lowest (although they keep on presenting differences with *Chain-ACO*). For instance, the average execution time of Munin1 would fall from 30140.60 to 22045.37 milliseconds or, in the case of HailFinder from 2643.33 to 1992.47 milliseconds.

6. CONCLUSIONS AND FUTURE WORK

The experimental study, as well as the experiments carried out in Section 3, confirm our starting hypothesis, as the use of a tree structure as surrogate model for ordering evaluation improves the results obtained when using a chain.

Also, we have tested an scheme for incorporating heuristic information to the ACO process which considers the absolute position of each variable in the network, and is function of the times that it is included in the optimal set of parents of other. However, some additional experimentation shows that this and more complex schemes for heuristic incorporation do not improve that used by *Chain-ACO*.

Another important contribution of this work, consisted in the modification of the way that a network is built from an ordering with *K2M*. By allowing some changes in the positions of the variables during the process, the number of candidate parents for each variable is maximized, and an improvement in the score can be obtained with almost nil extra cost in terms of time.
This modification is, furthermore, independent of the ACO algorithm, and can be used to improve the results of each algorithm which explores the space of orderings.

In conclusion, the successive application of the exposed improvements has produced a substantial improvement upon the *Chain-ACO* algorithm.

The main line of future work derived from this work consists of the search of an optimal tree by greedy-based techniques, such as GRASP (Chow and Liu's algorithm can be used with mutual information, but not with BDEu), and the construction of networks from this tree.

Another line would focus on efficiency, and would try to obtain an ordering in a fast-heuristic way, and build the compatible network by using the optimized procedure described in Section 4 of this paper.

Acknowledgments

This work was partially supported by FEDER funds and the Spanish Government (MINECO) through projects TIN2010-20900-C04-03 and TIN2013-46638-C3-3-P; and by Junta de Comunidades de Castilla-La Mancha (JCCM) through PEII-2014-049-P. We thank Jacinto Arias for his help with the statistical tests.

7. REFERENCES

[1] Juan I. Alonso-Barba, Luis delaOssa, and Jose M. Puerta. Structural learning of bayesian networks using local algorithms based on the space of orderings. *Soft Computing.*, 15(10):1881–1895, October 2011.

[2] S. Andreassen, F. V. Jensen, S. K. Andersen, B. Falck, U. Kjærulff, M. Woldbye, A. R. Sørensen, A. Rosenfalck, and F. Jensen. *MUNIN – an expert EMG assistant*, chapter 21. Computer-Aided Electromyography and Expert Systems, 1989.

[3] I. A. Beinlich, H. J. Suermondt, R. M. Chavez, and G. F. Cooper. The alarm monitoring system: A case study with two probabilistic inference techniques for belief networks. In *Second European Conference on Artificial Intelligence in Medicine*, volume 38, pages 247–256, Berlin, 1989. Springer-Verlag.

[4] J. Binder, D. Koller, S. J. Russell, and K. Kanazawa. Adaptive probabilistic networks with hidden variables. *Machine Learning*, 29(2–3):213–244, 1997.

[5] Rosa Blanco, Iñaki Inza, and Pedro Larrañaga. Learning Bayesian networks in the space of structures by estimation of distribution algorithms. *International Journal of Intelligent Systems*, 18(2):205–220, 2003.

[6] Eric Bonabeau, Marco Dorigo, and Guy Theraulaz. *Swarm Intelligence: From Natural to Artificial Systems.* Oxford University Press, Inc., New York, NY, USA, 1999.

[7] D.M. Chickering. Optimal structure identification with greedy search. *Journal of Machine Learning Research*, 3:507–554, 2002.

[8] G.F. Cooper and E. Herskovits. A Bayesian method for the induction of probabilistic networks from data. *Machine Learning*, 9:309–347, 1992.

[9] R. G. Cowell, A. P. Dawid, S. Lauritzen, and D. Spiegelhalter. *Probabilistic Networks and Expert Systems (Information Science and Statistics).* Springer, 2003.

[10] Rónán Daly and Qiang Shen. Learning Bayesian Network Equivalence Classes with Ant Colony Optimization. *J. Artif. Intell. Res. (JAIR)*, 35:391–447, 2009.

[11] L.M. de Campos and J.A. G. Learning Bayesian networks by ant colony optimisation: Searching in two different spaces. *Mathware and Soft Computing (en prensa)*, 2002.

[12] L.M. de Campos and J.M. Puerta. Stochastic local algorithms for learning belief networks: Searching in the space of the orderings. In *Symbolic and Quantitative Approaches to Reasoning with Uncertainty*, number 2143 in Lecture Notes in Artificial Intelligence, pages 228–239. Springer Verlag, 2001.

[13] Luis M. de Campos, Juan M. Fernández-Luna, José A. Gámez, and José M. Puerta. Ant colony optimization for learning bayesian networks. *International Journal of Approximate Reasoning*, 31(3):291 – 311, 2002.

[14] Janez Demšar. Statistical comparisons of classifiers over multiple data sets. *The Journal of Machine Learning Research*, 7:1–30, 2006.

[15] Milton Friedman. A comparison of alternative tests of significance for the problem of m rankings. *The Annals of Mathematical Statistics*, pages 86–92, 1940.

[16] David Heckerman, Dan Geiger, and David Maxwell Chickering. Learning Bayesian networks: The combination of knowledge and statistical data. *Machine Learning*, 20(3):197–243, 1995.

[17] A. Jensen and F. Jensen. Midas–an influece diagram for management of mildew in winter wheat. In *Proceedings of the 12th Annual Conference on Uncertainty in Artificial Intelligence (UAI-96)*, pages 349–356, 1996.

[18] K. Kristensen and I. A. Rasmussen. The use of a Bayesian network in the design of a decision support system for growing malting barley without use of pesticides. *Computers and Electronics in Agriculture*, 33:197–217, 2002.

[19] Pedro Larrañaga, Hossein Karshenas, Concha Bielza, and Roberto Santana. A review on evolutionary algorithms in bayesian network learning and inference tasks. *Information Sciences*, 233(0):109 – 125, 2013.

[20] Xavier Llorà, Kumara Sastry, Tian-Li Yu, and David E. Goldberg. Do not match, inherit: Fitness surrogates for genetics-based machine learning techniques. In *Proceedings of the 9th Annual Conference on Genetic and Evolutionary Computation*, GECCO '07, pages 1798–1805, New York, NY, USA, 2007. ACM.

[21] Pedro C. Pinto, Andreas Ngele, Mathus Dejori, Thomas A. Runkler, and Joo Miguel da Costa Sousa. Learning of bayesian networks by a local discovery ant colony algorithm. In *IEEE Congress on Evolutionary Computation*, pages 2741–2748. IEEE, 2008.

[22] Khalid M. Salama and Alex Alves Freitas. Learning bayesian network classifiers using ant colony optimization. *Swarm Intelligence*, 7(2-3):229–254, 2013.

[23] Marc Teyssier and Daphne Koller. Ordering-based search: A simple and effective algorithm for learning bayesian networks. In *UAI '05, Proceedings of the 21st Conference in Uncertainty in Artificial Intelligence*, pages 548–549, Edinburgh,Scotland, 2005 2005. AUAI Press.

[24] Ioannis Tsamardinos, Laura E. Brown, and Constantin F. Aliferis. The max-min hill-climbing Bayesian network structure learning algorithm. *Machine Learning*, 65(1):31–78, 2006.

[25] Frank Wilcoxon. Individual comparisons by ranking methods. *Biometrics bulletin*, pages 80–83, 1945.

[26] Yanghui Wu, John A. W. McCall, and David W. Corne. Two novel ant colony optimization approaches for bayesian network structure learning. In *Proceedings of the IEEE Congress on Evolutionary Computation, CEC 2010, Barcelona, Spain, 18-23 July 2010*, pages 1–7, 2010.

Genetically-regulated Neuromodulation Facilitates Multi-Task Reinforcement Learning

Sylvain Cussat-Blanc
University of Toulouse
21 Allée de Brienne
31042 Toulouse, France
cussat@irit.fr

Kyle I. S. Harrington
Beth Israel Deaconess Medical Center
Harvard Medical School
02215 Boston, MA
kharrin3@bidmc.harvard.edu

ABSTRACT

In this paper, we use a gene regulatory network (GRN) to regulate a reinforcement learning controller, the State-Action-Reward-State-Action (SARSA) algorithm. The GRN serves as a neuromodulator of SARSA's learning parameters: learning rate, discount factor, and memory depth. We have optimized GRNs with an evolutionary algorithm to regulate these parameters on specific problems but with no knowledge of problem structure. We show that genetically-regulated neuromodulation (GRNM) performs comparably or better than SARSA with fixed parameters. We then extend the GRNM SARSA algorithm to multi-task problem generalization, and show that GRNs optimized on multiple problem domains can generalize to previously unknown problems with no further optimization.

Categories and Subject Descriptors

I.2.6 [**Learning**]: Parameter learning

Keywords

Reinforcement learning; Gene regulatory network; Parameter control; Multi-task Learning; Neuromodulation

1. INTRODUCTION

Transfer and multi-task learning has recently been receiving attention within the reinforcement and machine learning communities [18, 31]. The ability to generalize between learnable tasks is a challenge that is far from fully solved, but is achievable, as evidenced by biological organisms capable of generalizing across multiple tasks. In this work we use an evolutionary algorithm to optimize gene-regulatory networks (GRNs) that dynamically tune the parameters of a reinforcement learning (RL) algorithm. This genetically-regulated neuromodulation (GRNM) extends previous results that showed GRNM can enhance the learning of agents beyond traditional fixed parameter RL [15]. We apply GRNM to additional problem classes, and show that GRNs evolved on agents learning a subset of problems can facilitate learning on previously unencountered problems.

This paper is organized as follows. First, we briefly summarize RL and explicate the SARSA algorithm used in this study. Then, an introduction to gene regulatory networks is given with the details of the computational model we use. Section 4 shows how we use the regulatory network for neuromodulation. Section 5 presents the four problems we use neuromodulation on followed by the results of GRNs trained specifically on each problem and the capacity of the GRNs to generalize their behavior to unknown problems.

GECCO '15, July 11–15, 2015, Madrid, Spain
© 2015 ACM. ISBN 978-1-4503-3472-3/15/07...$15.00
DOI: http://dx.doi.org/10.1145/2739480.2754730

2. REINFORCEMENT LEARNING

Reinforcement learning is a reward-based learning algorithm that allows agents to learn from experience. More formally, reinforcement learning (RL) is a mathematical framework for learning from a reward signal that is derived from Bellman's equation for optimal control [30]. One of the most important forms of RL is temporal-difference (TD) RL. TD-RL is a method for learning optimal behavior from changes in state and reinforcement by error prediction [28]. TD-RL agents learn an expected return that will be received after taking an action in any state. Strong correlations with this type of error predictive behavior have been found in studies of dopamine neurons [23].

TD-RL is used to solve Markov decision processes, which are an extension of Markov chains to problems framed in terms of state, action, and reward. Reward signals are encoded in a table which associates action preferences with states. The basic TD(γ) algorithm updates one state-action association at a timestep, which restricts sequence learning. Eligibility traces are used to associate reward with sequences of actions by reinforcing a weighted history of recent actions. In this study an online version of TD-RL, SARSA (short for, state-action-reward-state-action), is used. A review of reinforcement learning can be found in [30].

We include a few of the key equations from the SARSA algorithm. If we are in state s_t at time t, then we will take some action a_t which will bring us a reward r_t. This action will also cause us to transition to the state s_{t+1}. The SARSA algorithm learns a Q-function, which maps a value to each state-action pair (s_t, a_t). From each state multiple actions, A_t, may be taken. Given an optimal Q-function the best action to take is $argmin_{a_t \in A_t} Q(s_t, a_t)$.
The Q-function is approximated by SARSA with the following update rule

$$Q(s_t, a_t) \leftarrow Q(s_t, a_t) + \alpha[r_{t+1} + \gamma Q(s_{t+1}, a_{t+1}) - Q(s_t, a_t)] \quad (1)$$

where α is the learning rate, and γ is the discounting factor. Given only this update rule, it can be difficult to compute the Q-value for state-action pairs which indirectly contribute to obtaining a reward. This update method propagates information only to the preceding state-action pair, for those that are very distant from the reward, such as in the case of maze solving problems, this can require a large number of repeated trials. However, reward propagation can be partially alleviated by eligibility traces. Eligibility traces store an accumulating trace of state-action pairs. The "memory" of these state-action pairs can be tuned with the trace decay parameter λ. Eligibility traces are updated with

$$e_t(s,a) = \begin{cases} \gamma\lambda e_{t-1}(s,a) & \text{if } s \neq s_t \\ \gamma\lambda e_{t-1}(s,a) + 1 & \text{if } s = s_t \end{cases} \quad (2)$$

By combining the error predictive capabilities of SARSA with the state-action sequence memory of eligibility traces we can amplify the effects of our reward and speed up the learning process. When performing on-policy learning it is important to ensure that a sufficient amount of exploration occurs. To this end the ϵ-greedy method is used, where a random action is taken with $p(\epsilon)$, otherwise the agent's most preferred action is taken. However, the RL algorithm can still fail to capitalize on rarely experienced rewards.

3. GENE REGULATORY NETWORK

Artificial gene regulatory networks (GRNs) are a class of biologically-inspired algorithms. In living systems, GRNs are used within the cell to control DNA transcription and, correspondingly, the phenotypic gene expression. Although the inner workings of the cell are governed by a large collection of complex machines, simplified models of cells as entities with protein sensors and actuators both exhibit complex behavior and offer insights into natural systems [6]. These protein sensors represent receptor molecules localized to the cellular membrane which transduce external activity into excitatory and/or inhibitory regulatory signals. Cells can use external signals collected from protein sensors localized on the membrane to activate or inhibit the transcription of the genes. Computational models have been used in many developmental models of the literature [16, 9, 4] and to control virtual and real robots [32, 21, 17, 5].

Our model is based on Banzhaf's biologically-inspired model [1], a gene regulatory network is defined as a set of abstract proteins. Each protein has the following properties:

- The *concentration* is the quantity of each protein available in the network. This concentration influences the regulation of other proteins: the higher the concentration, the greater the effect on other proteins.
- The protein *tag* coded as an integer between 0 and p. The upper value p of the domain can be changed in order to control the precision of the GRN.
- The *enhancer tag* coded as an integer between 0 and p. The enhancer tag is used to calculate the enhancing matching factor between two proteins.
- The *inhibitor tag* coded as an integer between 0 and p. The inhibitor tag is used to calculate the inhibiting matching factor between two proteins.
- The *type* determines if the protein is an *input* protein, the concentration of which is given by the environment of the GRN and which regulates other proteins but is not regulated, an *output* protein, the concentration of which is used as output of the network and which is regulated but does not regulate other proteins, or a *regulatory* protein, an internal protein that regulates and is regulated by other proteins.

The dynamics of the GRN are calculated as follows. First, the affinity of a protein a to another protein b is given by the enhancing factor u^+_{ab} and the inhibiting u^-_{ab}:

$$u^+_{ab} = p - |enh_a - id_b| \quad ; \quad u^-_{ab} = p - |inh_a - id_b| \quad (3)$$

where id_x is the tag, enh_x is the enhancer tag and inh_x is the inhibiting tag of protein x.

The GRN's dynamics are calculated by comparing the proteins two by two using the enhancing and the inhibiting matching factors. For each protein in the network, the global enhancing value is given by the following equation:

$$g_i = \frac{1}{N}\sum_j^N c_j e^{\beta(u^+_{ij} - u^+_{max})} \quad ; \quad h_i = \frac{1}{N}\sum_j^N c_j e^{\beta(u^-_{ij} - u^-_{max})} \quad (4)$$

where g_i (or h_i) is the enhancing (or inhibiting) value for a protein i, N is the number of proteins in the network, c_j is the concentration of protein j and u^+_{max} (or u^-_{max}) is the maximum enhancing (or inhibiting) matching factor observed. β is a control parameter described hereafter.

The final modification of protein i concentration is given by the following differential equation:

$$\frac{dc_i}{dt} = \frac{\delta(g_i - h_i)}{\Phi} \quad (5)$$

where Φ is a function that keeps the sum of all protein concentrations equal to 1.

β and δ are two constants that set up the speed of reaction of the regulatory network. In other words, they modify the dynamics of the network. β affects the importance of the matching factor and δ affects the level of production of the protein in the differential equation. The lower both values, the smoother the regulation. Similarly, the higher the values, the more sudden the regulation.

4. NEUROMODULATION

In living organisms, neuromodulators are neuropeptides or small molecules, such as dopamine and serotonin. The production of these substances within the cell is controlled by gene regulatory networks. Neuromodulators change the behavior of neural networks within individual neurons, amongst neighboring neurons, or throughout the entire network. Neuromodulation has been found to be pervasive throughout the brain, and can have drastic consequences on the behavior of neurons and neuronal circuits [8, 19]. We have already noted that the temporal difference learning algorithm for error prediction has been observed in neural substrates [24]. An extensive review of computational models of neuromodulation can be found in [12], and some recent models are reviewed in [19]. In this study we extend work on the evolution of neuromodulation [15], focusing on the relationship between evolved neuromodulatory GRNs and reinforcement learning.

4.1 Regulating parameters

A number of algorithms have been introduced by the RL community for dynamically tuning parameters during learning and their convergence properties have been investigated [26]. However, in this study we study focus on a method inspired by neuromodulation both because of biological evidence linking reinforcement learning and neuromodulation, as well as previous findings that have demonstrated the robustness of GRNs to noise and their extensive adaptive capacity [22]. With the intention of focusing on the optimization of genetically-regulated neuromodulation, the physical mechanisms underlying neuromodulation are used as inspiration and the neuromodulation of reinforcement learning was optimized. Neuromodulation has been considered in the context of RL [10, 25, 11], but this previous work has not focused on the implications of neuromodulation on problem solving capacity. In this work we utilize the artificial gene regulatory network presented in the previous section to regulate the learning parameters of the SARSA algorithm. Three learning parameters are considered: the learning rate α, the discount factor γ and the memory depth λ.

To do so, the GRN uses three inputs that describe the current performance of the agent in the environment. They have been chosen to be problem-independent as one of our goals is to define a problem-independent neuromodulation architecture to minimize problem-specific adjustments. The first input describes the duration from the beginning of current episode: the concentration of this first input protein increases with the time spent in each learning episode. The concentration $C_{I_1}(t)$ of this input protein at time step t is calculated as follows:

$$C_{I_1}(t) = e^{-\frac{t^2}{t_{max}^2}} \tag{6}$$

where t_{max} is the expected duration of an episode. The second output protein's concentration $C_{I_2}(t)$ describes the quality of the current sequence of actions in term of rewards (smoothed over 25 steps to buffer the effect of sudden changes in reward signal):

$$C_{I_2}(t) = \frac{\sum_{s=1}^{25} \Big((25 - s) \times q_s(t-1) \Big)}{\sum_{s=1}^{25} s} \tag{7}$$

$$\text{with } q_s(t) = \begin{cases} 1 + 1000 \frac{Q.e}{Q.Q*e.e} & \text{if} \frac{Q.e}{Q.Q*e.e} > 0.4995 \\ 0 & \text{otherwise} \end{cases}$$

where e is the eligibility trace and Q is the Q-function, both described in Section 2. The aim of this input is to capture the quality of the current state history relative to previous experiences. Finally, the third input protein's concentration $C_{I_3}(t)$ informs the GRN about the 25-step smoothed average reward the agent can obtain in its current state:

$$C_{I_3}(t) = \frac{\sum_{s=1}^{24} \Big((25 - s) \times C_{I_3}(t-s) \Big) + 25 \times \sum_{r_e \in e} r_e}{\sum_{s=1} 25s} \tag{8}$$

where e is the eligibility trace. The formulae for GRN inputs involve multiple constants that were empirically determined to yield input values that are robust across multiple problems. This input encodes the frequency that the agent has reentered the same state.

In addition to these inputs, the GRN uses four output proteins to regulate the learning parameters:

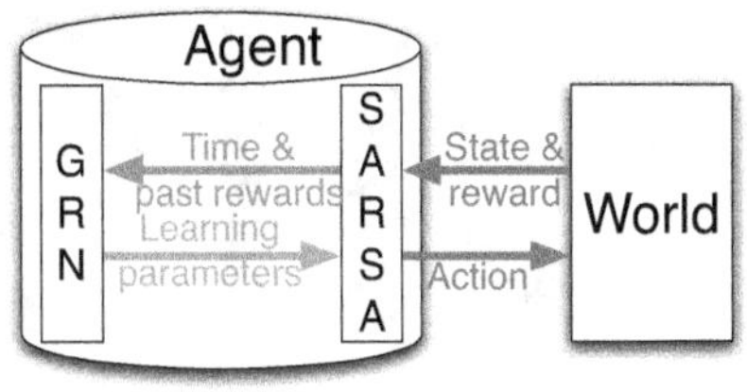

Figure 1: At every time step, SARSA updates the GRN inputs. The GRN returns updated learning parameters that are used by the SARSA algorithm.

- the output protein O_n, which concentration C_n normalizes the concentration of other outputs[1],
- the output protein O_α of concentration C_α, which provides the value for α to the SARSA algorithm with $\alpha = C_\alpha/(C_\alpha + C_n)$,
- the output protein O_γ of concentration C_γ, which provides the value for γ to the SARSA algorithm with $\gamma = C_\gamma/(C_\gamma + C_n)$,
- the output protein O_λ of concentration C_λ, which provides the value for λ to the SARSA algorithm with $\lambda = C_\lambda/(C_\lambda + C_n)$.

As depicted by figure 1, the GRN updates SARSA's learning parameters at every time step, before SARSA updates its internal variables and prediction. The GRN returns the learning parameters SARSA uses for its own decision step.

4.2 GRN Optimization

Before a gene regulatory network can be used for successful neuromodulation, the GRN is optimized for the ability to regulate SARSA parameters on one or multiple problems. In this paper, we use an evolutionary algorithm designed specifically for the evolution of GRNs called GRNEAT [3]. GRNEAT incorporates three key features: initialize with small networks, speciation of GRNs based upon a measure of similarity between networks, and an aligned crossover that preserves subnetwork architecture when recombining GRNs. This modified algorithm has been shown to converge faster and to better solutions than standard genetic algorithms. More details on GRNEAT can be found in [3].

During optimization, each GRN is evaluated independently on a given problem with 25 reruns in order to reduce the effect of stochasticity on fitness. As fitness is problem dependent, more detail is provided in the corresponding experiment sections. To avoid any memory bias, SARSA is completely reset before each evaluation. The parameters used for GRNEAT in this work are given by Table 1, and are consistent for all problems.

5. PROBLEMS

We have studied GRNM on four classic problems: Mountain Car, Maze, Puddle World and Acrobat. These problems are implemented within the RLPark software package [7]. These particular problems were chosen both because they represent classic benchmarks for RL and they represent a range of reward structures. Maze uses a discrete state-space,

[1]This is generally used in regulatory networks to obtain output values in [0, 1].

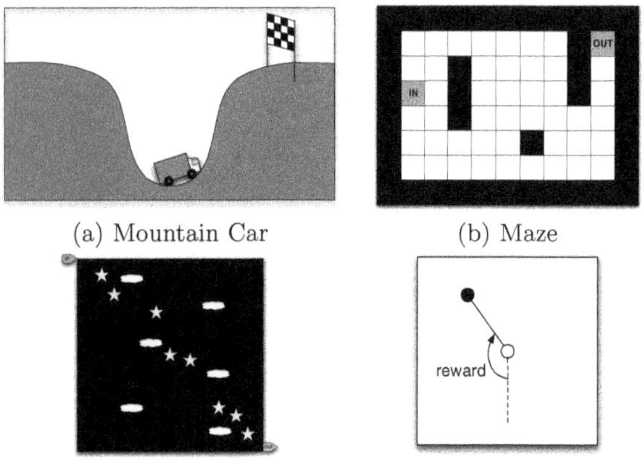

(a) Mountain Car (b) Maze (c) Puddle World (d) Acrobat

Figure 2: Schematics of test problems.

Parameter	value
Population size	500
Initial duplicates	19
Speciation threshold	0.15
Species min size	15
Selection	3-player tournament
Crossover rate	0.2
Mutation rate	0.8

Table 1: GRNEAT parameters used for evolution.

and agents only receive a one-shot reward upon completion. Mountain Car, Puddle World, and Acrobat problems all involve continuous state spaces and continuous reward signals. ϵ-greedy action selection with $\epsilon = 0.1$ is used in all problems for both fixed parameter SARSA and GRNM. In all cases agents do not have prior information about the specific task. Before detailing results obtained with GRNM, this section presents each problem.

5.1 Mountain Car

The Mountain Car problem was introduced by Moore to promote the broad applicability of dynamic programming [20]. In the mountain car problem, depicted in Figure 2(a), the agent is placed at the bottom of a valley with no initial velocity and must drive to the top of the right hill. The agent can take one of 3 actions: full thrust forward, full thrust in reverse, or no thrust. The difficulty of the task lies in the fact that the right hill is too steep to be climbed at full thrust, and thus the agent must first reverse up the left hill to gain sufficient momentum to climb the right hill. The agent experiences a negative reward for all time steps that it has not reached the top of the right hill, at which point the episode is completed. For evolution of GRNs, the fitness of an evaluation is given by the number of step necessary to complete a series of 25 episodes.

	α	γ	λ
Mountain car	0.071429	1.0	0.928571
Maze	1.0	0.928571	0.928571
Puddle world	0.057142	0.928571	0.5
Acrobate	0.05	0.928571	0.785714

Table 2: Fixed learning parameters for the SARSA algorithm obtained by parameter sampling.

5.2 Maze

Depicted in figure 2(b), the maze task was originally introduced by Sutton as an example problem for demonstrating the capabilities of initial reinforcement learning algorithms [27]. The maze is a 6 by 9 grid with 7 obstacles, a start, and a goal position. From any position, the agent may take any of 4 actions (right, left, up, and down); however, when the action would move the agent out-of-bounds or onto an obstacle, the agent remains in place. The only time a reward is received is when the agent reaches the goal, at which point the episode is completed. Although this problem and its variants have been studied by a number of researchers, of particular interest is Hanada's study which applies evolutionary programming to a multi-task version of Sutton's maze [14]. The fitness of a training run is given by the number of steps necessary to complete a series of 30 episodes.

5.3 Puddle World

The puddle world problem was introduced by Boyan and Moore [2], but was later presented in greater detail by Sutton [29]. As shown in figure 2(c), agents solving the puddle world task exist in a 2D continuous space. Agents may take 4 actions as in the maze problem (left, right, up, and down), but as opposed to the maze problem, actions in puddle world are stochastic. For these experiments the world is 100 by 100, and an agents action moves a unit distance $\pm$ noise taken uniformly from [-0.1,0.1]. The agent experiences a reward of -1 for each timestep until the episode is complete, and, if within either puddle, $-400 * d$, where d is the closest distance to a puddle's edge. The fitness is given by the average of rewards received during 40 episodes.

5.4 Acrobat

The acrobat problem has a long-standing history in robotics and control, some references to which may be found in [30]. The agent controls 2 segments with 2 joints, where the first joint represents attachment to the bar, and the second joint represents the waist of the acrobat. The agent can only control the second joint, and the corresponding actions are: apply a fixed amount of positive torque, apply a fixed amount of negative torque, or apply no torque. The agent is initialized in a downward vertical position and must reach an upward vertical position. The agent receives a reward of -1 for each timestep until the episode is complete. This problem is schemetized by figure 2(d). The fitness is given by the average of rewards received during 30 episodes.

6. GRNS FOR INDIVIDUAL PROBLEMS

In this first experiment, we have trained our GRNM model independently on each problem. To evaluate the gain provided by neuromodulation, we first determine the best fixed parameters to use with SARSA on each problem. We use combinatorial parameter sampling on α, γ and λ in $[0, 1]$ with 0.0714 steps (15 evaluations). Each evaluation is averaged on 10 replicates in order to average the randomness of the problems. At the end of the parameter sampling stage, we chose the best fixed learning parameters for a given problem by selecting the tuple with the highest fitness. These parameters are given in Table 2.

6.1 Mountain Car

Figure 3(a) plots the behavior of the best GRN obtained after 150 iterations. This figure plots the input proteins' concentrations and the three learning parameters calculated by the gene regulatory network. The GRN maintains almost constant parameter values over each episode time, except at the beginning where α and γ are increased. This reinforces learned values for the initial part of the agent's trajectory. In this experiment, it should also to be noticed that λ is kept at zero all over time, suggesting that on this simple problem sequence learning may not be necessary.

This GRN is then compared to the SARSA algorithm with fixed learning parameters on 100 independent reruns of mountain car with different random seeds. Figure 3(b) shows the results obtained for each episode averaged on the 100 runs. We can observe that GRNM trained on the mountain car (in green) beats the SARSA algorithm with fixed parameters (in red) on every episodes. More specifically, the first episodes (from 1 to 3) show that GRNM learns faster than the SARSA algorithm and later episodes (from 3 to 25) show that neuromodulation leads to agents that solve the problem faster than fixed-parameter SARSA. When comparing detailed results on Figure 5, the GRN-based neuromodulation gives better results on the mountain car problem when averaged on 100 independent runs.

6.2 Maze

The same procedure has been used to evolve a gene regulatory network to regulate SARSA algorithm's learning parameters on the Maze problem. Figure 3(c) presents the behavior of the best GRN obtained after evolution. The regulatory dynamics differ significantly from those obtained on the Mountain Car problem. This GRN starts with very high values for all learning parameters leading to a strong memorization of initial experiences. Then, upon discovering successful solutions, the learning rate α and the memory depth λ decrease to exploit the learned behaviors. γ is kept very high all along the simulation.

When compared to the fixed-parameter SARSA algorithm (Figure 3(d)), we can observe that GRNM is learning faster than the SARSA algorithm (episodes 2 to 5). However, the advantage turns to the fixed-parameter SARSA algorithm in the remaining episodes: the latter is doing slightly better than GRNM from episode 6 to the end. In an unpaired t-test fixed-parameter SARSA outperforms GRNM with $p = 0.0001$ on the Maze problem. Detailed results for the Maze problem are given by Figure 5.

6.3 Puddle World

Figure 3(e) presents the behavior of the best GRN obtained when neuromodulation is optimized on the puddle world problem. Once again, the GRN chooses to use higher learning parameters α and λ at the beginning of the simulation to learn from initial experiences faster. After this initial phase, the GRN increases the discounting factor and reduces the amount of memorization in order to better exploit learned experiences. This gives good results in comparison to fixed-parameter SARSA: as depicted in Figure 3(f), GRNM learns the value of states and actions faster and converges to an equivalent solution to fixed-parameter SARSA. When comparing the results in detail (Figure 5), neuromodulation obtains equivalent results when averaged on 100 independent runs but the standard deviation and worst result are better: the GRNM is capable of modulating the learning parameters when harder scenarios are encountered.

6.4 Acrobat

Figure 3(g) shows the regulation obtained with the best GRN evolved on the acrobat problem. The GRN finds learning parameters very close to the one obtained with parameter sampling for the fixed-parameter SARSA algorithm. However, in addition to finding these parameters, the GRN reduces these values all along the episodes, in particular α which decreases down to zero. As in the puddle world problem, the aim is to exploit more the results when an appropriate behavior is found by the SARSA algorithm. When compared to the fixed-parameter SARSA algorithm on this problem (Figure 3(h)), GRN-based neuromodulation both learns faster and finishes with a better behavior than the fixed-parameter SARSA algorithm. This is confirmed by results shown in Figure 5 in which the reward averaged on 100 independent runs is largely over with neuromodulation than with the fixed-parameter SARSA algorithm.

7. USING THE GRN EVOLVED ON MAZE

A powerful property of artificial gene regulatory networks is their capacity to generalize to unknown situations [22]. In the case of genetically-regulated neuromodulation, we considered the best GRN trained on the maze problem and tested it on other problems. We noticed that it performs well in comparison to the fixed-parameter SARSA algorithm: as presented in Figure 5, GRNM trained on maze (noted GRN_{mz}) obtains better results than the fixed-parameter SARSA algorithm on all other problems we have tested. In our opinion, the regulatory dynamics of this GRN are very generic: when the rewards start to increase, the learning rate is lowered to preserve previously learned experiences. This regulatory dynamic appears to be appropriate for most problems. However, this generic regulatory network does not beat GRNs trained on specific problems. This can be explained by the fact that optimizing the GRN on an individual problem allows the system to exploit problem-specific features, improving the quality of the parameter regulation.

Figure 4(a-c) shows the behavior of the GRN trained on the Maze problem and used on other problems. The behaviors are slightly different on each problem: the GRN is able to adapt to problem specificities. In particular, when the episodes are taking to much time, this GRN increases λ first and then α. It is also interesting to notice that the stabilized values of the learning parameters differ from a problem to another. For example, λ is kept around 0.8 on the mountain car problem, around 0.65 for the puddle world and the acrobat problems whereas it is equal to 0.7 on the maze problem. These values have to be compared to the best values obtained for fixed parameters in Figure 5: it shows the capacity of the GRN to approximate the best learning parameters to a problem without further learning.

When comparing to the fixed-parameter SARSA algorithm and GRNM optimized specifically on one problem (Figure 5), the GRN evolved on Maze outperforms fixed-parameter SARSA on Mountain Car and Acrobat but has poorer results on Puddle World. However, the worst-case is better than fixed-parameter SARSA on all problems, even Puddle World where the average reward is lower. Once again, this shows the capacity of GRNM to compensate learning parameters in harder scenarios.

8. EVOLVING A GENERIC GRN

Based on this observation, we have trained a new GRN on two problems instead of only one. The aim is to obtain a generic GRN that has been optimized for multiple problems. We have chosen to train the GRN on the Maze and the Mountain Car problems because of their differences in reward structure (reward is received once in Maze, and continuously in Mountain Car), as well as state-space (Maze uses a discrete state-space, while Mountain Car uses a continuous state-space). Figure 4(d-g) shows the behavior of the best GRN obtained. Comparable regulatory behavior can be observed on the different problems: at the beginning of each episode, λ is set up to a high value and then reduces until the end of the episode. However, the parameter values are regulated to different levels for each problem. The GRN might use the current step quality and the average state reward inputs to regulate these levels. These inputs provide the GRN with an estimation of the agent's progression in an episode. As the agent progresses further into an episode, the number of sequences of actions that could have led to any given state are almost always increasing, thus when the agent is learning values of states and actions later in an episode it appears to be useful to discount older actions and favor shorter and more recent sequences of actions.

We have compared this generic GRN to specific GRNs (optimized on each problem), to GRN trained on Maze and the best of from 3375 randomly-generated GRNs[2] (each random GRN is evaluated on one problem with the fitness function used to optimize the GRN previously). The same procedure as with prior experiments is used to evaluate these

[2] 3375 corresponds to the number of evaluations we used to obtain the fixed parameter for SARSA.

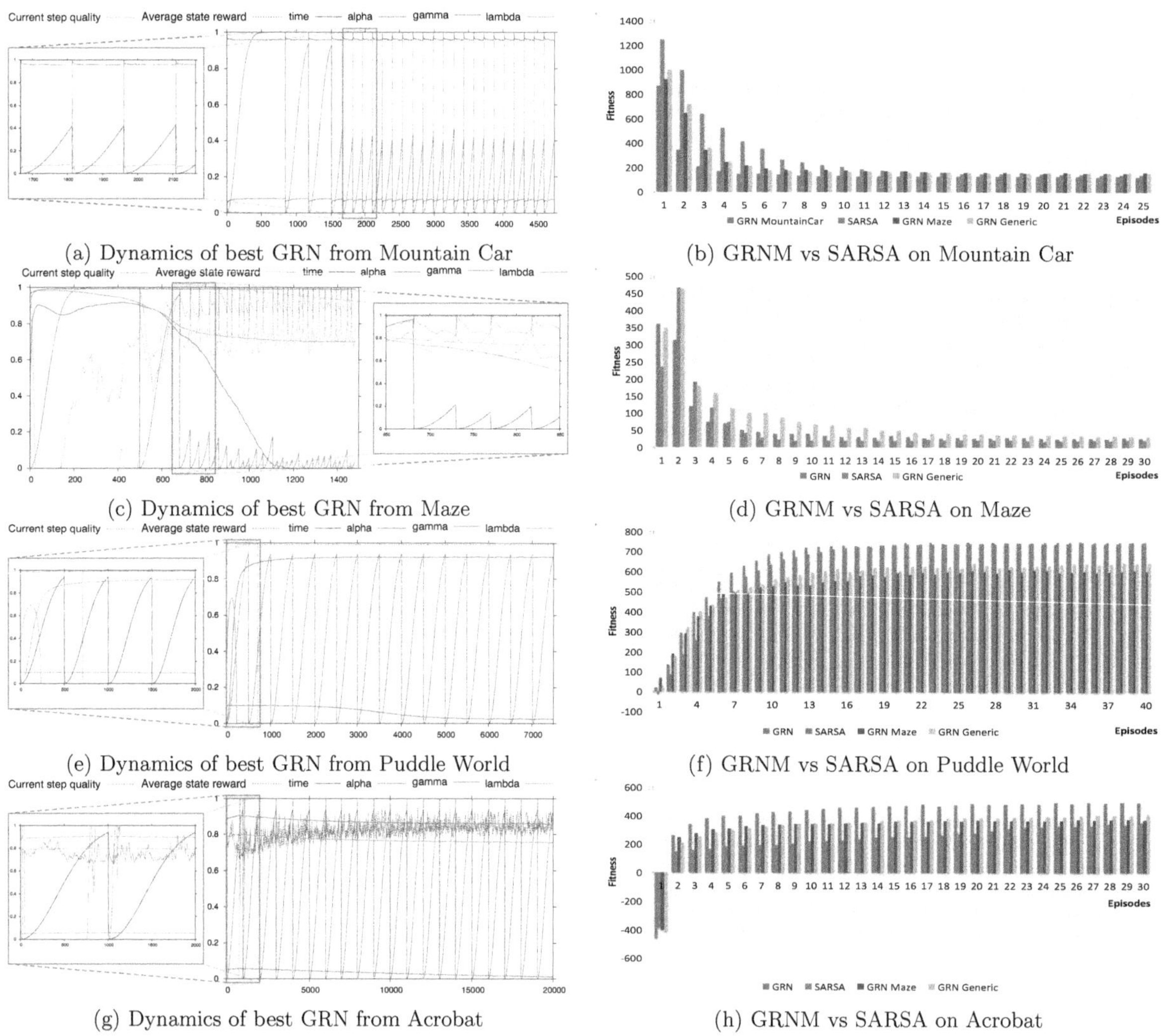

(a) Dynamics of best GRN from Mountain Car

(b) GRNM vs SARSA on Mountain Car

(c) Dynamics of best GRN from Maze

(d) GRNM vs SARSA on Maze

(e) Dynamics of best GRN from Puddle World

(f) GRNM vs SARSA on Puddle World

(g) Dynamics of best GRN from Acrobat

(h) GRNM vs SARSA on Acrobat

Figure 3: GRNs evolved on individual problems: (a,c,e,g) Regulation of the learning parameters of the best GRN obtained; (b,d,f,h) Comparison of the fitnesses per episode (abscissa) obtained by GRNM with a GRN trained on problem (green), with a GRN trained on maze (blue) for non-Maze problems, and with fixed-parameter SARSA algorithm (red). Results are averaged on 100 independent runs. Lower is better.

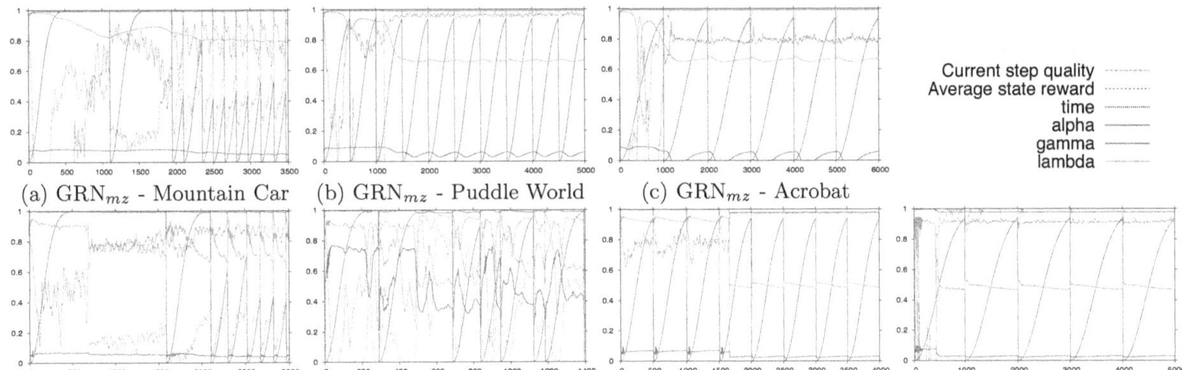

(a) GRN_{mz} - Mountain Car (b) GRN_{mz} - Puddle World (c) GRN_{mz} - Acrobat

(d) GRN_{g} - Mountain Car (e) GRN_{g} - Maze (f) GRN_{g} - Puddle World (g) GRN_{g} - Acrobat

Figure 4: (a-c) Behavior of the GRN trained on the Maze problem when used on other problems; (d-g) Behavior of the generic GRN when used on all problems.

GRNs on the different problems: the GRN is evaluated on 100 independent runs with different random seeds. Corresponding results are shown in Figure 5 as GRN_g for generic GRNs, and GRN_{rnd} for random GRNs. In all cases the generic GRN performs at least as well, or better than random GRNs. Interestingly, the generic GRN beats GRN_{mz} on the Puddle World and Acrobat problems but does not beat the GRNs specifically trained on these problems. The generic GRN and the GRN trained on Maze perform comparably on the Mountain Car problem, but the GRN trained on Maze is doing better on the Maze itself. This was expected since the GRN trained on Maze is specifically optimized for this problem whereas the generic GRN has been trained on two problems and thus its optimization was also affected by training on Mountain Car. Just as the GRN trained on Maze, the generic GRN beats the fixed-parameter SARSA algorithm on the Mountain Car and Acrobat problems. Both the Maze and Puddle World problems favor fixed-parameter SARSA. However, all GRNs do better in the worst-case scenarios due to the ability of GRNs to react to situations dynamically and avoid incorrect credit assignment in sequences of actions (for example, by varying λ).

9. CONCLUSION

In this paper, we employ gene regulatory networks to serve as neuromodulators of learning parameters for a reinforcement learning algorithm on four benchmark problems. We have evolved GRNs specifically on each task, which generally produced better or equivalent results to the standard fixed-parameter SARSA algorithm. In all cases, the worst-case scenario is always handled better by GRNM due to its ability to perform on-the-fly parameter adaptations which reduces complications of learning with fixed parameters, such as incorrect credit assignment in sequences of actions.

Additionally, the GRN evolved on the Maze problem as well as a generic GRN have been tested on the problems and offers encouraging results for multi-task learning in multiple problem domains. Once again, the worst-case scenario is consistently handled better by genetically-regulated neuromodulation with generic GRNs than with fixed-parameter algorithms, and generic GRNs evolved on alternative combinations of problems should be investigated. However, generic GRNs are not as good as GRNs specifically optimized for each task. Other inputs might be useful to the GRN for estimating the quality of the current neuromodulation and the quality of the agent behavior. The pursuit a generic GRN capable of generalizing the regulation of learning parameters across multiple tasks and problem domains would not only eliminate the need to search for additional GRNs, but also the parameter sampling phase commonly required for reinforcement learning applications.

As was noted in [25], neuromodulation is neither problem nor RL-algorithm specific, thus future work may investigate the application of genetically-regulated neuromodulation to alternative RL algorithms, such as Q-learning, as well as compare the performance and dynamics of GRNM to alter-

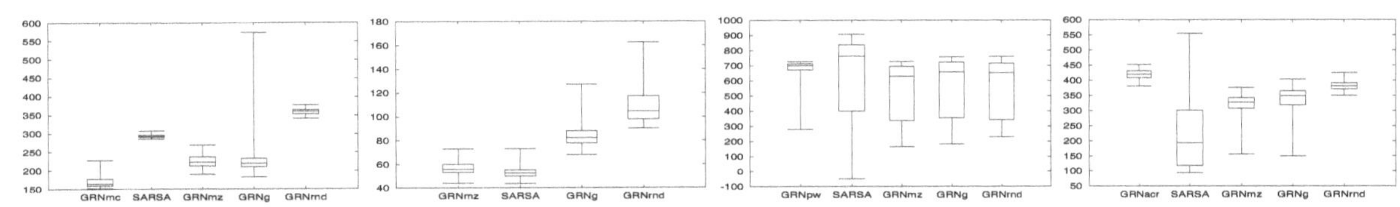

(a) Mountain Car (b) Maze (c) Puddle World (d) Acrobat

Figure 5: Detailed results of the 100 runs from the four problems with the best GRN trained on the specific problem, the SARSA algorithm with fixed parameters, the GRN trained on Maze (noted GRN_{mz} in the box plots), and a generic GRN trained both on the Maze and Mountain Car problems (noted GRN_g). Notice that, for the first two problems (Mountain Car and Maze), lower is better and for the two others (Puddle World and Acrobat), higher is better.

native methods of varying RL parameters. We have shown that a simple feedback controller can optimize community features of agent-based swarm simulations, the use of GRN-based neuromodulation is likely to further optimize these environmental controllers [13].

Acknowledgements: Kyle Harrington is supported by T32 HL07893 from the NHLBI of the NIH.

10. REFERENCES

[1] W. Banzhaf. Artificial regulatory networks and genetic programming. *Genetic Programming Theory and Practice*, pages 43–62, 2003.

[2] J. Boyan and A. Moore. Generalization in reinforcement learning: Safely approximating the value function. In *Advances in neural information processing systems*, pages 369–376, 1995.

[3] S. Cussat-Blanc, K. Harrington, and J. Pollack. Gene regulatory network evolution through augmenting topologies. *IEEE Transaction on Evolutionary Computation*, 2015, to be published.

[4] S. Cussat-Blanc, J. Pascalie, S. Mazac, H. Luga, and Y. Duthen. A synthesis of the Cell2Organ developmental model. *Morphogenetic Engineering*, 2012.

[5] S. Cussat-Blanc, S. Sanchez, and Y. Duthen. Controlling cooperative and conflicting continuous actions with a gene regulatory network. In *Conf. on Computational Intelligence in Games (CIG'12)*. IEEE, 2012.

[6] E. H. Davidson. The regulatory genome: gene regulatory networks in development and evolution. *Academic Press*, 2006.

[7] T. Degris. RLPark, 2014.

[8] A. Destexhe and E. Marder. Plasticity in single neuron and circuit computations. *Nature*, 431(7010):789–795, 2004.

[9] R. Doursat. Facilitating evolutionary innovation by developmental modularity and variability. In *Proc. of the 11th Conf. on Genetic and evolutionary computation*, pages 683–690. ACM, 2009.

[10] K. Doya. Metalearning and neuromodulation. *Neural Networks*, 15(4):495–506, 2002.

[11] K. Doya. Modulators of decision making. *Nature neuroscience*, 11(4):410–416, 2008.

[12] J. Fellous and C. Linster. Computational models of neuromodulation. *Neural computation*, 10(4):771–805, 1998.

[13] J. Gold, A. Wang, and K. Harrington. Feedback Control of Evolving Swarms. In *Proceedings of Artificial Life XIV*, pages 884–891, 2014.

[14] H. Handa. Evolutionary Computation on Multitask Reinforcement Learning Problems. In *Networking, Sensing and Control, 2007 IEEE Intl. Conf. on*, pages 685–688, 2007.

[15] K. I. Harrington, E. Awa, S. Cussat-Blanc, and J. Pollack. Robot Coverage Control by Evolved Neuromodulation. In *IJCNN 2013*, pages 543–550, 2013.

[16] M. Joachimczak and B. Wróbel. Evo-devo in silico: a model of a gene network regulating multicellular development in 3d space with artificial physics. In *Proc. of the 11th Intl. Conf. on Artificial Life*, pages 297–304, 2008.

[17] M. Joachimczak and B. Wróbel. Evolving Gene Regulatory Networks for Real Time Control of Foraging Behaviours. In *Proc. of the 12th Intl. Con. on Artificial Life*, 2010.

[18] H. Li, X. Liao, and L. Carin. Multi-task reinforcement learning in partially observable stochastic environments. *The Journal of Machine Learning Research*, 10:1131–1186, 2009.

[19] E. Marder. Neuromodulation of neuronal circuits: back to the future. *Neuron*, 76(1):1–11, 2012.

[20] A. Moore. Variable resolution dynamic programming: Efficiently learning action maps in multivariate realvalued state-spaces. In *Proc. of the Eighth Intl. Conf. on Machine Learning*, pages 333–337, 1991.

[21] M. Nicolau, M. Schoenauer, and W. Banzhaf. Evolving genes to balance a pole. *Genetic Programming*, pages 196–207, 2010.

[22] S. Sanchez and S. Cussat-Blanc. Gene regulated car driving: using a gene regulatory network to drive a virtual car. *Genetic Programming and Evolvable Machines*, 15(4):477–511, 2014.

[23] W. Schultz, P. Apicella, and T. Ljungberg. Responses of monkey dopamine neurons to reward and conditioned stimuli during successive steps of learning a delayed response task. *The Journal of Neuroscience*, 13(3):900–913, 1993.

[24] W. Schultz, P. Apicella, and T. Ljungberg. Responses of monkey dopamine neurons to reward and conditioned stimuli during successive steps of learning a delayed response task. *The Journal of Neuroscience*, 13(3):900–913, 1993.

[25] N. Schweighofer and K. Doya. Meta-learning in reinforcement learning. *Neural Networks*, 16(1):5–9, 2003.

[26] S. Singh, T. Jaakkola, M. Littman, and C. Szepesvári. Convergence results for single-step on-policy reinforcement-learning algorithms. *Machine Learning*, 38(3):287–308, 2000.

[27] R. Sutton. Integrated architectures for learning, planning, and reacting based on approximating dynamic programming. In *Proc. of the Seventh Intl. Conf. on Machine learning*, pages 216–224, 1990.

[28] R. S. Sutton. Learning to predict by the methods of temporal differences. *Machine learning*, 3(1):9–44, 1988.

[29] R. S. Sutton. Generalization in reinforcement learning: Successful examples using sparse coarse coding. *Advances in neural information processing systems*, pages 1038–1044, 1996.

[30] R. S. Sutton and A. G. Barto. *Introduction to reinforcement learning*. MIT Press, 1998.

[31] M. Taylor and P. Stone. Transfer learning for reinforcement learning domains: A survey. *The Journal of Machine Learning Research*, 10:1633–1685, 2009.

[32] J. Ziegler and W. Banzhaf. Evolving control metabolisms for a robot. *Artificial Life*, 7(2):171–190, 2001.

Simpler is Better: a Novel Genetic Algorithm to Induce Compact Multi-label Chain Classifiers

Eduardo C. Gonçalves
Institute of Computing
Universidade Federal Fluminense
Niterói, Brazil
egoncalves@ic.uff.br

Alexandre Plastino
Institute of Computing
Universidade Federal Fluminense
Niterói, Brazil
plastino@ic.uff.br

Alex A. Freitas
School of Computing
University of Kent at Canterbury
Kent, CT2 7NF, UK
A.A.Freitas@ukc.ac.uk

ABSTRACT

Multi-label classification (MLC) is the task of assigning multiple class labels to an object based on the features that describe the object. One of the most effective MLC methods is known as Classifier Chains (CC). This approach consists in training q binary classifiers linked in a chain, $\{y_1 \rightarrow y_2 \rightarrow ... \rightarrow y_q\}$, with each responsible for classifying a specific label in $\{l_1, l_2, ..., l_q\}$. The chaining mechanism allows each individual classifier to incorporate the predictions of the previous ones as additional information at classification time. Thus, possible correlations among labels can be automatically exploited. Nevertheless, CC suffers from two important drawbacks: (i) the label ordering is decided at random, although it usually has a strong effect on predictive accuracy; (ii) all labels are inserted into the chain, although some of them might carry irrelevant information to discriminate the others. In this paper we tackle both problems at once, by proposing a novel genetic algorithm capable of searching for a single optimized label ordering, while at the same time taking into consideration the utilization of partial chains. Experiments on benchmark datasets demonstrate that our approach is able to produce models that are both simpler and more accurate.

Categories and Subject Descriptors

I.2.6 [**Artificial Intelligence**]: Learning

Keywords

multi-label classification, genetic algorithms, classifier chains

1. INTRODUCTION

In recent years, multi-label classification (MLC) [25, 29] has become one of the most active research topics in the fields of data mining and machine learning. In this problem, each object of a dataset may belong to multiple class labels and the goal is to learn a system that can infer the correct labels of new, previously unseen, objects. A popular application is the classification of free text documents. For instance, an MLC system trained to infer movie genres according to their plots, could process a document containing the text summary of the Pedro Almodóvar's movie "Volver" and determine its genres as "Comedy", "Crime", and "Drama". Besides text classification, other modern applications of MLC include functional genomics (determining the multiple biological functions of genes), medical diagnosis (predicting the set of diseases a patient may develop) and direct marketing (recommendation of products for customers).

An important issue in MLC relates to the existence of dependence relationships among labels. For example, in the movie classification domain, intuitively a film is unlikely to be simultaneously considered as "Crime" and "Musical", since these two genres have a negative correlation. Analogously, the likelihood of a movie being labeled as "Crime" becomes stronger if it has been labeled as "Action" and "Thriller". Thus, it is expected that MLC methods capable of exploiting label dependencies should be more accurate. Indeed, a large number of recent proposals have concentrated efforts to tackle this issue by making use of diverse probabilistic techniques [13, 23, 24, 28].

In a different vein, the Classifier Chains (CC) method [22] employs a simpler non-probabilistic strategy to incorporate label dependencies into the classification process. In this approach, q binary classifiers are inserted at random order into a chain $\{y_1 \rightarrow y_2 \rightarrow ... \rightarrow y_q\}$, where each one is responsible for predicting a specific label in $\{l_1, l_2, ..., l_q\}$. The chain structure allows each binary classifier y_j to incorporate the labels inferred by the previous $y_1, ..., y_{j-1}$ classifiers as additional predictive information. Although the adopted principle is quite simple, a comprehensive empirical study [20] demonstrated that CC is able to outperform most of the other existing state-of-the-art MLC methods.

Nevertheless, the CC method suffers from two major drawbacks. First, it decides the label sequence at random. As demonstrated in [3], the use of distinct chain orderings can lead to large differences in the predictive accuracy of the model. Second, CC forces all labels to be present in the chain, despite the fact that some of them might carry redundant and irrelevant information. This might confuse the classification model instead of helping in discriminating the various other labels. To overcome these disadvantages, in this work we propose a novel Genetic Algorithm (GA) that performs a global search for an optimized chain (i.e., a label sequence that leads to an improvement on the predictive ac-

GECCO '15, July 11 - 15, 2015, Madrid, Spain
© 2015 ACM. ISBN 978-1-4503-3472-3/15/07...$15.00
DOI: http://dx.doi.org/10.1145/2739480.2754650

curacy of the CC model), by exploring partial chains with only a subset of labels. To the best of our knowledge, this is the first approach proposed with the explicit goal of finding an optimized partially chained model for MLC.

This paper is organized as follows. Section 2 gives a short overview on MLC. Section 3 reviews the original CC framework. Section 4 reviews work related to our proposal. Section 5 formally defines the concept of partially chained (PartCC) model for MLC. Section 6 describes the characteristics of our proposed GA. Section 7 reports the experimental results. Concluding remarks and future research directions are given in Section 8.

2. MULTI-LABEL CLASSIFICATION

The MLC problem can be defined as follows.

DEFINITION 1. *(Multi-label Classification Problem). Let* $X = \{A_1, ..., A_d\}$ *be a finite set of d predictive (input) attributes. Let* $L = \{l_1, ..., l_q\}$ *be a finite set of q possible class labels, where* $q \geq 2$*. Consider a training dataset* $\mathcal{D}$ *composed by N instances of the form* $\{(x_1, Y_1), (x_2, Y_2), ..., (x_N, Y_N)\}$*, where each* x_i *is a vector* $\{(x_1, ..., x_d)\}$ *that stores values for the d predictive attributes in X and each* $Y_i \subseteq L$ *is a subset of labels. The goal of the multi-label classification task is to learn a classifier (classification model)* $h(x) \rightarrow Y$ *from* $\mathcal{D}$ *that, given an unlabeled instance* $t = (x, ?)$*, predicts its set of labels (labelset) Y.*

The evaluation of MLC methods typically uses multiple performance measures, mainly because in MLC a result can be fully correct, fully wrong or partially correct. Hence, different performance measures provide the user with alternative analyses of the results, giving a better understanding about the actual predictive performance of a MLC method (an illustrative example is given in [11]).

In what follows, we introduce the measures used to assess the quality of the methods evaluated in our experiments. In the definitions, we use the following notation: n is the number of test instances; q is the number of labels; Y_i and Z_i represents, respectively, the actual and the predicted labelset of the ith test instance.

The Exact Match (EM), defined in Eq. 1, assesses the percentage of instances fully correctly predicted in the test set. Consider that $I(true) = 1$ and $I(false) = 0$.

$$EM = \frac{1}{n} \sum_{i=1}^{n} I(Y_i = Z_i) \quad (1)$$

Note that EM can deal with results that are both fully wrong and fully correct. However, it is unable to evaluate partially correct results. To cope with this issue, we also use the Accuracy (ACC), F-Measure (FM) and Hamming Loss (HL) measures, respectively defined in Eqs. 2, 3, 4. In Eq. 4, the expression $Y_i \triangle Z_i$ gives the symmetric difference between Y_i and Z_i. For EM, ACC and FM, greater values indicate better performance; whilst for HL, smaller values indicate better performance.

$$ACC = \frac{1}{n} \sum_{i=1}^{n} \frac{|Z_i \cap Y_i|}{|Z_i \cup Y_i|} \quad (2)$$

$$FM = \frac{1}{n} \sum_{i=1}^{n} \frac{2 \times |Z_i \cap Y_i|}{|Z_i| + |Y_i|} \quad (3)$$

$$HL = \frac{1}{n} \sum_{i=1}^{n} \frac{|Z_i \triangle Y_i|}{q} \quad (4)$$

3. CLASSIFIER CHAINS

Among several MLC methods proposed in the literature [20, 25, 29], the Binary Relevance (BR) is perhaps the simplest one. In this approach, the MLC problem is transformed into q independent binary classification problems. One binary classifier is separately trained to predict each label. To infer the labelset of a new object, the BR model simply aggregates the labels positively predicted by each of the independent classifiers. Figure 1 shows a BR model, viewed as a graph, in a problem with four labels. The node X represents the set of predictive attributes whereas the nodes l_1, l_2, l_3, l_4 represent the target labels. The directed edges from X to each of the four labels indicate that, in the BR approach, the binary classifiers responsible for the prediction of each label are trained using exclusively the attributes in X as the set of input attributes. Hence, all binary classifiers in the group are isolated from each other, being unable to exchange information at both the training and the classification steps.

The BR strategy has several advantages. First it is simple. Second, it is algorithm independent, i.e., it enables abstraction from the underlying base algorithm for binary classification. This is a major advantage, because different classifiers (such as decision trees, SVM, Bayesian methods, etc. [27]) are more or less effective in different application domains. Finally, BR scales linearly with q and can be easily parallelized. Nonetheless, an obvious and critical drawback lies in that the BR model completely ignores the possible correlations among labels, as the binary classifiers make decisions independently from each other. Thus, the method is more suitable for problems where only a small number of labels exhibit correlation with each other.

Proposed in [22], the Classifier Chains (CC) method can be seen as a direct extension of the BR approach, capable of exploiting label dependencies though. Similar to BR, the CC method involves training a group of q binary classifiers. Nevertheless, instead of being kept isolated from each other, these q classifiers are linked in a chain structure, which allows each one to pass their predictions to the other binary classifiers ahead in the chain. In order to better explain the CC method, consider the graph depicted in Figure 2, representing a CC model with four labels chained in the sequence $\{l_1 \rightarrow l_2 \rightarrow l_3 \rightarrow l_4\}$. The directed edges in the graph indicate that the binary classifier y_1, which is responsible for classifying the first label in the chain (l_1), will be trained using solely the attributes that compose the attribute set X as its input attributes. However, the binary classifier y_2, re-

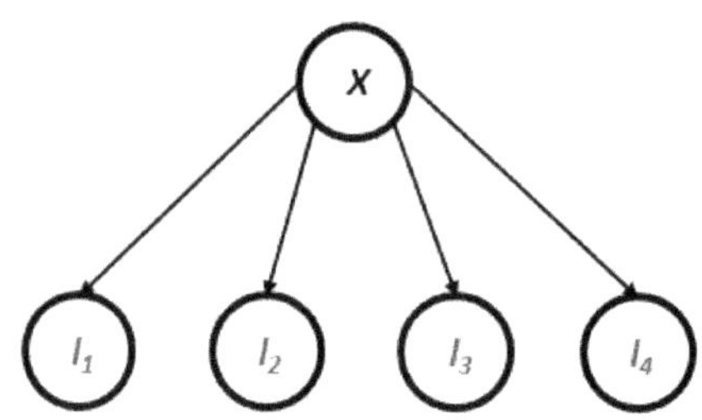

Figure 1: BR model

sponsible for the prediction of the second label in the chain (l_2), will be trained using X augmented with l_1 as the set of input attributes. Analogously, each subsequent classifier y_j will be trained using X augmented with the labels associated to the previous $j-1$ classifiers in the chain. Once the model is trained, the classification mechanism must be performed according to the chain sequence. To predict the labelset of a new object, q binary classifications are needed, with the process beginning at the first classifier in the sequence (y_1 in the example of Figure 2) and going along the chain. In this procedure, the classifier y_j predicts the relevance of label l_j, given the feature space augmented by the predictions carried out by the previous $j-1$ classifiers.

Although CC employs a direct and non-probabilistic approach to incorporate label dependencies into the classification model, it is considered one of the most effective MLC methods, in the sense that it has proven to be superior to state-of-the-art techniques in terms of predictive performance [20]. Besides this, CC still maintains most of the attractive characteristics of BR: it is algorithm independent, scales linearly with q and its training step can be easily parallelizable. Not surprisingly, CC has become one of the most adopted and representative frameworks for MLC [29].

4. RELATED WORK

A number of variations of the CC method have recently been proposed [3, 11, 16, 21, 24]. A common characteristic of these proposals is that they try to eliminate a key drawback in the original method: the fact that the label ordering is decided at random. In a recent study [3], an exhaustive experiment that compared the predictive performance of CC models built with thousands of distinct label orderings revealed that the differences in accuracy tend to be very large. The same study also revealed that, for many datasets, the original CC method (trained with a random order) might present a performance inferior to the BR method even in problems where most labels are correlated with each other. It is thus important to invest in algorithmic solutions to find an optimized chain order. Nonetheless, this is a difficult problem because of the enormous search space of $q!$ different possible label permutations.

Current extensions to the CC method make use of different approaches to solve the label sequence optimization problem (LSOP). The authors of the original CC model proposed the combination of random orders via an ensemble of classifier chains (ECC) in order to mitigate the effect of poorly ordered chains [22]. Differently, the approaches proposed in [3, 11, 16, 21] employ heuristic methods. In [16], the

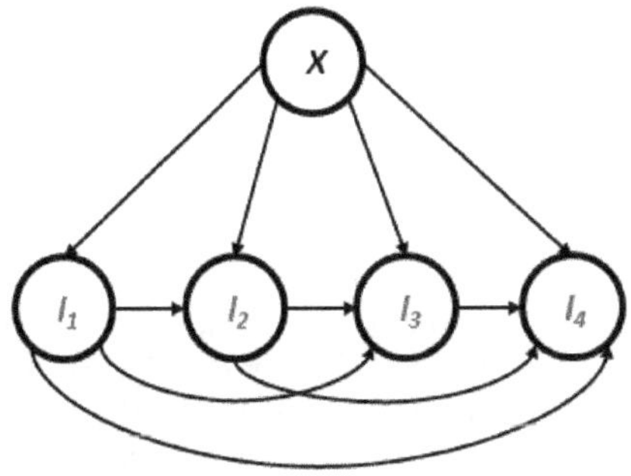

Figure 2: CC model

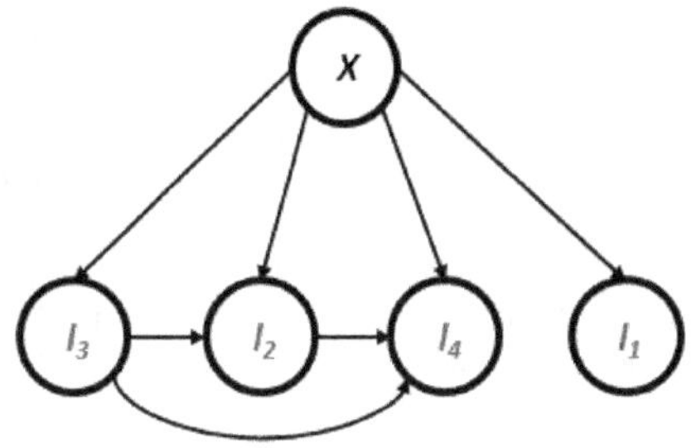

Figure 3: PartCC model

LSOP is addressed by performing a beam search over a tree in which every distinct path represents a different label permutation. The M2CC algorithm, described in [21], employs a double-Monte Carlo optimization technique to efficiently generate and evaluate a small population of distinct label sequences. The GACC method proposed in [11] performs a genetic algorithm search to solve the LSOP. In this technique, each chromosome represents a different label permutation. Crossover works by transferring sub-chains of random length between two individuals whilst mutation swaps pairs of labels of an individual. Finally, [3] proposes a lazy approach capable of searching for a distinct and more effective label sequence to each new instance t. In this strategy, for each instance in the training dataset, an effective label sequence is previously identified. At classification time, the label sequence for the new instance t is chosen based on the sequences associated with the instances in the training dataset that are more similar to t.

5. PARTIALLY CHAINED MODELS

The variations of the CC method aim at improving the model's effectiveness by handling the LSOP problem using different techniques. However, there is another important drawback in the original CC method that has been neglected in the literature. It corresponds to the fact that CC forces all labels to be present in the chain. None of the extensions have yet explored the idea of generating models defined by partial chains. In this context, the aim is to build a CC model in which one or more labels may be absent from the chain because their presence would lead to a decrease in the predictive accuracy. This is because some classifiers may pass redundant and irrelevant information, or wrongly predicted labels, along the chain, which might confuse the subsequent classifiers in the chain. Therefore, it might be interesting to remove these irrelevant or redundant labels from the chain structure (using independent binary classifiers for predicting each of them) and to create a partial chain with an optimized sequence using only the remaining labels.

An example of partially chained model (PartCC) for a MLC problem with four labels is shown in Figure 3. In this example, the classifiers associated to labels l_2, l_3 and l_4 are linked together in an optimized classifier chain model in the sequence $\{y_3 \rightarrow y_2 \rightarrow y_4\}$. The label l_1 is not in the chain. The intuition behind this representation is to indicate that l_1 will be treated by an independent binary classifier, because its presence in the chain would decrease the predictive accuracy of the multi-label classifier as a whole.

The PartCC model can be seen as an hybrid strategy between a BR model and a CC model using an optimized label sequence. Thus, it is expected to be effective in both situations: when the majority of the labels are dependent on each other and also in the converse case, when most labels are independent. More interestingly, since it deals with partial chains, it is capable of producing simpler, more compact multi-label chain classifiers, offering gains in terms of efficiency. Furthermore, a PartCC model is particularly suitable for problems that require the construction of comprehensible predictive models [9], as the shorter sequence is more realistic for the representation of true label dependencies in comparison with a full length sequence. Nonetheless, the problem of finding an optimized PartCC model is much more challenging than the traditional LSOP as the search space is composed by an ordinary BR model (where all labels are "disconnected") plus the models formed by all possible chain permutations of length 2 to q. Consequently, while the search space in the LSOP has size equal to $q!$, the size of the search space in the problem of optimizing PartCC models is much higher, being given by Eq. 5.

$$1 + \sum_{r=2}^{q} \frac{q!}{(q-r)!} \tag{5}$$

In this paper, a genetic algorithm for learning optimized PartCC models is proposed: GA for Optimizing Partially-Chained Models (GA-PartCC). To the best of our knowledge, this is the first method proposed with the following two explicit goals: (i) defining the most relevant labels to be chained and (ii) searching for an optimized sequence to place them in regard to the improvement of the classification accuracy. Our main motivations for presenting a solution based on the GA paradigm are as follows:

- GAs have been widely employed to solve a large number of classification problems in the most distinct contexts and application domains [1, 2, 5, 6, 8, 18].
- GAs are a global search method capable of effectively exploring the extremely large search spaces associated to the partially chained optimization problem. Due to this, GAs tend to cope better with attribute interactions than greedy methods [6, 8].
- GAs have been successfully applied to solve optimization problems where a candidate solution is represented as a permutation, like the classical traveling salesman problem (TSP) [17] and the vehicle routing problem (VRP) [19]. Note, however, that LSOP, as a classification problem, involve prediction and overfitting issues, unlike the TSP and VRP problems.
- As the CC and BR approaches, GAs are also easily parallelizable.

6. THE GA-PARTCC ALGORITHM

6.1 Representation and Initial Population

In GA-PartCC, individuals are represented by variable-length lists. Each candidate solution specifies both a subset of labels and the order they are placed into the chain. For instance, the model in Figure 3 is encoded as the list $[l_3, l_2, l_4]$. Similarly, the models in Figures 1 and 2 are respectively encoded as [ ] (empty list) and $[l_1, l_2, l_3, l_4]$.

We adopted a simplified controlled approach for generating the initial population. Let P be the population size. The first individual is an empty chain (i.e., a BR model) and the second individual constitutes a complete CC model with the default chain sequence (as the one shown in Figure 2). The remainder individuals are generated as follows. First, individual lengths are randomly drawn following a uniform distribution in the range $[2, q]$. As a consequence, $P-2$ chromosomes with distinct lengths will be generated. For each of these chromosomes, starting from an empty chromosome and from the leftmost allele, the chain sequence is defined by randomly selecting integer numbers (representing the label indexes) according to a uniform distribution in the range $[1, q]$. Repeated integers are not allowed in a chromosome.

6.2 Lexicographic Fitness Function

We adopted a multi-objective lexicographic approach [7] to determine the fitness of the candidate solutions. In this technique, two or more objectives with distinct predetermined priorities are taken into consideration to define the quality of each chromosome. Consider the following example. Let c_i and c_j be two candidate solutions. In the lexicographic approach used in GA-PartCC, when comparing two chromosomes, the GA first tries to determine which one is better considering the highest priority objective. If c_i is not better than c_j, and vice-versa, then both are compared considering the second objective. The process is repeated until either a winner is found or all the criteria have been tested (in the later case, if no winner was found, one of the chromosomes is randomly chosen as winner).

In GA-PartCC, we only consider two objectives: predictive accuracy (first priority) and model simplicity (second priority). To assess the predictive accuracy of a chromosome, we use the Quality (fitness) function defined in [3, 11]. This function simultaneously takes into account the measures of Exact Match, Accuracy and Hamming Loss, respectively defined in Equations 1, 2 and 4. The Quality of a chromosome c_i is computed as:

$$Quality(c_i) = \frac{(1 - HL) + ACC + EM}{3} \tag{6}$$

If two chromosomes have the same value for the Quality function, they must be compared with regard to model's simplicity (second objective). We consider a solution c_i simpler than c_j if c_i encodes a chain sequence shorter than the one encoded in c_j. The rationale lies primarily in the Occam's Razor principle [4] which states that "given two models with the same generalization error, the simplest one should be preferred because simplicity is desirable in itself". Indeed, as discussed in Section 5, a shorter model offers two other important advantages. First, it is more efficient, as it involves a smaller number of attributes. Second, it gives higher fidelity for representing label dependencies, since only the most relevant labels with regard to the classification problem are present in the chain.

By comparison with the simple use of a weighted formula to combine the two objective values, the lexicographic approach has the advantage of avoiding the specification of ad-hoc numeric weights; it requires only the specification of the relative priority of the objectives, which is well-defined in the context of classification (accuracy clearly has priority over the chain size). By comparison with the Pareto dominance-based approach for multi-objective optimization, the lexicographic approach has the advantages of being simpler and avoiding the issue of how to choose one single solution to be used in practice (out of all non-dominated solutions). Also, the usual Pareto approach would not allow us to specify that maximizing accuracy is more important than reducing the chain size, an important application-specific piece of knowledge that is naturally specified using the lexicographic approach.

The GA-PartCC follows the wrapper approach [6] in which the quality of an individual (candidate PartCC model) is determined by using the target MLC algorithm (i.e., the CC algorithm). The fitness function is calculated using only the training set, according to a holdout method that works as follows. First, the training set is partitioned into two mutually-exclusive subsets: building (2/3 split) and validation (1/3 split). Next, for each chromosome we build a PartCC model using only the building set, and then that model is evaluated with the validation set.

6.3 Selection Method

GA-PartCC uses the tournament selection method [6]. In this method, first k individuals are randomly drawn from the population, where k is a user-specified parameter called tournament size. Their fitness values are then compared according to the lexicographic approach presented in the previous subsection. The winner is the individual with the best lexicographic evaluation among the k participants. The selection procedure also implements elitism, in which a percentage of elite individuals are preserved from the previous generation according to their fitness values.

6.4 Genetic Operators

GA-PartCC implements crossover and mutation to deal with the two levels of representation encoded in the chromosomes (chain sequence and chain length).

The crossover operation consists in a modified version of the order crossover [5] method, which is often used in in GAs for permutation problems. The adaptation was necessary because the original method can deal only with chromosomes of the same length. In order to facilitate the explanation, consider the example shown in Figure 4. As the original method, our version of order crossover generates two children (represented by O_1 and O_2) from two parents (represented by P_1 and P_2). As shown in the figure, child O_1 must have the same length as P_2 and O_2 the same length as P_1. The crossover operates as follows. Two crossover points (represented by the two vertical thick lines in Figure 4) are chosen at random. The first step to generate O_1 is to copy the segment between the crossover points from P_1 into O_1 (Figure 4a). The second step consists in filling the remainder empty alleles in O_1 with genetic material from P_2 (Figure 4b). The procedure works as follows. Starting from the position next to the second crossover point (the fourth position in our example), the values that are present in P_2 but are not contained in O_1 are transferred to the empty alleles in O_1, wrapping around when the last position of both chromosomes is reached. O_2 is analogously generated.

The main advantages of the order crossover method used by GA-PartCC are the facts that it preserves the relative order in the parents in their children and always generates valid solutions. However, it does not create children with lengths difference form their parents' lengths, since the first child has the same length of the second parent and vice-versa. In order to increase the population's variability of length, in GA-PartCC, children resulting from crossover can

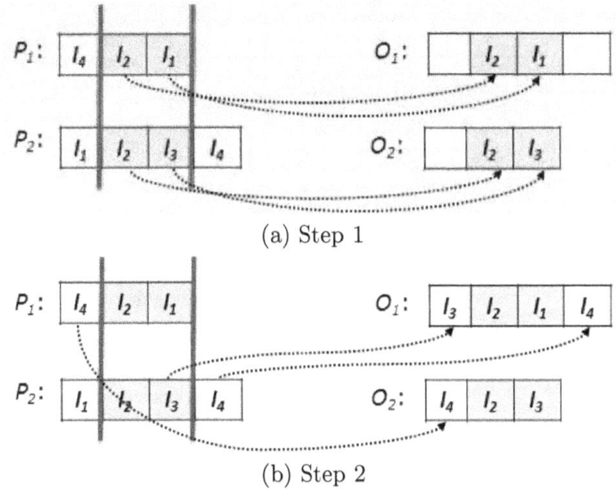

(a) Step 1

(b) Step 2

Figure 4: Adapted order crossover operation

be also subject to mutation, which consists in either inserting or removing a subchain. In the insertion procedure, a single insertion point is chosen at random in the current child. Next, a subchain with maximum length of 5% of q is randomly generated and inserted at that insertion point. The inserted sub-chain contains only labels that do not occur in the current child. The deletion procedure removes a segment between two randomly-chosen points.

7. EXPERIMENTS

7.1 Experimental Methodology

The performance of GA-PartCC was compared to the baseline methods BR and CC, and also against the GACC method [11], which can only deal with the optimization of full-length chains. We evaluated all methods using MULAN [26], an open-source package of Java classes for MLC that works on the top of the popular WEKA data mining tool [14]. The WEKA's J48 decision tree algorithm with default parameters was used as the base binary classification algorithm for all evaluated methods.

Table 1 presents the nine distinct benchmark datasets used in our experiments. In this table, the second column (q) presents the number of labels and the third (N) the number of instances. Observe that the datasets vary considerably in the number of labels, number of instances and application domain. Further information about the datasets can be found at the MULAN[1] and MEKA[2] repositories. The only exception is the "ces" dataset, described in [10].

The predictive performance of the algorithms was evaluated in terms of Accuracy, F-Measure, Hamming Loss and Exact Match. We used the well-known Friedman test and the Nemenyi post-hoc test to verify the statistical significance of the results at a confidence level of 95% [15]. As in the extensive evaluation of [20], a holdout evaluation was performed, where 2/3 of each dataset was used for learning the classifier and 1/3 for testing. We used the same training and test splits that come with the datasets.

As GACC and GA-PartCC algorithms are probabilistic

[1] http://mulan.sourceforge.net/datasets-mlc.html
[2] http://meka.sourceforge.net/#datasets

Table 1: Datasets used in the experiments

Dataset	q	N	Domain
birds	19	645	audio
cal500	174	502	music
enron	53	1702	text
genbase	27	662	genomics
llog	74	1,460	text
medical	45	978	text
thyroid	25	9,172	medical diagnosis
yeast	14	2,147	genomics
ces	17	903	social research

methods, the results reported are averaged over 10 executions with distinct seeds (except for the larger datasets "enron" and "llog" which were averaged over 5 executions). The results reported for CC are also averaged over 10 executions with distinct random seeds (5 executions for "enron" and "llog"). The parameters of the genetic algorithms were set by performing calibrating tests with three benchmark datasets obtained from the MULAN repository: emotions ($q = 6$, $N = 593$), scene ($q = 6$, $N = 2407$) and flags ($q = 7$, $N = 194$). These three datasets used for parameter calibration were not included in the experimental evaluation. The final settings are the following: number of generations: 50; population size: 200; crossover rate: 100%; mutation rate: 25%; tournament size: 2; elitist strategy: preserve the 2 best individuals at each generation. During the calibration tests, we observed the occurrence of overfitting, i.e., candidate solutions that have a high predictive accuracy on the training data, but do not generalize well for test instances [12]. To cope with this issue, we adopted the strategy of changing the building and validation sets at each generation of the GA by re-splitting the training set. It is worth reinforcing the fact that only the training set is used during the evolution process, as previously stated in Subsection 6.2.

7.2 Results

The results for the measures of Accuracy, F-Measure, Exact Match, and Hamming Loss are respectively shown in Tables 2, 3, 4 and 5. The best results for each dataset are highlighted in bold type. The rank obtained by each method in each dataset is presented in parenthesis. In the rows below Tables 2 and 3, the symbol $\succ$ represents a statistically significant difference between one or more methods. For instance, $\{a\} \succ \{b, c\}$ shows that the method a is significantly better than b and c.

The results presented in Tables 2 and 3 show that the GA-PartCC obtained the smallest rank sum (i.e., the best overall result) for both Accuracy and F-Measure. The Friedman test reported a significant difference between the evaluated methods. The Nemenyi post-hoc test indicated that GA-PartCC and GACC are significantly better than BR and CC for Accuracy and that GA-PartCC is significantly better than GACC, BR and CC for F-Measure.

Tables 4 and 5 show the results regarding the Exact Match and Hamming Loss measures. Although the Friedman and Nemenyi tests indicated that no statistically significant differences exist between the results of the four methods, note that the GA-PartCC obtained a competitive result, with the second smallest rank sum for both measures.

The GA-PartCC method was also evaluated with respect to the length of the chains associated to the best solutions. Table 6 shows the results averaged over the number of executions. Note that, for the datasets "llog" and "medical", the best models are on average composed by about half of the labels. For the other datasets, except "genbase", the best found models are, on average, composed by a large number of labels (but not all labels). This can be explained by the fact that in these datasets, a large number of labels exhibit dependence with each other. A notable exception is the dataset "genbase", in which the performance of the four evaluated methods is equivalent for all evaluation measures. In this case, the GA-PartCC method was consistent with the Occam's Razor principle, being able to choose the simplest model, an empty chain (equivalent to the BR model), as the best solution.

In summary, the results indicate that the proposed GA-PartCC method exhibits a very competitive performance, obtaining results significantly superior to the BR and CC methods according to two of the four evaluated measures of predictive accuracy. It was also significantly superior to GACC in one of the measures, and obtained competitive results in the other measures, yet with the advantage of generating simpler models than both CC and GACC.

8. CONCLUSIONS

This paper presented a novel method for multi-label classifier chains (CC) based on a genetic algorithm. This method, named GA-PartCC, differs from current extensions to the original CC model because it is capable of evaluating chain sequences that vary not only in the ordering but also in the length. In order to accomplish this task, GA-PartCC uses a variable-length list representation and a multi-objective lexicographic fitness function, taking into account two objectives: the model's accuracy and the model's size. In our experiments, GA-PartCC achieved statistically significantly better results than BR and CC in two of the four evaluated measures and a performance significantly superior to GACC in one of the measures, yet with the advantage of generating simpler models. None of the evaluated methods was significantly superior to GA-PartCC in any of the four performance measures.

As future research we plan to develop a memetic version of GA-PartCC. The idea is to identify, during the evolutionary process, groups of labels that tend to cause a decrease in the accuracy of most other labels when they take part into the chain. These labels could then be either removed from children resulting from crossover or placed in the last positions of these children. Similarly, groups of labels that tend to cause an increase in the predictive accuracy of other labels could be identified by the memetic procedure and placed in the first positions of new children.

9. ACKNOWLEDGMENTS

This work was supported by CAPES research grant BEX 1642/14-6 (E. C. Gonçalves).

10. REFERENCES

[1] M. P. Basgalupp, R. C. Barros, A. C. P. L. F. de Carvalho, A. A. Freitas, and D. D. Ruiz. Legal-tree: A lexicographic multi-objective genetic algorithm for decision tree induction. In *Proc. of the*

Table 2: Performance of BR, CC, GACC and GA-PartCC in terms of Accuracy.

Dataset	Accuracy			
	BR	CC	GACC	GA-PartCC
birds	**0.573** (1)	0.565 (4)	0.569 (2)	0.567 (3)
cal500	0.212 (4)	0.218 (3)	**0.224** (1)	0.222 (2)
enron	0.367 (4)	0.401 (3)	**0.409** (1)	0.405 (2)
genbase	**0.987** (2.5)	**0.987** (2.5)	**0.987** (2.5)	**0.987** (2.5)
llog	0.243 (2)	0.236 (4)	**0.249** (1)	0.242 (3)
medical	0.743 (3.5)	0.743 (3.5)	0.744 (2)	**0.748** (1)
thyroid	**0.984** (1.5)	0.983 (3.5)	0.983 (3.5)	**0.984** (1.5)
yeast	0.423 (3)	0.418 (4)	0.432 (2)	**0.440** (1)
ces	0.273 (4)	0.275 (3)	0.289 (2)	**0.292** (1)
rank sums	25.50	30.50	**17.00**	**17.00**
$\{GACC, GA\text{–}PartCC\} \succ \{BR, CC\}, and \{BR\} \succ \{CC\}$				

Table 3: Performance of BR, CC, GACC and GA-PartCC in terms of F-Measure.

Dataset	F-Measure			
	BR	CC	GACC	GA-PartCC
birds	**0.603** (1)	0.592 (4)	0.597 (2)	0.595 (3)
cal500	0.344 (4)	0.348 (3)	**0.356** (1)	0.355 (2)
enron	0.474 (4)	0.504 (3)	**0.507** (1.5)	**0.507** (1.5)
genbase	**0.991** (2.5)	**0.991** (2.5)	**0.991** (2.5)	**0.991** (2.5)
llog	0.261 (3)	0.252 (4)	**0.264** (1.5)	**0.264** (1.5)
medical	**0.773** (1.5)	0.769 (3.5)	0.769 (3.5)	**0.773** (1.5)
thyroid	0.990 (3.5)	0.990 (3.5)	0.990 (3)	**0.991** (1)
yeast	0.547 (3)	0.523 (4)	0.548 (2)	**0.550** (1)
ces	0.372 (4)	0.373 (3)	0.393 (2)	**0.397** (1)
rank sums	26.00	30.00	19.00	**15.00**
$\{GA\text{–}PartCC\} \succ \{GACC, BR, CC\}, and \{GACC, BR\} \succ \{CC\}$				

Table 4: Performance of BR, CC, GACC and GA-PartCC in terms of Exact Match.

Dataset	Exact Match			
	BR	CC	GACC	GA-PartCC
birds	0.486 (3)	0.485 (4)	**0.492** (1)	0.488 (2)
cal500	**0.000** (2.5)	**0.000** (2.5)	**0.000** (2.5)	**0.000** (2.5)
enron	0.086 (4)	0.125 (3)	**0.135** (1)	0.133 (2)
genbase	**0.975** (2.5)	**0.975** (2.5)	**0.975** (2.5)	**0.975** (2.5)
llog	0.199 (2)	0.198 (3.5)	**0.209** (1)	0.198 (3.5)
medical	0.651 (4)	0.665 (3)	0.670 (2)	**0.672** (1)
thyroid	0.903 (4)	0.941 (2.5)	0.941 (2.5)	**0.944** (1)
yeast	0.064 (4)	0.128 (3)	0.134 (2)	**0.136** (1)
ces	0.046 (3.5)	**0.049** (1)	0.047 (2)	0.046 (3.5)
rank sums	29.50	25.00	**16.50**	19.00
No statistically significant difference				

Table 5: Performance of BR, CC, GACC and GA-PartCC in terms of Hamming Loss.

Dataset	Hamming Loss			
	BR	CC	GACC	GA-PartCC
birds	**0.051** (2)	**0.051** (2)	**0.051** (1)	0.052 (4)
cal500	**0.163** (1)	0.176 (4)	0.173 (4)	0.170 (2)
enron	**0.054** (1.5)	**0.054** (1.5)	0.055 (3.5)	0.055 (3.5)
genbase	**0.001** (2.5)	**0.001** (2.5)	**0.001** (2.5)	**0.001** (2.5)
llog	**0.019** (2.5)	**0.019** (2.5)	**0.019** (2.5)	**0.019** (2.5)
medical	**0.011** (2.5)	**0.011** (2.5)	**0.011** (2.5)	**0.011** (2.5)
thyroid	**0.005** (1.5)	0.006 (3.5)	0.006 (3.5)	**0.005** (1.5)
yeast	**0.259** (1)	0.274 (3)	0.266 (3)	0.263 (2)
ces	0.192 (4)	0.191 (3)	**0.190** (1.5)	**0.190** (1.5)
rank sums	**18.50**	25.50	24.00	22.00
No statistically significant difference				

Table 6: Average length of the best chain determined by GA-PartCC

Dataset	q	avg length
birds	19	15.0
cal500	174	124.8
enron	53	52.0
genbase	27	0.0
llog	74	37.4
medical	45	20.2
thyroid	25	24.4
yeast	14	13.8
ces	17	13.7

2009 ACM Symposium on Applied Computing, SAC'09, pages 1085–1090, March 2009.

[2] L. Bull, E. Bernadó-Mansilla, and J. Holmes. Learning classifier systems in data mining: An introduction. In *Learning Classifier Systems in Data Mining*, volume 125 of *Studies in Computational Intelligence*, pages 1–15. Springer, 2008.

[3] P. N. da Silva, E. C. Gonçalves, A. Plastino, and A. A. Freitas. Distinct chains for different instances: An effective strategy for multi-label classifier chains. In *Proc. of the 2014 ECML/PKDD Conf., LCNS 8725*, pages 453–468, September 2014.

[4] P. Domingos. The role of occam's razor in knowledge discovery. *Data Mining and Knowledge Discovery*, 3(4):409–425, December 1999.

[5] A. E. Eiben and J. E. Smith. *Introduction to Evolutionary Computing*. SpringerVerlag, 2003.

[6] A. A. Freitas. *Data Mining and Knowledge Discovery with Evolutionary Algorithms*. Springer, 2002.

[7] A. A. Freitas. A critical review of multi-objective optimization in data mining: A position paper. *SIGKDD Explor. Newsl.*, 6(2):77–86, December 2004.

[8] A. A. Freitas. A review of evolutionary algorithms for data mining. In *Data Mining and Knowledge Discovery Handbook*, pages 371–400. Springer US, July 2010.

[9] A. A. Freitas. Comprehensible classification models: A position paper. *SIGKDD Explor. Newsl.*, 15(1):1–10, June 2013.

[10] E. C. Gonçalves. A human-centered approach for mining hybrid-dimensional association rules. In *Proc. of the 2014 Conf. on Information Fusion*, FUSION'14, pages 1–8, July 2014.

[11] E. C. Gonçalves, A. Plastino, and A. A. Freitas. A genetic algorithm for optimizing the label ordering in multi-label classifier chains. In *Proc. of the 25th Int'l Conf. on Tools with Artificial Intelligence*, ICTAI'13, pages 469–476, November 2013.

[12] I. Gonçalves and S. Silva. Balancing learning and overfitting in genetic programming with interleaved sampling of training data. In *Proc. of EuroGP 2013*, pages 73–84, April 2013.

[13] Y. Guo and S. Gu. Multi-label classification using conditional dependency networks. In *Proc. of the 22nd Int'l Joint Conf. on Artificial Intelligence*, IJCAI'11, pages 1300–1305, July 2011.

[14] M. Hall, E. Frank, G. Holmes, B. Pfahringer, P. Reutemann, and I. Witten. The weka data mining software: an update. *ACM SIGKDD Explor.*, 11(1):10–18, November 2009.

[15] N. Japkowicz and M. Shah. *Evaluating Learning Algorithms: A Classification Perspective*. Cambridge University Press, New York, 2011.

[16] A. Kumar, S. Vembu, A. K. Menon, and C. Elkan. Beam search algorithms for multilabel learning. *Machine Learning*, 92(1):65–89, July 2013.

[17] P. Larrañaga, C. M. H. Kuijpers, R. H. Murga, I. Inza, and S. Dizdarevic. Genetic algorithms for the travelling salesman problem: A review of representations and operators. *Artificial Intelligence Review*, 13(2):129–170, April 1999.

[18] E. Levy, O. E. David, and N. S. Netanyahu. Genetic algorithms and deep learning for automatic painter classification. In *Proc. of the 2014 Genetic and Evolutionary Computation Conference*, GECCO'14, pages 1143–1150, July 2014.

[19] P. Machado, J. Tavares, F. B. Pereira, and E. Costa. Vehicle routing problem: Doing it the evolutionary way. In *Proc. of the 2002 Genetic and Evolutionary Computation Conference*, GECCO'02, pages 690–696, July 2002.

[20] G. Madjarov, D. Kocev, D. Gjorgjevikj, and S. Džeroski. An extensive experimental comparison of methods for multi-label learning. *Pattern Recognition*, 45(9):3084–3104, September 2012.

[21] J. Read, L. Martino, and D. Luengo. Efficient monte carlo optimization for multi-label classifier chains. In *Proc. of the 38th Int'l Conf. on Acoustics, Speech, and Signal Processing*, ICASSP'13, May 2013.

[22] J. Read, B. Pfahringer, G. Holmes, and E. Frank. Classifier chains for multi-label classification. *Machine Learning*, 85(3):333–359, December 2011.

[23] A. E. Romero and L. M. de Campos. A probabilistic methodology for multilabel classification. *Intelligent Data Analysis*, 18(5):911–926, September 2014.

[24] L. E. Sucar, C. Bielza, E. F. Morales, P. H. Leal, J. H. Zaragoza, and P. Larrañaga. Multi-label classification with bayesian network-based chain classifiers. *Pattern Recogn. Lett.*, 41:14–22, May 2014.

[25] G. Tsoumakas, I. Katakis, and I. Vlahavas. Mining multi-label data. In *Data Mining and Knowledge Discovery Handbook*, pages 667–685. Springer, 2010.

[26] G. Tsoumakas, E. S. Xioufis, J. Vilcek, and I. P. Vlahavas. Mulan: A java library for multi-label learning. *Journal of Machine Learning Research*, 12:2411–2414, July 2011.

[27] M. J. Zaki and W. Meira Jr. *Data Mining and Analysis: Fundamental Concepts and Algorithms*. Cambridge University Press, New York, 2014.

[28] M.-L. Zhang and K. Zhang. Multi-label learning by exploiting label dependency. In *Proc. of the 16th ACM SIGKDD Int'l Conf. on Knowledge Discovery and Data Mining*, KDD'10, pages 999–1008, July 2010.

[29] M.-L. Zhang and Z.-H. Zhoug. A review on multi-label learning algorithms. *IEEE Trans. on Knowledge and Data Engineering*, 26(8):1819–1837, August 2014.

High-Dimensional Function Approximation for Knowledge-Free Reinforcement Learning: a Case Study in SZ-Tetris

Wojciech Jaśkowski, Marcin Szubert, Paweł Liskowski and Krzysztof Krawiec
Institute of Computing Science, Poznan University of Technology
Piotrowo 2, 60965 Poznań, Poland
{wjaskowski,mszubert,pliskowski,kkrawiec}@cs.put.poznan.pl

ABSTRACT

SZ-Tetris, a restricted version of Tetris, is a difficult reinforcement learning task. Previous research showed that, similarly to the original Tetris, value function-based methods such as temporal difference learning, do not work well for SZ-Tetris. The best performance in this game was achieved by employing direct policy search techniques, in particular the cross-entropy method in combination with handcrafted features. Nonetheless, a simple heuristic hand-coded player scores even higher. Here we show that it is possible to equal its performance with CMA-ES (Covariance Matrix Adaptation Evolution Strategy). We demonstrate that further improvement is possible by employing *systematic n-tuple network*, a knowledge-free function approximator, and VD-CMA-ES, a linear variant of CMA-ES for high dimension optimization. Last but not least, we show that a large systematic n-tuple network (involving more than 4 million parameters) allows the classical temporal difference learning algorithm to obtain similar average performance to VD-CMA-ES, but at 20 times lower computational expense, leading to the best policy for SZ-Tetris known to date. These results enrich the current understanding of difficulty of SZ-Tetris, and shed new light on the capabilities of particular search paradigms when applied to representations of various characteristics and dimensionality.

CCS Concepts

•Mathematics of computing → Evolutionary algorithms; •Computing methodologies → Reinforcement learning; Temporal difference learning; *Neural networks;* **•Applied computing → Computer games;**

Keywords

Reinforcement learning; covariance matrix adaptation; CMA-ES; VD-CMA; function approximation; knowledge-free representations; video games; n-tuple system

GECCO '15, July 11 - 15, 2015, Madrid, Spain

ISBN 978-1-4503-3472-3/15/07...$15.00

DOI: http://dx.doi.org/10.1145/2739480.2754783

1. INTRODUCTION

Evolutionary algorithms (EAs) implement a *generate-and-test* approach: candidate solutions are randomly perturbed and only then evaluated. This distinguishes them from the gradient-based approaches that modify candidate solutions in a directional way and so attempt to reduce the discrepancy between the current and the desired search state. By exploiting problems in such a way, the gradient-based methods may be more efficient at finding well-performing candidate solutions. On the other hand, by strictly following gradient when updating candidate solutions, they bias the search and may fail to exploit the uncharted parts of the search space. EAs are less biased in this sense and may so compensate for their inability to utilize the information on gradient.

The interplay between these aspects is particularly relevant for reinforcement learning (RL), the study of agents that issue actions that change the states of an environment and learn from the resulting delayed rewards. Within RL, EA-based techniques fall into the category of *direct policy search*, while examples of gradient-based learning techniques can be found among *value function-based methods* (which attempt to approximate the unknown underlying value of particular states). Value function-based methods prove spectacularly good in some problems (e.g., Backgammon [22]), while direct policy search fares very well in the others (e.g., Othello [8]).

Understanding the causes of these performance differences has been an important part of research agenda in RL [9]. There is partial evidence for many factors being involved here; Szita [16] suggested that policy representation (relying on function approximation), the presence of randomness, environment observability, and training regime are, among others, the critical factors. In this study, we focus on policy representation and, more specifically, on its dimensionality, meant as the number of variables/parameters that characterize candidate policies.

Value function-based methods derive an update rule for every variable of an agent's policy, and are by this token relatively insensitive to the their number. For instance, in some studies on Othello, the temporal difference learning algorithm, the classical value function-based RL method, proved very efficient when learning policies encoded by thousands of parameters [20]. At the same time, the results indicated inferior performance of EAs, which traversed the space of candidate solutions more slowly using conventional evolutionary search operators. However, we are currently witnessing the advent of EA techniques that are designed to handle high numbers of dimensions while capturing the interdependency between them. A notable representative of this trend is the CMA-ES (Covariance-Matrix Adaptation Evolution Strategy, [7]) approach; in particular, its recent variant, VD-CMA-ES [1], which avoids estimation of the entire covariance matrix and is thus particularly suitable to high-dimensional spaces. In this light, it is justified to ask: are these new generation EA techniques, when applied to RL problems, capable of equaling the performance of the value function-based methods for policy representations with a large number of parameters?

In this study we attempt to answer this question for SZ-Tetris [17], a difficult single-player stochastic game, which is a constrained variant of Tetris, one of the most common yardsticks in RL. Our contribution consists in bringing the evidence that CMA-ES is indeed able to attain the performance of value function-based methods, albeit at a larger computational cost. We also demonstrate the superiority of high-dimensional, domain-independent policy representations (systematic n-tuple networks) to handcrafted board features. Finally, using such a high-dimensional representation, we produce the best SZ-Tetris player to date, solving in this way the challenge posed recently by Szita and Szepesvári [17]:

> *Challenge #1: Find a sufficiently good feature set (semi-automatically or fully automatically). A feature set is sufficiently good if CEM (or CMA-ES, or genetic algorithms, etc.) is able to learn a weight vector such that the resulting preference function reaches at least as good results as the hand-coded solution.*

2. SZ-TETRIS

2.1 Game description

Tetris is a popular single-player stochastic video game created by Alexey Pajitnov in 1984. The game is played on a 10×20 board. During the game random *tetrominoes* – shapes composed of four connected square blocks – appear one-by-one at the top edge of the board and fall down the board. The objective of the game is to keep the board possibly clear by rotating and moving tetrominoes sidewise and so forming horizontal lines of blocks without any gaps. When at least one such line is created, it disappears, and the blocks above (if any) move down by the number of lines cleared. A point is awarded for each cleared line and the game ends when a tetromino extends beyond the top of the board when set in place.

The original Tetris had been a popular benchmark in RL [16], but it became hard to study when the best policies started achieving the level of tens of millions cleared lines on average [23]. Learning and evaluating such controllers is computationally expensive.

This is why Szita and Szepesvári [17] proposed to study SZ-Tetris, a variant of the original Tetris constrained to tetrominoes 'S' and 'Z'. SZ-Tetris was originally introduced by Burgiel [4] to prove that every Tetris game eventually ends with probability 1, regardless of the players's actions. 'S' and 'Z' tetrominoes are the most difficult ones to handle, which makes SZ-Tetris much harder than the original game. As a result, the computational cost of a single simulation is significantly lower. This facilitates experimentation and allows to measure performance of complex strategies with a reasonable accuracy as Tetris games typically have huge variance.

There are $2^{10\times 20}$ states in both Tetris and SZ-Tetris. In the latter one, regardless of the type of tetromino available, there are 17 possible actions in each move (9 vertical + 8 horizontal).

2.2 A Hand-Coded Controller

Surprisingly, from the computational intelligence point of view, the best SZ-Tetris controller to date has been a hand-coded player proposed as a baseline for other approaches [17]. The controller first divides the board into 5 blocks, each consisting of two adjacent columns. Throughout the game, the 'S' tetrominoes are placed vertically in the first or second block, while the 'Z' tetrominoes in the fourth or fifth block. The type of tetrominoes to be dropped in the third, middle block alternates with game progress. Initially, the player drops there the tetrominoes of the same type as the first tetromino that appeared in the game. Once the highest column on the board exceeds the height of 16[1], the type of tetrominoes for the middle block is flipped. The policy always drops a tetromino into the least occupied block of the compatible tetromino type.

According to Szita and Szepesvári [17], this heuristics, referred to in the following as *Hand-coded*, clears 182 rows on average, which is consistent with our implementation that achieves a score of 183.61 ± 1.4 (95% confidence interval), with the median score of 191.0.

2.3 State-Value Function and Action Selection

In every iteration of the game, given a state s of the board (a vector of $10 \times 20 = 200$ bits) and an incoming tetromino, a SZ-Tetris policy needs to choose the action (move) to be taken. As in many other reinforcement learning problems, one defines to this aim a *function approximator* f that captures the preference of board state in a real number. The direct *afterstates* of s are generated by simulating each of the 17 possible moves: 9 columns for a 2×3-tetromino dropped vertically, and 8 when rotated to 3×2 and dropped horizontally. Then, f is applied to each such *afterstate*, and the move leading to the state with the highest f is applied. Ties on f are resolved at random.

Note that, depending on the learning algorithm, f can be either a *state-value function*, which approximates the expected score from the given state or just a *state-preference function*, which absolute value has no interpretation.

Either way, the function f is the key determinant of policy performance and is usually based on a set of board *features*, either manually designed or defined in a generic, knowledge-free manner. The following subsections describe the classical expert-designed SZ-Tetris features and our proposal of knowledge-free features. Both these representations will be used in the experiments.

2.3.1 "Classical" Bertsekas & Ioffe (B&I) Features

In their early work on Tetris [2], Bertsekas *et al.* proposed the following set of features $\phi_i(s)$ of a board state (afterstate) s:

[1]This number was wrongly reported to be 15 in [17], but correct value of 16 appears in the code attached to the paper.

- The height h_k of the kth column of the board, $k = 1, \ldots 10$,
- The absolute difference $d_k = |h_k - h_{k+1}|$ between the heights of the kth and the $(k+1)$ column, $k = 1, \ldots 9$,
- The maximum column height max_h,
- The number of 'holes' on the board.

In total, this gives rise to $10+9+1+1 = 21$ features, and the state-value function f is defined as their linear combination:

$$f(s) = \sum_{i=1}^{21} w_i \phi_i(s),$$

Thus, an algorithm that learns to play SZ-Tetris using the B&I features searches a 21-dimensional space of weights w_i.

We find it important to note that the implementation used by Szita and Szepesvári [2] involved an additional end-game heuristic that was not explicitly described in the paper: the actions that immediately lead to terminal states are avoided unless there no other possibilities. Our preliminary experiments indicated that this seemingly minor modification has critical impact on performance when using B&I features[2], so we include it also in the implementation used in this study.

2.3.2 Systematic n-Tuple Network

An *n-tuple network* is a combinatorial structure originally proposed by Bledsoe and Browning [3] for pattern recognition and recently successfully adopted for Othello [12], Connect-4 [25] and the puzzle game 2048 [18]. It consists of m *n-tuples*, each representing a single board feature. The ith n-tuple consists of a list of n distinct board locations $(loc_{ij})_{j=1\ldots n}$ and an associated lookup table LUT_i that enumerates all possible states of the selected locations. For games with binary states of individual locations (like SZ-Tetris), the lookup table thus consists of 2^n entries, each holding a real number. Given a board state, the value of the feature is the entry of the lookup table addressed by the combined states of the board locations covered by the n-tuple. To keep the size of the lookup table within reasonable limits, n is typically low.

Formally, an n-tuple network implements a state-value function f as a sum of values returned by individual n-tuples f_i for a given state s:

$$f(s) = \sum_{i=1}^{m} f_i(s) = \sum_{i=1}^{m} LUT_i \left[\text{index}\left(s_{loc_{i1}}, \ldots, s_{loc_{in}}\right)\right],$$

$$\text{index}(\mathbf{v}) = \sum_{j=1}^{|\mathbf{v}|} v_j c^{j-1},$$

where $s_{loc_{ij}}$ is a board value at location loc_{ij}, $\mathbf{v}$ is a sequence of board values at those locations (the observed pattern), and c is the number of possible values in a board location, so that $0 \leq v_j < c$ for $j = 1 \ldots |\mathbf{v}|$. In the case of Tetris, $c = 2$ and values in $\mathbf{v}$ are 0 or 1 for empty and occupied locations respectively. See Fig. 1 for an illustration.

N-tuple networks mitigate the combinatorial explosion while capturing the utility of particular *combinations* of board

[2]Without it, we were not able to exceed 50 points with B&I features.

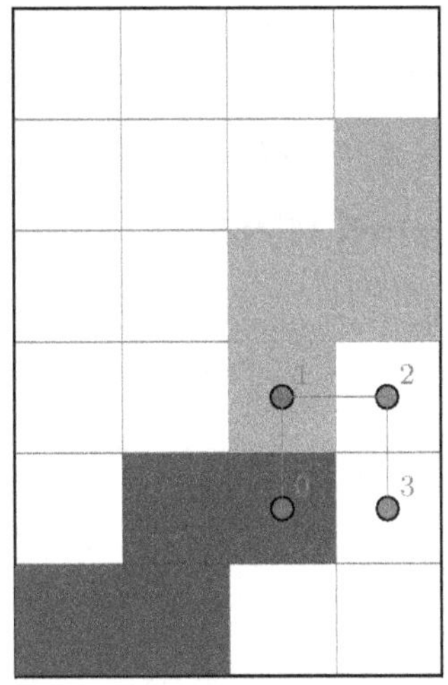

LUT

0123	value
0000	3.04
0001	−3.90
0010	−2.14
⋮	⋮
1100	−2.01
⋮	⋮
1110	6.12
1111	3.21

Figure 1: A 2×2-tuple on a small Tetris board. According to the values in its lookup table, for the given board state it returns −2.01.

states in a way that cannot be realized by the simpler linear representations.

Given the overwhelming number of n-ary combinations that can be formed from a board in most games, the locations of n-tuple are often drawn at random [11]. However, recently, it was found out that systematically placing n-tuples on the board leads to better performance [8] for Othello and avoids introducing additional variation into policy performance (the primary source of variation being game stochasticity and, in multi-player games, the opponents). Therefore, in this study we systematically cover the SZ-Tetris board by placing a same-shaped square n-tuples in all possible locations while allowing for overlaps. We consider two n-tuple shapes: 3×3 and 4×4. The former case gives rise to $(10-3+1)(20-3+1)/2 = 72$ unique n-tuple locations[3]. The lookup table of each such n-tuple has $2^{3\times3} = 512$ entries, so the total number of weights of such a systematic n-tuple network amounts to 36 864. In the latter case, there are 136 unique 4×4-tuple locations, and the total number of weights is thus $136 \times 2^{16}/2 = 4\,456\,448$. These are the numbers of parameters that define the strategies to be learned in Section 3.

Note that, with the n-tuple network, we did not use the end-game heuristic mentioned in Section 2.3.1. The preliminary tests have shown that it is not necessary for this function approximator.

2.4 Other approaches to SZ-Tetris

As we mentioned in Section 2.2 the best controller for SZ-Tetris was hand-coded by Szita and Szepesvári [17] and its mean score is about 183. In the same work, the authors experimented with learning weights for, among others, B&I features (see Section 2.3.1) and its discretized variants, but their best learned agent scores only 133 on average. More recently, Faußer and Schwenker [5] approached the game with a voting committee of TD(λ) agents achieving the av-

[3]The division by 2 is because we take board symmetry into account: given any two vertically mirrored afterstates, there is no rationale to prefer any of them, so f should grant them with the same value.

erage score of 150. Importantly, all these studies relied on hand-coded knowledge-based representations.

3. EXPERIMENTS AND RESULTS

3.1 Direct Policy Search Methods

In the first series of experiments[4], following the existing body of research about effective learning methods for Tetris [16], we use only direct policy search methods. In particular, we employ Cross-Entropy Method (CEM, [13]) and Covariance Matrix Adaptation Evolution Strategy (CMA-ES, [7]). Both methods can be classified as evolution strategies that work by maintaining, updating and sampling from a multivariate Gaussian probability distribution $\mathcal{N}(\mu, \Sigma)$. The simplest form of CEM, which we employ here, assumes that the covariance matrix Σ is a diagonal matrix. CMA-ES maintains and adapts the entire covariance matrix and features some additional adaptation mechanisms which CEM lacks. However, it was observed recently that CEM is just a special case of CMA-ES [14].

3.1.1 *Hand-Designed B&I Features*

In the first experiment we used the standard set of hand-designed Tetris B&I features, which implies learning taking place in a 21-dimensional parameter space (see Section 2.3.1). Following the initial study on SZ-Tetris [17], for CEM we used the selection rate 0.01[5] and population size of 1000. However, in contrast to that work, the fitness of an individual is an average number of cleared lines over 100 games, instead of just one game. In preliminary experiments, we have found that using such more precise evaluation is beneficial for the final performance.

For CMA-ES we used the standard version of the algorithm[6], also with the population size of 1000. What we, however, turned off was the step-size adaptation (step-size was set to 1), which we found harmful for the optimization process in the preliminary experiments.

We stop both algorithms after 200 generations (that is after $1000 \times 100 \times 200 = 20\,000\,000$ of games).

The performance obtained in 10 runs of the algorithms are shown in the left inset in Fig. 2. A single datapoint in the figure marks the performance of a best-of-generation solution. On average, CMA-ES performs slightly better than CEM (124.8 ± 13.1 vs. 117.0 ± 6.3 on average), but statistically there is no difference between these results. Interestingly, although most of the runs of CMA-ES cluster near the average of 124.8 points, one run found a policy that scores 180.6 ± 1.2 on average, equaling the SZ-Tetris record belonged to the hand-coded controller (cf. Section 2.2). To date, it was dubious whether this performance level can be achieved using the existing set of features (like the B&I ones) [17]. The achievement of this policy shows also that the employed direct policy search methods are prone to getting stuck in local minima, where significantly better optima exist. For reproducibility, below we show the weights of this best-performing controller:

h_1	h_2	h_3	h_4	h_5	h_6	h_7	h_8	h_9	h_{10}
70.8	-76.2	5.5	-2.4	-11.9	0.58	-15.7	60.3	72.2	-22.0
d_1	d_2	d_3	d_4	d_5	d_6	d_7	d_8	d_9	
7.3	-0.9	-41.8	-2.3	-44.4	0.75	-28.3	55.7	-56.2	
max_h	holes								
93.1	-55.5								

3.1.2 *Knowledge-Free Systematic n-Tuple Network*

An agent using the handcrafted B&I features can equal the performance of the hand-made heuristic agent. Is it possible to achieve the same level of performance without manually designing the features? In order to answer this question, we employ the 3×3-tuple networks presented in Section 2.3.2.

Knowledge-free approaches require longer learning than the knowledge-based ones. n-tuple networks are no exception to this rule. While the function involving B&I features have only 21 parameters, the 3×3-tuple network consists of 36 864 of them. Such a high number of parameters precludes the use of CMA-ES, since its time complexity depends on the square of the number of optimized parameters. Instead we used VD-CMA-ES [1], a new linear variant of CMA-ES, which maintains the covariance matrix implicitly in a form of $D(I + vv^{\mathrm{T}})D$, where D is a diagonal matrix of dimension n and v is a vector in $\mathbb{R}^n$. This expression cannot represent all possible covariance matrices, but is able to capture some dependencies between the variables in a compressed way, allowing so to apply the concepts of covariance matrix adaptation to highly dimensional spaces.

The course of learning is shown in the right inset of Fig. 2. Due to the large number of parameters, the learning is much slower; however, while the learning with the B&I features saturates quickly, VD-CMA-ES with n-tuples does not exhibit such a tendency, and even after 1000 generations, when we stopped the experiment, there is an observable potential for further growth. Most importantly, however, VD-CMA-ES using the n-tuple network surpasses CMA-ES with B&I features by a large margin (219.7 ± 2.8 vs. 124.8 ± 13.2). The best controller obtained by VD-CMA-ES scores 223.0 ± 1.4 points on average.

The experiment also shows that, despite CEM is a viable method for a small number of parameters, it performs poor in these high-dimensional spaces, being not able to find any agent that clears more than 20 lines.

3.2 Temporal Difference Learning

3.2.1 *Systematic 3×3-Tuple Network*

Szita and Szepesvári stated: *"There are many RL algorithms for approximating the value functions. None of them really work on (SZ-)Tetris, they do not even come close to the performance of the evolutionary approaches."* [17]. Indeed, when we applied the classical temporal difference learning TD(0) [15] to B&I features, the agent performance after 1 million training episodes was still close to 0 regardless of the exploration and learning rates.

This underperformance was puzzling, given that TD(0) has been found successful is so many various domains. We hypothesized that some peculiar properties of the B&I features could have prevented the algorithm from locating the well-performing policies. To verify this, we applied TD(0)

[4]The source code required to run the experiments along with the best obtained players is available at http://github.com/wjaskowski/gecco-2015-sztetris.

[5]Szita and Szepesvári [17] report to use the selection rate 0.1, but in the code repository referred from the paper selection rate was set to 0.01.

[6]https://code.google.com/p/cma-es/

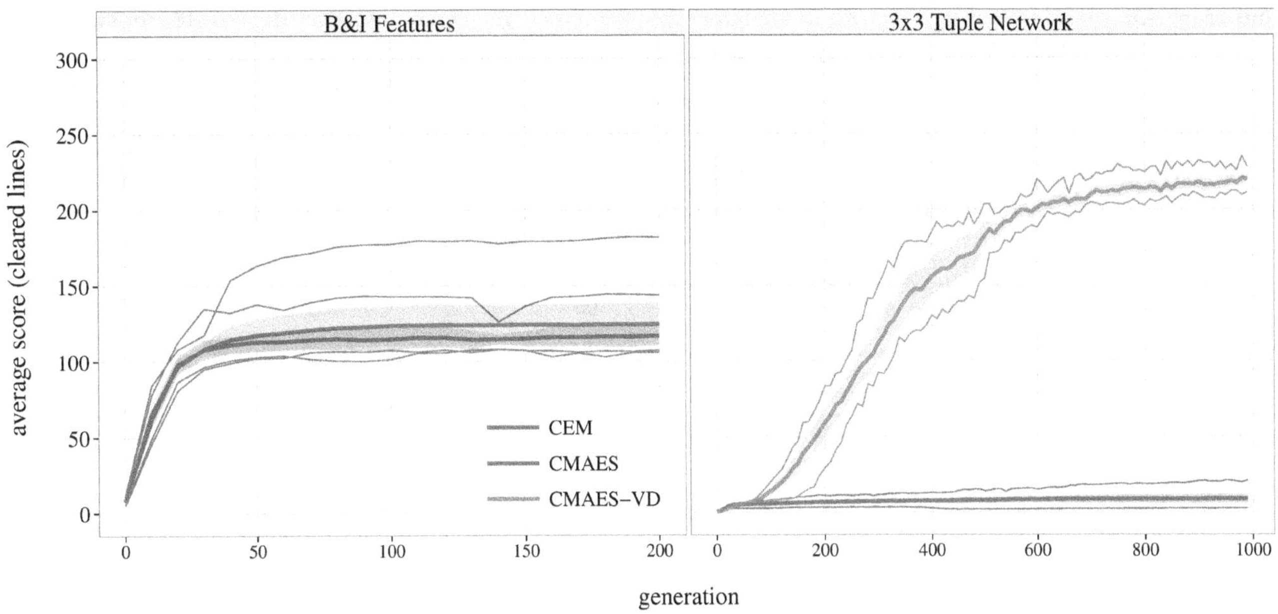

Figure 2: SZ-Tetris learning performance for different direct policy search methods and two state-value functions: the linear combination of Bertsekas & Ioffe features (left) and the 3×3 systematic n-tuple network (right). The thick curve plots the mean performance while the thin lines show the minimum and the maximum performance of 10 evolutionary runs. The 95% confidence interval around the mean has been marked as a shaded ribbon. The systematic n-tuple network was trained by VD-CMA-ES, which has linear time complexity in the function of the number of parameters (while CMA-ES's complexity is quadratic).

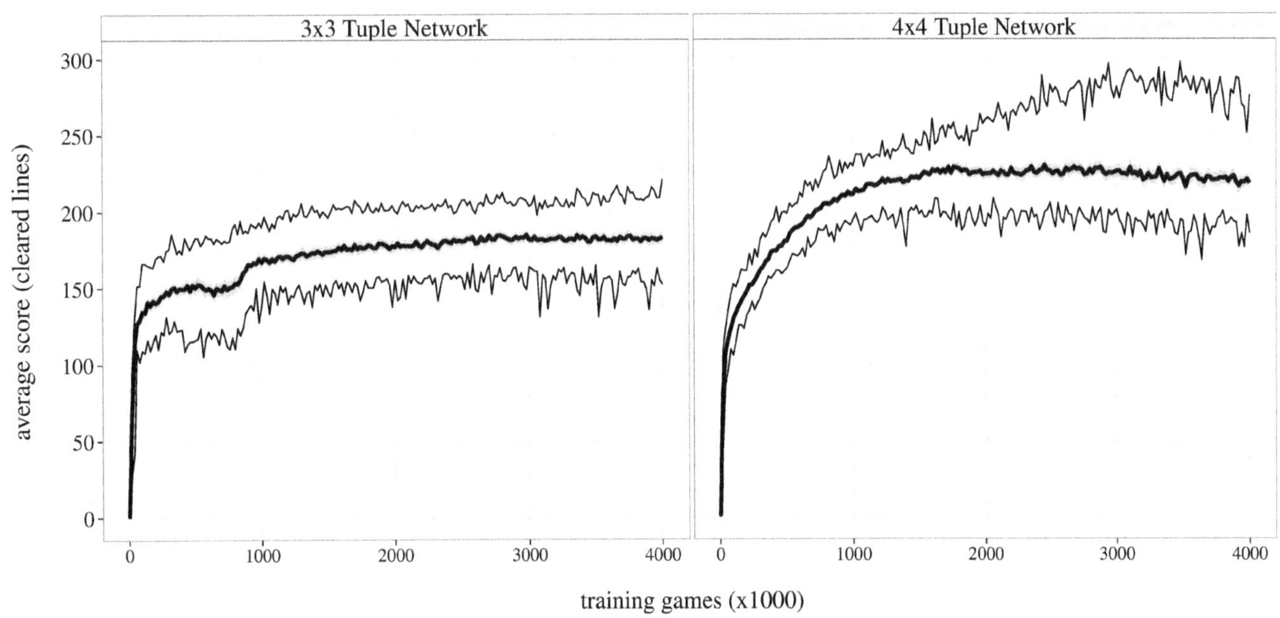

Figure 3: SZ-Tetris scores obtained by TD(0) agent in the function of the training games for 3×3 and 4×4-tuple network. The thick curve plots the average performance while the thin lines show the minimum and the maximum performance achieved in 50 runs. The 95% confidence interval around the mean has been marked in gray.

Table 1: **Comparison of the methods for SZ-Tetris. Method's average has been estimated based on the number of samples in 'Runs' column. Best agent performance has been estimated on 10 000 episodes. ± precedes 95% confidence interval delta.**

Algorithm	Evaluation Function	Features	Learning Games	Method's Average	Runs	Best Agent Score
Hand-coded [17]	-	-	-	-	-	183.6 ± 1.4
TD(0.5) committee [6]	MLP on B&I	10×1655	5 mln	-	-	ca. 150 [6]
CEM	B&I	21	20 mln	117.0 ± 6.3	10	146.4 ± 1.0
CMA-ES	B&I	21	20 mln	124.8 ± 13.1	10	180.6 ± 1.2
VD-CMA-ES	3×3-tuple network	36 864	100 mln	219.7±2.8	10	232.0 ± 1.4
TD(0)	3×3-tuple network	36 864	4 mln	183.3 ± 4.3	50	220.0 ± 1.3
TD(0)	4×4-tuple network	4 456 448	4 mln	218.0 ± 5.2	50	294.8 ± 1.4

to the 3×3-tuple network, using the learning rate $\alpha = 0.001$ and ϵ-greedy policy. ϵ was initialized by 0.1 and multiplied by 0.9 every 100 000 training episodes.

Figure 3 shows the results of 50 runs of TD(0). Its average score is significantly lower than the score obtained byVD-CMA-ES (183.3 ± 4.3 vs.219.7±2.8), but was achieved at a much lower computational expense (4 million vs. 100 million training episodes).

Nevertheless, n-tuples network is the first representation for which TD(0) works for this problem.

3.2.2 *Systematic* 4×4-*Tuple Network*

We treat the reasonably good performance achieved by TD(0) with the 3×3-tuple network as a sign of its capability to efficiently navigate in highly dimensional spaces. Given that the gradient-based update rule used by this algorithm operates on each parameter independently, there are no principal reasons why this could not hold in presence of even higher numbers of parameters.

In the right inset of Fig. 3, we present the performance of TD(0) applied to the systematic 4×4-tuple network. The learning proceeded here in a vast 4 456 448-dimensional search space, i.e., in a search space which dimensionality is of the same order as the number of learning episodes. Nevertheless, this apparently did not prevent TD(0) from excelling on this task. Although, its average performance of 218 ± 5.2 is similar to the one achieved by VD-CMA-ES using 3×3-tuple network 219.7±2.8, it was achieved using 25-times smaller computational budget (4 mln vs. 100 mln games). Short learning time made it possible to increase the number of independent runs to 50. This resulted in a strategy that clears an impressive 294.8±1.4 lines on average, i.e., reaching the level of play that has not been reported for SZ-Tetris to date.

4. DISCUSSION

To streamline our discussion, in Table 1 we summarize the experiments conducted in this paper and the relevant prior results on SZ-Tetris.

The arguably most important observation emerging from these results is the potential dwelling in high-dimensional knowledge-free representations. The systematic n-tuple networks proved versatile here in being not only good approximators of state-value function (when used with a gradient-based method of TD(0)), but also as state-preference functions (when evolved via direct policy search). In terms of average score, none of the configurations relying on handcrafted low-dimensional representations outperformed the policies equipped with n-tuple networks. We find this observation important, given that research on computer Tetris has been to date dominated by approaches that involve handcrafted features, sometimes sophisticated and deeply rooted in domain knowledge [24].

The efficiency of the knowledge-free representations is also conceptually stunning, when one realizes that a n-tuple network-based SZ-Tetris agent has no explicit knowledge on *any* aspects of the game that are essential for designing the handcrafted representations: the constraints resulting from board dimensions, the shapes of the tetrominoes, the 'mechanics' of tetrominoes fitting to each other, etc. Its entire perception of a game state boils down to a sum of a few dozen of numbers selected from lookup tables by a 200-bit board state. Yet despite this appalling ignorance, n-tuples manage to break the current performance records.

Ultimately however, the performance of a given policy depends also on the training algorithm. In this respect, the capacities of temporal difference learning methods are impressive, particularly for the most extensive 4×4 tuples, where it manages to learn supreme policies from a number of episodes that is comparable to the number of policy parameters (4 million episodes vs. 4 456 448 weights). This suggests that Szita's and Szepesvári's diagnosis that value function-based RL algorithms do not work for SZ-Tetris ([17], p.4) does not hold anymore. Well-performing policies can be efficiently found by temporal difference learning for SZ-Tetris once the underlying representation of state-value function is rich enough.

This is however not to say that gradient-based learning of value functions is destined to be always the pinnacle of performance. The local nature of search performed by such techniques incurs a measurable risk of missing even better candidate solutions. Despite the high-dimensional search space, VD-CMA-ES, which is a direct search method, was not only found to surpass TD(0) for 3×3-tuple network, but also to match the average score of TD(0) for a larger 4×4-tuple network. There are two factors that might have aid the direct policy search: not only the global, exploratory character of CMA-ES, but also the fact that the direct policy search seeks a state *preference* function, and so cares only about the ordering of state values, while the methods like TD(0) approximate state-value function and so insist on finding the right absolute state values. Because for any given state-value function, there are infinitely many state preference functions that select the actions in exactly the same way, finding a function that is good only with respect to the above ordering may be easier.

The price to pay for the potential of achieving better performance is computational expense. Whether gaining a few extra cleared lines in SZ-Tetris is worth investing 25-times greater computation time is a matter of context. If one is ultimately interested in finding that one best-of-all strategy, this may be the case. In this context, it might be tempting to consider hybrid approaches that leverage TD's capability to operate in high-dimensional spaces while maintaining some features of parallel global search. The evolutionary temporal difference learning we proposed and studied in [19, 10, 21, 20] seems to be a viable option for such an endeavor.

We conducted also preliminary behavioral analysis of the well-performing policies[7], trying to identify the key features that might have determined their performance. All learning algorithms compared here managed to more or less rediscover the essence of the hand-coded policy, i.e., they learned to stack the 'S' and 'Z' tetrominoes vertically in five separate blocks of width two. The best 4×4-tuple TD policy is more sophisticated. First of all, it does not stick to a fixed division into five blocks of width two, and can drop a tetromino vertically so that it fills in a single gap at arbitrary abscissa. It can also thoughtfully drop tetrominoes in horizontal position. Most interestingly, sometimes it makes a move that, at first sight, looks suboptimal and leaves a hole buried beneath the tetrominoes. Our analysis revealed, however, that, in a longer run, this makes it easier to dig up ('reopen') the holes and fill them in. More behavioral patterns emerged in the policies learned here, but their thorough analysis is beyond the scope of this paper.

On a more technical level, this study is, to the best knowledge of the authors, the first practical demonstration of the efficiency of VD-CMA-ES [1], the new variant of CMA-ES designed with high-dimensional representation in mind. Apparently, given many dimensions, it may be not necessary to capture all pairwise dependencies between them by maintaining the complete covariance matrix. Modeling only a fraction of that information can be sufficient to attain superior results. On the other hand, taking *some* interdependencies into account is essential, and discarding them altogether has detrimental effect, as witnessed by the inferior performance of CEM.

[7]Videos presenting exemplary games are available at http://github.com/wjaskowski/gecco-2015-sztetris.

5. CONCLUSIONS

In this study, we proposed a novel knowledge-free policy representation for the challenging reinforcement learning problem of SZ-Tetris and put it under extensive experimental scrutiny. The overall conclusion is that, by the virtue of high-dimensional systematic n-tuple network representation and appropriate learning algorithms, one can achieve at least the state-of-the-art level of performance in this game while being essentially completely ignorant about its nature. The peak demonstrator of validity of this stance is the best-to-date SZ-Tetris controller, which by clearing over 294 lines on average reaches a new quality of performance and conquers the hand-coded player, solving so the Challenge #1 posed by Szita and Szepesvári [17]. In authors' opinion, these results substantially enrich our current understanding of this game, and possibly similar RL tasks.

With this piece of work, we hope to pave the way towards a more routine use of knowledge-free representations in reinforcement learning tasks, whether approached with state-value-based function learning or with (evolutionary) direct policy search. As it follows from this study, both these approaches offer nowadays powerful algorithms that fare very well even when the number of variables to be simultaneously optimized is in the order of millions. By casting a learning task into a high-dimensional space, this project subscribes to the trend present in other branches of machine learning and computational intelligence, where, for instance, using thousands of features is nowadays common.

The computational overhead incurred by evolutionary search in huge spaces of knowledge-free representations may seem prohibitive. Note however that the statistics shown in Table 1 reflect only the machine-part of the effort invested in finding a solution. In focusing on the time spent on computation, we tend to ignore the human intellectual investment put into designing and validating hand-coded heuristics or handcrafted features. What is, for that instance, the machine-equivalent of the effort devoted by the authors of [17] to design their SZ-Tetris heuristics? If we had the means to take this human investment into account, the overall effort would possibly be not so favorable for knowledge-based approaches anymore.

Acknowledgment

This work has been supported by the Polish National Science Centre grant no. DEC-2013/09/D/ST6/03932. M. Szubert has been supported by the Polish Ministry of Science and Higher Education, grant no. 09/91/DSMK/0568. K. Krawiec acknowledges support from grant 09/91/DSPB/0572. The computations have been performed in Poznan Supercomputing and Networking Center.

6. REFERENCES

[1] Y. Akimoto, A. Auger, N. Hansen, and Others. Comparison-Based Natural Gradient Optimization in High Dimension. In *Genetic and Evolutionary Computation Conference GECCO'14*, 2014.

[2] D. P. Bertsekas and S. Ioffe. Temporal differences-based policy iteration and applications in neuro-dynamic programming. *Lab. for Info. and Decision Systems Report LIDS-P-2349, MIT, Cambridge, MA*, 1996.

[3] W. W. Bledsoe and I. Browning. Pattern recognition and reading by machine. In *Proc. Eastern Joint Comput. Conf.*, pages 225–232, 1959.

[4] H. Burgiel. How to lose at Tetris. *Mathematical Gazette*, 81:194–200, 1997.

[5] S. Faußer and F. Schwenker. Selective Neural Network Ensembles in Reinforcement Learning. In *European Symposium on Artificial Neural Networks*, pages 105–110, 2014.

[6] S. Faußer and F. Schwenker. Neural Network Ensembles in Reinforcement Learning. *Neural Processing Letters*, 41(1):55–69, 2015.

[7] N. Hansen and A. Ostermeier. Completely derandomized self-adaptation in evolution strategies. *Evolutionary computation*, 9(2):159–195, 2001.

[8] W. Jaśkowski. Systematic n-tuple networks for othello position evaluation. *ICGA Journal*, 37(2):85–96, June 2014.

[9] S. Kalyanakrishnan and P. Stone. Characterizing reinforcement learning methods through parameterized learning problems. *Machine Learning*, 84(1-2):205–247, 2011.

[10] K. Krawiec, W. Jaśkowski, and M. Szubert. Evolving small-board go players using coevolutionary temporal difference learning with archive. *International Journal of Applied Mathematics and Computer Science*, 21(4):717–731, 2011.

[11] S. Lucas. Learning to play Othello with n-tuple systems. *Australian Journal of Intelligent Information Processing*, 4:1–20, 2008.

[12] S. M. Lucas. Learning to play Othello with N-tuple systems. *Australian Journal of Intelligent Information Processing Systems, Special Issue on Game Technology*, 9(4):01–20, 2007.

[13] R. Y. Rubinstein and D. P. Kroese. *The cross-entropy method: a unified approach to combinatorial optimization, Monte-Carlo simulation and machine learning*. Springer Science & Business Media, 2004.

[14] F. Stulp and O. Sigaud. Path integral policy improvement with covariance matrix adaptation. *arXiv preprint arXiv:1206.4621*, 2012.

[15] R. S. Sutton. Learning to predict by the methods of temporal differences. *Machine learning*, 3(1):9–44, 1988.

[16] I. Szita. Reinforcement learning in games. In *Reinforcement Learning*, pages 539–577. Springer, 2012.

[17] I. Szita and C. Szepesvári. SZ-Tetris as a benchmark for studying key problems of reinforcement learning. In *Proceedings of the ICML 2010 Workshop on Machine Learning and Games.*, 2010.

[18] M. Szubert and W. Jaśkowski. Temporal difference learning of n-tuple networks for the game 2048. In *IEEE Conference on Computational Intelligence and Games*, pages 1–8, Dortmund, Aug 2014. IEEE.

[19] M. Szubert, W. Jaśkowski, and K. Krawiec. Coevolutionary temporal difference learning for othello. In *IEEE Symposium on Computational Intelligence and Games*, pages 104–111, Milano, Italy, 2009.

[20] M. Szubert, W. Jaśkowski, and K. Krawiec. On scalability, generalization, and hybridization of coevolutionary learning: a case study for othello. *IEEE Transactions on Computational Intelligence and AI in Games*, 5(3):214–226, 2013.

[21] M. Szubert, W. Wojciech Jaśkowski, and K. Krzysztof Krawiec. Learning Board Evaluation Function for Othello by Hybridizing Coevolution with Temporal Difference Learning. *Control and Cybernetics*, 2011.

[22] G. Tesauro. Temporal difference learning and td-gammon. *Communications of the ACM*, 38(3):58–68, 1995.

[23] C. Thiery and B. Scherrer. Building controllers for Tetris. *International Computer Games Association Journal*, 32:3–11, 2009.

[24] C. Thiery and B. Scherrer. Improvements on learning Tetris with cross entropy. *International Computer Games Association Journal*, 32, 2009.

[25] M. Thill, P. Koch, and W. Konen. Reinforcement Learning with N-tuples on the Game Connect-4. In C. A. C. Coello, V. Cutello, K. Deb, S. Forrest, G. Nicosia, and M. Pavone, editors, *Parallel Problem Solving from Nature - PPSN XII*, volume 7491 of *Lecture Notes in Computer Science*, pages 184–194. Springer, 2012.

Subspace Clustering Using Evolvable Genome Structure

Sergio Peignier
Université de Lyon
INSA-Lyon, CNRS, INRIA
LIRIS, UMR5205
F-69621, France
Sergio.Peignier@inria.fr

Christophe Rigotti
Université de Lyon
INSA-Lyon, CNRS, INRIA
LIRIS, UMR5205
F-69621, France
Christophe.Rigotti@insa-lyon.fr

Guillaume Beslon
Université de Lyon
INSA-Lyon, CNRS, INRIA
LIRIS, UMR5205
F-69621, France
Guillaume.Beslon@inria.fr

ABSTRACT

In this paper we present an evolutionary algorithm to tackle the subspace clustering problem. Subspace clustering is recognized as more difficult than standard clustering since it requires to identify not only the clusters but also the various subspaces where the clusters hold. We propose to tackle this problem with a bio-inspired algorithm that includes many bio-like features like variable genome length and organization, functional and non-functional elements, and variation operators including chromosomal rearrangements. These features give the algorithm a large degree of freedom to achieve subspace clustering with satisfying results on a reference benchmark with respect to state of the art methods. One of the main advantages of the approach is that it needs only one subspace clustering ad-hoc parameter: the maximal number of clusters. This is a single and intuitive parameter that sets the maximal level of details of the clustering, while other algorithms require more complicated parameter space exploration. The other parameters of the algorithm are related to the evolution strategy (population size, mutation rate, ...) and for them we use a single setting that turns out to be effective on all the datasets of the benchmark.

1. INTRODUCTION

Subspace clustering is recognized as more general and more difficult than clustering. A subspace clustering task searches for objects sharing similar feature values, and also at the same time searches for the subspaces where these similarities appear, while usual clustering only looks for groups of objects similar over the whole data space. Subspace clustering can be thought as *"similarity examined under different representations"* [Patrikainen and Meila, 2006] and is particularly useful when dealing with high dimensional spaces [Kriegel et al., 2009].

According to [Banzhaf et al., 2006], bio-inspired optimization algorithms could be improved by incorporating knowledge from molecular and evolutionary biology. A promising source of advances in optimization is one of the important phenomena in evolutionary biology: the dynamic evolution of the genome structure. Several studies showed for instance that an evolvable genome structure allows evolution to modify the effects that evolution principles (e.g., mutations) have on individuals, a phenomenon known as *evolution of evolution* [Hindré et al., 2012]. Evolvable genome structure can encompass various aspects, such as variable genome length or variable ratio of functional versus non-functional elements [Knibbe et al., 2007]. Among the state-of-the-art formalisms used for *in silico* experimental evolution and reviewed in [Hindré et al., 2012], two models enable genome structure evolution: [Knibbe et al., 2007] and [Crombach and Hogeweg, 2007], and have inspired key aspects of our work.

In this paper, we present Chameleoclust, an evolutionary subspace clustering algorithm that incorporates a genome having an evolvable structure. The genome is a *coarse-grained* genome, inspired on [Crombach and Hogeweg, 2007], and defined as a list of tuples of numbers. These tuples are mapped at the phenotype level to denote core point locations in different dimensions, which are then used to build the subspace clusters. In Chameleoclust, the genome also contains a variable proportion of non-functional elements as in [Knibbe et al., 2007], and is subject to local mutations and to large random rearrangements similar to those used in [Knibbe et al., 2007] and [Crombach and Hogeweg, 2007], namely: large deletions, duplications and translocations. The local mutations and rearrangements modify the genome elements but also the genome length and the proportion of non-functional elements. The key intuition in the design of the Chameleoclust algorithm is to take advantage of such an evolvable structure to detect various numbers of clusters in subspaces of various dimensions.

Chameleoclust is assessed using a reference framework for subspace clustering evaluation[Müller et al., 2009], and compared to state-of-the-art algorithms on both real and synthetic datasets. The experiments show that Chameleoclust obtains competitive results. Moreover, these results can be achieved with a single parameter related to the domain, i.e., the maximal number of clusters.

The rest of the paper is organized as follows. The next section introduces the proposed algorithm, and Sections 3 and 4 describe respectively the evaluation method and results. Section 5 presents the related work and we conclude with a summary in Section 6.

GECCO '15, July 11 - 15, 2015, Madrid, Spain

DOI: http://dx.doi.org/10.1145/2739480.2754709

2. Chameleoclust

Chameleoclust includes many bio-like features such as a variable genome length and organization, presence of both functional and non-functional elements, and variation operators including large chromosomal rearrangements. These features, inspired by the *in silico* experimental evolution formalisms of [Knibbe et al., 2007] and [Crombach and Hogeweg, 2007], give the algorithm a large degree of freedom by making the genome structure evolvable. Chameleoclust takes advantage of this structural flexibility to build subspace clustering with various number of clusters and in subspaces having different numbers of dimensions.

Dataset and clusters.

A dataset S is a set of objects described in $\mathbb{R}^D$ by D features (the coordinates of the objects). The size of S is the number of objects in S, and D is the number of dimensions (i.e., the dimensionality) of S. Each dimension is defined by a number from 1 to D and the set of all dimensions of the dataset is denoted $\mathcal{D} = \{1, \dots, D\}$. The algorithm takes as input a dataset S and a parameter c_{max} that is the maximal number of desired clusters. The algorithm outputs a subspace clustering in the form of a set of clusters, where each cluster is defined by a set of objects and a set of dimensions.

Overall clustering principle.

Each individual encodes in its genome a subspace clustering. More precisely a genome defines a set of so called *core points* located in various subspaces having possibly less than D dimensions. If the objects of the dataset tends to form groups around these core points, then a high fitness is associated to the corresponding individual. The reproduction (including selection and mutations) is performed for a whole generation in a synchronized way. After a given number of generations the process stops and the subspace clustering corresponding to the individual having the highest fitness is retained.

Preprocessing.

As in many typical clustering problems, the first step is to standardize the dataset to ensure that all features could have similar impact on the distance computation during the clustering. Thus each feature value x is replaced by its z-score: $z = \frac{x-\mu}{\sigma}$, where μ is the dataset mean and σ is dataset standard deviation for the given feature. After standardization, data values in different dimensions are independent of the offset and scale, and features have all the same zero mean and the same unitary dispersion. Finally the maximal value among all absolute values of the z-score of all features is computed and is noted x_{max} in the rest of the paper.

Genome structure.

A genome Γ is a list $[\gamma_1, \dots, \gamma_i, \dots, \gamma_n]$ of tuples of the form $\gamma_i = \langle g_i, c_i, d_i, x_i \rangle$, where $g_i \in \{0, 1\}$ indicates if γ_i is a functional element of the genome ($g_i = 1$) or not ($g_i = 0$), and c_i, d_i, x_i will be used to define the individual phenotype and have the following specific domains: $c \in \{1, \dots, c_{max}\}$, $d \in \{1, \dots, D\}$ and $x \in ValCoord$, with $ValCoord = \{j \times x_{max}/1000 \mid j \in \{-1000, \dots, 1000\}\}$, i.e. all values from $-x_{max}$ to x_{max} with step $x_{max}/1000$.

Phenotype.

A phenotype is simply a set of core points. Informally a core point is a specific point, around which objects can be grouped to form a subspace cluster. The number of core points cannot exceed the maximal number of desired clusters c_{max}. Each core point is identified by a number $c \in [1, c_{max}]$ and is denoted p_c. The intuition of the genotype-phenotype mapping is that each functional element of the genome $\langle 1, c, d, x \rangle$ is a contribution of value x to the location of core point p_c in dimension d. More precisely, let x_d be the coordinate of p_c for dimension d, then x_d is the sum of all the values x contained in a tuple of the form $\langle 1, c, d, x \rangle$ in the genomeΓ . The subspace associated to p_c (and for wich p_c is defined) is the set of dimensions $\mathcal{D}_{p_c} = \{d \mid \langle 1, c, d, x \rangle \in \Gamma \text{ for some } x\}$, i.e., the dimensions that contribute to p_c inΓ . Notice that the non-functional elements of Γ do not contribute to the phenotype.

For a given dataset $\mathcal{S}$, a phenotype Φ defines a subspace clustering of $\mathcal{S}$, by associating each object of $\mathcal{S}$ to the best matching core point in Φ. A non empty set of objects associated to a core point p_c forms a cluster in subspace $\mathcal{D}_{p_c}$. The precise definition of the notion of *best match* is given in paragraph *Fitness* here after.

Notice that the length of the genome can be different among individuals, leading to phenotypes containing different numbers of core points in various subspaces and thus defining subspace clustering models with different number of clusters in subspaces having different number of dimensions.

Mutation operators.

Each new genome is copied from a parent and modified by biologically inspired mutation operators of two kinds: Global rearrangements and point mutations. These operators are general mutation operators and are not guided by some criteria related to the subspace-clustering task. The model uses a single point mutation operator defined as follows for a genomeΓ.

- **Point substitution**: Let $\gamma_i \in \Gamma$ and $k \in \{1, 2, 3, 4\}$, both uniformly chosen, the k-th element of the tuple γ_i is replaced by a new random number drawn uniformly in its associated range:

$$\gamma_i \leftarrow \begin{cases} \langle \mathcal{U}(\{0,1\}), c, d, x \rangle & \textbf{if } k = 1 \\ \langle g, \mathcal{U}(\{1, \dots, c_{max}\}), d, x \rangle & \textbf{if } k = 2 \\ \langle g, c, \mathcal{U}(\{1, \dots, D\}), x \rangle & \textbf{if } k = 3 \\ \langle g, c, d, \mathcal{U}(ValCoord) \rangle & \textbf{if } k = 4 \end{cases}$$

  where $\mathcal{U}$ denotes the uniform random selection of a element in a set.

For the rearrangements, Γ is considered as being circular (as bacterial genomes). This means that the tuple γ_n is adjacent to the tuple γ_1. In order to define the possible rearrangements let us define three basic operators.

- Sublist extraction operator:

$$[\gamma_1, \dots, \gamma_n]_{i,j} = \begin{cases} [\gamma_i, \dots, \gamma_j] & \textbf{if } i < j \\ [\,] \text{ (the empty list)} & \textbf{if } i \geq j. \end{cases}$$

- List concatenation operator:

$$[\gamma_1, \dots, \gamma_n] + [\gamma'_1, \dots, \gamma'_m] = [\gamma_1, \dots, \gamma_n, \gamma'_1, \dots, \gamma'_m]$$

- Tuple merge operator M: Let $\gamma = \langle g, c, d, x\rangle$ and $\gamma' = \langle g', c', d', x'\rangle$, then four merges are defined depending on a merge index k:

$$M(\gamma,\gamma',k) = \begin{cases} \langle g, c', d', x'\rangle & \textbf{if } k = 1 \\ \langle g, c, d', x'\rangle & \textbf{if } k = 2 \\ \langle g, c, d, x'\rangle & \textbf{if } k = 3 \\ \langle g, c, d, x\rangle & \textbf{if } k = 4 \end{cases}$$

Rearrangements are responsible for changing the tuples positions, increasing or decreasing the genome length. In addition rearrangement breakpoints operate inside tuples, breaking them and recombining them according to the rearrangement operation, creating new tuples from old genetic material. The model uses three kinds of rearrangements: large deletions, large duplications and large translocations. For a rearrangement of a genome $\Gamma = [\gamma_1, \ldots, \gamma_n]$, a portion of$\Gamma$ bounded by two tuples $\gamma_i, \gamma_j \in \Gamma$ is considered, where i and j are uniformly chosen in $\{1, \ldots, n\}$. A breakpoint index is also uniformly chosen in $\{1, \ldots, 4\}$ to specify where the rearrangement limit is located within the bounding tuples. The three rearrangement operators can then be defined as follows:

- **Large deletions**: The segment between tuples γ_i and γ_j is excised.

  If $i \leq j$:

  $\Gamma \leftarrow \Gamma_{1,i-1} + M(\gamma_i, \gamma_j, k) + \Gamma_{j+1,n}$

  If $i > j$, because of genome circularity, we have:

  $\Gamma \leftarrow \Gamma_{j+1,i-1} + M(\gamma_i, \gamma_j, k)$

- **Large duplications** : The segment between tuples γ_i and γ_j is copied and inserted at the location of a third tuple γ_p (uniformly chosen).

  If $i \leq j$:

  $\Gamma \leftarrow \Gamma_{1,p-1} + M(\gamma_p, \gamma_i, k) + \Gamma_{i+1,j-1} + M(\gamma_j, \gamma_p, k) + \Gamma_{p+1,n}$

  If $i > j$, because of genome circularity, we have:

  $\Gamma \leftarrow \Gamma_{1,p-1} + M(\gamma_p, \gamma_j, k) + \Gamma_{j+1,n} + \Gamma_{1,i-1} + M(\gamma_i, \gamma_p, k) + \Gamma_{p+1,n}$

- **Large translocations**: The segment between tuples γ_i and γ_j is cut and inserted at the location of a third tuple γ_p (uniformly chosen) such that $p \notin [i, j]$ if $i \leq j$ and $p \notin [1, j] \cup [i, n]$ if $i > j$. Translocation can be defined with the two previous rearrangement operations. At first the segment between tuples γ_i and γ_j is duplicated at the location of the third tuple γ_p, and then it is deleted.

During the reproduction of an individual, the mutations stage is defined as follows. For each of the three kinds of rearrangement operations, the number of rearrangements per genome is drawn from a binomial law $\mathcal{B}(L, u_m)$ where L is the genome size and u_m is the mutation rate (same rate for all mutation operators). The rearrangements of the three kinds are then performed in a random order. Once rearrangements have been applied, the number of point substitutions per genome is drawn from a binomial law $\mathcal{B}(L', u_m)$ where L' is the genome size after applying the rearrangement operations, and then all these point substitutions are carried out.

Fitness.

For a given dataset $\mathcal{S}$, the fitness of a individual of phenotype Φ is related to the quality of the subspace clustering defined by Φ over $\mathcal{S}$. This quality measure is an internal measure based on a distance, and reflecting how the objects in $\mathcal{S}$ tend to form groups around core points ofΦ.

In [Beyer et al., 1999] and [Aggarwal et al., 2001] it has been shown that distance comparisons are less meaningful when dimensionality increases, this effect is called the *concentration effect* of the distances. Furthermore, distances do not have the same meaning in subspaces with different numbers of dimensions: It is not fair to compare distances calculated in subspaces with different dimensionality.

It has been shown in [Aggarwal et al., 2001] that the Manhattan distance is robust to the concentration effect. In the Chameleoclust algorithm, the distance used is the *Manhattan segmental distance* introduced in [Aggarwal et al., 1999] for the well known subspace clustering algorithm PROCLUS. It is a normalized version of the classic Manhattan distance to compare distances in subspaces with different number of dimensions. Let y_1 and y_2 be two points in a space over the set of dimension $\mathcal{D}$, and $y_{1,i}$ (resp. $y_{2,i}$) denotes the coordinate of y_1 (resp. y_2) in the dimension i of $\mathcal{D}$. Then, the Manhattan segmental distance is defined as:

$$d_{\mathcal{D}}(y_1, y_2) = \sum_{i \in \mathcal{D}} \frac{|y_{1,i} - y_{2,i}|}{|\mathcal{D}|}$$

The functions to evaluate the subspace clustering models corresponding to phenotypes and the fitness of the individuals are defined as follows.

- A function $\mathcal{E}(x, p_c)$ is used to assess the mismatch of the assignment of an object $x \in \mathcal{S}$ in space $\mathcal{D}$ to a core point p_c in subspace $\mathcal{D}_{p_c}$. The highest is $\mathcal{E}(x, p_c)$, the worst is the association of x to p_c. This function is defined by:

$$\mathcal{E}(x, p_c) = \frac{|\mathcal{D}_{p_c}| \cdot d_{\mathcal{D}_{p_c}}(x, p_c) + |\mathcal{D} \setminus \mathcal{D}_{p_c}| \cdot d_{\mathcal{D} \setminus \mathcal{D}_{p_c}}(x, \mathcal{O})}{|\,\mathcal{D}\,|}$$

  where $\mathcal{O}$ is the centroid of dataset $\mathcal{S}$, i.e., the origin of the coordinate system after the z-score standardization. The mismatch evaluation $\mathcal{E}(x, p_c)$ increases with the distance between the core point p_c and the object x (i.e., $d_{\mathcal{D}}(x, p_c)$). $\mathcal{E}(x, p_c)$ also increases if the subspace $\mathcal{D}_{p_c}$ has not enough dimensions to explain the shift of x with respect to $\mathcal{O}$ (i.e., $d_{\mathcal{D}' \setminus \mathcal{D}}(x, \mathcal{O})$).

- Each object $x \in \mathcal{S}$ is assigned to the core point $p_c \in \Phi$ for which $\mathcal{E}(x, p_c)$ is minimal (in the rare cases where several core points lead to the same minimal value, then one of them is chosen nondeterministically). Let $\mathcal{S}_{p_c}$ be the set of objects associated to p_c, then if $\mathcal{S}_{p_c}$ is not empty, the core point p_c defines the subspace cluster $\langle \mathcal{S}_{p_c}, \mathcal{D}_{p_c}\rangle$.

- Finally the fitness $\mathcal{F}$ can be defined as the opposite of the sum of the mismatches of the best possible assignments of the objects:

$$\mathcal{F} = -\sum_{p_c \in \Phi} \sum_{x \in \mathcal{S}_{p_c}} \mathcal{E}(x, p_c)$$

The fitness function $\mathcal{F}$ goes to 0 when the evaluation of the mismatches between objects and core points tends to 0 (perfect match), and is strongly negative when objects and core points are poorly related. Notice that a core point p_c with no associated object ($\mathcal{S}_{p_c} = \emptyset$) is not penalized, and its corresponding functional elements in the genome may then be preserved for further exploration.

Population.

Each individual can be perceived as an asexual artificial organism containing a single chromosome. The population evolves during T generations. At each generation the population is completely renewed but its size N remains constant over time. The following rank based selection method is used for reproduction. The individual of the current generation are ranked according to their fitness, in increasing order of performance (the worst has rank 0 and the best rank N). Then for each of the N individuals of the offspring generation, the parent of this individual is determined by a trial over a N classes multinomial law, where each class is associated to an individual of the current generation. For this multinomial law, a class associated to an individual α has a success probability $p_\alpha = (s-1)\frac{s^{N-r_\alpha}}{s^N-1}$ where r_α is the rank of the individual α and s the selection pressure parameter. In order to avoid the best fitness to decrease Chameleoclust uses an elitist selection method. More precisely, it always adds in the next generation an unchanged copy of the best current individual, and performs the random reproduction using only $N-1$ trials.

For the first generation, every initial individual is generated with a genome of size 100 containing random tuples of the form: $\langle g, \mathcal{U}(\{1, c_{max}\}), \mathcal{U}(\{1, D\}), \mathcal{U}(ValCoord)\rangle$, with $g = 1$ for 1/3 of them (functional elements) and $g = 0$ for the others (non-functional elements).

3. EXPERIMENTAL SETUP

Experimental protocol.

In order to evaluate and compare Chameleoclust to state-of-the-art algorithms, we used the evaluation framework of reference designed for subspace clustering and described in [Müller et al., 2009]. We clustered with Chameleoclust the same datasets and computed the same evaluation measures as recommended by [Müller et al., 2009]. We report in the Table 2 and Figure 3 the results given in [Müller et al., 2009] for the state-of-the-art algorithms, together with the results obtained for Chameleoclust.

In the framework of [Müller et al., 2009], as each algorithm requires several parameters (from 2 to 9), they are executed with many different parameter settings to explore the parameter space. Then, using an external labeling of the objects, only the subspace clusterings that are among the best (with respect to the external labeling) are retained. So, the results reported for these algorithms are in some sense the best possible subspace clusterings that could be achieved if we were able to find the most appropriated parameter values. Since generally no external labeling is available when we search for clusters, parameter tuning is most of the time a difficult task and these high quality subspace clusterings are likely to be hard to obtain.

An important point to notice, is that for Chameleoclust we did not perform any parameter optimization using external information. We simply ran Chameleoclust and took the subspace clustering defined by the individual of the last generation having the best fitness. Since the algorithm is non-deterministic, we ran it 10 times in the same conditions and report the minimal, maximal and mean values of the measures over these 10 runs. So, we compare clusterings effectively found by Chameleoclust to the best clusterings that could potentially be found by the other algorithms. All experiments were run on a quad-core Intel 2.67GHz CPU running Linux Ubuntu 14.04, and using a single core.

Datasets.

We studied Chameleoclust performances on real word data using the six benchmark datasets selected in [Müller et al., 2009] for their representativity: *breast, diabetes, liver, glass, shape, pendigits* and *vowel* (most of them coming from the UCI archive [Bache and Lichman, 2013]). These datasets have different dimensionalities and contain different numbers of objects. These objects are already structured in classes, and the class membership is used by quality measures to assess the cluster *purity*. However the number of classes does not necessarily reflect the number of subspace clusters, since even within a class the objects can form several clusters in different subspaces.

We also ran Chameleoclust on the 16 synthetic benchmark datasets provided by [Müller et al., 2009]. These datasets are particularly useful to study the algorithm performances, as the true clusters and their subspaces are known. They have different number of dimensions (5, 10, 15, 20, 25, 50 and 75), contain different number of objects (1500, 2500, 3500, 4500 and 5500), and various percentages of added noise (0, 10, 30, 50 and 70%). Each dataset contains 10 hidden subspace clusters.

For the real datasets we ran Chameleoclust using all objects, while for the synthetic dataset it was executed on random samples containing 20% of the objects to reduce the duration of the experiments. However, in both cases we used 100% of the objects for the evaluation of the clustering quality. This means that for a synthetic dataset after having computed a subspace clustering with 20% of the objects, then we associated 100% of the objects to the clusters (using the best matching core points). All datasets and additional material are made available by the authors of [Müller et al., 2009] at http://dme.rwth-aachen.de/openSubspace/evaluation.

Parameter setting.

We used the same setting of the evolution strategy parameters for **all** datasets: mutation rate $u_m = 0.005$, selection pressure $s = 0.8$, population size $N = 100$, and number of generations $T = 5000$. With 5000 generations the algorithm achieved a good convergence for fitness and genome length, as illustrated in Figure 1 and Figure 2. A single parameter needed to be changed: c_{max} the maximal number of subspace clusters that are built. However, this parameter does not require a fine tuning since Chameleoclust adapts the number of subspace clusters between 1 and c_{max}. It was set to 20 for all synthetic datasets and for three real datasets: *shape, pendigits* and *breast*. For the other real datasets, Chameleoclust was also tried with $c_{max} = 20$, but in this case the algorithm output exactly 20 subspace clusters. This meant that it did not succeed to regulate the number of subspace clusters because c_{max} was to small. Thus for these datasets the clusterings were repeated with $c_{max} = 100$ that turned out then to be a sufficient upper bound.

Evaluation measures.

In order to compare our algorithm to the others, we used the same standard evaluation measures for clusters and subspace clusters as [Müller et al., 2009]: entropy, accuracy, F1, RNIA and CE. We performed also the same simple transformation of entropy and RNIA, by computing $\overline{RNIA} = 1 - RNIA$ and $\overline{entropy} = 1 - entropy$ to have all evaluation measures ranging from 0 (low quality) to 1 (high quality). The three first measures (entropy, accuracy and F1) reflect how well objects that should have been grouped together were effectively grouped. The two last measures (RNIA and CE) take into account the way the objects are grouped and also relevancy of the subspaces found by the algorithm. For these measures, when the *true* dimensions of the subspace clusters are not known (for real datasets), then as in [Müller et al., 2009] all dimensions have been considered as relevant. We refer the reader to [Müller et al., 2009] for a detailed presentation of the evaluation measures.

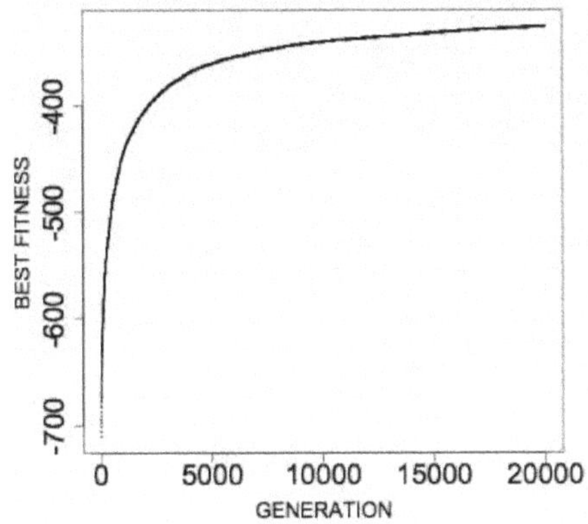

Figure 1: Average of the best fitness for 10 runs on one of the synthetic dataset (1500 objects, 10 dimensions, 0% noise).

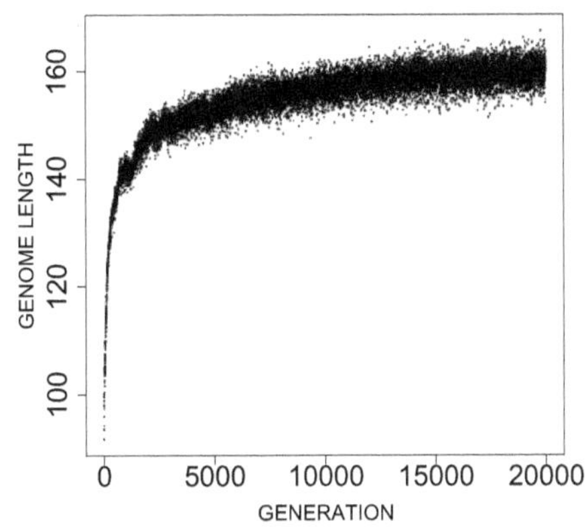

Figure 2: Average genome length of all individuals over 10 runs on one of the synthetic dataset (1500 objects, 10 dimensions, 0% noise).

4. EXPERIMENTAL RESULTS

Real dataset.

As aforementioned, we computed the minimum, the maximum and the mean of the evaluation measures over 10 standard runs of Chameleoclust, while for the other algorithms the measure values are taken from the best possible runs (the ones leading to the highest evaluation measures over the parameter space). Even though Chameleoclust has been executed on a computer (2.67GHz CPU) different from the one used by [Müller et al., 2009] (2.3GHz CPU), we report the runtimes, since at least their orders of magnitude can still be compared. We also give the number of subspace clusters found, the average dimensionality of these clusters, and their coverage (i.e., the percentage of objects of the dataset that were associated to clusters).

In order to illustrate the performances of Chameleoclust we focus on dataset *shape* in Table 2. For the sake of completeness the other results are given in Figure 3 . In Table 2, when an algorithm has a best possible run with a higher evaluation than Chameleoclust the result is highlighted in grey, and if the evaluation is similar to Chameleoclust then the result is simply emphasized in bold. The best possible runs of DOC and MINECLUS are observed with better results than standard runs of Chameleoclust for almost every quality measures, but they tend to split the dataset in more clusters (same behaviour also on the synthetic datasets) and have runtimes significantly higher than Chameleoclust. For PROCLUS and STAPC the best possible runs achieve better results than Chameleoclust for F1 and CE, but in these cases their coverage falls to about 80% to 90% leaving an important part of the dataset outside of the clusters. Looking at entropy many algorithms have best possible runs leading to a better $\overline{entropy}$ than Chameleoclust. However, in clustering tasks, the entropy cannot be interpreted regardless of the number of clusters, because usually the entropy quality measure tends to improve when the number of clusters increases. Indeed, by definition of the entropy measure, the best entropy is obtained for the extreme case where we have one cluster per object. Chameleoclust and three other algorithms (FIRES, P3C, STATPC) provide reasonable number of clusters with average quality entropy. As it can be expected, algorithms that increase importantly the number of clusters achieve higher entropy quality. Notice that Chameleoclust is the only one to obtain a reasonable number of clusters with a 100% coverage. Finally, the last row of the table shows the evaluations obtained when running Chameleoclust using only functional elements in the genome (i.e., g is constant and set to 1 in all genome elements $\langle g, c, d, x\rangle$). In this case we can observe a decrease of the performances that seems to advocate for the interest of the presence of both functional and non-functional elements, and that needs to be investigated further.

Figure 3 shows that for almost every dataset, the performances of Chameleoclust are reasonable with respect to the best possible runs of the other algorithms. Note that most of the time the number of classes within a dataset does not correspond to the number of clusters found by the algorithms. Indeed, predefined classes do not always form clusters. Consequently it is not surprising to obtain more clusters than classes. In some cases a few algorithms found a very large number of clusters (sometimes even more clusters than objects) and this is due to their ability to search for overlapping clusters. For all datasets, the number of clusters found by Chameleoclust is coherent with the number of clusters found by the other algorithms. Indeed Chameleoclust is able to adapt the number of clusters it produces and also their average dimensionality according to each dataset without specific parameter tuning, as summarized in Table 1.

Table 1: Average number of clusters and average dimensionality per cluster found for each dataset

Dataset	*NumClusters*	*AvgDim*
breast	15.2	5.32
diabetes	60.8	2.06
glass	34.8	2.67
liver	62.8	1.93
pendigits	17.5	5.61
shape	14.9	7.27
vowel	48.7	2.59

Synthetic data.

Chameleoclust was executed 10 times on each of the 16 synthetic datasets. For each dataset we kept the run reaching the highest fitness (for the best individual) among the 10 runs (notice that this selection is made without using any external labeling, but only the fitness values). Then for each evaluation measure, we plotted the measure value obtained with respect to the number of clusters found by each of the 16 selected runs. The results are shown Figures 4 to 8. For almost every synthetic dataset the number of clusters found by Chameleoclust is very close to the real number of clusters in the dataset (i.e., 10). Chameleoclust always found between 9 and 16 clusters, and for most of the datasets it found the exact number of clusters. As reported in [Müller et al., 2009] the other algorithms found between 5 and 50 clusters, excepted a few cases where much more clusters were found (up to more than several thousands). Among the other

Breast: 33 dimensions, 2 classes, 198 objects

	F1		*Accuracy*		*CE*		*RNIA*		*Entropy*		*Coverage*		*NumClusters*		*AvgDim*		*Runtime*	
	max	min	max	min	max	min	max	min	max	min	max	min	max	min	max	min	max	min
CLIQUE	0.67	0.67	0.71	0.71	0.02	0.02	0.40	0.40	0.26	0.26	1.00	1.00	107	107	1.7	1.7	453	453
DOC	0.73	0.61	0.81	0.76	0.11	0.04	0.84	0.07	0.46	0.27	1.00	0.80	60	6	27.2	2.8	1E+06	37515
MINECLUS	0.78	0.69	0.78	0.76	0.19	0.18	1.00	1.00	0.56	0.37	1.00	1.00	64	32	33.0	33.0	40359	29437
SCHISM	0.67	0.67	0.75	0.69	0.01	0.01	0.36	0.34	0.35	0.34	1.00	0.99	248	197	2.3	2.2	158749	114609
SUBCLU	0.68	0.51	0.77	0.67	0.02	0.01	0.54	0.04	0.27	0.24	1.00	0.82	357	5	2.0	1.0	5265	16
FIRES	0.49	0.03	0.76	0.76	0.03	0.00	0.05	0.00	1.00	0.01	0.76	0.04	11	1	2.5	1.0	250	31
INSCY	0.74	0.55	0.77	0.76	0.02	0.00	0.24	0.11	0.60	0.39	0.97	0.74	2038	167	11.0	4.4	134373	63484
PROCLUS	0.57	0.52	0.80	0.74	0.51	0.11	0.65	0.43	0.32	0.23	0.89	0.69	9	2	24.0	18.0	703	141
P3C	0.63	0.63	0.77	0.77	0.04	0.04	0.19	0.19	0.36	0.36	0.85	0.85	28	28	6.9	6.9	6281	6281
STATPC	0.41	0.41	0.78	0.78	0.16	0.16	0.33	0.33	0.29	0.29	0.43	0.43	5	5	33.0	33.0	5187	4906
Chameleoclust	0.64	0.58	0.8	0.76	0.15	0.09	0.32	0.23	0.31	0.25	1	1	18	12	12.08	4.61	566	523
mean	0.61		0.78		0.11		0.26		0.28		1		15.2		7.45		544	

Diabetes: 8 dimensions, 2 classes, 768 objects

	F1		*Accuracy*		*CE*		*RNIA*		*Entropy*		*Coverage*		*NumClusters*		*AvgDim*		*Runtime*	
	max	min	max	min	max	min	max	min	max	min	max	min	max	min	max	min	max	min
CLIQUE	0.70	0.39	0.72	0.69	0.03	0.01	0.14	0.01	0.23	0.13	1.00	1.00	349	202	4.2	2.4	11953	203
DOC	0.71	0.71	0.72	0.69	0.31	0.26	0.92	0.79	0.31	0.24	1.00	0.93	64	17	8.0	5.1	1E+06	51640
MINECLUS	0.72	0.66	0.71	0.69	0.63	0.13	0.89	0.58	0.29	0.17	0.99	0.96	39	3	6.0	5.2	3578	62
SCHISM	0.70	0.62	0.73	0.68	0.08	0.01	0.36	0.09	0.34	0.20	1.00	0.79	270	21	4.2	3.9	35468	250
SUBCLU	0.74	0.45	0.71	0.68	0.01	0.01	0.01	0.01	0.14	0.11	1.00	1.00	1601	325	4.7	4.0	190122	58718
FIRES	0.52	0.03	0.65	0.64	0.12	0.00	0.27	0.00	0.68	0.00	0.81	0.03	17	1	2.5	1.0	4234	360
INSCY	0.65	0.39	0.70	0.65	0.37	0.11	0.45	0.42	0.44	0.15	0.83	0.73	132	3	6.7	5.7	112093	33531
PROCLUS	0.67	0.61	0.72	0.71	0.34	0.21	0.78	0.69	0.23	0.19	0.92	0.78	9	3	8.0	6.0	360	109
P3C	0.39	0.39	0.66	0.65	0.56	0.11	0.85	0.22	0.09	0.07	0.97	0.88	2	1	7.0	2.0	656	141
STATPC	0.73	0.59	0.70	0.65	0.06	0.00	0.63	0.17	0.72	0.28	0.97	0.75	363	27	8.0	8.0	27749	4657
Chameleoclust	0.74	0.7	0.79	0.76	0.1	0.04	0.41	0.36	0.34	0.3	1	1	65	52	2.6	1.97	1956	1811
mean	0.72		0.77		0.07		0.38		0.32		1		60.8		2.24		1871	

Glass: 9 dimensions, 6 classes, 214 objects

	F1		*Accuracy*		*CE*		*RNIA*		*Entropy*		*Coverage*		*NumClusters*		*AvgDim*		*Runtime*	
	max	min	max	min	max	min	max	min	max	min	max	min	max	min	max	min	max	min
CLIQUE	0.51	0.31	0.67	0.50	0.02	0.00	0.06	0.00	0.39	0.24	1.00	1.00	6169	175	5.4	3.1	411195	1375
DOC	0.74	0.50	0.63	0.50	0.23	0.13	0.93	0.33	0.72	0.50	0.93	0.91	64	11	9.0	3.3	23172	78
MINECLUS	0.76	0.40	0.52	0.50	0.24	0.19	0.78	0.45	0.72	0.46	1.00	0.87	64	6	7.0	4.3	907	15
SCHISM	0.46	0.39	0.63	0.47	0.11	0.04	0.33	0.20	0.44	0.38	1.00	0.79	158	30	3.9	2.1	313	31
SUBCLU	0.50	0.45	0.65	0.46	0.00	0.00	0.01	0.01	0.42	0.39	1.00	1.00	1648	831	4.9	4.3	14410	4250
FIRES	0.30	0.30	0.49	0.49	0.21	0.21	0.45	0.45	0.40	0.40	0.86	0.86	7	7	2.7	2.7	78	78
INSCY	0.57	0.41	0.65	0.47	0.23	0.09	0.54	0.26	0.67	0.47	0.86	0.79	72	30	5.9	2.7	4703	578
PROCLUS	0.60	0.56	0.60	0.57	0.13	0.05	0.51	0.17	0.76	0.68	0.79	0.57	29	26	8.0	2.0	375	250
P3C	0.28	0.23	0.47	0.39	0.14	0.13	0.30	0.27	0.43	0.38	0.89	0.81	3	2	3.0	3.0	32	31
STATPC	0.75	0.40	0.49	0.36	0.19	0.05	0.67	0.37	0.88	0.36	0.93	0.80	106	27	9.0	9.0	1265	390
Chameleoclust	0.7	0.59	0.71	0.67	0.24	0.11	0.52	0.33	0.64	0.6	1	1	38	27	5.03	3.42	603	432
mean	0.62		0.68		0.19		0.46		0.62		1		34.8		4.17		544	

Liver: 6 dimensions, 2 classes, 345 objects

	F1		*Accuracy*		*CE*		*RNIA*		*Entropy*		*Coverage*		*NumClusters*		*AvgDim*		*Runtime*	
	max	min	max	min	max	min	max	min	max	min	max	min	max	min	max	min	max	min
CLIQUE	0.68	0.65	0.67	0.58	0.08	0.02	0.38	0.03	0.10	0.02	1.00	1.00	1922	19	4.1	1.7	38281	15
DOC	0.67	0.64	0.68	0.58	0.11	0.07	0.51	0.35	0.18	0.11	0.99	0.90	45	13	3.0	1.9	625324	1625
MINECLUS	0.73	0.63	0.65	0.58	0.09	0.09	0.68	0.48	0.33	0.16	0.99	0.92	64	32	4.0	3.7	49563	1954
SCHISM	0.69	0.69	0.68	0.59	0.04	0.03	0.45	0.26	0.10	0.08	0.99	0.99	90	68	2.7	2.1	31	0
SUBCLU	0.68	0.68	0.64	0.58	0.11	0.02	0.68	0.05	0.07	0.02	1.00	1.00	334	64	3.4	1.3	1422	47
FIRES	0.58	0.04	0.58	0.56	0.14	0.00	0.39	0.01	0.37	0.00	0.84	0.03	10	1	3.0	1.0	531	46
INSCY	0.66	0.66	0.62	0.61	0.03	0.03	0.42	0.39	0.21	0.20	0.85	0.81	166	130	2.1	2.1	407	234
PROCLUS	0.53	0.39	0.63	0.63	0.26	0.11	0.66	0.25	0.05	0.05	0.83	0.46	6	2	5.0	3.0	78	31
P3C	0.36	0.35	0.58	0.58	0.55	0.27	0.96	0.47	0.02	0.01	0.98	0.94	2	1	6.0	3.0	172	32
STATPC	0.69	0.57	0.65	0.58	0.23	0.01	0.58	0.37	0.63	0.05	0.77	0.71	159	4	6.0	3.3	1890	781
Chameleoclust	0.71	0.65	0.78	0.7	0.12	0.07	0.51	0.43	0.27	0.18	1	1	69	56	2.34	1.85	730	636
mean	0.68		0.75		0.10		0.46		0.21		1		62.8		2.04		703	

Pendigits: 16 dimensions, 10 classes, 7494 objects

	F1		*Accuracy*		*CE*		*RNIA*		*Entropy*		*Coverage*		*NumClusters*		*AvgDim*		*Runtime*	
	max	min	max	min	max	min	max	min	max	min	max	min	max	min	max	min	max	min
CLIQUE	0.30	0.17	0.96	0.86	0.06	0.01	0.20	0.06	0.41	0.26	1.00	1.00	1890	36	3.1	1.5	67891	219
DOC	0.52	0.52	0.54	0.54	0.18	0.18	0.35	0.35	0.53	0.53	0.91	0.91	15	15	5.5	5.5	178358	178358
MINECLUS	0.87	0.87	0.86	0.86	0.48	0.48	0.89	0.89	0.82	0.82	1.00	1.00	64	64	12.1	12.1	780167	692651
SCHISM	0.45	0.26	0.93	0.71	0.05	0.01	0.30	0.08	0.50	0.45	1.00	0.93	1092	290	10.1	3.4	5E+08	21266
SUBCLU	-	-	-	-	-	-	-	-	-	-	-	-	-	-	-	-	-	-
FIRES	0.45	0.45	0.73	0.73	0.09	0.09	0.33	0.33	0.31	0.31	0.94	0.94	27	27	2.5	2.5	169999	169999
INSCY	0.65	0.48	0.78	0.68	0.07	0.07	0.30	0.28	0.77	0.69	0.91	0.82	262	106	5.3	4.6	2E+06	1E+06
PROCLUS	0.78	0.73	0.74	0.73	0.31	0.27	0.64	0.45	0.90	0.71	0.90	0.74	37	17	14.0	8.0	6045	4250
P3C	0.74	0.74	0.72	0.72	0.28	0.28	0.58	0.58	0.76	0.76	0.90	0.90	31	31	9.0	9.0	2E+06	2E+06
STATPC	0.91	0.32	0.92	0.10	0.09	0.00	0.67	0.11	1.00	0.53	0.99	0.84	4109	56	16.0	16.0	5E+07	3E+06
Chameleoclust	0.7	0.51	0.73	0.59	0.4	0.25	0.6	0.47	0.67	0.56	1	1	19	14	7.44	4.64	12638	9760
mean	0.59		0.63		0.31		0.53		0.60		1		18		5.74		12284	

Vowel: 10 dimensions, 11 classes, 990 objects

	F1		*Accuracy*		*CE*		*RNIA*		*Entropy*		*Coverage*		*NumClusters*		*AvgDim*		*Runtime*	
	max	min	max	min	max	min	max	min	max	min	max	min	max	min	max	min	max	min
CLIQUE	0.23	0.17	0.64	0.37	0.05	0.00	0.44	0.01	0.10	0.09	1.00	1.00	3062	267	4.9	1.9	523233	1953
DOC	0.49	0.49	0.44	0.44	0.14	0.14	0.85	0.85	0.58	0.58	0.86	0.86	64	64	10.0	10.0	120015	120015
MINECLUS	0.48	0.43	0.37	0.37	0.09	0.04	0.62	0.34	0.60	0.46	0.98	0.87	64	64	7.2	3.6	7734	5204
SCHISM	0.37	0.23	0.62	0.52	0.05	0.01	0.43	0.11	0.29	0.21	1.00	0.93	494	121	4.3	2.8	23031	391
SUBCLU	0.24	0.18	0.58	0.38	0.04	0.01	0.39	0.04	0.30	0.13	1.00	1.00	10881	709	3.6	2.0	26047	2250
FIRES	0.16	0.14	0.13	0.11	0.02	0.02	0.14	0.13	0.16	0.13	0.50	0.45	32	24	2.1	1.9	563	250
INSCY	0.82	0.33	0.61	0.15	0.09	0.07	0.75	0.26	0.94	0.21	0.90	0.81	163	74	9.5	4.3	75706	39390
PROCLUS	0.49	0.49	0.44	0.44	0.11	0.11	0.53	0.53	0.65	0.65	0.67	0.67	64	64	8.0	8.0	766	766
P3C	0.08	0.05	0.17	0.16	0.12	0.08	0.69	0.43	0.13	0.12	0.98	0.95	3	2	7.0	4.7	1610	625
STATPC	0.22	0.22	0.56	0.56	0.06	0.06	0.12	0.12	0.14	0.14	1.00	1.00	39	39	10.0	10.0	18485	16671
Chameleoclust	0.45	0.37	0.49	0.42	0.11	0.08	0.42	0.36	0.47	0.43	1	1	56	31	3.02	2.66	2925	1947
mean	0.43		0.48		0.10		0.39		0.46		1		48.7		2.88		2618	

Figure 3: Result tables for six other real datasets

Table 2: Results for the Shape real dataset: 17 dimensions, 9 classes, 160 objects

	F1		*Accuracy*		*CE*		*RNIA*		*Entropy*		*Coverage*		*NumClusters*		*AvgDim*		*Runtime*	
	max	min	max	min	max	min	max	min	max	min	max	min	max	min	max	min	max	min
CLIQUE	0.31	0.31	**0.76**	**0.76**	0.01	0.01	0.07	0.07	0.66	0.66	**1.00**	**1.00**	486	486	3.3	3.3	235	235
DOC	0.90	0.83	**0.79**	**0.54**	**0.56**	**0.38**	0.90	0.82	0.93	0.86	**1.00**	**1.00**	53	29	13.8	12.8	2E+06	86500
MINECLUS	0.94	0.86	**0.79**	**0.60**	0.58	0.46	1.00	1.00	0.93	0.82	**1.00**	**1.00**	64	32	17.0	17.0	46703	3266
SCHISM	0.51	0.30	**0.74**	**0.49**	0.10	0.00	0.26	0.01	**0.85**	**0.55**	**1.00**	**0.92**	8835	90	6.0	3.9	712964	9031
SUBCLU	0.36	0.29	0.70	0.64	0.00	0.00	0.05	0.04	0.89	0.88	**1.00**	**1.00**	3468	3337	4.5	4.1	4063	1891
FIRES	0.36	0.36	0.51	0.44	0.20	0.13	0.25	0.20	0.88	0.82	0.45	0.39	**10**	**5**	7.6	5.3	63	47
INSCY	**0.84**	**0.59**	**0.76**	**0.48**	0.18	0.16	0.37	0.24	0.94	0.87	0.88	0.82	185	48	9.8	9.5	22578	11531
PROCLUS	0.84	0.81	0.72	0.71	0.25	0.18	**0.61**	**0.37**	0.93	0.91	0.89	0.79	34	34	13.0	7.0	**593**	**469**
P3C	0.51	0.51	0.61	0.61	0.14	0.14	0.17	0.17	0.80	0.80	0.66	0.66	**9**	**9**	4.1	4.1	140	140
STATPC	0.43	0.43	**0.74**	**0.74**	0.45	0.45	**0.55**	**0.55**	0.56	0.56	0.92	0.92	**9**	**9**	17.0	17.0	**250**	**171**
Chameleoclust	0.74	0.67	0.82	0.73	0.42	0.34	0.6	0.48	0.79	0.73	1	1	16	13	10	7.29	314	287
mean	0.71		0.79		0.38		0.54		0.76		1		15		8.26		309	
Only functional	0.73	0.53	0.8	0.66	0.45	0.18	0.65	0.28	0.77	0.62	1	1	15	9	11.33	3.78	366	159
mean	0.64		0.75		0.35		0.51		0.72		1		12		6.84		269	

algorithms, P3C is the one that gave the most often a number of clusters close to the real number, outputting between 6 and 16 clusters on these 16 synthetic datasets. Most of the evaluation measures for Chameleoclust are comparable to the ones reported in [Müller et al., 2009], keeping in mind that for the other algorithms only the best values of the evaluation measures over the parameter spaces were retained.

In addition, we give Figure 9 and Figure 10 the runtime of Chameleoclust with respect to the number of objects and number of dimensions of the synthetic datasets. The corresponding curves show that the algorithm scales rather linearly in both cases.

5. RELATED WORK

Many approaches have been investigated for subspace clustering in the literature using various clustering paradigms. The reader is referred for instance to [Kriegel et al., 2009], [Müller et al., 2009], and [Parsons et al., 2004] for detailed reviews and comparisons of the best methods and main categories:

- The cell-based approach, that defines clusters as hyper-rectangles laying in specific subspaces and containing more than a given number of objects. Clusters are usually constructed by discretizing the data space into axis-parallel cells and then aggregating promising cells. These selected cells are commonly the ones containing more objects than a threshold given as parameter. Other typical parameters are the number or the size of the cells.
- The density based approach, in which clusters are dense groups of objects in space. A cluster can have an arbitrary shape, but must be separated from the other clusters by low density regions. This approach defines dense regions as regions where within a given radius a number of objects exceeding a minimum threshold can be found. Clusters are built by joining together the objects from adjacent dense regions.
- The clustering-oriented approach, that usually defines properties of the targeted clustering such as the expected number of clusters or the cluster average dimensionality. According to these constraints, the objects are grouped together mainly using distance-based similarity. Most of these methods tend to build hyper-spherical shaped clusters in particular subspaces.

Even if many evolutionary clustering approaches exist [Hruschka et al., 2009] very few of them address the subspace clustering problem. An early approach was presented in [Sarafis et al., 2003], introducing a subspace clustering evolutionary algorithm that uses a rule-based representation to encode axis-parallel hyper-rectangular disjoint clusters. This algorithm is a member of the cell-based subspace clustering family. It uses task-specific mutation and recombination operators, and requires a non-evolutionary first stage to find promising clusters in 2D subspaces. More recently, in [Vahdat et al., 2010], a different evolutionary approach has been presented. It is also based on a first non-evolutionary clustering stage, used here to find a set

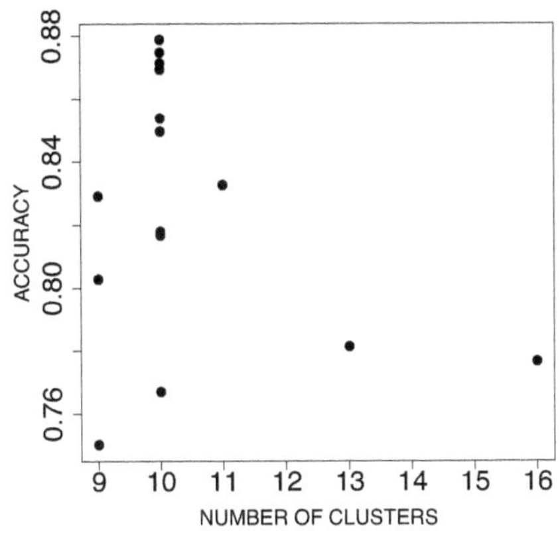

Figure 4: *Accuracy* and number of clusters for the best fitness among 10 runs for the 16 synthetic datasets.

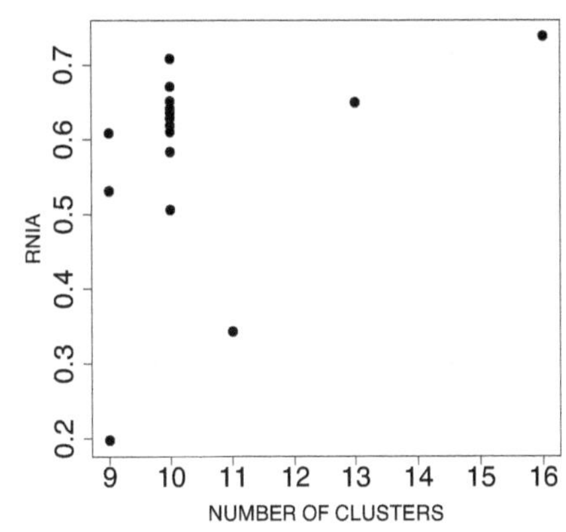

Figure 6: $\overline{RNIA}$ and number of clusters for the best fitness among 10 runs for the 16 synthetic datasets.

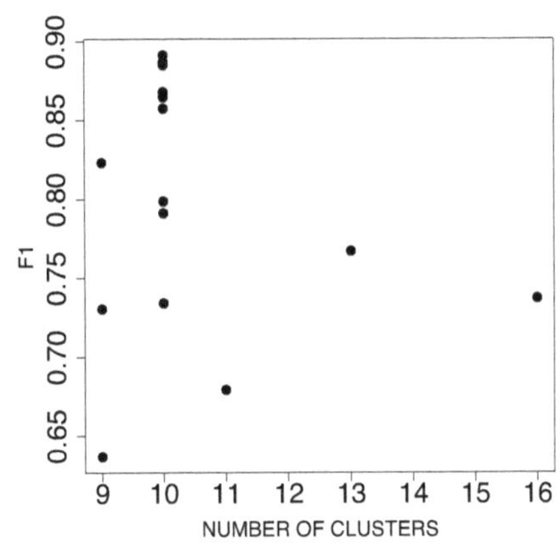

Figure 5: $F1$ and number of clusters for the best fitness among 10 runs for the 16 synthetic datasets.

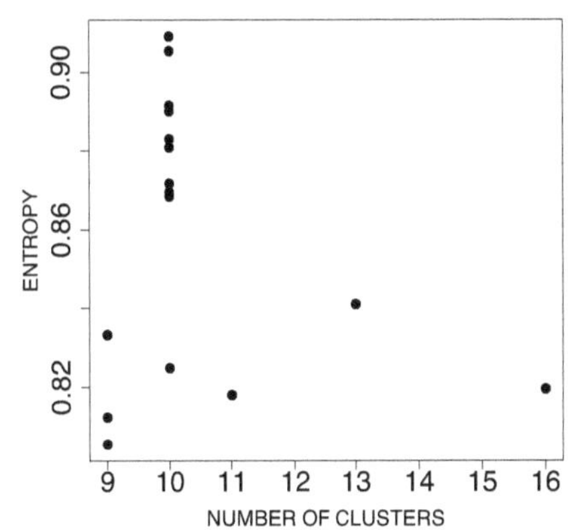

Figure 7: $\overline{Entropy}$ and number of clusters for the best fitness among 10 runs for the 16 synthetic datasets.

of cluster candidate positions in each dimension. Next, it uses a genetic algorithm to produce subspace clusters by combining the candidate positions found at the previous step. The final stage is then to run a second genetic algorithm to find the best combination of subspace clusters to form the whole clustering of the data. This approach is related to the clustering-oriented family. The Chameleoclust algorithm presented in this paper also falls into the clustering-oriented category, but it is a single stage fully evolutionary approach, without any preliminary stage to identified clusters in lower dimensional spaces. In addition it relies on generic bio-like mutation operations that are not specific to the subspace clustering task. Moreover, Chameleoclust has been compared to state-of-the-art subspace clustering algorithms using a reference framework and performed well, while requiring a single and easy to tune parameter (the maximal number of desired clusters).

6. CONCLUSION

In this paper, we presented Chameleoclust, an evolutionary algorithm for subspace clustering. Its key underlying principle is to use an evolvable genome structure to find various numbers of clusters in subspaces of various dimensionality. It was shown to be competitive with respect to state-of-the-art algorithms using an evaluation framework of reference. Directions for future work include: a deeper analysis of the benefits of the presence of the non-functional elements, the study of the stability of the parameters related to the evolution strategy (population size, mutation rate, ...), and the extension of the approach to try to take advantage of some crossover operations.

Acknowledgements

This research has been supported by EU-FET grant EvoEvo (ICT-610427).

7. REFERENCES

[Aggarwal et al., 2001] Aggarwal, C. C., Hinneburg, A., and Keim, D. A. (2001). On the surprising behavior of distance metrics in high dimensional space. In *Proc. of the 8th Int. Conf. on Database Theory*, pages 420–434. Springer.

[Aggarwal et al., 1999] Aggarwal, C. C., Wolf, J. L., Yu, P. S., Procopiuc, C., and Park, J. S. (1999). Fast algorithms for projected clustering. In *Proc. of the 1999 ACM SIGMOD Int. Conf. on Management of Data*, pages 61–72, New York, NY, USA.

[Bache and Lichman, 2013] Bache, K. and Lichman, M. (2013). UCI machine learning repository.

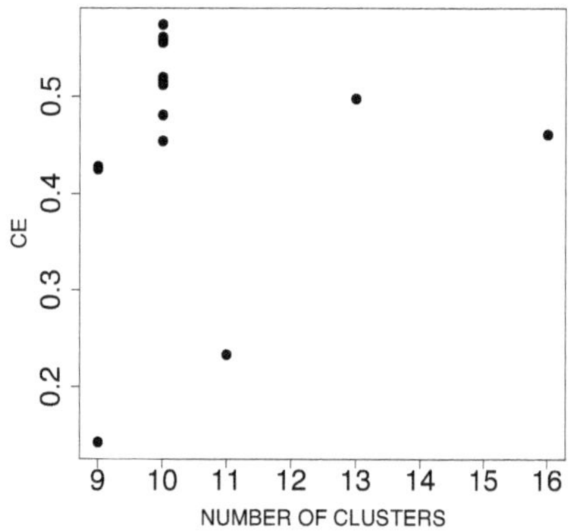

Figure 8: CE and number of clusters for the best fitness among 10 runs for the 16 synthetic datasets.

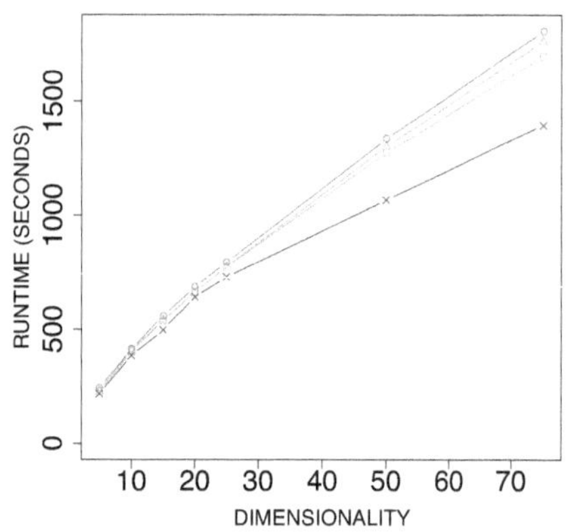

Figure 9: Runtime vs. dimensionality of the synthetic datasets. Maximal in red (circles), median in cyan (triangles), average in green (squares) and minimal in blue (crosses).

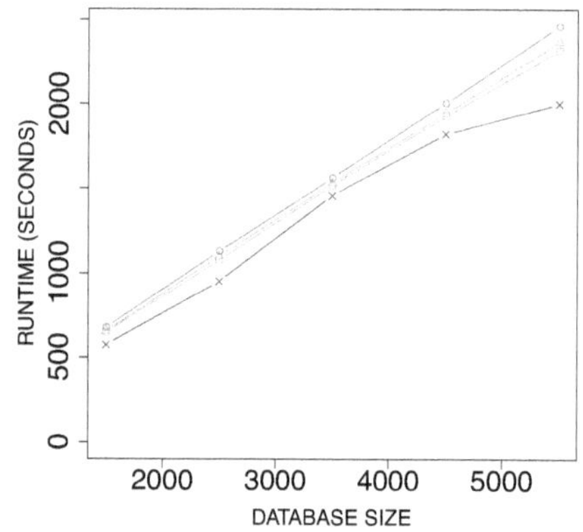

Figure 10: Runtime vs. number of objects of the synthetic datasets. Maximal in red (circles), median in cyan (triangles), average in green (squares) and minimal in blue (crosses).

[Banzhaf et al., 2006] Banzhaf, W., Beslon, G., Christensen, S., James, A., Képès, F., Lefort, V., Julian, F., Radman, M., and Ramsden, J. J. (2006). Guidelines: From artificial evolution to computational evolution: a research agenda. *Nature Reviews Genetics*, 7(9):729–735.

[Beyer et al., 1999] Beyer, K., Goldstein, J., Ramakrishnan, R., and Shaft, U. (1999). When is "nearest neighbor" meaningful? In *Proc. of the 7th Int. Conf. on Database Theory*, pages 217–235, London, UK.

[Crombach and Hogeweg, 2007] Crombach, A. and Hogeweg, P. (2007). Chromosome rearrangements and the evolution of genome structuring and adaptability. *Molecular Biology and Evolution*, 24(5):1130–9.

[Hindré et al., 2012] Hindré, T., Knibbe, C., Beslon, G., and Schneider, D. (2012). New insights into bacterial adaptation through in vivo and in silico experimental evolution. *Nature Reviews Microbiology*.

[Hruschka et al., 2009] Hruschka, E. R., Campello, R. J. G. B., Freitas, A. A., and de Carvalho, A. C. P. L. F. (2009). A survey of evolutionary algorithms for clustering. *IEEE Transactions on Systems, Man, and Cybernetics*, 39(2):133–155.

[Knibbe et al., 2007] Knibbe, C., Coulon, A., Mazet, O., Fayard, J.-M., and Beslon, G. (2007). A Long-Term Evolutionary Pressure on the Amount of Noncoding DNA. *Molecular Biology and Evolution*, 24(10):2344–2353.

[Kriegel et al., 2009] Kriegel, H.-P., Kröger, P., and Zimek, A. (2009). Clustering high-dimensional data: A survey on subspace clustering, pattern-based clustering, and correlation clustering. *ACM Transactions on Knowledge Discovery from Data*, 3(1):1:1–1:58.

[Müller et al., 2009] Müller, E., Günnemann, S., Assent, I., and Seidl, T. (2009). Evaluating clustering in subspace projections of high dimensional data. In *Proc. 35th Int. Conf. on Very Large Data Bases (VLDB 2009)*, volume 2, pages 1270–1281, Lyon, France.

[Parsons et al., 2004] Parsons, L., Haque, E., and Liu, H. (2004). Subspace clustering for high dimensional data: A review. *SIGKDD Explorations Newsletter*, 6(1):90–105.

[Patrikainen and Meila, 2006] Patrikainen, A. and Meila, M. (2006). Comparing subspace clusterings. *IEEE Transactions on Knowledge and Data Engineering*, pages 902–916.

[Sarafis et al., 2003] Sarafis, I. A., Trinder, P. W., and Zalzala, A. (2003). Towards effective subspace clustering with an evolutionary algorithm. In *Proc. of the 2003 Congress on Evolutionary Computation (CEC-2003)*, volume 2, pages 797–806.

[Vahdat et al., 2010] Vahdat, A., Heywood, M. I., and Zincir-Heywood, A. N. (2010). Bottom-up evolutionary subspace clustering. In *IEEE Congress on Evolutionary Computation*, pages 1–8.

Multiple Imputation for Missing Data Using Genetic Programming

Cao Truong Tran, Mengjie Zhang, Peter Andreae
School of Engineering and Computer Science
Victoria University of Wellington, PO Box 600, Wellington 6140, New Zealand
{cao.truong.tran, mengjie.zhang, peter.andreae}@ecs.vuw.ac.nz

ABSTRACT

Missing values are a common problem in many real world databases. Inadequate handing of missing data can lead to serious problems in data analysis. A common way to cope with this problem is to use imputation methods to fill missing values with plausible values. This paper proposes GPMI, a multiple imputation method that uses genetic programming as a regression method to estimate missing values. Experiments on eight datasets with six levels of missing values compare GPMI with seven other popular and advanced imputation methods on two measures: the prediction accuracy and the classification accuracy. The results show that, in most cases, GPMI not only achieves better prediction accuracy, but also better classification accuracy than the other imputation methods.

CCS Concepts

•**Computing methodologies → Genetic programming;** *Supervised learning by regression;* Classification and regression trees;

Keywords

Missing Data; Imputation Methods; Multiple Imputation; Regression; Genetic Programming

1. INTRODUCTION

Many real world databases suffer from an unavoidable problem of missing values for various reasons [19], [26]. For example, respondents in a social survey may refuse to answer some questions; in an industrial experiment, some results may be missing due to mechanical failures while collecting data; medical databases often contain missing values where almost every patient's record lacks some values because not all possible tests can be run on every patient.

Missing data causes a number of serious problems [4]. Although some methods of data analysis can deal with missing data, the majority of existing methods of data analysis require complete data. As a result, these data analysis methods cannot work immediately with original data containing missing values. Moreover, due to differences between missing data and complete data, missing data may cause biased results.

GECCO '15, July 11 - 15, 2015, Madrid, Spain

 ISBN 978-1-4503-3472-3/15/07...$15.00
DOI: http://dx.doi.org/10.1145/2739480.2754665

Several approaches have been proposed to handle the problem of missing values. A simple approach to missing values is to remove instances and/or attributes containing missing values. However, this method is only applicable when the data includes a small number of instances with missing values because if the data involves a relatively large number of missing values, removal might lead to a decrease in the information and serious bias during the inference. Another approach is to use imputation methods that fill missing values with plausible values. Imputation methods can often be applied even when data contains a large level of missing values. Therefore, imputation methods are a popular approach to missing values and a number of imputation methods have been developed [19], [26].

Regression analysis is a process to generate a mathematical function describing a relationship between a dependent variable and one or more independent variables to fit a given data. Regression-based imputation is an approach to imputing missing values. In regression-based imputation, a regression method is used to generate a regression function that is then used to estimate missing values from complete values. Many regression models have been used for imputing missing data, for example, linear or polynomial models are often used for imputing continuous attributes; log-linear models are often suitable for discrete attributes [10]. One of powerful imputation algorithms based on regression is MICE [31] that uses a number of regression methods such as Bayesian linear regression [21], classification and regression tree (CART) [6] and random forest regression [18].

Genetic programming (GP) is an evolutionary technique to generate solutions in the form of computer programs for a problem [17]. The ability of GP to learn the definition of a function itself from example data makes it an excellent choice for regression. Therefore, GP-based regression could be a promising research for imputation.

1.1 Research goals

The goal of this paper is to propose a multiple imputation algorithm using GP as a regression method (GPMI). GPMI is compared with other popular and advanced imputation methods on two measures –the prediction accuracy and the classification accuracy –to show that, in most cases,

1. GPMI can achieve better prediction accuracy than the other popular and advanced imputation methods ; and
2. GPMI can achieve better classification accuracy than the other popular and advanced imputation methods.

1.2 Organisation

The rest of the paper is organised as follows. Section 2 discusses related work. Section 3 introduces GPMI, the new multiple imputation for missing values using GP. Section 4 presents experiment design. Section 5 shows results and analysis. Section 6 draws conclusions and discusses potential future work.

2. RELATED WORK

This section discusses the background to our work including imputation methods, imputation evaluation and GP-based regression.

2.1 Imputation Methods

The goal of imputation of missing values is to fill missing values with plausible values [19]. Imputation methods can be divided into single imputation and multiple imputation methods (MI) [10]. Single imputation methods fill in a single value for each missing value, whereas MI methods replace each missing value with set of plausible values.

2.1.1 *Single imputation*

In single imputation methods, each missing value is substituted by one single value. The single imputation methods used in this paper include mean imputation, hot deck imputation and k-Nearest Neighbour (kNN) imputation.

Mean imputation fills in missing values in each feature with the average of the complete values in the same feature. This method maintains the mean of each feature, but it under-represents the variability in the data because all missing values in each feature have the same value [11].

In hot deck imputation, for each instance containing missing values, the most similar instance is found and then missing values are filled with complete values from this most similar instance. An advantage of this method is that it replaces missing values by real values from the data. However, this method ignores all global properties of the data, because it uses information of only the most similar instance [1].

Imputation based on kNN is a modified version of hot deck imputation. For each instance containing missing values, it finds the K most similar instances, and then fills missing values of the instance with the average of the values in the K most similar instances. Imputation based on kNN is typically better than mean imputation and hot deck imputation [5]. However, this method often suffers from a high computational cost because of having to search through all instances to find the K most similar instances of each instance containing missing values [11].

2.1.2 *Multiple imputation*

Figure 1 illustrates three main steps used in multiple imputation (MI). Firstly, missing data is imputed N times (N>1) to generate N different imputed data sets (complete data sets) using an imputation model that incorporates random variation. Secondly, the imputed data sets are analysed separately by using standard procedures for handling complete data. The second step provides N analysis results. Finally, the N analysis results are combined into a final result [24], [25], [27].

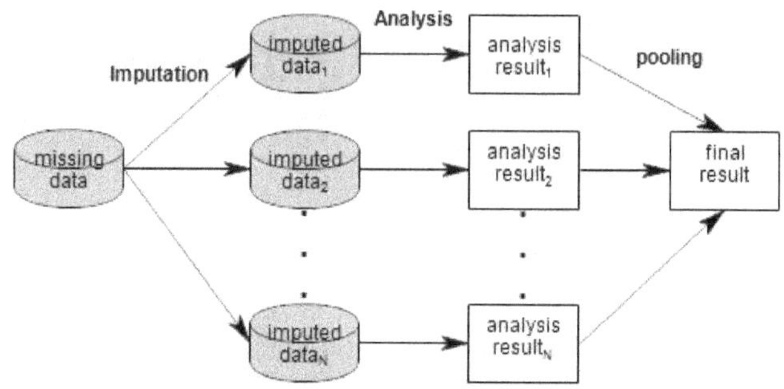

Figure 1: Main steps used in multiple imputation.

MI has become increasingly popular for several reasons. Firstly, although MI methods are computationally more expensive than single imputation methods, MI methods often reflect better uncertainty related to a particular model used for imputation [10]. Furthermore, many recent software developments have based on the the MI framework [13].

One of the most flexible and powerful MI methods is multivariate imputation by chained equations (MICE) [31]. Multiple imputation by chained equations is the first step to generate multiple imputed datasets in MICE. This imputation method uses a set of regression models to fill missing values. Initially, all missing values are filled with random complete values. After that, each attribute containing missing values is regressed on all other attributes in order to compute a better estimate for the attribute. The process is repeated several times for all attributes having missing values in order to generate a single imputed dataset. The whole procedure is repeated N times to generate N imputed data sets which then are used to calculate the final imputed data [33]. MICE software [7] makes it easy to use this method.

In this paper used four multiple imputation methods in MICE including multiple random sample imputation, multiple Bayesian linear regression imputation, multiple classification and regression trees (CART) imputation and multiple random forest regression imputation. In random sample imputation, missing values are filled by randomly picking a complete value from the same attribute. Bayesian linear regression [21] is a linear regression in which the statistical analysis is undertaken within the context of Bayesian inference. Classification and regression trees (CART) [6] is a decision tree learning technique that produces either classification or regression trees. CART uses the sum of squared errors as splitting criterion to build a regression tree. Random forest [18] is a learning method for both classification and regression. Random forest constructs a collection of decision trees and outputs the class that is the mode of the classes (classification) or mean prediction (regression) of the individual trees.

2.2 Imputation Evaluation

Two main approaches are often used to evaluate imputation methods: the prediction approach and the modelling approach [15].

The prediction approach is a primary measure to assess imputation methods [28], [29], [34]. The prediction approach evaluates how similar the imputed data is to the actual data. This approach is based on the assumption that the more similar imputed data is to the actual data, the better imputation is. The accuracy of prediction is evaluated by assessing the differences between actual values and imputed values.

Although the prediction capability is a popular and useful measure to assess imputation methods, it is not sufficient for inferring the effects of imputed values on the modeling tasks such as classification. In the modeling process, it is important that imputation methods must generate the imputed data which least distorts the relationships between attributes in the original data. These relationships can be explored by classification algorithms [15].

2.3 Genetic Programming-based Regression

Regression analysis is a process for estimating the relationship between a dependent variable and one or more independent variables. The estimation target is a regression function of the independent variables. Many techniques for doing regression analysis have been developed. These techniques can be subdivided into parameter regression and non-parametric regression. In parameter regression, the regression function is defined as a function of a finite number of unknown parameters. In contrast, in non-parametric regression, the regression function does not take a predetermined form, but is constructed according to information from the data. Regression analysis has been widely used for prediction and forecasting [16].

Symbolic regression is a type of regression analysis that searches the space of mathematical expressions to find the model that best fits a given dataset. Symbolic regression is non-parametric regression because it does not require a pre-specified model structure and attempts to discover both model structures and corresponding parameters. The original purpose of GP is to evolve computer programs that perform a user-defined task. Therefore, GP is an ideal choice for symbol regression. Recently, there has been a new research trend in using GP for symbol regression [3], [30].

To solve symbol regression using GP, initially, expressions are formed by randomly combining mathematical building blocks such as mathematical operators, functions, and constants. New equations are then formed by recombining previous equations using genetic programming. Conventional parameter regression techniques require a pre-defined model structure, and then they try to optimize parameters for the model structure. Therefore, conventional parameter regression techniques not only require domain knowledge to identify a pre-defined model structure, but also may be affected by human bias. In contrast, GP-based symbolic regression does not require priori assumptions, and instead it attempts to discover both model structures and model parameters. Although GP-based symbolic regression often takes much longer to discover an appropriate model structure and parameter than traditional regression techniques, the end result is likely to be a selection of high-scoring models [32].

3. MULTIPLE IMPUTATION USING GENETIC PROGRAMMING

Algorithm 1 shows the main body of our proposed imputation method based on GP. The input to the algorithm is a dataset containing missing values that need be imputed. Initially, the dataset is randomly imputed by using a random imputation method. The purpose of the initial step is to produce a temporary complete dataset that will be improved in the next steps. The outer loop in the algorithm iterates several times (MaximumIterations) to regress each feature containing missing values on other features. In the inner loop, for each the dth feature having missing values in original data (the data before being randomly imputed in the initial step), the dataset is divided into two subsets such that, the first subset (X_{dC}) contains instances having complete values in the dth feature in original dataset and the second subset (X_{dM}) contains instances having missing values in the dth feature in original dataset. GP then uses the first subset as a training set to discover a suitable function that regresses the feature on other features. After that the function is used to regress the feature in the second subset.

Algorithm 1: Imputation using Genetic Programming

```
Input: Dataset X with missing values
Output: Dataset X without missing values
Fill each missing value in data X by randomly
  picking up a complete value from the same attribute
while MaximumIterations is not reached do
    for d=1 to NumberOfFeature do
        if the d^th feature having missing values in
          original data then
            - Partition X into two subsets X_dC and
              X_dM such that X_dC contains instances
              that have complete values in the d^th
              feature in original data X; X_dM contains
              instances that have missing values in the
              d^th feature in original data X
            - Use GP and X_dC as a training set to
              build a function that regresses the d^th
              feature on other features
            - Apply the function to regress the d^th
              feature of X_dM on other features
            - Combine subset X_dC and subset X_dM to
              make new data X
        end
    end
end
return X
```

This algorithm incorporates random variation in the initial step, so different runs output different results. This algorithm is applied several times in the first step of multiple imputation process (in figure 1) to generate multiple imputed data sets. The imputed data sets are then analysed separately before being combined into a final result.

4. EXPERIMENT DESIGN

This section shows detailed experiment design including datasets, imputation methods, GP parameter settings, prediction accuracy evaluation and classification accuracy evaluation.

4.1 Datasets

The experiments used eight benchmark datasets selected from the UCI machine learning repository [2]. The selected datasets only have numerical features and include both binary and multiple classification tasks. Table 1 provides the main characteristics of each dataset including the number of examples, the number of features and the number of classes.

For each dataset, the missing completely at random mechanism (MCAR) [19] was used to introduce missing values in all features at six different levels: 5%, 10%, 20%, 30%, 40% and 50%. Therefore, from one complete dataset, six missing datasets were generated and a total of 48 missing datasets were used in the experiments.

Table 1: The datasets used in the experiments.

Name	#Instances	#Features	#Classes
Ionosphere	351	34	2
Iris Plant	150	4	3
Parkinsons	267	44	2
Seeds	210	7	3
SPECTF Heart	267	44	2
Vertebral Column	310	6	3
Wine Recognition	178	13	3
Yeast	1484	8	10

4.2 Imputation Methods

Table 2: The datasets used in the experiments.

Imputation methods	Single/ Multiple	abbrrev
Mean impuation	single	mean
Hot deck imputation	single	hd
kNN Imputation	single	kNN
Random sampling imputation	multiple	sample
Bayesian linear regression imputation	multiple	norm
Classification and regression tree imputation	multiple	cart
Random forest regression imputation	multiple	rf

4.3 Imputation Methods

The experiments compared GPMI to seven other imputation methods. Table 2 summaries all Benchmark imputation methods used in this paper. Mean imputation, hot deck imputation, kNN-based imputation were in-house implementations. The experiments used MICE's [7] implementation for the other four Benchmark imputation methods by setting their parameters as the default values. In the five multiple imputation methods, each attribute was repeatedly regressed on other attributes 30 times. With each missing dataset, each multiple imputation method was performed five times to procedure five imputed datasets before combining by calculating average of them to make a final imputed dataset.

4.4 GP settings

The implementation of GP in the experiment used the ECJ package [20]. The parameters of GP in GPMI were the same in all experiments and are shown in Table 3.

4.5 Prediction Accuracy Evaluation

Figure 2 shows steps to evaluate the prediction accuracy of imputation methods. Firstly, complete data is introduced

Table 3: The datasets used in the experiments.

Parameter	Value
Function set	+, -, x, / (protected division), exp, sin, cos, abs
Variable terminals	all features exept one feature being regressed
Constant terminals	Random float values
Population size	1024
Initialization	Ramped half-and-half
Generations	50
Crossover probability	60%
Mutation probability	30%
Reproduction rate	10%
Selection type	Tournament(size=7)

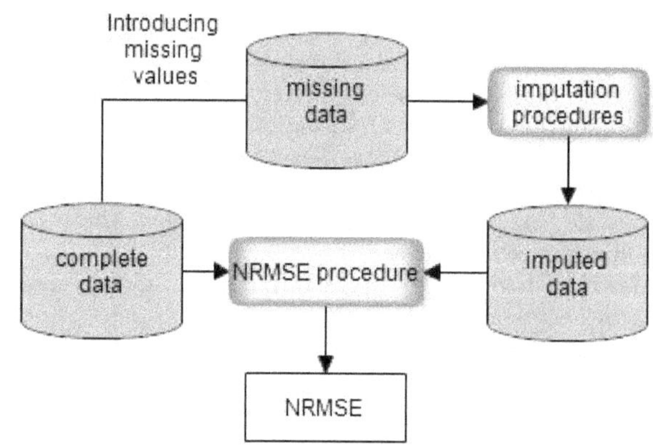

Figure 2: Measuring prediction accuracy

missing values to make missing data. After that, the missing data is substituted by using imputation methods to generate imputed data. Finally, the complete data is compared to the imputed data to evaluate differences. The experiements used the widely known Normalised Root Mean Square Error (NRMSE) to evalute the differences between the complete data and the imputed data.

4.6 Classification Accuracy Evaluation

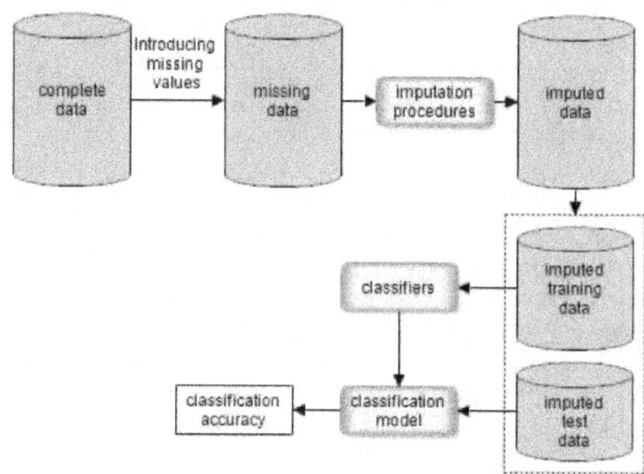

Figure 3: Measuring classification accuracy

Figure 3 shows steps to evaluate effects of imputation methods on classification. Missing values are firstly introduced in each dataset. Next, the missing values in the dataset were imputed using the eight imputation methods.

Each imputed dataset was then split into pairs of imputed training dataset and imputed test dataset. After that, the imputed training dataset was fed into classifiers to build classification models before being used to classify the imputed test dataset.

Table 4: The datasets used in the experiments.

Datasets	Classifiers				
	C4.5	NB	kNN	SVM	MLP
Ionosphere	94.57	95.68	95.91	96.24	**96.55**
Iris Plant	94.68	95.46	96.04	96.26	**96.64**
Parkinsons	84.47	69.53	89.71	87.35	**91.50**
Seeds	91.68	90.23	92.01	93.39	**95.09**
SPECTF Heart	85.17	71.34	73.73	80.44	**88.17**
Vertebral Column	81.02	82.70	77.20	76.38	**85.46**
Wine Recognition	93.06	**97.28**	92.89	96.81	97.14
Yeast	55.46	57.74	58.32	56.67	**58.55**

For each dataset, the best classifier was used to evaluate effects of imputation methods on classification. In order to find the best classifier for each dataset, five popular classifiers in the data mining community were used: C4.5 [23], Naive Bayes (NB) [22], k-Nearest Neighbors (kNN) [9], Support Vector Machine (SVM) [8] and Multilayer Perceptron (MLP) [14]. For the classifiers, WEKA's implementation [12] was used and all parameters were set to WEKA's defaults. Each complete dataset was classified by these classifiers to find the best classifier. Table 4 shows classification accuracy for eight datasets in the experiments. Table 4 shows that the best classifier for Wine Recognition data is NB. With the other datasets, MLP is the best classifier.

Because all datasets in the experiments have a relatively small number of examples, a ten-fold cross-validation approach was used to divide each imputed dataset into ten pairs of training set and test set. The process was repeated 30 times separately; therefore, each imputed dataset generated 300 different pairs of training set and test set. MLP is a stochastic classifier, so MLP was run 30 times for each pair of training set and test set.

5. RESULTS AND ANALYSIS

This section shows the prediction and classification accuracy of the eight imputation methods for the eight datasets with six levels of missing values. After that, analysis is presented to demonstrate how GPMI can achieve good prediction and classification accuracy.

5.1 Results

Figure 4 illustrates the Normalised Root Mean Square Error (NRMSE) of the eight imputation methods for the eight datasets with six levels of missing values. A smaller NRMSE is a better imputation. It is clear from figure 4 that, in most cases, GPMI achieves the smallest NRMSE compared to the other imputation methods.

Figure 5 shows average classification accuracy of the eight imputation methods for the eight datasets with six levels of missing values. The higher classification accuracy means the better imputation. Figure 5 shows that, in most all cases, GPMI achieves the highest classification accuracy compared to the other imputation methods.

In contrast, multiple random sample imputation gains both the worst NRMSE and the worst classification accuracy in most all cases. GPMI uses random sample imputation before applying GP as a regression tool. This means that GP plays a key role to help GPMI achieve both the best NRMSE and the best classification accuracy.

In short, figures 4-5 shows that, in most cases, GPMI not only achieves better prediction accuracy, but also better classification accuracy than the other imputation methods.

5.2 Analysis

To give a better picture of how GPMI can achieve better prediction and classification accuracy than the other imputation methods, this subsection analyses a dataset, namely, Seeds dataset with 20% of missing values.

Table 5: The datasets used in the experiments.

	f_1	f_2	f_3	f_4	f_5	f_6	f_7
f_1	1	0.99	0.61	0.95	0.97	-0.23	0.86
f_2	0.99	1	0.53	0.97	0.94	-0.22	0.89
f_3	0.61	0.53	1	0.37	0.76	-0.33	0.23
f_4	0.95	0.97	0.37	1	0.86	-0.17	0.93
f_5	0.97	0.94	0.76	0.86	1	-0.26	0.75
f_6	-0.23	-0.22	-0.33	-0.17	-0.26	1	-0.01
f_7	0.86	0.89	0.23	0.93	0.75	-0.01	1

Table 5 illustrates the correlation coefficient matrix of the complete Seeds dataset. It is clear from table 5 that some features have a strong linear relationship with other features. For example, the first feature has a strong linear relationship with the second feature, the fourth feature, the fifth feature and the seventh feature. In contrast, the sixth feature has a weak linear relationship with other features.

Table 6: The prediction accuracy (%) (with errors less than 10%) for f_1 and f_6 of Seeds Dataset with 20% missing values.

	mean	hd	kNN	sample	norm	cart	rf	GPMI
f_1	24.32	91.89	**100**	21.62	97.29	**100**	97.29	**100**
f_6	7.14	14.28	21.42	4.76	19.04	26.19	26.19	**53.33**

Table 6 shows the prediction accuracy of different imputation methods (with errors less than 10%) for the first feature and the sixth feature of Seeds Dataset with 20% missing values. It is clear from the table 6 that GPMI, kNN imputation and multiple CART imputation achieve the best prediction accuracy for the first feature. However, for the sixth feature, GPMI achieves 27.11% better than the second best imputations (multiple CART regression imputation and multiple random forest regression imputation). This means that GPMI is especially better than the other imputation methods for regressing missing values of a feature that has a non-linear relationship with other features.

In summary, GPMI can regress very well both missing values of a feature having a strong linear relationship with other features and missing values of a feature having a non-linear relationship with other features. These characteristic may help GPMI have better prediction and classification accuracy than the other imputation methods.

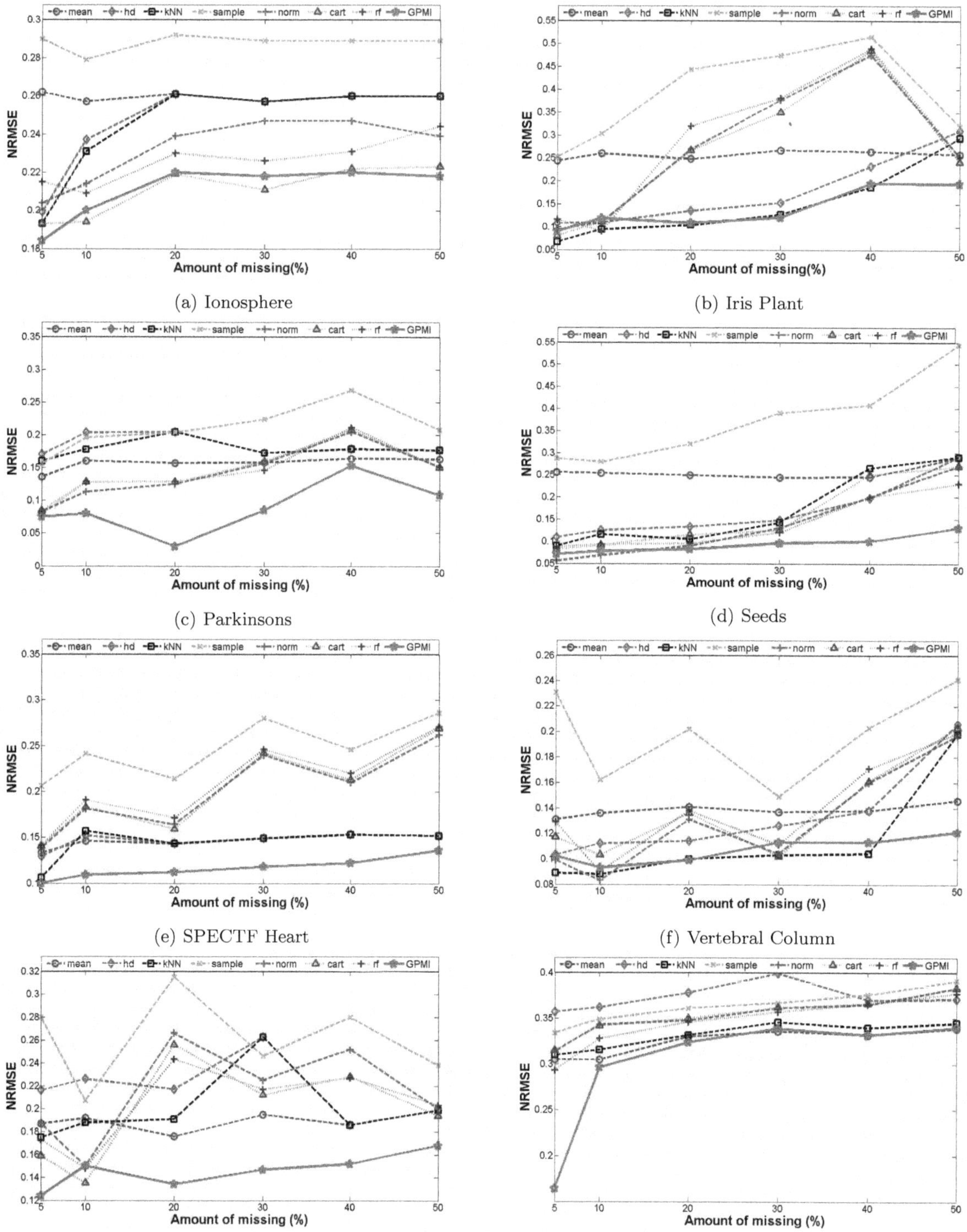

(a) Ionosphere (b) Iris Plant (c) Parkinsons (d) Seeds (e) SPECTF Heart (f) Vertebral Column (g) Wine Recognition (h) Yeast

Figure 4: Normalised Root Mean Square Error of the imputation methods

6. CONCLUSIONS AND FUTURE WORK

This paper proposed GPMI that is a multiple imputation method based on Genetic Programming (GP). GPMI uses GP as a non-parametric regression method to build mathematical functions that then regress missing values of one feature on other features. The experiments compared GPMI to seven other popular and advanced imputation methods (mean imputation, hot deck imputation, kNN imputation, multiple random sample imputation, multiple Bayesian linear regression imputation, multiple classification and regression tree (CART) imputation and multiple random forest imputation). The experiments on eight benchmark datasets with 6 levels (5%, 10%, 20%, 30%, 40%, 50%) of missing val-

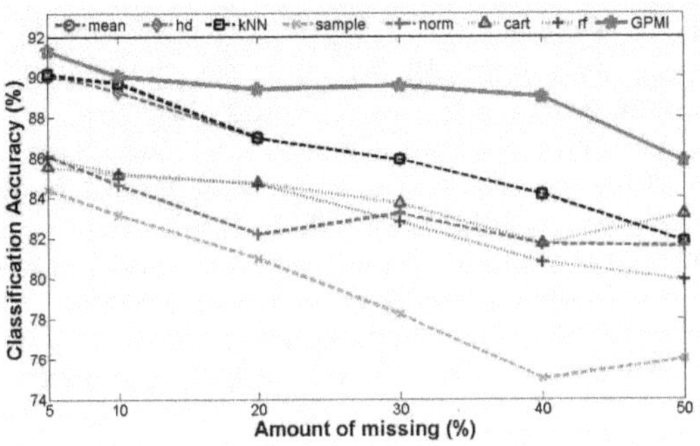

(a) Ionosphere

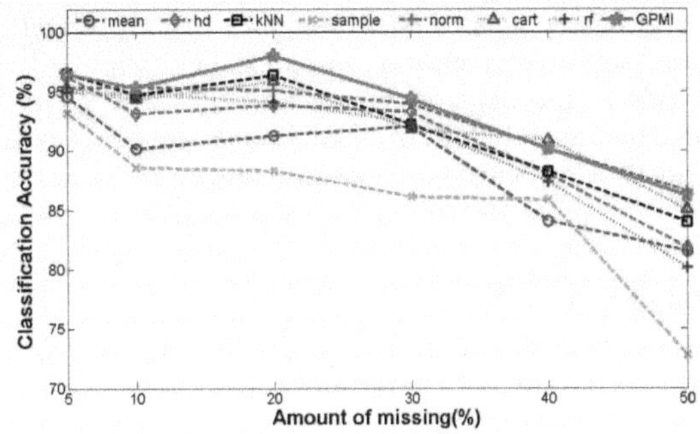

(b) Iris Plant

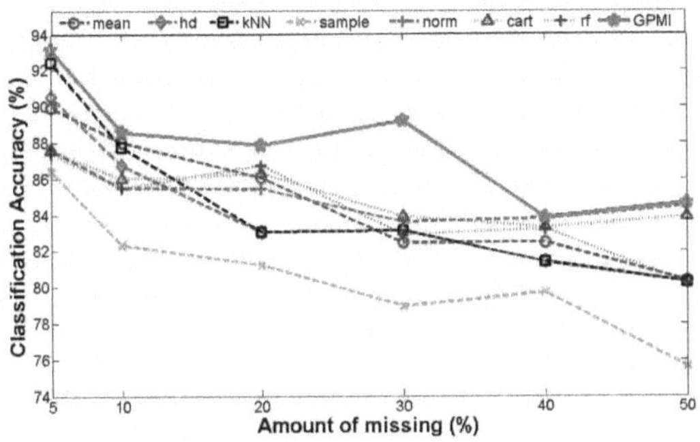

(c) Parkinsons

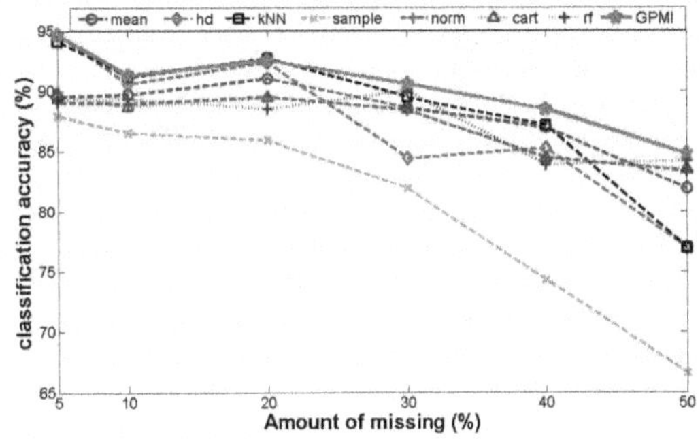

(d) Seeds

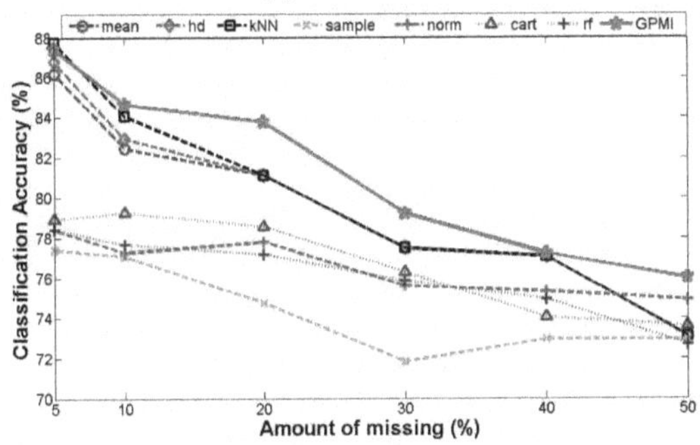

(e) SPECTF Heart

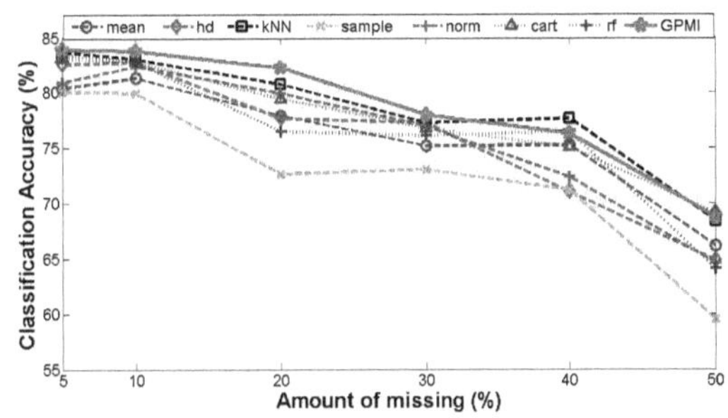

(f) Vertebral Column

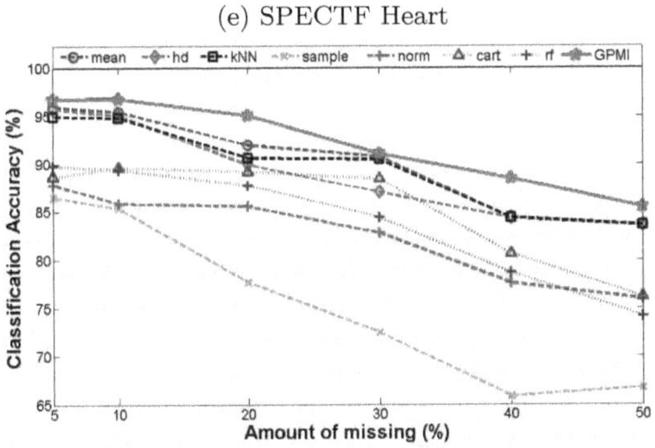

(g) Wine Recognition

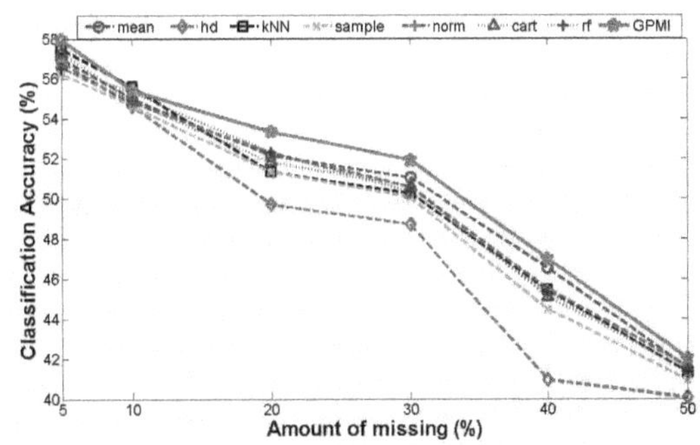

(h) Yeast

Figure 5: Average classification accuracy for imputed data

ues compared GPMI with the other imputation methods on two measures: prediction capability and classification accuracy. The empirical results showed that, in most cases, GPMI achieves better both prediction accuracy and classification accuracy compared to the other imputation methods.

The analysis shows that not only GPMI can impute very well missing values in a feature having a linear relationship with other features, but also it can impute quite well missing values in a feature having a non-linear relationship with other features. These features of GPMI may explain why GPMI can achieve good prediction and classification accuracy.

In this paper, GPMI used standard GP-based regression. Future work could apply advanced GP-based regression methods such as gradient descent GP to enhance GPMI. GPMI was compared to other imputation methods on missing *complete* at random data; therefore, another possible future work could compare GPMI to other imputation methods on other kinds of missing data such as missing at random data.

7. REFERENCES

[1] R. R. Andridge and R. J. Little. A review of hot deck imputation for survey non-response. *International Statistical Review*, 78:40–64, 2010.

[2] A. Asuncion and D. Newman. UCI machine learning repository. Available: http://www.ics.uci.edu/~mlearn/MLRepository.html, 2007.

[3] D. A. Augusto and H. J. Barbosa. Symbolic regression via genetic programming. In *Neural Networks, 2000. Proceedings. Sixth Brazilian Symposium on*, pages 173–178, 2000.

[4] J. Barnard and X.-L. Meng. Applications of multiple imputation in medical studies: from AIDS to NHANES. *Statistical Methods in Medical Research*, 8:7–36, 1999.

[5] G. E. Batista and M. C. Monard. A study of k-nearest neighbour as an imputation method. In *Hybrid Intelligent Systems - HIS*, pages 251–260, 2002.

[6] L. Breiman, J. Friedman, C. J. Stone, and R. A. Olshen. *Classification and regression trees*. CRC Press, 1984.

[7] S. Buuren and K. Groothuis-Oudshoorn. MICE: Multivariate imputation by chained equations in R. *Journal of statistical software*, 45:1–67, 2011.

[8] C. Cortes and V. Vapnik. Support-vector networks. *Machine learning*, 20:273–297, 1995.

[9] P. Cunningham and S. J. Delany. k-Nearest Neighbour classifiers. *Multiple Classifier Systems*, pages 1–17, 2007.

[10] A. Farhangfar, L. A. Kurgan, and W. Pedrycz. A novel framework for imputation of missing values in databases. *Systems, Man and Cybernetics, Part A: Systems and Humans, IEEE Transactions on*, 37:692–709, 2007.

[11] P. J. García-Laencina, J.-L. Sancho-Gómez, and A. R. Figueiras-Vidal. Pattern classification with missing data: a review. *Neural Computing and Applications*, 19:263–282, 2010.

[12] M. Hall, E. Frank, G. Holmes, B. Pfahringer, P. Reutemann, and I. H. Witten. The WEKA data mining software: an update. *ACM SIGKDD explorations newsletter*, 11:10–18, 2009.

[13] O. Harel and X.-H. Zhou. Multiple imputation: review of theory, implementation and software. *Statistics in medicine*, 26:3057–3077, 2007.

[14] K. Hornik, M. Stinchcombe, and H. White. Multilayer feedforward networks are universal approximators. *Neural networks*, 2:359–366, 1989.

[15] E. R. Hruschka, A. J. Garcia, E. R. Hruschka Jr, and N. F. Ebecken. On the influence of imputation in classification: practical issues. *Journal of Experimental & Theoretical Artificial Intelligence*, 21:43–58, 2009.

[16] D. Kleinbaum, L. Kupper, A. Nizam, and E. Rosenberg. *Applied regression analysis and other multivariable methods*. Cengage Learning, 2013.

[17] J. R. Koza. *Genetic Programming: On the Programming of Computers by Means of Natural Selection*. MIT Press, 1992.

[18] A. Liaw and M. Wiener. Classification and regression by randomforest. *R news*, 2:18–22, 2002.

[19] R. J. A. Little and D. B. Rubin. *Statistical Analysis with Missing Data*. Wiley-Interscience, 2002.

[20] S. Luke, L. Panait, G. Balan, S. Paus, Z. Skolicki, J. Bassett, R. Hubley, and A. Chircop. ECJ: A java-based evolutionary computation research system. *Downloadable versions and documentation can be found at the following url: http://cs. gmu. edu/eclab/projects/ecj*, 2006.

[21] T. Minka. Bayesian linear regression. Technical report, 3594 Security Ticket Control, 1999.

[22] K. P. Murphy. Naive Bayes classifiers. *University of British Columbia*, 2006.

[23] J. R. Quinlan. *C4.5: Programs for Machine Learning*. Morgan Kaufmann Publishers Inc, 1993.

[24] D. B. Rubin. Multiple imputation after 18+ years. *Journal of the American Statistical Association*, 91:473–489, 1996.

[25] D. B. Rubin. *Multiple imputation for nonresponse in surveys*. John Wiley & Sons, 2004.

[26] J. L. Schafer. *Analysis of incomplete multivariate data*. Chapman & Hall/CRC Monographs on Statistics & Applied Probability, 1997.

[27] J. L. Schafer. Multiple imputation: a primer. *Statistical methods in medical research*, 8:3–15, 1999.

[28] Q. Song and M. Shepperd. A new imputation method for small software project data sets. *Journal of Systems and Software*, 80:51–62, 2007.

[29] O. Troyanskaya, M. Cantor, G. Sherlock, P. Brown, T. Hastie, R. Tibshirani, D. Botstein, and R. B. Altman. Missing value estimation methods for dna microarrays. *Bioinformatics*, 17:520–525, 2001.

[30] N. Q. Uy, N. X. Hoai, M. O'Neill, R. I. Mckay, and E. Galván-López. Semantically-based crossover in genetic programming: application to real-valued symbolic regression. *Genetic Programming and Evolvable Machines*, 12:91–119, 2011.

[31] S. Van Buuren and K. Oudshoorn. Flexible multivariate imputation by MICE. Technical report, PG/VGZ/99.054: TNO Prevention and Health, Leiden, 1999.

[32] E. J. Vladislavleva, G. F. Smits, and D. Den Hertog. Order of nonlinearity as a complexity measure for models generated by symbolic regression via pareto genetic programming. *Evolutionary Computation, IEEE Transactions on*, 13:333–349, 2009.

[33] I. R. White, P. Royston, and A. M. Wood. Multiple imputation using chained equations: issues and guidance for practice. *Statistics in medicine*, 30:377–399, 2011.

[34] X. Wu and D. Barbará. Learning missing values from summary constraints. *ACM SIGKDD Explorations Newsletter*, 4:21–30, 2002.

Retooling Fitness for Noisy Problems in a Supervised Michigan-style Learning Classifier System

Ryan J. Urbanowicz
University of Pennsylvania
423 Guardian Dr.
Philadelphia, PA
19104-6021,USA
ryanurb@upenn.edu

Jason H. Moore
University of Pennsylvania
423 Guardian Dr.
Philadelphia, PA
19104-6021,USA
jhmoore@upenn.edu

ABSTRACT

An accuracy-based rule fitness is a hallmark of most modern Michigan-style learning classifier systems (LCS), a powerful, flexible, and largely interpretable class of machine learners. However, rule-fitness based solely on accuracy is not ideal for identifying 'optimal' rules in supervised learning. This is particularly true for noisy problem domains where perfect rule accuracy essentially guarantees over-fitting. Rule fitness based on accuracy alone is unreliable for reflecting the global 'value' of a given rule since rule accuracy is based on a subset of the training instances. While moderate over-fitting may not dramatically hinder LCS classification or prediction performance, the interpretability of the solution is likely to suffer. Additionally, over-fitting can impede algorithm learning efficiency and leads to a larger number of rules being required to capture relationships. The present study seeks to develop an intuitive multi-objective fitness function that will encourage the discovery, preservation, and identification of 'optimal' rules through accuracy, correct coverage of training data, and the prior probability of the specified attribute states and class expressed by a given rule. We demonstrate the advantages of our proposed fitness by implementing it into the ExSTraCS algorithm and performing evaluations over a large spectrum of complex, noisy, simulated datasets.

Categories and Subject Descriptors

J.3 [**Computer Applications**]:
Life and Medical Sciences[biology and genetics]

Keywords

classifier systems, multi-objective optimization, bioinformatics, pattern recognition and classification, multiple solutions

1. INTRODUCTION

Michigan-style learning classifier systems (LCS) offer a uniquely powerful and flexible approach to prediction, data mining, classification, and function approximation problems. One of the most important advantages of such rule-based algorithms is that they make few to no assumptions about the underlying pattern or patterns of association in the dataset. This is mainly due to how LCS distributes a learned solution over a population of human interpretable IF:THEN rules [16]. Previously, we developed an extended supervised tracking and classifying system (ExSTraCS) [13]. ExSTraCS is an LCS specialized to single-step supervised learning problems, a large category of problems that includes biomedical applications to which we have a particular interest in addressing (i.e. epidemiological and bioinformatic data mining and prediction). ExSTraCS sacrifices the ability to function on reinforcement learning problems in order to bolster performance in supervised learning domains with particular attention paid to learning efficiency, solution interpretability, and knowledge discovery in problems where the signal may be either clean or noisy. Real world applications such as those found in bioinformatics are typically noisy and may have a large number of potentially predictive attributes, complex patterns of association including epistasis (i.e. non-linear attribute interactions) and heterogeneity (i.e. independent associations with the same class/phenotypic endpoint).

More recently, ExSTraCS 2.0 was introduced, offering a new strategy to dramatically improve the scalability of Michigan-style LCS algorithms [17]. As a demonstration of this, ExSTraCS 2.0 solved the extremely complex 135-bit multiplexer problem 'directly' for the first time reported in the literature. This problem solution requires 135 predictive attributes involved in 128 heterogeneous 8-attribute epistatic interactions to predict the binary class of any instance with 100% accuracy. For a rough conceptual comparison of difficulty, consider that in the field of genetic epidemiology, researchers rarely even attempt to search for epistatic interactions that involve more than 2 or 3 attributes. Despite this success, specific performance drawbacks were identified in ExSTraCS 2.0 related to characterizing heterogeneous patterns of association in noisy simulated bioinformatics problems. It was proposed that this shortcoming could be attributed to the applied fitness metric. Specifically in modern Michigan-style LCS algorithms, fitness is generally based solely on rule accuracy, where (1) for supervised learning, accuracy refers to the proportion of 'matched' training instances for which the rule included the correct classification, and (2) for reinforcement learning, accuracy is a function of a rule's reward prediction error. Rule-accuracy is not

GECCO '15 July 11-15, 2015, Madrid, Spain

ACM ISBN 978-1-4503-3472-3/15/07.
DOI: http://dx.doi.org/10.1145/2739480.2754756

to be confused with training or testing accuracy which would be computed using the entire training or testing datasets.

The problem with a fitness metric based only on accuracy, is that an individual rule has little concept of what it means to be 'fit' in the context of the rule-population as a whole. Rule accuracy is a 'local' metric of rule value in that it only indicates value within the context of the subset of instances in the dataset that the rule matches. Rule accuracy does not necessarily indicate whether a rule is capturing useful generalizations in the dataset. For instance consider the situation where a rule matches only a single instance in the training dataset, and correctly classifies that instance. This rule would have a perfect accuracy. However, this rule likely represents an over-fit relationship identified in the training set that will have no useful predictive value in a testing dataset. In a clean problem, such as the standard multiplexer problems, implicit and explicit generalization pressures would help to eliminate such overfit rules in favor of equally accurate, but more general ones. This is not the case in noisy problems. Consider that in a noisy dataset, optimal rules can not achieve perfect rule accuracy. Instead, rules that are over-fit (i.e. additionally specify non-predictive attributes) will dominate, since overfit rules are likely to have accuracies closer to 1. When it comes to knowledge discovery within the rule population by means of manual rule inspection (i.e. identifying individual rules that capture the learned patterns of association), neither accuracy nor accuracy-based fitness can be used to rank the rule-population to identify the best rules. Instead, rule numerosity (i.e. the number of copies of a given rule stored in the rule population), serves as the only reasonable guide for ranking and identifying the best rules [19]. However, numerosity merely captures 'rule-value' indirectly and thus is not entirely reliable [9].

The strategy of 'fitness sharing' was implemented by Wilson as part of XCS in order to give individual rules a broader context of value [19]. Specifically, fitness sharing proportionally adjusts fitness so that rules with the highest accuracy within individual niches of the problem have the highest fitness. Bernado-Mansilla expanded their supervised learning LCS, called UCS [2] to include fitness sharing [7], noting some of it's performance trade-offs in supervised learning problems. In particular, fitness sharing was valuable at improving performance in class imbalance problems. However, fitness sharing still relies exclusively on accuracy, which we would expect to remain problematic in noisy problem domains, where the multi-objective balance between accuracy, and maximally (correctly) covering instances in the training data is critical to a global measure of rule value.

The most significant change to how rule fitness has been calculated in Michigan-style LCS algorithms involved the shift from strength-based fitness in ZCS [18] to accuracy-based fitness in XCS [19], proposed primarily in the context of reinforcement learning problems. Strength-based fitness relied on the predicted payoff that would be received when a given rule's action was chosen. However, accuracy-based fitness valued the accuracy of the payoff prediction rather than it's magnitude. This was a key to niching performance, allowing the algorithm to focus on and retain more than the strongest parts of the solution [4]. The development of UCS [2] included a new definition for accuracy-based rule fitness. In this supervised learning context, rule accuracy was simply the proportion of instances for which a rule predicted the correct class out of all those that it matched, and fitness was determined by a simple power function of this accuracy. This was the accuracy-based rule fitness adopted by ExSTraCS.

Since XCS, there have been relatively few attempts to develop an alternate fitness metric. Within Michigan-style LCSs, a class-sensitive accuracy/fitness metric was proposed to deal with class imbalance [6], a Bayesian classifier system was proposed to deal with noisy binary class problems [3], and a mutual information-based fitness developed for supervised learning and the discovery of default hierarchies [8] were all developed yielding mixed results. Within Pittsburgh-style LCSs there is no rule-level fitness, rather fitness is calculated at the level of the rule-set. Fitness research for this class of algorithms focused on the problem of balancing rule-set accuracy with parsimony (i.e. rule-generalization and set size). One Pittsburgh-style study proposed multi-objective learning classifier systems, and considered the use of a Pareto-front to better deal with noisy problems [5]. Notably a Pareto-front is typically intended for comparing complete solutions. Individual LCS rules do not constitute complete solutions therefore, as is, this approach does not appear to be applicable to Michigan-style LCS algorithms. However, this may make an interesting direction for future work. Another Pittsburgh-style study successfully developed a fitness metric that explicitly combined accuracy and the complexity of a rule set to promote generalization and reduce bloat. [1].

In the present study we propose a new multi-objective approach for calculating rule-level fitness for supervised learning Michigan-style LCS algorithm that combines (1) rule accuracy, (2) correct instance coverage, and (3) an adjustment for the combined state and class occurrence probabilities within a rule. We expect that the inclusion of instance coverage will help overcome the challenge of identifying heterogeneous and epistatic patterns in the context of noisy data by reflecting the value of having rules that are both accurate, and that are correctly applicable to a maximal number of instances. The adjustment for occurrence probabilities give rules that specify rare state combinations and/or rare classes (in the case of imbalanced data) a fitness boost to account for expected lower correct rule coverage. We believe that the development of a globally-minded fitness metric will not only speed up the effective discovery of optimal rules, but improve rule population interpretability, and the overall process of knowledge discovery. This proposed fitness strategy has been implemented and tested within the ExSTraCS 2.0 algorithm and evaluated over a spectrum of complex, noisy simulated genetic datasets concurrently modeling epistatic and heterogeneous patterns of association. We expect this new fitness metric to (1) eliminate the interpretability shortcomings previously identified in ExSTraCS 2.0 [17], (2) to further improve both global and manual knowledge discovery, and (3) promote more efficient learning. Additionally, we implemented and tested fitness-sharing as described in [7] to observe potential performance trade-offs in the context of the ExSTraCS algorithm and demonstrate that this mechanism alone is insufficient to address the problem of comparing global rule-value.

2. METHODS

In this section we briefly introduce (1) the ExSTraCS 2.0 algorithm along with some minor alterations designed to accommodate the new fitness metric, (2) our implementation of fitness-sharing (3) the multi-objective fitness metric with discussion of the logic behind the components, and (3) the simulated datasets and evaluation strategy applied to test this proposed fitness metric.

2.1 Algorithm

The ExSTraCS 2.0 algorithm [17] is a rule-based machine learning algorithm (or more specifically a Michigan-style LCS algorithm) that has been expanded and adapted to better suit the needs of real-world supervised learning problems wherein classification, prediction, data mining, and/or knowledge discovery is the goal. It is descended from a lineage of Michigan-style LCSs founded primarily on the architecture of XCS [19], the best-studied LCS to date. In descending chronological order, precursors of ExSTraCS 2.0 include ExSTraCS 1.0 [13], EK-UCS [14], AF-UCS [11], UCS [2], and XCS [19]. The features of ExSTraCS 2.0 that most differentiate it from UCS or XCS include: a rule specificity limit to address scalability issues [17], built-in rapid expert knowledge (EK) generation algorithms [13], EK guided covering and mutation for efficient learning and scalability [14, 17], attribute tracking and feedback for reusing useful attribute combinations and characterizing patterns of heterogeneity [11], built-in rule compaction strategies [9], and the consolidation of explore/exploit to perform simultaneously [12]. For a detailed description of the ExSTraCS 2.0 algorithm see [17]. For a complete software users guide see [10]. In this study the ExSTraCS 2.0 algorithm with our proposed multi-objective fitness will be referred to as ExSTraCS 2.1. Each version is available on *sourceforge.com*.

ExSTraCS 2.1 inherits all of the mechanisms and run parameters applied to ExSTraCS 2.0 [17] except for the following elements that have been updated to better suit the proposed multi-objective fitness strategy. First, we have eliminated class/endpoint mutation within the GA in order to ensure that all rules introduced to the rule-population match and correctly classify the current training instance. As a result of this, all rules now start out with a perfect fitness (i.e. fitness = 1) as they are initialized with perfect accuracy. As you will see in the next section, rules are also initialized with a maximum correct instance coverage. Second, once a given rule has had the opportunity to 'see' the entire training set we label that rule as 'epoch-complete'. Once this happens, the accuracy of that rule becomes fixed, and does not continue to change with experience, as any other fluctuations are the result of the random order of the training set. This brings consistency to how experience, or 'epoch-complete' rules are compared to one another through the fitness calculation. Lastly, to accommodate the constantly changing fitness estimate of 'inexperienced' rules introduced below we recalculate the fitness of every 'epoch-incomplete' rule whenever the matching phase occurs.

2.2 Fitness Sharing

We implemented fitness sharing into ExSTraCS 2.0 as described in [7], where this strategy had previously been implemented into UCS to evaluate it's effect within a supervised learning environment. In summary, rule-accuracy is calculated as previously described in ExSTraCS 2.0 [17], however fitness is no longer a simple power function of accuracy. Instead, whenever a match set is formed, a new accuracy metric k_r is first determined. If rule accuracy (A_r)is above some user defined threshold (A_0) than $k_r = 1$, otherwise:

$$k_r = \alpha(A_r/A_0)^{\nu} \tag{1}$$

As in [7], $\alpha = 0.1$, $A_0 = 0.999$, and we examine a value of 1 and 10 for ν. Next we calculated the relative accuracy (k'_r) of the rule to be the numerosity weighted ratio of k_r to the sum of all k_r in the current match set. Lastly, rule fitness is updated using the following equation:

$$F_r = F_r + \beta(k'_r - F_r) \tag{2}$$

In this way, rules that consistently have the highest accuracy within the match sets that it participates, will obtain the highest fitness values. We have implemented this into the original ExSTraCS 2.0 algorithm, as well as some test implementations combined with our proposed multi-objective fitness metric described below.

2.3 Multi-objective Fitness

In this section we detail the proposed multi-objective fitness metric. It includes three components; (1) an adjusted accuracy, (2) an adjusted ratio of correct instance coverage, and (3) an adjustment for a rule's combined state and class occurrence probabilities.

2.3.1 Accuracy Component

First we calculate the accuracy component (Ac_r). As we only want to value rule accuracy (A_r) that is greater than expected by random chance, we compare accuracy to the probability of picking the rule's class by chance (p_c). p_c need only be calculated once during the pre-processing phase of ExSTraCS. Using p_c rather than a constant accounts for class imbalance or the possibility of multiple class problems. If $A_r > p_c$ than a term we call useful accuracy (Au_r) is calculated as:

$$Au_r = A_r - p_c \tag{3}$$

Otherwise one of two alternative Au_r calculations are applied. In the special case where a rule is still relatively young (i.e. it has only had the opportunity to see less than 1000 learning iterations), and the second instance it matched happened yielded an incorrect classification, we do not want the rule to be assigned too low a value of Au_r. In order to protect young rules from having their accuracy cut in half on the second match of it's existence, useful accuracy is calculated as $Au_r = p_c/2$. We have somewhat arbitrarily chosen 1000 iterations as as reasonable rule-age cutoff ($AgeLimit_r$). If $A_r \leq p_c$ and this special case did not occur, than $Au_r = A_r/1000$. This yields a very small accuracy component. Next we scale Au_r so that it will range from 0-1 by dividing it by the maximum possible Au_r for a rule with this class (i.e. $1 - p_c$). Lastly we transform this scaled useful accuracy (Asu_r) using the following exponential function so that increases in Asu_r increase fitness with the greatest magnitude when closer to random class selection, than they are when they are close to perfect accuracy.

$$Ac_r = 2 * \frac{((1/(1 + exp(-5 * Asu_r))) - 0.5)}{0.98661429815} \tag{4}$$

This function yields Ac_r values between 0 to 1. The utilization of this transformation was inspired by our previous observation applying a higher ν to the fitness power function of accuracy led to worse performance in noisy problems [12]. This is due to the fact that at larger values of ν, any accuracy closer to 1 has a much heavier influence on fitness than a lower accuracy, leading to dramatic over-fitting in noisy problems. While it has been suggested that lowering the user specified parameter A_0, could help manage this problem in noisy domains, optimally setting this value is heavily problem dependent and would require either prior knowledge of the signal to noise ratio, or a potentially extensive and computationally expensive parameter sweep.

2.3.2 Correct Coverage Component

Next, we calculate the correct instance coverage component (Cc_r). Intuitively, we want to try to discover and preserve rules that capture an optimal balance of accuracy and instance coverage. However, if A_r was less than or equal to p_c (i.e. rule accuracy was lower than randomly choosing the correct class), we skip both the coverage and state probability adjustment described hereafter, and the final fitness only relies on Ac_r. This will encourage the deletion of such rules by the algorithm.

The correct instance coverage refers to the number of training instances that have been correctly covered by the current rule. In preliminary work we explored a number of terms introduced into the fitness function in an attempt to give a boost to rules that were more general, and thus correctly covered more instances. For instance, we considered rule specificity, match coverage, and correct coverage and found that they all end up overvaluing rules with low specificity at the expense of accuracy. Another challenge to consider when including coverage, is that as a rule's specificity increases, there is an expected reduction in the probability of a rule to be able to cover a given instance. Also, by not accounting for matching or correct covering based on prior probabilities, such coverage terms tended to yield misleading fitness metrics.

As a result, we came up with a term we call 'useful coverage' (Cr_r), which is essentially the coverage of a rule observed beyond what is expected by random chance. This is calculated similar to Au_r, and in-fact, the Cu_r term is somewhat of a combination of coverage and accuracy, since it's magnitude relies, in part, on A_r. Cu_r is calculated as:

$$Cu_r = Cc_r - (Cm_r * p_c) \tag{5}$$

where Cc_r is the correct coverage of the rule and Cm_r is the match coverage of the rule (i.e. the number of instances this rule matches in the training set). However, using raw coverage would be problematic, as it would make it harder for high order interactions to be detected, since they naturally will have a lower coverage due to compounding state probabilities. Therefore, we convert Cu_r into a coverage ratio Cr_r based on the largest Cu_r we have yet observed during training (Cu_{Ecmax}), where $Ecmax$ is the maximum for rules that have completed an epoch.

$$Cr_r = Cu_r / Cu_{Ecmax} \tag{6}$$

Note that a separate $Ecmax$ is stored and updated for each class to account for potential class imbalance. Also note, that we store a separate maximum useful coverage for rules that have not completed an epoch (Cu_{Eimax}). Note that every time fitness is calculated we check to see if either Cu_{Ecmax} or Cu_{Eimax} needs to be updated. This is where labeling of rules as epoch complete or incomplete becomes particularly important. Fundamentally, when training on a finite dataset, as is the assumption when using ExSTraCS, a point is reached where two groups of rules will exist in the population; i.e. those that have seen the entire dataset (epoch-complete), and those that have not, (epoch-incomplete). Once a rule has seen the entire dataset, accuracy is fixed and we can now directly compare such a rule with all other epoch-complete rules. In LCSs with a fitness based only on accuracy, comparing rule fitness's that are experienced vs. inexperienced is not a problem since a rule can have a very high accuracy from the start. However, when it comes to coverage, there can be a serious discrepancy between rules that are epoch-complete and those that are not. This unfairly biases experienced rules, such that epoch-incomplete rules may not survive long enough to see all the training instances and demonstrate their value.

To account for this in Cu_r, we adopt an extrapolation strategy to estimate Cu_r for an epoch-incomplete rule. If Cu_r is younger than this rule we extrapolate Cu_r up to the age of the current Cu_{Eimax} as follows:

$$Cuex_r = Cu_r * Age_{Eimax} / Age_r \tag{7}$$

where Age_{Eimax} is the age of the epoch-incomplete maximum useful coverage, and Age_r is the age of the current rule. If $Age_r > Age_{Eimax}$ we extrapolate Cu_{Eimax} as follows:

$$Cuex_{Eimax} = CU_{Eimax} * Age_r / Age_{Eimax} \tag{8}$$

In either case the larger of the two Cu values is set to Cu_{Eimax}, and Age_{Eimax} is left at the older age to which the extrapolation was performed. However, we do not allow very young rules to impact the value of Cu_{Eimax}. A rule must have $Age_r > AgeLimit_r$.

As with epoch-complete rules, we convert Cu_r into a coverage ratio Cr_r based on Cu_{Eimax} as follows:

$$Cr_r = Cu_r / Cu_{Eimax} \tag{9}$$

2.3.3 State/Class Probability Correction

Lastly, to obtain Cc_r we add an adjustment for the rule's combined state and class occurrence probabilities (Scp_r). First note that during the pre-processing state of ExSTraCS, we initially calculate and store the state frequencies for every discrete attribute in the dataset. For each rule we calculate Scp_r to be the product of all specified attribute state frequencies and p_c for the class given by that rule. Once this is calculated we check to see if Scp_r is the maximum or minimum among rules that have the same specificity (i.e. we separately store max and min Scp_r for rules with the same number of specified attributes. This helps to account for inherently smaller Scp_r values as rule specificity increases. Next, we calculate the adjustment as follows:

$$ScAdj_r = 1 - ((Scp_r - Scp_{min}) / Scp_{max}) \tag{10}$$

Keep in mind that the minimum and maximum Scp_r are for rules with the same specificity as the the current rule and that $ScAdj_r$ can have a value between 0 and 1. The idea here is that rarer state/class occurrence probabilities will yield and adjustment near 1 resulting in a fitness boost, while those that are maximally common will not impact fitness at all, leaving the Cc_r entirely up to correct coverage. Lastly we calculate Cc_r as follows:

$$Cc_r = Cr_r + (1 - Cr_r) * ScAdj_r * ScWeight \quad (11)$$

where $ScWeight = 0.5$. This new fitness constant indicates the fraction of coverage component that can be recovered by the $ScAdj_r$ term. If this value was set to 1, the rarest state/class combinations would always have an optimal correct coverage term (which would end up over-valuing rare state/class combinations.) This parameter might be tuned to improve performance on different problem domains.

We complete our calculation of rule fitness (F_r) to be an equally weighted combination of the average of the accuracy and correct coverage components.

$$F_r = (Ac_r + Cc_r)/2 \quad (12)$$

2.4 Evaluation

It was previously demonstrated that ExSTraCS 2.0 outperformed ExSTraCS 1.0 [17], which in turn had improved performance over AF-UCS and EK-UCS [13], which both had improved performance over XCS and UCS on similar complex noisy simulated genetic problems [12, 14, 11]. In the present study we compare and evaluate ExSTraCS with and without fitness sharing, as well as with and without the proposed multiobjective fitness function. Each implementations was run over the same set of 960 noisy (i.e. heritabilities of 0.1, 0.2, or 0.4), complex simulated genetic datasets with 20 discrete-valued attributes that were described and applied in [13, 17] and generated using GAMETES [15]. Each dataset concurrently modeled patterns of epistasis and heterogeneity where four of the attributes were predictive and 16 were non-predictive. 20 replicates of each dataset were analyzed and 10-fold cross validation (CV) was employed to measure average testing accuracy and account for over-fitting. ExSTraCS was run up to 200,000 learning iterations but performance was also evaluated after only 10,000 iterations. Pair-wise statistical comparisons were made using the Wilcoxon signed-rank tests. All statistical evaluations were completed using R. Comparisons were considered to be significant at $p \leq 0.05$. All analyses were performed using 'Discovery', a 2400 core Linux cluster available to the Dartmouth research community.

Comparisons were performed over a set of key performance metrics. Accuracy metrics were calculated as a respective 'balanced accuracy' to account for any imbalanced datasets. 'Both Power' is the ability to correctly identify both two-locus heterogeneous models. 'Single Power' is the ability to have found at least one. 'Co-occur. Power' indicates the ability to detect the correct heterogeneous pattern. Generality refers to classifier generality, or the average proportion of unspecified attributes across the classifier population. Macro Population refers to the number of unique classifiers in the classifier population. These metrics are described in greater detail in [17].

3. RESULTS AND DISCUSSION

We begin with a brief examination of fitness sharing incorporated into ExSTraCS. In previous work we implemented ExSTraCS with a fitness metric most similar to the one described in UCS [2]. A later version of UCS incorporating

Table 1: ExSTraCS 2.0: Original vs. Fitness Share

200,000 Iterations +QRF			
Performance Statistics	ExSTraCS ($\nu = 10$)		
	Original	Fitness Sharing	p
Train Accuracy	.7882	.9170	↑ ***
Test Accuracy	.6178	.5907	↓ ***
Both Power	.4052	.3115	↓ ***
Single Power	.7635	.6563	↓ ***
Both Co-Power	.0438	.0250	↓ *
Single Co-Power	.7771	.7042	↓ ***
Rule Generality	.8026	.7901	↓ ***
Macro Population	987.12	701.17	↓ ***
Run Time (min)	63.24	44.34	↓ ***

– No significant change
* $p < 0.05$ (Direction of change given by arrows)
** $p < 0.001$
*** $p << 0.001$

fitness sharing yielded some problem-specific advantages [7]. Table 1 summarizes the different performance metrics averaged over all 960 analyzed datasets (each run to times for cross validation) calculated after 200,000 learning iterations for ExSTraCS 2.0 with and without fitness sharing ($\nu = 10$). Overall, with the addition of fitness sharing, we observe significant decreases in average testing accuracy, rule generality, and all power metrics. A similar comparison was performed using fitness sharing ($\nu = 1$). The results are not included here, since the performance metrics yielded similar or significantly worse performance than fitness sharing with $\nu = 10$. Ultimately fitness sharing dramatically increased over-fitting within this particularly noisy problem domain, leading to the loss in predictive performance, as well as a large loss in solution interpretability. It seems that fitness sharing only exacerbated the accuracy-based fitness drawback within noisy problems.

Now we revert back to ExSTraCS 2.0 without fitness sharing and introduce our proposed multi-objective fitness. Table 2 summarizes the different performance metrics averaged over all 960 analyzed datasets (each run 10 times for cross validation) calculated after 10,000 and 200,000 learning iterations for ExSTraCS 2.0 without and with the proposed multiobjective fitness. Overall, with the addition of the multiobjective fitness function, we observe significant increases in average testing accuracy, Single Power, Both Co-Power, Single Co-Power, Macro-Population Size, and generality after 200,000 learning iterations. No significant change in the Both Power metric was observed. Significant overall decreases were observed for both training accuracy and run time. The observed increase in testing accuracy and decrease in training accuracy indicates an overall reduction in overfitting. As expected, the new fitness function is able to dramatically improve our ability to characterize heterogeneous patterns, evidenced by large significant increases in Both Co-Power. This is achieved while still managing to maintain or improve other critical performance metrics; namely testing accuracy and the three other power metrics. This supports the claim made previously in [17] that identified the loss in Both Co-Power to be a natural drawback to accuracy-based fitness in noisy problem domains. Also, in Table 1, note that after only 10,000 learning iterations the new fitness has largely and significantly outperformed the original fitness on all metrics with the exception of Both Power and run time. This suggests that the proposed multi-

Table 2: ExSTraCS 2.0: Original vs. Multiobjective Fitness

200,000 Iterations +QRF			
Performance Statistics	ExSTraCS		
	Original	New Fitness	p
Train Accuracy	.7882	.7463	↓ ***
Test Accuracy	.6178	.6215	↑ ***
Both Power	.4052	.4094	–
Single Power	.7635	.7833	↑ *
Both Co-Power	.0438	.2313	↑ ***
Single Co-Power	.7771	.8281	↑ ***
Rule Generality	.8026	.8118	↑ ***
Macro Population	987.12	1155.07	↑ ***
Run Time (min)	63.24	58.88	↓ **
10,000 Iterations			
Performance Statistics	ExSTraCS 2.0		
	Original	New Fitness	p
Train Accuracy	.7757	.7304	↓ ***
Test Accuracy	.6059	.6156	↑ ***
Both Power	.3771	.3479	↓ *
Single Power	.7688	.7885	↑ **
Both Co-Power	.0281	.1885	↑ ***
Single Co-Power	.7750	.8219	↑ ***
Rule Generality	.7776	.8104	↑ ***
Macro Population	1831.95	1616.09	↓ ***
Run Time (min)	2.52	2.58	↑ ***

– No significant change
* $p < 0.05$ (Direction of change given by arrows)
** $p < 0.001$
*** $p << 0.001$

objective fitness improves learning efficiency, obtaining better performance earlier. Furthermore, we believe that the significant average increase in macro population size indicates that a greater diversity of rules (of varying specificity) are being preserved in the rule population, since rules that were previously at an accuracy disadvantage are now given a fitness boost by the number of instances they correctly cover.

Additionally, upon manual rule inspection of rule populations evolved using the new fitness metric, we noted that when ranking rules by fitness, optimal rules that captured state combinations of the true separate underlying noisy epistatic models were typically ranked at or very close to the top. This was not true when using accuracy based fitness, where numerosity is the next best way to identify optimal rules. This observation became even more reliable when epoch-incomplete rules were excluded before fitness ranking. These observations suggest that this new fitness approach could be invaluable for the development of a much more effective rule compaction strategy that could be applied with little to no performance loss in noisy problem domains that we had previously observed with existing LCS rule compaction strategies [9].

To further characterize performance differences resulting from the new fitness, we explore performance differences when the 960 datasets are segregated by their heritability, sample size, architecture difficulty (i.e. hard (H), or easy (E)), and mix ratio. Figure 1 gives boxplot summaries of Co-Both Power, comparing ExSTraCS 2.0 with and without the new multi-objective fitness. Keep in mind that 'Sample Size' corresponds to the number of unique training instances in the original (pre-cross validation) datasets, and that heritability is inversely proportional to noise in the data. Note that the values summarized by each individual boxplot correspond to 20 replicate datasets evaluated using cross validation. We can see from these figures, that the new fitness consistently outperforms the original fitness. However similar plots for testing accuracy, and the other power metrics indicate some dataset-specific trade-offs between the new and original fitness metric that may be a useful target for ongoing investigation. While Co-Single Power, and testing accuracy is nearly universally better for all dataset combinations, for Both Power we observed losses for datasets with a 75:25 heterogeneous ratio and a larger sample size (see Figure 2). This may reflect that for certain datasets our multi-objective approach may be adding too much fitness bias based on correct coverage. Similarly for Single Power we observed losses for datasets with a 75:25 heterogeneous ratio, a larger sample size, and a smaller heritability (not shown).

4. CONCLUSIONS

In this work we have developed a new multi-objective fitness function designed, in particular, for supervised learning in Michigan-style learning classifier systems. Implementing this strategy into ExSTraCS 2.0, we found that this approach addressed previously identified shortcomings regarding the algorithm's rule interpretability and ability to characterize patterns of heterogeneity in the context of epistatic, noisy relationships between predictive attributes and class. While promising, this approach is not universally optimal. By de-emphasizing the importance of accuracy alone in the fitness function, this approach may not learn optimal solutions as quickly as accuracy-based LCS algorithms in 'clean' problems (i.e. no noise) typical of toy benchmark problems such as the multiplexer. However in the domain of bioinformatics, and most other real-world problems, the assumption of a 'clean' solution is often wildly unrealistic, making a fitness function that seeks a multi-objective balance of accuracy and correct instance coverage particularly critical to not only detecting the signal, but characterizing it.

Ongoing work will seek a parameter-free multi-objective fitness function, as well as one that better preserves Both Power and Single Power within the subset of 75:25 heterogeneous mix datasets identified in this study. Additionally we will test this approach on multiplexer problems and imbalanced data. This will help guide the ongoing development of an intuitive multi-objective fitness function. While the current study focused on discrete-valued attributes, we believe this approach can be easily expanded to continuous-valued attribute datasets as well. Lastly, we will follow up on the success observed in ranking rules by fitness during manual rule inspection, and pursue a new LCS rule compaction strategy that can dramatically reduce the rule population size while closely preserving or improving our set of performance metrics.

5. ACKNOWLEDGMENTS

This work was supported by NIH grants AI59694, LM009012, LM010098, EY022300, LM011360, CA134286, and GM103534. We also thank the reviewers for their constructive comments, especially towards the consideration of LCS fitness sharing. We thank Dartmouth College for access to their Discovery computing cluster during our move to the University of Pennsylvania.

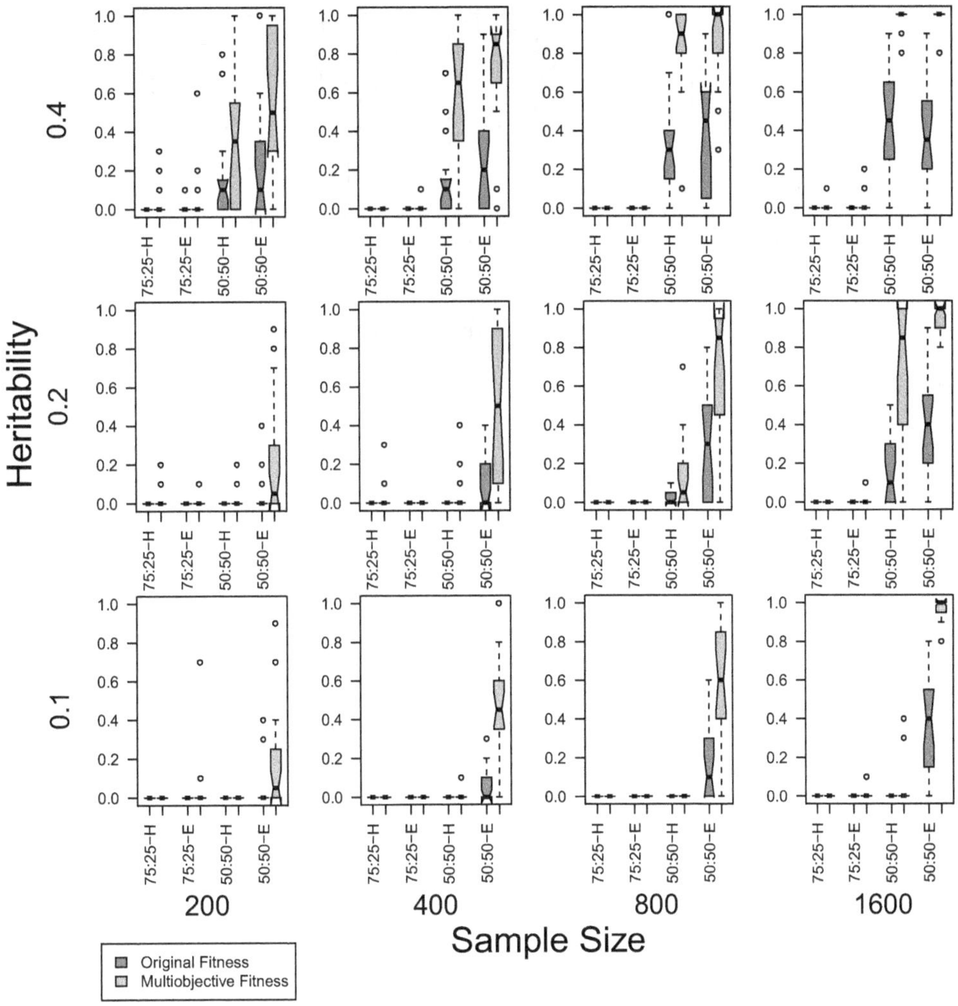

Figure 1: Comparing Co-Both Power after 200,000 iterations over all dataset combinations in the simulation study.

6. REFERENCES

[1] J. Bacardit and J. M. Garrell. Bloat control and generalization pressure using the minimum description length principle for a pittsburgh approach learning classifier system. In *Learning Classifier Systems*, pages 59–79. Springer, 2007.

[2] E. Bernadó-Mansilla and J. M. Garrell-Guiu. Accuracy-based learning classifier systems: models, analysis and applications to classification tasks. *Evolutionary Computation*, 11(3):209–238, 2003.

[3] H. Dam, H. Abbass, and C. Lokan. Bcs: a bayesian learning classifier system. Technical report, Citeseer, 2006.

[4] T. Kovacs. *Strength or accuracy? Fitness calculation in learning classifier systems.* Springer, 2000.

[5] X. Llorà and D. E. Goldberg. Bounding the effect of noise in multiobjective learning classifier systems. *Evolutionary Computation*, 11(3):279–298, 2003.

[6] A. Orriols and E. Bernadó-Mansilla. Class imbalance problem in ucs classifier system: fitness adaptation. In *Evolutionary Computation, 2005. The 2005 IEEE Congress on*, volume 1, pages 604–611. IEEE, 2005.

[7] A. Orriols-Puig and E. Bernadó-Mansilla. Revisiting ucs: Description, fitness sharing, and comparison with xcs. In *Learning Classifier Systems*, pages 96–116. Springer, 2008.

[8] R. E. Smith, M. K. Jiang, J. Bacardit, M. Stout, N. Krasnogor, and J. D. Hirst. A learning classifier system with mutual-information-based fitness. *Evolutionary Intelligence*, 3(1):31–50, 2010.

[9] J. Tan, J. Moore, and R. Urbanowicz. Rapid rule compaction strategies for global knowledge discovery in a supervised learning classifier system. In *Advances in Artificial Life, ECAL*, volume 12, pages 110–117, 2013.

[10] R. Urbanowicz. *ExSTraCS 2.1*, 2015 (accessed February 4, 2015).

[11] R. Urbanowicz, A. Granizo-Mackenzie, and J. Moore. Instance-linked attribute tracking and feedback for michigan-style supervised learning classifier systems. In *Proceedings of the fourteenth international conference on Genetic and evolutionary computation conference*, pages 927–934. ACM, 2012.

[12] R. Urbanowicz and J. Moore. The application of

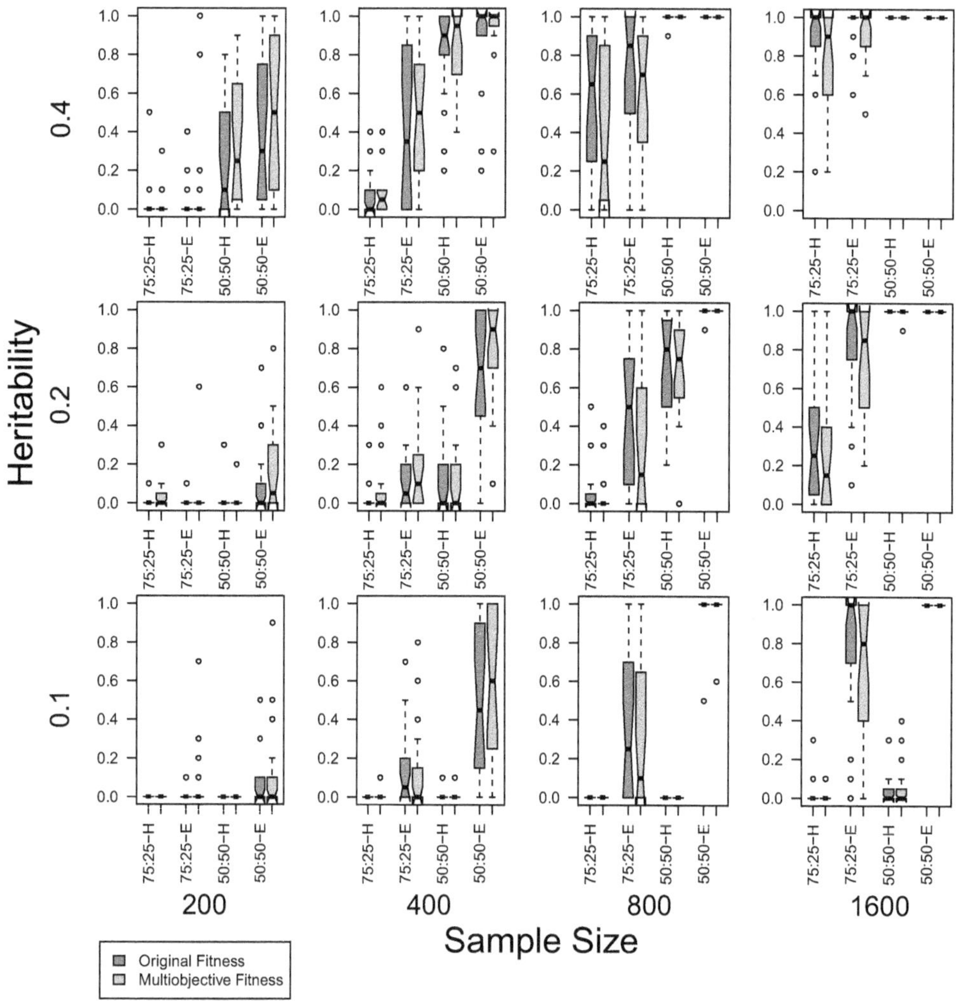

Figure 2: Comparing Both Power after 200,000 iterations over all dataset combinations in the simulation study.

michigan-style learning classifier systems to address genetic heterogeneity and epistasis in association studies. In *Proceedings of the 12th annual conference on Genetic and evolutionary computation*, pages 195–202. ACM, 2010.

[13] R. J. Urbanowicz, G. Bertasius, and J. H. Moore. An extended michigan-style learning classifier system for flexible supervised learning, classification, and data mining. In *Parallel Problem Solving from Nature–PPSN XIII*, pages 211–221. Springer, 2014.

[14] R. J. Urbanowicz, D. Granizo-Mackenzie, and J. H. Moore. Using expert knowledge to guide covering and mutation in a michigan style learning classifier system to detect epistasis and heterogeneity. In *Parallel Problem Solving from Nature-PPSN XII*, pages 266–275. Springer, 2012.

[15] R. J. Urbanowicz, J. Kiralis, N. A. Sinnott-Armstrong, T. Heberling, J. M. Fisher, and J. H. Moore. Gametes: a fast, direct algorithm for generating pure, strict, epistatic models with random architectures. *BioData mining*, 5(1):16, 2012.

[16] R. J. Urbanowicz and J. H. Moore. Learning classifier systems: a complete introduction, review, and roadmap. *Journal of Artificial Evolution and Applications*, 2009.

[17] R. J. Urbanowicz and J. H. Moore. Exstracs 2.0: description and evaluation of a scalable learning classifier system. *Evolutionary Intelligence*, pages 1–28, 2015.

[18] S. W. Wilson. Zcs: A zeroth level classifier system. *Evolutionary computation*, 2(1):1–18, 1994.

[19] S. W. Wilson. Classifier fitness based on accuracy. *Evolutionary computation*, 3(2):149–175, 1995.

A PSO Approach to Semivectorial Bilevel Programming: Pessimistic, Optimistic and Deceiving Solutions

Maria João Alves
FEUC, University of Coimbra / INESC Coimbra
Av Dias da Silva, 165, Coimbra
Portugal
+351 239 851 040
mjalves@fe.uc.pt

Carlos Henggeler Antunes
DEEC, University of Coimbra / INESC Coimbra
Polo 2, Coimbra
Portugal
+351 239 851 040
ch@deec.uc.pt

Pedro Carrasqueira
INESC Coimbra
Rua Antero de Quental, 199
Coimbra
Portugal
+351 239 851 040
pmcarrasqueira@net.sapo.pt

ABSTRACT

In a bilevel programming problem, the upper level decision maker (leader) decides first, but he must incorporate the reaction of the lower level decision maker (follower) in his decision. The existence of multiple objectives at the lower level gives rise to a set of lower level efficient solutions for each leader's decision, which poses additional difficulties for the leader to anticipate the follower's reaction. The optimistic approach assumes that the follower accepts any efficient solution, while the pessimistic approach considers that the leader prepares for the worst case. In this work, we first discuss the assumptions and implications of optimistic vs. pessimistic approaches in bilevel problems with multiple objective functions at the lower level (semivectorial bilevel problems) or at both levels. Three types of solutions are analyzed: the optimistic, pessimistic and deceiving solutions, the latter being a new solution concept introduced herein, which represents the worst outcome of a failed optimistic approach (i.e., when the leader believes that the follower will pursue his own interests but the follower does not react accordingly). Then we propose a particle swarm optimization algorithm to semivectorial bilevel problems, which aims to approximate these three types of solutions in a single run. Some experimental results of the algorithm are presented.

Categories and Subject Descriptors

I.2.8 [**Computing Methodologies**]: Artificial Intelligence – *problem solving, control methods, and search.*

General Terms

Algorithms, Management.

Keywords

Particle swarm optimization, multi-objective optimization, bilevel programming, pessimistic vs. optimistic approaches.

1. INTRODUCTION

Bilevel programs are useful to model hierarchical decision processes with two decision makers, the *leader* and the *follower*, each one controlling different sets of variables (x and y, respectively) and having their own objective functions subject to interdependent constraints. The decision process is sequential as the leader firstly sets the values of the variables x, and then the follower reacts already knowing the leader's decision. The follower chooses the y values that optimize his objective function on the feasible solutions restricted by the fixed x. The goal of the leader is to optimize his objective function, but he must incorporate into the optimization process the reaction of the follower because it also affects the leader's objective value and even the feasibility of the solution. This type of sequential decision-making situation appears in many aspects of resource planning, management and policy-making, including transportation network design and traffic management. For instance, in a road network design problem, a central agency plans and manages a network of roads (layout of streets, where to install traffic lights, etc.) and it intends to minimize investment and operational costs. However, it has to accommodate the traffic pattern formed by the individual decisions of the travelers, who want to minimize travel time, gasoline consumption, among other objectives. Thus, the central agency controls investment costs, but operational costs depend on traffic flows. Bilevel programs are very difficult to solve, even the linear case which is NP-hard [10].

A general bilevel programming problem with a single objective function at each level can be defined as follows:

$$\begin{aligned} &\text{"}\min_x\text{"} \quad F(x,y) \\ &s.t. \quad G(x,y) \le 0 \\ &\qquad y \in \arg\min_y \{ f(x,y) : g(x,y) \le 0 \} \end{aligned} \tag{1}$$

where $x \in \Re^{n_1}$ is a n_1-dimensional vector of upper level variables and $y \in \Re^{n_2}$ is a n_2-dimensional vector of lower level variables; $F(x, y)$ and $f(x, y)$ are the leader's and the follower's objective functions, respectively. Since the follower optimizes $f(x, y)$ after x has been selected, x assumes a constant vector whenever $f(x,y)$ is optimized. The follower's rational reaction set to a given x' is:

$$\Psi(x') = \left\{ y \in \Re^{n_2} : y \in \arg\min_y \{ f(x',y) : g(x',y) \le 0 \} \right\}$$

The feasible region for the bilevel problem (1), also called the *induced region*, is $IR = \{(x,y) \in \Re^{n_1+n_2} : G(x,y) \le 0,\ y \in \Psi(x)\}$. The *bilevel problem* is the leader's problem. Quotation marks have been added in "min" $F(x,y)$ due to the unclear definition of the objective function value $F(x, y)$ from the leader's point-of-view (who has control over x only) if the set of optimal solutions

GECCO '15, July 11 - 15, 2015, Madrid, Spain
 ISBN 978-1-4503-3472-3/15/07…$15.00
DOI: http://dx.doi.org/10.1145/2739480.2754644

of the lower level problem is not singleton [11]. Multiple optimal responses pose a problem to the leader, as he does not know which of them the follower will choose. This choice may affect significantly the leader's objective value and, consequently, his decision. In many studies this difficulty is avoided by just assuming that the solution of the lower level problem is unique. In other cases, an *optimistic* or a *pessimistic* approach is considered. The optimistic approach (the most common one) assumes that the leader is free to select the solution that suits him best among the optimal responses for the follower. In this case, the upper level optimization is taken with respect to x and y, meaning that the leader is able to influence the choice of the follower [11]. Thus, the problem can be written as:

$$\min_{x,y} \{F(x,y) : y \in \Psi(x), G(x,y) \le 0\}.$$

When cooperation between the leader and the follower is not allowed, or if the leader is risk-averse and wishes to bound the damage resulting from an undesirable selection of the follower, a pessimistic approach may be admitted. The leader prepares for the worst case, that is, he chooses a decision x which performs best in view of the 'worst' (globally optimal) follower response [18]. This leads to the following problem:

$$\min_{x} \left\{ \max_{y} \{F(x,y) : y \in \Psi(x)\} : G(x,y) \le 0 \right\}$$

A discussion of optimistic and pessimistic approaches in bilevel problems can be found in [10, 18], among others.

So far we have been referring to bilevel problems with a single objective function at each level. However, a bilevel problem may entail multiple objective functions at the upper, lower or both levels. Multiple objectives at one or both levels add further complexities, thus posing new challenges in handling such problems. Below we briefly refer to work on bilevel programming with multiple objectives at the lower level or at both levels (omitting studies on bilevel problems with multiple objectives only at the upper level).

Bilevel problems comprising a single objective at the upper level and a multiobjective lower level problem have been called *semivectorial bilevel* problems. This type of problem was first addressed by Bonnel [4], who provided necessary optimality conditions for an optimistic formulation. Solution approaches have been further proposed by Bonnel and Morgan [5], Ankhili and Mansouri [3], Zheng and Wan [19] and Calvete and Galé [6], all of them also concerned with the optimistic formulation. Liu et al. [14] developed necessary optimality conditions for the pessimistic formulation using a scalarization technique (which converts the lower level problem into a parameterized program), following an approach related to the Dempe et al.'s [12] for the optimistic formulation.

The bilevel problem with multiple objectives at both levels was addressed by Eichfelder [13], who presented new theoretical results for the nonlinear non-convex case and proposed an algorithm to bi-objective problems at both levels with one upper level variable. Deb and Sinha [8, 9] proposed multiobjective evolutionary algorithms, and Zhang et al. [20] and Carrasqueira et al. [7] presented algorithms based on particle swarm optimization (PSO). All these algorithms aim at approximating the whole Pareto front of the problem considering an optimistic formulation of the multiobjective bilevel problem. In addition, Ruuska and Miettinen [17] proposed a procedure to construct new evolutionary algorithms for optimistic multiobjective bilevel optimization. "*In the optimistic formulation, it is assumed that the follower accepts any efficient decision to the lower-level problem or, equivalently, chooses among the efficient decisions according to the leader's preference*" [17]. A different approach was adopted by Nishizaki and Sakawa [15] in their interactive procedure, who assumed that the leader has some subjective anticipation or belief of the follower's response. This anticipation may be optimistic, pessimistic or the leader knows the preference of the follower (arising from the past behavior of the follower).

In this paper, we discuss (in Section 2) the assumptions and implications of the optimistic and pessimistic approaches in multiobjective and semivectorial bilevel problems, drawing attention to the risk of assuming an optimistic approach in a real decision situation. Different kinds of solutions are analyzed through a numerical example and a new solution concept is introduced, which we call the *deceiving* solution. In Section 3 we propose an algorithm that uses PSO to approximate the pessimistic, optimistic and deceiving solutions to semivectorial bilevel problems. The PSO technique was chosen because it has already been successful in other bilevel problems, e.g. in [1] (which considers multiple objectives only at the upper level) and in [7]. Some experimental results of the algorithm are presented in Section 4. The paper ends with some conclusions in Section 5.

2. PESSIMISTIC VS. OPTIMISTIC APPROACHES IN MULTIOBJECTIVE AND SEMIVECTORIAL BILEVEL PROBLEMS

The optimistic and the pessimistic anticipation introduced by Nishizaki and Sakawa [15] for multiobjective bilevel problems clearly shows the difficulties of a bilevel decision process when multiple lower level objectives are considered. In case the follower has a single objective, it is often assumed that the rational response of the follower for a decision of the leader is deterministic. In case the set of optimal solutions of the lower level problem is not singleton (i.e. there are alternative optimal solutions), the most common approach is the optimistic one, which assumes that there may be some limited cooperation between the leader and the follower, so that the follower chooses an optimal solution that also benefits the leader (in an unselfish action) or the leader is able to make side payments that bias the follower's decision. When cooperation between the leader and the follower is not allowed, or the leader is risk-averse, a pessimistic approach can be admitted. Most theoretical and algorithmic contributions to bilevel programming relate to the optimistic formulation, as the pessimistic bilevel problem is perceived to be more difficult to solve. Also, the optimistic approach is adopted in almost all literature devoted to multiobjective or semivectorial bilevel problems.

There is, however, a major practical difference between the single objective case and when the follower has multiple conflicting objectives to be optimized. In the single-objective case, the reaction solutions are alternative optimal decisions to the follower with respect to a decision of the leader, i.e., they all attain the same value of the follower's objective function. In case of multiple objectives at the lower level, there is no single best objective value to the follower for each leader's decision, but rather a set of nondominated objective points (corresponding to a set of efficient/Pareto optimal solutions) in which a better value for one objective can only be attained if at least one of the other objectives is worsened. Therefore, a compromise solution taking into account the multiple objective functions must be selected. However, unless a scalar-valued utility function is assumed *a priori* (which turns the lower level problem into a surrogate single-objective one), the follower's decision may be very difficult to anticipate. This uncertainty on the behavior of the follower puts additional difficulties for the development of a procedure that can provide effective decision aid in bilevel problems with multiple objectives at the lower level [2]. The optimistic approach assumes that the follower is indifferent to all efficient solutions obtained for a given decision of the leader. But, is this assumption acceptable in most real decision problems?

Consider, for instance, a toll-setting problem. The owners of a highway system (leader) have to set tolls and they want to maximize total revenue. Users of highways (follower) want to minimize their travel costs and, simultaneously, minimize their travel times. Thus, the leader's decision should take into account these objectives of the follower and the decision should be such that tolls are not too high, otherwise fewer drivers would use the highways and this would generate smaller revenues for the leader. Suppose an extreme decision of the leader, in which tolls are set at the highest possible levels. For this decision, a set of efficient solutions for the follower can be obtained. At one extreme, we have the solution that minimizes cost, which may signify that users do not use highways; in this case, the revenue would be zero. At the other extreme, we have the efficient solution that minimizes time, which may represent an intensive use of highways by all users; this would be great for the leader, because the revenue would be the highest. The optimistic approach assumes that the follower is indifferent to these two opposite situations, which would take the leader to set very high prices for tolls. Of course this example is hypothetical and some concerns can be addressed by imposing additional constraints, but it illustrates the risk that one takes when adopting an optimistic procedure for decision support in a real multiobjective or semivectorial bilevel optimization problem.

In order to better illustrate the differences between the optimistic and the pessimistic solutions to a bilevel problem with multiple objective functions at the lower level, let us see a numerical example.

Example (Prob.1)

Consider the following semivectorial bilevel problem with two objectives at the lower level, which is an adaptation of Problem 3 in [8] by dropping the second upper level objective function.
Prob.1:

$$\begin{aligned} \min \quad & F(x,y) = (y_1-1)^2 + y_2^2 + x^2 \\ s.t. \quad & \min_y f_1(x,y) = y_1^2 + y_2^2 \\ & \min_y f_2(x,y) = (y_1 - x)^2 + y_2^2 \\ & s.t. \quad -1 \le y_1, y_2, x \le 2 \end{aligned}$$

where x and $y = (y_1, y_2)$ are, respectively, the upper level and the lower level variables.
For a fixed value of x, the efficient solutions to the lower level problem are given as follows: $\{(y_1, y_2) \in \Re^2 | y_1 \in [0, x], y_2 = 0\}$ for $0 \le x \le 2$ and $\{(y_1, y_2) \in \Re^2 | y_1 \in [x, 0], y_2 = 0\}$ for $-1 \le x \le 0$.
Let us denote by $\Psi_{Ef}(x)$ the set of efficient solutions to the lower level problem for a given x and by Ψ_{Ef} the union of $\Psi_{Ef}(x)$ for all x. Ψ_{Ef} is represented by the shaded area in figure 1, which shows a graph with axes y_1 and x because y_2 is 0 in all efficient solutions to the lower level problem. The level curves of $F(x,y)$ are also shown in figure 1 (circles centered in the point $(y_1, x) = (1,0)$).
Using an optimistic approach, the solution to the semivectorial bilevel problem is the one that optimizes the leader's objective function over the set of efficient solutions to the follower, assuming that the follower has no preferences among the efficient solutions obtained for each leader's decision x or that the follower will choose the solution that most benefits the leader. The optimistic optimal solution is the point **O** in figure 1, where $(x, y_1, y_2) = (0.5, 0.5, 0)$ and $(f_1, f_2) = (0.25, 0)$, $F = 0.5$.
Considering the pessimistic approach, the solution to the bilevel problem is the one that optimizes the leader's objective function over a subset of solutions formed by the worst options for the leader among the follower's efficient solutions for each x. This subset of efficient solutions, which are the "worst for the leader", is depicted in the bold line (left boundary of Ψ_{Ef}) in figure 1 and is denoted by $\Psi_{P\text{-}Ef}$. The solution that minimizes F over $\Psi_{P\text{-}Ef}$ is **P**, where $(x, y_1, y_2) = (0, 0, 0)$ and $(f_1, f_2) = (0, 0)$, $F = 1$. Note that **P** would be better than **O** to the follower, as **P** "dominates" **O** according to the follower's objective functions, but the follower could not choose **P** unless x was set to 0, and x is controlled by the leader. **P** is the pessimistic solution to this semivectorial bilevel problem. If the leader has no anticipation on the follower's reaction, the pessimistic approach represents the most conservative decision, while the optimistic decision is the most risky one.
Another solution that can be interesting to analyze is the outcome of a "failed optimistic" approach, i.e., when the leader believes that the follower will pursue his own interests but the follower does not act accordingly and chooses another efficient solution. The worst solution for the leader, given an optimistic x, provides an indication of the maximum risk the leader is taking if he adopts an optimistic approach. We will call this outcome the *deceiving solution* which is, in this example, the point **D** with $(x, y_1, y_2) = (0.5, 0, 0)$ and $(f_1, f_2) = (0, 0.25)$, $F = 1.25$.

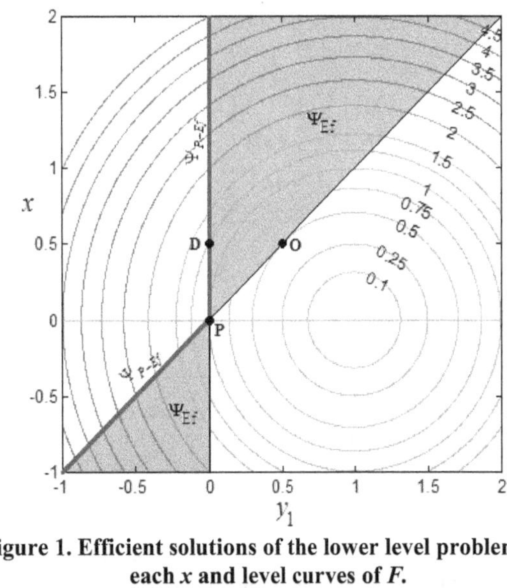

Figure 1. Efficient solutions of the lower level problem for each *x* and level curves of *F*.

To sum up, when dealing with a Bilevel Problem with Multiple Objectives at the Lower Level (BPMOLL), it can be interesting to know three types of solutions: the *optimistic* solution, the *pessimistic* solution and the *deceiving* solution (the new concept just introduced).

Consider the formulation of the BPMOLL with m objective functions at the lower level:

$$\begin{aligned} &\text{"min"}_{x} \quad F(x,y) \\ &s.t. \quad G(x,y) \leq 0 \qquad (2) \\ &\qquad y \in \arg\min_{y} \{(f_1(x,y),...,f_m(x,y)) : g(x,y) \leq 0\} \end{aligned}$$

Let $Y(x) = \{y \in \Re^{n_2} : g(x,y) \leq 0\}$ and let $\Psi_{Ef}(x)$ denote the set of efficient (Pareto optimal or nondominated) solutions of the lower level problem in (2) for a given x. Thus,

$\Psi_{Ef}(x) = \{y \in Y(x) : \text{there is no } y' \in Y(x) \text{ such that } f(x,y') \prec f(x,y)\}$

where $\prec$ denotes the dominance relation, i.e., $f(x,y') \prec f(x,y)$ iff $f_j(x,y') \leq f_j(x,y)$ for all $j=1,\ldots,m$, and $f_j(x,y') < f_j(x,y)$ for at least one j.

Concerning the BPMOLL:

- the *optimistic* solution, (x^o,y^o), is given by
  $$\min_{x,y} \{F(x,y) : y \in \Psi_{Ef}(x), G(x,y) \leq 0\}$$
- the *pessimistic* solution, (x^p,y^p), is given by
  $$\min_{x} \left\{ \max_{y} \{F(x,y) : y \in \Psi_{Ef}(x)\} : G(x,y) \leq 0 \right\}$$
- given the optimistic upper level decision x^o, the *deceiving* solution is $(x^d,y^d) = (x^o,y^d)$ where y^d is given by
  $$\max_{y} \{F(x^o,y) : y \in \Psi_{Ef}(x^o)\}.$$

Note that, if the upper level constraints only involve upper level variables, the selection of an x satisfying $G(x) \leq 0$ and then $y \in \Psi_{Ef}(x)$ results in a feasible solution to the problem. But, with $G(x,y) \leq 0$, the feasibility of a leader's solution may depend on the choice of the follower's solution. Since we assume that the follower's reaction cannot be anticipated, the feasibility of an upper level decision cannot also be anticipated. As a result, the *deceiving* solution may be infeasible to the leader, and this information can also be useful to the leader. On the other hand, it is worth noting that the pessimistic solution will be infeasible only if the lower level efficient solutions "worst for the leader" (one for each different leader's decision) are all infeasible.

3. PSO ALGORITHM TO APPROXIMATE THE PESSIMISTIC, OPTIMISTIC AND DECEIVING SOLUTIONS TO BPMOLL

The proposed algorithm is based on PSO and aims to provide three solutions to the BPMOLL: the *pessimistic*, *optimistic* and *deceiving* solutions, which are the outcome of the algorithm.

Consider the BPMOLL (2) including general constraints $G(x,y) \leq 0$ and $g(x,y) \leq 0$ and also bounds for the variables, which define the sets X and Y, respectively for x and y.

The outer cycle of the algorithm concerns the upper level search. For each upper level particle x^i, a subroutine *Lowerlevel-PSO*(x^i) is called to determine a set of (potentially) efficient solutions to the lower level problem polarized to the extreme values of F, the maximum and the minimum values. This set is denoted by $\Psi_{Ef}(x^i)$. Non-efficient lower level solutions are infeasible solutions to the bilevel problem, thus the quality of the solutions obtained for each $\Psi_{Ef}(x^i)$ is very important. Consequently, the population size and the number of iterations are higher in the lower level search than in the upper level search.

3.1 Algorithm steps

Let N be the size of the upper level population and T the number of iterations of the upper level cycle.

***Step* 1** – *Initialization of upper level search*

t =0

Randomly generate N vectors $x^i \in$ X to create a population of upper level solutions: $PopX_t = \{x^i, i=1,\ldots,N\}$.

For each x^i, i=1,…,N:

- Apply *Lowerlevel-PSO*(x^i) to obtain $\Psi_{Ef}(x^i) = \{y^{il}, l=1,\ldots,L_i\}$. In case $\Psi_{Ef}(x^i)=\varnothing$, x^i is perturbed in X (applying a uniform mutation operator) and the process is repeated.
- Candidate for *optimistic* solution: select the feasible y from $\Psi_{Ef}(x^i)$ with the best value of F using (3). If there is no solution in $\Psi_{Ef}(x^i)$ that satisfies the upper level constraints G, then the solution with smaller overall violation of G is chosen (taking into account the different orders of magnitude of the constraints).
  $$y^{io} \leftarrow \arg\min_{y^{il}} \{F(x^i,y^{il}) : y^{il} \in \Psi_{Ef}(x^i), G(x^i,y^{il}) \leq 0\} \qquad (3)$$
- Candidate for *pessimistic* and *deceiving* solutions: select the y from $\Psi_{Ef}(x^i)$ with the worst value of F using (4).
  $$y^{ip} \leftarrow \arg\max_{y^{il}} \{F(x^i,y^{il}) : y^{il} \in \Psi_{Ef}(x^i)\} \qquad (4)$$

Create two archives, O_t and P_t, with the selected y^{io} and y^{ip}, i =1,…,N, respectively:

$$O_t = \{(x^1, y^{1o}), (x^2, y^{2o}),\ldots,(x^N, y^{No})\}$$
$$P_t = \{(x^1, y^{1p}), (x^2, y^{2p}),\ldots,(x^N, y^{Np})\}$$

The archive P_t may contain solutions that are G-infeasible (i.e., do not satisfy constraints G) but, in general, all solutions in O_t are feasible (in the sense that they satisfy all constraints). Even though, the constraints G will be checked again for the selection of the optimistic solution in order to discard any (x^i, y^{io}) that came from a set $\Psi_{Ef}(x^i)$ with no feasible solutions.

Select the feasible solution o in O_t with the best F. This is the incumbent *optimistic* solution:

$o = (x^o,y^o) \leftarrow \arg\min \{F(x,y): (x,y) \in O_t, G(x,y) \leq 0\}$

Let k be the index of the selected solution in O_t such that $(x^o,y^o) = (x^k, y^{ko})$.

Select the feasible solution p in P_t with the best F. This is the incumbent *pessimistic* solution:

$p = (x^p,y^p) \leftarrow \arg\min \{F(x,y): (x,y) \in P_t, G(x,y) \leq 0\}$

If there is no feasible solution in P_t, the one with smaller overall violation of G is chosen.

The incumbent *deceiving* solution is the solution in P_t with index k (this solution may be infeasible):

$d = (x^d,y^d) = (x^k,y^{kp}) \in P_t$

In the next step, the upper level particles x will be moved according to the principles of PSO, but not all particles are oriented towards the same target: the first N/2 particles will follow a pessimistic approach while the others follow an optimistic one. Despite this division, only one archive $\Psi_{Ef}(x)$ is produced for each x and the sets O_t and P_t are built from the entire Ψ_{Ef}. The *personal best* (*pbest*) and the *global best* (*gbest*) particles used to guide the movement of the particles through the PSO process will be selected from P_t for the first N/2 particles (pessimistic approach) and from O_t for the other particles (optimistic approach).

Initialize velocity v_x^i, $pbest^i$ and $gbest^i$ for i=1,…,N:

$v_x^i \leftarrow 0$

$$pbest^i = \begin{cases} (x^i, y^{ip}) & \text{for } i \le N/2 \\ (x^i, y^{io}) & \text{for } i > N/2 \end{cases}$$

$$gbest^i = \begin{cases} p & \text{for } i \le N/2 \\ o & \text{for } i > N/2 \end{cases}$$

***Step* 2** – *Move upper level particles*

For each x^i, i=1,…,N:

- $v_x^i \leftarrow w.v_x^i + c_1.r_1\,(pbest^i(x) - x^i) + c_2.r_2\,(gbest^i(x) - x^i)$

  where w is the inertia weight, c_1 and c_2 are the cognitive and social coefficients, and $pbest^i(x)$, $gbest^i(x)$ are the x-parts of $pbest^i$ and $gbest^i$, respectively; r_1, r_2 = *random* (0, 1), drawn individually for each component of v_x^i.
- $x^i \leftarrow x^i + v_x^i$
- *Mutation*(x^i)
- If $x^i \notin$X, set each component of x^i out of bounds on the nearest bound (upper or lower bound).
- Apply the algorithm *Lowerlevel-PSO*(x^i) to determine $\Psi_{Ef}(x^i)$ as in *Step* 1.
- Select the solutions of $\Psi_{Ef}(x^i)$ with the best and the worst values of F, y^{io} and y^{ip}, respectively, using (3) and (4).

Hence, two archives O_{t+1} and P_{t+1}, are obtained:

$O_{t+1} = \{(x^1, y^{1o}), (x^2, y^{2o}),\ldots,(x^N, y^{No})\}$

$P_{t+1} = \{(x^1, y^{1p}), (x^2, y^{2p}),\ldots,(x^N, y^{Np})\}$

Update solutions o, p and d:

Let $o_{t+1} \leftarrow \arg\min\{F(x,y): (x,y) \in O_{t+1}, G(x,y) \le 0\}$. Let k be the index of o_{t+1} in O_{t+1}.

If $F(o_{t+1}) < F(o)$ then:

$o \leftarrow o_{t+1}$

$d \leftarrow (x^k, y^{kp}) \in P_{t+1}$

Let $p_{t+1} \leftarrow \arg\min\{F(x,y): (x,y) \in P_{t+1}, G(x,y) \le 0\}$. If there is no G-feasible solution in P_{t+1}, the one with the smallest overall violation of constraints G is chosen.

The following rule – which we will refer to as *Rule FG* – is applied to choose between p and p_{t+1} to set the new p:

If p and p_{t+1} are both G-feasible, then the new p is the one with lower F; otherwise, choose the solution p or p_{t+1} with smaller overall violation of G (which can be 0 if one of them is feasible).

Update $pbest^i$ and $gbest^i$, i=1,…,N:

for $i \le$ N/2 (*pessimistic* approach):

$pbest^i \leftarrow$ apply *Rule FG* between $pbest^i$ and (x^i, y^{ip})

$gbest^i \leftarrow p$

for $i >$ N/2 (*optimistic* approach):

$pbest^i \leftarrow$ apply *Rule FG* between $pbest^i$ and (x^i, y^{io})

$gbest^i \leftarrow o$

***Step* 3**

$t \leftarrow t+1$

If $t = T$, stop. Else, go to *Step* 2.

Return solutions o, p and d.

Let us now describe the steps of the algorithm *Lowerlevel-PSO*(x) whose outcome is $\Psi_{Ef}(x) = \{y^l,\ l=1,\ldots,L\}$ with $L \le L_{max}$, a maximum size defined *a priori*.

Lowerlevel-PSO(x)

Let N_l be the (maximum) size of the lower level population and T_l the number of iterations of the lower level PSO.

***Step L*.1** – *Initialization of the lower level population*

tl =0

Randomly generate N_l vectors $y^j \in$Y to form a population of lower level solutions for the given upper level x: $PopY_{tl} = \{y^j,\ j=1,\ldots,N_l\}$. For each y^j, check the constraints g and generate another $y^j \in$Y in case of g-infeasibility, considering a maximum of M trials (by default, $M = 2N_l$). Let N_l' be the number of g-feasible solutions obtained. If $N_l' = 0$, the algorithm stops returning $\Psi_{Ef}(x) = \emptyset$; otherwise, it continues with $N_l \leftarrow N_l'$ particles.

Initialize the velocity v_y^j and $pbest_y^j$ for each particle y^j, $j = 1,\ldots,N_l$:

$v_y^j \leftarrow 0$

$pbest_y^j \leftarrow y^j$

Initialize the archive $\Psi_{Ef}(x)$ with the nondominated y^j in $PopY_{tl}$ with respect to the lower level functions f.

***Step L*.2** – *Move lower level particles*

For each y^j, $j = 1,\ldots, N_l$

- Select $gbest_y^j$:

  As the goal is to find lower level efficient solutions near the extreme values of F (maximum and minimum), the $gbest_y^j$ is selected according to the following criterion: for the first half of the population (first $N_l/2$ elements), $gbest_y^j$ is randomly chosen among the 10% of the solutions with higher value of F; for the second half of the population, $gbest_y^j$ is randomly chosen among the 10% of the solutions with lower value of F. Hence, the first $N_l/2$ particles will be oriented to the *pessimistic* solution while the remaining ones will be oriented to the *optimistic* solution.
- $v_y^j \leftarrow w_l.v_y^j + c_{l1}.r_1\,(pbest_y^j - y^j) + c_{l2}.r_2\,(gbest_y^j - y^j)$

  where w_l is the inertia weight and c_{l1} and c_{l2} are the cognitive and social coefficients for the lower level search; r_1, r_2 = *random* (0, 1), drawn individually for each component of v_y^j.
- $y^j \leftarrow y^j + v_y^j$
- *Mutation*(y^j)
- If $y^j \notin$Y, set each component of y^j out of bounds on the nearest bound (upper or lower bound).
- Evaluate y^j according to f, F and g.
- Update $pbest_y^j$ in case (x, y^j) is g-feasible:

  If y^j dominates $pbest_y^j$, then $pbest_y^j \leftarrow y^j$; if y^j is nondominated with respect to $pbest_y^j$, a random selection between them is made to set the new $pbest_y^j$.

Update $\Psi_{Ef}(x)$ with the g-feasible solutions of the new population that are not dominated by any other element of the population and by any element of $\Psi_{Ef}(x)$. Delete from $\Psi_{Ef}(x)$ elements that become dominated. In case of $|\Psi_{Ef}(x)| > L_{max}$, the elements with the most central values of F (i.e. the most distant from the maximum and the minimum of F in $\Psi_{Ef}(x)$) are successively removed until L_{max} solutions remain in $\Psi_{Ef}(x)$.

***Step L*.3**

$tl \leftarrow tl$+1

If tl = Tl, stop. Else, go to *Step L*.2.

Return $\Psi_{Ef}(x)$.

In *Step* 1, before splitting the upper level population into two parts, P_t is rearranged in order that the first particles are G-feasible and the next ones are sorted by ascending order of the overall violation of constraints G. This sorting is replicated in O_t and $PopX_t$ to keep the correspondence with P_t, as the x^i part (in the i-th position) is the same in all archives. The purpose of this sorting is to preferentially use feasible *pbest* and *gbest* particles both in the pessimistic and the optimistic approaches. This order favors the fulfilment of constraints in the first half of P_t, the one used to select the guiding particles for the pessimistic approach, not harming the optimistic approach because solutions in O_t are generally feasible.

It is worthy of notice that, in a first attempt of the algorithm design, we did not consider a rigid division of the lower level population into two parts (pessimistic-oriented and optimistic-oriented) and the choice of each $gbest_y$ was made either from the top 10% or the bottom 10% of F. This option, however, led to very poor results for the *pessimistic* and *deceiving* solutions, which have been much improved with the strategy currently proposed.

In the next section we report some results of the algorithm. Different types of *mutation* for x^i and y^j (*Steps 2* and *L.2*) have been tested considering parts of the population with and without mutation, and uniform/non-uniform mutation.

4. EXPERIMENTAL RESULTS

We provide results on four illustrative problems for which we can determine exactly the *optimistic, pessimistic* and *deceiving* solutions. Thus, we can evaluate the quality of the approximations provided by the algorithm for these problems.

Prob. 1 – This problem is formulated above (in Section 2). It was used in the *Example* to illustrate the three types of solutions.

Sol.o: $(x, y_1, y_2) = (0.5, 0.5, 0)$, $(f_1, f_2) = (0.25, 0)$, $F = \mathbf{0.5}$
Sol.p: $(x, y_1, y_2) = (0, 0, 0)$, $(f_1, f_2) = (0, 0)$, $F = \mathbf{1}$
Sol.d: $(x, y_1, y_2) = (0.5, 0, 0)$, $(f_1, f_2) = (0, 0.25)$, $F = \mathbf{1.25}$

Prob. 2 – This is a generalization of the previous problem (problem 4 in [8]), which has one upper level variable (x) and k+1 lower level variables ($y_1, y_2, \ldots, y_{k+1}$). We have considered k =13.

$$\begin{aligned} \min \quad & F(x,y) = (y_1-1)^2 + \sum_{j=1}^{k} y_{j+1}^2 + x^2 \\ s.t. \quad & \min_y f_1(x,y) = y_1^2 + \sum_{j=1}^{k} y_{j+1}^2 \\ & \min_y f_2(x,y) = (y_1 - x)^2 + \sum_{j=1}^{k} y_{j+1}^2 \\ & s.t. \quad -1 \le y_1, y_2, \ldots, y_{k+1}, x \le 2 \end{aligned}$$

Sol.o: $(x, y_1, y_2, \ldots, y_{k+1}) = (0.5, 0.5, 0, \ldots, 0)$, $(f_1, f_2) = (0.25, 0)$, $F = \mathbf{0.5}$
Sol.p: $(x, y_1, y_2, \ldots, y_{k+1}) = (0, 0, 0, \ldots, 0)$, $(f_1, f_2) = (0, 0)$, $F = \mathbf{1}$
Sol.d: $(x, y_1, y_2, \ldots, y_{k+1}) = (0.5, 0, 0, \ldots, 0)$, $(f_1, f_2) = (0, 0.25)$, $F = \mathbf{1.25}$

Prob. 3 and *Prob. 4* – These problems are taken from problem 1 in [8] considering the first upper level objective function for *Prob. 3* and the second one for *Prob. 4*.

Prob. 3:

$$\begin{aligned} \min \quad & F(x,y) = y_1 - x \\ s.t. \quad & \\ & G_1(x,y) = 1 + y_1 + y_2 \ge 0 \\ & \min_y f_1(x,y) = y_1 \\ & \min_y f_2(x,y) = y_2 \\ & s.t. \\ & \quad g_1(x,y) = x^2 - y_1^2 - y_2^2 \ge 0 \\ & \quad -1 \le y_1, y_2 \le 1, \; 0 \le x \le 1 \end{aligned}$$

Prob. 4:

$$\begin{aligned} \min \quad & F(x,y) = y_2 \\ s.t. \quad & \\ & G_1(x,y) = 1 + y_1 + y_2 \ge 0 \\ & \min_y f_1(x,y) = y_1 \\ & \min_y f_2(x,y) = y_2 \\ & s.t. \\ & \quad g_1(x,y) = x^2 - y_1^2 - y_2^2 \ge 0 \\ & \quad -1 \le y_1, y_2 \le 1, \; 0 \le x \le 1 \end{aligned}$$

where x and $y = (y_1, y_2)$ are the upper level and the lower level variables, respectively. These problems have an upper level constraint with lower level variables, so there are lower level efficient solutions for a given x that are not feasible to the upper level problem. This constraint increases the difficulty of the problems.

Prob. 3
Sol.o: $(x, y_1, y_2) = (1, -1, 0)$, $(f_1, f_2) = (-1, 0)$, $F = \mathbf{-2}$
Sol.p = *Sol.d*: $(x, y_1, y_2) = (1, 0, -1)$, $(f_1, f_2) = (0, -1)$, $F = \mathbf{-1}$

Prob. 4
Sol.o: $(x, y_1, y_2) = (1, 0, -1)$, $(f_1, f_2) = (0, -1)$, $F = \mathbf{-1}$
Sol.p: all $(x, y_1, y_2) = (\alpha, -\alpha, 0)$ with $0 \le \alpha \le 1$, $(f_1, f_2) = (-\alpha, 0)$, $F = 0$
Sol.d: $(x, y_1, y_2) = (1, -1, 0)$, $(f_1, f_2) = (-1, 0)$, $F = \mathbf{0}$

The algorithm was implemented in Delphi for Windows and different types of *mutation* of x^i and y^j were experimented considering parts of the population with and without mutation, and uniform/non-uniform mutation. The probability of mutation of each variable was set to $1/n$ (n being the number of variables of the respective level) with a maximum of 0.2.

We considered the following parameters: $N = 20$; $N_l = 60$; $T = 50$; $T_l = 100$; $L_{max} = 30$. The PSO parameters were set as in [16]: w, w_l = *random* (0.1, 0.5); c_1, c_2, c_{l1}, c_{l2} = *random* (1.5, 2.0). Thirty independent runs were performed in each experiment.

Preliminary results seemed to indicate that better approximations for the pessimistic solutions are achieved with low degrees of mutation, while mutation is essential to obtain good optimistic solutions. So, the first three experiments considered the following mutation schemes, applied in both levels of the optimization process (i.e., for x and y):

- Exp. 1) *uniform mutation* for the whole population;
- Exp. 2) the first half of the population (*pessimistic*) does not suffer mutation and the second half of the population (*optimistic*) suffers *uniform mutation*;
- Exp. 3) an intermediate scheme between 1) and 2): the first half of the population (*pessimistic*) is divided into two equal parts, in which the first one does not suffer mutation and the second one undergoes *uniform mutation* such as in the *optimistic* part of the population.

We further performed another experiment including uniform and non-uniform mutation, in which the perturbation amounts decrease with the number of iterations. This is an adaptation of the mutation scheme employed in [16], which considers uniform + non-uniform + no mutation, applying each mutation operator to 1/3 of the population. We consider, however, different proportions of the population for each mutation operator:

- Exp. 4) first half of the population (*pessimistic*): ½ with no mutation and ½ with *non-uniform mutation*; second half of the population (*optimistic*): ½ with *uniform mutation* and ½ with *non-uniform mutation.*

The results of Experiments 1 to 4 are reported in Table 1, showing the average, the median and the interquartile range IQR (as a measure of statistical dispersion), of F, f_1 and f_2 over the 30 runs, for each of the three target solutions (*optimistic, pessimistic* and *deceiving*) in *Prob. 1* to *Prob. 4*. For space reasons, we omit the values of the decision variables. The Kruskall-Wallis test was used to test whether the medians of the F values among Experiments 1 to 4 (in the three types of solutions) are different, considering a significance level $\alpha = 0.05$. All differences in *Probs. 1, 2* and *4* were considered statistically significant except for the deceiving solution in *Prob. 1*. The results for *Prob. 3* are very similar in all experiments and the differences detected could not be concluded to be statistically significant.

Assessing the solutions in terms of the F value (i.e. its proximity to the exact one), we can observe that Exp. 2 provided in general the best approximation for the pessimistic solution, presenting better average and median F values than the other tests, with small statistical dispersion. Recall that Exp. 2 does not include mutation in the first half of the population, the one that is oriented to the pessimistic solution. The second half of the population (oriented to the optimistic solution) underwent mutation in all tests. We observe, however, that some mutation in the first part of the population (Exp. 1, 3 and 4) can also benefit the optimistic and/or deceiving solutions in some cases. Note that the different values and high interquartile ranges observed for f_1 in the pessimistic solution of *Prob. 4* do not mean instability of the algorithm, because all solutions $x = \alpha$, $y_1 = -\alpha$, $0 \leq \alpha \leq 1$, which lead to $f_1 = -\alpha$, are alternative pessimistic solutions.

Exp. 4 does not evidence an overall superiority with respect to the previous ones, namely in what concerns the approximation of the pessimistic solution for which the mutation scheme employed in Exp. 2 seems to be better. Therefore, no clear conclusions can be drawn about the use of *uniform* vs. *non-uniform* mutation operators.

Overall, the values presented in Table 1 show that the algorithm performed well in these four problems, being able to reach the exact values in some cases or closely approximate to them. The best solution approximations were obtained for *Prob. 3* and *Prob. 4* in all experiments and the worst case seems to be the computation of the optimistic solution of *Prob. 2*. The computational experiments suggest that better approximations for the pessimistic solution are obtained without mutation (or with low mutation rates) in contrast to the computation of the optimistic solution, which requires mutation.

Table 1. Average, median and interquartile range (in subscript) of the solutions obtained for *Problems 1 - 4*

		Optimistic solution			***Pessimistic solution***			***Deceiving solution***		
Prob.1		**F=0.5**	**$f_1 = 0.25$**	**$f_2 = 0$**	**F=1**	**$f_1 = 0$**	**$f_2 = 0$**	**F=1.25**	**$f_1 = 0$**	**$f_2 = 0.25$**
Exp. 1	Average	0.489	0.261	3E-4	0.973	0.036	0.009	1.243	3E-5	0.245
	Median $_{IQR}$	0.490 $_{0.006}$	0.257 $_{0.048}$	2E-4 $_{3E-4}$	0.994 $_{0.001}$	1E-5 $_{6E-6}$	2E-4 $_{4E-4}$	1.244 $_{0.042}$	1E-5 $_{2E-5}$	0.244 $_{0.041}$
Exp. 2	Average	0.493	0.255	1E-4	0.994	0.008	0.005	1.243	1E-5	0.245
	Median $_{IQR}$	0.493 $_{0.003}$	0.255 $_{0.035}$	7E-5 $_{8E-5}$	0.994 $_{8E-5}$	1E-5 $_{6E-7}$	1E-5 $_{6E-5}$	1.246 $_{0.036}$	5E-6 $_{7E-6}$	0.248 $_{0.035}$
Exp. 3	Average	0.489	0.264	2E-4	0.987	0.021	0.005	1.248	1E-5	0.249
	Median $_{IQR}$	0.489 $_{0.004}$	0.265 $_{0.032}$	2E-4 $_{2E-4}$	0.994 $_{0.001}$	1E-5 $_{3E-6}$	2E-5 $_{2E-4}$	1.249 $_{0.03}$	4E-6 $_{7E-6}$	0.252 $_{0.028}$
Exp. 4	Average	0.488	0.265	0.001	0.992	0.006	0.004	1.248	4E-6	0.250
	Median $_{IQR}$	0.489 $_{0.007}$	0.262 $_{0.044}$	2E-4 $_{3E-4}$	0.994 $_{2E-4}$	1E-5 $_{7E-7}$	5E-5 $_{3E-4}$	1.252 $_{0.043}$	3E-6 $_{4E-6}$	0.253 $_{0.044}$
Prob.2		**F=0.5**	**$f_1 = 0.25$**	**$f_2 = 0$**	**F=1**	**$f_1 = 0$**	**$f_2 = 0$**	**F=1.25**	**$f_1 = 0$**	**$f_2 = 0.25$**
Exp. 1	Average	0.398	0.382	0.065	0.824	0.033	0.023	1.282	0.056	0.255
	Median $_{IQR}$	0.402 $_{0.032}$	0.363 $_{0.114}$	0.065 $_{0.021}$	0.827 $_{0.043}$	0.031 $_{0.009}$	0.021 $_{0.012}$	1.266 $_{0.157}$	0.059 $_{0.028}$	0.240 $_{0.084}$
Exp. 2	Average	0.392	0.427	0.051	0.988	3E-4	0.001	1.222	1E-4	0.224
	Median $_{IQR}$	0.393 $_{0.021}$	0.435 $_{0.133}$	0.046 $_{0.031}$	0.990 $_{0.001}$	3E-5 $_{8E-5}$	3E-4 $_{0.001}$	1.223 $_{0.059}$	2E-5 $_{1E-5}$	0.223 $_{0.059}$
Exp. 3	Average	0.379	0.395	0.049	0.885	0.010	0.014	1.215	0.021	0.218
	Median $_{IQR}$	0.384 $_{0.062}$	0.400 $_{0.112}$	0.043 $_{0.025}$	0.892 $_{0.047}$	0.009 $_{0.006}$	0.006 $_{0.007}$	1.214 $_{0.105}$	0.016 $_{0.018}$	0.222 $_{0.071}$
Exp. 4	Average	0.365	0.413	0.051	0.981	0.002	0.004	1.208	0.008	0.209
	Median $_{IQR}$	0.364 $_{0.032}$	0.395 $_{0.138}$	0.044 $_{0.029}$	0.987 $_{0.010}$	7E-5 $_{0.002}$	0.001 $_{0.002}$	1.210 $_{0.075}$	0.005 $_{0.011}$	0.214 $_{0.078}$
Prob.3		**F= -2**	**$f_1 = -1$**	**$f_2 = 0$**	**F= -1**	**$f_1 = 0$**	**$f_2 = -1$**	**F= -1**	**$f_1 = 0$**	**$f_2 = -1$**
Exp. 1	Average	-1.998	-0.999	0.002	-1.002	-0.003	-0.999	-1.002	-0.003	-0.999
	Median $_{IQR}$	-2.000 $_{0}$	-1.000 $_{0}$	0.001 $_{0.002}$	-1.003 $_{0.001}$	-0.003 $_{4E-4}$	-1.000 $_{0}$	-1.003 $_{0.001}$	-0.003 $_{0.001}$	-1.000 $_{0}$
Exp. 2	Average	-1.997	-0.999	0.001	-1.001	-0.003	-0.999	-1.001	-0.003	-0.999
	Median $_{IQR}$	-2.000 $_{0}$	-1.000 $_{0}$	0.001 $_{0.001}$	-1.003 $_{0.001}$	-0.003 $_{5E-4}$	-1.000 $_{5E-6}$	-1.003 $_{0.001}$	-0.003 $_{0.001}$	-1.000 $_{4E-6}$
Exp. 3	Average	-1.999	-0.999	0.001	-1.002	-0.003	-0.999	-1.002	-0.003	-0.999
	Median $_{IQR}$	-2.000 $_{0}$	-1.000 $_{0}$	0.001 $_{0.001}$	-1.003 $_{0.001}$	-0.003 $_{0.001}$	-1.000 $_{5E-6}$	-1.003 $_{0.001}$	-0.003 $_{0.001}$	-1.000 $_{5E-6}$
Exp. 4	Average	-1.998	-0.999	0.001	-1.001	-0.003	-0.999	-1.001	-0.003	-0.999
	Median $_{IQR}$	-2.000 $_{0}$	-1.000 $_{0}$	0.001 $_{0.002}$	-1.003 $_{0.001}$	-0.003 $_{0.002}$	-1.000 $_{0.001}$	-1.003 $_{0.001}$	-0.003 $_{0.001}$	-1.000 $_{7E-6}$
Prob.4		**F= -1**	**$f_1 = 0$**	**$f_2 = -1$**	**F= 0**	**$-1 \leq f_1 \leq 0$**	**$f_2 = 0$**	**F= 0**	**$f_1 = -1$**	**$f_2 = 0$**
Exp. 1	Average	-1.000	0.002	-1.000	-0.047	-0.708	-0.047	-0.002	-1.000	-0.002
	Median $_{IQR}$	-1.000 $_{0}$	0.002 $_{0.002}$	-1.000 $_{0}$	-0.039 $_{0.011}$	-0.758 $_{0.268}$	-0.039 $_{0.011}$	-0.003 $_{4E-4}$	-1.000 $_{0}$	-0.003 $_{4E-4}$
Exp. 2	Average	-0.997	0.002	-0.997	-0.006	-0.888	-0.006	-0.003	-0.997	-0.003
	Median $_{IQR}$	-1.000 $_{0.005}$	0.001 $_{0.002}$	-1.000 $_{0.005}$	-0.006 $_{0.001}$	-0.930 $_{0.098}$	-0.006 $_{0.001}$	-0.003 $_{0.001}$	-1.000 $_{0.005}$	-0.003 $_{0.001}$
Exp. 3	Average	-0.999	0.002	-0.999	-0.029	-0.658	-0.029	-0.002	-0.999	-0.002
	Median $_{IQR}$	-1.000 $_{0}$	0.001 $_{0.002}$	-1.000 $_{0}$	-0.029 $_{0.008}$	-0.622 $_{0.211}$	-0.029 $_{0.008}$	-0.003 $_{0.001}$	-1.000 $_{4E-6}$	-0.003 $_{0.001}$
Exp. 4	Average	-0.999	0.002	-0.999	-0.013	-0.682	-0.013	-0.003	-0.999	-0.003
	Median $_{IQR}$	-1.000 $_{0}$	0.001 $_{0.002}$	-1.000 $_{0}$	-0.008 $_{0.007}$	-0.729 $_{0.390}$	-0.008 $_{0.007}$	-0.003 $_{0.001}$	-1.000 $_{5E-6}$	-0.003 $_{0.001}$

5. CONCLUSIONS

Most theoretical and algorithmic contributions to multiobjective or semivectorial bilevel problems adopt an optimistic approach. The optimistic approach assumes that the follower accepts any efficient solution to the lower-level problem, presuming that the follower does not have preferences, he chooses according to the leader's preferences or the leader is free to select the solution that suits him best among the efficient solutions to the follower. We believe, however, that this assumption is unrealistic in most practical decision situations. Therefore, the primary aim of this paper has been to discuss and point out the consequences of assuming an optimistic approach in a real decision situation. We have analyzed the *optimistic* and the *pessimistic* solutions, as well as introduced a new solution concept that we call the *deceiving* solution. The *deceiving* solution is the worst outcome from a failed optimistic approach, that is, it results when the leader makes an optimistic decision and the follower's reaction is against the interests of the leader.

In order to make a first assessment of the difficulty of computing these three types of solutions to semivectorial bilevel problems, we have developed an algorithm based on PSO intended to approximate the *optimistic*, *pessimistic*, and *deceiving* solutions in a single run. Some illustrative results were presented considering four semivectorial bilevel problems adapted from multiobjective bilevel problems available in the literature, for which we know the exact solutions. The computation of the *pessimistic* solution seemed to be the most sensitive one. Despite its preliminary nature, the experimentation reported here seems to indicate that better approximations for the pessimistic solutions are obtained without mutation (or with low mutation rates) in the PSO process, while mutation is essential to obtain good approximations for the optimistic solutions. We believe that additional improvements can be achieved for the computation of these solutions and we hope that this study can offer some insights into further investigation on this topic, namely in bilevel problems with multiple objectives in both levels. Indeed, we have already conducted some experiments with a modified and improved version of the algorithm proposed in [7] to compute the pessimistic Pareto optimal front to the leader.

6. ACKNOWLEDGMENTS

This work has been partially supported by QREN Mais Centro Program Project EMSURE (CENTRO 07 0224 FEDER 002004) and by FCT under project grant UID/MULTI/00308/2013.

7. REFERENCES

[1] Alves, M. J., and Costa, J. P. 2014. An algorithm based on particle swarm optimization for multiobjective bilevel linear problems. *Appl. Math. Comput.* 247, 547-561.

[2] Alves, M. J., Dempe, S., and Júdice, J. J. 2012. Computing the Pareto frontier of a bi-objective bi-level linear problem using a multiobjective mixed-integer programming algorithm. *Optimization* 61, 3, 335-358.

[3] Ankhili, Z., and Mansouri, A. 2009. An exact penalty on bilevel programs with linear vector optimization lower level. *Eur. J. Oper. Res.* 197, 1, 36-41.

[4] Bonnel, H. 2006. Optimality conditions for the semivectorial bilevel optimization problem. *Pac. J. Optim.* 2, 3, 447-468.

[5] Bonnel, H., and Morgan, J. 2006. Semivectorial bilevel optimization problem: penalty approach. *J. Optimiz. Theory App.* 131, 3, 365-382.

[6] Calvete, H. I., and Galé, C. 2011. On linear bilevel problems with multiple objectives at the lower level. *Omega* 39, 1, 33-40.

[7] Carrasqueira, P., Alves, M. J., and Antunes, C. H. 2015. A bi-level multiobjective PSO algorithm. In *Proceedings of EMO 2015*, LNCS 9018, Springer, 263-276.

[8] Deb, K., and Sinha, A. 2009. Solving bilevel multi-objective optimization problems using evolutionary algorithms. In *Proceedings of EMO 2009,* LNCS 5467, Springer, 110-124.

[9] Deb, K., and Sinha, A. 2010. An efficient and accurate solution methodology for bilevel multi-objective programming problems using a hybrid evolutionary-local-search algorithm. *Evol. Comput.* 18, 3, 403-449.

[10] Dempe, S. 2002. *Foundations of bilevel programming.* Springer.

[11] Dempe, S. 2009. Bilevel programming: implicit function approach. In Floudas and Pardalos (Eds), *Encyclopedia of Optimization*, vol. 2, 260-266.

[12] Dempe, S., Gadhi, N., and Zemkoho, A. B. 2013. New optimality conditions for the semivectorial bilevel optimization problem. *J. Optimiz. Theory App.* 157, 1, 54-74.

[13] Eichfelder, G. 2010. Multiobjective bilevel optimization. *Math. Program.* 123, 2, 419-449.

[14] Liu, B., Wan, Z., Chen, J., and Wang, G. 2014. Optimality conditions for pessimistic semivectorial bilevel programming problems. *J. Inequal. Appl.* 2014:41.

[15] Nishizaki, I., and Sakawa, M. 1999. Stackelberg solutions to multiobjective two-level linear programming problems. *J. Optimiz. Theory App.* 103, 1, 161-182.

[16] Reyes-Sierra, M. and Coello Coello, C.A. 2005. Improving PSO-based multi-objective optimization using crowding, mutation and ε-dominance. In *Proceedings of EMO2005*, LNCS 3410, Springer, 505–519.

[17] Ruuska, S., and Miettinen, K. 2012. Constructing Evolutionary Algorithms for Bilevel Multiobjective Optimization, In *IEEE Congress on Evolutionary Computation* (*CEC 2012*).

[18] Tsoukalas, A., Wiesemann, W., and Rustem, B. 2009. Global optimisation of pessimistic bi-level problems. *Lectures on Global Optimization* 55, 215-243.

[19] Zheng, Y., and Wan, Z. 2011. A solution method for semivectorial bilevel programming problem via penalty method. *Journal of Applied Mathematics and Computing* 37, 1-2, 207-219.

[20] Zhang, T., Hu, T., Guo, X., Chen, Z., and Zheng, Y. 2013. Solving high dimensional bilevel multiobjective programming problem using a hybrid particle swarm optimization algorithm with crossover operator. *Knowl.-Based Syst.* 53, 13-19.

Characterizing Pareto Front Approximations in Many-objective Optimization

Md Asafuddoula
University of New South Wales
Canberra, ACT 2610, Australia
Md.Asaf@adfa.edu.au

Tapabrata Ray
University of New South Wales
Canberra, ACT 2610, Australia
t.ray@adfa.edu.au

Hemant Kumar Singh
University of New South Wales
Canberra, ACT 2610, Australia
h.singh@adfa.edu.au

ABSTRACT

A Pareto Optimal Front (POF) provides the set of optimal trade-off solutions for multi-objective optimization problems. The characteristics of the POF, e.g. continuity, convexity, spread and uniformity are important in the context of decision making and performance assessment. Most of the existing metrics (hypervolume, inverted generational distance, coverage etc.) were originally designed for two or three objective optimization problems with an aim of assessing the quality of non-dominated solutions delivered by various algorithms. The metrics provide little information about the nature of the front and some of them (e.g. hypervolume) are computationally expensive for problems involving large number of objectives. For problems with more than three objectives, existing tools for visualization such as parallel plots, spider/radar plots and scatter plots also offer limited useful information in terms of the nature of the front. In this paper, we introduce an alternative scalar measure of diversity that is suitable for characterizing POF approximations of optimization problems with high number of objectives. The diversity is measured against a *Reference Pareto Front*, a set of points uniformly spread on the hyperplane with unit intercepts. We also illustrate that the computation of such a metric is a natural extension of decomposition based evolutionary algorithms which attempt to align solutions with the reference directions constructed using the Ideal point and uniformly distributed points on the hyperplane. In particular, the perpendicular distances between the uniformly distributed reference directions and their closest solutions in the non-dominated front provides information about the diversity, while the shortest distance of every solution from the hyperplane provides information about the convexity of the POF. The proposed metrics are illustrated using a number of test problems involving up to fifteen objectives.

Categories and Subject Descriptors

500 [**Mathematics of computing**]: Evolutionary algorithms

Keywords

Many-objective Optimization; Diversity; Hyperplane; Performance metrics

GECCO '15, July 11 - 15, 2015, Madrid, Spain

DOI: http://dx.doi.org/10.1145/2739480.2754701

1. INTRODUCTION

Multi-objective optimization refers to solving problems involving simultaneous maximization/minimization of two or more conflicting objectives. The problems containing more than four objectives are further differentiated as *many-objective* optimization (MaO) problems. The optimal designs for such problems are referred to as Pareto Optimal Set (POS) and the corresponding objectives form the Pareto Optimal Front (POF) in the objective space. In most cases, it is impossible to use exact optimization methods to identify POF due to the underlying complexities such as discontinuity, non-linearity and non-differentiability. Heuristic/metaheuristic search methods are preferred methods for solving such problems, and they deliver a non-dominated front (NDF) of solutions as an approximation of the POF.

Among the metaheuristic methods, population based approaches are preferred, since they inherently maintain a set of solutions that are evolved to converge to the POF. However, since such methods cannot guarantee optimality, design of metrics to assess the quality of solutions delivered by various population based algorithms has been an active area of research. A number of quality indicators [13, 15, 18, 24, 27] have been proposed to evaluate the performance of multi-objective optimizers mainly from three perspectives – (a) convergence, (b) uniformity and (c) spread. In order to assess convergence, indicators [4, 7, 19, 21, 22] typically need an optimal reference set which may not available for unknown problems. In order to assess uniformity, spacing measure [2, 8], uniform distribution measure [20], entropy measure [10] and clustering [23] based approaches have been proposed. In addition, there are also a number of other metrics, such as hypervolume [28], hyperarea ratio [19] and coverage difference [26]) which attempt to assess the NDF from all the three perspectives. While these indicators can give a good assessment of quality of solutions, their computational cost tends to be prohibitive for MaO problems, limiting their use.

Diversity is often used as a term to reflect a combination of uniformity and spread. In terms of diversity, G-Metric [17], Δ-Metric [8] and diversity measure (DM) [7] have been suggested in the literature. They originally considered bi-objective optimization and their performance is affected significantly when the number of objectives is increased [16]. In the context of MaO, diversity comparison indicator (DCI) [16] has been proposed recently. The method constructs an uniform grid and computes the contributions of solutions obtained by various algorithms to grids occupied by the solutions of the (approximate) Pareto Optimal Front (POF) obtained using combined non-dominated set. Although DCI can accurately rank various NDFs, it does not provide information about the nature of the fronts.

Apart from the above scalar metrics, visualization tools are regularly used to compare NDFs. Parallel coordinate plot [12], scatter plot [11], radar plot (RadViz) [14] are some of the commonly used ones. Once again, such plots do not offer much information about the nature of the NDFs.

In this paper, we introduce a new scalar measure of diversity derived from DCI, henceforth referred to as modified diversity indicator (M-DI). In M-DI, instead of computing the diversity of various NDFs relative to each other, the diversity is computed with respect to a *Reference Pareto front*, which is a set of uniformly distributed solutions on a hyperplane. Further, the nature of NDFs is characterized by two other measures, (a) shortest (normal) distance from a solution to the hyperplane (d_{hyp}) and (b) perpendicular distance between every reference direction and its closest solution (d_2). Since decomposition based evolutionary algorithms are being increasingly used for the solution of many objective optimization problems, we illustrate that the computation of the metrics discussed above follows as a natural extension.

The details of M-DI, d_{hyp} and d_2 computation are presented in Section 2. The differences between DCI and the proposed M-DI are also highlighted. In Section 3, we use bi-objective linear, convex and non-convex POFs to illustrate the principles of characterization. Thereafter, we compute the metrics based on solutions delivered by Decomposition Based Evolutionary Algorithm (DBEA) [1] and a Non-dominated Evolutionary Algorithm (NDEA) for DTLZ1 and DTLZ2 [9] problems involving 3, 5, 10 and 15 objectives and a 3-objective problem (DEB3DK [3]) with mixed (convex and non-convex) NDF. Subsequently, some limitations of the proposed metrics are highlighted. The final section summarizes the contributions.

2. PROPOSED METRICS

The central idea behind the development of the proposed metrics is to offer means to quantify diversity and gain understanding about the nature of the POF. The details of the computation of the metrics are presented in the following subsections.

2.1 Modified diversity indicator (M-DI)

As discussed earlier, our proposed M-DI indicator relies on the use of an *Reference Pareto front* (RPF), i.e., uniformly distributed set of reference points on the hyperplane with unit intercepts on each objective axis. In the context of decomposition based evolutionary algorithms (e.g. DBEA [1], NSGA-III [6]), these points are typically used to construct a set of uniform reference directions for decomposition. The points are generated using systematic sampling method introduced by Das and Dennis [5]. Thus the notion of RPF is inline with existing adopted practice of uniform reference direction generation mechanism as adopted in most standard decomposition based many objective optimization algorithms. The process of reference point generation is illustrated using a 2-objective optimization problem ($M = 2$) with an assumed spacing of $\delta = 0.05$ ($s = 20$) in Figure 1. The above process results in the generation of $W = 21$ reference points (W is computed using Equation 1).

$$W = {}^{(M+s-1)}C_s \quad (1)$$

We adopt a grid based scheme derived from diversity comparison indicator (DCI) [16] to quantify diversity against the Reference Pareto front. In DCI method, NDFs from various algorithms are collected together to identify a set of Pareto optimal solutions. The contribution of each algorithm is assessed against the combined Pareto optimal solutions using a grid defined by a "grid division" parameter. DCI is briefly presented below to highlight the differences with M-DI.

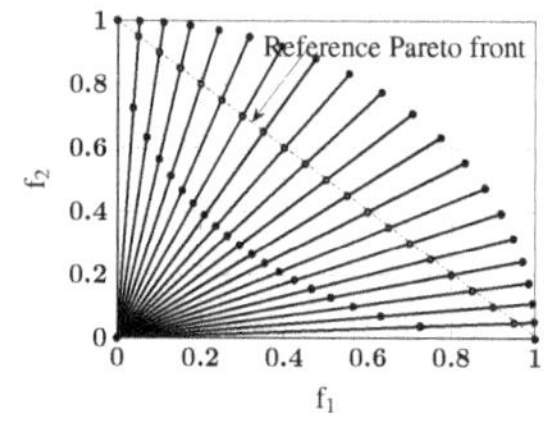

Figure 1: A *Reference Pareto front* for $M = 2$, $s = 20$

From the combined set of non-dominated solutions, the Nadir (np_k) and the Ideal (ip_k) points are identified. To construct grids, an updated Nadir point is used, with coordinates (ub_k) computed as follows:

$$ub_k = np_k + \frac{np_k - ip_k}{2 * s} \qquad k = 1, 2 \ldots M \quad (2)$$

The lower bounds (lb_k) of the objectives correspond to the Ideal point, where $k = 1, 2 \ldots M$ (number of objectives).

The coordinates of the hyper-boxes can be computed based on ub_k, lb_k and the s (as discussed in [16]). The solutions in combined non-dominated front obtained from all algorithms are assigned to their appropriate hyper-boxes ($h = \{h_1, h_2, ...\}$). For an approximation $\mathbf{P}$ obtained by a given algorithm, the grid contribution $CD(\mathbf{P}, h_1)$ to a hyper-box h_1 is computed as follows.

$$CD(\mathbf{P}, h_1) = \begin{cases} 1 - D(\mathbf{P}, h_1)^2/(M+1), & D(\mathbf{P}, h_1) < \sqrt{M+1} \\ 0, & D(\mathbf{P}, h_1) \geq \sqrt{M+1} \end{cases} \quad (3)$$

Here, $D(\mathbf{P}, h_1)$ represents the minimum Euclidean grid distance from the hyper-box h_1 to the hyper-boxes occupied by individuals of $\mathbf{P}$. Similarly, the grid contribution is computed for all other hyper-boxes with respect to the reference set. The final diversity measure (DCI) is computed as follows:

$$DCI = \frac{\sum_{i=1}^{|h|} CD(\mathbf{P}, h_i)}{|h|} \quad (4)$$

Assume two sets of Pareto front approximations $\mathbf{P}^1$ and $\mathbf{P}^2$ as shown in Figure 2(a). In this case $\mathbf{P}^2$ refers to the combined Pareto front and its DCI metric would be the highest (a value of 1). However, as one can observe that this value does not reflect uniform distribution of solutions in the objective space between the extremities of the front. In absence of any information regarding the nature of the POF, if a continuous front is assumed, RPF is likely to give best possible distribution of solutions.

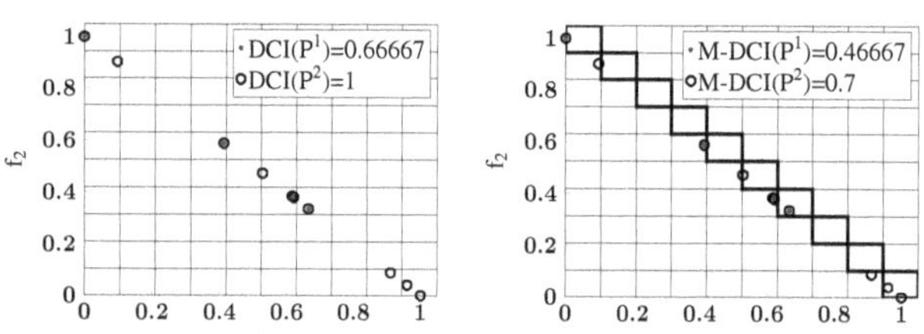

(a) (b)

Figure 2: (a) Diversity comparison using DCI (b) Modified diversity comparison using M-DI

In M-DI, the diversity is computed with respect to the RPF. The Nadir and Ideal point computations are the same as discussed above.

The number of reference points (W) on the RPF is related to the population size (N) used during the course of optimization. For example, a population of 90 used for a 3-objective optimization problem would mean use of 91 reference points on the RPF. Since the number of reference points obtained using the Das and Dennis's method [5] cannot match exact population sizes, the closest $W \geq N$ is used. The grid contribution $CD(\mathbf{P}, h)$ is computed as done in Equation 3, wherein h is the set of hyper-boxes occupied by the *Reference Pareto front*. The diversity metric M-DI is computed as follows: M-DI= $\frac{\sum_{i=1}^{|h|} CD(\mathbf{P},h_i)}{|h|}$.

Figure 2(b) shows the diversity metric computed using M-DI for the same two Pareto front approximations $\mathbf{P}^1$ and $\mathbf{P}^2$. One can clearly see that M-DI of $\mathbf{P}^2$ is 0.7000 while that of $\mathbf{P}^1$ is 0.4667 clearly indicating $\mathbf{P}^2$ is better than $\mathbf{P}^1$. At the same time, the value of $\mathbf{P}^2$is 0.7000 indicates that it still does not have a uniform diversity with respect to the RPF.

2.2 Perpendicular distance from a solution to the reference directions (d_2)

The distance of the closest solution to each reference direction provides important information about the diversity of the Pareto front approximations. The measure d_2 is illustrated in Figure 3.

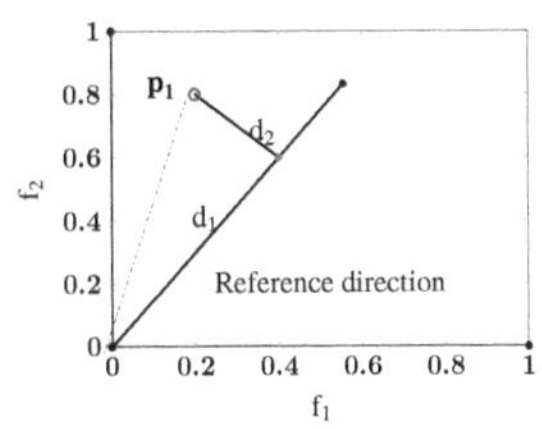

Figure 3: Perpendicular distance from a reference direction to an individual

Such a measure for a set of solutions $\mathbf{P}$={$\mathbf{p}_1$,$\mathbf{p}_2$,$\mathbf{p}_3$, ...$\mathbf{p}_N$} is computed as follows:

$$d_{1,i}^k = \mathbf{p}_i.\frac{\mathbf{w}^k}{||\mathbf{w}^k||} \quad (d_1 \text{ of solution } \mathbf{p}_i \text{ along } k^{th} \text{ direction}) \quad (5)$$

$$d_2(\mathbf{w}^k, \mathbf{P}) = \min_{i=1}^{N}(\sqrt{||\mathbf{p}_i||^2 - (d_{1,i}^k)^2} \quad (6)$$

It is to be noted that the set $\mathbf{P}$ contains normalized values using the identified Nadir and Ideal points. $d_{1,i}^k$ represents d_1 for $\mathbf{p}_i$ solution with respect to k^{th} direction and N is the number of solutions in $\mathbf{P}$.

2.3 Normal distance from a solution to the hyperplane (d_{hyp})

While the metric M-DI discussed above provides information about the diversity of the solutions with respect to the *Reference Pareto front*, it still does not offer any information about the nature of the front, for example its convexity. Identification of the nature of the front is critical in decision making, wherein the decision makers are often interested to identify solution(s) offering excellent trade-off (knees) [3]. The equation of a hyperplane is computed as shown below. For consistency, the solutions are normalized using the Nadir and Ideal points.

For any given non-dominated set of solutions $\mathbf{P}$, one can identify the extreme points (that result in the coordinates of the Nadir point) and construct a hyperplane (L). The generic equation of a plane in objective space can be written as:

$$a_1f_1 + a_2f_2 + ... + a_mf_M = 1 \quad (7)$$

where, f_1,f_2,....,f_M are the objectives and a_1, a_2,....,a_m forms the normal vector to the plane. The normal (i.e., shortest distance) d_{hyp} from a solution ($\mathbf{p}_1$) to this hyperplane can be calculated as follows.

$$d_{hyp}(\mathbf{p}_1, L) = \frac{a_1p_{11} + a_2p_{12} + ... + a_mp_{1m} - 1}{\sqrt{a_1^2 + a_2^2 + ... + a_m^2}} \quad (8)$$

For the normalized case considered here, all coefficients will become 1. A negative value of d_{hyp} indicates that the solution is below the hyperplane (convex region) and a positive value indicates that it resides above (non-convex region) the hyperplane. An value of $d_{hyp} = 0$ indicates that the point lies on the hyperplane itself. For example, assume three solutions $\mathbf{p}_1$=(0.2929, 0.2929), $\mathbf{p}_2$=(0.5000, 0.5000) and $\mathbf{p}_3$=(0.5000, 0.9000). The shortest distance from these solutions to the unit hyperplane would be -0.29288, +0.28284, 0 representing solution $\mathbf{p}_1$ below the hyperplane, solution $\mathbf{p}_2$ above the hyperplane and the solution $\mathbf{p}_3$ lies on the hyperplane.

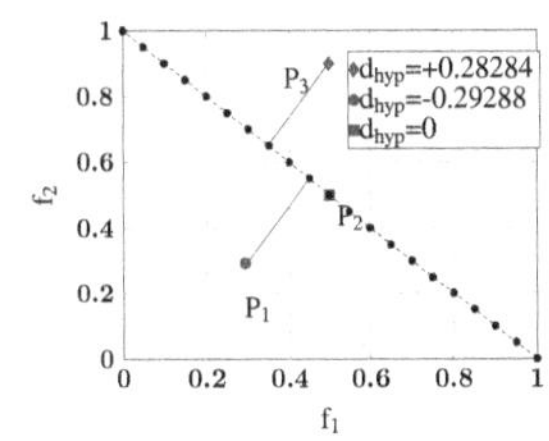

Figure 4: An example of normal from a solution to the hyperplane

Since a hyperplane is inherently constructed in most decomposition based evolutionary algorithms [1,6,25], computation of (d_{hyp}) does not incur any additional cost. *It is to be noted that while comparing two or more fronts, each front is normalized with respect to its own Ideal and Nadir points instead of a combined front, since d_{hyp} attempts to characterize nature of an individual front.* This is unlike other two metrics (M-DI and d_2) where normalization is based on Ideal and Nadir points of a combined non-dominated front.

3. RESULTS AND DISCUSSION

In this section, we analyze several NDFs using the metrics introduced in the previous section. First, the metrics are computed for three bi-objective POFs of artificially created linear, convex and non-convex fronts for illustration. Thereafter, the metrics are computed for NDFs delivered by DBEA and NDEA for two well-known benchmark functions, DTLZ1 and DTLZ2 [9] for 3, 5, 10 and 15-objective problems. Results for a problem with mixed Pareto front, DEB3DK [3], are also presented.

3.1 Illustrative Bi-objective Examples

The metrics M-DI, d_{hyp} and d_2 of the fronts are presented below in Figure 5. Take note that these solutions have been artificially constructed and used as a representative NDF.

The M-DI metrics for all three approximations are 1 indicating good diversity. As for the d_{hyp} metric, the values for the solutions are 0 for the linear front. For the convex front, such a value ranges

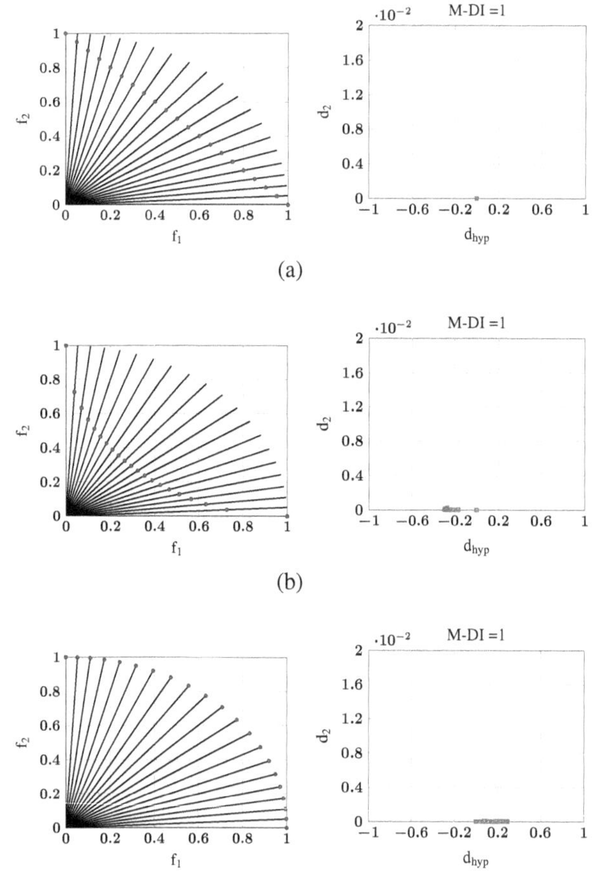

Figure 5: Pareto optimal fronts and their corresponding metrics (M-DI, d_{hyp} and d_2) (a) linear, (b) convex and (c) non-convex front for a 2-objective problem

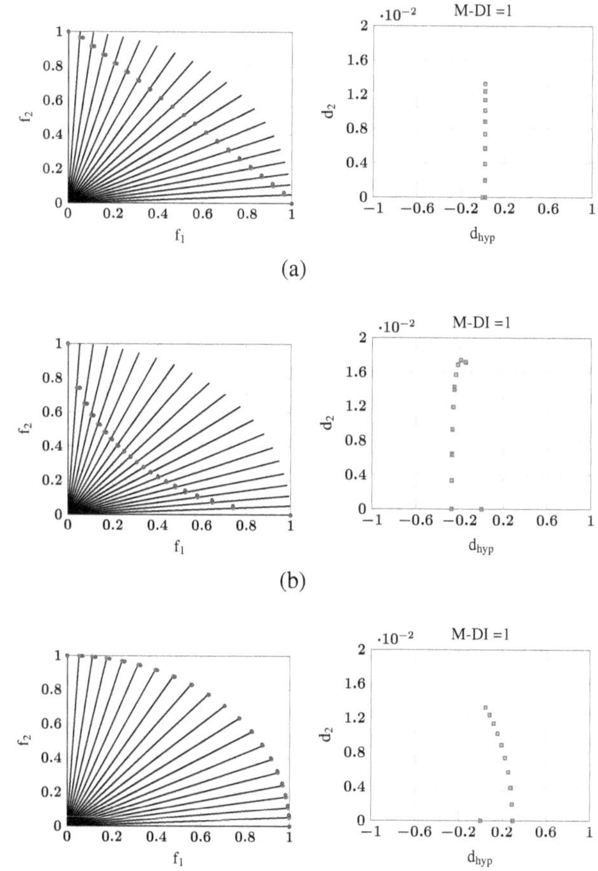

Figure 6: Pareto optimal fronts and their corresponding metrics (M-DI, d_{hyp} and d_2) (a) linear, (b) convex and (c) non-convex front for a 2-objective problem

between 0 to -0.29 while that for the non-convex front varies between 0 and 0.29. As mentioned before, positive range would indicate that the front is non-convex and a negative value would mean otherwise. One can also notice that the d_2 metrics are all 0 for all the approximations indicating perfect alignment with the reference directions.

In the event the points on the front are slightly offset (compared to the above) as illustrated in Figure 6, the M-DI and d_{hyp} metrics would remain roughly the same (since the solutions are still in their respective grids) with marginal variations in the d_2 metric.

3.2 Examples with three or more objectives

Having illustrated the behavior of the metrics bi-objective NDF, we next consider problems with ≥ 3 objectives. Instead of synthetically constructed solutions, we use the solutions delivered by two fundamentally different approaches: (a) decomposition based evolutionary algorithm (DBEA) [1] and (b) a non-domination based evolutionary algorithm (NDEA), which is same as NSGA-II [7] except minor modifications in binary tournament and simulated binary crossover to deal with with odd number of solutions in the population. Experiments are done on DTLZ1 and DTLZ2 problems with 3, 5, 10 and 15-objectives. While NDEA is not really designed to deal with problems involving many-objectives due to the limitations of non-dominated sorting, we use it in this study as a means to obtain a representative NDF. To generate the solutions uniformly on the hyperplane, systematic sampling [5] is adopted. Population sizes of 91, 126, 220 and 680 have been used for 3, 5, 10 and 15 objective problems respectively. These numbers correspond to the number of directions generated using the systematic sampling (Equation 1) with the number of divisions set as $s = 12, 5, 3, 3$, respectively. The probability of crossover is set to 0.9 and the probability of mutation is set to 0.1. The distribution index of crossover and mutation are set to $\eta_c = 30$ and $\eta_m = 20$ respectively. The population is evolved over 800, 1000, 1500 and 2000 generations for 3, 5, 10 and 15-objective problems respectively.

NDFs obtained by DBEA and NDEA for DTLZ1 and DTLZ2 problems with 3, 5, 10 and 15-objectives are normalized by the Ideal (which lies at origin for each problem) and Nadir points identified from the combined NDFs for each problem, shown in Table 1. Thereafter, the metrics M-DI and d_2 are computed based on the normalized NDF. Solutions worse than the Nadir point are eliminated in the calculation of these metrics. For d_{hyp} calculations, each front is normalized using its individual Ideal and Nadir points, as mentioned in previous section.

NDFs obtained by DBEA and NDEA for a 3-objective DTLZ1 are shown in Figure 7. One can see visually that the non-dominated solutions obtained by DBEA have a better spread and uniformity over the solutions delivered by NDEA. The M-DI metrics of DBEA

Table 1: Nadir points used for the normalization of the solutions of DTLZ problems

Problem	Obj.	Nadir point (combined) (used for M-DI and d_2)	Nadir point (DBEA) (used for d_{hyp})	Nadir point (NDEA) (used for d_{hyp})
DTLZ1	3	[0.5003, 0.5003, 0.5001]	[0.5003, 0.50026, 0.50013]	[0.40762, 0.36618, 0.50011]
	5	[185.7326, 185.4028, 107.7640, 0.5002, 7.5781]	[0.50007, 0.29845, 0.31028, 0.30845, 0.50015]	[185.73, 185.4, 107.76, 0.40557, 7.5781]
	10	[2.8612, 20.2230, 0.6383, 0.5035, 0.5589, 6.5558, 2.0277, 0.5036, 0.5035, 7.7312]	[2.8612, 20.223, 0.63825, 0.33112, 0.50325, 0.50491, 2.0277, 0.50364, 0.5035, 0.5016]	[0.0096505, 0.0043066, 0.15217, 0.0069722, 0.55888, 6.5558, 6.5195e-05, 0.44334, 1.584e-05, 7.7312]
	15	[0.3898, 0.4354, 0.4474, 0.5753, 1.5775, 0.4753, 9.3764, 0.4917, 0.4927, 0.5625, 0.4962, 0.4988, 0.5001, 0.5002, 4.5118]	[0.38977,0.43538, 0.44739, 0.41665, 0.29162, 9.3764, 0.49173, 0.31331, 0.48637, 0.49618, 0.33196, 0.50009, 0.34518, 0.50029]	[0.0095712, 0.11541, 0.032588, 0.57526, 1.5775, 0.32092, 0.017996, 0.4567, 0.1203, 0.56254, 0.013899, 0.28555, 0.055074, 0.41998, 4.5118]
DTLZ2	3	[1.0038, 1.0000, 1.0020]	[1.0038, 1, 1.0006]	[1.0026, 0.98699, 1.0001]
	5	[1.0070, 1.0009, 1.0002, 1.0008, 1.0132]	[1.007, 1.0009, 1.0002, 1.0008, 1.0003]	[0.97896, 0.94436, 0.98812, 0.96052, 1.0005]
	10	[1.0060, 1.9202, 1.0199, 1.0049, 1.0034, 1.0016, 2.6004, 2.3020, 2.0747, 1.9778]	[1.006, 1.013, 1.0126, 1.0049, 0.9108, 0.91252, 1.0046, 1.0023, 1.0015, 1.0121]	[0.3702, 1.9202, 1.0199, 0.026064, 0.68656, 0.20987, 2.5408, 1.3878, 1.8999, 0.4749]
	15	[2.5159, 2.3202, 2.7287, 1.8590, 2.7207, 2.2677, 2.7588, 2.4507, 2.2809, 1.0093, 2.3574, 1.5720, 3.0515, 2.3513, 3.0624]	[1.0114, 1.0082, 1.0104, 1.0115, 1.0058, 1.005, 1.0027, 1.0174, 1.0043, 1.0093, 1.0101, 1.0035, 1.0065, 1.0085, 1.0107]	[2.4981, 2.3202, 2.5754, 1.859, 2.668, 2.2447, 2.7588, 2.3957, 2.2703, 0.99712, 2.3574 1.5047, 3.0515, 2.1392, 2.8994]

Note: Ideal points for all above instances is at the origin ([0,0,...]).

and NDEA are 1 and 0.69231 confirming the visual observation. The d_{hyp} value for the solutions obtained by both algorithms are in the order of 1e-3 indicating that they lie on a linear front. The d_2 metric for DBEA solutions is 0, while for NDEA it spans between 0 and 0.19. Thus the solutions delivered by DBEA are perfectly aligned to the reference directions which also suggests that the front is likely to be continuous.

Figure 9 shows the non-convex NDFs for a 3-objective DTLZ2 problem as delivered by DBEA and NDEA. Once again, one can see visually that the non-dominated solutions obtained by DBEA have a better spread and uniformity over the solutions delivered by NDEA. The M-DI metrics of DBEA and NDEA are 0.99451 and 0.71978 respectively, confirming the visual observation. The d_{hyp} metric of the solutions obtained by DBEA span between 0 and 0.4 and that of NDEA span between 0 and 0.3. These positive values suggest that the front is non-convex. In terms of d_2 metric, DBEA obtains 0, while that of NDEA spans between 0 and 0.14. This clearly suggests that the solutions delivered by DBEA are perfectly aligned to the reference directions, while solutions delivered by NDEA deviate by a small margin. DCI metrics for both DTLZ1 and DTLZ2 are also shown in Figures 8 and 10. It is seen that while relative diversity of the two sets is captured correctly using DCI, the values do not give an idea of how good the overall diversity is.

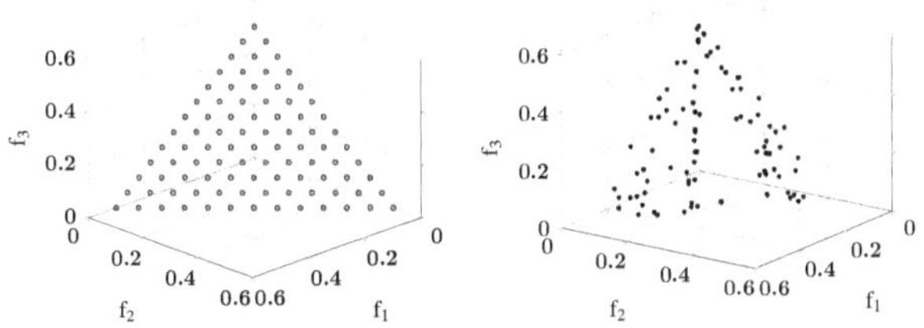

Figure 7: Non-dominated solutions obtained by DBEA and NSGA2 for DTLZ1 problem (3-objective)

Pareto front approximations for problems with larger number of objectives cannot be visually analyzed and hence we resort to the use of the above metrics for characterization. The Nadir and Ideal points used for normalization are mentioned in Table 1. The d_2 versus d_{hyp} metrics for the NDFs obtained using DBEA and NDEA for DTLZ1, 5, 10 and 15-objective are presented in Figures 11–12.

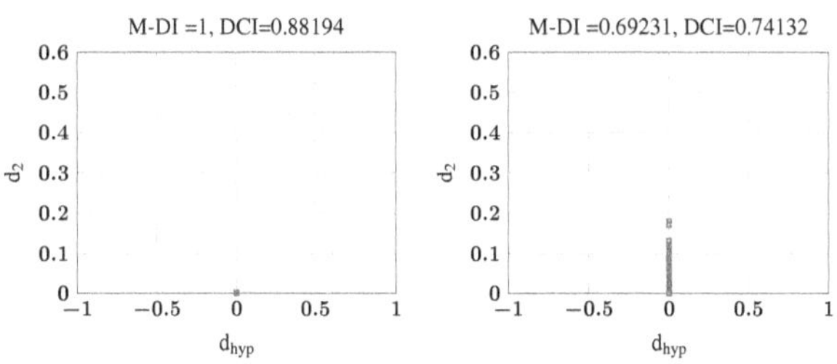

Figure 8: Metrics (M-DI, d_{hyp} and d_2) for the solutions obtained by DBEA and NDEA for DTLZ1 problem (3-objective)

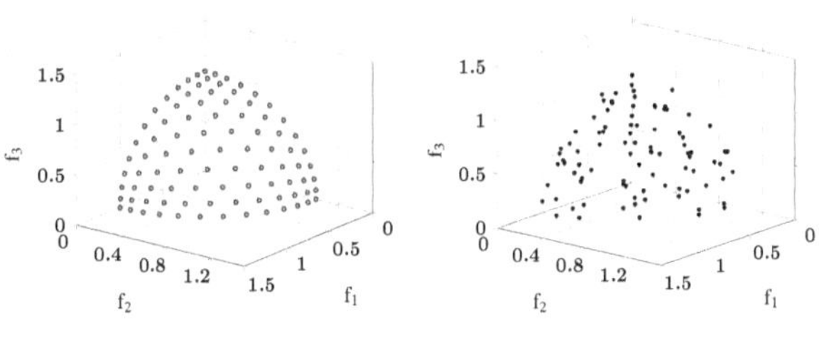

Figure 9: Non-dominated solutions obtained by DBEA and NDEA for DTLZ2 problem (3-objective)

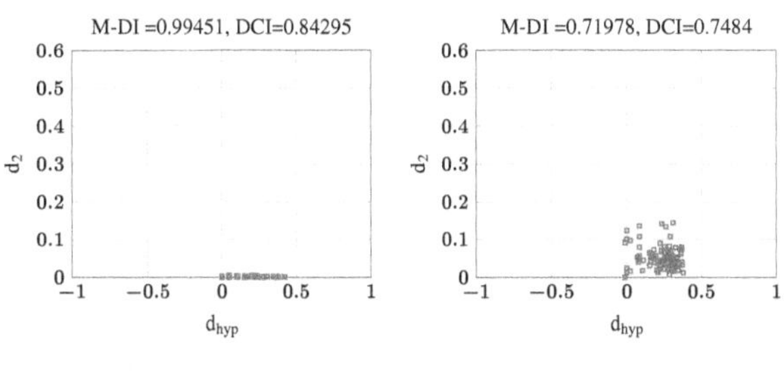

Figure 10: Metrics (M-DI, d_{hyp} and d_2) for the solutions obtained by DBEA and NDEA for DTLZ2 problem (3-objective)

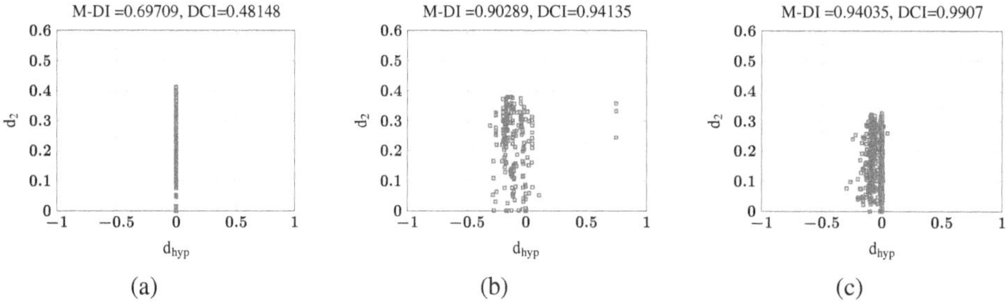

Figure 11: Metrics (M-DI, d_{hyp} and d_2) for 5, 10 and 15-objective DTLZ1 problem obtained by DBEA

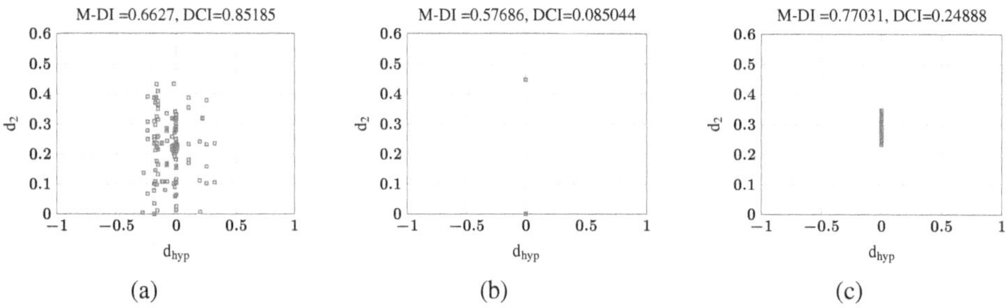

Figure 12: Metrics (M-DI, d_{hyp} and d_2) for 5, 10 and 15-objective DTLZ1 problem obtained by NDEA

The M-DI metric for the NDFs delivered by DBEA and NDEA for 5 objective problem are 0.6970 and 0.6627 respectively. The corresponding values for 10 and 15 objective problems are {0.90289, 0.57686} and {0.94035, 0.77031}. One can observe that the diversity of the solutions delivered by DBEA is better than that obtained using NDEA. In terms of the d_{hyp} metric, DBEA solutions obtain values close to 0 (for most of the solutions) for 5, 10 and 15 objective formulations. One can notice that such a measure for solutions delivered by NDEA has a greater variance. A value of 0 or nearly 0 suggests the presence of a linear front (if convergence is attained). In terms of d_2, solutions delivered by DBEA seems to me marginally better aligned than those obtained using NDEA. This is not surprising as NDEA would tend to use crowding to spread the solutions since most of them would be non-dominated with respect to each other. It is also important to highlight that several solutions delivered by NDEA were eliminated as they were dominated by Nadir computed based on the combined NDF.

For 5, 10 and 15 objective DTLZ2 problems, the Nadir and Ideal points used for normalization are mentioned in Table 1. The d_2 versus d_{hyp} metrics for Pareto front approximations obtained using DBEA and NDEA for DTLZ2, 5, 10 and 15 objectives are presented in Figures 13 and 14.

The M-DI metrics for the NDFs delivered by DBEA and NDEA for 5 objective problem are 1.0000 and 0.7619 respectively. The corresponding values for 10 and 15 objective problems are {0.93595, 0.69835} and {0.97132, 0.86020}. One can observe that the diversity of the solutions delivered by DBEA is better than that obtained using NDEA. In terms of the d_{hyp} metric, results of DBEA span between 0 and 0.55, -0.06 and 0.27, 0 and 0.23 for 5, 10 and 15 objective formulations. The results of NDEA span between -0.13 and 0.49, -0.14 and 0.43, -0.16 and 1 respectively for these problems. Positive span mostly indicates the front is non-convex, which is reflected in DBEA results. Since original front is non-convex, a substantial presence of negative d_{hyp} values in NDEA results indicates lack of convergence. In terms of d_2, solutions delivered by DBEA seem to be better aligned than those obtained using NDEA for 5 objective problem. One can also notice that the non-dominated solutions obtained by NDEA in Figure 14(b) seem to cover a partial Pareto front approximation, since they do not have uniform span on d_{hyp} metric compared to DBEA.

For comparison, DCI metric values are also presented for the above experiments in the respective figures. It is seen that for some cases, there could be mismatch in relative values of M-DI and DCI (e.g., 5-objective DTLZ1 and 15-objective DTLZ2 results). This may be due to the division size used for DCI which can affect the relative values of the metric [16].

3.3 Study of Mixed Shaped Pareto front Approximations

Lastly we present the results for a three objective optimization problem with mixed (convex/concave) front (DEB3DK) [3]. A population of 528 individuals are evolved for 1000 generations for both DBEA and NDEA. Results of a typical run are shown in Figure 15. One can observe visually a better distribution delivered by DBEA. The metrics are computed on the normalized set of solutions with the combined Nadir point as {16.52100, 8.12620, 8.97620}. For d_{hyp} calculation the individual Nadir points are {16.5210, 8.1262, 8.9762} and {15.9352, 7.8979, 8.7420} for DBEA and NDEA respectively. The Ideal points are at origin for both the algorithms. The M-DI values of DBEA and NDEA are 0.65199 and 0.55777. The d_{hyp} values for DBEA span between -0.00511 and 0.02784, while that of NDEA span between -0.00565 and 0.02341. The d_2 metric for both the sets span between 0 and 0.2. The d_{hyp} values span across positive and negative values indicates presence of a mixed front (if convergence is attained).

M-DI metric for DBEA shows better diversity. Also, more solutions are located below and above the hyperplane (Figure 16) compared to NDEA.

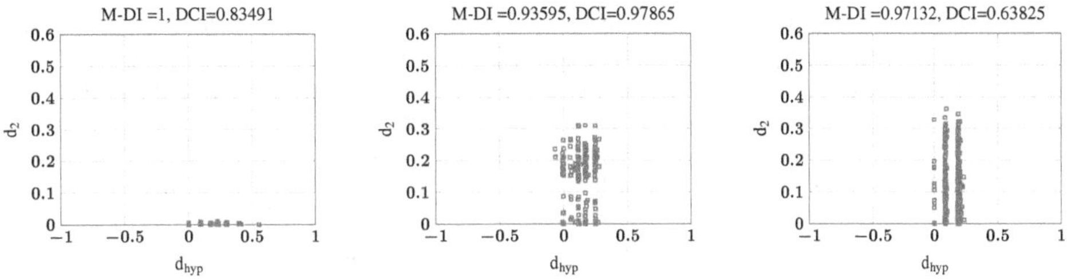

(a) (b) (c)

Figure 13: Metrics (M-DI, d_{hyp} and d_2) for 5, 10 and 15-objective DTLZ2 problem obtained by DBEA

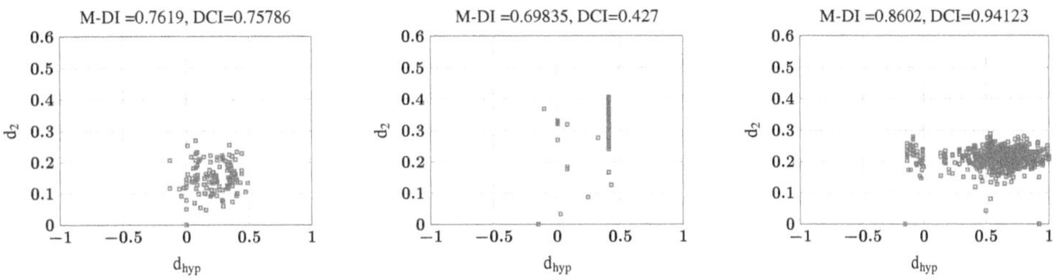

(a) (b) (c)

Figure 14: Metrics (M-DI, d_{hyp} and d_2) for 5, 10 and 15-objective DTLZ2 problem obtained by NDEA

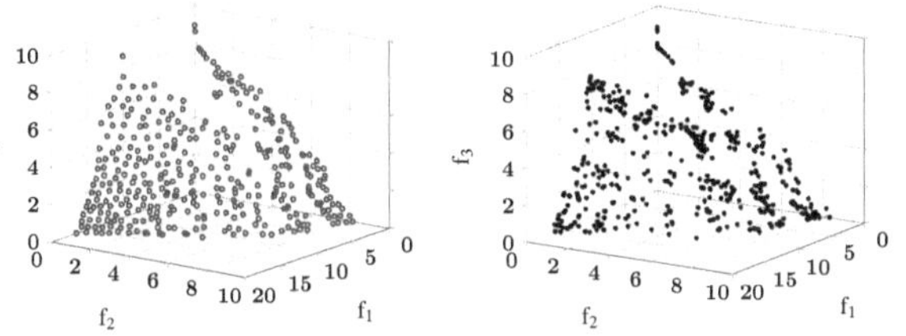

Figure 15: Non-dominated solutions obtained by DBEA and NDEA for DEB3DK problem

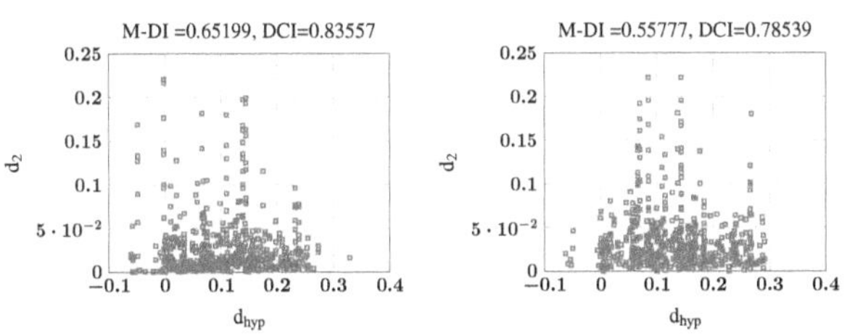

Figure 16: Metrics (M-DI, d_{hyp} and d_2) obtained by DBEA and NDEA for DEB3DK problem

4. LIMITATIONS

Before concluding the paper, it is important to highlight some limitations of the metrics presented. The *Reference Pareto Front* chosen here is a set of uniformly spaced points on a hyperplane with unit intercepts. Most decomposition based MaO algorithms [1,6,25] choose the reference directions by joining these reference points to the Ideal point. However, having a set of uniformly spaced reference points on the hyperplane does not translate to uniformity of solutions on the front itself which could be convex or non-convex as shown in Figure 17. This is particularly prominent when the POF contains large (nearly right-angled) concave or convex bulges. In absence of information about the exact nature of the front, use of such diversity based on projections on the reference hyperplane is adopted in this study. The absolute measure M-DI should also be used with caution for problems with disconnected fronts, although their relative values will be representative of the quality of solution sets. These limitations will be addressed in the future work by using a different way of generating reference directions and/or a different way of projecting them on the hyperplane.

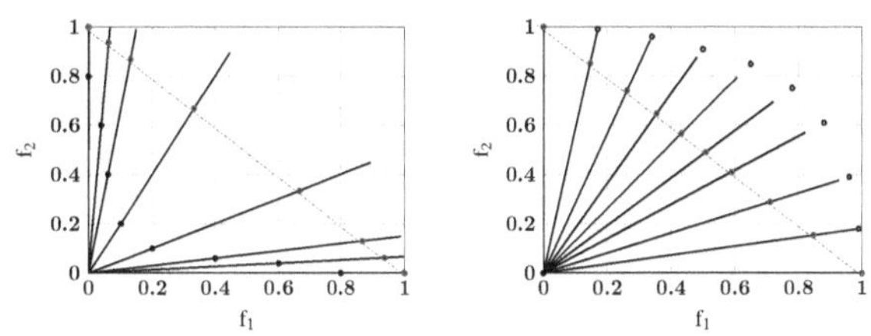

Figure 17: The solutions are uniformly distributed on convex/non-convex fronts but their projections on the reference plane (along the reference directions) are not.

5. CONCLUSIONS

A Pareto Optimal Front (POF) provides the optimal tradeoff information between conflicting objectives. Characterization of POF is important to decision makers. Existing metrics such as hypervolume, inverted generational distance, coverage etc., were originally designed to assess the quality of non-dominated fronts (NDFs) delivered by the algorithms, and provide little or no information about the characteristics of the front, such as convexity. For problems with more than three objectives, existing tools for visualization, e.g., parallel plot, spider/radar plot, and scatter plot also have limited use. In this paper, we introduce an alternative scalar measure of diversity that is suitable for characterizing NDFs for many objective optimization problems. The diversity is measured against an Reference Pareto Front. Two additional metrics, i.e., distance of solutions to the Reference Pareto Front (hyperplane) and distance of the closest solution to every reference direction provides useful information in terms of diversity of the NDF. Computation of such metrics does not incur any additional cost as the standard decomposition based algorithms commonly use these computations during the course of evolution. We illustrate the use of the proposed metrics to characterize problems with linear, convex, non-convex and mixed fronts for problems up to 15 objectives, and also highlight some limitations of the approach. Although limited in scope, the proposed metrics provide useful measures to characterize different Pareto fronts.

6. REFERENCES

[1] M. Asafuddoula, T. Ray, and R. Sarker. A decomposition based evolutionary algorithm for many objective optimization. *IEEE Transactions on Evolutionary Computation*, 2014. Available online.

[2] S. Bandyopadhyay, S. Pal, and B. Aruna. Multiobjective GAs, quantitative indices, and pattern classification. *IEEE Transactions on Systems, Man, and Cybernetics, Part B: Cybernetics*, 34(5):2088–2099, 2004.

[3] J. Branke, K. Deb, H. Dierolf, and M. Osswald. Finding knees in multi-objective optimization. In *Parallel Problem Solving from Nature - PPSN VIII*, volume 3242, pages 722–731. 2004.

[4] P. Czyzzak and A. Jaszkiewicz. Pareto simulated annealing–a metaheuristic technique for multiple-objective combinatorial optimization. *Journal of Multi-Criteria Decision Analysis*, 7(1):34–47, 1998.

[5] I. Das. and J. E. Dennis. Normal-bounday intersection: A new method for generating Pareto optimal points in multicriteria optimization problems. *SIAM J. Optim.*, 8(3):631–657, August 1998.

[6] K. Deb and H. Jain. An evolutionary many-objective optimization algorithm using reference-point-based nondominated sorting approach, part I: Solving problems with box constraints. *IEEE Transactions on Evolutionary Computation*, 18(4):577–601, 2014.

[7] K. Deb and S. Jain. Running performance metrics for evolutionary multi-objective optimization. In *Simulated Evolution and Learning (SEAL)*, pages 13–20, Singapore, 2002.

[8] K. Deb, A. Pratap, S. Agarwal, and T. Meyarivan. A fast and elitist multiobjective genetic algorithm: NSGA-II. *IEEE Transactions on Evolutionary Computation*, 6(2):182–197, 2002.

[9] K. Deb, L. Thiele, M. Laumanns, and E. Zitzler. Scalable multiobjective optimization test problems. In *IEEE Congress Evolutionary Computation*, pages 825–830, 2002.

[10] A. Farhang-Mehr and S. Azarm. An information-theoretic entropy metric for assessing multi-objective optimization solution set quality. *Journal of Mechanical Design*, 125(4):655–663, 2004.

[11] J. E. Fieldsend and R. M. Everson. Visualisation of multi-class roc surfaces. In *ICML Workshop ROC Anal. Mach. Learning*, pages 49–56, 2005.

[12] C. M. Fonseca and P. J. Fleming. Genetic algorithms for multiobjective optimization: Formulationdiscussion and generalization. In *5th International Conference on Genetic Algorithms*, pages 416–423, San Francisco, CA, USA, 1993. Morgan Kaufmann Publishers Inc.

[13] M. P. Hansen and A. Jaszkiewicz. Evaluating the quality of approximations to the nondominated set. In *Inst. Math. Modeling, Tech. Univ. Denmark, Kongens Lyngby, Denmark, Rep. IMM-REP-1998-7*, 1998.

[14] P. Hoffman, G. Grinstein, K. Marx, I. Grosse, and E. Stanley. DNA visual and analytic data mining. In *Proceedings Visualization '97.*, pages 437–441, Oct 1997.

[15] J. Knowles, L. Thiele, and E. Zitzler. A Tutorial on the Performance Assessment of Stochastic Multiobjective Optimizers. Technical report, ETH Zurich, Switzerland, 2006.

[16] M. Li, S. Yang, and X. Liu. Diversity comparison of pareto front approximations in many-objective optimization. *IEEE Transactions on Cybernetics*, 44(12):2568–2584, 2014.

[17] G. Lizarraga, A. Hernandez, and S. Botello. G-indicator: An M-ary quality indicator for the evaluation of non-dominated sets. volume 4827 of *Lecture Notes in Computer Science*, pages 118–127. 2007.

[18] T. Okahe, Y. Jin, and B. Sendhoff. A critical survey of performance indices for multi-objective optimisation. In *IEEE Congress on Evolutionary Computation*, pages 878–885, 2003.

[19] O. Schutze, X. Esquivel, A. Lara, and C. A. Coello Coello. Using the averaged hausdorff distance as a performance measure in evolutionary multiobjective optimization. *IEEE Transactions on Evolutionary Computation*, 16(4):504–522, 2012.

[20] K. Tan, T. Lee, and E. Khor. Evolutionary algorithms for multi-objective optimization: Performance assessments and comparisons. *Artificial Intelligence Review*, 17(4):251–290, 2002.

[21] D. Van Veldhuizen and G. Lamont. On measuring multiobjective evolutionary algorithm performance. In *IEEE Congress on Evolutionary Computation*, volume 1, pages 204–211, 2000.

[22] D. A. V. Veldhuizen and G. B. Lamont. Evolutionary computation and convergence to a pareto front. In *Stanford University, California*, pages 221–228. Morgan Kaufmann, 1998.

[23] J. Wu and S. Azarm. Metrics for quality assessment of a multiobjective design optimization solution set. *Journal of Mechanical Design*, 2000.

[24] G. Yen and Z. He. Performance metric ensemble for multiobjective evolutionary algorithms. *IEEE Transactions on Evolutionary Computation*, 18(1):131–144, 2014.

[25] Q. Zhang and H. Li. MOEA/D: A multiobjective evolutionary algorithm based on decomposition. *IEEE Transactions on Evolutionary Computation*, 11(6):712–731, 2007.

[26] E. Zitzler. *Evolutionary algorithms for multiobjective optimization: Methods and applications*. PhD thesis, Swiss Federal Inst. Technol. (ETH), Zurich, Dept. Info. Tech. Elect. Eng., Switzerland, 1999.

[27] E. Zitzler, J. Knowles, and L. Thiele. Quality assessment of pareto set approximations. In *Multiobjective Optimization*, volume 5252 of *Lecture Notes in Computer Science*, pages 373–404. 2008.

[28] E. Zitzler and L. Thiele. Multiobjective evolutionary algorithms: a comparative case study and the strength pareto approach. *IEEE Transactions on Evolutionary Computation*, 3(4):257–271, 1999.

Multi-objective Optimization with Dynamic Constraints and Objectives: New Challenges for Evolutionary Algorithms

Radhia Azzouz, Slim Bechikh, and Lamjed Ben Said
SOIE Laboratory, University of Tunis
Bardo, Tunis, Tunisia
azouzradhia@gmail.com, slim.bechikh@gmail.com, lamjed.bensaid@isg.rnu.tn

ABSTRACT

Dynamic Multi-objective Optimization (DMO) is a challenging research topic since the objective functions, constraints, and problem parameters may change over time. Several evolutionary algorithms have been proposed to deal with DMO problems. Nevertheless, they were restricted to unconstrained or domain constrained problems. In this work, we focus on the dynamicty of problem constraints along with time-varying objective functions. As this is a very recent research area, we have observed a lack of benchmarks that simultaneously take into account these characteristics. To fill this gap, we propose a set of test problems that extend a suite of static constrained multi-objective problems. Moreover, we propose a new version of the Dynamic Non dominated Sorting Genetic Algorithm II to deal with dynamic constraints by replacing the used constraint-handling mechanism by a more elaborated and self-adaptive penalty function. Empirical results show that our proposal is able to: (1) handle dynamic environments and track the changing Pareto front and (2) handle infeasible solutions in an effective and efficient manner which allows avoiding premature convergence. Moreover, the statistical analysis of the obtained results emphasize the advantages of our proposal over the original algorithm on both aspects of convergence and diversity on most test problems.

Categories and Subject Descriptors

I.2.8 [**Computing Methodologies**]: Artificial Intelligence – Problem Solving, Control Method, and Search.

General Terms

Algorithms, Design.

Keywords

Constraint handling, Multi-objective optimization, Dynamic optimization, benchmarks, self-adaptive penalty function.

GECCO '15, July 11 - 15, 2015, Madrid, Spain
© 2015 ACM. ISBN 978-1-4503-3472-3/15/07... $15.00
DOI: http://dx.doi.org/10.1145/2739480.2754708

1. INTRODUCTION

DMO Problems (DMOPs) involve the simultaneous optimization of several competing objectives subject to a number of given constraints where the objective functions, constraints and/or dimensions of the objective space and the design space may change over time. Many real-world engineering problems make part of this category of problems such as dynamic multi-objective scheduling and transportation problems, robot navigation, traffic signal control, program selection planning management and so forth. When dealing with such problems, the main difficulty lies on the fact that the optimal Pareto Front (PF) and the optimal Pareto Set (PS) may move over time. Moreover, as the constraints are also time-changing, the feasibility area would not remain unvariant which makes the task of optimization more difficult. Having such complex dynamic behaviors, solving this kind of problems needs to deal with mainly these issues: (1) evolving a near-optimal and diverse PF, (2) preserving the required diversity to ensure a high level of flexibility and (3) driving infeasible individuals toward feasible ones.

Applying Evolutionary Algorithms (EAs) to solve dynamic optimization problems has obtained great attention among many researchers. To the best of our knowledge, the earliest application of EAs to dynamic environments dates back to 1966 [15]. However, it was not until the late 1980s that the subject becomes a research topic. EAs were first applied to dynamic single-objective optimization problems. Several approaches have been proposed such as memory-based approaches [23], multipopulation approaches [4], predictive approaches [19], etc. When dealing with DMOPs, the task of optimization is much more difficult. In contrast to the single-objective case, there are few works dealing with DMOPs which include change prediction approaches [1, 8], memory-based approaches [3], and parallel approaches [17].

In real world, we often encounter problems that not only involve the optimization of several conflicting objectives simultaneously but also have a set of constraint conditions that must be satisfied. Several constraint handling techniques have been developed to be incorporated into EAs. Most of them are restricted to the single objective case [29]. Adapting constraint handling techniques to the multi-objective case is not yet highly explored. Nevertheless, some works have been established such as penalty functions-based techniques [27, 16], techniques based on maintaining the feasibility of solutions [14, 25], techniques based on some special ranking rules [11, 26], etc.

Despite the growing interest given to the use of EAs to solve dynamic optimization problems, most of the research was focused on the unconstrained or domain constrained problems (which are both regarded in this paper as unconstrained problems). Applying EAs to solve constrained DMOPs is not yet highly explored although this kind of problems is of significant importance in practice. Many real-world problems are constrained DMOPs such as optimal control problems, portfolio investment, chemical engineering design like the dynamic hydro-thermal power scheduling problem, dynamic scheduling and transportation problems such as the dynamic multi-objective vehicle routing problems and so forth. In fact, when dealing with such problems, the main difficulties consist on the need to not only efficiently handle the constraints but also rapidly and continually track the changing PF and drive infeasible solutions to feasible ones whenever the constraints change.

Motivated by the lack of attention on constrained DMOPs, we propose in this paper a set of dynamic constrained benchmark functions where the PF, the PS and the constraints are simultaneously time-dependent. The proposed test functions extend the static test suite developed in [12]. Moreover, we propose a new version of a basic dynamic constrained EA, which is DNSGA-II [13], where we replace the constraint dominance principle used to handle constraints by an adaptive penalty function-based technique proposed in [27]. In fact, this constraint dominance principle prefers feasible solutions over infeasible ones which may lead to the loss of some useful information about the infeasible region. This may cause a lack of diversity, mainly in dynamic environments, which leads inevitably to a premature convergence. Moreover, the adaptive penalty function adopted in this work may be useful for DMOPs since it adaptively regulates the penalty term relatively to the proportion of feasible solutions in current population. Thereby, we suppose that no further explicit actions would be needed whenever a change affects the feasible area. The remainder of this paper is organized as follows. Section 2 presents the literature review on this research area. Section 3 presents the proposed dynamic constrained test functions. Section 4 describes the proposed algorithm and details its building-blocks. Section 5 describes the experimental study. Finally, section 6 concludes the paper and gives some avenues for future research.

2. LITERATURE REVIEW

2.1 EAs for dynamic multi-objective optimization problems

When dealing with DMOPs, the multi-objective EA should be capable of attaining a fast convergence which also implies a rapid loss of diversity during the optimization process. Deb et al. [13] extended NSGA-II to handle DMOPs by introducing diversity at each change detection. One of the merits of this work is that it can also solve constrained DMOPs. When the behavior of the dynamic problem follows a certain trend, a prediction model may be used to exploit past information and anticipate the location of the new optimal solutions. Several works have been established using this approach such as the Feed-forward Prediction Strategy (FPS) [8], the Population Prediction Strategy (PPS) proposed recently by Zhou et al. [1], etc. Since the prediction may not be always successful, there is a need to combine such approach with a maintaining diversity mechanism. Moreover, this approach is suitable to only dynamic environments presenting a behavior that follows a certain trend. Several Memory-based approaches have been proposed in the literature. In [3], authors have presented a co-evolutionary multi-objective algorithm based on competitive and cooperative mechanisms to solve DMOPs using an emergent problem decomposition. More recently, Wang and Li [28] proposed new dynamic multi-objective test problems and a new Multi-Strategy ensemble MOEA (MS-MOEA) where the convergence speed is accelerated using a new offspring generation mechanism based on adaptive genetic and differential operators. The main drawback of memory-based approaches is that memory is very dependent on diversity and should, thus, be used in combination with diversity-preserving techniques. Another kind of approaches which is parallel approaches has also been used to solve DMOPs. Cámara et al. have proposed [17] a procedure for the adaptation of the Parallel Single Front Genetic Algorithm (PSFGA) to dynamic environments where the sequential algorithm is decomposed into several tasks that are run on different data distributed between several processors. The main drawback of this work is its sensitivity to the data decomposition. In [24] authors developed a Dynamic Orthogonal MOEA called DOMOEA, which presents a generalization of the Orthogonal MOEA (i.e., OMOEA-II) to dynamic environments. One of the disadvantages of this approach is that the statistical method used has been proven to be optimal for only additive and quadratic models. More recently, Deb [10] presented two different approaches that are usually used when resolving dynamic single-objective as well as multi-objective optimization problems. Moreover, an automated decision-making approach based on the utility function concept has been proposed. The majority of these works are based on some techniques that either detect or predict changes. Nevertheless, sometimes it is difficult or even impossible to detect these changes. Azzouz et al. have proposed the Multiple Reference Point-based Multi-Objective EA (MRP-MOEA) [20] that deals with dynamic problems with undetectable changes.

2.2 EAs for static constrained multi-objective optimization problems

Over the last decade, several constraint handling techniques have been developed to be incorporated into EAs. Most of them are restricted to the single objective case. Michalewicz and Schoenauer [29], roughly classified these techniques into four categories: (1) techniques based on the use of penalty functions, (2) techniques based on the preservation of the feasibility of solutions, (3) techniques based on the separation of objectives and constraints and (4) hybrid methods. As noted in [7], adapting constraint handling techniques to the multi-objective case is not yet largely explored. Some works have been established. We will briefly survey in the following the most interesting ones. In fact, the simplest and the most commonly used method is the use of penalty functions. The main idea behind it is to add a constraint violation measure to the objective function as a penalty term. If the penalty coefficients change with the generation number, the penalty function is said to be a dynamic (adaptive) penalty function. In 2009, Woldesenbet et al. [27] introduced a constraint handling technique based on adaptive penalty functions and distance measures by extending the corresponding version for the single objective constrained optimization. More recently in 2014, Jiao [16] proposed a modified objective function method with feasible-guiding strategy on the basis of NSGA-II. In fact, the objective function values of an individual are modified using its constraint violation values relatively to a feasibility ratio which is fed back from current population. Moreover, a feasible-guiding strategy is adopted to make use of preserved infeasible individuals and to evolve them towards feasible directions. A second approach consists on preserving the feasibility of solutions either by generating feasible individuals, or removing infeasible region from the search space, or repairing infeasible individuals and recovering them to feasible ones. Harada et al. [14] proposed a few efficient constraint-handling guidelines and designed a pareto descent repair operator that searches for feasible solutions out of infeasible individuals in the constraint function space. More recently in 2009, an infeasibility driven EA was proposed [25] to handle constraints by maintaining a small percentage of infeasible solutions close to the constraint boundaries. To make a separation between objectives and constraints, Fonseca and Fleming [5] suggested to treat constraints as high-priority objectives. They proposed to handle constraints by assigning high priority to constraints and low priority to objective functions, which allows searching the feasible solutions before searching the optimal solutions. One other constraint-handling technique consists on using some special ranking schemes or comparison rules to rank individuals. Deb et al. [11] proposed a constrained multiobjective EA based on the concept of constrained domination, which is also known as superiority of the feasible solution. Feasible solutions constrained dominates all infeasible solutions. When two feasible individuals are compared, the Pareto dominance is used while the level of constraints violation is used when comparing two infeasible individuals. In [26] authors proposed using three different non-dominated rankings of the population. The first ranking is obtained using the objective function values, the second is performed using the different constraints and the third is based on the combination of all objective functions and constraints. Then the algorithm will perform according to the predefined rules. Suganthan et al. [2] proposed a set of constraint-handling techniques to solve constrained problems. In this method, each constraint-handling technique has its own population.

2.3 EAs for dynamic constrained multi-objective optimization problems

Although DMO and constrained multi-objective optimization have received a focus separately, very few works have been done in solving constrained DMOPs. These works have been established mainly using artificial immune systems [30] and particle swarm optimization [9]. However, to the best of our knowledge, when using EAs, very few studies are available. One basic dynamic EA is proposed by Deb [13], which uses the constraint dominance principle used in NSGA-II to deal with constraints. However, since this principle prefers feasible solutions over infeasible ones, it often results in a premature convergence due to the loss of diversity over time.

3. DYNAMIC CONSTRAINED TEST FUNCTIONS

Deb et al. [12] proposed a set of static constrained multi-objective optimization problems (MOPs), denoted as CTP test problems, that challenge algorithms with different difficulties. We propose to modify this test suite into dynamic constrained MOPs that we denote as Dynamic CTP (i.e., DCTP), as follows:

DCTP1.

$$\begin{aligned} & Min(f_1(x,t), f_2(x,t)) \\ & f_1(x,t) = x_1 \\ & f_2(x,t) = t * g(x,t) * exp(-f_1(x,t)/g(x,t)) \\ & s.t.\ g(x,t) = 1 + \sum_{i=2}^{D}(x_i - sin(0.01\pi t)) \\ & c_1(x) = (f_2(x,t)/t) - (0.858 * exp(-0.541 * f_1(x,t)) \\ & c_2(x) = (f_2(x,t)/t) - (0.728 * exp(-0.295 * f_1(x,t)) \\ & x_i \in [0,1], \quad i = 1, 2, ..., D \end{aligned} \tag{1}$$

DCTP2 to DCTP8.

$$\begin{aligned} & Min(f_1(x,t), f_2(x,t)) \\ & f_1(x,t) = x_1 \\ & f_2(x,t) = t * g(x,t) * (1 - \sqrt{\frac{f_1(x,t)}{g(x,t)}}) \\ & s.t.,\ g(x,t) = 1 + \sum_{i=2}^{D}(x_i - sin(0.01\pi t)) \\ & c_j(x) = ((f_2(x,t)/t - e_j) * cos(\theta_j)) \\ & -(f_1(x,t) * sin(\theta_j)) \geq \\ & a_j * |sin[b_j * \pi * (((f_2(x,t)/t - e_j) * sin(\theta_j)) \\ & + f_1(x,t) * cos(\theta_j))^{c_j}]|^{d_j}, \quad j = 1, 2, ..., C \\ & x_i \in [0,1], \quad i = 1, 2, ..., D \end{aligned} \tag{2}$$

where D, C and t denote respectively the number of decision variables, the number of constraints and the time step. The settings of the different parameters is presented in table 1. These proposed benchmark functions present different challenges to the optimization algorithm since the PF, the PS and also the constraints change simultaneously over time. These characteritics make the task of optimization much more difficult than dynamic unconstrained problems. In addition, as presented in [12], these test functions present two kinds of tunable difficulties in a multi-objective optimization EA: (1) difficulty in the vicinity of the optimal PF where constraints do not make a major portion of the search space infeasible except near the optimal PF (the case of DCTP1 to DCTP5), and (2) difficulty in the entire search space where constraints produce different disconnected regions of feasible objective space (the case of DCTP6 to DCTP8). It is worth noting that the source code, the optimal PFs and the optimal PSs of these problems are shared via https://sites.google.com/site/slimbechikh/sourcecodes.

4. DYNAMIC PENALTY FUNCTION-BASED NSGA-II

4.1 Basic idea

Since dynamic constrained MOPs can be seen as static constrained MOPs for a short period after a change occurs, we can borrow ideas from the static constrained MOPs

	D	C	a	b	c	d	e	θ
DCTP1	30	-	-	-	-	-	-	-
DCTP2	30	1	0.2	10	1	6	1	$-0.2 * \pi$
DCTP3	30	1	0.1	10	1	0.5	1	$-0.2 * \pi$
DCTP4	30	1	0.75	10	1	0.5	1	$-0.2 * \pi$
DCTP5	30	1	0.1	10	2	0.5	1	$-0.2 * \pi$
DCTP6	30	1	40	0.5	1	2	-2	$0.1 * \pi$
DCTP7	30	1	40	5	1	6	0	$-0.05 * \pi$
DCTP8	30	2	a_1	b_1	c_1	d_1	e_1	θ_1
			40	0.5	1	2	-2	$0.1 * \pi$
			a_2	b_2	c_2	d_2	e_2	θ_2
			40	2	1	6	0	$-0.05 * \pi$

Table 1: Parameter settings

to deal with constraints in DMOPs. Thus, we propose to take advantge of a constraint handling technique that was proposed to deal with constraints in a static environment and that has presented promising results and to adopt it to dynamic problems. The basic idea behind our proposal is to integrate into an existing and very well known dynamic multi-objective EA a constraint-handling technique presenting an ability to not only handle constraints but also to preserve and drive prominent infeasible individuals towards feasible ones. By doing so, we suppose that the constraint-handling technique should be able to find feasible individuals and to mantain some infeasible solutions allowing to avoid premature convergence; while the dynamic EA would be able to ensure the diversity in the population and to track changing PFs. To this purpose, we choose to combine the basic dynamic EA DNSGA-II with the adaptive penalty function proposed in [27]. Moreover, we replace the constraint-dominance principle used in DNSGA-II by the standard Pareto dominance. The resulting algorithm is called Dynamic Constrained NSGA-II and is denoted as DC-NSGA-II. In the following, we give a brief description of DNSGA-II and the adaptive penalty function. Then, we describe the proposed algorithm DC-NSGA-II.

4.2 Dynamic NSGA-II: DNSGA-II

In [13], Deb et al. extended the NSGA-II procedure in order to handle DMOPs and track changing optimal PF. Firstly, they introduce a test to identify whether there is a change in the problem through randomly picking a few solutions from the parent population and re-evaluating their objective functions values and their constraints. Then, if a change is detected in the problem, the parent population is re-evaluated before merging it with child population. Moreover, diversity is introduced in a first version (DNSGA-II-A) through the replacement of $\zeta\%$ of the new population with new randomly created solutions. In the second version (DNSGA-II-B), diversity is ensured by replacing $\zeta\%$ of the new population with mutated solutions. One of the merits of these procedures is that they can also solve constrained DMOPs using the constraint-dominance principle. However, the main drawback of this principle is that it may lose some potential information of the infeasible region which may lead to a premature convergence. This is why in this work we propose to replace this constraint-handling technique by the use of an adaptive penalty function.

4.3 Constraint handling mechanism: An adaptive penalty function

In [27], a constraint handling technique for multiobjective EAs is proposed based on an adaptive penalty function and a distance measure. In fact, Constrained MOPs are converted into MOPs by using a modified objective functions that include distance measure and adaptive penalty. Both of them are constituted by combining adaptively the normalized constraint violations and the normalized objective functions relatively to a parameter r_f, which is decided by the proportion of feasible solutions in current population. Then, the modified objective functions are used in the nondominance sorting to facilitate the search of optimal solutions not only in the feasible space but also in the infeasible regions since this penalty function can make some infeasible solutions with good objective functions values and low constraint violation values be selected. The modified objective value $F_i(x)$ of the ith objective has two components: distance measure $d_i(x)$ and adaptive penalty $p_i(x)$. The two components are calculated as follows:

$$F_i(x) = d_i(x) + p_i(x) \tag{3}$$

$$d_i(x) = \begin{cases} v(x), & if\ r_f = 0 \\ \sqrt{\tilde{f}_i(x)^2 + v(x)^2}, & otherwise \end{cases} \tag{4}$$

$$p_i(x) = (1 - r_f)X_i(x) + r_f Y_i(x) \tag{5}$$

$$X_i(x) = \begin{cases} 0, & if\ r_f = 0 \\ v(x), & otherwise \end{cases} \tag{6}$$

$$Y_i(x) = \begin{cases} 0, & if\ x\ is\ a\ feasible\ solution \\ \tilde{f}_i(x), & if\ x\ is\ an\ infeasible\ solution \end{cases} \tag{7}$$

where $\tilde{f}_i(x)$, $v(x)$ and r_f represent respectively the ith normalized objective function value, the sum of the normalized constraints violation values and the feasibility ratio that calculates the ratio of the feasible individuals in current population. One of the merits of this adaptive penalty is its flexibility ensuring the efficiency of the use of infeasible individuals. As presented in [27] and with reference to equations 3, 4, 5, 6 and 7, we can state the following:

- If there are no feasible individuals in the population, the objective values will be totally disregarded allowing to find feasible individuals before looking for optimal solutions.
- If there are no infeasible individuals in the population, individuals will be compared based only on their objective functions values.
- If there are feasible individuals in the population, then individuals with both low objective functions values and low constraint violation values will be preferred
- If two individuals have close distance values, then the penalty term determines the dominant one. If r_f is small, the inividual closer to the feasible space will be dominant. If r_f is high, the individual with smaller objective functions values will be dominant. Otherwise, both individuals will be nondominant solutions.

4.4 Dynamic Constrained NSGA-II: DC-NSGA-II

The penalty function adopted in this work is self adaptive and it permits to guide the search either towards the feasibile area or the optimal region relatively to the current population. Such feature is highly recommended in dynamic environments. Thus, by incorporating it into a dynamic EA, we suppose that a diversity introduction mechanism would be sufficient to handle constraints changes affecting the feasible area and no further explicit actions would be needed. Thereby, we propose to integrate the adaptive penalty function into DNSGA-II, in its two versions (i.e., DNSGA-II-A and DNSGA-II-B). Moreover, we use the modified objective functions values in the nondominance ranking to replace the constraint dominance principle. This combination will permit to handle both changes of objective functions and constraints. Also, we propose to modify the diversity introduction mechanism. In fact, since accepting infeasible solutions may slow down convergence, we suggest to add a feasibility condition before incorporating any random or mutated solution into the population. This may prevents infeasible solutions to be integrated into the population. Thus, we propose to iterate over the procedure of generating a new solution randomly or by mutation until this solution is feasible or a fixed maximum number of iterations is reached. This will permit to control the new added solutions which should guide the rest of the population towards the new feasible regions. The flowchart of the proposed algorithm DC-NSGA-II is presented in figure 1. We denote by DC-NSGA-II-A and DC-NSGA-II-B respectively DC-NSGA-II where the diversity is introduced through the replacement of some individuals with randomly generated solutions and DC-NSGA-II where the diversity is introduced through the replacement of some individuals with mutated solutions.

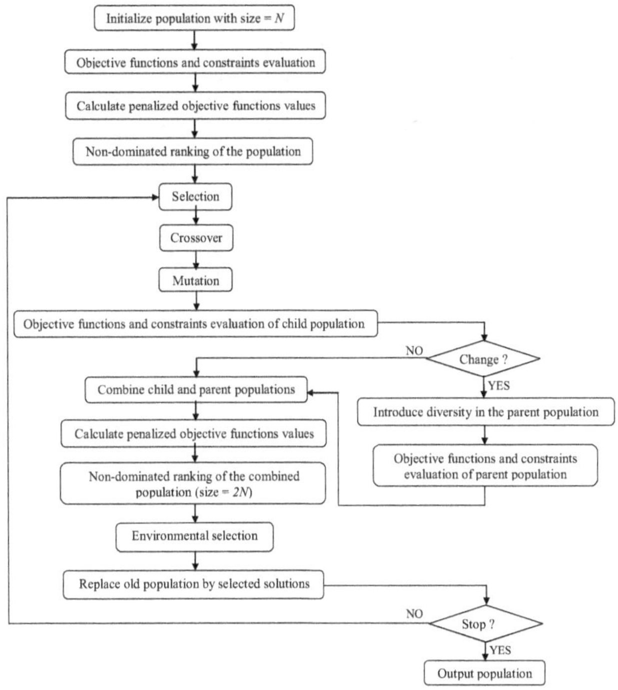

Figure 1: The flowchart of DC-NSGA-II.

5. EXPERIMENTAL STUDY

5.1 Performance metrics

5.1.1 *Convergence indicators*

We have opted to the use of the Inverted Generational Distance metric (IGD) [18] and the the HyperVolume (HV) Ratio metric ($HVRatio$) [6]. The IGD measures the gap between the optimal PF and the optimized one. The $HVRatio$ is the ratio between the HV of the obtained PF and the HV of the optimal one. The HV of a set A with respect to a RP ref denoted by $HV(A, ref)$ is the hyperarea of the set $R(A, ref)$. $HV(A, ref)$ measures how much of the objective space is dominated by A [6].

5.1.2 *Diversity indicator*

As a diversity indicator, we have used the maximum spread metric for dynamic environments (MS') introduced in [3].

In this work, for all performance indicators we use the mean indicator over time. Let θ be an indicator, the mean θ, denoted by $\overline{\theta}$, is calculated as follows

$$\overline{\theta} = \frac{1}{nbChanges} \sum_{i=1}^{nbChanges} \theta_i \quad (8)$$

where $nbChanges$ is the number of occured changes and θ_i is the value of θ computed before the occurence of the $(i+1)^{th}$ change.

5.2 Comparative Results

In this section, simulation results are presented using our proposed constrained DMOPs to assess the performance of the algorithms facing different difficulties. Moreover, we confronted our proposed algorithms, DC-NSGA-II-A and DC-NSGA-II-B to DNSGA-II-A and DNSGA-II-B respectively. For all the algorithms, we set the population size to 100 and all other parameters are set as in the original algorithm NSGA-II. For DC-NSGA-II versions, we set the maximum number of iterations before accepting an infeasible solution to be incorporated into the population at the step of diversity introduction to 5. The experiments are performed at a frequency of 10000 evaluations for each time step and with four test environments (t = 1, 2, 3, 4). For each experiment, thirty one independent simulation runs with randomly generated initial populations are conducted. For each test problem and each pair of algorithms, we perform a (two-sided) Wilcoxon test to decide whether or not the difference between the indicated median values (for each performance indicator) for the two algorithms is statistically significant on the considered problem instance. The results of the significance tests for the pairwise comparisons at level $\alpha = 0.05$ are presented in the form of (-: no significance) and (+: significance) respective appearence order of the algorithms.

Table 2 illustrates the obtained statistical results for the $\overline{IGD}$, $\overline{HVRatio}$ and $\overline{MS'}$ metrics. The PFs found by different algorithms after a single run for each test problem are drawn in figure 2. Relying upon table 2 and figure 2, we can infer the following conclusions. When observing the results of DCTP1, we can state that the optimal solutions found by DC-NSGA-II-A and DC-NSGA-II-B are widely spread and have respectively better convergence to the true PF than

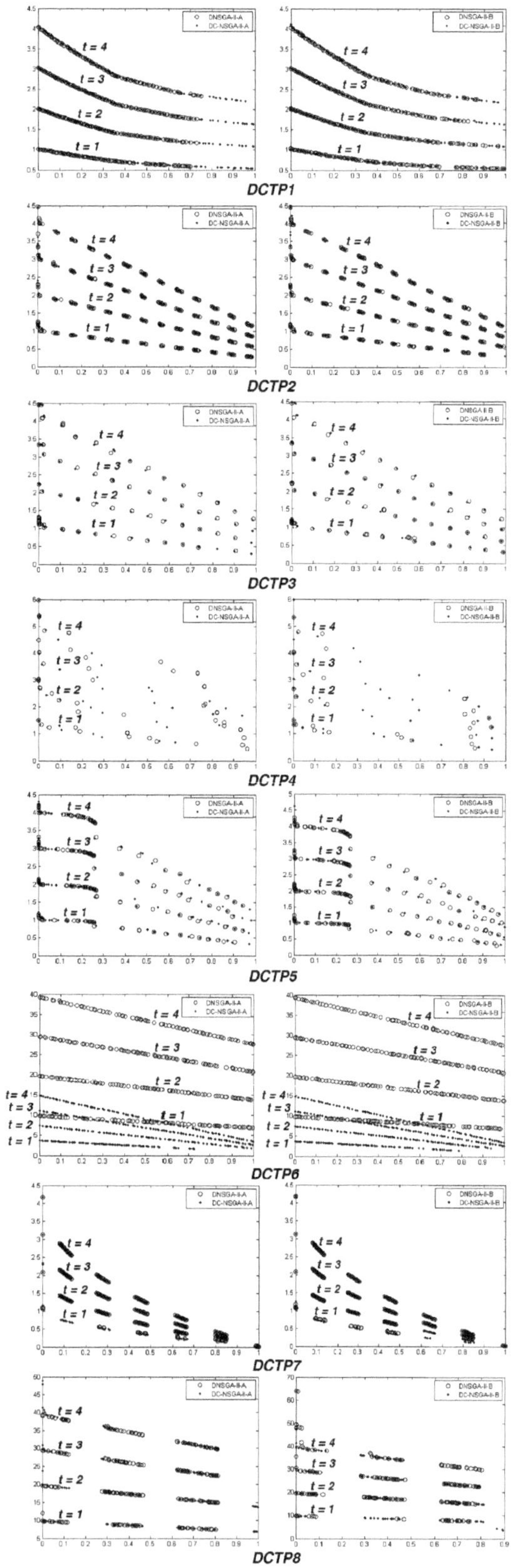

Figure 2: The obtained PFs using DNSGA-II-A, DC-NSGA-II-A (right), DNSGA-II-B and DC-NSGA-II-B (left).

DNSGA-II-A and DNSGA-II-B. The latter ones can only find a small part of the global PF and their obtained optimal solutions are very crowded. This indicates that they were not able to ensure a satisfactory diversity of the population. DC-NSGA-II-A has demonstrated a slightly better performance than DC-NSGA-II-B since random solutions ensure a higher level of diversity and do not give any attention to past optimal solutions. For DCTP2, since the constraint boundary is periodic, this test problem has a number of disconnected Pareto optimal regions at each time step. The experimental results demonstrate that using the penalty-based constrained handling method to keep infeasible solutions gives better results than only preferring the feasible ones. Moreover, the "*filtering*" mechanism used when applying the diversity introduction step promotes the performance of the proposed algorithms. DCPT3 is more difficult than DCTP2 since its disconnected feasible regions for each time step are constituted of only one Pareto optimal solution. With reference to the $\overline{IGD}$ metric, we may observe that our proposals have clearly better convergence than DNSGA-II versions to the global PF. The PF of DCTP4 is similar to that of DCPT3, but it is more complex because its Pareto optimal solutions are far from the constraint region. This is why we may observe the deterioration of the performance of the different algorithms. Nevertheless, the overall quality of the non-dominated solutions found by our proposals still is globally better than the ones obtained by any of the other algorithms. Concerning DCTP5, this test problem has a non-uniform PF which is constituted by a disjoint curve and some discrete points. The optimal solutions found by DC-NSGA-II-A are more approximate than all other algorithms with a satisfactory diversity of population. Moreover, as presented in figure 2, a discrete point near $f_1 = 0$ is still missed for the DNSGA-II versions. Although DCTP6 has a continuous optimal PF, its main difficulty is that its feasible objective space is presented in banded distribution. Thus, it is easy to be trapped in local optimal solutions. Figure 2 and table 2 clearly show that our proposed algorithms can converge to the true PF, while DNSGA-II versions are trapped in local PFs. This points out that their diversity of population should be improved further. When observing the obtained results on DCTP7 which has a disconnected optimal PF for each time step, we can see that the proposed algorithms get comparative performances, while DNSGA-II versions left a part of the disconnected optimal PFs. Finally, for DCTP8, where the feasible objective spaces are distributed in blocks, it was difficult to the different algorithms to avoid being trapped into local optimal PFs. This is because a very diversified population is needed to escape local optimal solutions which may not be the case when we deal with simultaneously time-dependent objectives and constraints. More advanced mechanisms should be used to solve such difficulty.

In summary, for the above test problems, our proposed algorithms behave globally better than the DNSGA-II versions with a statistical significance at level $\alpha = 0.05$. our proposals can not only track the time-varying PFs, but also find effectively the approximate Pareto optimal solutions with a satisfactory distribution. This is mainly due to the use of the adaptive penalty-based constraint handling technique which overcomes the disadvantage of infeasible individuals that always have worse rankings than feasible ones. Moreover, as the constraints change over time, feasible so-

	DC-NSGA-II-A			DC-NSGA-II-B			DNSGA-II-A			DNSGA-II-B		
	$\overline{IGD}$	$\overline{HVRatio}$	$\overline{MS'}$	$\overline{IGD}$	$\overline{HVRatio}$	$\overline{MS'}$	$\overline{IGD}$	$\overline{HVRatio}$	$\overline{MS'}$	$\overline{IGD}$	$\overline{HVRatio}$	$\overline{MS'}$
Md_1	**1,08E-02**	**9,86E+01**	**9,94E-01**	1,10E-02	9,85E+01	9,94E-01	2,13E-02	9,83E+01	9,33E-01	1,65E-02	9,84E+01	9,50E-01
Sd_1	**4,22E-04**	**1,79E-01**	**4,78E-03**	4,37E-04	1,35E-01	7,29E-03	1,38E-02	6,91E-01	4,39E-02	1,06E-02	4,72E-01	3,00E-02
Sg_1	**(+++)**	**(- - +)**	**(+++)**	(+++)	(- - -)	(+++)	(++ -)	(++ -)	(++ -)	(++ -)	(++ -)	(++ -)
Md_2	**5,00E-03**	**9,93E+01**	**9,99E-01**	5,10E-03	9,92E+01	9,99E-01	6,40E-03	9,89E+01	9,81E-01	6,20E-03	9,93E+01	9,99E-01
Sd_2	**2,19E-04**	**1,65E-01**	**3,45E-04**	5,45E-04	1,45E-01	8,37E-04	7,77E-03	4,46E-01	4,11E-02	3,62E-03	2,76E-01	2,31E-02
Sg_2	(- ++)	(- ++)	(- ++)	(- ++)	(- ++)	(- ++)	(+++)	(++ -)	(++ -)	(+++)	(++ -)	(++ -)
Md_3	**3,16E-02**	**9,57E+01**	9,84E-01	3,24E-02	9,56E+01	**9,88E-01**	5,19E-02	9,54E+01	9,32E-01	5,51E-02	9,55E+01	9,17E-01
Sd_3	**9,01E-03**	**2,98E-01**	1,73E-02	1,02E-02	3,46E-01	**2,62E-02**	4,47E-02	1,14E+00	5,74E-02	4,98E-02	1,89E+00	8,74E-02
Sg_3	**(- ++)**	**(- + -)**	(- ++)	(- ++)	(- - -)	**(- ++)**	(+++)	(+ - -)	(++ -)	(+++)	(- - -)	(++ -)
Md_4	1,73E-01	7,36E+01	7,91E-01	**1,58E-01**	**7,37E+01**	**8,44E-01**	3,01E-01	6,61E+01	6,43E-01	5,01E-01	6,05E+01	5,61E-01
Sd_4	1,48E-02	1,21E+00	4,79E-02	**2,83E-02**	**1,78E+00**	**5,86E-02**	1,71E-01	6,04E+00	1,13E-01	2,11E-01	8,42E+00	1,36E-01
Sg_4	(+++)	(- ++)	(- ++)	**(+++)**	**(- ++)**	**(- ++)**	(+++)	(++ -)	(++ -)	(+++)	(++ -)	(++ -)
Md_5	**8,90E-03**	**9,66E+01**	9,40E-01	9,30E-03	9,64E+01	**9,44E-01**	9,40E-03	9,62E+01	9,37E-01	9,10E-03	9,62E+01	9,18E-01
Sd_5	**5,89E-04**	**3,52E-01**	9,62E-03	8,45E-04	3,13E-01	**1,63E-02**	1,90E-03	2,15E+001	1,14E-01	2,23E-03	1,57E+00	7,03E-02
Sg_5	**(+++)**	(- ++)	(- ++)	(+ - -)	(- - -)	**(- - +)**	(+ - +)	(- - -)	(+ - -)	(+ - +)	(- - -)	(++ -)
Md_6	1,04E-01	9,50E+01	8,48E-01	**9,84E-02**	**9,53E+01**	**8,51E-01**	1,16E+01	0,00E+00	1,14E+00	1,16E+01	0,00E+00	1,14E+00
Sd_6	4,64E-02	1,87E+00	6,48E-02	**2,09E-01**	**8,77E+00**	**1,25E-01**	4,66E+00	3,88E+01	1,18E-01	3,44E-02	0,00E+00	5,03E-03
Sg_6	(- ++)	(- ++)	(+++)	**(- ++)**	**(- ++)**	**(+++)**	(++ -)	(++ -)	(++ -)	(++ -)	(++ -)	(++ -)
Md_7	**1,46E-02**	**9,85E+01**	**9,72E-01**	2,29E-02	9,84E+01	9,43E-01	2,68E-02	9,79E+01	9,13E-01	2,66E-02	9,78E+01	9,12E-01
Sd_7	**9,27E-03**	**5,85E-01**	**3,38E-02**	8,74E-03	7,49E-01	2,56E-02	2,45E-02	1,27E+004	4,67E-02	3,09E-02	1,58E+00	6,00E-02
Sg_7	**(+++)**	**(- ++)**	**(+++)**	(+++)	(- - -)	(+++)	(++ -)	(+ - -)	(++ -)	(++ -)	(+ - -)	(++ -)
Md_8	**1,19E+01**	1,94E+01	**2,73E-01**	1,23E+01	**1,95E+01**	2,71E-01	1,28E+01	1,87E+01	2,48E-01	1,23E+01	1,93E+01	2,59E-01
Sd_8	**1,50E+00**	6,53E+00	**1,01E-01**	3,71E+00	**1,87E+01**	1,81E-01	1,63E+00	9,97E+00	1,28E-01	3,08E+00	3,25E+00	4,68E-02
Sg_8	**(- - -)**	(- ++)	**(- ++)**	(- - -)	**(- - -)**	(- ++)	(- - -)	(- - -)	(++ -)	(- - -)	(- - -)	(++ -)

Table 2: Comparisons of statistical results of the non-dominated solutions found by the algorithms. Md_i, Sd_i, and Sg_i denote respectively the median value, the standard deviation value and the statistical significance for the $DCTP_i$ problem for $i = 1, 2, ..., 8$.

lutions at time t may not always remain feasible at time $t+1$ which makes discovering new feasible regions a difficult task. The use of a feasibility condition before incorporating any random or mutated solution guides the population towards the new feasible regions whenever a change takes place. When confronting our proposed versions, we can state that DC-NSGA-II-A has demonstrated a better performance than DC-NSGA-II-B on most test problems. This may be explained by the higher level of diversity ensured by the use of random solutions. This may help the algorithm to discover different search directions and to avoid giving any attention to past optimal solutions.

6. CONCLUSION

Motivated by the lack of attention on constrained DMOPs, we have proposed in this paper a set of test problems that extend a suite of static constrained MOPs where the PF, the PS and the constraints are simultaneously time-dependent. Moreover, we have proposed a new version of DNSGA-II to deal with dynamic constraints. We have replaced the constraint dominance principle by a more elaborated and self-adaptive penalty function. This allows searching for Pareto optimal solutions in both feasible and infeasible spaces. Besides, we have suggested to add a feasibility condition before incorporating any random or mutated solution into the population which may help the algorithm to find the prominent directions of the new feasible regions according to changing environments. The experimental results show that our algorithm is able to handle dynamic environments and to track changing PFs with time-varying constraints. Moreover, the obtained results have demonstrated the advantages of our proposals over the original DNSGA-II versions on both aspects of convergence and diversity on most test problems. This work may be extended in a number of ways. Firstly, as constraints changes can affect the feasibility area, some feasible solutions may become infeasible. Thus, elaborating a feasible guiding strategy that is able to guide these solutions towards the new feasible regions would be an interesting approach. Secondly, in addition to the challenging features characterizing constrained DMOPs, these problems may also suffer from multimodality [22]. More effective mechanisms may be proposed in this case to avoid being trapped into local optimal solutions. Moreover, other future directions for this work are: (1) integrating decision maker's preference information in dynamic optimization [21], and (2) making our algorithm into use to solve real world problems.

7. REFERENCES

[1] A. Zhou, Y. Jin, Q. Zhang, A population prediction strategy for evolutionary dynamic multiobjective optimization, IEEE Transactions on Cybernetics 44 (1) (2014) 40–53.

[2] B. Y. Qu, P. N. Suganthan, Constrained multi-objective optimization algorithm with an ensemble of constraint handling methods, Engineering Optimization 43 (4) (2011) 403–416.

[3] C. K. Goh, K. C. Tan, A competitive-cooperative coevolutionary paradigm for dynamic multi-objective optimization, IEEE Transcations on Evolutionary computation 13 (1) (2009) 103–127.

[4] C. Li, S. Yang, A general framework of multipopulation methods with clustering in undetectable dynamic environments, IEEE Transaction on Evolutionary Computation 16 (4) (2012) 556–577.

[5] C. M. Fonseca, P. J. Fleming, Multiobjective optimization and multiple constraint handling with evolutionary algorithms: Parti: a unified formulation, IEEE Transactions on Systems and Cybernetics-Part A: Systems and Humans 1 (28) (1998) 26 – 37.

[6] D. A. van Veldhuizen, Multi-objective evolutionary algorithms: classification, analyses, and new innovations, Ph.D. thesis, Graduate School of engineering Air University (1999).

[7] E. Mezura-Montes, C. A. C. Coello, Constraint-handling in nature-inspired numerical optimization: Past, present and future, Swarm and Evolutionary Computation 1 (4) (2011) 173 – 194.

[8] I. Hatzakis, D. Wallace, Dynamic multi-objective optimization with evolutionary algorithms: A forward-looking approach, in: Genetic and Evolutionary Computation Conference, 2006, pp. 1201–1208.

[9] J. Wei, L. Jia, A novel particle swarm optimization algorithm with local search for dynamic constrained multi-objective optimization problems, in: IEEE Congress on Evolutionary Computation (CEC), 2013, pp. 2436–2443.

[10] K. Deb, Single and multi-objective dynamic optimization: two tales from an evolutionary perspective, Tech. Rep. 2011004, Kanpur Genetic Algorithms Laboratory (2011).

[11] K. Deb, A. Pratap, S. Agarwal, T. Meyarivan, A fast and elitist multiobjective genetic algorithm: Nsga-ii, IEEE Transactions on Evolutionary Computation 6 (2) (2002) 182–197.

[12] K. Deb, A. Pratap, T. Meyarivan, Constrained test problems for multi-objective evolutionary optimization, in: Evolutionary Multi-Criterion Optimization, Vol. 1993, 2001, pp. 284–298.

[13] K. Deb, U. Rao, S. Karthik, Dynamic multi-objective optimization and decision-making using modified nsga-ii: a case study on hydro-thermal power scheduling, in: 4th International Conference on Evolutionary Multi-criterion Optimization, Vol. 4403, 2007, pp. 803–817.

[14] K. Harada, J. Sakuma, I. Ono, S. Kobayashi, Constraint-handling method for multi-objective function optimization: Pareto descent repair operator, in: 4th International Conference on Evolutionary Multi-criterion Optimization, 2007, pp. 156–170.

[15] L. J. Fogel, A. J. Owens, M. J. Walsh, Artificial Intelligence Through Simulated Evolution, 1966.

[16] L. Jiao, J. Luo, R. Shang, F. Liu, A modified objective function method with feasible-guiding strategy to solve constrained multi-objective optimization problems, Applied Soft Computing 14 (2014) 363–380.

[17] M. Camara, J. Ortega, F. de Toro, Parallel processing for multi-objective optimization in dynamic environments, in: IEEE International Parallel and Distributed Processing Symposium, 2007, pp. 1–8.

[18] M. Sierra, C. C. Coello, Improving pso-based multi-objective optimization using crowding, mutation and epsilon-dominance, in: 3rd International Conference On Evolutionary multi-criterion optimization, Vol. 3410, 2005, pp. 505–519.

[19] P. A. N. Bosman, Learning and anticipation in online dynamic optimization, in: Evolutionary Computation in Dynamic and Uncertain Environments, 2007, pp. 129–152.

[20] R. Azzouz, S. Bechikh, L. B. Said, A multiple reference point-based evolutionary algorithm for dynamic multi-objective optimization with undetectable changes, in: IEEE Congress on Evolutionary Computation (CEC), 2014, pp. 3168–3175.

[21] S. Bechikh, Incorporating decision maker's preference information in evolutionary multi-objective optimization, Ph.D. thesis, University of Tunis, Tunisia (2013).

[22] S. Wessing, M. Preuss, H. Trautmann, Stopping criteria for multimodal optimization, in: Parallel Problem Solving from Nature PPSN XIII, Vol. 8672, 2014, pp. 141–150.

[23] S. Yang, X. Yao, Population-based incremental learning with associative memory for dynamic environments, IEEE Transactions on Evolutionary Computation 12 (5) (2008) 542–561.

[24] S. Y. Zeng, G. Chen, L. Zheng, H. Shi, H. de Garis, L. Ding, L. Kang, A dynamic multi-objective evolutionary algorithm based on an orthogonal design, in: IEEE Congress on Evolutionary Computation, 2006, pp. 573–580.

[25] T. Ray, H. Singh, A. Isaacs, W. Smith, Infeasibility driven evolutionary algorithm for constrained optimization, in: Constraint-Handling in Evolutionary Optimization, Vol. 198, 2009, pp. 145–165.

[26] T. Ray, K. Tai, K. C. Seow, Multiobjective design optimization by an evolutionary algorithm, Engineering Optimization 33 (4) (2001) 399–424.

[27] Y. G. Woldesenbet, G. G. Yen, B. Tessema, Constraint handling in multi-objective evolutionary optimization, IEEE Transactions on Evolutionary Computation 13 (3) (2009) 514–525.

[28] Y. Wang, B. Li, Multi-strategy ensemble evolutionary algorithm for dynamic multi-objective optimization, Memetic Computing 2 (1) (2010) 3–24.

[29] Z. Michalewicz, M. Schoenauer, Evolutionary algorithms for constrained parameter optimization problems, Evolutionary Computation 4 (1) (1996) 1–32.

[30] Z. Zhang, S. Qian, Artificial immune system in dynamic environments solving time-varying non-linear constrained multi-objective problems, Soft Computing 15 (7) (2011) 1333–1349.

Finding the Trade-off between Robustness and Worst-case Quality

Juergen Branke
Warwick Business School
University of Warwick
Coventry, United Kingdom
juergen.branke@wbs.ac.uk

Ke Lu
Warwick Business School
University of Warwick
Coventry, United Kingdom
Ke.Lu@warwick.ac.uk

ABSTRACT

Many real-world problems are subject to uncertainty, and often solutions should not only be good, but also robust against environmental disturbances or deviations from the decision variables. While most papers dealing with robustness aim at finding solutions with a high *expected* performance given a distribution of the uncertainty, we examine the trade-off between the allowed deviations from the decision variables (tolerance level), and the worst case performance given the allowed deviations. A possible application are manufacturing tolerances, where an engineer can specify an allowed tolerance for manufacturing, but a low tolerance requirement incurs substantially higher manufacturing cost, whereas a high tolerance requirement usually means having to accept a lower worst-case quality of the solution.

More specifically, in this paper, we suggest two multi-objective evolutionary algorithms to compute the available trade offs between allowed tolerance level and worst-case quality of the solutions. Both algorithms are 2-level nested algorithms. While the first algorithm is point-based in the sense that the lower level computes a point of worst case for each upper level solution, the second algorithm is envelope-based, in the sense that the lower level computes a whole trade-off curve between worst-case fitness and tolerance level for each upper level solution.

Keywords

robustness; worst-case performance; tolerance level; envelope-based MOEA

1. INTRODUCTION

Many real-world optimization problems are subject to uncertainties that are practically impossible to avoid. For instance, in manufacturing, it is usually impossible to produce an item exactly following the design specifications, there are always some manufacturing tolerances. Typically, evolutionary algorithms aim to find a globally optimal solution. However, if such a solution is very sensitive to small variations of the decision variables or operating environment, in practice, people may prefer solutions that have perhaps slightly inferior quality but also have good *tolerance* to uncertainty. If a solution has tolerance to uncertainty in decision space, we can say it has good robustness. There are a number of different definitions for robust solutions [3], including having a good expected performance and a good worst-case performance.

A survey on robust design optimization has been provided by [1], [13] focuses on evolutionary algorithms in uncertain environments. To date, most of the papers using evolutionary algorithms (EAs) for robust design optimization search for solutions with a good *expected* performance given a distribution of possible disturbances of the decision variables. The main challenge then is to estimate the expected performance efficiently. One of the earliest approaches was probably [22] who suggested to simply disturb the decision variables randomly before evaluation. They show that for the limit case of infinite population sizes, this would lead the EA to search the landscape of expected fitness. To get more accurate estimates of the expected fitness also with small population sizes, researchers have proposed explicit averaging over multiple samples (e.g., [2, 23, 4]) or also to use surrogate functions to avoid costly fitness function evaluations [20]. [11] optimizes a "signal-to-noise ratio" rather than the expected fitness, which is basically a mean of squared fitness values, penalizing variance. Interestingly, [11] doesn't pre-specify the distribution of disturbances, but assumes equal distribution in an area that can also be set by the EA. So, the EA specifies a range for each decision variable, rather than a single value.

While most of the work on EAs for searching robust solutions assumes a single objective function, there are few papers that transfer these concepts to the multi-objective case [7, 8, 11, 21].

Some authors have also used multi-objective evolutionary algorithms (MOEAs) to examine the possible trade-off between solution quality and robustness, again with various definitions of robustness. In addition to the nominal (undisturbed) performance of a solution, [14] consider a variance measure, [19] consider an estimate of the gradient in the neighborhood, and [12] consider the maximum percentage degradation in fitness within a given neighborhood. In [16, 18, 17], robustness is considered as the maximum deviation from the specified decision variables that guarantees that the drop in performance from nominal to realized fitness is no more than some pre-specified threshold. [9] look at the

GECCO '15, July 11 - 15, 2015, Madrid, Spain

ISBN 978-1-4503-3472-3/15/07 . . . $15.00

DOI: http://dx.doi.org/10.1145/2739480.2754711

trade-off between performance and reliability, which is the probability of the solution being feasible.

To our knowledge, no one so far has studied the trade-off between robustness in the sense of acceptable deviation from specified decision variables (tolerance level), and worst-case quality, although this seems of great practical value. A possible reason may be that determining the worst case is itself a difficult optimization problem. In this paper, we tackle the tolerance/worst-case quality problem by suggesting and comparing two nested MOEAs.

The most similar previous approach is the inverse multi-objective robust evolutionary (IMORE) design optimization as proposed in [18] and further refined in [17]. IMORE computes the trade-off between nominal fitness (without disturbance) and robustness (here the tolerance level for decision variable disturbance such that the degradation in fitness is no more than a pre-set threshold). It is a three-level optimization approach: For each solution, the robustness is evaluated by solving a sequence of worst-case searches for different tolerance levels. Obviously, such a three-level search is computationally very expensive.

Our paper looks at a slightly different problem. Rather than searching for the trade-off between nominal performance and tolerance level given a constraint on degradation, we search for the trade-off between worst-case performance and tolerance level. This seems more intuitive and avoids the need to specify an allowable degradation before the optimization takes place.

We propose two different MOEAs for this problem, one of them point-based, the other one envelope-based, evolving a set of sets of solutions. While they are both nested, they only work on two levels rather than three as [17], which should make them more efficient. The two versions are compared empirically on a simple benchmark problem for which the optimal solution is known, and another problem taken from the literature. We also discuss the difficulty of performance metrics for this problem, and conclude that inverse generational distance [15] is a suitable metric.

The paper is structured as follows. First, we formally define the problem we want to solve. Then, in Section 3, we describe the two algorithms proposed to tackle the problem. The empirical evaluation on a simple benchmark problem can be found in Section 4. The paper concludes with a summary and a discussion of future work.

2. PROBLEM DEFINITION

We assume we are given an objective function $f(x)$ and an allowable range for $x \in [x^{\min}, x^{\max}]$. The optimization is not only over x, but the user can also set a tolerance level δ, and the goal is to identify the trade-off between tolerance level δ and worst case performance within the tolerance region $[x-\delta, x+\delta]$, which we assume to be symmetric around x. Without loss of generality assuming a maximization problem here, the two objectives we want to maximize are $f^w(x,\delta) = \min_y\{f(y)|y \in [x-\delta, x+\delta]\}$ and δ.

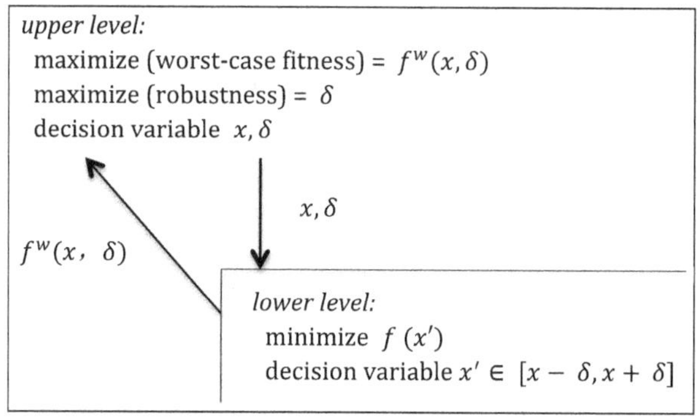

Figure 1: Point-based algorithm framework

To summarize, the aim is to identify all Pareto optimal solutions for the following 2-objective optimization problem:

$$\max \quad f^w(x,\delta) \tag{1}$$
$$\max \quad \delta \tag{2}$$
s. t.
$$x \in \quad [x^{\min}, x^{\max}] \tag{3}$$
$$\delta \in \quad [0, \min\{x - x^{\min}, x^{\max} - x\}] \tag{4}$$

Equation 4 ensures that the tolerance region can not exceed the allowed search space (e.g., a solution at the border of the feasible space can not have a tolerance lever greater than zero). Note that this is a nested optimization problem, as the calculation of $f^w(x,\delta) = \min_y\{f(y)|y \in [x-\delta, x+\delta]\}$ is itself an optimization problem.

An alternative formulation as bi-level optimization problem [10] would look as follows.

$$\max \quad f(x+\beta) \tag{5}$$
$$\max \quad \delta \tag{6}$$
s. t.
$$\beta = \quad \mathrm{argmin}\{f(x+\beta)|\beta \in [-\delta, \delta]\} \tag{7}$$
$$x \in \quad [x^{\min}, x^{\max}] \tag{8}$$
$$\delta \in \quad [0, \min\{x - x^{\min}, x^{\max} - x\}] \tag{9}$$

3. PROPOSED SOLUTION APPROACH

As mentioned before, we propose two alternative approaches to tackle this problem. Both algorithms are two level nested MOEAs. Worst-case fitness and robustness are the objectives to be maximized in the upper level. While the first algorithm is point-based in the sense that for each solution in the upper level the lower level returns a point of the worst case fitness, the second algorithm is envelope-based in the sense that for each solution in the upper level, the lower level obtains a whole trade-off front between worst-case fitness and tolerance level (and we call this front the "envelope"). In the following two subsections, we provide details of the two proposed algorithms.

3.1 The point-based nested MOEA

The idea of the point-based nested MOEA is relatively straightforward, the general structure is described in Figure 1, and the pseudocode for the upper and lower level are provided as Algorithm 1 and Algorithm 2, respectively. The

Algorithm 1 Pseudocode for upper level MOEA of point-based algorithm

```
1: procedure POINT-BASED MOEA
2:     Initialize parent population P (x, δ)
3:     Call lowerEA to evaluate each individual in P
4:     for j=1 to g do                    ▷ g is number of generations
5:         Non-dominate sort P
6:         Generate offspring population O by evolutionary
           operators
7:         Call lowerEA to evaluate each individual in O
8:         Get the union population U = P ∪ O
9:         Non-dominate sort U
10:        Select individuals to form the next generation
           parent population P
11:        Call lowerEA to re-evaluate each individual in the
           new next generation population P
12:    end for
13: end procedure
```

Algorithm 2 Pseudocode for lower level EA for point-based algorithm

```
procedure LOWEREA(x, δ)
    Initialize parent population P' such that each in-
    dividual is within [x − δ, x + δ]  ▷ (x, δ) is upper
    level individual
    Compute the fitness f(x') of each individual in P'
    for j=1 to g' do                   ▷ g' is number of generations
        Generate offspring population O' by evolutionary
        operators
        Compute the fitness of each individual in O'
        Get the union population U' = P' ∪ O'
        Sort U' according to fitness
        Select best individuals from U' to form the next
        generation parent population P'
    end for
return best individual in P'                           ▷ lowest f
end procedure
```

upper level simply optimizes the two objectives 1 and 2 as defined above, with x and δ as decision variables. We use an NSGA-II [6] type MOEA for this purpose. For evaluating the worst case function $f^w(x, \delta)$, the lower level EA is called. The lower level is a single objective EA that tries to identify the worst case within the tolerance region $[x - \delta, x + \delta]$ around the individual x.

Note that there is no guarantee that the lower level EA actually finds the true worst case for the given x and δ. If it doesn't, the individual looks more promising to the upper level than it actually is, and thus has a higher probability of surviving in the upper level from one generation to the next. Because NSGA-II is an elitist algorithm that always keeps the best solution, this could lead to a situation where the population fills up with solutions for which the true worst case has not been found, which is clearly undesirable. To prevent this from happening, we re-evaluate the population after every generation (Step 11 in Algorithm 1). If the worst case found in the re-evaluation is worse than the one found previously, it is adopted, otherwise it is discarded. This makes sure that individuals surviving over several iterations are tested again and again, ensuring that their worst-case fitness values are very accurate.

3.2 The envelope-based nested MOEA

The general structure of the envelope-based nested MOEA is shown in Figure 2, with the pseudocode for the upper and lower level described as Algorithm 3 and Algorithm 4, respectively. On the upper level, the envelope-based MOEA represents and individual only by x (not x and δ as the point-based MOEA introduced above). But in the objective space, each individual is actually represented by a partial Pareto front, which we call "envelope", that has been generated by the lower level MOEA. The idea is somewhat reminiscent to the envelope-based MOEA for portfolio optimization proposed in [5], which used parametric quadratic programming to generate an envelope on the lower level. In our case, the lower level MOEA generates a Pareto front of worst-case $f^w(x, \delta)$ vs. δ trade-off for a particular solution x from the upper level by running an MOEA with the minimization of $f(x')$ and $\delta = |x - x'|$ as the objectives and x' as decision variable. To ensure that the tolerance region only contains feasible individuals, x' is restricted to lie within $[x - \Delta, x + \Delta]$, where $\Delta = \min\{x - x^{\min}, x^{\max} - x\}$ is the minimum distance of x from either end of the feasible space. Note that given the minimization of $f(y)$ and δ as objectives, an individual with maximal tolerance level δ would be dominated by the solution representing the worst case solution within $[x - \Delta, x + \Delta]$ (unless the worst case is actually on the boundary of the feasible space). However, a decision maker would prefer this solution to the worst case solution, as it provides a larger tolerance level with the same worst case within the tolerance level. To resolve this issue, at the end of each lower level MOEA run, we add to the population an "artificial" individual with the worst fitness of all the individuals in the population, and the maximum allowed $\delta = \Delta$ (see Step 12 in Algorithm 4).

On the upper level we maximize $f^w(x, \delta)$ and δ. In each generation, all the envelopes are combined to form the overall Pareto front. Selection has to be done based on the envelopes. In our case, we use a similar procedure as the non-dominated sorting, where an individual/envelope is counted in the first rank if it has at least one point non-dominated in

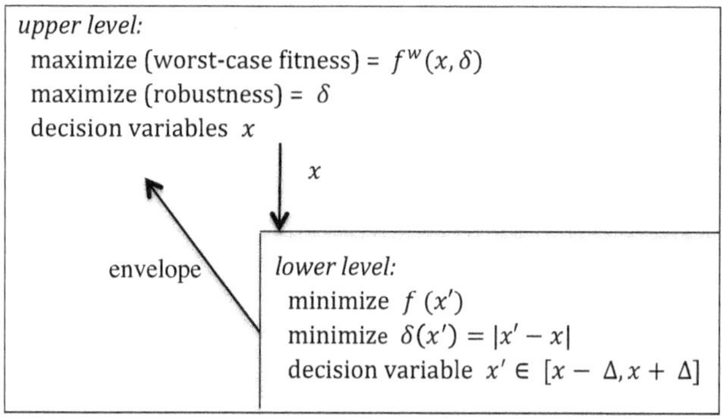

Figure 2: Envelope-based algorithm framework

the union of all envelopes. To rank individuals in the same non-domination front (done by crowding distance in NSGA-II), we have decided to equate the fitness of an envelope with its marginal hypervolume, i.e., the amount the hypervolume would reduce if this individual/envelope were removed from the population.

As in the point-based algorithm, a lower level run that does not identify the true (worst case) trade-off envelope might appear attractive on the upper level, and so all individuals are re-evaluated and the lower level is re-run in every generation. The new envelope is combined with the old one, and the best $(f(y), \delta)$ combinations are kept based on a non-dominated sorting and crowding distance calculations.

Algorithm 3 Pseudocode for upper level MOEA of envelope-based algorithm

procedure ENVELOPE-BASED MOEA
  Initialize parent population P (x)
  Call lowerMOEA to evaluate each individual P
  for j=1 to g **do** ▷ g is number of generations
    Non-dominate sort P, using marginal hypervolume as secondary selection criteria
    Generate offspring population O by evolutionary operators
    Call lowerMOEA to evaluate each individual in O
    Get the union population $U = P \cup O$
    Non-dominate sort U
    Select individuals to form the next generation parent population P
    Call lowerMOEA to re-evaluate each individual in the new next generation population P
  end for
end procedure

4. EMPIRICAL EVALUATION

In this section, we empirically compare the two proposed algorithms using a simple test function for which we can easily derive the optimum, and a test function taken from the literature.

Algorithm 4 Pseudocode for lower level MOEA of envelope-based algorithm

procedure LOWERMOEA(x)
  Initialize parent population P' (x', δ) ▷ x is upper level individual, $x' \in [x - \Delta, x + \Delta]$, $\Delta = \min(x - x^{\min}, x^{\max} - x)$
  Compute the objective values of each individual in P'
  for i=1 to g' **do** ▷ g' is number of generations
    Non-dominate sort P'
    Generate offspring population O' by evolutionary operators
    Compute the objective values of each individual in O'
    Get the union population $U' = P' \cup O'$
    Non-dominate sort U'
    Select individuals to form the next generation parent population P'
  end for
  Add to population individual $(\min\{f(P')\}, \Delta)$
end procedure

4.1 Test functions

4.1.1 Simple test function

We propose the following simple one-dimensional function $f(x)$, which is visualized in Figure 3:

$$f(x) = \begin{cases} \frac{5}{3}x - \frac{2}{3} & \textbf{if } 1 < x \leq \frac{5}{2} \\ -\frac{5}{3}x + \frac{23}{3} & \textbf{if } \frac{5}{2} \leq x \leq 4 \\ \frac{2}{3}x - \frac{2}{3} & \textbf{if } 4 < x \leq \frac{11}{2} \\ -\frac{2}{3}x - \frac{20}{3} & \textbf{if } \frac{11}{2} < x \leq 7 \end{cases} \quad 1.0 \leq x \leq 7.0$$

The function has two peaks. The corresponding true (f^w, δ) Pareto front can be derived as follows. The solution with the best worst-case fitness is clearly the solution at the highest peak ($x = 2.5$) with tolerance level $\delta = 0$. As the tolerance level is increased up to $\delta = 0.5$, the solution $x = 3.5$ remains the optimal solution, but the worst case obviously degrades down to approximately 2.7. If greater tolerance levels are desired, it is better to switch to solution $x = 5.5$. Although the peak is lower, it is also not as steep, which yields a better worst-case performance for larger tolerance regions. At $\delta = 1.5$, there is no solution that would not have $x = 4$ within its tolerance region $[x - \delta, x + \delta]$, and thus the worst case fitness drops to $f(4) = 1$. If this worst case is accepted, δ can be increased to 3 by choosing $x = 4$, which is the maximally robust solution. So, the Pareto set consists of all solutions $(x = 2.5, \delta \in [0, 0.5]), (x = 5.5, \delta \in [0.5, 1.5]), (x = 4, \delta = 3)$.

The true Pareto front is depicted in Figure 4 and can be described mathematically as follows.

$$f^w(\delta) = \begin{cases} -\frac{5}{3}\delta + 3.5 & \textbf{if } 0 \leq \delta \leq 0.5 \\ -\frac{2}{3}\delta + 3.0 & \textbf{if } 0.5 \leq \delta \leq 1.5 \\ 1.0 & \textbf{if } \delta = 3.0 \end{cases}$$

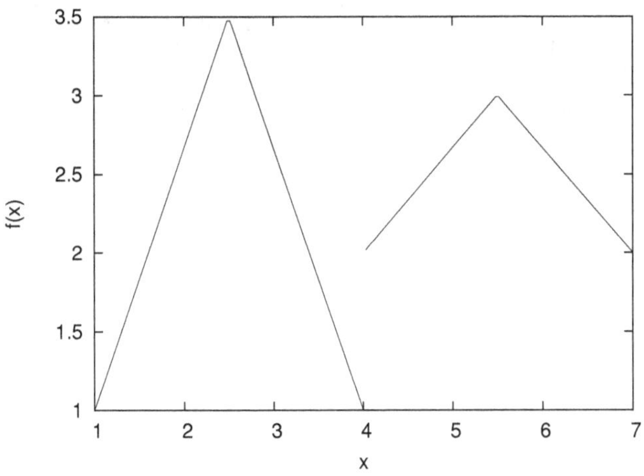

Figure 3: Test function

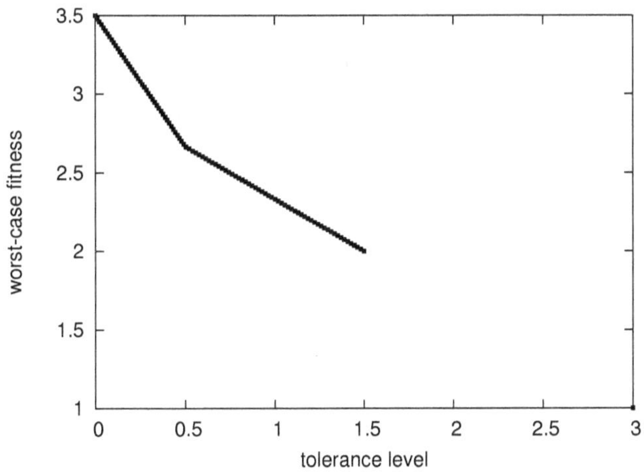

Figure 4: The true Pareto front between worst-case fitness and robustness of test function

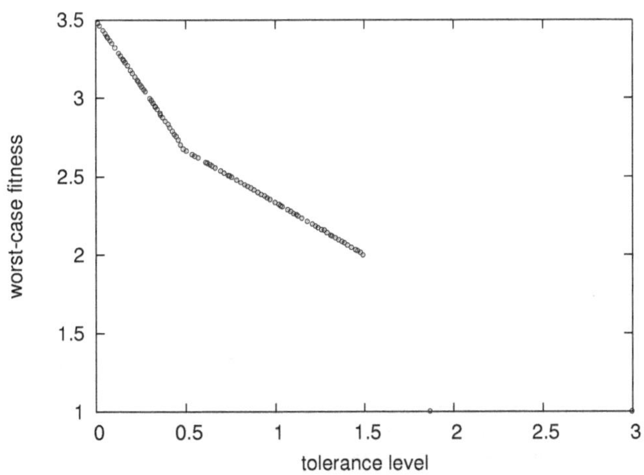

Figure 5: The trade-off between worst-case fitness and robustness of test function obtained by point-based MOEA

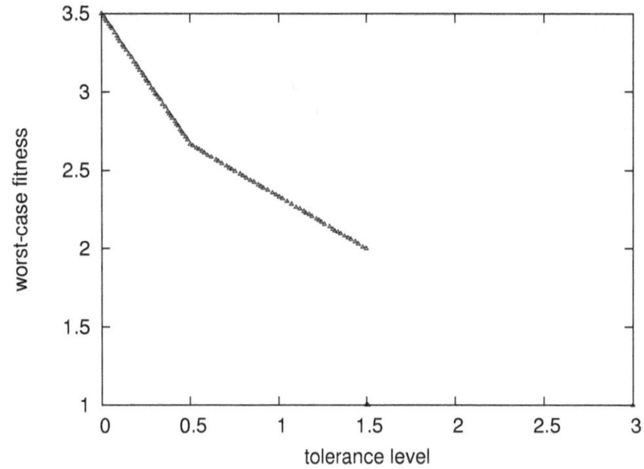

Figure 6: The trade-off between worst-case fitness and robustness of test function obtained by envelope-based MOEA

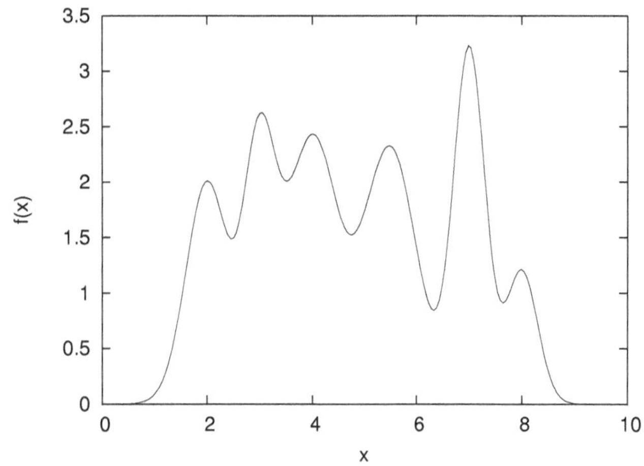

Figure 7: Test function from [18]

4.1.2 Test function from literature

The following test function has been taken from [18]. It has more local optima which makes it more interesting, but we do not know the true Pareto front for this function.

$$f(x) = 2e^{-(x-2)^2/0.32} + 2.2e^{-(x-3)^2/0.18} + 2.4e^{-(x-4)^2/0.5}$$
$$+2.3e^{-(x-5.5)^2/0.5} + 3.2e^{-(x-7)^2/0.18} + 1.2e^{-(x-8)^2/0.18}$$

where $0 \leq x \leq 10$

A plot of this function is shown in Figure 7.

4.2 Performance measure

The most widely used performance metric for multi-objective optimization is probably the Hypervolume [24]. However, in our case, the algorithm may find solutions on either side or the true Pareto front. If the lower level EA does not properly identify the worst case, then the information provided to the upper level EA is too optimistic, individuals will appear better than they are, and solutions to the upper right of the true Pareto front may appear (they do not actually exist, but the algorithm reports them as solution). On the

Table 1: Parameter setting for point-based and envelope-based MOEA

	point-based		envelope-based	
	upper	lower	upper	lower
popsize	100	40	40	100
max generations	250	40	100	100
crossover prob.	0.9	0.9	0.9	0.9
mutation prob.	1.0	0.9	1.0	1.0

other hand, even if the lower level EA computes the correct worst case, the upper level may not be able to find the best upper level solutions, in which case the results will appear towards the lower left of the true Pareto front. Hypervolume would count the former error (solutions perceived as too good) as benefit, and is thus not really suitable.

We therefore propose to use the inverted generational distance (IGD) metric [15]. This metric requires a number of targets along the true Pareto front, and then sums up the distances between each target and the closest point in the Pareto front approximation identified by the algorithm. We have chosen 100 equidistant points along the true Pareto front as targets. Because IGD tends to be smaller if the number of solutions in the Pareto front approximation is larger, and our two algorithm variants have different population sizes, we used crowding distance pruning to reduce the number of solutions returned by each algorithm to 100 before computing the IGD metric. Note that while IGD requires the true Pareto front to be known, this is only for evaluation of algorithm results and not needed for running the algorithm.

4.3 Parameters settings

We identified suitable parameter settings for each algorithm by some preliminary test runs. The number of solutions in the Pareto front approximation of the point-based algorithm corresponds to the number of individuals in the upper-level MOEA, whereas for the envelope-based MOEA, each individual in the upper level may contribute an entire envelope to the Pareto front approximation. Thus, clearly, the upper level population size of the point-based MOEA needs to be larger than for the envelope-based MOEA. On the other hand, the lower level population size needs to be larger for the envelope-based MOEA, as it needs to generate an entire envelope, rather than only search for a worst case. After some testing, we considered the parameter settings reported in Table 1 to be suitable. Note that these setting lead to the same total number of function evaluations for both algorithms.

Both algorithms on both levels use binary tournament for mating selection, arithmetic crossover, and Gaussian mutation with standard deviation of 1.

4.4 Test results

4.4.1 Simple test function

To evaluate the two algorithms proposed, we ran them 20 times on the simple test function introduced above and measured the IGD. Figures 5 and 6 show the final Pareto front approximation by the run with the median IGD of the point-based and envelope-based MOEAs, respectively. As can be seen, both algorithms find very good approximations to the Pareto front, clearly identifying all three parts that make up the front. The front of the envelope-based MOEA seems to be somewhat more evenly distributed.

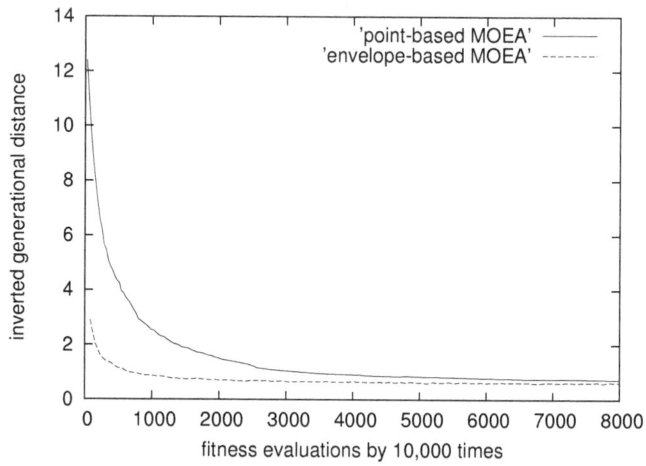

Figure 8: The comparison of inverted generational distance

Figure 8 shows the average IGD of each algorithm over the number of fitness function evaluations. This figure clearly demonstrates the superiority of the envelope-based approach. The algorithm shows a smaller IGD (better performance) from the beginning (2.91 vs. 12.4), converges more quickly, and maintains its advantage throughout the run, converging to a better solution.

On this problem, the envelope-based MOEA is computationally more time-consuming, presumably because the non-dominated sorting on the lower level is more complex. However, if function evaluations are expensive, this computational cost will be negligible, and the envelope-based MOEA will show its full advantage.

4.4.2 Test function from literature

We used the same parameters as above also on the test function proposed in [18]. Since we don't know the true Pareto front for this problem, we can not compute the IGD. However, Figures 9 and 10 show the Pareto front approximation obtained by the point-based MOEA and the envelope-based MOEA, respectively. Conclusions are similar as for the simple test function above. Both algorithms find a very similar front, which indicates that they have converged onto the true optimal Pareto front. Also, the extreme points (minimal tolerance level, $\max\{f^w(x,0)\} = \max\{f(x)\} = 3.23$ as well as maximal tolerance level, $\max\{f^w(x,5)\} = \min\{f(x)\} = 0$) have been identified correctly. Again, the front generated by the envelope-based approach seems to be more uniformly distributed.

5. CONCLUSION AND FUTURE WORK

In this paper, we investigated the trade-off between worst-case solution quality and tolerance level for a problem with uncertainty in the decision variable space. To solve this problem, we presented two nested multi-objective evolutionary algorithms. One is a point-based MOEA that, in the lower level, simply computes the worst-case performance of an upper level solution and tolerance level. With the envelope-based approach, for each solution, the inner level

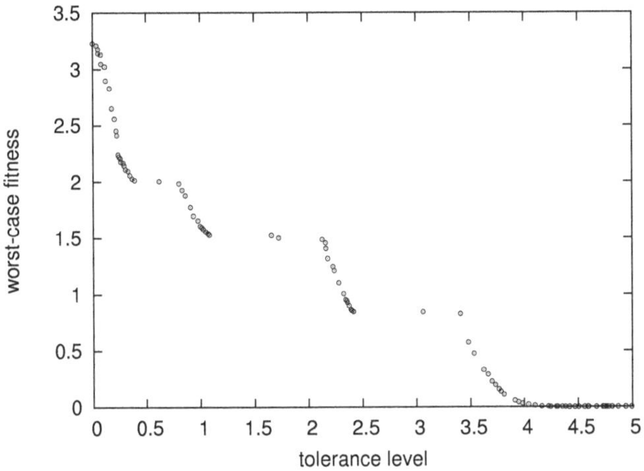

Figure 9: The trade-off between worst-case fitness and robustness of Lim's test function obtained by point-based MOEA

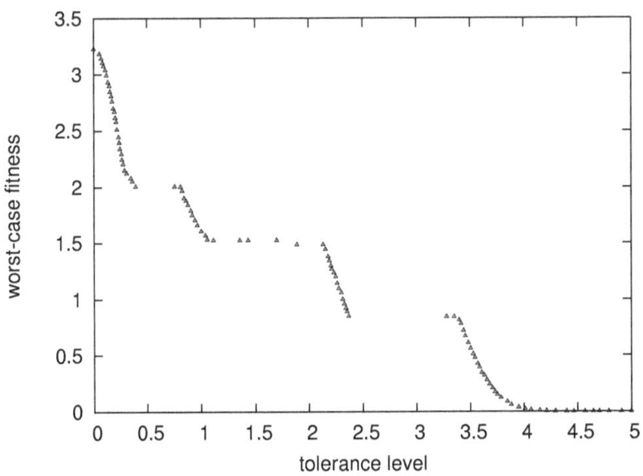

Figure 10: The trade-off between worst-case fitness and robustness of Lim's test function obtained by envelope-based MOEA

computes a trade-off envelope between worst-case fitness and tolerance level.

An empirical evaluation of both algorithms demonstrated that at least for the simple benchmark problems considered, both algorithms can find very good approximations to the true Pareto front. The envelope-based MOEA performed better than the point-based MOEA, with a lower inverse generational distance throughout the run, and a more even distribution of solutions along the front.

There are ample avenues for future work. Clearly the approaches should be tested on additional problems, including higher dimensional and multi-modal test problems or even a real-world problem. Also, the influence of the parameter settings should be studied more carefully.

6. REFERENCES

[1] H.-G. Beyer and B. Sendhoff. Robust optimization–a comprehensive survey. *Computer methods in applied mechanics and engineering*, 196(33):3190–3218, 2007.

[2] J. Branke. Creating robust solutions by means of evolutionary algorithms. In *Parallel Problem Solving from Nature—PPSN V*, pages 119–128. Springer, 1998.

[3] J. Branke. *Evolutionary Optimization in Dynamic Environments*. kluwer academic publishers, 2001.

[4] J. Branke. Reducing the sampling variance when searching for robust solutions. In *Genetic and Evolutionary Computation Conference (GECCO 2001)*, pages 235–242, 2001.

[5] J. Branke, B. Scheckenbach, M. Stein, K. Deb, and H. Schmeck. Portfolio optimization with an envelope-based multi-objective evolutionary algorithm. *European Journal of Operational Research*, 199(3):684–693, 2009.

[6] K. Deb, S. Agrawal, A. Pratap, and T. Meyarivan. A fast and elitist multi-objective genetic algorithm: NSGA-II. *IEEE Transactions on Evolutionary Computation*, 6(2):182–197, 2002.

[7] K. Deb and H. Gupta. Searching for robust pareto-optimal solutions in multi-objective optimization. *Lecture Notes in Computer Science*, 3410:150–164, 2005.

[8] K. Deb and H. Gupta. Introducing robustness in multi-objective optimization. *Evolutionary Computation*, 14(4):463–494, 2006.

[9] K. Deb, S. Gupta, D. Daum, J. Branke, A. K. Mall, and D. Padmanabhan. Reliability-based optimization using evolutionary algorithms. *Evolutionary Computation, IEEE Transactions on*, 13(5):1054–1074, 2009.

[10] K. Deb and A. Sinha. Solving bilevel multi-objective optimization problems using evolutionary algorithms. In *Evolutionary Multi-Criterion Optimization*, pages 110–124. Springer, 2009.

[11] B. Forouraghi. A genetic algorithm for multiobjective robust design. *Applied Intelligence*, 12(3):151–161, 2000.

[12] C. K. Goh and K. C. Tan. Evolving the tradeoffs between pareto-optimality and robustness in multi-objective evolutionary algorithms. In *Evolutionary Computation in Dynamic and Uncertain Environments*, pages 457–478. Springer, 2007.

[13] Y. Jin and J. Branke. Evolutionary optimization in uncertain environments-a survey. *Evolutionary Computation, IEEE Transactions on*, 9(3):303–317, 2005.

[14] Y. Jin and B. Sendhoff. Trade-off between performance and robustness: an evolutionary multiobjective approach. In *Evolutionary Multi-Criterion Optimization*, pages 237–251. Springer, 2003.

[15] J. Knowles and D. Corne. On metrics for comparing nondominated sets. In *Evolutionary Computation, 2002. CEC'02. Proceedings of the 2002 Congress on*, volume 1, pages 711–716. IEEE, 2002.

[16] M. Li, S. Azarm, and V. Aute. A multi-objective genetic algorithm for robust design optimization. In *Proceedings of the 7th annual conference on Genetic and evolutionary computation*, pages 771–778. ACM, 2005.

[17] D. Lim, Y.-S. Ong, Y. Jin, B. Sendhoff, and B. S. Lee. Inverse multi-objective robust evolutionary design. *Genetic Programming and Evolvable Machines*, 7(4):383–404, 2007.

[18] D. Lim, Y.-S. Ong, and B.-S. Lee. Inverse multi-objective robust evolutionary design optimization in the presence of uncertainty. In *Proceedings of the 2005 workshops on Genetic and evolutionary computation*, pages 55–62. ACM, 2005.

[19] B. Luo and J. Zheng. A new methodology for searching robust pareto optimal solutions with MOEAs. In *Evolutionary Computation, 2008. CEC 2008.(IEEE World Congress on Computational Intelligence). IEEE Congress on*, pages 580–586. IEEE, 2008.

[20] I. Paenke, J. Branke, and Y. Jin. Efficient search for robust solutions by means of evolutionary algorithms and fitness approximation. *Evolutionary Computation, IEEE Transactions on*, 10(4):405–420, 2006.

[21] A. Saha, T. Ray, and W. Smith. Towards practical evolutionary robust multi-objective optimization. In *Evolutionary Computation (CEC), 2011 IEEE Congress on*, pages 2123–2130. IEEE, 2011.

[22] S. Tsutsui and A. Ghosh. Genetic algorithms with a robust solution searching scheme. *Evolutionary Computation, IEEE Transactions on*, 1(3):201–208, 1997.

[23] D. Wiesmann, U. Hammel, and T. Back. Robust design of multilayer optical coatings by means of evolutionary algorithms. *Evolutionary Computation, IEEE Transactions on*, 2(4):162–167, 1998.

[24] E. Zitzler and L. Thiele. Multiobjective optimization using evolutionary algorithms-a comparative case study. In *Parallel problem solving from nature PPSN V*, pages 292–301. Springer, 1998.

Obtaining Optimal Pareto Front Approximations using Scalarized Preference Information

Marlon Braun
Institute AIFB, KIT, Germany
marlon.braun@kit.edu

Pradyumn Kumar Shukla
Institute AIFB, KIT, Germany
Institut für Mathematik, TU Clausthal, Germany
pradyumn.shukla@kit.edu

Hartmut Schmeck
Institute AIFB, KIT, Germany
hartmut.schmeck@kit.edu

ABSTRACT

Scalarization techniques are a popular method for articulating preferences in solving multi-objective optimization problems. These techniques, however, have so far proven to be ill-suited in finding a preference-driven approximation that still captures the Pareto front in its entirety. Therefore, we propose a new concept that defines an optimal distribution of points on the front given a specific scalarization function. It is proven that such an approximation exists for every real-valued problem irrespective of the shape of the corresponding front under some very mild conditions. We also show that our approach works well in obtaining an equidistant approximation of the Pareto front if no specific preference is articulated. Our analysis is complemented by the presentation of a new algorithm that implements the aforementioned concept. We provide in-depth simulation results to demonstrate the performance of our algorithm. The analysis also reveals that our algorithm is able to outperform current state-of-the-art algorithms on many popular benchmark problems.

Keywords

multi-objective optimization; scalarization method; preference-based approximation; electromagnetism-like mechanism

1. INTRODUCTION AND MOTIVATION

Multi-objective optimization focuses on finding solutions to problems that have multiple conflicting goals. Opposing aims lead to the problem not possessing a single solution attaining optimal values in each objective. Instead, we obtain a set of Pareto optimal solutions that can only be improved in one goal by deteriorating another objective at the same time. The image of the set of Pareto optimal solutions in the objective space is known as the Pareto optimal front [8].

Obtaining a closed form description of the Pareto front is often too difficult in practice [27]. Therefore, multi-objective optimization algorithms approximate the Pareto front by a finite set of points in its entirety to enable a decision maker to make an informed choice about the solution he finally implements. Such a decision maker usually already has a certain idea about which type of solutions he prefers, for example avoiding stark tradeoffs or extreme solutions. By incorporating his preferences into a search algorithm, we can generate more options that actually represent equitable candidate implementations [8].

Scalarization techniques articulate preferences by mapping the vector of objectives to real values, thereby imposing a total order on the objective space. Many calculation methods have been suggested in the literature [22]. Usually, these techniques are only capable of identifying a single point on the Pareto front. If only one solution is generated, however, we obtain no additional information about the composition of the Pareto front. There exists no possibility to assess how the option retrieved compares to other alternatives. It is well understood in economics and psychology, however, that human preferences change depending on the alternatives available [20]. One could argue that if the decision maker is able to specify a scalarization function that adheres to his preferences, there would be no need for obtaining other options. In practice however, the scalarization function may produce results that run counter-intuitive to the decision maker's expectations. The weighted sum method, for example, is only able to obtain boundary solutions on concave Pareto fronts [22].

Some scalarization techniques offer the possibility to vary given parameters to generate multiple solutions on the Pareto front. However, manipulating these parameters yields no guarantee for obtaining an approximation that actually adheres to the decision maker's preference. The weighted sum method's inability to find solutions on concave fronts amply demonstrates this circumstance. Other scalarization techniques have been used in conjunction with minimum threshold levels, underneath which all solutions are considered to be equal. Traditional evolutionary selection mechanisms have then been applied to find an approximation of the preferred set [11, 25]. Nevertheless, choosing a threshold level can be difficult. For a given threshold, the approximation of the remaining front does not prioritize solutions whose scalarization value is closer to the global optimum.

The observations in the two previous paragraphs necessitate the development of a mechanism that obtains a preference-driven approximation of the Pareto front. In order to quantify the quality of such an approximation, we require the definition of an optimal distribution of points. Defining

GECCO '15, July 11 - 15, 2015, Madrid, Spain

ACM ISBN 978-1-4503-3472-3/15/07...$15.00

DOI: http://dx.doi.org/10.1145/2739480.2754674

global diversity criteria has only recently seen increasing attention. Algorithms implementing traditional solving techniques such as the popular crowding distance metric [13] do not converge to an optimal distribution of points. One of the few, hence very popular global diversity criteria is hypervolume contribution [3]. Calculating hypervolume contributions however remains intractable in higher dimensions. Recent studies [28] have also shown that the optimal distribution of points depends on the chosen reference point. Reference point methods such as [21] or [12] are ill-suited for constrained problems or discontinuous Pareto fronts.

We propose an electrostatic potential energy inspired evolutionary algorithm to solve the aforementioned issues. To the best of our knowledge, [32] and [6] are till the present date the only attempts at designing an electromagnetism-inspired metaheuristic for solving multi-objective optimization problems. Both approaches assign charges to each solution based on their closeness to a randomly selected subset from an archive of non-dominated solutions. The charges are translated to force vectors, which are used to move solutions in the search space. The best solutions found are stored in an archive that uses clustering in [32] and crowding distance in [6] for pruning solutions.

The contributions of our work may be summarized in the following way:

- we propose a new mathematical notion for defining an optimal distribution of points according to a global diversity criterion. This notion can be combined with scalarized preference information to drive the distribution towards preferred subsets of the Pareto front,
- we develop a new algorithm for solving multi-objective optimization problems that implements aforementioned notion,
- a quantitative and qualitative study demonstrates the performance of our algorithm. We can show that our method outperforms current state-of-the-art algorithms in finding a diverse approximation to the Pareto front on many popular test problems.

The next section outlines some basic multi-objective optimization notions and presents the electrostatic energy based optimization concept. From this concept, we develop a multi-objective evolutionary algorithm in the subsequent section. Afterwards, the performance of our algorithm is evaluated. We first analyze its behavior under no preference articulation by assessing how its final population compares to an energy minimum distribution of points. We then compare its performance to other state-of-the-art algorithms. The evaluation section illustrates the example runs using various scalarization techniques whereas the concluding remarks at the end of the article show possible extensions.

2. AN ELECTROSTATIC ENERGY BASED OPTIMIZATION CONCEPT

Without loss of generality, we only consider minimization problems in this work. We minimize m objective functions $\mathbf{f}(\mathbf{x}) := (f_1(\mathbf{x}), \dots, f_m(\mathbf{x}))$ using n decision variables $\mathbf{x} := (x_1, \dots, x_n)$. The feasible search space is denoted by X and its image by $\mathcal{Y}$. Domination and Pareto optimality can then be defined in the following way.

DEFINITION 1 (DOMINATION [24]). *Let $\mathbf{x}^1, \mathbf{x}^2 \in X$ be given. $\mathbf{x}^1$ dominates $\mathbf{x}^2$, expressed as $\mathbf{x}^1 \succ \mathbf{x}^2$, if $f_i(\mathbf{x}^1) \leq f_i(\mathbf{x}^2)$ for all $i = 1, \dots m$ with strict inequality for at least one i.*

DEFINITION 2 (PARETO OPTIMALITY [24]). *A solution $\mathbf{x}^1 \in X$ is called* Pareto optimal *if no $\mathbf{x}^2 \in X$ exists so that $f_i(\mathbf{x}^2) \leq f_i(\mathbf{x}^1)$ for all $i = 1, \dots, m$ with strict inequality for at least one i.*

We denote the set of Pareto optimal solutions by X_p and its image, the Pareto front, by $\mathcal{Y}_p$. Next, we formally define scalarization functions.

DEFINITION 3 (SCALARIZATION FUNCTION). *A* scalarization function *is a map $W : \mathbb{R}^m \mapsto \mathbb{R}$.*

Our approach for approximating the Pareto front is founded on the physical phenomenon of electrostatic potential energy. In physics, charged particles interact by Coulomb forces with each other. In a closed system, these Coulomb forces induce an electrostatic potential energy. The energy that a given particle exhibits with respect to another particle is equal to the product of both their charges multiplied by Coulomb's constant and divided by their Euclidean distance to each other. The sum of all pairwise energies constitutes the energy of the system. Given a finite set of charges, there exists a distribution of particles that minimizes the energy of the closed system [19].

We translate the physical system to the optimization context. The Pareto front constitutes the closed system and a finite set of points on the front $\mathcal{S} = (\mathbf{x}^1, \dots, \mathbf{x}^N)$ represents the particles, with $|\mathcal{S}| = N$ and $\mathbf{x}^i \in X_p$ for all i. Charges are induced by the scalarization function. Our aim is to find an approximation to the Pareto front that minimizes the function

$$U(\mathcal{S}) = \sum_{i=1}^{N} \sum_{j=i+1}^{N} \frac{W(\mathbf{f}(\mathbf{x}^i)) \cdot W(\mathbf{f}(\mathbf{x}^j))}{\|\mathbf{f}(\mathbf{x}^i) - \mathbf{f}(\mathbf{x}^j)\|_2}. \tag{1}$$

THEOREM 1 (EXISTENCE OF MINIMUM). *Let W be continuous and $W(\mathbf{f}(\mathbf{x})) > 0$ for all $\mathbf{x} \in X_p$. Further let $\mathcal{Y}_p$ be compact and $|\mathcal{Y}_p| > N > 1$. Then, U attains its minimum on $\mathcal{Y}_p$.*

PROOF. The function U possesses a lower bound, since we require $W(\mathbf{f}(\mathbf{x})) > 0$ and because the denominator of U is positive. Let $\mathcal{P} := (\mathbf{y}^1, \dots, \mathbf{y}^N)$ with $\mathbf{y}^i \in \mathbb{R}^n$ for all i and $M := \{\mathcal{P} \mid U(\mathcal{P}) \leq \max_{\mathbf{x} \in X_p} N \cdot W(\mathbf{f}(\mathbf{x}))/\epsilon\}$ denote a lower level set with ϵ greater but close to zero. We obtain that the set $M \cap \mathcal{Y}_p$ is compact and that U is continuous on $M \cap \mathcal{Y}_p$, because W is continuous and the denominator of U never attains the value zero on $M \cap \mathcal{Y}_p$. Then, the conditions for the Weierstraß extreme value theorem are fulfilled [2]. □

Remark 1. Practically all non-degenerate real-valued optimization problems fulfill the requirements of Theorem 1. Unbounded or open Pareto fronts are seldom encountered in artificial or real problems. Deterministic and evolutionary methods alike struggle to approximate an unbounded Pareto front. The result of Theorem 1 can also be extended to integer-valued or mixed integer-real-valued objective functions. However, a formal proof goes beyond the scope of this paper.

Remark 2. The case, where no particular preference information is given, corresponds to choosing $W(\mathbf{f}(\mathbf{x})) = 1$. Such a scenario would result in finding a nearly equidistant approximation to the Pareto front.[1] Theorem 1 guarantees that such an approximation exists irrespective of the shape of the front, ignoring curvature and discontinuities.

The prerequisites for the function W in Theorem 1 are met by most common scalarization techniques [22]. Negative scalarization values can be rescaled to positive values for making them compatible with our approach. For illustrating the capabilities of our concept, we focus on four particular scalarization functions in this work. The sum of objectives and the Chebyshev method [22] are among the most prominent techniques in multi-objective optimization. The Nash bargaining solution [23] is a renowned tool in economics for choosing between Pareto optimal resource allocations. This technique was originally designed for maximization problems. Therefore, we reformulated the notion to make it compatible with minimization and to avoid scalarization values of zero. Finally, proper utility [25] is a concept that has only recently emerged. It is founded on the concept of proper Pareto optimality [18, 29] and describes desirability in terms of tradeoffs. Let $I := \{1, \ldots, m\}$ denote the set of objectives. The four methods are defined in the following way:

Sum of objectives:

$$W^s(\mathbf{f}(\mathbf{x})) = \sum_{i \in I} f_i(\mathbf{x}).$$

Chebyshev method:

$$W^c(\mathbf{f}(\mathbf{x})) = \max_{i \in I} (f_i(\mathbf{x}) - u_i^*)$$

with $u_i^* = \min_{\mathbf{y} \in X} f_i(\mathbf{y})$ and $\mathbf{u}^* = (u_1^*, \ldots, u_m^*)$ denoting the Utopia point.

Nash bargaining solution:

$$W^n(\mathbf{f}(\mathbf{x})) = \alpha \left(\max_{\mathbf{y} \in X_p} (N(\mathbf{y})) + \min_{\mathbf{y} \in X_p} (N(\mathbf{y})) \right) - N(\mathbf{x})$$

with

$$N(\mathbf{x}) = \prod_{i \in I} \left(u_i^{ndr} - f_i(\mathbf{x}) \right) \tag{2}$$

with $\alpha > 1$, $u_i^{ndr} = \max_{\mathbf{y} \in X_p} f_i(\mathbf{y})$ and $\mathbf{u}^{ndr} = (u_1^{ndr}, \ldots, u_m^{ndr})$ denoting the Nadir point.

Proper utility:

$$W^p(\mathbf{f}(\mathbf{x})) = \max_{\mathbf{y} \in X_p \setminus \{\mathbf{x}\}} \frac{\max_{i \in I}(f_i(\mathbf{x}) - f_i(\mathbf{y}))}{\max_{i \in I}(f_i(\mathbf{y}) - f_i(\mathbf{x}))}.$$

COROLLARY 1. *Let $\mathcal{Y}_p$ be compact and $|\mathcal{Y}_p| > N > 1$. Then, the function U attains its minimum on $\mathcal{Y}_p$ if W is chosen as either the Chebyshev method, proper utility, the Nash bargaining solution or the weighted sum method for $\mathcal{Y}_p \subset \mathbb{R}_+^m$.*

PROOF. Corollary 1 is a consequence of Theorem 1. □

[1] An exact equidistant approximation is not expected as points close to the boundary of the Pareto front naturally exhibit smaller energies compared to inner points, since neighboring solutions are not located in every direction.

3. ALGORITHMIC APPROACH

Finding the minimum of (1) for a given N is a highly difficult task as the problem formulation practically requires complete knowledge of the Pareto front. Additionally, the Jacobian of (1) possesses $N \cdot n$ entries. For this reason, an analytical or deterministic approach seems ill-advised to find the energy minimum in practice. This makes the evolutionary algorithm an ideal candidate for tackling the problem.

Devising an evolutionary strategy for obtaining the energy minimum provides two main challenges. First of all and obviously, the algorithm needs to converge towards the energy minimum state. This implies that the selection mechanism needs to assure the population's convergence to the Pareto front, while retaining the energy minimization focus at the same time. Secondly, once the optimal distribution has been attained, the population should remain at its current position if further search iterations are performed.

We pursue both goals by using a steady-state approach in combination with an archive mechanism. The interaction of both concepts fosters the population gradually converging towards an energy minimum state on the Pareto front, while remaining computationally tractable. We maintain a variable-sized archive A of non-dominated solutions attaining a maximum size of N that contains the currently best known minimum energy approximation. In each iteration, a new solution $\mathbf{p}$ is created by recombining parents from the archive and mutating the resulting offspring solution.[2] $\mathbf{p}$ is immediately discarded if it is dominated by or possesses the same objective values as any archive member. The newly created solution only enters the archive if either A has not reached its maximum size or if $\mathbf{p}$ can replace an archive member such that $\mathbf{p}$ reduces the overall energy of A.

An outline of the Electrostatic Potential Energy Evolutionary Algorithm (ESPEA) is provided in Algorithm 1. The function $e(\mathbf{a})$ calculates the energy the member $\mathbf{a}$ introduces into the archive:

$$e(\mathbf{a}) = \sum_{\mathbf{b} \in A \setminus \{\mathbf{a}\}} \frac{W(\mathbf{f}(\mathbf{a})) \cdot W(\mathbf{f}(\mathbf{b}))}{\|\mathbf{f}(\mathbf{a}) - \mathbf{f}(\mathbf{b})\|_2}. \tag{3}$$

The energy, $\mathbf{p}$ would introduce into the archive if it was to replace archive member $\mathbf{a}$, is given by

$$e_{-\mathbf{a}}(\mathbf{p}) = \sum_{\mathbf{b} \in A \setminus \{\mathbf{a}\}} \frac{W(\mathbf{f}(\mathbf{p})) \cdot W(\mathbf{f}(\mathbf{b}))}{\|\mathbf{f}(\mathbf{p}) - \mathbf{f}(\mathbf{b})\|_2}. \tag{4}$$

Step 13 encapsulates the replacement mechanism. As stated before, $\mathbf{p}$ can only replace an archive member if it decreases the overall energy of the archive. It may occur, however, that there exist multiple candidates for replacement. We have identified three different strategies for selecting the archive member to replace in this case. Let $A_>$ denote the subset of A consisting only of members that introduce more energy in lieu of $\mathbf{p}$, i.e. $A_> := \{\mathbf{a} \in A | e_{-\mathbf{a}}(\mathbf{p}) < e(\mathbf{a})\}$.

Best feasible position: $\arg\min_{\mathbf{a} \in A_>} e_{-\mathbf{a}}(\mathbf{p})$
Of all viable options, $\mathbf{p}$ replaces $\mathbf{a}$ such that it introduces the least energy possible into A.

Worst in archive: $\arg\max_{\mathbf{a} \in A_>} e(\mathbf{a})$
The new solution replaces the member that exhibits the highest energy of all elements in $A_>$.

[2] An exact formulation of the offspring generation method applied is provided in Section 4.

Algorithm 1: ESPEA

```
1  begin
2      Generate initial population P
3      Copy all non-dominated solutions in P to archive A
4      repeat
5          Generate a single new solution p
6          Remove all solutions from A dominated by p
7          if p ⊀ a ∧ f(p) ≠ f(a) ∀a ∈ A then
8              if |A| < N then
9                  A := A ∪ {p}
10             else
11                 Calculate e(a) for all a ∈ A
12                 Calculate e := (e_{-a^1}(p), ..., e_{-a^N}(p))
13                 update(A, p, e)
14     until stopping criterion
15     return A
```

Largest energy decrease: $\arg\max_{\mathbf{a}\in A_>}(e(\mathbf{a}) - e_{-\mathbf{a}}(\mathbf{p}))$
The energy difference before and after inserting $\mathbf{p}$ is maximized.

The three different selection mechanisms possess several advantages and disadvantages. Best feasible position (BFP) and worst in archive (WIA) put a very strong selection pressure on including only the best solutions into the archive. On the other hand, the total energy loss might only be marginal. The largest energy decrease (LED) builds a bridge between the two aforementioned approaches. However, considering the largest decrease might not remove the least favorable archive members in the long run.

A thorough mathematical proof for the convergence behavior of ESPEA goes beyond the scope of this paper. Whether convergence occurs, also depends on the scalarization function. However, we provide a formal tool, with which the stability of an archive given W can be calculated. We call an archive *evolutionary stable* if no new solution can supersede an existing archive member.

PROPOSITION 1. *Let* $E^+(\mathbf{a}) := \{\mathbf{p} \in X | e_{-a}(\mathbf{p}) < e(\mathbf{a})\}$ *denote the set of points that would decrease the energy of A if* $\mathbf{p}$ *was to supersede* $\mathbf{a}$ *and* $D(A) := \{\mathbf{p} \in X | \exists \mathbf{a} \in A : \mathbf{a} \succ \mathbf{p}\}$ *the set of points that are dominated by the archive A. A is* evolutionary stable *if* $\bigcup_{a\in A} E^+(\mathbf{a}) \subseteq D(A)$.

PROOF. A new solution $\mathbf{p}$ may only replace an archive member $\mathbf{a}$ if $e_{-\mathbf{a}}(\mathbf{p}) < e(\mathbf{a})$. According to Proposition 1, this is only the case if any archive member dominates $\mathbf{p}$. In this case however, $\mathbf{p}$ is automatically discarded before even being considered for insertion. □

CONJECTURE 1. *The ESPEA algorithm is evolutionary stable for the BFP, WIA and LED update mechanism if* $W(\mathbf{f}(\mathbf{x})) = 1$.

Remark 3. We base Conjecture 1 on an observation made in two dimensions for an archive of size three and a Pareto front consisting of an arbitrarily-shaped, continuous curve that has fixed boundary points. In this case, the energy minimum consists of the two boundary solutions of the Pareto front $\mathbf{x}^l$ and $\mathbf{x}^r$ and the solution $\mathbf{x}^m$, whose image lies on the Pareto front and has exactly the same distance from both boundary points. The complement of $E^+(\mathbf{x}^m)$ in $\mathcal{Y}$ (the image of those points that would introduce more energy into A than $\mathbf{x}^m$) consists of two circles having their centers at $\mathbf{f}(\mathbf{x}^l)$ and $\mathbf{f}(\mathbf{x}^r)$ intersecting $\mathbf{f}(\mathbf{x}^m)$. Aforementioned space overlaps into $D(A)$ resulting in all solutions that would introduce less energy into the archive being dominated by A. We believe that this observation may be generalized for an arbitrary number of points and objectives.

We would like to point out that other preference notions such as variable cone orderings [26] or tradeoff thresholds [5], effectively cropping the set of optimal solutions, can be implemented on top of ESPEA by changing the archive update mechanism in deciding if a solution is eligible to enter. Additional preferences information regarding diversity can also be encapsulated in the scalarization function.

Next, we analyze the complexity of ESPEA. Removing dominated solutions from the archive in Step 6 and checking if $\mathbf{p}$ is dominated by or if its objective values are equal to that of any archive member can be conducted at the same time. The worst case effort for this procedure lies in $O(mN)$ for an archive of size N. The computation effort for energy values in Step 11 and 12 hinges on the complexity of the scalarization function. As calculating the Euclidean distance requires an effort of $O(m)$, we gain a complexity of $O(N^2(m + O(W)))$ in Step 11. By exploiting the fact that energies are symmetric, we can halve the number of energy calculations, however this does not change the complexity class. An intelligent evaluation scheme in Step 12 allows us to reduce the effort for calculating the vector $\mathbf{e}$ to $O(N(m + O(W))$. All three update mechanism in Step 13 exhibit a computational complexity of $O(N)$. Therefore, the overall effort of a single ESPEA iteration lies in $O(N^2(m + O(W)))$. This circumstance makes the electrostatic energy approach computationally tractable in higher dimensions.

4. SIMULATION RESULTS

The computational analysis is split into two parts. In the first part, we assume no specific preferences, in order to benchmark the three archive update mechanisms presented in the previous section. We analyze how well each mechanism is suited to attain the energy minimum on a given set of widely used test problems. Thereafter, we compare ESPEA with state-of-the-art multi-objective evolutionary algorithms. The second part consists of the presentation of various representative example runs using the scalarization techniques presented in Section 2.

We implemented the ESPEA algorithm in the jMetal framework [15]. The code is publicly available and hosted as standalone project[3]. The following setup was used for performing the quantitative study. ESPEA employed SBX crossover [9] using a distribution index of 20 and a crossover probability of 0.9 in combination with binary tournament selection based on energy values if the archive had not reached its maximum size, yet. This way, we achieve an early selection bias towards the most promising solutions. Such a strategy was already successfully applied in the AMGA2 algorithm [31] in conjunction with the crowding distance metric. When the archive has reached its maximum size, we switch the crossover mechanism to differential evolution and select the

[3]http://sourceforge.net/projects/jmetalbymarlonso/

parents randomly. In recent years, differential evolution has proven to be one of the most competitive selection mechanisms [7]. In order to prevent an early genetic drift, when the archive is still small, we first utilize SBX. Parents are chosen randomly for the differential evolution, so that each solution on the Pareto front is given equal weight. We acknowledge, however, that there might exist better parent selection schemes that will be investigated in future studies. Polynomial mutation [10] using a distribution index of 20 and a mutation probability of one by the number of decision variables was used in all stages of the algorithm. We also used adaptive normalization in calculating Euclidean distances to mitigate the effect of different scales of individual objectives.

Reference points on the Pareto front were computed for each test problem of the study that served as approximate energy minima for a given population size. The final populations obtained by ESPEA using the different update mechanisms were compared against these reference points to assess ESPEA's performances. The reference points were created in the following way: We first obtained analytical function representations of the Pareto fronts of the test problems. Then, equidistant decision variables were used as starting points in conjunction with the MATLAB optimization toolbox, as they serve as good estimate for the energy minimum. The reference fronts and the code for generating them are contained in the online repository.

Using the approach outlined in the paragraph above limited our selection of test instances to continuous problems, whose analytical description of the Pareto front is known. Still, our final selection of eleven problems constitutes a representative sample of differing challenges. These are composed of convex and concave fronts, shallow and pronounced curvatures and Pareto fronts exhibiting multiple bulges. We employed a maximum archive size of 50 for two-dimensional problems, while three-dimensional problems were solved using an archive size of 100. Each ESPEA configuration was run 100 times on each test problem to provide a representative sample. 10,000 function evaluations were used on the 2D and 20,000 function evaluations on the 3D problems. The following tests suites were used in this study: DEB2DK, DO2DK [4], DTLZ [14], ZDT [34] and an instance of a Lamé hypersphere [16] with a curvature of 0.5.

Table 1: Median and IQR of IGD to minimum energy distribution.

	ESPEA BFP	ESPEA WIA	ESPEA LED
DEB2DK k1	$2.45e-3_{5.3e-4}$	$1.63e-3_{3.3e-4}$	$1.59e-3_{3.3e-4}$
DEB2DK k3	$5.02e-3_{2.8e-3}$	$1.54e-3_{2.8e-4}$	$1.62e-3_{2.4e-4}$
DO2DK k2 s1	$7.41e-4_{2.7e-3}$	$3.17e-4_{1.1e-5}$	$3.18e-4_{1.2e-5}$
DO2DK k4 s1	$6.57e-4_{2.6e-4}$	$3.35e-4_{1.5e-5}$	$3.34e-4_{1.3e-5}$
ZDT1	$1.12e-2_{1.9e-2}$	$1.62e-3_{3.3e-4}$	$1.63e-3_{2.7e-4}$
ZDT2	$7.62e-2_{2.6e-2}$	$1.22e-3_{3.6e-4}$	$1.27e-3_{3.3e-4}$
DTLZ1	$1.16e-2_{5.8e-3}$	$3.93e-3_{5.2e-4}$	$3.99e-3_{5.0e-4}$
DTLZ2	$9.37e-3_{1.8e-3}$	$5.47e-3_{2.3e-4}$	$5.53e-3_{3.2e-4}$
DTLZ3	$3.91e-1_{3.6e-1}$	$4.22e-1_{3.9e-1}$	$4.34e-1_{3.5e-1}$
DTLZ4	$9.44e-3_{5.9e-2}$	$6.11e-3_{6.2e-2}$	$1.22e-2_{6.2e-2}$
Lame 0.5	$3.58e-3_{2.9e-4}$	$2.56e-3_{1.7e-4}$	$2.57e-3_{1.8e-4}$

Table 1 lists medians and inter-quartile ranges of the inverted generational distance (IGD) metric [33]. Dark/light gray colored cells hint at the best/second-best result, respectively. The IGD metric reveals how close the final archive is to the reference set that constitutes the energy minimum. All archive update mechanisms are very capable of obtaining a close approximation to the energy minimum. DTLZ3 is the only problem, for which the inverted generational distance stays above the $10e-2$ threshold. We observe that WIA and LED exhibit a very similar performance, whereas BFP is outclassed on most problems. Interestingly, BFP obtains very good results on the problems DTLZ3 and DTLZ4, which are known to be difficult to solve.

Table 2: IGD. p-values of a multiple comparison of mean column ranks using Bonferroni adjusted p-values.

	ESPEA WIA	ESPEA LED
ESPEA BFP	0.0019	0.2642
ESPEA WIA		0.2642

We conducted a Friedman test in conjunction with Bonferroni correction to assess, whether the performance differences observed are significant across all tested problems. Table 2 lists the results. Only WIA's performance differs significantly from BFP. We would like to note, however, that the Bonferroni correction is very conservative and does only utilize ranks instead of absolute differences.

The distance between approximation and the ideal distribution of points is not the only performance indicator that should be considered in this context. Any approximation to the Pareto front exhibiting a small overall energy naturally constitutes a desirable result. Of course, such an approximation is required to have the full number of solution as requested by the user. The solutions retrieved should also be closely located to the Pareto front. We have already resolved the latter issue by showing that the approximations retrieved by ESPEA are close to the ideal distributions of points. Regarding the former issue, all three mechanisms were able to obtain the full number of solutions on all problems besides DTLZ3 in their median runs. However, even on DTLZ3, WIA and LED still obtained a median number of solutions of 97.5 and 92, respectively. BFP was only able to retrieve 69 solutions.

Table 3: Median and IQR of total energy values.

	ESPEA BFP	ESPEA WIA	ESPEA LED
DEB2DK k1	$7.17e+3_{5.7e+2}$	$5.68e+3_{2.8e+1}$	$5.67e+3_{1.8e+1}$
DEB2DK k3	$8.27e+3_{9.3e+2}$	$5.82e+3_{2.4e+1}$	$5.82e+3_{2.2e+1}$
DO2DK k2 s1	$7.27e+3_{9.0e+2}$	$5.03e+3_{3.4e+1}$	$5.03e+3_{3.2e+1}$
DO2DK k4 s1	$7.39e+3_{6.7e+2}$	$5.11e+3_{3.8e+1}$	$5.11e+3_{3.5e+1}$
ZDT1	$7.39e+3_{5.7e+2}$	$5.81e+3_{3.1e+1}$	$5.81e+3_{3.1e+1}$
ZDT2	$1.08e+4_{4.1e+3}$	$5.78e+3_{2.7e+1}$	$5.78e+3_{2.4e+1}$
DTLZ1	$1.96e+4_{5.5e+3}$	$1.12e+4_{2.3e+1}$	$1.12e+4_{2.8e+1}$
DTLZ2	$4.82e+4_{8.6e+4}$	$9.07e+3_{5.4e+1}$	$9.06e+3_{4.6e+1}$
DTLZ3	$6.74e+4_{5.3e+5}$	$1.38e+4_{2.3e+4}$	$1.40e+4_{1.3e+4}$
DTLZ4	$4.69e+4_{NaN}$	$9.22e+3_{1.6e+4}$	$9.21e+3_{1.6e+4}$
Lame 0.5	$1.68e+4_{1.1e+3}$	$1.38e+4_{4.2e+1}$	$1.37e+4_{5.4e+1}$

Table 3 lists medians and IQRs for the electrostatic potential energy values. BFP is clearly outperformed on all test instances. LED obtains the overall best results across all problems, however the actual performance difference compared to WIA is only marginal. In order to provide a complete picture, we also list the energy values of the optimal distributions calculated using the MATLAB software in Table 4. We observe that the approximations ESPEA produces come very close to the energy minima. On some test problems the approximations even attain a smaller energy value. This does not necessarily imply, however, that the optimal distributions obtained using MATLAB are approximated too roughly. Since the solutions generated by ESPEA may not reside exactly on the Pareto front, smaller energies may be attained, as energy is mainly a dispersion metric.

Table 4: Smallest known energy values for population sizes $N = 50$ on 2D and $N = 100$ on 3D problems.

	Minimum
DEB2DK k1	$5.63e+3$
DEB2DK k3	$5.78e+3$
DO2DK k2 s1	$5.30e+3$
DO2DK k4 s1	$5.37e+3$
ZDT1	$5.75e+3$
ZDT2	$5.75e+3$
DTLZ1	$1.23e+4$
DTLZ2	$9.05e+3$
DTLZ3	$9.05e+3$
DTLZ4	$9.05e+3$
Lame 0.5	$1.38e+4$

A Friedman test was conducted to assess, whether the observed performance differences are significant. The results are listed in Table 5. We observe that WIA and LED outperform BFP with high confidence. Based on these results, WIA and LED both appear as eligible options, whereas the use of BFP is discouraged. For the remainder of our study, we employed the WIA update strategy.

Table 5: ENERGY. p-values of a multiple comparison of mean column ranks using Bonferroni adjusted p-values.

	ESPEA WIA	ESPEA LED
ESPEA BFP	0.0017	0.0001
ESPEA WIA		1.0000

We opted to compare the performance of ESPEA to three state-of-the-art multi-objective evolutionary algorithms that also aim to obtain a predefined optimal distribution of points in a separate experiment. SMS-EMOA [3], MOEA/D [21] and NSGA-III [12] were chosen for this study. The first two algorithms are readily available in the jMetal framework, whereas NSGA-III was implemented from scratch. Algorithm configurations were taken from the respective original publications. MOEA/D weight vectors were obtained from the University of Essex homepage[4]. We employed 105 reference points for NSGA-III generated by the method suggested in [12]. ESPEA retained its configuration from the previous experiment. The same test problems as for the benchmark study were employed, since NSGA-III is recommended to be used with adaptive reference points on non-continuous Pareto fronts or constrained problems. Adaptive reference points, however, no longer prescribe an optimal distribution of points, which contradicts the approach of this study. We used a population size of 100 and 20,000 function evaluations on all problems.

[4]http://dces.essex.ac.uk/staff/qzhang/MOEAcompetition/CEC09final/code/ZhangMOEADcode/moead030510.rar

Table 6: Median IGD.

	ESPEA	SMS-EMOA	MOEA/D	NSGA-III
DEB2DK k1	$4.71e-5$	$4.88e-5$	$3.43e-4$	$1.27e-4$
DEB2DK k3	$4.68e-5$	$4.91e-5$	$3.65e-4$	$1.33e-4$
DO2DK k2 s1	$5.36e-5$	$6.04e-5$	$4.43e-4$	$4.03e-4$
DO2DK k4 s1	$5.43e-5$	$7.55e-5$	$4.33e-4$	$2.99e-4$
ZDT1	$4.56e-5$	$4.30e-5$	$3.35e-4$	$1.22e-4$
ZDT2	$4.43e-5$	$5.76e-5$	$4.24e-4$	$1.28e-4$
DTLZ1	$6.97e-4$	$4.41e-4$	$6.28e-4$	$7.00e-4$
DTLZ2	$6.91e-4$	$8.33e-4$	$7.71e-4$	$5.95e-4$
DTLZ3	$5.02e-2$	$4.34e-2$	$1.69e-2$	$5.74e-2$
DTLZ4	$6.97e-4$	$8.56e-4$	$1.00e-3$	$6.05e-4$
Lame 0.5	$2.64e-4$	$1.70e-4$	$2.92e-4$	$2.50e-4$

Table 6 lists median results for the IGD metric. IQR values were omitted for space limitations, but are readily available upon request. The reference fronts of DEB2DK and DO2DK were created by sampling 10,000 equidistant points and are contained in the online repository. Other reference fronts were obtained from the jMetal homepage[5]. The results clearly show that ESPEA excels on all test problems. ESPEA is among the top two performers on all but three test problems and scores five first places, the best value among all algorithms. It is noteworthy that the performance gap between ESPEA and the well established MOEA/D and NSGA-III becomes quite large on DEB2DK, DO2DK and the ZDT suite.

In the final part of this section, we present representative example runs of ESPEA on numerous test problems using the four scalarization techniques presented in Section 2. A population size of 50 and 100 were employed for 2D and 3D problems, respectively. The number of function evaluations corresponds to population size times 200.

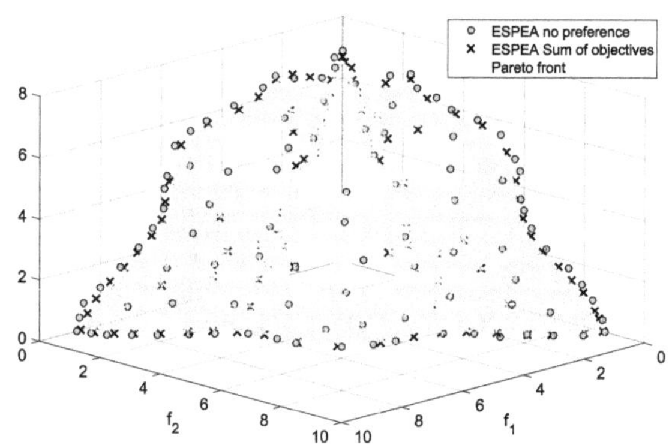

Figure 1: ESPEA example run on DEB3DK with $k = 2$ using the sum of objectives.

Figure 1 shows two example runs on the problem DEB3DK for $k = 2$ [4]. DEB3DK was omitted from our quantitative study, because its Pareto front features two distinct holes that prevent NSGA-III and MOEA/D from finding meaningful approximations without resorting to adaptive weight vectors/reference points. In order to demonstrate the effect of the sum of objectives charges, we also provide an ESPEA run using no preference information. We can observe that if no scalarization function is specified, solutions are distributed equally on the entire front. The sum of objectives introduces a strong focus on convex valleys. The

[5]http://jmetal.sourceforge.net/

Pareto front of DEB3DK features many convex and concave bulges. It is interesting to note that ESPEA using sum of objectives charges also captures points in concave regions, where the weighted sum method would fail.

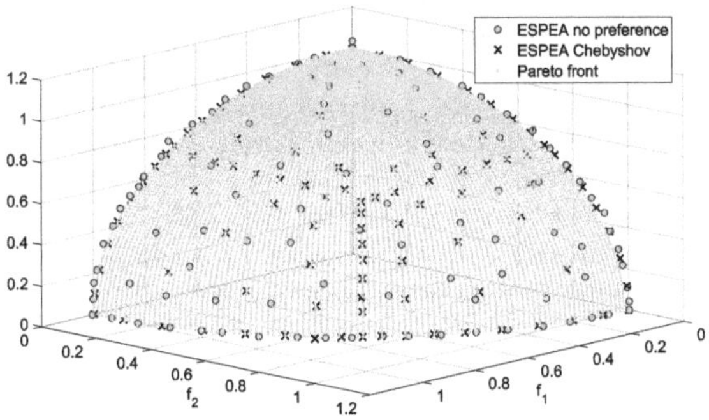

Figure 2: ESPEA example run on DTLZ4 using Chebyshev's method.

Chebyshev's method is illustrated in Figure 2 on DTLZ4. If no preferences are specified, solutions are equally distributed on the Pareto front. The Chebyshev technique retains the scope of the entire front, however we can spot a distinct intersection of three lines in the center of the figure. These three lines constitute exactly those points that minimize Chebyshev's scalarization function.

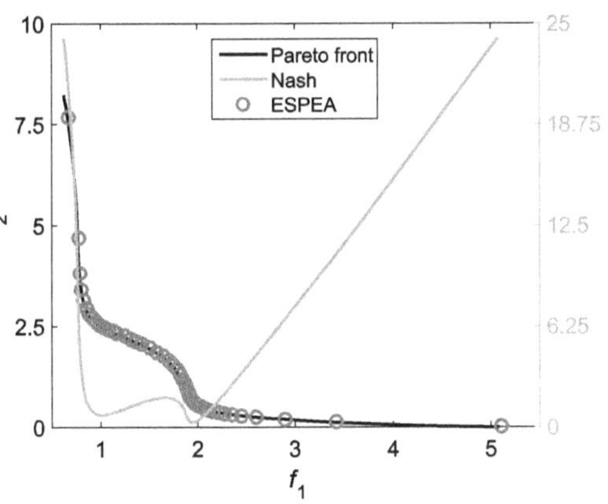

Figure 3: ESPEA example run on DO2DK with $k = 2$, $s = 1$ and $\alpha = 1.1$ using the Nash bargaining solution.

We choose DO2DK to illustrate the performance of ESPEA using the Nash bargaining solution. The current population was used to attain an estimate of the Nadir point and the minimum and maximum of (2). Figure 3 shows an ESPEA run on DO2DK and also the scalarization values for every point of the Pareto front. There is a stark focus of solutions on the barycenter of the curve as this region possesses the smallest scalarization values. Very few points are located on the near horizontal/vertical sections close to the boundary solutions. The Nash bargaining solution naturally avoids extreme points making these regions highly undesirable as indicated by the scalarization values.

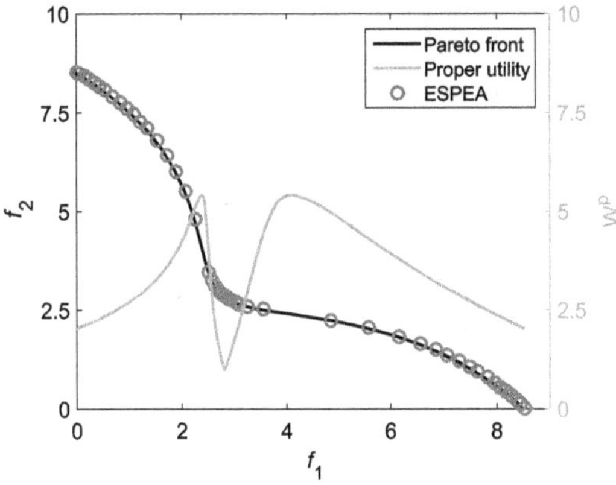

Figure 4: ESPEA example run on DEB2DK with $k = 1$ using proper utility.

Figure 4 illustrates the effect if proper utility values are set as charges. ESPEA places a heavy focus on the most favorable regions that are located at the convex valley in the center and at the boundary of the Pareto front. Utility values exhibit a sharp peak close to the global optimum, which is why ESPEA practically neglects these regions.

The search results presented in Figure 1 to 4 all present the decision maker with multiple solutions that are highly desirable with respect to his preferences. At the same time, a focus on the entire Pareto front is retained enabling him to make a comparison of his preferred solutions to other available options.

5. SUMMARY AND OUTLOOK

This paper has presented a new concept for defining an optimal distribution of points on the Pareto front. The optimal distribution can be biased towards preferred regions using scalarized preference information. We have presented the ESPEA algorithm, which implements aforementioned concept. A thorough computational study has revealed that ESPEA succeeds in obtaining these optimal distributions and compares well against state-of-the-art algorithms in finding an equidistant approximation to the Pareto front.

The electrostatic energy optimization concept offers many research questions that could be explored in subsequent studies. It would be especially of interest to formulate a coherent proof for Conjecture 1. In this light, it would make sense to further assess the evolutionary stability of ESPEA for arbitrary scalarization functions. Exact algorithms [17] for minimizing $U(\mathcal{S})$ could also be investigated. For this, set-based gradient of the $U(\mathcal{S})$ function needs to be computed [30]. Subsequent studies could also analyze ESPEA's performance on many-objective problems. Although one of ESPEA's great advantages is that it is parameter-free, it could make sense to employ a user-supplied parameter to strengthen or weaken the bias induced by the scalarized preference value. Apart from these, testing on real-world applications (such as [1]) is also intended.

6. REFERENCES

[1] Allerding, F., Premm, M., Shukla, P.K., Schmeck, H.: Electrical load management in smart homes using

evolutionary algorithms. In: Evolutionary Computation in Combinatorial Optimization, pp. 99–110. Springer (2012)
[2] Bertsekas, D.: Nonlinear programming. Athena scientific Belmont (1999)
[3] Beume, N., Naujoks, B., Emmerich, M.: SMS-EMOA: Multiobjective selection based on dominated hypervolume. European Journal of Operational Research **181**(3), 1653–1669 (2007)
[4] Branke, J., Deb, K., Dierolf, H., Osswald, M.: Finding knees in multi-objective optimization. In: PPSN VIII, pp. 722–731. Springer (2004)
[5] Braun, M.A., Shukla, P.K., Schmeck, H.: Preference ranking schemes in multi-objective evolutionary algorithms. In: R.H. Takahashi, K. Deb, E.F. Wanner, S. Greco (eds.) EMO, *LNCS*, vol. 6576, pp. 226–240. Springer (2011).
[6] Carrasqueira, P., Alves, M.J., Antunes, C.H.: An improved multiobjective electromagnetism-like mechanism algorithm. In: Applications of Evolutionary Computation, pp. 627–638. Springer (2014)
[7] Das, S., Suganthan, P.N.: Differential evolution: A survey of the state-of-the-art. Evolutionary Computation, IEEE Transactions on **15**(1), 4–31 (2011)
[8] Deb, K.: Multi-objective optimization using evolutionary algorithms, vol. 16. John Wiley & Sons (2001)
[9] Deb, K., Agrawal, R.B.: Simulated binary crossover for continuous search space. Complex Systems **9**(3), 1–15 (1994)
[10] Deb, K., Goyal, M.: A combined genetic adaptive search (GeneAS) for engineering design. Computer Science and Informatics **26**, 30–45 (1996)
[11] Deb, K., Gupta, S.: Understanding knee points in bicriteria problems and their implications as preferred solution principles. Engineering optimization **43**(11), 1175–1204 (2011)
[12] Deb, K., Jain, H.: An evolutionary many-objective optimization algorithm using reference-point based non-dominated sorting approach, part I: Solving problems with box constraints. Evolutionary Computation (2013)
[13] Deb, K., Pratap, A., Agarwal, S., Meyarivan, T.: A fast and elitist multiobjective genetic algorithm: NSGA-II. Evolutionary Computation, IEEE Transactions on **6**(2), 182–197 (2002)
[14] Deb, K., Thiele, L., Laumanns, M., Zitzler, E.: Scalable test problems for evolutionary multiobjective optimization. Springer (2005)
[15] Durillo, J.J., Nebro, A.J.: jMetal: A java framework for multi-objective optimization. Advances in Engineering Software **42**, 760–771 (2011)
[16] Emmerich, M.T., Deutz, A.H.: Test problems based on Lamé superspheres. In: Evolutionary Multi-Criterion Optimization, pp. 922–936. Springer (2007)
[17] Fischer, A., Shukla, P.K.: A levenberg–marquardt algorithm for unconstrained multicriteria optimization. Operations Research Letters **36**(5), 643–646 (2008)
[18] Geoffrion, A.M.: Proper efficiency and the theory of vector maximization. Journal of Mathematical Analysis and Applications **22**, 618–630 (1968)
[19] Halliday, D., Resnick, R., Walker, J.: Fundamentals of physics extended. John Wiley & Sons (2010)
[20] Kahneman, D., Tversky, A.: Prospect theory: An analysis of decision under risk. Econometrica: Journal of the Econometric Society pp. 263–291 (1979)
[21] Li, H., Zhang, Q.: Multiobjective optimization problems with complicated pareto sets, MOEA/D and NSGA-II. Evolutionary Computation, IEEE Transactions on **13**(2), 284–302 (2009)
[22] Marler, R.T., Arora, J.S.: Survey of multi-objective optimization methods for engineering. Structural and multidisciplinary optimization **26**(6), 369–395 (2004)
[23] Nash, J.F.: The bargaining problem. Econometrica: Journal of the Econometric Society pp. 155–162 (1950)
[24] Pareto, V.: Cours d'économie politique. Librairie Droz (1896)
[25] Shukla, P., Braun, M., Schmeck, H.: Theory and algorithms for finding knees. In: R.C. Purshouse, P.J. Fleming, C.M. Fonseca, S. Greco, J. Shaw (eds.) EMO, *LNCS*, vol. 7811, pp. 156–170. Springer Berlin Heidelberg (2013).
[26] Shukla, P.K., Braun, M.A.: Indicator based search in variable orderings: Theory and algorithms. In: R.C. Purshouse, P.J. Fleming, C.M. Fonseca, S. Greco, J. Shaw (eds.) EMO, *LNCS*, vol. 7811, pp. 66–80. Springer (2013).
[27] Shukla, P.K., Cipold, M.P., Bachmann, C., Schmeck, H.: On homogenization of coal in longitudinal blending beds. In: GECCO, pp. 1199–1206. ACM (2014)
[28] Shukla, P.K., Doll, N., Schmeck, H.: A theoretical analysis of volume based pareto front approximations. In: GECCO, pp. 1415–1422. ACM (2014)
[29] Shukla, P.K., Hirsch, C., Schmeck, H.: A framework for incorporating trade-off information using multi-objective evolutionary algorithms. In: PPSN XI, pp. 131–140. Springer (2010)
[30] Sosa Hernández, V.A., SchÃijtze, O., Emmerich, M.: Hypervolume maximization via set based newtons method. In: A.A. Tantar, et al. (eds.) EVOLVE, *Advances in Intelligent Systems and Computing*, vol. 288, pp. 15–28. Springer (2014).
[31] Tiwari, S., Fadel, G., Deb, K.: AMGA2: improving the performance of the archive-based micro-genetic algorithm for multi-objective optimization. Engineering Optimization **43**(4), 377–401 (2011)
[32] Tsou, C.S., Kao, C.H.: An electromagnetism-like meta-heuristic for multi-objective optimization. In: CEC, pp. 1172–1178. IEEE (2006)
[33] Van Veldhuizen, D.A., Lamont, G.B.: Evolutionary computation and convergence to a pareto front. In: Late breaking papers at the genetic programming 1998 conference, pp. 221–228. Citeseer (1998)
[34] Zitzler, E., Deb, K., Thiele, L.: Comparison of multiobjective evolutionary algorithms: Empirical results. Evolutionary computation **8**(2), 173–195 (2000)

Benchmarking Numerical Multiobjective Optimizers Revisited

Dimo Brockhoff
Inria Lille – Nord Europe
DOLPHIN Team
Villeneuve d'Ascq, France
dimo.brockhoff@inria.fr

Thanh-Do Tran
Inria Lille – Nord Europe
DOLPHIN Team
Villeneuve d'Ascq, France
thanh-do.tran@inria.fr

Nikolaus Hansen
Inria Saclay – Ile-de-France
TAO Team
Orsay, France
nikolaus.hansen@lri.fr

ABSTRACT

Algorithm benchmarking plays a vital role in designing new optimization algorithms and in recommending efficient and robust algorithms for practical purposes. So far, two main approaches have been used to compare algorithms in the evolutionary multiobjective optimization (EMO) field: (i) displaying empirical attainment functions and (ii) reporting statistics on quality indicator values. Most of the time, EMO benchmarking studies compare algorithms for fixed and often arbitrary budgets of function evaluations although the algorithms are any-time optimizers. Instead, we propose to transfer and adapt standard benchmarking techniques from the single-objective optimization and classical derivative-free optimization community to the field of EMO. Reporting *target-based runlengths* allows to compare algorithms with varying numbers of function evaluations quantitatively. Displaying *data profiles* can aggregate performance information over different test functions, problem difficulties, and quality indicators. We apply this approach to compare three common algorithms on a new test function suite derived from the well-known single-objective BBOB functions. The focus thereby lies less on gaining insights into the algorithms but more on showcasing the concepts and on what can be gained over current benchmarking approaches.

Categories and Subject Descriptors

G.1.6 [**Numerical Analysis**]: Optimization—*global optimization, unconstrained optimization*

Keywords

Benchmarking; Black-box optimization; Multiobjective optimization

1. A BRIEF OVERVIEW OF MULTIOBJECTIVE PERFORMANCE ASSESSMENT

Multiobjective optimization problems occur frequently in practice and several optimization algorithms are available that typically aim at finding a set of solutions that approximate the set of Pareto-optimal solutions with respect to the three criteria convergence, spread, and a good distribution [21]. In order to suggest well-performing algorithms to the practitioner, one needs to get insights into when and where algorithms have their strengths and weaknesses. Also for algorithm design, it is important to know where algorithms are failing in order to improve them while not introducing additional detrimental effects on the performance. Due to the difficulty of theoretical analyses, such investigations on algorithm performance are typically done by numerical experiments—in other words by *benchmarking*.

While in the early stages of (evolutionary) multiobjective optimization, visual comparisons of the resulting Pareto front approximations of algorithms have been used to draw conclusions, in recent years two complementary approaches have been developed to compare stochastic and set-based multiobjective optimization algorithms. The study of *Empirical Attainment Functions (EAFs)* [8], on the one hand, allows for graphical tools to visualize the (empirical) "probabilistic distribution of the outcomes obtained by a stochastic algorithm in the objective space" and the differences between algorithms in objective space [15]. On the other hand, most of the current studies in the EMO field use *quality indicators* such as the hypervolume- or ε-indicator to assess the quality of resulting solution sets [12, 20, 22]. Both the EAF approach and the idea of reporting quality indicators have in common that typical studies only report data for one or a few, often arbitrary, budgets of function evaluations[1].

Contrarily, in the single-objective blackbox optimization community, state-of-the-art benchmarking studies usually report (the distribution of) target-based runlengths[2] and illustrate them in so-called data and performance profiles [7, 16] which are also known as empirical cumulative distribution functions or empirical runtime distributions [11]. This has the advantage that the reported values are quantitative measurements on a ratio scale and, as runlengths, easily interpretable. For a specific problem difficulty, i.e., a target function value f_{target}, an algorithm $\mathcal{A}$ can be easily considered c times slower than an algorithm $\mathcal{B}$ if it takes c times longer to reach a function value of f_{target}. When comparing function (or indicator) values achieved at specific budgets,

GECCO'15, July 11–15, 2015, Madrid, Spain.
©2015 ACM. ISBN: 978-1-4503-3472-3/15/07 ...$15.00.
DOI: `http://dx.doi.org/10.1145/2739480.2754777`.

[1]In the case of combinatorial problems, where the view of the optimization problem as a blackbox is often violated, we also see studies that fix the computation time.

[2]Given a target function value f_{target}, the target-based runlength of algorithm $\mathcal{A}$ on function f is the number of function evaluations until $\mathcal{A}$ samples a solution s with $f(s) < f_{\text{target}}$.

however, the interpretation of reported indicator values is (at most) not intuitive. Another advantage of reporting target-based runlengths is that it allows to compare algorithms with different stopping criteria more naturally.

Related Benchmarking Studies.

Only very few studies started recently to also provide target-based runlengths when comparing multiobjective optimization algorithms and it is the main purpose of this paper to push forward this idea for benchmarking especially evolutionary multiobjective optimization algorithms. Custodio et al. [3] for example show performance profiles for the so-called purity indicator and two spread metrics as well as data profiles for purity while stochastic algorithms are displayed with respect to their worst, average, or best runs instead of displaying the full data distribution. In this benchmarking study, 100 test problems with different numbers of variables (from 2 till 30) and different numbers of objectives (2 and 3) are mixed within a plot while problems with lower search space dimension and less objectives are over-represented. Denysiuk et al. [5] mainly follow the standard way of showing ε- and hypervolume indicator values after a given budget of function evaluations and use performance profiles only briefly to show the distributions of the median values of both indicators. In another study, Denysiuk et al. [6] also use performance profiles to study the median values of the IGD indicator. Also in those two papers, the performance profiles aggregate over problems with different search space and objective space dimensions.

When looking at these few studies that use data and performance profiles for comparing multiobjective optimization algorithms, four concerns can be raised:

- The first study uses quality indicators that are not compliant with the Pareto dominance relation. This is also the case for the CEC'2009 competition [20].
- All studies mix problems of different search space dimensions and numbers of objective functions which does not allow for scalability analyses.
- On the contrary, typically different problem accuracies (or target difficulties) are not combined in a single plot, although this seems to make sense as on a single function, this allows to rediscover the algorithms' convergence plots (see also the next section for details).
- Most of the used test problems have characteristics for which it is at least questionable whether they are representative for real-world problems (e.g. are many of the often used problems separable or they contain distinctive distance- and position-related variables).

While benchmarking studies coming from the EMO field, such as the CEC'2007 competition [12], do typically use Pareto-dominance-compliant quality indicators, most of the recent studies in EMO report the achieved quality indicator values for a few (arbitrary) numbers of function evaluations instead of reporting (several) target-based runlengths. Many studies furthermore report results for a disproportionately high number of separable functions. Also scalability analyses with respect to the number of variables are rare though scalability with respect to the number of objectives gained recent interest, see for example [17]. As to the benchmark problems, several well-known test suites such as the DTLZ, WFG, and CEC 2009 problems (see e.g. [9]) are available and accepted in the community, but besides their mentioned deficiencies (separability, distance- vs. position-related variables, ...), they do not naturally suggest the distinction between problems and instances and, hence, their usage might have resulted in overfitting algorithms' performances to the few available problems in each benchmark suite.

In the case of single-objective blackbox optimization, most of the above concerns have been addressed by the recent and nowadays well-established Blackbox Optimization Benchmarking (BBOB) framework [10]. Here, aggregation of data is never performed over different search space dimensions in order to allow for statements on the scalability of algorithms with increasing dimension whereas runtimes for more than one target value are typically aggregated in single plots. Moreover, a large effort has been spent on the choice of the test problems in order to select 24 meaningful and yet understandable test problems which all offer a large number of randomly generated instances[3]. The problems exhibit a wide range of difficulties observed in practice. Except for one, no BBOB problem is fully quadratic and only five of them are separable.

Our Contributions.

Here, we build upon this BBOB framework by (i) using combinations of the 24 single-objective BBOB test functions to create bi-objective test problems, by (ii) recording runlengths to reach predefined target difficulties in terms of quality indicator differences to a reference set, and finally by (iii) using data profiles to illustrate their distribution while aggregating over target values, problems, and indicators. Further details on the experimental setup will be given in the following sections.

In order to showcase the idea of recording target-based runlengths and providing data profiles to visualize them, we compare three common EMO algorithms on a set of 300 BBOB-based bi-objective test problems and illustrate which new insights can be gained by the new benchmarking approach in Sec. 5.2. We thereby advocate the usage of an *external archive* of all non-dominated solutions found by an algorithm so far, as we believe this is relevant practice in bi-objective real-world applications where function evaluations are expensive. The usage of the external archive to define an algorithm's quality has the additional advantage that algorithms of different population sizes can be easily compared with each other.

Let us note that, by no means, our proposal is meant as a sole replacement of any current benchmarking exercise, but is expected to be complemented by other benchmarking and visualization efforts such as empirical attainment functions [8] or a rigorous (automated) identification of the algorithms' "search controls and failure modes" [9].

2. DATA PROFILES

When benchmarking (single-objective) blackbox optimization algorithms, the first step is typically to define a test problem which consists of (i) a test function such as SPHERE, ROSENBROCK, etc., (ii) a specific instance of this test function, e.g., a shifted or rotated version of the original test function, and (iii) a given target difficulty f_{target} to which the instance of the test function is supposed to be solved. Then, we run our algorithms of interest on this test problem and report and compare the algorithms' runtimes in terms

[3]In addition to these 24 noiseless problems, a benchmark suite with 30 noisy BBOB functions exists.

of the number of function evaluations until the problem's target function value is reached.[4]

Most of the time, we do not have a single test problem we are interested in but a whole test suite and if the number of test problems is large, it might be tedious to look at the single runtimes for each problem. Then, it often makes sense to aggregate the results in one way or the other. One standard way of doing this graphically is to display so-called *data profiles* [16]. A data profile is an empirical cumulative distribution function (ECDF) of the observed runtimes over all test problems in which we can read (on the y-axis) how many problems have been solved by each algorithm for a given budget (on the x-axis)[5]. More formally, a data profile for a solver s on a problem class $\mathcal{P}$ is defined as

$$d_s(\alpha) = \frac{1}{|\mathcal{P}|}\text{size}\left\{p \in \mathcal{P} \,\middle|\, \frac{t_{p,s}}{n_p} \leq \alpha\right\} \tag{1}$$

with $t_{p,s}$ being the observed runtime of solver s on problem p and n_p the number of variables of problem p [16]. Note that one can interpret the choice of p in Eq. 1 in two ways: either the problems are picked uniformly at random from $\mathcal{P}$ or the set of problems $\mathcal{P}$ is fixed beforehand and hence the choice of p is not always independent (for example if more than one target-based runlength is recorded for the same algorithm run). In the limit, however, both interpretations are equivalent. The idea behind having different instances of the same test function in a problem class is to allow for repetitions and statistically relevant results with respect to invariance properties of both stochastic and deterministic algorithms. Instead of running the same algorithm several times on the same instance, typically one (stochastic) algorithm run is performed on each instance, see e.g. [10].

The data profile approach has not only the advantage to display a large amount of data in a single plot that makes it easier to compare algorithms quickly (an algorithm is better if its data profile is more to the left and higher), but has also other important advantages:

Rediscovering convergence graphs: On a single function and when using a set of target values, plotting the data profile of a single run allows to rediscover the convergence graph (i.e. the best-so-far function value over time). The more target function values are defined, the closer the (vertically flipped) data profile is to the original convergence graph (where possibly the y-axis has to be rescaled accordingly). An illustration is shown in Fig. 1.

No constraint on the maximum number of function evaluations: Another beauty of the data profile approach is that algorithms can be compared even if they have not been run with the same number of function evaluations. The comparison is valid for runlengths up to the smallest budget among the compared algorithms.

Extracting information about function classes: Grouping different functions with similar properties to problem classes allows to extract information about on which types of problem algorithms are better and on which they are worse. In the single-objective BBOB testbed [10, 11], groups of separable or multimodal functions, for example, have been defined—between which one can see significant differences among the algorithms' performances.

[4]We report ∞ if the target has not been reached in the experiment.

[5]Solving a problem thereby means that the algorithm run has reached the problem's target precision.

All in all, data profiles are an important tool in state-of-the-art single-objective blackbox optimization benchmarking exercises that have been used already in a few derivative-free multiobjective optimization papers as indicated above. We are convinced that data profiles will also ease algorithm comparisons in the EMO field and consequently will lead to improved algorithms in practice. It will especially allow us to compare the performance of multiobjective algorithms over time while currently most studies (still) only look at a single or a few arbitrary budgets and report the quality values reached at those specific times. The additional advantage of displaying target-based runtimes is that the shown numbers are actually meaningful: It is easy to grasp that an algorithm that needs half as many function evaluations to solve a given problem is twice as efficient while knowing that the reached quality after the same budget is by a certain factor larger for one algorithm is usually difficult to interpret.

3. TRANSFERRING SINGLE-OBJECTIVE BENCHMARKING CONCEPTS TO THE MULTIOBJECTIVE SCENARIO

All we have to do to transfer the idea of data profiles to the multiobjective case is to define $t_{p,s}$ in Eq. 1 and, thus, more precisely what we define as a problem to be solved.

In the multiobjective case, k objective functions $f_i : X \to \mathbb{R}$ have to be simultaneously optimized (we assume, w.l.o.g., minimization here). If we assume the standard Pareto dominance relation $\prec$ is the underlying preference structure[6], the goal is to find (a subset or an approximation of) the Pareto set $\mathcal{P}_S = \{x^* \mid \nexists x \in X : x \prec x^*\}$. As usual, we call the image of $\mathcal{P}_S$ under $f = (f_1, \ldots, f_k)$ the Pareto front. Finding a subset or an approximation of the Pareto set is underspecified as such. Hence, we are typically interested in finding a solution set of as high quality as possible in as few function evaluations as possible where the quality of a solution set is given by a so-called quality indicator $I : 2^X \to \mathbb{R}$.

As a related issue, let us briefly discuss the difference between bounded and unbounded solution sets here. If we are interested in solution sets of a fixed size (of let us say μ), the optimization goal is to find a set of μ solutions among all sets of μ solutions that maximizes the quality indicator. For these optimal sets of μ solutions with respect to a quality indicator, the term *optimal μ-distribution* has been introduced [1]. If, on the other hand, an unbounded set with maximal quality indicator is sought, a good idea is to maintain an external archive of all non-dominated solutions found so far which, recently, even has been argued for when the the optimal μ-distribution is sought and can be extracted from the archive efficiently [2, 13].

Independent of whether an external archive is used or not, a problem p to define $t_{p,s}$ in the multiobjective case now consists of a given function per objective, a specific function instance per objective, a given quality indicator, and the target quality of the quality indicator. The quality indicator can thereby be computed with respect to a bounded or unbounded archive or as the indicator value of the best solution subset of size μ found so far. The value $t_{p,s}$ is then defined as the time to reach the given target indicator quality of problem p for solver s and the data profile can be plotted as in the single-objective case.

[6]We say solution x dominates solution y if $\forall 1 \leq i \leq k$: $f_i(x) \leq f_i(y)$ and $\exists 1 \leq i \leq k : f_i(x) < f_i(y)$ and write $x \prec y$.

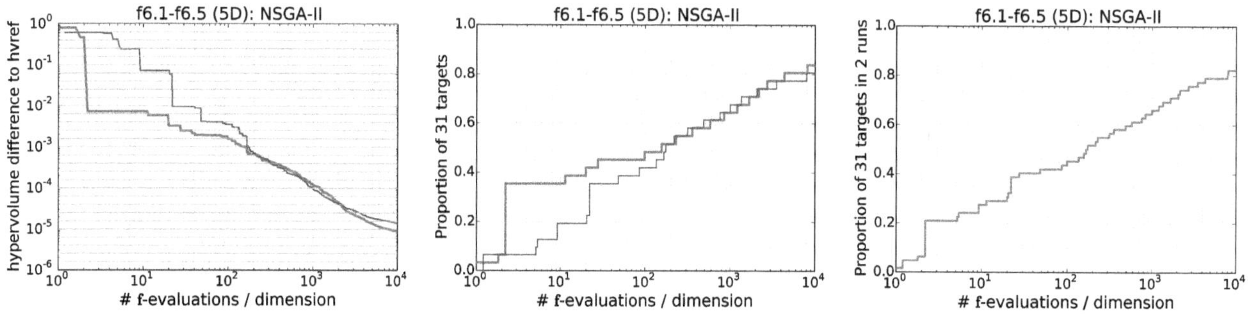

Figure 1: Recovery of convergence graphs using data profiles. The left plot shows the difference over time between the hypervolume indicator in two runs of NSGA-II to the hypervolume of the reference set on a combination of two instances (1 and 5) of the Attractive Sector function (f_6) in 5-D. The middle plot shows the corresponding data profile for each run individually using the 31 target values displayed as light (brown) horizontal lines on the left plot. The right plot shows the data profile, aggregated over the two runs.

As such, *multiobjective* data profiles do not only allow to aggregate results over several test functions and target difficulties but also over different quality indicators. However, one has to be careful that aggregating over different difficulties of the problems might bias the conclusions drawn from a data profile. This is evident when combining problems with different numbers of objective functions or search space dimensions—in particular if they are not uniformly distributed over the chosen problems. But also when combining results for several quality indicators, one should be careful to not introduce a strong bias, e.g., one should prevent that for one indicator significantly more target values are reached than for another indicator.

To not bias the implications made from a benchmarking exercise and to keep the test problems as close to real-world applications as possible is always an important and challenging task when designing a test problem suite. Hence, we rely here on an already established single-objective benchmark suite, the BBOB test problems [10, 11] and combine them to bi-objective problems by simply using all possible function combinations. Moreover, we use three well-known multiobjective optimization algorithms, namely NSGA-II [4], MOEA/D [19], and MO-CMA-ES [18], as a baseline to produce a reference set per problem instance, according to which the quality indicators are compared and the target difficulties are defined relatively. In the following, we will give some more details on this new multiobjective testbed.

4. GENERALIZING THE BBOB TESTBED TO MULTIOBJECTIVE OPTIMIZATION

The noiseless BBOB testbed [10] has 24 single-objective functions that are categorized into five groups: (1) five *separable* functions, (2) four *low or moderate condition* functions, (3) five *high condition* functions, (4) five *multi-modal* functions, and (5) five *multi-modal with weak global structure* functions. All functions are scalable in the number of decision variables. Typically, the testbed is used in dimensions 2, 3, 5, 10, 20, and sometimes 40. Importantly, all optima are known. Each of the functions has different *instances* in each dimension which are characterized by specific (random) transformations of the original function such as non-linear variable transformations or a rotation of the search space.

In order to generalize the noiseless BBOB testbed to a bi-objective one, and assuming that typical algorithms are invariant under permutations of the objective functions, we use all combinations of two BBOB functions f_i and f_j such that $1 \leq i \leq j \leq 24$ which gives $\binom{24}{2} + 24 = 300$ function combinations. The bi-objective instances are generated by choosing non-repetitive instances of the single-objective functions with the additional constraint that the two corresponding single-objective optima are different for each bi-objective function combination (across all 300 combinations and over dimensions 2, 3, 5, 10, 20, and 40). Here, we propose combining the five instances 2, 3, 7, 9, and 11 of the first objective function pairwisely with the five instances 4, 5, 8, 10, and 12 of the second objective function which guarantees that the single-objective optima are always different.

The above mentioned five function groups of the single-objective BBOB testbed result in natural—with the same argumentation as above—$\binom{5}{2} + 5 = 15$ groups of bi-objective test functions of which the first objective is chosen from a first function group and the second objective function is chosen from a second (potentially the same) function group. Since all but one function group have five elements, the 15 bi-objective function groups contain either $5 \cdot 5 = 25$ (10 groups), $5 \cdot 4 = 20$ (4 groups), or $4 \cdot 4 = 16$ (1 group) bi-objective problems. We have now, for example, a group of *separable–separable* bi-objective problems where separable functions are combined together or a *separable–multi-modal* group. Additionally, we can aggregate over all possible combinations of single-objective test functions, which will be denoted as *all functions–all functions* in the following plots.

Now we have a suite of multiobjective test problems with instances; what is missing is to define quality indicators and target values. As to the former, we use the two most popular and often recommended quality indicators of hypervolume and (additive) ε-indicator [22]. More precisely, we use the difference between the unary hypervolume indicator of the set of all non-dominated solutions found so far (in other words, the *archive*) and the hypervolume of a pre-computed *reference set* as well as the binary ε-indicator between the archive and the reference set. All objective vectors are scaled in the performance assessment step such that the known ideal and nadir points are at $(0,0)$ and $(1,1)$ respectively. At every new function evaluation, the archive and the hypervolume indicator difference are updated efficiently *on-the-fly*. The ε-indicator, for the time being, is computed from the stored non-dominated archive in a postprocessing step though a similar on-the-fly calculation is possible.

To compute the reference set for the indicators, we ran the algorithms NSGA-II (15 independent trials), MOEA/D (15 trials), and MO-CMA-ES (10 trials)[7] with population sizes of 1000, 1000, and 200 for $5{\cdot}10^5 D$, $5{\cdot}10^5 D$, and $10^5 D$ function evaluations, respectively. The non-dominated set of all evaluated solutions per test function instance is then used as the reference set.

As to the target values, 70 linearly spaced targets in the logarithmic scale from $10^{-0.1}$ to 10^{-7} were used for the hypervolume indicator and from $10^{-0.1}$ to 10^{-5} for the ε-indicator. To save disk space, we have used a thinning strategy that only writes *new* non-dominated solutions accumulated in the memory to disk when a new hypervolume target is hit. Non-dominated solutions generated after the previous target hit that are dominated at the time of the current target hit are explicitly discarded.

The usage of the external archive to define the performance of an algorithm in the bi-objective case is probably the most arguable part of our proposed benchmarking. However, note that in the bi-objective case, all obtained non-dominated objective vectors can be plotted easily to get an idea of the Pareto front and second, this approach allows to compare algorithms with different population sizes naturally. Moreover, the implementation of the archiving as well as the on-the-fly computation of the two indicator values is relatively cheap in the bi-objective case and does not add up much within the benchmarking (see Sec. 5.2). Note finally, that in the future, we plan to include also the extracted best subset of the archive of a specific size as performance measure, similar to [2, 13].

The proposed multiobjective BBOB test suite was implemented upon the COCO (COmparing Continuous Optimisers, [10]) platform and is available for download at `http://coco.gforge.inria.fr/GECCO2015-MOBBOB/`.

5. CASE STUDY ON THE MULTIOBJECTIVE BBOB TESTBED

In the remainder of the paper, we showcase what can be extracted from recorded data and demonstrate how the proposed multiobjective BBOB, by using data profiles, distinguishes from previous multiobjective benchmarking studies.

5.1 Experimental Setup

The three algorithms NSGA-II, MOEA/D, and MO-CMA-ES have been benchmarked on the proposed multiobjective testbed. Each algorithm was run once on each of the above mentioned 5 instances on every of the 300 bi-objective problems in dimensions 2, 3, 5, 10, and 20. All algorithms used a population size of 200. Since the employed implementations of NSGA-II and MOEA/D turned out to be fast compared to the Shark implementation of MO-CMA-ES, we allocated the same $10^5 D$ function evaluations for NSGA-II and MOEA/D while limiting the latter to $4{\cdot}10^4 D$ evaluations.

It should be noted that NSGA-II used the simulated binary crossover with a distribution index of 20 and a crossover rate of 1 and polynomial mutation, having a distribution index of 50 with a mutation rate of $1/D$. MOEA/D employed the differential evolution crossover of [14] with parameters $CR = 0.8$ and $F = 0.9$, and exactly the same mutation as of NSGA-II. In MOEA/D, a neighborhood size of 20 is used with a probability of 0.8 for selecting mating parents from the neighborhood. MO-CMA-ES uses the population-based notion of success within the generational evolutionary strategy (the $(\mu+\mu)$MO-CMA-ES^P version as in [18]).

We have also conducted an additional experiment to demonstrate the impact of the population size on the performance of NSGA-II, to which end we ran NSGA-II with population sizes of 48, 100, 148, 200, 500, and 1000 on the 5-D problems. All configurations were run up to $4{\cdot}10^5 D$ function evaluations except for those with large populations of 500 and 1000 individuals, which were run for $2{\cdot}10^5 D$ and $10^5 D$ function evaluations, respectively.

5.2 Experimental Results

The following paragraphs describe the results obtained from the benchmarking as displayed in Figures 2–6 and discuss the advantages gained over previous benchmarking efforts without the use of the archive, target-based runlengths, and data profiles. Due to space limitations, not all plots can be shown here but additional material is provided at `http://coco.gforge.inria.fr/GECCO2015-MOBBOB/`.

Possibility to Compare Algorithms with Different Population Sizes and Different Stopping Criteria: Figure 2 provides examples of data profiles displaying the performance of NSGA-II with different population sizes on three 5-D test functions. We clearly see that NSGA-II, when using a larger population size, becomes consistently slower in the beginning of the optimization (roughly by a factor of 6 between population sizes 48 and 1000). This is mostly related to the fact that the entire first generation resembles random search. The performance in the later stages of the search are less clear: whereas on the f_{12}–f_{21} combination, a larger population size clearly helps, the f_5–f_{11} example shows no trend. Note also that the algorithms displayed in Fig. 2 have been run for different numbers of function evaluations (indicated by big crosses at the evaluation budgets) which is a clear advantage of using the indicator values of all non-dominated solutions found as performance criterion.

Influence of Search Space Dimension: Figure 3 presents the data profiles of NSGA-II, MOEA/D, and MO-CMA-ES over five instances on the combinations of separable Ellipsoid (f_2) and separable Rastrigin (f_3) functions in dimensions 2, 3, 5, 10, and 20. Due to lack of space, only the individual-dimension plots for 2-D, 5-D, and 20-D are shown. It is, however, sufficient to realize the different behavior of the algorithms across dimensions. Accordingly, the aggregation over dimensions, as shown in the rightmost plot, turns out to be less interpretive. Indeed, without looking at the 2-D plot, it is hard to know from the aggregation plot that the hypervolume of MO-CMA-ES begins to approach that of the other algorithms in the 2–$4{\cdot}10^4$ functions evaluations range in 2-D. Because performance differences among algorithms might change drastically over dimensions, showing data profiles that aggregate over dimensions is usually not recommended. More informative, on the contrary, are scaling plots such as the ones in Fig. 4. Here, the expected running times [10] to hit the hypervolume target of 10^{-3} are plotted for all algorithms across five dimension values. NSGA-II is seen to scale better than the other algorithms on

[7]We employed the original implementations of NSGA-II in C from `http://www.iitk.ac.in/kangal/codes.shtml`, MOEA/D in C++ from `http://dces.essex.ac.uk/staff/zhang/webofmoead.htm`, and MO-CMA-ES in C++ from the Shark library at `http://image.diku.dk/shark`.

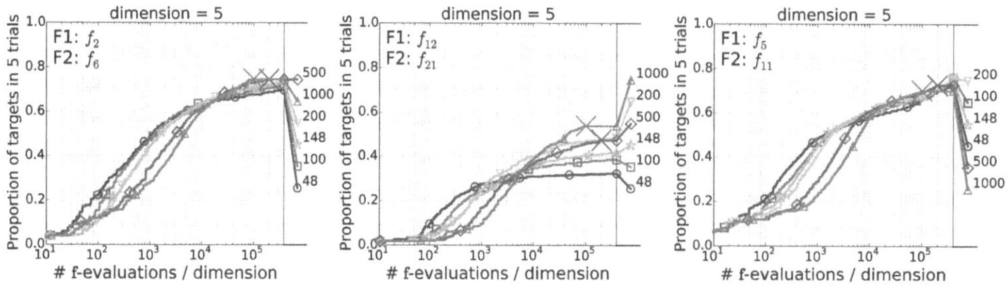

Figure 2: Comparison of six NSGA-II configurations using data profiles based on the hypervolume indicator. Each configuration goes with a different population size in $\{48, 100, 148, 200, 500, 1000\}$ and some of them have different run lengths. Cross signs indicate the function evaluation at which the algorithm was terminated.

the separable f_2-f_3 combination and solves the 20-D problem up to the given target while the other algorithms never hit this target within their allocated budget. Note that this behavior is specific to the separable functions shown here due to the fact that NSGA-II and MOEA/D's variation operators exploit separability while the MO-CMA-ES is invariant under rotations of the search space. Indeed, when a separable function is combined with a rotated, a high-condition, or a multi-modal function (Fig. 4, from left to right), the MO-CMA-ES is seen to scale significantly better than NSGA-II and MOEA/D, especially in the last case where only the MO-CMA-ES can solve the 10-D problem.

Aggregating Data over Test Functions: Looking at every single function combination and dimension is tedious, especially when 300 function combinations are involved. Thus, it is advisable to aggregate the data over all functions or a subset thereof to get a quick idea about performance differences first. Data profiles make this easy as can be seen in Fig. 5. The aggregation over all 300 function combinations looses most information (left) while the aggregation over functions with the same properties (middle and right) seems to be a good compromise and results in more pronounced, yet interpretable results. The overall picture in the left plot of Fig. 5, for example, tells us that NSGA-II outperforms the other two algorithms until about $6 \cdot 10^3$ function evaluations at which MO-CMA-ES takes the lead. MOEA/D seems dominated by NSGA-II at any budget of function evaluations. We can see that this is not the full picture if we focus on aggregations over function groups. If all objective functions are separable (Fig. 5, middle), the conclusions change drastically: NSGA-II becomes the dominating algorithm, outperforming the other two at any time. On the combination of moderate and multi-modal functions, however, even MOEA/D starts to outperform NSGA-II from around $5 \cdot 10^3$ function evaluations.

Aggregating Over Different Quality Indicators: Finally, data profiles also allow to aggregate performance over different indicators. In Figure 6, we show data profiles aggregating over hypervolume and ε-indicator on 5-D problems. The left-most and middle plots show the data profiles for individual indicators while the right-most plot shows the aggregated data over both indicators—exemplary for the combination of the Rosenbrock (f_8) and Weierstrass (f_{16}) functions. We observe that MO-CMA-ES is faster than the other two algorithms after about $4 \cdot 10^4 D$ function evaluations w.r.t. either of the two quality indicators. The superiority of MO-CMA-ES is then confirmed in the data profiles aggregating over both indicators.

Few Details on Timing, Data Storage and Thinning: Maintaining the archive of nondominated solutions and the computation of the indicators naïvely can be time consuming. In the case of only two objectives, however, both the archive and the hypervolume indicator value can be updated on-the-fly using appropriate data structures. Our implementation (in C) thus allows us to keep the additional overhead of the benchmarking small. Under a single core of the Intel i7-3520M CPU @ 2.9 GHz, running NSGA-II on an instance of the 300 combinations over 10^4 function evaluations, for example, takes 110 seconds without data logging, 119 seconds with logging nondominated solutions over time, and 120 seconds with logging nondominated solutions and computing the hypervolume indicator on-the-fly.

Once the actual algorithm runs are complete and the raw data is logged, a postprocessing script in Python enables us to automatically produce the plots as presented in this paper for the visual comparison of the algorithms. This script basically performs two major functions: processing the logged data to create a database of data profiles and plotting (and aggregating) these data profiles. Most of the postprocessing time lies in the extraction of data profiles. It takes, for example, about 12 minutes to build all data profiles for NSGA-II in 5-D and 3 minutes for the plotting.

Although the proposed data thinning results in significantly smaller data files than if all non-dominated points are recorded (typically 30% less), the amount of produced data for a typical benchmarking experiment is still quite large. This is unfortunately unavoidable if the unbounded external archive has to be stored. Running MO-CMA-ES resulted in the largest amount of data among the three tested algorithms. The corresponding amount of logged data when running MO-CMA-ES on five instances of all 300 test problems in dimensions 2, 3, 5, 10, and 20 is 3.8 GB compared to 2.2 GB for NSGA-II and 2.4 GB for MOEA/D. Though this amount is reasonable, given the cheap storage capacities these days, we plan to reduce this size further to ease the online distribution of algorithm data sets and to improve the ability to benchmark larger sets of algorithms.

6. CONCLUSIONS

Reporting the empirical cumulative distribution of target-based run lengths in so-called data profiles is a standard way to display and compare the performance of single-objective optimizers. Contrary, in the multiobjective case, most of the time, some statistics about the reached quality indicators for a certain budget (or a few budgets in number of function evaluations) are reported. In this paper, we argue in favor

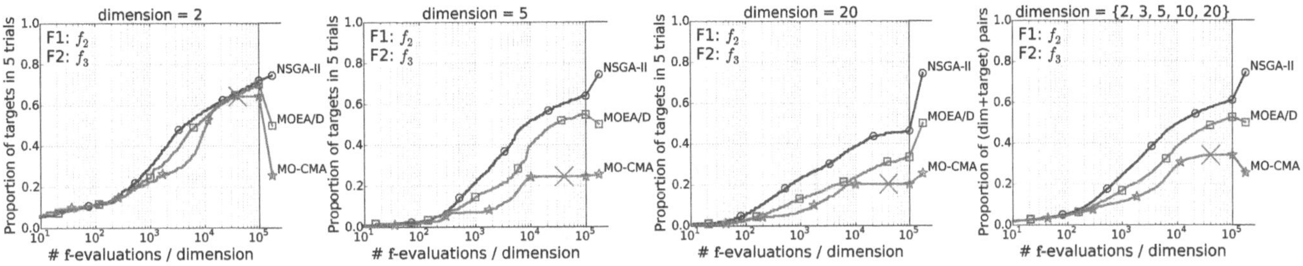

Figure 3: Influence of search space dimensions on the combination of separable Ellipsoid (f_2) and separable Rastrigin (f_3) functions w.r.t. the hypervolume indicator. The rightmost plot shows the aggregation of data profiles over all dimensions. Cross signs indicate the budget for MO-CMA-ES.

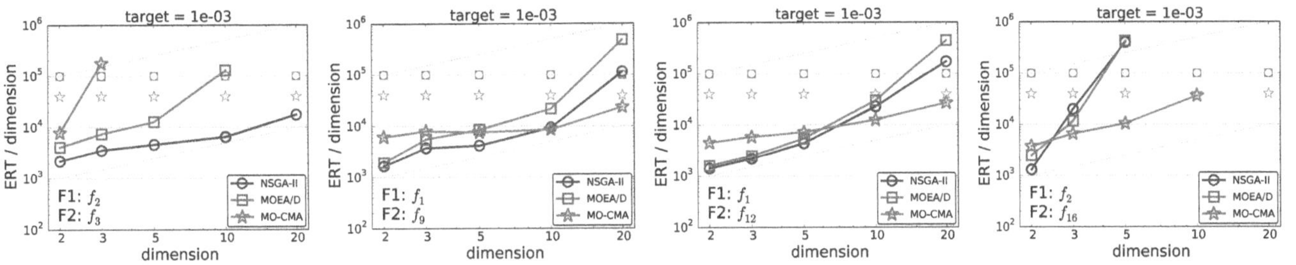

Figure 4: Expected running time (ERT, in number of f-evaluations) divided by dimension for the hypervolume target value 10^{-3} versus dimension. Light symbols give the maximum number of f-evaluations from the longest trial divided by dimension. Horizontal lines give linear scaling and slanted dotted lines give quadratic scaling.

of using data profiles also for benchmarking multiobjective optimizers and show how this can be achieved efficiently when combining the single-objective BBOB functions of [10, 11] to a bi-objective test suite. The proposed approach to performance assessment has several advantages:

- Reporting target-based runlengths instead of budget based quality indicator values makes the displayed values meaningful: it is for example easier to grasp that an algorithm takes twice as long to solve a certain problem than to understand what a quality indicator difference of a certain value means.
- Measuring the quality of an algorithm via an external archive allows to compare methods with different population sizes.
- Displaying empirical cumulative distribution functions aka data profiles allows to evaluate the algorithms over time (in an anytime setting) while no maximum number of function evaluations has to be prescribed.
- Using data profiles enables the aggregation of results over different targets, over different functions or function groups, and over different quality indicators.
- The use of well-established and well-understood single-objective test functions can help to explain performance differences of multiobjective optimizers but also to improve currently available algorithms for tackling the difficulties observed in practical applications.

The main disadvantage of the approach and the biggest challenge is that meaningful target f-values need to be defined to get meaningful problems.

Exploiting the described methodology for benchmarking state-of-the-art algorithms extensively and for designing new algorithms will be one of the obvious next steps. Extensions towards other quality measures that can be efficiently computed on-the-fly are planned. It is certainly interesting to additionally use the highest indicator value over all subsets of the archive with exactly μ solutions as a performance criterion as suggested in [2, 13].

Acknowledgments This work was supported by the grant ANR-12-MONU-0009 (NumBBO) of the French National Research Agency. TDT is further supported by an individual PhD grant of Inria.

7. REFERENCES

[1] A. Auger, J. Bader, D. Brockhoff, and E. Zitzler. Theory of the Hypervolume Indicator: Optimal μ-Distributions and the Choice of the Reference Point. In *Foundations of Genetic Algorithms (FOGA 2009)*, pages 87–102. ACM, 2009.

[2] K. Bringmann, T. Friedrich, and P. Klitzke. Two-dimensional Subset Selection for Hypervolume and Epsilon-Indicator. In *Genetic and Evolutionary Computation Conference (GECCO 2014)*, pages 589–596. ACM Press, 2014.

[3] A. L. Custódio, J. F. A. Madeira, A. I. F. Vaz, and L. N. Vicente. Direct multisearch for multiobjective optimization. *SIAM Journal on Optimization*, 21:1109–1140, 2011.

[4] K. Deb, A. Pratap, S. Agarwal, and T. Meyarivan. A Fast and Elitist Multiobjective Genetic Algorithm: NSGA-II. *IEEE Transactions on Evolutionary Computation*, 6(2):182–197, 2002.

[5] R. Denysiuk, L. Costa, and I. E. Santo. A New Hybrid Evolutionary Multiobjective Algorithm Guided by Descent Directions. *Journal of Mathematical Modelling and Algorithms*, 12:233–251, 2013.

[6] R. Denysiuk, L. Costa, and I. E. Santo. Many-Objective Optimization using Differential Evolution with Variable-Wise Mutation Restriction. In *Conference on Genetic and Evolutionary Computation (GECCO 2013)*, pages 591–598. ACM, 2013.

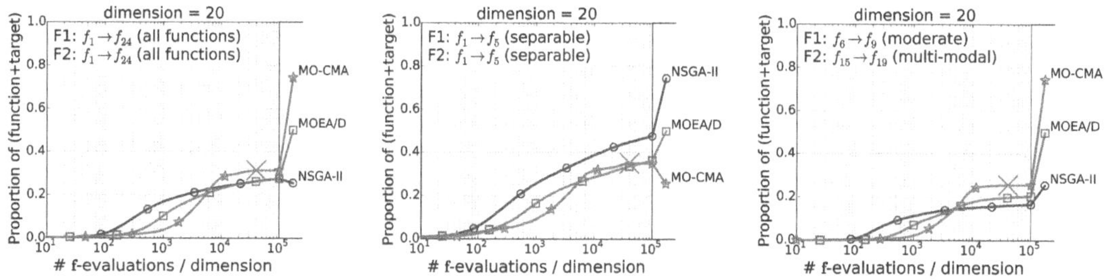

Figure 5: Hypervolume-indicator-based data profiles aggregating over all 300 problems (left), over all combinations of separable functions (middle), and over all combinations of moderate and multi-modal functions.

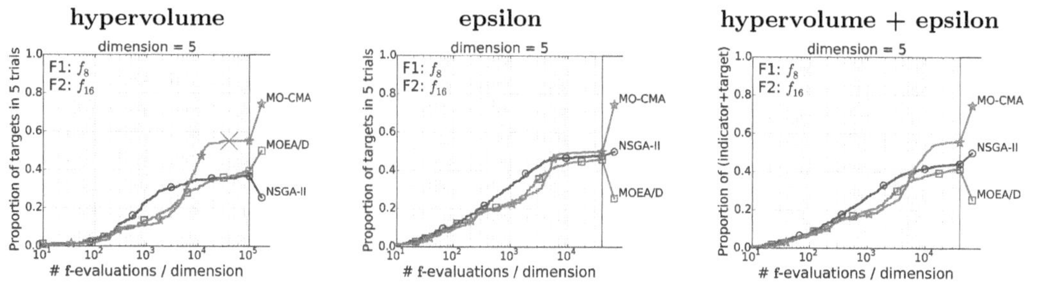

Figure 6: Data profiles of algorithm performances for the combination of Rosenbrock (f_8) and Weierstrass (f_{16}) functions in 5-D. The left and center plots show data profiles for the hypervolume and ε-indicator respectively, and the right plot shows the aggregation over both indicators.

[7] E. D. Dolan and J. J. Moré. Benchmarking Optimization software with Performance Profiles. *Mathematical Programming*, 91:201–213, 2002.

[8] V. Grunert da Fonseca, C. M. Fonseca, and A. O. Hall. Inferential Performance Assessment of Stochastic Optimisers and the Attainment Function. In *Evolutionary Multi-Criterion Optimization (EMO 2001)*, pages 213–225. Springer, 2001.

[9] D. Hadka and P. Reed. Diagnostic Assessment of Search Controls and Failure Modes in Many-objective Evolutionary Optimization. *Evolutionary Computation*, 20(3):423–452, 2012.

[10] N. Hansen, A. Auger, S. Finck, and R. Ros. Real-Parameter Black-Box Optimization Benchmarking 2009: Experimental Setup. Research Report RR-6828, INRIA Saclay, 2009.

[11] N. Hansen, A. Auger, R. Ros, S. Finck, and P. Posík. Comparing Results of 31 Algorithms from the Black-box Optimization Benchmarking BBOB-2009. In *GECCO workshop on Black-Box Optimization Benchmarking (BBOB'2010)*, pages 1689–1696, 2010.

[12] V. L. Huang, A. K. Qin, K. Deb, E. Zitzler, P. N. Suganthan, J. J. Liang, M. Preuss, and S. Huband. Problem Definitions for Performance Assessment of Multi-objective Optimization Algorithms. Technical report, Nanyang Technological University, 2007.

[13] T. Kuhn, C. M. Fonseca, L. Paquete, S. Ruzika, and J. R. Figueira. Hypervolume Subset Selection in Two Dimensions: Formulations and Algorithms. Technical report, University of Kaiserslautern, 2014.

[14] S. Kukkonen and J. Lampinen. Performance Assessment of Generalized Differential Evolution 3 with a Given Set of Constrained Multi-objective Test Problems. In *IEEE Congress on Evolutionary Computation (CEC 2009)*, pages 1943–1950, 2009.

[15] M. López-Ibáñez, L. Paquete, and T. Stützle. Exploratory Analysis of Stochastic Local Search Algorithms in Biobjective Optimization. In *Experimental Methods for the Analysis of Optimization Algorithms*, pages 209–222. Springer, 2010.

[16] J. Moré and S. Wild. Benchmarking Derivative-Free Optimization Algorithms. *SIAM J. Optimization*, 20(1):172–191, 2009.

[17] C. von Lücken, B. Barán, and C. Brizuela. A Survey on Multi-Objective Evolutionary Algorithms for Many-Objective Problems. *Computational Optimization and Applications*, 58(3):707–756, 2014.

[18] T. Voß, N. Hansen, and C. Igel. Improved Step Size Adaptation for the MO-CMA-ES. In *Conference on Genetic and Evolutionary Computation (GECCO 2010)*, pages 487–494. ACM, 2010.

[19] Q. Zhang and H. Li. MOEA/D: A Multiobjective Evolutionary Algorithm Based on Decomposition. *IEEE Transactions on Evolutionary Computation*, 11(6):712–731, 2007.

[20] Q. Zhang, A. Zhou, S. Zhao, P. Suganthan, W. Liu, and S. Tiwari. Multiobjective Optimization Test Instances for the CEC 2009 Special Session and Competition. Technical report, Univ. of Essex, 2009.

[21] E. Zitzler. *Evolutionary Algorithms for Multiobjective Optimization: Methods and Applications.* PhD thesis, ETH Zurich, Switzerland, 1999.

[22] E. Zitzler, L. Thiele, M. Laumanns, C. M. Fonseca, and V. Grunert da Fonseca. Performance Assessment of Multiobjective Optimizers: An Analysis and Review. *IEEE Transactions on Evolutionary Computation*, 7(2):117–132, 2003.

Fast Implementation of the Steady-State NSGA-II Algorithm for Two Dimensions Based on Incremental Non-Dominated Sorting

Maxim Buzdalov
ITMO University
49 Kronverkskiy ave.
Saint-Petersburg, Russia
mbuzdalov@gmail.com

Ilya Yakupov
ITMO University
49 Kronverkskiy ave.
Saint-Petersburg, Russia
iyakupov93@gmail.com

Andrey Stankevich
ITMO University
49 Kronverkskiy ave.
Saint-Petersburg, Russia
stankev@gmail.com

ABSTRACT

Genetic algorithms (GAs) are widely used in multi-objective optimization for solving complex problems. There are two distinct approaches for GA design: generational and steady-state algorithms. Most of the current state-of-the-art GAs are generational, although there is an increasing interest to steady-state algorithms as well. However, for algorithms based on non-dominated sorting, most of steady-state implementations have higher computation complexity than their generational counterparts, which limits their applicability.

We present a fast implementation of a steady-state version of the NSGA-II algorithm for two dimensions. This implementation is based on a data structure which has $O(N)$ complexity for single solution insertion and deletion in the worst case. The experimental results show that our implementation works noticeably faster than steady-state NSGA-II implementations which use fast non-dominated sorting.

CCS Concepts

•**Theory of computation** → **Mathematical optimization;** *Data structures design and analysis;*

Keywords

steady-state, multi-objective, NSGA-II, non-dominated sorting, incremental updates

1. INTRODUCTION

In the K-dimensional space, a point $A = (a_1, \ldots, a_K)$ is said to *dominate* a point $B = (b_1, \ldots, b_K)$ when for all $1 \le i \le K$ it holds that $a_i \le b_i$ and there exists j such that $a_j < b_j$. *Non-dominated sorting* of points in the K-dimensional space is a procedure of marking all points which are not dominated by any other point with the *rank* of 0, all points which are dominated by at least one point of the rank of 0 are marked with the rank of 1, all points which are dominated by at least one point of the rank $i-1$ are marked with the rank of i.

Many well-known and widely used multi-objective evolutionary algorithms use the procedure of non-dominated sorting, or the procedure of determining the non-dominated solutions, which can be reduced to non-dominated sorting. These algorithms include NSGA-II [5], PESA [4], PESA-II [3], SPEA2 [18], PAES [10], PDE [1], and many more. The time complexity of a single iteration of these algorithms is often dominated by the complexity of a non-dominated sorting algorithm, so optimization of the latter makes such multi-objective evolutionary algorithms faster.

In Kung et al [11], the algorithm for determining the non-dominated solutions is proposed with the running time complexity of $O(N \log^{K-1} N)$, where N is the number of points and K is the dimension of the space. It is possible to use this algorithm to perform non-dominated sorting: first, the non-dominated solutions are found and assigned the rank of 0. Then, these solutions are removed, the non-dominated solutions from the remaining ones are found and assigned the rank of 1. The process repeats until all the solutions are removed. This leads to the complexity of $O(N^2 \log^{K-1} N)$ in the worst case, if the maximum rank of a point in the result is $O(N)$.

Jensen [9] was the first to propose an algorithm for non-dominated sorting with the complexity of $O(N \log^{K-1} N)$. However, his algorithm was developed for the assumption that no two points share a common value for any objective, and the complexity was proven for the same assumption. The first attempt to fix this issue belongs, to the best of the authors' knowledge, to Fortin et al [7]. The corrected (or, as in [7], "generalized") algorithm works in all cases, and for the general case the performance is still $O(N \log^{K-1} N)$, but the only upper bound that was proven for the worst case is $O(N^2 K)$. Finally, Buzdalov et al in [2] proposed several modifications to the algorithm of Fortin et al to make the $O(N \log^{K-1} N)$ bound provable as well.

Evolutionary algorithms have a big advantage due to their great degree of parallelism, however, synchronous variants (which wait for evaluation of all individuals, then recompute their internal state) have only a limited applicability for distributed systems. Even on multicore computers an algorithm may have a poor performance if it spends big periods of time between fitness evaluations without using most of computer resources. To overcome these limitations, steady-state algorithms are developed, often with an intention to

GECCO '15 July 11-15, 2015, Madrid, Spain

ACM ISBN 978-1-4503-3472-3/15/07.

DOI: http://dx.doi.org/10.1145/2739480.2754728

become asynchronous. Particularly, a steady-state version of the NSGA-II algorithm was developed [13] which showed good convergence rate and high quality of Pareto front approximation. However, the running time of it is poor.

It is possible to perform incremental non-dominated sorting by doing a complete non-dominated sorting from scratch every time an element is added. However, running times become very high: $O(KN^2)$ for a single insertion when the fast non-dominated sorting [5] is used, or $O(N \log^{K-1} N)$ when the sorting from [2] is used. Thus, it is needed to develop new algorithms and data structures to handle incremental non-dominated sorting efficiently.

However, almost no such algorithms and data structures have been developed so far. To our best knowledge, the only paper which addresses this issue is a technical report by Li et al. [12]. In that report, a procedure called "Efficient Non-domination Level Update" is introduced, which has the complexity of $O(NK\sqrt{N})$ for a single insertion when solutions are spread evenly over layers. This procedure was shown experimentally to be quite efficient, however, the worst-case complexity for a single insertion is still $O(N^2K)$.

This paper briefly describes the incremental non-dominated sorting algorithm for the two-dimensional case ($K = 2$) which has worst-case insertion and deletion complexity of $O(N)$ and worst-case query complexity of $O(\log N)$. It is described in our previous paper [16] in more detail. We additionally modified it to support evaluation of the *crowding distance*, a density measure employed by the NSGA-II algorithm. After that, the steady-state version of the NSGA-II algorithm is presented. Various implementation details are discussed, and results of experiments are presented.

2. INCREMENTAL NON-DOMINATED SORTING ALGORITHM

In this section, we briefly describe the proposed incremental non-dominated sorting algorithm and the data structure which supports it. They are described in detail in [16] along with necessary proofs.

The choice of the Cartesian tree as an underlying balanced search tree is discussed in Section 2.1. The data structure design is described in Section 2.2. The procedure of solution lookup (finding which layer a solution belongs to) is described in Section 2.3. The procedure of solution insertion is described in Section 2.4. The procedure of querying the k-th solution (in some predefined order) together with its layer number and crowding distance is described in Section 2.5. The worst solution deletion is described in Section 2.6.

When discussing the runtime analysis, we denote by N the total number of solutions stored in the data structure and by M the current number of non-domination layers. For the sake of brevity, non-domination layers are called just "layers" in the rest of the paper.

2.1 Cartesian Trees

To implement the algorithm, we need to have a data structure for container of elements which performs the following operations in $O(\log N)$:

- search of an element in the container;
- split of the container by key into two parts (the elements less than the key and the elements not less than the key);
- merge of two containers C_1 and C_2 (every element from C_1 is not greater than every element from C_2).

```
structure SOLUTION
    – a solution to the optimization problem
    X : REAL – the first objective
    Y : REAL – the second objective
end structure
structure LLNODE
    – a node of a low-level tree
    L : LLNODE – the left child
    R : LLNODE – the right child
    V : SOLUTION – the node key
    P : LLNODE – the previous-in-order node
    N : LLNODE – the next-in-order node
    S : INTEGER – the subtree size
end structure
structure HLNODE
    – a node of a high-level tree
    L : HLNODE – the left child
    R : HLNODE – the right child
    P : HLNODE – the previous-in-order node
    N : HLNODE – the next-in-order node
    V : LLNODE – the node key
    S : INTEGER – the subtree size
    W : INTEGER – the sum of key sizes in the subtree
end structure
```

Figure 1: A pseudocode for the data structure

We will call data structures which fulfil these requirements "split-merge balanced search trees". There are several such data structures, including Cartesian Tree [15] and Splay Tree [14]. In the case of Cartesian Tree, the $O(\log N)$ bound holds *with high probability*, while Splay Tree has *amortized* $O(\log N)$ bounds. From the mentioned data structures, Cartesian Tree generally performs slightly better in practice, so we use it in an implementation of our algorithm.

2.2 Data Structure

The idea of the data structure is to arrange layers in a binary search tree (each tree node corresponds to a layer) in the increasing order of their numbers. Each layer, in turn, is represented by a binary search tree itself, where solutions are sorted in the increasing order of their first objective. Since for two different solutions a and b from the same layer it holds that either $a_X > b_X$ and $a_Y < b_Y$ or $a_X < b_X$ and $a_Y > b_Y$, solutions in each layer are effectively sorted in the decreasing order of their second objective as well.

For the sake of brevity, we denote the tree of layers as the "high-level" tree and every tree containing layer elements as a "low-level" tree. The pseudocode for the data structure is given in Fig. 1. The resulting data structure is presented in Fig. 2.

Note that the high-level tree can be an ordinary balanced tree, while every low-level tree should be a split-merge tree. However, to evaluate the number of a certain layer in $O(\log M)$, one needs to store the number of tree elements in a subtree in each node of the high-level tree. Additionally, to move between adjacent layers in $O(1)$, nodes should be augmented with pointers to the previous-in-order and the next-in-order nodes (which can be done without affecting $O(\log N)$ performance of basic operations).

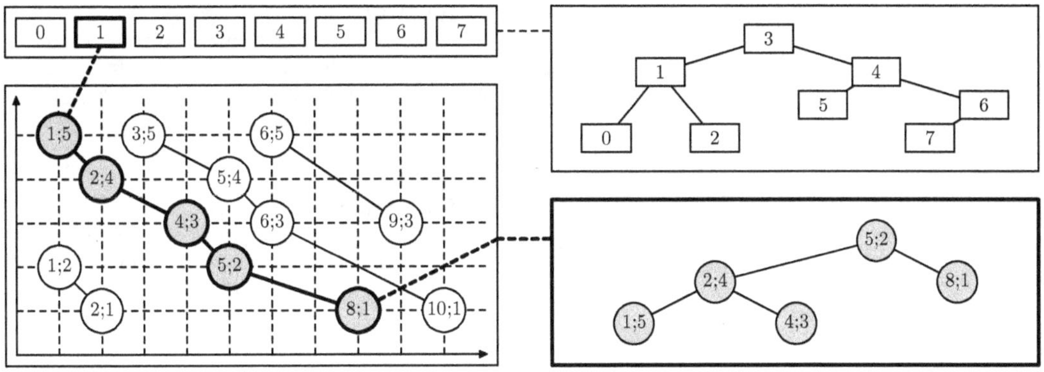

Figure 2: The data structure for the algorithm – the "tree of trees". Nodes of the "high-level" tree correspond to the layers. Each layer is, in turn, represented by a "low-level" tree, where nodes are sorted by the first objective. Note that layer numbers are not stored in nodes explicitly, they are just shown for convenience.

2.3 Lookup

Given a low-level tree T and a solution s, it is possible to find if s is dominated by at least one solution from T in $O(\log |T|)$. To do it, one needs to find a solution u from T such that $u_X \leq s_X$ and u_X is maximum possible, which can be done by traversing the tree T from its root. If u is found and dominates s, then a dominating solution from T is found, otherwise, no solution from T dominates s.

Using this algorithm, one can traverse the high-level tree and find a layer with the minimum number which does not dominate a certain solution s. The algorithm is presented in Fig. 3.

A rough estimation of the running time is $O(\log M \log N)$, where $O(\log M)$ is an estimation of the height of the high-level tree, and $O(\log N)$ is an estimation of heights of all low-level trees.

However, one can perform a better estimation using the following idea. There are $k = O(\log M)$ layers which were tested for domination. Let their sizes be $L_1 \ldots L_k$, and $L_1 + \ldots + L_k \leq N$. The running time for a layer of size L_i can be expressed as $O(1 + \log L_i)$ (we add extra 1 to handle a condition of $\log L_i = o(1)$). The total running time of a single lookup is:

$$O\left(k + \sum_{i=1}^{k} \log L_i\right).$$

Due to Cauchy's inequality, $\sum_{i=1}^{k} \log L_i \leq k \log(N/k)$, which finally gives the following complexity of a lookup operation:

$$O\left(\log M \left(1 + \log \frac{N}{\log M}\right)\right),$$

which, due to the fact that $M \leq N$ and $\log(N/\log M)$ is $\omega(1)$, can be simplified to:

$$O\left(\log M \log \frac{N}{\log M}\right).$$

When N is fixed and M varies, this expression reaches its maximum at $M = \Theta(N)$, yielding $O((\log N)^2)$ worst-case running time.

```
function LowLevelDominates(T, s)
    – returns whether any solution from T dominates s
    T : LLNode – the root node of the low-level tree
    s : Solution – the solution to test for domination
    B ← null – the best node so far
    while T ≠ null do
        if T.V.X ≤ s.X then
            B ← T
            T ← T.R
        else
            T ← T.L
        end if
    end while
    if B = null then
        return false
    end if
    return B.Y < s.Y or B.Y = s.Y and B.X < s.X
end function
function SmallestNonDominatingLayer(H, s)
    – returns the layer with the smallest index from H
    – which does not dominate s
    H : HLNode – the root node of the high-level tree
    s : Solution – the solution to find a layer for
    I ← 0 – the number of dominating layers so far
    B ← null – the best node so far
    while H ≠ null do
        if LowLevelDominates(H.V, s) then
            I ← I + H.S
            H ← H.R
            if H ≠ null then
                I ← I − H.S
            end if
        else
            B ← H
            H ← H.L
        end if
    end while
    return (B, I)
end function
```

Figure 3: A pseudocode for determining the smallest layer which doesn't dominate the given solution

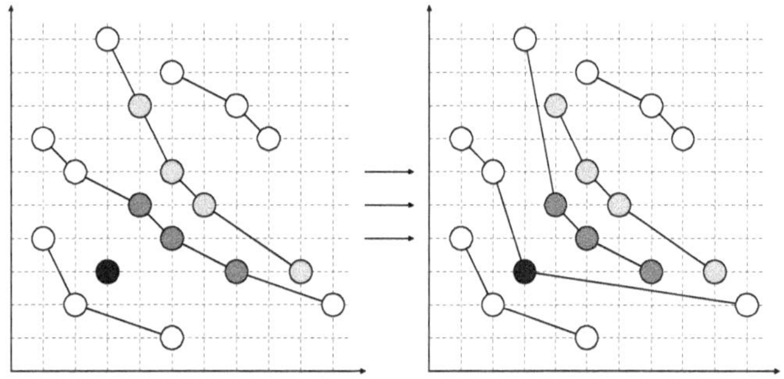

Figure 4: An example of the insertion process. Solutions which don't change their layer nodes (not numbers!) during the insertion process are white. A solution which is being inserted is black. Two clusters of solutions which together change their layer node are dark-gray and light-gray, correspondingly.

2.4 Insertion

Given a high-level tree H and a solution s, the insertion procedure updates H so that s is included in one of its low-level trees.

A key idea of fast implementation of insertion procedure is the fact that solutions who change their layers form contiguous pieces in their original layers and remain contiguous in their new layers as well. Fig. 4 illustrates an example of the insertion process.

The algorithm for a solution insertion is given in Fig. 5. It maintains a low-level tree which, at each stage, contains the solutions which needs to be inserted to the next layer. Initially it consists of the single solution which needs to be inserted. The layer to insert is initially found using the performing the SMALLESTNONDOMINATINGLAYER operation from Fig. 3.

The insertion algorithm works in iterations, each iteration pushes solutions to the layer that is immediately dominated by the layer of the previous iteration. On each iteration, the following operations are performed:

- The low-level tree of the current layer is split in three parts using the current pushed set of solutions C in the following way:
  - the "left part" T_L consists of all solutions from the current layer whose X coordinates are less than the smallest X coordinate of a solution from C;
  - the "middle part" T_M consists of all solutions from the current layer which are dominated by at least one solution from C;
  - the "right part" T_R consists of all solutions from the current layer whose Y coordinates are less than the smallest Y coordinate of a solution from C.
- The current layer is built by merging the trees T_L, C and T_R.
- If both T_L and T_R are empty, this means that the entire level was dominated by solutions from C. In turn, this means that a new layer consisting entirely of T_M should be inserted just after the current level. All remaining layers will effectively have their index increased by one. The insertion procedure stops here.

```
function SplitX(T, s)
    – splits a tree T into two trees L, R
    – such that for all l ∈ L holds l.X < s.X
    – and for all r ∈ R holds r.X ≥ s.X
    T : LLNode
    s : Solution
end function
function SplitY(T, s)
    – splits a tree T into two trees L, R
    – such that for all l ∈ L holds l.Y ≥ s.Y
    – and for all r ∈ R holds r.Y < s.Y
    T : LLNode
    s : Solution
end function
function Merge(L, R)
    – merges two trees L and R into a single one
    – given for any l ∈ L and r ∈ R holds l.X < r.X
    L : LLNode
    R : LLNode
end function
function Insert(H, s)
    – inserts a solution s into a high-level tree H
    H : HLNode
    s : Solution
    C ← new LLNode(s)
    (G, i) ← SmallestNonDominatingLayer(H, s)
    while G ≠ null do
        C_min ← a solution with minimum x from C
        C_max ← a solution with minimum y from C
        (T_L, T_i) ← SplitX(G.V, C_min)
        (T_M, T_R) ← SplitY(T_i, C_max)
        G.V ← Merge(T_L, Merge(C, T_R))
        if T_M = null then
            return – no more solutions to push down
        end if
        if T_L = null and T_R = null then
            – the current layer is dominated in whole
            – just insert pushed solutions as a new layer
            Insert new HLNode(T_M) after G
            return
        end if
        C ← T_M
        G ← G.N
    end while
    Insert new HLNode(C) after last node of H
end function
```

Figure 5: A pseudocode for insertion of a solution into a high-level tree

- If T_M is empty, the remaining layers should remain unchanged. The insertion procedure stops here.
- Otherwise, $C \leftarrow T_M$, and the insertion procedure continues with the next iteration.

If after the last iterations there are some solutions which were not inserted, a new layer is formed from them and is added as the last layer into the high-level tree.

We omit a long and rigorous proof of correctness of this algorithm for the sake of brevity. The running time of the insertion algorithm sums up from the running time of the lookup algorithm (which is $O(\log M \log(N/\log M))$) and from the total time spent in iterations. Assume that $P \leq M$ iterations were performed. Without losing generality, assume that the layers of sizes $L_1 \dots L_P$ were split in these iterations. Denote the sizes of their pairs after splits to be $L_1^L, L_1^M, L_1^R, \dots, L_P^L, L_P^M, L_P^R$. The value $L_0^M = 1$ corresponds to the initial set C consisting of the solution which is to be inserted. In i-th iteration, the following operations with $\omega(1)$ complexity were performed:

- finding minimum and maximum of C in $O(1+\log L_{i-1}^M)$;
- SPLITX in $O(1 + \log(L_i^L + L_i^M + L_i^R))$;
- SPLITY in $O(1 + \log(L_i^M + L_i^R))$;
- inner MERGE in $O(1 + \log(L_{i-1}^M + L_i^R))$;
- outer MERGE in $O(1 + \log(L_i^L + L_{i-1}^M + L_i^R))$.

In total, the sum of all numbers under logarithms does not exceed $4 \sum_{i=1}^{P} L_i$, and hence is $O(N)$. By Cauchy's inequality, the sum of all running times for all iterations is $O(P(1 + \log(N/P)))$. For a fixed N, this function has a maximum when $P = \Theta(N)$, which both gives us that $O(P(1+\log(N/P))) = O(M(1+\log(N/M)))$ and the worst-case running time of $O(N)$. The layer insertion operations which can happen at the end of the algorithm cost only $O(\log M)$ and thus don't change the estimations.

The total running time complexity for the insertion algorithm is:

$$O\left(M\left(1 + \log \frac{N}{M}\right) + \log M \log \frac{N}{\log M}\right).$$

2.5 Querying the k-th Solution

The NSGA-II algorithm features a selection operator based on binary tournament which considers every solution exactly twice. It does this by maintaining a permutation of indices $1 \dots N$, where N is the number of solutions in the population. When a solution is to be taken from the population, it takes an element E of this permutation which was not yet considered and takes a solution which is located at the position of E. When all elements of the permutation are considered, a new (random) permutation is generated instead.

To support this selection operator, we need to support an operation of querying the k-th solution in some predefined order ($1 \leq k \leq N$). Note that querying a random solution can be implemented using this operation (k is chosen randomly uniformly from the range $[1; N]$). Each query must return a solution, the number of layer it resides at, and the crowding distance of this solution in its layer.

To achieve this aim, we utilize node fields containing subtree sizes, and a field which stores the total size of all keys in the subtree of a high-level tree node. We use the lexicographical order on the solutions: first, the layer number is used to order the solutions, second, the abscissa is used to break ties.

Given k, the number of a solution in the lexicographical order, the first part of the query algorithm finds the layer in which this solution resides. This is done by traversing the high-level tree from the root and tracking the total size of keys in subtrees. The second part uses the same idea to find the solution inside the layer. The third part evaluates the crowding distance and constructs the query result. The algorithm is outlined on Fig. 6. The running time of this algorithm is straightforwardly $O(\log N)$.

```
structure QueryResult
    – the result of a query
    S : Solution – the solution
    L : Integer – the layer number
    C : Real – the crowding distance
end structure
function QueryLow(T, k, W, H, L)
    – finds k-th solution in a low-level tree T
    T : LLNode
    k : Integer
    W : Real – the abscissa difference
    H : Real – the ordinate difference
    L : Integer – the layer number
    if T.L ≠ null then
        if k ≤ T.L.S then
            return QueryLow(T.L, k, W, H, L)
        else
            k ← k − T.L.S
        end if
    end if
    if k = 1 then
        R ← new QueryResult
        R.S ← T.V, R.L ← L
        if T.P = null or T.N = null then
            R.C ← ∞
        else
            R.C ← |T.N.V.X − T.P.V.X| / W + |T.N.V.Y − T.P.V.Y| / H
        end if
        return R
    else
        k ← k − 1
    end if
    return QueryLow(T.R, k, W, H, L)
end function
function Query(T, k)
    – returns the k-th solution in a high-level tree T
    T : HLNode
    k : Integer
    L : Integer ← 0 – the layer number
    loop
        if T.L ≠ null then
            if k ≤ T.L.W then
                T ← T.L
                continue
            else
                k ← k − T.L.W, L ← L + T.L.S
            end if
        end if
        if k ≤ T.V.S then
            LL ← leftmost child of T.V
            RR ← rightmost child of T.V
            W ← |RR.V.X − LL.V.X|
            H ← |RR.V.Y − LL.V.Y|
            return QueryLow(T.V, k, W, H, L)
        end if
        k ← k − T.V.S, L ← L + 1, T ← T.R
    end loop
end function
```

Figure 6: A pseudocode for querying the k-th solution in lexicographical order

2.6 Deletion of the Worst Solution

In the NSGA-II algorithm, when the number of solutions exceeds the required population size, solutions are deleted from the population starting from the last layer. When one needs to retain some solutions in the last layer, they are deleted in the decreasing order of their crowding distances.

We have not invented an efficient data structure which locates the solution with the smallest crowding distance in a layer. So, to delete a single solution with the worst crowding distance from the last layer, we need to compute crowding distances for every solution in the layer and then delete the one with the smallest crowding distance. This can be done in $O(N)$.

3. EXPERIMENTS

To assess the performance of the proposed implementation, we performed experiments which are largely based on the experiments from [13]. The following benchmark problems are considered: ZDT1–ZDT4 and ZDT6 [17], DTLZ1–DTLZ7 [6], WFG1–WFG9 [8]. The parameters of these problems are the same as in the corresponding papers, except that we considered only two-dimensional versions of these problems.

The NSGA-II algorithm was implemented in as much compatible way to [13] as possible. Specifically, their implementation of the selection operator uses dominance comparison in the first step, unlike classical definition [5], which uses layer number comparison instead. A significant difference is that WFG problems in [13] were implemented using single-precision floating-point numbers, while we used double-precision numbers consistently.

We tested both generational and steady-state variants of the NSGA-II algorithm. Each of these variants was run using the proposed implementation, the ENLU approach [12] and the fast non-dominated sorting from [5]. For each combination, 100 runs were performed, each run had the computational budget of 25 000 evaluations as in [13]. In each run, the random seed for all operations related to evolutionary operators and to individual selection was derived from the number of the run. For other operations which require a random number generator, such as operations with Cartesian trees, a separate random number generator was used.

To assess quality of the results, we evaluated the hypervolume indicator [19] at the end of each run. To assess performance, we evaluated the wall-clock running time and the number of objective comparisons. Notably, each crowding distance evaluation was thought to use four objective comparisons. As the wall-clock time includes not only the time of non-dominated sorting, but the time of evolutionary operators and fitness function evaluations as well, we estimate the latter time by separately running evolutionary operators and fitness functions on randomly generated data and subtracting this time from the wall-clock time. For each mentioned measure we track the median and the interquartile range (IQR).

The source code for experiment reproduction is available both as supplementary materials to the paper and at GitHub[1]. We ran this code on a server with two Intel® Xeon® E5606 CPUs clocked at 2.13 GHz, having eight cores in total.

[1]https://github.com/mbuzdalov/papers/tree/master/2015-gecco-nsga-ii-ss

For each problem, medians and interquartile ranges for hypervolumes were correspondingly equal for all generational algorithms, and the same was true for all steady-state algorithms, so we are not presenting the results for hypervolumes. All other results of experiments are presented in Table 1.

One can see that the running times and the numbers of comparisons differ significantly. In all cases except one the proposed implementation (called INDS in the tables and further on) performs noticeably faster (in terms of wall-clock time) both with generational and with steady-state versions.

As the running time of Deb's fast non-dominated sorting is not input-sensitive, as follows from the algorithm, the number of comparisons as well as wall-clock times are almost equal for all problems, considering separately generational and steady-state NSGA-II variants. Two other approaches are clearly input-sensitive (for the steady-state case, the biggest time (0.12) is almost three times higher than the smallest time (0.042) in the case of ENLU).

The average operation complexity for INDS is expected to be higher than of the ENLU (due to usage of the tree-based data structure), and ENLU seems to be more complex than the fast non-dominated sorting as well. This made us interested in estimating the overhead imposed by using this or that algorithm, measured as the average wall-clock time **per objective comparison**. From the data presented in Table 1, we computed this ratio for all three algorithms separately for generational and steady-state variants. It appeared to be almost problem-independent. We give medians and interquartile ranges for these values (notation is the same as in Table 1):

- INDS(gen): median $4.07 \cdot 10^{-8}$, IQR $8.40 \cdot 10^{-10}$;
- ENLU(gen): median $1.39 \cdot 10^{-8}$, IQR $1.90 \cdot 10^{-10}$;
- debNDS(gen): median $8.97 \cdot 10^{-9}$, IQR $2.31 \cdot 10^{-11}$;
- INDS(ss): median $1.36 \cdot 10^{-8}$, IQR $1.87 \cdot 10^{-10}$;
- ENLU(ss): median $1.08 \cdot 10^{-8}$, IQR $2.00 \cdot 10^{-11}$;
- debNDS(ss): median $5.88 \cdot 10^{-9}$, IQR $1.58 \cdot 10^{-11}$.

We account the difference between generational and steady-state variants for different individual removal patterns (bulk removal in the first case and single element removal in the second case). According to the median values of average overhead, INDS is indeed the most expensive (approximately five times more work per single comparison than in fast non-dominated sorting), but it is not significantly worse than ENLU in this aspect. All differences are much smaller for the steady-state variant.

Finally, running times for the same algorithm on the same problem, but for two different NSGA-II variants (generational and steady-state) are very similar in the case of INDS and of ENLU (steady-state times never exceed generational times multiplied by two), but fast non-dominated sorting is slower by more than 10 times in the steady-state case. This removes a big complication of using steady-state multiobjective evolutionary algorithms in practice: while often being superior in terms of quality of results, they are no more slower in terms of running times – at least for biobjective problems.

Table 1: Results of experiments. Notation: "time" stands for the running time (in seconds), "cmp" for the number of comparisons, "med" for the median, "IQR" for the interquartile range. "INDS" is the proposed implementation, "ENLU" is the ENLU-based implementation, "debNDS" is the standard implementation which uses the Deb's fast non-dominated sorting, "gen" corresponds to the generational variant of the NSGA-II algorithm and "ss" to the steady-state variant. Gray cells denote minima of the running time and of the number of comparisons (for generational and steady-state variants separately).

Type	INDS(gen)		ENLU(gen)		debNDS(gen)		INDS(ss)		ENLU(ss)		debNDS(ss)	
	med	IQR	med	IQR	med	IQR	med	IQR	med	IQR	med	IQR
ZDT1												
time	$5.42 \cdot 10^{-2}$	$1.12 \cdot 10^{-2}$	$1.01 \cdot 10^{-1}$	$4.47 \cdot 10^{-3}$	$1.42 \cdot 10^{-1}$	$2.40 \cdot 10^{-3}$	$7.49 \cdot 10^{-2}$	$2.44 \cdot 10^{-2}$	$9.46 \cdot 10^{-2}$	$6.11 \cdot 10^{-3}$	$1.66 \cdot 10^{0}$	$2.47 \cdot 10^{-2}$
cmp	$1.13 \cdot 10^{6}$	$2.68 \cdot 10^{4}$	$6.53 \cdot 10^{6}$	$2.98 \cdot 10^{4}$	$1.08 \cdot 10^{7}$	$2.17 \cdot 10^{3}$	$3.70 \cdot 10^{6}$	$7.74 \cdot 10^{4}$	$7.64 \cdot 10^{6}$	$1.21 \cdot 10^{5}$	$2.58 \cdot 10^{8}$	$8.06 \cdot 10^{4}$
ZDT2												
time	$5.68 \cdot 10^{-2}$	$7.50 \cdot 10^{-3}$	$9.16 \cdot 10^{-2}$	$9.13 \cdot 10^{-3}$	$1.08 \cdot 10^{-1}$	$1.78 \cdot 10^{-2}$	$7.09 \cdot 10^{-2}$	$2.53 \cdot 10^{-3}$	$9.44 \cdot 10^{-2}$	$4.04 \cdot 10^{-3}$	$1.65 \cdot 10^{0}$	$4.88 \cdot 10^{-2}$
cmp	$1.15 \cdot 10^{6}$	$2.14 \cdot 10^{4}$	$6.10 \cdot 10^{6}$	$3.95 \cdot 10^{4}$	$1.07 \cdot 10^{7}$	$4.56 \cdot 10^{3}$	$3.30 \cdot 10^{6}$	$1.14 \cdot 10^{5}$	$6.90 \cdot 10^{6}$	$1.61 \cdot 10^{5}$	$2.57 \cdot 10^{8}$	$1.20 \cdot 10^{5}$
ZDT3												
time	$5.46 \cdot 10^{-2}$	$8.72 \cdot 10^{-4}$	$9.63 \cdot 10^{-2}$	$5.89 \cdot 10^{-3}$	$9.80 \cdot 10^{-2}$	$1.92 \cdot 10^{-3}$	$7.07 \cdot 10^{-2}$	$1.80 \cdot 10^{-3}$	$9.28 \cdot 10^{-2}$	$5.16 \cdot 10^{-3}$	$1.56 \cdot 10^{0}$	$1.31 \cdot 10^{-2}$
cmp	$1.12 \cdot 10^{6}$	$2.31 \cdot 10^{4}$	$6.32 \cdot 10^{6}$	$2.63 \cdot 10^{4}$	$1.08 \cdot 10^{7}$	$1.76 \cdot 10^{3}$	$3.38 \cdot 10^{6}$	$6.21 \cdot 10^{4}$	$7.14 \cdot 10^{6}$	$8.97 \cdot 10^{4}$	$2.57 \cdot 10^{8}$	$6.77 \cdot 10^{4}$
ZDT4												
time	$4.44 \cdot 10^{-2}$	$2.89 \cdot 10^{-3}$	$5.07 \cdot 10^{-2}$	$3.73 \cdot 10^{-3}$	$1.13 \cdot 10^{-1}$	$3.28 \cdot 10^{-3}$	$5.13 \cdot 10^{-2}$	$3.11 \cdot 10^{-3}$	$4.18 \cdot 10^{-2}$	$4.48 \cdot 10^{-3}$	$1.78 \cdot 10^{0}$	$5.24 \cdot 10^{-2}$
cmp	$1.07 \cdot 10^{6}$	$2.97 \cdot 10^{4}$	$3.41 \cdot 10^{6}$	$3.81 \cdot 10^{4}$	$1.07 \cdot 10^{7}$	$8.86 \cdot 10^{3}$	$2.05 \cdot 10^{6}$	$1.01 \cdot 10^{5}$	$3.68 \cdot 10^{6}$	$1.60 \cdot 10^{5}$	$2.56 \cdot 10^{8}$	$1.20 \cdot 10^{5}$
ZDT6												
time	$5.61 \cdot 10^{-2}$	$2.12 \cdot 10^{-3}$	$6.80 \cdot 10^{-2}$	$6.43 \cdot 10^{-4}$	$1.20 \cdot 10^{-1}$	$2.51 \cdot 10^{-3}$	$6.65 \cdot 10^{-2}$	$2.35 \cdot 10^{-3}$	$7.19 \cdot 10^{-2}$	$2.91 \cdot 10^{-3}$	$1.71 \cdot 10^{0}$	$3.26 \cdot 10^{-2}$
cmp	$1.12 \cdot 10^{6}$	$1.11 \cdot 10^{4}$	$4.52 \cdot 10^{6}$	$3.89 \cdot 10^{4}$	$1.07 \cdot 10^{7}$	$4.40 \cdot 10^{3}$	$2.64 \cdot 10^{6}$	$9.39 \cdot 10^{4}$	$5.29 \cdot 10^{6}$	$1.13 \cdot 10^{5}$	$2.56 \cdot 10^{8}$	$9.17 \cdot 10^{4}$
DTLZ1												
time	$4.67 \cdot 10^{-2}$	$5.04 \cdot 10^{-3}$	$5.66 \cdot 10^{-2}$	$3.19 \cdot 10^{-3}$	$1.13 \cdot 10^{-1}$	$2.86 \cdot 10^{-3}$	$4.88 \cdot 10^{-2}$	$3.08 \cdot 10^{-3}$	$5.21 \cdot 10^{-2}$	$5.21 \cdot 10^{-3}$	$1.69 \cdot 10^{0}$	$2.83 \cdot 10^{-2}$
cmp	$1.02 \cdot 10^{6}$	$2.27 \cdot 10^{4}$	$3.73 \cdot 10^{6}$	$5.80 \cdot 10^{4}$	$1.07 \cdot 10^{7}$	$7.87 \cdot 10^{3}$	$2.21 \cdot 10^{6}$	$2.02 \cdot 10^{5}$	$4.17 \cdot 10^{6}$	$2.42 \cdot 10^{5}$	$2.56 \cdot 10^{8}$	$2.19 \cdot 10^{5}$
DTLZ2												
time	$5.41 \cdot 10^{-2}$	$4.08 \cdot 10^{-3}$	$9.51 \cdot 10^{-2}$	$4.11 \cdot 10^{-3}$	$9.71 \cdot 10^{-2}$	$3.78 \cdot 10^{-3}$	$6.75 \cdot 10^{-2}$	$3.92 \cdot 10^{-3}$	$9.35 \cdot 10^{-2}$	$5.37 \cdot 10^{-3}$	$1.53 \cdot 10^{0}$	$2.15 \cdot 10^{-2}$
cmp	$1.09 \cdot 10^{6}$	$2.81 \cdot 10^{4}$	$6.24 \cdot 10^{6}$	$2.29 \cdot 10^{4}$	$1.08 \cdot 10^{7}$	$1.24 \cdot 10^{3}$	$4.19 \cdot 10^{6}$	$5.00 \cdot 10^{4}$	$7.91 \cdot 10^{6}$	$1.77 \cdot 10^{5}$	$2.58 \cdot 10^{8}$	$4.97 \cdot 10^{4}$
DTLZ3												
time	$4.30 \cdot 10^{-2}$	$1.83 \cdot 10^{-3}$	$5.37 \cdot 10^{-2}$	$4.27 \cdot 10^{-3}$	$1.13 \cdot 10^{-1}$	$9.16 \cdot 10^{-4}$	$4.18 \cdot 10^{-2}$	$2.07 \cdot 10^{-3}$	$4.78 \cdot 10^{-2}$	$4.52 \cdot 10^{-3}$	$1.94 \cdot 10^{0}$	$5.69 \cdot 10^{-2}$
cmp	$1.08 \cdot 10^{6}$	$3.78 \cdot 10^{4}$	$3.81 \cdot 10^{6}$	$1.11 \cdot 10^{5}$	$1.06 \cdot 10^{7}$	$8.25 \cdot 10^{3}$	$1.31 \cdot 10^{6}$	$1.06 \cdot 10^{5}$	$3.19 \cdot 10^{6}$	$1.02 \cdot 10^{5}$	$2.55 \cdot 10^{8}$	$1.07 \cdot 10^{5}$
DTLZ4												
time	$5.60 \cdot 10^{-2}$	$2.81 \cdot 10^{-3}$	$9.47 \cdot 10^{-2}$	$3.34 \cdot 10^{-3}$	$1.02 \cdot 10^{-1}$	$9.92 \cdot 10^{-3}$	$6.87 \cdot 10^{-2}$	$6.93 \cdot 10^{-3}$	$9.30 \cdot 10^{-2}$	$4.99 \cdot 10^{-3}$	$1.58 \cdot 10^{0}$	$5.08 \cdot 10^{-2}$
cmp	$1.08 \cdot 10^{6}$	$3.32 \cdot 10^{4}$	$6.21 \cdot 10^{6}$	$3.57 \cdot 10^{4}$	$1.08 \cdot 10^{7}$	$4.89 \cdot 10^{3}$	$3.95 \cdot 10^{6}$	$8.01 \cdot 10^{4}$	$7.67 \cdot 10^{6}$	$2.31 \cdot 10^{5}$	$2.58 \cdot 10^{8}$	$8.87 \cdot 10^{4}$
DTLZ5												
time	$5.36 \cdot 10^{-2}$	$2.49 \cdot 10^{-4}$	$9.30 \cdot 10^{-2}$	$1.24 \cdot 10^{-3}$	$9.66 \cdot 10^{-2}$	$3.03 \cdot 10^{-3}$	$6.76 \cdot 10^{-2}$	$4.36 \cdot 10^{-3}$	$9.40 \cdot 10^{-2}$	$4.35 \cdot 10^{-3}$	$1.54 \cdot 10^{0}$	$2.02 \cdot 10^{-2}$
cmp	$1.09 \cdot 10^{6}$	$3.29 \cdot 10^{4}$	$6.24 \cdot 10^{6}$	$2.29 \cdot 10^{4}$	$1.08 \cdot 10^{7}$	$1.24 \cdot 10^{3}$	$4.19 \cdot 10^{6}$	$5.26 \cdot 10^{4}$	$7.91 \cdot 10^{6}$	$1.77 \cdot 10^{5}$	$2.58 \cdot 10^{8}$	$4.97 \cdot 10^{4}$
DTLZ6												
time	$4.96 \cdot 10^{-2}$	$6.55 \cdot 10^{-3}$	$7.09 \cdot 10^{-2}$	$1.94 \cdot 10^{-3}$	$1.03 \cdot 10^{-1}$	$1.79 \cdot 10^{-3}$	$5.88 \cdot 10^{-2}$	$2.52 \cdot 10^{-3}$	$7.18 \cdot 10^{-2}$	$5.43 \cdot 10^{-3}$	$1.70 \cdot 10^{0}$	$1.96 \cdot 10^{-2}$
cmp	$1.16 \cdot 10^{6}$	$2.38 \cdot 10^{4}$	$5.17 \cdot 10^{6}$	$4.81 \cdot 10^{4}$	$1.07 \cdot 10^{7}$	$4.27 \cdot 10^{3}$	$2.90 \cdot 10^{6}$	$2.13 \cdot 10^{5}$	$5.95 \cdot 10^{6}$	$2.46 \cdot 10^{5}$	$2.57 \cdot 10^{8}$	$2.13 \cdot 10^{5}$
DTLZ7												
time	$5.64 \cdot 10^{-2}$	$4.39 \cdot 10^{-3}$	$9.43 \cdot 10^{-2}$	$3.82 \cdot 10^{-3}$	$1.02 \cdot 10^{-1}$	$1.80 \cdot 10^{-3}$	$7.06 \cdot 10^{-2}$	$2.16 \cdot 10^{-3}$	$9.07 \cdot 10^{-2}$	$2.93 \cdot 10^{-3}$	$1.59 \cdot 10^{0}$	$1.65 \cdot 10^{-2}$
cmp	$1.13 \cdot 10^{6}$	$2.07 \cdot 10^{4}$	$6.12 \cdot 10^{6}$	$2.86 \cdot 10^{4}$	$1.08 \cdot 10^{7}$	$1.85 \cdot 10^{3}$	$3.55 \cdot 10^{6}$	$6.15 \cdot 10^{4}$	$7.21 \cdot 10^{6}$	$1.32 \cdot 10^{5}$	$2.57 \cdot 10^{8}$	$6.50 \cdot 10^{4}$
WFG1												
time	$4.90 \cdot 10^{-2}$	$1.48 \cdot 10^{-3}$	$7.91 \cdot 10^{-2}$	$1.87 \cdot 10^{-3}$	$1.00 \cdot 10^{-1}$	$1.12 \cdot 10^{-3}$	$6.11 \cdot 10^{-2}$	$4.02 \cdot 10^{-3}$	$8.15 \cdot 10^{-2}$	$1.15 \cdot 10^{-2}$	$1.57 \cdot 10^{0}$	$2.80 \cdot 10^{-2}$
cmp	$1.07 \cdot 10^{6}$	$1.99 \cdot 10^{4}$	$5.48 \cdot 10^{6}$	$1.62 \cdot 10^{5}$	$1.07 \cdot 10^{7}$	$1.14 \cdot 10^{4}$	$2.94 \cdot 10^{6}$	$4.30 \cdot 10^{5}$	$6.27 \cdot 10^{6}$	$4.71 \cdot 10^{5}$	$2.57 \cdot 10^{8}$	$5.18 \cdot 10^{5}$
WFG2												
time	$5.94 \cdot 10^{-2}$	$2.67 \cdot 10^{-3}$	$1.04 \cdot 10^{-1}$	$5.11 \cdot 10^{-3}$	$1.02 \cdot 10^{-1}$	$1.87 \cdot 10^{-3}$	$9.73 \cdot 10^{-2}$	$4.72 \cdot 10^{-3}$	$1.23 \cdot 10^{-1}$	$8.75 \cdot 10^{-3}$	$1.54 \cdot 10^{0}$	$1.98 \cdot 10^{-2}$
cmp	$1.07 \cdot 10^{6}$	$3.65 \cdot 10^{4}$	$6.97 \cdot 10^{6}$	$6.68 \cdot 10^{4}$	$1.08 \cdot 10^{7}$	$2.14 \cdot 10^{3}$	$7.05 \cdot 10^{6}$	$1.25 \cdot 10^{5}$	$1.13 \cdot 10^{7}$	$1.64 \cdot 10^{5}$	$2.61 \cdot 10^{8}$	$8.74 \cdot 10^{4}$
WFG3												
time	$5.63 \cdot 10^{-2}$	$3.37 \cdot 10^{-3}$	$9.40 \cdot 10^{-2}$	$5.75 \cdot 10^{-4}$	$9.83 \cdot 10^{-2}$	$2.29 \cdot 10^{-3}$	$7.59 \cdot 10^{-2}$	$5.90 \cdot 10^{-3}$	$9.56 \cdot 10^{-2}$	$6.60 \cdot 10^{-3}$	$1.53 \cdot 10^{0}$	$1.72 \cdot 10^{-2}$
cmp	$1.07 \cdot 10^{6}$	$2.69 \cdot 10^{4}$	$6.16 \cdot 10^{6}$	$2.88 \cdot 10^{4}$	$1.08 \cdot 10^{7}$	$1.42 \cdot 10^{3}$	$4.98 \cdot 10^{6}$	$7.89 \cdot 10^{4}$	$8.69 \cdot 10^{6}$	$1.94 \cdot 10^{5}$	$2.59 \cdot 10^{8}$	$7.67 \cdot 10^{4}$
WFG4												
time	$5.34 \cdot 10^{-2}$	$1.46 \cdot 10^{-3}$	$9.22 \cdot 10^{-2}$	$2.35 \cdot 10^{-3}$	$9.90 \cdot 10^{-2}$	$1.19 \cdot 10^{-3}$	$7.51 \cdot 10^{-2}$	$4.20 \cdot 10^{-3}$	$9.78 \cdot 10^{-2}$	$3.68 \cdot 10^{-3}$	$1.53 \cdot 10^{0}$	$2.04 \cdot 10^{-2}$
cmp	$1.07 \cdot 10^{6}$	$2.11 \cdot 10^{4}$	$6.07 \cdot 10^{6}$	$5.90 \cdot 10^{4}$	$1.08 \cdot 10^{7}$	$2.56 \cdot 10^{3}$	$4.76 \cdot 10^{6}$	$1.92 \cdot 10^{5}$	$8.43 \cdot 10^{6}$	$2.49 \cdot 10^{5}$	$2.59 \cdot 10^{8}$	$1.85 \cdot 10^{5}$
WFG5												
time	$5.62 \cdot 10^{-2}$	$4.48 \cdot 10^{-3}$	$1.03 \cdot 10^{-1}$	$2.08 \cdot 10^{-3}$	$9.73 \cdot 10^{-2}$	$5.45 \cdot 10^{-3}$	$9.01 \cdot 10^{-2}$	$3.21 \cdot 10^{-3}$	$1.20 \cdot 10^{-1}$	$3.73 \cdot 10^{-3}$	$1.54 \cdot 10^{0}$	$1.60 \cdot 10^{-2}$
cmp	$1.08 \cdot 10^{6}$	$4.42 \cdot 10^{4}$	$7.10 \cdot 10^{6}$	$1.80 \cdot 10^{5}$	$1.08 \cdot 10^{7}$	$7.08 \cdot 10^{3}$	$6.71 \cdot 10^{6}$	$4.86 \cdot 10^{5}$	$1.11 \cdot 10^{7}$	$7.35 \cdot 10^{5}$	$2.61 \cdot 10^{8}$	$4.73 \cdot 10^{5}$
WFG6												
time	$5.46 \cdot 10^{-2}$	$3.50 \cdot 10^{-3}$	$9.19 \cdot 10^{-2}$	$6.80 \cdot 10^{-3}$	$1.01 \cdot 10^{-1}$	$3.19 \cdot 10^{-3}$	$6.92 \cdot 10^{-2}$	$2.74 \cdot 10^{-3}$	$9.29 \cdot 10^{-2}$	$7.66 \cdot 10^{-3}$	$1.53 \cdot 10^{0}$	$1.88 \cdot 10^{-2}$
cmp	$1.07 \cdot 10^{6}$	$1.97 \cdot 10^{4}$	$5.96 \cdot 10^{6}$	$7.38 \cdot 10^{4}$	$1.08 \cdot 10^{7}$	$4.13 \cdot 10^{3}$	$4.48 \cdot 10^{6}$	$3.28 \cdot 10^{5}$	$8.10 \cdot 10^{6}$	$4.59 \cdot 10^{5}$	$2.58 \cdot 10^{8}$	$3.29 \cdot 10^{5}$
WFG7												
time	$5.58 \cdot 10^{-2}$	$1.64 \cdot 10^{-3}$	$9.80 \cdot 10^{-2}$	$2.45 \cdot 10^{-3}$	$9.96 \cdot 10^{-2}$	$4.25 \cdot 10^{-3}$	$7.81 \cdot 10^{-2}$	$1.67 \cdot 10^{-3}$	$1.02 \cdot 10^{-1}$	$2.84 \cdot 10^{-3}$	$1.52 \cdot 10^{0}$	$1.63 \cdot 10^{-2}$
cmp	$1.06 \cdot 10^{6}$	$2.98 \cdot 10^{4}$	$6.38 \cdot 10^{6}$	$2.43 \cdot 10^{4}$	$1.08 \cdot 10^{7}$	$1.11 \cdot 10^{3}$	$5.53 \cdot 10^{6}$	$7.61 \cdot 10^{4}$	$9.47 \cdot 10^{6}$	$1.35 \cdot 10^{5}$	$2.59 \cdot 10^{8}$	$7.71 \cdot 10^{4}$
WFG8												
time	$5.50 \cdot 10^{-2}$	$4.76 \cdot 10^{-3}$	$8.04 \cdot 10^{-2}$	$1.46 \cdot 10^{-3}$	$1.08 \cdot 10^{-1}$	$1.40 \cdot 10^{-3}$	$4.79 \cdot 10^{-2}$	$3.04 \cdot 10^{-3}$	$6.28 \cdot 10^{-2}$	$6.48 \cdot 10^{-3}$	$1.52 \cdot 10^{0}$	$2.64 \cdot 10^{-2}$
cmp	$1.05 \cdot 10^{6}$	$4.14 \cdot 10^{4}$	$4.59 \cdot 10^{6}$	$1.25 \cdot 10^{5}$	$1.07 \cdot 10^{7}$	$8.61 \cdot 10^{3}$	$1.66 \cdot 10^{6}$	$1.32 \cdot 10^{5}$	$4.12 \cdot 10^{6}$	$1.61 \cdot 10^{5}$	$2.56 \cdot 10^{8}$	$1.23 \cdot 10^{5}$
WFG9												
time	$5.67 \cdot 10^{-2}$	$2.99 \cdot 10^{-3}$	$9.68 \cdot 10^{-2}$	$3.83 \cdot 10^{-3}$	$1.01 \cdot 10^{-1}$	$5.63 \cdot 10^{-3}$	$7.46 \cdot 10^{-2}$	$3.45 \cdot 10^{-3}$	$1.04 \cdot 10^{-1}$	$3.93 \cdot 10^{-3}$	$1.53 \cdot 10^{0}$	$1.56 \cdot 10^{-2}$
cmp	$1.06 \cdot 10^{6}$	$2.69 \cdot 10^{4}$	$6.23 \cdot 10^{6}$	$1.05 \cdot 10^{5}$	$1.08 \cdot 10^{7}$	$4.66 \cdot 10^{3}$	$4.91 \cdot 10^{6}$	$4.58 \cdot 10^{5}$	$8.56 \cdot 10^{6}$	$6.21 \cdot 10^{5}$	$2.59 \cdot 10^{8}$	$4.31 \cdot 10^{5}$

4. CONCLUSION

We proposed a new approach to implementation of steady-state multiobjective evolutionary algorithms for two dimensions. This approach is based on a data structure which is able to perform fast incremental non-dominated sorting and track other valuable data such as crowding distance. Experiments with the NSGA-II algorithm showed that the new approach offers running times similar to or better than those of generational versions while retaining the quality of steady-state versions.

This work was financially supported by the Government of Russian Federation, Grant 074-U01.

5. REFERENCES

[1] H. A. Abbass, R. Sarker, and C. Newton. PDE: A Pareto Frontier Differential Evolution Approach for Multiobjective Optimization Problems. In *Proceedings of the Congress on Evolutionary Computation*, pages 971–978. IEEE Press, 2001.

[2] M. Buzdalov and A. Shalyto. A provably asymptotically fast version of the generalized Jensen algorithm for non-dominated sorting. In *International Conference on Parallel Problem Solving from Nature*, number 8672 in Lecture Notes in Computer Science, pages 528–537. 2014.

[3] D. W. Corne, N. R. Jerram, J. D. Knowles, and M. J. Oates. PESA-II: Region-based Selection in Evolutionary Multiobjective Optimization. In *Proceedings of Genetic and Evolutionary Computation Conference*, pages 283–290. Morgan Kaufmann Publishers, 2001.

[4] D. W. Corne, J. D. Knowles, and M. J. Oates. The Pareto Envelope-based Selection Algorithm for Multiobjective Optimization. In *Parallel Problem Solving from Nature Parallel Problem Solving from Nature VI*, number 1917 in Lecture Notes in Computer Science, pages 839–848. Springer, 2000.

[5] K. Deb, A. Pratap, S. Agarwal, and T. Meyarivan. A Fast Elitist Multi-Objective Genetic Algorithm: NSGA-II. *Transactions on Evolutionary Computation*, 6:182–197, 2000.

[6] K. Deb, L. Thiele, M. Laumanns, and E. Zitzler. *Scalable Test Problems for Evolutionary Multiobjective Optimization*, pages 105–145. Springer, 2005.

[7] F.-A. Fortin, S. Grenier, and M. Parizeau. Generalizing the Improved Run-time Complexity Algorithm for Non-dominated Sorting. In *Proceeding of the Fifteenth Annual Conference on Genetic and Evolutionary Computation Conference*, GECCO '13, pages 615–622. ACM, 2013.

[8] S. Huband, P. Hingston, L. Barone, and R. L. While. A review of multiobjective test problems and a scalable test problem toolkit. *IEEE Transactions on Evolutionary Computation*, 10(5):477–506, 2006.

[9] M. T. Jensen. Reducing the Run-time Complexity of Multiobjective EAs: The NSGA-II and Other Algorithms. *Transactions on Evolutionary Computation*, 7(5):503–515, 2003.

[10] J. D. Knowles and D. W. Corne. Approximating the Nondominated Front Using the Pareto Archived Evolution Strategy. *Evolutionary Computation*, 8(2):149–172, 2000.

[11] H. T. Kung, F. Luccio, and F. P. Preparata. On finding the maxima of a set of vectors. *Journal of ACM*, 22(4):469–476, 1975.

[12] K. Li, K. Deb, Q. Zhang, and S. Kwong. Efficient non-domination level update approach for steady-state evolutionary multiobjective optimization. Technical report, 2014.

[13] A. J. Nebro and J. J. Durillo. On the effect of applying a steady-state selection scheme in the multi-objective genetic algorithm NSGA-II. In *Nature-Inspired Algorithms for Optimisation*, number 193 in Studies in Computational Intelligence, pages 435–456. Springer Berlin Heidelberg, 2009.

[14] D. D. Sleator and R. E. Tarjan. Self-adjusting binary search trees. *Journal of ACM*, 32(3):652–686, 1985.

[15] J. Vuillemin. A unifying look at data structures. *Communications of ACM*, 23(4):229–239, 1980.

[16] I. Yakupov and M. Buzdalov. Incremental non-dominated sorting with $O(N)$ insertion for the two-dimensional case. In *Proceedings of IEEE Congress on Evolutionary Computation*, 2015 (to appear).

[17] E. Zitzler, K. Deb, and L. Thiele. Comparison of multiobjective evolutionary algorithms: Empirical results. *Evolutionary Computation*, 8(2):173–195, 2000.

[18] E. Zitzler, M. Laumanns, and L. Thiele. SPEA2: Improving the Strength Pareto Evolutionary Algorithm for Multiobjective Optimization. In *Proceedings of the EUROGEN'2001 Conference*, pages 95–100, 2001.

[19] E. Zitzler and L. Thiele. Multiobjective evolutionary algorithms: A comparative case study and the Strength Pareto approach. *IEEE Transactions on Evolutionary Computation*, 3(4):257–271, 1999.

An Approach to Mitigating Unwanted Interactions between Search Operators in Multi-Objective Optimization

Chad M. Byers, Betty H.C. Cheng
BEACON Center for the Study of Evolution in Action
Department of Computer Science and Engineering
Michigan State University
East Lansing, Michigan, USA
{byerscha, chengb}@msu.edu

ABSTRACT

At run time, software systems often face a myriad of adverse environmental conditions and system failures that cannot be anticipated during the system's initial design phase. These uncertainties drive the need for dynamically adaptive systems that are capable of providing self-* properties (e.g., self-monitoring, self-adaptive, self-healing, etc.). Prescriptive techniques to manually preload these systems with a limited set of configurations often result in brittle, rigid designs that are unable to cope with environmental uncertainty. An alternative approach is to embed a search technique capable of exploring and *generating* optimal reconfigurations at run time. Increasingly, DAS applications are defined by multiple competing objectives (e.g., cost vs. performance) in which a *set* of valid solutions with a range of trade-offs are to be considered rather than a single optimal solution. While leveraging a multi-objective optimization technique, NSGA-II, to manage these competing objectives, hidden interactions were observed between search operators that prevented fair competition among solutions and restricted search from regions where valid optimal configurations existed. In this follow-on work, we demonstrate the role that niching can play in mitigating these unwanted interactions by explicitly creating favorable regions within the objective space where optimal solutions can equally compete and co-exist.

Categories and Subject Descriptors

I.2.8 [**Computing Methodologies**]: Machine Learning—*Machine Learning Approaches, Bio-inspired approaches, Genetic Algorithms*

Keywords

Decision making; Genetic Algorithms; Multi-objective optimization; Multiple solutions / Niching; Reference point-based niching; NSGA-III; Remote Data Mirroring

GECCO '15, July 11 - 15, 2015, Madrid, Spain

ISBN 978-1-4503-3472-3/15/07. . . $15.00

DOI: http://dx.doi.org/10.1145/2739480.2754698

1. INTRODUCTION

Intended to address the challenges posed by adverse environmental conditions and varying user requirements, dynamically adaptive systems (DASs) [18, 21] must reliably self-reconfigure at *run time* to avoid critical data and financial losses [17]. Emerging applications include the management of smart energy grids, traffic, and telecommunication systems that must cope with a myriad of system and environmental uncertainties (ex. node failures, link failures, etc.). Manual approaches to preload these systems with solutions are *prescriptive* in nature and often lead to brittle, rigid designs that are unable to scale or adapt to unanticipated conditions. An alternative approach is to embed a search process capable of exploring and *generating* new reconfigurations as the environment or high-level objectives/goals change. Evolutionary search techniques, such as genetic algorithms (GAs) [13, 15], provide one approach for DAS reconfiguration by harnessing biological principles of evolution to explore a *suite* of candidate solutions that often vary in their size, complexity, and the trade-offs made across the problem's dimensions. Previously [6], the underlying solution encoding was observed to have unintended interactions with specific evolutionary search operators, prohibiting search from returning solutions in valid regions of the objective space. This paper explores the use of niching to mitigate the negative effects of these unwanted interactions on solution set diversity.

In order to increase access to solutions throughout the objective space, a series of GA-based tools have been progressively developed, each of which required different levels of domain expertise: Weighted Plato [23], Targeting Plato [5], and NSGA-II Plato [6] that support dynamic reconfiguration for an industrial data mirroring (RDM) application. While the evolved solutions of these approaches were better than solutions generated manually, further inspection revealed that solutions were ill-fit for their intended environment, regions of the objective space were unreachable, or an exhaustive, trial-and-error-process would be necessary to yield desired solutions. Recently [6], hidden interactions were observed between a variable-length genome design and the diversity-preserving search operator of a popular multi-objective evolutionary algorithm (MOEA), NSGA-II[1], that significantly restricted search coverage in the objective space. This bias resulted from the violation of a key assumption that solutions' objective values are equally affected by mutation. More specifically, a variable-length genome design causes solutions with fewer elements to experience a greater change to their objective values when compared to more complex solutions. Since the diversity-preserving operator of NSGA-II prioritizes solutions located in sparsely populated regions, solutions with

[1]Non-dominated Sorting Genetic Algorithm [12]

fewer elements are more readily accepted due to their increased likelihood of escaping crowded regions. As a result, candidate solutions of varying size are unable to *globally* compete with one another in the same population.

To support a diverse set of optimal solutions where solution complexity is a key variable being explored, we propose that **niching** [25] be leveraged to mitigate unwanted, hidden interactions between search operators. Niching, in this work, refers to the process by which favorable regions are explicitly created and maintained in the objective space thereby partitioning a population into disjoint subpopulations. Niching enables fair competition during search since members of the same subpopulation, or niche, share similar objective values (e.g., complexity) and compete *locally* with one another. The ability to explicitly define niches within the objective space enables techniques that harness niching to drive search towards regions difficult to reach for other techniques.

We use the reference point-based niching operator of NSGA-III [10] to generate a diverse set of target configurations for an industrial RDM application where the number of solution elements (e.g., nodes, links, etc.) evolves freely over time. While this niching operator was intended to counteract the Curse of Dimensionality Problem [2] for high-dimensional applications, we demonstrate, in this work, its ability to successfully mitigate the hidden search interactions/bias present in NSGA-II and return diverse sets of Pareto-optimal configurations throughout the objective space. We compare NSGA-III's performance to previous Plato approaches in several key areas including overall search coverage and efficiency.

The remainder of this paper is organized as follows. In Sections 2 and 3, we provide background regarding RDM systems and an overview of preliminary investigations with the Plato approaches as well as their shortcomings. Next, Section 4 highlights three high-level properties necessary for search techniques used in DASs. We introduce NSGA-III's niching operator in Section 5 and discuss the key differences between NSGA-II and NSGA-III. Section 6 details our experimental design and results assessing NSGA-III's ability to provide these necessary high-level properties. Lastly, Section 7 overviews related work and we summarize our key findings and outline future directions for this work in Section 8.

2. BACKGROUND

In this section, we describe the application domain for a DAS, namely, remote data mirroring systems as well as the key elements and challenges in their design.

2.1 Remote Data Mirroring (RDM)

Remote data mirroring (RDM) systems [17] are widely deployed to offer file synchronization and reliability for critical data items distributed across a network in the presence of site/link failures [17]. In order to accomplish these objectives, RDM systems *copy* critical data residing at primary sites and *remotely store* (mirror) this data across secondary sites within the network. The design of an RDM solution, referred to as an **overlay network** [1], centers around two critical decisions: (1) the subset of network links to include from the underlying base network and (2) the type of RDM networking protocol utilized on each active link.

Two networking protocol types, *synchronous* and *asynchronous*, exist to balance the trade-offs associated with improving overall network bandwidth (performance) while mitigating the risk for greater potential data loss (reliability). A *synchronous* protocol ensures that each write operation of a critical data item is successfully applied and stored at the secondary site before subsequent write operations can proceed at the primary site. In contrast, *asynchronous* protocols *coalesce* write operations at the primary site over a specified length of time. After this length of time has elapsed, write operations are sent in batch form over the network to secondary sites and applied atomically. In Table 1, we present the elapsed time between each batch, the amount of potential data at risk (in GB), as well as the percentage of consumed network bandwidth for both synchronous (P1) and asynchronous (P2-P7) protocols.

In addition to its inherent DAS properties (e.g., self-* properties), the RDM problem encompasses a vast solution space where the set of all possible network designs is too large to manually enumerate. For a fully-connected network, the RDM problem's order of complexity comprises $2^{n(n-1)/2}$ network constructions, where n is the number of mirror sites.

Protocol Type	ID	Interval Length	Data at Risk (GB)	Bandwidth
Synchronous	P1	0 minutes	0.0	1.0
Asynchronous	P2	1 minute	0.35	0.9098
	P3	5 minutes	0.6989	0.8623
	P4	1 hour	1.7782	0.7271
	P5	4 hours	2.3802	0.5732
	P6	12 hours	2.8573	0.4380
	P7	24 hours	3.1584	0.3967

Table 1: Properties of RDM networking protocols [17].

3. PRELIMINARY INVESTIGATIONS

As part of an industrial collaboration, a series of genetic-algorithm based tools have been progressively developed in an effort to improve access to optimal solutions across the full range of dimensions in a RDM application.

3.1 Solution Encoding and Problem Objectives

For each of the three previous Plato approaches discussed in this paper (i.e. Weighted Plato, Targeting Plato, NSGA-II Plato), a genetic algorithm is integrated into the decision-making process of a RDM system in order to dynamically evolve reconfiguration plans, or overlay networks, that balance various objectives. An overlay network is internally represented as a vector containing N total elements. Each element maps to a specific connection (link) in the underlying base network and stores (1) a boolean flag for whether the connection is in use by the solution and (2) the specific RDM protocol used on the active connection. This solution encoding is subject to random mutation and crossover to generate new overlay network constructions.

During optimization of an RDM system, three orthogonal objectives (i.e. dimensions) are targeted: Cost (f_{cost}), Performance (f_{perf}), and Reliability (f_{reliab}). To quantify the optimization level that each network was able to achieve across these dimensions, we used the aggregate formulas given in Equations (1)-(6) that were derived from studies for optimizing data recovery systems [17]. In these equations, the vector ($\mathbf{x}$) corresponds to an evolved overlay network solution containing N total elements. For each vector element ($\mathbf{x}_i$) that maps to a unique link in the base network, the $\mathbf{x}_i^{flag}$ property indicates whether the link is active (1) or inactive (0) and $\mathbf{x}_i^{risk}$ and $\mathbf{x}_i^{bandwidth}$ indicate the data at risk and bandwidth consumed by the RDM protocol in use on the link, respectively. To calculate an overlay network's cost, the operational expense for activating an underlying network link is denoted as C_i. Similarly, the properties of particular RDM protocols, such as the amount of data at risk (ex. $P2^{risk}$), refer to those values given in Table 1. To remove the bias for search to favor dimensions with larger ranges of values, each objective function has been normalized between 0.0 and 1.0.

$$f_{cost}(\mathbf{x}) = \frac{\sum_{i=0}^{N} C_i x_i^{flag}}{\sum_{i=0}^{N} C_i} \quad (1)$$

$$f_{perf}(\mathbf{x}) = \frac{f_{efficiency}(\mathbf{x}) - P1^{bandwidth}}{P1^{bandwidth} - P7^{bandwidth}} \quad (2)$$

$$f_{efficiency}(\mathbf{x}) = \frac{\sum_{i=0}^{N} x_i^{bandwidth} x_i^{flag}}{\sum_{i=0}^{N} P1^{bandwidth} x_i^{flag}} \quad (3)$$

$$f_{reliab}(\mathbf{x}) = 0.5 \times f_{reliab1}(\mathbf{x}) + 0.5 \times f_{reliab2}(\mathbf{x}) \quad (4)$$

$$f_{reliab1}(\mathbf{x}) = 1.0 - \frac{\sum_{i=0}^{N} x_i^{flag}}{N} \quad (5)$$

$$f_{reliab2}(\mathbf{x}) = \frac{\sum_{i=0}^{N} x_i^{risk} x_i^{flag}}{\sum_{i=0}^{N} P7^{risk} x_i^{flag}} \quad (6)$$

For each of the preliminary investigations discussed in this section, the goal was to evolve overlay network solutions for a *fully-connected* RDM network containing 26 data mirrors. Each experimental run contained a population of 500 candidate solutions and employed tournament selection ($k = 5$), two-point crossover, and a 5% mutation rate for a total of 1,000 generations. To provide adequate statistical significance, a unique random seed was assigned to 30 replicate runs for each weight/target combination.

3.2 Weighted Plato

To guide evolutionary search towards solutions aligned with a user's high-level goals, a linear-weighted sum, shown in Equation (7), was used in Weighted Plato to prioritize problem objectives. During search, evolved network solutions whose characteristics maximized this linear-weighted sum, or fitness function, were considered to be aligned with the user's goals and selected by the genetic algorithm.

$$\text{Maximize} \quad \alpha_{cost}(1.0 - f_{cost}) + \alpha_{perf}(1.0 - f_{perf}) + \alpha_{reliab}(1.0 - f_{reliab}) \quad (7)$$

To evaluate how the relative prioritization of problem dimensions guided evolutionary search in the objective space [5], a diverse set of unique coefficient combinations were systematically generated by using an initial coefficient value of 0.0, an increment size of 0.10, and a requirement that the weighting coefficient values sum to 1.0. For each of these 66 unique coefficient combinations, the Weighted Plato reconfiguration tool was applied to dynamically generate an evolved overlay network optimized for the specific prioritization of problem objectives.

Experimental Results.

The Weighted Plato plot in Figure 1a shows the *combined* results from all 66 combinations where each three dimensional point corresponds to a returned solution's network measures. Although valid solutions were generated, three critical weaknesses were exposed. First, the solution surface where Pareto-optimal solutions reside was found to be non-convex causing a large number of valid solutions to be undetectable using a linear-weighted approach [7]. Second, after inspecting the qualities of returned solutions, we often found that solutions were optimized along a *single* dimension and misaligned with the user's weights and therefore, ill-fit for their intended environment. Third, linear-weighted sum approaches sacrifice exploration of the objective space in order to optimize a fitness function, and, as a result, a large number of coefficient combinations are necessary to achieve good search coverage.

3.3 Targeting Plato

To address the aforementioned challenges when using a linear-weighted approach, Targeting Plato [5] was developed, where a user specified the ideal *target values* for solutions to achieve along each objective. Candidate solutions in Targeting Plato were rewarded for their proximity to the ideal solution's target values as shown in Equation (8).

As before, we systematically generated various target configurations by starting each target measure at 0.0 with an increment size of 0.10 until the maximum boundary of 1.0 was reached within each dimension. We applied the Targeting Plato reconfiguration tool to generate an overlay network and plotted the *combined* solution set across all 1331 unique combinations in Figure 1b.

$$\text{Minimize} \quad |\tau_{cost} - (1.0 - f_{cost})| + |\tau_{perf} - (1.0 - f_{perf})| + |\tau_{reliab} - (1.0 - f_{reliab})| \quad (8)$$

Experimental Results.

We observed that Targeting Plato was not susceptible to the Pareto surface's non-convexity as solutions were successfully returned in interior regions where Weighted Plato was unable to previously reach, as shown in Figure 1b. To ensure that Pareto-optimal solutions were targeted during search, this approach requires that the target points be placed either on or beneath the Pareto surface. However, *apriori* knowledge of where the Pareto surface lies is rarely available causing a domain expert to rely on a trial-and-error approach with various target combinations. While Targeting Plato provided a more intuitive specification method for domain experts, this approach also collapsed the problem dimensions into a *single* objective function during optimization, similar to Weighted Plato. As such, the returned solution sets of these approaches often lacked diversity in their trade-offs, thus requiring costly iterations of search to be performed.

3.4 NSGA-II Plato

Two recurring observations with previous Plato-based studies were that (1) the objectives were often competing against, or in some cases negating, the effects of other objectives, or (2) complete knowledge of the fitness landscape was necessary to avoid suboptimal solutions. Despite only three objectives being present in the RDM application, multi-objective evolutionary algorithms (MOEAs) were explored next for their ability to manage competing objectives. As shown in Equation (9), each objective is optimized simultaneously in order to return a diverse set of Pareto-optimal solutions where each solution is optimal with respect to its associated trade-offs. These algorithms also do not require domain experts to specify desired solution qualities or to prioritize objectives to determine where solution trade-offs occur. Recently [6], a commonly-used MOEA named NSGA-II [12] was leveraged to mitigate the drawbacks of both Weighted Plato and Targeting Plato due to its incorporation of two operators: (1) non-dominated sorting and (2) a crowding-distance operator. Non-dominated sorting ensures that solutions approach true Pareto optimality by prioritizing solutions whose objective measures dominate the objective measures of other solutions in the population. To diversify the range of trade-offs found in the returned solution set, NSGA-II's crowding distance operator prioritizes solutions located in less crowded (i.e. novel) regions of the objective space.

$$\text{Minimize} \quad (f_{cost}, f_{perf}, f_{reliab}) \quad (9)$$

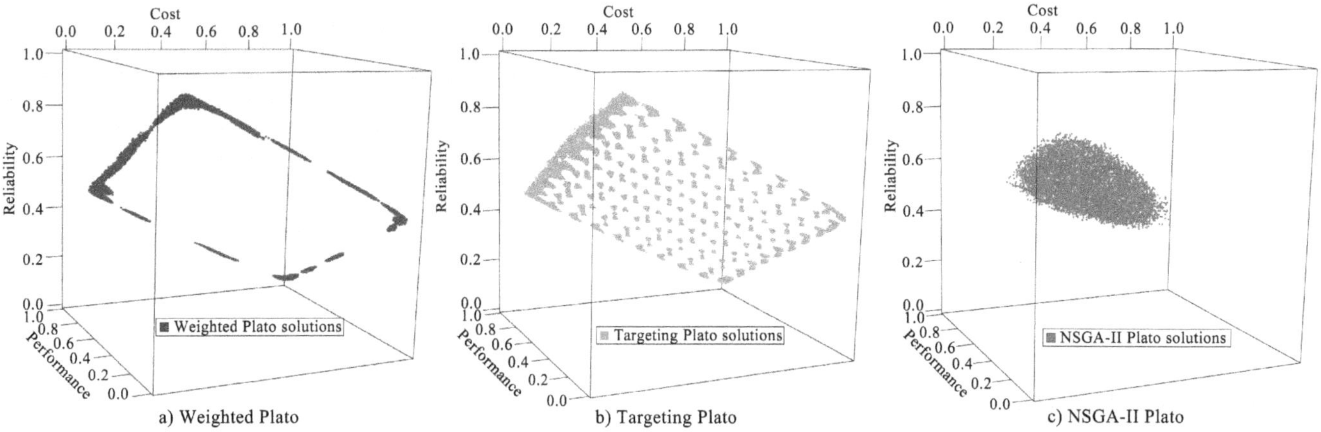

Figure 1: Returned solutions plotted within three-dimensional (Cost, Performance, and Reliability) objective space.

Experimental Results.
NSGA-II Plato was observed to overcome several shortcomings of Weighted Plato and Targeting Plato by returning solutions in non-convex regions without the requirement of domain-specific inputs (e.g., coefficients or target values) or complete knowledge of the Pareto surface. However, *hidden interactions* were discovered that restricted NSGA-II from regions of the objective space where valid, Pareto-optimal solutions were known to exist. Through an empirical study, these hidden search interactions were demonstrated to arise when solution objectives were unequally affected by mutation. In the context of the RDM application, solution objectives were unequally affected by mutation due to a variable-length genome design used to freely evolve overlay networks of various sizes and complexities. As shown in Figure 1c, NSGA-II Plato's search was biased towards regions associated with low Cost values as these solutions contain few network links and thus their objective values experience greater changes during mutation. Since NSGA-II's crowding-distance operator prioritizes solutions located in sparsely-populated regions of the objective space, solutions whose objective values experience greater change are favored since they are less likely to become more crowded over time.

4. DESIRED SEARCH PROPERTIES

Given the observed weaknesses of previous Plato approaches, we highlight three high-level abilities needed for search techniques used in the dynamic reconfiguration of DAS systems: (1) the ability to return a *diverse* solution set, (2) the ability to return *non-dominated, Pareto-optimal* solutions, and (3) the ability to *manage non-uniform mutational effects* to solution objectives. For each of these abilities, we provide a working definition, describe its importance for DAS reconfiguration, and summarize whether the ability was supported in previous Plato approaches (Table 2).

4.1 Diverse Solution Set

Solution set diversity, or "spread," represents the degree of coverage a search technique is able to achieve in the objective space. Maintaining a diverse population preserves a variety of open, parallel search avenues to explore, thus lowering the barrier of probabilistically discovering a global optima, if multiple paths to such optima exist. While a diverse population may slow convergence on newly discovered optima due to its spread, this property also reduces the likelihood of search becoming trapped in local optima. For applications, such as RDM, that require a DAS to respond to a variety of environmental and system uncertainties, a highly diverse solution set offers (1) a range of trade-offs for both domain users and automated tools to consider as well as (2) a method to indirectly probe the range of achievable objective values given current conditions.

In both the original Weighted Plato and Targeting Plato, the quality of an evolved solution was collapsed into a single fitness value, and, as a result, search often converged upon *one* particular solution type that optimized this value. The returned solution sets of these approaches often lacked diversity, and good coverage could only be achieved by exhaustively varying search parameters over many search iterations. In addition, non-convex Pareto surfaces prevent Weighted Plato from returning a large number of solutions. While the crowding-distance operator of NSGA-II Plato is normally capable of driving search towards sparsely-populated areas of the objective space, hidden interactions with solutions whose objective values are unequally affected by mutation were observed to disrupt this mechanism. Therefore, NSGA-II only supports solution set diversity when these interactions are not present in the optimization problem.

4.2 Non-Dominated, Pareto-Optimal Solutions

For applications defined by multiple orthogonal (conflicting) objectives, a solution is *Pareto-optimal* if no single objective can be improved further without sacrificing its quality along another objective. While Pareto optimality can be assessed for a solution in isolation, non-domination is assessed relative to other members of the *aggregate* solution set, or population. A solution B is said to "dominate" another solution C when solution B is no worse than solution C within each respective objective and solution B improves upon at least one of solution C's objective values. The ability to return an increasing majority of non-dominated solutions is a desirable search property since these solutions are irreplaceable by other population members thus helping to minimize search "waste" (i.e., dominated solutions) and improve search efficiency. However, since minor changes may easily produce new, non-dominated solutions, this ability alone does not guarantee a broad range of trade-offs, thus underscoring the importance of solution set diversity.

Linear-weighted sum techniques, such as Weighted Plato, can be used to seek Pareto-optimal solutions, however, non-convex regions of the objective space remain undetectable and, as demonstrated, returned solutions may be misaligned with the user's goals and therefore ill-fit for their intended environment. While Targeting Plato overcame these weaknesses, *apriori* knowledge of the Pareto surface's location is necessary to avoid returning suboptimal

	Desired Search Property		
	Seeks Diverse Solution Set (Coverage)	**Seeks Non-dominated (Pareto-optimal) solutions**	**Manage non-uniform mutational effects on solution objectives**
Weighted Plato (Weighted Sum)	No	**Yes**	N/A
Targeting Plato (Ideal Solution)	No	**Yes**	N/A
NSGA-II Plato (Crowding Distance)	**Yes**	**Yes**	No

Table 2: The desired search properties supported by previous Plato approaches.

solutions causing a domain expert to often rely on a trial-and-error approach using various target combinations. By constantly prioritizing solutions that improve upon the objective values of other population members, NSGA-II Plato is able to seek and return non-dominated, Pareto optimal solutions, however, these solutions were not representative of the overall objective space.

4.3 Manage Non-Uniform Mutational Effects

Finally, in order to handle combinatorial optimization problems, such as our RDM application, we seek evolutionary search techniques that can successfully mitigate the non-uniform effects of mutation on solution objectives as a direct result of hidden interactions recently observed [6]. In this empirical study, a variable-length genome caused solutions' objective values to be disproportionately affected by mutation and as a result, solutions with fewer elements experienced greater changes to their objective values during mutation thus conferring an advantage for escaping crowded regions. These hidden interactions between NSGA-II's crowding-distance operator and mutation prevented fair competition among solutions and biased search towards regions containing smaller solutions. In various application domains, the number of solution elements is often a free variable evolved to explore different designs and their associated trade-offs. Therefore, properly managing this interaction is critical for search techniques used for DAS. Moreover, a variable-length genome design is but one specific example by which objective values may vary disproportionately during search.

Both Weighted Plato and Targeting Plato approaches do not contain a mechanism, such as the crowding-distance operator, that explicitly rewards solutions based on their location relative to one another. As a result, these approaches are not susceptible to non-uniform mutational effects.

5. LEVERAGING NICHING

In biology, an ecological niche [22] often refers to a specific role, function, or area that an organism inhabits within an ecosystem as a result of the distribution of resources, predators, and/or competitors. When space within a population of competing individuals is limited, evolution via natural selection often drives organisms to enter unique niches in order to minimize competition thus allowing a more diverse overall population to co-exist. Similarly, in evolutionary search, a niching operator *creates* regions where individuals can locally compete by segmenting the population into distinct subpopulations and is useful when *simultaneously* targeting multiple optima and/or when solution set diversity is difficult to achieve due to convergence.

5.1 NSGA-III

In many-objective (four or more objectives) optimization problems, two critical issues arise: (1) the search space volume increases exponentially, due to the Curse of Dimensionality problem [2], making it difficult to effectively explore new regions, and (2) the majority of the population's open slots become occupied with non-dominated solutions causing evolutionary search to slow down dramatically [10]. To address these issues, Deb and Jain recently developed a new MOEA named NSGA-III [10] that incorporated the concept of **niching** during search by replacing NSGA-II's crowding-distance operator with a *reference point-based niching* operator.

We propose a new alternative role for NSGA-III's niching operator, namely, to manage non-uniform mutational changes to solution objectives. In applications where variable-length genomes are used, solutions cannot globally compete with one another due to inequity created by differing solution sizes. Niching promotes fair competition among solutions by ensuring that solutions *locally* compete with others based on similar objective values thereby building equity between solutions back into the optimization algorithm. In addition, the ability to explicitly define niche locations in the objective space allows NSGA-III to produce a selective pressure for search to enter regions previously difficult to reach by NSGA-II.

To understand the key differences between the diversity-preserving mechanisms of NSGA-II (*crowding-distance*) and NSGA-III (*niching*), we describe the distinct process used by each operator to select solutions for subsequent iterations of search. We begin, however, with an overview of shared core functionality found in both NSGA-II and NSGA-III approaches. At the start of each generation, a parent population (**P**) containing N individuals is used to generate an offspring population (**Q**) of equal size using standard genetic operators such as crossover and mutation. Next, these two populations are merged into one combined population (**R**) where all $2N$ solutions are sorted into a series of disjoint, non-dominated sets called *fronts*. Solutions are iteratively placed into successive fronts (ex. F_1, F_2, etc.) if they are non-dominated with respect to remaining, unsorted solutions. To select for truly Pareto-optimal solutions, fronts are sequentially added based on their non-domination level until the population capacity, N, is matched or exceeded. If the population capacity is matched upon adding the last front (F_L), no further operations are necessary and the next generation begins again using this newly generated population. If adding the last front (F_L) causes the population capacity to be exceeded since only K slots remain, then additional steps must be taken to determine which solutions from F_L will fill these remaining unoccupied slots. The two distinct diversity-preserving mechanisms, crowding-distance and reference point-based niching, used to make this decision are discussed below.

Crowding Distance Operator (NSGA-II).

In the NSGA-II implementation used in NSGA-II Plato [6], a *crowding-distance* operator calculated each solution's nearest neighbor distance based on all of the problem objectives. Since solutions that maximized this distance measure were more likely to be located in novel regions of the objective space, the top K solutions of F_L filled the remaining slots in the new population. This diversity-preserving mechanism is intended to expand overall coverage by driving search towards sparsely-populated regions of the objective space. However, this mechanism can be disrupted when solution objectives are disproportionately affected by mutation.

Reference-Point Based Niching Operator (NSGA-III).

In NSGA-III, the *reference point-based niching* operator starts with a set of reference points, or niches, that either (1) have been generated in a structured manner, such as being uniformly distributed, or (2) pre-determined and supplied by the user. Next, solutions from previously added fronts (i.e., $F_1 \ldots F_{L-1}$) are *associated* to a unique niche. To associate a solution to a specific niche, a reference line is projected from the origin through each niche's reference point, and the perpendicular distance between a solution and each reference line is calculated. Afterwards, each solution is associated with the niche whose reference line has the closest perpendicular distance. To fill the remaining K slots in the next generation's population, the niche with the least associated solutions (excluding niches with no associated solutions) is chosen and the solution in F_L with the closest perpendicular distance to this niche's projected reference line is added to the population. After this solution has been associated with the niche, this selection process repeats until all remaining K slots are filled.

6. EXPERIMENTAL DESIGN AND RESULTS

We assess whether niching can provide the three high-level desired properties for DAS by using NSGA-III for the dynamic reconfiguration of an industrial RDM application. In this application, NSGA-III must evolve overlay network solutions for a *fully-connected* RDM network containing 26 data mirrors, causing the optimization problem to be non-trivial based on the large number of unique network constructions possible (i.e., 7×2^{325}).

Each evolutionary run contained a population of 500 candidate solutions that employed tournament selection ($k = 5$), two-point crossover, and a 5% mutation rate for a total of 1,000 generations, equating to roughly 4 minutes of wall-clock time. To provide adequate statistical significance, we used 30 replicate runs with a unique random seed assigned to each run. We used Das and Dennis's [8] systematic approach to generate a uniformly distributed grid of reference points in the objective space on a normalized hyperplane in $N - 1$ dimensions. The granularity of this reference grid's resolution can be specified by the domain expert based on the number of intervals (p) along each of the hyperplane's edges. The total number of reference points (H) for an M-objective problem is given by Equation (10). In our RDM application where solutions were to be optimized along three objectives ($M = 3$), each of the 2D hyperplane's edges was divided into 20 intervals ($p = 20$), producing a total of 231 unique uniformly-distributed reference points.

$$H = \binom{M+p-1}{p} \tag{10}$$

Diverse Solutions and Mitigating Non-Uniform Effects.

To assess solution set diversity due to niching, we visually inspected the search coverage for each replicate run using NSGA-III Plato. In order to demonstrate that each run consistently achieved the same level of coverage, solutions from an individual run were assigned the *same*, unique color along a red-blue gradient (i.e., $Run_1 = Red \ldots Run_{30} = Blue$). Using niching, we observed that a significantly large region of the Pareto surface was consistently found and returned by each experimental run when compared to the achieved coverage of previous Plato approaches (Figure 1). As such, the even distribution of each run across the full objective space has yielded an overall purple coloring of the combined results. More importantly, solutions of varying sizes and complexities were evolved, maintained, and returned. This result demonstrates that niching was able to overcome and mitigate the hidden search bias caused by non-uniform changes to solution objectives, a critical property for maximizing the number of different DAS designs as well as their associated trade-offs.

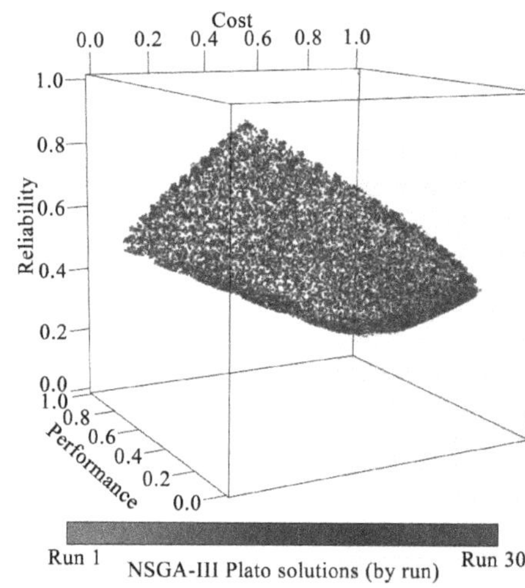

Figure 2: The returned solutions for NSGA-III Plato plotted within three-dimensional objective space.

To quantify and compare the search volume for each of the Plato approaches, we used the *hypervolume indicator* [27] to measure the volume dominated by Pareto-optimal solutions in the final population. The percentage of the objective space's total hypervolume that is dominated by a *single* run across the different Plato approaches is summarized in Figure 3.

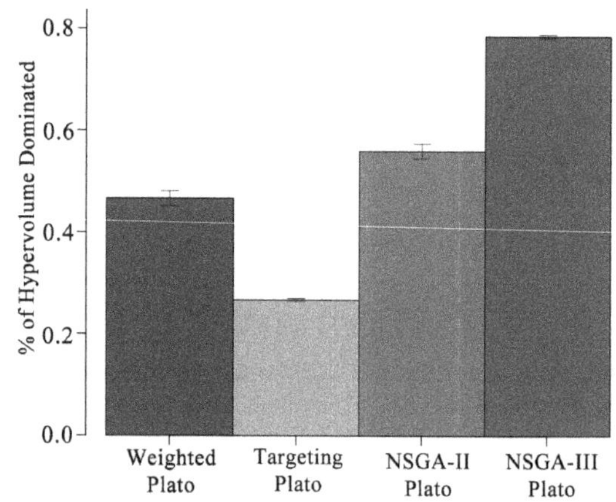

Figure 3: Average percentage of the hypervolume dominated by each Plato approach's solutions

By leveraging niching, NSGA-III achieved a significant increase ($p \ll 0.01$) in average search coverage that was 1.6-1.7 times greater than the average Weighted Plato run, 2.9-3.0 times greater than the average Targeting Plato run, and 1.4 times greater than the average NSGA-II Plato run. However, due to the non-convex Pareto surface, Weighted Plato could not achieve equivalent search coverage, even with multiple runs, since the interior of this surface is unreachable by linear-weighted approaches. Using numerous target value combinations, Targeting Plato could achieve comparable search coverage, however, this is computationally expensive and requires *complete* knowledge of the Pareto surface's location to ensure sub-optimal solutions are not returned. Similar to Weighted Plato, the NSGA-II Plato approach could not achieve equivalent search coverage due to the non-uniform changes to solution objectives during mutation that restricts search to a limited region of the Pareto surface.

7. RELATED WORK

The hidden search bias caused by non-uniform changes to solutions' objective values was only discovered recently [6] and therefore, to the best of the authors' knowledge, the use of reference point-based niching to mitigate this issue has not been previously presented in the literature. The key factor that enabled reference point-based niching to overcome this hidden search bias was that niches were *explicitly defined* and maintained during search. Alternative niching strategies [25] often rely on niches to *dynamically emerge* in the objective space based on solution properties.

In **sharing** and **clearing** strategies [14, 16, 24], a resource (e.g., objective value or fitness) is apportioned to individuals within a user-defined niche radius (threshold) in either the solution or design space. In these strategies, niches emerge as solutions are driven towards sparsely-populated regions to avoid sharing and competing for their niche's resource with more population members. However, these strategies may be biased against solutions whose objective values experience little variation as these solutions more rapidly acquire niche members. **Clustering** operators [25], such as k-means, can be used in place of a niche radius for allocating individuals into k niches based on their proximity to a centroid, however, offline analysis of this approach demonstrated that this approach was unsuccessful at mitigating the search bias.

In **crowding** strategies [9, 12], competition takes place between parents and offspring for inclusion in the next generation's population, where offspring crowd out the most similar individual from a randomly selected subset of user-specified size, often referred to as the crowding factor. In these strategies, niches emerge as solutions are driven away from other members to lower the probability of being selected for replacement. Using NSGA-II, we observed [6] that crowding strategies remain susceptible to search bias as parents whose objectives experience high variation are likely to be more dissimilar to their offspring and therefore may be prioritized during search.

Similarly, the **ϵ-dominance** [11] strategy expands the range of objective values considered to be *dominated* by a particular solution by adding a small value (ϵ) to each objective measure. Niches emerge as solutions are driven away from other members to lower the probability of being placed into a dominated front. However, this strategy is vulnerable to similar hidden interactions since it requires niches to be dynamically created by solutions as opposed to explicitly being defined. Once a solution becomes truly Pareto-optimal, neighboring solutions must be able to mutate outside the range of objective values considered to be dominated which may be difficult in regions where these values experience less variation, thus biasing search against these regions.

Reference grid niching strategies typically divide the objective space into subspaces either through an explicit distribution of niches (e.g., NSGA-III) or by allowing niches to emerge from solution properties. The Pareto Archived Evolutionary Strategy (PAES) [19] performs the latter by recursively bisecting the range of current objective values to determine whether to archive a solution. One potential shortcoming of this strategy, however, is that the degree to which a solution is crowded affects the archival of solutions. Since archived solutions whose objective values experience less variation become crowded more rapidly, these solutions may be frequently selected by PAES for replacement and biased against. In contrast, reference grid strategies that explicitly define niches, such as NSGA-III, are not susceptible to the level of crowding within a niche, and therefore the niches are preserved by keeping at least one associated member in subsequent generations of search.

8. CONCLUSIONS

The experiments in this paper have demonstrated the value of *reference point-based niching* for applications defined by two key features: (1) solution set diversity is a priority and (2) objective values of solutions are unequally affected by mutation. Multi-objective genetic algorithms, such as NSGA-II, often seek to return a *diverse* set of Pareto-optimal solutions and may incorporate search operators (e.g., crowding-distance) that are responsive to the distances that solutions mutate in the objective space. When solutions' objective values are disproportionately affected by mutation, however, these operators are biased towards solutions whose objective values experience greater changes due to their ability to escape into less crowded, novel regions of the objective space.

Reference point-based niching mitigates this issue by performing two key functions. First, niches are *explicitly* created and maintained uniformly throughout the objective space in regions difficult for search to reach. The solutions in these regions may either be too difficult to construct by random mutation alone or biased against due to smaller changes to their objective values. Niching produces a strong selective pressure for solutions to find sparsely populated niches in order to minimize competition and increase their chances of survival into the next generation. As a result, solutions are constantly driven to equally spread across the objective space resulting in the significant observed increase in search coverage (i.e. diversity) when compared with previous approaches. Second, reference point-based niching ensures that only solutions with similar properties (i.e. solution size or Cost) are localized within the same niche promoting fair competition among solutions.

Although the variable-length genome design in the RDM application caused non-uniform changes to solution objectives, this scenario is only one of many different ways that this hidden search bias may manifest itself in an application. For example, if the mapping between solution elements and problem objectives changes over time, then solutions whose objectives are mapped to fewer elements will experience greater changes to their objectives, and, as a result, these solutions may be preferred during search. Alternatively, if an objective's granularity is non-uniform, then a search bias may exist for solutions in more coarse-grained regions of the objective that experience more variation. Moreover, if the granularities between objectives are different, then solutions able to optimize along the coarser objective more easily may be prioritized. Objective function granularity has been recently highlighted [20] as an important future research area for its effects on search dynamics and performance. These issues are exacerbated further in dynamic optimization problems (DOPs) [4] as both the Pareto surface and granularity of objectives change over time thus underscoring the importance of niching.

Our results provide a key insight into niching features useful for overcoming this hidden bias to aid researchers exploring multi-objective optimization in domains sharing similar qualities. In general, our future work aims to explore problem and solution characteristics that cause evolutionary search techniques to be either well-suited or counterproductive to multi-objective optimization. Future directions include (1) exploring adaptive methods for distributing reference points, (2) designing a formal benchmark problem for studying both spatial and temporal changes to objective granularity, and (3) evaluating alternative niching strategies' performance on this problem such as ϵ-dominance as well as hypervolume-based approaches such as IBEA [26] and SMS-EMOEA [3].

9. ACKNOWLEDGMENTS

We gratefully acknowledge Professor Kalyanmoy Deb for his help introducing us to NSGA-III and his feedback on this work. This work has been supported in part by NSF grants IIP-0700329, CCF-0820220, DBI-0939454, CNS-0854931, CNS-0915855. Any opinions, findings, or conclusions expressed in this material are those of the author(s) and do not necessarily reflect the views of the National Science Foundation or other sponsors.

10. REFERENCES

[1] D. Andersen, H. Balakrishnan, F. Kaashoek, and R. Morris. Resilient overlay networks. *SIGOPS Oper. Syst. Rev.*, 35(5):131–145, Oct. 2001.

[2] R. Bellman. *Dynamic Programming*. Princeton University Press, Princeton, NJ, USA, 1st edition, 1957.

[3] N. Beume, B. Naujoks, and M. Emmerich. SMS-EMOA: Multiobjective selection based on dominated hypervolume. *European Journal of Operational Research*, 181(3):1653–1669, September 2007.

[4] J. Branke, T. Kaubler, C. Schmidt, and H. Schmeck. A multi-population approach to dynamic optimization problems. In *In Adaptive Computing in Design and Manufacturing*, pages 299–308. Springer, 2000.

[5] C. Byers and B. H. C. Cheng. Mitigating uncertainty within the dimensions of a remote data mirroring problem. Technical Report MSU-CSE-14-10, Computer Science and Engineering, Michigan State University, East Lansing, Michigan, September 2014.

[6] C. Byers, B. H. C. Cheng, and K. Deb. Unwanted feature interactions between the problem and search operators in evolutionary multi-objective optimization. In *Proceedings of the 8th International Conference on Evolutionary Multi-Criterion Optimization*. Springer-Verlag, 2015 (full paper - to appear).

[7] I. Das and J. Dennis. A closer look at drawbacks of minimizing weighted sums of objectives for pareto set generation in multicriteria optimization problems. *Structural optimization*, 14(1):63–69, 1997.

[8] I. Das and J. E. Dennis. Normal-boundary intersection: A new method for generating the pareto surface in nonlinear multicriteria optimization problems. *SIAM J. on Optimization*, 8(3):631–657, Mar. 1998.

[9] K. A. De Jong. *An Analysis of the Behavior of a Class of Genetic Adaptive Systems*. PhD thesis, Ann Arbor, MI, USA, 1975. AAI7609381.

[10] K. Deb and H. Jain. An evolutionary many-objective optimization algorithm using reference-point-based nondominated sorting approach, part i: Solving problems with box constraints. *Evolutionary Computation, IEEE Transactions on*, 18(4):577–601, Aug 2014.

[11] K. Deb, M. Mohan, and S. Mishra. Evaluating the epsilon-domination based multi-objective evolutionary algorithm for a quick computation of pareto-optimal solutions. *Evol. Comput.*, 13(4):501–525, Dec. 2005.

[12] K. Deb, A. Pratap, S. Agarwal, and T. Meyarivan. A fast and elitist multiobjective genetic algorithm: NSGA-II. *Trans. Evol. Comp*, 6(2):182–197, Apr. 2002.

[13] D. E. Goldberg. *Genetic Algorithms in Search, Optimization and Machine Learning*. Addison-Wesley Longman Publishing Co., Inc., Boston, MA, USA, 1st edition, 1989.

[14] D. E. Goldberg and J. Richardson. Genetic algorithms with sharing for multimodal function optimization. In *Proceedings of the Second International Conference on Genetic Algorithms on Genetic Algorithms and Their Application*, pages 41–49, Hillsdale, NJ, USA, 1987. L. Erlbaum Associates Inc.

[15] J. H. Holland. Genetic algorithms. *Scientific American*, July 1992.

[16] J. Horn, N. Nafpliotis, and D. Goldberg. A niched pareto genetic algorithm for multiobjective optimization. In *Evolutionary Computation, 1994. IEEE World Congress on Computational Intelligence., Proceedings of the First IEEE Conference on*, pages 82–87 vol.1, Jun 1994.

[17] K. Keeton, C. Santos, D. Beyer, J. Chase, and J. Wilkes. Designing for disasters. In *Proceedings of the 3rd USENIX Conf. on File and Storage Technologies*, pages 59–62, Berkeley, CA, USA, 2004.

[18] J. O. Kephart and D. M. Chess. The vision of autonomic computing. *Computer*, 36(1):41–50, Jan. 2003.

[19] J. D. Knowles and D. W. Corne. Approximating the nondominated front using the pareto archived evolution strategy. *Evol. Comput.*, 8(2):149–172, June 2000.

[20] K. McClymont. Recent advances in problem understanding: Changes in the landscape a year on. In *Proceedings of the 15th Annual Conference Companion on Genetic and Evolutionary Computation*, GECCO '13 Companion, pages 1071–1078, New York, NY, USA, 2013. ACM.

[21] P. K. McKinley, S. M. Sadjadi, E. P. Kasten, and B. H. C. Cheng. Composing adaptive software. *Computer*, 37(7):56–64, July 2004.

[22] A. T. Peterson, J. Soberon, R. G. Pearson, R. P. Anderson, E. Martinez-Meyer, M. Nakamura, and M. B. Araujo. *Ecological Niches and Geographic Distributions (MPB-49)*. Monographs in Population Biology. Princeton University Press, 2011.

[23] A. J. Ramirez, D. B. Knoester, B. H. C. Cheng, and P. K. McKinley. Applying genetic algorithms to decision making in autonomic computing systems. In *Proceedings of the 6th International Conference on Autonomic Computing*, ICAC '09, pages 97–106, New York, NY, USA, 2009. ACM.

[24] V. Seydi Ghomsheh, M. Khanehsar, and M. Teshnehlab. Improving the non-dominate sorting genetic algorithm for multi-objective optimization. In *Computational Intelligence and Security Workshops, 2007. CISW 2007. International Conference on*, pages 89–92, Dec 2007.

[25] O. Shir. Niching in evolutionary algorithms. In G. Rozenberg, T. Back, and J. Kok, editors, *Handbook of Natural Computing*, pages 1035–1069. Springer Berlin Heidelberg, 2012.

[26] E. Zitzler and S. Kunzli. Indicator-based selection in multiobjective search. In *in Proc. 8th International Conference on Parallel Problem Solving from Nature (PPSN VIII*, pages 832–842. Springer, 2004.

[27] E. Zitzler, L. Thiele, M. Laumanns, C. M. Fonseca, and V. G. da Fonseca. Performance assessment of multiobjective optimizers: An analysis and review. *Trans. Evol. Comp*, 7(2):117–132, Apr. 2003.

MOEA/VAN: Multiobjective Evolutionary Algorithm Based on Vector Angle Neighborhood

Roman Denysiuk
Algoritmi R&D Center
University of Minho
Campus de Gualtar
4710-057 Braga, Portugal
roman.denysiuk@algoritmi.uminho.pt

Lino Costa
Department of Production and Systems Engineering
University of Minho
Campus de Gualtar
4710-057 Braga, Portugal
lac@dps.uminho.pt

Isabel Espírito Santo
Department of Production and Systems Engineering
University of Minho
Campus de Gualtar
4710-057 Braga, Portugal
iapinho@dps.uminho.pt

ABSTRACT

Natural selection favors the survival and reproduction of organisms that are best adapted to their environment. Selection mechanism in evolutionary algorithms mimics this process, aiming to create environmental conditions in which artificial organisms could evolve solving the problem at hand. This paper proposes a new selection scheme for evolutionary multiobjective optimization. The similarity measure that defines the concept of the neighborhood is a key feature of the proposed selection. Contrary to commonly used approaches, usually defined on the basis of distances between either individuals or weight vectors, it is suggested to consider the similarity and neighborhood based on the angle between individuals in the objective space. The smaller the angle, the more similar individuals. This notion is exploited during the mating and environmental selections. The convergence is ensured by minimizing distances from individuals to a reference point, whereas the diversity is preserved by maximizing angles between neighboring individuals. Experimental results reveal a highly competitive performance and useful characteristics of the proposed selection. Its strong diversity preserving ability allows to produce a significantly better performance on some problems when compared with stat-of-the-art algorithms.

Categories and Subject Descriptors

I.2.8 [**Artificial Intelligence**]: Problem Solving, Control Methods, and Search–*Heuristic methods*

Keywords

Multiobjective optimization; Evolutionary multiobjective optimization; Multiobjective evolutionary algorithms; Performance assessment

GECCO '15, July 11 - 15, 2015, Madrid, Spain

DOI: http://dx.doi.org/10.1145/2739480.2754722

1. INTRODUCTION

In practice, the simultaneous optimization of multiple objectives has become widespread. Without loss of generality, a multiobjective optimization problem (MOP) with m objectives and n decision variables can be formulated as:

$$\begin{array}{ll} \text{minimize:} & \boldsymbol{f}(\boldsymbol{x}) = (f_1(\boldsymbol{x}), f_2(\boldsymbol{x}), \ldots, f_m(\boldsymbol{x}))^{\mathrm{T}} \\ \text{subject to:} & \boldsymbol{x} \in \Omega \end{array} \tag{1}$$

where $\boldsymbol{x}$ is the decision vector, $\Omega \subseteq \mathbb{R}^n$ is the feasible decision space, and $\boldsymbol{f}(\boldsymbol{x})$ is the objective vector defined in the attainable objective space $\Theta \subseteq \mathbb{R}^m$.

In multiobjective optimization, the Pareto dominance relation is usually used to define the concepts of optimality. For two solutions $\boldsymbol{x}$ and $\boldsymbol{y}$ from Ω, a solution $\boldsymbol{x}$ is said to dominate a solution $\boldsymbol{y}$ (denoted by $\boldsymbol{x} \prec \boldsymbol{y}$) if for all $i \in \{1, \ldots, m\}$ $f_i(\boldsymbol{x}) \leq f_i(\boldsymbol{y})$ and there exists at least one objective such that $f_j(\boldsymbol{x}) < f_j(\boldsymbol{y})$.

A solution $\boldsymbol{x}^* \in \Omega$ is Pareto optimal if and only if:

$$\nexists \boldsymbol{y} \in \Omega : \boldsymbol{y} \prec \boldsymbol{x}^*. \tag{2}$$

In the presence of multiple conflicting objectives, there is a set of optimal solutions, known as the Pareto optimal set. For MOP (1), the Pareto optimal set (or Pareto set for short) is defined as:

$$\mathcal{PS} = \{\boldsymbol{x}^* \in \Omega \,|\, \nexists \boldsymbol{y} \in \Omega : \boldsymbol{y} \prec \boldsymbol{x}^*\}. \tag{3}$$

For MOP (1) and the Pareto set $\mathcal{PS}$, the Pareto optimal front (or Pareto front for short) is defined as:

$$\mathcal{PF} = \{\boldsymbol{f}(\boldsymbol{x}^*) \in \Theta \,|\, \boldsymbol{x}^* \in \mathcal{PS}\}. \tag{4}$$

Since it is often not possible to obtain the whole Pareto set, solving (1) is usually understood as approximating the Pareto set by obtaining a set of solutions that are as close as possible to the Pareto set and as diverse as possible.

Evolutionary algorithms (EAs) have become popular in solving MOPs. Similarly to single-objective counterparts, multiobjective evolutionary algorithms (MOEAs) draw inspiration from natural evolution. Natural selection is responsible for adaptation of species to their environment, giving extra survival and reproduction probability to the most fitted individuals. EAs usually mimic this process by assigning fitness values to population members and sampling the population, according to these values. Although it can be relatively easy in the single-objective case, it is not so straightforward in multiobjective optimization. Therefore, selection is a major issue in the design of MOEAs.

Based on the fitness assignment and selection, most modern MOEAs can be classified into three major categories: dominance-, scalarizing- and indicator-based algorithms. Dominance-based MOEAs use the concept of the Pareto dominance. To guide the search, the dominance relation between population members and the population diversity can be incorporated in a scalar fitness value [21]. Another common approach is to perform two stage selection, ranking and selection individuals according to nondomination levels and applying diversity preserving mechanism when the last accepted level cannot be completely accommodated [3]. Due to a low selection pressure in high dimensional objective spaces, the performance of dominance-based algorithms severely deteriorates when the number of objectives is increased [15]. This issue can be addressed by modifying the dominance relation [16, 19] or the diversity preserving mechanism [5, 6, 12]. For some other problems, the dominance relation provides a high selection pressure [11], which can be harmful for search due to the loss of diversity. Scalarizing-based approaches incorporate traditional mathematical techniques [14] based on the aggregation of multiple objectives into a single parameterized function. A scalar fitness value is assigned to each population member, with an individual representing a solution to the corresponding single-objective function. MOEAs relying on scalarization produce promising results for many-objective problems [9] and in terms of balancing the convergence and diversity [11]. Though this balance cannot be ensured on some other problems [13]. To use scalarizing functions, a set of weight vectors usually must be provided in advance, which is not easy for all the cases. To guide the search, indicator-based approaches employ performance indicators, such as the ϵ or hypervolume indicators. A scalar fitness value is assigned to each population member, reflecting its quality with respect to the convergence and diversity [20]. Indicator-based MOEAs are successful in dealing with many-objective problems [17]. The difficulty in their application arises from the high computational cost. For example, the time required for calculating the hypervolume grows exponentially with the number of objectives [18], limiting significantly its applicability. Approximating the hypervolume requires the compromise between accuracy and complexity [1].

This study suggests a selection scheme that does not rely on the aforementioned fitness assignment strategies. The proposed framework shares some similarities with MOEA/D, being different in several ways. MOEA/VAN does not require a prior information in terms of weight vectors, alleviating user's burden. Its selection scheme is adaptive and solely based on interactions between individuals in the current population. The concept of the similarity is defined based on the angle between objective vectors. MOEA/VAN attempts to maintain the population as diverse as possible, according to the defined measure. One of the two most similar individuals in the population is removed, according to the convergence. As a result, less selection pressure and higher diversity are expected, which can be beneficial for search.

The remainder of this paper is organized as follows. Section 2 describes the proposed framework. Section 3 reports results of the experimental study, including experimentation with different configurations and comparison with state-of-the-art algorithms. Section 4 concludes the study and outlines some possible future work.

2. PROPOSED FRAMEWORK

Multiobjective evolutionary algorithm based on vector angle neighborhood (MOEA/VAN) solves a multiobjective optimization problem by minimizing distances between population members and a reference point while maximizing angles between neighboring individuals. Contrary to MOEAs, which minimize a weighted distance to a reference point [11], MOEA/VAN does not require a set of weight vectors to be provided beforehand.

During the search, MOEA/VAN maintains the population, P, of size μ and a reference point, $\boldsymbol{z}$, composed of the lowest objective values found so far. Each individual in P is represented by the decision vector $\boldsymbol{x}$, the vector of objective functions $\boldsymbol{f}$, the vector of translated objectives $\tilde{\boldsymbol{f}}$ calculated as:

$$\tilde{f}_j = f_j - z_j \quad \forall j \in \{1, \ldots, m\} \tag{5}$$

and the vector $\boldsymbol{\theta}$ containing all the angles between the current individual and the other population members. During the evolution, translated objective values, $\tilde{\boldsymbol{f}}$, are used. The angle between the individuals a and b is computed as:

$$\theta = \arccos\left(\frac{\langle \tilde{\boldsymbol{f}}_a, \tilde{\boldsymbol{f}}_b \rangle}{\|\tilde{\boldsymbol{f}}_a\| \|\tilde{\boldsymbol{f}}_b\|}\right) \tag{6}$$

where $\langle \cdot, \cdot \rangle$ denotes the dot product and $\| \cdot \|$ denotes the Euclidean norm.

The convergence is ensured by minimizing the p-norm of each individual:

$$\|\tilde{\boldsymbol{f}}\|_p = \left(\sum_{j=1}^{m} |\tilde{f}_j|^p\right)^{\frac{1}{p}}. \tag{7}$$

For preserving diversity, one of the two most similar individuals in the population is removed after generating offspring. As the similarity measure defying the concept of the neighborhood, the angle between individuals is used. The smaller the angle, the closer (or more similar) individuals. It is important to note that the length of vectors and the distance between them do not play a major role for defining similarity. Due to these features, it is expected that the selection would be particularly useful for maintaining diversity and not be affected by the curse of dimensionality.

In this study, the real representation for individuals is used. An offspring individual, $\boldsymbol{y}$, is produced using a differential evolution (DE) operator that works as follows $\forall j \in \{1, \ldots, n\}$:

$$y_j = \begin{cases} x_j^i + F \times (x_j^{r1} - x_j^{r2}) & \text{with probability } CR \\ x_j^i & \text{with probability } 1 - CR \end{cases} \tag{8}$$

The polynomial mutation is applied on the offspring as follows $\forall j \in \{1, \ldots, n\}$:

$$y_j = \begin{cases} y_j + \sigma_j \times (ub_j - lb_j) & \text{with probability } p_m \\ y_j & \text{with probability } 1 - p_m \end{cases} \tag{9}$$

where lb_j and ub_j are the lower and upper bounds of the j-th variable, respectively,

$$\sigma_j = \begin{cases} (2u_j)^{1/(1+\eta_m)} - 1 & \text{if } u_j \leq 0.5 \\ 1 - (2 - 2u_j)^{1/(1+\eta_m)} & \text{otherwise} \end{cases} \tag{10}$$

and $u_j \in [0, 1]$ is a uniform random number. To ensure feasibility, individuals are repaired as:

$$y_j = \min\{\max\{y_j, lb_j\}, ub_j\} \quad \forall j \in \{1, \ldots, n\}. \tag{11}$$

The outline of MOEA/VAN is given as follows:

Input:

- CR - crossover probability;
- F - scaling factor;
- p_m - mutation probability;
- η_m - mutation distribution index;
- δ - probability for mating pool;
- T - neighborhood size for mating selection;
- K - neighborhood size for environmental selection;
- p - parameter defining p-norm;
- μ - population size;
- $maxEval$ - maximum number of function evaluations.

Output:

- $\{\boldsymbol{x}^1, \ldots, \boldsymbol{x}^\mu\}$ - approximation to the Pareto set;
- $\{\boldsymbol{f}(\boldsymbol{x}^1), \ldots, \boldsymbol{f}(\boldsymbol{x}^\mu)\}$ - approximation to the Pareto front.

Step 1 Initialization

Step 1.1 Randomly generate initial population.

Step 1.2 Initialize a reference point, $\boldsymbol{z}$, as $\forall j \in \{1, \ldots, m\}$: $z_j = \min_{1 \le i \le \mu} f_j(\boldsymbol{x}^i)$

Step 1.3 Translate objective vectors using (5).

Step 1.4 Compute the angles between all the population members using (6).

Step 2 Mating selection

Step 2.1 Uniformly at random select a population member (say the i-th individual is selected).

Step 2.2 With probability δ, select two different individuals $r1$ and $r2$ from the T closest individuals, or with probability $(1 - \delta)$ select these individuals from the whole population.

Step 3 Variation

Step 3.1 Generate an offspring, $\boldsymbol{y}$, using a differential evolution (DE) operator.

Step 3.2 Apply polynomial mutation on the offspring.

Step 3.3 Repair the offspring.

Step 4 Update

Step 4.1 For each $j \in \{1, \ldots, m\}$, if $f_j(\boldsymbol{y}) < z_j$, then set $z_j = f_j(\boldsymbol{y})$.

Step 4.2 If $\boldsymbol{z}$ was updated in Step 4.1, translate objectives for $P \cup \boldsymbol{y}$. Otherwise, translate objectives for $\boldsymbol{y}$.

Step 4.3 If $\boldsymbol{z}$ was updated in Step 4.1, compute the angles between all the members of $P \cup \boldsymbol{y}$. Otherwise, compute the angles between $\boldsymbol{y}$ and all the members of P.

Step 5 Environmental selection

Step 5.1 If $\boldsymbol{y}$ is better for at least one objective comparing with each of K closest individuals in the population, go to Step 5.2. Otherwise, go to **Step 6**.

Step 5.2 Find two closest individuals from $P \cup \boldsymbol{y}$, and remove individual having larger $\|\tilde{f}\|_p$.

Step 6 If the maximum number of function evaluations is reached, then stop. Otherwise, go to **Step 2**.

3. EXPERIMENTAL VALIDATION

This section presents and discusses results of the experimental study carried out to validate the proposed approach. The experimental study is divided into two parts, which are devoted to handling different problem characteristics. For experiments, GDE3 [10], MOEA/D [11] and IBEA [20] are used within the JMetal framework [7]. The major reason for choosing these algorithms is that they are established state-of-the-art algorithms and represent the main trends to the fitness assignment and selection in MOEAs – namely the dominance-, scalarizing- and indicator-based strategies. Hence, they serve as an important reference for evaluating the proposed approach, where the main novelty is the selection mechanism.

3.1 Complicated Pareto Sets

In this part, two sets of challenging problems from [11] and [13] are adopted, which are referred in the following as the LZ09 and LGZ test suites, respectively. These problems pose significant difficulties for MOEAs in terms of obtaining well distributed approximations. First, experiments are conducted to estimate the effects of major control parameters in MOEA/VAN. Then, the performance of MOEA/VAN is compared with state-of-the-art algorithms.

3.1.1 Experimental Setup

The values of δ, T, K and p for MOEA/VAN are determined in parametrization study. Some general parameters are as shown in Table 1. The remaining settings are as follows. Thirty independent runs are performed with a population size of $\mu = 300$, running for 1.5×10^5 and 3×10^5 function evaluations on the LZ09 and LGZ problems, respectively. These settings are as suggested in [11] and [13].

MOEA/VAN	MOEA/D	GDE3	IBEA
$CR = 1.0$	$CR = 1.0$	$CR = 1.0$	$\eta_c = 20$
$F = 0.5$	$F = 0.5$	$F = 0.5$	$p_c = 0.9$
$\eta_m = 20$	$\eta_m = 20$	$\eta_m = 20$	$\eta_m = 20$
$p_m = 1/n$	$p_m = 1/n$	$p_m = 1/n$	$p_m = 1/n$
	$\delta = 0.9$		
	$T = 20$		

Table 1: Parameter settings for the algorithms.

As the performance measure, the inverted generational distance (IGD) indicator [2] is used. This indicator can be referred as the distance from the Pareto front, $\mathcal{PF}$, to an approximation set [23], A. IGD can be defined as:

$$I_{IGD} = \frac{\sum_{a' \in \mathcal{PF}} d(\boldsymbol{a}', A)}{|\mathcal{PF}|} \tag{12}$$

where $d(\boldsymbol{a}', A)$ is the minimum Euclidean distance between $\boldsymbol{a}'$ and the points in A. IGD can measure both the diversity and convergence of A. The smaller the value of I_{IGD}, the better the quality of A. For calculating IGD, 1,000 uniformly distributed points along the Pareto front are generated for each problem. For statistically sound conclusions, the Wilcoxon rank sum test is performed at significance level of 0.05 [8].

3.1.2 Parametrization Study

MOEA/VAN relies on the setting of δ, T during the mating selection and K, p during the environmental selection.

δ \ T	10	20	30	40
0.7	5.67	3.33	8.78	10.33
0.8	5.78	4.67	7.11	10.67
0.9	9.33	5.56	7.00	9.56
1.0	13.22	11.33	11.33	12.33

(a) LZ09 test suite

δ \ T	10	20	30	40
0.7	9.57	8.14	11.43	13.57
0.8	8.71	5.00	9.71	12.71
0.9	8.43	2.71	6.43	10.71
1.0	11.57	2.43	6.00	8.86

(b) LGZ test suite

δ \ T	10	20	30	40
0.7	7.38	5.44	9.94	11.75
0.8	7.06	4.81	8.25	11.56
0.9	8.94	4.31	6.75	10.06
1.0	12.50	7.44	9.00	10.81

(c) LZ09 and LGZ test suites

Table 2: Mean ranks for different values of δ and T.

p \ K	0	1	5	300
1.0	4.78	3.44	6.78	11.78
2.0	5.00	3.67	7.22	12.33
10.0	9.22	5.78	10.11	13.44
∞	10.00	7.33	11.11	14.00

(a) LZ09 test suite

p \ K	0	1	5	300
1.0	7.00	2.71	7.71	15.14
2.0	6.43	2.14	8.29	14.14
10.0	7.43	4.00	9.00	14.29
∞	8.43	5.71	9.14	14.43

(b) LGZ test suite

p \ K	0	1	5	300
1.0	5.75	3.13	7.19	13.25
2.0	5.63	3.00	7.69	13.13
10.0	8.44	5.00	9.63	13.81
∞	9.31	6.63	10.25	14.19

(c) LZ09 and LGZ test suites

Table 3: Mean ranks for different values of p and K.

These are the major control parameters that determine the performance of the algorithm. To investigate the sensitivity of MOEA/VAN to these parameters, the following experiments are performed.

First, the performance of MOEA/VAN is studied for $\delta \in \{0.7, 0.8, 0.9, 1.0\}$ and $T \in \{10, 20, 30, 40\}$. Table 2 shows the results with respect to IGD. It can be seen that MOEA/VAN is not very sensitive to these parameters, with $T = 20$ being the best choice. Concerning δ, results indicate that MOEA/VAN must focus more on exploration for LZ09 and exploitation for LGZ.

Further, the performance of MOEA/VAN is studied for $p \in \{1, 2, 10, \infty\}$ and $K \in \{0, 1, 5, 300\}$. The obtained results are presented in Table 3. These results also indicate that MOEA/VAN is not very sensitive to the choice of p and K, with $K = 1$ being the best setting for the LZ09 and LGZ suites along with $p = 1$ and $p = 2$ that are notably better than other values. Based on the obtained results, in the following experiments, MOEA/VAN is used with $\delta = 0.9$, $T = 20$, $p = 2$ and $K = 1$.

3.1.3 Comparison Study

The main focus of this study is to evaluate the competitiveness of the selection scheme used in MOEA/VAN when dealing with problems that pose significant challenge for many MOEAs to obtain a well converged and distributed approximations. Table 4 shows the results obtained on the LZ09 and LGZ problems. The results indicate that MOEA/D dominates the other algorithms on the LZ09 problems. It should be noted that MOEA/VAN also provides a highly competitive performance on these instances. MOEA/VAN always performs better than GDE3 and IBEA. Also, it is statistically better than the other three algorithms on F6. This can be further confirmed when looking at Figure 1, which shows approximation sets with the best IGD values obtained by MOEA/VAN. From the plots, it is clear that MOEA/VAN is able to obtain adequate approximations for all these problems. Concerning the LGZ problems, MOEA/VAN clearly outperforms all the other algorithms, being statistically better with respect to IGD on all the instances.

To explain the much better performance of MOEA/VAN on the LGZ suite, 10^4 points are randomly generated in the decision space using the Latin hypercube sampling. Figure 2 illustrates their mapping into the objective space for F1. The plot suggests a significant bias in the fitness landscape. A large number of points are located close to the corner point of the Pareto front. Whereas points that occupy intermediate regions of the objective space are far away from the Pareto front and are dominated by those points in

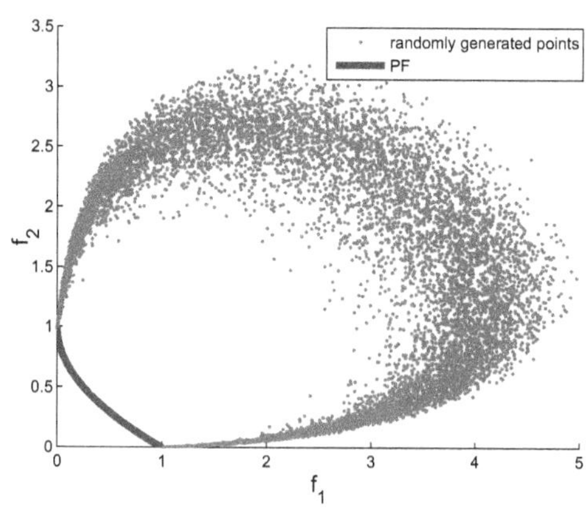

Figure 2: Image of 10^4 evenly distributed points in the decision space for LGZ1.

	MOEA/VAN	MOEA/D	GDE3	IBEA
F1	2.15e-03 (9.1e-05)^{III,IV}	1.31e-03 (7.7e-06)^{I,III,IV}	2.19e-03 (1.0e-04)^{IV}	6.77e-03 (7.4e-04)
F2	4.40e-03 (9.5e-04)^{III,IV}	2.75e-03 (2.8e-04)^{I,III,IV}	4.23e-02 (5.2e-03)^{IV}	1.12e-01 (1.5e-02)
F3	9.20e-03 (1.1e-02)^{III,IV}	2.69e-03 (4.2e-03)^{I,III,IV}	3.66e-02 (2.7e-03)^{IV}	5.48e-02 (2.9e-02)
F4	1.00e-02 (5.6e-03)^{III,IV}	6.46e-03 (9.9e-03)^{I,III,IV}	3.62e-02 (3.4e-03)^{IV}	7.14e-02 (4.3e-02)
F5	1.56e-02 (6.4e-03)^{III,IV}	1.22e-02 (5.4e-03)^{I,III,IV}	3.53e-02 (4.4e-03)^{IV}	3.96e-02 (1.5e-02)
F6	3.11e-02 (5.3e-04)^{II,III,IV}	4.69e-02 (8.9e-03)^{III,IV}	1.14e-01 (2.3e-02)^{IV}	5.33e-01 (4.6e-02)
F7	1.99e-03 (1.1e-04)^{III,IV}	1.34e-03 (2.1e-05)^{I,III,IV}	3.94e-01 (0.0e+00)	1.98e-01 (9.1e-02)^{III}
F8	3.78e-03 (5.8e-03)^{III,IV}	1.71e-03 (1.8e-03)^{I,III,IV}	3.94e-01 (0.0e+00)	2.07e-01 (4.5e-02)^{III}
F9	4.42e-03 (2.1e-03)^{III,IV}	3.85e-03 (2.1e-03)^{I,III,IV}	4.50e-02 (7.8e-03)^{IV}	1.20e-01 (6.7e-02)

(a) LZ09 test suite

	MOEA/VAN	MOEA/D	GDE3	IBEA
F1	1.62e-02 (3.6e-03)^{II,III,IV}	3.52e-01 (1.4e-02)^{III,IV}	3.60e-01 (1.1e-02)	3.58e-01 (5.7e-03)
F2	3.55e-03 (1.3e-02)^{II,III,IV}	2.08e-01 (6.3e-02)^{III,IV}	3.55e-01 (0.0e+00)^{IV}	3.55e-01 (5.6e-17)
F3	5.68e-03 (1.9e-02)^{II,III,IV}	4.33e-01 (2.2e-02)^{III}	5.02e-01 (7.1e-02)	4.55e-01 (6.6e-02)^{III}
F4	1.38e-02 (1.1e-02)^{II,III,IV}	2.25e-01 (7.8e-03)	2.18e-01 (3.7e-02)^{II}	2.22e-01 (7.4e-03)^{II}
F5	1.54e-02 (2.0e-03)^{II,III,IV}	3.18e-01 (7.6e-03)	3.03e-01 (2.6e-02)^{II}	2.45e-01 (2.6e-02)^{II,III}
F6	5.79e-02 (2.6e-03)^{II,III,IV}	3.19e-01 (8.5e-08)	3.19e-01 (2.6e-02)^{II,IV}	3.19e-01 (7.1e-06)^{II}
F7	1.20e-01 (4.7e-03)^{II,III,IV}	4.01e-01 (2.0e-02)^{IV}	4.01e-01 (3.2e-06)^{IV}	4.04e-01 (1.0e-03)

(b) LGZ test suite

Table 4: Median and interquartile range of the IGD indicator. The superscripts I, II, III and IV indicate whether the respective algorithm performs statistically better than MOEA/VAN, MOEA/D, GDE3 and IBEA, respectively.

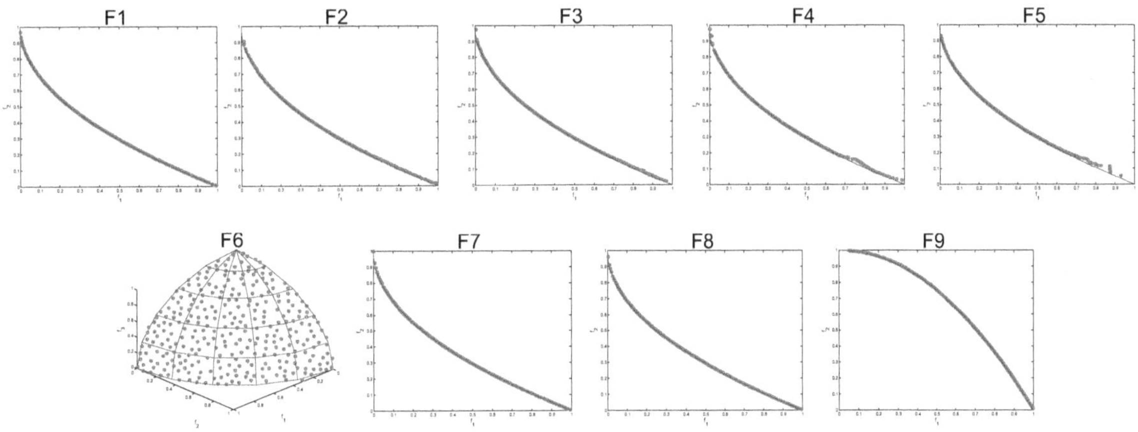

Figure 1: Approximation sets for the LZ09 test suite obtained by MOEA/VAN.

the extreme regions of the Pareto front. From the earliest generations, individuals located in the corner regions will be highly favored by the majority of selection schemes. The high selection pressure will filter out individuals in the other regions. The number of population members located close to the corner points of the Pareto front will grow, resulting in the severe loss of diversity and the stagnation of the population. Such circumstances require selection to tread the convergence and diversity equally.

Figure 3 presents the best approximations in terms of IGD obtained by all the algorithms for the LGZ problems. As expected, due to a poor ability to keep diversity in the above outlined environmental conditions, MOEA/D, IBEA and GDE3 located only those solutions that are close to the boundaries of the Pareto front. Whereas the remaining optimal regions are left unexplored, for the majority of cases.

On the other hand, MOEA/VAN is able to produce adequate approximations for all the instances. This is due to the proposed selection scheme that attempts to maximize angles between individuals, thereby forcing the uniform distribution of the population over the objective space. To replace some population member, a better converged individual must appear in the same region of the objective space. This guarantees that diverse individuals are not lost even though they appear unpromising comparing with other individuals, as exploitation of their diversity plays a crucial role for the population to evolve. Another nice feature of the MOEA/VAN selection scheme is that it is completely adaptive, being solely defined by the interplay between population members and the existing environment. Though it worth mentioning that the uniform distribution of angles does not guarantee the uniform distribution of approximation set, which can be largely influenced by the Pareto front geometry.

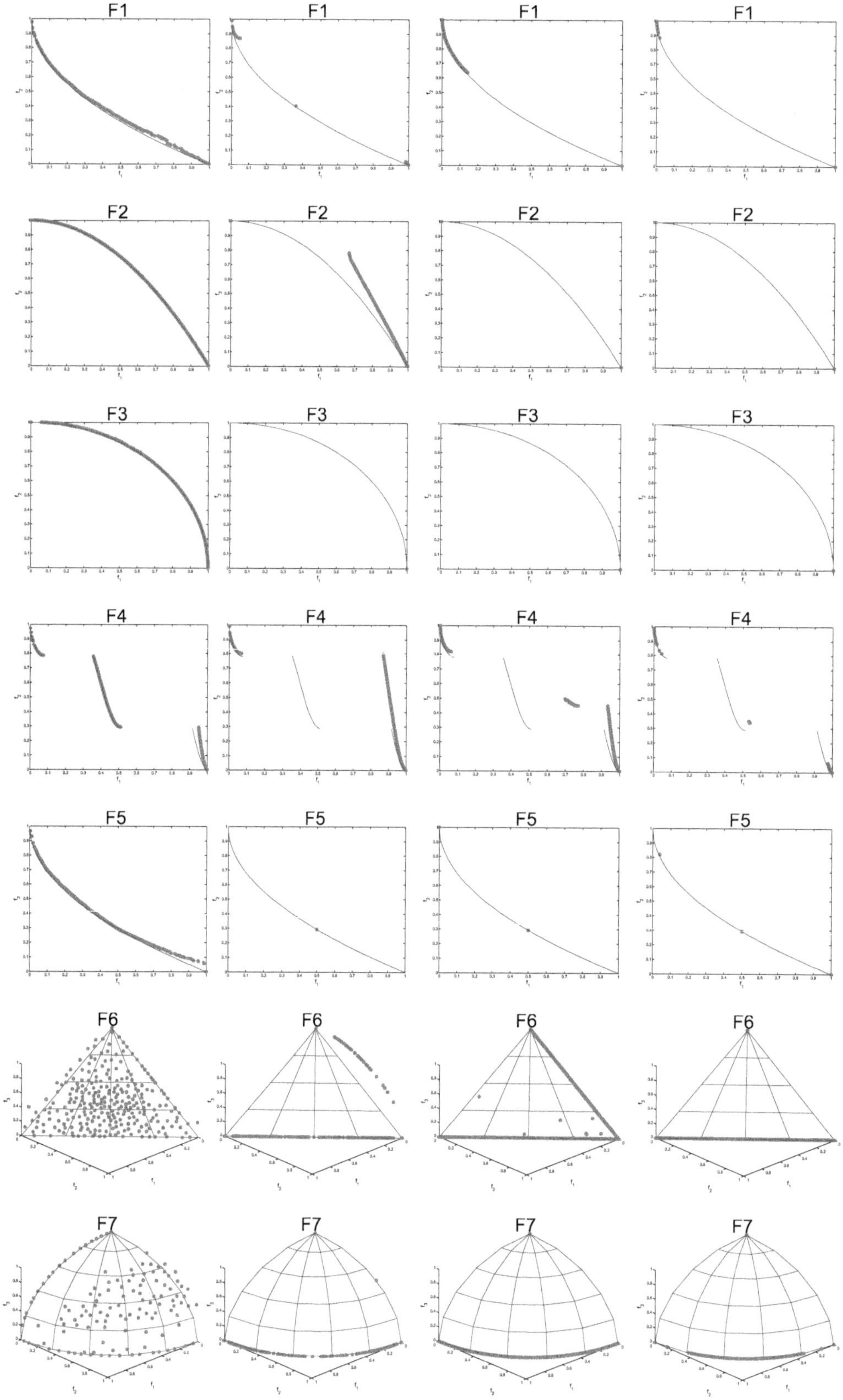

Figure 3: Approximation sets for the LGZ test suite obtained by MOEA/VAN, MOEA/D, GDE3 and IBEA, left to right.

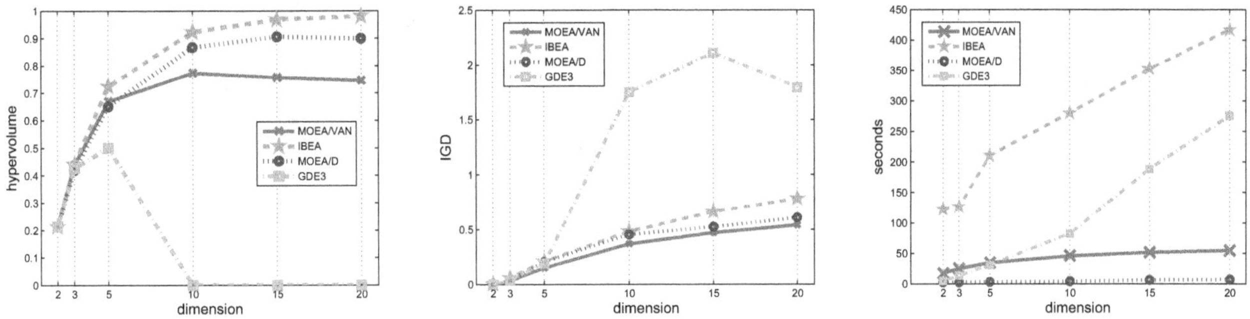

(a) HV (the higher the better) (b) IGD (the lower the better) (c) run time

Figure 4: Results for many-objective optimization.

3.2 Many-Objective Optimization

The issue of scalability of MOEAs has drawn considerable attention in recent years because many state-of-the-art algorithms face significant difficulties in dealing with many-objective problems, whereas those are widespread in practice. In the following, the performance of MOEA/VAN is studied in high dimensional objective spaces, adopting the DTLZ2 problem [4] for this purpose.

3.2.1 Experimental Setup

For the performance comparison, all algorithms are run on the DTLZ2 problem with the fixed number of decision variables, $n = 30$, ranging from 2 to 20 objectives. The population size is as in the previous experiments. The stopping criterion for state-of-the-art MOEAs is 500 generations, with MOEA/VAN run for equivalent number of function evaluations.

The outcomes are assessed using the IGD and hypervolume (HV) indicators. The hypervolume [22] can be defined as the Lebesgue measure, Λ, of the union of hypercuboids in the objective space:

$$I_H = \Lambda\left(\bigcup_{\boldsymbol{a}\in A}\{f_1(\boldsymbol{a}'),\ldots,f_m(\boldsymbol{a}') : \boldsymbol{a} \prec \boldsymbol{a}' \prec \boldsymbol{r}\}\right) \quad (13)$$

where $A = \{\boldsymbol{a}_1, \ldots, \boldsymbol{a}_{|A|}\}$ denotes a set of nondominated solutions and $\boldsymbol{r}$ is a reference point. The higher I_H, the better performance. For calculating the HV indicator, the nadir point is used as a reference point. Solutions that do not dominate the nadir point are discarded. If there is no solution dominating the nadir point, then the hypervolume of A is equal to zero. Solutions used to calculate the hypervolume are normalized using the ideal and nadir points [14].

3.2.2 Comparison Study

Figure 4 summarizes the results obtained for many-objective optimization. The graphical representation of the median values of the HV and IGD indicators are shown in Figures 4a and 4b, respectively. These plots reveal that the performance of MOEA/VAN is comparable with those produced by the established many-objective optimizers (IBEA and MOEA/D). Whereas the performance of GDE3 severely deteriorates when the number of objectives is increased. MOEA/VAN tends to maintain a uniform distribution of individuals in the population, this feature allows to obtain the best performance in terms of IGD up to 20 objectives (Figure 4b). With respect to the hypervolume, which is a biased indicator, IBEA achieves the best results followed by MOEA/D with the decomposition method based on the Chebyshev metric (Figure 4a). Nonetheless, it is clear that the selection in MOEA/VAN can guide the search in high dimensional objective spaces. Figure 4c presents the mean computational time consumed by the algorithms. This figure shows that MOEA/VAN consumes less time than IBEA and more time than MOEA/D. In turn, GDE3 works faster when the number of objectives is small and slower for high dimensional spaces. It can be seen that the computational time does not grow sharply with the number of objectives, as it is for IBEA and GDE3. The main computational burden in the selection of MOEA/VAN is incurred when a reference point has been updated and the update of angles between individuals is required, though it can be negligible in real-world applications. Thus, the obtained results appear encouraging for the use of MOEA/VAN in many-objective optimization.

4. CONCLUSIONS

Balancing the convergence and diversity is an important issue that must be taken into consideration when designing evolutionary algorithms for solving multiobjective optimization problems. This paper proposed a new selection scheme for evolutionary multiobjective optimization. To provide convergence, individuals in the population seek to minimize their distances to a reference point defined by the lowest objective values found during the search. After generating an offspring, closest neighbors in the population are compared to remove the inferior one with respect to convergence. As similarity measure that defines the concept of neighborhood, the angle between objective vectors is used.

MOEA/VAN is validated by performing the experimental study using test suites with different characteristics and state-of-the-art algorithms. The obtained results indicate that MOEA/VAN is not very sensitive to the choice of major control parameters, with the default settings being suggested. The results of the comparison study reveal a highly competitive performance of MOEA/VAN. Clear advantages of the proposed selection are observed on problems where the ability to keep diversity plays a crucial role. Also, encouraging results are obtained for problems with high dimensional objective spaces. Further attractive feature of the proposed selection is that it is completely adaptive and the need for user's interaction is minimized.

As future work, it is intended to address limitations of the proposed approach and further exploit its strengths. The selection in MOEA/VAN can face difficulties in handling problems with disconnected or degenerated Pareto fronts. One possible way to overcome this is to maintain an archive with nondominated solutions found during the search. Also, it would be interesting to investigate the MOEA/VAN framework combined with other offspring generating strategies and to design a more elaborate mating selection procedure. Further, MOEA/VAN can be extended from a steady-state to generation variant, as well as the adaptation of control parameters is another promising research direction.

5. ACKNOWLEDGMENTS

This work has been supported by FCT - Fundação para a Ciência e Tecnologia in the scope of the project: PEst-OE/EEI/UI0319/2014.

6. REFERENCES

[1] J. Bader and E. Zitzler. HypE: An algorithm for fast hypervolume-based many-objective optimization. *Evolutionary Computation*, 19(1):45–76, 2011.

[2] P. A. N. Bosman and D. Thierens. The balance between proximity and diversity in multiobjective evolutionary algorithms. *IEEE Transactions on Evolutionary Computation*, 7(2):174–188, 2003.

[3] K. Deb, A. Pratap, S. Agarwal, and T. Meyarivan. A fast and elitist multiobjective genetic algorithm: NSGA-II. *IEEE Transactions on Evolutionary Computation*, 6(2):182–197, 2002.

[4] K. Deb, L. Thiele, M. Laumanns, and E. Zitzler. Scalable test problems for evolutionary multi-objective optimization. Technical Report 112, Swiss Federal Institute of Technology, Zurich, Switzerland, 2001.

[5] R. Denysiuk, L. Costa, and I. Espírito Santo. Many-objective optimization using differential evolution with variable-wise mutation restriction. In *Proceedings of the Conference on Genetic and Evolutionary Computation*, GECCO'13, pages 591–598, 2013.

[6] R. Denysiuk, L. Costa, and I. Espírito Santo. Clustering-based selection for evolutionary many-objective optimization. In *Parallel Problem Solving from Nature*, PPSN'14, pages 538–547, 2014.

[7] J. J. Durillo and A. J. Nebro. jMetal: A Java framework for multi-objective optimization. *Advances in Engineering Software*, 42(10):760–771, 2011.

[8] S. García, D. Molina, M. Lozano, and F. Herrera. A study on the use of non-parametric tests for analyzing the evolutionary algorithms' behaviour: A case study on the CEC'2005 special session on real parameter optimization. *Journal of Heuristics*, 15(6):617–644, 2009.

[9] E. J. Hughes. Evolutionary many-objective optimisation: Many once or one many? In *Proceedings of the IEEE Congress on Evolutionary Computation*, CEC'05, pages 222–227, 2005.

[10] S. Kukkonen and J. Lampinen. GDE3: the third evolution step of generalized differential evolution. In *Proceedings of the IEEE Congress on Evolutionary Computation*, CEC'05, pages 443–450, 2005.

[11] H. Li and Q. Zhang. Multiobjective optimization problems with complicated Pareto sets, MOEA/D and NSGA-II. *IEEE Transactions on Evolutionary Computation*, 13(2):284–302, 2009.

[12] M. Li, S. Yang, and X. Liu. Shift-based density estimation for Pareto-based algorithms in many-objective optimization. *IEEE Transactions on Evolutionary Computation*, 18(3):348–365, 2014.

[13] H.-L. Liu, F. Gu, and Q. Zhang. Decomposition of a multiobjective optimization problem into a number of simple multiobjective subproblems. *IEEE Transactions on Evolutionary Computation*, 18(3):450 – 455, 2014.

[14] K. Miettinen. *Nonlinear multiobjective optimization*, volume 12 of *International Series in Operations Research and Management Science.* Kluwer Academic Publishers, 1999.

[15] R. C. Purshouse and P. J. Fleming. Evolutionary many-objective optimisation: An exploratory analysis. In *Proceedings of the IEEE Congress on Evolutionary Computation*, CEC'03, pages 2066–2073, 2003.

[16] H. Sato, H. E. Aguirre, and K. Tanaka. Controlling dominance area of solutions and its impact on the performance of MOEAs. In *Proceedings of the Conference on Evolutionary Multi-Criterion Optimization*, EMO'07, pages 5–20, 2007.

[17] T. Wagner, N. Beume, and B. Naujoks. Pareto-, aggregation-, and indicator-based methods in many-objective optimization. In *Proceedings of the Conference on Evolutionary Multi-Criterion Optimization*, EMO'07, pages 742–756, 2007.

[18] L. While, P. Hingston, L. Barone, and S. Huband. A faster algorithm for calculating hypervolume. *IEEE Transactions on Evolutionary Computation*, 10(1):29–38, 2006.

[19] S. Yang, M. Li, X. Liu, and J. Zheng. A grid-based evolutionary algorithm for many-objective optimization. *IEEE Transactions on Evolutionary Computation*, 17(5):721–736, 2013.

[20] E. Zitzler and S. Künzli. Indicator-based selection in multiobjective search. In *Proceedings of the Conference on Parallel Problem Solving from Nature*, PPSN'04, pages 832–842, 2004.

[21] E. Zitzler, M. Laumanns, and L. Thiele. SPEA2: Improving the strength pareto evolutionary algorithm. Technical Report 103, Computer Engineering and Networks Laboratory (TIK), ETH Zurich, Zurich, Switzerland, 2001.

[22] E. Zitzler and L. Thiele. Multiobjective optimization using evolutionary algorithms - A comparative case study. In *Proceedings of the Conference on Parallel Problem Solving From Nature*, PPSN'98, pages 292–304, 1998.

[23] E. Zitzler, L. Thiele, M. Laumanns, C. M. Fonseca, and V. G. da Fonseca. Performance assessment of multiobjective optimizers: An analysis and review. *IEEE Transactions on Evolutionary Computation*, 7(2), 2003.

Greedy Hypervolume Subset Selection in the Three-Objective Case

Andreia P. Guerreiro
apg@dei.uc.pt

Carlos M. Fonseca
cmfonsec@dei.uc.pt

Luís Paquete
paquete@dei.uc.pt

CISUC, Department of Informatics Engineering
University of Coimbra
Pólo II, P-3030 290 Coimbra, Portugal

ABSTRACT

Given a non-dominated point set $X \subset \mathbb{R}^d$ of size n and a suitable reference point $r \in \mathbb{R}^d$, the Hypervolume Subset Selection Problem (HSSP) consists of finding a subset of size $k \leq n$ that maximizes the hypervolume indicator. It arises in connection with multiobjective selection and archiving strategies, as well as Pareto-front approximation post-processing for visualization and/or interaction with a decision maker. Efficient algorithms to solve the HSSP are available only for the 2-dimensional case, achieving a time complexity of $O(n(k + \log n))$. In contrast, the best upper bound available for $d > 2$ is $O(n^{\frac{d}{2}} \log n + n^{n-k})$. Since the hypervolume indicator is a monotone submodular function, the HSSP can be approximated to a factor of $(1 - 1/e)$ using a greedy strategy. Such a greedy algorithm for the 3-dimensional HSSP is proposed in this paper. The time complexity of the algorithm is shown to be $O(n^2)$, which considerably improves upon recent complexity results for this approximation problem.

Categories and Subject Descriptors

F.2.2 [**Analysis of Algorithms and Problem Complexity**]: Nonnumerical Algorithms and Problems—*Geometrical problems and computations*

Keywords

Hypervolume Indicator; Subset Selection; Submodular Function; Greedy Algorithms

1. INTRODUCTION

Multiobjective optimization consists of finding solutions that minimize, without loss of generality, a vector of $d > 1$ objective functions, $f(x) = (f_1(x), ..., f_d(x))$. Each solution x is an element of a decision space, and is mapped onto a point in a d-dimensional objective space. Due to conflicting objectives, there is usually no ideal solution to a multiobjective optimization problem, but multiple Pareto-optimal solutions. In this paper, only the points in objective space are considered.

Let u and v be two points in objective space. Point u is said to weakly dominate point v, denoted $u \leq v$, if $u_i \leq v_i$ for all $i = 1, ..., d$, and to dominate v if, in addition, $u \neq v$. If neither $u \leq v$ nor $v \leq u$, then u and v are said to be incomparable, or mutually non-dominated. A point is said to be Pareto-optimal if no other point dominates it, and the set of all Pareto-optimal points is called the Pareto-Front.

Quality indicators map a set of n (mutually non-dominated) points onto a real value, and are used to evaluate the quality of discrete Pareto-front approximations. Due to its seemingly unique properties [1], the hypervolume indicator [17, 12] is used extensively, both in performance studies and in multiobjective selection and archiving strategies. Unfortunately, the hypervolume indicator becomes computationally demanding as the number of objective dimensions grows. Its time complexity is $\Theta(n \log n)$ in up to 3 dimensions [3], but, for general d, the best upper bound known to date is $O(n^{d/3}\text{polylog}\, n)$ [7]. So far, the fastest algorithms in practice [10, 16] are asymptotically slower than this.

The problem of selecting k out of n points that maximize the hypervolume indicator commonly arises in multiobjective selection and archiving. This is known as the Hypervolume Subset Selection Problem (HSSP) [2], and algorithms to solve it exactly are available only for 2 dimensions, with $O(n(k + \log n))$-time complexity [6, 13]. For $d > 2$, the equivalent problem of determining a subset of $n - k$ points that contribute the least hypervolume to the original set can be solved in $O(n^{\frac{d}{2}} \log n + n^{n-k})$ [5].

Since the hypervolume indicator is a monotone submodular function [15], and the HSSP consists of maximising it subject to a cardinality constraint, an $(1 - 1/e)$-approximation to the hypervolume of an optimal subset may be obtained with an (incremental) greedy strategy [14]. Based on this result, Friedrich and Neumann [9] show that a particular EMO algorithm (GSEMO) obtains such an approximation in an expected $O(n^2(k + \log n))$ number of steps, for any number of dimensions. However, their analysis does not take into account the time required to compute the hypervolume of the subsets evaluated in the process.

Greedy heuristics for the HSSP were also considered by Bradstreet *et al.* [4],who studied both incremental strategies, where k points are selected one at a time so as to maximize the increase in hypervolume at each step, and decremental strategies, where $n - k$ points are removed one at a time

GECCO '15, July 11 - 15, 2015, Madrid, Spain

DOI: http://dx.doi.org/10.1145/2739480.2754812

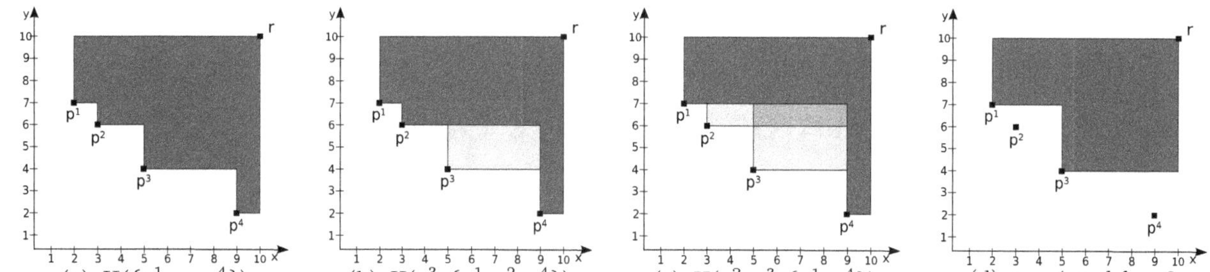

(a) $H(\{p^1, ..., p^4\})$ (b) $H(p^3, \{p^1, p^2, p^4\})$ (c) $H(p^2, p^3, \{p^1, p^4\})$ (d) $n = 4$ and $k = 2$

Figure 1: Two-dimensional examples: (a) hypervolume indicator, (b) hypervolume contribution, (c) joint hypervolume contribution, and (d) hypervolume subset selection problem – optimal subset.

from the original set, so as to minimize the loss of hypervolume in each step. The decremental case was also considered by Bader and Zitzler [2], and was analyzed by Bringmann and Friedrich [5], who showed that it may be very far from optimal for $n - k > 1$.

In this paper, an incremental greedy algorithm for the HSSP in 3 dimensions is proposed, providing a $(1 - 1/e)$-approximation to the optimal subset in $O(n^2)$-time. The next section introduces relevant definitions, and reviews an existing approach to the computation of 3-dimensional hypervolume contributions in linear time. In Section 3, the general strategy is outlined first, and the simpler 2-dimensional case is considered before the main algorithm proposed is described in detail. Experimental results are presented in Section 4, and are followed by some concluding remarks.

2. PRELIMINARIES

The following definitions are useful in stating the problem of interest and explaining the algorithm proposed. Illustrative examples are given in Figures 1(a)–(d).

Definition 1. **(Hypervolume Indicator)** Given a point set $\mathrm{S} \subset \mathbb{R}^d$ and a reference point $r \in \mathbb{R}^d$, the hypervolume indicator of S is the measure of the region weakly dominated by S and bounded above by r, i.e.

$$H(\mathrm{S}) = \lambda(\{q \in \mathbb{R}^d \mid \exists p \in \mathrm{S} : p \leq q \wedge q \leq r\})$$

where λ denotes the Lebesgue measure.

A fixed reference point is assumed throughout the paper.

Definition 2. **(Hypervolume Contribution)** Given a point $p \in \mathbb{R}^d$, a point set $\mathrm{S} \subset \mathbb{R}^d$, and a reference point $r \in \mathbb{R}^d$, the (hypervolume) contribution of p to S is:

$$H(p, \mathrm{S}) = H(\mathrm{S} \cup \{p\}) - H(\mathrm{S})$$

In some cases, such as when determining the decrease in the contribution of a given point $p \in \mathbb{R}^d$ to a set $\mathrm{S} \subset \mathbb{R}^d$ due to the addition of another point $q \in \mathbb{R}^d$ to S, it is also useful to consider the contribution dominated simultaneously and exclusively by two points:

Definition 3. **(Joint Hypervolume Contribution)** The joint hypervolume contribution of $p, q \in \mathbb{R}^d$ to $\mathrm{S} \subset \mathbb{R}^d$ is:

$$H(p, q, \mathrm{S}) = H(\mathrm{S} \cup \{p \vee q\}) - H(\mathrm{S})$$

where $\vee$ denotes the *join*, or component-wise maximum.

Moreover, a point $q \in \mathrm{S}$ is said to delimit the contribution of a point $p \in \mathbb{R}^d$ to a point set $\mathrm{S} \subset \mathbb{R}^d$, iff $H(p, q, \mathrm{S}\backslash\{q\}) > 0$. For example, in Figure 1(b), the contribution of p^3 is delimited only by p^2 and p^4. Finally, the HSSP problem is formally defined as [2]:

Problem 1. **(Hypervolume Subset Selection Problem (HSSP))** Given a point set $\mathrm{S} \subset \mathbb{R}^d$ and an integer $k \in \{0, 1, \ldots, |\mathrm{S}|\}$, find a subset $\mathrm{A} \subset \mathrm{S}$ such that:

$$H(\mathrm{A}) = \max_{\substack{\mathrm{B} \subset \mathrm{S} \\ |\mathrm{B}|=k}} H(\mathrm{B})$$

2.1 Computing hypervolume contributions

The efficient computation of hypervolume contributions in 3 dimensions is an important aspect of the greedy algorithm for the HSSP developed in this work. In HV4D [10], an algorithm for hypervolume computation in 4 dimensions, the 3-dimensional contribution of each new point visited in the main loop is computed in linear time. This is achieved using a dimension-sweep approach based on another algorithm by Emmerich and Fonseca [8] for the problem of computing all contributions in 3 dimensions. A simplified version of that approach, which does not explicitly use a box-division of the contribution, is described next using Figure 2 for illustration. It will be referred to as IHV3D.

Given a point $p \in \mathbb{R}^3$ and a set $\mathrm{S} \subset \mathbb{R}^3$ of n points, IHV3D computes the contribution $H(p, \mathrm{S})$ by sweeping the points $q \in \mathrm{S}$ such that $q_z > p_z$ in ascending order of the z coordinate, and partitioning the 3-dimensional contribution in horizontal slices. The contribution of p is the sum of the volumes of all slices. The volume of a slice is the area of the base of that slice multiplied by its height. The height of a slice is the absolute difference between the two consecutive points defining that slice. The base is delimited by the projection onto the (x, y)-plane of the first point defining that slice and all points below it in z. Thus, S is split into two sets, $\mathrm{S}^1 = \{q \in \mathrm{S} | q_z \leq p_z\}$ and $\mathrm{S}^2 = \{q \in \mathrm{S} | q_z > p_z\}$. In addition, a set of points whose projections on the (x, y)-plane delimit the area exclusively dominated by p in each iteration, S', is maintained. This set of mutually non-dominated points is initialized with such points in S^1 to represent the base of the first slice.

Both the splitting of S and the initialization of S' are performed in linear time. In the example of Figure 2(a), $\mathrm{S}^1 = \{s^1, ..., s^7\}$, $\mathrm{S}^2 = \{s^8, ...s^{12}\}$ and $\mathrm{S}' = \{s^2, ..., s^7\}$. Note that at most two points in S' are not dominated by p on the (x, y)-plane, one above and to the left, and another below and to the right (s^2 and s^9 in the example).

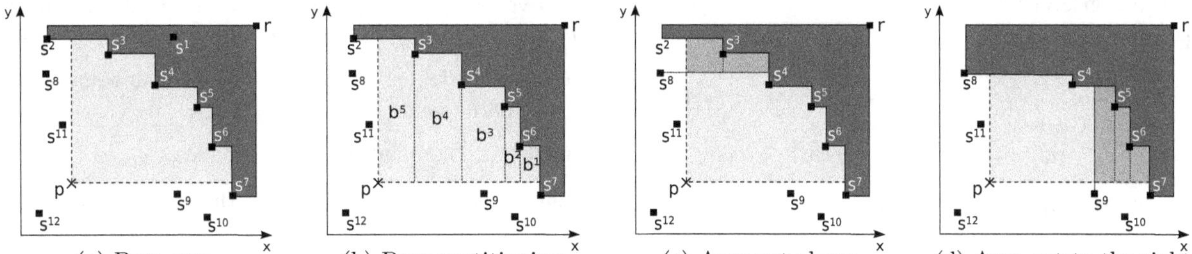

(a) Base area (b) Base partitioning (c) Area cut above (d) Area cut to the right

Figure 2: Example of the computation of the contribution $H(p, \mathrm{S})$ where $\mathrm{S} = \{s^1, ..., s^{12}\}$. It is assumed that $s^1_z < ... < s^7_z < p_z < s^8_z < ... < s^{12}_z$.

Algorithm 1 gHSS(X, k, r)

Require: $\mathrm{X} \subset \mathbb{R}^d$, $k \in \mathbb{N}^+$, $r \in \mathbb{R}^d$

```
1: S ← {}
2: for all q ∈ X do
3:    q.c ← H(q, S)
4: for i = 1..k do
5:    p ← argmax_{q∈X}{q.c}
6:    X ← X\{p}
7:    for all q ∈ X do
8:       q.c ← q.c − H(p, q, S)
9:    S ← S ∪ {p}
10: return S
```

The area of the base of the first slice is computed by adding up the areas of the non-overlapping rectangles into which the base is partitioned (see Figure 2(b)) as the points in S′ are visited in ascending order of y. Then, the points in S^2 are visited in ascending order of z. For each new point, the volume of the current slice is computed and the area of its base is updated to obtain the base area of the next slice. In the example, the first point visited is s^8. Therefore, the area of the base of the bottom slice is multiplied by $s^8_z - p_z$. Then, the base area is updated by subtracting the area of the region that is now dominated also by s^8 (see Figure 2(c)). This area is computed by visiting the points in S′ that are dominated by s^8 on the (x, y)-plane. In the example, these are points s^2 and s^3, which are subsequently replaced in S′ by s^8. Hence, S′ becomes $\mathrm{S}' = \{s^8, s^4, ..., s^7\}$. The procedure for s^9 is similar (see Figure 2(d)). Visited points that do not dominate part of the region dominated by p are skipped (e.g. s^{10}).

The algorithm continues until a point in S^2 that dominates p on the (x, y)-plane is found, s^{12} in the example. The volume of the last slice is computed by multiplying the current base area by $(s^{12}_z - s^{11}_z)$. In IHV3D, all sets are implemented as sorted lists, and sentinels are used to ensure that limiting points such as s^2, s^7 and s^{12} always exist. IHV3D has an amortized $O(n)$ time complexity because each point in S is visited once when it is added to S′ and a second time when it is removed from S′, and all operations on S′ are performed in constant time.

3. GREEDY HSS ALGORITHM

In this section, a general greedy algorithm [4] for the Hypervolume Subset Selection Problem is explained. Subsequently, specialized algorithms for 2 and 3 dimensions are proposed.

3.1 General Case

Given a non-dominated point set $\mathrm{X} \subset \mathbb{R}^d$, where $|\mathrm{X}| = n$, the greedy algorithm for Problem 1 chooses $k \leq n$ points from X and stores them in S, one at a time, always selecting the point that contributes the most hypervolume to the set of points already chosen. For that reason, gHSS (Algorithm 1) first computes the contribution of each point $q \in \mathrm{X}$ to the initially empty set S (line 3) and stores it in $q.c$. Afterwards, the algorithm picks the point p in X with maximal contribution (line 5). Then, it updates the contribution of the remaining points in X to $\mathrm{S} \cup \{p\}$ (line 8), i.e., it removes the portion of the contribution of each $q \in \mathrm{X}$ that is dominated by p. Finally, it moves p from X to S (lines 6 and 9). Lines 5 to 9 are repeated until S contains k points.

It is clear from Definition 3 that, in the absence of an efficient algorithm to compute the Joint Hypervolume Contribution (line 8), an algorithm for the Hypervolume Indicator can be used to determine this quantity. Furthermore, line 8 could simply recompute the whole contribution $H(q, \mathrm{S} \cup \{p\})$. Updating the contributions of all points p in a set X to the corresponding sets $\mathrm{X} \backslash \{p\}$ under single-point changes to X can already be performed efficiently in 2 dimensions [11]. The following sections show how $H(p, q, \mathrm{S})$ can be efficiently computed in the 2- and 3-dimensional cases.

3.2 2-dimensional Case

The algorithm proposed in this section (gHSS2D) deals with the particular case of gHSS in 2 dimensions. In this case, a simple procedure can be used to update the contributions of the unchosen points in line 8 of Algorithm 1. Assume that points in $\mathrm{X} \cup \mathrm{S}$ are always kept sorted in ascending order of the y-coordinate (and in descending order of the x-coordinate). Therefore, every point $q \in \mathrm{X} \cup \mathrm{S}$ needs to keep the information of the next and of the previous point in $\mathrm{X} \cup \mathrm{S}$ which is determined once by sorting X in a pre-processing step.

Because a contribution is represented by a rectangle, every $q \in \mathrm{X}$ stores its contribution ($q.c$) and also the upper point currently bounding it. All upper points are initially set to the reference point. Let t^1 and t^2 be the closest points in S to the left and to the right of p, respectively. Then, for each point p chosen, the points to its left are visited, in ascending order of coordinate y, until t^1 is reached. Similarly, the points to its right are visited until t^2 is reached. Every point $q \in \mathrm{X}$ between t^1 and p has the upper point previously set

Algorithm 2 gHSS3D(X, k, r)

Require: $\mathrm{X} \subset \mathbb{R}^d$, $k \in \mathbb{N}^+$, $r \in \mathbb{R}^d$
1: X is sorted in *ascending* order of all dimensions
2: $\mathrm{S} \leftarrow \{(r_x, -\infty, -\infty), (-\infty, r_y, -\infty), (-\infty, -\infty, r_z)\}$
3: **for all** $q \in \mathrm{X}$ **do**
4: $\quad q.c \leftarrow (r_x - p_x) \times (r_y - p_y) \times (r_z - p_z)$
5: **for** $i = 1..k$ **do**
6: $\quad$ initialize $q.v$ to 0 **for all** $q \in \mathrm{X}$
7: $\quad p \leftarrow \mathsf{argmax}_{q \in \mathrm{X}}\{q.c\}$
8: $\quad \mathrm{X} \leftarrow \mathrm{X} \backslash \{p\}$
9: $\quad \mathrm{X}' \leftarrow \mathrm{X}$
10: $\quad$ **for all** $o \in \{(x,y,z), (z,x,y), (y,z,x)\}$ **do**
11: $\quad\quad (x, y, z) \leftarrow o$// Change coordinate order
12: $\quad\quad \mathrm{X}^1 \leftarrow \{q \in \mathrm{X}' \mid p^* \leq q^* \vee p_z \geq q_z\}$
13: $\quad\quad \mathrm{X}^2 \leftarrow \{q \in \mathrm{X}' \mid p^* \geq q^* \vee p_z \leq q_z\}$
14: $\quad\quad \mathrm{S}^1, \mathrm{S}^2 \leftarrow \mathsf{split}_z(\mathrm{S}, p_z)$
15: $\quad\quad \mathsf{jointContributions1}(p, \mathrm{S}^1, \mathrm{S}^2, \mathrm{X}^1, r)$
16: $\quad\quad \mathsf{jointContributions2}(p, \mathrm{S}^1, \mathrm{S}^2, \mathrm{X}^2, r)$
17: $\quad\quad \mathrm{X}' \leftarrow \mathrm{X}' \backslash (\mathrm{X}^1 \cup \mathrm{X}^2)$
18: $\quad$ **for all** $q \in \mathrm{X}$ **do**
19: $\quad\quad q.c \leftarrow q.c - q.v$
20: $\quad \mathrm{S} \leftarrow \mathrm{S} \cup \{p\}$
21: **return** S

to (t_x^2, t_y^1) and therefore, the quantity $H(p, q, \mathrm{S})$ is $(t_x^2 - p_x) \times (t_y^1 - q_y)$ and their upper point is set to (p_x, t_y). The points $q \in \mathrm{X}$ between p and t^2 have $H(p, q, \mathrm{S}) = (t_x^2 - q_x) \times (t_y^1 - p_y)$ and their upper point is set to (t_x^2, p_y).

The time complexity of gHSS2D is $\Theta(n(k + \log n))$ because the initial sorting costs $\Theta(n \log n)$-time and, for each point p chosen, up to n contributions have to be computed, each in constant time. A worst case example is the set of n points $\{(-i, -2^{n-i+1} + 1) \mid i \in \{1, ..., n\}\}$ with $r = (0, 0)$. Note that gHSS2D and the exact algorithms [6, 13] have similar time complexities. However, the greedy version should be easier to implement and, because it is very simple and uses simple data structures, it is very fast in practice.

3.3 3-dimensional Case

The algorithm that deals with the particular case of gHSS in 3 dimensions (gHSS3D) is presented in this section. This section starts by defining the data structures, some notation and procedures used by the algorithm. Then, the algorithm itself and, in particular, the update of the contribution of points in X computed in line 8 of Algorithm 1, are detailed. This section finishes with a discussion of the time-complexity of gHSS3D.

3.3.1 Data structures and procedures

gHSS3D uses doubly linked lists to maintain the sets of points sorted as well as sentinels to ensure that there is always a point in the limiting conditions. Algorithm 2 keeps both sets X and S sorted in ascending order of all coordinates. Each point $q \in \mathrm{X}$ keeps some information associated such as the area ($q.a$), volume ($q.v$), height ($q.z$) and the contribution ($q.c$). The first three values are temporary values that are used to compute the volume $H(p, q, \mathrm{S})$ which will be subtracted from the contribution of q, $q.c$. The value $q.z$ indicates the value of the third coordinate up to which volume $q.v$ has been updated, and $q.a$ keeps the area dominated at height $q.z$. p^* and S^* will denote the projections of p and S onto the (x, y)-plane, respectively.

Given $\mathrm{X}, \mathrm{S} \subset \mathbb{R}^3$ represented by sorted lists and the points $p, q \in \mathbb{R}^3$ and $h \in \mathbb{R}$, the following procedures are available.

next$_y(p, \mathrm{S})$ The point following p in S with respect to coordinate y, for $p \in \mathrm{S}$.

head$_y(\mathrm{S})$ The point $q \in \mathrm{S}$ with the least q_y.

min$_y(p, \mathrm{S})$ The point $q \in \mathrm{S}$ with the least $q_y > p_y$ such that $q_x \leq p_x$.

addFirst$_y(p, \mathrm{S})$ Add point p to S where p becomes $\mathsf{head}_y(\mathrm{S})$.

minima(S) Return the points that are not dominated in the (x, y)-plane , i.e., $\{q \in \mathrm{S} \mid \nexists t \in \mathrm{S} : t^* \leq q^*, t \neq q\}$.

split$_y(\mathrm{S}, h)$ Given $h \in \mathbb{R}$, split S in two sets, S^1 and S^2 such that $\mathrm{S}^1 = \{q \in \mathrm{S} \mid q_y \leq h\}$ and $\mathrm{S}^2 = \{q \in \mathrm{S} \mid q_y > h\}$ and return S^1 and S^2.

area(p, S) The quantity $H(p^*, \mathrm{S}^*)$.

updateVolume(X, h) Given $h \in \mathbb{R}$, for each point $q \in \mathrm{X}$, update its volume, save it in $q.v$ and update $q.z$, i.e., compute $q.v \leftarrow q.v + q.a \times (h - q_z)$ and set $q.z \leftarrow h$.

initializeBases$(\mathrm{X}, p, \mathrm{S})$ For each point $q \in \mathrm{X}$, compute $H(p^*, q^*, \mathrm{S}^*)$ and save it in $q.a$.

updateAreas$(p, \mathrm{X}, \mathrm{S})$ For each $q \in \mathrm{X}$ compute $q.a \leftarrow q.a - H(p^*, q^*, \mathrm{S}^*)$.

Procedures next, head, min, addFirst and split are also available for coordinates x and z and, apart from split and min, they all run in constant time. All procedures that modify or return a subset of a given sorted set guarantee that the returned sets are also sorted according to the coordinate used for sweeping the points. These procedures may also guarantee that those points are sorted according to other coordinates, if needed. More information about those procedures will be given in the next sections. Note that, if a set of non-dominated points on the (x, y)-plane is sorted in ascending order of one coordinate, then it is also sorted according to the other coordinate, but in descending order.

split_y has a cost of $O(|\mathrm{S}^2|)$ because it is the cost of finding the break point by sweeping points in descending order of coordinate y. The remaining procedures have linear cost w.r.t. the total size of the received sets, i.e., either $O(|\mathrm{X}|)$, $O(|\mathrm{S}|)$ or $O(|\mathrm{S}| + |\mathrm{X}|)$. Both initializeBases and updateAreas will be explained in more detail in Section 3.3.3.

3.3.2 Main loop of gHSS3D

gHSS3D follows the same working principle as gHSS, but instead of updating the contributions of points in X one by one (lines 7 and 8 in Algorithm 1), it divides the (x, y, z)-space into 8 octants with a common vertex at p, and updates the contributions of the points in each pair of opposite octants at the same time (lines 9 to 17 in Algorithm 2).

The two octants corresponding to the region that dominates p and the region dominated by p are ignored because they do not contain any points. The remaining three pairs of octants are all updated in the same way, except that a different coordinate order is considered for each pair. The order is set in such a way that a different dimension is used as the z-coordinate in each case (lines 10-17 of Algorithm 2).

Given a coordinate order $o \in \{(x, y, z), (z, x, y), (y, z, x)\}$, the two octants considered when order o is selected, are those

Algorithm 3 jointContributions2$(p, \mathrm{S}^1, \mathrm{S}^2, \mathrm{X}^2, r)$

1: $\mathrm{S}' \leftarrow \{q \in \mathsf{minima}(\mathrm{S}^1) \mid p^* \leq q^*\} \cup \{\min_x(\mathrm{S}^1), \min_y(\mathrm{S}^1)\}$
2: $p.a \leftarrow \mathsf{area}(p, \mathrm{S}')$
3: $u \leftarrow p$
4: $\mathrm{L} \leftarrow \mathrm{X}^2 \cup \mathrm{S}^2$
5: $q \leftarrow \mathsf{head}_z(\mathrm{L})$
6: **while** $q \in \mathrm{X}^2$ **or** $q^* \nleq p^*$ **do**
7: **if** $q \in \mathrm{S}^2$ **then**
8:   **if** $q_x \leq p_x$ **then**
9:    $\mathrm{S}', \mathrm{T} \leftarrow \mathsf{split}_y(\mathrm{S}', q_y)$
10:    $p.a \leftarrow p.a - \mathsf{area}(p \vee q, \mathrm{T} \cup \{\mathsf{head}_x(\mathrm{S}')\})$
11:    $\mathsf{addFirst}_x(q, \mathrm{S}')$
12:   **else**
13:    $\mathrm{S}', \mathrm{T} \leftarrow \mathsf{split}_x(\mathrm{S}', q_x)$
14:    $p.a \leftarrow p.a - \mathsf{area}(p \vee q, \mathrm{T} \cup \{\mathsf{head}_y(\mathrm{S}')\})$
15:    $\mathsf{addFirst}_y(q, \mathrm{S}')$
16:   $\mathsf{updateVolume}(\{u\}, q_z)$
17:   $u.a \leftarrow p.a$
18: **else**
19:   $\mathsf{updateVolume}(\{u\}, q_z)$
20:   $q.a \leftarrow p.a$
21:   $q.z \leftarrow q_z$
22:   $q.prev \leftarrow u$
23:   $u \leftarrow q$
24: $q \leftarrow \mathsf{next}_z(q, \mathrm{L})$
25: $\mathsf{updateVolume}(\{u\}, q_z)$
26: $vol \leftarrow 0$
27: **while** $u \neq p$ **do**
28: $vol \leftarrow vol + u.v$
29: $u.v \leftarrow vol$
30: $u \leftarrow u.prev$

that contain sets $\mathrm{X}^1 \subseteq \mathrm{X}$ and $\mathrm{X}^2 \subseteq \mathrm{X}$, defined as follows. X^1 contains the points in X that are dominated by p in the first two dimensions of o, but are equal to or better than p in the third one. X^2 contains the points in X that dominate p in the first two dimensions of o but are equal to or worse than p in the third one. Lines 9 and 17 guarantee that no point in X is updated more than once, in case there are points with repeated coordinates, i.e., points on the boundary between two octants. The computation of $q.v = H(p, q, \mathrm{S})$ for $q \in \mathrm{X}^1$ and $q \in \mathrm{X}^2$ is detailed in Algorithms 4 and 3, respectively.

3.3.3 Update contributions of points in X

Figure 3(a) gives the base example that will be used to help explain the update of contributions of points in sets X^1 and X^2. In this explanation, let us consider only the case when the order considered is $o = (x, y, z)$. In such case, X^1 and X^2 are $\mathrm{X}^1 = \{q^1, q^3, q^4\}$ and $\mathrm{X}^2 = \{q^6, q^7\}$. The update procedure for the remaining coordinate orders is similar.

The update procedure will be explained first for X^2 and then for X^1. In both cases, the algorithms are built upon IHV3D (explained in Section 2). Therefore, Algorithm 2 splits S into S^1 and S^2. In this case only, function split takes $O(n)$-time as it has to guarantee that S^1 and S^2 are sorted according to all dimensions. Set S' is also maintained along the execution of both Algorithm 4 and 3, and is initialized as the subset of S^1 that delimits the area dominated by p. In the example, we have that $\mathrm{S}^1 = \{s^1, ..., s^7\}$, $\mathrm{S}^2 = \{s^8, ...s^{10}\}$ and $\mathrm{S}' = \{s^3, ..., s^7\}$ (initial set).

In the case of X^2 ($\mathrm{X}^2 = \{q^6, q^7\}$), all those points dominate p in (x, y)-plane and have higher z-coordinate. Therefore, if X^2 is sorted in ascending order of z, then, given any $q \in \mathrm{X}^2$ and its previous point u in X^2, the joint contribution of q with p is equal to the joint contribution of u with p above the value q_z of coordinate z. Moreover, the contribution of q when it is $\mathsf{head}_z(\mathrm{X}^2)$, is equal to the contribution of p above the value q_z of coordinate z. In the example of Figure 3(a), the joint contribution of q^7 with p is equal to the joint contribution of q^6 with p for $z \geq q^7_z$. The joint contribution of q^6 with p is equal to the contribution of p for $z \geq q^6_z$. Hence, for each $q \in \mathrm{X}^2$, Algorithm 3 stores the previous point $u \in \mathrm{X}^2$ in $q.prev$.

Algorithm 3 behaves just like IHV3D, i.e., uses S' to maintain the points delimiting the area of p at height $z = q_z$ and sweeps S^2 in ascending order of z in order to update the area of p and compute the slice volume (lines 8 to 15). Additionally, the algorithm sweeps X^2 along with S^2 in ascending order of the z-coordinate by merging the two lists (line 4). The algorithm records u, the last point from X^2 visited (except the first initialization of u which is a sentinel) and updates its volume (line 16) and area (line 17) when the area of p ($p.a$) is updated. Whenever the current point $q \in \mathrm{X}^2 \cup \mathrm{S}^2$ belongs to X^2, the volume simultaneously dominated by u and p bounded below by u_z becomes bounded above by q_z (line 19) and stays associated to (and only to) u. The contribution of p above q_z becomes associated to q (lines 20 and 21) and q is set as the new u (line 23). In that way, each part of the contribution p (a consecutive set of slices) is associated to a single point of X^2. When the first point from S^2 that dominates p in the (x, y)-plane is found, the volume of the last point from X^2 is updated (line 25). Then, $q \in \mathrm{X}^2$ are visited again but in descending order of the z-coordinate and their volumes are accumulated and added to the next visited points (lines 27 to 30).

Algorithm 4 jointContributions1$(p, \mathrm{S}^1, \mathrm{S}^2, \mathrm{X}^1, r)$

1: $\mathrm{S}' \leftarrow \{q \in \mathsf{minima}(\mathrm{S}^1) \mid p^* \leq q^*\} \cup \{\min_x(\mathrm{S}^1), \min_y(\mathrm{S}^1)\}$
2: $\mathrm{X}' \leftarrow \{q \in \mathrm{X}^1 \mid p^* \leq q^*$ **and** $\nexists t \in \mathrm{S}' : t^* \leq q^*\}$
3: $\mathsf{initializeBases}(\mathrm{X}^1, p, \mathrm{S}^1)$
4: $\mathrm{L} \leftarrow \mathrm{S}^2$
5: $q \leftarrow \mathsf{head}_z(\mathrm{L})$
6: **while** $q^* \nleq p^*$ **do**
7: **if** $q_x \leq p_x$ **then**
8:   $\mathrm{S}', \mathrm{T} \leftarrow \mathsf{split}_y(\mathrm{S}', q_y)$
9:   $t \leftarrow \mathsf{head}_x(\mathrm{S}')$
10:   $\mathrm{X}', \mathrm{A} \leftarrow \mathsf{split}_y(\mathrm{X}', q_y)$
11:   $\mathrm{B} \leftarrow \{u \in \mathrm{X}' \mid u_x < t_x\}$
12:   $\mathsf{updateVolume}(\mathrm{A} \cup \mathrm{B}, q_z)$
13:   $\mathsf{updateAreas}_y(p \vee q, \mathrm{B}, \mathrm{T} \cup \{\mathsf{head}_x(\mathrm{S}')\})$
14:   $\mathsf{addFirst}_x(q, \mathrm{S}')$
15: **else**
16:   $\mathrm{S}', \mathrm{T} \leftarrow \mathsf{split}_x(\mathrm{S}', q_x)$
17:   $t \leftarrow \mathsf{head}_y(\mathrm{S}')$
18:   $\mathrm{X}', \mathrm{A} \leftarrow \mathsf{split}_x(\mathrm{X}', q_x)$
19:   $\mathrm{B} \leftarrow \{u \in \mathrm{X}' \mid u_y < t_y\}$
20:   $\mathsf{updateVolume}(\mathrm{A} \cup \mathrm{B}, q_z)$
21:   $\mathsf{updateAreas}_y(p \vee q, \mathrm{B}, \mathrm{T} \cup \{\mathsf{head}_y(\mathrm{S}')\})$
22:   $\mathsf{addFirst}_y(q, \mathrm{S}')$
23: $q \leftarrow \mathsf{next}_z(q, \mathrm{L})$

In the case of points $q \in \mathrm{X}^1$, Algorithm 4 uses a set $\mathrm{X}' \subseteq \mathrm{X}^1$ that will be used along its execution to keep the

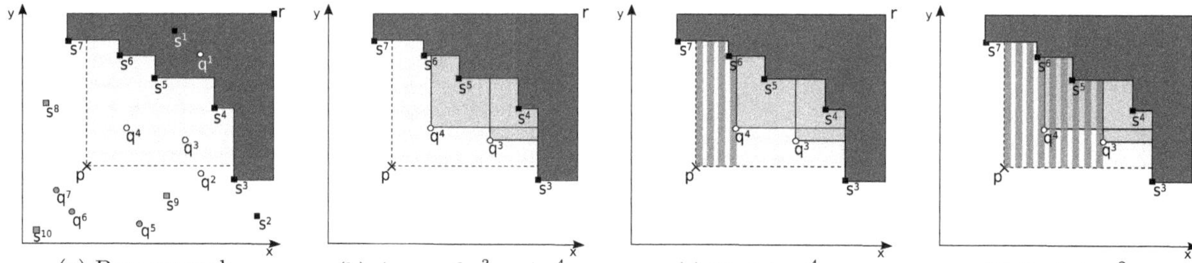

(a) Base example (b) Areas of q^3 and q^4 (c) Update $q^4.a$ (d) Update $q^3.a$

Figure 3: Example where $\mathrm{X} = \{q^1, ..., q^7\}$ (circles), $\mathrm{S} = \{s^1, ..., s^{10}\}$ (squares) and p is the last point picked from X and that will be added to S. Consider that the squares and circles painted gray have higher z coordinate than p and the remaining ones have lower z coordinate than p. Moreover, consider that when $\mathrm{X} \cup \mathrm{S}$ is sorted in ascending order of the z coordinate, the following point order is obtained: $q^1, s^1, ..., s^7, q^2, ..., q^4, p, s^8, q^5, q^6, s^9, q^7, s^{10}$.

points of X^1 whose common contribution with p is still being computed. X' is initialized, in linear time, with the points in X^1 that need to be updated, i.e., those points such that $q^* \in \mathrm{X}^{1*}$ is not dominated by S'^* ($\mathrm{X}' = \{q^3, q^4\}$). The computation of $H(p, q, \mathrm{S})$ for each $q \in \mathrm{X}'$ has two main steps, the computation of the base area of the volume $H(q \vee p, \mathrm{S}')$ (line 3) and the area updates (lines 13 and 21). Figures 3 and 4 will be used as examples, respectively.

Figure 3(b) shows the base areas of q^3 and q^4, to be computed. They overlap partially, and are depicted in medium gray. The base areas are initialized in linear time by computing $H(p^*, \mathrm{S}'^*) - H(p^*, \mathrm{S}'^* \cup \{q^*\})$, for each $q \in \mathrm{X}'$. The area of points in X' are initialized with $H(p^*, \mathrm{S}'^*)$ which was previously computed in line 2 of Algorithm 3 in linear time. The value $H(p^*, \mathrm{S}'^* \cup \{q^*\})$ is computed in two sweeps. Points in $q \in \mathrm{S}' \cup \mathrm{X}'$ are first visited in ascending order of x and the area dominated by p between p_x and each q_x is computed in a cumulative way. When a point from X' is visited, the area accumulated so far is subtracted from the area of that point. In Figures 3(c) and 3(d), the striped area is the accumulated area that is subtracted to q^4 and q^3, respectively. The remaining area to be subtracted, i.e., the area between p_y and q_y to the right of p_x, is computed in an analogous way by sweeping points in $\mathrm{S}' \cup \mathrm{X}'$ in ascending order of the y-coordinate. Note that in the second sweep it is also necessary to add to $q.a$ the area bounded below by p and above by q, for each $q \in \mathrm{X}'$, as it was subtracted twice.

Figure 4 shows the update of the areas of points in X^1 (lines 13 and 21). The update of volumes are performed in lines 12 and 20. This corresponds to the cases where a point of S' cuts above area dominated by p (lines 7 to 14 and s^8 in Figures 4(a) and 4(b)) or to the right (line 16 to 22 and s^9 in Figure 4(c) and 4(d)). Points $q \in \mathrm{S}^2$ are visited in ascending order of z-coordinate, as in IHV3D. Looking at the case of $q = s^8$, Algorithm 4 first removes from S' ($\mathrm{S}' = \{s^3, ..., s^7\}$) the set T in $O(|\mathrm{T}|)$-time. T contains the points in S' with higher y-coordinate than s^8_y ($\mathrm{T} = \{s^5, ..., s^7\}$ and S' becomes $\mathrm{S}' = \{s^3, s^4\}$), through function split. T is kept sorted according to the y-coordinate. Similarly, set A is removed from X' ($\mathrm{X}' = \{q^3, q^4\}$)in $O(|\mathrm{A}|)$-time, also through split (line 10). Set A^* contains the points dominated by q^*, i.e., those that have no more contribution above q_z ($\mathrm{A} = \{\}$). Finally, the areas of the points in X' to the left of the point that delimits q at right ($t = s^4$) have to be updated, therefore, those points are stored in B (line 11, $\mathrm{B} = \{q^3, q^4\}$). The volumes of points in $\mathrm{B} \cup \mathrm{A}$ are updated in $O(|\mathrm{A}| + |\mathrm{B}|)$-time (line 12). Then, in procedure updateAreas (line 13), points $u \in \mathrm{B} \cup \mathrm{T}$ are visited in descending order of coordinate x. For each u visited, the area dominated by $p \vee q$ to the right of u is accumulated. Whenever the visited point u belongs to B, the area computed so far is subtracted from $u.a$. Therefore, the update of the areas of points in B costs $O(|\mathrm{A}| + |\mathrm{B}|)$. At last, q is added to S' ($\mathrm{S}' = \{s^8, s^4, s^3\}$).

When q is below p ($q_y \leq p_y$), the procedure is analogous. Note that in the example of Figure 4(c), $q = \{s^9\}$ and $\mathrm{A} = \{q^3\}$, therefore, q^3 is removed from X' and its volume is updated. Therefore X' becomes $\{q^4\}$, then $t = s^8$, $\mathrm{B} = \{q^4\}$, and at the end of that iteration $\mathrm{S}' = \{s^8, s^9\}$ and $\mathrm{X}' = \{q^4\}$ (Figure 4(d)). Algorithm 4 finishes when the first point q that dominates p in the (x, y)-plane is found.

3.3.4 Time-complexity

Algorithm 2 (gHSS3D) sorts points in $O(n \log n)$-time and initializes their contributions in linear time. Then, it updates the contributions of points in X k times by sweeping them considering three different coordinate orders. For each coordinate order, the points of two disjoint sets are updated, X^1 and X^2 in Algorithms 4 and 3, respectively. Lines 11 to 14 and 17 have linear cost, while Algorithm 3 (line 16) has amortized linear time. Algorithm 4 (line 15) has amortized $O(n^2)$-time, but the amortization is along the entire execution of Algorithm 2.

Algorithm 3 inherits IHV3D's time complexity. As IHV3D, it computes the base area of p in linear time (line 2). Afterwards, points in S are only swept once when they are added to S' (line 1, 11 or 15) and once again if they are removed from S' (lines 9 and 13) and used to update the area of p (lines 10 and 14). Points in X^2 are used in constant time operations in the first while loop (lines 16 to 25) and are all visited once again, to update their volumes (lines 27 to 30).

The time-complexity of Algorithm 4 is analyzed by considering all calls (a maximum of n) from Algorithm 2. The analysis shows that, some steps amortize to $O(n)$-time for each call of Algorithm 4, while others are worse than linear in one call but result in $O(n^2)$-time across the n possible calls. In the latter case, Algorithm 4 guarantees that each point is compared against all other points a constant number of times.

Algorithm 4 also guarantees that each point is visited only if its area or volume has to be updated or if it delimits the contribution of the area being computed. The operations

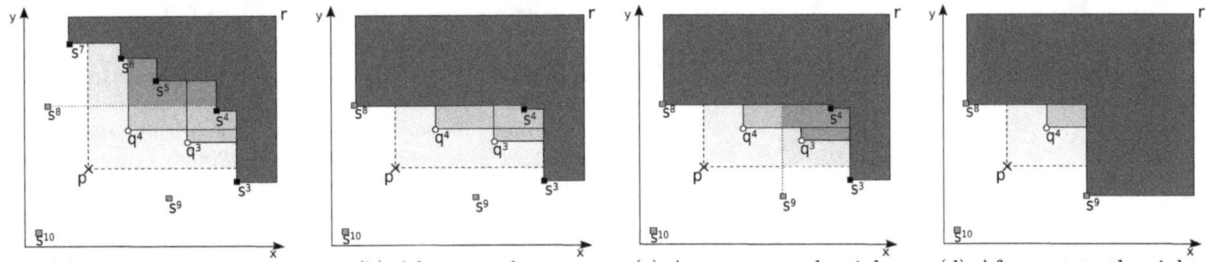

(a) Areas cut above (b) After cut above (c) Areas cut to the right (d) After cut to the right

Figure 4: Example of Algorithm 4 when points from S^2 are used to update the areas of points in X^1.

performed to maintain S′ (lines 8, 16, 14 and 22) are the same as in Algorithm 3, therefore, these operations amortize to linear time. As with S′, points from X^1 are added once to X′ (line 2) and are removed once from X′ (line 10 or 18). Therefore, maintaining X′ also amortizes to linear time. It remains to explain how many times points in $\mathrm{B} \subset \mathrm{X}'$ are visited. Constructing B has a cost $O(|\mathrm{B}|)$, and procedure updateAreas has a cost of $O(|\mathrm{B}| + |\mathrm{T}|)$. Since the points in T were previously removed from S′, they are used by updateAreas only once. However, in the worst case, B is equal to X′ in every iteration, and points are never removed from X′. This means that procedure updateAreas has a cost of $O(n)$, leading to $O(n^2)$-time complexity over $|\mathrm{S}^2|$ iterations.

Basically, the role of updateAreas is to compare each point in X with points in S. However, along gHSS3D execution, each point in X is compared, in this procedure, against each point in S just once, amortizing all of its executions, and of updateVolume, to $O(n^2)$. The reason is that a point $u \in \mathrm{X}^1 \subseteq \mathrm{X}$ is only compared to a point $s \in \mathrm{S}^2 \subset \mathrm{S}$ if s delimits the contribution of u (i.e., $H(u, s, \mathrm{S}\backslash\{s\}) > 0$). These points are compared only because the region where s delimits the contribution of u is dominated by p. Therefore, after p is added to S, the point s will not delimit the contribution of u anymore. This is because $p \leq (u \vee s)$ and $p_z \leq s_z$, which means that u has no contribution w.r.t. $\mathrm{S} \cup \{p\}$ above the value p_z of coordinate z ($H(u, s, (\mathrm{S} \cup \{p\})\backslash\{s\}) = 0$). Consequently u will not be compared again with s. In the example of Figure 4, neither q^3 or q^4 will be compared against s^8 or s^9 in any future execution of procedure updateAreas. Therefore, Algorithm 2 has amortized $O(n^2)$-time complexity.

4. RESULTS

The proposed algorithms, gHSS2D and gHSS3D, were implemented in C and compiled with gcc version 4.7.2. All tests were run on an Intel(R) Core(TM) i7-3612QM CPU @ 2.10GHz with 6 MB of cache and 8 GB of RAM.

The first results (see Figure 5) concern approximation quality. The results produced by gHSS2D were compared against those obtained with the exact algorithm by Bringmann *et al.* [5], HypSSP. Regarding gHSS3D, optimal results were obtained by adapting the HSSP ILP formulation by Kuhn *et al.* [13] to the 3-dimensional case, and solving it with the GNU Linear Programming Toolkit. Figure 5 shows the ratio between the hypervolume indicator values of the approximate and exact solutions for various sets, for growing values of k. Spherical fronts consisted of points randomly located on the positive quadrant/orthant of a unit circle/sphere with centre at the origin of the coordinate axes. Linear fronts were such that $0 \leq x_i \leq 1$ for $i = 1, 2$ and $i = 1, 2, 3$, respectively, and $\sum_i x_i = 1$ in both cases. The reference point was set to $(1, 1)$ and $(1, 1, 1)$ for 2 and 3 dimensions, respectively.

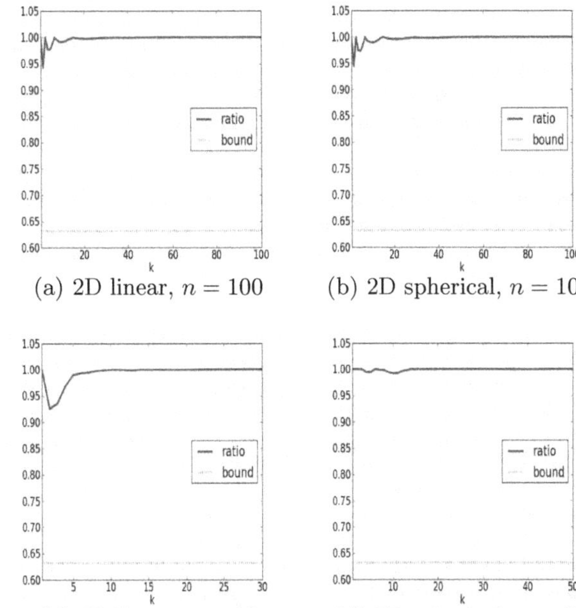

(a) 2D linear, $n = 100$ (b) 2D spherical, $n = 100$ (c) 3D linear, $n = 30$ (d) 3D spherical, $n = 50$

Figure 5: The ratio between the hypervolume indicator of the approximated and the exact solutions for a fixed set size n and variable subset size k.

The hypervolume ratio between the greedy and the optimal solution was always found to be greater than 0.93, which is much better than the theoretical bound of $(1 - 1/e) \simeq 0.63212$. Moreover, the approximation ratio was lower for smaller values of k. For $k \geq n/2$, the ratio was found to be either 1 (an optimum was found) or very close to 1.

The second set of experiments concerned runtime. Figure 6 shows the behaviour of gHSS2D and gHSS3D for growing set size n and $k = n/2$. The average runtimes of 13 runs on spherical fronts with the same characteristics described above is depicted (other fronts produced similar results). Figure 6 clearly shows the quadratic growth of the runtime of both algorithms. Still, selecting $k = 5000$ out of $n = 10000$

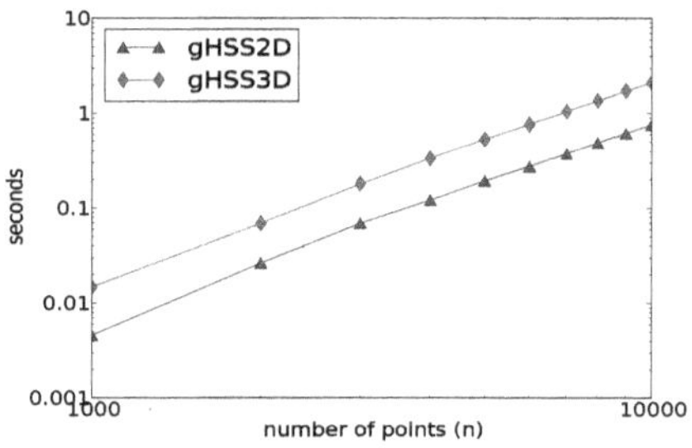

Figure 6: Runtime of gHSS2D and gHSS3D for spherical data sets for $n = 1000$ to $n = 10000$ and where $k = n/2$.

points was performed in less than 1 second in 2 dimensions, and in about 2 seconds in the 3-dimensional case.

5. CONCLUDING REMARKS

In this paper, greedy algorithms for the HSSP in two and three dimensions were proposed, providing a $(1 - 1/e)$-approximation to the optimal solution in each case. The two-dimensional version, gHSS2D, has a worst-case time complexity of $\Theta(n(k + \log n))$, which is similar to the complexity of exact algorithms for the same problem [6, 13]. However, it does have the advantage of being very simple to implement and very fast in practice. The $O(n^2)$ time complexity of the three-dimensional version, on the other hand, is considerably lower than that of the corresponding exact algorithm, which is $O(n^{\frac{d}{2}} \log n + n^{n-k})$. In practice, gHSS3D was at most 3 times slower than gHSS2D on the spherical data sets used for testing.

Regarding the quality of the approximation, the results obtained experimentally were much better than the guaranteed approximation factor, staying within at least 0.93 of the optimal values, in comparison to the theoretical $(1 - 1/e) \simeq 0.63212$. Therefore, gHSS3D should provide an interesting alternative to much more computationally expensive exact algorithms for hypervolume-based multiobjective selection and/or archiving in the three-objective case.

Acknowledgments

A. P. Guerreiro acknowledges Fundação para a Ciência e a Tecnologia (FCT) for Ph.D. studentship SFHR/BD/77725/2011, co-funded by the European Social Fund and by the State Budget of the Portuguese Ministry of Education and Science in the scope of NSRF–HPOP–Type 4.1–Advanced Training. This work was partially supported by the iCIS project (CENTRO-07-ST24-FEDER-002003) which is co-financed by QREN, in the scope of the Mais Centro Program and European Union's FEDER.

6. REFERENCES

[1] A. Auger, J. Bader, D. Brockhoff, and E. Zitzler. Theory of the hypervolume indicator: Optimal μ-distributions and the choice of the reference point. In *Foundations of Genetic Algorithms (FOGA 2009)*, pages 87–102, New York, NY, USA, 2009. ACM.

[2] J. Bader and E. Zitzler. Hype: An algorithm for fast hypervolume-based many-objective optimization. *Evol. Comput.*, 19(1):45–76, Mar. 2011.

[3] N. Beume, C. Fonseca, M. López-Ibáñez, L. Paquete, and J. Vahrenhold. On the complexity of computing the hypervolume indicator. *IEEE Trans. Evol. Comput.*, 13(5):1075–1082, Oct 2009.

[4] L. Bradstreet, L. While, and L. Barone. Incrementally maximising hypervolume for selection in multi-objective evolutionary algorithms. In *IEEE CEC 2007*, pages 3203–3210, Sept 2007.

[5] K. Bringmann and T. Friedrich. An efficient algorithm for computing hypervolume contributions. *Evol. Comput.*, 18(3):383–402, Sept. 2010.

[6] K. Bringmann, T. Friedrich, and P. Klitzke. Two-dimensional subset selection for hypervolume and epsilon-indicator. In *Conference on Genetic and Evolutionary Computation*, GECCO '14, pages 589–596, New York, NY, USA, 2014. ACM.

[7] T. M. Chan. Klee's measure problem made easy. In *Proc. 54th IEEE Symposium on Foundations of Computer Science (FOCS)*, pages 410–419, Los Alamitos, CA, USA, 2013. IEEE Computer Society.

[8] M. Emmerich and C. Fonseca. Computing hypervolume contributions in low dimensions: Asymptotically optimal algorithm and complexity results. In *EMO 2011*, volume 6576 of *LNCS*, pages 121–135. Springer, 2011.

[9] T. Friedrich and F. Neumann. Maximizing submodular functions under matroid constraints by multi-objective evolutionary algorithms. In *PPSN XIII*, volume 8672 of *LNCS*, pages 922–931. Springer International Publishing, 2014.

[10] A. P. Guerreiro, C. M. Fonseca, and M. T. M. Emmerich. A fast dimension-sweep algorithm for the hypervolume indicator in four dimensions. In *CCCG 2012*, pages 77–82, 2012.

[11] I. Hupkens and M. Emmerich. Logarithmic-time updates in SMS-EMOA and hypervolume-based archiving. In *EVOLVE IV*, volume 227 of *Advances in Intelligent Systems and Computing*, pages 155–169. Springer, 2013.

[12] J. D. Knowles, D. W. Corne, and M. Fleischer. Bounded archiving using the Lebesgue measure. In *IEEE CEC '03*, volume 4, pages 2490–2497, 2003.

[13] T. Kuhn, C. M. Fonseca, L. Paquete, S. Ruzika, and J. Figueira. Hypervolume subset selection in two dimensions: Formulations and algorithms. Technical report, Technische Universität Kaiserslautern, 2014.

[14] G. Nemhauser, L. Wolsey, and M. Fisher. An analysis of approximations for maximizing submodular set functions–I. *Mathematical Programming*, 14(1):265–294, 1978.

[15] T. Ulrich and L. Thiele. Bounding the effectiveness of hypervolume-based $(\mu + \lambda)$-archiving algorithms. In *Learning and Intelligent Optimization*, volume 7219 of *LNCS*, pages 235–249. Springer, 2012.

[16] L. While, L. Bradstreet, and L. Barone. A fast way of calculating exact hypervolumes. *IEEE Trans. Evol. Comput.*, 16(1):86–95, 2012.

[17] E. Zitzler and L. Thiele. Multiobjective optimization using evolutionary algorithms – A comparative case study. In *PPSN V*, volume 1498 of *LNCS*, pages 292–301. Springer, 1998.

Improved Metaheuristic Based on the R2 Indicator for Many-Objective Optimization

Raquel Hernández Gómez
Computer Science Department
CINVESTAV-IPN
México, D.F. 07360
rhernandez@computacion.cs.cinvestav.mx

Carlos A. Coello Coello
Computer Science Department
CINVESTAV-IPN
México, D.F. 07360
ccoello@cs.cinvestav.mx

ABSTRACT

In recent years, performance indicators were introduced as a selection mechanism in multi-objective evolutionary algorithms (MOEAs). A very attractive option is the $R2$ indicator due to its low computational cost and weak-Pareto compatibility. This indicator requires a set of utility functions, which map each objective to a single value. However, not all the utility functions available in the literature scale properly for more than four objectives and the diversity of the approximation sets is sensitive to the choice of the reference points during normalization. In this paper, we present an improved version of a MOEA based on the $R2$ indicator, which takes into account these two key aspects, using the achievement scalarizing function and statistical information about the population's proximity to the true Pareto optimal front. Moreover, we present a comparative study with respect to some other emerging approaches, such as NSGA-III (based on Pareto dominance), Δ_p-DDE (based on the Δ_p indicator) and some other MOEAs based on the $R2$ indicator, using the DTLZ and WFG test problems. Experimental results indicate that our approach outperforms the original algorithm as well as the other MOEAs in the majority of the test instances, making it a suitable alternative for solving many-objective optimization problems.

Categories and Subject Descriptors

I.2.8 [**Computing Methodologies**]: Artificial Intelligence—*Problem Solving, Control Methods, and Search.*

Keywords

Multi-objective optimization; performance measures; genetic algorithms.

1. INTRODUCTION

A wide variety of real-world problems require the simultaneous optimization of several (often conflicting) objectives, whose solution involves finding a set of trade-off solutions. These are called Multi-objective Optimization Problems (or MOPs) and for solving them, Multi-objective evolutionary algorithms (MOEAs) have been proven effective [2], especially when no gradient information is assumed. An important trend in MOEAs is the incorporation of performance indicators as a selection mechanism. This has been mainly motivated by the fact that Pareto-based selection schemes do not perform properly when dealing with MOPs having four or more objectives (the so called many-objective optimization problems [11]).

The indicator that has been most commonly adopted in the selection mechanism of a MOEA has been the hypervolume [22], being the only unary indicator known to be Pareto compliant. However, its drawback is that its computational cost grows exponentially as the number of objectives increases. An alternative is the $R2$ indicator [8], which is correlated with the hypervolume [19], but requires a much lower computational cost. Moreover, the use of the $R2$ indicator is recommended [13] for many-objective problems, since it simultaneously evaluates convergence and diversity of an approximation set. One of the first MOEAs that have been proposed based on this indicator is the Many Objective Metaheuristic Based on the $R2$ indicator (MOMBI) [9]. Nevertheless, in some test instances it experimented loss of diversity for high dimensionality. In this paper, we address this problem and propose an improved version, called MOMBI-II. Furthermore, we provide a comparative study with respect to other recent MOEAs, such as Δ_p - Differential Evolution (Δ_p-DDE) [16], which is based on the Δ_p indicator; the Nondominated Sorting Genetic Algorithm III (NSGA-III)[4], which relies on Pareto dominance and a niching strategy; and three MOEAs based on the $R2$ indicator: $R2$-IBEA [15], $R2$-MOGA [7] and the original MOMBI.

The remainder of this paper is organized as follows. Section 2 introduces basic concepts that will be used in the paper. Section 3 presents an overview of emerging MOEAs that can handle many-objective problems. Section 4 describes in detail our proposal. Then, we present the experimental results in Section 5. Our conclusions and some paths for future research are provided in Section 6.

GECCO '15, July 11 - 15, 2015, Madrid, Spain

DOI: http://dx.doi.org/10.1145/2739480.2754776

2. PRELIMINARIES

The formal definition of a MOP is given by:

$$\text{Minimize} \quad \vec{f}(\vec{x}) := (f_1(\vec{x}), f_2(\vec{x}), \ldots, f_m(\vec{x})) \qquad (1)$$

$$\text{subject to} \quad x \in \mathcal{S}, \qquad (2)$$

where $\vec{x}$ is the *decision variable vector*, $\mathcal{S} \subset \mathbb{R}^n$ is the *feasible region set* and $\vec{f}(\vec{x})$ is the vector of m (≥ 2) *objective functions* ($f_i : \mathbb{R}^n \to \mathbb{R}$).

The aim is to seek from among the set of all numbers which satisfy the constraints functions defined in equation (2) the particular set $\vec{x}^*$ which yields the optimum values of all the objective functions. In the following, we provide concepts related to Pareto optimality. Unless otherwise stated, let be $\vec{x}, \vec{y} \in \mathcal{S}$.

Definition 1. A decision vector $\vec{x}$ is *Pareto optimal* if there does not exist another decision vector $\vec{y}$ such that $f_i(\vec{y}) \leq f_i(\vec{x})$ for all $i \in \{1, \ldots, m\}$ and $f_j(\vec{y}) < f_j(\vec{x})$ for at least one index j.

Definition 2. The *Pareto Optimal Set* $\mathcal{P}^*$ is defined by:

$$\mathcal{P}^* := \{\vec{x} \mid \vec{x} \text{ is Pareto optimal}\}.$$

Definition 3. The *Pareto Optimal Front* $\mathcal{PF}^*$ is given by:

$$\mathcal{PF}^* := \{\vec{f}(\vec{x}) \in \mathbb{R}^m \mid \vec{x} \in \mathcal{P}^*\}.$$

Definition 4. A solution $\vec{x}$ is said to *weakly dominate* a solution $\vec{y}$ (denoted by $\vec{x} \preceq \vec{y}$), if and only if $\forall i \in \{1, \ldots, m\}$, $f_i(\vec{x}) \leq f_i(\vec{y})$.

Definition 5. A solution $\vec{x}$ is said to *dominate* a solution $\vec{y}$ (denoted by $\vec{x} \prec \vec{y}$), if and only if $\vec{x} \preceq \vec{y} \wedge \vec{f}(\vec{x}) \neq \vec{f}(\vec{y})$.

Definition 6. A vector of decision variables $\vec{x} \in X$ is *nondominated* with respect to the set $X \subseteq \mathcal{S}$ if there does not exist another vector $\vec{y} \in X$ such that $\vec{f}(\vec{y}) \prec \vec{f}(\vec{x})$.

Definition 7. The set of *nondominated solutions* relative to the set X is expressed by $\{\vec{x} \in X \mid \vec{x} \text{ is nondominated}\}$.

The Pareto optimal front of a multi-objective optimization problem is bounded by two special vectors:

Definition 8. The *ideal objective vector* $\vec{z}^* \in \mathbb{R}^m$ minimizes all objective functions. Each ith-component is defined as $z_i^* = \min_{\vec{x}} f_i(\vec{x})$.

Definition 9. The *nadir objective vector* $\vec{z}^{nad} \in \mathbb{R}^m$ is constructed using the worst values of $\mathcal{PF}^*$. Each ith-component is defined as $z_i^{nad} = \max_{\vec{x} \in \mathcal{P}^*} f_i(\vec{x})$.

A utility function $u : \mathbb{R}^m \to \mathbb{R}$ is a model of the decision maker's preference that maps each objective vector into a scalar value. Given an approximation set A, and a set of utility functions U, the unary $R2$ indicator [1] is defined as:

$$R2(A, U) = \frac{1}{|U|} \sum_{u \in U} u^*(A), \tag{3}$$

where $u^*(A) = \min_{\vec{a} \in A}\{u(\vec{a})\}$ is the best utility value obtained in the set A.[1]

[1]For simplicity, we have applied the dual property: $\min \vec{z} = -\max(-\vec{z})$, and we also assume that the utility functions are non-negative.

3. PREVIOUS RELATED WORK

In this section, we review some recently created MOEAs that were designed for many-objective optimization problems.

Δ_p-DDE [16] uses the Δ_p indicator [18] as the selection mechanism of differential evolution. Since this semi-metric requires knowledge about the Pareto optimal front, Δ_p-DDE employs an echelon form of the nondominated individuals. The complexity of this MOEA is dominated by the building of the reference set, which is exponential with respect to the number of objectives and the quality of the outcome sets is influenced by a resolution parameter.

The Nondominated Sorting Genetic Algorithm III (NSGA-III) [4] is similar to the original NSGA-II algorithm [5], which ranks individuals using a nondomination criterion. But, the maintenance of diversity is aided by a set of weight vectors. The main advantage of this MOEA is the uniformity of its distributions. However, its implementation is not trivial, being sensitive to the construction of a hyper-plane.

The $R2$ Indicator Based Evolutionary Algorithm ($R2$-IBEA) [15] is an extension of IBEA [23], which eliminates Pareto dominance and performs a selection guided by an exponential amplification of a binary version of the $R2$ indicator. The set of normalized weight vectors is generated using a hypervolume-based approach. The reference point is dynamically updated according to the extent of current solutions in objective function space.

The $R2$ Multi-Objective Genetic Algorithm ($R2$-MOGA) and $R2$ Multi-Objective Differential Evolution ($R2$-MODE) [7] incorporate the $R2$ indicator to a modified version of the nondominated sorting method of NSGA-II [5], in order to separate individuals into layers. This approach is coupled to two different search algorithms, resulting in two MOEAs. The set of weight vectors is generated at each generation using a random approach. A reference point is updated per generation using the utopian point.[2]

The Many-Objective Metaheuristic Based on the $R2$ Indicator (MOMBI) [9] is another example of a MOEA based on the $R2$ indicator, which is easy to implement and does not require Pareto dominance (in the following sections we will discuss more about it).

These three $R2$ approaches adopt the weighted Tchebycheff functions as their utility functions.

4. OUR PROPOSED APPROACH

In this section we describe, in order of importance, the main limitations of the original MOMBI. First, we analyze the scalability of some utility functions. Then, we provide a mechanism to update the reference points during normalization. Finally, we introduce MOMBI-II, including a brief analysis of its computational complexity.

4.1 Scalability of Utility Functions

There are several possible utility functions, the majority of which have been borrowed from mathematical programming. The most popular is the Weighted Tchebycheff (WT) metric [12], which is of the form:

$$u_{tch}(\vec{v} : \vec{r}, \vec{w}) = \max_{i \in \{1, \cdots, m\}} \{w_i |v_i - r_i|\}, \tag{4}$$

where $r \in \mathbb{R}^m$ is a reference point, $\vec{w}$ is a weight vector such that $w_i \geq 0$ for all $i \in \{1, \cdots, m\}$ and $\sum_{i=1}^m w_i = 1$. The

[2]$z_i^{**} = z_i^* - \epsilon_i$ for all $i \in \{1, \cdots, m\}$, where $\epsilon_i > 0$ is a relatively small but computational significant scalar.

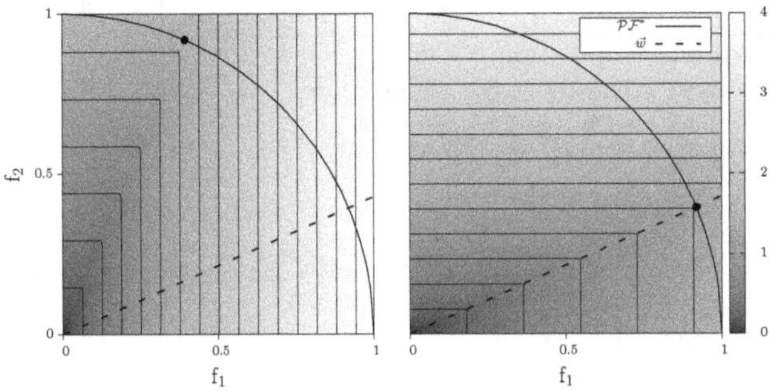

Figure 1: Contour lines of the WT (left) and ASF (right) metrics for the weight vector $\vec{w} = (0.7, 0.3)$.

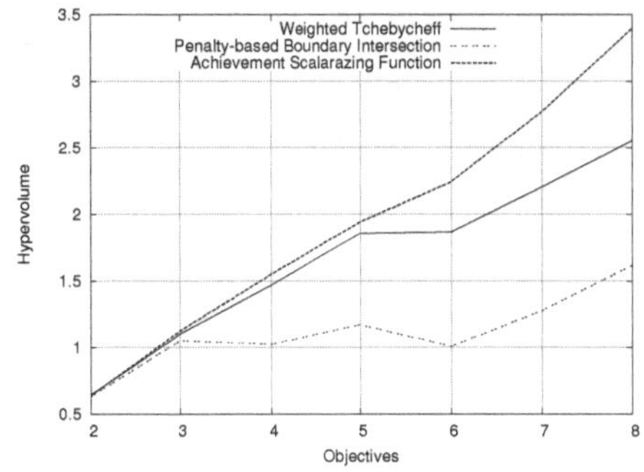

Figure 2: Average hypervolume for MOEA/D using three different scalarizing functions from 2 to 8 objectives on the DTLZ3 test problem.

minimization of this metric produces weakly Pareto optimal solutions. The geometric interpretation of equation (4) is presented in Figure 1. It is interesting to observe that the contour lines are incongruent with the weight vector.

Another important metric is the Penalty-based Boundary Intersection (PBI) [21]:

$$u_{pbi}(\vec{v} : \vec{r}, \vec{w}) = d_1 + \theta d_2, \tag{5}$$

$$d_1 = \frac{||(\vec{v} - \vec{r})^T \vec{w}||}{||\vec{w}||}, \tag{6}$$

$$d_2 = \left|\left| \vec{v} - \left(\vec{r} + d_1 \frac{\vec{w}}{||\vec{w}||} \right) \right|\right|, \tag{7}$$

where $\theta > 0$ is a penalty parameter. The minimization of the PBI metric produces Pareto optimal solutions much better uniformly distributed than those obtained by equation (4).

A metric that has been scarcely studied in MOEAs is the achievement scalarizing function (ASF) [20], defined as[3]:

$$u_{asf}(\vec{v} : \vec{r}, \vec{w}) = \max_{i \in \{1, \cdots, m\}} \left\{ \frac{|v_i - r_i|}{w_i} \right\}, \tag{8}$$

Its minimization produces weakly Pareto optimal solutions. Note that the weight vector agrees with the contour lines of Figure 1.

When these metrics are incorporated into a MOEA, a set of weight vectors is required in order to exploit its population-based nature. Usually, the Simplex-Lattice Design (SLD) method [17] is the most preferred. In this case, the distribution of the vectors is equally spaced over a simplex, producing more points at the boundary than at the center. This could explain the distinctive distribution generated by MOEAs based on the WT metric, such as MOEA/D [21] or MOMBI, where solutions are biased from the center of the Pareto front to a few boundary points, since this metric optimizes the opposite weight vectors.

In the following, we examine the scalability of these three metrics applied to the well-known MOEA/D on the DTLZ3 test problem [6]. We performed 30 independent runs of each instance from 2 to 8 objectives, adopting the same parameter settings used in [9]. To assess performance, we employed the hypervolume indicator.

In Figure 2, we present our experimental results. Here, for two and three objectives all the metrics gave very similar results. However, as the number of objectives increases, the performance of PBI and the WT metrics degrades. In contrast, the ASF metric obtained the maximum hypervolume for many-objective problems.

It is important to mention that the only difference between the WT and ASF utility functions is the weight parameter. Thus, the former can derive congruent results, if we change the vectors in such a way that each component is the reciprocal of those generated by the SLD method[4]. However, we decided to incorporate the ASF metric into MOMBI-II and left for future research the design of other weight vectors.

4.2 Update of Reference Points

In the original version of MOMBI each objective function was normalized using the following expression:

$$f_i'(\vec{x}) = \frac{f_i(\vec{x}) - z_i^{min}}{z_i^{max} - z_i^{min}} \quad \forall i \in \{1, \cdots, m\}, \tag{9}$$

where $\vec{z^{min}}$ and $\vec{z^{max}}$ are the ideal and nadir objective vectors, respectively, taken from the current population.

Some problems with this approach were that the true ideal vector of the feasible region was never retained, and in consequence, boundary solutions of the Pareto optimal front were missing. In multi-frontal problems, the nadir objective vector was always an outlier, causing a poor distribution in the approximation sets. In high dimensionality, it could happen that the ideal and the nadir vectors were close, flattening some objectives and thus causing MOMBI to lose diversity. Also, the constant update of these vectors made the population unstable in the final generations.

In order to overcome these drawbacks, we update the reference points in a smarter way, taking into account statistical information of previous generations. The idea is to monitor the nadir point of the parents population at each generation, determining how close are the individuals from the true Pareto front. A high variance means that solutions are far away, which strongly biases the location of the point. A low variance means that solutions are close, thus, small movements must be done. This mechanism can serve as a cut-off of objective space, since outliers are removed.

In Algorithm 1, we present the pseudo-code of this technique. Here, we use a data structure called *record* that stores

[3]We consider the absolute value from its original definition.

[4]The restriction of normalization is dropped without affecting weak Pareto dominance [12]. In order to avoid indeterminate form, a computational big scalar can be taken instead.

Algorithm 1 Update Reference Points

Require: $\vec{z}^{min}$, $\vec{z}^{max}$, population P, num. objectives m
Ensure: $\vec{z}^{min}$ and $\vec{z}^{max}$

1: Update vectors $\vec{z}^*$ and $\vec{z}^{nad}$
2: $z_i^{min} \leftarrow \min\{z_i^{min}, z_i^*\} \quad \forall i \in \{1, \cdots, m\}$
3: Store $\vec{z}^{nad}$ in record
4: Obtain vector of variances $\vec{v} \in \mathbb{R}^m$ for $\vec{z}^{nad}$ from *record*
5: **if** $\max_{j\in\{1,\cdots,m\}} v_j > \alpha$ **then**
6: $\quad z_i^{max} \leftarrow \max_{j\in\{1,\cdots,m\}} z_j^{nad} \quad \forall i \in \{1, \cdots, m\}$
7: **else**
8: $\quad$ **for all** $i \in \{1, \cdots, m\}$ **do**
9: $\quad\quad$ **if** $|z_i^{max} - z_i^{min}| < \epsilon$ **then**
10: $\quad\quad\quad z_i^{max} \leftarrow \max_{j\in\{1,\cdots,m\}} z_j^{max}$
11: $\quad\quad\quad$ Mark z_i^{max}
12: $\quad\quad$ **else if** $z_i^{nad} > z_i^{max}$ **then**
13: $\quad\quad\quad z_i^{max} \leftarrow 2z_i^{nad} - z_i^{max}$
14: $\quad\quad\quad$ Mark z_i^{max}
15: $\quad\quad$ **else if** $v_i = 0$ **and** z_i^{max} has not been marked recently **then**
16: $\quad\quad\quad$ Obtain the maximum value a for z_i^{nad} from record
17: $\quad\quad\quad z_i^{max} \leftarrow (z_i^{max} + a)/2$
18: $\quad\quad\quad$ Mark z_i^{max}
19: **return** $\vec{z}^{min}$ and $\vec{z}^{max}$

the nadir vector of a few generations. We also need the parameter α, which is the threshold of variances for the vector $\vec{z}^{nad}$, and the parameter ϵ, which is a tolerance threshold. In line 1, the ideal and nadir objective vectors are updated using Definitions 8 and 9. In line 2, if $\vec{z}^{min}$ is improved, then it is updated. In lines 3 and 4, the nadir vector is kept in *record* and its vector of variances, for each objective, is estimated. If the maximum variance of all objectives is high, then $\vec{z}^{max}$ is updated using the maximum objective of the nadir vector (lines 5 and 6). Otherwise, from lines 8 to 18, each component of $\vec{z}^{max}$ is examined. If the absolute difference between its ith value and z_i^{min} is less than ϵ, then it is marked and updated, using the maximum objective of $\vec{z}^{max}$. Otherwise, if the ith value of the nadir vector is greater than the component, then it is expanded and marked. Otherwise, if the variance is zero and z_i^{max} has not been marked yet, then it is marked and averaged between its previous value and the maximum value stored for it in *record*. In all cases, the mark lasts the same number of generations that *record* is kept. The total complexity of this algorithm can be done in $\mathcal{O}(|P|m)$, where $|P|$ denotes the population size.

4.3 MOMBI-II

In this subsection, we introduce MOMBI-II (Many-Objective Metaheuristic Based on the $R2$ Indicator II), which is inspired on a Genetic Algorithm.

The $R2$ ranking procedure (see Algorithm 2) remains almost with no changes. Solutions that optimize the set of weight vectors are chosen and placed on top such that they get the first rank (the best). Such points will then be removed and a second rank will be identified in the same manner. The process will continue until all the solutions had been ranked. When two individuals contribute with the same utility value, then we choose as tiebreaker the one with the lower Euclidean distance. This eliminates weak-Pareto solutions. The ASF metric is adopted as our utility function. The notation assumes that each individual p contains the vector of objective functions $p.\vec{f}$, the hierarchy of the individual $p.rank$ and $p.\mu$, the current utility value for a weight vector $\vec{w}$. The complexity of the algorithm is $\mathcal{O}(|W||P|(\log|P| + m))$.

Algorithm 2 $R2$ Ranking Algorithm

Require: Population P, set of weight vectors W
Ensure: Ranking of the population

1: $p.rank \leftarrow p.\mu \leftarrow \infty \quad \forall p \in P$
2: **for all** $\vec{w} \in W$ **do**
3: $\quad$ **for all** $p \in P$ **do**
4: $\quad\quad p.\mu \leftarrow u_{asf}(p.\vec{f} : \vec{0}, \vec{w})$
5: $\quad$ Sort P w.r.t. the fields μ and L_2 in increasing order
6: $\quad rank \leftarrow 1$
7: $\quad$ **for all** $p \in P$ **do**
8: $\quad\quad p.rank \leftarrow \min\{p.rank, rank\}$
9: $\quad\quad rank \leftarrow rank + 1$

Algorithm 3 Main Loop of MOMBI-II

Require: MOP, stopping criterion, set of weight vectors W
Ensure: Pareto set approximation

1: Initialize population P_i, $i \leftarrow 1$
2: Evaluate population P_i
3: Calculate the L_2-norm of objectives for P_i
4: Set $\vec{z}^{min} \leftarrow \vec{z}^*$ and $\vec{z}^{max} \leftarrow \vec{z}^{nad}$
5: **while** termination condition is not fulfilled **do**
6: $\quad$ Perform parent selection
7: $\quad$ Generate offspring P_i' using variation operators
8: $\quad$ Evaluate population P_i'
9: $\quad$ Calculate the L_2-norm of objectives for P_i'
10: $\quad$ Normalize objective functions for $P_i \bigcup P_i'$
11: $\quad$ Execute $R2$ ranking algorithm $(P_i \bigcup P_i', W)$
12: $\quad$ Reduce population $P_{i+1} \leftarrow \{P_i \bigcup P_i'\}$
13: $\quad$ Update reference points $(\vec{z}^{min}, \vec{z}^{max}, P_{i+1}, m)$
14: $\quad i \leftarrow i + 1$
15: **return** P_i

The main loop of MOMBI-II is presented in Algorithm 3. The normalization step in line 10 is performed using equation (9). The criteria for population reduction takes into account the rank of each individual and the Euclidean distance. Next, we determine the complexity of this approach. Parent selection is performed in $\mathcal{O}(|P|)$, as well as the offspring generation. The evaluation of the population, the calculation of the norm, the update of reference points and the normalization is done in $\mathcal{O}(|P|m)$ each. As seen before, the ranking procedure takes $\mathcal{O}(|W||P|(\log|P|+m))$ and the reduction can be performed in $\mathcal{O}(|P|\log|P|)$. Therefore, the overall complexity of MOMBI-II at each generation is $\mathcal{O}(|W||P|(\log|P| + m))$ and the storage is $\mathcal{O}(|P|m)$.

5. EXPERIMENTAL RESULTS

In this section, we first describe the parameters used to compare the performance on 3, 5 and 10 objectives of Δ_p-DDE, NSGA-III, $R2$-MOGA, $R2$-IBEA[5], MOMBI-II and MOMBI. With the aim of evaluating the impact of only one improvement in the proposed MOEA, we considered another version, named MOMBI-ASF, which incorporates the ASF metric and the normalization is done as in the original algo-

[5]Ten objectives were excluded from the study, since this MOEA is scalable up to 5 objectives [15].

Table 1: **Parameters adopted in the study.**

m	Weights		$\lvert P\rvert$	Δ_p-DDE	WFG	
	H	H_{ref}		r	n	k
3	12	66	92	10	24	4
5	5	30	126	4	47	8
10	3	10	220	3	105	18

rithm. Then, we establish the adopted performance metric in the experiments, the test problems and finalize with the discussion of the results.

5.1 Parameters Settings

The parameters were identical for all the algorithms (see Table 1). The set of weight vectors was generated using the SLD method. Its cardinality is given by the combinatorial number:

$$|W| = \binom{H+m-1}{m-1}, \tag{10}$$

where m represents the number of objectives and H is a proportionality parameter. The population size $|P|$ was the same as the number of weight vectors, except for 3 objectives (in this case, it was increased by 1 to fulfill the requirement of adopting even numbers in the binary tournament selection). For Δ_p-DDE, the p-norm was set to 1, the parameters F and C were both established to 0.5 and the resolution of the reference set r varied according to the objectives as shown in Table 1. In the genetic algorithms, the variation operators were simulated binary crossover (SBX) and polynomial-based mutation [3]. As suggested in [4], the crossover rate and its distribution index were set to 1.0 and 30, respectively. The mutation rate was set to $1/n$ (here, n represents the number of variables) and its distributed index was set to 20. All these MOEAs were implemented using real-numbers encoding and their source code was provided by their authors, except for NSGA-III.

For MOMBI-II, the parameters ϵ and α were set to $1e-3$ and 0.5, respectively. These values were determined from an analysis of several samplings. We observed that they are independent of the dimensionality and the problem to be solved. As an example, we show in Figure 3(a) the median values of the Δ_2 indicator (see next subsection for its definition) for 30 independent runs of DTLZ1 with 5 objectives. Similarly, the *record* size (used for tracing the variance of the nadir vector) was set to 5 generations. It can be appreciated from Figure 3(b), that low values of the indicator are achievable using this value and it is computationally less expensive than if we perform the normalization at every generation.

5.2 Performance Measure

We selected the Δ_p [18] as a performance assessment measure. This indicator simultaneously evaluate proximity to the Pareto optimal front and spread of solutions along it. Given an approximation set A and a discretized Pareto optimal front $\mathcal{PF}$ of a MOP, the Δ_p indicator is defined as:

$$\Delta_p(A,\mathcal{PF}) = \max\left(\left(\frac{\sum_{i=1}^{|A|} d_i^p}{|A|}\right)^{\frac{1}{p}}, \left(\frac{\sum_{i=1}^{|\mathcal{PF}|} e_i^p}{|\mathcal{PF}|}\right)^{\frac{1}{p}}\right), \tag{11}$$

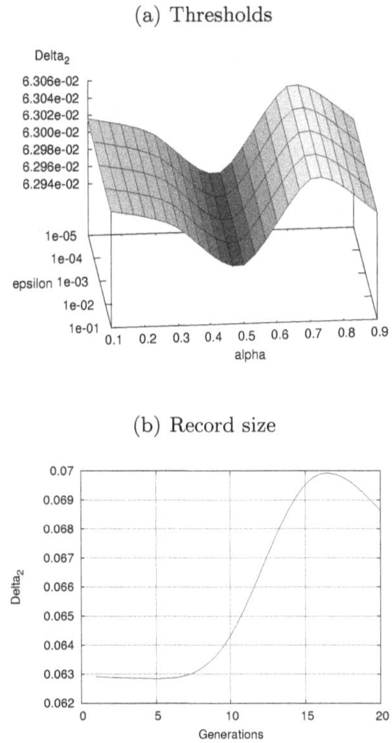

Figure 3: Parameter sampling in MOMBI-II for the DTLZ1 with 5 objectives.

where d_i is the Euclidean distance from $a_i \in A$ to its nearest member in $\mathcal{PF}$ and e_i is the Euclidean distance from $pf_i \in \mathcal{PF}$ to its nearest member in A. Small values of Δ_p are preferred.

Since this indicator requires that $\mathcal{PF}$ is known, we sampled it for each type of geometry in the adopted test problems by generating a set of weight vectors using the SLD method and then finding the intersection point of $\mathcal{PF}$ with the lines defined between the origin and the weight vectors. The number of points in $\mathcal{PF}$ is defined by equation (10), using the parameter H_{ref} of Table 1.

5.3 Test Problems

For comparison purposes, we select four normalized problems of the Deb-Thiele-Laumanns-Zitzler (DTLZ) set [6]. These are DTLZ1, with a linear and multi-frontal Pareto front and the others with a concave geometry: DTLZ2, DTLZ3 (multi-frontal) and DTLZ4 (biased). We also include in the study two problems of the Walking-Fish-Group (WFG) set [10], which are concave with different scale in each objective. Such instances are WFG6 (non-separable) and WFG7 (biased). Their properties make these two problems much harder to solve for MOEAs. The number of decision variables and position-related (k) parameters are specified in Table 1.

5.4 Discussion of Results

We performed 30 independent runs of each of the 7 MOEAs compared on all the test instances adopted. With the aim of comparing the performance of all algorithms among themselves in a pairwise fashion, the Wilcoxon rank sum test (one-tailed) with the Bonferroni correction [14] was applied

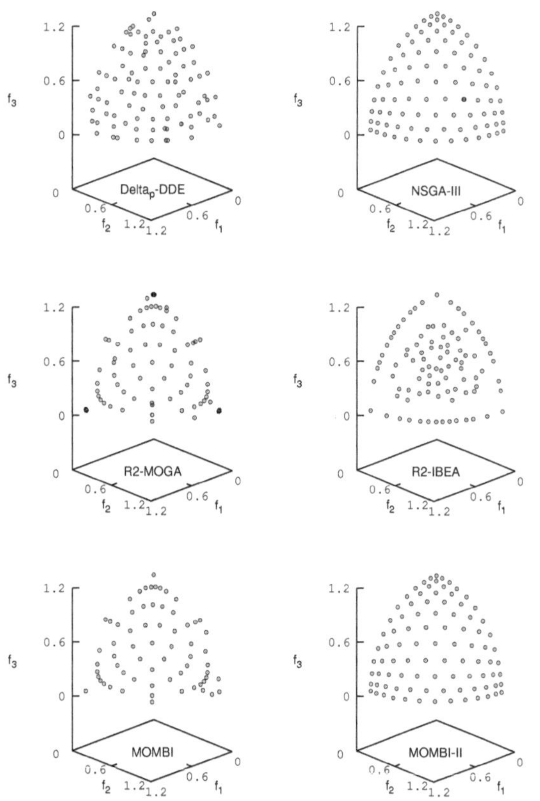

Figure 4: Pareto fronts produced by MOEAs on DTLZ3 for 3 objectives.

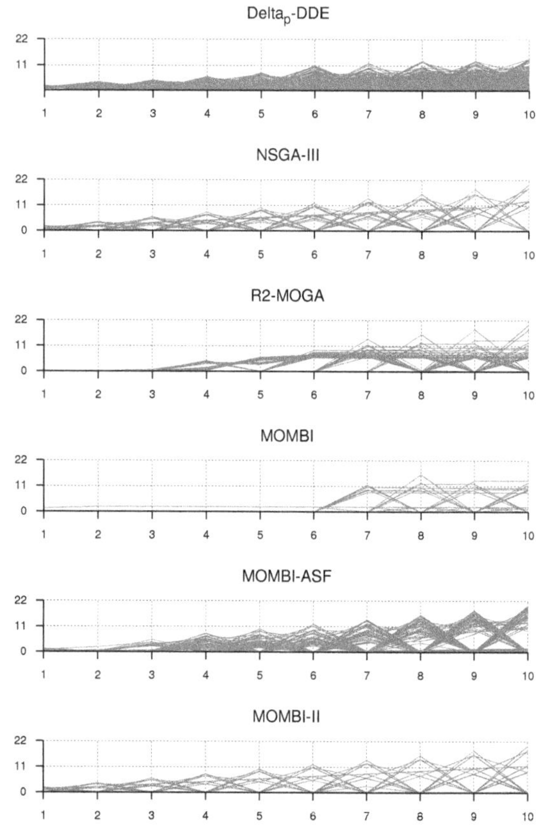

Figure 5: Parallel coordinates of the approximations obtained by MOEAs on WFG7 for 10 objectives.

to the Δ_2 indicator values. Experimental results appear in Tables 2 and 3. Examples of the Pareto fronts, corresponding to the median values, are depicted in Figures 4 and 5.

The best algorithm was MOMBI-II, outperforming the other MOEAs in 96.1% of the tests. It was followed by NSGA-III with 65.7%, both Δ_p-DDE and MOMBI-ASF with 52%, $R2$-IBEA with 26.4%, $R2$-MOGA with 18.6% and in last place is MOMBI with 5.9%.

MOMBI-II tied on two instances for 3 objectives with MOMBI-ASF and NSGA-III, producing almost identical results. On WFG6 and WFG7 for 10 objectives, MOMBI-II lost against Δ_p-DDE. As can be seen in Figure 4, the distributions of the Pareto fronts produced by MOMBI-II are more uniform than those generated by Δ_p-DDE and the other MOEAs based on the $R2$ indicator.

NSGA-III faced difficulties on multi-frontal problems for 10 objectives, being unable to reach the true Pareto front in some cases. In general, this algorithm produced similar results to those generated by MOMBI-II.

Δ_p-DDE experimented the same difficulties as NSGA-III on multi-frontal problems. Surprisingly, it won on WFG6 and WFG7 for ten objectives. Here, we suspect that differential evolution is able to produce better solutions than SBX and polynomial-based mutation. An advantage of Δ_p-DDE is that it explores more regions for many-objective problems than those algorithms based on weight vectors.

The performance of MOMBI-ASF was poor, being unable to beat NSGA-III. This indicates that the mechanism for updating the reference points plays an important role in MOMBI-II, specially for many-objective problems.

The solutions generated by $R2$-IBEA have a strong bias to the center of the Pareto front than to its edges, being similar to those generated by the hypervolume-based algorithms.

In $R2$-MOGA and MOMBI the WT metric presented difficulties in convergence in high dimensionality problems.

6. CONCLUSIONS AND FUTURE WORK

In this work, we have introduced an improved version of a MOEA based on the $R2$ indicator (called MOMBI-II), which substitutes the weighted Tchebycheff metric by the achievement scalarizing function, since the former presents difficulties for many-objective problems. Moreover, we developed a mechanism to update the reference points, required during the normalization process of the objective functions, using statistical information of the population proximity to the true Pareto optimal front. This is an important aspect since the diversity is sensitive to the choice of such points.

Experimental results indicate that the new version outperformed MOMBI, Δ_p-DDE, NSGA-III, $R2$-MOGA and $R2$-IBEA in more than the 96% of the test instances. Therefore, we believe that MOMBI-II is a suitable alternative for solving many-objective optimization problems.

It is worth noticing that the solutions produced by MOMBI-II are uniformly distributed in objective space, being similar to those generated by NSGA-III. However, MOMBI-II requires much less computational effort and the source code is in the public domain.

Much more work is still required. We are interested, for example, in studying the scalability of some other utility functions available in the literature and in incorporating a mechanism to handle constraints, in order to solve real-world problems.

Acknowledgments

The first author acknowledges support from CONACyT and CINVESTAV-IPN to pursue graduate studies in Computer Science. The second author gratefully acknowledges support from CONACyT project no. 221551.

7. REFERENCES

[1] D. Brockhoff, T. Wagner, and H. Trautmann. On the Properties of the $R2$ Indicator. In *2012 Genetic and Evolutionary Computation Conference (GECCO'2012)*, pages 465–472, Philadelphia, USA, July 2012. ACM Press. ISBN: 978-1-4503-1177-9.

[2] C. A. Coello Coello, G. B. Lamont, and D. A. Van Veldhuizen. *Evolutionary Algorithms for Solving Multi-Objective Problems*. Springer, New York, second edition, September 2007. ISBN 978-0-387-33254-3.

[3] K. Deb and R. B. Agrawal. Simulated Binary Crossover for Continuous Search Space. *Complex Systems*, 9:115–148, 1995.

[4] K. Deb and H. Jain. An Evolutionary Many-Objective Optimization Algorithm Using Reference-Point-Based Nondominated Sorting Approach, Part I: Solving Problems with Box Constraints. *Evolutionary Computation, IEEE Transactions on*, 18(4):577–601, Aug 2014.

[5] K. Deb, A. Pratap, S. Agarwal, and T. Meyarivan. A Fast and Elitist Multiobjective Genetic Algorithm: NSGA–II. *IEEE Transactions on Evolutionary Computation*, 6(2):182–197, April 2002.

[6] K. Deb, L. Thiele, M. Laumanns, and E. Zitzler. Scalable Test Problems for Evolutionary Multiobjective Optimization. In A. Abraham, L. Jain, and R. Goldberg, editors, *Evolutionary Multiobjective Optimization. Theoretical Advances and Applications*, pages 105–145. Springer, USA, 2005.

[7] A. Diaz-Manriquez, G. Toscano-Pulido, C. Coello, and R. Landa-Becerra. A Ranking Method Based on the $R2$ Indicator for Many-Objective Optimization. In *Evolutionary Computation (CEC), 2013 IEEE Congress on*, pages 1523–1530, 2013.

[8] M. P. Hansen and A. Jaszkiewicz. Evaluating the Quality of Approximations to the Non-dominated Set. Technical Report IMM-REP-1998-7, Technical University of Denmark, March 1998.

[9] R. Hernandez Gomez and C. Coello Coello. MOMBI: A New Metaheuristic for Many-Objective Optimization Based on the $R2$ Indicator. In *Evolutionary Computation (CEC), 2013 IEEE Congress on*, pages 2488–2495, 2013.

[10] S. Huband, L. Barone, L. While, and P. Hingston. A Scalable Multi-objective Test Problem Toolkit. In C. A. Coello Coello, A. Hernández Aguirre, and E. Zitzler, editors, *Evolutionary Multi-Criterion Optimization. Third International Conference, EMO 2005*, pages 280–295, Guanajuato, México, March 2005. Springer. Lecture Notes in Computer Science Vol. 3410.

[11] H. Ishibuchi, N. Tsukamoto, and Y. Nojima. Evolutionary Many-Objective Optimization: A Short Review. In *2008 Congress on Evolutionary Computation (CEC'2008)*, pages 2424–2431, Hong Kong, June 2008. IEEE Service Center.

[12] M. Kaisa. *Nonlinear Multiobjective Optimization*. Kluwer Academic Publishers, Boston, 1st edition, 1999.

[13] J. Knowles and D. Corne. On Metrics for Comparing Nondominated Sets. In *Congress on Evolutionary Computation (CEC'2002)*, volume 1, pages 711–716, Piscataway, New Jersey, May 2002. IEEE Service Center.

[14] R. G. Miller. *Simultaneous Statistical Inference*. Springer-Verlag, New York, 1981.

[15] D. H. Phan and J. Suzuki. R2-IBEA: R2 Indicator Based Evolutionary Algorithm for Multiobjective Optimization. In *Evolutionary Computation (CEC), 2013 IEEE Congress on*, pages 1836–1845, 2013.

[16] C. A. Rodríguez Villalobos and C. A. Coello Coello. A New Multi-Objective Evolutionary Algorithm Based on a Performance Assessment Indicator. In *2012 Genetic and Evolutionary Computation Conference (GECCO'2012)*, pages 505–512, Philadelphia, USA, July 2012. ACM Press. ISBN: 978-1-4503-1177-9.

[17] H. Scheffé. Experiments with Mixtures. *Journal of the Royal Statistical Society. Series B (Statistical Methodology)*, 20:344–360, 1958.

[18] O. Schütze, X. Esquivel, A. Lara, and C. A. Coello Coello. Using the Averaged Hausdorff Distance as a Performance Measure in Evolutionary Multiobjective Optimization. *IEEE Transactions on Evolutionary Computation*, 16(4):504–522, August 2012.

[19] S. Wessing and B. Naujoks. Sequential Parameter Optimization for Multi-Objective Problems. In *Evolutionary Computation (CEC), 2010 IEEE Congress on*, pages 1–8, July 2010.

[20] A. Wierzbicki. The Use of Reference Objectives in Multiobjective Optimization. In G. Fandel and T. Gal, editors, *Multiple Criteria Decision Making Theory and Application*, volume 177 of *Lecture Notes in Economics and Mathematical Systems*, pages 468–486. Springer Berlin Heidelberg, 1980.

[21] Q. Zhang and H. Li. MOEA/D: A Multiobjective Evolutionary Algorithm Based on Decomposition. *IEEE Transactions on Evolutionary Computation*, 11(6):712–731, December 2007.

[22] E. Zitzler. *Evolutionary Algorithms for Multiobjective Optimization: Methods and Applications*. PhD thesis, Swiss Federal Institute of Technology (ETH), Zurich, Switzerland, November 1999.

[23] E. Zitzler and S. Künzli. Indicator-based Selection in Multiobjective Search. In X. Y. et al., editor, *Parallel Problem Solving from Nature - PPSN VIII*, pages 832–842, Birmingham, UK, September 2004. Springer-Verlag. Lecture Notes in Computer Science Vol. 3242.

Table 2: **Median and standard deviation of the Δ_2 indicator for 3 and 5 dimensions. In each case, the outperformance relation among algorithms is shown, using a significance level of $\alpha = 0.5$ (for example, Δ_p-DDE performs significantly better than $R2$-MOGA and MOMBI on DTLZ1 for 3 objectives). The two best values are shown in gray scale, where the darker tone corresponds to the best value. The number of generations appears within parentheses in the first column.**

Problem	Δ_p-DDE 1	NSGA-III 2	$R2$-MOGA 3	$R2$-IBEA 4	MOMBI 5	MOMBI-ASF 6	MOMBI-II 7
3 Objectives							
DTLZ1 (400)	0.0252±8.60e-4 3,5	0.0220±2.25e-1 1,3,4,5	0.0352±7.00e-4 5	0.0239±2.01e-4 1,3,5	0.0361±1.32e-4 –	0.0225±6.10e-4 1,3,4,5	0.0212±9.48e-5 1,2,3,4,5,6
DTLZ2 (250)	0.0680±2.31e-3 3,4,5	0.0585±1.67e-4 1,3,4,5,6	0.0804±9.67e-4 4,5	0.0821±2.42e-3 –	0.0824±1.83e-2 –	0.0589±6.00e-4 1,3,4,5	0.0583±5.37e-4 1,3,4,5,6
DTLZ3 (1000)	0.0672±2.86e-1 3,4,5	0.0588±6.27e-4 1,3,4,5,6	0.0800±7.72e-1 4	0.0853±3.36e-3 –	0.0806±1.29e-2 4	0.0594±9.25e-3 1,3,4,5	0.0579±1.86e-4 1,2,3,4,5,6
DTLZ4 (600)	0.0685±1.87e-3 3,4,5	0.0584±3.42e-1 1,3,4,5,6	0.0829±1.50e-1 –	0.0833±2.40e-1 –	0.0827±1.50e-1 –	0.0947±1.58e-1 –	0.0578±1.12e-1 1,2,3,4,5,6
WFG6 (400)	0.3474±2.35e-2 3,4,5	0.2545±3.23e-3 1,3,4,5	0.3836±9.37e-3 5	0.3900±2.69e-2 5	0.4117±6.37e-3 –	0.2497±3.41e-3 1,2,3,4,5	0.2487±2.85e-2 1,2,3,4,5
WFG7 (400)	0.2799±1.15e-2 3,4,5	0.2420±9.81e-4 1,3,4,5	0.3878±1.11e-2 5	0.3831±2.14e-2 5	0.4073±6.03e-3 –	0.2418±2.21e-3 1,3,4,5	0.2402±1.18e-3 1,2,3,4,5,6
5 Objectives							
DTLZ1 (600)	0.0677±2.86e-3 3,5,6	0.0668±1.34e-3 1,3,4,5,6	0.1190±6.22e-4 5	0.0686±4.98e-4 3,5,6	0.1199±2.12e-2 –	0.0730±5.03e-3 3,5	0.0629±2.62e-4 1,2,3,4,5,6
DTLZ2 (350)	0.2113±2.69e-3 3,4,5	0.2092±1.32e-4 1,3,4,5,6	0.3376±5.32e-4 5	0.2271±2.16e-3 3,5	0.3397±2.51e-4 –	0.2107±3.69e-3 3,4,5	0.2051±7.87e-4 1,2,3,4,5,6
DTLZ3 (1000)	0.2117±7.44e+1 3,4,5,6	0.2098±6.89e-3 1,3,4,5,6	0.3379±1.02e-3 5	0.2252±3.65e-3 3,5	0.3402±8.10e-2 –	0.2136±4.30e-3 3,4,5	0.2049±9.29e-4 1,2,3,4,5,6
DTLZ4 (1000)	0.2146±2.97e-3 3,4,5,6	0.2091±1.91e-1 5	0.3368±7.38e-2 5	0.2281±7.33e-2 3,5,6	0.3396±8.80e-2 –	0.2644±1.00e-1 3,5	0.2038±1.18e-1 1,2,3,4,5,6
WFG6 (750)	1.3321±3.05e-2 3,4,5	1.2564±2.46e-3 1,3,4,5,6	3.3935±1.19e-1 –	1.4415±3.73e-2 3,5	2.3444±1.90e-2 3	1.2619±1.42e-2 1,3,4,5	1.2416±3.18e-3 1,2,3,4,5,6
WFG7 (750)	1.3953±1.92e-2 3,4,5	1.2657±1.66e-2 1,3,4,5,6	2.3404±1.60e-2 5	1.4255±2.67e-2 3,5	2.4201±7.19e-2 –	1.3384±2.46e-2 1,3,4,5	1.2477±4.76e-3 1,2,3,4,5,6

Table 3: **Median and standard deviation of the Δ_2 indicator for 10 objectives (continuation).**

Problem	Δ_p-DDE 1	NSGA-III 2	$R2$-MOGA 3	MOMBI 5	MOMBI-ASF 6	MOMBI-II 7
DTLZ1 (1000)	9.9311±7.45e+0 –	0.2113±2.78e+0 1	0.1569±1.32e-1 1,5,6	0.1647±9.54e-3 1,6	0.2087±2.74e-2 1	0.1235±1.08e-2 1,2,3,5,6
DTLZ2 (750)	0.4208±3.92e-3 2,3,5,6	0.4290±2.59e-1 3,5,6	0.6355±1.84e-2 5	0.6633±3.37e-2 –	0.4703±1.70e-2 3,5	0.4156±3.25e-4 1,2,3,5,6
DTLZ3 (1500)	512.7180±1.02e+2 –	0.9053±2.20e+0 1	0.6714±1.97e+0 1	0.6885±3.66e-2 1,2	0.4777±6.93e-2 1,2,3,5	0.4151±4.65e-2 1,2,3,5,6
DTLZ4 (2000)	0.4417±3.76e-3 3,5	0.4280±1.29e-1 1,3,5	0.6419±2.47e-2 5	0.6804±1.53e-2 –	0.4329±2.26e-2 1,3,5	0.4148±4.98e-2 1,2,3,5,6
WFG6 (2000)	4.6238±8.11e-2 2,3,5,6,7	4.8552±5.55e-3 3,5,6	7.3007±4.91e-1 5	7.6871±3.62e-1 –	5.2036±4.38e-2 3,5	4.7527±6.55e-3 2,3,5,6
WFG7 (2000)	4.5544±8.74e-2 2,3,5,6,7	4.9397±9.26e-1 3,5,6	7.7848±3.87e-1 5	7.8535±3.91e-1 –	5.8264±4.89e-1 3,5	4.7688±3.13e-2 2,3,5,6

Parallel Multi-Objective Evolutionary Design of Approximate Circuits

Radek Hrbacek
Brno University of Technology, Czech republic
Faculty of Information Technology
ihrbacek@fit.vutbr.cz

ABSTRACT

Evolutionary design of digital circuits has been well established in recent years. Besides correct functionality, the demands placed on current circuits include the area of the circuit and its power consumption. By relaxing the functionality requirement, one can obtain more efficient circuits in terms of the area or power consumption at the cost of an error introduced to the output of the circuit. As a result, a variety of trade-offs between error and efficiency can be found. In this paper, a multi-objective evolutionary algorithm for the design of approximate digital circuits is proposed. The scalability of the evolutionary design has been recently improved using parallel implementation of the fitness function and by employing spatially structured evolutionary algorithms. The proposed multi-objective approach uses Cartesian Genetic Programming for the circuit representation and a modified NSGA-II algorithm. Multiple isolated islands are evolving in parallel and the populations are periodically merged and new populations are distributed across the islands. The method is evaluated in the task of approximate arithmetical circuits design.

Categories and Subject Descriptors

B.6.0 [**Hardware**]: Logic Design—*General*; I.2.8 [**Computing methodologies**]: Artificial intelligence—*Problem Solving, Control Methods, and Search*

Keywords

Cartesian Genetic Programming; Parallel Evolutionary Algorithms; Multi-objective Optimization; Cluster; Combinational Circuit Design; Approximate Circuits

1. INTRODUCTION

While evolutionary design of digital circuits has been well established in the past, the correct functionality has always been an essential requirement put on the circuits. The other parameters, like the area, delay or power consumption, have been considered as secondary and have not been optimized as long as a fully working solution has been found. Recently, power efficiency has become the most important parameter of many real circuits. At the same time, a wide range of applications capable of tolerating imperfections (e.g. multimedia) has spread out. As a consequence, a new research field has been brought into being – the *approximate computing* [3].

The approximate digital circuits are designed in such a way that the functionality specification is not fully met in exchange for savings in terms of area, delay, power consumption etc. Although the circuit is not working properly, it can still be suitable for applications in which certain level of error is not recognizable (e.g. human perception and multimedia applications). Moreover, in some cases (e.g. low battery), the users could knowingly tolerate even more inaccuracy in order to extend the battery life.

After the first manual attempts to circuit approximation suffering from low scalability and efficiency [2, 7], a new class of systematic methods has been developed. The Systematic methodology for Automatic Logic Synthesis (SALSA) uses a quality function which decides whether a predefined quality constraint is met. The algorithm is allowed to modify the circuit as long as the quality constraint is not exceeded [19]. Another approach, Substitute-and-Simplify (SASIMI), looks for signal pairs having similar values with a high probability. By substituting one signal for the other, a part of the circuit can be removed resulting in area and power savings at the cost of an error introduced to the output [18].

The aforementioned methods have to be applied repeatedly with different error constraints if a set of trade-offs is demanded. In this paper, we propose a multi-objective evolutionary design approach which is capable of providing a whole set of trade-offs between a set of conflicting objectives. The proposed method is based on Cartesian Genetic Programming (CGP), widely used for the design of digital circuits, and a modified NSGA-II algorithm providing the multi-objective approach.

Since the evolutionary design is very computationally demanding [6], much emphasis has been put to the parallel implementation of the method. In order to make full use of a computer cluster, a spatially structured evolutionary algorithm has been introduced to the design process.

The proposed method has been evaluated in the task of approximate arithmetical circuits design with respect to three objectives – error, area and latency.

GECCO'15, July 11-15, 2015, Madrid, Spain.
Copyright 2015 ACM 978-1-4503-3472-3/15/07 ...$15.00.
http://dx.doi.org/10.1145/2739480.2754785

2. EVOLUTIONARY DESIGN OF DIGITAL CIRCUITS

In our previous work, we used Cartesian genetic programming to either design digital circuits from scratch [6] or to optimize existing circuits [14]. CGP, a branch of genetic programming, has been introduced by Miller [9]. While GP uses tree representation, an individual in CGP is represented by a directed acyclic graph of a fixed size. The candidate solution can have multiple outputs and intermediate results can be reused, which makes CGP very suitable for the design of digital circuits, e.g. arithmetic and logic circuits, digital filters, cryptography related Boolean functions, etc. [10, 5].

CGP uses a fixed-sized cartesian grid of $n_r \times n_c$ nodes interconnected by a feed-forward network (see Figure 1). Node inputs can be connected either to one of n_i primary inputs or to an output of a node in preceding l columns. Each node has a fixed number of inputs n_{ni} (usually $n_{ni} = 2$) and can perform one of the functions from the set Γ. Each of n_o primary circuit outputs can be connected either to a primary input or to a node's output. The area and delay of the circuit can be constrained by changing the grid size and the l-back parameter.

The genotype is of fixed length, whereas the phenotype is of variable length depending on the number of inactive nodes, i.e. nodes whose output is not used by any other node or primary output. This implies the existence of individuals with different genotypes but the same phenotypes, which is usually referred to as neutrality [20]. It was shown that for certain problems the neutrality significantly reduces the computational effort and helps to find more innovative solutions [8].

CGP uses a simple mutation based $(1 + \lambda)$ evolutionary strategy as a search mechanism. The population size $1 + \lambda$ is mostly very small, typically, $\lambda = 4$. The initial population is constructed either randomly (evolutionary design) or by mapping of a known solution to the CGP chromosome (evolutionary optimization). In each generation, the best individual is passed to the next generation unmodified along with its λ offspring individuals created by means of point mutation operator. In case more individuals with the best fitness exist, a randomly selected one is chosen. The mutation rate m is usually set to modify up to 5 % randomly selected genes.

In the case of digital circuit evolution, the fitness function usually corresponds to the quality of the candidate circuit measured as the number of correct output bits compared to a specified truth table (i.e. the Hamming distance). In order to obtain a fully working circuit, all combinations of input values have to be evaluated. For a circuit with n_i inputs and n_o outputs, 2^{n_i} test vectors need to be fetched to the primary inputs and $n_o \cdot 2^{n_i}$ output bits have to be verified so as to compute the fitness value.

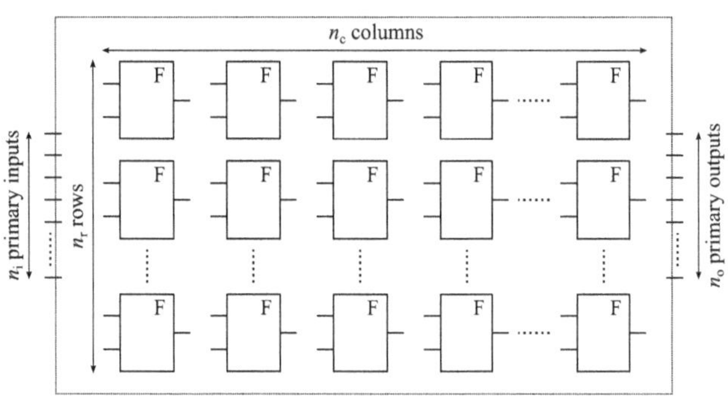

Figure 1: Cartesian genetic programming scheme.

The fitness calculation is computationally very intensive, since the number of test vectors grows exponentially with the number of primary inputs. Recently, it has been sped up by applying parallelism at various levels (data, thread, process) [6, 5] or by introducing formal methods, e.g. SAT solvers [14] or Binary Decision Diagrams (BDD) [16].

Besides the correct functionality, the demands placed on current digital circuits include the area of the circuit and its power consumption. The power consumption of digital circuits consists of two major components – the static and the dynamic power dissipation. The dynamic dissipation occurs while changing the state of the gates and thus it is highly dependent on the character of the gate's input signals. On the contrary, the static power consumption is rather constant and depends on the area of the circuit. The static dissipation has been substantially reduced by introducing the CMOS technology, which uses complementary connected transistors. However, with the decreasing size of the semiconductor technology process, the static dissipation is increasing due to rising leakage currents and is becoming the major component of the power consumption. Therefore, when evolving digital circuits with respect to the power consumption, the area of the circuit can be used to estimate the power consumption [13].

Another important characteristic of a digital circuit is the latency, i.e. the interval between the stimulation of the inputs and the response on the outputs. The latency can be determined by finding the longest path from the inputs to the outputs with respect to particular latencies of the gates along the path. Since the propagation delay of a gate differs for different transitions on the inputs, computing the total circuit latency would require simulating all possible input transitions on the whole circuit. The number of different transitions N_t grows rapidly with the number of primary inputs n_i: $N_t = 2^{n_i} \cdot (2^{n_i} - 1)$. Applying all these combinations is computationally intensive, therefore, an estimation must be used instead. In this paper, we assign each node function a fixed latency. When computing the overall circuit latency, the longest path from an input to an output considering the latencies of all gates along the path is considered.

2.1 Approximate circuits

Many computer systems or programs have the ability to tolerate some loss of accuracy or quality in the computational process and still produce meaningful and useful results. Significant area or energy-efficiency improvements can be achieved by relaxing the functionality requirement. For example, the growing popularity of portable multimedia devices offers a great scope for approximate computation, since human perception is limited and the users are ready to tolerate degraded quality of the multimedia content (e.g. video playback) in exchange for longer battery life. Automatic approximate computing techniques are being developed to speed up the design process and to find the trade-offs between the resources being shrunk (e.g. energy, time, area) and the inaccuracy of the computation.

Recently, several single-objective evolutionary approaches to design approximate circuits have been introduced [12]. Different error metrics have been utilized, starting with the

Hamming distance and introducing new metrics more suitable for arithmetical circuits, e.g. the worst case error, mean absolute error, relative error etc. [15]. In this paper, we use a compromise error metric which penalizes both the mean error and the isolated deviations – the mean squared error:

$$f_{\text{mse}} := \frac{\sum_{\forall i}\left(O^{(i)}_{\text{orig}} - O^{(i)}_{\text{approx}}\right)^2}{2^{n_i}}, \quad (1)$$

where $O^{(i)}_{\text{orig}}$ is the decimal representation of the i-th circuit correct output and $O^{(i)}_{\text{approx}}$ is the individual's i-th output. The choice, which error metric to use, always depends on a concrete application.

Although several attempts to use multi-objective evolutionary algorithms exist [11], recent techniques have been based mainly on multi-phase single-objective approaches [15] or have used constrained resources in order to find approximate circuits with smaller area or power consumption [12, 17].

3. MULTI-OBJECTIVE CGP

Unlike the single-objective optimization, which enables to compare any two candidate solutions and decide which one is better, the multi-objective optimization leads to the existence of a whole range of trade-off solutions, if the objectives are conflicting. In the case of digital circuits design, the better the circuit works, the larger area and power consumption it has.

Many multi-objective evolutionary algorithms have been proposed, most of them are based on the idea of *Pareto dominance.* The solution p *dominates* the solution q if p is no worse than q in all objectives and p is strictly better than q in at least one objective. The principle can be seen in Figure 2, the Pareto optimal solutions are not dominated by any other solutions and form the so called *Pareto front.*

3.1 NSGA-II and its modifications

One of the most popular multi-objective evolutionary algorithms is the Non-dominated Sorting Genetic Algorithm II (NSGA-II) [1]. It is based on sorting individuals according to the dominance relation into multiple fronts. The first front F_0 contains all Pareto optimal solutions. Each subsequent front F_i is constructed by removing all the preceding fronts from the population and finding a new Pareto front. Each solution is assigned a *rank* according to the front it belongs to, the solutions from the front F_i have the rank equal to i. The NSGA-II fast non-dominated sort (see Algorithm 1) is very efficient, the overall complexity is $\mathcal{O}(MN^2)$, where N is the population size and M is the number of objectives.

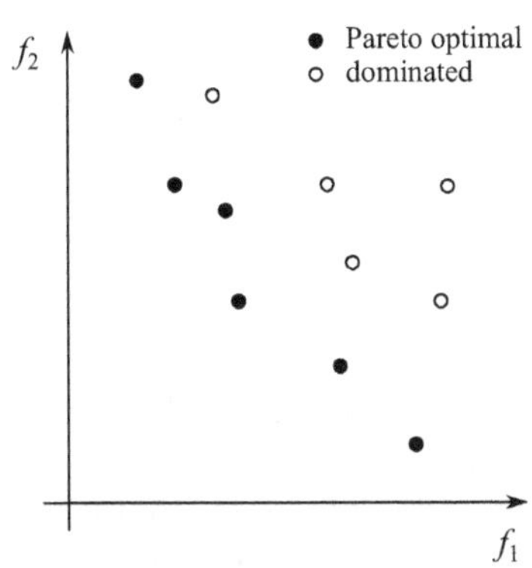

Figure 2: Pareto optimal and dominated solutions.

```
fast-non-dominated-sort(P)
foreach p ∈ P do
    F0 = ∅
    Sp = ∅
    np = 0
    foreach q ∈ P do
        if p ≺ q then
            Sp = Sp ∪ {q}
        end
        else if q ≺ p then
            np = np + 1
        end
    end
    if np = 0 then
        p_rank = 0
        F0 = F0 ∪ {p}
    end
end
i = 0
while Fi ≠ ∅ do
    Q = ∅
    foreach p ∈ Fi do
        foreach q ∈ Sp do
            nq = nq − 1
            if nq = 0 then
                q_rank = i + 1
                Q = Q ∪ {q}
            end
        end
    end
    i = i + 1
    Fi = Q
end
F = (F0, F1, ...)
return F
```

Algorithm 1: Fast non-dominated sort.

The solutions within the individual fronts are sorted according to the *crowding distance* metric, which helps to preserve a reasonable diversity along the fronts [1]. The crowding distance is the average distance of two solutions on either side along each of the objectives. The boundary solutions are assigned an infinite crowding distance, which ensures that these solutions will dominate the inner solutions (see Algorithm 2).

```
crowding-distance-assignment(P)
l = |I|
foreach p ∈ P do
    p_dist = 0
end
foreach objective m do
    P = sort(P, m)
    P[0]_dist = ∞
    P[l − 1]_dist = ∞ for i in 1 to l − 2 do
        P[i]_dist = P[i]_dist +
            (P[i + 1]_m − P[i − 1]_m)/(f_m^max − f_m^min)
    end
end
```

Algorithm 2: Crowding distance assignment.

Any solution from the front F_i always dominate any solution from $F_j, j > i$. Within the fronts, solutions with higher crowding distance are preferred.

Most real applications require to be able to constraint the solutions on particular objectives. NSGA-II offers a simple way to handle the constraints and keep the algorithm complexity low. Each solution can be either *feasible* or *infeasible*, the infeasible solutions are assigned a *constraint violation* according to the Algorithm 3. The constraints on the objective m are denoted by $\langle c_m^{\min}, c_m^{\max} \rangle$.

constraint-violation-assignment(P)
foreach $p \in P$ **do**
  $p_{\text{constr\_viol}} = 0$
  foreach *objective* m **do**
    if $p_m < c_m^{\min}$ **then**
      $p_{\text{constr\_viol}} = p_{\text{constr\_viol}} + (c_m^{\min} - p_m)/f_m^{\max}$
    end
    if $p_m > c_m^{\max}$ **then**
      $p_{\text{constr\_viol}} = p_{\text{constr\_viol}} + (p_m - c_m^{\max})/f_m^{\max}$
    end
  end
end

Algorithm 3: Constraint violation assignment.

When comparing two solutions, a feasible solution is always preferred. If both solutions are infeasible, the solution with smaller constraint violation is better. In the opposite case, when both solutions are feasible, the dominance depends on the rank and the crowding distance.

Since the original NSGA-II algorithm was based on a genetic algorithm, there must have been changes to use it with CGP [4, 11]. Firstly, due to the absence of the crossover operator in CGP, the offspring population is constructed only using mutation. Secondly, the crowding distance is often not sufficient for CGP to maintain the diversity of the population. The neutrality present in CGP causes a premature convergence, the Pareto fronts are flooded by individuals that are genotypically distinct but phenotypically identical. We propose to introduce a new *equivalence rank*, which enables to put the equivalent solutions in an order and preserve the neutrality character of the CGP. The principle can be seen from Algorithm 4. At the beginning, the population is randomly shuffled. Then, for each individual, the equivalence rank of all individuals (except for already processed ones) with the same fitnesses is incremented.

equivalence-rank-assignment(P)
foreach $p \in P$ **do**
  $p_{\text{eq\_rank}} = 0$
end
random_shuffle(P)
$Q = P$
foreach $p \in P$ **do**
  $Q = Q \setminus \{p\}$
  foreach $q \in Q$ **do**
    if $p \equiv q$ **then**
      $q_{\text{eq\_rank}} = q_{\text{eq\_rank}} + 1$
    end
  end
end

Algorithm 4: Equivalence rank assignment.

When comparing two individuals, the individual with a lower equivalence rank always dominates the other one. Two individuals with the same equivalence rank are compared using the standard constrained-domination rules. As a consequence, none of the fronts contains individuals with the same fitness and the dominance relation among the individuals with the same fitness is random.

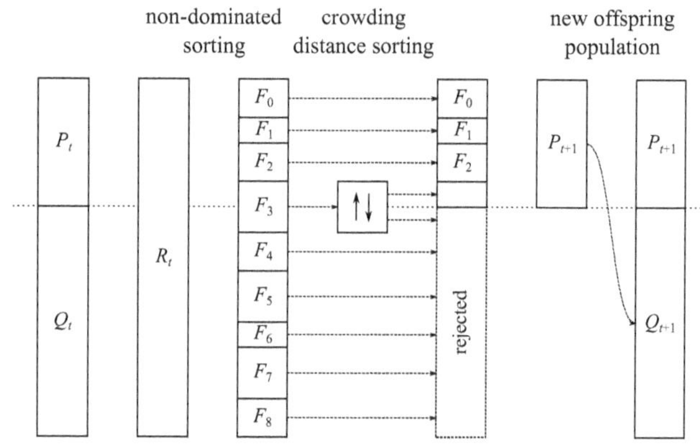

Figure 3: NSGA-II algorithm scheme.

Unlike the original NSGA-II algorithm, which uses a population of parents P and an offspring population Q, both of size N, our modification enables us to set the offspring size independently. In each generation, N_{p} individuals are selected as parents and N_{q} offspring individuals are created by means of mutation. Besides the tournament selection, we use a new deterministic selection mechanism, which cyclically takes the individuals from the parent population P and creates mutants.

The aforementioned principles make the multi-objective approach even more similar to the standard CGP. The overall algorithm works as follows:

nsga-ii(P_t, Q_t)
$R_t = P_t \cup Q_t$
equivalence-rank-assignment(R_t)
constraint-violation-assignment(R_t)
$F =$ fast-non-dominated-sort(R_t)
$P_{t+1} = \emptyset$
$i = 0$
while $|P_{t+1}| + |F_i| \leq N_{\text{p}}$ **do**
  crowding-distance-assignment(F_i)
  $P_{t+1} = P_{t+1} \cup F_i$
  $i = i + 1$
end
crowding-distance-assignment(F_i)
sort(F_i, $\prec_{\text{n}}$)
$P_{t+1} = P_{t+1} \cup F_i\,[0 : (N_{\text{p}} - |P_{t+1}| - 1)]$
$Q_{t+1} =$ create-offspring(P_{t+1})
$t = t + 1$

Algorithm 5: Modified NSGA-II.

In each generation t, the populations P_t and Q_t form an unified population R_t. The individuals in R_t are assigned the equivalence rank and the crowding distance. Then, the Pareto fronts are identified and the new parental population P_{t+1} is filled with the individuals from the first fronts until P_{t+1} is not overcrowded. The individuals from the last used Pareto front are sorted using the crowding distance and a fraction of them is selected just to fill the population P_{t+1} (Figure 3).

4. PARALLEL MULTI-OBJECTIVE CGP

The evolutionary design is a very computationally demanding approach. In order to reduce the design time, one has to deal with a parallel implementation of the fitness function or search algorithm modifications. In our previous work, we have introduced parallelism at various levels (instruction, data, thread and process) to the CGP and sped up the design process significantly [6, 5]. However, the work was focused on single-objective design of (non-approximate) digital circuits having several specifics, e.g. small population size or the Hamming distance as the fitness function.

In the case of approximate arithmetical circuits, the fitness function (Equation 1) is much more computationally demanding and the implementation much less efficient. On the other hand, the population size of the multi-objective approach is much bigger, which makes the parallel processing of the individuals more efficient.

Besides the parallel implementation of the fitness evaluation, additional speed-up can be achieved by employing spatially structured evolutionary algorithms. Since CGP does not use any crossover operator, there is not a large scope of methods. However, a simple isolated islands model with a periodical exchange of the best individuals across the islands has been confirmed to be beneficial [6].

We propose to extend the multi-objective approach by introducing the isolated islands model. Unlike the single-objective case, the multi-objective algorithm requires to exchange the whole population. The Algorithm 6 is very similar to the single-population case, the only difference is that each G_r generations the populations are unified across the islands and a common Pareto front is identified on each island. Since the equivalence rank is assigned randomly to the individuals with the same fitness, the Pareto fronts on individual islands are phenotypically identical, but genotypically distinct. This principle should avoid the algorithm to converge prematurely and help to preserve the diversity across the populations.

```
nsga-ii-islands(P_t, Q_t)
R_t = P_t ∪ Q_t
if t mod G_r = 0 then
  | R_t = MPI_Allgather(R_t)
end
equivalence-rank-assignment(R_t)
constraint-violation-assignment(R_t)
F = fast-non-dominated-sort(R_t)
P_{t+1} = ∅
i = 0
while |P_{t+1}| + |F_i| ≤ N_p do
  | crowding-distance-assignment(F_i)
  | P_{t+1} = P_{t+1} ∪ F_i
  | i = i + 1
end
crowding-distance-assignment(F_i)
sort(F_i, ≺_n)
P_{t+1} = P_{t+1} ∪ F_i [0 : (N_p − |P_{t+1}| − 1)]
Q_{t+1} = create-offspring(P_{t+1})
t = t + 1
```

Algorithm 6: NSGA-II with the isolated islands model.

5. EXPERIMENTAL RESULTS

In this section, experiments regarding the multi-objective design of arithmetical circuits are presented and the proposed modifications to the NSGA-II algorithm are examined. All experiments were performed on a computer cluster of 180 nodes with the following hardware configuration: 2× 8-core Intel E5-2665, 64 GB RAM, connected by Infiniband links. Each node was fully loaded with 16 threads, the evaluation of the population was parallelized using OpenMP.

The circuits were design with respect to 3 objectives – the mean squared error (as defined in Equation 1), the area of the circuit (approximate number of transistors considering common CMOS gates) and the latency (see Section 2). The CGP parameters were set similarly to the single-objective case [6], i.e. $\Gamma = \{\mathtt{BUF}, \mathtt{NOT}, \mathtt{AND}, \mathtt{OR}, \mathtt{XOR}, \mathtt{NAND}, \mathtt{NOR}, \mathtt{XNOR}\}$ and the mutation rate was set to 5 %, we used a linear CGP ($n_r = 1$). The number of columns was $n_c = 800$ in the case of the 4-bit multiplier and $n_c = 100$ in the case of the adder. All experimental results were obtained by running 100 independent evolutionary runs.

5.1 Selection type

In Section 3.1, we have proposed a modification to the NSGA-II selection mechanism – a new deterministic selection. Furthermore, the offspring size N_q is not necessarily equal to the parental population size N_p. In order to draw a comparison between the original tournament selection and the new deterministic selection, a number of experiments were carried out, the task was to design a combinational 4-bit multiplier.

The parental population size was set to $N_p = 50$ and the offspring size was $N_q \in \{50, 60, \ldots, 150\}$, the generation count was $G = 5000$. The same experiments were run for both tournament and deterministic selection.

The results can be seen in Figure 4. The quality of the resulting Pareto front was measured in terms of the Pareto front size (number of individuals) and the best error achieved. No matter how imperfect such comparison is, some trends can be inferred. The tournament selection is beneficial in the

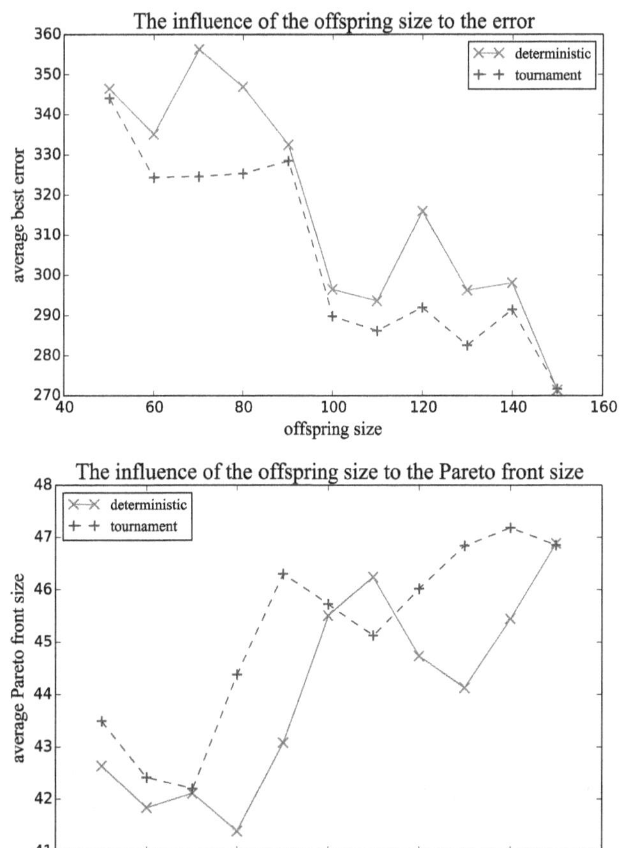

Figure 4: The influence of the offspring size.

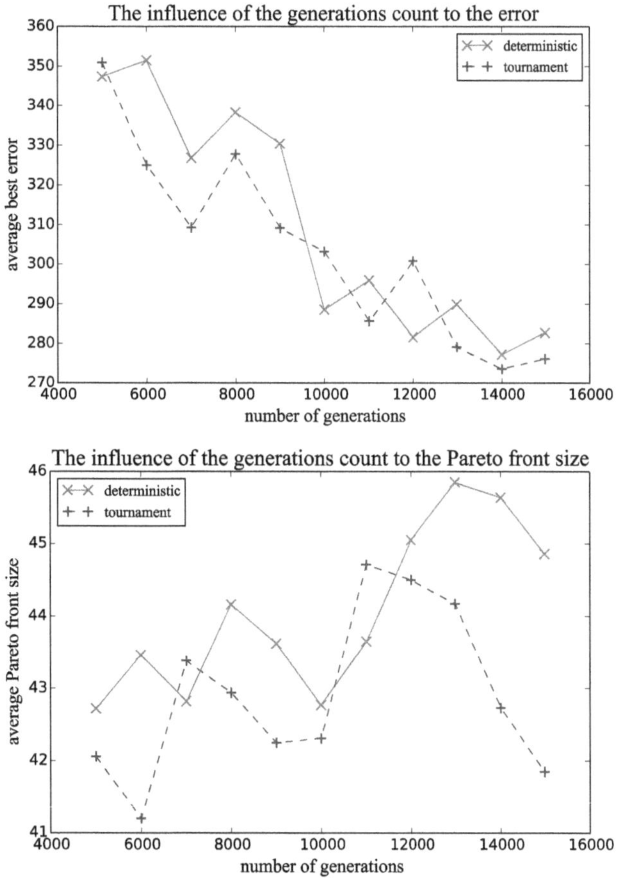

Figure 5: The influence of the number of generations.

cases, when N_q is not an integer multiple of N_p. Otherwise, both selection types evince about the same performance.

Similarly to the single-objective case, one can adjust the number of generation and the population size so as the computational effort is the same. In our second experiment, the population size was fixed ($N_p = 50$, $N_q = 50$), but the number of generations was $G \in \{5000, 6000, \ldots, 15000\}$.

As can be seen in Figure 5, there is no conclusive difference between the two selection types. However, when comparing with the previous experiment (Figure 4), increasing the offspring size seems to be slightly more advantageous than increasing the number of generations.

5.2 Number of Islands

Recently, we have shown that a spatially structured evolutionary algorithm can speed up the evolutionary design of combinational circuits in comparison with a single-population process [6]. The Figure 6 shows the influence of the number of islands on the mean error achieved during the evolutionary design of a 4-bit multiplier. The single-population approach was compared to the multiple islands model with 2, 4 and 8 islands. The populations (each of $N_p = 100$ parental and $N_q = 100$ offspring individuals) were exchanged every $G_r = 500$ generations across the islands. It can be seen that increasing the number of islands significantly reduces the mean error during the whole evolutionary process. The more islands, the less generations is needed to achieve comparable results.

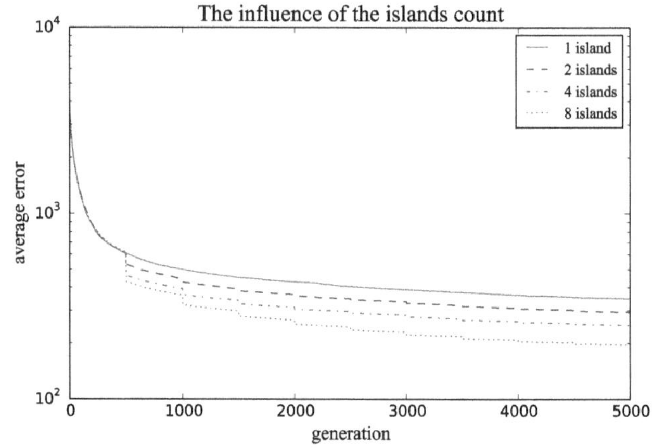

Figure 6: The influence of the number of islands.

5.3 Examples of Evolved Circuits

In this section, the proposed multi-objective approach is demonstrated on two examples of arithmetical circuits. Figure 8 shows the Pareto front of approximate 4-bit multipliers obtained after 1000000 generations. The population size was set to $N_p = 100$ parental and $N_q = 300$ offspring individuals and tournament selection was used to create the offspring population. Eight islands were exchanging the populations every $G_r = 1000$ generations. At the end of the evolution, 66 trade-off solutions were found having the mean squared error from 46.16 to 153.75, the area from 0 to 512 transistors and the latency from 0 to 19 gates. The extremely erroneous solutions are not shown in the Pareto front in Figure 8. Table 1 shows the output errors for all input combinations.

The same experimental setup was used for the design of combinational 4-bit adders. Since combinational adders are much less complex circuits than the multipliers, the number of generations was set to 100000. The resulting Pareto front can be seen in Figure 9, Table 2 shows the output errors for the individual with the lowest error. In comparison with the multiplier, the error is significantly smaller and the circuit has much smaller area (70 transistors) and latency (3 gates). The wiring diagram is depicted in Figure 7.

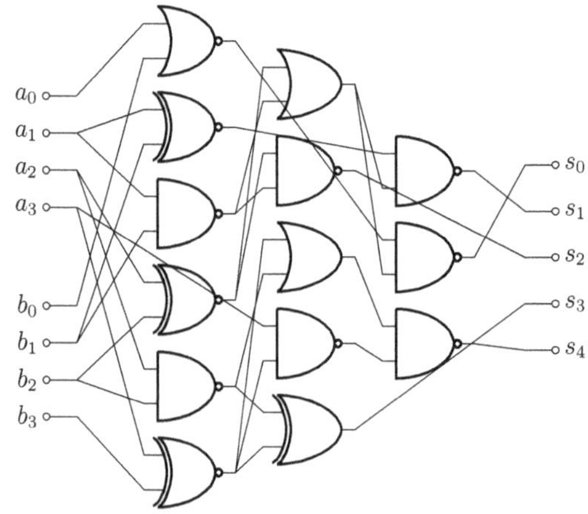

Figure 7: The best 4-bit adder diagram.

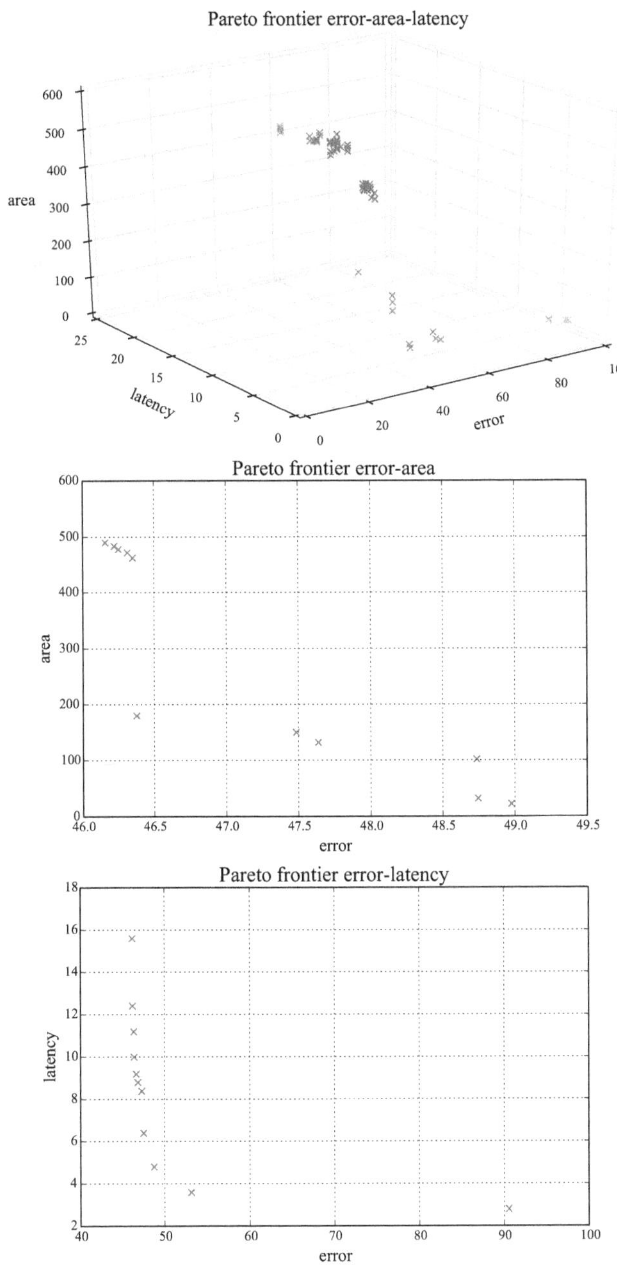

Figure 8: Combinational 4-bit multiplier.

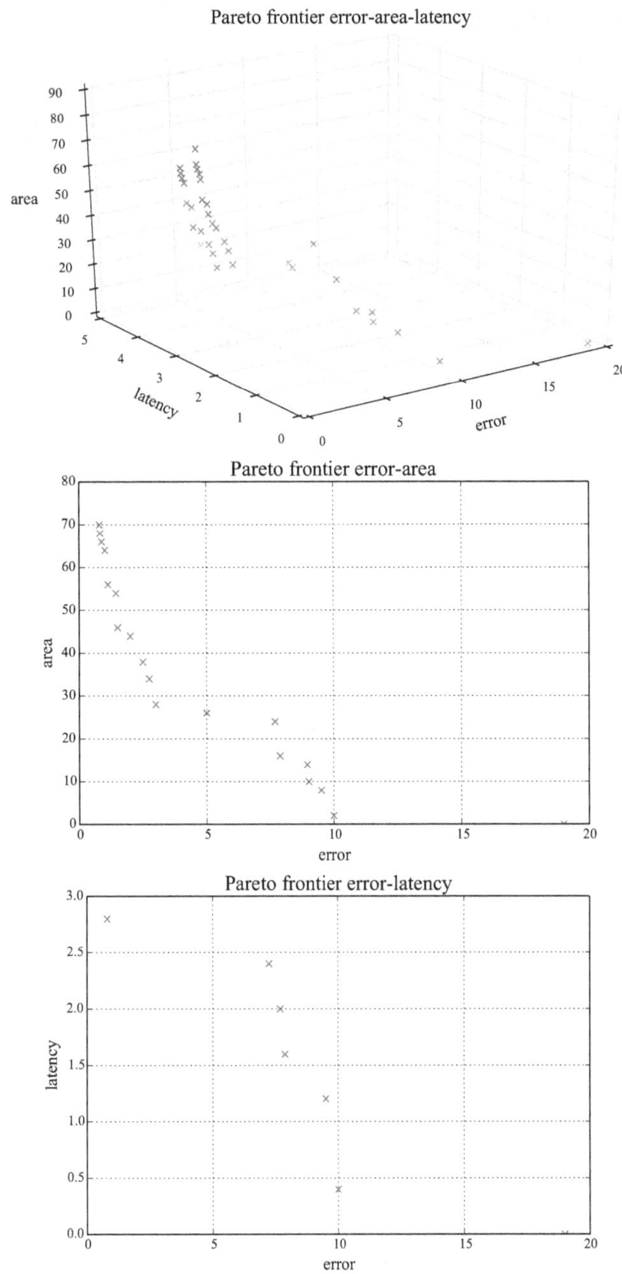

Figure 9: Combinational 4-bit adder.

·	0	1	2	3	4	5	6	7	8	9	10	11	12	13	14	15
0	0	0	0	0	0	0	0	0	0	0	0	0	0	0	0	0
1	0	-1	0	-1	0	-1	0	-1	0	-1	0	-1	0	-1	0	-1
2	0	2	0	1	0	2	0	1	0	2	0	1	0	2	0	1
3	0	1	1	-2	0	0	-3	-6	0	1	1	-2	-5	-8	-11	-14
4	0	0	0	0	0	1	0	3	0	0	0	0	0	0	0	0
5	0	-1	0	0	0	-2	0	-4	-1	2	-3	-8	-5	-2	-7	-12
6	0	-1	0	-3	0	1	-5	-11	0	-1	0	-3	8	2	4	1
7	0	0	1	-6	0	-4	-11	-18	-1	0	-7	-14	0	1	-3	-10
8	0	0	0	0	0	0	0	0	0	0	0	0	0	0	0	0
9	0	1	0	1	0	-1	2	0	0	-3	0	-4	3	-6	1	-8
10	0	2	0	1	0	-3	3	-7	0	3	-5	-15	0	-3	-13	-23
11	0	3	0	-2	0	-8	-3	-14	0	-4	-15	-26	-5	-16	-27	-38
12	0	0	0	-5	0	0	8	4	0	0	0	-5	16	4	0	1
13	0	1	0	-8	0	-2	2	1	-1	-6	-3	-16	4	-1	2	-4
14	0	-1	3	-11	0	-7	0	-3	0	-1	-13	-27	8	1	-5	-19
15	0	0	1	-14	0	-12	-3	-10	-1	-8	-23	-38	0	-4	14	-1

Table 1: Error table for the best multiplier.

+	0	1	2	3	4	5	6	7	8	9	10	11	12	13	14	15
0	0	0	0	0	0	0	0	0	0	0	0	0	0	0	0	0
1	0	-1	0	-1	0	-1	0	-1	0	-1	0	-1	0	-1	0	-1
2	0	0	0	0	0	0	-1	-2	0	0	0	0	0	0	-1	-2
3	0	-1	0	-1	0	-1	-2	-3	0	-1	0	-1	0	-1	-2	-3
4	0	0	0	0	0	0	0	0	0	0	0	0	0	0	0	0
5	0	-1	0	-1	0	-1	0	-1	0	-1	0	-1	0	-1	0	-1
6	0	0	-1	-2	0	0	0	0	0	0	-1	-2	0	0	0	0
7	0	-1	-2	-3	0	-1	0	-1	0	-1	-2	-3	0	-1	0	-1
8	0	0	0	0	0	0	0	0	0	0	0	0	0	0	0	0
9	0	-1	0	-1	0	-1	0	-1	0	-1	0	-1	0	-1	0	-1
10	0	0	0	0	0	0	-1	-2	0	0	0	0	0	0	-1	-2
11	0	-1	0	-1	0	-1	-2	-3	0	-1	0	-1	0	-1	-2	-3
12	0	0	0	0	0	0	0	0	0	0	0	0	0	0	0	0
13	0	-1	0	-1	0	-1	0	-1	0	-1	0	-1	0	-1	0	-1
14	0	0	-1	-2	0	0	0	0	0	0	-1	-2	0	0	0	0
15	0	-1	-2	-3	0	-1	0	-1	0	-1	-2	-3	0	-1	0	-1

Table 2: Error table for the best adder.

6. CONCLUSIONS

Recently, a new application area for evolutionary algorithms has emerged, EAs have been confirmed to be competitive in the task of approximate circuits design [17]. The evolutionary design is a computationally demanding task, therefore, several approaches to speed up the entire process have been proposed [6].

In this paper, a new multi-objective evolutionary method for designing approximate digital circuits has been presented. The method is based on the well-known NSGA-II algorithm modified in order to be more suitable for the use with CGP. Besides a parallel implementation of the population fitness evaluation, a simple spatially structured algorithm is introduced for the purpose of speeding up the evolutionary process.

The proposed method has been evaluated in the task of approximate combinational multiplier and adder design. In comparison with existing methods, the multi-objective approach enables to obtain a set of Pareto optimal solutions in a single run.

In our future research, we will focus on increasing the scalability of the method in order to be able to design more complex circuits. For that purpose, the fitness function needs to be accelerated.

7. ACKNOWLEDGMENTS

This work was supported by the Czech Science Foundation project 14-04197S. The author thanks the IT4Innovations Centre of Excellence for enabling these experiments.

8. REFERENCES

[1] K. Deb, A. Pratap, S. Agarwal, and T. Meyarivan. A fast and elitist multiobjective genetic algorithm: Nsga-ii, Apr. 2002.

[2] V. Gupta, D. Mohapatra, A. Raghunathan, and K. Roy. Low-power digital signal processing using approximate adders. *Computer-Aided Design of Integrated Circuits and Systems, IEEE Transactions on*, 32(1):124–137, Jan 2013.

[3] J. Han and M. Orshansky. Approximate computing: An emerging paradigm for energy-efficient design. In *Test Symposium (ETS), 2013 18th IEEE European*, pages 1–6, May 2013.

[4] J. Hilder, J. Walker, and A. Tyrrell. Use of a multi-objective fitness function to improve cartesian genetic programming circuits. In *Adaptive Hardware and Systems (AHS), 2010 NASA/ESA Conference on*, pages 179–185, June 2010.

[5] R. Hrbacek. Bent functions synthesis on xeon phi coprocessor. In *Mathematical and Engineering Methods in Computer Science*, LNCS 8934, pages 88–99. Springer Verlag, 2014.

[6] R. Hrbacek and L. Sekanina. Towards highly optimized cartesian genetic programming: From sequential via simd and thread to massive parallel implementation. In *GECCO '14 Proceedings of the 2014 conference on Genetic and evolutionary computation*, pages 1015–1022. Association for Computing Machinery, 2014.

[7] P. Kulkarni, P. Gupta, and M. Ercegovac. Trading accuracy for power with an underdesigned multiplier architecture. In *VLSI Design (VLSI Design), 2011 24th International Conference on*, pages 346–351, Jan 2011.

[8] J. Miller and S. Smith. Redundancy and computational efficiency in cartesian genetic programming. *Evolutionary Computation, IEEE Transactions on*, 10(2):167–174, 2006.

[9] J. Miller and P. Thomson. Cartesian genetic programming. In *Genetic Programming*, volume 1802 of *Lecture Notes in Computer Science*, pages 121–132. Springer Berlin Heidelberg, 2000.

[10] J. F. Miller, editor. *Cartesian Genetic Programming.* Natural Computing Series. Springer Verlag, 2011.

[11] J. Petrlík and L. Sekanina. Multiobjective evolution of approximate multiple constant multipliers. In *IEEE International Symposium on Design and Diagnostics of Electronic Circuits and Systems 2013*, pages 116–119. IEEE Computer Society, 2013.

[12] L. Sekanina and Z. Vasicek. Approximate circuits by means of evolvable hardware. In *2013 IEEE International Conference on Evolvable Systems (ICES)*, Proceedings of the 2013 IEEE Symposium Series on Computational Intelligence (SSCI), pages 21–28. IEEE Computer Society, 2013.

[13] L. Sekanina and Z. Vasicek. Evolutionary computing in approximate circuit design and optimization. In *1st Workshop on Approximate Computing (WAPCO 2015)*, pages 1–6, 2015.

[14] Z. Vasicek and L. Sekanina. Formal verification of candidate solutions for post-synthesis evolutionary optimization in evolvable hardware. *Genetic Programming and Evolvable Machines*, 12(3):305–327, 2011.

[15] Z. Vasicek and L. Sekanina. Evolutionary design of approximate multipliers under different error metrics. In *17th IEEE Symposium on Design and Diagnostics of Electronic Circuits and Systems*, pages 135–140. IEEE Computer Society, 2014.

[16] Z. Vasicek and L. Sekanina. How to evolve complex combinational circuits from scratch? In *2014 IEEE International Conference on Evolvable Systems Proceedings*, pages 133–140. Institute of Electrical and Electronics Engineers, 2014.

[17] Z. Vasicek and L. Sekanina. Evolutionary approach to approximate digital circuits design. *IEEE Transactions on Evolutionary Computation*, 99(99):1–13, 2015.

[18] S. Venkataramani, K. Roy, and A. Raghunathan. Substitute-and-simplify: A unified design paradigm for approximate and quality configurable circuits. In *Design, Automation Test in Europe Conference Exhibition (DATE), 2013*, pages 1367–1372, March 2013.

[19] S. Venkataramani, A. Sabne, V. Kozhikkottu, K. Roy, and A. Raghunathan. Salsa: Systematic logic synthesis of approximate circuits. In *Design Automation Conference (DAC), 2012 49th ACM/EDAC/IEEE*, pages 796–801, June 2012.

[20] T. Yu and J. Miller. Finding needles in haystacks is not hard with neutrality. In *Genetic Programming*, volume 2278 of *Lecture Notes in Computer Science*, pages 13–25. Springer Berlin Heidelberg, 2002.

A Study on Performance Evaluation Ability of a Modified Inverted Generational Distance Indicator

Hisao Ishibuchi
Osaka Prefecture University
Sakai, Osaka, Japan 599-8531
+81-72-254-9350
hisaoi@cs.osakafu-u.ac.jp

Hiroyuki Masuda
Osaka Prefecture University
Sakai, Osaka, Japan 599-8531
+81-72-254-9198
hiroyuki.masuda@ci.cs.osakafu-u.ac.jp

Yusuke Nojima
Osaka Prefecture University
Sakai, Osaka, Japan 599-8531
+81-72-254-9198
nojima@cs.osakafu-u.ac.jp

ABSTRACT
The inverted generational distance (IGD) has been frequently used as a performance indicator for many-objective problems where the use of the hypervolume is difficult. However, since IGD is not Pareto compliant, it is possible that misleading Pareto incompliant results are obtained. Recently, a simple modification of IGD was proposed by taking into account the Pareto dominance relation between a solution and a reference point when their distance is calculated. It was also shown that the modified indicator called IGD$^+$ is weakly Pareto compliant. However, actual effects of the modification on performance comparison have not been examined. Moreover, IGD$^+$ has not been compared with other distance-based weakly Pareto compliant indicators such as the additive epsilon indicator and the D1 indicator (i.e., IGD with the weighted achievement scalarizing function). In this paper, we examine the effect of the modification by comparing IGD$^+$ with IGD for multiobjective and many-objective problems. In computational experiments, we generate a large number of ordered pairs of non-dominated solution sets where one is better than the other. Two solution sets in each pair are compared by the above-mentioned performance indicators. We examine whether each indicator can correctly say which solution set is better between them.

Categories and Subject Descriptors
Mathematics of computing ~ Evolutionary algorithms

Keywords
Evolutionary multiobjective optimization, solution set comparison, many-objective optimization, inverted generational distance.

1. INTRODUCTION
Many-objective optimization has been a hot topic in the field of evolutionary multiobjective optimization (EMO). Since the well-known Pareto dominance-based EMO algorithms such as SPEA [30], SPEA2 [28] and NSGA-II [7] do not always work well on many-objective optimization problems, a number of new EMO algorithms and modifications of existing ones have been proposed in the literature [13], [22]. Difficulties in evolutionary many-objective optimization are related to various aspects such as the search for Pareto optimal solutions, the approximation of the Pareto front by a limited number of solutions, the presentation of obtained solutions to the decision maker, the choice of a single final solution, and the monitoring of the search behavior of EMO algorithms. It is also difficult to evaluate an obtained set of non-dominated solutions of a many-objective optimization problem.

In the EMO community, the hypervolume [29] has been used to evaluate a set of obtained non-dominated solutions. This is mainly because no other Pareto compliant unary indicator is known [27], [31]. The hypervolume has also been used to evaluate the fitness of each solution in indicator-based EMO algorithms such as SMS-EMOA [2] and HypE [1]. High performance of those algorithms has been reported for many-objective problems [1], [23]. However, it is not easy to use the hypervolume when the number of objectives is large (e.g., more than 10) and the number of non-dominated solutions is large (e.g., more than 1000). This is because a long computation time is still needed to calculate the hypervolume of a large number of non-dominated solutions in a high-dimensional objective space whereas some fast algorithms have been proposed for efficient calculation [4], [24], [18].

Recently the inverted generational distance (IGD) has often been used to evaluate solution sets of many-objective problems [17], [25]. To the best of our knowledge, the term "inverted generational distance (IGD)" was first used in 2004 [5], [20]. Similar ideas have been used in the literature since 1998 [6], [9] where the weighted achievement scalarizing function was used for distance calculation from each reference point to the nearest solution. This type of IGD was referred to as D1 in [9] and denoted as $D1_R$ in [9], [16]. However, the Euclidian distance has been usually used in IGD for performance evaluations in the literature since 2003 [3], [14]. One advantage of IGD as a performance indicator over the hypervolume is its computational efficiency. Since IGD is based on the distance calculation between two points in the objective space, its calculation is usually very efficient even in the case of many-objective optimization.

One well-known flaw of the Euclidian distance-based IGD in comparison with the hypervolume is the lack of the Pareto compliant property [27], [31]. This flaw is illustrated in Fig. 1 where two solution sets $A = \{\boldsymbol{a}_1, \boldsymbol{a}_2, \boldsymbol{a}_3\}$, $B = \{\boldsymbol{b}_1, \boldsymbol{b}_2, \boldsymbol{b}_3\}$ and a reference point set $Z = \{z_1, z_2, z_3\}$ are given in a two-dimensional objective space. Since every solution in B is dominated by at least one solution in A, we can say that A is a better solution set than B from the viewpoint of Pareto dominance. However, the dominated solution set B is evaluated as being better than A if we use the Euclidian distance-based IGD in Fig. 1 for comparing A and B.

Another difficulty of IGD is its dependency on the specification of a reference point set. In Fig. 2, we show another example with

GECCO '15, July 11 - 15, 2015, Madrid, Spain
© 2015 ACM. ISBN 978-1-4503-3472-3/15/07…$15.00
DOI: http://dx.doi.org/10.1145/2739480.2754792

two solution sets A, B and a reference point set Z. The solution set A is evaluated as being better in Fig. 2 by the Euclidian distance-based IGD. In Fig. 3, four reference points z_4, z_5, z_6 and z_7 are added to Z in the example in Fig. 2. After this modification of Z, the solution set B is evaluated as being better by IGD in Fig. 3 while A is evaluated as being better in Fig. 2.

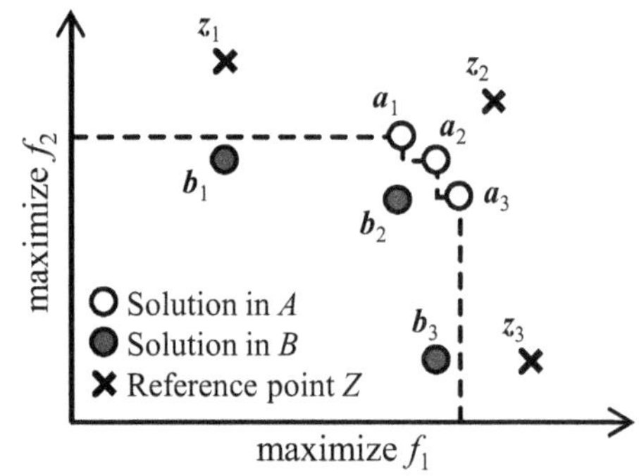

Figure 1. Pareto incompliant example where two solution sets $A = \{a_1, a_2, a_3\}$ and $B = \{b_1, b_2, b_3\}$ are evaluated by IGD using a reference point set $Z = \{z_1, z_2, z_3\}$.

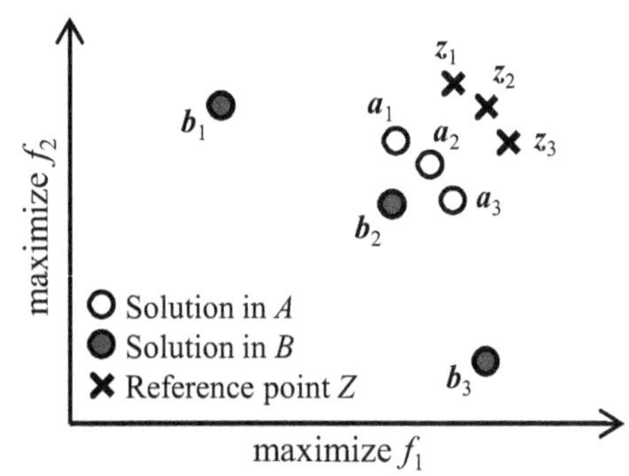

Figure 2. Another example with two solution sets $A = \{a_1, a_2, a_3\}$, $B = \{b_1, b_2, b_3\}$, and a reference point set $Z = \{z_1, z_2, z_3\}$.

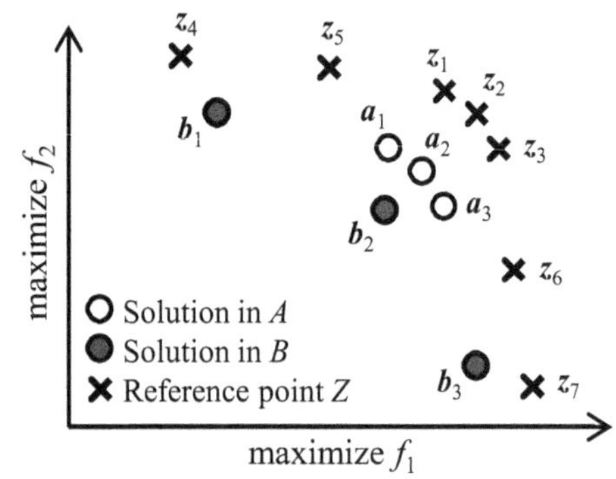

Figure 3. Addition of four reference points to Z in Fig. 2.

To remedy these difficulties of IGD, a simple modification of the distance calculation has been proposed in [11]. The proposed idea, which is explained in Fig. 4 for the solution set $A = \{a_1, a_2, a_3\}$, is to calculate the distance from each reference point z_i to the dominated region by the solution set instead of the distance to the nearest solution. The modified indicator, which is called IGD$^+$, is the average length of the three dotted lines in Fig. 4. It should be noted that the two solution sets A, B and the reference point set Z in Fig. 4 are the same as those in Fig. 1. As we explained in Fig. 1, the dominated solution set B was evaluated as being better than A by IGD. Such a Pareto incompliant result is not obtained by IGD$^+$ in Fig. 4 where the solution set A is evaluated as being better than B. If we use IGD$^+$ in Fig. 2 and Fig. 3, the solution set A is evaluated as being better than B. It should be noted that B is evaluated as being better than A in Fig. 3 by IGD. It was also shown that IGD$^+$ is weakly Pareto compliant in [12].

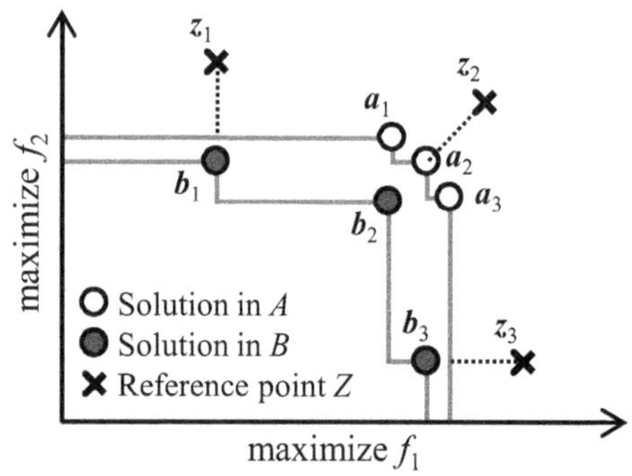

Figure 4. Illustration of the basic idea of IGD$^+$.

Whereas the effect of using IGD$^+$ instead of IGD is clear in Figs. 1-4, its practical usefulness is still unclear. This is because these examples were intentionally created for illustration purposes. For example, the diversities of the two solution sets A and B are unusually different in each figure. The solution set A has a similar diversity to the reference point set Z in Fig. 2 whereas B is similar to Z in the other figures. All examples in [11], [12] are somewhat similar to these examples in Figs. 1-4 intentionally generated for illustrating the flaws of IGD. Similar situations to Figs. 1-4 are not likely to happen frequently in performance comparison of non-dominated solution sets obtained by EMO algorithms.

The aim of this paper is to examine the effect of using IGD$^+$ instead of IGD for performance comparison of EMO algorithms on many-objective test problems. We also compare IGD$^+$ with other weakly Pareto compliant unary indictors such as the additive epsilon [31] and D1 [9].

This paper is organized as follows. In Section 2, we explain IGD, IGD$^+$, the additive epsilon and D1. The concept of the Pareto compliance [27] is also explained in Section 2. In Section 3, we report experimental results where pairs of non-dominated solution sets are searched from multiobjective knapsack problems and DTLZ2 with 2-10 objectives. In each pair of solution sets, one set is better than the other in the sense of Pareto dominance (more specifically, with respect to the relation "better" in [31]). Using those pairs of solution sets, the discrimination ability of each indicator is examined. Experimental results demonstrate the effect of using IGD$^+$ instead of IGD. High discrimination ability of D1 is also demonstrated. Finally this paper is concluded in Section 4.

2. MULTIOBJECTIVE OPTIMIZATION

In this section, we briefly explain a multiobjective optimization problem, Pareto dominance relation between solutions, Pareto dominance relation between solution sets, performance indicators, and the concept of Pareto compliance.

2.1 Multiobjective Optimization Problems

Let us consider the following m-objective maximization problem:

$$\text{Maximize } \boldsymbol{f}(\boldsymbol{x}) = (f_1(\boldsymbol{x}), f_2(\boldsymbol{x}), \ldots, f_m(\boldsymbol{x})), \quad (1)$$

$$\text{subject to } \boldsymbol{x} \in \boldsymbol{X}, \quad (2)$$

where $\boldsymbol{f}(\boldsymbol{x})$ is an m-dimensional objective vector, $f_i(\boldsymbol{x})$ is its i-th objective to be maximized ($i = 1, 2, \ldots, m$), $\boldsymbol{x}$ is the decision vector, and $\boldsymbol{X}$ is the feasible region in the decision space.

2.2 Pareto Dominance between Solutions

Let $\boldsymbol{x}$ and $\boldsymbol{y}$ be two feasible solutions of the maximization problem in (1)-(2). When the following relations hold, we say that $\boldsymbol{x}$ is dominated by $\boldsymbol{y}$:

$$\forall i,\ f_i(\boldsymbol{x}) \le f_i(\boldsymbol{y}) \text{ and } \exists j,\ f_j(\boldsymbol{x}) < f_j(\boldsymbol{y}). \tag{3}$$

This Pareto dominance relation is denoted as $\boldsymbol{x} \prec \boldsymbol{y}$:

$$\forall i,\ f_i(\boldsymbol{x}) \le f_i(\boldsymbol{y}) \text{ and } \exists j,\ f_j(\boldsymbol{x}) < f_j(\boldsymbol{y}) \quad \Leftrightarrow \quad \boldsymbol{x} \prec \boldsymbol{y}. \tag{4}$$

When the following relation holds, we say that $\boldsymbol{x}$ is weakly dominated by $\boldsymbol{y}$:

$$\forall i,\ f_i(\boldsymbol{x}) \le f_i(\boldsymbol{y}). \tag{5}$$

This weak Pareto dominance relation is denoted as $\boldsymbol{x} \preceq \boldsymbol{y}$:

$$\forall i,\ f_i(\boldsymbol{x}) \le f_i(\boldsymbol{y}) \quad \Leftrightarrow \quad \boldsymbol{x} \preceq \boldsymbol{y}. \tag{6}$$

If a feasible solution $\boldsymbol{x}$ is not dominated by any other feasible solutions of the multiobjective problem in (1)-(2), $\boldsymbol{x}$ is called a Pareto optimal solution. Its projection $\boldsymbol{f}(\boldsymbol{x})$ in the objective space is also often referred to as a Pareto optimal solution. The set of all Pareto optimal solutions is the Pareto optimal solution set. The projection of all Pareto optimal solutions (i.e., the Pareto optimal solution set) to the objective space is called the Pareto front.

If a feasible solution $\boldsymbol{x}$ is not dominated by any other feasible solutions in a solution set A, $\boldsymbol{x}$ is called a non-dominated solution in the solution set A. If all solutions in A are non-dominated solutions in A, A is called a non-dominated solution set.

2.3 Pareto Dominance between Solution Sets

Let us denote two non-dominated solution sets by $A = \{\boldsymbol{x}_1, \boldsymbol{x}_2, ..., \boldsymbol{x}_{|A|}\}$ and $B = \{\boldsymbol{y}_1, \boldsymbol{y}_2, ..., \boldsymbol{y}_{|B|}\}$ where $|A|$ and $|B|$ are the number of solutions in A and B, respectively. These two non-dominated solution sets are also denoted using the corresponding solutions in the objective space as $A = \{\boldsymbol{a}_1, \boldsymbol{a}_2, ..., \boldsymbol{a}_{|A|}\}$ and $B = \{\boldsymbol{b}_1, \boldsymbol{b}_2, ..., \boldsymbol{b}_{|B|}\}$ where $\boldsymbol{a}_i = \boldsymbol{f}(\boldsymbol{x}_i)$, $i = 1, 2, ..., |A|$ and $\boldsymbol{b}_j = \boldsymbol{f}(\boldsymbol{y}_j)$, $j = 1, 2, ..., |B|$.

In Hansen & Jaszkiewicz [9] and Zitzler et al. [31], relations between solution sets were discussed for solution set comparison. In this paper, we use the Pareto dominance relation, the weak Pareto dominance relation, and the relation "better" between two solution sets.

The Pareto dominance relation $A \prec B$, which means that the non-dominated solution set $A = \{\boldsymbol{x}_1, \boldsymbol{x}_2, ..., \boldsymbol{x}_{|A|}\}$ is dominated by $B = \{\boldsymbol{y}_1, \boldsymbol{y}_2, ..., \boldsymbol{y}_{|B|}\}$, was defined as follows [31]:

$$\forall \boldsymbol{x}_i \in A,\ \exists \boldsymbol{y}_j \in B : \boldsymbol{x}_i \prec \boldsymbol{y}_j \quad \Leftrightarrow \quad A \prec B. \tag{7}$$

The weak Pareto dominance relation $A \preceq B$, which means that A is weakly dominated by B, was defined as follows [31]:

$$\forall \boldsymbol{x}_i \in A,\ \exists \boldsymbol{y}_j \in B : \boldsymbol{x}_i \preceq \boldsymbol{y}_j \quad \Leftrightarrow \quad A \preceq B. \tag{8}$$

This weak Pareto dominance relation holds even when the two solution sets are the same (i.e., $A = B$). In order to represent the case where the weak Pareto dominance relation holds for different non-dominated solution sets A and B (i.e., the case where B is better than A), the relation "better" was proposed as follows [31]:

$$A \preceq B \text{ and } A \ne B \quad \Leftrightarrow \quad A \lhd B. \tag{9}$$

From these definitions, the following relation holds:

$$A \prec B \quad \Rightarrow \quad A \lhd B \quad \Rightarrow \quad A \preceq B. \tag{10}$$

The left-hand side of (9) can be rewritten as

$$\forall \boldsymbol{x}_i \in A,\ \exists \boldsymbol{y}_j \in B : \boldsymbol{x}_i \preceq \boldsymbol{y}_j \text{ and } \exists \boldsymbol{x}_i \in A,\ \exists \boldsymbol{y}_j \in B : \boldsymbol{x}_i \prec \boldsymbol{y}_j. \tag{11}$$

That is, at least one solution $\boldsymbol{y}_j$ in the solution set B is needed to be better than a solution $\boldsymbol{x}_i$ in A in order that B is better than A.

2.4 Performance Indicators

Since the Euclidean distance in the objective space has been used in the generational distance (GD) and the inverted generational distance (IGD) in recent studies on evolutionary many-objective optimization [17], [25], we use the Euclidean distance whereas GD was originally proposed in a more general form [21]. For further discussions on GD and IGD, see Schuetze et al. [19].

Each of GD and IGD evaluates the distance between a solution set and the Pareto front in a different manner. We assume that a non-dominated reference point set $Z = \{\boldsymbol{z}_1, \boldsymbol{z}_2, ..., \boldsymbol{z}_{|Z|}\}$ is given in the objective space as an approximation of the Pareto front. The GD of a non-dominated solution set $A = \{\boldsymbol{a}_1, \boldsymbol{a}_2, ..., \boldsymbol{a}_{|A|}\}$ is the average distance from each solution to the nearest reference point:

$$GD(A) = \frac{1}{|A|} \sum_{i=1}^{|A|} \min_{\boldsymbol{z}_j \in Z} d(\boldsymbol{a}_i, \boldsymbol{z}_j), \tag{12}$$

where $d(\boldsymbol{a}_i, \boldsymbol{z}_j)$ is the Euclidean distance between $\boldsymbol{a}_i$ and $\boldsymbol{z}_j$.

The IGD of $A = \{\boldsymbol{x}_1, \boldsymbol{x}_2, ..., \boldsymbol{x}_{|A|}\}$ is the average distance from each reference point to the nearest solution:

$$IGD(A) = \frac{1}{|Z|} \sum_{j=1}^{|Z|} \min_{\boldsymbol{a}_i \in A} d(\boldsymbol{a}_i, \boldsymbol{z}_j). \tag{13}$$

In Fig. 5 (a), we show the contour lines of the Euclidean distance from the reference point $\boldsymbol{z}$ in the objective space for the case of a two-objective maximization problem. In Fig. 5 (a), a solution $\boldsymbol{a}$ is dominated by a solution $\boldsymbol{b}$. However, if the Euclidean distance is used, the solution $\boldsymbol{a}$ has a shorter distance to the reference point $\boldsymbol{z}$ than the solution $\boldsymbol{b}$. In this case, a singleton solution set $A = \{\boldsymbol{a}\}$ is evaluated as being better than another singleton solution set $B = \{\boldsymbol{b}\}$ by GD and IGD with a singleton reference point set $Z = \{\boldsymbol{z}\}$.

In IGD$^+$, the distance between a reference point $\boldsymbol{z} = (z_1, z_2, ..., z_m)$ and a solution $\boldsymbol{a} = (a_1, a_2, ..., a_m)$ is calculated in the objective space for our m-objective maximization problem as follows:

$$d_{IGD^+}(\boldsymbol{a}, \boldsymbol{z}) = \sqrt{\sum_{k=1}^{m} (\max\{z_k - a_k, 0\})^2}. \tag{14}$$

If the solution $\boldsymbol{a}$ is dominated by the reference point $\boldsymbol{z}$, $d_{IGD^+}(\boldsymbol{a}, \boldsymbol{z})$ is the same as the Euclidean distance $d(\boldsymbol{a}, \boldsymbol{z})$ since $a_k \le z_k$ holds for all k's in (14). When $\boldsymbol{a}$ and $\boldsymbol{z}$ are non-dominated with each other, only those objectives with $a_k \le z_k$ are used in the distance calculation in (14). That is, if the solution $\boldsymbol{a}$ is better than the reference point $\boldsymbol{z}$ with respect to some objectives, those objectives are not used in the distance calculation in (14). The contour lines of the distance from $\boldsymbol{z}$ measured by (14) are shown in Fig. 5 (b). In the dominated region by $\boldsymbol{z}$ (i.e., in the lower-left region of $\boldsymbol{z}$), the contour lines of $d_{IGD^+}(\boldsymbol{a}, \boldsymbol{z})$ in Fig. 5 (b) are the same as those of the Euclidean distance in Fig. 5 (a). However, the contour lines of $d_{IGD^+}(\boldsymbol{a}, \boldsymbol{z})$ in Fig. 5 (b) are parallel to an axis of the objective space in the non-dominated region with respect to $\boldsymbol{z}$. As a result, the singleton solution set $B = \{\boldsymbol{b}\}$ is correctly evaluated as being better than $A = \{\boldsymbol{a}\}$ by IGD$^+$ with $Z = \{\boldsymbol{z}\}$ in Fig. 5 (b).

In the D1 indicator [9], the weighted achievement scalarizing function was used to measure the distance from the reference point $\boldsymbol{z} = (z_1, z_2, ..., z_m)$ to the solution $\boldsymbol{a} = (a_1, a_2, ..., a_m)$ as

$$d_{D1_R}(\boldsymbol{a}, \boldsymbol{z}) = \max_k \{\lambda_k (z_k - a_k)\}\,, \tag{15}$$

where λ_k is a weight for the kth objective defined as $\lambda_k = 1/R_k$ with R_k being a range of the kth objective in the reference point set Z [9]. The difference among IGD, IGD$^+$ and D1 is only in their distance calculation. The D1 indicator can be written in the same manner as IGD and IGD$^+$ as follows:

$$D1_R(A) = \frac{1}{|Z|} \sum_{j=1}^{|Z|} \min_{\boldsymbol{a}_i \in A} d_{D1_R}(\boldsymbol{a}_i, \boldsymbol{z}_j)\,. \tag{16}$$

The contour lines of the distance in the D1 indicator are shown in Fig. 5 (c) for $(\lambda_1, \lambda_2) = (1, 1)$. In Fig. 5 (c), $B = \{\boldsymbol{b}\}$ is correctly evaluated as being better than $A = \{\boldsymbol{a}\}$ by D1 with $Z = \{\boldsymbol{z}\}$.

Whereas all IGD, IGD$^+$ and D1 evaluate a solution set A using the average distance from each reference point to its nearest solution over all reference points, the additive epsilon indicator $I_{\varepsilon+}$ uses the maximum distance in the following manner [31]:

$$I_{\varepsilon+}(A, Z) = \inf_{\varepsilon} \{\forall \boldsymbol{z}_j \in Z, \exists \boldsymbol{a}_i \in A : \boldsymbol{a}_i + \boldsymbol{\varepsilon} \succeq \boldsymbol{z}_j\}\,, \tag{17}$$

where $\boldsymbol{\varepsilon}$ is an m-dimensional vector of ε: $\boldsymbol{\varepsilon} = (\varepsilon, \varepsilon, .., \varepsilon)$.

For the case of $Z = \{\boldsymbol{z}_1, \boldsymbol{z}_2\}$, the contour lines of $I_{\varepsilon+}(\{\boldsymbol{a}\}, \{\boldsymbol{z}_1, \boldsymbol{z}_2\})$ are written in Fig. 5 (d) as bold red lines. Thin lines and dotted lines can be viewed as distances from $\boldsymbol{z}_1$ and $\boldsymbol{z}_2$ measured by the weighted achievement scalarizing function with $(\lambda_1, \lambda_2) = (1, 1)$, respectively. The red bold lines in Fig. 5 (d) correspond to the larger distance from $\boldsymbol{z}_1$ and $\boldsymbol{z}_2$. It should be noted that the additive epsilon was originally proposed as a binary performance indicator to compare two solution sets A and B as $I_{\varepsilon+}(A, B)$ [31].

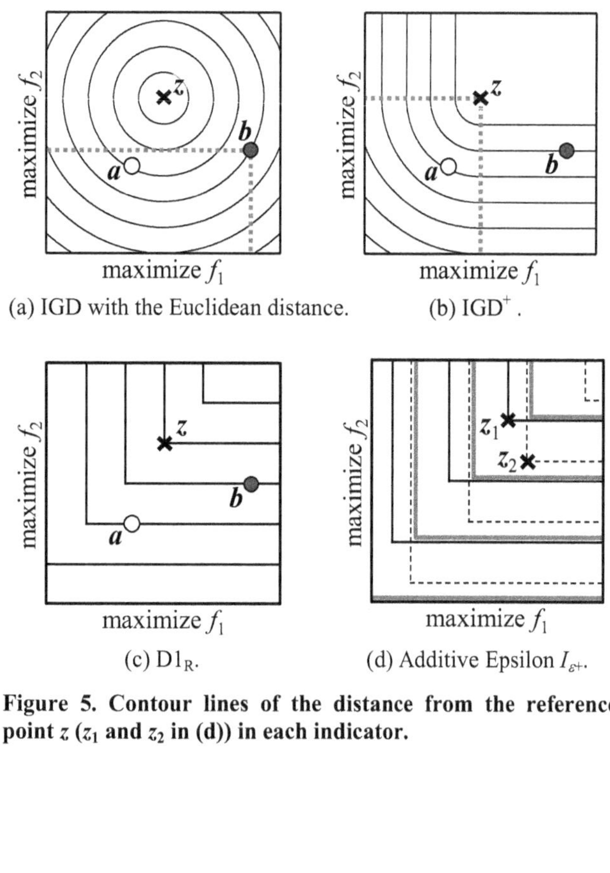

(a) IGD with the Euclidean distance. (b) IGD$^+$. (c) D1$_R$. (d) Additive Epsilon $I_{\varepsilon+}$.

Figure 5. Contour lines of the distance from the reference point $\boldsymbol{z}$ ($\boldsymbol{z}_1$ and $\boldsymbol{z}_2$ in (d)) in each indicator.

2.5 Pareto Compliance

In [9], [27], [31], comparison of solution sets has been discussed in detail. Let us assume that we have two non-dominated solution sets A and B. A unary performance indicator $I(.)$ is called "Pareto compliant" when the following relation holds for arbitrary pairs of non-dominated solution sets A and B [27]:

$$\text{If } A \lhd B \text{ then } I(A) > I(B)\,, \tag{18}$$

where we assume that smaller values of $I(.)$ means better solution sets as in the case of all the performance indicators explained in the previous subsection. Whenever a non-dominated solution set B is better than another non-dominated solution set A in the sense of the better relation " $\lhd$ " in Section 2, a Pareto compliant indicator always correctly says that B is better than A. For the best of our knowledge, only the hypervolume is known as a Pareto compliant unary indicator [27].

As shown in Fig. 5 (a), GD and IGD are not Pareto compliant. They cannot always correctly say which is better between an arbitrary pair of two non-dominated solution sets A and B with $A \lhd B$. For some pairs of A and B with $A \lhd B$, GD and IGD incorrectly say that A is better than B. Such a Pareto incompliant evaluation result is not obtained from IGD$^+$, D1 and $I_{\varepsilon+}$. That is, the following relation holds for arbitrary pairs of non-dominated solution sets A and B when IGD$^+$, D1 and $I_{\varepsilon+}$ are used as $I(.)$:

$$\text{If } A \lhd B \text{ then } I(A) \geq I(B)\,. \tag{19}$$

For arbitrary pairs of non-dominated solution sets A and B with $A \lhd B$, IGD$^+$, D1$_R$ and $I_{\varepsilon+}$ never say that A is better than B. However, for some pairs of A and B with $A \lhd B$, these indictors say that the two solution sets A and B have the same performance: $I(A) = I(B)$ whereas $A \lhd B$. That is, the two solution sets are evaluated as being equivalent while $A \lhd B$ holds. This issue will be further discussed in the next section.

In this paper, we use the additive epsilon $I_{\varepsilon+}$ as a unary indicator in order to compare it with other unary indicators such as IGD$^+$ and D1. However, as we have already mentioned, $I_{\varepsilon+}$ was originally proposed as a binary indicator to compare two non-dominated solution sets A and B in [31] where both $I_{\varepsilon+}(A, B)$ and $I_{\varepsilon+}(B, A)$ were used to compare A and B. When the additive epsilon is used as a binary indicator, it is Pareto compliant [31].

3. COMPUTATIONAL EXPERIMENTS

In our computational experiments, we first search for a number of ordered pairs of non-dominated solution sets (A, B) where $A \lhd B$ holds between A and B. Then each performance indicator is applied to A and B to check whether it can correctly say that B is better than A. As test problems, we use DTLZ2 with a continuous concave Pareto front and multiobjective knapsack problems with a convex Pareto front. These two test problems are used because it was reported in [15] that the shape of the Pareto front (i.e., concave or convex) had a dominant effect on the consistency among performance indicators.

3.1 Two-Objective DTLZ2

As many-objective test problems, the DTLZ test suite [8] has been used in the literature. We apply NSGA-II to a two-objective 11-variable DTLZ2 problem 100 times under the following setting:

String: Real-number string of length 11,
Crossover: SBX with the probability 0.8,
Mutation: PM with the probability $1/n$ where n is the string length,

Population size: 100,
Termination condition: 500 generations.

From a single run of NSGA-II, a series of 500 non-dominated solution sets $\{S_1, S_2, ..., S_{500}\}$ is obtained where S_t is a set of non-dominated solutions in the tth population. From the series of these 500 solution sets, we extract an ordered series of solution sets with respect to the relation better $\lhd$ in the following manner.

Let the first solution set S_1 be the current solution set. The current solution set S_1 is compared with the next solution set S_2 to examine whether $S_1 \lhd S_2$ holds. If $S_1 \lhd S_2$ holds, the current solution set S_1 is replaced with S_2, and the new current solution set S_2 is compared with the next solution set S_3 to examine whether $S_2 \lhd S_3$ holds. If $S_1 \lhd S_2$ does not hold, S_2 is removed from the series of the solution sets, and the current solution set S_1 is compared with the next solution set S_3. The comparison of the current solution set S_i with the next solution set S_j is iterated until the last solution set S_{500} is examined. If $S_i \lhd S_j$ holds, the current solution set S_i is replaced with S_j, and S_j is compared with the next solution set S_{j+1}. If $S_i \lhd S_j$ does not hold, S_j is removed, and S_i is compared with S_{j+1}. In this manner, we extract a series of ordered non-dominated solution sets.

Let N be the number of obtained ordered non-dominated solution sets. Those solution sets are renumbered as $S_1, S_2, ..., S_N$ where $S_1 \lhd S_2 \lhd ... \lhd S_N$ holds. From this series, we extract $(N-1)$ pairs of solution sets (S_t, S_{t+1}) with $S_t \lhd S_{t+1}$ where $t = 1, 2, ..., N-1$.

This procedure is applied to each of 100 runs of NSGA-II on the two-objective DTLZ2 problem. Then we have 2193 pairs of ordered non-dominated solution sets (A_i, B_i) with $A_i \lhd B_i$, $i = 1, 2, ..., 2193$. Two solution sets A_i and B_i in each of the obtained 2193 pairs are compared using each performance indicator. The reference point set Z in each indicator is generated by uniformly sampling 200 points along the known true Pareto front.

Experimental results are summarized in Table 1. Table 1 shows the percentage of correctly evaluated pairs ($I(A_i) > I(B_i)$), pairs incorrectly evaluated as being equivalent ($I(A_i) = I(B_i)$), and pairs with totally inconsistent evaluations ($I(A_i) < I(B_i)$).

In Table 1, about 2% of evaluation results by GD and IGD are Pareto incompliant: A_i is evaluated as being better than B_i whereas B_i is better than A_i. Those pairs are correctly evaluated by IGD$^+$. That is, the modification of the distance calculation in IGD$^+$ improves the quality of IGD as a performance indicator. Good results are also obtained from D1 with the weighted achievement scalarizing function for the distance calculation. In Table 1, about 9% of pairs are incorrectly evaluated as being equivalent by $I_{\varepsilon+}$. This may be because $I_{\varepsilon+}(A, Z)$ calculates the maximum distance between the two non-dominated solution sets A and Z whereas the other indicators calculate the average distance between them.

Table 1. Results on the 2193 pairs of ordered non-dominated solution sets of the two-objective DTLZ2 problem.

Indicator	Correct $I(A_i) > I(B_i)$	Equivalent $I(A_i) = I(B_i)$	Inconsistent $I(A_i) < I(B_i)$
GD	98.04%	0.00%	1.96%
IGD	97.95%	0.00%	2.05%
IGD$^+$	100.00%	0.00%	0.00%
D1	100.00%	0.00%	0.00%
Additive ε	91.24%	8.97%	0.00%

3.2 Many-Objective DTLZ2

In the same manner as in the previous subsection, we apply NSGA-II to DTLZ2 with 4, 6, 8 and 10 objectives. After 100 runs on each test problem, we obtain the following number of pairs of ordered non-dominated solution sets for each test problem:

145 pairs for the four-objective DTLZ2 with 13 variables,
0 pairs for the six-objective DTLZ2 with 15 variables,
0 pairs for the eight-objective DTLZ2 with 17 variables,
0 pairs for the ten-objective DTLZ2 with 19 variables.

The number of obtained pairs of ordered non-dominated solution sets severely decreases from 2193 for the two-objective DTLZ2 problem by increasing the number of objectives. This is because (i) most solutions become non-dominated with each other by increasing the number of objectives and (ii) each population has a large diversity throughout the 500 generations from a random initial population to the last population at the 500th generation.

Since no pair of ordered non-dominated solution sets is obtained for many-objective DTLZ2 test problems with 6-10 objectives, we only report experimental results on the four-objective DTLZ2 problem here. The reference point set is generated by randomly sampling 1000 points on the entire Pareto front. Experimental results are summarized in Table 2 in the same manner as in Table 1. In Table 2, the same result is obtained by IGD, IGD$^+$ and D1.

Table 2. Results on the 145 pairs of ordered non-dominated solution sets of the four-objective DTLZ2 problem.

Indicator	Correct $I(A_i) > I(B_i)$	Equivalent $I(A_i) = I(B_i)$	Inconsistent $I(A_i) < I(B_i)$
GD	97.93%	0.00%	2.07%
IGD	100.00%	0.00%	0.00%
IGD$^+$	100.00%	0.00%	0.00%
D1	100.00%	0.00%	0.00%
Additive ε	93.79%	6.21%	0.00%

3.3 Two-Objective Knapsack Problem

Multiobjective knapsack problems have been frequently used as discrete test problems in the EMO community since Zitzler & Thiele [30]. We use the two-objective 500-item knapsack problem in [30] in our computational experiment. NSGA-II is applied to this test problem 100 times under the following setting:

String: Binary string of length 500,
Crossover: Uniform crossover with the probability 0.8,
Mutation: Bit-flip mutation with the probability 1/500,
Constraint handling: Greedy repair in [30],
Population size: 100,
Termination condition: 2000 generations.

From 100 runs of NSGA-II, we obtain 47993 pairs of ordered non-dominated solution sets (A_i, B_i) with $A_i \lhd B_i$. As the reference points, we use all the known 1427 Pareto optimal solutions. Evaluation results of the 47993 pairs of ordered non-dominated solution sets are summarized in Table 3.

In Table 3, many inconsistent results (18.20%) are obtained by GD. IGD also generate inconsistent results for 5.21% pairs of solution sets. Such an inconsistency is removed by the use of IGD$^+$. This observation shows the effect of the modification of the distance calculation. However, about 17.6% pairs of A_i and B_i with $A_i \lhd B_i$ are evaluated as being equivalent by IGD and IGD$^+$.

Table 3. Results on the 47993 pairs of ordered non-dominated solution sets of the two-objective 500-item knapsack problem.

Indicator	Correct $I(A_i) > I(B_i)$	Equivalent $I(A_i) = I(B_i)$	Inconsistent $I(A_i) < I(B_i)$
GD	81.80%	0.00%	18.20%
IGD	77.22%	17.58%	5.21%
IGD$^+$	82.41%	17.59%	0.00%
D1	99.96%	0.04%	0.00%
Additive ε	14.83%	85.17%	0.00%

One question in Table 3 is the difference in the number of pairs with $I(A_i) = I(B_i)$ between IGD$^+$ and D1. As we have already shown in Fig. 5, these two indicators have similar contour lines of the distance from a reference point (see Fig. 5 (b) and Fig. 5 (c)).

In Fig. 6, we show an example of two non-dominated solution sets A_i and B_i with $A_i \lhd B_i$, which are correctly evaluated by D1 as $D1_R(A_i) > D1_R(B_i)$ and incorrectly evaluated by IGD$^+$ as $IGD^+(A_i) = IGD^+(B_i)$. The difference between these two solution sets is only two solutions highlighted by a red circle in Fig. 6 (a) and Fig. 6 (b). These two solutions are contributed to the calculation of $D1_R(A_i)$ and $D1_R(B_i)$. However, they are not contributed to $IGD^+(A_i)$ and $IGD^+(B_i)$, which leads to $IGD^+(A_i) = IGD^+(B_i)$.

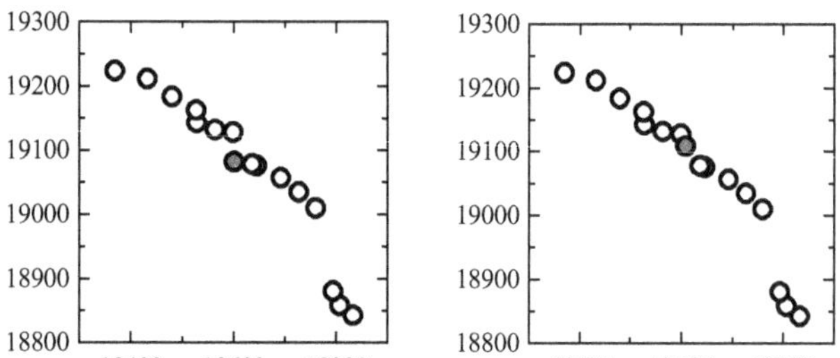

(a) Solution set A_i. (b) Solution set B_i.

Figure 6. Two non-dominated solution sets A_i and B_i for which $A_i \lhd B_i$, $D1_R(A_i) > D1_R(B_i)$ and $IGD^+(A_i) = IGD^+(B_i)$ hold.

Fig. 6 suggests that more solutions are used in the calculation of D1 than that of IGD$^+$. To examine this issue, we calculate the average number of solutions in A_i and B_i used for the calculation of each indicator in Table 3. The following results are obtained:

GD: 33.4 solutions (all solutions in A_i and B_i),
IGD: 13.3 solutions,
IGD$^+$: 13.3 solutions,
D1: 33.0 solutions,
Additive ε: 1.0 solution.

Since GD is the average distance over all solutions, 33.4 is the average number of solutions in A_i and B_i. Since the maximum distance is calculated in the additive ε, $I_{\varepsilon+}$ depends on only a single solution. Whereas the other indicators calculate the average distance, more solutions are used for the calculation of D1 than IGD and IGD$^+$. This may be the reason for the difference in the percentages of $I(A_i) = I(B_i)$ between IGD$^+$ and D1 in Table 3.

The next question is why more solutions are used for the calculation of D1 than IGD$^+$. The reason can be explained by the difference in the distance calculation between these two indicators. In Fig. 7, we explain the dependency of the nearest solution on the distance calculation in each performance measure. In Fig. 7 (b), a different solution is chosen as the nearest solution for each reference point (i.e., all the three solutions in Fig. 7 (b) are used in the calculation of D1). However, in Fig. 7 (a), the solution $\boldsymbol{a}_2$ is not chosen as the nearest solution for any reference points ($\boldsymbol{a}_3$ is chosen as the nearest solution for z_2 and z_3). As a result, only the two solutions $\boldsymbol{a}_1$ and $\boldsymbol{a}_3$ are used in the calculation of IGD$^+$. As illustrated in Fig. 7 (a), a non-dominated solution at a locally concave location is not likely to be selected as the nearest solution of a reference point when the Euclidean distance is used and the reference points are not close to the obtained solutions.

To examine this issue, we show in Fig. 8 a Voronoi diagram for the three solutions in Fig. 7 using the Euclidean distance and the weighted achievement scalarizing function. In Fig. 8 (a), the solution $\boldsymbol{a}_2$ has a triangular territory in its right-upper region. Only when a reference point is in this triangular territory, $\boldsymbol{a}_2$ is selected as its nearest solution. The same solution $\boldsymbol{a}_2$ has a belt-like territory in its right-upper direction in Fig. 8 (b).

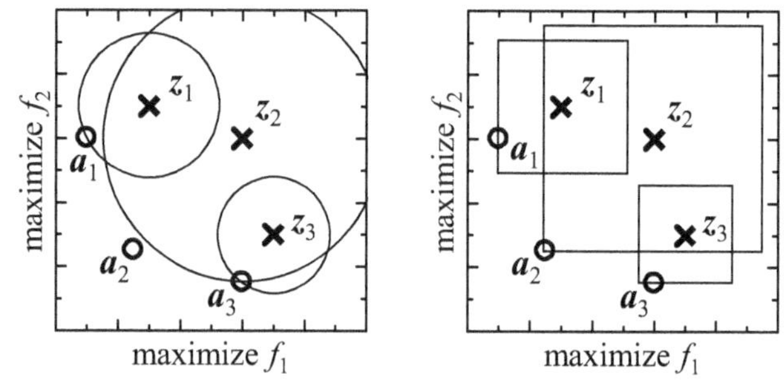

(a) IGD$^+$. (b) D1.

Figure 7. Contour line corresponding to the distance from each reference point to its nearest solution.

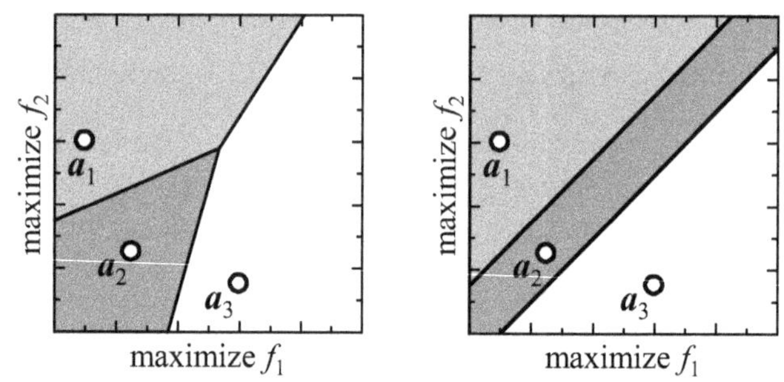

(a) IGD$^+$. (b) D1.

Figure 8. Voronoi diagram for the three solutions in Fig. 7.

3.4 Many-Objective Knapsack Problems

In the same manner as in the previous subsection, we perform computational experiments on 500-item multiobjective knapsack problems with 4-10 objectives. We use the same four-objective 500-item problem as in [30]. Multiobjective knapsack problems with more than four objectives are generated by adding objectives to the four-objective problem. The added objectives are randomly generated as in [30]. Pairs of ordered non-dominated solution sets are selected from 100 runs on each test problem. Reference points are specified by choosing non-dominated solutions among the merged population of all the selected pairs of solution sets and the final populations of 100 runs on each test problem.

In Table 4, we show the number of obtained pairs of ordered non-dominated solution sets (A_i, B_i) with $A_i \lhd B_i$, and the number of reference points in the reference point set for each test problem. In

Tables 5-8, experimental results are summarized in the same manner as in Table 3. From the comparison of Table 3 with Tables 5-8, we can see that much better results are obtained in Tables 5-8 than Table 3. Among the examined indicators, the best results are obtained by D1.

Table 4. The number of pairs of ordered non-dominated solution sets and the number of reference points.

Problem	(A_i, B_i)	Reference points
Two-Objective	47993	1427
Four-Objective	4704	2259
Six-Objective	1913	3780
Eight-Objective	1030	4938
Ten-Objective	624	5084

Table 5. Results on the four-objective knapsack problem.

Indicator	Correct $I(A_i) > I(B_i)$	Equivalent $I(A_i) = I(B_i)$	Inconsistent $I(A_i) < I(B_i)$
GD	98.15%	0.00%	1.85%
IGD	99.30%	0.60%	0.11%
IGD$^+$	99.36%	0.64%	0.00%
D1	100.00%	0.00%	0.00%
Additive ε	53.93%	46.07%	0.00%

Table 6. Results on the six-objective knapsack problem.

Indicator	Correct $I(A_i) > I(B_i)$	Equivalent $I(A_i) = I(B_i)$	Inconsistent $I(A_i) < I(B_i)$
GD	99.53%	0.00%	0.47%
IGD	99.53%	0.47%	0.00%
IGD$^+$	99.53%	0.47%	0.00%
D1	100.00%	0.00%	0.00%
Additive ε	71.20%	28.80%	0.00%

Table 7. Results on the eight-objective knapsack problem.

Indicator	Correct $I(A_i) > I(B_i)$	Equivalent $I(A_i) = I(B_i)$	Inconsistent $I(A_i) < I(B_i)$
GD	99.32%	0.00%	0.68%
IGD	98.74%	1.26%	0.00%
IGD$^+$	98.54%	1.46%	0.00%
D1	100.00%	0.00%	0.00%
Additive ε	78.54%	21.46%	0.00%

Table 8. Results on the ten-objective knapsack problem.

Indicator	Correct $I(A_i) > I(B_i)$	Equivalent $I(A_i) = I(B_i)$	Inconsistent $I(A_i) < I(B_i)$
GD	99.36%	0.00%	0.64%
IGD	96.96%	3.04%	0.00%
IGD$^+$	96.63%	3.37%	0.00%
D1	100.00%	0.00%	0.00%
Additive ε	81.09%	18.91%	0.00%

4. DISCUSSIONS AND CONCLUSIONS

We examined the distance calculation in the IGD indicator. We also compared distance-based indicators through computational experiments and obtained the following observations:

(i) Inconsistent evaluation results by IGD were actually obtained and removed by using IGD$^+$ instead of IGD.

(ii) Best evaluation results with respect to the Pareto compliance were obtained by D1 among GD, IGD, IGD$^+$, D1 and $I_{\varepsilon+}$.

The first observation supports the use of IGD$^+$ instead of IGD. This observation is consistent with theoretical discussions in [12]. The use of IGD$^+$ instead of IGD was also suggested in [11] by comparing them with respect to the sensitivity to the specification of reference points. The second observation may need further studies using other test problems and other EMO algorithms. This is because the best indicator depends on the setting of experiments. Whereas we used the Voronoi diagram in Fig. 8 to explain the best results by D1 in Table 3 (and Fig. 7), the same diagram can be used to explain the advantage of IGD$^+$ over D1 if the reference points are much closer to the three solutions in Fig. 7. Actually a different observation can be obtained from the same experiment on a different test problem. In Table 9, we show experimental results on a two-objective WFG1 problem [10]. The best results are obtained from IGD$^+$ in Table 9. Table 10 shows experimental results on the same WFG1 problem by MOEA/D with the weighted Tchebycheff function [26]. In Table 10, the best results are obtained from IGD$^+$. However, good results are also obtained by all indicators. These observations suggest the necessity of further studies of each indicator.

Table 9. Results on the 11782 pairs of ordered non-dominated solution sets of a two-objective WFG1 problem (NSGA-II).

Indicator	Correct $I(A_i) > I(B_i)$	Equivalent $I(A_i) = I(B_i)$	Inconsistent $I(A_i) < I(B_i)$
GD	83.58%	0.00%	16.42%
IGD	96.92%	0.87%	2.21%
IGD$^+$	99.13%	0.87%	0.00%
D1	98.50%	1.50%	0.00%
Additive ε	50.53%	49.47%	0.00%

Table 10. Results on the 1672 pairs of ordered non-dominated solution sets of a two-objective WFG1 problem (MOEA/D).

Indicator	Correct $I(A_i) > I(B_i)$	Equivalent $I(A_i) = I(B_i)$	Inconsistent $I(A_i) < I(B_i)$
GD	98.56%	0.00%	1.44%
IGD	98.56%	0.00%	1.44%
IGD$^+$	100.00%	0.00%	0.00%
D1	99.70%	0.30%	0.00%
Additive ε	98.92%	1.08%	0.00%

5. REFERENCES

[1] Bader, J. and Zitzler, E. 2011. HypE: An algorithm for fast hypervolume-based many-objective optimization. *Evolutionary Computation* 19, 1 (Spring 2011) 45-76.

[2] Beume, N., Naujoks, B., and Emmerich, M. 2007. SMS-EMOA: multiobjective selection based on dominated hypervolume. *European Journal of Operational Research* 180, 3 (September 2007) 1653-1669.

[3] Bosman, P.A.N. and Thierens, D. 2003. The balance between proximity and diversity in multiobjective evolutionary algorithms. *IEEE Trans. on Evolutionary Computation* 7, 2 (April 2003) 174-188.

[4] Bradstreet, L., While, L., and Barone, L. 2008. A fast incremental hypervolume algorithm. *IEEE Trans. on Evolutionary Computation* 12, 6 (December 2008) 714-723.

[5] Coello, C.A.C. and Sierra, M.R. 2004. A study of the parallelization of a coevolutionary multi-objective evolutionary algorithm. *Lecture Notes in Computer Science 2972: MICAI 2004* (April 2004) 688-697.

[6] Czyzak, P. and Jaszkiewicz, A. 1998. Pareto simulated annealing - A metaheuristic technique for multiple-objective combinatorial optimization. *Journal of Multi-Criteria Decision Analysis* 7, 1 (January 1998) 34-47.

[7] Deb, K., Paratop, A., Agarwal, S., and Meyarivan, T. 2002. A fast and elitist multiobjective genetic algorithm: NSGA-II. *IEEE Trans. on Evolutionary Computation* 6, 2 (April 2002) 182-197.

[8] Deb, K., Thiele, L., Laumanns, M., and Zitzler, E. 2002. Scalable multi-objective optimization test problems. *Proc. of 2002 Congress on Evolutionary Computation* (Honolulu, USA, May 12-17, 2002) 825-830.

[9] Hansen, M.P. and Jaszkiewicz, A. 1998. Evaluating the quality of approximations of the non-dominated set. *Technical Report IMM-REP-1998-7*, Technical University of Denmark.

[10] Huband, S., Hingston, P., Barone, L., and While, L. 2006. A review of multiobjective test problems and a scalable test problem toolkit. *IEEE Trans. on Evolutionary Computation* 10, 5 (October 2006) 477-506.

[11] Ishibuchi, H., Masuda, H., Tanigaki, Y., and Nojima, Y. 2014. Difficulties in specifying reference points to calculate the inverted generational distance for many-objective optimization problems. *Proc. of 2014 IEEE Symposium on Computational Intelligence in Multi-Criteria Decision-Making* (Orlando, USA, December 9-12, 2014) 170-177.

[12] Ishibuchi, H., Masuda, H., Tanigaki, Y., and Nojima, Y. 2015. Modified distance calculation in generational distance and inverted generational distance. *Lecture Notes in Computer Science 9019: EMO 2015, Part II* (Springer, Berlin, March-April 2015) 110-125.

[13] Ishibuchi, H., Tsukamoto, N., and Nojima Y. 2008. Evolutionary many-objective optimization: A short review. *Proc. of 2008 IEEE Congress on Evolutionary Computation* (Hong Kong, China, June 1-6, 2008) 2424-2431.

[14] Ishibuchi, H., Yoshida, T., and Murata, T. 2003. Balance between genetic search and local search in memetic algorithms for multiobjective permutation flowshop scheduling. *IEEE Trans. on Evolutionary Computation* 7, 2 (April 2003) 204-223.

[15] Jiang, S., Ong, Y., Zhang, J., and Feng, L. 2014. Consistencies and contradictions of performance metrics in multiobjective optimization. *IEEE Trans. on Cybernetics* 44, 12 (December 2014) 2391-2404.

[16] Knowles, J.D. and Corne, D.W. 2002. On metrics for comparing non-dominated sets. *Proc. of 2002 Congress on Evolutionary Computation* (Honolulu, May 12-17, 2002) 711-716.

[17] Li, M., Yang, S., and Liu, X. Shift-based density estimation for Pareto-based algorithms in many-objective optimization. *IEEE Trans. on Evolutionary Computation* 18, 3 (June 2014) 348-365.

[18] Russo, L.M.S. and Francisco, A.P. 2014. Quick hypervolume. *IEEE Trans. on Evolutionary Computation* 18, 4 (August 2014) 481-502.

[19] Schuetze, O., Esquivel, X., Lara, A., and Coello, C.A.C. 2012. Using the averaged Hausdorff distance as a performance measure in evolutionary multiobjective optimization. *IEEE Trans. on Evolutionary Computation* 16, 4 (August 2012) 504-522.

[20] Sierra, M.R. and Coello, C.A.C. 2004. A new multi-objective particle swarm optimizer with improved selection and diversity mechanisms. *Technical Report of CINVESTAV-IPN* (November 23, 2004).

[21] Van Veldhuizen D.A. 1999. Multiobjective evolutionary algorithms: Classifications, analyses, and new innovations. Ph.D. Thesis, Graduate School of Engineering, Air Force Institute of Technology, Wright-Patterson AFB, USA (1999)

[22] von Lücken, C., Barán, B., and Brizuela, C. 2014. A survey on multi-objective evolutionary algorithms for many-objective problems. *Computational Optimization and Applications* 53, 3 (July 2014) 707-756.

[23] Wagner, T., Beume, N., and Naujoks, B. 2007. Pareto-, aggregation-, and indicator-based methods in many-objective optimization. *Lecture Notes in Computer Science 4403: Evolutionary Multi-Criterion Optimization - EMO 2007*, (Springer, Berlin, March 2007), 742-756.

[24] While, L., Bradstreet, L., and Barone, L. 2012. A fast way of calculating exact hypervolumes. *IEEE Trans. on Evolutionary Computation* 16, 1 (February 2012) 86-95.

[25] Yang, S., Li, M., Liu, X., and Zheng, J. 2013. A grid-based evolutionary algorithm for many-objective optimization. *IEEE Trans. on Evolutionary Computation* 17, 5 (October 2013) 721-736.

[26] Zhang, Q. and Li, H. 2007. MOEA/D: A multiobjective evolutionary algorithm based on decomposition. *IEEE Trans. on Evolutionary Computation* 11, 6 (December 2007) 712-731.

[27] Zitzler, E., Brockhoff, D., and Thiele, L. 2007. The hypervolume indicator revisited: On the design of Pareto-compliant indicators via weighted integration. *Lecture Notes in Computer Science 4403: EMO 2007* (Springer, Berlin, March 2007) 862-876.

[28] Zitzler, E., Laumanns, M., and Thiele, L. 2001. SPEA2: Improving the strength Pareto evolutionary algorithm. *TIK-Report*, No. 103, ETH Zurich.

[29] Zitzler, E. and Thiele, L. 1998. Multiobjective optimization using evolutionary algorithms - A comparative case study. *Lecture Notes in Computer Science 1498: Parallel Problem Solving from Nature - PPSN V* (September 1998) 292-301.

[30] Zitzler, E. and Thiele, L. 1999. Multiobjective evolutionary algorithms: A comparative case study and the strength Pareto approach. *IEEE Trans. on Evolutionary Computation* 3, 4 (November 1999) 257-271.

[31] Zitzler, E., Thiele, L., Laumanns, M., Fonseca, C.M., and da Fonseca, V.G. 2003. Performance assessment of multiobjective optimizers: An analysis and review. *IEEE Trans. on Evolutionary Computation* 7, 2 (April 2003) 117-132.

A Performance Comparison Indicator for Pareto Front Approximations in Many-Objective Optimization

Miqing Li
Department of Computer Science
Brunel University London
Uxbridge UB8 3PH, U. K.
miqing.li@brunel.ac.uk

Shengxiang Yang
School of Computer Science and Informatics
De Montfort University
Leicester LE1 9BH, U. K
syang@dmu.ac.uk

Xiaohui Liu
Department of Computer Science
Brunel University London
Uxbridge UB8 3PH, U. K.
xiaohui.liu@brunel.ac.uk

ABSTRACT

Increasing interest in simultaneously optimizing many objectives (typically more than three objectives) of problems leads to the emergence of various many-objective algorithms in the evolutionary multi-objective optimization field. However, in contrast to the development of algorithm design, how to assess many-objective algorithms has received scant concern. Many performance indicators are designed in principle for any number of objectives, but in practice are invalid or infeasible to be used in many-objective optimization. In this paper, we explain the difficulties that popular performance indicators face and propose a performance comparison indicator (PCI) to assess Pareto front approximations obtained by many-objective algorithms. PCI evaluates the quality of approximation sets with the aid of a reference set constructed by themselves. The points in the reference set are divided into many clusters, and the proposed indicator estimates the minimum moves of solutions in the approximation sets to weakly dominate these clusters. PCI has been verified both by an analytic comparison with several well-known indicators and by an empirical test on four groups of Pareto front approximations with different numbers of objectives and problem characteristics.

CCS Concepts

•Computing methodologies → Heuristic function construction; •Applied computing → Multi-criterion optimization and decision-making; •Theory of computation → *Bio-inspired optimization;*

Keywords

Multi-objective optimization; many-objective optimization; performance assessment indicator

GECCO'15, July 11-15, 2015, Madrid, Spain.

DOI: http://dx.doi.org/10.1145/2739480.2754687

1. INTRODUCTION

Over the past decade, many-objective optimization has attracted great attention and gradually developed into an independent research topic in the evolutionary multiobjective optimization (EMO) field [9, 17]. In the last five years, a wide variety of many-objective optimization techniques have been proposed, ranging from the modification of Pareto-based algorithms [22] and the introduction of decomposition-based and indicator-based algorithms [1, 5] to the design of new optimizers specially for many-objective problems [11, 31, 32, 34].

However, in contrast to the development of algorithm design, how to assess and compare many-objective optimizers has received scant concern [21]. Many performance indicators are designed in principle for any number of objectives, but in practice are invalid or infeasible when assessing Pareto front approximations (i.e., solution sets obtained by population-based search algorithms) with high dimensions. In general, the difficulties of performance indicators in assessing high-dimensional Pareto front approximations can be summarized as follows.

- *Ineffectiveness of Pareto dominance.* Since the portion of the space that a solution dominates decreases exponentially with the number of objectives, most solutions in different approximation sets are likely to be incomparable under the criterion of Pareto dominance. This can lead to the ineffectiveness of many performance indicators based on the comparison of solutions' Pareto dominance relation, such as the *coverage* [36] and *G*-metric [26].

- *Rapid increase of time or space requirement.* The time or space required by some performance indicators increases exponentially with the number of objectives, such as the *hypervolume* [36], *hyperarea radio* [29], and *diversity measure* [6]. This can affect their application in many-objective optimization.

- *Difficulties of parameter setting.* Purshouse and Fleming [27] have shown that the *sweet-spot* of algorithm parameter setting that produces good results could shrink markedly in many-objective optimization. This could also apply to parameter setting of performance indicators. In general, the sensitiveness of assessment results to an indicator's parameter(s) increases with the number of objectives. Two high-dimensional approximation sets could return completely contrary results when assessed by an indicator with slightly different settings of its parameter(s) [21].

- *Difficulties of the substitution of Pareto front.* Many performance indicators require a reference set as a substitution of the Pareto front, such as GD [29] and IGD [2]. However, to represent a higher-dimensional Pareto front, exponentially more points are needed. As shown by Ishibuchi et al [14], insufficient points can easily lead to an inaccurate or even misleading assessment result.

In this paper, we propose a performance comparison indicator (PCI) to assess high-dimensional Pareto front approximations, attempting to overcome the above difficulties. PCI can be partially viewed as an integration of two effective performance indicators, IGD$^+$ [16] and the *binary ϵ-indicator* [37]. Like IGD$^+$, when comparing an individual p with an individual q, PCI only considers the objectives where p is inferior to q. Like the binary ϵ-indicator, PCI considers the comparison of multiple approximation sets, providing relative quality for these sets. This can avoid theoretical limitations of unary performance indicators [37]. Moreover, PCI uses a reference set constructed by the tested approximation sets themselves, rather than one specified by the user. More importantly, unlike many performance indicators (such as IGD, IGD$^+$, and the *average Hausdorff Distance* [28]) which compare each point in the reference set with the approximation set, the proposed indicator divides points in the reference set into many clusters and estimates the minimum move of the approximation sets to weakly dominate these clusters.

Note that this paper focuses on the comparison of Pareto front approximations rather than on search algorithms, that is, we assume that for each algorithm only one run is performed. In addition, without loss of generality, we consider minimization MOPs throughout this paper. The rest of this paper is organized as follows. Related work is reviewed in Section 2. Section 3 is devoted to the description of the proposed indicator. Analytic and empirical studies are carried out in Section 4 and Section 5, respectively. Finally, Section 6 concludes the paper.

2. RELATED WORK

Despite the difficulties in assessing high-dimensional Pareto front approximations, some effort has been made. Jaimes and Coello [18] measured the Tchebycheff distance of an approximation set to the "knee" of the Pareto front in many-objective optimization. This measurement is based on the assumption that, in the absence of particular preference information, the decision maker may have more interest in the knee of a problem's Pareto front. Recently, Li et al [21] proposed an indicator to compare the diversity of approximation sets. They put all approximation sets into a grid environment and calculated the contribution of each set to those nonempty hyperboxes. A problem in these indicators is that they only focus on one particular aspect of the performance of approximation sets, failing to provide a general evaluation of the sets' performance.

On the other hand, some classic performance indicators which measure the overall quality of approximation sets have been frequently used to test and compare many-objective optimizers [10, 24, 30]. Examples are the hypervolume [36], ϵ-indicator [37], and IGD [2] (also its variation IGD$^+$ [16]).

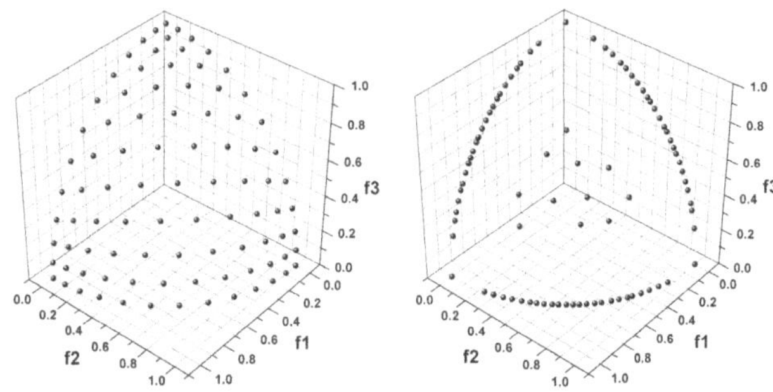

(a) MOEA/D (b) IBEA

Figure 1: An example that HV prefers the knee and boundary points on the Pareto front, where two sets of Pareto optimal solutions on DTLZ2 are obtained by MOEA/D and IBEA. The solution set with better distribution (obtained by MOEA/D) has a worse (lower) HV result, as given in Table 1.

Table 1: HV results of the two sets in Figure 1 under different reference points. The range of DTLZ2's Pareto front is $[0, 1]$ for all objectives.

Reference point	MOEA/D	IBEA
(1.0, 1.0, 1.0)	4.1413E–1	4.1525E–1
(1.1, 1.1, 1.1)	7.4484E–1	7.4596E–1
(1.2, 1.2, 1.2)	1.1418E+0	1.1430E+0
(1.4, 1.4, 1.4)	2.1578E+0	2.1590E+0
(1.7, 1.7, 1.7)	4.3268E+0	4.3280E+0
(2.0, 2.0, 2.0)	7.4138E+0	7.4150E+0
(2.5, 2.5, 2.5)	1.5039E+1	1.5040E+1
(3.0, 3.0, 3.0)	2.6414E+1	2.6415E+1

Next, we will briefly discuss their pros and cons, especially when assessing high-dimensional approximation sets.

The hypervolume (HV) indicator [36] calculates the volume of the objective space enclosed by an approximation set and a reference point. HV has good theoretical properties and can give a general evaluation of the set, but its computational complexity increases exponentially with the number of objectives. These lead to its dominant application in the 2- or 3-objective problems. While the Monte Carlo method can largely reduce the time cost [1, 3], how to choose a proper reference point in the HV calculation is an important issue [19] and its difficulty also increases with the number of objectives. In addition, the HV indicator generally prefers the knee and boundary points of the Pareto front to well-distributed ones. Figure 1 gives such an example, where we consider two sets of Pareto optimal solutions[1] obtained by two well-known EMO algorithms, MOEA/D [33] and IBEA [35], on test problem DTLZ2 [8]. Table 1 gives the HV results of these two solution sets with various settings of the reference point. As shown, the solution set with better distribution (obtained by MOEA/D) has a worse (lower) HV evaluation value than its competitor, regardless of the choice of the reference point.

The unary ϵ-indicator [37] measures the minimum factor ϵ for an approximation set such that any point in a reference set is ϵ-dominated [20] (additively or multiplicatively) by at

[1]Here, the number of DTLZ2's decision variables n is set to $m-1$ (m is the number of objectives) to ensure that all solutions produced by the algorithms are Pareto optimal.

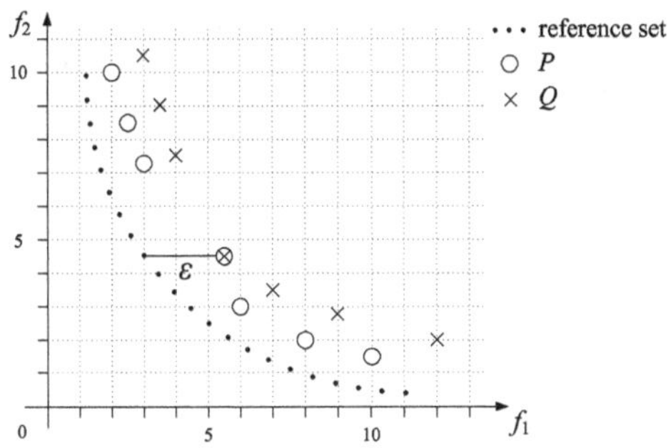

Figure 2: An example that the unary additive ϵ-indicator fails to distinguish between two approximation sets. P and Q have the same evaluation result ($\epsilon = 2.5$).

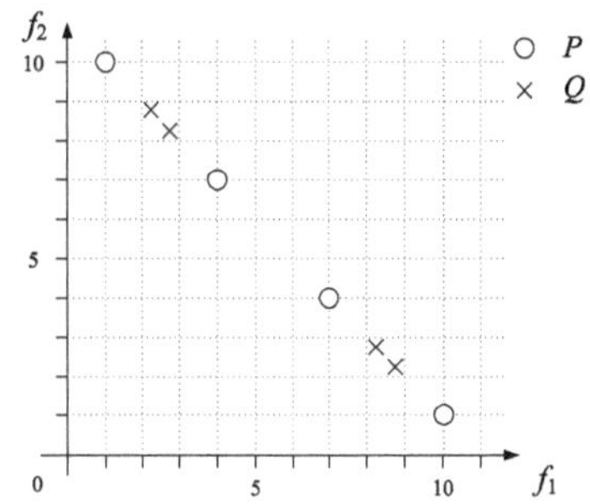

Figure 3: An example that IGD and IGD$^+$ fails to reflect the performance difference between approximation sets, where the reference set is constructed by the approximation sets themselves. P and Q have the same IGD and IGD$^+$ evaluation results (0.884 and 0.625 respectively).

least one solution in the approximation set. One weakness in the ϵ-indicator is that its evaluation value is only related to one particular solution in an approximation set, which could lead to an inaccurate estimation of the set's performance. Figure 2 gives an example that the unary additive ϵ-indicator fails to distinguish between approximation sets (P and Q). As can be seen from the figure, P clearly outperforms Q, but the two sets have the same evaluation result.

Zitzler et al [37] also presented a binary ϵ-indicator and stated its desirable features, such as being free from the limitations of unary performance indicators, having a low computational cost, and representing natural extension to the evaluation of approximation schemes in theoretical computer science. However, the ϵ-indicator (both unary and binary) only considers one particular objective of the problem (i.e., the objective where the considered approximation sets have the biggest difference), ignoring the difference on the others. This unavoidably leads to an information loss, especially for optimization problems with many objectives. Consider two 10-objective solutions, $p = (0, 0, 0, ..., 0, 1)$ and $q = (1, 1, 1, ..., 1, 0)$. p performs better on nine objectives and q does better only on the last objective, but they have same evaluation result ($\epsilon = 1$).

IGD [2] calculates the average Euclidean distance from each point in a reference set (a substitution of the Pareto front) to its closest solution in an approximation set. This overcomes the ϵ-indicator's problem of only returning one particular objective value of one particular solution. However, one weakness of IGD is its non-compliance with the Pareto dominance relation. Ishibuchi et al [16] presented several examples that an approximation set P could obtain a worse IGD result than an approximation set Q even if P Pareto-dominates Q. This even happens when the reference set is exactly the Pareto front. In fact, a reference set with sufficient, well-distributed points can only reduce the possibility of this misleading result, rather than eliminating it completely.

To solve this problem, Ishibuchi et al [15, 16] proposed a modified IGD (IGD$^+$), only considering the superior objective values of the reference point to the solution of the approximation set in their distance calculation. This can enable the indicator to be weakly Pareto compliant[2] [16]. However, like IGD, IGD$^+$ also needs a reference set specified by the user. While IGD$^+$ alleviates the severe sensitivity of IGD to the reference set, different reference sets can cause IGD$^+$ to prefer different approximation sets. This may lead to inconsistent evaluation results among these sets. In fact, how to specify a proper preference set in many-objective optimization is a challenging issue [15]; this also applies to artificial test functions with a known Pareto front, given that exponentially increasing points are needed to accurately represent a higher-dimensional Pareto front.

For an MOP with an unknown Pareto front, a practical method of constructing a reference set is to use the nondominated solutions of all solutions in the considered approximation sets. This method is widely used in many-objective optimization [12, 15]. However, in this method, there is no information about the location and distribution of the points in the reference set. Some points could be far away from the Pareto front, like the *dominance resistant solutions*[3] [8, 13] which are preserved more likely in a higher-dimensional objective space. Some points could be located closely or even overlapping, and this will result in some areas overcrowded and some others empty. Overall, such a reference set with an arbitrary distribution of nondominated solutions can significantly decrease the accuracy of the evaluation result. Figure 3 gives an example that with the reference set constructed by the tested approximation sets, IGD and IGD$^+$ fail to reflect the performance difference between the sets. As shown, the points of the reference set are not well distributed, which leads to the result that P with uniformly-distributed solutions has the same evaluation value as Q whose solutions concentrate in two small areas.

3. PROPOSED METHOD

As indicated before, the binary ϵ-indicator directly considers the performance difference of approximation sets, but only returns one particular objective value of one particular solution; IGD$^+$ (or IGD) considers the whole approximation set and multiple (or all) objectives, but requires a reference

[2]For a weakly Pareto compliant indicator I, if a set P weakly dominates a set Q, then $I(P)$ is not worse than $I(Q)$ [37].

[3]Dominance resistant solutions in a set are the solutions with a quite poor value in at least one of the objectives but with (near) optimal values in some others, and thus are nondominated in the set.

set which is hard to specify in many-objective optimization. So, an intuitive idea of developing an indicator is to consider their combination, that is, using the calculation method of IGD$^+$ to directly compare two approximation sets (i.e., two approximation sets are viewed as mutual reference sets in the IGD$^+$ calculation). This indicator, though, also suffers from the effect of a poorly-distributed reference set, e.g., still failing to distinguish between the approximation sets in Figure 3. In fact, since each point (regardless of its location) in the reference set is equally treated in the evaluation, the areas with many similar (or duplicate) points have more effect than the same-size ones with few points on the evaluation result. This naturally leads such an indicator to prefer an approximation set having similar distribution with the considered reference set. In addition, since a binary indicator manipulates only two approximation sets, many comparisons are required when more than two approximation sets are involved ($\binom{n}{2}$ comparisons for n sets).

Given the above, this paper presents a performance comparison indicator (PCI), capable of assessing multiple approximation sets (any number) in a single run. PCI constructs a reference set by using all the tested Pareto front approximations and assesses each approximation on the basis of this reference set. Rather than dealing with each point in the reference set, PCI divides all points into many clusters according to their distribution (the method of the division will be explained later), and considers the relationship between the clusters and solutions in the approximation set. Specifically, PCI measures the minimum move distance of one solution to weakly dominate[4] all points in a cluster, as defined as follows.

Definition 1 (Dominance Distance of a point to a point set): Let p be a point and Q be a set of points $\{q_1, q_2, ..., q_k\}$ ($k \geq 1$). The dominance distance $D(p,Q)$ of p to Q is defined as the minimum move of p in the objective space such that p weakly dominates all points in Q. It can be calculated as

$$D(p,Q) = \sqrt{\sum_{i=1}^{m}(p^{(i)} - d(p^{(i)},Q))^2} \tag{1}$$

$$d(p^{(i)},Q) = \begin{cases} \min\{q_1^{(i)}, q_2^{(i)}, ..., q_k^{(i)}\}, & \text{if } p^{(i)} > \min\{q_1^{(i)}, q_2^{(i)}, ..., q_k^{(i)}\} \\ p^{(i)}, & \text{otherwise} \end{cases}$$

where $p^{(i)}$ denotes the objective value of point p in the ith objective and m is the number of objectives.

Dominance distance $D(p,Q)$ only considers the objectives where Q performs better than p (i.e., the best value of the points in Q is better than that of p), regardless of the advantage of p over Q. This can lead to the indicator free from the effect of poorly-converged reference points, such as the dominance resistant solutions. The range of $D(p,Q)$ is from 0 to ∞; the smaller the better. If p performs slightly worse than Q in only few objectives, $D(p,Q)$ will be small. Only when p weakly dominates all points in Q, $D(p,Q) = 0$.

Note that when Q has only one point q, the dominance distance of p to Q becomes $D(p,q)$, i.e., the minimum move of p to weakly dominate q in the objective space. This method has already been used in the area to measure the difference between two solutions. IGD$^+$ used this measure to replace the Euclidean distance in the IGD calculation, making the indicator compliant with weak Pareto dominance. Li et al [22] adopted a similar principle to improve solutions' density estimation, enabling Pareto-based algorithms to be suitable for many-objective problems. In fact, $D(p,Q)$ can also be viewed as the dominance distance of p to a point, q_{ideal}, constructed by the best value of each objective for all k points in Q.

In contrast to IGD and IGD$^+$ which consider each point in the reference set, PCI replaces a set of similar points with an imaginary (ideal) point constructed by themselves. This avoids the overlapping effect of similar points and also takes into account the superiority of these points on each objective. In fact, the dominance distance of a point to a set of points is larger than or equal to the maximum dominance distance of the point to all members in the set, but is smaller than their summation, i.e., $\max\{D(p,q_1), ..., D(p,q_k)\} <= D(p,Q) < D(p,q_1) + ... + D(p,q_k)$. The proof is omitted here for lack of space.

Given that the dominance distance of a point to a cluster reflects the advantage of the cluster over the point, one may think to use this dominance distance to consider all clusters in the reference set to assess an approximation set. However, this evaluation may lead to an inaccurate result when in a cluster there is more than one solution from the assessed approximation set. To explain this, we introduce the following definition.

Definition 2 (Dominance Distance of a point set to another): Let P be a set of points and Q be a set of points. The dominance distance $D(P,Q)$ of P to Q is defined as the minimum total distance of the move of points of P in the objective space such that for any point $q \in Q$, there is at least one point $p \in P$ that weakly dominates q.

The dominance distance of two sets reflects their performance difference. If P (weakly) dominates Q, then $D(P,Q) = 0$.

In the proposed indicator, since the reference set consists of all the approximation sets, a cluster can contain points from different approximation sets. Let a cluster C be comprised of P and Q, where $P = \{p_1, ..., p_i\}$ is from the assessed approximation set and $Q = \{q_1, ..., q_j\}$ from other approximation sets. Apparently, $D(P,C) = D(P,Q)$. When $i = 1$, $D(P,C)$ is the dominance distance of p_1 to the ideal point of C. When $i \geq 2$, $D(P,C)$ could be smaller than $\min\{D(p_1,C), ..., D(p_i,C)\}$.

Figure 4 gives an example to illustrate this situation. Consider the dominance distance of three solution sets P_1 ,P_2, and P_3 to three clusters C_1 ,C_2, and C_3, respectively in the figure, where $P_1 \in C_1, P_2 \in C_2, P_3 \in C_3, P = P_1 \cup P_2 \cup P_3$. For P_1 which has only one solution, $D(P_1,C_1)$ is the dominance distance of the solution to the cluster, ($D(P_1,C_1) = (0.5^2 + 0.5^2)^{0.5} \approx 0.707$). For P_2 which has two solutions, $D(P_2,C_2)$ is the dominance distance of the upper solution to the ideal point of the two Q solutions, and this is smaller than the minimum of the dominance distance of the two single P_2 solutions to the cluster ($0.559 < \min\{1.031, 1.25\}$). Cluster C_3 gives an extreme situation where no move of the P_3 solutions is needed to weakly dominate all solutions in the cluster (i.e., $D(P_3,C_3) = 0$), but the dominance distance of the two single P_3 solutions to the cluster is 1.0.

From the above, it is clear that for a cluster $C = P \cup Q$ ($P = \{p_1, ..., p_i\}, i \geq 2, Q = \{q_1, ..., q_j\}$), the required move

[4]For two solutions p and q, p weakly dominates q ($p \preceq q$) if and only if p is not worse than q in all objectives.

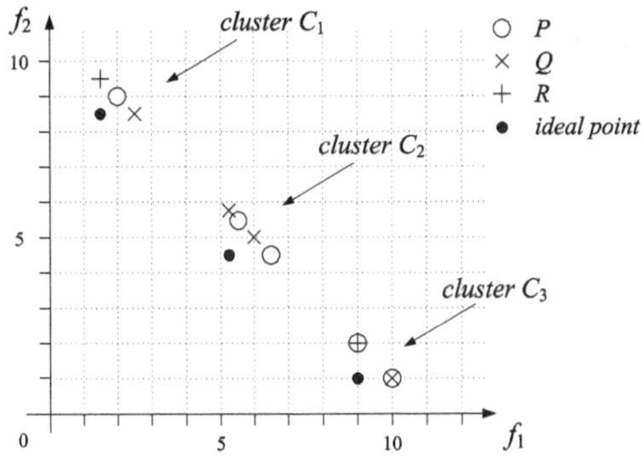

Figure 4: An example that the dominance distance of a set of solutions to a cluster can be smaller than the minimum of their single dominance distance to the cluster. For three sets P_1 ,P_2, and P_3 ($P_1 \in C_1, P_2 \in C_2, P_3 \in C_3, P = P_1 \cup P_2 \cup P_3$), their dominance distance to C_1, C_2 and C_3 is 0.707, 0.559 and 0.0, respectively, while the minimum of their single solution's dominance distance to C_1, C_2 and C_3 is 0.707, 1.031 and 1.0, respectively.

of P to weakly dominate C can be (much) smaller than the minimum move of any one point in P to weakly dominate C. This is because the points in C can be "divided and conquered" by multiple solutions in P. However, how to determine $D(P, C)$ (i.e., the minimum move of $\{p_1, ..., p_i\}$ to weakly dominate $\{q_1, ..., q_j\}$) could be quite time consuming; there are i^j possibilities for $p_1, p_2, ..., p_i$ to divide $q_1, q_2, ..., q_j$. Here, we approximately measure it by

$$D'(P, C) = \max\{\min\{D(p_1, q_1), \dots, D(p_i, q_1)\}, \dots, \min\{D(p_1, q_j), \dots, D(p_i, q_j)\}\} \quad (2)$$

when $i \geq 2$. This only requires $i \times j$ comparisons. Although $D'(P, C) \leq D(P, C)$, their difference is generally slight when the size of C is small. In the example of Figure 4, $D'(P_2, C_2) = 0.5 < D(P_2, C_2) = 0.559$ and $D'(P_3, C_3) = D(P_3, C_3) = 0$.

Algorithm 1 gives the main procedure of the proposed indicator. It is necessary to mention here that we normalize approximation sets before the evaluation, in order to make PCI be able to deal with MOPs with non-commensurable objective functions. Specifically, the range of an MOP's Pareto front is used to implement the normalization if it is available; otherwise, the boundary of the constructed reference set is done. From Algorithm 1, it can be seen that PCI treats the clusters differently. For a cluster where the number of solutions from the assessed approximation set is less than two, PCI takes account of the minimum move of one solution in the approximation set to weakly dominate the cluster (step 8), on the basis of Eq. (1). Otherwise, PCI estimates the minimum move of the set's solutions in the cluster to weakly dominate the cluster by Eq. (2) (step 10).

An important issue in the proposed indicator is to cluster the points in the reference set before assessing approximation sets (step 2). Here, we use a greedy method to stepwise merge points according to their dominance distance. Algorithm 2 gives the details of clustering. A threshold σ is required in this clustering. We set σ to be the interval (in the sense of the dominance distance) of two neighboring

Algorithm 1 Performance Comparison Indicator (PCI)

Require: $P^1, P^2, \dots, P^{pn}$ (tested approximation sets)
1: $S \leftarrow \mathit{NondominanceSelection}(P^1, P^2, \dots, P^{pn})$
/* Finding out the nondominated solutions of the mixed set consisting of all the approximation sets */
2: $(C_1, C_2, ..., C_{cn}) \leftarrow \mathit{Clustering}(S)$
/* Clustering the points in S according to Algorithm 2 */
3: **for all** $P^i \in \{P^1, P^2, \dots, P^{pn}\}$ **do**
4: $\quad \mathrm{PCI}(P^i) \leftarrow 0$
5: $\quad$ **for all** $C_j \in \{C_1, C_2, \dots, C_{cn}\}$ **do**
6: $\quad\quad P^i_j \leftarrow P^i \cap C_j$
7: $\quad\quad$ **if** $|P^i_j| < 2$ **then**
8: $\quad\quad\quad \mathrm{PCI}(P^i) \leftarrow \mathrm{PCI}(P^i) + \min\{D(p^i_1, C_j), ..., D(p^i_n, C_j)\}$
/* Finding out the minimum dominance distance of one solution in $P^i = \{p^i_1, ..., p^i_n\}$ to C_j */
9: $\quad\quad$ **else**
10: $\quad\quad\quad \mathrm{PCI}(P^i) \leftarrow \mathrm{PCI}(P^i) + D'(P^i_j, C_j)$
/* Estimating the dominance distance of P^i_j to C_j */
11: $\quad\quad$ **end if**
12: $\quad$ **end for**
13: $\quad \mathrm{PCI}(P^i) \leftarrow \mathrm{PCI}(P^i)/cn$
14: **end for**
15: **return** $\mathrm{PCI}(P^1), \mathrm{PCI}(P^2), \dots, \mathrm{PCI}(P^{pn})$

Algorithm 2 *Clustering*(S)

Require: $S = \{s_1, s_2, \dots, s_{sn}\}$, σ (threshold)
1: $(p_1, p_2, ..., p_{pn}) \leftarrow \mathit{FindSortPair}(S, \sigma)$
/* Find all pairs of solutions in S satisfying that $\max\{D(s_i, s_j), D(s_j, s_i)\} \leq \sigma$ where s_i and s_j are the two solution of a pair, and then sort the pairs in the ascending order according to $\max\{D(s_i, s_j), D(s_j, s_i)\}$ */
2: $C_1 \leftarrow s_1, C_2 \leftarrow s_2, ..., C_{sn} \leftarrow s_{sn}$ /* Cluster initialization */
3: **for all** $p \in \{p_1, p_2, \dots, p_{pn}\}$ **do**
4: $\quad (C_m, C_n) \leftarrow \mathit{Locate}(p)$ /* Let C_m and C_n be clusters which the two solutions of pair p fall into */
5: $\quad$ **if** $m \neq n$ **then**
6: $\quad\quad$ **if** $\forall s_i \in C_m, s_j \in C_n : D(s_i, s_j) < \sigma \wedge D(s_j, s_i) < \sigma$ **then**
7: $\quad\quad\quad C_m \leftarrow C_m \cup C_n$
8: $\quad\quad\quad C_n \leftarrow \emptyset$
/* Merging two clusters if the dominance distance of any two solutions in them is not larger than σ */
9: $\quad\quad$ **end if**
10: $\quad$ **end if**
11: **end for**
12: **return** $\{C_1, C_2, ..., C_{cn}\} : |C_i| > 0$

points in the normalized hyperplane with ideal distribution of N points, where N is the size of the reference set. In this case, $\sigma = 1/h$ and $N = \binom{m-1+h}{m-1}$, where h denotes the divisions along each objective and m is the number of objectives. Since $(h+m-1) \times (h+m-2) \times ... \times (h+1) \approx (h+m/2)^{m-1}$, σ can be approximately obtained by

$$\sigma \approx \frac{1}{\sqrt[m-1]{N(m-1)!} - (m/2)} \quad (3)$$

4. COMPARISON WITH POPULAR PERFORMANCE INDICATORS

Table 2 summarizes the properties of PCI and some popular performance indicators. As seen, PCI and the ϵ-indicator perform similarly in terms of many aspects, such as neither specifying a reference set nor requiring parameter setting in the evaluation. Only difference between them shown in the table is that PCI is capable of dealing with more than two

Table 2: Properties of some performance indicators

Indicators	Convergence	Diversity	Number of sets	Time complexity	Pareto compliant	Reference set specification	Parameter setting
Coverage [36]	√		binary	quadratic	weakly	no	no
DCI [21]		√	arbitrary	quadratic	no	no	yes
HV [36]	√	√	unary	exponential	yes	no	yes
ϵ-indicator [37]	√	√	unary/binary	quadratic	weakly/yes	no	no
IGD [2]	√	√	unary	quadratic	no	yes	no
IGD$^+$ [16]	√	√	unary	quadratic	weakly	yes	no
PCI	√	√	arbitrary	quadratic	weakly or yes*	no	no

*PCI is Pareto compliant when two approximation sets are considered, but weakly Pareto compliant when more sets are involved. The proof is omitted due to the limit of the space.

Table 3: Evaluation results of PCI and the peer indicator (HV, ϵ-indicator, or IGD$^+$) on the approximation set instances in Figures 1–3. The reference point 1.1 is used in the HV calculation of Figure 1's instance. A better result is highlighted in boldface.

Two sets	Peer indicator	PCI
Fig. 1(a) vs Fig. 1(b)	0.7448 vs **0.7460** (HV)	**0.0159** vs 0.0170
P vs Q in Fig. 2	2.5 vs 2.5 (ϵ-indicator)	**0.0000** vs 0.1204
P vs Q in Fig. 3	0.625 vs 0.625 (IGD$^+$)	**0.0648** vs 0.0926

approximation sets in a single run. In fact, one significant weakness of the ϵ-indicator to other performance indicators, as indicated before, is its return only being the difference on one particular objective of one particular solution for two approximation sets.

Like IGD$^+$, PCI only considers the inferiority of solutions in the evaluation. However, one difference is that PCI considers the comparison between a point to a point set (or two point sets), which could be viewed as a more general case of two-points comparison in IGD$^+$. In addition, since the reference set in PCI consists of the tested approximation sets, the evaluation result of one approximation set depends entirely on its performance difference with other sets. In contrast, in IGD$^+$ the reference set is specified, and the evaluation result of the approximation sets not only depends on their performance difference but also could be largely affected by the reference set (such as its distribution).

Finally, Table 3 gives the evaluation results of PCI and the peer indicators on the approximation sets in Figures 1–3. As shown, compared with HV, ϵ-indicator and IGD$^+$, the proposed indicator can accurately reflect the difference of solution sets in terms of uniformity, convergence and diversity, respectively.

5. EXPERIMENTAL STUDIES

In this section, we verify the proposed indicator by assessing Pareto front approximations obtained by six established multiobjective algorithms, NSGA-II [7], AR [4, 25], IBEA [35], MOEA/D-TCH [33], MOEA/D-PBI [33], and SPEA2+SDE [22]. These algorithms are representative in terms of both convergence and diversity in dealing with many-objective problems.

A crossover probability $p_c = 1.0$ and a mutation probability $p_m = 1/n$ (where n is the number of decision variables) are used. The crossover and mutation operators are simulated binary crossover (SBX) and polynomial mutation with both distribution indexes 20. The population size is set to 100 (or approximately 100 for MOEA/D due to its property [33]) and the termination criterion is $30,000$ evaluations.

To start with, we consider a tri-objective MOP, DTLZ1 [8], whose Pareto front is the positive part of a hyperplane satisfying $f_1 + f_2 + f_3 = 0.5$. Here, we ease the difficulty of the problem by using $g = \sum_{i=m}^{n}(x_i - 0.5)$ in DTLZ1 [8] in order to focus on the diversity verification of the indicator.

Figure 5 shows the approximation sets of the six algorithms as well as the corresponding PCI result. As can be seen from the figure, the solutions of MOEA/D-PBI are perfectly distributed over the whole Pareto front, thus having the best evaluation result. Although the solution sets of SPEA2+SDE, IBEA, and NSGA-II cover the triangle, their uniformity is different, which is consistent with the PCI results. The solution set of MOEA/D-TCH is of great regularity, but fails to cover the boundary region of the Pareto front, thus leading to a worse PCI than the above four sets. The solutions of AR only concentrate around three extreme points and obtain the worst PCI value.

To examine the proposed indicator on MOPs with an irregular Pareto front, we introduce the test problem DTLZ7 [8]. The tri-objective DTLZ7 has a disconnect Pareto front consisting of four regions with both convex and concave shapes. Figure 6 gives the approximation sets and the evaluation results. As shown, the set of SPEA2+SDE and NSGA-II is located in the four optimal regions, with a nearly equal number of solutions. The solutions of the two MOEA/D algorithms are mainly distributed in the bottom region of the Pareto front, and IBEA and AR fail to find all the four regions. It is clear that the PCI results confirm the observations. The solution set with a lower PCI value means that it performs better regarding the combined performance in finding multiple Pareto optimal regions and in maintaining solutions' uniformity and diversity in each region.

Next, we consider a four-objective MOP, Rectangle problem [23]. The Rectangle problem has two interesting features: 1) its Pareto optimal solutions lie in a rectangle in the two-variable decision space and 2) they are similar (in the sense of Euclidean geometry) to their images in the four-dimensional objective space. These make the visual examination of Pareto front approximations feasible by observing their behavior in the decision space. Figure 7 shows the approximation sets and the evaluation results on an instance of the Rectangle problem where the search range and Pareto optimal range of x_1 and x_2 are $[-0.2, 1.2]$ and $[0, 1]$, respectively. As can be seen, the performance of these approximation sets is consistent with the PCI results. SPEA2+SDE and IBEA have a set of well-converged and well-distributed solutions, thus having better PCI results than the other four algorithms. IBEA obtains a slightly worse PCI value than SPEA2+SDE, with more solutions being located onto the boundary of the optimal region. MOEA/D-TCH, NSGA-II and MOEA/D-PBI perform similarly in terms of con-

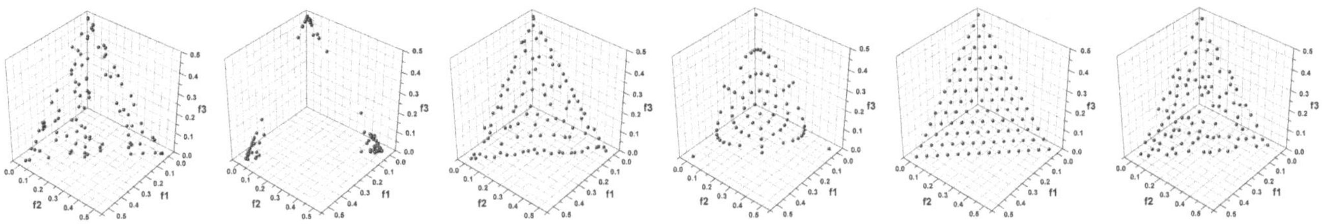

(a) NSGA-II PCI = 0.0417 | (b) AR PCI = 0.1619 | (c) IBEA PCI = 0.0305 | (d) MOEA/D-TCH PCI = 0.0434 | (e) MOEA/D-PBI PCI = 0.0270 | (f) SPEA2+SDE PCI = 0.0291

Figure 5: Approximation sets of the six algorithms and their PCI result on the tri-objective DTLZ1.

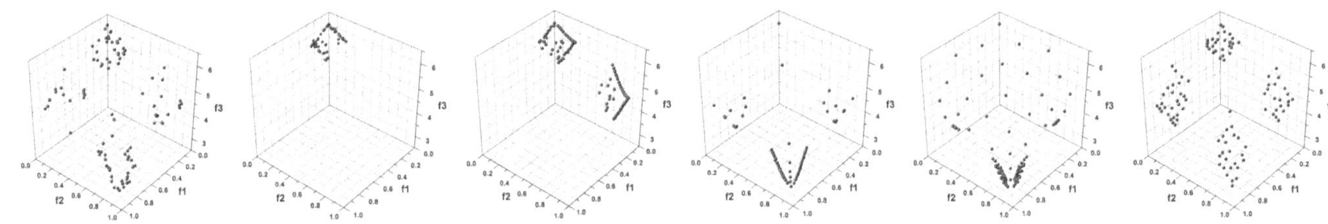

(a) NSGA-II PCI = 0.0346 | (b) AR PCI = 0.2564 | (c) IBEA PCI = 0.1045 | (d) MOEA/D-TCH PCI = 0.0638 | (e) MOEA/D-PBI PCI = 0.0483 | (f) SPEA2+SDE PCI = 0.0163

Figure 6: Approximation sets of the six algorithms and their PCI result on the tri-objective DTLZ7.

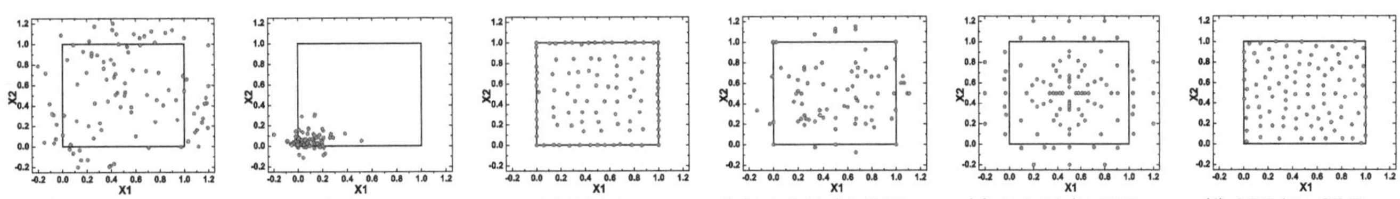

(a) NSGA-II PCI = 0.0692 | (b) AR PCI = 0.4147 | (c) IBEA PCI = 0.0506 | (d) MOEA/D-TCH PCI = 0.0666 | (e) MOEA/D-PBI PCI = 0.0798 | (f) SPEA2+SDE PCI = 0.0498

Figure 7: Approximation sets of the six algorithms in the two-variable decision space and their PCI result on the four-objective Rectangle problem, where the Pareto optimal solutions in the decision space are similar to their images in the objective space in the sense of Euclidean geometry.

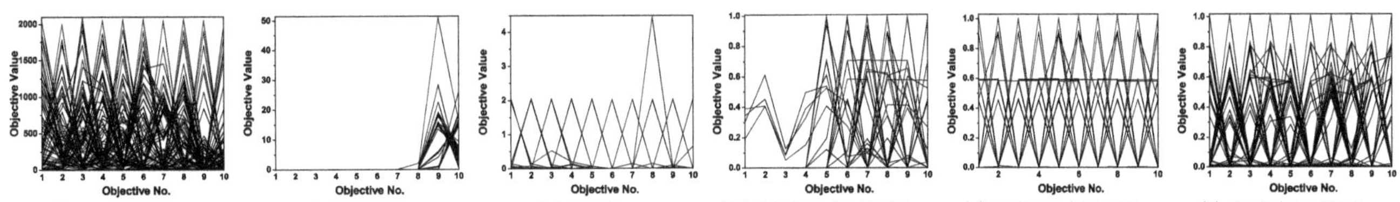

(a) NSGA-II PCI = 236.07 | (b) AR PCI = 11.820 | (c) IBEA PCI = 1.0058 | (d) MOEA/D-TCH PCI = 0.2218 | (e) MOEA/D-PBI PCI = 0.0936 | (f) SPEA2+SDE PCI = 0.0845

Figure 8: Parallel coordinate plot of approximation sets of the six algorithms and their PCI result on the ten-objective DTLZ3.

vergence and diversity. Among them, MOEA/D-TCH has fewer solutions out of the optimal rectangle and MOEA/D-PBI has many solutions concentrated into the center of the rectangle. This leads to the difference of their PCI results. All solutions of AR are located around the lower left corner of the rectangle and thus have the worst evaluation result.

Finally, the 10-objective DTLZ3 is used to verify PCI in assessing approximation sets for high-dimensional challenging MOPs. DTLZ3 has a vast number of local optimal fronts ($3^{10}-1$) and a global one satisfying $f_1^2+f_2^2+...+f_m^2=1$ in the range $f_1, f_2, ..., f_m \in [0,1]$. Figure 8 shows the approximation sets by parallel coordinates as well as the corresponding evaluation results. As shown, the solutions of only three algorithms SPEA2+SDE, MOEA/D-PBI, and MOEA/D-TCH can converge into the optimal front. SPEA2+SDE and MOEA/D-PBI achieve a good balance between convergence and diversity, while MOEA/D-TCH fails to cover the whole Pareto front. Almost all solutions of IBEA converge into the boundary of a local optimum ($f_1^2+...+f_{10}^2=2$), and most of AR's solutions concentrate around two boundary points of a local optimum ($f_1^2+...+f_{10}^2=20$). NSGA-II completely fails to approach the optimal front, with the upper boundary of its solutions exceeding 2000 on each objective. The PCI results clearly reflect the performance of the approximation sets. A set with a lower DCI value means that it performs better with respect to the tradeoff between convergence and diversity.

6. CONCLUSIONS

This paper presents a performance comparison indicator (PCI) to assess Pareto front approximations of population-based search algorithms. PCI evaluates the relative quality of approximation sets to a reference set which is constructed by themselves. The points in the reference set are clustered according to their distribution, and PCI estimates the minimum moves of one solution (or a set of solutions) in one approximation set to weakly dominate these clusters. The proposed indicator can be practical, especially in many-objective optimization, given its combined evaluation of convergence and diversity, (weak) compliance with Pareto dominance, applicability for any number of approximation sets, no need of a specified reference set, and no requirement of parameter setting in the assessment.

7. REFERENCES

[1] J. Bader and E. Zitzler. HypE: An algorithm for fast hypervolume-based many-objective optimization. *Evol. Comput.*, 19(1):45–76, 2011.

[2] P. A. N. Bosman and D. Thierens. The balance between proximity and diversity in multiobjective evolutionary algorithms. *IEEE Trans. Evol. Comput.*, 7(2):174–188, 2003.

[3] K. Bringmann, T. Friedrich, C. Igel, and T. Voß. Speeding up many-objective optimization by Monte Carlo approximations. *Artif. Intell.*, 204:22–29, 2013.

[4] D. W. Corne and J. D. Knowles. Techniques for highly multiobjective optimisation: some nondominated points are better than others. In *Proc. 9th Genetic Evol. Comput. Conf. (GECCO)*, pages 773–780, 2007.

[5] K. Deb and H. Jain. An evolutionary many-objective optimization algorithm using reference-point-based nondominated sorting approach, part I: Solving problems with box constraints. *IEEE Trans. Evol. Comput.*, 18(4):577–601, 2014.

[6] K. Deb and S. Jain. Running performance metrics for evolutionary multi-objective optimization. Technical Report 2002004, KanGAL, Indian Institute of Technology, 2002.

[7] K. Deb, A. Pratap, S. Agarwal, and T. Meyarivan. A fast and elitist multiobjective genetic algorithm: NSGA-II. *IEEE Trans. Evol. Comput.*, 6(2):182–197, 2002.

[8] K. Deb, L. Thiele, M. Laumanns, and E. Zitzler. Scalable test problems for evolutionary multiobjective optimization. In A. Abraham, L. Jain, and R. Goldberg, editors, *Evolutionary Multiobjective Optimization. Theoretical Advances and Applications*, pages 105–145. Berlin, Germany: Springer, 2005.

[9] P. Fleming, R. Purshouse, and R. Lygoe. Many-objective optimization: An engineering design perspective. In *Proc. 3rd Int. Conf. Evol. Multi-Criterion Optimiz. (EMO)*, pages 14–32. 2005.

[10] D. Hadka and P. Reed. Diagnostic assessment of search controls and failure modes in many-objective evolutionary optimization. *Evol. Comput.*, 20(3):423–452, 2012.

[11] Z. He, G. G. Yen, and J. Zhang. Fuzzy-based Pareto optimality for many-objective evolutionary algorithms. *IEEE Trans. Evol. Comput.*, 18(2):269–285, 2014.

[12] E. J. Hughes. MSOPS-II: A general-purpose many-objective optimiser. In *Proc. 2007 IEEE Congr. Evol. Comput. (CEC)*, pages 3944–3951, 2007.

[13] K. Ikeda, H. Kita, and S. Kobayashi. Failure of Pareto-based MOEAs: does non-dominated really mean near to optimal? In *Proce. 2001 IEEE Congr. Evol. Comput. (CEC)*, volume 2, pages 957–962, 2001.

[14] H. Ishibuchi, N. Akedo, and Y. Nojima. Behavior of multi-objective evolutionary algorithms on many-objective knapsack problems. *IEEE Trans. Evol. Comput.*, 19(2):264–283, 2015.

[15] H. Ishibuchi, H. Masuda, Y. Tanigaki, and Y. Nojima. Difficulties in specifying reference points to calculate the inverted generational distance for many-objective optimization problems. In *Proc. 2014 IEEE Symp. Comput. Intell. in Multi-Criteria Decision-Making*, pages 170–177, 2014.

[16] H. Ishibuchi, H. Masuda, Y. Tanigaki, and Y. Nojima. Modified distance calculation in generational distance and inverted generational distance. In *Proc. 8th Int. Conf. Evol. Multi-Criterion Optimiz. (EMO)*, pages 110–125, 2015.

[17] H. Ishibuchi, N. Tsukamoto, and Y. Nojima. Evolutionary many-objective optimization: A short review. In *Proc. 2008 IEEE Congr. Evol. Comput. (CEC)*, pages 2419–2426, 2008.

[18] A. L. Jaimes and C. A. Coello Coello. Study of preference relations in many-objective optimization. In *Proc. 11th Genetic Evol. Comput. Conf. (GECCO)*, pages 611–618, 2009.

[19] J. Knowles and D. Corne. Properties of an adaptive archiving algorithm for storing nondominated vectors. *IEEE Trans. Evol. Comput.*, 7(2):100–116, 2003.

[20] M. Laumanns, L. Thiele, K. Deb, and E. Zitzler. Combining convergence and diversity in evolutionary multiobjective optimization. *Evol. Comput.*, 10(3):263–282, 2002.

[21] M. Li, S. Yang, and X. Liu. Diversity comparison of Pareto front approximations in many-objective optimization. *IEEE Trans. Cybern.*, 44(12):2568–2584, 2014.

[22] M. Li, S. Yang, and X. Liu. Shift-based density estimation for Pareto-based algorithms in many-objective optimization. *IEEE Trans. Evol. Comput.*, 18(3):348–365, 2014.

[23] M. Li, S. Yang, and X. Liu. A test problem for visual investigation of high-dimensional multi-objective search. In *Proc. 2014 IEEE Congr. Evol. Comput. (CEC)*, pages 2140–2147, 2014.

[24] M. Li, S. Yang, X. Liu, and R. Shen. A comparative study on evolutionary algorithms for many-objective optimization. In *Proc. 7th Int. Conf. Evol. Multi-Criterion Optimiz. (EMO)*, pages 261–275, 2013.

[25] M. Li, J. Zheng, K. Li, Q. Yuan, and R. Shen. Enhancing diversity for average ranking method in evolutionary many-objective optimization. In *Proc. 11th Int. Conf. Parallel Problem Solving From Nature (PPSN)*, pages 647–656, 2010.

[26] G. Lizárraga-Lizárraga, A. Hernández-Aguirre, and S. Botello-Rionda. G-Metric: an M-ary quality indicator for the evaluation of non-dominated sets. In *Proc. 10th Genetic Evol. Comput. Conf.*, pages 665–672, 2008.

[27] R. C. Purshouse and P. J. Fleming. On the evolutionary optimization of many conflicting objectives. *IEEE Trans. Evol. Comput.*, 11(6):770–784, 2007.

[28] O. Schütze, X. Esquivel, A. Lara, and C. A. C. Coello. Using the averaged Hausdorff distance as a performance measure in evolutionary multi-objective optimization. *IEEE Trans. Evol. Comput.*, 16(4):504–522, 2012.

[29] D. A. Van Veldhuizen. *Multiobjective evolutionary algorithms: Classifications, analyses, and new innovations.* PhD thesis, Department of Electrical and Computer Engineering, Graduate School of Engineering, Air Force Institute of Technology, Wright-Patterson AFB, Ohio, 1999.

[30] T. Wagner, N. Beume, and B. Naujoks. Pareto-, aggregation-, and indicator-based methods in many-objective optimization. In *Proc. 4th Int. Conf. Evol. Multi-Criterion Optimiz. (EMO)*, pages 742–756. 2007.

[31] R. Wang, R. C. Purshouse, and P. J. Fleming. Preference-inspired co-evolutionary algorithms for many-objective optimisation. *IEEE Trans. Evol. Comput.*, 17(4):474–494, 2013.

[32] S. Yang, M. Li, X. Liu, and J. Zheng. A grid-based evolutionary algorithm for many-objective optimization. *IEEE Trans. Evol. Comput.*, 17(5):721–736, 2013.

[33] Q. Zhang and H. Li. MOEA/D: A multiobjective evolutionary algorithm based on decomposition. *IEEE Trans. Evol. Comput.*, 11(6):712–731, 2007.

[34] X. Zhang, Y Tian, and Y. Jin. A knee point driven evolutionary algorithm for many-objective optimization. *IEEE Trans. Evol. Comput.*, 2014, in press.

[35] E. Zitzler and S. Künzli. Indicator-based selection in multiobjective search. In *Proc. 8th Int. Conf. Parallel Problem Solving from Nature (PPSN)*, pages 832–842. 2004.

[36] E. Zitzler and L. Thiele. Multiobjective evolutionary algorithms: A comparative case study and the strength Pareto approach. *IEEE Trans. Evol. Comput.*, 3(4):257–271, 1999.

[37] E. Zitzler, L. Thiele, M. Laumanns, C. M. Fonseca, and V. G. da Fonseca. Performance assessment of multiobjective optimizers: An analysis and review. *IEEE Trans. Evol. Comput.*, 7(2):117–132, 2003.

Improving Robustness of Stopping Multi-objective Evolutionary Algorithms by Simultaneously Monitoring Objective and Decision Space

Md Shahriar Mahbub
Fondazione Bruno Kessler
Trento, Italy
University of Trento
Trento, Italy
mahbub@fbk.eu

Tobias Wagner
Institute of Machining Technology (ISF)
TU Dortmund, Germany
wagner@isf.de

Luigi Crema
Fondazione Bruno Kessler
Via Sommarive 18, I-38123
Trento, Italy
crema@fbk.eu

ABSTRACT

Appropriate stopping criteria for multi-objective evolutionary algorithms (MOEA) are an important research topic due to the computational cost of function evaluations, particularly on real-world problems. Most common stopping criteria are based on a fixed budget of function evaluations or the monitoring of the objective space. In this work, we propose a stopping criterion based on monitoring both the objective and decision space of a problem. Average Hausdorff distance (AHD) and genetic diversity are used, respectively. Two-sided t-tests on the slope coefficients after regression analyses are used to detect the stagnation of the AHD and the genetic diversity. The approach is implemented for two widely used MOEAs: NSGA-II and SPEA2. It is compared to a fixed budget, the online convergence detection approach, and the individual monitoring of each space on four bi-objective and two three-objective benchmark problems. Our experimental results reveal that the combined approach achieved significantly better results than the approaches considering only one of the spaces. In particular, we find that the combined consideration runs longer and hence more robustly ensures a well-approximated Pareto front. Nevertheless, on average 29% and 17% function evaluations are saved for NSGA-II and SPEA2, respectively, compared to standard budget recommendations.

Categories and Subject Descriptors

I.2.8 [**Artificial Intelligence**]: Problem Solving, Control Methods, and Search-Heuristic methods

Keywords

Multi-objective optimization, stopping criteria, performance assessment

1. INTRODUCTION

GECCO '15, July 11 - 16, 2015, Madrid, Spain
© 2015 ACM. ISBN 978-1-4503-3472-3/15/07... $15.00
DOI: http://dx.doi.org/10.1145/2739480.2754680

Virtually all the engineering fields have to deal with optimization problems. Most practical problems encounter multiple contradictory objectives; therefore, the problems need to be considered as multi-objective optimization problems. Multi-objective evolutionary algorithms (MOEA) have become a common technique for optimizing real-world optimization problems [15]. Unlikely to a single-objective optimization where the goal is to find one optimal solution, a MOEA generates a set of non-dominated solutions. The representation of the solutions in objective space is called Pareto front. A MOEA should find the Pareto front [2] by using minimum computational cost. Since function evaluations (FE) of most real-world optimization problems are costly, FE occupy the lion's share of total computational cost of an optimization algorithm. Therefore, finding an appropriate stopping criterion is an important task to minimize computational cost. To save wasteful function evaluations, it is necessary to spot the stagnation or convergence of an algorithm. Until now, almost all MOEAs are stopped after a certain number of function evaluations [15]. However, specifying this number for a practical problem without any prior knowledge is quite difficult. Therefore, in the last few years some techniques for detecting convergence of MOEAs have been proposed [15, 13, 1, 7, 11, 8].

Most proposed techniques are based on investigating the objective space of a problem. Our approach is based on the simultaneous monitoring of the objective and the decision space. Simultaneous stabilization of indicators on both spaces provides a more robust stopping criterion, as it is shown later that an algorithm runs longer when a decision space indicator is combined with an objective space indicator. In this context robust refers to the repeatability of the stopping decision with regard to the stochastic indicator measurements. Additionally, the proposed approach does not require any prior knowledge with regard to thresholding parameters that have to be set. The convergence is detected by analyzing the trends of the two indicators. A two-sided t-test on the slope coefficients is used to detect the stagnation of the linear trend.

The remainder of the paper is organized as follows. In section 2, we briefly describe the state of the art criteria for stopping MOEAs. Section 3 presents the details of our proposed method. Experimental results are reported and discussed in section 4. Conclusions and future work will be described in section 5.

2. STATE OF THE ART

Deb and Jain [3] were first to propose two metrics, *convergence* and *diversity*, that can be monitored online. The stopping decision of a MOEA depends on the visual inspection of the metrics. At that time, no automatic convergence detection method was proposed. Inspired from the stopping criterion of a single objective evolutionary algorithm (EA), Rudenko and Schoenauer [11] proposed a stability measure. It is based on the density of non-dominated solutions. By studying the dynamics of NSGA-II [4], the authors experimentally showed that the algorithm converges when the maximum crowding distance [4] stagnates. The user needs to provide a threshold and the algorithm stops when the standard deviation of the maximum crowding distance falls below the threshold for a pre-defined number of generations.

Martí et al. [8] proposed a stopping method called MGBM criterion. The authors proposed an indicator named *mutual dominance rate (MDR)* that is basically a measurement of how many non-dominated solutions of one generation dominate the non-dominated solutions of the successive generation. They used a simplified Kalman filer to gather evidences about when to stop. A MOEA is stopped when the a-posteriori estimation of MDR falls below a pre-defined threshold.

Goel and Stander [7] use an external achieve to propose a new indicator, named *consolidation ratio(CR)*. The archive keeps non-dominated solutions and in each generation, the archive is updated. CR is the ratio of the number of solutions of the previous generation that are still present in archive with regard to the size of the archive. Two different stopping criteria are proposed: *fixed threshold approach* and *utility-function based approach*. In the fixed threshold approach, a MOEA is stopped when CR falls below the pre-defined threshold. For the other approach, the utility of evolving extra generation is calculated and the algorithm terminates when the utility falls below the utility threshold.

Bui et al. [1] suggest a stability measure named *dominance-based quality (DQ)* which is based on the dominance relation of a solution with its neighbouring solutions. The basic idea is that the number of dominating neighbouring solutions will decrease over time as a solution moves towards the Pareto front. To measure DQ of a solution, the authors use additional function evaluations and a Monte Carlo simulation approach. The authors do not provide any suggestions about the convergence value of DQ. However, it is obvious that $DQ = 0$ is a powerful stopping criterion and with the help of visual inspection, the stagnation of an algorithm can be identified.

Trautmann et al. [13] and Wagner et al. [15] apply a statistical approach to solve the problem. In [15], the authors propose two different statistical tests on three performance indicators (PI) (i.e., hypervolume, R2 and additive epsilon) to detect convergence. One of the tests is a *one-sided χ^2-variance test* for measuring the significance of the variances of PIs compared to pre-defined threshold. Another proposed test is the *two-sided t-test* for detecting stagnation by analyzing slope coefficients of different PI trends. A MOEA is stopped when any of the two tests detects convergence (i.e., p-value lower/above the critical level depending on the test).

Roche et al. propose a stopping criterion based on the loss of population diversity in the decision space [10]. The authors propose a formula to determine the time, when the diversity falls below a threshold. The authors also propose a statistical procedure to confidently stop an EA. However, without prior knowledge about the decision space of a problem, it is very difficult to set the threshold. The method is validated only on single objective problems. In contrast, as we are dealing with MOEAs (population consists of a set of solutions covering a Pareto front, not converging towards a single solution), the population always has certain diversity. Hence, in our context, it is more important to detect the moment in time, when the solutions covering the decision space are no longer moved. Therefore, it is preferable to detect stagnation of the diversity value instead of the value falling below a certain threshold.

3. PROPOSED METHODOLOGY

Most of the studies we have discussed above require an objective-space based indicator which has to fall below an user-defined threshold to stop. Additionally, some recent studies also address the stagnation of multiple objective-space based indicators using statistical tests. In contrast to these approaches, our proposed method is based on the simultaneous monitoring of two metrics; one in objective space and another one in decision space. To get a better stopping/convergence method, our primary assumption is that indicators on these two spaces (i.e., objective and decision) should stabilize concurrently. A stagnation of indicators in objective space (e.g., hypervolume [19], epsilon [20] and so on) does not mean that the algorithm could not improve later. The individuals of a population may contain enough diversity to generate better children in later generations. Therefore, by concurrently monitoring the two spaces, a more robust stopping criterion could be developed. *Average Hausdorff distance* [12] and *diversity* [16] metrics are used to monitor the objective and decision space, respectively. In the field of MOEA, diversity usually refers to population diversity in the objective space; however in this paper, we use the term *diversity* to refer to decision space diversity.

Average Hausdorff distance.

Classical Hausdorff distance is a widely used metric to measure the distance between two sets. It is the maximum distance among all the distances form every point of one set to the closest point in the other set. Therefore, the original version of Hausdorff distance is not a suitable metric for measuring the convergence of multi-objective optimization algorithms [12]. The main reason is that a set with an outlier is largely penalized compared to a set without any outlier when measuring distance from a reference set. That is not compatible with the stochastic nature of MOEAs. The situation with outliers can be improved by averaging the distance between the set and reference set. Therefore, average Hausdorff distance (AHD) is proposed by Schutze et al. in [12] by exploiting generational distance (GD) and inverted generational distance (IGD), as GD and IGD both inherently measure average distance between two sets. Let $A = \{a_1, a_2 \ldots, a_n\}$ and $B = \{b_1, b_2, \ldots, b_m\}$ are two finite sets. GD is defined as follows:

$$GD(A,B) = \frac{1}{n}\Big(\sum_{i=1}^{n} dis(a_i,B)^p\Big)^{\frac{1}{p}} \quad (1)$$

Where $dis(a_i, B) = \inf_{b_i \in B} \|a_i - b_i\|$ and $\|.\|$ refers to a Euclidean norm. The indicator suffers the problem that a large candidate set having many similar solutions may reduce the GD value. Therefore, it becomes difficult to compare candidate sets with different numbers of solutions (e.g., larger and smaller candidate sets). To avoid this problem, the authors of [12] propose a slightly modified version of GD by taking the power mean of average distances.

$$GD(A,B)_p = \left(\frac{1}{n}\sum_{i=1}^{n} dis(a_i,B)^p\right)^{\frac{1}{p}} \quad (2)$$

Now, the larger candidate set does not always have good GD value. Moreover, the penalizing effect of outliers can be controlled though p. The same approach is applied on IGD [12].

$$IGD(A,B)_p = \left(\frac{1}{m}\sum_{i=1}^{m} dis(b_i,A)^p\right)^{\frac{1}{p}} \quad (3)$$

Finally, the average Hausdorff distance is defined as follows:

$$AHD_p(A,B) = max(GD_p(A,B), IGD_p(A,B)) \quad (4)$$

For small p values, the set with outliers are less penalized than the classical Hausdorff distance. Larger p values have more penalizing effects. Moreover, when $p = \infty$, the AHD is deduced to Hausdorff distance.

Diversity.

There are many possible techniques to measure the genetic diversity of a population. Two popular methods are Hamming distances among all pairs of chromosomes and Shannon entropy on gene frequencies [16]. The authors of [16] argue that the underlying mechanisms of all diversity measurements are similar. Fundamentally, population diversity is a measurement of how individuals of a population are different to each other.

Considering P is a population of n individuals and $\{x_{i,1}, x_{i,2}, \ldots, x_{i,l}\}$ are l chromosomes of an arbitrary i^{th} individual. The diversity of the kth chromosome is based on all possible distances between the chromosomes of the individuals. It can be written in the following way [16]:

$$Div_k^2(P) = \frac{1}{2}\sum_{i=1}^{n}\sum_{j=1}^{n} dis(x_{i,k}, x_{j,k}) \quad (5)$$

Summing up over all the chromosomes, the equation (5) becomes

$$Div^2(P) = \frac{1}{2}\sum_{k=1}^{l}\sum_{i=1}^{n}\sum_{j=1}^{n} dis(x_{i,k}, x_{j,k}) \quad (6)$$

By using some algebraic manipulation, the diversity can be written in the following form:

$$Div^2(P) = n^2\sum_{k=1}^{l}\left(\overline{x_k^2} - \overline{x_k}^2\right) \quad (7)$$

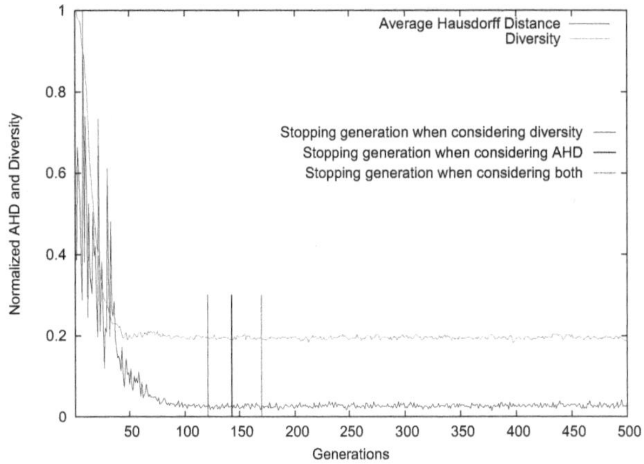

Figure 1: Normalized AHD and diversity are represented by black and blue trends. Three vertical lines with three different colors indicate the stopping generations for three different approaches.

Where $\overline{x_k} = \frac{1}{n}\sum_{i=1}^{n} x_{i,k}$ and $\overline{x_k^2} = \frac{1}{n}\sum_{i=1}^{n} x_{i,k}^2$. Finally, omitting constants and applying a monotone transformation, diversity is defined as follows [16]:

$$Div(P) = \frac{1}{l}\sqrt{\sum_{k=1}^{l}\left(\overline{x_k^2} - \overline{x_k}^2\right)} \quad (8)$$

Figure 1 illustrates the values of two metrics on the ZDT1 [17] problem when solved by NSGA-II. In the figure, the values of AHD and diversity are normalized to show both metrics in the same plot. The figure illustrates that after some time the metrics stabilize. There are still some random fluctuations, but no significant increasing or decreasing trends can be found.

The reason for the remaining perturbations can be explained by diversity controlling mechanism. Most classical MOEAs, such as NSGA-II [4] and SPEA2 [18], have a mechanism to maintain diversity in the objective space (e.g., crowding distance, archive truncation). The perturbations reflect that some individuals are moved from a crowded region to a less crowded region by means of the diversity controlling mechanism. Figure 2 illustrates the Pareto fronts of the 140th and 141th generation. The region covered by a rectangle illustrates the behaviour discussed before. Within the zoomed view in the upper part of the figure, one can see the re-positioning of an individual in the 140th generation marked by '+', which is marked by '□' in the 141th generation. Therefore, if the trend (figure 1) stabilizes for a longer time, we conclude that significant improvements are unlikely.

To detect stability, a regression analysis is performed. More specifically, a two-sided t-test is carried out to check the significance of the decreasing linear trend [15]. Using the test, it is possible to measure the slope (β) of the indicator values using a least-squares method [15]. Moreover, a statistical hypothesis test (i.e., t-test) is carried out to determine the significance of β. Since we want to detect the disappearance of the trend (i.e., $\beta = 0$), the statement for the hypothesis test can be expressed as:

$$H_0 : \beta = 0 \text{ vs } H_1 : \beta \neq 0 \quad (9)$$

Consequently, we try to detect the generation where the null hypothesis cannot be rejected anymore. Figure 1 shows the

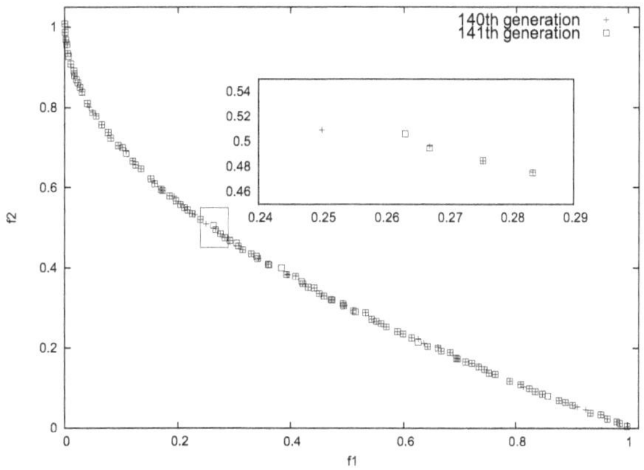

Figure 2: Pareto fronts extracted by NSGA-II for two consecutive generations.

stopping generations (three vertical lines) when the test is applied individually and concurrently on different metrics (i.e., AHD and diversity). It is clear from preliminary results that each metric stabilizes at different time. Moreover, by considering two metrics simultaneously, the algorithm stops later. Hence, it is possible to detect convergence more robustly by monitoring the objective and decision space concurrently.

Algorithm 1 presents the details of the proposed method. There are four intuitive parameters that need to be specified. The user has to provide a significance level (α) for the statistical test. Mainly two values are found: 0.05 (standard) and 0.1 (conservative) [15]. A user needs to specify the number of previous generations (*nGenLT*), for which *AHD* and *Diversity* values are considered in order to estimate the slope of the linear regression model. The next parameter (*nGenUnCh*) is the number of preceding generations for which no significant improvement can be obtained (i.e., H_0 cannot be rejected, *p*-value>α). Finally, the last parameter (*MaxGen*) is the number of maximum allowable generations. *AHD* and *Diversity* are calculated for each generation (step 9 and 10). After *nGenLT* generations, *p*-values for AHD and diversity are calculated (step 12 and 13). To calculate *p*-values for corresponding metrics the previous *nGenLT* metric values are considered. A MOEA will be stopped when either the algorithm already evolved for *MaxGen* generations or the *p*-values for both metrics (*AHD* and *Diversity*) are larger than α for the previous *nGenUnCh* generations (step 15).

4. EXPERIMENTS AND RESULTS

A number of experiments has been conducted to analyze the performance of the proposed MOEA stopping criterion. For the experiments, we have selected two widely used MOEAs (i.e., NSGA-II [4] and SPEA2 [18]) and six benchmark problems (*ZDT1, ZDT2, ZDT3, ZDT4, DTLZ2, DTLZ5*) [17, 5] providing different characteristics of the Pareto fronts. All the problems of the ZDT family are bi-objective, whereas DTLZ2 and DTLZ5 are three-objectives problems. Our concurrent approach will be compared with an individual monitoring of each space. Additionally, it will be compared with a state-of-the-art stopping criterion, called *online convergence detection (OCD)* [15]. To run OCD, the framework proposed in [14] is used. Finally, a comparison with standard budget recommendations will be presented.

4.1 Experimental settings

The proposed methodology is implemented in jMetal [6], a multi-objective meta-heuristic framework developed in JAVA. The framework contains a large set of implemented meta-heuristics including NSGA-II and SPEA2, as well as many benchmark problems. Table 1 shows the standard parameter settings for our experiments. Moreover, we have used simulated binary crossover [2], polynomial mutation [2] and binary tournament selection [2] for both of the algorithms. Additionally, we set $nGenLT = 30$, $nGenUnCH = 10$ and $\alpha = 0.05$ for the experiments. $p = 2$ is used to calculate AHD. For each problem, the algorithms independently run *30* times. Moreover, for each run, we let the algorithms evolve *500* generations. The reason of letting the algorithms to run more than standard *MaxGen* (table 2) is that we want to investigate when exactly the proposed stopping method is activated. Finally, we have used the following parameters in the variance test of OCD for the three indicators: $\epsilon_{HV} = 1e^{-4}$, $\epsilon_R = 1e^{-6}$ and $\epsilon_{Epsilon} = 2e^{-4}$.

Table 1: Parameter settings for NSGA-II and SPEA2

	NSGA-II	SPEA2
Population size	100	100
Archive Size	–	100
Crossover probability	0.9	0.9
Mutation Probability	$1/l$	$1/l$
Distribution Index	20	20

4.2 Evaluation metrics

To evaluate our proposed method, we have defined four metrics/indicators. The first indicator is the difference between the hypervolumes (HV) [19] achieved by the different approaches ($HV_i : i \in \{AHD, Div, AHD{+}Div, OCD\}$) and the HV achieved after the standard *MaxGen* (i.e., $HV_i - HV_{std}$), we call the difference HV_d. In the same manner, differences between the epsilon [20] indicator values ($eps_d = eps_{std} - eps_i : i \in \{AHD, Div, AHD{+}Div, OCD\}$) are computed. The Pareto reference fronts provided by the jMetal framework [1] are used to calculate the epsilon indicator. Negative HV_d values corresponds to a smaller HV achieved when the algorithm is stopped by the approach compared to the standard *MaxGen*. In contrast, negative eps_d values mean the epsilon indicator is larger when the algorithm is stopped by the approach than the one standard *MaxGen*. Therefore, HV_d and eps_d values close to 0 indicate a good approximation of the Pareto front. The standard stopping generations for the different problems can be found in table 2. Additionally, we want to measure the percentage of the HV [9] of true Pareto front obtained by an algorithm at the time the algorithm is stopped by the combined approach ($AHD + Div$). The calculation is done by taking the ratio between the HV achieved by the algorithm and the HV of the true Pareto front (i.e., $HV_{per} = \frac{HV_{AHD+Div}}{HV_{tPF}}$). We again use the Pareto-reference fronts provided by jMetal framework. We will also report the average number of function evaluations (*NoSFE*) saved for each problem. The *NoSFE* will be calculated by

[1]http://jmetal.sourceforge.net/problems.html

Algorithm 1 Algorithm for detecting stopping generation

Require:
α ▷ Significance level for statistical test
$nGenLT$ ▷ Number of previous generations considered for calculating slope of linear regression model
$nGenUnCh$ ▷ Number of previous generations the p-values remain unchanged ($pVal_j > \alpha, j \in \{AHD, Div\}$)
$MaxGen$ ▷ Maximum number of allowed generations
$i = 0$
repeat
  $i \leftarrow i + 1$
  $AHD[i] \leftarrow$ AHD between Pareto front of ith and $(i-1)^{th}$ generation
  $Div[i] \leftarrow$ Diversity of ith generation
  if $i > nGenLT$ **then**
    $pAHD[i] \leftarrow pValue$ based on regression analysis of the previous $nGenLT$ values of AHD
    $pDiv[i] \leftarrow pValue$ based on regression analysis of the previous $nGenLT$ values of Div
  end if
until $i \geq MaxGen$ **or** $(\forall_j \in \{i, i-1, \ldots, i - nGenUnCh\} : pAHD[j] > \alpha \wedge pDiv[j] > \alpha)$

$(MaxGen - Gen_{AHD+Div}) * PS$, where $Gen_{AHD+Div}$ is the stopping generation number of the combined approach and PS is the population size.

Table 2: Standard maximum allowed number of generations for different problems [15]

Problem	ZDT family	DTLZ2	DTLZ5
Standard *MaxGen*	200	300	200

Table 3: Means and standard deviations of the evaluation metrics on the different problems for our proposed approach

Problem	Evaluation metrics	NSGA-II mean	NSGA-II SD	SPEA2 mean	SPEA2 SD
ZDT1	NoSFE	5527	2382	643	1153
	HV_d	-5.89E-03	3.54E-03	-6.24E-04	1.19E-03
	eps_d	-3.06E-03	3.33E-03	-5.40E-04	1.21E-03
	HV_{per}	0.979285	0.005466	0.986092	0.001775
ZDT2	NoSFE	2793	1887	0	0
	HV_d	-2.68E-03	2.04E-03	0.00E+00	0.00E+00
	eps_d	-1.63E-03	2.38E-03	0.00E+00	0.00E+00
	HV_{per}	0.966308	0.006051	0.957989	0.042851
ZDT3	NoSFE	5077	2427	1427	2509
	HV_d	-4.36E-03	2.88E-03	-3.46E-03	1.40E-02
	eps_d	-4.71E-03	4.35E-03	-5.37E-03	2.38E-02
	HV_{per}	0.984483	0.00566	0.983046	0.027052
ZDT4	NoSFE	777	1864	953	2582
	HV_d	-2.30E-02	6.62E-02	-4.03E-02	1.29E-01
	eps_d	-2.04E-02	6.17E-02	-7.41E-02	2.42E-01
	HV_{per}	0.925081	0.109336	0.874061	0.185557
DTLZ2	NoSFE	18323	2410	15173	6152
	HV_d	-3.13E-03	7.17E-03	-3.85E-03	4.81E-03
	eps_d	3.52E-03	3.21E-02	-2.45E-03	1.18E-02
	HV_{per}	0.790937	0.011261	0.857519	0.008931
DTLZ5	NoSFE	3113	3467	2767	4192
	HV_d	-8.90E-05	2.66E-04	-4.36E-04	7.50E-04
	eps_d	-2.66E-04	1.83E-03	-6.47E-04	1.58E-03
	HV_{per}	0.969181	0.003113	0.968569	0.00784

4.3 Discussion

Figure 3 and 4 present comparisons of the four different stopping approaches with respect to the stop generation (StopGen), HV_d and eps_d on the different test scenarios. Each row of the figures presents a problem and each column presents the performance with regard to a particular indicator. Horizontal lines in the plots of the first column indicate the standard *MaxGen*. Moreover, horizontal lines in the plots of the second and third columns are drawn to indicate the zero level for the corresponding indicators.

It is clear from the figures that for all the problems and algorithms, the combined approach runs longer than the individual approaches. At the same time, the combined approach has a better performance with regard to the Pareto front approximation. It is interesting to point out that there is no clear winner between AHD and Div. Therefore, relying on a particular space may detect converge prematurely. This clarifies the fact that the simultaneous monitoring of both spaces is more reliable to detect the convergence of an algorithm.

The figures also illustrate that the algorithms run much longer for OCD than for the combined approach on all ZDT problems. However, on DTLZ problems, the algorithms with OCD stop earlier. In contrast, using our method the algorithms stop more reliably with well-approximated Pareto fronts. Therefore, the simultaneous monitoring approach is more consistent, whereas OCD is not so stable when confronted with different problems.

In this paragraph, we will compare our method ($AHD + Div$) with standard budget recommendations (table 2). Table 3 reports the means and standard deviations of the respective indicator values. We have found very well approximated Pareto fronts for all problems and both algorithms, except on *ZDT4*. The means and standard deviations of HV_d and eps_d are very low for all these problems.The good quality Pareto fronts are found while also obtaining reasonably good *NoSEF*s. The only exception is *ZDT2* for SPEA2, where the proposed method does not converge before *MaxGen*. Very good percentages of true HVs (HV_{per}) are obtained. HV_{per} has reached over 95% for all the problems, except *DTLZ2* and *ZDT4*. HV_{per}s are considerably low (0.7916) for NSGA-II and SPEA2 (0.8557) on the *DTLZ2* problem. However, please note that the average HV_{per}s are 0.7976 and 0.8657 for standard *MaxGen* for NSGA-II and SPEA2, respectively. Therefore, there is almost no difference in terms of achieved HV_{per} when comparing our method with standard *MaxGen*. Nevertheless, sometimes the method detects convergence prematurely on the *ZDT4* problem. It should be noted that the *ZDT4* problem has 21^9 local Pareto fronts. Finally, in comparison to standard

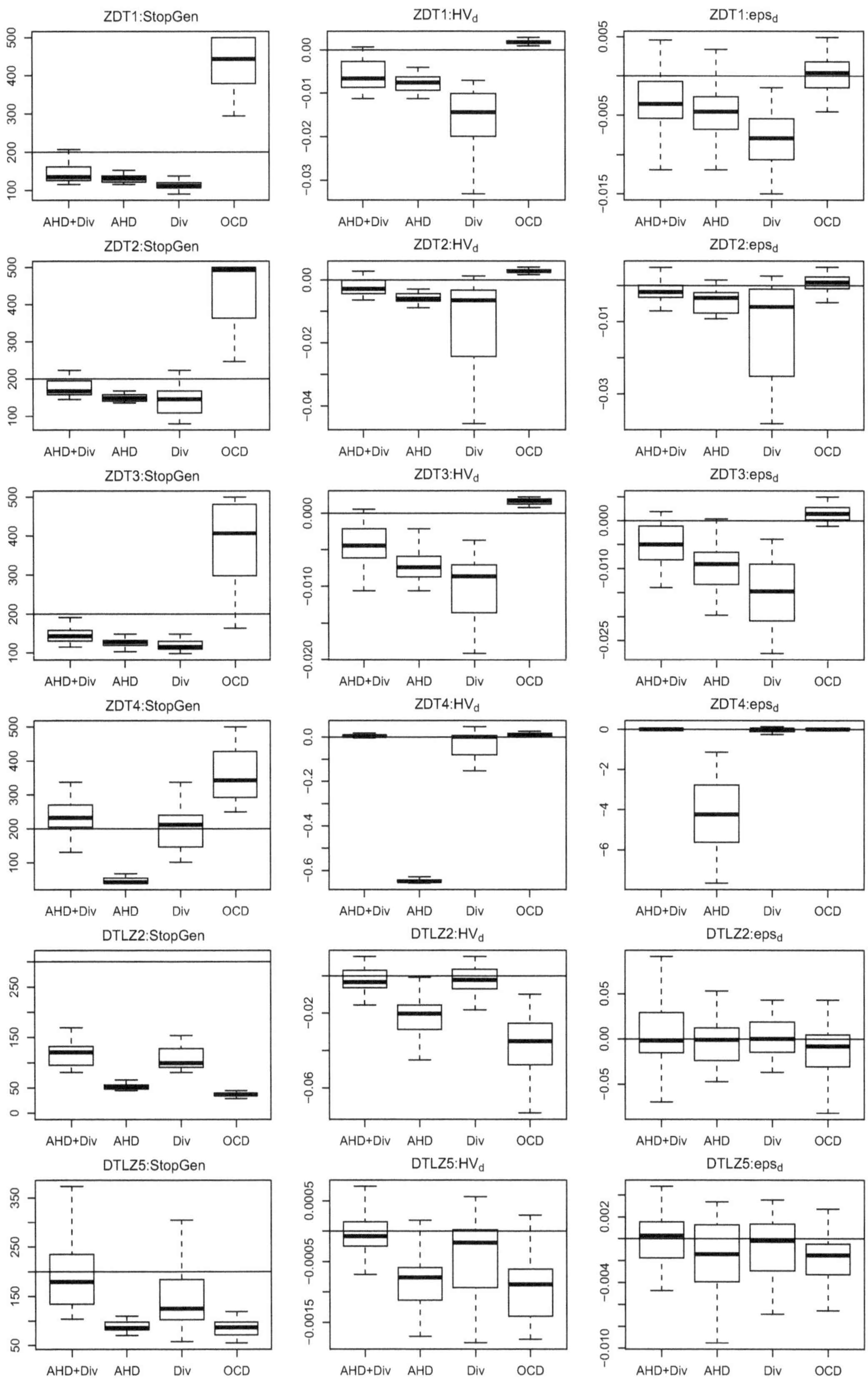

Figure 3: Boxplots for *stopping generation*, HV_d and eps_d on the different problems for NSGA-II

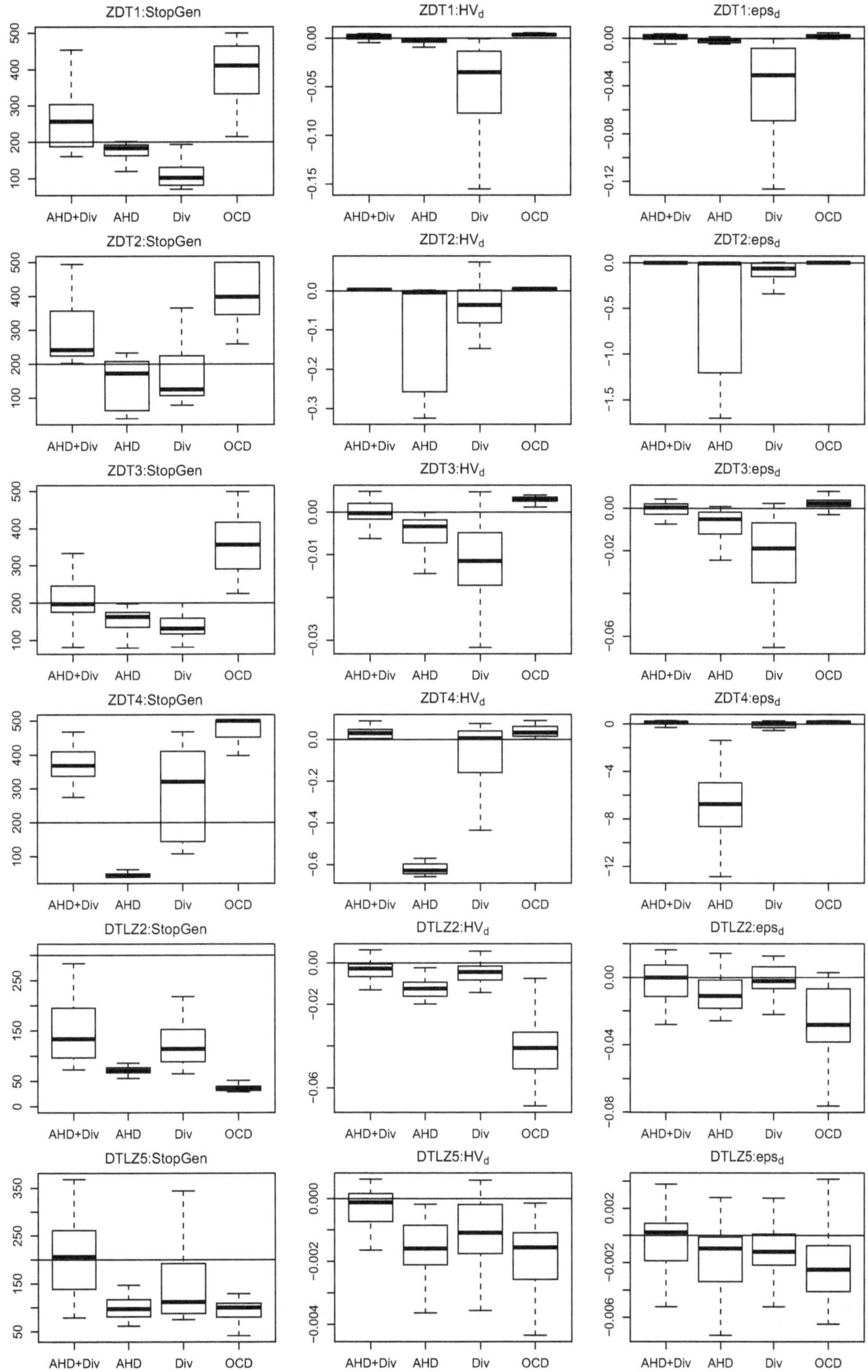

Figure 4: Boxplots for *stopping generation*, HV_d and eps_d on the different problems for SPEA2

budget recommendation, on average our proposed method saves 29% and 17% of function evaluations for NSGA-II and SPEA2, respectively.

5. CONCLUSION AND FUTURE WORK

In this paper, we have shown that the simultaneous monitoring of the objective and decision space of a problem, can improve the robustness of stopping MOEA. Two metrics have been proposed for the different spaces. The stagnation has been detected by a two-sided t-test on the regression coefficients estimated from the matrices in the two spaces.

We have validated our method by investigating the performance on six different benchmark problems for two well-established MOEAs. Our proposed method performs consistently well for all problems, also compared to state-of-the-art stopping criteria. Additionally, on average a decent number of function evaluations has been saved compared to fixed budget recommendations without losing significant approximation accuracy.

In future work, we will investigate the combination of monitoring the decision space diversity with other objective space metrics, such as the hypervolume.

6. REFERENCES

[1] L. T. Bui, S. Wesolkowski, A. Bender, H. A. Abbass, and M. Barlow. A dominance-based stability measure for multi-objective evolutionary algorithms. In *IEEE Congress on Evolutionary Computation*, pages 749–756. IEEE, 2009.

[2] K. Deb. *Multi-objective optimization using evolutionary algorithms*, volume 16. John Wiley & Sons, 2001.

[3] K. Deb and S. Jain. Running performance metrics for evolutionary multi-objective optimizations. In *Proceedings of the Fourth Asia-Pacific Conference on Simulated Evolution and Learning (SEAL'02)*, pages 13–20, 2002.

[4] K. Deb, A. Pratap, S. Agarwal, and T. Meyarivan. A fast and elitist multiobjective genetic algorithm: NSGA-II. *IEEE Transactions on Evolutionary Computation*, 6(2):182–197, 2002.

[5] K. Deb, L. Thiele, M. Laumanns, and E. Zitzler. Scalable test problems for evolutionary multiobjective optimization. In *Evolutionary Multiobjective Optimization*, Advanced Information and Knowledge Processing, pages 105–145. Springer London, 2005.

[6] J. J. Durillo and A. J. Nebro. jMetal: A Java framework for multi-objective optimization. *Advances in Engineering Software*, 42:760–771, 2011.

[7] T. Goel and N. Stander. A non-dominance-based online stopping criterion for multi-objective evolutionary algorithms. *International Journal for Numerical Methods in Engineering*, 84(6):661–684, 2010.

[8] L. Martí, J. García, A. Berlanga, and J. M. Molina. An approach to stopping criteria for multi-objective optimization evolutionary algorithms: the MGBM criterion. In *IEEE Congress on Evolutionary Computation*, pages 1263–1270. IEEE, 2009.

[9] A. J. Nebro, J. J. Durillo, C. A. C. Coello, F. Luna, and E. Alba. A study of convergence speed in multi-objective metaheuristics. In *Parallel Problem Solving from Nature–PPSN X*, pages 763–772. Springer, 2008.

[10] D. Roche, D. Gil, and J. Giraldo. Detecting loss of diversity for an efficient termination of EAs. In *15th International Symposium on Symbolic and Numeric Algorithms for Scientific Computing (SYNASC)*, pages 561–566, 2013.

[11] O. Rudenko and M. Schoenauer. A steady performance stopping criterion for Pareto-based evolutionary algorithms. In *6th International Multi-Objective Prpgramming and Goal Programming Conference*, 2004.

[12] O. Schutze, X. Esquivel, A. Lara, and C. A. Coello Coello. Using the averaged Hausdorff distance as a performance measure in evolutionary multiobjective optimization. *IEEE Transactions on Evolutionary Computation*, 16(4):504–522, 2012.

[13] H. Trautmann, T. Wagner, B. Naujoks, M. Preuss, and J. Mehnen. Statistical methods for convergence detection of multi-objective evolutionary algorithms. *Evolutionary computation*, 17(4):493–509, 2009.

[14] T. Wagner, H. Trautmann, and L. Martí. A taxonomy of online stopping criteria for multi-objective evolutionary algorithms. In *Proceedings of the 6th International Conference on Evolutionary Multi-criterion Optimization*, EMO'11, pages 16–30. Springer, 2011.

[15] T. Wagner, H. Trautmann, and B. Naujoks. OCD: Online convergence detection for evolutionary multi-objective algorithms based on statistical testing. In *Evolutionary Multi-Criterion Optimization*, volume 5467 of *Lecture Notes in Computer Science*, pages 198–215. Springer, 2009.

[16] M. Wineberg and F. Oppacher. The underlying similarity of diversity measures used in evolutionary computation. In *Genetic and Evolutionary Computation-GECCO 2003*, pages 1493–1504. Springer, 2003.

[17] E. Zitzler, K. Deb, and L. Thiele. Comparison of multiobjective evolutionary algorithms: Empirical results. *Evolutionary Computation*, 8(2):173–195, 2000.

[18] E. Zitzler, M. Laumanns, and L. Thiele. SPEA2: Improving the strength pareto evolutionary algorithm. Technical Report TIK-Report No. 103, Computer Engineering and Networks Laboratory (TIK), Swiss Federal Institute of Technology (ETH), Zurich, 2001.

[19] E. Zitzler and L. Thiele. Multiobjective evolutionary algorithms: a comparative case study and the strength pareto approach. *IEEE Transactions on Evolutionary Computation*, 3(4):257–271, 1999.

[20] E. Zitzler, L. Thiele, M. Laumanns, C. M. Fonseca, and V. G. Da Fonseca. Performance assessment of multiobjective optimizers: An analysis and review. *IEEE Transactions on Evolutionary Computation*, 7(2):117–132, 2003.

On Maintaining Diversity in MOEA/D: Application to a Biobjective Combinatorial FJSP

Juan José Palacios Alonso
University of Oviedo
Department of Computer Science, 33204, Gijón (Spain)
palaciosjuan@uniovi.es

Bilel Derbel
Université Lille 1, CRIStAL (CNRS UMR 9189), Inria Lille Nord Europe
59655 Villeneuve d'Ascq Cedex (France)
bilel.derbel@lifl.fr

ABSTRACT

MOEA/D is a generic decomposition-based multiobjective optimization framework which has been proved to be extremely effective in solving a broad range of optimization problems especially for continuous domains. In this paper, we consider applying MOEA/D to solve a bi-objective scheduling combinatorial problem in which task durations and due-dates are uncertain. Surprisingly, we find that the conventional MOEA/D implementation provides poor performance in our application setting. We show that this is because the replacement strategy underlying MOEA/D is suffering some shortcomes that lead to low population diversity, and thus to premature convergence. Consequently, we investigate existing variants of MOEA/D and we propose a novel and simple alternative replacement component at the aim of maintaining population diversity. Through extensive experiments, we then provide a comprehensive analysis on the relative performance and the behavior of the considered algorithms. Besides being able to outperform existing MOEA/D variants, as well as the standard NSGA-II algorithm, our investigations provide new insights into the search ability of MOEA/D and highlight new research opportunities for improving its design components.

Keywords

EMO, decomposition-based EA, fuzzy scheduling

1. INTRODUCTION

Multiobjective optimization problems (MOPs) are a natural and very frequent outcome in several application fields like logistics, planning, green-IT, clouds, etc. They are used to model a problem where one wants to optimize several, *a priori*, conflicting objectives. In practice, it is unlikely to find a solution which is able to optimize all target objectives simultaneously at the same time. Hence, solving a MOP turns out to finding a whole set of solutions; each one exhibiting a different compromise between objectives — which would allow a decision maker to choose among afterward.

More formally, a multi-objective optimization problem can be defined by a set of $M \geq 2$ objective functions $f = (f_1, f_2, \ldots, f_M)$, and a set X of feasible solutions in the *decision space*, where X is a discrete set in the combinatorial case. Let $Z = f(X) \subseteq \mathbb{R}^M$ be the set of feasible outcome vectors in the *objective space*. To each solution $x \in X$ is then assigned exactly one objective vector $z \in Z$, on the basis of the vector function $f : X \rightarrow Z$ with $z = f(x)$. Without loss of generality, in a maximization context, an objective vector $z \in Z$ is dominated by an objective $z' \in Z$, denoted by $z \prec z'$, iff $\forall m \in \{1, 2, \ldots, M\}$, $z_m \leq z'_m$ and $\exists m \in \{1, 2, \ldots, M\}$ such that $z_m < z'_m$. By extension, a solution $x \in X$ is dominated by a solution $x' \in X$, denoted by $x \prec x'$, iff $f(x) \prec f(x')$. A solution $x^\star \in X$ is termed *Pareto optimal*, if there does not exist any other solution $x \in X$ such that $x^\star \prec x$. The set of all Pareto optimal solutions is called the *Pareto set*. Its mapping in the objective space is called the *Pareto front*. One of the most challenging task in multi-objective optimization is to identify a minimal complete Pareto set, i.e., one Pareto optimal solution for each point from the Pareto front. This task is usually intractable for several optimization problems and one seeks instead a good *Pareto front approximation*.

In this context, we are interested in evolutionary multiobjective optimization (EMO) methods which have been shown to be well-applicable for a broad range of MOPs while being particularly accurate in finding high quality approximations [5, 4]. The EMO methods encompass several algorithms relying on different concepts and having seemingly different properties. Besides the well-established class of Pareto-dominance based algorithms, e.g. NSGA-II [6], we can report a recent and growing interest in the so-called *aggregation-based* algorithms, and especially the MOEA/D (multiobjective evolutionary algorithm based on decomposition) framework [19]. MOEA/D decomposes a given MOP into a number of single-objective optimization subproblems; Each single-objective optimization problem is defined by a scalarizing function using a different weight vector.

The original idea of MOEA/D is to define a neighborhood relation between subproblems and to solve each problem using standard evolutionary operators (crossover, mutation) as in the single-objective setting, but cooperatively based on the solutions computed at the neighboring subproblems. Each time a subproblem is considered, some parents are selected among neighbors in order to generate a new offspring which could replace the solutions of neighboring subproblems if an improvement is observed. As such, we claim that the selection and replacement components in MOEA/D are critical when evolving the population since it implies an

GECCO '15, July 11 - 15, 2015, Madrid, Spain

DOI: http://dx.doi.org/10.1145/2739480.2754774

intensification-diversification trade-off — which is known to be a key ingredient in the success of any evolutionary algorithm. When applying MOEA/D for continuous MOP, this claim is rather well known and it was previously shown how to deal with this issue by designing MOEA/D variants that can improve on the conventional one [13]. For combinatorial problems, this issue is relatively less studied and one can only find few systematic investigations on the subject [16]. In this paper, we are specifically interested in the applicability of MOEA/D for a particular combinatorial optimization problem, namely, a bi-objective job shop scheduling problem with uncertainty. In this context, our contribution can be summarized in the three following points:

- We found that the previous claim is verified for the bi-objective combinatorial problem that we are tackling. In particular, we analyze the behavior of conventional MOEA/D and elicit its relative performance when compared to NSGA-II, considered as a baseline standard Pareto-dominance based algorithm. We illustrate how MOEA/D can in fact suffer from a loss in population diversity and premature convergence.
- We investigate the efficiency of existing mechanisms to deal with this issue, and we elicit their relative impact on performance. We illustrate how they can improve to some extent the performance of MOEA/D by avoiding solution duplication and hence increasing diversity.
- We propose a novel replacement strategy as an alternative to existing mechanisms. We show that besides being extremely simple, the so-obtained MOEA/D variant is successful in significantly improving the runtime performance. More importantly, the experimental study and the results obtained in this paper have the primary goal of providing a comprehensive analysis of MOEA/D in an attempt to unify our understanding of its algorithmic components; and thus to better grasp the future design challenges and research questions.

We also notice that although our results are with respect to a particular combinatorial optimization problem, which is challenging *per se*, the newly proposed mechanism is generic and fully compatible with MOEA/D viewed as a problem-independent EMO framework. Accordingly, we structure the paper following a step-by-step presentation allowing us to state our findings in an incremental manner. In the remainder, we first start by describing and formulating, in Section 2, the bi-objective fuzzy job shop scheduling problem we are interested in. In Section 3, we discuss the applicability of conventional MOEA/D, and we provide a brief analysis of its behavior compared to NSGA-II. In Section 4, we recall some existing variants of MOEA/D and we introduce the newly proposed strategy in order to deal with diversity issues. In Section 5, we provide our experimental results and analyze our findings. In Section 6, we conclude the paper and discuss some open research directions.

2. BACKGROUND ON THE FJSP

The *job shop scheduling problem* (*JSP*) consists in scheduling a set of jobs $J = \{J_1, \ldots, J_n\}$ on a set of physical resources or machines $M = \{M_1, \ldots, M_m\}$, subject to a set of constraints. There are *precedence constraints*, so each job J_i, $i = 1, \ldots, n$, consists of m tasks $\{\theta_{i1}, \ldots, \theta_{im}\}$ to be sequentially scheduled. Also, there are *capacity constraints*, whereby each task θ_{ij} requires the uninterrupted and exclusive use of one of the machines $\eta_{ij} \in M$ for its whole processing time p_{ij}. We can also consider due-date constraints, where each job has a maximum completion time and all its tasks must be scheduled to finish before this time. A feasible schedule is an allocation of starting times S_{ij} for each task θ_{ij} such that all constraints hold. The objective is to find a schedule which is *optimal* according to some criterion, e.g. the *makespan* or the delay w.r.t. the due-dates is minimal.

2.1 Uncertain durations

In real-world situations, it is often to find that some factors are unknown in advance and only some uncertain information is available. In the case of task processing times, an expert may be able to roughly estimate them based on his own experience. This knowledge is modeled using fuzzy intervals or fuzzy numbers, which have been extensively studied in the literature (cf. [8]). The simplest model of a fuzzy interval is a *triangular fuzzy number* or TFN, given by an interval $[a^1, a^3]$ of possible values and a most plausible value a^2 in it. That is, for a TFN A, denoted $A = (a^1, a^2, a^3)$, the membership function is determined as follows:

$$\mu_A(x) = \begin{cases} \frac{x-a^1}{a^2-a^1} & : a^1 < x \le a^2 \\ \frac{x-a^3}{a^2-a^3} & : a^2 < x < a^3 \\ 0 & : x \le a^1 \text{ or } a^3 \le x \end{cases} \tag{1}$$

This model has been extensively used in the fuzzy scheduling literature [1]. However, when TFNs are to be used to extend the job shop to handle uncertainty, two issues must be addressed: the establishment of an order relation between TFNs and the means of extending the arithmetic operations of addition and maximum to work with TFNs (so to compute starting and completion times).

The fact that there is no natural total ordering in the set of TFNs makes concepts like "minimal makespan" ambiguous. The membership function of a fuzzy number can be interpreted as a possibility distribution on the real numbers; this allows to define its expected value, given for a TFN A by $E[A] = \frac{1}{4}(a^1 + 2a^2 + a^3)$. This induces a total ordering $\le_E$ in the set of fuzzy intervals [9], where for any two fuzzy intervals A and B, $A \le_E B$ iff $E[A] \le E[B]$. The expected value coincides with the *neutral scalar substitute* of a fuzzy interval and can also be obtained as the centre of gravity of its *mean value* or using the *area compensation* method [7].

Regarding arithmetic operations, for the fuzzy job shop (*FJSP*), we need two operations on fuzzy numbers, the sum and the maximum. These are obtained by extending the corresponding operations on real numbers using the *Extension Principle*. In the case of the sum, for any pair of TFN A and B, the resulting expression is $A + B = (a^1 + b^1, a^2 + b^2, a^3 + b^3)$. However, computing the resulting expression of the maximum is cumbersome, if not intractable. For the sake of simplicity and tractability of numerical calculations, it is fairly common in the literature following [9], to approximate the result of this operation. So for any two TFNs A, B, if F denotes their maximum and $G = (\max\{a^1, b^1\}, \max\{a^2, b^2\}, \max\{a^3, b^3\})$ its approximated value, it holds that F and G have identical support and modal value. The most immediate consequence of this result in terms of scheduling is that, given a schedule, the makespan of all its possible realizations is contained within the support of the fuzzy makespan.

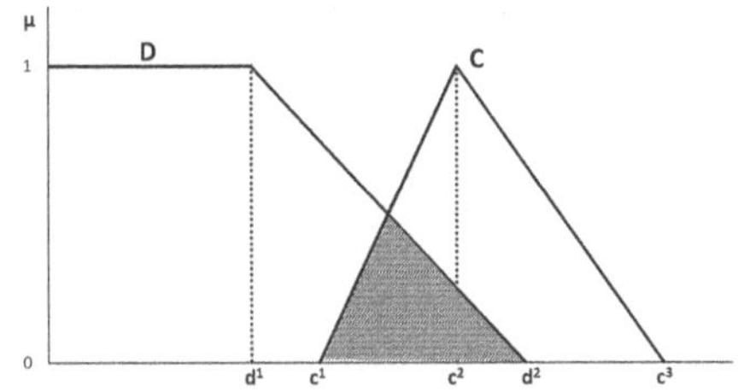

Figure 1: Intersection between a TFN and the due-date.

2.2 Flexible due dates

In the case in which due dates exist in real situations, they are often flexible: a customer is satisfied if his job finishes before a preferred due-date d^1 and after this time his satisfaction decreases until a limit due-date d^2, after which he is completely unsatisfied. A natural approach to modeling such satisfaction degrees is the use of a fuzzy set $D = (d^1, d^2)$ with linear decreasing membership function as follows:

$$\mu_D(x) = \begin{cases} 1 & : x \leq d^1 \\ \frac{x-d^2}{d^1-d^2} & : d^1 < x < d^2 \\ 0 & : d^2 \leq x \end{cases} \quad (2)$$

According to [7], this expresses a flexible threshold "less than" and the satisfaction degree of the customer for the job finishing at time x. However, in our case the completion time of the jobs is not a real number x, but a TFN. When the completion time of a job J_i is a TFN C_i, the degree to which D_i is satisfied is usually measured by the *agreement index* (AI) [12, 14] computed as follows (see Fig. 1):

$$AI(C, D) = \frac{Area(C \cap D)}{Area(C)} \quad (3)$$

Here the flexible due date D is completely satisfied when $AI = 1$ and unsatisfied when $AI = 0$.

2.3 The bi-objective optimization problem

Having established how to model uncertain duration times and flexible due-dates, it is possible to find a schedule for a given FJSP instance and compute a fuzzy makespan, $C_{max} = \max C_i$, a TFN indicating the time when all jobs are finished. It is also possible to measure for every job $J_i, i = 1, \ldots, n$, to what degree its completion time C_i satisfies the flexible due-date D_i, as given by the agreement index $AI_i = AI(C_i, D_i)$. Our target is to minimize C_{max} and maximize the different AI_i, which shall be aggregated as to have an overall measure. In this paper we shall consider the optimization of the average AI (AI_{av}) together with the makespan. The problem can be formulated as follows:

$$\text{minimize } C_{max} = \max_{i=1\ldots n} C_i \quad (4)$$

$$\text{maximize } AI_{av} = 1/n \sum_{i=1}^{n} AI_i \quad (5)$$

subject to:

$$A_i = AI(C_i, D_i),\ 1 \leq i \leq n \quad (6)$$

$$C_i = \max_{j=1\ldots m} C_{ij},\ 1 \leq i \leq n \quad (7)$$

$$C_{ij} = S_{ij} + p_{ij},\ 1 \leq i \leq n, 1 \leq j \leq m \quad (8)$$

$$S_{ij} \geq C_{ij-1},\ 1 \leq i \leq n, 2 \leq j \leq m \quad (9)$$

$$S_{ij} \geq C_{lm} \vee C_{ij} \leq S_{lm}, \forall l, m,\ l \neq i \vee m \neq j : \eta_{ij} = \eta_{lm} \quad (10)$$

Algorithm 1: The conventional MOEA/D [19]

Input: $\{\lambda^1, \ldots, \lambda^N\}$: weight vectors w.r.t sub-problems;
$\mathcal{B}(i)$: the neighbors of sub-problem $i \in \{1, \ldots, N\}$;
$P = \{x^1, \ldots, x^N\}$: the initial population

```
while NOT STOPPING CONDITION do
    for i ∈ {1,...,N} do
        // Mating selection
        (k, ℓ) ← rand(B(i));
        // Variation
        y ← CROSSOVER_MUTATION_REPAIR(x^k, x^ℓ);
        z* ← UPDATE_REFERENCE_POINT(z*, y);
        // Environmental replacement
        shuffle(B_i);
        for j ∈ B_i do
            if g^te(y, λ^j) < g^te(x^j, λ^j) then x^j ← y;
```

In the rest of this paper, we use the fuzzy job shop instances proposed in [11]. These were obtained by fuzzyfying 12 well-known benchmark problems for deterministic job shop which are considered hard to solve: FT10 (size 10×10), FT20 (20 × 5), La21, La24, La25 (15 × 10), La27, La29 (20 × 10), La38, La40 (15 × 15), and ABZ7, ABZ8, ABZ9 (20 × 15). The task durations are generated from each original problem following [9], so they become symmetric TFNs where the modal value is the original duration. The due date d_i for each job J_i is defined following [2]: first, we define a generic due date $d_i = TF \sum_{j=1}^{m} p_{ij}^2$, where TF is a tightness factor; then, we use two different tightness factors to have the points that define the satisfaction function: d_i^1, with TF = 1.3, and d_i^2, with TF = 1.7.

3. MOEA/D APPLIED TO THE FJSP

In this section, we briefly review the conventional MOEA/D algorithm as originally described in [19] and we discuss its applicability for the bi-objective FJSP. Generally speaking, MOEA/D falls in the class of decomposition based EMO algorithms [10] which aim is to search for good solutions in multiple regions of the Pareto front. For this purpose, the original MOP is *decomposed* into a number of *scalarized* single-objective *sub-problems*. Different scalarizing functions have been proposed so-far [17]. In this paper, we use the weighted Tchebycheff (g^{te}) function which is to be minimized:

$$g^{te}(x, \lambda) = \max_{i \in \{1,2\}} \lambda_i \cdot |z_i^\star - f_i(x)|$$

where $\lambda = (\lambda_1, \lambda_2)$ is a positive weighting coefficient vector and $z^\star = (z_1^\star, z_2^\star)$ is a reference point.

Let $(\lambda^1, \ldots, \lambda^N)$ be a set of N uniformly distributed weighting coefficient vectors defining N sub-problems to be optimized. For each sub-problem $i \in \{1, \ldots, N\}$, the goal is to approximate the solution x with the best scalarizing function value $g^{te}(x, \lambda^i)$. For that purpose, MOEA/D maintains a population $P = (x^1, \ldots, x^N)$, each individual corresponding to a good-quality solution for one sub-problem. For each sub-problem $i \in \{1, \ldots, N\}$, a set of neighbors $\mathcal{B}(i)$ is defined by considering the T closest weight vectors (including i). To evolve the population, sub-problems are optimized iteratively as sketched in the high level template of Algorithm 1 where we omit some details for the sake of conciseness. At a given iteration corresponding to one sub-problem i, two solutions are selected at random from $\mathcal{B}(i)$, and an offspring solution y is created by means of variation oper-

Table 1: Comparing MOEA/D *vs.* NSGA-II. Average indicator value and the standard deviation (in parentheses, with a multiplicative factor of 10^{-1}) are reported.

instance	Hypervolume Indicator		Epsilon Indicator	
	MOEA/D	NSGA-II	MOEA/D	NSGA-II
ABZ7	$0{,}382_{(0,38)}$	$0{,}423_{(0,32)}$	$0{,}179_{(0,39)}$	$0{,}141_{(0,32)}$
ABZ8	$0{,}373_{(0,31)}$	$0{,}428_{(0,35)}$	$0{,}218_{(0,33)}$	$0{,}164_{(0,36)}$
ABZ9	$0{,}349_{(0,44)}$	$0{,}415_{(0,33)}$	$0{,}244_{(0,47)}$	$0{,}180_{(0,35)}$
FT10	$0{,}549_{(0,48)}$	$0{,}591_{(0,39)}$	$0{,}199_{(0,50)}$	$0{,}163_{(0,40)}$
FT20	$0{,}203_{(0,24)}$	$0{,}241_{(0,18)}$	$0{,}110_{(0,23)}$	$0{,}076_{(0,18)}$
La21	$0{,}427_{(0,33)}$	$0{,}449_{(0,37)}$	$0{,}158_{(0,34)}$	$0{,}142_{(0,40)}$
La24	$0{,}429_{(0,36)}$	$0{,}456_{(0,39)}$	$0{,}181_{(0,38)}$	$0{,}162_{(0,40)}$
La25	$0{,}440_{(0,30)}$	$0{,}445_{(0,32)}$	$0{,}163_{(0,32)}$	$0{,}165_{(0,33)}$
La27	$0{,}228_{(0,24)}$	$0{,}254_{(0,29)}$	$0{,}184_{(0,26)}$	$0{,}166_{(0,33)}$
La29	$0{,}235_{(0,31)}$	$0{,}254_{(0,27)}$	$0{,}201_{(0,36)}$	$0{,}190_{(0,30)}$
La38	$0{,}608_{(0,51)}$	$0{,}683_{(0,34)}$	$0{,}199_{(0,48)}$	$0{,}132_{(0,31)}$
La40	$0{,}618_{(0,45)}$	$0{,}691_{(0,36)}$	$0{,}204_{(0,43)}$	$0{,}145_{(0,35)}$

ators, e.g., mutation and crossover. Then, for every sub-problem $j \in \mathcal{B}(i)$, if y improves over j's current solution x^j then y replaces it. The algorithm continues looping over sub-problems until a stopping condition is satisfied.

From the previous description, we can see that MOEA/D is an extremely simple algorithm where only the variation step (line 4) needs to be expanded when applied to a particular problem. Specifically for the FJSP, there exist several well-established operators from the literature which might be applied. In this paper, solutions are encoded using permutations with repeated elements. This is a permutation of the set of tasks, each being represented by its job number. A given permutation is decoded into its associated schedule using an insertion strategy in the schedule-generating scheme [18]. We thereby use one of the most popular crossover operators for the JSP, the Generalized Order Crossover (GOX), and inversion as mutation strategy.

To assess the performance of the so-obtained algorithm, we consider a Pareto-dominance EMO method as a plausible alternative, namely, we use the well-known NSGA-II algorithm [6]. For completeness, we recall that in contrast to MOEA/D, the NSGA-II algorithm is based on a nondominated-sorting and crowding-distance estimation procedure for comparing qualities of different solutions, which serve for mating selection and environmental replacement. For fairness, we use the same mutation and crossover operators for both algorithms. We thereby conduct a first set of experiments using the previously described instances. Both MOEA/D and NSGA-II are run 30 independent times using the following setup: the population size is set to 100, the probability to apply crossover (resp. mutation) is set to 1 (resp. 0.1) and the stopping criterion is fixed to $5 \cdot 10^4$ function evaluations. Since the neighborhood size T is believed to have strong impact on performance, we tested a broad range of T-values in order to finely tune MOEA/D. Due to lack of space, we only show in this section the results obtained with the best value, namely, $T = 5$. Later, we will discuss further the impact of this parameter — for now we just focus on MOEA/D tuned with the best paramater setting.

We use the hypervolume[1] (to be maximized) and the epsilon indicators (to be minimized) [20] in order to appreciate the relative performance of the two designed approaches. Our findings are summarized in Table 1, where gray cells indicate that the algorithm in the corresponding column

[1]the reference point is set to the worst objective values ever observed in any run.

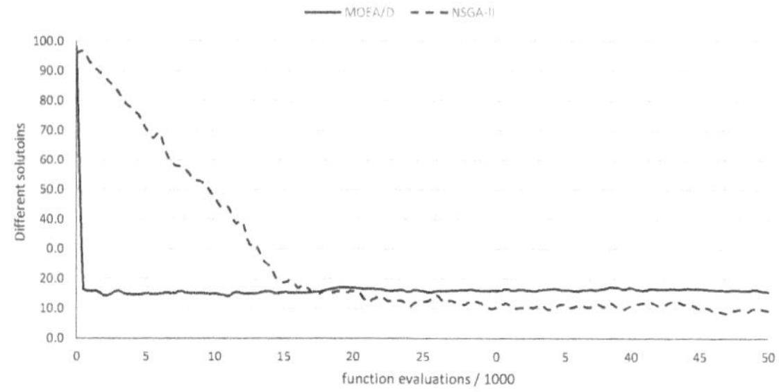

Figure 2: Evolution of the percentage of different objective vectors in the population.

is significantly better than the other one using a statistical t-test with confidence 0.05. We can see that NSGA-II is outperforming MOEA/D in all but one instance for both indicators. To understand this huge difference between the two approaches, we show in Fig. 2 the evolution of the average number of different solutions (in the objective space) in the population maintained by both approaches as a function of the number of function evaluations for instance La29 (similar observations were verified for the other instances). We observe that NSGA-II is able to maintain more different solutions than MOEA/D in the first stages of the run; or equivalently, that the number of copies in MOEA/D population is increasing very abruptly. We clearly attribute this to the fact that as soon as a good solution is found in MOEA/D, it will immediately replace all solutions from the neighbor subproblems. Although this strategy could speed-up convergence, it obviously prevents the genetic operators to produce improving offsprings in diversified regions in the objective space. Hence, we can argue that this replacement strategy is seemingly very aggressive, thus killing population diversity and leading to a premature convergence of MOEA/D.

Actually, the previous discussion holds for the original replacement component of MOEA/D which was first described in [19]. It is in fact important to grasp the algorithm behavior without necessarily being in a horse-racing condition, which might lead to diminish our understanding of the key ingredients towards a successful application. Having identified this weakness, we describe in the next section some existing alternatives together with our own proposal.

4. MAINTAINING DIVERSITY IN MOEA/D

Based on our observations, we are willing to provide improved variants of MOEA/D for the FJSP by addressing the raised diversity issue. In the following, we first review two variants (MOEA/D-n_r and MOEA/D-**ss**) which we believe to be the best existing alternatives from the literature. We then describe our own proposal MOEA/D-RO, a relatively simple variant that we will show to be extremely effective.

MOEA/D-n_r [13] : **Parametrizing the number of replacements.** Two modifications are proposed in [13] in order to better control the replacement and the selection components of conventional MOEA/D. The first one concerns the number of replacements that are allowed when an improving offspring is found. More specifically, once a new offspring has been generated for a given subproblem i in line 4, this offspring can only replace a maximum number of n_r other solutions in the T-neighborhood $\mathcal{B}(i)$ of subproblem i, where $n_r \leq T$ is a user-defined (typically small) parameter — the 'for loop' in line 7 is then modified accordingly. The

n_r parameter can be viewed as a mean to control how many solutions can be discarded from the population when a high quality offspring improving simultaneously several subproblems is found. The second modification described in [13] concerns the choice of parents in the mating selection step in line 3. Instead of systematically choosing parents from only the T-neighborhood at every iteration, an additional parameter $\delta \in [0, 1]$ is introduced in order to allow parent selection from the whole population with probability $1 - \delta$, i.e., at every iteration, the neighbors of a subproblem are defined by solely its T-neighborhood with probability δ, or using the whole population with a probability $1-\delta$ (typically δ is set to a high value). The δ parameter can be viewed as a mean to increase diversity among parents which might potentially results in increasing the diversity and the accuracy of generated offsprings. These two modifications are mostly studied for continuous MOPs and we are only aware of few related investigations in the combinatorial setting, e.g., [3].

MOEA/D-**xy** [16] **: A generational approach.** Specifically for the combinatorial case, a recent study was conducted in [16] where the authors advocated for the design of new replacement and selection strategies within the MOEA/D framework. The main idea developed therein is that since subproblems are processed in an iterative manner in conventional MOEA/D, as well as in its variants [13], once a solution gets replaced in a given iteration, it is definitively discarded and gets no chance to produce an offspring eventhough it could be potentially beneficial. Accordingly, the authors proposed to adopt a generational approach in which all individuals in the population are evolved simultaneously before the replacement can take place. They consequently described four variants denoted MOEA/D-**xy** with $\mathbf{x}, \mathbf{y} \in \{\mathbf{s}, \mathbf{c}\}$. The components of the so-denoted couple $(\mathbf{x}, \mathbf{y})$ correspond respectively to the selection and the replacement strategies; and the notation **s** (resp. **c**) refers to a so-called *selfish* (resp. *collective*) variant. A systematic study of these variants showed the superiority of MOEA/D-**ss** (when the crossover operator is not disabled) over conventional MOEA/D and its variants [19, 13]. Consequently, we only retain this variant as a competing algorithm for the problem we are tackling[2]. This variant introduces the following modifications. First, for each subproblem i, generate a new offspring y^i by fixing the first parent to be the current solution x^i and by selecting the second one from the remaining subproblems in the T-neighborhood of i. This is performed for *all* subproblems *before* any replacement is performed. Then, an offspring y^i can only replace the *current* solution x^i of the subproblem from where it was originated. Once the replacement is performed the next generational round is performed and so until termination. This variant is termed selfish because each subproblems privileges its own solution in the reproduction phase, and it also does not include its neighbors in the replacement phase.

MOEA/D-RO **: Recursive opportunistic replacement.** This strategy is our own contribution and it can be viewed as a very intuitive answer to the question of how to maintain population diversity. More specifically, we explicitly check diversity of conventional MOEA/D locally at the neighborhood level, and we manage to design a non-oblivious re-

[2]Our tuning experiments have also confirmed its adequacy, we do not include the results due to lack of space.

Table 2: Performance of MOEA/D and MOEA/D-n_r depending on the neighborhood size T for instance La29.

	T	MOEA/D		MOEA/D-$n_r = 1$		MOEA/D-$n_r = 2$	
		δ=1.0	δ=0.9	δ=1.0	δ=0.9	δ=1.0	δ=0.9
Hypervol.	5	0.235	0.225	0.252	**0.258**	0.249	0.244
	25	0.235	0.239	**0.274**	0.264	0.252	0.255
	50	0.233	0.233	0.269	0.277	0.267	0.262
	75	0.238	0.240	0.264	**0.278**	0.257	0.268
	100	0.225	0.213	0.278	**0.288**	0.253	0.255
Epsilon	5	0.201	0.212	0.183	**0.176**	0.184	0.191
	25	0.204	0.199	**0.160**	0.172	0.184	0.181
	50	0.207	0.207	0.168	**0.157**	0.167	0.174
	75	0.200	0.198	0.172	**0.155**	0.178	0.167
	100	0.215	0.228	0.158	**0.145**	0.184	0.183

placement. First, we simply do not allow an offspring to replace a solution if there already exists a solution having the same objective values in the corresponding neighborhood. Moreover, every time this condition is satisfied and the replacement is activated with respect to an offspring, say y, and a neighboring subproblem solution, say x^j, we do the following. The offspring y becomes the new current solution for subproblem j, but the previous solution x^j is not discarded if it can improve the solution of other neighbors. Hence, we recursively check whether there is an opportunity that solution x^j replaces a solution j' in the neighborhood $\mathcal{B}(j)$ of subproblem j. If such a solution is found, a new replacement is activated and so on until no improvement is observed. Notice that with this strategy we do maintain diversity but we also attempt to improve convergence since we heuristically check whether a solution can serve for some subproblems before discarding it from the population.

In the remainder of this paper, we shall provide a comprehensive study allowing us to understand the impact of each of the previously described variants.

5. EXPERIMENTAL RESULTS

As previously, we use the same crossover and mutation operators and the same maximum budget of $5 \cdot 10^4$ function evaluations. In all reported tables, we use the same format by putting the best average indicator value in bold and having gray cells indicating that no significant differences can be reported w.r.t. the best with confidence 0.05. Unless stated explicitly the population size is set to 100.

5.1 Tuning MOEA/D

We start examining the relative performance of MOEA/D with respect to the MOEA/D-n_r variant to which it is more related and which was the first introduced to deal with diversity issues. In Table 2 we illustrate the influence of different parameters: T, nr and δ for instance La29, having similar results with the other instances (not reported here because of space limitations). In general, we appreciate that MOEA/D is not very sensible to the neighborhood size T. In fact, we can say that small neighborhood sizes help to delay the premature convergence just a little bit, but they don't overcome the issue. On the other hand, MOEA/D-n_r performs better with a large neighborhood size (for instance, 100 when $nr = 1$). This may sound shocking, but it is not so if we take into account that the nr parameter helps to control the diversity through a less aggressive replacement and the large neighborhood size allows to mate very different solutions. Finally, regarding the δ parameter, it turned out that running the algorithms without using it or using it with a quite standard value (0.9), have no statistically significant

Table 3: Comparing MOEA/D ($T = 5$) *vs.* MOEA/D-n_r ($T = 100$) for different nr values ($\delta = 1.0$).

instance	Hypervolume Indicator			Epsilon Indicator		
	MOEA/D	MOEA/D-$n_r = 1$	MOEA/D-$n_r = 2$	MOEA/D	MOEA/D-$n_r = 1$	MOEA/D-$n_r = 2$
ABZ7	$0{,}382_{(0{,}38)}$	$\mathbf{0{,}435}_{(0{,}35)}$	$0{,}406_{(0{,}33)}$	$0{,}179_{(0{,}39)}$	$\mathbf{0{,}128}_{(0{,}37)}$	$0{,}156_{(0{,}34)}$
ABZ8	$0{,}373_{(0{,}31)}$	$\mathbf{0{,}446}_{(0{,}33)}$	$0{,}425_{(0{,}33)}$	$0{,}218_{(0{,}33)}$	$\mathbf{0{,}144}_{(0{,}34)}$	$0{,}165_{(0{,}34)}$
ABZ9	$0{,}349_{(0{,}44)}$	$\mathbf{0{,}425}_{(0{,}41)}$	$0{,}404_{(0{,}45)}$	$0{,}244_{(0{,}47)}$	$\mathbf{0{,}167}_{(0{,}42)}$	$0{,}188_{(0{,}48)}$
FT10	$0{,}549_{(0{,}48)}$	$\mathbf{0{,}617}_{(0{,}45)}$	$0{,}596_{(0{,}44)}$	$0{,}199_{(0{,}50)}$	$\mathbf{0{,}135}_{(0{,}46)}$	$0{,}154_{(0{,}47)}$
FT20	$0{,}203_{(0{,}24)}$	$\mathbf{0{,}238}_{(0{,}20)}$	$0{,}227_{(0{,}22)}$	$0{,}110_{(0{,}23)}$	$\mathbf{0{,}079}_{(0{,}18)}$	$0{,}089_{(0{,}20)}$
La21	$0{,}427_{(0{,}33)}$	$\mathbf{0{,}470}_{(0{,}27)}$	$0{,}447_{(0{,}33)}$	$0{,}158_{(0{,}34)}$	$\mathbf{0{,}119}_{(0{,}29)}$	$0{,}142_{(0{,}34)}$
La24	$0{,}429_{(0{,}36)}$	$\mathbf{0{,}472}_{(0{,}47)}$	$0{,}460_{(0{,}34)}$	$0{,}181_{(0{,}38)}$	$\mathbf{0{,}141}_{(0{,}48)}$	$0{,}153_{(0{,}34)}$
La25	$0{,}440_{(0{,}30)}$	$\mathbf{0{,}472}_{(0{,}35)}$	$0{,}464_{(0{,}38)}$	$0{,}163_{(0{,}32)}$	$\mathbf{0{,}136}_{(0{,}37)}$	$0{,}142_{(0{,}38)}$
La27	$0{,}228_{(0{,}24)}$	$\mathbf{0{,}270}_{(0{,}29)}$	$0{,}259_{(0{,}26)}$	$0{,}184_{(0{,}26)}$	$\mathbf{0{,}142}_{(0{,}35)}$	$0{,}154_{(0{,}29)}$
La29	$0{,}235_{(0{,}31)}$	$\mathbf{0{,}278}_{(0{,}31)}$	$0{,}253_{(0{,}32)}$	$0{,}201_{(0{,}36)}$	$\mathbf{0{,}158}_{(0{,}34)}$	$0{,}184_{(0{,}35)}$
La38	$0{,}608_{(0{,}51)}$	$\mathbf{0{,}706}_{(0{,}36)}$	$0{,}687_{(0{,}33)}$	$0{,}199_{(0{,}48)}$	$\mathbf{0{,}112}_{(0{,}31)}$	$0{,}131_{(0{,}29)}$
La40	$0{,}618_{(0{,}45)}$	$\mathbf{0{,}684}_{(0{,}41)}$	$0{,}679_{(0{,}46)}$	$0{,}204_{(0{,}43)}$	$\mathbf{0{,}147}_{(0{,}37)}$	$0{,}150_{(0{,}44)}$

differences for any of the three configurations described in the table. We attribute this to the fact that the parameter δ can only help to diversify the search in the selection step, which is completely annealed if either the population becomes very little diverse due to the aggressive replacement of MOEA/D or if the neighborhood size T is set to a large value in the case of MOEA/D-n_r with a small nr parameter.

In Table 3 we show the performance of the three algorithms for all the instances. Based on the previous analysis, we only show results with a small T-value for MOEA/D (namely, $T = 5$), and a large value for MOEA/D-n_r (namely, $T = 100$). Also based on the lack of differences between using δ or not, we remove this parameter from all configurations. We can appreciate in the table that MOEA/D-n_r clearly outperforms MOEA/D in both indicators and for all instances. This behavior is due to the less aggressive replacement strategy which allows the algorithm to keep more diversity. Regarding the best value for the nr parameter, we obtain the best results for all instances when $nr = 1$, even though in some of them the differences with respect to the use of $nr = 2$ are not statistically significant. Due to this, we shall fix $nr = 1$ and $T = 100$.

5.2 Comparative analysis

Overall performance. In the following we analyze the behavior of the remaining strategies, i.e., MOEA/D-**ss** and MOEA/D-RO. In Table 4, where we also include NSGA-II as a baseline reference approach, we can see that for all instances except for FT20, the newly proposed MOEA/D-RO strategy provides the best results for both indicators. However, the differences between this algorithm and the already existing MOEA/D-**ss** are not statistically significant, but there is a huge difference between them when examining more carefully their runtime behavior as discussed in the following.

Runtime behavior. In Fig. 3, we provide a sample extracted from our data to illustrate this claim. In the first sub-figure, the Y-axis represents the average hypervolume obtained by each algorithm, while the X-axis measures the number of calls to the evaluation function (in the logarithmic scale). We remark that the behavior observed for instance La29 is seemingly the same for all the other instances, except for instances La21 and FT20 for which the behavior is slightly different (not shown in the figure due to space limitations).

Overall, even though MOEA/D-**ss** and MOEA/D-RO obtain similar hypervolume values at the end of the $5 \cdot 10^4$ function evaluations, we see that the evolution of both in time is different. For MOEA/D-RO, MOEA/D-n_r, and even NSGA-II, they obtain good results even with a short amount of function evaluations, while MOEA/D-**ss** is much slower converging to good results. Actually, in the first stages MOEA/D-**ss** performs worse than MOEA/D-n_r, but it is able to outperform it (and also MOEA/D-RO for instance FT20) after a given number of evaluations. The only exception to this is for La21, where MOEA/D-n_r remains better than MOEA/D-**ss**. In the right part of Fig. 3, we see the number of different objective vectors that are maintained within the population during the evolution of the algorithms. The MOEA/D-RO has a 100% of different solutions, as expected by taking T equal to the population size, but what is more interesting is that MOEA/D-**ss** offers more diversity than MOEA/D-n_r. In our judgment, this is what makes this strategy better in the long term, as in the first iterations of the algorithm it is more focused on keeping the diversity that will allow it to reach better solutions at the end.

EAF analysis. In order to have a more clear information about the relative performance of the different competing strategies, we compare the sets of solutions obtained by each pair of the algorithms by means of the empirical attainment functions (EAFs) [15]. The EAF provides the probability, estimated from several runs, that an arbitrary objective vector is dominated by, or equivalent to, a solution obtained by a single run of the algorithm. The difference between the EAFs for two different algorithms enables to identify the regions of the objective space where one algorithm performs better than another. The magnitude of the difference in favor of one algorithm is plotted within a gray-colored graduation as illustrated in Fig. 4. First of all, we can appreciate that the solutions obtained with MOEA/D-RO dominate those obtained by the MOEA/D-**ss** and MOEA/D-n_r in almost every region of the front. Furthermore, none of the algorithms are able to obtain solutions dominating those obtained by MOEA/D-RO. Interestingly, we can observe a specific feature for the NSGA-II algorithm that we were not able to elicit from the previous indicator based results. In fact, we can appreciate that it is quite good finding solutions in the middle part of the front. We hence argue that the decomposition nature of the MOEA/D algorithms makes solutions spread much better, thus forcing the population to stay spread even at the extreme parts and thus investing the running resources at looking for good solutions along all the front, while NSGA-II is focusing its "efforts" in finding good solutions in the middle part, especially if a loss in diversity occurs at the early stage of the optimization process.

Table 4: Overall comparisons of competing algorithms ($T = 100$, $nr = 1$, $\delta = 1$ when it holds).

instance	Hypervolume Indicator				Epsilon Indicator			
	MOEA/D-n_r	MOEA/D-ss	MOEA/D-RO	NSGA-II	MOEA/D-n_r	MOEA/D-ss	MOEA/D-RO	NSGA-II
ABZ7	0,435$_{(0,35)}$	0,446$_{(0,27)}$	**0,456**$_{(0,30)}$	0,423$_{(0,32)}$	0,128$_{(0,37)}$	0,112$_{(0,28)}$	**0,106**$_{(0,34)}$	0,141$_{(0,32)}$
ABZ8	0,446$_{(0,33)}$	0,459$_{(0,32)}$	**0,477**$_{(0,33)}$	0,428$_{(0,35)}$	0,144$_{(0,34)}$	0,129$_{(0,34)}$	**0,112**$_{(0,34)}$	0,164$_{(0,36)}$
ABZ9	0,425$_{(0,41)}$	0,435$_{(0,35)}$	**0,445**$_{(0,38)}$	0,415$_{(0,33)}$	0,167$_{(0,42)}$	0,156$_{(0,38)}$	**0,148**$_{(0,48)}$	0,180$_{(0,35)}$
FT10	0,617$_{(0,45)}$	0,634$_{(0,41)}$	**0,643**$_{(0,42)}$	0,591$_{(0,39)}$	0,135$_{(0,46)}$	0,117$_{(0,43)}$	**0,109**$_{(0,47)}$	0,163$_{(0,40)}$
FT20	0,238$_{(0,20)}$	**0,249**$_{(0,20)}$	0,243$_{(0,23)}$	0,241$_{(0,18)}$	0,079$_{(0,18)}$	**0,068**$_{(0,18)}$	0,073$_{(0,20)}$	0,077$_{(0,18)}$
La21	0,470$_{(0,27)}$	0,456$_{(0,29)}$	**0,478**$_{(0,33)}$	0,449$_{(0,37)}$	0,119$_{(0,29)}$	0,132$_{(0,32)}$	**0,112**$_{(0,34)}$	0,142$_{(0,40)}$
La24	0,472$_{(0,47)}$	0,491$_{(0,30)}$	**0,507**$_{(0,36)}$	0,456$_{(0,39)}$	0,141$_{(0,48)}$	0,122$_{(0,30)}$	**0,108**$_{(0,34)}$	0,162$_{(0,40)}$
La25	0,472$_{(0,35)}$	0,485$_{(0,30)}$	**0,494**$_{(0,32)}$	0,445$_{(0,32)}$	0,136$_{(0,37)}$	0,120$_{(0,30)}$	**0,115**$_{(0,38)}$	0,165$_{(0,33)}$
La27	0,270$_{(0,29)}$	0,274$_{(0,22)}$	**0,279**$_{(0,28)}$	0,254$_{(0,29)}$	0,142$_{(0,35)}$	**0,134**$_{(0,24)}$	0,134$_{(0,29)}$	0,166$_{(0,33)}$
La29	0,278$_{(0,31)}$	0,283$_{(0,32)}$	**0,300**$_{(0,31)}$	0,254$_{(0,27)}$	0,158$_{(0,34)}$	0,148$_{(0,34)}$	**0,134**$_{(0,35)}$	0,190$_{(0,30)}$
La38	0,706$_{(0,36)}$	0,709$_{(0,36)}$	**0,721**$_{(0,30)}$	0,683$_{(0,34)}$	0,112$_{(0,31)}$	0,111$_{(0,34)}$	**0,101**$_{(0,29)}$	0,132$_{(0,31)}$
La40	0,684$_{(0,41)}$	0,697$_{(0,35)}$	**0,726**$_{(0,31)}$	0,691$_{(0,36)}$	0,147$_{(0,37)}$	0,135$_{(0,34)}$	**0,109**$_{(0,44)}$	0,145$_{(0,35)}$

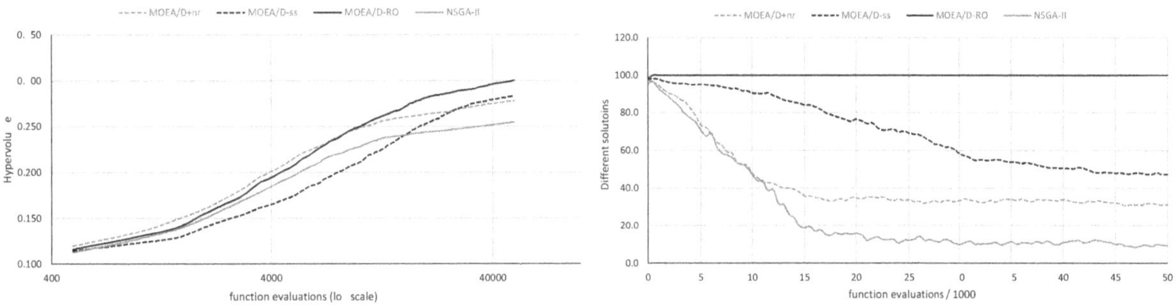

(a) Hypervolume evolution for La29 (b) Diversity evolution for La29

Figure 3: Evolution of the hypervolume (% of different solutions in the population) depending on the number of evaluations

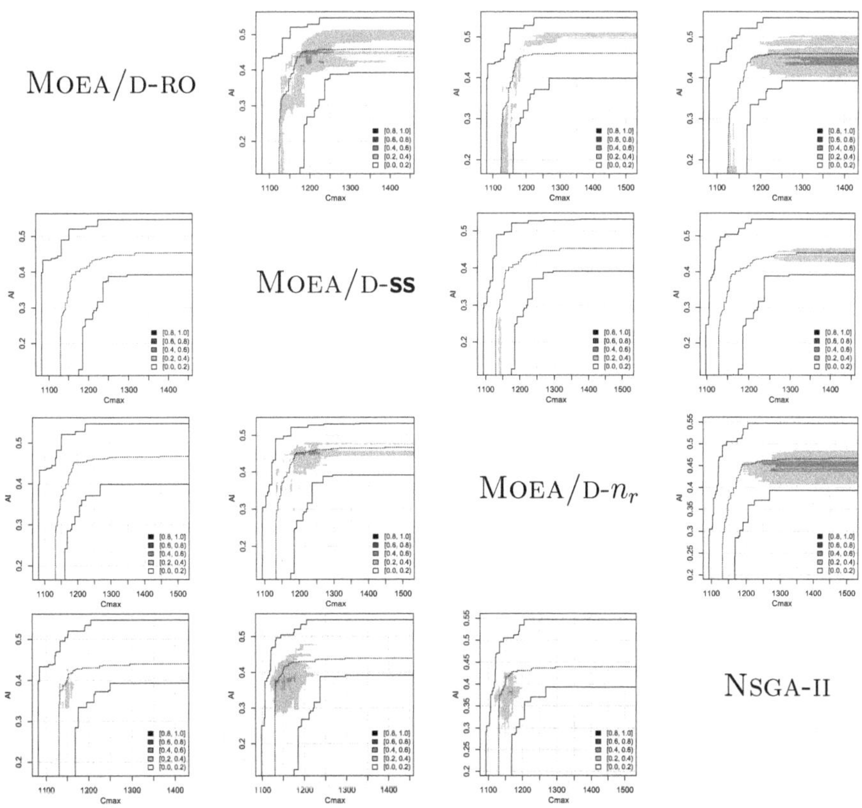

Figure 4: Comparison of MOEA/D-RO, MOEA/D-ss, MOEA/D-n_r, and NSGA-II using the EAF differences. Results are for instance La21. The plot in row i and column j shows the areas where algorithm i improves over algorithm j.

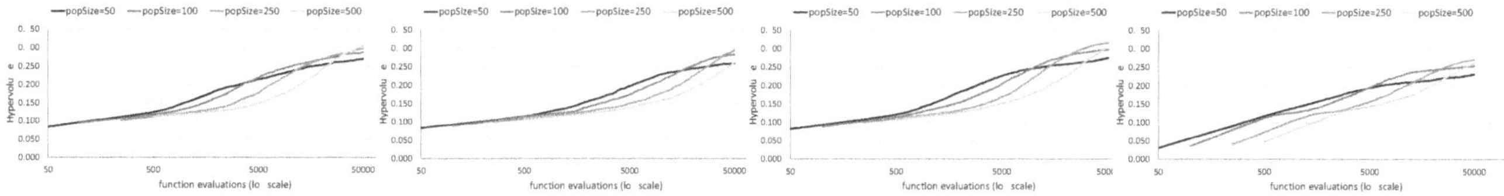

Figure 5: Runtime evolution of the hypervolume using different population sizes for instance La29 and different algorihtms. From Left to right: MOEA/D-RO, MOEA/D-**ss**, MOEA/D-n_r, NSGA-II.

Impact of population size. When a diversity issue is found in some algorithm, it is a common practice to increase the population size as to have a larger pool of solutions to evolve. To further study the influence of this parameter on the considered MOEA/D variants, in Fig. 5 we plot their runtime behavior using four different population sizes 50, 100, 250 and 500; but keeping as stopping criterion the same number of function evaluations. Even though the figure shows the results for instance La29, the behavior is the same for the other instances. We observe that increasing the population size is a good option if one has a large budget, but in case of having a short budget of time it is much better to have small population sizes and let the algorithm converge for more iterations. Furthermore, this behavior is common for all the tested algorithms, which indicates that all of them scale consistently in a similar way. Finally we can confirm that the MOEA/D-**ss** is the slowest algorithm converging, even when using larger the population size.

6. CONCLUSION

In this paper, we addressed some diversity issues of MOEA/D variants applied to the FJSP. The MOEA/D-n_r and MOEA/D-**ss** algorithms proposed in the literature are good alternatives, as they improve the performance of MOEA/D, but they can be improved substantially as illustrated by the proposed MOEA/D-RO variant independently of the available budget. We also confirmed that all MOEA/D variants perform very competitive compared to the Pareto-dominance based algorithm NSGA-II. However, it was interesting to observe that NSGA-II is able to find better solutions than MOEA/D-n_r and MOEA/D-**ss** in the medium part of the front, while the MOEA/D variants are all better at finding good solutions at the extremes of the front due to the nature of the MOEA/D framework.

It is our hope that the new findings elicited by the throughout analysis presented in this paper would enhance our understanding of the main ingredients for designing highly efficient decomposition-based algorithm. In particular, it would be interesting to conduct similar investigations for other combinatorial problems and to study more deeply the behavior of MOEA/D when additionally plugging local search based operators.

7. REFERENCES

[1] S. Abdullah and M. Abdolrazzagh-Nezhad. Fuzzy job-shop scheduling problems: A review. *Information Sciences*, 278:380–407, 2014.

[2] M. Andresen, H. Bräsel, M. Mörig, J. Tusch, F. Werner, and P. Willenius. Simulated annealing and genetic algorithms for minimizing mean flow time in an open shop. *Mathematical and Computer Modelling*, 48:1279–1293, 2008.

[3] P. C. Chang, S. H. Chen, Q. Zhang, and J. L. Lin. MOEA/D for flowshop scheduling problems. In *CEC*, pages 1433–1438, 2008.

[4] C. A. Coello Coello, G. B. Lamont, and D. A. Van Veldhuizen. *Evolutionary Algorithms for Solving Multi-Objective Problems*. 2007.

[5] K. Deb. *Multi-Objective Optimization using Evolutionary Algorithms*. John Wiley & Sons, 2001.

[6] K. Deb, S. Agrawal, A. Pratap, and T. Meyarivan. A fast and elitist multiobjective genetic algorithm: NSGA-II. *IEEE TEC*, 6(2):182–197, 2002.

[7] D. Dubois, H. Fargier, and P. Fortemps. Fuzzy scheduling: Modelling flexible constraints vs. coping with incomplete knowledge. *European Journal of Operational Research*, 147:231–252, 2003.

[8] D. Dubois and H. Prade. *Possibility Theory: An Approach to Computerized Processing of Uncertainty*. Plenum Press, New York (USA), 1986.

[9] P. Fortemps. Jobshop scheduling with imprecise durations: a fuzzy approach. *IEEE Transactions of Fuzzy Systems*, 7:557–569, 1997.

[10] I. Giagkiozis, R. C. Purshouse, and P. J. Fleming. Generalized Decomposition. In *EMO*, pages 428–442, 2013.

[11] I. González Rodríguez, C. R. Vela, A. Hernández-Arauzo, and J. Puente. Improved local search for job shop scheduling with uncertain durations. In 19th *Inter. Conf. on Automated Planning and Scheduling*, pages 154–161, 2009.

[12] A. Kaufmann and M. Gupta. *Introduction to Fuzzy Arithmetic*. Van Nostrand Reinhold, New York, 1991.

[13] H. Li and Q. Zhang. Multiobjective optimization problems with complicated pareto sets, MOEA/D and NSGA-II. *IEEE TEC*, 13(2):284–302, 2009.

[14] L. D. Long and A. Ohsato. Fuzzy critical chain method for project scheduling under resource constraints and uncertainty. *International Journal of Project Management*, 26(6):688–698, 2008.

[15] M. López-Ibáñez, L. Paquete, and T. Stützle. In T. Bartz-Beielstein, M. Chiarandini, L. Paquete, and M. Preuss, editors, *Experimental Methods for the Analysis of Optimization Algorithms*, chapter 9, pages 209–222. Springer.

[16] G. Marquet, B. Derbel, A. Liefooghe, and E.-G. Talbi. Shake them all! Rethinking selection and replacement in MOEA/D. In *PPSN XIII*, pages 641–651. 2014.

[17] K. Miettinen. *Nonlinear Multiobjective Optimization*. Kluwer, Boston, MA, USA, 1999.

[18] J. J. Palacios, C. R. Vela, I. González-Rodríguez, and J. Puente. Schedule generation schemes for job shop problems with fuzziness. In *ECAI*, pages 687–692, 2014.

[19] Q. Zhang and H. Li. MOEA/D: A multiobjective evolutionary algorithm based on decomposition. *IEEE TEC*, 11(6):712–731, 2007.

[20] E. Zitzler, L. Thiele, M. Laumanns, C. M. Fonseca, and V. Grunert da Fonseca. Performance Assessment of Multiobjective Optimizers: An Analysis and Review. *IEEE TEC*, 7(2):117–132, 2003.

Incorporating User Preferences in MOEA/D through the Coevolution of Weights

Martin Pilát
Charles University in Prague
Faculty of Mathematics and Physics
Malostranské náměstí 25
118 00 Prague, Czech Republic
Martin.Pilat@mff.cuni.cz

Roman Neruda
Institute of Computer Science
Academy of Sciences of the Czech Republic
Pod Vodárenskou věží 271/2
182 07 Prague, Czech Republic
roman@cs.cas.cz

ABSTRACT

The resulting set of solutions obtained by MOEA/D depends on the weights used in the decomposition. In this work, we use this feature to incorporate user preferences into the search. We use co-evolutionary approach to change the weights adaptively during the run of the algorithm. After the user specifies their preferences by assigning binary preference values to the individuals, the co-evolutionary step improves the distribution of weights by creating new (offspring) weights and selecting those that better match the user preferences. The algorithm is tested on a set of benchmark functions with a set of different user preferences.

Categories and Subject Descriptors

I.2.8 [**Artificial Intelligence**]: Problem Solving, Control Methods, and Search—*heuristic methods*; G.1.6 [**Mathematics of Computing**]: Optimization—*global optimization*

Keywords

evolutionary algorithms, multi-objective optimization, coevolution, MOEA/D

1. INTRODUCTION

Multi-objective evolutionary algorithms have gained a lot of attention in the recent decades and they are considered to be among the best multi-objective optimizers. Currently, decomposition-based multi-objective algorithms [17, 3] are becoming more popular, mainly because they outperform the more traditional domination based algorithms when solving many-objective problems. The decomposition-based algorithm transform the multi-objective problem into a set of single-objective problems by using a set of weights or reference vectors. The single-objective subproblems are then solved all at once.

GECCO '15, July 11 - 15, 2015, Madrid, Spain
 ISBN 978-1-4503-3472-3/15/07... $15.00
DOI: http://dx.doi.org/10.1145/2739480.2754801

The weights used by the algorithm directly affect the resulting non-dominated set. Thus, it should be possible to incorporate user preferences into the search by means of altering the weights. In this work, we take this approach and show that co-evolution of weights can be used as a mean to incorporate user preferences into the MOEA/D algorithm [17].

The way the user has to use to specify the preferences can affect the usability of the approach. If the user has to assign specific preference values to each individual in the population it is much more difficult than assigning only binary values (whether the individual is preferred or not). The later case is also more general and allows for interactive evolution – the user is presented the set of solutions found so far and selects those they like. The algorithm uses this selection to guide the search towards the preferred area of the search space. In the present paper, we propose an approach which can deal with such a binary preferences, thus generalizing the ways in which preferences can be specified.

We consider the multi-objective optimization problem defined as the tuple $\langle D, O, f, g\rangle$, where D is the decision space, O is the objective space, usually $O \subseteq \mathbb{R}$, $f = \{f_1, \dots, f_m\}$ is a set of m objective functions $f_i : D \to O$ which should be minimized, and $g = \{g_1, \dots, g_k\}$ represents a set of k constraints $g_i : D \to \mathbb{R}$ with the feasible set being defined as $g_i(x) \leq 0$. The goal of multi-objective optimization is to find an approximation of the Pareto set, i.e. such set of feasible solutions from the decision space that there is no other feasible solution which would be better in all objectives than some solution from the Pareto set. We say that the approximation is well-converged, if the found solutions are close to the Pareto set, and we say that it is well-spread if for each solution in the Pareto set, there is a close solution in the set returned by the algorithm.

The main goal of this work is to demonstrate a co-evolutionary approach to incorporating of binary user preferences into MOEA/D. We describe an extension of MOEA/D with the co-evolution of weights – cwMOEA/D – and illustrate its performance on a set of benchmark problems with different types of Pareto fronts and with two different types of user preferences. In this work, we also investigate, how the changing of the weights affects the convergence speed of the MOEA/D algorithm and how it affects the number of individuals found in the preferred region of the Pareto front. We also discuss how the proposed algorithm could be extended to provide even better results.

In the next section, we describe the work most related

to this contribution in more detail, Section 3 is devoted to the description of the algorithm, in Section 4 we describe the experiments and discuss the performance of the algorithm and, finally, in Section 5 we provide some directions for future research.

2. RELATED WORK

The Multi-objective Evolutionary Algorithm Based on Decomposition (MOEA/D) [17] is based on the idea of the decomposition of the multi-objective problem into a set of single-objective subproblems. The decomposition is based on a set of weights each of which corresponds to a single subproblem. Very often, the so called Tchebycheff decomposition is used. Given a weight vector $\lambda = \langle\lambda_1, \ldots, \lambda_n\rangle$, the corresponding subproblem is defined as

$$\text{minimize } g^{te}(x|\lambda, z^*) = \max_{1\leq i\leq m} \lambda_i|f_i(x) - z_i^*|,$$

where z^* is a reference point chosen as the minimum of objective function values found during the evolution. The main advantage of this approach is that it works regardless of the shape of the Pareto front, while other decomposition approaches (like the weighted sum approach) only work for convex Pareto fronts.

Apart from being used for the decomposition, the weights are also used to define neighborhoods of the subproblems. These subproblems are then solved all at once. In each generation, a new individual is generated and evaluated using its own set of weights. It is compared to its parent and in case the offspring is better it replaces the parent. Moreover, it is also compared to other individuals in its neighborhood and is allowed to replace some of them.

Different sets of weights in MOEA/D lead to different resulting sets of solutions found by the algorithm and therefore, it is crucial to set the weights in such a way to provide as good results as possible. Some research has been already done in this direction. Jiang *et al.* [9], for example, proposed a method for symmetric Pareto fronts, which aims at producing such weight vectors, that the hyper-volume of the resulting non-dominated set is maximized. They describe the shape of the Pareto front as $f_1^p + f_2^p = 1$, for some p estimated from the current non-dominated set and seek the optimal set of intersection points by the Simplex Method.

Qi *et al.* [14] created a method for sampling the weight vectors and obtained better spread of solutions. Moreover, the vectors are adjusted later in the process of evolution to obtain even better distribution of the solutions. The adjustment is again based on the geometrical properties of the current non-dominated set.

A slightly different approach to decomposition is used in NSGA-III [3]. The algorithm uses reference points instead of weight vectors to guide the search. The reference points are used inside a secondary sorting criterion. The individuals from the same non-dominated set which are closer to the lines defined by the origin and a reference point are preferred. In an extension of NSGA-III for constrained optimization [8], reference points are removed from the parts of search space which do not satisfy the constraints, and new reference points are generated in those parts of search space which do. The reference points are generated in such a way, to provide equal spread of solutions on the whole Pareto front.

Although the goal of most multi-objective algorithms is to provide the approximation of the whole Pareto front, in practice only an interesting part of the front is often required. Thus, it is important, to provide a way for the user (decision maker) to supply their preferences to the algorithm. If the algorithm is able to respect these preferences, it can focus on interesting parts of the Pareto front and use the computational resources more effectively (e.g. provide more solutions in the preferred area). There have been many attempts to integrate user preferences into multi-objective evolutionary algorithms. Branke [1] in his work describes many different ways how to provide preference information to multi-objective evolutionary algorithm. Among these are: the scaling of objectives, additional constraints, providing a reference point, and limiting the potential trade-offs. Each of these approaches can be useful in different situations, depending on which type of preferences is more natural in the given case.

More specifically, Molina *et al.* [12] created an algorithm based on g-dominance. The algorithm uses a reference point and prefers individuals which either dominated the reference point or are dominated by the point. This leads to the preference of an interesting part of the Pareto front.

Mohammadi *et al.* [11] proposed the R-MEAD2 algorithm. Similarly, to MOEA/D, this algorithm is also based on decomposition, however, R-MEAD2 is guided by a user specified reference point and the goal is to provide Pareto optimal solutions close to this reference point. To this end, the weights are adjusted during the evolution.

Another group of algorithms is based on interactive evolution, such algorithms use the feedback of a decision maker to create a value function which models the decision maker's preferences. For example, Deb and Kumar [4] proposed a technique based on Light Beam Search combined with evolutionary algorithm. In this technique, the decision maker is asked to provide local preferential information, which is used to build an outranking relation that is in turn used to reflect the decision makers preference during selection in the evolutionary algorithm.

Sinha *et al.* [15] proposed a technique which, apart from incorporating the preferences to the search also tries to minimize the number of queries to the decision maker. The algorithm queries the decision maker only after "significant progress is made". The progress is measured by the distance between an ideal point and the points in the current population. The decision maker is asked to choose the best point from a set of presented points.

In the next section, we propose a novel framework for the incorporation of user preferences - cwMOEA/D. Although, the cwMOEA/D algorithm is based on MOEA/D and is based on the changing of the weights used in the algorithm, and therefore it cannot be easily used in conjunction with algorithms which do not use decomposition (like the traditional NSGA-II [5]), it provides a way to incorporate most of the above described preference-based approaches into the popular and effective MOEA/D algorithm. Compared to the above mentioned algorithms, the new framework is more general – it expects only binary preference, i.e. each point is either preferred or not. It is trivial to implement most of the reference point based approaches (like the g-dominance) in cwMOEA/D. The interactive approaches, which aim at learning a value function, can also be implemented in the proposed framework in a simple way – after the points are evaluated with a given approach, they can be ranked some

Algorithm 1 cwMOEAD/D

```
Require: n: population size
Require: δ: probability of neighborhood operators
1: λ ← InitUniformWeights()
2: InitNeighborhood(λ)
3: P ← InitPopulation();
4: z* ← InitIdealPoint(P)
5: while termination criterion not met do
6:     Par ← ∅                          ▷ saved parent population
7:     Off ← ∅                          ▷ saved offspring population
8:     for all parent ∈ P do            ▷ in random order
9:         r ← RandomNumber(0,1)
10:        if r ≤ δ then                ▷ as in MOEA/D
11:            child ← PerformNeighborhoodOperators()
12:        else                         ▷ as in MOEA/D
13:            child ← PerformGlobalOperators()
14:        end if
15:        Evaluate(child)
16:        Par ← Par ∪ {parent}         ▷ save parent
17:        Off ← Off ∪ {child}          ▷ save offspring
18:        z* ← UpdateReference(child)  ▷ as in MOEA/D
19:        UpdateProblem(child)         ▷ as in MOEA/D
20:    end for
21:    λ ← UpdateWeights(λ, Off ∪ Par)
22: end while
```

Algorithm 2 UpdateWeights(λ,P)

```
pref ← EvaluateUserPreference(P)   ▷ provided by user
childWeights ← MutateWeights(λ, pref)
rPref ← RefinePreference(pref, P)
for i ← 1 to Length(λ) do
    OldIndex ← AssingIndividual(λ[i],P)
    NewIndex ← AssingIndividual(childWeights[i],P)
    if rPref[NewIdx] < rPref[oldIdx] then
        λ[i] ← childWeights[i]
    end if
end for
return λ
```

Algorithm 3 MutateWeights(λ,pref)

```
Require: σ_p: std. dev. for preferred individuals
Require: σ_n: std. dev. for not-preferred individuals
childWeights ← ∅
for i ← 1 to Length(λ) do
    if pref[i] < 0 then               ▷ preferred individual
        childWeights[i] ← GaussianMutation(λ[i],σ_p)
    else
        childWeights[i] ← GaussianMutation(λ[i],σ_n)
    end if
end for
return childWeights
```

Algorithm 4 RefinePreference(pref, P)

```
Require: m: the number of closest individuals in Eq. 1
rPref ← ∅
pInds ← {P[i]|pref[i] < 0}            ▷ preferred individuals
for i ← 1 to Length(P) do
    if pref[i] > 0 then
        rPref[i] ← min_{p∈pInds} |p, P[i]|
    else          ▷ average distance to m nearest neighbors
        rPref[i] ← AvgDstMNN(pInds\{P[i]}, P[i], m)
    end if
end for
return rPref
```

and a number of the best may be flagged as preferred points, the rest as not-preferred.

3. ALGORITHM DESCRIPTION

In this work, we incorporate user preference handling into the original MOEA/D algorithm. In order to do so, we add a co-evolutionary step. In this step, the weights used in the decomposition are adjusted in such a way that the algorithm looks for solutions more preferred by the user. The user needs to specify their preference in a form of function which evaluates the solutions. This function shall return a negative number for preferred solutions and a positive number otherwise. The algorithm does not depend on the particular value, but only on the sign. This makes specifying user preferences easier, and, in fact, the same approach can be used even in the interactive setting, where the user selects preferred solutions as they are offered to them by the algorithm. The new algorithm – cwMOEA/D – is described in more detail in the rest of this section.

The main loop of the algorithm (cf. Algorithm 1) closely matches the main loop of MOEA/D [17]. There are only two additions: during each iteration, the parents and new offspring are saved (lines 6-7 and 16-17), in order to have more evaluated individuals for the selection of weights; and after each MOEA/D iteration, the adaptation of weights is performed (line 21).

3.1 User Preference Specification

We assume, the user provides their preference as a function, $p : D \to \{-1; 1\}$, where D is the decision space of the problem at hand. This does not in any way limit the preferences to the decision space. The preference function can first evaluate the objective functions and use them to compute the preference later. In fact, the algorithm uses the preference function after all the individuals have already been evaluated, so the objective values are available for all individuals and do not be re-evaluated again. We use the objective space D in the definition of preference function only in order to make the function more general.

Such a general specification of user preference leads to an important advantage – it can be used to express most of the ways, how preferences can be specified. For example, if the user wants to limit the trade-off between the objectives such, that

$$l \leq \frac{f_1(x)}{f_2(x)} \leq h,$$

for some real bounds h and l, they can use the following preference function:

$$p(x) = \begin{cases} -1 & \text{if } l \leq \frac{f_1(x)}{f_2(x)} \leq h; \\ 1 & \text{otherwise.} \end{cases}$$

The disadvantage of such a preference function is that it provides only a binary information. Such information is not very suitable for use with evolutionary algorithms, and therefore we first refine the preference (cf. Algorithm 4). Let $P_p = \{x \in P | p(x) \leq 0\}$ is the set of preferred individuals

Algorithm 5 AssingIndividual(λ,P)
1: idx $\leftarrow \arg\min_{i\in\{1,\ldots,\text{Length}(P)\}}$DecompFitness($P[i]$,$\lambda$)   2: **return** idx

Figure 1: Example of refined user preference. The user prefers individuals which lie between the two dashed lines. The red points correspond to individuals, the green points to their refined preference (the distance was multiplied by 5 for negative individuals to make the differences more visible).

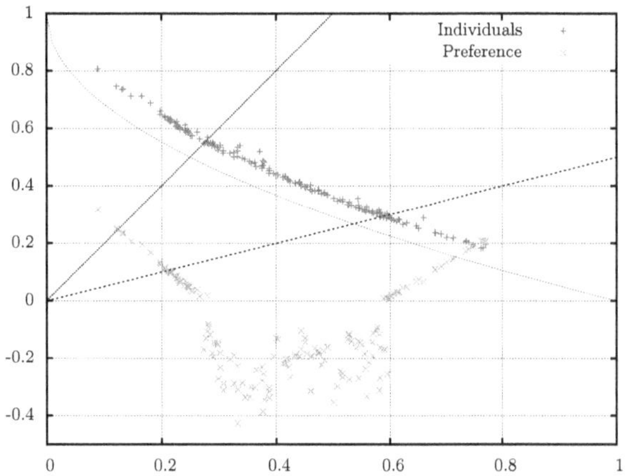

from population P and $P_n = \{x \in P | p(x) > 0\}$ is the rest of individuals. Now, the refined preference function

$$p^*(x) = \begin{cases} |x, P_p| & x \in P_n \\ -|x, P_p|_m & x \in P_p \end{cases} \tag{1}$$

where $|x, P_p|$ is the distance of individual x to the closest preferred individual, and $|x, P_p|_m$ is the average distance of x to the m closest preferred individuals (except x itself). Thus, the refined preference p^* is positive, if the original preference is positive and it is negative, if the original is negative. Moreover, not-preferred individuals closer to preferred individuals are preferred over those further from the preferred ones. For the preferred individuals, the refined preference favors those, which are further from other preferred individuals. An example of such a refined preference is presented in Figure 1. The figure was obtained by running the cwMOEA/D algorithm (further described below) on the ZDT1 [18] problem for 20,000 function evaluations. The average distance to the five closest individuals was used to compute the refined preference for the preferred individuals.

3.2 Co-evolution of Weights

The algorithm aims at updating the weights in such a way, that they better match the user preferences specified by the preference function. To this end, a co-evolutionary step is added into the MOEA/D algorithm (cf. Algorithm 2). After each iteration of the algorithm, new weights are generated by means of mutation (line 2). We use simple Gaussian mutation with different standard deviation for preferred and not-preferred individuals (cf. Algorithm 3). After the mutation, the user preference is refined (line 3 of Alg. 2), and the selection of the weights is performed (lines 4-10).

The selection always compares each weight with its offspring (the weight obtained by mutation from the parent weight), this ensures that the weights do not change much and, mostly, that the neighborhoods in MOEA/D change only slowly.

We use the refined user preference function to select the weight. The only problem is, that the function is defined over the individuals in the population and not the weights. Therefore, we need to match the weights with the individuals. To this end, we define the *assigned individual* x to weight w as

$$x = \arg\min_{x\in P} g(x|w),$$

where P is the population and $g(x|w)$ is the fitness of the individual x given the weight w (cf. Algorithm 5). Thus, each weight is assigned to the individual, for which it provides the best (lowest) fitness. Once the individuals have been assigned, both to the parent and to the offspring weight, the preferences of the assigned individuals are compared, and the weight which corresponds to the individual with lower preference is selected. Note that we do not need to compute the assignment in the mutation of the weights (which also depend on the user preference), as MOEA/D keeps the individuals matched to the weights of the subproblem the individuals optimize. However, we need to compute the assignment in the selection step, as the newly generated weight may be far from the original one, and thus may better correspond to a different individual.

4. EXPERIMENTS AND DISCUSSION

We have implemented the algorithm in the jMetal framework [6] and the source codes are available as supplementary materials. In all the experiments presented in this section, we use the population size of 100 individuals. The offspring are created using a differential crossover operator [13] and polynomial mutation [2]. The parameter δ which controls the percentage of genetic operations performed on the neighborhood and globally was set to $\delta = 0.9$ (i.e. 90 percent of the operations are performed in neighborhoods). The size of the neighborhood was set to 20, and each offspring can replace at most 2 other individuals in its neighborhood. These are the default settings from the jMetal framework and correspond to the settings used in [10]. The same settings were also used for MOEA/D in cases, where cwMOEA/D is compared to MOEA/D. After preliminary experiments, we have set the number of closest individuals used in the preference refinement procedure of preferred individuals to $m = 5$. This value provides good compromise, as the refined value is local, yet not too noisy. The parameters σ_p and σ_n (the standard deviations for the mutations of weights for preferred and not-preferred individuals respectively) were set to $\sigma_p = 0.001$ and $\sigma_n = 0.01$. The reasons for this setting are detailed in the next section.

4.1 The Effect of the Mutation of Weights

Before we show, how the algorithm works for different user preferences, we first investigate the setting of the two standard deviations for the mutation of weights and we provide reasons for using different standard deviation for preferred and not-preferred individuals.

To this end, we run the algorithm on the ZDT1 [18], WFG1, WFG2, and WFG4 [7] problems and report the generational distance (GD) [16] of the population with respect

Figure 2: Comparison of convergence speed for different standard deviation in the mutation of the weights. Median (line) and first and third quartile (error-bars) from 15 independent runs.

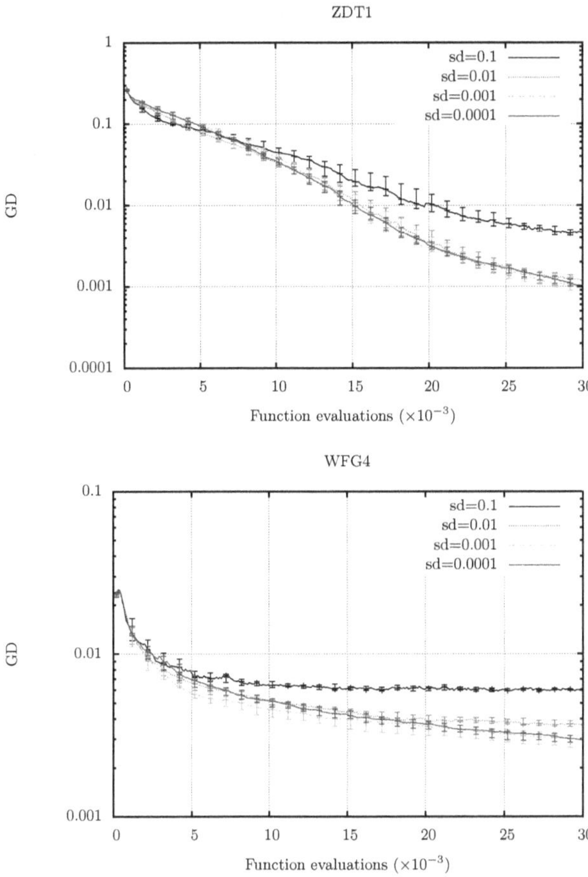

Figure 3: Comparison of the number of preferred individuals for different standard deviation in the mutation of the weights. Median (line) and first and third quartile (error-bars) from 15 independent runs.

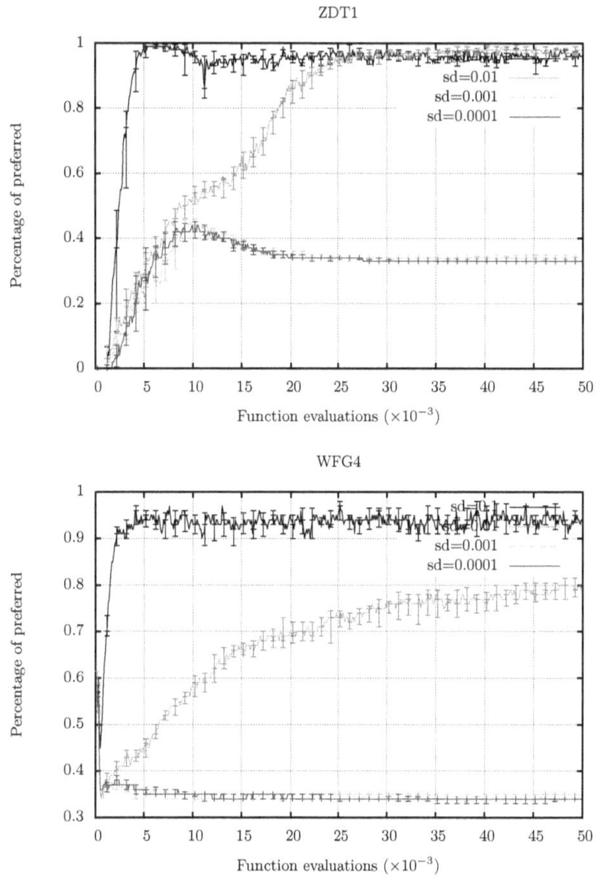

to a reference set. The generational distance measures the average distance of each individual in the population to the closest individual in the reference set, as such, the indicator only measures the convergence of the population, but does not in any way reflect the spread. Moreover, we also count the ratio of preferred individuals among the individuals in the population.

The results for the dependence of the generational distance after a given number of evaluations on the standard deviation is presented in Figure 2. We can see, that with higher standard deviation, the convergence is slower. The difference is most pronounced for standard deviation equal to 0.1. This is not surprising, as the larger standard deviation means larger changes in the weights and it is difficult for the algorithm to react to such a dynamic environment.

Figure 3 on the other hand shows the percentage of preferred individuals in the population. We can see that for small standard deviations, the weights are not sufficiently adjusted to react to the user preference. For ZDT1, standard deviation of at least 0.01 is required to ensure most of the individuals are preferred. For WFG3, this number seems to be even larger.

The previous experiments show that for fast convergence we need small standard deviations in the weight mutation, and for large number of preferred individuals we need large values of standard deviation. This is the main reason, we use different standard deviation for preferred and not-preferred individuals. In the rest of the experiments, we use standard deviation of 0.01 for not-preferred individuals and of 0.001 for the preferred ones.

4.2 Limited trade-off

In this section, we provide the results of experiments with limited trade-off between two objectives. The preference is specified as

$$0.5 \leq \frac{f_1(x)}{f_2 x} \leq 2.$$

In this case, the preferred area is a continuous part of the Pareto front (in case the Pareto front itself is continuous). We let the algorithm run for 150,000 function evaluations, with population size of 100 individuals, and the standard deviation for weight mutation set as described in the previous section (i.e. 0.01 for not-preferred individuals and 0.001 for the preferred ones). The initial weights were generated uniformly, and the Tchebycheff decomposition was used to define the subproblems. We made 15 independent runs of the algorithms and show the population in the last genera-

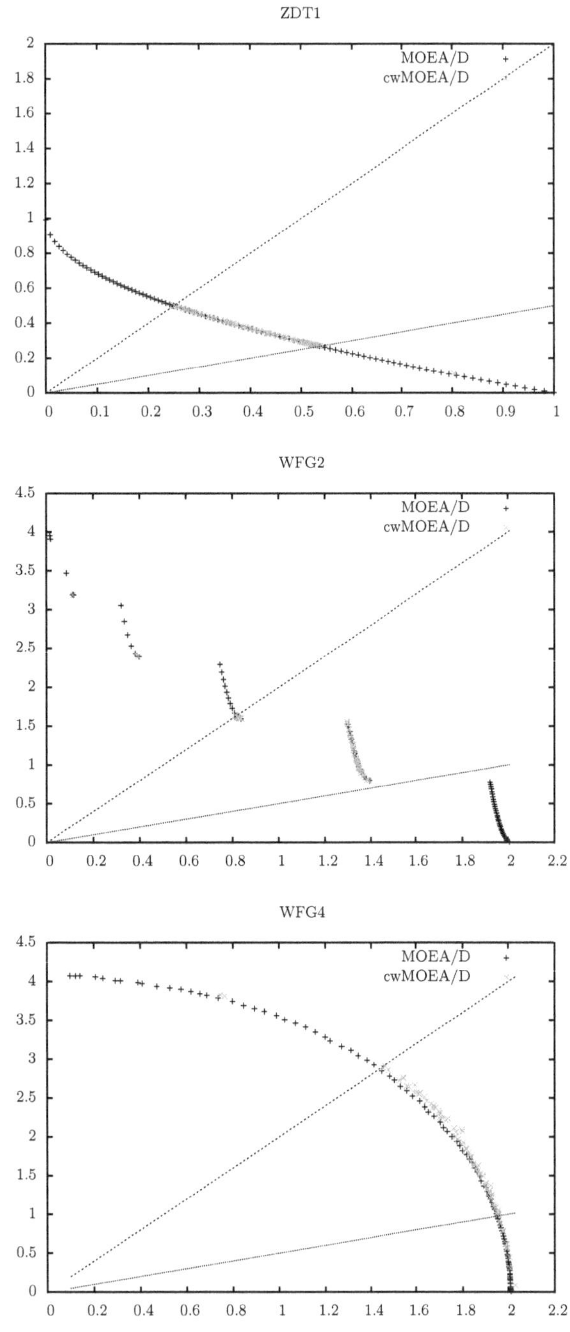

Figure 4: The resulting populations after 150,000 evaluations for the ZDT1, WFG2, and WFG4 problems. Population with median hyper-volume from 15 independent runs is plotted.

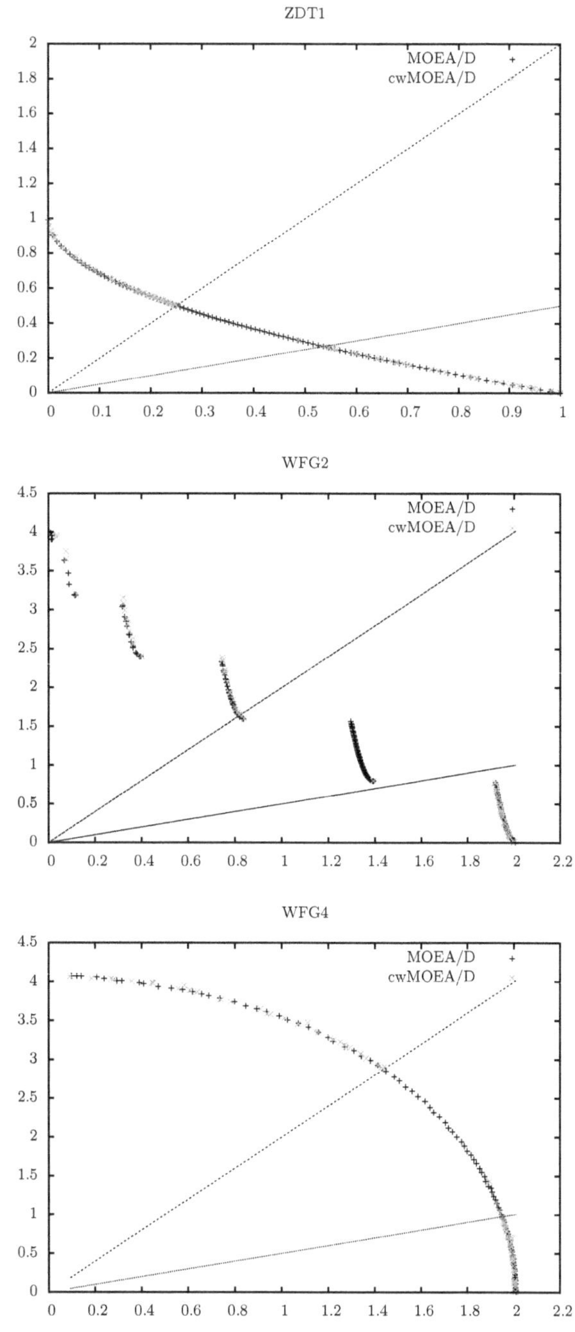

Figure 5: The resulting populations after 150,000 evaluations for the ZDT1, WFG2, and WFG4 problems. Population with median hyper-volume from 15 independent runs is plotted.

tion with median hyper-volume (of the preferred individuals) in the plots in Figure 4. For comparison, we also show the set of solutions found by MOEA/D without any user preferences.

To demonstrate the results, we have chosen three benchmark problems with different properties. ZDT1 is a simple problem with convex Pareto front, WFG2 is a more complicated problem with non-continuous Pareto front and WFG4 has concave Pareto front.

The results show, that the algorithm is able to adjust the weights in such a way that the user preference is met. Most of the solutions correspond to the preferred ones. However, in all cases there are a few solutions outside the preferred zone.

For ZDT1, the algorithm found a good spread of preferred

solutions converged close to the Pareto front. There is also only one solution outside of the preferred zone.

The WFG2 problem provides and interesting challenge as its Pareto front is not continuous. We can see that the algorithm found the correct parts of the Pareto front and that the solutions are well spread and converged. However, there are a few solutions on the extreme ends of some of the other non-continuous parts of the fronts. The algorithm was not able to change some of the weights enough to ignore these parts. The number of such solutions is low and it does not harm the overall performance much. Also, there are a lot of solutions on the small preferred part on the boundary of the preferred area.

For the WFG4 problem, we can see that the algorithm again moved most of the solutions to the preferred area. In comparison to the other test problems, there are more not-preferred individuals in this set of solutions. Also, the solutions are slightly worse converged compared to MOEA/D without user preferences.

Overall, the algorithm found a large number of well-spread and converged solutions, however, the distribution is not as uniform as the one found by MOEA/D.

4.3 Non-continuous preference

Apart from testing a continuous preference, it may also be interesting to test some non-continuous preference, i.e. such that there are at least two preferred areas in the objective space. To this end, we invert the preference we used in the previous section. Now, the preferred solutions are those, where

$$\frac{f_1(x)}{f_2(x)} < 0.5 \text{ or } \frac{f_1(x)}{f_2(x)} > 2.$$

Such a preference poses new challenge, the algorithm now should divide the weights into two groups instead of grouping them together. We again show the results on the ZDT1, WFG2, and WFG4 benchmark functions in Figure 5. The parameters of the algorithm are the same as in the previous section, the only part that changed is the user preference.

We can again see that the algorithm is able to respect the user preference and most of the solutions are in the preferred areas. In all cases, the solutions are well-converged and spread, however, we can observe that each of the two parts of the preferred space contains different number of solutions.

For the ZDT1 benchmark, we can see that the algorithm found more solutions in the upper part of the search space than in the lower part, however, both parts contain more solutions than what MOEA/D was able to find.

The cwMOEA/D algorithm was able to find all the preferred part of the non-continuous Pareto front of the WFG2 problem, this time, the density of solutions is higher in the lower part, and the upper part is slightly under-represented.

Finally, for WFG4, the algorithm again correctly found the two preferred parts of the Pareto front, but again, the upper part contains less solutions than the lower part.

The differences between the number of solutions in the upper and lower part of the preferred area can be explained by the way the algorithm converges toward the Pareto front. If there are more solutions in one part of the preferred area in the beginning, it is difficult for the algorithm to move them to the other part. Such a move would require large changes in the weights and the algorithm is not able to make such changes in its presents form. It could be beneficial to make more aggressive selection of the weight which would allow the algorithm to move the weight further. For example, the weights can be compared to other weights than just its parents. This would allow the algorithm to remove the weight from the over-represented area and move it to the under-represented one. However, such an aggressive move might require re-computation of the neighborhoods for the underlying MOEA/D algorithm. Such an extension is left as a future work.

4.4 Discussion

In the experimental section, we presented the results of the algorithm only for the problems with two objectives, however, the approach is general and does not depend on the number of objectives. We left the experiments with more than two objectives as a future work. We will also investigate, how the number of objectives affects the required magnitude of the weights mutation.

The same approach can also be used to handle constrained problems – the solutions which do not satisfy the constraints can be flagged as not-preferred and the algorithm will automatically lead the search to the areas which do satisfy the constraints. The testing and evaluation of cwMOEA/D for constrained multi-objective optimization is also left as a future work.

5. CONCLUSION AND FUTURE WORK

We have developed a co-evolution-based algorithm which incorporates user preferences into MOEA/D – cwMOEA/D. The experiments have shown that the algorithm is able to find well-spread and converged solutions in the area of the search space specified by the user. This leads to more effective use of computational resources as uninteresting areas of the space are not examined. The larger number of interesting solutions found by the algorithm allow the decision maker to choose from a wider set of possibilities.

We have also found several directions for future work. The solutions are not as regularly spread as those found by MOEA/D, it may be beneficial to look for ways, which would make the solution set more regularly spread. A better mutation of the weights may be useful to reach this goal. We have also observed that in case of non-continuous preference, some parts of the preferred space may contain more individuals than other. It may be interesting to improve the selection of the weights in such a way that a weight from the over-represented can "move" to the under-represented part. We will also compare cwMOEA/D to different preference-based methods and experiment with the possibilities of constrained handling based on the ideas from cwMOEA/D.

Acknowledgments

This work has been supported by Czech Science Foundation project no. P103-15-19877S.

6. REFERENCES

[1] J. Branke. Consideration of partial user preferences in evolutionary multiobjective optimization. In J. Branke, K. Deb, K. Miettinen, and R. Slowinski, editors, *Multiobjective Optimization*, volume 5252 of *Lecture Notes in Computer Science*, pages 157–178. Springer Berlin Heidelberg, 2008.

[2] K. Deb. *Multi-objective optimization using evolutionary algorithms*, volume 16. John Wiley & Sons, 2001.

[3] K. Deb and H. Jain. An evolutionary many-objective optimization algorithm using reference-point-based nondominated sorting approach, part I: Solving problems with box constraints. *Evolutionary Computation, IEEE Transactions on*, 18(4):577–601, Aug 2014.

[4] K. Deb and A. Kumar. Light beam search based multi-objective optimization using evolutionary algorithms. In *Evolutionary Computation, 2007. CEC 2007. IEEE Congress on*, pages 2125–2132. IEEE, 2007.

[5] K. Deb, A. Pratap, S. Agarwal, and T. Meyarivan. A fast and elitist multiobjective genetic algorithm: Nsga-ii. *Evolutionary Computation, IEEE Transactions on*, 6(2):182–197, 2002.

[6] J. J. Durillo and A. J. Nebro. jMetal: A java framework for multi-objective optimization. *Advances in Engineering Software*, 42(10):760–771, 2011.

[7] S. Huband, P. Hingston, L. Barone, and L. While. A review of multiobjective test problems and a scalable test problem toolkit. *Evolutionary Computation, IEEE Transactions on*, 10(5):477–506, 2006.

[8] H. Jain and K. Deb. An evolutionary many-objective optimization algorithm using reference-point based nondominated sorting approach, part II: Handling constraints and extending to an adaptive approach. *Evolutionary Computation, IEEE Transactions on*, 18(4):602–622, Aug 2014.

[9] S. Jiang, Z. Cai, J. Zhang, and Y.-S. Ong. Multiobjective optimization by decomposition with pareto-adaptive weight vectors. In *Natural Computation (ICNC), 2011 Seventh International Conference on*, volume 3, pages 1260–1264, July 2011.

[10] H. Li and Q. Zhang. Multiobjective optimization problems with complicated pareto sets, MOEA/D and NSGA-II. *Evolutionary Computation, IEEE Transactions on*, 13(2):284–302, April 2009.

[11] A. Mohammadi, M. Omidvar, X. Li, and K. Deb. Integrating user preferences and decomposition methods for many-objective optimization. In *Evolutionary Computation (CEC), 2014 IEEE Congress on*, pages 421–428, July 2014.

[12] J. Molina, L. V. Santana, A. G. Hernández-Díaz, C. A. C. Coello, and R. Caballero. g-dominance: Reference point based dominance for multiobjective metaheuristics. *European Journal of Operational Research*, 197(2):685–692, 2009.

[13] K. Price, R. M. Storn, and J. A. Lampinen. *Differential evolution: a practical approach to global optimization*. Springer Science & Business Media, 2006.

[14] Y. Qi, X. Ma, F. Liu, L. Jiao, J. Sun, and J. Wu. MOEA/D with adaptive weight adjustment. *Evolutionary Computation*, 22(2):231–264, June 2014.

[15] A. Sinha, P. Korhonen, J. Wallenius, and K. Deb. An interactive evolutionary multi-objective optimization algorithm with a limited number of decision maker calls. *European Journal of Operational Research*, 233(3):674–688, 2014.

[16] D. A. Van Veldhuizen and G. B. Lamont. Evolutionary computation and convergence to a pareto front. In J. R. Koza, editor, *Late Breaking Papers at the Genetic Programming 1998 Conference*, University of Wisconsin, Madison, Wisconsin, USA, 22-25 July 1998. Stanford University Bookstore.

[17] Q. Zhang and H. Li. MOEA/D: A multiobjective evolutionary algorithm based on decomposition. *Evolutionary Computation, IEEE Transactions on*, 11(6):712–731, Dec 2007.

[18] E. Zitzler, K. Deb, and L. Thiele. Comparison of multiobjective evolutionary algorithms: Empirical results. *Evol. Comput.*, 8(2):173–195, June 2000.

Analysis of Objectives Relationships in Multiobjective Problems Using Trade-Off Region Maps

Rodrigo L. Pinheiro
ASAP Research Group
School of Computer Science
The University of Nottingham
rzp@cs.nott.ac.uk

Dario Landa-Silva
ASAP Research Group
School of Computer Science
The University of Nottingham
jds@cs.nott.ac.uk

Jason Atkin
ASAP Research Group
School of Computer Science
The University of Nottingham
jaa@cs.nott.ac.uk

ABSTRACT

Understanding the relationships between objectives in many-objective optimisation problems is desirable in order to develop more effective algorithms. We propose a technique for the analysis and visualisation of complex relationships between many (three or more) objectives. This technique looks at conflicting, harmonious and independent objectives relationships from different perspectives. To do that, it uses correlation, trade-off regions maps and scatter-plots in a four step approach. We apply the proposed technique to a set of instances of the well-known multiobjective multidimensional knapsack problem. The experimental results show that with the proposed technique we can identify local and complex relationships between objectives, trade-offs not derived from pairwise relationships, gaps in the fitness landscape, and regions of interest. Such information can be used to tailor the development of algorithms.

Categories and Subject Descriptors

G.1.6 [**Optimisation**]; I.2.8 [**Problem Solving, Control Methods, and Search**]

Keywords

multiobjective fitness landscape analysis; trade-off region maps; fitness landscape visualisation

1. INTRODUCTION

It is important to understand the relationships between objectives in multiobjective optimisation problems (MOPs) because this can help to tailor the search according to the multiobjective fitness landscape. This is particularly when tackling large real-world MOPs with many objectives (more than two). In the multiobjective optimisation literature, the focus is often on MOPs that exhibit strong conflict relationships between objectives as this is part of the motivation for applying multiobjective techniques. However, the conflict relationship between objectives could be local rather than global. A *global conflict relationship* would hold throughout most, if not all of, the search space. On the other hand, a *local conflict relationship* would hold in a restricted region of the search space, e.g. the objectives could be in conflict early in the search but not conflicting later. This was discussed by Knowles and Corne [1] in the context of the multiobjective quadratic assignment problem. Castro-Gutierrez et al. [2] studied the objectives' relationships in multiobjective vehicle routing problems.

As the number of objectives increases, composite relationships between objectives might emerge, i.e. relationships between objectives (conflicting or otherwise) that are not global but localised and more complex. Several techniques have been previously applied for the analysis and visualisation of relationships between objectives in MOPs. These include parallel coordinates, scatter-plots (which both involve graphical representations), Kendall correlation [3] (a quantitative metric), and statistical measures [4], among others. Purshouse and Fleming [5] discussed these techniques in their research into the relationships between objectives in MOPs. Other works that have used some of these techniques include Castro-Gutierrez et al. [2] on multiobjective vehicle routing problems, and Ishibuchi et al. [6] on many-objective problems with correlated objectives. One limitation of these techniques is that they are most suited to identify only pairwise relationships between objectives.

In this work, we propose a technique to analyse and visualise global and local relationships between many objectives in order to achieve a clearer understanding of the fitness landscape in a MOP. The technique requires a set of non-dominated solutions to be supplied (which can be obtained in any way) and uses Karnaugh maps [7] to visualise composite relationships between many objectives. The technique also uses correlation and scatter-plots to complement the analysis. The technique involves four steps: analyse global pairwise relationships between objectives in the given non-dominated set, estimate the range of values for each objective, identify objective trade-offs using Karnaugh region maps, and identify local relationships between objectives using scatter-plots. This technique seeks to analyse the objectives' relationships from multiple perspectives in order to better understand the fitness landscape in many-objective combinatorial optimisation problems, which are well known for having irregular and difficult to assess fitness landscapes.

Section 2 surveys some related work. Section 3 provides the motivation for this work. Section 4 describes the proposed technique while experimental results applying the proposed technique to several instances of the multiobjective

GECCO '15, July 11 - 15, 2015, Madrid, Spain

ISBN 978-1-4503-3472-3/15/07...$15.00

DOI: http://dx.doi.org/10.1145/2739480.2754721

multidimensional 0-1 knapsack problem [8, 9] are presented in Section 5. Our main observation is that different instances of the same problem may exhibit very different relationships between objectives. Finally, Section 6 concludes the paper.

2. RELATED WORK

Better understanding of fitness landscapes has been beneficial in multiobjective combinatorial optimisation (MOCO) problems. For example, Garrett and Dasgupta [10] [11] adapted single-objective landscape analysis techniques (distribution of optima, fitness distance correlation, ruggedness, random walk analysis and analysis of the geometry of the solution space) for tailoring multiobjective evolutionary algorithms. They applied such techniques to quadratic assignment and generalised assignment problems with two objectives. They concluded that the performance of hybrid algorithms benefits from using knowledge of the fitness landscape. Castro-Gutierrez et al. [2] used the objectives' pairwise dependency correlation analysis proposed by Purshouse and Fleming [5] to assess the conflicting nature of objectives in multiobjective vehicle routing problems.

Brownlee and Wright [12] proposed a visualisation technique to evaluate the quality of a non-dominated set based on a ranking of the objectives. However, this technique may not be suitable for large solution sets as it is based on the individual analysis of solutions. Other visualisation techniques include objective wheels, bar graphs and colour stacks as explored by Anderson and Dror [13].

Verel et al. [14] adapted single-objective landscape analysis techniques to set-based multiobjective problems with objective correlation. Later, Verel et al. [15] conducted a study on the landscape of local optima in such problems. Verel et al. [16] proposed to carry out *a priori* analysis of a problem by evaluating the problem size, its epistasis, the number of objectives and the correlation values between objectives, to suggest the best way to tackle it. They concluded that, depending on the problem features, different types of algorithms (scalar or Pareto approach) and sizes of the solution archive should be employed.

Walker et al. [17] reviewed different methods (scatter plots, parallel coordinates and heat maps) to visualise solution sets for many-objective problems. They also proposed two techniques: a data mining visualisation tool to plot a convex graph, and a new similarity measure of solutions to plot them in a two-dimensional space.

Giagkiozis and Fleming [18] proposed a technique to estimate the Pareto front of a continuous optimisation problem, and then use the estimated front to obtain values for the decision variables of interesting solutions. They proposed using a multiobjective algorithm to obtain an initial solution set, which is then used to calculate a projection matrix of the optimal Pareto set. They tested their technique on convex benchmark problems.

Tusar and Filipic [19] presented a comprehensive survey and assessment on several visualisation techniques for many-objectives approximation sets. They also presented a visualisation method that uses orthogonal projections of a section and applied it to four-dimensional approximation sets.

It is clear that understanding the fitness landscape of multiobjective optimisation can help to develop better solution methods. It is also clear that the analysis and visualisation of objectives' relationships, particularly in combinatorial landscapes with many objectives, is a topic of interest for researchers. The technique proposed in this paper seeks to make a contribution in this area.

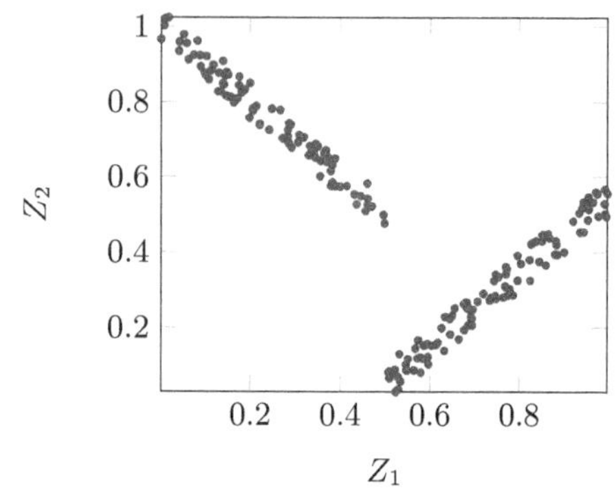

Figure 1: Example of complex relationship between two objectives Z_1 and Z_2 in a 3-objective optimisation problem.

3. OBJECTIVES RELATIONSHIPS IN MULTIOBJECTIVE OPTIMISATION

The focus of this research is to investigate the relationship between objectives in MOPs by analysing the non-dominated approximation set and its coverage of the solution space. We use the concepts of conflict, harmony and independence between objectives as proposed by Purshouse and Fleming [5].

Results from some existing techniques to assess the conflicting nature of objectives can be deceiving. The literature includes studies of pairwise relationships between objectives [2, 6, 20]. However, analysis techniques such as Kendall correlation [3] only manage to identify *global relationships* between objectives. Figure 1 shows a Pareto-front between two maximisation objectives, Z_1 and Z_2, in a scenario with three objectives (we omit the scatter-plots for Z_3). Clearly, when $Z_1 < 0.5$, the objectives are conflicting while when $Z_1 > 0.5$ the objectives are harmonious. However, if the number of solutions with Z_1 lower than 0.5 is roughly the same as the number of solutions with Z_1 higher than 0.5, simply applying the Kendall correlation technique would result in a correlation value close to 0. The conclusion could be drawn that the objectives are independent, when in reality there may be *local relationships* that could be exploited.

Some existing techniques might not reveal trade-offs which result from *composite relationships* between two and more objectives. Figure 2a lists a set of non-dominated fitness vectors for three maximisation objectives and Figure 2b shows their scatter-plot matrix and correlation values. We can observe that high values (51-100) appear simultaneously only in up to two of the three objectives. Two points in Figure 2a have only one good objective value. Four points are good for only Z_1 and Z_2. Three points are good for only Z_1 and Z_3, and the remaining points are good for only Z_2 and Z_3. No solution present has values higher than 50 for all three objectives simultaneously. The scatter plot and correlation values do not help us to appreciate the three-way trade-off. Likewise, we can see that the correlation values do not indicate any strong pairwise correlation.

Hence, to better analyse and visualise the multiobjective nature of optimisation problems, we need techniques that help us to identify global, local and composite relationships

$(45, 68, 85), (6, 63, 99), (34, 64, 95),$
$(28, 100, 48), (98, 47, 69), (48, 62, 79),$
$(72, 24, 90), (82, 79, 16), (36, 100, 97),$
$(100, 87, 41), (98, 19, 87), (85, 57, 50),$
$(88, 20, 73), (91, 48, 99), (94, 31, 70),$
$(56, 49, 59), (75, 93, 1), (38, 84, 85),$
$(45, 78, 47)$

(a) Non-dominated points.

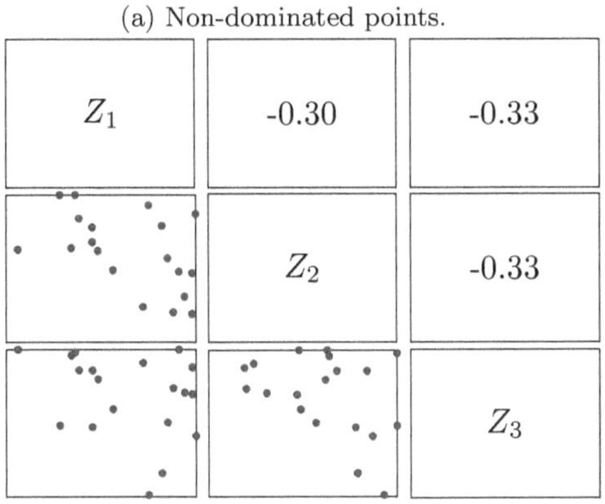

(b) Scatter-plot matrix and correlation coefficients.

Figure 2: Three-way conflicting objectives

between objectives as well as interesting trade-offs in the fitness landscape.

4. A FOUR STEPS ANALYSIS AND VISUALISATION TECHNIQUE

We propose a four-step technique to analyse and visualise objectives relationships. It requires some knowledge of the problem domain (the desirable range of objective values) and an approximation set of non-dominated solutions, which could be obtained using any multiobjective algorithm (*MOA*), such as those available in frameworks like JMetal [21] and ParadiseEO [22]. The quality of the approximation set given may affect the conclusions from the analysis because inaccurate ranges and scatter plots could lead to inaccurate observations, thus combining the results from the application of a number of well-accepted MOAs may be wise.

The scope of our technique is to aid the study of a subset of problem instances, to aid in tailoring an algorithm for solving other problem instances. Our aim in this work is to investigate the suitability of our technique, hence we test it on scenarios for which good algorithms are known. Although the approach requires some instances to be solved beforehand, the increased understanding of the problem should help in identifying the strengths and weaknesses of novel algorithms. Solution of these many-objectives problems are computationally expensive thus any help in tailoring fast techniques that can provide good-enough results has value, and this technique may allow a user to identify similarities between instances which could be exploited.

Each step in the proposed technique aggregates some information about the relationship between objectives, the coverage of the feasible solution space and the trade-offs in the fitness landscape. The four steps are described here and are illustrated by applying them to benchmark instances of the multiobjective multidimensional knapsack problem.

Step 1 – Global Pairwise Relationship Analysis:

First, the Kendall correlation values [3] are calculated, as in [5], to identify global pairwise relationships. Strongly conflicting correlations (values < -0.5) immediately indicate that a trade-off surface exists, whilst strongly harmonious correlations (values > 0.5) indicate that objectives could be aggregated or clustered. Correlation values showing that objectives are independent indicate that the data is not globally dependent, but do not imply the absence of local trade-offs in the fitness landscape. If independence is detected, the problem could be decomposed by separating the decision variables according to the objectives, to solve each objective (or groups of objectives) separately as such an approach provides improved performance [23].

Step 2 – Objective Range Analysis:

Here, the range (difference between best and worst values) is calculated for each objective in the given approximation set. Then, using problem domain knowledge the objectives which are interesting for further exploration are identified. A *meaningful objective* is an objective with a range which is large enough so that solutions can be classified into different quality categories regarding that objective value (e.g. good to bad, high to low, etc). Analogously, a *non-meaningful objective* is an objective with a range so small that the variability in the solution quality regarding that objective is considered negligible, thus not worth exploring further.

One way to deal with non-meaningful objectives is to ignore them during the optimisation. It is possible that by optimising the other objectives, the non-meaningful ones will present acceptable values within their small range anyway. Having a small range on the given approximation set does not mean that the range will be small across the entire solution space. The non-meaningful objective could be removed, the MOA re-executed and the ranged recalculated for the excluded objective. If the new solution set still exhibits only a small range for the excluded objective, it can be safely ignored. Another way to deal with non-meaningful objectives is to combine or cluster them [20].

Step 3 – Trade-off Regions Analysis:

We apply a quantitative method, namely Karnaugh maps [7], to classify the solution space into regions to help with the identification of trade-offs and the complex relationships between objectives. A Karnaugh map is a method for simplifying boolean algebra expressions using a truth table. The map has 2^i cells where i is the number of variables. The cells are labelled with binary numbers following the Grey code, meaning that any two adjacent cells differ in one bit. Hence, in a three variable scenario, the cells adjacent to cell 0 (000_2) are cells $1(001_2)$, $2(010_2)$ and $4(100_2)$. Karnaugh maps make it easy to visualise patterns that are used to group boolean variables.

In this step, for each objective Z_i where $(i = 1, 2, \ldots m)$, we define a threshold t_i such that values above t_i (maximisation problem) are considered good or acceptable, and values below t_i are considered inadequate. These t_i can be set using some knowledge of the problem domain or empirically – for example, using the average value for each objective as its threshold. Next, we classify each objective value in each solution as good (↑) or bad (↓). Finally, we draw a *region map* similarly to a Karnaugh map, but showing the count of solutions in each region rather than 0-1 output variables, and using solutions classifications (labelled ↑ and ↓) instead of the input variable values. The map is built with 2^m regions such that each region represents a single combination of good and/or bad objectives. We number the regions r_k using a binary encoding such that the least significant digit represents Z_1 and the most significant digit is Z_m, $\uparrow = 0$ and $\downarrow = 1$. For instance, the region $Z_3^{\downarrow}$, $Z_2^{\uparrow}$ and $Z_1^{\downarrow}$, would be region r_5, since binary 101_2 is 5.

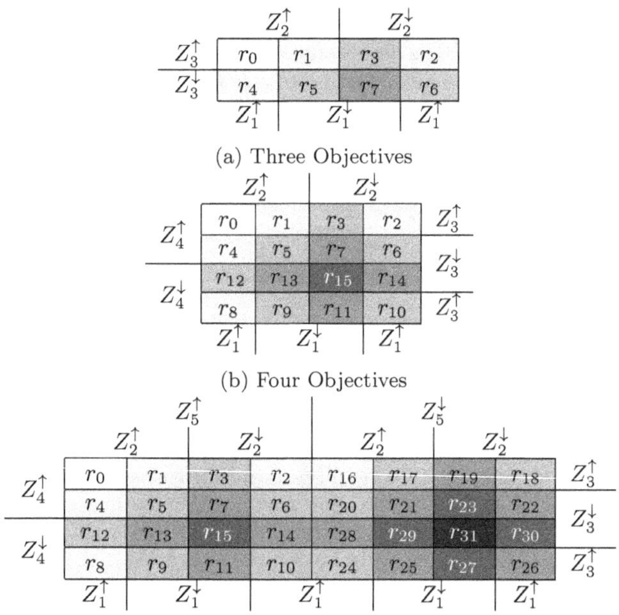

(a) Three Objectives

(b) Four Objectives

(c) Five Objectives

Figure 3: Region map schematics.

Figure 3 presents the region map schematics for 3, 4 and 5 objectives. Each region is identified with the r_k. Regions with the same number of good solutions are highlighted with the same shade of grey in such a way that lighter tones represents a higher number of good solutions while darker tones represents fewer good solutions.

The main advantage of the region map is that we can easily identify which objectives simultaneously present good values and the existence of trade-offs. If the region r_0 is not empty, then we have solutions with acceptable values in all objectives, meaning that the problem could potentially be tackled with single-objective algorithms. A range analysis on the solutions in this region could provide additional information on which approach is appropriate. On the contrary, when most solutions fall into region r_{2^m-1}, it means that the thresholds may have been set too high and should be lowered for more accurate results. When there are no solutions in r_0, but there are solutions scattered across the regions, there are trade-offs and the map can be used to visualise them.

Step 4 – Multiobjective Scatter-plot Analysis:

The last step is an analysis using scatter plots. First, for each instance we normalise the values of all objectives. Then, we select an objective and draw a scatter plot of all remaining objectives against the selected objective. Finally, we can combine all scatter plots into a single one. By visually inspecting this combined graph we can identify local relationships (conflicts and harmony), interesting patterns, gaps in the solution space, and well-spread trade-offs or isolated regions. This information can help us to tailor a solution algorithm by directing the search towards the regions of interest. When the landscape of the solution space is consistent throughout all instances analysed in this way, we could have a clearer idea of what type of solutions to expect when solving unseen instances.

When picking an objective for this process, it is preferable to select one that has a wider range of values rather than being concentrated in only a small range, otherwise the resulting graph may be more difficult to read. It may be interesting to test different objectives in order to spot which provide more useful information, or, if multiple objectives provide different insights, all of them could be considered instead of only one.

The next section presents experimental results from applying the proposed analysis and visualisation technique to five sets of benchmark instances of the multiobjective multidimensional knapsack problem.

5. SAMPLE ANALYSIS

In order to illustrate the analysis technique we apply it to different scenarios of the multiobjective multidimensional knapsack problem (MOMKP) [8]. We aim to show that within the same problem, the proposed technique can identify multiple scenarios with distinct multiobjective natures.

In the MOMKP, we have n items ($i = 1, \dots, n$) with m weights w_j^i ($j = 1, \dots, m$) and p profits c_k^i ($k = 1, \dots, p$). A set of items must be selected to maximise the p profits while not exceeding the capacities W_j of the knapsack. This problem can be formulated as follows:

$$\begin{array}{lll} \text{maximise} & \sum_{i=1}^{n} c_k^i x_i & k = 1, \dots, p \\ \text{subject to} & \sum_{i=1}^{n} w_j^i x_i \leq W_j & j = 1, \dots, m \\ & x_i \in 0, 1 & i = 1, \dots, n \end{array}$$

We considered five MOMKP datasets, each with five instances, all with $m = 4$, $p = 4$, $n = 1000$ and $W_j = 50000$. The first four datasets were generated following the guidelines in Bazgan et al. [9] and are as follows:

- **Set A**: Independent random instances where $w_k^i \in_N [1, 1000]$ and $c_k^i \in_N [1, 1000]$.
- **Set B**: Uncorrelated harmonious instances where $w_k^i \in_N [1, 1000]$, $c_1^i \in_N [1, 1000]$ and $c_k^i \in_N [max\{c_{k-1}^i - 100, 1\}, min\{c_{k-1}^i + 100, 1000\}]$ for $k = (2, 3, 4)$.
- **Set C**: Uncorrelated conflicting instances where $w_k^i \in_N [1, 1000]$, $c_1^i \in_N [1, 1000]$ and $c_k^i \in_N [max\{900 - c_{k-1}^i, 1\}, min\{1100 - c_{k-1}^i, 1000\}]$ for $k = (2, 3, 4)$.
- **Set D**: Correlated conflicting instances where $w_1^i \in_N [max\{900 - |c_1^i - c_4^i|, 1\}, min\{1100 - |c_1^i - c_4^i|, 1000\}]$, $w_k^i \in_N [max\{900 - |c_k^i - c_{k-1}^i|, 1\}, min\{1100 - |c_k^i - c_{k-1}^i|, 1000\}]$, $c_1^i \in_N [1, 1000]$ and $c_k^i \in_N [max\{900 - c_{k-1}^i, 1\}, min\{1100 - c_{k-1}^i, 1000\}]$ for $k = (2, 3, 4)$.

Set A contains only independent objectives. In set B all objectives are harmonious. Set C contains three pairs of conflicting objectives, (Z_2, Z_1), (Z_3, Z_2) and (Z_3, Z_4), while the weights are uncorrelated. Set D has conflicting objectives, as set C, but the weights are correlated to the objective values. The fifth set X was generated using data from a real-world home health-care scheduling problem.

Set A	A1	A2	A3	A4	A5	Mean
Z_1-Z_2	-0.15	-0.33	-0.21	-0.39	-0.49	-0.314
Z_1-Z_3	-0.02	0.09	-0.43	-0.34	0.11	-0.118
Z_1-Z_4	-0.21	0.09	-0.18	0.20	0.07	-0.006
Z_2-Z_3	-0.30	-0.37	0.17	0.01	-0.42	-0.182
Z_2-Z_4	0.06	-0.22	-0.17	-0.41	-0.09	-0.166
Z_3-Z_4	-0.25	-0.20	-0.22	-0.26	0.19	-0.148

Set C	C1	C2	C3	C4	C5	Mean
Z_1-Z_2	-0.96	-0.97	-0.98	-0.98	-0.98	**-0.974**
Z_1-Z_3	0.93	0.95	0.95	0.96	0.96	**0.950**
Z_1-Z_4	-0.93	-0.92	-0.92	-0.97	-0.95	**-0.938**
Z_2-Z_3	-0.96	-0.96	-0.97	-0.97	-0.96	**-0.964**
Z_2-Z_4	0.95	0.92	0.93	0.96	0.94	**0.940**
Z_3-Z_4	-0.98	-0.94	-0.95	-0.97	-0.97	**-0.962**

Set D	D1	D2	D3	D4	D5	Mean
Z_1-Z_2	-0.92	-0.92	-0.94	-0.94	-0.94	**-0.932**
Z_1-Z_3	0.88	0.84	0.88	0.87	0.87	**0.868**
Z_1-Z_4	-0.84	-0.84	-0.87	-0.87	-0.87	**-0.858**
Z_2-Z_3	-0.87	0.90	-0.91	-0.90	-0.90	**-0.896**
Z_2-Z_4	0.82	0.86	0.87	0.87	0.87	**0.858**
Z_3-Z_4	-0.92	-0.93	-0.93	0.92	-0.92	**-0.924**

Set X	X1	X2	X3	X4	X5	Mean
Z_1-Z_2	-0.26	-0.29	-0.13	-0.24	-0.32	-0.248
Z_1-Z_3	-0.13	-0.24	-0.27	-0.25	-0.27	-0.232
Z_1-Z_4	-0.29	-0.12	-0.29	-0.21	-0.07	-0.196
Z_2-Z_3	-0.25	-0.13	-0.26	-0.23	-0.19	-0.212
Z_2-Z_4	-0.13	-0.28	-0.22	-0.11	-0.27	-0.202
Z_3-Z_4	-0.24	-0.23	-0.14	-0.21	-0.18	-0.200

Table 1: Results for the pairwise relationship analysis (1.0 is completely harmonious, -1.0 is completely conflicting).

For each instance we run a single-objective genetic algorithm on each objective alone, then both NSGAII [24] and MOEA/D [25] algorithms on each pair and triple of objectives. We then combined all the obtained non-dominated solutions into an archive. We randomly drew from the archive half of the individuals for the initial population and the other half were randomly generated. We performed three runs for the MOEA/D and three runs for the NSGA-II with all objectives. The approximation non-dominated set was formed with all non-dominated solutions which were found in the process. Both NSGAII and MOEA/D used a population of 200 individuals, binary tournament selection and half uniform crossover [26] for 1500000 function evaluations. Overall, we obtained non-dominated sets with approximately 900 solutions for set A, 3 for set B, 550 for set C, 1500 for set D and 2500 solutions for set X.

Only a few non-dominated solutions were found for set B, the objectives there are strongly harmonious. Therefore, when maximising one of the objectives, the other objectives are also maximised. The data is therefore not enough for some of the analysis steps. However, the results are presented for completeness and illustrate that the number

Set A		A1	A2	A3	A4	A5	Mean
	Max	105269	105591	98845	109048	98562	103463.0
Z_1	Min	81507	84910	72393	82400	78259	79893.8
	Range	22.6%	19.6%	26.8%	24.4%	20.6%	22.8%
	Max	105565	102067	101879	107485	106290	104657.2
Z_2	Min	84618	78862	75194	78073	82345	79818.4
	Range	19.8%	22.7%	26.2%	27.4%	22.5%	23.7%
	Max	100267	105755	106024	110554	102331	104986.2
Z_3	Min	76363	80682	78207	82257	77085	78918.8
	Range	23.8%	23.7%	26.2%	25.6%	24.7%	24.8%
	Max	107607	110827	105888	103686	106472	16895.4
Z_4	Min	84932	88405	75817	76770	86274	82439.6
	Range	21.1%	20.2%	28.4%	26.0%	19.0%	22.9%

Set B		B1	B2	B3	B4	B5	Mean
	Max	103713	n/a	104141	111900	n/a	106584.7
Z_1	Min	102748	n/a	104107	111622	n/a	106159.0
	Range	0.9%	n/a	0.1%	0.2%	n/a	0.4%
	Max	104952	n/a	107233	113620	n/a	108601.7
Z_2	Min	104410	n/a	106638	113496	n/a	108181.3
	Range	0.5%	n/a	0.6%	0.1%	n/a	0.4%
	Max	106633	n/a	109010	113821	n/a	109821.3
Z_3	Min	106274	n/a	108175	113479	n/a	109309.3
	Range	0.3%	n/a	0.8%	0.3%	n/a	0.5%
	Max	107347	n/a	108361	113926	n/a	109878.0
Z_4	Min	107025	n/a	107324	113663	n/a	109337.3
	Range	0.3%	n/a	1.0%	0.2%	n/a	0.5%

Set C		C1	C2	C3	C4	C5	Mean
	Max	109142	105928	114773	115084	112290	111443.4
Z_1	Min	34911	33631	35449	35317	33157	34493.0
	Range	68.0%	68.3%	69.1%	69.3%	70.5%	69.0%
	Max	111124	109863	110290	114339	112559	111635.0
Z_2	Min	37928	36764	33189	30491	32431	34160.6
	Range	65.9%	66.5%	69.9%	73.3%	71.2%	69.4%
	Max	109775	104817	113400	115214	112467	111134.6
Z_3	Min	35859	33066	35326	35508	33004	34552.6
	Range	67.3%	68.5%	68.8%	69.2%	70.2%	68.9%
	Max	109569	108055	109242	113106	113391	110272.6
Z_4	Min	38774	37107	34277	32074	34062	35258.8
	Range	64.6%	65.7%	68.6%	71.6%	69.4%	68.0%

Set D		D1	D2	D3	D4	D5	Mean
	Max	186945	190209	188157	170337	179792	183088.0
Z_1	Min	58152	65554	69709	53810	64747	62394.4
	Range	68.9%	65.5%	63.0%	68.4%	64.0%	65.9%
	Max	180305	188813	197847	183889	191691	188509.0
Z_2	Min	64198	58680	68608	55859	63604	62189.8
	Range	64.4%	68.9%	65.3%	69.6%	66.8%	67.0%
	Max	185349	189131	187175	169153	180283	182218.2
Z_3	Min	56697	63717	68430	52449	67272	61713.0
	Range	69.4%	66.3%	63.4%	69.0%	62.7%	66.1%
	Max	182878	188835	196048	182326	190441	188105.6
Z_4	Min	66673	61884	70145	59158	66344	64840.8
	Range	63.5%	67.2%	64.2%	67.6%	65.2%	65.5%

Set X		X1	X2	X3	X4	X5	Mean
	Max	29105	30825	29173	29906	30536	29909.0
Z_1	Min	4930	3703	5317	4685	4429	4612.8
	Range	83.1%	88.0%	81.8%	84.3%	85.5%	84.6%
	Max	28885	30180	29314	28990	31422	29758.2
Z_2	Min	4706	4506	5024	4027	4190	4490.6
	Range	83.7%	85.1%	82.9%	86.1%	86.7%	84.9%
	Max	299949	29488	28154	31445	30055	29818.2
Z_3	Min	4096	4288	4298	4652	4102	4287.2
	Range	86.3%	85.5%	84.7%	85.2%	86.4%	85.6%
	Max	30040	30478	30063	31103	29206	30178.0
Z_4	Min	5075	3749	3673	4334	4563	4278.8
	Range	83.1%	87.7%	87.8%	86.1%	84.4%	85.8%

Table 2: Results for the objective ranges analysis.

of solutions obtained can have a major impact on the analysis and that, it is important to have a comprehensive set, with enough well-spread solutions.

5.1 Application of the Proposed Technique

Step 1 - Global Pairwise Relationships Analysis. The results for this step are in Table 1. Note that coeffi-

	$Z_2^{\uparrow}$		$Z_2^{\downarrow}$		
$Z_4^{\uparrow}$	01.2%	05.9%	07.9%	06.3%	$Z_3^{\uparrow}$
$Z_4^{\uparrow}$	04.0%	06.5%	07.2%	08.6%	$Z_3^{\downarrow}$
$Z_4^{\downarrow}$	4.7%	11.2%	00.5%	08.0%	$Z_3^{\downarrow}$
$Z_4^{\downarrow}$	02.8%	06.7%	08.7%	10.0%	$Z_3^{\uparrow}$
	$Z_1^{\uparrow}$	$Z_1^{\downarrow}$	$Z_1^{\downarrow}$	$Z_1^{\uparrow}$	

(a) Set A

	$Z_2^{\uparrow}$		$Z_2^{\downarrow}$		
$Z_4^{\uparrow}$	45.0%	10.0%	11.7%	00.0%	$Z_3^{\uparrow}$
$Z_4^{\uparrow}$	00.0%	00.0%	00.0%	00.0%	$Z_3^{\downarrow}$
$Z_4^{\downarrow}$	13.3%	00.0%	00.0%	15.0%	$Z_3^{\downarrow}$
$Z_4^{\downarrow}$	00.0%	00.0%	05.0%	00.0%	$Z_3^{\uparrow}$
	$Z_1^{\uparrow}$	$Z_1^{\downarrow}$	$Z_1^{\downarrow}$	$Z_1^{\uparrow}$	

(b) Set B

	$Z_2^{\uparrow}$		$Z_2^{\downarrow}$		
$Z_4^{\uparrow}$	00.0%	00.2%	00.3%	00.6%	$Z_3^{\uparrow}$
$Z_4^{\uparrow}$	00.0%	49.9%	01.9%	00.3%	$Z_3^{\downarrow}$
$Z_4^{\downarrow}$	00.0%	00.9%	00.8%	00.4%	$Z_3^{\downarrow}$
$Z_4^{\downarrow}$	00.0%	00.2%	00.8%	43.5%	$Z_3^{\uparrow}$
	$Z_1^{\uparrow}$	$Z_1^{\downarrow}$	$Z_1^{\downarrow}$	$Z_1^{\uparrow}$	

(c) Set C

	$Z_2^{\uparrow}$		$Z_2^{\downarrow}$		
$Z_4^{\uparrow}$	00.0%	00.0%	00.0%	00.0%	$Z_3^{\uparrow}$
$Z_4^{\uparrow}$	00.0%	55.6%	04.7%	00.0%	$Z_3^{\downarrow}$
$Z_4^{\downarrow}$	00.0%	04.4%	09.9%	01.8%	$Z_3^{\downarrow}$
$Z_4^{\downarrow}$	00.0%	00.0%	01.0%	22.6%	$Z_3^{\uparrow}$
	$Z_1^{\uparrow}$	$Z_1^{\downarrow}$	$Z_1^{\downarrow}$	$Z_1^{\uparrow}$	

(d) Set D

	$Z_2^{\uparrow}$		$Z_2^{\downarrow}$		
$Z_4^{\uparrow}$	00.0%	00.0%	05.9%	00.0%	$Z_3^{\uparrow}$
$Z_4^{\uparrow}$	00.0%	06.2%	10.0%	05.9%	$Z_3^{\downarrow}$
$Z_4^{\downarrow}$	07.9%	15.4%	04.7%	15.0%	$Z_3^{\downarrow}$
$Z_4^{\downarrow}$	00.0%	07.1%	15.4%	06.4%	$Z_3^{\uparrow}$
	$Z_1^{\uparrow}$	$Z_1^{\downarrow}$	$Z_1^{\downarrow}$	$Z_1^{\uparrow}$	

(e) Set X

Table 3: Results for the trade-off regions analysis.

cient values for set B are not provided for the reason given above. The table presents the individual pairwise correlation value for each combination of objectives. As expected for fully independent objectives, set A has values close to 0. The values for sets C and D are also predictably close to either 1 or -1 indicating global conflicting or harmonious relationships. Set X has values similar to A – they do not reveal a strong global relationship between objectives as they are closer to 0 than to 1 or -1. Also, in set X it is not possible to decompose the decision variables according to the objectives, as every item has all weights and values above zero.

Step 2 - Objective Range Analysis. The results for this step are in Table 2. Considering set B, it can be seen, that the set presents small ranges of less than 0.3% on average. In this dataset all objectives are harmonious and the solutions found are all located in a small region of the solution space. These few solutions dominated all other solutions explored. Both sets C and D present similar results to each other with large ranges for each objective (over 60%). This is expected since these are instances with conflicting objectives and present global trade-offs. The large ranges mean that while we have solutions with good values for a given objective, at least one other objective has poor value.

Finally, we highlight that while the global pairwise relationship analysis (step 1) hinted that sets A and X were similar, the difference between them now becomes clear with the results from step 2. In set A, each objective range is around 24.0% of the maximum value – the smallest ranges excluding the harmonious instances – whilst in set X the ranges go up to 84.9%, the largest range found. Thus, we can see that the ranges for set X are closer to those for set D, a conflicting scenario with global trade-offs.

Step 3 - Trade-Off Regions Analysis. The results for this step are in Table 3. For each instance we computed the number of solutions in each region and the map shows the average percentage for each set. We set the range threshold to 1% above the mean value found for each objective, thus considering a value slightly above the average to be good. We can observe that on set A the front is well distributed as we have solutions in all regions, scattered throughout the solution space, as a result of the independent objectives. Additionally, note that we have solutions both in r_0 and r_{15}. This is due to the map presenting the combined results for all five instances in that set, and in some instances we have solutions in r_0 only and in other instances in r_{15} only.

In sets C and D we clearly identify the global relationships. There are no solutions with good values in all objectives and most instances present no solution with good values in three objectives. The majority of the solutions are situated where Z_1 and Z_3 alone have good values and where Z_2 and Z_4 alone have good values, as these are the harmonious pairs. Additionally, we can observe that almost no solutions are present in conflicting areas. For instance, where Z_1 and Z_2 present good values simultaneously. Moreover, solutions in conflicting areas should be close to the chosen threshold.

The set X does not contain solutions in r_0 and there are no solutions in regions r_1, r_2, r_4 and r_8, meaning that no high values can be simultaneously found for three or more objectives. We can find good values simultaneously only for up to two objectives. The map for set X resembles the ones for sets C and D in the sense that we can clearly see that there are several regions without solutions. Thus, we have trade-offs to present to the decision-maker. This means that the decision-maker has to choose between up to two good objective values to the detriment of the remaining objectives, since all of the regions containing solutions have at most two simultaneously good values.

Step 4 - Multiobjective Scatter Plot Analysis. This analysis was performed for each instance and Figure 4 presents the results for all instances of each set combined. We can see in Figure 4a that although instances in dataset A are completely random, all of them show similar landscapes with a high concentration of solutions towards the $(1, 1)$ corner. Moreover, no local relationships can be identified, which is expected as the data is completely random.

On sets C and D we can clearly see the trade-off regions. Also, there is a noticeable gap in the solution space when Z_1 is in the range from 0 to 0.5 and when the remaining objectives are in the range from 0 to 0.4, approximately. Moreover, the landscape of the solution space appears to be similar for all instances of each of the sets C and D.

Since the data was uniformly generated (these gaps are unlikely to arise from the data itself) and could represent limitations in the solution algorithms, indicating that they did not explore the entire front. It is well known that the performance of some MOEAs is limited when the number of objectives is more than three [27].

Set X presents a unique scenario, as we can identify patterns and gaps in the solution space. The first feature worth

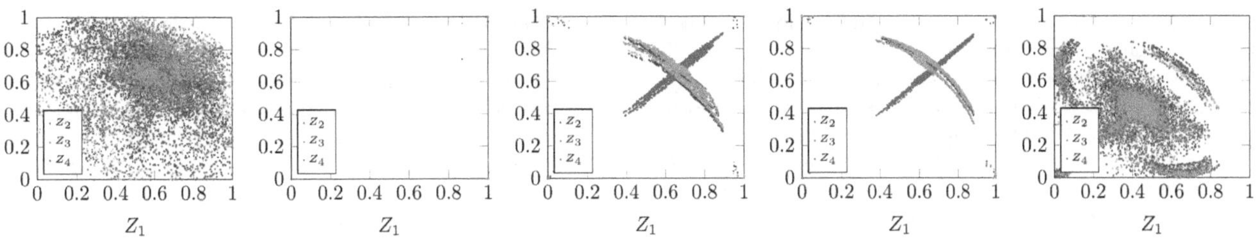

(a) Set A (b) Set B (c) Set C (d) Set D (e) Set X

Figure 4: Results for the trade-off regions analysis.

noticing is that there is a lack of solutions with values within [0.85, 1]. Again, this is due to limitations of the solution algorithms. However, we can see that the size of the gap is small, confirming that instances with strongly conflicting objectives present a bigger challenge to the algorithms. We can also identify several local relationships. When Z_1 ranges from 0.5 to 0.8, the three remaining objectives simultaneously conflict and harmonise. Knowing that only two simultaneous objectives present high values (from the region map analysis), we can conclude that whenever Z_1 increases, only one of the other objectives simultaneously increases too.

5.2 Discussion

With the proposed analysis and visualisation technique, we can better understand the multiobjective nature of the problem instances considered. Looking at only the correlation coefficients, we could conclude that: sets A and X do not present interesting multiobjective traits, that set B is inconclusive and that sets C and D present conflicting and harmonious objectives. However, by applying our analysis and visualisation technique we can reach a more comprehensive understanding of these instance sets.

As fully random instances, dataset A does not present relevant global or local pairwise relationships according to the global pairwise analysis (step 1) and the multiobjective scatter plot analysis (step 4). Additionally, the objective range analysis (step 2) shows that even though there is a large set of non-dominated solutions, these are concentrated in a reasonably small area of the search space. For this dataset we can use the information from the trade-off region maps to interact with the decision-maker to identify which regions are of more interest and then use single-objective optimisation algorithms to find solutions in that region. Since we have solutions in all of the regions of the map, any objective vector could provide an adequate solution.

Set B presents a completely harmonious case and by analysing the ranges and bearing in mind that the algorithms found just a handful of solutions, we can assume that a single-objective algorithm aiming to maximise any of the objectives could provide a reasonable good solution.

Sets C and D present similar scenarios, hence the correlation between weights and coefficients does not impact on the nature of the problem. The entire solution set represents a huge trade-off. We also notice that the algorithms found it very difficult to expand along the front and that they mainly explored the region surrounding the intersection of the trade-off. Nonetheless, by perceiving that all instances in these sets have similar landscapes and by knowing the approximate boundaries of each objective (by applying single-objective algorithms to each objective alone), we can estimate the landscape of solutions for other instances in those sets. Therefore, we could direct the search to the regions of interest after presenting the expected trade-offs to the decision-maker. However, if it is imperative to use an *a posteriori* approach, the global pairwise analysis and the scatter plots provide sufficient information to make feasible the grouping of harmonious objectives.

Finally, set X presents a quite different picture. By only evaluating the global pairwise analysis (step 1) we conclude that there is no strong pairwise relationship between objectives. However, the objectives range analysis (step 2) shows that in fact we have non-dominated solutions that vary greatly in quality. This is an indication of the existence of trade-offs (as we can see by comparing this set with sets C and D). The trade-off region analysis (step 3) showed the existence of overall trade-offs as it is not possible to have solutions with good values in more than two objectives simultaneously. Finally, the multiobjective scatter plot analysis (step4) identified local relationships between objectives and gaps in the solution space, pointing to the existence of local conflicts. Therefore, instances in dataset X exhibit a distinctive multiobjective nature perhaps with interesting options for a decision-maker. A sound possibility to tackle this problem would be to use the region map to identify the regions of interest and then locate those regions in the scatter plot. In case a selected region contains a local conflict, we can use the algorithm proposed by [1] to reach the trade-off front and then expand through it.

6. CONCLUSION

We proposed a technique that uses correlation, trade-off region maps and scatter-plots as tools for the analysis and visualisation of objectives' relationships in multiobjective optimisation problems. The technique consists of four steps: 1) evaluate the global correlation values, 2) compute the range of values for all objectives, 3) compute the distribution of solutions in the different trade-off regions, and 4) conduct a scatter-plot analysis of the objectives.

We applied the proposed technique to five sets of instances for the multiobjective multidimensional knapsack problem. The proposed technique helps to identify features such as local and complex relationships between objectives, trade-offs not derived from pairwise relationships, gaps in the fitness landscape and regions of interest. Different conclusions can be reached about the objectives relationships, for different instances even though they are scenarios from the same problem. We also discussed how the analysis and visualisation technique could be used to better understand the fitness landscape of the problem in hand.

Future work includes applying the proposed technique to other optimisation problems to validate further. It is also important to study the impact that the initial approximation set provided has on the accuracy of the analysis. Finally, we intend to investigate how the components of this technique, such as the trade-off region map, could be employed during the optimisation process for a many-objectives algorithm, to direct the search towards regions of interest.

7. REFERENCES

[1] J. Knowles and D. Corne. Towards Landscape Analyses to Inform the Design of Hybrid Local Search for the Multiobjective Quadratic Assignment Problem. In *Soft Computing Systems: Design, Management and Applications*, pages 271–279, Amsterdam, 2002.

[2] J. Castro-Gutierrez, D. Landa-Silva, and J. Moreno Perez. Nature of real-world multi-objective vehicle routing with evolutionary algorithms. In *Systems, Man, and Cybernetics (SMC), 2011 IEEE International Conference on*, pages 257–264, 2011.

[3] M. G. Kendall. A new measure of rank correlation. *Biometrika*, 30(1/2):81–93, 1938.

[4] M. Khabzaoui, C. Dhaenens, and E.-G. Talbi. A multicriteria genetic algorithm to analyze DNA microarray data. In *Evolutionary Computation (CEC), IEEE Congress on*, pages 1874–1881, 2004.

[5] R. C. Purshouse and P. J. Fleming. Conflict, harmony, and independence: Relationships in evolutionary multi-criterion optimisation. In *Evolutionary Multi-Criterion Optimization*, volume 2632 of *LNCS*, pages 16–30. 2003.

[6] H. Ishibuchi, N. Akedo, H. Ohyanagi, and Y. Nojima. Behavior of EMO algorithms on many-objective optimization problems with correlated objectives. In *Evolutionary Computation (CEC), 2011 IEEE Congress on*, pages 1465–1472, June 2011.

[7] M. Karnaugh. The Map Method for Synthesis of Combinational Logic Circuits. *Trans. AIEE. pt. I*, 72 (9):593–599, 1953.

[8] T. Lust and J. Teghem. The multiobjective multidimensional knapsack problem: a survey and a new approach. *CoRR*, abs/1007.4063, 2010.

[9] C. Bazgan, H. Hugot, and D. Vanderpooten. An efficient implementation for the 0-1 multi-objective knapsack problem. In *Experimental Algorithms*, volume 4525 of *LNCS*, pages 406–419. 2007.

[10] D. Garrett and D. Dasgupta. Multiobjective landscape analysis and the generalized assignment problem. volume 5313 of *LNCS*, pages 110–124. 2008.

[11] J. D. Garrett. *Multiobjective Fitness Landscape Analysis and the Design of Effective Memetic Algorithms*. PhD thesis, Memphis, TN, USA, 2008.

[12] A.r E.I. Brownlee and J. A. Wright. Solution analysis in multi-objective optimization. In *First Building Simulation and Optimization Conference, Loughborough, UK*, 2012.

[13] R. K. Anderson and M. Dror. An interactive graphic presentation for multiobjective linear programming. *Applied mathematics and computation*, 123:229–248, 2001.

[14] S. Verel, A. Liefooghe, and C. Dhaenens. Set-based multiobjective fitness landscapes: A preliminary study. In *Proceedings of the 13th Annual Conference on Genetic and Evolutionary Computation*, GECCO '11, pages 769–776, New York, NY, USA, 2011.

[15] S. Verel, A. Liefooghe, L. Jourdan, and C. Dhaenens. Pareto local optima of multiobjective NK-landscapes with correlated objectives. In *Evolutionary Computation in Combinatorial Optimization*, volume 6622 of *LNCS*, pages 226–237. 2011.

[16] S. Verel, A. Liefooghe, L. Jourdan, and C. Dhaenens. On the structure of multiobjective combinatorial search space: MNK-landscapes with correlated objectives. *European Journal of Operational Research*, 227(2):331 – 342, 2013.

[17] D. J. Walker, R. M. Everson, and J. E. Fieldsend. Visualizing mutually nondominating solution sets in many-objective optimization. *Evolutionary Computation, IEEE Transactions on*, 17(2):165–184, 2013.

[18] I. Giagkiozis and P.J. Fleming. Pareto front estimation for decision making. *Evolutionary Computation, MIT Press*, Apr 2014.

[19] T. Tusar and B. Filipic. Visualization of pareto front approximations in evolutionary multiobjective optimization: A critical review and the prosection method. *Evolutionary Computation, IEEE Transactions on*, 19(2):225–245, April 2015. ISSN 1089-778X. .

[20] X. Guo, Y. Wang, and X. Wang. Using objective clustering for solving many-objective optimization problems. *Mathematical Problems in Engineering*, 2013.

[21] J. J. Durillo and A. J. Nebro. jMetal: A java framework for multi-objective optimization. *Advances in Engineering Software*, 42:760–771, 2011.

[22] S. Cahon, N. Melab, and E.G. Talbi. ParadisEO: a framework for the reusable design of parallel and distributed metaheuristics. *Journal of heuristics*, 10: 357–380, 2004.

[23] R. C. Purshouse and P. J. Fleming. An adaptive divide-and-conquer methodology for evolutionary multi-criterion optimisation. In *Evolutionary Multi-Criterion Optimization*, volume 2632 of *LNCS*, pages 133–147. 2003.

[24] K. Deb, A. Pratap, S. Agarwal, and T. Meyarivan. A fast and elitist multiobjective genetic algorithm: NSGA-II. *Evolutionary Computation, IEEE Transactions on*, 6(2):182–197, 2002.

[25] Q. Zhang and H. Li. MOEA/D: A multiobjective evolutionary algorithm based on decomposition. *Evolutionary Computation, IEEE Transactions on*, 11 (6):712–731, 2007.

[26] L. J. Eshelman. The chc adaptive search algorithm: How to have safe search when engaging in nontraditional genetic recombination. In *FOGA'90*, pages 265–283, 1990.

[27] I. Giagkiozis and P.J. Fleming. Methods for many-objective optimization: An analysis. Research Report No. 1030, November 2012.

A New Framework for Self-adapting Control Parameters in Multi-objective Optimization

Xin Qiu
NUS Graduate School for Integrative Sciences and Engineering
National University of Singapore, Singapore
qiuxin@u.nus.edu

Weinan Xu
Department of Electrical and Computer Engineering
National University of Singapore, Singapore
pumpkinxu@163.com

Jian-Xin Xu
Department of Electrical and Computer Engineering
National University of Singapore, Singapore
elexujx@nus.edu.sg

Kay Chen Tan
Department of Electrical and Computer Engineering
National University of Singapore, Singapore
eletankc@nus.edu.sg

ABSTRACT

Proper tuning of control parameters is critical to the performance of a multi-objective evolutionary algorithm (MOEA). However, the developments of tuning methods for multi-objective optimization are insufficient compared to single-objective optimization. To circumvent this issue, this paper proposes a novel framework that can self-adapt the parameter values from an objective-based perspective. Optimal parametric setups for each objective will be efficiently estimated by combining single-objective tuning methods with a grouping mechanism. Subsequently, the position information of individuals in objective space is utilized to achieve a more efficient adaptation among multiple objectives. The new framework is implemented into two classical Differential-Evolution-based MOEAs to help to adapt the scaling factor F in an objective-wise manner. Three state-of-the-art single-objective tuning methods are applied respectively to validate the robustness of the proposed mechanisms. Experimental results demonstrate that the new framework is effective and robust in solving multi-objective optimization problems.

Categories and Subject Descriptors

I.2.8 [**Artificial Intelligence**]: Problem Solving, Control Methods, and Search—*Heuristic methods*; G.1.6 [**Numerical Analysis**]: Optimization

GECCO '15, July 11 - 15, 2015, Madrid, Spain

 ISBN 978-1-4503-3472-3/15/07...$15.00

DOI: http://dx.doi.org/10.1145/2739480.2754714

Keywords

Multi-objective optimization, Parameter tuning, Differential Evolution

1. INTRODUCTION

Multi-objective Evolutionary Algorithms (MOEAs) are favored approaches for solving optimization problems with multiple conflicting objectives. A good volume of work has been undertaken to extend powerful Single-objective evolutionary algorithms, including Differential Evolution (DE) [21] and Particle Swarm Optimization (PSO) [12], into Multi-objective Optimization (MO) [16, 5]. According to previous empirical studies [6, 3, 20, 17], the success of DE and PSO in solving a particular problem is very closely related to the fine-tuning of their control parameters. To enhance the optimization performance, many methods were proposed to help adapt these parameters intelligently [3, 19, 27, 10, 11, 25, 23]. However, most of the efficient tuning mechanisms are restricted to Single-objective Optimization (SO), and little attention has been devoted to the adaptation of control parameters in MO. Actually, the parametric sensitivity issue may become more challenging since multiple objectives may have disparate requirements for the parametric setup. Self-adaptation of control parameters from the perspective of objective space is still a research gap. To fill the above niche, a new parameter adaptation framework for multi-objective optimization is developed in this paper. The proposed framework is able to make use of existing single-objective tuning methods during multi-objective optimization. The optimal parametric setups will be estimated in an objective-wise manner, and the positions of individuals in objective space will be considered in order to achieve a more efficient adaptation. Implementations with three state-of-the-art SO adaptation methods and two classical MOEAs demonstrate that the proposed framework is effective and robust in solving MO problems.

The rest of this paper is organized as follows. Section 2 reviews the previous work in parameter adaptation for DE briefly and introduces the basic ideas of three adaptation methods involved in later experiments. Section 3 describes the technical details of the proposed framework and explains the underlying rationales. Section 4 presents the experimental results for evaluation of the new mechanisms. Concluding remarks and future work are summarized in Section 5.

2. BACKGROUND

2.1 Parameter adaptation for DE

Typically, the self-adaptation methods for control parameters in DE can be classified into three main categories:

1) Randomization Strategy

A randomization model is pre-defined, and new parameters will be generated based on the probability in which this randomization model is distributed. This kind of strategies do not take any feedback from evolutionary search into account [27]. Two successful examples are jDE [3], and SaNSDE [24].

2) Statistical Strategy

These approaches will update parameter value as a statistical model such as normal distribution or Cauchy distribution. With the information acquired from evolutionary search, the mean value of the distributions will be updated so that the control parameters will be real-time tuned. JADE [27], MDE_pBX [10], and SaDE [19] are representative algorithms in this class.

3) Coevolution Strategy

Control parameters are combined with the individuals as the chromosome, and undergo mutation and crossover altogether with individuals. Since the process of evolution is to search the optimal solution, control parameters will also evolve to better values, and these values can be propagated to more offspring [27]. SPDE [1] and DESAP [22] belong to this category.

Among all the existing adaptive DE variants, the tuning methods applied in jDE [3], JADE [27], and MDE_pBX [10] present overall good performances [6]. In this paper, all of them will be implemented into the proposed framework independently. There are two control parameters in classical DE, namely, scaling factor F and crossover probability Cr. Compared to Cr, the overall performance of DE depends more heavily on the selection of F [26, 7], which has a big role in controlling the searching step of the optimization process. Therefore, the empirical study in this paper will focus on adapting the scaling factor F using the new framework. The following subsections introduce the adaptation mechanisms of F in jDE, JADE, MDE_pBX, respectively.

2.2 jDE

In jDE, all the control parameters are applied at the individual level. The new control parameters for each individual $X_{i,G}$, where i is the index of the solution in population and G is the number of current generation, are generated as

$$F_{i,G+1} = \begin{cases} F_l + rand_1 \times F_u & \text{rand}_2 < \tau_1 \\ F_{i,G} & \text{rand}_2 \geq \tau_1 \end{cases} \quad (1)$$

where $rand1$ and $rand2$ are uniform random values $\in [0,1]$. F_l and F_u are the lower bound and upper bound for the new generated parameter values. τ_1 represent the probability to adjust scaling factor F.

The contribution of parameter tuning in jDE is that the self-tuning formula is quite simple and easy to manipulate. It outperforms traditional DE and some other self-tuning methods like FADE [15] in handling single-objective problems [3].

2.3 JADE

Similar to jDE, the principle for adaptation mechanism in JADE is that better control parameters tend to generate individuals which are more likely to survive, and better individuals help to propagate their associated paremeters. In JADE, F is encoded into each individual, and the associated F for each solution is updated as follows:

$$mean_L(S_F) = \frac{\sum_{F \in S_F} F^2}{\sum_{F \in S_F} F} \quad (2)$$

$$\mu_F = (1-c) \times \mu_F + c \times mean_L(S_F) \quad (3)$$

$$F_i = randc_i(\mu_F, 0.1) \quad (4)$$

where S_F is the set of successful F values in previous generation. More specifically, for any F_i, if the child solution $X_{i,G+1}$ replaces its parent solution $X_{i,G}$, this F_i will be stored in the set S_F. $randc_i(\mu_F, 0.1)$ refers to a Cauchy distribution generator with location parameter μ_F and scale parameter 0.1. The location parameter μ_F of the Cauchy distribution is initialized as 0.5 and then updated at the end of each generation via the above formula. c is a positive constant between 0 and 1.

Cauchy distribution is applied instead of normal distribution or uniform distribution because it is more helpful to diversify the F values in current population, thereby avoiding premature convergence which often occurs with highly concentrated parameter values. According to [27], the tuning method in JADE is very effective in solving single-objective problems.

2.4 MDE_pBX

The parameter adaptation schemes in MDE_pBX are inspired by those used in JADE algorithm [10], but the former ones have their own distinctive characteristics. At every generation, the scaling factor F_i associated with each individual is independently generated via the following process:

$$\omega_F = 0.8 + 0.2 \times rand(0,1) \quad (5)$$

$$mean_{Pow}(F_{success}) = \sum_{x \in F_{success}} (x^n / |F_{success}|)^{1/n} \quad (6)$$

$$F_m = \omega_F \times F_m + (1-\omega_F) \times mean_{Pow}(F_{success}) \quad (7)$$

$$F_i = Cauchy(F_m, 0.1) \quad (8)$$

where $F_{success}$ stores the successful F values in previous generation and is formed via the same way as S_F in JADE. $Cauchy(F_m, 0.1)$ is a random number sampled from a Cauchy distribution with location parameter F_m and scale parameter 0.1. $rand(0,1)$ stands for a uniformly distributed random number in (0,1) and $meanPow$ stands for the power mean. ω_F is a weight factor varies randomly between 0.8 to 1. n is fixed as 1.5.

The main differences between adaptation mechanisms in MDE_pBX and JADE are the dynamic weight and power mean calculation. The experimental results in [10] show that the tuning approach of MDE_pBX performs better than those in jDE and JADE over a wide variety of single-objective problems.

3. PROPOSED FRAMEWORK

3.1 Overview of the framework

Based on our above review, many researchers have already investigated the adaptation of control parameters in SO and proposed numerous efficient schemes. In contrast, parameter adaptation in MO received less attention and the development of related methods is insufficient. When solving MO problems, more than one objective needs to be optimized simultaneously and each of them may have disparate parametric requirements. This intrinsic difference between SO and MO causes the difficulty in directly applying SO adaptation approaches into MO problems. To overcome this issue, we propose a new framework that can extend existing single-objective adaptation approaches into MO. The aim of the proposed framework is to effectively adapt the control parameters from an objective-based perspective.

During implementation of the new framework, optimal control parameters for each objective will be estimated via corresponding estimation groups (formed by selected individuals), where SO adaptation schemes are applied. Based on the estimation results, the parameter values for remaining individuals will be produced according to their current positions in objective space. Considering the different structures of MOEAs, two versions are designed for more efficient and convenient implementation of the proposed framework. One is the general version, which can be implemented in dominance-based MOEAs [8, 9, 13], indicator-based MOEAs [2] and other population-based MOEAs. Another is the decomposition-based version, which shows high efficiency when used with decomposition-based MOEAs [28, 14]. Detailed descriptions of the proposed framework will be provided in the next subsections.

Algorithm 1 Procedure of General Version

Random Initialization
for $g = 1, 2, \cdots, G_{\max}$ **do**
  Reproduction operations (e.g., Crossover, Mutation)
  Update of successful F sets if needed
  Survival Selection
  for each objective k, $k = 1, 2, \cdots, M$ **do**
    Clear corresponding estimation group.
    Sorting the population w.r.t the fitness values in kth objective.
    for each individual i, $i = 1, 2, \cdots, N$ **do**
      The rank of individual $X_{i,g}$ is recorded as $r^k_{i,g}$.
      if $r^k_{i,g} \leq 10\% \cdot N$ **then**
        $X_{i,g}$ is added into the estimation group for kth objective.
      end if
    end for
  end for
  for each individual i, $i = 1, 2, \cdots, N$ **do**
    if individual $X_{i,g}$ is among any estimation groups **then**
      Perform selected single-objective adaptation method to adapt $F_{i,g}$
    end if
  end for
  for each objective k, $k = 1, 2, \cdots, M$ **do**
    Calculate the arithmetic mean of associated F values in estimation group for kth objective. Denote it as F^{ref}_k.
  end for
  for each individual i, $i = 1, 2, \cdots, N$ **do**
    if individual $X_{i,g}$ is not within estimation groups **then**
      $S_i = 1/r^1_{i,g} + 1/r^2_{i,g} + \cdots + 1/r^M_{i,g}$.
      $F_{i,g} = \frac{(F^{ref}_1/r^1_{i,g} + F^{ref}_2/r^2_{i,g} + \cdots + F^{ref}_M/r^M_{i,g})}{S_i}$.
    end if
  end for
end for

3.2 General Version

3.2.1 Basic Structure

In the proposed framework, control parameters are applied at the individual level. Each solution has its own associated parameters. The introduced mechanisms will be performed after survival selection, which is always at the end of each generation. For a better interpretation, we divide the framework into three phases.

The first phase is grouping, during which particular individuals need to be selected to form the estimation groups. The target of estimation groups is to estimate the optimal parametric setups for each objective. Thus, those individuals which place obviously more weight on optimizing one of the objectives are preferred. In order to picking up the individuals with above-mentioned properties, a sorting procedure is performed among the population based on their fitness values on each separate objective. Since the different objectives are commonly conflicting to each other, higher ranking in one objective indicates higher weight on optimizing this objective. Based on our preliminary tests for group size, the individuals that rank among top 10% within one objective will be recorded as the estimation group for this objective.

The second phase is adaptation. In this phase, the parameter values of the individuals in estimation groups will be adapted using single-objective adaptation schemes. Depending on the procedures of the utilized schemes, additional modifications may be needed for a more efficient implementation. For instance, the adaption mechanisms in JADE and MDE_pBX involve the selections of successful F values, which are supposed to have different definitions in SO and MO. During implementations of the proposed framework, separate sets are created for each objective to store their corresponding successful F values. More specifically, if the offspring outperforms the parent in kth objective, the F value associated with the parent will be recorded as a successful F value for kth objective. After that, adaptation mechanisms are performed for the estimation groups of each objective using the corresponding successful parameter sets.

The last phase is hybridization. Arithmetic mean of all the control parameter values associated with the members in one estimation group is computed as the estimated optimal parameter value for corresponding objective. Suppose we are adapting the scaling factor F in DE, then the estimated values are symbolized by F^{ref}_k, where $k = 1, 2, \ldots, M$ and M is the total number of objectives. With the estimated optimal parametric setups for each objective, the parameter values for remaining individuals can be generated according to their positions in objective space, which may reveal the

Algorithm 2 Procedure of Decomposition-based Version

Random Initialization
for each individual i, $i = 1, 2, \cdots, N$ **do**
  Assignment of weight vector $\lambda^i = (\lambda_1^i, \lambda_2^i, \ldots, \lambda_M^i)$
end for
for $g = 1, 2, \cdots, G_{\max}$ **do**
  Reproduction operations (e.g., Crossover, Mutation)
  Update of successful F sets if needed
  Survival Selection
  for each objective k, $k = 1, 2, \cdots, M$ **do**
    Clear corresponding estimation group.
    Sorting the population w.r.t the assigned weights on kth objective.
    for each individual i, $i = 1, 2, \cdots, N$ **do**
      The rank of individual $X_{i,g}$ is recorded as $rw_{i,g}^k$.
      if $rw_{i,g}^k \leq 10\% \cdot N$ **then**
        $X_{i,g}$ is added into the estimation group for kth objective.
      end if
    end for
  end for
  for each individual i, $i = 1, 2, \cdots, N$ **do**
    if individual $X_{i,g}$ is among any estimation groups **then**
      Perform selected single-objective adaptation method to adapt $F_{i,g}$
    end if
  end for
  for each objective k, $k = 1, 2, \cdots, M$ **do**
    Calculate the arithmetic mean of associated F values in estimation group for kth objective. Denote it as F_k^{ref}.
  end for
  for each individual i, $i = 1, 2, \cdots, N$ **do**
    if individual $X_{i,g}$ is not within estimation groups **then**
      $F_{i,g} = \lambda_1^i \times F_1^{ref} + \lambda_2^i \times F_2^{ref} + \cdots + \lambda_M^i \times F_M^{ref}$.
    end if
  end for
end for

weights on optimizing each objective. In order to extract the position information in objective space, the concept of "sub-rank" is employed. Sub-rank is defined as a vector comprising the ranks of an individual in each seperate objective among current population. For example, if the sub-rank of one individual is (1, 1) in a two-objective problem, it means that this individual has the best fitness value for both objectives. Now we symbolize the sub-rank for individual $X_{i,g}$ by $R_{i,g} = (r_{i,g}^1, r_{i,g}^2, \ldots, r_{i,g}^M)$, where i is the index for this individual and g is the number of current generation. Following the assumption that we are adapting F in DE, the $F_{i,g}$ associated with $X_{i,g}$ will be updated as below:

$$S_i = 1/r_{i,g}^1 + 1/r_{i,g}^2 + \cdots + 1/r_{i,g}^M \tag{9}$$

$$F_{i,g} = \frac{(F_1^{ref}/r_{i,g}^1 + F_2^{ref}/r_{i,g}^2 + \cdots + F_M^{ref}/r_{i,g}^M)}{S_i} \tag{10}$$

It is notable that the parameter values associated with parents are always used in reproduction operations (e.g., crossover and mutation), and the offspring will inherit parents' associated control parameters before conducting survival selection.

To present a clear picture of how proposed framework operates, pseudo-codes of the implementation procedure (adapting F) are provided in Algorithm 1.

3.2.2 *Underlying Rationale*

The fundamental principle for individual-level parameter adaptation is that suitable control parameters tend to make their associated solutions more likely to survive and better solutions help to propagate their associated parameters [3, 27]. Therefore, the distribution of parameter values for one estimation group, which emphasize more on optimizing one particular objective, may reveal the parametric requirement of this objective. Calculation of the arithmetic mean within one estimation group is a reasonable way to approximate the optimal parameter values for corresponding objective. The advantages of considering all the parameter values within one group include making the estimation more reliable and alleviating the influence of possible outliers.

The role of adaptation phase is to help our framework exploring effective control parameters. Since the members in estimation groups focus much more on optimizing one particular objective, employing a single-objective tuning method that is proved to be effective will facilitate a more efficient adaptation for this objective. The parametric sensitivity issue for a MO problem has be converted into several single-objective tuning tasks. The adapted control parameters reveal the parametric requirements for each objective, thereby providing useful information for further analysis.

During the hybridization phase, all the individuals except for those in estimation groups will be assigned with new control parameters based on their sub-ranks. As per (10), a relatively higher rank in kth objective will lead to a larger weight on corresponding F_k^{ref}, which reflects the preferred parametric setup of kth objective, during the calculation of new parameter values. In other words, the different weights on optimizing each objective are reflected during the parametric trade-off among different objectives. Each individual will utilize the most proper parametric setup for its current region in objective space and keep exploring with the existing weights on optimizing each objective. As a result, the diversity of the population is better maintained and the efficiency of exploration is improved.

3.3 Decomposition-based Version

The implementation of the general version will introduce additional sorting procedures, which has $O(MNlogN)$ computational complexity. M is the total number of objectives and N is the population size. The purpose of these sortings is to calculate the sub-ranks so that the weights on optimizing each objective can be decided. Actually in decomposition-based MOEAs, each individual has already be assigned with a weight vector that decides its optimization weights. To reduce the unnecessary time complexity of the framework, a simplified version for decomposition-based MOEAs is developed. Similar to the general version, the decomposition-based version is also divided into three phases.

In the grouping phase, the members of estimation groups are decided based on their weight vectors. The individuals with the highest 10% weights on one particular objective are selected to form the estimation group for this objective. The adaptation phase in decomposition-based version is identical with that in general version.

Table 1: Mean and Standard Deviation of the IGD Values for General Version (30 runs)

Problems	NSGA-II -jDE	NSGA-II JADE	NSGA-II MDE_pBX	NSGA-II -DE
	Mean(Std)	Mean(Std)	Mean(Std)	Mean(Std)
UF1	0.0619	0.0696	0.0662	0.0603
(2-obj)	(0.0082)	(0.0104)	(0.0077)	(0.0162)
UF2	**0.0391**	**0.0405**	**0.0375**	0.0429
(2-obj)	**(0.0041)**	**(0.0035)**	**(0.0029)**	(0.0047)
UF3	**0.0957**	**0.121**	**0.1053**	0.1515
(2-obj)	**(0.0213)**	**(0.0333)**	**(0.0261)**	(0.0271)
UF4	**0.0694**	**0.0698**	**0.0673**	0.0723
(2-obj)	**(0.0065)**	**(0.0068)**	**(0.0066)**	(0.0078)
UF5	1.141	1.11	1.0741	0.8494
(2-obj)	(0.2105)	(0.2243)	(0.2038)	(0.1698)
UF6	**0.3808**	**0.3993**	**0.393**	0.4181
(2-obj)	**(0.0674)**	**(0.0841)**	**(0.091)**	(0.0819)
UF7	**0.0291**	**0.0344**	**0.028**	0.0389
(2-obj)	**(0.0032)**	**(0.0058)**	**(0.0035)**	(0.0422)
UF8	**0.131**	**0.1483**	**0.1443**	0.152
(3-obj)	**(0.0324)**	**(0.0373)**	**(0.0248)**	(0.03)
UF9	**0.1891**	**0.1931**	0.1995	0.1938
(3-obj)	**(0.0762)**	**(0.0653)**	0.0598	(0.0646)
UF10	**0.8013**	**0.8238**	**0.9876**	2.4308
(3-obj)	**(0.0954)**	**(0.1469)**	**(0.1704)**	(0.1848)

Table 2: Mean and Standard Deviation of the IGD Values for Decomposition-based Version (30 runs)

Problems	MOEA/D -jDE	MOEA/D JADE	MOEA/D MDE_pBX	MOEA/D -DE
	Mean(Std)	Mean(Std)	Mean(Std)	Mean(Std)
UF1	**0.042**	**0.0431**	**0.0422**	0.0475
(2-obj)	**(0.0078)**	**(0.0073)**	**(0.0099)**	(0.0372)
UF2	**0.0245**	**0.0236**	**0.0239**	0.0426
(2-obj)	**(0.0044)**	**(0.0061)**	**(0.0033)**	(0.0316)
UF3	**0.0943**	**0.0994**	**0.0706**	0.1513
(2-obj)	**(0.0667)**	**(0.0626)**	**(0.0402)**	(0.0688)
UF4	**0.0758**	**0.0825**	**0.0746**	0.0866
(2-obj)	**(0.0114)**	**(0.0171)**	**(0.0104)**	(0.0104)
UF5	**0.6891**	**0.6867**	**0.6577**	0.7643
(2-obj)	**(0.1603)**	**(0.1719)**	**(0.1747)**	(0.1307)
UF6	**0.3791**	**0.3712**	**0.3641**	0.4386
(2-obj)	**(0.2551)**	**(0.2275)**	**(0.2048)**	(0.2206)
UF7	**0.0267**	**0.0671**	**0.0409**	0.1018
(2-obj)	**(0.0398)**	**(0.1177)**	**(0.0747)**	(0.1648)
UF8	0.0964	0.0926	**0.0902**	0.0911
(3-obj)	(0.0193)	0.0183	**(0.0183)**	(0.0124)
UF9	0.1335	0.1085	0.1174	0.1065
(3-obj)	(0.0445)	(0.0484)	(0.0472)	(0.0452)
UF10	0.5899	0.5917	0.6447	0.5826
(3-obj)	(0.1273)	(0.1236)	(0.1181)	(0.0716)

During the hybridization phase, the sub-ranks in the general version are replaced by weight vectors. Suppose that the weight vector assigned to individual $X_{i,g}$ (outside estimation group) is $(\lambda_i^1, \lambda_i^2, \ldots, \lambda_i^M)$, then the associated parameter (e.g., $F_{i,g}$) will be generated as below:

$$F_{i,g} = \lambda_1^i \times F_1^{ref} + \lambda_2^i \times F_2^{ref} + \cdots + \lambda_M^i \times F_M^{ref} \quad (11)$$

The detailed structure of the decomposition-based version (adapting F) is demonstrated in Algorithm 2.

4. EMPIRICAL STUDY

4.1 Numerical Benchmarks

10 representative benchmark problems from CEC-09 Special Session and Competition [29] are selected to evaluate the performance of the proposed framework. Numerous types of Pareto Optimal Front are covered including convex, non-convex, disconnected points, disconnected lines, straight line, discontinuous surfaces and continuous surface. With these benchmarks, whether the framework is capable to handle different kinds of problems will be validated.

4.2 Experimental Setup

In the following experiments, the proposed general version and decomposition-based version are implemented into NSGA-II-DE [14] and MOEA/D-DE [14], respectively. The scaling factor F in these two MOEAs will be adapted via the new framework. The single-objective adaptation methods in jDE, JADE, MDE_pBX are employed respectively in the adaption phase as stated in Section.3. Thus, totally 6 variants of the proposed framework are tested, namely, NSGA-II-jDE, NSGA-II-JADE, NSGA-II-MDE_pBX, MOEA/D-jDE, MOEA/D-JADE, MOEA/D-MDE_pBX. The performances of the proposed variants are compared with those of original NSGA-II-DE and MOEA/D-DE. Recommended parametric setups in the original literatures are utilized for all the above algorithmic components (F values are fixed as 0.5 in original NSGA-II-DE and MOEA/D-DE). For all the testing algorithms, the population size is fixed as 100 for 2-objective benchmarks, 300 for 3-objective benchmarks, and the maximum number of function evaluations is set to 5×10^4 for 2-objective problems, 15×10^4 for 3-objective problems. Inverted Generational Distance (IGD) [4] is selected as the quantitative metric to evaluate the performance of algorithms in terms of both convergence and diversity. All of the simulations were done on an Intel (R) Core (TM) i7 machine with 16-GB RAM and 3.40-GHz speed.

4.3 Effectiveness of the Proposed Framework

Table 1 and Table 2 show the mean and standard deviation of the IGD values over 30 independent runs of each algorithm on each benchmark. The entries that outperform original NSGA-II-DE or MOEA/D-DE in terms of mean value are marked in boldface.

From Table 1, the general version of the proposed framework is able to improve the optimization performance of original NSGA-II-DE in most problems except for UF1 and UF5. For UF1, actually the recommended F value 0.5 in original NSGA-II-DE is already close to the optimal setting. The adaption in our framework may employ some less efficient parameter values, which lead to the relatively slower convergence speed compared to original NSGA-II-DE. The shape of POF in UF5 is disconnected points, which will lead to clustering of the population. As a result, the sub-ranks utilized in the general version cannot reveal the true positions of individuals in objective space. The efficiency of the proposed mechanisms is thus deteriorated. When the performances among three proposed variants are compared, no obvious difference is observed in most benchmarks and improvement over original NSGA-II-DE is achieved by all of them. This implies that the proposed framework is not sensitive to the selection of single-objective adaptation methods and is able to successfully apply them in solving multi-objective problems.

Based on the results in Table 2, the decomposition-based version presents better performance than original MOEA/D-DE in all the 2-objective problems. More specifically, all the three variants of decomposition-based version achieved superior results over original MOEA/D-DE in solving UF1-UF7. There is a significant difference between decomposition-based version and general version in optimizing UF5. It is because the individuals in decomposition-based version have been assigned with fixed weight vectors, which will decrease the chance of clustering during optimization. Another notable pattern is that no significant improvement is achieved by the decomposition-based version in solving 3-objective problems. This may result from the unevenly assignment of weight vectors for 3-objective problems in MOEA/D as described in [18]. The effectiveness of parameters generated in hybridization phase will be alleviated because of this issue.

4.4 Behaviors of the Proposed Framework

In order to further investigate the detailed behaviors of the proposed framework, the movement of F_k^{ref} and the number of successful F values during optimization are presented in this subsection.

Figure 1 plots the F_k^{ref} values over generations for each objective on UF3 and UF10. All the 6 variants are tested for comparison. As stated before, F_k^{ref} actually represents the estimated optimal F values for kth objective. From Figure 1, the estimated results show different patterns among three single-objective adaptation methods. The distributions of F_k^{ref} values in jDE-based variants are obviously more widespread compared to those of JADE-based and MDE_pBX-based variants. This is because the tuning mechanisms in jDE involves a uniform randomization process, which will generate a wide variety of values. The F_k^{ref} values for JADE-based variants will converge more easily. This implies that the adaptation mechanisms in JADE is relatively weak in exploring new parameter values. The MDE_pBX-based variants presents a good trade-off between exploitation and exploration during adaptation of parameter values. From the perspective of MOEAs, the behaviors of the general version and the decomposition-based version provide similar patterns, which result from the same underlying rationales of these two versions. From the perspective of problems, all the objectives in UF3 and UF10 have the similar parametric requirements. It is difficult to observe the difference between multiple objectives. Actually this is common for the existing MO benchmark problems, which do not intentionally set disparate parametric requirements for each objective.

Figure 2 plots the number of successful F values over generations for each objective on UF3 and UF10. An F value is defined to be "successful" for kth objective when the associated offspring outperforms its parent in kth objective. The total number of successful F values for each objective in one generation will thus reveal the efficiency of adopted adaptation mechanisms on optimizing corresponding objectives. From Figure 2, the general version presents higher number of successful F values than the decomposition-based version in most cases. This indicates that the employment of sub-ranks help increase the efficiency of the adaptation. The patterns among different objectives are almost the same within one problem. It reflects that there is no bias in the proposed framework during the optimization of multiple objectives. A decreasing trend can be observed in most plots. This is because the improvement of population quality during later optimization stage becomes more difficult compared with earlier stages. All the three single-objective adaptation methods present similar results when implemented in the general version. However, the MOEA/D-MDE_pBX variant shows significantly higher overall success rate on UF3 compared with the other two decomposition-based variants. The previous results in Table 2 also demonstrate that MOEA/D-MDE_pBX performs significantly better than the jDE-based and JADE-based variants in solving UF3. This implies that the successful tuning of F values plays an very important role in improving the performance of algorithms.

5. CONCLUSIONS

This paper has proposed a new framework for self-adapting control parameters in multi-objective optimization. The proposed mechanisms are able to employ existing SO adaptation methods for optimizing multiple objectives. Efficient adaption from an objective-based perspective is achieved by utilizing position information in objective space. Successful implementations with two types of MOEAs and three exiting SO tuning approaches validate the effectiveness of the proposed framework.

In future work, designing a mechanism for dynamically switching among different SO adaptation methods is expected to further enhance the robustness of the framework. Introduction of more tuning approaches and implementation into more MOEAs will also be considered.

6. ACKNOWLEDGMENTS

This work was supported by the Singapore Ministry of Education Academic Research Fund Tier 1 under the project R-263-000-A12-112.

7. REFERENCES

[1] H. A. Abbass. The self-adaptive pareto differential evolution algorithm. *Congress on Evolutionary Computation 2002*, 1:831–836, 2002.

[2] J. Bader and E. Zitzler. Hype: An algorithm for fast hypervolume-based many-objective optimization. *Evolutionary Computation*, 19(1):45–76, March 2011.

[3] J. Brest, S. Greiner, B. Boskovic, M. Mernik, and V. Zumer. Self-adapting control parameters in differential evolution: A comparative study on numerical benchmark problems. *Evolutionary Computation, IEEE Transactions on*, 10(6):646–657, Dec 2006.

[4] C. A. C. Coello and N. C. Cortes. Solving multiobjective optimization problems using an artificial immune system. *Genetic Programming and Evolvable Machines*, 6(2):163–190, 2005.

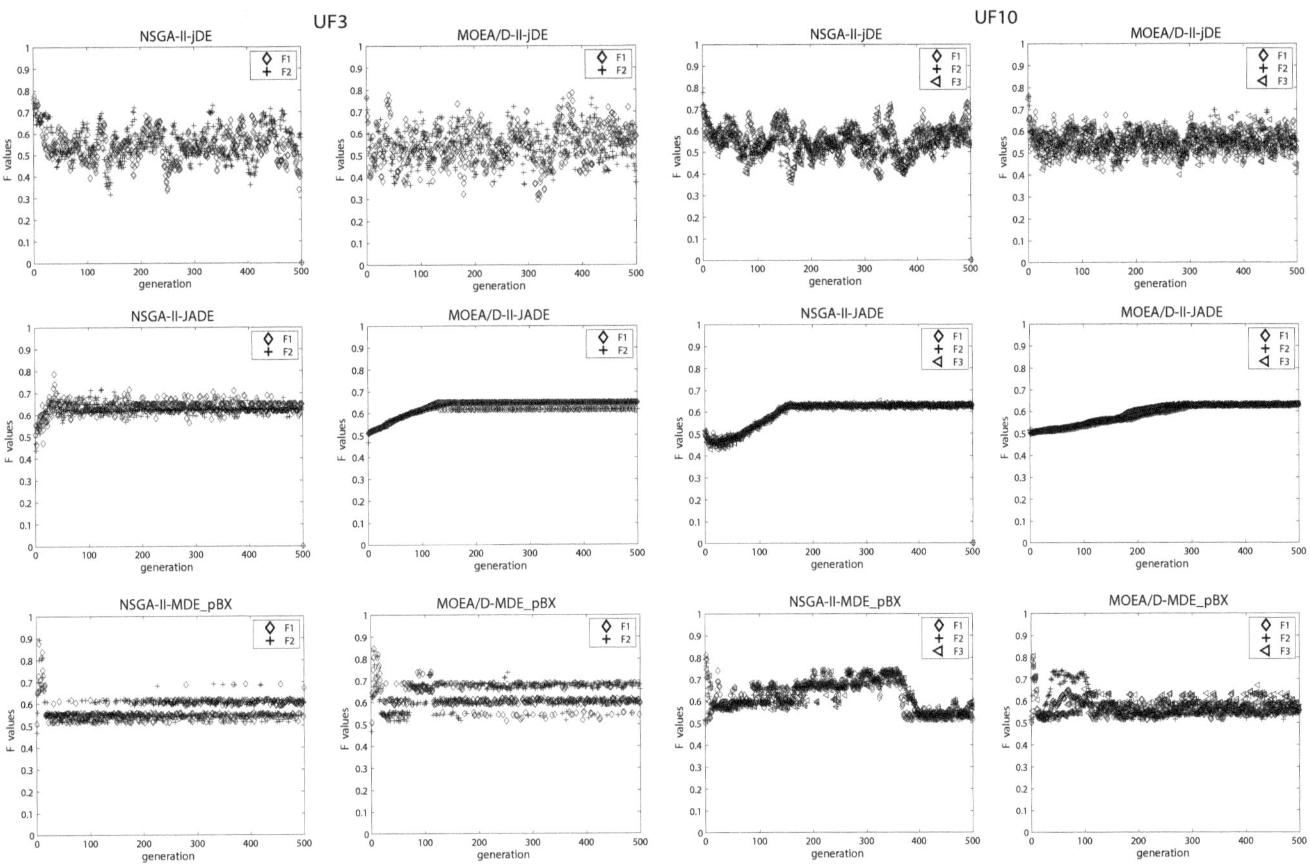

Figure 1: This figure plots the F_k^{ref} values over generations for each objective on UF3 (2-objective) and UF10 (3-objective). Vertical axis indicates the values for each F_k^{ref}, and horizontal axis represents the number of current generation. Different symbols are utilized to differentiate the F_k^{ref} for each objective.

[5] C. A. C. Coello and M. Reyes-Sierra. Multi-Objective Particle Swarm Optimizers: A Survey of the State-of-the-Art. *International Journal of Computational Intelligence Research*, 2, 2006.

[6] S. Das and P. N. Suganthan. Differential evolution: A survey of the state-of-the-art. *Evolutionary Computation, IEEE Transactions on*, 15(1):4 –31, feb. 2011.

[7] S. Dasgupta, S. Das, A. Biswas, and A. Abraham. On stability and convergence of the population-dynamics in differential evolution. *AI Commun.*, 22(1):1–20, 2009.

[8] K. Deb, A. Pratap, S. Agarwal, and T. Meyarivan. A fast and elitist multiobjective genetic algorithm: NSGA-II. *Evolutionary Computation, IEEE Transactions on*, 6(2):182–197, 2002.

[9] A. W. Iorio and X. Li. Solving rotated multi-objective optimization problems using differential evolution. *Advances in Artificial Intelli-gence, Proceedings*, 3339:861–872, 2004.

[10] S. Islam, S. Das, S. Ghosh, S. Roy, and P. Suganthan. An adaptive differential evolution algorithm with novel mutation and crossover strategies for global numerical optimization. *Systems, Man, and Cybernetics, Part B: Cybernetics, IEEE Transactions on*, 42(2):482–500, April 2012.

[11] N. Iwasaki, K. Yasuda, and G. Ueno. Dynamic parameter tuning of particle swarm optimization. *IEEJ Transactions on Electrical and Electronic Engineering*, 1(4):353–363, 2006.

[12] J. Kennedy and R. Eberhart. Particle swarm optimization. In *Neural Networks, 1995. Proceedings., IEEE International Conference on*, volume 4, pages 1942–1948 vol.4, Nov 1995.

[13] S. Kukkonen and J. Lampinen. GDE3: The third evolution step of generalized differential evolution. *IEEE Congress on Evolutionary Computation (CEC'2005)*, 1:443–450, 2005.

[14] H. Li and Q. Zhang. Multiobjective optimization problems with complicated pareto sets, MOEA/D and NSGA-II. *Evolutionary Computation, IEEE Transactions on*, 13(2):284–302, 2009.

[15] J. Liu and J. Lampinen. A fuzzy adaptive differential evolution algorithm. In *TENCON '02. Proceedings. 2002 IEEE Region 10 Conference on Computers, Communications, Control and Power Engineering*, volume 1, pages 606–611, Oct 2002.

[16] E. Mezura-Montes, M. Reyes-Sierra, and C. A. C. Coello. Multi-objective optimization using differential evolution: A survey of the state-of-the-art. *Advances in Differential Evolution , Studies in Computational Intelligence*, 143:173–196, 2008.

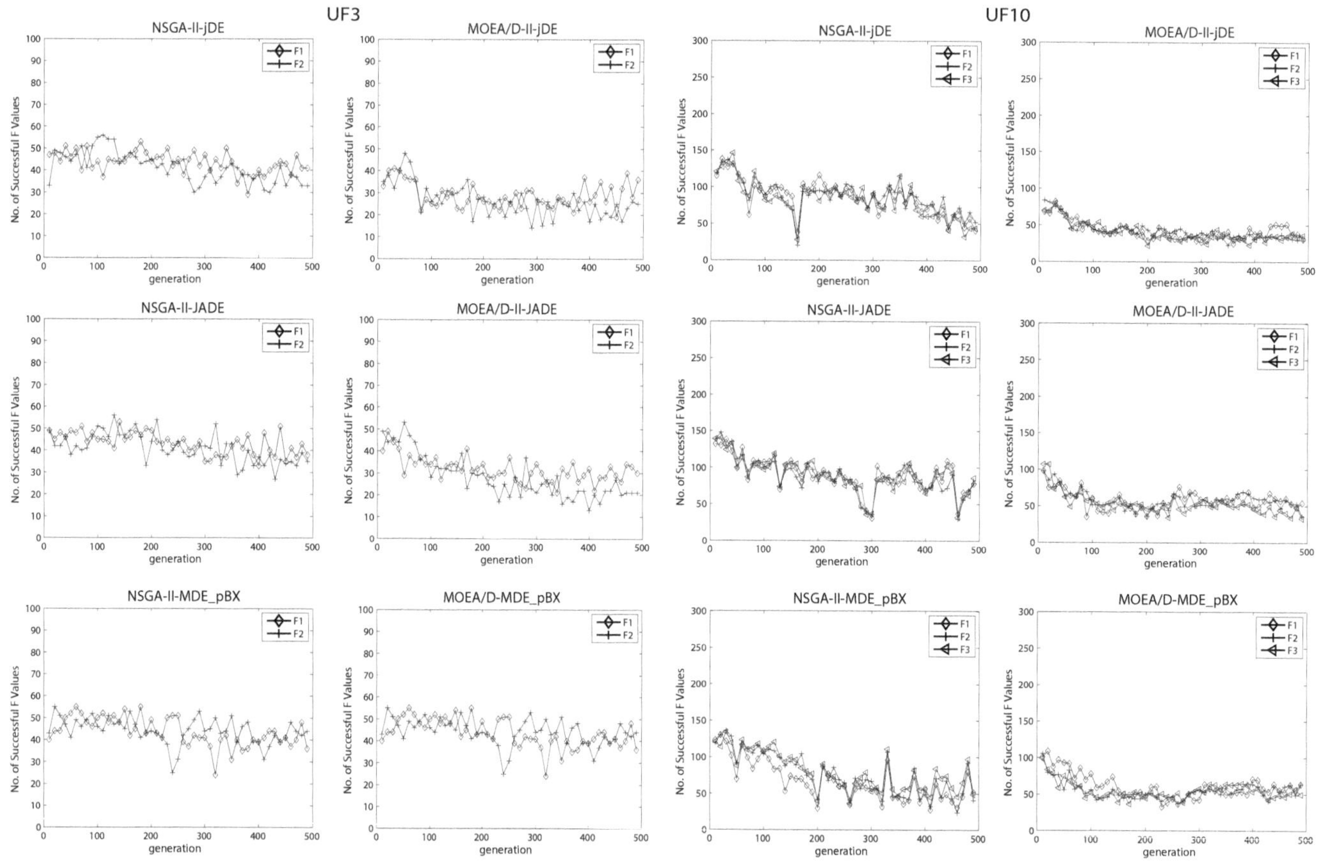

Figure 2: This figure shows the number of successful F values over generation for each objective on UF3 (2-objective) and UF10 (3-objective). Vertical axis indicates the number of successful F values for corresponding objectives, and horizontal axis represents the number of current generation. The different scales of vertical axes are due to the different population size for UF3 and UF10.

[17] M. E. H. Pedersen and H. Laboratories. Good parameters for particle swarm optimization. In *Technical Report*, 2010.

[18] Y. Qi, X. Ma, F. Liu, L. Jiao, J. Sun, and J. Wu. Moea/d with adaptive weight adjustment. *Evolutionary Computation*, 22(2):231–264, 2014.

[19] A. K. Qin, V. L. Huang, and P. Suganthan. Differential evolution algorithm with strategy adaptation for global numerical optimization. *Evolutionary Computation, IEEE Transactions on*, 13(2):398–417, April 2009.

[20] Y. Shi and R. Eberhart. Fuzzy adaptive particle swarm optimization. In *Evolutionary Computation, 2001. Proceedings of the 2001 Congress on*, volume 1, pages 101–106 vol. 1, 2001.

[21] R. Storn and K. V. Price. Differential evolution - a simple and efficient heuristic for global optimization over continuous spaces. *Golbal Optimization, Journal of*, 11, no. 4:341–359, 1997.

[22] J. Teo. Exploring dynamic self-adaptive populations in differential evolution. *Soft Computing*, 10(8):673–686, 2006.

[23] G. Xu. An adaptive parameter tuning of particle swarm optimization algorithm. *Applied Mathematics and Computation*, 219(9):4560 – 4569, 2013.

[24] Z. Yang, K. Tang, and X. Yao. Self-adaptive differential evolution with neighborhood search. In *Evolutionary Computation, 2008. CEC 2008. (IEEE World Congress on Computational Intelligence). IEEE Congress on*, pages 1110–1116, June 2008.

[25] K. Yasuda, K. Yazawa, and M. Motoki. Particle swarm optimization with parameter self-adjusting mechanism. *IEEJ Transactions on Electrical and Electronic Engineering*, 5(2):256–257, 2010.

[26] D. Zaharie. On the explorative power of differential evolution. In *Proc. 3rd Int. Workshop Symbol. Numer. Algorithms Sci. Comput.*, Timisoara, Romania, Oct. 2-4 2001.

[27] J. Zhang and A. Sanderson. Jade: Adaptive differential evolution with optional external archive. *Evolutionary Computation, IEEE Transactions on*, 13(5):945–958, Oct 2009.

[28] Q. Zhang and H. Li. MOEA/D: A multiobjective evolutionary algorithm based on decomposition. *Evolutionary Computation, IEEE Transactions on*, 11(6):712–731, 2007.

[29] Q. Zhang, A. Zhou, S. Zhao, P. N. Suganthan, W. Liu, and S. Tiwari. Multiobjective optimization test instances for the CEC 2009 special session and competition. *Technical Report*, 2008.

Multi-Objective BDD Optimization with Evolutionary Algorithms

Saeideh Shirinzadeh[1] Mathias Soeken[1,2] Rolf Drechsler[1,2]

[1] Department of Mathematics and Computer Science, University of Bremen, Germany
[2] Cyber-Physical Systems, DFKI GmbH, Bremen, Germany
{saeideh,msoeken,drechsle}@cs.uni-bremen.de

ABSTRACT

Binary Decision Diagrams (BDDs) are widely used in electronic design automation and formal verification. BDDs are a canonical representation of Boolean functions with respect to a variable ordering. Finding a variable ordering resulting in a small number of nodes and paths is a primary goal in BDD optimization. There are several approaches minimizing the number of nodes or paths in BDDs, but yet no method has been proposed to minimize both objectives at the same time.

In this paper, BDD optimization is carried out as a bi-objective problem using two aforementioned criteria. For this purpose, we have exploited NSGA-II which has been proven to fit problems with a small number of objectives. Furthermore, the algorithm is facilitated with an objective priority scheme that allows to incorporate preference to one of the objectives.

Experimental results show that our multi-objective BDD optimization algorithm has achieved a good trade-off between the number of nodes and the number of paths. Comparison of the results obtained by applying priority to the number of nodes or paths with node and path minimization techniques demonstrates that the proposed algorithm can find the minimum of the preferred objective in most cases as well as lowering the other objective simultaneously.

Categories and Subject Descriptors

I.2.8 [**Artificial Intelligence**]: Problem solving, Control methods and Search—*Heuristic methods*; J.6 [**Computer-Aided Engineering**]: Computer-aided design (CAD)

Keywords

Multi-objective optimization; genetic algorithm; BDD optimization

GECCO '15, July 11 - 15, 2015, Madrid, Spain
© 2015 ACM. ISBN 978-1-4503-3472-3/15/07...$15.00
DOI: http://dx.doi.org/10.1145/2739480.2754718

1. INTRODUCTION

Binary Decision Diagrams (BDDs) are graph based data structures that allow a compact and canonical representation of Boolean functions [5, 6]. BDDs are extensively used in VLSI CAD for synthesis and verification [11]. Moreover, *Artificial Intelligence* (AI) benefits from BDDs, e.g., in software model checking [13], sparse-memory applications [19], and enhancing search methods [14].

All these applications exploit BDD optimization with respect to the number of nodes in the graph. Many VLSI CAD applications map BDDs directly to target circuits, and therefore, a smaller BDD results in smaller chip area [10]. Also the number of one-paths, i.e., paths to logical 1, is influential in several applications. As an example, in formal verification using SAT-solving, the number of required steps to solve a SAT problem can be measured by the number of paths in BDDs [24]. In logical synthesis it has been shown that a reduction in the number of paths enhances the minimization of *Disjoint-Sum-of-Product* representations which can be directly extracted from BDDs [30, 22].

Many approaches have been developed for BDD optimization that aim at minimizing the number of nodes. Exact minimization techniques can be classified as a group of these approaches. Although, exact methods can guarantee to find the optimal BDD, they suffer from a high order of complexity and run-time [11]. Hence, there is a strong motivation to employ heuristics regardless that the optimum is not guaranteed. Dynamic reordering based approaches have been widely used for this purpose. They tackle the BDD minimization problem by determining a promising variable ordering in a reasonable amount of time [25]. Simulation-based approaches such as evolutionary algorithms have also been proposed to get a higher degree of minimization. Few techniques using dynamic reordering and evolutionary computation have been developed for minimizing the number of one-paths in BDDs [15, 17]. In this paper the BDD optimization problem is conducted with respect to both criteria addressing significant cost metrics. The proposed *Multi-Objective BDD optimization* (MOB) algorithm minimizes the number of nodes and one-paths at the same time without any loss of quality compared to a single objective method. The proposed approach is also capable of handling specific applications' preferences where either nodes or one-paths are of higher importance.

2. BACKGROUND

This section describes concepts of multi-objective optimization and BDDs and briefly introduces state-of-the-art BDD optimization approaches.

2.1 Basic Concepts

2.1.1 Multi-Objective Optimization

An arbitrary optimization problem with m objectives can be defined as

$$\min \mathbf{f}(\mathbf{x}) = (f_1(\mathbf{x}), f_2(\mathbf{x}), \ldots, f_m(\mathbf{x}))^{\mathrm{T}},$$

where solution $\mathbf{x} = (x_1, x_2, \ldots, x_n)^{\mathrm{T}}$ is described as a decision vector from the decision space $\Omega \subseteq \mathbb{R}^n$, and $\mathbf{f} : \Omega \to \Lambda$ is a set of m objective functions which evaluates a specific solution by mapping it to objective space $\Lambda \subseteq \mathbb{R}^m$.

Let $\mathbf{x}, \mathbf{y} \in \Omega$, then the *Pareto-dominance*, denoted by $\prec$, can be defined as

$$\mathbf{x} \prec \mathbf{y} :\Leftrightarrow \exists j \in \{1, 2, \ldots, m\} : \\ f_j(\mathbf{x}) < f_j(\mathbf{y}) \wedge \forall i \neq j : \ f_i(\mathbf{x}) \leq f_i(\mathbf{y}).$$

According to the definition above, an optimal solution, also called *non-dominated* is a solution that is not dominated by any other solution. The set of optimal solutions is the so-called *Pareto set*, denoted by $\omega \subseteq \Omega$. It must fulfill the property

$$\forall p \in \omega : \nexists q \in \Omega : q \prec p.$$

The *Pareto front* λ is defined as the image of the Pareto set in the objective space, i.e, $\lambda = f(\omega) \subseteq \Lambda$. Finding a well converged set of solutions to the Pareto set is the goal of a *Multi-Objective Evolutionary Algorithm* (MOEA). The final output of a MOEA is a set of non-dominated solutions, so-called *Pareto set approximation*.

2.1.2 Binary Decision Diagrams

Binary Decision Diagrams (BDD) can provide a compact graph representation for most of the practical relevant Boolean functions. The main reason of the compactness of BDDs is that such functions often have common *subfunctions* where for a given function $f(x_1, x_2, \ldots, x_n)$ its subfunctions are $f(0, x_2, \ldots, x_n)$ and $f(1, x_2, \ldots, x_n)$ as well as their subfunctions and so on. A function $f(x_1, \ldots, x_n)$ is called a *bead* if it depends on its first variable, or in other words, if its truth table representation is not of the form $\alpha\alpha$ for any bitstring α of length 2^{n-1} [20]. The nodes of a BDD for a Boolean function f are all subfunctions of f which are beads. The size of a BDD can further be reduced with complemented edges such that a subfunction and its complement can be represented by the same node [3].

It can be easily seen that the set of subfunctions changes when the order of input variables is changed. In fact the *variable ordering* of a BDD can have a significant impact on the number of nodes in a BDD, referred to as N, and also the number of *one-paths*, referred to as P, which are all paths from the start vertex to the 1-terminal that have an even number of complemented edges (including the complement of the start vertex). As an example, the function

$$\bar{x}_1\bar{x}_2\bar{x}_3 \vee \bar{x}_1 x_2 x_4 \vee x_1 x_2 \bar{x}_3 \bar{x}_4 \vee x_1 \bar{x}_2 x_3 x_4$$

from [15] and depicted in Fig. 1 has its minimal number of nodes, $N = 5$, for the variable ordering $x_4 < x_3 < x_3 < x_1$. The minimal number of one-paths, $P = 4$, is obtained for the variable ordering $x_2 < x_1 < x_4 < x_3$.

Improving the variable ordering to find a BDD with at most N nodes is known to be NP-complete [2] and several

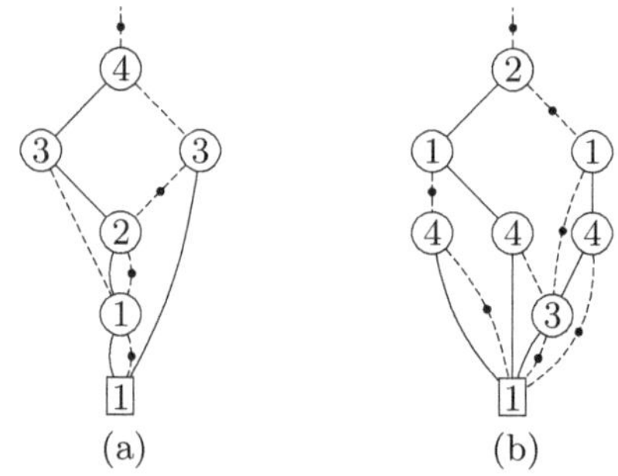

Figure 1: BDDs for the function $\bar{x}_1\bar{x}_2\bar{x}_3 \vee \bar{x}_1 x_2 x_4 \vee x_1 x_2 \bar{x}_3 \bar{x}_4 \vee x_1 \bar{x}_2 x_3 x_4$

heuristics have been proposed that are illustrated in the next section.

2.2 Related Work

BDD optimization techniques aim to find an optimal variable ordering which leads to the minimum BDD with respect to the optimization criterion. There are several approaches for exact minimization guaranteeing to find the minimal BDD [12, 16, 18]. Nevertheless, high complexity of the exact methods is a reason for heuristic methods to be of higher interest. Sifting [25] is a well known node minimization algorithm based on a hill-climbing framework. The technique is based on a rule that swaps two adjacent variables in a BDD without changing the function. Sifting uses this feature by moving each variable downwards and upwards in the variable order. The BDD size resulting from reordering every variable is recorded during this procedure and finally the variable is moved back and fixed to the position where the BDD with the minimum number of nodes was found. Results obtained by sifting can be far from the optimum when the number of inputs increases. Employing approaches such as *Simulated Annealing* (SA) and *Evolutionary Algorithms* (EAs) for BDD node minimization, the number of nodes can even decrease to half of that achieved by sifting for large circuits [1, 9]. Since SA has been used for comparison with MOB in our experimental studies, its framework is briefly discussed in the following. At first, a variable ordering is generated randomly and the nodes of the resulting BDD are counted. Before a termination criterion is satisfied, a randomly chosen ordering is accepted instead of the current variable permutation if it leads to a BDD with a lower number of nodes. Otherwise, the new variable ordering might be accepted in a probabilistic manner. In fact, SA allows to accept a variable ordering with a certain probability in order to make the algorithm capable of escaping a local minimum.

The majority of BDD optimization approaches are based on node minimization, however it has been proven that the number of BDD paths are also important in some applications such as SAT-solving or synthesis [11]. *Modified Sifting* (MS) [15] is a BDD optimization method aiming at minimizing the number of one-paths. The framework of MS is the same as sifting with the objective being set to the number of one-paths. Similar to sifting, MS examines just a few possibilities of the whole search space that makes it faster compared to simulation based methods such as SA and EA. Consequently, the BDDs found by MS might have a considerable higher number of one-paths than the optimum when the number of variables increases. An EA for BDD path minimization was proposed in [17]. EA has a better performance than MS for the same reasons mentioned above. EA applies roulette wheel mating selection for creating an offspring with a cardinality of half of the current population. In each iteration, after employing variation operators the offspring is produced and then the new population is created by combining the offspring with the best half of the individuals in the current population.

All of the BDD optimization techniques explained above optimize BDDs with respect to one of the cost metrics. An approach introduced in [21] employs sifting and MS separately and then stores the number of nodes and one-paths returned by both methods. Thereafter, a comparison operator checks the node counts found by two approaches. If they are equal, the optimized BDD is characterized by the BDD found by MS. Otherwise, the same scenario is repeated for equal one-path counts but the BDD found by sifting is selected this time. In the case that both objectives in the BDDs found by two methods are different, the user is supposed to choose between the resulting BDDs. Indeed, the algorithm introduced in [21] chooses between results obtained by sifting and MS instead of a multi-objective optimization.

3. MULTI-OBJECTIVE BDD OPTIMIZATION

3.1 Overview

The proposed multi-objective BDD minimization approach is a non-dominated sorting based algorithm structurally similar to NSGA-II [7] with variation operators specifically designed for escaping invalid variable permutations. NSGA-II has been shown excellent performance on problems with two or three objectives. However, as a Pareto-dominance algorithm it fails to rank solutions in the presence of many objectives. Since BDD optimization is characterized as a bi-objective problem in this paper, NSGA-II would be sufficient and more reasonable than paying high penalties when using many objective optimization approaches, e.g., [28].

In order to keep the paper self-contained, a brief explanation of the relation employed by NSGA-II to rank a population is given. According to non-dominated sorting, all individuals should be assigned to a level of dominance that is equal to their overall fitness values used for ranking the population. To find all members of the first non-dominated front, each individual should be compared with every other individual in the population to find if it is non-dominated. This procedure can be completed by exploiting a fast non-dominated sorting scheme to find all levels of dominance. Fast non-dominated sorting decreases computational complexity by counting the number of individuals which dominate or are dominated by each individual in the population. To preserve a well-distributed optimal set, density of individuals is also considered besides non-domination rank in the selection process. The density estimation metric so-called crowding distance is calculated to discriminate between individuals belonging to the same non-dominated front. Thus, between two individuals with different non-dominated ranks, the individual with lower rank is preferred. Otherwise, the individual with greater value of crowding distance is preferred in the case of equal ranks.

The general framework of the MOB algorithm is described in Algorithm 1. First, a random parent population P_0 of size N is initialized. Each individual of the population is characterized by a permutation of the variable indices of the BDD. Objective values are assigned to the population by counting the number of nodes and one-paths. Then, the population is sorted based on non-domination. Steps 6–18 are iterated until the stopping criterion is satisfied. After applying binary tournament, recombination, and mutation operators an offspring Q_t of size equal to the parent population is created in step 6. To ensure elitism, Q_t is combined with the current population P_t resulting in a new population R_t. In step 9, non-dominated sorting is employed to classify R_t into different non-domination levels (F_1, F_2, and so on). Thereafter, individuals are added to P_{t+1} starting from the first non-dominated front F_1. This procedure is continued to fill population P_{t+1} with subsequent non-dominated fronts until their sizes are smaller than the free available slots in P_{t+1} (step 17), formally expressed as

$$P_{t+1} \leftarrow P_{t+1} \cup F_i[1 : (N- \mid P_{t+1} \mid)].$$

Otherwise, the lesser crowded individuals in the current front F_i are chosen after sorting the front according to the crowding distance.

Algorithm 1 Framework of the general MOB

1: $P_0 \leftarrow$ InitializePopulation
2: CountNodesOne-paths(P_0)
3: $\{F_1, F_2, \ldots\} \leftarrow$ Non-dominated-sort(P_0)
4: $t \leftarrow 0$
5: **while** the stopping criterion is not met **do**
6: $\quad Q_t \leftarrow$ MakeOffspringPopulation(P_{t+1})
7: $\quad$ CountNodesOne-paths(Q_t)
8: $\quad R_t \leftarrow P_t \cup Q_t$
9: $\quad \{F_1, F_2, \ldots\} \leftarrow$ Non-dominated-sort(R_t)
10: $\quad P_{t+1} \leftarrow \emptyset$
11: $\quad i \leftarrow 1$
12: $\quad$ **while** $|P_{t+1}| + |F_i| \leq N$ **do**
13: $\quad\quad P_{t+1} \leftarrow P_{t+1} \cup F_i$
14: $\quad\quad i \leftarrow i + 1$
15: $\quad$ **end while**
16: $\quad$ CrowdingDistanceSort(F_i)
17: $\quad P_{t+1} \leftarrow P_{t+1} \cup F_i[1 : (N - |P_{t+1}|)]$
18: $\quad t \leftarrow t + 1$
19: **end while**

3.2 Variation Operators

In this section, the employed variation operators are introduced. The offspring population is produced by recombination and mutation operators. Recombination includes specific crossover operators which avoid omissions and duplication in variable indices. Indeed, the employed crossover operators ensure that the permutations remain valid. Three crossover operators are used in the proposed BDD optimization algorithm including partially matched crossover, inversion and reproduction. Partially matched crossover PMX [23] is performed by randomly choosing two crossover points which break two parents in three sections. Two children are produced by combination of sections from both parents such that each previously used variable index is substituted for a new one to guarantee valid permutations. Inversion introduced in [17] breaks each parent into three sections by choosing two random positions. Then, one child is produced from each parent by inverting the order of indices in a randomly chosen part. The last employed crossover operator only copies each parent with no genetic change. That means the created children are identical to their parents.

After recombination, three mutation operators all described in [17] are employed such that one of them might affect a child according to given probabilities. The first operator exchanges two random variable indices of the individual. The second operator applies the first mutation technique twice on the same permutation. In the third mutation operator a position is chosen randomly and its content is exchanged with an adjacent index.

3.3 Priority

In many real world applications, one or more objectives are of higher level of significance. In such optimization problems, although it is desirable to minimize all objectives, it is preferred to escape penalties for objectives with higher priorities as a cost of improving lesser important criteria. Hence, the proposed MOB optimization approach is equipped with the ability to handle priority in order to meet requirements of specific applications. For instance, the number of nodes is more important than the number of one-paths in formal verification. On the other hand, the number of paths are regarded as an influential objective in SAT-solving.

Several techniques have been developed to model priorities in a multi-criteria optimization problem. Weighted sum is a widely used classical method that is able to handle objective priorities. It scalarizes the set of objectives into a fitness value by multiplying each objective with a user supplied weight. For a solution $\mathbf{x} \in \Omega$, the fitness function $f(\mathbf{x})$ is given by

$$f(\mathbf{x}) = \sum_{i=1}^{m} w_i.x_i.$$

It is obvious that larger coefficients, denoted by ω_i, represent higher objective priorities in the fitness value. Another approach so-called *priority preferred* is proposed in [26]. It incorporates a lexicographic ordering of objectives with relation *preferred* that is a refinement of Pareto-dominance [8]. In this work, the model explained in [26] is adapted to non-domination instead of *preferred*. Let $p = \{p_1, p_2, \ldots, p_m\}$ be a priority vector determining priorities assigned to the objectives for an m-objective problem. Each component p_i, $i \in \{1, 2, \ldots, m\}$ can adopt values from the set $\{1, 2, \ldots, n\}$, $n \leq m$ (n is equal to m in case that all objectives have different priorities). Considering a minimization problem, we assume that a lower value of p_i means objective i is of higher priority. Given two solutions $\mathbf{x}, \mathbf{y} \in \Omega$, $\mathbf{x}|_j$ and $\mathbf{y}|_j$ represent subvectors of $\mathbf{x}$ and $\mathbf{y}$ only including objective functions with priority of j, priority-dominance is defined as

$$\mathbf{x} \prec_p \mathbf{y} :\Leftrightarrow \exists j \in \{1, 2, \ldots, n\} : \mathbf{x}|_j \prec \mathbf{y}|_j \wedge \\ \forall k < j : \mathbf{y}|_k \not\prec \mathbf{x}|_k.$$

More informally, the relation defined above employs Pareto-dominance to compare objective functions with equal priorities. In other words, $\mathbf{x}$ priority-dominates $\mathbf{y}$ if there is a subvector of objective functions with identical priority in $\mathbf{x}$ that dominates the corresponding subvector in $\mathbf{y}$, and at the same time $\mathbf{x}|_j$ is not dominated by any subvector of priority value higher than j in $\mathbf{y}$.

Priority-dominance can be defined more simply in the bi-objective BDD optimization problem. In this case, the

Algorithm 2 Priority-dominance

```
1: GetPriorityVector(p) ▷ To determine priority subvectors
2: for all x ∈ Ω do
3:     S_x ← ∅                ▷ Set of individuals dominated by x
4:     n_x ← 0   ▷ The number of individuals dominating x
5:     for all y ∈ Ω do
6:         i ← 1
7:         while i ≤ 2 do
8:             if x|_i ≺ y|_i then
9:                 S_x ← S_x ∪ {y}
10:            else if y|_i ≺ x|_i then
11:                n_x ← n_x + 1
12:            else
13:                i ← i + 1
14:            end if
15:        end while
16:    end for
17: end for
```

priority vector consists of two values, i.e., 1 for objective with higher significance and 2 for the other objective. The priority subvector for each individual is equal to the corresponding objective function representing the number of nodes or one-paths. The procedure to compare individuals according to a given priority vector is described in Algorithm 2. In steps 6–13, an individual $\mathbf{x}$ is compared with $\mathbf{y}$ based on priority-dominance. For this purpose, relation dominance is applied to the corresponding objective functions with high priority in $\mathbf{x}$ and $\mathbf{y}$. Obviously, if these values are different $\mathbf{x}$ priority-dominates or is priority-dominated by $\mathbf{y}$. Otherwise, the other objective is taken into account to discriminate between individuals. In order to determine the non-domination front for each individual, two entities are also calculated in parallel with the comparisons. S_x represents the set of solutions which are dominated by individual $\mathbf{x}$, and n_x is the number of individuals dominating $\mathbf{x}$. Thereafter, these entities can be used for fast non-domination sorting as described in [7].

4. EXPERIMENTAL RESULTS

4.1 Experimental Setup

In order to evaluate the performance of MOB and compare it with other discussed existing approaches, several experiments are carried out on a benchmark set including 25 Boolean functions. The functions are taken from ISCAS89 [4] and LGSynth91 [29] benchmark sets with a range of input variables from 7 to 54. MOB has been run 30 times independently for each function. In all experiments, the population size is set to 100 and the algorithm terminates after 1000 iterations. Similarly to EA, the probabilities of crossover operators are set to 0.98, 0.01, and 0.01 for PMX, inversion and reproduction, respectively. Three mutation operators have an overall probability of $1/n$, where n is the number of variables of the BDD. The CUDD package [27] is used for BDD representation and comparison of results with node minimization approaches.

4.2 Performance Assessment

To evaluate the performance of the general MOB algorithm, statistical studies have been performed on the final populations for all thirty runs of each function. Complete statistics representing the average values, the smallest and

Table 1: Descriptive statistics for MOB

Function	Inputs	Outputs	Min		Mean		Median		Max	
			N	P	N	P	N	P	N	P
s1196	32	31	611	2581	677.37	2922.21	675	2857	1014	4333
s1238	32	31	627	2518	707.34	2827.9	679	2806	1057	4479
s1488	14	25	373	352	396.17	365.45	402	357	464	517
s208	18	9	50	53	59.52	62.67	60	61	63	202
s27	7	4	10	16	10	16	10	16	10	16
s298	17	20	74	70	74.51	73.4	74	74	77	74
s344	24	26	104	330	104.73	331.45	104	330	110	346
s382	24	27	121	230	138.73	255.82	136	247.5	208	332
s386	13	3	109	57	114.16	64.89	113	65	133	82
s400	24	27	121	230	142.147	252.05	135	247	188	332
s444	24	27	119	230	134.95	261.88	132	258	188	340
s510	25	13	146	153	149.49	166.78	150	159	156	183
s526	24	27	116	157	128.74	164.15	129	161	147	197
s641	54	42	461	1512	533.51	1594.76	527	1593	604	1793
s713	54	42	435	1523	527.23	1647.11	517	1627	631	1936
s820	23	24	221	146	224.94	157.13	224	151	240	180
s832	23	24	220	146	224.75	158.37	225	152	235	179
alu4	14	8	564	1372	573.19	1428.55	572	1372	644	1599
clip	9	5	75	214	75	214	75	214	75	214
misex1	8	7	35	34	35.4	35.24	35	36	37	36
sao2	10	4	81	97	84.43	102.15	85	102	96	111
t481	16	1	21	841	21.94	903.31	21	841	32	1009
cordic	23	2	43	9440	49.41	20260.62	47	25797	82	34393
misex3	14	14	480	1973	545.74	2120.83	536	2056	751	3046
seq	41	35	1208	1766	1275.76	1901.32	1270	1883	1461	2301
$\sum$			6425	26041	7009.16	38288.04	6933	43462.5	8703	58230

the greatest observations of results are shown in Table 1. It is worth mentioning that for a function with four or more number of variables, a BDD minimal in both metrics of nodes and paths does not exist necessarily [15]. Thus, the values of nodes and one-paths achieved by MOB might represent the real optimum for one or both objectives or even none of them. Indeed, with no priority to nodes or one-paths, results shown in Table 1 are supposed to express a good trade-off between objectives.

In order to analyze the descriptive statistics of results obtained by the general bi-objective MOB, we assume the minimum found for each objective as a metric roughly estimating the optimal value. Statistics of the number of nodes (N) and one-paths (P) shown in Table 1 demonstrate that the average values represented by mean and median are closer to the minimum of the number of nodes and paths rather than the maximum values found in the whole runs. For instance, for function s1196 mean values for the number of nodes and one-paths are only 10.86% and 13.22% greater than their minimum values, respectively. The worst observations of the number of nodes and one-paths are 70.37% and 67.88% greater than minimums found for the corresponding objectives. This property in the first three statistics is especially apparent for the functions resulting in larger BDDs in size and number of paths. Considering the effect of maximum number of nodes and one-paths on worsening their average values, the discussion above reflects the fact that the final populations are of high quality in comparison with the best ever found values. In general, the number of nodes and paths of the BDDs found by MOB are mostly spread over values expressing an optimal BDD which indicates the quality of results.

4.3 Comparison of Results

As discussed before, the number of nodes or one-paths of BDDs resulting by the general MOB algorithm does not represent the optimum value for each objective necessarily. Instead, the minimum BDD, either in the number of nodes or paths, is accessible for a single-objective method. Therefore, in order to make a fair comparison the results of MOB with priority to the number of nodes or one-paths are compared with the introduced node or path minimization methods, respectively. For this purpose, the BDDs possessing the smallest values for the preferred objective in all 30 runs are chosen as the results of the prioritized MOBs shown in Table 1 and Table 2.

In Table 2, the BDDs found by node minimization techniques discussed in Section 2.2, sifting and SA, are compared to the optimum BDDs obtained by MOB with priority to the number of nodes. It can be easily concluded from the table that the number of BDD nodes found by sifting for the 25 benchmark circuits are far away from the values returned by the two other approaches except for a few cases. However, sifting obtains smaller one-path counts than the compared methods for a couple of functions that is an unintended result of lower capability of finding the minimized BDDs. On the other hand, SA shows high performance by achieving BDDs with the minimum number of nodes for most of the functions. Considering all results shown in Table 2, MOB with priority to the number of nodes shows obviously higher quality than

Table 2: Comparison of results with priority to the number of nodes with existing node minimization approaches

Function	Sifting [25]		SA [1]		MOB	
	N	P	N	P	N	P
s1196	642	**3511**	600	4079	**599**	3907
s1238	642	**3511**	600	4079	**599**	3909
s1488	391	551	**369**	582	373	**407**
s208	61	**79**	**41**	1867	**41**	1867
s27	**10**	17	**10**	17	**10**	**16**
s298	78	**73**	**74**	74	**74**	74
s344	**104**	**330**	**104**	**330**	**104**	**330**
s382	121	**315**	**119**	332	**119**	332
s386	123	70	**110**	65	**110**	**58**
s400	121	315	**119**	332	121	**292**
s444	161	447	**119**	**332**	**119**	**332**
s510	165	206	148	192	**146**	**181**
s526	141	368	**113**	207	115	**189**
s641	629	2164	408	2883	**385**	**2671**
s713	629	2164	408	2883	**389**	**2617**
s820	258	184	**221**	180	**221**	**177**
s832	258	184	**221**	180	**221**	**151**
alu4	804	2876	**564**	**1430**	**564**	**1430**
clip	87	326	**75**	275	**75**	**214**
misex1	**35**	39	**35**	39	**35**	**36**
sao2	86	**97**	**81**	130	**81**	111
t481	**21**	1009	**21**	1009	**21**	**841**
cordic	43	38482	43	38482	**42**	**27329**
misex3	602	2654	**478**	3485	**478**	**3408**
seq	2163	62587	**1193**	2265	**1193**	**2259**
$\sum$	8325	122559	6274	65729	**6235**	**53228**

Table 3: Comparison of results with priority to the number of one-paths with existing one-path minimization approaches

Function	MS [15]		EA [17]		MOB	
	N	P	N	P	N	P
s1196	1523	2874	1142	**2508**	**1087**	2509
s1238	1523	1874	1105	**2508**	**1064**	2509
s1488	500	369	410	**352**	**408**	**352**
s208	**62**	**53**	**62**	**53**	**62**	**53**
s27	13	**16**	11	**16**	**10**	**16**
s298	91	**70**	88	**70**	**76**	**70**
s344	**104**	**330**	**104**	**330**	**104**	**330**
s382	**152**	238	188	**230**	188	**230**
s386	158	61	121	**57**	**113**	**57**
s400	152	238	190	**230**	**188**	**230**
s444	**154**	243	188	**230**	188	**230**
s510	184	170	159	**153**	**155**	**153**
s526	153	162	**138**	**156**	**138**	157
s641	768	1700	911	**1444**	**611**	1447
s713	768	1700	1458	**1447**	**616**	1452
s820	310	155	250	**146**	**230**	**146**
s832	310	155	249	**146**	**230**	**146**
alu4	621	1545	597	**1372**	**572**	**1372**
clip	127	262	**75**	**214**	**75**	**214**
misex1	42	**34**	37	**34**	**36**	**34**
sao2	102	99	100	**97**	**86**	**97**
t481	35	1009	50	**841**	**21**	**841**
cordic	**49**	30093	171	**8332**	73	9440
misex3	946	2303	727	1976	**577**	**1973**
seq	1398	1841	1499	**1744**	**1391**	**1744**
$\sum$	10245	47594	10030	**24684**	**8299**	25802

the other two methods with respect to both metrics. The sum of results for the whole benchmark set obtained by MOB reveals a decrease of 2090 and 39 in the number of nodes in comparison with sifting and SA. Moreover, MOB with priority to the number of nodes finds BDDs with noticeably lower one-path counts for the majority of the benchmark functions. To make a more precise comparison, the sum of the number of one-paths in MOB is 97.36% and 19.02% smaller than the corresponding values in sifting and SA, respectively. Indeed, MOB with priority to the number of nodes finds better minimized BDDs than the well known node minimization techniques besides achieving a large reduction in the number of one-paths.

Since the number of nodes are assumed to be of higher importance in this experiment, finding minimal BDDs in size is the principal goal of the MOB with priority to the number of nodes. Nonetheless, there are three functions for which MOB fails to find the BDD representations with minimum number of nodes obtained by SA. For functions *s1488*, *s400*, and *s526*, BDDs found by MOB have in total 8 more nodes than the three BDDs resulted by SA. On the other hand, the sum of one-path counts for the mentioned functions shows a decrease of 233 compared to the total number of one-paths in the corresponding BDDs found by SA. Considering the fact that MOB with priority to the number of nodes is a multi-objective algorithm, finding BDDs with a small increase in the node counts as a fair cost of reducing the number of paths is acceptable.

Table 3 shows the comparison of results obtained by MOB with priority to the number of one-paths with BDDs found by MS and EA. It can be clearly seen that results obtained by MS are dominated by EA and MOB. Therefore, the quality of BDDs optimized by EA and MOB are compared in the following. According to the table, MOB has found the minimum number of one-paths that were also found by EA for the majority of benchmark circuits. However, for a few functions BDDs obtained by MOB have higher one-path counts than the corresponding BDDs by EA. For functions *s1196*, *s1238*, *s641*, and *s713* the BDDs found by MOB show few increases in the numbers of one-paths while the node counts are considerably lowered. Only the function *cordic* shows a high difference between the numbers of one-paths resulted by EA and MOB. The BDD representing *cordic* found by MOB is 13% larger than the BDD resulted by EA with respect to the number of one-paths. It is also worth mentioning that the number of nodes in the BDD found by MOB for the function *cordic* is decreased to less than half of the nodes in the BDD found by EA. Although MOB has almost failed to find the minimal BDD wih respect to the significant objective for *cordic*, it has compensated this failure with a fair reduction in the other objective. For function *misex3*, MOB has even found a BDD noticeably smaller in size with a lower number of one-paths compared to the BDD obtained by EA.

The total number of one-paths obtained by MOB is almost equal to half of the one-paths achieved by MS with a reduction of 18.99% in the number of nodes. In comparison with EA, MOB shows an increase of 4.52% in the one-path counts that is mainly caused by result of *cordic*. Also, MOB has 17.26% less BDD nodes compared to EA for the whole benchmark set. Although, the results obtained by MOB are slightly worsened in the number of one-paths compared to EA, MOB has noticeably lowered the number of BDD nodes. In general, it is fair to say that MOB with priority to the number of one-paths shows a high performance with respect to both objectives in comparison with existing node minimization techniques.

In order to have a thorough assessment on the experimental results, multiplication of the number of nodes and one-paths is considered as a metric representing the quality of BDDs. In fact, a lower *Node-One-Path-product* (NOP) means a better trade-off between both optimization criteria. The values of NOPs obtained by all types of MOB and the other methods are shown in Table 4. According to the table, the general MOB with no priority has achieved the minimum sum of all NOP values among all other approaches that reveals its high performance as a multi-objective technique. The sum of NOP values of the general MOB is decreased to 92.78%, 27.02%, 43.84%, and 32.28% of the corresponding values in sifting, SA, MS, and EA, respectively. Moreover, the two other versions of MOB have also considerable lower NOP sums than that of node or path minimization methods. In other words, priority based MOB types find a good trade-off that is usually the minimal BDD with respect to the objective of higher importance besides reducing the value of the other objective. To evaluate the effect of priority on MOB, sum of results with priority to nodes and one-paths are respectively compared to the sum of median values of nodes and one-paths obtained by the general MOB. The integration of results shown in Tables 1, 2, and 3 describes that after applying priority to the number of nodes and one-paths, MOB has achieved 10.06% and 40.63% less BDD nodes and one-paths than the general MOB. Since one-path counts are spread over a larger range than nodes, results of MOB with priority to the number of one-paths show higher level of BDD abstraction in respect to one-paths. In general, incorporating priority with MOB has improved the performance of the algorithm with respect to the user preferred objective in addition to preserving favorable multi-objective features.

5. CONCLUSION

Since many applications in electronic design automation and formal verification successfully use BDDs, their optimization is of high interest. The existing BDD optimization approaches either target the number of nodes or the number of paths. In this paper, we have proposed a bi-objective evolutionary algorithm to find minimal BDDs in both cost metrics. The proposed approach also benefits from an objective priority facility allowing the user to give higher importance to one of the optimization criteria according to the application's requirements. Experimental results show that the multi-objective BDD optimization approach is able to find more compact BDDs considering both objectives in comparison with the existing BDD optimization methods.

Acknowledgments

This work was supported by the German Research Foundation (DFG) (DR 287/23-1) within a Reinhart Koselleck project and by the University of Bremen's graduate school SyDe, funded by the German Excellence Initiative.

6. REFERENCES

[1] B. Bollig, M. Löbbing, and I. Wegener. Simulated annealing to improve variable orderings for OBDDs. In *Int'l Workshop on Logic Synth*, 1995.

[2] B. Bollig and I. Wegener. Improving the variable ordering of OBDDs is NP-complete. *IEEE Transactions on Computers*, 45(9):993–1002, 1996.

[3] K. S. Brace, R. L. Rudell, and R. E. Bryant. Efficient implementation of a BDD package. In *Proceedings of the 27th annual Design Automation Conference (DAC)*, pages 40–45, 1990.

[4] F. Brglez, D. Bryan, and K. Kozminski. Combinational profiles of sequential benchmark circuits. In *IEEE International Symposium on Circuits and Systems*, pages 1929–1934, 1989.

[5] R. E. Bryant. Graph-based algorithms for Boolean function manipulation. *IEEE Transactions on Computers*, 35(8):677–691, 1986.

[6] R. E. Bryant. Binary decision diagrams and beyond: Enabling technologies for formal verification. In *Proceedings of IEEE/ACM International Conference on Computer-Aided Design (ICCAD)*, pages 236–243, 1995.

[7] K. Deb, A. Pratap, S. Agarwal, and T. Meyarivan. A fast and elitist multi-objective genetic algorithm: NSGA-II. *IEEE Transactions on Evolutionary Computation*, 6(2):182–197, 2002.

[8] N. Drechsler, R. Drechsler, and B. Becker. Multi-objective optimisation based on relation *Favour*. In *Proceedings of the first International Conference on Evolutionary Multi-Criterion Optimization (EMO)*, volume 1993, pages 154–166, 2001.

[9] R. Drechsler, B. Becker, and N. Göckel. A genetic algorithm for variable ordering of OBDDs. In *IEE Proceedings of Computers and Digital Techniques*, volume 143(6), pages 364–368, 1996.

[10] R. Drechsler, J. Shi, and G. Fey. Synthesis of fully testable circuits from bdds. *IEEE Transactions on CAD of Integrated Circuits and Systems*, 23(3):440–443, 2004.

[11] R. Ebendt, G. Fey, and R. Drechsler. Advanced BDD optimization. Springer, 2005.

[12] R. Ebendt, W. Günther, and R. Drechsler. An improved branch and bound algorithm for exact BDD minimization. *IEEE Transactions on CAD of Integrated Circuits and Systems*, 22(12):1657–1663, 2003.

[13] S. Edelkamp and T. Mehler. Byte code distance heuristics and trail direction for model checking Java programs. In *Workshop on Model Checking and Artificial Intelligence (MoChArt)*, pages 69–76, 2003.

[14] S. Edelkamp and F. Reffel. OBDDs in heuristic search. In *Lecture Notes in Computer Science*, volume 1504, pages 81–92. Springer, 1998.

[15] G. Fey and R. Drechsler. Minimizing the number of paths in BDDs: Theory and algorithm. *IEEE Transactions on CAD of Integrated Circuits and Systems*, 25(1):4–11, 2006.

[16] S. J. Friedman and K. J. Supowit. Finding the optimal variable ordering for binary decision diagrams. In *Proceedings of the 24th ACM/IEEE Design Automation Conference (DAC)*, pages 348–356, 1987.

[17] M. Hilgemeier, N. Drechsler, and R. Drechsler. Minimizing the number of one-paths in BDDs by an

Table 4: Comparison of Node-One-Path-products (NOPs)

Function	Sifting [25]	SA [1]	MS [15]	EA [17]	MOB priority to one-paths	MOB priority to nodes	MOB general
s1196	2254062	2447400	4377102	2864136	2727283	2340293	**1906860**
s1238	2254062	2447400	4377102	2771340	2669576	2341491	**1889888**
s1488	215441	217341	184500	144320	143616	151811	**142065**
s208	4819	76547	**3286**	**3286**	**3286**	76547	**3286**
s27	170	170	208	176	**160**	**160**	**160**
s298	5694	5476	6370	6160	**5320**	5476	5476
s344	**34320**	**34320**	**34320**	**34320**	**34320**	**34320**	**34320**
s382	38115	39508	36176	43240	43240	39508	**33082**
s386	8610	7150	9638	6897	6441	**6380**	**6380**
s400	38115	39508	36176	43700	43240	35332	**32562**
s444	71967	39508	37422	43240	43240	39508	**33082**
s510	33990	28416	31280	24327	23715	26426	**23562**
s526	51888	23391	24786	21528	21666	21735	**20640**
s641	1361156	1176264	1305600	1315484	884117	1028335	**806837**
s713	1361156	1176264	1305600	2109726	894432	1018013	**802382**
s820	48246	39780	48050	36500	33580	39117	**33222**
s832	48246	39780	48050	36354	33580	33371	**32928**
alu4	2312304	806520	959445	819084	**784784**	806520	**784784**
clip	28362	20625	33274	**16050**	**16050**	**16050**	**16050**
misex1	1365	1365	1428	1258	**1224**	1260	1260
sao2	**8342**	10530	10098	9700	**8342**	8991	**8342**
t481	21189	21189	35315	42050	**17661**	**17661**	**17661**
cordic	1654726	1654726	1474557	1424772	689120	1147818	**686774**
misex3	1597708	1665830	2178638	1436552	1138421	1629024	**1116951**
seq	135375681	2702145	2573718	2614256	2425904	2694987	**2305520**
$\sum$	148829734	14721153	19132139	15867306	12648099	12575456	**10744074**

evolutionary algorithm. In *IEEE Congress on Evolutionary Computation (CEC)*, pages 1724–1731, 2003.

[18] N. Ishiura, H. Sawada, and S. Yajima. Minimazation of binary decision diagrams based on exchanges of variables. In *Proceedings of IEEE/ACM International Conference on Computer-Aided Design (ICCAD)*, pages 472–475, 1991.

[19] R. M. Jensen, E. A. Hansen, S. Richards, and R. Zhou. Memory-efficient symbolic heuristic search. In *Proceedings of the 16th International Conference on Automated Planning and Scheduling (ICAPS)*, pages 304–313, 2006.

[20] D. E. Knuth. *The Art of Computer Programming*, volume 4A. Addison-Wesley, 2011.

[21] K. Lu, Y. Ramin, Y. Edwin, and K. Constantinos. Structural optimization of reduced ordered binary decision diagrams for SLA negotiation in IaaS of cloud computing. In *Proceedings of the 10th International Conference on Service-Oriented Computing*, pages 268–282, 2012.

[22] A. Mishchenko and M. Perkowski. Fast heuristic minimization of exclusive-sums-of-products. In *5th Int'l Workshop on Applications of the Real-Muller Expansion in Circuit Design*, 2001.

[23] I. Oliver, D. Smith, and J. Holland. Study of permutation crossover operators on the traveling salesman problem. In *Proceedings of the second International Conference on Genetic Algorithms*, pages 224–230, 1987.

[24] S. Reda, R. Drechsler, and A. Orailoglu. On the relation between SAT and BDDs for equivalence checking. In *Proceedings of the International Symposium on Quality Electronic Design*, pages 394–399, 2002.

[25] R. Rudell. Dynamic variable ordering for ordered binary decision diagrams. In *Proceedings of IEEE/ACM International Conference on Computer-Aided Design (ICCAD)*, pages 42–47, 1993.

[26] F. Schmiedle, N. Drechsler, D. Große, and R. Drechsler. Heuristic learning based on genetic programming. *Genetic Programming and Evolvable Machines*, 3(4):363–388, 2002.

[27] F. Somenzi. CUDD: CU Decision Diagram package release 2.5.0. University of Colorado at Boulder, 2012.

[28] A. Sülflow, N. Drechsler, and R. Drechsler. Robust multi-objective optimization in high dimensional spaces. In *Proceedings of the 4th International Conference on Evolutionary Multi-Criterion Optimization (EMO)*, pages 715–726, 2006.

[29] S. Yang. Logic synthesis and optimization benchmarks user guide: Version 3.0. Microelectronics Center of North Carolina (MCNC), 1991.

[30] Y. Ye and K. Roy. A graph-based synthesis algorithm for AND/XOR networks. In *Proceedings of the 34th Design Automation Conference (DAC)*, pages 107–112, 1997.

Empirical Study of Multi-objective Ant Colony Optimization to Software Project Scheduling Problems

Jing Xiao
School of Computer Science
South China Normal University
Guangzhou 510631, China
xiaojing@scnu.edu.cn

Mei-Ling Gao
School of Computer Science
South China Normal University
Guangzhou 510631, China
galy108@163.com

Min-Mei Huang
School of Public Administration
South China Normal University
Guangzhou 510006, China
huangmm@scnu.edu.cn

ABSTRACT
The Software Project Scheduling Problem (SPSP) focuses on the management of software engineers and tasks in a software project so as to complete the tasks with a minimal cost and duration. It's becoming more and more important and challenging with the rapid development of software industry. In this paper, we employ a Multi-objective Evolutionary Algorithm using Decomposition and Ant Colony (MOEA/D-ACO) to solve the SPSP. To the best of our knowledge, it is the first application of Multi-objective Ant Colony Optimization (MOACO) to SPSP. Two heuristics capable of guiding the algorithm to search better in the SPSP model are examined. Experiments are conducted on a set of 36 publicly available instances. The results are compared with the implementation of another multi-objective evolutionary algorithm called NSGA-II for SPSP. MOEA/D-ACO does not outperform NSGA-II for most of complex instances in terms of Pareto Front. But MOEA/D-ACO can obtain solutions with much less time for all instances in our experiments and it outperforms NSGA-II with less duration for most of test instances. The performance may be improved with tuning of the algorithm such as incorporating more heuristic information or using other MOACO algorithms, which deserve further investigation.

Categories and Subject Descriptors
I.2.8 [**Artificial Intelligence**]: Problem Solving, Control Method, Search-Heuristic methods.

General Terms
Algorithms, Performance, Experimentation, Management.

Keywords
Software Project Scheduling; Multi-objective Optimization; Ant Colony Optimization; Automatic Software Project Management; MOEA/D; NSGA-II.

1. INTRODUCTION
Nowadays, with the booming development of software industry, the software project is becoming more and more complicated. To make a project successful, a software project manager must consider how to plan, schedule, and monitor tasks and employees more efficiently. However, it's very difficult and time-consuming for people to manage these tasks manually. Therefore, it's valuable to pay special attention to the research of computer aided tools to improve the software project management. Generally, the Software Project Scheduling Problem (SPSP) [1] focuses on finding an optimal allocation of employees to tasks according to the resources and Task Precedence Graphs (TPGs). SPSP is NP-hard [2].

Ant colony optimization (ACO) is a bionic intelligence optimization algorithm that was initially proposed by Dorigo [3] for handling single-objective optimization problems. ACO has been applied to a lot of optimization problems in operations research such as resource constraint project scheduling problems [4], flow shop problems [5, 6] and job shop scheduling problems [7]. The employee allocation model of SPSP was first designed by Alba and it has been solved by Genetic Algorithm (GA) in [1]. Later Chicano [8] solved the SPSP using multi-objective metaheuristic algorithms including NSGA-II, SPEA2, PAES, MOCell and GDE3. And Luna [9] performed a scalability analysis of multi-objective metaheuristics. In addition, there are a few papers to solve the SPSP with Ant Colony Optimization (ACO). Xiao and Ao [2] proposed the original application of single-objective combinatorial ant colony optimization to SPSP. Afterwards, Crawford [10] proposed a max-min ant system algorithm to solve SPSP.

As ACO has been successfully applied to a variety of combinatorial optimization problems [11], it has soon been extended to multi-objective optimization problems [12, 13]. Multi-objective optimization problems are those with several, typically conflicting criteria for evaluating solutions. Even though we can't define the uniform priori preference of the objectives in all environments, we can try to get some optimal solutions that might be the best in a special case. Therefore, differing from single-objective optimization problems, each multi-objective optimization algorithm maintains a non-dominated archive and outputs all the non-dominated solutions at the end of the algorithm.

Many people have been working on the Multi-Objective Ant Colony Optimization (MOACO). The literature can be divided into two categories: the one is MOACO algorithms and their applications [12,13,14,15,16,17,18]; the other is the analysis of alternative design choices [19,20,21] of MOACO. There are many classical MOACO algorithms, such as BicriterionAnt [17], Multiple Ant Colony System [14], Pareto Ant Colony Optimization [15], COMPETants [16] and several mACO Variants [18]. In addition, with the successful application of Multi-Objective Evolutionary Algorithms based on Decomposition (MOEA/D) [22], the MOEA/D-ACO [23] has been proposed. MOEA/D-ACO is an algorithm framework that decomposes a multi-objective optimization problem into series of single-objective optimization problems where each ant is used to

GECCO '15, July 11 - 15, 2015, Madrid, Spain
 ISBN 978-1-4503-3472-3/15/07…$15.00
DOI: http://dx.doi.org/10.1145/2739480.2754702

tackle one single-objective sub-problem. Ants are divided into some groups and each ant has a few of neighbors. These groups and neighborhoods are computed according to the corresponding weight vectors λ. In MOEA/D-ACO, every ant uses different heuristic information and each group uses a different pheromone matrix.

In this paper, we use the MOEA/D-ACO framework to propose an algorithm for solving SPSP. We compare the proposed algorithm with NSGA-II [8] to evaluate its performance. As MOACO has been successfully applied to solving a variety of problems, the application of MOACO to SPSP is meaningful.

The rest of this paper is organized as follows. In Section 2, we describe the model of the Software Project Scheduling Problem addressed previously. Section 3 gives the details of our MOEA/D-ACO algorithm for SPSP. After that, the methodologies and experimental results that employ MOEA/D-ACO and NSGA-II are shown in Section 4. Section 5 concludes our work and outlines the future work.

2. SOFTWARE PROJECT SCHEDULING

We cite the formulation of SPSP proposed by Alba in [1]. Therefore, we focus on dedications of employees to tasks. Each employee has a set of skills, a salary and maximum degree of contribution to the project. And each task has a set of prerequisite skills and a required effort.

Here, we define the resources in SPSP. First, every employee is denoted as e_i, where i varies from 1 to E; and E is the number of employees. Then, we define skills of employee e_i as $e_i^{skills} \subseteq SK$, where SK means the set of all skills of the project; salary of employee i is denoted as e_i^{salary}, and the maximum dedication is represented as e_i^{max} .

Second, each task is denoted as t_j, where j varies from 1 to T, and T is the number of total tasks. Thus, the set of required skills of task t_j is defined as $t_j^{skills} \subseteq SK$, and the corresponding effort is defined as t_j^{effort} .

In addition, all tasks must be performed following the TPGs. TPG is defined as a directed acyclic graph G(V,E), where V is a set of vertices mapping tasks and E is a set of edges indicating the completing sequences of tasks. If there is a directed edge (t_j, t_k) among the vertices v_i and v_j, it means that the task t_j must be completed before the task t_k starts. Figure 1 provides an example of the SPSP model.

Then, we can describe solutions of SPSP according to the elements of problem instances. As every employee may have a dedication to each task, we use a matrix $M=(m_{ij})$ of size E×T to represent a solution, where m_{ij} is the dedication of employee e_i to task t_j and $m_{ij} \geqslant 0$. If $m_{ij}=0$, it means that employee e_i doesn't perform to the task t_j. Some constraints need to be set for guaranteeing the feasibility of solutions. On the one hand, all required skills of each task must be included in the total skills of all employees participating in the task. On the other hand, no employee can contribute to the project with a degree exceeded his/her maximum dedication. When the solution meets these two constraints, the project could be successfully scheduled.

After obtaining a solution, we calculate the duration of each task; then compute the start time and end time according to the TPGs. Afterwards, build the Gantt Diagram of the scheduling and calculate the duration of the project. After that, cost of the project can be computed with the salary, work time and dedication of the employees.

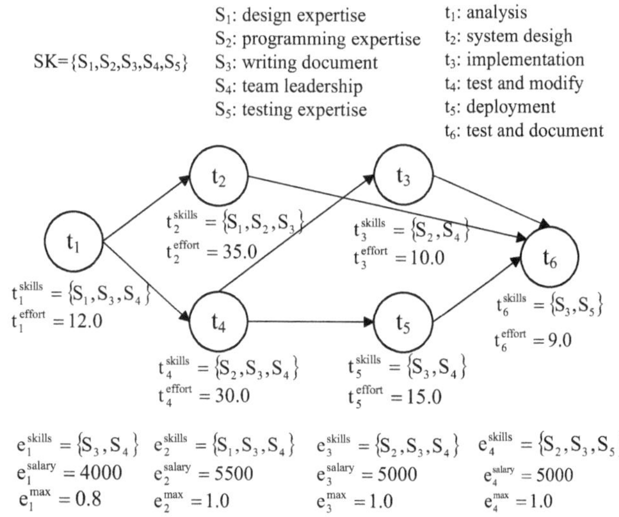

Figure 1. An example of SPSP model

Taking the objectives and constraints into account, we evaluate the quality of a solution by following three metrics: feasibility of a solution, project duration and project cost. In order to compute project duration P_{dur}, we must get duration of each task, denoted with t_j^{dur} . It is calculated as follows:

$$t_j^{dur} = \frac{t_j^{effort}}{\sum_{i=1}^{E} m_{ij}} \tag{1}$$

Then, by combining the duration time and the TPG we can get the starting time and ending time of each task. If one task has no prior-precedence tasks in the TPG, its starting time is zero. Otherwise, it will start until all prior-precedence tasks are finished. Obviously ending time can be easily calculated with the duration time and starting time. The calculation is described as the following formulas:

$$t_j^{start} = \begin{cases} 0 & \text{if} \forall k \neq j, (t_k, t_j) \notin E \\ \text{Max}\left\{ t_k^{end} \mid (t_k, t_j) \in E \right\} & \text{else} \end{cases} \tag{2}$$

$$t_j^{end} = t_j^{start} + t_j^{dur} \tag{3}$$

After that, we can build a Gantt Diagram for this scheduling of the project. And the finish time of the last task in the Gantt Diagram is the duration of the project. It can be described as follows:

$$P_{dur} = \text{Max}\left\{ t_j^{end} \mid \forall k \neq j, (t_j, t_k) \notin E \right\} \tag{4}$$

The project cost P_{cost} can be calculated as sum of all corresponding remunerations of employees. Remuneration of each employee is calculated using correlative salary, dedication and duration of tasks. We describe it by the following equation.

$$P_{cost} = \sum_{j=1}^{T} \sum_{i=1}^{E} e_i^{salary} \cdot m_{ij} \cdot t_j^{dur} \tag{5}$$

In addition, in order to get some meaningful solutions, we must check the feasibility of solutions. At first, the required skills of a task must be included in the set of skills of employees who perform the task. The skills are represented as follows:

$$t_j^{skills} \subseteq \bigcup_{\{i \mid m_{ij}>0\}} e_i^{skills} \quad \forall j \in \{1,2,\ldots,T\} \tag{6}$$

Secondly, to check the overwork of each employee, we need to compute workload of an employee at any time *t*, which is defined as follows:

$$e_i^{work}(t) = \sum_{\{j \mid t_j^{start} \le t \le t_j^{end}\}} m_{ij} \tag{7}$$

Thirdly, according to the workload and related maximum dedication, we calculate overwork of an employee as:

$$e_i^{over} = \int_{t=0}^{t=P_{dur}} \text{ramp}\left(e_i^{work}(t) - e_i^{max}\right) dt \tag{8}$$

where ramp(x) is a function defined as:

$$\text{ramp}(x) = \begin{cases} 0, & \text{if } x \le 0 \\ x, & \text{if } x > 0 \end{cases} \tag{9}$$

Finally, the total overwork of a project is the sum of all employees' overwork.

$$P_{over} = \sum_{i=1}^{E} e_i^{over} \tag{10}$$

In this paper, we aim to obtain Pareto-based solutions to minimize project cost (Equation (5)) and project duration (Equation (4)) using multi-objective ACO algorithm.

3. MOEA/D-ACO for SPSP

The MOEA/D-ACO is a multi-objective ant colony optimization algorithm proposed by L. Ke and Q. Zhang [23]. In order to apply MOACO to solve SPSP, we need to not only build the construction graph for ants but also design the pheromone and heuristic information. Different from single-objective optimization problems, we need to manage the non-dominated solutions in a multi-objective optimization algorithm. In this section, we describe the process of applying MOEA/D-ACO to solve SPSP.

3.1 Construction graph

The first step to apply ACO to solve the SPSP is to transform the dedication of employees to tasks into the ants' foraging path graph. Because any employee can have a dedication (can be zero) to any task, each task needs to be split up to construct an ant's foraging path graph. The graph presents the associated employees and their dedication to the task which is described in Figure 2. An ant travels from the start node via the column 1, column 2, … , column E to the end node in the directed graph. According to the path that selected by an ant, we can get the dedication of every employee to the task. So, after an ant goes through all tasks in the TPG, a candidate solution of the instance is obtained.

There are *V* nodes in each column of the graph indicating that a task is split into several parts. And *V* is calculated as follows:

$$V = Unit^{-1} + 1 \tag{11}$$

where *Unit* is the minimum degree of an employee's dedication to a task. In other words, the dedications of employees to tasks are multiplication of *Unit*. The value of *Unit* can be set manually.

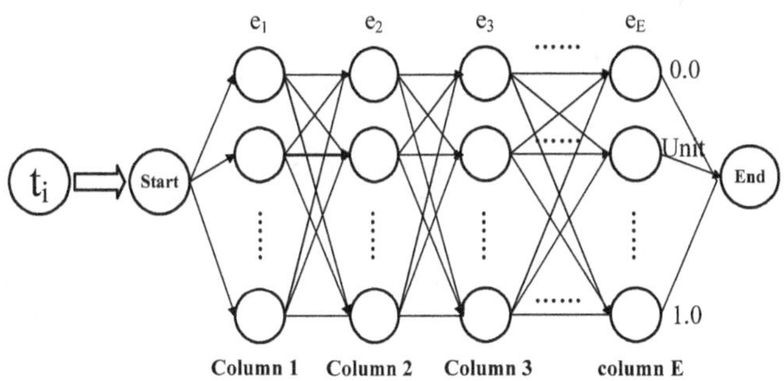

Figure 2. Construction graph of task t_i

The process of splitting a task into a graph can be described as follows:

(a) Generate a node as start node and insert it into the column 0.

(b) Construct *j* nodes as the candidate dedications of the first employee to the task, and insert them into the column 1.

(c) Construct nodes as (b) for other employees.

(d) Generate a node and insert it into the column E+1 as the end node.

(e) Construct edges between any neighbor columns.

Note that, there is only one node per column that can be passed by an ant when it forages a path. It means every employee has a dedication (can be zero) to a task.

3.2 Algorithm description

Since MOEA/D-ACO is based on decomposition, and the methods for decomposing a multi-objective optimization into a series of single-objective subproblems may have different influence on the performance. We adopt both the Weighted Sum Approach and Tchebycheff Approach previously used in [23].

The procedure of MOEA/D-ACO for SPSP is described as follows:

Input:

- Instances of SPSP.
- Number of ants, N.
- Number of groups.
- Size of neighbors, T. It means each ant has T neighbors.
- Basic parameters of ACO, such as α, β and ρ.

Output:

- Set of non-dominated solutions (Pareto Set), PS.

Step 1) Initialization.

Step 1.1) Set PS = Ø.

Step 1.2) Set Initial values of pheromones as 1.

Step 2) Construction solutions.

Step 2.1) Generation S^i. Each ant *i* constructs a new solution S^i according to the probabilistic matrix computed by the associated pheromone and heuristic information.

Step 2.2) Evaluation S^i. Calculate both cost and duration of S^i. And assess the feasibility of S^i.

Step 3) Update.

Step 3.1) Update of PS. If there is no solution in PS that dominates S^i, add S^i to PS, and remove those dominated by S^i from PS.

Step 3.2) Update of pheromone matrices. For each ant *i*, if S^i is just be added to PS, update the pheromone information of the ant's group.

Step 3.3) Update of the best solution x^i of subproblem *i*. If x^i is dominated by the best solution S^α generated by the neighbors of ant *i*, set $x^i = S^\alpha$.

Step 4) Stopping. If the termination criterion is met, stop and output the PS. Otherwise, go to the next generation (Step 2).

3.3 Pheromone and Heuristic information

As we all know, pheromone and heuristic information are very important in ant colony algorithms. Various problems or algorithms may require different expression and management of pheromone and heuristic information.In this section, we describe the settings and update strategy of pheromone and heuristic information in MOEA/D-ACO for SPSP.

3.3.1 Pheromone management

According to the MOEA/D-ACO framework, ants in the same group share one pheromone matrix. Therefore, all the pheromone operations in this paper are performed in groups.

Firstly, at the beginning of the algorithm, the pheromones on all edges of the construction graph are initialized as value 1.

Secondly, for all solutions that are constructed by ants in group *j* and used to update the non-dominated solutions PS in Step 3.1, we update the pheromone (Step 3.2) by the following equations.

$$\tau^j_{k,l} = \rho\tau^j_{k,l} + \sum_{x \in PS} \frac{1}{f(x \mid \lambda^j)} \tag{12}$$

$\tau^j_{k,l}$ represents the pheromone of group *j* on the edge marked by *k* and *l*, and ρ is the persistence rate of the old pheromone trail. $f(x|\lambda^j)$ is the objective function of solution *x*, and it can be calculated with Weighted Sum Approach as equation (13) or Tchebycheff Approach as equation (14):

$$f^W\left(x|\lambda^j\right) = \sum_{i=1}^{m} \lambda^j_i \cdot f_i(x) \tag{13}$$

where λ^j is the weight vector of group *j*, and $f_i(x)$ is the value of the *i* th objective.

$$f^T\left(x|\lambda^j\right) = \underset{1 \le i \le m}{Max}\left\{\lambda^j_i(f_i(x) - \underset{x \in \Omega}{Min}(f_i(x)))\right\} \tag{14}$$

where Ω is the set of solutions obtained in this run.

Thirdly, we set a max pheromone τ_{max} and a min pheromone τ_{min}. The two pheromone values are calculated at each generation with equation (15) and equation (16):

$$\tau_{max} = \frac{Num + 1}{(1-\rho)\ f_{min}} \tag{15}$$

where *Num* is the number of non-dominated solutions found in Step 3.1.

$$\tau_{min} = \theta\tau_{max} \tag{16}$$

θ is a control parameter whose value is in (0,1).

Then, the pheromone values are normalized to keep in the range from τ_{min} to τ_{max}.

3.3.2 Heuristic information

In MOEA/D-ACO framework, each ant has a heuristic information matrix and it's related to the ant's weight vector λ^i. In order to apply this algorithm to solve the SPSP, the calculation of heuristic information is described as following:

$$\eta^i_{k,l} = \frac{1}{\sum_{j=1}^{m} \lambda^i_j C^j_{k,l}} \tag{17}$$

where $\eta^i_{k,l}$ express the heuristic information of ant *i* on the edge marked by *k* and *l*, and $C^j_{k,l}$ is the information related to the edge. *m* is the number of objectives.

In this work, we adopt two heuristics to enhance the search ability of ants. When an ant travels on graph to construct a solution, the heuristic information on the edges makes a great influence on the ant's path selection. If ant *i* selects an edge ended with a node at column *k* and row *l*, the dedication of employee e_k to the task is equal to *l*Unit*. And the heuristic $\eta^i_{k,l}$ is calculated as follows:

(1) Allocated Dedication and the Salary of an employee (H1). This strategy means that the heuristic information is related to both the dedication of corresponding employee who has already performed in other tasks and the salary of the employee. That is to say, the $C^j_{k,l}$ in equation (17) is the dedication of employee e_k to other tasks or the salary of the employee.

(2) Total Dedication and Allocated Dedication (H2). This heuristic strategy means that the heuristic information is related to both the total dedication that the task requires and the Allocated Dedication. Therefore, $C^j_{k,l}$ in equation (17) is the total dedication that the task requires or the dedication of employee e_k to other tasks.

The probabilistic matrix is calculated by the pheromone and heuristic information as follows:

$$ProM_{k,l} = \left[\tau^i_{k,l} + \varepsilon \times In(x^i(k,l))\right]^\alpha \cdot \left(\eta^i_{k,l}\right)^\beta \tag{18}$$

where α, β and □ are three parameters that express the influence of pheromone and heuristics, and $In(x^i,(k,l))$ is a function whose value equals to 1 if the edge marked by *k* and *l* is in the solution x^i or 0 otherwise.

4. COMPUTATIONAL EXPERIMENTS

In this section we present the results of experiments to assess the performance of the MOEA/D-ACO algorithm for SPSP. In this paper, we compare the effectiveness of using MOEA/D-ACO with that using NSGA-II to solve the SPSP.

The algorithm was implemented in the C++ language using Microsoft Visual Studio 2010 and all experiments were run on an Intel CORE i5, 3.30GHz, 8GB of RAM PC running Windows 7 Ultimate.

In order to have a general research, we use a total of 36 randomly generated instances [1]. There are four groups, and each group has 9 instances with different number of employees or tasks. In the first two groups, the total number of skills is not defined while the tasks and employees have two separate ranges. Instances in the later two groups just have a fixed number of total skills: 5 or 10. In this paper, we define instances in the first group (G1) as Ee_Tt_p5. For example, the instance 5e_10t_p5 has 5 employees,

10 tasks, and the number of skills of employees varies from 4 to 5. Similarly, the instance in second group (G2) is Ee_Tt_p7 where the number of skills of employees varies from 6 to 7. Instances in the later two groups (G3 and G4) are defined as Ee_Tt_gS. For example, the instance 10e_20t_g10 means that there are 10 employees, 20 tasks, and a total of 10 skills. All instances are presented in Table 1, and the benchmarks can be downloaded from [24].

Table 1. Experimental Instances

Group	task / employee	10	20	30
G1 (4-5skills)	5	5e_10t_p5	5e_20t_p5	5e_30t_p5
	10	10e_10t_p5	10e_20t_p5	10e_30t_p5
	15	15e_10t_p5	15e_20t_p5	15e_30t_p5
G2 (6-7skills)	5	5e_10t_p7	5e_20t_p7	5e_30t_p7
	10	10e_10t_p7	10e_20t_p7	10e_30t_p7
	15	15e_10t_p7	15e_20t_p7	15e_30t_p7
G3 (5skills)	5	5e_10t_g5	5e_20t_g5	5e_30t_g5
	10	10e_10t_g5	10e_20t_g5	10e_30t_g5
	15	15e_10t_g5	15e_20t_g5	15e_30t_g5
G4 (10skills)	5	5e_10t_g10	5e_20t_g10	5e_30t_g10
	10	10e_10t_g10	10e_20t_g10	10e_30t_g10
	15	15e_10t_g10	15e_20t_g10	15e_30t_g10

4.1 Methodology

We implemented MOEA/D-ACO algorithm by referencing to the MOEA/D-ACO_TSP code developed by L.Ke and Q.Zhang, which is publicly available at the website [25]. NSGA-II algorithm used in this paper was adapted from the source code of NSGA-II, which is created by Kalyanmoy Deb and is freely available at [26].

In order to perform a meaningful study, we set the parameters in MOEA/D-ACO and NSGA-II as similar as possible. The parameter settings in this paper for MOEA/D-ACO are shown in Table 2 while those for NSGA-II are given in Table 3. Two algorithms were run 10 times for each instance and we take the average values.

Table 2. Parameter settings of MOEA/D-ACO

Parameter	Setting
Number of Ants	24
Number of generations	3000
Number of Groups	3
Size of Neighbors	10
Alpha	1
Beta	2
Pheromone trail evaporation	0.98

Table 3. Parameter settings of NSGA-II

Parameter	Setting
Population Size	72 individuals
Generations	1000
Selection Operator	Elitist selection
Crossover Operator	Simulated binary crossover, P_c=0.9
Mutation Operator	Polynomial mutation, P_m=1.0/L

L is the individual length (=number of employees × number of tasks).

4.2 Experimental Results

4.2.1 Parameters tuning of MOEA/D-ACO for SPSP

Since ACO algorithms are sensitive to the setting of parameters, we carried out a series of experiments to find the proper values of parameters α, β, ρ. Also the ant number N is a special parameter of ACO, we need different numbers of ants in various problems. We set α=1 and empirically define the values of β, ρ and N.

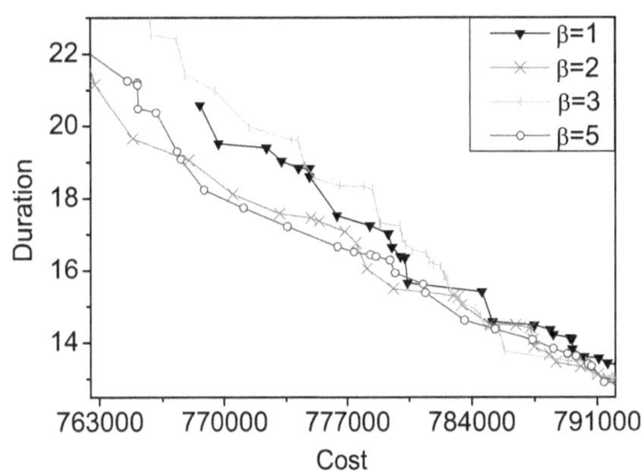

Figure 3. Results using different values of β

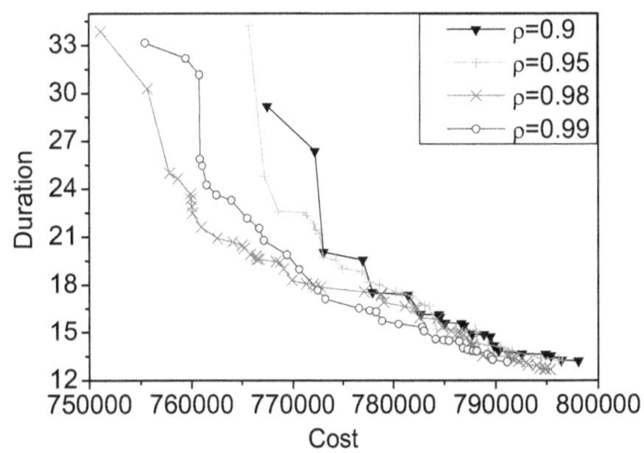

Figure 4. Results using different values of ρ

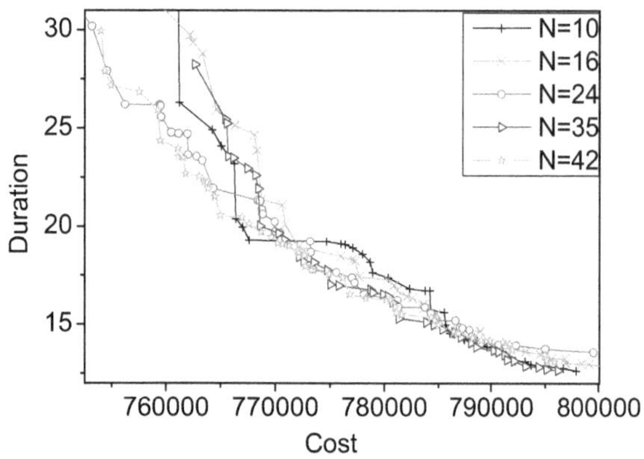

Figure 5. Results using different values of N

We used the 5e_10t_p5 instance with Unit=1/7 to tune the parameters while the heuristics strategy adopted is H1. In order to guarantee the independence of experiments, we performed all the tests by varying one variable and fixing others. The initial setting of parameters are ρ=0.95, N=24.

The results shown in Figure 3 indicate that results obtained with β=2 and β=5 are better. Here, we set β=2 in later experiments.

Figure 4 illustrates the results obtained with different values of ρ. The figure reveals that the results in MOEA/D-ACO are especially sensitive to the value of ρ and we can get the best results while ρ=0.98.

In Figure 5, there are results generated by changing the number of ants. It demonstrates that the results obtained with parameters N=24 and N=42 are better. In order to obtain good results with shorter time, we set N=24.

According to the analysis above, we adopted α=1, β=2, ρ=0.98 and N=24 for our experiments.

4.2.2 Comparing the MOEA/D-ACO with NSGA-II

A total of 36 publicly instances were used to make a comparison of performance between the MOEA/D-ACO and NSGA-II. We performed experiments of MOEA/D-ACO by using both heuristics strategies H1 and H2, which are the two common used methods of decomposition called Weighted Sum Approach and Tchebycheff Approach. In our experiments, we found that MOEA/D-ACO using heuristics H1 is better adopted with Weighted Sum Approach (denoted as MOEA/D-ACO_H1), and MOEA/D-ACO using heuristics H2 is better adopted with Tchebycheff (denoted as MOEA/D-ACO_H2).

We first analyze the obtained Pareto Front (PF) of our experiments. Take consideration of clarity and the space constraints, we selected the representative results to show the features of the algorithms. The Reference Pareto Front (RPF) is the best solutions obtained in all experiments.

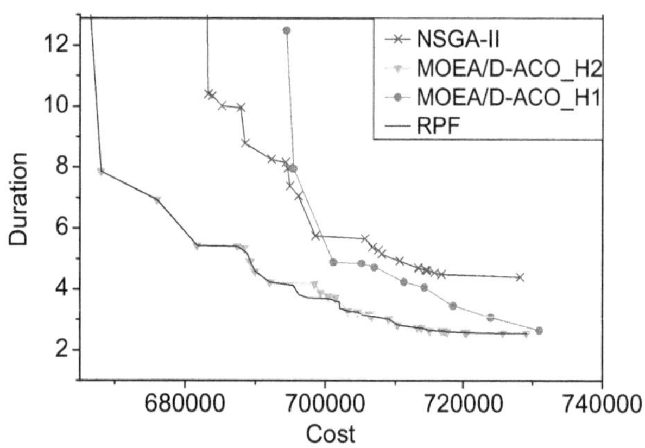

Figure 6. PF of the algorithms for instance 15e_10t_g10

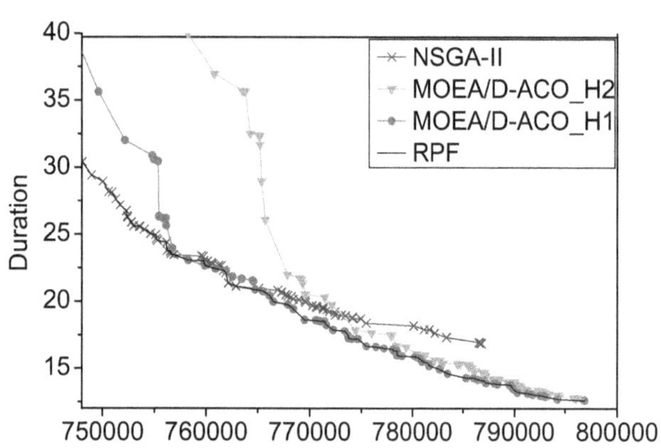

Figure 7. PF of the algorithms for instance 5e_10t_p5

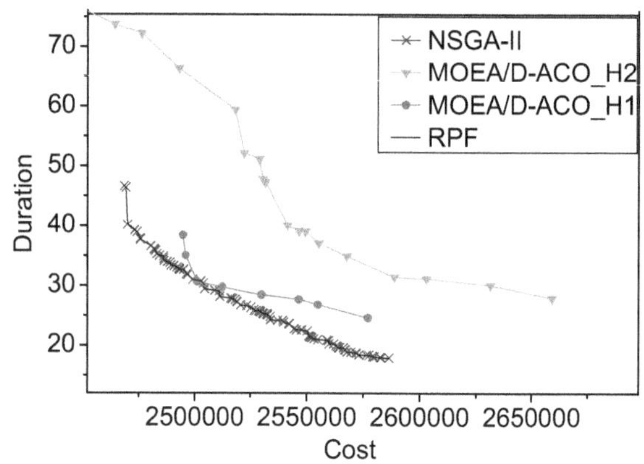

Figure 8. PF of the algorithms for instance 10e_20t_p7

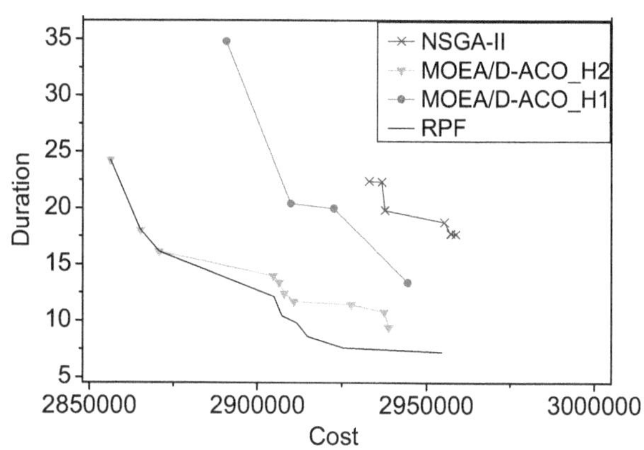

Figure 9. PF of the algorithms for instance 15e_30t_g10

In Figure 6, we can observe that the solutions of MOEA/D-ACO-H2 are better than those of NSGA-II for 15e_10t_10g. And MOEA/D-ACO outperforms NSGA-II for other instances: 10e_30t_g5, 10e_10t_g10 and 15e_20t_g10.

The results shown in Figure 7 indicate that MOEA/D-ACO can obtain solutions that have smaller duration for the instance of 5e_10t_p5. We also find the same result for instances 10e_10t_p5, 10e_20t_p5, 15e_10t_p5, 15e_30t_p5, 10e_10t_p7, 15e_10t_p7, 15e_30t_p7, 10e_10t_g5, 15e_10t_g5, 15e_20t_g5, 15e_30t_g5 and 5e_10t_g10.

However, it also shows that NSGA_II outperforms the current setting of MOEA/D-ACO for instance 10e_20t_p7 as shown in the Figure 8. And we find the same result for the following 11 instances: 5e_20t_p5, 10e_30t_p5, 15e_20t_p5, 5e_10t_p7, 5e_20t_p7, 10e_30t_p7, 5e_10t_g5, 5e_20t_g5, 5e_30t_5 and 10e_20t_g5.

We also observe that both MOEA/D-ACO and NSGA-II can find several solutions when the problem is complex, but the solutions that MOEA/D-ACO obtained are better than those by NSGA-II for instance 15e_30t_g10 as shown in Figure 9. It is the same case for instances of 5e_20t_g10, 10e_20t_g10, 10e_30t_g10 and 5e_30t_p5.

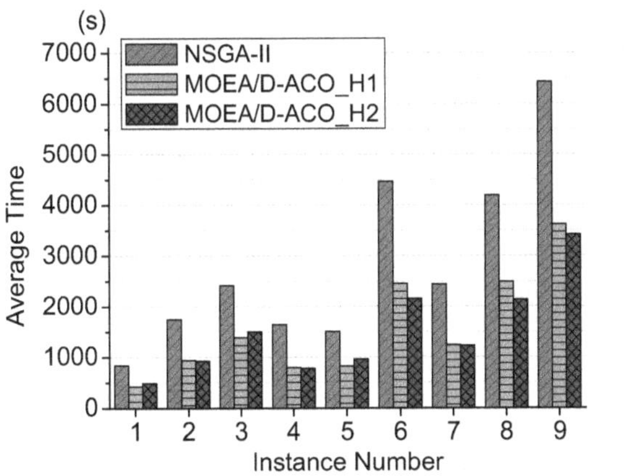

Figure 10. Average running time of the algorithms for G1

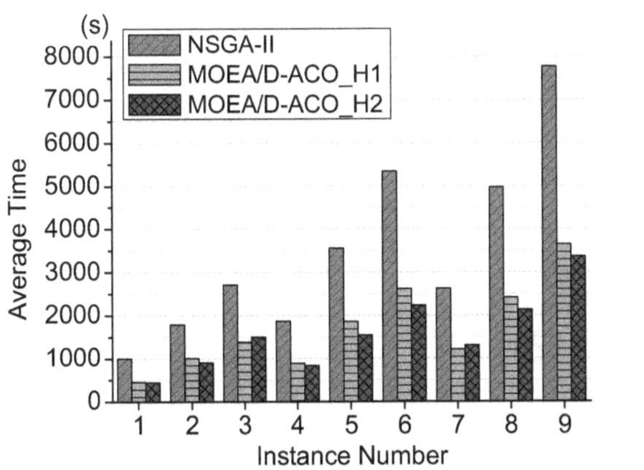

Figure 11. Average running time of the algorithms for G2

It is found that MOEA/D-ACO can't find solutions for the instance 5e_30t_g10 and 5e_30t_p7 during our 10 runs while the NSGA-II can obtain a small number of solutions.

We also make a comparison of running time of the algorithms. From Figure 10 to Figure 13, we demonstrate that MOEA/D-ACO consumes much less time for all instances than NSGA-II. The time is average value obtained from 10 runs.

5. CONCLUSIONS

This paper proposes a new approach to solve the Software Project Scheduling problems (SPSP) using a Multi-objective Ant Colony Optimization (MOACO) Algorithm called MOEA/D-ACO. The representative design we presented, such as the construction graph, the methods of decomposition and the two heuristics strategies, can provide a good reference for applying other MOACO algorithms to SPSP.

We present the process of parameters tuning for the MOEA/D-ACO algorithm for SPSP to get a better setting. Then, the test results of MOEA/D-ACO algorithm for a total of 36 publicly instances are given and compared with those results using NSGA-II in two ways.

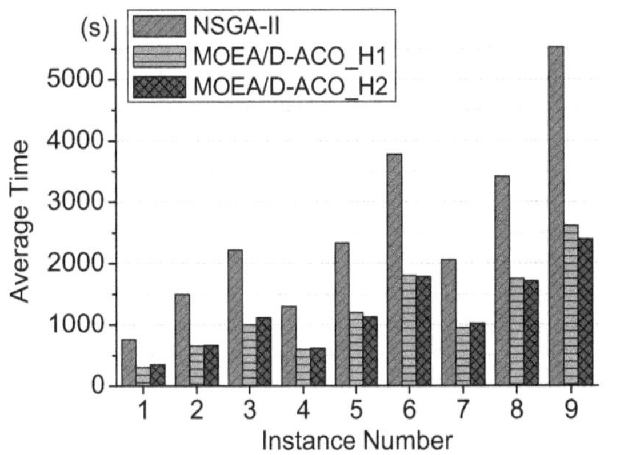

Figure 12. Average running time of the algorithms for G3

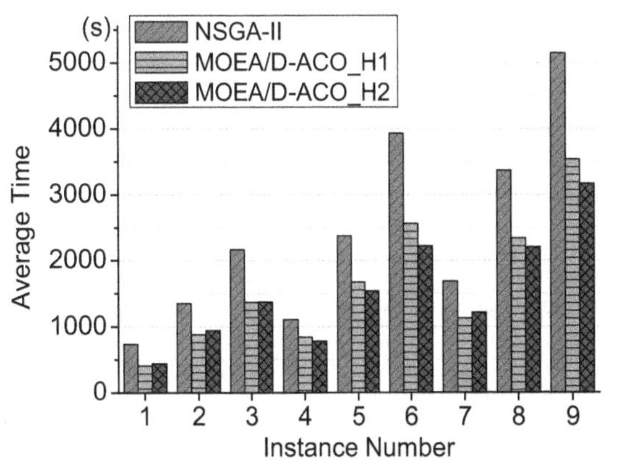

Figure 13. Average running time of the algorithms for G4

First, an analysis of obtained Pareto Front of the algorithms indicates that for the current setting of MOEA/D-ACO, NSGA-II is better at solving more complex and larger instances. MOEA/D-ACO can outperform NSGA-II in several instances and obtain solutions with less project duration. Software project managers could choose the appropriate algorithm according to the real world requirement of emphasis on duration or cost.

Second, the comparison of running time of the algorithms shows that MOEA/D-ACO can solve the SPSP with much shorter time than NSGA-II for all instances.

Since an ACO algorithm depends a lot on the heuristic information it uses, therefore, applying better heuristic strategies in our algorithm or employing other MOACO algorithms may solve the SPSP more successfully, which deserves further research. In addition, the hybrid algorithms that combine MOACO and GA may also be one of our future works.

6. ACKNOWLEDGMENTS

This work was partially supported by the National Natural Science Foundation of China (NSFC) projects No. 61202296 and 71102146, the National High-Technology Research and Development Program ("863" program) of China under Grant No. 2013AA01A212, the Natural Science Foundation of Guangdong Province project No. S2012030006242 and the Key Areas of Guangdong-HongKong Breakthrough project No. 2012A090200008. The authors thank the anonymous reviewers for their helpful advices to improve this paper.

7. REFERENCES

[1] E.Alba, and JF.Chicano. Software project management with GAs. *Information Sciences*,177(11),2380-401,2007.

[2] J.Xiao, X.T.Ao, and Y.Tang.Solving software project scheduling problems with ant colony optimization.*Computer and Operation Research*,40(1),3346,2013.

[3] M.Dorigo,V.Maniezzo ,and A.Colorni. AntSystem: Optimization by colony of cooperating agents. *Systems, Man, and Cybernetics, Part B: Cybernetics, IEEE Transactions on*, 26(1), 29-41,1996.

[4] D. Merkle, M. Middendorf and H. Schmeck. Ant colony optimization for resource-constrained project scheduling. *IEEE Transactions on Evolutionary Computation*,6(4),333-346,2002.

[5] T. Stützle. An ant approach to the flow shop problem. *Proceedings of the 6th European Congress on Intelligence Techniques & Soft Computing*, 3: 1560-1564, 1998.

[6] B. Yagmahan, M. M. Yenisey. Ant colony optimization for multi-objective flow shop scheduling problem. *Computers & Industrial Engineering*, 54((3): 411-420, 2008.

[7] L. N. Xing, Y. W. Chen, P. Wang et al. A knowledge-based ant colony optimization for flexible job shop scheduling problems. *Applied Soft Computing*, 10(3): 888-896, 2010.

[8] J.F.Chicano,F.Luna,A.j.Nebro,and E,Alba. Using multi-objective metaheuristics to solve the software project scheduling problem. *Proceedings of the 13th annual conference on Genetic and evolutionary computation.* GECCO'11,1915-1922,2011.

[9] F.Luna, L.Gonzalez-Alvarez, F.Chicano, and A.Vega-Rodriguez. The software project scheduling problem: A scalability analysis of multi-objective metaheuristics. *Applied Soft Computing* ,136-148,2014.

[10] B.Crawford, R.Soto,F.Johnson,E.Monfroy,and F.Paredes. A Max-Min Ant System algorithm to solve the Software Project Scheduling Problem. *Expert Systems with Applications*,41,6634-6645,2014.

[11] M.Dorigo and T.Stützle. Ant colony optimization:Overview and recent advances. *In Handbook of metaheuristics.* Springer US.page 227-263,2010.

[12] D.Angus and C.Woodward. Multiple objective ant colony optimization. *Swarm Intelligence*,3(1),69-85,2009.

[13] T.Stützle, M.lópez-Ibáñez,and M.Dorigo. A concise overview of applications of ant colony optimization.*Wiley Encyclopedia of Operations Research and Management Science*,896-911,2011.

[14] B.Barán and M.Schaerer. A multiobjective ant colony system for vehicle routing problem with time windows. *In Applied Informatics*,97-102,2003.

[15] K.F.Doerner, W.J.Gutjahr, R.F.Hartl, C.Strauss, and C.Stummer. Pareto ant colony optimization:A metaheuristc approach to multi-objective portfolio selection. *Annals of Operations, Research*,131(1-4),79-99,2004.

[16] K.F.Doerner, R.F.Hartl,and M.Reimann. Are CompetAnts more competent for problem solving? The case of a multiple objective transportation problem, *Central European Journal for Operations Research and Economics,*11(2),15-141,2003.

[17] S.Iredi, D.Merkle,and M.Middendorf. Bi-criterion optimization with multicolony ant algorithms. *Evolutionary Multi-Criterion Optimization,*359-372,2001.

[18] I.Alaya,C.Solnon, and K.Ghédira. Ant colony optimization for multiobjective optimization problems. *International Joumal on computer science*, 450-457,2010.

[19] M.López-Ibáñez,L.Paquete,and T.Stützle. On the design of ACO for the biobjective quadratic assignment problem. *Ant Colony Optimization Swarm Intelligence*,Springer Berlin Heidelberg,214-225,2004.

[20] M.López-Ibáñez,and T.Stützle.The impact of design choices of multi-objective ant colony optimization algorithms on performance: an experimental study on the biobjective TSP. *Proceedings of the 12th annual conference on Genetic and evolutionary computation*,GECCO'12,1-78,2010.

[21] M.López-Ibáñez,and T.Stützle. An experimental analysis of design choices of multi-objective ant colony optimization algorithms. *Swarm Intelligence*,6,207-232, 2012.

[22] Q. Zhang and H.Li. MOEA/D: A Multiobjective Evolutionary Algorithm based on Decomposition. *IEEE Transactions on Evolutionary Computation,*11(6),712-731,2007.

[23] L. Ke and Q. Zhang. MOEA/D-ACO:A Multiobjective Evolutionary Algorithm Using Decomposition and Ant Colony. *IEEE Transaction on Cybernetics*,2168-2267,2012.

[24] E.Alba and J.Francisico. 2005. Available from http://tracer.lcc.uma.es/problems/psp/generator.html .

[25] L. Ke and Q. Zhang. 2012. Available from http://cswww.essex.ac.uk/staff/zhang/ .

[26] Kanpur Genetic Algorithms Laboratory. Original Implementation (for windows and linux). Available from http://www.iitk.ac.in/kangal/codes.shtml.

Improved Sampling of Decision Space for Pareto Estimation

Yiming Yan
Department of Automatic Control and Systems Engineering
The University of Sheffield
Sheffield, UK, S1 3JD
yiming.yan@sheffield.ac.uk

Ioannis Giagkiozis
Department of Automatic Control and Systems Engineering
The University of Sheffield
Sheffield, UK, S1 3JD
i.giagkiozis@sheffield.ac.uk

Peter J. Fleming
Department of Automatic Control and Systems Engineering
The University of Sheffield
Sheffield, UK, S1 3JD
p.fleming@sheffield.ac.uk

ABSTRACT

Pareto Estimation (PE) is a novel method for increasing the density of Pareto optimal solutions across the entire Pareto Front or in a specific region of interest. PE identifies the inverse mapping of Pareto optimal solutions, namely, from objective space to decision space. This identification can be performed using a number of modeling techniques, however, for the sake of simplicity in this work we use a radial basis neural network. In any modeling method, the quality of the resulting model depends heavily on the *training* samples used. The original version of PE uses the resulting set of Pareto optimal solutions from any multi-objective optimization algorithm and then utilizes this set to identify the aforementioned mapping. However, we argue that this selection may not always be the best possible and propose an alternative scheme to improve the resulting set of Pareto optimal solutions in order to produce higher quality samples for the identification scheme in PE. The proposed approach is integrated with MAEA-gD, and the resulting solutions are used with PE. The results show that the proposed method shows promise, in that there is measurable improvement in the quality of the estimated PE in terms of the coverage and density.

Categories and Subject Descriptors

H.4 [**Information Systems Applications**]: Miscellaneous; D.2.8 [**Software Engineering**]: Metrics—*complexity measures, performance measures*

Keywords

Local search; Metaheuristics; Neural networks; Surrogate model/fitness approximation; Machine learning

GECCO '15, July 11 - 15, 2015, Madrid, Spain
© 2015 ACM. ISBN 978-1-4503-3472-3/15/07...$15.00
DOI: http://dx.doi.org/10.1145/2739480.2754713

1. INTRODUCTION

Real world problems often have multiple competing objectives that are to be optimized simultaneously, see [5, 3, 13, 27] to mention but a few. However, when multiple competing objectives are considered there no longer exists a single optimal solution. Rather, there exists a set of optimal solutions. This set is the minimal (maximal) set of the feasible objective vectors when all objectives are to be minimized (maximized). This introduces a subtle yet important difficulty, as in practice, only one solution can be selected at a given time. Therefore, a reduction of this optimal set is required. The process of reduction is context sensitive and most often requires the aid of a decision-maker (DM). Broadly speaking, there are 3 ways that the DM can be involved in the optimization process, i) *a-priori* preference articulation [23, p. 114], ii) interactive preference articulation (see for example [4, 24, 21]), and, iii) *a-posteriori* preference articulation [23, p. 77]. In *a-priori* preference articulation the DMs preferences are distilled into a utility function which can then be incorporated within the optimization process to reduce the multi-objective problem to a single objective problem [23, p. 115]. Interactive preference articulation methods involve the DM throughout the optimization process, and, *a-posteriori* preference articulation methods rely on the production of a *representative* optimal set from which the DM can select a single solution. For problems where there is a clear way to construct a utility function, *a-priori* methods are preferable as their computational requirements are lower than both alternatives. This is because only one problem is considered at a time, while in *a-posteriori* and interactive preference articulation methods a set of optimal points must be maintained [23, p. 115]. However, the creation of a utility function that accurately represents the DMs preferences is a challenging task. Interactive preference articulation methods can offer an alternative, which can be computationally more efficient than *a-posteriori* methods, since the optimization algorithm will have a progressively more restricted search space to explore. These methods however require a substantial time investment from the DM. Lastly, when there is no clear way for a utility function to be defined and the DM cannot be continuously involved with the optimization process, then *a-posteriori* preference articulation methods are preferable. For a more detailed exposition on methods and specific algorithms employed in decision-making the reader is referred to [25] and [23].

A-posteriori preference articulation can be summarized as follows:

Problem Formulation The analyst, using specifications described by the DM formulates an optimization model, which could be a mathematical programming formulation or a data-driven model, etc.

Solution Process Subsequently, based on the properties of the problem, the analyst identifies a suitable algorithm (e.g. gradient-based or evolutionary algorithms) to solve the optimization model.

Decision Making Based on the information provided from the algorithm, the DM can, i) make their decision if the solutions provided by the algorithm are desirable, ii) reformulate the model and repeat the process, or, iii) choose another algorithm and repeat the process.

One caveat with *a-posteriori* preference articulation methods is that computational resources impose a practical limit on the size of the *representative* optimal set that can be produced by the algorithm. This reveals an underlying meta-trade-off, namely, the size of the representative optimal set and the satisfiability of the DM, to wit, the larger the size of the representative set the more likely it is that a solution that will match the DMs preferences will be identified, albeit simultaneously the more expensive the optimization process becomes.

Pareto Estimation (PE) was introduced to alleviate some of these problems in the *a-posteriori* decision-making paradigm [6, 7]. In general, PE utilizes a set of candidate Pareto optimal solutions generated by an algorithm to identify the relationship between objective space and decision space. This can then be employed to generate more Pareto optimal solutions on the entire Pareto front or in specific regions, see for example in [6]. PE was shown to produce promising results on standard test problems with 2 and 3 objectives [6, 7]; particularly, a real world portfolio optimization example is also presented in [6] where the authors illustrate the ability of PE to increase the density of Pareto solutions within the regions of interest of a DM. Further development of PE includes [20, 19], where the authors extend PE to increase the density of multi-modal solutions of an MOP by using clustering analysis and employing PE for every cluster separately. Although in previous studies PE was used at the end of the optimization procedure, this is not a requirement, and, as we show in this work can in fact be beneficial to be incorporated in the algorithm. A recent work using similar ideas as PE employs Gaussian models to actively manage solutions during the optimization with promising results, opening a new dimension of application for Pareto estimation [1].

As is the case with all methods that are based on data-driven models, the performance of PE is contingent upon the quality of the Pareto set approximation produced by the optimization algorithm, for instance see [22]. In this work, we present an initial numerical study on the effect that the *quality* of samples has on the resulting PE model and its performance. In principle, for any interpolation method, Shannon's theorem (see [17] for a review) places a lower bound on the number of samples required for the complete determination of the function. However, the *placement* of these samples in the domain of the function is also very important, this placement is the object of study of optimal sampling [22].

The remainder of this work is organized as follows. In Section 2, we introduce a general formulation of multi-objective problems and the original Pareto estimation method. Section 3 presents a motivating example to better illustrate the basis for this work, i.e. generating better candidates of Pareto optimal solutions for PE by redistributing the solutions in the population. In Section 4 we demonstrate our methodology using MAEA-gD introduced in [10, 9]. Lastly, in Section 6, we conclude, summarize and reflect on future research directions based on this work.

2. BACKGROUND

2.1 Multi-Objective Optimization

Without loss of generality, a (continuous) multi-objective optimization problem can be defined as follows,

$$\begin{aligned} \min_{x} \quad & \mathbf{F}(\mathbf{x}) = (\, f_1(\mathbf{x}), f_2(\mathbf{x}), \ldots, f_k(\mathbf{x})\,) \\ \text{subject to} \quad & \mathbf{x} \in \mathbf{S} \subseteq \mathbb{R}^n, \end{aligned} \tag{1}$$

where $\mathbf{F}$ is a vector of scalar objective functions f_i with $i \in \{1, 2, \ldots, k\}$, k is the number of objectives, n is the number of decision variables, $\mathbf{x}$ is an n-dimensional vector of decision variables, $\mathbf{S}$ is the feasible region of $\mathbf{x}$ and $\mathbf{S}$ is an subset of the n-dimensional real space. For any $\mathbf{x} \in \mathbf{S}$, there exists a vector $\mathbf{z} = \mathbf{F}(\mathbf{x})$, which is an objective vector corresponding to the decision vector $\mathbf{x}$. The set of all possible objective vectors resulting from decision vectors in the feasible region are denoted as $\mathbf{Z}$, namely $\mathbf{Z} = \{\mathbf{z} \in \mathbb{R}^k \,|\, \mathbf{z} = \mathbf{F}(\mathbf{x}), \quad \forall \mathbf{x} \in \mathbf{S}\}$. A decision vector $\mathbf{x}^* \in \mathbf{S}$ is said to Pareto-dominate a decision vector $\mathbf{x}$, if and only if $f_i(\mathbf{x}^*) \leq f_i(\mathbf{x})$ for all $i \in \{1, \ldots, k\}$ and $f_i(\mathbf{x}^*) < f_i(\mathbf{x})$ for at least one i. A decision vector $\mathbf{x}^* \in \mathbf{S}$ is said to be Pareto optimal if it is not dominated by any other decision vectors in $\mathbf{S}$. For an objective vector $\tilde{\mathbf{z}} = (\tilde{f}_1, \ldots, \tilde{f}_k) \in \mathbf{Z}$, if there is no other objective vector $\mathbf{z} = (f_1, \ldots, f_k) \neq \mathbf{z}$, such that $f_i \leq \tilde{f}_i$ for all $i \in \{1, \ldots, k\}$ and $f_i < \tilde{f}_i$ for at least one i, we also say this objective vector $\tilde{\mathbf{z}}$ is non-dominated. The set of all non-dominated objective vectors in $\mathbf{Z}$, denoted as $\mathcal{P}$, is called the Pareto Front (PF). The decision vectors corresponding to $\mathcal{P}$ is denoted as $\mathcal{D}$. Optimization algorithms in the *a-posteriori* decision-making paradigm strive to obtain an approximation of the PF. In the remainder of this work we also denote the PF approximation as $\mathcal{P}$.

2.2 Pareto Estimation

In general, PE attempts to identify a relationship from the objective space to the decision space (inverse mapping) and then utilize this relationship to produce more Pareto solutions on the entire PF or in a specific region of the PF. To identify this relationship, the set of Pareto optimal objective vectors, $\mathcal{P}$, is first transformed into a projected set, $\tilde{\mathcal{P}}$. One element in $\mathcal{P}$ is mapped exactly to one element in $\tilde{\mathcal{P}}$, namely this transformation can be described as a function

$$\Pi^{-1} : \mathcal{P} \mapsto \tilde{\mathcal{P}}.$$

In the identification of the inverse mapping points in the projected space, $\tilde{\mathcal{P}}$, are used in lieu of $\mathcal{P}$, and, the motivation for this is to simplify the use of the resulting inverse mapping [7]. Elements in $\tilde{\mathcal{P}}$ are easily obtained and manipulated and therefore new samples are obtained in this space rather than the actual PF, whose topology is mostly unknown. One potential projection is to first normalize the objective vectors in $\mathcal{P}$ by

$$\tilde{z}_i = \frac{z_i - z_i^\star}{z_i^{nd} - z_i^\star}, \quad (2)$$

where $\mathbf{z}^\star$ is the ideal objective vector and $\mathbf{z}^{nd}$ is the nadir objective vector [23, pp. 15-16], which can be estimated from $\mathcal{P}$, and then project $\tilde{\mathbf{z}}_i$ onto the $(k-1)$-simplex, to produce the $\tilde{\mathcal{P}}$. The $(k-1)$-simplex is defined by $\{\mathbf{e}_1, \ldots, \mathbf{e}_{k-1}\}$, where $\mathbf{e}_i$ is a vector with a one in the ith position and zeros in the rest. Following the projection, the relationship from $\tilde{\mathcal{P}}$ to the decision vectors $\mathcal{D}$ is identified, namely,

$$\tilde{F}_{\mathcal{P}} : \tilde{\mathcal{P}} \mapsto \mathcal{D}. \quad (3)$$

It is clear that a composite of Π^{-1} and $\tilde{F}_{\mathcal{P}}$ provides the relationship from the objectives to the decision variables,

$$\tilde{F}_{\mathcal{P}}(\Pi^{-1}(\mathcal{P})) = \mathcal{D}.$$

This procedure is illustrated in *Fig. (1)*. Since it is very

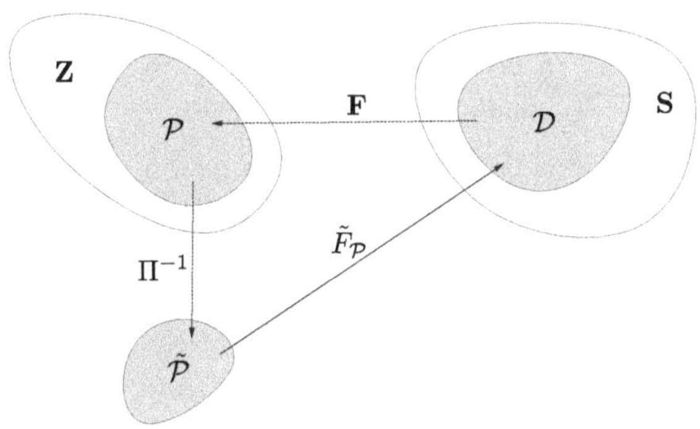

Figure 1: Pareto Estimation Method [7]

difficult, if not impossible, to mathematically derive the relationship $\tilde{F}_{\mathcal{P}}$, some meta-modeling method is used to identify this relationship approximately. Considering computational efficiency, the Radial Basis Function Neural Network (RBFNN) can be employed and the performance is promising [7]. A promising alternative to RBFNNs appear to be Gaussian processes, see for example [1].

With a set of evenly spaced samples, $\mathcal{E}$ as an input, $\tilde{F}_{\mathcal{P}}$ is able to generate a set of decision variables $\mathcal{D}_{\mathcal{E}} = \tilde{F}_{\mathcal{P}}(\mathcal{E})$ and this set of decision variables can then be used to generate the corresponding Pareto optimal objective vectors. If $\mathcal{E}$ is sampled in the entire projected objective space $\tilde{\mathcal{P}}$, PE will generate more solutions on the entire PF. Alternatively, if $\mathcal{E}$ is sampled in a specific region, then PE will be able to provide more solutions in a specific region of the PF.

For a given projection Π^{-1} and a meta-modeling method (e.g. RBFNN) for identifying the mapping $\tilde{F}_{\mathcal{P}}$, the quality of the identified relationship $\tilde{F}_{\mathcal{P}}$ from PE is mainly affected by the training data, i.e. the approximation of Pareto optimal solutions generated from the algorithm that is employed to solve a given MOP. Therefore the question we seek to answer is the following: How to manipulate the placement of the population during the optimization, so as to produce better data samples for PE, and therefore improve the quality of the resulting PE model and its performance, whilst ensuring that the convergence rate of the algorithm is not reduced. In the following section, we reflect on these questions and explore methods to address this problem.

3. MOTIVATING EXAMPLE

Consider the process of identifying $\tilde{F}_{\mathcal{P}}$ as the process of interpolating a function, whose domain is $\mathcal{D}$, using the candidate Pareto optimal solutions as samples. It was argued in the introduction that for a fixed number of samples their position can be an important in the quality of the resulting interpolations of the same function. To better understand the importance of sampling, let us consider the following example in *Fig. (2)*. In the example shown in *Fig. (2)*, we

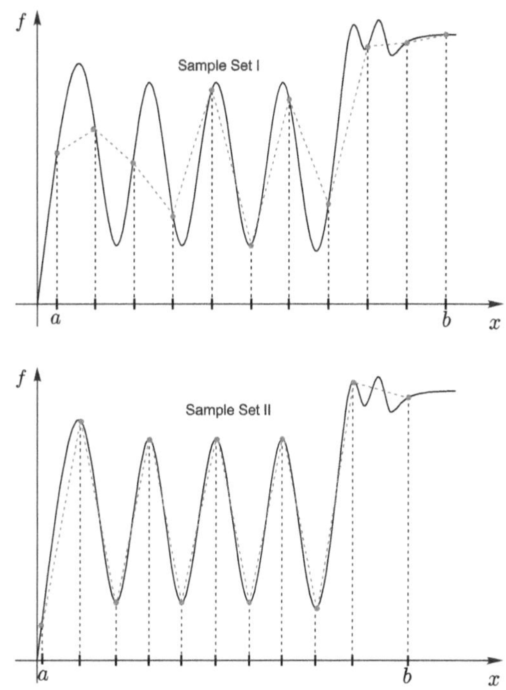

Figure 2: Piecewise linear interpolation (red dashed lines) of a function, $f(x)$, using two different sample sets (red dots).

assume that a piecewise linear interpolation function is used to obtain an approximation of the function f (black solid line). We compare the interpolations from two sample sets, Sample Set I and Sample Set II. Both sets contain 11 samples but the positions of the samples are different. It is clear that Sample Set II better approximates the function $f(x)$ when compared with Sample Set I. Samples from Sample Set I are evenly spaced, but due to the location of the samples, in particular the first four points from the left-hand side, the variation of the function is not sufficiently captured. Sample Set II is obtained by a left shift of the position of all samples within (a, b) in Sample Set I and a few other sample relocations. By doing this, Sample Set II produces a model that is more representative of the underlying function $f(x)$.

The above example illustrates that the topology of a function can be better interpolated if the high variation (and high amplitude) regions of the function are well sampled. The variation of a function can be measured by its *frequency* and *amplitude*. By amplitude of a function, we mean the distance from the 'top of a crest' or the 'bottom of a trough' to a baseline (or base hyperplane in a space of more than two dimensions); in the above example, we can consider a line that horizontally passes thorough the 'center' of the function as the base line which can be estimated by the mean of the samples. We consider the regions with high frequency and amplitude as the *high variation regions*. Therefore, if we can identify the high variation regions of a function and allocate more samples there, we can produce better interpolation of a function.

Using the same line of reasoning we expect that if we distribute samples so as to capture most of the variations in decision space, we should be able to obtain a better approximation of the mapping $\tilde{F}_{\mathcal{P}}$, defined in (3) and therefore produce a better estimate of the PF using PE. Specifically, we break down our method into three parts.

1. Manipulate the current population to identify a model that maps from the objective space to the decision space. This process is identical to the PE method, and can be considered as building a *local approximate* of the mapping $\tilde{F}_{\mathcal{P}}$ using currently available information. This model is regarded as a local approximate because the current population may not be close enough to the actual PF and therefore can only provide partial information of the actual mapping. Quality of the local approximate improves, as the algorithm approaches the PF.
2. Utilize the local approximate of $\tilde{F}_{\mathcal{P}}$ to identify the areas in the decision space that are more 'important' for obtaining better topology of the Pareto optimal solution set in the decision space. Since $\tilde{F}_{\mathcal{P}}$ maps $\tilde{\mathcal{P}}$ to $\mathcal{D}$, the domain of the function is the projected space $\tilde{\mathcal{P}}$. This implies that we have to identify the areas of $\tilde{F}_{\mathcal{P}}$ that present more geometrical changes in the decision space and then find the corresponding regions in the projected objective space $\tilde{\mathcal{P}}$. This can be achieved by as follows: first we evenly sample the projected space, then use these samples and the local estimate of $\tilde{F}_{\mathcal{P}}$ to generate new decision vectors, and finally identify the regions according to certain measure of the geometrical changes (frequency and amplitude) of $\tilde{F}_{\mathcal{P}}$. In this work, we simply use the density of decision vectors as the measure. Alternative methods will be explored in future research.
3. Reallocate the position of the samples in the projected objective space, with more samples presenting in the areas identified above and generate the corresponding weighting vectors to the new samples using generalized decomposition (see Section 4.1).

To have consistently more samples in the identified areas in successive generations, the change of samples' locations in $\tilde{\mathcal{P}}$ need to be *transformed* to affect the search of the algorithm. For decomposition-based algorithm, for instance, we could transform these changes to alter the direction of corresponding weighting vectors; see next section for an algorithm that incorporate the above idea into a decomposition based algorithm.

4. MAEA-GD/RD

Decomposition-based multi-objective optimization methods have steadily increased in popularity in the last decade, see for example [15, 12, 26]. These methods transform (1) into a set of single-objective subproblems with the help of a scalarizing function and a set of weighting vectors. These subproblems are subsequently solved simultaneously to produce an approximation of the Pareto optimal set.

4.1 Generalized Decomposition

Given a measure for the quality of distribution of points on the Pareto front and a scalarizing function, generalized decomposition (gD) can be used to create a set of weighting vectors that will result in sub-problems that produce a set of solutions that are optimally distributed according to the given measure [10]. The optimality of the resulting distribution is contingent on the convergence of the sub-problems and knowledge of the Pareto front geometry *a-priori* to the solution of the problem. Nevertheless, it has been shown that when the PF geometry is unknown *a-priori*, which is most often the case, assuming an affine PF geometry still produces results that are several orders of magnitude better, in the selected measure, than commonly used alternative methods [9].

Generalized decomposition obtains weighting vectors by solving the following program:

$$\begin{aligned} &\min_{\mathbf{w}} G(\mathbf{w}, \mathbf{F}(\mathbf{x})), \\ &\text{subject to } \sum_{i=1}^{k} w_i = 1, \\ &\text{and } w_i \geq 0, \forall\, i \in \{1, \ldots, k\}. \end{aligned} \tag{4}$$

The assumption in (4) is that $G(\mathbf{w}, \mathbf{F}(\mathbf{x}))$ is a convex function with respect to the weighting vectors. This is the case for all ℓ_p-norm based scalarizing functions which are most commonly employed in decomposition-based optimization algorithms (see for example [16, 14, 18, 26]), a family that also includes the widely used Chebyshev decomposition as a limiting case [9].

4.2 MAEA-gD

MAEA-gD is a many objective optimization evolutionary algorithm based on generalized decomposition introduced in [10]. MAEA-gD is similar to MOEA/D [26], however, there are two significant differences, i) the neighborhood is based on distance in objective space and not weighting vector space, and, ii) generalized decomposition is used to generate the weighting vectors, see [10]. The main concepts in the algorithm are summarized as follows.

Step 1 Initialization

1. Generate N evenly distributed points on the $(k-1)$-simplex, where N is the size of population. We refer to this set as reference PF.
2. Utilize generalized decomposition, (4) to generate the set of weighting vectors, $\{\mathbf{w}_1, \ldots, \mathbf{w}_N\}$, using the reference PF.
3. For each point in the reference PF, find the T closest weighting vectors. Set $\mathcal{A}(i) = \{i_1, \ldots, i_T\}$, where $\mathbf{w}_{i_1}, \ldots, \mathbf{w}_{i_T}$ are T closest neighbors of $\mathbf{w}_i$.
4. Generate an initial population of size N, either randomly or by a problem-specific method.

Step 2 Update

For $i = 1, \ldots, N$, **do**

1. Randomly select two indices from the neighborhood $\mathcal{A}(i)$ and generate a new population $\mathbf{x}_i^{\text{new}}$ using genetic operators.
2. Evaluate $\mathbf{z}_i^{\text{new}} = \mathbf{F}(\mathbf{x}_i^{\text{new}})$.
3. Update population in the neighborhood $\mathcal{A}(i)$.

Step 3 Stopping Criteria
Terminate the algorithm if the stopping criteria are satisfied. Otherwise go to **Step 2**. Here we use number of iterations as the stopping criterion.

Step 4 Output the non-dominated solutions.

4.3 MAEA-gD with Sample Redistribution

By sample redistribution, we mean the reallocation of samples in the current population in objective space, so that more samples are present in regions where higher quality topological information is more likely to be obtained and used to improve the identification of $\tilde{F}_{\mathcal{P}}$. To achieve this, in the context of a decomposition based algorithm, we choose to alter the direction of the weighting vectors, which will guide the algorithm to generate samples in the desirable regions. This change however means that this re-sampling procedure cannot be performed on every iteration as this has the potential risk of stalling the algorithm convergence rate [8]. To minimize the impact to algorithm convergence, the sample redistribution is performed every $K = 10$ iterations. Furthermore, this *delay* also allows the algorithm to adapt the current solutions towards the new target solutions.

For every K iterations of MAEA-gD, the non-dominated decision and objective vector sets, $\mathcal{D}$ and $\mathcal{P}$, respectively, are used by the following redistribution algorithm.

Step 1: First, using (2), we normalize $\mathcal{P}$. Subsequently, the normalized $\mathcal{P}$ is projected onto the $(k-1)$-simplex. This results in $\tilde{\mathcal{P}} = \Pi^{-1}(\mathcal{P})$, as described in *Sec. 2.2*. In contrast with [7], in this work Π^{-1} is a radial projection. Namely, all elements in $\tilde{\mathbf{z}} = \mathbf{z}/\|\mathbf{z}\|_1$, where $\|\cdot\|_1$ is the ℓ_1-norm. With this projection the edge effects observed in [7] are removed and all points on the PF can be reached.

Step 2: $\tilde{\mathcal{P}}$ and $\mathcal{D}$ are used as the input and output, respectively, in the training of a RBFNN.

Step 3: Generate N evenly spaced vectors $\mathcal{E} = \{\bar{\mathbf{e}}_i\}, \forall i = 1, \ldots, N$, within the $(k-1)$-simplex, as described in [7]. Here N is the population size.

Step 4: Use $\mathcal{E}$ as the input to the RBFNN trained in **Step 2** to obtain estimates of decision vectors, $\mathcal{D}_{\mathcal{E}} = \{\bar{\mathbf{x}}_i\}, \forall i = 1, \ldots, N$.

Step 5: Compute the average distance from one vector to all others in $\mathcal{D}_{\mathcal{E}}$, namely $\forall i = 1, \ldots, N$, compute $d_i = \sum_{t=1, t\neq i}^{N} \|\bar{\mathbf{x}}_i - \bar{\mathbf{x}}_t\|_2/N$, where $\|\cdot\|_2$ is the ℓ_2-norm. Denote the index set $\mathcal{B} = \{b_j\}, \forall j = 1, \ldots, T$, where $d_{b_1}, \ldots, d_{b_T}$ are the T smallest average distances.

Step 6: Utilize the generalized decomposition method [10] to transform $\mathcal{E}$ to weighting vectors $\bar{\mathbf{W}} = \{\bar{\mathbf{w}}_i\}, \forall i = 1, \ldots, N$. Set $M = \sum_{j=1}^{T} d_{b_j}$ and assume the current set of weighting vectors for MAEA-gD is $\mathbf{W}$. In the following, we update the weighting vectors.

For $j = 1, \ldots, T$, **do**

6.1 Compute $s_j = (M - d_{b_j})/\sum_{t=1}^{T}(M - d_{b_t})$. Here, s_j, is a measure of the relative variation, i.e. the higher the value of s_j, the more variation in the neighborhood of $\bar{\mathbf{x}}_{b_j}$.

6.2 Calculate $n_j = \lfloor N \cdot s_j \rfloor$, where $\lfloor a \rfloor$ means the largest integer not greater than a. Note that $\sum_{t=1}^{T} n_t \leq N$.

6.3 Assume $\tilde{\mathbf{z}}_p, \forall p = 1, \ldots, n_j$, are the n_j closest vectors, in $\tilde{\mathcal{P}}$, of $\bar{\mathbf{e}}_{b_j}$, $\mathbf{w}_p \in \mathbf{W}$ is the weighting vector corresponding to $\tilde{\mathbf{z}}_p$, and $\bar{\mathbf{w}}_{b_j} \in \bar{\mathbf{W}}$ to $\bar{\mathbf{e}}_{b_j}$ Update weighting vectors for MAEA-gD by setting $\mathbf{w}_p = (1-\alpha)\mathbf{w}_p + \alpha\bar{\mathbf{w}}_{b_j}$, where α is in $(0, 1)$. Here we choose $\alpha = 0.05$. A small α value avoids large changes in the weighting vectors, and, therefore large changes in the sub-problems. This is aimed to counter the effect that varying weighting vectors have on algorithm convergence [8].

We refer to the algorithm MAEA-gD with sample redistribution as MAEA-gD/RD.

5. NUMERICAL EXPERIMENTS

In this section, we perform numerical tests to investigate the potential merit of the proposed methodology. by comparing the quality of the Pareto optimal solutions from PE based on the estimate of optimal decision vectors and objective vectors generated by algorithms MAEA-gD and MAEA-gD/RD respectively. Every algorithm is run 50 times, using a different seed in the random number generator on every run. The size of the population for both MAEA-gD and MAEA-gD/RD is 465 and both algorithms have 400 iterations. For each algorithm on every run, the approximation of the Pareto optimal set is obtained and subsequently PE is used to generate an estimated PF. For the estimation we employ the Pareto Estimation Toolbox from [6] and 3240 estimated Pareto optimal solutions are generated. For the test problems, we choose WFG6-9 [11] with 3 objectives and 24 variables, and DTLZ1-2 [2] with 3 objectives and 10 variables. To compare the quality of the estimated solutions obtained using PE from MAEA-gD and MAEA-gd/RD, we employ the following three measures.

- Inverted Generational Distance (IGD). IGD measures the distance from elements of one set to the actual PF of the test problem. In this test, we employ the the ratio of two IGD values, $D_R(\bar{P}_E, \hat{P}_E)$, defined as the ratio of the distance from $\bar{P}_E$ to the actual PF over that from the $\hat{P}_E$ to the actual PF, where $\bar{P}_E$ is the Pareto estimate generated by PE based on the solutions from MAEA-gD, and $\hat{P}_E$ from MAEA-gD/RD.
- Mean Distance to Nearest Neighbor. This metric measures the density of the solutions on a PF. Also, we employ the ratio $S_R(\bar{P}_E, \hat{P}_E)$ in our test, which is the ratio of the mean distance to the nearest neighbor in $\bar{P}_E$ divided by that in $\hat{P}_E$.
- Coverage Metric (C-Metric). C-metric (ranging from 0 to 1 inclusive) measures the ratio of non-dominated points between two sets of Pareto solutions, namely higher value of $C(\bar{P}_E, \hat{P}_E)$ indicates that $\bar{P}_E$ have more dominating points; higher value of $C(\hat{P}_E, \bar{P}_E)$ indicates the opposite. It is worth mentioning that $C(\bar{P}_E, \hat{P}_E)$ does not have to equal 1- $C(\hat{P}_E, \bar{P}_E)$ and so both values are presented in the test.

For details and mathematical formulation of the three measures, please refer to [7, Section V].

In Table 1 we summarize the ratios of the IGD values $D_R(\bar{P}_E, \hat{P}_E)$ and the mean distance to the nearest neighbor $S_R(\bar{P}_E, \hat{P}_E)$ for the selected 3-objective problems. Values for $D_R(\bar{P}_E, \hat{P}_E) > 1$ indicate that $\bar{P}_E$ produces a better IGD value than $\hat{P}_E$, namely $\bar{P}_E$ is closer to the actual PF than $\hat{P}_E$. From the results of $D_R(\bar{P}_E, \hat{P}_E)$ in Table 1, we can see that, for all 6 test problems, the values of $D_R(\bar{P}_E, \hat{P}_E)$ are close to or greater than one. This implies that, the the quality of the estimated PF, $\hat{P}_E$, from the optimal solutions of

MAEA-gD/RD, is at least as good as $\bar{P}_E$ from MAEA-gD, in terms of coverage and the distance to the actual PF. Regarding $S_R(\bar{P}_E, \hat{P}_E)$, the value of $S_R(\bar{P}_E, \hat{P}_E) > 1$ means that the average distance of the neighboring solutions is smaller in $\hat{P}_E$ compared to $\bar{P}_E$. Since the new fronts from $D_R(\bar{P}_E, \hat{P}_E)$ have similar coverage, a smaller average distance to the nearest neighbor in $\hat{P}_E$ indicates more evenly distributed solutions on the estimated PF. It can be seen by the results in Table 1, that MAEA-gD/RD has superior performance in comparison to PE applied on MAEA-gD, in 4 out of 6 problems, with only marginally inferior results on WFG6 and DTLZ2.

In Table 2, we present the values of C-Metric, $C(\bar{P}_E, \hat{P}_E)$ and $C(\hat{P}_E, \bar{P}_E)$, for the selected test problems. $C(\hat{P}_E, \bar{P}_E) > C(\bar{P}_E, \hat{P}_E)$ indicates that larger proportion of solutions in $\hat{P}_E$ dominates the solutions in $\bar{P}_E$; for $C(\hat{P}_E, \bar{P}_E) < C(\bar{P}_E, \hat{P}_E)$, the converse is true. The results suggest that, except for WFG6, MAEA-gD/RD improves Pareto estimation when compared with the estimation that results by using MAEA-gD. The reason for this improvement, although a welcome byproduct, is still an open question which we plan on investigating further in future work. A potential explanation could be that when altering the location of samples, our method implicitly performs local search on a surrogate model of the inverse of the objective function. Therefore, the updating procedure we use may also be improving algorithm convergence as on every K iterations a redistribution takes place.

The plots in *Fig. (4)* show the normalized local density of the estimated PF from PE for problems WFG7 and DTLZ2. The density is estimated based on the average distance from each Pareto optimal solution to its five nearest neighbors on the PF and is regularized between $[0, 1]$, where 0 is the smallest relative distance and hence highest density (densest, marked with warm color), and 1 represents the sparest, marked with color of cooler tones. Higher density translates to a larger number of Pareto optimal solutions in a neighborhood. It can be observed that the density of Pareto optimal solutions on the estimated PF obtained from the MAEA-gD/RD is slightly more uniform across the estimated PF, as there are fewer color variations when compared with the results obtained using MAEA-gD. See for example the bright yellow areas on the edges for both test problems for MAEA-gD/RD fade and dissolve into their neighborhood compared with these ares for MAEA-gD. This indicates that the resulting estimated solutions on the PF obtained by MAEA-gD/RD are more evenly distributed.

In *Fig. (3)* the final distribution of solutions on the Pareto front is illustrated for MAEA-gD and MAEA-gD/RD. At

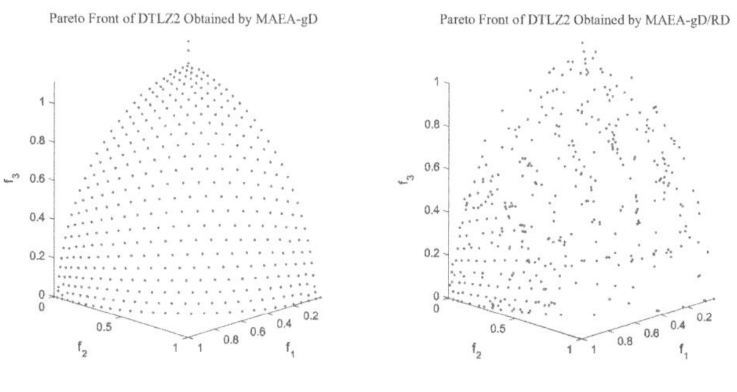

Figure 3: Pareto Front obtained from MAEA-gD and MAEA-gD/RD on DTLZ2

this point, it could be argued that the distribution of solutions from MAEA-gD/RD is *obviously* inferior. However, we argue that this is not in fact the case as better model for Pareto estimation has been identified using this distribution (for this problem) of solutions, which in turn can be used to create any desirable distribution in certain regions or across the PF. Furthermore, the distribution of the approximated Pareto optimal set in MAEA-gD/RD gives us information about the location of regions of high variation. This information can be leveraged by the analyst to produce more robust solutions, for example by requesting points from PE that are below a certain sensitivity threshold.

6. CONCLUSIONS

PE is a novel method of improving the density of a given approximate Pareto optimal solutions on the entire PF or in a specific region in which the DM is interested. In this paper, we present a method for improving the quality of the estimated Pareto optimal solutions from PE by allocating more samples in areas of high variation thus acquiring better topological information of the relationship between the projected objective vectors, $\tilde{\mathcal{P}}$, and decision vectors.

As the performance of PE is contingent upon the quality of the Pareto set approximation produced by the optimization algorithm, in this work, we present an initial numerical study on the effect that the quality of samples has on the resulting PE model, $\tilde{F}_{\mathcal{P}}$ and its performance. Given that in real world problems the objective function is usually computationally more expensive than the optimization algorithm, improvements in the PE model can result in better utilization of the available samples, therefore resulting in a more efficient use of computational resources.

In this work we explored a potential direction for improving the utilization of the information obtained from a MOEA

Table 1: $D_R(\bar{P}_E, \hat{P}_E)$ and $S_R(\bar{P}_E, \hat{P}_E)$ values of the Pareto estimate sets from MAEA-gD, $\bar{P}_E$ and MAEA-gD/RD, $\hat{P}_E$.

	$D_R(\bar{P}_E, \hat{P}_E)$			$S_R(\bar{P}_E, \hat{P}_E)$		
Problem	min.	mean	std.	min.	mean	std.
WFG6	0.6865	**1.0288**	0.1743	0.6163	0.9489	0.1195
WFG7	0.6744	0.979	0.1744	0.9775	**1.025**	0.0204
WFG8	0.7902	0.989	0.0829	0.9609	**1.0087**	0.0225
WFG9	0.6315	**1.0149**	0.1883	0.6756	**1.0416**	0.207
DTLZ1	0.9338	**1.0005**	0.0139	0.0061	**1.9934**	4.5145
DTLZ2	0.225	**1.593**	1.1893	0.9726	0.9924	0.0106

Table 2: C-Metric values of the Pareto estimate sets from MAEA-gD, $\bar{P}_E$ and MAEA-gD/RD, $\hat{P}_E$.

	$C(\bar{P}_E, \hat{P}_E)$			$C(\hat{P}_E, \bar{P}_E)$		
Problem	min.	mean	std.	min.	mean	std.
WFG6	0.0280	**0.6023**	0.2384	0.0573	0.4378	0.2413
WFG7	0.0004	0.0314	0.0305	0.0240	**0.1317**	0.0713
WFG8	0.1688	0.4073	0.0941	0.3077	**0.4191**	0.0661
WFG9	0.2306	0.5378	0.1726	0.2936	**0.6942**	0.1835
DTLZ1	0.0000	0.2572	0.4138	0.0000	**0.4779**	0.4931
DTLZ2	0.0000	0.0160	0.0355	0.0000	**0.0884**	0.0829

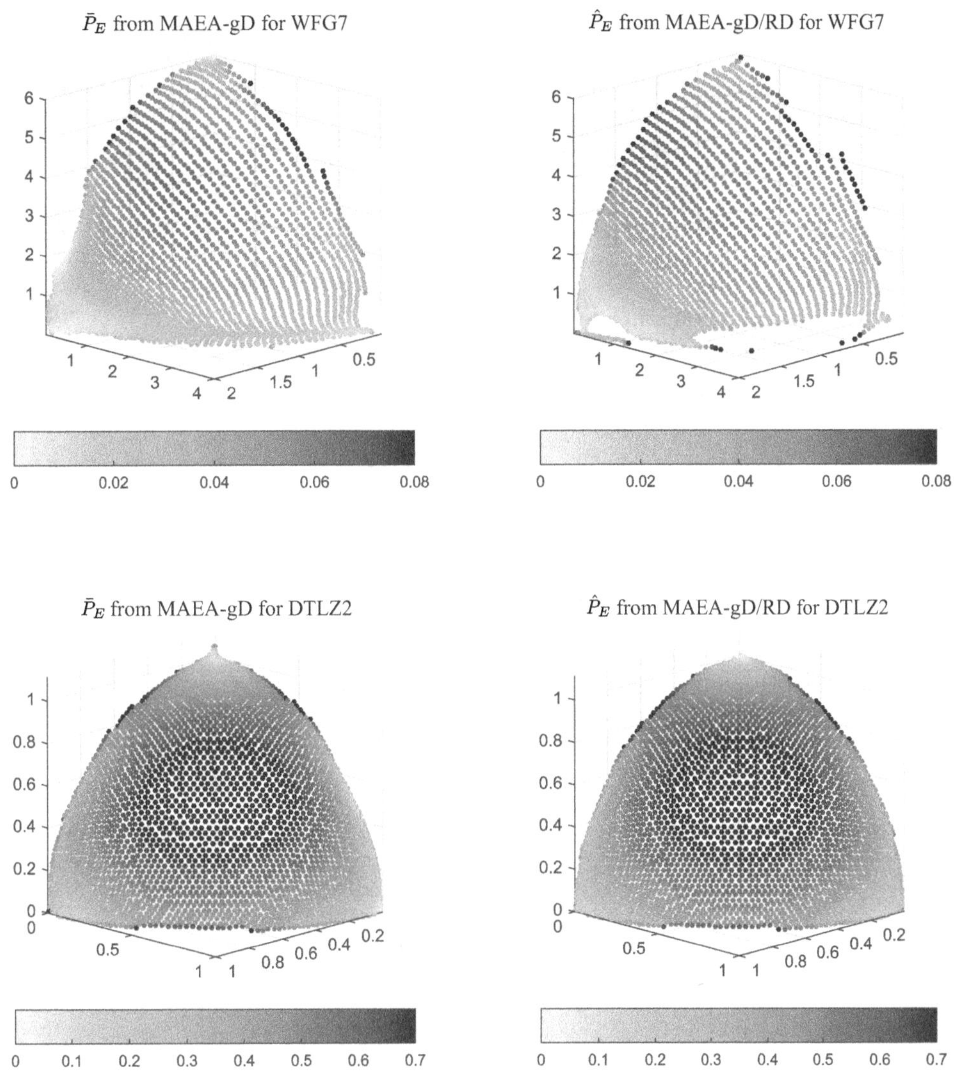

Figure 4: Density maps for WFG7 and DTLZ2. The color changes from bright yellow to dark blue as the the density decreases. Here 0 stands for the smallest distance and therefore highest density, and 1 for the sparsest.

to better estimate the PF using PE. The preliminary numerical results in *Sec. 5*, i.e. the statistics of three different measures and also the density plots, suggest that the proposed method can be useful for the production of better samples for PE which can be used to create a higher quality model of the inverse mapping, i.e. the mapping from the objective space to the decision space.

Nevertheless, despite the apparent superior performance of the method presented in this work in comparison with the original version of Pareto estimation [7], there is a number of open questions that need to be further investigated. As mentioned in the introduction real-world problems are usually multi-objective, and, often more than 3 objectives (many-objective problems) are involved. However, the scalability of PE to many-objectives has not been explored. This can have significant practical implications. Another issue is that the statistical results suggest that the solutions from PE and PE with the presented improved sampling strategy seem to produce superior solutions to the original approximation of the Pareto front generated from the algorithm. Although this result is a positive by-product, it should be further investigated as better understanding of the root cause for this behavior can suggest currently unforeseen improvements to PE. Lastly, we envisage that the obtained results could be further improved by exploring more better techniques for identifying high variation regions in decision space. These improvements can also lead to a method for identifying robust solutions, if the used robustness measures are based on the sensitivity of the inverse mapping.

7. ACKNOWLEDGMENTS

This work was supported by Jaguar Land Rover and the UK-EPSRC grant EP/L025760/1 as part of the jointly funded Programme for Simulation Innovation.

8. REFERENCES

[1] R. Cheng, Y. Jin, K. Narukawa, and B. Sendhoff. A multiobjective evolutionary algorithm using gaussian processbased inverse modeling. *IEEE Transactions on Evolutionary Computation*, PP(99), 2015.

[2] K. Deb, L. Thiele, M. Laumanns, and E. Zitzler. Scalable multi-objective optimization test problems. In *Congress on Evolutionary Computation*, volume 1, pages 825 –830, may 2002.

[3] C. Erbas, S. Cerav-Erbas, and A. Pimentel. Multiobjective optimization and evolutionary algorithms for the application mapping problem in multiprocessor system-on-chip design. *IEEE Transactions on Evolutionary Computation*, 10(3):358–374, 2006.

[4] C. Fonseca and P. Fleming. Multiobjective Optimization and Multiple Constraint Handling with Evolutionary Algorithms. I. A Unified Formulation. *IEEE Transactions on Systems, Man and Cybernetics, Part A: Systems and Humans*, 28(1):26–37, 1998.

[5] C. Fonseca and P. Fleming. Multiobjective Optimization and Multiple Constraint Handling with Evolutionary Algorithms. II. Application Example. *IEEE Transactions on Systems, Man and Cybernetics, Part A: Systems and Humans*, 28(1):38–47, 1998.

[6] I. Giagkiozis and P. Fleming. Increasing the Density of Available Pareto Optimal Solutions. Research Report No. 1028, Department of Automatic Control and Systems Engineering, The University of Sheffield, November 2012.

[7] I. Giagkiozis and P. J. Fleming. Pareto front estimation for decision making. *Evolutionary Computation*, 22(4):651–678, 2014.

[8] I. Giagkiozis, R. Purshouse, and P. Fleming. Towards understanding the cost of adaptation in decomposition-based optimization algorithms. In *IEEE International Conference on Systems, Man and Cybernetics*, pages 615–620, Oct 2013.

[9] I. Giagkiozis, R. Purshouse, and P. Fleming. Generalized decomposition and cross entropy methods for many-objective optimization. *Information Sciences*, Available Online:1–25, Jun. 2014.

[10] I. Giagkiozis, R. C. Purshouse, and P. J. Fleming. Generalized decomposition. In *Evolutionary Multi-Criterion Optimization*, volume 7811 of *Lecture Notes in Computer Science*, pages 428–442. Springer Berlin Heidelberg, 2013.

[11] S. Huband, P. Hingston, L. Barone, and L. While. A Review of Multiobjective Test Problems and A Scalable Test Problem Toolkit. *IEEE Transactions on Evolutionary Computation*, 10(5):477–506, 2006.

[12] E. Hughes. Multiple Single Objective Pareto Sampling. In *Congress on Evolutionary Computation, 2003*, volume 4, pages 2678–2684. IEEE, 2003.

[13] E. Hughes. Radar waveform optimisation as a many-objective application benchmark. In *Evolutionary Multi-Criterion Optimization*, volume 4403 of *Lecture Notes in Computer Science*, pages 700–714. Springer Berlin / Heidelberg, 2007.

[14] E. Hughes. Many-objective directed evolutionary line search. In *Proceedings of the 13th annual conference on Genetic and evolutionary computation*, pages 761–768. ACM, 2011.

[15] A. Jaszkiewicz. On the Performance of Multiple-Objective Genetic Local Search on the 0/1 Knapsack Problem - A comparative Experiment. *IEEE Transactions on Evolutionary Computation*, 6(4):402–412, 2002.

[16] A. Jaszkiewicz. Do Multiple-Objective Metaheuristics Deliver on Their Promises? A Computational Experiment on the Set-Covering Problem. *IEEE Transactions on Evolutionary Computation*, 7(2):133–143, 2003.

[17] A. J. Jerri. The shannon sampling theoremâĂŤits various extensions and applications: A tutorial review. *Proceedings of the IEEE*, 65(11):1565–1596, 1977.

[18] Y. Jin, T. Okabe, and B. Sendho. Adapting Weighted Aggregation for Multiobjective Evolution Strategies. In *Evolutionary Multi-Criterion Optimization*, pages 96–110. Springer, 2001.

[19] R. Kudikala, I. Giagkiozis, and P. Fleming. Estimation of pareto optimal solutions for multi-objective multi-modal problems. In *19th International Conference on Soft Computing, MENDEL*, 2013.

[20] R. Kudikala, I. Giagkiozis, and P. Fleming. Increasing the density of multi-objective multi-modal solutions using clustering and pareto estimation techniques. In *The 2013 World Congress in Computer Science Computer Engineering and Applied Computing*, 2013.

[21] M. Luque, K. Miettinen, P. Eskelinen, and F. Ruiz. Incorporating preference information in interactive reference point methods for multiobjective optimization. *Omega*, 37(2):450–462, 2009.

[22] A. McBratney, R. Webster, and T. Burgess. The design of optimal sampling schemes for local estimation and mapping of of regionalized variablesâĂŤi: Theory and method. *Computers & Geosciences*, 7(4):331–334, 1981.

[23] K. Miettinen. *Nonlinear Multiobjective Optimization*, volume 12. Springer, 1999.

[24] M. Sun, A. Stam, and R. Steuer. Interactive multiple objective programming using tchebycheff programs and artificial neural networks. *Computers & Operations Research*, 27(7):601–620, 2000.

[25] C. Vira and Y. Haimes. *Multiobjective Decision Making: Theory and Methodology*. Number 8. North-Holland, 1983.

[26] Q. Zhang and H. Li. MOEA/D: A Multiobjective Evolutionary Algorithm Based on Decomposition. *IEEE Transactions on Evolutionary Computation*, 11(6):712–731, 2007.

[27] Z. Zhang. Multiobjective optimization immune algorithm in dynamic environments and its application to greenhouse control. *Applied Soft Computing*, 8(2):959–971, 2008.

An Experimental Investigation of Variation Operators in Reference-Point Based Many-Objective Optimization

Yuan Yuan, Hua Xu, Bo Wang
State Key Laboratory of Intelligent Technology and Systems
Tsinghua National Laboratory for Information Science and Technology
Department of Computer Science and Technology, Tsinghua University, Beijing 100084, P.R.China
yyxhdy@gmail.com, xuhua@tsinghua.edu.cn, wbthu@outlook.com

ABSTRACT

Reference-point based multi-objective evolutionary algorithms (MOEAs) have shown promising performance in many-objective optimization. However, most of existing research within this area focused on improving the environmental selection procedure, and little work has been done on the effect of variation operators. In this paper, we conduct an experimental investigation of variation operators in a typical reference-point based MOEA, i.e., NSGA-III. First, we provide a new NSGA-III variant, i.e., NSGA-III-DE, which introduces differential evolution (DE) operator into NSGA-III, and we further examine the effect of two main control parameters in NSGA-III-DE. Second, we have an experimental analysis of the search behavior of NSGA-III-DE and NSGA-III. We observe that NSGA-III-DE is generally better at exploration whereas NSGA-III normally has advantages in exploitation. Third, based on this observation, we present two other NSGA-III variants, where DE operator and genetic operators are simply combined to reproduce solutions. Experimental results on several benchmark problems show that very encouraging performance can be achieved by three suggested new NSGA-III variants. Our work also indicates that the performance of NSGA-III is significantly bottlenecked by its variation operators, providing opportunities for the study of the other alternative ones.

Categories and Subject Descriptors

I.2.8 [**Artificial Intelligence**]: Problem Solving, Control Methods, and Search—*Heuristic methods*; G.1.6 [**Numerical Analysis**]: Optimization

Keywords

Many-objective optimization, NSGA-III, Differential evolution, Variation operators, Reference-point

GECCO '15 July 11–15, 2015, Madrid, Spain
© 2015 ACM. ISBN 978-1-4503-3472-3/15/07...$15.00
DOI: http://dx.doi.org/10.1145/2739480.2754655

1. INTRODUCTION

Recently, many-objective optimization problems (MaOPs) have stirred great interest in evolutionary multi-objective optimization (EMO) community. This is largely due to the fact that most of existing well-established multi-objective evolutionary algorithms (MOEAs), e.g., non-dominated sorting genetic algorithm II (NSGA-II) [8], which are effective for solving multi-objective optimization problems (MOPs) fail to show satisfactory performance in handling many (four or more) objectives. The main reason is that almost all the solutions in the population become non-dominated with the number of objectives increasing, leading to the severe loss of Pareto-based selection pressure towards the Pareto front (PF) [18]. To address this difficulty, some efforts, e.g., [32, 18, 2, 7, 31], have been done in the literature, which are providing valuable insights into this area.

In this paper, we would like to experimentally investigate the variation operators in reference-point based many-objective optimization. The motivation comes from the following two aspects. On the one hand, the recent progresses [7, 31] on reference-point many-objective algorithms have shown that this category of techniques do deserve to be highlighted in many-objective optimization. However, almost all the related algorithms in this regard adopted the conventional genetic operators to reproduce solutions, leaving room for the investigation of the other alternative variation operators, e.g., differential evolution (DE) [26]. On the other hand, several recent studies [24, 14, 17] have shown that the issue of performing an effective search in the decision space should be addressed more carefully when handling many objectives. Nevertheless, it is well known that pure genetic operators may not be powerful enough to achieve a good balance between exploration and exploitation in the decision space for some complex problems [30].

In view of the above two aspects, it would be very interesting and essential to have a look at how the other variation operators influence the performance of reference-point based many-objective algorithms on MaOPs and to what extend. To this end, we focus on a typical algorithm falling into this class, i.e., NSGA-III [7], and study the effect of several kinds of variation operators on its search performance. Our contribution is reflected in the following aspects: 1) To our knowledge, this is the first report to introduce DE operator into the recently proposed NSGA-III (NSGA-III-DE). In addition, we also examine the effect of two main control parameters on the performance of NSGA-III-DE. 2) Two other NSGA-III variants (NSGA-III-2S and NSGA-III-HVO) with new reproduction mechanisms are developed based on the

the experimental analysis of the search behavior of NSGA-III and NSGA-III-DE, both of which can achieve significant performance improvement over NSGA-III and NSGA-III-DE. 3) Since the official code implementation of NSGA-III has not been released and the original NSGA-III paper [7] failed to give all the details of its normalization procedure, it is a non-trivial task to well implement NSGA-III and obtain comparable results to those in that paper. Chiang [6] provided a C++ implementation, but this implementation performs very bad on problems with 8 and higher number of objectives. As supplementary material of this paper, we make our NSGA-III implementation available, which appears to show the similar performance to the official implementation in most cases.

This paper continues with the following parts. Section 2 introduces the background knowledge of this study. Section 3 describes the target algorithms to be investigated in our experiments. Section 4 provides the extensive experimental results and discussions. Finally, our conclusions are drawn in Section 5.

2. BACKGROUND

2.1 Reference-Point Based Many-Objective Optimization

Reference-point based many-objective optimization [7, 31] is a class of recent promising techniques for solving MaOPs. Slightly different from the decomposition-based MOEAs, the reference-point based MOEAs perform the predefined multiple targeted search by means of multiple predefined reference points instead of multiple search directions, which can effectively alleviate several difficulties in handling many objectives [7]. Along this research direction, NSGA-III may be one of the most representative algorithms.

The basic framework of NSGA-III remains similar to the well-known NSGA-II with significant changes in the selection mechanism in the last accepted non-domination level. NSGA-III has two distinct features, i.e., niching procedure and adaptive normalization. In terms of the form, the niching procedure replaces the crowding distance operator in NSGA-II, intending to maintain the diversity in the high-dimensional objective space. The main motivation behind this is that the crowding distance used in NSGA-II tends to favor dominance resistant solutions [16], posing potential detrimental effect upon the convergence of NSGA-II on MaOPs. In NSGA-III's niching procedure, the normalized objective space is first divided into a number of clusters aided by a set of well-distributed reference lines, and each solution can be classified into a sole cluster represented by a specific reference line. When executing the selection, the solutions locating on the non-domination levels ahead of the last accepted one are definitely selected for the next generation and they are already allocated into respective clusters; in the last accepted front, the solutions associated with a cluster with the smaller number of solutions have higher priority to be chosen. The adaptive normalization is designed to effectively handle problems having a PF whose objective values may be differently scaled. This task is essentially equivalent to estimate the nadir point during the optimization process. In NSGA-III's adaptive normalization, the extreme point in each objective axis is first identified and all these extreme points are used to construct a linear hyperplane; the intercepts of the hyperplane with objective axes constitute the nadir point. Overall, the principle of NSGA-III is to emphasize non-dominated solutions yet close to a set of supplied reference points in the normalized objective space.

Very recently, Yuan *et al.* [31] proposed an improved NSGA-III procedure called θ-NSGA-III, which aims to enhance the convergence of NSGA-III by exploiting the fitness evaluation scheme in MOEA/D but still inherit the strength of diversity preservation in NSGA-III. Similar to NSGA-III, θ-NSGA-III also conducts the partition of normalized objective space and clustering process using reference lines, but the difference mainly lies in the environmental selection phase. In θ-NSGA-III, instead of Pareto-dominance, the solutions are ranked by the non-dominated sorting procedure based on a new dominance relation, i.e., θ-dominance, which not only prefers the solutions with better fitness values in each cluster but also ensures that the solutions distribute as evenly as possible between these clusters.

Prior to NSGA-III and θ-NSGA-III, there were also some studies, e.g., [13, 22], that suggested to guide the multi-objective search using multiple reference points. Nevertheless, these developed algorithms may have potential design defects or failed to verify their effectiveness on MaOPs.

2.2 Differential Evolution

DE is a simple but powerful evolutionary algorithms (EAs) for global optimization, which has been successfully applied in various areas, e.g., [4, 29]. DE evolves a population of N candidate individuals, each of which is a n-dimensional real-valued parameter vector and is denoted as $X_{i,G} = [x_{1,i,G}, x_{2,i,G}, \ldots, x_{n,i,G}]^{\mathrm{T}}$, where $i = 1, 2, \ldots, N$ and G is the current generation. DE consists of three main operators: mutation, crossover, and selection. The mutation operator is to construct a mutant vector $V_{i,G} = [v_{1,i,G}, v_{2,i,G}, \ldots, v_{n,i,G}]^{\mathrm{T}}$. It is well known that there exists several different mutation schemes of DE. In this paper, we adopt the DE/rand/1 scheme illustrated as follows:

$$V_{i,G} = X_{r_1^i,G} + F \cdot (X_{r_2^i,G} - X_{r_3^i,G}) \tag{1}$$

The indices r_1^i, r_2^i and r_3^i are mutually different integers randomly chosen from the range $[1, N]$ and are also different from the based vector index i; F is a scale factor typically lying in the interval $[0.4, 1]$. After the mutation operator, the crossover operator is to generate a trial vector $U_{i,G} = [u_{1,i,G}, u_{2,i,G}, \ldots, u_{n,i,G}]^{\mathrm{T}}$ by exchanging the components between the target vector $X_{i,G}$ and the mutant vector $V_{i,G}$. DE can use two kinds of crossover methods, i.e., exponential or binomial. This paper adopts the binomial crossover described as follows:

$$u_{j,i,G} = \begin{cases} v_{j,i,G}, & \text{if } rand(0,1) \le Cr \text{ or } j = q \\ x_{j,i,G}, & \text{otherwise} \end{cases} \tag{2}$$

The crossover probability Cr is a constant real number taken from the interval $[0, 1]$; q is an integer randomly chosen from $[1, n]$ which ensures that $U_{i,G}$ gets at least one component from $V_{i,G}$. The selection operator is to decide whether or not $U_{i,G}$ is the member of the population for the next generation. For single-objective optimization, the selection can be described as

$$X_{i,G+1} = \begin{cases} U_{i,G}, & \text{if } f(U_{i,G}) \le f(X_{i,G}) \\ X_{i,G}, & \text{otherwise} \end{cases} \tag{3}$$

where $f(X)$ is the objective function to be minimized.

Until now, DE has been extended extensively to handle multiple objectives in the literature [21]. It should be specially mentioned that a MOEA/D version [33] with DE operator won the CEC 2009 MOEA competition. Recently, a number of researchers [10, 7, 3] have started to investigate the performance of DE on MaOPs.

Note that, the selection operator in the original DE, i.e., Eq. (3), cannot be directly used in multi or many-objective optimization. Thus DE operator in MOEAs generally refers to the procedure of obtaining $U_{i,G}$ based on $X_{i,G}$ only including mutation and crossover.

2.3 Variation Operators in Multi and Many-Objective Optimization

In the field of EMO, most of studies, e.g., [8, 34], focus on the environmental selection phase, i.e., how to select solutions to survive in the next generation. However, like single-objective EAs, it is also very important for a MOEA to maintain the balance between exploration and exploitation in the decision space, which is normally achieved by variation operators. Indeed, in multi-objective optimization, the exploration/exploitation dilemma is exacerbated by the contrary goals of convergence and diversity in the objective space [27].

To enhance the search ability of MOEAs in the decision space, a few studies [5, 20] suggested new variation operators for MOPs. Besides this, another line of research in this respect is to synthesize the effect of several existing variation operators. This is based on the fact that different variation operators generally have strength in certain problem landscapes and even fit different courses of optimization process. Thus the synergetic combination of them is expected to have complementary advantages in the search ability. In the past few decades, this general idea has been made use of by many researchers in multi-objective phase. Vrugt *et al.* [28] proposed to simultaneously use different variation operators to create offsprings in NSGA-II, where the adaptive offspring creation is designed to favor the operators that exhibit the highest reproductive success. Tan *et al.* [27] presented an adaptive variation operator that exploits the chromosomal structure of binary representation and synergizes the function of crossover and mutation. Elhossini *et al.* [12] suggested a hybridization of particle swarm optimization (PSO) and genetic operators to handle MOPs, where genetic operators are modified to preserve the information used by PSO. Some recent similar works can be referred in [14, 23, 19, 25]. Moreover, it is worth mentioning that the category of these methods generally use the adaptive control mechanisms to coordinate the selection of different variation operators.

Within the many-objective domain, the research on the influence of variation operators is relatively rare. But recent studies have indicated that this issue may deserve special attention when handling many objectives. Sato *et al.* [24] found that the genes in true Pareto set (PS) become noticeably diverse as the number of objective is increased and claimed that the conventional variation operators might become too disruptive and decease their effectiveness in this case. Based on the analysis, the authors further suggested Controlling the maximum number of Crossed Genes (C-CG) in crossover operators, which could significantly improve the search performance of several MOEAs on MaOPs. Ishibuchi *et al.* [17] observed that the clear performance improvement on many-objective knapsack problems is obtained when the parent-offspring distance is small. To further verify this observation, the authors implemented a distance-based crossover operator where the parent-offspring distance is specified as a user-defined parameter.

3. TARGET ALGORITHMS

The original NSGA-III uses the simulated binary crossover (SBX) and polynomial mutation [1] to produce the offsprings. We hereafter call it NSGA-III-SBX to distinguish it notably from the other concerned NSGA-III variants in this paper, i.e., NSGA-III-DE, NSGA-III-2S and NSGA-III-HVO.

NSGA-III-DE replaces SBX in NSGA-III-SBX with DE operator, which is the only difference between the two. In Algorithm 1, we describe how to produce the offspring population Q by the current population P in NSGA-III-DE.

Algorithm 1 Reproduction in NSGA-III-DE

$P \leftarrow \{X_{1,G}, X_{2,G}, \ldots, X_{N,G}\}$
$Q \leftarrow \emptyset$
for $i \leftarrow 1$ to N **do**
  $U_{i,G} \leftarrow$ DEOperator($X_{i,G}$)
  $Y_{i,G} \leftarrow$ PolynomialMutation($U_{i,G}$)
  $Q \leftarrow Q \cup Y_{i,G}$
end for
return Q

NSGA-III-2S is a two-stage algorithm, simply combining NSGA-III-SBX and NSGA-III-DE. In NSGA-III-2S, NSGA-III-DE runs in the first half of generations and NSGA-III-SBX runs in the remaining generations.

NSGA-III-HVO employs a strategy hybridizing three different variation operators, i.e., SBX, DE operator, and polynomial mutation. One operator is randomly selected from the three whenever an offspring solution is to be produced. In Algorithm 2, we describe the procedure of producing the offspring population Q using the current population P in NSGA-III-HVO. It needs to be further explained that Step 6 first randomly chooses an integer $r^i \in [1, N]$ and $r^i \neq i$, and then executes the SBX to $X_{i,G}$ and $X_{r^i,G}$.

Algorithm 2 Reproduction in NSGA-III-HVO

1: $P \leftarrow \{X_{1,G}, X_{2,G}, \ldots, X_{N,G}\}$
2: $Q \leftarrow \emptyset$
3: **for** $i \leftarrow 1$ to N **do**
4:   Randomly choose an integer $k \in [1, 3]$
5:   **if** $k = 1$ **then**
6:     $Y_{i,G} \leftarrow$ SBXCrossover($X_{i,G}$)
7:   **else if** $k = 2$ **then**
8:     $Y_{i,G} \leftarrow$ DEOperator($X_{i,G}$)
9:   **else**
10:     $Y_{i,G} \leftarrow$ PolynomialMutation($X_{i,G}$)
11:   **end if**
12:   $Q \leftarrow Q \cup Y_{i,G}$
13: **end for**
14: **return** Q

Note that, we only focus on NSGA-III and its variants in this paper due to space limitation, but the similar experimental observations and conclusions can be obtained based on θ-NSGA-III.

4. EXPERIMENTAL STUDIES

4.1 Experimental Setup

To test the considered algorithms, we adopt two groups of test problems in our experiments. The problems in the first group are all normalized problems including DTLZ 1-4 [9]. The second group contains three scaled problems, i.e., scaled DTLZ 1-2 [7] and WFG6 [15]. The scaled DTLZ 1-2 are the modifications of DTLZ1 and DTLZ2, respectively. To illustrate, if the scaling factor is 10^i, the scaled DTLZ1 modify the objective functions of the original DTLZ1 as follows

$$f_i \leftarrow 10^{i-1} f_i,\ \ i = 1, 2, \dots, m \tag{4}$$

where m is the number of objectives. In our experiments, we hereafter call scaled DTLZ1 and DTLZ2 as SDTLZ1 and SDTLZ2 for short.

All the used problems can be scaled to any number of objectives and decision variables. We consider the number of objectives $m \in \{3, 5, 8, 10, 15\}$. For DTLZ 1-4 and SDTLZ 1-2, the total number of decision variables is given by $n = m + k - 1$, k is set to 5 for DTLZ1 and SDTLZ1, 10 for DTLZ 2-4 and SDTLZ2 as recommended in [9, 7]. For WFG6, according to [15], the number of decision variables n is set to 24, and the position-related parameter is set to $m-1$. The scaling factors used for SDTLZ 1-2 with different number of objectives are consistent with those in [7].

To evaluate the target algorithms, the inverted generational distance (IGD) is used as the performance metric. We use the way suggested in [7] to compute IGD. IGD can measure both convergence and diversity of a solution set and smaller value means better performance.

For the parameter settings, each of the considered algorithms adopts the same setting of population size and the maximum number of generations (MaxGen) with that in the original NSGA-III study [7] for different problem instances. The parameters used for three variation operators are shown in Table 1. In Section 4.2 we will also investigate the effect of parameters F and Cr on the performance of NSGA-III-DE.

Table 1: Parameter settings for variation operators.

Variation Operator	Parameter	Value
SBX	Crossover probability (p_c)	1.0
	Distribution index for crossover (η_c)	30
DE	Scale factor (F)	0.5
	Crossover probability (Cr)	0.1
Polynomial mutation	Mutation probability (p_m)	$1/n$
	Distribution index for mutation (η_m)	20

All the target algorithms are implemented in the jMetal framework [11], and perform 20 independent runs for each test instance. The source code for reproducing experiments described in this paper is available at http://learn.tsinghua.edu.cn:8080/2012310563/NSGAIIIStudy.rar.

4.2 Effect of Parameters On NSGA-III-DE

There are two typical control parameters in NSGA-III-DE: F and Cr. In this subsection, we focuss on the effect of each of the two parameters on the performance of NSGA-III-DE. DTLZ1, DTLZ3, SDTLZ2, and WFG6 problems with 5, 8, 10 and 15 objectives are used for the illustration purpose.

To examine the effect of F, we fix Cr to 0.1 and vary F between 0.4 and 1 with a step size 0.1. Figure 1 presents how the performance of NSGA-III-DE varies over the change of F in terms of medium IGD. From Figure 1, F exerts similar influence to NSGA-III-DE for DTLZ1, DTLZ3 and SDTLZ2 problems, where IGD fluctuates with the variation of F and the fluctuation is small except on 5-objective DTLZ1. For WFG6 problem, IGD slowly grows larger with the increasing of F on 5, 8 and 10-objective instances, whereas it shows fluctuation on 15-objective instance.

With regard to Cr, we investigate the situation $Cr \in [0, 1]$ with a step size 0.1, where F is set to 0.5. Figure 2 shows the effect of Cr on the medium IGD obtained by NSGA-III-DE. As can be seen from Figure 2, the performance of NSGA-III-DE is very much influenced by Cr on DTLZ1, DTLZ3 and SDTLZ2 problems, where IGD rises sharply as the increasing of Cr from the overall perspective. As for WFG6 problem, the variation tendency of IGD is basically consistent with that on the other three problems, but the variation range is much smaller.

In summary, we can obtain some insights on the influence of F and Cr. NSGA-III-DE can generally achieve the relatively stable performance over a wide range of F values on most of concerned problem instances, and $F = 0.5$ seems to be a good choice for NSGA-III-DE in most cases. In contrast to F, the performance of NSGA-III-DE is normally much more sensitive to Cr. Small Cr value, i.e., $Cr \in [0, 0.1]$, is recommended according to the results, and large Cr value usually leads to particularly poor performance of NSGA-III-DE. Recall that Cr controls how many variables in expectation are changed in a population member. Thus, it means that NSGA-III-DE obtains good performance when the child solution inherits the most of information from the parent solution. It is interesting to note that this observation is similar to that in [24], where the performance improvement is reported for many-objective 0/1 knapsack problems by exchanging only a small number of genes between two parents when producing the child solution.

4.3 NSGA-III-DE vs. NSGA-III-SBX: Exploration vs. Exploitation

In this subsection, we will conduct the comparison of search behavior between NSGA-III-DE and NSGA-III-SBX on MaOPs. Specifically, we would like to know which algorithm is better at exploration and which one is better at exploitation in the search space. To understand this is very helpful for designing more effective variation operators. Note that, here we do not carry out a detail performance comparison on different problem instances between the two algorithms, which will be further done in Section 4.4.

To examine the exploration ability of NSGA-III-DE and NSGA-III-SBX, we use 5-objective DTLZ2 as an illustration. First, a population is randomly generated for this problem instance. Then, both NSGA-III-DE and NSGA-III-SBX use this population as the initial population and run for a number of generations. Figure 3 shows the evolutionary trajectories of IGD over generations for NSGA-III-DE and NSGA-III-SBX. From Figure 3, both of the two algorithms decrease IGD value in a similar manner in the initial evolutionary stage, but NSGA-III-DE manages to find better IGD value after about 40 generations. This phenomenon demonstrates that NSGA-III-DE could locate the promising search regions more quickly than NSGA-III-SBX by randomly distributed solutions in the decision space. In Figure 4, we further plot the parallel coordinates of decision vari-

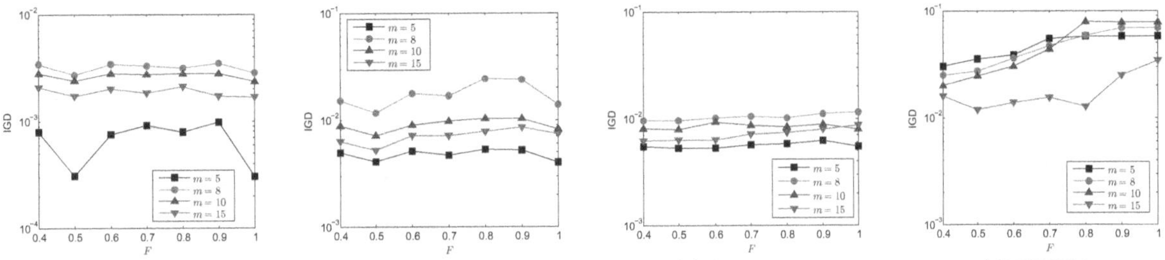

(a) DTLZ1 (b) DTLZ3 (c) SDTLZ2 (d) WFG6

Figure 1: Examination of the influence of F ($Cr = 0.1$) on IGD of NSGA-III-DE for the considered test problems with varying number of objectives m. The figures show the medium IGD of 20 independent runs each.

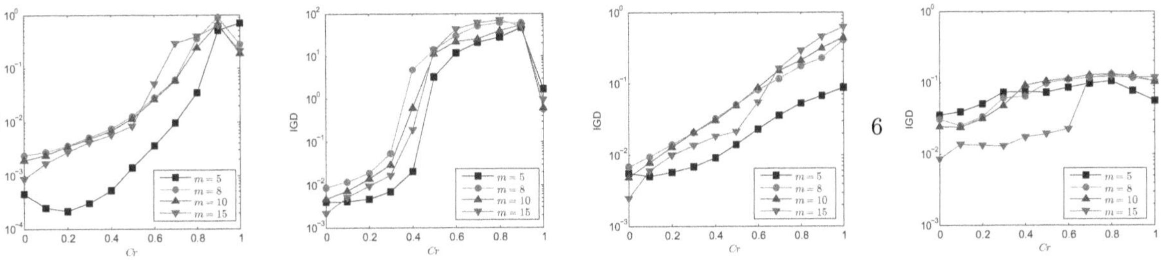

(a) DTLZ1 (b) DTLZ3 (c) SDTLZ2 (d) WFG6

Figure 2: Examination of the influence of Cr ($F = 0.5$) on IGD of NSGA-III-DE for the considered test problems with varying number of objectives m. The figures show the medium IGD of 20 independent runs each.

able values for one population obtained by NSGA-III-DE and NSGA-III-SBX after MaxGen/2 = 135 generations, respectively. Since the PS of 5-objective DTLZ2 is

$$x_j = \begin{cases} [0,1], & j = 1,2,3,4 \\ 0.5, & j = 5,6,\ldots,14 \end{cases} \tag{5}$$

it is clear from Figure 4 that NSGA-III-DE converge faster to the PS compared with NSGA-III-SBX in the early stage of evolution. Based on the above observations, NSGA-III-DE may perform the exploration in the search space more effectively than NSGA-III-SBX.

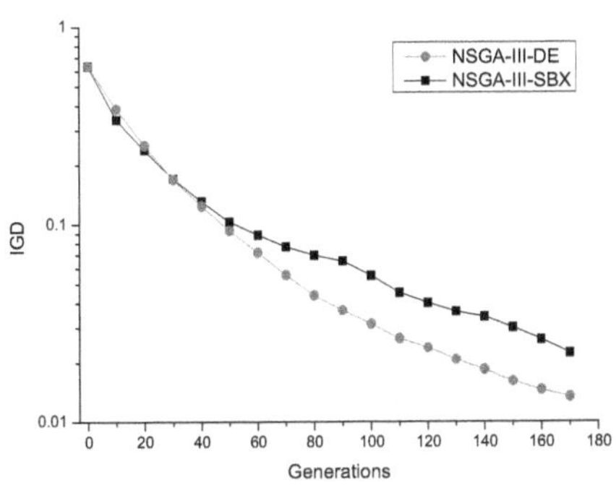

Figure 3: Evolutionary trajectories of IGD over generations for NSGA-III-DE (NSGA-III-SBX) on 5-objective DTLZ2. The initial population is a randomly generated population.

In order to investigate the exploitation ability, we do a similar experiment but the initial population is a population close to the PF that can be obtained by any many-objective optimizer. We run NSGA-III-DE and NSGA-III-SBX respectively on this initial population, and Figure 5 describes the evolutionary trajectories of IGD over generations. It can be seen from Figure 5 that the situation is quite different from that in Figure 3. In this case, NSGA-III-SBX could reduce IGD value with elapse of generations more quickly than NSGA-III-DE from the beginning. Because the initial population itself is an elite population, NSGA-III-SBX has stronger ability than NSGA-III-DE to further refine good solutions, which demonstrates its superiority over NSGA-III-DE in performing the exploitation in the search space.

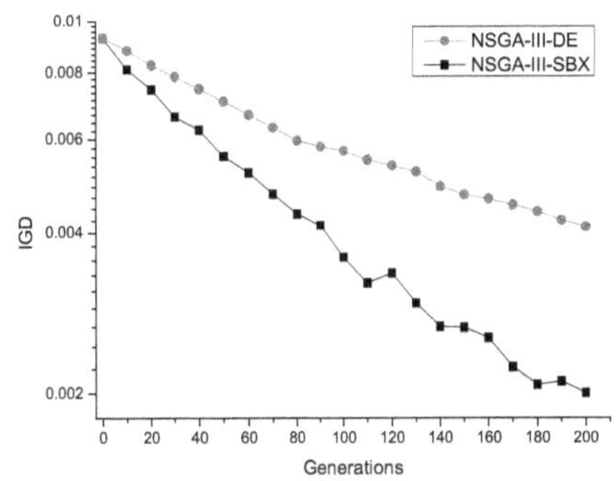

Figure 5: Evolutionary trajectories of IGD over generations for NSGA-III-DE (NSGA-III-SBX) on 5-objective DTLZ2. The initial population is a population close to the PF.

Many studies have shown that it is beneficial to adopt a "exploration first, exploitation later" strategy to extract necessary information about the search space before exploitation starts [27], thus it is expected to achieve a better

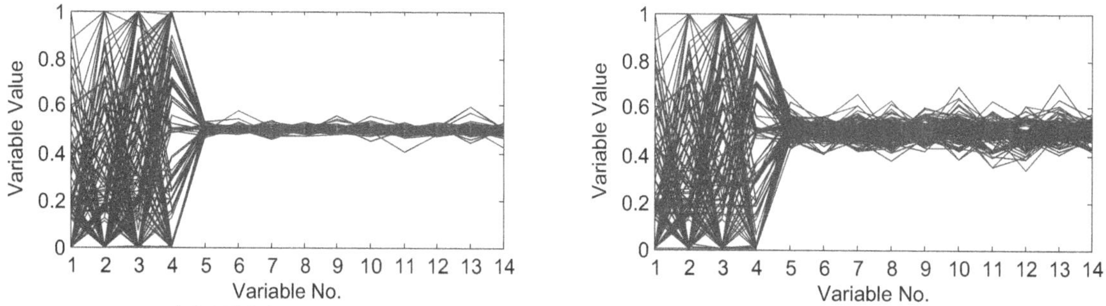

(a) NSGA-III-DE (b) NSGA-III-SBX

Figure 4: Parallel coordinates of the decision variable values of one population for 5-objective DTLZ2. The population is obtained by running NSGA-III-DE (NSGA-III-SBX) after 135 generations on the same randomly generated initial population.

performance if NSGA-III-DE is run first then NSGA-III-SBX, which is the motivation of the development of NSGA-III-2S. Moreover, since NSGA-III-SBX and NSGA-III-DE show complementary advantages, it is natural to synthesize the effect of these variation operators to enhance the search performance, which is the main purpose of NSGA-III-HVO. Later, we will verify the effectiveness of NSGA-III-2S and NSGA-III-HVO.

4.4 Comparison Between NSGA-III Variants

In this subsection, all the target algorithms are tested on the two groups of problems. Table 2 shows the comparison results on normalized problems, and Table 3 on scaled problems. As mentioned before, our NSGA-III-SBX is an "unofficial" implementation of NSGA-III, we also list the results from the original NSGA-III paper [7] for comparison. Note that, althoug NSGA-III was tested on WFG6 in [7], the authors did not indicate the setting of number of variables for this problem. Thus we do not use the original NSGA-III's results on WFG6 here. In the following paragraphs, we will describe these comparison results in detail.

For DTLZ 1-3 and SDTLZ1 1-2 problems, the comparison situations are similar. NSGA-III-DE generally performs better than NSGA-III-SBX except few exceptions (3-objective DTLZ2 and SDTLZ2). Either of NSGA-III-2S and NSGA-III-HVO exhibits clear advantage over both NSGA-III-SBX and NSGA-III-DE. To be specific, NSGA-III-2S outperforms NSGA-III-SBX on all these instances; and it is obviously better than NSGA-III-DE in most cases except on 15-objective instances and 5-objective DTLZ1 (S-DTLZ1), where they achieve the very close performance. NSGA-III-HVO shows much better performance compared with NSGA-III-SBX and NSGA-III-DE on nearly all the instances, whose IGD values on some instances, e.g., 5-objective DTLZ3, are even one or two orders of magnitude less. In addition, NSGA-III-HVO is also superior overall to NSGA-III-2S, which usually obtains better IGD results except on DTLZ2 (SDTLZ2) with 3 and 5 objectives.

For DTLZ4 problem, NSGA-III-DE performs worst on all the instances. NSGA-III-2S performs better than NSGA-III-SBX on 3 and 5-objective instances, but is outperformed by NSGA-III-SBX on 8 and 10-objective instances. On 15-objective instance, their is only slightly performance difference between NSGA-III-2S and NSGA-III-SBX. NSGA-III-HVO achieves the best performance on all the instances except 8-objective one, where NSGA-III-SBX performs best.

Table 2: Best, median and worst IGD values for all the considered NSGA-III variants on normalized test problems. Best performance is shown in bold.

Problem	m	NSGA-III[†]	NSGA-III -SBX	NSGA-III -DE	NSGA-III -2S	NSGA-III -HVO
DTLZ1		4.880E-04	8.901E-04	5.639E-04	2.091E-04	**8.715E-05**
	3	1.308E-03	2.186E-03	6.893E-04	2.822E-04	**1.406E-04**
		4.880E-03	2.070E-02	9.174E-04	**5.693E-04**	8.024E-04
		5.116E-04	7.601E-04	2.513E-04	2.843E-04	**5.560E-05**
	5	9.799E-04	1.991E-03	3.767E-04	3.416E-04	**8.053E-05**
		1.979E-03	4.493E-02	4.630E-04	9.292E-04	**1.047E-04**
		2.044E-03	3.386E-03	2.478E-03	1.730E-03	**9.321E-04**
	8	3.979E-03	4.704E-03	2.985E-03	2.150E-03	**1.314E-03**
		8.721E-03	1.175E-02	3.395E-03	3.098E-03	**2.557E-03**
		2.215E-03	2.867E-03	2.245E-03	1.733E-03	**1.023E-03**
	10	3.462E-03	4.488E-03	2.623E-03	2.158E-03	**1.137E-03**
		6.869E-03	2.343E-02	4.027E-03	3.742E-03	**3.394E-03**
		2.649E-03	2.849E-03	1.667E-03	1.246E-03	**5.448E-04**
	15	5.063E-03	5.769E-03	1.972E-03	2.019E-03	**8.728E-04**
		1.123E-02	3.275E-02	2.063E-02	3.645E-02	3.733E-02
DTLZ2		1.262E-03	1.213E-03	3.756E-03	**1.099E-03**	1.304E-03
	3	**1.357E-03**	2.043E-03	4.354E-03	1.401E-03	1.632E-03
		2.114E-03	8.355E-03	4.782E-03	**1.892E-03**	2.065E-03
		4.254E-03	4.752E-03	5.137E-03	**2.275E-03**	2.601E-03
	5	4.982E-03	6.415E-03	5.750E-03	**2.825E-03**	3.209E-03
		5.862E-03	9.040E-03	6.608E-03	**3.030E-03**	4.117E-03
		1.371E-02	1.486E-02	8.245E-03	6.592E-03	**5.680E-03**
	8	1.571E-02	1.737E-02	1.009E-02	8.155E-03	**7.197E-03**
		1.811E-02	2.105E-02	1.222E-02	9.850E-03	**9.038E-03**
		1.350E-02	1.558E-02	7.727E-03	6.125E-03	**4.502E-03**
	10	1.528E-02	1.745E-02	8.527E-03	7.005E-03	**5.361E-03**
		1.697E-02	2.545E-02	9.491E-03	8.248E-03	**6.549E-03**
		1.360E-02	1.591E-02	5.457E-03	5.745E-03	**3.585E-03**
	15	1.726E-02	1.984E-02	6.587E-03	6.875E-03	**4.792E-03**
		2.114E-02	2.358E-02	8.683E-03	8.403E-03	**6.080E-03**
DTLZ3		9.751E-04	1.203E-03	1.947E-03	2.475E-04	**1.207E-04**
	3	4.007E-03	4.809E-03	2.540E-03	2.977E-04	**2.511E-04**
		6.665E-03	1.714E-02	3.189E-03	**3.307E-04**	1.696E-03
		3.086E-03	4.175E-03	4.150E-03	8.566E-04	**4.658E-04**
	5	5.960E-03	8.056E-03	4.702E-03	1.086E-03	**5.585E-04**
		1.196E-02	2.390E-02	5.715E-03	1.281E-03	**7.871E-04**
		1.244E-02	1.530E-02	1.075E-02	8.474E-03	**4.304E-03**
	8	2.375E-02	3.219E-02	1.317E-02	1.115E-02	**5.154E-03**
		9.649E-02	1.130E-01	1.497E-02	1.607E-02	**1.284E-02**
		8.849E-03	9.217E-03	7.426E-03	4.892E-03	**2.541E-03**
	10	1.188E-02	1.516E-02	8.426E-03	6.140E-03	**2.975E-03**
		2.083E-02	2.825E-02	9.466E-03	7.790E-03	**4.615E-03**
		1.401E-02	1.689E-02	4.767E-03	4.844E-03	**1.993E-03**
	15	2.145E-02	4.019E-02	5.799E-03	6.312E-03	**3.506E-03**
		4.195E-02	8.801E-02	1.048E-02	8.108E-03	**7.010E-03**
DTLZ4		2.915E-04	3.815E-04	3.084E-03	3.471E-04	**2.716E-04**
	3	5.970E-04	9.040E-04	3.697E-03	4.156E-04	**3.470E-04**
		4.286E-01	3.704E-03	4.223E-03	6.204E-04	**4.414E-04**
		9.849E-04	**6.464E-04**	5.076E-03	6.947E-04	6.624E-04
	5	1.255E-03	1.099E-03	6.298E-03	9.227E-04	**8.746E-04**
		1.721E-03	1.972E-03	7.422E-03	1.375E-03	**1.151E-03**
		5.079E-03	**3.581E-03**	1.663E-02	5.026E-03	4.500E-03
	8	7.054E-03	**4.844E-03**	1.941E-02	6.426E-03	5.315E-03
		6.051E-01	**5.698E-03**	2.128E-02	7.750E-03	6.367E-03
		5.694E-03	**3.834E-03**	1.148E-02	5.639E-03	3.925E-03
	10	6.337E-03	4.703E-03	1.434E-02	6.553E-03	**4.361E-03**
		1.076E-01	5.656E-03	1.525E-02	7.492E-03	**5.054E-03**
		7.110E-03	5.514E-03	8.543E-03	5.830E-03	**3.093E-03**
	15	3.431E-01	7.312E-03	1.014E-02	7.367E-03	**4.936E-03**
		1.073E+00	1.053E-02	1.151E-02	1.015E-02	**6.651E-03**

[†] The results are taken from the original NSGA-III paper [7].

Table 3: Best, median and worst IGD values for all the considered NSGA-III variants on scaled test problems. Best performance is shown in bold.

Problem	m	NSGA-III†	NSGA-III -SBX	NSGA-III -DE	NSGA-III -2S	NSGA-III -HVO
SDTLZ1		3.853E-04	1.342E-03	9.805E-04	4.629E-04	**1.559E-04**
	3	1.214E-03	5.843E-03	1.465E-03	5.899E-04	**2.329E-04**
		1.103E-02	4.925E-02	1.748E-03	8.159E-04	**6.576E-04**
		1.099E-03	2.580E-03	3.156E-04	5.353E-04	**1.197E-04**
	5	2.500E-03	1.914E-02	7.398E-04	6.748E-04	**1.771E-04**
		3.921E-02	9.925E-02	8.775E-04	1.327E-03	**2.458E-04**
		4.659E-03	1.545E-02	4.706E-03	3.753E-03	**2.220E-03**
	8	1.051E-02	1.564E-01	5.590E-03	4.763E-03	**3.099E-03**
		1.167E-01	2.213E-01	7.022E-03	7.559E-03	**5.614E-03**
		3.403E-03	2.143E-02	4.423E-03	3.756E-03	**2.045E-03**
	10	5.577E-03	1.911E-01	5.104E-03	4.228E-03	**2.792E-03**
		3.617E-02	2.369E-01	5.809E-03	**5.236E-03**	6.893E-03
		3.450E-03	8.456E-03	2.910E-03	2.919E-03	**8.961E-04**
	15	6.183E-03	1.493E-02	4.000E-03	4.110E-03	**2.098E-03**
		1.367E-02	9.362E-02	**4.777E-03**	7.548E-02	7.987E-02
SDTLZ2		1.347E-03	1.368E-03	3.629E-03	**1.078E-03**	1.471E-03
	3	2.069E-03	2.304E-03	4.188E-03	**1.392E-03**	1.764E-03
		5.284E-03	6.520E-03	4.779E-03	2.346E-03	**1.999E-03**
		1.005E-02	1.163E-02	5.029E-03	**2.465E-03**	2.499E-03
	5	2.564E-02	4.682E-02	5.871E-03	**2.744E-03**	3.259E-03
		8.430E-02	1.200E-01	6.242E-03	**3.317E-03**	4.306E-03
		1.582E-02	2.212E-02	9.162E-03	**6.053E-03**	6.649E-03
	8	1.788E-02	4.128E-02	1.022E-02	8.473E-03	**8.330E-03**
		2.089E-02	2.273E-01	1.117E-02	**9.417E-03**	1.333E-02
		2.113E-02	2.335E-02	7.653E-03	6.499E-03	**4.460E-03**
	10	3.334E-02	5.988E-02	8.314E-03	7.171E-03	**6.617E-03**
		2.095E-01	1.511E-01	8.646E-03	**7.573E-03**	1.010E-02
		2.165E-02	2.243E-02	5.279E-03	5.523E-03	**3.407E-03**
	15	2.531E-02	3.526E-02	6.703E-03	6.848E-03	**5.112E-03**
		4.450E-02	1.209E-01	**7.568E-03**	8.447E-03	8.424E-03
WFG6		–	2.531E-02	2.944E-02	**1.932E-02**	2.269E-02
	3	–	2.989E-02	4.688E-02	2.943E-02	**2.919E-02**
		–	3.913E-02	6.458E-02	4.107E-02	**3.561E-02**
		–	2.696E-02	3.375E-02	2.669E-02	**2.296E-02**
	5	–	3.409E-02	4.512E-02	**3.127E-02**	3.201E-02
		–	4.030E-02	6.201E-02	3.884E-02	**3.821E-02**
		–	2.682E-02	**1.789E-02**	2.142E-02	1.999E-02
	8	–	3.531E-02	3.322E-02	3.167E-02	**3.159E-02**
		–	3.987E-02	5.299E-02	**3.824E-02**	4.033E-02
		–	3.004E-02	**2.102E-02**	2.262E-02	2.785E-02
	10	–	3.785E-02	3.249E-02	**3.106E-02**	3.158E-02
		–	4.453E-02	4.719E-02	4.067E-02	**3.954E-02**
		–	3.882E-02	8.346E-03	**7.599E-03**	2.109E-02
	15	–	5.479E-02	**1.572E-02**	2.129E-02	4.297E-02
		–	3.057E-01	**3.723E-02**	4.552E-02	7.829E-02

† The results are taken from the original NSGA-III paper [7].

As for WFG6 problem, NSGA-III-SBX outperforms NSGA-III-DE on 3 and 5-objective instances, whereas NSGA-III-DE has an advantage over NSGA-III-SBX on the remaining instances. NSGA-III-HVO shows performance at par with NSGA-III-2S and they are better than both NSGA-III-SBX and NSGA-III-DE except on 15-objective instance, where NSGA-III-DE exhibits superiority over the others.

It is worth noting that, compared with the results from the original NSGA-III paper [7], our NSGA-III-SBX can provide similar IGD performance except on SDTLZ1; the developed NSGA-III-2S and NSGA-III-HVO can generally obtain clearly better results.

To have statistically sound conclusions, Wilcoxon signed-rank test at a 5% significance level is further conducted on IGD results obtained by any two competing algorithms. Table 4 summarizes the significant test. In this table, Alg_1 vs. Alg_2, 'B' ('W') means that the number of instances on which the results of Alg_1 are significantly better (worse) than those of Alg_2, and 'E' indicates the number of instances where there exists no statistical significance between the results of two. From Table 4, NSGA-III-DE shows certain advantages over NSGA-III-SBX on the consider instances; NSGA-III-2S generally performs better than its two individual components, i.e., NSGA-III-SBX and NSGA-III-DE; NSGA-III-HVO is overall the best performing algorithm among the target algorithms.

Table 4: Summary of significant test between any two algorithms.

Alg_1 vs. Alg_2	B	W	E
NSGA-III-DE vs. NSGA-III-SBX	25	9	1
NSGA-III-2S vs. NSGA-III-SBX	30	3	2
NSGA-III-2S vs. NSGA-III-DE	27	1	7
NSGA-III-HVO vs. NSGA-III-SBX	34	1	0
NSGA-III-HVO vs. NSGA-III-DE	32	1	2
NSGA-III-2S vs. NSGA-III-HVO	7	23	5

5. CONCLUSION AND FUTURE WORK

This is a primary study to investigate the effect of variation operators in reference-point based many-objective optimization, and more specifically in NSGA-III. In this study, we have suggested three new NSGA-III variants: NSGA-III-DE, NSGA-III-2S and NSGA-III-HVO. Extensive experimental results have shown that all of them are compared favourably with the original NSGA-III on the considered problem instances, implying that the performance of NSGA-III is significantly bottlenecked by its variation operators.

Our current work can be extended in the following directions. First, in NSGA-III-2S and NSGA-III-HVO, we just adopt naive methods to combine variation operators and it is possible to further enhance their search performance by introducing adaptive operator selection mechanisms [19, 25]. Second, as NSGA-III-DE has shown the competitive performance to the original NSGA-III, there exist research opportunities in combing NSGA-III with other alternative variation operators, e.g., particle swarm optimization (PSO). Last, it is meaningful and challenging to do theoretical analysis to support some interesting experimental observations about the effect of variation operators, e.g., it is generally suitable for NSGA-III-DE to use small Cr values.

Acknowledgment

This work is supported by National Basic Research Program of China (973 Program) (Grant No. 2012CB316301), National Natural Science Foundation of China (Grant No. 61175110), National S&T Major Projects of China (Grant No. 2011ZX02101-004), and National Banking Information Technology Risk Management Projects of China.

6. REFERENCES

[1] R. B. Agrawal, K. Deb, and R. B. Agrawal. Simulated binary crossover for continuous search space. *Complex Systems*, 9:1–34, 1994.

[2] J. Bader and E. Zitzler. HypE: An algorithm for fast hypervolume-based many-objective optimization. *Evolutionary Computation*, 19(1):45–76, 2011.

[3] S. Bandyopadhyay and A. Mukherjee. An algorithm for many-objective optimization with reduced objective computations: A study in differential evolution. *IEEE Transactions on Evolutionary Computation*, in press.

[4] H. Cai, C. Chung, and K. Wong. Application of differential evolution algorithm for transient stability constrained optimal power flow. *IEEE Transactions on Power Systems*, 23(2):719–728, 2008.

[5] T.-M. Chan, K.-F. Man, S. Kwong, and K. Tang. A jumping gene paradigm for evolutionary multiobjective optimization. *IEEE Transactions on Evolutionary Computation*, 12(2):143–159, 2008.

[6] T.-C. Chiang. A C++ implementation of NSGA-III. http://web.ntnu.edu.tw/~tcchiang/publications/nsga3cpp/nsga3cpp.htm

[7] K. Deb and H. Jain. An evolutionary many-objective optimization algorithm using reference-point based non-dominated sorting approach, Part I: Solving problems with box constraints. *IEEE Transactions on Evolutionary Computation*, 18(4):577–601, 2014.

[8] K. Deb, A. Pratap, S. Agarwal, and T. Meyarivan. A fast and elitist multiobjective genetic algorithm: NSGA-II. *IEEE Transactions on Evolutionary Computation*, 6(2):182–197, 2002.

[9] K. Deb, L. Thiele, M. Laumanns, and E. Zitzler. Scalable multi-objective optimization test problems. In *IEEE Congress on Evolutionary Computation*, pages 825–830, 2002.

[10] R. Denysiuk, L. Costa, and I. Espírito Santo. Many-objective optimization using differential evolution with variable-wise mutation restriction. In *Proceeding of the 2013 Conference on Genetic and Evolutionary Computation*, pages 591–598, 2013.

[11] J. J. Durillo and A. J. Nebro. jmetal: A java framework for multi-objective optimization. *Advances in Engineering Software*, 42(10):760–771, 2011.

[12] A. Elhossini, S. Areibi, and R. Dony. Strength pareto particle swarm optimization and hybrid EA-PSO for multi-objective optimization. *Evolutionary Computation*, 18(1):127–156, 2010.

[13] J. R. Figueira, A. Liefooghe, E.-G. Talbi, and A. P. Wierzbicki. A parallel multiple reference point approach for multi-objective optimization. *European Journal of Operational Research*, 205(2):390–400, 2010.

[14] D. Hadka and P. Reed. Borg: An auto-adaptive many-objective evolutionary computing framework. *Evolutionary Computation*, 21(2):231–259, 2013.

[15] S. Huband, P. Hingston, L. Barone, and L. While. A review of multiobjective test problems and a scalable test problem toolkit. *IEEE Transactions on Evolutionary Computation*, 10(5):477–506, 2006.

[16] K. Ikeda, H. Kita, and S. Kobayashi. Failure of Pareto-based MOEAs: does non-dominated really mean near to optimal? In *IEEE Congress on Evolutionary Computation*, pages 957–962, 2001.

[17] H. Ishibuchi, Y. Tanigaki, H. Masuda, and Y. Nojima. Distance-based analysis of crossover operators for many-objective knapsack problems. In *Parallel Problem Solving from Nature*, pages 600–610, 2014.

[18] H. Ishibuchi, N. Tsukamoto, and Y. Nojima. Evolutionary many-objective optimization: A short review. In *IEEE Congress on Evolutionary Computation*, pages 2419–2426, 2008.

[19] K. Li, A. Fialho, S. Kwong, and Q. Zhang. Adaptive operator selection with bandits for a multiobjective evolutionary algorithm based on decomposition. *IEEE Transactions on Evolutionary Computation*, 18(1):114–130, 2014.

[20] M. Li, S. Yang, K. Li, and X. Liu. Evolutionary algorithms with segment-based search for multiobjective optimization problems. *IEEE Transactions on Cybernetics*, 44(8):1295–1313, 2014.

[21] E. Mezura-Montes, M. Reyes-Sierra, and C. A. C. Coello. Multi-objective optimization using differential evolution: a survey of the state-of-the-art. In *Advances in differential evolution*, pages 173–196, 2008.

[22] H. J. Moen, N. B. Hansen, H. Hovland, and J. Tørresen. Many-objective optimization using taxi-cab surface evolutionary algorithm. In *Evolutionary Multi-Criterion Optimization*, pages 128–142, 2013.

[23] A. J. Nebro, J. J. Durillo, M. Machín, C. A. C. Coello, and B. Dorronsoro. A study of the combination of variation operators in the NSGA-II algorithm. In *Advances in Artificial Intelligence*, pages 269–278, 2013.

[24] H. Sato, H. E. Aguirre, and K. Tanaka. Genetic diversity and effective crossover in evolutionary many-objective optimization. In *Learning and Intelligent Optimization*, pages 91–105, 2011.

[25] V. A. Shim, K. C. Tan, and H. Tang. Adaptive memetic computing for evolutionary multiobjective optimization. *IEEE Transactions on Cybernetics*, in press.

[26] R. Storn and K. Price. Differential evolution–a simple and efficient heuristic for global optimization over continuous spaces. *Journal of global optimization*, 11(4):341–359, 1997.

[27] K. C. Tan, S. C. Chiam, A. Mamun, and C. K. Goh. Balancing exploration and exploitation with adaptive variation for evolutionary multi-objective optimization. *European Journal of Operational Research*, 197(2):701–713, 2009.

[28] J. A. Vrugt and B. A. Robinson. Improved evolutionary optimization from genetically adaptive multimethod search. *Proceedings of the National Academy of Sciences*, 104(3):708–711, 2007.

[29] Y. Yuan and H. Xu. Flexible job shop scheduling using hybrid differential evolution algorithms. *Computers & Industrial Engineering*, 65(2):246–260, 2013.

[30] Y. Yuan and H. Xu. Multiobjective flexible job shop scheduling using memetic algorithms. *IEEE Transactions on Automation Science and Engineering*, 12(1):336–353, 2015.

[31] Y. Yuan, H. Xu, and B. Wang. An improved NSGA-III procedure for evolutionary many-objective optimization. In *Proceedings of the 2014 Conference on Genetic and Evolutionary Computation*, pages 661–668, 2014.

[32] Q. Zhang and H. Li. MOEA/D: A multiobjective evolutionary algorithm based on decomposition. *IEEE Transactions on Evolutionary Computation*, 11(6):712–731, 2007.

[33] Q. Zhang, W. Liu, and H. Li. The performance of a new version of MOEA/D on CEC09 unconstrained mop test instances. In *IEEE Congress on Evolutionary Computation*, pages 203–208, 2009.

[34] E. Zitzler, M. Laumanns and L. Thiele. SPEA2: Improving the strength Pareto evolutionary algorithm. *Technical Report TIK-Report 103*, Swiss Federal Institute of Technology, Zurich, Germany, 2001.

Injecting CMA-ES into MOEA/D

Saúl Zapotecas-Martínez
Shinshu University
Faculty of Engineering
4-17-1 Wakasato, Nagano,
380-8553, Japan
saul.zapotecas@gmail.com

Bilel Derbel
Univ. Lille, CRIStAL
Inria Lille Nord-Europe
Villeneuve d'Ascq, France
bilel.derbel@univ-lille1.fr

Arnaud Liefooghe
Univ. Lille, CRIStAL
Inria Lille Nord-Europe
Villeneuve d'Ascq, France
arnaud.liefooghe@univ-lille1.fr

Dimo Brockhoff
INRIA Lille Nord-Europe
Dolphin Team
Villeneuve d'Ascq, France
dimo.brockhoff@inria.fr

Hernán E. Aguirre
Shinshu University
Faculty of Engineering
4-17-1 Wakasato, Nagano,
380-8553, Japan
ahernan@shinshu-u.ac.jp

Kiyoshi Tanaka
Shinshu University
Faculty of Engineering
4-17-1 Wakasato, Nagano,
380-8553, Japan
ktanaka@shinshu-u.ac.jp

ABSTRACT

MOEA/D is an aggregation-based evolutionary algorithm which has been proved extremely efficient and effective for solving multi-objective optimization problems. It is based on the idea of decomposing the original multi-objective problem into several single-objective subproblems by means of well-defined scalarizing functions. Those single-objective subproblems are solved in a cooperative manner by defining a neighborhood relation between them. This makes MOEA/D particularly interesting when attempting to plug and to leverage single-objective optimizers in a multi-objective setting. In this context, we investigate the benefits that MOEA/D can achieve when coupled with CMA-ES, which is believed to be a powerful single-objective optimizer. We rely on the ability of CMA-ES to deal with injected solutions in order to update different covariance matrices with respect to each subproblem defined in MOEA/D. We show that by cooperatively evolving neighboring CMA-ES components, we are able to obtain competitive results for different multi-objective benchmark functions.

Categories and Subject Descriptors

I.2.8 [**Computing Methodologies**]: Artificial Intelligence—*Problem Solving, Control Methods, and Search.*

Keywords

Multi-objective Optimization; Decomposition-based MOEAs; Covariance Matrix Adaption Evolution Strategy.

GECCO '15, July 11 - 15, 2015, Madrid, Spain
© 2015 ACM. ISBN 978-1-4503-3472-3/15/07... $15.00
DOI: http://dx.doi.org/10.1145/2739480.2754754

1. INTRODUCTION

A multi-objective optimization problem (MOP) refers to the situation where several conflicting objectives are to be optimized simultaneously. In such a setting, solving a MOP consists in finding a whole set of solutions providing both good and diverse compromises with respect to the corresponding objectives. Computing such a set is actually a challenging task for which one can find different methodological frameworks and different algorithmic concepts. Evolutionary algorithms (EA) are particularly well-suited in order to compute an accurate approximation of the so-called Pareto set, that is the set of the best achievable objective trade-offs. Generally speaking, multi-objective EAs can be classified in different classes, ranging from dominance-based algorithms [4], indicator-based algorithms [19], and aggregation-based algorithms [12, 17]. In this paper, we are interested in the MOEA/D (multi-objective optimization based on decomposition) framework for which we can witness a growing interest from the community due to its simplicity and to its effectiveness when applied to a broad range of multi-objective optimization problems.

One can find several variants and implementations of MOEA/D, which are all based on seemingly the same concept. Instead of attempting to directly solve the MOP as a whole, all MOEA/D variants decompose the original MOP into several single-objective subproblems, and solve them cooperatively. More specifically, a set of weighting coefficient vectors is used to define different scalarized subproblems for which one solution is maintained and evolved over time. In this respect, any single-objective optimizer can be potentially plugged into MOEA/D as search engine for the single-objective subproblems. This has been done for example with polynomial mutation and SBX crossover [17] as well as differential evolution (DE) [14], where the latter is believed to be among the best performing implementations [14]. However, this inclusion of single-objective optimizers might not always be straightforward due to two additional specificities of the MOEA/D framework related to the *cooperativity* among the search process of the scalarized problems.

Instead of solving every subproblem independently, MOEA/D defines a neighborhood relation among them, and allows solutions to be exchanged between neighboring problems in two ways. On the one hand, the currently best-known solution of a neighboring problem can be employed to change ones own search distribution, e.g., by using them as parents in a crossover operator. On the other hand, newly generated solutions are also allowed to be actively transferred to a neighboring subproblem in order to replace its current best solution. On an abstract level, we can say that in MOEA/D, the single-objective optimizers applied at each subproblem are not only acting selfishly to improve the solution of their own problem by "stealing information" from others, but they also behave in an altruistic way by helping to improve the solutions of their neighbors.

In this paper, we investigate new opportunities offered by the flexibility of MOEA/D in incorporating novel single-objective optimizers. More specifically, we explore the strengths of the well-established CMA-ES (Covariance Matrix Adaption Evolution Strategy) algorithm considered as a state-of-the-art optimizer for single-objective blackbox continuous problems [9]. Our interest in combining the CMA-ES with MOEA/D stems from two sources. On the one hand, CMA-ES has been shown experimentally to be among the best-performing single-objective blackbox algorithms on the well-established BBOB testbed, with typically superior performance to DE variants and other numerical optimizers—especially when the problems are difficult and the budgets are not too small [7]. On the other hand, a recent paper by Hansen [6] shows that external solutions can be easily *injected* into the algorithm to gain from good candidate solutions that are not sampled directly from the algorithm itself. Both aspects together make the CMA-ES with injection a highly interesting candidate to be used within MOEA/D and its cooperative optimization in which solutions are exchanged between single-objective subproblems.

In this paper, we therefore propose a novel variant of MOEA/D where CMA-ES is used as the core single-objective evolution engine and where the injection idea allows to incorporate information from neighboring scalarizing problems into the search distributions. We show that by appropriately injecting solutions coming from the CMA-ES sampling process into neighboring subproblems, we can derive novel effective variation mechanisms which are compatible with the decomposition-based concepts used with the MOEA/D framework. To assess the validity of our approach, we conduct an experimental study where, in particular, we analyze the performance of the proposed MOEA/D-CMA algorithm compared to MOEA/D-DE using the CEC 2009 box-constrained benchmark functions. Besides being able to obtain competitive results, the investigations conducted in this paper highlight promising alternatives for designing novel efficient multi-objective optimization algorithms falling in the class of aggregation-based EAs.

Note that already several multi-objective versions of the CMA-ES algorithm exist [10, 11] which, however, do not resemble the framework of MOEA/D but instead aim at maximizing the hypervolume of a solution set in the framework of indicator-based algorithms. These algorithms are not in the focus of this paper although a numerical comparison would be interesting for the future.

The rest of this paper is organized as follows. In Section 2, we review some basic concepts related to multi-objective optimization as well as to the MOEA/D framework. In Section 3, we recall the main algorithmic components of the single objective CMA-ES as well as the idea of injection that will serve as a basis towards its successful incorporation into MOEA/D. In Section 4, we describe our proposed MOEA/D-CMA approach and discuss its design components in detail. In Section 5, we describe our experimental study and discuss our main findings. Section 6 finally concludes the paper and discusses related open research directions.

Algorithm 1: General Framework of MOEA/D

Input:
N: the number of subproblems to be decomposed;
W: a well-distributed set of weight vectors $\{\mathbf{w}^1, \ldots, \mathbf{w}^N\}$;
T: the neighborhood size.
Output:
P: the final approximation to PS.

$\mathbf{z} = (z_1 = +\infty, \ldots, z_k = +\infty)^\intercal$;
Generate a random set of solutions $P = \{\mathbf{x}^1, \ldots, \mathbf{x}^N\}$ in Ω;
for $i = 1, \ldots, N$ **do**
    $B_i \leftarrow \{i_1, \ldots, i_T\}$, such that: $\mathbf{w}^{i_1}, \ldots, \mathbf{w}^{i_T}$ are the T closest weight vectors to $\mathbf{w}^i$;
    $z_j \leftarrow \min(z_j, f_j(\mathbf{x}^i))$; // for $j = 1, \ldots, k$
while *stopping criterion is not satisfied* **do**
    for $\mathbf{x}^i \in P$ **do**
        Reproduction: Randomly select two indexes k, l from B_i, and then generate a new solution $\mathbf{y}$ from $\mathbf{x}^k$ and $\mathbf{x}^l$ by using genetic operators.
        Mutation: Apply a mutation operator on $\mathbf{y}$ to produce $\mathbf{y}'$.
        Update of $\mathbf{z}$: $z_j \leftarrow \min(z_j, f_j(\mathbf{x}^i))$; // for $j = 1, \ldots, k$
        Update of Neighboring Solutions: For each index $j \in B_i$, if $g(\mathbf{y}'|\mathbf{w}^j, \mathbf{z}) < g(\mathbf{x}^i|\mathbf{w}^j, \mathbf{z})$, then set $\mathbf{x}^j = \mathbf{y}'$;
return $P = \{\mathbf{x}^1, \ldots, \mathbf{x}^N\}$;

2. BASIC CONCEPTS

2.1 Multi-objective Optimization

Assuming minimization, a continuous multi-objective optimization problem (MOP), can be stated as:

$$\underset{\mathbf{x} \in \Omega}{\text{minimize}} \quad \mathbf{F}(\mathbf{x}) = (f_1(\mathbf{x}), \ldots, f_k(\mathbf{x}))^\intercal \tag{1}$$

where $\Omega \subset \mathbb{R}^n$ defines the decision space and $\mathbf{F}$ is defined as the vector of the objective functions where each $f_j : \Omega \rightarrow \mathbb{R}$ ($j = 1, \ldots, k$) is the function to be minimized. In this paper we consider the box-constrained case, i.e., $\Omega = \prod_{i=1}^{n}[a_j, b_j]$. Therefore, each variable vector $\mathbf{x} = (x_1, \ldots, x_n)^\intercal \in \Omega$ is such that $a_i \leq x_i \leq b_i$ for all $i \in \{1, \ldots, n\}$. In order to describe the concept of optimality in which we are interested, the following definitions are introduced [15].

Definition 1. *Let* $\mathbf{x}, \mathbf{y} \in \Omega$, *we say that* $\mathbf{x}$ dominates $\mathbf{y}$ *(denoted by* $\mathbf{x} \prec \mathbf{y}$*) with respect to the problem defined in equation* (1) *if and only if:* 1) $f_i(\mathbf{x}) \leq f_i(\mathbf{y})$ *for all* $i \in \{1, \ldots, k\}$ *and* 2) $f_j(\mathbf{x}) < f_j(\mathbf{y})$ *for at least one* $j \in \{1, \ldots, k\}$.

Definition 2. *Let* $\mathbf{x}^\star \in \Omega$, *we say that* $\mathbf{x}^\star$ *is a* Pareto optimal *solution, if there is no other solution* $\mathbf{y} \in \Omega$ *such that* $\mathbf{y} \prec \mathbf{x}^\star$.

Definition 3. *The* Pareto optimal set PS *is defined by:* $PS = \{\mathbf{x} \in \Omega | \mathbf{x} \text{ is a Pareto optimal solution}\}$ *and its image* $PF = \{\mathbf{F}(\mathbf{x}) | \mathbf{x} \in PS\}$*) is called* Pareto front PF.

2.2 MOEA/D

The Multi-Objective Evolutionary Algorithm Based on Decomposition (MOEA/D) [17], transforms a MOP into several scalarizing subproblems. Therefore, an approximation of the Pareto set is obtained by solving the N scalarizing subproblems in which a MOP is decomposed.

Considering $W = \{\mathbf{w}^1, \ldots, \mathbf{w}^N\}$ as the well-distributed set of weighting coefficient vectors, MOEA/D seeks the best solution to each subproblem defined by each weight vector using the Penalty Boundary Intersection (PBI) approach [17], which is in the form:

$$\text{minimize:} \quad g^{pbi}(\mathbf{x}|\mathbf{w}^i, \mathbf{z}) = d_1 + \theta d_2 \tag{2}$$

such that

$$d_1 = \frac{|(\mathbf{F}(\mathbf{x}) - \mathbf{z})^\intercal \mathbf{w}|}{\|\mathbf{w}\|} \text{ and } d_2 = \left\|(\mathbf{F}(\mathbf{x}) - \mathbf{z}) - d_1 \frac{\mathbf{w}}{\|\mathbf{w}\|}\right\|$$

where $\mathbf{x} \in \Omega \subset \mathbb{R}^n$ and $z_j = \min\{f_j(\mathbf{x})|\mathbf{x} \in \Omega\}$ for $i = 1, \ldots, N$ and $j = 1, \ldots, k$. Since $\mathbf{z} = (z_1, \ldots, z_k)^\intercal$ is unknown, MOEA/D states each component z_j by the minimum value for each objective f_j found during the search, for $j = 1, \ldots, k$.

In MOEA/D, a neighborhood of a weight vector $\mathbf{w}^i$ is defined as a set of its closest weight vectors in W. Therefore, the neighborhood of the weight vector $\mathbf{w}^i$ contains all the indexes of the T closest weight vectors to $\mathbf{w}^i$.

Throughout the evolutionary process, MOEA/D finds the best solution to each subproblem maintaining a population of N solutions $P = \{\mathbf{x}^1, \ldots, \mathbf{x}^N\}$ where $\mathbf{x}^i \in \Omega$ is the current solution to the ith subproblem. Algorithm 1 presents the general framework of MOEA/D, however, for a more detailed description of this algorithm the interested reader is referred to [17].

3. CMA-ES

The Covariance Matrix Adaptation Evolution Strategy (CMA-ES, [9]) is one of the state-of-the-art numerical blackbox optimization algorithms available—outperforming other algorithms especially for difficult functions and larger budgets [7]. To minimize a function $f : \mathbb{R}^n \to \mathbb{R}$, CMA-ES iteratively samples λ solutions from a multivariate normal distribution, parameterized by a mean vector $\mathbf{m}_\tau \in \mathbb{R}^n$, a step size $\sigma_\tau > 0$, and a covariance matrix $\mathbf{C}_\tau \in \mathbb{R}^{n \times n}$ at time step τ. After the evaluation and ranking of the λ candidate solutions, their relative steps (between the sampled points and the old mean, sorted according to the solution's objective function value) are used to update the parameters of the sampling distribution. This loop of sampling and sample distribution update is repeated until any of several stopping criteria is met.

More concretely, the CMA-ES version, employed in this paper and following [5], works as follows. In the initialization step at $\tau = 0$, the mean $\mathbf{m}_0$ is typically sampled uniformly at random in a bounded search domain $[a, b] \in \mathbb{R}^n$, the initial covariance matrix $\mathbf{C}_0$ is chosen as the identity matrix, and the evolution paths $\mathbf{p}_\rho$ and $\mathbf{p}_c$ are set to $\mathbf{0} \in \mathbb{R}^n$.

At each iteration, CMA-ES then samples $\lambda \geq 1$ candidate solutions $\mathbf{x}^i \in \mathbb{R}^n$ $(1 \leq i \leq \lambda)$ according to a multivariate normal distribution ($\mathbf{x}^i \sim \mathcal{N}(\mathbf{m}_\tau, \sigma_\tau^2 \mathbf{C}_\tau) \sim \mathbf{m}_\tau + \sigma_\tau \cdot \mathcal{N}(\mathbf{0}, \mathbf{C}_\tau)$).

The candidate solutions $\mathbf{x}^i$ are evaluated with respect to the objective function $f : \mathbb{R}^n \to \mathbb{R}$ and ranked according to f-values where we use the notation $\mathbf{x}^{i:\lambda}$ for the ith best solution (i.e. $f(\mathbf{x}^{1:\lambda}) \leq \cdots \leq f(\mathbf{x}^{\mu:\lambda}) \leq f(\mathbf{x}^{\mu+1:\lambda}) \leq \cdots \leq f(\mathbf{x}^{\lambda:\lambda})$.

The new mean vector is computed via *weighted recombination* of the μ best candidate solutions as:

$$\begin{aligned} \mathbf{m}_{\tau+1} &= \textstyle\sum_{i=1}^{\mu} \omega_i \mathbf{x}^{i:\lambda} \\ &= \mathbf{m}_\tau + \textstyle\sum_{i=1}^{\mu} \omega_i (\mathbf{x}^{i:\lambda} - \mathbf{m}_\tau) \end{aligned} \tag{3}$$

where the positive (recombination) weights $\omega_i > 0$ with $\sum_{i=1}^{\mu} \omega_i = 1$ are typically chosen linearly on the log-scale with $\mu \leq \lambda/2$.

The step size σ_τ is updated using *cumulative step size adaptation* (CSA). The evolution path (or search path) $\mathbf{p}_\sigma$ is thereby firstly updated as:

$$\mathbf{p}_\sigma \leftarrow (1 - c_\sigma)\mathbf{p}_\sigma + \sqrt{1 - (1 - c_\sigma)^2}\sqrt{\mu_{\text{eff}}}\mathbf{C}_\tau^{-1/2} \frac{\mathbf{m}_{\tau+1} - \mathbf{m}_\tau}{\sigma_\tau} \tag{4}$$

with the help of which the step size is finally updated as:

$$\sigma_{\tau+1} = \sigma_\tau \times \exp\left(\frac{c_\sigma}{d_\sigma} \times \left(\frac{\|\mathbf{p}_\sigma\|}{E\|\mathcal{N}(\mathbf{0}, \mathbf{I})\|} - 1\right)\right) \tag{5}$$

where $c_\sigma^{-1} \approx n/3$ is the backward time horizon for the evolution path $\mathbf{p}_\sigma$ and larger than one, $\mu_{\text{eff}} = \left(\sum_{i=1}^{\mu} \omega_i^2\right)^{-1}$ is the variance effective selection mass and $1 \leq \mu_{\text{eff}} \leq \mu$ by definition of ω_i, $\mathbf{C}_\tau^{-1/2} = \sqrt{\mathbf{C}_\tau^{-1}}$ is the unique symmetric square root of the inverse of $\mathbf{C}_\tau$, and d_σ is a damping parameter usually close to one. For $d_\sigma = \infty$ or $c_\sigma = 0$ the step size remains unchanged. Note that the step size σ_τ is increased if and only if $\|\mathbf{p}_\sigma\|$ is larger than the expected step length of a fully random sample:

$$\begin{aligned} E\|\mathcal{N}(0, I)\| &= \sqrt{2}\,\Gamma((n+1)/2)/\Gamma(n/2) \\ &\approx \sqrt{n}\,(1 - 1/(4\,n) + 1/(21\,n^2)) \end{aligned} \tag{6}$$

and decreased if it is smaller. For this reason, the step size update tends to make consecutive steps $\mathbf{C}_\tau^{-1}$-conjugate, in that after the adaptation has been successful, $\left(\frac{\mathbf{m}_{\tau+2} - \mathbf{m}_{\tau+1}}{\sigma_{\tau+1}}\right)^{\lambda} \mathbf{C}_\tau^{-1} \frac{\mathbf{m}_{\tau+1} - \mathbf{m}_\tau}{\sigma_\tau} \approx 0$ holds.

Finally, the covariance matrix is updated by means of *rank-one* and *rank-μ* updates for which, again, the respective evolution path is firstly updated as:

$$\mathbf{p}_c \leftarrow (1 - c_c)\mathbf{p}_c + \mathbf{1}_{[0, \alpha\sqrt{n}]}(\|\mathbf{p}_\sigma\|)\sqrt{1 - (1 - c_c)^2}\sqrt{\mu_{\text{eff}}} \frac{\mathbf{m}_{\tau+1} - \mathbf{m}_\tau}{\sigma_\tau} \tag{7}$$

which is used to update the covariance matrix as:

$$\begin{aligned} \mathbf{C}_{\tau+1} = {} & (1 - c_1 - c_\mu + c_s)\mathbf{C}_\tau + c_1 \underbrace{\mathbf{p}_c \mathbf{p}_c^\intercal}_{\texttt{rank-one update}} \\ & + \underbrace{c_\mu \sum_{i=1}^{\mu} \omega_i \frac{\mathbf{x}^{i:\lambda} - \mathbf{m}_\tau}{\sigma_\tau} \left(\frac{\mathbf{x}^{i:\lambda} - \mathbf{m}_\tau}{\sigma_\tau}\right)^\intercal}_{\texttt{rank-}\mu\texttt{ update}} \end{aligned} \tag{8}$$

where $^\intercal$ denotes the transpose and $c_c^{-1} \approx n/4$ is the backward time horizon for the evolution path $\mathbf{p}_c$ and larger than one, $\alpha \approx 3/2$ and the indicator function $\mathbf{1}_{[0, \alpha\sqrt{n}]}(\|\mathbf{p}_\sigma\|)$ evaluates to one iff $\|\mathbf{p}_\sigma\| \in [0, \alpha\sqrt{n}]$ or, in other words, $\|\mathbf{p}_\sigma\| \leq \alpha\sqrt{n}$, which is usually the case. The constant $c_s = (1 - \mathbf{1}_{[0, \alpha\sqrt{n}]}(\|\mathbf{p}_\sigma\|)^2)\, c_1 c_c (2 - c_c)$ makes partly up for the small variance loss in case the indicator is zero, $c_1 \approx 2/n^2$ is the learning rate for the rank-one update of the covariance matrix and $c_\mu \approx \mu_{\text{eff}}/n^2$ is the learning rate for the rank-μ update of the covariance matrix and must not exceed $1 - c_1$.

This completes an iteration of CMA-ES which continues with the sampling of new solutions and updates of the sample distribution parameters until a stopping criterion is met (see Sec. 4 for details). For a more detailed description, the interested readers are referred to [5].

CMA-ES with Injection. If external solutions are available to CMA-ES, for example from a gradient step or from evaluating a meta-model of the (expensive) objective function, these solutions can be directly used in the update of the sampling distribution's parameters. The only change to make the above algorithm work when handling such "injections" of solutions—as argued in [6]—is to restrict the distance between injected solution and previous mean and to rescale the corresponding search step accordingly before taking it into account in the updates of mean, step size, and covariance matrix.

Procedure `Initialize`($\langle \mathbf{p}_c^i, \mathbf{p}_\sigma^i, \mathbf{C}^i, \mathbf{m}^i, \sigma_i, \tau_i \rangle, \mathbf{x}^i, \sigma_{\text{init}}$)

$\mathbf{p}_c^i \leftarrow \mathbf{p}_\sigma^i \leftarrow \mathbf{0}$; `// Initial cumulative paths`
$\mathbf{C}^i \leftarrow \mathbf{I}$; `// Initial covariance matrix`
$\mathbf{m}^i \leftarrow \mathbf{x}^i, \sigma_i \leftarrow \sigma_{\text{init}}$; `// Initial mean and sigma`
$\tau_i \leftarrow 0$; `// Initial iteration`

4. MOEA/D-CMA

The proposed MOEA/D with Covariance Matrix Adaption Evolution Strategy (MOEA/D-CMA) is given in the template of Algorithm 2. As we can see, the proposed approach consists in an initialization step, recombination step and a specific CMA evolution process. In the following, we will provide a step-by-step description of the different components involved in our proposed approach.

Preliminary Considerations and Initialization. MOEA/D-CMA decomposes the problem (1) into N single-objective optimization subproblems. It is in fact based on MOEA/D in the sense that it updates a neighborhood of solutions which solves a set of neighboring subproblems. However, instead of using genetic operators (crossover and mutation), each subproblem evolves the parameters of a multivariate normal distribution and samples according to this distribution, as presented in Section 3. Therefore, analogously to MOEA/D, MOEA/D-CMA employs a well-distributed set of weight vectors $W = \{\mathbf{w}^1, \ldots, \mathbf{w}^N\}$ to define the set of single-objective subproblems to be optimized cooperatively. Each weight vector $\mathbf{w}^i$ defines a scalarized function by using the PBI approach (equation (2)). However, the use of other scalarized functions is also possible, see for example those presented in [15]. Each of the subproblems is then solved by a CMA-ES instance, involving a mean vector, step size, covariance matrix, and the corresponding cumulation paths as presented in Section 3. The ith individual is thereby denoted by the six-tuple $\langle \mathbf{p}_c^i, \mathbf{p}_\sigma^i, \mathbf{C}^i, \mathbf{m}^i, \sigma_i, \tau_i \rangle$ with τ_i being an iteration counter.

Let us consider $P = \{\mathbf{x}^1, \ldots, \mathbf{x}^N\}$ as the set of initial random solutions generated in the feasible search space Ω. At the beginning, the reference point $\mathbf{z}$ is set with infinite values and then, its jth component is updated with the minimum value of the jth objective function f_j found along the optimization process. Analogously to MOEA/D, a neighborhood B_i which contains the indexes of the T closest weight vectors to $\mathbf{w}^i$ is defined. Each solution in P defines the initial mean of each CMA-ES's search distribution. The covariance matrices, step sizes and evolution paths are initialized the same for each subproblem as shown in procedure `Initialize`.

Recombination. In **Step 1** of Algorithm 2, the ith subproblem generates a set of solutions $\mathbf{V}^i$ by using the multivariate normal distribution which is in the form $\mathcal{N}(\mathbf{m}^i, \sigma_i^2 \mathbf{C}^i)$[1]. It is worth noticing that the new solutions in $\mathbf{V}^i$ could be located outside of the feasible region. In this case, we substitute each infeasible solution by its closest vector in the feasible region, which is denoted by $\mathbf{V}^i_{\text{rep}}$. If the solution is feasible we set $\mathbf{v}_{\text{rep}} = \mathbf{v}$, this procedure is referred to as `Repair` in Algorithm 2.

After sampling new candidate solutions, we update the neighboring solutions maintained at each subproblem. For this purpose we adopt the update mechanism proposed in MOEA/D-DE [14], where a maximum number of replacements n_r (lines 20–21) and a dynamic selection of neighborhood (line 18) are employed. In this way, the probability of losing diversity is reduced and the preservation of the best solutions to each neighboring subproblem is maintained during the sampling procedure.

It is important to note that in order to avoid stagnation and allow for restarts of the single optimization runs in each subproblem, we adopt a reset procedure denoted by `ResetCriteria` in line 12. This procedure first checks the following four criteria taken from the literature (e.g., see [1]):

1. `NoEffectCoord.` Reset if adding 0.2-standard deviations in any single coordinate does not change $\mathbf{m}^i$ (i.e. m_j equals $m^i_j + 0.2\sigma c_{j,j}$ for any $j = 1, \ldots, n$).
2. `NoEffectAxis.` Reset if adding a 0.1-standard deviation vector in any principal axis direction of $\mathbf{C}^i$ does not change $\mathbf{m}^i$. More formally, stop if $\mathbf{m}^i$ equals $\mathbf{m}^i + 0.1\sigma\sqrt{d_{jj}}\mathbf{b}_j$, where $j = (\tau \mod n) + 1$ and d_{jj} and $\mathbf{b}_j$ are the jth eigenvalue and eigenvector of $\mathbf{C}^i$, with $||\mathbf{b}_j|| = 1$, respectively.
3. `TolXUp.` Stop/Reset if $\sigma \cdot \max(\text{diag}(D))$ increased by more than 10^4.
4. `ConditionCov.` Stop/Reset if the condition number of the covariance matrix exceeds 10^{14}.

Therefore, if the components of the ith tuple satisfies one of the above criteria, the tuple $\langle \mathbf{p}_c^i, \mathbf{p}_\sigma^i, \mathbf{C}^i, \mathbf{m}^i, \sigma_i, \tau_i \rangle$ is reset using the same `Initialize` procedure as introduced previously. It is worth noticing that with each reinitialization, we reset the step size σ_i to the initial value divided by a factor of two, and using the current best solution for this subproblem as the new initial mean before continuing. More precisely, the ith mean is set as $\mathbf{m}^i = \mathbf{x}^i$ and $\sigma_i = \sigma_{\text{init}}/2$.

Evolution Strategy. After performing the recombination and replacement stage, we consider to evolve and update the components of every single CMA-ES optimizer at each single-objective subproblem. This is the main aim of **Step 2**. Generally speaking, we adopt a variant of the original CMA-ES presented in [6], where the injection of external solutions into the evolution of the covariance matrix is possible. As it was pointed out by Hansen [6], the injection of solutions in the evolutionary process of CMA-ES could improve the adaptation of the matrix if the injected solutions provide sufficient information about the fitness landscape. Our main concern is then to design an accurate injection mechanism which can deal in a proper way with our multi-objective setting.

We argue that, under some assumptions, from the Karush-Kuhn-Tucker conditions, it can be deduced that the PS of a continuous MOP with k objectives forms a $(k-1)$-dimensional piecewise continuous manifold in decision variable space [15]. It means that an optimal solution of the scalarizing problem defined by a weight vector $\mathbf{w}^p$ is close to the one defined by another weight vector $\mathbf{w}^q$ $(p \neq q)$, if $\mathbf{w}^p$ and $\mathbf{w}^q$ are close to each other.

We hypothesize that during the search, the sample distribution of each subproblem converges to the region in which the optimal solution to each subproblem is located. Therefore, considering continuous MOPs and having the reference to the neighboring candidate solutions to each subproblem, the solutions to be injected are chosen precisely from this neighborhood. With that, a set of promising solutions are injected while eventually optimizing each separate subproblem.

[1]Note that the sampling is implemented via an Eigen decomposition of the covariance matrix into $\mathbf{C}^i = \mathbf{BDB}^{-1}$ and then sampling according to $\mathbf{m}^i + \sigma^i \mathbf{BD}\mathcal{N}(\mathbf{0}, \mathbf{I})$ with $\mathbf{B}$ an orthonormal basis of eigenvectors and $\mathbf{D}$ a diagonal matrix containing the corresponding positive eigenvalues.

Algorithm 2: MOEA/D-CMA+I

Input:
N: the number of subproblems to be decomposed;
W: a well-distributed set of weight vectors $W = \{\mathbf{w}^1, \ldots, \mathbf{w}^N\}$;
T: the neighborhood size.
Output:
P: the final approximation to PS;

1 INITIALIZATION
2 $\mathbf{z} = (z_1 = +\infty, \ldots, z_k = +\infty)^\intercal$;
3 Generate a random set of solutions $P = \{\mathbf{x}^1, \ldots, \mathbf{x}^N\}$ in Ω;
4 **for** $i = 1, \ldots, N$ **do**
5 $\quad z_l = \min(z_l, f_l(\mathbf{x}^i))$; // for $l = 1, \ldots, k$
6 $\quad B_i \leftarrow \{i_1, \ldots, i_T\}$, such that: $\mathbf{w}^{i_1}, \ldots, \mathbf{w}^{i_T}$ are the T closest weight vectors to $\mathbf{w}^i$;
7 $\quad$ `Initialize` $(\langle \mathbf{p}_c^i, \mathbf{p}_\sigma^i, \mathbf{C}^i, \mathbf{m}^i, \sigma_i, \tau_i \rangle, \mathbf{x}^i, \sigma_{\text{init}})$
8 EVOLUTION STRATEGY
9 **while** *stopping criterion is not satisfied* **do**
10 $\quad$ **Step 1.** REPRODUCTION AND REPLACEMENT
11 $\quad$ **for** $i = 1, \ldots, N$ **do**
12 $\quad\quad$ `ResetCriteria` $(\langle \mathbf{p}_c^i, \mathbf{p}_\sigma^i, \mathbf{C}^i, \mathbf{m}^i, \sigma_i, \tau_i \rangle, \mathbf{x}^i, \sigma_{\text{init}}/2)$;
13 $\quad\quad \mathbf{V}^i = \mathbf{V}^i_{\text{rep}} = \emptyset$;
14 $\quad\quad$ **for** $j = 1, \ldots, \lambda$ **do**
15 $\quad\quad\quad \mathbf{V}^i \leftarrow \mathbf{V}^i \cup \{\mathbf{v}^j\}$, where $\mathbf{v}^j \leftarrow\sim \mathcal{N}(\mathbf{m}^i, \sigma_i^2 \mathbf{C}^i)\}$;
16 $\quad\quad\quad \mathbf{V}^i_{\text{rep}} \leftarrow \mathbf{V}^i_{\text{rep}} \cup \{\mathbf{v}^j_{\text{rep}}\}$, where $\mathbf{v}^j_{\text{rep}} \leftarrow$ `Repair` $(\mathbf{v}^j)$;
17 $\quad\quad\quad z_l \leftarrow \min(z_l, f_l(\mathbf{v}^j_{\text{rep}}))$; // for $l = 1, \ldots, k$
18 $\quad\quad\quad$ **if** *rand*() $< \delta$ **then** $\pi \leftarrow B_i$ **else** $\pi \leftarrow \{1, \ldots, N\}$;
19 $\quad\quad\quad c \leftarrow 0$;
20 $\quad\quad\quad$ **foreach** $l \in \pi$ **do**
21 $\quad\quad\quad\quad$ **if** $g^{pbi}(\mathbf{v}^j_{rep}|\mathbf{w}^l, \mathbf{z}) < g^{pbi}(\mathbf{x}^l|\mathbf{w}^l, \mathbf{z})$ *and* $c < n_r$ **then**
$\quad\quad\quad\quad\quad \mathbf{x}^l \leftarrow \mathbf{v}^j_{\text{rep}}$ and $c \leftarrow c + 1$;
22 $\quad$ **Step 2.** COVARIANCE MATRICES ADAPTATION
23 $\quad$ **for** $i = 1, \ldots, \ldots, N$ **do**
24 $\quad\quad$ **if** *rand*() $< \delta$ **then** $\pi \leftarrow B_i$ **else** $\pi \leftarrow \{1, \ldots, N\}$;
25 $\quad\quad \mathbf{Q} \leftarrow \mathbf{V}^i$;
26 $\quad\quad$ 2.1. INJECTING SOLUTIONS
27 $\quad\quad$ **foreach** $j \in \pi$ **do**
28 $\quad\quad\quad \mathbf{Q} \leftarrow \mathbf{Q} \cup \{\mathbf{v}^\star\}$, such that: $\mathbf{v}^\star = \arg\min_{\mathbf{v} \in \mathbf{V}^j_{\text{rep}}} g(\mathbf{v}|\mathbf{w}^i, \mathbf{z})$;
29 $\quad\quad$ 2.2. COVARIANCE MATRIX ADAPTATION
30 $\quad\quad \mathbf{y}^j \leftarrow \dfrac{\mathbf{q}^{j:|Q|} - \mathbf{m}^i}{\sigma_i}$ where:
$\quad\quad f_{\text{fit}}(\mathbf{q}^{1:|Q|}|\mathbf{w}^i, \mathbf{z}) \leq \cdots \leq f_{\text{fit}}(\mathbf{q}^{\mu:|Q|}|\mathbf{w}^i, \mathbf{z}) \leq \cdots$ and $\mathbf{q}^j \in Q$;
31 $\quad\quad \mathbf{y}^j \leftarrow \alpha_{\text{clip}}\left(c_y, \|(\mathbf{C}^i)^{-1/2}\mathbf{y}^j\|\right) \times \mathbf{y}^j$, if $\mathbf{q}^{j:|Q|}$ was injected;
32 $\quad\quad \Delta\mathbf{m} \leftarrow \sum_{j=1}^{\mu} \omega_j \mathbf{y}^j$;
33 $\quad\quad \mathbf{m}^i \leftarrow \mathbf{m}^i + c_m \sigma_i \Delta\mathbf{m}$;
34 $\quad\quad \mathbf{m}^i_{\text{rep}} \leftarrow$ Repair$(\mathbf{m}^i)$;
35 $\quad\quad$ `UpdateStepSize` $(\mathbf{C}^i, \Delta\mathbf{m}, \mathbf{p}_\sigma^i, \sigma_i)$;
36 $\quad\quad$ `UpdateCovarianceMatrix` $(\mathbf{C}^i, \mathbf{p}_c^i, \Delta\mathbf{m}, \mathbf{y}^1, \ldots, \mathbf{y}^\mu)$;
37 $\quad\quad \tau_i \leftarrow \tau_i + 1$;
38 $\quad\quad$ **for** $l \in \pi$ **do**
39 $\quad\quad\quad$ **if** $g^{pbi}(\mathbf{m}^i_{rep}|\mathbf{w}^l, \mathbf{z}) < g^{pbi}(\mathbf{x}^l|\mathbf{w}^l, \mathbf{z})$ **then** $\mathbf{x}^l \leftarrow \mathbf{v}^j_{\text{rep}}$;
40 **return** $P \leftarrow \{\mathbf{x}^1, \ldots, \mathbf{x}^N\}$;

Injecting Solutions. In **Step 2** of Algorithm 2, the set $\mathbf{Q}$ denotes the set of candidate solutions to be injected in the adaptation of the covariance matrix. This set of solutions, in fact, contains the samples, generated by the ith subproblem, and the best solution for the ith scalarized subproblem (defined by $\mathbf{w}^i$) found among the samples $\mathbf{V}^j$ (for $j \in B_i$). Since we are injecting (hypothetically) promising solutions, we consider the repaired solutions $\mathbf{V}^j_{\text{rep}}$. Note that the samples $\mathbf{V}^i$ are the samples given by the ith subproblem and $i \neq j$.

To obtain a ranking among the to-be-injected solutions, the sorting is carried out by using the definition of an auxiliary fitness function adopted from [8], which allows us, to deal with the box-constrained case, and it is stated as follows.

$$f_{\text{fit}}(\mathbf{q}^j|\mathbf{w}^i, \mathbf{z}) = g^{pbi}(\mathbf{q}^j_{\text{rep}}|\mathbf{w}^i, \mathbf{z}) + \alpha\|\mathbf{q}^j - \mathbf{q}^j_{\text{rep}}\|^2 \tag{9}$$

It is worth noticing that line 31 is introduced as part of the updated process of the CMA-ES with injection [6], where $\alpha_{\text{clip}}(c, x) = 1 \wedge \frac{c}{x}$ and the notation $a \wedge bc + d$ refers to the minimum of a and $bc + d$. In this way, the tuple $\langle \mathbf{p}_c^i, \mathbf{p}_\sigma^i, \mathbf{C}^i, \mathbf{m}^i, \sigma_i, \tau_i \rangle$ is updated by means of equations provided by [6], which are referred to as the `UpdateStepSize`. More precisely, the step size σ_i and the corresponding evolution path $\mathbf{p}_c^i$ are updated according to the following equations.

$$\mathbf{p}_\sigma^i \leftarrow (1 - c_\sigma)\mathbf{p}_\sigma^i + \sqrt{c_\sigma(2 - c_\sigma)\mu_{\text{eff}}}(\mathbf{C}^i)^{-1/2}\Delta\mathbf{m} \tag{10}$$

$$\sigma_i \leftarrow \sigma_i \times \exp\left(\Delta_\sigma^{\max} \wedge \frac{c_\sigma}{d_\sigma}\left(\frac{\|\mathbf{p}_\sigma^i\|}{E\|\mathcal{N}(\mathbf{0}, I)\|} - 1\right)\right) \tag{11}$$

The covariance matrix is updated by the procedure `UpdateCovarianceMatrix` by using Equation (8). However, because we are injecting a set of solutions, the learning path $\mathbf{p}_c^i$ is updated by means of the following equation.

$$\mathbf{p}_c^i \leftarrow (1 - c_c)\mathbf{p}_c^i + h_\sigma\sqrt{c_c(2 - c_c)\mu_{\text{eff}}}\Delta\mathbf{m} \tag{12}$$

In fact, as it is shown in [6], Equations (10), (11) and (12) differ from Equations (4), (5) and (7), by introducing the parameter $\Delta\mathbf{m}$ and $\Delta_\sigma^{\max}$. Note however, that using $\Delta_\sigma^{\max} = +\infty$ and $\Delta\mathbf{m} = \frac{\mathbf{m}_{\tau_i} - \mathbf{m}_{\tau_i - 1}}{\sigma_i}$, the original equations of CMA-ES are recovered. It is also possible to inject an arbitrary mean, which shifts the current mean $\mathbf{m}^i$ by means of additional equations. In the study presented herein, we focused only on the injection of already evaluated solutions. However, the injection of a determined mean, is indeed, a possible path for future research.

In the remainder, our proposed approach is denoted as MOEA/D-CMA+I as exactly described in Algorithm 2; however, we shall also consider a second variant of this algorithm, denoted by MOEA/D-CMA, by taking off the injection mechanism, i.e., $\mathbf{Q} = \mathbf{V}^i$ and $\Delta_\sigma^{\max} = +\infty$.

5. EXPERIMENTAL STUDY

In order to analyze the efficiency of the proposed approach *with* and *without* injection, i.e. MOEA/D-CMA+I and MOEA/D-CMA, we compare its performance against two competing algorithms: (i) the conventional *Multi-Objective Evolutionary Algorithm based on Decomposition* (MOEA/D) [17], and (ii) an improved variant of MOEA/D which uses differential evolution operators and a dynamic neighborhood selection. The corresponding algorithm is called MOEA/D-DE [14]. In this section, the benchmark problems and the performance assessment design adopted in our analysis are presented.

5.1 Experimental Setup

We consider the continuous MOPs with complicated Pareto sets proposed in [18], and extracted from the CEC 2009 special session and competition on the performance assessment of multi-objective optimization algorithms. This benchmark test suite has been specifically designed to resemble complicated real-life optimization problems. The MOPs therein present different properties in terms of separability, multi-modality, and shape of the Pareto front, i.e. convexity, concavity, discontinuities, gaps, etc. More particularly, we consider all box-constrained functions UF1–F10 under their original setting [18], with UF1–UF7 being two-objective problems and UF8–UF10 being three-objective problems. Notice that, for all of them, the number of variables is $n = 30$, and the Pareto fronts lie in the hyper-box $[0, 1]^k$, where k denotes the number of objective functions for the problem under consideration.

All the competing algorithms considered in this study were compared by following the performance assessment experimental setup recommended in [13].

Relative Hypervolume Deviation. The first performance measure indicates the relative hypervolume achieved by the Pareto set approximation given by an algorithm. This Relative Hypervolume (RHV) deviation can be computed by:

$$RHV(A) = \frac{HV(R) - HV(A)}{HV(R)} \tag{13}$$

where HV is the hypervolume indicator [20], A is an approximation set and R is a reference set for the instance under consideration. The reference vector is set to $(2, \ldots, 2)^{\intercal}$. In this quality indicator, a lower value means a better approximation set.

Inverted Generational Distance. The Inverted Generational Distance (IGD, [3]) indicates how far a given Pareto front approximation is from a reference set. Let R be the true Pareto front, the IGD for a set of approximated solutions A is calculated as:

$$IGD(A) = \tfrac{1}{|R|} \textstyle\sum_{i=1}^{|R|} d_i \tag{14}$$

where $d_i = \min_{j=1}^{|A|} \sqrt{\sum_{l=1}^{k} (f_l(i) - f_l(j))^2}$ and k is the number of objective functions. A value of zero in this performance measure, indicates that all the solutions obtained by the algorithm are on the true Pareto front.

Both performance measures (i.e. RHV and IGD) are computed by using the reference sets available at: http://dces.essex.ac.uk/staff/qzhang/moeacompetition09.htm.

5.2 Parameter Setting

As we mentioned before, we consider two variants of the proposed MOEA/D-CMA paradigm. The first version exactly maps to the one presented in Algorithm 2 (i.e. MOEA/D-CMA+I). The second version, denoted by MOEA/D-CMA, corresponds to the same framework, but without performing the phase where solutions are injected to the neighboring subproblems. That is, **Step 2.1** is not performed in Algorithm 2, i.e. $\mathbf{Q} = \mathbf{V}^i$. This shall allow us to appreciate by how much the search process can actually benefit from injecting solutions sampled from neighboring subproblems.

Besides these two versions, we also consider the conventional MOEA/D [17] as well as the more sophisticated MOEA/D-DE [14] in our comparative study. For all competing algorithms, the set of weighting coefficient vectors is generated following a simplex-lattice design [16]. The settings of N and $W = \{\mathbf{w}^1, \ldots, \mathbf{w}^N\}$ are controlled by a parameter H. More precisely, let $\{\mathbf{w}^1, \ldots, \mathbf{w}^N\}$ be the set of weight vectors. Each individual weight w_j^i, such that $i = 1, \ldots, N$ and $j = 1, \ldots, k$, can take a value from $\left\{\frac{0}{H}, \frac{1}{H}, \ldots, \frac{H}{H}\right\}$. Therefore, the number of vectors in W is given by $N = C_{H+k-1}^{k-1}$, where k is the number of objective functions. In this work, we set $H = 99$ for two-objective problems, and $H = 19$ for three-objective problems, that is 100 and 210 weight vectors for MOPs having two and three objectives, respectively.

To fix the parameters of MOEA/D-CMA+I and MOEA/D-CMA, we essentially get inspired by the standard setting values suggested in [5], which are summarized in Table 1. However, following our

Table 1: Parameters for MOEA/D-CMA

$\lambda = 4 + \lfloor 3 \ln n \rfloor$	$\mu = \lfloor \frac{\lambda}{2} \rfloor$
$\omega_i = \dfrac{\ln\left(\frac{\lambda+1}{2}\right) - \ln i}{\sum_{j=1}^{\mu} \left(\ln\left(\frac{\lambda+1}{2}\right) - \ln j\right)}$ for $i = 1, \ldots, \mu$	
$\mu_{\text{eff}} = \sum_{i=1}^{\mu} (\omega_i^2)^{-1}$	$c_y = \sqrt{n} + 2n/(n+2)$
$c_m = 1$	$c_\sigma = \frac{\mu_{\text{eff}}+2}{n+\mu_{\text{eff}}+3}$
$c_c = \frac{4}{n+4}$	$d_\sigma = 1 + c_\sigma + 2\max\left(0, \sqrt{\frac{\mu_{\text{eff}}-1}{n+1}} - 1\right)$
$c_1 = \frac{\alpha_{\text{cov}} \min(1, \lambda/6)}{(n+1.3)^2+\mu_{\text{eff}}}$	$c_\mu = 1 - c_1 \wedge \alpha_{\text{cov}} \frac{\mu_{\text{eff}}-2+1/\mu_{\text{eff}}}{(n+2)^2+\alpha_{\text{cov}}\mu_{\text{eff}}/2}$
$\alpha_{\text{cov}} = 2$	$\Delta_\sigma^{\max} = 1$

empirical observations, we reduce the population size λ to be the same as μ. Nonetheless, the adjustment of the λ parameter, is indeed, one important open issue that would deserve to be investigated. The remaining parameters required by the MOEA/D framework are set as follows: $T = 20$, $\eta_c = \eta_m = 20$, $P_c = 1$ and $P_m = 1/n$; which represent respectively the neighborhood size, crossover index (for Simulated Binary Crossover (SBX)), mutation index (for Polynomial-Based Mutation (PBM)), crossover rate and mutation rate. Finally, the parameter θ in the PBI approach was set to $\theta = 5$. For MOEA/D-DE, we adopted the set of parameters given in [14]. More precisely, the differential factor was set as $F = 0.5$, the crossover ratio was set as $CR = 1$, the maximum number of replacements was set as $n_r = 2$, and $\delta = 0.9$.

We define the initial step size as $\sigma_{\text{init}} = \frac{1}{4} \times (U_b - L_b)$, where U_b and L_b are the upper- and the lower-bounds in the search space. Since we consider the problems with the same boundaries in all dimensions, the decision variables of the original CEC 2009 test functions are simply rescaled without modifying the shape of the PS or the PF. Finally, the auxiliary fitness function was computed with $\alpha = 1 \times 10^{-5}$.

For each MOP, we performed 30 independent runs and we measure the performance of the algorithms after $N \times 1\,000$ and $N \times 2\,000$ fitness function evaluations.

5.3 Numerical Results

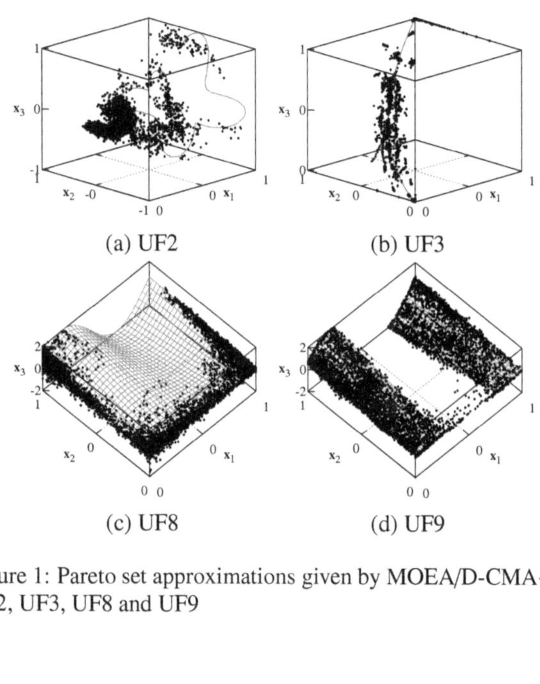

(a) UF2 (b) UF3

(c) UF8 (d) UF9

Figure 1: Pareto set approximations given by MOEA/D-CMA+I in UF2, UF3, UF8 and UF9

Table 2: Comparison of the competing algorithms with respect to the relative hypervolume deviation (RHV) and to the inverted generational distance (IGD). The first number stands for the average indicator-value (lower is better). The number in brackets stands for the standard deviation. Bold values correspond to the best average indicator-value for the instance and the indicator under consideration. Underline values correspond to algorithms that are *not* statistically outperformed by any other algorithm for the instance and the indicator under consideration with respect to a Mann-Whitney non-parametric statistical test with a p-value of 0.05 by using a Bonferroni correction [2].

	RHV				IGD			
	MOEA/D-CMA+I	MOEA/D-CMA	MOEA/D	MOEA/D-DE	MOEA/D-CMA+I	MOEA/D-CMA	MOEA/D	MOEA/D-DE
Fitness function evaluations = N x 1000								
UF1	**0.058** (0.01)	0.177 (0.01)	0.216 (0.07)	0.105 (0.05)	**0.003** (0.01)	0.012 (0.01)	0.009 (0.04)	0.005 (0.03)
UF2	**0.065** (0.03)	0.100 (0.02)	0.101 (0.04)	0.081 (0.04)	**0.004** (0.02)	0.007 (0.01)	0.007 (0.03)	0.005 (0.03)
UF3	**0.125** (0.04)	0.227 (0.04)	0.325 (0.02)	0.213 (0.07)	0.008 (0.02)	0.014 (0.02)	0.012 (0.01)	**0.008** (0.02)
UF4	**0.054** (0.00)	0.075 (0.00)	0.085 (0.01)	0.081 (0.01)	**0.002** (0.00)	0.003 (0.00)	0.002 (0.00)	0.003 (0.00)
UF5	0.742 (0.11)	0.951 (0.05)	**0.435** (0.04)	0.488 (0.08)	0.223 (0.40)	0.315 (0.39)	**0.128** (0.25)	0.143 (0.29)
UF6	0.387 (0.08)	0.391 (0.03)	0.405 (0.07)	**0.318** (0.09)	0.024 (0.07)	**0.015** (0.01)	0.021 (0.05)	0.018 (0.08)
UF7	**0.050** (0.02)	0.120 (0.02)	0.379 (0.05)	0.176 (0.14)	**0.002** (0.00)	0.008 (0.01)	0.020 (0.05)	0.009 (0.08)
UF8	0.074 (0.04)	0.093 (0.03)	0.167 (0.12)	**0.074** (0.05)	0.007 (0.02)	0.009 (0.01)	0.010 (0.07)	**0.005** (0.02)
UF9	0.086 (0.04)	0.092 (0.02)	0.223 (0.02)	**0.082** (0.02)	0.007 (0.03)	0.007 (0.01)	0.009 (0.01)	**0.006** (0.02)
UF10	0.918 (0.07)	0.988 (0.04)	**0.510** (0.11)	0.525 (0.05)	0.046 (0.13)	0.077 (0.21)	0.022 (0.05)	**0.019** (0.03)
Fitness function evaluations = N x 2000								
UF1	**0.051** (0.02)	0.157 (0.02)	0.205 (0.07)	0.075 (0.04)	**0.003** (0.01)	0.011 (0.02)	0.008 (0.04)	0.003 (0.02)
UF2	**0.056** (0.02)	0.082 (0.01)	0.092 (0.03)	0.062 (0.03)	**0.004** (0.02)	0.005 (0.01)	0.006 (0.03)	0.004 (0.03)
UF3	**0.085** (0.04)	0.199 (0.03)	0.325 (0.02)	0.122 (0.07)	0.006 (0.02)	0.013 (0.01)	0.012 (0.01)	**0.004** (0.03)
UF4	**0.051** (0.00)	0.072 (0.00)	0.074 (0.01)	0.076 (0.01)	**0.002** (0.00)	0.003 (0.00)	0.002 (0.00)	0.003 (0.00)
UF5	0.738 (0.11)	0.882 (0.06)	0.424 (0.05)	**0.406** (0.06)	0.221 (0.40)	0.275 (0.35)	**0.123** (0.26)	0.128 (0.41)
UF6	0.363 (0.11)	0.331 (0.04)	0.392 (0.04)	**0.314** (0.10)	0.023 (0.09)	**0.013** (0.01)	0.021 (0.05)	0.018 (0.08)
UF7	**0.041** (0.02)	0.117 (0.01)	0.369 (0.06)	0.140 (0.14)	**0.002** (0.00)	0.007 (0.01)	0.019 (0.05)	0.007 (0.08)
UF8	0.054 (0.03)	0.074 (0.02)	0.163 (0.13)	**0.042** (0.03)	0.006 (0.01)	0.008 (0.01)	0.010 (0.07)	**0.004** (0.01)
UF9	0.074 (0.04)	**0.059** (0.02)	0.162 (0.03)	0.071 (0.03)	0.006 (0.03)	0.006 (0.01)	0.008 (0.02)	**0.006** (0.02)
UF10	0.909 (0.07)	0.962 (0.05)	0.510 (0.11)	**0.462** (0.06)	0.045 (0.11)	0.057 (0.16)	0.022 (0.05)	**0.017** (0.04)

Our results are summarized in Table 2, where we can see the relative performance of the four competing algorithms using two different stopping conditions and for the two quality indicators described above. Notice that we can read two informations in Table 2. We put in bold the best average indicator-value obtained among all algorithms. We also perform a Mann-Whitney non-parametric statistical test between each pair of algorithms in order to determine whether a given algorithm is significantly outperformed by any other. If *no* other algorithm is statistically better than the algorithm under consideration, then the corresponding indicator-value is underlined in the table. Several interesting observations can be extracted from Table 2. First, we can see that there are no significant differences between the behavior of the algorithms when considering different stopping conditions. This hopefully informs that all algorithms are rather ranking in the same manner independently of the available function-evaluation budget. More interestingly, the results of Table 2 allows us to validate the accuracy of the introduced approach from several perspectives.

When comparing MOEA/D-CMA+I with MOEA/D-CMA, we can see that MOEA/D-CMA is outperformed by MOEA/D-CMA+I for all instances except for UF6 when using the IGD indicator. This indicates that the way in which solutions are injected from neighboring subproblem into the single-objective CMA-ES engine, and the way in which CMA-ES is taking care of those solutions when adapting its components, is drastically improving the search when compared to the straightforward version where CMA-ES is plugged within MOEA/D to simply sample new points independently at every subproblem. Notice however, that the MOEA/D-CMA version exhibits, in the worst case, very comparable performance with respect to conventional MOEA/D, and the more advanced MOEA/D-CMA+I algorithm is outperforming the conventional version of MOEA/D in almost all instances expect for instance UF5 and UF10. This indicates that the variation operator induced by the MOEA/D-CMA algorithm is performing well. This is confirmed when looking at the relative performance of MOEA/D-CMA+I with respect to MOEA/D-DE which is known to perform extremely well on these benchmark functions. We can see that there is no algorithm that is performing better in all the considered instances and that the difference is most of the time not statistically significant. Notice also that the difference between the two algorithms is more pronounced for the last 3 instances UF8, UF9 and UF10, in favor of MOEA/D-DE—these instances are actually the three-objective problems considered in our experiments. For the bi-objective instances, MOEA/D-CMA+I appears to be relatively competitive compared to MOEA/D-DE.

In Fig. 1, we show the Pareto set approximations obtained by our proposed MOEA/D-CMA+I for the UF2, UF3, UF8 and UF9 problems. As we can see, the benchmark functions exhibit complicated shapes and depending on the considered instance, the algorithm has some potential in accurately approaching the true Pareto set. This is actually a common behavior for the other competing algorithms as well which is to be attributed to the particular difficulty of some of the considered instances.

We recall that the main purpose of this paper is to investigate at what extent the CMA-ES single-objective optimizer could be appropriately integrated within the MOEA/D framework and what are the benefits one can obtain. As such, we can conclude from the previous set of experiments that injecting accurately solutions from neighbors plays a crucial role to this end. We can also conclude the newly proposed MOEA/D-CMA+I algorithm is a promising candidate to solve hard and complicated optimization problems. In fact, the CMA-ES optimizer enjoys several attractive properties, such as invariance and robustness, which are not verified by several other evolutionary operators. Hence, the experimental study presented in this paper, and the relatively good performance that MOEA/D-CMA+I is able to obtain can be viewed as a first promising step towards the establishment of highly accurate algorithms.

6. CONCLUSIONS AND FUTURE WORK

In this paper, we consider the single-objective CMA-ES algorithm as a plausible optimizer to be incorporated into the MOEA/D framework. We proposed to assign to each subproblem, obtained by decomposition, a single CMA-ES engine and to profit from the solutions of the neighboring subproblems in order to adapt the CMA-ES components accordingly. We thereby rely on the ability of CMA-ES to deal with external solutions in order to derive novel variation operators for the MOEA/D framework. The experimental study conducted in this paper allows us to validate the proposed approach and to show its effectiveness. Besides, the presented algorithm opens the road to further challenging research questions. In fact, the proposed approach is to be viewed as a first step enlightening how the CMA-ES algorithm can specifically be used as a single-objective optimizer when solving multi-objective problems; and this is thanks to the basic concepts introduced by MOEA/D and the ability of CMA-ES of handling external solutions. It is worth noticing that different strategies to take into account the sampled solutions from neighbors could be investigated in the future. Furthermore, it would be insightful to study more deeply the behavior of the so-obtained strategies when considering other benchmark functions. This would enable to fully appreciate the strength of the CMA-ES algorithm on a broad range of problems with different properties. It is our hope that the contribution of this paper can serve as a starting point to derive more powerful aggregation-like EMO methods based on the well established CMA-ES algorithm.

7. REFERENCES

[1] A. Auger and N. Hansen. A restart CMA evolution strategy with increasing population size. In B. McKay et al., editors, *CEC'2005*, volume 2, pages 1769–1776, 2005.

[2] C. E. Bonferroni. Teoria statistica delle classi e calcolo delle probabilita. *Pubblicazioni del R Istituto Superiore di Scienze Economiche e Commerciali di Firenze*, 8:3–62, 1936.

[3] C. A. Coello Coello and N. Cruz Cortés. Solving Multiobjective Optimization Problems using an Artificial Immune System. *Genetic Programming and Evolvable Machines*, 6(2):163–190, June 2005.

[4] K. Deb, A. Pratap, S. Agarwal, and T. Meyarivan. A Fast and Elitist Multiobjective Genetic Algorithm: NSGA–II. *IEEE Transactions on Evolutionary Computation*, 6(2):182–197, April 2002.

[5] N. Hansen. The CMA evolution strategy: a comparing review. In J. Lozano, P. Larranaga, I. Inza, and E. Bengoetxea, editors, *Towards a new evolutionary computation. Advances on estimation of distribution algorithms*, pages 75–102. Springer, 2006.

[6] N. Hansen. Injecting external solutions into CMA-ES. Technical report, INRIA, 2011.

[7] N. Hansen, A. Auger, R. Ros, S. Finck, and P. Posík. Comparing results of 31 algorithms from the black-box optimization benchmarking BBOB-2009. In J. Branke et al., editors, *GECCO workshop on Black-Box Optimization Benchmarking (BBOB'2010)*, pages 1689–1696. ACM, July 2010.

[8] N. Hansen, S. Niederberger, L. Guzzella, and P. Koumoutsakos. A method for handling uncertainty in evolutionary optimization with an application to feedback control of combustion. *IEEE Transactions on Evolutionary Computation*, 13(1):180–197, 2009.

[9] N. Hansen and A. Ostermeier. Completely Derandomized Self-Adaptation in Evolution Strategies. *Evolutionary Computation*, 9(2):159–195, 2001.

[10] C. Igel, N. Hansen, and S. Roth. Covariance matrix adaptation for multi-objective optimization. *Evolutionary Computation*, 15(1):1–28, 2007.

[11] C. Igel, T. Suttorp, and N. Hansen. Steady-state selection and efficient covariance matrix update in the multi-objective cma-es. In *Evolutionary Multi-Criterion Optimization*, pages 171–185. Springer Berlin Heidelberg, 2007.

[12] H. Ishibuchi and T. Murata. Multi-Objective Genetic Local Search Algorithm. In T. Fukuda and T. Furuhashi, editors, *Proceedings of the 1996 International Conference on Evolutionary Computation*, pages 119–124, Nagoya, Japan, 1996. IEEE.

[13] J. Knowles, L. Thiele, and E. Zitzler. A Tutorial on the Performance Assessment of Stochastic Multiobjective Optimizers. 214, Computer Engineering and Networks Laboratory (TIK), ETH Zurich, Switzerland, feb 2006. revised version.

[14] H. Li and Q. Zhang. Multiobjective Optimization Problems With Complicated Pareto Sets, MOEA/D and NSGA-II. *IEEE Transactions on Evolutionary Computation*, 13(2):284–302, April 2009.

[15] K. Miettinen. *Nonlinear Multiobjective Optimization.* Kluwer Academic Publishers, Boston, Massachuisetts, 1999.

[16] H. Scheffé. Experiments With Mixtures. *Journal of the Royal Statistical Society*, Series B (Methodological), 20(2):344–360, 1958.

[17] Q. Zhang and H. Li. MOEA/D: A Multiobjective Evolutionary Algorithm Based on Decomposition. *IEEE TEVC*, 11(6):712–731, December 2007.

[18] Q. Zhang, A. Zhou, S. Zhao, P. N. Suganthan, W. Liu, and S. Tiwari. Multiobjective Optimization Test Instances for the CEC 2009 Special Session and Competition. Technical Report CES-487, University of Essex and Nanyang Technological University, 2008.

[19] E. Zitzler and S. Künzli. Indicator-based selection in multiobjective search. In *PPSN VIII*, pages 832–842. Springer, 2004.

[20] E. Zitzler and L. Thiele. Multiobjective Optimization Using Evolutionary Algorithms – A Comparative Case Study. In A. E. Eiben, editor, *PPSN V*, pages 292–301, Amsterdam, September 1998. Springer-Verlag.

Author Index

www.ingramcontent.com/pod-product-compliance
Lightning Source LLC
LaVergne TN
LVHW080102011026
849160LV00013B/1018